Brill's
New Pauly

ANTIQUITY
VOLUME 5

EQU-HAS

Brill's New Pauly

Brill's
Encyclopaedia of the Ancient World
New Pauly

Edited by
Hubert Cancik and
Helmuth Schneider

English Edition
Managing Editor *Christine F. Salazar*

Assistant Editors *Simon Buck, Tina Chronopoulos, Tina Jerke, Ingrid Rosa Kitzberger, Claudia Kunze, Sebastiaan R. van der Mije, Astrid Möller, Antonia Ruppel* and *Reinhard Selinger*

ANTIQUITY
VOLUME 5

EQU-HAS

BRILL
LEIDEN - BOSTON
2004

Koninklijke Brill NV incorporates the imprints Brill Academic Publishers, Martinus Nijhoff Publishers and VSP.

Originally published in German as DER NEUE PAULY. Enzyklopädie der Antike. Herausgegeben von Hubert Cancik und Helmuth Schneider.

Cover design: TopicA (Antoinette Hanekuyk)
Front: Delphi, temple area
Spine: Tabula Peutingeriana

Translation by protext TRANSLATIONS B.V.

Data structuring and typesetting:
pagina GmbH, Tübingen, Germany

The publication of this work was supported by a grant from the GOETHE-INSTITUT INTER NATIONES.

ISBN (volume) 90 04 12268 0
ISBN (set) 90 04 12259 1

This book is printed on acid-free paper.

PRINTED IN THE NETHERLANDS

Table of Contents

Notes to the User

Arrangement of Entries

The entries are arranged alphabetically and, if applicable, placed in chronological order. In the case of alternative forms or sub-entries, cross-references will lead to the respective main entry. Composite entries can be found in more than one place (e.g. *a commentariis* refers to *commentariis, a*).
Identical entries are differentiated by numbering. Identical Greek and Oriental names are arranged chronologically without consideration of people's nicknames. Roman names are ordered alphabetically, first according to the *gentilicium* or *nomen* (family name), then the *cognomen* (literally 'additional name' or nickname) and finally the *praenomen* or 'fore-name' (e.g. *M. Aemilius Scaurus* is found under *Aemilius*, not *Scaurus*).
However, well-known classical authors are lemmatized according to their conventional names in English; this group of persons is not found under the family name, but under their *cognomen* (e.g. Cicero, not Tullius). In large entries the Republic and the Imperial period are treated separately.

Spelling of Entries

Greek words and names are as a rule latinized, following the predominant practice of reference works in the English language, with the notable exception of technical terms. Institutions and places (cities, rivers, islands, countries etc.) often have their conventional English names (e.g. *Rome* not *Roma*). The latinized versions of Greek names and words are generally followed by the Greek and the literal transliteration in brackets, e.g. *Aeschylus* (Αἰσχύλος; *Aischýlos*).
Oriental proper names are usually spelled according to the 'Tübinger Atlas des Vorderen Orients' (TAVO), but again conventional names in English are also used. In the maps, the names of cities, rivers, islands, countries etc. follow ancient spelling and are transliterated fully to allow for differences in time, e.g. both Καππαδόκια and *Cappadocia* can be found. The transliteration of non-Latin scripts can be found in the 'List of Transliterations'.
Latin and transliterated Greek words are italicized in the article text. However, where Greek transliterations do not follow immediately upon a word written in Greek, they will generally appear in italics, but without accents or makra.

Abbreviations

All abbreviations can be found in the 'List of Abbreviations' in the first volume. Collections of inscriptions, coins and papyri are listed under their *sigla*.

Bibliographies

Most entries have bibliographies, consisting of numbered and/or alphabetically organized references. References within the text to the numbered bibliographic items are in square brackets (e.g. [1.5 n.23] refers to the first title of the bibliography, page 5, note 23). The abbreviations within the bibliographies follow the rules of the 'List of Abbreviations'.

Maps

Texts and maps are closely linked and complementary, but some maps also treat problems outside the text. The authors of the maps are listed in the 'List of Maps'.

Cross-references

Articles are linked through a system of cross-references with an arrow → before the entry that is being referred to.
Cross-references to related entries are given at the end of an article, generally before the bibliographic notes. If reference is made to a homonymous entry, the respective number is also added.
Cross-references to entries in the *Classical Tradition* volumes are added in small capitals.
It can occur that in a cross-reference a name is spelled differently from the surrounding text: e.g., a cross-reference to Mark Antony has to be to Marcus → Antonius, as his name will be found in a list of other names containing the component 'Antonius'.

List of Transliterations

Transliteration of ancient Greek

α	a	alpha
αι	ai	
αυ	au	
β	b	beta
γ	g	gamma; γ before γ, ϰ, ξ, χ: n
δ	d	delta
ε	e	epsilon
ει	ei	
ευ	eu	
ζ	z	z(d)eta
η	ē	eta
ηυ	ēu	
θ	th	theta
ι	i	iota
ϰ	k	kappa
λ	l	la(m)bda
μ	m	mu
ν	n	nu
ξ	x	xi
ο	o	omicron
οι	oi	
ου	ou	
π	p	pi
ϱ	r	rho
σ, ς	s	sigma
τ	t	tau
υ	y	upsilon
φ	ph	phi
χ	ch	chi
ψ	ps	psi
ω	ō	omega
ʽ	h	spiritus asper
ᾳ	ai	iota subscriptum (similarly ῃ, ῳ)

In transliterated Greek the accents are retained (acute ′, grave ‵, and circumflex ˆ). Long vowels with the circumflex accent have no separate indication of vowel length (makron).

Transliteration of Hebrew

א	a	alef
ב	b	bet
ג	g	gimel
ד	d	dalet
ה	h	he
ו	w	vav
ז	z	zayin
ח	ḥ	khet
ט	ṭ	tet
י	y	yod
כ	k	kaf
ל	l	lamed
מ	m	mem
נ	n	nun
ס	s	samek
ע	ʿ	ayin
פ	p/f	pe
צ	ṣ	tsade
ק	q	qof
ר	r	resh
שׂ	ś	sin
שׁ	š	shin
ת	t	tav

Pronunciation of Turkish

Turkish uses Latin script since 1928. Pronunciation and spelling generally follow the same rules as European languages. Phonology according to G. Lewis, Turkish Grammar, 2000.

A	a	French a in *avoir*
B	b	b
C	c	j in *jam*
Ç	ç	ch in *church*
D	d	d
E	e	French ê in *être*
F	f	f
G	g	g in *gate* or in *angular*
Ğ	ğ	lengthens preceding vowel
H	h	h in *have*
I	ı	i in *cousin*
İ	i	French i in *si*
J	j	French j
K	k	c in *cat* or in *cure*
L	l	l in *list* or in *wool*
M	m	m

N	n	n
O	o	French o in *note*
Ö	ö	German ö
P	p	p
R	r	r
S	s	s in *sit*
Ş	ş	sh in *shape*
T	t	t
U	u	u in *put*
Ü	ü	German ü
V	v	v
Y	y	y in *yet*
Z	z	z

Transliteration of Arabic, Persian, and Ottoman Turkish

ء, ا	ʾ, ā	ʾ	ʾ	hamza, alif
ب	b	b	b	bāʾ
پ	–	p	p	pe
ت	t	t	t	tāʾ
ث	ṯ	s̱	s̱	ṯāʾ
ج	ǧ	ǧ	ǧ	ǧīm
چ	–	č	č	čim
ح	ḥ	ḥ	ḥ	ḥāʾ
خ	ḫ	ḫ	ḫ	ḫāʾ
د	d	d	d	dāl
ذ	ḏ	ẕ	ẕ	ḏāl
ر	r	r	r	rāʾ
ز	z	z	z	zāy
ژ	–	ž	ž	že
س	s	s	s	sīn
ش	š	š	š	šīn
ص	ṣ	ṣ	ṣ	ṣād
ض	ḍ	ḍ	ḍ	ḍād
ط	ṭ	ṭ	ṭ	ṭāʾ
ظ	ẓ	ẓ	ẓ	ẓāʾ
ع	ʿ	ʿ	ʿ	ʿain
غ	ġ	ġ	ġ	ġain
ف	f	f	f	fāʾ
ق	q	q	q, k	qāf
ك	k	k	k, g, ñ	kāf
گ	–	g	g, ñ	gāf
ل	l	l	l	lām
م	m	m	m	mīm
ن	n	n	n	nūn
ه	h	h	h	hāʾ
و	w, ū	v	v	wāw
ى	y, ī	y	y	yāʾ

Transliteration of other languages

Akkadian (Assyrian-Babylonian), Hittite and Sumerian are transliterated according to the rules of RLA and TAVO. For Egyptian the rules of the Lexikon der Ägyptologie are used. The transliteration of Indo-European follows Rix, HGG. The transliteration of Old Indian is after M. Mayrhofer, Etymologisches Wörterbuch des Altindoarischen, 1992ff. Avestian is done according to K. Hoffmann, B. Forssman, Avestische Laut- und Flexionslehre, 1996. Old Persian follows R.G. Kent, Old Persian, ^{2}1953 (additions from K. Hoffmann, Aufsätze zur Indoiranistik vol. 2, 1976, 622ff.); other Iranian languages are after R. Schmitt, Compendium linguarum Iranicarum, 1989, and after D.N. MacKenzie, A Concise Pahlavi Dictionary, ^{3}1990. For Armenian the rules of R. Schmitt, Grammatik des Klassisch-Armenischen, 1981, and of the Revue des études arméniennes, apply. The languages of Asia Minor are transliterated according to HbdOr. For Mycenean, Cyprian see Heubeck and Masson; for Italic scripts and Etruscan see Vetter and ET.

List of Illustrations and Maps

Illustrations are found in the corresponding entries. ND means redrawing following the instructions of the author or after the listed materials.
RP means reproduction with minor changes.

Some of the maps serve to visualize the subject matter and to complement the articles. In such cases, there will be a reference to the corresponding entry. Only literature that was used exclusively for the maps is listed.

Lemma Title AUTHORS Bibliography

List of Authors

Aigner-Foresti, Luciana, Vienna	L. A.-F.
Albiani, Maria Grazia, Bologna	M. G. A.
Alonso-Núñez, José Miguel, Madrid	J. M. A.-N.
Ambühl, Annemarie, Basle	A. A.
Ameling, Walter, Jena	W. A.
Andreau, Jean, Paris	J. A.
Angeli Bertinelli, Maria Gabriella, Genova	M. G. A. B.
Auffarth, Christoph, Tübingen	C. A.
Baatz, Dietwulf, Bad Homburg	D. BA.
Badian, Ernst, Cambridge, MA	E. B.
Baltes, Matthias, Münster	M. BA.
Bär, Jürgen, Berlin	J. BÄ.
Barceló, Pedro, Potsdam	P. B.
Baudy, Dorothea, Konstanz	D. B.
Baumbach, Manuel, Heidelberg	M. B.
Beck, Hans, Cologne	HA. BE.
Belke, Klaus, Vienna	K. BE.
Berger, Albrecht, Berlin	AL. B.
Berschin, Walter, Heidelberg	W. B.
Binder, Vera, Gießen	V. BI.
Birley, A. R., Düsseldorf	A. B.
Blech, Michael, Madrid	M. BL.
Bleckmann, Bruno, Bern	B. BL.
Bloch, René, Princeton, NJ	R. B.
Bobzien, Susanne, Oxford	S. BO.
Böck, Barbara, Berlin	BA. BÖ.
Bonatz, Dominik, Freiburg	DO. BO.
Bonfante, Larissa, New York	L. B.
Bowie, Ewen, Oxford	E. BO.
Brandes, Wolfram, Frankfurt/Main	W. BR.
Brändle, Rudolf, Basle	R. BR.
von Bredow, Iris, Stuttgart	I. v. B.
Brehmer, Bernhard, Tübingen	B. BR.
Bremmer, Jan N., Groningen	J. B.
Brentjes, Burchard, Berlin	B. B.
Briese, Christoph, Randers	CH. B.
Bringmann, Klaus, Frankfurt/Main	K. BR.
Brisson, Luc, Paris	L. BR.
Brock, Sebastian P., Oxford	S. BR.
Brodersen, Kai, Newcastle and Mannheim	K. BRO.
Brown, Christopher, London, Ontario	CH. BR.
Büchli, Jörg, Zürich	J. BÜ.
Burford Cooper, Alison, Ann Arbor	A. B.-C.
Burian, Jan, Prague	J. BU.
Calboli, Gualtiero, Bologna	G. C.
Calboli Montefusco, Lucia, Bologna	L. C. M.
Calmeyer-Seidl, Ursula, Berlin	U. SE.
Campbell, J. Brian, Belfast	J. CA.
Camporeale, Giovannangelo, Florence	GI. C.
Carroll-Spillecke, Maureen, Cologne	M. C.-S.
Cartledge, Paul A., Cambridge	P. C.
Cassin, Barbara, Paris	B. C.
Chaniotis, Angelos, Heidelberg	A. C.
Cholidis, Nadja, Berlin	N. CH.
Christes, Johannes, Berlin	J. C.
Christmann, Eckhard, Heidelberg	E. C.
Clinton, Kevin, Ithaca N. Y.	K. C.
Colbow, Gudrun, Munich	G. CO.
Colpe, Carsten, Berlin	C. C.
Courtney, Edward, Charlottesville, VA	ED. C.
de Libero, Loretana, Hamburg	L. d. L.
Decker, Wolfgang, Cologne	W. D.
Degani, Enzo, Bologna	E. D.
Deißmann-Merten, Marie-Luise, Freiburg	M. D. M.
den Boeft, Jan, Leiderdorp	J. d. B.
Detel, Wolfgang, Frankfurt/Main	W. DE.
Di Marco, Massimo, Fondi (Latina)	M. D. MA.
di Mattia, Margherita, Rome	M. d. M.
Dierichs, Angelika, Münster	AN. DI.
Dietz, Karlheinz, Würzburg	K. DI.
Docter, Roald Frithjof, Gent	R. D.
Domhardt, Yvonne, Zürich	Y. D.
Dominicus, Brigitte, Diersdorf	B. DO.
Dorandi, Tiziano, Paris	T. D.
Döring, Klaus, Bamberg	K. D.
Dörrie †, Heinrich, Münster	H. D.
Dräger, Paul, Trier	P. D.
Drew-Bear, Thomas, Lyon	T. D.-B.
Dreyer, Boris, Göttingen	BO. D.
Duchesne-Guillemin, Jacques, Lüttich	J. D.-G.
Ducrey, Pierre, Lausanne	PI. DU.
Duridanov, Ludmil, Freiburg	L. D.
Eck, Werner, Cologne	W. E.
Eder, Walter, Bochum	W. ED.
Egelhaaf-Gaiser, Ulrike, Gießen	UL. EG.-G.
Ego, Beate, Osnabrück	B. E.
Eigler, Ulrich, Trier	U. E.
Eleuteri, Paolo, Venice	P. E.
Elvers, Karl-Ludwig, Bochum	K.-L. E.
Engelmann, Helmut, Cologne	HE. EN.
Engels, Johannes, Cologne	J. E.
Errington, Robert Malcolm, Marburg/Lahn	MA. ER.
Euskirchen, Marion, Bonn	M. E.
Falco, Giulia, Athens	GI. F.
Fantuzzi, Marco, Florence	M. FA.
Felber, Heinz, Leipzig	HE. FE.
Fell, Martin, Münster	M. FE.
Feucht, Erika, Heidelberg	E. FE.
Flaig, Egon, Greifswald	E. F.
Flamant, Jaques, Venelles	J. F.
Flury †, Peter, Munich	P. FL.
Folkerts, Menso, Munich	M. F.

Fornaro, Sotera, Sassari S. FO.
Forssman, Bernhard, Erlangen B. F.
Förtsch, Reinhard, Cologne R. F.
Frank, Karl Suso, Freiburg K.-S. F.
Franke, Thomas, Bochum T. F.
Frateantonio, Christa, Gießen-Erfurt C. F.
Frede, Dorothea, Hamburg D. FR.
Freis, Helmut, Saarbrücken H. F.
Freitag, Klaus, Münster K. F.
Fröhlich, Roland, Tübingen RO. F.
Funke, Peter, Münster P. F.
Furley, William D., Heidelberg W. D. F.
Fusillo, Massimo, L'Aquila M. FU.
Galsterer, Hartmut, Bonn H. GA.
Gamauf, Richard, Vienna R. GA.
García-Ramón, José Luis, Cologne J. G.-R.
Gargini, Michela, Pisa M. G.
Gärtner, Hans Armin, Heidelberg H. A. G.
Gatti, Paolo, Triento P. G.
Gehrke, Hans-Joachim, Freiburg H.-J. G.
Giaro, Tomasz, Frankfurt/Main T. G.
Giovè Marchioli, Nicoletta, Triest N. G.
Giuffrida, Claudia, Catania C. GIU.
Gizewski, Christian, Berlin C. G.
Gödde, Susanne, Münster S. G.
Gottschalk, Hans, Leeds H. G.
Graf, Fritz, Princeton, NJ F. G.
Grafton, Anthony, Princeton, NJ AN. GR.
Graßl, Herbert, Salzburg H. GR.
Groß-Albenhausen, Kirsten, Frankfurt/Main K. G.-A.
Gruber, Joachim, Erlangen J. GR.
Gschnitzer, Fritz, Heidelberg F. GSCH.
Gulletta, Maria Ida, Pisa M. I. G.
Günther, Linda-Marie, Bochum L.-M. G.
Gutsfeld, Andreas, Münster A. G.
Guyot, Peter, Hildesheim P. GU.
Haas, Volkert, Berlin V. H.
Haase, Mareile, Erfurt M. HAA.
Hadot, Ilsetraut, Limours I. H.
Haebler, Claus, Münster C. H.
Harder, Ruth Elisabeth, Zürich R. HA.
Harmon, Daniel P., Seattle D. P. H.
Hauser, Stefan R., Berlin S. HA.
Heider, Ulrich, Cologne U. HE.
Heinrichs, Johannes, Bonn JO. H.
Heinz, Marlies, Freiburg M. H.
Heinze, Theodor, Geneva T. H.
Herz, Peter, Regensburg P. H.
Hild, Friedrich, Vienna F. H.
Hintze, Almut, Cambridge A. HI.
Höcker, Christoph, Kissing C. HÖ.
Höckmann, Olaf, Mainz O. H.
Hoesch, Nicola, Munich N. H.
Högemann, Peter, Tübingen PE. HÖ.
Hoheisel, Karl, Bonn KA. HO.
Hönle, Augusta, Rottweil A. HÖ.
Hossenfelder, Malte, Graz M. HO.
Hübner, Wolfgang, Münster W. H.
Huff, Dietrich, Berlin D. HU.
Hünemörder, Christian, Hamburg C. HÜ.
Hunger, Hermann, Vienna H. HU.
Hunter, Richard, Cambridge R. HU.
Hurschmann, Rolf, Hamburg R. H.
Huß, Werner, Munich W. HU.
Inwood, Brad, Toronto, ON B. I.
Jameson, Michael, Stanford MI. JA.
Jansen-Winkeln, Karl, Berlin K. J.-W.
Job, Michael, Marburg/Lahn M. J.
Johne, Klaus-Peter, Berlin K. P. J.
Johnston, Sarah Iles, Columbus S. I. J.
Kalcyk, Hansjörg, Petershausen H. KAL.
Kaletsch, Hans, Regensburg H. KA.
Kammerer-Grothaus, Helke, Bremen H. K.-G.
Käppel, Lutz, Kiel L. K.
Karttunen, Klaus, Helsinki K. K.
Kearns, Emily, Oxford E. K.
Kessler, Karlheinz, Emskirchen K. KE.
Kienast, Dietmar, Neu-Esting D. K.
Kierdorf, Wilhelm, Cologne W. K.
King, Helen, Reading H. K.
Klose, Dietrich, Munich DI. K.
Knauf, Ernst Axel, Bern E. A. K.
Köckert, Matthias, Berlin M. K.
Kohler, Christoph, Bad Krozingen C. KO.
Kramolisch, Herwig, Eppelheim HE. KR.
Krampe, Christoph, Bochum C. KR.
Krasser, Helmut, Gießen H. KR.
Krauss, Rolf, Berlin R. K.
Kuchenbuch, Ludolf, Hagen LU. KU.
Kuhn, Christina, Kassel CH. KU.
Kühne, Hartmut, Berlin H. KÜ.
Kuhrt, Amélie, London A. KU.
Kunz, Heike, Tübingen HE. K.
Küppers, Jochem, Düsseldorf J. KÜ.
Kutsch, Ernst, Vienna ER. K.
Kytzler, Bernhard, Durban B. KY.
Lafond, Yves, Bochum Y. L.
Lakmann, Marie-Luise, Münster M.-L. L.
Lange, Armin, Tübingen AR. L.
Latacz, Joachim, Basle J. L.
Le Bohec, Yann, Lyon Y. L. B.
Leisten, Thomas, Princeton, NJ T. L.
Leppin, Hartmut, Frankfurt/Main H. L.
Leschhorn, Wolfgang, Völklingen W. L.
Ley, Anne, Xanten A. L.
Lezzi-Hafter, Adrienne, Kilchberg A. L.-H.
Liebermann, Wolf-Lüder, Bielefeld W.-L. L.
Lienau, Cay, Münster C. L.
von Lieven, Alexandra, Berlin A. v. L.
Link, Stefan, Paderborn S. L.
Lintott, A. W., Oxford A. W. L.
Liwak, Rüdiger, Berlin R. L.
Lohmann, Hans, Bochum H. LO.
Losemann, Volker, Marburg/Lahn V. L.
Lundström, Steven, Berlin S. LU.
Luzzatto, Maria Jagoda, Florence M. J. L.

Macuch, Maria, Berlin	M. MA.	Rathbone, Dominic, London	D. R.
Maharam, Wolfram-Aslan, Munich	W.-A. M.	Redies, Michael, Berlin	M. R.
Manganaro, Giacomo, Sant' Agata li Battiata	GI. MA.	von Reibnitz, Barbara, Basle	B. v. R.
Manthe, Ulrich, Passau	U. M.	Renger, Johannes, Berlin	J. RE.
Marek, Christian, Zürich	C. MA.	Rhodes, Peter J., Durham	P. J. R.
Markschies, Christoph, Heidelberg	C. M.	Richmond, John A., Blackrock, VA	J. A. R.
Martini, Wolfram, Gießen	W. MA.	Riederer, Josef, Berlin	JO. R.
Matthaios, Stephanos, Nikosia	ST. MA.	Riedweg, Christoph, Zürich	C. RI.
Maul, Stefan, Heidelberg	S. M.	Rist, Josef, Würzburg	J. RI.
Mehl, Andreas, Halle/Saale	A. ME.	Rix, Helmut, Freiburg	H. R.
Meier, Mischa, Bielefeld	M. MEI.	Robbins, Emmet, Toronto, ON	E. R.
Meiser, Gerhard, Halle/Saale	GE. ME.	Röllig, Wolfgang, Tübingen	W. R.
Meißner, Burkhard, Halle/Saale	B. M.	Rosenberger, Veit, Augsburg	V. RO.
Meister, Klaus, Berlin	K. MEI.	Rudolph, Kurt, Marburg/Lahn	KU. R.
Michel, Simone, Hamburg	S. MI.	Ruffing, Kai, Marburg/Lahn	K. RU.
Miller, Martin, Berlin	M. M.	Runia, David T., Parkville	D. T. R.
Mlasowsky, Alexander, Hannover	A. M.	Rüpke, Jörg, Erfurt	J. R.
Mohr-Sigel, Dorothea, Tübingen	D. SI.	Sallaberger, Walther, Leipzig	WA. SA.
Mommsen, Heide, Stuttgart	H. M.	Sallares, Robert, Manchester	R. SA.
Montanari, Ornella, Bologna	O. M.	Sallmann, Klaus, Mainz	KL. SA.
Muckensturm-Poulle, Claire, Besançon	C. M.-P.	Salomone Gaggero, Eleonora, Genova	E. S. G.
Müller, Walter W., Marburg/Lahn	W. W. M.	Salzman, Michele Renée, Riverside, Ca	M. SA.
Müller-Kessler, Christa, Emskirchen	C. K.	Sancisi-Weerdenburg, Helen, Utrecht	H. S.-W.
Narcy, Michel, Paris	MI. NA.	Sartori, Antonio, Milan	A. SA.
Naso, Alessandro, Udine	A. NA.	Šašel Kos, Marjeta, Ljubljana	M. Š. K.
Nesselrath, Heinz-Günther, Göttingen	H.-G. NE.	Savvidis, Kyriakos, Bochum	K. SA.
Neudecker, Richard, Rome	R. N.	Sayar, Mustafa H., Cologne	M. H. S.
Neumann, Günter, Münster	G. N.	Schaffner, Brigitte, Basle	B. SCH.
Niehoff, Johannes, Budapest	J. N.	Schaller, Bernd, Göttingen	BE. SCH.
Nielsen, Inge, Hamburg	I. N.	Schanbacher, Dietmar, Dresden	D. SCH.
Niemeyer, Hans Georg, Hamburg	H. G. N.	Schaus, Gerald P., Waterloo, Ontario	G. P. S.
Nissen, Hans Jörg, Berlin	H. J. N.	Scheer, Tanja, Rome	T. S.
Nünlist, René, Providence, RI	RE. N.	Scheibler, Ingeborg, Krefeld	I. S.
Nutton, Vivian, London	V. N.	Scherf, Johannes, Tübingen	JO. S.
Oettinger, Norbert, Augsburg	N. O.	Scheuer, Hans Jürgen, Göttingen	HA. J. S.
Olshausen, Eckart, Stuttgart	E. O.	Schiemann, Gottfried, Tübingen	G. S.
Onken, Björn, Kassel	BJ. O.	Schindler, Claudia, Tübingen	C. SCHI.
Osborne, Robin, Oxford	R. O.	Schmidt, Ernst-Günther, Leipzig	E.-G. S.
Oswald, Renate, Graz	R. OS.	Schmidt, Margot, Basle	MA. SCH.
Padgett, J. Michael, Princeton	M. P.	Schmidt, Peter Lebrecht, Konstanz	P. L. S.
Pahlitzsch, Johannes, Berlin	J. P.	Schmitt-Pantel, Pauline, Paris	P. S.-P.
Palermo, Dario, Catania	DA. P.	Schmitz, Winfried, Bielefeld	W. S.
Pappa, Anna, Ioannina	A. P.	Schneider, Helmuth, Kassel	H. SCHN.
Pappalardo, Umberto, Naples	U. PA.	Schnelle, Udo, Halle/Saale	U. SCHN.
Paulus, Christoph Georg, Berlin	C. PA.	Scholz, Udo W., Würzburg	U. W. S.
Pekridou-Gorecki, Anastasia, Frankfurt/Main	A. P.-G.	Schön, Franz, Regensburg	F. SCH.
Pera, Rossella, Genova	R. PE.	Schönbeck, Hans-Peter, Halle/Saale	H.-P. S.
Petraccia Lucernoni, Maria Federica, Milan	M. F. P. L.	Schönig, Hanne, Halle/Saale	H. SCHÖ.
Pingel, Volker, Bochum	V. P.	Schottky, Martin, Pretzfeld	M. SCH.
Plath, Robert, Erlangen	R. P.	Schulte-Altedorneburg, Jörg, Marburg/Lahn	J. S.-A.
Platz-Horster, Gertrud, Berlin	G. PL.	Schulzki, Heinz-Joachim, Freudenstadt	H.-J. S.
Plontke-Lüning, Annegret, Jena	A. P.-L.	Schürmann, Astrid, Mannheim	AS. S.
Pollmann, Karla, St. Andrews	K. P.	Schwarcz, Andreas, Vienna	A. SCH.
Portmann, Werner, Berlin	W. P.	Schwemer, Anna Maria, Tübingen	A. M. S.
Prayon, Friedhelm, Tübingen	F. PR.	Schwertheim, Elmar, Münster	E. SCH.
Prescendi, Francesca, Geneva	FR. P.	Schwindt, Jürgen Paul, Bielefeld	J. P. S.
Pressler, Frank, Freiburg	F. P.	Schyboll, Achim, Schliengen	ACH. S.
Raaflaub, Kurt A., Rhode Island	K. RA.	Seidlmayer, Stephan Johannes, Berlin	S. S.

Selzer, Christoph, Frankfurt/Main	C.S.
Senff, Reinhard, Bochum	R.SE.
Siebert, Anne Viola, Hannover	A.V.S.
Smolak, Kurt, Vienna	K.SM.
Sonnabend, Holger, Stuttgart	H.SO.
Spickermann, Wolfgang, Bochum	W.SP.
Stahlmann, Ines, Berlin	I.ST.
Stanzel, Karl-Heinz, Tübingen	K.-H.S.
Stegmann, Helena, Bonn	H.S.
Stein-Hölkeskamp, Elke, Cologne	E.S.-H.
Steinbauer, Dieter, Regensburg	D.ST.
Steinhart, Matthias, Freiburg	M.ST.
Strauch, Daniel, Berlin	D.S.
Streck, Michael P., Munich	M.S.
Strobel, Karl, Klagenfurt	K.ST.
Strothmann, Meret, Bochum	ME.STR.
Stumpf, Gerd, Munich	GE.S.
Talbert, Richard, Chapel Hill, NC	RI.T.
Thür, Gerhard, Graz	G.T.
Thüry, Günther E., Salzburg	G.TH.
Tinnefeld, Franz, Munich	F.T.
Todd, Malcolm, Exeter	M.TO.
Tomaschitz, Kurt, Vienna	K.T.
Toral-Niehoff, Isabel, Freiburg	I.T.-N.
Tosi, Renzo, Bologna	R.T.
Touwaide, Alain, Madrid	A.TO.
Treidler, Hans, Berlin	H.T.
Uggeri, Giovanni, Florence	G.U.
Umbach, Kathrin, Kassel	K.UM.
Ungefähr-Kortus, Claudia, Alten-Buseck	C.U.-K.
von Ungern-Sternberg, Jürgen, Basle	J.v.U.-S.
Uthemann, Karl-Heinz, Amsterdam	K.U.
van Wickevoort Crommelin, Bernhard, Hamburg	B.v.W.C.
Vassis, Ioannis, Athens	I.V.
Veigel, Isabell, Berlin	IS.V.
Versnel, Hendrik S., Warmond	H.V.
Visser, Edzard, Basle	E.V.
Voß, Wulf Eckart, Osnabrück	W.E.V.
Wachter, Rudolf, Heidelberg	R.WA.
Wagner, Jörg, Tübingen	J.WA.
Wagner-Hasel, Beate, Darmstadt	B.W.-H.
Walde, Christine, Basle	C.W.
Waldner, Katharina, Erfurt	K.WA.
Walser †, Gerold, Basle	G.W.
Wandrey, Irina, Berlin	I.WA.
Wartke, Ralf-B., Berlin	R.W.
Wehgartner, Irma, Würzburg	I.W.
Weiß, Peter, Kiel	P.W.
Weißenberger, Michael, Greifswald	M.W.
Welwei, Karl-Wilhelm, Bochum	K.-W.WEL.
Wiegels, Rainer, Osnabrück	RA.WI.
Wierschowski, Lothar, Oldenburg	L.WI.
Wiesehöfer, Josef, Kiel	J.W.
Will, Wolfgang, Bonn	W.W.
Willvonseder, Reinhard, Vienna	R.WI.
Wirbelauer, Eckhard, Freiburg	E.W.
Wittke, Anne-Maria, Tübingen	A.W.
Wülfing, Peter, Cologne	P.WÜ.
Wyrwa, Dietmar, Bochum	D.W.
Zahrnt, Michael, Kiel	M.Z.
Zaminer, Frieder, Berlin	F.Z.
Ziegler, Sabine, Würzburg	S.ZI.
Ziegler †, Konrat, Göttingen	K.Z.
Zimmermann, Bernhard, Freiburg	B.Z.
Zingg, Reto, Basle	RE.ZI.

Equisetum Because of their mode of growth, since antiquity four different leafless or small-leaved species of plant bear the name *equisetum, equisaeta, cauda equina* or *caballina*, ἱπποχαίτη (*hippochaítē*) or ἵππουρις (*híppouris*), horsetail or mare's-tail. This is true of: *Equisetum L.* and *Hippochaete Milde*, equisetum, shave grass or scouring rush; of *Ephedra L.*, ἔφεδρον (*éphedron*) or ἵππουρις, the jointfir members of the *Gymnospermae*, some of them climbers; also of water-plants in the case of the candelabra alga *Chara*, still called *E. foetidum* in the 16th cent. by C. BAUHIN; finally of *Hippuris L.*, mare's-tail. Plin. HN 26,132 recommends a broth of *equisaetum* for swellings of the spleen in runners. He reports its use for the stemming of bleeding (26,133). Dioscorides (4,46 [1. 203f.] and [2. 388f.]) prescribes the juice to be drunk as a remedy against haemorrhage and dysentery, and describes it as a diuretic.

1 WELLMANN, 2 2 BERENDES. C.HÜ.

Equites Romani
A. DEFINITION B. KINGDOM AND EARLY REPUBLIC C. MIDDLE AND LATE REPUBLIC D. PRINCIPATE

A. DEFINITION
The term *equites Romani* (*ER*) originally described the mounted contingent of the Roman citizenry; in the course of the history of the Republic it came to denote the second rank (*ordo*) after that of the senators; it thus concerned citizens from whom mounted service was no longer required, but who were definitely entitled to serve as officers in the army. This evolutionary process is not clearly described in any of the sources, and is at present the subject of some controversy.

B. KINGDOM AND EARLY REPUBLIC
Later Roman authors tell us that equestrians in the early period were called *celeres* or *trossuli* (Plin. HN 33,35–36). Livy numbers them at 300 (1,15,8). When, according to Roman tradition, Servius Tullius organized the *comitia centuriata*, he is said to have created 18 → *centuriae*, in which citizens of the highest census class were enrolled (Liv. 1,43,9; Dion. Hal. Ant. Rom. 4,18,1; 4,20,3). Six of these *centuriae* were named after the original *tribus* of the Ramnes, Titienses and Luceres, and termed the *sex suffragia* (Cic. Rep. 2,36; 2,39; Liv. 1,36,2; 1,36,7–8; Fest. 452). The senators and their sons are supposed to have served and voted in these six *centuriae*. The *equites* were provided with money for the purchase of a horse (hence the term *equus publicus*); they further received from widows an annual contribution to pay for the horse's fodder: the so-called *aes equestre* and *aes hordiarium* (Liv. 1,43,9; Fest. 71,91). The complicated structure of the *comitia centuriata*, falsely ascribed by tradition to Servius Tullius, was at any rate valid for the Roman army of the 4th cent. BC. With the growth of the Roman population, we should expect an increase in the number of equestrian *centuriae* in line with that of the 170 *centuriae* of foot-soldiers. According to Polybius (2,24,14), evidently based on census in 225 BC the equestrian forces of Rome and Campania comprised 23,000 men in all, of whom some 3,000 came from Campania. Researchers assume that the majority of the remaining 20,000 equestrians were not members of the 18 equestrian centuries, as membership of these was linked to the *aes equestre*, which was granted only to a small number of citizens: Cato postulated that no more than 2,200 equestrians should receive the *aera equestria* (ORF 8, fr. 85–86). Accordingly, up until 225 BC most equestrians were probably not provided with an *equus publicus*, but had to buy and maintain their own horse. The few indications that equestrians served *equis suis* or *equis privatis* (with one's own horse), however, relate to special circumstances, and cannot be generally applied (Liv. 5,7,5; 27,11,14–15).

C. MIDDLE AND LATE REPUBLIC
After the Second Punic War, the military significance of the Roman cavalry diminished greatly, as now increasing recourse could be had to the more effective contingents of Numidian, Spanish and Gaulish riders. But, especially in the late Republic, Roman citizens still provided mounted military service, for the most part as officers or on special service (Sall. Iug. 65,4; Cic. Planc. 32; Caes. B. Gall. 1,42,6; 7,65,5). During this period, the *equites* acquired greater self-confidence as an *ordo*, clearly distinguished from the Senate and senators. One reason for this was the rise of the → *publicani*, whose leading figures were *equites* (Liv. 43,16,1–4; Cic. Planc. 32; Cic. Rab. Post. 3); another was their active participation as *iudices* in the *quaestiones perpetuae* (judges in the permanent courts of law), either to the exclusion of senators or in conjunction with them (Plin. HN 33,34; CIL I[2] 583, 13ff.; Cic. Verr. 1,38): their high social standing also found expression in the post-Sullan period in the *lex Roscia* (67 BC), which allotted the first 14 rows at the theatre to the *equites* (Hor. Epist. 1,57–67); this measure was later confirmed by the *lex Iulia theatralis* of Augustus (Plin. HN 33,32). The census for *equites* at a level of 400,000 sesterces is also mentioned for the first time in association with the Augustan statute, although a census at that level for the *ordo equester* is probable at the latest for the period after the Second Punic War (Liv. 24,11,7). In any case, wealth of that order was only a necessary condition for enrolment in the 18 equestrian centuries, and by no means a sufficient one. The high standing of the ER still resided in the fact that physical and moral aptitude was a primary consideration for enrolment by the *censor*; it could also

depend on family origin (Cic. Planc. 32; Nep. Att. 1,1): this was important, esp. for young men who were still in *patria potestas* and had no wealth of their own.

It is not possible to determine precisely the legal status of the *equites* and the relationship between the *ordo equester* and the *ordo senatorius* for the period of the late Republic; the initial difficulty lies in interpreting Cicero's brief remark (Cic. Rep. 4,2) about the *plebiscitum reddendorum equorum* (129 BC). The text is generally understood to mean that this law required senators to relinquish their *equus publicus*. The term *ER equo publico* continued to be used in the late Republic (Cic. Phil. 6,13). The prevailing opinion since MOMMSEN is that, besides the small group of *equites equo publico*, which comprised the 18 equestrian centuries, there was also a larger group of Roman citizens who, on grounds of wealth, were permitted to serve on horseback and were called *ER*. NICOLET [3] has it that only the *equites equo publico* were real *ER*, and the others had the status of *equites* only for census purposes (Cic. Q. Rosc. 42). A third possibility is that the *ER* are to be understood as including all the *equites* of the equestrian centuries, while *equites equo publico* refers to a more precisely defined group within the centuries. It is in any case clear that the term *ER*, as well as being used for those who were registered as *equites* in the civic lists, also referred to citizens who, while not being registered as *equites*, could demonstrate a degree of wealth corresponding to the census for *equites*. Cicero accordingly regards the *tribuni aerarii* in the courts of the late Republic as *equites*.

Although many *equites* during the late Republic participated in commercial activities and in the *societates publicorum*, and lent money on a large scale, their role in society cannot adequately be described on the exclusive basis of such activities; nor may an economic contrast be constructed in this way between *equites* and senators. *Equites* in the same way as senators were very often large-scale landowners, and their estates were a necessary basis for many of their commercial activities. Thus Sex. Roscius Amerinus possessed 13 estates on the Tiber (Cic. S. Rosc. 20), and T. Pomponius Atticus, too, had large estates in Italy and Epirus (Nep. Att. 14,3).

D. PRINCIPATE

Augustus sought to cope with the problems of the late Republic, and in particular the marked increase in the number of citizens qualifying for the equestrian census, by reinforcing the prestige of the *equites equo publico*, who now numbered 5,000 (Dion. Hal. Ant. Rom. 16,13,4; Plin. HN 33,31; Suet. Aug. 38,3), especially by the expedient of public ceremonies such as the *transvectio* on 15 July of each year. *IIIviri* were also appointed to review the list of *ER*. In the lists of jurors, the *equites equo publico* were distinguished from the other *equites* (Tabula Hebana 8,11–12,57). In a statute of AD 23, Tiberius attempted to redefine the right of the *equites* to wear the golden ring. This right, alongside the privilege of occupying the first 14 rows at the theatre, was accorded to those who could demonstrate free descent for three generations and wealth of 400,000 HS (Plin. HN 33,32). During the early Principate, the political significance of the *ordo equester* increased appreciably. One reason for this was the high number of individuals who could lay claim to the rank of an *eques*; Strabo (3,5,3; 5,1,7) informs us that 500 *equites* lived in Gades and Patavium respectively. *Equites* not only served as officers in the army, but also took on important positions in the administration of the Imperium Romanum; as procurators, they had responsibility for the possessions and finances of the *princeps*, and they could become *praefectus Aegypti* or praetorian prefect. Although there was no established career ladder for *equites*, as a rule they progressed from the ranks of the military and relatively modest civil posts to higher positions commanding corresponding levels of remuneration. During the 3rd cent. AD, all the higher ranks in the Roman army and many posts in the civilian administration that had previously been the preserve of senators were opened up to *equites*; their importance was underlined by titles such as *vir eminentissimus*.

1 G. ALFÖLDY, Die Stellung der Ritter in der Führungsschicht des Imperium Romanum, in: ALFÖLDY, RG, 162–209 2 P. A. BRUNT, The Equites in the Late Republic, in: Id., The Fall of the Roman Republic, 1988, 144–193 3 C. NICOLET, L'ordre équestre à l'époque républicaine, 1966 4 H. G. PFLAUM, Les carrières procuratoriennes équestres sous le Haut-Empire romain, 1960/1 (Supplement, 1987) 5 A. STEIN, Der röm. Ritterstand, ein Beitrag zur Sozial- und Personengeschichte des röm. Reiches, 1927 6 T. P. WISEMAN, The Definition of 'Eques Romanus' in the Late Republic and Early Empire, in: Historia 19, 1970, 67–83. A.W.L.

Equites singulares From the 2nd cent. BC at the latest, Roman commanders had an elite unit composed of mounted troops and foot soldiers, its members drawn from the contingents of the Italian *socii*, as was the case with the → *extraordinarii*. Towards the end of the Republic the elite units were recruited from the → *auxilia*; it is unknown whether these, too, had a particular name. Similar units appear to have existed at the beginning of the Principate. During the German campaign of Germanicus (AD 11–14), Fabricius Tuscus commanded an *ala praetoria*, by which is probably meant the commander's elite mounted troop. During the course of the 1st cent. AD, the term *singulares* came into use to describe such units: an *ala singularium* is attested for the year AD 70 (Tac. Hist. 4,70,2); this unit had probably already been constituted under the *principes* from the Julio-Claudian family.

The function of the *equites singulares* (*ES*) – as also that of the *pedites singulares* – was to protect holders of high office in the provinces (i.a. provincial governors of consular or praetorian rank, the *praefectus Aegypti*, proconsuls, legionary legates, procurators exercising the functions of a governor, as well as city prefects, praetorian prefects and tribunes of the praetorian cohorts). They formed part of the elite unit that was stationed at the governor's residency in the capital city of a province and accompanied the governor as he carried out the duties of his office; they could also perform the function of a police force, and individual *ES* also delivered diplomatic dispatches. On campaigns, the *ES* escorted the commander and at the same time served as a tactical unit of the army.

Provincial governors recruited *ES* from the ranks of the *alae* and cohorts of the provincial *auxilia*, or, if they were administering a province without standing troops, from those of a neighbouring province; a soldier serving as a *singularis* continued to be registered in his original unit, and might very well return to it subsequently. The size of units of the *ES* varied. In provinces where one or more legions were stationed, a unit could probably be equal in size to the *alae*, while in other circumstances the *ES* were made up of far smaller units. The *ES* were commanded by a legionary centurion with the title *praepositus* or *curam agens*, or, in provinces where no legions were stationed, perhaps by a *decurio*.

The *ES* bore the same weapons as the mounted troops of the *auxilia* (Jos. BI 3,96–97); they neither had a particular rank nor received additional payment. Nevertheless, great prestige was associated with service as *eques singularis*. Upon returning to their units, *singulares* were normally not promoted; some, however, advanced to becoming *decurio* or *centurio* of *auxilia* in their province.

The units of the *ES* were well-trained and well-led troops. They might be sent to other provinces if the military situation required it. Thus in the 2nd and 3rd cents. AD the *ES* from Moesia Superior were sent to Mauretania (CIL VIII 3050). If the *ES* remained for some time in their new posting, they could become regarded as an independent unit; in some cases a new, permanent *ala* of auxiliaries was formed from an old unit of *ES*, as with the *ala I Ulpia singularium* constituted by Trajan and long stationed in Syria during the 2nd cent. AD (ILS 9471). There is however no clear indication that the *ES* were a kind of tactical mobile reserve, and thus forerunners of the regular field army of the 4th cent. The *ES* still existed in late antiquity, although their function appears to have changed: they practically became civil officials.

The *ES Augusti* were the mounted unit of the personal bodyguard of the *princeps*; this unit was probably formed under the Flavians with a strength of 500 men, later to be increased to 1,000. The *ES Augusti* were recruited from auxiliary *alae* throughout the empire, but Germans and Pannonians predominated. They were stationed in Rome, where they eventually had their own camp (ILS 2180–2214).

→ Ala; → Auxilia; → Extraordinarii; → Cavalry

1 P. A. Brunt, C. Fabricius Tuscus and an Augustan Dilectus, in: ZPE 13, 1974, 161–185 2 M. Speidel, Die ES Augusti, 1965 3 Id., Guards of the Roman Armies, 1978.

J.CA.

Equitius. Relatively rare Roman family name (for derivation: Varro, Rust. 2,1,10).

[1] **E., L.** Adventurer of uncertain origins, who in 102 BC represented himself as the son of the people's tribune Ti. → Sempronius Gracchus, killed in 133. He was acknowledged neither by the censor, Q. Caecilius [I 30] Metellus Numidicus, nor by the sister of Gracchus. As a follower of L. Ap(p)uleius [I 11] Saturninus, in 100 he stood for the post of people's tribune for 99, but was himself killed during the unrest that led to the death of Appuleius.

J. Lea Beness, T. W. Hillard, The Death of L. Equitius on 10. December 100 B.C., in: CQ N.S. 40, 1990, 269–272; B. L. Twyman, The Day Equitius Died, in: Athenaeum N.S. 67, 1989, 493–499.

K.-L.E.

[2] Flavius E. came from Pannonia. In AD 364 he was *tribunus scholae primae scutariorum*, and after the death of Iovianus for a time imperial candidate. He was then loyal to Valentinian I, in 364 became *comes rei militaris per Illyricum* and in 365 *comes et magister utriusque militum per Illyricum* (Amm. Marc. 26,1,4; 1,6; 5,3; 5,10f.; Cod. Theod. 7,1,8). He was engaged in strengthening frontier defences in the north (ILS 762; 774f.). Although he had enjoyed little success against the Quadi in 373 (Amm. Marc. 30,6,2), he became consul (with Gratian) in 374. With Merobaudes, in 375 he was instrumental in the army in obtaining the acclamation of Valentinian II as emperor ([Aur. Vict.] Epit. Caes. 45,10; Zos. 4,19). PLRE 1, 282 E. (2).

W.P.

Equizeto Town in *Mauretania Sitifensis*, at a road junction south-west of Sitifis: the modern Ouled-Agla or Lecourbe; in Tab. Peut. 2,1 referred to as *Equeheto*. The town was a *municipium* by the time of Alexander Severus at the latest [1. 567 no. 29]. Inscr.: CIL VIII 2, 8810–8825; 9045; 10427–10430; Suppl. 3, 20606; Suppl. 4, 22658,5.

1 Bull. Archéologique du Comité des Travaux Historiques, 1897.

AAAlg, folio 15, no. 91.

W.HU.

Equus see → Constellations

Equus October (*October equus*). A chariot race was held every year on the Ides of October on the → Campus Martius in Rome (Fest. 190 L.; Plut. Quaest. Rom. 97), and the right-hand horse of the victorious team (but cf. [2]) killed. The horse's head was (previously?) wrapped in bread (*panibus*) or – if we follow the conjecture in [5] – with cloths (*pannibus*). After the animal had been killed with spears, the inhabitants of the Roman quarters of Via Sacra and Subura fought for the head, which was then either carried to the → Regia (Via Sacra) or hung from the *turris Mamilia* (Subura), while the tail (euphemism for the genitalia?) was cut off and carried to the Regia, so that the blood could drip onto a hearth (Paul. Fest. 246 L.).

Details and attributions of its significance to priests remain obscure. Even in antiquity, several interpretations were suggested: (1) commemoration of the fall of Troy or revenge for the Greek subterfuge of the wooden horse (Timaeus of Tauromenium, FGrH 566 F 36); (2) sacrifice to → Mars, the god of war (cf. Fest. 190 L.); (3) association with the growth of the crops (see Paul. Fest. 246 L.).

1 C. AMPOLO, La città arcaica e le sue feste. Due ricerche sul Septimontium e l'Equus October, in: Archeologia laziale 4, 1981, 233–240 2 F. COARELLI, Il campo Marzio, vol. 1, 1997, 61–73 3 G. DEVEREUX, The Equus October Ritual Reconsidered, in: Mnemosyne 23, 1970, 297–301 4 G. RADKE, October equus, in: Latomus 49, 1990, 343–351 5 U.W. SCHOLZ, Studien zum altital. Marskult und Marsmythos, 1970, 89–167. A.V.S.

Er (Ἤρ; *Êr*). From Pamphylia; the son of Armenius; subject of the eschatological myth in Plat. (Resp. 10,614b ff.): having fallen in war, E. was discovered undecayed after 10 days; when on the 12th day he was about to be burned on the pyre, he came back from the afterlife and, as he had been instructed, reported on his descent or *katabasis* to the Underworld, with the court of the dead, punishments and rewards, the spindle of Ananke, the casting of lots by Lachesis. Ancient tradition already associates the E. myth with the Orient: in Clem. Al. (Strom. 5,14,103,2ff.) and Procl. (in Pl. Resp. 2,109,7ff. KROLL) E. is replaced by Zoroaster, but this relates to a polemic tendency, going back to Aristoxenus of Tarentum and Colotes, to characterize Plato as a plagiarist dependent on the Orient; Plato's sources perhaps include Pythagorean (not Orphic) conceptions as well as folklore [1. 137ff.; 2. 195, 248; 1. 307,1]. Association with the legend handed down by 9th-cent. Armenian historians (Moses Chorenaçi, Ps.-Agathangelus), telling the story of the Armenian king Ara, son of Aram, whom Semiramis desires in vain, kills in battle and in vain tries to bring back to life by means of demons [1. 138ff.; 3. 658f.; 4. 243ff.] is unclear; but Plato could be using the oriental name E. (Suda s.v.E.; Lc 3,28) and the marginal Pamphylians (instead of Armenians) to indicate the 'folkloric' (πᾶσι φύλοις) and 'fantastic' aspect of his myth ([5. 108]; otherwise [1. 138ff.]).
→ Ananke; → Elysium; → Afterlife, concepts of; → Katabasis; → Moira; → Pamphylia; → Semiramis; → Underworld; → Zoroaster

1 J. KERSCHENSTEINER, Platon und der Orient, 1945 2 WILAMOWITZ 2 3 J. MARQUART, Beiträge zur Gesch. und Sage von Eran, in: ZDMG 49, 1895, 628–672 4 K. KERÉNYI, Die griech.-oriental. Roman-Lit. in rel.-gesch. Beleuchtung, [3]1973 5 K. REINHARDT, Platons Mythen, 1927. P.D.

Erannoboas (Ἐραννοβόας; *Erannobóas*). Tributary of the Ganges according to Arr. Ind. 4,3 and Plin. HN 6,65; Middle Indian Hiraññāha, another name for Śoṇa, the modern Son; although the latter is mentioned separately by both authors as Sonus (Σῶνος; *Sônos*). Ancient Palibothra/Pāṭaliputra was situated at the confluence of the Son and the Ganges. K.K.

Eranos (ἔρανος; *éranos*). Etymology uncertain; the word originally meant 'a meal for friends' (Hom. Od., Pind.). The cost was borne in common by the participants. Collections made among friends in order to present a gift to one of them were also called *éranoi*; to give gifts in return was merely customary, not a statutory obligation (Theophr. Char. 17,9). Two legal institutions developed on this basis:

[1] A kind of collective wealth. Funds (*eisphoraí*) collected by a group of individuals (*plērōtaí*, Dem. Or. 21,184f.) were applied to a particular purpose (payment of a fine, payment of a ransom, purchase out of slavery) in favour of a beneficiary. The fund was named after the initiator of its collection: this was often the beneficiary himself. The funds were transferred to the beneficiary purely as an interest-free loan for the purpose stipulated; the members of the fund could take an action for return of the amount (but see Pl. Leg. 11,915e).

[2] A particular type of private association was also called *eranos*; see → Associations.
→ Loan

A. BISCARDI, Diritto greco antico, 1982, 157; H.-A. RUPPRECHT, Unt. zum Darlehen im Recht der graeco-ägypt. Papyri, 1967, 3f.; Id., Einführung in die Papyruskunde, 1994, 118f. G.T.

Eraricus, Erarich (Ἐράριχος; *Eráríchos*). A Rugian, AD 541 king of the Ostrogoths in succession to Ildibad. Officially, E. negotiated with Justinian a withdrawal of the Goths to the region north of the Po, but secretly he offered to abandon the whole of Italy in return for a large sum of money and the status of *patricius*. While his ambassadors were still negotiating, E. was eliminated after having reigned for only five months; his successor was Totila (Procop. Goth. 3,2; Jord. Rom. 378f.; Chron. min. 2,106f. MOMMSEN). M.MEI. and ME.STR.

Eras

A. DEFINITION AND ORIGIN B. CALCULATION C.1 'DYNASTIC' ERAS C.2 LOCAL ERAS OF THE HELLENISTIC PERIOD C.3 ERAS OF THE ROMAN PERIOD

A. DEFINITION AND ORIGIN

The term era describes a regular, continuous series of years beginning from a generally recognized starting point (epoch). Unlike dating based on → eponyms and the counting of the years of a reign (see below), as required for lists of officials or of rulers, knowledge of the year as counted within an epoch makes the conversion of year-numbers possible. The etymology of the word era is disputed (perhaps from the pl. of *aes* with change of declension). In Spanish inscriptions *aera* or *era* (ἔρα; *éra*) appears as a synonym for *anno* accompanying numbers of Spanish eras, but to describe the sequence of years it is not used until Isid. Orig. 5,36,4 [4.77f.; 9. 374–376]. Inscriptions, coins, weights and more rarely papyri are frequently dated according to 'political' eras based on political-historical events. 'Literary', 'scholarly' or 'astronomical' eras on the other hand (e.g. the dating of Olympiads, Roman reckonings of time *ab urbe condita*, the era of Nabonassar) are infrequently to be found in public documents. 'Sacral' eras, invented by chronographers and theologians for the dating of biblical events, were not used in official dating until late on (e.g. 'Byzantine Creation Era' from 1.9.5009 BC, Christian Era) [3. 207–226; 10. 189–194, 250–253].

Eras arose from the system of dating according to years reigned (already early on in Egypt and Mesopotamia), adopted from the Achaemenid and Phoenician kings by Alexander the Great (subsequently also used under Philip III/V, the Ptolemies, the Attalids, the Cappadocian, Paphlagonian, Galatian and Jewish kings) [6. 12–21]. The first dynastic era (see below) was the 'Seleucid Era', created when the successors of Seleucus I continued his system of counting the Babylonian satrapal years. As eras are associated with regular, set years, the first local eras also arose in places where the length of the year was regulated by the standard Babylonian cycle (→ Time-reckoning). Supposed early eras, which have been inferred from the numbers on coins at Tyre (era of Azemilcus 349/8?), Sidon (era of Abdalonymus 333/ 2?), Akko (era of Alexander 332/1) and Messana in Sicily (5th cent.), are disputed [6.10].

B. Calculation

The exact starting date of an era depends on the local → calendar. As eras were usually introduced some time after the political event from which they were reckoned, either the previous or the following New Year's Day could be defined as the beginning of Year 1. Only rarely does the epochal year correspond exactly to a Julian year. Thus when converting dates dual year-numbers (e.g. 6/5) should normally be given, having regard for possible alterations of the calendar in the Roman period. The conversion formula for the BC period is: epochal year (given below) – year-number + 1 (in reckoning across the change from BC to AD the 1 is omitted); in the AD period: epochal year + year-number – 1.

C.1 'Dynastic' eras

The most widely applied was the Seleucid era, to be reckoned in the western Seleucid kingdom and in the Greek cities (with New Year in autumn) from 312/11, in the east (Babylonian calendar with New Year in spring) from 311/10. Inscriptions and coins of the Seleucids and local coins of Greek cities are dated according to this, in some instances until the 3rd cent. AD (Akko-Ptolemais, Alexandria/Troad, Antioch, Apamea, Ascalon, Berytus, Byblos, Damascus, Emesa, Laodicea ad mare, Orthosia, Seleucia Pieria, Tripolis etc.), inscriptions into the Middle Ages in Syria (Apamea, Damascus, Dura-Europus, Emesa, Hatra, Cyrrhestice, Orthosia, Palmyra, Tripolis etc.), less often in Palestine, Arabia, Commagene, Asia Minor (e.g. in the Pontic kingdom), coins of the kings of Characene and Elymaeis as well as coins and documents of the Parthian kingdom [2. 781f.; 6. 22–43; 7. 53–57].

The Seleucid era was imitated by the Parthian 'Arsacid era' from 248/7 (Greek-Maced.) or 247/6 (Babylon.) [2. 782], by the Bithynian royal era from 297/6 (from 149/8 on coins), by the Pontic royal era of Mithridates VI from 297/6 (from 96/5 on coins; also the 'era of the conquest of Asia' from 89/8). The Pontic era was adopted in the Bosporan kingdom under Mithridates VI (on coins and in inscriptions until the 5th cent.) [6. 44–64]. Eras of the Indo-Bactrian kings and the Sacae [13. 494–502], as well as the Sassanid era from AD 226/7 (only in Syrian texts), are disputed [2. 783; 3. 210f.].

C.2 Local eras of the Hellenistic period

Eastern cities relinquished earlier modes of dating and dated 'freedom eras' from the deposition of local kings (cf. 'era of the people' in Phoenician inscriptions), thus Tyre 275/4, Sidon mid 3rd cent. BC, Citium/ Cyprus 311/10, Lapethus/Cyprus 307/6 [14]; or from the winning of autonomy and freedom from Seleucid or Ptolemaean overlordship, thus Aradus and its allies Marathus, Balanea, Paltus, Carne, Simyra, Gabala 259/8, Perge, Sillyon, Aspendus and Phaselis 221/0 or a little later, Ariassus/Pisidia 189/8?, again Tyre 126/5, Sidon 112/11, Seleucia Pieria 109/8, Tripolis *c.* 105–95, Ascalon 104/3, Laodicea ad mare and Berytus 81/0. Akko-Ptolemais in the Roman period remembered its re-foundation as Antioch by means of an era beginning in 174/3, just as in the mid 1st cent. BC Apamea, Bithynion, Nicaea, Nicomedia, Prusa and Tios commemorated their incorporation into the kingdom of Bithynia in 282/1 with an era [6. 191–197, 390–392; 11; 12]. Local eras are restricted to the territory of the particular city; eras seldom migrate to neighbouring communities. Multiple datings according to different eras (up to four) are attested, especially in the Roman period.

C.3 Eras of the Roman period

Many Greek cities (probably independently of Roman influence) began eras from their incorporation into the Roman realm. Not 'provincial eras', but local eras with differing epochal years are the 'Pompeian era' in Syria, Phoenicia and Judaea with the epochal years 66/5 (Antioch, Apamea, Arethusa), 64/3 (Abila, Byblos?, Dion?, Dora?, Gadara, Hippus, Canatha?, Nysa-Scythopolis, Orthosia, Tripolis?), 63/2 (Akko-Ptolemais?, Gerasa, Pella, Philadelphia) and 61/0 (Gaba?, Gaza, Raphia; tentatively Botrys, Chalcis and Demetrias) [7. 74–135; 11; 12], in Bithynia-Pontus the 'Lucullan era' from 71/0 (Abonutichus, Amastris, Sinope), the 'inner Paphlagonian era' from 6/5 (Gangra, Caesarea, Neoclaudiopolis, Pompeiopolis), the era of Amasea and Sebastopolis (3/2 BC), Comana (AD 34/5), Cerasus, Neocaesarea, Sebaste, Trapezus and Zela (64/5), Nicopolis (71/2); in the east the eras of Samosata (*c.* 71/2) and Edessa (213/14). Only in Macedonia (148/7), Mauretania (AD 40) and Arabia with Adraa, Bostra, Medaba, Petra, Rabbathmoba (106/7) [7. 146–304] do we find unified 'provincial eras' dating from the foundation of the province; also in Galatia (25/4), except in Tavion (21/0), but not in Asia (only local freedom eras from 134/3 on coins from Ephesus and Sardis?). The 'Sullan era' (85/4) was established in Lydia, Phrygia, eastern Caria, Mysia, Ilium and the area around Cibyra after Sulla's Mithridatic War [3. 213 f.; 6]. It remains unclear whether inscriptions from the Peloponnese (Aegina, Andania, Argos, Epidaurus, Corone, Lycosura, Mantinea, Megalopolis, Pagae, etc.) are dated according to the Macedonian era (148/7) or an Achaean era (*c.* 146 BC).

Multiple changes in Roman rulers, their administrative measures and grants of autonomy led in the 1st cent. BC to numerous new eras either replacing former eras or (on political grounds) amending them in the short term: the 'Pompeian era' only in the Near East (see above) and Cilicia (new settlements at Alexandria, Epiphaneia and Mopsus in 68/7, at Mallus in 67/6; re-foundation of Soli-Pompeiopolis 66/5) [15], perhaps in Berenice/Cyrenaica (68/7); the 'Caesarean era' after the battle of Pharsalus in Antioch/Syria (49/8), Akko-Ptolemais (49/8), Laodicea/Syr. (48/7), Ephesus with the Caystrus valley (48/7), Apollonis/Lydia (48/7), Aegeae/Cilicia (47/6), Gabala (46/5); the 'era of M. Antonius' in Rhosus (42/1), Apamea/Syria (41/0), Thessalonica (41/0), Leucas/Syria (38/7?), Balanea (37/6), as well as the 'era of Cleopatra' in Akko-Ptolemais, Berytus, Chalcis?, Orthosia and Tripolis (37/6); the 'Actian era' in Macedonia with Thessalonica and Philippi? (32/1), in Thessaly (32/1?), Achaea with Epidaurus, Corinth, Messene, Pherae/Messenia, Tegea (31/0), in Asia Minor in Apollonis/Lydia, Philadelphia, Sardis?, Aezani?, Bageis, Daldis, Characeni and Samos (31/0), in Syria in Antioch, Apamea, Arethusa, Botrys, Byblos, Doliche?, Gabala, Gadara?, Laodicea, Seleucia and Tripolis (31/0), in Commagene (31/0) and Cyrenaica (31/0); era of the 'rule of Augustus' in Egyptian papyri (30/29) [3. 213–217; 6. 423–428; 11; 12].

During the Roman Imperial period inscriptions and coins are sometimes dated for the year of the reign or the emperor's *tribunicia potestas* [1. 39 f.; 6. 18–21; 7. 335–338, 357–380], sometimes from old eras (e.g. Seleucid, Sullan) or new eras based on foundations and renamings of cities (Anazarbus 19/8, Augusta 20/1, Balanea *c.* 48/9, Irenopolis/Cilicia *c.* 51/2, Flaviopolis/Cilicia 73/4, Hadriania and Hadrianoi/Mysia 130–133, Caesarea Panias *c.* 3/2, Capitolias *c.* 97/8, Neapolis/Palestine 72/3, Philippopolis/Arabia *c.* 244/5, Sebaste/Palestine 25/4, Tiberias *c.* 19/20), on the promotion to *colonia* (Emerita/Spain *c.* 25 BC, Laodicea ad mare 197/8, Samos *c.* 20/19?, Sinope 45 BC) or other manifestations of imperial favour (Amisus 32/1, Cibyra 24/5, Laodicea ad mare 194/5), often connected with an imperial visit (Diospolis *c.* 199/200, Eleutheropolis 200/1, Laodicea/Phrygia 128/9).

Cities dating their own eras from a visit by Hadrian were Athens, Epidaurus, Hermione, Tegea, Troezen (124/5) and Gaza (130/1); Epidaurus had an era of the 'institution of the Olympieion and the foundation of the Panhellenion' (131/2). A particular case is the 'era of the apotheosis of Augustus' in Samos (14/5) [6. 377 f.]. Some local eras are unexplained: e.g. Chersonesus Taurice (*c.* 25/4), Dionysopolis/Phrygia (152/3), Paphos (182/3), Termessus (*c.* 72/1?), Tyras (56/7) and the Thessalian era from AD 10/11; uncertain also is the nature of the era on coins from Viminacium (239 or 240: foundation of the colony?; also interpreted as the era of the province of Moesia Superior) and the era of Dacia (246/7).

Eras are rare in the west. It remains to be explained whether the Spanish era from 38 BC (in Christian inscriptions from the Iberian peninsula from the 5th to the 11th cents.) is to be identified with the era on pagan inscriptions from north-western Spain or arose only with the Christian calculation of Easter [9]. The few eras of Italy (eras of the foundation of Rome, of Interamna *c.* 672 BC, of the colony of Puteoli *c.* 194 BC, supposed eras of Feltria 39 BC, Patavia *c.* 173 BC, Mediolanum [5] and Praeneste) are probably purely antiquarian in nature. In Carthage, besides later eras from the conquest by the Vandals (439) and by Byzantium (533), we know of sacral eras of the priesthood of the Cereres (*c.* 44–38) and the provincial cult (*c.* 70–72). The (originally astronomical) 'era of Diocletian' (284/5) becomes established in Egypt and Palestine in the 6th cent. [7. 314–318].

The Christian era is based on 6th-cent. calculations of the dates of Easter by the Roman monk Dionysius Exiguus, who equated the 248th year of Diocletian with year 532 *domini nostri Iesu Christi*. The Christian era (*ab incarnatione Domini* and similar) spread from learned writings (e.g. → Cassiodorus) and from Easter tables, in Anglo-Saxon documents from the 7th cent. and in the Frankish kingdom from the 8th cent. onwards. The counting of years before Christ did not come into use until the end of the 18th cent. [16].

1 Bickerman, ²1963 2 Id., Time-Reckoning, in: Cambridge History of Iran 3, 1983, 778–791 3 V. Grumel, Chronologie, 1958 4 W. Kubitschek, Grundriß der ant. Zeitrechnung, 1928 5 W.V. Harris, Era of Patavium, in: ZPE 27, 1977, 283–293 6 W. Leschhorn, Ant. Ären, 1993 (with further lit.) 7 Y.E. Meimaris, Chronological Systems in Romano-Byz. Palestine and Arabia, 1992 (lit.) 8 O. Mœrkholm, Era of the Pamphylian Alexanders, in: ANSMusN 23, 1978, 69–75 9 O. Neugebauer, Spanish Era, in: Chiron 11, 1981, 371–380 10 Samuel 11 H. Seyrig, Les ères de quelques villes de Syrie, in: Syria 27, 1950, 5–50 12 Id., Les ères pompéiennes des villes de Phénicie, in: Syria 31, 1954, 73–80 13 W. Tarn, Greeks in Baktria and India, ²1955 14 J. Teixidor, Ptolemaic Chronology in the Phoenician Inscr. from Cyprus, in: ZPE 71, 1988, 188–190 15 R. Ziegler, Ären kilik. Städte, in: Tyche 8, 1993, 203–219 16 A.-D. von den Brincken, Beobachtungen zum

Aufkommen der retrospektiven Inkarnationsära, in: Archiv für Diplomatik 25, 1979, 1–20. W.L.

Erasinides (Ἐρασινίδης; *Erasinídēs*). Athenian *strategos*. In 409 BC he petitioned that Thrasybulus of Calydon be honoured with a golden wreath for the killing of the oligarch Phrynichus (IG I[3] 102). Elected *strategos* in the spring of 407, in 406 E. was encircled with Conon at Mytilene, but was able to fight his way through by ship to Athens (Xen. Hell. 1,6,16–22). E. commanded a squadron at the sea-battle at the Arginusae, and subsequently urged a rapid attack on the Spartan fleet lying off Mytilene (Xen. Hell. 1,6,29–38; 7,29). Owing to the failure to rescue shipwrecked survivors, the *strategoi* were dismissed from office. Upon his return E. was charged with embezzlement and dereliction of duty, and arrested. E. and seven other *strategoi* were sentenced to death in an → *eisangelia* action for their failure to rescue the shipwrecked survivors, and executed (Xen. Hell. 1,7; Diod. Sic. 13,101).

R.A. Bauman, Political Trials in Ancient Greece, 1990, 69–76. W.S.

Erasinus (Ἐρασῖνος; *Erasînos*). Name of several rivers in Greece, listed by Strabo (8,6,8): at Eretria in Euboea, Brauron in Attica, Bura in Achaea and in the south-western part of the plain of Argos. The last-named river, which is only some 5 km long but carries abundant water, takes the underground outflow from Lake Stymphalus, 35 km distant as the crow flies: this was already known in antiquity (Hdt. 6,76,1), and has now been confirmed by experiment.

R. Baladié, Le Péloponnèse de Strabon, 1980, 103ff. F.GSCH.

Erasistratus (Ἐρασίστρατος; *Erasístratos*)

A. Life B. Work C. Teaching 1. Anatomy 2. Physiology 3. Nosology D. Influence

A. Life

Physician, born in the 4th–3rd cent. BC at Iulis on Ceos; the son of Cleombrotus, physician to Seleucus I, and Cretoxene; brother and nephew to other physicians (fr. 1–8 Garofalo). Information on his education is contradictory, but, if we ignore Eusebius when he tells us that E. attained the zenith of his career in 258 BC, a link with Theophrastus and the Peripatos appears possible [7]. The professional practice of his father and E.'s own association with Chrysippus of Cnidus and Aristogenes, another Seleucid physician, make it probable that he practised for a while at the Seleucid court. It would, however, be precipitate to conclude from these indications and from the apocryphal tale of the healing of Antiochus [2] I *c.* 294 (fr. 24–28) that he practised exclusively at Antioch [2; a contrary opinion in 5], as all the ancient reports of anatomical experiments suggest Alexandria as the place where they occurred (the dedication of a cure for gout to a Ptolemaic king, fr. 239, by no means proves that E. lived for a long time in Egypt [3. 21]). His dissections in part presuppose the results of Herophilus, and are to be dated to the 280s or later. E. is said to have committed suicide with hemlock in order to put an end to the pain caused by an incurable ulcer in his foot. He was buried at Mycale (fr. 3,1).

B. Work

E. wrote treatises on fevers, dropsy, bloodletting, gout, pharmacology and dietetics as well as texts on hygiene and on the 'general principles of medicine'. → Galen still knew some of these texts in the 2nd cent. AD, and quotes them verbatim. But reconstruction of the teachings of E. is made difficult by the fact that information on his writings derives mainly from opponents or from Galen, who placed overmuch emphasis on the value of E.'s anatomy to the detriment of his other teachings [6; 8].

C. Teaching

1. Anatomy

E. continued the work of → Herophilus, the investigation of human anatomy; he certainly performed vivisection, even if it is a matter of dispute whether it was on human beings or on animals. He traced the course of the nerves into the cerebellum (fr. 288, 289) and gave the most exact description of the valves of the heart (fr. 201; [5. 195–231; 6. 205–217; 9. 536–582]). He distinguished sensory from motor nerves, and recognized the origin of veins and arteries in the heart, although he believed that only veins normally held blood. When E. nevertheless found blood in the arteries, which according to him contained *pneuma*, he explained this by pathological changes or the escape of *pneuma:* he thought that the resulting vacuum sucked blood from other parts of the body. E.'s dissections were complemented by clever experimentation (fr. 42 A, 49, 52, 53) and by autopsies (fr. 251, 280). E. emphasized the importance of constant practice in every kind of investigation, so as to be better able to deal with illnesses (fr. 247).

2. Physiology

E. regarded the body as a kind of machine, and rejected many explanatory models based on teleological conceptions [5. 195–231]. He demonstrated that muscle-size increases owing to work performed, not work to be performed. E. understood nutrition and respiration as separate activities, and in his attempts at explaining them pores played an important role, their size varying according to the distribution of the particles of matter. The pulse results from the mechanical motion of the *pneuma* distributed through the arteries by the heart, the contraction of the heart causing the arteries to dilate. Hunger arises when the stomach continues to work after all food has already been broken down and distributed. A threefold system of vessels, comprising a network of nerves, veins and arteries (fr. 86, 87), constitutes the basic structure and material of the entire body. This system agglomerates to itself other organs, such as for example the lungs, from depositions of nutriments. Bile is extracted from the blood through filtration by the liver, serous fluids through attraction by the kidneys (fr. 140). E.'s use of explanatory models derived from contemporary natural science and technology is particularly striking.

3. Nosology

Although E. was a strong advocate of causative explanation, he rejected qualitative explanatory models such as warmth and cold in favour of mechanical causes such as obstruction (fr. 198), or, in the case of dropsy, cirrhosis of the liver. He distinguished two kinds of paralysis, both of them caused by the infiltration of fluid into the nerve-canals and subsequent obstruction to the flow of *pneuma* (fr. 212). He especially emphasized the desirability of avoiding *plethora*, i.e. an excess of blood, which might lead to gout, inflammation and various kinds of fever. E. rejected phlebotomy as a curative measure, relying instead on dietetic and medicinal procedures, especially the reduction of nutrition to the point of a starvation diet when a *plethora* was suspected. But his therapeutic methods may have been less radical than Galen would have us believe [8].

D. Influence

E. was soon regarded as one of the most significant doctors of antiquity, and occupied a prominent place in the list of Dogmatist physicians (→ Dogmatists). Until the late 2nd cent. AD in Rome [1. 100–106] and even in Spain [10], physicians may be found who feel committed in various ways to the teachings of E. E.'s anatomical experiments encouraged Galen to imitate him, and his emphasis on the body as a mechanism may have influenced → Asclepiades [6] of Bithynia.

1 P. Brain, Galen on Bloodletting, 1986 2 P. M. Fraser, The Career of Erasistratus of Ceos, in: Rendiconti dell'Istituto Lombardo 103, 1969, 518–537 3 I. Garofalo, Erasistrati Fragmenta, 1988 4 C. R. S. Harris, The Heart and the Vascular System in Ancient Greek Medicine, 1973 5 G. E. R. Lloyd, A Note on Erasistratus of Ceos, in: JHS 95, 1995, 172–175 6 J. N. Longrigg, Greek Rational Medicine, 1993 7 J. Scarborough, Erasistratus, Student of Theophrastus, in: BHM 59, 1985, 515–517 8 W. D. Smith, Erasistratus' Dietetic Medicine, in: BHM 56, 1982, 398–409 9 F. Solmsen, Kleine Schriften, 1968 10 Hispania epigraphica 4, 1994, 65 n. 146 11 J. N. Longrigg, s.v. E., Dictionary of Scientific Biography 4, 382–386 12 M. Wellmann, s.v. E. 2), RE 5, 333–351. V.N.

Erastus (Ἔραστος; *Érastos*) from Scepsis. 4th cent. BC; a pupil of Plato, he took part in the philosophical delegation to Hermias at Assos (Didymus, In Demosthenem commenta V 54 = F 7 Lasserre). According to Philod. Index academicorum VI 10–12, E. like Asclepiades of Phleius was the author of a text 'Memories (*Apomnēmoneúmata*) of Plato', otherwise unknown.

F. Lasserre, De Léodamas de Thasos à Philippe d'Oronte. Témoignages et fragments, 1987. K.-H.S.

Erato (Ἐρατώ; *Eratṓ*).

[1] One of the nine → Muses; daughter of Zeus and Mnemosyne (Hes. Theog. 78; Apollod. 1,13). Attribution of a sphere of activity, as in the case of the other Muses, emerged only gradually. Plato i.a. assigns her to the sphere of the erotic, on account of her name (Phdr. 259d); but she is above all the Muse of love-lyric, and is appealed to in this connection by poets (cf. Verg. Aen. 7,37; Ov. Ars am. 2,16; 425). She is portrayed i.a. on the François Vase (570 BC) and on the Basle *lekythos* (together with → Thamyris and → Klio).

A. Queyrel, s.v. Mousa, LIMC 6.1, no. 121 and no. 81 (other portrayals nos. 17–18, 93). R.B.

[2] Armenian queen. She came to the throne as sister-wife and co-regent to Tigranes IV after the death of her father Tigranes III, which occurred shortly before 6 BC. Augustus failed in an attempt to install their uncle Artavasdes III in place of the ruling couple, who were under Parthian influence; E. did not abdicate until her brother was killed in AD 1 while countering a barbarian attack. Between AD 13 and 15 she briefly ruled again alone as the last representative of the Artaxiad dynasty.

M.-L. Chaumont, L'Arménie entre Rome et l'Iran I, in: ANRW II 9.1, 1976, 71–194; M.-L. Chaumont, s.v. Armenia and Iran II, EncIr. 2, 422; M. Pani, Roma e i Re d'Oriente da Augusto a Tiberio, 1972; M. Schottky, Media Atropatene und Groß-Armenien in hell. Zeit, 1989; Id., Parther, Meder und Hyrkanier, AMI 24, 1991, 70f.; A. Stein, s.v. Erato (9), RE 6, 355f. M.SCH.

Eratocles (Ἐρατοκλῆς; *Eratoklês*). Head of a school of harmonics opposed on three occasions by Aristoxenus (5f. Meibom).

A. D. Barker, Hoi kaloumenoi harmonikoi: the predecessors of Aristoxenus, in: PCPhS 24, 1978, 1–21. F.Z.

Eratosthenes (Ἐρατοσθένης; *Eratosthénēs*).

[1] An Athenian of rich family. In 411 BC he was serving as a trierarch in the Hellespont, but left his ship in order to support the oligarchs in Athens (Lys. 12,42). After the capitulation of Athens in the Peloponnesian War (404 BC), E. belonged to an action group – the five ephors – working for an oligarchic coup. After the abolition of the democratic order, E. was on the ruling committee of the Thirty, and after its overthrow of that of the Ten (Lys. 12,43–48; 54; Xen. Hell. 2,3,2). After the victory of the democrats in 403, and after being called to account judicially for their actions, E. and Pheidon remained in Athens (Aristot. Ath. Pol. 39,6; And. 1,90). As during the oligarchy E. had been involved in arrests, one of whose victims had been Polemarchus, brother of Lysias, in 403 E. was arraigned for murder by Lysias, but acquitted (Lys. 12).

G.A. Lehmann, in: Ant. und Universalgesch. FS H.E. Stier, 1972, 201–233. W.S.

[2] of Cyrene
A. Life B. Scientific work C. Philological works D. Assessment

A. Life
The librarian at Alexandria (after Apollonius [2] and before Aristophanes [4], cf. POxy. 1241) is said to have lived for some 80 years (cf. Suda ε 2898, Ps.-Lucian Macrobii 27), but the information to hand is not without contradictions: the birth-date given in the Suda (126th Ol. = 276–3 BC) cannot be reconciled with Str. 1,2,2, according to which he is supposed to have been a pupil of the Stoic Zeno, who died in 262/1 (which puts E.'s birth back at least ten years). After a period in Athens he is supposed to have been summoned to Alexandria by Ptolemy III (thus after 246 BC), but he is also said to have been a pupil of Callimachus, although during these years the great poet was already near to death. He was also reckoned to be the pupil of other prominent masters: in Cyrene that of the grammarian Lysanias, in Athens of the Academician Arcesilaus and the Stoic heretic Ariston [7] (cf. Ath. 7,281c).

B. Scientific work
The extensive works of E. survive only in fragments and the testimony of others. Theon of Smyrna used a *Platōnikós* from his pen, probably a dialogue inspired by the cosmological conceptions of Plato (esp. the *Tímaios*). A spurious letter in his name, written by Eutocius from Ascalon, provides information on his activities as a mathematician (cf. Archim. 3, 98ff. H.; Wilamowitz and Wolfer nevertheless regarded the dedicatory epigram accompanying the letter as authentic, which supports the hypothesis that E. was teacher to the later Ptolemy IV Philopator): worthy of mention are his investigations on the duplication of the cube, on the mean proportions (his work *On the mean proportions*, Περὶ μεσοτήτων, appears to have adopted the Pythagorean theory of the three mathematical means, cf. Pappus 7 S. 636, 24f. Hultsch), and especially on the identification of prime numbers (by the method of the so-called 'sieve of E.'). His fame as a mathematician, which he already enjoyed in his lifetime, is demonstrated by the fact that Archimedes dedicated his treatise *Méthodos* to him.

The extant prose work entitled *Constellations* (Καταστερισμοί; *Katasterismoí*) is probably the epitome of an astronomical work giving the mythological origin of the names of the constellations. E. certainly had an intense interest in geography; in this connection, the three books *Geōgraphiká* are the most noteworthy (we have extracts from them via Strabo): the first two books were devoted to the history of the discipline and to various specific investigations; the third was on the map of the world (Hipparchus is said to have polemicised against this), a closing section containing descriptions of individual countries. He not only used mathematical method to approach various geographical problems, but also suggested a system of lines of longitude and latitude (even though his calculations were for the most part erroneous); he recognised the theoretical feasibility of circumnavigating the Earth.

Of especial significance is his work *On the measurement of the Earth* (Περὶ ἀναμετρήσεως τῆς γῆς): his calculation of the circumference of the Earth involved measuring the difference in the incidence of the sun's rays as observed at the cities of Syene (the modern Assuan) and Alexandria, both lying on approx. the same meridian (he assumed that the Earth is a perfect sphere); his result was 252,000 stadia (*c.* 45,460 km), certainly a good approximation. A further calculation, in which he achieved a result very close to the actual value, concerned the angle of the ecliptic.

According to Pfeiffer, E. was the founder of the ancient science of critical chronography. He developed its principles in the *Chronographíai* (Χρονογραφίαι); these comprised a comprehensive chronological survey on the basis of the Olympic victors' lists and (for the prior period) the list of Spartan kings (E. began with the capture of Troy and divided all history up to the death of Alexander the Great into ten epochs). E. wrote two further specialist works: the *Olympionikai* (Ὀλυμπιονῖκαι, a precise reconstruction of the Olympic victors' lists) and *On the eight-year cycle* (Περὶ τῆς Ὀκταετηρίδος), a calendar problem. Even though E. had history begin with Homer, thus contradicting his own principle that unverifiable myths should be given no consideration, his radical criticism of Homer as a historical and geographical source is significant, for he had no truck with allegorical interpretations: in his view, one could not expect a poetic work, designed to entertain, to evince scientific verisimilitude and the intention to instruct.
Musical theory: see end of article.

C. Philological works
We possess fragments and testimony of E.'s poetic production, which certainly included an epic *Hermês* and an elegiac *Ērigónē*. In relation to his philological work, Pfeiffer's claim that with him the spirit and methods of science began to influence philology cannot be confirmed. We know that E.'s interests were especially directed towards comedy (he wrote at least twelve volumes 'On the Old Comedy'/Περὶ τῆς ἀρχαίας κωμῳδίας); in this area he along with Euphronius and Dionysiades continued the work of Lycophron. His lexical verdicts perhaps evince a certain strictness of attitude: thus he regarded Pherecrates' comedy *Metallês* (Μεταλλῆς) as spurious because it featured an irregular use of εὐθύς. According to the Suda, → Aristophanes [4] of Byzantium was his pupil: the latter displayed a rather less strict attitude to particular lexical problems than his master, but he shared his high regard for Pherecrates, whom both placed on the same level as the triad of Eupolis, Cratinus and Aristophanes. In lyrical analysis too, E. achieved remarkable insights: of particular significance is his attribution of a popular hymn to Pallas to Lamprocles (PMG 735; but cf. Page ad l.). He fur-

ther compiled two *Onomastika* (with the titles Ἀρχιτεκτονικός, *Architektonikós* and Σκευογραφικός, *Skeuographikós*); according to Clement of Alexandria, who quotes him along with Antidorus of Cyme and Praxiphanes (Strom. 1,16,79,3), he also wrote Γραμματικά (*Grammatiká*; but according to Suet. Gramm. 10 he called himself not *grammatikós* but *philólogos*). Finally, the *Explanationes in artem Donati* of Servius have it that he elucidated the pronunciation of the circumflex (this in relation to spoken accents: it does not mean that he used diacritical marks before Aristophanes of Samothrace).

D. Assessment

E. had a truly encyclopaedic spirit. Spiteful tongues among his contemporaries gave him the nickname 'pentathlete' (*Péntathlos*) and 'the runner-up' (*Bē̃ta*), to indicate that he did not occupy the first rank in any of the areas to which he turned his attention. Pfeiffer emphasizes that he was a scientist rather than a poet and philologist. In fact he was one of the most prominent figures of his time, and in many regards his ideas represent a link between the Peripatos and Alexandrianism.

Editions: H. Berger, Die geogr. Fragmente des E., 1880; K. Strecker, De Lycophrone Euphronio Eratosthene comicorum interpretibus, 1884; Ps.-Eratosthenis Catasterismi, rec. A. Olivieri (MythGr III/1), 1897; CollAlex 58–68; FGrH II 1010–21 (no. 241); SH 397–99; A. Rosokoki, Die Erigone des E., 1995.

Bibliography: G. Bernhardy, Eratosthenica, 1822; E. Maass, Analecta Eratosthenica, 1883; G. A. Keller, E. und die alexandrinische Sterndichtung, 1946; E. P. Wolfer, E. von Kyrene als Mathematiker und Philosoph, 1954; R. Pfeiffer, History of Classical Philology, I, 1968, 152–70. R.T.

In his theory of music, E. distinguishes between *diástēma* and *lógos* (e.g. 2 to $^1/_2$ and $^1/_2$ to 2 represent the same interval, but not the same relationship [1]). His division of the three tonic families on the basis of number-theory and harmony [2] (→ Music II) indirectly attests to a coming-together of Pythagorean number-theory and the system of → Aristoxenus.

1 I. Düring, Porph. Komm. zur Harmonielehre des Kl. Ptol., 1932, 91,4ff.; but cf. 92,24f. 2 Id., Harmonielehre des Kl. Ptol., 1930, 70ff. 3 Id., Ptol. und Porph. über die Musik, 1934, 85ff., 177 4 MSG 416f. F.Z.

[3] **Scholastikos.** Writer of epigrams of the Justinian period (2nd half of the 6th cent. AD), of whose epigrams at least five from the 'Kyklos' of Agathias are extant (disputed are Anth. Pal. 5,243f.; 246; 7,601; they may only with difficulty be attributed to him). These are erotic (5,242; 277; the first poem is uncommonly obscene), dedicatory (6,77f.) and epideictic (9,444) epigrams that may no longer be described as carefully written. It is not improbable that he is the writer of a hypothesis regarding Theoc. 12. (cf. [1]).

1 A. S. F. Gow, Theocritus, I, 1952, LXXXIIIf. E.D.

Ercavica Celtiberian settlement. The origin of the name is uncertain: it may be Celtiberian ([1. 1485] or Basque [2. 72]). Despite being attested in several sources, the precise location of E. cannot be established ([3]: on the Cabeza del Griego west of Cuenca? A contrary view is [2. 331,5]; cf. also CIL II p. 419, 425). It belonged to the *conventus* of Caesaraugusta (Plin. HN 3,24; CIL II 4203). The *nobilis et potens civitas* ('noble and mighty city') surrendered in 179 BC without resistance to the *propraetor* Tib. Gracchus (Liv. 40,50,1). It was a *municipium* (coins: [4. 109]) and had Latin rights of citizenship (Plin. HN 3,24). Other mentions: Ptol. 2,6,57; Geogr. Rav. 4,44 p. 312,2 *Erguti*. Mentioned during the West Gothic period (in the form *Aravica*, *Iravica*) as the seat of a bishop [5].

1 Holder, 1 2 A. Schulten, Numantia 1, 1914 3 E. Hübner, s.v. E., RE 6, 397f. 4 A. Vives, La moneda hispánica, 1926 5 Fontes Hispaniae Antiquae 9, 1947, s.v. Aravica.

Tovar, 3, 1989, 215f. P.B.

Erchia (Ἐρχία; *Erchía*). Attic *mesogeia* deme of the Aegeis phyle; the modern Spata. Seven (six) → bouleutai, eleven after 307/6 BC. Xenophon (Diog. Laert. 2,48) and Isocrates (Steph. Byz. s.v. E.) were *demótai* of E.; Alcibiades possessed 300 *plethra* (*c.* 26.5 ha.) of land in E. The *lex sacra* of E. from Pussiri south of Spata (SEG 21, 541; [1–7]) lists 59 annual sacrifices at a total cost of 547 drachmas. 21 of the 46 cults are generally situated in the territory of E. (Ἐρχι, Ἐρχιᾶ, Ἐρχιᾶσιν): one on the *agora* of E.; nine of them ἐμ Πάγῳ, i.e. on a hill at E., which Vanderpool [5] assumes to be the Tzumba Sideri; eight cults ἐμ Πόλει Ἐρχιᾶ(σιν), on the fortress or acropolis of E., probably the deme-centre (= Magula in Spata?). Inscriptions also attest a *demarchos* for E. (l. 58), a herald (l. 54) who also functioned as priest, a Delphinion (A l. 26), a Pythion (A l. 54f.), a *hecaterion* (B l. 8), two peak cults ἐπὶ τõ Ἄκρο (D l. 4f., 8f.) and an *agora* (E l. 50f.).

1 G. Daux, La grande démarchie. Un nouveau calendrier sacrificiel d'Attique (Erchia), in: BCH 87, 1963, 603–634 2 S. Dow, The Greater Demarkhia of E., in: BCH 89, 1965, 180–213 3 A. Hollis, Epops in the Erchian sacred calendar and the 'Aetia' of Callimachus, in: E. M. Craik (ed.), Owls to Athens. Essays on classical subjects presented to K. Dover, 1990, 127–130 4 M. Jameson, Notes on the Sacrificial Calendar from E., in: BCH 89, 1965, 154–172 5 E. Vanderpool, The Location of the Attic Deme E., in: BCH 89, 1965, 21–26 6 D. Whitehead, Index s.v. E. 7 Id., The 'Greater Demarchy' of E., in: The Ancient World 14, 1986, 57–64.

Traill, Attica 5, 15f., 41, 59, 104, 110 no. 41, table 2. H.LO.

Erebos see → Underworld

Erechtheus (Ἐρεχθεύς; *Erechtheús*). Mythical king of Athens, with an important cult on the Athenian Acropolis. It is difficult to classify E. as a hero or a god: his cult title in the earlier period is Poseidon E. (e.g. IG I³ 873; Eur. Erechtheus fr. 65,93–4), but he was ascribed a human past, and as a phyle hero (→ Eponymos) has equal status with the other nine (although in the canonic order of phyles he is listed first). There is much cross-contamination between E. (written Erichtheus on the → Marmor Parium) and → Erichthonius; whether the two were originally identical has not yet been clarified. In the mythology as it developed further they are certainly separate, although prior to Euripides' *Erechtheus* (423 BC) this was perhaps not universally so clear-cut. According to early sources, E. is supposed to have been born out of the earth (Hom. Il. 2,546–551 and Hdt. 8,55). Euripides (Ion 267ff.) provides the version that later became generally accepted: E. was a direct descendant of earth-born Erichthonius, son of → Pandium and brother of → Butes. Another tradition, linking him with North Africa instead of Athens, made him the son of Nemesis of Rhamnus (Suda, s.v. Ῥαμνουσία Νέμεσις). E. married Praxithea, and as king led Athens to victory over the Eleusinians, killing their leader, Poseidon's son → Eumolpus. In Euripides' tragedy on this theme, the victory was made possible by the voluntary sacrifice of E.'s daughter; but E. himself was killed by Poseidon in revenge for Eumolpus. Despite the disunity of Attica, assumed in the story, E. represents the prototype of Athenian courage in war, and, along with → Cecrops, the archetypal character of the Athenians, who in poetry were often called *Erechtheidai*.

G.W. Elderkin, The cults of the Erechtheion, in: Hesperia 10, 1941, 113–124; K. Jeppesen, The theory of the alternative Erechtheion, 1987; E. Kearns, The heroes of Attica, 1989, 113–115, 160, 210f.; U. Kron, Die zehn att. Phylenheroen, 1976, 32–83, 249–259; Id., s.v. E., LIMC 4.1, 923–51; N. Loraux, Les enfants d'Athéna, ²1990, 45–57; Id., L'invention d'Athènes, 1981, 135–153; J. Mikalson, E. and the Panathenaia, in: AJPh 97, 1976, 141–153; M.L. West, The Hesiodic Catalogue of Women, 1985, 106f. E.K.

Ereike (ἐρείκη; *ereíkē* is first mentioned in Aesch. Ag. 295 and Theophr. Hist. pl. 1,14,2). The genus *Erica* comprises *c.* 500 species, most of all African shrubs and trees. In the maquis of Greece, however, only three species of the *Ericaceae* family are represented, amongst them the brier *Erica arborea l.* which grows like a tree and flowers in spring; in contrast, the popular honey flora, mentioned by Pliny (HN 11,42) and Dioscorides (1,88 [1. 82] and 1,117 [2. 106]), belongs to the autumn flowering ones. In Italy, on the other hand, eleven species are native. According to Dioscorides and Pliny (HN 13,114; 24,64), the brier is reputed to be effective against snake bites. The French name *bruyère* refers to pipe bowls made from the fine-grained wood of the brier.

1 Wellmann 1 2 Berendes. C.HÜ.

Ereleuva (Erelieva, Hereleuva). *Concubina* of the Amal Thiudimer, mother of → Theoderic the Great (Iord. Get. 269); for the legal position of marriage [1. 262]; for her origins, Anon. Val. 58: Gothic lady; but differing [1. 263]: possibly of provincial Roman origin. E. accompanied her son on his military campaigns (Malchus fr. 18, FHG 4, 130) and was honoured for that by Ennodius (Ennod. MGH (AA) 7,208). At a Catholic baptism, she was given the name Eusebia (Anon. Val. 58) and maintained contact with Pope Gelasius by correspondence (MGH (AA) 12,390, no. 4f., AD 495/96). PLRE 2, 400 (*Erelieva quae et Eusebia*).

1 H. Wolfram, Die Goten, ³1990. M.MEI. and ME.STR.

Eresus (Ἔρεσος; *Éresos*). City on the west coast of Lesbos (Str. 13,2,4; Plin. HN 5,139; Ptol. 5,2,29; Mela 2,101), 4 km south of today's town of Eresos near Skala Eresou. Few archaeological remains: ring wall of the acropolis, port facilities from the 5th/4th cents. BC, relics of the Hellenistic city wall, Roman cisterns; early Christian churches from the 5th cent., i.a. a basilica of St. Andrew. At the location of the ancient acropolis, there are the ruins of a Byzantine-Genoan castle. E. was the home town of the Peripatetics Theophrastus and Phaenias, and probably also of the lyricist Sappho.

As a member of the → Delian League in 428 BC, E. took part in the unsuccessful uprising of the Lesbian towns against Athens, prosecuted by Mytilene (Thuc. 3,18,1; 35). After being encouraged by exiles from Methymna, then controlled by Sparta to secede (Thuc. 3,100,3) in 412 BC, Thrasybulus achieved the return of E. to Athens' side in 389 BC (Diod. Sic. 14,94,3f.). In 377 BC, a member of the 2nd → Athenian League (IG II/III² 43, B 21 [1. 257]). Around 350 BC, establishment of a tyrannis (Hermon, Heraius, Apollodorus) which in 343 BC was ended by Philip II (subsequently cultic honours: altars for Zeus Philippios). A new tyrannis in 336 BC (Agonippus and Eurysilaus: Dem. Or. 17,7), in 334 suspended for a while, in 333 reinstalled with the aid of the Rhodian Memnon, who served the Persian court (Diod. Sic. 17,29,2). Final overthrow of the tyrannis in 332 by Hegelochus, the general of Alexander [4] the Great (Dem. Or. 17,7; Arr. Anab. 3,2,3ff.). After 316 BC, E. belonged to the kingdom of Antigonus [1] Monophthalmus (in 306, the time of the confirmation of the so-called tyrant law [2. 2]), from Ptolemy IV, it belonged to his kingdom (IG XII 2,527). Only a few reports from Roman times.

1 StV 2² 2 Welles.

H. Berve, Die Tyrannis bei den Griechen 1, 1967, 336–338; R. Koldewey, Die ant. Baureste der Insel Lesbos, 1890; H. Pistorius, Beitr. zur Gesch. von Lesbos im 4. Jh. v. Chr., 1913. H.SO.

Eretria (Ἐρέτρια; *Erétria*).

[1] City on Euboea

A. Location B. History C. Institutions D. Minting E. Religion F. Archaeological Monuments

A. Location

E. lies on the SW coast of → Euboea, at a distance of *c.* 20 km from the main town of Chalcis, across from Oropus on the mainland. First mentioned by Hom. Il. 2,536 (for the origin of the name E. cf. Str. 10,1,8). Aegilia belonged to the territory of E. (Hdt. 6,107; IG I[2] 376).

B. History

The earliest settlement goes back to Neolithic times and to the Early and Middle Bronze Age. The excavations on the acropolis of E. also yielded finds of the Late Bronze Age (i.e. of Mycenaean times). The neighbouring Lefkandi shows a continuity of settlement from the beginnings of the Bronze Age into the 10th/9th cents. BC. It was possibly the mother town of Chalcis and also of E. In the 8th cent., the town experienced an important upswing as is demonstrated by the architectural and material legacy of this time. However, this upswing can be shown not only for the city itself, but for various places of the Mediterranean region: numerous finds prove the presence of Euboean merchants in the Chalcidice, at the Syrian-Phoenician coast and in southern Italy (Ischia/Pithecussae, Cumae). The vigourous contacts of the Euboeans with the East and the West possibly reach back into Mycenaean times, as is suggested by finds from Lefkandi/Toumba. During the Great Colonization, E. played an important role, as did Chalcis. Thus, Mende (Thuc. 4,123,1) and Methone (Plut. Quaest. Graec. 293B) were founded by E. The city reinforced its influence over the Cyclades islands Andros, Ceos and Tenos (Str. 10,1,10). The war that broke out between Chalcis and E. over the Lelantine Plain located between the two cities probably dates back to the 8th cent. BC, but possibly only to the 7th or the 6th cent. Thucydides (1,15,3) describes it as the first war in which two important coalitions of Greek cities clashed. The rules of war, in particular the prohibition of hurling and missile weapons, are evidence of a society ruled by the aristocracy, the 'horse breeders' (*hippobótai* in Chalcis) and 'knights' (*hippeîs* in E.). According to Hdt. 5,99, the assistance given to Miletus in the → Ionian Revolt was the reason why the Persians in 490 BC first attacked E. E. was taken, set fire to and part of the population was enslaved (Hdt. 6,101). In 446, E. came under Athenian dominance (Thuc. 1,114,3). E. liberated itself in 411 and, in the 4th cent., experienced a time of prosperity which can be seen in its urban development. E. was ruled by various tyrants, later by the philosopher Menedemus. From the time of Philip II, the city at times came under Macedonian dominance. E. had suffered due to the → Chremonidean War (268/7–262/1). With the conquest by Roman troops in 198 BC, the city was destroyed once again (Liv. 32,16f.). Its existence is documented into Byzantine times; thereafter, E. was abandoned gradually, probably because of the unhealthy climate because of the nearby swamps.

C. Institutions

E. was ruled by *próbouloi* and *stratēgoí*, as well as by a council (*boulḗ*). The Ionian origin of the population is reflected in the existence of probably six tribes, of which two are known: Mecistis and Narcittis. The extensive area of E. was subdivided into about 60 demes, which were divided into five *choroí* (districts) of *c.* 12 demes each.

D. Minting

From the 6th cent. until probably 446 BC, E. minted a first series of coins in its own name featuring a cow licking its hind leg, and an octopus on the reverse. In the 4th/3rd cents. BC, the minting of the Euboean League replaced the city's mintings, but in the 2nd cent., it was resumed sporadically.

E. Religion

Apollo Daphnephoros was the main deity of E. Great importance was also attributed to the sanctuary of Artemis Amarysia, located *c.* 15 km east of E., as can be seen both from texts and archaeological finds. A temple of Dionysus, a sanctuary of Isis, a sanctuary of Hercules and a thesmophorium have been uncovered. The cult of Asclepius and of Hygieia is documented only by inscriptions and statues.

F. Archaeological Monuments

Thanks to the excavations carried out since 1885, the most important ancient monuments of E. are known. In the sanctuary of Apollo, a series of temples dating back to the 8th cent. was discovered under the ruins of the great Doric temple from the 6th cent. BC. The residential buildings of the 4th cent. are particularly well preserved. Apart from a theatre, two gymnasiums and several temples, E. boasted a city wall as early as archaic times, which was fully rebuilt in the 4th cent. and surrounded the city area as well as the acropolis. Finds from the necropoleis from archaic, classical and Hellenistic times, discovered at the end of the 19th cent., as well as from the Macedonian chamber graves, are scattered amongst museums in the whole world.

Eretria, Ausgrabungen und Forsch., 10 vols. since 1968; K. Schefold, P. Auberson, Führer durch E., 1972; O. Picard, Chalcis et la Confédération eubénne, 1979; P. Bruneau, Le sanctuaire et le culte des divinités égyptiennes à Erétrie, 1975; D. Knoepfler, Sur les traces de l'Artémision d'Amarynthos près d'Erétrie, in: CRAI, 1988, 382–421; Id., ΕΡΕΤΡΙΑΣ ΓΗ, Acts of the Copenhagen Polis Centre 4, 1997; for excavation reports see AD, AE, AK, BCH, Ergon, Praktika. PI.DU.

[2] City on the northern slope of the Othrys mountains near today's Tsangli at the transition from the Crocium plain (Κρόκιον πεδίον; *Krókion pedíon*) into the valley of the → Enipeus [2], where the roads from the plain (coming from Halus or Thebae in the Phthiotis) branched to Pharsalus, Scotussa or Pherae. E. is mentioned several times in connection with military actions of the 2nd Macedonian War (Liv. 32,13; 33,6 = Pol. 18,20). E. was destroyed by Philip V in 198 BC.

I. Blum, Die Stadt E. in Thessalien, in: Topographie antique et géographie historique en pays grec, 1992, 157–229; F. Stählin, Das hellen. Thessalien, 1924, 174.
HE.KR.

Eretrian School see → Elis and Eretria, School of

Eretria Painter Attic red-figured vase painter, active around 440–415 BC; named after an → *epínētron* from Eretria, today in Athens (NM). More than half of his numerous surviving works are decorations on drinking bowls which he produced together with three other painters at the same time as the pre-eminent Penthesilea workshop. While his pictures of athletes and youths tend to be of the conventional type, the pictures of horsemen, Amazons and satyrs are pointing beyond the stereotypes of the age. Once, the Eretria Painter (EP) gives figures of a *thiasos* the names of islands, probably after a literary example (Warsaw, Mus.). In addition, he painted closed vessel types in at least six other workshops, while adapting to their style in each case. A pair of jugs belongs to his early work which indicates connections to the → Codrus Painter (Palermo, MN and Agrigento, Mus. arch.). On kantharoi of the 'Hercules type', Trojan themes can be found (Paris, CM; Tarent, NM). For Apollonia [2] Pontice, he painted on a Thracian form, one of the few representations of that people from classical times (Sozopol, Mus.). The subtlety of the figures, the originality of the composition, the inclination to deal with female subject matters find their full expression only on the late choes and 'belly-shaped' lekythoi; here, his style reflects familiarity with the circles of the → Aeson and → Meidias Painters. Famous are his Anthesteria pictures; in one of them, father and son, called Prometheus and Epimetheus, celebrate Dionysus Liknites (Athens, NM). On 'belly-shaped' lekythoi, the EP also used the white-ground technique, such as in the middle band of the squat lekythos (New York, MMA), which represents the dark sides in the life of a woman in contrast to the scenes on the eponymous *epínētron*.

Beazley, ARV² 1247–1255; Id., Paralipomena, 469–470; Id., Addenda², 353–355; A. Lezzi-Hafter, Der E., 1988; J.H. Oakley, The Achilles Painter, 1997, 108 with n. 178; Id., W. D. E. Coulsen, O. Palagia, Athenian Potters and Painters, 1997, 353–369, 473–490.
A.L.-H.

Eretum Town of the Sabini (Str. 5,3,1; 11 [1. 479]) at the *via Salaria*, 18 miles away from Rome, where the *via Nomentana* branches off (Tab. Peut. 5,5; It. Ant. 306,5). Being situated near the border of Rome, E. was involved in many disputes in the time of the Roman kings (Liv. 3,26,2; 29,7; 38,3; Dion. Hal. Ant. Rom. 3,32; 59; 4,3; 51; 5,45; 11,3 [2. 435–437]). Finally, E. was incorporated into Nomentum (Liv. 3,26,2; 29,7; 38,3; 42,3; Dion. Hal. Ant. Rom. 11,3,2) and assigned to the *tribus Clustumina*. E. is modern Casa Cotta di Montelibretti [3. 57]. There is a necropolis nearby (end of 7th cent.–beginning of 3rd cent. BC).

1 Nissen, 2 2 L. Pareti, Storia di Roma, 1, 1952 3 P. Santoro, La città sabina di E., in: Enea nel Lazio, 1981.

Civiltà arcaica dei Sabini nella valle del Tevere, 1973/4; M.P. Muzzioli, s.v. E., Enciclopedia Virgiliana 2, 1985, 363f.
A.SA.

Ergasterion

I. Ancient Orient II. Greece

I. Ancient Orient

In the palace economies (→ *oîkos* economy) of the Ancient Orient, certain mass products were made for the requirements of (large) patrimonial households themselves, but also for exchange in long distance trade with large *ergasteria* (factories) in which often several hundred, sometimes far more than a thousand male or female workers were employed. Their wages were normally paid in kind as daily rations; their social status was equivalent to patrimonial subjects, required to perform compulsory service. The best evidence for *ergasteria* comes from southern Babylonia at the time of the 3rd dynasty of Ur (21st cent. BC [1; 2]; → Mesopotamia) and from → Mari on the middle Euphrates (18th cent.) [3]. In the *ergasteria* of southern Mesopotamia, mainly textiles and grain products were processed for the requirements of aristocratic households. In special factories, prestige objects were manufactured for the ruler's household and for furnishing the temples. The organization of work in the *ergasteria* was based on that found in craftsmen's workshops, i.e. without advanced division of labour.

→ Work

1 The Assyrian Dictionary of the University of Chicago N, s.v. neparum 2 J.-P. Grégoire, Les grandes unités de transformation des céréales, in: P.C. Anderson (ed.), Préhistoire de l'Agriculture, 1992, 321–339 3 M. van de Mieroop, Crafts in the Early Isin Period, 1987 4 J. Renger, Review to AOAT 3, in: JNES 32, 1973, 261–265.
J.RE.

II. Greece

From Classical Greece up to Byzantine times, the *ergasterion* (ἐργαστήριον; *ergastḗrion*) was a place where people worked; the term could be used for a smithy, a laundry, the workshop of a carpenter, for a brothel, a butcher's shop, a plant for the smelting of silver as well as the workshop of a cabinet-maker or a sculptor. Very often, it refers to a shop where the products of a craftsman were sold (therefore, IG II[2] 1013,9 lists sales guidelines for *ergasteria* and other establishments). Only few craftsmen required more than a place for their simple and often portable tools, space to work, as well as a location to store material and their products. An *ergasterion* was thus no more than an empty and covered area which, in the most favourable case, was surrounded by walls and equipped with a lockable door. Many craftsmen worked under modest conditions in their own houses such as in the Athenian street of the marble workers, where sculptors, makers of terracotta figures, cobblers and smiths lived and worked in simple rooms. Even if the owner of the *ergasterion* was not active himself in the workshop, nevertheless, the craftsmen were often accommodated in his house as, for example, the 30 cutlers and the 20 cabinet-makers occupied with the manufacture of beds, who belonged to the father of Demosthenes and of whom it is said that they had been παρ' ἡμῖν (*par hēmîn*, 'with us') and had then been led ἐκ τῆς οἰκίας (*ek tês oikías*; 'out of the house') (Dem. Or. 27,24–25). The 120 slaves, who belonged to the father and brother of Lysias and produced weapons, lived in an *ergasterion* which was directly adjacent to their (= owners') house (Lys. 12,8). The workshop of Pasion, in which probably 60 to 70 men worked, could have been located directly next to his house (Dem. Or. 36,4; cf. also IG II[2] 2496: tenancy of a workshop with an adjacent residential house).

About the value and the level of revenues from individual larger *ergasteria*, information can be found in the Attic orators: the two *ergasteria* of his father, mentioned by Demosthenes, together are supposed to have been worth 23,000 drachmas and to have brought in 4,200 drachmas per year (3,000 drachmas for the *ergasterion* where swords were made and 1,200 drachmas from the furniture workshop); the value of the raw materials stored in the two workshops is reported to be an additional 8,000 drachmas (Dem. Or. 27,9–10). A workshop owned by Pasion, where shields were produced, secured an income for its owner in the amount of 6,000 drachmas per year (Dem. Or. 36,4; 36,11).

The occupation of smiths, potters and miners required permanent installations such as a forging furnace, kilns, sludge basins for clay, ore washing tables and smelting furnaces which could not be erected or installed in residential buildings. The installations in Attica for processing ore were called *ergasteria* in the sales lists of the πωλῆται (*pōlē̂tai*) and also in the Attic orators; archaeological excavations show that these installations had been carefully constructed for the purpose of extracting silver. Other craftsmen also required specially constructed *ergasteria*, e.g. for sculptors employed in the construction of temples. The *ergasterion* owned by Phidias in Olympia was a solid stone building, in which there was enough space for work on the statue of Zeus. The statue of Asclepius and the sculptures for the pediment of the temple at Epidaurus (370 BC) were also made in an *ergasterion* with stone walls and a tiled roof. The sculptors and stone masons who were employed in the construction of the Parthenon and the Erechtheion had their workshops on the Acropolis.

The term *ergasterion* could also refer to just the workers, independently of the building in which they were deployed. Underlying this use of the term was the recognition that, while the building was by no means unimportant, the work itself was the decisive factor for the production of craftwork. It is for just this reason that Demosthenes refers to two *ergasteria* which do not consist of buildings but of the cutlers and the bed manufacturers. In this case, the craftsmen were slaves; but if the term *ergasterion* was used to mean 'workshop', no conclusions can be drawn as to the legal status of the craftsmen.

→ Crafts, trades; → Slavery

1 A. Burford, The Greek Temple Builders at Epidauros, 1969 2 Id., Craftsmen in Greek and Roman Society, 1972 3 C.E. Conophagos, Le Laurium antique, 1980 4 M.I. Finley, Land and Credit in Ancient Athens, 1952 5 A. Mallwitz, Olympia und seine Bauten, 1972, 255–266 6 P.V. Stanley, The Value of Ergasteria in Attica: A Reconsideration, in: Münstersche Beitr. zur ant. Handelsgesch. 9, 1990, 1–13.

A.B.-C.

Ergastulum Refers to a room in which tied-up slaves had to spend the night; it also refers to a group of bound slaves. With the acquisition of larger numbers of slaves during the Roman expansion in the 2nd and 1st cents. BC, the Roman slave owners were more frequently confronted with the fact that slaves fled or became violent against their owners. The result was an increased occurrence of slaves being tied up, who also had to do their work in that condition (*compediti* or *vincti*). This phenomenon becomes clear both in Cato as well as in Varro without the word *ergastulum* being used, which, however, already appears in Cicero (Clu. 21; Sest. 134). Slaves tied up for punishment also came under a special legal category; they could not obtain Roman citizenship as a result of manumission (Gaius 1,13–15).

In Columella (1,6,3), *ergastulum* is referred to as an underground room in which slaves who had been chained by their master as punishment had to spend the night; it had to be high enough that the windows could not be reached by them. Such *ergastula* have been found in excavations of *villae rusticae*, e.g. near Gragnano in Italy [2; 3. 240f.]. For the *ergastulum*, according to Columella (1,8,17), there was a special overseer (*ergastularius*, cf. CIL X 8173). But Columella (1,8,16ff.) advises landholders to exercise strict control over the overseers so that the tied-up slaves receive all the necessary provisions and do not become dangerous as a result of overly strict treatment.

In many passages of ancient literature, *ergastulum* is understood to mean a gang of tied-up slaves who were deployed exclusively in agriculture, principally in vineyards (thus e.g. Plin. HN 18,36; Juv. 14,24; cf. Ov. Pont. 1,6,31). According to Apuleius (Apol. 47), such an *ergastulum* comprised a gang of 15 tied-up slaves. However, the *ergastulum* was not the place where tied-up slaves carried out their work [1. 249ff.]. During the turmoil of the Civil Wars, even freemen and deserters were forcibly taken into *ergastula* so that Augustus and, on his orders, Tiberius intervened against it (Suet. Aug. 32,1; Tib. 8). According to HA Hadr. 18,10, Hadrian reportedly abolished the *ergastula* as slave prisons; however, this is unlikely. During the course of the 1st cent. AD, the number of *ergastula* probably declined for the simple reason that, due to the development of slavery, fewer tied-up slaves were used in agriculture; whether the phenomenon disappeared altogether cannot be ascertained.

1 R. ETIENNE, Recherches sur l'ergastule, in: Actes du colloque 1972 sur l'esclavage, 1974, 249–266 2 M. DELLA CORTE, in: NSA 1923, 275ff. 3 FLACH 4 MARTINO, WG, 129ff., 259ff. 5 THÉDENAT, in: DS II 1,810f.

W.E.

Erginus (Ἐργῖνος; *Ergînos*). Mythical king of Orchomenus in Boeotia, son of Clymenus and → Budeia or Buzyge. When Menoeceus' chariot driver, the Theban Perieres, killed E.'s father during the feast of Poseidon, E. made Thebes pay tributes. The young Hercules, however, liberated Thebes from this tribute in a fight in which E. was defeated (Paus. 9,17,1–4; 37,1–4; schol. Il. 16,572; Apollod. 2,67–69; Eur. HF 220–221; Diod. Sic. 4,10,5). The fight of E. against Hercules is depicted on a Hadrianic relief [1]. He is likely to be identical with the Argonaut E., son of Clymenus or Poseidon, who despite his advanced age won in a running competition during the funeral games for Thoas on Lemnos (Pind. Ol. 4,19–27; Herodorus FGrH 31 F 55; Apoll. Rhod. 1,185–187 with schol.; Callim. Fr. 668).

1 R. VOLLKOMMER, s.v. E., LIMC 3.1, 819, no. 1.

R.B.

Ergocles (Ἐργοκλῆς; *Ergoklês*). Athenian *strategos*. In 404/3 BC, he joined the democrats in Phyle. In 390/89, he operated as a *strategos* together with Thrasybulus in the Hellespont and on the coast of Asia Minor. After his return, he was indicted for embezzlement, bribery and abuse of authority and sentenced to death; his assets were confiscated (Lys. 28). Since the embezzled money was never found, there were suspicions that Philocrates, trierarch and treasurer under E., had taken possession of this money (Lys. 29).

W.S.

Ergotimus (Ἐργότιμος; *Ergótimos*). Attic potter who, around 570–560 BC, worked together with the black-figured vase painter → Clitias. Their main work, signed jointly, is the so-called François Vase in Florence, a monumental volute crater (→ Vessels, shapes and types of), which, for the first time, displays spirally coiled jug handle volutes which are supported on top of the vessel rim. Apart from that, E. has signed an unusual stand as well as two delicate 'Gordion cups', an experimental, transitional form between → Siana cups and → Little-master cups. A footless 'button-handle cup' in Berlin is not by Clitias, as such being the only one of E.'s signed works. As 'son of E.', Eucheirus later signed several Little-Master cups.

BEAZLEY, ABV, 76–80 (162); BEAZLEY, Addenda², 21f. (47); Id., Little-Master Cups, in: JHS 52, 1932, 185–186; H. E. SCHLEIFFENBAUM, Der griech. Volutenkrater, 1991, 53–54; E. SIMON, Die griech. Vasen, 1976, 52–57.

H.M.

Erianthes (Ἐριάνθης; *Eriánthēs*). Theban commander of the Boeotian triremes at Aigospotamoi. His statue, therefore, stood on the Spartan victory monument in Delphi (Paus. 10,9,9) [1. 14f.]. After the capitulation of Athens, his demand to destroy the city was rejected in Sparta (Xen. Hell. 2,2,19; Plut. Lys. 15). When the Thebans in 395 BC endeavoured to form an alliance with Athens, they attempted to interpret the action by E. as having been carried out by him without authority (Xen. Hell. 3,5,8).

1 J.-F. BOMMELAER, Lysandre de Sparte, 1981.

K.-W.WEL.

Erica see → Ereike

Ericea (Ἐρίκεια/*Eríkeia*, from ἐρείκη/*Ereíkē*, 'brier'?). Attic *asty*(?)-deme of the Aegeis phyle, one *bouleutes* (after 307/6 BC two). Its location determined to be near Kypseli as the finding-place of a decree (IG II², 1215, beginning of the 3rd cent. BC) in which an unknown deme honours a donor for the repairs to cultic installations.

TRAILL, Attica 16, 39 with n. 10, 59, 70, 74 n. 10, 110 no. 42, table 2; WHITEHEAD Index s.v. E.

H.LO.

Ericepaeus (Ἠρικεπαῖος; *Ērikepaîos*). Deity which is mentioned in Orphic poetry and the associated Bacchian mysteries; the late etymology of 'life-giver' (ζωοδοτήρ; *zōodotḗr*) cannot be verified (Malalas, Chronogr. 4,91; cf. Suda 660 s.v. Orpheus). The name is first mentioned with certainty in the papyrus Gurôb 1, a Dionysian mysteries text of the late 3rd cent. BC [1]; an earlier reference in a gold leaflet from Pherae is uncertain [2]. E. then becomes important in various Neoplatonic writings of the so-called rhapsodic theogony of Orpheus. Here, E. is one of the names of the primeval being Phanes Metis E., who was born from an egg (Orph. Fr. 60; 65; 81; 85; 167).

An altar of Imperial times from Hierocaesarea in Lydia is dedicated to Dionysus E., whereby the dating, according to a hierophant, leads to the Bacchic mysteries [3]; however, the relationship of this text to Orphic poetry is under dispute: it is not clear whether it adopts a local, Lydian cult name of Dionysus (as in → Hipta) or whether the mysteries cult of Dionysus, just as in nearby Smyrna (LSAM 84), is more likely to be dependent on the Orphic poems.

1 M. WEST, The Orphic Poems, 1983, 170f. 2 P. CHRISOSTOMOU, Ἡ Θεσσαλικὴ θεὰ Ἐννοδία ἢ Φεραία θεά,

thesis 1991, 372 3 J. KEIL, A. VON PREMERSTEIN, Denkschriften der Akad. der Wiss. Wien 52, 1908, 54 no. 112. F.G.

Erichthonius (Ἐριχθόνιος; *Erichthónios*).

[1] Important figure of Athenian mythology; his birth from the earth is said to have taken place on the Acropolis and symbolized the autochthonal nature of Athenians. E.'s relation to the very similar sounding → Erechtheus is problematic; most of the early texts (e.g. Hom. Il. 2,546–51) speak of Erechtheus, not E., as the one born of the earth, and an original cult of E., which would differ from the one of Erechtheus, cannot be detected. In Euripides (Ion 267ff.) and amongst the historians of local Attic history, the two figures are differentiated genealogically; in the 5th cent., they generally have their own identity because of the myths told about them: Erechtheus is the adult king of war while for E. birth and childhood are emphasized. When Hephaestus tried, without success, to rape Athena, his semen dropped on her thigh; she wiped it off with a piece of wool (ἔριον, *érion*) and threw it to the ground (χθών, *chthṓn*); the earth received the semen and bore E. whom she later entrusted to Athena (this episode was a popular theme on red-figured vases). Athena in turn passed the child on to → Aglaurus, Pandrosus and Herse, the daughters of Cecrops; she had put the child into a basket together with snakes and forbade the girls to open it. When all or only two of them ignored the order, they had such a fright that they jumped from the Acropolis to their death. In all probability, this myth is related to the difficult-to-interpret rite of the → Arrhephoroi on the Acropolis.

A further version, which made E. the son of king Canaus' daughter Atthis and Hephaestus (Apollod. 3,187), appears to be intent on giving a rational explanation for his birth from the Attic earth (Ἀτθὶς γῆ, *Atthìs gê*). In local history and mythography, too, E.'s biography extended beyond his childhood: he became king and founded a dynasty. In Apollodorus (3,187), he expelled Amphictyon, married Prasithea/Praxithea (a further mix-up with Erechtheus) and begot a son → Pandium. The deeds that were most frequently attributed to him are the foundation of the → Panathenaea (e.g. Hellanicus FGrH 323a F 2) and – probably associated with that – the invention of the cart (Marmor Parium 10, cf. Verg. G. 3,113–4).

C. BÉRARD, Anodoi, 1974, 34–8; U. KRON, s.v. E., LIMC 4.1, 923–51; E.H. LOEB, Die Geburt der Götter in der griech. Kunst, 1979, 165–181, 334–44; N. LORAUX, Les enfants d'Athéna, ²1990, 35–73; J. MIKALSON, Erechtheus and the Panathenaia, in: AJPh 97, 1976, 141–53; N. ROBERTSON, The Origins of the Panathenaea, in: RhM 128, 1985, 231–95. E.K.

[2] Son of the Trojan → Dardanus and of → Bateia, husband of → Astyoche or Callirhoe (Apollod. 3,140; Dion. Hal. Ant. Rom. 1,62). For family tree see → Dardanidae. According to Aesch. fr. 368 TGF, E. is a son, not a grandson of Zeus. E. was possibly entered into the Trojan list of kings due to Attic influence [1] (cf. Str. 13,604).

1 ESCHER, s.v. E., RE 6, 440.

Eridanus (Ἠριδανός/*Ēridanós*, Latin *Eridanus*).

[1] Mythical river in the (north) west (northern Italy, south of France or Spain), son of → Oceanus and → Tethys (Hes. Theog. 338). → Phaeon plunged into the E. from his sun wagon and his sisters (→ Heliades) were turned into black poplars on the banks of the E., and their tears into amber (Eur. Hipp. 736–741; Ov. Met. 2,324; 365; Hyg. Fab. 152; 154). Since Hesiod, the E. is associated with the creation of amber (Hes. fr. 150,23–24 M-W). In attempts at geographical localizations, one thought of the Rhône et al. principally of the Po (possibly already Pherecydes FGrH 3 F 74; Plin. HN 37,31–32). Accordingly, E.-Padus is a motif of the Roman river god iconography [1]. Hdt. 3,115 and Str. 5,1,9, of course, denied the existence of the E. In Verg. Aen. 6,659, the E. belongs to the Underworld (for E. as a constellation see → Constellations).

1 E. SIMON, s.v. E.1, LIMC 3.1, 821–822.

F. BÖMER, P. Ovidius Naso met. 1–3 (comm.), 1969, 322–323.

[2] Athenian river (Pl. Criti. 112a; Str. 9,1,19; Paus. 1,19,5).

G. G. BELLONI, s.v. E. 2), LIMC 3.1, 822–823. R.B.

Erigon (Ἐριγών; *Erigṓn*). Largest tributary of the → Axius, flows through the Macedonian regions of Lyncestis, Pelagonia and Derriopus, mouth near Stobi; today's Crna Reka.

F. PAPAZOGLOU, Les villes de Macédoine, 1988, 292. MA.ER.

Erigone (Ἠριγόνη; *Ērigónē*).

Name of two similar figures of Attic mythology:

[1] Daughter of → Icarius, who had given Dionysus a hospitable reception and, for this, had received as a present the knowledge of making wine. When Icarius, on behalf of Dionysus, tried to introduce viticulture, he was killed by the farmers who thought they had been poisoned after they had drunk unblended wine. E. was led to her father's body by the dog Maera and thereupon hanged herself from a tree. Dionysus punished the Athenians with an epidemic of hangings amongst their girls, whereupon the → Aiora festival was established as atonement, the story being the aition of the festival. Icarius, E. and the dog Maera were removed to a place among the stars. The literary form of the story goes back to Eratosthenes' short epic E. [1] (Hyg. Poet. Astr. 2,149–209; Apollod. 3,191–192; Hyg. Fab. 130; Nonnus, Dion. 47,34–264).

[2] Daughter of Aegisthus and Clytaemnestra. Her fate is related differently. According to Dictys 6,4, she hanged herself out of grief over → Orestes' acquittal. According to Hyg. Fab. 122, Orestes wanted to kill E., but Artemis removed her to Attica and made her a priestess.

1 A. Rosokoki, Die E. des Eratosthenes, 1995.

W. Burkert, Homo necans, 1972, 247; 267–268; Burkert, 255; 363–364; R.M. Gais, s.v. E. 2, LIMC 3.1, 824–825; E. Pochmarski, s.v. E. 1, LIMC 3.1, 823–824. R.B.

Erigyius (Ἐρίγυιος; *Erígyios*). From Mytilene, resident of Amphipolis together with his brother → Laomedon, older than Alexander [4] and was banished in 337/6 BC together with others of his friends from younger days. As the only one of this group he was quickly given a command over troops, led the Greek cavalry near → Issus and → Gaugamela, and later appears as a trusted adviser of the king. He also took on special military tasks, thus e.g. against → Satibarzanes, whom he killed in single combat (Arr. Anab. 3,28,3; Curt. 7,4,32–38). He died in the winter of 328/7 and was buried with the highest honours (Curt. 8,2,40).

Berve 2, no. 302; Heckel 209f. E.B.

Erineus (Ἐρινεός, Ἐρινεόν; *Erineós, Erineón*). Apart from Boium, Cytenium and Acyphas/Pindus, one of the towns, reportedly founded by → Dorus, of the middle Greek Doris. Reference passages: Tyrateus fr. 2 West; Hdt. 8,43; Scyl. 62; Scymn. 592ff.; Diod. Sic. 4,67,1; Str. 9,4,10; 10,4,6; Conon, FGrH 26 F 1,27; Plin. HN 4,28; Ptol. 3,14,14; Aristid. 12,40; Steph. Byz. s.v. E.; schol. Pind. Pyth. 1,121; schol. Aristoph. Plut. 385; schol. Lycoph. Alex. 980). As the only historical event, a raid by the Phocians on E. in 458/7 BC is documented (Thuc. 1,107,2; Diod. Sic. 11,79,4). E. is to be localized directly northwest of today's Kastelli at the northern side of the valley exit of ancient Pindus (today's Kanianitis).

E. W. Kase et al. (ed.), The Great Isthmus Corridor Route, 1991; Müller, 488; D. Rousset, Les Doriens de la Métropole, in: BCH 113, 1989, 199–239; Id., Les Doriens de la Métropole, in: BCH 118, 1994, 361–374. P.F.

Erinna (Ἤριννα; *Érinna*). Poet and author of a work known in antiquity as the 'Distaff' (Ἠλακάτη; *Ēlakátē*), a poem of 300 hexameters (Anon. Anth. Pal. 9,190,3). Eusebius indicates that her creative time was between 353 and 352 BC (= Ol. 106.4 or 107.1). The Suda, which erroneously made her into Sappho's contemporary, names several possible places of origin; the most probable being the island of Telos since she writes in Doric with the occasional Aeolism. The literary similarities with the works of → Asclepiades and → Theocritus actually give rise to the assumption that this poet wrote no earlier than the 3rd cent. BC. The preserved remainders of *c.* 54 verses, which supplement the few quotations (SH 402–[406]), were published in 1929 (SH 401). Here, E. describes the experiences of her childhood, which she shared with Baucis, and laments the death of her girlfriend, which occurred soon after her marriage, a fact we learn about from another source (Erinna Anth. Pal. 7,712). The papyrus mentions the distaff (ἀλακάταν; *alakátan*) of the title (l. 39). It is not certain whether this is Moira's distaff (cf. anon. Anth. Pal. 7,12,4), a distaff of the poet herself (cf. anon. Anth. Pal. 9,190,5) or a distaff given by E. as a present to Baucis (cf. Theoc. 28). The number 19 ἐννεα[και]δέκατος; *ennea[kai]dékatos* (l. 37) appears to be the source for the assumption that E. composed the poem at the age of 19 years (anon. Anth. Pal. 9,190,4; Asclepiades Anth. Pal. 7,11,2); according to the Suda (η 521 Adler), she is also said to have died at this age. Two verses, quoted by Athenaeus (SH [404]), are part of a → propemptikon which is possibly addressed to Baucis who is known from the 'Distaff' and who is embarking on a sea voyage [3. 101–107]. The authenticity of the epigrams attributed to E. is being disputed (SH 403); even the 'Distaff' has been referred to as a fake.

1 FGE 343–346 2 GA I.2, 281f. 3 J. Rauk, E.'s Distaff and Sappho Fr. 94, in: GRBS 30, 1989, 101–116 4 M. L. West, E., in: ZPE 25, 1977, 95–119. E.R.

Erinys (Ἐρινύς; *Erinýs*). Etymology uncertain (Chantraine 2,371, cf. [1; 2. 83–4]). E. is already mentioned in → Linear B (KN 200 = Fp 1, 208 = V 52, cf. ⟨Fs 390⟩; [1]) in connection with other deities such as Zeus, Athene, Paeon and Poseidon. Later, the name appears both in the singular as well as in the plural ('Erinyes'). Mostly, the Erinyes are daughters of Night (Aesch. Eum. 69; 322 *et passim*) or they originate from drops of blood shed during Uranus' castration (Hes. Theog. 185), which indicates their connection with crime within a family, in particular patricide; cf. [2. 84–5]. Although the Erinyes are usually referred to as virgins (Aesch. Eum. 68–70; Soph. Aj. 835; Verg. Aen. 6,280), some myths make E. the mother of the horse Arion (by Poseidon) or of Despoina (Paus. 8,25,2–10, cf. 8,42; Callim. Fr. 652; schol. Hom. Il. 23,346 Dindorf = Thebaïs fr. 6b; 6c EpGF, cf. [3. 143–45; 4]). Like Demeter, with whom E. is identified in some versions of the Arion myth, the Erinyes sometimes have the power to destroy or to foster fertility of any kind (Aesch. Eum. 903–15 and *passim*, [3.142–47]). In Roman myths, the Erinyes appear as → Furiae (Cic. Nat. D. 3,46; cf. Verg. Aen. 3,331; for the representations of a different kind in art cf. [5. 1. 24–90]). Their individual names, in Greek as well as in Latin, are Megaera ('envious one'), Tisiphone ('avenger of murder') and Allecto (the 'irreconcilable one'): Apollod. 1,3 [2. 123–24].

In Homer, many of the characteristic traits of the Erinyes in later literature appear for the first time: they live in the Underworld (Hom. Il. 9,571f.; cf. Aesch. Eum. 395–6), vouch for oaths (Hom. Il. 19,259f.; cf.

Hes. Op. 803f.), carry out curses (Il. 9,454–56; 571f.; cf. Aesch. Eum. 421; Soph. Aj. 835–44), bring about madness or blindness (Hom. Od. 15,233–34; cf. Aesch. Eum. 329–32; Verg. Aen. 7,323–53) and punish offences, in particular crimes within a family (Hom. Od. 2,134–36; cf. Aesch. Cho. 1048–62; Eum. 94–177; Apollod. 3,87; Eur. Med. 1389; [3. 148]). In Aeschylus (Eum. 273–5; 339–40) and later, it is also said that they punish malefactors in the Underworld (Verg. Aen. 6,605–07; cf. Hom. Il. 3,276ff. and 19,259); in Apulian vase painting of the late 4th cent. BC, they are often depicted punishing criminals [5. 58–72; 6. 3.1. 828–29]. According to the oldest and most widespread theory, the Erinyes represent the angry dead who return in order to punish the living [8. 206; 9]. The identification of the Erinyes with the dead is probably true in general; however, the record of E. in Linear B (as a goddess) and her connection to Demeter make a modification of this thesis necessary [3]. Another familiar opinion sees the Erinyes as personified curses [10. 438–9].

At least since classical times, 'Erinyes' is only one of several names for goddesses who were also called Eumenides (the 'well-meaning ones') or *semnaì theaí* ('honoured goddesses') and who had places of worship at several locations in Greece; during worship, the euphemistic names were used [7; 8; 9]. The Erinyes were also associated with other groups of goddesses such as → Moira and → Praxidice [2. 86–91]. In a curse tablet E. is asked to force the → *áhoros* or *biaiothánatos* ('he who died prematurely or by violence') to be obedient (PGM IV,1417; IG (= CIA) 3[3], tab. def. 108). In ancient art, the Erinyes are generally depicted with wings, snake-like hair, hunting-boots and in a short chiton; sometimes they carry torches or whips [5. 1. 24–34; 6]. Aeschylus (Eum. 46–59), who provides the first literary description of their appearance, compares them with Gorgons and Harpies.

→ Moira; → Vanth

1 G. Neumann, Wortbildung und Etym. von E., in: Die Sprache 32, 1986, 43–51 2 E. Wüst, s.v. E., RE Suppl. 8, 82–166 3 S. I. Johnston, Penelope and the Erinyes: Od. 20,61–82, in: Helios 21/2, 1994, 137–159 4 Id., Xanthus, Hera and the Erinyes: Il. 19,400–419, in: TAPhA 122, 1992, 85–98 5 C. Aellen, A la recherche de l'ordre cosmique, 1994 6 H. Sarien, s.v. E., LIMC 3.1, 825–43 and 3.2, 595–606 7 A. Henrichs, Namenslosigkeit und Euphemismus. Zur Ambivalenz der chthonischen Mächte im att. Drama, in: H. Hofmann, A. Harder (ed.), Fragmenta Dramatica, 1991, 161–201 8 H. Lloyd-Jones, Erinyes, Semnai Theai, Eumenides, in: E. M. Craik (ed.), Owls to Athens, 1990, 203–11 9 A. Henrichs, Anonymity and Polarity: Unknown Gods and Nameless Altars at the Areopagos, in: Illinois Classical Studies 19, 1994, 27–58 10 Farnell, Cults, vol. 5.

S.I.J.

Eriphus (Ἔριφος; *Ériphos*). Poet of the Middle Comedy of whom three titles of works and seven fragments have still survived. In the Μελίβοια (*Melíboia*), E. appears to have taken up verses of → Antiphanes [1] and varied them (fr. 2; cf. Antiphanes fr. 59); in Πελταστής (*Peltastḗs*), a *miles gloriosus* probably appeared (fr. 6 [2. 326f.]).

1 PCG V, 1986, 178–182 2 H.-G. Nesselrath, Die att. Mittlere Komödie, 1990.

H.-G.NE.

Eriphyle (Ἐριφύλη; *Eriphýlē*). Daughter of Talaus; sister of → Adrastus and wife of the seer → Amphiaraus in Argus, who were reconciled after a feud and were willing to submit to E.'s judgement in case of future quarrels. Amphiaraus, in anticipation of his death, refused to take part in Adrastus' campaign against Thebes. Bribed by → Polyneices with Harmonia's necklace, E. forced him to participate. He instructed his sons to avenge him regarding E. (Hom. Od. 11,326f.; Stat. Theb. 4,187–213; Apollod. 3,60ff.). During the campaign of the → Epigoni against Thebes, E. let herself be bribed once again and persuaded her son → Alcmaeon to join the campaign (Apollod. 3,81; 86; Diod. Sic. 4,66,2f.). After his return, he punished E. (Verg. Aen. 6,445f.).

E. Bethe, s.v. E., RE 6, 460–463; A. Lezzi-Hafter, s.v. E. 1, LIMC 3.1, 843–846.

R.HA.

Eris (Ἔρις; *Éris*). Personification of (often warlike) strife, Latin → Discordia; in allegorical genealogy interpreted as sister of → Ares (Hom. Il. 4,441) or as daughter of → Nyx (Hes. Theog. 224ff., together with other negative 'abstracta'). In the Iliad, E. (alone or in association with Ares and other personifications) triggers the fighting (Hom. Il. 11,3ff.; 4,439ff.). The post-Homeric *Cypria* make E. the person actually responsible for the Trojan War due to her instigating the judgement of Paris at the wedding of Peleus and Thetis (Cypria argum. p. 38 Bernabé; the motif of the golden apple is Hellenistic). This negative image of E., adopted by Hesiod himself (Hes. Theog. 225), is later modified by him (Op. 11ff.) in that he contrasts it with a positive E. ('competition'). Both aspects are inherent in the Homeric conception of E. [1] and possibly an Indo-European heritage [2]. – The early Greek epic refers to pictorial representations of E. with striking frequency (Hom. Il. 5,740; 18, 535 = Hes. Sc. 156; 148), probably due to the influence of oriental or orientalizing art. The identification of such representations of E. is made particularly difficult by the mythological context being absent quite often (exception: judgement of Paris).

1 J. Hogan, E. in Homer, in: Grazer Beiträge 10, 1981, 21–58 2 B. Mezzadri, La double E. initiale, in: Métis 4, 1989, 51–60.

H. Giroux, s.v. E., LIMC 3.1, 846–850; H. A. Shapiro, Personifications in Greek Art, 1993, 51–61.

RE.N.

Eristic see → Sophists

Ermanaric, (H)ermanaricus (also Ermenrichus, Hermenerig). King of the East Goths who, as the first historically documented → Amal, already belongs to the 10th generation of the Amal family tree (Iord. Get. 79 from Cassiodorus). He was the youngest son of Achiulf, brother of Ansila, Ediulf and Vultuulf, and was regarded as the founder of the 'younger' family line which, in AD 515, rejoined the 'older' line, founded by Vultuulf, as a result of the marriage of → Eutharicus with → Amalasuntha (Iord. Get. 79–81). Around AD 370, E. ruled over an extensive empire with its core in southern Russia, but numerous peoples, stretching as far the Baltic region, were connected with it, with varying degrees of dependency (cf. Iord. Get. 116ff.). However, E.'s kingdom collapsed quickly when, in *c.* 375, the Huns crossed the Don; E. took his own life and the other Goths were subjected or withdrew (Amm. Marc. 31,3,1–3). PLRE 1, 283.

P. HEATHER, Cassiodorus and the Rise of the Amals, in: JRS 79, 1989, 103–128; H. WOLFRAM, s.v. E., RGA 7, 510–512; Id., Die Goten, ³1990, 95ff. M.MEI. and ME.STR.

Eroeadae (Ἐροιάδαι; *Eroiádai*).

[1] Attic *asty*(?)-deme (IG II², 1927) of the phyle Hippothontis, one *bouleutes* (after 307/6 BC: two). Only this E. (not E. [2]) is mentioned by Harpocr., Hsch. and Steph. Byz. s.v. E. Presumably located near Chaidari (there is the finding place of IG II², 1867, 6090). Ὀρε(ι)άδαι; *Ore(i)ádai* (SEG 13,115; SEG 17, 98; IG II², 2776 l. 52 [1. 82]) is possibly a variant of E. based on vowel metathesis [2. 171f.].

1 S.G. MILLER, A Roman Monument in the Athenian Agora, in: Hesperia 41, 1972, 50–95 2 P. SIEWERT, Die Trittyen Attikas und die Heeresreform des Kleisthenes, 1982 3 TRAILL, Attica 52, 59, 70, 110 no. 43, 125, table 8 4 Id., Demos and Trittys, 1986, 137 with n. 36.

[2] Attic *asty*(?)- or *mesogeia*-deme of the phyle Antiochis, one *bouleutes*. Harpocr., Hsch., Steph. Byz. s.v. E. mention only E. [1]. Location unknown.

TRAILL, Attica 54, 70, 110 no. 44, 125 no. 6, table 10; Id., Demos and Trittys, 1986, 139. H.LO.

Eros (Ἔρως; *Érōs*).

[1] Greek personification of love as sexual desire (Latin Amor, Cupido). Usually, E. is regarded as being the son of → Aphrodite, in whose sphere of influence he represents a central figure. → Ares is named as his father (Simon. fr. 43B). Not mentioned in Homer, E.'s image in archaic poetry is developed into an expression of the complex and contradictory experience of individual love [1]: 'limb-loosening' conquerer of gods and men (Hes. Theog. 121f.), he is simultaneously golden-haired (Anac. fr. 14B) and gold-winged (Aristoph. Av. 1738), but also irresistible like a storm (Sappho fr. 47); this antinomy is expressed in the image of the childlike-irresponsible (Alcm. fr. 38), of the 'bittersweet' (Sappho fr. 130) god. Other analyses of the effect of love construct a plurality of Erotes (Pind. Nem. 8,5f.; Bacchyl. 9,73) or they represent him, together with → Himeros and → Pothos ('longing'), with the → Charites ('grace') and with → Peitho ('persuasion'), as helpers and companions of Aphrodite; this occurs in particular in red-figured Attic vase painting, where E. is consistently depicted as a winged ephebe [2]. Then, in Hellenistic poetry and art, the image of the god as a childlike and playful boy dominates, who acts without any kind of innate responsibility. Plato splits the figure into a 'reasonable' (*sṓphrōn*) part and one 'causing offence' (*aischrós*) (Symp. 180) or positions (Phdr. 255D) E. and Anteros as complementary figures [3].

Alongside this image, there is a different one, first encountered in Hesiod, in cosmological and philosophical reflections. As the basic power of theogonic and cosmogonic events, conceived in genealogical form, E. is a primeval power in Hesiod which, together with → Gaia and → Tartarus ('earth' and 'depth of the earth') is created out of chaos without parents (Theog. 116–122) [4]. In → Acusilaus and → Parmenides, E. similarly is a primeval power. In the former, he is the son of → Nyx and → Aether (9 B 1 DK), in the latter, he is installed as the 'first of the gods' by the original female demon (28 B 13 DK). Orphic poetry adopts this in various, complex images [5]; in the detailed cosmogony of Aristophanes (Av. 692–716), shaped by Orphic ideas, the creator-god E. originates from a cosmic egg produced by Nyx. Plato, in the myth of Phaedrus (Symp. 178B), playfully falls back on the cosmogonic original god ('the oldest of the gods') and makes him the son of Penia and Poros, 'poverty' and 'abundance'. Later systematization attempts to sort out various genealogies and aspects by a split into three figures (Cic. Nat. D. 3,60). Gnostic speculations in turn develop the cosmogonic and Platonic suggestions further [6; 7] (→ Gnosis).

In worship, E. usually occurs together with → Aphrodite, in whose sphere of influence, concerned with love and marriage, he belongs; sanctuaries solely dedicated to him are rare. An exception is the cult in the Boeotian → Thespiae, where E. was worshipped in the form of a stone monument (Paus. 9,27,1); whether this cult is as ancient as Pausanias, based on that representation, thinks it is, is uncertain [8; 9].

E. in Latin is equivalent to Amor and Cupido, but having purely literary functions; both names are used synonymously [10].

1 F. LASSERRE, La figure d'E. dans la poésie grècque, 1946 2 H. A. SHAPIRO, Personifications in Greek Art. The Representation of Abstract Concepts 600–400 B.C., 1993, 110–124 3 C. OSBORNE, E. unveiled. Plato and the God of Love, 1994 4 A. BONNAFÉ, E. et Eris. Mariages divins et mythe de succession chez Hésiode, 1985 5 C. CALAME, E. initiatique et la cosmogonie orphique, in: PH. BORGEAUD (ed.), Orphée et Orphisme. En l'honneur de J. Rudhardt, 1991, 227–248. 6 M. TARDIEU, Trois mythes gnostiques. Adam, E. et les animaux d'Égypte dans un écrit de Nag Hammadi (II, 5), 1974 7 M.J. EDWARDS,

Gnostic E. and Orphic Themes, in: ZPE 88, 1991, 25–40 8 B. NEUTSCH, Vom Steinmal zur Gestalt. Zum Wandel griech. Götterbilder am Beispiel Hermes, E. und Aphrodite, in: B. OTTO, F. EHRL (ed.), Echo. Beiträge zur Arch. des mediterranen und alpinen Raums, 1990, 245–262 9 SCHACHTER 1, 217 10 A. FLIEDNER, Amor und Cupido. Untersuchungen über den römischen Liebesgott, 1974.

W. STROBEL, E. Ein Versuch seiner bildlichen Darstellungen, 1952; A. GREIFENHAGEN, Griech. Eroten, 1957; S. FASCE, E. La figura e il culto, 1977; J.-P. VERNANT, Un, deux, trois. E., in: M.-M. MACTOUX, E. GENY (ed.), Mélanges P. L'Evêque 1, 1988, 293–306; V. PIRENNE-DELFORGE, E. en Grèce – dieu ou démon?, in: J. RIES, H. LIMET (ed.), Anges et démons, Actes du Colloque de Liège et Louvain-la-Neuve, 1989; N. BLANC, F. GURY, s.v. E., LIMC 3.2, 609–727. F.G.

[2] Imperial freedman and personal secretary, originator of the conspiracy which in AD 275 led to the murder of Aurelianus [3] (Aur. Vict. Caes. 35,8, not referred to by name; Zos. 1,62,1; Zon. 12,27; SHA Aur. 36,4; 37,2, under the name 'Mnesteus', probably because of a translation error; PIR³, 85). A.B.

Erotianus Greek grammarian, middle or end of the 1st cent. AD, author of a glossary of Hippocratic words, which he dedicated to → Andromachus [4 or 5], a doctor at the imperial court in Rome [2; 3]. The alphabetic structure of the glossary, in its surviving form, does not go back to E. since, in his preface (9), he expressly emphasizes that he had explained the words in the sequence of their appearance in *c.* 37 Hippocratic texts which in turn could be classified into 1) semiotic, 2) physiological-aetiological, 3) therapeutic texts, 4) miscellaneous, 5) texts on the art of medicine such as *Iusiurandum*, *Lex* and *De vetere medicina* [5]. Such a general classification scheme probably goes back to → Bacchius [1], 3rd cent. BC, even though individual details most probably do not come from him. In addition, E. demonstrates his familiarity with other Hellenistic scholars and glossarists [4; 6. 488–495]. Unintelligible terms from the Hippocratic works he explains by referring back to poetic and non-medical prose as well as to other medical texts. His remark that *Prorrhētikón II* was not written by Hippocrates, represents the earliest evidence of an authenticity debate on the Hippocratic texts [5. 234]. E. had the aim to make → Hippocrates available again and to recommend his works as literature of high quality, in particular for those doctors whose knowledge was on a par with that of Hippocrates. E.'s glossary was used directly and indirectly by a large circle of readers. For Diogenianus and Hesychius, it represented the main source of early medical terms [2. 547f.], and even though Galen in his own Hippocratic glossary mentions E. only once (19,108), he is indebted to him far more than this single reference suggests.

EDITION: 1 E. NACHMANSON, Erotiani Vocum Hippocraticarum Collectio, 1918.

BIBLIOGRAPHY: 2 L. COHN, s.v. Erotianos, RE 6, 543–548 3 H. GÄRTNER, s.v. Erotianos, KlP 2, 363–364 4 J. ILBERG, Das Hippokratesglossar des E., in: Abh. sächs. Akad. Wiss. 14, 1893, 101–147 5 E. NACHMANSON, Erotianstudien, 1917 6 SMITH 7 STADEN 8 H. STEPHANUS, Dictionarium medicum, 1564. V.N.

Eroticism

I. LITERATURE II. ART

I. LITERATURE

A. INTRODUCTION B. THE NATURE OF EROS C. TAMED EROTICISM D. ROMAN LOVE LIFE E. THE NOVEL

A. INTRODUCTION

Sexual desire is one of the main subjects of ancient literature. Its representation in Greek and Roman texts includes a range of motifs (e.g. the → ekphrasis of the lover or the → paraklausithyron) which can also be found in the literature of the Near East (cf. the Song of Songs) and Egypt. Whether these congruencies are based on transcultural transfers or rather on parallel developments can usually not be determined. Since constructs of desire and love (if not also these feelings themselves) are dependent on traditional patterns and social conventions of individual cultures, the forms of the literary representations of → *érōs* (ἔρως, ἔρος) or *amor* are also stylised to a high degree: they use familiar metaphors (e.g. fire, injury) and, time and again, refer to a few 'classical' texts. Thus, for example, → Sappho was soon established as the female erotic poet *par excellence* (although almost the entire erotic literature of antiquity emanates from male authors). This literary stylizing of eroticism does not mean a lack of imagination and neither merely the realisation that desire is just as universal as it is unique when experienced by each person; rather, the 'classical' texts contributed to the cultural interpretation of eroticism. Therefore, literary representations of *érōs/amor* are actually normative and potentially didactic. They defy categorization according to genre or time of origin; descriptions of *amor* in Latin literature are strongly influenced by Greek models, for example.

The physical aspects of eroticism and sexuality can be found in the relevant genres, described in a very direct language: in iambic poetry (→ Hipponax; Catullus; Horace, 'Epodes'), in the Old → Comedy, in → epigrams (→ Martialis; *carmina* → *Priapea*), in → satire and in some → novels (→ Lollianus; Apuleius). The genres of high literature (epic, lyric poetry, rhetoric) avoid clear obscenities (such as βινεῖν, *bineîn*; *futuere*, etc.) and refer to the sex drive and sex act with circumlocutions and euphemisms. The actual erotica of ancient literature encompass a range from crude sexuality of, e.g., the → *mimos* (cf. e.g. Herodas 5) to the highly refined pornography of the → Second Sophistic where even the sexual act itself becomes a theme of scholarly debate (cf. Ps. Lucian Erotes; Ach.Tat. 2.35–38), and to the burlesque voyeurism in Nonnus' *Dionysiaka*. The Latin poetry of late antiquity (*Anthologia Latina*, the → Pervigilium Veneris or → Maximianus' elegies) includes particularly numerous erotic themes and thus anticipates the medieval lyric tradition.

B. The nature of Eros

In archaic epics, *érōs* (etymology unknown) is associated with any physical pleasure or a need to be satisfied (hunger, thirst, lament etc.); in the sexual area, *érōs* is the sudden, urgent desire by a man to unite with a particular woman, which is normally triggered by the sight of her beauty (cf. Hom. Il. 3,441–446; 14,312–338; 16,181–186; Hom. Od. 18,212f.; Hom. h. Aphrod. 144–154). 'Love at first sight', a frequent but not altogether universal motif of ancient literature, is a later expression of this concept, primarily in narrative texts: *érōs* radiates from the eyes of the beautiful person and attacks the victim through his eyes (e.g. Ach.Tat. 1,9,4). Since the beginnings of archaic lyric poetry, this motif of being overpowered can also be found in a pederastic context.

Érōs banishes all caution and reason (νόος, *nóos*; φρένες, *phrénes*; cf. Pl. Phdr. 238b-c; Theophr. fr. 115: Ἔρως δέ ἐστιν ἀλογίστου τινὸς ἐπιθυμίας ὑπερβολή, '*Érōs* is an excess of irrational desire') as well as any normal perception: lovers are proverbially blind *vis-à-vis* the faults of the loved one (cf. e.g. Pl. Leg. 5,731e5f.). *Érōs* causes deep distress and the loss of self-control (μανία, *manía*; οἶστρος, *oîstros* etc., cf. Ibycus, PMG 286: *érōs* as a storm): it is an involuntary compulsion (ἀνάγκη, *anánkē*; cf. Pl. Phdr. 240c-e; Xen. Cyr. 5,1,12) from which an escape is only possible occasionally. Love is never an unalloyed pleasure (cf. Sappho fr. 130: γλυκύπικρον ἀμάχανον ὄρπετον, 'the bittersweet, untamable animal'). For that reason and because the intrusion of *érōs* indicates a lack of something (the missing 'other') which is necessary for happiness, the concept of love is pitted against the favoured idea of self-reliance and independence (αὐτάρκεια, *autárkeia*) of the individual. This latter concept is dissolved by *érōs* (the 'limb-loosening', λυσιμελής, *lysimelḗs*) (cf. Hes. Theog. 121, Sappho fr. 130) in that he makes free men into 'slaves' no longer capable of making decisions (cf. the *servitium amoris* of Roman → elegies).

Since *érōs* cannot be controlled, it operates outside social institutions and norms, and actually against them (cf. Soph. Ant. 781–800). Thus, for example, the *érōs* felt by Paris for Helena characterizes his 'marriage' to her as a transgression (cf. Phaedra's *érōs* for her stepson Hippolytus and Apul. Met. 4,30,4: ⟨*amor*⟩ *omnium matrimonia corrumpens*, 'love spoils the marriage of all'). Since *érōs* corrodes body and mind, it is often represented as a disease (νόσος, *nósos*, Latin *pestis*) and described in quasi-medical language (cf. the initial scene of *Hippolytus* by Euripides). The search for a remedy (φάρμακον, *phármakon*) threads its way through the whole of ancient literature (e.g. Theoc. 11, Catull. 76, Ov. Rem. am., Longus 2,7,7). Here, the power of *érōs* appears similar to the ambivalent gifts of Dionysus (for this ambiguity cf. Anacreon PMG 376: μεθύων ἔρωτι, 'drunk with love'; Eur. Hipp. 525–544; Eur. Med. 627–34; Eur. IA 543–557). Both are often mentioned together (cf. Anacreon PMG 357; Eur. Bacch. 402–416), primarily in the social context of the → symposium.

Amongst the most impressive records of the idea of *érōs* as a painful obsession are the subliterary magic spells from late Hellenism and the Imperial period, many of which have remained intact on Egyptian papyri: with the aid of love spells, men attempt to arouse mad lust in the desired woman: 'Make ⟨her⟩ love me with gut-consuming passion (ἔρωτι σπλαγχνικῷ) ... When she wants to sleep, place thorns under her and barbs on her brow' (PGM 36,149–153). Such violent and often sadistic fantasies reveal the extreme form of a specifically male projection of eroticism onto women who were regarded as emotionally more unstable than men and thus were regarded as being especially vulnerable to the attacks of *érōs* (just as to being seized by Dionysus, cf. the Maenads, → *Mainades*). In satirical literature, this attitude is crystallized in the image of the sex-obsessed woman (e.g. Aristoph. Lys.; Juv. 6). Women thus require strong social control; the 'works of Aphrodite' are placed in antithesis to those of Athena (weaving and other domestic crafts), the true female area of activity (cf. Hom. h. Aphrod. 1–15; Hor. Carm. 3,12).

The destructive potential of female desire was already recognized in classical Greek literature, most of all in Attic tragedies (cf. also Gorg. Helena 15–19), and used as a literary theme. But, especially from Hellenistic and Roman times, there are (from the pen of male authors) detailed descriptions of the psychological and physical suffering of women seized by *érōs/amor* (Theoc. 2; Apoll. Rhod. 3–4; Dido in Vergil; Ovids *Heroides* etc.)

C. Tamed Eroticism

Two of the literary strategies used to tame this dangerous power deserve special consideration:

A series of prose texts predominantly from the 4th cent. BC channel pederastic eroticism into socially or philosophically productive avenues by emphasizing, as the elegies of → Theognis had done before, their educational function in teaching ἀρετή (*aretḗ*, 'virtue') (cf. Xen. Symp. 8; Ps. Demosth. Erotikos). Typical in them is the distinction between the 'heavenly' love for the soul of the other and the common striving for purely physical satisfaction (this distinction, advocated by Plato's Socrates, had its effects for a long time, e.g. it reached into the tradition of novel writing, see below). Prominent amongst the texts are the brilliant discussions on eroticism (τὰ ἐρωτικά, *tá erōtiká*) in Plato's *Symposium* and *Phaedrus*; they influenced these themes throughout the entire rest of antiquity, principally the extensive narrative or para-philosophical treatment of eroticism in the Second Sophistic and, facilitated by late

Platonism, in the Christian literature.The latter saw in Plato's ideas a pagan version of *érōs*, which could be given a new spiritual expression as a result of either ignorance or deliberate misunderstanding.

Plato reinterpreted the confusion of the lover and his longing for the loved one as a striving for metaphysical knowledge. In the *Symposium*, he has the comedy writer → Aristophanes [3] narrate a myth: originally, human beings were double (just like Siamese twins), but the gods divided them into two halves each in order to curtail their exuberance. Therefore, *érōs* is the search of individuals for their male or female counterpart; when this counterpart is found, the individual would like to spend the rest of his/her life with that person, being reunited into a whole now. This mythological model explains both the power of the erotic drive as well as the special happiness of those who can remain in a lifelong bond of φιλία (*philía*, 'friendship').

(2) Since the 4th cent. BC, a widespread plot structure can be found in comedy (in → Menander; Plautus; Terence; cf. Eubulus fr. 40 KASSEL-AUSTIN; Alexis fr. 20 KASSEL-AUSTIN): a young man, gripped by *érōs*, falls in love with a young woman and/or rapes her; finally, this leads to marriage. Here, the power of eroticism is reinterpreted and employed for the socially sanctioned purposes of marriage, having children and the continuity of the → *oîkos*.

D. ROMAN LOVE LIFE

The Hellenistic epigram and Roman poetry, especially Catullus, the elegies of → Propertius, → Tibullus, → Ovidius, also → Virgilius (Eclogae and Aen. 4), probe the semi-paradox that the lover is constantly 'possessed' by a demonic power which causes a crippling paranoia (cf. Ter. Eun. 72f.; Catull. 85). *Amor* suppresses *consilium*, the clear reasoning of the upright citizen (Ter. Eun. 57f.; Prop. 1,1,6). The elegiac model of love, the 'war service of love' (*militia amoris*, cf. Ov. Am. 1,9: *militat omnis amans*), is contrasted with the traditional Roman core values – supported in epics – of political and military honour (cf. Prop. 2,1); it represents the Roman equivalent of the threat posed by *érōs* to the social institution of the Greek polis. Catullus' erotic poetry proved to be particularly effective. His reflections on parallels and differences between sexual love (*amor*) and the longing caused by the death of a brother, are amongst the most innovative and most moving poetic renditions of the theme (Catull. 65; 68; cf. also Catull. 72,3f.).

Ovid's *Ars amatoria* provides concrete instructions for an intimate life with the respective opposite sex: Book 1–2 for men, Book 3 for women. In this didactic poetry, which *i.a.* is part of the tradition of pornographic manuals (Philaenis), the play (*ludus*) of love is given rules. In the erotodidaxis of Roman (cf. Ov. Am. 1,4; Tib. 1,4) and later Greek literature (cf. Ach.Tat. 1,9–11; Alciphron; Aristaenetus), *érōs/amor* is no longer an overpowering, irrational force, but an art (τέχνη, *téchnē*; *ars*) the tactics of which one can learn.

E. THE NOVEL

In the Greek and Roman novel of the Imperial period, the *érōs* of ancient literature celebrates its last triumphs. A pair of lovers (not always married) is being separated; the two suffer incredible trials while they – just as the two mythological halves in Plato's *Symposium* – are looking for each other all over the world. This faithfulness, which is always rewarded in the end, and the high value placed on chastity and marriage (especially in Heliodorus' *Aethiopiaca*) are reminiscent of contemporary Christian ideals. This contrasts with the purely physical, painful longing caused amongst the less virtuous co-actors by the beauty of the pair. The 'Odyssey' is a critical model here, not only as the prototype of all travel narratives: the story of the longing of the wandering Odysseus for his faraway wife (cf. Hom. Od. 5,82–84; 156; 158) and the happy – also sexual – reunion with her (Hom. Od. 23,295f.) anticipates the narrative erotic energy which leads the listener and the reader to the end of the work and finally directs the figures of the novel into each other's arms. In → Petronius' *Satyrica*, this narrative pattern is reversed in a parodying manner by juxtaposing the unfaithfulness of most of the figures in the novel and their constant hunt for sexual pleasures with the downright absurd romantic self-dramatization of Encolpius.

A special place in ancient erotic literature is taken up by → Longus' 'Daphnis and Chloe'. This novel abandons the convention of love at first sight and thus gains space for new topics: the growth of love and sexuality between two teenagers as well as the relationship between human constructs of *érōs* and the practices of nature.

G. BINDER, B. EFFE (ed.), Liebe und Leidenschaft. Histor. Aspekte von E. und Sexualität, 1992; R.D. BROWN, Lucretius on Love and Sex, 1987; A. CARSON, Eros the Bittersweet, 1986; K.J. DOVER, Greek Homosexuality, 1978; P. FLURY, Liebe und Liebessprache bei Menander, Plautus und Terenz, 1968; M. FOUCAULT, Histoire de la sexualité, vol. 2–3, 1984; M. FUSILLO, Il romanzo greco. Polifonia ed eros, 1989; S.D. GOLDHILL, Foucault's Virginity, 1995; D.M. HALPERIN, J.J. WINKLER, F.I. ZEITLIN (ed.), Before Sexuality, 1990; D.F. KENNEDY, The Arts of Love, 1993; D. KONSTAN, Sexual Symmetry: Love in the Ancient Novel and Related Genres, 1994; F. LASSERRE, La figure d'Eros dans la poésie grecque, 1946; J.C. MCKEOWN, Ovid: Amores, 1987; C. OSBORNE, Eros Unveiled: Plato and the God of Love, 1994; E. ROHDE, Der griech. Roman und seine Vorläufer, [3]1914; A. SIEMS (ed.), Sexualität und E. in der Ant., 1988; P. VEYNE, L'élegie érotique romaine: l'amour, la poésie et l'occident, 1983; J.J. WINKLER, The Constraints of Desire, 1990; F.I. ZEITLIN, Playing the Other. Gender and Society in Classical Greek Literature, 1996. R.HU.

II. ART

The following article provides an overview of research, the inventory of motifs and representations of eroticism in the fine arts of the Greeks and Romans. Due to the complexity of the subject matter, no general or literary references in relation to individual points can be given; in various details, the article is indebted to the works in the bibliography below.

A. Definition B. State of research C. Basic motifs D. Representations

A. Definition

Eroticism as a fundamental expression of human communication pervades all manifestations and relationship forms of love. Eroticism, derived from → *érōs* (ἔρως, ἔρος), encompasses the spiritual and physical, is the spiritual-psychological development of sexuality, plays consciously or unconsciously with physical charms. In Latin *amor*, the phenomenon is only partly covered; the facets of meaning in *libido* (pleasure, charm, desire, lechery) subsume an eroticism that is closely connected with → sexuality. Here, the latter is understood to mean sexuality without erotic complications in the totality of all modes of behaviour which are related to the sexual act/sexual gratification in human beings and animals. In contrast to the sexuality of an animal, human eroticism does not exclusively serve the purpose of procreation, but as a component of personality is oriented towards the physical as well as the spiritual-psychological. The ability of human beings to act both in a spiritual-psychological and in a physical-sensual way, forbids on the one hand using 'eroticism' and 'sexuality' as synonymous, but permits on the other hand to conceptually exchange both terms because of the parallelism of eroticism and sexuality. Eroticism can belong to → pornography, which primarily deals with sexual acts as they are portrayed today in literature, photography and film.

B. State of research

Research on eroticism in Greek and Roman art demonstrates a concentration in certain areas: anthropology, sociology, religion, ancient texts (s. I above), surviving monuments (fine art), history of reception. Examinations of individual topics are predominant, works providing an overview are rare. Some publications do not give exact descriptions of what makes a representation erotic, instead they offer a time-specific interpretation/current research analysis which, at a secondary level, is based on the sculptural or pictorial work and evaluates it in a way that supports the intended reading. Based on a difficult selection of images, any overall treatment of eroticism must consider the scale from moderately erotic to lacking decency because this very juxtaposition of openly expressed and subliminally operating sensuality creates a basis for the stimulation which the ambivalent term eroticism refers to. The basic experience of eroticism, which primarily occurs as a result of looking, feeling and touching, is based on the biologically attractive; this can, but need not, be beautiful. Any contact with erotic images depends on personal erotic sensibility. Written as well as verbal expressions regarding eroticism betray individual perception. An absolute, neutral consideration of eroticism is impossible.

Most of the investigations into eroticism discuss Greek and Roman monuments of the Mediterranean basin together, which leads to improper generalizations. Things Greek cannot be transferred without reservations to things Roman although there are threads of tradition leading from things Greek to things Roman. All erotica of ancient Italy are to be evaluated before the background that the development of art there in the 1st millennium BC largely rests on the interaction with different cultures, most of all the Greek. Together with Hellenism, Rome also adopted erotic art, combined it with its own approach and developed it further.

Erotic representations in diverse materials and dimensions run through the art genres (sculpture, relief, painting, mosaic). The frequency of the medium used for eroticism differs between the Greeks and Romans. Their images become manifest in: statues/groups of statues; reliefs as individual pieces or as decorations on utensils (mainly drinking vessels, lamps, mirrors, cut stones, coins); vases (vessel painting); buildings (wall paintings, floor mosaic). Special research has recorded erotic symbols, e.g. from the vegetable world. Due to the random occurrence of finds, the interpretation of archaeological monuments related to eroticism is characterized, for Greek and Roman examples, by the difficulty of having to work on items that happen to be available.

It remains a research objective to systematically record all collection activities regarding erotic art. For Greek and Roman antiquity, C. Johns [1] carried out pioneering work in this regard.

C. Basic motifs

Eroticism has basic motifs which are determined less by the relevant culture than by the reception on the part of the viewer who, moulded by education and guided by religion, views things according to his/her predisposition, dependent on and specific to the respective gender, and who is psychologically sensual and can be sexually stimulated in a physical sense. The following motifs are characteristic of Greek and Roman images even though they do not consistently correspond:

Nudity; interplay between nudity and being clothed: frequently, for men, there is a coat where the edge follows an arc under his genitals and, for women, a robe leaving part or all of her breast uncovered; furthermore, transparent materials over prominent parts of the body and erogenous zones. Pose: a woman/a man is presented in three-quarter view in a reclining pose, which inevitably evokes a sensual understanding of physicality. An arm moved back over the head brings about an association of relaxation, comfort, sleep, opening up to a person opposite and leads the viewer's gaze to the body. Rear view: the curved buttock is deliberately provocative. Erection: sexual arousal is shown. Posture and eye contact: woman/man or youth/man approach each other in the course of which they may establish intimately longing eye contact. Dance: soft or temperamental dancing steps have an erotic effect. Performance: acrobatic jumps/tricks favour sexual desires. Chase: the interested male, often with an erect penis, chases a youth or a woman. Resistance: playful withdrawal by the wooed/desired one intensifies the longing of the person opposite. Embrace: a heterosexual couple/homosexual pair of men embrace each other intimately. Kiss of a pair (woman and man or youth and man respectively). Manual touch: erotic-sexual stimulation of the partner by touching/stroking of the primary and secondary sexual organs. Sexual union: heterosexual couples have frontal or dorsal (*a tergo*) intercourse. Various other coitus positions, also fellatio and cunnilingus, occur between two persons or in a group. Thigh intercourse: a man rubs his genitals between the thighs of his partner. Self-gratification: male masturbation is shown. Auxiliary objects: jewellery on bare skin, loose strands in otherwise well-styled hair and rich hair all indicate female attractiveness.

Certain gestures are to be ascribed to the group of basic erotic motifs as lesser classification units which, dependent on the pictorial content, can be read as erotic codes (→ Gestures). Exemplary: if a hand touches the point of the chin of the desired opposite person, it signals consent; an arm stretched out towards a partner means that sexual animation is approved of or that sensual desire is rejected; if a woman's hand takes holds of the corner of a robe with the tips of her fingers, it creates a coquettish setting.

D. Representations

The basic motifs of eroticism listed under C. run through reality and myths with varying intensity in a rich range of themes. They occur amongst gods, heroes, human beings, mythical creatures, animals, plants, even in the area of death. The context of a representation can co-determine or cause its erotic effect. Erotic figures of Greek mythology reappear manifold in the Roman one, which itself produced hardly any new mythological figures of primary erotic characterization.

An individual person (goddess/god, woman/man, heroine/hero) may have an erotic effect by being partly covered or nude, even if the latter imparts heroic qualities: ideal → nudity does not preclude sensual perception. Free-standing sculptures (Roman copy after Greek original and Roman creation) are a source of erotic signals (nude body surface, see-through robe, narrow breast band). Parts of coats cover the thighs of seated women in a way that emphasizes the pubic area. Unrealistic robe formations stress the erotic.

In the case of the deities → Priapus, → Aphrodite/Venus and → Dionysus/Bacchus, eroticism is tangible most frequently. Priapus, with exaggerated displays of erections, becomes the quintessence of the erotic-sexual. Around Aphrodite/Venus, vulgar eroticism only occurs within the circle of her admirers from the milieu of prostitutes, and around Dionysus/ Bacchus, it is confined to his followers. Thus, gross eroticism is not a theme directly associated with Aphrodite/Venus and Dionysus/Bacchus. In mythology, the *thiasos* of Dionysus exhibits the erotic-sexual image content most with significantly more pairs engaged in intercourse than among Bacchus' entourage in Roman monuments. Randy → Satyrs and → Sileni, most represented in Greek vase painting, are depicted less lecherously in Roman art, e.g. on sarcophagus reliefs, although their sexual interest in their companions seems just as carnal as that of their Greek counterparts. It can be deduced from systematic investigations that the → Pans in Roman art are clearly erotically superior to the Satyrs (one should take note, e.g., of their activities with goats). Roman Dionysiac representations show sensually more restrained images than their Greek equivalents. The Satyrs, popular in Greek art, though they can only be called erotic with reservations, who masturbate alone or in a group, are not shown in Roman art; there, one can find dwarf-like, deformed or old men instead, with excessively large penises.

→ Hercules, as a protagonist of the male world of heroes, offers erotic representations of his amorous adventures. → Leda, seduced by Zeus in the shape of a swan, is a popular material for eroticism in Roman art. The entire realm of heroes offers significantly more erotic facets, though.

Eroticism in 'everyday' life depicts especially scenes at → banquets. Some images depict → hetaerae at drinking orgies in sensual body presentations with moderate eroticism, many present hetaerae or prostitutes and men during erotic-sexual interaction (courting, kiss, foreplay, coitus), arranged as a pair situation or group activity. These monuments depict women during performances for the sexual animation of symposiasts, for example dancing with imitations of male genitals. It is not always possible to determine whether an erotic act is taking place at a drinking orgy or in a brothel. Negotiations between a prostitute and her suitor, expressed with a purse held by the man, are only found on Attic vase paintings. While Attic vessels (end of 6th cent./1st quarter of 5th cent. BC) are rich in direct erotica, the vase painting of Southern Italy (end of 5th cent./4th cent. BC), which was influenced by Greek art, only portrays modest lovemaking activities. There are no Greek wall paintings containing eroticism that can be evaluated. Roman-Campanian wall paintings (1st cent. AD) from Pompeii clearly display erotica; they decorated private houses, baths and brothels. Reliefs on lamps and terra sigillata of the entire *imperium romanum* offer numerous coitus representations.

In the Greek and Roman world, all female partners in images of eroticism are to be regarded as prostitutes: enhancing men's quality of life, they guarantee those sensual pleasures for men which are based on a consensus between prostitution and social norms. Some representations strikingly reflect women being disadvantaged and, at times, violence is eroticized. In Greek and

Roman art, artistically rendered love acts follow similar arrangements of frontal and dorsal intercourse while lying down, squatting or standing. There are pictures of couples where the woman carries out fellatio on the man. A statistical evaluation may reveal that sexual intercourse in a standing position occurs more often on Greek monuments than on Roman ones. Sexual foreplay appears less varied in Roman than in Greek erotica. Women, painted on Attic vases as desirable beauties (as individuals, to be associated with a private picture), are missing in Roman art, likewise images of women in obscene performances during drinking orgies. Brothel scenes in Roman art exclusively show coitus, fellatio, rarely cunnilingus.

The homosexual love scene, a reflection of → paederasty, on Attic vases (6th/5th cents. BC) presents a motif repertoire similar to that of heterosexual relations between couples, i.e. it shows eroticism as being sexually congruent. Roman art shows love between men only occasionally. Greek vase paintings with masturbating men do exist, but there are no equivalents in Roman art.

The penis appears as an independent, often winged object which, on religious and mythological monuments of the everyday world, is the epitome of an omnipresent potency, while the combinations of the phallus with other elements, forming absurd images, are more diverse in Roman than in Greek art. However, phallus birds (phallus head on bird body) occur more often in Greek art. Phallic symbolism, associated with manifestations of carnal love, sexual desires and pictorial beauty, can be received as erotic when viewed.

Extreme sexual situations are documented in Greek vase painting (6th cent. BC): animals in intercourse with mythical creatures or human beings. Such images of superficially erotic nuances with humorous to satirical elaboration are hardly equivalent to the brutal scenes on Roman lamp reliefs where a four-legged creature copulates with a woman.

Eroticism in the area of death becomes visible in women on Greek grave stelae where physical beauty combines with passing gifts and eye contact between those saying farewell. → Sirens and → Sphinx, in some Greek vase pictures to be interpreted as erotic death demons, are only partially equivalent to Roman sphinxes with voluptuous busts (sarcophagus and architectural decoration).

Occasionally, developments from Greek to Roman iconography of eroticism are concretizations. A lecherous Greek Satyr in a vase painting, who longingly creeps up on Dionysus' sleeping companion, becomes a servant of Bacchus in a Roman sarcophagus relief who suppresses his sexual interest and leads his master to the slumbering Ariadne. Often, reception patterns and paths of tradition can only be recognized associatively. Motif traditions elucidated by scholarly knowledge are rare and can only be documented by great research efforts. The occasionally expressed view that the pictorial language of eroticism developed from Greek simplicity to Roman diversity cannot be maintained because turbulent orgies full of drastic love acts in the middle of a → *klínē*, lamps and drinking vessels on Attic vases are not a suitable pattern for quietly reclined, almost featureless couples in a row on Roman terra sigillata. Without hair-splitting hypotheses, Graeco-Hellenistic mosaics cannot be made into models for erotica in Roman mosaics. Statements regarding a development from Greek to Roman image concepts in eroticism can at best be made via statistical investigations.

A glance at all preserved reliefs shows: Roman glyptic articles are more numerous than Greek ones. The most extensive groups of Roman artefacts are lamps and terracotta utensils. Eroticism on Roman stone reliefs (decorative disc/brothel sign) or metal tokens (means of payment in brothels) is without Greek parallels.

The following observations are applicable to all representations of eroticism in Greek and Roman art: there is more subdued sensuality than vulgar carnality whereby the ambiguous basic tendency (soft tenderness, demanding desire) and thus the complex effects of eroticism are recognised. Eroticism attaches itself firmly to religion and deity. Eroticism, as a matter-of-fact component of life is rarely hidden. Nevertheless, in images of heterosexual couples, wives are never portrayed, but usually hetaerae/prostitutes, even in a wall painting in the living area of a Pompeian married couple or on a vessel amongst the household utensils of married Athenians. The social acceptance of extramarital love-interests varied in the centuries from which the pictorial media containing eroticism have survived. The erotic art of antiquity expresses primeval human experiences of manifold passions by way of many formal languages that are subject to workshop-specific and period-related style criteria.

→ Pornography; → Sexuality; → EROTICA

1 C. JOHNS, Sex or Symbol. Erotic Images of Greece and Rome, 1982, 15–35

J. BOARDMAN, E. LA ROCCA, Eros in Griechenland, 1976; J. BOARDMAN, The Phallos-Bird in Archaic and Classical Greek Art, in: RA 1992, 227–242; O.J. BRENDEL, The Scope and Temperament of Erotic Art in the Graeco-Roman World, in: T. BOWIE, CH. CHRISTIANSON (ed.), Stud. in Erotic Art, 1970, 3–69; A. DIERICHS, E. in der Kunst Griechenlands, [2]1997; Id., E. in der Röm. Kunst, 1997; K.J. DOVER, Greek Homosexuality, 1978; G. FEMMEL, CH. MICHEL, Die Erotica und Priapea aus der Sammlung Goethes, 1990; R. FLACELIÈRE, L'amour en Grèce, 1960; M. GRANT, A. MULAS, Eros in Pompeji. Das Geheimkabinett des Mus. von Neapel, 1975; P. GRIMAL, L'amour à Rome, 1988; A. HERMANN, H. HERTER, s.v. Dirne, RAC 3, 1149–1213; H. HERTER, s.v. Genitalien, RAC 10, 1–51; Id., s.v. Phallos, RE 19, 1938, 1681–1748; R. HURSCHMANN, Symposienszenen auf unterital. Vasen, 1985; L. JACOBELLI, Le pitture erotiche delle terme suburbane di Pompei, 1995; C. JOHNS, Sex or Symbol. Erotic Images of Greece and Rome, 1982 · E.C. KEULS, The Reign of the Phallus, 1985; M.F. KILMER, Greek Erotica on Attic Red-Figured Vases, 1993 · D.M. KLINGER, Erot. Kunst in der Ant./Erotic Art in Antiquity, vol. 7, 1983;

G. KOCH-HARNACK, Knabenliebe und Tiergeschenke. Ihre Bed. im päderastischen Erziehungssystem Athens, 1983; Id., Erotische Symbole. Lotosblüte und gemeinsamer Mantel auf ant. Vasen, 1989; T. LAQUEUR, Making Sex. Body and Gender from Greeks to Freud, 1990; A. LESKY, Vom Eros der Hellenen, 1976; H. LICHT, Sittengesch. Griechenlands, vol. 2: Das Liebesleben der Griechen, 1926; suppl. vol: Die E. in der griech. Kunst, 1928; J. MARCADÉ, Eros Kalos. Studie über die erotischen Darstellungen in der griech. Kunst, 1962; Id., Die Liebe in der Kunst der Etrusker und Römer. Roma Amor, 1977; G. L. MARINI, Il Gabinetto Segreto del Museo Nazionale di Napoli, 1971 · M. C. MARKS, Heterosexual Coital Position as a Reflection of Ancient and Modern Cultural Attitudes, 1978; M. MEYER, Männer mit Geld, in: JDAI 102, 1988, 87–125; CH. MILES, J. NORWICH, Liebe in der Ant., 1997; D. MOUNTFIELD, Erot. Kunst der Ant., 1982; I. PESCHEL, Die Hetäre bei Symposion und Komos in der att.-rf. Vasenmalerei des 6.–4. Jh. v. Chr., 1989; C. REINSBERG, Ehe, Hetärentum und Knabenliebe, [2]1993; A. RICHLIN (ed.), Pornography and Representation in Greece & Rome, 1992; A. K. SIEMS (ed.), Sexualität und E. in der Ant., 1988; B. SIMONETTA, R. RIVA, Le Tessere Erotiche Romane, 1981; A. STEWART, Art, Desire and the Body in Ancient Greece, 1997, 156–181; F. SUTTON, The Interaction between Men and Women Portrayed on Attic Red-figure Pottery, 1981; V. VANOYEKE, La prostitution en Grèce et à Rome, 1990; A. VARONE, Erotica Pompeiana. Inscrizioni d'amore sui muri di Pompei, 1994; G. VORBERG, Glossarium Eroticum, 1932; Id., Ars Erotica Veterum. Das Geschlechtsleben im Alt., 1926/1968; K.-W. WEEBER, Flirten wie die alten Römer, 1997. AN.DI.

Erucius Italian family name (possibly originating in Etruria, SCHULZE, 112, 170), attested from the 1st cent. BC but not of any significance until the 2nd cent. AD. K.-L.E.

[1] Sex. E. Clarus. Son of the E. Clarus named in Pliny (Ep. 2,9,4), grandson of the later Praetorian prefect Septicius Clarus; father or grandfather of E. [2]. Pliny supported him in the early stages of his career. He took part in Trajan's Parthian War, in which he conquered Seleucia probably in AD 116. He consequently received a suffect consulate in AD 117. Under Pius he became *praef. urbi*, in 146 *cos. ord. II*; he died in February or March of that year [1]. He had an interest in literature from his youth. PIR[2] E 96.

1 VIDMAN, FO[2], 50.

[2] C. E. Clarus. Son or grandson of E. [1]. *Cos. ord.* in 170; probably shortly afterwards, consular legate of Syria Palaestina. Married to Pomponia Triaria. PIR[2] E 95.

RAEPSAET-CHARLIER, No. 642.

[3] C. Iulius E. Clarus Vibianus. Son of E. [2]. He was probably of patrician rank (cf. AE 1954, 139). In AD 192 Commodus is said to have considered having him and Pompeius Falco murdered, as the consuls designated for 193, and that, among other things, led to Commodus' own murder. In AD 193 *cos. ord.* Executed by Septimius Severus for not being prepared to take action against the supporters of Albinus. His son was E. [4]. PIR[2] E 97.

[4] C. E. Clarus. = C. Iulius Rufinus Laberius Fabianus Pomponius Triarius E. Clarus Sosius Priscus. Son of E. [3], of patrician rank; honoured in Diana Veteranorum. AE 1954, 139.

W. ECK, RE Suppl. 14, 117; E. CHAMPLIN, in: AJPh 100, 1979, 298ff. W.E.

Ervig, Ervigius King of the West Goths, AD 680–687. As *comes* at the court of Wamba, E. was not free of involvement in the latter's deposal and he had himself anointed king without any election. In 681 he had a new version of the law of the West Goths issued. His policy of strengthening the kingship came to grief in 683, when he was obliged to make concessions to the aristocracy at the 13th Council of Toledo. In 687, seriously ill, he designated his bitter rival Egica as his successor. M.MEI. and ME.STR.

Eryce (Ἐρύκη; *Erýkē*). Town in Sicily (Steph. Byz. s.v. 'E., s.v. Παλική), located most probably in the mountainous area [1] of Ramacca [2].

1 V. TARTARO, La montagna di Ramacca e l'antica città di E., 1980 2 E. PROCELLI, s.v. Ramacca, BTCGI 14, 549–554. GI.F.

Erycius (Ερύκιος; *Erýkios*) Author of 14 epigrams in the 'Garland' of Philippus: dedicatory, funerary and epideictic epigrams treating traditional (often bucolic, cf. Anth. Pal. 6,96; 255; 7,174 etc.) themes with remarkable elegance. Internal evidence assigns him to the 2nd half of the 1st cent. BC and suggests that he probably visited Rome (cf. 6,96,2 Ἀρκάδες ἀμφότεροι and Verg. Ecl. 7,4 *Arcades ambo*). The heading of 7,230 attests to his having come from Cyzicus (that of 7,397, Ἐρυκίου Θετταλοῦ, seems to confirm the existence of a second E.); he is possibly identical with the Hellenistic epic writer of the same name (cf. SH 407).

GA II,1, 244–255; 2, 278–288. E.D.

Erymanthian Boar see → Hercules

Erymanthus (Ἐρύμανθος; *Erýmanthos*).

[1] A mountain range extending up to 2,224 m in height and consisting of several chains stretching north-east to south-west; located in the north-western Peloponnese in the border area between → Elis and → Achaea, the earlier north-western mountain border of → Arcadia. Composed of layers of limestone, it drops away sharply for over 25 km in the north-west towards the flysch hills of Voundoukia; today also Olonos. The setting for one of the 12 labours of Hercules, the slaying of the Erymanthian boar (cf. Soph. Trach. 1097); Artemis' hunting ground (Hom. Od. 6,102).

1 A. PHILIPPSON, Der Peloponnes, 1892, 280ff. 2 PHILIPPSON/KIRSTEN, 3, 201ff.

[2] Right tributary of the → Alpheius [1], rises in the Lampea range and flows into the Alpheius a little below Ladon (Pol. 4,70,8ff. Str. 8,3,12; 32); today also Doana.

1 A. PHILIPPSON, Der Peloponnes, 1892, 280ff. 2 PHILIPPSON/KIRSTEN, 3, 208. C.L. and E.O.

Erysichthon (Ἐρυσίχθων; *Erysíchthōn*: 'tearing up the earth' or 'protector of the country'). Mythical figure whose story is best known through Callimachus' 6th hymn to Demeter. According to it, he was a Thessalian, son of Triopas. He felled a grove that was sacred to Demeter even though the goddess in human form had warned him against it. As punishment for that he was made eternally hungry; he used up all he owned trying to assuage his hunger. Callimachus portrayed him as an unmarried youth; in other versions, including the earliest (Hes. fr. 43a M-W), he had a daughter Mestra, whose lover Poseidon had lent her the power to change into any shape she wished; she supported her father by allowing herself to be sold off in various animal shapes, escaping and returning to be sold yet again. The Hesiodic poem differs from later accounts in that it makes Mestra, and thus E. as well, Athenian. That suggests an identification with a figure that otherwise seems completely different, namely that of the Attic E., usually (or at least later) identified as the son of → Cecrops who died young and childless. E. probably enjoyed a hero cult for a while at Prasiae on the eastern coast of Attica, where his grave was located (Paus. 1,31,2). His mythical function, possibly principally under Phanodemus' influence (FGrH IIIb no. 325 F2), was establishing the Athenian relationship with Delos.

W. BURKERT, Structure and history in Greek mythology and ritual, 1979, 134–6; D. FEHLING, E. oder das Märchen von der mündlichen Überlieferung, in: RhM 115, 1972, 173–196; U. KRON, s.v. E., LIMC 4.1, 14–21; N. ROBERTSON, The ritual background of the E. story, in: AJPh 105, 1984, 369–408. E.K.

Erythea (Ἐρύθεια; *Erýtheia*). One of the → Hesperids (Hes. fr. 360; Apollod. 2,114). According to schol. Apoll. Rhod. 4,1399, the mythical island E. ('Red Country') on which → Geryoneus lived (Hes. Theog. 290) is named after her. According to Paus. 10,17,5 (after him Steph. Byz. s.v. E.), E. was Geryoneus' daughter and the mother of → Norax by Hermes. E. was usually thought to be in the area of Gadera or Tartessus (Stesichorus fr. 184 PMGF 1; Pherecydes FGrH 3 F 18b; Ephorus FGrH 70 F 129a; Philistides FGrH 11 F 3; Hdt. 4,8). This view was challenged by Hecataeus (FGrH 1 F 26). R.B.

Erythrae (Ἐρυθραί; *Erythraí*).

[1] Boeotian city mentioned as early as Hom. Il. 2,499 (Plin. HN 4,26; Steph. Byz. s.v. E.) on the northern slope of the → Cithaeron range east of Plataeae and Hysiae. Other references: Eur. Bacch. 751; Thuc. 3,24,2; Xen. Hell. 5,4,49; Paus. 9,2,1. According to Str. 9,2,12 mother city of the Ionian E. [2]. Before the battle of Plataeae (479 BC) the Persian camp stretched along the Asopus from E. over Hysiae to Plataeae, while the Greek army took up position initially at the foot of the Cithaeron range and then moved over Hysiae to Plataea (Hdt. 9,15; 19; 22; 25; Diod. Sic. 11,29,4). At the beginning of the Peloponnesian War the population of the unfortified E., which belonged to one of the areas of the Boeotian League dependent on Thebes, was evacuated to Thebes (Hell. Oxy. 19,3,387; 20,3,438; Str. 9,2,24). E. has been located east of today's Erythrai (previously: Kriekouki) either near today's abandoned settlement of Katsoula *c.* 4 km away, north of the Agia Triada church [2; 4] or near today's abandoned *metochi* of the Meletios monastery *c.* 8 km away, west of today's Dafni (previously: Darimari) beneath the mountain Kastron [1; 3].

1 FOSSEY, 116–119 2 MÜLLER, 491–493
3 PRITCHETT, IV, 89–91; V, 99–101 4 P.W. WALLACE, Strabo's Description of Boiotia, 1979, 55f. P.F.

[2] One of the 12 Ionian cities forming the → Panionium, on the Western coast of Asia Minor opposite Chios north of today's Çeşme on the bay of Ildır (Hdt. 1,142). According to the myth of its founding (Diod. Sic. 5,79; Paus. 7,3,7), E. owes its origins to Cretans, but on the evidence of the earliest inscriptions the inhabitants spoke an Ionian dialect. Lydian and Persian domination alternated. Taking part in the Ionian Revolt with eight ships, E. joined the Hellenic symmachy in 479 BC and subsequently the → Delian League; the enormously high contribution paid by the city attests to its wealth, which E. was able to preserve even in the 4th cent. In the Hellenistic period, Ptolemaic, Seleucid and Attalid influence in E. alternated several times over. When the province of Asia was constituted in 129 BC, E. was probably able to maintain the status of a free city for some time.

E.'s favourable siting for settlement – the 85 m high hill of the acropolis, the harbour protected by the offshore islands – is still readily recognizable today, but essentially all that remains of the buildings in E. is the over 4 km long ring wall from the Hellenistic period, together with the vestiges of the theatre; anything else was carried off in the 19th cent. for nearby buildings. The excavations by E. AKURGAL have considerably extended our knowledge of the city, especially of its early period; the most important finds are displayed in the museum of Izmir.

ARCHAEOLOGY: E. AKURGAL, Ancient Ruins of Turkey, 1979; Id., Eine ephesische Elfenbeinstatuette aus E., in: M. KANDLER et al. (ed.), Lebendige Altertumswiss., FS H.

Vetters, 1985, 43–49; O. BINGÖL, Der erste Wanddekorationsstil in E., in: AA 1988, 501–522; C. BAYBURTLUOGLU, E., 2 vols., 1975/77.
INSCRIPTIONS: IEry; SEG 26, 1282; 30, 1327–1331; 31, 969–971; 32, 1145; 33, 963; 36, 1039; 37, 917–955.
RELIGION: GRAF.
MONETARY SYSTEM: PH. P. BETANCOURT, Bronze Hoard from E., in: ANSMusN 1972, 23–39. HE.EN. and E.O.

Erythraean paean A → paean to → Asclepius in dactyls preserved in an inscription from Erythrae [2] (*c.* 380–360 BC), sung by the community during the sacrifice in the Asclepius cult as an appeal for good health; the inscription contains three other paeans with cult directions. Probably composed as early as the 5th cent. BC, the paean remained popular (numerous inscriptions) in many places until the Imperial period.
→ Metre

F. GRAF, Nordion. Kulte, 1985, 250–257; L. KÄPPEL, Paian, 1992, 189–200; 370–374 (with text, translation, bibliography). L.K.

Erythra thalatta (Ἐρυθρὰ θάλαττα; *Erythrà thálatta*).
[1] A sea (Ionian Ἐρυθρὴ θάλασσα, 'Red Sea') frequently mentioned from Herodotus until late antiquity, corresponding roughly in its normal extent to the north-western Indian Ocean (today's Arabian Sea), while today's Red Sea and Persian Gulf were regarded as κόλποι (*kólpoi*) of the *Erythra thalatta* (ET). Later on, however, this name undoubtedly covered an area much further eastwards; even the term *Periplus maris erythraei* to describe the coast stretching from within today's Red Sea to South-east Asia, attests to the name ET being applied far into the Indian Ocean, at least around its coastal sections. Curt. 8,9,6 confirms this when he has the Indus and the Ganges flowing into the *Rubrum mare*. The ET originated in today's Persian Gulf; that goes back to Herodotus (Hdt. 1,1; 180; 189; 3,30; 93; 4,37; 6,20 and *passim*), and to Xenophon as well (Cyr. 8,6,20; 8,1). Herodotus called today's Red Sea Ἀράβιος κόλπος (*Arábios kólpos*, Hdt. 2,11; 102; 158; 4,39; 42f.). Herodotus was not familiar with the name Ἰνδικὸν πέλαγος (*Indikòn pélagos*), but in the 5th cent. BC the term ET probably covered the Strait and the Gulf of Oman as well, thereby beginning the name's extension eastwards. In any case the 'Islands of the Banned' (Hdt. 7,80; [1]), close to the Strait of Oman, were then part of the ET. The colour red, ἐρυθρός (*erythrós*), referred to in the name, derives from some coral shelves in the Persian Gulf and, further on, from the appearance of the neighbouring Arabian Desert; the ET was the sea of the 'red land' (Str. 16,4,20). As an explanation, the mythical connection with a King Erythra(u)s (Mela 3,72; Curt. 8,9,14; Plin. HN 6,107; Steph. Byz. s.v. Ἐρύθρα), is quite worthless. That other sources of late antiquity also applied the name ET at least as far as India is shown *i.a.* by Eustathius on Dionysius Periegetes 1088 [2], according to which the Indus quickly alters its course southwards, opposite (κατεναντίον) the ET, and this sea is at the same time called Ἐρυθραῖος ὠκεανός (*Erythraîos ōkeanós*). Of all the sources the *Periplus maris rubri* represents not only the longest sea journey but also the greatest geographical extent of the name ET. At the same time there are indications of a retrograde development in which the ET is finally restricted to the area corresponding to today's Red Sea, a process that was already discernible in → Agatharchides, who essentially understood the ET as today's Red Sea. The fact that biblical sources (→ Erythra thalatta [2]) applied the name 'Red Sea' to the northernmost section of today's Red Sea (cf. also Diod. Sic. 1,33,8f.) allows us to surmise with some justification that – even before Hdt. – the whole Red Sea was once so called, its name being just as physically well founded in its southern section, through the proximity of the Arabian Desert and the presence of coral, as in the Persian Gulf. Red Sea, Persian Gulf, Arabian Sea and parts of the Indian Ocean are the seas and sub-seas to which the name ET was applied in antiquity, even if never at any stage to all.
[2] 'Red Sea' in biblical transmission (1 Macc 4,9; Acts 7,36; Hebr 11,29 and passim) means only the northernmost part of today's Red Sea, also known as the 'Sea of Reeds' (Hebrew *yam sūf*).

1 W. SIEGLEN, Schulatlas zur Gesch. des Alt., 7 2 GGM 2, 397f.

TAVO B V 1–3. H.T. and B.B.

Eryx (ὁ Ἔρυξ/*ho Éryx*, Lat. *Eryx*, *Erucus*, *Erycus*).
[1] High, isolated mountain in western Sicily (751 m), now Monte San Giuliano. Settled even in prehistoric times, with a famous sanctuary to the probably Phoenician goddess of E., identified as Aphrodite by the Greeks, later (Thuc. 6,2,3) became a polis of the → Elymaeans. The attempt by Dorieus to establish a Greek colony (around 510 BC) ended in his destruction by the Phoenicians and the Elymaeans of Segesta (Hdt. 5,43–46), to whom E. was already subject at that time – as in 416 when they encouraged the Athenians to undertake the great Sicilian expedition, with the inducement of the temple treasures which were allegedly at their disposal (Thuc. 5,46). With only brief interruptions (conquest by → Pyrrhus in 278/7: Diod. Sic. 23,21; Plut. Pyrrhus 22) E. then became one of the strongest Carthaginian bases until the end of the 1st Punic War. In the Roman period the temple, held to have been founded by Aeneas for his mother Venus, was held in high regard and the inhabitants, *Venerii servi*, among whom there were also *hierodouloi*, enjoyed special standing: Diod. Sic. 4,83; Str. 6,2,6; Cic. Div. Caec. 55; Cic. Verr. 2,3 *passim*. Restoration of the dilapidated temple by Tiberius (Tac. Ann. 4,43,4: AD 25), as also attested by Claudius (Suet. Claud. 25,5). Afterward the cult seems to have been abandoned. Plin. HN 3,91 includes the *Erycini* amongst the *stipendiarii*. The ring walls of the town of S. Giuliano on the peak of E. are largely of ancient ori-

gin, otherwise the remains are of no significance. Inscriptions: IG XIV 281–286; CIL X 7253–7262; 8042,1. Many coins: HN 138 [1; 2]. K.Z.

Excavations that were carried out in the 1930s in the extreme south-east of mount S. Giuliano led to identification of the course of the ancient wall and to recovery of ceramics as well as architectonic features (probably from the famous *témenos*). Since then research has more recently concentrated on recording the different building stages (from the Elymian period through the later renovations of the Roman and medieval periods), likewise on the Punic-Hellenistic necropoleis outside the Porta Trapani (3rd cent. BC) [3] and the collection of materials from late antiquity and the Middle Ages [4]. Two new inscriptions from the Hellenistic period have been found (CIS 1, 3776: Carthage and Cagliari) attesting to the widespread distribution, beyond the island, of the Venus cult of E. even in the Punic period [5].

1 A. Tusa Cotroni, Sicilia Archaeologica 3, 1968, 33 2 P.R. Franke, M. Hirmer, Die griech. Mz., 1964, pl. 69 3 S. De Vido, s.v. Erice, BTCGI 7, 356ff. 4 F. Maurici, Erice, in: Giornate Internazionali di Studi sull'area elima, Gibellina 1991, 1992, 443–461 5 A.M. Bisi, s.v. Erice, EAA, II Suppl. 1971–1994 II, 1994, 497. GI.F.

[2] Eponymous hero of the mountain and city of E. [1], founder of the temple there. He is a son of → Poseidon (Apollod. 2,111; Tzetz. schol. Lycoph. 1232) or of → Butes [1] and Aphrodite. On return from the Geryoneus adventure, Hercules defeats and slays him in the wrestling match for the prize of cattle or of E.'s land. That was the basis for Heracleid Dorieus' [1] claim to the land (Hdt. 5,43; Diod. Sic. 4,23; Paus. 3,16,4; 4,36,4; Verg. Aen. 5,392–420; 759–761).

I. Krauskopf, s.v. E., LIMC 4.1, 22; G.K. Galinsky, s.v. E., EV 2, 364–365; R.J.A. Wilson, Sicily under the Roman Empire, 1990, 283–285. R.B.

Eryximachus (Ἐρυξίμαχος; *Eryxímachos*) Son of → Acumenus, Athenian doctor and Asclepiad, 5th cent. BC. As a friend of the sophist Hippias (Pl. Prt. 315A) and of Phaedrus (Pl. Phdr. 268A; Symp. 177A), he plays an important part in Plato's *Symposium*, in which he delivers a long speech in honour of Eros (185E–188E). His slightly pedantic manner earns him only the good-natured laughter of the invited guests but contemporary parallels to his linking of natural philosophy and medicine can be found in the *Corpus Hippocraticum*. V.N.

Esagil (Esagila). 'House whose top is high', Sumerian name for the temple complex dedicated to the principal Babylonian deity → Marduk in the centre of → Babylon, which encompasses besides the Marduk temple at ground level, also called E., the temple-tower (→ Tower of Babel) belonging to it, a great number of sanctuaries of various gods and large courtyard areas with utility rooms. In the ground-level temple there were the valuable cult images of Marduk and his wife Zarpanitum, who had her own chambers at her disposal there. The seven-storey, 92 m high temple-tower (→ Ziggurrat), surrounded by a square wall with sides 400 m in length, was erected on a surface of 92 m × 92 m and was topped with a small temple that was reached by a monumental flight of external stairs [1]. The tower bore the Sumerian name Etemenanki ('house, foundation of heaven and earth') and symbolized the axis of the world (→ Babylon). According to the → *Enūma elīš*, the gods of the world had constructed E. for Marduk, at the conclusion of creation, on the spot which had been creation's starting-point. Tending to these gods and their king Marduk was the most important cult duty of the Babylonian king.

Babylonian descriptions of E. [2; 3] and the details given by Herodotus (1,181–183) are of great importance as scant remains have been uncovered from the Marduk temple buried under a 21 m high hill of debris. Its outlines have been deduced from underground tunnels. Only the later building stages of E. are known, although E. is epigraphically attested from as early as the early 2nd millennium BC.

To demolish Babylon's claim to be the centre of the cosmos, → Sanherib and → Xerxes had the Marduk temple razed. Alexander the Great, who wanted to revive the claim to world domination that E. symbolized, ordered E. to be rebuilt. Antiochus [2] I continued the construction work. E. survived until the Parthian period. (See also map.)

1 H. Schmid, Der Tempelturm Etemenanki in Babylon, 1995 2 A.R. George, Babylonian Topographical Texts, 1992 3 Id., The Bricks of Esagil, in: Iraq 57, 1995, 173–197.

W. von Soden, Die babylon. Königsinschr. und die Frage nach dem Baubeginn von Etemenanki, in: ZA 86, 1996, 80–88; F. Wetzel, F.H. Weissbach, Das Hauptheiligtum des Marduk in Babylon, 1938.
For the maps: A.R. George, Babylonian Topographical Texts, 1992; U. Finkbeiner, B. Pongratz-Leisten, Beispiele altoriental. Städte. Babylon zur Zeit des neubabylon. Reiches, TAVO B IV 19, 1993; H. Schmid, Der Tempelturm Etemenanki in Babylon, 1995. S.M.

Eschatology

A. Term and subject matter
B. Graeco-Roman domain C. Hebrew Bible and Hellenistic Judaism D. Christianity
E. Reception

A. Term and subject matter

The term eschatology (from the Greek ἔσχατος/ *éschatos*, 'last'), initially a term for the 'doctrine of last things'(*tà éschata* sc. *prágmata*) as the final part of all theological outlines of Christian dogma, is to be found first in the 17th cent. as a neologism coined by Protestant theologians (Ph.H. Friedlieb, 1644; A. Calow, 1655–1677), and after D.F. Schleiermacher it replaced the older title *De novissimis*. In fact, though, the

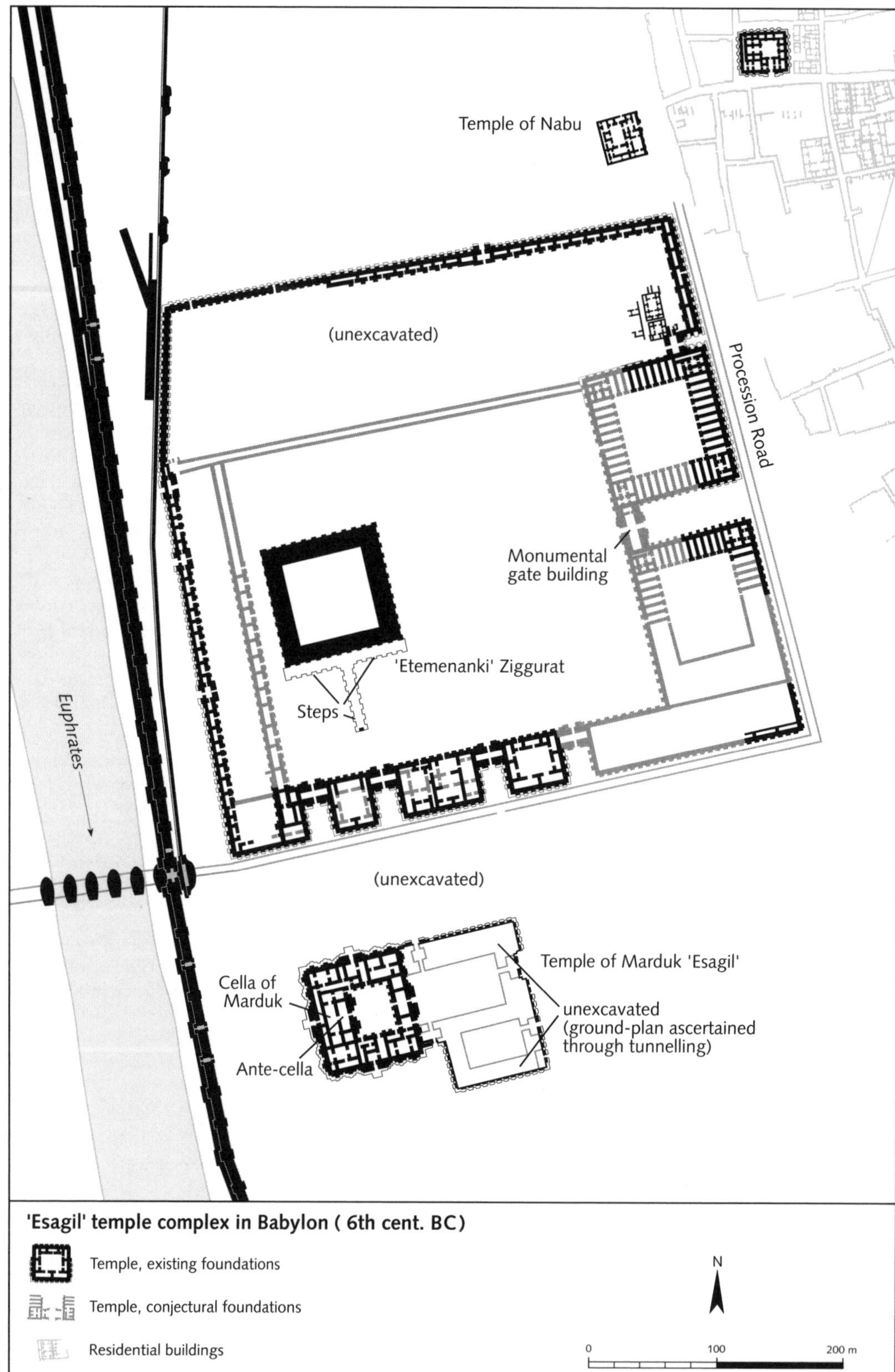

'Esagil' temple complex in Babylon (6th cent. BC)

question of the *éschata* (Sir 7,36; Orig. *Perì archôn* 1,6,1; GCS 22,78,21f.) had often been asked back in antiquity. Eschatology is used in various contexts in religious studies:

a) Individual eschatology is generally understood as synonymous with concepts of the → afterlife (→ death, immortality, metempsychosis/migration of the → soul, judgement of the dead). b) Collective eschatology enquires into the final destiny of a group, a people, humanity (final judgement, destruction or final attainment of salvation). c) Cosmological eschatology includes beliefs of the world's eternity, of its cyclical destruction or renewal but also of a non-recurring course of history (end of an epoch, a global era); in keeping with the various cosmogonies, it often assumes their motifs, e.g. return of chaos, birth of a new cosmos, global conflagration, assumption of a thousand-year period for salvation (possibly linked to a saviour- or Messiah-figure). Creation and re-creation, dawn of history and the world's end are bound up with each other. Eschatology can be closely linked with cult in a periodic program, e.g. festivals at New Year and those related to the rhythm of vegetation or *rites de passage*. Frequently, especially in Judaism, Christianity and Islam, eschatology is the subject of visionary-prophetic, revelatory (apocalyptic) literature. Divinatory practices (casting lots, dream and oracles) were supposed to clarify the future and show how present experiences relate to eschatology. Eschatology can be part of the theology or philosophy of history (historical events as a – purposeful – divine plan).

B. Graeco-Roman domain

In Graeco-Roman antiquity, eschatology appeared as a theme in various forms and genres (e.g. as physical theories, mythical or historical stories, collections of oracles, account of visions, travel to heaven or Hades) and natural philosophy.

1. Homer and Hesiod 2. Philosophy 3. Historiography 4. Virgil 5. Individual Eschatology in Mysteries and Cult 6. Oracular practice

1. Homer and Hesiod

Homer's individual eschatology describes death as a common to all destiny, as the power of the → Moira, without any hope for an afterlife; the meeting-place of *all* dead souls is → Hades, where they lead a joyless, empty shadow-existence. Immortality is an attribute of the gods. At the same time, in the *Iliad* a collective eschatology is discernible in the fall of Troy that is anticipated by Hector (Il. 6,448f.) and Andromache (Il. 24,728ff.), a paradigm for the end of a people.

A doctrine of ages of the world (→ Eras; → Period, era) or a division into periods comparable to the cosmology of the Ancient Orient is first encountered in → Hesiodus (about 700 BC); a theory of decadence lies at the heart of his historical view of the history of mankind (doctrine of the ages of different metals, Op. 109–176), though without any contemplation of the end of the world or the world's original state. The decline of the ages follows a non-cyclical succession of five phases; the first, the 'Golden Age', became a model for a large number of ancient utopias; the last, portrayed as a future, disastrous 'Iron Age' (Op. 178–180), is actually the poet's 'here and now'.

2. Philosophy

→ Anaximander of Miletus (*c.* 550 BC) was already describing the world's 'coming into being' and 'ceasing to be' (γένεσις and φθορά) in terms of 'necessity', 'justice', 'order', 'time' (A 9 DK). → Heraclitus of Ephesus (6th/5th cents. BC), for whom fire represents the beginning and end of all things (A 1 DK), links cosmology and individual eschatology: the human soul is a spark from the eternal fiery substance of the ether into which the soul ascends on the death of the human; the → Stoa will later pick up these thoughts (Sen. Ep. 65,24: death as *ekpýrōsis* of the body; similarly Varro Ant. fr. 8; 23; § 18).

Along with shaping the doctrine of periods and cycles into a blueprint for a philosophy of history (Tim. 39d, Plt. 269f), individual eschatology plays an important part in → Plato's (427–348/7 BC) philosophy: the soul of the individual, eternal and participating in the Ideas, strives to return to its divine origin (and, linked to that, a devaluation of the troublesome body as 'grave of the soul', Pl. Phd. 67c); in the afterlife the soul experiences the judgement of the dead, purification and punishments that are its due (cf. myth of → Er, Plt. 10,614b–621). The cycle of births through reincarnation continues until man is 'completely pure' by virtue of his philosophical life, i.e. his soul, completely liberated from the body enters the family of gods.

→ Epicurus (341–270 BC) thought differently: his radical outline of an absolute end in 'nothing' (cf. Epist. 3; § 124 Diog. Laert.; Lucr. 3,840) aims at freeing men from the fear of death and the afterlife. As an extension of Heraclitus' thought, the concept of global destruction as purification (ἡ διὰ πυρὸς κάθαρσις) is especially evident in the early Stoa, with a subsequent restoration of the old order (παλιγγενεσία, ἀποκατάστασις, *renovatio mundi*) or the concept of a succession of different worlds (SVF fr. 627; Sen. Dial. 6,26).

3. Historiography

Similar to the pattern in Hesiod, epochs serve to depict history, e.g. in → Eratosthenes, → Apollodorus [7] of Athens, Castor of Rhodes; → Varro, → Censorinus [4], → Augustinus. In that way world history can be arranged with the help of number symbolism (Varro, Plutarch, Arnobius, Eusebius) or can be related to the human ageing process (cf. Cic. Rep. 2,3; 2,21; 3,34; Vell. Pat. 1,7). In → Polybius the history of peoples reach their peak in the 'exclusive dominance' of the Romans (cf. also Hdt. 1,95); and it is with elements of collective eschatology that Polybius sketches the destruction of Carthage, with its parallels in the Greek archetype of Troy.

4. VIRGIL

In Virgil as well, history ends with the era of bliss of Roman rule. With him, political theology becomes historical teleology (Verg. Aen. 1,279: Rome's universal rule, *imperium sine fine*, in peace and justice as the goal of history). Likewise, Aeneas' journey through the Underworld (Aen. bk. 6) not only depicts individual eschatology with Orphic-Pythagorean motifs (see below; judgement of the dead, places of punishment, Elysium, Aen. 6,645ff.; cf. Aen. 6,724ff.) but also contains collective eschatology in its depiction of future Roman society, as does the description of the shield (Aen. 8,625–731).

In the return of the Golden Age (Verg. Ecl. 4) the Hesiodic world-age myth undergoes a positive shift: Virgil links the picture of cosmic renewal to a 'final period' with the new consul's assumption of office, with motifs of bucolic nature und utopia, as well as the announcement of a 'child Messiah' bringing peace and hope. The political relevance of such eschatology lies in the fact that, with the title of *Augustus* conferred on Octavian in 27 BC, the beginning of a new era was launched: Virgil represents the collective eschatology of victors to justify political dominance.

5. INDIVIDUAL ESCHATOLOGY IN MYSTERIES AND CULT

Theories of the relationship between soul and the divine generally work from the premise that the soul's divine element is pressing for a return to its origin and is striving for a (at least temporary) reunification with the god, after its consummation into the sublime. Being human is thus regarded as an intermediate stage aiming at post-mortal or transhuman existence. That hope finds expression in → burial and mourning rites, cult of the dead and funerary symbols. The initiate can on the other hand experience an emotional anticipation of the *éschata*, of fulfilment in the *epopteia* ('vision') of the Mysteries: becoming free and released from fear of death, → epiphany of the deity, realization of the hidden truth (Soph. fr. 753; Pind. fr. 137). The Demeter hymn (→ Mysteries) offers members of the cult community, i.e. the initiated, the prospect of a happier lot in the afterlife than it does for the uninitiated (5,480ff.), but happier in this life, too, and this is based on insight into the connection between life and death, between the dying and reawakening of Nature (cf. Demeter-Kore-myth).

A similar link between life (transhuman existence) and death (human constraint) also takes place in the → Dionysus cult. In consecration, as someone 'who is in God' (*éntheos*), the devotee experiences the god as a liberator and, in ecstasy, experiences the progress to the divine ('qualitative' eschatology). The spirit of *enthousiasmos* (of belonging to the god) is more extensively developed in the Orphic tradition (→ Orphism, Orphic poetry), which is linked to the Dionysian, so that it takes on the 'divinity of the soul'. Thus wisdom consists of recognizing oneself as divine. In the initiate's consecration the day of actual death is anticipated and interpreted as the beginning of real life, that of the soul. In Orphic thought, a deceased person will become a god (gold tablet A4, Thurii) and take part in the symposium of the blessed. Earthly existence has the character of penitence. The concept of migration of the soul (→ Soul, migration of the) is an important feature of this eschatology; the number of reincarnations is dependent on moral qualification, determined by a judgement of the dead, and can be influenced by morally responsible behaviour.

6. ORACULAR PRACTICE

At the start of his 'world history' Diodorus [18] (80–*c.* 29 BC) inserts an explicit mythology and typography of Hades (Diod. Sic. 1,2; motifs, however, already present in pre-Hellenistic Greek literature, e.g. Aesch. Telephus; Aristoph. Ran.; Pl. Phd.; in the Latin sphere, Verg. Aen. 6; parodied in the 'Dialogues of the Dead' of Lucian). Accounts of heroes (Orpheus, Aeneas, Hercules) who went down into the Underworld provided information about the afterlife. Oracle caverns that were believed to offer access to the Underworld were sometimes linked to cult activity (at → Lebadea, attested until the Roman Imperial period; → Ephyra [3], Lake Avernus). Necromancy as a source of information about the future and the afterlife (as early as Hom. Od. 11) was, however, rejected by Heliodorus (end of bk. 6) as basically prohibited and 'not serious'.

C. HEBREW BIBLE AND HELLENISTIC JUDAISM

In the Hebrew Bible expectations of the future do not present any unified system (for a discussion of the concept [3. 655; 8. 569]). In the 'OT' eschatology refers fundamentally and primarily to the future of Israel. Eschatology is linked to the pattern of history. An essential element of eschatological discussions before classical prophecy is the pledge to deliver the Promised Land to Israel. God's guidance is manifest in the founding of David's kingdom and future salvation is also bound up with David's line. This expectation of salvation is shaken by the sermons of the scriptural prophets from Amos to Ezechiel who announce a harsh judgement. The fall of Israel and the experience of exile reveal the reality of that judgement.

From the period of exile onwards, the central focus is on a prophecy that looks to the start of a new period of grace (Hos., Ez. 36f.; Joel, Deutero-Zachariah, Is. 24–27). Increasingly, the future and history of nations and the earth, and the purpose and end of history *per se* are given thematic prominence (cf. Joel 1,15; 4,14; Dan. 2; 7). This eschatology is characterized by dualistic-apocalyptic motifs: world powers as opponents of the kingdom of God (Babylon: Dan. 7; Assur: Is. 15,5ff.; Nah: → Edom as code for Rome); natural phenomena and miraculous signs on the day of judgement; different religious or political Messiah-figures; restoration of the people of Israel and the Temple; pilgrimage to Zion. Together with the extension to all nations, there can also be observed a restrictive focussing on only one group (→ Essenes, Pharisees, Qumran, Zelots) as recipients of salvation. The division of history into periods (Dan. 7,2–14; Eth. En. 93 or 91,12–17, *c.* 170 BC), from the 'earliest times' to the 'final period' is later reduced to two ages of the world, 'this one' and the coming 'aeon' (e.g. 1 QS 3,13–4,26; 4 Ezra 7,26ff.; Is. 65,17; 66,2). Linked to the belief in resurrection, in the sense of a reunion of the individual's body and soul in eternal salvation or damnation, this two-period doctrine is also relevant to the individual eschatology of Hellenistic-Roman Judaism and has a formative effect on all other eschatological statements in Judaism, Christianity and Islam. Source material for Jewish eschatology in the Hellenistic-Roman period derives from a great variety of apocalypses (Eth. En., Ezra, Apoc. Baruch), apocrypha, pseudepigraphic literature, the Qumran literature, Philo, Josephus, as well as the Rabbinical tradition.

D. Christianity

Both individual (death and individual judgement, heaven, hell) and cosmological eschatology (Christ's return, end of the world, Judgement Day, eternal life) are represented in Christianity. That said, NT eschatology (cf. Mk 13, Hebr, 2 Pet., Rev) is by no means homogeneous; what is new is the link with Christology. For Jesus and the Synoptists the focus is the proclamation of the Kingdom of God, which through the agency of Jesus has an effect even on the present. The message of redemption in the death of Jesus (Mk; Paul, 1. Cor 15, 2. Cor 5; Jesus as the end of the law and thus of history, Rom. 10,4) underlines the certainty that the believer's present existence is already eschatologically qualified for the future glory that accompanies the resurrection of the dead and is completed with the return of Jesus Christ (*parousia*). Luke divides the course of the whole of the history of salvation into three epochs: the period of Israel, the period of Jesus as the historical midpoint, the period of the Church up to the *parousia*. Judaism's wavering between national and universal expectation is resolved in favour of a universalist interpretation.

John's gospel essentially abandons the traditional apocalyptic and adopts an eschatology of the present (judgement not as a cosmological drama but in mankind's attitude towards Jesus). Unlike the Revelation of John, which predicts an end in the near future (details of the final day, apocalyptic symbols) and interprets the community's current plight (under Domitian) as part of the concluding battle between God and the opposing powers with the eschatological goal of the 'new heaven' and the 'new earth' (Apoc. 21; before that, a thousand-year kingdom and world judgement, Apoc. 20,1–10; eschatology as a socially stabilising factor for a group).

Under the influence of Hellenistic ideas the eschatology of the early Church quickly experienced a strong process of individualization; life after death and physical immortality move to centre stage. Eschatology that is now understood as applying only to the afterlife leads to a devaluation of the world, the development of a Christian Platonism, and has a regime-stabilizing effect. The eschatology of → Origenes represents the fallen world's return to God through Christ's humanity, in a cosmic process of purification and education (the purgatory motif). Later on, individual eschatological themes were given functional value: e.g. the belief in physical resurrection of the dead, in conflict with → Gnosticism; the prospect of justice and hell as an ethical-moral motivation (→ Tertullianus; → Lactantius); especially in the West, division of the world into periods is clearly linked to imperial chronology; also discernible are a chiliastic modification of the Roman ideology of state and emperor, and interpretation of the millennium as the period of the Church (Tyconius; Augustine).

E. Reception

In the Judaism of the Middle Ages eschatological ideas are arranged in the framework of a philosophically and cabalistically oriented theology; Maimonides strictly separates the period of the Messiah's rule, as the last days of this world, from the final state of salvation that was thought of as being in the afterlife. Islamic eschatology emphasizes salvation as being in the afterlife and recognizes an individual judgement of the dead. An apocalyptic description of the events at the end of the world can be found in the short early suras of the Koran. For Christian theologians of the Middle Ages the eschatological pronouncements of Augustine and Gregory the Great were especially influential.

1 H. Cancik, s.v. E., HRWG 2, 341–343 2 Id., The End of the World, of History and of the Individual in Greek and Roman Antiquity, in: J. Collins (ed.), Encyclopaedia of Apocalypticism 1, 1998, 84–125 3 C.-M. Edsman, A. Jebsen, R. Meyer et al., s.v. E., RAC 2, 650–689 4 G. Kittel, s.v. ἔσχατος, THWNT 2, 694f. 5 G. Sauter, Einführung in die E., 1995 6 Th. Söding, G. Greshake, K. Hoheisel et al., s.v. E., LThK 3, 859–880 7 H. Sonnemans, Seele. Unsterblichkeit – Auferstehung. Zur griech. und christl. Anthropologie und E., 1984 8 K. Thraede, s.v.E., RAC 6, 559–564. D.SI.

Ešmūn Old Phoenician deity, probably a → healing deity (> *šmn*, 'Oil'), interpreted by the Greeks as → Asclepius and also as → Apollo. An important sanctuary of the cult of Esmun, which was widespread around the Mediterranean, was situated near Ṣidon (*Bustān aš-Šaiḫ*). In Tyrus, Esmun was associated with → Melqart.

1 E. Lipiński, s.v. E., DCPP, 158–160 2 R. Stucky, Die Skulpturen aus dem E.-Heiligtum bei Sidon: griech., röm., kypr. und phönik. Statuen vom 6. Jh. v.–3. Jh. n. Chr., 1993. C.K.

Esna (Old Egytpian *Jwnyt*, later (*Tꜣ*)–*Snj*). Place in Upper Egypt, *c.* 60 km south of Luxor on the western bank of the Nile. Named in Greek λάτων (πόλις) after the latus fish, much venerated in cult practice. Today's city E. stands on the old settlement, therefore only the temple (9 m beneath today's level) is accessible. The first reference to E. comes from the 1st intermediate period; E. did not become significant, however, until the New Kingdom as the departure point for a caravan route to Nubia. The principal deity was the ram Chnum (→ Chnubis), whose temple is E.'s most significant monument. It was begun under the later Ptolemies (VI/VIII); the hypostyle room, the only part accessible today, dates from the 1st cent. AD and was decorated under the emperors Claudius to Decius (middle of the 1st–middle of the 3rd cent. AD; names of most of the Caesars can still be found). It contains the most recent body of hieroglyphic inscriptions, remarkable for an especially elaborate writing system. In the Christian era E. was a bishopric. It is the birthplace of → Pachomius, founder of Egyptian monasticism.

S. Sauneron, LÄ 2, 30–33. K.J.-W.

Espionage Procuring information about the political and military situation of the enemy played an important part in Greek and Roman warfare (cf. Thuc. 6,32,3 f.). Aside from statements made by deserters, → prisoners of war, or even merchants (cf. Caes. Gall. 4,20,3 f.) and travellers, army commanders and politicians made use of the knowledge gained by spies. In Greek texts, spies are referred to as κατάσκοποι/*katáskopoi*, although the distinction between espionage and military intelligence is murky (Hdt. 7,145 f.; Thuc. 6,63,3). In Caesar, spies (*speculatores*) are distinguished from → *exploratores* (Caes. Gall. 2,11,2; cf., however, 5,49,8). The term *speculator* is also used for foreign spies (Liv. 22,33,1). One must, however, take into consideration that the *speculatores*, who belonged to the → *principales* of each legion in the late Republic and Principate, also had to fulfill other duties (tombstone of a *speculator*: AE 1945,88).

Espionage is first mentioned in Homer: the Trojan Dolon secretly tries to board Agamemnon's ship in order to eavesdrop on the Greeks (Hom. Il. 10,314–459; Odysseus in Troy: Hom. Od. 4,242–258). Although the activities of spies are hardly ever documented, the measures taken against espionage indicate that it was regarded as a serious danger. In Rhodes, for instance, entering the station of the fleet was punishable by death (Str. 14,2,5). The commander Chares [1] caught spies in his camp by forcing each soldier to name his unit (Polyaenus, Strat. 3,13,1). Delegations were often used for espionage and for investigating the land of the enemy (Alexander [4]: Arr. Anab. 4,1,2).

According to Procopius [3], Rome had always used espionage (Procop. Pers. 1,21,11): P. Cornelius [I 71] Scipio used the negotiations prior to a battle in Africa (203 BC) for spying on the enemy camp (Liv. 30,4,1–3; cf. also 30,29,2 ff.). Espionage was even used in the Civil War (Bell. Hisp. 13; 20). Captured spies had to face severe punishments; thus, a Carthaginian spy had his hands cut off (Liv. 22,33,1), and in the civil War, slaves that were discovered to be *speculatores* were crucified, soldiers were beheaded (Bell. Hisp. 13; 20; cf. Suet. Aug. 27,3). The specialized literature of Greece and Rome deals with espionage only briefly (Frontin. Str. 1,2; Onasander 10,9; Veg. Mil. 3,22,13). For the procurement of political relevant information within the Imperium Romanum, the → *frumentarii* were used in the 2nd and 3rd cents. AD, and in late antiquity, the → *agentes in rebus*.

→ Curiosi; → Secret police; → Communications

1 N. J. E. Austin, N. B. Rankov, Exploratio, 1995, 54–60. BJ.O. and K.UM.

Esquiliae General term for the hills Cispius and Oppius in → Rome (Varro, Ling. 5,49). Here was the end of the plateau that extended to the Anio; and from it important aqueducts (Anio vetus 270 BC, Aqua Marcia 144 BC, Aqua Claudia and Anio novus AD 52) led into the city. The Anio novus that was incorporated into the Porta Maggiore is particularly impressive.

A hasty and exhaustive redevelopment started in 1870/71 caused large-scale exposure and destruction, with which the documentation process could not keep pace; as a result, the considerable number of finds, plans and photographs are not much of a guide to the correlation of the finds. Tradition (Varro, Ling. 5,49) portrays the E. as uninhabited in the earlier period, interspersed with groves of individual *sacraria* and covered with houses of kings like Tarquinius Superbus (Solin. 1,26). The region was said to have been added to the city by Servius Tullius (Liv. 1,44,3). The territory outside the wall was organized as a *pagus* (CIL VI 3832 = 31577). In the late Republican period E. and Fagutal still formed the second region of the city (Varro, Ling. 5,50; Fest. 344), only to be divided up in the Augustan reform (7 BC) into the third (Oppius), fourth (Fagutal) and fifth (Cispius) regions. Only the last of these retained the name.

Fundamental to the settlement history is the separation between those parts lying within the Servian Wall, with a residential settlement, and the areas beyond the Wall, where extensive necropoleis were situated in the Republican period, but the topographic transition between the two functions remains unexplained. No later than the Augustan period, beginning with Maecenas, the zone outside the wall was occupied by a series of parks belonging to the aristocracy. Horace mentions a cemetery of Republican Rome with mass graves for the poor (Hor. Sat. 1,8,10) but its identification with the variously located *puticuli* (Varro, Ling. 5,25) has not been entirely settled. The latter were at times linked to a necropolis that was attested from the 8th to the 1st cents. BC and was closed in the Augustan period. What has been transmitted to us is simply that the *horti Maecenatis* (Hor. Sat. 1,8,7f.; Carm. 3,29,5f.; Epod. 9,3; Suet. Aug. 72,2; Nero 38,2) were sited on a necropolis for paupers and that Maecenas was able to stroll over it, just as he could over the rampart, or *agger*, of the Servian Wall (Hor. Sat. 1,8,10). In a similar situation, partly buried in the *agger*, lies the so-called Auditorium of Maecenas from the period around 40 BC, which as an extant building conveys a snapshot of the high quality of the architecture and of its fittings. In this demonstrative incorporation of a city wall into a residential district, a widespread phenomenon in Augustan Italy (cf. the Augustan suburban dwellings of Herculaneum and Pompeii), there was perhaps to be found a a conscious demonstration of the rule of domestic peace in Italy that had been created by Augustus. The *horti Maecenatis* constituted an important centre within Augustan Rome. Virgil's house (Donat., Vita Ver. 13) was also in the neighbourhood or even within the complex (Hor. Sat. 2,6,30; Epist. 2,2,65); likewise the houses of Horace and Propertius and Horace's grave (Suet., fragm. p. 298). Other aristocratic parklands were established – the *horti Epaphroditiani, Lamiani, Maiani, Lolliani and Pallantiani* (→ Rome). They all gradually passed into the imperial domain. Especially rich and high-quality sculptural furnishings were found here, some of which have ended up in the Palazzo dei Conservatori. A large number of sanctuaries, divine precincts and public places are mentioned in literature, with no possibility of fixing their location and often with only their mention as a *terminus ante quem*.

C. Buzzetti, in: LTUR 3, 1995, 234–235; Richardson, 146. R. F.

Essedarius, Essedum see → War chariot

Essenes

A. Etymology B. Ancient Sources C. The Qumran finds D. History

A. Etymology

The name E. (Ἐσσηνοί, Ἐσσαῖοι; Essēnoí, Essaîoi) was probably applied by outsiders to the community that it describes. It represents an attempt to render in Greek the Aramaic *ḥ^{a}sayya*ʾ (*ḥsyh* is Qumranic, now attested in the non-Essene *Aramaic Levi Document*: *wlʾ mtmḥʾ šm ḥsyh mn kwl ʿmhʾ lʿlm*, 'and the name of the devout will not be extinguished in eternity'; 4 Q 213a 3–4 6). The Hebrew *ḥāsîd* that has the same meaning as the Aramaic *ḥ^{a}sayya*ʾ is also found, as part of a place-descriptor of the settlement of Qumran that had at that time been destroyed, in a letter dating to AD 134/5 (*mṣd ḥsydym*, 'fortress of the devout'; Murabbaʿat [= Mur] 45 6) – and this tends to corroborate the etymology suggested (cf. [4. vol. 2, 164]).

B. Ancient Sources

Until modern times the E., as a Jewish religious party, were known to us only from Greek and Latin sources (mainly → Philo of Alexandria, Quod omnis probus liber sit 75–91; Pro Iudaeis defensio [Euseb. Praep. evang. 8,11; cf. Phil. De vita contemplativa on the Therapeutae]; Jos. BI 2,119–161, Ant. Iud. 18,11 and 18–22; Plin. HN 5,73; Hippolytus, Refutatio 9,18,2–28,2; other textual sources in [1; 7]). The picture emerges of a community of about 4,000 people (Phil. Quod omnis probus liber sit 75; Jos. Ant. Iud. 18,20) scattered throughout Palestine. As well as the large number of its members (cf. the Pharisees numbered about 6,000), the reports mentioning Essene seers and interpreters of dreams (Jos. BI 1,78; 2,111–113, Ant. Iud. 13,311–313; 15,371–379; 17,345–348), as well as the Zealot military commander called 'John the Essene' (Jos. BI 2,567) confirm that the E. were not a 'sect' in the sense of a fringe group having no influence on public life [36; 35]. The picture emerges of an egalitarian group (though with a strict hierarchical structure) characterized by communal property, common work programs, communal meals and the idea of purity. According to Jos. Ant. Iud. 18,19 (Latin translation and epitome!; cf. Phil. Quod omnis probus liber sit 75) the E. did not participate in Jerusalem's sacrificial cult. Moses, the Torah and scriptural exegesis (Jos. BI 2,136; 145; 152; Phil. Quod omnis probus liber sit 80–82) stood at the centre of Essene belief. As well as a branch living in an unmarried state, Josephus mentions a second group that accepted marriage and intercourse solely for the purpose of procreation (BI 2,160f.). Spiritually the E. were noted for their belief in destiny and the doctrine of the soul's immortality (Jos. Ant. Iud. 18,18; cf. 13,172; 15,373, BI 2,154–158). The depiction in Philo and Josephus is tendentious and influenced by Greek attitudes (see e.g. the description of the E. as a philosophical school similar to the Pythagoreans: Jos. Ant. Iud. 18,11). The account by Pliny the Elder (HN 5,73) is interesting from a geographical perspective as he describes the E. as a group settled on the Western bank of the Dead Sea north of ʿEn Gedi.

The Egyptian group of the *Therapeutae* described by Philo in De vita contemplativa may be considered as either influenced by the E. or as a splinter group of the E.

C. The Qumran finds

Even before the Qumran finds, Ginzberg [21] postulated that the Damascus Document (= CD) found in the → Geniza of the Cairo Ezra-Synagogue and later at → Qumran was Essene in origin [21]. The settlement and textual finds at Qumran were first ascribed to the E. by Sukenik [6] (1948). The Essene origin of part of the Qumran MSS is suggested by theological concordance (determination, life after death, central significance of the Torah) and lifestyle parallels (communal meals, purifying baths, hierarchical structure, three-year 'probationary period' for new members, communal property, monogamy, no spitting in assembly, oil as carrier of impurity; see *i.a.* [35; 36; 38]). Through the pottery found there, an ostrakon recently found in Qumran [17] and a fr. that documents the application of halakhic regulations from the community rules of Qumran (for 4 Q477 see [18]), the settlement of Ḫirbet Qumran is inseparably linked with the MSS finds.

The Essene texts of Qumran sketch a portrait of radical Torah-observance, a dualistic world vision and a community marked by short-term eschatological expectancy and seeing itself as the only legitimate remnant of God's chosen people who had by then fallen into transgression. In their church services the E. experienced communion with the angels. Their view of history was based on predestination and on the division of history into epochs. The concept of two Messiahs is interesting from an eschatological point of view. As well as to the Davidic Messiah, it looked to a priestly → Messiah (1 QS IX 11; CD XII 23; XIV 19; XIX 10; 4 Q test; cf. CD XX 1) and was probably influenced by Zach 4.

Consistent with the notion of being a remnant, there can be found, along with the lexeme *yaḥad* ('new'), self-descriptive terms like 'people of the new covenant' (*hbryt hḥdšh*; CD VI 19; VIII 21; XIX 33; XX 12; applying to an earlier stage of the E.) or simply 'the league' (*hbryt*; e.g. 1 QS I 18.20.24 and *passim*). Because of the key importance of dualism and → eschatology the Qumran community has been repeatedly characterized as apocalyptic (see e.g. [15; 22]), however the complete absence of apocalypses in the Essene texts argues against this (cf. [14; 33; 35]). The central role of Torah observance, the theme of purity and calendary issues, as well as the great importance of the priests, all suggest instead that the E. were a group determined by priests. That is shown especially clearly in 1 QSa II 11–22 where, in the eschatological assembly of God's community, the priests take precedence over the Messiah both on entry and during the meal. It may finally have also been a consequence of the priestly influence on the Essene community that it adhered to the old, solar cult calendar that had not been in use since the → Hasmonaean period (for the different solar and lunisolar calendars in the 'astronomical book of Enoch' [astr En = 1 Hen 72–82], 'Book of Jubilees' [Jub] and the calendar texts from Qumran see [8; 27, vol. 3, 53ff.]).

Essene texts are regarded essentially as scriptural exegesis: two of the most important community rules (for the Essene → Halakha see [29; 31]) bear the title *mdrš [h]twrh h'ḥrwn* ('definitive exegesis of the Torah'; see in the Damascus Document MSS from Cavern 4: 4 QD[a] 11 20f. par 4 QD[e] 7 II 15) and *mdrš lmśkyl 'l 'nšy htwrh hmtndbym lhšyb mkl r' wlhḥzyq bkl 'šr ṣwh* 'Directions for the instructor for all men of the Torah who have dedicated themselves to turn from evil and to cling fast to everything that he has commanded'; see in the MSS of community rules from Cavern 4: 4 QS[b] 5 1 par 4 QS[d] 1 I 1). The community's history and its eschatological hopes are depicted in consecutive interpretations of the texts of the prophets and of the psalms (consecutive pesharim) or in interpretations of thematically compiled written quotations (thematic pesharim). Both thematic and consecutive pesharim were thus regarded as inspired and capable of scriptural exegesis only in following the 'teacher of justice' (1 QpHab II 1–11; VII 3–5). The Essenes also tended to compose their poetic-liturgical literature from quotations from, and allusions to, the Scriptures (→ Exegesis).

D. History

(For the history of the E. see [34; 35; 13]): The ancient accounts about the E., the excavations and the Essene texts from Qumran allow a sketchy reconstruction of the Essene movement. The main literary sources are the short outline of origins in CD I 5ff. and the eschatological realization of Biblical texts in the history of the E. through Pešarim: After the Maccabean Jonathan, following the Hellenistic high priests Jason, Menelaus, Alcimus and an interim predecessor whose name has not survived (on that see [35]), was appointed high priest in 152 BC (1 Macc 10,15–21), his predecessor left the Temple with a following from the priestly group and joined a Chassidic priestly group calling itself 'the new covenant'. That group probably left the Temple 20 years earlier at the time of the so-called Hellenistic religious reforms. From the union of the two groups there developed the Essene community (the fact that Josephus mentions the E. for the first time during Jonathan's regime, in Ant. Iud. 13,171–173, would support that historical genesis; cf. [11]). The causes for the 152 BC schism were the lunar calendar used by Jonathan and the fact that he was not an Oniad and thus not of the priestly family that alone was supposed to provide the high priest. In the Essene texts of Qumran, Jonathan's predecessor is described only as 'teacher of justice'. The doctrinal songs that he composed in the *Hodayot* and the account in 1 QpHab XI 4–8, *i.a.*, document the conflicts and crises associated with the schism. The Sadducean religious party developed later from those priests who stayed with the Temple.

Quite soon after the creation of the E. a dispute arose over the correct interpretation of the Torah. Under the leader whom the E. called a 'man of derision' and 'man of lies', a group split off from the E. They were described as those 'who interpret aiming for smooth things' (*'šr drš bḥlqwt* or *dwršy ḥlqwt*, CD I 18 and *passim*). As the term involves a play on words on the central beliefs of Pharisaism (→ Halakhah and → Midrash) and as the group so described was in 4 QpNah 3–4 I 6f. connected with the persecution of Pharisees by → Alexander [16] Iannaeus [30], the schism mentioned in CD I 12ff. may well have brought about the birth of Pharisaism.The halakhic and calendary issues of contention with the Pharisees were impressively set out in an early letter from the Essene community to the high priest in Jerusalem (4 QMMT).

As attested by the ancient sources in their reports of the Essene movement having 4,000 members (see above), the E. quickly developed into a relatively large religious party whose influence should in no way be underestimated (cf. [36; 35]). Structural preconditions in Qumran, the (several!) encampments mentioned at CD VII 6 (and *passim*), Philo (Quod omnis probus liber sit 75) and Josephus (BI 2,124 Ant. Iud. 18,19) suggest, in contrast to Pliny (HN 5,17) that the Essene movement was not restricted to the settlement at Qumran or the Dead Sea. In excavations at 'En el-Ghuweir, Ḥiam el-Sagha and Jerusalem, graves have been found resembling those in the cemeteries of Qumran, thus pointing to Essene settlements outside Qumran [39]. Little is known of the further course of Essene history. Reference to the persecution of Pharisees by the Hasmonean ruler Alexander [16] Iannaeus (4 QpNah 3–4 I 6f.), together with a fr. interpreted as an undelivered message of greetings to him (4 Q448), makes it possible that there was a rapprochement with the Hasmonaeans during his period in office (103–76 BC). The legendary account of an E.'s prediction of Herod the Great's rule (Jos. Ant. Iud. 15,375–378) could hint at political influence on that king. The end of the Essene movement can probably be set during the 1st Jewish War (AD 60–70 or 74) – the archaeological finds at Qumran and the account of Essene martyrs in Jos. BI 2,152f. both point to that. The fact that a Zealot military commander was called John the Essene (Jos. BI 2,567), together with Roman persecution of the E., makes it not improbable that the E. took part in the Zealot liberation struggle. The E., who were actually pacifist, would thus have seen it as the final struggle, described in the rule of war, against the powers of darkness. Whether remnants of the Essene movement were absorbed into early Christianity and Rabbinical Judaism is a matter of contention but cannot be ruled out altogether.

EDITIONS: 1 A. ADAM, CH. BURCHARD, Ant. Berichte über die E., [2]1972 2 K. BEYER, Die aram. Texte vom Toten Meer, vol. 1–2, 1984–1994 3 J.H. CHARLESWORTH (ed.), The Princeton Theological Seminary Dead Sea Scrolls Project, vol. 1ff., 1991ff. 4 Discoveries in the Judean Desert, vol. 1ff., 1955ff. (= DJD 1ff.) 5 F. GARCÍA MARTÍNEZ, E. J. C. TIGCHELAAR, The Dead Sea Scrolls Study Edition, vols. 1–2, 1997/8 6 E. L. SUKENIK, The Dead Sea Scrolls of the Hebrew University, 1955 (Hebr. 1948) 7 G. VERMES, M. D. GOODMAN, The Essenes According to the Classical Sources, 1989.

LITERATURE: 8 M. ALBANI, Zur Rekonstruktion eines verdrängten Konzepts: Der 364-Tage-Kalender in der gegenwärtigen Forschung, in: Id. et al. (ed.), Studies in the Book of Jubilees, 1997, 79–125 9 T. S. BEALL, Josephus' descriptions of the Essenes illustrated by the Dead Sea Scrolls, 1988 10 R. BERGMEIER, Die Essener-Berichte des Flavius Josephus, 1993 11 O. BETZ, s.v. E. und Therapeuten, TRE 10, 386–391 12 CH. BURCHARD, Bibliogr. zu den Hss. vom Toten Meer, vol. 1–2, 1957–1965 13 PH. R. CALLAWAY, The History of the Qumran Community, 1988 14 J. CARMIGNAC, Qu'est-ce que l'Apocalyptique? Son emploi à Qumrân, in: Revue de Qumran 10, 1979–1981, 3–33 15 J. J. COLLINS, Apocalypticism in the Dead Sea Scrolls, 1997 16 F. M. CROSS, The Ancient Library of Qumran, [3]1995 17 F. M. CROSS, E. ESHEL, Ostraca from Khirbet Qumrân, in: IEJ 47, 1997, 17–28 18 E. ESHEL, 4Q477: The Rebukes by the Overseer, in: Journal of Jewish Studies 45, 1994, 111–122 19 H.-J. FABRY, s.v. Qumran, Neues Bibellexikon, in print 20 F. GARCÍA MARTÍNEZ, D. W. PARRY, A Bibliography of the Finds in the Desert of Judah 1970–95, 1996 21 L. GINZBERG, Eine unbekannte jüd. Sekte, 1922 22 M. HENGEL, Judentum und Hellenismus, [2]1973 23 B. JONGELING, A Classified Bibliography of the Finds in the Desert of Judah 1958–1969, 1971 24 A. LANGE, H. LICHTENBERGER, s.v. Qumran, TRE 28, 45–79 25 W.S. LASOR, Bibliography of the Dead Sea Scrolls 1948–1957, 1958 26 E. LOHSE, Die Texte aus Qumran, [3]1981 27 J. MAIER, Die Qumran E.: Die Texte vom Toten Meer, vol. 1–3, 1995/6 28 J. T. MILIK, Ten Years of Discovery in the Wilderness of Judaea, 1959 29 L. H. SCHIFFMAN, The Halakhah at Qumran, 1975 30 Id., Pharisees and Sadducees in Pesher Nahum, in: M. BRETTLER, M. FISHBANE (ed.), Minḥah le-Naḥaum, FS Nahum M. Sarna, 1993, 272–290 31 Id., Reclaiming the Dead Sea Scrolls, 1994 32 Id. and J.C. VANDERKAM (ed.), Encyclopedia of the Dead Sea Scrolls, 2000 33 H. STEGEMANN, Die Bed. der Qumranfunde für die Erforschung der Apokalyptik, in: D. HELLHOLM (ed.), Apocalypticism in the Mediterranean World and the Near East, [2]1989, 495–530 34 Id., Die Entstehung der Qumrangemeinde, thesis Bonn 1971 35 Id., Die Essener, Qumran, Johannes der Täufer und Jesus, [4]1994 36 Id., The Qumran Essenes – Local Members of the Main Jewish Union in Late Second Temple Times, in: J. TREBOLLE BARRERA, L. VEGAS MONTANER (ed.), The Madrid Qumran Congress, 1992, 83–166 37 G. STEMBERGER, Pharisäer, Sadduzäer, E., 1991 38 J. C. VANDERKAM, The Dead Sea Scrolls Today, 1994 39 B. ZISSU, śdh 'qbrym ḥpwrym' bbyt ṣpp' – ʿdwt ʾrkyʾwlwgyt lqhylt ʾysyym?, in: A. FAUST (ed.), New Studies on Jerusalem. Proceedings of the Second Conference, 1996, 32–40.

AR.L.

Estate register In contrast to the → land register that existed – probably based on an Old Egyptian model [1] – in Ptolemaic and Roman Egypt (and, in antiquity, possibly only there) as a safeguard for private property transactions, the primary purpose of estate registers (ER) and similar registers was the levy of land taxes as well as the administration of state leases. Thus, almost inevitably, they were just as widespread as those very forms of state income. A prerequisite for starting up archives or books with records of the size and location of properties is a knowledge of surveying techniques and the availability of a profession of → surveyors. However, we lack a direct transmission of an ER (*forma*) for ancient Rome and Italy where our knowledge of this profession is by far the best. From a much earlier period a so-called 'estate register-text' of Urnammu (ruler of Ur in Mesopotamia 2111–2094 BC) mentions the precisely surveyed district borders of his kingdom. In other respects as well, ER were apparently widespread in Mesopotamia and possibly even in general use [2. 57]. ER in Egypt are treated *i.a.* in the 'Official regulations for the vizier' from the middle of the 2nd millennium BC [5]. According to it the most senior official in the whole kingdom had the responsibility, amongst other things, for proceedings concerning fields, checking the survey results and administering the ER and boundary maps. At first glance it is therefore all the more astounding that technical evidence of an ER is completely lacking for the Ptolemaic period in Egypt. That is precisely the reason that the land register (*bibliothḗkē enktḗseōn*) was originally regarded as an ER (cf. also [3. 75]). In the Ptolemaic period, however, a separate ER may have been superfluous, as on the one hand the authorities could access the land register at any time and on the other hand, because of a specific registration (*katagraphḗ*), transactions involving property (and other objects) were registered by them anyway [4. 184ff.].

→ Apographe

1 S. ALLAM, Publizität und Schutz im Rechtsverkehr, in: Id. (ed.), Grund und Boden in Altägypten, 1994, 31–44 2 H. SAUREN, Zum Beweis des Eigentums an Grund und Boden in Mesopotamien, ibid., 45–64 3 H.A. RUPPRECHT, Kleine Einführung in die Papyruskunde, 1994 4 WOLFF 5 K. SETHE, Urkunden der 18. Dyn., vol. 4 (G. STEINDORFF et al., Urkunden des ägypt. Alt. IV), [2]1961 (repr.), 1103–1117.

G.S.

Este Culture The term Este culture is applied broadly to the Iron Age population group of the Veneti in the period between 1000 und 300 BC (chronological table in → Golasecca culture), whose material legacy from the area between the Po, Lake Garda, the north-eastern arc of the Alps and the Adriatic indicates a relatively homogeneous group at a similar stage of development. The name is taken from the necropoleis of the most important settlement of the early period, today's Este. Other centres were situated in Padua and, especially in the early phase, at Frattesina di Fratte Polesine. Sanctuaries at Este, San Pietro Montagnon and Caldevigo have been attested because of the votive offerings. Evidence of links to the Etruscan, Hallstatt and Golasecca cultures has been established many times over. The most significant testimony to the cultural achievement is the 'situla art', whose embossed figurative jewellery illustrates the early Veneti's conception of the world. Typical ceramic forms are vessels with black and red horizontal sectioning and boot-shaped vessels.

→ Etruscan archaeology; → Golasecca culture; → Hallstatt culture; → Hoard(find)s; → Venetia; → Veneti; → Villanova culture

O.-H. FREY, Die Entstehung der Situlenkunst, 1966; A. Neppi Modona (ed.), Este e la civiltà paleoveneta a cento anni dalle prime scoperte. Atti dell' XI Convegno dell'Istituto di Studi Etruschi ed Italici (Este-Padova 1976), 1980; G. FOGOLARI, A.L. PROSDOCIMI, I Veneti antichi, 1987; A.M. CHIECO BIANCHI, I Veneti, in: G. PUGLIESE CARRATELLI (ed.), Italia omnium terrarum alumna, 1988, 1–98.

C.KO.

Esther (Ester). The Hebrew Book of Esther, dated to either the end of the Persian or the beginning of the Hellenistic period, recounts (a) the decision that the Persian King Ahasverus (485–465 BC) is said to have taken (cf. especially 3,13), at the urging of the anti-Jewish Haman, one of his most influential officials, to eliminate his kingdom's Jews, and (b) the salvation of the Jews, in which a major part was played by the Jewish E., who had entered the court without being recognized, as the kings' consort. The book, the historical background of which is fictitious, is the basis of the legend for the Purim festival (Feast of Lots). As God is not explicitly mentioned at any stage as having intervened in the events, the book's theological character and its intended message pose a problem that has been much debated to this day. The theological message is clearly sets out in the book's Greek translation, which, according to the colophon at its end, claims to have been finished in Jerusalem 'in the fourth year of the reign of Ptolemy and Cleopatra' (10,31), and thus has to be dated to 114 or 78/7 BC, and which extends the Hebrew narrative (the so-called 'Additions to E.', which according to Protestant tradition belong to the → Apocrypha but according to Catholic tradition are an integral part of the canon). It refers unambiguously to the people's salvation through the intervention (5,1; 8,12q), of God who responded to his supplicants' prayers (4,17a-i; 4,17k-z; 5,1a; 1,1h-k; 10,3f). In both of the similarly embellished Aramaic translations of the book, probably originating in the 6th and 7th cents. (*Targūm Rīšōn* and *Targūm Šēnī*), that trend is expanded further. The anti-Jewish Haman here appears as a representative of the Roman Empire.

→ Bible

H. BARDTKE, Zusätze zu Ester, Jüd. Schriften aus hell.-röm. Zeit I/1, 1973, 15–62; O. KAISER, Einleitung in das Alte Testament. Eine Einführung in ihre Ergebnisse und Probleme, [5]1984, 202–211; J. V.D. KLAAUW, J. LEBRAM, s.v. Ester, TRE 10, 1982, 391–395 (all with extensive bibliographies).

B.E.

Estimation In many ancient political communities, the right of full citizenship, the active or passive right to vote, the assignment to certain arms of service, and the act of splitting the cost of financial services by the state between the citizens, were all contingent upon economical ability and thereby indirectly dependent upon social status. These rights and duties were assigned on the basis of an estimation. Ancient political theory regarded the requirement of meeting certain qualifications concerning assets and income for the right of citizenship and the right to vote as the mark of an oligarchical constitution, and referred to such a constitution as *politeía apò timēmátōn* (Pl. Resp. 550c-d) or as → *timokratía* (Aristot. Eth. Nic. 1160a 33–37). In Athens, → Solon established four classes of estimation (*télos*) according to the amount of agricultural yields, and these classes were the basis for determining political rights. In the → Delian League, the term estimation was used for determining the contingents of ships and the financial contributions of the members (→ *phóros*).

In republican Rome, the → *censores* conducted an estimation (→ *census*) of the Roman citizens every five years. The citizens' assets determined their assignment to the different arms of service of the army (*classes*; cf. Servius → Tullius) and therefore the weight of their vote in the respective → *centuria* during votes in the → *comitia centuriata*. In the Roman provinces, estimations were conducted to determine the amount of taxation.

→ Census; → Eisphora; → Hippeis; → Pentakosiomedimnoi; → Status; → Taxes; → Thetes; → Time; → Zeugitai

L. FOXHALL, A View from the Top. Evaluating the Solonian Property Classes, in: L. G. MITCHELL, P. J. RHODES (ed.), The Development of the Polis in Archaic Greece, 1997, 113–136; C. NICOLET, The World of the Citizen in Republican Rome, 1980, 49–88; W. SCHMITZ, Reiche und Gleiche, in: W. EDER (ed.), Demokratie, 573–597. W. S.

Estrangelā The term *estrangelā* (deriving from the Greek στρογγύλος/*strongýlos*, 'rounded') refers to the pattern of Syriac script in the oldest manuscripts (5th–8th cents., still common up to the 13th cent. but rarely used thereafter).

E. HATCH, An Album of Dated Syriac Manuscripts, 1946, 24–27. S.BR.

Esus Celtic god whose identification with a Roman god is uncertain. Whereas Luc. 1,444ff. ranks E. with → Teutates and → Taranis as the three principal Celtic gods, the (later) schol. on Lucanus identify E. with either Mars or Mercury. That E. cannot be Mercury is made clear from the side panel of the Mercury altar at Trier [1. VI 4929]: it shows E. felling trees in the company of a bull and three cranes, similar to a scene on a monument in Paris. This detailed representation on the Nautae Parisiaci memorial [1. IV 3133] shows a god on one panel and gives his name as *ESVS*, on the next panel it shows a bull *TARVOS* (*sic*) *TRIGRANVS* carrying three cranes on his back and head. The myth that had taken shape pictorially here as early as the 1st cent. AD is, however, no more comprehensible than the character of E.

1 ESPÉRANDIEU, Inscr.

IHM, s.v. E., RE 6, 694ff,; W. DEONNA, in: Ogam 10, 1958, 3ff.; P.M. DUVAL, Études celtiques VII, 1, 1958, 50ff.; J. DE VRIES, Kelt. Religion, 1961, 97ff.; P.M. DUVAL, in: TZ 36, 1973, 81ff.; M. LE GLAY, s.v. E., LIMC 4.1, 25. M.E.

Esuvii (Esubii). Tribe in Gallia Celtica, later Lugdunensis, between the lower Seine and the Loire. Caesar (Gall. 2,34; 3,7; 5,24; 5,53) mentions it as one of the tribes of Aremorica (Bretagne) between the Coriosolites and the Aulerci in the area of Sées (Orne). Y.L.

Esuvius

[1] Imperator Caesar C. Pius E. Tetricus Augustus. He came from a noble (Aur. Vict. Caes. 33,14), certainly (because of the name E.) Gallic family and, even before his elevation to Augustus, was senator and governor of Aquitania, when Victorinus ruled over the rebel Gallic empire (Eutr. 9,10). After Victorinus was murdered, he was proclaimed emperor by the military, probably in the spring of AD 271, and clothed in the purple in Bordeaux (Eutr. ibid.; [Aur. Vict.] Epit. Caes. 35,7; Iohannes Antiochenus, FHG 4, 598, 152,1). He ruled over Gaul (ILS 567, other inscriptions see below [1; 2]) and Britain [3], but not Spain (despite SHA Clod. 7,5). He held the consulate three times, and the *tribunicia potestas* (not recognized in Rome) four times [4]. He had coins minted in Trier and Cologne. In 273(?) he elevated his eponymous son E. [2] to Caesar (Aur. Vict. Caes. 33,14). From the very beginning he was on the defensive against Germans invading across the Rhine. The *praeses provinciae Belgicae* Faustinus revolted against E. in Trier (Aur. Vict. Caes. 35,4). When Aurelianus [3] advanced against Gaul in 274 with a strong army, E. betrayed his troops just before the impending battle on the Catalaunian Fields (at Châlons) and surrendered without a battle (Eutr. 9,13,1. Zos. 1,61,2). With his son and → Zenobia, E. was paraded in triumph (Eutr. 9,13,2), but still received other high offices; he became *corrector Lucaniae* (Aur. Vict. Caes. 35,5) and reached old age (Eutr. 9,13,2). The *vita* (SHA Tyr. Trig. 24) is largely fictitious.

1 I. KÖNIG, Die gallischen Usurpatoren, 1980 2 J.F. DRINKWATER, The Gallic Empire, 1987 3 The Roman Inscriptions of Britain 1, 1965, 2224–6 4 RIC 5/2 399–418.

KIENAST, [2]1996, 247f. A.B.

[2] C. Pius E. Tetricus Caesar. Son of E. [1]; elevated to Caesar in AD 273 (?), *princeps iuventutis* in 274(RIC 5/2 424 no. 281) and *cos.* (in Gaul) (ESPÉRANDIEU, Inscr. 656). Paraded with his father in Aurelianus' [3] triumph, he nevertheless later occupied the highest offices (Aur. Vict. Caes. 35,5). A.B.

Etanna *Civitas* of the Allobroges in Gallia Narbonensis on the left bank of the Rhône, *statio* on the Vienne-Geneva road (Tab. Peut.). Identified with Yenne or Etain near Yenne. Flourished from the 2nd to 6th cents. AD. Inscriptions: CIL 12,305.

P. DUFOURNET, Le réseau routier gallo-romain de Vienne à Genève et la position des stations d'E. et de Condate, Archéologie, 1965, 35–72. Y.L.

Eteagoras (Ἐτεαγόρας; *Eteagóras*). Writer of comedy in the 3rd cent. BC; one comedy is epigraphically attested to have won the Lenaea. Neither the titles nor fragments of his plays have survived.

PCG V, 183. H.-G.NE.

Etemenanki see → Esagil

Etenna (Ἔτεννα; *Étenna*). Pisidian mountain town in the Side hinterland, today's Sirtköy. Coins assure that it was already established in the early Hellenistic period. E. provided mercenaries (epigraphically attested), fought with a large contingent on the side of Achaeus [5] against Selge (Pol. 5,73,3) in 218 BC and was probably a target in Antiochus III's Pisidian campaign in 193 BC (Liv. 35,13,5). In the Imperial period it belonged to the province Lycia-Pamphylia; it was the suffragan diocese of Side in late antiquity; it went into decline in the 12th cent. AD. Relatively extensive coin-minting [1], with a crescent-shaped sword as its coat of arms.

1 AULOCK 2, 30–32, 75–95.

J. NOLLÉ, Zur Gesch. der Stadt E. in Pisidien, in: E. SCHWERTHEIM (ed.), Forsch. in Pisidien, 1992, 61–141. P.W.

Eteobutadae (Ἐτεοβουτάδαι; *Eteoboutádai*, 'ancient/true Butadae'). Attic *génos* that claimed descent from the hero Butes [1] and probably originated as a cult association in the territory of → Butadae. Since the Eteobutadae are already attested during the archaic period, its members – contrary to what the name suggests – could not have taken their name after the creation of the Cleisthenic deme Butadae. They provided the priestess of → Athena Polias (Aeschin. Leg. 147) and the priests of Poseidon Erechtheus (Plut. Lycurgus 47 f.). Lycurgus [9] belonged to the *génos* of the Eteobutadae.
→ Genos; → Ismenias [5]; → Lycurgus [7]

F. BOURRIOT, Recherches sur la nature du genos, 2, 1976, 1304–1347, 1362; R. C. SMITH, The Clans of Athens and the Historiography of the Archaic Period, in: Echos du Monde Classique 29, 1985, 51–61; K.-W. WELWEI, Athen, 1992, 94, 224, 240. H. LO.

Eteocles (Ἐτεοκλῆς; *Eteoklês*, 'genuine fame' cf. [1]).
[1] Theban hero, son of → Oedipus and his mother Iocasta (Epicaste); in the *Oedipodea* (fr. 2 PEG I; → Epic cycle) Euryganeia is the mother. The feud with his brother → Polyneices, recounted as early as Homer (Il. 4,376–398), stemmed from the curse uttered by their father after both sons had insulted him (Thebais fr.2–3 PEG I; Attic tragedy: Aesch. Sept.; Soph. OT; Soph. OC; Soph. Ant.; Eur. Phoen.). E. broke the agreement under which rule was to alternate annually between him and Polyneices and forced the latter into exile, whence Polyneices with six other military commanders launched a campaign against Thebes. In the ensuing battle the two brothers killed each other. Aeschylus portrays E. primarily as a responsible and patriotic prince [2], whereas E. is depicted as tyrannical in Eur. Phoen. E.'s son and successor was Laodamas (Apollod. 3,55–74; 83; Hyg. Fab. 67–70; Stat. Theb.; Paus. 9,5,10–13; 9,25,2). Paus. 9,18,3 mentions sacrifices on the graves of both brothers on the road to Chalcis. The oldest extant representation of E. and the death at each other's hands is to be found on the → Cypselus Chest (Paus. 5,19,6) [3].

1 KAMPTZ, 88; 193 2 A. J. PODLECKI, The Character of E. in Aeschylus' Septem, in: TAPhA 95, 1964, 283–299 3 I. KRAUSKOPF, s.v. E., LIMC 4.1, 28 no. 4.

H. H. BACON, The shield of E., in: E. SEGAL (ed.), Oxford Readings in Greek Tragedy, 1983, 24–33; J. A. JOHNSON, E. and the posting decisions, in: RhM 135, 1992, 193–197; I. KRAUSKOPF, s.v. E., LIMC 4.1, 26–37; A. LESKY, E. in den Sieben gegen Theben, in: Id., Gesammelte Schriften, 1966, 264–274.

[2] King in Boeotian Orchomenus, son of Evippe and the river-god Cephisus. He was regarded as the founder of the cult of the three → Charites, said to be stars fallen from heaven (Hes. fr. 71; Paus. 9,34,9; 35,1; 38,1). R.B.

Eteo-Cretan In Hom. Od. 19, 176 the Ἐτεόκρητες (*Eteókrētes*) are described as the 'real, true Cretans' of the five peoples inhabiting Crete. That may well have been the situation in the poet's time (8th cent BC.) but not that of the 2nd millennium. In a commentary on that point Str. 10,4,6 names the πολίχνιον Πρᾶσος (*políchnion Prâsos*; 'the small town *Prā́sos*') in the east of the island as the area occupied by the Eteo-Cretans (EC). That is suggestive of an area to which they had retreated. Diod. Sic. 5,64,1 describes the EC as αὐτόχθονες (*autóchthones*; 'autonomous').

Texts (without exception fragmentary and short) from the 7th–4th cents. BC, probably of an official nature, have been found at → Praesus and Drerus; held to be EC, these texts used the Greek alphabet but were in a non-Greek language. So far they remain the only sample and remain incomprehensible. EC was perhaps more widespread in Crete in earlier times.
→ Greece, languages; → Pre-Greek languages

Y. DUHOUX, L'étéocrétois. Les textes – la langue, 1982. G.N.

Eteo-Cyprian The non-Indo-European, still unintelligible language of the Eteo-Cyprians, whose name, like that of the Eteo-Cretans, is applied to the non-Greek population of Cyprus [1. 49ff.]. Textual evidence, *c.* 7th–3rd cents. BC and for the most part from → Am(m)athus [3], was written in the → Cypriot Script, also used by the Greeks, the symbols for which have the same pronunciation in both languages, as demonstrated by the spelling of proper names in the → bilingual inscription of Amathus:
1) *a-na · ma-to-ri · u-mi-e-sa- : i-mu-ku-la-i-la-sa-na · a - ri - si - to - no - se · a - ra - to - wa - na - ka - so - ko - o - se*
2) *ke-ra-ke-re-tu-lo-se ·? ta-ka- : na-?–?–so-ti · a-lo · ka-i-li-po-ti*
1) Ἡ πόλις ἡ Ἀμαθουσίων Ἀ ρ ί σ τ ω : ν α; *Hē pólis hē Amathousíōn Arístōna*
2) Ἀ ρ ι σ τ ώ ν α κ τ ο ς εὐπατρίδην; *Aristṓnaktos eupatrídēn* [2. 206–209].
→ Cypro-Minoan scripts

1 KSd 2 MASSON.

MASSON, 85–87; M. EGETMEYER, WB zu den Inschr. im kypr. Syllabar, 1992, 302–322. A.HI.

Eteonicus (Ἐτεόνικος; *Eteónikos*). Spartan, campaigned under Astyochus against Lesbos in 412 BC (Thuc. 8,23); as → harmost of Thasos he was forced out by an anti-Spartan faction in 410 (Xen. Hell. 1,1,32). After the Spartan defeat at Arginusae in 406, E. took his ship and troops safely to Chios and stationed them there until Lysander's arrival (Xen. Hell.1,6,26; 35–38; 2,1,1–6; 10; Diod. Sic. 13,97,3; 100,5). He held a command at Aigospotamoi (405) (Diod. Sic. 13,106,5; Paus. 10,9,10). E. later conquered the Thracian coast (Xen. Hell. 2,2,5) and in 400 was in Byzantium, where he met Xenophon (Xen. An. 7,1,12–20). In the Corinthian war, from Aegina, he disrupted Athenian trade in *c.* 390 (Xen. Hell. 5,1,1f. 13). M.MEI.

Eteonus (Ἐτεωνός; *Eteōnós*). Boeotian city on the northern slope of Cithaeron, described in Hom. Il. 2,497 as πολύκνημος (*polýknēmos*, 'with many mountain forests'); renamed in the classical period as Σκαφ(λ)αί/Σκάρφη (*Skaph(l)ai/Skárphē*); References: Str. 7,3,6; 9,2,24; Plin. HN 4,26; Stat. Theb. 7,266; Steph. Byz. s.v. E.; inscriptions in [2. 84f.]. E. belonged to one of the regions in the Boeotian League under the control of Thebes (Hell. Oxy. 19,3,387; 20,3,438). The tomb of Oedipus was visible in the Demeter sanctuary (Lysimachus of Alexandria, FGrH 382 F 2). E.'s location is a contentious issue [1; 3].

1 Fossey, 130f. 2 M.H. Hansen, An Inventory of Boiotian Poleis in the Archaic and Classical Periods, in: Id., Introduction to an Inventory of Poleis, 1996, 73–116 3 P.W. Wallace, Strabo's Description of Boiotia, 1979, 89–91. P.F.

Etesiai The cool, strong winds blowing from the north to the north-east each year from the middle of July (rising of Sirius) for about 40 days (different duration [1. 714]) were called ἐτησίαι (or βορέαι, *boréai*). These winds blowing from the → Propontis were then a considerable obstacle to navigation on the Black Sea. Isidorus (Orig. 13,11,15) mentions them as north winds that return each year, though without giving any specific timeframe. They were characterized as lashing the waves of the sea, making the sea dark, healthy, dry, and taking the edge off the summer heat. There were also winter *etesiai,* clear, fine-weather southerly winds that were named οἱ λεγόμενοι Λευκόνοτοι ('the so-called *leukónotoi*') (Aristot. Mete. 2,5,362a 14). According to many ancient theories, the *etesiai* bottled up the waters of the rising Nile (Hdt. 2,20; Lucr. 6,712–718; Thales in Sen. Q Nat. 4,2,22ff.) and caused rainfall in Ethiopia (cf. Hdt. 2,22). According to Aristotle (Mete. 2,5,361b 24) its 'precursor' winds were called πρόδρομοι (→ *pródromoi*), in 362a 23 he also calls the ὀρνιθίαι (*ornithíai*), after the winter solstice, weak *etesiai*. Schmidt [2] explains their geophysical causes.

1 A. Rehm, s.v. Etesiai, RE 6, 713–717 2 G. Schmidt, s.v. Winde, RE 8 A, 2212–2214. C.HÜ.

Ethics

A. Background B. The Socratic beginnings C. Plato D. The early Academy and Aristotle E. The Cynic Tradition F. The Quietistic Tradition and Epicureanism G. Stoicism H. Later Platonism

A. Background

In antiquity ethics was the concern to establish what disposition of character is best for mankind. That consideration began with the Homeric ideal of 'being a speaker of words and a doer of deeds' (Hom. Il. 9,443). Critical thought about character made progress in the 5th cent. BC, often embedded deeply in a political context. The earliest research on man's character concentrated most of all on his role as a citizen. Democritus' work 'On rest' seems by contrast to have focussed on the private and personal aspect.

B. The Socratic beginnings

The real tradition of ethical thought in antiquity began with → Socrates: he abandoned natural philosophy and paved the way for discussion on the nature of the good life. His concentration on the best possible state of the soul brought with it the risk of an individual's conflict with the values of a larger social group and even of his family. One branch of Socratic philosophy, the → Cynic school, developed this side of his thought in particular. The search for man's individual → happiness was also an invitation to consider a refined hedonism; Aristippus [3] and the → Cyrenaic school were thus able to claim to have been inspired by Socrates. Even more central to Socrates' concept of man's character and goodness (ἀρετή, *aretḗ*) was his concern for long-term stability. In keeping with the tradition that man's success and contentment (εὐδαιμονία, *eudaimonía*) could be judged only on the basis of one's whole life ('Call no-one happy before he is dead '), Socrates preferred to ask how one was supposed to live than to enquire into the correctness of individual actions. The concept of human *aretḗ* was based on the thought that the character is a stable condition that requires planning and control and that form of intellectual competence that is associated with technical, craft, skills. Such craft skills (τέχναι, *téchnai*) require the knowledge of relevant objects (including virtues) and the self-control (σωφροσύνη, → *sōphrosýnē*) necessary to translate that knowledge into action.

A further feature of Socratic ethics is the confidence that possession of such qualities will suffice to achieve human goals. Given that conviction, factors that are beyond the individual's rational control must be minimized; that applies equally to the meaning of moral happiness (in contrast to the traditions reflected in drama and poetry). A large part of Socratic ethics follows from that: the importance of a definition of virtues (*aretaí*); the tendency to identify virtue with knowledge and to regard the virtues as mutually dependent; the denial of 'weak will'; the assertion that no-one knowingly behaves falsely other than as a consequence of intellectual error; and the thesis that virtue in itself suffices to confer happiness.

C. Plato

It is difficult to distinguish Plato's contribution to ethics from that of Socrates. The most important differences derive from → Plato's having committed himself to separate ideas as the basis of knowledge (including moral knowledge) and having divided man's soul into three parts (reason, motivation and desires). This *tripartite* division conflicts with Socrates' implicit theory of *unity*. Plato was also more convinced than Socrates of the immortality of the soul, and of the possibility of reward after death and of reincarnation. Whereas Socrates had an ambivalent attitude towards hedonism, Plato rejected enjoyment/pleasure (ἡδονή, *hēdonḗ*) as an essential part of a happy life. Finally, he conceded the existence of elements that transcend man's nature: in maintaining (Tht. 176b), that 'assimilation to god' is worth man's striving for, he is explicitly expressing the theme of transcendence found in his dialogues. This passage was to become a source of ethical doctrine for the later Platonic tradition.

D. The early Academy and Aristotle

In the next generation, ethics was recognized as a branch of philosophy in its own right. The subdivision of philosophy into logic, physics and ethics, as advocated by the Platonic pupil Xenocrates of Chalcedon, was adopted by → Aristotle and the Hellenistic schools. Aristotle defined ethics as part of politics and composed at least two versions of his lecture on ethics; of those two the 'Nicomachean Ethics' was by far the most influential. The central doctrines of Aristotelian ethics are based on thought processes that are developed in Eth. Nic. 1, the clearest formal interpretation of ancient eudaimonism. Aristotle advances the thesis that the good life is an active life (βίος πρακτικός, *bíos praktikós*) in harmony with our nature and our natural functions. Understanding man's nature enables the understanding of his characteristic advantages (i.e. the virtues). The soul combines rational and non-rational components. The rational component can achieve the intellectual virtues, which can be divided into practical and theoretical, while the non-rational component can follow the dictates of practical reason and is the main seat of the virtues of character. These are defined as intermediate conditions between two extremes (= μεσότης/*mesótēs*, μέσον/*méson*). A great part of Aristotelian ethics consists of an analysis of both intellectual and moral virtues. Other important themes are the role of friendship (φιλία, *philía*) in the good life and the balance between the private and the official. The most hotly debated question in Aristotle's ethical theory is the relationship between theoretical and practical activity (→ Theory; → Practice).

E. The Cynic Tradition

Socrates also inspired the Cynic movement, whose most influential figure was → Diogenes [14] of Sinope. The Cynics emphasized the individual's moral and intellectual autonomy; hence their characteristic activity of confrontationally exposing conventional moral concepts. That became a source of inspiration for moral reformers, satirists and even other philosophers.

F. The Quietistic Tradition and Epicureanism

The Democritean tradition (→ Democritus) and the hedonistic side of Socratic philosophy gave rise to various quietistic forms of ethical theory. The Cyrenaics traced their origin back to → Aristippus [3] the Elder. They saw their goal in life as striving for immediate gratification. Similarly, in the Pyrrhonian tradition (→ Pyrrhon), pure repose is a general goal in life, and the determined abandonment of intellectual pressures is a means to that end.

By contrast the Epicurean form (→ Epicureanism) of hedonism remains within the eudaimonic framework shared with Plato, Aristotle and the Stoics. The idea of a good life is here founded on an explicit theory of man's nature (including the atomistic basis), according to which, its basic striving is to be free from any suffering of the soul and from any bodily pain (→ *ataraxía*). Reason's task was to increase what was understood as pleasure and to reduce pain, and all of that in the context of a coherent plan covering the entire lifespan. An explicit theory of political and social relationships is an integral part of Epicurean ethics, although it assigns them only an instrumental significance.

G. Stoicism

Stoic ethics remained Socratic in many points where Plato and Aristotle departed from Socrates. They advocated rational planning for the whole of one's life and, as the basis for their view of that goal (τέλος/*télos*, *finis*), took a distinctly different concept of man's nature. A cosmological theory was an expressly integral element of the Stoic concept of a proper and satisfying way of life. In its early years the Stoic school was inclined towards Cynic themes in its political philosophy but, throughout its history, maintained the importance of practical activity and social commitment.

Also featuring in its doctrine: formalizing a Socratic view of value in which moral diligence and related qualities were regarded as important and not to be compared to more profane advantages such as health and wealth; embarking on a life free of passions (πάθος/*páthos*, *affectus*; → Affects); and a model of moral freedom of choice, combining the absolute pre-eminence of rationally definable principles with a contextual flexibility. As the Stoic goal in life was formulated as 'living according to Nature' and Nature was both immanent and divine, the tension between naturalism and transcendence remained in finely-balanced equilibrium in Greek ethics.

H. LATER PLATONISM

In later Platonism (→ Middle Platonism; → Neoplatonism) the transcendental themes of Platonic ethics moved into the foreground. Even Plato's own works had encouraged the combining of a radical discontent towards life in the material world with ethical theory. Stoicism juxtaposed the philosophical ideal of the wise man who was not distracted by life's vagaries. That combination led to a concept in late antiquity of philosophical perfection that adopted and nevertheless transcended the moral and practical qualities underpinning Greek ethical theory and practice.

→ Friendship; → Happiness; → Pleasure; → Virtue; → PRACTICAL PHILOSOPHY

J. ANNAS, The Morality of Happiness, 1993; S. BROADIE, E. with Aristotle, 1991; J. DILLON, An ethic for the late antique sage, in: L. GERSON (ed.), The Cambridge Companion to Plotinus, 1996, 315–335; M. FORSCHNER, Die stoische Ethik, ^{2}1995; B. INWOOD, E. and Human Action in Early Stoicism, 1985; A. KENNY, The Aristotelian E., 1978; P. MITSIS, Epicurus' Ethical Theory, 1988; B. WILLIAMS, Shame and Necessity, 1993. B.I.

Ethiopian Geʿez, the classical language of Ethiopia, actually belongs to the southern branch of Semitic languages. It was spoken by the tribes Agʿazjan and Ḥabašāt, which had migrated into Abyssinia from South Arabia, founded the kingdom of → Axum and in the middle of the 4th cent. AD were converted to Christianity by missionaries. The earliest evidence is stone inscriptions (Axum inscriptions, Maṭara obelisk 4th cent. AD).

From the 9th cent. until the present Geʿez has been used only as a literary and church language. Related Semitic languages are Tigriña and Tigre in the north, and Argobba, Harari, Gafat and Gurage in the south. Amharic, the official language of Ethiopia, replaced Geʿez in the south. The → alphabet (26 characters) is an extension of the Old Southern Arabic one but is written from left to right. The original Semitic stock of consonants was sharply reduced.

E. BERNARD, A. J. DREWES, R. SCHNEIDER, Recueil des inscriptions de l'Éthiopie des périodes pré-axoumite et axoumite, 1991; E. ULLENDORFF, The Semitic Languages of Ethiopia, 1955. C.K.

Ethnarchos The title *ethnarchos* was given by the Romans to both Hyrcanus II (63–40 BC) and the son of Herod, Archelaus (4 BC-AD 6) (Hyrcanus II by Caesar 47 BC cf. Jos. Ant. Iud. 14,192ff.; Archelaus by Augustus after Herod's death, cf. Jos. Ant. Iud. 17,317). Formal expression was thus given to the designated person's rule over the Jewish people, while at the same time deliberately avoiding the title of king (cf. Jos. Ant. Iud. 20,244). The head of the Jewish community in Alexandria, who is said to have been able to operate as the ruler of a sovereign state, also bore that title (Jos. Ant. Iud. 14,117). According to Philo, the office was replaced by a council of elders (In Flaccum 74).

I. GAFNI, s.v. E., Encyclopedia Judaica 6, 945f.; P. SCHÄFER, Gesch. des Judentum in der Antike. Die Juden Palästinas von Alexander dem Großen bis zur arab. Eroberung, 1983, 97, 116. B.E.

Ethnic names Ethnic names of all kinds (e.g. Κρῆτες, Κορίνθιοι, *Campānī, Ligurēs*) have been passed down to us in abundance from Graeco-Roman antiquity, as have *ktetika* to describe objects or abstract concepts (κρητικός, κορινθιακός, *campānicus*, *ligustīnus*). Ethnic names (EN) can act as place names (Λοκροί, *Tarquiniī*) and as personal names (Mycenaean dat. *i-ja-wo-ne /Iāwonei/*). As in the case of place names, progenitors were also invented in antiquity for EN (Ἕλλην, Δῶρος, Αἴολος, Ἰταλός; → Aeolus [1], → Dorus, → Hellen, → Italus). Among the ethnic names two types can be differentiated:

(1) EN that show a link with the region in which the tribe lived or from which it had spread out. In general they are based on the place name (the base word is often unfathomable), or vice versa (Θετταλοί, *Campānī* > Θετταλία, *Campānia*; cf. also the place name Βοῖον (ὄρος) > EN Βοιωτοί > place name Βοιωτία), and are formed with suffixes, e.g. **-i̯o-* (e.g. Ἀργεῖοι from the place name Ἄργος) and **-(V)no-* (*Rōmā-nī, Tusculānī, Praenest-īnī*; Greek -[ι]ωος and -ᾶνός in the EN of Lower Italy and Asia Minor, e.g. Ταραντῖνοι, Σαρδιανοί). In Greek **-ēu̯-* (Hom. and later), **-(ī)tā-*, **-(i)ā/ōtā-* are used and often take the place of **-i̯o-*, cf. Μυκηναῖος > Μυκανεύς, Mycenaean *ro-u-si-jo/Lousios/* > Λουσ-ιάτας from the place name Λοῦσοι; the following are somewhat relic-like: **-ān-*, *-ant-*, *-u̯on-* (e.g. Αἰνιᾶνες, Ἄβαντες, Ἰάονες). In the Italian area: **-ko-* (*Faliscī* from the place name *Faleriī*), also **-ko-lo-* (*Tusculī* from *Tu(r)scī*); **-ensi-* (often in foreign EN, *Carthāgin-i-*), **-(V)ti-*(Etruscan?: *Camertēs* from the place name *Camer[-īnum]*). Different forms for an EN are possible (e.g. *Vols-cī*: Ὄλσοι; *Sabīnī, Sabellī, Samnītēs* from **sab-n-īno-, *sab-en-lo-, *sab-n-īti-* from the place name *Samnium* [2]).

(2) EN that indicate themes based on self-naming (a-e) or naming by other peoples (f): (a) membership of one's own clan: *Suēbī* (Germanic) from Indo-European **s(u̯)e-b*^{h}*(o)-*, 'of one's own type' (Gothic *sibja*, 'clan'), *Teutisci* (: *diutisk*, 'belonging to the people [Gothic *þiuda*]'). (b) Entirety (cf. *Alemanni*): Πάμφυλοι, Αἰολεῖς (: αἰόλος 'mobile, colourful'). (c) Animal names: *Hirpīnī* or *Pīcentēs* from Samnite *(h)irpus* 'Wolf' and Lat. *pīcus* (place name *Pīcēnum*); *Bruttiī*, Βρέττιοι, *Frentānī* 'deer people' (Messap. βρένδον· ἔλαφον, place name *Brundisium* [modern Brindisi]). (d) Place of residence: *Aequī* : *Aequīculī* (: *aequus* 'flat', place name *Aequum Tuticum*). (e) Terms of praise, e.g. 'strong' (old Lat. *Forctēs* 'fortēs' from **b*^{h}*r̥ĝ*^{h}*-ti-*, cf. also **b*^{h}*r̥ĝ*^{h}*-n̥t-*, 'high': *Burgundiī* [Germanic], *Brigantēs* [Gallic]). (f) Insulting names, e.g. 'incomprehensible' (Παφλαγόνες for the Greeks of Asia Minor, cf. παφλάζειν, 'to stutter'; βάρβαροι).

EN (like place names) have often spread out from an original area, e.g. the Ἕλληνες originally inhabited the Phthiotis, the *Italī* (Ἴταλοι) the Greek area around the Gulf of Tarentum (: place name *Ϝιταλία after a *u̯*-less Greek variant of ἔτε/αλον: *uitulus*, 'calf'). Consequently general EN are also used to denote a region, cf. Ἀχαιοί, Αἰολεῖς to Ἀχαία, Αἰολίς). The EN Πελασγοί (originally in Dodona and Thessaly) has developed the meaning 'pre-Greek ' or 'ancient' [1].

Many Greek and Italic tribes took on pre-Greek and pre-Italic EN; others were also named by neighbouring peoples, so there are cases of multiple naming, e.g. Etruscan Ῥασέννα/*Rasna* : Greek Τυρσηνοί/Τυρρηνοί: Lat. *Etruscī/Tu(r)scī*. A classic example: the Greeks, who called themselves Ἕλληνες (in Homer also Ἀχαιοί, Δαναοί, Ἀργεῖοι), were called *Graecī*, *Graiī* by the Italic peoples after the first Greek tribe (Γραικοί, Γραῆς [Dodona], place name Γραική, Γραῖα [Oropus, Eretria]) they met, and correspondingly they were called *Yaunā* (ancient Persian: Ἰάονες) by the Iranians, and *Aḫḫii̯au̯a-* (for Ἀχαιοί) by the Anatolians.
→ Geographical names; → Onomatology; → Word formation

1 J. L. García Ramón, Pelasgos y micénicos en Tesalia, in: Zephyrus 26/27, 1976, 473–478 2 H. Rix, Sabini, Sabelli, Samnium, in: BN 8, 1957, 127–143 (= Id., KS, 2001, 106–122).

G. B. Pellegrini, Toponimi ed etnici dell'Italia antica, in: Prosdocimi, 79–127; E. Risch, Ein Gang durch die Gesch. der griech. ON, in: MH 14.2, 1965, 63–74 (= Id., KS, 1981, 133–144); M. Sakellariou, Peuples préhelléniques d'origine indo-européenne, 1977 (collection of material); F. Solmsen (ed. by E. Fränkel), Idg. EN als Spiegel der Kulturgesch., 1922, 95–110. J. G.-R.

Ethnikon (Modern term, from ἐθνικός/*ethnikós*, 'belonging to an *éthnos*'; ethnic). Scholarly term in epigraphy for the designation of origin of a person mentioned outside his native polis or region. The ethnikon (cf. Str. 14,2,18) identifies affiliation with the inhabitants of a particular polis (e.g., *Korínthios*) or a particular region (e.g., *Boiōtós*, *Sikeliṓtēs*). The phenomenon is well attested: the ethnikon was also applied to women, citizens of destroyed or no longer existing poleis retained their ethnikon, and on occasion it designated a town without the status of a polis (e.g., *Naukratítēs* before the period of Alexander). This demonstrates that a local and especially a tribal ethnikon (as eventually also *Thrax*, *Galátēs*) did not principally define political affiliation in the sense of citizenship but origin in a geographical or topographical sense.
→ Ethnos

M. H. Hansen, City-Ethnics as Evidence for Polis Identity, in: Id., K. Raaflaub (ed.), More Studies in the Ancient Greek Polis, 1996, 169–196; E. Risch, Zur Gesch. der griech. Ethnika, in: MH 14, 1957, 63–74. L.-M. G.

Ethnography see → Anthropology

Ethnos (ἔθνος; *éthnos*, pl. ἔθνη/*éthnē*) has multiple meanings in Greek and refers to different types of groups, e.g., warrior bands (Hom. Il. 3,32) or large ethnic groups (Hdt. 1,101). From the classical period, *ethnos* was often juxtaposed to the term → *pólis* (cf. Hdt. 5,2; 8,108; regarding Aristotle's [6] discussion of *éthnē*: [1; 2]). For some time research considered the polis ('city state') as the highest developmental phase of the state in Hellas, while *éthnos* ('tribe') supposedly constituted an earlier and more primitive form [3]. The current view is more complex both in terms of chronology and structure because it considers parallel developments and different living conditions [4]. It thus becomes evident that geographically scattered intra-Hellenic (large) *éthnē*, such as the Achaeans, Ionians and Dorians, never were primordial tribes in the meaning of communities of descent whose origins should be sought in an age before the migration into Hellas. Rather, their genesis is now dated to the 8th/7th cents. BC [5; 6]. However, there is still considerable controversy regarding the development of a sense of affiliation and shared traits in cult, calendar system, institutions etc. (→ Dorieis; → Iones).

Apart from the large *éthnē*, many smaller *éthnē*, such as the Aetolians, Boeotians, Thessalians, etc., which are already mentioned in Homer, existed in Greece. Like the *póleis*, these *éthnē* were also involved in a process of differentiation since the archaic period, with differing 'segments' forming in the *éthnos* depending on size, form and structure. While these sub-units largely remained autonomous, at the federal state level organizational forms such as the federal assembly, council, officials, etc. as well as federal laws that made collective action possible, particularly in military and foreign policy, developed. However, this process did not happen at the same time and with the same intensity in all *éthnē*. In a federal state the citizens had double citizenships at the levels of member state and federation (→ *sympoliteía*). Many *koiná* (→ *koinón*) succeeded in integrating territories not belonging to the *éthnos* (cf. the incorporation of Calydon into the Achaean League before 389 BC, see → Achaeans [1] B.3., Xen. Hell. 4,6,1; [7]). Some *éthnē* are found up to the Roman Imperial period, even though form and functions had changed in the context of the Roman province.

1 P. Funke, Die Bed. der griech. Bundesstaaten in der polit. Theorie und Praxis des 5. und 4. Jh. v. Chr., in: W. Schuller (ed.), Polit. Theorie und Praxis im Altertum, 1998, 60–71 2 G. A. Lehmann, Ansätze zu einer Theorie des griech. Bundesstaates bei Aristoteles und Polybios, 2001 3 V. Ehrenberg, Der Staat der Griechen, [2]1965 4 P. Funke, Stamm und Polis. Überlegungen zur Entstehung der griech. Staatenwelt in den Dunklen Jahrhunderten, in: J. Bleicken (ed.), Colloquium aus Anlaß des 80. Geburtstages von A. Heuss, 1993, 29–48 5 C. Ulf, Griech. Ethnogenese versus Wanderungen von Stämmen und Stammstaaten, in: Id. (ed.), Wege zur Genese griech. Identität, 1996, 240–280 6 J. Hall, Ethnic Identity in Greek Antiquity, 1997 7 H. Beck, Polis und Koinon, 1997, 59 f.

H.-J. GEHRKE, Ethnos, Phyle, Polis, in: P. FLENSTED-JENSEN et al. (ed.), Polis and Politics. Studies in Ancient Greek History, 2000, 159–176; F. GSCHNITZER, Stammes- und Ortsgemeinden im alten Griechenland, in: Id. (ed.), Zur griech. Staatskunde, 1969, 271–297; J. HALL, Hellenicity. Between Ethnicity and Culture, 2001; J. A. O. LARSEN, Greek Federal States, 1968; I. MALKIN (ed.), Ethnicity and the Construction of Ancient Greek Identity, 2001; R. PARKER, Cleomenes on the Acropolis, 1998; C. TANCK, Arche – Ethnos – Polis, 1997. K. F.

Ethopoeia (ἠθοποιία/*ēthopoiía*; Lat. *ethopoeia*, *notatio*). *Ethopoeia* means the representation of the character (→ *êthos*) of an orator or another person by (imitative) speech (→ *mímēsis*), which may be effected as speech without dialogue, → dialogue or → monologue. In ancient rhetorical theory, *ethopoeia* has been included from Aristotle as a reproducible quality among technical means of persuasion with which the speaker may introduce himself as an insightful, virtuous and benevolent person. Roman rhetoric introduced further refinements: the forensic orator had to present his own *ēthos* and in a more moderate form that of his client (Rhet. Her. 4,63–65; Cic. De or. 2,184). The possible combinations of *êthos* and → *páthos* were correlated with the → *genera dicendi*; *ethopoeia* as a moderate arousal of emotions was equivalent to the middle style. In schools of rhetoric *ethopoeia* was practiced by role playing in which historical or fictional personages were assumed. Depending on the mixture of *êthos* and *páthos*, *ethopoeia* was differentiated as ethically calm, pathetically moved and 'mixed'. In varying definitions *ethopoeia* was classified as a word figure (Rutilius [II 6] in Quint. Inst. 9,3,99) or a thought figure (ibid. 9,2,58; → Figures). The delimitation of *ethopoeia* against → personification (I. A.) and *sermocinatio* (fictional dialogue) is uncertain, and its obvious proximity to fictionalization techniques in literature was already noted in antiquity (ibid. 3,8,49–54).

→ Progymnasma; → Speech/oration II; → Rhetoric VI. A.2.

LAUSBERG, §§ 820–825; G. NASCHERT, s. v. Ethopoeia, HWdR, 1512–1516. C. W.

Ethos (ἦθος; *êthos*, character) was primarily a philosophical concept and as such concerned man's free actions with regard to specific moral criteria. It was accordingly the result of a decision to behave in a certain way and it conferred merit upon the actor depending on the degree to which that behaviour corresponded to the relevant ideal of virtue. In the literary field, *ethos* served to characterize the different people in a work, whereas in rhetoric it had from the earliest times a fundamental function for persuading and convincing. In Greek rhetoric *ethos* involved the orator as well as his adversary, in Roman rhetoric it included the person of the *reus*, i.e. the client for whom the orator was speaking. Aristotle regarded *ethos* as one of the three features of 'artistic evidence' (πίστεις ἔντεχνοι) and he bemoaned the fact that some teaching authors had not taken into account the persuasive power of the 'orator's integrity' (ἐπιείκεια τοῦ λέγοντος; → *argumentatio*) (Rhet. 1356a1f.). In Aristotle's view the orator appeared to be 'credible' (ἀξιόπιστος, 1356a4ff.) in the eyes of his audience precisely through the effect of the *ethos* that he displayed at the very moment he spoke, as he showed good will, virtue and understanding in his speech (1378a6ff.). The orator's *ethos* certainly also proved to be useful in the epideictic genre (1366a 25ff.) and in legal speeches, but it was especially effective in the *genus deliberativum* (1377b 24ff.).

Along with this *ethos* that had a rationally persuasive effect on the audience, there appeared another form that aimed at stirring the emotions. Cicero's *conciliare* is primarily based on that moderate stirring of emotions (→ *captatio benevolentiae*) caused by the orator's skilful display of his own *mores* and those of his client (De or. 2,182ff.; Or. 128). Contrary to Aristotle's '*ethos* of the orator', it is far more a question here of pre-existing qualities such as the *dignitas hominis*, the *res gestae*, and the *existimatio vitae*. It is, however, just this *patronus-cliens* combination that allows Cicero to give a double illustration of the *ethos* of the orator who creates an *ethos* by depicting (*exprimere*) the client's *mores* in a particularly measured *elocutio* and *actio*, thus allowing him as he speaks to appear *probus, bene moratus, bonus vir* (De or. 2,182–184). Quint. Inst. 6,2,8ff. later adopted this doctrine of Cicero's.

→ Captatio benevolentiae; → Epideixis; → Pathos

L. CALBOLI MONTEFUSCO, Cicerone, De oratore: la doppia funzione dell'E. dell'oratore, in: Rhetorica 10, 1992, 245–259; W. FORTENBAUGH, s.v. E., in: HWdR vol. 2, 1516–1525; C. GILL, The E./Pathos Distinction in Rhetorical and Literary Criticism, in: CQ 78, 1984, 149–166; J. SPRUTE, E. als Überzeugungsmittel in der aristotelischen Rhet., in: G. UEDING (ed.), Rhet. zwischen den Wissenschaften, 1991; J. WISSE, E. and Pathos from Aristotle to Cicero, 1989; M. H. WÖRNER, Das Ethische in der Rhet. des Aristoteles, 1990. L.C.M.

Etruscan

A. SOURCES AND SCRIPT B. METHODOLOGY C. LANGUAGE

A. SOURCES AND SCRIPT

E. is known to us from roughly 9,000 texts from the period 700 BC to AD 10, as well as from *c.* 40 glosses. With the exception of a → *liber linteus* on the bindings on an Egyptian mummy, containing the fragment of a description of a ritual, all the texts are inscriptions: funerary, ownership, votive, gift and manufacturing inscriptions and annotations on paintings. Most come from Etruria itself, others from neighbouring regions, a small number from outside Italy. The script uses an alphabet taken from a pre-700 BC Western Greek prototype (X = *ks*, not k^h) and is in turn the origin of the Latin alphabet (C = *k* as in E., which had no voiced consonants, not *g* like the Greek γ). There is therefore no problem with reading the texts phonetically.

B. Methodology

E. is certainly no longer an unknown or even enigmatic language. However, as we have not come across any well-known language to which E. is related, ready access to a comparison of words and forms ('etymological' method) is restricted to the marginal area of loan words (e.g. Latin *satelles* from E. *zatlaθ*, E. *pruχum* from Greek προχοῦν [acc.] 'pitcher'). In general, in working from short texts, one has to try to determine the 'message' of a text from its context, dissect this into elements, correlate the elements to the words of the text

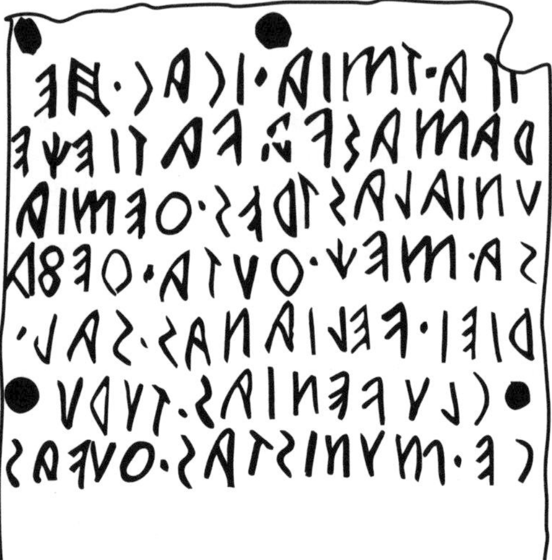

Text sample: opening lines of the dedicatory inscription Pyrgi A

$^{1}{}_{1}$*ita.* $_{2}$ *tmia.* $_{3}$*ica*$_{4}$*c.* $_{5}$*he*^{2}*ramaσva* $_{6}$*vatieχe* $_{7}{}^{3}$*unialas*$_{8}$*. tres* $_{9}$*Θemia*^{4}*sa* $_{10}$*meχ*$_{11}$*. Θuta*$_{12}$*. Θefa*^{5}*riei*$_{13}$*. velianas.* $_{14}$*sal* $_{15}{}^{6}$*cluvenias*$_{16}$*. turu*^{7}*ce.* ...

$_{1\text{-}5}$subject, nominative: [suffix] *-0;*
$_{1;3}$demonstrative pronouns; $_{4}$conjunction; $_{5}$plural: *-(χ)va;* $_{6}$preterite passive: *-χe;* $_{7}$ablative II: *-al-as;* $_{8}$ *-tra ?* abl.I: *-^{i}s;* $_{9}$preterite participle: *-sa;* $_{10}$ablative III: *-0;* $_{11}$uninflected adjective ; $_{12}$ *-i* uncertain; $_{13}$gentile name; genitive I: *-s;* $_{14}$predicative; $_{15}$attribute, gen.I; $_{16}$preterite active: *-ce.*

»$_{1}$This ~$_{2}$cult room $_{4}$and $_{3}$these $_{5}$statues $_{6}$were wished for $_{7}$by Juno $_{8}$?. $_{9}$having built $_{10}$from $_{11}$[his] own $_{10}$patrimony $_{12}$Tiberius $_{13}$Veliana $_{16}$dedicated (this) $_{14}$as ? $_{15}$of ?. ...«

The numbers in superscript refer to the lines of the right-to-left inscription, while the subscript ones refer to the syntactic analysis. H.R.

and check against occurrences in all the other texts ('combinatorial' method); archaeology, linguistics and knowledge of text structures in historically adjacent languages can help this process. The few longer texts are only partly intelligible using that approach, but the majority of shorter texts are almost completely intelligible. Our knowledge of the vocabulary is also fragmentary; our knowledge of the grammar on the other hand is considerable.

C. Language

The E. phonology contains four vowels and no voiced consonants; the value of θ, χ and φ is a matter of conjecture. Morphologically, E. is (still) largely agglutinative: case and number of a noun, for example, are each indicated by a suffix: *clan* 'son', genitive *clen-s*, plural *clen-ar*, gen. pl. *clinii-ar-as*; loc. in *-i* (*zilc-i* 'in ? office') can also be formed from the genitive: *clen-ar-as-i* at the sons' place. Nominative and accusative are differentiated pronominally, *mi* : *mi-ni* 'I' : 'me'. The verb shows tense and voice but not person and number, *am-e* : *am-ce* 'is/am' : 'was'; *mene-ce* 'made', passive *mena-χe*. The meaning of some words is clearly discernible (*puia* 'wife', *θu zal ci* 'one, two, three', but can only be approximate or vague in others (*zusle* 'a sacrificial animal', *alce* perhaps 'gave').

→ Glossography; → Italy: alphabetical scripts; → Italy: languages; → Personal names: Rome and Italy; → Lemnos-Stele

Editions: CIE, 1893ff. (not yet completed); M. Pallottino (ed.), Testimonia linguae etruscae, ²1968 (Selection); ET.

Literature: M. Pallottino, Etruscologia, ⁷1984, 402–517 (Ger.: Id., Etruskologie, 1988, 379–487, 506–509); H. Rix, Schrift und Sprache, in: M. Cristofani (ed.), Die Etrusker, 1985, 210–238; L. Agostiniani, Contribution à l'étude de l'épigraphie et de la linguistique étrusques, in: Lalies 11, 1992, 37–74.

Bibliography with reproductions: Editio: CIE, 6314 (with photos); H. Rix (ed.), Etr. Texte, 2 vols., 1991, no. Cr 4.4.; Literature: M. Cristofani, Sulla dedica di Pyrgi, in: E. Acquara (ed.), Studi in onore di S. Moscati, 1996, 1117–1126. H.R.

Etruscan vase painting see → Pontic, Red-figured, Black-figured vases

Etrusci, Etruria (Tusci), the Etruscans.
I. History II. Archaeology III. Religion IV. Language

I. History
A. Name B. History of their influence and history of research C. Sources D. Geographic Territory E. Origins F. Beginnings G. Natural resources and Economy H. 8th/7th Centuries I. 6th/5th Centuries J. 4th/3rd Centuries and End

A. Name
A people in Italy who, between the 9th and 1st cents. BC, created the highest form of civilization in the Western Mediterranean before Roman civilization prevailed over the same territory. Various popular names were applied to the E.: *Rasna* (or Graecized *Rasenna*) in Etruscan sources, *Tyrrhenoi* or *Tyrsenoi* in Greek sources, *Turskus* in Umbrian sources and *Etrusci*, *Tusci* or *Lydii* (according to Hdt. 1,94 because of their possible origin in *Lydia*) in Lat. sources.

B. History of their influence and history of research
The extraordinarily diverse resources of the region that they inhabited and the consequential leading role that they played in world trade, their high cultural level, their model character and the competence with which the Romans credited them in science and cult practices, the glory of being a 'very old people distinct from all others by virtue of their language and customs' (Dion. Hal. Ant. 1,30,2) are the main reasons for a form of myth developing around the E., even in antiquity.

That myth resurfaced with Humanism and in the Renaissance, when the E. were cited in Tuscany and Latium – principally in Florence and Viterbo – as a model for social and moral renewal and were adopted into the political and cultural programs of a large number of princes (cf. the Medici family in Tuscany). The literary tradition of the E. was quoted (Liv., Pliny the Elder), but E. monuments were also highly esteemed (cf. Cosimo. I de' Medici and his art collection with the bronze statues 'Minerva', 'Chimaera', 'Arringatore'). Later research by the classical scholars of the 18th cent. (F. Buonarotti, A.F. Gori, S. Maffei, G.B. Passeri, M. Guarnacci) who took up E. culture should be seen in that perspective (*i.a.* inscriptions, language, religion, art). Between the 18th cent. and the first decades of the 19th, E. studies began to be put on a historical basis (L. Lanzi, G. Micali in Italy, K.O. Müller in Germany). Specialists in a great number of disciplines (art, religion, history, epigraphy, language, topography, natural history) studied the E. but did not go beyond their own field of research. Their research results, for all their quality, were thus unable to offer a comprehensive insight into the world of the E. In the transition from multidisciplinary to interdisciplinary practice, modern Etruscology has developed as a science of its own.

C. Sources
Epigraphical-linguistic, historiographical-literary, archaeological, onomastic und toponomastic sources are available. Of these, archaeological sources, which are closely linked to the epigraphical, are the most abundant and the most informative. For that reason Etruscology is often regarded as an archaeological and not a historical discipline. Apart from problems inherent in some sources, we must also be clear about some factors that are a fundamental obstacle to the work of the Etruscologist: the complete destruction of the literary and historiographical output of the E. themselves and also of the classical literary works on the E. (such as the *libri rerum Etruscarum* of Verrius Flaccus or the Τυρρηνικά (*Tyrrhēniká*) of Emperor Claudius), the infrequent and haphazard way in which ancient writers convey information about the E., the difficulties involved in understanding the Etruscan language, the fact that, until a few decades ago, too little attention was paid to their settlements during excavation, the occasional revival of imaginative hypotheses that, first advanced by scholars in the 15th–16th and 18th cents., are no longer tenable, and finally the large number of misleading dilettantic publications on the world of the E.

D. Geographic Territory
The region in which E. civilization developed is bounded in the north by the Arno basin up to the Tuscan-Emilian → Appenninus, in the south and east by the Tiber, and in the west by the *mare Tyrrhenum*. The E. first expanded from there in the 9th cent. BC, heading towards the areas around Salerno and Bologna (→ Bononia [1]). Numerous E. settlements from the 6th and 5th cents. have been found in the Po valley and in → Campania; but between the end of the 5th and the 4th cents. they were driven out by Gauls or → Samnites. According to E. evidence and later records, smaller E. communities were also found in various Italian regions among indigenous tribes (for example in Latium, Romagna, Liguria and Piedmont), as well as in several areas of the Mediterranean (Languedoc, Corsica, Carthage and Egypt).

E. Origins
The origin of the E. has been an issue debated over a long period, from antiquity onwards. Hellanicus (FGrH 4 F 3 in Dion. Hal. Ant. Rom. 1,28,3) and Anticlides (FGrH 140 F 21 in Str. 5,2,4) thought the E. to be Pelasgians who had immigrated from the Aegean, Hdt. 1,94 had Lydian information according to which the E. came from Lydia, Dion. Hal. Ant. Rom. 1,30 by contrast regarded them as autochthonous. In the 15th cent., Annio from Viterbo advanced the hypothesis, surviving until the 18th cent., that they originated in Israel. In the past 200 years, mainly on the basis of ancient sources claiming an E. identification with the Raeti (Liv. 5,33,11; Plin. HN 3,133; Iust., Pomp. Trog. epit. 20,5,10; Steph. Byz. s.v. Ῥαιτοί) and by analogy

with prehistoric Italian-E. cultures, it has been argued instead that the E. migrated from Central Europe. All these theories lose credibility because of the same fundamental prejudice: namely, that of assuming the E. people to have already been in existence, in Italy or outside it, even before their history had actually begun. Each of these theories comes up with historically established information that does not, however, contribute to a definitive solution to the problem because it has to be put in the context of (and compared with) the equally historically established results of other theories. It thus follows that the compelling conclusions of specific theories can only be of any real value if (taking up the suggestion by M. PALLOTTINO) the question of origins is replaced by a question about evolution, as to how, for example, different ethnic and cultural communities merged and thus created a new people. This development might have taken place in the E. region between the end of the Bronze Age and the beginning of the Iron Age (between the 10th and the beginning of the 9th cents. BC). For in the middle decades of the 9th cent. the Villanova culture prevailed, lasting throughout the whole of the 8th cent. and representing the first hallmarks of E. civilization. At the same time, in various other regions of the Italian peninsula, those other peoples (Veneti, Picentes, Umbri, Sabini, Latini, Samnites, Dauni, etc.), were establishing themselves who, together with the E., were to leave their mark on Italian history in the 1st millennium BC.

F. BEGINNINGS

The only evidence of the Villanova culture is archaeological in character. The population increase is remarkable. Because the building materials used were not very durable, we know almost nothing of the dwellings. The settlements – in some cases integrated into those of the late Bronze Age without any break in continuity, in others newly erected – are usually to be found on a site offering natural protection – as a rule, in southern E., on a plateau ringed by a river and, in northern E., on the summit of a hill. The form of settlement is a village of a few hundred to a couple of thousand inhabitants; some of these villages lying at most 1 to 2 km distant from one another belong to the settlement nucleus that in the course of a few centuries will be transformed into a metropolis. The dwelling is a hut in a circular or quasi-circular shape with walls and roofs made from wood or other perishable material (branches, twigs, hay, mud), with the interior consisting of a single room and a central fireplace. We know substantially more about the necropoleis: wide urn-fields with graves mostly of the *tomba a pozzetto type* (→ Funerary architecture) for the cremation rite or, also, from the 8th cent. BC, graves for a burial rite. In the first case the urn is a vase in double bowl or hut shape. The grave furnishings, less rich in the initial period, more so in the later period, contained objects indicating gender and social status: razor blades or weapons as grave furnishings for men, necklaces or sewing equipment for women.

G. NATURAL RESOURCES AND ECONOMY

The process of forming the E. people was already complete by the start of the Villanova period. That is convincingly demonstrated by the resources available to the inhabitants of E. E. was a fertile land 'offering everything imaginable' (Diod. Sic. 5,40,3), well suited to agriculture that had been carried out intensively from the 9th/8th cents. BC, thanks to the use of iron in tool-manufacture and to the introduction of the plough. Add to that the fact that large forests with tall trees offered very good wood (Str. 5,2,5), as well as the salt from salt mines (Volterra) and the saltworks along the Tyrrhenian coast. On top of that came the output from the mines in the Colline Metallifere on the island of Elba und in the Tolfa mountains (iron, copper, tin, zinc, lead), popular trading commodities (Plin. HN 33,1). No less important were other products like wool from sheep and goats, pork (one of the oldest E. representations: herdsman with pigs on the Plikasna situla from Clusium, middle of the 7th cent. BC) or tuna (cf. Str. 5,2,6–7: observation posts on heights along the coast at Populonia and Porto Ercole).

H. 8TH/7TH CENTURIES

In the course of the 8th cent., thanks to its natural resources and manufactures, E. belonged to a wide trading network: northern European, Sardinian, Phoenician and Euboean items have been found in the graves. The main items used in exchange for these imports were, then as later on, minerals and metals. It cannot be ruled out that activities and practices linked to those foreign products might have been imported with them. That is the case, for example with the Euboean geometrically decorated bowls that were probably imported with Euboean wine; and with the wine the relevant drinking practices would have been introduced as well, along with the rationale for these ceremonies. The development of which we are conscious here goes beyond the mere exchange of wares and is laden with cultural implications. People will also have migrated from the point of sale of these foreign products and organized the trade or manufacture on the spot of products similar to the imports. It was along with the economic and cultural flow of trade from Euboean territory that the Greek → alphabet reached E.

The large trading networks expanded yet again in the 1st half of the 7th cent. From northern Europe via north Italy came → amber, from the eastern Mediterranean Corinthian and Ionian products were introduced from the Middle East: as well as the banqueting vessels there now came containers for perfume and ornamental objects. The materials from which these objects were fashioned were gold, silver and ivory, as well as fine ceramics. These imports fundamentally altered two facets of life: → banquets and → hygiene. Lifestyle became more luxurious, suggesting lasting wealth. The monumental tumulus tomb (in Vetulonia, in Marsiliana d'Albegna), the creation of which points to gentilician social structure, is the visible expression of an

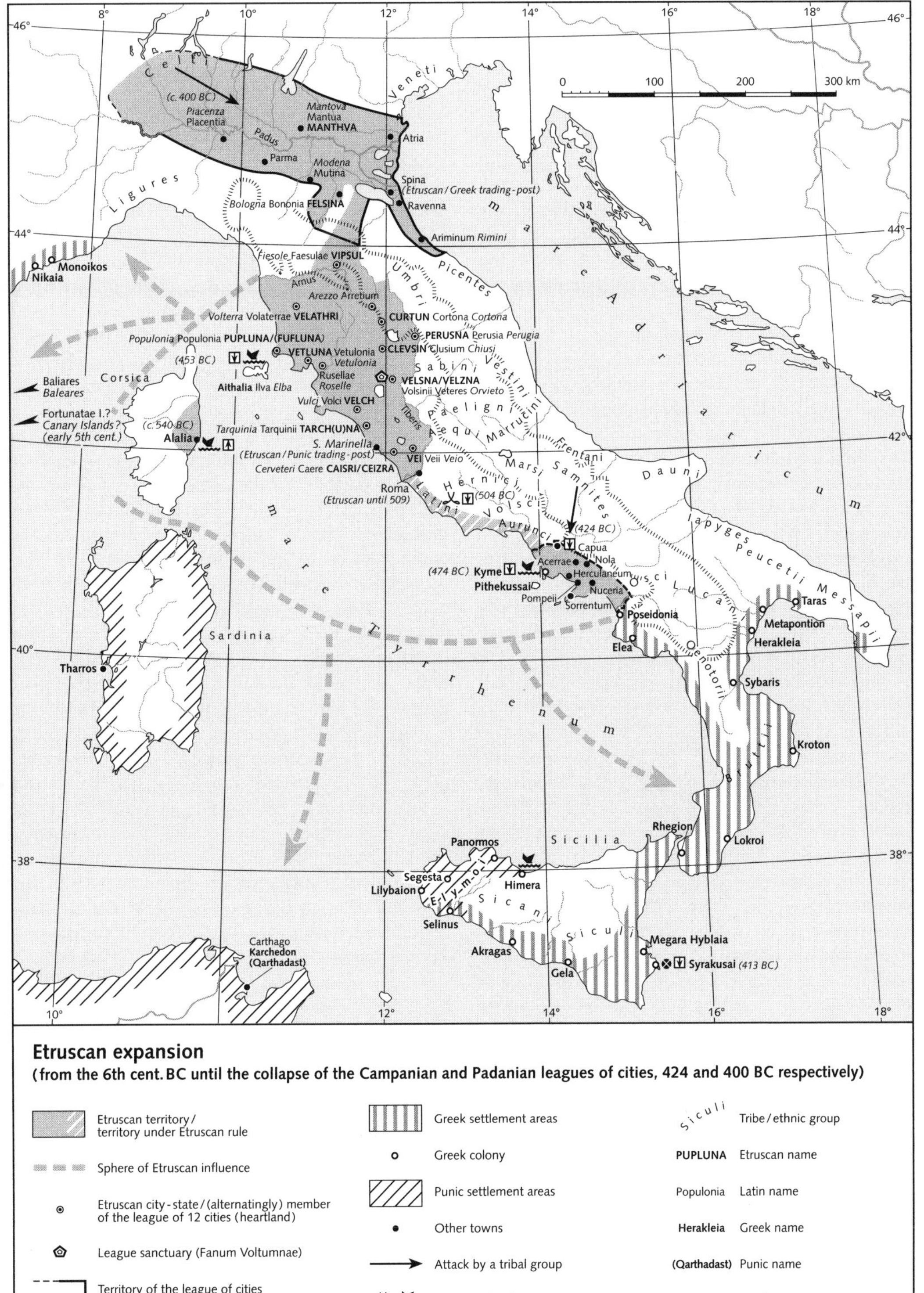

Etruscan expansion

(from the 6th cent. BC until the collapse of the Campanian and Padanian leagues of cities, 424 and 400 BC respectively)

- Etruscan territory / territory under Etruscan rule
- Sphere of Etruscan influence
- Etruscan city-state / (alternatingly) member of the league of 12 cities (heartland)
- League sanctuary (Fanum Voltumnae)
- Territory of the league of cities in the Padus region, 6th cent. BC
- Territory of the Campanian league of cities, 6th cent. BC
- Greek settlement areas
- Greek colony
- Punic settlement areas
- Other towns
- Attack by a tribal group
- Land / sea battle
- Siege
- Etruscan victory (in some cases together with their allies) / Etruscan defeat
- Siculi — Tribe / ethnic group
- **PUPLUNA** — Etruscan name
- Populonia — Latin name
- **Herakleia** — Greek name
- **(Qarthadast)** — Punic name
- *Populonia* — Modern name
- Appenine

aspiring aristocratic class. Even the manner of living changed: people switched from huts to houses with a rectangular plan and stone foundations, divided into several rooms. Once again, from the same sources as the foreign imports, craftsmen turned up in E. and produced locally the same objects as those being imported. Many imported containers were filled (perfumes, oils) and then earmarked for use at ceremonies (feasts, banquets) requiring a large supply of goods like oil and wine. Production of these items was begun in E. at the end of the 8th and the beginning of the 7th cent. BC, no doubt at the initiative of those specialized peasants who had streamed in from outside, attracted by the commercial demand of a rich, local clientele.

The immigrant master craftsmen, however, must have contributed to artistic development, to sculpture (→ Sculpting, technique of) and painting. This phenomenon is alluded to in ancient literature (Plin. HN 35,16, 152). In this production artists turned to foreign styles, themes and iconographic patterns that were nevertheless adapted to the ideology of the local (aristocratic) communities. Various E. items, mostly in bronze, were exported to a number of regions in Central and northern Europe and indicate for us today the existence of far-reaching trade links that probably included consumer goods and raw materials but yet cannot be quantified or identified with any accuracy.

It must in conclusion be stressed that E. was not uniformly affected by this process of renewal. Instead the process was more pronounced in the centres with high economic potential or with good overseas links, and within those centres more strongly evident amongst the representatives of the social groups in power. The increase in production of items destined for internal and external markets led to the development of an ever wider social layer of specialized artisans and small business proprietors, who all contributed to and benefited from the prosperity. A new – democratic – class began to infiltrate and displace the old aristocratic order, zealously striving to carve a clearly defined and decisive position for itself, even in politics. The city reflected the new social power-sharing – especially in new building projects undertaken no longer for individuals but for the whole community: e.g. straight-running roads, the creation of structures for political (squares) or religious (sanctuaries) gatherings, paving of public sites, the installation of sewerage systems and city walls, the development of necropoleis etc. The city thus became a political community and the nucleus of social order in E. Political, economic and military activities proceeded on the basis of individual cities, just as in the Greek *póleis*. In the last decades of the 7th and in the 1st half of the 6th cent., economic production in E. increased both in range and quality. Wine, oil and derivative products (perfumes, ointments) were exported on a large scale, principally to the western Mediterranean (Provence, Languedoc, the Iberian coast of Catalonia as far as Gibraltar, North Africa, Corsica, Sardinia, Campania and Sicily).

I. 6th/5th Centuries

The main suppliers of foreign goods in the 6th and in the first decades of the 5th cent. BC were the Phocaeans, the Athenians and Aeginetans. The *mare Tyrrhenum* (Tyrrhenian Sea) was now the stage for large competing trade interests between the Phocaeans, E. and Carthaginians. The clash between E. and Carthaginians, on the one hand, and Phocaeans on the other in the sea battle at Alalia (→ Aleria) around 540 BC (Hdt. 1,166f.) led to a division of areas of influence (→ Corsica to the E., Sardinia to the Carthaginians and South Gaul and southern Italy to the Phocaeans), without there being any interruption in the commercial and cultural exchanges between E. and Greece. Furthermore, trade-goods and master craftsmen arrived in E. from Greece. Greeks built up businesses and developed artistic traditions of quality: for example the → Caeretan hydriae in Caere, black-figured ceramics in Vulci, and frescoes in Tarquinia. After the battle of Alalia, as a consequence of which trade links with South Gaul became increasingly difficult, commercial traffic left E. for continental Europe over the Po Valley and exports included not only bronze vessels (part of the whole wine trade) but probably wine as well. The trading partners were Celtic nobles influenced by the E. in this way.

In 509 BC the E. lost control over Rome and in 504 (battle of → Aricia), upper Latium as well. At the start of the 5th cent. BC their attempt to colonize the Lipari islands and the 'Happy Islands' failed (Diod. Sic. 5,20,4). In 474 BC they were defeated by the Syracusans in the naval battle at Cumae (→ Cyme), in 453 BC they were again defeated by the Syracusans to the north of their ore-mines (Elba, Populonia): a crisis then arose in the large southern coastal cities of Caere, Tarquinia and Vulci, while Populonia in the north, as the centre of a large mining region, possibly supported by Syracuse, gained in influence. The blockade of the southern harbours between the 2nd half of the 5th and the 4th cent. BC was followed by a drop in ceramic production, a large part of which was intended for E. markets. That led to the immigration of Attic masters into the Pontus region, southern Italy and into E. itself. This crisis affecting the coastal cities benefited the agriculturally oriented towns in the E. hinterland along the Tiber valley (Veii, Falerii, Volsinii, Clusium, Cortona, Arretium – cf. the wheat supplies to Rome in 492, 440, 433 and 411 BC, and the wine, oil and dried fruit exports from Clusium to Gaul in the first years of the 4th cent.: Liv. 5,33,1–6; Dion. Hal. Ant. Rom. 13,10; Plut. Camillus 15,3–4). In these cities there arose potters' workshops and sculpture schools influenced by the great Greek art of the Classical period (cf. the red-figured vases of Falerii, the temple sculptures in Falerii and Volsinii/Orvieto).

The E. attempt (from Tarquinia?) to engage in naval power politics, with a modest contingent in the Athenian force besieging Syracuse in 413 BC, failed. The last blow dealt by the Syracusans against E. naval power was the plundering of the sanctuary and harbour at

Pyrgi in 384 BC. Possibly linked to those events is the fact that in the coastal cities in the 2nd half of the 4th cent. BC there sprang up a new land-owning aristocracy that turned its attention to the hinterland, resettled the region of the cliff necropoleis (Tuscany, → Blera/Bieda, Norcia, → Castel d'Asso, S. Giovenale, S. Giuliano, Sovana) and thus revitalized an area abandoned at the end of the 6th cent. BC. Evidence of this socio-economic trend is quite substantial, chamber graves decorated with frescoes in Vulci ('tomba François') and Tarquinia (e.g. *tombe dell'Orco, degli Scudi*), with stucco in Caere (*tomba dei Rilievi*) and Tarquinia (*tomba della Mercareccia*).

J. 4th/3rd Centuries and End

In the early 4th cent. BC the Roman conquest of Veii (396 BC) at the end of a decades-long war meant the beginning of Roman penetration into E. Many cities built or rebuilt their city walls because of the imminent Roman threat. After the capture of Veii, Rome conquered the neighbouring cities of Capena and Falerii and established two Latin *coloniae*, Sutrium (383 BC) and Nepete (373 BC) in that territory. The conquest of Veii and the establishment of colonies introduced Rome's enduring presence in E. For its long-standing policy of friendship with Rome, Caere became *civitas sine suffragio* – after the Gallic siege throughout the 4th cent. After the war with Rome (358–351 BC) Tarquinia negotiated a 40-year armistice that was renewed in 308. In 310 BC the Romans defeated the E., and in 283, the E. and the Gallic Boii at Lake Vadimonis. In 302 BC the aristocracy in Arretium received help from Rome against a slave uprising. In 294 BC Volsinii, Perusia and Arretium negotiated various armisticies with Rome. In 293 BC Rusellae was conquered by the consul L. Postumius Megellus, and in 280 BC Vulci and Volsinii surrendered to the consul T. Coruncianus. In 273 BC the *colonia* → Cosa was established in the territory of the Vulci, and in 264 BC Volsinii was destroyed by the consul M. Fulvius Flaccus and the inhabitants transferred to a new settlement (Volsinii Novi); the same fate befell Falerii in 241 BC.

Meanwhile, instead of fighting, the E. were seeking to find a place for themselves in Roman life and politics. When a Roman expedition was being prepared to campaign against Hannibal in Africa, several E. cities (Caere, Populonia, Tarquinia, Volterra, Arretium, Perusia, Clusium and Rusellae) contributed provisions from their own produce (Liv. 28,45,14–18). In addition, many members of the E. lower orders enlisted in the Roman army, others from the higher levels pursued political careers in Rome without abandoning their links to their home-towns (cf. the → Caecinae from Volterra, the Tarquitii from Caere). The E. accepted the establishment of Roman *coloniae* in their homeland (Castrum Novum in 264 BC, Alsium in 247, Fregenae in 245, Pyrgi in 191, Saturnia in 183, Gravisca in 181), as well as the construction of major roads (cf. the *viae Aurelia, Clodia, Cassia, Flaminia, Amerina*) that helped deployment of Roman troops, even when they partly followed existing E. roads. Colonies and roads are clear elements of Romanization. The statue of the 'Arringatore (Orator)' (2nd cent. BC, Florence, MA) is the expression of this new state of affairs: the clothing, the footgear and the descriptive, portrait-like execution indicate the opening-up to the Roman world, while the E. inscription on the edges of the toga demonstrate its E. cultural origins.

In the 3rd/2nd cents. Rome and E. followed the same cultural trends: take for example the Greek myths from the Trojan and Theban cycles, which belong as much to the repertoire of archaic Latin tragedy as to the decoration on E. ossuaries. With the end of the Social Wars and the *lex Iulia de civitate* (90–88 BC) the residents of *Italia antiqua*, and thus the E. as well, gained the *civitas Romana*. That officially put an end to regional Italian cultures, and the new unitary Roman State was established, with Latin as the official language. The divine cults of the E. were only of historic-cultural significance in the 1st cent. BC and in the Imperial period: some tomb inscriptions were bilingual, using Latin and E., documents with E. religious teaching were translated into Latin; Verrius Flaccus and the Emperor Claudius composed works on the E.; Roman art collectors gathered *Tyrrhena sigilla* (Hor. Epist. 2,2,180–183); there were attempts to have young patricians adopt the *Etrusca disciplina*, so as to avoid having this art practised by incompetent people just for the sake of money (Cic. Div. 1,92); on special occasions haruspices of E. origin were consulted – even into the 6th cent. AD (Procop. Goth. 8,21,16).

L. Banti, Il mondo degli Etruschi, [2]1969 (Engl. tr.: Etruscan Cities and their Culture, 1973); J. Heurgon, La vie quotidienne chez les Etrusques, [2]1979; M. Torelli, Storia degli Etruschi, 1981; M. Cristofani (ed.), Gli Etruschi. Una nuova immagine, 1984 (Die Etrusker [2]1995); Id. (ed.), Civiltà degli Etruschi, 1985; A. Maggiani (ed.), Artigianato artistico in Etruria, 1985; G. Camporeale (ed.), L'Etruria mineraria, 1985; G. Colonna (ed.), Santuari d'Etruria, 1985; S. Stopponi (ed.), Case e palazzi d'Etruria, 1985; A. Carandini (ed.), La romanizzazione dell'Etruria: il territorio di Vulci, 1985; P. Barocchi (ed.), L'Accademia etrusca, 1985; F. Borsi(ed.), Fortuna degli Etruschi, 1985; G. Pugliese Carratelli (ed.), Rasenna, 1986; M. Pallottino, Etruskologie, [7]1988; Id. (ed.), Gli Etruschi e l'Europa, 1992. GI.C.

Maps: Die Etrusker und Europa, exhibition cat. Berlin, 1993; M. Cristofani (ed.), Die Etrusker, 1995; F. Prayon, Die Etrusker, 1996; K. v. Welck, R. Stupperich (ed.), Italien vor den Römern, 1996.

II. Archaeology

A. Definition B. Cultural/general C. Art D. Reception/Antiquity

A. Definition

E. archaeology covers the entire E. legacy, including linguistic evidence and the literary transmission by the Greeks and Romans [12; 40]. Research is traditionally based on the interpretation of monuments. While E. studies (*etruscologia*) in Italy have a tradition extending back to the Renaissance and represent a discipline encompassing all aspects of E. culture [38], outside Italy it is a subdivision of separate subjects such as Classical archaeology, Pre- and Proto-History, Ancient History, Classical philology and Comparative Linguistics. The chronological framework for E. archaeology extends from the final phase of the Bronze Age (proto-Villanova 11th/10th cents. BC) up to the end of the Romanization of Etruria in the early 1st cent. BC. The division into different cultural and artistic periods generally follows the Greek terminology (Archaic, Classical, Hellenism), however in Etruria the → Villanova culture [2] corresponds to the geometric period (9th/8th cents.), and the archaic period lingers on into the 5th cent. BC ('subarchaic style').

Geographically, E. archaeology encompasses the E. heartland between the Arno and the Tiber, as well as the colonized territories of the Po valley (Mantua) and Campania (Capua) and the adjacent regions of Italic tribes who were culturally partly Etruscanized (especially Latium), including early Rome [21; 46]. Like Greek archaeology, E. archaeology distinguishes between individual city states and the cultural achievements of each region (e.g. Tarquinia: tomb paintings, Vulci: toreutics [1]), in that, apart from rich tomb finds, the latter increasingly involve sanctuaries and residential settlements [7; 47]. In contrast to older, Graecocentric research, what is now of primary interest is specifically E., both in its own evolution and as an integral component of the multicultural world of the Mediterranean [38; 42; 53].

B. Cultural/general

In keeping with the definition of E. archaeology as a field of cultural knowledge, all subjects are included, from geology, geography and topography [49] through to economics and trade [11. 68–99], internal and external history [45. 15–76; 56], state, society and family [11. 100–135; 30; 45. 80–156; 52], as well as religion and culture, the study of which, on the basis of the extensive, written (*disciplina Etrusca*, → Divination VII) and archaeological transmission (→ Haruspices: bronze liver from Piacenza [54]), assumes a particularly important role [11. 136–167; 34; 41; 45. 159–237].

C. Art

1. Architecture 2. Sculpture 3. Tomb paintings 4. Burial offerings 5. Ceramics, Minor arts, Toreutics

1. Architecture

Determining factors for E. culture and art were, on the one hand, the favourable climatic and geographic conditions that promoted agriculture and trade (with coastal metropoles like Cerveteri, Tarquinia, Vulci) and, on the other, the geological advantages offered by the rich mineral deposits and their exploitation [11. 68–87; 22] in the surrounding areas (Populonia, Vetulonia), the Monti Metalliferi (Volterra, Massa Marittima) and the Tolfa mountains (Monte Rovello, Castellina del Marangone). Also decisive for creative activity were the volcanic formations in southern Etruria, in so far as the softer tufa stone and the harder nenfro and limestone were to determine the figurative forms in → sculpture [48]. The location of settlements established, mainly for reasons of fortification, on rounded mountain peaks, can be deduced from the extensive necropoleis, and frequently also, in cases of continuity of settlement, from the remains of surrounding walls and city gates (Volterra, Perugia). Features of urbanization and infrastructure (roads, drainage, cisterns) [4; 45. 371–530; 55], as well as the development of residential architecture from modest beginnings to multi-storied apartment blocks, *insulae*, are known to us through large-scale excavations (especially at S. Giovenale, Acquarossa, Marzabotto) and replicas in tombs (see below) [49]. The development of residential architecture follows similar patterns to those in Greece (oval houses, *langraum*, and *breitraum* houses), but the preference for axial and symmetrical room layouts, together with a concern for comfort led to significant original innovations such as the atrium house [7; 43; 46].

The necropoleis have been particularly well excavated, with their chamber graves imitating the interior of a domestic dwelling; in northern Etruria these graves are constructed from stone blocks, while in the south, hypogean forms chiselled in the tufa rock predominate [43; 49]. Despite regional variations the round tumulus grave over a shaped base and earth mound, with an entrance (*dromos*), cross-shaped outline layout and homelike interior (especially Cerveteri) can be termed the common evolutionary trend for the early period (7th/6th cents. BC). In the 6th/5th cents., flat tomb façades predominate (the 'cube-' and 'aedicula grave' types: Cerveteri, Blera, Populonia), with the exterior and the internal divisions clearly based on the contemporary dwelling. From the 4th/3rd cents. façade tombs predominate, often with elements of temple architecture (Sovana: Tomba Ildebranda, Norchia: gable graves) [37], along with rich, genteel graves imitating the internal division with an atrium (Cerveteri: Tomba dei Rilievi; Perugia: grave of the Volumni) [3; 49]; → Funerary architecture.

Sacral architecture is much more varied than the typical temple style known since Vitruvius (4,7) as 'Tuscan', with its rear *cellae*, deep colonnaded entrance hall and wooden, stucco-decorated roof (examples: Veio, Portonaccio and Pyrgi, Temple A). To that must be added Greek-influenced building forms like the temple with circular central hall and only one *cella* (Pyrgi, Temple B) or, from the early 6th cent. BC, monumental court complexes (Murlo; Cerveteri, Montetosto), and buildings with aisles (Acquarossa) with sacral or public function. As in the residential dwelling, the tomb and → temple, the paratactical, tripartite room arrangement is characteristic [7; 47]. The temple pediments in the early period

The Etruscan heartland: settlements and production centres (8th – 2nd cents. BC)

- City state
- Other settlement
- Important sanctuary
- Port
- Fortification wall
- Metalworking
- Chamber tombs (rock-cut)
- Chamber tombs (constructed)
- Tomb paintings
- Tomb sculpture (7th/6th cents.)
- Sarcophagi (6th – 3rd cents.)
- Urns (4th – 1st cents. AD)
- AG Silver
- CU Copper
- FE Iron
- PB Lead
- SN Tin
- ZN Zinc
- Territories of the city-states (in part largely hypothetical)
- Historical coastline
- Cerveteri Modern name
- **Gravisca** Ancient name
- ▲ Mountain

are 'open'; only the front beam having relief decoration in clay (antepagment of Pyrgi [47 with fig.179–181]; 'closed' pediment reliefs with Greek myths appear only in the Hellenistic period: → Telamon [24]); also typically E.-Italian is the arrangement of clay statues of gods on the ridge of temple roofs (Murlo, Veio, Satricum [17]). Striking as an individual design is the 'Tuscan' → column with capital (abacus, torus, leaf garland), smooth shaft and the base with a shaped bulge (Vitruvius 4,7). The Tuscan column, derived from the proto-Doric wooden capital in Greece and known from the beginning of the 6th cent. BC in temples, tombs and houses had, moreover, a form-shaping influence on funerary architecture (tumuli and cube-tombs) and altars [44]. As excavations in harbour sanctuaries like Pyrgi and Gravisca show, temples and altars were an element of extensive complexes with a large number of sacral and profane buildings as well as sacrificial and drainage ditches for votive offerings and discarded building decorations [7; 17]. The variety of deities worshipped in a single sanctuary is remarkable, including Greek and Semitic deities, like Uni-Astarte, as well as E. deities [25; 36] in Pyrgi.

2. SCULPTURE

In contrast to the situation in Greece and Rome, marble was used only rarely; what was used predominantly was clay (sacral areas) and stone (funerary areas), as well as bronze as votive sculpture for memorials like the 'Arringatore (Orator)' in Florence [9; 18]. Thus, in 264 BC, after the capture of Volsinii/Orvieto, 2,000 statues were pillaged and transported to Rome (Plin. HN 34,34). In tomb-sculpture (with 'images' of the deceased) extending back to the 7th cent. BC, indigenous Villanova traditions (head and canopic urns) can be seen along with Oriental influences ('Oriental phase': seated portraits in Ceri and Cerveteri [10]) and, from the 6th cent., strongly Greek stylistic elements (Vetulonia, Pietrera; Vulci), also discernible in temple and votive sculpture that began in the 6th cent. BC and continued until ending in the 2nd/1st cents. BC [13; 47; 48]. A specifically E. feature is the special emphasis given to the head, through its size or the exaggeration of individual features in comparison to the rather sketchy reproduction of the body (Apollo of Veio [47 with fig. 118–119]), preservation of archaic stylistic forms, also termed 'sub-archaic style' (antepagment of Pyrgi), and from the 4th cent. BC the juxtaposition of naturalistic ('Apollo' of Falerii; urn of a couple in Volterra [48 with fig. 240–241, 286–287]) and abstract stylistic elements disregarding bodily proportions, like the overlong bronze statue of the 'Ombra della Sera' in Volterra [45. 638–676]. The E. did not strive for individual portraits, as in Roman art of the Imperial period [9; 26].

Along with free-standing sculpture, relief art was very highly developed, with a large number of local traditions, as in the archaic limestone reliefs, each having funerary origins, in Chiusi [32] and the Hellenistic sarcophagic and urn-reliefs from Tarquinia (nenfro), Volterra (alabaster), Chiusi (limestone) or Siena (clay), whose mythical iconographic themes are not only very relevant to the reconstruction of Greek mythological motifs but are also a source of information on technical questions (workshops), as well as for social and political information [27; 36].

3. TOMB PAINTINGS

Etruria is host to the most significant → grave paintings in the Mediterranean from the 1st millennium BC: thanks to the geologically advantageous qualities of the volcanic tufa rock and the concern for richly decorated chamber graves, local centres for grave painting established themselves, especially from the 6th cent. BC, in Tarquinia, Chiusi and Orvieto (with precursors in Cerveteri and Veio). The principal themes in Tarquinia were originally aspects of the funeral rites (Tomba degli Auguri [50 with fig. 13–22]) and the funeral wake (Tomba dei Leopardi [50 with fig. 105]), and then, from the 4th cent. BC, representations of the afterlife (Tomba dell'Orco [50 with fig. 127–134]) and funeral processions, often with the participants and the deceased mentioned by name. The Tomba François in Vulci (4th cent. BC) is an important case in point, with the duels of historical figures of the 6th cent. BC, including the Aulus brothers and Gaius Vibenna from Vulci, as well as Mastarn identical to King Servius Tullius from Rome [51]. The wall paintings reflect the dominant style of Greek vase-painting of the time, initially Corinthian, Ionian and Attic, and in the Hellenistic period, southern Italian in particular. Grave paintings are of central importance for onomastics, representations of the afterlife, and funeral customs, as well as for details such as dress [5], decoration and utensils, but going well beyond all that, by virtue of the thematic, iconographic and stylistic proximity to Greek pictorial motifs, also for our knowledge of Greek wall paintings, which have been largely destroyed. F.PR.

4. BURIAL OFFERINGS

In E. thinking, observance of funeral rites was of central importance for the deceased's well-being in the afterlife and, as well as in costly funerary architecture, this was also reflected in the burial offerings.

From the beginning of the 9th to the middle of the 8th cent. only personal objects were buried with the deceased's ashes in the → Villanova culture urns: almost all graves belonged to the same social class. Amongst the burial offerings were also libation vessels, which were broken after being used in the burial ritual.

From as early as *c.* 750 BC members of the aristocracy were buried in their own graves, which, in addition to personal possessions, contained metal objects indicating the dead person's social rank (e.g. shields of thin brass, water canteens and horse-bits of bronze). In the so-called Oriental phase (end of the 8th – 7th cents. BC) the propensity to highlight the social status of the person buried gained in importance. In the chamber tombs under monumental tumuli imported articles from the eastern Mediterranean (Syria, Palestine, Cyprus) were found as status symbols: *i.a.* gold jewellery, ostrich egg shells, carved ivory, vases of precious metals.

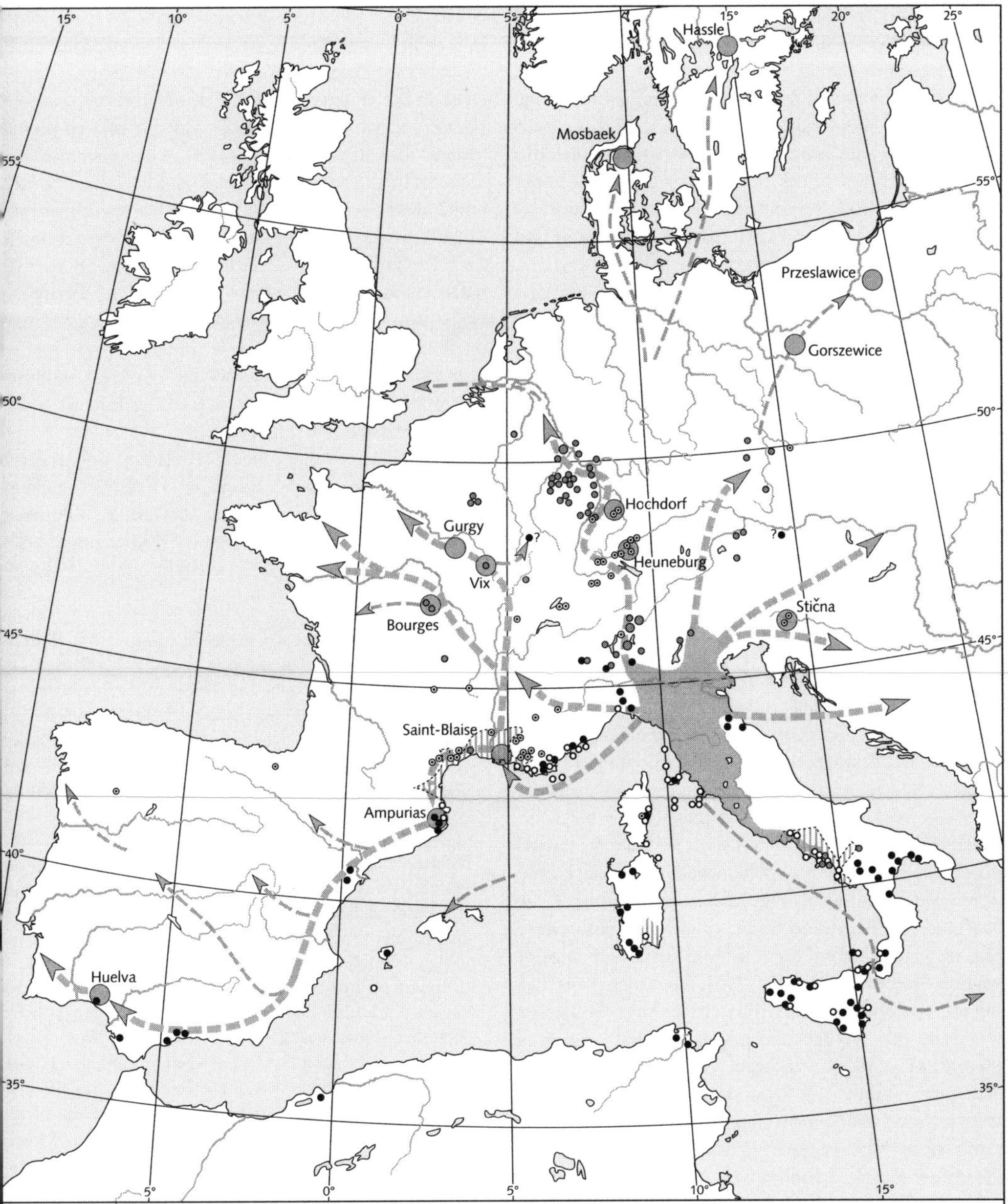

Hassle
Mosbaek
Przeslawice
Gorszewice
Hochdorf
Gurgy
Heuneburg
Vix
Bourges
Stična
Saint-Blaise
Ampurias
Huelva

Etruscan exports (7th – 5th cents. BC)

Main routes for the distribution of Etruscan products

Distribution area of bucchero ware (7th/6th cents. BC):

• Single find

 Strong concentration

○ Distribution area of wine amphorae (7th/6th cents. BC)

Distribution area of bronze beaked pitchers (6th/5th cents. BC):

1-2

3 or more

⊙ Distribution area of bronze bowls with beaded rims (6th/5th cents. BC):

•? Identification uncertain

0 150 300 450 600 750 km

The phenomenon of 'princely graves' continued until about the middle of the 6th cent. BC, a time when there was much change in E. necropoleis. As in Greece, new social classes had developed in the cities and in the process the previously prevailing clear distinction began to converge in both → funerary architecture and in grave offerings. Greek pottery was especially popular; around 550 the importation of Corinthian pottery was replaced with Attic. In the 3rd and 4th cents. graves were again furnished with expensive drinking and dining equipment, mostly of indigenous manufacture. These vases reproduce standardized forms. A.NA.

5. Ceramics, Minor arts, Toreutics

From the modest, dark brown → impasto ware of the Villanova period arose → bucchero pottery in the 7th cent. BC, distinguished by the quality of its black clay, the elegance of vessel shapes and its incised and relief decoration. In general, painted Greek ceramics had been imported in large quantities since the 8th cent. BC (especially from Corinth and Athens) and had been imitated in Etruria, in part by Greeks themselves (7th cent.: the potter and painter Aristonothus; 6th cent.: style of the → 'Caeretan hydriae'), but mostly by locals at a rather low level artistically (e.g. Italo-geometric, Italo-Corinthian, E.-black-figured) [35]. Individual styles, like the so-called → Pontic vases, boast particularly original graphic motifs and are important testimony to the fact that Greek myths were known in Etruria [33].

In the minor arts it was not unusual for the E. to outdo their instructors, Phoenicians and Greeks in particular: carved → ivory, gold jewellery in the highly developed techniques of granulation and filigree, as well as gems and cameos [1; 14; 57]. E. → toreutics were also of prime quality, especially in Vulci, with bronze wagons decorated in relief [30], bronze vessels and utensils (tripods, candelabra), frequently decorated with figurative statuettes as grip or lid [27], as well as the type of → mirrors decorated with mythical themes etched or in relief [22]. From the 5th cent. BC bronzes were an important export item for Italy and the region north of the Alps (beaked pitchers with figurative handles [14; 15]). The metal caskets known as → cists, the iconography of which is very informative about everyday life and Greek myths, mark the final phase of E. toreutics. However, the focal point of production shifted to Latium (see Ficoroni cist [20]), and Etruscan artistic creativity is absorbed by Roman-dominated Hellenistic-Italic art. Minting of coins took place independently of Lower Italy and Rome, with the main centres in northern Etruria (Populonia, Volterra) [8].

D. Reception/Antiquity

Apart from their role as upholders of culture for the neighbouring Italian tribes, the E. took part indirectly in the development of Celtic toreutics, through the export into the region north of the Alps of bronze vessels with figurative ornamentation, and of imitations and perhaps also as the transmitters of Mediterranean construction technique (Heuneburg: clay brick wall) [16]. The German runic script was derived from the E. alphabet via intermediate points in the Alps [15. 411–441]. In the archaic period the effect on Rome was preponderant: in robes of office, and symbols of power (purple toga, *lituus*, *sella curulis*), in urbanization and construction techniques (Tuscan temple; *atrium* house), in the plastic arts (Zeus cult image in the Jupiter temple, Lupa?), perhaps also in onomastics [25; 37]. From the early Roman Republic, E. influence dropped off sharply but remained firm in memory (Posidonius, Vitruvius) or, because of its origin, was described as 'Tuscan', like the three-cell temple that was the building model for the Capitolia and its capitals or the → atrium with its unsupported roof. For the revival of E. culture since the Renaissance see → Etruscology.

→ Acquarossa; → Blera/Bieda; → Caere; → Castellina del Marangone; → Ivory carvings; → Falerii; → Graviscae; → Marzabotto; → Murlo, Norchia; → Perusia; → Populonia; → Pyrgi; → Saena; → Satricum; → Sovana; → Tarquinii; → Veii; → Volaterrae; → Volsinii; → Etruscology

1 L. Banti, Die Welt der Etrusker, 1960 2 G. Bartoloni, La cultura villanoviana, 1989 3 H. Blanck, G. Proietti, La Tomba dei Rilievi di Cerveteri, 1986 4 A. Boethius, J. B. Ward-Perkins, Etruscan and Roman Architecture, 1970, 25–95 5 L. Bonfante, Etruscan Dress, 1975 6 Id. (ed.), Etruscan Life and Afterlife, 1986 7 S. Stopponi (ed.), Case e palazzi d'Etruria, Exhibition catalogue Siena, 1985 8 F. Catalli, Monete etrusche, 1990 9 G. Colonna, Il posto dell'Arringatore nell'arte etrusca di età ellenistica, in: SE 56, 1989/90, 99–119 10 Id., F. W. von Hase, Alle origini della statuaria etrusca: La Tomba delle Statue presso Ceri, in: SE 52, 1984, 13–59 11 M. Cristofani (ed.), Die Etrusker, [2]1995 12 Id. (ed.), Dizionario della civiltà etrusca, 1985 13 Id., I bronzi degli Etruschi, 1985 14 M. Cristofani, M. Martelli, L'oro degli Etruschi 15 L. Aigner-Foresti (ed.), Etrusker nördl. von Etrurien, Symposium Wien, 1992 16 Die Etrusker und Europa, exhibition catalogue Berlin, 1992 17 E. Rystedt et al. (ed.), Deliciae Fictiles. Proc. of the First International Conference on Central Italic Architectural Terracottas, 1993 18 T. Dohrn, Der Arringatore, 1968 19 Id., Die etr. Kunst im Zeitalter der griech. Klassik, 1982 20 Id., Die Ficoronische Ciste, 1972 21 Enea nel Lazio, Exhibition catalogue Rome, 1981 22 G. Camporeale (ed.), L'Etruria mineraria, Exhibition catalogue Portoferraio et al., 1985 23 U. Fischer-Graf, Spiegelwerkstätten in Vulci, 1980 24 B. v. Freytag gen. Löringhoff, Das Giebelrelief von Telamon, 1986 25 Die Göttin von Pyrgi, Kolloquium Tübingen, 1981 26 G. Hafner, Männer- und Frauenbildnisse aus Terrakotta im Museo Etrusco Gregoriano, in MDAI(R) 73/74, 1966/67, 29–51 27 R. Herbig, Die jüngeretr. Steinsarkophage, 1952 28 S. Haynes, Etruscan Bronzes, 1985 29 H. Hencken, Tarquinia and Etruscan Origins, 1968 30 J. Heurgon, Die Etrusker, 1972 31 U. Höckmann, Die Bronzen aus dem Fürstengrab von Castel S. Mariano, 1982 32 J.-R. Jannot, Les reliefs archaïques de Chiusi, 1984 33 I. Krauskopf, Der thebanische Sagenkreis und andere griech. Sagen in der etr. Kunst, 1974 34 Id., Todesdämonen und Totengötter im vorhell. Etrurien, 1987 35 M. Martelli (ed.), La ceramica degli Etruschi,

1987 36 F.-H. MASSA-PAIRAULT, Recherches sur l'art et l'artisanat étrusco-italiques à l'époque hellénistique, 1985 37 J. P. OLESON, The Sources of Innovation in Later Etruscan Tomb Design, 1982 38 M. PALLOTTINO, Etruskologie, [7]1988 39 Id., It. vor der Römerzeit, 1987 40 A. J. PFIFFIG, Einführung in die Etruskologie, 1972 41 Id., Religio etrusca, 1975 42 F. PRAYON, Die Etrusker. Gesch., Religion, Kunst, 1996 43 Id., Frühetr. Grabund Hausarchitektur, 1975 44 Id., Zur Genese der tuskanischen Säule, in: Vitruv-Kolloquium, 1984, 141–162 45 G. PUGLIESE CARRATELLI (ed.), Rasenna. Storia e civiltà degli Etruschi, 1986 46 M. CRISTOFANI (ed.), La grande Roma dei Tarquini, Exhibition catalogue Rome, 1990 47 G. COLONNA (ed.), Santuari d'Etruria, Exhibition catalogue Arezzo, 1985 48 M. SPRENGER, G. BARTOLONI, Die Etrusker. Kunst und Gesch., 1977 49 S. STEINGRÄBER, Etrurien, 1981 50 Id. (ed.), Etr. Wandmalerei, 1985 51 F. BURANELLI (ed.), La Tomba François di Vulci, Exhibition catalogue Rome, 1987 52 M. TORELLI, Die Etrusker, Gesch., Kultur, Gesellschaft, 1988 53 O. W. v. VACANO, Die Etrusker in der Welt der Ant., 1957 54 L. B. VAN DER MEER, The Bronze Liver of Piacenza, 1987 55 J. B. WARD-PERKINS, Etruscan Energeering, in: Hommages à A. Grenier, 1962, 1636–1643 56 K. W. WEEBER, Gesch. der Etrusker, 1979 57 P. ZAZOFF, Die ant. Gemmen, 1983, 214–259. F.PR.

BURIAL OFFERINGS: B. D'AGOSTINO, Tombe 'principesche' dell'orientalizzante antico da Pontecagnano, in: Monumenti Antichi dell'Accademia dei Lincei, s. Miscellanea, vol. II.1, 1977; G. COLONNA, L'ideologia funeraria e il conflitto delle culture, in: Archeologia laziale 4 (Quaderni di Archeologia Etrusco-Italica 5), 1981, 229–232; M. A. CUOZZO, Prospettive teoriche e metodologiche nell'interpretazione delle necropoli: la post-processual archaeology, in: Annali. Istituto orientale di Napoli, n.s. 3, 1996, 1–37; G. PIANU, La standardizzazione, in: M. CRISTOFANI (ed.), Civiltà degli Etruschi, 1985, 326–338. A.NA.

MAPS: M. CRISTOFANI, Economia e società, in: G. PUGLIESE CARATELLI (ed.), Rasenna, Storia e civiltà degli Etruschi, 1986, 79–156 (with p. 120 fig. 9, p. 126 fig. 11); Die Welt der Etrusker, exhibition catalogue Berlin, 1988; Die Etrusker und Europa, exhibition catalogue Berlin, 1993; F.-W. v. HASE, Il bucchero etrusco a Cartagine, in: M. BONGHI JOVINO (ed.), Produzione artigianale ed esportazione nel mondo antico il bucchero etrusco, 1993, 187–194, especially 188; Id., Ägäische, griech. und vorderoriental. Einflüsse auf das tyrrhenische Mittelitalien, in: JRGZ 35, 1995, 239–286; W. KIMMIG, Die griech. Kolonisation im westl. Mittelmeergebiet und ihre Wirkung auf die Landschaften des westl. Mitteleuropa, in: JRGZ 30, 1983, 7–78, especially 39, 41; M. MILLER, Befestigungsanlagen in It. vom 8. bis 3. Jh. v. Chr., 1994; F. PRAYON, die Etrusker, 1996; K. v. WELCK, R. STUPPERICH (ed.), Italien vor den Römern, 1996. F.PR.

III. RELIGION

A. INTRODUCTION B. GODS AND MYTHOLOGY
C. AFTERLIFE D. RITUALS

A. INTRODUCTION

In antiquity the E. were regarded as a people who were very serious and especially meticuluous in their religious observance (Liv. 5,1,6). The particular connection with the transcendental was expressed, on the one hand, in their never abandoned mystical interpretation of natural phenomena (Sen. Q Nat. 2,32,1), and on the other, in the very large number of temples, grave sites and votive offerings. Differences in the concepts of → afterlife, burial and cremation can be assigned to regional variation. Secondary sources offer a one-sided view of E. religion: texts of prophecy that had political significance for Rome (→ Divination VII.) and were observed by the E. upper class (Tac. Ann. 11,15,1) have survived. We are, on the other hand, ill-informed about popular religion.

B. GODS AND MYTHOLOGY

According to the legendary account, the E. received their doctrine from the gods (Cic. Har. resp. 10,20) or from the wise child Tages (Cic. Div. 2,23,50) and the nymph Vegoia (Serv. Aen. 6,72,5). As a revelatory and recorded religion it is typologically closer to the Ancient Oriental rather than Greek or Roman religion. Over time the E. religion underwent an inner evolution that cannot be reconstructed in detail, and it also adopted foreign (Greek and Oriental) beliefs. E. prophecy and cosmogony have significant parallels in the Ancient Orient; likewise, motifs of Oriental origin appear in the calendar of → Nigidius Figulus on meteorological omens. Gods of Greek origin, like Apollo, are known from the 6th cent. BC; the E. name Ap(u)lu (< Apollo in the Latin form) is attested in the 1st half of the 5th cent. [2]. Tinia, Turan, Σeθlans, Culsans, Turms etc. are of more obscure origin but probably belong to the oldest core of Etruscan religion going back to the 2nd millennium.

In an early phase of E. religiosity, Nature was considered to have a soul: veneration of conically-shaped stones is iconographically attested in the 5th and 3rd cents. BC in Tarquinia (tomb 'del letto funebre', around 460 [5. no. 82]) and Volterra (urn reliefs [6. pl. LII, 15]). From archaic, aniconic, levels of E. religiosity derive non-corporeal entities whose gender and number are varied and uncertain. Their names are unknown, their Latin terms *dei superiores et involuti* (Sen. Q Nat. 2,41,2), *dei consentes* (Arnob. 3,40) or *complices* (Arnob. ibid.) do not cast any light on their nature. They were hierarchically superior to the high god Tinia (Sen. Q Nat. 2,45,3), who had to obtain their approval before casting dangerous or destructive lightning bolts (Sen. Q Nat. 2,41,1–2).

Uni and Men(e)rva, Maris and Neθuns go back to the 10th cent. as individualized deities of common Italian origin [3]. In the following two cents. clearly developed gods emerge from that original, not very individualized world of deities. In the 7th cent. the E. pantheon had gods who supervised Nature and its phenomena, the fundamental events in human life and human activities: heaven (Tinia) and Nature (Fufluns, Turan), birth (Θalna) and death (Vanθ, Culsans), war (Laran), and crafts (Σeθlans) etc. Altogether 38 names of gods have been noted just on the model liver of Piacenza (3rd cent., ET Pa4.2).

Under the influence of Greek religion, E. gods were represented anthropomorphologically from the 6th cent.; similarly, Greek views of deities were integrated, either with a change in character while name and appearance were preserved (around 530 Apulu was a demon of death and like Artumes < Artemis a god of fertility [2]) or with a correlation with functionally similar E. deities: thus Tinia with Zeus/Jupiter, Uni with Hera/Juno, Fufluns with Dionysus/Bacchus, Σeθlans with Hephaestus/Vulcanus, Turms with Hermes/Mercurius, Neθuns with Poseidon/Neptune and Turan with Aphrodite/Venus. It was not uncommon for independent E. beliefs to merge with Greek myths: Menerva, who was close to Athena, was a lightning-throwing goddess (ES III 153) [7]. In the obscurity of the early period a many-faceted young spirit of the earth, Voltumna, was said to hold sway as the principal E. deity (Varro, Ling. 5,46) and was venerated in Volsinii (Prop. 4,2,3); he was later identified with Tinia. Only after Tinia's identification (by the priesthood ?) with the functionally similar Zeus (ET Ta 3.2) in the 6th cent. BC did a schism take place with the original Voltumna-Tinia and this was also reflected in the iconography; from the 5th cent. Tinia was held to be similar to Zeus. In Seneca's later description (Q Nat. 2,45,1–3) Tinia was accorded the attributes of the most senior deity, with power over gods and men.

Whether or not there was an original E. mythology can be answered, cautiously, in the affirmative, by virtue of the representations of animal beings and demon wolves [6. pl. x 5; 6]. Greek myths were adopted from the 8th–7th cents. BC but their representation on vases was initially only incidental decoration and did not at that stage imply that the foreign religion had been adopted; the iconography of Greek myths was transformed by the addition of E. deities (Hercle and Menerva, ES II 153) [7]. It is in the area between legend and myth that we find the grey youth Tages (see above), who revealed himself in Tarquinia to a farmer called Tarchon (Lyd. De ostentibus 4,20) and was said to have handed over to him the holy precepts of the *Etrusca disciplina*. The legend developed in Tarquinia, the normative character of the *Etrusca disciplina* can be attributed to a priesthood that, in a period that we cannot more precisely determine, was seeking to anchor in myth, and thus consolidate, its primary role for maintaining the *Etrusca disciplina*. Another mythical figure is the monstrous Olta, who was said to have destroyed the fields of Volsinii before being struck by lightning summoned by King Porsenna (Plin. HN 2,54,140).

Vegoia's 'prophecy' (Gromatici veteres 350,17–351, 11 LACHMANN) contains references to an Etruscan cosmogony, a fairly long fragment of which was reproduced by the Suda (s.v. τυρρηνία χώρα); it was elaborated in the style of Sumerian-Babylonian literature: a deity orders the chaos of the basic elements and creates the world of his own free will over a period of 12,000 years.

C. Afterlife

The E. believed in a life after death and therefore sought to immortalize the image and name of the deceased in painting and inscription: the corpse was buried, together with domestic equipment, in a specially constructed dwelling, the grave; if the corpse was cremated, the remains were stored in anthropomorphic vessels (canopi of Chiusi [8]) or house urns. E. funerary architecture and wall paintings indicate the existence of two different and probably not contemporaneously developed concepts: according to one, the immaterial part, the soul, lived on in the grave; according to the other, it undertook a journey into the afterlife. Important traces of the Dionysus-cult (ET Ta 1.184 and many others; Liv. 39,3–19) indicate the existence of a religion of mysteries. In the Imperial period an E. doctrine of salvation presaged a deification of the soul through special rites (Arnob. 2,62); whether Orphic-Pythagorean or Christian influence played a part in that doctrine is an open question for the time being. Several images from the 6th cent. BC show deceased people travelling to the afterlife on a seahorse or a bird (Tarquinia, Tomba dei Tori, around 550 [5. 120]). Originally the object of the journey was probably Elysium or the Islands of the Blessed; this Ancient Oriental belief was in the same way familiar to Greek eschatology (Hom. Od. 4,561–8). In the 2nd half of the 6th cent. the belief emerged that the deceased journeyed to the kingdom of the dead on foot, on horse, or on a wagon; demons brought him down from the earth or waited for him at the gate to the Underworld [6. pl. CXXVII a;b]. Here a large number of demons (Charu, Thuchulcha) and demonesses (Vanθ) [9] were at work, inducting the deceased; their ugly but still human appearance was regarded as a tangible expression of the fear of death and of the pain of those left behind [4].

Greek and western Greek influence in southern Etruria grew stronger from the second half of the 5th cent. (Vulci, Tomba François, around 330; Tarquinia, Tomba dell' Orco II, 3rd cent. [5. no. 178,94]). In the Underworld there then were to be found Aita (~Hades) and Φersipnai (~Persephone) (Orvieto, Tomba Golini II, middle of the 4th cent. BC [5. no. 33]); the Greek contribution to this belief might have been superficial though, as the rulers of the E. Underworld bore distinctly non-Greek features. Even in other respects the doctrine of afterlife continues to convey an unmistakable E. content even if figures in the E. afterlife are characterized by Greek stylistic elements (Vanθ-representation in the grave of Anina, Tarquinia, 280–150 BC [5. no. 40]).

D. Rituals

Prayer and sacrifice: the formally meticulous ritual recorded on the bindings of the Zagreb mummy provides for a large number of sacrifices of wine and bread, as well as prayers, on certain days of the month, for specific gods who are mentioned by name. E. rituals for founding cities were adopted by Rome (Liv. 1,44,2ff.).

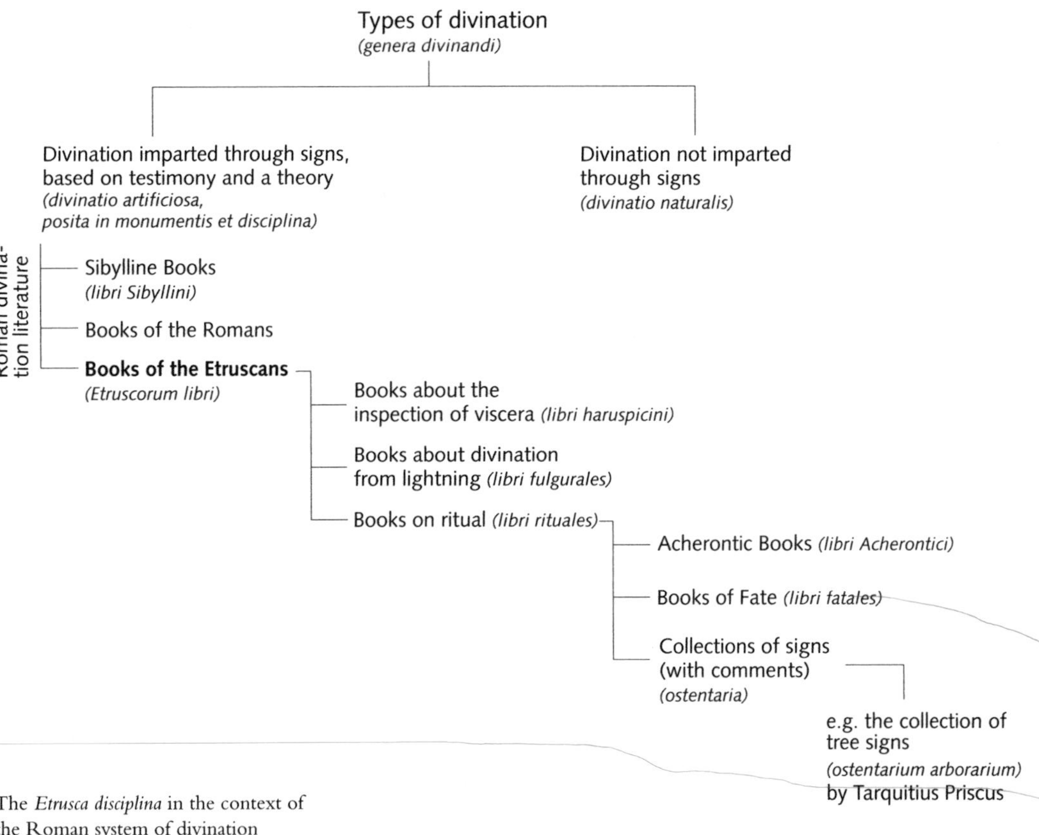

The *Etrusca disciplina* in the context of the Roman system of divination

The books of the Etruscans were transmitted as part of the Roman literature on divination. Its tripartition into Sibylline books, books of the Romans and books of the Etruscans reflected the tripartition of the Roman system of religion into *Graecus ritus* (Greek rite), *patrius ritus* (indigenous rite) and *Etrusca disciplina* (Etruscan discipline).

M. HAA.

Common E. cult ceremonies were supposed to have taken place on a periodic basis (Liv. 5,1). The annual ceremony of hammering the nail to mark the passing of the year took place in the Nortia sanctuary of Volsinii. Of the E. Bacchanalia we know scarcely any more than the fact of its existence as attested by Livy (39,9,1ff.). Magical rites are also to be included among their practices [1]: magical lightning (Sen. Q Nat. 2,33; Plin. HN 2,54,140), likewise talismans and amulets for using or warding off supernatural powers: the metal caps that had a positive effect (*bullae*, Juv. 1,5,164; Macrob. Sat. 1,6,9), as well as lead tablets, with the text of curses, that had a negative effect (ET Vt 4.1 and many more).

The *netvis*, Latin *haruspex* (ET Um 1.7; Cic. Div. 1,14,24; 2,53,109; → *haruspices*) was guardian of the *Etrusca disciplina*, soothsayer, celebrant of cult activities, and thus executor of the will of the gods. The *trutnvt*, Latin *fulgur(i)ator* (ET Um 1.7; Cic. Div. 2,53,109) was responsible for interpreting lightning. There were other priestly offices as well (*maru, cepen*: ET s.v.); Livy (5,1,5) mentions a *sacerdos*. Unusual Latin terms for priests (CIL XI 1848 in Arretium) are probably translations of E. priestly offices. As well as the liturgical accessories for the cult site (incense burners, crozier, sacrificial axe and knives), cult statues should be mentioned; difficult to distinguish in a formal sense from votive statues of gods, they are nevertheless amply attested in literature: e.g. in the *liber linteus zagrabiensis*, a calendar-based ritual text from the bindings on the Zagreb mummy mentioned above (middle of the 2nd cent.; ET I.).

We do not know when the E. authors composed the written text of the *Etrusca disciplina* attributed to Tages (Cic. Div. 2,23,50). There were probably original versions in individual cities (Cic. Div. 1,44,100). The corpus contained the teaching on the reading of entrails (*libri haruspicini*: Cic. Div. 1,33,72) and the interpretation of lightning (*libri fulgurales*: Cic. ibid.), as well as procedures for founding cities, dedicating sanctuaries and dividing up fields (*libri rituales*: Cic. ibid.). The ritual books included the doctrine on the afterlife (*libri acheruntici*: Arnob. 2,62; Serv. Aen. 8,398,20) and the interpretation of miracles (*ostentaria*: Macrob. Sat. 3,7,2). According to E. belief, the gods express their will through signs (Cic. Har. resp. 10,20).

The highest duty of the E. priesthood was to determine from which god the sign came, for what purpose the god sent it, what the sign meant and, if negative, how it could be expiated (Cic. Cat. 3,8,19). An essential precondition was the careful and deliberate observation of divine signs visible in the lightning bolts shot by nine of the gods (Plin. HN 2,52,137f.; Sen. Q Nat. 2,40f.), and as revealed in the livers of sacrificed animals (ES CCXXIII) and other omens. Observation of weather signs underwent a 'scientific' elaboration in Etruria and was more highly esteemed than haruspicy (Sen. Q Nat. 2,33f.). Ornithoscopy was likewise known in Etruria but less widespread than in Rome and among the Umbrians. Interpreting the future was bound up with the belief that the heavens were divided into 16 precisely defined regions (Cic. Div. 2,18,42; Plin. HN 2,55,143), in which the gods had their seat from which they sent signs to mankind to express their will (Fest. 454 L.; Mart. Cap. 1,41ff.). Division of the heavens was then conceptually translated to the earth and the liver (cf. the bronze liver of Piacenza): deviations from the norm, in heaven, in the liver or on the earth, signified that the god residing in the corresponding region of heaven was now revealing himself.

The E. religion was not confined to Etruria. Some practices were adopted by Roman cult, though they generally underwent substantial internal change. In Rome the interpretation of lightning, liver and prodigies remained in the hands of E. *haruspices* (Dion. Hal. 4,59–61; Cic. Har. resp. 9,18), who were brought from Etruria expressly for this purpose (Cic. Cat. 3,19). The Roman state took care not to let the doctrine of → *haruspices*, as *Etrusca disciplina* (→ Divination VII) part of official Roman religion (Cic. Div. 1,41,92; Tac. Ann. 11,15), disappear. It had a resurgence under Emperor Alexander Severus (HA Alex.27,6). Emperor Constantine was the first to interfere seriously with the activities of the *haruspices* (Cod. Theod. 9,16,1) but he was not able to eliminate them completely. The last reference to *haruspices* appeared in AD 408 (Zos. 5,41); E. soothsayers were mentioned as late as Procopius (BG 8,21,16).

→ ETRUSCOLOGY; → Tarquitius Priscus

1 PFIFFIG, 12ff. 2 I. KRAUSKOPF, s.v. Apollon/Aplu, LIMC 2.1, 335ff. 3 H. RIX, Rapporti onomastici fra il panteon etrusco e quello romano, in: Gli Etruschi e Roma, Atti in onore di M. Pallotino, 1981, 104ff. 4 M. PALLOTTINO, Etruskologie. Gesch. und Kultur der Etrusker, 1988, 310 5 S. STEINGRÄBER, Etr. Wandmalerei, 1985 6 G. KÖRTE, I rilievi delle urne etrusche. III, 1916 7 G. COLONNA, s.v. Athena/Menerva, LIMC 2.1, 1050ff.; 1066ff. 8 R. GEMPELER, Die etr. Kanopen, 1974 9 I. KRAUSKOPF, Todesdämonen und Totengötter im vorhell. Etrurien, Biblioteca di studi etruschi 16, 1987. 10 E. GERHARD, G. KÖRTE, Etr. Spiegel, 1884–1897 (= ES) 11 L. MAGGIANI, Wiss. und Rel., in: M. CRISTOFANI (ed.), Die Etrusker, 1995, 136 ff 12 H. RIX, G. MEISER et al., Etr. Texte I–II, Scripta Oralia 23 A 6, 1991 (= ET) 13 E. SIMON, Etr. Kultgottheiten, in: M. CRISTOFANI (ed.), Die Etrusker, 1995, 152ff. 14 C. O. THULIN, Die etr. Disziplin, I–III, 1905–1909.

FIG.-BIBLIOGRAPHY: Ancient Sources: Cic. Div. I; A. BOUCHÉ-LECLERCQ, Histoire de la divination dans l'antiquité IV: Divination italique, 1882, 3–115; C. THULIN, Die Etr. Disciplin I–III, 1905–1909, repr. 1968, especially I, 1–12; H. CANCIK, Libri fatales. Röm. Offenbarungslit. und Geschichtstheologie, in: D. HELLHOLM (ed.), Apocalypticism in the Mediterranean World and the Near East, conf. Uppsala 1979, 1983, 549–576; C. GUITTARD, Contribution des sources littéraires à notre connaissance de l'Etrusca disciplina: Tarquitius Priscus et les arbores infelices, in: H. HERES, M. KUNZE (ed.), Die Welt der Etrusker, colloquium Berlin 1988, 91–99. L.A.-F.

IV. LANGUAGE

→ Etruscan

Etruscus Author of an artistically refined epigram on a fisher that is rich in effective antitheses: his boat helped him to survive yesterday but today it serves as his funeral pyre (Anth. Pal. 7,381, cf. Antiphilus, Anth. Pal. 7,635). It is part of the 'Garland' of Philippus. All that is known of its poet is that he was a 'Messenian' (Μεσσήνιος; *Messēnios*) but it is unclear in the lemma whether he was from Messenia or Messina.

GA II,1, 254f.; 2, 288. E.D.

Etymander Longest river (1,000 km) of the Persian core provinces → Arachosia and → Drangiana (modern Helmand Rūd), now inside Afghanistan. Today the Helmand no longer reaches the lake basin of Daryāče-ye Sīstān, but disappears in swamps because some of its water is diverted for irrigation. Arr. Anab. 4,6,6 reports that this river flows through the territory of the Εὐεργέται (*Euergétai*, → Ariaspae). Plin. HN 6,92 calls the river the *Erymandus*. Curt. 8,9,10 erroneously located the river in India with the name *Ethymantus*.

Barrington Atlas 3 H3 6 A3 (Erymandos); TAVO A IV 4, A VIII 2/3, B VII 6. H.T.

Etymologica

I. ANTIQUITY II. THE 5TH–8TH CENTS. III. THE ETYMOLOGICUM GENUINUM IV. OTHER BYZANTINE ETYMOLOGICA

I. ANTIQUITY

The interest of the Greeks in etymology was linked from the 5th cent. through to the Alexandrian period to philosophical speculation on the origins of language (which reached its peak in Plato's *Cratylus*) as well as research, especially by the Sophists, on the origin of individual poetic and especially Homeric 'glosses' for the purpose of determining their true (ἔτυμος; *étymos*) meaning. The earliest treatise is the writing of Heraclides Ponticus 'On Etymologies' (Περὶ ἐτυμολογιῶν; *Perì etymologiôn*, which is a chapter from 'On words'/Περὶ ὀνομάτων; *Perì onomátōn*). Systematic research was first conducted by the Stoics (e.g., → Chrysippus of Soli, Περὶ τῶν ἐτυμολογικῶν πρὸς Διοκλέα in 7 vols.), who assumed an anomalistic concept of language and developed a complex system of derivation by starting with the 'first' substantives and verbs to represent the language as a whole. The objective of analogistic Alexandrinism was different: e.g., Apollodorus [7] and Demetrius Ixion were concerned with etymology but the most mature representative was → Philoxenus. They all postulated a development that occurred in a context of precise standards of analogy formation occurring from monosyllabic roots and not original words.

II. The 5th–8th cents.

The first real etymological lexica were written in late antiquity in the 5th cent. AD, especially by Orion and Orus. Only a few excerpts and fragments of these small collections are preserved. Orion incorporated materials from Soranus, Herodianus (both 2nd cent. AD), Heraclides Ponticus and Philoxenus. However, Orus primarily used → Philoxenus.

The lexicon *Haimōdeîn* (Αἱμωδεῖν), and those of Methodius and Anastasius Sinaites as well as the 'Ecloges' of the Cod. Baroccianus 50 are from the 6th to 8th cents., while the *E. Parvum* is from the 9th cent.

III. The Etymologicum Genuinum

The fourth phase is represented by encyclopaedic works called etymologica that were compiled from the time of Photius: since Reitzenstein the first of these has been called the *Etymologicum Genuinum* (but *Etymologicum Magnum Genuinum* by Lasserre-Livadaras). According to tradition, Photius himself wrote it and its completion is dated to 13 May 865 or 882. Two versions of the codices copied in the 10th cent. in South Italy are preserved. Version A, preserved in the Cod. Vaticanus Graecus 1818, is largely mutilated; version B of the Cod. Laurentianus S. Marci 304 is more complete (only the first page is missing) but is entirely illegible in some sections. This work is a compilation from many sources (Choeroboscus, Orus, Herodianus, Theognostus, Orion, Methodius, the → epimerismi on Homer, the epimerismi on the Psalms, the exegetic traditions on all major authors and the problematic lexicon *Rhētorikón* (Ῥητορικόν), which is closely related to Photius. Numerous etymologies were derived from it in later centuries.

IV. Other Byzantine Etymologica

Regarding the relationships between these works and their various editions, it must be kept in mind that these works were copied and interpolated for practical purposes. The differences between different works and editions are to some extent very small. In particular, the *E. Magnum* of the mid 12th cent. (already with this title in Eust. 834,46 and 1443,65, renamed by Lasserre-Livadaras to *E. Magnum auctum*) belongs into this tradition. It is the most impressive work of its type and was compiled by using a multitude of sources (including the *E. Gudianum*). Only seven manuscripts in two groups are preserved.

The *E. Symeonis* (named after the grammarian to who it is attributed), of which three editions are known, must also be dated into the 12th cent., but perhaps a little earlier than the *E. Magnum*. Two manuscripts (Parmensis Gr. 2139 of the 14th cent. and Vindobonensis Phil. Gr. 131 of the 2nd half of the 13th cent.) transmit abbreviated versions, three others a more extensive version (Laurentianus S. Marci 303 (of 1291) and Vossianus Gr. 20 (13th cent.) represent the so-called *Megálē grammatikḗ* which fills the gap from the beginning to the gloss ἄβαλ (*ábal*) with the help of the *E. Magnum*. Vaticanus Gr. 1276, called the *E. Casulanum* (after the monastery of S. Nicola in Casola), stands alone. Finally, in Voss. Gr. 20 (whose variants are listed in the appendix of the *E. Magnum* edited by Gaisford) glosses from the *E. Magnum* were entered in the margin, interlined and placed in a supplementary section (starting at f. 210[r]). The lexicon of Pseudo-Zonaras (13th cent.) is also important – it is based on the *E. Genuinum* (in a better version than that of our codices) and the *E. Symeonis* (in a version similar to Vaticanus Gr. 1276). The *E. Genuinum* was repeatedly used by Eustathius in his commentary on the *Iliad* and *Odyssey*, which was written before 1175, and is one of the many sources of the *E. Gudianum* (named after the Danish humanist M. Gude [17th cent.], the owner of Cod. Guelpherbytanus Gr. 29–30). Of the *E. Gudianum*, the Codex Vat. Barberinus Gr. 70 (11th cent.) from Otranto is preserved and all other versions are derived from it. They are divided into four groups. The first group, which consists of three manuscripts of the 13th cent. and two of the 15th, is quite faithful to Vat. Barb. 70. The second group is limited to the Parisinus Suppl. Gr. 172 (the *E. Sorbonicum*) of the 13th cent. The third group is extensively cross-contaminated by the *E. Genuinum* and consists of the Vaticanus Gr. 1708 (12th cent.) and the *E. Cretense*, of which many copies are preserved. Finally, the fourth group is based on a copy of the *E. Cretense*, which has been subjected to many later interpolations, especially from the lexicon of Cyrillus (the oldest codex is Vindob. Phil. Gr. 158 of the 13th cent., one of the worst is the Guelpherbytanus Gr. 29–30 of 1293, of which the edition of Sturz is a diplomatic transcription). There obviously were numerous exchanges between the traditions derived from the *E. Genuinum* and the *E. Gudianum*. While interpolations from the *E. Genuinum* are already found in the Vat. Barb. 70, the *E. Gudianum* is one of the sources of the *E. Symeonis* and the *E. Magnum*.

Editions: 1 Etymologicum Genuinum et Etymologicum Symeonis (β), ed. G. Berger, 1972 2 Etymologicum Gudianum quod vocatur rec. E. A. De Stefani, I (α-β), II (β-ζ), 1909–20 3 Etymologicum Magnum, ed. Th. Gaisford, 1848 4 Etymologicum Magnum Genuinum. Symeonis Etymologicum una cum Magna Grammatica. Etymologicum Magnum auctum synoptice ediderunt F. Lasserre, N. Livadaras, I (α-ἀμωσογέπως), 1976, II (ἀνά-βώτορες), 1992 5 E. Miller, Mélanges de littérature grecque, 1868, 11–340 6 Etymologicum Parvum quod vocatur, ed. R. Pintaudi, 1973 7 Etymologicum Graecae linguae Gudianum ed. F. G. STURZIUS, 1818 8 Orionis Thebani Etymologicon, ed. F. G. STURZIUS, 1820 9 I. Zonarae Lexicon ex tribus codicibus manuscriptis, ed. I. A. H. TITTMANN, I–II, 1808 10 Die Fragmente des Grammatikers Philoxenos, ed. C. THEODORIDIS, 1976. LIT: 11 K. ALPERS, Bericht über Stand und Methode der Ausgabe des Etymologicum Genuinum, 1969 12 Id., Zonarae Lexicon, RE X A, 732–63 13 C. CALAME, Etymologicum Genuinum. Les citations de poètes lyriques, 1970 14 A. CELLERINI, Introduzione all' Etymologicum Gudianum, 1989 15 R. REITZENSTEIN, Gesch. der griech. Etymologika, 1897 16 Id., s.v. Etymologika, RE IV 1, 807–17. R.T.

Etymology (ἐτυμολογία, literally 'science of the true meaning of a word'; Latin *etymologia*). Modern linguistics ([1]; cf. [2]) considers etymology the study of word formation processes [3] and the shifts in sound and meaning in the prehistory of words from which it attempts to gain insight into the relationships of words and languages. By contrast, ancient etymology attempted an interpretative determination of the 'actual' meaning (ἔτυμον/*étymon*) of (proper) names or words, which did not preclude the correct analysis of a composite or derivative. Etymology was introduced as a grammatical discipline by → Philoxenus [8] of Alexandria – without lasting success – and as a philosophical method no later than → Chrysippus [2], but was already practiced by poets [4] and sophists (without being called 'etymology') since the Homeric epics.

I. FROM HOMER TO THE SOPHISTIC II. PLATO AND ARISTOTLE III. HELLENISM IV. LATIN ETYMOLOGY

I. From Homer to the Sophistic

Homespun interpretation of proper names (especially of deities), e.g., by apposition or a relative clause, was already practiced by Homer (cf. [5]), e.g., *Odysseús* was related to *odýresthai* ('to wail') or *odýssesthai* ('to be wroth'; cf. Hom. Od. 1, 55 and 62). It was poetically elaborated by the tragedians (*Zeus*, genitive *Zēnós* from *zên*, 'to live', Aesch. Suppl. 584). The → rhapsodes who commented on Homer and Hesiod, such as → Theagenes [2] of Rhegium, elaborated this allegorically, while the Sophists systematized poetic exegesis in the interest of a critical ὀρθοέπεια/*orthoépeia* ('correct language'; e.g., *phlégma* must mean inflammation, not slime, because it was derived from *phlégein*, 'to burn'; Prodicus Fr. 84 B 4 DK) – this was a serious approach to semantics (cf. → Linguistic theory).

II. Plato and Aristotle

The language theory of Heraclitus' student → Cratylus, which assumed a 'natural' name of things, was used by Plato [1] in the eponymous dialogue as the base for a → philosophy of language[6] operating with the dialectic of *phýsei – thései* (Pl. Crat. 390d 7–e3: 'by nature – through naming'). Assuming that everything manifests its specific nature in an autonomous word field and, second, that the name (ὄνομα/*ónoma*) with an additional element pf predication (ῥῆμα/*rhêma*) was only a human means of understanding but which has been altered by use, it should be possible to derive the original name (πρώτη φωνή/*prṓtē phōnḗ*) given by a knowledgeable name giver and with it the original meaning of the word, i.e., the nature of what was named. However, varying means of access that are phonologically different but semantically equivalent (language differences!) are possible. Thus Astyanax, 'city ruler', expresses the same as Hector, '(city) preserver'.

The guiding thought of this operation is not the relationship between words but the meaning sought: *phrónēsis* ('thinking') is not placed, as would appear obvious, with *phroneîn* 'to think' (Pl. Crat. 411d 4–6), but with *phorâs nóēsis* or *phorâs ónēsis* ('understand/promote a process'); *ónoma* ('name') with *on* ('being'). Endings, prefixes and suffixes were considered to be autonomous *rhḗmata*, and composites were not differentiated from derivatives. Instead of regular laws of sound change, arbitrary 'embellishments' of language were used to explain word changes, so that in the individual case the congruence between thing and name could become imperfect, even unrecognizable. A chance hit is, for example, *zygón* with *dyogón* ('double steering' = 'draft team': Pl. Crat. 418d 8). → Aristotle [6], whom Dion [I 3] of Prusa (Or. 53,1) claimed as the inventor of grammar and textual criticism, did little to extend Plato's approach (matter-name-model), but he nevertheless included several etymological interpretations in his poetics, rhetoric and hermeneutics despite his more teleological than backwards-oriented thought.

III. Hellenism

Of → Chrysippus [2] the book title *Perì tôn etymologiôn* is attested (SVF 2 p. 9, 13 f.), but whether it only intended to confirm Stoic teachings by means of interpreting Homer remains speculation. The etymological research of → Crates [5] of Mallus with an allegorical foray into natural philosophy (e.g., a cosmological interpretation of Homer's shield description) also appears to have been less groundbreaking than once assumed [7]. His attested writings mostly serve → textual criticism and exegesis of Homer, as do the works of the Alexandrians → Aristophanes [4] of Byzantium, → Eratosthenes [2] of Cyrene and → Aristarchus [4] of Samothrace. To the Alexandrian grammarians a lexicographic recording of the etymological stock was important, especially in the *Rhēmatikón* of → Philoxenus [8], who initiated the tradition of the → Etymologica (which were later strongly expanded by semantic material).

IV. Latin etymology

→ Crates' [5] lecture in Rome in 168 BC may have inspired the linguistic research of L. Aelius [II 20] Stilo Praeconinus and → Aurelius Opilius, which was then reflected in → Cicero (e.g. Cic. Top. 2,35) and → Varro [2] (*De lingua Latina* is our main source of Hellenistic etymology) [8; 9]. To have a free hand in historical-antiquarian etymologization, Varro to some extent assumed a profound change of words due to age (*vetustas*), misnomer (*falsa impositio*) – e.g., the notorious *etymologiae e contrario* ('from the opposite') such as *canis quod non canit*, approximately: 'dog' (*canis*) because he doesn't 'sing' (*canit*) – and letter manipulation (*interpolatio*: 'addition'/*additio*, 'ommission'/*demptio*, 'exchange'/*traiectio* and 'replacement'/*commutatio*; also vowel 'shortening and lengthening'/*correptio* and *productio*). In this respect, Varro attached himself to Plato's *Kratýlos* and Chrysippus but at the same time scuttled evidently sensible derivations. This resulted in an antithetics of (etymological) *anomalía* ('iregularity') of forms metastatically anchored in traditional language and (systematic and grammatical) *analogía* ('regularity') of inflection and word formation. The (Stoic) partition of word groups according to place-matter-time-motion was likewise counterproductive.

However, Varro's differentiation of four phases of etymology by degree of evidence is significant: (1) composites easily explained by anyone; (2) explanations only apparent to trained → grammarians; (3) difficult poetic words that only philosophers are able to probe; (4) the 'sanctuary and royal initiations' (*adyton et initia regis*) of the 'original names' given by the *onomatothétes* (Latin *impositor verborum*, approximately: 'the original word designer') [10]. Unfortunately, these principles are not consistently applied.

Thus, the *lusus originationis* ('word explanation game') prevailed later despite the warnings of Cicero (Nat. Deor. 3,62), → Quintilian [1] (Inst. 1,6,32–38) and → Gellius [6] (11,15,8). It is especially visible in → Donatus [3], → Servius [2], → Macrobius [1], the Mythographus Vaticanus (→ Mythographi Vaticani) and largely also in the lexicons of → Verrius [1] Flaccus (in Festus [6]) and → Nonius [III 1], less among the *Grammatici Latini* (→ Grammarians), of whom only Diomedes [4] (GL 1,322,25), Pompeius [III 1] (GL 5,95,5 etc.), Donatianus (GL 6,275,14), → Cassiodorus (GL 7,215,31) and → Martianus Capella mentioned *etymologia* as a discipline (but did not engage in it). Only → Isidore [9] of Seville attempted towards the end of late Antiquity to collect, categorize by material and define the entire knowledge of the Romans in the *Etymologiae* [11]. The result was an encyclopaedia but not a linguistic work (→ Encyclopaedia).

→ Etymologica; → Grammarians; → Philosophy; → Language philosophy; → Stoicism; → ETYMOLOGY; → ONOMASTIC ETYMOLOGY

1 M. JOB, s. v. E., DNP 13, 1057 f. 2 R. THURNEYSEN, E., eine akad. Rede (1905), in: R. Schmitt (ed.), E., 1977, 50–73 3 E. WÖLFFLIN, Die Etymologien der lat. Grammatiker, in: ALLG 8, 1893, 430 4 E. RISCH, Namensdeutungen und Worterklärugen bei den ältesten griech. Dichtern, in: Eumusia. FS E. Howald, 1949, 72–91 (= Id., KS, 1981, 294–313) 5 PFEIFFER, KPI, ch. 2 6 K. BARWICK, Probleme der stoischen Sprachlehre und Rhetorik (Abh. der sächsischen Akad. der Wiss., Philol.-Histor. Klasse 49.3, 1957), 70–79 7 H. J. METTE, Parateresis, 1952, 2–48 8 S. ROESCH, Le rapport de res et verbum dans le De lingua Latina de Varron, in: M. BARATIN et al. (ed.), Conceptions latines du sens et de la signification, 1999, 65–80 9 R. SCHRÖTER, Studien zur varronischen E., 1. Teil (AAWM 12, 1959), 1960 10 W. PFAFFEL, Quartus gradus etymologiae, 1981 11 C. CODOÑER, ¿'Origines' o 'Etymologiae'?, in: Helmantica 45, 1994, 511–527.

KL. SA.

Euangelion The term εὐαγγέλιον (*euangélion*) has been attested since Homer (Od. 14,52f.; 166f.), where it is the messenger's reward for good news. In Plut. Demetrius 17; Philostr. VA 5,8, *euangelion* stands for news of victory, in Plut. Sertorius 11,8 *euangelion* is the message itself, and *euangelion* could also mean joyful political and private messages (Cic. Att. 2,3,1). In the → imperial cult *euangelion* had a religious meaning. In the inscription of Priene (OGIS II 458) both the announcement of the blessings coming with the emperor and the joyful messages of the occasion of the blessing are called *euangélia* (pl.). Philo (Legatio ad Gaium 18.99.231) and Josephus (BI 4,618.656) also attest to the use of *euangelion* in the context of the Hellenistic ruler cult. News of the elevation of Vespasian to emperor is called εὐαγγέλια (*euangélia*) by Josephus; each town celebrated this good news and sacrificed in the new emperor's honour.

The Hebrew noun בְּשֹׂרָה (*b^esorah*) in the OT following common usage describes the 'messenger's reward for news of a victory' (2 Sam 4,10; 18,22) or the 'news of a victory' (2 Sam 18,20. 25. 27; 2 Kg 7,9). In the LXX the substantive *euangelion* merely appears in the plural (2 Kg 4,10), also the feminine ἡ εὐαγγελία (*hē euangelía*), which should be translated as 'happy news' (cf. 2 Sam 18,20. 22. 27; 2 Kg 7,9). Unlike the verb εὐαγγελίζεσθαι (*euangelízesthai*) the noun *euangelion* has no theological meaning in the OT tradition. Nor were *euangélion*/*euangelízesthai* or a Hebrew or Aramaic equivalent part of the annunciation of the historical → Jesus because the quote from Is. 61,1 LXX in Mt 11,5/Lc 7,22 presumes a post-Easter Christology. The historical root of the NT tradition of the *euangelion* term probably lies in Hellenistic ruler worship. The early congregations attached themselves to beliefs current in their surroundings but also fundamentally differed from the *euangélia* of their surroundings because of this singular *euangelion*. In → Paul *euangelion* appears as a non-literary term that signifies the living spoken word of the salvational message (cf. 1 Thess 1,9b–10; 1 Cor 15,3b–5; Rom 1,3b–4a). The transition from the non-literary concept of *euangelion* to the literary genre of the → Gospels is evident in the Gospel of Mark. The *euangelion* of Jesus Christ becomes the *euangelion* about Jesus Christ (cf. Mk 1,1), which is now announced in the new literary genre of the gospel/*euangelion*. From the 1st half of the 2nd cent., the word *euangelion* is also a term for a book (cf. Didache 11,3; 15,3f.; 2nd Letter of Clement 8,5; Just. Apol. I 66,3). At about the same time the gospel headings, where *euangelion* clearly means a book, came into being.

H. Frankemölle, Evangelium. Begriff und Gattung, 1988 G. Strecker, s.v. εὐαγγέλιον, Exegetisches WB zum NT II, 176–186 J. Schniewind, Euangelion 1.2, 1927/1931 G. Friedrich, s.v. εὐαγγέλιον, ThWB II, 435–446 P. Stuhlmacher, Das paulinische Evangelium, 1968.

U.SCHN.

Euboea (Εὔβοια; *Eúboia*).

[1]

I. Location II. Economy III. History

I. Location

The largest Greek island other than Crete extends parallel to the eastern coast of central Greece (Locris, Boeotia and Attica). E. is about 160 km long, about 5.5 to 50 km wide and has an area of 3,580 km². It is separated by a strait from the mainland which narrows at its centre to a 40-m wide channel, the → Euripus [1]. Since the 5th cent. BC several bridges linked E. at this point to the mainland. Because of its steep cliffs the east coast is almost inaccessible with Cyme and Cerinthus being the only ports. All other ports were located on the protected, more accessible west coast. The most important were → Chalcis [1] on the Euripus and Carystus near the southern tip of E. The interior of E. is largely taken up by a shale and limestone mountain range. Geographically it is the south-eastern continuation of Ossa and Pelion. The highest mountain is the Dirphys (1,746 m). The south of the island is characterized by a continuation of the Attic crystalline shale and marble mountains. It is a low, infertile and sparsely settled, rolling country in the far south in which the Ocha once more rises to 1,398 m. At the NW tip of E. lies Cape Cenaeum with a Zeus sanctuary, at the NE tip the Artemis temple made famous by the naval battle of 480 BC. Cape Geraestus forms the SW tip and Cape Caphereus, which was particularly feared by mariners, is found in the SE. In the middle of the east coast, Cape Chersonesos separates central from south E.

II. Economy

Apart from agriculture, viticulture, horticulture and fruit-growing, livestock breeding was important in antiquity. Several towns had a cow as a symbol on their coins and in antiquity its name was also explained as 'rich in cattle'. However, fish catching and purple fishery were also important trades. The large forests especially in the north supplied wood for commercial use. Chalcis, → Eretria [1] and Cyme were important crafts centres (pottery and metallurgy). The commercial significance of the island is reflected in the widespread use of the Euboean system of measures and weights. Marble and asbestos from Styra and Carystus and medicinal earths from Chalcis and Eretria were much prized. Salt was another export article. Strabo (10,1,9) mentions copper and iron mining but they remain unproven [1. 243ff.].

III. History

A. Early period to the end of the 5th cent. BC B. 4th Cent. BC to the Roman Imperial Period C. Byzantine period

A. Early period to the end of the 5th cent. BC

Colonists from Thessaly inhabited E. in early antiquity. Hellopieis and Perrhaebi (Scymn. 578; Str. 9,5,17) settled in the N, the Abantes in the W and in the S the Dryopes (Hdt. 8,46,4; Thuc. 7,57,4; Scymn. 577; Diod. Sic. 4,37,2; Paus. 4,34,11). So far, there have only been a few prehistoric finds. In the historical period the inhabitants were Ionians (→ Iones) who settled without any recognizable traces of tribal affiliation in individual city states. Hom. Il. 2,536ff. names seven cities. Apart from Eretria and Chalcis, they were Histiaea, Cerinthus, Dion, Carystus and Styra. Also to be mentioned are Histiaea-Oreos in the NW, Athenae-Diades (later Athenitae), Aedepsus with its hot mineral springs, Orobiae and Aegae, Dystus in the south, which later became a deme of Eretria like Styra. In the lists of the → Delian League are recorded Diacrioe, Grynchae, later a deme of Eretria, and Posideion, later a deme of Histiaea. In the 2nd → Athenian League Arethusa also appears as a member. E. attained its greatest significance in the early period when numerous colonies were founded by Chalcis, Eretria and Cyme. Settlements were founded on the coasts of Thrace, in Italy, Sicily and the islands of the Aegean. The war of the two cities over the Lelantine Plain, the plain at the mouth of the Lelantus, ended with victory for Chalcis but weakened both towns in the end. In 506 BC Athens defeated Chalcis and subsequently settled 5,000 Attic cleruchs in this plain, which was in such demand because of its fertility. In 490 BC the Persians conquered and destroyed Eretria and Carystus. Eretria, though restored, never again reached its former power. After the Persian wars, Athens again controlled the island. An uprising was suppressed in 446 by Pericles. In 411 another uprising was more successful because Athens was encumbered due to circumstances relating to the Peloponnesian war. An Euboean league was founded to which only Chalcis and Eretria initially belonged. During the Corinthian war E. sided with Athens and Thebes. Many Euboean towns also belonged to the 2nd Athenian League.

B. 4th Cent. BC to the Roman Imperial Period

After the battle of Leuctra in 371 there was a brief association with Thebes, but in 357 BC the island rejoined the Athenian League. There was another secession in 349 and a renewed alliance with Athens in 341. After the battle of → Chaeronea in 338 E. was annexed to Macedonia. From 308 to 304 E. was a member of the Boeotian League. In 196 the Romans occupied the island and declared it free. Subsequently, Chalcis became the headquarters of Antiochus III, later of Archelaus, the general of Mithridates VI. After 146 E. was severely punished for participating in the uprising against Rome and became a tributary. During the Roman Imperial period the island was part of the province of Achaea. H.KAL.

C. Byzantine period

The island and the *póleis* A(e)depsus, Chalcis, Porthmus and Carystus, which were mentioned in Hierocles (644,10f.; 645,6–8) and Constantine Porphyrogennetus (De thematibus 90; 95 Pertusi), belonged to the diocese of *Macedonia* from the mid 4th cent. and, with the introduction of the → theme system in the 7th cent., to the *théma Hellás* (θέμα Ἑλλάς). A 'bishop of E.' (= Chalcis?) participated in 325 in the council of Nicaea [2. 239]. Bishops are attested in Chalcis after 457/8 [3. 89,36], but about the same period also in Carystus [3. 89,32] and in 553 in Porthmus [4. 22, 33, 136f.]. All were subject to Corinth but after the elevation of Athens to *mētrópolis* (about 900), Aulon and Oreos are named together with Euripus (the mediaeval name of Chalcis), Carystus and Porthmus as suffragan bishoprics of Athens. Having been less affected by the ravages of the 5th cent., E. economically remained an essential part of the early and middle Byzantine state. E.W.

In 1209 E. was divided into three baronies (Chalcis, Carystus and Oreos) and was subject to Verona. After 1366 the Venetians became the masters of E. and in particular took control of the port towns. The interior was divided among numerous Frankish nobles. It was in this period that the name Negroponte, which might refer either to the bridge across the Euripus or is a corruption of the name Euripus, was coined. Negroponte became a Venetian kingdom, briefly came under Genoese influence before being occupied by the Turks in 1470. H.KAL.

1 O. Davies, Roman mines in Europe, 1935. 2 H. Gelzer, H. Hilgenfeld, O. Cuntz (ed.), Patrum Nicaenorum Nomina, 1898 3 E. Schwartz (ed.), Acta Conciliorum Oecumenicorum II,5 4 E. Chrysos, Die Bischofslisten des V. Ökumenischen Konzils (553), 1966.

J. Boardman, Early Euboean pottery and history, in: ABSA 52, 1957, 1ff.; P. A. Brunt, Euboia in the time of Philip II., in: CQ 19, 1969, 245ff.; L. Bürchner, s.v. *Lēlanton Pedíon*, RE XII 2, 1889f.; C. Bursian, Geogr. von Griechenland 2, 1868, 395ff.; J. B. Bury, The Lombards and Venetians in Euboia, in: JHS 7, 1886, 309ff.; Id., The Lombards and Venetians in Euboia, in: JHS 8, 1887, 194ff.; J. D. Carpenter, D. Boyd, The Dragon-Houses of Southern Euboia, in: AJA 29, 1976, 250ff.; H.-J. Gehrke, Zur Rekonstruktion antiker Seerouten, in: Klio 74, 1992, 98ff.; F. Geyer, Top. und Gesch. der Insel Euboia, 1, 1903; Id., Euboia in den Wirren der Diadochenzeit, in: Philologus 85, 1930, 175ff.; C. Marek, Euboia und die Entstehung der Alphabetschrift bei den Griechen, in: Klio 75, 1993, 27ff.; A. Philippson, s.v. Euboia, RE VI 1, 851ff.; Id., Euboia, 1907; Philippson/Kirsten, 1, 561ff., 641ff. (bibliography); L. H. Sackett, Prehistoric Euboia, in: ABSA 61, 1966, 33ff.; E. Sapouna-Sakellaraki, Un dépot de temple et le sanctuaire d'Artémis Amarysia en Eubée, in: Kernos 5, 1992, 235–263 ; L. A. Tritle, Eretria, Argoura, and the road to Tamynai, in: Klio 74, 1992, 131ff.; M. B. Wallace, Herodotos and Euboia, in: Phoenix 28, 1974, 22ff.; Id., The Euboean league and its coinage, in: Numismatic notes and monographs 134, 1956; J. Koder, Negroponte, 1973; J. Koder, s.v. Euboia, LMA 4, 66–68; T. E. Gregory, N. P. Ševčenko, s.v. Euboia, ODB 2, 736f.; J. Koder, F. Hild, TIB 1, 1976, passim. H.KAL. and E.W.

[2] Fortified settlement on Sicily [1], founded with the intention of controlling the large territory of Leontini. The oligarchs of Leontini attempted in vain in 490 BC to protect E. from Aenesidamus, who conquered and destroyed it. Recently, it is preferred [3; 4; 5] to assume that E. [2] was situated on the Monte S. Mauro di Caltagirone [6] rather than at Licodia Eubea.

1 C. Camassa, s.v. Eubea di Sicilia, BTCGI 7, 391–397 2 Ph. Cluverius, Sicilia antiqua cum minoribus insulis ei adiacentibus. Sardinia et Corsica, Lugduni Batavorum 1619, 378–387 3 G. Manganaro, La caduta dei Dinomenidi, in: Annali dell' Ist. Italiano di Numismatica 21/22, 1974/5, 21 4 Id., Segnalazioni di epigrafia greca, in: Kokalos 14/15, 1968/9, 199 n. 16, 201 n. 24 5 M. Frasca, È anonima la città greca di Monte S. Mauro di Caltagirone?, in: PdP 52, 1997, 407–417 6 F. Frisone, s.v. Monte S. Mauro, BTCGI 10, 1992, 487–498. GI.F.

Euboean Vase Painting see → Geometric vase painting.

Euboeus (Εὔβοιος; *Eúboios*). Poet of parodies from Paros. According to Ath. 15,698a, he was a contemporary of Philippus and particularly despised the Athenians. Alexander of Pleuron praised him together with → Boeotus of Syracuse in an elegy (Ath. 15,699c). From preserved fragments it appears that E. parodied the elevated tone of the epic in Homeric hexameters while making craftsmen his subject (Ath. 15, 699a). The influence of this type of epic → parody on the *poesis ludibunda* may be traced through to Horace.

SH 410–412; A. Meineke, Analecta Alexandrina, 1843, 230–233; R. Schröter, Horazens Satire 1, 7 und die antike Eposparodie, in: Poetica 1, 1967, 8–23. C.S.

Eubuleus (Εὐβουλεύς; *Eubouleús*). E., 'the good advisor', was a central figure of the myth represented in the secret rites of the Eleusinian mysteries: he returned → Kore from the Underworld. In images he bears torches and stands between Thea and Theos (as Persephone and Hades are called in the mysteries) before Kore's return, or he stands beside Kore after her return [1]. In related myths (which are not shown in the cult) he is a swineherd (Orph. fr. 51), the son of Dysaules and the brother of → Triptolemus, who reports to Demeter what happened to Kore. In one version of the episode his pig is swallowed up by the earth together with Kore and this was used to explain why piglets are thrown into pits (fr. 50) at the → Thesmophoria. However, E. was not among the gods honoured at the Attic Thesmophoria [1].

Outside of Attica, E. appears a) as an epithet of Zeus as a fertility deity and was worshipped in this form at local Thesmophoria, b) as euphemistic appellation of Hades and c) as the name of an 'Orphic' Underworld deity equated with Dionysus [2].
→ Mysteries

1 K. CLINTON, Myth and Cult: the Iconography of the Eleusinian Mysteries, 1992, 51–63, 71–73, 78–91 2 F. GRAF, Eleusis und die orphische Dichtung Athens in vorhellenistischer Zeit, 1974, 171–174. K.C.

Eubulides (Εὐβουλίδης; *Euboulídēs*).
[1] **E. from Miletus.** Member of the → Megarian school. The time when E. lived (mid 4th cent. BC) is determined by his intense attacks against Aristotle, which are repeatedly mentioned in the sources. In part these are personal attacks (Euseb. Praep. evang. 15,2,5), in part criticism of certain logical theorems by Aristotle (Eubulides, SSR vol. 4, p.88). Possibly, Aristotle may in turn have discussed the teachings of E. There is evidence that Aristotle was thinking of E. or at least people near him [1] when in the 'Metaphysics' () he rejected the opinion of those 'who claim like the Megarians that something only has potential when it is active (i.e., to be active in the respective sense), but that it does not have potential when it is inactive'. E. was mostly famous in his own time and later as a master of inventing and using conclusions and paradoxes. In the preserved sources he is associated with several conclusions circulating under specific names including the famous 'Liar' (ψευδόμενος; *pseudómenos*), whose original formulation probably was about as follows: 'If you say that you are lying and say it truly, are you lying or telling the truth?' (Cic. Acad. 2,95), and the 'Heap' (*sōrítēs*, σωρίτης): 'With which additional grain will a number of individual grains become a heap?' (cf. Cic. Acad. 2,49).
→ Logic

1 G. GIANNANTONI, Die Philosophenschule der Megariker und Aristoteles, in: K. DÖRING, TH. EBERT (ed.), Dialektiker und Stoiker, 1993, 155–165, here: 155–161.

EDITIONS: K. DÖRING, Die Megariker. Komm. Sammlung der Testimonien, 1972, II 1.; SSR II B, also vol. IV 88. BIBLIOGRAPHY: K. DÖRING, Euboulids, in: GGPh² 2.1, § 17 D (with bibliography). K.D.

[2] Comedy writer of the 4th cent. BC (uncertain), one fragment of whose Κωμασταί(*Kōmastaí*, 'The Night Owls') is preserved.

1 PCG V, 186. H.-G.NE.

[3] Comedy writer of the 3rd cent. BC, who once won at the Lenaea [1. test.]. No work or fragment is preserved.

1 PCG V, 187. H.-G.NE.

Recurring name in an Athenian family of sculptors:
[4] E. II (to distinguish him from his grandfather and grandson) is famous as the creator of the seated statue of Chrysippus around 208–204 BC. It was identified in copies because of the *porrecta manu* ('counting with the fingers') gesture. The associated portrait head is not clearly identified from a coin of Soli because it may depict Aratus.
[5] E. III, the grandson of E. II, son of → Eucheir II, with whom he signed honorary statues. For the Dionysus sanctuary in the Kerameikos he created and dedicated about 150 BC a marble group of deities of which the head of Athena is preserved together with the bronze helmet that was put on it.

G. BECATTI, Attika, in: RIA 7, 1940, 14–16, 28–33; H. BRUNN, Gesch. der griech. Künstler, 1, 1857, 551–552; P. MORENO, Scultura ellenistica, 1994, 553–555; J. J. POLLITT, Art in the Hellenistic Age, 1986, 165 Fig.; OVERBECK, No. 2235–2244 (sources); A. STEWART, Attika, 1979, 50–52. R.N.

Eubulus (Εὔβουλος; *Eúboulos*).
[1] E., son of Spintharus of the deme Probalinthus, *c.* 400 to before 330 BC, possibly identical with the Athenian who in 369 applied for permission for Xenophon to return (Ister FGrH 334 F 32) and a thesmothete attested in Athens about 370/69 (SEG 19,133,4). If that is the case, he was a member of the Areopagus. After 354/3 he achieved significant political influence in Athens as an administrator of the *theorikon* treasury, and because of his abilities as an orator, his membership in the Areopagus and good contacts to the Council of the 500. In the age of E., the ἐπὶ τὸ θεωρικόν (*hoi epì tò theōrikón*) was a committee of magistrates elected for four-year terms (Aristot. Ath. Pol. 43,1). Their multiyear term of office, considerable expertise and mandate by election gave them a strong position among the democratic offices without violating their fundamental principles because all magistrates involved in finances were subject to strict controls and the public assembly retained the decision-making powers. Beyond the administration of the *theorika*, the *theorikon* treasury attracted additional functions of other treasuries and magistrates after 354. It supervised the leasing of mines, financing of public building projects and roads as well as the monies for the navy. Finally, the *theorikon* administrators together with the council of the 500 controlled the finances of the polis (Aeschin. In Ctes. 25; Schol. Aeschin. In Ctes. 24; Schol. Dem. Or. 1,1; Harpocration and Suda s.v. Theorika; IG II/III² I 1, 223 C 5 = Agora 15,34). E. supported *c.* 348 a law to prohibit applying for a change of the distribution key of the polis' finances in the *ekklesia* and transferring surplus to the *stratiotikon* instead of the *theorikon* treasury (Schol. Dem. Or. 1,1; Lib. hypothesis ad Dem. Or. 1,4). In external and military policy E. advocated a course of cautious restraint as precondition of financial consolidation, but supported political and military involvement by Athens if vital interests of the polis appeared endangered, e.g., in 352 at Thermopylae or later on Euboea. In 347/6 E. proposed sending Athenian delegates out to create an alliance against → Philippus II (Dem. Or. 19,304). From 346 to 340 the *ekklesia* passed on E.'s initiative *psephismata* on Athenian poli-

cies in northern Greece (Dem. Or. 18,70; 75). But the foreign policy dispute between E. and the rhetors around Demosthenes intensified. In 343 E. supported Aeschines when he was charged because of dishonest embassy. After 338 a law by Hegemon (Aeschin. In Ctes. 25) drastically limited the powers of the *theorikon* treasury and E. stopped playing an important political role. The resistance of Hypereides against honours for E. about 331/30 (Hyp. fr. 104–106 JENSEN) may be considered to be repayment for E.'s politics before Chaeronea. E. was to a significant degree responsible for the financial recovery of the polis, whose annual revenues he increased from *c.* 130 to 400 talents. Under his influence numerous public building projects were begun, the economic activity in the Attic mining district and the port of Piraeus recovered and the navy and its infrastructure were strengthened (IG II/III² II 1, 1627, 354; 1628, 524; 1629, 1001; 1631, 231; Plut. Mor. 812F; Din. 1,96; Schol. Aeschin. Leg. 8; Harpocration s.v. Eubulus).
→ Athens; → Theorikon; → Demokratia

J.J. BUCHANAN, Theorika, 1962; G.L. CAWKWELL, Eubulus, in: JHS 83, 1963, 47–67; DEVELIN No. 1113; J. ENGELS, Studien zur polit. Biographie des Hypereides, ²1993, 59–67 and 194f.; A. FRENCH, Economic Conditions in Fourth-Century Athens, in: G&R; 38, 1991, 24–40; HANSEN, Democracy 263f., 289f.; H. LEPPIN, Zur Entwicklung der Verwaltung öffentlicher Gelder im Athen des 4. Jh. v. Chr., in: EDER, Demokratie 557–571; A. MOTZKI, Eubulos von Probalinthos und seine Finanzpolitik, 1903; PA 5369; E. RUSCHENBUSCH, Die Einführung des Theorikon, in: ZPE 36, 1979, 303–308. J.E.

[2] The son of Euphranor, an important author of the Attic Middle → Comedy. The Suda [1. test. 1] dates him to the 101st Olympiad (= 376–372 BC, on the basis of a Dionysian victory? [2. 8]); in the inscribed list of Lenaean victors he is two places behind → Anaxandrides and two ahead of → Antiphanes [1] [1. test. 3], which also points to the 370s. Allusions to contemporary events in his fragments extend at least from the 360s to the 330s [3. 196]. E. won six times at the Lenaea [1. test. 3]. He also had some of his plays performed by Aristophanes' son Philippus [1. test. 4]. The number of his plays is said to be 104 [1. test. 1]; 58 play titles are attested, of these 28 or 29 have a mythical topic. Often these mythical pieces are parodies, especially of the tragedies of Euripides (*Antiópē*, *Aúgē*, *Bellerophóntēs*, *Danáē*, *Ixíōn*, *Íōn*, *Mḗdeia*, *Oidípous*, *Oinómaos*, *Phoínix*), but also those of other ancient tragedians (*Mysoí*/'The Mysians', *Prókris*). To what extent E. parodied Euripides is not evident from the few fragments [1 on fr. 6,2].

Occasionally, lyrical verse sequences are preserved that may have been sung by a chorus (fr. 102f. 137), and some fragments have roughly aeschrological traits of the Old Comedy (fr. 10. 52. 61. 118. 140); some traits point towards the New Comedy: some titles indicate important roles for slaves (*Ankylíōn*, *Kampylíōn*, *Sphingokaríōn*, *Parmeniskos*), others for prostitutes (*Klepsýdra*, *Nánnion*, *Neottís*, *Plangṓn*), others could easily be imagined in the repertoire of authors of the New Comedy (*Anasōzómenoi*, *Pámphilos*, *Pannychís*, *Psáltria*, *Títthai*/*Títthē*), and fr. 69 strongly indicates a recognition motif. Apart from outspoken slaves (42. 119. 123), speak parasites (72), cooks (14. 75) and pimps (67; cf. *Pornoboskós*). In several fragments E. is explicitly attested as a writer of the Middle Comedy, only the Suda calls him a 'borderline case between the Old and the Middle Comedy', which perhaps indicates the coexistence of heterogeneous elements [3. 60f.].

1 PCG V, 1986, 188–273 2 R.L. HUNTER, Eubulus, The Fragments, 1983 3 H.-G. NESSELRATH, Die att. Mittlere Komödie, 1990. H.-G.NE.

Eucharides Painter Attic vase painter, active *c.* 495–475 BC, named after a → *kalos*-inscription on an early stamnos in Copenhagen. The majority of his works are red-figured but like his teacher, the Nikoxenos Painter, he also worked in the black-figured technique, e.g., on some Panathenaic prize amphorae. His red-figure images decorate large craters and amphorae but also lekythoi and bowls, the latter generally only being painted on the inside. Early stamnoi establish a link to the Tyszkiewicz Painter and there are indications that he worked in the same workshop as the painters in the succession of Syleus (→ Syleus Painter). His characteristic style is coarse and angular, being pervaded by archaic strength. Apart from genre and Dionysian scenes, he painted rarer mythological themes: Danae and Perseus, Heracles and Eurytus, Apollo and Tityus, the death of Argus and Actaeon.

BEAZLEY, ABV, 395–398; BEAZLEY, ARV², 226–232, 1637, 1705; J.D. BEAZLEY, The Master of the Eucharides-Stamnos in Copenhagen, in: ABSA 18, 1911–1912, 217–233; E. LANGRIDGE, The Eucharides Painter and his Place in the Athenian Potters' Quarter, 1993. M.P.

Eucheir (called E. II). A sculptor in Athens, the son of → Eubulides [4], called Eubulides II. Together with his son → Eubulides [5], also called Eubulides III, he signed honorary statues and votives in Attica, Euboea and Megara during the 1st half of the 2nd cent. BC. His Hermes in Phenea, which Pausanias described, is perhaps depicted on coins.

G. BECATTI, Attika, in: RIA 7, 1940, 14–17; H. BRUNN, Gesch. der griech. Künstler, 1, 1857, 551–552; LOEWY, 134, 135, 222–227; P. MORENO, Scultura ellenistica, 1994521, 554 R.N.

Eucheria *Versus Eucheriae poetriae* ('Verses of the poetess E.') is the title of an → epigram in 16 elegiac distichs in the Cod. Paris. Lat. 8071 (Thuaneus; 9th cent.); this text is found, sometimes incomplete and without title, in other codices of the 9th–12th cents. It is a catalogue of monstrous associations of 'noble' and 'base' objects; the meaning of these associations is clarified in the concluding distichon, which speaks of the absurdity of a man of low birth being a suitor of E. It is conceivable that the name was secondarily interpreted as the poetess' name. The text was probably written about the 5th cent. AD because the masculine form of the name, Eucherius, is well attested in this period (PLRE 1,288; 2,404–406). It was probably written in southern Gaul because the Gallic word for owl, *cavannus* (V. 29), occurs. However, *lingonicum aes* (V. 9) appears to derive from Mart. 1,53,3 (formally also the reference text). A secure *terminus ante quem* is offered by the quote of v. 31 in the grammar of → Iulianus of Toledo (2nd half of the 7th cent.).

Anth. Lat. 390 (386 SHACKLETON-BAILEY) M. MARCOVICH, A. GEORGIADOU, E.'s Adynata, in: Illinois Classical Studies 13, 1988, 165–174. K.SM.

Eucherius

[1] Flavius E. was an uncle of emperor Theodosius I (Them. Or. 16,203d). He is possibly identical with the *comes sacrarum largitionum* of AD 377–379 (Cod. Theod. 1,32,3; 10,20,9). In 381 he was consul (Them. ibid.). He was still alive in 395 (Zos. 5,2,3). PLRE 1, 288 E. (2). W.P.

[2] Flavius E., the son of → Stilicho and Serena, born AD 389 in Rome. He first lived in Constantinople, then at the court of → Honorius, where he became *tribunus et notarius*. In 400 he became engaged with → Galla [3] Placidia, the daughter of Theodosius I. In the course of the anti-Germanic riots after the death of → Arcadius in 408, Stilicho was suspected of wanting to elevate his son as the Augustus of the East and was murdered. E. fled to Rome where he sought refuge in a church but was soon killed. PLRE 2, 404f. H.L.

[3] As a monk of the island monastery of Lérins off the south coast of France he wrote two didactic letters (*De laude eremi* [2] and *De contemptu mundi* [3]) as well as two exegetic works (*Formulae spiritalis intellegentiae* and *Instructiones*) [4]. As bishop of Lyon (434–450) he wrote the *Passio Acaunensium martyrum* [1] (i.e., the martyrology of the soldiers of the Theban Legion). The *Passio* [5. 261–265], which is filled with rhetorical figures and motifs (*situs loci*, c. 5; *laudatio* c. 11) and was written observing the rules for clausulae, centres on the declaration to the emperor, a work of 'Constantinian' imperial theology. No later than in 515 the *Passio* was read publicly each year on 22 September in St. Maurice (MGH AA 6/2, p.145).

EDITIONS: 1 B. KRUSCH, MGH Scriptores rer. Merov. 3, 1886, 32–41 2 S. PRICOCO, 1965 3 Id., 1990 4 C. WOTKE, CSEL 31, 1894 (complete edition).
BIBLIOGRAPHY: 5 W. BERSCHIN, Biographie und Epochenstil im lat. Mittelalter, 1, 1986. W.B.

Euclea (Εὔκλεια; *Eúkleia* = 'good reputation'). Cultic name of → Artemis (Soph. OT 159–161), but also a deity in her own right next to → Eunomia (Paus. 1,14,5; Bacchyl. 13,183–185SM; IG 3.1,277; 623; 733; 738). The relationship of Euclea and Artemis is difficult to define. Plut. Aristides 20,6–8,331e reports that E. was generally equated with Artemis (but according to others E. is the daughter of Hercules and Myrto). The cult of E. Artemis allegedly was particularly popular in Boeotia (sanctuary in Plataeae) and Locris. A sanctuary of E. Artemis is also attested for Thebes (Paus. 9,17,1–2). Plutarch is the only source for her being worshipped in Locris. According to [1], E. is an epithet of Artemis that took on a life of its own, but according to [2] E. was originally an independent deity who was later identified with Artemis. An E. festival (Εὔκλεια; *Eúkleia*) was held in Corinth (Xen. Hell. 4,4,2) and Delphi (Syll.[2] 438, 64) [3]. Regarding the iconography cf. [4; 5; 6].

1 NILSSON, GGR 493–494 2 R. HAMPE, Eukleia u. Eunomia, in: MDAI(R) 62, 1955, 107–123 3 NILSSON, Feste 237–238 4 A. KOSSATZ-DEISSMANN, s.v. Eukleia, LIMC 4.1, 48–51 5 L. KAHIL, s.v. Artemis, LIMC 2.1, 677 No. 729 6 H. A. SHAPIRO, Personifications in Greek Art, 1993, 70–78.

D. C. BRAUND, Artemis Eukleia and Eur. Hipp., in: JHS 100, 1980, 184–185; SCHACHTER 1, 102–106. R.B.

Eucles (Εὐκλῆς; *Euklês*). Son of a Dionysius, successor of Zeno as head of the δωρέα (*dōréa*) of Apollonius near Philadelphia in 248 BC until its dissolution in 243.

C. ORRIEUX, Les archives d'Euclès et la fin de la dôréa du dioecète Apollonios, in: CE 55, 1980, 229–239. W.A.

Euclidas (Εὐκλείδας; *Eukleídas*; Paus. 2,9,1; 3: Epicleidas).

[1] Spartan king *c.* 227–222 BC, son of Leonidas II, Agiad. His brother Cleomenes III elevated him as king after the murder of the Eurypontid Archidamus III to formally preserve the double monarchy. Tradition attributes the Spartan catastrophe against Antigonus [3] Doson (222) at Sellasia to his tactical incompetence. E. was killed in this battle (Plut. Cleom. 11,5; 28,3; 6f.; Phil. 6; Paus. 2,9,1; 3; Pol. 2,65–68). M.MEI.

[2] Syracusan die cutter, who signed tetradrachms, small silver nominals and bronzes around 410–400 BC and now and then to about 385, occasionally also alternating with → Eumenus and → Evaenetus. His style is very fine and he is considered the originator of 'en face' cut obverse portraiture.

→ Evaenetus; → Eumenus; → Tetradrachmon

R. WEIL, Die Künstlerinschr. der sicilischen Münzen, in: 44. Winckelmannsprogramm der Arch. Ges. zu Berlin, 1884, 17–18; L. FORRER, Biographical dictionary of medallists 2, s.v. Eukleidas, 1904, 30–35; L. TUDEER, Die Tetradrachmenprägung von Syrakus in der Periode der signierenden Künstler, in: ZfN 30, 1913, 1–292, esp. 220ff.; H. A. CAHN et al., Griech. Münzen aus Großgriechenland und Sizilien, Basle, AM Ludwig collection, 1988, 130ff. A.M.

Euclides (Εὐκλείδης; *Eukleídēs*).

[1] Athenian archon in 403/2 BC. During his year in office Athens made a new start following the Oligarchy

of the Thirty (e.g., see And. 1,87–94) and, among others, officially adopted the Ionian alphabet (Theopomp. FGrH 115 F 155).

DEVELIN 199; LGPN 2, Εὐκλείδης (9). P.J.R.

[2] **of Megara.** Student of Socrates, founder of the → Megarian School; born between 450 and 435, probably died early in the 360s. In Plato's *Phaedon* (59c) E. is named among those present at the death of Socrates. It is also credibly attested that Plato and some unnamed Socratics retreated to his house at Megara after the death of Socrates (Diog. Laert. 2,106; 3,6). However, the reasons for, and immediate circumstances of, this retreat are uncertain. E. composed six dialogues with the titles *Lamprías*, *Aischínēs*, *Phoínix*, *Krítōn*, *Alkibiádēs* and *Erōtikós*.

A tradition that is most clearly evident in Cic. Acad. 2,129 claims E. taught that 'good is only that which was one and the same and always remained the same', and, therefore, classified him in the succession of the → Eleatic School. As K.v. FRITZ [1] has demonstrated, this tradition is an ahistorical construct. Only the review of the key thoughts of E.'s philosophy by Diog. Laert. 2,106 is reliable: E. 'was of the opinion that good is one but given many names; sometimes it is called insight (φρόνησις/*phrónēsis*), sometimes god, sometimes reason (νοῦς/*noûs*) etc. However, he cancelled the opposite of good by denying its existence '. This review clearly demonstrates that E. closely adhered to his teacher → Socrates in his philosophy: the three theses of his work, first, that good is one, second, that insight and reason are only alternative names for good, and third, that the opposite of good does not exist (which apparently must be understood to mean that evil is only mistaking good), unmistakably pick up the three basic convictions of Socrates, first, that what one should strive for is good in various manifestations as just, pious, etc., second, that whoever knows good will do it of necessity, and third, that whoever does evil, only does it, because they are mistaken and erroneously consider bad for something good.

Other knowledge of E.'s philosophical views relates to logic. Diog. Laert. 2,107 relates that E. 'did not attack proofs at their premises but at their concluding sentence'; also, that he rejected the analogy procedure that Socrates preferred as an unfit means of argumentation.

1 K. v. FRITZ, s.v. Megariker, RE Suppl. 5, 707–724, esp.: 707–716 (shortened version in: Id., Schriften zur griech. Logik, 1978, vol. 2, 75–92, esp.: 75–64).

EDITIONS: K. DÖRING, Die Megariker. Kommentierte Sammlung der Testimonien, 1972, I 1.; SSR II A.
BIBLIOGRAPHY: K. DÖRING, Eukleides, in: GGPh² 2.1, § 17 A (with bibliography); GUTHRIE III, 1969, 499–507. K.D.

[3] **(Euclid)**
A. LIFE B. WORKS C. LATER RECEPTION D. THE 'SECTIO CANONIS'

A. LIFE

Little is known for certain about the life of E. According to comments in → Proclus (in Euc. 1, p. 68,6–20 FRIEDLEIN) and → Pappus, he was younger than the scholars around Plato and his immediate students whose research he used and older than → Archimedes [1] (*c.* 287–212) who assumes E.'s theorems to be known This makes scholars assume his main period of activity to about 300 BC (regarding this issue cf., e.g., [15. 414f.]). He worked and taught in Alexandria (Pappus 7,35, p. 678,10–12 HULTSCH). Already in late antiquity and throughout the Middle Ages he was confused with the philosopher → E. [2] of Megara.

B. WORKS

The largest and most important work, which made E. the 'mathematics teacher of all nations and generations', is the 'Elements' (Στοιχεῖα; *Stoicheîa*) in 13 bks. Large parts of it are based on other mathematicians, e.g., the Pythagoreans, → Theaetetus and → Eudoxus [1] [13; 20; 25; 26; 29]. E.'s significance is to have summarized the knowledge of his predecessors and arranged it in a systematic order. The 'elements' of his teaching structure are (unprovable) definitions (ὅροι, *hóroi*), postulates (αἰτήματα, *aitḗmata*) and axioms (κοιναὶ ἔννοιαι, *koinaì énnoiai*). Based on them, E. derives theorems (θεωρήματα, *theōrḗmata*) and construction problems (προβλήματα, *problḗmata*), which he proves by strictly deductive methods. For this purpose, he uses a consistent scheme throughout the work. Proven sentences and solutions are used for other proofs with the sentences on which the proof rests being presumed as givens without specific reference.

The 'Elements' may be subdivided into planimetric (bks 1–6), arithmetic (bks 7–9) and stereometric (bks 11–13) books. Bk. 1 treats plane geometry up to the theorem of → Pythagoras (1,47), bk. 2 'geometrical algebra', bks 3–4 elementary circles with in- and circumscribed polygons. Bk. 5 contains the theory of proportions founded by Eudoxus, which may also be applicable to irrational dimensions, and book 6 its applications. Bks 7–9 present the theory of natural numbers, which derives from the Pythagoreans, including the proof that there is an infinite number of primary numbers (9,20), and the postulate on generating perfect numbers (9,36). Bk. 10, which is particularly voluminous, is a special treatise on different types of irrationality, which may arise as solutions to squared equations. Bk. 11 treats elementary postulates of stereometry while bk. 12 discusses volume determinations according to Eudoxos. Bk 13, which is based on Theaetetus (like bk. 10), teaches the relationships between a sphere and the regular polyhedrons it can incorporate and, as the climax of the entire work, proves that there are only five such bodies. Bk. 14 was added by → Hypsicles, and bk. 15 in the 6th cent. AD.

Lesser writings preserved in Greek:

1) The *Data* (Δεδομένα; *Dedoména*, Ed. [1. vol. 6], German trans.[6]) amends the first books of the 'Elements' and examines which parts of a figure are predetermined if others parts are given. Particularly interesting are the problems that deal with plane geometry. With their help the Greeks were able to solve square equations geometrically.

2) The 'Optics' ('Οπτικά, *Optiká*, Ed. [1. vol. 7], French translation [7]; cf. also [21]) are the earliest Greek treatise in which the laws of geometric perspective were deduced. It consists of 58 propositions.

3) The *Phainómena* (Φαινόμενα, Ed. [1. vol. 8], English translation [10]) treats those elements of spherical geometry that are required for spherical astronomy. The *Phainómena* closely adheres to the sphaerics of → Autolycus [3] and in turn supplied → Theodosius' writings with materials.

4) The *Sectio canonis* (Κατατομὴ κανόνος; *Katatomḕ kanónos* [1. vol. 8]) represents the foundation of mathematical music theory using proportionality theory in the manner of the Pythagoreans (cf. D.).

5) A treatise on mirrors (Κατοπτρικά, *Katoptriká*) attributed to E. is considered to be a later compilation [21].

The following works of E. are lost or, in any case, not preserved in Greek:

6) The treatise *Perì diairéseōn* (Περὶ διαιρέσεων) treats the division of geometric figures by means of lines into sections that satisfy predetermined conditions. The text is lost but all 36 postulates and four complete proofs exist in an Arabic translation [30. 233–247; 8; 28. 118].

7) The three books of *Porísmata* (Πορίσματα) are mentioned in Pappus (7, p. 648–660 HULTSCH) and Proclus (In Euc. 1, p. 212,12f., 301,21ff. FRIEDLEIN). Even in antiquity there was no clarity regarding the meaning of the term *pórisma*. Presumably, the treatise contained characterizations of lines and circles as geometric loci, with the aid of which complex geometric construction problems could be solved.

8) The 'Surface Loci' (Τόποι πρὸς ἐπιφανείᾳ, *Tópoi pròs epiphaneía*) treated surfaces in space, probably the surfaces of rotating bodies, as geometric loci.

9) In the *Pseudária* (Ψευδάρια), E. described different types of false conclusions in mathematics and juxtaposed them with valid conclusions.

10) The four bks of the *Kōniká* (Κωνικά) contained a study of conical sections that was probably based on the (also lost) work of → Aristaeus [2]. Their content was probably similar to the first three bks of → Apollonius' *Kōniká* [13].

11) E. presumably also wrote treatises on mechanics. There are medieval Latin texts with titles such as *De levi et ponderoso* or *De gravi et levi*, *De canonio* or *De ponderibus*, some of which were translated from Arabic and which may derive from E. [28. 120; 16. 24–30; 22].

C. LATER RECEPTION

Already in antiquity there were commentaries on E.'s main work, the 'Elements', specifically by → Heron, Pappus, Proclus and → Simplicius. The manuscripts of the 'Elements' are almost all derived from the revision made by → Theon of Alexandria (4th cent. AD). Only Vaticanus Graecus 190 (10th cent.) as well as some papyrus fragments [2] and Arabic testimonials are based on older traditions. The translation by Boethius was created about 500 but has only been preserved in fragments in several texts. Apart from several translations (especially in the 9th cent. by al-Ḥaǧǧāǧ and Isḥāq b. Ḥunain), innumerable excerpts, reworkings and commentaries (of which the version of aṭ-Ṭūsī (13th cent.) was the most common) existed in the Arabic countries. Apart from Arabic there were translations into Persian, Hebrew, Syriac and Armenian. During the 12th cent. the 'Elements' were translated three times from Arabic into Latin. (Adelhard of Bath, Hermann of Carinthia, Gerard of Cremona). However, two rewritings were more important: the so-called version II, probably by Robert of Chester (about 1140) and the edition of Campanus (before 1260; printed in 1482 and repeatedly later), which is based on it. In the 16th cent., Latin editions (B. Zamberti, F. Commandino) predominated even after the publication of the Greek *editio princeps* (1533). The earliest printed vernacular editions were produced by N. Tartaglia (1543), J. Scheubel (1555), W. Holtzmann (1562), P. Forcadel (1564) and H. Billingsley (1570). Heiberg [1] compiled the definitive Greek edition.

The most interesting parts of E.'s 'Elements' throughout the ages were the 5th postulate ('parallels postulate'), the theory of proportionality in vol. 5 and the representation of irrationalities in vol. 10. Attempts to prove the parallels postulate led in antiquity, the Middle Ages and the early modern periods to the finding of sentences that were equivalent to the 5th postulate and finally in the early 19th cent. to the insight that mathematically consistent geometries are possible that do without the parallels postulate ('non-Euclidian geometry'). Regarding the history of transmission of the 'Elements' see especially [17; 18; 24; 28] and the bibliography [12].

→ Rationality; → Mechanics; → Physics; → Proportion; → Pythagorean School

EDITIONS AND TRANSLATIONS: 1 I.L. HEIBERG, H. MENGE (ed.), Euclidis opera omnia, 8 vols., 1883–1916 (with Latin trans.; republished by E.S. STAMATIS, 1969–1977) 2 E. TURNER et al., Euclid, Elements 1, Definitions 1–10 (P. Mich. III 143), in: YClS 28, 1985, 13–24 3 TH. L. HEATH, The thirteen books of Euclid's Elements, 3 vols., ²1925 (reprint 1956; free Engl. translation with commentary and introduction) 4 C. THAER, Euklid. Die Elemente, 1933–1937 (reprinted since 1962) 5 M. CAVEING, B. VITRAC, Les éléments. Traduits du texte de Heiberg, 1990–1994 (so far 2 vols.) 6 C. THAER, Die Data von Euklid, 1962 7 P. VER EECKE (ed.), Euclide, L'Optique et la Catoptrique, 1938 (French trans.) 8 R.C. ARCHIBALD, Euclid's Book on Divisions of Figures, 1915

9 A. BARBERA, The Euclidean Division of the Canon: Greek and Latin sources. New critical texts and translations, 1991 10 J.L. BERGGREN, R.S.D. THOMAS, Euclid's Phaenomena: A translation and study of a Hellenistic treatise in spherical astronomy, 1996.
BIBLIOGRAPHIES: 11 P. RICCARDI, Saggio di una Bibliografia Euclidea, 1887–1893 (reprint 1974) 12 M. STECK, M. FOLKERTS, Bibliographia Euclideana, 1981.
BIBLIOGRAPHY: 13 B. ARTMANN, Euclid's Elements and its Prehistory, Apeiron 24(4), 1991, 1–47 14 F. BECKMANN, Neue Gesichtspunkte zum 5. Buch Euklids, Archive for History of Exact Sciences 4, 1967/8, 1–144 15 I. BULMER-THOMAS, s.v. Euclid, Dictionary of Scientific Biography 4, 1971, 414–437 16 M. CLAGETT, The Science of Mechanics in the Middle Ages, 1959 17 M. FOLKERTS, Probleme der Euklidinterpretation und ihre Bedeutung für die Entwicklung der Mathematik, in: Centaurus 23, 1980, 185–215 18 M. FOLKERTS, Euclid in Medieval Europe, 1989 19 D.H. FOWLER, An invitation to read Book X of Euclid's Elements, in: Hist. Math. 19, 1992, 233–264 20 W.R. KNORR, The Evolution of the Euclidean Elements, 1975 21 A. LEJEUNE, Euclide et Ptolémée. Deux stades de l'optique géométrique grecque, 1948 22 E.A. MOODY, M. CLAGETT, The medieval science of weights, 1952 23 I. MUELLER, Philosophy of mathematics and deductive structure in Euclid's Elements, 1981 24 J. MURDOCH, Euclid: Transmission of the Elements, Dictionary of Scientific Biography 4, 1971, 437–459 25 E. NEUENSCHWANDER, Die ersten vier Bücher der Elemente Euklids. Unt. über den mathematischen Aufbau, die Zitierweise und die Entstehungsgesch., in: Archive for History of Exact Sciences 9, 1973, 325–380 26 Id., Die stereometrischen Bücher der Elemente Euklids. Unt. über den mathematischen Aufbau und die Entstehungsgesch., in: Archive for History of Exact Sciences 14, 1975, 91–125 27 P. SCHREIBER, Euklid, 1987 28 F. SEZGIN, Gesch. des arabischen Schrifttums, 5, 1974, 83–120 29 A. SZABÓ, Anfänge der griech. Mathematik, 1969 30 F. WOEPCKE, Notice sur des traductions arabes de deux ouvrages perdus d'Euclide, in: Journal Asiatique 4, ser. 18, 1851, 217–247. M.F.

D. THE 'SECTIO CANONIS'

The *Sectio canonis* (Κατατομὴ κανόνος; *Katatomḕ kanónos*) is an important mathematical-harmonic treatise (primary) in the Pythagorean tradition (probably about 300 BC), which has been attributed to E. since antiquity (in manuscripts erroneously also to → Cleonides) but the author is disputed [6. 14–22]. Contents: a) introduction to acoustics (differences in pitch are defined in quantitative terms more or less by motion or air bursts). b) Analysis of intervals (*diastḗmata*) composed according to number theory ('multiple', 'superparticular'), presented in the style of E.'s *Elementa* in eleven propositions and proofs. c) Problems of interval composition (12–18). d) Two canon divisions for determining the 'immutable' system and supplementary sound scales (19–20). The treatise, which may depend on a lost work on music by E. (cf. Procl. in Euc. 69), is also preserved in two other versions, with the introduction and §§ 17ff. [9] missing in Porphyry and §§ 10ff. in Boethius (*De institutione musica* 4,1f.).

EDITIONS.: 1 MSG, 115–166 2 I.L. HEIBERG, H. MENGE (ed.), Euclidis opera omnia, vol. 8, 1916, 158–183 (with Latin translation) 3 TH.J. MATHIESEN, An annotated translation of E.'s Division of a monochord, in: Journal of Music Theory 19, 1975, 236–258 4 A. BARKER, The Euclidean Sectio canonis, in: Greek Musical Writings, II, 1989, 190–208 (English translation and commentary) 5 L. ZANONCELLI, La manualistica musicale greca, 1990, 31–70 (with Italian translation and commentary) 6 A. BARBERA, The Euclidean Division of the Canon, 1991 (Edn. of all versions with an English translation and commentary).
BIBLIOGRAPHY: 7 A. BARKER, Methods and aims in the Euclidean Sectio canonis, in: JHS 101, 1981, 1–16 8 W. BURKERT, Weisheit und Wissenschaft, 1962, 421–423 9 I. DÜRING, Komm. zur Harmonielehre des Klaudios Ptolemaios, 1932, 90, 92,29–93,2 10 F.R. LEVIN, Unity in E.' Sectio canonis, in: Hermes 118, 1990, 430–443 11 E. PÖHLMANN, Musiktheorie in späten Sammelhss., in: A. BIERL, P.v. MÖLLENDORFF (ed.), FS H. Flashar, 1994, 182–194, especially 191–193 12 B.L. VAN DER WAERDEN, Die Pythagoreer, 1979, 378f., 382f., 405–411. F.Z.

[4] Aristot. Poet. 1458b7ff. quotes two metrically anomalous hexameters (fr. 1–2 WEST) by a E. (Εὐκλείδης ὁ ἀρχαῖος; *Eukleídēs ho archaîos*) to mock the tendency of some poets towards arbitrary prosodic lengthening. Identification with E. [1], the archon of 403 BC[1], or E. [2] of Megara [2] is very doubtful; WILAMOWITZ [3] assumes that it is the bibliophile mentioned in Ath. 1,3a. [5] suspects a comedian (thus already in [4]) or a iambographer.

1 I. BYWATER, Aristoteles on the Art of Poetry, 1909, 297 2 A. GUDEMAN, Aristoteles' Περὶ ποιητικῆς, 1934, 375f. 3 U.v. WILAMOWITZ, KS 4, 1962, 366 4 A. ROSTAGNI, Aristotele. Poetica, [2]1945, 134 5 M.L. WEST, IEG II[2] 63. M.D.MA.

[5] Sculptor from Athens. He created several images of deities in the Peloponnese. Pausanias saw marble statues he made of Demeter, Aphrodite, Dionysus and Eileithyia in Bura. The head and arm are preserved of his acrolithic cult figure of Zeus in Aegira, which is attested by Pausanias as well as on coins. The dating (early 4th to 2nd cents. BC) is based on stylistic criteria and disputed, but classicistic tendencies rather point to the 2nd cent. BC. Therefore, E. must be unrelated to the stone-mason mentioned in the testament of Plato.

G. BECATTI, Attika, in: RIA 7, 1940, 25–28; OVERBECK, No. 1147–1148 (sources); R.R.R. SMITH, Hellenistic sculpture, 1991, 240, fig.; R. TRUMMER, Zwei Kolossalköpfe aus Aigeira, in: AntPl 22, 1993, 141–155. R.N.

Eucrates (Εὐκράτης; *Eukrátēs*).
[1] Athenian *strategos* in 432/1 BC (IG I[3] 365.5), participated in a campaign to Macedonia. W.W.
[2] *Choregos* and *strategos* in Athens. The brother of → Nicias. In 415 BC accused of the mutilation of the Herms but released (And. 1,47; 66). In 412/1 in Thrace as *strategos*. In 405/4 again *strategos*, he resisted to-

gether with other generals the peace terms negotiated by Theramenes during the blockade of Athens and, therefore, was executed by the Thirty (Lys. 13,13–38; 18,4–8). His oldest son attempted to avoid the confiscation of his wealth in a court case of 403 (Lys. 18).

W.S.

Eucratides (Εὐκρατίδης; *Eukratídēs*). The son of Heliocles and Laodice, overthrew Demetrius I of Bactria and India about 170 BC on behalf of his cousin Antiochus IV and made himself 'great king'. About 150 (?) E. was murdered by his son. Soon after E.'s death the Bactrian kingdom came to an end due to external attacks (HN 838f.; Str. 11,9,2, 11,11,2; 15,1,3; Iust. 41,6,1–5

The Cambridge History of Iran 3, 1984; A.N. LAHIRI, Corpus of Indo-Greek Coins, 1965; A.K. NARAIN, The Indo-Greeks, 1957; W.W. TARN, The Greeks in Bactria and India, ²1951; WILL; G.WOODCOCK, The Greeks in India, 1966.

A.ME.

Euctemon from Athens. Astronomer, meteorologist and geographer, is named together with → Meton as the discoverer of the 19-year lunisolar cycle. Together they observed, in the last third of the 5th cent. BC, solstices and equinoxes, the anomaly of solar movements and the length of the solar year, also the rising and setting of the planets 'in Athens, on the Cyclades, in Macedonia and in Thrace' (Ptol. Phaseis p. 67,6 HEIBERG, cf. Anon. a. 379 CCAG V 1 [1904] p. 205,6 ἐν Ἀθήναις (*en Athḗnais*) and Avienus Ora maritima 350 *Atheniensis* or 337 *Amphipolis urbis incola*). In Athens E. observed the solstice of 432 (Ptol. Syntaxis 3,1 p. 205,21) and probably participated in the reform of the Attic calendar. His meteorology is dated by A.REHM [4. 140] after the beginning of the Sicilian expedition in 415. His → parapegma (calendar with weather information) notes the *pháseis* in greater detail than that of Meteon, i.e., the heliacal and acronycal rising and setting of the fixed stars as well as *episēmasíai*, i.e., the regular change in the weather on certain days, which is more localized than the phases. He was the first in Greece to use the zodiac as the reference timetable (→ Ecliptic). To an extent recognizable, his geography is, among other, concerned with the western Mediterranean even though direct observation is unlikely.

His *episēmasía* and astronomical observations were used especially by Pseudo-Theophrastus *De signis* [4. 122–140], Valens, Ptolemy in the *Phaseis* and Iohannes Lydus, his geography by Avienus.

EDITIONS: A.REHM, Das Parapegma des E., 1913, 14–27.
BIBLIOGRAPHY: 1 H.BERGER, Gesch. der wiss. Erdkunde der Griechen, ²1903, 240–242 2 A.REHM, s.v. Euktemon 10), RE IV 1, 1060f. 3 Id., RE Suppl. 7, 175–198 4 Id., Parapegmastudien, 1941 5 W.GUNDEL, H.G. GUNDEL, Astrologumena, 1966 6 B.L. VAN DER WAERDEN, Die Astronomie der Griechen, 1988, 79–82.

W.H.

Eudaemon (Εὐδαίμων; *Eudaímōn*). Correspondent of → Libanius (Ep. 167; 255; 633) and his 'fraternal' friend for over thirty years (cf. Ep. 108; 132; 164; 315; 632; 826; 1057), from Pelusium in Egypt, born before AD 337 (probably *c.* 314/24: [2. 279]), died before AD 392. According to the Suda (ε 3407) a 'grammarian' (but he may also have taught rhetoric), author of a Τέχνη γραμματική/*Téchnē grammatikḗ* ('Grammar') and an Ὀνοματικὴ ὀρθογραφία/*Onomatikḕ orthographía* ('Orthography of Names') (cf. Lib. Ep. 255,7, regarding E.'s opinion on the vocative of Ἡρακλῆς/*Heraklês*), which was used by Stephanus of Byzantium and in the Etymologica [1]; also a poet and lawyer in Elusa (in 357), where he was in the pay of the emperor, likewise in Antioch and Constantinople. Not to be confused with the younger E., a rhetoric teacher, who also belonged to the circle of Libanius [2. 400–403; 3. 121–132].

1 L.COHN, s.v. Eudaimon (8), RE VI 1, 885 2 R.A. KASTER, Guardians of Language, 1988, 113, 154, 211, 230, 279–282 3 O.SEECK, Die Briefe des Libanius, 1906, 131 4 Libanios, Briefe, ed. by G.FATOUROS, T.KRISCHER, 1980, 274.

S.FO.

Eudamidas (Εὐδαμίδας; *Eudamídas*).

[1] Spartan, the brother of Phoebidas. E. was supposed to lead a campaign in 382 BC together with Amyntas of Macedonia against Olynthus, but was defeated because of his weak forces and probably killed (Xen. Hell. 5,2,24f.; Diod. Sic. 15,20f.; Dem. Or. 19,264). Maybe he is identical with the early 4th-cent. ephor mentioned in IG V 1, 1232.

[2] E. I, Spartan king, Eurypontid, the son of Archidamus III, since 331 or 330 successor of his brother Agis III (Plut. Agis 3,3). E. supposedly supported a more peaceful policy, especially towards Macedonia, despite the resistance of large parts of the *damos* (Paus. 3,10,5). He died before 294.

[3] E. II, Spartan king, grandson of the above, the son of Archidamus IV, father of the reform king Agis IV, who succeeded him in 244 (Plut. Agis 3,3).

M.MEI.

Eudamus (Εὔδαμος; *Eúdamos*).

[1] Macedonian general (*dux Thracium* in Curt. 10,1,21), appointed in 323 BC by Alexander [4] the Great as military commander together with Taxiles (Arr. Anab. 6,27,2). He slew Porus and took 120 elephants west when he followed the call of Eumenes [1] together with other eastern satraps in 317 BC (Diod. Sic. 19,14). He fought under Eumenes and was killed together with him by Antigonus [1] (Diod. Sic. 19,27–44). According to BERNARD, the so-called Porus coins perhaps go back to him as the 'elephant general' [1].

1 P.BERNARD, Le monnayage d'Eudamos, in: Orientalia Iosephi Tucci memoriae dicata (Serie Orientale Roma 56,1), 1985, 65–94.

K.K.

[2] Rhodian, together with → Pamphilidas in 190 BC the successor of the nauarch → Pausistratus against

Antiochus III (Syll.[3] 673; Liv. 37,12,9; cf. App. Syr. 27/133 'Eudoros'), was inclined towards peace negotiations in Eleia (Pol. 21,10,5) [1. 133] and victorious at Side and Myonesus (Liv. 37,22,3–4; 23,8–24,11; 29,6.9) [1. 80]. E. advised the Romans to take Patara (Liv. 37,24,13).

[3] Rhodian nauarch, left Tenedus to a Macedonian fleet in 168 BC (Liv. 44,28,3) [1. 142].

1 H.H. Schmitt, Rom und Rhodos, 1957. L.-M.G.

Eudemus (Εὔδημος; *Eúdemos*).

[1] Sculptor in Miletus. He signed a male seated statue of the 1st half of the 6th cent. BC, one of the earliest → Branchidae of Didyma.

Fuchs/Floren, 373–375; Loewy, No. 3; K. Tuchelt, Die archaischen Skulpturen von Didyma, 1970, 77–78, 121. R.N.

[2] **of Cyprus.** A friend of → Aristotle of about the same age, participated, as a follower of Dion [I 1], in the overthrow of Dionysius II and was killed in the fighting that followed Dion's death, probably in 353 BC. Aristotle dedicated the dialogue Εὔδημος ἢ περὶ ψυχῆς ('Eudemus or About the Soul') to him, in which, starting from a dream of E., the immortality of the soul was proved developing the ideas of Plato's *Phaedon* (fr.37–48 Rose[3], 56–66 Gigon). We know nothing of E.'s own philosophical interests, but he was probably a member of the → Academy for some time.

W.W. Jaeger, Aristoteles, 1923, 37ff.; W. Spoerri, Prosopographica, in: MH 23, 1966, 44ff. H.G.

[3] **of Rhodes** Student of Aristotle, born before 350 BC.
A. Life B. Writings C. Tradition

A. Life

After the death of his teacher, E. founded a school in his native town but maintained a scientific correspondence with → Theophrastus in Athens. Besides Theophrastus, he was the only one to attempt to continue Aristotle's philosophy as a whole, but emphasized logic and natural philosophy. He must have lectured on ethics but no ethical fragments are preserved under his name, perhaps because in antiquity Aristotle's so-called 'Eudemian Ethics' was considered a work of E.

B. Writings

In logic the following are certain: the *Analytiká* (fr. 9–244) and *Perì léxeōs* ('On linguistic expression', fr. 25–9). In the Analytics E. is almost always mentioned together with Theophrastus and appears to have followed most of his innovations, for example, the introduction of five 'indirect' modi of the first syllogistic figure (fr.17) and the *in peiorem* rule for modal syllogisms (fr. 11) as well as the formation of the theory of hypothetical syllogisms (fr. 21–3). The assumption of [1. 125] that these innovations were still inspired by Aristotle is worth considering. E.'s *Perì léxeōs* was more independent because it was more oriented towards logic than the writings of the same name by Aristotle (Rh. 3 = 1425b–1426b) and Theophrastus, which both dealt with the stylistic aspects of language. A treatise on categories is incorrectly attributed to E. by later sources (fr. 7–8, cf. [2]), but the theory itself was taken for granted by him: the only fragment of his book *Perì gonías* ('On angles') contains proof that the term 'angle' belongs to the category of 'quality' (fr. 30).

The best-known is his 'Physics' (*Physiká*), in which he treats the same materials as Aristotle in bks 1–6 and 8 of his physics lectures. E. appears to be the first to unite the parts of this lecture into a single systematic treatment. The deviations in material from his teacher are few but the presentation, despite abridgements, is broader and more oriented towards the didactic representation than research. Only one comment by E. on metaphysics is preserved (fr. 124); reports that he was somehow involved in the editing of Aristotle's writings (fr. 3, cf. fr. 124) require clarification. Also, a number of animal tales, mainly relating to animal psychology (fr. 125–32), bear his name.

E.'s contributions to the history of science are significant: 'Research in Geometry' (Ἱστορίαι γεωμετρικαί; *Historíai geōmetrikaí*; fr. 133–41), 'Research in Arithmetic' (Ἀριθμητικαί; *Arithmētikaí*; fr. 142), 'Research in Astronomy' (Ἀστρολογικαί; Astrologikaí; fr. 143–149) and perhaps also a history of theology (fr. 150, without indicating the title). These works appear to have been of a purely historical and doxographical nature, i.e., the word ἱστορία (*historía*) had its modern meaning in this context – 'history'. Like Menon's Ἰατρικά (*Iatriká*; 'Medical Topics') and the 'teachings of the natural philosophers' (Φυσικῶν δόξαι; *Physikôn dóxai*) by Theophrastus, they belong into the framework of an attempt inspired by Aristotle to summarize the scientific results of interest to philosophy. Presumably they were already written during Aristotle's life time.

C. Tradition

After E., Rhodes produced several renowned Peripatetics, among them Pasicles (E.'s nephew and presumed author of bk. α of the Aristotelian Metaphysics), → Praxiphanes, → Hieronymus and → Andronicus [4]. This indicates a certain after-effect in E.'s home polis but probably his school did not survive his death. Otherwise, he was almost unknown in the Hellenistic period. Writers depending on Hellenistic sources, such as Cicero, Arius Didymus, Diogenes Laertius and Sextus Empiricus, never mention him. Only the commentators of the early Imperial period recognized his value in explaining and developing Aristotelian philosophy. Galen wrote a commentary on E.'s *Perì léxeōs* (*De libris propriis*, p. 42 and 47 K.]), while Alexander [26] of Aphrodisias, Themistius, Simplicius and Philoponus quote him regularly.

→ Aristotelianism

1 I.M. BOCHENSKI, La logique de Theophraste, 1947
2 H.B. GOTTSCHALK, Did Theophrastus write a 'Categories'?, in: Philologus 131, 1987, 245–253.

FRAGMENTS: WEHRLI, Schule, 8, ²1969; H.B. GOTTSCHALK, Addenda Peripatetica, in: Phronesis 18, 1973, 98.
BIBLIOGRAPHY: F.WEHRLI, RE Suppl. 11, 895–901; F.WEHRLI, GGPh² 3, 1983, 530ff; J.BODNÁR, W.FORTENBAUGH (ed.), Eudemos of Rhodes, 2002 H.G.

[4] Greek anatomist of the 3rd cent. BC (Gal. 18A,7), author of a treatise on anatomy. He studied glands in the abdominal cavity, especially parts of the pancreas (Gal. 4,646), and the nervous system. However, the attribution of a papyrus fragment (Pack² 2346) on nerves to him is by no means certain. He described the uterus in detail and discussed the blood vessel layout of the embryo (Sor. Gyn. 1,57). His teaching on bones was not without errors (Rufus Nom. part. 73), but on the whole reliable. He produced useful observations on the *processus styloideus* of the temporal bone, the small carpal and tarsus bones and the joints of hands and feet.
→ Medicine V.N.

[5] The author of 16 elegiac verses (= SH 412 A) on producing antidotes against poisonous animals, which was used by Antiochus [10] VIII of Syria (Θηριακὴ Ἀντιόχου τοῦ Φιλομήτορος; cf. Plin. HN 20,264). They were transmitted by Asclepiades Pharmakion and Heras ap. Galen. 14,185 and 201 KÜHN. The equation with the Methodist E. by [1] for apparently chronological reasons is problematic. However, he might be the otherwise unknown 'elder E.' (πρεσβύτερος; *presbýteros*), who is mentioned in Gal. 13,291,10; see [2].

1 M.WELLMANN, s.v. Eudemos (18), RE VI 1, 904f.
2 C.FABRICIUS, Galens Exzerpte aus älteren Pharmakologen, 1972, 245f. M.D.MA.

[6] Follower of the physician → Themison, early 1st cent. AD. As physician and alleged lover of Livia, the wife of Drusus the Younger, (Plin. HN 29,20), he became involved in the murder of Drusus in AD 23 (Tac. Ann. 4,3,11). His observations on rabies, which he considered the acute opposite of chronic melancholy, are referred to by Caelius Aurelianus (Acut. 3,11–16). E. described at least one case of rabies in a colleague and recommended bloodletting, hellebore and bleeding. For heart ailments he recommended an enema with cold water. Perhaps he is identical with E. [5], who as the author of a pharmacological book recorded a theriac recipe in verse by Antiochus [10] VIII of Syria, which incidentally could also be read as a stone inscription in the Asclepius temple of Cos (Gal. 14,185; 201; Plin. HN 20,264), but this is not certain ([1]).
→ Medicine

1 C.FABRICIUS, Galens Exzerpte aus älteren Pharmakologen, 1972, 245f. V.N.

[7] Peripatetic, born about AD 100, one of the first teachers and advisors of the physician Galen (Gal. De praenotatione ad Epigenem 2,14,605–13 KÜHN) when he still lived in Pergamum. Later he moved to Rome, where he had contact with an influential circle of high-ranking admirers of Aristotle. There Galen met him again during his first stay; he cured the 63-year old E. of a dangerous fever and as a result was introduced to his circle.

ZELLER, 3,1, 806 and 855; PIR³ s.v. 109 (not all passages quoted there refer to E.); R.B. TODD, Alexander of Aphrodisias on Stoic Physics, 1976, 4. H.G.

[8] Rhetor of an uncertain period from Argos, probably identical to the E. named by Ioannes Doxopatres in the Hermogenes scholia (6,384 WALZ). He composed an alphabetically arranged lexicon (λέξεων ῥητορικῶν συναγωγή; *léxeōn rhetorikôn synagōgḗ*), of which excerpts in different versions are preserved (Paris. gr. 2635; Vindob. gr. 132; Laur. 38,59) and that the Suda cites as its source.

EDITIONS: C.BOYSEN, 1891, in: K.LATTE, H.ERBSE, Lexica Graeca Minora, 1965, 12–38. M.W.

Eudocia (Εὐδοκία; *Eudokía*).
[1] **Aelia Eudocia.** Original name Athenais. Came from a traditional background in Athens (her father was the rhetor Leontius) and had an excellent education. Allegedly at the instigation of → Pulcheria, she married → Theodosius II on 7 June 421; she was baptized for this purpose and given the name Aelia E. She was considered pious and increasingly exerted an influence on her husband, pushing aside Pulcheria. In 422 she gave birth to → Eudoxia [2] and before 431 to Flaccilla. In 423 she became Augusta. In 438 she went on a pilgrimage to Jerusalem. In about 441 her confidant Cyrus (city prefect and consul in 441) was deprived of power and in this way she also lost her influence. Between 441 and 443 she went to Jerusalem where she lived an ascetic life and promoted the construction of churches and city walls until she died on 20 October 460. The extent to which her withdrawal was forced owing to differences with the advisers of Theodosius II or voluntary (the result of the piety of the empress) is a contentious matter. After the Council of Chalcedon in 451 she supported the Monophysites – who had been condemned there – until she turned to orthodoxy in 455 because of personal disappointments. E. wrote works of literature dealing with both secular and religious subjects [1].

In the Byzantine period a veritable E. novel appeared that centred particularly on her 'discovery' by Pulcheria and an alleged love affair with → Paulinus ('apple affair'); F.GREGOROVIUS depicted her life in literary form [2].

1 A.LUDWICH (ed.), 1897, cf. CPG 3, 6020–6025
2 F.GREGOROVIUS, Athenais, 1881.

PLRE 2, 408f.; A.A. CAMERON, The Empress and the Poet, in: YClS 27, 1982, 217–289, 270ff.; K.G. HOLUM, Theodosian Empresses, 1982, 112ff. H.L.

[2] Elder daughter of Licinia → Eudoxia [2] and the western Roman emperor Valentinianus III (Procop. Vand. 1,5,3; Evagrius, Historia ecclesiastica 2,7; Zon. 13,25,27), born in AD 438 or 439. In 455 she had to marry the emperor Palladius, son of the emperor Petronius Maximus (Hydatius Lemiensis 162) although she had been engaged to be married to Huneric – the son of the king of the Vandals, Geiseric (→ Geisericus) – since 442/3 (Merobaudes carm. 1,17f.). After the conquest of Rome in 455 by the Vandals, Geiseric took her with him to Africa, together with her mother and sister Placidia, where she married Huneric in 456 (Procop. Vand. 1,5,6). Hilderic (→ Hildericus) was born of this marriage and from 523 he was king of the Vandals (Zon. 13,25,29). After staying in Africa for 16 years she went to Jerusalem where she died shortly afterwards (471/2; Zon. ibid.).

A. Demandt, Die Spätantike, 1989, Index s.v. E.; PLRE 2, 407f. E. 1. M.MEI. and ME.STR.

Eudorus (Εὔδωρος; *Eúdōros*).

[1] One of the five leaders of the → Myrmidons under Achilles. A son of Hermes and → Polymele, he was brought up by his grandfather Phylas after Polymele later married the Actorid Echecles. His aptitude for fighting, being a fast runner, is strongly emphasized (Hom. Il. 16,179–186) but apart from this, the *Iliad* is silent on his fate. Eust. Od. 1697,56 reports of his death at the hands of Pyraechmes at the first clash with the Trojans (cf. also Eust. Od. 1053,54).

R. Janko, The Iliad. A Commentary, Vol. 4 (Bk. 13–16), 1992, 342–344; W. Kullmann, Die Quellen der Ilias, Hermes ES 14, 1960, 126; 132–133. R.B.

[2] **of Alexandria.** Platonic philosopher of the 1st cent. BC, he is considered the first representative of so-called → Middle Platonism. His varied interest in philosophy and science is reflected in numerous writings that continued to be influential right through to the time of → Simplicius (6th cent. AD). E. wrote a 'classification of the teachings of the philosophers', of which Stobaeus (2,42,7ff. Wachsmuth-Hense) preserved the section about ethics, and a commentary on Plato's *Timaeus* that is repeatedly cited by Plutarch [1. 48, 211]. It is uncertain whether the critical remarks on the Aristotelian theory of categories [1. 256] and the emendation of a spelling mistake in the 'Metaphysics' of Aristotle [2] originate from commentaries by E. on these works. A paper by E. on the Pythagorean theory of principles (Simpl. In phys. 121,10 Diels) demonstrates his great interest in this philosophy. E. also wrote a work about astronomy – perhaps a comm. on → Aratus [4] [1. 290[4]] – and a geographical work 'About the Nile' [1. 290]. E. was possibly the first to attribute to Plato the wording regarding the ultimate aim (*telos*) ὁμοίωσις θεῷ κατὰ τὸ δυνατόν ('to become like God so far as possible') and to have shown this in his dialogues [1. 382]. With regard to the question of the origin of the world in Plato's *Timaeus*, he was of the opinion that the world had neither come into being nor was it perishable.

1 Dörrie/Baltes III, 1993 2 P. Moraux, Eine Korrektur des Mittelplatonikers E. zum Text der Metaphysik des Aristoteles, in: Beiträge zur Alten Gesch. und deren Nachleben, FS F. Altheim, ed. by R. Stiehl and H. Stier, 1969, 492–504.

Fragments: C. Mazzarelli, in: RFN 77, 1985, 197–209, 535–555.
Bibliography: J. Dillon, The Middle Platonists, 1977, 115–135; H. Dörrie, Der Platoniker E. von Alexandrien, in: Hermes 79, 1944, 25–38 = Platonica minora 1976, 297–309; Moraux II, 1984, 509–527.
M.BA. and M.-L.L.

Eudoxia (Εὐδοξία; *Eudoxía*)

[1] Wife of Arcadius, Augusta from AD 400 onwards; see → Aelia [4].

[2] **Licinia E.** Born in AD 422; daughter of → Theodosius II and → Eudocia [1]. From 424 engaged to be married to → Valentinianus III , from 437 married. Two daughters: → Eudocia [2] and → Placidia. 439 Augusta. Promoted the building of churches in Rome. It is hard to judge the extent of her influence on the court but presumably it was dominated by her mother-in-law → Galla [3] Placidia. Pope → Leo the Great encouraged her in 450, after the 'Robber Synod ' to intervene in favour of orthodoxy by taking up the matter with her father Theodosius II (her letter: Leo Magnus, epist. 57 = PL 54,967/8–971/2). In 455 Petronius Maximus, who had instigated the murder of her husband, forced her to marry him. The (improbable) rumour went about that in revenge she summoned the Vandals to Italy. Their king Geiseric (→ Geisericus) took her together with her daughters to Africa and forced Eudocia to marry his son Huneric (→ Hunericus). In 462 she was handed over to Constantinople where she met Daniel Stylites. Nothing is known about the rest of her life. PLRE 2,410–412. H.L.

Eudoxias (Εὐδοξιάς; *Eudoxiás*). City of *Galatia II*, named after the wife of Arcadius or the daughter of Theodosius II, probably Hamamkarahisar (Arslani [1. 447–464]) at the foot of the → Dindymum ([2. 129] incorrectly attributes this area to Germia); documented to have been a bishopric from 451 onwards (Hierocles, 698,2).

1 M. Waelkens, Germa, Germokoloneia, Germia, in: Byzantion 49, 1979 2 Mitchell 2.

K. Belke, Germia und E., in: W. Hörandner et al., Byzantios. FS H. Hunger, 1984; Belke, 163. K.ST.

Eudoxus (Εὔδοξος; *Eúdoxos*).

[1] **of Cnidus.** One of the most important ancient mathematicians and astronomers, he was presumably born in 391/390 BC (on the problem of dating see [7. 137–139]). He studied mathematics with → Archytas [1] and

medicine with → Philistion. At the age of 23 he went to Athens and it is said that, among other things, he attended lectures there with → Plato. At the expense of his Cnidian friends, presumably in 365/4 [11], E. went with a letter of recommendation from → Agesilaus [2] to king → Nectanebus in Egypt. He lived there for over a year acquiring the astronomical knowledge of the priests of Heliopolis and is said during this period to have written a work entitled Ὀκταετηρίς (*Oktaetērís*) about the eight-year calendar cycle. Around 362, E. founded a school in Cyzicus. At times he stayed at the court of → Maussolus. When E. left Cyzicus just before 350 [7. 140]) and went to Athens, many of his pupils followed him, among these being → Menaechmus and → Deinostratus. There are varying reports about his relationship with Plato. Certainly E. did not enter the Academy, but information regarding hostility between E. and Plato is probably based on a dramatization of their scientific differences. E. spent the last years of his life in Cnidus where he died at the age of 53, i.e. presumably in 338/7, a highly revered man.

The topics covered by the lectures and writings of E. ranged from theology and philosophy to geography, astronomy, physics and pure mathematics. None of his writings are extant; the fragments and testimonies were collected by LASSERRE [7].

E. made a significant contribution to Greek mathematics. Significant parts of bk. 5 (theory of proportions), bk. 6 (geometrical applications of the theory of proportions) and bk. 12 (volume computation) of the 'Elements' of Euclid can be traced back to E. (→ Euclides [3]). The definition of ratio invented by him (so-called 'Archimedean axiom': Euc. 5, Def. 4) and the brilliant definition of the correspondence of proportions based on it (Elem. 5, Def. 5) are of fundamental significance. With their help E. was able to expound a new theory of proportions that – as opposed to the old Pythagorean theory presented in bk. 7 of the 'Elements' – is also applicable to incommensurable magnitudes, for example to diagonals and the side of the square or pentagon. The method of exhaustion developed by E. is based on the divisive form of the so-called 'Archimedean axiom' (formulated in Euc.10,1); with the help of the method of exhaustion, infinitesimal problems, e.g. the determination of the volume of figures not defined by straight lines, could be solved mathematically correctly. Using this method, E. proved with exactitude the most important theorems in Euc. 12 (ratio of the area of a circle or the volume of a sphere to the radius; volume of the pyramid and the cone). After E. the method of exhaustion was used by the Greeks for all infinitesimal tasks; it also meets today's requirements of mathematical rigour.

E. also solved in a purely geometrical manner the problem of the → duplication of the cube ('Delian Problem'; generally: discovery of two mean proportionals) by sectioning two curves; it is not known which curves were involved (fr. D 24–29 LASSERRE, with comm. [7. 163–166]).

According to the ideas of the Pythagoreans and also Plato, perpetual movements could only rotate in a uniform manner. This created the task of tracing the complicated motion of the planets back to combinations of rotations. E. solved the problem by declaring that the apparent movements of the planets (including the moon and sun) around the earth worked on a system of 27 homocentric spheres rotating around the earth as the central point. This system described by E. in his work Περὶ ταχῶν (*Perí tachôn*) was reconstructed by SCHIAPARELLI from information in Aristotle and Simplicius ([13]; more recent presentations in [9; 2; 8; 10]; fragments in fr. F 121–126, D 6–15 LASSERRE). The furthermost sphere bears the fixed stars; the others serve to explain the movement of the sun, the moon and the five planets. For each of the planets, four spheres are necessary whilst three are required for the sun and moon respectively. The concentric spherical shells that are nested in each other rotate with varying speed and direction on different axes. The apparent loop movement of an outer planet visible from the earth results, with a suitable selection of the speeds and axis angles, in a figure-of-eight (hippopede) that can also be described as the diameter of a sphere with a thin cylinder touching the sphere. By combining the hippopede with a movement going the length of the → ecliptic, the movement of the planet can be ascertained in relation to the fixed stars. The complicated movements of the planets with their anomalies are therefore traced back to uniform circular movements. The homocentric system of E. was improved by → Callippus, adopted by Aristotelian physics and in this way was influential right through to the 16th cent., even though this model was unable to explain the changing brightness of the planets because the distances between the planets and the earth always remain the same.

E.'s Φαινόμενα (*Phainómena*) and his Ἔνοπτρον (*Énoptron*) – which to a large extent is identical with the former (fr. F 1–120 LASSERRE) – for which E. also used his observations of fixed stars was widely influential. The work of → Aratus [4] is based upon these writings.The lost work Περὶ ἀφανισμῶν (*Perì aphanismôn*, fr. F 127–128 LASSERRE) was probably concerned with the way in which stars become invisible – the determination of which was indispensable for the establishment of calendars. An astronomical calendar treatise extant on papyrus and known by the title *Eudoxi Ars Astronomica* was not the work of E. but does contain a lot that can be traced back to him and that is related to his work *Oktaetērís* about the eight-year calendar cycle (fr. F 129–269 LASSERRE).

In his great geographical work Γῆς περίοδος (*Gês períodos*, [3]; fr. F 272–373 LASSERRE), E. systematically described the inhabited world in the manner of → Hecataeus. The spherical shape of the earth, its most important circles and points (tropics, equator, poles and meridian) as well as the external light of the moon were well known to him.

E.'s theory that pleasure (ἡδονή, *hēdonḗ*) was the greatest good was discussed by Plato in the *Philebos* and in particular by Aristotle (Eth. Nic. 10; see in this regard [6] and [12] where the close connection between E.'s scientific and moral philosophy is demonstrated). With regard to the Ideas, E. was of a quite different opinion from Plato. The theory of Ideas – in conjunction with the theory of Proportions – also has a part to play in E.'s explanation of colours: each manifestation of colour is based on the proportion of pure colours contained in it; the purest colours correspond to the simplest number ratios and produce the greatest pleasure [1. 3, 389–410].

→ Calendar; → Proportion; → Duplication of the cube; → Geography; → Ideas, theory of

1 O. BECKER, E.-Studien I–IV, Quellen und Stud. zur Gesch. der Mathematik, Astronomie und Physik, Abt. B, 2, 1933, 311–333, 369–387; 3, 1936, 236–244, 370–410 2 D.R. DICKS, Early Greek astronomy to Aristotle, 1970, 151–189 3 F. GISINGER, Die Erdbeschreibung des E. von Knidos, 1921 4 TH. L. HEATH, A history of Greek mathematics, I, 1921, 322–335 5 G.L. HUXLEY, s.v. Eudoxus of Cnidus, Dictionary of Scientific Biography 4, 1971, 465–467 6 H. KARPP, Unt. zur Philos. des E. von Knidos, 1933 7 F. LASSERRE, Die Fr. des E. von Knidos, 1966 8 E. MAULA, Studies in Eudoxus' homocentric spheres, 1974 9 O. NEUGEBAUER, On the hippopede of Eudoxus, in: Scripta Mathematica 19, 1953, 225–229 10 J.D. NORTH, The hippopede, in: A. VON GOTSTEDTER (ed.), Ad radices, 1994, 143–154 11 G. DE SANTILLANA, Eudoxus and Plato. A Study in Chronology, in: Isis 32, 1947, 248–262 12 W. SCHADEWALDT, E. von Knidos und die Lehre vom unbewegten Beweger, in: Satura, 1952, 103–120 13 G.V. SCHIAPARELLI, Die homocentrischen Sphären des Eudoxus, des Kallippus und des Aristoteles, Abhandlungen zur Gesch. der Mathematik 1, 1877, 101–198 14 B.L. VAN DER WAERDEN, Erwachende Wiss., 1956, 292–313.

M.F.

[2] Comic poet of the 3rd or 2nd cent. BC from Sicily who won three times at the → Dionysia and five times at the Lenaea [1. test. 1]. However, the inscription that records the victory of a comic poet at the Dionysia in 181 BC should be completed with the name of → Archicles rather than that of E. [1. test. *2]. Two play titles and two fragments are extant.

1 PCG V, 274f.

H.-G.NE.

[3] **of Cyzicus.** Greek seafarer who at the time of Ptolemy VIII, Cleopatra II and Ptolemy IX went on expeditions to India (Posid. in Str. 2,3,4), eastern and western Africa. E. is said to have attempted to circumnavigate Africa (Nep. in Mela 3,90; 92; Plin. HN 2,169; 6,188).

F. JACOBY s.v. E. 6), RE 6, 929f.; J.H. THIEL, E. of Cyzicus, 1967; R. HENNIG, Terrae Incognitae, vol. 1, [2]1944, 271–278.

K.BRO.

Euergetes (εὐεργέτης; *euergétēs*, 'benefactor'). An honorary title bestowed by Greek communities upon people who rendered particularly outstanding services to them. There is evidence of this term with this meaning from the 5th cent. BC (cf. Hdt. 8,136), but *euergesia* as an aspect of the ideal of generosity of the Greek aristocracy can be traced back to the Homeric period (→ Euergetism). In Athens the work of individual citizens for the polis in the 5th cent. was still primarily regulated by → liturgies and it was expected of one as a service to the collective (cf. still Aristot. Eth. Nic. 4,1119b 19ff.); and although in the 4th cent. certain people were especially honoured for their services, as a rule only non-Athenians received the title E. [5. 19ff., esp. 24ff.]. But from the 3rd cent. until late antiquity there are many, in particular epigraphical testimonies regarding honours bestowed on citizens of outstanding merit – *euergétai* – in their *poleis*. Hellenistic rulers often had the epithet Euergetes and used the *euergesia*, which they considered to be among the virtues of rulers, as an instrument or programme in their dealings with Greek *poleis* [cf. for instance 2. 366f., No. 297, l. 41ff.; 1]; the Romans copied them in this. The endowment of buildings, schools, grain etc. brought the donors honours and recognition; the Euergetes could be honoured through honorary inscriptions, statues, festivals, processions etc. and from *c.* 150 BC onwards sometimes even with cults. Some Greek communities honoured the Romans as a whole as *koinoì euergétai* (κοινοὶ εὐεργέται) [3. 117ff., esp. 124ff.].

1 K. BRINGMANN, The King as Benefactor, in: A. BULLOCH, E.S. GRUEN (ed.), Images and Ideologies, 1993, 7–24 2 K. BRINGMANN, H.v. STEUBEN (ed.), Schenkungen hellenistischer Herrscher an griech. Städte und Heiligtümer, vol. 1, 1995 3 J.-L. FERRARY, Philhellénisme et impérialisme, 1988 4 PH. GAUTHIER, Les cités grecques et leurs bienfaiteurs, 1985 5 F. QUASS, Die Honoratiorenschicht in den Städten des griech. Ostens, 1993 6 P. VEYNE, Le pain et le cirque, 1976 7 M. WÖRRLE, P. ZANKER (ed.), Stadtbild und Bürgerbild im Hellenismus, 1995.

M.MEI.

Euergetism

I. GENERAL POINTS II. GREECE III. ROME

I. GENERAL POINTS

The concept is derived from Greek → *euergétēs* (benefactor) and was coined as a scholarly term by A. BOULANGER following the example of the comparable modern Greek *euergetes* [13. 22]. It refers to a central phenomenon in the ethics of reciprocity specific to Graeco-Roman civilization that is part of the ethnological and socio-anthropological concept of gift exchange. In the spirit of strict → reciprocity every act that was related to a person or group of persons, positive as well as negative, had to be repaid; the good deed (εὐεργεσία/*euergesía* or *beneficium*) had to be answered by corresponding thanks (χάρις/*cháris*, εὐχαριστία/*eucharistía* or *gratia*) on which one could count and which one could pin expectations on. Social reputation (τιμή, 'honour') was dependent upon following such rules. In this way *euergesía* was an essential element of all social relationships, from the individual and intimate sphere of friendship and love to the relations between people and gods; there is also evidence of the term *euergesía* from the 5th cent. BC for the area of interstate relationships [8]. Euergetism was therefore a decisive element in the recognition of a higher social position, voluntary and obligatory well-doing being inseparably intertwined. Rich individuals acted as benefactors and were honoured for it, whereas the honours made them more willing to perform further good deeds and were at the same time one of the reasons why a strongly hierarchical system remained essentially stable for many centuries.

II. Greece

In archaic and Classical Greece this system of rules can be shown from the sources (cf. esp. Aristot. Rh. 1,5,1361a 28–b 2). From the last third of the 4th cent. onwards, euergetism was the basis for the permanent dominance of a class of persons of high standing in the Greek cities that characterized Hellenism and the Principate [10]. The working of this system of social and political reciprocity was an essential prerequisite for the vitality of the civilization of the ancient cities. The work of the *euergétai* particularly involved the maintenance of good relationships with the Hellenistic rulers, and later with the Romans. Euergetism was also important as an element of the rule of the Hellenistic monarchs. Special services for the cities, such as the 'liberation' of a polis, could result in divine honours for the kings [6]. This is the background of early Hellenistic euhemerism, which regarded the gods as deified former benefactors (FGrH 63, cf. [11]). With the growing decline of power on the part of the Hellenistic monarchy in the 2nd cent. BC, there was an increase in the importance of persons of high standing within the city and of Rome, Roman aristocrats and ultimately of the Roman *principes* [4; 12].

III. Rome

As the leading role of the aristocracy in Rome was traditionally much more firmly fixed than in Greece [3], euergetism did not become important there until the 2nd cent. with the decline in the clientele and as a result of the availability of considerable financial resources owing to Roman expansion. It then became an important element of political and social practices and was firmly integrated into the system of obligation – *beneficium* and *gratia* – manifesting itself especially in the *ambitus* (competition in the election campaign [7. 51–76]). It now became quite a normal and typical part of a career not just to pay out sums of money but also to organize lavish games. Like the Hellenistic monarchs, the Roman *principes* also used euergetism and the expectations associated with it as a legitimation strategy, of which 'bread and circuses' (*panem et circenses*, Juv. 10,81; [13. 441–632; 2. 38–93]), i.e. providing food for the populace of the city of Rome and entertaining them with games (with the emperor present) became a particularly important part. In relation to the entire empire, the *princeps* – as in the Republican period, the Romans as a whole – now appeared to be the benefactor of humanity. In addition there developed in the cities of the western half of the empire, the Roman *municipia* and colonies, a system of rule by notables that in all essentials paralleled that which existed in the Greek east: generosity expressed in services to the community was the basis for social reputation and power here as well. As it was also a matter of competition, there was a risk that conspicuous generosity placed excessive demands on the potential of the local elites so that the *princeps* had to impose rules (cf. the correspondence between Trajan and Pliny, Ep. 10). Under additional burdens (e.g. tax increases and growing military demands) the system could begin to waver. This was increasingly the case in the 3rd cent. AD and it gradually led to state regulatory mechanisms that dissolved the characteristic balance between voluntary service and obligation: Euergetism was transformed on the one hand into a system of taxes and levies and on the other hand was integrated into the patronage of late antiquity [9].

1 K. Bringmann, H. von Steuben (ed.), Schenkungen hellenistischer Herrscher an griech. Städte und Heiligtümer, vol. 1, 1995 2 E. Flaig, Den Kaiser herausfordern. Die Usurpation im Röm. Reich, 1992 3 E. Flaig, Politisierte Lebensführung und ästhetische Kultur. Eine semiotische Untersuchung am röm. Adel, in: Histor. Anthropologie 1, 1993, 193–217 4 Ph. Gauthier, Les cités grecques et leurs bienfaiteurs (IVe-Ier siècle avant J.-C.), 1985 5 H.-J. Gehrke, Der siegreiche König. Überlegungen zur hell. Monarchie, in: AKG 64, 1982, 247–277 6 C. Habicht, Gottmenschentum und griech. Städte, ²1970 7 M. Jehne (ed.), Demokratie in Rom? Die Rolle des Volkes in der Politik der röm. Republik, 1995 8 P. Karavites, Euergesia in Herodotus and Thucydides as a Factor in Interstate Relations, in: Revue Internationale des Droits de l'Antiquité 27, 1980, 69–79 9 J.-U. Krause, Das spätant. Städtepatronat, in: Chiron 17, 1987, 1–80 10 F. Quass, Die Honoratiorenschicht in den Städten des griech. Ostens, 1993 11 M. Sartori, Storia, utopia e mito nei primi libri della Bibliotheca historica di Diodoro Siculo, in: Athenaeum 62, 1984, 492–536 12 J. Touloumakos, Zum röm. Gemeindepatronat im griech. Osten, in: Hermes 116, 1988, 304–324 13 P. Veyne, Bread and Circuses, 1980.

H.-J.G.

Eugam(m)on (Εὐγάμ(μ)ων; *Eugám(m)ōn*). Epic poet of Cyrene to whom is attributed the two-volume → Telegonia. According to Eusebius (in Jer. Chron. 102,1 Helm), the epic was written during the period of the 53rd Olympiad = 568–565 BC and is supposed (Clem. Al. strom. 2,442,4f.) to have been identical to a book of → Musaeus about the Thesprotians: E. allegedly drew upon this without naming his source (Paus. 8,12,5 likewise mentions a *Thesprotís*). The *Telegonia* described the post-Odyssean journeys of Odysseus to Elis, to Thesprotia because of the prophecy of Tiresias (cf. Hom. Od. 11,121), his battle against the Bryges and his return to Ithaca. E. also told of Telegonus, Odysseus' and Circe's son who looked for his father, did not recognize him and killed him (cf. also the form of this motif in the Lay of Hildebrand).

EpGF 71–73 and 95; M. DAVIES, The Epic Cycle, 1989, 87–94; A. HARTMANN, Unt. über die Sagen vom Tod des Odysseus, 1917; R. MERKELBACH, Untersuchungen zur Odyssee, in: Zetemata 2, 1951, 220–230. C.S.

Euganei Name given to a people from the eastern, Venetian part of the Po plain who withdrew to the mountainous interior of the country when the → Veneti came from the east (cf. the Paphlagonian immigrants in Liv. 1,1,2f.). There they mixed with the Raeti and later were frequently confused with them [1. 486f.; 3. 101f.]. Cato (HRR fr. 41) mentions 34 *oppida* of the E., among these the → Camunni, Trumplini and Stoeni (uncertain), while for others the Camunni were Raeti (Str. 4,6,8) and the Stoeni were Ligures (Acta Triumphalia for the year 637; Str. 4,6,6; Steph. Byz. s.v. Στουῖνος). → Verona, the point where the valley intersected with the mountains, was in the area of the Raeti and the E. alike (Plin. HN 3,130). The attribution of → Aquileia (Sil. Pun. 8,605; 12,216; Mart. 13,89,1), → Altinum (Martial. 4,25,4; 10,93,1), → Patavium (Juv. 8,15) and Aponus (Luc. 7,193) to the territory of the E. is to be considered as literary inaccuracy.

1 NISSEN, Vol. 1 2 L.A. PROSDOCIMI, La lingua, in: G. FOGOLARI, A.L. PROSDOCIMI (ed.), I Veneti antichi, 1988 3 R. DE MARINIS, La popolazioni alpine di stirpe retica, in: G. PUGLIESE CARRATELLI (ed.), Italia omnium terrarum alumna, 1987 4 L. PARETI, Storia di Roma, vol. 1, 1952. A.SA.

Eugenes (Εὐγενής; *Eugenḗs*) Writer of an epigram in iambic trimeters about a work of art that represents the old, drunken → Anacreon (Anth. Plan. 308): a very faithful, ambitious imitation of two poems by Leonidas of Tarentum (Anth. Plan. 16,306f.; the expression 'swan of Teos', Τήιον κύκνον, in v. 2 is an allusion to Antipater of Sidon 7,30,1). The epigram may be from the beginning of the Imperial period. About the poet, whose name is very rare, nothing is known.

FGE 110f. E.D.

Eugenius (Εὐγένιος; *Eugénios*).
[1] Flavius Eugenius. Roman usurper in AD 392–394. He was a Christian, a teacher of grammar and rhetoric in Rome and he became *magister scrinii* for Valentinian II around 392 (Zos. 4,54,1). On 22 August 392 he was elevated to the position of emperor by Arbogast (Socr. 5,25; Sozom. Hist. eccl. 7,22,4). Constantly controlled by Arbogast, he first sought an agreement with Ambrosius and Theodosius I (Ambr. Epist. 57; Zos. 4,54f.; ILS 790). He was not acknowledged by Theodosius, so he allied himself in Italy with the non-Christian senators under the leadership of Nicomachus Flavianus. On 5/6 September 394 he was defeated and killed by Theodosius on the river Frigidus (Philostorgius, Historia ecclesiastica 11,2; Socr. 5,25; Oros. 7,35). PLRE 1, 293 E. (6). W.P.

[2] of Augustopolis (Phrygia Salutaris), grammarian in Constantinople under Anastasius I (AD 491–518), predecessor of Stephanus of Byzantium, the only author who cites him (s.v. Ἀνακτόριον); the Suda (ε 3394) provides a muddled catalogue of his works: 1) on metrics, regarding the 'colometry of the lyrical parts in Aeschylus, Sophocles and Euripides, from 15 tragedies': testimonies regarding the selection of tragedians in the Byzantine period [4; 5], possibly a metrical comm. (an analogous work is that of Heliodorus about Aristophanes [cf. 2; 5; 6. 168–169]); 'to what extent is the Palimbaccheus a paean?' (part of a larger work?); 2) on orthography: 'on the question of how the temple names are spelt' (cf. → Horapollon); 'on words that end in –ια'; 3) on lexicography: Παμμιγὴς λέξις (*Pammigès léxis*; 'Varied expressions', probably identical with the συλλογὴ λέξέων/*syllogḕ lexéōn* cited by Steph. Byz.); 4) poetry in iambic trimeters; quoted in the praef. of the Suda as a source.

1 L. COHN, s.v. E., RE 6, 987–988 2 J. IRIGOIN, in: La philol. grecque (Entretiens XL), 1993, 80–81 3 R.A. KASTER, Guardians of Language, 1988, 282 4 A. WARTELLE, Histoire du texte d' Eschyle, 1971, 355–356 5 G. ZUNTZ, An Inquiry into the Transmission of the Plays of Euripides, 1965, 30 6 O. HENSE, Heliodoreische Unt., 1870. S.FO.

[3] Bishop of Carthage. Pressured by the emperor Zeno, King Huneric accepted the selection of E. as Bishop of Carthage after the office had been forcibly vacant for 24 years; he held the office from AD 480/1–505. E. defended the Catholic faith during the rule of the Arian Vandals. For the bishops' synod of Carthage in 484 he wrote the *Liber fidei catholicae* (Victor Vitensis, Historia persecutionis Africanae provinciae 2,56–101). As a result he was persecuted and exiled by Hunneric. In 487 he was able to return to Carthage but was later banished again by King Thrasamund in 497(?). E. died in 505 in exile in Albi/southern France. Apart from the above-mentioned *Liber* there is evidence of two letters to King Huneric (Victor Vitensis 2,41–42) and a pastoral letter to the community at Carthage (Greg. Tur. Franc. 2,3). Cf. Gennadius, vir. ill. 94.
→ Arianism; → Vandals

A. MANDOUZE, Prosopographie chrétienne du Bas-Empire 1, 1982, 362–64.; V. SAXER, Saints anciens d'Afrique du Nord, 1979. K.-S.F.

[4] Cleric at the royal court of the Visigoths who wrote in Latin, 646–657 as E. II. Archbishop of Toledo. The book of prose attested to by his successor Ildefons has been lost. In addition to letters and possibly some hymns [3. 120, 220, 237], a collection of poems related to the tradition of late antiquity is extant. It comprises occasional and didactic poetry, genre pieces, epitaphs, a humorous poem with words split up (in the style of Lucilius) and personal lyric poetry. The verse structure (esp. of the Sapphic verses) is often accentuated. For King Chindaswinth, E. revised the works of → Dracon-

tius [3] (*Satisfactio, De laudibus Dei 1*). E. influenced the Carolingian poets and also Petrus Damiani (11th cent.).

EDITION: 1 F. VOLLMER, MGH AA 14, 231–290 (27–131: revision of Dracontius).
BIBLIOGRAPHY: 2 BRUNHÖLZL, 1,95 f. 522 3 J. PÉREZ DE URBEL, El origen de los himnos mozárabes, in: Bulletin hispanique 28, 1926 4 W. PFEIFFER, The Change of Philomela, 1985. K.SM.

Eugippius As abbot of Castellum Lucullanum (now San Severino) near Naples, around 511 E. wrote the *Commemoratorium vitae S. Severini* [1; 3; 4], in which the prophetic appearance of the ascetic Severin († 482) in the Roman Danube provinces is described. Using classical stylistic elements [6. 174–181], E. recounts one *exemplum* after another; the number of chapters – 46 – is perhaps intended symbolically. This is supported by the remarkably full presentation of a corresponding exegesis of the name Adam (A=1; Δ=4; A=1; M=40: total 46) in the *Excerpta ex operibus S. Augustini* [6. 182; 3], an → Augustinus textbook carefully compiled by E. from over 300 excerpts, which Cassiodorus recommended for study (Inst. 1,23). E. also wrote a *Regula* [5].

EDITIONS: 1 T. MOMMSEN, W. BULST, Commemoratorium vitae S. Severini, 1948 2 P. KNÖLL, CSEL 9/1, 1885 (Excerpta) 3 R. NOLL, Vita S. Severini, 1963 4 T. RÉGERAT, 1991 5 F. VILLEGAS, A. DE VOGÜÉ, CSEL 87, 1976 (*Regula*).
BIBLIOGRAPHY: 6 W. BERSCHIN, Biographie und Epochenstil im lat. Mittelalter, 1, 1986. W.B.

Eugnostus (Εὔγνωστος; *Eúgnōstos*) The name of the author of a letter ('The blessed E. to his people') that has twice been passed down to us in the Coptic library of Nağʿ Ḥammādī (III 70,1–90,13 and, in a much worse condition, V 1–17). The letter, which was probably written in the late 1st or in the early 2nd cent. AD, contains – following the rejection of the philosophical teachings regarding the rulership of the world – a cosmogony described as a revelation of the 'God of Truth' that considers the 'forefather of the universe', only negatively predictable, to be the reason for creation and an androgynous 'immortal human being' by the name of 'Nous/Pansophos Sophia' to be the beginning of creation. The letter certainly contains little Christian thought (for instance the wording 'Son of Man' who is also called 'Saviour') was however not revised before the end of the 2nd cent. to form what is now clearly a Christian-Gnostic work, 'Sophia Jesu Christi'.
→ Gnosis, Gnostics, Gnosticism

M. KRAUSE, in: Id., K. RUDOLPH, Die Gnosis, Vol. 2: Koptische und mandäische Quellen, 1971, 32–45 (translation). F.G.

Eugraphius Latin grammarian and author of a Terence comm. that is also included with various Terence MSS. He may have lived in the 6th cent. AD: he used the Terence comm. of → Donatus [3]. The *Commentum* of E. mainly consists of notes of a rhetorical type, sometimes only of paraphrasing. In the Middle Ages E.'s name appears to have been unknown but there are traces of his comm. in the glossaries and scholia to Terence.

EDITION: P. WESSNER, 1908 (repr. 1963).
BIBLIOGRAPHY: Id., E., RE 6, 990–991; SCHANZ/HOSIUS 4,2, 240–242; HLL § 706. P.G.

Euhemerus (Εὐήμερος; *Euémeros*) of Messene (it is unknown to which Messene this refers; some testimonials attest to other cities of birth). Of his work, the Ἱερὰ ἀναγραφή (*Sacra historia*), the résumé in the 'Historical Library' of → Diodorus [18] Siculus (5,41–46 and 6,1) and various testimonies and fragments have been passed down to us. E. pretended to have gone on a number of trips on behalf of King Cassander (305–297 BC). He told particularly of his visit to an archipelago: on the biggest island, Panchaea, he saw a temple dedicated to Zeus that stood in the middle of an idyllic landscape (the whole island was exceptionally fertile). Inside the temple an inscription on a pillar told of the history of the cult of the gods of Olympus: these had been mortals who had been deified because of their extraordinary services to human civilization. The rest of the work was dedicated to the description of the social structure of Panchaea. It had three classes (priests and artisans, farmers, soldiers and shepherds) and a strict collective economy that only allowed a person's house and garden to be privately owned.

It is not easy to assign this work to any particular literary genre. As the type of the first-person narrative used to describe an imaginary journey [1], a topos since time immemorial, has been linked with the representation of an alternative type of life, the term 'utopian novel' has been suggested, which is also suitable for the lost works of → Theopompus, → Hecataeus of Abdera and above all → Iambulus [2]. Because we do not have the text itself, the relationship between the fictitious and theoretical components cannot be determined with certainty; but the fact that Lucian in the 'True History' made the whole of the historiographic, ethnographic and utopian literature that presents reports about fantastic journeys as personal experiences into the object of a satirical pastiche is evidence of the vividness of these lost works. The genre did not again achieve comparable vividness until the modern period with works ranging from *Utopia* by Thomas Morus (who coined the term that is now commonly used) and Tommaso Campanella's *Città del Sole* to Swift and Butler's *Erewhon*.

The name E. has always been linked with the rationalist interpretation of myths; it is therefore hard to differentiate between the original body of thought of E. and euhemerism. Precursors of this humanistic view can be found in → Prodicus and in → Hecataeus of Abdera (the latter had however dealt with Egyptian religion). It can be inferred from Diodor's excerpt, however, that E.'s position is more differentiated than the simple assertion that the gods were human by nature (see the differentiation between ἀίδιοι and ἐπίγειοι θεοί in Diod. Sic. 6,1,1–2 ap. Euseb. Praep. evang. 2,2,52–3 = T 25 WINIARCZYK) [3]. With regard to the utopian components (which was occasioned the term 'ancient communism' [4. 274–275]), the borrowing from Plato is obvious (esp. *Critias*), even if it is clear that E. was not a systematic thinker. Undoubtedly there is a direct relationship with the Hellenistic practice of the deification of rulers, as Ptolemy I practised in the case of Alexander the Great, Ptolemy II in that of Ptolemy I (283 BC) and finally for himself and his wife Arsinoe (in 270); the work of E. is generally dated to 280 BC. It cannot be said with such certainty whether this relationship is of a polemical nature, an alternative society being designed without rulers and a ruler's cult.

A negative, conservative reaction to the work of E. is to be found in the 1st iambus of → Callimachus (fr. 191); the Latin translation (very probably in prose) by → Ennius ensured wide distribution of E.'s works in Roman culture, from Lucretius to Cicero and Virgil and the polemical reactions of the Christians, particularly in the *Divinae Institutiones* of Lactantius.

→ EUHEMERISM; → Novel; → Utopia

1 P.B. GOVE, The Imaginary Voyage in Prose Fiction, 1961 2 B. KYTZLER, Zum utopischen Roman der klass. Ant., in: H. HOFMANN (ed.), Groningen Colloquia on the Novel, 1, 1988, 7–16 3 R.J. MÜLLER, Überlegungen zur Ἱερὰ ἀναγραφή des E. von Messene, in: Hermes 121, 1993, 276–300 4 R. v. PÖHLMANN, Gesch. der sozialen Frage und des Sozialismus in der ant. Welt II, 31925.

R. BICHLER, Zur histor. Beurteilung der griech. Staatsutopie, in: Grazer Beiträge 11, 1984, 179–206; H. BRAUNERT, Die heilige Insel des E., in: RhM 108, 1965, 255–268; J. FERGUSON, Utopias of the Classical World, 1975; M. FINLEY, Utopianism Ancient and Modern, in: The Critical Spirit (Essays in honor of H. Marcuse), 1967, 3–20; H. FLASHAR, Formen utopischen Denkens bei den Griechen (Innsbrucker Beiträge zur Kulturwiss., Issue 3), 1974; F. JACOBY, s.v. E., RE 6, 952–72; G. VALLAURI, Origine e diffusione dell'evemerismo nel pensiero classico, 1960; M. WINIARCZYK (ed.), Euhemeri Messenii Reliquiae, 1991; M. ZUMSCHLINGE, E. staatstheoretische und staatsutopische Motive, thesis 1976. M.FU.

Eulaeus (Εὐλαῖος; *Eulaîos*).

[1] One of the main rivers of the area of Susiana (Arr. Anab. 7,7; Diod. Sic. 19,19,1; Plut. Eumenes 14; Str. 15,3,4; 22; Plin. HN 6,100; 31,35 et al.) on which the metropolis Susa was also situated; it appears in the Hellenistic period as the Greek polis with the name Σελεύκεια ἡ πρὸς τῷ Εὐλαίῳ(Seleucia on the E.). It is indeed certain that E. was named after the river name *Ulaï* that appears in Mesopotamian and Biblical testimonials; however the identification of E. and the other rivers of Susiana passed down from antiquity (→ Choaspes [1], Pasitigris, Kopratas, Hedyphon, Aduna) with rivers of the present day (Karḫe, Āb-e Dēz, Šūr Rūd, Kārūn etc.) is still a matter of debate. The reason for this is both the lack of clarity of ancient nomenclature itself and presumably also hydrographical changes in this region.

G. LE RIDER, Suse sous les Séleucides et les Parthes, 1965, 263–267; P. HÖGEMANN, Der Ausbau von Elam zur Seeprovinz unter Dareios. I. (522/21–486 v. Chr.) und ihr Zustand zur Zeit Alexanders des Großen in den Jahren 325 und 324 v. Chr., in: Stuttgarter Kolloquium zur histor. Geogr. des Altertums 2, 1984 und 3, 1987, 1991, 133–147. J.W.

[2] Eunuch of Macedonian origin, τιθηνός (*tithēnós*, 'foster-father') and from 176–169 BC ἐπίτροπος (*epítropos*, 'manager') of Ptolemy VI; he was held responsible by the court for the disaster of the 6th Syrian War, which is why reports about him are seriously distorted. (PP 6,14607). W.A.

Eulogius (Εὐλόγιος; *Eulógios*). Perhaps the person to whom was dedicated the lexicon of Hesychius (6th cent. AD [4; 1. 358]; but [5] dates E. to the period between Theodosius of Alexandria ([4th cent. AD] and Choeroboscus [9th cent. AD]) and who is known through the citations in the *Etymologicum Magnum* and in the *Etymologicum Gudianum*. He is also the source of some Homeric epimerisms [2; 3]. E. was a grammarian and his nickname was *Scholastikós*; he was the author of a didactic book about morphology in 'Questions and Answers' (Ἀπορίαι καὶ λύσεις, 'Difficulties and Solutions'; EM 638,18), and of a work that was not of an elementary nature (like the → Epimerismi), but of a scientific nature [1. 358–359], part of which bore the title 'On irregular words ' (Περὶ δυσκλίτων ῥημάτων) (EM 809,34–37).

1 R. REITZENSTEIN, Gesch. der griech. Etym., 1897, 351–370 (with fragments) 2 Epimerismi Homerici, Pars Prior, ed. A.R. DYCK, 1983, 31 3 Epimerismi Homerici, Pars Altera, ed. A.R. DYCK, 1995, 48 4 Hesychii Alexandrini Lexicon ... recensuit M. SCHMIDT, 1862, CLXXXVII 5 Hesychii Alexandrini Lexikon, ed. K. LATTE, 1953, VII. S.FO.

Eumaeus (Εὔμαιος; *Eúmaios*). The faithful swineherd of → Odysseus (Hom. Od., esp. Bks. 14–17; 20–22); son of a king, he was abducted as a child owing to the betrayal of a Phoenician maid and was sold. Hardworking, caring, pious and unconditionally faithful to his absent master, E. represents the type of the loyal vassal. The meeting with Telemachus on E.'s farm, in accordance with Athena's directive (Hom. Od. 13,404), marks the beginning of Odysseus's homecoming within Ithaca. From there E. accompanies the beggar Odysseus back to the palace, arranges a conversation with → Penelope and helps him to kill the suitors. RE.N.

Eumares (Εὐμάρης; *Eumárēs*). Painter in Athens. He was considered to be the inventor of the distinction between male and female figures, probably by means of the skin colour, and of a new flexibility of the bodies. If he can be correctly associated with this stage of development achieved around 600 BC, he cannot be equated with the bearer of this common artist's name who appears as the father in a signature of → Antenor and his brother and who himself placed his signature on a work on a base of the Acropolis around 520 BC.

FUCHS/FLOREN, 295; OVERBECK, No. 388 (sources); A.E. RAUBITSCHEK, Dedications from the Athenian Akropolis, 1949, No. 51, 197, 244, 108; I. SCHEIBLER, Griech. Malerei der Ant., 1994, 55, 59, 71. R.N.

Eumedes (Εὐμήδης; *Eumḗdēs*). Comic poet of the 3rd cent. BC – two victories at the Lenaea are attested for him in an inscription; on the list of prize-winners his name is entered after that of → Diodorus [10], the brother of → Diphilus [5] [1st test.]. Of his Σφαττόμενος (*Sphattómenos*; 'The Tormented One') only one fragment in an extremely poor condition is extant.

1 PCG V, 277. H.-G.NE.

Eumelus (Εὔμηλος; *Eúmēlos*).

[1] Son of → Admetus and → Alcestis. He led (only) 11 ships from Pherae against Troy (Hom. Il. 2,711–715) [1]. Although he had the best horses (Hom. Il. 2,763–767), he did not win the chariot race at the funeral games for Patroclus, as Athena broke the yoke of his chariot (Hom. Il. 23,391–397). Achilles nevertheless awarded him a prize (23, 533–538). According to Apollod. epit. 5,5, he is said to have won at the funeral games for Achilles although Q. Smyrn. 4,522–544 does not agree (cf. in this regard [2]). According to Hom. Od. 4,797, his wife was Iphthime, a sister of Penelope. It appears that E. has not been visually represented. [3].

1 E. VISSER, Homers Katalog der Schiffe, 1997, 670–681 2 W. KULLMANN, Die Quellen der Ilias, Hermes ES 14, 1960, 112 3 J.-R. GISLER, s.v. E., LIMC 4.1, 54–55.

[2] Father of → Agron [1].

[3] Father of → Botres. R.B.

[4] Spartocid king, 310/309–304/3 BC, father of Spartocus III. As a son of → Paerisades I, he was initially co-regent with his brothers Satyrus and Prytanis (IOSPE 2,1; 2). After the victories over them, he revived the 'old order' and the → *ateleia* in Panticapaeum. E. was very active in foreign policy: he liaised with the cities of Asia Minor, accepted refugees from → Callatis in Psoa, planned a coalition of the Black Sea countries against → Lysimachus, successfully fought pirates and annexed new territories (Diod. Sic. 20,22–25).

→ Spartocides

V.F. GAJDUKEVIČ, Das Bosporanische Reich, 1971, 85ff. I.v.B.

[5] Early Greek man of letters from Corinth, supposedly from the nobility of the Bacchi(a)des and a son of Amphilytus (Paus. 2,1,1 = T 1 BERNABÉ = T 1 DAVIES), about whose life time, type of literary production and number of works neither ancient nor modern research has any precise knowledge. From the different estimates regarding his life time (at least five, see the Testimonies in BERNABÉ and DAVIES) one would arrive at the 2nd half of the 8th cent. BC: 'obviously too early' BETHE [1. 1080]. According to the various quotations and references, some of which may be from the Hellenistic era but most from the Imperial era, E.'s works included:

(1) Epics of different natures: (a) mythological: a *Titanomachía* as well as an *Eurōpía* (three fragments of which only one has the author's name, ὁ τὴν Εὐρωπίαν πεποιηκὼς Εὔμηλος, to which [2. 346, n. 28] remarks: 'how easily the definite name is added'), (b) antiquarian-historical: the *Korinthiaká* from which 10–15 references have been passed down to us (among these three hexametric – only one with the name of the author –, the others in prose, according to Paus. 2,1,1 from a Κορινθία συγγραφή – for which he doubts the authorship of E. just as much as he does for the epic; in this regard [1. 1080]: '... to E. the Corinthian epic is unanimously [apart from Pausanias] attributed, just because ancient tradition knows of no other Corinthian writer besides him'), and a 'Homecoming of the Greeks' (Νόστος Ἑλλήνων; DUBIA 1 DAVIES p. 103), the author of which is stated by the source (a Pindar scholion) to be a Corinthian by the name of Eumolpus, which has been changed by conjecture to 'Eumelus', (c) a *Bougonía*, of which we know nothing further.

(2) a *Proshódion* (processionary song for sacrifices) to Delian Apollo in the Aeolian dialect (fr. 696 PMG, probably in hexameters [3] that E. is said to have written for the Messenians and that Pausanias who cites two verses from it considers to be the only credible work written by E. (T 8 BERNABÉ; cf. [2. 344]). – In view of this situation regarding the sources, BETHE's sceptical overall assessment [1. 1080] regarding E. (in agreement with WILAMOWITZ) is understandable enough: '... epics without names have been linked to names without epics on the basis of some assumptions or connections that mostly cannot be checked'.

1 E. BETHE, s.v. E., RE 6, 1080f. 2 U. v. WILAMOWITZ-MOELLENDORFF, Homerische Unt. (Der epische Cyclus), Philol. Unt. 7, 1884 3 C.M. BOWRA, Two Lines of Eumelus, in: CQ 13, 1963, 145f. J.L.

Eumeneia (Εὐμένεια; *Euméneia*).

[1] Town in the south of Phrygia (modern Işıklı), founded by Attalus II in the name of his brother Eumenes II (Steph. Byz. s.v. E.), close to the Maeander at the foot of a mountain. The numerous inscriptions from E. and its surroundings are mainly from the Roman period and are mostly tomb inscriptions; for the necropoleis that were intensively depleted by the farmers were located on the lower slopes of the mountain whilst the city centre in the plain is probably today at the bottom of the

lake which is traversed by the river at this point. E. had originally been established by colonists from Argus (coins: Εὐμενέων Ἀχαιῶν; *tribus Herais, Argeias*); there were Jewish and Christian communities. Minting of coins from the 2nd cent. BC to Gallienus. In the Roman period it was the location of a garrison (*cohors Claudia Sugambrum equitata*, later *cohors I Raetorum* that was likewise partly cavalry); it was still the site of a garrison in the late Imperial period (tomb inscription of a mounted archer δρακωνάρις, *drakōnáris*); in the Byzantine period it was a fortress and suffragan bishopric of Laodicea in the province of Phrygia Pacatiana.

TH. DREW-BEAR, Nouvelles inscriptions de Phrygie, 1978, 16–19, 53–114; BELKE/MERSICH, 251f.; M. CHRISTOL, TH. DREW-BEAR, in: Y. LE BOHEC (ed.),La hiérarchie de l'armée romaine sous le Haut-Empire. Actes du Congrès de Lyon (15–18 septembre 1994), 1995, 62–68; L. ROBERT, Epitaphes d'Eumeneia de Phrygie, in: Hellenica XI–XII, 1960, 414–439. T.D.-B.

[2] see → Tomi

Eumenes (Εὐμένης; *Euménēs*).

[1] * 362/1, Son of Hieronymus of Cardia, from 342 onwards chancellor for the Macedonian king Philip II and then for Alexander III, for whom he kept the *ephemerides* (Nep. Eumenes 1,4–6; Plut. Eumenes 1,4; Arr. Anab. 7,4,6; Ath. 10,434b). In 326, E. was *strategos* on a military mission in north-western India and then he was the trierarch of the Indus fleet (Arr. Anab. 5,24,6, Ind. 18,7; Curt. 9,1,19). At the mass wedding in Susa in 324, E. was probably the only Greek to receive a noble Iranian as his wife: Artonis, the sister of Alexander's wife Barsine (Plut. Eum. 1,7; Arr. Anab. 7,4,6). After Hephaestion's death, E. succeeded Perdiccas as hipparch (Nep. Eum. 1,6; Plut. Eum. 1,5). In the disputes after the death of Alexander in June 323 he was on the side of Perdiccas and when positions were allocated in Babylon, he was one of only a few Greeks to be given a satrapy, Cappadocia and Paphlagonia that had not been conquered by Alexander; he was then appointed by the regent of the empire, Perdiccas, as the authorized *strategos* of the armed forces in Cappadocia and Armenia and he defeated Perdiccas' opponent Craterus in Cappadocia in spring 320.

After Perdiccas' failure and death on the Nile, E., like Perdiccas' other supporters, was banished by the military meeting in summer 320 in Triparadeisus (Nep. Eum. 2–3; Diod. Sic. 18,3,1; 29–32; 37; Plut. Eum. 3,3; Curt. 10,10,3; Iust. 13,4,16; 8). After a one-year siege by Antigonus [1] Monophthalmos who had been dispatched against him, E. escaped from Nora near the Taurus mountains and subsequently fought against him as 'the authorized *strategos* of Asia' for the new regent of the empire Polyperchon. Through a cult with the insignia of Alexander, E. consolidated his precarious position as a Greek amongst the Macedonian soldiers. E.'s advocacy of the unity of the empire created by Alexander (Nep. Eum. 7; Diod. Sic. 18,39ff.; 60f.; Plut.

Eum. 11f.; Polyaenus, Strat. 4,8,2; Iust. 14,1f.) may also have spoken in his favour. E. was driven away by Antigonus via Syria and Babylonia to Iran, pitched an undecided battle against him in Paraetacene, but lost the battle in Gabiene and was handed over by his own troops to the victor in winter 316/5 and executed (Nep. Eum. 8ff.; Diod. Sic. 18,62f.; 73; 19,12–44; Plut. Eum. 16–19; Iust. 14,3f.).

BENGTSON 1, 1937, 171ff.; BERVE 2, 156–158; P. BRIANT, D'Alexandre le Grand aux Diadoques, in: REA 74, 1972, 32–73 and 75, 1973, 43–81; R.M. ERRINGTON, From Babylon to Triparadeisos, in: JHS 90, 1970, 49–77; Id., Diodorus Siculus and the Chronology of the Early Diadochoi, in: Hermes 105, 1977, 478–504; WILL. A.ME.

[2] **E. I.** Of Pergamum, son of E., adopted like his cousin Attalus [3] by his paternal uncle, Philetaerus; he succeeded him as ruler of Pergamum in 263 BC (IG XI 4,1107; OGIS 266; SEG 35,409; Str. 13,4,2). With his victory in 262/1 over Antiochus [2] I at Sardeis, E. established his independence from the Seleucids with whom he was however on friendly terms from then on. E. was allied with Ptolemy II without becoming his dependant. E. increased the size of the Pergamene kingdom, which was still small, but he paid tributes to the Galatians (OGIS 266: place names; Liv. 38,16,14; Str. 13,4,2). E. influenced the self-government of the city of Pergamum through *strategoi* appointed by him; the city honoured him with games, the Eumeneia. E. sponsored science. He died in 261 (Str. 13,4,2; Diog. Laert. 4,38; 5,67).

[3] **Eumenes II Soter.** Of Pergamum, eldest son of Attalus [4] I. (cf. [1]). He reigned from 197 BC onwards, for a short period as co-regent with his father, after his father's death alone [2]. Like his father and with the constant and active support of his brother Attalus [5] (II), E. advocated the freedom of the Greeks, trusted in co-operation with Rome, from which he profited for the first time as early as 197/6, and extended his rule at the cost of neighbouring monarchies. In 194 he rejected an alliance offer from Antiochus [5] III, instead urging the Romans to make war on him, supported them in 191 in the naval battle at Corycus, then in their crossing of the Hellespont and himself contributed to the joint victory over Antiochus at the beginning of 189 at Magnesia (Syll.[3] 595; 605; Pol. 21,3b; 8; Liv. 34,26,11; 29,4; 30,7; 35,13,6ff.; 17,1; 36,42,6–43,4; 37,39ff.; 53,13; App. Syr. 31; 33f.).

After negotiations skilfully conducted by him in Rome, primarily against the remonstrances of the Rhodians, E. acquired in 188, in consequence of the Roman-Seleucid peace of Apamea and as a Roman gift, large parts of what had previously been Seleucid Asia Minor, including the coastal towns of Ephesus, Tralleis and Telmessus. His enormously enlarged kingdom now stretched from the Thracian Chersonesus to the south-eastern Mediterranean and the Taurus mountains; it was the strongest power in Asia Minor (Pol. 21,18ff.; 46; Liv. 37,52ff.; 38,39,8; 14ff.; Str. 13,4,2). After a war against the Galatians and against King Prusias I of Bithynia (186–183), E. managed to increase his territory thanks to Roman intervention and despite the maritime defeat he suffered against Hannibal who was working for Prusias ([1]; Nep. Hann. 10; Iust. 32,4). In 183, E. entered into military assistance treaties with 31 Cretan towns (ICret. 4, 179 = [3]). In the war against Pharnaces of Pontus (182–179) in which there was a clash between the various interests of E. and Rhodes, E. won additional territories. In 175 he supported Rome's candidate Antiochus [6] IV as successor to the throne of Seleucus IV (OGIS 248; Pol. 25,2; 27,7; App. Syr. 45). After accusations against the Macedonian king Philip V (esp. 186/5), E. stirred up opinion against his successor Perseus in 172 in Rome, warning of Macedonian influence in Greece (Liv. 42,11ff.; Val. Max. 2,2,1; App. Mac. 11).

When E. had been attacked on the home journey at Cirrha, probably at Perseus' orders, and was considered dead, his brother Attalus [5] (II) took over rule and married E.'s wife Stratonice, but relinguished both after E. arrived in Pergamum alive (Diod. Sic. 29,34,2; Liv. 42,16; Plut. Mor. 489E-F). The brothers continued their joint policy. In the war of the Romans against Perseus (171–168), E. was unsuccessful in the sieges of Cassandria and Demetrias (Liv. 44,12,4). His dispute with the Roman consul Marcius Philippus and the attempts by Perseus to build closer ties with him made the Romans suspicious of him for years to come and caused them, albeit futilely, to incite his brother Attalus against E. (Pol. 29,4ff.; 30,1ff.; 31,1; 32,1; Liv. 44,24f.; 45,19f.; Vell. Pat. 1,9,2; App. Mac. 18). In 167/6, E. wanted to justify his policy in Rome, but the Senate refused to hear him and also did not allow him to rule over the Galatians whom he had successfully fought, instead declaring them independent in 166 (WELLES 55ff.; Pol. 29,6,3f.; 30,20; 31,2; 6; Iust. 38,6,4). E. continued to support Greek towns with endowments and their sympathy for him even increased because of his difficult position with the Romans; among these were Athens, Delphi, Miletus, Rhodes and Calauria. In Pergamum he erected many buildings and by creating the library made the city into a centre of Greek culture and scholarship (IG IX 1^2 1,179; 183; OGIS 297; WELLES 48; cf. 52f.; SEG 36, 1046–1048; Pol. 31,6,6; 31,31; Vitr. De arch. 5,9,1; Str. 13,4,2). E. celebrated in particular his victories over the Galatians by reorganizing the Nicephoria (Syll.[3] 629) and through the construction – not completed by him – of the 'Pergamum altar' to Zeus [4]. E.'s successor was his brother Attalus [5] II, whose successor Attalus [6] III was the son of E. (according to SEG 39, 1180,68) or of Attalus II.

[4] Eumenes (III) of Pergamum. Ruler name of Aristonicus [4].

1 M. SEGRE, in: RFIC 60, 1932, 446 2 G. PETZL, Inschr. aus der Umgebung von Saittai, in: ZPE 30, 1978, 249–276, esp. 263ff. No. 12 = SEG 28,902 3 G. DUNST, in: Philologus 100, 1956, 305–311 4 TH.-M. SCHMIDT, in: B. ANDREAE et al., Phyromachos-Probleme, 1990, 141–162.

R.E. ALLEN, The Attalid Kingdom, 1983; BENGTSON 2, 1944, 195ff.; G. DAUX, Delphes au IIe et au Ier siècle, 1936, 272ff., 497ff.; C. HABICHT, Athen in hellenistischer Zeit, 1994, 183ff.; GOSHAWK; E.V. HANSEN, The Attalids of Pergamum, 1971; H.-J. SCHALLES, Unt. zur Kulturpolitik der pergamenischen Herrscher im 3. Jh. v. Chr., 1985; K. STROBEL, Die Galater, 1996; B. VIRGILIO, Fama, Eredità e Memoria degli Attalidi di Pergamo, in: Studi ellenistici 4, 1994, 137–71; WILL. A.ME.

[5] In 169/8 BC E., as the envoy of Ptolemy VI and VIII, requested from the Achaean League assistance against Antiochus [6] IV; he is documented *c.* 163 as an officer of this name.

E. OLSHAUSEN, Prosopographie der hell. Königsgesandten vol. 1, 1974, 71f. no. 49. W.A.

Eumenids see → Erinys

Eumenus (Εὔμενος; *Eúmenos*). One of the earliest Syracusan stamp cutters, manufactured around 415–400 BC, initially influenced by Sosion, predominantly tetradrachmas of varying quality. E. signed alternately with Sosion, Phrygillus, Evaenetus and Euth[...]. In the older research he is occasionally referred to as Eumenes. → Evaenetus; → Phrygillus; → Sosion; → Tetradrachmon

R. WEIL, Die Künstlerinschr. der sicilischen Münzen, in: 44. Winckelmannsprogramm der Arch. Ges. zu Berlin, 1884, esp. 5–7; L. FORRER, Biographical dictionary of medallists 2, 1904, 35–38, s.v. E.; L. TUDEER, Die Tetradrachmenprägung von Syrakus in der Periode der signierenden Künstler, in: ZfN 30, 1913, 1–292, esp. 219f.; H.R. BALDUS, Das Oeuvre des Stempelschneiders Eumenos von Syrakus im Lichte der frühen Leukaspisdrachmen, in: Chiron 2, 1972, 37–55; H.A. CAHN et al., Griech. Münzen aus Großgriechenland und Sizilien, AM Basel Sammlung Ludwig, 1988, 130f. A.M.

Eumolpus (Εὔμολπος; *Eúmolpos*, 'the one who sings well'). Mythical progenitor of the Eumolpids, the Eleusinian family from whom the → hierophant and other priests of the Eleusinian → Mysteries derived. He first appears in the Homeric hymn to Demeter (154; 475) as one of the rulers of Eleusis who were initiated into the Mysteries by the goddess. In the opinion of the Eumolpids, E. was the son of Poseidon (Paus. 1,38,2; Aristid. 22,4 and *passim*) and the first hierophant (FGrH 10 fr. 13; schol. Aeschin. 3,18). On visual representations he holds a sceptre; his iconography therefore resembles that of the hierophant [1], who with his melodious voice played the part of E. (IG II^2 3639,3–4).

According to Apollod. 3,201ff., his mother → Chione, the daughter of Boreas, threw him into the sea because of the disgrace; this was perhaps an aition of the 'baptism' of the hierophant, a ritual by which he handed over his former name to the sea (IG II^2 3811). The various ancient genealogies of E. and his adventures in Ethiopia and Thrace mostly attempted to identify the Eleusinian hierophant as the Thracian king of the same name who led the Eleusinians against Athens (Eur. Erechtheus). This aspect is obviously not older than the 5th cent. BC and it is perhaps also an invention of Euripides (cf. [2]). Another tradition customary in Athens held E. to be the son of the poet → Musaeus (FGrH 10 fr. 13 [3]). Cf. also → Exegetai.

1 K. Clinton, Myth and Cult: the Iconography of the Eleusinian Mysteries, 1992, 75–78 2 Id., The Author of the Homeric Hymn to Demeter, in: OpAth 16, 1986, 46, n. 24 3 F. Graf, Eleusis und die orphische Dichtung Athens in vorhell. Zeit, 1974, 17–18 4 O. Kern, s.v. E., RE 16, 1117–1120. K.C.

Eunapius (Εὐνάπιος; *Eunápios*). Greek sophist and historian from Sardeis (*c.* AD 347–414) [8. 2–4], who, apart from a comprehensive philosophical and rhetorical eduction by → Chrysanthius and → Prohaeresius also possessed excellent medical knowledge and the favour of → Oribasius. In his writings E. was a determined opponent of Christianity, to which, an adherent of → Julian [11] the Apostate (Fr. 1,95–101 Blockley), he opposed the concept of a restored Greek → *paideía*.

Of the 'Histories' (Ἱστορικὰ ὑπομνήματα/*Historikà hypomnémata*, 14 vol.) that he wrote at the suggestion of Oribasius (Fr. 15,16–18 Blockley), only fragments are preserved. Some insight is provided by the works of later readers such as → Zosimus [5], who according to Photius (Phot. Bibl. Cod. 98) only rephrased E. [4. 2; 2. 19–74, 119–178]. E.'s 'Histories' were convceived as a continuation of Herennius → Dexippus' [2] work (fr. 1,90–95) and treated the events from AD 270 to 404 (Phot. Bibl. Cod. 77), with fr. 72 Blockley indicating an extension to AD 414 [6. 165], which therefore must be assumed to be the *terminus post quem* for E.'s death. The 'Histories' possibly appeared in continuous fascicles [7. 157] and were edited twice (Phot. Bibl. Cod. 77), with the νέα ἔκδοσις/*néa ékdosis* ('new edition'), probably arranged by E. himself ([4. 2–3] however, [1] disagrees), containing less material hostile to Christianity [6]. However, an exact dating of the two editions is not possible [8. 10–11]. Apart from Zosimus [5], the work was particularly used by ecclesiastical historians such as → Philostorgius and → Sozomenus (however [5]) as a source; its relationship to the history of → Ammianus Marcellinus is disputed [4. 24–25].

Probably after completing the first part of the 'Histories', E. wrote in 396 or 399 [8. 9; 3] the 'Lives of the Sophists' (βίοι σοφιστῶν/*Bíoi sophistôn*). This completely preserved work was structured following → Philostratus' [5] (B.2.) model of the same name, and contains 24 biographies of varying length of Neoplatonists, Sophists and physicians esp. of the 4th cent. AD. This collection of portraits, for which E. often resorted to oral sources and his own experience [8. 23–32], may be read as a programmatic approach to contrast Christian saints with the idealized image of pagan intellectuals but also as the author's self-representation, who as philosopher, Sophist and physician combines the qualities of these three groups in himself and thus becomes the model of the new scholar.

Editions: 'Histories': FHG 4, 7–56; R. C. Blockley, The Fragmentary Classicising Historians of the Later Roman Empire, vol. 2, 1983, 1–150 (with English translation and commentary). 'Lives of the Sophists': G. Giangrande, Eunapii Vitae Sophistarum, 1956; W. C. Wright, Philostratus and Eunapius: The Lives of the Sophists, 1921 (reprint 1998; with English translation).

Bibliography: 1 A. Baker, Eunapius' Νέα Ἔκδοσις and Photius, in: GRBS 29, 1988, 389–402 2 A. Baldini, Ricerche sulla storia di Eunapio di Sardi, 1984 3 T. M. Banchich, The Date of Eunapius' *Vitae Sophistarum*, in: GRBS 25, 1984, 183–192 4 R. C. Blockley, The Fragmentary Classicising Historians of the Later Roman Empire, vol. 1, 1981 5 D. F. Buck, Did Sozomen Use Eunapius' *Histories*?, in: MH 56, 1999, 15–25 6 W. R. Chalmers, The ΝΕΑ ΕΚΔΟΣΙΣ of Eunapius' Histories, in: CQ 47, 1953, 165–170 7 W. R. Chalmers, Id., Eunapius, Ammianus Marcellinus, and Zosimus on Julian's Persian Expedition, in: CQ 54, 1960, 152–160 8 R. J. Penella, Greek Philosophers and Sophists in the Fourth Century AD, 1990. M. B.

Euneus (Εὔνηος; *Eúnēos*).

[1] Lemnian ruler, son of Hypsipyle (→ Lemnian women) and of Jason (Apollod. 1,115; Hyg. Fab. 15), brother of → Thoas [2], grandson of → Thoas [1] and great-grandson of → Dionysus. In the Trojan War he assisted both the Achaeans and the Trojans. While he was sending wine-laden ships to the former (Hom. Il 7,467–469), he bought freedom for Priamus' son Lycaon who was a prisoner of war (Hom. Il 23,746–747). – In Athens there was a 'musicians' guild' (*génos musikṓn*) by the name of Euneidai whose progenitor E. is said to have been (Hsych. s.v. Εὐνεῖδαι).

G. Berger-Doer, s.v. E. et Thoas, LIMC 4.1, 59–62; G. W. Bond, Eur. Hypsipyle, 1963, 20; P Oxy. 6,28.

[2] (Eunaeus). Son of Clytius. Trojan, killed by Camilla (Verg. Aen. 11,666–669).

G. Garbugino, s.v. E., EV 2, 423–424. R.B.

Eunicus (Εὔνικος; *Eúnikos*) Poet of Attic Old Comedy, of whom we have two play titles (and two fragments, the second uncertain). For a play about hetaerae, Ἄντεια/*Ánteia* (test. ii), Philyllius is also cited as the author while for the Πόλεις/*Póleis* Philyllius and Aristophanes are also named as authors.

1 PCG 5, 278f. H.-G.NE.

Eunomia (Εὐνομία, Εὐνομίη; *Eunomía, Eunomíē*). Personification of good order. Along with → Dike and → Eirene she is one of the three → Horae (Hes. Theog. 901–902), the daughters of Zeus and Themis. Only in Alcman (PMG 64) is E. the daughter of Promatheia ('foresight, consideration') and sister of → Tyche and

→ Peitho. In her role as the guardian of peace (cf. Pind. Pyth. 5,66–67: *eunomía apólemos*, 'unwarlike E.'), E. is praised particularly in times of crisis (Tyrtaeus IEG fr. 1–4; Solon IEG fr. 4, 32–39); in the 5th cent. (in the Peloponnesian War) E. became a political catchword [1], which is also reflected in the iconography [2]. In Athens she was worshipped in a cult together with → Euclea [3]; for Aegina cf. Bacchyl. 13,182–189SM.

1 G. Grossmann, Polit. Schlagwörter aus der Zeit des Peloponnesischen Krieges, 1950, 30–89 2 A. Kossatz-Deissmann, s.v. E., LIMC 4.1, 62–65 3 R. Hampe, Eukleia u. E., in: MDAI(R) 62, 1955, 111f.

M. Ostwald, Nomos and the Beginnings of Athenian Democracy, 1969, 62–85; H. A. Shapiro, Personifications in Greek Art, 1993, 79–85. R.B.

Eunomius (Εὐνόμιος; *Eunómios*). Bishop of Cyzicus († about AD 394). Of lowly origins, E., who was connected with the bishops Aetius of Alexandria and Eudoxius of Antioch, became Bishop of Cyzicus about AD 360. Following opposition he gave up his office. With the death of Aetius (367), E. became the sole leader of the church community of the Anhomoiousians (→ Arianism) which had broken away from the imperial church. He was exiled repeatedly. Only a few of his writings are extant, among these being the Ἀπολογητικός (*Apologētikós*) that was written about 360 and the work that was written in 378 as a response to the criticism of → Basilius [1] of Caesarea – Ἀπολογία ὑπὲρ ἀπολογίας (*Apología hypèr apologías*). Uncertain from the point of view of historical derivation, E., building on his theory of language [3], represents a heightened Arian position ('transcendentalism carried to extremes' [2. 526]).

Edition: 1 R. P. Vaggione, E. The Extant Works, 1987. Bibliography: 2 A. M. Ritter, s.v. E., TRE 10, 525–528 3 K.-H. Uthemann, Die Sprache der Theologie nach E. von Cyzicus, in: ZKG 104, 1993, 143–175. J.RI.

Eunomus (Εὔνομος; *Eúnomos*).
[1] Young cup-bearer and relative of King Oeneus. Hercules punches E. for his clumsiness, killing him, and then goes into voluntary exile in Trachis at the court of King Ceyx (Hellanicus FGrH 4 F 2; Apollod. 2,150).
[2] Spartan king of the clan of the Eurypontids. Perhaps the name was however only inserted on the royal list as a personification of → Eunomia [1]. Hdt. 8,131 places E. between → Polydectes and → Charillus, Paus. 3,7,2 between → Prytanis and Polydectes. According to Plut. Lycurgus 1,8, 40a-b, he was usually regarded as → Lycurgus' father (but by Simonides as a brother of Lycurgus and a son of Prytanis). As such it is said that he was murdered with a kitchen knife during the unrest that preceded the Lycurgan legislation. Dion. Hal. Ant. Rom. 2,49,4 took a different view again, regarding him as a nephew of Lycurgus.

1 P. Cartledge, Sparta and Lakonia, 1979, 104; 344. R.B.

Eunones King of the Aorsi, supported C. → Iulius Aquila and → Cotys I against → Mithridates IX. However after the capture of Uspe, he received the latter but handed him over later on the condition that his life would be spared (Tac. Ann. 12,15–20).
→ Aorsi

V. F. Gajdukevič, Das Bosporanische Reich, 1971, 342f. I.v.B.

Eunostidae (Εὐνοστίδαι; *Eunostídai*).
[1] Attic deme (?) of the phyle Ptolemais, first attested to in 201/0 BC (IG II² 2362), cf. the inscriptions of 108/7 BC (IG II² 1036 l. 37; [1. 159; 2]). In AD 154/5 (IG II² 2067) and AD 173/4 (IG II² 2103) ephebes of the phyle Ptolemais from Εὐν and Εὐ, respectively, are mentioned. Position unknown.

1 C.A. Hutton, The Greek Inscriptions at Petworth House, in: ABSA 21, 1914/16, 155–165 2 Traill, Attica 90, 114 No. 12. H.LO.

[2] Phratry in Naples, adopted from Cyme (ILS 6188), named after Eunostus, the hero of Tanagra; this is how the assumption that the E. originally came from Boeotia and had come to Cyme with the colonists of → Euboea [1] is to be understood. Under Hadrian, the phratry, retaining the old name, took on, in conjunction with the Antinous cult (→ Antinous [2]), the additional title of *Antinoítai*; it is also conceivable that the *E. Antinoítai* is the name of a new phratry [1. 107]; [2].

1 M. Garducci, L'istituzione della fratria, in: Memorie Accademia dei Lincei, Ser. 6,8, 1938, 65–135
2 E. Miranda, Iscrizioni greche d'Italia, 1990, 62f. no. 137a. U.PA. and H.SO.

Eunostus (Εὔνοστος; *Eúnostos*). Son of Pasicrates (?), at the end of the 4th and the beginning of the 3rd cent. BC he was the city king of Soli on Cyprus; under unknown circumstances he married Eirene [2] after 307. PP 6,14508. W.A.

Eunuchs Εὐνοῦχος (*Eunoûchos*, from ὁ τὴν εὐνὴν ἔχων, 'the one who supervises the bed') is the term for a male rendered infertile through castration. The word is found for the first time in Hipponax fr. 39,3 D; there are numerous synonyms, the most common being *spádōn* (from σπάω, 'tear out'), perhaps for the first time in Theophrastus (= Hier. Adversus Iovinianum 1,47), then in the Septuagint. The Latin language has adopted the Greek expressions. – The origin of the practice of castrating young boys before or during puberty in order to use them as slaves for domestic service is uncertain but it was probably related to the development of polygamy (eunuch as 'guardian of the harem'). For the Greeks it was initially an Oriental custom: in the 6th and 5th cents. BC Ionian Greeks were castrated as a 'tribute' or as prisoners of war and sent to Persia. The fact that this practice was later adopted and continued by the Graeco-Roman monogamous society can only be understood within the framework of the representative aspect of slavery: keeping slaves always meant prestige for the master; eunuchs who were particularly rare and expensive slaves attested to the particularly high social prestige of the owner. That is why in Athens we first find eunuchs as luxury slaves in the private houses of Callias (Pl. Prt. 314c) while in Rome they are first found at the house of Maecenas (Sen. Ep. 114,6). In late antiquity an upper-class household without eunuchs was inconceivable and since the 2nd cent. these had mostly been 'foreigners' (ban on castration in the Roman empire from the time of Domitian onwards). The classical duties of the eunuchs were: caring for the bedchamber, serving at meals, at bathing, physical care and dressing, raising children, and guarding property and the house. Stigmatized for life by castration (appearance, voice), the eunuchs were a marginalized group in society: as 'effeminate' men who could not meet the social norm of differentiation between the gender roles, they were on the one hand constantly rejected in Graeco-Roman antiquity, but on the other hand they were occasionally desired as 'catamites' for the very reason that they had androgynous characteristics (e.g. by Alexander the Great, Nero, Domitian).

Eunuchs in the household of a ruler reigning with absolute power could assume important political roles as court eunuchs that went beyond serving their master. Greek sources point to an institutionalized, hierarchically classified group of court eunuchs at the Persian court at the latest from the time of Xerxes I with a 'head eunuch' at the top who mostly acted politically against representatives of the aristocracy to stabilize central power. Alexander [4] the Great took over the court eunuchs of Darius III and incorporated them into his house servants; they were part of the external image of court ceremony but did not come to the fore in politics. At the Seleucid court and the court of Ptolemy there was a circle of eunuchs who personally surrounded the ruler and could certainly influence him but did not play any external political role as a group. Here there were no politically important offices reserved for eunuchs; only sporadically did they stand out politically, an example of this being Aristonicus, the leader of the army under Ptolemy V, and the court eunuchs who as rearers and guardians of princes managed the business of government for their wards (Eulaeus in 176–169 BC for Ptolemy VI, Potheinus in 51–48/7 BC for Ptolemy XIII, Ganymedes in 48/7 BC for Arsinoe IV). The Roman Principate had no institutionalized group of court eunuchs but among the imperial freedmen who had since the time of Claudius been increasingly used for administration there were time and again individual eunuchs, many of whom also performed the role of procurator or even took on military missions, such as Posides under Claudius and Pelago under Nero.

Diocletian widened the role of the court eunuchs and established them as a group of court servants within the *sacer comitatus*. The first time we read about them is in connection with the great persecution of the Christians in 303. There is evidence for the first time under Constantine of the office of → *praepositus sacri cubiculi* (*PSC*) that afterwards formed the institutional framework for the power of the highest court eunuch. From the late 4th cent. onwards, the *PSC* was equal in prestige and privilege with the top of the civil government and military leadership. Under the *PSC* there developed in the late 4th cent. and in the 5th cent. AD further court offices that were exclusively reserved for eunuchs and that corresponded with the classical tasks of a eunuch. Of all court officials the *PSC* was closest to the emperor himself. In this way he acquired monopoly over information transmission between the latter and his immediate political associates and this formed the basis of his power and wealth. Because of the lack of family ties and the stigma of castration which prevented him from developing close ties with the aristocracy, the absolute dependence of the court eunuchs on the *princeps* was a given fact; their loyalty resulting from this and the experience gained from the permanent performance of their office meant that they became for the *princeps* an instrument, with the help of which he was able to stabilize his own position in the case of conflicts with the army leadership and the aristocracy. Striking examples are the eunuchs Eusebius, *PSC* under Constantine II 337–361, Eutropius, *PSC* under Arcadius 395–399, Chrysaphius, *primicerius sacri cubiculi* and then *spatharius* (head bodyguard) under Theodosius II 441–450.

In the Byzantine period the institution of the eunuchs was preserved in the tradition of late antiquity; this also applies to their entanglement in dynastic and palace intrigues.

→ Castratio; → Spado

1 A. Demandt, Die Spätantike, 1989, 241f., 294f. 2 J. E. Dunlap, The Office of the Grand Chamberlain in the Later Roman and Byzantine Empire, in: Univ. of Michigan Studies (Human. Series) 14, 1924, 161ff. 3 P. Guyot, E. als Sklaven und Freigelassene in der griech.-röm. Ant., 1980 4 K. Hopkins, The Political Power of Eunuchs, in: Id., Conquerors, 172–196 (= Id., PCPhS 189, 1963, 62–80) 5 Jones, LRE 6 D. Schlinkert, Der Hofeunuch in der Spätantike: ein gefährlicher Außenseiter?, in: Hermes 122, 1994, 342–359 7 R. Scholl, Alexander d.Gr. und die Sklaven am Hofe, in: Klio 69, 1987, 114ff. P.GU.

Eunus (Εὔνους; *Eúnous*). Syrian, leader of the slave revolts in Sicily in 141–132 BC. He gathered together 400 slaves and conquered Enna; other towns joined the rebellion. Favoured by the good portent of his name ('well disposed') and his talent for prophecy [2. 28–29], as a result of his success he was chosen to be king in the Hellenistic manner; he called himself Antiochus (Diod. Sic. 34,2,24; [3]) and took on the traditional insignia of rule, although this indicates his desire for unity rather than a national uprising. After the first battles with the Praetorian armies (MRR 1, 482–86) between 141 and 134, Rome sent the consuls L. Calpurnius [III 1] Piso Frugi (133) and P. Rutilius (132) to fight against the

rebellious slaves who in the meantime numbered 20,000. E. was taken captive by the victorious Romans and died of disease (in Rome: Plut. Sulla 36,6; in Morgantina: Diod. Sic. 34/35,2,22–23).
→ Damophilus [1]

1 W.R. Bradley, Slavery and Rebellion in the Roman World, 1989, Index s.v. E. 2 F. Kudlien, Sklaven-Mentalität im Spiegel antiker Wahrsagerei, 1991 3 G. Manganaro, Ancora sulle rivolte 'servili' in Sicilia, in: Chiron 13, 1983, 405–409 4 W.Z. Rubinsohn, Die großen Sklavenaufstände in der Antike, 1993. ME.STR.

Euodus

[1] Imperial freedman who had great influence over Tiberius in the last year of his life. PIR² E 114.

[2] Imperial freedman who commanded the soldiers in 48 who were to kill Messalina, the wife of Claudius. PIR² E 115. W.E.

[3] Imperial freedman, the teacher of Caracalla; the honours that he was to receive from the Senate for his role in the fall of C. → Fulvius [II 11] Plautianus in AD 205 were cancelled by Severus because of his low rank (Cass. Dio 77,6,1). After the death of Severus in 211, Caracalla killed him. A.B.

[4] Evodus (Εὔοδος; *Eúodos*) Epigrammatic poet of the Imperial age (1st or 3rd cent. AD), of whom Planudes preserved two short poems, of altogether three hexameters, in the form of riddles (Anth. Pal. 16,116 and 155): the first describes a centaur, the second the phenomenon of the echo, which is int. al. referred to as the 'residue (τρύγα; *trýga*) of the voice' and the 'tail of the word'. E.D.

Euonymon (Εὐώνυμον; *Euṓnymon*). Attic *asty* deme of the phyle Erechtheis, ten (from 307/6 BC twelve) *bouleutai*. Its location has been pinpointed to 'Trachones' (modern Alimos) on the Leophoros Vouliagmenis because of epigraphical evidence. There are also Mycenaean tombs [1] and a late geometric necropolis [2; 6. 7]. E. had a northern border with Alopece, an eastern one with Hymettus, whilst in the south it bordered on Aexone and in the west on Halimus. North of the airport is the theatre of E. with an orthogonal prohedria from the 5th cent. BC that in the latter part of the 4th cent. was equipped with a new prohedria and a theatre out of breccia [3. 16f.; 4; 5; 6. 219f.]. The deme which honoured in IG II² 2829 *Charinos Charonidou* could be E. [6. 392, 429].

1 M. Benzi, Ceramica micenea in Attica, 1975, 173, 179ff., 184, 192 2 J.M. Geroulanos, Grabsitten der ausgehenden geometrischen Zeit im Bereich des Gutes Trachones, in: MDAI(A) 88, 1973, 1–54 3 H.R. Goette, Griech. Theaterbauten der Klassik, in: E. Pöhlmann (ed.), Stud. zur Bühnendichtung und zum Theaterbau der Antike, 1995, 9–48 4 H. Lohmann, Zur baugesch. Entwicklung des antiken Theaters, in: G. Binder (ed.), Das antike Theater, 1998 5 Travlos, Attika 6f. 6 Whitehead, Index s.v. E.

Traill, Attica 15, 38, 59, 63, 66f., 110 no. 45, table 1; Id., Demos and Trittys, 1986, 125. H.LO.

Eupalamus Father of → Daedalus [1].

Eupalinus of Megara, son of Naustrophus, as an → architect and engineer, presumably under the tyrant → Polycrates, was responsible for the construction of a → water supply system for the town of → Samos (modern Pythagoreion on the island of Samos) described by Herodotus (3,60) as one of the great feats of Greek engineering; there is no evidence of further work by E. The system that was rediscovered in 1853 consists of four building complexes connected with each other: a fountainhead building situated high in the mountain (→ Wells) with a great covered water reservoir, a pipeline *c.* 840 m long that follows the natural slope and that is likewise covered, the 1,036 m long tunnel with an average height of 1.80 m and a width of the same dimensions that passes through Mount Kastro with the separately incorporated channel running into it (with an artificial incline of an average 0.36%) and the 620 m long city pipeline located fully underground which fed the water into a → cistern under the theatre.

The tunnel in particular, which with a slight zigzag advanced from both sides at the same time and had numerous extant measurement markings, has assisted with research into ancient measurement and levelling techniques, although no one has been able to establish with absolute certainty how this edifice was constructed from an engineering perspective; the only certainty is that for the measurement of the tunnel E. did not use any of the foot measurements primarily asserted in metrological research (→ Building trade; → Measures). The dating of the construction of the water pipeline to between 550 and 530 BC is based on ceramic fragments that were found in front of the tunnel entrances and that obviously form the waste from the first cleaning of the tunnel pipeline performed about 530 BC; among these are fragments of a → Little-Master cup from 540/530 BC.

H. Kienast, Der Tunnel des E. auf Samos, in: Architectura 7, 1977, 97–116; Id., The Tunnel of E. at the Island of Samos, in: Ancient Technology. conference Athens 1987, 1990, 38–45; Id., Die Wasserleitung des E. auf Samos, Samos 19, 1995; H. Svenson-Evers, Die griech. Architekten archaischer und klassischer Zeit, 1996, 50–58 (bibliography.). C.HÖ.

Eupator Ti. Julius E., king of the → Regnum Bosporanum, from AD 154/5 to *c.* 174, follower of → Rhoemetalces. Coins to 170. Roman vassal, financially supported by the Romans (Lucian, Alex. 57). As the first king of the Bosporus he had a Sarmatic sign as his emblem. Most of the inscriptions come from → Panticapaeum where his residence was located (IOSPE 2, 422, 438 et al.).

V.F. Gaidukevič, Das Bosporanische Reich, 1971, 348 n. 42; 351. I.v.B.

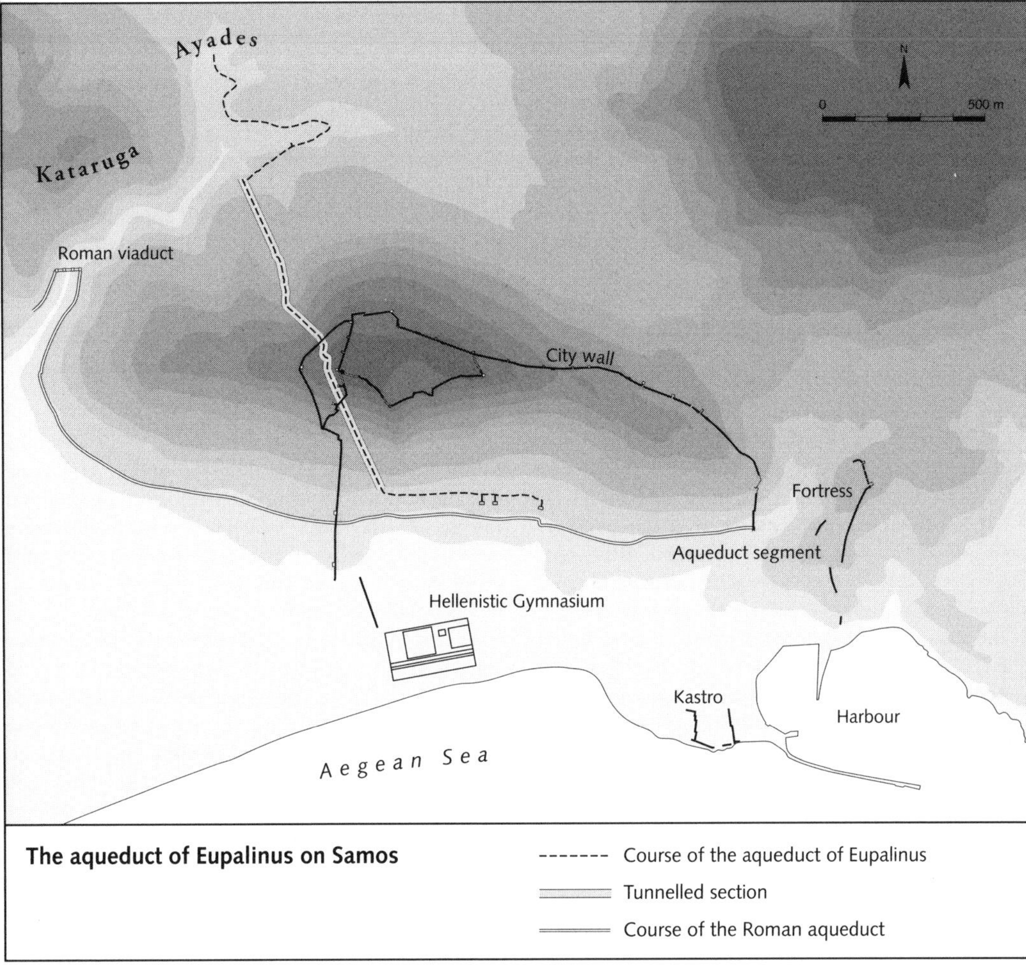

The aqueduct of Eupalinus on Samos

Eupatoria

[1] The town established by Mithridates the Great in Pontus at the confluence of the Iris (modern Yeşilırmak) into the Lycus (modern Kelkit Cayı) had without a fight opened the gates to the Romans under Lucullus in 71 BC in the 3rd Mithridatic War; as a result it was totally destroyed by the king four years later. The reconstruction had not yet been completed when Pompey captured E. in 65 BC and, renamed Magnopolis, incorporated it into the large territorium as one of 11 towns of the newly established Roman province of → *Bithynia et Pontus* (Str. 12,3,30; App. Mith. 561; [3. 27–44; 4. 43; 1. 263]). The town is mentioned for the last time in Pliny the Elder (Plin. HN 6,3,8 [2. 52–54]).

1 L. Ballesteros Pastor, Mithrídates Eupátor, 1996
2 C. Marek, Stadt, Ära und Territorium in Pontus-Bithynia und Nord-Galatia (IstForsch 39), 1993
3 Olshausen/Biller/Wagner 4 V. Tscherikover, Die hellenistischen Städtegründungen, 1927. E.O.

[2] see → Cercinitis

Eupatorium (εὐπατόριος; *eupatórios*, Dioscorides 4,41; [1. 198f.] and [2. 386]; *eupatoria*, Plin. HN 25,65). This plant of the Rosaceae species *Agrimonia eupatoria L.*, the agrimony with yellow inflorescence (cf. [3. fig. 222]), was considered by Dioscorides to be a valuable medicine for dysentery, liver complaints and snake bites. Pliny does not support the name variant *hepatoria* being derived from liver complaints [4] (nor the synonymous description ἡπατῖτις (*hēpatîtis*) in the recensio Vindobonensis of Dioscorides); allocating the *regia auctoritas* to the plant is an allusion to → Mithridates VI Eupator of Pontus (around 132–66 BC). In the Middle Ages the name eupatorium was passed to other medicinal plants e.g. the labiate *Teucrium scorodonia L.*, sage germander, and especially to the composite flower, the hemp agrimony [3rd. fig. 221] or water hemp and common basil (*herba regia*) *Eupatorium cannabinum L.*, which perhaps goes back to Avicenna.

1 M. Wellmann (ed.), Pedanii Dioscuridis de materia medica, vol. 2, 1906 (repr. 1958) 2 J. Berendes (ed.) Des Pedanios Dioscurides Arzneimittellehr, 1902 (repr. 1970) 3 H. Baumann, Die griech. Pflanzenwelt, 1982
4 H. Garms, s.v. Eupatorium, KlP 2, 1967, 430. C.HÜ.

Eupatridai (Εὐπατρίδαι; *Eupatrídai*). The term is a collective name initially for the nobility in Athens and it means descendants 'of good fathers'. It reflects an important phase in the development of the social elite into an aristocracy, a phase in which there was less emphasis or not sole emphasis on the aspects of habitus, life style and wealth that were originally constitutive for the Greek nobility but rather an emphasis on aristrocratic descent that marked a clearer distinction. The E. consisted of lineages (γένη, *génē*) that were defined by patrilineal descent and did not form any clans. Their role in ancient times remains unclear; there is evidence of an Eupatrid on a tombstome (IG I[3] 1513 = XII 9, 296 of Eretria, about the 3rd quarter of the 6th cent. BC). Other mentions are later constructs (Aristot. Ath. Pol. 13,2; Plut. Thes. 25,1ff.; 32,1). It is most likely that they had certain privileges like membership of the Areopagus (Androtion FGrH 324 F 3; Philochorus FGrH 328 F 20); Eupatrids were involved in the battle against tyranny after the assassination of Hipparchus (PMG 907). Since classical times their prerogatives were limited to the hereditary tenure of certain priestly offices as well as to the office of the phyle kings that remained relevant to cult (Poll. 8,11). In addition there was also a lineage in Athens (γένος; *génos*) by the name of *Eupatridai*, attested to from Hellenistic times in functions (esp. the office of the → *exēgētaí*, 'interpreters') within the framework of the cult of the Delphic Apollo. It seems very likely that this did not go back to older times. – *Eupatridai* is also used in Athens in later sources as a term to describe members of the aristocracy, esp. frequently as a translation of Lat. → *patricius*.

1 F. Bourriot, Recherches sur la nature du génos, 1976 2 Davies 3 E. Stein-Hölkeskamp, Adelskultur und Polisgesellschaft, 1989 4 I. Toepfler, Att. Genealogie, 1889, repr. 1973. H.-J.G.

Euphanes (Εὐφάνης; *Euphánēs*). Writer of Middle Comedy who is entered on the list of victors of the Lenaea directly before → Alexis [1. test. 1] and for whom two play titles and two fragments are attested; fr. 1 from the Μοῦσαι (*Moûsai*; 'The Muses') presents a number of contemporary Athenian gluttons.

1 PCG V, 280f. H.-G.NE.

Euphantus of Olynthus (TrGF 1, 118; FGrH 74), end of the 4th, beginning of the 3rd cent. BC; according to Diog. Laert. 2,110 teacher of → Antigonus [2] Gonatas, to whom he dedicated a work 'On the Rule of Kings' (Περὶ βασιλείας; *Perì basileías*). Writer of a history of the Diadochi period and of several successful tragedies. B.Z.

Euphemia

[1] E. Aelia Marciana. Only daughter of the emperor Marcianus, married Anthemius [2] in *c.* AD 453 who was later emperor in the west and had four sons and a daughter with him. In 467 she was elevated to *Augusta*. Her fate after the execution of her husband in 472 is unknown.

PLRE 2, 423f. No. 6.; P. Grierson, M. Mays, Catalogue of Late Roman Coins, 1992, 260f.

[2] Originally a slave of 'Barbarian' origin by the name of Lupicina, concubine, later the wife of the emperor Iustinus I. The endowment of the Euphemia church in the quarter *tà Olybríou* (τὰ 'Ολυβρίου) in Constantinople is incorrectly attributed to her. She lies buried with her husband in the monastery *tà Augoústēs* (τὰ Αὐγούστης) in Constantinople.

A. Berger, Unt. zu den Patria Konstantinupoleos, 1988, 496f., 654f.; PLRE 2, 423 No. 5. F.T.

Euphemism is the concealing description of a thing that can have disastrous effects if directly named or that can give offence. The word euphemism as a substantive belongs to εὐφημίζω, εὐφημέω (*euphēmízō*, *euphēméō*) 'to pronounce words with a good portent' (technical term since the Alexandrian grammarians).

Fear (esp. in the case of religious or superstitious euphemism) and shame are psychological factors in euphemism. Forms of euphemism: stand-in words (words that generalize as in e.g. *membrum*, words that suggest or paraphrase; also metaphors or foreign words), antiphrasis (ἀριστερός; *aristerós*), ellipsis (e.g. in oaths νὴ τόν; *nḕ tón*) etc. The most important areas of application: names of gods and demons (*Eumenides*, *Manes*; Christian: *hostis* etc. for 'devil'), topics like dying, death, killing (*abire*, cf. ThlL I, 68, 49ff.), sexuality, sexual organs, prostitutes and disease.
→ Gods, names of

I. Opelt, Euphemismus, RAC 6, 947–964 (examples, bibliography). P.FL.

Euphemus (Εὔφημος; *Eúphēmos*). In older myth, the son of Poseidon and of the Boeotian Mecionice of Hyrie (Hes. fr. 253 M.-W.); husband of the sister of Hercules, Laonome, with the ability to walk on water (probably all in Hes. fr. 253), Argonaut (Apollod. 1,112), chariot victor at the funeral games for Pelias (Cypselus chest, Paus. 5,17,9), (illegitimate) progenitor of the Battiads whom he sired with an (anon.) Lemnian woman, i.e. first ancestor of the kings of Cyrene (cf. Βάττος ... Εὐφημίδης τῶν Μινυέων, instead of MSS Εὐθυμίδης, Hdt. 4,150,2). Pindar (Pyth. 4) is of a different opinion; according to his story (initial idea: Hdt. 4,179) the Argonaut campaign only took place for the purpose of the establishment of Cyrene by Delphi: E., now the son of Poseidon who had moved to Taenarum and of the aristocratic daughter of Tityus Europe (Pind. Pyth. 4,43ff.; Apoll. Rhod. 1,179ff.), receives from Eurypylus-Trito (Pind. Pyth. 4,28ff.) on the return from Colchis in the Libyan desert a clod of earth as a pledge for a settlement in the 4th generation; however this clod gets lost (i.e.-– has to be lost as the Doric migration that took place

then did not reach Libya). Medea therefore prophecies at Thera (Pind. Pyth. 4,9ff.) that there will not be a settlement until the 17th generation (the historical time of the establishment of Cyrene in 631 BC; it is possible to ascertain this numerically, as the Argonaut Hercules cites the Spartan king-list). E. then sired the (now legitimate) first ancestor of the Battiads (with Lamache) at Lemnos (moved by Pind. to the return journey so that E. can stay there); from there the Euphemids migrate via Sparta to Thera, Cyrene's historical *mātrópolis* (Pind. Pyth. 4,20; 50ff.; 251ff.; cf. also Hdt. 4,147ff.; Apoll. Rhod. 4,1537ff.; 1731ff.).
→ Battus; → Battiads

P. Dräger, Argo pasimelousa I, 1993, 228–92. P.D.

Euphorbion (εὐφόρβιον; *euphórbion*, *euphorbea*). Name given to the gum resin (Plin. HN 25,77f.) of the cactus-like species of spurge (*Euphorbia resinifera*, *beaumeriana* and *antiquorum*) which King Juba II of Mauretania found in the Atlas Mountains and is said to have named after his personal physician Euphorbius. Dioscorides 3,82 [1. 98f.] and 3,86 [2. 320f.] however mentions a king of the Libyans of the same name as the person who coined the name. According to Isidorus (Orig. 17,9,26), the name *euphorbium* is derived from the sharpening of the eye-sight through its sap – euphorbium allegedly caused good vision as well as curing snake bite. The plant genus itself was called τιθύμαλλος (*tithýmallos*, Theophr. Hist. pl. 9,15,6) or τιθύμαλλον (*tithýmallon*, Dioscorides 4,164 [1. 309–313] and 4,162 [2. 458–460]); seven species were differentiated [3. fig. 228, 233].

1 M. Wellmann (ed.) Pedanii Dioscuridis de materia medica, vol. 2, 1906 (repr. 1958) 2 J. Berendes (ed.) Des Pedanios Dioscurides Arzneimittellehr, 1902 (repr. 1970) 3 H. Baumann, Die griech. Pflanzenwelt, 1982. C.HÜ.

Euphorbus (Εὔφορβος; *Eúphorbos*). Hero in the *Iliad* on the Trojan side, son of Panthoos and Phrontis [1]. Together with Hector he killed Patroclus (Il. 16,806–815); Menelaus killed him in a counter-strike (Il. 17,9–60) [2]. His shield was kept at the Heraeum of Argus (Paus. 2,17,3). → Pythagoras considered himself to be an incarnation of E. (Heraclid. Pont. fr. 89 Wehrli/Schule; Callim. Fr. 191,59–63 Pfeiffer; Diog. Laert. 8,1,4; Ov. Met. 15,160–163 etc.) [3; 4].

1 P. v. d. Mühll, Kritisches Hypomnema zur Ilias, 1952, 255 2 L. Kahil, s.v. E., LIMC 3.1, 69 3 W. Burkert, Lore and Science in Ancient Pythagoreism, 1972, 138–141 4 F. Bömer, P. Ovidius Naso. Metamorphosen, bks. 14/15, 1986, ad locum. C.A.

Euphorion (Εὐφορίων; *Euphoríōn*).
[1] A figure invented by Ptolemy Chennus (Phot. 149a): E., a winged son of Achilles and Helena, is killed on the island of Melos by a bolt of lightning from Zeus whose love he does not reciprocate. The nymphs who bury the corpse are changed into frogs by Zeus. In Goethe's Faust (2nd Part), E. appears as the son of Faust and Helena.

K.-H. Tomberg, Die Kaine Historia des Ptolemaios Chennos, 1967, 108. R.B.

[2] **of Athens.** Tragedian, son of Aeschylus. He won prizes on four occasions with tragedies by his father (Suda ε 3800, see also DID C 8). He won the Dionysia of 431 BC, beating Sophocles and Euripides (DID C 12), probably with his own tragedies [1. 56].

1 H. Hoffmann, Chronologie der attischen Tragödie, 1951.

Mette, 18 and 162; TrGF 12. F.P.

[3] Greek author with varied interests, born in Chalcis between 275 and 268 BC. According to details from the Suda, he studied writing under → Archebulus of Thera (= Archebulus apud Heph. 28,14?) and philosophy under Lacydes (head of the Academy after 241/240 BC) and Prytanis (Peripatetic who was still alive in 222) in Athens. According to Helladius (Phot. 279,532b 18 B. = T 3 van Groningen [= v.G.]) he obtained Athenian citizenship. He became the lover of Nicaea, the wife of Alexander [9]. He became rich, perhaps as a result of this relationship (cf. Plut. Mor. 472d = T 6 v. G.); he then went to the court of Antiochus III the Great in Syria who entrusted to him the management of the library of Antiochia.

With regard to the philological-historical work of E., little more is known than the titles of several prose works: 'Historical treatise' (Ἱστορικὰ ὑπομνήματα; *historikà hypomnḗmata*), a work about the vocabulary of Hippocrates; 'On the Aleuadae', 'On the Isthmian Games', 'On the Lyricists'. *Hēsíodos* (Ἡσίοδος) was a hexametric poem about the death of the poet who was depicted as a hero (like Eratosthenes' *Anterinýs?*), if F 23 v. G. is to be attributed to this work. With regard to some poems of which only the titles are known, it is only possible to hypothesize on the basis of extant testimonies. For the titles for which there is no relationship with mythological figures or for which no such relationship is known, no hypothesis appears to be satisfactory: *Apollódōros* (Ἀπολλόδωρος), *Artemídōros* (Ἀρτεμίδωρος), *Dēmosthénēs* (Δημοσθένης); *Klḗtōr* (Κλήτωρ), *Xénios* (Ξένιος), *Polycharēs* (Πολυχάρης), 'answers to Theodoridas' (Ἀντιγραφαὶ πρὸς Θεοδορίδαν). In *Aléxandros* (Ἀλέξανδρος) the etymology of the Cilician town of Soli was discussed: was it a work about Alexander the Great who stayed there or rather a court poem dedicated to the husband of Nicaea, or a mythological epyllion about Paris, in the same onomastic fashion that made Lycophron use the title *Alexándra* (Ἀλεξάνδρα) for his poem about Cassandra? Similarly, with the *Hippomédōn meízōn* (Ἱππομέδων μείζων) one thinks either of a mythological epyllion or an encomiastic poem.

The following were certainly mythological-aetiological epyllia: 1. *Ánios* (Ἄνιος): the son or descendant of Apollo, father of Elais, Spermos and Oinos, who brought forth olives, wheat and wine. 2. *Diónysos* (Διόνυσος): an aetiological treatise on customs, cults, origins of towns that can be linked with Dionysus. As almost all the fragments relate to Greece, the triumphal march with which the god captured the Greek towns for his cult perhaps represents the leitmotif (cf. also Nonnus, Dion. 44–47). 3. *Diónysos kechēnṓs* (Διόνυσος κεχηνώς, 'Dionysus with the open mouth'): the aition of the foundation of this cult on Samos (cf. Plin. HN 8,21,57f.) must have been at this poem's centre; Eratosthenes also appears to have written about it, cf. Ael. NA 7,48. 4. *Ínachos* (Ἴναχος) and/or *Istíē* (Ἰστίη): a work with a dual title or two separate works about the aition of the foundation of the Macedonian capital city Aegae by Caranus of Argus. 5. *Hyákinthos* (Ὑάκινθος): in the centre was the aetiology of the flower; in F 44 v. G., E. explicitly recalls the traditional version, its origin in the blood of Ajax; in F 47 v. G. the wounded Adonis is mentioned, without doubt because his blood gives rise to another flower, the anemone or the rose. 6. *Philoktḗtēs* (Φιλοκτήτης (F 48 v. G.): Philoctetes lying on the beach on the point of death is rescued on Lemnos by the shepherd Iphimachus; the Greeks had left him there after he was bitten by a snake. In F 49 v.G. he founds Crimisa in the Crotoniatis after his arrival in Italy and there he introduces the cult of Apollo Alaeus (an additional extremely rare myth that is obviously in the aetiological style). 7. *Mopsopía ḕ Átakta* (Μοψοπία ἢ Ἄτακτα) was probably a colourful collection (συμμιγεῖς ἱστορίαι) explains the Suda; cf. in addition Philetas' *Átaktoi glṓssai*) of myths that were at least partially of aetiological relevance and connected with Attica.

The three works that belong to the genre of curse poetry were also in catalogue form. The *Chiliádes* (Χιλιάδες; 5 bks.) contained, according to Suda, examples of punishments that were unavoidable even if they followed long after the wrong was committed. They were meant to remind those who had stolen from the poet the money entrusted to him that immense punishment awaited them. 'Curses or the Cup Thief' (Ἀραὶ ἢ Ποτηριοκλέπτης) was also a list of the cruel sufferings of mythical figures which E. wants to befall the thief of a drinking-cup (F 10 v.G.).

'The Thracian' (Θρᾶξ; *Thrâix*) is the best-known poem because of the papyrus fragments: in SH 415 E. wishes that one of his enemies – perhaps the murderer of a guest (cf. c. I C, 19 and II, 11 and 25f.; the inhospitable nature of the Thracians was notorious) – should experience the terrible loves of obscure mythological figures (Clymenus and Harpalyce, Semiramis, Trambelus and Apriate); the impetus for wishing that his enemy would suffer shipwreck was the mention of Apriate in the waves: E. had a predilection known in antiquity for erudite incomprehensibility; this is confirmed by the extant fragments. It is demonstrated in the choice of themes (predilection for shorter myths for which aetiological poetology was an ideal form), and also on the narrative level in the presentation of myths and their characters by means of short, sometimes almost enigmatic allusions, e.g. F 11 v. G., and in selected descriptions using weird epithets or patronymics, e.g. F 48, 3 v. G., as well as on the lexical level (in his studied preference for rare words). Typically the Greek authors who demonstrate the most points in common with E. (Callimachus, Alexander Aetoleus, Lycophron, Nicander, Parthenius, Nonnus) are likewise characterized by particular erudition.

In the 1st cent. BC, E. was particularly famous in Rome where – no less than Callimachus – he became the symbol for and model of the 'new' writing that countered that of Ennius and national ancient poetry on a monumental scale (cf. Cic. Tusc. 3,19,45). The elegiac poet Cornelius Gallus still defines his *carmina* as *Chalcidico ... condita versu* (Verg. Ecl. 10,50f.; probably rather an allusion to E. than to the incomprehensible Theocles of Naxos or Eretria, the inventor of the elegy, according to Suda ε 772). Philargyrius, Servius and Probus ad T 14 v. G. also unanimously describe Gallus as an imitator of the elegiac poet and as his translator into Latin. In spite of this, only two epigrams in distichs by E. are extant (Anth. Pal. 6,279 and 7,651), whilst all the fragments preserved for us are hexametric. It is probable that the only reason why E. is referred to as an elegiac poet is that Gallus made use of him [1].

1 F. JACOBY, Zur Entstehung der röm. Elegie, in: RhM 60, 1905, 70 n.

EDITIONS: F. SCHEIDWEILER, 1908; CollAlex; L.A. DE CUENCA, 1976; B.A. VAN GRONINGEN, 1977 (with comm.); SH (papyrus fragments).
BIBLIOGRAPHY: F. DELLA CORTE et al., E. e i poeti latini, in: Maia 17, 1965, 158–176; L. ALFONSI, E. e l'elegia, in: Miscellanea di studi alessandrini in memoria di A. Rostagni, 1963, 455–468; A. BARIGAZZI, Il Dionysos di E., in: ibid., 416–454; J.A. CLÚA, E.'s Dionysos, in: Prometheus 17, 1991, 111–124; Id., El Jacinto de E. y el problema del élegos, in: Emerita 59, 1991, 39–51; K. LATTE, Der Thrax des E., in: Philologus 90, 1935, 129–155; G. SCHULTZE, Euphorionea, 1888; F. SKUTSCH, s.v. E., RE VI, 1174–1190; P. TREVES, E. e la storia ellenistica, 1955; C. TUPLIN, Cantores E., in: Papers of the Liverpool Latin Seminar, 1976, 1–23; L.C. WATSON, Cinna and E., in: SIFC 54, 1982, 93–110; L.C. WATSON, Arae: the Curse Poetry of Antiquity, 1991.
M.FA.

Euphranor (Εὐφράνωρ; *Euphránōr*).
[1] Important sculptor, painter and art critic (→ Art, theory of) in Athens with his acme in 364–361 BC. As paintings the 'Battle of Mantinea' (362 BC), the 'Apotheosis of Theseus' and 'Twelve Gods in the Stoa Eleutherios' are described and 'Democracy and Demos' and 'Odysseus' are mentioned. E. described his 'Theseus' as 'meat-nourished' in contrast to the 'rose-nourished' one by → Parrhasius. Ancient art critics emphasized the versatility and *dignitas* of his representation of the gods and are probably oriented towards the lost *volumina de symmetria et coloribus* of E. They justified and at the same time made more difficult the recognition of his sculpture, much of which later went to Rome. None of

the numerous images of the gods that have been passed down in copies to us can be recognized with confidence as his work. The identifications of 'Leto with the Twins' with a type in Rome or of 'Philip and Alexander on the Quadriga' with the so-called 'Alexander Rondanini' are mostly rejected. Only the cult image of Apollo Patroos from the temple on the Athenian Agora is generally recognized in an original marble torso found there.

LIPPOLD, 260–261; OVERBECK, No. 1109, 975, 1073, 1074, 1191, 1704, 1726–1728, 1785–1806 (sources); O. PALAGIA, E., 1980; I. SCHEIBLER, Griech. Malerei der Antike, 1994, 72–74, 98, 117, 153, 155, 162; STEWART, 287–288; H. A. THOMPSON, Buildings on the West side of the Agora, in: Hesperia 6, 1937, 90–115; L. TODISCO, Scultura greca del IV secolo, 1993, 91–103. R.N.

[2] Commander of the Rhodian ships in Caesar's fleet, who fought off the coast of Alexandria and died in February 47 in the naval battle of Canopus (Bell. Alex. 11; 13; 15f.; 25). W.W.

Euphrates

[1] Stoic philosopher from Syrian Tyre (born *c.* AD 40). He married into the family of Pompeius Iulianus, moved to Rome and was perhaps under the patronage of the emperor. Under Hadrian he committed suicide in 118 BC. The skilful protreptic orator (→ Protreptics) did not allow himself to be infected by the Cynic fashion and supported moderation and rationalism in philosophical as well as political matters. His resistance to Neo-Pythagorean and Chaldaean tendencies and his professional jealousy brought him into conflict with → Apollonius [14] of Tyana. Main sources: Philostr. VS 1,7,2 (487f.); 1,25,5 (536), VA 5,33; 37, Epist. Apollonii 14–18, 50–52; Plin. Ep. 1,10; Cass. Dio 69,8,3; Epict. 3,15,8; 4,8,17–20.

M. FREDE, E. of Tyre, in: R. SORABJI (ed.), Aristotle and After (BICS Suppl. 68), 1997, 1–11. B.I.

[2] The longest river in the Middle East of *c.* 2,760 km, attested to since the 3rd millennium BC as Sumerian *Buranuna*, Akkadian *Purattu*/ *Purantu*, Biblical *Pərāṯ*, Arabic *al-Furāt*.

Modern Kara-Su that is still called E. in its lower reaches near Erzerum and the Murat-Su join above modern Malatya to form the actual E. Ancient authors regard the Murat-Su (*Arsanias*, Plin. HN 5,84; Plut. Lucullus 31; Assyrian *Arsania*) as only a tributary. Herodutus is the first to name the source of the E. in Armenia (1,180ff.; cf. among others Plin HN 5,84; Ptol. 5,12,3; Dionys. Per. 978). Mentioned are also the Abos mountain range close to the source of the Araxes (→ Araxes) near Erzerum (Str. 11,14,2), and the Pyxurates as a source (Plin. HN 5,83). The deep cleft of the E. as it cuts through the Taurus mountain range made it a natural border line. In this way it formed the eastern border of → Cappadocia and → Commagene. From the time of Vespasian, the Cappadocian and the Euphrates *limes* ran there [3]. Important crossings were at → Melitene (Malatya) and → Samosata (Samsat).

North of Zeugma the E. reaches Mesopotamia. From there the river is navigable, although it is quite dangerous in stormy weather and hampered locally by the strong meandering of the river bed. Routes along the banks often facilitated faster communication. In places ranges of hills stretch down to the river bank. The section between Zeugma and the bend in the Euphrates near Meskene formed a natural border between the ancient Oriental states of Mesopotamia and northern Syria, between Romans and Parthians, and the same applied to the Assyrian, Persian and Roman provincial organization (cf. e.g. the Aramaic provincial term *eber nāri*, 'over the river' for Syria). East of the E. however, stretches a wide steppe area so that the left bank was often still fully or partly controlled by northern Syria. The most important crossing from the Hellenistic time onwards was → Zeugma/Seleucea that became more important than the more southerly crossing at → Karchemish (modern Ǧarābulus), a small state and trading centre of the 3rd–1st millennia BC. The Assyrian gateway to northern Syria (9th–7th cents. BC) was situated at → Til Barsip (Tall Aḥmār). An additional crossing in ancient times was at Qalʿat Naǧm.

At Eski Meskene (ancient *Emar*, Greek *Barbalissos*/ *Balis*), the final point of the trade route leading from Babylonia to northern Syria, the E. turns in a southeasterly direction. Larger tributaries are the Nahr al-Balīḫ, at the mouth of which the ancient town of Tuttul and in Graeco-Roman times → Nicephorium/Callinicum (near modern Raqqa) lay, and the → Ḫabur with Circesion. As important roads also ran along these tributaries and steppe routes from Syria reached the middle E. via → Palmyra (Tadmor) and from the Arabian peninsula, there were always important trading towns there. The entire section of the river was an often rapidly changing, strongly fortified border zone between Assyria and Babylonia and the Roman or Byzantine Imperium and the Parthians/Sassanids. In the 3rd millennium BC right up to its destruction by → Ḫammurapi of Babylon (17th cent. BC), the kingdom of → Mari (Tall Ḥarīrī) controlled the trade on the E., while in the middle of the 2nd millennium it was controlled by the city of Terqa (Tall ʿAšāra), capital city of Ḫana. The Assyrian residence of the governor Ḫindānu (Tall al-Ǧābirīya) in the 8th/7th cents. BC was the end of a caravan track from → Saba and → Teima. Similar roles until its destruction by → Sapor I were held by the Hellenistic, Parthian and Roman → Dura-Europus. South of the mouth of the Ḫabur lie islands in the E. from which traffic could be controlled at least from the beginning of the 1st millennium BC, the greatest of these being modern "ʿĀna', (Assyrian, Babylonian, Palmyrian, Persian and Greek or Latin sources), with date palm cultivations, the centre of a small state in the 9th/8th cents. BC, also modern Ǧazīrat Talbīs (Assyrian Talbiš; Isid. Charax, Mans. Parth. [stathmoì Parthikoí] 1, Θιλαβοῦς (*Philaboûs*), supposedly with Parthian treasure), Ǧazīrat Baiǧān (Assyrian, Parthian and Roman fortress), etc. Alexander the Great used ships at

Thapsacus (Dibsi) (Arr. Anab. 3,7,1). Julian's campaign was also accompanied by a fleet (Amm. Marc. 23,3,9). There is no evidence however of a permanent Roman E. fleet. The office of a *dux ripae* is known from Dura-Europus [7. 3,30ff.]. Ancient Babylonian texts from Mari [4] attest to measurements of the water level of the E. and its tributaries as well as the side canals serving as retention pools for irrigation and as means of transport. Important ancient canals ran between the mouth of the Ḫābūr and the E. and between Dura-Europus and modern Abu Kamāl.

After al-Ḥīt (ancient Itu) with its asphalt sources, the E. enters alluvial, central Babylonia at Fallūǧaū and divides into several side branches that are permanently changing. The high salt content results here in a strong increase in the salination of the soil that increases from north to south. Flooding after the melting of the snow in the north was a regular occurrence so channels, damming and drainage of the water of the E. were therefore the prerequisite for the intensive agrarian use of Babylonia. Most of the larger Babylonian centres were located on the branches of the E. and on the side canals, e.g. → Babylon. Goods were to a large extent transported by ship. Where the E. and the Tigris came together, canals united the two river systems e.g. the → Naarmalcha (Babylonian *nr̄ šarri*) that flows into the Tigris at Seleucea that is often wrongly distinguished in ancient authors from another 'royal river'. Near Babylon was the mouth of the Palacottas (Babylonian *Pallukattu*) that was sailed by Alexander (Arr. Anab. 7,21). In astronomical cuneiform texts of the Seleucid and early Parthian period from Babylon there are many notes with dates regarding the water level and observations of particular hydrological phenomena [5].

In the south of Mesopotamia the E., dividing into several branches, winds through a wide swamp area (Ḥōr) and joins the Tigris at al-Qurna. The reconstruction of its earlier course is a contentious issue as flooding catastrophes greatly changed the landscape and the coastline of the Persian Gulf. One branch of the E. appears to have temporarily facilitated direct access to the Gulf. The ancient authors had no clear ideas about its course and speculate about its disappearance in the swamps or often have it flowing, separate from the Tigris, into the Gulf or as in Herodotus 1,180, into the Red Sea (cf. among others Str. 11,14,7; 15,3,5f.; 16,4,1; Mela 3,77; Arr. Anab. 5,5,5; 7,7,5).

Lucullus made offerings to the E. when he crossed it (Plut. Lucullus 24,5). In addition to indications of regional cult worship of the river god E. (→ River gods), e.g. coins (Samosata), paintings from Dura-Europus, the relief of Ayni (in Zeugma) and the mosaic of Tall Masʿūdīya (inscription: βασιλευς ποταμος Ευφρατης and Syrian *prt mlkʾ*; → Bilingual inscriptions), there are often allegorical representations of the E. on Roman mosaics and on Imperial Roman coins [1].

→ Limes; → Euphrates frontier

1 J. Balty, LIMC 4.1, 70–74 2 F. R. Chesney, Narrative of the E.-Expedition, 1868 3 H. Hellenkemper, Der Limes am nordsyrischen Euphrat, in: Stud. zu den Militärgrenzen Roms II, 1977, 461–471 4 B. Lafont, Nuit dramatique à Mari, in: J.-M. Durand, Mémoires de NABU (Nouvelles assyriologiques brèves et utilitaires) 1, 1992, 93–105 5 A. Sachs, H. Hunger, Astronomical Diaries I–III, 1988ff. 6 F. Weissbach, s.v. Euphrat, RE VI 1, 1195–1215 7 Dura Report IX.

K.KE.

Euphrates frontier (Roman) The Euphrates was part of the extensive Roman defence system that stretched from the Black Sea to the Red Sea and that was meant to fortify Asia Minor with Pontus, Cappadocia and Armenia, parts of the Caucasus, the central Euphrates region, Syria and Palestine against attacks from Iran and Mesopotamia. The river was originally the demarcation line and political frontier between Rome and the Parthian empire before it became a military zone that was kept under surveillance and that – as the most recent research [1] has emphasized – by no means was of a purely defensive nature but served at the same time as a line of communications and supplies for military operations. The Euphrates therefore never became a political and military border in the actual sense (apart from partial sections in the north; treaties of Iovianus in AD 363 and Theodosius II in 422). The incorporation of Mesopotamia as part of the Roman empire remained a mere incident. The Romans could ultimately only hold northern Mesopotamia and Osrhoene in the southern bend of the Euphrates. The actual border zone formed a surveillance and defence line with a mixed population on both sides and a Romanized upper class. The Roman frontier system should therefore be regarded as a zone [1] with changing spheres of influence that remained open to east-west trade and that could not disrupt the deeper-lying continuing traditions.

The role of a frontier line already mirrors the Archaemenid satrap classification and could be seen in the offer of Darius III to Alexander [4] the Great in 333 BC to divide the empire. The uniform political area with its urbane civilization (cities established under Seleucus I) was also preserved under the Seleucids, who however with the loss of Mesopotamia (142–139 BC) to the Parthians were limited to Syria situated west of the Euphrates (unsuccessful campaign of Antiochus VII in 129 BC). With the appearance of the Romans (Sulla in 96 BC) the central Euphrates served as the demarcation line between both great powers and as a border for the province of Syria that was newly created by Pompey in 64 BC west of the bend in the Euphrates. This partition line was also used as a basis for the negotiations with the Parthians in 20 BC (surrender to Augustus of the ensigns taken at Carrhae in 53 BC) and despite the operations of Corbulo in the sixties of the 1st cent. AD was retained until the campaigns of Trajan (114–117). In view of the war of retribution that had still not been fought, it remained merely a provisional border. The claim to Armenia and the so-called client states as well as the competing claim of the Parthians was in keeping with this. The original border security system based on diplomacy and mobile intervention troops (legions distributed throughout Antioch, Laodicea, Cyrrhus and Rhaphaneai) had possibly already been abolished in the Flavian period. The incorporation of the frontier states located in front of it (Pontus, Cappadocia, Commagene and Armenia Minor) led to the setting up of new provinces and the stationing of Roman legions directly on the Euphrates, although the river was very hard to secure in view of the diverse options for crossing it – the relevant bridges, roads and fortifications (Satala, Melitene, Samosata and Zeugma). In view of possible surprise attacks by the mobile Iranian armies (Sapor I, middle of the 3rd cent. AD), the Roman offensives of the 2nd cent. (Marcus Aurelius and Lucius Verus) and the Severan period pushed through to the Tigris and the Chaboras and under Septimius Severus led to the establishment of two provinces (Osrhoene and Mesopotamia). The defence concept – with the pushing forward of the eastern frontier with an extensive defence system (→ Limes) without a fixed border – continued to remain tied to the Euphrates as 'an obstacle to approaches' [2] and required the increasing military presence of Rome that grew from the original three to four legions and up to eight legions between the Black Sea and the Gulf of Aqaba as well as two additional legions for Mesopotamia. The towns acted as temporary bases for military operations (Soura, Dura-Europus, Hatra). After temporary losses in the 3rd cent. AD (invasions of the Sassanids, conquest of the Imperium Palmyrenum by 273) the peace treaty under Diocletian in 297 preserved Roman rule over the *regiones Transtigritanae*. In the middle of the 4th cent. AD the legions moved back from eastern Mesopotamia to Constantia (loss of Nisibis in 363). Under Theodosius, Armenia was partitioned (AD 395). In the 5th and 6th cents. solid border fortresses (Amida, Singara, Nisibis, Zenobia, Resapha and Oriza) secured the *limes* and the territory in front of the Euphrates zone for a long time into the Byzantine period.

1 C. R. WHITTAKER, Frontiers of the Roman Empire, 1994 2 J. WAGNER, Die Römer an Euphrat und Tigris, AW 16, 1985 (special issue).

Reports of the International Congresses of Roman Frontier Studies since 1949; P. FREEMANN, D.L. KENNEDY (ed.), The Defence of the Roman and Byzantine East, 1986; D.L. KENNEDY, The Roman Army in the East, 1996; F. MILLAR, The Roman Near East, 1993. B.v.W.C.

Euphron (Εὔφρων; *Eúphrōn*).

[1] Sculptor from Paros who worked in Athens in the middle of the 5th cent. BC. Based on the evidence from extant sculpture pedestals, he created votive reliefs. The bearded head of a herm dedicated in Piraeus is extant.

JEFFERY, 363, no. 29; C. KAROUZOS, En feuilletant les vieilles publications, in: BCH 70, 1946, 263–270; A. E. RAUBITSCHEK, Dedications from the Athenian Akropolis, 1949, no. 298, 304. R.N.

[2] After the conquest of Sicyon by Epaminondas in 369 BC and the stationing of a Theban garrison, pro-Spartan E. was successful with the help of the Arcadians and Argivians and of the *dēmos* of Sicyon in a democratic coup (in 368 according to Diod. Sic. 15,70,3 [2. 243f.], in 366 according to Xen. Hell. 7,1,44 [3. 370–372]). He was elected *stratēgós* and equipped 2,000 mercenaries with means attained through confiscations (Xen. Hell. 7,2,11). When the Theban garrison and the returned commanders rebelled against the tyranny (Xen. Hell. 7,1,46) of E., he fled, but in 366 captured Sicyon with Athenian mercenaries. He was killed in Thebes, where he had then requested help against the ruling oligarchs (Xen. Hell. 7,3,4–5, cf. [1. 104, 215; 4. 22 A.74]) and later buried at the market-place of Sicyon.

1 H. BECK, Polis und Koinon, 1997 2 J. BUCKLER, The Theban Hegemony 371–362 BC, 1980 3 H.-J. GEHRKE, Stasis, 1985 4 M. JEHNE, Koine Eirene, 1994. ME.STR.

[3] After the death of Alexander [4] the Great in 323 BC, E., the grandson of E. [2], expelled the Macedonian garrison in Sicyon, restored democracy and after the alliance with Athens, joined in the Lamian War (Diod. Sic. 18,11,2). After being defeated, E. was killed when the garrison returned. The Athenians honoured him with an inscription in 318/17 (Syll.³ 317). ME.STR.

[4] Writer of New Comedy (1st half of the 3rd cent. BC, fr. 8 mentioning the politician Callimedon may perhaps even go back to the 4th cent.). Five titles and eleven fragments are extant; four of them have gnomic content; in four of them speak (fr. 1; 8; 9; 10) cooks who either invite their assistants to put as much of the meals in their own pockets as possible (fr. 9), or praise them for it (fr. 1).

1 PCG V, 282–292. H.-G.NE.

[5] Son of Hacoris, Hellenized Egyptian of noble birth; in the 6th Syrian War he was probably on the side of Antiochus [6] IV.

W. CLARYSSE, Hakoris, an Egyptian nobleman and his family, in: AncSoc 22, 1991, 240–243. W.A.

Euphronius (Εὐφρόνιος; *Euphrónios*).

[1] Writer of Old Comedy who in 458 BC won the Great → Dionysia [1. test. 1. 2]. Neither titles nor fragments are extant.

1 PCG V, 293. H.-G.NE.

[2] Attic vase painter and potter of the late archaic period who is considered like → Phintias and → Euthymides to belong to the group of 'pioneers' who helped red-figure vase painting achieve its breakthrough. E. worked as a painter between 520 and 500 BC for the potters Euxitheus and Cachrylion and primarily decorated types of vessels that were used at the symposium, esp. chalice craters and bowls. Several psykters, stamnoi, pelikai, amphoras, hydriae, a volute crater and a

plate are also known to be his work, a total of a good 50 vases or vase fragments, 11 of which are signed by him. Influenced in his early years by the older vase painter → Oltus, E. soon developed his own distinctive style. Characteristic of his work are large powerful figures with strong dynamics and at the same time with careful and very close attention to detail and a tendency towards ornamental flourish and a marked interest in the anatomical structure of the human body, which is represented often in complicated poses and movements with all the muscles, tendons and folds of skin. His extensive mythological images of monumental proportions are characterized by drama and emotionalism; the focus of these is often Hercules (chalice crater in Paris, LV, with a wrestling match between Hercules and Antaeus, volute crater in Arezzo, with Hercules in the Battle of the Amazons, etc.). His New York crater with the retrieval of the body of Sarpedon by Thanatos and Hypnos from the Trojan battle field (New York, MMA) is also famous. The everyday images for which E. mainly selected palaistra scenes, symposium scenes, and komos scenes are simpler but no less progressive in the spatial representation of moving figures (e.g. psykter in St. Petersburg depicting a symposium with hetaerae, chalice crater in Berlin with athletic scene). Name captions are frequent in E.; his preferred *kalos* name is Leagrus.

About 500 BC E. appears to have given up painting. From the time after this and up to about 470 BC however, a good 20 cups and a lidded vase with an *Euphrónios epoíēsen* signature are extant; these are painted by various vase painters, among these by → Onesimus, → Duris and the → Pistoxenus painter. Other cups can be attributed to the potter E. because of their shape. Presumably E. became the owner of a potter's workshop that specialized in the manufacture of cups. A votive offering given by E. in about 480 BC to the Athenian Acropolis (fragments of its marble base are preserved) attests to the degree of affluence which he had attained.

BEAZLEY, ARV², 13–17; BEAZLEY, Addenda², 152–153; Euphronios der Maler, exhibition catalogue Berlin 1991; Euphronios und seine Zeit, Proceedings of a conference at Berlin, 19–20 April 1991, 1992; M. ROBERTSON, The Art of Vase-Painting in Classical Athens, 1992, 21–35. I.W.

[3] Greek poet and grammarian, end of 3rd cent. BC; born in Cherrhonesus near Cyrene according to Heph. p. 56; Pelusium in the Nile delta is mentioned by CollAlex 176,3. E. was the teacher of Aristophanes [4] of Byzantium (Suda s. v. Ἀριστοφάνης Βυζάντιος). He composed commentaries on Attic comedy [2]; he wrote → priapea (Georgios Choiroboskos, commentary in Heph. P. 241 CONSBRUCH; cf. Str. 8,382). The only fragment preserved in this meter (Glyconeus and Pherecrateus, cf. → Metre V, table) speaks of 'young Dionysus' (CollAlex 176 f., V.1: νέου Διονύσου), i.e., Ptolemy [7] IV. Philopator (thus Proverbia Bodleiana GAISFORD 907 [1]; cf. Clem. Alex. Protrepticus p. 16; 22).

1 W. BÜHLER, Zenobii Athoi proverbia, vol. 1, 1987
2 K. STRECKER, De Lycophrone, Euphronio, Eratosthene comicorum interpretibus, thesis Greifswald 1884. W. D. F.

Euphrosyne (Εὐφροσύνη; *Euphrosýne*, 'cheerfulness'). One of the → Charites (Hes. Theog. 909; Pind. Ol. 14,14; Apollod. 1,13). In Hyg. Poet. Fab. praef. E. is a daughter of Erebos and → Nyx (cf. Gratia in Cic. Nat. D. 3,44). In Orph. H. 3,5 E. is an epithet of Nyx.

K.-H. TOMBERG, E.B. HARRISON, s.v. Charis, Charites, LIMC 3.1, 191–203. R.B.

Eupithius (Εὐπίθιος; *Eupíthios*). Writer of an epigram that consists of an expressive curse of Herodian's work 'The General Pronunciation of Greek' (Ἡ καθόλου προσῳδία; *hē kathólou prosōidía*) (Anth. Pal. 9,206). The otherwise unknown poet was, as we gather from the heading, an Athenian; he should either be considered a contemporary of Herodian (2nd half of the 2nd cent. AD) or lived after him. E.D.

Eupolemus

[1] Jewish-Hellenistic historian (mid 2nd cent. BC), probably identical with the E. mentioned in 1 Macc 8,17; in Palestine he wrote a work Περὶ τῶν ἐν τῇ Ἰουδαίᾳ βασιλέων ('On the Kings of Judea'). Fragments are extant because of the excerpts of → Alexander [23] Polyhistor in Euseb. Praep. evang. and Clem. Al.: → Moses was the 'first sage', first legislator and inventor of the script which was passed down to the Phoenicians and Greeks by the Jews (F 1). E. describes the succession of rule by the prophets from Moses to Samuel, then the succession of the kings, esp. the great kingdom of → David in anachronistic form. The temple building of → Salomo is arranged with a fictive correspondence between him, Pharaoh Vaphres and Suron of Tyrus (cf. 2 Chr 2,2–5) who supported it with money and workers. The temple was called ἱερὸν Σολομῶνος (*hieròn Solomônos*), and from this the name of the city Hierosolyma was derived for Jerusalem. The reason for the destruction of the temple is given as the decline into idolatry. Nebuchadnezzar, instigated by the prophecy of → Jeremiah, went on a military campaign against the Jews and destroyed the temple. Jeremiah also brought to safety the Ark of the Covenant with the tables of the law. E. is an early source of the Jewish legends about the building and destruction of the temple (cf. 2 Macc 2,4–8). Like the older Jewish-Hellenistic authors he makes great efforts with chronology and proving the age of Jewish written records.

→ Artapanus; → Demetrius [22]; → Jerusalem

FGrH III C 2 no. 723; N. WALTER, Fragmente jüd.-hell. Historiker (Jüd. Schriften aus hell.-röm. Zeit 1,2), 1980, 93–108; SCHÜRER 3,1, 517–521; G.E. STERLING, Historiography and Self-definition, 1992, 207–222.

[2] Ps.-E., the 'Samaritan Anonymus' (1st half of 2nd cent. BC), should be distinguished from 'Jewish E.' [1]. His Samaritan origin can be seen from the fact that → Abraham is accepted and revered by Melchisedech on Mount Garizim in the sanctuary of the Samaritans (cf. Gen 14). Ps.-E. presents Abraham as the purveyor of culture; the latter teaches the Phoenicians and the Egyptians astrology that goes back to → Henoch who is identified with → Atlas [2]. → Noah is euhemeristically equated with the king of Babel, Belos/Kronos, depending on → Berosus.

→ Baal; → Euhemerism; → Samaria

FGrH 3 C 2 no. 724; N. Walter, Fragmente jüd.-hell. Historiker (Jüd. Schriften aus hell.-röm. Zeit 1,2), 1980, 137–143; Schürer 3,1, 528–531; G. E. Sterling, Historiography and Self-definition, 1992, 187–206. A.M.S.

Eupolis (Εὔπολις; *Eúpolis*). Apart from Aristophanes and Cratinus, the most important writer of Attic Old Comedy, son of Sosipolis.

A. Life B. Work

A. Life

E. is said to have already begun his performances at the age of 17 [1. test. 1]; varying times for his debut are stated: in 429 [1. test. 2a], 427 [1. test. 6a], 426 [1. test. 6b] or between 427 and 424 BC [1. test. 7. 8]. The epigraphical lists of the winners at the Dionysia and the Lenaea show that he began his performances about the same time as → Aristophanes (or shortly before him): in the former he is listed directly after Aristophanes, in the latter directly before him [1. test. 11, 12]. The constant rivalry with Aristophanes [cf. 1. test. 16 = fr. 89; test. 17 = fr. 65; test. 18 = fr. 62; 3] ended with the relatively early death of E. about which there were soon various versions. Probably E. lost his life in the naval war against the Spartans at the Hellespont through shipwreck [1. test. 1 with n.]. An adventurous version (that can already be read in Duris of Samos) that has Alcibiades drowning E. in 415 during the voyage of the Athenian expedition fleet to Sicily because he had been mocked by him [1. re *Báptai*, test. ii-vi], was already refuted by Eratosthenes on the basis that E. was still writing plays even after 415 [1. test. 3].

B. Work

E. is said to have written a total of 17 [1. test. 1] or 14 [1. test. 2a] plays. 16 play titles are attested if the Αὐτόλυκος (*Autólykos*), which E. revised and performed a second time (test. ii), is counted twice. E. won seven times, three victories being at the Lenaea [1. test. 1, 12]. In his first play Προσπάλτιοι (*Prospáltioi*; 'The Prospaltians'; fr. 259,4), the inhabitants of the Attic deme Prospalta are obviously ridiculed for their love of bringing lawsuits (test. ii). At the Lenaea of 425 he came third with Νουμηνίαι (*Numēníai*) that is only known by its title. About the same time as Aristophanes' 'Equites' (or somewhat earlier? [cf. 2. 17]) it appears that Χρυσοῦν γένος (*Chrysoûn génos*; 'The Golden Age') was staged, at the time when Cleon was building up his power to the greatest extent; under this 'ruler' the Athenians were obviously represented ironically as such (cf. fr. 316). It is probable that Μαρικάς (*Marikás*) was performed at the Lenaea of 421 (fr. 211); under this name (that was meant to insinuate the barbaric origin, cf. test. v), E. attacked the politician Hyperbolus (cf. Cleon as Paphlagonian in Aristophanes' 'Equites'). At the Dionysia of the same year, E. with the Κόλακες (*Kólakes*, 'Flatterers') came first, beating Aristophanes' 'Peace'; central to the play (that could have inspired Plato to write *Prōtagóras*, cf. test. ii) was ridicule of the rich man Callias who had recently inherited his father's estate and so had become the desired target of numerous 'flatterers' who represented themselves in the *parabasis* (fr. 172), and amongst whom Protagoras (fr. 157f.) and probably also other Sophists figured prominently.

In the following year E. had Demostratus as director (cf. Callistratus and Philonides in Aristophanes) perform the first *Autólykos* (the date of the second is unknown). The Πόλεις (*Póleis*) of the years 422 and 420 brought the allied city-states of Athens onto the stage as chorus and they obviously (like the chorus in the 'Birds' of Aristophanes) appeared individually in the *parodos* (fr. 245–247). As the general Phormion plays an important role in the Ταξίαρχοι (*Taxíarchoi*), the play was probably not written too long after his death (in 428, cf. however [2. 22–24]); the grumpy Phormion (cf. fr. 268,14f.) had to deal here with the effeminate (fr. 271f.) god Dionysus himself as a recruit (fr. 274). In Βάπται (*Báptai*), perhaps performed in 416 or 415 and said to have brought down upon E. the wrath of Alcibiades (see above), it is obvious that a number of well-known Athenians (fr. 90–92) was the subject of gossip in connection with an orgiastic cult (cf. test. ii). In the play Δῆμοι (*Dêmoi*) that was probably staged in 412 ([2. 24–27] argues for 416) E. dramatized a strange notion that competes with the fantasy of Aristophanes' 'Frogs': when (because of the Decelean War?) the longing of the Athenians for the great statesmen of their past grows, the brave Pyronides (= the General Myronides) brings the four most important statesmen (Solon, Miltiades, Aristides and Pericles) back to the light of day from the Underworld so that they can assist the city again. In a papyrus the end of the *parabasis* is extant, according to which the great deceased appeared on the stage (fr. 99); the famous and often quoted description of Pericles' rhetorical talents perhaps comes from the first half of the play (fr. 102).

As far as can be seen, E.'s work certainly matched that of Aristophanes in many respects; ancient critics attributed to him a great wealth of ideas and 'elegance' in the conception and design of comic situations [1. test. 34], as well as a sharpness of political and personal mockery equal to that of Cratinus [1. test. 2a, 42]. E.'s works were discussed by critics in the Alexandrian period and remnants of such commentaries from the first centuries of the common era are extant [1. test. 48]; in the Imperial period he was considered to be a major source of good old Attic writing [1. test. 41], and Galen wrote three books about his πολιτικὰ ὀνόματα (*politikà onómata*; 'words in general use'), but E. came off worse in relation to Aristophanes in the occurring limitation of texts used for school lessons.

1 PCG V, 294–539 2 I.C. STOREY, Dating and re-dating E., in: Phoenix 44, 1990, 1–30 3 K. SIDWELL, Authorial collaboration? Aristophanes' *Knights* and E., in: GRBS 34, 1993, 365–389. H.-G.NE.

Eupyridae (Εὐπυρίδαι; *Eupyrídai*). Attic *mesogeia* deme of the phyle Leontis, two *bouleutai*. E. with the neighbouring deme Cropidae and Peleces formed the cult association of Trikomoi (Steph. Byz. s.v. E.; [1. 112; 2. 184f.[46]]). As Archidamus moved through Cropidae to Acharnae in 431 BC (Thuc. 2,19), E. can be estimated to lie north of the Aegaleus near Kamatero. From there originates the decree IG II[2] 1362 to protect the trees in the sanctuary of Apollo Erasitheus [2], and from Hagios Saranta to the west of Menidi come the tomb inscriptions IG II[2] 6146.

1 S. SOLDERS, Die außerstädtischen Kulte und die Einigung Attikas, 1931 2 WHITEHEAD, Index s.v. E.

TRAILL, Attica 46, 62, 68, 110 no. 46, table 4; Id., Demos and Trittys, 1986, 131. H.LO.

Euricus, Euric (also Eurichus, Euarix). King of the Visigoths in AD 466–484, son of Theoderic I, succeeded to the throne after the murder of his brother Theoderic II (Iord. Get. 190; Hydatius Lemiensis 237). E.'s reign was marked by the constant endeavour to expand the area of his kingdom (originally Aquitania II, Novempopulana and parts of Narbonensis I) and to weaken the dependence on Rome, which is clear from the termination of the → *foedus* with the Romans. From 468 he advanced against the Suebi and in the following years conquered almost the entire Iberian peninsula. His attempt to cross the Loire was thwarted by Romans and Franks despite a victory over the Bretons. However his advances into the southern Gallic area east of the Rhône resulted in the annihilation of a Roman army (in 471). Initially the Burgundians hindered E. in his further conquests in the Provence and he also met with resistance from the local aristocracy in the Auvergne (→ Ecdicius), but Iulius Nepos finally had to acknowledge his conquests in 475. In the negotiations with the imperial envoy, Bishop Epiphanius [2], E. now demanded the title *amicus*. When he took possession of the southern Provence in 476/7 the kingdom of the Visigoths achieved its greatest expansion (Iord. Get. 237–244; Ennod. MGH (AA) 7,95).

E. was also an active lawmaker (Isid. Historia Gothorum 35), but the codification of Visigothic law (*Codex Euricianus*) is likely to go back to his son and successor Alaric [3] II [1. 43ff.]. The strict Arian E. certainly maintained contact with dignitaries of the Catholic Church, but attempted to infiltrate their organization e.g. through the ban on filling vacant bishoprics (Greg. Tur. Franc. 2,25; Sid. Apoll. Epist. 7,6,6f.).

1 H. NEHLSEN, s.v. Codex Euricianus, RGA 5, 42–47.

PLRE 2, 427f.; V. BURNS, The Visigothic Settlement in Aquitania, in: Historia 41, 1992, 362–373; K.F. STROHEKER, Eurich, König der Westgoten, 1937; H. WOLFRAM, Die Goten, [3]1990, 186ff. M.MEI. and ME.STR.

Euripides

[1] The Attic Tragedian.

A. BIOGRAPHY B. PLAYS C. DRAMATURGIC COMPOSITION AND THEOLOGY D. TEXTUAL TRADITION AND LEGACY

A. BIOGRAPHY

The most important evidence comes from the *vita* passed down to us in several MSS, the → Marmor Parium, the → Suda, Gell. NA 15,20 and the *vita* by → Satyrus. Only a few details of E.'s life can be considered certain: born between 485 and 480 BC on Salamis, son of a Mnesarchus or Mnesarchides. He took part in the Great Dionysia for the first time in 455, achieving his first victory in 441. During his lifetime he won first prizes in the tragic agon four times; he was awarded the prize for the fifth time posthumously when his son → Euripides [4] performed his trilogy ('Iphigenia at Aulis', 'Bacchae', 'Alcmaeon in Corinth'). In 408 he went to the Macedonian court of Archelaus in Pella where he died in 406 shortly before the Great Dionysia. When → Sophocles heard the news of the death of E., he had the chorus appear for the proagon without their wreaths.

→ Aristophanes, who best knew the works of E. and was their sharpest critic, pinpoints in his parodies ('Acharnians', 'Thesmophoriazusae', 'Frogs') significant qualities of E.'s tragedies: the making of tragedy into a bourgeois genre (cf. 'Electra'), the questioning of the heroic (e.g. 'Hercules'), the proximity of language and thought to the Sophists, the presentation of female passion ('Medea', 'Hippolytus'), the dominance of → intrigue as part of the structure (cf. Aristoph. Thesm. 94) and the proximity to 'new music' (particularly in the → monodies).

From the notice in the Suda (ε 3695) that E. participated in the agon 22 times we can deduce that he wrote 88 plays; in addition there are the plays not performed in Athens – 'Archelaus' and 'Andromache'. As there is definite evidence of relatively few satyr plays by E., he probably often replaced the final satyr play with a tragedy with a good ending, as in the case of 'Alcestis'. The plays with a definite date ('Alcestis' 438, 'Medea' 431, 'Hippolytus' 428, 'Trojan Women' 415, 'Helen' 412, 'Orestes' 408, 'Iphigenia at Aulis' and 'Bacchae' posthumously after 406) provide a framework for dating, so that the others can be classified with the help of metric analysis (steady increase of resolutions in the iambic trimeter [1]) ('Heraclidae' between 431 and 428, 'Andromache', 'Hecuba', 'Hiketidae' between 430 and

420, 'Electra' and 'Heracles' between 419 and 416, 'Trojan Women', 'Iphigenia among the Taurians', 'Phoenician Women', 'Cyclops' between 415 and 408, 'Rhesus' probably not authentic).

B. Plays

1. Alcestis 2. Medea 3. Hippolytus (*stephanēphoros*) 4. Heracles 5. Electra 6. Suppliant women and Heraclidae 7. Andromache 8. Hecuba and the Trojan Women 9. Phoenician Women and Orestes 10. Iphigenia among the Taurians, Ion, Helen 11. Iphigenia at Aulis 12. Bacchae 13. Cyclops 14. Rhesus 15. Fragments

1. Alcestis

Performed in 438 in place of the satyr play after the 'Cretan Women', 'Alcmaeon in Psophis' and 'Telephus'; 2nd place in the agon after Sophocles. What is different about the situation compared to the Alcestis dramas of → Aeschylus and → Phrynichus is that Alcestis does not die on her marriage day for her husband but after years of happy marriage. The play is divided into two parts, clearly marked by the departure of the chorus in V. 741–746: a) In V. 1–746 Alcestis is the focus; dramatic scenes show her leaving Admetus and the children and her death. b) The 2nd part (V. 747–1163) presents the effects on Admetus: too late (940) and exposed to social constraints (hospitality to Heracles), he realizes the meaninglessness of life without Alcestis. The two parts are held together by Heracles who appears in 476 and brings Alcestis back to Admetus. The burlesque quarrel between Thanatos (death) and Apollo in the prologue (1–76), the character of Heracles and the non-tragic turn for the better from sorrow to happiness (cf. the hypothesis) underline its satyr-play-like nature.

2. Medea

Performed in 431 as the 1st play with the tragedies *Philoctetes* and *Diktys* and the satyr play *Theristae*; 3rd place in the agon after Euphorion and Sophocles. As early as antiquity, it was a contentious issue whether the innovative idea that Medea – and not the Corinthians – kills her children herself comes from E. or from → Neophron; the arguments presented tend to support E. [2]. By returning to the older form of the two-actor play, E. emphasizes the dominance of the protagonist and the weakness of the men surrounding her (Creon, Jason, Aegeus). From the prologue discussing her to the *exodos*, she is present and through her intelligence and cleverness (δεινότης, *deinótēs*; σοφία, *sophía*) controls the men who come to her – particularly in the two supplication scenes in which, humbly requesting, she obtains from Creon (271ff.) the postponement of exile by one day, necessary for her revenge on Jason, and a promise of asylum from Aegeus (663ff.). Considerations of content and staging technique make it probable that vv. 1056–1080 are not the work of E [3]. Aristotle (Poet. 1454a37– 1454b2; 1461b20f.) criticizes the lack of motivation in the conclusion to the tragedy (Medea's flight on the snake chariot) and the Aegeus scene (663ff.).

3. Hippolytus (*stephanēphoros*)

Performed in 428, 1st place in the agon. Revision of the 1st Hippolytus play (*Hippólytos kalyptómenos*) in which Phaedra herself declared Hippolytus her love and Hippolytus concealed his head in shame (cf. the hypothesis). The tragedy is structured on a divine framework: In the prologue (1–57) Aphrodite announces that Hippolytus must die because of the contempt he shows her and that she will use Phaedra as the instrument of her revenge; in the *exodos* (1283ff.) Artemis promises to kill Aphrodite's lover (→ Adonis) to restore her honour (τιμή; *timḗ*) (1420–1422). The humans are mere chess pieces in the divine game although they initially provoke divine revenge because of their one-sided behaviour, their hubris. The only ray of hope remains the reconciliation between the human characters (Hippolytus and Theseus in the *exodos*).

4. Heracles

Performed in *c.* 416. The tragedy is clearly divided into two sections. a) V. 1–814 depict the return of the hero – threatened by the usurper Lycus – awaited with great longing by his family; he immediately takes revenge on Lycus. b) The 2nd part (815–1428), introduced by a 2nd prologue of Iris and Lyssa, who on behalf of Hera are to strike Heracles with madness (822–874), presents the fall of the hero: in a fit of madness he murders his wife and children. The 'Heracles' contains a further development of the theology of the 'Hippolytus': in the disputes of the gods, the humans – even demigods like Heracles – are mere playthings. Even Lyssa cannot see any sense in Hera's plan (843ff.). Human friendship remains the glimmer of hope (Theseus, 1163ff.). What is clear is that the heroic status is taken away from Heracles (particularly V. 622ff.) as a means of eliciting sympathy.

5. Electra

E.'s depiction of characters in a decidedly unheroic light can be seen especially clearly in the play 'Electra' that was probably written shortly before the 'Heracles': Electra lives in the country as the wife of an impoverished nobleman, plagued by the cares of everyday life (especially V. 404ff.). Aegisthus is characterized as a jovial, overly trusting host who kindly invites in his murderers (774ff.), Clytaemestra is presented as a woman who had for a long time repented of her deed and who wishes to be reconciled with her daughter (cf. especially V. 1057; 1106; 1123 in contrast to Soph. El. 622). In this way the justification for the matricide is questioned, especially as Orestes, driven by Electra to commit the deed, is plagued by doubt (962ff.), and the Dioscuri in the → *exodos* rebuke Apollo's order to commit matricide as foolish and ill-considered (1245f., 1302). A debatable issue is the priority of the 'Electra' plays of E. and Sophocles. As E. engages directly with Aeschylus' 'Choephoroi' (particularly in the → anagnorisis 524ff., in which Electra rationalistically refutes

Aeschylus' signs of recognition), the sequence Aesch. Cho., E. El., Soph. El. (as a response to E.) is certainly conceivable.

6. Suppliant woman and Heraclidae

In the two *hiketeia* plays (performed in the twenties) the praise of Athens that also repeatedly resounds in other plays is the focal point: Athens, represented by its 'democratic' king Theseus (cf. also Eur. HF; Soph. OC), brings salvation to the weak and proves itself to be the place of refuge for those seeking protection, and in this way is fully in keeping with the ideology of the epitaphs.

7. Andromache

(420s): → Aristophanes [4] of Byzantium praises in his hypothesis some sections of the play as a success (among these the prologue and Andromache's → *threnos* in elegiac distichs), but describes the play overall as second-rate. The compositional flaws stem from the fact that the play is based on two myths: a) the story of Andromache, the woman given as booty to Neoptolemus, who is married to Orestes' sister Hermione; b) the quarrel between Orestes and Neoptolemus. The plot is held together by Neoptolemus who does not himself appear in the play. The danger to which Andromache is exposed in the 1st part by Hermione and Menelaus corresponds in the 2nd part to the isolation of Hermione who is rescued by Orestes (802ff.). The final part presents the effect on the aged Peleus of the news that Neoptolemus has been murdered by Orestes in Delphi (1047ff.).

8. Hecuba and the Trojan Women

In two tragedies about the Peloponnesian War, in which 'Hecuba' (performed in the 420s) and the 'Trojan Women' (performed in 415 as the 3rd play after 'Alexander' and 'Palamedes', 2nd place in the agon), E., like → Aeschylus in the 'Persians', presents the consequences of military defeat from the point of view of those defeated. He presents the Trojan royal family as an example of a fall from the height of power. The victor too, however, will not enjoy his success: Cassandra foresees in a vision Agamemnon's fate (Tro. 307ff.; cf. Aesch. Ag. 1072ff.) and Poseidon and Athena already announce in the prologue (Tro. 1–97) that they want to punish the Greeks on their homeward journey for their hubris in victory by subjecting them to thunderstorms.

9. Phoenician Women and Orestes

The'Phoenician Women' (performed in *c.* 411) and 'Orestes' (performed in 408) show the influence of internal political crisis in Athens as well as the effect of the power struggle between the radical democrats and the oligarchs. Both tragedies present the change of traditional customs and laws described by Thuc. 3,82 (καθεστῶτες νόμοι; *kathestôtes nómoi*). In contrast to Aesch. Sept., E. does not create the chorus of 'Phoenician Women' with the collective of the Thebans concerned but with a group of Phoenician girls who are present in the action as uninvolved spectators. In this way he foregrounds all the more the quarrel between the brothers. As opposed to Aeschylus, the status of Polyneices is enhanced to a certain degree, as the unlawfulness of Eteocles' claim to rule becomes clear. An innovation on the part of E. is also the attempt at reconciliation by Iocaste who is not heeded in the escalation of violence. As a positive character E. invented Menoeceus, Creon's son who voluntarily dies rescuing the polis. In 'Orestes' the effect of internal political crisis becomes even clearer: Orestes, Pylades and Electra form, as was common in polis life, a political club (*hetairía*: 804; 1072; 1079) to assert themselves against the unscrupulous Menelaus by taking Hermione hostage (cf. the criticism of the unnecessarily bad character of Menelaus in Aristot. Poet. 1454a 28f.; 1461b 21). Although Menelaus admits defeat in order to save the life of his daughter (1617), the three want to set the palace on fire (1618): violence and hatred take on an impetus of their own. Only Apollo as the *deus ex machina* brings the plot to the end predetermined by myth (1625ff.).

10. Iphigenia among the Taurians, Ion, Helen

'Iphigenia among the Taurians' (*c.* 414), 'Ion' (*c.* 413) and 'Helen' (performed in 412 together with the 'Andromeda'), which were written about the same time, form a group that is closely connected by content and structure. The structure of the plays is determined by the close link between → *anagnorisis* and → *intrigue* used by E. in ever new varieties. In IT the *anagnorisis* is caused by the letter read out by Iphigenia (769ff.) to ensure that Pylades could deliver the news to Orestes even if the letter got lost (cf. the criticism by Aristot. Poet. 1454a 7). In 'Ion' there is a double *anagnorisis*: on the basis of Apollo's intrigue, King Xuthus believes Ion to be his son (510ff.). The conspiracy against Ion's life hatched as a result by his mother Creusa fails (1106ff.); only now does it come to actual *anagnorisis* between Ion and Creusa with the aid of signs of recognition (1395ff.). In the 'Helen' E. applies the version of the myth that goes back to → Stesichorus – Helen is carried away to Egypt by Zeus, and the Trojan War was fought for a phantom. The *anagnorisis* of Helen and Menelaus who ended up in Egypt threatens to fail, since the insecure Menelaus does not trust the Egyptian Helen. Only the arrival of a messenger who reports the disappearance of the phantom (εἴδωλον; *eídōlon*) (597ff.) prevents the failure of the *anagnorisis*. This in turn provokes an intrigue that serves either the purpose of liberation (IT, Hel.) or of revenge (Ion, cf. El.).

11. Iphigenia at Aulis

Performed posthumously (in 405 – *c.* 400) together with 'Alcmaeon in Corinth' and 'Bacchae' (see below 12.) by E.'s son E. [4]. E. foregrounds a human behaviour that he revealed in the earlier tragedies through secondary roles: the readiness for self-sacrifice of young people who have accepted their fate (cf. Polyxena in Hec.; Menoeceus in Phoen.). Iphigenia, who was enticed to Aulis by Agamemnon on the false pretence that she was to marry Achilles, voluntarily dies for the common good in the *exodos* (1368ff.).

12. Bacchae

The plot of the play involves the victorious return of the god Dionysus to his homeland Thebes (1ff.), his epiphany as a god (576ff.) and the punishment of the enemy of the god (*theomáchos*) Pentheus who, walking in the mountains (*oreibasía*; cf. 660ff.), is torn apart by his mother Agave who is under the delusion that she is killing an animal (1168ff.). The entire play, embedded in the framework plot of a *theomáchos* tragedy (cf. Aesch. 'Bassaridae' [TrGF III p. 138f.], *Pentheus* [TrGF III p. 298f.]), is a dramatization of Dionysian rites (*oreibasía*, *ōmophagía*, *sparagmós*; the *parodos* is conceived of as a → *dithyrambos*). The interpretation is controversial (extreme positions: celebration of the cult of Dionysus or sharp criticism of the consequences of irrationalism?) [4]. In a literary sense the 'Bacchae' are a return to the cult origins of the genre of → tragedy (Dionysus myth, *dithyrambos*) and so are in keeping with the archaizing tendency of these years [5].

13. Cyclops

E.'s only extant satyr play (dating controversial, probably written between 411 and 408) is a dramatization of the → Polyphemus episode (Hom. Od. 9). In contrast to the Homeric model, Polyphemus in E. is put into a humorous tension between monster and man with pretensions of education (316ff.: Parody of Sophistic theories concerning the right of the stronger). The special charm of the play is the combination of rudimentary form (chorus of the Satyrs, Silenus), Homeric myth and modern themes.

14. Rhesus

The question of authenticity is still contentious. Although is not possible to clarify this completely, the arguments do not tend to support E.'s authorship. 'Rhesus', a 'night play', is a dramatization of the → Doloneia (Hom. Il. 10). The changing sequences of scenes with the different *dramatis personae* achieve effective dramaturgy – fully in the sense of → Astydamas' *dictum* that the audience had to be entertained by diversion (TrGF I 60 F 4).

15. Fragments

The popularity of E. in the 4th and 3rd cents. BC means that there are a large number of fragments (*c.* 1,300, many on papyrus) extant (TrGF V Kannicht, in preparation), and there are also a large number of hypotheses extant on papyrus. An idea of the plot and the content of several plays can be gained on the basis of the fragments ('Antiope', 'Erechtheus', 'Phaethon', 'Alexander', 'Archelaus', 'Hypsipyle', 'Cresphontes').

C. Dramaturgic composition and theology

If in Aeschylus man was still part of a world order full of meaning, the laws of which he could experience on his sorrowful path 'learning through suffering' (πάθει μάθος; *páthei máthos*) through divine grace (χάρις; *cháris*), he is in E.'s works a plaything of the gods who are too remote from human experience for man in his meaningless suffering to be able to understand them. Like human beings, the gods are driven to protect their honour: for Aphrodite and Artemis (Hipp.), Hera (HF), Athena (Tro.) and Dionysus (Bacch.) it is as with Medea a matter of the restoration of their honour. Their actions can therefore also be exposed to criticism (cf. Lyssa in HF 846ff., Castor in El. 1245, 1302, Cadmus in Bacch. 1348), their plan can even be frustrated by humans as in the 'Ion'.

D. Textual tradition and legacy

1. Textual tradition 2. Legacy

1. Textual tradition

If E. was not exactly spoilt by success in his lifetime, he became the tragedian *par excellence* in the 4th cent. after old tragedies were admitted to the Great Dionysia (Aristot. Poet. 1453a29 ὁ τραγικώτατος; *ho tragikṓtatos*). The consequence of this popularity is a large number of actor interpolations that got into the text prior to the compilation of the state copy by → Lycurgus (um 330). Of the Alexandrian philologists, → Aristophanes [4] of Byzantium concerned himself with E. as with Aeschylus and Sophocles.The works of E. were passed down to the Middle Ages in two groups: a) 10 plays that have → scholia that go back to Aristophanes of Byzantium and → Didymus [1] of Alexandria (Alc., Andr., Hec., Hipp., Med., Or., Rhes., Tro., Phoen., Bacch. [schol. not extant]). Of this so-called 'Selection' the philologists of the 13th/14th cents. only edited and commentated on Hec., Or., Phoen.: more than 200 MSS; edition of Demetrius Triclinius (1280–1340) extant in the autograph (Angel. gr. 14). b) 9 plays without scholia (Hel., El., Heracl., HF, Suppl. IA, IT, Ion, Cyc.) that are part of an alphabetically arranged edition of E. and were not combined with the 1st group to form a complete edition until Triclinius: Laurentianus plut. 32, 2 (L), beginning of the 14th cent., with corrections by Triclinius; Palatinus gr. 287 (P), around 1340, copy of L. Ed. princeps: I. Lascaris, Florence around 1494, followed by the Aldine of M. Musurus, Venice 1504.

2. Legacy

The popularity of E. in the 4th and 3rd cents. resulted in dramatists having to come to grips in a productive manner with the classics who were constantly being staged at that time. E. not only made a mark on their material (cf. Carcinus, TrGF I 70 F 1e, Medea; Eubulus, Ion, fr. 36–38 PCG; Medea, fr. 64 PCG) and their style (gnomic), but – as a result of the pattern of *anagnorisis* and intrigue (see above under B.10.) dominating his late work – provided a plot structure that characterized plays from the New → Comedy onwards. To a particular extent he influenced Roman tragedy of the Republic (cf. Ennius, Med.) and the Augustan period (Ov. Med., cf. also Ov. Met. 7, 1–424; Epist. 12), and with → Seneca as connecting link, French tragedy of the 17th cent.

The German classics of the 18th cent. had a high regard for E.: prompted by Wieland who had translated 'Helen' and 'Ion', Schiller rendered 'Iphigenia at Aulis'

(1789) and scenes from the 'Phoenician Women' (in 1789, revised in 1803) into German, with the aim of acquiring the 'Greek style'. Schiller admired E. particularly for the 'collision of passions' presented in his tragedies and the 'endless diversity' of his work, behind which there always shone through, however, a 'unity of the same human form' (letter to Lotte von Lengefeld and Karoline von Beulwitz dated 4 December 1788). The representation of female passion, behind which the 'beauty of character' paled, was also praised by F. Schlegel ('Treatise on the Female Characters in the Works of the Greek Writers', 1794). Goethe also productively discussed E. and also stressed the effectiveness of E.'s works on stage (Conversations with Eckermann, dated 28 March 1827), and, like Schiller, he translated resp. paraphrased scenes from E. ('The Bacchae of E.': 1827; 'Phaethon, Tragedy of E.' – Attempt at a restoration from fragments: 1823) in his 'Iphigenia on Tauris' (in 1779 in rhythmized prose, in 1786 in verses, in 1802 first performance using Schiller's revision). In the play that Schiller calls 'astonishingly modern and un-Greek' (letter to Körner dated 21 January 1802), Goethe departs – in a few points that are however significant – from Euripides' 'Iphigenia among the Taurians': King Thoas is a considerate ruler who pressures Iphigenia to marry him. Hurt by her refusal, he orders her to sacrifice two young men who have just appeared (Orestes and Pylades). In a scene which no longer bears any similarity to the *anagnorisis* driven to extremes in E., Orestes reveals his identity to his sister. Likewise the rescue does not take place as it does in E. through Athena as the *dea ex machina* (Eur. IT 1345ff.); rather Thoas relieves the Greeks of free will after Iphigenia has revealed to him the cunning trick that was not invented by her, as in E., but by Pylades. Overcome by Iphigenia's 'purity', Thoas forgoes his pleasure and so professes his belief in 'Humanity'.

After the frosty reception of E. that set in already in Goethe's time (cf. Conversations with Eckermann dated 28 March 1827: Goethe defends E. against the criticism of Schlegel), as is clearly expressed in Nietzsche's 'Birth of Tragedy' (*chap.* 12: E. as the representative of 'aesthetic Socratism'), E. experienced a renaissance in the 20th cent.: influenced by the World Wars, tragedies like 'Hecuba' and 'Trojan Women' were highly topical. Man can see no higher meaning in his suffering any more but finds himself thrown into an absurd world in the sense of existentialist philosophy [6] (cf. F.Werfel, Preliminary Remarks regarding 'Trojan Women', 1915) in which he must assert himself and develop his full potential (cf. J.Anouilh, Médée, 1948). The conflict between the sexes and the plumbing of the depths of the female psyche in particular are points of departure that are foregrounded in the contemporary reception of E.: e.g. in Hugo von Hofmannsthal's 'Ägyptische Helena' (as an opera with music by Richard Strauss, Dresden 1928); in Helen and Menelaus male and female identity, Orient and Occident are contrasted with each other in an archetypal manner. R. Liebermann's opera 'Freispruch für Medea' (Hamburg 1995) goes even further in this direction: Medea does not kill her children but refuses the power-hungry Jason a son and heir. In Colchis she is integrated into an ancient oriental community of women infiltrated by Jason with the Greeks as destructive western conquerors. In a comparable manner, Christa Wolf in 'Medea: Stimmen' (1996) also rehabilitates the heroine: Medea is the victim of the career ambitions of Jason who leaves her to marry the Corinthian heiress to the throne, Glauce. In Christa Wolf, Medea does however not become a perpetrator through Jason's unfaithfulness: Glauce commits suicide and the angry Corinthian mob kills Medea's children. Fruitful starting-points for contemporary discussions are the following topics: E. as a writer who critically analyzes or even destroys tradition, makes the conflict between the sexes a theme, who critically reflects upon his poetic creations, E. – in the full sense of Aristophanes – as a writer in the period of decadence following the peak of the classical period.

1 M. Cropp, G. Fick, Resolutions and chronology in E., 1985 (BICS Suppl. 43) 2 B. Gauly et.al. (ed.), Musa tragica, 1991, 60f. 3 B. Manuwald, Der Mord an den Kindern, in: WS n.F. 17, 1983, 27–61 4 E. Lefèvre, E.' Bakchai und die politische Bedeutung seines Spätwerks, in: DRAMA 3, 1995, 156–181 5 B. Zimmermann, Gattungsmischung, Manierismus, Archaismus, in: Lexis 3, 1989, 25–36 6 K. Reinhardt, Die Sinneskrise bei E., in: Die Neue Rundschau 68, 1957, 615–646 (= in: E. Schwinge, E., 1968, 507–542).

Text, fragments: J. Diggle, 3 vols., Oxford 1981, 1984, 1994 cf. Studies on the text of E., 1981; Euripidea, 1994); E.-edition of the Bibliotheca Teubneriana (almost complete); A. Nauck, B. Snell, Tragicorum Graecorum Fragmenta, 1964, 363–716 with a supplement by B. Snell; C. Austin, Nova Fragmenta Euripidea in papyris reperta, 1968.

Commentaries:
Alc.: A.M. Dale, 1954; D.J. Conacher, 1988.
Andr.: P.T. Stevens, 1971.
Bacch.: E.R. Dodds, ²1960.
Cyc.: R. Seaford, 1984; R.G. Ussher, 1978.
El.: J.D. Denniston, 1939; M.J. Cropp, 1988.
Hec.: C. Collard, 1991.
Hel.: A.M. Dale, ²1993; R. Kannicht, 2 vols., 1969.
Heracl.: J. Wilkins, 1993.
HF: U.v. Wilamowitz-Moellendorff, 3 vols., ²1895 (repr. 1959); G.W. Bond, 1981.
Supp.: C. Collard, 2 vols., 1975.
Hipp.: W.S. Barrett, 1964.
Ion: U.v. Wilamowitz-Moellendorff, 1926; A.S. Owen, 1939.
IA: W. Stockert, 1991.
IT: M. Platnauer, 1938.
Med.: D.L. Page, ²1952.
Or.: W. Biehl, 1965; C.W. Willink, 1986; M.L. West, 1987.
Phoen.: E. Craik, 1988; D.J. Mastronarde, 1994.
Tro.: K.H. Lee, 1976; A.S. Barlow, ¹1986, ⁴1993; W. Biehl, 1989.
Commentaries on the fragments: Andromeda: F. Bubel, 1991. Antiope: J. Kambitsis, 1972. Archelaus/Cresphontes: A. Harder, 1985. Hypsipyle: G.W.

BOND, 1963. W.E.H. COCKLE, 1987. PHAETHON: J. DIGGLE, 1970. PEIRITHOUS/PALAMEDES: D.F. SUTTON, 1987. TELEPHUS: E. HANDLEY, J. REA, BICS Suppl. 5, 1957.
BIBLIOGRAPHY: P. BURIAN, Directions in Euripidean criticism, 1985; A. PIPPIN BURNETT, Catastrophe survived. E.' plays of mixed reversal, 1971; H. ERBSE, Studien zum Prolog der Euripideischen Tragödie, 1984; W.H. FRIEDRICH, E. und Diphilos, 1953; R.E. HARDER, Die Frauenrollen bei E., 1993; M. HOSE, Studien zum Chor bei E., 2 vols., 1990/91; M. HOSE, Drama und Ges. Studien zur dramatischen Produktion in Athen am Ende des 5. Jh., 1995; N.C. HOURMOUZIADES, Production and imagination in E., 1965; K. MATTHIESSEN, E. Die Tragödien, in: G.A. SEECK (ed.), Das griech. Drama, 1979, 105–154; J. LATACZ, Einführung in die griech. Tragödie, 1993, 250–383; A. LESKY, Die tragische Dichtung der Hellenen, [3]1972, 275–522; U. PETERSEN, Goethe und E. Unt. zur E.-Rezeption in der Goethezeit, 1974; E.R. SCHWINGE, E. (Wege der Forschung), 1968; CH. SEGAL, E. and the Poetics of Sorrow, 1993; B. SEIDENSTICKER, Palintonos Harmonia. Stud. zu komischen Elementen in der griech. Tragödie, 1982, 89–241; T.B.L. WEBSTER, The Tragedies of E., 1967; B. ZIMMERMANN, Die griech. Tragödie, [2]1992, 94–138. B.Z.

[2] Older than E. [1]. He wrote 12 dramas and won twice in the agon (cf. DID A 3a).

TrGF I 16.

[3] Nephew of E. [2]. Writer of an 'Orestes', a 'Medea' and a 'Polyxena'.

TrGF I 17.

[4] Son of E. [1]. He performed the 'Bacchae', 'Iphigenia at Aulis' and 'Alcmaeon in Corinth' posthumously. B.Z.

Euripus
[1] (Εὔριπος ὁ Χαλκιδικός; *Eúripos ho Chalkidikós*). This strait, 9 km in length between Chalcis on Euboea and Boeotia, with three narrows, lies at the approximate mid-point of the sound between → Euboea and the Greek mainland (Anon. in GGM 1,105 § 29: ἡ τῶν Εὐβοέων θάλαττα). Originally, two channels ran through the most northerly narrows at Chalcis, one at the western shore, 0.5 m deep and 15 m wide, bounded on the seaward side by a reef, and with a navigable channel at the eastern shore, some 5 m deep and 18 m wide (since 1892 these narrows have been fundamentally transformed: the reef blown up and the channel widened to 30 m, deepened to 8 m). Owing to the different times at which the tides from the NW and SE reach this point, the current at the narrows changes direction four to six times daily (speed of the current up to 14.82 km/h) ([1]; the term E. thus designates an unstable person: Diogenianus 3,39). In 411 BC the E. was spanned by a wooden bridge two *plethra* (*c.* 66 m) in length, from the time of Alexander the Great fortified with towers, gates and walls (Diod. Sic. 13, p.1; 47,3; Str. 1,1,17; 9,2,2; 8; 10,1,2; 8).

1 C. LIENAU, Griechenland, 1989, 113 2 PHILIPPSON/KIRSTEN 1, 553ff. E.O.

[2] Town in Acarnania on the south coast of the Gulf of Ambracia. Located on the basis of Scyl. 34 and the lists of *theorodokoi* (IG IV[2] 95 l. 15; SEG 36, 331 l. 28–30) at modern Paliambela (Rouga), or, preferably, Loutraki.

D. STRAUCH, Die Umgestaltung NW-Griechenlands unter röm. Herrschaft, 1996, 282f. D.S.

Euromus (Εὔρωμος; *Eurōmos*). Town in the Carian interior (Str. 14,1,8; 2,22; Steph. Byz. s.v. E.; Plin. HN 5,109), 22 km south of the former Gulf of Latmia (the modern Bafa or Çamiçi gölü), 3 km south of Selimiye at the northern end of the Mylasa plateau; today's Ayaklı. In the 5th cent. as *H(K)yromos* a member of the → Delian League. The town was probably not called *E.*, often also *Eúropos,* until after the 4th cent. BC. Sympolitically linked with its περιπόλιοι (*peripólioi*, 'neighbouring towns'; Str. loc. cit.) of Olymus, Chalcetor (the modern Karakuyu tepe) to the SW, Hydae to the south, subsequently also Mylasa. In 197 under Macedonian occupation (since 201/0, Pol. 18,2,3; 44,4; Liv. 33,30) and called *Phílippoi*, E. together with Iasus and Pedasa, and with the agreement of Philip V who had just been defeated, concluded a treaty with Zeuxis, a *strategos* of Antiochus III, in the hope (to be dashed in 188) of escaping the impending annexation of Caria by Rhodes. Liberated in 196 from the Macedonians, in 167 from the Rhodians by Rome (Pol. 30,5,11–15); in 129 BC, E. belongs to the province of Asia.

To the south-east of the town wall (round tower, beginning of the 3rd cent. BC) there is a temple of Zeus Lepsi(y)nos (Λέψινος/Λέψυνος) from the Hadrianic period; 16 columns with fragments of architraves (on the column shafts *pínakes* with the names of patrons) of its *peristasis* have remained standing since antiquity, to its eastern frontage an altar, to the SW chamber tombs; in the area of the town an agora, a theatre, thermal baths. Turkish excavations established i.a. a Hellenistic and archaic predecessor structure to the temple (terracotta roof tiles with figurative frieze), dedicated to the local Carian divinity.

Türkiye-Türkei road map, Turkish Ministry of Defence/Kartographischer Verlag Ryborsch, Obertshausen bei Frankfurt/Main 1994, sheet 2; G.E. BEAN, Kleinasien 3, 1974, 45ff.; M. ERRINGTON, Antiochos III., Zeuxis und Euromos, in: EA 8, 1986, 1–8; W. KOENIGS, Westtürkei, 1991, 229f.; A. LAUMONIER, Cultes indigènes en Carie, 1958, 164ff.; MAGIE 2, 749, 908f., 952; E. MEYER, s.v. Euromos, RE Suppl. 15, 97; S. PÜLZ, Zur Bauornamentik des Zeustempels von Euromos, in: MDAI(Ist) 39, 1989, 451ff.; ROBERT, Villes, 59f. H.KA.

Europe/Europa (Εὐρώπη; *Eurṓpē*).
[1] Originally reserved for the female mythological figure (→ E. [2]; cf. Hes. Theog. 357, 359), as a geographi-

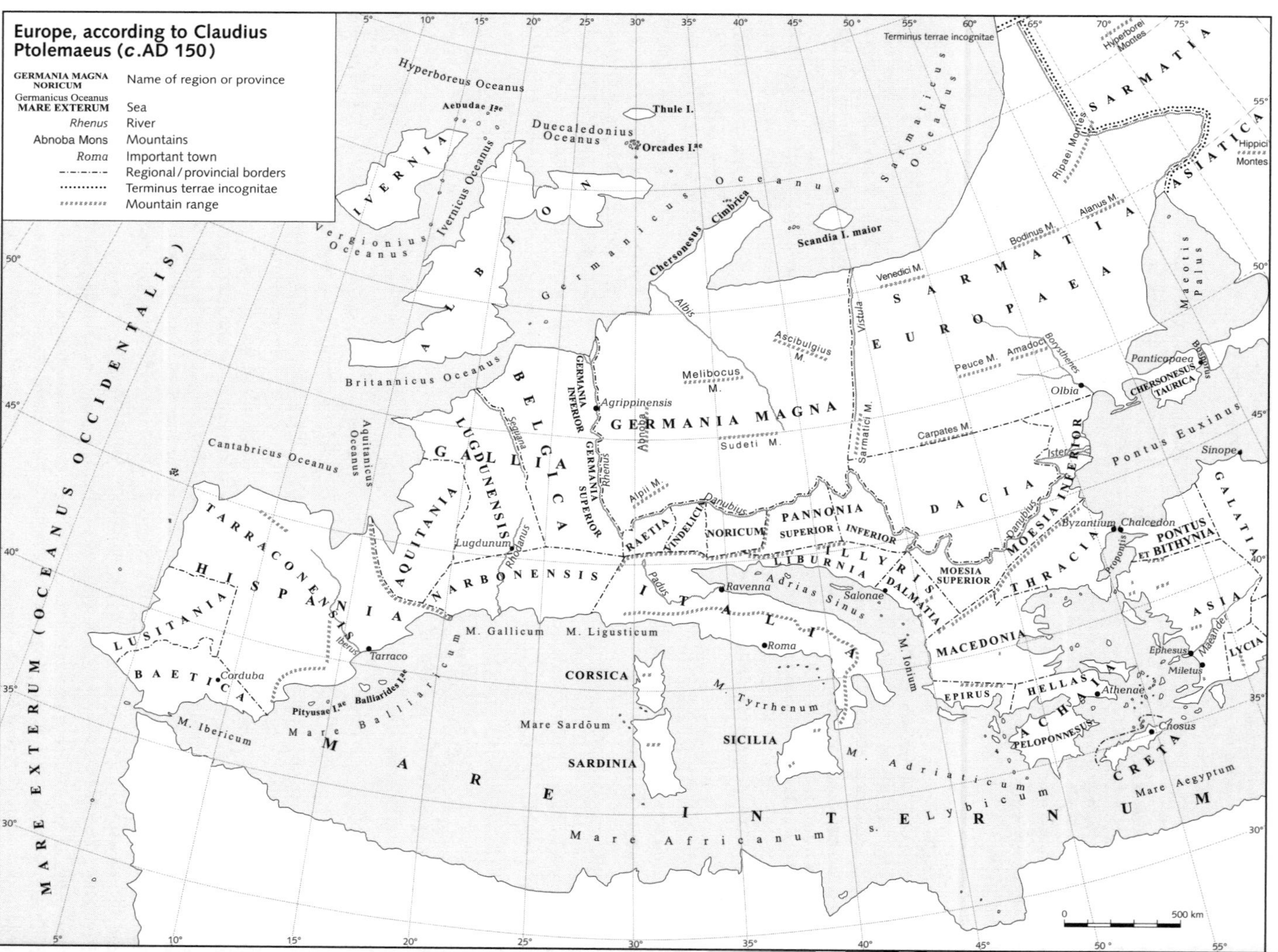
Europe, according to Claudius Ptolemaeus (c.AD 150)
GERMANIA MAGNA NORICUM — Name of region or province
Germanicus Oceanus MARE EXTERUM — Sea
Rhenus — River
Abnoba Mons — Mountains
Roma — Important town
Regional / provincial borders
Terminus terrae incognitae
Mountain range
Hyperboreus Oceanus
Aebudae I.ae
Thule I.
Duecaledonius Oceanus
Orcades I.ae
Terminus terrae incognitae
Sarmaticus Oceanus
Germanicus Oceanus
Scandia I. maior
Chersonesus Cimbrica
IVERNIA
Ivernicus Oceanus
Vergionius Oceanus
ALBION
Britannicus Oceanus
Aquitanicus Oceanus
Cantabricus Oceanus
MARE EXTERUM (OCEANUS OCCIDENTALIS)
GALLIA
BELGICA
LUGDUNENSIS
AQUITANIA
NARBONENSIS
Lugdunum
Rhodanus
Seguana
GERMANIA INFERIOR
GERMANIA SUPERIOR
Agrippinensis
Rhenus
Abnoba
GERMANIA MAGNA
Albis
Melibocus M.
Ascibulgius M.
Sudeti M.
Alpii M.
Danubius
RAETIA
VINDELICIA
NORICUM
PANNONIA SUPERIOR
PANNONIA INFERIOR
ILLYRIS
LIBURNIA
DALMATIA
Salonae
Vistula
Venedici M.
Sarmatici M.
SARMATIA EUROPAEA
Bodinus M.
Alanus M.
Ripaei Montes
Hyperborei Montes
SARMATIA ASIATICA
Hippici Montes
Maeotis Palus
Peuce M.
Amadoci
Borysthenes
Olbia
Panticapaea
Bosporus
CHERSONESUS TAURICA
Carpates M.
DACIA
Ister
MOESIA INFERIOR
MOESIA SUPERIOR
Pontus Euxinus
Sinope
GALATIA
Byzantium
Chalcedon
Propontis
PONTUS ET BITHYNIA
THRACIA
MACEDONIA
ASIA
Maeander
Ephesus
Miletus
LYCIA
EPIRUS
HELLAS
ACHAIA
Athenae
PELOPONNESUS
Chosus
CRETA
Mare Aegyptum
HISPANIA
TARRACONENSIS
LUSITANIA
BAETICA
Corduba
Tarraco
Iberus
Pityusae I.ae
Balliarides I.ae
M. Ibericum
Mare Balliaricum
M. Gallicum
M. Ligusticum
ITALIA
Padus
Ravenna
Roma
Adrias Sinus
M. Ionium
CORSICA
SARDINIA
Mare Sardōum
M. Tyrrhenum
SICILIA
M. Adriaticum
MARE INTERNUM
Mare Africanum
Libycum
0 500 km

al term E. initially referred to central Greece (cf. Hom. I. ad Apollinem 251, 291) and the Thracian-Mace-onian north (cf. Hdt. 6,43; 7,8), as opposed to the 'eloponnese in the south, the Ionian Islands in the west nd the Aegean islands, and separated from the Asiatic ind-mass by the Aegean Sea, the Hellespont, Propon-is, the Bosporus and Pontus Euxinus.

As awareness grew during the 'great colonisation' hat the Black Sea/Pontus Euxinus was enclosed to the ast (Mimnermus in the 7th cent. still has it differently; f. Str. 1,2,40), the frontier between E. (used with in-reasing frequency to describe all land outside Asia, cf. Iecat. in Hdt. 4,36) and Asia became problematic; for ere the two regions were not clearly distinguished rom one another: the eastern frontier of E. was set at he Tanais (Hdt. 4,45,2; Str. 1,4,7; 7,4,5; 11,1,1), at the ea of Azov/Maeotis (Hdt. 4,45,2; Str. 7,4,5), at the Cimmerian Bosporus (cf. Hecat. FGrH 1 F 212; Hdt. .,45,2; Str. 7,4,5; Aisch. Prom. 733–735, 790), at the 'hasis (Hdt. 4,45,2), in the Caucasus between Pontus Euxinus and the Caspian Sea/Kaspia Thalatta (Str. ,4,7), at the Araxes (Hdt. 4,40) and at the Kaspia Tha-atta (Hdt. 4,40). While the frontier to the south with .ibya – assigned sometimes to Asia (Agathemerus 2,2; all. Iug. 17; Luc. 9,411), but sometimes to E. (Sil. Pun. .,195), sometimes seen as its own continent (Hdt. 2,16; .,42; Cic. Nat. D. 2,165) – was readily defined by the *negálē thálassa* (Hdt. 4,8; 42f.), the western frontier by he Atlantic Ocean (Hdt. 1,202), Herodotus (4,45) had o clear notion of the northern frontier of E., and for a ong time the north of E. remained unknown to the ncient world (cf. Pol. 3,37). Knowledge of Scandinavia lid not come until Pliny (HN 4,95; 104) and Ptolemy 2,11,33f.; 8,6,4). But even then the size of E. was over-stimated: for Pliny (HN 6,210) E. is the largest of the hree continents, taking up 5/12 of the entire world's sur-ace. Other references: Str. 2, 5,25–27; Plin. HN 3f.; Mela 1,15–19; 3,1–35.

Although otherwise seldom used ideologically, in he context of the conflict between the Greeks and the Achaemenid realm (5th/4th cents. BC, cf. e.g. Hdt. 1,3f.; Diod. Sic. 11,62; [4]) the concept of E. acquired olitical overtones. However close the cultural rela-ions between Europe and the world of the Near East, he preconception inexorably developed of a cultural listinction between E. and Asia; this was reinforced by he romanized culture of the Germanic and West-Slavic uccessor states, against the background of an ever nore pronounced exclusion of the Greek-Byzantine East in the western psyche. Stages in this process were he division of imperial jurisdictions between the tri-umvirs Caesar and Mark Antony in 40 BC by the merid-an running north to south through Scodra (App. B Civ. 5,65), the succession arrangements after the death of Theodosius the Great in AD 395 (Ambr. Obit. Theod. 5; Claud. Carm. 1,7,151ff.), and the Great Schism of 16.7.1054 [2].

1 A. FORBIGER, Hdb. der alten Geogr. 3, ²1877 2 A. MICHEL, Humbert und Kerullarios, 2 vols., 1924/1930 3 M. NINCK, Die Entdeckung von Europa durch die Griechen, 1945 4 H. BERVE, Der Europa-Begriff in der Ant., in: E. BUCHNER, P. R. FRANKE (ed.), Gestaltende Kräfte der Ant., ²1966, 467–484 5 K. GOLDAMMER, Der Mythos von Ost und West, 1962 6 A. SCHOENING, Germanien in der Geogr. des Ptolemaeus, 1962.

MAPS: H. KIEPERT, Formae Orbis Antiqui, XXXVI, 1911. E.O.

[2] Daughter of → Phoenix, of the king of Sidon or Tyre, or of → Agenor and Argiope, Cassiopeia, Perimede or Telephassa; sister of → Cadmus (Hom. Il. 14,321f.; Hes. fr. 140MW; Bacchyl. 17,31SM; Hyg. Fab. 178; Paus. 7,4,1); in Hes. Theog. 357 she is referred to as an Oceanid. Zeus falls in love with her, transforms into a bull, and, as E. is picking flowers on the seashore, abducts her to Crete, where he couples with her. She bears → Minos, → Rhadamanthys and according to later sources also → Sarpedon (Hes. fr. 140MW; Bacchyl. fr. 10SM; Hyg. Fab. 106). In Crete she marries king → Asterius, who brings up her sons (Hes. fr. 140MW; Apollod. 3,5). Zeus gives her the bronze watchman Talos, a dog that never misses its prey and a spear that always hits its target (Apoll. Rhod. 4,1643; Ov. Met. 7,681ff.; Poll. 5,39). Her father sends Cadmus or all her brothers in vain to seek her (Hdt. 4,147; Apollod. 3,2). An epic *Eurṓpē* is ascribed to Eumelus (schol. Hom. Il. 6,131 DINDORF, but otherwise in Paus. 9,5,8; 4,4,1); Stesichorus (fr. 195 PMGF; schol. Eur. Phoen. 670) and Simonides (fr. 562 PMG) too are each said to have written a work with this title. In Aeschylus' *Káres* or *Eurṓpē* (TrGF 3F99) E. awaits news of her son Sarpedon. Aeschylus and Acusilaus (FGrH 2F29) saw the bull as having been sent by Zeus, which would fit its later becoming a constellation (Eur. Phrixus fr. 820 TGF), while according to Hesiod and Bacchylides (schol. Il. 12,292; 307) Zeus himself changes into a bull and then perhaps reassumes human form on Crete. The latter version is followed by most later authors (Mosch. 2; Hor. Carm. 3,27,25ff.; Ov. Met. 2,846–851; Apollod. 3,1ff.; Lucian Dialogi Marini 15).

E. had a cult at Gortyn on Crete as E. → Hellotis, the Hellotia being celebrated here annually in her honour (Theophr. Hist. pl. 1,9,5; Plin. HN 12,11; Ath. 15,22,678b). Coins from Gortyn from the 5th cent. onwards certainly bear the image of Europa. A Boeotian version of the legend mentions a cave in which Zeus is supposed to have hidden E., who is here referred to as daughter of Tityus and mother of Euphemus (Pind. Pyth. 4,46; Apoll. Rhod. 1,179–184; Paus. 9,19,1); in Lebadea Demeter bears the epithet E. (Paus. 9,39,4). E. is later also identified with → Astarte as worshipped in Sidon (Lucian Syria dea 4).

W. BÜHLER, Europa, 1968; J. ESCHER, s.v. E. 1, RE 6,1287–1298; M. ROBERTSON, s.v. E. 1, LIMC 4.1,76–92; M. SORDI (ed.), L'Europa nel mondo antico, in: Contributi dell' Istituto di storia antica 12, 1886, 1–48.

FIG.: M. ROBERTSON, s.v. E. 1, LIMC 4.2, 32–48; E. ZAHN, Europa und der Stier, 1983. R.HA.

Eurotas (Εὐρώτας; *Eyrṓtas*, 'the abundantly-flowing'). The 82 km-long river (mythological derivation from king E. in Paus. 3,1,1f.) rises with its source-streams on the flat valley-watershed of the Alpheius between Mt. Parnon and Mt. Taygetus on the Asea plain, and in the north-western foothills of the Arcadian Mt. Parnon (the presumption of subterranean links in the region of its source between the E. and Lake Taka, made in Paus. 8,44,4, is improbable), and, following a tectonic depression ('the E. trough'), enters the 18 km-long and *c.* 10 km-wide Laconian basin north of Sparta. In its winding, superimposed course and in parts narrow gorge it penetrates hilly country of up to 516 m, composed of neogene conglomerates and limestone, and flows into the Gulf of Laconia east of Gythium, forming a formerly malarial flood plain (of Helus: Str. 8,5,2) of *c.* 50 km². The E. flows for the entire year, but, depending on the climate and owing to heavy demands on its waters (*c.* 120 km² are irrigated by the waters of the E.), its volume varies greatly with the seasons. In antiquity the E. was often unfordable (Pol. 5,22,2).

PHILIPPSON/KIRSTEN 3,2, 1959, 446–463. C.L. and E.O.

Eurus (Εὖρος/*Eûros*, Lat. *Eurus*). One of the four cardinal winds (Hom. Od. 5,295f.; Verg. Aen. 1,85f.) also used to refer to the different points of the compass. In Hesiod, however (Theog. 379f.), E. is missing. [1]. At first in the Greek world all easterly winds (cf. the Hom. four-winds model [2. 2353, fig. 15]) were called *Eúroi* (Ps.-Aristot. De mundo 4,394b 20); but especially the E. as neighbour to the → Notus, the south wind (Aristot. Mete. 2,6,363b 21–23), blows from the point of winter sunrise, and is accordingly often called the south-east wind (*Eurónotos*, otherwise ESE); on the Athenian 'Tower of the Winds' too, E. is an intermediate wind from the SE [4]. But the → Apheliotes (in Lat. called *solanus*) on the twenty-four point wind-rose (Vitr. De arch. 1,6,10) blows directly from the east. There then follow to the south between it and the E. the *Ornithiae* and the *Eurocircias*. In Vitr. De arch. 1,6,11 the E. derives its name from the fact that it emerges from the morning winds (*quod ex auris procreatur*). Areas of habitation to the east or south-east were regarded as healthy. Otherwise the E. was described sometimes as rain-bearing, but sometimes as dry (Ptol. Tetr. 1,10), or – as Aristotle has it (Mete. 2,6,364a 24f.) – as warm, at first dry and then wet. Pliny (HN 2,119–121) in his history of the wind-rose states that the E. is synonymous with the Roman *Volturnus* (ESE). When he takes up the theme again (HN 18,338), he mentions that in Italy and Gaul, because of the dry and warm properties of the E., beehives and vineyards should be set out to the east.

Just as beneficial effects could also be looked for from other wind-gods, the Spartans called on E. as 'saviour of Sparta' (PMG 858; [5]).
→ Winds

1 M.L. WEST, Hesiod Theogony, 1966, 2271 2 W.BÖKER, s.v. Winde, RE 8 A, 2211–2387 3 A.REHM, s.v. Euros, RE 6, 1311ff. 4 E.SIMON, s.v. Venti, LIMC 8.1 188f. no. 12 5 BURKERT, 272. C.HÜ. and R.F

Euryale (Εὐρυάλη; *Euryálē*).
[1] One of the → Gorgons (Hes. Theog. 276; Pind. Pyth 12,20; Apollod. 2,40).
[2] Mother of → Orion (Eratosth. Katasterismoi 32; Hyg. Poet. Astr. 2,34; Apollod. 1,25). R.B

Euryalus (Εὐρύαλος; *Euryálos*, 'far-voyaging' [1. 71 195]); the name of several heroes, usable in hexameters.

1 KAMPTZ.

[1] An Argive hero, son of Mecisteus from Argos. He is mentioned both as one of the → Argonauts (Apollod 1,113) and one of the Epigoni (sons of the seven heroes who fought in vain against Thebes; Apollod. 3,82; Paus. 2,20,5). E. marches against Troy with Diomedes and Sthenelus (Hom. Il. 2,566; 6,20–28 *aristeia*; Apollod. 1,103; Paus. 2,30,10). At the funerary games for Patroclus he is defeated in the boxing competition by Epius (Hom. Il. 23,677–699). According to Quint Smyrn. 4,472–494 he was an occupant of the Trojan Horse, and took part in the funerary games for Achilles E. was depicted as one of the Epigoni in a statuary group at Delphi (Paus.10,10,4), and figured as a wounded warrior in the *Ilioupersis* of Polygnotus (Paus. 10,25,6).

M.PIPILI, s.v. Euryalos 2, LIMC 4.1, 94–95; W.KULLMANN, Die Quellen der Ilias, Hermes ES 14, 1960, 90; 148–151.

[2] A Phaeacian, son of Naubolus. He excels in beauty and in wrestling. When he mocks → Odysseus, who does not wish to take part in the games, Odysseus rebukes him and E. apologizes (Hom. Od. 8,115–185; 396–400).
[3] Son of → Odysseus and of Euippe in Epirus. When he visits his father on Ithaca he is killed by Odysseus at the behest of the suspicious Penelope, before he can make himself known. Sophocles used the story in his *Euryálos* (Parthenius 3; TrGF 4, 194).
[4] Trojan, a companion of Aeneas, remarkable for his youthful beauty. Thanks to the help of his friend → Nisus he wins the running race (Verg. Aen. 5,294–361). On a scouting expedition against the Rutulians the pair kill many enemies, but eventually are killed together (Verg. Aen. 9,177–445).

M.BELLINCIONI, s.v. Euryalos, EV 2, 424–426. R.B

Eurybates (Εὐρυβάτης; *Eurybátēs*, 'the long-striding' [1. 77]). Descriptive name of two heralds.

1 KAMPTZ.

[1] Herald to Agamemnon (Hom. Il. 1,320; Ov. Epist. 3,9–10). Together with Talthybius he takes → Briseis

rom the tent of Achilles and brings her to Agamemnon. He is frequently depicted in this function [1].

1 E. ZERVOUDAKI, s.v. Euryalos 1, LIMC 4.1, 95–97.

[2] Quick-witted herald to Odysseus, who treasures him despite his ugliness (Hom. Od. 19,244–248; Hom. Il. 2,184). He was perhaps depicted in the *Ilioupersis* of Polygnotus at Delphi (Paus. 10,25,4; 8) [1].

1 E. ZERVOUDAKI, s.v. Euryalos 2, LIMC 4.1, 97. R.B.

Eurybiades (Εὐρυβιάδης; *Eurybiádēs*). Spartan commander of the fleet of the Greek confederation of 481 BC at the battles of Artemisium and Salamis in 480. After the Persians had overcome Leonidas' position at Thermopylae, E. took timely measures to lead the Greek fleet through the narrow sound of Euripus into Attic waters (Hdt. 8,4–21). At Salamis, against the vigourous protests of most leaders of the Greek naval contingents, he followed Themistocles' plan to give battle to the Persian fleet in the Bay of Salamis (Hdt. 8,49; 57ff.; 74; 79), but after the victory did not accept Themistocles' advice to pursue the Persian fleet to the Hellespont and there destroy the bridges of ships (Hdt. 8,108).

J.F. LAZENBY, The Defence of Greece 490–479 B.C., 1993, 117–203. K.-W.WEL.

Euryclea (Εὐρύκλεια; *Eurýkleia*, the 'widely-famed' [1], *Euryclia*). Daughter of Ops, from childhood the trusted servant in the house of → Odysseus. She recognizes him by a scar when she is washing the beggar's feet (Hom. Od. 1,429; 2,345–347; 19,350–507; Hyg. Fab. 125,20; 126,7) [2].

1 KAMPTZ, 37 2 O. TOUCHEFEU, s.v. Eurykleia, LIMC 4.1, 101–103.

G. RAMMING, Die Dienerschaft in der Odyssee, PhD thesis 1973. R.B.

Eurycleides (Εὐρυκλείδης; *Eurykleídēs*). Son of Micion from Cephisia; the most significant Athenian statesman of the 2nd half of the 3rd cent. BC: treasurer of the war-chest 244/3 BC (?), *strategos* of hoplites *c.* 245/240 (?), eponymous *archon* 240/239 (?) (IG II/III² I 2 1300; II 1 1705; Syll.³ 491; 497) [1. 118–127]; in 229 BC E. together with his brother → Micion in cooperation with → Diogenes [1] became the liberator of Athens from Macedonian rule, and subsequently the mentor of a strict policy of neutrality, distanced from → Aratus [2] and in friendship with the Ptolemies (cf. Plut. Arat. 41,3; Pol. 5, 106); supposedly poisoned by → Philippus V (Paus. 2,9,4), E. died in unknown circumstances between 210 and 201. In 229 E. sponsored an *agon* for Demeter and Kore, and initiated the symbolically fecund state cult of Demos and the Charites, whose family priesthood passed to his descendants [2. 177–195]. E.' was one of the leading families in Athens during the 2nd cent. [1. 179–182].

1 C. HABICHT, Studien zur Gesch. Athens in hell. Zeit, 1982 2 HABICHT. L.-M.G.

Eurycles (Εὐρυκλῆς; *Euryklês*). Son of the noble Spartan Lachares, who was executed by Antonius for piracy (Syll.³ 786; Plut. Ant. 67,2ff.). E. consequently fought on Octavian's side at Actium; as C. Iulius E. he received Roman citizenship, the island of Cythera and a dynastic position in Sparta (Plut. ibid.; Str. 8,5,1; 8,5,5; cf. [1]). On a journey to Judaea, E. as intermediary deepened the rift between king Herod and his sons. Awarded with 50 talents, by dint of similar intrigues he obtained further sums from Archelaus of Cappadocia (Jos. Ant. Iud. 16,301; 306; 309ff.; BI 1,513ff.). Upon his return E. attempted to gain influence over the → Eleutherolakones, built a gymnasium in Sparta and a luxurious bath in Corinth, appeared as a benefactor in Gytheum and was honoured in Asopos and Athens (Paus. 3,14,6; 2,3,5; IG V 970; Syll.³ 787). E. was arraigned twice under Augustus – i.a. by a descendant of Brasidas (Plut. Mor. 207F) – for having caused unrest in Achaea and plundered the cities. Eventually (perhaps in connection with Tiberius' *secessio* to Rhodes) he was condemned and banished (Jos. BI 1,531; Ant. Iud. 16,310). He was rehabilitated after his death (before 2 BC?), as demonstrated by the subsequent feasts of *Euryclea* in Gytheum and Sparta (SEG 11,922f.; IG V 1,71b 53ff.; 86,30f.; 168,13; 550; 664). His son C. Iulius Laco acquired the same post as his father (Syll.³ 789). Several generations of the family appear during the Imperial period, and a link was formed i.a. with the house of Commagene [2; 3].

1 G. W. BOWERSOCK, Eurycles of Sparta, in: JRS 51, 1961, 112–118 2 A.J.S. SPAWFORTH, Babilla, the Eurylids, and memorials for a Greek magnate, in: ABSA 73, 1978, 249–260 3 A.R. BIRLEY, in: ZPE 116, 1997, 210ff. and 237ff., Appendix 2 with genealogy.

A.S. BRADFORD, A Prosopography of Lacedaemonians, 1977, 178ff. and 256; P. CARTLEDGE, A. SPAWFORTH, Hellenistic and Roman Sparta, 1989, 97ff.; S. GRUNAUER-VON HOERSCHELMANN, Die Münzprägung der Lakedaimonier, 1978, 63ff.; 162ff.; 73ff.; 171ff.; H. LINDSAY, Augustus and Eurycles, in: RhM 135, 1992, 290–297. D.K.

Eurydamas (Εὐρυδάμας; *Eurydámas*, 'the far-conquering'); the name of several heroes, usable in hexameters.

[1] Father of Abas and Polyidus. Aged Trojan who had the gift of prophesying from dreams, but could not foretell the death of his sons by the hand of Diomedes (Hom. Il. 5,148–151 with schol.; Tzetz. Homerica 66).

[2] Suitor to Penelope (Hom. Od. 18,297); he was killed by Odysseus (Hom. Od. 22,283).

[3] Supposed inventor of the Thessalian custom of dragging a murderer around the grave of his victim (Aristot. fr. 166 ROSE). R.B.

Eurydice (Εὐρυδίκη; *Eurydíkē*).

[1] Frequently occurring name of Greek heroines, initially that of the wife of Aeneas in the → Cypria (Paus. 10,26,1; catalogue [1. 193]). The best-known is the wife of → Orpheus; the myth is told by → Vergilius (Georg. 4,453–527) and → Ovidius (Met. 10,1–147; 11,1–66) in the form that has since become canonical: E. died of a snakebite on the day of her marriage; through the power of his songs Orpheus was able to persuade the rulers of the Underworld to return E. to him, on condition that he should not look back at her during their return from the Underworld. Orpheus broke the condition and lost E. a second time. Iconographically, the myth has come down to us via an Attic relief of the 5th cent., extant in copies [2]. The first literary mentions (Eur. Alc. 357; Isoc. Or. 11,8) deal only with Orpheus' power to bring back the dead; Pl. Symp. 179d relates that only a vision of E. was shown to Orpheus. Hellenistic authors appear not to speak of Orpheus' failure (Hermesianax, fr. 7,1–14 POWELL, where Argiope in mentioned in place of E.; Moschus 3,130); this is probably a tendentious alteration of the traditional myth, to whose typology Orpheus' failure is fundamental [3; 4; 5].

1 D. LYONS, Gender and Immortality. Heroines in Ancient Greek Myth and Cult, 1997 2 G. SCHWARZ, s.v. E., LIMC 4.2, 50f. 3 J. HEURGON, Orphée et E. avant Virgile, in: Mélanges d'Archéologie et d'Histoire 49, 1932, 6–60 4 F. GRAF, Orpheus. A poet among men, in: J. BREMMER (ed.), Interpretations of Greek Mythology, 1988, 80–106 5 C. RIEDWEG, Orfeo, in: S. SETTIS, (ed.), I Greci. Storia, Cultura, Arte, Società 2,1, 1996, 1251–1280.

F.G.

[2] From the royal house of Lyncestis; wife of → Amyntas [3] of Macedonia (from 390 BC), mother of → Alexander [3], → Perdiccas and → Philippus II. She appears to have supported → Ptolemaeus Alorites against Alexander, and married him after he had killed Alexander and made himself king (hence probably the horror story in Iustin. 7,5,4–8, according to which she tried to kill Amyntas and murdered Alexander and Perdiccas). When → Pausanias, supported by → Olynthus, invaded Macedonia, she called upon → Iphicrates for aid (described rhetorically in Aeschin. Leg. 2,26–29). She probably died during the time of Perdiccas.

HM 2, 182f.

[3] Daughter of → Amyntas [4] and → Cyn(n)ane; birth-name Hade(i)a. Born *c.* 337 BC, she was brought up as a warrior by her mother, and after the death of Alexander [4] in 322 taken by her to Asia Minor, where, after → Alcetas [4] had murdered Cynnane, she married the feeble-minded Philip III (see → Arridaeus [4]), took the 'royal name' E., and began to reign in Philip's name. Held by → Antipater [1] at Triparadeisus, after his death she allied herself with → Cassander against → Polyperchon and → Olympias. Abandoned by her troops in Cassander's absence, she was captured along with Philip. Philip was murdered and E. forced by Olympias to commit suicide. Cassander buried the royal couple at → Aegae [1], perhaps in the so-called tomb of Philip II (Arr. Succ. 22–3.33; Diod. Sic. 18,39; 19,11.35).

[4] E., daughter of → Antipater [1], married → Ptolemaeus *c.* 320 BC and bore him → Ptolemaeus Keraunos, → Meleager, → Lysandra and → Ptolemais. Displaced from Ptolemaeus' side by → Berenice [1], she fled to Miletus, where after a long engagement → Demetrius [I 2] married Ptolemais (287) before his last campaign.

[5] E., daughter of → Lysimachus; married → Antipater [2] (perhaps only after → Cassander's death). When Antipater was ousted by → Demetrius [I 2] in 293 BC she fled with him to Lysimachus, who, however, after allying himself with → Pyrrhus, murdered Antipater and had E. thrown into captivity (Iust. 16,2,4).

J. SEIBERT, Histor. Beiträge zu den dynastischen Verbindungen in hell. Zeit, 1967 (see index).

E.B.

Euryganea (Εὐρυγάνη, -εια; *Eurygánē, -eia*). In the → *Oidipódeia* of the Cyclic Epics the second wife of → Oedipus, after → Iocaste (Epicaste) commits suicide upon discovery of her incest. From her come the children that are elsewhere ascribed to Jocasta (Oedipodea, argumentum; fr. 2 PEG I; Apollod. 3,55).

R.B.

Eurylochus (Εὐρύλοχος; *Eurýlochos*).

[1] Close relation and ambivalent companion of → Odysseus. He is the only one not to accept the invitation of → Circe, and so escapes being transformed into a pig (Hom. Od. 10,205–274; Apollod. Epit. 7,14–15; Ov. Met. 14,287). When E. later incites the companions against Odysseus, he is threatened with punishment by death (Hom. Od. 10,429–448). Together with → Perimedes he takes part in the sacrifice to the dead before Odysseus enters the Underworld (ibid. 11,23–24); according to Paus. 10,29,1 the scene was depicted in the *Nekyia* of Polygnotus. The pair bind Odysseus tighter when they sail past the Sirens (ibid. 12,195–196). E. eventually brings about his own downfall and that of the companions, when he induces the latter to slaughter the cattle of Helios (ibid. 12,339–352).

O. TOUCHEFEU, s.v. E.1, LIMC 4.1, 103.

R.B.

[2] Spartiate; in 426 BC after the Athenians had been defeated by the Aetolians he was to join the latter in the capture of Naupactus. But the *polis* was secured in time by Demosthenes [1], and E. had to withdraw. He thereupon planned an attack on the Amphilochi and the Acarnanians in the company of the Ambracians, but after joining the Ambracians he was defeated and killed at Olpae by Demosthenes (Thuc. 3,100–109). M.MEI.

Eurymachus (Εὐρύμαχος; *Eurýmachos*; for the name cf. [1]). Son of Polybus; one of the most respected of → Penelope's suitors (Hom. Od. 1,399). In the suitors' board games he is often the victor (Ath. 1,17 a b). He is killed by Odysseus, in spite of offering him atonement (Hom. Od. 22,44–88). Cf. also Aesch. 179 TrGF.

1 KAMPTZ, 72. R.B.

Eurymedon (Εὐρυμέδων; *Eurymédōn*, 'far-prevailing' [2]). The name of several heroes, usable in hexameters. [1] King of the → Giants, by his daughter Periboea grandfather of Nausithous the son of Poseidon, ancestor of the Phaeacian kings. E. brought himself and his people to ruin (Hom. Od. 7,58–60 with schol. and Eust.). According to → Euphorion fr. 99 POWELL (schol. Hom. Il. 14,295–296) he raped Hera, whereupon she bore → Prometheus. For this Zeus later hurled E. into the Tartarus.

1 F. VIAN, s.v. E.1, LIMC 4.1, 105 2 KAMPTZ 84, 195.

[2] Chariot driver to Agamemnon (Hom. Il. 4,228 with schol.). Upon returning from Troy he was murdered by Aegisthus along with his master (Paus. 2,16,6).
[3] Servant to Nestor (Hom. Il. 8,114; 11,620 with schol.). R.B.
[4] Athenian commander in the Peloponnesian War. Sent in 427 BC to support the democrats in Corcyra, he tolerated their massacre under the oligarchs (Thuc. 3,80–85). After the attack on Tanagra in 426, in the spring of 425 he commanded the fleet that sailed to Sicily, enabling → Demosthenes [1] to establish himself at Pylos. After the capture of Sphacteria by Cleon, E. travelled via Corcyra, where a campaign waged with the democrats against the oligarchs ended in a further bloodbath, to Sicily (Thuc. 4,46). His arrival caused the Sicilians to conclude the peace of Gela, so that the Athenian fleet had to return home. Because of dashed hopes for the subjection of Sicily, E. was condemned for alleged corruption (Thuc. 4,58–65) in Athens. He was not *strategos* again until 414, when he took funds to the Athenian army in Sicily, and with Demosthenes further reinforced it. After the failed storming of Epipolae in 413 even E. was unable to accomplish immediate withdrawal from Sicily against the opposition of Nicias. He perished when the Athenian fleet was destroyed in the great harbour of Syracuse (Thuc. 7,42f.; 52,2).

H.-J. GEHRKE, Stasis, 1985, 88–93; D. KAGAN, The Peace of Nicias and the Sicilian Expedition, 1981. W.S.

[5] After the Cestrus the most voluminous river in the east of Pamphylia (the modern Köprü Çayı), rising in the Taurus and flowing to the south past Selge and → Aspendus to the sea. Already in its first mention by Scylax (GGM 1,75) described as navigable as far as Aspendus. Other references: Xen. Hell. 4,8,30; Arr. Anab. 1,27; Str. 12,7,3; Plin. HN 5,96. Well known for the battle of the E., in which the Athenians under Cimon defeated the Persian army and fleet in 465 BC (Thuc. 1,100,1; Diod. Sic. 11,61,1; [1. 194f.]). A crude, comically obscene reference to the defeat of the Persians at the E. occurs on an Attic red-figured cup with inscription [2].

1 H. BENGTSON, Griech. Gesch. (HbdA III,4), [4]1969 2 K. SCHAUENBURG, ΕΥΡΥΜΕΔΩΝ ΕΙΜΙ, in: MDAI(A) 90, 1975, 97–121, pl. 25. W.MA.

[6] At present unlocated city near Tarsus in Cilicia (Steph. Byz. 286). W.MA.

Eurymedusa (Εὐρυμέδουσα; *Eurymédousa*). Maidservant to → Nausicaa (Hom. Od. 7,8). R.B.

Eurynome (Εὐρυνόμη; *Eurynómē*). Daughter of Oceanus; with Thetis she hid → Hephaestus for nine years after he had been expelled from Olympus by Hera (Hom. Il. 18,398ff.). In Hes. (Theog. 358), E. comes next to Metis in the catalogue of the → Oceanids (337; Apollod. 1,8 mother Tethys), next to Metis and Themis in the catalogue of the wives of Zeus as mother of the → Charites (907ff.; Apollod. 1,13), as which Call. (fr. 6 Pf.) calls her Τιτηνιάς (*Titēniás*) (participant in the battle with the giants on the Pergamum Altar: inscr. from Pergamum 110). Like the Song of Orpheus (Apoll. Rhod. 1,503ff.), this reflects a tradition according to which the 'far-prevailing' and her husband Ophion as ruler of the gods were thrown into Oceanus by Cronus and Rhea (Orph. fr. 29, probably Pherec. Syr. [1]). Cult of E. in Arcadian Phigalia, with sanctuary and *xoanon*, where E. was depicted as a mermaid and popularly identified with Artemis (Paus. 8,41,4ff.). Of 11 other bearers of the name, the best-known is Penelope's housekeeper (Hom. Od. 17,495).

1 WILAMOWITZ Vol. 2, 198.

WILAMOWITZ Vol. 1, 216f. P.D.

Euryphon of Cnidus Greek physician, mid 5th cent. BC. The story recounted in Sor. Vita Hipp. 5, that E. cured Perdiccas II of Macedonia of an illness caused by unrequited love, arose comparatively late and is rather fantastical. According to Galen (17a,886), he provided the most important contributions to the so-called 'Cnidian Sentences', which have survived only in fragments [1. 65–66; 2. 14–26]. In the opinion of some ancient scholars some of his works, especially those dealing with dietetics, were taken up into the Hippocratic Corpus (Gal. 6,473; 7,960; 16,3).

E. regarded diseases as the result of residues of food that, in his opinion, rise to the head. If the stomach is empty and clean before the next meal, digestion functions normally (Anonymus Londinensis 3,7). Galen (2,900; 15,135–136) includes him in a list of physicians well-versed in anatomy, doubtless referring to E.'s naming of the parts of the body and his differentiation of veins and arteries rather than to a definite practice of dissection [3. 1343]. E. believed that pleurisy, of whose symptoms he gave a reliable description, also affected the lungs (Cael. Aurel., Acut. 3,144, cf. 2,96). Although his cures also included herbs and gruel, they relied essentially on drastic bleeding, cutting and burning (Gal. 11,149; 18A, 149). His treatise on → gynaecology was esp. significant [2. 152–154], so that his recommendations in cases of retention of the placenta or prolapse of the womb (for the latter, to tie the patient for 24 hours head-downwards to a ladder), and his tests for the ability to conceive were cited until well into the 2nd cent. AD (Sor. 4,71; 4,85; 1,35). He rejected the generally held opinion that a premature foetus in the 7th month of pregnancy was capable of surviving, fixing the age of survivability at the 8th month (Censorinus, DN 7,5). His most famous saying was that time had been his greatest teacher (Stob. Ecl. 1,8,40).

1 H. GRENSEMANN, Knidische Medizin, Part I, 1975 2 J. JOUANNA, Hippocrate. Pour une Archéologie de l'École de Cnide, 1974 3 M. WELLMANN, s.v. Euryphon, RE 5, 1342–1344. V.N.

Eurypontids (Εὐρυπωντίδαι; *Eurypōntídai*). Spartan royal house, whose representatives according to Herodotus (6,51) were supposed to have less prestige than the royal house of the Agiads. In fact the E. provided important kings such as Archidamus II, Agesilaus II, Agis II, III and IV. Its eponym was the fictitious figure of Eurypon, a descendant of Heracles in the sixth (Hdt. 8,131; Str. 8,366) or seventh generation (Plut. Lycurgus 1; Paus. 3,7,1). The list of E., like that of the Agiads, is unusable historically for the period prior to the early 6th cent. BC.

→ Agiads

E.I. MCQUEEN, The Eurypontid House in Hellenistic Sparta, in: Historia 39, 1990, 163–181; P. PORALLA, Prosopographie der Lakedaimonier bis auf die Zeit Alexanders d. Gr., [2]1985, 149–165. K.-W.WEL.

Euryptolemus (Εὐρυπτόλεμος; *Euryptólemos*). Cousin and close friend of Alcibiades [3] and related to the younger Pericles. In 408 BC, E. and → Diotimus [1] were sworn witnesses to the contract in Chrysopolis between Pharnabazus and Alcibiades and were members of an Athenian delegation to Susa. As a result of a shift in the Persian court in favour of the Spartans, the delegation was detained for quite some time (Xen. Hell. 1,3,12f.; 1,4,1–7). In the Arginusae trial E. argued, first by → *paranómōn graphḗ*, which he was obliged to withdraw, and then in a public speech, for the arraigned commanders to be given a proper legal trial (Ps.-Pl. Ax. 369 A; Xen. Hell. 1,7,12–34).

R.A. BAUMAN, Political Trials in Ancient Greece, 1990, 70–74; DAVIES, 377f. W.S.

Eurypylus (Εὐρύπυλος; *Eurýpylos*).

[1] Son of Euaimon; a Thessalian and suitor to Helen (Apollod. 3,131), a warrior at Troy: leader of 40 ships (Hom. Il. 2,734ff.); wounded by Paris (11,575ff.), healed by Patroclus (11,809ff; 15,390ff.); stranded in Libya on the journey home (Lycoph. Al. 901f. with schol.).

[2] Son of → Telephus son of Heracles; king of the Mysians; sent to the aid of Troy (Acusilaus FGrH F 40) by his mother → Astyoche, sister of Priam (Apollod. 3,146), whom Priam had bribed with the golden vine (cf. Ilias parva, EpGF fr. 6). He kills Machaon and Nireus (Ilias parva, EpGF fr. 7; Hyg. Fab. 113), is killed by Neoptolemus along with many Ceteians (Mysians) (Hom. Od. 11,519ff.; Apollod. Epit. 5,12).

[3] Son of Poseidon and Astypalaea; king of the Meropes on Cos (Hom. Il. 2,677); during a storm raised by Hera (14,250ff.; 15,26ff.) he prevents Heracles from landing as he returns from Troy, and Heracles kills him and his sons (Apollod. 2,137f.); Heracles fathers Thessalus by E.'s daughter Chalciope (Apollod. 2,166; Pherec. FGrH F 78).

[4] According to Pind. (Pyth. 4,20ff.), a son of Poseidon who, in the likeness of → Trito (in Apoll. Rhod. 4,1551ff. as Trito himself) hands the Argonaut Euphemus a clod of Libyan sand; in the Hell. period he becomes the king of Libya (Acesander FGrH F 4; his genealogy F 1; cf. Phylarchus FGrH F 15) during whose reign the nymph Cyrene kills a rampaging lion (Akesandrus FGrH F 4, cf. Callim. H. 2,92 [1. 282ff.]).

[5] Hero of Patrae, in Paus. (7,19,9) identified with the Thessalian E. [1], elsewhere with E. son of Dexamenus king of Olenus; his cult legend (Paus. 7,19–20): from the booty of Troy E. received the chest containing the statue of Dionysus Aisymnetes, at the sight of which he went mad; after consulting the oracle at Delphi he came to Patrae; his arrival put an end to the traditional human sacrifice to Artemis Laphria, and at the same time to his madness, thus fulfilling two oracles [2. 374–380].

1 P. DRÄGER, Argo pasimelousa, vol. 1, 1993
2 WILAMOWITZ, Vol. 1. P.D.

Eurysaces (Εὐρυσάκης; *Eurysákēs*). In Athenian tradition a son of → Ajax (Soph. Aj. 340; 575). E.'s name ('broad shield') reflects an attribute of his father (cf. Astyanax, Neoptolemus, Telemachus). He had a sanctuary in the city deme of Melite, where he is supposed to have settled after he and his brother Philaeus had handed their hereditary homeland of Salamis to the Athenians (Plut. Solon 83d). The story is doubtless a transparent political invention. The circumstance attendant on it was E.'s office as priest in the *Salaminioi* lineage. Sophocles wrote a tragedy 'E.', which is lost.

W.K. FERGUSON, The Salaminioi of Heptaphylai and Sounion, in: Hesperia 7, 1938, 1–68 (esp. 15–17); O. TOUCHEFEU, s.v. E., LIMC 4.1, 111–2. E.K.

Eurysthenes (Εὐρυσθένης; *Eurysthénēs*).

[1] Legendary Spartan king, according to tradition a son of Aristodemus, descendant of Heracles. E. was held to be the progenitor of the Agiads (Hdt. 4,147; 6,52; 7,204; Cic. Div. 2,90). Hellanicus (FGrH 4 F 116) makes him author of the Spartan constitution, along with his brother Procles, ancestral father of the Eurypontids; Ephorus ascribes to him the dividing-up of the

Lacedaemonian settlement districts (FGrH 70 F 117). But claims such as these are the expression of various attempts to explain and classify the peculiarities of Spartan society in a historical-mythological context. The same applies to the allegedly abiding struggle between E. and his brother (Paus. 3,1,7), to which is attributed the state of strife between the Spartan royal houses, and in the final analysis also the very creation of the list of kings, which is entirely worthless for the early period.

[2] Descendant of the Spartan king Damaratus, Agiad, who was deposed in 491 BC and fled to the Persians. In 399 together with his brother Procles he ruled Pergamum and its environs (Xen. Hell. 3,1,6). M.MEI.

Eurystheus (Εὐρυσθεύς; *Eurystheús*). Mythical ruler of Argos. He was the antagonist of → Heracles, and charged him with the twelve labours. The rivalry between the two had been caused by Hera: after Zeus had declared that a son of his blood would be born that very day, and would rule over all that he surveyed, Hera delayed → Alcmene's labour and accelerated that of the wife of Sthenelus, who was a Perseid and therefore a descendant of Zeus (Hom. Il. 19,95–133). In some versions of the myth, at that moment Hera and Zeus agreed that Heracles would owe service to E., and would later be immortal. It was thus as a mortal that, following the instructions of the Delphic oracle, Heracles came into E.'s service, either to atone for having murdered his own children in a fit of madness (e.g. Apollod. 2,73) or simply because E. ordered it. The setting of seemingly insoluble tasks by a tyrannical ruler is a frequent motif in Greek mythology, but in significance Heracles' labours go far beyond their predecessors. Vases depict E. hiding terrified in a barrel as Heracles brings him the Erymanthian boar. → Cerberus being dragged off to the upper world is also depicted on some vases. Upon Heracles' death E. began to seek out Heracles' children, and pursued them throughout Greece. According to an Athenian myth (Eur. Heracl., cf. Hdt. 9,27), the Athenians protected the Heraclidae and defeated the Argives led by E. It was believed that E. was buried in Pallene or at Gargettus; according to another version, his head was cut off and brought to Alcmene, who put out the eyes with weaving-pins (in Str. 8,6,19 the head was buried separately in Tricorythus). That Euripides should have invented the entire story of E.' burial in Attica appears improbable, but the interpretation of the myth that makes E. a heroic saviour of Athens against the Doric descendants of the Heraclidae possibly began with him.

→ Doric Migration

W. Felten, s.v. E., LIMC 5.1, 43–8; E. Kearns, The heroes of Attica, 1989, 49–50; J. Wilkins, Euripides: Heraclidae, 1993, XI–XXXV, 190–1; G. Zuntz, The political plays of Euripides, 1955, 81–88. E.K.

Eurytion (Εὐρυτίων; *Eurytíōn*). Frequently used name of heroes and → centaurs.

[1] Thessalian centaur; in the house of Peirithous, while drunk on wine, he violates Peirithous' bride → Hippodamia, whereupon the Lapiths disfigure him; this leads to the conflict between → Lapithae and centaurs. The suitor → Antinous [1] holds E.'s fate up before Odysseus as a warning (Hom. Od. 21,295–304). Later too, E. as leader of the centaurs is frequently represented as a terrifying example (Thgn. 1,542).

[2] Peloponnesian centaur, son of Ixion. He flees from Heracles into the → Pholoe mountains, and is later killed by him in the house of → Dexamenus (Hyg. Fab. 33; Apollod. 2,83–87).

[3] → Geryoneus' herdsman on the island of Erythea; killed by Heracles (Hes. Theog. 293; Hellanicus FGrH 4 F 110; Apollod. 2,106). Illustrations frequently show him in the fight between Heracles and his master.

[4] King of Phthia; son of Actor; killed unintentionally by his son-in-law → Peleus at the Calydonian Hunt (Apollod. 1,70; 3,163).

[5] Companion of Aeneas; son of Lycaon; brother of Pandarus. At the funeral games in honour of → Anchises he wins the second prize for archery (Verg. Aen. 5,495–544).

L. Polverini, s.v. Eurizione, EV 2,435. R.B.

Eurytius Crater Early Corinthian columned crater of *c.* 600 BC from Cerveteri (Paris, LV), in which new figurative and decorative forms are combined with the highest-quality illustrations in the black-figured style and polychrome line-drawings. Obverse: the only Corinthian example of the feast given by → Eurytus [1] for → Heracles (copious name-labels); reverse: battle (outside Troy?). Below the handles a novel 'kitchen scene' and an early depiction of the suicide of Ajax. In addition, friezes of herons and animals and a deer hunt.

Amyx, CVP 147, 558f. no. 12; Amyx, Addenda, 43; M. Denoyelle, Chefs-d'oeuvre de la céramique Greque dans les collections du Louvre, 1994, 38f. no. 14; B. Fehr, Oriental. und griech. Gelage, 1971, 28–31; E. Simon, Die griech. Vasen, [2]1981, pl. XI; S.R. Wolf, Herakles beim Gelage, 1993, 11f. M.ST.

Eurytus (Εὔρυτος; *Eúrytos*).

[1] Ruler of Oechalia, mentioned in Hom. Il. 2,596; 730. The location of Oechalia is unclear (on the Peloponnese?). In Hom. Od. 21,20ff., Iphitus the son of E., while searching for his horses in Messenia, gives Odysseus his father's great bow (with which Odysseus later kills the suitors), and on his search is later murdered by Heracles. E. himself is killed by Apollo, whom he challenges to an archery competition (Od. 8,224–228). He plays an important role in the non-extant early epic 'The Capture of Oechalia' (Οἰχαλίας ἅλωσις; *Oichalías hálōsis*) by → Creophylus. Soph. Trach., where Heracles kills E. as well as Iphitus in order to gain possession

of E.'s daughter → Iole, doubtless refers to this poem. Here, Oechalia lies in Euboea.

M. DAVIES, Sophocles *Trachiniae*, 1991, xxii-xxxvii. E.R.

[2] Pythagorean from Croton (Iambl. VP 148), Metapontum (ibid. 266f.) or Tarentum (ibid. 267; Diog. Laert. 8,46). He is regarded as a pupil of → Philolaus (Iambl. VP 139 and 148; cf. [1]; according to ibid. 104 even a pupil of Pythagoras!) and teacher of the last Pythagoreans of the 'mathematical' school (→ Echecrates [2] of Phleius), of Archytas and Plato (Apul. De Platone et eius dogmate 1,3; Diog. Laert. 3,6); he may therefore have been born *c.* 450/440 BC [1. 4], and lived at least into the first two decades of the 4th cent. We learn from Aristotle (Metaph. 1092b 10–13; also Alex. Aphr., CAG 1, S. 826f. and Syrianus, CAG 6.1, S. 187f.) and Theophrastus (Metaph. 6a 19–22, cf. [2]) that E. assigned particular numbers to living beings and plants, his classification residing in the corresponding number of reckoning-stones it took to outline the form of the particular being or plant [3]. Regarding the neo-Pythagorean forgery 'On fate', ascribed to one Eurysus in the MSS, cf. [4].
→ Pythagorean School

1 C.A. HUFFMAN, Philolaus of Croton, 1993, 4–7 2 A. LAKS, Eurytus in Theophrastus' Metaphysics, in: W. FORTENBAUGH, R.W. SHARPLES (ed.), Theophrastean Studies on Natural Science, Physics and Metaphysics, Ethics, Religion and Rhetoric, 1988, 237–243 3 W.K. C. GUTHRIE, A History of Greek Philosophy I, 1962, 273–275 4 H. THESLEFF, The Pythagorean Texts of the Hellenistic Period, 1965, 87f. C.RI.

Eusebeia (εὐσέβεια; *eusébeia*). With *eusebeia* the Greeks characteristically conceptualized religion in a different way from the Romans with their *religio* or modern research with its 'beliefs of the Hellenes' or 'Greek religion' [1]. *Eusebeia* remained a part of the social value-system, in which the gods had no exclusive place. Factually and to some extent chronologically, three spheres may be distinguished:

1. In the *polis*, *eusebeia* describes a relationship of belonging and authority with regard to one's own parents, the *polis* and its norms, and the gods (Lys. 6. 33; Isoc. Or. 7. 30; Pl. Resp. 615 c); it requires careful dealing (also *eulábeia*) and loyalty. For overstepping this norm, → *asébeia*, one could be arraigned and punished with extreme severity (cf. Pl. Euthphr.). In some trials the attempt was made to prove political dissent as denial of the gods (even of the *polis*); *asebḗs* and *átheos* become synonymous.

2. Thus begins a philosophical-theological discourse, in which philosophers and their pupils see themselves as leading a religious life on the one hand, but on the other hand criticize traditional religion, whose anthropomorphic gods are corrupt, immoral and not omniscient. In order to construct foundations for ethical behaviour that no longer relate to the traditional system of the *polis*, but can claim universal validity, pantheistic or transcendent theologies arise. Recognition of the correct gods (or *gnō̂sis*) is part of *eusebeia*. Treatises *Perì eusebeías* (Περὶ εὐσεβείας) associate the destruction of traditional religion with the construction of one that is philosophically grounded; thus Theophrastus, Philodemus, or Cicero in *De natura deorum*.

3. In middle and late antiquity *eusebeia* becomes the individual virtue of bourgeois decency of love-patriarchalism, in the political sphere the ruler's claim to virtue and a salutation for the (Christian) emperor, which, however, included the claim to veneration [3].
→ Asebeia; → Atheism

1 E. FEIL, Religio, in: Forschungen zur Dogmen- und Kirchengesch. 36, 1986, 32–49 2 W. PÖTSCHER (ed.), Theophrastos περὶ εὐσεβείας, Philosophia antiqua 11, 1964 3 D. KAUFMANN-BÜHLER, s.v. Eusebeia, RAC 6 (1966), 985–1052 (esp. 1023–1048).

BAUER/ALAND 659f.; J. VAN HERTEN, Θρησκεία, εὐλάβεια, ἱκέτης. PhD thesis, Utrecht 1934; J. C. BOLKESTEIN, Ὅσιος en Εὐσεβής. Bijdrage tot de godsdienstige en zedelijke terminologie van de Grieken, PhD thesis, Utrecht 1936; W. J. TERSTEGEN, Εὐσεβής en Ὅσιος in het grieksch taalgebruik na de IVe eeuw, PhD thesis, Utrecht 1941; W. FAHR, Θεοὺς νομίζειν: Zum Problem der Anfänge des Atheismus bei den Griechen, Spudasmata 26, 1969; BURKERT, 408–412; D. OBBINK (ed.), Philodemus, On Piety, 1996. C.A.

Eusebia
[1] from Thessalonica; perhaps the daughter of Eusebius [1]. From about AD 352 she was the second wife of Constantius II (Julian Or. 3,109a-b, 110d). She was held to be unusually beautiful (Amm. Marc. 18,3,2), and is supposed to have exercised a strong influence on the emperor (cf. Amm. Marc. 21,16,16), to such an extent as to arouse the suspicion of her contemporaries ([Aur. Vict.] Epit. Caes. 42,20). On her advice Julian, of whom she was very fond (cf. Julian Or. 3,117a–118c), was elevated to the rank of Caesar (Amm. Marc. 15,2,8; 8,3). In around 360 she died childless (Amm. Marc. 16,10,18; 21,6,4). Julian wrote a panegyric in her honour *c.* 356/7 (Or. 3). PLRE 1, 300f.
→ Iulianus Apostata W.P.
[2] Baptismal name of → Ereleuva.

Eusebius (Εὐσέβιος; *Eusébios*).
[1] **Flavius Eusebius.** Mention is made in the statute Cod. Theod. 11,1,1 of AD 360 of the former *cos. et mag. equitum et peditum* Eusebius. This probably refers to *cos.* E. of 347, who may perhaps be identified as the father of the empress Eusebia [1] (cf. Julian Or. 3,107d–110d). PLRE 1, 307f. Eusebius (39).
[2] **Eusebius.** Son of E. [1]. Like his brother Hypatius, he enjoyed the patronage of his sister → Eusebia [1] (cf. Julian Or. 3,116a). In AD 355 he was *consularis Hellesponti*, 356 *consularis Bithyniae* (Lib. Ep. 457–459), and in 359 *consul* with his brother (Amm. Marc. 18,1,1). In 371/2 both were suspected of having imperial ambitions, unjustly punished and later rehabili-

tated (Amm. Marc. 29,2,9–11). PLRE 1, 308f. Eusebius (40).

[3] **Eusebius.** Eunuch, *praepositus sacri cubiculi* under Constantius II, perhaps from as early as AD 337 (Phot. Bibl. 256; Socr. 2,2,5–6) until 361. The orthodox and the followers of Julian were suspicious of the all-powerful Arian E. (Athan. Epist. ad Iov.; Lib. Or. 18,152). In 354/5 he led the proceedings against the Caesar Gallus and his followers (Amm. Marc. 14,11,21; 15,3,2). In 355 he tried in vain to persuade Liberius of Rome to condemn Athanasius (Athan. Hist. Ar. 35ff.). In 359 he influenced the synods of Ariminum and Seleucia in accordance with the anti-Nicene policy of the emperor (Sozom. Hist. Eccl. 4,16,22). At the end of 361 he was condemned to death by the extraordinary court instituted by Julian at Chalcedon, and executed (Amm. Marc. 22,3,12; Socr. 3,1,46). PLRE 1, 302f. Eusebius (11).

[4] **Eusebius.** Pupil of Libanius, AD 355–361 influential at the court of Constantius II (Lib. Ep. 73; 437; 669). Perhaps *magister scrinii c.* 360 (Lib. Ep. 218). PLRE 1, 303f. Eusebius (15).

[5] **Eusebius.** of Antioch, pupil of Libanius (Lib. Or. 1,258). In AD 388 he took part in a delegation to the court of Arcadius (Lib. Ep. 878–880 i.a.). He wrote panegyrics to Theodosius I and to Arcadius (Lib. Or. 1,258). He may possibly be identified with the *praef. Augustalis* E. of 385 or 387 (cf. PLRE 1, 305 Eusebius 23 and 24). W.P.

[6] **Eusebius.** Eunuch, in AD 409 *praepositus sacri cubiculi* to Honorius; as such briefly very influential after the death of → Stilicho. Soon put to death at the instigation of the *magister equitum* Allobich. PLRE 2, 429. H.L.

[7] **Eusebius of Caesarea.** Born shortly after 260, for his entire lifetime E. was closely associated with Caesarea in Palaestina (→ Caesarea [2] Maritima). Decisively influenced by the presbyter Pamphilus, he soon became the latter's most important collaborator. His first works (i.a. a first edition of the 'Chronicle' and the 'Ecclesiastical History') were written at this time. After the 'Great Persecution' during the years AD 303–313, E. became bishop of Caesarea. As a 'clever ecclesiastical politician' [7. 56] of great eloquence and diplomatic skill, he played an essential but not always successful role in Church controversies of his time. He sought in vain an understanding with → Arius (→ Arianism). Excommunicated because of this, he defended himself successfully at the council of Nicaea (325), and won the favour of the emperor → Constantinus [1]. He subsequently contended against Eustathius [5] of Antioch (deposed *c.* 330), presided over the synod of Tyre (335) directed against → Athanasius, and at the behest of the emperor wrote texts against Marcellus of Ancyra (*Contra Marcellum*; *De ecclesiastica theologia*). E. died between 337 and 340, on 30 May.

Works (selected): 'not an especially original thinker' [8. 538], E. contributed considerably, with learning and a thorough knowledge of sources, in a large number of writings on many themes (CPG 3465–3507; cf. [5]). The dating of many works is disputed (list [7. 188–191]). Prominent among the historical writings are the two-part 'Chronicle', the so-called *Vita Constantini* (panegyric with speeches appended) and the 'Ecclesiastical History' (several stages of writing: bks. 1–7: up to 280; bks. 8–9: Great Persecution; bk. 10: period after 312/313; cf. [2. 129–164], a contrary view in [3]). Here for the first time E. depicts the history of the people of God in the *oikoumene*, making constant comparisons with the normative tradition of the Apostles. The double work *Praeparatio/Demonstratio evangelica*, written between 312 and 322, is apologetic in character. Beholden to Origen, the *Eclogae propheticae* and the comprehensive commentaries on Is. and the Psalms have a significant exegetic aspect

Theology and influence: drawing on biblical roots and sources in Origen and the mid-Platonic writers, E. develops an impressive 'apologetic, historical and cultural-theological system' [7. 57], which becomes a guiding influence for Byzantine imperial theology in its interpretation of the Christian emperor as a divine ruler in the tradition of Christ. E., who transmits many of Origen's texts in his writings, tries in vain to tread a middle way – inspired by → Dionysius [52] of Alexandria [8. 540] – between Arian and Nicene theology. Many eastern and western writers continue and translate the 'Ecclesiastical History'.

1 H.W. Attridge, G. Hata (ed.), Eusebios, Christianity and Judaism, 1992 (Bibliogr. 761–780) 2 T.D. Barnes, Constantine and Eusebios, 1981 3 R.W. Burgess, The Dates and Editions of Eusebius' Chronici canones and Historia ecclesiastica, in: The Journal of Theological Studies 48, 1997, 471–504 4 E. des Places, Eusèbe de Césarée commentateur, 1982 5 Quasten 3, 309–345 6 D. Timpe, Was ist Kirchengesch.?, in: W. Dahlheim et al. (ed.), FS Robert Werner, 1989, 171–204 7 F. Winkelmann, E. von Kaisareia, 1991 8 D.S. Wallace-Hadrill, s.v. E. von Caesarea, TRE 10, 537–543. J.RI.

[8] **Eusebius.** Bishop of Nicomedia and leading exponent of the Origenist tradition in the Arian struggle († AD 341).

Initially bishop of → Berytus, the pupil of Lucianus of Antioch became bishop of Nicomedia, the seat of → Licinius, before 318. Closely connected to the court, in the burgeoning dispute over the Egyptian presbyter → Arius [3] and his teaching on the trinity (→ Arianism) E. stood unreservedly behind Arius. In numerous letters (i.a. to Paulinus of Tyre: CPG 2045) he supported Arius' case against that of his bishop Alexander of Alexandria, and had him declared orthodox by a local synod in Bithynia. Notwithstanding, a short time later at the council of Nicaea (325) E. signed the condemnation of Arius. Three months after the council he was nevertheless banished to Gaul by the emperor Constantine [1] for his continued support of the Arians and his close relations with Constantia, the widow of Licinius. After a written declaration of his orthodoxy, E. was rehabilitated at the so-called second synod of Nicaea of 327/8

[1. 177f.]. As an influential adviser to Constantine, he subsequently obtained the deposition of a series of bishops who adhered to the Nicene orthodoxy: 329 → Eustathius [5] of Antioch, 335 → Athanasius of Alexandria, 336 → Marcellus of Ancyra. He also succeeded in obtaining the reconciliation of Arius (synod of Jerusalem 335). On the occasion of a Gothic legation to the court *c.* 336, E. consecrated Ulfila as a bishop. He likewise baptized the dying Constantine († 22.5.337) in Nicomedia.

E.'s influence increased still further under Constantius II, who favoured the Arians. In 338 he was able to take up the bishopric of Constantinople, which he had long aspired to. The conflicts concerning the Nicaenum, primarily fought around the person of Athanasius and the theology of Marcellus of Ancyra, abruptly flared up again. Under the aegis of E., a synod in Antioch in 339 again deposed Athanasius, replacing him by military force with Gregorius of Cappadocia. To resolve the problem, Julius I of Rome, who was on the side of Athanasius and Marcellus, but whose approval was also sought by the Eusebian bishops, suggested an ecumenical synod, but this was sharply rejected by E. (reconstruction of the letter in [5. 297–300]). E. died in the middle of 341.

E.'s person and influence are for the most part evaluated from a negative point of view determined by Athanasius (references [5. 27]). On the other hand, the *Epistula ad Constantiam* (CPG 3503), which is probably to be ascribed to E., gives a more complex picture of his character.

1 CPG 2045–2056 (Ed.) 2 R.P.C. Hanson, The Search for the Christian Doctrine of God. The Arian Controversy 318–381, 1988, 27–32 and passim 2 A. Lichtenstein, Eusebios von Nikomedien, 1903 3 R. Lorenz, Das vierte Jh. (O), 1992, C111–C155 4 C. Luibhéid, The Arianism of Eusebius of Nicomedia, in: Irish Theological Quarterly 43, 1976, 3–23 5 E. Schwartz, Gesammelte Schriften 3, 1959 6 M. Spanneut, s.v. Eusebios, DHGE 15, 1466–1471.

J.RI.

[9] Eusebius. Bishop of → Emesa († *c.* AD 359). Born in Edessa, after periods in Palaestine, Antioch [1] and Alexandria [1], from 335 E. operated again in Antioch as a priest and teacher of scripture. After 341 bishop of Syrian Emesa. Of his many writings (Jer. Vir. ill. 91), 29 homilies in Latin have survived along with diverse exegetical fragments. Orientated towards → Eusebius [7] of Caesarea, E. represented a subordinationist teaching on incarnation, resting on Arian principles (→ Arianism), and anticipating later tendencies typical of the Antiochene School (→ Antiochene School).

Editions: CPG 3525–3543; B.M. Buytaert, Eusèbe d'Emèse, Discours conservé en Latin 1–2, 1953, 1957 (in: CPG 3525–3543).
Bibliography: B.M. Buytaert, L'Héritage littéraire d'Eusèbe d'Emèse, 1949; M.F. Wiles, The theology of Eusebius of Emesa, in: Studia patristica 19, 1989, 267–280.

J.RI.

[10] Eusebius of Dorylaeum. This layman of Constantinople (probably a rhetor and lawyer) appeared as early as AD 428 as the first public opponent of his patriarch → Nestorius and the latter's denial of the title of *theotókos* (Evagrius, Hist. Eccl. 1,9). In his written protest, which he attached to the church door (CPG 2, 5940: *diamartyría/contestatio*), he was the first to echo Nestorius and → Paulus of Samosata. In 448 he became bishop of → Dorylaeum in Phrygia. At the sitting of 8 November 448 of the synod of Constantinople (σύνοδος ἐνδημοῦσα), E. presented a written charge of heresy (ACO II 1/1, 100–145) against the Monophysite archimandrite → Eutyches [3], and as a consequence was excommunicated at the synod of Ephesus on 8 August 449. He appealed i.a. to pope → Leo I (ACO II 2/1, 79–81), and at the council of → Chalcedon was successful in obtaining the final condemnation of Eutyches.

E. Schwartz, Acta Conciliorum Oecumenicorum (= ACO) I 1/1, 102f. or I/3, 18f.; M. Tetz, Zum Streit zw. Orthodoxie und Häresie an der Wende des 4. zum 5. Jh., in: Id., Athanasiana, 1995, 275–289.

C.M.

[11] Eusebius of Alexandria. 'Eusebius of Alexandria 'is the name attached to a collection of 22 (or 24) lectures (CPG 3, 5510–5532 = BHG 635a-z) on various themes, which, on the basis of the *Vita* (BHG 635) added to them, may have been written at the end of the 5th cent. The author of the *sermones* is portrayed as a supposed successor of → Cyrillus of Alexandria, allegedly designated by Cyril himself. The author of the *Vita* is perhaps also the author of parts of the collection, which may originate from the area of Syria/Palestine. There exists a Latin version of three of the sermons (Vetus Latina 1/1, 454: Frede).

G. Lafontaine, Les homélies d'Eusèbe d'Alexandrie, 1966; J.C. Thilo, Über die Schriften des Eusebius von Alexandrien, 1832; Th. Zahn, Skizzen aus dem Leben der Alten Kirche, [3]1907, 321–330.

C.M.

[12] Eusebius of Vercellae. born *c.* AD 283 on Sardinia; *lector* in Rome, first bishop of Vercellae, participant in various synods; banished to the east in 355, he returned under emperor → Iulianus, campaigned enthusiastically against → Arianism and died 1 August 371 in Rome. Three letters survive: 1. to → Constantius [2] II in reply to a letter from the emperor urging him to attend the Milan synod of 354; 2. to his diocese, reporting to it on events during his exile; 3. to → Gregorius of Elvira, praising his strength of his faith. Lost to us are a translation of the commentaries on the Psalms by → Eusebius [7] of Caesarea and the commentary on the Psalms by → Origenes. Attribution of the 7 bks. *De trinitate* is disputed.

Edition: V. Bulhart, CCL 9, 1957.
Bibliography: J. Doignin, in: HLL, § 584; R. Klein, Constantius II. und die christl. Kirche, 1977, esp. 145–148.

J.GR.

[13] **Eusebius Gallicanus.** Name introduced by BARONIUS for a collection of Latin sermons surviving under the name of E. [9] of Emesa (CPL 966); if we take seriously the notes of Caesarius of Arles to the lemmata of his homilies, they may be traced back to the works of → Faustus Reiensis, to whom the 34th sermon certainly belongs.

EDITIONS: A. HAMMAN, PL Suppl. 3, 1963, 545–699 (–709); F. GLORIE, CCL 101–101B, 1970–1971.
BIBLIOGRAPHY: G. MORIN, La collection gallicane dite d'Eusèbe d'Émèse ..., in: ZNTW 34, 1935, 92–115; J. LEROY, L'œuvre oratoire de S. Fauste de Riez, 1954; Id., F. GLORIE, 'Eusèbe d'Alexandrie', source d''Eusèbe de Gaule', in: Sacris Erudiri 19, 1969/70, 33–70. K.U.

Eustathius (Εὐστάθιος; *Eustáthios*).

[1] **from Caria.** Rhetor of the 4th cent. AD; studied in Athens and later settled in Tyre. He held many offices in the imperial administration, and used them to enrich himself (i.a.: *rationalis summarum per orientem*), in 388 he was *consularis Syriae*. He was at first a friend of → Libanius (panegyric: Lib. Or. 44), later his enemy (diatribe: Or. 54, cf. also Or. 1,271–275). There is no other witness apart from Libanius. M.W.

[2] Neoplatonic philosopher and rhetor, probably from the school of → Iamblichus. He appears to have taken over leadership of the school from Iamblichus' successor → Aedesius, presumably in Pergamum (Eunapios, Vit. Soph. 6,4,6ff.). In AD 358, owing to his rhetorical gifts, he was sent by Constantius II as an ambassador to the Parthian king Sapor (Amm. Marc. 17,5,15). Among his admirers are → Libanius (Epist. 123 FÖRSTER) and emperor → Iulianus, who invited him to this court (Epist. 76 HÖRTLEIN = 34 BIDEZ-CUMONT). He was married to the philosophically trained Sosipatra (Eunapios Vit. Soph. 6,6,5), and died before 390. L.BR.

[3] Greek rhetor of the 4th and 5th (?) cents. AD, author of a lost commentary on → Hermogenes' teaching on *staseis* (εἰσήγησις εἰς τὰς στάσεις), and perhaps also on his work περὶ εὑρέσεως (cf. WALZ 2,545 and 7,704). In his opinions E. mainly followed → Minucianus the elder. and → Porphyrius; he is often cited by later Byzantine rhetors.

FRAGMENT: H. RABE, De Christophori commentario in Hermogenis librum περὶ στάσεων, in: RhM 50, 1895, 244–248. M.W.

[4] Probably born in Constantinople; lived from *c.* AD 1115 to *c.* AD 1195; initially a monk and deacon at the Hagia Sophia and at the same time a teacher of rhetoric, then (from *c.* 1175 or 1179) archbishop of Thessalonica. His speeches, letters and other occasional writings ([1]; among them an eyewitness account of the capture of Thessalonica by the Normans in 1185 [2], as well as critical texts on monasticism) show him to be a highly educated and deeply religious person. By his impressive commentaries (παρεκβολαί), not only on Homer (*Iliad* [3] and *Odyssey* [4]), but also on Pindar ([5]; only the proem is extant) and Dionysius Periegetes [6] he distinguishes himself as a versatile scholar and one of the most significant classical philologists of the Byzantine period.

1 TH. L. F. TAFEL, Eustathii metropolitae Thessalonicensis Opuscula, 1832 2 S. KYRIAKIDIS, Eustazio di Tessalonica. La espugnazione di Tessalonica, 1961 3 M. VAN DER VALK, Eustathii archiepiscopi Thessalonicensis commentarii ad Homeri Iliadem pertinentes I–IV, 1971–1987 4 G. STALLBAUM, Eustathii archiepiscopi Thessalonicensis commentarii ad Homeri Odysseam I–II, 1825/6 5 A. KAMBYLIS, Eustathios von Thessalonike. Prooimion zum Pindarkomm., 1991 6 GGM II, 201–407.

L. COHN, s.v. Eustathios 18), RE 6, 1452–1489; N.G. WILSON, Scholars of Byzantium, 1983, 196–204; A. KAZHDAN, S. FRANKLIN, Studies on Byzantine Literature of the Eleventh and Twelfth Centuries, 1984, 115–195. I.V.

[5] Bishop of Antioch († before 360/1 [2]). Initially bishop of Beroea [3] in Syria, E. sided with Alexander of Alexandria and became bishop of Antioch in 324/5 [1] (a synod there under Ossius of Cordoba) after the death of Philogonius. As a proponent of orthodoxy and bitter opponent of Arius and his teaching at the council of Nicaea in 325, he soon lost imperial support because of the ascendancy of → Arianism at court, was suspected of → Sabellianism, and in 330/1 [1] banished to Thrace. Of his numerous writings, besides fragments in florilegia and *catenae*, *De engastrimytho* against the Origenist exegesis has survived entire. His dualist Christology anticipates later Antiochene formulations.

1 R. P. C. HANSON, The Fate of Eustathius of Antioch, in: ZKG 95, 1984, 171–179 2 R. LORENZ, s.v. Eustathios, TRE 10, 543–546.

EDITION: CPG 3350–3398. J.RI.

[6] Bishop of Sebaste († *c.* 377/380). The first monastic ascetic, he was elevated to bishop of Armenian Sebaste before AD 357; E. is regarded as the founder of monasticism in Asia Minor (Sozom. Hist. Eccl. 3,14,31). His theological opinions were changeable (Homoeousian, from 360 tending towards orthodoxy); the criticism of the Church implied by the enthusiastic asceticism he represented (radical adoration of the cross combined with harsh criticism of church officialdom and the Church) caused repeated conflicts (deposition, followers condemned at Gangra in 340). Resistance against the divinity of the Holy Ghost (→ Pneumatomachoi) led to a rift with his close friend and pupil → Basilius [1] of Caesarea in 373. None of E.'s writings survive.

1 J. GRIBOMONT, S. Basile et le monachisme enthousiaste, in: Irénikon 53, 1980, 123–144 2 W.-D. HAUSCHILD, s.v. Eustathios, TRE 10, 547–550. J.RI.

[7] On the evidence of the prologue addressed to a deaconess named Syncletia, probably also mentioned in → Sedulius, an otherwise unknown author of this name wrote a Latin translation of the nine homilies of → Basilius [1] the Great on the Hexaemeron (CPG 2, 2835). As

it is cited by → Augustinus (Gen. ad litt. 1,18), it must originate prior to 400, thus a few years after the death of Basil (379). E. possibly came from Italy. E.A. DE MENDIETA and ST. Y. RUDBERG produced a critical edition in 1958 (TU 66).

B. ALTANER, Eustathius, der lat. Übers. der Hexaemeron-Homilien Basilius des Großen, in: Id., Kleine patristische Schriften, TU 83, 1967, 437–447. C.M.

[8] of Epiphania [2]/Coele-Syria, lived in the 5th cent. and wrote a twelve-volume digest of world history (χρονικὴ ἐπιτομή). The three-volume first part extended to the fall of Troy, the second in nine books from Aeneas to AD 503 (Evagrius, Hist. Eccl. 5,24). It is cited in the Suda (s.v. Eustathius); but the work had already been used in the 6th cent. by Malalas and Evagrios Scholastikos (→ Evagrius [2]). The attempt to attribute considerable portions of Evagrius to E. [4] could not be sustained.

EDITIONS: 1 FGH 4, 138–142 2 L. DINDORF, Historici graeci minores 1, 353–363.
BIBLIOGRAPHY: 3 G. GARITTE, s.v. Eustathe d'Epiphanie, DHGE 16, 24–26 4 L. JEEP, Quellenuntersuchungen zu den griech. Kirchenhistorikern, in: Jbb. für klass. Philol. Suppl. 14, 1885, 53–178 (esp. 159–161). C.M.

Eustochius Evodus (Εὐστόχιος; *Eustóchios*) from Alexandria. He encountered → Plotinus towards the end of the latter's life (*c.* AD 269), who converted him to philosophy. E. also acted as Plotinus' physician, accompanied him on his last journey, and was with him when he died (Porphyrius V. Plot. 7). V.N.

Eutecnius (Εὐτέκνιος; *Eutéknios*). The famous Cod. Vindobonensis med. gr. 1 (late 5th cent. AD) with the herbal of Pedanius Dioscorides also contains prose paraphrases on → Nicander's *Thēriaká* and *Alexiphármaka* [4; 2; 5]. A remark in a manuscript attributes them to a 'rhetor' (σοφιστής; *sophistḗs*) by the name of E., who is to be dated sometime between the 3rd and 5th cents. AD [3. 34–37]; without any solid proof, the following anonymous paraphrases are also attributed to the same E.: on → Oppianus' [4; 6] *Halieutiká* (from 3,605) and, from as early as C. GESNER in 1555, on → Dionysius' [29] *Ixeutiká* [1; 7]. The assignment of the paraphrase on the *Kynēgetiká* [8], transmitted in the best MS, to E. is equally uncertain. For the correlation of the scholia to Oppianus (still in the edition by E.C. BUSSEMAKER, 1849) with the paraphrase, cf. [11].

EDITIONS: 1 A. GARZYA, Dionysii Ixeuticon seu De aucupio libri tres, 1963 2 M. GEYMONAT, Paraphrasis in Nicandri Alexipharmaca, 1976 3 I. GUALANDRI, Paraphrasis in Nicandri Theriaca, 1968 4 Id., Incerti auctoris in Oppiani Halieutica paraphrasis, 1968 5 M. PAPATHOMOPOULOS, Paraphrasis in Nicandri Theriaca et Alexipharmaca, 1976 6 Id., Paraphrasis in Oppiani Halieutica, 1976 7 Id., Paraphrasis in Oppiani ixeutica, 1976 8 O. TÜSELMANN, Paraphrasis in Oppiani Cynegetica, 1900.
BIBLIOGRAPHY: 9 L. COHN, s.v. E., RE 6, 1492 10 F. FAJEN, Hs. Überlieferung und sog. E.-Paraphrase der Halieutika des Oppian, 1979 11 A. LUDWICH, Aristarchs Homer. Textkritik, II, 1885, 597–599. S.FO.

Euterpe (Εὐτέρπη; *Eutérpē*; cf. τέρπειν; *térpein*, 'giver of joy'). One of the nine → Muses, the daughter of Zeus and → Mnemosyne (Hes. Theog. 77; Apollod. 1,13; Orph. H. 76,8; schol. Apoll. Rhod. 3,1 b). Later texts describe flute playing as her particular responsibility (Hor. Carm. 1,1,33; schol. Eur. Rhes. 346; schol. Hes. Theog. 76). According to Apollodorus of Athens (FGrH 244 F 146) and Heraclid. fr. 159 WEHRLI, E. was impregnated by Strymon and gave birth to → Rhesus (cf. Apollod. 1,18; schol. Hom. Il. 10,435; Serv. Aen. 1,469). Images of her as Euturpa can be found on Etruscan mirrors from the 4th cent. BC [1; 2]. Tiepolo and Böcklin used her as a motif in their paintings.

1 M. BONAMICI, s.v. Mousa (in Etruria), LIMC 6.1, 683–685 no. 10–13 2 C. DE SIMONE, Die griech. Entlehnungen im Etruskischen, 1968–1970, 1,64; 2,27.

A. QUEYREL, s.v. Mousa, LIMC 6.1, 661 no.18; 671 no.121 (François-Vase). R.B.

Eutharicus, Eutharic Grandson of Berimund of the Amal dynasty, called to Italy by Theoderic the Great in AD 515 and married to → Amalasuntha in order to secure the succession (Iord. Get. 298). He was later adopted by Justin as his son-at-arms, received Roman citizenship; at the assumption of his consulate in 519 – on the occasion of which Cassiodorus had written a speech (MGH AA 12,465ff.) and probably also compiled his chronicle –, he was called Flavius E. Cillica (CIL VI 32003). When he responded rigourously to religious unrests in Rome in 520, his popularity declined; overall, his attitude was anti-Catholic (Anon. Vales. 80). He was killed soon after, in 522/3, thus rendering unnecessary the regulations regarding Theoderic's succession which had been confirmed by Constantinople.

PLRE 2,438; H. WOLFRAM, Die Goten, [3]1990, Index s.v. E. M.MEI. and ME.STR.

Eutherius (Εὐθήριος; *Euthḗrios*).
[1] An Armenian pagan eunuch, who had come to the court of Constantine I as a slave, later served under Constans, and under Julian rose to *praepositus sacri cubiculi* (AD 356–360). In Milan in 356/7, E. appeared before Constantius II to defend Julian against Marcellus' accusations (Amm. Marc. 16,7,2f.); after Julian had been made Augustus in 360, he became his envoy with Constantius (Amm. Marc. 20,8,19; 9,1–4; Zos. 3,9,3f.); In 361, Julian recalled him once again to his court (Julian. Ep. 10 WRIGHT). Later, he retired to Rome. Ammianus Marcellinus expressed his highest admiration for E. (16,7,2–10).

PLRE 1, 314f., E. no. 1.; H. SCHOLTEN, Der Eunuch in Kaisernähe, 1995, 214. M.MEI.

[2] Bishop of → Tyana in the 1st half of the 5th cent. AD. As an ardent supporter of → Nestorius, he opposed the anathematisms of → Cyrillus of Alexandria. In 431, the Council of → Ephesus excommunicated him. He joined → Iohannes of Antioch, but opposed the developing reconciliation between Iohannes and Cyrillus. When this came about in 433, E. parted from Iohannes. In consequence, he lost his office and was sentenced to exile in Scythopolis (→ Beisan).

M. TETZ, Eine Antilogie des E. von Tyana, (Patristische Texte und Studien, 1), 1964. K.SA.

Euthias (Εὐθίας; *Euthías*). Attic comic poet, who came second in a contest around the mid 4th cent. BC [1. test.]. Of his plays, neither titles nor fragments are extant.

1 PCG V, 540. H.-G.NE.

Euthycles (Εὐθυκλῆς; *Euthyklês*). Poet of the late Old Comedy (?). Two titles of plays and two fragments are extant.

1 PCG V, 541f. H.-G.NE.

Euthycrates (Εὐθυκράτης; *Euthykrátēs*).

[1] E., an Olynthian, allegedly accepted bribes from → Philipus II in 348 BC to betray his home polis, thus bearing part of the guilt for its destruction. Because of this, E. was ostracized by Athens (Diod. Sic. 16,53,2; Dem. Or. 8,40; 9,56; 18,295; 19,265–267; Hyp. fr. 76 JENSEN). In *c.* 345–343, he acted as *syndikos* for the Delians in their dispute with the Athenians regarding the *prostasía* of the Delphi sanctuary. → Demades' application to lift E.'s ostracism and even to honour him as an Athenian *próxenos* led to → Hypereides probably taking legal action in early 336 BC (Hyp. fr. 76–86 JENSEN).

→ Demosthenes; → Olynthus

J. ENGELS, Studien zur polit. Biographie des Hypereides, [2]1993, 80; 136–142; H. WANKEL, Demosthenes Rede für Ktesiphon über den Kranz, 1976, 336–338; W. WILL, Callidus emptor Olynthi: Zur polit. Propaganda des Demosthenes und ihrer Nachwirkung, in: Klio 65, 1983, 51–80. J.E.

[2] Sculptor from Sicyon, son and pupil of → Lysippus. Of his numerous works that are known – mostly groups centring around Alexander –, none has been identified within the extant corpus of sculptures.

G. CRESSEDI, EAA 3, 548–549, s.v. E. 1; OVERBECK, no. 1341, 1509, 1516, 1522–1525 (sources). R.N.

[3] Comic poet, who in the 3rd cent. BC apparently enjoyed two successes at the Lenaea.

1 PCG V, 543. H.-G.NE.

Euthydemus (Εὐθύδημος; *Euthýdemos*).

[1] Athenian *strategos* of 418/17 BC. He took part in the Sicilian campaign, during which in 414/13 both he and Menander became commanders to serve alongside Nicias. They were defeated before → Demosthenes [1] even arrived. They failed in their attempt to force their departure out of Syracuse's great harbour (Thuc. 7,16,1; 69,4; Diod. Sic. 13,13,2–4; Plut. Nicias 20).

D. KAGAN, The Peace of Nicias and the Sicilian Expedition, 1981. W.S.

[2] **E. I.** Greek king of Bactria at the end of the 3rd cent. BC. According to Pol. 10,49; 11,39, he hailed from Magnesia. In *c.* 225, E. overthrew Diodotus II of Bactria; he was himself defeated by Antiochus [5] III, but retained his independence. Demetrius [10] I was his son (Str. 11,11,1), as was probably E. [3] II. A large number of his coins have been found in Afghanistan and Central Asia. It is likely that he ruled for a long period. He seems to have been the last of the Greeks whose rule also encompassed Sogdiana. On Agathocles' [7] memorial coins, he was named *theós*.

P. BERNARD, Fouilles d'Aï Khanoum 4, 1985, 131ff.; BOPEARACHCHI 47–49, 154–161. K.K.

[3] **E. II.** Greek king of Bactria in the early 2nd cent. BC, only known from his coins. These show him as belonging to the Euthydemids; he was probably a son of E. [2] I and a younger brother of Demetrius [10] I. Perhaps he was only a viceroy of the latter.

BOPEARACHCHI 55f., 168–171. K.K.

[4] Sophist, depicted in Plato's eponymous Socratic dialogue as a representative of eristics, i.e. the art of achieving victory in a discussion by any means. Because of a certain agreement within the source material (particularly Pl. Crat. 386d; Aristot. Soph. el. 177b12, and Rh. 1401a 26), it is generally assumed that E. was a historical figure, as was his brother Dionysodorus. The brothers were born in Chios and later exiled from Thurii; in 416 BC, they came to Athens to become professional teachers of *aretḗ* ('excellence', 'virtue'). The sophisms which they employ in Plato's dialogue in order to refute the arguments of the other participants, were for the most part based on the homonymy and ambiguity of words; they provided Aristotle with a number of examples for his 'Sophistic Refutations'.

M. CANTO, L'Intrigue philosophique, 1987; G. GROTE, Plato and the Other Companions of Socrates, 1875, 1, 519–564; M. NARCY, Le Philosophe et son double, 1984; R. K. SPRAGUE, Plato's Use of Fallacy, 1963. B.C.

[5] Athenian physician. Heraclides of Tarentum mentions him as the author of a book on the names and medicinal properties of various vegetables. His familiarity with a forged treatise by Hesiod (Ath. 3,116a) suggests that he might have lived in the Hellenistic period, perhaps in the 2nd cent. BC. He also wrote about the art of cooking and about salted fish (cf. Ath. 12,516c;

3,116a; 3,118b; 7,307b), but it is likely that Athenaeus received this information second-hand. V.N.

[6] see → Socratics.

Euthymenes of Massalia (Ευθυμένης; *Euthyménēs*). Greek seafarer, probably of the 6th–5th cents. BC, who sailed along the north-western African Atlantic coast to the mouth of a big river (Senegal?), where he noticed areas of fresh water within the ocean, and where the → Etesians periodically caused the river water to rise; this together with the fauna of that region, which was similar to that of Egypt (crocodiles, hippopotami), led E. to conclude that the river must be the upper course of the Nile, rising from the ocean. In line with Thales, he saw explained the periodic flooding of the Nile as a consequence of the Etesians.

His work, probably a → periplous (cf. Marcianus of Heraclea, epit. 2, GGM 1, 565), is lost; only his thesis regarding the annual inundation of the Nile, which may have already been known to Herodotus (via Hecataeus?) (Hdt. 2,20f.; Hecat. FGrH 1 F 278), appears repeatedly in doxographies; cf. Anonymus Florentinus 5 (FGrH 647 F 1,5); Aet. Placita philosophorum 4,1,2 (p. 384ff. DIELS, DG = FGrH 647 F 2,2); Lydus, Mens. 4,68 p. 145 WUENSCH; Sen. Q Nat. 4a,2,22; Plut. Mor. 897f.

FHG 4, 408–409 (obsolete); DIELS, DG, 226–228; F. JACOBY s.v. E. 4, RE 6, 1907, 929f.; W. ALY, Die Entdekkung des Westens, in: Hermes 62, 1927, 299–341 (esp. 305–307); R. HENNIG, Terrae Incognitae, vol. 1, [2]1944, 80–85; J.O. THOMSON, History of Ancient Geography, 1948, 77. K.BRO.

Euthymides (Εὐθυμίδης; *Euthymídēs*) Attic red-figured vase painter of the late Archaic period (510–500 BC). An Athenian citizen, he included in his signature his father's name Polias, who is probably identical with the sculptor Pollias, known from ancient written sources. Alongside → Euphronius [2], with whom he was in artistic competition (cf. his well-known inscription ΗΟΣ ΟΥΔΕΠΟΤΕ ΕΥΦΡΟΝΙΟΣ on the amphora in Munich, SA 2307), E. was the most important painter within the 'Pioneer' group of artists. He exceeded Euphronius in his grasp of spatiality and the plastic representation of the human body; his style of drawing was more sweeping, his obsession with detail less than Euphronius'. His preferred medium for decoration were large amphoras, but he is also known to have painted hydrias, a volute-krater, a psykter, a plate, as well as two bowls (extant in fragments). His unpretentious, lifelike, and often humorous pictures are filled with a few large figures, whose internal relationships he portrayed masterfully. He liked to write, and generally gave his figures names, which he took either from myths or from within his own sphere of life. No black-figured vessels of his are transmitted, but it is possible that two large votive tablets from the Athenian Acropolis were his work, one of them showing a black-figured image of Athena, the other decorated with a warrior in coloured contour drawing. The → Cleophrades Painter is thought to be his pupil. The discovery in New York of a signature *Euthymídes epoíēsen* on the foot of an early 5th cent. BC oinochoe, which had not been painted by E., has led to the assumption that in his later years E., same as Euphronios [2], had become the owner of a workshop.

BEAZLEY, ARV[2], 26–30; BEAZLEY, Addenda[2], 155–156; M. ROBERTSON, The Art of Vase-Painting in Classical Athens, 1992, 29–35, 56–60; M. WEGNER, Euthymides und Euphronios, 1979. I.W.

Euthymius (Εὐθύμιος; *Euthýmidos*) **I of Constantinople** (b. *c.* AD 834 in → Seleucia, d. 917). After a period as monk on the Bithynian → Olympus, he transferred to the monastery of St. Theodorus outside Constantinople. As the father confessor of Emperor → Leo VI, he became abbot of the monastery of Psamathias, which the emperor had built for him specifically. After the deposition of the patriarch of Constantinople, → Nicolaus I Mysticus, he assumed that office; in agreement with the other patriarchs and contrary to Byzantine canon law, he gave his exceptional consent to the emperor's fourth marriage (tetragamy controversy). After Leo's death, he was deposed and forced into exile. His followers seceded from the imperial Church. This schism continued to the end of the 10th cent. In 921, E. was rehabilitated posthumously.

P. KARLIN-HAYTER, Vita Euthymii patriarchae Constantinopolitani, 1970. K.SA.

Euthynai (εὔθυναι; *eúthynai*). The term *euthynai* ('straightening out') was used specifically in reference to the audits of the official conduct of administrators after their departure from office. In Athens, this procedure was split into two parts: on the one hand, there was the *lógos* ('statement of accounts'), which looked into the way officials handled public funds, carried out by a committee of ten *logistaí* ('auditors') plus one *synḗgoros* each ('legal advisor') ([Aristot.] Ath. Pol. 54,2), and on the other the *euthynae* in a stricter sense, offering the opportunity of passing complaints of any nature regarding the conduct of public servants, under the scrutiny of a committee of ten *eúthynoi* ('organizers'), each assisted by two *páredroi* ('assessors') ([Aristot.] Ath. Pol. 48,3–4). If the *logistaí* or the *eúthynoi* considered a case serious enough and in need of legal clarification, they transferred it to a jury court as an indictment.

Comparable procedures are documented for numerous other Greek states, and the same procedures can frequently also be found in settlements under Athenian influence. However, an accounting procedure called *mastráa* is documented in Elis in the 1st half of the 5th cent., [1. 31]; a decree from Corcyra from the 2nd cent. BC, sets out a very detailed accounting procedure (IG IX 1[2], 694). A decree from Tomi stipulates that any military commander who was appointed in a particular emergency should be exempted from public accounting (IScyth. Min. 2, 2).

1 C.D. Buck, Greek Dialects, ³1955.

On Athens: M. Piérart, Les ΕΥΘΥΝΟΙ Athéniens, in: AC 40, 1971, 526–573. P.J.R.

Euthynteria (Εὐθυντήρια; *euthyntēria*) Rare ancient Greek architectural technical term; according to IG II², 1668, l. 15–18 (*syngraphe* of Philo's arsenal), *euthynteria* described the levelled top of the foundations, the base for the rising walls of a building; from the *euthynteria* rose the → orthostates. Modern archaeological terminology customarily uses the term *euthynteria* in a more general sense in Greek columned buildings, referring to the top and thus the first levelled layer of the foundations, which is just proud of the soil level and upon which the → krepis rises.

W. Dörpfeld, Die Skeuothek des Philon, in: MDAI(A) 8, 1883, 151; Ebert, 11, 14; A. Linfert et al., Die Skeuothek des Philon im Piräus, 1981, 18–19; W. Müller-Wiener, Griech. Bauwesen in der Ant., 1988, 78–79, 87, 135–136. C.HÖ.

Euthyphron (Εὐθύφρων; *Euthýphrōn*). Athenian seer, a character in Plato's eponymous dialogue: Socrates, who has been summoned to court, meets E., who wants to see his father prosecuted for manslaughter by criminal negligence, because he has allowed a slave to die who had been guilty of murder. Socrates' reservations about this way of action lead to a debate on the nature of piety. E. is also mentioned in Pl. Crat. 396d; 399e; 428c.

M.L. McPherran, Socratic Piety in the E., in: H.H. Benson (ed.), Essays on the Philosophy of Socrates, 1992, 220–241; A. Tulin, Dike phonou: The Right of Prosecution and Attic Homicide Procedure, 1996; L. Versényi, Holiness and Justice. An Interpretation of Plato's E., 1982. R.B.

Eutocius (Εὐτόκιος; *Eutókios*) The mathematician E. of Ascalon was presumably born around 480 BC; the widespread assumption that he was a pupil of the architect → Isidorus of Miletus is hardly plausible [1. 488]. He wrote commentaries on three works of → Archimedes [1] (*Perì sphaíras kaì kylíndrou*, Περὶ σφαίρας καὶ κυλίνδρου, *kýklou métrēsis*, κύκλου μέτρησις, *Perì epipédōn isorrhopiôn*, Περὶ ἐπιπέδων ἰσορροπιῶν, text editions [3. 1–319]) as well as on the first four books of Apollonius' *Kōniká* (Κωνικά) [13] (dedicated to → Anthemius [3], text edition [4. 168–361]). The commentaries are based on excellent sources and contain valuable material, e.g. on the attempts by Greek mathematicians to solve the problem of → duplication of the cube and dividing the sphere.

1 I. Bulmer-Thomas, s.v. Eutocius of Ascalon, Dictionary of Scientific Biography 4, 1971, 488–491 2 Th.L. Heath, A History of Greek Mathematics, II, 1921, 540f. 3 J.L. Heiberg (ed.), Archimedis opera, 3, ²1915 (repr. 1972) 4 Id. (ed.), Apollonii Pergaei quae graece exstant, 2, 1893 5 P. Tannery, Eutocius et ses contemporains, Mémoires scientifiques, 2, 1912, 118–136. M.F.

Eutolmius Illustrius (Εὐτόλμιος Ἰλλούστριος; *Eutólmios Illoústrios*). Epigrammatic poet, honoured with the titles *vir illustris* and *scholastikós*. Five of his poems are extant, probably originating from Palladas' *Syllogḗ*: the epigrammatic epitaphs Anth. Pal. 7,608 and 611 (elegant imitations of Bianor 7,644 and Parmenion 7,184), the anathematic epigram 6,86 (whose lapidary brevity was seemingly parodied by Palladas), and the epideictic epigram 9,587, a single distich, describing a θερμοχύτης; *thermochýtēs* ('a vessel, out of which warm beverages were poured'). E.D.

Eutresis (Εὔτρησις; *Eútrēsis*). Boeotian settlement near the modern Leuctra. The settlement mound, Arkophodi by its modern name, was on the road from Thespiae to Plataea. The settlement was already of importance in the early Greek period and was also mentioned in Homer's catalogue of ships (Il. 2,502). Later, despite its allegedly famous Apollo oracle, it became no more than a dependent settlement within the territory of Thespiae. Source references: Hell. Oxy. 19,3,387; 20,3,438; Str. 9,2,28; Steph. Byz. s.v. E.

Fossey, 149–154. K.F.

Eutropia

[1] Wife of Emperor Maximianus. Mother of Maxentius and Fausta ([Aur. Vict.] Epit. Caes. 40,12). After AD 324, she spent some time as a Christian pilgrimess in Palestine and drew Constantine's attention to the desecration of the holy place of Mambre (Eus. Vita Const. 3,52).

[2] Half-sister of Constantine. Mother of Nepotianus, who in AD 350 was declared Augustus in Rome. B.BL.

Eutropius

[1] Author of a Latin historical work, which according to its dedication was written at the instruction of Emperor Valens. The text indicates that the author had taken part in Julian's Persian campaign (10,16,1). In the *intitulatio* of a MS, he is referred to as a *magister memoriae*. It is still questionable whether he is identical with another Eutropius of the 2nd half of the 4th cent., whose name appears in other sources: possibly he was *proconsul Asiae* in 371/2, *praef. praet. Illyrici* in 380–1, and *consul posterior* in 387. The historical work, referred to as *breviarium* in the MSS, provides in ten short books an outline of the history of Rome from the foundation of the city to Jovian's death in AD 364. His account is distinguished by its brevity and clarity. His reports concentrate almost entirely on armed conflicts. The author provides extensive evaluations, while striving for balance and impartiality. His language is probably deliberately simple, because it was the aim of his work to provide in an easily accessible form a quick

general account of Roman history. Some of his turns of phrase (8,8,4; 9,4) suggest that E. was not a Christian; however, this does not prevent him from painting a positive picture of Constantius II (10,15,1) nor from criticizing Julian's excessive hostility towards Christians (10,16,3). He used the epitome of Livy's work as his source up to the Imperial Period. His use of Suetonius as a source was only indirect, through the so-called Enmann's → *Kaisergeschichte*, which E. then followed up to the rule of Diocletian. Contemporary history was mainly based on his own knowledge. The short historical compendium was a very popular genre in the 2nd half of the 4th cent. (Aurelius Victor, Ps.-Aurelius Victor, Festus). E.'s work was at least twice translated into Greek and used by Jerome, Orosius, and Isidore. In the Middle Ages, two sequels were written (Paulus Diaconus, Landolfus Sagax). Its use as a school textbook continued into the modern era.

EDITIONS: MGH AA 2 DROYSEN; C. SANTINI (ed.), Eutropii breviarium ab urbe condita, [2]1992; F.L. MÜLLER, Eutropii Breviarium ab urbe condita, 1995 (with translation and commentary).
BIBLIOGRAPHY: PLRE 1, 317 E. (2); H.W. BIRD, Eutropius: His Life and Career, in: Echos du monde classique 32, 1988, 51–60; G. BONAMENTE, Giuliano l'Apostata e il breviario di Eutropio, 1986; M.P. SEGOLINI et A.R. CORSINI (edd.), Eutropii Lexicon, 1982; V. HAEHLING, 211–237; A. MOMIGLIANO, Pagan and Christian Historiography in the Fourth Century A.D., in: Id. (ed.), The Conflict Between Paganism and Christianity in the Fourth Century, 1963, 79–99. W.P.

[2] According to SHA Clod. 13,2, E. was a Dardanian of noble descent, who supposedly married a niece of Emperor Claudius [III 2] Gothicus. Emperor Constantius I is supposed to be a son of this marriage. This reference has to be seen within the context of Constantine's efforts at establishing his own noble descent (cf. Pan. Lat. 6 (7),2–4). PLRE 1, 316 E. (1).

[3] Son of a *colonus*, who studied rhetoric and jurisprudence. In AD 389, he became *consularis Syriae*. He is only known from Libanius' or. 4, which was directed against him. PLRE 1, 318 E. (3). W.P.

[4] *Praepositus sacri cubiculi* in the east from AD 395 to 399, *cos.* 399, *patricius*. A eunuch of unfree origin, who had already occupied a position of trust under → Theodosius I; after the deposal of the *praef. praet.* → Rufinus in 395, he rose to central importance under Arcadius. However, he incurred the enmity of the Empress → Eudoxia [1] as well as ecclesiastical circles. After his initial co-operation with → Stilicho, he later became his opponent and supported → Gildo's secessionary movement in Africa. He was overthrown in 399 by → Gaenas and eventually executed. He was severely criticized, not least after his downfall, particularly forcefully in the two invectives by → Claudianus [2], which should be used with extreme caution. For that reason the extent to which he had actually been able to exert large-scale political influence remains a matter of contention [1. 98f.; 2. 6f.] (PLRE 2, 440–444).

1 J.H.W.G. LIEBESCHUETZ, Barbarians and Bishops, 1990, 93ff. 2 AL. CAMERON, J. LONG, Barbarians and Politics at the Court of Arcadius, 1993. H.L.

Eutyches (Εὐτύχης; *Eutýchēs*).

[1] Gem-cutter of the 1st cent. AD, signed as 'son of → Dioscorides of Aegeae' the rock crystal with a bust of Athena (Berlin, SM), in the style of the Athena of Velletri.
Athena of → Velitrae; → Intaglio; → Gem and cameo cutters

ZAZOFF, AG, 317[70], 331 pl. 92,3; AGD II, Berlin 169 pl. 80 and 81 no. 456. S.MI.

[2] (Eutyc(h)ius, MSS), Latin grammarian of the 4th cent. AD, a pupil of → Priscianus and author of an *Ars de verbo*, probably identical with the eponymous grammarian, whose *Excerpta De adspiratione* → Cassiodorus used in his *Orthographia*. The *Ars* (2 bks.) partially follows on from Priscianus and provides mainly superficial and schematic descriptions of the flections of the verb, whereas the *Excerpta* seem to come from a more detailed work. Judging by the frequent use in glossaries, E.'s work was well known in medieval times (e.g. by Malsacanus, Micon, as well as Anon. ad Cuimnanum), with commentaries written by Sedulius Scottus and Remigius of Auxerre.

EDITIONS: GL 5,447–488 (Ars); GL 7,199,5–202,17 (Exc.).
BIBLIOGRAPHY: G. GOETZ, s.v. E. 6, RE 6, 1529; SCHANZ/HOSIUS 4,2,238–240. P.G.

[3] The 'heresiarch', Monophysite monk (d. after 454). A follower of → Cyrillus of Alexandria since the Council of Ephesus in AD 431, E., in his position as abbot of the monastery of St. Job in Constantinople, was able to exert considerable influence at court through his godson Chrysaphius. His Christology, focussed on individual Cyrillian phrases (Acta Conciliorum Oecumenicorum 2/1,1,143: 'after the incarnation, I confess to a single nature'), became the starting-point of → Monophysitism. Charges by → Eusebius [10] of Dorylaeum led to a legally unsatisfactory doctrinal trial in November 448 [1], which ended with his denouncement as a heretic. Rehabilitated in 449 by a synod called to Ephesus by Theodosius II ('Robber Council of Ephesus'), E. was once again deposed and exiled by the Council of Chalcedon in 451.

1 G. MAY, Das Lehrverfahren gegen E. im November des J. 448, in: Annuarium historiae conciliorum 21, 1989, 1–61 2 H.-J. SIEBEN, s.v. E., LThK[3] 3, 1023f. (literature). J.RI.

Eutychianus

[1] According to Malalas (p. 332,9ff.) a Roman officer from Cappadocia, who recorded his eyewitness account of Julian's Persian campaign of AD 363 in an annalistic history (FHG 4,6). Both the character and his work may well be fictitious (cf. FGrH II B 226, p. 638f.). PLRE 1, 319 E. (39). W.P.

[2] *Praef. praet.* (*Illyrici?*) in AD 396/7.; *praef. praet. Orientis* between 397 and 399; II in 404/5; *cos.* in 398. His identification with Typhus as in Synesius De prov., → Caesarius [3], is contentious. If that identification is correct, he was be a brother of → Aurelianus [4], *comes sacrarum larg. c.* 388/9 and *praef. praet. Orientis*.

PLRE 1,319–321; DELMAIRE, 115ff.; v. HAEHLING, 78f. H.L.

Eutychides (Εὐτυχίδης; *Eutychídēs*) Sculptor and painter from Sicyon, pupil and son of → Lysippus. His acme was dated to 296–293 BC. His fame is based on the bronze statue – known in many replicas and copies – of Tyche of Antioch on the Orontes, which he created not long after the city's refoundation in 300 BC. It is one of the keystones for the chronology of Hellenistic sculpture, and was trendsetting in its composition in the round and its iconography of personifications of cities. E.'s work was much praised for his veristic and detailed representation of textile surfaces. His personification of → Eurotas was seen as 'fluid'. It is uncertain whether a Dionysus statue, owned by Asinius Pollio, was made by E. or a homonymous artist of around 100 BC.

J.C. BALTY, LIMC 1, 840–851, s.v. Antiocheia; T. DOHRN, Die Tyche von Antiochia, 1960; B. FEHR, Lectio graeca, lectio orientalis. Überlegungen zur Tyche von Antiocheia, in: Visible Religion 7, 1990, 83–92; OVERBECK, no. 1516, 1530–1536 (sources); P. PROTTUNG, Darstellungen der hell. Stadttyche, 1995, 43–115; B.S. RIDGWAY, Hellenistic sculpture, 1, 1990, 233–237; STEWART 201–202, 298. R.N.

Eutychius Proculus Latin grammarian of the 2nd cent. AD from Sicca Veneria in Africa. Teacher of → Marcus Aurelius (cf. SHA Aur. 2,3. 5), who elevated him to the proconsular career. His works are lost. It is unlikely that E. is identical with the (probably fictitious) grammarian Proculus, to whom SHA trig.tyr. 22,14 attributes an (even more probably fictitious) treatise with the title of *De peregrinis regionibus*.

A. KAPPELMACHER, s.v. E. 1, RE 6, 1534f.; SCHANZ/HOSIUS 3,174; A.R. BIRLEY, Some Teachers of M. Aurelius, in: Bonner Historia-Augusta-Colloquien 1966/7, 1968, 39f.; H.G. PFLAUM, La valeur de la source, ibid. 1968/9, 1970, 204. P.G.

Eutychus Donkey driver with a donkey by the name of Nicon, whom Octavian met before the battle of Actium and who became an *omen*. Octavian had a brazen image erected of E. and his donkey (Suet. Aug. 96,2; Plut. Antonius 65.5), which was later transferred to Constantinople, but was destroyed in 1204 (Niketas Choniates 6 [PG 139,1049,1ff.]).
→ Omen D.K.

Euxenides (Εὐξενίδης; *Euxenídēs*). Comic poet, whose plays were reputedly performed in Athens at the time of Epicharmus (still before the Second Persian War) [1. test.]; nothing of them has survived.

1 PCG V, 544. H.-G.NE.

Evadne (Εὐάδνη; *Euádnē*, 'the pleasing one').
[1] Daughter of Poseidon and Pitane, the daughter of the river god Eurotas, who was brought up by the Arcadian king → Aepytus [1]. She secretly gave birth to Apollo's son → Iamus, the ancestor of the prophetic clan of the Iamidae in Olympia, and abandoned him in a bed of violets (Pind. Ol. 6,28–73) [1; 2].
[2] Daughter of Iphis (Apollod. 3,79) or Phylacus (Hyg. Fab. 243,3; 256). She threw herself on the burning funeral pyre of her husband → Capaneus to stay united with him in death; for that reason, she was seen as a model of conjugal faithfulness (Eur. Supp. 980–1701). Aeneas catches sight of E. in the *lugentes campi* of the Underworld (Verg. Aen. 6,447) [3; 4].

1 U. v. WILAMOWITZ-MOELLENDORFF, Isyllos, 1886, 178 2 H.W. PARKE, The Oracles of Zeus, 1967, 174–185 3 R.G. AUSTIN, P. Vergili Maronis Aeneidos liber sextus, 1977, 158–160 4 G. GARBUGINO, s.v.E., EV 2, 437. R.B.

Evaenetus (Εὐαίνετος; *Euaínetos*). The most famous and best of the Syracusan coin-engravers, who in the latter third of the 5th cent. BC initially worked in Catana and also in Camarina, and then from *c.* 410 BC in Syracuse. Alongside splendid dekadrachmas, E. also signed smaller silver denominations as well as gold and bronze coins, occasionally taking turns with Euclidas and Eumenus.
→ Dekadrachmon; → Euclidas; → Eumenus

R. WEIL, Die Künstlerinschr. der sicilischen Münzen, in: 44. Winckelmannsprogramm der Arch. Ges. zu Berlin, 1884, esp. 10–12; L. FORRER, Biographical Dictionary of Medallists 2, s.v. E., 1904, 41–50; L. TUDEER, Die Tetradrachmenprägung von Syrakus in der Periode der signierenden Künstler, in: ZfN 30, 1913, 1–292, esp. 222ff.; J. LIEGLE, E. Eine Werkfolge nach Originalen des Staatlichen Münzkabinetts zu Berlin, in: 101. Winckelmannsprogramm der Arch. Ges. zu Berlin, 1941; H.A. CAHN et al., Griech. Münzen aus Großgriechenland und Sizilien, AM Basel Sammlung Ludwig, 1988, 130ff. A.M.

Evaeon (Εὐαίων; *Euaíōn*). Tragedian, son of → Aeschylus (Suda αι 357); his name appears on a number of vessels (450–440 BC), sometimes with the patronym or respectively the addition καλός (*kalós*), see [1].

1 BEAZLEY, ARV² 1579 2 TrGF 13.

Evages (Εὐάγης; *Euágēs*). Comic poet, life dates unknown, from the island of Hydrea (near Troezen). It is supposed that E. started out as an uneducated shepherd, but then turned into a comic poet of good repute [1. test.].

1 PCG V, 183. H.-G.NE.

Evagon (Εὐάγων/*Euágōn*, in MSS also as Εὐγαίων/*Eugaíōn*, Εὐγέων/*Eugéōn*). Of Samos, hailed by Dionysius of Halicarnassus as one of the earliest of the Greek historiographers (De Thucydide 5) and the first

Samian historian (last third of the 5th cent. BC), the author of *Hôroi Samíōn*, which was still referred to by Aristotle; Thucydides, too, used it. In the course of a 2nd cent. BC territorial dispute with Priene, the Samians cited an old border agreement (early 7th cent.), mentioned by E. – who thus is one of the earliest local historians who did not only write about myths, but also about historical events (IPriene 37, 118ff. = FGrH 535 F 3). M.MEI. and ME.STR.

Evagoras (Εὐαγόρας; *Euagóras*).

[1] E. I. (*c.* 435–374/3 BC), from *c.* 411 Greek king of Salamis in Cyprus. Apart from Greeks, Salamis was from the 9th/8th cents. also inhabited by Phoenicians. Other cities were even ruled by Phoenician kings, such as Citium, Amathus and Soli. However, there were no ethnic tensions. The cultural differences themselves began to blur in the early 4th cent. BC. Both Greek and Phoenician kings were equally receptive to the culture of the Greek motherland, esp. that of Athens. The Anatolian dynasties, even the satraps and, more surprisingly perhaps, the court of the Great King, were all more or less Hellenized.

It is important to take this into account for a proper evaluation of Isocrates Or. 9 (*Evagoras*, a 'speculum regum', EDER). Isocrates struck ethnic, nationalistic, and patriotic notes; he portrayed the Phoenicians as barbarians and styled E. as a bringer of culture (Isoc. Or. 9,47). However, it was neither E.'s aim to strengthen the Greek element (Isoc. Or. 9,51, cf. FGrH 688 F 30: Greeks as enemies) nor to weaken the Phoenicians, and neither did he perceive the Persians as arch-enemies. Up to 391, he thought highly of his status as a vassal. This is not contradicted by his open admiration for Athens (Isoc. Or. 9,53). The first half of his rule (411–391) was dedicated to securing his power in Salamis – there are no indications of a properly organized polis. He then tried to expand his rule to the entire island (Diod. Sic. 14,98,1). The latter was impossible to achieve without Persian consent.

Probably in the belief that he would be rewarded with the rule of the entire island, E. supported – also as a friend of Athens – Conon in assembling a Persian fleet against the common enemy Sparta (Isoc. Or. 52–56; Xen. Hell. 2,1,29). However, Artaxerxes II did not go along with that plan: for strategic reasons, there should be no unification of Cyprus under E.'s rule (Diod. Sic. 14,98,3). This led to revolt and war in the second half of his rule (391–380 or 379). He entered into an alliance with Athens as well as with Acoris [2] of Egypt (Theopomp. FGrH 115 F 103). For a time, both Phoenicia and Cilicia were under his protectorate (Diod. Sic. 15,2,3). However, E. finally suffered defeat at Citium and was put under siege in Salamis, but he was given back his city kingdom (Diod. Sic. 15,3–4; 8–9,2). He continued to reign as a vassal up to his violent death in 374/3.

E. A. COSTA, E.I. and the Persians, in: Historia 23, 1974, 40–56; F. G. MAIER, in: CAH² 6, 1994, 312–317.

[2] E. II. Probably a grandson of E. [1] I, prior to 351 BC Persian vassal of Salamis. Because of his sympathies with Persia, E. was driven out by Cypriot insurgents, but the Persians made him king of Sidon; from there he was deposed because of incompetence in office; he fled back to Cyprus, where he was captured and executed (Diod. Sic. 16,46,3). PE.HÖ.

Evagrius (Εὐάγριος; *Euágrios*)

[1] Ponticus. Religious writer and monastic spiritual leader (AD 345–399). Born in the Pontic Ibora, he was a pupil of → Gregorius of Nazianzus; after periods spent in Constantinople (ordination to deacon) and Jerusalem, he stayed in the Egyptian anchorite community of Kellia (Nitrian desert) from 383 as a much sought-after spiritual advisor. Posthumously condemned as an Origenist (553 Council of Constantinople), his few extant works are frequently transmitted ps.-epigrapically (esp. Neilus of Ancyra). Apart from Bible commentaries, based on the Alexandrian exegesis (Ps, Ecc, Prov), they comprised mainly ascetic treatises (Λόγος πρακτικός [*Lógos praktikós*], *Kephalaia gnostica*, *Epist. ad Melaniam* i.a.). In these, he describes on the basis of the experiences of the Egyptian monks a possible way to a perception of divinity through contemplation and purging of all passion. Through the early translation of his works, also into the languages of the Christian Orient, E. became an imparter of monastic spirituality in the East (Palladius, Maximus Confessor) as well as in the West (Iohannes Cassianus).

EDITION: CPG 2430–2482.
BIBLIOGRAPHY: G. BUNGE, Origenismus-Gnostizismus: Zum geistesgesch. Standort des E., in: Vigiliae Christianae 40, 1986, 24–54; E.A. CLARK, The Origenist Controversy, 1992, 283, s.v. E.; A. GUILLAUMONT, s.v. E., TRE 10, 565–570. J.RI.

[2] of Antioch. Bishop of Antioch (*c.* 320 to 394). E. was initially employed as a public servant in Antioch, but left his home town after meeting bishop → Eusebius of Vercellae, whom he then followed to Italy for about 10 years. Highly regarded at the court of Valentinian II, he came down firmly on the side of Pope → Damasus in the latter's dispute with Ursinus. E. left Rome in *c.* 373, entrusted by Damasus with a conciliatory note to → Basilius [1] of Caesarea regarding the Meletian schism. After his arrival in Antioch, E., a friend of Jerome's, joined sides with the minority around bishop Paulinus, whom he succeeded in office in *c.* 388. E. is the author of a Latin adaptation of the *Vita Antonii* (*c.* 370, CPG 2101).

G. J. M. BARTELINCK, Einige Bemerkungen über Euagrius' von Antiochien Übers. der *Vita Antonii*, in: Revue bénédictine 82, 1972, 98–105; M. SPANNEUT, s.v. 3. E., DHGE 16, 102–107. J.RI.

[3] Scholasticus. (Evagrius of Epiphaneia). E. was born in *c.* AD 537 in → Epiphaneia [2]/Koile Syria and died after 594 in → Antioch [1], where he had worked as a lawyer, as indicated i.a. by his epithet σχολαστικός/ *scholastikós*. He served as secretary to Patriarch Gregorius of Antioch (570–593). E. is the last of the ancient Greek Church historians in the tradition of → Eusebius [7] of Caesarea. After Gregorius' death, E. wrote a history of the Church in six volumes, dealing with the period between 431 and 594. It is not an official history; like the works of → Socrates and → Sozomenus, whose tradition it was meant to continue, it followed the order of the emperors. E. sympathized with Neo-Chalcedonism; he offers important documents and distinguishes himself with the critical evaluation of his sources.

J. BIDEZ, L. PARMENTIER, Euagrius, The Ecclesiastical History, 1898 (repr. 1964); A. J. FESTUGIÈRE, Evagre. Histoire ecclésiastique, Byzantion 45, 1975, 188–471; P. ALLEN, Evagrius Scholasticus, the Church Historian, 1981; A. DE HALLEUX, s.v. Evagre, DHGE 16, 1495–1498. C.M.

[4] *Praef. praet. Orientis*, documented only through several – albeit difficult to date – laws of AD 326 (Cod. Theod. 9,3,2 etc.), 329–331 (ibid. 12,1,1 etc.) and 336 (ibid. 12,1,22). It is improbable that he continuously held this office in this period. PLRE 1, 284f. E. (2). W.P.

Evander (Εὔανδρος; *Eúandros*).

[1] Arcadian-Roman hero (Greek Euandros), according to Paus. 8,43,1ff. the son of Hermes and an Arcadian nymph (Themis, Nicostrate: Plut. Quaest. Rom. 278B-C), or alternatively the prophesying → Carmentis from Pallantium. In Hes. fr. 168MW, he is a son of Echemus of Tegea and Tyndareus' daughter Timandra, Hellenism makes him the son of the Italian → Sibyl. Banished because of his involvement in a popular uprising or the murder of one of his parents (Serv. Aen. 8,51), E. arrived in Italy about 60 years before the Trojan War (Dion. Hal. Ant. Rom. 1,31–33;40), where he was given a friendly reception by the indigenous king → Faunus. E. founded the first settlement on the Palatine (allegedly named after the Arcadian Pallantium: cf. e.g. Pol. 6,11a). According to Cato (in Solin. 2,7f.; Verg. Aen. 8,562), E. had won that territory in battle from the king of Praeneste. As cultural hero, E. taught to the indigenous population the alphabetic script (Tac. Ann. 11,14) as well as the use of musical instruments; he also introduced 'Arcadian' cults (Lupercus, Ceres, Neptunus Equester, Victoria: Dion. Hal. Ant. Rom. 1,33). Together with Hercules, who had just defeated the giant → Cacus, E. founded the Hercules cult at the Ara Maxima in Rome (Verg. Aen. 8,185ff.; Liv. 1,7,3ff.). E. supported → Aeneas, when he arrived from Troy, against the Latins, in which fight his son → Pallas was killed.

In Rome E. was given a cult at the Porta Trigemina (Dion. Hal. Ant. Rom. 1,32,2), and his grave was supposedly on top of the Palatine hill (Eust. on Dionys. Per. 347); it is likely that his cult in Pallantium, where a temple and a marble statue were dedicated to him, only dates back to the Roman Imperial period (Paus. 8,44,5). It has not yet been possible to establish convincing evidence for a historical foundation of the E. legend (e.g. a Mycenaean settlement on the Palatine). From the 3rd cent. BC at the latest, the Romans used the E. myth in their encounter with the eastern Greek world to legitimize their own Greek (i.e. non-Barbarian) roots.

→ Hercules; → Pallantium

G. G. BELLONI, s.v. E., LIMC 4.1, 40–41; D. BRIQUEL, Les traditions sur l'origine de l'écriture en Italie, in: RPh 62, 1988, 251–271; J. ESCHER, s.v. E., RE 6, 839–842; M. JOST, Sanctuaires et cultes d'Arcadie, 1985, 537; P. M. MARTIN, Pour une approche du mythe dans sa fonction historique. Illustration: le mythe d'Éuandre, in: Caesarodunum 9, 1974, 132–151; P. WEIZSÄCKER, s.v. E., ROSCHER 1.1, 1393–95.

[2] Lycian king, son-in-law of → Bellerophon and father of → Sarpedon, an ally of the Trojans (Diod. Sic. 5,79). T.S.

[3] **from Phocaea.** Philosopher of the 3rd/2nd cents. BC, whose name appears in a list of successors to → Lacydes after the latter's premature departure from the scholarchate of the Academy (Suda, s.v. Plato; Philod. Index academicorum M 10–21). Some references (esp. Diog. Laert. 4,60) seem to indicate that E. occupied a position of prominence alongside → Telecles (cf. Apollod. Chronicle 7–9 DORANDI).

→ Academy K.-H.S.

[4] (**C. Avianus**) Sculptor, toreutic artist, restorer in Athens; freedman of M. Aemilianus Avianius. In *c.* 50 BC, Cicero purchased some sculptures from him for his villas. Mark Antony took him to Alexandria in 36 BC, from where he returned to Rome in 30 BC as a prisoner of war. Augustus commissioned him to complete → Timotheus' statue of Artemis. R.N.

Evandridas (Εὐανδρίδας; *Euandrídas*). Tragedian, son of Hestiaeus; according to an inscription from *c.* 200 BC (GVI 2018), found in Miletus, he lived exactly to the age of 80 [1. 185 B].

1 A. REHM, R. HARDER, Didyma II, 1958 2 TrGF 116. F.P.

Evangelus (Εὐάγγελος; *Euángelos*). Comic poet of the 3rd cent. BC (uncertain), of whose Ἀνακαλυπτομένη (*Anakalyptoménē*) a fragment in trochaic tetrameters has survived: the master of the house and a cook make preparations for a wedding.

1 PCG V, 184f. H.-G.NE.

Evanthes (Εὐάνθης; *Euánthēs*). It is not known when he wrote his *hymnos* to Glaucus, in which he portrayed him as a son of Poseidon and the nymph Nais, and in which the god of the sea fell in love with → Ariadne, after Theseus had abandoned her (Ath. 7, 296c).

SH 194. C.S.

Evanthius Latin grammarian, who worked in Constantinople during the 1st half of the 4th cent. AD. Extant of his works are a treatise entitled *De fabula* or *De comoedia* (regarding the title see Rufin. Gramm. 6,554,4), which is contained in the preface to → Donatus' [3] commentary on Terence. The first three chapters of this preface are undoubtedly by E., whereas there is considerable uncertainty regarding the fourth. It is almost certain, however, that E. also commented on Terence's individual comedies, and that these commentaries were widely used by Donatus; it is even quite likely that Donatus used parts of them verbatim in his own commentaries, as in the case of *De fabula*.

P.L. SCHMIDT, in: HLL, § 526.2. P.G.

Evarchidas (Εὐαρχίδας; *Euarchídas*). Syracusan coin-engraver, who at the end of the 5th cent. BC signed tetradrachmas together with Phrygillos.
→ Tetradrachmon

L. FORRER, Biographical Dictionary of Medallists 2, s.v. E., 1904, 50–51; L. TUDEER, Die Tetradrachmenprägung von Syrakus in der Periode der signierenden Künstler, in: ZfN 30, 1913, 1–292, esp. 36ff., 228. A.M.

Evaretus (Εὐάρετος; *Euáretos*). Tragedian, who came second in the Dionysia of 341 BC with *Teûkros*, *Achilleús*, and a further unknown play (DID A 2a,7), and third in the Dionysia of 340 with *Alkméōn* and a further unknown play (DID A 2a, 26).

METTE, 91f.; TrGF 85. F.P.

Evenor

[1] (Εὐήνωρ; *Euḗnōr*). Athenian sculptor. Three bases on the Acropolis bear his signature, dating from around 490–470 BC. One of these is linked, not without controversy, to the so-called Angelitus' Athena (Athens, AM Inv. no. 140).

A.E. RAUBITSCHEK, Dedications from the Athenian Akropolis, 1949, no. 14, 22, 23.; B.S. RIDGWAY, The Severe Style in Greek Sculpture, 1970, 29–30, fig. 39. R.N.

[2] Greek physician from Argos in Acarnania; he lived in Athens, and received Athenian citizenship in 322/1 BC. His main work, comprising at least five bks., deals with therapeutics (Cael. Aurel. Chron. 3,122); it is contentious whether his gynaecological observations, including his recommended therapy for prolapse of the uterus and retention of the placenta, came from the same work or a separate one dedicated specifically to gynaecology. In the case of pleuritis, he thought that the lungs themselves were most affected (Cael. Aurel. Acut. 2,96), febrile illnesses he explained with an abnormal increase in innate heat, and he operated on oedematous patients to relieve them of excess fluid (Cael. Aurel. chron. 3,122). He had great confidence in the healing powers of water, esp. water from cisterns and most of all the water from the Amphiaraos sanctuary (Ath. 2,46 d). V.N.

Evenus (Εὔηνος, Εὐηνός; *Eúēnos*, *Euēnós*)
[1] of Paros
A. PERSONAL DATA B. LATER RECEPTION

A. PERSONAL DATA

Eratosthenes distinguishes between two elegiac poets from Paros, both named E. (Harpocr. s.v. Εὔηνος 139,15 DINDORF), others maintain that there had only been one [1]. Plato mentions an E. of Paros, a poet and 'philosopher' (Pl. Phd. 60d; 61b), a teacher of political rhetoric around 400 BC (Pl. Ap. 20a-b), who had 'discovered' a number of tropes (Pl. Phdr. 267a). Both his language and the subject matter of some of the extant fragments, e.g. moderation in drinking (2 GENTILI-PRATO/WEST, possibly a reply to → Critias 4 G.-P. = 6 W., 18ff.), fit in with the sophist E. of the late 5th cent. BC, the teacher of → Philistus (Suda s.v. Φίλιστος), who found a connection between grammar and music (Quint. 1,10,17). However, chronicles date the apex of his work to 456 BC (Hieron. Chron. 80,1 = 111,12 HELM; Georgius Syncellus 254c).

Of three presumably complete Theognidea addressed to Simonides (vv. 467–496; vv. 667–682; [1341 op.] 1345–50), vv. 467–96 can be attributed to E. with certainty, because Theognis v. 472 = 7 G.-P./8 W. (πᾶν γὰρ ἀναγκαῖον χρῆμ' ἀνιηρὸν ἔφυ) is quoted in Aristot. Metaph. 1015a 29f. and Eth. Eud. 1223a 31f. (with πρᾶγμα instead of χρῆμα) as E.'. It is likely that the other two were also written by E., possibly also vv. 903–30, which are addressed to Democles [2]. However, it is possible that the addressee was not Simonides of Ceos (d. 468 BC), but another Simonides, possibly also of Paros, if vv. 667–682 are indeed a request for protection regarding an E. in exile [3]. The older E. in Eratosthenes as well as the *floruit* of 456 BC may both be consequences of the identification of Simonides with the eponymous poet from Ceos.

B. LATER RECEPTION

Pherecrates, fr. 162 PCG (Chiron), quoted vv. 467ff. in an Attic theatre in *c.* 420 BC; Plato and Aristotle assume that their readers are aware of E.'s works. It is likely that in the 2nd cent. AD, only his *Erōtiká* were known: Artemidorus [6] knew the *Erōtiká*, addressed to Eunomus (Artem. 1,4), and Epictetus (in Arrian, Epicteti Dissertationes 4,9,6) considered E. as risqué as → Aristides [2] (cf. Ausonius, Cento Nuptialis 10 p. 168f. PRETE). It is possible that Maximus of Tyre 38,4 knew E. from Plato, but Ath. 428c-d quotes Thgn. vv. 477–486 as verses written by Theognis himself, as does Stob. 3,18,14 regarding vv. 479–486.

1 A. GARZYA, Eueno di Paro, in: Giornale italiano di filologia 6, 1953, 310–320 = Studi sulla lirica greca, 1963, 75–89 2 Q. CATAUDELLA, Theognidea 903–930, in: RhM 99, 1956, 40ff. 3 B. VAN GRONINGEN, Theognis, Le premier livre, 1966, 267–269.

EDITIONS: GENTILI/PRATO 2, 1985; IEG. E.BO.

[2] Epigrammatic poet of the 'Garland' of Philippus (Anth. Pal. 4, 2, 13), under whose name 11 poems have come to us, nearly all of them epideictic and at times of remarkable quality (e.g. 9,122; 251; 11,49; epigram 9,75 = EpGr 1106 KAIBEL was also found on a wall in Pompeii). However, it is impossible to trace them back to a single poet: 9,251 (the only one within a sequence of epigrams by Philippus) is marked as 'by E. the grammarian' (Εὐήνου γραμματικοῦ), 9,62 'by E. of Sicily' (Εὐ. Σικελιώτου), 9,75 'by Evenus of Ascalon' (Εὐ. Ἀσκαλωνίτου), and 9,602 'by Evenus of Athens' (Εὐ. Ἀθηναίου). The assumption that some of the epigrams were written by E. [1] of Paros, the famous 5th. cent elegiac (such as 11,49 = Evenus eleg. fr. 2 WEST), has got a good claim to a certain degree of probability.

GA II,1, 254–261; 2, 289–294. E.D.

[3] Important river in Aetolia, carrying a lot of water, originally named Lycormas (Str. 7,7,8; 10,2,5), modern name also Phidaris; it rises on the north-western slopes of Mt. Corax within the territory of the Bomieis (Str. 10,2,5), flows through a number of narrow gorges (therefore not navigable inland) and finally in a wide delta south of Calydon into the Gulf of Patras.

C. ANTONETTI, Les Étoliens, 1990; PHILIPPSON/KIRSTEN 2,2, 304f., 307, 314–317. D.S.

Evergides Painter Anonymous Attic bowl painter of the late 6th cent. BC, named after the potter Euergides; however, he also worked for the potter Chelis (bowl Paris, LV Inv. G 15 [1. 91, no. 51]), possibly for other potters as well. His *c.* 150 extant bowls are mainly painted with genre images (scenes depicting athletics, horses, chariots, as well as symposium and komos scenes), as well as mythological (Hercules, Theseus, Peleus-Thetis, Ajax-Achilles playing board games, etc.) and Dionysian topics; fabulous creatures (griffin, sphinx, Pegasus) appear alongside the bowl handles. A bowl from the Athenian Acropolis (Athens, NM Inv. Akr. 166 [1. 92, no. 64]) depicts Athena amongst vase painters and metal-working artisans; two other → bilingual vases (Paris, LV Inv. G 16 [1. 94, no. 94] and Naples, MN Inv. H 2609 [1. 9, no. 2]) are the result of a collaboration with → Epictetus [1].

1 BEAZLEY, ARV², 35, 87–106, 1624–1626, 1700 2 BEAZLEY, Paralipomena, 330, 509 3 BEAZLEY, Addenda², 170–171 4 H.J. BLOESCH, Formen att. Schalen, 1940, 51–53 5 J. BOARDMAN, Athenian Red Figure Vases. The Archaic Period, 1979, 56, 58, 60–61 6 B. COHEN, Attic Bilingual Vases and their Painters, 1978, 437–438 7 M. ROBERTSON, The Art of Vase-painting in Classical Athens, 1992, 38, 52–57, 268. R.H.

Everyday crockery Modern archaeological term for the coarser ceramics in everyday use, a definition blurred by the fact that black glaze ceramics, → terra sigillata, and sometimes even painted fine ceramics were put to everyday use. However, as a pottery product, everyday crockery is clearly distinguishable from the latter three. The handle, rim, and foot profiles are less clearly defined; the outside of vessels is mostly unslipped or only thinly glazed and perfunctorily decorated. In contrast with frequently exported fine ceramics, this is mostly pottery produced for local markets only (→ Pottery, production of). It was generally used for domestic purposes and in agriculture [1], in trade [2], on markets [3], and in long-distance trade (→ Transport amphorae). The repertoire of forms ranged from heavy tubs, barrels, mortaria to lighter wares such as hydrias, jugs, small amphorae, cooking vessels [4], including numerous special forms for specific purposes, such as funnels, measuring jugs [5], beehives [1. 397–412], stands, colanders and sieves. In all historical periods, pottery for everyday use was produced in large quantities, and its shards are the staple commodity of most archaeological excavations. In the 19th cent., such finds were largely disregarded, esp. if they had been found alongside painted ceramics, but nowadays, their study opens up insights into various socio-economic aspects [6].
→ Vessels, shapes and types of; → Black burnished ware; → Clay vessels

1 J.E. JONES, A.J. GRAHAM, L.H. SACKETT, An Attic Country House, in: ABSA 68, 1973, 355–452 2 H.S. GEORGIOU, Ayia Irini: Specialized Domestic and Industrial Pottery, in: Keos 6, 1986 (Bronze Age) 3 M. LANG, M. CROSBY, Weights, Measures and Tokens, in: Agora 10, 1964, 39–64 4 B. SPARKES, The Greek Kitchen, in: JHS 82, 1962, 121–137; 85, 1965, 162–163 5 F.W. HAMDORF, Karpometra. Olympia Berichte 10, 1981, 192–208 6 D.P.S. PEACOCK, Pottery in the Roman World: An Ethno-Archaeological Approach, 1982.

B.A. SPARKES, L. TALCOTT, Black and Plain Pottery, in: Agora 12, 1970; W. GAUER, Die Tongefäße aus dem Brunnen unterm Stadion-Nordwall, OlF 8, 1975; Amphores romaines et histoire économique. École française de Rome, 1989; I. BALD ROMANO, Hell. Deposit from Corinth, in: Hesperia 63, 1994, 57–104. I.S.

Evetes (Εὐέτης; *Euétēs*).
[1] Tragedian, whose plays were performed in Athens at the time of → Epicharmus (486/5 or 485/4 BC; cf. Suda ε 2766; see also [1.34]). A victory at the Dionysia soon after 484 is transmitted (DID A 3a, 12).

1 H. HOFFMANN, Chronologie der att. Tragödie, 1951.

TrGF 6. F.P.

[2] Comic poet; his only transmitted play title *Epíklēros* ('The Heiress') can hardly be made to fit in chronologically with the observation in the Suda (ε 2766) that a playwright named E. had his plays performed in Athens at the same time as → Epicharmus, unless this E. is identical with the tragedian E. [1] (TrGF 6 [2]).

1 PCG V, 276 2 TrGF 345. H.-G.NE.

Evocati In the 2nd cent. BC, Roman soldiers had to serve in the military for up to six years, followed by a further 16 years, during which as *evocati* they had to be available to be called up again. During the civil wars in the final years of the Roman Republic, military leaders frequently tried to talk experienced soldiers into returning to their units. Troops recruited in that manner were referred to as *evocati*. In rank, *evocati* stood above simple soldiers, but below the *centuriones*. They either formed a special unit, or they were integrated into existing units. Frequently, it was the promises of loot and advancement which enticed soldiers to return to service in the legions.

In 44 BC, the young C. Caesar (the future Augustus) appealed that a great number of veterans, whom Caesar hat settled in Campania, return to serve under him (Cass. Dio 45,12); in the early years of the Principate, *evocati* were occasionally used in the same way as in the Republic. Thus, a lot of soldiers were called up again in AD 6 in consequence of the Pannonian revolt (Velleius 2,111,1). Augustus, however, created a special unit of *evocati*, who like the *centuriones* carried a staff (Cass. Dio 55,24,8; CIL VI 3419). These *evocati* were soldiers, who stayed on in the army after the completion of their regular service, either as volunteers or on order of the *princeps*. The term *evocatus* referred to a specific military rank; *evocati* are evident into the 3rd cent. AD. Towards the end of the 1st cent. AD, many of the *evocati* came from the Praetorian units; they had completed their 16 years of service. Those remaining in Rome were presumably answerable to the *praefectus praetorio*; however, the special role of the *princeps* is clearly expressed in the title *evocatus Augusti*, which many *evocati* bore.

It is likely that an *evocatus* could expect to rise to *centurio* or even further advancement: 'C. Cusp(ius) Secundus swore his oath as an *evocatus* ... and fulfilled it as a *centurio*' (CIL III 3470; ILS 2453). However, some *evocati* never advanced any further: e.g. Pellartius Celer served for 27 years as an *evocatus* (AE 1952,153). Within locations of the army administration, *evocati* were responsible for special military and technical duties. *Evocati* received higher decorations than simple soldiers, thus emphasizing their rank. J.CA.

Evocatio The appeal to the deities of a besieged city to leave it and take up new residence in Rome (Plin. HN 28,18; Serv. Aen. 2,351). The best and until recently only reliable example was the *evocatio* of Juno Regina from the Etruscan city of Veii in 396 BC (Liv. 5,21,3–7; cf. 5,22,7; 23,7; 31,3), resulting in → Camillus' resettlement of the cult on the Aventine hill in Rome. However, the historical reliability of such legendary reports from Rome's early history (cf. [1. 193–200; 2. 162f.]) is no less controversial than the authenticity of later *evocationes*. Particularly the much discussed *evocatio* of Juno from Carthage in 146 BC (Serv. Aen. 12,841) raises many doubts [3. 47–50]. Undoubtedly, the formula in question (*carmen*) in Macrob. Sat. 3,9,7 contains old and authentic elements, but it refers to the goddess in a masc. pl. form instead of a female deity (however, Liv. 5,21,5 already referred to *deos evocatos* in relation to Veii, cf. [4. 42ff.; 5. 157ff.]). Another argument against the authenticity is also that the reception of the city goddess Juno (Caelestis) in Rome only took place much later. However, an inscription from Isaura Vetus in Cilicia (AE 1977, 816) [6] leads to a new interpretation: The inscription probably refers to an *evocatio* in *c.* 75 BC, but points to a change in ritual: The goddess is no longer taken to Rome, but is given a new cult in her place of origin.

Another kind of *evocatio*, which survived into the later periods (Ulp. Dig. 1,8,9,2), was used in private cult rituals in order to cleanse a location from any associated religious obligations.

1 J. Piccaluga, Terminus, 1974 2 J. Rüpke, Domi militiaeque, 1990 3 R. E. A. Palmer, Roman Religion and Roman Empire, 1974 4 V. Basanoff, E., 1947 5 J. Hubaux, Rome et Véies, 1958 6 J. Le Gall, in: Mélanges J. Heurgon I, 1976, 519–24.

M. Beard, J. North, S. Price, Religions of Rome, 1997; A. Blommart, Les processus d'introduction des dieux étrangers à Athènes et à Rome, 1997; Latte, 43, 125, 200, 346; G. Wissowa, Religion und Kultus der Römer, [2]1912 (repr. 1971), 44, 383f. H.V

Exactor The term *exactor* has two different meanings: on the one hand, *exactores* worked as supervisors and controllers in various sectors, on the other hand, within the Roman financial administration, an *exactor* was a debt collector.

As evident in one of Pliny's letters (Plin. Ep. 9,37,3), on large estates *exactores* supervised that the *coloni* carried out their work correctly. In the building trade and in public building projects, *exactores* are epigraphically attested (CIL VI 8480 = ILS 1601; 8481; 8673; 8677 = ILS 1628; CIL XII 3070 = ILS 4844); in these instances, they were charged with the inspection of the buildings. It was quite common for an *exactor* to be a slave or freedman of the building sponsor. In a metaphorical sense, the term *exactor* was used for someone supervising the study of pupils (Quint. Inst. 1,3,14; 1,7,34) as well as for a magistrate supervising the execution of a death sentence (Liv. 2,5,5). Even the 'king of the bees' was referred to as the *exactor* of the work of the other bees (Sen. Clem. 1,19,2). In mints, there is documentary evidence of *exactores auri*, *argenti*, *aeris* (CIL VI 42; 44 = ILS 1635). It is probably correct that these *exactores* were assumed to be imperial officials who controlled the minting process.

In the later years of the Republic and during the Principate, *exactores* acted as debt collectors at the request of the creditors. In private service (Dig. 40,5,41,17), the work of an *exactor* was distinguished from that of a → *coactor*, in the service of the *princeps* as well as in public service from that of the → *susceptor*. During the Principate, an *exactor* was never just an ordinary tax collector; it was his task to collect money owed to the community or any extraordinary contributions (Caes. B Civ. 3,32,4; CIL VI 8434 = ILS 1523).

As late as the 4th cent. AD, *exactores* regularly acted on behalf of the Roman empire; generally, they were rich → *curiales*, who were responsible for the collection of taxes and who ranked highly amongst the → *curia*. Throughout the 4th cent. AD, a number of imperial decrees were issued that dealt with sanctions against *exactores* who abused their position (Cod. Theod. 11,1,3; 11,7,1; 11,8,1; 12,6,22).

1 E. BERNAREGGI, Familia monetalis, in: Numismatica e antichità classiche, 1974, 177–191 2 L. DE SALVO, I munera curialia nel IV secolo, in: Atti del X° Convegno internazionale dell'Accademia Romanistica Costantiniana, 1995, 291–318 3 C. LEPELLEY, Quot curiales tot tyranni, L'image du décurion oppresseur du Bas-Empire, in: E. FRÉZOULS (ed.), Crise et redressement dans les provinces européennes de l'Empire, 1983, 143–156 4 J.D. THOMAS, The Office of Exactor in Egypt, in: Chronique d'Egypte, 34, 1959, 124–140. J.A.

Exagium (ἐξάγιον, στάγιον; *exágion, stágion*). Originally a Hellenistic coin weight (in Babylon with a weight of 17,00 g), the *exagium* is predominantly a coin weight for the *solidus* subsequent to Constantine's reforms (AD 312); within the Greek speaking population, it even became a synonym for the latter and was distorted to *stágion*. The equation was made easier by the fact that the *solidus* and the *exagium* had a weight of $^1/_{72}$ of a *libra* (= 4.55 g), but the weight of the latter was reduced in the Byzantine era (from the 9th cent.: 4.43 g).

Exagia take the shape of round or square bronze discs, which in the 4th and 5th cents. AD bear the bust of the current emperor and sometimes the location of the mint as well as the abbreviated legend *exagium solidi*. In the Byzantine period, *exagia* bear silver encrusted inscriptions referring to the weight, e.g. II SOL(idi) XII, i.e. two ounces = 12 *solidi*, thus equating one ounce with six *solidi*. However, *exagia* did not have a clearly defined weight.

F. HULTSCH, Griech. und röm. Metrologie, 1882, 327; SCHRÖTTER, 184; W. TRAPP, Kleines Handbuch der Maße, Zahlen, Gewichte und der Zeitrechnung, 1992, 212f. A.M.

Exaleiptron (ointment container) see → Vessels, shapes and types of

Exarchate The term refers to those Byzantine territories in Italy and North Africa which after the reorganization under → Mauricius (AD 582–602) were administered by an exarch (ἔξαρχος; *éxarchos, patricius et exarchus*). As a direct representative of the emperor, the exarch – similar to the later theme structure; → Theme – exercised both civilian and military power and could intervene in Church politics (e.g. by confirming the election of a pope). This unusual concentration of power was the result of fighting against the attacks by Slavs, Avars, and Persians, tying up resources as well as soldiers in the east. Administration und defence of the western territories thus relied largely on local resources, which were almost entirely at the disposal of the exarch.

The exarchate of Ravenna, first documented in 584, comprised the Byzantine possessions in mainland Italy, which remained after the Langobardian incursion of 568, thus including Rome, but not Sicily. Battles against the Langobards created a constant demand in soldiers from local resources; however, they acted in local interests rather than imperial ones. This led to a weakening of the powers of the exarch in the 7th and 8th cents., which was not fundamentally reversed by Emperor Constans' [2] II campaign against the Langobards and his short visit to Rome in AD 663. In the course of the 8th cent., the influence of the exarch decreased further, because the Byzantine territories were concentrated in southern Italy, and thus received support from the Sicilian theme. The Langobardian capture of Ravenna in 751 spelled the end of the exarchate and Byzantine rule in central Italy, which was later to become the centre of the papal state.

An exarch of Carthage is first mentioned in 591 (Gennadius); in the early 7th cent., this office is held by Heraclius, father of the eponymous emperor. The danger of concentrating so much power in the hands of the exarch is demonstrated by Gregorius' attempted usurpation in 646/7; Byzantine rule in Africa ended with the Arab capture of Carthage (698) and Septem (Ceuta, 711).

G. OSTROGORSKY, Geschichte des byz. Staates, [3]1963, 68, 98ff., 118, 141f. M.MEI.

Exauctorare The verb *exauctorare* refers to the judicial act, by which a Roman military commander could release a soldier or an entire unit from their oath of allegiance. Such an act could be carried out at certain times defined in law, in the Republican era for example following a victory, at the time of the Principate at the end of a soldier's compulsory military service (Suet. Aug. 24,2; Suet. Tib. 30; Tac. Ann. 1,36,4; Tac. Hist. 1,20,6). In exceptional circumstances, this might be linked with a reward (CIL XVI 17): the release from the oath was then complimented with the award of a diploma – the released soldiers thus became → veterans. Frequently, *exauctorare* meant a punishment, less for individual soldiers than for complete units (Suet. Vit. 10,1; SHA Alex. Sev. 12,5). The unit was then dissolved and its name erased from inscriptions (CIL III 186 = ILS 2657; 206 = ILS 5865; VIII 17953; 17954 etc.). This form of punishment, which was similar to the *ignominiosa* → *missio*, was more common during the Principate than the Republic. The soldiers themselves, however, remained in the army and were distributed to other units.

1 W. ECK, H. WOLFF (ed.), Heer und Integrationspolitik, 1986 2 O. FIEBIGER, s.v. e., RE 6, 1553 3 Y. LE BOHEC, Troisième Légion Auguste, 1989, 55; 591

4 S. Link, Konzepte und Privilegierung röm. Veteranen, 1989. Y.L.B.

Exceptio In the Roman formulary procedure, *exceptio* (objection, literally 'exception') refers to a special defence plea by the defendant. It can refer to the trial as a whole, but its particular usage was as a corrective measure in an → *actio* based on the *ius civile*. In the fomula, the *exceptio* appears as a negative conditional clause, which follows the plaintiff's claim summarized in the → *intentio*, and precedes the condemnation formula (→ *condemnatio*). Worded as a negative condition for the *condemnatio* and thus an exception from the conditions for condemnation – therefore its name –, an *exceptio* was as a rule included in the formula by the praetor at the request of the defendant. This measure ensures the inclusion of the procedurally important defendant's plea into the formula by acknowledging the facts of relevance to the *actio*, but also by citing particular circumstances which oppose a condemnation. Thus it is possible for the *promissor*, accused on the basis of a stipulatory promise, to cite the missing valuation of a loan by employing the *exceptio doli* (*si in ea re nihil dolo malo Auli Agerii factum sit neque fiat*, 'if in this case as a result of the plaintiff's evil intent nothing has happened nor happens'), or claim an informal agreement on a waiver, settlement, or moratorium with the *exceptio pacti conventi* (*si inter Aulum Agerium et Numerium Negidium non convenit, ne ea pecunia peteretur*, 'if no agreement has been reached between plaintiff and defendant that this money will not be demanded') (cf. Gai. Inst. 4,116; 119). The *promissor* under fear can claim the *exceptio metus* (Gai. Inst. 4,117: Ulp. Dig. 44,4,4,33).

In the face of the action by an owner based on the *rei vindicatio*, who had sold a *res mancipi*, but never formally mancipated it, but only informally traded it, the buyer can defend himself as a 'bonitary' owner by citing the *exceptio rei venditae et traditae*, a special case of the *exceptio doli* (cf. chapter D. 21,3). An owner according to civil law faced with the *actio Publiciana* is entitled to the *exceptio iusti dominii* (*si ea res possessoris non sit, si non suus esset*, if this object does not belong to the possessor/is not his) (cf. Dig. 6,2,17; 6,1,72; 44,4,4,32; 21,3,2). The owner, who withdraws his sales mandate to the → *procurator* after the sale, but prior to the actual handing over (→ *traditio*) of the goods, thus preventing the purchaser from taking possession of his property according to the *ius civile*, is countered with the *exceptio si non auctor meus ex voluntate tua vendidit* ('if my guarantor did not sell with your permission') (cf. Dig. 6,2,14). If a pawned item has been sold with the agreement of the pawnee, the purchaser can defend himself against the *actio Serviana pignus* by the *creditor* with the *exceptio si non voluntate creditoris veniit* ('if the item was not sold with the agreement of the creditor') (Dig. 20,6,8,9). *Exceptiones* can permanently block an *actio* or obstruct it for a limited period. Thus one can distinguish between *exceptiones peremptoriae* (*perpetuae*) and *dilatoriae* (*temporales, temporariae*) (cf. Gai. Inst. 4, 120–125). In all of these cases, an *exceptio* is based on the *ius honorarium* and on *aequitas*. The *ius civile*, for example, forms the basis for the *exceptio legis Cinciae* to ward off actions regarding the enforcement of prohibited donations (Paulus Vat. 310). Special procedural pleas are the *exceptio rei iudicatae vel in iudicium deductae* in case of a renewed action regarding the same matter at issue (Gai. Inst. 4,107), also the *exceptio praeiudicii* in order to prevent for example that a certain legal status in an action is subject to a preliminary decision, e.g. the legal status of heirs in an action outside of the *hereditatis petitio* (Gai. Inst. 4, 133).

The procedural defence against an *exceptio* is the *replicatio*. For example, the bonitary owner whose action is based on the *actio Publiciana* can dismiss the *exceptio iusti dominii* of the owner according to civil law with the *replicatio rei venditae et traditae* (reply regarding an object that is sold and handed over) (Dig. 44,4,4,32). A *replicatio* can then be countered with a *duplicatio*, this in turn with a *triplicatio* etc. On the other hand, there is no requirement for an *exceptio* from the outset, if the action can be judged in good faith (*bona fides*). *In bonae fidei iudiciis exceptiones insunt* (law suits based on good faith already comprise *exceptiones*).

With the decline of the formulary procedure in Late Antiquity, *exceptiones*, too, lost their unique place within the legal process. From then on, the term generally applied to any plea by the defendant. The term *exceptio* still had the same unspecified meaning within the context of the early modern German common civil law action. In the 19th cent., Savigny drew a distinction between the Roman *exceptio* and the plea within the modern framework of legal action. In Windscheid's view, the plea is the opposite of a substantial claim. In contrast, the plea with its two variations modelled on the Roman *exceptiones*, i.e. the peremptory and the dilatory plea, is still one of the fundamental terms used in substantial civil law. In this sense, the Latin term *exceptio* is still in common use, as e.g. in *exceptio doli* as the defence of fraud.

→ Aequitas; → Creditor; → Dolus; → Pactum; → Stipulatio

M. Kaser, K. Hackl, Das röm. Zivilprozeßrecht, [2]1997, 256–265, 582–586 H. Honsell, Th. Mayer-Maly, W. Selb, Röm. Recht, [4]1987, 506–561 Wieacker, RRG, 458f. O. Lenel, Edictum perpetuum, [3]1927, repr. 1956, 501–513 Id., Über Ursprung und Wirkung der Exceptionen, 1876, repr. 1970 F. Eisele, Die materielle Grundlage der E., 1871 M. Kaser, 'Ius honorarium' and 'ius civile', in: ZRG 101, 1984, 1–114 R. Knütel, Die Inhärenz der e. pacti im bonae fidei iudicium, in: ZRG 84, 1967, 133–161 A. Wacke, Zur Lehre vom pactum tacitum und zur Aushilfsfunktion der e. doli, in: ZRG 90, 1973, 220–261; 91, 1974, 251–284 K. Hackl, Praeiudicium im klass. röm. Recht, 1976 H. Ankum, Pap. D. 20,1,3 pr.; 'Res iudicata' and Full and Bonitary Ownership, in: Estudios en homenaje a J. Iglesias, 1988, 1121–1149. C.KR.

Exceptor General meaning: 'speedwriter' (*excipere*, 'to record'; Greek synonym ταχύγραφος/*tachýgraphos*, → Tachygraphy), specific meaning: an important subaltern official in the civil and military administration of the provinces (in late antiquity also in diocesan and prefecturial administration) besides auditors (→ *numerarius*), actuaries (e.g. → *actarius*) and archivists and registrars. The task of the exceptor was to record protocols and to draw up or copy administrative or legal records (Cod. Iust. 10,12,2 – *exceptores et ceteri officiales*: Cod. Iust. 12, tit. 49 *De numerariis, actuariis et chartulariis et adiutoribus scriniariis et exceptoribus sedis excelsae ceterorumque iudicum tam civilium quam militarium*). There were special bureaux for this purpose in the central offices of the empire (*ab* → *epistulis*; *a* → *libellis*; *a memoria* etc.).

JONES, LRE, 587f. C.G.

Excerpta Barbari A medieval Latin MS. (Parisinus Latinus 4884) contains the translation (*c.* AD 700) of the Alexandrian version of a Christian world chronicle, which, because of its Vulgar Latin language, has been known as the 'E.B.' since J. J. SCALIGER; it is based on a Greek version from the 5th cent. AD. The extant text, which ends in 387, is divided into three sections: a world chronicle from Adam to Cleopatra (p. 184–280 FRICK); a list of rulers from the Assyrians to the Roman emperors (until Anastasius, 491–518; the conclusion is possibly a later insertion; p. 280–330) and a chronicle of *fasti* from Caesar to the year 387, which is linked to part 1 and ends abruptly (p. 330–370); the pages dealing with the *fasti* from Domitian to Diocletian have been lost, cf. p. 354. Notes from a town chronicle of Alexandria have been inserted into the last section, thus indicating the origin of the document.

EDITIONS: C. FRICK, Chron. min., 1892, 183–371 (including an attempt at re-translation into Greek); Part 3 in TH. MOMMSEN, Chron. min. 1, 1892, 272–298.
BIBLIOGRAPHY: C. FRICK, Chron. min. 1892, LXXXIII–CCIX; F. JACOBY, s.v. E.B., RE 6,2, 1566–1576. P.L.S.

Excerpta Valesiana Two different historiographic texts dating from late antiquity, which H. VALESIUS first edited in 1636 from what is today called the Cod. Berol. Phill. 1885 (9th cent.). The first excerpt (a), entitled *Origo Constantini imperatoris*, comes from a collection of biographies of emperors (mid 4th cent.) and outlines the life of emperor Constantine [1] I from the year 305. The second (b), an excerpt *ex libris chronicorum* (6th cent.), covers the era from 474 to 526, in particular the rule of Theoderic; the tradition of the text is contributed to by the Palatinus Latinus 927 (12th cent.).

EDITIONS: J. MOREAU/V. VELKOV, E.V., [2]1968, 1–10 (a), 10–29 (b); I. KÖNIG, 1987 (a), (with commentary); Id., 1997 (b).
BIBLIOGRAPHY: P. L. SCHMIDT, in: HLL, § 535 (a); J. N. ADAMS, The text and language of a vulgar Latin chronicle, 1976 (b). P.L.S.

Excubiae see → Vigiliae

Excursus (*excursus*). Interruption as a form of expansion and at the same time linguistic embellishment (*ornatus*) in narrative texts; also with the function of providing evidence of a statement in the main text: Polybius (18,35) uses an *excursus* about Aemilius Paulus as evidence of the incorruptability of the generals of Ancient Rome; at the same time he also uses this *excursus* to provide a contrast to Titus Flaminius, who is portrayed in the main text. In rhetorical terminology, the *excursus*, generally synonymous with *egressio, excursio, digressus/io* and παρέκβασις/*parékbasis*, belongs to the complex of digression from the subject (*genus expatiandi*, Quint. Inst. 4,3,1). Quintilian deals with the *excursus* in the chapter *De egressione* (Inst. 4,3,1–17). In the context of court speeches, he categorizes the *excursus* as superfluous to the five usual *partes orationis* (4,3,14). As example he mentions the praise of Sicily in the Verrines (Cic. Verr. 2,1). Quintilian also emphasizes the basic difficulty arising from use of the *excursus* for → *amplificatio*: it must be appropriate in the context and must not interrupt the presentation (Inst. 4,3,6).

The *excursus* is rarely explicitly defined as such. Thucydides refers to ἐκβολὴ τοῦ λόγου (*ekbolè toû lógou*; 1,97,2) in explaining the interpolation about the → Pentekontaetia. Sometimes the *excursus* is marked by a introductory phrase (e.g. Sall. Iug. 95,2: Sulla excursus). In the concluding phrase, the metaphor of return is often used (e.g. Pol. 18,36; Cic. Verr. 2,3,69). Occasionally the fiction of an independent speech can be found (Cic. Tusc. 5,66). However, there are not necessarily any limits on *excursi*, either in terms of their linguistic marking or their scope. Thus, Tacitus' *Germania* can be interpreted as an *excursus* [1] that has been handed down separately.

Excursi are a means of emphasizing the elaborated character of a literary text. Theoretically, they can be found in every genre, even in poetry (e.g. excursus on the annual rise of the Nile in Luc. 10,194–331), but particularly dating from Herodotus' *lógoi* in → historiography. In this context the influence of Hellenistic historiography is of particular importance (e.g. Theopompus' *excursus On the Demagogues of Athens* in the 10th book of the *Philippica*). *Excursi* can also be found in philosophical texts (Cic. Tusc. 5,64–66 on Archimedes' tomb) and scientific texts (e.g. the *excursus* on the larch in Vitr. De arch. 2,9,15–17). Sometimes epitomators refer to the deletion of the *excursus* from the original text in the foreword (e.g. Ianuarius Nepotianus in the Val. Max. epitome). – It is difficult to distinguish the *excursus* from other forms of interruption of the narrative flow. Pliny draws a parallel between the *excursus* and the → Ekphraseis in the *Aeneid* and the *Iliad* (Ep. 5,6,43). In epic poetry, Odysseus' tales (Hom. Od. 9–12) and those of Aeneas (Verg. Aen. 2–3) about their odysseys and also episodes such as the story of Hypsipyle in Statius (Theb. 5,17–498) are related to the *excursus*.

1 A.A. LUND, Tacitus Germania, 1988, 17f.

L. ECKARDT, Excursus und Ekphraseis bei Lucan, diss. Heidelberg 1936; M.v. POSER, Der abschweifende Erzähler, 1969. U.E.

Excusatio often denotes a situation in which a certain behaviour that would usually result in punishment or require compensation, remains without consequences (e.g. Paulus Dig. 13,7,16,1). In legal terminology, *excusatio* is used in particular to denote the opportunity for someone chosen for a public office (*honos*), someone affected by a burden in public interest (→ *munus*) and especially someone called to be a guardian (→ *tutela*) to excuse themselves with reference to their specific circumstances. Individual judgements by the responsible magistrates and the emperors probably eventually resulted in the creation of a system of reasons for excuses such as that presented by Modestinus (3rd cent.) in his *libri de excusationibus*. Some reasons for the use of the *excusatio*: being over 70 years old, having a large number of children of one's own (in Rome 3, in Italy 4, and in the provinces 5), three current guardianships, enmity with the ward's father. Members of certain professional groups could also excuse themselves from guardianships, as could those suffering from a physical infirmity making them unfit for the task. The guardian against his will had 50 days to pursue the claim of *excusatio* (Cod. Iust. 5,62,6).

A. GUZMAN, Dos estudios en torno a la historia de la tutela romana, 1976; M. PENTA, *Potioris nominatio* ed *excusatio* tra consuetudine e legislazione imperiale, in: Index 18, 1990, 295–316. R.WI.

Execias (Ἐξηκίας; *Exēkías*). Important potter and vase painter in the Attic black figure tradition, active between 550 and 530 BC. His potter's mark has been preserved on 15 vessels, with three of these bearing his artist's signature: neck amphora in Berlin [1. no. 12] and the belly amphorae in the Vatican [1. no. 8] and in Tarento [2]. A further 30 works in a similar style are attributed to E. The extant vase paintings must have been produced within a short time, because the → *kalos* name Onetorides can be found on the earlier as well as the later works. E.'s potter's mark on two earlier amphorae from the → E group provide evidence that he worked in this workshop, although he very soon outgrew it. He rather tended to model his paintings on those of → Nearchus. E. created new versions of several types of vessels (neck amphora, belly amphora type A, eye bowl and cup crater), and his strong, precise designs had a decisive influence on the following generation of potters. His placement of decoration and design of ornamentation were benchmarks for a long period of time. With his vase paintings, E. provided new means of expression for figurative art. Although he only had the limited means of expressive of black figure painting, he ventured into mental and spiritual areas that were previously reserved for poetry. He achieved this with new pictorial ideas and many expressive individual motifs, which are placed in careful relation to each other within well thought-out compositions. In the 'Suicide of Aias' on an amphora in Boulogne [1. no. 9], it is not the accomplished act which is portrayed, which was traditional until then, but its preparation, expressing the thoughts and emotions of the determined hero. On the eye bowl in Munich [1. no. 21], Dionysius is reclining like a drinker in a sailing boat, around whose mast a big vine has grown: an image revealing the essence of the god. The board-game between Achilles and Aias on the amphora in the Vatican [1. no. 8] is also a new pictorial motif showing the contrasting characters of the two first heros before Troy, and probably not, as is often supposed, the illustration of a lost episode of the epic.

E.'s main works were created with great technical skill; the figures, in their refined dignity, recall the sculpture of that era. In his work E. left his own unique stamp also on well-known scenes. He had a particular interest in Trojan themes, with an apparent predilection for → Aias. Aside from vases, E. also painted large clay pinakes, destined for the decoration of tomb monuments. Fragments in Berlin can be completed to a series of at least 15 tablets with pictures of the lamentation of the dead and the funeral procession. The vivid scenes and the overall design of this frieze are on a par with panel painting.

1 W. TECHNAU, E., 1936 2 F.G. LO PORTO, in: Atti del 16. Convegno di Studi sulla Magna Grecia, 1977, 730 pl. 101.

BEAZLEY, ABV, 143–149, 686f.; BEAZLEY, Paralipomena, 59–61; BEAZLEY, Addenda², 39–42; Id., The Development of Attic Black-Figure, 1951, 63–72; J. BOARDMAN, Exekias, in: AJA 82, 1978, 11–25; H. MOMMSEN, Exekias I: Die Grabtafeln, 1997; M. ROBERTSON, A History of Greek Art, 1975, 131–135. H.M.

Executor In the mancipation will of Roman law (→ Testament) the testator assigned his property by → *mancipatio* to a 'purchaser of the family' (*familiae emptor*). The latter may possibly have acted as an executor in the archaic period but there is no reference to it in any of the sources [1. 108, 679; 3. 1014]. In Classical Roman law of the 1st–3rd cents. AD, execution of wills existed as a separate institution only in embryonic form: by → *fideicommissum* an heir or legatee might be obligated to release the estate or a portion of it to another party, or by instruction (→ *mandatum*) someone might be given the duty of executing the will. The executor was not established in law as a fully developed institution until late antiquity [2; 3. 1015–1016].

1 KASER, RPR, vol. 1, 693 2 KASER, RPR, vol. 2, 485
3 B. KÜBLER, s. v. T., RE 5 A, 1013–1016. U. M.

Exedra

A. Terminology and definition
B. Graeco-Roman exedras C. Christian exedras

A. Terminology and definition

Exedra is a latinized Greek word (ἐξέδρα = outdoor seat), which started to be used by the Romans in the Republican era. On the basis of written sources, the exedra can be defined as a space open to the elements and generally having (two) columns *in antis*. An exedra could have benches and was sometimes decorated with statues of deities or commendable citizens. They had either a rectangular or semicircular ground plan, with the rectangular form being more common; in many cases there was a portico in front.

B. Graeco-Roman exedras

Exedras are found in widely differing contexts, in the Greek era, however, they were most frequently built together with a → gymnasium. Their function there was as places for conversation and discussion. Evidence of this function is provided in the section of Vitruvius dealing with the Palaestra (5,11,2), where the main room, the Ephebeum, is described as a large, rectangular exedra equipped with seats. Behind porticos there were other large exedras, also provided with seating, where philosophers, rhetors, and other learned men could sit and debate. There is archaeological evidence of exedras in Greek gymnasiums, Roman → thermal baths, and in connection with public porticos and shrines. A dedication in the form of a mosaic inscription provides proof of the existence of this type of exedra in the shrine to the Syrian gods on Delos (IDélos 2288). It was situated opposite the theatre, opened on to a portico and provided access to a space behind – an oikos. The exedra in Pompey's portico near his theatre-temple was very well known (Plut. Brutus 14; 17). It was the venue for meetings of the Senate and housed a statue of Pompey. There is also evidence that there were exedras in the villas of wealthy Romans (e.g. Cic. Fam. 7,23,3), and, according to Vitruvius (7,3,4), they were even integrated into ordinary houses. Definitive evidence is provided by papyruses from Egypt, in which the main area of a house is termed an exedra; this was always situated on the ground floor near the entrance. There is also archaeological evidence of exedras in houses in Olynthus, Priene, Pompeii, on Delos, and elsewhere. The majority of these exedras opened on to an inner courtyard sometimes lined with columns.

C. Christian exedras

In the sacred architecture of the early Christian era, the term exedra indicates a completely open space usually integrated into a church building. Gradually, the exedra came to be equated with the → apse in the choir of a church, where there was also seating. It is for this reason that exedra is often used in modern literature as the technical term for a semicircular room.

F.W. Deichmann, s.v. E., RAC 6, 1165–1174; J. Delorme, Gymnasion, 1960, 325–329; G. Hornbostel-Hüttner, Studien zur römischen Nischenarchitektur, 1979; F. Luckhard, Das Privathaus im ptolemischen und römischen Ägypten, 1914, 77–80; I. Nielsen, Thermae et Balnea, [2]1993, 165 et passim; S. Settis, 'Esedra' e 'ninfeo' nella terminologia architettonica del mondo romano, in: ANRW I 4, 661–745; B. Tamm, Auditorium and Palatium, 1963, 147–188; S. Freifrau von Thüngen, Die freistehende griechische Exedra, 1994. I.N.

Exegesis (ἐξήγησις; *exḗgēsis*)

A. Judaism B. Christianity

A. Judaism

The Jewish exegesis, which started within the biblical texts themselves in the form of explanatory glossaries and extrapolations in antiquity served to bring up to date the traditions of the sacred scriptures (→ Bible). In early Judaism, biblical stories were retold (known as the 'Rewritten Bible'), e.g. the 'Book of Jubilees' (*c.* mid

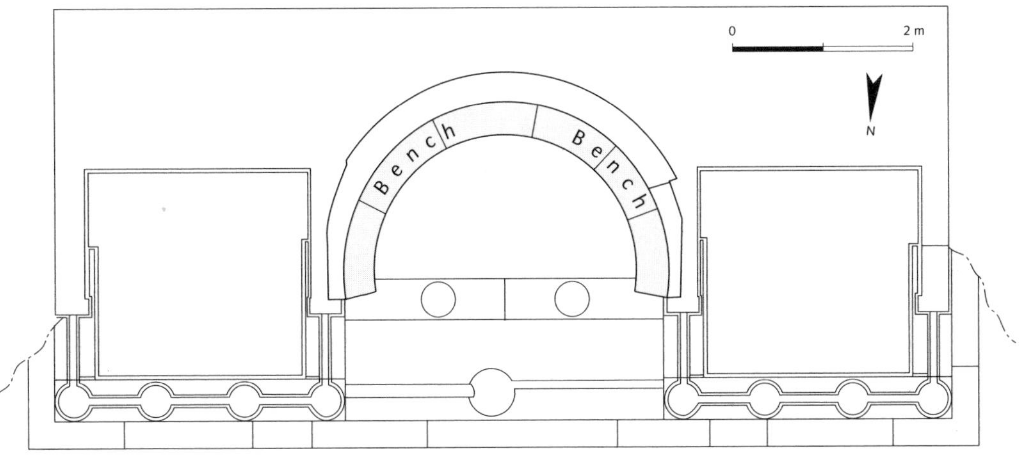

Tenos, fountain exedra (Hellenistic); top view

2nd cent. BC) or the *Liber Antiquitatum Biblicarum* (*c.* end of the 1st cent. AD). These retellings fill in narrative gaps in the biblical text, reconcile contradictions, and also add their own explanations in order to emphasize independent theological views.

In → Qumran, this type of exegesis is represented by the *Genesis Apocryphon* (*c.* 100 BC). Apart from this, the Pešer ('interpretation') genre is found here too. A distinction is made between continuous *pešarim*, which give a running interpretation of the text of the Bible and relate it to the fate of the community (e.g. *Nahum-Pešer*; *Habakkuk-Pešer*), and thematic *pešarim*, which combine different verses (e.g. 4Q Flor). The various rules of the community are also – according to the title of the Damascus document – an Halachic (→ Halakhah) interpretation of the Torah.

The first representative of the Hellenistic exposition of the Bible, for which the allegorical interpretation plays an important role in terms of the harmonization of the Torah with Greek philosophical tradition, is Aristoboulus, who wrote a pedagogic text for the young Ptolemy VI Philometor (180–145 BC). However, his work has only been preserved in a few fragments in → Eusebius [7] of Caesarea. This allegorical interpretation is developed to its fullest extent in → Philo of Alexandria's interpretation of the Pentateuch, where the correspondence between imparted law and natural law is illustrated and the allegorical interpretation is seen as the way to true knowledge of God (cf. the works *De opificio mundi*; *De Abrahamo*; *De Iosepho*; *Legum allegoriae*).

Finally, a large part of the → Rabbinical literature produced in the centuries after the destruction of the temple can be termed Biblical exegesis, where numerous *Midrašim* perform running interpretations of the biblical text in a narrative form – explaining it and making it topical in the interests of both paraenesis and edification. The reversion to biblical tradition and interpretation also plays an important role for the → Halakhah. Hermeneutic rules were developed for each of the areas of Halakhah and → Haggadah, rules which in turn are closely linked to Greek rhetoric. A large proportion of the → Targum, i.e. the Aramaic translation of the Bible, can also be ascribed to the Jewish biblical exegesis.

M. Hengel, Judentum und Hellenismus. Studien zu ihrer Begegnung unter besondere Berücksichtigung Palästinas bis zur Mitte des 2. Jh. v.Chr., 31988, s.v. Exegese, Philo von Alexandrien; G. Stemberger, Gesch. der jüdischen Literatur. Eine Einführung, 1977, 35–38, 54, 60, 80–95; Id., Einleitung in Talmud und Midrasch, 81992 (on hermeneutics: 25–40). B.E.

B. Christianity

Initially, the Christians simply took over the OT from → Judaism and adapted its tradition of interpretation (→ Philo). From the 2nd cent., however, disputes with synagogues and heretics made clarifications necessary. Then → Iustinus related the testimony of the prophets to Jesus Christ as Messiah and → Eirenaeus [2] was the first theological writer to link church tradition and exegesis with reference to the general meaning of faith (*regula fidei*). The first culmination point was → Origenes, who is seen as the advocate of the threefold meaning of Scripture (De principiis 4,2,4f.; expanded on in Cassian. Conlationes patrum 14,8 on the fourfold meaning; verse: *littera gesta docet, quid credas allegoria/moralis quid agas, quo tendas anagogia*). The opposite of this direction with its focus on → allegoresis (→ Eusebius [7] of Caesarea, → Cyrillus of Alexandria) was a tradition of literalism originating in Antioch [1] (→ Diodorus [20] of Tarsus, → Theodorus of Mopsuestia). The exegesis of late antiquity found expression in scholia (occasional brief remarks), *quaestiones et responsiones* (explanation of problematic points in the text), and the *libri commentarii* (continuous systematic commentaries) constructed according to a set scheme [1. 418f.]. In the 6th cent. the → Catenae, a collection of exegetical excerpts, were added. The first commentary in Latin was written around 300 by → Victorinus of Poetovio (now Ptuj). Important Western exegetes are → Hieronymus, → Ambrosius of Milan, → Augustinus and Pope Gregory (→ Gregorius) I.

1 A. Di Berardino, B. Studer (ed.), Storia della teologia, vol. 1, 1993, 413–436 2 H. Graf Reventlow, Epochen der Bibelauslegung, vol. 1, 1990, 104–195; vol. 2, 1994, 9–118 3 H.J. Sieben, Exegesis Patrum, 1983 (bibliography). J.RI.

Exegetai (ἐξηγηταί/*exēgētaí*, from the Greek ἐξηγέομαι/*exēgéomai*, 'interpret, expound'). In general terms, the advisors, interpreters, and leaders; specifically the expounders of the originally oral tradition of sacred law in Athens. There were three categories of *exegetai* who enjoyed lifelong office: the *Eumolpidṓn*, appointed from among the Eumolpidae; the *Pythóchrēstoi*, appointed by the Delphic oracle, and the *Eupatridṓn* selected by the demos (people) from the → Eupatridae. [1. 24–40; 2. 34–52]. The *exegetai Eumolpidṓn* were responsible for the correct observance of the Eleusinian cult (IG I3 78 l. 36f.; Lys. 6,10; And. 115f.; [3; 4. 83; 5. 161–169; 6. 53f., 296]). In the 5th cent., the whole family may have had collective responsibility for the interpretation of sacred law, whereas later the task was carried out by a council of two or three *exegetai*. [2. 19–23, 37–42; 3. 89–92; 6. 295f.]. There still is dispute about the timing of the introduction of the offices of the *exegetes Pythóchrēstos* and the *exegetes Eupatridṓn* (under Solon (early 6th cent. BC) [1. 21f.; cf. 6. 220] or in 403 BC [2. 18–33; 7. 164–174; 4. 115]), the number of the *exegetai Pythóchrēstoi* in the classical era [1. 27–41; 7. 162–164], and about their being fed in the → Prytaneion (IG I3 131, 440/32). These non-Eleusinian *exegetai* provided information about cult regulations at the request of private individuals and the demos, in particular as regards ritual cleansing and sacrifices (Pl. Euthphr. 4 cd; Leg. 958 d; Demosth. 47,70; Isaeus 8,38f.; Theophr. Char. 16,6; IG II2 403; SEG 26, 121 l.

13f.; [1. 41–51; 2. 29, 43, 63f.; 8]); it is uncertain whether disregarding their interpretation was punishable [6. 53f.]. The literature of sacred law (*Exegetika*), known since the 4th cent., arose in part from their activities (FGrH 323 F 14; FGrH 352–356) [9. 6–12]. In several places outside Athens, *exegetai* were entrusted with different duties, such as the *exēgētḗs* (or *periēgētḗs*) in Olympia, who belonged to the cult personnel and probably functioned as a 'tourist guide' (Syll.[3] 1021 I. 20; Paus. 5,15,10), and the *exegetai* who were responsible for the municipal administration of Alexandria [10. 102–104].

→ Eleusis; → Eumolpus

1 F. JACOBY, Atthis, 1949 2 J. H. OLIVER, The Athenian Expounders of the Sacred and Ancestral Law, 1950 3 K. CLINTON, The Sacred Officials of the Eleusinian Mysteries, 1972 4 R. S. J. GARLAND, Religious Authority in Archaic and Classical Athens, in: ABSA 79, 1984, 75–123 5 M. OSTWALD, From Popular Sovereignty to the Sovereignty of Law, 1986 6 R. PARKER, Athenian Religion: A History, 1996 7 J. H. OLIVER, Jacoby's Treatment of the E., in: AJPh 75, 1954, 160–174 8 F. BOURRIOT, Recherches sur la nature de genos, 1976, 407–423 9 A. TRESP, Die Fragmente der griechischen Kultschriftsteller, 1914 10 D. DELIA, Alexandrian Citizenship during the Roman Principate, 1991. A.C.

Exempla see → Valerius [III 5] Maximus; → Rhetoric V.

Exercitatio A frequent repetition of a certain activity (γυμνασία, προγύμνασμα, μελέτη) to the point of habit (Rhet. Her. 1,3; Cic. De or. 2,358), the aim of which was to acquire or hone a skill – either physical or intellectual. The literature of rhetoric is mainly concerned with the latter. It envisioned daily practice in writing, reading, and speaking (Quint. Inst. 10,7,27; cf. Cic. Brut. 309), which was designed to amplify the natural talent of youths who wanted to become orators (Quint. Inst. 1 pr. 27) and enabled the learning of the individual rules to become habitual (Quint. Inst. 2,4,17; cf. the connection between *exercitatio* and *consuetudo* e.g. in Cic. De or. 1,81; 2,32), so that this constant practice allowed the speaker to improvise without the listener noticing this *ex tempore dicendi facultas* (Quint. Inst. 10,7,1) (Cic. De or. 1,152; Orat. 200; Quint. Inst. 10,7,7). Conceived as a necessary supplement to the duality of educational factors *ars/doctrina* and *natural ingenium* (theory and aptitude), the *exercitatio* had already been considered by the old Sophists to fall within the well-known triad φύσις (*phýsis*), τέχνη (*téchnē*) or ἐπιστήμη (*epistḗmē*), and μελέτη (*melétē*; own talent, technical direction, practice), and was so later by Isocrates (Antid. 187; Adv. soph. 14ff.), Plato (Phdr. 269d), and Aristotle (Diog. Laert. 5,18). Cicero ascribes enormous importance to *exercitatio* from Inv. 1,2 on (cf. e.g. De or. 1,148ff.; 2,232; Brut. 25), the author of *Rhetorica ad Herennium* concludes his didactic work with an emphatic application of *exercitatio*. (4,69). Quintilian, who prizes it as the most effective method of learning (Inst. 2,17,13), dedicates a large amount of space to detailing the various exercises. *Exercitatio* was not limited to school exercises but required lifelong practice and was linked to the *partes rhetorices* (→ officia orationis), the *partes orationis* (parts of speech) and the → *genera causarum*. Writing was especially necessary for the *exercitatio* (Cic. De or. 1,150, Quint. Inst. 10,3,4–10,5,15), particularly translation from Greek into Latin and paraphrases of progressively more difficult texts. Regarding the *memoria*, the orator could improve his memory through various exercises (Rhet. Her. 3,39; Cic. De or. 1,157; Quint. Inst. 11,2,40). In presentation, the *exercitatio* played a particularly important role in nurturing the voice (Rhet. Her. 3,20; Quint. Inst. 11,3,22) and teaching the use of body language in achieving the appropriate emphasis (Rhet. Her. 3,27; Quint. Inst. 11,3,29).

→ Education; → Progymnasma

1 B. APPEL, Das Bildungs- und Erziehungsideal Quintilians nach der Institutio oratoria, 1914 2 S. F. BONNER, Roman Declamation in the Late Republic and Early Empire, 1969 3 Id., Education in Ancient Rome, 1977 4 L. CALBOLI MONTEFUSCO, Quintilian and the Function of Oratorical exercitation, in: Latomus 55, 1996, 615–625 5 A. N. CIZEK, Imitatio et tractatio, 1994 6 G. FUNKE, Gewohnheit, in: Archiv für Begriffsgeschichte 3, 1958, 99–118 7 H. I. MARROU, Histoire de l'éducation dans l'antiquité, 1948 8 J. MURPHY, Quintilian, On the Teaching of Speaking and Writing, 1987 9 P. SHOREY, Φύσις, Μελέτη, Ἐπιστήμη, in: TAPhA 39, 1908, 185–201 10 T. VILJAMA, From Grammar to Rhetoric, in: Arctos 22, 1988, 179–201. L.C.M.

Exhaireseos dike (ἐξαιρέσεως δίκη; *ex(h)airéseōs díkē*). In Athens, anyone who claimed that someone else was his slave needed no special authority in order to 'lead away' (ἄγειν, *ágein*) the person concerned. A third party could then intervene and 'free' (ἐξαιρεῖσθαι or ἀφαιρεῖσθαι εἰς ἐλευθερίαν, *ex(h)aireîsthai / aphaireîsthai eis eleutherían*; Aeschin. in Timarchum 62; Demosth. Or. 59,40; Lys. 23,9) the captive with an act of formalized violence. The captor then had to free the captive, although only on receipt of surety, and could then proceed against the third party arguing *exhaireseos dike*. If he won the case, the slave belonged to him and the accused had to pay a fine, of which half was payable to the state. It is possible that the beginning of the Great Law Code of → Gortyn could be interpreted in this sense.

A. KRÄNZLEIN, Eigentum und Besitz im griechischen Recht, 1963, 159ff.; A. R. W. HARRISON, The Law of Athens I, 1968, 178ff.; A. MAFFI, in: Symposion 1995, edited by G. THÜR, J. VÉLISSAROPOULOS, 1997, 17–25. G.T.

Exheredatio Disinheritance. Archaic Roman law allowed the appointment of an inheritor in a will probably only when there was no *suus heres* (family heir). Later, it became possible to appoint one among several

→ *sui heredes* as an heir and to disinherit the rest. In the historical era there were no limits on the disinheritance of *sui*, but this had to be expressly stated in the will. Sons had to be disinherited by name, other *sui* (wife – *uxor in manu* –, grandchildren, great-grandchildren etc. of both sexes) could be disinherited *inter ceteros* (as a group without stating their names); if this form of disinheritance was not followed, the will was completely ineffective in case of the → *praeteritio* ('passing over') of sons, whereas *ceteri* passed over received one share of the inheritance where *sui* had been nominated or half of the inheritance where there were *extranei* (heirs outside the family). If the correct form was followed, disinheritance was automatically effective (Dig. 28,2; Cod. Iust. 6,28). From the beginning of the Imperial period, a child who had been formally disinherited for no stated reason could obtain a quarter of his legal inheritance by → *querela inofficiosi testamenti* (contesting the will). From the *querela* developed the Justinian right to a compulsory share of an inheritance, which is preserved in modern inheritance law (Dig. 5,2; Cod. Iust. 3,28).
→ Succession, law of II E; → Postumus

1 HONSELL/MAYER-MALY/SELB, 463ff. 2 Kaser, RPR I, 705ff.

U.M.

Exilarch The Exilarch (Aramaic *rēš alūṯā*, 'Head of the diaspora') was the leader of the Babylonian Jews and the official representative at the court of the Parthian king in the Talmudic and Gaonic periods (*c.* 3rd–10th cents. AD). This institution, which claimed its origins in the House of David, was probably introduced during the administrative reforms of Vologaeses. I. (AD 51–79) [3]. The first certain details about the office date from the 3rd cent. (cf. yKil 9,4ff [32b]). The Exilarch had authority primarily in juridical and legal judgments. As his competence in matters pertaining to religious law was far less than that of the rabbis, there were often attacks from this quarter. There are also reports of disputes with the Palestinian patriarchs.

1 E. BASHAN, s.v. E., in: Encyclopedia Judaica 6, 1023–1034 2 M. JACOBS, Die Institution des jüdischen Patriarchen. Eine quellen- und traditionskritische Studie zur Geschichte des Judentums in der Spätantike, in: Texte und Studien zum antiken Judentum 52, 1995, 225–231 3 J. NEUSNER, History of the Jews in Babylonia I, 1965, 50–58, 97–112; II, 1966, 92–125; III, 1968, 41–49; IV 1968, 73–124 4 G. STEMBERGER, Das klassische Judentum. Kultur und Geschichte der rabbinischen Zeit, 1979, 73–79.

B.E.

Exile, literature of A distinction must be made between the two types of literature of exile: texts describing the fate of exiles or refugees and those written by exiles themselves, which detail their experiences and feelings. Examples of the first category are → Odysseus, → Aeneas, and → Oedipus and the second → Cicero, → Ovidius, and → Seneca.

In Homer's epics, the subject is addressed (Hom. Il. 9,648) and reflected on (Od. 15,343–5), as it is in early Greek lyric poetry (i.a. Tyrtaeus fr. 6 D = Hor. Carm. 3,2,13; Alc. 24 D; Thgn. 1197–1202 = Verg. Ecl. 1,70 f.). The *locus classicus* is Eur. Phoen. 357–442, the analytical dialogue between Polynices and Jocasta about the key aspects of the suffering of refugees; in a similar vein there are also Isoc. Or. 19,23–27 and 14,46–50. The subject also has its place in the Hellenistic → diatribe in various *de exilio* texts as in Teles, Musonius, Dion Chrys. 13, Plut. Mor. 599a–607f, Favorinus, Cass. Dio 38,18–29, Cic. Tusc. 5,105–109 and Paradoxa Stoicorum 18,27–32, as well as Sen. Dial. 12.

The problematic nature of being away from one's homeland is best detailed in prose in Cicero's letters from his time in banishment and in poetry in the works of Ovid written in exile; even Vergil thematized the sorrowful experiences of exile in Ecl. 1 (cf. Catal. 3 and 8) and in various characters in the *Aeneid*.

E. DOBLHOFER, Exil und Emigration, 1987; H. FROESCH, Exul poeta, in: H.-J. GLÜCKLICH (ed.), Lateinische Literatur, heute wirkend, 1987, 1,51–64; G.D. WILLIAMS, Banished Voices. Readings in Ovid's Exile Poetry, 1995.

B.KY.

Exilium Term used both for banishment and for the place of banishment. During the era of the Twelve Tablets (5th cent. BC), it was probably already permissible for the perpetrator of a capital offence to avoid the punishment (blood revenge) by voluntarily exiling himself from Roman territory. In the *iudicium populi* (trial in the People's Court) the accused had the option of voluntarily going into exile up to the point of sentencing; after this the magistrate responsible for enforcing the judgment could sanction the escape. There were arrangements with some towns regarding the acceptance of exiles. Initially these were places without Roman citizenship in Latium (e.g. Tibur, Praeneste) or Greek Neapolis (Naples), later outside Italy. If the flight into exile was followed by → *aqua et igni interdictio*, the accused then lost their citizenship and their assets, and if they returned they were subject to the death penalty. This same practice was common in → *quaestio* trials. *Exilium* usually replaced the enforcement of the death penalty against *honestiores*, and was therefore viewed as a punishment. *Exilium* was first provided as a legal punishment (*poena legis)* in the *lex Tullia de ambitu* (63 BC). In the Imperial period, *exilium* was replaced by permanent → *deportatio*, and temporary → *relegatio*; the term *exilium* was used by lawyers to refer to both. The experience of *exilium* resulted in numerous literary discussions (e.g. in Cicero, Ovid, Seneca; → Exile, literature of).

G. CRIFÒ, Ricerche sull' 'e.' nel periodo repubblicano I, 1961 (also M. FUHRMANN, in: ZRG 80, 1963, 451–457); Id., L'esclusione dalla città, 1985; E. DOBLHOFER, Exil und Emigration, 1987,; E.L. GRASMÜCK, E., 1978, 62–148; E. LEVY, Die römischen Kapitalstrafe, in: Gesammelte Schriften 2, 1963, 334–347; MOMMSEN, Strafrecht, 68–73. R.GA.

Exitus illustrium virorum Sub-genre encompassing works which have as their theme the literary stylization of the deaths of famous men, generally the victims of tyranny: the stoically stylized deaths of Cato (Plut. Cato min. 68ff.) and Seneca (Tac. Ann. 15,60ff.) reflect this influence. The genre also covers the thematization of the deaths of rulers or generals. The name derives from Plin. Ep. 8,12,4, where he writes of the *exitus illustrium virorum* of one Titinius Capito. Cicero refers to rhetoric as context when he compiles *Exitus clarissimorum virorum nostrae civitatis* as *exempla consolationis* ('consoling examples') (Div. 2,22). This also explains the closeness to *exempla* collections (→ Valerius Maximus). There are close links with the *Teleutaí* genre (3rd–2nd cents. BC), for which the archetype is the death of Socrates. However, the description in Xenophon of the death of Cyrus and his last words is also significant (Cyr. 8,7,6–28). The collections of *novissima verba* ('last words') are also closely related, as are the → *acta sanctorum/martyrum*, which are not limited to Judaeo-Christian literature, and descriptions of the demise of the tormentors.

A. RONCONI, s.v. E.I.V., RAC 6, 1558–1568. U.E.

Exkoubitai (ἐξκουβῖται). Military guard unit for the protection of the emperor, created by → Leo I the Great. This military unit was put together in order to prevent any inefficiency of the *tágma tôn scholôn*, and was commanded by a *comes* (known as the *comes excubitorum*), who had considerable influence with the emperor, particularly during the 6th and 7th cents. From the 8th cent. the *comes* was replaced by the *domesticus*, who according to BURY [3. 57] was of lower rank. To this guard unit belonged also other officers such as *topotērētḗs*, *chartulárioi*, *scríbōnes*, a *prōtomandátōr*, *drakōnárioi* and *skeuophóroi*. The soldiers of the *exkoubitai* unit received more pay than the norm, as their physical superiority was obvious and a recruitment requirement.

1 J. F. HALDON, Byzantine Praetorians, 1984 2 A. KAZHDAN, s.v. Domestikos ton exkoubiton, ODB 1, 646f. 3 J. B. BURY, The Imperial Administrative System in the Ninth Century, with the Revised Text of the Kletologion of Philotheos, 1911. A.P.

Exodos (ἔξοδος, generally 'departure', 'end'). According to Aristot. Poet. 1452b 21f., the *exodos* is the part of a tragedy which is not followed by a chorus (→ Stasimon) (concluding act). Moving from this broad definition, it probably makes more sense to define the *exodos* in a narrower sense as the exit of the chorus at the end of a drama (cf. Aristoph. Vesp. 582). The most frequent form in tragedy is the '*ecce* conclusion': the deed and the doer are presented in a pathos-laden concluding scene (initially usually indirectly by means of a messenger's report [→ Messenger scenes]), the events are interpreted and generalized and there is a glimpse into the future (e.g. Aesch. Pers. 908ff.; Aesch. Sept. 861ff.; Soph. Trach. 971ff.; Soph. Ant. 1155ff.; Soph. OT 1223ff.; Eur. Med. 1293ff.; Eur. Hipp. 1151ff.; Eur. HF 910ff.; Eur. Bacch. 1024ff.). Less frequently, the plot takes a new turn in the *exodus* and is brought to a conclusion only in the last scenes of the play (e.g. Aesch. Eum. 778ff.; Aesch. Prom. 907ff.; Soph. Aj. 1223ff.; Soph. El. 1398ff.; Soph. Phil. 1218ff.; Eur. Alc. 1006ff., Eur. IT 1284ff., Eur. Hel. 1512ff.). A hybrid form can be found in Euripides (Eur. Ion 1106ff.; Eur. Phoen. 1308ff.; Eur. Or. 1549ff.). In comedy, the *exodus* represents the peak of the exemplification scenes which show the triumph of the comic hero, and often ends with a *komos* (Aristoph. Ach., Eccl.), wedding procession (Aristoph. Pax, Av.), or a lively dancing scene (Aristoph. Vesp., Lys.).

G. KREMER, Die Struktur des Tragödienschlusses, in: W. JENS (ed.), Die Bauformen der griechischen Tragödie, 1971, 117–141; B. ZIMMERMANN, Untersuchung zur Form und dramatischen Technik der Aristophanischen Komödien II, 1985, 75–90. B.Z.

Exomosia (ἐξωμοσία), literally 'denial on oath of knowledge'. 1) In the procedural law of Athens, witnesses could avoid the obligation to appear in court (and confirm evidence which had been pre-formulated by one of the two parties in the case) by swearing ceremonial oaths out of court to the effect that they 'did not know' the facts in question. The *exōmosía* did not entail any legal sanctions, only positive testimony in court could be sued for (→ *pseudomartyríōn díkē*). There is evidence of a similar system recorded as *apōmosía* in the indemnity contract of Stymphalus (IPArk 17,13), which should not be confused with the Athenian → *hypōmosía*, sometimes called *exōmosía*. 2) In Athens it was possible to avoid the obligation of taking on an office, particularly an envoyship, by swearing a formal *exōmosía* on the grounds of poverty, illness, or other significant reasons.

A. R. W. HARRISON, The Law of Athens II, 1971, 139f.; G. THÜR, Beweisführung vor den Schwurgerichtshöfen Athens, 1977, 140, 317; G. THÜR, H. TAEUBER, Prozeßrechtliche Inschrifte der griechischen Poleis. Arkadien, 1994, 239f. G.T.

Exorcism In the strict sense, this is the ritual driving out of a demon (→ Demons), who is causing an illness in the person possessed. The process primarily involves the use of verbal rites (ἐπῳδαί, *carmina*) (Isid. Orig. 6,19,55: *sermo increpationis in diabolum ut excedat*): the exorcist makes verbal contact with the demon and forces it to leave the person. The Greek root ἐξορκίζειν (*ex(h)orkízein*), which originally merely meant 'to swear' (dating from Demosthenes; ἐξορκισμός; *ex(h)orkismós*, 'oath', Pol. 6,21,6), is understood in this context as 'to conjure out'.

In this sense, exorcism in the Graeco-Roman world from the Hellenistic era onwards was affected particularly by Egyptian but also by Jewish influences. An exorcism runs according to a set course [1; 2. 78–82]: the exorcist must make the demon speak by calling it by name (using a vague formula if necessary: PGM IV 1240) and by ritual (PGM XIII 243; a dumb demon in Mk 9,25). By this he invokes a powerful god, usually with a name formed of magical incantations (see PGM IV 1228–1264; 3009–3086). Professional exorcists can also talk to the demon in foreign languages (Lucian. Philopseudes 34,15; Hier. Vita Hilarionis 18). The demon must identify itself by name or by displaying its influence (Mk 5,9). It can manifest its departure by entering an object and destroying it (cf. the Jewish exorcist Eleazar before Vespasian: Jos. Ant. Iud. 8,45–47; Apollonius of Tyana: Philostr. VA 4,20; Jesus and the swineherd of Gerasa: Mk 5,12f.; Lc 8,29). The magic papyruses are a particularly good source of detailed exorcism rites and the relevant incantations [2. 9–15].

In Jewish exorcism the powerful name used is that of the 'God of Abraham, Isaac, and Jacob' (Orig. contra Celsum 4,33). In the NT, Mark (from the exorcism in the synagogue at Capernaum: Mk 1,21–28) presents → Jesus several times as an exorcizing healer. However, while Jesus banishes demons in the name of his own authority, his successors do it in his name – from Paul's healing of someone possessed (πύθων, *pýthōn*: Acts 16,16) to the saints (e.g. Athan. Vita Antonii 63,637). Although the name of Jesus (PGM IV 3021) is even used by Jewish (Acts 19,13f.) and pagan exorcists.

In some pagan and also some Christian reports it is possible to detect a certain distrust of the mechanical rite. This is also obvious in the criticism of Celsus (in Orig. contra Celsum 4,33). Miracle men such as → Apollonius [14] of Tyana or his brahman teacher do not need a formula, but seek to converse with the demon (Philostr. VA 4,25; 3,28), as does Hilarion (Hier. Vita Hilarionis 18). Saint Antonius even prays with the possessed (Athan. Vita Antonii 64,637). This, however, is theological fiction; in practice, the exorcism formula is used constantly and successfully to heal the sick [3].

In a broader sense, the term exorcism is used to mean the curing of any illnesses and disturbances caused by demonic or magical influences. There is good evidence of these types of rites in various collections from the Ancient Orient [4]. Demonic possession was a common explanation of madness in Greece in the 5th cent. BC (see Soph. Trach. 1235; Eur. Hipp. 141–144) and cathartic rituals including special diets (→ Epilepsy: Hippoc. De morbo sacro 18,6) or dance and music (Pl. Leg. 7,790d-e) were used to cure it. Magic bonds (→ Defixio) as a cause of speech defects and otherwise inexplicable problems were recognized from the 5th cent. onwards; they are released by a specialist, known as the 'deliverer' (ἀναλύτης, *analýtēs*) about whose rites nothing is known, but which are probably cathartic, as well as having the aim of destroying the binding magic (Poll. 7,188, according to Magnes Lydoi fr. 4 PCG V; Phot. 1548, according to Men. Heros fr. 5 Sandbach; Hsch. s.v. περικαθαίρων). This technique is also recorded in the chronicles of the lives of Christian saints. Infrequently, this type of magic is resolved through a polis ritual [5].

It is not always possible to clearly distinguish exorcisms, which are curative, from rites and amulets, which are to prevent demonic attacks: although the two areas are in theory distinguishable, the ritual practice of both is very similar, with closely linked formulae and rites [6]. The use of incantations (*epoidaí*) in medicine is a completely separate matter [7] and does not concern demonic involvement. There are records of this type of incantation from the time the blood from Odysseus' thigh wound was staunched (Hom. Od. 19,457f. [8]); Plato counts them as legitimate medical techniques (Resp. 426b), as do the Pythagoreans (Porph. Vita Pythagorae 30). Galen used Homeric verses (Alexander Trallianus 2,474; Iambl. VP 29,164).

1 C. Bonner, The Technique of Exorcism, in: Harvard Theological Review 36, 1943, 39–49 2 J. Tambornino, De antiquorum daemonismo, 1909 3 P. Brown, The Holy Man, in: Id., Society and the Holy in Late Antiquity, 1982, 83 4 J. Bottéro, Mythes et rites de Babylone, 1985, 65–112; 163–219 5 F. Graf, An Oracle against Pestilence from a Western Anatolian Town, in: ZPE 92, 1992, 267–278 6 R. Kotansky, Greek Exorcistic Amulets, in: M. Meyer, P. Mirecki (ed.), Ancient Magic and Ritual Power, 1995, 243–277 7 W.D. Furley, Besprechung und Behandlung. Zur Form und Funktion von ΕΠΩΔΑΙ in der griechischen Zaubermedizin, in: Philanthropia kai Eusebeia. FS A. Dihle, 1994, 80–104 8 R. Renehan, The Staunching of Odysseus' Blood. The Healing-Powers of Magic, in: AJPh 113, 1992, 1–4.

P. Canivet, A. Adnés, Guérisons miraculeuses et exorcismes dans l'Histoire Philotée, in: RHR 171, 1967, 53–82; 149–179; D. C. Duling, Solomon, Exorcism, and the Son of David, in: Harvard Theological Review 68, 1975, 235–252; R. Merkelbach, Exorzismen und jüdisch-christlich beeinflußte Texte, in: Abrasax. Ausgewählte Papyri religiösen und magischen Inhalts 4, 1996; P.A. Rodewyk, Die dämonische Besessenheit in der Sicht des Rituale Romanum, 1963; K. Thraede, s.v. E., RAC 7, 44–117.

F.G.

Exordium In the construction of a speech, the *exordium* represented the first part (*principium*, *pro(h)oemium*, Greek *prooímion*). It had three objectives: to inform the listeners, to attract their attention, and to obtain their goodwill by preparing them for the rest of the speech (Cic. Inv. 1,20). This principle, which is already obvious in Aristot. Rhetorica ad Alexandrum 1436a 33ff., remained a constant of Latin and Greek rhetoric into late antiquity. The inspiration for the content of the *exordium* came from the nature of the speaker, the opponent, and the judge, as well as the case itself (Aristot. Rh. 1415a 26f.; Cic. De or. 2,321). Quint. Inst. 4,1,6f. adapted this to Roman legal practice and distinguished the person of the *actor causae* from that of the *litigator*, raising the number of the *personae* to four. The use of the *exordium* hinged on the nature of the *causa*; it could therefore be omitted in *genus honestum* (*éndoxon*) (Aug. 148,30ff. HALM), because the listener was already well-disposed towards the speaker. The *exordium* was also superfluous if the listeners were already informed about the subject (in the *genus deliberativum*, Aristot. Rh. 1415b 34f.; in simple and unambiguous cases). On occasion, the *vis prohoemii* could be desirable at various moments during the course of the speech, and the *exordium* was then called a *merikón* (Fortunatianus, Ars rhet. 127,2f. CALBOLI MONTEFUSCO). In terms of form, the *exordium* had to be proportional to the case in length and complexity (Cic. De or. 2,320; Quint. Inst. 4,1,62) and had to have enough of a connection with the rest of the speech in order to form a coherent structure. The speaker had to exercise a certain amount of restraint in his choice of words in the *exordium* as regards embellishment and presentation (Cic. Orat. 124; Quint. Inst. 4,1,55ff.), because the impression of exaggerated affectation made both the speech and the speaker less credible (Cic. Inv. 1,25). The *insinuatio* was a specialized form of the *exordium*.

→ Partes orationis; → Rhetoric

E.W. BOWER, ΕΦΟΔΟΣ and insinuatio in the Greek and Latin Rhetoric, in: CQ 52, 1958, 224–230; G. CALBOLI, Due questioni filologiche, in: Maia 23, 1971, 115–128; L. CALBOLI MONTEFUSCO, E., Narratio, Epilogus, 1988; J. CHRISTES, Realitätsnähe und formale Systematik in der Lehre vom E. der Rede, in: Hermes 106, 1978, 556–573; F.P. DONNELLY, A Function of the Classical E., in: Classical Weekly 5, 1911–1912, 204–207; CH. KÖHLER, Die Proömientechnik in Ciceros Reden, 1968; C. LOUTSCH, L'exorde dans les discours de Cicéron, 1994; R. VOLKMANN, Die Rhetorik der Griechen, [2]1885. L.C.M.

Exoteric/Esoteric see → Philosophical literature, genres of

Exoules dike (ἐξούλης δίκη). In Athens, a charge of 'expulsion' was a criminal charge. It was available to privileged claimants (e.g. the successful creditor in a lawsuit) against debtors who resisted, by formally expelling the creditor, the justified seizure of property by the creditor's formalized use of force. The expelled party could raise the charge of *e.d.*; if he could justify his action, the expeller was sentenced to a fine of double the value of the land. It was divided between the claimant and the state, in accordance with a law of → Solon's.

E. RABEL, Δίκη ἐξούλης und Verwandtes, in: ZRG 36, 1915, 340–380; A. KRÄNZLEIN, Eigentum und Besitz im griechischen Recht, 1963, 166; A.R.W. HARRISON, The Law of Athens I, 1968, 311f. G.T.

Expeditio The basic meaning of the Latin verb *expedire* is 'to remove the foot from its bond', in a military context it means 'to make ready', 'to make ready for battle'. *Expeditio* is the term for a hunt (Arnob. 3,21: *venationum praepotens* [...] *in expeditionibus Diana*), but especially for a campaign against an enemy and thus originally for only a part of warfare (*bellum*), as suggested by the division of the *expeditio* into march and battle (Liv. 3,12,5: *egregia facinora nunc in expeditionibus, nunc in acie*). *Expeditio* as the term for operations within a larger war is found in inscriptions of the Principate, for example, the *expeditio per regnum Decebali regis Dacorum* of C. Velius [5] Rufus in AD 89 in the context of the *bellum Marcomannorum Quadorum Sarmatarum*, of the 1st Pannonian War under Domitian [1] (AE 1903,368) or the *expeditio Burica* (CIL III 5937) probably in the context of the 2nd Marcomannic War (178–180) of Marcus [2] Aurelius. After the 1st cent. AD, *expeditio* could be the term for the whole war in a similar manner as *bellum*.

In inscriptions, *expeditio*, especially in association with the name of an adjective derived from the name of a hostile people (e.g., *expeditio Germanica*), attests to the emperor's personal participation in the campaign. The first epigraphical occurrence of *expeditio* refers to Caligula's sham campaigns (CIL III 6809=ILS 2696). Claudius' [III 1] campaign against Britain may also have been called *expeditio Britannica* (CIL XIII 5125, fragmentary); the next campaign led by a ruler was the *expeditio Germanica* of Domitian [1] (CIL XIV 3612= ILS 1025). The meaning of *expeditio* is particularly evident in the case of the → Jewish Wars. The 1st Jewish War (AD 66–71), which was led by Vespasian before his elevation as princeps and later by Titus [3] as deputy of the princeps, was called the *bellum Iudaicum* but never the *expeditio Iudaica*. The 2nd Jewish War (132–135), in which Hadrian personally participated, was also called the *expeditio Iudaica* (e.g., CIL VI 1523 = ILS 1092; VI 3505). The literary sources support this impression (e.g., Suet. Tib. 37,4; Suet. Claud. 17,1).

The differential frequency of the epigraphical testimonials for *expeditio* and *bellum* are remarkable. In the 1st cent. AD, six occurrences for *expeditio* are juxtaposed by 52 for *bellum*, while in the 2nd cent. up to Antoninus [1] Pius there are 20 occurrences for *expeditio* and 37 for *bellum*. However, a change is noticeable under Marcus [2] Aurelius: *expeditio* occurs in 25 cases, *bellum* in 14 cases; under the Severans *expeditio* clearly predominates with 21 occurrences against one occurrence for *bellum*. Later epigraphical attestations are rare because of the general decline of inscriptions. The increased use of *expeditio* is a significant indicator that the princeps personally looked after the fortunate outcome of wars. Finally, the → *felicitas* of the princeps, his fortunate victoriousness, is reflected in formulas attested from the time of Marcus Aurelius such as *expeditio felicissima II Germanica* (CIL V 2155=ILS 1574); by contrast, *bellum felicissimum* is not attested. The Greek equivalent to *expeditio* is στρατεία/*strateía* (AE 1958,15; Cass. Dio 60,21,2).

→ Armies III.

1 G. ALFÖLDY, Bellum Mauricum, in: Chiron 15, 1985, 91–109 2 V. ROSENBERGER, Bella et expeditiones, 1992. V. RO.

Experience (ἐμπειρία, *empeiría*, or πεῖρα, *peîra*). An epistemological faculty, which mediates between perception and knowledge or skill and is related to memory even in its earliest recorded mention by Anaxagoras (Anaxag. frg. 59 B 21b DK). Plato makes an explicit distinction between experience on the one and knowledge (ἐπιστήμη/*epistḗmē*) and skill (τέχνη/*téchnē*) on the other hand, because it is not focused either on generalities or on causes; rather it represents a familiarity with individual facts, which is linked to habit and makes possible a well-ordered life (cf. Pl. Grg. 448c; 463a; Resp. 409b; 422c; 582a; Phdr. 270b; Leg. 720c; 857c; 938a). Aristotle arranges these ideas very precisely: experience consists of the knowledge of a finite number of similar individual facts originating from perception and kept in the memory, the similarity of which is expressly registered in the framework of their induction. In this respect, experience presents a plausible, if not logically cogent basis for universal statements (cf. Aristot. An. post. 2,19,100a; Metaph. 1,1,980b–981b; Phys. 7,3,247b20f.). Similarly, the Stoics determine experience as a mass of comparable sensory ideas (SVF II 83; and SVF I 216; III 4,12–14: A good life rests on experience). The empirical medical school of Hellenism (→ Empiricists) expanded the term 'experience' (*empeiría* or *peîra*) to include knowledge of that which happens occasionally, often, or regularly and is based on individual observations (see [1]).

1 J. Barnes, Medicine, Experience and Logic, in: Id. et al.(ed.), Science and Speculation, 1982.

L. Bourgey, Observation et expérience chez Aristote, 1955; P.H. and E.A. DeLacy, Philodemus: On Methods of Inference, ²1978.

W.DE.

Expiatory rites reestablished a state between the gods and humans as it existed before a knowing or unknowing failing of humans. Expiatory rites (ER) are strategies for handling ill fortune and generate a community spirit among those in whose name they are performed.

In the Greek world ER were practiced in the archaic and classical period (→ Purification), but can also be proven for later times. When a small town in Lydia was visited by an epidemic in the 2nd cent. AD, a delegation was sent to the → oracle of → Clarus [1]. → Apollo commanded that the houses be sprinkled with a mixture of water from seven sources and demanded as his reward a statue that represented him as an archer [1. 396–399].

The Romans used ER to restore divine favour (→ *pax deorum*). It was only rarely clear to the Romans at which deity to direct the expiatory rite to. According to Cato Agr. 139 before pruning trees a pig was to be sacrificed to the deity thought to be present at the location with the phrase *si deus si dea es* ('whether you be god or goddess'); the expiatory rite was performed in this case before the fault. This type of piacular sacrifice (→ *piaculum*) is described, for example, in the *commentarii* ('Records') of the → *Arvales fratres*. At official level ER were used at the beginning of the year to expiate the prodigies of the previous year. Just as the → *prodigium* violated boundaries, the expiatory rite served to symbolically restore them. The essential part of ER for prodigia were → sacrifices and → processions of which there were numerous variants: a procession of all citizens of a town (→ *lustratio*), a procession of select persons through the town, sacrifices at all cultic images, a feast together with the images of the deities (→ *lectisternium*). Hails of stones were expiated with a nine-day feast (*novendiale sacrum*); hermaphrodites were thrown into the sea (cf., e.g., Liv. 27,11,1–6). In special cases, there was resort to → human sacrifices: a pair of Gauls and a pair of Greeks respectively were buried alive in the Forum Boarium at Rome in 228, 216 and 114/13 BC. If a → Vestal broke her vow of chastity, she was also buried alive.

Even though several Roman ER can be broadly understood as → scapegoat rituals (→ *pharmakós* [2]), only one such ritual in the narrow sense is attested: in 101 BC a goat with burning torches on its horns was chased out of Rome (Obseq. 44a).

→ Ritual

1 R. Merkelbach, J. Stauber (ed.), Steinepigramme aus dem griech. Osten, vol. 1, 1998.

M. Beard, Re-Reading (Vestal) Virginity, in: R. Hawley, B. Levick (ed.), Women in Antiquity, 1995, 166–177; A. Bendlin, s. v. Reinheit/Unreinheit, HrwG 4, 412–416; A. Chaniotis, Illness and Cures in the Greek Propitiatory Inscriptions and Dedications of Lydia and Phrygia, in: Ph. van der Eijk et al. (ed.), Ancient Medicine in Its Socio-Cultural Context, 1995, 323–344; B. MacBain, Prodigy and Expiation, 1982; R. Parker, Miasma, ²1996; V. Rosenberger, Gezähmte Götter, 1998.

V. RO.

Exploration, voyages of Voyages of exploration served to open up new routes and thus also new geographical spaces, which – even though they may long have been known to other peoples – still had to be discovered for the Graeco-Roman peoples of the Mediterranean; this explains why most of these voyages took place comparatively early. The opening up of routes across the Mediterranean and its subsidiary seas and the associated coastal regions was already accomplished in prehistoric times and perhaps became the subject of myths (→ Odysseus; → Argonautae).

Historically evident discoveries thus refer to routes and regions outside these regions, which were opened by pure chance or on voyages of exploration either in the interest of the discoverer, or by order of states or rulers: It is said that early in the 5th cent. BC, a merchant by name of → Colaeus accidentally discovered the sea route to → Tartessus. Seemingly in his own interest, the Greek seafarer → Euthymenes went on a voyage of exploration along the west coast of Africa (6th/5th cents. BC), as did → Pytheas to the British (?) isles in the northern seas (4th cent. BC); with the help of his own observations, the Greek merchant → Hippalus was able to discover – probably in the 2nd/1st cents. BC – that a direct sea route to India was possible during the monsoon season (Peripl. m.r. 57).

On 'state' orders, the Carthaginian 'king' → Hanno explored the west coast of Africa, probably in the 5th cent., roughly concurrent with Himilko's exploration of the (British?) tin islands (Plin. HN 2, 169; Avien. 117; 383; 412). In an official mission for the Egyptian Pharaoh Necho II (610–595 BC), Phoenicians explored the possibility of circumnavigating Africa from the east (Hdt. 4,42); → Scylax explored the Indian Ocean for the Persian king Darius I (522–486 BC), Sataspes for Darius' successor Xerxes. I (485–465 BC) the circumnavigation of Africa (Hdt. 4,43). For Alexander the Great. (336–323 BC), → Nearchus and others explored the Persian Gulf, for Seleucus. I and his successors, Patrocles explored the Caspian Sea, and Demodamas the lands beyond the Syr Darja (Plin. HN 6,49) as well as → Megasthenes parts of India. Parts of India were also the target of explorations by Dionysius on behalf of Ptolemy I (282–246 BC) (Plin. HN 6,58), and on behalf of Ptolemy III (246–222 BC) Simmias went to Ethiopia and southern Arabia (Diod. Sic. 3,18). During the reign of the later Ptolemies, → Eudoxus explored India and the circumnavigation of Africa. Between 26 and 24 BC, L. → Aelius [II 11] Gallus explored Arabia for Augustus, and between 25 and 21 BC C. → Petronius the Sudan.

During the Roman Imperial period ([1. 97–101]), when most of the *oikoumene* was known, there is occasional evidence of exploratory expeditions (however, cf. [2. 1351]), e.g. in the Sudan on behalf of Nero (AD 54–68) (Plin. HN 6,181).

This list of voyages of exploration may seem extensive, but this must not mask the fact that it is not a strong characteristic of ancient cultures systematically to expand their geographical knowledge for practical (military or economic) interests.

→ Travel

1 C. Nicolet, L'inventaire du monde, 1988 2 R.J. A. Talbert, Review of C. Nicolet, in: American Historical Review 94, 1989.

R. Hennig, Terrae Incognitae 1, ²1944 (use with caution); O. Seel, Ant. Entdecker-Fahrten, 1961; M. Cary, E.H. Warmington, The Ancient Explorers, 1963 (= Id., Die Entdeckungen der Ant., 1966); J.S. Romm, The Edges of the Earth in Ancient Thought, 1992; N.J.E. Austin, N.B. Rankov, Exploratio, 1995. K.BRO.

Exploratores *Exploratores* were the scouts of the Roman army. They reconnoitred the movements and deployments of the enemy as well as the terrain and positions of camps. In the early years of the Principate, soldiers selected from the → *auxilia* were commandeered from their units for a certain length of time to act as scouts. In the Dacian War (AD 105–106), Ti. Claudius Maximus, then serving in an *ala*, was selected by Trajan himself as a scout and brought the *princeps* the head of King Decebalus. In the mid 2nd cent. there is evidence of small reconnaissance units called *explorationes*. They were commanded by prefects or *praepositi* and often named after the region in which they served, such as the *Exploratio Seiopensis* from Seiopa in upper Germania (CIL XI 3104). A group of scouts could also be called a *numerus* (CIL III 14207; 14210). There is evidence of the deployment of reconnaissance units in Britain, Gaul, Germania, Pannonia and northern Africa. In other parts of the Imperium individual soldiers in the military units were probably detailed as *exploratores*. Scouts were generally mounted, although 5 of the 15 soldiers that were *exploratores* in Dura-Europus for the *Cohors XX Palmyrenorum* in AD 219 were infantry (P. Dura, 100).

Large armies in action on the battlefield had a special unit of mounted *exploratores*, probably commanded by a *praepositus*, which rode ahead of the marching column and were stationed near the gate in military camps (Arr. Tact. 1,1; Ps.-Hyg., De Mun. Cast. 24,30). Pseudo-Hyginus describes an army, consisting of three legions and the auxiliary troops, which had 200 *exploratores* attached to it. Vegetius and other authors of military handbooks emphasized the importance of efficient reconnaissance (Veg. Mil. 3,6; cf. Onasander 6,7).

1 N. Austin, B. Rankov, Exploratio, 1995 2 M. Speidel, in: JRS 60, 1970, 142–153. J.CA.

Expositio totius mundi et gentium and *Descriptio totius mundi* are the titles of two anonymous free Latin adaptations of a lost anonymous Greek commercial-geographical text, written in AD 459/460. This work written by an Orthodox covers Asia, Europe, and Africa as far as Egypt including the islands, and offers colourful details about the characteristics, products, trading habits, and lives of the various peoples.

GGM 2, 513–528; GLM, 104–126; J. Rougé, E., SChr 124, 1966; F. Martelli, Introduzione alla E., 1982; J. Drexhage, Die E., in: Münstersche Beiträge zur antiken Handelsgeschichte 2.1, 1983, 3–41. K.BRO.

Exposure, myths and legends of There are many peoples around the world with examples of myths and legends of exposure in their history; they differ very little in terms of structure, particularly in the case of the myths regarding origins or derivations from animals, which are very widespread in European and Asian peoples. In these myths the progenitor, the first king or the hero of a tribe is either himself the offspring of an animal (often of a wolf) or is suckled by an animal (most often a wolf or dog). Myths and legends of exposure are also told mainly about mythical kings, seers, or the founders of kingdoms or cities; they are often only known in local traditions and are sometimes re-enacted there in the cult of the god or hero concerned.

The following elements, with variations, can be found in all myths and legends of exposure: the abandonment of a newborn, the child of a god or a king, either by the mother (e.g. in the case of → Zeus, → Iamus, and → Parthenopaeus), out of shame or fear of her own father (i.a. in the case of Asclepius in Epidaurus' version, Paus. 2,26,3–7, → Linus, → Hippothoon, and → Miletus), or by the child's father, warned by bad prophecies from an oracle or dreams (→ Oedipus, → Paris), or by the grandfather (→ Cyrus; Dionysus in the myth of Brasiae, Paus. 3,24,3ff.). The exposure is frequently linked to ancient mythical locations such as mountains and caves (Zeus), trees (→ Romulus and Remus), springs (→ Atalante, → Caeculus) or waters (→ Sargon, → Moses); the place where the abandonment took place often has cult significance as the sanctuary of a god. The story of exposure at sea in a box also occurs frequently (e.g. in the cases of → Perseus and → Telephus, Hecat. 1,29). The exposed child is usually fed by (wild) animals, by wolves (Miletus, Romulus and Remus) and dogs (→ Neleus; Cyrus according to Ael. VH 12,42), by goats (Zeus; → Aegisthus), deer (Telephus), horses (Hippothoon), and bears (Atalante, Paris), or it is looked after by birds (→ Cycnus, Aechmagoras). In other variations, the infant's divine father protects his exposed child (as Apollo does Asclepius, → Ion, → Anius, Hercules and Aechmagoras). The child, in a conflicted state between misfortune and luck, between being exposed with no protection and the prospect of an auspicious future, is generally found by shepherds and is brought up in lowly circumstances. Precious offerings occasionally point to the noble origins and help to find the real parents again (Daphnis and Chloe, Longus 1,1–6; 4,30–36; Hippothoon). The name of the foundling contains testimony to the place where it is found, so Miletus is abandoned under a yew tree ([σ]μῖλαξ; *[s]mîlax*), Iamos is placed on violets (schol. Apoll. Rhod. 1,85), or the name recalls the animal wet-nurse (Aegisthus was fed by a goat, Cycnus was rescued by swans) or refers to the fate of the child (Oedipus). The exposed children often grow faster than their contemporaries (Zeus) and are superior to them in terms of strength, intelligence, and beauty (Paris, Oedipus, Daphnis, and Chloe). Once grown up, they win their own kingdoms or found cities (Miletus, Cydon, Romulus) or cults, and punish those who did them or their mothers wrong.

Stories often tell of the abandonment of pairs of twins (Romulus and Remus; → Aeolus and Boeotus, → Amphion and Zethus, → Lycastus and Parrhasius, → Pelias and Neleus i.a.). This perhaps has its roots in the ancient institution of the double kingship [1. 73–74]. In antiquity, the birth of twins was always seen as numinous; it was supposed that there had been two inseminations: one by a human and one by a divine father (Plin. HN 7,48f.). It was for this reason that twins were viewed as divine beings who often had supernatural powers.

Original versions of the individual myths and sagas are rare. The more recent variants, particularly those by historians, demonstrate attempts at rationalization; such as the wolf being reinterpreted as a *lupa*, a prostitute (Plut. Romulus 4; Liv. 1,4,7), or the dog as a woman called Cyno (Cyrus, Hdt. 1,110f.). Many myths of exposure survive in legends and folk tales. Myths and legends of exposure were also applied to historical figures, whose abandonment, rescue, and rise (from lowly origins) to high positions of power were seen as particular signs of divine favour, and were used to legitimate claims to power (→ Agathocles, → Cypselus of Corinth, → Ptolemaeus I Soter, → Constantinus the Great, the ruler of the → Sassanids, the mother of Charlemagne, Theoderic, Dietrich of Bern, Wolfdietrich, and others). In the field of cults there was a close link between the custom of individual peoples and their mythical origins (→ Lupercalia). Initiation rites, (ritual) battles, and the procession of groups ('alliances') of young men obviously reflect their role in myths and legends of exposure [cf. 1. 29–44]. It seems that the cult-related wearing of masks had great significance. The animal mother or animal nurse was often depicted on the standards and weapons of the tribe or people who regarded the exposed child as the hero of their origins [1. 45–49].

1 G. Binder, Die Aussetzung des Königskindes. Kyros und Romulus, 1964.

W. Burkert, Antike Mysterien, [2]1991; M. Huys, The Tale of the Hero who was exposed at Birth in Euripidean Tragedy, 1995; M. Klisches, Der Stern als Geburtssymbol, Einzelne Vorformen und ähnliche Zeichen, 1992; W. Speyer, Der numinose Mensch als Wundertäter, in: Kairos NF 26,3–4, 1984, 129–153; W. Speyer, Die Verehrung der Heroen, des göttlichen Menschen und des christlichen Heiligen, Analogien und Kontinuitäten, in: P. Dinzelbacher, D.R. Bauer (ed.), Heiligenverehrung in Geschichte und Gegenwart, 1990; H. Usener, Die Sintflutsagen, 1899; A. Wirth, Danae in christlichen Legenden, 1892.

R.OS.

Extispicin see → Divination; → Omen

Extraordinarii The *extraordinarii* were soldiers from allied Italian cities, serving in the army of early Rome as elite units of infantry and cavalry. Twelve prefects appointed by the consuls selected the best soldiers from the contingents of the alliance – around a third of the cavalry and a fifth of the infantry – in order to make up the *extraordinarii* (Pol. 6,26,6). Some *extraordinarii* were entrusted with the special task of accompanying the consuls and acting as their bodyguard. They also took part in battles as regular troops; in 209 BC they fought under M. Claudius Marcellus in the campaign against Hannibal in Apulia (Liv. 27,12,14). In Gaul in 194 BC, the consul Ti. Sempronius Longus gave them the order to repel the enemy troops who had invaded the camp (Liv. 34,47,3). In Polybius' plan of a military camp, cavalry, volunteers, and some infantry, selected from the ranks of the *extraordinarii* to constantly accompany the consuls, were stationed on the *via principalis* opposite the *forum* and the *quaestorium* (Pol. 6,31). The remaining *extraordinarii*, infantry, cavalry, and other auxiliary units were stationed on a road running parallel to the *via principalis*, behind the general's tent (*praetorium*), the *forum* and the *quaestorium*. It is unlikely that the *extraordinarii* continued to exist later than the 2nd cent. BC.

1 Liebenam, s.v. E., RE 6,2, 1696–1698 2 A.R. Neumann, s.v. Equites E., RE Suppl. 11, 652. J.CA.

Ex(s)uperantius

[1] see → Iulius E.

[2] Originally from Poitiers; after internal unrest in AD 417, he tried to restore order in Aremorica. In 424/5 *praef. praet. Galliarum*, he was beaten to death during a mutiny in Arelate. PLRE 2, 448. H.L.

Exuviae (from *exuere*, 'take off, remove'). In addition to its profane meaning ('discarded items of clothing, captured weapons, stripped animal hide'), *exuviae* (cf. ThlL s.v. *exuviae*) is used to signify the attributes of the gods that are paraded on festive occasions (Plin. HN 7,145; Suet. Aug. 94,6; Apul. Met. 9,4; 11,10; 11,29). In the *pompa circensis* (festive → procession through the → circus) they were taken on special carts (*tensae*) to the → *pulvinar* (Fest. 500: *vehiculum quo exuviae deorum ludicris circensibus in circum ad pulvinar vehuntur*). In Val. Max. 1,1,16 (Lactant. Div. inst. 2,16,16), a boy holds Jupiter's *exuviae*. Images on *denarii* from the time of L. Rubrius Dossenus (87/86 BC), showing the cart with Jupiter's thunderbolt and Juno and Minerva with birds [1; 2], are a reference to the *exuviae* in the *pompa circensis* [3].

1 H.A. Grueber, Coins of the Roman Republic in the British Museum, 1970, 1,311 no. 2448–2458 2 E.A. Sydenham, The Coinage of the Roman Republic, 1952, no. 705–707 3 Latte, 249 n. 2.

M. Malavolta, s.v. E., EV 2, 449–450; A. Piganiol, Recherches sur les jeux romains, 1923, 26; 31. R.B.

Eye see → Physics [VII]

Ezechiel

[1] see → Prophets

[2] (Ἐζεκίηλος, Ἐζεκιῆλος; *Ezekíēlos, Ezekiêlos*). Judaeo-Hellenistic tragedian, who probably lived in Alexandria (or see [5]). The draft of the *Exagōgḗ*, the only known work of E., of which 5 fragments (269 trimeters) have been preserved, can be dated to the period between *c.* 240 BC (*terminus post quem*: origin of the Septuagint) and 100 BC (*terminus ante quem*: evidence from → Alexander [23] Polyhistor). The preserved verses (the most complete tragedy fragments after Euripides) were handed down in the *Praeparatio Evangelica* (9,28,1–29,16) of → Eusebius [7] of Caesaria, who quotes them from the work *Perì Ioudaíōn* (Περὶ Ἰουδαίων, 'On the Jews') by Alexander Polyhistor (FGrH 273 F 19). Verses 7–40a and 50b–54 were also handed down by Clement of Alexandria (Strom. 1,23,155,2–7; 156,1f.) and verses 256–269 by Eustathius [5] of Antioch (PG 18, 729 D). The subject of the *Exagōgḗ* is the Exodus of the Israelites from Egypt, as

told in Ex 1–15. The prologue and the four scenes which have been preserved can be arranged into five acts [3]. The division into acts, whether there was a chorus, and whether it was a piece to be performed or read are questions still unresolved [2; 9]. In a deviation from the rules of classical tragedy, there is no unity of place and time. In addition to the influence of the tragedies of Euripides (and also those of Aeschylus), which E. follows in terms of style and metre [3; 5], he also draws heavily on the language and content of the Septuagint [1]. In addition, E. refers to traditions of the Jewish exegesis of the Bible [1; 4] and does not shrink from including additional remarks regarding himself and the plot.

Editions: 1 H. Jacobson, The Exagoge of Ezekiel, 1983 2 R. Kannicht, B. Gauly et al., Musa Tragica, 1991, no. 128 3 TrGF 1, no. 128.

Bibliography: 4 H. Jacobson, Mysticism and Apocalyptic in E.'s Exagoge, in: Illinois Classical Stud. 6, 1981, 272–293 5 K. Kuiper, De Ezechiele poeta Iudaeo, in: Mnemosyne 28, 1900, 237–280 6 G. Vermes et al., The history of the Jewish people in the age of Jesus Christ (175 B.C.–A.D. 135) 3, 1986, 563–566 (English revised translation by E. Schürer, Die Geschichte des jüdischen Volkes im Zeitalter Jesu Christi, 1890ff.) 7 B. Snell, Die Jamben in Ezechiels Moses-Drama, in: Glotta 44, 1966, 25–32 8 P.W. van der Horst, Moses' Throne Vision in E. the Dramatist, in: Journal for Jewish Studies 34, 1983, 21–29 9 E. Vogt, Tragiker E., in: W.G. Kümmel (ed.), Jüdische Schriften aus hellenistisch-römischer Zeit. 4: Poetische Schriften, 1983. I.WA.

Eznik of Kolp (Kołp). Pupil of → Mesrop. His student colleague Koriwn gives some details about E.'s biography in the Vita of Mesrop. According to him, in around AD 406 E. goes to → Edessa [2] (= Urfa) on behalf of his teacher and Katholikos → Sahak in order to learn Syriac and to translate works by the Syrian church fathers into Armenian. Together with Koriwn he brought around 435 Greek biblical manuscripts, manuscripts by the church fathers, and the Acts of the Synods of → Nicaea and → Ephesus from → Constantinople to Armenia. Based on this material, he and Sahak undertook a revision of translations already in existence.

As Bishop of Bagrewand he took part in the Synod of Artašat (449), which spoke out against the reintroduction of Zoroastrianism. In addition to a letter to Mesrop, of which only fragments are still in existence, the detailed treatise *De deo* or 'Against the sects' (written 441–448) has also been preserved – the first original works in the Armenian language. The treatise, which is partially dependent on Greek authors (→ Epiphanius of Salamis, → Hippolytus, → Basileus [1] the Great and → Ephraim), is directed against pagan Greek philosophy and rejects the contemporary sects such as the Marcionites (→ Marcion), Manichaeans (→ Mani), and the Zoroastrians (→ Zoroaster). The essence of God, the problem of evil, and free will are all dealt with in detail. → Armenia; → Armenians, Armenian literature; → Armenian; → Syria

EDITIONS: M. MINASSIAN, Čark' ənddēm 'Atandoc', 2 vols., 1992.
BIBLIOGRAPHY: V. INGLISIAN, RAC 7, 118–128. K.SA.

Ezra

[1] A priest (Ezra 7,1–5; 7,12), who, on behalf of the Persian high king → Cyrus II, promulgated a legal code that was binding for the members of the Jerusalem cult (Ezra 7). According to theological history, E. came to Jerusalem in 458 or 398 BC with authority for the temple (Ezra 7:7), solved the problem of mixed marriages there (Ezra 9f.) and later gave a definitive reading of the Torah (Neh 8–10). The description 'E. the scribe' (Ezra 7:11; Neh 8:1 et passim) resulted in E. being regarded as a champion for Jewish scribes and a pioneer for the canonical literature (4 Ezra 14:18–48).

A. H. J. GUNNEWEG, Esra, 1985; W. TH. IN DER SMITTEN, Esra-Quellen, Überlieferung und Geschichte, Studia Semitica Neerlandica 15, 1973. R.L.

[2] 3 E. (LXX: 1 Esdr; Vulg.: 3 Esdr) contains 2 chronicles 35–36, Ezra and Neh 7:72–8,13a in slightly differing orders, and also the 'contest' among Darius' three pages (3:1–5; 3:6). Probably originally written in Hebrew-Aramaic, 3 E. is preserved in a good Greek translation dating from the mid-2nd cent. BC and another translation into the language of the old church. Jos. Ant. Iud. 11,1–157 uses 3 E. as a source and is also familiar with its special material.
→ Apocryphal literature

EDITIONS: R. HANHART, Esdra Liber I, Septuaginta VIII,1, 1974; R. WEBER et al., Biblia sacra iuxta vulgatam versionem II, 1983, 1910–1930.
TRANSLATIONS, COMMENTARIES: K.-F. POHLMANN, 3. Esra-Buch, JSHRZ I 5, 1980.
BIBLIOGRAPHY: SCHÜRER, III 2, 708–718. A.M.S.

[3] 4 E. (Vulg.: 4 Esdr), an → apocalypse written in Hebrew-Aramaic (?) in around AD 100; has survived only in Latin, Syriac and other translations. These are all based on a Greek translation, which, like the Hebrew original, has been lost. 4 E. is one of the most important sources for Jewish theology at the end of the 1st cent. AD and supersedes all other early Jewish apocalyptic writings in terms of the theological clarity of the argumentation. The destruction of Jerusalem and the temple by the Romans (AD 70) is reflected on by the fictitious author from the time of exile E. against the background of the destruction by the Babylonians (586 BC). E.'s prophetic revelations are presented in seven parts, three dialogues with an angel or God and four visions. The theological themes centre on the question of theodicy, God's justness in the face of the triumph of the heathens over the pious, the course of world history in terms of the teaching of the four kingdoms (12,11 Daniel), the function of the law, the eschatological judgment, the appearance on Earth of the heavenly Jerusalem, the Messianic Period, at the end of which the Messiah will die (7:29), the end of this world and the coming of the next, and the Last Judgment. At the end, E. is transported into Heaven like Enoch and Elijah (→ Elias), after restoring the law destroyed when the temple was burned. In prophetic inspiration he dictates the 24 canonical and a further 70 apocryphal books. E. is seen as a new → Moses.
→ Apocryphal literature; → Pseudepigraphic literature

EDITIONS: R. WEBER et al., Biblia sacra iuxta vulgatam versionem II, 1983, 1934–1967.
TRANSLATION, COMMENTARY: J. SCHREINER, 4. Esra-Buch, JSHRZ V 4, 1981; M. E. STONE, Fourth Ezra, Hermeneia, 1990.
BIBLIOGRAPHY: SCHÜRER, III 1, 294–307. A.M.S.

[4] The additional Christian chapters to 4 Ezra (1–2 and 15–16) in the Latin version are counted as 5 Ezra and 6 Ezra. 5 Ezra (4 Ezra 1–2) consists of a judgment speech against Israel (*c.* 2nd half of the2nd cent. AD); 6 Ezra (4 Ezra 15–16), which dates from *c.* 3rd cent. AD, contains predictions of judgments pronouncements on the worldly kingdoms and exhortations to steadfastness under persecution.
→ Apocryphal literature, Pseudepigraphic literature

EDITIONS: R. WEBER et al., Biblia sacra iuxta vulgatam versionem II, 1983, 1931–1934, 1967–1974.
TRANSLATION, COMMENTARY: H. DUENSING, A. DE SANTOS OTERO, in: W. SCHNEEMELCHER, Neutestamentliche Apokryphen II, [5]1989, 581–590. A.M.S.

F

F (linguistics) The use of the sixth letter of the alphabet Ϝ was restricted at an early stage in Greek, as the sound designated by it (*u̯* at the opening of the syllable) was already no longer available in the decisive Ionic-Attic language at the beginning of written records; in other dialects Ϝ is however still frequently attested (→ Digamma). For the aspirated articulation that originated from **su̯-* there was in Greek the spelling ⟨ϜH⟩ [3. 23]. It was used in Italy for the fricative sound /f/ [1], in Etruscan and Venetian alternately with ⟨HF⟩, also in early Latin *FHE:FHAKED* (Fibula Praenestina, CIL I[2] 3). As the letter F in Latin only appeared in this digraph FH – for /u̯/ ⟨V⟩ was used everywhere –, the H could be regarded as superfluous and could be left off; consequently F on its own come to stand for the unvoiced sound /f/ that at least in the Imperial period was spoken in a labiodental manner.

Latin /f/ [2. 163–173] arose in inherited words particularly through the media of aspirates in the initial sounds of words: *fero* < **bher-*; *fūmus* < **dhūmo-*; *formus* 'warm' < *g^{w}*hormo-*; *fu-d-* < **ĝhu-d-* (in *fundo*; cf. χέω χυτός; *chéō chytós*); cf. also *frīgus* < **srīgos* (ῥῖγος; *rhîgos*). Almost only by keeping this *f-* after joining words did *f* also became a medial sound: *per-fero*, *cōn-fundo*; with the assimilation *af-fero*, *dif-fero*. On the other hand, the different type of *-f-* in *rūfus* < **rou̯dho-* must be based on borrowing.

Greek φ was pronounced [ph] in pre-Christian times; Latin *f* at that time still had no exact counterpart in Greek. Φ e.g. in Φάβιος (*Phábios*) is therefore initially based on sound substitution [2. 162].

→ P; → V (linguistics)

1 M. Lejeune, Notes de linguistique italique XXI, in: REL 44, 1966, 141–181 2 Leumann 3 Wachter. B.F.

Faba see → Beans

Faberius Roman surname (Schulze, 161).

F., private secretary (*scriba*, γραμματεύς; *grammateús*) of Caesar; identical to the F. mentioned frequently by Cicero in spring 45 BC who had been given a loan by Cicero, the repayment of which involved irregularities that only Atticus could rectify (Cic. Att. 12–15). After the murder of Caesar, F. helped M.→ Antonius [I 9] to falsify the decrees of the dictator (App. B. Civ. 3,16; Cic. Att. 14,18,1). He probably died shortly afterwards.

H.P. Benöhr, Fabianum negotium, in: ZRG 106, 1986, 275–320; O.E. Schmidt, Der Briefwechsel des M. Tullius Cicero von seinem Proconsulat bis zu Caesars Ermordung, 1893, 289–308. K.-L.E.

Fabia

[1] **F.** Two daughters of the patrician Ambustus with the same name. The younger one had married the plebeian Licinius Stolo whilst the older one had married the patrician Ser. Sulpicius, who was able to hold high state offices because of his origin. When the messenger announced his arrival by knocking loudly on the front door, the younger F. was startled and the older one mocked her. Traditionally the incident is said to have led to the offended sister pressing her plebeian husband to allow access to the highest state offices to plebeians as well, which was finally achieved through the admission of plebeians to the consulate in the *leges Liciniae Sextiae* in 367 BC (Liv. 6,34,6–11; Flor. 1,17,1–4; Vir. ill. 20,1f.; Cass. Dio 7 fr. 29,1f.). cf. [1. 15,17].

[2] **F.** Half-sister of Terentia (Ascon. In orationem in toga candida p. 82 Kiessling-Schoell) – the wife of Cicero, Vestal before 78 to 53 BC (Cic. Fam. 14,2,2). She was indicted for alleged incest with Catiline but was acquitted (Sall. Catil. 15,1) [1. 61, 63f.; 2. 265].

1 R.A. Bauman, Women and Politics in Ancient Rome, 1992 2 D. Balsdon, Die Frau in der röm. Antike, 1979, Index s.v. ME.STR.

[3] **F. Agrippina.** Daughter of a consul, either of Fabius [II 1 or 2], PIR[2] F 74.

[4] **F. Balbin[a]** Named in the will of Domitius [II 25] Tullus amongst the recipients of a legacy.

Raepsaet-Charlier, 305 no. 349; G. di Vita-Evrard, in: Epigrafia Juridica Romana, 1989, 163.

[5] **F. Numantina.** Perhaps the daughter of Fabius [II 14] Maximus. Married to Sex. Appuleius [II 4], *cos. ord.* AD 14 and to M. Plautius Silvanus; in 24 she was indicted for magical practices against him but she was acquitted; to her son Sex. Appuleius [II 5], who died young, she erected the tomb in Luna, CIL XI 1362 = ILS 935.

Syme, AA, 417f.; Raepsaet-Charlier, 308f. no. 353; PIR[2] F 78.

[6] **F. Orestilla.** Supposedly the wife of Emperor Gordian I, HA Gord. 17,4; probably a fictitious person.

PIR[2] F 79; R. Syme, Emperors and Biography, 1971, 4; 169f. W.E.

Fabianus

[1] Pope from AD 236 to 250, a Roman, divided the church of Rome into seven districts headed by deacons; from these later developed (12th cent.) the churches headed by cardinals. F. is mentioned in Euseb. Hist. eccl. VI,29, Jer. Ep. 84,10, Cypr. Ep. 9,1, Novatianus (Cypr. Ep. 30,5).

MGH AA 9/1,75; LThK[3] vol. 3, 1146f. RO.F.

[2] **Papirius F.** Philosopher and rhetor, see → Papirius

Fabius Roman patrician family name, probably derived from Etruscan *fapi* [1. 162]. According to ancient etymology, however, either from *faba* '(broad)bean' ('legume grower': Plin. HN 18,10; [2]) or from the original 'Fodius', 'Fovius' ('wolf pit hunter': Plut. Fabius 1,2; Fest. 77 L.) because the Fabii with the Quinctii originally appointed the priesthood of the Luperci; the → Lupercalia were also the family celebration of the Fabii (Ov. Fast. 193ff.). Early Imperial pseudogenealogy, which perhaps arose in the literary circle of Fabius [II 14], traced the family back to Hercules (Plut. and Fest. ibid.; Ov. Fast. 2,237 etc.). The family had since the 5th cent. BC belonged with the Aemilii, Claudii, Cornelii and Valerii to the great patrician noble families of the Roman Republic. The rural *tribus* Fabia was called after it (probably on the left-hand bank of the Tiber, north of Rome and south of the Cremera [3. 40f.]). The family tree of the early Republican branches of the → Vibulani and Ambusti cannot be reconstructed with certainty. Their family history, especially the importance of the Fabii in the 5th cent. BC in connection with the catastrophe at the Cremera in 477 (→ F. [I 37]), was chronicled by Q.F. [I 35] Pictor and particularly by the younger Annalists. The most important family since the 4th cent. had been the Maximi. When they were under threat of dying out at the beginning of the 2nd cent., Q.F. Maximus (*praet.* 181) adopted sons from the families of the patrician Aemilii (F. [I 23]; through his brother there was also a connection to the Cornelii) and the Servilii, who were also patrician (F. [I 29]). In the 1st cent. AD the patrician line finally died out. Later bearers of the widespread name no longer have anything to do with this branch. In the 1st cent. the building activity of F. [I 22] and his commission to T. → Pomponius Atticus to write a special history of these families, especially, however, the proper names of F. [II 13–15], testify to the intense interest in the history of the family and the *gentes* connected with it. Rare first names: Caeso (which in the patrician family only appears in relation to the Fabii and Quinctii) and Numerius.

1 Schulze 2 Walde/Hofmann 1,436 3 L. Ross Taylor, The Voting Districts of the Roman Republic, 1960.

Family tree of the younger Fabii: Münzer, Groag, s.v. F., RE 6, 1777f.; G. V. Sumner, The Orators in Cicero's Brutus, 1973, 30–32.

I. Republican period II. Imperial period

I. Republican period

[I 1] Perhaps people's tribune in 64 BC (MRR 2,162), pushed through the *lex Fabia,* that stipulated the maximum number of attendants of candidates for office (→ *ambitus*) (Cic. Mur. 71).

P. Nadig, Ardet ambitus, 1997, 45–48.

[I 2] Originator of a law, the date of which cannot be fixed but that was first mentioned in 63 BC by Cicero (Rab. perd. 8); it forbade any claim to property rights concerning humans (→ *plagium*) regarding free men, freedmen and their slaves.

[I 3] **F., C.** Praetor in 58 BC, proconsul in Asia as the successor to T. Ampius [I 2] Balbus 57 (MRR 2, 203; coin minting: [1]). Not identical with F. [I 4] (MRR 3, 86).

1 G. Stumpf, Numismatische Untersuchungen zur Chronologie der röm. Statthalter in Kleinasien, 1991, 23–28.

[I 4] **F., C.** 54–49 BC legate of Caesar in Gaul and in the Civil War, in which he distinguished himself on many occasions. In 49 he occupied the passes of the Pyrenees with three legions before the Pompeians arrived and also fought in Spain (Caes. B Civ. 1,37; 40); he probably died soon afterwards. It is uncertain whether he, as the people's tribune, was the originator with his colleagues of an agrarian law, the *lex Mamilia Roscia Peducaea Alliena Fabia* [1. no. 54], that was dated to 55 [2. 74, n. 72]; the text is probably part of Caesar's agrarian law of 59 [3].

1 M. Crawford (ed.), Roman Statutes 2, 1996 2 M. Gelzer, Caesar, 61960 3 M. Crawford, The lex Iulia agraria, in: Athenaeum N.S. 66, 1989, 179–190.

[I 5] **F., Q.** Aedile before 266 BC, he was handed over in that year by Rome together with Cn. Apronius [I 2] because of an assault on envoys from Apollonia but he was sent back by that city (MRR 1,200).

[I 6] **F. Ambustus, C.** Consul in 358 BC, he was beaten by the Tarquinii; 307 Romans are said to have been captured and sacrificed by the enemy (Liv. 7,12,6; 15,9f.). It can be assumed that he suffered the same fate as F. [I 37] at the Cremera.

[I 7] **F. Ambustus, C.** In 315 BC *magister equitum* of the dictator Q.F. [I 28] Maximus Rullianus (Liv. 9,23,6–17), probably a fabrication [1. 175, n. 3].

1 Mommsen, Public Law 2.

[I 8] **F. Ambustus, K.** Quaestor in 409 BC, consular tribune in 404 (war against the Volscans), in 401, 395, 390 (?); → F. [I 12].

[I 9] **F. Ambustus, M.** Son of F. [I 8], consular tribune in 381, 369 BC. According to Livy he initiated for personal motives with his plebeian son-in-law C. → Licinius Stolo and L. Sextius the admission of plebeians to the consulate (6,34,5–11). In 363 censor (?).

[I 10] **F. Ambustus, M.** According to annalistic tradition, F. Ambustus, M. as *cos I* was victorious against the Hernicians in 360 BC (MRR 1,120), and as *cos. II* defeated the Faliscans and Tarquinians in 356 (MRR 1,123), whilst as *cos. III* he conquered Tibur in 354 and took revenge on the Tarquinii for the murder of Romans (→ F. [I 6]); supposedly he also entered into the first treaty with the Samnites (Liv. 7,19,1–4; Diod. Sic. 16,45,8; InscrIt 13,1,69). As *interrex* in 355 and 351 he is said to have prevented, as a dedicated patrician, the election of plebeian consuls (unsuccessful as a dictator in 351, Liv. 7,17,10–12; 22,2f.; 10f.). *Magister equitum*

The Fabii Maximi and their family connections (4th cent. BC to 1st cent. AD)

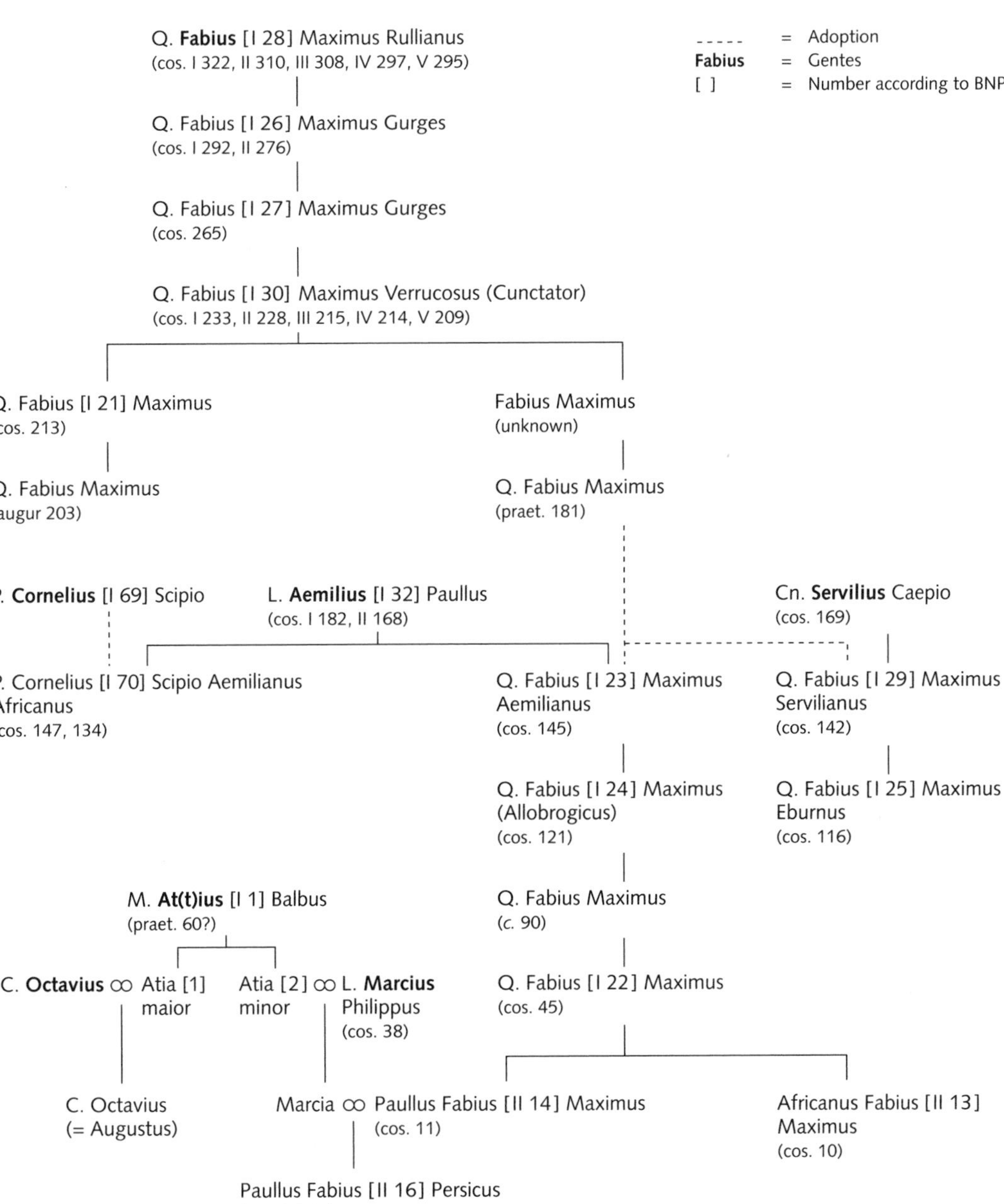

in 322, *princeps senatus* from an uncertain point in time onwards (Plin. HN 7,133).

[I 11] F. Ambustus, N. (Cn.?) Consular tribune in 406 BC, conquered the Volscan city of Anxur (Liv. 4,59,3–10); perhaps an envoy in 398 to the Oracle of Delphi (MRR 1,86); in 391 with his brothers he was an envoy to the Celts (→ F. [I 12]); consular tribune in 390 (MRR 1,94).

[I 12] F. Ambustus, Q. is said with his two brothers F. [I 8] and [I 11], according to annalistic tradition, to have provoked the conquest of Rome by the Gauls: in 391 BC, sent as envoys to Clusium that was under threat from the Celts, they involved themselves in the war illegally and killed a Celtic leader. When the Celts demanded that the brothers be handed over, the people elected them as consular tribunes for 390; then the Celts attacked Rome, which led to the defeat of the Romans at Allia and the conquest of Rome (Liv. 5,24–36; older, different version in Diod. Sic. 14,113).

Th. Mommsen, Röm. Forschungen 2, 303–307; E. Meyer, KS 2, 312–314.

[I 13] F. Buteo, M. (Cognomen: 'goshawk', 'buzzard'; exact meaning not clarified). Consul in 245 BC with C. Atilius [I 11] Bulbus, fought in Sicily against Carthage (supposedly naval victory and shipwreck off the coast of Aegimurus, Flor. Epit. 1,18,30f.). Censor in 241; in 218 he or F. [I 30] led the Roman delegation to Carthage to declare war (MRR 1,241). In 216, he as the oldest censor became the dictator at the end of the year in order to supplement the Senate after the battle of Cannae (Liv. 23,22f.; MRR 1,248).

[I 14] F. Buteo, N. Brother of [I 13]. As consul in 247 BC he unsuccessfully laid siege to Drepanum on Sicily (MRR 1,216). In 224 he was *magister equitum*.

[I 15] F. Buteo, Q. In 188 BC quaestor (?) in Spain, in 181 praetor in Gallia Cisalpina; there in 180 he was propraetor and head of a three-man council for the establishment of a Latin *colonia* in the area of Pisae (Liv. 40,36,13; 43,1); in 168 he reconciled border disputes between the colonists and Pisae (Liv. 45,13).

[I 16] F. Dorsuo, C. (or K.) (Cognomen 'long back'), perhaps pontifex in 390 BC; During the siege of Rome by the Gauls, he went down from the Capitol, made a sacrifice at the destroyed Temple of Vesta and returned unscathed (Cassius Hemina fr. 19 HRR in App. Celt. 6; Liv. 5,46; 52; MRR 1,96).

[I 17] F. Dorsuo, M. As consul in 345 BC he captured the Volscan fortress of Sora with his colleague Ser. Sulpicius Camerinus (Liv. 7,28,6). K.-L.E.

[I 18] F. Gallus, M. Roman Epicurean and friend of Cicero (Cic. Fam. 7,24–26 and 9,25,2–3); under Cassius [I 10] governor of Damascus. He owned a villa in Herculaneum. In 45 BC through a eulogy to Cato Uticensis (Cic. Fam. 7,24–26), who had recently died, he openly opposed Caesar. Cicero provides ample evidence that he turned to Epicureanism (Fam. 7,26,1; 9,25,2), but he was probably only superficially interested in it.

C.J. Castner, Prosopography of Roman Epicureans, [2]1991, 34f. T.D.

[I 19] F. Hadrianus, C. Marian, mint master in 102 BC (?, RRC 322); as praetor in 85 or 84 he drove Q. Caecilius [I 31] Metellus Pius out of Africa, and from 83–82 he was propraetor there (for the dating see MRR 2,69; 3,86) because of his cruelty he was burnt to death in his house by the citizens of Utica who were in revolt (Cic. Verr. 2,1,70).

[I 20] F. Labeo, Q. (Cognomen: 'thick lips'). Quaestor in 196 BC, praetor and propraetor in 189/8; as a commander of the Roman fleet, he attempted in vain to prevail upon the Cretans to hand over the Roman prisoners; he destroyed 50 war ships of Antiochus [5] III off the coast of Patara in Lycia and captured Telmessus, made a votive offering to Apollo on Delos (IDelos 442B l. 103 = ILS 8765) and celebrated a naval triumph (Pol. 21,46,3; Liv. 37,60; 38,39; InscrIt 13,1,81; bow of the ship on the coin of his grandson Q.F. Labeo 124, RRC 273). In 184 he was a member of a three-man council for the establishment of the colonies of Potentia and Pisaurium, he was consul in 183 in Liguria where he remained until 182 with an extended *imperium*. Pontifex since 180; he probably also became a member in 167 of a ten-man council for the reorganization of Macedonia. He also had a literary education (Cic. Brut. 81; Suet. Vita Ter. 4).

[I 21] F. Maximus, Q. Son of F. [I 30], the 'Cunctator'. In 217 BC he served under his father, in 216 he was a war tribune, in 215 he was curule aedile, in 214 praetor (in Apulia) and in 213 consul; the unusually rapid succession of offices without particular successes probably goes back to the influence of his father who also accompanied him as a legate (Liv. 22,44,9ff.). In battle he won Arpi in Apulia and held it in 212. Later he was also legate (209–8) and envoy (207); he died before his father who delivered his funeral oration that was probably also read by Cicero (Cato 12 and *passim*).

[I 22] F. Maximus, Q. in 59 BC successfully charged C. Antonius [I 2] (*cos.* in 63) for his involvement in the conspiracy of Catilina. As curule aedile in 57, proud of belonging to the three families of the Aemilii, Cornelii and Fabii, he renovated the triumphal arch of his grandfather F. [I 24] Maximus (Allobrogicus), the → Fornix Fabianus (Cic. Vatin. 28; ILLRP 392a-c), and with his colleague Q. Caecilius [I 32] Metellus Pius Scipio he induced T. → Pomponius Atticus to write the family history of the Aemilii, Cornelii and Fabii Maximi (Nep. Att. 18,4). He was probably praetor in 48, and as Caesar's legate in Spain he captured Munda in 45. As a reward he ultimately received the suffect consulate in 45 (from 1 October to 31 December) and a triumph, but he died on his last day in office. His sons were: F. [II 13 and 14].

M. Gelzer, Caesar [6]1960, Index s.v. F.

[I 23] F. Maximus Aemilianus, Q. Son of L. Aemilius [I 32] Paullus and hence the older brother of P. Cornelius [I 70] Scipio Aemilianus, adopted by the grandson of F. 'Cunctator' [I 30], Q.F. Maximus (*praet.* 181). In 168 BC he fought as a boy under his father at Pydna and brought the victory message to Rome; in 167 he was again in the Balkans as legate. In 154 he was an envoy to Pergamum, in 149 he was praetor (Sicily). As consul in 145 with L. Hostilius Mancinus and in 144/3 as proconsul he re-organized the Roman army in Spain and had several successes against → Viriatus. In 134–132 he was the legate for his brother Scipio outside Numantia; he died before his brother in about 130.

[I 24] F. Maximus (Allobrogicus), Q. Son of F. [I 23]. As quaestor in 134 BC he perhaps supplied to his uncle P. Cornelius [I 70] Scipio volunteers to Spain (App. Ib. 84); in 129 he held the funeral oration for Scipio that was written by C. Laelius (Cic. De or. 2,341). He was probably praetor in 124 and propraetor in 123 in Spain; by order of C. Sempronius Gracchus he was rebuked by the Senate for exploiting the provincials (Plut. C. Gracchus 6,1). In 121 he was consul with L. Opimius in Gallia Transalpina; with his predecessor Cn. → Domitius [I 3] Ahenobarbus he ended the war against the

Allobrogians and Arvernians, and in 120 or slightly later he triumphed and erected a victory monument on the battle field at the mouth of the Isère and a triumphal arch at the Forum Romanum (→ Fornix Fabianus; Cic. Font. 36; InscrIt 13,1,83; Str. 4,185; MRR 1,520f.); the cognomen Allobrogicus is attested from the 1st cent. AD onwards. He or F. [I 25] was the envoy to Crete in 113 and censor in 108; he probably died before 100.

[I 25] F. Maximus Eburnus, Q. Probably the son of F. [I 29]; quaestor (?) in 132 BC (Sicily), mint master (?) in 127 (RRC 265), not praetor until 119 and consul in 116 with C. Licinius Geta, in 115–114 proconsul in Macedonia (?, MRR 3, 87), in 113 perhaps envoy and in 108 censor (→ F. [I 24]). He had his son killed for his illicit sexual practices, was condemned for it and went into exile in 104 (Val. Max. 6,1,5; Oros. 5,16,8).

[I 26] F. Maximus Gurges, Q. (Cognomen, according to Macrob. Sat. 3,13,6 supposedly 'spendthrift'), son of F. [I 28] Rullianus. *Tribunus militum* in 297 BC; As aedile in 295 he built the Temple of Venus Obsequens *ad circum maximum* using money from fines (Liv. per. 11). Consul I in 292, proconsul in 291 (triumph over the Samnites in 290), censor 289?, consul II in 276 and triumph again over the Samnites, Lucanians and Bruttians (InscrIt 13,1,75), in 273 leader of the delegation to Ptolemy II Philadelphus (MRR 1,197); consul III in 265 (?, → F. [I 27]).

[I 27] F. Maximus Gurges, Q. Son of [I 26] and father of the 'Cunctator', F. [I 30]. He (probably not his father) was consul in 265 BC and died in office after being wounded in Volsinii (MRR 1,201).

[I 28] F. Maximus Rullianus, Q. (Cognomen Rullianus not clarified), son of F. [I 10], the most important family member in the 4th cent. BC, whose role in the Samnite Wars was greatly embellished in the later tradition (partly in a retrospective view of the career of F. [I 30]). In 331 aedile; in 325 as the *magister equitum* of the dictator L. Papirius Cursor he won a victory over the → Samnites in disobedience of his orders; the fact that he was condemned to death by the dictator for it but was pardoned only through the will of the people of Rome is meant to explain the anomaly regarding constitutional law (Liv. 8,30–35,10). As *cos. I* in 322 some of the sources attribute to him the victory and triumph over the Samnites (Liv. 8,40,1–3). In 315 he fought as dictator unsuccessfully against the Samnites at Lautulae and laid siege to Sora (Liv. 9,22–24), in 313 he is said as dictator II to have conquered Nola and Fregellae (Diod. Sic. 19,101,37). In 310 as *cos. II* he defeated the Etruscans and in 308 as *cos. III* fought against the Samnites and other tribes, in 297 as *cos. IV* he fought again in Samnium (MRR 1,161; 164; 175). In 295 as *cos. V* with P. Decius [I 2] Mus, his plebeian colleague of the last three consulates who sacrificed himself in battle, he won the decisive battle at Sentinum over the allied Samnites and Celts, as a result of which Central Italy fell firmly into Roman hands. As censor in 304 he restricted the acceptance of citizens who owned no property to the four municipal *tribus* again (Liv. 9,46,14f.). K.-L.E.

[I 29] F. Maximus Servilianus, Q. Son of Cn. → Servilius Caepio, adopted by Q. Fabius Maximus (*praet.* in 181 BC); in 142 he achieved the consulate (MRR 1, 474). Perhaps already in 142 [1], certainly as proconsul from 141 onwards, he fought against → Viriatus. After initial successes and conquests he got into difficulty in 140 and concluded a peace *aequis condicionibus* that was, however, ignored by his successors (cf. esp. App. Ib. 283–294; Liv. per. 53/54: in this regard [2.]). F. was → pontifex and wrote a work about religious law in at least 12 bks. (Macrob. Sat. 1,16,25), as well as a historical work (*Annales*) of which only 2 fragments about the early Roman period are known (HRR 1^2 117f.: fr. 3 has been attributed wrongly to him).

1 A.E. Astin, The Roman Commander in Hispania Ulterior in 142 B.C., in: Historia 13, 1964, 245–254
2 H. Simon, Roms Kriege in Spanien, 1962, 118–128.
W.K.

[I 30] F. Maximus Verrucosus, Q. (Cognomen Verrucosus: 'warty'), the so-called Cunctator ('hesitator'), son of F. [I 27], great-grandson of [I 28], the most important Roman politician in the 2nd Punic War. As consul I in 233 BC with M. Pomponius he triumphed over the Ligurians and dedicated a temple to Honos (Cic. Nat. 2,61). He was the most prominent opponent of the reforms of C. Flaminius [I 1] and also attempted to hinder his rise. Censor in 230, *cos. II* in 228, dictator in 221 (?). In 219 opponent of immediate declaration of war on Carthage; he or F. [I 13] was leader in 218 of the famous delegation that delivered the Roman ultimatum. After the defeat at Lake Trasimene in 217 he became dictator as a result of the decision of the people. In principle F. avoided an open battle against Hannibal and this is the origin of his later nickname 'Cunctator' (following Ennius [Ann. 363Sk.]: *unus homo nobis cunctando restituit rem)*; the attempt to surround Hannibal in Campania, however, failed. Dissatisfied with the conduct of the war, Rome gave the commander of F.'s cavalry, M. Minucius Rufus, equal authority to act. The latter confronted Hannibal, was beaten and only rescued by F. himself. The defeat of the consuls of 216 at Cannae demonstrated the correctness of F.'s strategy: in 215 he became *cos. suff.* (dedication of the Temple of Venus Erucina) and also pushed through (using questionable means) his re-election to *cos. IV* in 214 although he achieved nothing decisive; he secured the election of his son F. [I 21] to *cos.* in 213 and was also his legate. As *cos. V* in 209 he captured Tarentum and destroyed it. In 205 he opposed the plan of P. Cornelius [I 71] Scipio to wage war on Africa. He also held the funeral oration for his son and probably died in 203.

Conscious of power, F. championed his own political interests (he was *princeps senatus* in 209 and 204) and as a representative of the old patrician aristocracy, sought to fend off the claims of the plebeian *nobiles;* for this purpose he also used his position as augur (supposedly from 265) and from 216 simultaneously his position as pontifex – an honour that was not achieved again until Caesar.

Main sources: Pol. 3,86ff.; Liv. 21–30; Plut. Fabius Elogium: InscrIt 13,3, no. 80.

[I 31] F. Pictor, C. Had the temple of Salus decorated with paintings in 304 BC and as a result is said to have been given the cognomen Pictor (Cic. Tusc. 1,4; Plin. HN 35,19).

[I 32] F. Pictor, C. Probably the elder son of F. [I 31] and the brother of F. [I 33], consul in 269 BC. According to Plin. HN 33,44, he is said to have introduced silver minting to Rome.

[I 33] F. Pictor, N. Envoy in 273 BC (cf. F. [I 26]), consul in 266, celebrated two triumphs.

[I 34] F. Pictor, N. Described by Cicero as an expert on law and history (Cic. Brut. 81), perhaps identical to F. Pictor, who wrote a work about religious law and annals in Latin (HRR 1, 112–116).

E. BADIAN, in: JRS 57, 1967, 228; SCHANZ/HOSIUS 1,174.

K.-L.E.

[I 35] F. Pictor, Q. Probably son of C.F. [I 32] Pictor [4], first Roman historian; patrician [3. 227–230]. He took part in the Ligurian campaign of 233 (or possibly 223) BC (fr. 24 P.), also the campaign against the *tumultus Gallicus* of 225 (fr. 23 P.). Probably F. was a senator only of praetorian rank (Pol. 3,9,4), when after the defeat at Cannae in 216 BC he was sent as envoy to Delphi to ask the oracle (Liv. 22,57,5; 23,11,1–6; Plut. Fabius Maximus 18).

The work that probably comprises several books (Pol. 3,9,3) written in Greek (Dion. Hal. Ant. Rom. 1,6,2) and is quoted by Latin authors (fr. 3; 24; 27 P.) as *Annales* (→ Annalists) has been lost apart from a few testimonia that speak of Italian (and Sicilian?: fr. 2; 3A P.) ancient history with Hercules, Lanuvinus and Aeneas and 'much later' (i.e. according to the kings' list of Alba in accordance with the Eratosthenian chronology) of Romulus, Remus and the founding of Rome [4] and goes up to 217 (fr. 26 P.)/216 BC (App. Hann. 116). According to Dion. Hal. Ant. Rom. 1,6,2 [6. 932–940], the work consisted of a detailed prehistory and a history of the foundation of Rome (this can be taken literally in [5. 161–165] as opposed to [6. 940]), the 'archaeology' that is told in a manner that is somewhere between approximation and irregularity (period of the Monarchy; Early and Middle Republic) and a contemporary history from the 1st Punic War onwards ([9] re Pol. 1,14,1) that is again very detailed. Whether the work was written during (*c.* 210 BC [3. 237]) or after the 2nd Punic War (*c.* 200 [2. 3f.]) and where it ended (after 209 BC: [9] re Pol. 10,2,1–20,8; before 213 BC: [3. 236]) is a contentious matter. The assessment of the interdependence of the sources that have mostly only been reconstructed – Diocles of Peparethus for the *ktisis* (Plut. Rom. 3); perhaps Timaeus; Philinus of Agrigentum for the 1st Punic War (Pol. 1,14,3; 15,12); additionally, Roman oral traditions [8], public (*annales*, → *commentarii* of the *pontifices*) and private, esp. Fabian family archives (as a result on occasions somewhat weighted towards the Fabians) – determines the evaluation of the achievement and the work's bias: the main goal of this portrayal of Roman history – that was certainly not balanced in form and content – was surely not the projection of Roman great power politics onto the beginning [1] that resulted in an all too heavy emphasis on Roman greatness and victoriousness [6] or conspicuous disinterest in Roman conquests in the east [5], but rather to correct the previous depictions – which had been hostile to Rome – and to represent Roman civilization and its history for the Greek-speaking cultural world of the Mediterranean Sea area in order to stress its analogy with Greek culture.

EDITIONS: HRR, pp. 5–39; cf. FGrH 809 B.W. FRIER, Roman Historiography ..., thesis Princeton 1970, 152–225.

BIBLIOGRAPHY: 1 A. ALFÖLDI, Early Rome and the Latins, 1964, 123–175 (cf. Röm. Frühgesch., 1976, 48–82) 2 E. BADIAN, The early Historians, in: T.A. DOREY (ed.), Latin historians, 1966, 1–6 3 B.W. FRIER, Libri Annales Pontificum Maximorum, 1979, 227–253 4 G. MANGANARO, Una biblioteca storica nel ginnasio a Tauromenium nel II sec. a. C., in: La Parola di Passato 29, 1974, 389–409 5 K.E. PETZOLD, Zur Gesch. der röm. Annalistik, in: W. SCHULLER (ed.), Livius, 1993, 151–188 6 D. TIMPE, Fabius Pictor und die Anfänge der röm. Historiographie, in: ANRW I.2, 928–969 7 Id., Mündlichkeit und Schriftlichkeit als Basis der frühen röm. Überlieferung, in: J. VON UNGERN-STERNBERG, H. REINAU (ed.), Vergangenheit in mündlicher Überlieferung, 1988, 266–286 8 J. VON UNGERN-STERNBERG, Überlegungen zur frühen röm. Überlieferung ..., ibid. (no. 7), 237–265 9 F. WALBANK, A Comm. on Polybios, 1957–1979.

U.W.S.

[I 36] F. Sanga, Q. Senator, learned in 63 BC as patron of the Allobrogian envoys of the plans of the Catilinarians (→ Catilina) and reported them to Cicero (Sall. Catil. 41,4f.). In 58 he supported Cicero, who had been exiled.

[I 37] Fabii Vibulani. The history of the family is closely connected with the famous tale of the destruction of the Fabii at the river Cremera in 477 BC: according to the annalistic tradition, the three brothers Q., K. and M. Fabius alternately held a consulate position between 485 and 479 (Q. 485, 482, died in 480; K. 484, 481, 479; M. 483, 480). When the constant attacks of the residents of Veji on Roman territory increased in 479, the Fabii decided, under the leadership of the Consul K.F., to secure the border at the Cremera on their own initiative and for this purpose to muster the entire clan (supposedly 306 relatives) with the clients and vassals. In 477 the Fabii were enticed into an ambush by the Vejentines and killed; only one son who was a minor survived in Rome and he alone perpetuated the lineage (Liv. 2,48–50; Diod. Sic. 11,53,6; Dion. Hal. Ant. Rom. 9,20–22), → F. [I 38].

The historical aspect of this familial and patriotically presented episode is the fact that in the Early Republic the great *gentes* still had the option of waging independent warfare (although this probably had to be acceptable to the entire state).

B. LINKE, Von der Verwandtschaft zum Staat, 1995, 157f.; J.-C. RICHARD, Historiographie et Histoire: L'expérience des Fabii à la Crémère, in: EDER, Staat, 174–199; D. TIMPE, Das Kriegsmonopol des röm. Staates, in: EDER, Staat, 383.

[I 38] **F. Vibulanus, Q.** Son of M.F. [I 37] Vibulanus, in a non-historical sense regarded as the progenitor of the later Fabii; consul on several occasions (I 467, II 465, III 459 BC). According to tradition, he fought against the Aequians, *praefectus urbi* (462, 458), and from 450 to 449 was one of the most highly respected decemvirs. In 449 he fought the Sabines (Liv. 3,1,41,9; Dion. Hal. Ant. Rom. 10,58).

[I 39] **F. Vibulanus (Ambustus), Q.** Son of F. [I 38], consul in 423 BC, consular tribune in 416, 414, *cos. II* in 412. K.-L.E.

II. IMPERIAL PERIOD

[II 1] **C.F. Agrippinus.** Senator who perhaps came from Ostia. Praetorian governor of Thrace before AD 148 (THOMASSON, Laterculi I 164); *cos. suff.* 148. F. [II 2] was his descendant. PIR² F 20.

[II 2] **C.F. Agrippinus.** Consular governor of Syria Coele in AD 218/219; killed there by Elagabalus, PIR² F 19; cf. PIR² F 17. Descendant of F. [II 1]; Clodius [II 2] could be his descendant on his daughter's side of the family.

[II 3] **Q.F. Barbarus Antonius Macer.** *Cos. suff.* together with Licinius Mucianus about AD 64; F. [II 4] was his descendant.

W. ECK, RE Suppl. XIV, 117.

[II 4] **Q.F. Barbarus Valerius Magnus Iulianus.** Praetorian legate of *legio III Augusta* in Africa under Nerva, *cos. suff.* in AD 99; descendant of F. [II 3]. PIR² F 23.

[II 5] **Q.F. Catullinus.** Perhaps the son of F. [II 4]. Praetorian legate of *legio III Augusta* in AD 128 when Hadrian visited the legion; *cos. ord.* in 130; *curator operum publicorum.*

THOMASSON, Fasti Africani 145; PIR² F 25.

[II 6] **L.F. Cilo Septiminus Catinius Acilianus Lepidus Fulcinianus.** Senator of the Iberian peninsula. His long *cursus honorum* is passed down to us in CIL VI 1408/9 = ILS 1141/2 and AE 1926, 79 with variations. His career began under Marcus Aurelius; under Commodus he was legion commander, proconsul of Narbonensis, *praefectus aerarii militaris*, praetorian governor of Galatia, etc. As the designated consul he buried → Commodus,who had been murdered on 31 Dec. AD 192; *cos. suff.* 193. Supporter of Septimius Severus, who appointed him during the Civil War against Pescennius Niger in the east. Legate of Pontus-Bithynia, Moesia superior and Pannonia superior (197–201). At the latest in 203 he was city prefect in Rome, and in 204 he became *consul ordinarius II*. In the conflict between Caracalla and Geta he tried to mediate but got into danger himself. Only when the city cohorts intervened in his favour did Caracalla support F. [1]. Severus had given him a large *domus* in the municipal Roman *regio* XII.

1 K. H. DIETZ, Caracalla, Fabius Cilo und die Urbaniciani, in: Chiron 13, 1983, 381ff.

LTUR II 95f.; CABALLOS, Senadores I, 132ff.; PIR² F 27.

[II 7] **C.F. Fabianus Vetilius Lucilianus.** Praetorian governor of Numidia and designated consul under Severus Alexander.

THOMASSON, Fasti Africani 183f.; PIR² F 29.

[II 8] **F. Fabullus.** A simple soldier who on the 15th Jan. AD 69 cut off the head of the Emperor Galba. PIR² F 31.

[II 9] **M.F. Fabullus.** was probably a *homo novus* and came from the Iberian peninsula. He was *legatus Augusti pro praetore provinciae Africae* probably under Nero in an extraordinary function, later legate of the *legio XIII Gemina* and in AD 69 of the *legio V Alaudae.*

CABALLOS, Senadores I, 135f.; PIR² F 30; 32.

[II 10] **P.F. Firmanus.** Son of a Lucius who came from the *tribus Quirina*, perhaps from Spain. Legate, perhaps in Africa; *cos. suff.* with L. Tampius Flavianus in AD 44 or 45 [1. 180f., 188; 2. 32, 242].

1 N. FERCHIOU, Quelques inédits de Furnos Maius, in: A. MASTINO (ed.), Africa Romana 2, 1985, 179–188
2 G. CAMODECA, L'archivio Puteolano dei Sulpicii, 1992.

[II 11] **L.F. Iustus.** Senator and *amicus* of Tacitus, who dedicated to him his *Dialogus* [1. 110ff.]; also linked with Pliny the Younger; Aquilius Regulus asked F. to mediate between him and Pliny. Probably legion commander in AD 96/7 (Plin. Ep. 1,5,8), *cos. suff.* in 102 as the successor of Licinius Sura. Consular governor of Moesia inferior in 105 – *c.* 108 (AE 1981, 746), of Syria in 108/9 – *c.* 112 [2. 341ff., 346ff.; 3. 217].

1 R. SYME, Ten Studies in Tacitus, 1970 2 W. ECK, Jahresund Provinzialfasten der senatorischen Statthalter von 69/70 bis 138/139, in: Chiron 12, 1982, 281–362
3 R. SYME, Danubian Papers, 1971.

CABALLOS, Senadores I, 139ff.; PIR² F 41.

[II 12] **M.F. Magnus Valerianus.** His career is preserved in CIL XI 2106 = ILS 1138 up to the command over the *legio I Italica. Cos. suff.* under Commodus, in AD 193 *curator operum locorumque publicorum*; in 204 he participated in the Secular Games as *XVvir sacris faciundis* [1. 238f.].

1 KOLB, Bauverwaltung.

PIR² F 43.

[II 13] **Africanus F. Maximus.** Son of Q. F. Maximus, *cos.* in 45 BC, patrician. In 10 BC *cos. ord.*, member of the *septemviri epulonum*, proconsul of Africa perhaps in 6/5 BC (AE 1955, 40); brother of F. [II 14].

THOMASSON, Fasti Africani, 23f.; PIR² F 46.

[II 14] **Paullus F. Maximus.** Brother of F. [II 13]; patrician; born probably in 46 BC. Closely connected with Augustus, married to Marcia, a cousin of Augustus. As *quaestor Augusti* he accompanied the *princeps* to the east between 22 and 19 BC. *Cos. ord.* in 11, proconsul of Asia probably in 10/9–9/8 BC. At that time he implemented a reform of the calendar in the province: the new year in Asia began on the birthday of Augustus. In about 3 BC he was governor in Hispania Tarraconensis. Pontifex and *frater Arvalis*. Influential political adviser of Augustus; supporter of Horace and particularly Ovid. In the early summer of AD 14 he accompanied Augustus on a visit to Planasia where Agrippa [2] Postumus was interned; because he passed the information on to his wife (and so to Livia), he incurred the wrath of Augustus. So he probably committed suicide before Augustus' death.

SCHEID, Recrutement, 84ff.; VOGEL-WEIDEMANN, 336ff.; SYME AA, 403ff.; PIR² F 47. W.E.

[II 15] **F. Mela.** Jurist in the Augustan period, contemporary of → Antistius [II 3] Labeo [3], known only because of 33 indirect citations in Justinian's Digests [1]. According to the citation of Africanus, Dig. 46,3,39 pr., F. wrote a work consisting of at least 10 books, probably primarily about honorarium law [2].

1 O. LENEL, Palingenesia iuris civilis 1, 1889, 691ff. 2 C. FERRINI, Opere II, 1929, 14ff. 3 R. A. BAUMAN, Lawyers and Politics in the Early Roman Empire, 1989, 38. T.G.

[II 16] **Paullus F. Persicus.** Son of F. [II 14] and Marcia. *Frater arvalis* in place of his father in AD 15, later *sodalis Augustalis* and pontifex. Quaestor of Tiberius, *cos. ord.* in 34. Proconsul of Asia probably in 43/4 where he rearranged the financial administration in Ephesus, IEph. Ia No. 17–19. *Curator alvei Tiberis* under Claudius; in 48 he is mentioned in Claudius' speech about the '*ius honorum*' of the Gauls (CIL XIII 1668 = ILS 212). He probably died before Claudius. Seneca describes him as a degenerate aristocrat (Ben. 2,21,4f.; 4,30,2), but his judgement is probably biased.

VOGEL-WEIDEMANN, 334ff.; SCHEID, Recrutement, 110ff.; SYME, AA, 417; PIR² F 51.

[II 17] **Q.F. Postuminus.** *Cos. suff.* in AD 96, VIDMAN, FO² 45. In 97 he held a speech in the Senate for Publicius Certus. In *c.* 102–104 he was consular legate of Moesia inferior ([1. 338]; AE 1981, 745); proconsul of Asia in *c.* 111/2 [1. 351].

1 W. ECK, Jahres- und Provinzialfasten der senatorischen Statthalter von 69/70 bis 138/139, in: Chiron 12, 1982, 281–362.

[II 18] **F. Priscus.** He perhaps came from Tarraco and was legate of the *legio XIV Gemina* in AD 70 in Mogontiacum; wars against rebellious Gallic tribes.

CABALLOS, Senadores I, 143; PIR² F 55. W.E.

[II 19] **F. Rusticus.** Young friend of Seneca (Tac. Ann. 13,20,2), probably from Spain [1. 203; 2. 179; 293]. He wrote – probably in the Flavian period – a historical work that → Tacitus used as an important source for the Neronian period (cited Ann. 13,20,2; 14,2,2; 15,61,3), presumably also for the year of four emperors; Tacitus had a high regard for F.'s style (Agr. 10,3), but criticizes his bias for Seneca. F. is probably the anonymous historian upon whom Quintilian (Inst. 10,1,104) lavishes praise [1.; 2. 293]. If he is identical to the recipient of a legacy by the same name in the will of → Dasumius [1] [1. 203; 3. 201], he was still alive in AD 108 and moving in the circles of Tacitus and Pliny the Younger (→ Plinius [2]).

FRAGMENTS: HRR 2, 112f.

1 BARDON 2, 203f. 2 SYME, Tacitus, 179, 289–294. 3 J. WILKES, Julio-Claudian Historians, in: CW 65, 1971/2, 177–203, esp. 201. W.K.

[II 20] **L.F. Tuscus.** *Cos. suff.* in AD 100 (VIDMAN, FO² 45), he perhaps came from Baetica.

CABALLOS, Senadores I 145; ECK, RE Suppl. XIV 117.

[II 21] **F. Valens.** He came from Anagnia, of equestrian origin; accepted into the Senate. In AD 68 he was legate of the *legio I* in Germania. In December 68 he negotiated with Vitellius, whom he acclaimed Imperator on the 2nd Jan. 69 with his legion. The latter made him the commander of the army in the war against Galba/Otho. F. was one of the victors in the battle of Bedriacum. For this he received a suffect consulate in Sept. 69. He is said to have been involved in the defense against the Flavians but he was caught and executed by the Flavians in Urbinum. Tacitus provides a description of his personality (Hist. 3,62).

G. ALFÖLDY, Die Legionslegaten der röm. Rheinarmeen, 1967, 8f.; PIR² F 68. W.E.

Fable

I. ANCIENT ORIENT II. GREEK LITERATURE III. LATIN LITERATURE

I. ANCIENT ORIENT

No evidence exists of there being a term for the fable itself either in the Sumerian or the Akkadian fable. The fable is a short, fictitious story with an inherent moral, the characters of which are personified animals. Reduced to the moral, several fables have attained the status of a proverb. The fable has its origin in oral literature; it represents a simple form of the allegory. Rank disputes/tenzons (main protagonists: personified animals, natural phenomena and cultural objects) in which no allegory is present in the plot should be distinguished from the fable [1; 2. 150ff.]. The first written textual evidence for the Sumerian fable comes from the 1st half of the 2nd millennium BC and was part of the ancient Babylonian school curriculum ([3. 19f.]; for the rhetorical purpose of the fable [4. 30off]). Other fables are 'Donkey and Dog', 'Lion and Goat', 'Ten Wolves' and 'Dog and Fig' [5]. The Sumerian fable 'Heron and Tortoise' [6. 51ff.] is to be found in the Akkadian fable of 'Eagle and Snake' (incorporated into the Akkadian Etana myth) and is the oldest Akkadian fable set down in writing (ancient Babylonian period). In addition, other Akkadian animal stories from the 1st millennium BC are extant [2; 7–11].

The fable spread from Mesopotamia to the neighbouring countries. The Sumerian fable 'Heron and Tortoise' – in Akkadian 'Eagle and Snake' – was known in Egypt, Syria and Greece [8. 70ff.]. The Akkadian tale of the 'Fox' is considered to be the forerunner of 'Reynard de Vos'. Aesop's fable of 'The Mosquito and the Elephant' has its equivalent in the Akkadian fable of the same name; the Sumerian fable of 'Dog and Fig' is a precursor of Aesop's fable of 'The Fox and the Grapes'.

1 B. ALSTER, Living Waters, 1990, 1ff. 2 W.G. LAMBERT, Babylonian Wisdom Literature, 1960 3 E.I. GORDON, Sumerian Proverbs, 1959 4 R.S. FALKOWITZ, The Sumerian Rhetoric Collection, 1984 5 E.I. GORDON, Sumerian Animal Proverbs and Fables, in: JCS 12, 1958, 1–21, 43–75 6 G. GRAGG, The Fable of the Heron and the Turtle, in: AfO 24, 1973, 51–72 7 R.J. WILLIAMS, The Literary History of a Mesopotamian Fable, Phoenix 10, 1956 8 E. EBELING, Die babylon. F. und ihre Bed. für die Literaturgesch. (Mitt. der Altoriental. Ges. II/3), 1927 9 R.J. WILLIAMS, A Stubborn Faith, 1956, 3ff. 10 B. ALSTER, Paradoxical Proverbs and Satire in Sumerian Literature, in: JCS 27, 1975, 201–230 11 R.S. FALKOWITZ, La Fable, 1984, 1ff.

BA.BÖ.

II. Greek Literature

A. Form and Structure B. Terms C. Content D. Fable collections

A. Form and Structure

Any Greek text that can be classified as a fable is always characterized by three elements (cf. Theon, Progymnasmata 72,27ff.): (A) the narrative form, (B) the freely invented content (the indirect message) and (C) the paraenetic function (the 'moral') which is expressed explicitly and which has general value (the direct message). Of two texts that are similar to each other e.g. Hom. Il. 2,307–18 and Corpus Fabularum Aesopicarum (= CFA) 255, only the second one is a fable. Moreover, (C) is so important that it determines (B) in the sense that the fictitious elements must reflect real mechanisms of social life. As the plot in (B) has to be probable, the element of invention is not exemplified to such a great extent in it as in its characters: in general it features animals with human behaviour (including the ability to speak), less frequently people who talk to animals, and from time to time plants that also talk. If (C) appears in the form of a → gnome, an anecdote with exclusively human protagonists can also be a fable (as early as the 5th cent. BC, cf. Aristoph. Vesp. 1427ff.).

In the Aesopian phrase (→ Aesop), some animals are still related to mythical symbols (the lark as a primeval bird, the sacred scarabee, the eagle of Zeus). Characters in the fables can also be personifications of human feelings (Plat. Phd. 60b; Plut. Mor. 112a; 609f.) or ancient beings such as the Earth or Charybdis as well as gods and demigods (Zeus, Prometheus) as addressees of the protests of the animals (cf. the animal delegations to Zeus in the Aesopian tradition in Callim. Fr. 192) or as responsible for the human failings that are the focus of the original Aesopian fables. In the 6th cent. BC, greater probability is bestowed upon the element (B) through the Aesopian idea that the history of the world is divided up into two periods: a first period in which 'birds, fish and four-legged animals' spoke like people, and a second period in which the insolence of the animal delegations brought down upon them the wrath of Zeus, initiating the current world in which only humans can speak (Callim. Fr. 192). Recurring wording in the Aesopian tradition (from Xen. Mem. 2,7,13 to Max. Tyr. Or. 19,2) and the fact that there is no evidence of talking plants in the original Aesopian tradition (→ Aesopus) confirm the reliability of Callimachus' report. Incidentally Callim. Fr. 194 attributes a fable with talking plants (a typical motif of the fable of the ancient Middle East, → *ainos* [2]) to the 'ancient Lydians'. Texts from wisdom sayings like the tale of → Ahiqar did however promulgate the fable type with talking plants from at least the 5th cent. BC onwards ([9. 55]; Anth. Pal. 9,3).

In the archaic phase (7th/6th cents. BC), (A) can be extended through direct speeches (cf. the archaic *aînos* in Callim. Fr. 194; Archil. IEG fr. 175–181; the *lógos* of Aesop in the *Vita Aesopi* 135–139 PERRY); in the systematic collections of 'Aesop's' fables there are hardly any considerable variations in length that can still be observed. Only in the literary fable (e.g. Phaedr. 4, 19; Babr. 95) does the archaic type of (A) appear from time to time.

Mostly (C) follows upon (B), but it can also precede it. In both cases it may be a → gnome (in the technical sense) that is sometimes spoken by the last speaker, generally an animal. The fact that a gnome could be given to an animal for utterance (as in Hes. Op. 210–11) was the subject of complaint by Aristarchus [4] of Samothrace (schol. vet. in Hes. ad loc., p. 76 PERTUSI) but the archaic example left its traces in the collections of Aesop (cf. Phaedr. 1, 26, 12; PRyl. 493, 129–30). If (C) precedes (B) it is called *promýthion* whereas if it follows it, it is called *epimýthion*; the latter represents the older form, evidence for which is already to be found in Hes. Op. 202–11 and in the fables of Stesichorus and Aesop mentioned by Aristot. Rh. 1393b [2]. Throughout the entire history of the Greek (and Latin) fable, a varying combination of both forms of the element (C) is to be observed; *epimýthion* and *promýthion* can be found in fables in ancient collections (PRyl. 493; Phaedrus) as well as in later collections (Aphthonius) side by side with each other so that it cannot be asserted [13] that the *epimýthion* gradually replaced the *promýthion*. The systematic collections have a tendency to introduce element (C) with a number of stereotypical phrases.

B. Terms

The Greeks called the fable *aînos* (αἶνος), *lógos* (λόγος), *mŷthos* (μῦθος) [12. 123ff.]. With the term *aînos* (only used in archaic times), they emphasized the paraenetic and admonishing role (C) (cf. Hes. Op. 202–11, Theon, Progymnasmata 73,33f. and Suda αι s.v. αἶνος). The term *lógos* used from the 6th cent. onwards stressed element (A) (→ Aesop). The term *mŷthos* that was applied from the 5th cent. onwards to the non-Aesopian fable (Aeschyl. TrGF 139) and from Plato (Phd. 60c) onwards was also applied to the Aesopian one, emphasized element (B). In schools during the Imperial period, the term *mŷthos* dominated (cf. the *Mythíamboi* of Babrius or the *Dekamythía* of Nikostratus), and ultimately replaced the term *lógos* at the beginning of the Byzantine period. The term *parádeigma* (Aristot. Rh. 1393a 27) is frequently attested to in its Latin translation *exemplum* (e.g. Phaedrus). A successful fable becomes part of the inherited tradition of all people in the form of the proverb (→ *paroimia*): (A) and (B) are reduced to a minimum and (C) remains unspoken insofar as it is known to everyone.

C. Content

The majority of the oldest fables serve to describe types of political behaviour and mechanisms of power. Hes. Op. 210–11 addresses rulers (*basileîs*), the *aînoi* of Archilochus threaten traitors with revenge (IEG fr. 172–81; 185–87), Stesichorus tells his *lógos* directed against tyrants to the inhabitants of a Sicilian town (Aristot. Rh. 1393b), Aesop in a fable directs his tale at the citizens of an Ionian town (Aristot. ibid.), Semonides of Amorgus describes in a fable the politician who fishes in the cloudy waters (IEG fr. 8–9; cf. Aristoph. Equ. 864ff.), the great king Cyrus of Persia addresses in his fable the Greek envoys (Hdt. 1,141). The Attic → skolion about a crab and a snake (PMG 892; CFA 211) admonishes political traitors. Timocreon of Rhodes, a famous skolion author, reminds the Athenian Themistocles of a fable of Aesop (PMG 729 = CFA 17).

The symposium was the preferred medium for disseminating the best-known (also non-Greek) fable motifs amongst the Greek elites (Plut. Mor. 147b). The depiction of typical fable animals on seals (scarabees, ram's heads, crustaceans etc.), on shield emblems [16. 112ff.] and old pieces of money from the poleis, the animal symbolism in the speech of the Oracle (cf. the satire of Aristoph. Pax 1063–86) and on archaic monuments (frogs, a palm and water snakes on the Cypselus monument in Delphi; Plut. Mor. 399f) indicate the socio-cultural background that favoured the dissemination of the fable wherever Greek elites were influential (cf. the allusions in Ion of Chios fr. 38,36 TrGF and Pl. Phd. 82a).

The fact that the fable accompanied envoys, politicians and traders on their journeys led the Greeks to the conclusion as early as the 1st half of the 5th cent. that many fables were of other geographical origin and hence did not originate from Aesop. Aeschylus (TrGF 139) knows of Libyan fables, Timocreon of Rhodes mentions Carian and Cypriot fables (PMG 734; 730), and Aristoph. Vesp. 1427ff. refers to a Sybaritic fable. The Assyrian (for the Greeks 'Syrian', Babr. Prolog II 2) fables of Ahiqar were known in Athens in the 5th cent. [9. 30ff., 55ff.] and were first edited in written form by Democrites, then by Theophrastus. The Peripatetic → Chamaileon even named the author of the Libyan fable (Hsch. s.v. λιβυκοί λόγοι II 595,46 Latte). The *Progymnásmata* (e.g. Theon 73, 1ff.) then drew upon this material. Although the Aesopian model of the demegoric fable, again recommended by Aristot. Rh. 1393b, still had a certain vitality in the political battle [4. 400] (Plut. Phocion 9,1; Plut. Demosthenes 23, 5; but cf. the rejection of this model by Demades in CFA 63), the fable in the 4th cent. BC, particularly the authors' fables whose history can be traced, is now the legacy of ancient (not only Greek) cultures and becomes the subject of scholarly collections e.g. of riddles (*gríphoi*), proverbs (→ Clearchus of Soloi) or sayings of the Seven Sages (Demetrius [4] of Phalerum).

D. Fable collections

The first stage in the series of 'Aesop's' collections that stretch right through to the Byzantine period is the collection (*synagōgḗ*) of *lógoi Aisṓpeioi* in a single book compiled by the Peripatetic → Demetrius [4] of Phalerum (about 300 BC) (Diog. Laert. 5,80–81). The adjective *Aisṓpeioi* refers to the fact that here not only the fables of Aesop were collected (that made up a small group, cf. Phaedr. Prolog IV 11–12) but also all the fables related to the Aesopian type, i.e. the Libyan, Carian, Sybaritic, Lydian, 'Syrian' etc., the prerequisite being that they possessed all the elements of the fable (A+B+C), cf. Theon Progymnasmata 73,1–15. The collection of the sayings of the Seven Sages by Demetrius (F 10,3 DK) suggests that the fables were compiled under categories of the type 'the Phrygian (?) Aesop said' (Theon, ibid. 73,5–6). It is hard to say what criteria were applied for their classification within the individual groups. If PRyl. 493 (beginning of the 1st. cent. AD) is directly linked with the collection of Demetrius [3. 26–8], the subgroups were perhaps categorized according to whether the fables dealt with plants, animals and humans, heroes and gods, etc.

With regard to the 'moral', the systematic style of the collection has certainly contributed to establishing a limited number of initial phrases that are encountered with few variants in the entire history of fable collections whether they be in verse or in prose [13]. Through the status of the compiler the collection that got into the library of Alexandria became the authoritative scholarly text for successive centuries [14. 325]. Hellenistic writing that knew not only about the fables of Aesop but also of ancient Lydian fables (Callim. Fr. 192; 194) and that reproduces the 'Syrian' fables in verse form (fable of Ahiqar: Leonidas of Tarentum, Anth. Pal. 9,99 [14. 322]) offers a geographical perspective on the fable that can be explained from the point of view of a student of Theophrastus. Clear thematic and stylistic correspondances e.g. between → Phaedrus and Plutarch and between Ennius and → Babrius can be explained by the presence of an authoritative collection [14. 321ff.]. The prooemia of the fables, which are told by → Maximus of Tyre in the 2nd cent. AD (Or. 19,2; 32,1; 15,5; 36,1) leave us with echoes of the symbolism of the fables of Demetrius amongst which are mixed Callimachian reminiscences (for Or. 36,1 cf. Callim. Fr. 192,15–17). The same echoes are to be found in the prologues of Babrius. Himerius in the 4th cent. AD (Or. LXVI 1, cf. Aes. F 432) still boasts of drawing upon the collection of Demetrius [14. 302]. A modest but important channel of dissemination for fables were the various collections meant for rhetoric exercises in the Greek and Latin schools of the Imperial period [8] that appeared at intervals between the 2nd cent. AD and late antiquity (cf. the 16f. of Ps.-Dositheus in CFA II pp. 120–9 or the 40 *mŷthoi* of the rhetor → Aphthonius of late antique times in CFA II pp. 133–51). The fable – mentioned by Ps.-Hermog. Progymnasmata p. 2,15f. Rabe and only attested to in late ancient Syrian collections – about monkeys that found a city leads us to the conclusion that the corpus of so-called 'Fables of Syntipas' (*c.* 60f.) that is extant in a Byzantine edition (CFA II pp. 155–83; Aes. pp. 529–50), was also used at the rhetorical schools of the Imperial period. Between these two parallel paths for passing down the tradition, the rhetorical of the small collections (to which PKöln II 64 from the 2nd cent. AD also belongs, cf. Theon, Progymnasmata 75,9–10) and the scholarly one of the Demetrian collection, scholars have placed the *Dekamythía* ('Ten Types of *mŷthoi*') of the Sophist → Nicostratus that was compiled at the beginning of the 2nd cent. AD and that (cf. Aes. T 81–2) extended the boundaries of the fable by accepting 'dramatic' fables (cf. the tragedy passus in Phaedr. 4,7). Fables such as the 12th one of Babrius bring us to the assumption that he was influenced by the *Dekamythía*.

Under the pressure of the new comprehensive reference works (*Dekamythía*, *Mythíamboi* of → Babrius) the non-alphabetically arranged collection of Demetrius (unlike that of Babrius), which did not have any of the new materials which had been used in schools for centuries, gradually came to look like an antiquarian work: it had had its day as a reference book. At this point in time (late antiquity according to [1. 78–9], 9th/10th cents. according to [7]) the compilation of the best-known collection of Aesop's fables was commenced, the so-called *Collectio Augustana* (= CFA I, c. 230f., cod. G and Pa from the 11th cent., Pb from the 13th.). The *cod. Parisinus* Pa, which has been wrongly underestimated, even though it is in an extremely poor condition, has passed down to us the original prooemium (Aes. T 1) that announces the intention of the editor to bring the *mŷthoi* of 'Lydian' Aesop into the special section of a *bibliothḗkē* that also contains collections of *kephálaia* from tragedies, apophthegmata, gnomes and allegories (*parabolaí*): a Byzantine encyclopaedic project that, perhaps also in imitation of Demetrius, subjected the entire treasure of Greek fables to alphabetic reorganization so as to pass it down to later generations.

→ Ainos; → Aesop; → Babrius

Aesopi Fabulae, I & II, 1925, ed. E. Chambry; Aesopica I, 1952 (= 1980), ed. B. E. Perry (= Aes.; T = Testimonia; F = Fabulae); Corpus Fabularum Aesopicarum, I & II, 1959–70, edd. A. Hausrath, H. Hunger (= CFA). M.J.L.

III. Latin Literature

In Latin literature, the fable is present from the very beginning through its recourse to Greek literary forms and collections. It contains its paraenetic and admonishing function and serves to speak the truth in a veiled manner. For this purpose it is either fitted into heterogeneous contexts and exemplifies a certain occurrence or fact or it stands on its own and is aimed at a → *gnṓmē*.

The first fable that can be found in Latin literature was given poetic form by → Ennius in his *Saturae* (→ Satire) (Enn. Sat. 21–58 V.): According to → Gellius (2,29), Ennius passed on the advice of the 'crested lark' through the *apologus Aesopi*: *ne quid exspectes amicos, quod tute agere possies*, 'do not expect from friends what you are capable of doing yourself' (Gell. NA 2,29,20 = Enn. Sat. 58 V.; for the relationship between Enn., Babr. 88 and Avianus 21 cf. [25. 155–162, 236f.; 27]). → Lucilius then fits into his *Saturae* the fable of the 'sick lion' whose summons is not adhered to by the fox as all the tracks only lead into the cave (Lucil. fr. 980–989 Marx = 1074–1083 Krenkel). From the fragmentary text that has been passed down to us, we cannot determine whether Lucilius, like the early Greek → iambographers, wishes to personally attack and mock others. Following on from Lucilius, → Horatius in his *Saturae* and *Epistulae* (Hor. Sat. 2,1,62–65; Epist. 1,1,73–75: allusion to the fable of the 'sick lion'; cf. later also Sen. Dial. 8,1,3) uses the fable frequently in order to mock behaviour in an urbane and entertaining tone, enunciate a truth in a veiled manner or to instruct people in a popular philosophical vein. In addition to allusions to fables (Hor. Sat. 2,3,186; 199; 2,5,55f.; Epist. 1,3,18–20; 1,20,14–16), Horace elaborates four fables in detail (Sat. 2,3,314–320: 'Cattle and Puffed-up Frog'; 2,6,79–117: 'Town Mouse and Country Mouse'; Epist. 1,7,29–33: 'Fox with Bloated Belly'; 1,10,34–41: 'Horse and Master'); most of these fables are introduced in the context of a carefully critical consideration by Horace of his relationship with Maecenas [23; cf. as a whole 18].

Within Latin prose we rarely encounter fables for exemplification and as rhetorical means of persuasion (all passages in [3. 37; 21. 1732ff.]). The report of → Livius (2,32,5–12) stands quite alone: he stated that Menenius Agrippa had prevailed upon the rebellious

Plebeians to return to the town in a speech with the fable of 'The Stomach and the Limbs' (Oriental origin; in the case of Livy, the fable was probably communicated through the younger Annalists [24. 142f.]). Livy himself describes this form of the art of oration as not in keeping with the period and repugnant (Liv. 2,32,8; [cf. 29. 77f.]). → Quintilianus (Inst. 5,11,19) confirms this judgement after he has already elsewhere (Inst. 1,9,2) assigned the Aesopian fable to early school instruction and so had expressly named the area in which the fable was most at home in Rome during the Imperial period (additional theoretical thoughts on the designation of the fable and its relationship to the proverb in Quint. Inst. 5,11,20f.).

The Greek freedman → Phaedrus, who in the first third of the 1st cent. AD with his poetic fable collection in 5 books (only book 1 is almost completely extant) self-confidently and with great poetic ambitions (cf. esp. Phaedr. 1 prol., 2 prol.) started the ancient small genre of fable poetry, clearly has a different view of the function and intention of the fable. He uses the potential for personal invective and the veiled criticism of political conditions – known since the beginnings of the fable in Greece – to an extent not otherwise encountered in antiquity (cf. programmatically Phaedr. 3 prol.), but nonetheless feels obliged to set himself the primary goal of providing popular philosophical instruction in an entertaining form, as also pursued by Horace (Sat. and Epist.). Phaedrus initially takes his material from a Hellenistic collection of prose fables (possibly those of Demetrius [4] of Phalerum or from a comparable collection: [13. 391ff.; 14. 325ff.]), but in the course of his writing he frees himself from this: he uses for instance → apophthegmata, anecdotes and novellas from other sources or invents his own materials (literature on Phaedr.: [3. 55f.]). Phaedrus appears to have had little success with his high poetic standards and also with his unmistakably critical tones (he is only mentioned in Mart. 3,20,5 and Avianus praef. 14 GUAGL.). → Seneca (consol. ad Polyb. 8,3) and Quintilian (Inst. 5,11,19) obviously consciously overlook him in their comments on Aesop's fables [26].

→ Avianus, who at the beginning of the 5th cent. AD presented a collection of 42 fables in distichs, made the second great contribution to Latin fable poetry. They are distinguished by a clear tendency towards generally valid moralizing and didacticism and – in contrast to those of Phaedrus – are free of critical overtones of social and political circumstances. Avianus to a large extent takes his material from → Babrius, whose *Mythíamboi* had had great success in Graeco-Roman schooling in the Imperial period – probably directly, not via the mediation of Latin paraphrases of Babrius no longer available to us, such as the Latin prose version of a Greek *Aesopia trimetria* by the teacher of rhetoric Iulius Titianus (turn of the 2nd/3rd cents. AD), of which only Auson. Epist. 16,2,78–81 SCH. (= 9b,78–81 GREEN) reports [cf. 25; 3. 69–79].

It was also in late antiquity (probably in the 4th/5th cents. AD) that the sole prose collection of Aesop's fables in Latin came into existence and it is passed down to us in four recensions that are clearly different from each other and whose relationship to each other has been judged controversially in research [31; 32; 28. 404–431; 1. 2, 473–509; 20. 61–67; 3. 105–116]. The author of an accompanying letter under the pseudonym → Romulus, passed down to us in two recensions, maintains that he translated the fables by Aesop himself into Latin. The preserved text shows however that the collection is in large part a Phaedrus prose paraphrase and that further materials were added in later recensions to an original version that only has recourse to Phaedrus (origin about the middle of the 4th cent. AD) – especially in the final part, for instance from the collection of Pseudo-Dositheus. The Phaedrus paraphrases do preserve a certain independence of content: in a comparable manner to Avianus, they tend towards general moralizing and didacticism and tone down the social criticism of the model [20. 61–67; 26. 26–28; 30].

The wide distribution accorded the fable throughout the entire Middle Ages and went on to influence the modern era, was based almost exclusively on the poetic fable collection of Avianus and the prose collection of 'Romulus'; these for their part indirectly passed down Babrius and Phaedrus and in this way established their collection as a keystone of the European tradition of the fable. The original fables of Phaedrus were not rediscovered until the time of the Humanists, with the *editio princeps* Pithous (1596), based on the cod. Pithoeanus saec. IX as the main bearer of the incomplete Phaedrus tradition, representing the decisive step in the wide dissemination of the fables of Phaedrus in modern times (for the Latin revisions in the Middle Ages of Avianus and 'Romulus' [22]; the complicated communication processes, the meaning of revisions and the passing down to the national languages, the contribution of school and sermons to the wide dissemination and general availability of the fable in the Middle Ages etc. is presented in [20]; the material is presented in [19]).

J.KÜ.

→ FABLE

1 F.R. ADRADOS, Historia de la fábula greco-latina I–III, 1979–87 2 J. DALFEN, Die ὕβρις der Nachtigall. Zu der F. bei Hesiod, in: WS 107, 1994/5, 157–77 3 N. HOLZBERG, Die ant. F., 1993 4 S. JEDRKIEWICZ, Sapere e paradosso nell' antichità: Esopo e la favola, 1989 5 T. KARADAGLI, F. und Ainos, 1981 6 F. LASSERRE, La fable en Grèce dans la poésie archaique, in: Entretiens XXX, 1984, 61–103 7 M.J. LUZZATTO, La datazione della Collectio Augustana di Esopo, in: Jb. der österr. Byzantinistik 33, 1983, 137–77 8 Id., Note su Aviano e sulle raccolte esopiche greco-latine, in: Prometheus 10, 1984, 75–94 9 Id., Grecia e Vicino Oriente: tracce della 'Storia di Ahiqar', in: Quaderni di Storia 36, 1992, 5–84 10 Id., Esopo, in: S. SETTIS (ed.), I Greci, II 1, 1996, 1307–24 11 K. MEULI, Herkunft und Wesen der F., in: Id., Gesammelte Schriften II, 1975, 731–56 12 M. NOJGAARD, La fable antique, I, 1964 13 B.E. PERRY, The origin of the

epimythion, in: TAPhA 71, 1940, 391–419 14 Id., Demetrius of Phalerum and the Aesopic fables, in: TAPhA 93, 1962, 287–346 15 Id., Babrius and Phaedrus, 1965 16 J. Spier, Emblems in archaic Greece, in: BICS 37, 1990, 107–29 17 W. Wienert, Die Typen der griech.-röm. F., 1925. 18 F. della Corte, Orazio favolista, in: Opuscula 11, 1988, 35–41 19 G. Dicke, K. Grubmüller, Die F. des MA und der frühen Neuzeit. Ein Katalog der dt. Versionen und ihrer lat. Entsprechungen, 1987 20 K. Grubmüller, Meister Esopus, 1977 21 A. Hausrath, s.v. F., RE 6, 1704–1736 22 L. Hervieux, Les fabulistes latins depuis le siècle d'Auguste jusqu' à la fin du moyen âge, 5 vols., 1893/4 (repr. 1970) 23 N. Holzberg, Die F. von Stadtmaus und Landmaus bei Phaedrus und Horaz, in: WJA N.F. 17, 1991, 229–239 24 L. Koep, s.v. F., RAC 7, 129–154 25 J. Küppers, Die F. Avians, 1977 26 Id., Zu Eigenart und Rezeptionsgesch. der ant. F.-Dichtung, in: E. Könsgen (ed.), Arbor amoena comis, 1990, 23–33 27 C.W. Müller, Ennius und Aesop, in: MH 33, 1976, 193–218 28 M. Nojgaard, La fable antique, vol.2: Les grands fabulistes, 1967 29 P.L. Schmidt, Polit. Argument und moralischer Appell: Zur Historizität der ant. Fabel im frühkaiserzeitl. Rom, in: Der Deutschunterricht 31,6, 1979, 74–88 30 K. Speckenbach, Die F. von der F., in: Frühma. Studien 12, 1978, 178–229 31 G. Thiele, Der Lat. Äsop des Romulus und die Prosa-Fassungen des Phädrus, 1910 32 C.M. Zander, Phaedrus solutus vel Phaedri fabulae novae XXX, 1921. M.J.L. and J.KÜ.

Fabrateria

[1] F. Vetus. Town of the Hernici on the Trerus (modern Sacco) near Frosinone (→ Frusino) in *Latium adiectum* (*regio I*), called *F. Vetus* from the end of the 2nd cent. BC, near the church of Santa Maria del Fiume near Ceccano (cf. CIL X p. 552, 5647–5661; EEpigr 8, 888f.). As a Volscian town, it was involved in Rome's disputes with the Samnites (Liv. 8,19,1) in 330. Initially *civitas sine suffragio*, then *municipium*, *tribus Tromentina* (CIL X 5657); under *dictatores*, later administered by *IV viri* and *decuriones*. Cult of Ceres and Hercules. Centuriation area.

[2] F. Nova. Roman *colonia* founded as *F. Nova* in 124 BC by C. Gracchus 18 km to the south-east in place of → Fregellae (destroyed in 125: Vell. 1,15,4) on the *via Latina* where the Liris meets the Trerus at La Civita near San Giovanni Incarico. Administered by *II viri*. Later *municipium*, *tribus Tromentina* (CIL X 5582). Archaeology: 3.2 km long ring wall; amphitheatre [1].

1 L. Crescenzi, L'anfiteatro di S. Giovanni in Carico, in: Archeologia Laziale 7, 1985, 109–111.

G. Colasanti, Fregellae, 1906; A. Nicosia, F. Nova, 1977; S. Antonini, F. Vetus, 1988; P.G. Monti, Un nuovo contributo alla ricostruzione della centuriazione romana nel Lazio meridionale, in: Terra dei Volsci, Contributi, 1992, 1. G.U.

Fabri In the military context *fabri* were craftsmen of the Roman army who were under the command of the *praefectus fabrum*. According to Livy (1,43,3), they initially formed two independent cohorts; at the latest from the time of Caesar onwards they were classified as soldiers of the legion (Caes. B Gall. 5,11,3). Vegetius (2,11) mentions the *tignarii*, *structores*, *carpentarii*, *ferrarii* and *pictores* (carpenters, bricklayers, cartwrights, smiths and painters) as some of the *fabri*. It was their duty to set up the winter camp and to produce or repair catapults and siege machines. However, the *fabricae* (→ *fabrica, fabricenses*) – also mentioned by Vegetius – who produced the weapons belong to late antiquity. Moreover the army had brickyards, pottery works and lime works. It is uncertain whether soldiers only had a supervisory role there or worked there themselves. In Britain there is evidence from the end of the 1st/beginning of the 2nd cent. AD of a *fabricie(n)sis leg(ionis) XX V(aleriae) V(ictricis)* (CIL VII 49 = ILS 2429). The unusual choice of words in a military context could refer to a civilian artisan in the army. Otherwise a term like *miles tector* was common (CIL XIII 5209; 11803 = ILS 9183).

1 G. Alföldy, Inschr. aus den Kalkbrennereien der niedergermanischen Legionen in Iversheim (Kr. Euskirchen), in: Epigraphische Studien 5, 1968, 17–27 2 H. von Petrikovits, Die Spezialgebäude röm. Legionslager, in: Id., Beiträge zur röm. Gesch. und Arch. von 1931–1974, 1976, 519–545 3 Id., Röm. Militärhandwerk. Arch. Forschungen der letzten Jahre, in: Ibid., 598–611 4 E. Sander, Der praefectus fabrum und die Legionsfabriken, in: BJ 162, 1962, 139–161. L.WI.

Fabrica, fabricenses Originally *fabrica* only refers to the finished work (ThlL VI 12ff.), but later it primarily refers to the place where something was manufactured.

Fabricae as production centres for equipment first appear in the direct military environment [11]. The first five *fabricae* with civilian employees were established in the Orient under Diocletian (Ioh. Mal. 307,21ff.). Not. Dign. Or. 11,18ff. and Not. Dign. Occ. 9,15ff provide an overview of the stock at the end of the 4th cent. The *fabricae* were subordinate to the *praefectus praetorio* (Cod.Theod. 10,22,2) up to *c.* 388, then to the *magister officiorum* (Cod.Theod. 10,22,3) who regularly posted → *agentes in rebus* as *principes fabricarum* (Cod. Theod. 10,22,3). The *magister officiorum* also had jurisdiction over the *fabricenses* and their families (Cod. Iust. 11,10,6). Sometimes they were administered by a joint *scrinium fabricarum* together with the *barbaricarii* (Cod. Iust. 12,20,5): *scrinio fabricarum et barbar⟨icar⟩um*. There is no express mention of their own *scrinium fabricensium* until 539 (Iust. Nov. 85,3). The role of the *scrinium armorum* (Lydus, Mag. 3,5) is unclear. In the east the *fabricae* were administered by four *subadiuvae fabricarum* (Not. Dign. Or. 11,44), while in the west they were administered by an unknown number of them (Not. Dign. Occ. 9,43).

The regional classification of the *fabricae* depended on the availability of raw materials (metals, charcoal) and the large army groups of the *comitatenses*. There was therefore a distinction between the actual *fabricae* whose job was to manufacture weapons and other institutions under state control that likewise produced high quality goods and were subordinate to the *comes sacrarum largitionum* (Not. Dign. Or. 13,16–20; Not. Dign. Occ. 11,45–77) or *comes privatarum* (Not. Dign. Occ. 12,26f.). The *fabricenses* were treated like soldiers which also included retirement as the term *veteranus in fabrica* demonstrates (CIL V 8742). The *fabricenses* were tattooed like *tirones* (Veg. Mil. 2,5) on the arms (Cod. Theod. 10,22,4) to prevent them from fleeing. It is unknown what the tattoos looked like and what their content was. The *fabricenses* were personally free but like other groups (*navicularii, pistores, suarii*) they were bound by their duties. They had ownership rights over their workshops and work tools that they could bequeath to their heirs (for the law of succession of the *fabricenses* cf. Theod. Nov. 6,3) but had limited mobility and were incorporated in the local organization of the *fabricenses* (*corpus fabricensium*) that had collective liability (Cod. Iust. 11,10,5) and inheritance rights (Theod. Nov. 6,3). The work of the *fabricenses* was certainly attractive for → *curiales* [1] (Cod. Iust. 11,9,4), as they were exempt from billeting soldiers (Cod. Theod. 7,8,8 = Cod. Iust. 12,40,4) and municipal burdens (Cod. Iust. 11,10,6). For the use of their labour and their specialized knowledge *fabricenses* received *annonae* as wages (cf. Iust. Nov. 85,3).

The material necessary for their work (metal; Cod.Theod. 10,22,2) was supplied as was fuel (charcoal; Cod.Theod. 11,16,15; 11,16,18) and was not allowed to be substituted for money (Cod. Theod. 10,22,2). For this purpose the *fabricenses* produced work that was precisely delineated and free of charge for the state. This does not appear to exclude the possibility of additional private financial activity and in the same way not all representatives of relevant occupations were automatically recorded as *fabricenses* (Iust. Nov. 85,3 pr.). Military organization is exemplified by the rank descriptions *praepositus* (CIL V 8697), *tribunus* (Amm. Marc. 14,8,18 and passim), *primicerius* (Cod.Theod. 10,22,3 for 2 years), *biarchus* (CIL V 8754), *ducenarius* (Foss), *centenarius* (Diehl 508). The local *fabricenses* appear as a rule rather to have been organizational amalgamations of smaller workshops but not to have been large closed operational units.

1 N. Charbonnel, La condition des ouvriers dans les ateliers impériaux aux IVe et Ve siècles, in: F. Burdeau, N. Charbonnel, M. Humbert, Aspects de l'empire romain, 1964, 61–95 2 Clauss, 51–54 3 R. Delmaire, Les institutions du Bas-Empire romain de Constantin à Justinien. I. Les institutions civiles palatines, 1995 4 A. Demandt, Die Spätant., 1989 5 C. Foss, The fabricenses ducenarii of Sardis, in: ZPE 35, 1979, 279–283 6 S. James, The fabricae, in: J.C. Coulston (ed.), Military equipment and the identity of Roman Soldiers, 1988, 257–331 7 Jones, LRE, 834–836 8 C.P. Jones, Stigma. Tattooing and branding in Graeco-Roman antiquity, in: JRS 77, 1987, 139–155, esp. 149. 9 J. Karayannopulos, Das Finanzwesen des frühbyz. Staates, 1958 10 J.H.W.G. Liebeschütz, From Diocletian to the Arab conquest. Change in the Late Roman Empire, 1990 11 H. von Petrikovits, Beitr. zur röm. Gesch. und Arch. I. 1931–1974, 1976, 519–545; 598–611; 612–619 12 E. Sander, Der Praefectus Fabrum und die Legionsfabriken, in: BJ 162, 1962, 139–161 13 L. Wierschowski, Heer und Wirtschaft. Das röm. Heer der Prinzipatszeit als Wirtschaftsfaktor, 1984 14 St. Williams, Diocletian and the Roman recovery, 1985.

P.H.

Fabricius Roman plebeian *nomen gentile*, probably not from *faber* ('smith'), but from Etruscan *hapre* like Faberius and others. [1; 2]. Perhaps the family immigrated to Rome [3], in the 3rd cent. BC it became part of the nobility with F. [I 3] but was unable to maintain this status in the 2nd cent. In Rome there was a *compitum Fabricium* (Fest. 180L) or a *vicus Fabrici* (ILS 6073) between Caelius and Palatine, perhaps named after the place of residence of F. [I 3] [4], and the *pons Fabricius*, → F. [I 1].

1 Schulze, 161f.; 258 2 E. Fraenkel, s.v. Namenwesen, RE 16, 1670 3 Münzer, 62; 413 4 G. Pisani Sartorio, s.v. Copitum Fabricium, in: LTUR 1, 1993, 315f.

I. Republican period II. Imperial period

I. Republican period

[1] **F., L.** In 62 BC probably people's tribune (MRR 2, 141, n. 8; 174) and *curator viarum* (Cass. Dio 37,45,3), completed the *pons Fabricius*, the stone bridge between the left bank and the island of the Tiber (CIL VI 1305 = ILS 5893 = ILLRP 379; illustration in Nash 2, 189f.).
[2] **F., Q.** supported Cicero's recall in 57 BC as people's tribune (MRR 2, 202).
[3] **F. Luscinus, C.** (for the cognomen, 'the one-eyed', see [1]). *Homo novus* who rose to power in the war against the Samnites and → Pyrrhus: he was consul I in 282 BC, consul II in 278 and censor in 275 (in each case together with Q. Aemilius [I 30] Papus). In 282 he fought against the Samnites, Bruttians and Lucanians and was granted a triumph (MRR 1,189). Thurii which he liberated set up a statue of honour to him in Rome (Plin. HN 34,32). In 280 together with Papus and P. Cornelius [I 27] Dolabella, he negotiated with Pyrrhus the release of Roman captives from the battle of Heraclea which he secured in 279 despite the failure of the peace treaty. In 278 he fought against the Lucanians, Bruttians, Tarentinians and Samnites and was granted another triumph. As censor in 275 he forced P. Cornelius [I 62] Rufinus out of the Senate because he owned 10 pounds of silver crockery (Liv. Epit. 14; Val. Max. 2,9,4, & numerous others). He was accorded the extraordinary honour of being buried inside the city (Cic. Leg. 2,58). In the later tradition F. Luscinus was considered to be an example of modesty, severity and generosity; his negotiations with Pyrrhus (he is said to have warned him that he was to be assassinated by a confidant, Gell. NA 3,8; Cic. Off. 1,40; 386; Cic. Fin. 5,64 and others) and his lifestyle were the subject of countless anecdotes.

1 WALDE/HOFMANN 1, 838.

CAH 7,2, ²1989, Index s.v.

[4] **F. Luscinus, C.** probably the grandson of F. Luscinus [I 3], in 195 BC praetor urbanus (Liv. 33,42,7; 43,5) and in 190 legate of the consul L. Cornelius [I 72] Scipio Asiagenes (Liv. 37,4,2). K.-L.E.

II. IMPERIAL PERIOD

[II 1] **C.F. Tuscus.** Son of a Gaius, of the Tribus Aniensis. His home was Alexandria Troads in the province of Asia. In the Augustan-Tiberian period he took on several equestrian services in the army and was involved in levying of troops conducted by Augustus/Tiberius in Rome, perhaps because of the defeat of Varus. Finally he was *praefectus equitum* in Germania under Germanicus (AE 1973, 501).

DEVIJVER, PME, F 18; DEMOUGIN, Prosopographie, 189f. no. 216.

[II 2] **A. Didius Gallus F. Veiento.** Senator, probably adopted by A. Didius [II 2] Gallus [1. 119]. Under Nero as praetorian he was forced out of the Senate because he published pamphlets against senators. Under Vespasian he was in the Senate again; his powerful position can be seen from his three consulates: in AD 74?, 80, 83?, and his three priestly offices. He was a member of the *consilium* Domitians, also mentioned in Juvenal (4, 113; 123ff.). With his wife Attica he perhaps accompanied Domitian in 88/9 on the campaign against Antonius [II 15] Saturninus. Under Nerva he continued to have an influence on the emperor and the Senate.

1 SALOMIES, Nomenclature.

SYME, RP VII, 532ff.; PIR² F 91. W.E.

Fabulla Wife of a certain Asiaticus, mentioned in the will of Domitius [II 25] Tullus as the recipient of a legacy (AE 1976, 77); she is presumably identical to the F. mentioned in Apollonius [14] of Tyana as the wife of Valerius, proconsul of Asia (Epist. 58). The latter is perhaps identical to Valerius Asiaticus, *cos.* in AD 94, proconsul of Asia 108/9 [1. 292ff.]. In this case the Letter of Apollonius would be fictitious. Cf. PIR² F 92.

1 W. ECK, Zum neuen Fr. des sog. Testamentum Dasumii, in: ZPE 30, 1978, 277–295. W.E.

Fabullus Friend of → Catullus, recipient of the poem of invitation of Catull. 13, mostly mentioned together with Veranius: from Hispania Citerior they send Catullus a serviette (Catull. 12,14ff., cf. Catull. 9); about the time of his journey to Bithynia (57/6 BC) they are part of the cohors of a governor Piso (probably L. Calpurnius [I 19] Piso Caesoninus) and are disappointed, just as Catullus, in their financial expectations (Catull. 28 and 47). So this probably concerns two different journeys of the pair, the first one (in 60/59) probably being a private venture, especially if F. came from Spain. SYME [2. 300–304] considers an earlier stay of Piso there too, while WISEMAN [3. 38ff.], not very plausibly, assumes that there was only one journey (to Spain in 57/6) and posits another Piso.

1 C.L. NEUDLING, A Prosopography to Catullus, 1955, 65f. 2 SYME, RP I 3 T.P. WISEMAN, Catullan Questions, 1969. P.L.S.

Facial expression FE means the expressive motions of the entire face (moods) or parts of it that spontaneously indicate a momentary human mood or are deliberately assumed with the intention of making a particular expression. FE's are often situation-related and supplemented by → gestures (→ Gestus) or even only become comprehensible through the latter. On the stage individual characters were shown with differing FE's (→ Masks, → Mimos). FE's were also a means of providing a person (e.g. a philosopher, poet or ruler) with certain characteristics and character traits (→ Portraiture, cf. Cic. Pis. 1; Cic. Sest. 19; Ter. An. 855–857). In painting → Polygnotus supposedly was the first to portrait people with open mouths and visible teeth. → Sculpture adopted this artistic means of expression (cf. Xen. Mem. 3,10,1–8).

In the course of this development, a change in the meaning of certain FE's occurred. FE's may already be observed in archaic art, e.g. in the grimace of → Gorgo (bared teeth, furrowed nose and contracted forehead as signs of wildness) and the 'Archaic Smile' as an expression of youthful beauty (cf. e.g. Hom. H. ad Venerem 17) or liveliness. The dying and the slain bear this smile (especially kouroi and korai, → statues; → sculpture). In battle scenes the mouth is represented slightly opened from late Archaic art onwards to symbolize the defeated and exhausted (e.g. → Amazons, → Giants, Persians, etc.). However, the opponent has a closed mouth as an expression of self-control and discipline. In a funerary context the open mouth may be a sign of mourning ([1. pl. 3], → Mourning, → Gestures, → Gestus) or respect. However, towards the late 6th cent., this expression turns into an expression of superiority and victory (cf. Anth. Pal. 16,54). The furrowed forehead is initially an expression of wildness and lack of control, but then becomes a sign of internal excitement and reflection. The form of the eyebrows altered from their position at rest can mean several things: slanted, raised brows stand for suffering, high-raised brows indicate mad attack, laterally raised brows that drop off to the base of the nose portray dignity and imperious authority.

Under Hellenism, the Roman republic and in the Imperial period, a canon of FE's developed for characterizing rulers and politicians, which also served as a guideline for private art. It includes traits like reflectiveness, dynamic energy, self-control, strictness, tense determination by means of a 'strict expression', determined look, furrowed forehead, flared nostrils, drawing together of the eyebrows, open (or closed) mouth as the main image formulas.

→ Gestures; → Gestus; → Sculpture; → Portraiture

1 MDAI(A) 29, 1904.

B. FEHR, Bewegungsweisen und Verhaltensideale, 1979; L. GIULIANI, Bildnis und Botschaft. Hermeneutische Untersuchungen zur Bildniskunst der röm. Republik, 1986; H. KENNER, Weinen und Lachen in der griech. Kunst, 1960; H. P. LAUBSCHER, Fischer und Landleute, 1982; W. MARTINI, Die archa. Plastik der Griechen, 1990, 83–85; G. SITTL, Die Gebärden der Griechen und Römer, 1890. R.H.

Factiones

I. REPUBLIC II. IMPERIAL PERIOD

I. REPUBLIC

In Rome the permanent or temporary union between people who were mostly of high rank so as to preserve or assert similar interests. Initially used in the sense of a kinship connection (Plaut. Trin. 452; 466; 490), *factiones* gain a pejorative meaning in the late Roman Republic ('clique', 'coterie' in [1. 103 and passim]) as the term for an oligarchical group (Cic. Rep. 1,68; Caes. B Civ. 3,82f.) that was mostly reproached for moral inferiority (Sall. Iug. 31,15) and always for striving for power (*dominatio*). For instance, political fellow travellers (*Syllana f.*: Ps.-Ascon. 255), conspirators (Sall. Catil. 32,2), the union between Caesar, Crassus and Pompey in 60 BC (cf. Cic. Att. 2,3,3f.) or even the → *optimates* (Cic. Rep. 3,23) were called *factiones*.

The union of the powerful (*principes, potentes*) was, aside from → *amicitia* and *clientela* (→ *cliens*), part of the regular fabric of aristocratic politics, however the late Republican role of the *factiones* is hardly comparable with the political ties observable since the end of the war against Hannibal (as [1. 104–110] assumes), but was an expression of crisis [2. 162–167]. The pursuit of politics of the *factiones* ends with the Republic; in the Imperial period the meaning of the word changes (see II below).

1 M. GELZER, Die Nobilität der röm. Republik, [2]1984
2 CHR. MEIER, Res publica amissa, [2]1980.

R. SEAGER, Factio: Some Observations, in: JRS 62, 1972, 53–58. W.ED.

II. IMPERIAL PERIOD

Organizations operated by equites without which *circenses* (→ Circus [II]) are inconceivable in Imperial Rome. For the circus games they supplied everything necessary: chariot drivers with personnel, horses and payments in kind. The directors (*domini factionum*) were equites, and they were efficient and so self-confident that at the time of Nero they could still dictate their conditions to those holding the games (Suet. Nero 22). As is still the case today at soccer games, the spectators recognized the *factiones* competing against each other by their colours: blue = *venetus*, green = *prasinus*, red = *russatus*, white = *albatus*. Two additional *factiones* and colours introduced by Domitian (purple = *purpureus*, gold = *aureus*; Suet. Dom. 7) did not outlast this emperor. The short tunics of the chariot drivers, the decoration for the horses and probably also the chariot boxes were kept in the colour of the party [1]; the spectators therefore saw a 'colourful procession' (*discolor agmen*, Ov. Am. 3,2,78). Although *circenses* had been celebrated in Rome from the time of the kings on, no author before Pliny (Plin. HN 8,160) mentions the *factiones* and their colours. This is explained by the fact that the *circenses* did not gain their special importance until under Caligula.

In the Augustan period only enthusiasts and experts in the equestrian sport attended the circus (Ov. Am. 3,2,1). Around the turn of the 1st to the 2nd cent. AD the situation changed markedly (Plin. Ep. 9,6): it was not the quickness of the horses nor the skill of the chariot drivers that, according to Pliny, interested the audience but merely the 'jersey' (Lat. *pannus* = cloth), i.e. the colour of the tunics worn by the racing drivers; the decision on a colour is made without any *ratio*. Pliny does not mention any individual colour, obviously the favour of the masses was still evenly distributed. Only the imperial court was unambiguously set on blue and green; this is attested to by Suetonius' biographies (Suet. Calig. 55; Nero 22; Vit. 7), Marcus Aurelius (1,5), the SHA (Lucius Verus 4,8; 6,2) and Cassius Dio (59,14,6; 73,17; 78,10,2; 80,14,2). The predilection of the emperor for blue and green that was initially probably coincidental tends to explain why these *factiones* were predominant at the circus towards the end of the 2nd cent. For the emperors informed their favourites of their liking for them in an extravagant way: Caligula had the racetrack sprinkled with vermilion and malachite (Suet. Calig. 18); Nero, as a chariot driver, wore a malachite-green tunic, and to match it, the racetrack was dyed with malachite (Plin. HN 33,90); Vitellius, a supporter of the Blues, established *stabula* for the chariot drivers (Tac. Hist. 2,94,3). Highly qualified chariot drivers, e.g. the *miliarii* Gutta Calpurnianus and Diocles, were still in the 2nd cent. winning themselves victory palms in the colours of all four *factiones*. This did not prevent the Whites and Reds in the course of the Imperial period from being classified later with the greater *factiones*, initially in an alternating combination, finally in Constantinople in the combination green/red, blue/white [2. 45–73]. The way in which this relationship was organized 'is something of a puzzle' [2. 70], but it certainly is connected with the fact that all four *factiones* were reconstituted during the Imperial period from independent companies into organizations in the service of the emperor.

This development was completed in the 4th cent. AD, as the Codex Theodosianus demonstrates. Imperial decrees now regulated the duties of the *factiones* very precisely, e.g. how worn-out racehorses were to be treated, which horses were allowed to be sold, how the naming was to be done, who had to supply feed to the individual *factiones* etc. (Cod. Theod. 15,10,1; 15,10,2). In inscriptions from the late 3rd cent., victorious chariot drivers are named repeatedly as *domini* of the *factiones* with the title *factionarius*. The declaration of legal incapacity of the *factiones* was unavoidable: the monopoly for the equipping of the *circenses* could not remain in private hands. The smaller *factiones* received not just colours but also their own *stabula* in the *regio* 9 at the Circus Flaminius [3; 4]. As is still the case today, *stabulum* was an all-embracing term for the equestrian sport (comparable with the modern term 'racing stable'). The fact that the *factiones* of the 4th cent. AD primarily worked for the emperor can be demonstrated by the case of the city prefect Symmachus. He himself acquired the racehorses for the *circenses* that his son as the praetor (in AD 401) had to equip. In his letters he does not mention *factiones* once [2. 8].

Emperor Constantine I took on the Roman circus organization of his period for Constantinople: trained staff in the imperial service were responsible for the preparation and running of the *circenses*; as in Rome, there was a two-way division into blue and green and the Whites and Reds were allocated to these. For the two groups two stables were built, the Dihippion to the north-west of the hippodrome [5]. The term *factiones* never appears in Byzantine sources and actually there were no longer any *factiones* in their original form. Among the notorious 'Circus parties' (modern term) of the eastern Roman empire it is thought that there were rabid supporters of the circus colours who are described in the sources as μέρη (*mérē*), δῆμοι (*dêmoi*), στασιῶται (*stasiôtai*) ('divisions', 'groupings', 'party followers'). They have nothing to do with the organization of the *circenses*. 'There is a deceptive line of continuity between the Blues and Greens of Rome and Constantinople' [2. 309].

1 K. Parlasca, in: Helbig, vol. 3, No. 2470
2 A. Cameron, Circus-Factions, 1976 3 H. Jordan, Ch. Hülsen, Top. der Stadt Rom im Altertum 1, 1–3, 1878, 551 4 F. Coarelli, Rom, 1974, 248 5 W. Müller-Wiener, Bildlex. zur Top. Istanbuls, 1977, 232.

A. Demandt, Die Spätantike, 1989; L. Friedländer, Die Spiele, in: J. Marquart (ed.), Röm. Staatsverwaltung 3, 1885, 511–524; Humphrey; P. Veyne, Brot und Spiele, 1988, 596–631. A.HÖ.

Fadius Roman *nomen gentile*, attested to from the 1st cent. BC (Schulze, 132; 516).
I. Republican period II. Imperial period

I. Republican period

[1] **F., T.** Quaestor in 63 BC; in 57 as plebeian tribune he supported the recall of Cicero (Cic. P. Red. Sen. 21; Ad Q. Fr. 1,4,3; Att. 3,23,4). In 52 he was exiled for unknown reasons (Cic. Fam. 5,18).

Syme, RP 2, 594 (Name).

[2] **F. Gallus, M.** the Epicurean, M. → Fabius [I 18] Gallus. K.-L.E.

II. Imperial period

[II 1] **L. F. Rufinus** *Cos. suff.* in AD 113; belonged to Pliny's circle. PIR² F 100.

[II 2] **C. F. Rufus** Probably the son of F. [II 1]; *cos. suff.* in 145. PIR² F 101. W.E.

Faenius Rufus, L. Eques who in AD 55 became *praefectus annonae* through the support of Agrippina [3] and was held in high esteem by the people of Rome. Appointed by Nero in 62 to the position of *praefectus praetorio* along with Tigellinus; when the latter accused him of having had a relationship with Agrippina and Nero mistrusted him, he joined the Pisonian conspiracy. After it was uncovered, he was executed. It is still very uncertain whether the *horrea Faeniana* go back to him (CIL VI 37796).

H. Pavis d'Escurac, La préfecture de l'annone, 1976, 322; PIR² F 102. W.E.

Faesulae Town in northern Etruria (*regio VII*) on a rise above Florence north of the Arno, modern Fiesole. Etruscan name Vipsl [1. 675ff.]. Mentioned by Pol. 2,25,6 in relation to the Celtic invasion of 225 BC. In 217 Hannibal marched from F. to Lake Trasimena (Pol. 3,80; 82). In the Social War, F. was destroyed by L. Porcius Cato (Flor. 2,6,11). Later F. was a Sullan veteran colony (Cic. Cat. 3,14; Sall. Catil. 28), *tribus Scaptia*. In 63 BC the town sided with Catilina (Sall. Catil. 24).

Stilicho defeated the Goti there in AD 405 under Radagais (Oros. 7,37); in 539 occupied by Belisarius (Procop. Goth. 2,24). Diocese from the 5th cent. onwards Archaeology: few remains from the Iron Age; city wall from the 3rd cent. BC later restored (2,570 m long) [2]; Etruscan-Roman temple with an altar; next to it, a well preserved theatre and thermal baths; characteristic funerary steles from the 6th cent. BC onwards. From the 3rd cent. onwards necropolises on the Bargellino. Roman aqueduct from Montereggi. Langobardian cemetery at the theatre [3]. Archaeological museum. Epigraphical evidence: CIL XI p. 298f., 1543–1576.

1 M. Pallottino, Testimonia Linguae Etruscae, ²1968
2 M. Morciano, La lettura delle mura di F., in: Journal of Ancient Topography 4, 1994, 161–176 3 O. von Hessen, Die langobardischen Grabfunde aus F., 1966.

M. Lombardi, F., 1941; A. De Agostino, F., 1954; P. Bocci, Nuovi scavi del tempio di Fiesole, in: SE 29, 1961, 411–415; Id., F., in: NSA 1961, 52–62; M. Fuchs, Il teatro romano di F., 1986; M. Salvini, F., 1990. G.U.

Fagifulae Town of the Samnites Pentri (*regio IV*) on a hill to the right of the Tifernus. In 217 BC won back from the Carthaginians by Q. Fabius Maximus (Liv. 24,20,5). *Municipium, tribus Voltinia* (Plin. HN 3,107; CIL IX p. 237). Its location was pinpointed at the Church of Santa Maria di Faífula (Faífoli) near Montágano north of Campobasso. Epigraphical evidence: CIL IX 2551–2561; EEpigr 8, 109.

A. DEGRASSI, Quattuorviri, in: Id., Scritti vari 1, 1962, 150ff.; G. DE BENEDETTIS, F., in: S. CAPINI (ed.), Samnium. Archeologia del Molise, 1991, 259f. G.U.

Fagus see → Beech

Faience The term faience describes earthenware with a coating of pewter glaze that looks like porcelain and was produced for the first time in Spain in the 13th cent. AD and traded via Mallorca (*Majolica*), although it got its name from earthenware manufactured from the 16th cent. onwards in northern Italian Faenza that borrowed from Chinese porcelain.

In the archaeological literature faience is a common but incorrect term for a glass-like, silicated, glazed or unglazed product of chalky to sandy consistency (hence more accurately termed siliceous ceramics). Its base material consists as a rule of ground quartz sand, sodium carbonate, sodium hydrogen carbonate and lime, colour-giving additives and coincidental impurities that can be shaped by mixing with water and small amounts of potter's clay and serves as a carrier for coloured glazes. During the firing of the object, a thin, natural glaze initially arises through the glazing of the surface. The characteristic, powerfully colourful, hard, artificial glazing is produced from the same base substances and, depending on the desired colour, traces of iron (red/green/black), manganese (brown/dark red/green), antimony (yellow), copper (blue/green), calcium (blue) or lime (white) as well as plant ash; it comes about after an additional firing, the so-called glazing firing. The components of the base substance and glazing can vary greatly from region to region depending on the origin and age of the faience but they remain unchanged over long periods of time.

Faience is one of the oldest and, because of the easy availability of the base substances, also one of the cheapest of the artificially produced man-made materials. The earliest known evidence of faience comes from Egypt and Mesopotamia and goes back to the 2nd half of the 4th millennium BC. From the early Bronze Age onwards, faience was used in Egypt, in the Middle East, in Mycenae and on Crete, as well as from the late Bronze Age onwards in northern Syria, in Cyprus and in the eastern Mediterranean to produce artisan products of high artistic quality. In addition to pearls and amulets there were statuettes of animals and humans, a variety of open and closed vessels and inlay work for jewellery and furniture as well as wall decorations and tiles.

During the 1st half of the 7th cent. the production of faience with an Oriental influence in the form of figurative balsamaria, 'pilgrim bottles' and miniature pots for the eastern and central Mediterranean market began on Rhodes, situated on the eastern edge of the Aegean and on the trade route from the Phoenician Levant and Cyprus to the west. From the outset, production was closely connected with the Phoenician perfume industry that had also been established in Rhodes from the middle of the 8th cent.

From the end of the 7th cent. onwards Rhodian faience production was expanded through products from Naucratis. Here was discovered not just a production centre with mines for extracting raw materials and for further processing of prepared material, but also clay models, scarab seals, amulets, figurative pendants with Egyptian and Greek features (cats, naked women, deities, flute and lyre players) as well as ointment and perfume containers of Corinthian and Rhodian shape (→ Aryballoi [2] and head vases, partly with Egyptian name cartouches) that had been very widely distributed from here throughout the entire Mediterranean.

BIBLIOGRAPHY AND MAPS: K. GALLING, s.v. Fayence, Biblisches Reallex., 154ff.; R.J. CHARLESTON, Roman Pottery, 1955; J.V. NOBLE, The Technique of Egyptian Fayence, in: AJA 73, 1969, 435–439; D. BURR THOMPSON, Ptolemaic Oinochoai and Portraits in Fayence, 1973; H. HODGES, Artifacts, 1976; B. NOLTE, s.v. Fayence, LÄ 2, 138–142; J. DAYTON, A. DAYTON, Minerals, Metals, Glazing, and Man, 1978, 25f., 35–38, 434f.; V. WEBB, Archaic Greek Fayence, 1978 (with extensive bibliography); P. VANDIVER, F. Vessels, in: Egypt's Golden Age: The Art of Living in the New Kingdom 1558–1085 B.C. exhibition catalogue Boston, 1982, 140f.; A. KACZMARCZYK, R.E.M. HEDGES, Ancient Egyptian F. An Analytical Survey of Egyptian F. from Predynastic to Roman Times, 1983; J. RIEDERER, Arch. und Chemie – Einblicke in die Vergangenheit. exhibition catalogue Berlin, 1987, 199–201; M.S. TITE, I.C. FREESTONE, M. BIMSON, Egyptian F.: An Investigation of the Methods of Production, in: Archaeometry 25,1, 1983, 17–27; P.T. NICHOLSON, Egyptian Fayence and Glass (Shire Egyptology Series 18), 1993, 9–17.; CH.B.

Faiyum Large oasis *c.* 80 km south-west of Cairo with a lake in the north. Name from Egyptian *pꜣ-jm* ('the sea', older names *tꜣš*, 'lake land' and *š-rsj*, 'southern lake', Greek ἡ λίμνη (*hē límnē*) or Κροκοδιλοπολίτης νομός (*Krokodilopolítēs nomós*), from 256/5 onwards Ἀρσινοίτης νομός/*Arsionoïtēs nomós*). The capital city Šdjt (→ Arsinoe [III 2]) is mentioned early but it was not until the 12th Dynasty that F. was developed through dam construction, especially under Amenemhet III (*c.* 1853–1808) who was still considered a local hero in Roman times. The chief god was always the crocodile god Sobek (*Sbk*; cf. Str. 17,811; Hdt. 2,69; 2,148). There are hardly any sources until the Greek conquest. The F. was primarily used for hunting and fishing. Through new dams (lake at the entrance to F.) and irrigation of the edges of the desert by → Ptolemaeus II, intensive agricultural use became possible; Greek soldiers settled in *c.* 30–40 new villages. In late antiquity most of these settlements were given up; countless Demotic and Greek papyri have been found there.
→ Heracleopolis magna

D. ARNOLD, s.v. Fajjum, LÄ 2, 87–93. K.J.-W.

Glazing techniques

1. Self-glazing through efflorescence of the salts in the drying process

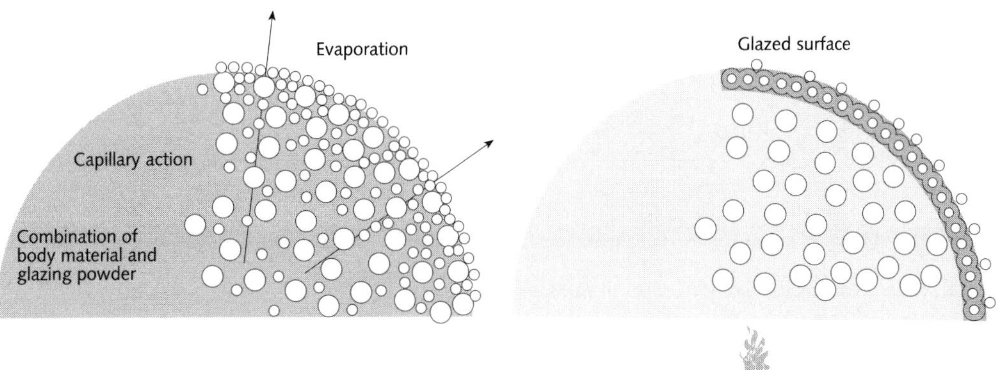

2. Self-glazing by immersion in glazing powder for firing

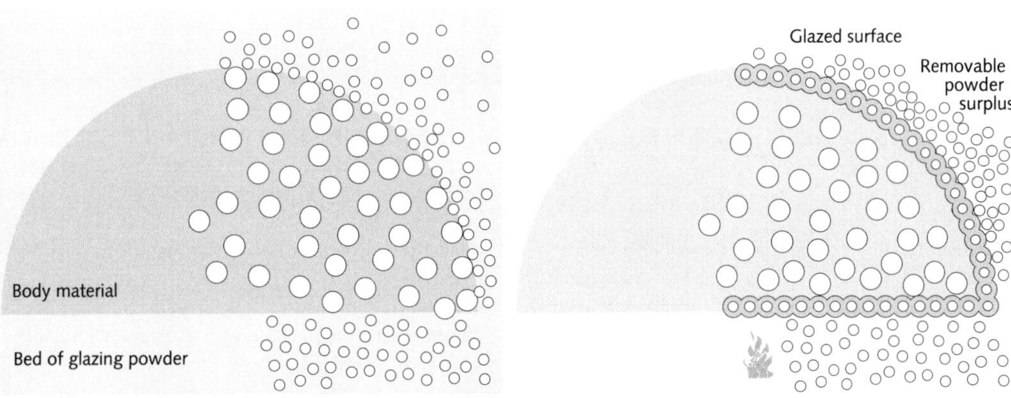

3. Application of glazing after drying (by immersion, pouring on or coating)

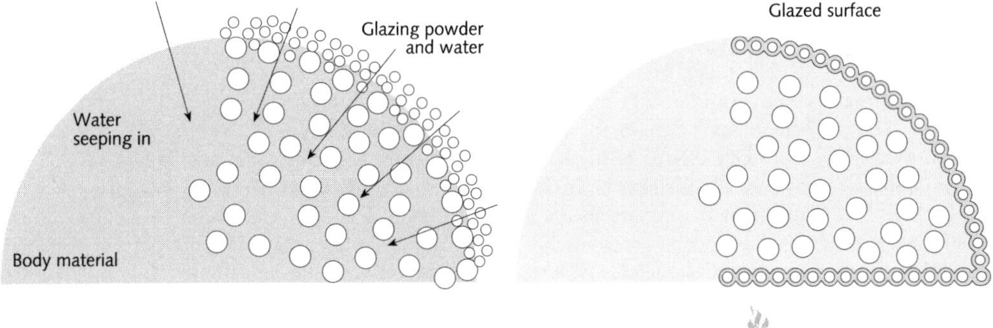

Quartz sand

Alkaline salts

Firing

Quartz particles merging with the alkaline salts because of chemical reaction

The formed object is dried and subsequently fired. During firing, the alkaline salts contained in the glazing powder act as a melting agent on the quartz particles of the body material. The merged quartz particles form the glaze.

M. HAA.

Falacrinae, Falacrinum Settlement of the Sabini (*regio IV*) at the sources of the Avens in the area of Reate on the border with Picenum. Station of the *via Salaria* (It. Ant. 307; Tab. Peut. 5,4), near the church of S. Silvestro in Falacrino in Collicelle (Cittareale, Rieti). Birth place of Vespasianus (Suet. Vesp. 2,1). Inscriptions.: CIL IX, p. 434.

NISSEN vol. 2, 468; N. PERSICHETTI, Viaggio archeologico della via Salaria, 1893, 79f. G.U.

Falarica see → Pilum

Falcata Modern technical term derived from *falcatus* ('sickle-shaped') that describes the cutting and stabbing weapon of the Iberian foot soldier that was about 60 cm long and had a slightly crooked back, an s-shaped curved blade and a pommel bent downwards with bird or horse head ends. The distribution of the falcata, which goes back directly to the Italian cutting swords and is attested from the 2nd half of the 5th cent. at the latest to the 1st cent. BC, is concentrated in the Hispanic south-east (→ Contestani(a), → Bastetani).
→ Sword

F. OUESADA SANZ, Arma y simbolo: la f. iberica, 1992. M.BL.

Falcidius Italian personal name (SCHULZE 272).

F., C. (P.?), people's tribune in 41 BC and originator of one of the last known plebiscites (*lex Falcidia*), which prescribed that a testator could only leave so many legacies as allowed the heir to remain with a quarter of the inheritance (*quarta Falcidiana*) (Dig. 35,2; Gai. Inst. 2,227).

KASER, RPR 2, 756f. K.-L.E.

Falcons While ἱέρακες generally denotes goshawks and ἰκτῖνοι harriers, only the kestrel (*Falco tinnunculus*) is identifiable among falcons. Aristophanes calls it Κερχνῇς (Av. 1181 in Ael. NA 12,4), Aristotle κεγχρίς (Hist. an. 6,2,559a 26; *cenchris*, Plin. HN 10,143f.). According to Aristot. Hist. an. 6,1,558b 28–30, it lays four or more red eggs (as well Plin. HN 10,143f.), has a crop (Hist. an. 2,17,509a 6) and drinks a fair bit (8,3,594a 1f.). Pliny claims that the *tinnunculus* is a friend of domestic pigeons whom it defends against goshawks (HN 10,109). Like Pliny, Columella (8,8,7) relates a recommendation by Democritus: the pigeons can be permanently bound to their loft by placing four clay pots holding a young falcon each under the corners of the loft. According to Plin. HN 29,127 the dung of the *cenchris* reduces the white spots in the human eye. Nicander (in Antoninus Liberalis 9) has the Muses transform a daughter of Pierus (→ Pierides) into this bird [1. 135].
→ Birds of prey

1 D'ARCY W. THOMPSON, A Glossary of Greek Birds, 1936, repr. 1966. C.HÜ.

Falerii

[1] Capital city of (non-Etruscan) Falisci in southern Etruria on a tuff spur of the eastern Monti Cimini between two righthand tributaries of the Tiberis (Vicano and Fosso Maggiore). Founded by the Argive hero → Halesus (Ov. Fast. 4,73), according to others a Chalcidian foundation (Iust. 20,1,13). Had its own Italic dialect (Str. 5,2,9; [1; 2; 3]). Cult of the Sabine Juno Curitis; likewise Sabine: the cult of Janus Quadrifrons (Serv. Aen. 7,607); additional cults: Minerva, Mars, Apollo on the Mons Soracte that was situated in the city area. In the 5th cent. BC F. was initially allied with → Fidenae (Liv. 4,17; 18; 32), then with → Veii (Liv. 5,8; 17; 18); in 394 F. was captured by Camillus (Liv. 5,26f.). In the 4th cent. F. was allied with the Tarquinii (Liv. 7,16). In 351 BC a 40-year ceasefire was signed with Rome which was changed in 343 into a *foedus* (Liv. 7,22; 38). F. revolted against Rome in 293 (Liv. 10,45) and 241 (Pol. 1,65); destroyed by the Romans in 241, F. lost 15,000 residents and half its territory (triumph of Q. Lutatius Cerco in 240, CIL I², p. 47; Zon. 8,18). Transplanted from the hill – that was hard to capture – to the plain 5 km to the west (→ F. [2] Novi). In the Middle Ages F. was resettled (Viterbo); modern Civita Castellana.

The town originally lay on the Vignale to the north-east of the modern town (temple terracottas from ancient times). F. spread over the area of the later Medieval settlement, surrounded by a tuffstone wall in *opus quadratum* (northern gate in the monastery of Santa Maria del Carmine). In the district of Celle there is a possible temple of Juno Quiritis (Dion. Hal. Ant. Rom. 1,21; Ov. Fast. 6,49). Necropolises (beginning of the 7th–3rd cent. BC) are situated on the hills of Montarano and Celle in the north-east as well as in Penna and Valsiarosa to the south-west of the town. Ovid in the *Amores* describes F. as the home of his wife (Am. 3,13).

[2] F. Novi. Modern name of the town on the *via Amerina* between Nepet and Horta (Tab. Peut. 5,4) where F. was reestablished in 241 BC. *Municipium, tribus Horatia.* Under the Gracchi or the Triumviri [7. 217,5] *colonia Iunionia Faliscorum*. The town was the home of the poet Annius. Colony under Gallienus. Centre of linen production; cattle-raising. Since the 5th cent. a bishopric. In the 11th cent. the inhabitants left F. and returned to Civita Castellana (F. [1]). F. was situated close to the church of Santa Maria di Fàlleri.

Archaeology: the city wall of 240–230 BC that is almost triangular is well preserved (over 2 km long, 9 gates, 50 towers); F. has a regular ground plan with a main west-east axis and *insulae* (1 *actus*) [6]; forum, theatre (Fortuna statue in the Museum of Antiquities Berlin; Sileni in the Louvre); outside the walls there is an amphitheatre; *via sacra, via Augusta.* Necropolises in the south and in the east (Tre Camini, Pratoro), mausoleums in the east and the north. Christian catacombs [4].

F. is probably not identical to Aequum Faliscum that is probably situated at Grotta Porciosa [5].

1 G. Giacomelli, La lingua falisca, 1963 2 Id., Il Falisco, 1978, 505–542 3 G. Maetzke (ed.), La civiltà dei Falisci, 1990 4 E. De Louet, F., in: Bullettino d'Archeologia Cristiana 3, 1880, 69–71 5 O. Cuntz, Aequum Faliscum, in: Jahresh. 2, 1899, 87f. 6 F. Castagnoli, Ippodamo, 1956, 84 7 F. Blume, K. Lachmann (ed.), Die Schriften der röm. Feldmesser 2 vols., 1848ff.

F. Barnabei, A. Cozza, A. Pasqui, Antichità del territorio Falisco, in: Monumenti degli Scavi di Antichi dell' Accademia dei Lincei 4, 1894, 5–104; M. Taylor, H. C. Bradshaw, Architectural Terra-cottas from two temples at F.V., in: PBSR 8, 1916, 1–34; L. A. Holland, The Faliscans in prehistoric times, in: Papers of the American Academy in Rome 5, 1925; B. Götze, Ein röm. Rundgrab in F., 1939; M. Frederiksen, J. B. Ward-Perkins, The Ancient Road Systems of the Central and Northern Ager Faliscus, in: PBSR 25, 1957, 67–136; C. Battisti, L'antica F., in: L'Universo 45, 1965, 845–854; G. Pulcini, F. veteres, F. novi, Civita Castellana, 1974; T. W. Potter, A Faliscan Town in South Etruria, 1976, 33f.; I. Di Stefano Manzella, F. Novi negli scavi degli anni 1821–1830, in: Memorie della Pontificia Accademia romana di Archeologia 12,2, 1979; Id., Supplementa Italica, N.S. 1, 1981, 101–176; BTCGI 5, 1987, 323–368; A. Comella, I materiali votivi di F., 1986; Id., Le terrecotte architettoniche del santuario dello Scasato a F.: scavi 1886–1887, 1993; M. Andreussi, s.v. Falisci, EV 2, 457f. G.U.

Falesia Harbour on the Etruscan coast opposite Ilva (modern Elba), 12 miles south of Populonia (It. Ant. 501; *Faleria*, Rut. Namat. 1,371, should be corrected to Falesia [2]). In the Middle Ages Porto di Felesa [1], modern Piombino (Livorno).

1 G. Targioni Tozzetti, Relazione d'alcuni viaggi fatti in diverse parti della Toscana 4, 1751, 250
2 R. Gelsomino, Nota a Rut. Nam. 1,371, in: Rivista di Cultura Classica e Medioevale 15, 1973, 35–47. G.U.

Faliscan is sketchily known as a result of *c.* 280 inscriptions primarily from Falerii that are generally fragmentary (Civita Castellana; after the destruction in 241 BC, Falerii Novi, modern S. Maria di Falleri). They begin around 650 BC (Old F.) with a few longer texts [2. no. 241–243], become more numerous from the 5th cent. onwards (Middle Faliscan; generally stereotypical except for [2. no. 244] *foied vino pipafo/pafo, cra carefo = hodie vinum bibam, cras carebo*). New Faliscan (from 240 BC onwards) shows a strong Latin influence. In the 2nd cent. BC the language disappears. About two thirds of the texts are funerary, the remainder (mostly on vessels) are primarily owners' inscriptions and votive inscriptions; barely a quarter contain appellative wording.

The Faliscan alphabet is derived from the southern Etruscan one but has preserved *D O X*/ks/. For missing *B G* there is *P* and (generally) *C*, respectively, for /f/ the symbol ↑ (from → Digamma). As in the oldest Etruscan and Latin inscriptions, [2 no. 241] uses *K* before *a*, *C* before *e i*, *Q* before *o u* (*karai sociai eqo*).

Faliscan is closely related to Latin. As in the latter, it shows (as opposed to Oscan-Umbrian/Sabellian) preservation of proto-Indo-European k^w (*cuando*; Sabellian > *p*); *-ai* in the nominative plural 1st declension (*sociai*, Sabellian *-as*); accusative singular *med* 'me' (Sabellian *meom*); labial future (*care-f-o*, Sabellian *-s-*) etc.; re the vocabulary cf. *f/hileos, -a* versus Oscan *puklo-* 'son', *futir* 'daughter'. Divergences arise partly through the preservation of the older sound (fricative representation of b^h as β [>F<] [as in Prenestinian Latin] versus Lat. *b*; dative singular 2nd declension *-oi* versus Lat. *-ō*); partly through changes in Faliscan: *au* > *ou* > *o*: *pola*; d^h > δ > β (>F<): *efiles* = *aediles* [root $*h_2a\hat{i}d^h$-]; *f* > *h* (since Middle Faliscan; *hilea*, gloss. *haba* = *faba*; hypercorrect *foied* [s.o.] < $*g^h\hat{o}\hat{i}$-$d\hat{i}\bar{e}d$). Faliscan therefore varies from municipal Roman Latin not much more than the Latin dialects (for which there is little evidence). However, because of its early separation from these dialects by the Etruscan language (probably at the end of the 2nd millennium), it should for the historical period no longer be classified as belonging to the Latin dialect continuum: the *nomen Latinum* does not include the Faliscans (and so was not constituted until after the Faliscans were separated from it).

Sources: 1 CIE 8001–8600 2 Vetter, 277–331.
Bibliography: 3 G. Giacomelli, La lingua falisca, 1963 4 Id., Il Falisco, in: Prosdocimi, 505–542 5 G. Maetzke (ed.), La civiltà dei Falisci. Atti del XV Convegno di Studi Etruschi ed Italici, 1990 6 R. E. Wallace, B. D. Joseph, On the Problematic *f/h* Variation in Faliscan, in: Glotta 69, 1991, 84–93. GE.ME.

Falisci Tribe north-east of Rome between the Monti Cimini and the Tiber, culturally closely connected with the Latins and Etruscans. The capital city was → Falerii (Civita Castellana), and there were also towns called → Narce (Fescennium?), → Capena, Nepi (→ Nepete) and Sutri (→ Sutrium). From the 8th cent. BC Falerii and Narce flourished under the influence of Etruscan → Veii. The fossa burials (→ Funerary architecture) contain not just Italian bronze and clay wares but also Oriental imports (northern Syrian seals and Assyrian bronze bowls with cuneiform inscriptions, both from Falerii); from the end of the 7th cent. there is evidence of chamber tombs. The mountain → Soracte (major deity Soranus) and the temple in Falerii (Celle, Vignale, Sassi Caduti) with rich terra-cotta decorations were cultural centres from the 6th cent. In the 4th cent. an important ceramics industry was founded in the tradition of Attic red-figured vase painting (Aurora Painter and others). With the conquest of Falerii (in 241 BC) the cultural and political dominance of Rome began.
→ Faliscan

G. Colonna, I F., in: G. Pugliese Carratelli (ed.), Italia omnium terrarum alumna, 1988, 522–524; G. Maetzke (ed.), La civiltà dei F. Atti del XV Convegno di Studi Etruschi ed Italici, 1990. A.NA.

Falsification (of texts)

A. The term B. Ancient and classical period C. Hellenistic period D. Roman Republic E. Imperial period and late antiquity

A. The term

The falsification of texts is almost as old as writing itself. Long before the origin of Greek literature, Egyptian scribes had falsely maintained that the texts written by them were word-for-word copies of older, more authoritative originals (ANET 414; 495). Jewish and Etruscan priests emphasized the mysterious circumstances under which prophetic and legal scripts had turned up, obviously brought to light by the hand of the divine [1; 2].

Not every adulteration of a text is a falsification. In many religious traditions authors have expressed themselves through the role of a divine or prophetic person without making the formal claim to have also written the text in question themselves with all its linguistic and stylistic details [3; 4; 5]. Genuine falsifications can (cf. [6]) only occur in a culture that has a clear concept of authorship and in which, as a result, the attributing of a work to a real or even fictitious author who did not write it represents a conscious attempt to deceive the reader whose expectation is that it is authentic [6].

B. Ancient and classical period

In the course of the 8th and 7th cents. BC, Greek writers and artists had a clear concept of artistic individuality. In the 6th and 5th cents. BC when the Ionian philosophers developed new research methods in respect of the universe and its past, new questions about the authenticity of historical tradition and literary texts were asked – e.g. regarding Homer's authorship of several poems in the → Epic Cycle which Herodotus denied in one instance while doubting it in another (2,117; 4,32). Solon and Peisistratus were suspected of having inserted non-original verses in the Homeric text in order to accentuate Athens' importance in prehistory (Str. 9,1,10). Genuine works or parts of works by a certain author were – borrowing from the legal terminology for family relationships – described either as 'natural children' (*gnḗsioi*) or as 'illegitimate children' or 'bastards' (*nóthoi*).

The existence of this terminology is indicative of a trend: from the falsification of texts that in Greek temples and cities was a normal means of filling gaps in the historical and religious records to an ingenious tradition of conscious artistic faking in the 6th and 5th cents. BC. This required creativity and considerations of two kinds: the forger had to imagine how a text that was written at a chronological or geographical distance had to look; he also had to explain why the text was still extant and how he had acquired it. → Acusilaus of Argus maintained, for example, that his mythography was in keeping with the truth as he had taken it from bronze tablets that his father had discovered in his garden (Suda s.v. Ἀκουσίλαος; *Akousílaos*). → Ctesias justified the value of his representation of Persian history through his alleged use of official documents (Diod. Sic. 2,32,4).

The increasing refinement of falsification techniques led to double-edged results: Herodotus, for example, believed in the age of several three-legged stools with inscriptions that he had seen in Thebes, as the verses on them were written with letters which he considered to be 'Cadmean'. The use of an ancient script in this case made a late text successfully appear to be old (5,59–61). The historian → Theopompus (4th cent. BC) used the same argument in the opposite direction: the Peace of Callias from the 5th cent. had to be a falsification as it had been written in the Ionian alphabet that had not been used in Athens before the end of the cent. (FGH 115 F 154).

C. Hellenistic period

During the Hellenistic period literary forgery flourished. The stiff competition between the great libraries of Alexandria, Pergamum and Pella (→ library) drove up prices for the works of the great Greek writers and in order to cover the need for new acquisitions, forgers created many non-genuine works in prose and verse (cf. Gal. 15,105; 17,1,607 Kuhn). The Alexandrian philologists developed lavish aids of criticism (such as the *Pínakes* of → Callimachus) to protect the reader from deception. Their efforts were only partly successful: in the corpus of the Attic orators, many works were passed on that were condemned by Caicilius of Caleacte and other philologists. The collection of the works of Hippocrates contained a number of scripts in the 2nd cent. AD that Galen considered to be non-genuine both for stylistic reasons and reasons of content [7].

Although non-genuine oracles had already been circulating amongst the Greeks for hundreds of years, the aggressive competition between the schools of belief that characterized the Hellenistic world stimulated the production of non-genuine works to a new extent and created a new level of intellectual ambition. One or more Greek-speaking Jews, presumably in the 2nd cent. BC, for example, forged perfectly the work that is today known as the Aristeas Letter. The letter, a complete fiction, itself contained documents to support its credibility: no extant Greek falsification from such an early period of time shows such a systematic effort to use techniques of textual criticism to recreate the past. Similar efforts were made in the mass production of non-genuine religious scripts and Sibylline prophecies. The distribution of such works led by the 1st cent. AD at the latest to academics and historians developing several groundrules for critical investigation. Josephus, for example, argued that the official records kept by priests were more credible than the scripts of individuals like those of the Greek historians (Contra Apionem 1,130; 1,107; 1,28).

D. Roman Republic

Sibylline prophecies flourished in spite of Cicero's objection that they did not go back to the inspiration of prophetesses but were the conscious invention of authors. Likewise literary fakes were created without a clear motive. Varro estimated that 109 of the 130 works of Plautus in circulation in his age (1st cent. BC) were not genuine. As this example shows, Roman scholars quickly followed the model of the Greeks, compiling lists of works held to be genuine on the basis of stylistic criteria etc. [8].

E. Imperial period and late antiquity

The growing spread of Christianity accelerated the production of non-genuine documents, like, for example, the alleged correspondence between Jesus and King Agbar preserved in the archives of Edessa; these were included in the 'church history' of Eusebius (1,13; 2,16), the first detailed collection of documents about the history of early Christianity. Adherents of other revelations likewise produced forged scripts – pseudonymous works which apply the standard method of forgers in order to make the work credible, the statement that they were actually written by the alleged authors. In this way, one of these texts that allegedly originated from the Egyptian sage Hermes Trismegistus (→ Hermes E) described its Greek translation clearly as inadequate to the distinctive language of the Egyptian original (16,2).

The production and proof methods for fakes crossed religious and cultural boundaries. Julius Africanus, an experienced literature academic and librarian who was extremely well acquainted with the common practices of falsification, applied all ancient scientific testing methods in a detailed letter to Origenes in order to show that the history of Susanna and the Eldest in the LXX text of the Book of Daniel could not be authentic. Origenes' energetic response found plausible counter-arguments to every objection [9]. At the same time the pagan scholar Porphyrius attempted, using similar criteria to those of Africanus, to prove the non-genuine nature of the entire Book of Daniel. All the techniques of the forgers and the criticism of forgery are to be found in the → *Historia Augusta* (4th cent. AD), the most complex, splendid and least explicable fake of ancient times.

Polished literary falsifications and their sophisticated critical exposure have in the ancient tradition completely consumed the efforts of famous intellectuals. The forgers and critics who worked in a dialectical relationship to each other created methods of imagining the past and analyzing documents; these methods continued to be used in modern research as well. In spite of this, the motives for the literary falsifications of antiquity and the period that followed often remained obscure.

→ Falsification

1 J. Leipoldt, S. Morenz, Heilige Schriften, 1953 2 W. Speyer, Bücherfunde in der Glaubenswerbung der Antike, 1970 3 N. Brox, Falsche Verfasserangaben, 1975 4 J.J. Collins, The Apocalyptic Vision of the Book of Daniel, 1977 5 D.G. Meade, Pseudonymity and Canon, 1988 6 W. Speyer, Die literarische Fälschung im heidnischen und christl. Altertum, 1971 7 W. Smith, The Hippocratic Tradition, 1979 8 J.E.G. Zetzel, Latin Textual Criticism in Antiquity, 1981 9 N. De Lange (ed.), Origen, Lettre à Africanus sur l'histoire de Suzanne, 1983 10 A. Momigliano, Secondo contributo alla storia degli studi classici, 1960, 105ff. 11 R. Syme, Ammianus and the Historia Augusta, 1968 12 Id., Emperors and Biography, 1971 13 T.D. Barnes, The Sources of the Historia Augusta, 1978.

AN.GR.

Falsum In Roman law the crime of forgery. Gell. NA 20,1,53 calls the false bearing of a witness, which according to the XII Tables was punishable with death, *testimonium falsum*. However this probably had nothing to do with the criminal acts for which Sulla (probably in 81 BC) introduced a public suit (*quaestio de falso*) in the *lex Cornelia testamentaria nummaria* (Dig. 48,10). The jurisprudence of the Imperial period dealt not just with the forging of wills and the counterfeiting of coins as Sulla's law but also for example with the bribing of witnesses and judges and with supposititious children. Simple document forging was presumably subjected by a decision of the Senate to punishment according to the *lex Cornelia* (Ulp. Coll. 8,7,1; Inst. Iust. 4,18,7). According to the *lex Cornelia*, *falsum* was a capital offence (→ *capitale*) and so could be punished with death. It is probable that the condemnation of freemen to deportation developed in the Imperial period from the → *aqua et igni interdictio* – which was imposed perhaps only additionally (Inst. Iust. 4,18,7: *poena in servos ultimum supplicium ..., in liberos vero deportatio*).

R. Rilinger, Humiliores-Honestiores, 1988, 142–156.

G.S.

Fama (Greek Φήμη (*Phḗmē*): Hesiod; cf. Ὄσσα (*Óssa*): Homer). Personification of public speech from the point of view of its origin, increase and effect as rumour and (good or bad) defamation of character. Like → Peitho and → Eris she is part of a group of figural concepts of the communicative power and momentum dynamism of language to which is accorded attributes of the divine and the demonic. Her threatening nature comes from the fact that through the many voices of her speech the difference between fiction and truth and between diametrically opposed values is confused and rendered powerless (cf. Ach.Tat. 6,10,4–5, where she is called a daughter of the *Diabolḗ* ('slander')). Barely demonstrable in traces of ritual practice (Paus. 1,17,1), F. is attested to almost exclusively as a didactically or epically conceived allegory [1; 5]. In the earliest evidence where she is mentioned by name, Hesiod calls her a deity because, once uttered, she is immortal (Op. 760–764). In a mythological context Verg. Aen. 4,173–197 provides her with a genealogical connection as the last-born of the generation of the → Giants. Typical of of F.'s origin is her immense growth in size and strength while she moves forward: initially she is small and fearful but grows with raging rapidity into a monster that fills out the space between the earth (the maternal Gaia) and the sky (the father Uranus). As opposed to *Ossa*, the rumour spread by Zeus (Hom. Il. 2,93f.; Od. 24,413f.), F., through her middle position between human and divine living space, potentially threatens both spheres. In Val. Fl. 2,117–125 she is therefore held down by Jupiter so that she can only spread fear in the earthly region.

Whenever a succinct ekphrasis of F. has been passed down to us, she is described as winged. According to Virgil, her body is covered with as many eyes, mouths, tongues and ears as it has feathers (otherwise [2]). In Stat. Theb. 3,425–431, as the vanguard of Mars and his war chariot, she wears thorns and a Scythian helmet; according to Claudian she has a pair of black wings (De bello Gothico 5,201). Only Ovid with his depiction of F. (Met. 12,39–63) directly tackles the problem of her latency by making her purely acoustic being indirectly visible in the structure of her bronze palace in a central place between heaven, sea and earth: F.'s *domus*, whose countless openings are open to day and night in order to gather the voices of the world, represents all the characteristics of the incorporeal F. herself. Her courtly state, composed of personified levels of intensity of public speech (*rumores*, *confusa verba*, *susurri*) and her mass psychological effects (*credulitas*, *error*, *vana laetitia*, *consternati timores*, *seditio repens*) represents a phenomenology of rumour in the forecourts of power.

1 F. Bömer, P. Ovidius Naso, Met. B. 12f., 1982, 24f. 2 R. R. Dyer, Vergil's Fama: A new interpretation, in: G & R 36, 1989, 28–32 3 W. Fauth, Die F. bei Vergil und Ovid, in: Anregung 11, 1965, 232–238 4 H. Kauffmann, s.v. F., Reallexikon zur dt. Kunstgesch., vol. 6, 1425–1445 5 A. S. Pease, Aeneidos lib. IV, 1935, 211ff.

HA.J.S.

Fames (Greek λιμός/*limós*). Personification of hunger; also called the most powerful of the Furies (→ Furiae) (Serv. Aen. 6,605) who arouses a voracious appetite that cannot be assuaged (in Plaut. Stich. 155–170 the never sated parasite describes F. as his mother). She is often listed in the catalogue of the great evils that populate the entrance to the Underworld (Verg. Aen. 6,273–281; Sen. Herc. f. 650ff.; Claud. Carm. 3,30ff.). Ovid (Met. 8,796–822) has F. – brilliantly represented as a figure who is emaciated and close to death herself – living in the desolate area of the Caucasus.

F. Bömer, P. Ovidius Naso, Met. 8–9, 1977, 235f.

B.SCH.

Family

I. Ancient Orient II. Egypt III. Iran, Sassanid period IV. Greece and Rome

I. Ancient Orient

The family in Mesopotamia was organized in a patrilineal manner; remnants of matrilineal family structures are to be found in Hittite myths, among the Amorite nomads of the early 2nd millennium BC and the Arab tribes of the 7th cent. BC. As a rule monogamy was predominant; marriage to concubines with lesser rights was possible, while there is evidence of polygamy particularly in the ruling families. The family consisted of a married couple and their children although it is not possible to obtain any reliable details about how many children each family had. Unmarried brothers of the head of the family could be part of the family.

The role of the family as a mutually supportive community depended on the economic conditions and structures of an agrarian society. All family members were required to work, particularly in times in which agricultural production was determined through the allocation of fields (*c.* 6 ha, sufficient for the subsistence of one family) to subjects obligated to work. If there were no children, adoption – mostly of freed slaves or agnatic members of the family – served as provision for old age. Family membership had consequences with regard to succession claims. Real and fictitious genealogies (→ genealogy) legitimated status and property and ownership rights. There is evidence in the 3rd and 2nd millennium BC of fratriarchal forms of succession to the throne in Babylonia, Elam and Assyria. Artisan occupations and positions within institutional households were family-linked. Family names were customary in Babylonia (not in Assyria!) from the 8th/7th cents. BC.

→ Work; → Marriage; → Woman; → Social structure

J.N. Postgate, Early Mesopotamia, 1992, 88–108 (Household and Family); C. Wilcke, Familiengründung im alten Babylonien, in: E. W. Müller (ed.), Geschlechtsreife und Legitimation zur Zeugung, 1985, 213–317.

J.RE.

II. Egypt

In Egypt people usually married within the same social groups. Marriages between cousins, uncle and niece, and more rarely between half-siblings by the same father were allowed. Marriage between full siblings common in the Ptolemaic period seldom occurred in the time of the pharaohs. A man was supposed to marry as soon as he could support a family. In the upper class this was after he had completed his education, i.e. at about the age of 20. Girls married after reaching puberty at 12 to 14 years of age. The man asked the father for the hand of the bride in marriage and if he had died he asked the mother or an uncle. They signed the contract which they kept or entrusted to a third party or a temple archive. From 536 BC onwards the marriage contracts that have been passed down to us are signed by the partners themselves. They set out the rights of the wife and her children in the case of a divorce. Both partners could request a divorce and remarry. As a third of the possessions of a man usually went to the wife and two thirds to their joint children, divorce was very hard for a man. If the wife was at fault, she forfeited her rights to her husband but kept her own possessions over which she had free right of disposal.

Single marriage was usual. If a man could afford it, he could in the time of the pharaohs also have several wives or have intercourse with dependent women. The children of the first wife were however his main heirs. Adultery with a married woman was not allowed. Literary texts mention the death penalty for adultery, and court files mention the threat of cutting off the nose and ears, one hundred lashes or exile to the mines. We read nothing about the administering of the punishments. In the late period there is evidence of the imposition of high fines and of banishment from the community in the case of priests. If a woman was unable to clear herself through an oath, her husband could disown her.

Poorer couples could live in the home of the parents of the husband (patrilocal). More rarely they lived in the home of the wife's parents or the husband contented himself with visiting her (matrilocal). If he could afford it, the husband was supposed to establish his own household (neolocal). Literary texts, household lists, the description of the wife as the mistress of the house and the size of the houses indicate small families. The wife and children could be held liable for misdemeanours of the husband.

The Egyptian terms for the family certainly indicate that there were originally larger units. A husband was expected to love his wife and respect her in the household but not accord her any power. Depictions show that married couples jointly participated in banquets; they were accompanied to family events by their children. In the Old Kingdom (2700–2190 BC) children occasionally took part in the funerary banquet of the parents. A middle- or upper-class man had an ardent desire for his son to succeed him in his office. However aptitude and the consent of the king were necessary for this. In this way many offices were able to stay in certain families for many generations. If a king wanted to destroy the power of a family, he could refuse his consent. Children were supposed to look after their sick or aged parents, see to their burial and perform the cult of the dead. If they were not prepared to do so, they could lose their inheritance or part of their inheritance.

→ Woman

E. Feucht, Das Kind im Alten Ägypten, 1995.

E.FE.

III. Iran, Sassanid period

The head of the family under the Sassanids (3rd–7th cent. AD) was the master of the house (*kadag-xwadāy*) and it was his responsibility to represent the family legally and socially to the outside and to look after his dependent wife and children.

Under Sassanid family law there were three different forms of marriage contracted for different purposes: 'full entitlement' marriage (*pādixšāy*), 'auxiliary marriage' (*čagar*) and 'common marriage' (*xwasrāyūn/ēn*). In full entitlement marriage the wife was the mistress of the house (*kadag-bānūg*); she was subject to the marital authority of the husband and had a claim to part of his estate when he died. The children of this type of marriage were considered legitimate offspring of the father and had inheritance rights. If the master of the house was infertile or died childless, the mistress of the house was obligated to bear children for him by another man. For this purpose 'auxiliary marriage' – in which the wife was neither subject to the marital authority of the husband nor entitled to inherit his property – to a close relative of the first husband or any other man was contracted. The children of this union were considered from a legal point of view to be the children of the first husband. This 'supposititious child' (*strīh*) meant to prevent childlessness was very widespread towards the end of the Sassanid period amongst the wealthy. If the master of the house did not leave a wife with full entitlements, other people from his family group too could be given the duty of fathering children (as *stūr*). In 'common marriage' a wife entered into a marriage on her own authority, without the consent of her guardian. Although it was accepted as a legally valid marriage, the wife remained – as opposed to the case of the full entitlement form of marriage – in the guardianship of her father or brother and did not move to the family group of the husband. The marriages referred to could also be entered into temporally. There is also evidence of incestual marriages that were regarded in Zoroastrianism as especially commendable.

M. Macuch, Inzest im vorislam. Iran, in: AMI 24, 1991, 141–154; Id., Rechtskasuistik und Gerichtspraxis zu Beginn des 7. Jh. in Iran, 1993; Id., Das sasanid. Rechtsbuch 'Mātakdān i hazār dātistān' (Part 2), 1981; A. Perikhanian, The Book of a Thousand Judgements, 1997.

M.MA.

IV. Greece and Rome

A. Greece

1. General: Questions and definitions

For the modern term 'family' there is no precise equivalent in Greek; the closest to it is the word οἶκος or οἰκία (→ *oíkos, oikía* = house, household). To the extent that this refers to a body of persons, the members were as a rule the father of the family, his wife, their joint children and the slaves of the household (Aristot. Pol. 1253b 2ff.); thus, family concerns the nuclear family as the everyday community living together (ibid. 1252b 13f.). It was at the same time an economic unit: ideally and typically the household of a farmer with a team of oxen (Hes. Op. 405) – with a husband, wife, children and farm workers who performed specific tasks, with the wife restricted to the domestic sphere (Xen. Oec. 7,22ff.).

The father had the dominant role. He was the master of all family members (κύριος, → *kýrios*) without having the permanent authority of a → *pater familias*: a son left this subordinate position at the latest when he established his own household and took on the *oíkos*, which often caused conflict – frequently the father retired to a special part of the estate. The father of the family represented the entire family culturally and legally. In this respect the family represents a strict patrilineal union. The family was an integral part of the polis ('each polis is made up of houses, *oikíai*', Aristot. Pol. 1253b 1f.), because the prerequisite for the legal status of a citizen had been associated with being the offspring of a legally valid union – at Athens since the so-called Bastard Law of Pericles of 451 BC, it had been restricted to a marriage between two citizens. The family was therefore also the subject of legislation by the polis since the preservation and protection of the family and its members was of utmost importance as was the settling of possible conflicts between families. Particularly inheritances caused conflicts.

2. Internal structures

The essential element of the *oíkos* was the marital union between a man and his wife (Aristot. Pol. 1253b 9f.); the → marriage that was in principle monogamous consisted legally of an agreement (→ *engýēsis*) between the father or the guardian of the bride and the bridegroom. The wedding itself was conducted ceremonially in the social sphere as the change from one *oíkos* to the other: the bride was conspicuously led from the former house to the new house and received there by the mother of the groom, carrying with her as she went a torch with the hearth fire of her old family to the new home. There she walked around the hearth fire (→ Wedding customs and rituals). At Athens, the → phratria was informed of the change (Isaeus 3,76; 8,18; Dem. Or. 57,43; 57,69; Poll. 3,42; Hsch. s.v. γαμηλία; *gamēlía*). Correspondingly, in the case of divorce (→ Marriage), the wife returned to her old family or to the *oíkos* of her guardian.

As the protection of the continued existence of the family was a significant religious, political, social and economic matter, great importance was attached to fathering (Dem. Or. 59,122) and to the upbringing of children. The religious acceptance of the newborn child into the family was – in Athens – likewise marked by walking around the hearth fire on the 5th resp. 10th day after birth (*amphidrómia* – friends of the parents carried the newborn child around and it was named; Aristoph. Lys. 757 with Schol.; Pl. Tht. 160e with Schol.) and the social and political registration of the child by notification at the phratria which at the same time involved recognition on the part of the father. To his children the father was the master (*kýrios*), but his authority was curbed by social norms and laws that served to protect the children from certain actions (e.g. selling them into slavery [8. F 26]). While the sons achieved their political majority when they completed the → *ephēbeía* and so also had the right to establish their own households, the daughters remained under the authority of their father until his death, and after that they were subject to the authority of their closest male collateral relative (e.g. brother, father's brother) – unless they moved to another *oíkos* through marriage. Parents and children also had to support each other financially and this included providing for their parents in old age, to which according to Solon they were only obligated if the parents had ensured that they had received an education and hence had appropriate finances (Aristoph. Av. 1353ff.; Dem. Or. 24,107; Plut. Solon 22,1; Ael. NA 9,1; Diog. Laert. 1,55; Lib. Or. 11,14). The aspect of the continuation of the family unit particularly showed in generational change, i.e. in the law of succession (→ Succession, law of) and in the cult of the dead (→ Dead, cult of the). When the father died, the sons inherited his property in equal shares (Isaeus 6,25). In Athens the daughters had no right of inheritance but they did have a claim to a dowry (→ *proíx*), as laid down in the → marriage contracts (Hsch. s.v. ἐπίδοσις); however in other areas of Greece daughters also shared in the estate. If there were no male heirs, the family assets passed to an 'hereditary daughter' (→ *epíklēros, patroûchos*) who had to marry her closest male relative according to the rules of the → *anchisteía* and for this to occur any marriage union already in existence was dissolved. The actual heir was then a son (or the sons) of this union, a grandson of the testator. This prevented the transfer of the *oíkos* to an outside *oíkos* master (the – possible – husband of the daughter of another family) and the continuity of the *oíkos* in the old family was protected. This continuity was also expressed by the obligations of the children to their deceased parents, from the performance of the burial itself (laying out in the house, funeral lament, funeral procession from the house to the burial place) to regular sacrifices for the dead and judicial measures, e.g. acts of revenge for wrong that had been done to the parents or relatives. Characteristically such obligations corresponded very precisely with the line of succession. At the same time they show how the *oíkos* was integrated into wider family relationships.

3. External integration

Aside from the distinctive emphasis on continuity, the Greek family was characterized by a great deal of autonomy. It was not firmly embedded in overarching familial organizations that formed fixed associations (for instance clans or kinship groups). Thus we consider the wider surroundings of the family particularly with a view to the rights and obligations that certain persons had in relation to the head of a family. This concerned the *anchisteía* (ἀγχιστεία), a circle of relatives that reached as far as the children of male first cousins (in other words, the grandsons of the uncle). They had rights and duties with regard to the inheritance (including the marriage of the 'hereditary daughter') in a graduated order (whereby the male or agnatic line ranked ahead of the female or cognatic line) as well as obligations to support and take revenge (IG I[3] 104, 13–25; Isaeus 7,22; 8,34; 11,2; 11,11f.; Dem. Or. 43,27; 43,43; 43,51; 43,57).

The latter also applied to those related by marriage (sons-in-law or fathers-in-law, brothers-in-law: IG I[3] 104, 22) who, regardless of the family ties existing between them, often formed a closer circle of friends; it also applied to the members of the → phratria (φράτερες (*phráteres*), φράτορες (*phrátores*), cf. IG I[3] 104, 18 and 23) who can be understood as the wider family descendants (for instance through tracing their lineage back to a common ancestor who as a rule was a mythical one) and who were important for the control of citizen status (in the case of births), although apart from certain worship practices they did not act as a fixed political and social grouping. Neither are the 'lineages' (*génē*) to be understood as comprising larger family groups with common property and collective organizational forms.

4. Variations

Because of the evidence, our knowledge essentially relates to Athens in the classical period (5th/4th cents. BC). It is probable, though, that the regulations applying there were very widespread. But there were also considerable differences: in the law of → Gortyn – and it would not have been much different in the rest of Crete – there was also a right of inheritance for daughters, allowing them to inherit half the male portion of the inheritance, or the dowry could be regarded as a share of the inheritance (ICret 4,72, 4,48ff.), and generally women had their own property that was not accessible to their husbands. There were also corresponding rules for hereditary daughters (ibid. 5,9ff.; 7,27ff.; 4,76 B 1ff.). In addition, in view of these in particular, there were also certain rights for cognatic relatives. There are good reasons for the assumption that the legal position in Sparta was similar. Certainly the family structure in Sparta was marked to a great extent by the distinctive integration of Spartan individuals into the polis community: the boys were withdrawn from the supervision of their fathers from the age of 7 through the system of → *agōgḗ*. Furthermore the women, apart from the ownership rights that have been mentioned, had a strong position in the management of the entire family assets and through polyandry that was occasionally practised, e.g. the 'lending' of fertile wives to friends, this could also be extended to several properties (*kláro*i).

In the Hellenistic period it can be seen – in any case in the marriage contracts primarily originating in Egypt – that the nuclear family itself had a more important role in relation to the great weight attached to patrilineal descent (the dowry no longer fell to the father of the bride); in addition the leeway of the wife increased and she could enter into a marriage contract herself (even if this required the consent of her *kýrios*).

→ Marriage; → Woman; → Friendship

1 F. Bourriot, Recherches sur la nature du genos, 1976 2 Busolt/Swoboda I 3 M. Dettenhofer, Die Frauen von Sparta. Gesellschaftliche Position und polit. Relevanz, in: Klio 75, 1993, 61–75 4 S. Hodkinson, Land Tenure and Inheritance in Classical Sparta, in: CQ 36, 1986, 378–406 5 N. M. Kennell, The Gymnasium of Virtue, 1995 6 W. K. Lacey, The Family in Classical Greece, 1968 7 C. Reinsberg, Ehe, Hetärentum und Knabenliebe im ant. Griechenland, 1989 8 E. Ruschenbusch, ΣΟΛΩΝΟΣ ΝΟΜΟΙ (Historia Einzelschr. 9), 1966, F 26–31; 47–58 9 C. Vatin, Recherches sur le mariage et la condition de la femme mariée à l'époque hellénistique, 1970 10 R. F. Willets, The Law Code of Gortyn, 1967.

H.-J.G.

B. Rome

1. Definition

In Roman society the legally recognized, legitimate family was differentiated from the natural family to which belonged concubinage often caused by marriage prohibitions. The sources mainly provide information about the legitimate family and here it primarily concerns the family in the upper classes although there were also relationships similar to families in the lower classes and even amongst the slaves. In law *familia* denotes, first, all people who were subject to the *potestas* (authority) of the → *pater familias* – the wife, daughters, sons and their families, and the slaves (*iure proprio plures personae, quae sunt sub unius potestate aut natura aut iure subiectae*), as well as the entire possessions of this community (Dig. 50,16,195,2, Kaser, RPR 22f.). Ulpianus even includes not just the slaves but also the freedpersons and *alieni* (those subject to external authority) (Dig. 47,8,2,14); second, it denotes all agnates (→ *agnatio*) who were fathered by a common progenitor (Dig. 50,16,195,4). The wife is only included in this definition if she had entered into a marriage *in manu* which had already become rare in the Republic. Outside the legal sphere, the term *familia* could however also be used for groups linked by friendship such as the *cohors* of the governor or even select groups like the *familia Caesaris*. This fact alone shows that the term *familia*, based on the social and political structures of Rome, eludes the modern categories of the term family that initially includes the members of a household, i.e. the wife and children and possibly the additional relatives.

Nor does the term → *domus* find an equivalent in the modern family: on the one hand it referred to the space in which a family group lived, but it also meant the family group itself, i.e. the spouses, children and slaves; whilst the term *familia* in its broader sense could include agnatic kinship, *domus* in the wider sense included both agnatic and cognatic kinship, exemplified in the Principate by the *domus Caesaris*. Finally, *domus* could also signify the assets of a family that were necessary to maintain its social status. Added to this is the fact that the term *familia* and hence also agnatic descent, expressed in the name, played a greater role in the Republican period – because of the special political structures – than in the Principate, in which the splendid representation that manifested itself in the *domus* (as the space) became more and more important. To sum up, we could say that the Romans did not create a concept that would be applicable to the modern family – parents and children – but rather that a wider network of relationships was considered to be the nucleus of society.

2. FAMILY AS A SOCIAL UNIT

The social unit that was under the authority of the *pater familias* could theoretically consist of more than two generations but in reality it mostly comprised parents and children in addition to the household slaves. The community did not intervene in this unit until the Principate and before this the law primarily regulated the relationships between families, as can be seen in the dotal law and the law of succession and later in the guardianship law, i.e. the law only became effective in the formation and dissolution of a family. With the → *patria potestas* ('authority of the father of the household'), the *pater familias* had full right of disposal over the people in the family, regardless of their ages, and over their communal possessions. He decided who was to be accepted into and dismissed from the family community. Children born to him required his recognition after the → birth; likewise he was able to remove children from the family community through → *emancipatio* and he could also remove his wife through divorce or accept strangers into the family group through → adoption or adrogation. He also had the authority to punish the members of his family community although this authority was restricted because it involved the co-operation of a household court consisting of relatives and friends. He alone was therefore originally legally capable of acting or legal subject, i.e. *sui iuris*. The *patria potestas* excluded the children and the wife from property and claims; they were *alieni iuris*, but they were legally competent with the exception of women who required the formal consent of a tutor for any business transaction (→ *tutela*). Even sons who had their own wives remained subject to the *patria potestas* while the father was still alive, although at the same time they could exercise all the political rights of a citizen and even occupy the highest offices.

From this we can assume that limits applied to the rigid exercising of the rights of the *patria potestas*: these rights were limited by the expectation that the holder of the rights acted in the interests of the family community and represented the family members subordinate to his *potestas* in public; on the other hand, however, the *pater familias* also had to act in the interests of the *res publica*, the community. This explains why the father in individual cases took advantage of his authority to use capital punishment if a son was guilty of a political crime. Otherwise, that a woman married *in manu* could already request a divorce early in the marriage and leave the household community qualifies the strict rule of the *pater familias*. Moreover, as early as the Republican period, the legal relationships between family members changed in favour of those subject to the *patria potestas*. The sons received a *peculium* (separate property) and the strict *manus* marriage was superseded early by the *manus*-free marriage; in particular, however, the wife, if she was *sui iuris*, could freely dispose over her property. With the beginning of the Principate, family matters were increasingly regulated by the law. The marriage laws of Augustus not only made adultery a crime but they also intervened in the right of free disposal over deceased estates. In addition marriage options of the senatorial rank were limited, the aim being to delimit it against the lower ranks.

3. WEDDING

The legal prerequisite for the existence of a family was a *iustum* → *matrimonium*, i.e. a marriage between two sexually mature persons willing to marry, linked by → *conubium*, the aim being to produce offspring. There was however a prohibition on the marriage of relatives closer than 6th cousins and this existed not just in the agnatic but also in the cognatic line; this also applied to adopted sons who, although theoretically not related by blood, were counted as members of the new kinship group. In some cases the son of the mother's brother was however adopted; Scipio Aemilianus (*cos.* in 147 BC) and M. Cato Licinianus (*praetor designatus* in 152 BC) are examples of this. As the names of the wives have only rarely been passed down to us, we cannot exclude the possibility that adopted sons more frequently came from the cognatic kinship group and therefore that the marriage prohibitions extended to them. Scipio Aemilianus also married the daughter of his father's sister, possibly a reference to the preference for marriages amongst *cognati* who were further removed than 6th cousins. Under Emperor Claudius this restriction was reduced to the marriage of relatives not closer than 4th cousins.

The wedding was a purely private act whereby the woman either went over to the *potestas* of her husband (*conventio in manum*) or remained in the *potestas* of her father; where applicable, she continued to be *sui iuris*. Associated with marrying was the → *dos* (dowry) that was available in marriage for maintaining the wife but which had to be given to the wife after a possible divorce so that she could finance her upkeep and enter into a further marriage. When a woman entered into *manus* marriage, she became a member of the family of her husband (*filiae loco*) but she continued to bear the name of the → *gens* from which she came, with the addition of the praenomen of her father or husband in the genitive case. The alliances between aristocratic families, whether it be through adoption or marriage, always manifested themselves through the name. The laws that related to marriage and the position of the wife were primarily relevant in succession and therefore were particularly applicable to the marriages in the upper class. During the Principate, jurists were increasingly occupied with families that did not have a *iustum matrimonium* as a prerequisite, e.g. if one partner had lesser rights, but here too they only involved themselves to alleviate or facilitate heritability and testamentary capacity for mothers or children out of these relationships.

4. Family and public

The patriarchal nature of Roman society, expressed in the patronage which the aristocrats accorded to their clientele, also characterized the relationship between the individual members of a *domus*: in both cases there was a hierarchy that on the one hand was determined by *auctoritas* ('authority') and *obsequium* ('obedience'), and on the other hand by reciprocal *fides* ('reliability') and duty of care. But other values were also crucially important for the *domus*: *Concordia* ('harmony'), that should predominate between the marriage partners, mutual respect that the partners owed each other, *pietas* ('respect') of the children for their parents and *caritas* ('respect') of the children for their children (Cic. ad Brut. 20,2) are values that were likewise applicable to the political organization. And as in an aristocratic family, grownup sons together their fathers sought to continue the achievements of their *gens* for the *res publica*, the wife too, as a representative of her *gens* and as a *matrona*, carried out roles in public although she was excluded from political participation. *Matronae* performed cult duties and as a collective they were also consulted in the Republican period with regard to the financial support of the community; in individual cases women also tried to have a great influence on politics (cf. for instance Liv. 34,1–8,3). In the Principate the *conventus matronarum* was limited to a small circle of aristocratic ladies who were primarily concerned with etiquette.

5. Family in Religion and Cult

In religious law the family was certainly a closed community. Here we should distinguish between domestic worship and the actual cult of the family: all members of a household community together worshipped Vesta, the hearth goddess, together with the *di* → *penates*, the protection gods of household property, as well as the *lar familiaris* (in the Principate the → *lares familiares*) and the → *genius* of the household master who simultaneously appears as the *genius domus* or *familiae* (CIL X 6302). The members of the family took an oath on the *genius* of the master of the household. Everyone who was subordinate to the *potestas* of the *pater familias* took part in the cult of the *divi parentes*, the parent gods (three generations of individual ancestors) and *di manes* (underground forces); only the *in manu* wife was accepted into the cult community of the *sacra familiae*.

6. Inheritance rules

If the *pater familias* died, his sons and daughters who were under his *potestas* inherited his estate in equal portions. His lineage ended if he had no children and – unlike in Greece for instance – no arrangements were made for the perpetuation of his house (epiclerate; Jewish levirate). The agnates and fellow members of the gens and from the praetor's edict → *bonorum possessio* in the late Republic onwards also the cognates up to 6th/7th cousins then became the heirs. Until the end of the 3rd cent. BC the *pater familias* could divide up his entire *patrimonium* (property) by will through legacies to non-family members and through manumissions (Gaius inst. 2,224), without leaving anything in his will to his sons whom he had to disinherit explicitly and later also to all his male offspring. In the period that followed, the attempt was made, with the *lex Furia* and in 169 BC with the *lex Voconia*, to limit this power to dispose by will, which however was not fully successful until the *lex Falcidia* in 40 BC that ensured the heirs a quarter of the estate. In the aristocratic upper class, it was therefore not guaranteed that the property would remain in the family. Marriage, legacies and adoptions were not means of guaranteeing the estate but should rather be regarded as ways of creating political alliances. In any case the lack of willingness to produce offspring was regarded as a problem; Augustus attempted through the *ius trium liberorum* ('three children law') to motivate upper class families to raise children.

7. Family as household community

The *domus* as an internal space provided a framework for diverse activities and for the special position of the family: in the atrium the master of the house was greeted every day by his *clientes* (→ *cliens, clientes*), and as the cabinets were there with the *imagines* (ancestor masks) of the ancestors who had rendered outstanding services to the *res publica* (Plin. HN 35,6), the merits and the dignity of the family were obvious to everyone entering the house. This impression was further strengthened by the stemmata that adorned the walls including the complete agnatic and cognatic kinship (Plin. HN 35,6; Suet. Galba 2).

It is very hard for us to imagine the nature of the emotional ties between the members of a household community set up in such a manner, especially as the extant funeral inscriptions contain wording that is frequently repeated. The children in many cases grew up with the children of slaves, and often when they were young, were raised by slaves, which undoubtedly led to emotional bonds, especially as the absence of the father, the frequent divorces from the Middle Republic onwards and also a comparably high mortality during birth made the development of emotional ties to the parents more difficult. Overall the closer and wider *domus* evoked a strong feeling of solidarity that was also able to cover half-brothers and half-sisters and their children. We can assume from the various descriptions for relatives on the maternal and paternal side (*matertera* – the sister, *avunculus* – the mother's brother; *amita* – the sister, *patruus* – the father's brother) that originally they had differing roles that are still partly comprehensible in the cult. In connection with the marriage prohibitions that applied to agnatic and cognatic relatives alike, this appears to support the view that with the development of the political system, an originally existent cognatic system of kinship receded because of the emphasis on agnatic structures and the *patria potestas* (cf. Gai. Inst. 1,156), although it never completely disappeared and in the Principate period it was increasingly taken into account again.

→ Agnatio; → Cognatio; → Marriage; → Woman; → Gens; → Kinship, relatives; → FAMILY

1 J. ANDREAU, H. BRUHNS (ed.), Parenté et stratégies familiales dans l'antiquité romaine, 1990 2 M. BETTINI, Antropologia e cultura romana, 1988 3 K. R. BRADLEY, Discovering the Roman family, 1991 4 S. DIXON, The Roman family, 1992 5 R. KERTZER, P. SALLER (ed.), The family in Italy from antiquity to the present, 1991 6 D. B. MARTIN, The construction of the ancient family. Methodical considerations, in: JRS 86, 1996, 39–60 7 J. MARTIN, Zur Anthropologie von Heiratsregeln und Besitzübertragung, in: Historische Anthropologie 1, 1993, 149–162 8 B. RAWSON (ed.), Marriage, divorce and children in ancient Rome, 1991 9 Id., (ed.), The family in ancient Rome, 1986 10 Id., P. WEAVER (ed.), The Roman family in Italy, 1997 11 R. P. SALLER, Patriarchy, property and death in the Roman family, 1994 12 B. D. SHAW, Seasons of death, in: JRS 86, 1996, 100–138 13 Y. THOMAS, A Rome: pères citoyens et cités des pères, in: A. BURGUIÈRE et al. (ed.), Histoire de la famille I, 1986, 195–229 (Gesch. der Familie I, 1996). M.D.M.

C. FAMILY, REPRESENTATIONS OF

1. ARCHAIC AND CLASSICAL GREECE

In the area of conflict between the → private and the public sphere, the explicitly pictorial representation of the family in Greek art as the union between a husband, his wife and close relatives remained for several generations a motif that ran counter to the private sphere and therefore is initially a rare exception; more often, on the other hand, there are representations of the family in Etruscan art (sarcophagus lid e.g. in Rome, VG). Greek-Ionian statue groups like that of → Geneleus from the Heraeum of → Samos (mid 6th cent. BC) are in the eastern Asia Minor tradition; they show the proud head of the family as the ruler and 'owner' of his wife and children and, in a completely analogous manner to the pictorial presentation of luxurious fittings and furnishings, hunting dogs or expensive riding horses, served to demonstrate wealth and social prestige. The youthful Kore statues (→ Sculpture) in sanctuaries (like for instance the Acropolis in Athens) acted as a type of detail in the work: they too embodied, in a statuesque, cipher-like reduction, from the ancient aristocratic life of the 6th cent. BC the aspect 'family with a fine daughter', as in real life it publicly presented itself at festivals and celebrations in the sanctuary or in the procession; a complete and non-reduced pictorial representation is seen on a painted wooden votive tablet in Athens (NM, Corinthian, about 540 BC). Equally rare are non-mythical family scenes in Attic vase painting, mostly in the context of the 'warrior's departure' (e.g. white-ground lekythos in Berlin, Museum of Antiquities, about 470 BC). Occasionally victors' statues in Greek sanctuaries are shaped through later additions into family groups (statue of Theopompus I and the Diagorides statue in Olympia).

On the late classical, multiple-figured Attic funerary reliefs in Athens we do not find the theme of the family in the sense of a kinship group but the *oikía* (οἰκία; → *oíkos*) as a patriarchally ruled household community with wife, children, slaves and material possessions still essentially on the same level. In ever new details that do not provide a complete picture until we survey many statues on site, we find (aside from honouring the deceased) the theme of the state, the polis as the nucleus of the citizens' values – a phenomenon that transfers the private sphere to the public sphere whilst at the same time becoming a mirror to a late classical society that is intent on a retreat into the domestic sphere and on turning away from public and political activity.

2. HELLENISTIC PERIOD

Without a direct connection, neither in content nor typology, with the archaic and classical Greek forms, the first depictions of the family arise in the early Hellenistic period within the context of monarchical-dynastic concepts of rule; the mode of representation often mixes together in a complex manner the aspects of the 'living family', 'ancestors' and 'genealogical derivation' or 'relationship to the world of the gods' (and in this idiosyncratic way probably refers back to earlier Oriental-Egyptian pictorial concepts of the representation of rulers). Early examples that continue the artistic form of the honouring statue of the commander embedded in the political-social context of the polis, though with an already clear dynastic emphasis, were to be found on the Acropolis in Athens (monument for Conon and Timotheus; monument for Pandeites and Pasicles, 2nd half of the 4th cent. BC). The Anathema of the Thessalian tetrarch → Daochus II that was dedicated after 336 BC at Delphi shows the ruler, his son and the male ancestors from four generations in a pose that makes them look like heroes, together with the image of an unspecifically transmitted god (perhaps Apollo); what is suggested here is the eternal existence of his dynasty at the same time as its legitimation as a result of the achievements of the past and its harmonious agreement with the Greek gods as guarantor for a good future.

The so-called Philippeion in Olympia, begun by Philip II of Macedon in 338 BC as a monument for the victory at Chaeronea and finished under Alexander [4] the Great, presented in a temple-like form of construction borrowed from the Greek → tholos the ruler Alexander, his parents Philip and Olympias as well as his grandparents Amynthas and Eurydice in extremely lavish gold-ivory statues built by the sculptor → Leochares. The monument placed in the most prominent position at the entrance to the Altis became a prototype for the celebration of Hellenistic ruling families. Adaptations of such visualizations of people are sometimes to be found in a less luxurious form as a special means of representation in the private sphere as well e.g. in the portrait statues of the married couple Cleopatra and Dioscurides on Delos (138 BC) or as votive offerings in sanctuaries ('Aetolian family monument' and the statue to Phoenix, Epicteta and her sons, both in Delphi, 3rd cent. BC).

3. Rome

In the Roman Imperial period from Augustan times on, well thought-out representations of the imperial family were a pictorial cipher for constancy and continuity and through purposeful celebration or by leaving out individual people, they were also a common method of providing propaganda regarding the succession. The pictorial media were primarily state reliefs (frieze of the → Ara Pacis Augustae), coins and cameos (Gemma Augustea in Vienna, KM; Grande Camée de France in Paris, BN). During the reign of the adoptive emperors of the 2nd cent. AD various monuments display the imperial family as a framework for adoption processes (e.g. on the so-called adoption plate of the Parthian monument from Ephesus in Vienna, KM). The establishment of a new family-related dynasty by the Roman emperor Septimius Severus is intensively publicized – as a reaction to the turmoil surrounding succession to the throne that preceded his rule and hence as a proclaimed end to a perceived crisis – in practically all pictorial media of this period (coins, engraved gems and cameos, state reliefs etc.) by means of the harmonious representation of the emperor, his wife Julia Domna and his sons Caracalla and Geta (cf. esp. the Egyptian panel in Berlin, Museum of Antiquities, with the erased Geta following his → *damnatio memoriae*). Representations of the imperial family from late antiquity mostly belong to the context of the court ceremonial (e.g. the family of Justinian on the mosaics of S. Vitale in Ravenna); such ceremonial contexts are imitated by family depictions of the aristocracy, e.g. on the ivory diptychon of Eucherius (after AD 396, Monza, Diocesan Museum).

Family representations that belong in a narrower sense to the private sphere are to be found more extensively in the pictorial world of Roman antiquity than in the Greek one. Those on Roman funerary reliefs of the later Republic and the early Imperial period primarily present the theme of the family as a legal factor in the life of the citizens and outline the status of the owner of the tomb as a freedman who can act autonomously (e.g. funerary relief of Publius Aiedius in Berlin, SM, 1st cent. AD; family funerary relief in Copenhagen, NCG, late 1st cent. BC). Funerary reliefs with representations of the family from later periods often show the passing of the 'father's authority' to the son ('parental pair pillar', 3rd cent. AD, in Trier). The representations of married couples on Roman golden glasses that were mostly additionally decorated with drinking sayings refer to the private sphere (e.g. golden glass fragment in Rome, MV). Finally there are numerous painted representations of the family in the Christian catacombs (e.g. the family of Theotecnus from the 6th cent. AD in the Ianuarius catacomb in Naples).

J. Bergemann, Demos und Thanatos. Unt. zum Wertesystem der Polis im Spiegel der attischen Grabreliefs des 4. Jh. v.Chr., 1997; A. Borbein, Die griech. Statue des 4. Jh. v.Chr., in: JDAI 88, 1973, 79–90; B. Fehr, Bewegungsweisen und Verhaltensideale ..., 1979; Id., Kouroi e korai, in: S. Settis et al., I Greci. Storia, Cultura, Arte, Società, vol. 1, 1996, 810–813; Ch. Habicht, Ein kaiserliches Familiendenkmal aus Lindos, in: ZPE 84, 1990, 113–120; B. Hintzen-Bohlen, Die Familiengruppe. Ein Mittel zur Selbstdarstellung hellenistischer Herrscher, in: JDAI 105, 1990, 129–154; H.J. Kienast, Die Basis der Geneleos-Gruppe, in: JDAI(A) 107, 1992, 29–42 · A. McCann, The Portraits of Septimius Severus (Memoirs of the American Academy in Rome 30), 1968; A. Mlasowsky, Nomini ac fortunae: Die Sukzessionspropaganda der röm. Kaiser von Augustus bis Nero im Spiegel der Reichsprägung und der archäologischen Quellen, in: JDAI 111, 1996, 249–388; H. Möbius, Zweck und Typen der röm. Kaiserkameen, in: ANRW II 12.3, 32–88; A. Rawdan, Die Darstellung des regierenden Königs und seiner Familienangehörigen in den Privatgräbern der 18. Dyn., 1969; U. Rössler-Köhler, Die rundplastische Gruppe der Frau Pepi und des Mannes Ra-Schepses. Bemerkungen zur Ikonographie von Familiendarstellungen des Alten Reiches, in: MDAI(K) 45, 1989, 261–274; L. Schneider, Zur sozialen Bedeutung der archaischen Korenstatuen (Hamburger Beitr. zur Arch., suppl. 2), 1975; D. Soechting, Die Porträts des Septimius Severus, 1972; H.v. Steuben, Die Geneleosgruppe in Samos, in: Armagani. FS für J. Inan, 1989, 137–144; W. Trillmich, Familienpropaganda der Kaiser Caligula und Claudius, 1978; P. Zanker, Grabreliefs röm. Freigelassener, in: JDAI 90, 1975, 267–315. C.HÖ.

V. Early Middle Ages

All matters regarding the family in the centuries between the political collapse of the Roman empire and the Carolingian foundation of western and central Europe are inextricably connected with the spatially and temporally unclear genesis and spread of the European marriage and household model that is evidenced only in a later period. It concerns the husband-centred, nuclear family household that was based on late marriage of a couple almost the same age and servants not related through kinship but belonging to the household. The cluster of very different developments has not to date produced any valid picture of structural change in the family as a key pattern for social relationships.

From the 4th cent. AD onwards, church and state inbreeding prohibitions were introduced (for instance levirate, and niece and cousin marriage) that were extended far into the Middle Ages. The weakening of the classical → *patria potestas* had already begun earlier: important patriarchal powers over the wife and the *familia* had to a large extent been taken away from the → *pater familias* and as a Christian he lost his role as household priest and became like his wife a member of the local Christian community. In theology (patristics) and church law (council, synods) sexual ethics were on the one hand determined by toleration of sexual intercourse within marriage oriented solely towards procreation and on the other hand by the requirement of lifelong chastity. For all social groups and classes indissoluble monogamy was declared to be compulsory. Of fundamental consequence was ultimately a new understanding of kinship: aside from blood kinship through birth and marriage, spiritual kinship brought about by rebirth through baptism with all its possibilities for supplementing or overlapping relationship options gained importance.

These late Roman and Christian/clerical circumstances, requirements and provisions were confronted with the various grouping habits of the gentes within the areas that the mass migration of peoples called into being. They are most clearly reflected in the relevant passages from the Leges Barbarorum of the early Middle Ages. Within the context of the different forms of settlement, merging of populations and mission, differing family constellations formed between marriage and clan for which however the same trends apply: the gradual transition from clan (not the so-called Germanic *Sippe*) to lineage, the ruralization and shrinking of households to nuclear family-focussed units with slaves or servants, interclass marriage with variable rank-related bequeathing of the estate and the spread of types of relationship that could offer diverse protection (parochial avowals of friendship and brotherhood, manorial *familia*).

However the details uncovered to date by research with regard to the early Middle Ages mostly concerns specific individual cases. It is not until the 9th cent. that we can – in cases where the sources passed down to us allow us a more exact insight – discern in outline the contours of the Ancient European pattern of the husband-dominated family or household, both amongst the aristocracy and the peasant cottagers.

→ Family

1 W. Affeldt et al. (ed.), Frauen im Früh-MA, 1990 2 A. Burguiere et al. (ed.), Histoire de la famille, 1, 1986 3 J. Goody, The development of the family and marriage in Europe, 1983 4 A. Guerreau-Jalabert, Spiritus et caritas. Le baptême dans la société médiéval, in: F. Heritier-Auge, E. Copet-Rougier (ed.), La parenté spirituelle, 1996, 133–203 5 J. Hajnal, European Marriage Patterns in Perspective, in: D. V. Glass, D. E. C. Eversley (ed.), Population in history, 1965, 101–143 6 D. Herlihy, Medieval households, 1985 7 R. Le Jan, Famille et pouvoir dans le monde Franc (VIIe – Xe siècle), 1995 8 J. U. Krause, Familien- und Haushaltsstrukturen im spätant. Gallien, in: Klio 73, 1991, 537–562 9 M. Mitterauer, Historisch-anthropologische Familienforsch. Fragestellungen und Zugangsweisen, 1990 10 A. C. Murray, Germanic Kinship Structure, 1983 11 P. L. Reynolds, Marriage in the Western Church, 1994 12 S. F. Wemple, Women in Frankish Society. Marriage and the Cloister 500–900, 1981.

LU.KU.

Family planning Although a distinction was made in ancient gynaecology between abortion and contraception (Sor. 1,60), the corresponding methods and practices cannot be precisely separated the one from the other. On the one hand, conception was regarded as a process, and its interruption at an early stage of pregnancy was certainly regarded as contraceptive; on the other hand, in view of deficiencies in understanding as to the point of conception, a device used as a contraceptive could also produce an abortion. → Child Exposure must also be regarded as a form of family planning.

If Hippocratic medicine laid appreciably less emphasis on contraception than on the aim of encouraging conception, it did in *mísy* (copper ore) recommend a substance that was capable of preventing conception for a year (Hippoc. Mul. 1,76; Nat. Mul. 98). At the same time, however, ancient doctors held the mistaken opinion that the fertile days of the cycle were those immediately before and after menstruation, and advised women to abstain from sexual relations during this period (Sor. 1,61). Antiquity knew of a multitude of contraceptive methods, ranging from highly effective preventive pessaries soaked in vinegar, oil or cedar resin to supposedly magical amulets. Some of these methods, esp. most of those taken orally, certainly also had the effect of producing an abortion. Whether the extremely infrequent mention of *coitus interruptus* is to be regarded as a sign of rarity, or, on the contrary, of habitual use, remains disputed. Soranus recommends not only coital and post-coital techniques for preventing the semen from penetrating deep into the uterus, but also vaginal douches and cold drinks (Sor. 1,61ff.). The level of fertility in marriage (or the interval between two births) was also influenced by maternal breast-feeding, sometimes combined with post-natal sexual abstinence.

There is intense discussion among scholars as to the aims and extent of contraception in ancient times. For a long time the thesis was held that the extensive practice of family planning ('family limitation') as a particular form of birth-control was a phenomenon of the modern age, and depended on the general availability of effective contraceptive methods; this view was opposed by those who, pointing out a supposed decline in population during the Early Principate, expressed the view that over the course of time a profound knowledge of reliable contraceptive methods evolved among women, and that this knowledge was applied extensively and successfully to limit family size. This assumption has now been contradicted on the basis of a precise evaluation of household censuses in Egypt. Knowledge about effective contraception was probably gained in non-marital circumstances, and spread from there (via medical texts and by → midwives) to upper-class and possibly also poorer families, its purpose being less the intentional limitation of family size than the protection of the mother's health. The conclusion appears to be that family planning was practised to an extent and in a manner that could not have had a decisive effect on natural fertility.

Contraception – unlike abortion and the exposure of children – was seldom condemned; it is, however, the case that in the philosophical literature the production of children is regarded as the most important purpose of marriage (Pl. Leg. 783d–784d; Musonius Rufus 12f.). Despite being condemned by individual Church Fathers, contraceptive practices were not subject to ecclesiastical punishment.

→ Abortifacients; → Abortion

1 E. EYBEN, Family Planning in Graeco-Roman Antiquity, in: AncSoc 11/12, 1980/81, 5–82 2 M.-T. FONTANILLE, Avortement et contraception dans la médecine gréco-romaine, 1977 3 B.W. FRIER, Natural Fertility and Family Limitation in Roman Marriage, in: CPh 89, 1994, 318–333 4 K.M. HOPKINS, Contraception in the Roman Empire, in: Comparative Studies in Society and History 8, 1965/66, 124–151 5 J.M. RIDDLE, Contraception and Abortion from the Ancient World to the Renaissance, 1992. J.W.

Fan (ῥιπίς, *rhipís*; *flabellum*). Fans were used in the Orient and in Egypt from ancient times as symbols of status. The fan probably did not reach Greece until the 5th cent. BC; Eur. Or. 1426–1430 (first mention) still calls the fan 'barbaric', but it quickly became one of a woman's most important accoutrements (cf. Poll. 10,127); she would either cool herself with it or have a female servant fan her (cf. the *flabellifera* in Plaut. Trin. 252 and the *flabrarius* as her male counterpart in Suet. Aug. 82). On Greek vases and terracotta ('Tanagra figurines') fans are very often depicted in women's hands. Their shape and the material of which they were made scarcely figure in ancient literature; Eur. Or. 1426–30 talks of a circular structure of feathers, in Hesychios (s.v. ῥιπίς) it is woven from bulrushes, but leather, raffia, straw etc. might also be used. There is the heart-shaped blade-fan with a short handle, which, especially on the terracotta figurines, is variously coloured or ornamented; and there is the feathered fan, comprising a long staff with a sometimes ornamented head from which the individual feathers stand out separately from one another. In Etruscan art too, the blade-fan and the feathered fan are common. Here we find original (metal) fans; also a rectangular one from a male burial. Etruscan ivory hands as fan-holders should also be mentioned.

In Rome, feathered fans made of peacock feathers (according to Ath. 6,257b and Prop. 2,24,11) are depicted, if only rarely. In the Later Imperial period two further forms occur: the flag fan, of which specimens in straw survive, and the circular wheel-fan comprising two handles for opening and closing, the fan-blade lying folded between them; fragments of the latter variant, which was evidently popular in the northern provinces of the Roman empire, have also survived (York).

Whisks made of peacock-feathers should also be mentioned. A distinction should be made between these fans and those used to kindle fires (e.g. Aristoph. Ach. 669; 888, Anth. Pal. 6,101;306; → Household equipment).

E. DIEZ, Flabella, in: AA, 1955, 58–69; E. DIEZ, TH. KLAUSER, W. PANNOLD, s.v. F., RAC 7, 217–236; T. SCHILP, Zur Rekonstruktion eines röm. Fächers (?), in: Mainzer Zschr. 73/4, 1978/9, 365–366; A. ROMUALDI, in: Etrusker in der Toskana, Ausst.-Kat. Hamburg, 1987, 234–235, no. 32; Die Etrusker und Europa. Ausst.-Kat. Paris-Berlin 1992/3, 127, no. 89–92. R.H.

Fannia

[1] In 88 BC, F. hid the ostracized C. Marius in her house in Minturnae, after he had helped her to win back her dowry in a divorce case in 100 BC against C. Titinius (Val. Max. 8,2,3; Plut. Marius 38,3–9). K.-L.E.

[2] Full name perhaps Clodia F. Daughter of the senator and Stoic Clodius [II 15] Thrasea Paetus and of Arria [2]. Wife of Helvidius Priscus, whom she accompanied into exile under Nero and Vespasian. Herennius Senecio wrote a biography of her husband at her request, for which Domitian banished her. After Domitian's death Pliny supported her in her attempt to avenge her stepson Helvidius.

RAEPSAET-CHARLIER 232f. no. 259; PIR² F 118. W.E.

Fannius Plebeian nomen (SCHULZE 266; 424), attested historically from the beginning of the 2nd cent. BC. K.-L.E.

I. REPUBLICAN PERIOD II. IMPERIAL PERIOD

I. REPUBLICAN PERIOD

[I 1] **F.M. f., C.** Roman senator and historian (in Cic. Brut. 99 falsely differentiated from a relative). F. distinguished himself in 146 BC with Ti. Gracchus at the storming of Carthage (Plut. Gracchi 4,6), fought in 141 as *tribunus militum* in Spain (App. Ib. 287), was the son-in-law of C. → Laelius and heard → Panaetius (Cic. Brut. 100f.). In 122 he attained the consulacy, supported by C. Gracchus (→ Sempronius) (MRR 1, 516), but in a sensational speech turned against Gracchus' citizenship policy (ORF4 no. 32, fr. 1–5). Probably after 120 he wrote a historical work in at least 8 bks., which in spite of its title *Annales* perhaps dealt only with contemporary history. Fragments show a concern for internal politics and verbatim speeches by leading politicians (HRR I², 140 fr. 5: Q. → Caecilius [I 27] Metellus Macedonicus).

M. → Iunius Brutus produced an → epitome to the work (Cic. Att. 12,5,3); Sallust valued it for its truthfulness (Hist. 1,4 M.).

FRAGMENTS: HRR I² 139–141.
BIBLIOGRAPHY: E. BADIAN, Early Historians, in: Latin Historians, 1966, 1–38, esp. 14f.; F. CASSOLA, I Fanni in età repubblicana, in: Vichiana 12, 1983, 84–112, esp. 86–96; SCHANZ/HOSIUS 1, 198–200; G.V. SUMNER, The Orators in Cicero's Brutus, 1973, 53–55. W.K.

[I 2] **F., C.** In 61 BC a co-prosecutor of P. Clodius [I 4] Pulcher, in 59 he opposed Caesar as people's tribune (Cic. Sest. 113; Vatin. 16 i.a.) and was accused by L.

→ Vettius of conspiracy against Pompey (Cic. Att. 2,24,3); subsequently probably *aedile* and praetor. On Pompey's side in the Civil War, he was to take over as governor of Sicily with propraetorian *imperium*, but then in 49/8 went to fill the same position in Asia (coinage: [1. 35–40]; legend *pr[aetor]* or *pr[o praetore]*). Cicero in 48 believed, probably wrongly, that he was dead (Att. 11,6,6), as in 43 a F. is mentioned as a Senate delegate to Sex. Pompeius (Cic. Phil. 13,13). He joined the latter, was ostracized, fled with him to Sicily (App. B Civ. 4,354), and achieved high office under him; he did not go over to M. Antonius [I 9] in Asia until 35 (App. B Civ. 5,579). He was pontifex from 57 at the latest (Cic. Har. resp. 12; cf. coinage [1]).

1 G. Stumpf, Numismatische Untersuchungen zur Chronologie der röm. Statthalter in Kleinasien, 1991.

[I 3] F., L. Follower of C. Flavius [I 6] Fimbria; in 85 BC he fled with L. Marius to Mithridates VI, with whom in 79 he established the association with Q. Sertorius in Spain (Cic. Verr. 2,1,87; Ps.-Ascon. 244St.). In 73 he fought as Mithridates' commander against Rome, and returned to Rome after 72 through the mediation of L. Licinius Lucullus (App. Mith. 286–290). 68/7 legate in the army of Lucullus (Cass. Dio 36,8,2).

[I 4] F., M. Plebeian *aedile* and mint master in 86 BC (RRC 351), then a judge, in 80 praetor and chairman of the court for murder cases (Cic. Rosc. Am. 11f.).

[I 5] F. Chaerea, C. Perhaps a freedman. His slave Panurgus had been trained by the actor Q. → Roscius and then murdered by Q. Flavius from Tarquinii. Upon complaining, F. and Roscius received damages, but (probably 76 BC) took each other to court, F. being represented by P. Saturius, Roscius by Cicero (*Pro S. Roscio comoedo*).

[I 6] F. Strabo, C. Praetor by 164 BC at the latest; as consul in 161 with M. Valerius Messalla he promulgated the *lex Fannia* limiting the expenditure devoted to banquets (Gell. NA 2,24,3; Plin. HN 10,139; Ath. 6,108; Macrob. Sat. 3,17,5), and expelled Greek philosophers and orators from Rome (Gell. NA 15,11,1). In 158 he led a legation to Illyria (Pol. 32,18,3f.), and in 154 one to Pergamum (Pol. 33,9,3).

E. Baltrusch, Regimen morum, 1989, 81–85. K.-L.E.

II. Imperial period

[II 1] F. Caepio. Participated in a conspiracy against Augustus, according to Cassius Dio in 22 BC (54, 3). The conspiracy being betrayed, he fled; accused by Tiberius, Augustus' stepson, he was condemned in his absence. A slave betrayed him, and he was executed. PIR² F 117; L 218; Syme, AA 387ff. W.E.

Fanum (Etymology: *d^hh_1s-no-; but Oscan-Umbrian fēsnā < stressed form *d^heh_1s- [1]). Generic expression for the holy place (*locus sacer*, Liv. 10,37,15) consecrated to the deity by the *pontifices* (Varro, Ling. 6,54; Fest. 78 L.; → *pontifex*). Initially designating the location without regard for the form and function of the cult site contained within the sacred precincts (e.g. grove, spring, cave, temple, altar etc.). Later, *fanum* really comes to mean only the ancient sanctuary as opposed to the temple (*aedis*) as an architectural entity. Attempts to differentiate *fanum* from → *delubrum* are dubious. The places where the couches (*lecti*) for the → *lectisternium* were set up are also called *fanum*. The selection of places for *lecti* as well as that of the locations for the *fanum* in a newly-founded city is called *fanum sistere* (Fest. 476 L.). *Fanum sistere* can also be used in the sense of *locum consecrare* ('make a place sacred'). The opposite is *profanare* (= 'make profane again') (Fest. 256 L.; 295 L.; Macrob. Sat. 3,3,4). The meaning is extended to designate as *fana* the temples of non-Roman, mostly oriental gods. From this is derived *fanaticus* ('appertaining to the sacred' > 'held by the deity') as a term for the personnel belonging to the temples of oriental gods (→ Bellona, Juv. 4,123; → Isis, CIL VI 2234; → Mater magna, CIL VI 490). *Fanum* is also sometimes found as a component of ancient place-names, as in Fanum Voltumnae, Fanum Martis, Fanum Fortunae.

1 Walde/Hofmann I, 454.

H. Jordan, Über die Ausdrücke aedes, templum, fanum, delubrum, in: Hermes 14, 1879, 577f. A.V.S.

Fanum Fortunae Umbrian harbour-city north of the mouth of the Metaurus (*regio VI*), where the *via Flaminia* reaches the Adriatic coast; the modern Fano (Pesaro; It. Gaditanum 95; It. Ant. 126; It. Burd. 615; Tab. Peut. 5,2). The name derives from the cult of Fortuna. F. had the status of a *municipium*, *tribus Pollia*. The city was occupied by Caesar after his crossing of the Rubicon (Caes. B Civ. 1,11,4); under Augustus it was the veterans' colony of *Iulia Fanestris* (CIL XI 6232); *basilica* of Vitruvius (5,1,6–10; [1; 2]). In the 4th cent. AD F. was *colonia Flavia Fanestris*. Destroyed by Vitigis in AD 545 (Procop. Goth. 3,11; 25). A triumphal arch of Augustus survives, along with the city walls dated by CIL XI 6218f. to AD 9; restored by Constantine; round watchtowers. The *via Flaminia* formed the main axis of the city, which has an orthogonal plan. For the Early Christian phase see [3].

1 F. Pellati, La basilica di Fano e la formazione del trattato di Vitruvio, in: RPAA 23–24, 1947/8, 153–174 2 J. Prestel, Des M. Vitruvius Pollio Basilika zu F.F., 1900 3 G. Binazzi, Regio VI. Umbria (Inscriptiones Christianae Italiae 6), 1989, 192–198.

N. Alfieri, Per la topografia storica di F.F., in: Rivista Storica dell'Antichità 6–7, 1976/7, 147–171; N. Dolci, Le fogne romane di F., 1979; F. Battistelli, A. Deli, Immagine di F. romana, 1983; BTCGI 7, 1989, 410–415; N. Alfieri, L'urbanistica di F.F., in: Id., F. Milesi, F. romana, 1992, 77–86. G.U.

Fan Ye Chinese author of a dynastic history that contains i.a. information on the geography of the Parthian empire and on contacts between the Parthians and the Chinese. Born AD 398 into a family of Chinese imperial officials, F. himself held the posts of administrative district officer and general in the imperial guard. Implicated in a conspiracy under emperor Wen (Sung Dyn.), he was executed in AD 446, which prevented the completion of his 100–chapter 'History of the later Han Dynasty (AD 25–220)', *Hou Hanshu* (10 chs. 'basic annals', *benji* of emperors and empresses, 80 biographical chs. *liezhuan*, and 10 historical treatments of individual subject-areas). The modern edition, based on that of Sima Biao (240–306) supplemented in the 12th cent. by eight monographs in 30 chapters, is fundamental to an understanding of the late Han period. In the absence of documentary evidence, F. relied on secondary material, but linguistically and stylistically he adapted it in a remarkable manner. For information on the lands to the west, in particular the Parthian empire (*Anxi*) between AD 91 and 123, we mainly have to thank a report by Ban Yong to the emperor.

H. Bielenstein, The Restoration of the Han Dynasty, in: Bull. of the Museum of Far Eastern Antiquities 26, 1954, 3–209; 31, 1959, 1–287; 39, 1967, 1–198; 51, 1979, 1–300; E. Chavannes, Les pays d'occident d'après le Heou Han Chou, in: T'oung Pao[2] 8, 1907, 148–219; M. Kordosis, China and the Greek World, 1992; D. D. Leslie, K. H. J. Gardiner, The Roman Empire in Chinese Sources, Rome 1996; H. Schmidt-Glintzer, Gesch. der chines. Lit., 1990, 131–133. J.W.

Far Originally probably 'corn' in the sense of grain [1]. In the historical period, however, the name applied especially to spelt as opposed to common wheat (*triticum*). Synonyms are *ador* and *alicastrum*; evidently a short form of *far adoreum*. Plin. HN 18,82 maintains that the zones of cultivation for *far* (emmer) and ζειά/*zeiá* (ζέα/*zéa*) are mutually exclusive. According to Dion. Hal. Ant. Rom. 2,25,2, however, these two kinds of grain, along with *arinca* (ὄλυρα; *ólyra*) as grown in Gaul, Italy and elsewhere, are identical. 3 kinds of the highly cold-resistant (Plin. HN 18,83, cf. Columella 2, 8,5) *far* (= *semen adoreum*) are mentioned in Columella 2,6,3 (*Clusinum*; *vennuculum rutilum et candidum*; *halicastrum* = *semen trimenstre*, the best in weight and quality). All may be identified with the tetraploid emmer (*Triticum dicoccum Schübler*), as the original diploid einkorn (*Triticum monococcum L.*, τίφη/*típhē* or ζέα ἁπλῆ/*zéa haplē*) probably occurred only in Asia Minor, and hexaploid spelt or dinkel (*Triticum spelta L.*) only in SW Germany and Switzerland (where it is today again cultivated). In the Imperial period the Romans consistently called spelt *spelta* or *scandula* (*brace*, *bracis* and *spica* are uncertain). Until the 2nd cent. BC *far* was the chief grain grown by the Romans; after roasting (Ov. Fast. 1,693) it was not suitable for baking into bread, but only for producing porridge (*puls*, Plin. HN 18,83; cf. Plaut. Mostell. 828: *pultiphagi barbari*). When *triticum* was later introduced as a bread-grain (perhaps from Greece), it gradually displaced both *far* and *puls*. The *pistores*, from being producers of hulled grain (*alicae*; cf. Plin. HN 22,128) from *far* by pounding it in mortars (Plin. HN 18,107f.: *pistores qui far pisebant*; Serv. Aen. 1,179), consequently became millers and bakers. The early Greeks on the other hand lived on barley (κριθή/*krithḗ*, *hordeum*) and its products (ἄλφιτα/ *álphita* = *polenta* and μᾶζα/*mâza)*, not from *far* and *puls*, but in Rome the latter in the form of *mola salsa* (Plin. HN 18,7 and 31,89) and *libum* (unleavened loaves with cheese, Cato Agr. 75) and *puls fitella* (sacrificial porridge, Plin. HN 18,84) always retained its significance as sacrificial food, as did barley in Greece (cf. Val. Max. 2,5,5).

1 Walde/Hofmann.

N. Jasny, The Wheats of Classical Antiquity, 1944. C.HÜ.

Farfarus Left-hand tributary of the Tiber in the region of the Sabini (Ov. Met. 14,330; Sil. Pun. 4,182); Latinized as *Fabaris* (Verg. Aen. 7,715; Vibius Sequester 148), the modern Farfa; it flows by Trebula Mutuesca.

Nissen vol. 2, 478; M. P. Muzzioli, s.v. Fabaris, EV 2, 451. G.U.

Farmers

I. Greece II. Rome

I. Greece

No Greek term corresponds exactly to the English word farmer. The Greek word γεωργός (*geōrgós*) described someone who cultivated the land, whether landowner, simultaneously proprietor and farmworker, or merely a farmworker (Xen. Oec. 5,4); it thus applied to rich and poor, citizen and non-citizen, slave or free man. The relatively unusual term αὐτουργός (*autourgós*) meant someone who worked for himself or with his own hands, and was restricted to free men; although it means 'men who have no leisure' (Thuc. 1,141,3–5), it related neither solely to people of low social status nor to farmworkers [1. 168–73]. Neither of these terms has the pejorative meaning expressed by the word ἄγροικος (*ágroikos*; Theophr. Char. 4). These lexicographical considerations are important to our perception of Greek farmers and their self-image. Rich and poor farmers stood up for each other, for they had basic interests in common. In the case of Athens, this can be seen in Xen. Ath. Pol. 2,14 and Aristoph. Eccl. 198, where the rich and the farmers, unlike the poor, opposed the formation of a fleet. Small farmers were not regarded as a social class dominated or exploited by outsiders, or having their own cultural tradition, as one expects of the classical farmer [3. 142].

Although it is probable that most citizens of most *poleis* owned land, the γεωργός (*geōrgós*) was a sufficiently conspicuous figure to fill the title role in both the old and the new comedy. He is characterized by a profound attachment to the land he cultivates, but that attachment does not remain unaffected by resentment at low returns (Men. Georgos 35–39; cf. Xen. Cyr. 8,3,38), and by his often surly aversion (Aristoph. Plut. 903) to involving himself in politics (Aristoph. Georgoi fr. K-A). Aristotle consequently regarded a democracy of farmers as a particular kind of constitution: in his opinion, it was the best form of democracy, as the citizens had no leisure and concerned themselves little with politics (Pol. 1318b6–1319a19). But the farming life was also reputed to have positive influences on the citizenry. Thus Xenophon in the *Oeconomicus* maintained that agriculture provided the prospect of riches, good health and happiness, and that it therefore represented the best possible occupation for a free man. Xenophon may have been concerned to emphasize the advantages of a man who enjoys leisure – leisure being the prerequisite for service in the cavalry and for athletic pursuits – but farmers were generally regarded as the backbone of the hoplite armies (Aristot. Pol. 1291a30).

The farmer was by no means an ignorant figure. Hesiod in his *Erga* ('Works and Days') established a tradition by which agriculture was seen as an occupation demanding a high degree of expert knowledge, and Xenophon's *Oeconomicus* was only one (and perhaps the least systematic) of the numerous treatises on agriculture written in classical Athens. Xenophon in his work clearly tends to the view that the working methods of farmers depend merely on common sense, but Aristotle appears to express a widespread opinion when he emphasizes the many kinds of knowledge that a farmer must possess (Aristot. Pol. 1258b12–20). In literature from Homer onwards, the farmer's skills provided the stuff of similes; from Hesiod's time, moreover, the occupation of farming is seen from the point of view of morality.

Recent archaeological surveys have contributed to our knowledge of the various lifestyles of farmers in different regions and epochs of antiquity. The degree of social isolation of people living on the land did not depend solely on wealth: it varied from place to place and from period to period. For reasons that are often hard to explain, settlement in villages or in scattered farms was widespread. A series of classical landscapes (Boeotia, southern Argolis, Kea) seem to have contained many farms that were isolated or clustered in small groups; the same applies at least to particular areas of Attica. In such circumstances, a landowner's opportunity to participate in the political or social life of the city depended on his degree of prosperity, and on whether, like Ischomachus in Xenophon, he could afford a second house in the city and an estate manager (ἐπίτροπος; *epítropos*) to oversee the work of the slaves on the farm. Although Menander in the *Dyskolos* refers to the isolation of farmers, we should not make too much of this: the highly varying demands for labour during the course of the year afforded an opportunity for leisure, making it possible to be absent from the farm for days at a time; but this also necessitated recourse to relatives and neighbours to share the work.

→ Agrarian structure; → Agrarian writers

1 A. Burford, Land and Labor in the Greek World, 1993 2 T. Gallant, Risk and Survival in Ancient Greece. Reconstructing the Rural Ancient Economy, 1991 3 R. Osborne, Demos. The Discovery of Classical Attika, 1985 4 S. Pomeroy, Xenophon, Oeconomicus: A Social and Historical Commentary, 1994 5 S. Todd, Lady Chatterley's Lover and the Attic Orators: The Social Composition of the Athenian Jury, JHS 110, 1990, 146–173.

R.O.

II. Rome

There are various Latin words to express the meaning of our term 'farmer': *Agricola* signified a person who worked on the land, while *colonus*, which might initially have had a similar meaning, eventually referred to the smallholder; *assiduus*, on the other hand, meant a landowner on a small scale, but whose estate (*census*) qualified him for military service and a privileged electoral status. Terms such as *agrestis*, *rusticus* and *paganus* expressed the contempt of the city-dweller for country people.

The aristocrats of Early Rome employed non-Roman slaves on their estates rather than dependent workers (*nexi*), thus contributing to the growth of the smallholder farmer class, from which Rome's big armies could be recruited. In this way, the Roman Republic in its own conception became a commonwealth of independent small farmers. The political moral of this ideal is contained in the *praefatio* to Cato's *De agricultura* (mid 2nd cent. BC): agriculture is morally irreproachable, socially accepted and from an economic point of view low in risk; farmers (*agricolae*) also make the best soldiers and are least inclined to subversive ideas. The myth of the early peasant commanders such as → Cincinnatus and M'. Curius Dentatus, whom → Cato sought to emulate by working together with his slaves from time to time, is also to be seen in this light. In fact, the Roman Republic made great efforts between the 4th and the early 2nd cents. BC to maintain and increase the numbers of the *assidui* by founding colonies and redistributing the conquered lands of Italian peoples. The settlement programmes carried out during the period between the Gracchi (→ Gracchus) and Augustus were in many respects a continuation of this policy, although now it was public Roman land that was being redistributed.

In Roman literature, aristocratically orientated as it was, apart from a few sentimental or moralizing texts there is hardly any realistic information on the daily life of Roman farmers. Even Virgil's *Georgica* may only to a limited degree be characterized as a realistic description of the smallholder farming economy in Upper Italy. The agronomic handbooks, among them that of the elder Cato, are concerned with the management of wealthy estates dependent on slave labour; although they also provide information on elements of farming practice and rural knowledge (including folk medicine), they tell us very little about freeborn smallholders and harvest workers, who were also employed by the owners of large estates. But the annalistic records often lists the size of the plots allocated by state settlement programmes; as a rule (with the exception of the Latin *coloniae* of the early 2nd cent. BC and the land distributed by the Gracchi), these measured between seven and ten *iugera* (1.8 to 2.5 ha). We are speaking here of plots suited to a peasant subsistence economy: the farms were not big enough to support an ox or to feed a large family. It is highly probable that legumes and vegetables rather than grain were cultivated on this land. The effect of such settlement programmes was that sons entered the army in the hope of a new allotment of land. In time, the size and constitution of individual families and the distribution of property ownership within them began to change. The structure of land distribution, originally conceived with a view to equality, had to crumble under the pressure of socially conditioned and market-based transactions such as the division of inherited estates, marriage, sale, or leasing. While the properties of some farmers expanded, others were forced into casual labour or migrated to the cities. Paid labour and taxation meant contact with the money economy, even for poor smallholder farmers. Surveys and excavations have shown that widely scattered settlements were very frequent in the whole of Italy, not just in the colonies. Those very small, unspectacular farmsteads that have been excavated may be associated with the subsistence economy, but this kind of structure seldom leaves archaeologically detectable traces; more cases are known of larger and more comfortable farmhouses, and installations for the production of olive oil or wine. These probably belong to larger farms capable of employing slaves and oxen, and as a rule producing surpluses.

The social class represented by the 'farmers' of Republican Italy was not static. It possessed a high degree of social mobility, and included landless workers as well as families in process of becoming *domus nobiles*. The formation of a standing army during the Principate and the end of popular voting finally made it superfluous to secure the existence of free farmers by political measures. Leasing became ever more widespread, and eventually with the colonate a system arose that bound the tenant to the soil; but the free smallholder farmer never disappeared entirely. Although the concept of private property furthered the small-farm economy in the provinces, the *imperium romanum* had no official policy for encouraging small farmers. Many testimonies to the social situation of small farmers stem from the provinces: thus the moralizing description of country life in the Euboean speech of Dio Chrysostom (Or. 7), or the extant documents on papyri from Roman Egypt, among which the archive of Cronion from the early 2nd cent. AD (P. Cronion) and the archive of Aurelius Isidorus from the late 3rd and early 4th cents. AD (P.Cair.Isid.) are of especial significance.

→ Agrarian structure (Rome); → *colonatus*; → Agriculture (Rome); → Subsistence farming

1 J.K. Evans, Plebs rustica. The Peasantry of Classical Italy II. The Peasant Economy, in: AJAH 5, 1980, 134–173 2 J.M. Frayn, Subsistence Farming in Roman Italy, 1979 3 K. Greene, The Archaeology of the Roman Economy, 1986 (ch. 4, 5) 4 W.E. Heitland, Agricola. A Study of Agriculture and Rustic Life in the Greco-Roman World from the Point of View of Labour, 1921 5 W. Scheidel, Grundpacht und Lohnarbeit in der Landwirtschaft des römischen Italien, 1994. D.R.

Farnus see → Ash (tree)

Farrago was a mixed crop (mixed mash, *Mengkorn*, *Mischel*, *méteil*, *mistura*), used for food into the 20th cent. AD, but already in antiquity relegated for the most part to use as cattle fodder; thus *farrago* served as green or dry fodder as well as forage for draught animals (Fest. 81 L.) and domestic animals. It consisted of the threshings of emmer (*ex recrementis farris*, Plin. HN 18,142) and weed-seeds, of which many accompany this spelt-wheat; *farrago* could also be sown mixed with vetch seed (Varro, Rust. 1,31,5; Plin. HN 18,142). Columella had a high regard for *farrago hordeacea* (2,7,1f.; 2,10,31; 11,2,99); veterinarians preferred *farrago triticea* (Veg. Mulomedicina 1,22,7). Like other fodder crops (*siliqua*, *vicia*, *lupinum*, *avena*), *farrago* was sown at the end of September (Columella 11,2,71; cf. 2,10,24), and could be frequently grazed very early in the year or harvested in May (Varro, Rust. 1,31,4; Columella 2,10,31). It was regarded as a concentrated feed, and considered to be cleansing (Varro, Rust. 1,31,5; Verg. G. 3,205). The form *ferrago* was already known to Varro (Rust. 1,31,5: *ferro caesa ferrago dicta*); Juvenal used the word in a transferred sense for mixed forms in literature (1,86). In this sense it was adopted into modern languages from the 17th cent. (English; French; Spanish: *fárrago*; Italian: *farragine*).

1 G. Comet, Le paysan et son outil, 1992, 252f. 2 A. Ernout, Philologica III, 1965, 136–138 3 T.L. Makrey, in: D.R. Harris, G.C. Hillman (ed.), Foraging and Farming, 1989, 589–593 4 F. Olck, s.v. f., RE 6.2, 1999f. E.C.

Fas is to be understood as 'that which is divinely sanctioned'; its opposite is *nefas*. The adjective *fastus* is derived from it. *Fas* and *nefas* appear at first with verbs (e.g. *fas est*), later also as nouns in expressions such as *contra fas*. The derivation is disputed: 1. from **fēs-/*fas<*d^h(e)h$_1$s-* as *festus*, *feriae*, *fanum*; 2. from **fā<*b^{h}eh$_2$-* as *fari*, *fama*, *fabula*, *fatum* [1]. The relationship between *fari* and the adj. *fastus* was already recognised by Varro (Ling. 6, 29–30; 53). According to [2] *fari* indicates the existence of the utterance removed from the speaker and from its meaning, and in this sense *fas* means 'that which is sanctioned by divine edict'.

The opposition of → *ius*, the law of humans, to *fas*, the law of the gods (Serv. Georg. 1,269) is not tenable for the older period [3]: *fas* cannot be equated with *iura divina* [4]. The distinction rests rather on the normative character of the terms: *fas* signifies everything that is free from religious prohibition, and – in contrast to *ius* – not necessarily that which must be done or is statutory. [5] has it that *fas* functions as a complementary term to *sacrum*. Written in upper case, F (*fas*) and N (*nefas*) in calendars indicate the character of the day [6].

1 Ernout/Meillet, s.v. f. 2 É. Benveniste, Le vocabulaire des institutions indo-européennes, vol. 2, 1969, 133ff. 3 A. Magdelain, Essai sur les origines de la sponsio, 1943 4 H. Fugier, Recherches sur l'expression du sacré dans la langue latine, 1963, 127ff. 5 Latte, 38–39 6 G. Wissowa, Rel. und Kultus der Römer, 1912, 438.

H. van den Brink, Ius Fasque, 1968; P.M. de Carvalho, Note de sémantique latine: Fas, fastus – feriae, festus etc., in: REA 73, 1971, 319–326; C. A. Peeters, Fas et nefas, 1945, 159ff. FR.P.

Fasces Bundle of rods made of elm or birch, held together by red straps. The *fasces*, more than likely of Etruscan origin, were carried in front of supreme Roman magistrates (→ *Consul*, → *Praetor*) by public servants (*lictores*; → *Lictor*) as a symbol of their authority (→ *Imperium*). Outside of Rome (cf. → *Pomerium*), an axe was placed in the centre of the *fasces* as symbol of absolute military authority over Roman, as well as allied and provincial, soldiers [1. 196 f.; 2. 119 f.]. The → *dictator* was allotted 24 *fascia*, the two consuls 12 each, the praetors 6 each, and the promagistrates 12 (proconsul) or 6 (propraetor) [2. 120 f.]. The → *princeps* had 12 *fasces* decorated with laurel (*laureati*) [1. 201]. The *fasces* accompanied a bearer of the *imperium* everywhere he went, even in his house, at the theatre or at the baths (not, however, at the *lupanar*, 'brothel' [1. 207]). As *insignia imperii* (*dignitatis insignia*: Cic. Ad Q. Fr. 1,1,13; 'symbol of authority/dignity of office'), they served to clear the way for public officials, to summon citizens to appear in court (→ *vocatio in ius*), to arrest (*prensio*), to chastize (*verberatio*), or at executions [1. 208]. However, the magistrate's absolute authority (→ *coercitio*) was limited within the municipal area of Rome (*domi*) via the → *provocatio*. A magistrate of lower rank had to lower his *fasces* before an official of higher rank. Scandalous behaviour which led to an → *abrogatio* or → *abdicatio* could result in the *fasces* being broken. [3]. In the late Roman Republic, *fasces* were often attacked and damaged in the public assembly [4].

Besides those holding the *imperium*, the → *flamen Dialis* and the → Vestals were also accompanied by a *lictor*, in the ruler cult, Livia [2] and Agrippina [3] minor each received two *fasces* (Tac. Ann. 1,14; 13,2). In the modern period, the *fasces* primarily play a role as political symbol of republican freedom and constitution, state unity and continuity, but also as symbol for unrestricted authoritarian force. During the French Revolution, they symbolized, together with the liberty cap, the liberation from absolutism and the new republican order. In the USA, the *fasces* especially represent national unity (e.g. *Washington Monument*; *Lincoln Memorial*) and the republican constitution (e.g. rostrum of the House of Representatives with bronze *fasces*). In Italy in 1919, *fasces* found their way onto the flag of Mussolini's *fasci di combattimento*, in 1926–1942 they were also an official state symbol, and on the war flag of the *Repubblica Sociale Italiana* (1943–1945). Mussolini himself appeared in public accompanied by lictors, for example in Tripoli (→ Fascism). Even in the early 21st cent., there are, among other examples, *fasces* on US stamps, on the French state seal, on EU passports, on the flag of the canton of St. Gall, and on the Ecuadorian flag.

→ Fascism

1 Th. Schäfer, Imperii insignia, 1989 2 W. Kunkel, Die Magistratur, 1995 3 L. de Libero, Zerbrochene Rutenbündel, zerschlagene Amtsstühle, in: M. Hundt (ed.), Gesch. als Verpflichtung. FS R. Postel, 2001, 1–28 4 G. Laser, Populo et scaenae serviendum est, 1997, 218–225. L. D. L.

Fascia see → Ornament

Fasciae Bandages, bindings, straps of different kinds were made of various materials (felt, leather, linen, wool), and could be white or coloured. *Fasciae* as a category includes the straps of the bed (*lectus*, → *kline*) on which the mattress was laid, → swaddling cloths (σπάργανα, *spárgana*) and *fasciae crurales*, bindings designed to protect the lower legs (*fasciae tibiales*) or thighs (→ *feminalia*) against the cold. The use of *fasciae* was regarded as unmanly, and for men was restricted to invalids, but even Augustus (Suet. Aug. 82,1) and Pompey (Cic. Att. 23,1; Val. Max. 6,2,7) wore such *fasciae*. *Fasciae crurales* were part of the equipment of hunters and herdsmen. There were also *fasciae pedules*, which were pulled over the feet and shoes; surgical bandages are also called *fasciae*, and *fasciae pectorales* were women's breast-bindings. These were worn against the skin, and served to cover the breasts or to support them; in the latter case they were fastened beneath the breasts. When tightly bound, they were supposed to prevent excessive growth of the breasts. A similar purpose was served by the *mamillae* or → *strophium*. Pictorial representations of *fasciae pectorales* are not very common in Greek and Roman art; on occasion, the addition of supporting straps over the shoulders conveys the impression of a modern brassière (→ Bathing costume). The leather straps, supporting the short → *tunica* of chariot drivers (*agitatores*), were also called *fasciae*.

→ Bathing costume; → Clothing R.H.

Fascinum see → Magic

Fasti

A. The term B. Qualification of days C. Dissemination D. Magistrate lists

A. The term

Formed as an adjective from the Latin *fās* ('divine right'; no etymological link with **fēs* or **făs* and their derivative terms *fēriae*, *fēstus* and *fānum* can be demonstrated [11. 134]), *fastus* in technical language is found only in association with *dies*, and in Rome then signifies those days on which certain public acts were held to be permitted. This concept gave a calendrical digest of such days – among which the *dies fasti* predominate – the name *fasti*. As regards both name and graphic form, the word displaced all other competing terms for → calendar in Rome. The common, continuously extended process from the Late Republican period by lists of magistrates for each year could – *pars pro toto* – as a whole be termed *fasti*, even when the interest lay in the list itself. Modern use of the word as a technical term for such lists, and by extension lists of other kinds, is not a linguistic practice found in antiquity.

Historically, *fasti* appear in Rome from the end of the 4th cent. BC, when Cn. Flavius, a *scriba* (*pontificius*?) of Ap. → Claudius [I 2] Caecus is supposed to have published alongside trial-formulae a complete survey of impending court hearings (Liv. 9,46; Cic. Mur. 25; Plin. HN 33,17), thus, in the context of the reform programme of Claudius, establishing public and notably senatorial control over traditional institutions such as the priesthood of the *pontifices*, who had previously determined the statutory and political quality of the days on an individual basis [20. 246ff.]; in view of the lack of alternative terms for calendar, the fact that a calendar in written form probably existed from the time of the Early Republic, but without containing *fasti*-related information, led already in the Late Republic to confusion as to the historical development of the concept (Cic. Att. 6,1,8).

B. Qualification of days

The only example of *fasti* from the Republican period, the mural of the *fasti Antiates*, derives from a probably private context in the Latin coastal town of Antium. Here, the days are differentiated by the initials *F, N, NP, EN, C* and some other more specialized marks; this arises from the necessity to assign to each day of the year, systematically and in written form, its own statutory character; the fact that the conceptualization used here is broadly lacking in extant remains of sacral literature has led to doubts as to the great age of particular rules [10], and even of the entire system [20].

The determination of *dies fasti* (*F*) and *nefasti* (*N*) is fundamental. Discussion of the calendar by antique authors (Varro, Ling. 6,12–34; Macrob. Sat. 1,12–16) centres around the (problematic, see above) etymology *fās* and *fari*, and characterises the *dies nefasti* as those days on which the praetor may not pronounce the initiating formula for trials, *do, dico, addico* (Varro, Ling. 6,29f.); by analogy, no popular assemblies (→ *comitia*) could take place. The rulings concern important 'interfaces' of interaction between the *populus* and the magistrature; they do not impinge on the military, economic or private sphere. With the transformation of most *dies fasti* into *dies comitiales* (C) [10. 106–111], which must have occurred before the *lex Hortensia* of 287 BC [20. 279], there was once again a distinction between the political sphere (*comitia* and from 287 probably also *concilia plebis*; otherwise [10] after [7. 23]) and the private legal sphere, opening up at least to the latter the *nundinae* and normally also the *kalendae* and *nonae* and the following day in each case.

Other distinctions have religious motives behind them: concealed behind the initials *NP* are the → *feriae*; extensive restrictions to activities applied to these days on religious grounds, and they were regarded as the property of divinities named in each case. The meaning of the abbreviation, which no antique source provides, is disputed: against *nefas feriarum publicarum* (or similarly [10. 76]: *dies nefasti publici*), current since at least [4. 438], we now have the suggestion [20. 259] of *N(efas) P(iaculum)*, referring to the stereotypical exhortation *piaculum esto!* against infringements of the *feriae* rules ([16. 227; 19. 18] are unacceptable). On three days, the qualification changes from *N* to *F* only upon completion of a particular act: *Q(uando) R(ex) C(omitiavit) F(as)* (24 March and May), similarly *Q(uando) St(ercus) D(elatum) F(as)* (15 June): the latter upon completion of the cleansing of the temple of Vesta. Still more complex is the situation with regard to the days marked *EN*, which are deemed *nefas* morning and evening, but *fas* between the killing of the sacrificial animal in the day's central ritual and completion of its preparation. The antique term *dies intercisi* (Varro, Ling. 6,31 and passim) in association with the related fragmentary formula of Verrius Flaccus (*fasti Praenestini* on 10 January: *[endo] pro in ponebatur*) has led to the suggestion, impossible from the point of view of historical linguistics [9], but generally accepted, that the abbreviation's meaning is *dies en(do)tercisi*; under the assumption of a haplography, *Endoitio Exitio Nefas* is suggested [20. 268f.].

C. Dissemination

At least from the time of Cicero, *fasti* may have been widely disseminated in the form of scrolls (see Ov. Fast. 1,657; Cic. Att. 4,8a,2), later in the form of codices (→ Chronographer of 354). More striking is their frequent appearance as a large mural decoration for private apartments; such are the *fasti Antiates maiores* from the 60s of the 1st cent. BC and – all in the city of Rome – the *fasti plateae Manfredo* (shortly before 19 BC), the probably Tiberian *fasti Viae Graziosa* and the immense *fasti* porticus painting [12; 15] from the late Antonine or Severan period (*c.* the last third of the 2nd cent. AD). Still to be explained, however, is the rapid dissemination of *fasti* in the form of inscriptions on marble, often several square metres in size, during the

Early Principate. The following *fasti* inscriptions have survived, for the most part in fragmentary form (in chronological order, in so far as this can be established; + indicates the certain existence, ? the possible existence of accompanying magistrate lists):

EARLY AUGUSTAN:
F. fratrum Arvalium (early 20s, 1st cent. BC?; Rome) +
F. Pinciani (*c.* 20 BC; Rome) +
F. Lateranenses (early Augustan?; Rome) ?

AUGUSTAN:
F. Sabini (after 19 BC; regio Sabina) ?
F. Caeretani (Caere) +
F. Esquilini (no later than 7 BC; Rome) +
F. Maffeiani (Rome)
F. Nolani (Nola) ?
F. Paulini (Rome) ?
F. Ostienses (definitely before AD 2; Ostia) +
F. Oppiani (late 1st cent. BC; Rome) ?
F. magistrorum vici (*c.* 7 BC; Rome) +

LATE AUGUSTAN:
F. Viae Ardeatinae (Rome) ?
F. villae Maxentii (Augustan?; Rome) ?
F. Palatii Urbinatis (Augustan?; Urbinum Metaurense?) ?
F. Venusini ([before] AD 4; Venusia) +
F. Cuprenses (early 1st cent. AD; Cupra Maritima) +
F. Praenestini (AD 6/9; Praeneste) +
F. Vallenses (after AD 7; Rome) +
F. Tusculani (or Tiberian?; Tusculum) ?

EARLY IMPERIAL PERIOD (POSSIBLY STILL AUGUSTAN):
F. Capuani (Capua)
F. Quirinales (Rome) ?
F. Fandozziani (Rome) ?
F. Viae Lanza (Rome) ?
F. Viae Tiburtinae (Rome) ?
F. Tarentini (Calabria?) ?

TIBERIAN:
F. Sorrinenses maiores (or late Augustan?; Sorrina) ?
F. Farnesiani (or late Augustan?; Rome?) ?
F. insulae Tiberinae (or late Augustan?; Rome) ?
F. Vici Iugarii (or late Augustan?; Rome) ?
F. Viae Principe Amedeo (Tiberian?; Rome) ?
F. Foronovani (Tiberian?; Forum novum/Sabina)
F. Vaticani (Rome) ?
F. Verulani (Verulae) ?
F. Amiterni (Amiternum) +
F. Allifani (Allifae/Campania)
F. Tauromenitani (Tiberian?; Tauromenium/Sicilia) +
F. Viae dei Serpenti (after AD 23; Rome) ?
F. Antiates maiores (AD 31?; Antium) +

POST-TIBERIAN:
F. Pighiani (under Caligula; Rome?) ?
F. aedis Concordiae (date uncertain; Rome) ?
F. Sorrinenses minores (Claudian?; Sorrina)
F. Tusculani (late 1st cent.?; Tusculum)
F. Lanuvini (2nd cent.; Lanuvium) ?
F. Guidizzolenses (2nd cent.?; Brixia; with → *feriale*)

On the grounds of their content, since [4] *fasti* have been read as a religious document, copies of a pontifical original in the city of Rome. This 'synoptic' reading has hindered the analysis of particular examples; it only apparently corresponds to the perspective of *fasti*-commentators in antiquity (authors of *libri fastorum* commentaries – not calendars in book-form – are i.a. Ovid and Verrius Flaccus; these must be distinguished from systematic *De anno* treatises; works in [1. xxv-xxvi]). With the exception of the *fasti Praenestini*, which contain commentaries by → Verrius Flaccus, in the context of the actual calendar form, there is an absence of any specific reference to a locality or group. This rules out any use as group-related → *feriale*; the numerous errors also speak against a centrally supervised legal document [20. 165ff.]. More credible is the interpretation of the lavish reproductions that quickly spread through Middle Italy and even to regions still using a (Greek) luni-solar calendar (Tauromenium) as a mark of loyalty to Augustus as a personification of Roman tradition: from the final years of the life of Caesar, imperial feast-days enter the Roman festive calendar and even the *fasti*. It is even possible to see in the speed of change in the number of imperial feast-days a motive for the marked reduction in the occurrence of inscribed *fasti* in the mid 1st cent. AD [20. 417ff.].

As a genre the *fasti* remained attractive, even though from the end of the 1st cent. AD the now obsolete name-giving element for the days was replaced by *dies festi* and *feriae* in the sense of 'holidays'. The 'Chronographer of 354', dedicated to a Christian, shows how *fasti* could become a component of a Christian entity, as yet with no intrusion into the calendar text; with the enforcement of the Julian calendar, the form of the *fasti* too was taken over by the Church as the custodian of the calendar tradition in the Middle Ages; the style of the *fasti* still characterizes modern western calendars. Individual evidence for the influence of the antique *fasti* is provided by the *fasti* of → Polemius Silvius of AD 448/9 (*fasti* as a framework for antiquarian/calendarian scholarship) and the *calendarium marmoreum* from Naples (9th cent.), a marble tablet more than 5 m wide, which in 12 monthly sections assigns at least one saint to each day [5].

D. Magistrate lists

A different course of development was followed by the list component of the *fasti*; although this could remain linked to the calendar proper up to the 'Chronographer of 354', as early as the Augustan period it could also appear separately (*fasti Capitolini*). Seen as a whole, magistrate lists not only offered the opportunity for simply projecting forward and thus updating the document until it took on the form of a Chronicle (→ *fasti Ostienses*; *consularia*; → Chronicles), but also for its taking on a more specific character by complementing the list of *consules* and *censores* of the city of Rome with that of local or collegiate magistrates, or of those presiding over associations [22] (e.g. in the *fasti magistrorum vici*).

Using the *fasti Antiates maiores*, whose list of consuls and censors may have begun *c.* 170 BC, it is possible to trace such catalogues back to the time of M. Fulvius Nobilior [21]; the widely held assumption of the existence of older *fasti*, based perhaps on the mention of the (presumably fictitious) *libri lintei* (cf. [13]), has met with criticism [21]. It is certain that in the 2nd and 1st cents. BC chronological consul lists constituted a major medium for the 'reconstruction' of a past, notably that of the Early Republic, that at the same time satisfied personal claims by its connections to family histories (→ Genealogy). In this connection, 'Fastenkritik' (*fasti* criticism) has become an important method for the scientific reappraisal of early Roman history; the existence of name-bearing individuals and entitlements to the consulacy and other leading offices (and the implications for constitutional history; → Consul, → Consular Tribune) down to the 4th cent. BC are subjects of fundamental uncertainty [8; 17; 18]; isolated cases of falsification must also be assumed for the ensuing period (comprehensive analysis and radical criticism: [23]).

→ *feriae*; → *feriale*; → Genealogy; → Calendar

Editions: 1 T. Mommsen, CIL 1²,1 (calendars) 2 InscrIt 13,1, 1949 (magistrate lists) 3 InscrIt 13,2, 1963 (calendars; for new discoveries see no. 20).

Bibliography: 4 G. Wissowa, Rel. und Kultus der Römer, ²1912 5 D. Mallardo, Il calendario marmoreo di Napoli, in: Ephemeris Liturgica 58, 1944, 116–177; 59, 1945, 233–294; 60, 1946, 7–26 6 L.R. Taylor, New Indications of Augustan Editing in the Capitoline Fasti, in: CPh 46, 1951, 73–80 7 Id., Forerunners of the Gracchi, in: JRS 52, 1962, 19–27 8 R. Werner, Der Beginn der röm. Republik, 1963 9 M.E.H. Hermans, Endotercisus, in: MH 21, 1964, 173–176 10 A.K. Michels, The Calendar of the Roman Republic, 1967 (repr. 1978) 11 É. Benveniste, Indoeurop. Institutionen, 1993 (French 1969) 12 F. Magi, Il calendario dipinto sotto Santa Maria Maggiore, 1972 13 J. Pinsent, Military Tribunes and Plebeian Consuls, 1975 14 R.T. Ridley, Fastenkritik, in: Athenaeum 58, 1980, 264–298 15 M.R. Salzman, New Evidence for the Dating of the Calendar at Santa Maria Maggiore in Rome, in: TAPhA 111, 1981, 215–227 16 P. Brind'Amour, Le calendrier romain, 1983 17 K.J. Hölkeskamp, Die Entstehung der Nobilität, 1987 18 J. Bleicken, Gesch. der röm. Republik, ³1988 19 G. Radke, F. Romani, 1990 20 J. Rüpke, Kalender und Öffentlichkeit, 1995 21 Id., F., in: Klio 77, 1995, 184–202 22 Id., Gesch.-Schreibung in Listenform, in: Philologus 141, 1997, 65–85 23 F. Mora, F. e schemi cronologici, 1998.

J.R.

Fastidius Bishop in Britain in the 5th cent. AD; according to Gennadius (vir. ill. 57) author of two texts: *De vita Christiana (ad Fatalem)* and *De viduitate servanda*. His adherence to the Pelagians (→ Pelagius), named in → Prosper Tiro's *Chronicon* of 429 (MGH AA 9,1, 472), is not proven. Leaving aside the *Epistula ad Fatalem* (cf. CPL 763) used in sermon 20 of → Caesarius of Arles (CPL 1008), any attribution of texts, including the so-called *Corpus Caspari* (CPL 732–736), is disputed.

F.G. Nuvolone, s.v. F., Dictionnaire de Spiritualité 12, 2912–2914.

K.U.

Fasti Ostienses Marble calendar extant in fragmentary form, with added list of Roman consuls and suffect consuls as well as Ostia's *duumviri*. The list is expanded by substantial reports from Rome and Ostia, thus acquiring the character of a chronicle. While only fragments of the calendar covering three months are comprehensible, parts of these provide highly detailed notes on the various feasts, and the historiographical component regarding the magistrature makes the *Fasti Ostienses* (FO) one of our most important Latin inscriptions. The fragments cover – with gaps – the period from 49 BC to AD 175. Compilation of the FO probably began before AD 2 [1. 174]; it may have been begun at about the time of Sulla [2. 144], and was continued for nearly two cents. If we take the Roman pontifical annals [3] as a model, the *pontifex Volcani* was probably entrusted with its maintenance, which means that the FO might originally have served as wall-cladding for a temple of Vulcan, which has not been precisely located [2. 147f.]. The substantially consistent sequence of documentation – Roman city magistrates, historical remarks, local office-holders – leads to the assumption that entries were always made at one and the same time at the beginning of the following year; only in exceptional cases do we find an addition made later [2. 144f.]. Apart from the inclusion of local officials and events, the main emphasis is on events in Rome and at the imperial court: deaths, births, gifts of money, triumphs, temple-dedications and games take up a large part of the document. The *acta diurna populi Romani* may have served i.a. as a source for the recorded events, which are often precisely dated [4]. On grounds of the thoroughness and diversity of the information given, the FO stand close in status to literary texts such as the *breviaria* of Roman history (e.g. that of → Velleius Paterculus) [3].

Editions: 1 InscrIt 13.1, 173–241 (list of officials); 13.2, 104–106 (calendar) 2 FO² (list of officials only).

Bibliography: 3 J. Rüpke, Gesch.-Schreibung in Listenform, in: Philologus 141, 1997, 65–85 4 A. Stein, Die röm. Staatszeitung und die F.O., in: HZ 149, 1934, 294–298.

B.BR.

Fat see → vol. 6, Addenda

Fate

A. General B. Graeco-Roman Philosophical Theories of Fate

A. General

As can be seen from the multitude of names – some of them impersonal – for the powers of fate in Homer (→ *aísa*, *aísimon*, → *anánkē*, → *moîra(i)*, *móros*, *mórsimon*, → *némesis*, *pepromén̄ē*), these are not personal deities, but rather explain inescapable events, such as the early death of prominent heroes. Even the gods' ability to assert their authority was limited when faced with this 'lot' [1; 2].

B. Graeco-Roman Philosophical Theories of Fate

In early Greek philosophy the question of human destiny is replaced, in → Heraclitus [1], in → Empedocles [1] or in → Atomism, by that of natural order and its laws. A link between mythical powers of fate and a generally rational natural order was established by → Plato [1]: in the 10th bk. of the 'Politeia' (Pl. Resp. 161c) the → Moirai, as daughters of → *Anánkē* (→ Necessity), are guarantors of both a harmonious world order and the self-determined choices of individuals. → Aristotle [6], though he did develop a comprehensive theory of causation, consciously avoided deriving from it a comprehensively functioning 'world mechanism'[3].

In Hellenism, the Stoics (cf. → Stoicism) set in opposition to the Atomism of → Epicurus, with its purely mechanistic explanation of infinite worlds, a comprehensive theory of fate through a spiritual-physical power that forms the entire world (*heimarménē*, Latin *fatum*). The divine → *lógos* [1], which was designated equally as Zeus, fate, necessity and providence (*prónoia*, Latin *providentia*), permeates and ordains the entire world as → *pneûma* (a mixture of air and → fire). This *pneûma* holds the world together in its entirety, while also determining, by its different degree of density, the consistency and behaviour of individual things [4; 8]. The interaction of the various pneumatic powers also constitutes human fate in the sense of an unbroken chain of causation (cf. the etymological derivation of *heimarménē* from *eírein* = 'connect', or from *heirmós aitiṓn* = 'causal link'). Providence is not an inescapable destiny (→ Predestination, theory of), but an 'administration' (*dioíkēsis*) of the world that is tied to preconditions (*confatalia*, Cic. Fat. 30), that can also be predicted on the basis of certain signs and that justifies → divination as a science (*mantikḗ*, Lat. *divinatio*) (Cic. Div. 2,130; Cic. Fat. 11–17; Sext. Emp. Adversus math. 9,132) [8].

The divine *pneûma* also determines the inner nature of human beings. Thus, for the opponents of the Stoics, the otherwise assumed moral autonomy of the individual becomes a problem. Cicero's works 'On Fate' (*De fato*) [5] and 'On Divination' (*De divinatione*), as well as Alexander [26] of Aphrodisias' treatise 'On Fate' (*Perì heirmaménēs*) testify to a centuries-long polemic and corresponding defensive strategies of the Stoics [6; 7]. Added to the problem of free will was that of the justice of providence (→ Theodicy).

The Stoic theory of fate was not a unified doctrine [8]. Although primary sources are not extant (except for → Seneca [2] the Younger, who saw himself as allied to Stoicism but often went his own way), secondary sources reflect different positions and strategies, also in regard to the severity of the deterministic ideas, predictability, theory of causation and the autonomy of the individual. There is a lengthy development between the theories of → Chrysippus [2], brilliant for its logic and physics, the representatives of the Middle Stoa, such as → Panaetius [4] and → Posidonius [3] of Rhodes, and members of the Late Stoa who were almost exclusively interested in ethical questions (self-determination and compatibility with fate), such as → Epictetus [2] and → Marcus [2] Aurelius [9]. Above all, the question of free will and the indeterminacy of the future strongly influenced early Christian theologians; besides Iustinus Martys (*Apologia*), Eusebius (Pr. EV. 6), and Augustinus, these also include Origen (*Contra Celsum*, *De principiis*) or Tertullian (*Apologeticum*) [10] and continued to be important during the Middle Ages and into the modern era [3].

→ Predestination, theory of; → Will

1 W. C. Greene, Moira: Fate, Good and Evil in Greek Thought, 1948 2 E. R. Dodds, The Greeks and the Irrational, 1951 3 W. L. Craig, The Problem of Divine Foreknowledge and Future Contingents from Aristotle to Suarez, 1988 4 S. Samburski, The Physics of the Stoics, 1957 5 R. W. Sharples (ed.), Cicero: On Fate, 1991 (with Engl. transl. and comm.) 6 Id. (ed.), Alexander of Aphrodisias, On Fate, 1983 (with Engl. transl. and comm.) 7 A. Zierl (ed.), Alexander von Aphrodisias, Über das Schicksal, 1995 (with German transl. and comm.) 8 S. Bobzien, Determinism and Freedom in Stoic Philosophy, 1998 9 W. Theiler, Tacitus und die antike Schicksalslehre, 1946 M. Kranz, s. v. Schicksal, HWPh 8, 1275–1289

D. FR.

Fates see → Parcae; → Moira

Fatima (Fāṭima). Daughter of → Muhammad and his first wife Ḫadīǧa; wife of the future Caliph ʿAlī b. Abī Ṭālib (→ Ali), mother of al-Ḥasan and al-Ḥusain; she is the only daughter of the prophet to be universally venerated by Muslims, who ascribe extraordinary powers to her. Especially among the → Shiites and the Ishmaelites she is regarded as a miraculous woman, in whom Christian (equated with the Virgin Mary) and gnostic traits (F. as the incarnation of light) come together. Little is known about the historic F.

H. Lammens, Fāṭima et les filles de Mahomet. Notes critiques pour l'étude de la Sīra, 1912; L. Massignon, La notion du voeu et la dévotion musulmane à Fāṭima, in: Studi orientalistici in onore di Giorgio Levi della Vida II, 1956, 102–126; L. Veccia Vaglieri, s.v. F., EI² 2, 841b–850a.

I.T.-N.

Faunus Roman god of the outdoors, early identified with the Greek → Pan. In poetry and especially in the figurative arts the two generally coincide: F., lover of the → Nymphs (Hor. Carm. 3,18,1) and insatiable erotomaniac [1], comes from Hellenistic mythology. F. does not have his own iconography [2; 3]. Like Pan, he is associated with forest and mountains as well as with goats and sheep. More his own is his role as originator of nightmares and numinous voices (and then generally as a seer), his association with the → *Lupercalia* and his integral place in the line of original Italian kings. It is not clear whether the much more frequent pl. *Fauni* (attested since Enn. Ann. 207) is modelled on the Greek pl. *Panes* or stands alone.

A. Faunus as god of the outdoors B. Cult C. Mythology

A. Faunus as god of the outdoors

F., like Pan, belongs firmly to uncivilized nature outside the city and beyond the cultivated zone (Verg. Aen. 10,551); in this sense he is autochthonous (Verg. Aen. 8,314), and is associated with → Silvanus. He is accordingly the god of small animals, with whom as *Inuus* he is sexually engaged (Serv. Aen. 6,775); in his own mythic creation Ovid integrates this into the aetiology of the *lupercalia* (Fast. 2,423–446). The connected derivation of the name from *favere*, 'to be favourably disposed' (Serv. Auct. Georg. 1,10), is certainly not tenable, as such an attribute is unattested; just as false is the modern conception of F. as a wind-god (Favonius: [4]). As the god of 'wild nature' F. appears in various impish or ghostly roles. He is capable of frightening people and attacking them (Dion. Hal. Ant. Rom. 5,16,2f.) while remaining unseen (certain female dogs can see F.: Plin. HN 8,42,151), and while inducing a kind of possessed state he can bring nightmares (Serv. Aen. 6,775); certain folk-medicinal preparations are ascribed with healing powers (Plin. HN 25,10,29; 30,24,84). Ennius (Ann. 207) associates *Fauni* with the *vates*; their prophetic voices might be heard at the crisis of battle (Cic. Div. 1,45,101), but are so frequent (Cic. Nat. D. 3,6,15) that the usual antique etymology for the name F. derives it from *fari* in the sense of 'prophesy' (Varro, Ling. 7,36). As the god of such voices he is also called *Fatuus* and *Fatuclus* (Serv. Aen. 6,775). More common than *Fatuus* is *Fatua*, identified with *Fauna* (in the *libri pontificales*, Labeo in Macrob. Sat. 1,12,21) and portrayed as an ecstatic prophetess (Iust. 43,1,8). – In literature, F. becomes an oracular god; his incubatory oracle at Albunea is described by Virgil after his own invention (Aen. 7,81–91, cf. Ov. Fast. 4,649–668 [5. 176 n. 2]), while Calpurnius relates one of F.' oracular texts inscribed in the bark of a tree (Ecl. 1,33–88).

B. Cult

In Rome, F. has his sanctuary outside the → *pomerium* and beyond the firm ground on the Tiber island; the temple was built using fines from the *pecuarii* ('cattle breeders'), and dedicated on 13 February, 194 BC (Liv. 33,42,10; 34,53,3f.). Immediately afterwards, on 15 February, came the → *Lupercalia* (*fasti Esquilini*; Ov. Fast. 2,193f.); F. is regarded as the god of this feast, and is accordingly firmly associated with Arcadian → Pan Lykaios (Dion. Hal. Ant. Rom. 1,80,1 according to Aelius Tubero fr. 3 Peter; Liv. 1,5,2). The god is associated with the 'savage and primitive brotherhood' of the *luperci* (Cic. Cael. 26). It is as a result of this association rather than on grounds of it that the *Lupercal* on the Palatine became the grotto of F. Augustine is probably referring to the *Lupercalia* when he maintains that Romulus began the cult of F. in Rome (Civ. 4,23). Evidence for a private cult of F. is in fact entirely absent; it is possible that in this respect he is replaced by Silvanus [6], with whom, however, he is only later identified (Ps.-Aur. Vict. Origo gentis Romanae 4,6). – It is difficult to determine the extent to which the rural feasts of F. in poetry reflect a real cult and not a Hellenistic idealization of rural life (Hor. Carm. 1,4,11; 3,18,1–16; Calp. Ecl. 5,24–31).

C. Mythology

F. regularly appears in myth as the ancient king of the → Aborigines and son of → Picus (Verg. Aen. 7,48); both occur as *numina silvestria* ('forest gods') and *di agrestes* ('rural gods') (Ov. Fast. 3,303; 315) in the period preceding the foundation of the city; the woodpekker (*picus Martius*) is also linked with F. in folk-belief (Plin. HN 25,10,29). It is possible that the Ps.-Hesiodian Agrius already represents the Hellenization of F. [7. 48]; in later traditions he is host in Rome to Heracles in place of → Evander (Derkyllos FGrH 288 F 2). F. is closely associated with his female counterpart *Fauna*, who is regarded as his wife or daughter. We have no evidence of a cult of *Fauna*, but she is regularly identified with → Bona Dea, → Ops and → Maia (Macrob. Sat. 1,12,21).

1 E. Fantham, Sexual comedy in Ovid's Fasti, in: HSPh 87, 1983, 185–216 2 P. Pouthier, P. Rouillard, F. ou l'iconographie impossible, in: L. Kahil et al. (ed.), Iconographie classique et identités régionales, 1986, 105–110 3 Id., s.v. F., LIMC 8.1, 582f. 4 L. Luschi, Cacu, Fauno e i venti, in: SE 57, 1991, 109–117 5 R. Heinze, Vergils ep. Technik, 31928 6 G. Wissowa, Rel. und Kultus der Römer, 1912, 213 7 T.P. Wiseman, Remus. A Roman Myth, 1995.

J. Gagé, Énée, F. et le culte de Silvain 'Pélasge', in: MEFRA 73, 1961, 69–138; Latte, 83f.; E.C.H. Smits, F., 1946; T.P. Wiseman, The god of the Lupercal, in: JRS 85, 1995, 1–22; G. Wissowa, Rel. und Kultus der Römer, 1912, 208–216. F.G.

Fausta Flavia Maxima F., daughter of Emperor Maximian and Eutropia; when still a minor, at the end of AD 307, she was married to Constantinus [1] in order to reinforce the alliance between Maximian and Constantine, after the former had returned to politics. Mother of three emperors: Constantinus [2], Constantius [2] and Constans [1]. At the end of 324 she was elevated with Helena to the rank of Augusta, but a little later, in circumstances that remain unexplained, killed by order of her imperial husband.

PLRE 1, 325f.; J.W. Drijvers, Flavia Maxima F., in: Historia 41, 1994, 500–506. B.BL.

Faustina

[1] Annia Galeria Aurelia F. Daughter of Marcus Aurelius and F. [3]. Born probably AD 151 [1. 108, 247;

2. 161], married to Cn. Claudius [II 62] Severus, *cos. II* 173. Her son was Ti. Claudius [II 65] Severus Proculus, *cos. ord.* 200. PIR² C 1028.

1 A.R. BIRLEY, Marcus Aurelius, ²1988 2 W. AMELING, Die Kinder des Marc Aurel..., in: ZPE 90, 1992, 147–166.

[2] **Annia Galeria F.** Wife of Emperor → Antoninus [1] Pius. Daughter of → Annius [II 15] Verus, *cos. III* AD 126 and Rupilia F. By her marriage with Antoninus Pius she had four children, of whom only F. [3] outlived the parents. After Pius' accession to power she received the name Augusta. She died before 24 October 140; on that same day she was deified by senatorial decree; before 13 November honoured with a *funus censorium* and buried in the *Mausoleum Hadriani* (ILS 349). A temple was built in her honour on the edge of the *Forum Romanum* (ILS 348). A foundation for the maintenance of the *puellae Faustinianae* was instituted in her memory. [1. 403ff.].

PIR² A 715.

1 L. VIDMAN, in: Sodalitas. Scritti Guarino I, 1984.

W.E.

[3] **Annia Galeria F.** Wife of Emperor Marcus Aurelius. Daughter of F. [2] and → Antoninus [1] Pius. Born 16 February *c.* AD 130 [2. 34f.]. By command of Hadrian betrothed to L. Verus on 25 February 138; after Hadrian's death the betrothal was dissolved, and a new one entered into with Marcus Aurelius, Pius' other adoptive son. Married by April 145; to celebrate the occasion, coins were minted bearing the couple's portraits, and on the same day a *congiarium* was probably given to the *plebs* of the city of Rome (FO² 50).

In the course of her long marriage she bore in all at least fourteen children, of whom only a small number outlived her [2. 247f.; 5]. Her *fecunditas* ('fertility') is celebrated on coins. Her first daughter, Domitia F., was born on 30 November 147; on 1 December F. received the name Augusta, and Marcus Aurelius the *tribunicia potestas* (FO² 51). Many of the children born to her in subsequent years died shortly after birth, the latter generally being recorded on coins. The children and their mother were also often mentioned in the exchange of letters between Fronto and Marcus Aurelius, along with everyday events and illnesses [4. Index, S. 279]. In 161 her daughter Lucilla was betrothed to L. Verus, co-ruler to Marcus Aurelius; the marriage took place in 164. Her son Commodus, the later emperor, was born on 31 August 161, and *c.* 170 her last daughter Vibia Aurelia Sabina.

During the war against the Marcomanni F. was in Carnuntum with her husband, perhaps in reaction to rumours that she had affairs with men, notably gladiators. While there she brought influence to bear in the case against Herodes Atticus. In 174 after the victory over the Quadi she was honoured with the title *mater castrorum* – perhaps also as a compensation for her unlooked-for sojourn on the Danube. According to Cassius Dio (71,22,3) and HA Aur. (24,6) F. is supposed to have encouraged the governor of Syria, Avidius [1] Cassius, to take power and to marry her in the event of her husband's death. The report probably merits its belief. Avidius was proclaimed emperor in 175 – on grounds of a false report of Marcus' death. This rebellion collapsed after a few months, but Marcus Aurelius went east, accompanied by F.

F. died at the end of 175 / beginning of 176 in Halala, a village in Cappadocia, which was elevated to city status as Faustinopolis. The Senate made her *diva*; her death was commemorated on coins, and a charitable foundation instituted to her *memoria*: *novae puellae Faustinianae*. These measures were probably taken by Marcus Aurelius with the intention of countering rumours about her. His mourning of her may have been philosophically restrained, but nevertheless genuine. Contrary to widely-held tradition, in his 'Contemplations' (εἰς ἑαυτόν) he portrays her in a favourable light.

BIBLIOGRAPHY: 1 PIR² A 716 2 A.R. BIRLEY, Marcus Aurelius, ²1988 3 RIC III 268ff. 4 M.P. VAN DEN HOUT (ed.), Fronto. Epistulae, 1988 5 W. AMELING, Die Kinder des Marc Aurel, in: ZPE 90, 1992, 147–166.
PORTRAITS: 6 FITTSCHEN-ZANKER III 20ff. no. 19ff. 7 K. FITTSCHEN, Die Bildnistypen der Faustina Minor ..., 1982.

W.E.

[4] Third and last wife of Emperor Constantius [2] II from the beginning of AD 361 (Amm. Marc. 21,6,4). The usurper → Procopius subsequently gained the sympathy of the troops by forcing her and her daughter Constantia [3] to accompany him on his campaign (Amm. Marc. 26,7,10; 9,3). PLRE 1, 326. K.G.-A.

Faustinupolis see vol. 6, Addenda

Faustus Supposedly an ancient Latin praenomen (Liber de praenominibus 4), but historically only attested (with meaning 'The Fortunate') for F. Cornelius [I 87] Sulla, the son of the dictator Sulla and his descendants (→ Cornelius [II 57] and [II 60]). Epithet of the Anicii (→ Anicius [II 2–6]); also a favourite name for slaves.

SALOMIES, 28; H. SOLIN, Die stadtröm. Sklavennamen, 1, 1996, 82–85; SYME, AA, Stemma XVI.

K.-L.E.

[1] **Anicius Acilius Glabrio F.** Scion of the most important late Roman senatorial family who became *praefectus urbi Romae* three times under Honorius and Valentinian III, in AD 437/8 and 442 *praefectus praetorio Italiae Africae et Illyrici* (ILS 1283), and in 438 consul. On 25 December of that consular year the Senate gathered in his house to receive the just completed Codex Theodosianus from him (Cod. Theod. 1,2,1–4).

PLRE 2, 452–454; A. CHASTAGNOL, Fastes de la Préfecture de Rome, 1962, 286–289; J. HARRIES, J. WOOD, The Theodosian Code, 1993, 19–22.

K.P.J.

[2] **Flavius Anicius Probus F. iunior Niger.** Consul in AD 490, was sent as *magister officiorum* probably in

491 by → Theoderic to Constantinople to have his rule legalized (Anon. Valesianus 11,53; 12,57). Although he remained there to about 493, he was unsuccessful. In 503–505/6 he was *quaestor palatii* and in 507–512 *praefectus praetorio* in the Ostrogothic kingdom. → Ennodius sent him many letters between 501 and 512.

PLRE 2, 454–456; I. König, Aus der Zeit Theoderichs d. Gr., 1997, 127, 138f.; J. Moorhead, Theoderic in Italy, 1992. K.P.J.

[3] **F. Reiensis.** Bishop of Reii (Riez), born shortly before AD 410 in Britain, monk on the island of Lerinum (modern Lérins, off the southern coast of France), after 434 the third abbot there, after about 460 bishop of Riez, in 477–484/5 banned by Euric, died about 495. Venerated as a saint in Provence (feast day: 28 Sept.). At the synods of Arles and Lyon (about 475) and in the 3-vol. *De gratia dei* (CPL 961), he turned against the predestinationism of Lucidus. By emphasizing the fundamental potential of a fallen human to be good (*possibilitas boni*), which must precede (outward) mercy, F. was suspected of being a Pelagian (→ Pelagius) after 519, especially by → Johannes Maxentius and → Fulgentius of Ruspe. The 2nd Synod of Oranges (529) under Caesarius of Arles was directed against F.'s teachings though without mentioning F. Gennadius defended F.'s teachings (Vir. ill. 86) of mercy and Sidonius Apollinaris composed an eucharisticon for F. (Carmen 16). In a letter (Epist. 3 CSEL 21 = 20 MGH AA 8) F. expounded the physicality of angels and the soul to emphasize the different nature of God, which caused → Claudianus [4] Mamertus to write his treatise *De statu animae* (CPL 983). The homiletic writings of F. (CPL 965–975a) in revised form were preserved especially in → Eusebius [13] Gallicanus and the large sermon collections of → Caesarius [4] of Arelate.

Editions: On CPL 961–977 cf. A. Hamman, PL Suppl. 3, 1963, 492–545.
Bibliography: É. Griffe, Les sermons de F.R., in: BLE 61, 1960, 27–38; C. Tibiletti, F.R. nei giudizi della critica, in: Augustinianum 21, 1981, 567–587; Id., Polemiche in Africa contro i teologi provenzali, in: Augustinianum 26, 1986, 499–517; Th. A. Smith, De gratia, 1990. K.U.

[4] **Faustus of Byzantium.** His large work 'History of Armenia', which narrated the history of Greater Armenia during the 4th cent. AD in classical Armenian, was attributed to F. at an early point in time. Lazar of P'arpec'i (5th cent.), who considered his own work the third history of Armenia (after → Agathangelus [2] and F.), attests F.'s epithet, which supposedly referred to the location of his literary activity. In fact, however, F.'s epithet is derived from the misunderstood title of his treatise *Buzandaran Patmut'iwnk'* ('Historical Commentary'), which resulted in 'Byzantium' or 'Buzanda'/'Podandos' becoming a locational attribution. The author was an Armenian cleric, who assumed a united Armenia in the 4th cent.

His work, which was originally written in Greek (before the invention of Armenian writing) is only preserved in an Armenian version of the 2nd half of the 5th cent. and only consists of four of the originally 6 volumes. This work is the only basic source for the history of Armenia in the 4th cent. → Procopius used it for recounting regional events (Procop. Pers. 1,5,9–40 and Procop. Aed. 3,1,6 depend on 4,52ff. and 5,7 of F.'s treatise). The work shows the author to have been familiar with the country and language and to have been conscientious in carefully and objectively narrating the events of this period, especially concerning power struggles between the nobility and the ecclesiastical leadership.
→ Armenia; → Armenian

M. Lauer, Des F. Geschichte Armeniens, 1879 (edition); N. G. Garsoïan, The Epic Histories attributed to P'awstos Buzand (Buzandaran Patmut'iwnk'), 1989 (edition and bibliography). K.SA.

Faventia A town of eastern Aemilia located on the *via Aemilia* (Itin. Gaditanum 90; It. Ant. 100; 126; 287; It. Burd. 616; Tab. Peut. 4,5) at the crossing of the Anemo (Lamone), modern Faenza. Late Republican foundation (augural name), *municipium*, *tribus Pollia* [5. 93]. In 82 affected by the Civil War (Liv. Epit. 88; Vell. Pat.2,28; App. B Civ. 1,91). Famous for wine (Varro Rust. 1,2,7) and linen production (Plin. HN 19,9). Early Christian diocese. Prehistoric settlement on the Colle di Persolino; 6th-cent. BC settlement in the Piazza d'Armi. From the Roman period: an orthogonal plan, oriented towards the *via Aemilia*; city walls of *opus quadratum*. F. extended beyond its walls in the Imperial period. Augustan and late Roman mosaics [1]. F. was a traffic node between Ravenna and Classis in the north and Etruria in the south (It. Ant. 283) [2; 3]. Centuriated territory. The → *cardo maximus* followed an extension of the present-day Corso Garibaldi; *villae* [4].

1 G.V. Gentili, Mosaici augustei e tardoromani, in: V. Righini (ed.), Un museo archeologico per F., 1980, 419–501 2 A. Mosca, La via Faventina, in: N. Alfieri (ed.), La viabilità tra Bologna e Firenze nel tempo (Atti del Convegno ... 28 settembre – 1° ottobre 1989), 1992, 179–188 3 Id., Via Quinctia, in: Journal of Ancient Topography 2, 1992, 91–108 4 P. Monti, Le ville romane del Faentino, in: G.C. Susini (ed.), La villa romana, 1971, 75–102 5 W. Kubitschek, Imperium Romanum tributim discriptum, 1889.

G. Rossini, Le antiche iscrizioni romane di F., 1938; A. Medri, F. romana, 1943; G.C. Susini (ed.), Studi Faentini in mem. di mons. G. Rossini, 1966; V. Righini (ed.), Un museo archeologico per F., 1980; Id. (ed.), Archeologia a F., 1990. G.U.

Favonius Rare Roman family name, occurring in Latium (Schulze 563).

[1] **F., M.** He came from the municipal elite and was a follower of M. → Porcius Cato (Uticensis), whose political and personal intransigence he attempted to imi-

tate, leading to envy and numerous electoral defeats. In 61 BC he attacked P. Clodius [I 4] Pulcher, in 60 he unsuccessfully charged Q. Caecilius [I 32] Metellus Pius Scipio. In the 50s he opposed Caesar, Pompey and Crassus in vain. He became aedile in 53 or 52 and praetor in 49 (after an election defeat). In the Civil Wars he bitterly opposed an agreement with Caesar (Cic. Fam. 7,15,2) but while fighting alongside Pompey he remained critical of him and other members of the Senate (Plut. Pompeius 60; 67). After Pompey's death, Caesar pardoned F. He then kept aloof of politics and the conspiracy against Caesar (Plut. Brutus 12,2). However, he did join Caesar's murderers, was captured at Philippi and executed.

C.F. Konrad, Notes on Roman Also-Rans, in: J. Linderski (ed.), Imperium sine fine, 1996, 123 (lit.). K.-L.E.

[2] **F. Eulogius.** A *Disputatio de somnio Scipionis scripta* is preserved with the name F. E. and dedicated to a Superius, *consularius provinciae Byzacenae* (Subscriptio). This F.E. is identified with the E. whom Augustine mentions, in connection with a dream *apud Mediolanum*, i.e., between AD 384 and 386 (Aug. De cura pro mortuis gerenda 11,13), as a former student who had become a rhetor in Carthage. F.'s work consists of two parts of differing length: a manual (2–19) of arithmetic dedicated to the numbers 1–9 (following Cic. Rep. 6,12), and an introduction to music theory (21–27), which is essential for understanding Cicero's explanation of the harmony of the spheres (Rep. 6,18). The factual content is very basic and permits neither the establishment of its relationship to the commentary of → Macrobius nor an identification of the sources; perhaps F.E. used the Virgil commentary of → Marius Victorinus. It cannot be determined whether or not F.E. was a Christian.

Edition: A. Holder, 1901.
Translations: R.E. van Weddingen, 1957 (French); L. Scarpa, 1974 (Italian).
Bibliography: S. Gersh, Middle Platonism and Neoplatonism 2, 1986, 743–745; M. Sicherl, s.v. F.E., RAC 7, 636–640. J.F.

Favorinus Rhetorician with philosophical interests, author of → Buntschriftstellerei, a representative of the → Second Sophistic, born about AD 80–90 in Arelate. His life is recounted in Philostr. VS 1,8 and the Suda (also s.Gell. NA 16,3,1 et passim). He was described as a hermaphrodite (Philostr.: ἀνδρόθηλυς, εὐνοῦχος; *andróthēlys, eunoûchos*; Polemon in Förster Scriptores physiognomonici 1,160,10: *sine testiculis natus*, cf. [6]). He was trained in Massalia, heard Dio Chrysostom speak in Rome (?) and became an acclaimed speaker. In Ephesus he was involved in a protracted quarrel with → Polemon and later temporarily lost Hadrian's favour. His treatise Περὶ φυγῆς (*Perì phygês*), with local reference to Chios, indicates banishment, but since this is otherwise unknown in the remainder of the biographic tradition, it may have been a fiction [8]. Reconciled with the emperor, he lived (as an *eques*: [Dion. Chrys.] 37,25) in Rome until his death in the mid 2nd cent. Among his students and friends were → Herodes Atticus, → Gellius, → Fronto and → Plutarchus (who dedicated *De primo frigido* to him). Being equally fluent in Greek (which he preferred) and Latin, he was well versed in both literatures. The beauty of his expression was widely acclaimed. His philosophical leanings were towards the Academy and the Sceptics.

Of numerous works, three are preserved; some among the speeches in the corpus of Dio Chrysostom (the attribution is only definite for *Perí phygês*): 1. [Dion Chrys.] Or. 37, the *Korinthiakós*, full of 'petty groping for effects' [13], delivered in Corinth, regarding F.'s volatile relationship with that town; 2. [Dion Chrys.] or. 64, 'On Fortune' (Περὶ Τύχης; *Perì Týchēs*), attributed to F. by J. Geel and A. Sonny [3]; 3. 'On banishment' (probable title Περὶ φυγῆς; *Perì phygês*): extensive remains on a papyrus published in 1931 [4], refutation of the four reasons why people fear banishment: longing for home, longing for friends and relatives, the desire for wealth and honour and the feeling of a lack of freedom. The anthology 'Memorabilia' (Ἀπομνημονεύματα; *Apomnēmoneúmata*) in at least 5 books and 'Colourful History' (Παντοδαπὴ ἱστορία; *Pantodapḕ historía*) in 24 books were used by → Diogenes [17] Laertius. Of about 20 other treatises, some of which were philosophical ('The Tropes of the Pyrrhonians', 10 books; 'Plutarch or about the elementary teachings (?) [διάθεσις; *diáthesis*] of the Academy'; 'Against Epictetus'), of which only the titles and fragments are preserved.

1 A. Barigazzi (ed.), F. di Arelate, Opere, 1966 2 E. Mensching (ed.), F. von Arelate, Fr., 1st part 1963 (no more have been published) 3 A. Sonny, Ad Dionem Chrysostomum analecta, 1896, 219ff. 4 M. Norsa, G. Vitelli (ed.), Il papiro vaticano gr. 11. Φαβωρίνου περὶ φυγῆς, 1931 5 B. Häsler, F. Über die Verbannung, 1935 6 H.J. Mason, F.' disorder: Reifenstein's syndrome in antiquity, in: Janus 66, 1979, 1–13 7 Ch.K. Callanan, A. Bertini Malgarini, Übersehene F.-Frg. aus einer Oxforder Hs., in: RhM 129, 1966, 170–183 8 S. Swain, F. and Hadrian, in: ZPE 79, 1989, 150–158 9 G. Anderson, The Second Sophistic, in: D.A. Russell (ed.), Antonine Literature, 1990, 91–110 10 A. Barigazzi, F. di Arelate, in: ANRW II 34.1, 556–581 11 E. Amato, Studi su F.: Le orazioni ps.-crisostomiche, 1995 12 M.-L. Lakmann, F. v. Arelate, in: Vir bonus dicendi peritus. FS A. Weische, 1997, 233–243 13 E. Norden, Die ant. Kunstprosa, [2]1909, 423. E.-G.S.

Febris Personification of malarial fever. The inhabitants of Rome, which was originally located in a swampy area where malaria posed a real threat, built F. sanctuaries at an early time (Cic. Leg. 2,28; Aug. Civ. 3,25). A main sanctuary on the Palatine (Plin. HN 2,16; Cic. Nat. D. 3,63; Ael. VH 12,11) and other temples on the Quirinal and near the *Mariana monumenta* (Esquiline?) are known (Val. Max. 2,5,6). In the Quirinal sanctuary, persons afflicted by the fever dedicated *re-*

media that had been attached to their disease-stricken bodies (Val. Max. 2,5,6). Apart from F., personifications of the tertian and quartan fevers, *Tertiana* (CIL 7,999) and *Quartana* (CIL 12,3129), are attested in the late period. F. is one of the deities bringing misfortune that were worshipped in a cult to keep them inactive (cf. → Robigalia). The worship of F. and other 'negative deities' was already rejected by Cicero (Nat. D. 3,25) and cited as arguments against paganism by Christian authors (Aug. Civ. 2,14; Min. Fel. 25; Lactant. Div. inst. 1,20,17). Seneca made F. the only faithful deity accompanying emperor Claudius into the Other World (Apocol. 6).
→ Fever B.SCH.

Fecunditas Personification of fertility, which was only created in association with the imperial family. When → Poppaea Sabina gave birth to a daughter of Nero in AD 63, the Senate resolved to dedicate a temple to F. (Tac. Ann. 15,23). Since the reign of Antoninus Pius, F. was pictured on the obverse of coins. She is often depicted with children in her arms or at her side, occasionally also with a cornucopia [1].

1 T. GANSCHOW, s.v. F., LIMC 8.1 (Suppl.), 583ff. B.SCH.

Felicissimus Head of the treasury under Aurelianus [3] (SHA Aurelian. 38,3), who incited the workers to forge coins in AD 271 or 274. When this became known, he organized an uprising on Caelius Mons, which imperial troops were able to put down only with heavy losses. F. was killed in the process (Eutr. 9,14; Aur. Vict. Caes. 35,6; [Aur. Vict.] Epit. Caes. 35,4; Suda s.v. μονιτάριοι). Polemius Silvius (Chron. min. 1, 521f. MOMMSEN) lists him among the usurpers.

PIR² F 140; PLRE 1, 3311; KIENAST, ²1996, 238. T.F.

Felicitas The Roman goddess F., usually depicted as a wreathed figure with a cornucopia and herald's staff (*caduceus*) [1], is the personification of good luck and success that supposedly endures unlike → Fortuna (Val. Max. 7,1). She received her first temple in Rome, which was built with booty from the Spanish campaigns of L. Lucinius Lucullus (Cass. Dio 43,21,1; 76,2), shortly after 146 BC in the Velabrum area (Suet. Iul. 37). Another temple (together with Venus Victrix, Honos and Virtus) was built by Pompey in 55 BC on top of his theatre, where a sacrifice was celebrated annually on 12 August (CIL I² 1 p. 217; 244; 324). Other sacrifices were held on 1 July and 9 October for the Capitoline F. (CIL I² 1 p. 214; 245). A cult site is also attested on the Field of Mars (CIL I² 1 p. 252,11). F. originally allotted a good fate to commanders with military accomplishments. From the dictator Sulla, who called himself → *felix*, to the Imperial period she gained in importance. Caesar had a temple built for her at the site of the old *curia* of Faustus Sulla (Cass. Dio 44,5,2) and used her name as a watchword at the battle of Thapsus (Bell. Afr. 83). The emperors then transformed her into *F. Augusta*, who was intended to personify the continued happy state of the *Imperium Romanum*. They practised her cult, donated altars and statues (CIL I² 1 p. 229; Suet. Tib. 5) and often had her image depicted on coins until the Constantinian period (1st half of the 4th cent. AD). F. could also signify fertility (CIL IV 1454).

1 T. GANSCHOW, s.v. F., LIMC 8.1 (Suppl.), 585–591.

H. ERKELL, Augustus, F., Fortuna, 1952, 45–128; E. WISTRAND, Felicitas imperatoria, 1987. B.SCH.

Felix Roman cognomen ('The Fortunate One'), in the Republican period initially an epithet of the dictator L. Cornelius [I 90] Sulla and his descendants (Cornelius [II 59–61]); in the Imperial period, as a name invoking luck, one of the most common cognomina and the most common slave name.

DEGRASSI, FCIR 252; KAJANTO, Cognomina 29, 272f.; H. SOLIN, Die stadtröm. Sklavennamen 1, 1996, 86–93. K.-L.E.

[1] Gem-cutter of the Roman Republican period, probably a contemporary of → Dioscurides [8], named together with → Anteros in an inscription as a *gemari de sacra via* [1. 44 and note 40]. He signed the famous sardonyx showing the theft of the Palladion and the ownership inscription of Calpurnius Severus in Greek writing, Oxford, AM [1. Plate 39,1f.; 2. 287 note 126 (bibliography), Plate 81,4].
→ Gem cutting

1 M. L. VOLLENWEIDER, Die Steinschneidekunst und ihre Künstler in spätrepublikanischer und augusteischer Zeit, 1966 2 ZAZOFF, AG. S.MI.

[2] Under Constantius II he was initially a *notarius*, then after Julian's usurpation in AD 360 he was assigned to him as *magister officiorum* (Amm. Marc. 20,9,5). In 362, Julian promoted him to *comes sacrarum largitionum* (Cod. Theod. 9,42,5; 11,39,5). Under Julian's influence he turned away from Christianity (Lib. Or. 14,36). He died as soon as in 362/3 (Amm. Marc. 23,1,5). PLRE 1, 332 (F. 3). W.P.

[3] Roman senator from the circle of Symmachus (correspondence: Epist. 5,47–54), pagan. Influential with → Eugenius [2] but did not fall out of favour: under Honorius from AD 395/6 to 397 *quaestor sacri cubiculi*, in 398 *praefectus urbi Romae*.

PLRE 2, 458f.; V. HAEHLING 398f. H.L.

[4] F. I. Pope in 268–273, Roman, mentioned in Eus. HE 7,30,23. He re-established the ecclesiastical communion with Antioch after the dispute over Paul of Samosata. Emperor Aurelian commanded that Antioch's episcopal see should belong to the contender with connections to the 'bishops of Italy and Rome'.

L. DUCHESNE (ed.), Liber pontificalis, vol. 1, 1886 (reprint 1955), CXXV; 158.

[5] **F. II.** Counterpope (355–358), favoured by emperor Constantius II as a friend of the Arians (→ Arianism) while Liberius (352–366) went into exile. However, the people rejected F. who had to leave Rome after Liberius' return (358). Considered a true pope since the 6th cent. and celebrated as a martyr due to a case of mistaken identity (29 July).

L. DUCHESNE (ed.), Liber pontificalis, vol. 1, 1886 (reprint 1955), CXXIIIff.; 211; H. JEDIN (ed.), Handb. der Kirchengesch., vol. II/1, 1973, 258f. RO.F.

[6] **Flavius Constantius F.** Imperial general in the West, AD 425–430, → Valentinianus III and → Galla [3] Placidia appointed him *magister utriusque militiae* after the suppression of the usurpation of Iohannes (ILS 1293; 1298; Chron. min. 2,21 MOMMSEN). He was able to reconquer Pannonia from the Huns in 427, fought the *comes Africae* → Bonifatius [1], became *consul* in 428, but was defeated in the power struggle with general → Aetius [2] and slain by soldiers in Ravenna (Chron. min. 1,301, 473; 2,22, 77f.; Iohannes Antiochenus fr. 201 FHG IV 614f.).

PLRE 2, 461f.; A. DEMANDT, s.v. magister militum, RE Suppl. 12, 653f. K.P.J.

[7] Learned → Manichean, known from his dispute with → Augustinus. Augustine challenged him to leave Hippo or engage in a public debate, which was held in December 404. F. declared himself defeated and abjured Manichaeism (cf. Aug. Contra Felicem, CSEL 25,2). F. is presumably the *conversus ex Manichaeis*, who reported all Manichaeans known to him (PL 42,518). RO.F.

Fel Temp Reparatio coins see → Maiorina

Fencing see → Sports

Fenestella Roman historian of the early Imperial period. The exact dates of his life are uncertain: according to Jerome he died at the age of 70 in AD 19 (Chron. p. 172 HELM), according to Pliny only 'late in the reign of Tiberius' (*novissimo Tiberii Caesaris principatu*; HN 33,146). F. wrote an annalistic history in more than 22 books (Fr. 21 PETER from book 22 [= HRR 2, 85f.] relates to 57 BC) that extended from the early Roman period to the late Republic and perhaps even included the Augustan period (Fr. 24 PETER [= HRR 2, 86]). The fragments betray an extraordinary interest in learned antiquarian questions (etymology, constitutional law, cultural history, even details of literary history). Therefore, Seneca included F. among the *philologi* (Ep. 108,31). The assumption of separate writings on the history of luxury and Cicero's life [5] are generally rejected today [1. 61; 2. 148[1]; 6. 596]. It is uncertain whether F. also composed poems (only claimed in Jer. Chron.).

F.'s work was esteemed for its *diligentia* (cf. Lactant. Div. inst. 1,6,14) and wealth of material. It was especially used by → Asconius Pedianus (beyond the quotes [4]), → Plinius the Elder and → Plutarchus (on the extent [3]). Diomedes (GL 1,365,7) knew of *epitomae* in at least 2 vols.

FRAGMENTS: HRR 2, 79–87; ACCORNERO (see below), 70–81.

BIBLIOGRAPHY: 1 P. ACCORNERO, F., in: Atti Torino 112, 1978, 43–88 2 BARDON 2, 147f. 3 G. DELVAUX, L'annaliste Fénestella et Plutarque, in: Les Ét. classiques 57, 1989, 127–146 4 B. MARSHALL, Asconius and F., in: RhM 123, 1980, 349–354 5 R. REITZENSTEIN, Ein verkanntes Werk F.s, in: FS J. Vahlen, 1900, 409–424 6 SCHANZ/HOSIUS 2[4] 595f. W.K.

Fennel (*feniculum* first in Plaut. Pseud. 814, MLat. *feniculum* or *fenuclum*, μάραθ(ρ)ον; *márath(r)on*). An umbellifer (*Umbelliferae*) introduced from the eastern Mediterranean. It differs from the closely related → dill (*anethum*) because of its size and its being perennial. As a vegetable and an astringently scented herb (cf. e.g., Plin. HN 19,186), it was particularly grown in the wine-growing areas of Germany [1. 26] (sown in February in Italy according to Pall. Agr. 3,24,9). The well-known Attic village Marathon is probably named for its fennel fields rather than a local hero of the same name (Plut. Thes. 32; Paus. 1,16). Wreaths of fennel were woven for the Dionysus cult and some mysteries (Demosth. 18,260). Its juice was used in ophthalmology. It was extracted from the stem, fresh seed or root, dried in the sun and admixed to honey (Plin. HN 20,254; other applications: 20,43; 20,256f. et passim; also Dioscurides 3,70 p. 2,81 WELLMANN = 3,74 p. 308f. BERENDES). A herbal wine prepared with fennel was also popular (Pall. Agr. 11,14,6).

→ Spices

1 G.E. THÜRY, J. WALTER, Condimenta. Gewürzpflanzen in Koch- und Backrezepten aus der röm. Ant., 1997. C.HÜ.

Fenni According to Tacitus 'an uncivilized and very poor' (*mira feritas, foeda paupertas*) but 'happy' (*beatius arbitrantur*) northern people of hunters, whose classification as Germans or Sarmatians was left uncertain (Tac. Germ. 46). They undoubtedly were identical with the *Phínnoi* (Φίννοι) in northern Scandinavia, who were considered 'neighbours' of the Goths (Ptol. 2,11,16: Hs. X; 3,5,8; cf. Jord. Get. 3,22: *mitissimi*), but not Suomi Finns, who were only named thus in the 2nd half of the 12th cent. Because of the customs described in Tac. Germ. 46, the F. have been equated with the Sami (Lapps) but this is disputed.

H.H. BARTENS, s.v. Finnische Völker, RGA 9, 70–77; A.A. LUND, Kritischer Forsch.-Ber. zur *Germania* des Tacitus, in: ANRW II 33.3, 1989–2222, esp. 2182–2188. K.DI.

Fenugreek *Trigonella foenum-graecum L.* (βούκερας, αἰγόκερας, τῆλις; *boúkeras, aigókeras, têlis*) is an annual cultivar of the Mesopotamian species *Tr. Hauss-*

knechtii (not the Mediterranean *Trigonella gladiata*), with a tangy fragrance that was used medicinally and as fodder. As seed finds of *c.* 3000 BC near Cairo show, fenugreek was cultivated in ancient Babylonia and Egypt, (Egyptian *šbt*, Arabic *ḥulba*) from where it was exported. Dioscurides 2,102 ([1. 176f.] = 2,124 [2. 206f.]) recommends the meal produced from the seed as a tonic and for cleansing as well as using an infusion against female ailments. Plin. HN 24,184–188 provides several similar recipes for *silicia*, citing for example Diocles of Carystus. Fenugreek was also much used in the Middle Ages.

1 M. Wellmann (ed.), Pedanii Dioscuridis de materia medica 1, 1908, reprint 1958 2 J. Berendes (ed.), Des Pedanios Dioskurides Arzneimittellehre übers. und mit Erl. versehen, 1902, reprint 1970. C.HÜ.

Fenus nauticum The Roman and Hellenistic maritime loan (cf. the titles *De nautico fenore* Dig. 22,2 and Cod. Iust. 4,33). The name is first encountered late in the 3rd cent. AD in a statement of Diocletian and Maximian (Cod. Iust. 4,33,4) and meant both the loan principle and the maritime interest. Classical jurists called the loan object the *mutua pecunia nautica* (Cerv. Scaevola Dig. 45,1,122,1) or *pecunia traiecticia*. It is defined by Modestinus as *pecunia quae trans mare vehit* (Dig. 22,2,1). The loan served to facilitate financing the export and import of goods by the sea. The *fenus nauticum* is equivalent to the δάνειον ναυτικόν (*dáneion nautikón*), an institution of Greek maritime law adopted by the Romans during the conquest of the Mediterranean region in the Republican period. The Greeks had the δάνειον ἑτερόπλουν (*dáneion heteróploun*) for simple sea travel to the destination and the δάνειον ἀμφοτερόπλουν (*dáneion amphoteróploun*) for the voyage to and from the destination. An insight into the situation of the 4th cent. BC is provided by the maritime loan documents recorded in the corpus of Demosthenes' speeches, e.g., in the oration 'Against Lacritus' (Dem. Or. 35). The acceptance of Greek practice during the 2nd cent. BC is attested in Plutarch's report on the maritime loan of Cato Maior (Plut. Cato maior 21,5–7). It is a matter of debate whether the Tabulae Pompeianae 13 and 34 of AD 38 and 52 refer to a *fenus nauticum*.

It is characteristic of the *fenus nauticum* that in the ordinary loan (*mutuum*) the creditor bears the maritime risk (*periculum maris*). In the event of a typical peril of the sea, such as ship-wreck, the debtor (if he has not violated the agreement) is not required to repay the loan. In this respect the maritime loan has an insurance-like function. The risk of the creditor is matched on the other hand by the *usurae maritimae*, i.e., 'maritime interest' of an unlimited rate (cf. Paul. Sent. 2,14,3). Justinian finally limited annual interest to 12 % (Cod. Iust. 4,32,26,2). A probably typical example of details in a draft contract is represented by the maritime loan of Callimachus (Dig. 45,1,122,1) (see [6]). Its appraisal by Scaevola is based on a loan stipulation document in the form of a *chirographum* with the following statements:

location at which the agreement was concluded (Berytus), destination of the voyage (Brundisium), duration of the loan (200 days), latest date of beginning the return voyage (*intra idus Septembres*), immediate repayment in case the contract is exceeded, in which case an accompanying slave is authorized to collect, and pledging the financed goods as collateral. The interest was included in the total sum to be repaid, already prepaid or included in the deadline agreement as a discount. It is uncertain if the interest agreement was binding in a maritime loan without a stipulation. This form was probably as customary as a special contract penalty promise (*poena pecuniae traiecticiae*) in case of late repayment (cf. Dig. 22,2,9; 44,7,23).

The ancient *fenus nauticum* was further developed by medieval and modern maritime laws. In the Statute of Marseilles (1253) it is called *mutuum portandum in aliquod viagium ad fortunam vel resigum ipsius mutuantis*. The *Ordonnance de la marine* of 1681 mentions the '*contrat à grosse aventure*' or '*à retour de voyage*' *among the 'contrats maritimes*' (Livre III, Titre V; also cf. Art. 311 Code de Commerce 1808: '*contrat à la grosse*'). This contract is the equivalent to the *Bodmerei* (derived from *Boden*, *Bodem* in the meaning of bottom of the ship) of Dutch, German and North European maritime laws. The object of the *Bodmerei* agreement is the ship and its load as collateral with the stipulation that the loan provider bears the risk for the objects subject to the *Bodemerei* agreement (cf. §§ 679ff. of the Handelsgesetzbuch [HGB, Commercial Law Code] of 1900, repealed in 1972). *Bodmerei* payments are mentioned in §§ 779, 803 HGB as objects of a maritime insurance agreement. Provisions such as 'no arrival, no sale' – as found in the American 'Uniform Commercial Code' of 1956 – are likewise part of the *fenum nauticum* tradition.

→ Loan; → Mutuum; → Naufragium; → Poena; → Stipulatio

1 L. Goldschmidt, Unt. zur l. 122 § 1 D. de V.O. (45,1), 1855 2 J. Rougé, Recherches sur l'organisation du commerce maritime en Méditerranée sous l'empire Romain, 1966, 345–360 3 Martino, WG, 152–158 4 G. Purpura, Testimonianze storiche ed archeologiche di traffici marittimi di libri e documenti, in: Annali del Seminario Giuridico dell' Università di Palermo 44, 1996, 369–375 5 H. Ankum, Quelques observations sur le prêt maritime dans le droit romain préclassique et classique, in: S. Adam (ed.), Symbolès, 1994, 105–113 6 C. Krampe, Der Seedarlehensstreit des Callimachus, in: Collatio iuris Romani, Études Hans Ankum, 1995, 207–222 7 P. Gröschler, Die tabellae-Urkunden aus den pompejanischen und herkulanischen Urkundenfunden, 1997 (= Freiburger Rechtsgesch. Abh., N.F., vol. 26), 160–162 8 K. Tanev, F. n., in: Orbis Iuris Romani, 1998. C.KR.

Fer(i)culum Occasionally *feretrum* (e.g., Ov. Met. 3,508; 14,747), the name for various types of devices employed for carrying goods. In particular, it refers to the racks on which objects were presented during processions (triumphs, funerals etc.), e.g., booty, prisoners, images of deities etc. (Suet. Caes. 76). The *ferculum* was also used to transport the deceased and objects to be interred or cremated (Stat. Theb. 6,126). *Ferculum* was also the name for the trencher (→ Household equipment), the flat bowl in which foods were served during meals (e.g., Petron. Sat. 39,1; 39,4 passim; Prop. 4,4,76; Apul. Met. 2,19,3; Hor. Sat. 2,6,104).

W. HILGERS, Lat. Gefäßnamen, in: BJ, 31. Suppl. 1969, 180–181; E. KÜNZL, Der röm. Triumph, 1988, 74–80; J. KÖHLER, Zur Triumphalsymbolik auf dem Feldherrnsarkophag Belvedere, in: MDAI(R) 102, 1995, 371–379. R.H.

Ferentinum Mountain top town (404 m) of the Hernici in *Latium adiectum* on the *via Latina*, 24 miles from Anagnia and 7 miles from Frosinone, modern Ferentino (Frosinone) on the Trerus (modern Sacco; It. Ant. 305; Tab. Peut. 6,2). Occupied by Volsci in 413, later returned to the Hernici (Liv. 4,51ff.); in 361 conquered by the consul Licinius Calvus (Liv. 7,9). It remained loyal to Rome during the Hernici uprising in 306 but suffered severe devastation in 211 from Hannibal. After 195 BC in possession of the *ius Latii* (Liv. 34,42,5). During the Gracchian reforms there were excesses of Roman magistrates (Gell. NA 10,3,5); *municipium*, *tribus Publilia*; *IV viri* are recorded [1. 19, 22]. In the Imperial period *Ferentinates Novi* are attested in inscriptions (CIL X 5825; 5828), which indicates the existence of a *colonia*. Episcopal see since the 4th cent.

Archaeological finds: the Roman city walls with gates and towers are preserved; acropolis with fortifications of Sulla's period (CIL X 5837–5840) on massive walls with projection and battlements (Vescovado); Republican period market; theatre; sulphur baths. The rock tomb of A. Quintilius from the time of Trajan is located before the Porta Maggiore (CIL X 5853).

1 W. KUBITSCHEK, Imperium Romanum tributim discriptum, 1889.

T. ASHBY, F., in: MDAI(R) 24, 1909, 1–58; A. BARTOLI, F., F. novum, F. maius, in: RPAA 26, 1950/1, 153–156; Id., F., in: Rendiconti Acc. Lincei 9, 1954, 470–506; G. GULLINI, I monumenti dell' Acropoli di Ferentino, in: ArchCl 6, 1954, 185–216; H. SOLIN, Regio I, F., in: Supplementa Italica 1, 1981, 23–69; R. GELSOMINO, F. nel sistema viario romano, 1986; C. BIANCHI, F. in Hernicis, 1989; A.M. RAMIERI, F. dalle origini all'alto medioevo, 1995; L. QUILICI, S. QUILICI, Opere di assetto territoriale ed urbano, 1995. G.U.

Ferentis, Ferentium Town in southern Etruria (*regio* VII), attested in the 8th/6th cents. BC on an outlier of the Poggio San Francesco (305 m), modern Ferento, 9 km north of Viterbo, on an elevation between eastern tributaries of the Tiber. In the Roman period relocated to the Northeast on the other side of the river (306 m; Pianicara). Its territory was distributed under the Gracchi [1. 216]; *municipium*, *tribus Stellatina*. The *gens Salvia* as well as Otho (Tac. Hist. 2,50; Suet. Otho 1,1) and Flavia Domitilla (Suet. Vesp. 3) came from F. The town decayed in the later Imperial period; it was an episcopal see to the 7th cent. In 1172 it was destroyed by Viterbo.

Archaeological finds include remains of earthworks, the city walls on a mountain slope have fallen, regular town layout, an Augusteum in the forum (CIL XI 7431), a theatre in the southwestern part of the town (its statues are in the Florentine museum) and large baths. An amphitheatre is located in the northeast, Etruscan necropoleis on the Poggio del Talone, Roman ones near Pianicara (funerary monument of the *gens Salvia*) and a subterranean Christian funerary system near S. Eutizio. Several Roman bridges are preserved in the territory of F. Finds and inscriptions in the Museo Civico in Viterbo.

1 F. BLUME, K. LACHMANN (ed.), Die Schriften der röm. Feldmesser, 2 vols., 1848ff.

A. GARGANA, F., guida degli scavi, 1935; Id.., Il teatro di F., 1937; R. ROSSI DANIELLI, F., 1959; C.F. GIULIANI, Bolsenae F., in: Quaderni dell' Istituto di Topografia Antica dell' Università di Roma 2, 1966, 67–70; P. GIANNINI, F., 1971; BTCGI 7, 1989, 427–443; P. PENSABENE, Il teatro romano di F., 1989; Id., Monumenti medievale a F., in: Rivista di Studi Liguri 59/60, 1993/4, 267–296. G.U.

Feretrius An epithet of → Jupiter of uncertain meaning, which already caused etymological speculation during antiquity, reflecting antiquarian and political interests. These related the name and cult of the god to each other. Derivations ranged from *ferre* (*arma*: Prop. 4,10,47; Liv. 1,10,5–6; cf. R. Gest. div. Aug. 19: *tropaiophóros*; *pacem*: Fest. 81 L.) and *feretrum* (rack on which captured weapons were carried during the triumph: Plut. Marcellus 8) to *ferire* (*ense ducem*: Prop. 4,10,46; Jupiter who 'strikes' with his lightening bolt: Plut. Marcellus 8; *ferire foedus* [*sc. fetiales*], cf. Fest. 81 L.).

The sanctuary of Jupiter F. on the Capitol was considered the oldest temple of Rome (Liv. 1,10,7); supposedly founded by Romulus, it required restoration (delapidated, without roof: Nep. Att. 20,3) by Augustus. The temple inventory included the *sceptrum*, the *lapis silex* and the *spolia opima*. The cult of Jupiter F. combined two components: 1. → *dedicatio* of the *spolia opima* ('fat booty furnishings'): the dedication of armour captured in single combat from the enemy leader was performed only by Romulus, A. Cornelius Cossus and M. Claudius Marcellus (cf. Fest. 204 L.). This rare ritual act enhanced the prestige of individuals and acquired political significance under Augustus (cf. Liv. 1,10,7; 4,20; Cass. Dio 51,24,4). 2. Of greater significance to the cultic practice was Jupiter F. as a god of oath. The → *fetiales* swore upon the *sceptrum* and concluded alliances among states with the *lapis silex*, a flint to which divine powers were ascribed probably because of its great age and durable material (Fest. 81 L.). There is no evidence of a cultic veneration of the stone in the historical period (not even in Serv. Aen. 8,641). But even in the Imperial period the most solemn formula for an oath was on many occasions: [*per*] *Iovem lapidem* ('by Jupiter the Stone'; Gell. NA 1,21,4).

S.J. HARRISON, Augustus, the poets and the spolia opima, in: CQ 39, 1989, 408–414; SIMON, GR, 108; 242 · L.A. SPRINGER, The Cult and Temple of Iuppiter F., in: CJ 50, 1954/55, 27–32. HE.K.

Feriae The Latin word for 'holiday'; grammatically plural, it is often used as if in the singular (cf. *Kalendae, Nonae, Idus, nundinae*). Its ancient form (Paul Fest. 76 L., 323 L.[1]) is *fesiae* (cf. the etymologically related *festus*). *Dies feriatus* is frequently used as a synonym. Offerings and prescribed rituals could form a regular part of certain holidays. Generally, the main characteristic of *feriae* was the cessation of all profane activities.

Corresponding to the *sacra* (Fest., 284 L.), *feriae* fell into two broad categories: *feriae privatae* and *feriae publicae*. *Feriae privatae* referred to family or personal occasions such as birth, death, or any of the rites of passage. Important *gentes*, such as the Iulii, Claudii, and Aemilii, had their own special holidays (Macrob. Sat. 1,16,7). The term *feriae* could even apply to individuals who for some reason were obliged to make a → *piaculum* or an *expiatio* (ibid.).

Feriae publicae were state rituals which were observed by the entire population or a certain group within society. *Feriae stativae* were annual rituals which were always celebrated on the same day; *feriae conceptivae* were celebrated on dates set annually by the state priests. *Feriae imperativae* referred to extraordinary holidays, which magistrates with *imperium* could order under special circumstances for the atonement of *prodigia* and catastrophes, or the celebration of victories.

Serv. Georg. 1,268 emphasizes that on these days, activities dedicated to the gods (including rituals or liturgies) took precedence over human labour. The atmosphere was supposed to be one of harmony and peace, described in Cic. Leg. 2,55 as *quieti dies* of the gods. On *feriae*, citizens were supposed to refrain from (legal) disputes (Cic. Div. 1,102; cf. Isid. Nat. 1,4). Acts of physical violence committed on *feriae* required particular atonements (Macrob. Sat. 1,15,21). In theory at least, a *feriatus dies* was supposed to be a day of rest for slaves and masters alike. Cicero (Leg. 2,19) recommends that a master celebrate a *feriatus dies* with those of his slaves who deserve to rest (2,29), as soon as all reasonably appropriate jobs were completed (see also Tib. 2,1,5 and 23f.; Ov. Fast. 1,665–670). At the → *saturnalia, feriae servorum* (CIL 1^2,269), slaves enjoyed the privilege of fools. According to Cato's expositions (Agr. 138) even working animals were granted a certain reprieve from their toils, unless those absolutely essential: human survival – thus a possible interpretation of these rules – depends on the successful execution of an appropriate task at the appropriate time. Labour, particularly agricultural labour, is symptomatic of human mortality, and thus always inappropriate during *feriae*, when the presence of immortals was called upon (see Tib. 2,1,1–10; Catull. 64,384–388, cf. vv. 38–42; [4. 58–68]).

Alongside movable *feriae* and those ordered in reaction to current events [6. 204f.], there were at least *feriae publicae* at set dates (cf. Columella 2,12,9), amongst them all of the Ides, the Kalends of March, June, and October as well as the *Nonae Caprotinae*. Because of their high number, the Romans tried to reconcile *religio* with practical necessities, esp. within the field of agriculture. Learned discussions and interpretations were devoted to the question, what kind of work might be permitted or forbidden during *feriae publicae*. As a general rule, undertakings on a larger scale were forbidden, esp. if they required any breaking of the soil (thus touching the chthonic sphere) or any involvement with the dead (and thus the Underworld). Permitted were labours on a lesser scale, whose qualities were aimed at healing or furthering growth (such as spreading manure or certain methods of cultivation), and which increased the enjoyment of the day or formed part of the ritual. Amongst the permitted labours were those which had to do with sun or with light (such as laying out apples, pears, and figs for drying: Columella 2,21,3). There were special regulations for traders and craftsmen who continued to work through many of the holidays. However, it was seen as important that the sight of these men hard at work did not disturb the festivities. Fest. 292 L. provides a description of the *praeciamitatores*, who walked ahead of the *flamines* (and probably also other priests, cf. the *calatores* in Serv. Georg. 1,268) through the city, and called on everyone to cease working, before the priests themselves went past.

In the Imperial age, the casuistic interpretation of religious laws gave a wider scope (cf. Verg. G. 1,268–275 with Varro in Serv. Auct. Georg. 1,270 and Columella 2,21,2). The past tense used by Macrobius in his lecture (Sat. 1,16,9–11) indicates that at the beginning of the 5th cent. AD these rules were obsolete. Farmers' almanacs as well as the → *feriale Duranum* of the 3rd cent. AD provide evidence of the wide range and variety within local and institutional regulations; in contrast with the Republican era, legal procedures could continue on *feriae*, provided that both parties to the conflict were in agreement (Ulpian Dig. 2,12,6; [6. 210f.] for the subsequent period). Early attempts to reduce the ever-increasing number of *feriae* were undertaken by Claudius (Cass. Dio 60,17,1) and Vespasian (Tac. Hist. 4,40), a trend which was to continue throughout the Imperial period.

1 G. WISSOWA, Religion und Kultus der Römer, ^{2}1912, 432–449 2 Id., s.v. F., RE 6, 2212–2213 3 C. JULLIAN, s.v. F., DS 2, 1042–1066 4 P. BRAUN, Les Tabous des F., in: Année sociologique 3, 1959, 49–125 5 K. NICOLAI, 'Feiertage und Werktage im röm. Leben ...', in: Saeculum 14, 1963, 194–220 6 F.M. DE ROBERTIS, Lavoro e lavoratori nel mondo romano, 1963, repr. 1979, 200–211 7 A.K. MICHELS, The Calendar of the Roman Republic, 1967, 61–83 8 D.P. HARMON, The Family (Public) Festivals of Rome, in: ANRW II 16.2, 1592–1603 (1440–1468). D.P.H.

Feriae Latinae was the annual celebration of the league of Latin towns on the Albanus mons, in honour of → Jupiter Latiaris. The organization of the festival lay with Rome; all information regarding the foundation of the celebration, its changes and development refers to its mythical ancient history (Dion. Hal. Ant. Rom. 4,49; 6,95; Plut. Camillus 42,5 p. 151; Str. 5,3,2 p. 229). These → *feriae conceptivae* (Varro, Ling. 6,25) were of great political importance: Roman consuls had to set the date for this festival immediately after their accession to office, and only after its completion were they allowed to take the field (Liv. 21,63,5; 8; 22,1,6; 44,19,4; Cass. Dio 46,33,4). Rome, in line with the other Latin cities, was represented by all of its officials, a young man of noble descent was appointed *praefectus urbi feriarum Latinarum causa* (CIL VI 1421; Cass. Dio 49,42,1; 53,33,3). Hostilities were suspended for the duration of the celebration (Dion. Hal. Ant. Rom. 4,49,2; Macrob. Sat. 1,16,16f.). Remains of → *fasti* dating from the Imperial age have been found on the Albanus mons (InscrIt XIII,1,143ff.).

The celebration took the form of a → *lustratio* (Cic. Div. 1,17–18), i.e. a ritual involving a procession, a common practice in events with the aim of furthering social integration. At the *feriae Latinae*, milk was given as an initial offering (Cic. loc. cit.); The sacrificial animal was originally a white bull (Arnob. 2,68), later also a reddish one. The distribution of its meat was of great symbolic significance: Rome provided the animal for the cultic sacrifice, and the representatives of all of the Latin communities had to plead for their share (*carnem petere*: Varro, Ling. 6,25; Cic. pro Planc. 23) – a clear symbol of Rome's claim to hegemony (Dion. Hal. Ant. Rom. 4,49,3). The return gifts of the Latini were less prestigious: lambs, cheese, milk, and such like (Dion. Hal. ibid.). Their subordinate status was further emphasized by the fact that their representatives offered a prayer for Rome, *populo Romano Quiritium* (Liv. 41,16,1). The correct execution of the ritual was meticulously observed; any disruptions necessitated a repeat (*instauratio*), as was the case when the Lanuvium magistrate forgot to pray for the people of Rome (ibid.), when the representatives from Ardea (Liv. 32,1,9) or respectively Laurentum (Liv. 37,3,4) protested because they had not received an adequate share of the sacrificial meat, or when a sudden change in the weather interrupted the *feriae Latinae* (Liv. 40,45,2). The successful completion of the solemnities was signalled by the sacrificial fire, which shone from the mountain top far into the night (Luc. 1,550; 5,402).

More difficult to grasp are references to the festive custom of *oscillatio* (Fest. 212 L.; Schol. Bobiensia in Cic. Planc. 23), as well as to other – possibly concurrent – events in the participating towns, such as the chariot race on the Capitol, in which the winner received a draught of absynthium (Plin. HN 27,45). Alleged human sacrifices at the *feriae Latinae* are part of Christian propaganda from the 2nd cent. AD (Tatianus 29; Tert. Apol. 9; Min. Fel. 30,4; Prudent. Contra Symmachum 1, 396).
→ Alba Longa; → Latin League; → Sacrifice

LATTE, 144ff.; B. LIOU-GILLE, Naissance de la langue latine. Mythe et culte de fondation, in: RBPh 74, 1996, 73–97; D. SABBATUCCI, La religione di Roma antica, 1988, 305ff.; CH. WERNER, De feriis Latinis, 1888. D.B.

Feriale

A. TERM B. SOCIAL STRUCTURES C. EXAMPLES

A. TERM

Feriale is the term used in the title of a Campanian inscription of AD 387, containing a list of seven annually celebrated rituals (InscrIt 13,2,283). From this text, known as the *feriale Campanum*, historians now apply this term to similar compilations within the Latin sphere: In contrast with actual calendars (→ *fasti*), *ferialia* do not list all of the days within a year, but only those associated with certain specific rituals. It makes sense to extend the academic application of the term *feriale* to include comparable written compilations in other cultures [13. 525], thus replacing the term 'sacrificial calendar', as the latter provides no indication whether feast days are marked as special within a (complete) calendar, or whether only pertinent days are contained within a list. Since *ferialia* served a specific purpose and were targeted (only) at a certain specified group, there was a general requirement for the list of dates to be preceded by some explanatory introductory lines. Form-critically, it thus makes sense also to apply the term *feriale* to texts embedded within other genres (altar laws, testaments, ritual texts).

B. SOCIAL STRUCTURES

In contrast with the more descriptive genre of the *fasti*, *ferialia* are more normative in character. A *feriale* sets out the calendrically prescribed religious obligations for a certain group or sometimes for a certain community or location. It could be targeted at the relatives of a deceased who were bound by his testament (as set out in a grave inscription) to a regular cult of the dead; it could also be directed at the members of an association, whose statutory celebrations and commemorations formed part of a *lex collegii* (e.g. CIL 14,2112) or were displayed as graffito on the walls of the clubhouse (→ *schola*) (text: [4. 625–630]; see also [13. 530f.]; it is possible that the *feriale Cumanum*, InscrIt 13,2,279, was used by a *collegium* of *seviri Augustales*; cf. [1]). Religious obligations of Roman military units could have been set out in a service instruction, as palpable in the → *feriale Duranum*. No *ferialia* of larger priestly colleges are extant; the *acta* of the → *Arvales fratres* are excerpts from the minutes of meetings and do not contain any prescriptive texts.

There is no known written *feriale* pertaining to a larger community or settlement. In view of the great number and variability of cultic obligations within a single polis – the consequence of a polytheistic system –, which would have had to be canonized in such a document, oral communication, in form of monthly (Varro, Ling. 6,28) or annual announcements, was a far more suitable medium. It is quite possible that in more complex local societies weekly (→ Week) or rather monthly patterns (for Athens see [8. 13–24]) were of greater importance, whereas voluntary associations within a polis (such as clubs) had a particular need to develop patterns of activity which were compatible with the rhythm of the community as a whole. Communities, even under the rule of the Roman *imperium*, enjoyed considerable freedom in defining their own *ferialia*. The late Republican *lex Ursonensis* (CIL 1^2,594 = ILS 6087) even granted to *coloniae civium Romanorum* complete freedom regarding the setting of festival dates (ch. 64); without specifying any dates, the legal framework from Rome merely stipulated three *ludi* for the *trias capitolina* (Jupiter, Juno, and Minerva) plus one holiday dedicated to Venus with her close foundation links to Caesar (ch. 70f.). In the Imperial age, feast days (*dies natalis, dies imperii*), particularly those of the ruling dynasty, became increasingly obligatory in character; they did not only provide an important framework for the way that towns and cities structured their own calendars [13. 515ff., 544f.], but also for private religious activities [7].

C. Examples

1. Etruscan: The *tabula Capuana* dates from the early 5th cent. BC. The extant fragment (probably pertaining to spring and summer) contains calendrically ordered detailed instructions on how to carry out various rituals (mainly sacrifices) for a number of different deities. In each case, it names the priests and/or groups in charge; geographically, their activities extend beyond Capua (most recently in [14]). Dating from the Late Republican period, a comparable, but even more extensive ritual text in the form of a *feriale* is found in the → *liber linteus* of the mummy bindings of Agram [12; 9; 6. 103–110].

2. Greek: Of particular importance – alongside regulations contained within extensive sacral laws – are the independent *ferialia* of the Attic demes [3] with their at times very precise descriptions of cultic obligations. Their particular focus is on the regulation of the financial burdens associated with a cult [2; 10. 185–208]; in the *feriale* from Erchia (SEG 21,541), the list of festivals is even ordered in columns according to which of five private institutions was to be responsible for the cost.

3. Roman: It seems that initially, in competition with the complete calendars of the *fasti, ferialia* did not develop as an independent and stable epigraphical form. However, also worth noting, apart from the already mentioned important inscriptions of the (late Augustan) *feriale Cumanum*, and the *feriale Campanum* as well as the → *feriale Duranum*, are the *fasti Guidizzolenses*, a fragmentary extant inscription, found near Brixia: it combines a number-based calendric scheme (designed as a perpetual calendar) with a *feriale*, listing seven feast days for the 2nd half of the year; most likely, it dates from the 2nd or 3rd cent. AD and is the only known example of a combination of a *feriale* with a calendar (in written form only evident in Roman culture) [13. 160–164]. The → Chronographer of AD 354 already contains Christian *ferialia* in the form of lists of *dies depositionis* or respectively *natales*, i.e. the dates of the deaths/ burials of martyrs and thus their new birthdays. From a design point of view, combining these dates (fixed in the Julian calendar – solar year) with the Easter celebrations (determined by the lunar cycle) proved problematic, leading to the medieval *computus* documents (long-term graphic diagrams for the calculation of the Christian calendar [11]).

→ Calendar

Bibliography: 1 T. Mommsen, Das Augusteische Festverzeichnis von Cumae, in: GS 4, 1906, 259–270 2 M. Jameson, Notes on the Sacrificial Calendar from Erchia, in: BCH 89, 1965, 154–172 3 St. Dow, Six Athenian Sacrificial Calendars, in: BCH 92, 1968, 170–186 4 P. Castrén, Graffiti di Bolsena, in: MEFRA 84, 1972, 623–638 5 F. Graf, Zum Opferkalender des Nikomachos, in: ZPE 14, 1974, 139–144 6 A. J. Pfiffig, Religio Etrusca, 1975 7 P. Herz, Unt. zum Festkalender der röm. Kaiserzeit nach datierten Weih- und Ehreninschr., 2 vols., thesis Mainz 1975 8 D. Mikalson, The Sacred and Civil Calendar of the Athenian Year, 1975 9 F. Roncalli, Carbasinis voluminibus implicati libri, in: JDAI 95, 1980, 227–264 10 D. Whitehead, The Demes of Attica 508/7–ca. 250 B.C., 1986 11 A. Borst, Computus, 1990 12 I. Edlund-Berry, Etruscans at Work and Play, in: Kotinos. FS E. Simon, 1992, 330–338 13 J. Rüpke, Kalender und Öffentlichkeit, 1995 14 M. Cristofani, Tabula Capuana, 1995.

Editions: InscrIt 13,2,279ff. only offers (apparently) independent Lat. *ferialia*; LSCG 1f.; 7; 17f.; 20; 62; 96; 128; 151; 165; 169 (Greek).

J.R.

Feriale Duranum The *feriale Duranum* is a papyrus found during excavations in 1931/32 in the garrison town of Dura-Europus (prov. Mesopotamia) with a calendar of feast days dating from the rule of Severus Alexander, which was originally intended for official use by the *cohors XX Palmyrenorum* (2/3 extant, from beginning of January to the end of September). Alongside date and reason for a particular festival, it also contained information on what kind of sacrificial animal was to be used. It has been possible to identify with a sufficient degree of certainty about three quarter of the festivals listed: 1. Apart from topical feast days of the ruling emperor Severus Alexander *(dies imperii, dies Caesaris)* and those of his closest family, there are also dynastically relevant celebrations such as the *dies natales* and *dies imperii* of his deified predecessors and their wives (esp. Severi, and Antonines). The continued celebration of the birthday of the (not deified) Germanicus on 24 May remains an enigma. – 2. A cluster of festivals with particular relevance to the military (*rosaliae signorum*, day of discharge). – 3. A number of feast days traditionally celebrated in the city of Rome (Mars Pater, Quinquatria, *dies natalis urbis Romae, circenses Martiales*, Vestalia, Neptunalia, *circenses Salutares*), in addition to the New Year's celebrations on 1 January and the *nuncupatio votorum* on 3 January. It has to be assumed that the lost part of the *feriale Duranum* also contained Saturnalia, Augustalia, and the Armilustrium, alongside a number of *dies natales*. The *feriale* is evidence of the official army religion, which does not take into account the actual ethnic or religious composition of the troops (absence of all Oriental cults) and claims validity across the entire empire. In its basic outline, it is likely to date back to the Julio-Claudian period, but like all official festival calendars, it underwent a process of constant actualization.

EDITION: R.O. FINK, Roman military records on papyrus, 1971, no. 117 (older literature).
BIBLIOGRAPHY: C. HOPKINS, The discovery of Dura-Europos, 1979; R.O. FINK, A.S. HOEY, W.F. SNYDER, The F.D., in: YClS 7, 1940, 1–221 (first publication); W.F. SNYDER, Public anniversaries in the Roman empire, in: ibid., 223–317; A.D. NOCK, The Roman army and the Roman religious year, in: Harvard Theological Review 45, 1952, 187–252; J.F. GILLIAM, The Roman military feriale, in: Harvard Theological Review 47, 1954, 183–196; P. HERZ, Unt. zum Festkalender der röm. Kaiserzeit nach datierten Weih- und Ehreninschriften, 2 vols., 1975; Id., Kaiserfeste der Prinzipatszeit, in: ANRW II 16.2, 1978, 1135–1200; TH. PEKÁRY, Das Opfer vor dem Kaiserbild, in: BJ 186, 1986, 91–103; D. FISHWICK, Dated inscriptions and the F.D., in: Syria 65, 1988, 349–361 = The imperial cult in the Latin West II,1, 1991, 593–608; O. STOLL, Die Fahnenwache in der röm. Armee, in: ZPE 108, 1995, 107–118; Id., Excubatio ad signa, 1995. P.H.

Fern Pliny names three species of fern – *felix, dryopteris,* and *polypodium* –, all of which are characterized by the absence of flowers and seeds. Plin. HN 27,78–80 describes two varieties of *felix*, one of which the Greeks on account of its pinnae referred to as πτέρις (*ptéris*) or respectively βλάχνον (*bláchnon*) and male (perhaps *Aspidium filix mas L.*, the Male or Shield Fern, cf. Dioscorides 4,184 p. 2,332f. WELLMANN = 4,183 p. 471f. BERENDES), the other as female fern θηλυπτερίς (*thēlypterís*) or respectively νυμφαία πτέρις (*nymphaía ptéris*; Dioscorides 4,185 p. 2,333 WELLMANN = 4,184 p. 472 BERENDES).

The roots of both were thought to be good pig fodder. Only three-year old plants should be dug up and then used i.a. as a laxative or vermifuge. Women were not advised to take either variety, because both were thought to cause miscarriages or infertility. The *dryopteris* in Plin. HN 27,72 (= Dioscorides 4,187 p. 2,335 WELLMANN = 4,186 p. 473 BERENDES) is probably identifiable as Oak Fern (*Polypodium dryopteris L.*). Because of its caustic effect (*vis caustica*), Pliny recommends it for hair removal. Plin. HN 26,58 (= Dioscorides 4,186 p. 2,334 WELLMANN = 4,185 p. 472f. BERENDES) describes *polypodium* or *filicula* as a species of fern which grows on rocks or underneath old trees, probably *Polypodium vulgare L.* The juice of its roots, used as a food supplement, should remedy constipation and purge both bile and phlegm. Occasionally, fern was also used to fertilize fields (Plin. HN 17,54). Palladius sees fern as nothing but a common weed which ought to be eradicated (Agric. 6,3,3, and 8,1,1). C.HÜ.

Feronia Name of a goddess with several cult-places in central Italy, which were all located outside of municipal centres, as well as a sacred spring in Aquileia. The etymology of her name is as uncertain as the origins of the cult. In line with Varro, Ling. 5,74, modern scholars assume that F. was a Sabine deity. In contrast with earlier assumptions, Etruria is now generally rejected as the cult's place of origin [1. 309; 2. 407]. The archaeological findings in particular support the notion of its Sabine roots, because all of her sanctuaries are located within Sabine territory or territories under Sabine influence (Amiternum, Capena, Pisaurum, Tarracina, Trebula Mutuesca).

The most important cult-places were in Capena/Mons Soracte and Tarracina: Excavations during the 1950s in → Capena (in the sanctuary of → *lucus Feroniae*) produced numerous terracotta votive offerings, in the shape of various limbs and body parts, as well as figurines of farm animals. Whereas body parts point to F. as a healing deity, the animal figures were seen as a confirmation of the 'agrarian character' of this goddess, to whom, according to Liv. 26,11,9, the inhabitants of Capena sacrificed the first fruits of each harvest (for more information on the annual fair, which took place on the occasion of this sacrifice and which was attended by both Sabini and Latini, cf. Dion. Hal. Ant. Rom. 3,32,1; for the religious → ecstasy of those involved in the cult, who walked barefoot across hot coals, cf. Str. 5,226 and Varro in Serv. Aen. 9,787). The cult continued beyond the foundation of the Sullan colony of Lucus Feroniae; in the Imperial period, a building dedicated to the ruler cult was integrated into the sanctuary [3. 168].

In the sanctuary of → Tarracina, manumission of slaves took place: candidates, their head shorn, had to sit on a stone seat, from which they rose after the ceremony, wearing a → *pilleus* (= hat and also the sign of a freedman) – according to Serv. Aen. 8,564, the seat bore the inscription *Bene meriti servi sedeant, surgant liberi.*

Age and form of the F. cult in Rome itself are uncertain. The only known aspects are the day of foundation of the sanctuary on the Campus Martius (13 November, CIL I² p. 335, cf. also [4. 197]) and a never clearly defined connection with freedmen (Liv. 22,1,18 mentions a donation by freedwomen for a votive offering to F. as part of a → *prodigium* ordered by the Senate in 217 BC).

1 PFIFFIG 2 G. DUMÉZIL, La rel. romaine archaïque, 1966 3 SCHEID, Collège 4 SCULLARD.

P. LONGO, F. Un culto sabino nel territorio volsco, in: La valle Pontina nell'antichità: Atti del convegno, 1990, 59–62; RADKE, 124ff.; A.M. SGABINI MORETTI, Statue e ritratti onorari da Lucus Feroniae, in: Rendiconti della Pontificia Accademia 55–56, 1982–84, 71–109. C.F.

Ferrandus Deacon in Carthage, d. AD 546/547, pupil and friend of bishop → Fulgentius of Ruspe, whose *vita* he wrote soon after the latter's death in 532 (though his authorship is not universally recognized). F. compiled the first anthology (*Breviatio canonum*) of North African canon law (a summary of synodal decisions in 232 canons). Also extant are 14 of his letters, mainly dealing with theological questions (Monophysitism, Three-Chapter Controversy).

PL 65,117–150; 67,949–963; 88,817–830; LThK², 4,87; H. Jedin (ed.), Hdb. der Kirchengesch., vol. II/2, 1975, 188. RO.F.

Ferreolus Gallic aristocrat, grandson of the consul of 381 AD Afranius Syagrius, related by marriage through his wife Papianilla to → Sidonius Apollinaris (Sid. Apoll. Epist. 1,7,4; 7,12,1f.; Carm. 24,35–38). As *praefectus praetorio Galliarum*, he supported → Aetius [2] in 451 in the repulse of the Huns, protected Arelate from the Goths in 452/3, and granted tax concessions in Gaul (Sid. Apoll. Epist. 7,12,3). In 469, he came to Rome as an envoy of his homeland to raise charges against Arvandus, his successor in office (Sid. Apoll. Epist. 1,7,4; 9).

PLRE 2, 465f.; J. Harries, Sidonius Apollinaris and the Fall of Rome, 1994. K.P.J.

Ferret A domesticated form of the polecat (*Mustela putorius furo*), specially bred to hunt for rabbits in their underground burrows, a member of the genus *Mustela* of the weasel family (*Mustelidae*). Plin. HN 8,218 mentions the existence of ferrets (under the name of *viverra*) on the Balearic Islands. Isid. Orig. 12,2,39 is the first to transmit the description *furo*, derived from *furvus* ('dark'). The earliest detailed description is provided by Thomas of Cantimpré 4,42 ([1. 135f.] *c.* AD 1240). He notes the similarity of the *furunculus* (popularly known as *furetus*) with the polecat (*putorius*), the colour of its fur ranging from white to yellowy (*buxeus*), its size, which was larger than that of a weasel, and its ferocious hunting instinct and bloodlust at the young age of only 80 days. His observations on the fertility of ferrets (30-day gestation, broods of 7–8 young, who are blind for the first 40 days after birth) also stem from a reliable source. The organotherapeutic preparations which follow the quotation from Thomas in Albertus Magnus 22,101 [2. 1403] originate at least partially from the 12th/13th-cents. Latin version of Ps.-Rhazes, ch. 20 [3. 577].
→ Marten

1 H. Boese (ed.), Thomas Cantimpratensis, Liber de natura rerum, 1973 2 H. Stadler (ed.), Albertus Magnus, de animalibus, 1920 3 Rasis, De facultatibus partium animalium, in: Abubetri Rhasae ... opera exquisitiora, Basileae 1544. C.HÜ.

Fertile crescent see → Mesopotamia

Fertilizer Fertilizer was used in ancient agriculture in order to preserve or improve the fertility of the soil used for cultivation; the choice of fertilization method in each case depended crucially on the social environment, economic conditions, climate, and local traditions. Even though intensive soil cultivation was seen as more important than fertilization (Cato Agr. 61,1: *Quid est agrum bene colere? Bene arare. Quid secundum? Arare. Tertio? Stercorare*), agrarian writers wrote about this problem at great length. It was one of the fundamental problems for ancient agriculture that an insufficient supply of forage crops made it impossible to keep stabled cattle on a larger scale. Since cattle herds were left to graze woodland pastures during the summer, most of the valuable manure was lost to fertilization. Because of this situation, it was necessary to keep fields fallow every other year (Pind. Nem. 6,10–12; Verg. G. 1,71f.; Columella 2,10,7; Plin. HN 18,187; 18,191).

The use of animal manure as fertilizer is already evident in Homer (Hom. Od. 17,296–300); Xenophon emphasizes the importance of fertilization, and Theophrastus provides a synopsis of the manure of various animals (Xen. Oec. 20,10; Theophr. Hist. pl. 2,7,4). Cato, Varro, and Virgil all advise on fertilization and the preparation of a midden (*stercilinum*: Cato Agr. 5,8; Varro, Rust. 1,13,4, Columella 1,6,2; on fertilization, cf. also Cato Agr. 29; 36; 37,2; Varro, Rust. 1,7,8; 1,19,3; 1,23,3; 1,38; Verg. G. 1,71–93, Plin. HN 17,42–57). Based on his observation of decreasing fertility of the soil – explained by his contemporaries partly as a result of exhaustion, partly as that of the aging process of the earth as a whole – Columella stipulates the requirement of frequent, timely, and moderate fertilization in order to increase yields (Colum. 2,1,7: *licet enim maiorem fructum percipere si frequenti et tempestiva et modica stercoratione terra refoveatur*). According to Columella, three groups of fertilizers were of particular importance for agriculture: bird manure, human excrement, and cattle dung (Columella 2,14,1: *quod ex avibus, quod ex hominibus, quod ex pecudibus*; cf. Columella 8,9,4; Varro, Rust. 1,38); pigeon manure was valued particularly highly. It was considered necessary to store animal manure for a year prior to using it. Different types of fertilizer were used for the fertilization of fields, olive groves, and vineyards. The main justification for keeping cattle on large estates was the fact that they would also produce copious amounts of manure (Columella 6, praef. 2; 8,1,2; cf. Varro, Rust. 1,2,21; 2, praef. 5). If no animal dung was available, plant material could also be used to set up a *stercus*, i.e. a compost heap (Cato Agr. 37,2; Columella 2,14,6).

A particular fertilization process was the sowing of lupins which were then ploughed under immediately after cutting, thus enriching the soil with the nitrogen fixed in their roots (Columella 2,13; 11,2,44; cf. Cato Agr. 37,2; Varro, Rust. 1,23,3; Plin. HN 17,54; 18,133–136). In Gallia Cisalpina, ash was used as a fertilizer; for its production, stubble fields or the dung of the draught animals were burned (Plin. HN 17,49; cf. Verg.

G. 1,84f.; for Greece: Xen. Oec. 18,2). The use of marl as a fertilizer was already known to Varro, but only described in detail by Pliny: it was mainly used in Gaul and Britain, and seems to have been restricted to certain regions; marl is a crumbly combination of limestone and clay, which was sometimes mined (Varro, Rust. 1,7,8; Plin. HN 17,42–48). Even though crop rotation as a means of preserving the fertility of the soil was known (Verg. G. 1,73–76; Plin. HN 18, 191), it was not generally attributed with any great importance.
→ Agrarian writers; → Grain

1 M.-C. Amouretti, Le pain et l'huile dans la Grèce antique, 1986, 62–63 2 A. Burford, Land and Labor in the Greek World, 1993, 122–124 3 F. Olck, s.v. Düngung, RE 5, 1756–1776 4 M.S. Spurr, Arable Cultivation in Roman Italy c.200 B.C.-c. A.D. 100, 1986, 126–132 5 K.D. White, Roman Farming, 1970, 110–145.

E.C.

Fer(c)tum see → Strues

Fescennini versus Improvized songs, sung at weddings, which fall into the category of quite commonly found apotropaic obscenity. The custom even continued in Christian times. The reason for the (unproven) etymological derivation of the name from *Fescennia* or *-ium*, a Faliscan town in southern Etruria, is unclear. An alternative derivation from *fascinum* (Paul Fest. 76; cf. 76, where he offers the form *Fescemnoe*) is linguistically impossible. Literary versions are found in → Catullus 61,119ff. (alluding to the bridegroom's previous homosexual relations), and also → Claudianus [2], *De nuptiis Honorii Augusti* (the only sexual reference here alludes to the wedding night). → Annianus, too, wrote a number of *Fescennini versus* (Courtney 387; 390). Hor. Epist. 2,1,145 uses *Fescennina licentia* in an non-technical sense to describe the trading (cf. Liv. 7,2,7) of insults in a boisterous atmosphere. As a general insult, but probably with sexual content, Octavian wrote *Fescennini versus* against Pollio (Macrob. Sat. 2,4,21).

G. Wissowa, s.v. F.v., RE 6, 2222f. ED.C.

Festival dress It is safe to assume that the dress worn at private and public festivals differed in colour or adornment from everyday wear; women in → Sybaris, for example, who were to partake in one of the municipal festivities, received a year's notice in order to prepare their attire accordingly (Ath. 12,521c; Plut. Mor. 147e). A public appearance called for a clean attire (cf. Pl. Symp. 174a). On some festive occasions, a cloak was worn, referred to as ξυστίς (*xystís*) (Aristoph. Lys. 1190, Nub. 70; Theoc. 2,74; Plut. Alcibiades 32,2). The 'Phoenician' red chitons, worn by the Athenian metics for the Panathenaean procession (→ Panathenaea), were also seen as a kind of festival dress (e.g. Phot. s.v. σκάφας; *skáphas*). Brides sometime wore purple at their weddings, but generally, there is more evidence of both bride and groom being dressed in white (Eur. Alc. 923). Similar rules were applied in Rome, e.g. regarding the assumption of the *toga virilis* as well as other festivals (Ov. Fast. 4,619; 5,355), cultic acts (Ath. 4,149e), sacrifices, or the *pompa* (see → Procession) of a certain god, but also *pompa circensis*, when laurel wreaths were frequently also worn (Cass. Dio 62,4,1f.). According to Mart. 14,1, it was a notable exception that a *synthesis* (actually a house or dinner dress) was worn in public at the Saturnalia. Also worth noting are the saffron-coloured robes worn by the girls about to be ordained into the service of → Artemis Brauronia, as well as the purple dress of the → *Hellanodikai* of the Olympic Games and also the black robe worn by the judges at the Nemean Games. For the occasion of the → *adventus Augusti*, sources confirm that white dress was worn, including at times by officers (Tac. Hist. 2,89,2, cf. Plut. Pompeius 40,2f.), and in this context it is also worth mentioning the special robes of the triumphator (→ Triumph). The compulsory wearing of the → *toga* in the theatre, the circus, or when appearing in front of the emperor, can also be seen as one aspect of festival dress (e.g. Mart. 2,29; 5,19; Juv. 11,204; SHA Comm. 16; SHA Sev. 1; SHA Hadr. 22,2; cf. Juv. 1,96; Mart. 5,22 and *passim* regarding the appearance of clients). However, it is a peculiarity rather than a case of festival dress when on the occasion of the arrival of M. → Antonius [I 9] citizens dressed up as maenads, satyrs, and Pans (Plut. Antonius 24,3).
→ Ceremonial Dress; → Clothing; → Mourning dress

E. Künzl, Der röm. Triumph, 1988, 85–90; Mommsen, Staatsrecht III, 215–221; O. Nussbaum, s.v. Geleit, RAC 9, 908–1049; A. Pekridou-Gorecki, Mode im ant. Griechenland: Textile Fertigung und Kleidung, 1989, 121–123; H. Rühfel, Kinderleben im klass. Athen, 1984, 115.

R.H.

Festivals; Feasts

I. The Ancient Orient II. Egypt III. Greece 1. Public nature and communication 2. 'Festival culture' 3. Criticism and continuity in Early Christianity 4. Categories based on cultural studies 5. Types of Greek festivals 6. Elements of complex rituals 7. Feast and religion 8. Feasts as loci of the identity of social groups 9. Regulations: verbal instructions and written fixation 10. Feast and poetry 11. Agons 12. Feast and market; economic aspects

I. The Ancient Orient

The ancient Mesopotamian calendar was based on the phases of the lunar cycle and was observed in the cult on a monthly basis (1st, 7th, 15th day). Annual feasts were frequently associated with the agrarian cycle (sowing, harvest), whereby regional differences must be drawn into consideration (e.g., irrigation vs. rainfed agriculture). Non-cyclical feasts were generally related to the ruler (crowning, temple and palace construction, war, death). In the family sphere, major stages in the life cycle (marriage, death) were celebrated, while annual family festivals honoured the ancestors.

The key actor in a feast was the king: in the cult he represented his country before the deity and the blessing for the land was granted to him. Priests and cult personnel supported the king in a more or less active role. The people probably only experienced feasts of the official cult as processions. The hierarchical social order with its divine legitimization constituted an essential element of ancient Oriental feasts. Festivals provided the framework for royal representation; high officials and foreign delegates were hosted as guests to the feast and given gifts to honour and confirm their loyalty and to demonstrate the mutual relationship. As is attested especially for one-time events (e.g., temple and palace dedications), festivals provided relief for the population, e.g., through a break from work and especially food distribution.

Apart from feasts at state sanctuaries under direct patronage of the king, there were local ones at which the provincial governor or some equivalent was the head celebrant. These local festivals were occasionally integrated into the state calendar (e.g., through the presence of the king). In Babylonia deities travelled to cult centres in the context of a feast. Social groups defined by feasts are rarely encountered but there were, e.g., feasts for women. Family feasts were held especially in the context of the ancestor cult. A legal connection could be strengthened by a banquet after concluding a sale or agreement.

The ruler provided the facilities required for the feast (festival houses) and cult objects (e.g., a boat, cult vessels). The king or local ruler was responsible for the festival costs, the temple contributed from its assets but levies could also be raised.

The festival rites included: recital of hymns, prayers or laments with the respective gestures, music and dance; libations, bloody and bloodless sacrifices, with very little being known about the further distribution of food (banquet); processions, especially by boat in Babylonia; robing and bathing the statue of the deity.

Ritual texts have been preserved in quantity since the 2nd millennium. A part of cuneiform literature (myths, hymns, prayer) belongs to the world of the festivals although attribution is often impossible. The recitation of Sumerian lamentations in the 2nd and 1st millennia, when Sumerian had died out as a spoken language, deserves notice; in a comparable manner hymns in languages other than Hittite were presented during Hittite festive prayers (especially in Hattian, Luwian, Palaic).

The main sources are expense axxounts for the cult, as well as, for the 2nd–1st millenia, ritual texts; there are also references in literary texts, royal inscriptions and letters.

→ Akītu festival; → Hieros gamos; → New Year's celebration

M. E. Cohen, The Canonical Lamentations of Ancient Mesopotamia, 1988; Id., The Cultic Calendars of the Ancient Near East, 1993; V. Haas, Gesch. der hethit. Rel., 1994; B. Pongratz-Leisten, Ina šulmi īrub (BaF 16), 1994; J. Renger, Isinnam epēšum. Überlegungen zur Funktion des F. in der Gesellschaft, in: A. Finet (ed.), Actes de la XVIIe Rencontre Assyriologique Internationale, 1970,; W. Sallaberger, Der kultische Kalender der Ur III-Zeit, 1993.

WA.SA.

II. Egypt

In chronological terms, Egyptian festivals of a sacred character may be divided into two groups: cyclical monthly feasts and annual feasts. Monthly feasts were scheduled according to the phases of the moon and celebrated in the seclusion of the temple while annual feasts were scheduled according to the solar year and usually were procession festivals. Monthly festivals were one-day events, annual festivals lasted several days. Festivals of superregional significance must be separated from those of regional or local importance, which could, however, develop into imperial festivals. Hdt. 2,59–63 reported on some Egyptian local festivals at the centre of which stood the local deity. Some festivals combined two or three of four fundamental aspects of meaning: the cycle of nature, divine/mythical, royal/theological and funerary (royal and private). Other, sometimes unique, feasts were determined by the monarchical dogma and the cult of the king (ascension to the throne, crowning, renewal celebration, temple foundation, mourning feast, victory celebration). There also were private feasts (birth, death, ancestor worship).

In theory, the head of the feast was the Pharaoh, but he only appeared in person at the most important festivals. High-ranking civil servants and priests represented him, assisted by ordinary priests, officials and groups of dancers, singers, rowers etc. Recitations, ritual acts (e.g., at the image of the deity), cult games, music and dance, offering of sacrifices (e.g., food, drink, flowers), incense and libations characterized the cultic activities, particularly movements of the divine image with its entourage during processions inside the temple under exclusion of the people and outside with their participation. Thus, the feast created an important contrast to the serenity and seclusion of the sacred routine. Processional festivals were a locus of a) communication between different social groups and communication with the dead, and b) self-representation of the actors (the king, high officials, priests, also acrobats, dancers, musicians) in the deity's entourage. Feasts were the only form of participation in the cult of the deities as a significant aspect of religious life open to the people.

The processional festival as the most important form required its own festive architecture (halls of appearance, gates, station sanctuaries, procession roads) and cult instruments (barques, shrines). The economic aspect is reflected in the huge quantities of foodstuffs supplied to the temple and its redistribution to officials and feast participants (as symbols of abundance).

The mostly domestic and private 'beautiful day' must be distinguished from the religious festival. It is a spontaneous festival and not fixed in the calendar though it may be triggered by a religious festival. It is illustrated by banqueting scenes in tombs of the 15th/14th cents. BC as an aesthetic staging that was made emphatically sensual and erotic with music, dance, meals and drink. These feasts united members of the upper classes.

Late feast calendars based on a year of 365 days provide detailed instructions regarding the course of religious festivals. The composition of festival literature and writings is personified by the lector priest who, as master of the feast rolls, performed the recitations and thus formed the framework of the event. It belonged to the 'beautiful day' feast that toasts were composed while the harpers' songs mourned the transitoriness of all things earthly (e.g., the unpleasant lot of the dead) and called for enjoyment of the feast. This contradiction to the core of the Egyptian world-view may be interpreted as an independent existentialist dimension of the feast.

New Kingdom sources (1530–1070 BC) show a clear sacralization of the earthly world in the festival, which is the locus of pronounced proximity to the gods, so that the deceased will wish to participate in the feast and his active participation in the feast during his lifetime emphasizes his state of initiation.

H. ALTENMÜLLER, s.v. Feste, LÄ 2, 171–191; J. ASSMANN, Der schöne Tag. Sinnlichkeit und Vergänglichkeit im Altägypt. Fest, in: W. HAUG, R. WARNING (ed.), Das Fest, 1989, 3–28; Id., Das ägypt. Prozessionsfest, in: Id., T. SUNDERMEIER (ed.), Das F. und das Heilige, 1991, 105–122; Id., Geheimnis, Gedächtnis und Gottesnähe, in: Id. et al. (ed.), Thebanische Beamtennekropolen, 1995, 281–293; A. GRIMM, Die altägypt. Festkalender in den Tempeln der griech.-röm. Epoche, 1994; A. J. SPALINGER, The Private Feast Lists of Ancient Egypt, 1996. HE.FE.

III. GREECE

1. PUBLIC NATURE AND COMMUNICATION

Festivals were loci of communication and one of the key occasions on which the public was constituted in the Greek polis [1]. They united various social groups and thus created their identity, ranging from girls of the same age to the Pan-Hellenic public. The festival public comprised more than the public in the political sense defined as free adult men [2. 582; 3]. The function of festivals usually included a religious element but it was never exclusive. A classification by deity (unchallenged since [4]) or restriction to the 'religious significance' [5] reduces the manifold variety that the feasts offered for divine service, communal eating, performances, dance, self-presentation and experience of the social community that one belongs to as well as the roles into which its members are introduced and in which they were confirmed by the feast. Similar considerations apply to Rome and the empire's towns, including the representation of Rome's rule over the towns and their acceptance or rejection (see → Ludi; → Ruler cult).

2. 'FESTIVAL CULTURE'

Cultural critics who accuse modern industrial society of being incapable of celebrating feasts [6] are tempted to construct Antiquity as a contrasting festival culture. In this ideological confrontation the Dionysiac and orgiastic aspect or a return to creative chaos are made out as the alternative to modernism [7; 8]; in another line of the debate the childlike and playful or agonistic aspect of the Greeks stands in the foreground [9; 10; 11; 12]. Both arguments belong to a debate about the retreat of the Church and neo-pagan laicism since the French Revolution [13; 14; 15; 16; 17] and are rooted in the cultural criticism of the Reformation [18; 19; 20].

3. CRITICISM AND CONTINUITY IN EARLY CHRISTIANITY

When the apologetic programme for 'Antiquity and Christianity' sees the typical ancient feast in the representation of the Dionysus cult in Euripides' *Bacchae* [21. 750], it places itself in the tradition of the early Church's criticism of festivals. Theologians warned that the devil entered into soul at festivals and that one should stay away from them (Tert. De spectaculis 14–27; Aug. Conf. 3,2) [22]. Simultaneously, Christians as citizens were dependent on the public nature and calendar of festivals, so they took over the municipal feasts. Existing feast programmes were changed or renamed [23; 24; 25]. The temple closures of the 4th cent. exempted festivals (Cod. Theod. 16,10,3; 17; 19). Cultural criticism led to changes and discontinuities in the rituals but not to their abolition. Usually only their reason and meaning changed.

Christian cultural criticism only continued ancient cultural criticism: in Judaism it was emphasized by the feast monopoly of the Jerusalem temple (Am 5,21; Ez 8;14;22), its destruction in 70 and the Roman occupation in AD 133 (spiritualized and eschatologized in Hebr 12,22) [21. 754f.; 26; 27; 28]. It was less pronounced among the Greeks but very familiar, as in the 'Odyssey' (Hom. Od. 20,165–358; 21,144–147; cf. 22,310 [29. 293f.; 477–501]) and in Plato (Plat. Leg. 2,653cd [30]).

4. CATEGORIES BASED ON CULTURAL STUDIES

The scholarly analysis of ancient festivals culture has suffered from being pressed between the positivistic accumulation of source material on the one hand and a polemic or apologetic construction on the other. The sources for ancient feasts are familiar from lexicons of late antiquity containing etymological speculation or comment on contemporary allusions (scholia). It was only the diaspora Greeks of Alexandria [31] and the Roman public who did not know the feast from practice. Contemporaries imbued the feast as experienced jointly by poet and public with a meaning, parodied or exalted it (e.g., Hom. H. 4,100–141), but this does not permit a reconstruction of the actual practice. Literature reflects festival ideology but provides no ritual instructions, s. 9. [32; 33]. In modern festival theory the juxtaposition of feast and routine ('the ordained escape' from the tread-mill [34]; bi-dimensionality of routine as against the creation of, or search for, meaning [35]) conceals the sense and motivation which festivals lend to normality. Playful inversion during feasts usually affirms the normal order [29. 1–37, 573–589]; rules limit the playful element, with the strictest application at the beginning and end of the feast. However, an interaction precedes the game: this year's actors are next year's spectators and so on [36]. Therefore, the function of feasts within society's internal order, in the interplay with other communication networks, such as marriage rules, exchanges, legal and political gatherings, requires elucidation. With increased fixing of the procedural rules ('state'), they partially change the function without entirely entering into the self-representation of power ('secularization') [37; 38].

5. Types of Greek Festivals

Although the manuals by Nilsson and Deubner interpreted festival rituals as 'originally' agrarian magic and fertility (in the tradition of Mannhardt and Frazer), with an almost exclusive validity [5. IV and repr. 1995, VII* (F. Graf); 39], social and political significance universally proved to be the decisive level of significance [40; 41; 42; 43; by contrast 31]. However, more differentiated types remained associated with various functions of the polis: the New Year's festival; the festival of the admission of adolescents among adults ('initiation'); women's feasts; military feasts (such as the Karneia in Sparta, s. Demetrius in Ath. 4,141e-f). They range from an occasional feast such as the *epitaphios* to the annual celebration of a victory over the neighbouring polis, which maintains the town's identity and image of the enemy over generations (e.g., Marathon, cf. Hdt. 6,105–112; Paus. 8,48,4f.) [44; 45; 46; 47] Seasonal and agrarian events took a back-seat to social context.

6. Elements of complex rituals

Four sections can be distinguished in the course of a festival: procession, including masked parades; sacrifices and banquets; chorus and dance; agons (→ Competitions, artistic, vol. 4 Addenda) [41. 163–178; 48]. Differing designs give feasts their specific character. However, organizers also borrowed elements across feast types because they were attractive. The introduction of new rituals (e.g., the weapons dance [49]) into an already complex ritual is almost unlimited, except perhaps by economy [50; 51]. Myths attempted to bind rituals together through narrative sequencing but without the necessity of completeness [29. 202–276]. Feasts often lasted more than a day, often three days, but each day kept its character and name. Longer feast periods such as the preparation of the → Panathenaia [41. 346–354] or seasonal focal points such as the Dionysian festivities in late winter may be observed but the documentation does not allow them to be viewed as deliberate units.

7. Feast and Religion

As early as the Mycenaean period, the calendar was organized according to deities and the months named according to the feasts of deities [52; 53; 54]. However, it does not appear to have been theologically organized (as in the 'ecclesiastical year'). Furthermore, almost no feast was exclusively associated with one deity while inversely feasts of the same type were associated with several deities. That feasts may be older than their association with particular deities of the Greek *polis* panthea has been known for some time [55; 56]. It is more important to note the place and time of origin than to theologize, i.e., to search for essential associations in the identity of the deity and 'its' feasts. The internal structure in the pantheon of the polis was decisive, as were the relationships and delimitations towards the outside [57]. No clear differences arise from the linguistic differentiation of feast/celebration, mourning/rejoicing, religious/profane: ἑορτή (*heortḗ*), πανήγυρις (*panḗgyris*) (or simply ἀγορά [*agorá*]), παννυχίς (*pannychís*), θεοξένια (*theoxénia*) [58; 59]. When Plato had the gods establish feasts and assigned them an ethical and religious purpose (Plat. Leg. 2,653cd), he attempted to give them a justification beyond human licence and in particular that of the democratic majority. Feasts became the communicative locus in which religion confronted society in nomothetic terms and the poet took on the functions of the theologian. However, religion was not separated out; the feasts belonged to the particular social groups; even 'state cults' did not form a closed organized group except that financing was the responsibility of the public purse [60]. Feasts were always celebrated collectively; individual life cycles were celebrated collectively on a fixed day in the context of age and gender classes, reflected in the feast of a divine or heroic representative of the social group (for example, Artemis as a girl, as in Brauron). Group identity was constructed by genealogical derivation from a common, fictional ancestor (e.g., Ion, the son of Apollo, as the ancestor of the Ionians: Eur. Ion 1553–1605) or reflected the rules exercized in a myth of how they became established 'at the initial occasion' (cf. Hes. Theog. 555–557), but not as a positive origin myth with a deity creating the order (*in illo tempore* – e.g., [8]) that would have made them immutable but rather as a didactic paradigm [61]).

8. Feasts as loci of the identity of social groups

As with Greek polis society in general, its religion reflects the low importance of kinship compared to associations [62; 63; 64]. The latter required periodic affirmation in feasts to define, recall and demonstrate the limits, the rules and the links to other groups and neighbouring poleis (often through playful inversion). The polis is the level of reference [65] beneath which the family, the phratry, the phyle and the neighbourhood, men, women and adolescents each celebrated their feasts; above the polis level were agrarian associations in central and supralocal sanctuaries; finally, Pan-Hellenic feasts defined the Greeks and how they differed from the barbarians [66]. Herodotus' claim (Hdt. 2,49–58) that the Greeks inherited the names of the gods and feasts from Egypt should be considered as an argument for their long tradition rather than a historical conclusion. Direct borrowing from the Orient cannot be documented even in the Bronze Age (→ Adonis), but a reworking of the experiences of Oriental feasts is evident [67. 121–132; 68]. The celebration of the same feasts by linguistically distinct Ionians and Dorians (e.g., the Anthesteria and Karneia) is a sign of the desire to belong.

9. Regulations: verbal instructions and written fixation

Publicly accessible stone and metal calendars (also in the demes of Athens, not just a central state calendar, like the one edited by Nicomachus around 400 BC on the royal stoa) assured that the dates of the various feasts could be known and checked in advance, which groups must furnish and finance them, what sacrificial animal was required, so that it would be known and could be checked [69. beginning with Solon Fr. 81–86 Ruschenbusch; 70; 71]. In the Hellenistic period, documents of foundation fulfilled the function of public recollection of the original purpose of the foundation and its author (*euergétēs*) [37; 72]. Another kind of inscription represents the significance of the polis' deity by naming the delegates invited to the festival from 'all over the world', the *theōroí,* or their hosts in the polis [73; 74; 75]. The invitation was announced by heralds together with a truce (*ekecheiría*) [21. 767–785]. Thus, feasts were able to delay wars; on the other hand, a town's festival could be used for an attack (Thuc. 5,82,2f.; Pomp.Trog. 43,4). By contrast, it was agreed in the Peace of Nicias (422/21 BC) that free access to the Pan-Hellenic sanctuaries, which had been disrupted by the war, should be available again (Thuc. 5,18; cf. the comical inversion in Aristoph. Av. 188–193). The programme of the festival was also announced by heralds; regulations determined the acts of participants and visitors, on occasion in great detail [76; 77].

10. Feast and Poetry

The festive community is the audience for poetry that was first presented, then written [78; 79]; even Herodotus' 'Histories' were first published verbally at a feast. The functional incorporation of early Greek 'literature' was selective, it extended from liturgical forms such as *hýmnos klētikós*, *paián*, *epiníkion*, *thrênos* and *epithalámion* to the grand epic [29. 277–291] and the tragedy, which combines several genres [80]. In each case, the feast is more than just the occasion to compose poetry; it is the setting for poets and listeners [81]. The shared experience of ritual performance and its significance made the unity of poet and audience real. Since the religious meaning is only one of several, an emancipation of liturgy from religious origins cannot be considered the norm of development. Even advanced drama contains liturgical pieces [82; 83]. However, ritual rigour and exact repetition of hieratically fixed texts were not demanded but instead distinctiveness and imagination in the interpretation because the festival programmes required a competition of performances and the selection of a victor [84; 85].

11. Agons

Thus, poets were subjected to the same terms, much as dancers (cf. Antiph. Or. 6), musicians and athletes, at a specifically defined point, temporally, spatially and socially, so that with better preparation they would be able to find the audience's taste and gain recognition as victors. These agons (→ Competitions, artistic, vol. 4 Addenda) were organized by disciplines as well as the age and gender of competitors [86]. To some extent professionalism emerged. However, the support of the social groups (town quarters, demes etc.) was more decisive in assuring the space for preparation for one of their own, than the value of the (possible) prizes for the victor.

12. Feast and market; economic aspects

Feasts were also economically significant, by promoting and enabling more than normal – both in qualitative and quantitative terms – consumption [87; 88]: the town or rather its social groups enhance prestige by commissioning artists, expensive materials (such as are represented by the bronze works and vessels of workshops that travelled from festival to festival [89; 90]), expensive buildings, quantitative and qualitative escalation against competitors; an infrastructure for the festival-related tourism was required; markets associated with the feasts became necessary to keep certain elements available for the feast (such as wine decanters for the Choai feast, cf. → Anthesteria; Aristoph. Ach. 719–1234; Thuc. 6,44,2f.) [91]. By contrast, a significant economic burden did not arise from the number of feast days (e.g., eighty in classical Athens, but up to 200 in Imperial Rome) because participation was not required and rest from work was not enforced or locally restricted, especially because in any case the feasts fell into periods of less work [92].

Pericles considered festivals one of the characteristics of Athens' superiority over other poleis (Thuc. 2,38; 1,70); the 'aged oligarch' sensed economic interests (Xen. Ath. Pol. 3,2; 3,8) [2. 569]. Feasts provided the opportunity to demand top performance from Greek culture. Only they provided the challenge.

→ Feast; → Festival; → Feast culture

1 B. Gladigow, Struktur der Öffentlichkeit und Bekenntnis in polytheistischen Rel., in: H.G. Kippenberg, G.G. Stroumsa (ed.), Secrecy and Concealment (Studies in the History of Religions 65), 1995, 17–35 2 C. Meier, Zur Funktion der Feste in Athen im 5. Jh. v.Chr., in: W. Haug, R. Warning, Das F., 1989 3 J. Henderson, Comic hero versus political élite, in: A.H. Sommerstein et al. (ed.), Tragedy, Comedy and the Polis, 1993, 307–320 4 C. Robert, in: GGA 161, 1899, 524f. 5 Nilsson, Feste, S. III–V 6 W. Gebhardt, F., Feier und Alltag, 1987 7 R. Caillois, L'homme et le Sacré, [2]1949, dt. 1988 8 M. Eliade, Le mythe de l'éternel retour, 1949, 227f. 9 J.G. Herder, Auch eine Philos. der Gesch. zur Bildung der Menschheit, 1774 = Bibliothek Dt. Klassiker 105, 1994, 85 10 J. Burckhardt, Griech. Kulturgesch. 4, [3]1902, 61–168 11 J. Huizinga, Homo ludens, 1938, 20–33, 75–79 12 G. Dörr, s.v. Agon/agonal, HrwG 1, 1988, 415–417 13 M. Ozouf, La fête révolutionnaire: 1789–1799, 1976 14 U. Raulff, Ein Historiker des

20. Jh.: Marc Bloch, 1995, 323–345, 397–401 15 C. A. Lobeck, Aglaophamus, 1829 16 F. Nietzsche, Geburt der Trag., 1872, c. 1 17 H. Cancik, Nietzsches Ant., 1996, 50–63, 107–121 18 J. Heers, Fêtes des fous et Carnevals, 1983 19 H.-D. Altendorf, P. Jezler (ed.), Bilderstreit, 1984 20 M. Maurer, F. und Feiern als histor. Forschungsgegenstand, in: HZ 253, 1991, 101–130 21 T. Klauser, s.v. F., RAC 7 22 F. v. d. Meer, Augustinus der Seelsorger, 1951, 72–83 23 H. Usener, Das Weihnachtsfest, 1899 24 T. Baumeister, s.v. Höhenkult, RAC 15, 986–1015 25 J. Rüpke, Kalender und Öffentlichkeit, 1995, 471–484 26 T. Klauser, Der Festkalender der Alten Kirche, in: H. Frohnes, U. W. Knorr (ed.), Kirchengesch. als Missionsgesch. 1, 1974, 377–388 27 E. Otto, T. Schramm, F. und Freude, 1977 28 M. Hengel, A. M. Schwemer (ed.), Königsherrschaft Gottes und himmlischer Kult, WUNT 55, 1991 29 C. Auffarth, Der drohende Untergang, 1991 30 H. Yunis, A New Creed, 1988, 29–58 31 G. Baudy, Das alexandrinische Erntefest, in: Mitt. für Anthropologie und Religionsgesch. 6, 1991, 5–110 32 A. Henrichs, Greek Maenadism from Olympias to Messalina, in: HSPh 82, 1978, 121–160 33 J. Bremmer, Greek Maenadism reconsidered, in: ZPE 55, 1984, 267–286 34 S. Freud, Totem und Tabu 1912/13, Studienausgabe 9, 1974, 425 35 J. Assmann, Der zweidimensionale Mensch, in: J. Assmann, Th. Sundermeier (ed.), Das F. und das Heilige, 1991, 13–30 36 W. Puchner, Brauchtumserscheinungen im griech. Jahreslauf und ihre Beziehungen zum Volkstheater, 1977, 342 37 A. Chaniotis, Sich selbst feiern?, in: M. Wörrle, P. Zanker (ed.), Stadtbild und Bürgerbild im Hell., Vestigia 47, 1995, 147–172 38 J. Köhler, Pompai. Untersuchungen zur hell. Festkultur, Europ. Hochschulschriften 38. 61, 1996 39 Deubner 40 W. Burkert, Homo necans, 1972 41 Burkert 42 B. Gladigow, in: GGA 235, 1983, 1–16 43 H. S. Versnel, Transition and Reversal in Myth and Ritual, 1993, 16–89 44 W. K. Pritchett, The Greek State at War vol. 3, 1979, 154–229 45 W. Burkert, Krieg, Sieg und die olympischen Götter der Griechen, in: F. Stolz (ed.), Rel. zu Krieg und Frieden, 1987, 69–87 46 R. Lonis, Guerre et rel. à l'époque classique, 1979 47 A. J. Holladay, M. D. Goodman, Religious Scruples in Ancient Warfare, in: CQ 36, 1986, 151–171 48 C. Calame, Morfologia e funzione della festa nell' antichità, in: AION, sezione filologico-letteraria 4/5, 1982/83, 3–21 49 S. H. Lonsdale, Dance and Ritual Play in Greek Rel., 1993, 137f. 50 C. Calame, Mythe et rite en Grèce: des catégories indigènes?, in: Kernos 4, 1991, 179–204 51 B. Gladigow, s.v. Ritual, HrwG 4, 1998 52 B. D. Meritt, The Athenian Year, 1961, 204–206 53 C. Trümpy, Untersuchungen zu den altgriech. Monatsnamen und Monatsfolgen, Bibliothek der klass. Alt.wiss. 2.98, 1997 54 C. Trümpy, Nochmals zu den myk. Fr-Täfelchen, in: SMEA 27, 1989, 191–234 55 E. Meyer, Gesch. des Alt. 1.2, 1913, 732 56 Schlesier, 112 57 Graf, 367–372 and passim 58 J. D. Mikalson, The Heorte of Herotology, in: GRBS 23, 1982, 213–221 59 L. Ziehen, s.v. Panegyris, RE 18, 581–583 60 S. B. Aleshire, Towards a Definition of 'State Cult' for Ancient Athens, in: R. Hägg (ed.), Ancient Greek Cult Practice from the Epigraphical Evidence, 1994, 9–16 61 J. Bremmer, What is a Greek myth?, in: J. Bremmer (ed.), Interpretations of Greek Mythology, 1987, 1–9 62 K. W. Welwei, Ursprünge genossenschaftlicher Organisationsformen in der archa. Polis, in: Saeculum 39, 1988, 12–23 63 E. Stein-Hölkeskamp, Adelskultur und Polisgesellschaft, 1989 64 P. Schmitt-Pantel, La cité au banquet, Collection de l'École Française de Rome 157, 1992 65 W. Burkert, Die ant. Stadt als Festgemeinschaft, in: P. Hugger, W. Burkert (ed.), Stadt und F., 1987, 25–44 66 C. Morgan, Athletes and Oracles: the transformation of Olympia and Delphi in the eighth century BC, 1990 67 W. Burkert, Herodot über die Namen der Götter, in: MH 42, 1985 68 S. P. Morris, Daidalos and the Origins of Greek Art, 1992 69 R. Parker, Athenian Rel., 1996, 43–53 70 Whitehead, 176–208 71 M. H. Jameson, D. R. Jordan, R. D. Kotansky, A Lex Sacra from Selinous (Greek, Roman, and Byzantine Monographs 11), 1993 72 M. Wörrle, Stadt und F., 1989 73 A. Plassart, Inscriptions de Delphes, in: BCH 45, 1921, 1–85 74 P. Charneux, Liste argiennes de théorodoques, in: BCH 90, 1966, 156–239, 710–714 75 S. Miller, The Theorodokoi of the Nemean Games, in: Hesperia 57, 1988, 147–163 76 κάπηλοι-Inschr. von Samos SEG 27, 1977, 545 77 Andania: Syll.[3] 736; Amorgos: Syll.[3] 981 78 W. Rösler, Dichter und Gruppe, 1980 79 J. Herington, Poetry into Drama, 1985 80 W. Burkert, Wilder Ursprung, 1990, 13–39 81 R. Kannicht, Thalia, in: W. Haug, R. Warning, Das F., 1989, 29–52 82 A. Henrichs, Warum sollte ich tanzen?, 1996 83 A. M. Bowie, Aristophanes, 1993 84 Pickard-Cambridge/Gould/Lewis 85 J. Henderson, The Demos and the Comic Competition, in: J. J. Winkler, F. I. Zeitlin (ed.), Nothing to do with Dionysos?, 1990, 271–313 86 D. G. Kyle, Athletics in Athens, [2]1993 87 C. Auffarth, Hera und ihre Stadt Argos, 1995, ch. 4 88 V. Lanternari, La grande festa, (1959) [2]1976 89 Ch. Risberg, Metal Working in Greek Sanctuaries, in: T. Linders, B. Alroth (ed.), Economics of Cult in the Ancient Greek World, Boreas 21, 1992, 33–40 90 M. Guggisberg, Terrakotten von Argos, in: BCH 112, 1988, 167–227, 235–243 91 L. de Ligt, P. W. de Neeve, Ancient Periodic Markets: Festivals and Fairs, in: Athenaeum 66, 1988, 391–416 92 H. Kloft, Arbeit und F.: Ant., in: P. Dinzelbacher (ed.), Europ. Mentalitätsgesch., 1993, 326–336.

J. D. Mikalson, The Sacred and Civil Calendar of the Athenian Year, 1975; A. Mommsen, Heortologie, 1864; new as: F. der Stadt Athen im Alt., 1898; Nilsson, Feste; E. Simon, Festivals of Attica, 1983. C.A.

IV. Rome
see → Ludi

Festus

[1] see → Marcius Festus

[2] **Iulius F. Hymetius.** served around AD 350 as *corrector Tusciae et Umbriae*, later as *praetor urbanus* and *consularis Campaniae cum Samnio* (before 355). In 362, he became *vicarius urbis Romae* (Cod. Theod. 11,30,29), and from 366 to 368 *proconsul Africae* (Cod. Theod. 9,19,3; his entire career: ILS 1256). As *proconsul*, he helped to alleviate a famine in Carthage, and in this context was sentenced to a fine as a result of being falsely accused of fraud (Amm. Marc. 28,1,17f.). In around 370/1, the Senate exiled him to Dalmatia on a charge of high treason (Amm. Marc. 28,1,19–23), but he was rehabilitated after the death of Valentinianus I

(ILS 1256). Neither he nor his wife Praetextata were Christians (Jer. Ep. 107,5). PLRE 1, 447 (Hymetius).

[3] F. hailed from Tridentum (modern Trento). He was *consularis Syriae* (AD 365 or 368), *magister memoriae*, and from 372 to 378 *proconsul Asiae* (his career in Amm. Marc. 29,2,22). In the latter role, he ordered the execution of the pagan philosophers Coeranius (Amm. Marc. 29,2,25) and Maximus (Lib. Or. 1,158). According to pagan tradition, he died on a 3rd January (probably 380), after visiting a temple of Nemesis (Eunap. VS 7,6,11–13). It is possible that he is identical with the eponymous author of a *breviarium*, who had also been a *magister memoriae*. PLRE 1,334 (F. 3). W.P.

[4] **F. Rufius.** Author of a → *breviarium* of Roman history. The general view amongst scholars is that this F., who in one strand of the transmitted text bears the family name Rufius, is identical with the *F. quidam Tridentinus* of Amm. Marc. 29,2,21f. [1]. According to Ammianus, he came from humble origins, but with the support of Maximus rose rapidly under Valens, whom he accompanied to the east in AD 364. There he became administrator for Syria; in *c.* 370, he succeeded Eutropius first as *magister memoriae*, then in 372 as *proconsul* of Asia. He died in 380, after his recall.

His *breviarium* presupposes knowledge of the work of his predecessor → Eutropius [1]. F., too, concludes his account in 364 with Jovian's surrender of Nisibis. However, he views events from an entirely new angle: Rome's expansion and its politics at its eastern border (chs. 15–30) are reported chronologically and form the main part of his work, almost as an exemplum for a new Persian War. The introduction provides only a brief, non-chronological general synopsis of Roman history by epochs (ch. 2), and the acquisition of its western provinces. Time and again, most emphasis is placed on administrational aspects. His main source is Eutropius, supplemented by Florus as well as a further source of the group of Livy epitomes.

1 B. Baldwin, F. the Historian, in: Historia 27, 1978, 197–217 2 J.W. Fadie, The Breviarium of F., 1967.

U.E.

[5] **Flavius Rufius Postumius F.** became *consul* in AD 472, later *patricius* and *caput senatus*; in 497, he was sent to Constantinople, and succeeded in having → Theoderic's rule in Italy recognized by → Anastasius [1]. He returned to the king with the *ornamenta palatii* (Anon. Valesianus 12,64). In the Laurentian Schism after 498, he was against Symmachus and for Laurentius, whom he granted asylum (Lib. Pontificalis ed. Duchesne 1, 46; 260).

PLRE 2, 467–469; I. König, Aus der Zeit Theoderichs d. Gr., 1997, 132, 156–61; J. Moorhead, Theoderic in Italy, 1992.

K.P.J.

[6] **Sex. Pompeius F.** Author of an alphabetic encyclopaedia *De verborum significatione*, an abridgement (cf. p. 242,28ff. L.) of the eponymous work by the late Augustan antiquarian → Verrius Flaccus. The name of its addressee (Artorius Rufus) points to southern Gaul, the moderately archaizing style of the work to the latter half of the 2nd cent. AD. Verrius' originally about 80 bks. were abridged to 20, with obsolete lemmata removed altogether; of the remainder, lemmata of specific interest in conjunction with the history of language were set aside for a planned second volume (see below). This division of each letter into two topical sections parts dates back to Verrius himself ([1. 2ff.]; for criticism of Verrius see [1. 7ff. 104ff.]). In late antiquity, it was still quite rare for the encyclopaedia to be used in competition with Verrius' full version, but from the 6th to 8th cents., F. became part of the repertoire of the glossographical tradition. During the Middle Ages, the use of the text (probably transmitted via the Monte Cassino monastery) remained rather scant and limited to Italy, where its epitome by the Carolingian scholar → Paulus Diaconus (Monte Cassino, *c.* 787) even lost the examples of archaic Latin contained in the original. F. himself only became known again in 15th-cent. Rome after the discovery of the archetype, Naples IV. A.3 (end of the 11th cent., the extant copy fragmentary and damaged), especially through Pomponio Leto and Angelo Poliziano. According to p. 242,30ff., F. had intended to compile those parts of Verrius' material which were mainly concerned with the history of language in a shorter treatise entitled *Priscorum verborum cum exemplis*, a work, which may have been used by Nonius [13. 239].

→ Glossography

Editions: J.J. Scaliger, 1575/6 (comm.) C.O. Müller, [2]1880 E. Thewrewk, 1889 W.M. Lindsay, 1913 Id., Gloss. Lat. 4, 1930, 71–467.

Bibliography: 1 R. Reitzenstein, Verrianische Forschungen, 1887 2 A. Simonelli, S.P.F. negli studi dell'ultimo trentennio, in: Orpheus 12, 1991, 171–203 3 G. Goetz, CGL 1, 1923, 10ff. (also P. Wessner, ibid., 309–369) 4 W.M. Lindsay, H.J. Thomson, Ancient Lore in Medieval Latin Glossaries, 1921, Vff. 5 Lindsay 1930, 75ff. 6 K. Neff, De Paulo Diacono Festi epitomatore, 1891 7 W. Strzelecki, Quaestiones Verrianae, 1932, 3ff. 8 F. Bona, Contributi allo studio della composizione del De verborum significatu di Verrio Flacco, 1964, 30ff. 9 R. Bianchi, Due citazioni attribuite a F., in: Atti e memorie dell'Arcadia 3,7, 1980/81, 235–262 10 S. Lanciotti, Una stranezza del Vat. Lat. 3369, in: Studi Urbinati 62, 1989, 221–251 11 W. Bracke, La première 'edition' humaniste du De verborum significatione, in: Revue d'histoire des textes 25, 1995, 189–215 12 A. Grafton, Joseph Scaliger 1, 1983, 134–160 13 P.L. Schmidt, in: HLL § 440.

P.L.S.

Fetiales Roman priests, who formed a → *collegium* of 20 life-time members. They were co-opted from Rome's noble families (Dion. Hal. Ant. Rom. 2,72). Their name was linked with *foedus* (Serv. Aen. 1,62), *fides* (Varro, Ling. 5,86), and *ferire* (Fest. 81 L.). According to tradition, the founder of this *collegium* was either Numa (Dion. Hal. Ant. Rom. 2,72,1; Plut. Numa 12,4–13,67f–

68c; Camillus 18,137b-f), Tullus Hostilius (Cic. Rep. 2,31), or Ancus Marcius (Liv. 1,32,5; Ps. Aur. Vict. De viris illustribus 5,4; Serv. Aen. 10,14).

The *fetiales* upheld the *ius fetiale* (Cic. Off. 1,36; Liv. 9,9,3), i.e. the sacral aspect of juridic relations between peoples [1; 2]. They conveyed diplomatic decisions by the Senate: a *fetialis* was the *publicus nuntius populi Romani* (Liv. 1,32,6). *Fetiales* always acted in pairs: the *verbenarius* and the *pater patratus*. A detailed description of the role of the *fetiales* is found in Livy's report on the war between Romans and Albans (Liv. 1,24,3ff.): After the *verbenarius* had touched the *pater patratus* with a bunch of sacred herbs which had been picked on the *arx*, the *patres patrati* of both nations met to enter into a *foedus*; they struck down a piglet with a stone, invoking Jupiter to strike the tribe who broke this oath in the same way that the sacrificial animal was slain. If an oath had been broken, the *fetiales* of the aggrieved nation would approach the *fetiales* of the other nation and demand satisfaction (*rerum repetitio*). In the case of a successful demand, the *pater patratus* handed the perpetrators over to the opposing side. Failing this, the Senate of the injured people would declare war after an interval of 33 days (Liv. 1,32,5ff.). As a declaration of war, the *pater patratus* threw a spear (→ *hasta*), which had been dipped in blood, into enemy territory and recited a ritual formula (Liv. 1,32,12ff.) [3]. In overseas wars, this rite was carried out symbolically in Rome itself: the *pater patratus* threw the spear into a piece of land near the temple of → Bellona, symbolizing the enemy territory; this happened e.g. when Augustus declared war on Mark Antony and Cleopatra (Cass. Dio 50,4,5), and also, when in AD 178 Marcus Aurelius declared war on the Scythians [4].

1 G. Dumézil, Remarques sur le ius fetiale, in: REL 34, 1956, 93–108 2 C. Saulnier, Le rôle des prêtres fétiaux et l'application du »ius fetiale« à Rome, in: Revue historique du droit français et étranger 58, 1980, 171ff. 3 J. Bayet, Le rite du fécial, in: MEFRA 52, 1935, 39–76 4 J. Rüpke, Domi militiae, 1990, 105ff.

M. Beard, J. North, Pagan Priests. Rel. and Power in the Ancient World, 1990, 17ff.; 177ff.; J.H.W.G. Liebeschuetz, Continuity and Change in Roman Rel., 1979, 62ff.; J. Scheid, Les prêtres officiels sous les empereurs julio-claudiens, in: ANRW II 16.1, 610–654; L. Schumacher, Die vier hohen röm. Priesterkollegien unter den Flaviern, den Antoninen und den Severern, 69–235 n.Chr., in: ANRW II 16.1, 655–819; Th. Wiedemann, The fetiales, in: CQ 36, 1986, 478–490; G. Wissowa, Rel. und Kultus der Römer, 1912, 550ff. FR.P.

Fever (πυρετός/*pyretós*, Lat. *febris*) strictly refers to a symptom only, i.e. a raise in body temperature, but all ancient medical authors frequently use this term to refer to a specific illness or class of illness. In modern diagnostic usage, the term covers a variety of conditions; thus the identification of any ancient 'fever' without any further sub-classification or other description of symptoms is bound to fail. Such aids to identification could consist of observations regarding the periodicity of fever attacks, as in the *febris tertiana* or *febris quartana*, when episodes of high temperature alternate with those of normal body temperature, or those of characteristic symptoms such as the ἠπίαλος πυρετός (*ēpíalos pyretós*; shivering fits), where the raise in temperature is preceded by shaking and dazedness, or the καῦσις (*kaûsis*), a burning sensation pervading the entire body, coupled with a feeling of coldness at the body surface.

Febrile illnesses were extremely common, esp. → malaria; the Romans invoked the personified goddess → Febris (and, in the Imperial period, Quartana and Tertiana, CIL 7,99; 12,3129) in order to ward off or heal such fever attacks. Malaria fever with its periodic progress also provided the model for the ancient notion of the course of a disease, namely onset, aggravation to the point of crisis, finally remission or cure. Fevers, which were easy to diagnose by touch or observation, were also classified according to the bodily fluids which were thought to play a part in the course of a disease (cf. melancholic fever), but also according to whether they affected the entire body as in the case of hectic fever or typhus. The latter variations were considered the more dangerous ones, whereas *febris quartana* was seen as far less harmful. Bilious fever was so common during the summer season that Galen and Hippocratic authors even described it as part of the body's natural metabolism. The Hippocratic tradition frequently associated any fever leading to an acute disease with bile. Such diseases were explained with an overheating of the body, which in turn could be traced back to external causes such as exposure to the sun, or internal causes such as gluttony or the blockage of pores, resulting in a malfunction of the 'coction process'. Therapeutic measures included purgation and phlebotomy, which should have resulted at least in a temporary lowering of the temperature, further a reduction diet and careful nursing – esp. during the crisis.

→ Galen; → Hippocrates

1 W.F. Bynumy, V. Nutton, Theories of Fever from Antiquity to the Enlightenment, 1981 2 M.D. Grmek, Les maladies à l'aube de la civilisation occidentale, 1983 3 R. Sallares, The Ecology of the Ancient Greek World, 1991. V.N.

Fibrenus Left tributary of the Liris in Latium in the region between Sora and Arpinum, modern Fibreno. At its mouth was the location of Cicero's *villa* (Cic. Leg. 2,6), remains of which are thought to be recognizable in the abbey of San Domenico near Isola del Liri.

Nissen vol. 2, 670. G.U.

Fibula (Lat. *fibula*, from *figibula*; *figere*, 'tack', 'pin'), a multi-part clasp used in clothing. Because of the wide range of types and decor, fibulae provide one of the most important guides for the differentiation and chronology of prehistoric and primitive cultures. For the various types and cultures, see → Needle. F.PR.

Fictio *Fictio*, rooted in Roman jurisprudence, describes a technique still used in modern legal practice in order to arrange sanctions for different circumstances from those originally addressed by the law through working on the assumption that both sets of circumstances are identical, even though in reality they are not. This concept developed from the religious rule stating *simulacra pro veris accipiuntur* ('images are accepted as reality'): Priests as the first legal experts in Rome's early history transferred the concept expressed in this religious rule to the legal sphere. This was to the benefit of the legal framework because it allowed the preservation of existing legal forms and procedures while at the same time answering the demand to consider and decide upon entirely new facts and circumstances. Within the Roman legal system, *fictio* was thus an important tool for the advancement of the law. For that reason, it was mainly used by the → praetor.

Early examples are legal transactions concerning changes in personal status, such as the formal → *emancipatio* with its three (fictitious) sales, or the *adrogatio* (→ Adoption) with its pretence that the adoptee 'was born by the father and the mother of this family' (*ex eo patre matreque familias natus esset*, Gell. NA 5,19,9). However, *fictiones* were predominantly used in legal formulae. There is early evidence of praetors, inserting into certain charges the formula *si civis esset* ('as if he was a citizen'), in order to make it possible for a non-citizen to charge with theft or damage to property (*actio furti* and *actio legis Aquiliae*) (Gai. Inst. 4,37). A different fiction applied to the possessor, who had purchased an object, but could not become its owner, because it was not in the vendor's ownership, and who would otherwise have had to wait for a year to acquire it by usucaption: for the intervening period, the purchaser would enjoy the same protection, 'as if he had already owned it for a year' (*anno possedisset*, cf. Gai. Inst. 4,36).

Jurists are guided by the same motivation as the praetors in their use of *fictiones*: If for a partner in a business, for example, a certain condition (→ *condicio*) is disadvantageous (but essential to the success of the business) and if he then deliberately prevents this condition from occurring, the case is to be treated, as if the condition had actually occurred, according to Julian and Ulpian (Dig. 35,1,24; 50,17,161). The same principle still applies in the modern German civil code (§ 162 Bundesgesetzbuch).

WIEACKER, RRG, 324f.; DULCKEIT/SCHWARZ/WALDSTEIN, 164. G.S.

Fictores ('moulders of sacrificial cakes', bakers). They assisted the → *pontifices* (*fictores pontificum*: CIL VI 1074; 10247) and the Vestals (*fictores virginum Vestalium*: CIL VI 786; 2134; Varro, Ling. 7,44, Cic. Dom. 139), their office, according to Ennius (Ann. 115), dated back to Numa. The *fictores* baked the sacrificial cakes (*liba*) – a task which they may have taken over from the Vestal virgins – and sometimes they were also present at the sacrifices themselves. Cf. *strufertarii* (Fest. 85 L.), who offered → *strues* and *fertum*.

M. IHM, s.v. F., RE 6, 2271; LATTE, 410; F. FLESS, Opferdiener und Kultmusiker auf stadtröm. histor. Reliefs, 1995, 21 n. 11 pl. 4,1; A.V. SIEBERT, Instrumenta sacra, 1998. A.V.S.

Ficulea Town in Latium, north-east of Rome on the *via Ficulensis* (Liv. 3,52,3), subsequently the *via Nomentana* [1. 43], localized near Casale di Marco Simone Vecchio. It was originally founded by Aborigines (Dion. Hal. Ant. Rom. 1,16), then by the Prisci Latini; captured by Tarquinius Priscus (Liv. 1,38,4); *municipium* (Plin. HN 3,64). Atticus (Cic. Att. 12,34) and Martial (6,27,2) owned estates near F.

1 A. NIBBY, Analisi storico-topografico-antiquaria della carta dei dintorni di Roma 2, 1837.

L. QUILICI, S. QUILICI GIGLI, F., 1993. G.U.

Fideicommissum The *fideicommissum* (literally: 'entrusted in faith'), which from the 2nd cent. BC (Ter. Andr. 290–298) appeared alongside the *legatum* (legacy), was a request of the testator to an heir or legatee to pass on the inheritance in part or total to a third party. Since a *fideicommissum* was not subject to the same restrictions as the civil law of succession, it was used to make a bequest to a person who would otherwise not be eligible to be an heir or to receive a legacy (non-citizens; women according to the *lex Voconia*, → Succession, law of II D; the unmarried and the childless according to the *lex Papia*, → *caducum*), or it was used to exceed the limitation of legacies to three quarters of the entire estate, as imposed by the *lex Falcidia* (→ *legatum*). Such requests could be incorporated within a testament or recorded independently, esp. in form of a codicil by a person who made no testamentary disposition (→ *codicilli*); there was no set formula. A *fideicommissum* was not legally enforceable, but in line with the tradition of succession, its fulfilment was expected (if at all possible). If a testator wanted to make certain that his wishes were going to be fulfilled, he had to name the person to whom he wanted to make a bequest as his heir or legatee, while observing the limitations imposed by law. Under Augustus, *fideicommissa* became legally enforceable (Inst. Iust. 2,23,1; 25 pr.); thus, it became possible to testate enforceably and without limitations. The *senatus consultum Pegasianum* (under Vespasian), however, granted *fideicommissa* equality in status with legacies in respect of the *leges Falcidia* and *Papia*; Justinian standardized all types of bequest (Cod. Iust. 6,43,2).

The ancient rule in civil law – *semel heres semper heres* ('once an heir, always an heir') – excluded in principle an inheritance in fee tail or by substitution; the *fideicommissum hereditatis*, however, made it possible to transfer the inheritance to a third party, thus allowing that party to enjoy the economic position of being an heir (while the appointed heir remained formally the *heres*, without retaining his inheritance). In such cases, the testator would order his heir (or a fideicommissioner) to transfer the inheritance (or a part thereof) after a specified period or upon the fulfilment of a certain condition. The heir was then obliged to sell his inheritance for the symbolic sum of 1 HS to the fideicommissioner and transfer it → *in iure cessio*; in the course of this action, the heir promised by way of a → *stipulatio* that he would pass on all future profits from his inheritance, whereas the fideicommissioner promised to pay all unpaid debts of the estate. In practical terms, the position of the fideicommissioner was thus comparable to that of substitute heir. As the heir continued to be personally liable for the debts of the estate, he could take recourse in the *stipulatio*, but bore the risk of the fideicommissioner becoming insolvent.

For that reason, many heirs chose to waive their inheritance (→ *abstentio*), thus also voiding any *fideicommissum*. It was for that reason that the *senatus consultum Trebellianum* (AD 55) stipulated that any claims and debts associated with heirship would as a matter of course pass on to the fideicommissioner. However, there were still heirs who waived their rights, because an inheritance encumbered with a *fideicommissum hereditatis* held no attraction for them. Therefore, the *senatus consultum Pegasianum* specified that an heir could be forced to accept and subsequently pass on his inheritance; if he did that voluntarily, he would receive a quarter of the inheritance in compensation. However, the *senatus consultum Pegasianum* again specifically excluded the transfer of claims and debts in cases of voluntary acceptance of an inheritance; thus heir and fideicommissioner were once more forced to use *stipulationes* in order to safeguard their positions, as in the case of partial legatees (→ *legatum*) (Gai. Inst. 2,247–259). This created an unsatisfactory legal situation, which was only rectified in AD 533 by combining the advantages of both the *senatus consultum Trebellianum* and the *Pegasianum* (transfer of the liability for debts of the estate to the fideicommissioner; the entitlement of the heir to a quarter of the estate) and revoking the disadvantages of the *senatus consultum Pegasianum* (Inst. 2,23,7). The Justinian *Trebellianum* applied in Common Law, where the universal *fideicommissum* (*fideicommissaria* → *substitutio*) was used to appoint substitute heirs.

→ Succession, law of II. G.

1 Honsell/Mayer-Maly/Selb, 496ff. 2 D. Johnston, The Roman Law of Trusts, 1988 3 Kaser, RPR I, 757ff.; II 549ff., 563f. 4 U. Manthe, Das senatus consultum Pegasianum, 1989 5 P. Voci, Diritto ereditario romano II [2]1963, 223ff. U.M.

Fidelis (Φιδέλιος; *Phidélios*) of Milan. Lawyer in Rome and in AD 527/8 *quaestor palatii* of the Ostrogoth king → Athalaricus (Cassiod. Var. 8,18f.). In 536, he was sent to → Belisarius on behalf of the citizens of Rome and pope Silverius, in order to hand over the city (Procop. Goth. 1,14,5). In 537/8, he served as *praefectus praetorio* for the Eastern Roman Empire. In 538, he fell into the hands of the Goths near Ticinum, who killed him as a traitor (Procop. Goth. 1,20,19f.; 2,12,27f.; 34f.).

PLRE 2, 469f.; Stein, Spätröm. R. vol. 2, 348, 354. K.P.J.

Fidenae Latin town on a hill left of the Tiber along the *via Salaria* (Tab. Peut. 5,5), five (Dion. Hal. Ant. Rom. 2,53) or six (Eutr. 1,4,19) miles from Rome. It was settled from the Iron Age onwards [1], and took part in the *feriae Latinae* on *mons Albanus* (Plin. HN 3,69). During the 5th cent., it was allied with Veii (Liv. 4,17ff.). At the time of Horace (Epist. 1,11,8), it was almost completely abandoned. The collapse of the wooden amphitheatre in AD 27 claimed many victims, the majority of them visitors from Rome (Tac. Ann. 4,63; Suet. Tib. 40). Tufa was quarried within the territory of the town (Vitr. De arch. 2,7,1). Ruins between Villa Spada (residential quarter) and Castel Giubileo (*arx*).

1 A.M. Bietti Sestieri, F., in: Archeologia Laziale 10, 1990, 115–120.

Nissen 2, 604ff.; G. Garbugino, s.v. F., EV 2, 509; L. Quilici, S. Quilici Gigli, F., 1986. G.U.

Fidenas Roman cognomen ('victor over Fidenae'), transmitted for the Sergii and Servilii of the early Republican era (5th/4th cents. BC); the *dictator* Q. → Servilius Priscus allegedly captured the town of Fidenae in Latium in 435 and subsequently was given the epithet (Liv. 4,45,5).

Kajanto, Cognomina 181; F. Münzer, s.v. Servilius, RE II A 2, 1789f.; 1803f.; W. Reichmuth, Die lat. Gentilicia, 1956, 55. K.-L.E.

Fidentia Augural name of a town in the western Aemilia (*regio VIII*) on the *via Aemilia* (It. Ant. 288; It. Burd. 616; Tab. Peut. 4,3) on the crossing of the river Stirone, in the Middle Ages Borgo San Donnino, from 1927 Fidenza (Parma). It was founded as a *municipium* in the 2nd cent. BC; during the Civil War, it was besieged by Lucullus in 82 BC (Plut. Sulla 17; Vell. Pat. 2,28; Liv. Epit. 88). It later declined to become *vicus Fidentiola* (It. Ant. 99; 127).

A. Aimi, Storia di F., 1982; M. Calvani Marini, F., 1977; M. Catarsi, Il territorio fidentino nell'antichità, in: G. Ferrarini, C. Cropera (ed.), F., 1994, 12–55; P.L. Dall'Aglio, Agiografia e topografia antica, in: Journal of Ancient Topography 1, 1991, 57–70. G.U.

Fides

I. Religion II. Law III. Christian

I. Religion

F. is the cultically venerated personification of faith and veracity [1]. According to Varro (Ling. 5,74), she had been adopted in Rome from the Sabini; her cult is still in evidence at the end of the 2nd cent. AD (Tert. Apol. 24,5). F. is depicted as a woman, her head adorned with a garland or veil, dressed in a → *chitṓn* and *péplos* [2]. She appears frequently in poetry, but rarely in prose. She was considered to be a very ancient deity (Sil. Pun. 1,329f.; 2,484ff.) and therefore referred to as *cana* (Verg. Aen. 1,292). According to Agathocles *Perì Kyzíkou* (Fest. 328 L.), the legendary foundation of her temple on the Palatine dates back to Rhome, the granddaughter of Aeneas. However, most sources (Liv. 1,21,4; Dion. Hal. Ant. Rom. 2,75,3; Plut. Numa 16,1,70f.) name → Numa as the founder of both the temple and the cult. In historical times, the temple of *F. publica* or *populi Romani* was situated on the Capitol, close to the temple of Jupiter (Cic. Off. 3,104). It was built by Atilius [I 14] Calatinus between 258 and 247 BC, then in 115 BC restored and extended by Aemilius [I 37] Scaurus (Cic. Nat. D. 2,61) [3]. On the walls of the temple or nearby, international treaties and military diplomes were on display. Dion. Hal. Ant. Rom. 5,68,4 reports that sacrifices took place throughout the year. The anniversary of the temple on 1 October was ritually celebrated (Fast. Amiterni CIL I,1², p. 245; Fast. fratrum Arvalium CIL I,1², p. 214): on this day, the → *flamines maiores* drove to her temple in a covered carriage, their right hands covered to the fingers with a white cloth (Liv. 1,21,4; Serv. Aen. 1,292; 8,636). This shrouding is so characteristic for the cult of F. that the goddess herself is frequently described as being 'shrouded in a white cloth' (Hor. Carm. 1,35,21–22: *albo rara F. colit velata panno*). According to Livius (loc. cit.), the covered hand symbolizes that faith needs to be protected and the right hand, in which faith is held, is sacred (*sacrata*), and according to Servius (loc. cit.; cf. also Mythographi Vaticani 2,89) that faith needs to be kept hidden. Apparently, this ritual was designed to put the right hand, given to seal solemn agreements and alliances, under F.'s special protection: The goddess was to protect faithful alliances and guard against unfaithful ones.

1 G. Wissowa, Rel. und Kultus der Römer, 1912, 133–134 2 D.E.M. Nash, s.v. F., LIMC 4.1, 132ff. 3 G. Freyburger, F. Études sémantique et religieuse depuis les origines jusqu'à l'époque augustéenne, 1986, 229ff.

J.H.W.G. Liebeschuetz, Continuity and Change in Roman Rel., 1979, 175ff.; G. Piccaluga, F. nella religione romana, in: ANRW II 17.2, 703–735; Radke, 128.

FR.P.

II. Law

Fides became one of the most important legal concepts in Rome. In Cicero's words (Off. 1,23), it constitutes no less than the fundamental basis of → justice (*fundamentum iustitiae*). In this context, *fides* is defined as the constancy and veracity of a word once given and the agreed content (*dictorum conventorumque constantia et veritas*). The closest equivalent to Roman *fides* in modern legal terminology is the concept of trust ([1. 4] following on from [2]). By contrast, classifying *fides* as a mere expectation [cf. 3. 148] may have the advantage of potentially describing a wider range in meaning, but also the distinct disadvantage of socio-ethical blandness. Whereas the equivalent Greek concept of πίστις (→ *pístis*) firmly remains within the socio-ethical sphere of friendship (cf. Aristot. Eth. Nic. 1162b 31), it was the integration of *fides* into positive law, which gave to the Roman heritage its special quality and lasting influence, esp. in post-antique Europe.

It is almost impossible to reconstruct the earliest roots of *fides* within the Roman code of law [4. 506]. At any rate, the Twelve Tables (8,21) already threaten punishment for any *patronus* violating his obligation to protect and be loyal to his → *cliens*; as early as the 5th cent. BC, this relationship is thus very clearly defined as a legal and not a social one. Romans emphasized throughout the essential significance of *fides* within this relationship. There are some common factors between the relationship of *patronus* and *cliens* and the → *deditio* of Roman international law (*ius gentium*), which resulted in the surrendering nation or tribe entering into a kind of client relationship with Rome. It is this latter aspect of *fides* which has been more closely examined in recent years [1; 3]. The normativity of international law is based on *fides*. For that reason, a betrayal of the *fides publica*, of the trust which the state laid claim to also in relations with non-Romans, could result in the extradition (*noxae deditio*, → *noxa*) of the Roman lawbreaker to the victims of his transgression.

From the time of Plautus, it became more common to find *fides* qualified as *bona fides* ('good faith', or more modern: trust, cf. [5. 33]). The greatest effect of this formula was to provide a basis for an entirely novel way of looking at the laws governing private obligations: From the 2nd cent BC, it was a generally acknowledged principle that, on the basis of *bona fides*, informal agreements regarding purchases, rentals, services, business transactions, and those concerning cooperation within a company as a whole, were legally binding. Their fulfilment was legally enforceable with a *bonae fidei* → *iudicium* (cf. [4. 441ff., 449, 453ff.] for a differentiated view). For that reason, it suggests itself to see the difference between simple *fides* and *bona fides* in the 'objectivation' of the former [1. 43f.]: a legal instrument, which allowed private citizens to enter into agreements in the confidence that they would be adhered to, developed into a criterium for judgement by an organ of the state, i.e. the → *praetor*. The *praetor peregrinus* may have played a leading role in this, as, in contrast with the more formal transactions of the → *ius civile*, the informal obligations *ex fide bona* had generally been open to non-Romans from the outset. However, the greatest impact of *ex fide bona* transactions was on legal dealings between Roman citizens, where their great practicability increasingly displaced other more formal contracts. Some types of *bonae fidei iudicia* (e.g. → *fiducia*, etymologically clearly based on *fides*) were even restricted to Roman citizens only.

Still in the period of the Roman Republic, the aspect of *fides* as part of *bonae fidei iudicia* once again acquired new meaning: it became a legal standard to determine the content of obligations. This new demand on the loyalty of partners within an obligation was even able to reverse the original meaning of *fides* – i.e. the strict adherence to a verbal agreement – and include a 'reasonable relaxation of the severity of the claims of one of the parties' [4. 506]. Judgements by a *praetor* and a → *iudex* thus enjoyed a high degree of flexibility: It was possible to base the defence of a debtor on the malicious behaviour of the creditor (→ *exceptio*, → *dolus*), and similarly to take into account informal (secondary) agreements (→ *pactum*). There is probably no other sphere in which the sense of justice and practicability within Roman jurisprudence had greater scope for development than in the deliberations of *praetores* interpretating *bonae fidei iudicia*.

The modern principle of good faith in European laws of obligation (e.g. § 242 Bundesgesetzbuch) is based on the Roman concept of *bona fides*, in the same way as the modern legal concept of 'good faith' as the basis for the acquisition of real rights is rooted in Roman law: Even though Roman law did not know of a formal legal transaction allowing acquisition by an unentitled person, it knew the concept of acquisition by usucaption (→ *usucapio*) – and for this, *bona fides* was an essential precondition in respect of the (in reality non-existent) entitlement of the seller. It seems to have been developed as a measure of effective usucaption at about the same time that *bonae fidei iudicia* became the prevalent form of transaction. For that reason, it is not too far-fetched to assume an internal link between the two, i.e. the preservation of trust as the ethos of a developed system of legal transactions.

1 D. Nörr, Die F. im röm. Völkerrecht, 1991 2 R. Heinze, F., in: Hermes 64, 1929, 140–166 3 D. Nörr, Aspekte des röm. Völkerrechts, 1989 4 Wieacker, RRG 5 L. Lombardi, Dalla 'f.' alla 'bona f.', 1961.

C. Becker, s.v. F., RAC 7, 801–839; M. Bretone, Storia del diritto romano, ³1989, 98–101; M. Kaser, Ius gentium, 1993, 35ff., 126; D. Nörr, Mandatum, f., amicitia, in: D. Nörr, S. Nishimura (ed.), Mandatum und Verwandtes, 1993, 13–37.

G.S.

III. Christian

Latin-speaking Christendom translated → *pístis* (πίστις) as *fides*. The term, with its sense of 'trust' or 'trustworthiness', thus gave the Christian concept of faith a strong moral/legal connotation. Thus, in the Latin-speaking Western Church, faith (*fides*) emerged in clear opposition to knowledge (Tert. De praescriptione 7,13: 'When we believe, there is nothing more we desire to believe), while in the Eastern Church the two were closely interconnected (e.g., Clem. Al. Strom. 5,1,3: 'There is neither knowledge, γνῶσις/*gnôsis*, without faith, *pístis*, nor faith without knowledge'). In → Novatianus, → Cyprianus [2] and → Lactantius [1], *fides* often signifies Christianity as a whole, the old meaning of 'allegiance' still being felt. Not until → Augustinus does the synthesis succeed: although he also gives priority to faith (he likes to quote Is. 7,9 in LXX: 'If you do not believe, you will not understand'), he now expressly differentiates between the content and the act of faith (Aug. Trin. 13,2,5: *aliud sunt ea, quae creduntur, aliud fides qua creduntur* – 'the things that one believes are one thing, the faith with which one believes them is another'). This made Augustine fundamental for all of Western theology.

→ Pistis

D. Lührmann, s.v. Glaube, RAC 11, 1981, 48–122 (bibliography); S. G. Hall, s.v. Glaube IV. Alte Kirche, TRE 13, 1984, 305–308; H. Vorster, s. v. Glaube, HWdPh 3, 1974, 628–643; E. Tielsch, Die Wende vom antiken zum christl. Glaubensbegriff, in: Kantstudien 64, 1973, 159–199.

J.BÜ.

Fiducia Term for 'fiduciary agreement', (e.g. Paulus, Sent. 2,13,1) also for the object held in trust. *Fiducia* could be found in various aspects of Roman civil law: In the law of persons, there was the *coemptio* of women (a form of → *mancipatio*, Gai. Inst. 3,113), not only for the purpose of marriage (*matrimonii causa*), but also in the context of the transference of property on trust (*fiduciae causa*), e.g. in order to avoid one kind of guardianship (→ *tutela*) and to establish a different one (of a *tutor fiduciarius*) (Gai. Inst. 1,114; 115). The law of persons and obligations (entitlement to damages) are linked in the fiduciary *noxae deditio* (→ *noxa*, → *noxalis actio*, cf. Papin. Coll. 2,3,1).

In the law of property, *fiducia* is found as a security trust for a loan (*fiducia cum creditore contracta*, a *fiducia* in agreement with the creditor), but, especially in times of uncertainty, also as an administrative trust (*fiducia cum amico contracta*, a *fiducia* with a friend: Gai. Inst. 2,59f.). The trust agreement (*fiducia contracta*) follows on from a *mancipatio* or → *in iure cessio* (Gai. Inst. 2,59; 3,201; Isid. Orig. 5,25,23). The *formula Baetica* provides evidence of a *mancipatio* with a *pactum conventum* (agreement) on a trust (1st/2nd cents. AD, FIRA III no. 92), with *fidi fiduciae causa* as an ancient formula, cf. e.g. Plaut. Trin. 117 and 142. The fiduciary is obliged to *fides* (Cic. Top. 10,41). Even though he is formally the owner, he undertakes in the trust agreement to deal with the entrusted property in a certain manner, e.g. to hand it back to the trustor: in case of a security trust, once the debts are redeemed (*mancipatio Pompeiana* of AD 61, p.3, l. 1ff., FIRA III no. 91), in case of a → *donatio mortis causa* (gift in case of death), if the intended recipient has already died (Papin. Dig. 39,6,42 pr. with *traditionibus* instead of *mancipationibus* and *bona fide* instead of *fiducia*). The *actio fiduciae*, a *bonae fidei* → *iudicium* (Gai. Inst. 4,62) with the consequent → *infamia* (Gai. Inst. 4,182), deals with the obligation to revert the property to the original owner. If the trustor came into property (again), he could restore his ownership by *usureceptio* (see also → *usucapio*; Gai. Inst. 2,59f.). Prior to the reacquisition, he could – in the same way as a proprietor – bequeath the item in question *per praeceptionem* (in anticipation) (Gai. Inst. 2,220). Other than through redemption (1) of the secured loan, a *fiducia* also ends if no payments have been received, even though the secured claim was due (2): The creditor is then within his rights to realize the property. These two possible ends of a *fiducia* are confirmed by the *formula Baetica* with these words: *usque eo is fundus eaque mancipia fiduciae essent, donec* (1) *ea omnia pecunia persoluta* (2) *fidesve L. Titi soluta liberataque esset* ('this property and this *mancipia* are going to be subject to this *fiducia*, (1) until all the money has been paid, or (2) the obligation of L. Titius to *fides* expired', l. 9ff.). In the following, the *formula* substitutes the normally to be expected 'expiry' with the fiduciary's right to sell (l. 11ff.): If the proceeds of the sale were less than required, the remainder of the debt would remain, if they were higher, the creditors would pass on the surplus (FIRA III no. 91 p.3 l. 12ff.). Later, this was accepted as a matter of course: *fiducia* is based on the principles of the law of lien (Gai. Inst. 2,60: *contrahitur ... pignoris iure ...*). The acceptance of children as lien or *fiducia* was punishable with → *deportatio* (Paulus, Sent. 5,1,1).

Fiducia is also found in the law of succession. An heir charged with a → *fideicommissum* was known as a *heres fiduciarius*, the inheritance he was obliged to hand over as *hereditas fiduciaria* (Iavolenus Dig. 36,1,48 (46); Ulp. Dig. 12,1,9,1).

In his → *Corpus iuris*, Justinian had *fiducia* removed from the law of property, together with *mancipatio* and *in iure cessio*. The *fiducia cum creditore contracta* was replaced with → *pignus*, e.g. in Dig. 10,2,28 (cf. Gai. Inst. 2,220), and the place of the *fiducia cum amico contracta* was taken by *mandatum* (mandate) – in itself already based on → *amicitia* (Paul. Dig. 17,1,1,4): Dig. 17,1,27,1 (with *tradidero* instead of *mancipavero*) and ibid. 30 (with *mandati* instead of *fiducia*).

KASER, RPR I 47, 79, 83, 324, 415, 460–463; II 275, 313; Id., Studien zum röm. Pfandrecht, 1982; A. MANIGK, s.v. F., RE 4, 2287–2316; G. NOORDRAVEN, De f. in het Romeinse recht 1988 (review: F.B.J. WUBBE, in: ZRG 108, 1991, 515–523). D.SCH.

Fig The fig has been indigenous to southern Europe since at least the Neolithic period, as documented by fruit discoveries from Lerna, the Argolid and the Bronze Age at the Mincio. The first literary references are in the Odyssey (e.g. Hom. Od. 11,588; 12,103). The fig is represented by two deciduous species of the genus *Ficus* of the *Moraceae*: (a) *Ficus carica L.* as ἐρινεός (*erineós*), the goat fig as a wild form besides to the συκῆ (*sykê*), the cultivated eating fig that was pollinated by a male plant (*caprificus*) of (a). (b) the sycamore or mulberry fig, *Ficus sycomorus L.* (συκόμορος, συκόμορον; *sykómoros, sykómoron* in Theophr. Hist. pl. 4,2,1–2 and Dioscorides 1,127 p. 1,116f. WELLMANN = 1,181–182 p. 145f. BERENDES). On the occasion of Alexander's campaign to India, Theophrastus learned of the evergreen giant fig *Ficus bengalensis* (Banyan) with prop roots (Hist. pl. 1,7,3 and 4,4,4; cf. Diod. Sic. 17,90; Str. 15,1,694; Plin. HN 12,22f. etc. [3. 158–190]). We do not know whether the species *Ficus benjamina* and *magnoloides* that are often cultivated today in southern Italy were already known in antiquity. The rubber plant tree (*Ficus elastica Roxb.*), a common indoor plant in central Europe, was introduced later.

The sycamore fig (in Plin. HN 13,56f. *ficus aegyptia*) provided the wood for mummy cases. Its tapped latex was recommended by Dioscorides e.g. for stomach troubles and snake bites and in Pliny was used like rennet in the production of cheese (HN 16,181). The eating figs, of which there were various types (Plin. HN 15,68–72), were cultivated everywhere in the Mediterranean as fruits (a very detailed account in Plin. HN); the fruits which are still preferably dried nowadays (ἰσχάς; *ischás* first according to Alexis in Ath. 3,75b, cf. Ath. 14,652 b ff.; Plin. HN 15,82) are produced through artificial pollination with the pollen of the goat fig (ἐρινασμός; *erinasmós, caprificatio*) using fig wasps, ψῆνες (*psenes, culices* Plin. HN 15,80) (the method is mentioned e.g. in Hdt. 1,93, Aristot. Hist. an. 5,32,557 b 25–31, Theophr. Hist. pl. 2,8,1–4 and Caus. pl. 2,9,5, Plin. HN 15,79–81 and Ath. 3,76 d-e [1]). In Plin. HN 15,74f. an anecdote about a fig fruit (*pomus*) from Carthage refers to the demand of the older Cato to destroy the Punic capital city. Medical use is mentioned by Dioscorides (1,128 p. 1,117–120 WELLMANN = 1,183–186 p. 147–150 BERENDES) and Plin. HN 23,117–130 (and *passim*).

In religion and myth figs played a particular role: a sacred fig tree grew between Athens and Eleusis as a supposed present from Demeter to Phytalus (Paus. 1,37,2). The Capitoline she-wolf is said to have suckled Romulus and Remus under an old fig tree (Plin. HN 15,77); the *ficus ruminalis* is therefore named after the *rumis* = nipple of the animal. Other known fig trees are mentioned there too. Figs, as well as grapes, are linked with Dionysus: one of his epithets (like that of Plato [2. 151]) was φιλόσυκος (*philósykos*; 'fig enthusiast'). Connections existed also to Hermes and Priapus (Hor. Sat. 1,8,1ff.).

→ Fruit; → Pomiculture

1 F. OLCK, s.v. Feige, RE 6, 2100–2151 2 H. BAUMANN, Die griech. Pflanzenwelt, 1982 3 H. BREZL, Botanische Forschungen des Alexanderzuges, 1903. C.HÜ.

Figulus Roman cognomen ('Potter'), attested to in the *fasti* of the Republican period for the family of the Marcii and the writer P. → Nigidius Figulus.

KAJANTO, Cognomina 322. K.-L.E.

Figura etymologica see → Figures

Figures (Lat. *figura*; Greek σχῆμα/*schêma*; French *figure*).
A. Overview B. Terminology C. Historical outline D. Definitions E. Questions of the functional-pragmatic approach

A. Overview

Figures are formal phenomena of language beyond the grammatical primary structure. In rhetoric they are treated in the context of → *elocutio* under the category *ornatus* (decoration) and are mostly defined as deviations from normal language usage; if they are few in number, it is considered as paucity of expression (Quint. Inst. 9,3,3). The theory of figures assumes that there is a raw framework of arguments in simple words that has to be clad and ornamented. This procedure will occur in a variety of forms depending on the type of text (poetry, court oration etc.) and speech situation and will take into consideration the recipients' horizon of expectation which will be different in each case. The use and recognition of figures requires culturally generated knowledge: a commonly used figure must first be recognized and isolated so that it can be accepted into the convention of the rhetorical classifications.

The theory of figures, which shows an uninterrupted continuity through the Middle Ages to modern times, appears either as part of more widely ranging rhetoric manuals or in separate representations. Two approaches can be differentiated: the logical-structural approach dominant in ancient rhetoric aims at collecting, naming and classifying figures, while the functional-pragmatic approach analyses the functions and effects of the figure within the framework of steering the recipients, both with regard to the production and interpretation of texts. The logical-structural view was documented in such a large number of figure taxonomies (often with diagrams) that they were equated with rhetoric itself: they range from pragmatic treatment to over-precise subdivisions [1]. Rhet. Her. 1,1,1 and Quint. Inst. 9,1,22 already warned against rhetoric as an art that is practiced remote from reality, a practice which was to discredit the theory of figures in particular after the 18th cent., as it was argued that lay people too speak in figures without instruction and can be impressed by these. It was this very observation that led to the rehabilitation of the theory of figures by modern structuralism, which evaluates rhetoric generally as an attempt to develop a timeless system of strategies of expression valid for all languages, not based on linguistic systematical grammar [15]. The theory of figures in the context of handbooks of rhetoric, poetics and stylistics can therefore be regarded as a cornerstone of modern linguistics and semiotics, particularly of the branch of linguistics that deals with the relationship between form and content of language and the questions of infinite sentence generation (Rhet. Her. 4,43,56; Quint. Inst. 9,1,16). The universal applicability of the theory of figures had already been addressed by Cic. Opt. Gen. 5,14, and answered in the negative: the system of figures known from Greek rhetoric cannot be applied without modifications to Latin which is structured differently. Rhet. Her. 4,10 also dispenses with rendering the Greek terminology in Latin and therefore uses a descriptive model suitable for Latin. This transformation of the theory of figures can also be observed in regard to modern European languages that are also often modelled after the stylistics of Latin. A modern compendium in the spirit of ancient rhetoric is provided by Lausberg although this work is controversial [7] because of its theoretical one-sidedness – the figures are mostly classified only according to one criterion [9]

B. Terminology

The phenomenon of surface structuring of language was noticed early in poetry but it was not referred to by the term *figura* until much later. The Greek expression *schêma* (Cic. Brut. 275; Quint. Inst. 9,1,1) was possibly used in this sense from the time of → Theophrastus. Rhet. Her. speaks of *verborum exornatio* and *sententiarum exornatio* (4,13,18); Cicero already uses *figurae*, but not yet as a part of his terminology (Opt. Gen. 14); in other works he speaks of *lumina orationis* (Orat. 135), *conformatio verborum* and *conformatio sententiarum* (De or. 3,96). Quintilian explains the term *figura* – used as a self-evident *terminus technicus* – as a metaphorical explanatory aid in which the human body is used as an analogy of language (10,1,10): language without figures corresponds to the resting or even lifeless body that is less responsive than one in motion (i.e. with figures), conveying vividness and expressiveness. This image already encapsulates today's problem of evaluating any form of language as a figurative means of expression. Moreover it correlates with the wider use of *figura* denoting the three → *genera dicendi* (Rhet. Her. 4,11; Cic. De or. 3,212). In modern poetics, all types of poetic coding, even poetry as such, are regarded as figures [7. 304]. *Schêma* and *figura* remained in use beyond the Middle Ages, although the figure, as the more commonly used concept, made it into the national languages.

C. Historical outline

Aristotle's Rhetoric does not yet draft any clear system figures but shows only different options and effects of speech ornamentation with regard to word use, arrangement and rhythm that deviate from normal speech usage. Outstanding theoreticians of the theory of figure in particular were → Anaximenes [2], → Theophrastus, who dealt with the figure within the context of his *Lexis* (*Perì léxeōs*), and → Gorgias the Younger, whose work is known at least roughly through the translation of → Rutilius Lupus.

The first Latin rhetoric, the → *Rhetorica ad C. Herennium*, on which most medieval and modern theories of figure are based, refers to unspecified Greek models which the anonymous author simplifies in applying them to the Latin language (4,10). He presents 65 figures (45 figures of expression, 20 figures of content;

4,18; 4,69), under which he also subsumed the → tropes since they are also figurative speech. Quint. Inst. 9,1,25 in his treatment of the figure follows Cicero (De or. 3,201ff.) who, he says, takes a middle path between extreme classification and practical approach and attempts to classify the figure into various supergroups. As important authors of later theories of figure, the following can be mentioned: Ps.-Demetrius, → Alexander [25], → Hermagoras, Phoibammon, Marius Plotius → Sacerdos, → Charisius [3], → Diomedes [4] and → Donatus' [3] grammatical work *Ars Maior*, whose reception was the most lasting, aside from the Rhet. Her.[14] (details on the history of the figure in [10]).

D. Definitions

In the history of rhetorics the definitions of the figure comprised heterogeneous phenomena. The dichotomous model subdivides the figure into figures of thought and figures of words without taking into account the tropes (Cic. De or. 3,200); the trichotomous classification subdivides into tropes (which are evaluated as one-word figures), figures of thought and figures of words (Rhet. Her. 4). The individual assessment resulted in an only moderately stable, but nevertheless tradition-forming system of classification, with the trichotomous model having the greater after-effect. The constant factor of both models is the subdivision into figures of expression, which in turn are divided into grammatical and rhetorical figures, and figures of thought.

(I) Figures of expression or figures of words (*figurae verborum* or *figurae elocutionis*: Quint. Inst. 9,3) are breaks in the normal sentence pattern (Cic. Orat. 135). (1) Grammatical figures (Quint. Inst. 9,3,2) are the result of the infringement of the grammatical rules of work usage and sentence construction, for instance, barbarism (colloquialism, graecism etc.) or soloecism (infringement of syntactical correctness). (2) The rhetorical word figures are differentiated according to three categories of change (*quadrupertita ratio*); already Quintilian demonstrates a consciousness that figures are not based only on the principle of deviation but also on 'the choice, made on the basis of considerations outside of language, from among the formal options provided by language' [7. 296]: a) omission (*detractio/diminutio*) of words that are otherwise indispensable in the syntax, as in the case of the zeugma or the ellipsis, calls for tacit supplementation by the recipients; b) addition (*adiectio*) refers in particular to all figures of accumulation and repetition of words, sounds or the combination of the two; they serve predominantly to boost the affect. These include anaphera, epanalepsis, epiphora, anadiplosis, climax, symploche, polyptoton (*figura etymologica*), paronomasia, synonymia, polysyndeton and asyndeton; c) transpositions (*transmutatio*) are conscious changes in normal word order, like parallelism, → antithesis, chiasm and hyperbaton (often combined with homoioteleuton and homoioptoton) and anastrophe.

(II) Figures of thought or sense (*figurae sententiae*: Quint. Inst. 9,2) relate to the conduct of thoughts, not word or sentence construction. The figures of thought, which are classified differently in the various rhetorics, form an open group. Some of them should be regarded as bordering on tropes or in other classifications should be allocated even totally to the tropes that follow the 4th category of change (*immutatio*, substitution). The possibility of a precise differentiation between the figures of expression and those of thought has been doubted: Cicero (De or. 3,200) postulated that the difference between the two categories was that a figure of expression was destroyed if a word was taken away from it; on the other hand, figures of thought, which he thought more important, (Orat. 136) remain the same even in a different formulation. Quintilian modified this to the effect that a figure of thought can be expressed through various figures of word although this was like splitting hairs because often neither could be separated from each other with regard to the effect (Inst. 9,1,15). The figures of thought include those of address and question and those that refer to the matter (evidence, → comparison) or are addressed to the audience (rhetorical question, licence).

E. Questions connected with the functional-pragmatic approach

A central problem of the theory of figure that was also seen in a differentiated manner in the rhetoric of antiquity, is the contribution of ornamentation to the conveying of content, i.e. the relationship between surface and deep structure. The discussion of this question is not confined to the functional-pragmatic approach but is always also a by-product of the system of classification. Even Aristotle noted in his Rhet. (3,11,15 = 1413a) the emotive, affect-boosting influence of surface phenomena which also supports the process of perception and of memorizing what had been said [7. 326]. This is the beginning of the emotive-functional model that occurs in later theories. Cicero (as also e.g. Isoc. Or. 12,2; Rhet. Her. 4,32) warned against showing off and against speech ornamentation gaining greater importance than content. Not least the disregard of this warning resulted in modern criticism of rhetoric. Aside from stimulating emotion, the author of Rhet. Her. considers the generation of credibility an important function of the figure (4,41), Quintilian, on the other hand, the variety that increases the audience's attention (Inst. 9,1,11; 9,1,21). However, he also attributes an intrinsic value to the *ornatus* (Inst. 8,3,61; cf. Cic. Orat. 138) within the aesthetic of reception (cf. Cic. Brut. 275; De or. 3,190–208), especially as the recipient is pleased by the figure and is therefore more prepared to agree to what is said.

Following ancient rhetoric, figures cannot only be regarded as an aid to persuade or instruct: whoever attempts to express himself, must always draw on figures or figurative language, because language is not a mere materialization of thought but also adds something. In recent research on the figure, the fundamentally figurative nature of language is emphasized and figurativeness is regarded as an intrinsic feature of language. In view of the modern research results, the potential of ancient observations should also be revisited.

→ FIGURES, THEORY OF

1 R. BARTHES, Das semiologische Abenteuer, 1988, 15–101 2 D. BREUER, Rhet. Figur, in: C. WAGENKNECHT (ed.), Zur Terminologie der Lit.-Wiss., 1988, 223–238 3 J. DUBOIS et al., Rhétorique générale, 1970 (Ger. 1974) 4 G. GENETTE, Figures, 1966 5 K.H. GÖTTERT, Einführung in die Rhet., 1991, 40–65 6 J. KNAPE, s.v. Elocutio, HWdR 2, 1022–1083 7 Id., s.v. Figuren-Lehre, HWdR 3, 289–342 8 M. LANDFESTER, Die Kunstsprachen, 1997 9 LAUSBERG, §§ 453–1082 10 J. MARTIN, Antike Rhet., 1974, 248–315 11 H.F. PLETT, Die Rhet. der Figuren, in: Id., Rhet., 1977, 125–165 12 J. RICHTER-REICHHELM, Compendium scholare troporum et figurarum, 1988 13 G.O. ROWE, s.v. Style, Handbook of Classical Rhetoric in the Hellenistic Period 330 B.C.-A.D. 400, ed. S.E. PORTER, 1997, 121–158 14 U. SCHINDEL, Die lat. Figuren-Lehre des 5.-7. Jh. und Vergils Donatkomm., 1975 15 T. TODOROV, Théories du symbole, 1977 (Ger. 1995).

C.W.

Figurine vases Vases worked three-dimensionally using a combination of techniques; figurine vases made by coroplasts, often originating from the same moulds as the statuettes (terracottas). Precursors in Anatolia, Egypt and the Ancient Orient. Greek figurine vases of clay (birds, cattle, horses) in greater numbers from the 14th cent. BC. [1]. Vast production of ointment vessels with glazed clay painting in the 7th–6th cents. BC e.g. in Corinth [2], Rhodes [3] and Boeotia: complete figures, busts, heads, limbs, animals, animal protomes, hybrid monsters, fruits [4]. In Athens the head vessels of Charinus and of more recent workshops come into being from 500 BC [5]; in a parallel manner Sotades manufactures rhyta with three-dimensional groups (Amazon on horseback, camel driver, black man and crocodile) [6]. A type of Attic lekythoi and small jugs from the 4th cent. BC are decorated with colourfully conceived groups of figures (Eros-Aphrodite, Boreas-Oreithyia, Dionysus, winged beings) [7]. Hellenistic figurine vases as a rule merely have a black or red coating and are rarely glazed [8]. The motifs are figures of gods, black boys, actors and caricatures [9; 10]. Several Imperial period workshops in North Africa retain Alexandrian-Hellenistic types of grotesques [11]. – Figurine vases were primarily used as votive offerings or as objects deposited with corpses in graves while in the Imperial period they also served as luxury vessels of glass, bronze and precious metal.

→ Askos; → Rhyton; → Sotades Painter; → Terracottas

1 M.A. GUGGISBERG, Frühgr. Tierkeramik, 1996 2 W.R. BIERS, Mass Production, in: Hesperia 63, 1994, 509–516 (Technik) 3 J. DUCAT, Les vases plastiques rhodiens, 1966 4 S.A. IMMERWAHR, The Pomegranate vase, in: Hesperia 58, 1989, 297–410 5 J.D. BEAZLEY, Charinos, in: JHS 49, 1929, 38–78 6 L. KAHIL, Un nouveau vase plastique du potier Sotades, in: RA 1972, 271–284 7 M. TRUMPF-LYRITZAKI, Gr. Figurenvasen, 1969 O. DEUBNER, Boreas und Oreithyia. Eine attische Figuren-Lekythos, in: Boreas 2, 1979, 53–58 8 K. PARLASCA, Kleinasiatische Terrakotten mit Bleiglasur, in: MDAI(Ist) 40, 1990, 198–199 9 M. SGUAITAMATTI, Vases plastiques hellénistiques de Grande Grèce et de Sicile, in: Numismatica e Antichità classiche 20, 1991, 117–146 10 R.A. LUNSINGH SCHEURLEER, Finally Awake, in: BABesch 68, 1993, 195–202 11 J.W. SALOMONSON, Der Trunkenbold und die Trunkene Alte, in: BABesch 55, 1980, 65–134 12 M. BARBERA, Il tema della caricatura in alcune forme vascolari di età imperiale, in: BABesch 67, 1992, 169–182.

R.H. HIGGINS, Cat. of Terracottas Brit. Museum 1, 1954, 43–60, 2, 1959; I. RICHTER, Das Kopfgefäß, 1967; E. REEDER WILLIAMS, Figurine Vases from the Athenian Agora, in: Hesperia 47, 1978, 356–401; E. WALTER-KARYDI, Die Themen der ostionischen figürlichen Salbgefäße, in: Münchner Jahrbuch der bildenden Kunst 36, 1985, 7–16.

I.S.

Filocalus, Furius Dionysius Roman calligrapher of the 4th cent. AD who possibly created the monumental upper-case letter alphabet of the late Latin inscriptions [2; 3]. His earliest attested work is the → Chronographer of 354 [4]. Later he wrote the inscriptions of the → Epigrammata Damasiana; to Pope → Damasus' epitaph for the martyr Eusebius, F. added his name, describing himself as *cultor* and *amator* (admirer and personal friend) of this pope. Therefore F. was probably an esteemed if not aristocratic Christian. It seems likely that he should be identified with the F. who together with a Melania, probably the aristocratic ascetic → Melania the Elder, is mentioned in Anth. Lat. 120 [1].

1 A. CAMERON, F. and Melania, in: CPh 87, 1992, 140–144 2 A. FERRUA, Epigrammata Damasiana, 1942 3 Id., F., l'amante della bella lettera, in: Civiltà cattolica 1, H. 2125, 1939, 35–47 4 M. SALZMAN, On Roman Time, 1990.

M.SA.

Filter Filters were used for straining and filtering water, wine, oils, perfume, vinegar, honey and liquid medicine. For this purpose various materials were used: linen cloths, bast weave, ash, clay or wood. Greek and Roman antiquity knew different filtering vessels (ἠθμός/*hēthmós*, ὑλιστήρ/*hylistḗr*, *colum*, *infundibulum*, *saccus* etc.), including the superb Macedonian devices of the Hellenistic period, as well as the metal ladles with the sieve-like bottom and the wine sieves mainly known from the Roman Imperial period (Hildesheim silver find, treasure find from Kaiseraugst, and many more), furthermore Etruscan oenochoes with a sieve opening or a conical opening or clay ladles. The Daunian 'drain vessels' (→ Daunian vases) with a perforated mouth also belong here.

R. PETROVSZKY, Studien zu röm. Bronzegefäßen mit Meisterstempeln, 1993; Pompeji wiederentdeckt, exhibition cat. Hamburg 1993, 191, no. 89; J. VOKOTOPOULOU, Führer durch das Arch. Museum Thessaloniki, 1996, 161, 208, 211.

R.H.

Fimbria Roman cognomen ('fringe', 'curl'), attested in the Republican period in the family of the Flavii, also in the Imperial period.

KAJANTO, Cognomina 223. K.-L.E.

Fimbriae (κροσσοί/*krossoí*; θύσανοι/*thýsanoi*). These were actually the thread ends left at the edge of the cloth that – with several knotted together or hanging individually – decorated materials of all kinds such as cloths, blankets and clothes. They could also be worked separately and sewed on. Thus, for example, the ταραντῖνον (*tarantînon*), a luxury garment, or the *rica*, a Roman head scarf, are explicitly defined as trimmed with *fimbriae* (Fest. 288,10; Non. 549,9). The Oriental and Egyptian garments already show evidence of *fimbriae*; they are also documented in Greek, Etruscan and Roman art; extant cloths also have *fimbriae*.

W.H. GROSS, s.v. F., KlP 2, 548; U.MANDEL, Zum Fransentuch des Typus Colonna, in: MDAI(ist) 39, 1989, 547–554; W.SCHÜRMANN, Zur Deutung der Fransentücher im hell.-röm. Ägypten, in: Beiträge zur Ikonographie und Hermeneutik, FS N. Himmelmann, 1989, 297–330; A.STAUFFER, Textilien aus Ägypten aus der Sammlung Bouvier, exhibition cat. Fribourg 1992. R.H.

Finches As neither Greeks nor Romans paid much attention to many small songbirds, there is no clear evidence of them either. Medieval miniatures show both colourful finch species quite frequently (chaffinch e.g. [2. fig. 37 b]; goldfinch e.g. [2. fig. 10, 11 a-b, 15, 42, 44]).

1) Chaffinch (*Fringilla coelebs L.*), σπίζα/*spíza*, σπιζίον/*spizíon*, σπίνος/*spínos*, φρυγίλος/*phrygílos* (Aristoph. Av. 763), ποικιλίς/*poikilís* (interpretation uncertain, Aristot. Hist. an. 8[9],1,609a 6f.), *fring(u)illa* (*-us* Mart. 9,5,7). A songbird with a melancholic-sounding (Mart. ibid.) song (*fringulire*, *friguttire* Varro, Ling. 7,104; Paul Fest. p. 90). In the early morning it was considered as an omen for a storm (Avien. Arati Phaenomena 1761). In the summer it prefers warm areas, in the winter cool ones (Aristot. Hist. an. 8[9],7,613b 3–5). It hangs (Soph. fr. 398 NAUCK²) head first in the hedges (which would rather point to the siskin) and like other species, lives on seeds and worms (Aristot. Hist. an. 7(8),3,592b 16f.). It is humorously identified by Aristophanes (Av. 875) with the god of fertility → Sabazius.

2) Thistle finch, goldfinch (*Carduelis carduelis*), ἀκανθίς/*akanthís*, ἀκανθύλλις/*akanthýllis*, ἀστραγαλῖνος/*astragalînos*, *acanthis*, *acalanthis*, *carduelis*, *cardelis* (Petron. Sat. 46). According to → Dionysius [29] 3,2 [1. 39] it was caught like the chaffinch (*spínos*) with glue make of mistletoe (ἰξός/*ixós*). The bird lives in a meagre manner and is unsightly but sings forcefully (Aristot. Hist. an. 8(9),17,616b 31f.; cf. Theoc. 7,141; Verg. G. 3,338; Calp. 6,7; Paul Nol. 23,12). The *acanthis*, a 'very small bird' (*avis minima*) with 12 eggs (Plin. HN 10,175) is probably rather a species of titmouse. As the finch like other birds and like the donkey lives on thistles, it is supposed to live in enmity with it according to Aristot. Hist. an. 8(9),2, 610 a 4ff. (= Plin. HN 10,205; Ael. NA 4,5). In Rome, as is still the case in southern countries today, people liked to keep it in a cage and even train it because it was a cheerful singer (Plin. HN 10,116; cf. Petron. Sat. 46). A daughter of the Macedonian tribal hero Pierus is supposed to have been transformed into this finch (Antoninus Liberalis 9). Aristophanes (Av. 872) describes the goddess Artemis as a thistle finch, although the allusion is unclear.

1 A.GARZYA (ed.), Dionysii Ixeuticon libri, 1963
2 B.YAPP, Birds in medieval manuscripts, 1981. C.HÜ.

Fines, ad Fines

[1] modern Vinxt. Town at the place (near Sinzig) where the road between Bonn and Remagen reaches the border between Germania inferior and superior (*Obrinkas* Ptol. 29,2; 8f.; cf. *Abrinkas* Marcianus 2,28, < Celt. **aber* 'mouth'). Altars to the *(Nymphae) Fines* have been found there and, on both sides, inscriptions by *beneficiarii* and soldiers (CIL XIII 7713; 7724; 7731f.).

C.B. RÜGER, Germania Inferior, 1968, 47–49. K.DI.

[2] modern Pfyn near Frauenfeld (Switzerland), *vicus* of the 1st–3rd cent. in Raetia on the border with Germania superior (previously Gaul, later Maxima Sequanorum); 300 m south-east of it there was a late Roman fortress high above the river Thur from *c.* AD 300 (1,5 ha.) that probably existed until the mid 5th cent.

TIR L 31,18; J.BUERGI, Pfyn. Ad Fines, in: Arch. der Schweiz 6, 1983, 146–160; W.DRACK, R.FELLMANN, Die Römer in der Schweiz, 1988, 470f.; J.GARBSCH, P.KOS (ed.), Das spätröm. Kastell Vemania bei Isny, 1, 1988, 118; M.HARTMANN, Bemerkungen zu den Mz.-Funden aus Pfyn, in: SM 42, 1992, 126–129. K.DI.

[3] see → Ad Fines

Finger ornaments see → Jewellery

Finis Border, particularly between properties (e.g. Celsius, Dig. 41,2,18,2). The boundary stone (→ *terminus*) was sacred; anyone who ploughed it out of the ground was cursed (*sacer*; Paul Fest. 505,20f. L.) together with the team of oxen, according to a regulation ascribed to → Numa Pompilius. The fields were separated by a 5 feet wide ridge that according to the Twelve Tablets (tab. VII 4) could not be acquired (see → *usucapio*) (Cic. Leg. 1,12,55f.).

The border adjustment suit (*actio finium regundorum*) was an *actio in personam* (personal suit) and yet it was *pro vindicatione rei* (on handing over, Paul Dig. 10,1,1). It concerned in particular rural properties, occasionally also large gardens in Rome (*controversia de fine*, Paul Dig. 10,1,2 pr.; Ulp. Dig. 10,1,4,10), as well as unequal allocations in assigned areas (*controversia de modo*, Mod. Dig. 10,1,7, → *adsignatio*). With the co-operation of the → surveyors, the judge had to initially determine the old border; if this failed, he reset the border, where necessary through another area. Through → *adiudicatio* (judicial arrangement) he granted new property; at the same time he imposed an equalization payment on the beneficiary (Ulp. Dig. 10,1,2,1; Gai. ibid. 3). The judge had to consider distances between the borders which the Twelve Tablet Law had set for buildings and cultivated areas according to the model of the Solonic Law (Gai. Dig. 10,1,13).

Furthermore *finis* occurs as a country border (*f. provinciae, f. patriae*, Dig. 1,18,15; 47,18,1,1). In a figurative sense *finis* is used in regard to legal remedy (*actio*, Dig. 47,4,1,2), a legal concept (*culpa lata*, Dig. 50,16,223) or a behaviour (*deliberare*, Gai. Inst. 2,164). Furthermore *finis* is found in the sense of a sum (Gai. Inst. 4,57), amount (Dig. 50,16,124) or end (*litium, vitae*, Dig. 41,10,5 pr.; 36,1,67,1).

FLACH, 25–28; KASER, RPR I, 138, 142f., 409f.; II, 272, 593; O. BEHRENDS, Bodenhoheit und privates Bodeneigentum im Grenzwesen Roms, in: Die röm. Feldmeßkunst, AAWG 193, 1992, 192–284; R. KNÜTEL, Die actio finium regundorum und die ars gromatica, ibid., 285–310; on both, review F. STURM, in: ZRG 114, 1997, 548–55; F.T. HINRICHS, Zur Gesch. der Klage finium regundorum, in: ZRG 111, 1994, 242–279. D.SCH.

Fire (πῦρ; *pŷr*, Lat. *ignis*).
A. PRODUCTION B. GREEK MYTHOLOGY
C. GREEK CULT D. GREEK PHILOSOPHY
E. ROMAN RELIGION

A. PRODUCTION

In practical life the Greeks had already been using fire since Homeric times for cooking, smithing, sacrificing, firing ceramics, for cremation, heating, lighting, as a signal, as a weapon, for cleaning and for extracting ore. People rubbed sticks (πυρεῖα/*pyreîa*, Theophr. De igne 64 COUTANT) against each other or hit appropriate stones in order to ignite a fire, and as a source of fire, they kept a permanently burning oil lamp or a glowing → narthex staff (Hes. Theog. 567).

B. GREEK MYTHOLOGY

Corresponding to the human division of labour, female and male gods developed who were responsible as donators or patrons for the various duties related to fire: → Hestia, the hearth goddess, held a central position in the home and state (→ Prytaneion or temple) [1], and through her chastity and her tie to the hearth (cf. H. Hom. 5,29f.) she embodied the behaviour desired of a wife or daughter. → Hephaestus, god of the artisan fire, as well as the Telchines, the → Daktyloi Idaioi, were responsible for metal and ceramic work requiring fire. People partly made a connection on a mythical level between smithing and volcanic fire by locating the divine blacksmith's shop in underground caves or in volcanoes (Hephaestus on Lemnos: Hom. Il. 1,593; in Thetis' cave: Hom. Il. 18,398–400; Cyclopes in Aetna: Callim. H. 3,46f., the volcanic nature of Aetna was attributed to the fire-spitting monster → Typhon who had been taken prisoner by Zeus: Pind. Ol. 4,11f.) [2; 3]. With the divine gift of heavenly fire a complex of myths taken up on two occasions by Hesiod was connected (Theog. 535f.; Erg. 47f.): When gods and humans once separated, (ἐκρίνοντο; *ekrínonto*), the Titan son → Prometheus attempted to deceive Zeus with a distribution of the sacrificial meat that was favourable to humankind. Furious about it, Zeus withheld fire from humans; Prometheus stole it and gave it to the humans; therefore he received agonizing punishment. Zeus punished the humans by handing over → Pandora who brought into the world a jar full of evils [15. 181–201]. This complex of myths conceals several traits of Greek marriage, as with the handing over of a bride from the house of her father to that of the bridegroom fire is also passed over in the form of a torch procession after a common meal [4] (→ Marriage).

C. GREEK CULT

From the cooking ritual, key cult actions developed in Greek religion: the torch run (→ *lampadedromía*) to bring new fire – pure from the point of view of the cult – to a new open hearth; the burnt offering itself, with a distinction made between the fire of annihilation (holocaust) and the sacrificial meal shared with the gods (*thysía*); *amphidrómia* to acquaint a newborn child with the home hearth. Torch light was a highly significant element of nightly celebrations (*pannychís*), played a central role in the main act of the Eleusinian → Mysteries in the Telesterion and gave its name to the night celebration on the → Parnassus (*phánai*). From the burnt offering explicit fire festivals developed, e.g. the Daedala, celebrated in honour of Zeus and Hera near Plataia [5; 15. 201f.] (→ Hera), or the sacrifices for → Artemis Laphria in Patrai [15. 116–141] with a huge fire.

In connection with cremation, fire attained an eschatological dimension: as a 'passport' to the Underworld, the Homeric hero received his 'share of fire' (e.g. Hom. Il. 23,75f.). A river Pyriphlegethon, 'blaze', encircled the afterlife; the Eleusinian *mystes*, to whom had been granted the enlightenment of the → *epopteía*, had been promised a happier fortune in the afterlife. According to myth, Hercules, Asclepius and Semele achieved deification through their deaths by flame. The content and store of knowledge of the Orphian Derveni papyrus suggested a link between cremation, cosmology and the belief in an afterlife [6]. Fire in the form of a 'baptism with fire' offered the chance to already attain higher spheres during one's lifetime: in the Homeric Hymn (2,239f.) Demeter would have made prince → Demophon [1] immortal through nightly fire baptism had she not been interrupted in the process; esp. in the → Dionysus cult there is evidence of rites that imply a handling of fire without pain or being burnt (Eur. Bacch. 757f.; fire-walking in the cult of Artemis Perasia: Str. 12,2,7). Possibly the Anastenaria, the fire-walking still practised today in northern Greece, goes back to it [7; 15. 212f.]. The idea that earthly existence could be transcended by fire is based on its purifying power [8], for the elimination or overcoming of the body gave rise to hope for an incorporeal existence (Iambl. Myst. 5,12).

D. Greek philosophy

In philosophy fire also played an important and diverse role. In the course of early Ionian speculation about the origin and composition of the cosmos, → Heraclitus made fire the basic substance and symbol of the universe (12 B 30f. DK: 'The cosmos is an eternally living fire that extinguishes itself in degrees and flares up in degrees'; 12 B 90 DK: all things can be exchanged for a corresponding value in fire, just as goods are exchanged for money) [9]. → Empedocles [1] made fire, under the term 'Helios' or 'Hephaestus', one of the four 'roots' (ῥιζώματα/ *rhizṓmata*) of his cosmogony (together with air, water and earth) that unite into new material or dissolve under the influence of two cosmic forces – love and strife (φιλία/*philía*; νεῖκος/ *neîkos*).

These four basic substances became fixed components of the Theory of the Four Elements (→ Elements, theory of the) for the universe (in Aristotle five elements: the heavenly ether was in principle different from the four sublunar elements), which sought to explain the physical world in a twofold manner: on the one hand, all living creatures and inanimated objects were a mixture of these four elements with fire as the warming, life-giving one; on the other hand, the cosmos itself consisted (according to the most common geocentric view) of a round core of earth surrounded by concentric layers of water, air and – on the outermost edge – ether (= fire). The glowing heavenly bodies represented concentrations of ether. However, a contrasting image is found in many Pythagoreans (→ Pythagorean School) who declared that fire was the central hearth of the universe around which circled our planet earth and the other heavenly bodies (ἑστία τοῦ παντός: Philolaus in Aetius [2] 2,7,7 Diels, DG) [10]; this 'world hearth' was at the same time the seat and centre of power of Zeus who controlled the world (Διὸς φυλακήν, Simpl. cael 230a 9). Among the Stoics (→ Stoicism) ethereal fire was closely linked with the logos of the world (→ Logos): 'creative fire' (πῦρ τεχνικόν (*pŷr technikón*) was supposed to be responsible for the origin of the universe; Zeus steered the world with fiery lightning (see Cleanthes, Zeus hymn fr. 1,10 CollAlex); the universe was dissolved in fire at regular intervals (ἐκπύρωσις/*ekpýrōsis*) [11].

E. Roman religion

Here the eclipsing of an indigenous substratum by foreign (esp. Greek) influence is noticeable. An old fire cult of → Cacus and his sister Caca (cf. Serv. Aen. 8,190: *in quo ei (sc. Cacae) pervigili igne sicut Vestae sacrificabatur*) located on the Palatine appears to have been continued in a similar form through the cult of the state hearth celebrated in honour of → Vesta (= Ἑστία/ *Hestía*) in the small round building close to the *regia*; the priestesses of Vesta (Vestals) were responsible for watching over an eternally burning fire (*ignis inextinctus*: Ov. Fast. 6,297) [12]. Although the Vestals were obligated to remain chaste during their term in office, there is a link between the birth legends of several state founders (esp. Romulus, but also Servius Tullius, Caeculus [13; 14]) with an extra-marital union between a Vestal and a divine father. It does not seem to be out of the question to link the protective gods of a Roman house, the → Penates, to the *penus* (chamber / safe) meant for the storing of special sacred relics in the Vesta sanctuary. The ancient Italian fire god Volcanus (probably an Etruscan name; → Volcanus) originally had a closer relationship with vulcanism (cf. the cult centres in Puteoli: Str. 5,4,6; Mutina: Plin. HN 2,240) than Hephaestus, with whom he was later increasingly identified as the god of the artisan fire and the blacksmith's craft. At the Volcanalia festival in August, living fishes from the Tiber were thrown into the fire for him (cf. Varro, Ling. 6,20). His epithets Mulciber and Quietus as well as the association with → Stata Mater ('who brings the flames to a standstill') indicate an important function of the god in banning of the danger of an annihilating blaze.

→ Energy; → Hearth

1 L. Gernet, The Anthropology of Ancient Greece (English trans. by J. Hamilton, Blaise Nagy), 1981, 322–39 2 M. Détienne, La cité et son autonomie. Autour d'Hestia, in: Quaderni di storia 11.22, 1985, 59–78 3 M. Delcourt, Héphaistos ou la légende du magicien, [2]1982 ([1]1957) 4 L. Séchan, Le mythe de Prométhée, [2]1985 ([1]1951) 5 L. Prandi, L'Heraion di Platea e la festa dei Daidala, in: M. Sordi (ed.), Santuari e politica nel mondo antico, 1983, 82–94 6 G.W. Most, The fire next time. Cosmology, allegoresis, and salvation in the Derveni Papyrus, in: JHS 117, 1997, 117–35 (esp. p. 131–134) 7 L.M. Danforth, Firewalking and Religious Healing. The Anastenaria of Greece and the American Firewalking Movement, 1989 8 K.P. Hatzijoannou, Η χρήση του καθάρσιου πυρός για τον εξαγνισμό και την αθανασία στον ελληνικό χώρο, in: Ἡ Ἐπιστιμονικὴ ἐπετηρὶς τῆς φιλοσοφικῆς Σχολῆς τοῦ Ἀριστοτελίου Πανεπιστιμίου Θεσσαλονίκης, Τμήμα φιλοσοφίας 12, 1973, 53–69 9 C. D. C. Reeve, Ekpyrosis and the priority of fire in Heraclitus, in: Phronesis 27, 1982, 299–305 10 W. Burkert, Weisheit und Wissenschaft: Studien zu Pythagoras, Philolaos und Platon, 1962, 315–335 11 A.A. Long, Heraclitus and Stoicism, in: Philosophía 5–6, 1975–1976, 133–53 12 H. Hommel, Vesta und die frühröm. Religion, in: ANRW 1.2, 397–420 13 A. Brelich, Vesta, 1949, 95–103 14 H.J. Rose, De virginibus Vestalibus, in: Mnemosyne 54, 1926, 440–448 (for the cult) 15 W.D. Furley, Studies in the use of fire in ancient Greek religion, 1981.

M. Delcourt, Pyrrhos et Pyrrha. Recherches sur les valeurs du feu dans les légendes helléniques, 1965; W. Burkert, Neues F. auf Lemnos: Über Mythos und Ritual, in: Id., Wilder Ursprung. Opferritual und Mythos bei den Griechen, ed. by G.W. Most, 1990, 60–76.

W.D.F.

Fire-brigades

I. General II. Republican Rome III. Late Antique Rome and Constantinople IV. Ostia and Puteoli V. The Rest of Italy and the Provinces

I. General

Organized fire-brigades were necessary in larger cities of the Roman Empire; in smaller settlements, help from neighbours was a matter of course (Sen. Controv. 5,5; Sen. Clem. 1,25,5). Efforts were focussed on smothering smaller fires started from open fires (→ Hearth and → lighting) before the fire spread and developed enough heat and consequent draft to become a conflagration. This danger was especially acute in areas where houses were built very close together; during the Imperial period, specific minimal distances between buildings were stipulated in building codes. Fires were fought using buckets of water (*hamae*: Juv. 14,305), blankets soaked in vinegar (*centones*: cf. Dig. 33,7,12,18), pickaxes (*dolabra*: Dig. 1,15,3,3) as well as fire hoses and pumps (*siphones*: cf. Plin. Ep. 10,33,2); which had only a limited capacity [6. 365 f.]. Sources documenting organized fire-fighting in Greece during pre-Roman times are not known.

II. Republican Rome

The *tresviri nocturni* (→ *viginti(sex)viri*) were charged with fire safety and with fighting fires. With the help of slaves, they kept watch at night. The → *aediles* could also be charged with fighting fires (Dig. 1,15,1). During a major fire in 67 BC, the consuls had to intervene (Cic. Pis. 26). In 21 BC, M. Egnatius [II 10] Rufus established a private fire brigade while an aedile. After a major fire in AD 6, Augustus created a fire-brigade, the → *vigiles* (Suet. Aug. 30,1; cf. Cass. Dio 55,26,4 f.).

III. Late Antique Rome and Constantinople

During the reign of the emperor Valentinianus [1] I (364–375), the military organization of the *vigiles* was dismantled [2. 250–262]. Members of professional organizations (→ *Collegium* [1]) were forcibly recruited for fire-fighting, the so-called *collegiati* (Cod. Iust. 11,18). This can be inferred from the parallel development in → Constantinople (Notitia urbis Constantinopolitanae 2,25–28). Here in the year AD 409, 14 *vicomagistri* guarded the regions of the city and used 560 *collegiati* to fight fires (Cod. Iust. 4,63,5). As late as the 6th cent. AD in Rome, if a fire broke out the cry of *omnes collegiati, concurrite!* ('Come here, all *collegiati*!', Lydus, Mag. 1, 50) could be heard.

IV. Ostia and Puteoli

Rome's food supply depended on harbours. For this reason, emperor Claudius [III 1] (41–54) stationed one cohort (→ *cohors*) in → Ostia and one in → Puteoli, presumably → *urbanae cohortes*. In the → Year of four emperors (AD 69), these cohorts were withdrawn. Emperor Trajan [1] (98–117) enlarged Ostia to be the main harbour of Rome. His successor Hadrian had a barracks built there and stationed a → *vexillatio* (→ Ensigns) of *c.* 400 → *vigiles* under the command of two tribunes and four centurions, who were replaced every four months (CIL XIV 4500; 4503–4505). The last evidence for this unit is from AD 241–244. (CIL XIV 4398).

V. The Rest of Italy and the Provinces

Associations (→ Professional associations) of craftsmen who were drawn upon to fight fires (Plin. Ep. 10,33) are documented for many cities in Italy and the western provinces. Specifically responsible for this were the *centonarii* (fire-fighters equipped with *centones*, 'fire mats'; cf. *collegium centonariorum* CIL V 5128 *et passim*). Those not connected with the trade, and honorary members, were also allowed in the associations.

In the year AD 110, Trajan forbade the establishment of a *collegium fabrorum* to fight fires in Nicomedia, because he feared that a political club would develop out of this association (Plin. Ep. 10,34). During a fire in Smyrna in AD 150, the *strategos* commanded the populace to provide fire-fighting equipment (Ps.-Pionios, Vita Polycarpi 28: [8]). This has lead to the conclusion that there were no associations to fight fires in the eastern provinces [9].

→ Fire; → Vigiles; → Housing conditions

1 F. M. Ausbüttel, Untersuchungen zu den Vereinen im Westen des Reiches, 1982 2 A. Chastagnol, La préfecture urbaine à Rome au Bas-Empire, 1960 3 P. Kneissl, Die fabri ... in den Städten Italiens und der westlichen Prov., in: R. Günther, St. Rebenich (ed.), E fontibus haurire. Beitr. zur röm. Gesch. und ihren Hilfswissenschaften, 1994, 133–146 4 R. Lafer, Omnes collegiati concurrite. Brandbekämpfung im Imperium Romanum, 2001 5 O. Robinson, Fire Prevention at Rome, in: RIDA 24, 1977, 377–388 6 R. Sablayrolles, Libertinus miles. Les cohortes des vigiles, 1996 7 H. Vetters, Zu römerzeitlichen Bauvorschriften, in: F. Krinzinger et al. (ed.), Forschungen und Funde. FS B. Neutsch, 1980, 477–485 8 F. X. Funk, F. Diekamp, Patres Apostolici, vol. 2, 1913, 443, 8–11 9 A.H. M. Jones, The Greek City from Alexander to Justinian, ²1966, 215.

H. F.

Firmicus Maternus, Iulius Came from a respected family, not necessarily of senatorial rank, probably from Syracuse, his later place of residence. Educated in Latin as well as Greek, he gave up work as an attorney in Rome during his work on the *Matheseos libri VIII*. Written between the end of AD 334 and the beginning of 337 for his friend Lollianus Mavortius, governor of Campania and proconsul of Africa, it represents the most comprehensive astrological handbook in Latin. In bk. 1, which is Neoplatonically inspired, F. defends astrology as a mystery of salvation and throughout the remainder, interrupted by prayers, he offers the technical explanations, mostly in Lat. terminology. After his conversion to Christianity, it was certainly the same

Firmicus Maternus who between 343 and 350 in *De errore profanarum religionum* exposed the gods of the 'heathens' as dubious humans (2–17), and the symbols and rites of the (Neoplatonically elevated) mystery cults, which can be compared to the Christian ones, as diabolic mimics of the latter (18–27). He called for general conversion (28f.) and was the first to call upon the emperors (using a Florilegium that was originally meant to prevent the Christians from apostasy in the persecution around 250; Cypr. De fortitudine 2–5) to eradicate violently the non-Christian cults. – The *Consultationes Zacchaei et Apollonii* were incorrectly attributed to him by G. MORIN. For lost or announced works [1. 88].

MATH.: W. KROLL, F. SKUTSCH, 1897–1913 (reprint 1968) P. MONAT, 1992 (vols. 1–2) J.R. BRAM, 1975 (Engl. trans.)
DE ERRORE: R. TURCAN, 1982 A. PASTORINO, 1956 (²1969) K. ZIEGLER, 1953.
BIBLIOGRAPHY: 1 W.F. HÜBNER, A. WLOSOK, in: HLL § 515 2 K. ZIEGLER, s.v. F.M., RAC 7, 946–959 3 A. QUACQUARELLI, La sicilianità di F.M., i suoi Matheseos libri e la cultura cristiana delle scienze nel 4° secolo, in: Vetera Christianorum 25, 1988, 303–342 4 J.M. VERMANDER, Un arien d'occident méconnu: F.M., in: Bulletin de Littérature Ecclésiastique 81, 1980, 3–16 5 K. HOHEISEL, Das Urteil über die nichtchristl. Religionen im Traktat De errore ... des Iul. F.M., diss.Bonn 1972 6 G. BLASKÓ, Grundlinien der astrologischen Weltanschauung nach der Mathesis des F.M., diss. Innsbruck 1956. KA.HO.

Firmillianus Important bishop of → Caesarea in Cappadocia (died in AD 268). Shortly after 230 he became bishop and around 250 he instigated the deposition of bishop Fabius of → Antioch [1] who was inclined towards Novatianus. In the dispute on the baptism of heretics, the close friend of → Origenes sided with → Cyprianus [2] of Carthage and opposed the Roman bishop Stephanus I. Informed by Cyprianus, he replied in autumn 256 [1. 248] with a letter originally written in Greek (Cypr. epist. 75 [CCL 3C,582–604]) in which he rejected Stephanus's demands to give up the baptism of heretics and his authoritarian-primatial conduct in the sharpest tone ([1. 250], with terms like *audacia*, *stultitia* etc.). Excommunicated by Stephanus (Euseb. Hist. eccl. 7,5,4), F. presided over the first synod against → Paulus of Samosata and died on the way to the second meeting.

1 G.W. CLARKE, The Letters of St. Cyprian of Carthage. vol. 4, 1989 (Ancient Christian Writers 47), 246–276 (Bibliogr.) 2 P. NAUTIN, s.v. Firmilien, DHGE 17, 249–252. J.RI.

Firmum Picenum Settlement from the early Iron Age; town in the Picenum, *regio V*, on a rise (319 m) on the right bank of the Tinna, modern Fermo (Ascoli P.), 8 km from the Adriatic coast where the harbour was situated (Φίρμον Πικηνόν· ἐπίνειον ... Κάστελλον, Str. 5,4,2 or *castellum Firmanorum*, Plin. HN 3,111). In 264 BC it was a colony with *ius Latii* (Vell. Pat. 1,14,7), five *quaestores*. In the war with Hannibal it sided with Rome, in the Social War it was a Roman base (App. B Civ. 1,47). After the civil wars, veterans of the 4th legion were settled in F.P. (CIL IX 5420; [2. 226,2]). In the wars against the Gothi it was a Byzantine town. From the period of the Latin *colonia* there is a city wall in *opus quadratum* with restoration from the Augustan period; temple and early Christian remains under the cathedral (6th cent., F.P. attested as a bishopric); theatre and cisterns [1]. Inscriptions: CIL IX, p. 508.

1 P. BONVICINI, Le cisterne romane di F., 1972 2 F. BLUME, K. LACHMANN (ed.), Die Schriften der röm. Feldmesser, 2 vols., 1848ff.
NISSEN vol. 2, 423–425; G. NAPOLETANI, F. nel Piceno, 1907; L. POLVERINI (ed.), F.P., 1987; L. PUPILLI, F., Antiquarium, 1990; G. BINAZZI, Picenum (Inscriptiones Christianae Italiae 10), 1995, 24–29. G.U.

Firmus

[1] Senator attested in a fragmentary inscription from Arretium, CIL XI 1834 = ILS 1000. According to [1] based on AE 1967, 355, the name should be C. Petillius Q. f. Pom. Firmus. As *tribunus* of *legio IV Flavia* he took part in a campaign and then received *dona militaria*. He was *quaestor Vespasiani* and was honoured by the Senate with *ornamenta praetoria*. Perhaps a son of → Petillius Cerialis [2. 81ff.].

PIR² F 159.
1 BOSWORTH, in: ZPE 39, 1980, 267ff. 2 T. FRANKE, Die Legionslegaten der röm. Armee ..., 1991. W.E.

[2] A businessman from Seleucia who became rich and powerful through his wide-ranging trade (as far as India). As an ally of Zenobia he organized a revolt of the Alexandrians in AD 273 that led to the disruption of the grain supply to Rome. Aurelianus [3] was able to suppress the revolt (SHA Quadr. tyr. 3–6; Aurel. 32,1–3; Prob. 24,7; Zos. 1,61,1).

PIR² F 162; PLRE 1, 339 F. 1; KIENAST, ²1996, 238. T.F.

[3] Son of the Moorish prince Nubel, brother of Gildo and of Mascezel (Amm. Marc. 29,5,2; 6; 11). Accused of having killed his third brother Zammac (Amm. Marc. 29,5,1f.), he became the leader of an uprising of Moorish tribes against the *comes Africae*, Romanus (Amm. Marc. 29,5,3; [Aur. Vict.] Epit. Caes. 45,7). Around AD 372 he was made emperor by Roman troops (Amm. Marc. 29,5,20; Zos. 4,16,3). He supported the Donatists (Aug. Contra epist. Parmeniani 1,10,16). In 374–375 he was defeated by the *magister militum* Theodosius, the father of the later emperor Theodosius I, and committed suicide (Amm. Marc. 29,5,4–55). PLRE 1,340 (F. 3). W.P.

First Philosophy see → Metaphysics

Firuz see → Perozes [1]

Firuzabad (Fīrūzābād). Town 110 km south of Širāz, Iran. In the plain of F. surrounded by mountain crests, the minor prince Ardašīr Papakan, founder of the Sassanid empire before AD 224, built his circular-shaped town Ardašīr Ḫurra which became his princely seat. In so doing he triggered the power struggle with the Parthian Great King of Iran, Artaban IV (AD 213–224), whose successful outcome is extolled by two rock reliefs in the entrance gorge to the plain. The fortified palace above the gorge was built before, and the larger palace in the plain was built after the decisive battle. A partially preserved tower building in the centre of the circular town probably had not just symbolic significance but also a practical role in the radially-concentric division of the land of the plain. The Būyid ʿAḍud ad-Daula (AD 949–983) changed the name, which had been shortened to Gōr, to F.

D. Huff, Architecture sassanide, in: Splendeur des sassanides: l'empire perse entre Rome et la Chine (224–642). Exhibition cat. Musées royaux d'Art et d'Histoire, 1993, 45–61; P. Schwarz, Iran im Mittelalter nach den arab. Geographen, 1969, 56–59; L. Vanden Berghe, Bibliographie analytique de l'Iran ancien, 1979, 70–71. D.HU.

Fiscus In the time of the late Republic the word *fiscus* on the one hand referred to a container for storing money, on the other hand it already referred to public funds that were placed at the disposal of a promagistrate in the province (Cic. Verr. 2,3,197). Furthermore *fiscus* also meant the private assets of a Roman citizen. In the Principate period the *fiscus* was the cashier's office of the *princeps*; as he alone could dispose of the *fiscus*, he could also exercise considerable influence over politics by using these finances. This already applies to Augustus who spent large sums of money on distributing land and providing for soldiers and who financially supported the *aerarium* through payments from his own assets (R. Gest. div. Aug. 16f.). Tiberius was still making strict delineations between the administration of his private assets and his public duties (Tac. Ann. 4,15,2). Although *fiscus* and *aerarium* are repeatedly compared with each other in the literature (Tac. Ann. 2,47,2; 6,17,1; Plin. Pan. 36; 42,1), it remains unclear how the functions of *fiscus* and *aerarium* should be differentiated precisely. Public earnings also went into the *fiscus*, such as confiscated assets (*bona damnatorum*; *bona caduca* and *vacantia*) or taxes from the provinces (Gaul: Suet. Aug. 40,3); the earnings from Egypt, on the other hand, went into the *aerarium*, according to Velleius Paterculus (Vell. Pat. 2,39,2). Although Seneca still upheld the fiction that the *fiscus* was a private fund of the *princeps* (Sen. Ben. 7,6,3), according to Tacitus it was irrelevant whether money was allocated to the *aerarium* or to the *fiscus* (Tac. Ann. 6,2,1). In Seneca and Pliny the private assets of the *princeps* appear as *patrimonium*, in Pliny they are separated from the public assets, the *imperium* (Sen. Ben. 7,6,3; Plin. Pan. 50,2; cf. already R. Gest. div. Aug. 17,2). As the influence of the *princeps* on the use of money of the *aerarium* increased constantly, the separation of both funds ultimately became politically irrelevant. From the mid 3rd cent. AD the term *fiscus* comprised all earnings and possessions of the Imperium Romanum, although the development cannot be outlined exactly.
→ Aerarium

1 P. A. Brunt, The *F.* and its Development, in: Id., Roman Imperial Themes, 1990, 134–162 2 F. Millar, The Emperor in the Roman World, 1977, 188–190; 197–200 3 Id., The F. in the First Two Centuries, in: JRS 53, 1963, 29–42. H.SCHN.

Fiscus Iudaicus The special tax of two drachmas per person imposed on the Jewish population after the conquest of Jerusalem (AD 70) by Vespasianus (Jos. BI 7,218). The *fiscus iudaicus* (*FI*) replaced the half-shekel tax levied for the Jewish Temple and was regarded as a punitive measure as it was diverted to the temple of Jupiter Capitolinus in Rome. Under Domitianus the *FI* was collected rigourously as a measure for preventing conversions (Suet. Dom. 12,2) [3; 4; 7], but already under Nerva the collection was eased off [1; 4]. The levying of the *FI* is attested until the mid 3rd cent. AD (Orig. Epist. ad Africanum 14).

1 M. Goodman, Nerva, the *Fiscus Judaicus* and Jewish Identity, in: JRS 79, 1989, 40–44 2 C. J. Hemer, The Edfu Ostraka and the Jewish Tax, in: Palestine exploration quarterly 105, 1973, 6–12 3 G. Vermes et al. (ed.), The history of the Jewish people in the age of Jesus Christ (175 B.C.-A.D. 135) 2, 1979, 271–273; 3, 1986, 122f. (rev. Engl. trans. of E. Schürer, Die Gesch. des jüd. Volkes im Zeitalter Jesu, [1]1890ff.) 4 P. Schäfer, Judeophobia. Attitudes towards the Jews in the Ancient World, 1997, 113–116 5 E. M. Smallwood, The Jews under Roman Rule. From Pompey to Diocletian, 1976 6 M. Stern, Greek and Latin Authors on Jews and Judaism 2, 1980, no. 320 7 L. A. Thompson, Domitian and the Jewish Tax, in: Historia 31, 1982, 329–342. I.WA.

Fish dishes (and seafood) Overall term for meals prepared from fish, crustaceans and molluscs. The large range of varieties of fish and seafood in the Mediterranean was very different, depending on the season and area of the catch; consumer taste also changed over time. Of the large number of species used for fish dishes (cf. the catalogues in Plin. HN 9,43–104; Ath. 3,30–36; 7,277–330; 8,355–358; Auson. Mos. 75–149) we should emphasize not only → tuna but particularly → crustaceans, → molluscs, → snails and → cuttlefish that were a more important part in the diet of antiquity than today. At the beginning of the 4th cent. AD top quality sea fish cost on average twice as much as pork (CIL III 2, p. 828 5,1; 2; cf. p. 827 4,1); large specimens were traded at unimaginable prices (Plut. Symp. 4,4,668). Freshwater fish that was less highly regarded by gourmets and only eaten in inland areas not close to the sea (cf. however Plin. HN 9,68) was much cheaper than saltwater fish (CIL III 2, p. 828 5,3–4).

As fish does not keep for a long time without cooling, preserved fish like salted or fermented fish (the latter in the form of the slushy *hallex* or the liquid *garum*; Plin. HN 31,94–95) was widespread in the ancient world. The preserves of saltwater fish were the most common; they were much cheaper than fresh fish (CIL III 2, p. 827 3,6–7; p. 828 5,5).

About two thirds of the fish dishes known from antiquity were made from saltwater fish and seafood, the remainder from freshwater fish. Preparation: fish and seafood were grilled (Apicius 10,1,6–9; 11–13) or boiled (Apicius 10,1,2–5), but only rarely fried. Salted fish was soaked first (Apicius 9,11–13). In haute cuisine sometimes very complicated sauces came with the fish dishes (Apicius 10,1). In the 1st cent. BC fish dishes were the subject of specialized literature which is no longer extant (cf. e.g. Dorion; → Epaenetus). For the lower classes, cheap fresh, salted or fermented fish served as a side dish with their main meal, a mush of pulses or bread made of barley or wheat (Aristoph. Equ. 678–679); in coastal regions fish was considered to be the epitome of a side dish (Ath. 7,276e-f; Plut. Symp. 4,4,667f). In better circles seafood, smaller fish and high quality preserved fish were served as an hors d'oeuvre; on the other hand, larger fish (incidentally a more desired luxury product than fish [Plut. Symp. 4,4,2,668]) were as a rule served as the main course. Fish dishes were more essential in the diet of coastal inhabitants than nowadays. But also in areas further away from the sea, fish, especially in a preserved form, was a food that was affordable for a relatively wide spectrum of classes (Ter. An. 369). Fresh high quality fish from a certain size onwards (e.g. moray, red barbel, sturgeon), however, always remained reserved for the rich (Plin. HN 9,67–68; Ath. 7,302e) who had a high regard for fish dishes as a mark of haute cuisine (Juv. 4). Therefore, fish meals were to a large extent socially distinctive.

J. André, L'alimentation et la cuisine à Rome, [2]1981, 95–113; A. Dalby, Siren Feasts. A History of Food and Gastronomy in Greece, 1996; J. Engemann, s.v. Fisch, Fischer, Fischfang, RAC 7, 959–1097; E. Fournier, s.v. Cibaria, DS 1,2, 1162–1168; N. Purcell, Eating Fish. The Paradoxes of Seafood, in: J. Wilkins, D. Harvey, M. Dobson (ed.), Food in Antiquity, 1995, 132–149; J. Wilkins, Social Status and Fish in Greece and Rome, in: G. Mars, V. Mars (ed.), Food, Culture and History, vol. 1, 1993, 191–203. A.G.

Fishes Aristotle had a knowledge of fish (ἰχθύς; *ichthýs*, Pl. ἰχθύες; *ichthýes*), the modern class of vertebrates, as a sub-group of aquatic animals (ἔνυδρα; *énydra*) that was almost even better than his knowledge of birds, and he provides about 133 names in the *Historia animalium*. Of these however many sea fish must remain unidentified. He was informed by experienced fishermen whom he questioned, for example, at the rich fish market in Athens. He clearly distinguishes the cartilagenous fish that are phosphorescent in the dark as σελάχη (*seláchē*; of σέλας, *sélas*, 'light') [1. 55], namely → sharks and rays (→ Electric ray) from the common bony fish, and he distinguishes among the latter according to their habitats *thaláttia* (sea fish) and *potámia* (river fish) as well as according to sea zones, such as the shore area, the stony bottom and the depths. Major passages in Aristotle: Hist. an. 2,13,504b 13–505b 4 (external features); 4,8,533a 25–534b 10 (ability to smell); 4,10,536b 32–537b 3 (sleeping and waking); 4,11,538a 1–b 2 (parthenogenesis in the → eel, sexual differences); 5,5,540b 6–541a 3 (procreation); 5,9, 542b 32 5,11,543b 31 (spawning seasons); 6,10,564b 14 – 6,12,566b 6; 6,13,567a 17 – 6,17,571b 2 (details of viviparity and oviparity); 7(8),2,591a 7–592 a 29 (means of nutrition) 7(8),13, 597 b 31–599a 3 (migrations); 7(8),15, 599b 2–600a 10 (hibernation); 7(8),19, 601b 9– 7(8),20,603a 11 (?) (growth and diseases); 8(9),2,610b 1–19 (friends and enemies) and 8(9),37, 620b 10–621b 28 (special features). The mammals that also live in the water like the → dolphin and the → whale, however, are not always clearly distinguished from the fish. Viviparity in cartilaginous fish was well known to Aristotle.

Plin. HN bk. 9 and 32, without any distinction between fish and water mammals, provides equally extensive material; like Aristot. Hist. an. 2,14,505b 18–22 he mentions the only 'legendary fish', the *echenais/echeneis = remora* (Plin. HN 9,79 and 32,2–6; cf. Ael. NA 2,17 [1. 59f.]). This fish originated in the desire to explain the currents of the Black Sea that impaired navigation and were barely predictable. Additional important sources of the ancient knowledge of fish are – apart from Aelianus [2] – Athenaeus [3], who among other things cites fragments from Aristotle's students Clearchus of Soli and the zoologist Dorion, as well as Oppian's *Halieutika* and Ovid's homonymous didactic poem. Amongst the Romans, the breeding of fine fish in special fish ponds (details in Colum. 8,16–17) was especially important for luxury dining [2. 2,339ff.] from 100 BC onwards.

For the religious significance of the fish see → Ichthys.

1 R. Strömberg, Studien zur Etymologie und Bildung der griech. Fischnamen, 1943 2 Keller. C.HÜ.

Fishing, Fishing trade

I. Ancient Orient II. Egypt III. Greece and Rome

I. Ancient Orient

Especially in the south of Mesopotamia with its river courses, canals and swamps, fish greatly supplemented the diet; in addition there was fish breeding in ponds for fresh fish. Fishing was mainly done with fish traps and nets and more rarely with spears. The catch was measured by numbers of fish or by volume, but hardly ever according to weight. Preserved fish too (dried, smoked, salted) served as food, and was also suitable for trade

with the mountainous countries in the east that were rich in raw materials. Sea fishing (with nets) in the Persian Gulf did not play an important part. For the use of waters, silver instead of fish was paid to the state in the 3rd and in the 1st half of the 2nd millennium.
→ Fish dishes

R.K. Englund, Organisation und Verwaltung der Ur III-F., 1990; A. Salonen, Die Fischerei im alten Mesopot. (Annales Academiae Scientiarum Fennicae Ser. B, Tom. 166), 1970; M. Van de Mieroop, Society and Enterprise in Old Babylonian Ur, 1992, 181–183. WA.SA.

II. Egypt

From Egyptian prehistory, fish was the most important protein-containing food for the majority of the population. Finds of parts of catching implements, pictorial sources in tombs and written evidence provide information about fishing in the Nile and in the waters of the → Delta [1] and the → Faiyum; we can assume that fishing was carried out in the sea. Fishing with drag nets and fish traps in particular was economically important. Fishermen are represented as simple people; images depicting the owners of the tombs fishing with spears or rods have religious connotations or illustrate a state of leisure. Fresh and dried or salted fish served as goods for redistribution and trade.

D.J. Brewer, R.F. Friedman, Fish and Fishing in Ancient Egypt, 1989; D. Sahrhage, Fischfang und Fischkult im alten Ägypten, 1997. HE.FE.

III. Greece and Rome

In the epics of Homer fishing is mostly mentioned in similes (e.g. Il. 16,406ff.; Od. 12,251ff.; 22,384ff.). The heroes prefer to eat meat and only catch fish if they are ravenously hungry (Hom. Od. 12,330ff.; 4,368f.). Nevertheless Odysseus emphasizes wealth of fish as one of the blessings of a land ruled by a just king, along with prosperity in grain, fruit and cattle (Hom. Od. 19, 108ff.). At an early time, fishing guaranteed food and was carried out both in the sea – mostly close to the coast – and in rivers or lakes. The methods of catching that are listed systematically by Plato in the *Sophistḗs* (Pl. Soph. 219a–221c), vary according to the species of fish, the reasons for and times of catching. The fishermen used fish hooks of varied size and shape made of bone, horn, bronze or copper; multiple hooks were used to catch larger fish or for fishing on the bottom of the sea; the fishing line was made of horse hair or flax, and fishing was also done without a rod (Opp. Hal. 3,76ff.). Greek fishermen made bait out of colourful woollen threads and this proved its worth for fishing in the sea (Ael. NA 15,10) and in Macedonian rivers (Ael. NA 15,1). For spearing the fish, long spears, harpoons or multi-pronged forks were used and the trident was used particularly in tuna fishing (Aristoph. Vesp. 1087; Opp. Hal. 3,88ff.). Fishing with fish traps, mostly with barrel-like spanned nets plaited from bulrush or reed (Plin. HN 21,114), the entrances of which were shaped like a funnel so that the fish went in but could not get out again, yielded greater dividends than fishing with a rod and line, harpoon or trident (Opp. Hal. 4,53ff.). The most important tool was the net (Opp. Hal. 3,80ff.). A throw net, thrown out by one person and immediately drawn in again, was frequently used; this was a solid purse seine woven from thick cords that was held open by an iron hoop attached to its edge and drawn with ropes. There were also dragnets that were made heavy with rocks or lead at the bottom in order to keep them in a vertical position; cork pieces kept a net on the surface (Aesch. Cho. 506f.); in this way the dragnet widened into a wide pocket while the fishermen pulled the net along from the boats (Verg. G. 1,142). On Euboea fishermen went fishing at night with torch light (cf. Pl. Soph. 220d), using dolphins as 'helpers' (Opp. Hal. 5,425ff.). Even fishing with poison was practised (Opp. Hal. 4,647–693).

The catching of tuna fish is described in detail in ancient literature (Plin. HN 9,44–53; Ael. NA 15,5; Opp. Hal. 3,620–648; Philostr. Imag. 1,13). It was known that tuna moved through the Mediterranean Sea in large schools during certain seasons (May to October; Aristot. Hist. an. 599b). At the corresponding places on the coast, tuna guards initially kept watch for the approach of schools of fish (Aristoph. Equ. 313) and then also directed the fishing boats. There is evidence of such tuna guards for the Etrurian coast and for North Africa (Str. 3,2,7; 5,2,6; 5,2,8; 17,3,16). Numerous fishermen often worked together to catch the tuna (cf. also St. 1,2,16: swordfish). Aristotle describes midsummer fishing on the Bosporus during the so-called 'turning' of the sea (Hist. an. 600a) when Sirius rises. In winter fishermen caught sturgeons in the Black Sea, which were the size of dolphins (St. 7,3,18); the inhabitants of the Pontus areas put up their tents on the ice for fishing and fished in the holes in the ice (Aristot. Mete. 348b).

Fishing could certainly contribute to the wealth of a town; this applies for instance to Byzantium (Plin. HN 9,50f.; Tac. Ann. 12,63). The most important extant work on fishing is the extensive *Halieutiká* by Oppian written in hexameters (5 bks., late 2nd cent. AD) that not only describes the species of fish and their way of life (Hal. 1–2) but also provides comprehensive information on fishing. Passed down to us only in fragments is a book about fishing by Ovid attested to in Pliny (Plin. HN 32,11–13). In the Anthologia Graeca there are informative epigrams on the life of the fishermen (Anth. Gr. 6,4f.; 6,23–30; 6,33; 6,38; 6,89f.; 6,105; 6,230).

1 H.-G. Buchholz et al., Jagd und Fischfang (ArchHom J), 1973 2 T. Gallant, A Fisherman's Tale, 1985 3 H. Höppner, Halieutika, 1931, 109ff. CH.KU.

Fish-plate Archaeological research regards the fish-plate (FP) as a plate that is decorated with paintings almost exclusively of fish and other marine animals (mussel, cuttlefish, prawn, shrimp, electric ray, seahorse and many more); other motifs are rare (e.g. grasshopper, head of a woman or purely floral ornament). FP have a wide standing ring and a handle of varying height. Their dish, with an edge bent round to the outside, inclines in a trough shape towards the deepened centre. As a ceramic workpiece, this plate shape is already known for the late archaic period, but it was not until almost the end of the 5th cent. BC that it was decorated with the main motif after which it was named. The production reached its height in the western Greek ceramic centres (with the exception of Lucania) around 350 BC, from which over 1,000 examples are known; it ended around 300 BC. The question of a secular, sepulcral or cultic function of the FP is unsolved, but a lead table from Miletus with dishes and a FP with fish arranged on it in the shape of a circle seems to support its secular use as an eating plate [1.pl. 21]; its use in *kóttabos en lekánēi* (→ Kottabos) is uncertain. The later Hellenistic black-varnished plates are related in shape.

1 W. Schiering, Milet: Eine Erweiterung der Grabung am Athenatempel, in: MDAI(Ist) 29, 1979, 100–101.

I. McPhee, A.D. Trendall, Greek Red-figured Fish-plates, AK 14. Beih., 1987; Id., Addenda to Greek Red-figured Fish-plates, in: AK 33, 1990, 31–51; R. Lindner, Att. F., in: AA, 1985, 251–254; N. Kunisch, Griech. F., 1989; N. Eschbach, Bewohner des Meeres, in: W. Martini, W. Hornbostel, Bilder der Hoffnung. Jenseitserwartungen auf Prunkgefäßen Süditaliens, exhibition cat. Gießen-Hamburg 1995, 64–65, no. 25; R. Hurschmann, Die unterital. Vasen des Winckelmann-Instituts der Humboldt-Universität zu Berlin, 1996, 21–22, no. 6; S.J. Rotroff, Hellenistic Pottery, in: Agora 29, 1997, 417–418, no. 1713–1719.

R.H.

Fissi dies see → Fasti

Fist-fighting (πυγμή, πύξ; *pygmḗ*, *pýx*; *pugilatio*, *pugilatus*). There is already evidence of the discipline in the pre-Greek period (Egypt [1. N 1–2]; Mesopotamia [2. fig. 69; 3. 16f.]) and it was also practised in ancient marginal cultures (Etruria [4. 181–268]; representation on *situlae* [4. 168–174; 185f.; 226–231]; Lucania [5. 54f.]). In the early Greek Aegean area impressive documents from Thera (fresco of the so-called 'boxing princes') [6. pl. 38; 7. 43–45] and the depiction on a rhyton from Hagia Triada [6. pl. 106f.; 7. 43–45] [8] provide evidence of its existence. The oldest literary description of a boxing match – which is followed by countless others in the epic right through to the *Dionysiaká* of Nonnus [9] – is to be found in the *Iliad* (Hom. Il. 23,651–699) within the context of the funerary games for Patroclus, where the athletes, girded and equipped with leather straps (ἱμάντες; *himántes*), are involved, after trading verbal provocations, in a fierce exchange of blows. Its bloody end that occurs when the loser is incapable of fighting, is characteristic of the rigour of this discipline that could only be escaped by withdrawing from the registration for the event or by giving up (ἀπαγορεύειν) [10. 10]. As the event was not divided into weight classes (although probably into age groups), a tall heavy fighter had the best chance of winning (Philostr. *Perì gymnastikês* 34). Nevertheless there were athletes who placed greater emphasis on technique than on fighting strength (e.g. Hippomachus in Paus. 6,12,6; Melancomas in Dion Chrys. Orationes 28,29; cf. Verg. Aen. 5,430f.).

There was no time limit or break in the fighting; the limit on the period of action of the fighting pair was occasionally determined by putting up barriers [2. fig. 81f.] or by attaching them to each other [7. 44 and fig. 10f.]. Onomastus of Smyrna, the first fist-fighting winner in Olympia (23rd Olympic Games = 688 BC) [11. no. 29], is said to have written the first rules. The view, frequently expressed in secondary literary in an exaggerated manner, that only blows to the head were allowed, is not convincing [12. 293f.]; it is of course undoubtedly the case that these were the most effective. The image used in satirical epigrams of the boxer disfigured beyond recognition who loses his inheritance as a result (Anth. Pal. 11,75 [13. 204–209]) was probably quite often realistic. A faithful image of a fist-fighter marked by the fight and bleeding marks from numerous wounds caused by the blows is presented by the late Hellenistic bronze statue in a sitting position of the so-called 'Seated Boxer' that was created in the tradition of the image of Hercules, the ideal for all athletes [14. 150–174; 201–203]. The participation of the upper class in fist-fighting, for which there is ample evidence for the Archaic and Classical periods, should also be regarded as applicable to later periods [15. 73f.; 78f.]. The Rhodian aristocratic family of the Diagorides that produced four Olympic victors in the 5th cent. BC in three successive generations is an illustrious example of the way in which the aristocracy participated in this discipline [16. 136–138]. Because of the risk of injury, training was done with padded boxing gloves (σφαῖραι; *sphaîrai*) and head protection (ἀμφωτίδες; *amphótides*) and involved working out with the sand bag (κώρυκος; *kṓrykos*) and shadow-boxing (σκιαμαχεῖν; *skiamacheîn*) [12. catalogue s. vv.]. The most famous fist-fighter in antiquity was Theogenes from the island of Thasos, who had a total of 1,300 victories (including the successes in the → pankration) and remained undefeated in his special discipline for 22 years [17. no. 37].

In Rome there was not just a Greek fist-fighting tradition but Rome had its own as well, also in the form of group fights (*pugiles catervarii*) [18. 1313f.] for which Augustus had a predilection (Suet. Aug. 45,2). Here too, with the *caestus* [19; 2. 75–79; passages and literature: 11. 277], a brutal boxing glove was developed that had metal parts (and often to protect the fist-fighter from blows, it also had bandages stretching over the upper arms). Its punching effect considerably surpassed that of the effective leather straps (ἱμάντες ὀξεῖς; *himántes oxeîs*) that in Greece superseded the simple leather straps from the 4th cent. BC [2. 68–70].

1 W. Decker, M. Herb, Bildatlas zum Sport im Alten Äg., 1994 2 M. Poliakoff, Combat Sports in the Ancient World, 1987 3 R. Rollinger, Aspekte des Sports im Alten Sumer, in: Nikephoros 7, 1994, 7–64 4 J.-P. Thuillier, Les jeux athlétiques dans la civilisation étrusque, 1985 5 A. Pontrandolfo, A. Rouveret, Le tombe dipinte di Paestum, 1992 6 S. Marinatos, M. Hirmer, Kreta, Thera und das myk. Hellas, 1959, repr. 1986 7 S. Laser, Sport und Spiel (ArchHom T), 1987 8 J. Coulomb, Les boxeurs minoëns, in: BCH 105, 1981, 27–40 9 F. Fiedler, Der F. in der griech. Dichtung, in: Stadion 18, 1991, 1–67 10 M. Poliakoff, Studies in the Terminology of Greek Combat Sports, ²1986 11 L. Moretti, Olympionikai, 1957 12 G. Doblhofer, P. Mauritsch, U. Schachinger, Boxen (Quellendokumentation zur Gymnastik und Agonistik im Alt. 4), 1995 13 L. Robert, Les épigrammes satiriques de Lucillius sur les athlètes. Parodie et réalités, in: Entretiens 14, 1968, 181–295 14 N. Himmelmann, Herrscher und Athlet, 1989 15 H. W. Pleket, Zur Soziologie des ant. Sports, in: MededRom 36, 1974, 57–87 16 W. Decker, Sport in der griech. Ant., 1995 17 J. Ebert, Epigramme auf Sieger an gymnischen und hippischen Agonen, 1972 18 E. Mehl, J. Jüthner, s.v. Pygme, RE Suppl. 9, 1306–1352 19 J. Jüthner, s.v. caestus, RE 3, 1319–1321.

W. Rudolph, Olympischer Kampfsport in der Ant., 1965.

W.D.

Fistula see → Water-pipes

Fixed stars

I. Ancient Orient II. Greece and Rome

I. Ancient Orient

Sumerian and Akkadian languages do not distinguish between fixed stars and planets: for both MUL or *kakkabu* is used. Nevertheless the movement of the planets in relation to the fixed stars was known. Individual fixed stars certainly rarely had their own names (e.g. Li_9-si_4 = Antares), but most were grouped into → constellations. According to their position in the sky, they were initially roughly organized in the so-called → astrolabia (earliest example around 1100 BC), then more precisely in the astronomical compendium MUL.APIN (around 1000 BC) [1]: the 'paths' of the gods Enlil, Anu and Ea correspond to sections of the horizon in the east over which the fixed stars rise [2. 31]. MUL.APIN also classifies the fixed stars according to their rising and setting in the course of the year. In the observational texts of the 1st millennium BC, the positions of the moon and the planets are shown relative to certain fixed stars close to the ecliptic, the so-called normal stars [3. 43–50]. → Astronomy; Zodiac

1 H. Hunger, D. Pingree, MUL.APIN, An Astronomical Compendium in Cuneiform, 1989 2 E. Reiner, D. Pingree, Babylonian Planetary Omens 2, 1981, 17f. 3 A.J. Sachs, Babylonian Observational Astronomy, in: F.R. Hodson (ed.), The Place of Astronomy in the Ancient World, 1974, 43–50 4 E. Weidner, s.v. F. RLA 3, 72–82.

H.HU.

II. Greece and Rome

According to the Greek concept, the fixed stars, the Greek term is ἀπλανής (= *aplanḗs inerrans, inerrabilis*) *sc.* ἀστήϱ (*astḗr*), were 'attached' (*[in-, ad]-fixae*) like nails (Anaximenes A 14 DK: ἥλων δίκην καταπεπηγέναι), to the inside of the hollow sphere of the sky. In contrast to the planets, they only participate in the apparent daily rotation of the sky, and they are the fastest at the equator and reduce down to zero towards the poles. The misleading term 'fixed' is to be found in the literature from the time of Seneca (Nat. 7,24,3: *fixum et immobilem populum*).

In Homer's *Iliad* we find the Pleiades, Hyades, Orion and the She-Bear (= Plough), whilst in the *Odyssey* we also encounter Bootes. The circum-polar stars assisted seafarers with navigation: the Phoenicians used the more precise Little Bear closer to the pole whilst the Greeks used the Great Bear (Arat. 37–44). The daily rotation helped to determine the time at night and the annual rising and setting was a means of dividing up farm work. Eight phenomena were differentiated: the apparent or actual rising and setting, in each case in the evening (acronychal) or in the morning (heliacal). Together with weather signs (ἐπισημασίαι; *episēmasiai*) (esp. those of the Pleiades, Capella and Sirius) they were recorded on → parapegmata. As a harbinger of a storm Arcturus speaks the prologue in the Plautinian *Rudens*. Eudoxus' *Katasterismoí* enumerate individual fixed stars within the individual constellations but do not give details of positions (documented in Hyg. Poet. Astr. 3). Eudoxus of Cnidus noted risings of fixed stars or whole constellations in common with parts of the → ecliptic upon which are based the influential *Phainómena* of → Aratus [4]; both are criticized by Hipparchus.

There is evidence for Eudoxus' catalogues of fixed stars (the number of 1,080 fixed stars given by the anonymous writer of the Commentatorium in Aratum Reliquiae p. 128,13 Maass – which only applies to the definite constellations – is certainly an overestimate). The catalogue of Hipparchus [1; 4] which was written as a result of the observation of a nova in 134 BC and is partly extant probably comprised *c.* 760–850 stars. The declination (= distance to the celestial equator) and the co-culmination (= length of the simultaneously culminating degree of the ecliptic) served as co-ordinates. Because this method depends on latitude, it was superseded in the early modern age by equatorial longitude. According to their position, the fixed stars are classified into three groups: on the *c.* 12° wide band of the ecliptic, north or south of it. For the following periods, the catalogue of Ptolemy (Syntaxis 7,5–8,1; then Hephaestion of Thebes, Apotelesmatika 1,3–5) became important – with 1,022 stars according to his own addition that were classified into six size classes – 15 of the first size, 45 of the second, 208 of the third, 474 of the fourth, 217 of the fifth, 49 of the sixth and 5 nebulous ones (νεφελοειδεῖς), as well as the Coma Berenice. As a rule, Ptolemy adds 2°4' to the longitudes of his predecessor, based on his precession value (→ ecliptic) being too high. In the *Apotelesmatika* (1,9) he establishes the κρᾶσις (*krâsis*; 'mixture') of the fixed stars or parts of constellations mostly according to the temperament of two planets (the nebulous fixed stars are like the moon). Although the colour of the fixed stars was probably a starting point [3], mythological speculations also played a part [7]. The catalogue of Theon of Alexandria records in his Πρόχειροι κανόνες ('Handy Tablets') only the fixed stars of the ecliptic – starting at Regulus; for other anonymous records with interpretations see CCAG V 1 (1904), 212–226. A record (later also expanded) of the 30 brightest fixed stars of first or second size [3. 77–82] remained particularly influential. Firm. Math. 6,2 emphasizes the four *stellae regales* that are aligned according to the four areas of the world: Aldebaran and Antares that as two of the six reddish stars (ὑπόκιρροι; *hypókirrhoi*) are said already in the catalogue of the *Sýntaxis* to lie exactly opposite each other, as well as Regulus and Fomalhaut.

The distance and size of the fixed stars were discussed but to a large extent underestimated. That is why astronomers were also unable to observe the parallax (with the exception of the moon). Astronomers even took into consideration the motion of the fixed stars but were unable to put this theory into practice. The representation of their shape as a sphere analogous to that of the sun, moon and earth came close to postulating a perfect supralunar world unlike hypotheses of cone or pyramid shapes. Fire was the substance of the fixed stars; however, it was debated whether this fire as the ethereal πέμπτη οὐσία (*pémpt-́e ousia* → quinta essentia) could be separated from the earthly one or not. Because of the fiery nature of the fixed stars they were regarded as divine, and to some extent also as the manifestation of the immortal part of human souls after death.

→ Astrology; → Astronomy; → Euctemon; → Calendar; → Milky Way; → Constellations; → Zodiac

1 F. Boll, Die Sternkataloge des Hipparch und des Ptolemaios, Bibliotheca Mathematica III 2, 1901, 185–195 2 Id., s.v. F., RE 6, 2407–2431 3 Id., Ant. Beobachtungen farbiger Sterne, 1916 4 H. Vogt, Versuch einer Wiederherstellung von Hipparchs Fixsternverzeichnis, in: Astron. Nachr. 224, 1925, 17–32 5 S. Feraboli, Sulle tracce di un catalogo stellare preipparcheo, in: Mosaico (FS U. Albini), 1993, 75–82 6 H. Hunger, D. Pingree, MUL. APIN, An Astronomical Compendium in Cuneiform, 1989 7 W. Hübner, Astrologie et myth. dans la Tétrabible de Ptolémée d'Alexandrie, in: Sciences exactes et sciences appliquées à Alexandrie, 1998. W.H.

Flaccinator Roman cognomen, → Folius [I 2–3].

Flaccus Roman *cognomen* ('floppy-eared'), probably originally an individual *cognomen*, in the Republican period especially widespread in the senatorial families of the Fulvii, Norbani and Valerii, and in the Imperial period also among numerous other families. Nickname of the poet Q. → Horatius F.

Degrassi, FCap. 144; Degrassi, FCIR 252; Kajanto, Cognomina 240. K.-L.E.

[1] **Statilius F.** Writer of epigrams. The *cognomen* F. is often mentioned in combination with the *nomen* Statilius (Στατύλλιος Φλάκκος; *Statýllios Phlákkos*). He lived at the beginning of the 1st cent. AD, if the Latin version of Anth. Pal. 7,542 is actually the work of Germanicus. There is no proof of his being identical to the Epicurean Statilius who fell in battle at Philippi (42 BC) nor is there evidence of his identification with the F. whose death we are reminded of in Sen. Ep. 63.1. It is sheer hypothesis to assign his 14 epigrams (6,165 should perhaps be attributed to another F., cf. FGE 46–49) to the 'Garland' of Philippus. The mostly conventional poems – love, anathematic, funerary and epideictic epigrams – nonetheless demonstrate *hapax legomena* (cf. 6,196), excentric themes (9,37 and 117) as well as sophisticated variations on the same theme (12,25–27, cf. Tullius Laureas 12,24; perhaps also 9,44–45).

GA II 1,422–431; 2,451–457. M.G.A.

[2] Poet from Patavium (Mart. 1,76,2; 10,48,5), friend of Martial (Mart. 1,61,4), toured Cyprus in AD 93/4 (Mart. 8,45,1; 7f.; 9,90,9). M.MEI. and ME.STR.

Flacilla Aelia Flavia F. First wife of the emperor Theodosius I; three children were born of the marriage contracted in *c.* AD 376: the later emperors → Arcadius and → Honorius as well as → Pulcheria. In 379 F. was appointed *Augusta*. The committed supporter of Nicene Christianity (Sozom. Hist. eccl. 7,6; Theod. Hist. eccl. 5,19) was considered pious and charitable. When she died in 386 in Skotumis (Thrace), Gregorius [2] of Nyssa held the funerary oration (PG 46, 877–892). Her statue was erected in the Senate building (Them. Or. 19,228b). PLRE 1, 341f. K.G.-A.

Flamines Roman priests who with the → pontifex, the → rex sacrorum and the → Vestals form the *collegium pontificum* and are part of the *collegia maiora*. They are responsible for the cult of individual deities (Cic. Leg. 2,20). Three *flamines maiores* perform the rites of the cult of the old state gods Jupiter (*flamen Dialis*), Mars (*flamen Martialis*) and Quirinus (*flamen Quirinalis*); there are also twelve *flamines minores* (Volcanalis, Cerialis, Carmentalis, Portunalis, Volturnalis, Palatualis, Furrinalis, Floralis, Falacer, Pomonalis and two additional unknown ones). According to tradition, the old priestly office goes back to → Numa (Varro, Ling. 7,45; Cic. Rep. 2,26; Liv. 1,20,2). The *flamines* were appointed by the *pontifex maximus*. The three *flamines maiores* came from Patrician lineages (Cic. Dom. 38; Fest. 137 L.; Tac. Ann. 4,16) [1]. Their office was for life although the *flamen Dialis* had to give it up after the death of the *flaminica*, his wife (Gell. NA 10,15,22; Plut. Quaest. Rom. 50,276e-f).

The *flamen Dialis* is described as 'celebrating every day' (*cotidie feriatus*, Gell. NA 10,15,16) and never separated himself from his religious role: he always wore the *toga praetexta* – in contrast to the two other *flamines maiores* who only wore it while they were on duty (Serv. Aen. 8,552) – and a cap made of leather from an animal sacrificed to Jupiter, on the top of which was a little wooden rod wrapped around with woollen thread (Gell. NA 10,15,32; Serv. Aen. 2,683; Fest. 9 L.). He had at his disposal the → *sella curulis* (Liv. 1,20,2; 27,8,8; Plut. Quaest. Rom. 113,291b-c) and a → *lictor* (Fest. 82 L.). He had to be the offspring of parents who had contracted marriage through → *confarreatio* and he himself had to be in a marriage of such kind (Tac. Ann. 4,16; Serv. Aen. 4,103; 374). Numerous prohibitions prevented him from being ritually unclean (Gell. NA 10,15 according to Fabius Pictor; see also Plut. Quaest. Rom. 109–112,289f–291b) [2]: Among other things, he was not allowed to mount a horse (Plin. HN 28,146; Plut. Quaest. Rom. 40,274b-e; Fest. 71 L.), see an army (Fest. 295 L.), swear an oath, wear a ring, see a person in chains (Serv. Aen. 2,57) or have a knot on him (Fest. 72 L.), nor could he touch, see or refer to yeast, raw meat, goat, dog, ivy (Fest. 72 L.) or beans (Plin. HN 18,119) and he was not allowed to leave his bed for longer than two nights; he also had to avoid all contact with death and graves. Other bans related to his hair and nails. The *flamen Dialis* sacrificed a sheep at the Ides (Ov. Fast. 1,587f.; Macrob. Sat. 1,15,16) and celebrated *confarreatio* (Serv. Georg. 1,31) with the *pontifex maximus*. With the *flaminica* he took part in the purification rites in February (Ov. Fast. 2,21ff.), the → *lupercalia* (Ov. Fast. 2,282f.) – with the unsolved problem of how this is consistent with the dog sacrifice of the festival (Plut. Quaest. Rom. 68,280b-c) and the presence of the goat that was sacrificed by the *luperci* and whose hide was worn in the form of a belt (Plut. Romulus 21,6ff., 31bff.; Fest. 75 L.) – and he participated in the → *vinalia* (Varro, Ling. 6,16) [3]. The description of the *flamen Dialis* as a 'living and sacred statue of the god' (Plut. Quaest. Rom. 111, 200a-d) induced the interpretation of DUMÉZIL that his significance (and that of the other *flamines maiores*) was related to his nature – mediator between people and gods – rather than his actions [4; 5].

The *flaminica* was involved in the office of her husband and was likewise affected by the bans. Her marriage to the *flamen* was indissoluble (e.g. Ov. Fast. 6,232). She wore a red dress, sandals made from the hide of a sacrificial animal and a head-scarf with a twig from an *arbor felix* (Gell. NA 10,15,28; Serv. Aen. 4,137). With uncombed and unadorned hair (Gell. NA 10,15,30) she went to the → *argei*; at the → *nundinae* she sacrificed a ram to Jupiter in the Regia (Macrob. Sat. 1,16,30) [6].

Less has been passed down to us regarding the other two *flamines maiores*. The *flamen Martialis* sacrificed a victorious horse to Mars on 15th October. The *flamen Quirinalis* made sacrifices on 25th April (→ *Robigalia*) to Robigus (Ov. Fast. 4,907ff.), on 21 August (→ *Consualia*) with the Vestals he sacrificed to Consus (Tert. De spectaculis 5,7), and on 23rd December (→ *Larentalia*) with the *pontifex maximus* he made sacrifices at the tomb of → Acca Larentia (Gell. NA 7,7,7; Macrob. Sat. 1,10,15). Together the *flamines maiores* performed the rite of → Fides. At festivals the *flamines* were forbidden to see people working (Macrob. Sat. 1,16,9).

Not much is known about the *flamines minores*. In any case, the gods assigned to them were among the oldest ones in the Roman religion. Presumably the number of *flamines minores* was reduced in the course of time: Augustine (Civ. 2,15) only mentions the three *flamines maiores*. In the Imperial period the priesthood was expanded by the *flamines Augustorum*, i.e. the *flamines* of the deified emperors and empresses [7].

1 TH. MOMMSEN, Röm. Forschungen, vol. 1, 1879, 78 2 F. GRAF, Plutarco e la religione romana, in: I. GALLO (ed.), Plutarco e la religione, 1996, 269–283 3 DUMÉZIL, 195f. 4 DUMÉZIL, 572 5 J. SCHEID, Le flamine de Jupiter, les Vestales et le général triomphant, in: Le temps de la reflexion 7, 1986, 213–230 6 N. BOELS, Le statut religieux de la flaminica Dialis, in: REL 51, 1973, 77–100 7 D. FISHWICK, Flamen Augustorum, in: HSPh 74, 1970, 299–312.

M. BEARD, J. NORTH, Pagan Priests. Rel. and Power in the Ancient World, 1990, 17ff.; 177ff.; J.H.W.G. LIEBESCHUETZ, Continuity and Change in Roman Rel., 1979, 301ff.; J. SCHEID, Les prêtres officiels sous les empereurs julio-claudiens, in: ANRW II 16.1, 610–654; L. SCHUMACHER, Die vier hohen röm. Priesterkollegien unter den Flaviern, den Antoninen und den Severern, 69–235 n.Chr., in: ANRW II 16.1, 655–819; J.H. VANGGAARD, The Flamen, 1988. FR.P.

Flamingo (*Phoenicopterus ruber L.*, φοινικόπτερος; *phoinikópteros, phoenicopterus*). Wader named after its partly scarlet red wings; distinctive, shy brooding bird in north Africa and southern Asia, today also in the Camargue (southern France). It was first mentioned as a rare import by Aristophanes (Av. 270ff.) and also by Cratinus (fr. 114 KOCK = 108 EDMONDS). The observation of huge flocks made by the Alexander-historian Cleitarchus (FGrH 137 F 21) is reflected tendency (without naming the flamingo explicitly) in Ael. NA 17,23. The Romans regarded it highly as a delicacy (Cels. 2,18; Juv. 11, 139; two recipes in Apicius 6,1), especially its large tongue (Sen. Ep. 110,12; Plin. HN 10,133 with reference to Apicius; Mart. 13,71; Suet. Vit. 13,2). According to Mart. 3,58,14, it was fattened at Baiae. Caligula had a preference for it on certain days as a sacrificial animal for his own divinity (Suet. Calig. 22,3). There are extant depictions of it on mosaics, etc. [1. 2,212; cf. 2,235 and pl. 119].

1 KELLER 2 TOYNBEE, Animals in Roman Life and Art, 1973 C.HÜ.

Flamininus Rare Roman cognomen, derived from *flamen* and designating the son of a *flamen*, in the Republican period it became hereditary in a branch of the patrician family of the Quinctii. The most important bearer of the name is T. → Quinctius Flamininus (*cos.* in 198 BC).

H. Gundel, s.v. Quinctius, RE 24, 1038; J. Reichmuth, Die lat. Gentilicia, 1956, 74. K.-L.E.

Flaminius Roman plebeian gentile name (occupational designation, derived from the priestly office of the *flamen* [1]). Bearers of the name have emerged from the 3rd cent. BC. But the family is probably older, as can be seen from the place names *campus Flaminius* and *prata Flaminia* (Varro, Ling. 5,154; Liv. 3,54,15; 3,58,7) that can, however, also be interpreted as 'property of the *flamines*' (Oros. 5,18,27; [2]). Via Flaminia → F. [1].

1 Schulze 108; 332 2 F. Coarelli, s.v. Campus Flaminius, LTUR 1, 1993, 219.

[1] F., C. *Homo novus* who was successful in his career despite the resistance of a large part of the nobility. Senatorial historiography – represented by Polybius and Livy, who base their work on Q. → Fabius Pictor, and the sources dependent on them – paints a picture of a benevolent demagogue; in later popular tradition he is considered to be a precursor of the Gracchi (Cic. Acad. 2,13). As people's tribune in 232 BC he allegedly – against the fierce resistance of the Senate under the leadership of Q. Fabius [I 30] Maximus Verrucosus – introduced a law providing for the distribution of the → *ager Gallicus* (the territory of the Senones between Sena Gallica and Ravenna conquered by Rome) to needy individual Roman settlers (as *ager viritanus*, i.e. an assignation *viritim*) (Pol. 2,21; Cic. Cato 11; Brut. 57 etc.). Polybius describes this settlement as the reason for the attack by the Gauls in 225 and for a 'change for the worse among the people'.

As praetor in 227 he was the first regular governor to successfully administer Sicily (cf. Liv. 33,42,8). As consul in 223 he defeated – together with his colleague P. Furius [I 27] Philus – the Gallic Insubres on the other side of the Po (Pol. 2,32f.); because of his alleged disregard for unfavourable omens, the Senate initially did not want to recognize his consulate and also refused him a triumph but he then performed this with the consent of the people (Liv. 21,63,2; Plut. Marcellus 4). He was probably commander of the cavalry in 221 for his political opponent Q. Fabius Maximus; both of them had to give up their offices because of a religious *faux-pas*. In 220 together with L. Aemilius [I 27] Papus he was censor (Liv. 23,23,5); they limited the registration of freedpersons to only four tribus (Liv. per. 20). F. built the *via Flaminia* from Rome to Ariminum, probably in order to create a link to the newly settled *ager Gallicus*, and erected on the Field of Mars the *circus Flaminius* [1] that still existed right through to Late Antiquity. In 218 he supported the *lex Claudia* (according to Livy he was the only senator to do so), which greatly restricted the sea trade of senators (Liv. 21,63,3).

In the Second Punic War he was consul again in 217 although he did not take up his office in Rome but in Ariminum, for which he was reproached for disregarding the auspices; he is said to have continued to fail to take unfavourable omens into consideration (Liv. 21, 63; 22,1,5ff.; Cic. Div. 1,77f. et al.). F. took control of the army at Arretium but Hannibal avoided him and when he advanced, he was ambushed in the morning mists of 21st June at Lake Trasimene. The entire army was destroyed, F. fell in battle and his corpse was not found (Pol. 3,80–85; Liv. 22,4–7 etc.). According to Ovid (Fast. 6,765–768), the day of the battle was considered as a *dies ater*. F.'s career shows that contrary to senatorial tradition the entire Senate was not against him – rather he probably had support amongst the plebeian nobility; the image of a 'democratic' leader of the people has been exaggerated in modern times.

1 A. Viscogliosi, s.v. Circus Flaminius, LTUR 1, 1993, 269–272.

R. Develin, C.F. in 232 BC, in: AC 45, 1976, 638–643; Id., The Political Position of C.F., in: RhM 122, 1979, 268–277; A.M. Eckstein, Senate and General, 1987, 10–17; 31; R. Feig Vishnia, State, Society and Popular Leaders in Mid-Republican Rome 241–167 BC, 1996, 11–48; L. Oebel, C.F. und die Anfänge der röm. Kolonisation im *ager Gallicus*, 1993; J. v. Ungern-Sternberg, The End of the Conflict of the Orders, in: Social Struggles in Archaic Rome, 1986, 352–377.

[2] F., C. Son of F. [1], in 209 BC quaestor of P. Cornelius [I 71] Scipio (Africanus); in 196 as curule aedile he distributed grain at a reduced price that had been made available to him by the Sicilians in fond memory of his father (Liv. 33,42,8). In 193 he was praetor in Hispania citerior where he fought successfully against the Celtiberians until 190. As consul in 187 he defended his former colleague M. Fulvius Nobilior against the reproaches of his colleague in office M. Aemilius [I 10] Lepidus (Liv. 38,43,8–44,3). He fought successfully in Liguria and built a road from Bononia to Arretium (Liv. 39,2,1–11). From 183 he was a member of a three-man committee for the establishment of the *colonia* Aquileia that went ahead in 181 (Liv. 39,55,6; 40,34,2f.).

[3] F., C. In 67 BC curule aedile, in 66 judge at the *quaestio de sicariis* ('court for treacherous murder'), perhaps identical to the C. F., who at the end of 63 was host to Catiline near Arretium (Sall. Catil. 36,1). K.-L.E.

Flanona (modern Plomin/Croatia); town on the eastern coast of the peninsula of Histria in Liburnia, province of Dalmatia. An earlier Liburnian fortress above the bay of F. gave the entire bay of Kvarner the name: *sinus Flanaticus* (Plin. HN 3,139; Artemidorus in Steph. Byz. s.v. Φλάνων). F. probably became a *municipium* under Augustus (rather than under Tiberius), and *tribus Claudia* and *Sergia* (AE 1973, 477) are attested; the Aquilii were one of the foremost families. The residents are called *Flanonienses Vanienses* in Pliny (HN 3,130). In the late 2nd cent. AD, F. was called *res publica Flanatium* when Cn. Papirius Secundinus of Pola as *curator* supervised the affairs of F. (InscrIt X 1,88 = CIL V 60). In F. Constantius II had Gallus killed in AD 354 (Socr. 2,34,3f.). F. is not mentioned by the Geographus of Ravenna, possibly because of its minor significance in Late Antiquity. Scattered Roman remains are extant. The Liburnian nature of F. is reflected in the names and in the cults of the indigenous goddesses Sentona, Ica, Iria (Venus) and Minerva Flanatica; the latter goddess was also worshipped in the region of Parentium (InscrIt X 2,94).

Š. Mlakar, Istra u antici, 1962, 37f.; J.J. Wilkes, Dalmatia, 1969. M.Š.K.

Flavia

[1] F. Domitilla. Daughter of Flavius Liberalis of Ferentum in Etruria [2. 210, 1447]. First mistress of the *eques* Statilius Capella; she later married → Vespasianus. The sons Titus, Domitian and a daughter Flavia [2] were born of the marriage ([Aur.Vict.] Epit. Caes. 10,1; 11,1). Initially subject only to Latin law, she later received Roman citizenship when her father became *adsertor*. She died before Vespasian came to power on 1 July AD 69 (Suet. Vesp. 3) and was not deified. A sesterce minting from 80/1 commemorates her: RIC 2, p. 134, nos. 153–154; BMCRE 2, p. 270f. nos. 226–229 [1. nos. 367; 2. 210, 621; 3]. PIR² F 416.

[2] F. Domitilla. Daughter of F. [1] and Vespasian, her husband was probably Q. Petillius Cerialis Caesius Rufus [4. 67f.]. After her death before 1 July AD 69 she appears on coins as *Diva* and *Augusta* (RIC 2, p. 124 nos. 69–73; BMCRE 2, 246 nos. 136–138, p. 249 no. 148, p. 251 no. 14, p. 312 no. 68). A *sacerdos divae Domitillae* (CIL V 2829 = ILS 6692) and a temple in Ferentum (AE 1962, 272; AE 1963, 83) are also known. [1. no. 368; 2. 261; 3]. PIR² F 417.

[3] F. Domitilla. Daughter of F. [2]. Her husband was T. Flavius Clemens, *cos.* in AD 95, a cousin of Domitian. In 95 both were indicted and sentenced by Domitian for a lack of religious orthodoxy (Suet. Dom. 15,1). F. was exiled to Pandateria (according to Cass. Dio 67,14,2) or to Pontia (according to Euseb. Hist. eccl. 3,18,4, where she is incorrectly described as the niece of Clemens). They were outlived by seven children (CIL VI 8942 = ILS 1839); the two surviving sons were named Vespasian and Domitian by Domitian and raised by Quintilianus (Quint. Inst. 4, praef. 2). It is not certain whether F. was a Christian (Eus. loc. cit.) or a Jew. She endowed a cemetery (Coemeterium D.) on the *via Ardeatina* (her gravestone CIL VI 10098 = ILS 5172 [1. no. 369; 3]). PIR² F 418.

1 Raepsaet-Charlier 2 Vogel-Weidemann
3 H. Temporini, Die Frauen am Hofe Traians, 1979
4 Birley. ME.STR.

[4] F. Pollitta. *Clarissima femina* of Sardes where she was active as benefactress in AD 211. AE 1993, 1505. W.E.

[5] F. Titiana. Daughter of T. F. (Claudius) Sulpicianus, wife of Pertinax [1. 267], whose death in AD 193 she survived (SHA Pert. 13,7). Despite the opposition of Pertinax to elevating her to the position of *Augusta* (Cass. Dio 73,7,1; SHA Pert. 5,4; 6,9 cf. in this regard [2. 34,169]), there are inscriptions that describe her as such (ILS 410). Her son is P. Helvius Pertinax.

Raepsaet-Charlier no. 383; PIR² F 444.

1 Birley 2 H. Temporini, Die Frauen am Hofe Traians, 1979. ME.STR.

Flavian Dynasty Modern term for two series of Roman emperors in the 1st and 3rd/4th cents. AD, who were descended from the same family: one series of succession was founded in AD 69 by T. Flavius → Vespasianus (69–79) and was continued to AD 96 by his sons → Titus [3] (79–81) and → Domitianus [1] (81–96); the other series, which is occasionally called the 'Second Flavian Dynasty', was founded by the house of Flavius Valerius → Constantinus [1] I, which fictively began with (Flavius) → Claudius [III 2] Gothicus (268–270) and ended with the death of Flavius Claudius → Iulianus [11] (360–363). The term 'dynasty' here expresses the *de facto* transfer of rule within the same family over a period of time but not a succession based on family membership or authorization that is legally secure (→ Usurpation III).

With Vespasian, in contrast to all earlier emperors (including those of the → Year of the Four Emperors) an Italic family (from Sabinian Reate) that was not part of the ancient Roman nobility ('of obscure origin', *obscura...ac sine ullis maiorum imaginibus*: Suet. Vesp. 1,1) ascended to power. It could only be traced back two generations to a grandfather of Vespasian (Flavius Petro), a → *centurio*, but then experienced a rapid ascent with the father, who was already an *eques* (→ Flavius [II 39]) and his sons who pursued senatorial careers (the brother → Flavius [II 40] Sabinus was a *praefectus urbi*). Vespasian based his legitimization on the powers of his '»good«' predecessors Augustus, Tiberius [1] and Claudius [III 1], which he had conferred upon himself with a → *lex de imperio*, as well as making it clear that 'his sons or no one', *aut filios sibi successores aut neminem* (Suet. Vesp. 25) would succeed him. The succession was without problems in both cases because it had been well prepared for by the sons' (especially Titus') participation in the duties of the → ruler. Both sons had no sons of their own, so that the Flavian Dynasty (FD) was extinguished in AD 96 with the murder of Domitian, who was hated by many senators because of his arrogant style of governing (→ *senatus* III.).

Despite its short duration of only 27 years (69–96), the emperors of the FD managed to suppress unrest in the empire (Iudaea, → Jewish Wars; Batavi, → Batavian revolt), secure the borders on the Rhine, Danube and in the East, solidify the empire's → infrastructure through road construction, restore the finances and improve the quality of the imperial administration. Through generous granting of Roman → citizenship (→ *civitas* B.) to individuals and entire communities across the empire by the Flavian rulers, the name *Flavius* – similar to *Claudius* – spread and was still common in late antiquity to indicate possession for centuries of Roman citizenship.

When founding the 2nd FD, Flavius Valerius Constantinus [1] I deliberately (probably not before AD 310) set himself apart from membership in the family of the Herculii (→ Diocletianus; → *tetrárchēs* IV with stemma) and via his father Flavius Valerius Constantius [1] fictively traced his family back to Claudius [III 2] Gothicus (268–270; SHA Clod. 7,8: *Flavius Claudius*; SHA Aur. 17,2); Constantius [1] as the son of a freely invented cousin of Claudius becomes his grand-nephew (SHA Clod. 9,9; cf. stemma of the family of → Constantinus [1]). Constantinus [1] (306–337) planned to pass on power within his family (Crispus [1], Caesar in 317, executed 326; Constantinus [2], Caesar in 317; Constantius [2], Caesar in 324; Constans [1], Caesar in 333), probably as a tetrarchy with the participation of Dalmatius [2], a (half-)nephew from the marriage of his father with → Theodora [1]. However, the latter was killed after the death of Constantinus [1] (together with his father and other relatives from Theodora's line), so that Constantinus [2] (337–340), Constans [1] (337–350) and Constantius [2] (337–361) shared the imperial government.

Only after the death of Constans (350) did Constantius draw grandsons of Theodora more closely into the family by marrying them to his sisters and elevating them as Caesars: first Constantius [5] Gallus (in 351 marriage to → Constantina and elevation as caesar) and after his execution (354) Julian [11] (in 355 marriage to Helena [3] and elevation as caesar). In 361, Julian was proclaimed caesar by his troops in Gaul and after the unexpected death of Constantius in the same year became sole ruler without a fight (361–363). Because none of the marriages produced children, the 2nd FD came to an end with Julian's death during a campaign against the Persians. W. ED.

Flavianus

[1] *Praefectus praetorio* with (Geminius) Chrestus in AD 222 or 223. When upon the insistence of Julia Mamaea, Domitius → Ulpianus was put in charge by Severus Alexander as praetorian prefect, the guard mutinied, so Ulpianus had F. and Chrestus killed (Cass. Dio 80,2,2; Zos. 1,11,2). PIR² F 180. T.F.

[2] **Virius Nicomachus F.** Dominant figure of the non-Christian aristocracy in Rome in the last quarter of the 4th cent. AD. He had a close friendship with Q. Aurelius → Symmachus, from whom numerous letters to him are extant (Symmachus, Ep. 2,1–91). In 364/5 he was *consularis Siciliae*, in 377 *vicarius Africae* and he possibly supported the Donatists there (Aug. Epist. 87,8). He stood up for the concerns of Leptis Magna (Amm. Marc. 28,6,28). In 382/3 (or 389/390) he was *quaestor sacri palatii* and in 390 *praefectus praetorio Italiae, Illyriae et Africae*. He supported the usurpation of Eugenius [2], who again appointed him *praefectus praetorio* (in 393–4) and in 394 promoted him to the rank of consul (cf. the list of offices ILS 2947). At the age of sixty he killed himself because of Eugenius' defeat against Theodosius I (5. 9. 394) (Rufin. 11,33).

The anonymous Christian defamatory poem *carmen contra paganos* (also *carmen adversus Flavianum*, Text: Anth. Lat., ed. F. Bücheler, A. Riese, I 1, no. 4, p. 20–25), written about 394/5, was probably directed against him. He translated Philostratus' biography of Apollonius of Tyana into Latin (Sidon. Epist. 8,3,1) and wrote *Annales* (ILS 2948) (also lost) that he dedicated to Theodosius I and that possibly were used by Ammianus Marcellinus as source. Even Christians remembered him with great respect (Ambr. Obit. Theod. 4; ILS 2948). Macrobius has him appear in the *saturnalia* (cf. Sat. 1,1,4). He was the father of F. [3].

PLRE 1, 347–349; J. J. O'Donnell, The Career of Virius Nicomachus F., in: Phoenix 32, 1978, 129–143; Th. Grünewald, Der letzte Kampf des Heidentums in Rom?, in: Historia 41, 1992, 462–487. W.P.

[3] **Nicomachus F.** Son of the well-known head of the pagan senatorial aristocracy in Rome (→ F. [2]), he was *proconsul Asiae* in AD 382/3 and *praefectus urbi Romae* in 393–4 under the usurper → Eugenius [2] (Symmachus, Ep. 2,24; 7,104). After his death and the suicide of his father, he fled and sought asylum in a church and converted to Christianity (Aug. Civ. 5,26,1). Rehabilitated under Honorius, he was city prefect of Rome again from 399 to 400 and in 408 (Symmachus, Ep. 4,4; 7, 93; Cod. Iust. 2,15,1). In 414 he was despatched to Africa to reorganize affairs (Cod. Theod. 7,4,33). As *praefectus praetorio Italiae Illyrici et Africae* in 431/2 he achieved the vindication of the reputation of his father (ILS 2948). He was involved in the revision of the 1st Livy decade (*subscriptio* to Liv. bks. 6–8), → Symmachus sent him the letters 6,1–81.

PLRE 1, 345–47; A. Chastagnol, Fastes de la Préfecture de Rome, 1962, 239–44; v. Haehling 323f. K.P.J.

Flavia Solva Town in Noricum, modern Wagna near Leibnitz. *Municipium* (Plin. HN 3,146) from the time of Vespanian; destroyed by the invasion of Marcomanni around AD 170, built up again after that. Orthogonal street system with *insulae*, burial area (from Late Antiquity, on the Frauenberg).

E. Hudeczek, F.S., in: G. Christian (ed.), Leibnitz, 1988, 21–54; M. Hainzmann, E. Pochmarski, Die römerzeitlichen Inschr. und Reliefs von Schloß Seggau bei Leibnitz, 1994. H.GR.

Flavinium Town in the *regio VII* (Etruria) at the southern foot of the → Soracte (Verg. Aen. 7,696; Serv. Aen. ad 1; Sil. 8,490) where according to Sil. 13,85 the Capenas (modern Gramiccia?) caused floods. G.U.

Flaviopolis Town to the north-east of Cilicia Pedias, assumed on the basis of inscriptions and the remains of buildings to lie close to Kadirli. F. was founded by Vespasian in AD 73/4 during the rebuilding of Cilicia, and conquered by the Sassanid king Šapur I in AD 260.

H.T. Bossert, U.B. Alkim, Karatepe, Kadirli and its environments, 1947, 17–22; M.Gough, s.v. F., PE, 330; Hild/Hellenkemper, s.v. Phlabias, 378f. M.H.S.

Flavius Roman plebeian gentile name, derived from the individual *cognomen Flavus* ('the blond one') through the suffix of affiliation *-ius*, abbreviated form *Fl.* The bearers of the name that was already common in the Republican period were initially politically unimportant; F. [I 5] was the first one to attain to Roman nobility. In the Imperial period the name was spread further in the Roman empire as a result of the granting of citizenship by the Flavian Emperors Vespasian, Titus and Domitian (AD 68–96). In Late Antiquity (4th–6th cents.) F. was initially *gentilicium* of the family of → Constantinus I (so-called 2nd Flavian Dynasty). Germanic generals also on occasion made F. part of their names when they commenced work in the service of Rome. Especially in the east of the empire, F. was considered during this period to be a term of courtesy that was placed in front of the individual aristocratic name so it was not really part of the name (often in the dating of the consuls).

Bagnall 36–40; Schulze 167.

I. Republican period II. Imperial period

I. Republican period

[I 1] F., C. In 57 BC attested to as the friend of Cicero's son-in-law C. Calpurnius [I 20] Piso, in 46 recommended by Cicero to M. Acilius [I 9] Caninus (Fam. 13,31). In 44 he attempted to obtain from the Roman *equites* under the leadership of Atticus funds for the murderers of Caesar (Nep. Att. 8,3). In 42 as *praefectus fabrum* of Brutus he fell in battle at Philippi and he was deeply mourned by the latter (Plut. Brutus 51,2); not identical to the mint master in 43–42 under Brutus, C.F.Hemic[...], *legatus pro praetore* (RRC 504). K.-L.E.

[I 2] F., Cn. [1]. As the scribe of the censor Appius Claudius [I 2] Caecus, he is said to have published in 304 BC the collection of judicial forms (*legis actiones*) mentioned by Pomponius (Dig. 1,2,2,7), *ius Flavianum* and the court calendar (*dies fasti*), which has been interpreted (Cic. Mur. 25; Liv. 9,46,5; Plin. HN 33,17) as a breach of the monopoly of pontifical jurisprudence and the beginning of its laicization [2].

1 MRR I, 168 2 Wieacker, RRG 524ff. T.G.

[I 3] F., L. As people's tribune he unsuccessfully applied in 60 BC for a law providing for the distribution of land in favour of the veterans of Pompey (Cic. Att. 1,18,6; 19,4; Cass. Dio 37,49f.). As praetor in 58 he came into conflict with P. Clodius [I 4] Pulcher because the latter had abducted the Armenian prince Tigranes, whose guarding had been entrusted to F. by Pompey (Ascon. 47f.; Cass. Dio 38,30,1f.). Perhaps identical with the F. whom Caesar intended as administrator for Sicily in 49 (Cic. Att. 10,1,2).

E. Badian, The Auctor of the lex Flavia, in: Athenaeum 55, 1977, 233–238.

[I 4] F., M. As secretary (*scriba*, i.e. possibly *pontifex minor*) he was involved in the reform of the calendar by Caesar in 46 BC (Macrob. Sat. 1,14,2f.).

J. Rüpke, Kalender und Öffentlichkeit, 1995, 372f.

[I 5] F. Fimbria, C. *Homo novus* who was people's tribune and (at the latest in 107 BC) praetor and who together with C. Marius was consul in 104. Probably after the administration of a province he was indicted by M. Gratidius [I 2] for extortion but he was acquitted (Cic. Font. 24; 26; Brut. 168). In 100 he was one of the staunch opponents of L. Appuleius [I 11] Saturninus (Cic. Rab. perd. 21); he died before 91. Cicero paid tribute on several occasions to his political stance and his talent for rhetoric (Planc. 12; Brut. 129 etc.).

[I 6] F. Fimbria, C. Son of F. [I 5], supporter of C. Marius and L. Cornelius [I 18] Cinna in the Civil War. On behalf of Cinna he entered into an alliance with the Samnites in 87 BC (Granius Licinianus p. 16 Criniti). During the capture of Rome F. had several members of the nobility murdered. (Liv. per. 80; Flor. 2,9,14; Aug. Civ. 3,27) and attempted to assassinate the *pontifex maximus* Q. → Mucius Scaevola (Cic. S. Rosc. 33; Val. Max. 9,11,2). In 86, as legate, he accompanied the consul L. → Valerius Flaccus to the east in order to eliminate L. Cornelius [I 90] Sulla but he soon fell out with him. After a mutiny by the army in which Flaccus was killed, F. assumed supreme command. Successful as commander but unscrupulous (destruction of Ilium), he conquered Bithynia and encircled Mithridates VI in Pitane, but L. → Licinius Lucullus, fleet commander for Sulla, let him escape by sea. After the Peace of Dardanus (in 85) between Mithridates and Sulla, the latter attacked F., whose army deserted. F. committed suicide (Liv. per. 82f.; detailed account in App. Mithr. 203–249; MRR 2, 56; 59; 3, 92). His troops had to continue to serve under Lucullus and could not return to Italy until 67.

A. Keaveney, Sulla, 1982, Index s.v. F.

[I 7] F. Pusio, C. Roman *eques*, in 91 BC a fierce opponent of the *lex iudiciaria* of the people's tribune M. → Livius Drusus (Cic. Clu. 153); perhaps murdered by a slave (Val. Max. 8,4,2). K.-L.E.

II. Imperial period

[II 1] T. F. Abascantus. Imperial freedman, *ab epistulis* for Domitian, whose work is described by his *amicus* Statius (Stat. Silv. 5,1,81ff.; CIL VI 8598f.) who accompanied Domitian on campaigns (Stat. Silv. 5,1,127ff.). In about AD 95 he erected to his wife Priscilla a magnificent marble tomb on the *via Appia* on the river Almo which was still not finished a year after her death (Stat. Silv. 5,1,222ff.; CIL VI 2214.). PIR² F 194.

[II 2] F. Aelianus. Consular legate of Pannonia inferior in AD 228; perhaps identical with the Flav[ius...]ian[us], governor of Germania inferior in 231. Eck, Statthalter 213; PIR² 196.

[II 3] F. Antiochianus. Senator from the east of the empire, perhaps from Phrygia, IGR 4, 893. *Cos. ord. II* in AD 270, PIR² F 203. Perhaps related to F. [II 4].

[II 4] F. Antiochus. *Cos. suff.* in an unknown year before AD 244/249; there is evidence that he was consular governor of Syria Coele during this period [1]. Perhaps the father of F. [II 3].

1 Dura Europos. Final Report 5, 1, 1959, 173ff. no. 38.

[II 5] M. (F.) Aper. Senator of Gaul who was promoted at least to the rank of praetor; probably the father of F. [II 6]. Introduced by Tacitus as an interlocutor in *Dialogus*, Syme, RP II 701f.; VI 226f.; PIR² A 910; F 206.

[II 6] [M.] F. Aper. Senator who in AD 105 intervened in the Senate; at that time he was probably of consular rank, perhaps *cos. suff.* in 103, probably the son of F. [II 5], father of F. [II 7]. Syme, RP VI 226f.; Vidman, FO² 46. 98.

[II 7] M. F. Aper. Son of F. [II 6]. Governor of Lycia-Pamphylia in AD 125, *cos. ord.* in 130.

W. Eck, in: Chiron 13, 1983, 160ff.; Wörrle, Stadt und Fest, 1988, 35ff.; PIR² F 208.

[II 8] M. F. Aper. *Cos. suff.* in *c.* AD 155/160, *cos. ord. II* in 176; son of F. [II 7], Alföldy, Konsulat 194; PIR² F 209.

[II 9] T. F. Aper Commodianus. *Cos. suff.* before AD 222, consular governor of Germania inferior in 222 and 223. Eck, Statthalter 207f.; PIR² F 210.

[II 10] F. Archippus. Philosopher who came from Prusias in Bithynia. He was sentenced to the mines by proconsul Velius (or Vettius) Paulus in about AD 79/80 for forging a testament, but was later restored to favour and given privileges by Domitian before 86; presumably he was also granted Roman citizenship at that time. Under Trajan he was indicted by Pliny because he insisted on his immunity to arrest. Trajan confirmed that he had this immunity just as Nerva had already done previously (Plin. Ep. 10,58–60). An indictment brought by him against Dio [I 3] Chrysostom was unsuccessful (Plin. Ep. 10,81f.).

C. P. Jones, The Roman World of Dio Chrysostom, 1978, 100ff.

[II 11] T. F. Artemidorus. Citizen of Adana and Antioch in Syria. Victorious as a pancratiast, also at the first Capitoline Agon under Domitian, PIR² F 221.

[II 12] Q. F. Balbus. Proconsul of Achaia (IGLS XIII 9074); praetorian governor of Arabia probably under Caracalla or Elagabalus, then *cos. suff.* PIR² F 227.

W.E.

[II 13] F. Boethus. of Ptolemais in the province of Syria Palaestina, patron of Galen (Gal. 2,215; 19,13). *Consul suffectus* before AD 163 (Gal. 2,215), left Rome before 166 as *legatus proconsularis* for his home province. He held this office until his death (Gal. 19,16). His wife and his son Cyrillus were among the patients of Galen during his first stay in Rome (Gal. 14,641; 635). As an enthusiast of philosophy and literature (Gal. 14,5) and as a pupil of Alexander of Damascus and a friend of the philosopher Eudemus, he preferred Aristotelian philosophy (Gal. 14,625; 612). Eager to learn, he took part in Galen's sections and had the records copied for later evaluation (Gal. 14,630). In response to his request, Galen wrote at least nine mostly anatomical treatises, among these being *De usu partium* and *De placitis Hippocratis et Platonis*. F. Boethus took these writings with him to Palestine or had them sent there.

→ Galen of Pergamum

V.N.

[II 14] F. Caper. Grammarian around AD 200. His writings, particularly *De Latinitate*, represent the branch of Roman grammar that since → Verrius Flaccus contrasted the more recent language trend with the older one and endeavoured to establish a linguistic norm through orthoepy (application of correct grammatical forms, word choice in erudite language) as well as in orthography. In his rejection of extreme analogistic definition and archaizing narrow conduct of thought, F. Caper steers a mid-course and endeavours at the same time to register the linguistic peculiarities of the *veteres*.

Works: 1. *De dubiis generibus*, a compilation of nouns with changing grammatical gender, was probably intended as a preliminary work for *De Latinitate* and was model for Nonius, bk. 3 (*De indiscretis generibus*), and *Anonymus De dubiis nominibus* (GL 5,567–594). – 2. F. Caper's major work *De Latinitate* was set out in the manner of the usual *artes* with the sequence of the parts of speech and attempted to pick out from a large number of individual pieces of evidence the correct style, grammatical gender, (inflection) form or means of expression. The Anon. in Char. 1,15; Prisc. 6 as well as Ps.-Probus, *De nomine* convey an impression of the original. The prerequisite for his work were the *Dubii sermonis libri* of → Pliny the Elder, which F. Caper brought up to date according to the direct precursors Probus, Terentius Scaurus and Caesellius Vindex. Beginning with → Iulius Romanus, F. Caper's materials were used by the artigraphic tradition interested in scholarly detail (Diomedes; Priscianus, especially bks. 3–10), the lexicographical tradition (Arusianus Messius) and the commentary tradition (Servius) and, as it were, were absorbed to the detriment of the original. Remnants of extracts are extant in Late Antiquity with the script in the name of F. Caper *De orthographia* (GL 7,92–107) blending together with the prose version of a grammatical didactic poem and F. Caper's first work in *De verbis dubiis* (GL 7,107–112) – 3. Nor should we doubt the existence of *Commentarii in Ciceronem*, at least in relation to the orations (cf. Hier. Adversus Rufinum 2,9).

G. KEIL, De F.C. grammatico, in: Dissertationes philologicae Halenses 10, 1889, 245–306; L. JEEP, Priscianus, in: Philologus 68, 1909, 1–51; A. HOELTERMANN, De F.C. grammatico, 1913; K. BARWICK, Remmius Palaemon, 1922, 191ff.; W. STRZELECKI, De F. C. Nonii auctore, 1936; Id., De Ps.-Capri 'orthographia', 1949; P.L. SCHMIDT, in: HLL, § 438. 492.1. P.L.S.

[II 15] **T. F. Claudianus.** *Cos. suff.* in AD 179 (AE 1990, 1023 = RMD III 185). Possibly CIL VI 1413 refers to him. PIR² F 236.

[II 16] **T. F. Clemens.** Son of F. [II 41]. Younger cousin of Domitian, born before AD 69 as he was presumably on the Capitol during the wars with the Vitellians. Married to Flavia [II 3] Domitilla, with whom he had several children (seven perhaps). Two of his sons were designated by Domitian as his own successors, which is why he gave them the names Vespasianus and Domitianus. In 95 he was *cos. ord.* together with Domitian (VIDMAN, FO² 45). Later in 95 he was executed by Domitian; the reason was supposedly impiety. Whether this meant that he had leanings towards Judaism or Christianity remains unclear; he cannot have been a baptized Christian. PIR² F 240.

[II 17] **L. F. Cleonaeus.** According to CIL VI 31808 (= [1] = CIL VI 41123) *VII vir epulonum*; presumably in the period of Marcus Aurelius. If CIL VI 1545 = 41124 also refers to him, he was promoted to the consulate and to the *cura alvei Tiberis*.

1 G. CAMODECA, in: EOS 1,539ff.

[II 18] **T. F. Coelianus.** *Cos. suff.* in AD 289, presumably from May to August, CIL X 4631= InscrIt XIII 1, p. 269; W. ECK, in: ZPE 118, 1997, 275ff. PIR² F 246.

[II 19] **T. F. Constans.** As *praefectus praetorio, eminentissimus vir*, he dedicated an altar in Cologne to the goddess Vagdavercustis; he possibly came from the colony [1. n. 19]. Perhaps identical to the procurator of Dacia inferior in AD 138 PIR² F 247.

1 W. ECK, in: EOS 2, 545.

[II 20] **T. F. Damianus.** Citizen of Ephesus, Sophist who according to Philostratus built fine buildings in his home town (Philostr. VS 2,23) where he died at the age of 70. His sarcophagus was also found there. Three of his sons, T. F. Damianus, T. F. Phaedrus and T. F. Vedius Antoninus, were consuls at the beginning of the 3rd cent. AD.

PIR² F 253; H. HALFMANN, in: EOS 2, 629; C. SCHULTE, Die Grammateis von Ephesos, 1994, 184ff.

[II 21] **T. F. Decimus.** *Cos. suff.* probably at the beginning of the rule of Septimius Severus, proconsul of Africa in AD 209 THOMASSON, Fasti Africani 82.

[II 22] **[T.] F. Decimus.** *Cos. suff.* probably in Nov./Dec. AD 289 (CIL X 4631= InscrIt XIII 1, p. 269).

W. ECK, in: ZPE 118, 1997, 275ff.

[II 23] **(F.) Domitianus.** Son of F. [II 16]. Domitian designated him with his older brother F. [II 48] Vespasianus as his successors although both were still very young. → Quintilianus was their teacher. PIR² F 257. 397.

[II 24] **F. Earinus.** Castrated favourite of Domitianus. Came from Pergamum, imperial freedman. PIR² F 262.

[II 25] **T. F. Geminus.** *Eques* in the Severan period. After the *militia equestris*, he was procurator for the census in Belgica and governor of Alpes Atrectianae and Vallis Poenina.

F. BÉRARD, in: Gallia 52, 1995, 347ff.

[II 26] **T. F. Italicus.** Equestrian governor of Dacia inferior inAD 133 (AE 1962, 255 = RMD I 35). PFLAUM Suppl. 42f.

[II 27] **F. Iulianus.** Praetorian legate of Cilicia in AD 217 (AE 1954, 8); under Elagabalus he was praetorian legate of Arabia.

W. ECK, RE Suppl. 14, 120f.; PIR² F 295.

[II 28] **F. Iuvenalis.** Praetorian prefect under Didius [II 6] Iulianus, then also under Septimius Severus; perhaps he came from Africa.

A. BIRLEY, Septimius Severus: The African Emperor, 1988, 102f.; PIR² F 300.

[II 29] **T. F. Longinus Q. Marcius Turbo.** *Eques*, probably adopted by the Hadrian praetorian prefect Marcius Turbo. After the *militia equestris*, he was quaestor for Aelius Caesar in AD 137; after the praetorship, he was legionary legate and governor of Lugdunensis. In *c.* 149 he was *cos. suff.*; in 151/2 *curator operum publicorum*; about 154/156 governor of Moesia inferior.

KOLB, Bauverwaltung 208f.; PIR² F 305. W.E.

[II 30] **F. Manlius Theodorus.** → Theodorus

[II 31] **F. Maternianus.** Probably *eques*, deputy of the praetorian prefect in Rome, when Caracalla stayed in the east. He warned the emperor by letter about Macrinus, who had asked the magi about the future, which was considered to be high treason. As the letter was intercepted, Macrinus had F. killed at a later time. PIR² F 317.

[II 32] **F. Mon[tanus] Maximil[lianus?]** Proconsul in Asia in the 3rd cent. AD, IEph. III 698.

[II 33] **T. F. Pergamus.** Imperial freedman; procurator on Corsica, in Narbonensis, in the regio Syriatica and in the province of Asia, IEph. III 855. 855A.

[II 34] **T. F. Philinus.** *Cos. suff.* in the early 3rd cent. AD. He came from Thespiae. AE 1953, 51.

C. P. JONES, in: GRBS 21, 1980, 378f.; W. ECK, RE Suppl. 14, 121; PIR² F 331.

[II 35] **T. F. Piso.** *Eques.* He took part in the imperial *consilium* regarding the citizenship of the Zegrenses prince Aurelius Iulianus in AD 177, AE 1971, 534. *Praefectus annonae* in 179, AE 1973, 126; *praefectus Aegypti* in 182, PFLAUM, Suppl. 47f.

[II 36] [?F]l. Postumus. Consular governor of Tres Daciae in *c.* AD 211/213 AE 1978, 678; PISO, FPD 168f.

[II 37] F. Ranius Pollio Flavianus. Son of the legate of Asia F. Pollio Flavianus; the family came from Africa. AE 1993, 1734; 1748.

PIR[2] F 340; W. ECK, RE Suppl. 14, 121; M. CORBIER, in: EOS 2,708f.

[II 38] P. F. Pudens Pomponianus. Senator who came from Thamugadi and was promoted to the rank of proconsul of Crete and Cyrenae. SEG 36, 1464; M. LE GLAY, in: EOS II 772; PIR[2] F 346.

[II 39] (F.) Sabinus. Son of T. F. Petro of Reate in the land of the Sabines. Initially active in the levying of taxes in Asia, he later worked as a money-lender amongst the Helvetians. It is uncertain whether he was of equestrian rank. Married to Vespasia Polla. His sons were F. [II 40] and the later emperor → Vespasianus. PIR[2] F 351; DEMOUGIN 245f.

[II 40] T. F. Sabinus. Son of F. [II 39] and Vespasia Polla, elder brother of the later emperor Vespasianus. According to Tacitus Hist. 3,75,1 (to AD69), he was in the service of the *res publica* for 35 years. Whether this means that his career began in 34 is uncertain; in any case he was born before AD 9. Involved as legionary legate in the Britannian campaign of Claudius [III 1] (BIRLEY 224), *cos. suff.* probably in 47 [1; 2. 263]. For six years he was governor of Moesia; probably designated to conduct the census in Gaul, but he was then appointed city prefect in 61 (he may perhaps have already held the office at an earlier time). Deposed by Galba in 68, reappointed by Otho, he also remained in this office under Vitellius. Even after his brother Vespasian was elevated to emperor, Vitellius left him in this role. In late autumn 69, F. negotiated his abdication with Vitellius; when the plan failed, there were fights between the city cohorts under Sabinus and the Vitellians on the Capitol and during these battles Sabinus was killed on 19th or 20th Dec. Early in 70 he received a *funus censorium*, CIL VI 31293. His son was F. [II 38]. A daughter married Caesennius [3], *cos. ord.* in 61.

1 S. PANCIERA, in: EOS 1 609ff. 2 G. CAMODECA, L'archivio puteolano dei Sulpicii, 1992.

[II 41] T. F. Sabinus. Probably the son of F. [II 40]. As designated consul in AD 69, he was commander of Othonian troops; association with Vitellius; *cos. suff.* from April to the end of June 69; in 72 *cos. suff. II. Curator operum publicorum* under Titus or shortly beforehand. His sons were F. [II 16] and [II 42]. KOLB, Bauverwaltung 155; PIR[2] F 354.

[II 42] T. F. Sabinus. Probably the son of F. [II 41]; brother of F. [II 16]. During the battles against the Vitellians he was on the Capitol. Married to Iulia, Titus' daughter. In AD 82 he was *cos. ord.* together with Domitian; later executed by the latter; the reasons are unclear.

C. P. JONES, The Roman World of Dio Chrysostom, 1978, 46f.; B. W. JONES, The Emperor Domitian, 1992, 44ff.; PIR[2] F 355.

[II 43] F. Scaevinus. Senator who took part in the Pisonian conspiracy against Nero but was betrayed by his slaves. PIR[2] F 357.

[II 43a] F. Severinus. Governor of the province of Lycia-Pamphylia, married to a certain Dracilla; possibly, according to [1], living as early as Antoninus [1] Pius' time, but more probably no earlier than the 2nd half of the 3rd cent. AD.

1 S. ŞAHIN, Inschr. von Perge, vol. 1, 1999, 157. W. E.

[II 44] L. F. Silva Nonius Bassus. Senator of Urbs Salvia. Related to → Salvius Liberalis, perhaps also to the Flavian imperial house. Accepted into the Senate under Nero, and included among the praetorians by Vespasian und Titus, legate of the province of Judea, where he conquered the fortress of Masada in April AD 73 or 74. In 81 *cos. ord.* He built the amphitheatre in Urbs Salvia.

W. ECK, Senatoren von Vespasian bis Hadrian, 1970, 93ff.; Id., in: Picus 12/13, 1992/93, 87ff.; H. M. COTTON, in: ZPE 78, 1989, 157ff.; M. F. FENATI, Lucio Flavio Silva Nonio Basso e la città di Urbisaglia, 1995.

[II 45] T.F. (Claudius) Sulpicianus. Probably came from Hierapytna on Crete. Senator, *frater Arvalis* at least from AD 170/176; *cos. suff.* under Marcus Aurelius, *proconsul Asiae* under Commodus (SEG 30, 1349). CIL VI 31712 (cf. Addenda in CIL VI suppl. VIII to 31712) refers to him. Father-in-law of Pertinax, who made him city prefect in 193. When he endeavoured to claim the imperial honours after the latter's death himself, Didius [II 6] Iulianus was successful; F. lost the office of city prefect. He was probably killed by Septimius Severus in 197 because he was a supporter of Clodius [II 1] Albinus.

HALFMANN 187f.; SCHEID, Collège 87f., 410ff.; PIR[2] F 373.

[II 46] Q. F. Tertullus. *Cos. suff.* in AD 133, proconsul of Asia in 148/9. AE 1981, 845 = RMD II 100; PIR[2] F 376.

[II 47] F. Ulpianus. Praetorian governor of Cilicia in AD 202 (THOMASSON, I 291); *cos. suff.*; consular governor of Moesia inferior in *c.* 210–212/3.

D. BOTEVA, in: ZPE 110, 1996, 244f.

[II 48] (F.) Vespasianus. → F. [II 23]. W.E.

Flavus Roman *cognomen* ('golden yellow', 'blond', probably named after the hair colour), in the Republican period for C. Alfius [I 6] F., the family of the Decimii, Sp. → Larcius F. and L. → Lucretius Tricipinus F.

KAJANTO, Cognomina 227. K.-L.E.

[1] Brother of → Arminius, of the Cheruscan tribal aristocracy. Son of → Segimerus, son-in-law of the Chatti princeps Actumerus (Tac. Ann. 11,16,1), father of → Italicus [1. 201f.]. F. remained on the side of Rome after AD 9. There is evidence of deployments under → Tiberius (in which he lost an eye) and → Germanicus (AD 16) and of military honours; his exact career is uncertain. Tacitus sets the 'traitor' F. against the *liberator* Arminius in the fictitious oration of disputation about the Weser: F. praises the *magnitudo Romana*. Arminius praises the freedom of the fathers (Tac. Ann. 2,9f.). In AD 47 F. is also called an *explorator* (Tac. Ann. 11,16,3), i.e. probably a 'spy' [2. 43]. As a counter-image to the 'liberator' Arminius, the 'collaborator' F. is depicted from the time of Humanism in nationalistic representations of the Roman-Germanic conflict.

1 A. BECKER, Rom und die Chatten, 1992 2 D. TIMPE, Arminius-Studien, 1970 3 Id., s.v. F., RGA 9, 174f.

V.L.

Flax see → Linen

Flea (ψύλλα, ψύλλος; *psýlla*, *psýllos*, *pulex*). Of the almost 2,000 species, evidence has been found to date in archaeological discoveries of antiquity for the following [2]: (a) the human flea *Pulex irritans L.*; (b) the dog flea *Ctenocephalides canis Curt.*; (c) the rat and mouse flea *Nosopsyllus sp.* For all three species there are flea remains of fleas from the 2nd–4th cents. AD (excavations in England). Ancient literature, on the other hand, does not distinguish between species but only according to hosts (which does not allow for a clear delineation of the species as fleas are not limited to individual hosts). The authors mention the flea of fowl (Columella 8,5,3; Varro, Rust. 3,9,8); the flea of dogs (Columella 7,13,2; Gp. 19,3,2; Varro, Rust. 2,9,14); and particularly the flea as human parasite [1. 241; 4. 102–104; 5. 278]. Poor home hygiene assists with its proliferation, and it is of medical interest as a carrier of the plague and flea-borne typhus. Antiquity, however, had no health concerns about the flea [5. 278]; people only regarded it as annoying and particularly as a nightly disturber of the peace. Back scratchers (Mart. 14,83), magic and primarily plant preparations ([1. 241f.; 4. 102f.; 5. 278] were used against the flea and the itch caused by its bites; cf. [6] regarding a testimony wrongly attributed to the flea hunt). Aristotle in particular writes about the zoology of the flea (e.g. Part. an. 1,4,683a 33–36 to the saltatory legs). The Aristotelian theory of the abiogenesis of the animal in dust and Isidor's false derivation of the word *pulex* from *pulvis* (Orig. 12,5, 15) originated in the observation regarding the connection between the flea plague and dust.

1 I. C. BEAVIS, Insects and Other Invertebrates in Classical Antiquity, 1988, 240–242 2 A.R. HALL, H.K. KENWARD, Environmental Evidence from the Colonia, The Archaeology of York 14, 6, 1990 3 KELLER, 2,400–401 4 W. RICHTER, s.v. Floh, RE Suppl. 15, 101–104 5 G.E. THÜRY, Zur Infektkette der Pest in hell.-röm. Zeit, in: FS 75 Jahre Anthropologische Staatssammlung München 1902–1977, 1977, 275–283 6 Id., Flohjagd mit der Lampe?, in: Arch. der Schweiz 17, 1994, 120–122.

G.TH.

Flevum Germanic name ('the flooding, streaming [body of water]') for the most northerly branch of the delta of the Rhine: Plin. HN 4,101 (*Flevum ostium*); Mela 3,24 (*lacus Flevo*, formerly Zuidersee, modern IJsselmeer); cf. Ptol. 2,11,12. Tac. Ann. 4,72,3 mentions a Roman *castellum Flevum* besieged by Frisii in AD 28, the locality of which is pinpointed in Velsen [1]. It is debatable whether the *Flevi* in the Laterculus Veronensis 13 are derived from F. [2; 3].

→ Rhenus

1 J.-M. A. W. MOREL, A. V. A. J. BOSMAN, Velsen-Noord Spaarndammer polder, in: Archeologische Kroniek van Holland 1, 1989 (1990), 311–314 2 O. BREMER, Ethnographie der german. Stämme, ²1904, 146
3 SCHÖNFELD, 88.

G. NEUMANN, s.v. F., RGA 9, 191.

K.DI.

Flora Italian goddess whose worship in places other than Rome is attested to in various towns in central Italy (Agnone, Amiternum, Furfo, Pompeii). The blossom (*flos*) to which her name refers is related by the ancient sources to grain (Aug. Civ. 4,8), wine (Lactant. Div. inst. 1,20,7) or any flowering (Fast. Praenestini on 28th April). It is not just in Rome that she is closely connected to → Ceres: in Agnone she is called *F. Cerialis* (dat. *Fluusaí Kerríiai*), in Rome her main temple is situated directly with those of Ceres and Liber [1]. She is connected with → Robigus, the deity that protects people from black rust in cereals (Varro, Rust. 1,1,6) and is identified with Demeter's daughter → Kore (Plin. HN 36,4,23; Ampelius, Liber memorialis 9,11).

F.'s cult in Rome is old as she has her own *flamen Floralis* (Varro, Ling. 7,45), and there is nothing to confirm the modern view that she was introduced from Greece [2; 3]. According to Varro, Titus Tatius dedicated her first altar (Ling. 5,74): even if this is mythical aetiology, it indicates the Roman view of the high age of her cult. Her oldest temple was situated on the Quirinal [4], and she was given a second one near to the Circus Maximus in conjunction with the introduction of the → Floralia in 238 BC on the recommendation of the Sibylline Books (Tac. Ann. 2,49) [5]: The day of foundation was 28 April (Fast. Praenestini); Augustus organized a new building that Tiberius dedicated on 13 August (Fast. Allifani). Her main festival, the → Floralia (28 April), was erotic and sumptuous by nature which suits the character of a deity of future abundance.

1 H. LE BONNIEC, Le culte de Cérès à Rome, 1958, 195–202 2 G. WISSOWA, Religion und Kultus der Römer, 1912, 197f. 3 F. ALTHEIM, Terra Mater, 1931, 132–146 4 F. COARELLI, s.v. F., templum, LTUR 2, 254 5 E. PAPI, s.v. F., aedes, LTUR 253f.

P. MINGAZZINI, Due pretese figure mitiche. Acca Larenzia e F., in: Athenaeum 2, 1947, 140–165; V. HOŠEK, s.v. F., LIMC 4.1, 137–139.

F.G.

Floralia Celebrated in honour of 'mother → Flora', these were the → *ludi* (Cic. Verr. 2,5,36) which ran from the birth date of the temple on 28 April (Verrius Flaccus, *Fasti Praenestini* for this date; Ov. Fast. 4,947) to early May (Ov. Fast. 5,183ff.). F. are also attested to for Pisaurum (CIL XI 6357), Alba Fucens (CIL IX 3947) and Cirta (CIL VIII 6958) (see also the Agnone bronze [1]). The peasant calendars (→ *menologia*) and the *Fasti Venusini* record for 3 May a sacrifice to Flora that was meant to relate to the F. [2. 197[4]; 3]. According to myth, the Sabine Titus Tatius had already erected an altar to Flora (Varro, Ling. 5,74). But according to Plin. HN 18,286 and Vell. Pat. 1,14,8, the F. were not institutionalized until the 3rd cent. BC, and according to Ov. Fast. 5,329, they were celebrated each year from 173. They were considered to be a folksy 'plebeian' festival.

The F. marked an important phase in the development of grain, namely the flowering time (Varro, Antiquitates 172 CARDAUNS in Aug. Civ. 4,8). The harvest yield depended on its undisturbed course and successful pollination (cf. Verrius Flaccus, *Fasti Praenestini* to this date) (Ov. Fast. 5,261ff., also with reference to wine, olives etc.). The inconspicuous blooming of the most important plants for economic purposes was made manifest through lavish floral decoration (→ roses on the tables, wreaths: see esp. Ov. Fast. 5,194; 335f.; 359f.). The *florifertum* mentioned in Paul. Fest. 81 L. and the flora described by Lucr. 5,739f. that were used to sprinkle the path for → Ceres with pigments and scents lead us to the conclusion that there was a flower and grain procession to the sanctuary [2. 198]. Additional ritual elements are, among other things, a hare and goat hunt held in the circus (Ov. Fast. 5,371ff.; Mart. 8,67,4) as well as the scattering of legume seeds (peas, beans) amongst the people (Pers. 5,177–79 with schol.; Hor. Sat. 2,3,182), with clear allusions to the sexual aspect of the flower festival that also has as the subject the myth of the conception of Mars by Juno that is also told by Ov. Fast. 5,229ff. If the festival was also generally considered to be boisterous and happy and the listed spectacles were attributable to the minor muse (Ov. Fast. 5, 331ff.), the erotic side could, however, only be realized within the context of social conventions or even by professional providers of favours in a deputizing manner who celebrated a festival on this day and proved to be particularly permissive (Sen. Ep. 97,8 etc.).

→ Ceres; → Grain

1 VETTER, 147 2 G. WISSOWA, Religion und Kultus der Römer, [2]1912, 197f. 3 LATTE, 73f.

F. BÖMER, P. Ovidius Naso. Die Fasten 2: Kommentar, 1958, to Ov. fast. 5, 183ff.; W. W. FOWLER, The Roman Festivals of the Period of the Republic, 1908, 91ff.; H. LE BONNIEC, Le culte de Cérès à Rome. Des origines à la fin de la République, 1958, 196ff. D.B.

Florence Painter Attic red-figured vase painter of the early classical period, active *c.* 465 – 455 BC; according to BEAZLEY 'brother' of the Boreas Painter. Artists from the workshop, in which the 'painter of London E 489' was also active, painted predominantly column craters of average quality; among them the outstanding centauromachy on the eponymous vase in Florence (AM) is an exception. Further subject areas are komos, symposium, 'warrior's farewell' and Dionysus' entourage. His figures tend to be stiff and lacking in grace, and the compositions show little originality.

BEAZLEY, ARV[2], 536, 540–545, 1658; E. PARIBENI, s.v. Pittore di Firenze, EAA III, 701. M.P.

Florentia

[1] City in North-Etruria, *regio VII*, on the right bank of the Arnus below → Faesulae, modern Florence. Settlement from the Villanova period [3]. Roman colony, possibly founded in the 40s or 30s of the first cent. BC (Tac. Ann. 1,79,1; [6. 1,213]), *tribus Scaptia* [5. 84]. The choice of site for its founding was made favourable by a ford over the Arnus, used from the time of the Villanova culture, where the *via Cassia (*It. Ant. 285; Tab. Peut. 4,2), the *via Quinctia* (Tab. Peut. 4, 2) and the two trans-Apennine roads to → Bononia [1] (possibly the *via Flaminia 'minor'* from 187 BC) and to → Faventia (so-called v*ia Faventina*, It. Ant. 284) crossed [1; 2]. In the 4th cent. the city was mentioned as the seat of the c*orrector Tusciae* F. Tuscorum (Tab. Peut. 4,2; Cod. Theod. 9,1,8).

Archaeological findings: city wall (480 × 420 m) with four gates and round towers. Below S. Maria in Campidoglio a c*apitolium* on the paved main forum, today Cinema Gambrinus. Temple of Isis, theatre, baths, *castellum aquarum,* and an amphitheatre outside the city wall. Aqueduct from the Val Marina. In 393 Ambrosius dedicated the church to St. Laurence; not far from it S. Felicita with a graveyard. Findings and inscriptions in the Museo Archeologico. *Centuriatio* orientated to the West *secundum naturam* [4].

1 A. MOSCA, La via Faventina, in: N. ALFIERI (ed.), La viabilità fra Bologna e Firenze, 1992, 179–188 2 Id., Via Quinctia, in: Journal of Ancient Topography 2, 1992, 91–108 3 L. A. MILANI, F. Tomba italica a pozzo del centro di Firenze, in: NSA 1892, 458–468 4 F. CASTAGNOLI, La centuriazione di F., in: L'Universo 28, 1948, 367ff. 5 W. KUBITSCHEK, Imperium Romanum tributim discriptum, 1889 6 F. BLUME, K. LACHMANN (ed.), Die Schriften der röm. Feldmesser, 2 vols., 1848ff.

A. K. LAKE, The Archaeological Evidence for the 'Tuscan Temple', in: Memoirs of the American Academy in Rome 12, 1935, 89–149, esp. 93–98; G. MAETZKE, F., 1941; Id., F., in: NSA 1948, 60–99; C. HARDIE, The Origin and Plan of Roman Florence, in: JRS 55, 1965, 122–140; W. V. HARRIS, Rome in Etruria and Umbria 1971, 342f.; E. MENSI, La fortezza di F. e il suo territorio in epoca romana, 1991. G.U.

[2] City in western Aemilia (*regio VIII*) on the *via Aemilia* between → Fidentia and Placentia (It. Ant. 288), probably founded in the 2nd cent. BC (augural name), modern Fiorenzuola d'Arda. Inscription: CIL XI p. 203.

E. OTTOLENGHI, Fiorenzuola e dintorni, 1903. G.U.

Florentiana (Φλωρεντίανα; *Phlōrentíana*: Procop. Aed. 4,4,1–3). Roman fortress on the Danuvius (Danube) near the mouth of the Timacus (modern Timok). Originally in Moesia Superior, from AD 271 in Dacia Ripensis, probably modern Florentin near Vidin in Bulgaria. The fortress, destroyed in late antiquity, was rebuilt at the time of Justinian for strategic reasons.

V.I. VELKOV, Die thrak. und dak. Stadt in der Spätant., 1959, 75 (Bulgarian with German summary); TIR L. 34, 1968, 59 (bibliography). J.BU.

Florentinus

[1] Came from a Gaulish family; correspondent of Symmachus (Epist. 4,50–57), probably a pagan. In AD 379 he probably held the notary's office. It is doubtful whether he is identical with the homonymous *comes sacrarum largitionum* [1. 100–103]; in 395 *quaestor sacri cubiculi*; from 395 to 397, thus for an unusually long time, attested as *praefectus urbi Romae*, proved successful during a famine. Claudian [2] dedicated the second book of *De raptu Proserpinae* to him (praef. 50).

1 DELMAIRE.

PLRE 1, 362; V. HAEHLING, 397f. H.L.

[2] Greek author (probably from the first third of the 3rd cent. AD) of Γεωργικά (*Geōrgiká*) of at least eleven bks. (Gp. 9,14,1), which are based on the Quintilii and in turn provided the source – according to p. 3 B. and numerous quotations and chapter details – for the Γεωπονικά (→ Geoponica). The work is typical of the late flourishing of specialized literature in the Rome of this era.

E. ODER, Beiträge zur Gesch. der Landwirtschaft bei den Griechen, in: RhM 45, 1890, 59–99, esp. 83ff.; S. GEORGOUDI, Des chevaux et des boeufs dans le monde grecque, 1990, 38–42, 54f. P.L.S.

[3] Known only by his cognomen, author of a comprehensive textbook *Institutiones* (12 bks.) from the period after Antoninus Pius (late 2nd cent. AD). F., never quoted in the legal literature of the Principate period and neither attested as an official nor as a respondent, was probably active only as a law teacher [2], possibly in the provinces [3]. His textbook was used in late antiquity for teaching in eastern law schools (schol. Sinaitica 35 FIRA) and in drafting Justinian's *Digesta* and *Institutiones* [1].

1 F. WIEACKER, Textstufen klass. Juristen, 1959, 199ff. 2 SCHULZ, 127, 189 3 D. LIEBS, Jurisprudenz, in: HLL 4, 1997, 206f. T.G.

Florentius

[1] **Flavius F.** Was *praefectus praetorio Galliarum* from AD 357 to 360. At his instigation, Constantius [2] II had his auxiliary troops withdrawn from Gaul, which resulted in Julian's elevation (Julian. Ep. 282c; Amm. Marc. 20,4,2). In 360 Constantius appointed him *praefectus praetorio Illyrici* and in 361 honoured him with the consulate (Amm. Marc. 21,6,5). After Julian's victory he was sentenced to death *in absentia* by the Commission of Calchedon (Amm. Marc. 22,3,6). He is probably identical to the homonymous *comes* of Constantius who, on the orders of the emperor, attempted to persuade Athanasius to return to Alexandria in 346 (Athan. Hist. Ar. 22). PLRE 1, 365 (F. 10).

[2] Originated from Antioch [1] (Lib. Ep. 113), under Constantius [2] II he was *magister officiorum* from AD 359 to 361 (cf. Amm. Marc. 20,2,2). In 361 the Commission of Calchedon, instigated by Julian, banished him to an island in Dalmatia (Amm. Marc. 22,3,6). Apparently he was later rehabilitated (Lib. Ep. 1164) and is possibly identical to the homonymous *praefectus praetorio Galliarum* of 367: PLRE 1,363 (F. 3), cf. S. 364 (F. 5). W.P.

[3] Governor of Cilicia and later, in AD 392–393 in Syria, where his cruel administration induced → Libanius to give a defamatory speech against him (Lib. Or. 46).

PLRE 1, 364f.; O. SEECK, Die Briefe des Libanius, 1966, 158f.

[4] **Flavius F.** From Syria; was *praefectus urbi Constantinopolitanae* in AD 422 (Cod. Theod. 6,8,1), *praefectus praetorio Orientis* from 428 to 430 and again in 438–439 (Cod. Theod. 15,8,2; Cod. Iust. 1,19,8; 9,27,6; Nov. Theod. 3) and *consul* in 429. He became *patricius* from 444 to 448. As an orthodox Christian (Theod. Epist. 47; 89) he took part in the Synods of Constantinople in 448–449 and in the Council of Calchedon in 451 (Acta Conc. Oecumenicorum II 1,1,55; 138f.; 145; 148).

PLRE 2, 478–480; A. GRILLHEIMER, H. BACHT, Das Konzil von Chalkedon 2, 1954, 214–216. K.P.J.

Florianus see → M. Annius [II 4] F.

Florilegium Probably only in neo-Latin equivalent of Greek *anthología* (→ anthology) and thus the term for collections of short independent texts or quotations. With Christian authors the usual expression is *flores*. *Florida* was already used as the term for a collection by Appuleius (→ Ap(p)uleius [III]). Comparable ancient metaphorical terms are Greek *anthologiká*, *leimōnes*, *pandéktai*, *strōmateís* (cf. Gell. NA pr.), Latin *coniectanea*, *prata*, *silvae*, and also *excerpta*, *electa*, etc. Christian *florilegia* of biblical texts enjoyed great popularity since Cyprianus' *testimonia*, the Church Fathers themselves (esp. Augustine, Gregory [3] the Great) soon became the object of *florilegia*. As early as the Middle Ages there was a new flourishing of the *florilegium* of secular ancient writings. A history of *florilegium* literature (and its significance for the tradition of numerous ancient authors) has not yet been written.

H. CHADWICK, s.v. F., RAC 7, 1131–1160; E. RAUNER, F., in: LMA 4, 566–69. J.P.S.

Florus Roman cognomen ('blond', 'radiant', with ablaut, related to *flavus* [1]), in the Republican period epithet of C. Aquilius [I 11] F. and L. Mestius F.

1 WALDE/HOFMANN 1, 513f.

KAJANTO, COGNOMINA 233f. K.-L.E.

[1] **P. Annius F.** Under the cognomen Florus (in conjunction with the family name Annius or Ann(a)eus and the first name P. or L.) four works or groups of works are known: 1. the introduction to a dialogue *Vergilius orator an poeta* (P. Annius F.), 2. and 3. fragment of a correspondence (Charisius, Gramm. 66,10f.; 157,21f. B.) and an exchange of poetry (cf. also Anth. Lat. 238–246; 75; 84–87SHB) with Hadrian (Annius F.) and 4. an *Epitome de Tito Livio* (L. Anneus F.). The identity of the person behind this is generally acknowledged today; L. Ann(a)eus, the name of both Senecas, may have been passed on from him. The biography results from *Vergilius orator* 1–3: originating from Africa, as a young man F. was defeated in one of the Capitoline poetry *agones*, organized from AD 86 onwards by Domitian and still carried out in 90 and 94, by the emperor himself. After long travels as a wandering orator (to Sicily, Crete, Rhode, Egypt, Rome and Gaul), F. settled as a teacher of literature in Tarraco, where he was in his fifth year of teaching at the time of the dialogue (102 or 106, cf. 1,9). His friendly relations with Hadrian suggest a later stay in Rome; his historical work also falls into the later years of Hadrian, according to Epit. 1, praef. 1ff..

The *Epitome*, praising the greatness of Rome, is based on a comparison – probably conveyed by Varro – of the Roman historical epochs with the four ages of man (pr. 4–8), only three of which (the time of the kings = *infantia*; conquest of Italy up to 264 BC = *adulescentia*; conquest of the whole world up to Augustus = *iuventas*), but not the *senectus* = Imperial period are sketched in close detail – and indeed more rhetorically than historically. The main source is Livy, probably directly; the traditional assumption that he used a comprehensive epitome by Livy from the 1st cent. AD has recently been contested with good reasons. The historical work was written essentially for the educated, non-senatorial upper class of the Latin half of the empire, as can be seen from the emphases of the depiction: the concise handling of the 700–year history of the deeds (= wars) of Rome up to Augustus starts with *A Romulo tempora regum septem*; starting with the *Bellum Etruscum* (1,4), 68 wars follow up to the last chapter (2,34: *Pax Parthorum et consecratio Augusti*). The series of wars is interrupted twice in bk. 1, which contains only foreign wars up to the conquest of Gaul by Caesar, by retrospectives (*anacephalaeoses* 1,2; 47) and a general chapter *De seditionibus* (1,17) on the internal crises (attempts at dictatorship and secessions). Bk. 2 begins with the Gracchi and lists the ensuing civil wars up to Actium; the series of civil wars is not continued until Augustus (2,22–33). The history seems to concentrate on wars and world domination, cf. 2,33,59; 2,34,64. This is the reason for F.'s dissatisfaction with the Augustan peace policy continued by Hadrian and with the Imperial period in general, which appears to him to be marked by *inertia Caesarum* (pr. 8).

From late antiquity (Ampelius, Festus, Orosius, Augustine, Iordanes) the *Epitome*, together with other surveys, played its part in conveying knowledge of Roman history. The work reached the Middle Ages, via an archetype from late antiquity, in two versions, also of late antiquity, of two bks. with inserted titles or four books – in numerous codices (together with Livy's Periochae). Particularly in Humanism – Petrarch had the text and used it in particular in the *Historia Iulii Caesaris* – F. was drawn on to fill the gaps in the Livy tradition. The *Epitome* was also a much-used textbook in the modern era and was still widely read up to the 19th cent., but it fell victim to the pressure of historicism and positivism from the middle of the 19th cent.

EDD.:
EPITOME: P. JAL, Vol. 1/2, 1967; E. MALCOVATI, ²1972; C. FACCHINI TOSI, 1990 (Praefatio).
POEMS: S. MATTIACCI, I frammenti dei poetae novelli, 1982, 54–63; C. DI GIOVINE, 1988; COURTNEY, 375–386.
ENCYCLOPAEDIA: M. L. FELE, 1975.
BIBLIOGRAPHY: S. LILLIEDAHL, F.-Studien, 1928; P. STEINMETZ, Unters. zur röm. Lit. des 2. Jh., 1982, 121–138; J. M. ALONSO-NUÑEZ, Die polit. und soz. Ideologie des F., 1983; M. D. REEVE, The Transmission of F., in: CQ 38, 1988, 477–491; 41, 1991, 453–483; L. BESSONE, F., in: ANRW II.34,1, 80–117; Id., La storia epitomata, 1996; M. HOSE, Erneuerung der Vergangenheit, 1994, 53–140; K. SALLMANN, in: HLL § 462.

[2] Is named in Sen. Controv. 9,2,23f. as the instigator of a *sententia inepte tumultuosa* attributed to M. Porcius Latro. He is not identical to the addressee of Hor. Epist. 1,3; 2,2 or the orator mentioned in Quint. Inst. 10,3,13. P.L.S.

Flour (Greek ἄλευρον/*áleuron*, Lat. *farina*). Fine-grained to powdery product resulting from grinding, crushing or pounding certain grains or seeds. The most important source product in the Greek period was barley (Ath. 3,111e–112a) and in the Roman period it was wheat (Plin. HN 18,74; 85–90); depending on the region, flour was also made from millet (Gal. De alimentorum facultatibus 1,15) and rye (Plin. HN 18,141) and in areas with no grain cultivation or in times of emergency even from starch-containing fruits such as beans or acorns (Plin. HN 16,15; 18,117).

Flour was differentiated according to its degree of fineness and purity. In the Roman Imperial period, for example, fine flour with only small proportions of bran (*flos*; *pollen*), medium-fine, relatively pure flour (*siligo*; *similago*) and coarse cooking flour with high proportions of bran (*cibarium*, Plin. HN 18,86–90) were known. As milling and sieving techniques were not very far advanced, the quality of the flour was not the same as today's; it went off quickly because the starch-containing inside of the grain could not be completely separated from the outside layers rich in oil. Even fine flour had a relatively high proportion of bran and was darkish in colour. Furthermore, flour was always slightly contaminated with rubbings from the millstones.

In the kitchen flour was mainly used for baking. The finer types of flour were used for cakes and fine bread, while the coarse flour formed the basis of the 'bread of poorer quality' (*panis secundarius*; cf. Suet. Aug. 76,1). Flour was also used for mushy mixed beverages (Hom. Il. 11,640) and to thicken sauces (Apicius 3,11,1). In cult, flour was of great significance as a food offering; in medicine it was used predominantly for poultices to reduce inflammation and swelling (Celsus, artes 4,6; 5,27,13; Dioscorides, De materia medica 2,85–86 WELLMANN).

→ Bakeries; → Grain; → Mill

J. ANDRÉ, Essen und Trinken im alten Rom, 1998; A. DALBY, Essen und Trinken im alten Griechenland, 1998; A. MAU, s.v. Bäckerei, RE 2, 2734–2743; L. A. MORITZ, Grain-Mills and Flour in Classical Antiquity, 1958. A.G.

Fly As μυῖα (μῦα; *myîa*, *mŷa*; Lat. *musca*), which Aristotle attributed to the dipterans (δίπτερα; *díptera*), not only the housefly, but also the gadfly or blind fly (also κυνόμυια; *kynómyia*) and the bluebottle were conceived. In Aristotle, Pliny and Lucian (*Muscae Encomium* = 'Praise of the Fly') usually the housefly is referred to, but the sting of the gadfly (Aristot. Hist. an. 1,5,490a 20; 4,7,532a 21; Plin. HN 11,100; Lucian. *Muscae Encomium* 6) and its buzzing during flight (Aristot. Hist. an. 4,9,535 b 9–11; Plin. HN 11,266) are also mentioned. Homer (Il. 2,469; 16,639–641; 4,131) alludes to the gadflies persistently flying around cattle, milk cans and small children, as well as around corpses which are supposedly devoured by the 'worms' of bluebottles (Il. 19,25ff.; cf. also Theophr. Char. 25,5; Paus. 10,28,7). Their maggots were known (σκώληκες; *skōlēkes*, Aristot. Hist. an. 5,1,539b 11; 5,19,552a 21); Plin. HN 10,190: *vermiculus*), but nothing was known about their very small eggs or pupae. Aristotle's description of their procreation is wrong (Hist. an. 5,8,541b 34ff.). Their intrusiveness and impudence were almost proverbial (Phaedr. 5,3; Ael. NA 7,19; Horapollon 1,51), similarly their craving for sweets (Hom. Il. 16,641; Aesop. 292f.). The fly was also regarded as courageous (Hom. Il. 17,750; Lucian. *Muscae Encomium* 5), sometimes stupid (Plin. HN 29,106), sometimes clever (Lucian. ibid.). Various kinds of fly-flaps (μυισόβη/*myisóbē*, *muscarium*: Aristoph. Equ. 60; Vesp. 597; Men. Fr. 437 KÖRTE[2]; Syll[3] 367; Mart. 3,82,12 and passim) were used to protect against flies, as well as plant juices and chemicals (Columella 7,13,1; Plin. HN 20,184; 24,53; 25,61 and 34,167; Gp. 13,12). Flies were hunted by spiders (Aristot. Hist. an. 1,1,488a 18; Nic. Ther. 735; Plin. HN 29,87) and wasps (Aristot. Hist. an. 8(9),42,628b 34ff.; Plin. HN 11,72).

Their supposedly tough life gave them demonic power (Apul. Met. 2, 22; cf. Eurynomos in Paus. 10,28,7). The apotropaic god Myiodes later became Zeus Apomyios (Paus. 5,14,1; Plin. HN 29,106; Ael. NA 5,17) and Myiagros (Paus. 8,26,7; Plin. HN 10,75; cf. [1. 441], whom KELLER [2. 2,449] identified with Beelzebub, 2 Kgs 1,2). Hercules had to protect his temple in the Forum boarium in Rome against flies (Plin. HN 10,79; Plut. Quaest. Rom. 90). The impudence of flies led to the introduction of Myia as the portrayal of the parasite (Antiphon fr. 195 CGF; Plaut. Poen. 690ff.; Anth. Pal. 16,9; Apoll. Rhod. 4,1453). A comic verse in Lucian. Muscae Encomium 11 mentions a hetaira Myia. Flies on cameos were said to protect against the evil eye [cf. 3. pl. 29,29–30 and 39 also pl. 24,37). Plin. HN 34,83 (cf. 36,43) mentions a depiction in miniature art. In proverbs the following phrases are found: 'making an elephant out of a fly' (Lucian. Muscae Encomium 12), 'a fly in the brain' (Phaedr. 4,23) and 'as much as a fly' (i.e. almost nothing) in Herondas 1,15 (cf. Suet. Dom. 3,1). In Lucian. Muscae Encomium 10 a myth about metamorphosis is mentioned.

→ Insects

1 NILSSON, Feste 2 KELLER 3 F. IMHOOF-BLUMER, O. KELLER, Tier- und Pflanzenbilder auf Münzen und Gemmen des klass. Alt., 1889, repr. 1972. C.HÜ.

Flycatcher This songbird family is represented in the Mediterranean by only two varieties: (a) the grey (*Muscicapa striata Pall.*) and (b) the collared flycatcher (*M. albicollis Temminck*). The two were not distinguished in antiquity, thus it is impossible to identify them either in zoological records or in ancient illustrations (for instance on mosaics [1. vol. 2, 119]). The ancient name συκαλλίς/*sykallís*, *ficedula* is based on the assumption, already indirectly refuted by Aristotle (Hist. an. 8(9),3,592b 21f. and 28f.) that it eats figs. Aristotle's contention that the μελαγκόρυφος (the titmouse) turns into a *sykallís* at a certain time (Hist. an. 8(9),49b,632b 31ff.; cf. Gp. 15,1 and Plin. HN 10,86) rather applies to the twin types of marsh tit (*Parus palustris L.*) and black-capped chickadee(*Parus atricapillus L.*); Alexander of Myndes in Ath. 2,65b supports this interpretation. It is undisputed that the flycatcher was held in high estimation as a delicacy (Epicharmus in Ath. 2,65 b; Lucil. 978 M., along with turtle doves; Petron. Sat. 33; Juv. 14,9; Mart. 13,49; Favorinus in Gell. NA 15,8; Poll. 6,77). In the *Edictum Diocletiani* 4,36 the top prices for ten flycatchers were laid down as forty denarii as opposed to sixty for ten thrushes. Dioscurides 2,56 p. 1,138 WELLMANN = 2,60 p. 169 BERENDES recommends their meat for improving the eyesight.

1 KELLER. C.HÜ.

Flying fox (Badul) see → Bat

Fodder The extent and type of animal husbandry in ancient → agriculture was essentially determined by the availability of fodder, which in turn was dependent on the respective geomorphologic and climatic conditions. Thus, Boeotia was famous in the Homeric period for its meadows rich in green fodder (ποίη/*poíē*; Hom. Il. 2,503; H. Hom. 3,243; 4,190); fodder was also available from fallow fields and woodlands; in addition there were pastures (λειμών/*leimṓn*; Hom. Il. 2,461–469). Specifically, Homer mentions a type of clover (λωτός/*lōtós* (→ lotus) and wild → parsley (σέλινον/*sélinon*; Hom. Il. 2,776) as fodder. → Pigs were pastured in woodlands and fed with acorns and cornelian cherry (Hom. Od. 14,1 f.; 10,242 f.). → Grain (Hom. Il. 5,195 f.) was used to feed horses; geese were also fed wheat (Hom. Od. 19,536 f.). Storing hay for working animals was already recommended by Hesiod (Hes. Op. 606 f.).

In the classical, Hellenistic and Roman periods, pastures were the most important source of fodder. Because of the hydrological and climatic circumstances of the Mediterranean region, summer pasture was scarce in the lowlands because only naturally and artificially irrigated meadows could be used for this purpose. Animals were increasingly taken to upland pastures for this purpose (Soph. OT 1131–1139). Indications of a seasonal migration of herds (→ Transhumance) are found in Crete and later in Italy (Varro, Rust. 2,2,9; 2,5,11; 2,10,3; Columella 6,22,2). Despite the importance of pasturing, feeding is known from the Hellenistic period. In particular, pigs were fattened for the market with barley, millet, → figs, acorns, wild pears and → cucumbers, while → cattle received as their usual fodder grain, grass, → vegetables, vetches, ground → beans and bean straw. Barley, figs, spent brewer's grain and elm leaves were also used for fattening cattle; → horses, → mules and → donkeys were given grass, grain and → clover, and → sheep received olive twigs, vetches and bran (Aristot. Hist. an. 595a–596a).

The Roman → agrarian writers provide detailed instructions for feeding the oxen used as draught animals, who were fed during work periods in their stables and rarely pastured in the open (Cato Agr. 30; 54; Columella 6,3,4–8; 11,2,99–101); fodder is also mentioned for horses (Columella 6,27,8; 6,27,11), donkeys (Columella 6,37,9), sheep (Cato Agr. 30,2; Columella 7,3,19–22; Pall. Agric. 12,12, 1–3), pigs (Columella 7,9,5–9; Pall. Agric. 3,26,3), → dogs (Columella 7,12,10), poultry (Columella 8,4,1; 8,4,3: chickens; 8,8,1 f.; 8,8,6; 8,9,2 f.: pigeons; 8,10,3–5: thrushes; 8,11,1 f.; 8,11,6; 8,11,14 f.: peafowl; 8,14,2; 8,14,10; 8,15,6: ducks and geese), → fish (Columella 8,17,12–15) and kept game (Columella 9,1,5–8). Many animals such as horses, cattle, sheep, goats and pigs were kept almost exclusively in herds in the open, on pastures and in woodlands without feeding, especially during the summer (Columella 6,27,1 f.; Varro, Rust. 2,5,11; Columella 7,2,3; 7,6,1; 7,9,6). Additional fodder stored for the winter was used to make up for the paucity of green fodder.

Fodder plants were cultivated on estates (Cato Agr. 27), but also as a mixed sowing (*farrago*). The importance of barley as a fodder plant is noticeable (Plin. HN 18,74). Because fodder such as barley and lupines served as human food in times of need (Columella 2,9,14; 2,10,1, 2,10,22), livestock was often slaughtered in times of harvest failures (Quint. Decl. 12,6). Availability of fodder was also very important for using draught animals: cattle and horses were unaffordable for smallholders because of the high fodder costs. Therefore, Columella praises the Arcadian donkey because of its frugal needs (Columella 7,1).

The availability of fodder was a logistical problem in military operations and the provisioning of the standing army (→ Logistics) of the late Republic and the Principate (Caes. B Gall. 1,16,2; 2,2,2; 7,14,2; 7,16,3; cf. Veg. Mil. 3,1,5; 3,3). The necessity of supplying the frontier armies with fodder had a significant impact on agricultural development in the north-western provinces.

→ Meat, consumption of; → Stables, keeping of animals in; → Zoo; → Husbandry

1 A. CHANIOTIS, Milking the Mountains. Economic Activities on the Cretan Uplands in the Classical and Hellenistic Period, in: Id. (ed.), From Minoan Farmers to Roman Traders, 1999, 181–220 2 H.-J. DREXHAGE, Preise, Mieten/Pachten, Kosten und Löhne im röm. Ägypten bis zum Regierungsantritt Diokletians, 1991, 313–326 3 ISAGER/SKYDSGAARD, 83–96 4 G. KRON, Roman Ley-Farming, in: Journal of Roman Archaeology 13, 2000, 277–287 5 W. RICHTER, Die Landwirtschaft im homerischen Zeitalter (ArchHom 2), 1968 6 J. P. ROTH, The Logistics of the Roman Army at War (264 B. C.A. D. 235), 1999, 61–67; 125–130 7 M. SCHNEBEL, Die Landwirtschaft im hell. Ägypten, 1925, 342–352 8 O. STOLL, Terra pecorum fecunda, in: Id., Röm. Heer und Gesellschaft, 2001, 421–451 9 WHITE, Farming, 199–223 10 WHITTAKER 11 L. WIERSCHOWSKI, Heer und Wirtschaft, 1984, 151–173. K. RU.

Foederati Roman name for partners in treaties with Rome, who were independent subjects in international law. The parties to the treaties were geographically in direct contact with the *Imperium Romanum* or were counted as part of it. Proculus calls all *foederati externi* (Dig. 49,15,7), but at the time of the Republic there were *foederati* on provincial soil (Cic. Verr. 5,51). The term has purely political implications, locating it geographically at the borders of the empire is inadequate.

From the Principate period treaties were made by the emperor or a representative [9. 92, 112], as a → *foedus* as it were, which, however, did not always establish a *foederati* relationship (cf. Cass. Dio 72,18,1). The treaty was signed with due solemnity and conditions were variable [9. 90]. It is still difficult to draw up a formulation (for late antiquity [5]). The contractual relationship was based on principles such as → *amicitia*, → *societas*, → *pax*, → *hospitium*. A *foedus* always depended on the actual strength of Rome [9. 81f.]. → *Deditio* as a preliminary was desired by the Romans, but not essential. In the course of policies of expansion at the time of the Principate, Rome made use of the *foederati* for both defensive and offensive purposes (cf. Vell. Pat. 2,105,1; 2,106,1; Cass. Dio 72,11; *Inscriptions latines d'Afrique* 609).

The → Constitutio Antoniniana and the army reform of → Gallienus, reacting in part to growing pressure from outside, prepared border policies which were intensified in late antiquity. For instance, the *foedus* of → Constantinus [1] with the Goths in 332 [1. 54–59, 113f.] secured the Danube border for *c.* 50 years and procured Gothic influx for Rome for undertakings in the east (on treaties of this period see [5. 175ff.]). The defeats against the Persians (treaty between → Iovianus and → Sapor II in 363) also weakened Rome in the west. The arrangement with the Gothic leagues of → Fritigern on the Danube (376) became ineffective as a result of the battle of Adrianopolis (378). The *foedus* between → Theodosius I and the Goths (3 Oct. 382) pointed in a new direction. After the *deditio* they all together were resettled as *gentiles* belonging to the empire in the area of Dacia ripensis and Moesia II. Since the Roman population was not relocated, the institute of → *hospitalitas* regulated their relationship with the new settlers. The → *conubium* was denied to the Gothic population. They were considered to be autonomous, were not liable to taxes and received payments. They had to supply military assistance under Roman supreme command.

The treaty was a model for future settlements of *foederati* on imperial territory [1. 138ff.; 5. 293f. with bibliography]. Rome was forced to make concessions in the treaties with Alaric (→ Alaricus [2]) from 392 to 402–403. Defence against pressing polyethnic leagues towards the south in 391–392 under Alaric's command led to the *deditio* of the Goths and a *foedus* confirming the arrangements of 382, which probably brought Alaric recognition as king of the Goths [8. 150ff.]. The *foedus* with → Arcadius (397) contains his appointment as *magister militum per Illyricum*. Settlement of the Goths took place in Macedonia (*Emathia Tellus*), where Alaric was also given civil rulership (Claud. in Eutropium 2,214–218; De bello Gothico 496f.; 535–539 [8. 149f.]). The Goths were largely autonomous and their duty was to defend the borders of the territory which also financed them. The form of financing and settlement is generally disputed [5. 296–8]. There is a strong argument for the application of the *hospitalitas* well documented for Theoderic I (treaty with Honorius in 418–419) in conjunction with financing by granting tax shares (*sors*; Procop. Goth. 1,1,4ff.; 28; [2; 3]). The *foedus* of 397 became a precedent. Subsequently Alaric's battles in Italy and Athaulf's (→ Ataulfus) campaign to Aquitania show an increasing tendency towards independence of the Goths of Alaric or Visigoths who abandoned the *foederati* relationship and became an autonomous power factor in the empire. The Roman relationship to the Huns under → Attila, and later to → Theoderic the Great (treaties of 478, 483, 487/8; [5. 185f.; 8. 271ff.]), developed similarly.

From the 5th cent. Roman barbarian troops recruited privately and later regularly were also called *foederati*. In the 6th cent. they were under a *comes foederatorum* (→ *comes*) and received military payments (*annonae foederaticiae*). (*bucellarii*, Olympiodorus fr. 7, [4. 665]).

1 P.A. Barceló, Roms auswärtige Beziehungen unter der Constantinischen Dynastie (306–363), 1981 2 J. Durliat, Le salaire de la paix sociale dans le royaumes barbares, in: H. Wolfram, A. Schwarcz (ed.), Anerkennung und Integration, 1988, 21–72 3 W. Goffart, Barbarians and Romans A.D. 418–584, 1980 4 Jones, LRE, vol. 2 5 R. Schulz, Die Entwicklung des röm. Völkerrechtes im 4. und 5. Jh. n.Chr., 1993 6 A. Schwarcz, s.v. Foederati, RGA 8, 290–299 7 B. Stallknecht, Untersuchungen zur röm. Außenpolitik in der Spätantike, 1969 8 H. Wolfram, Die Goten, ³1990 9 K.H. Ziegler, Das Völkerrecht der röm. Republik, in: ANRW I 2, 68–114.

U.HE.

Foedus Ceremonial treaty of peace and friendship between Rome and another state which is placed under the protection of the gods. By contrast to a truce (*indutiae*) the *foedus* was drawn up for the long term (*pia et aeterna pax*). The result of the *foedus* was a → *societas* or an → *amicitia*, Rome's partners were → *foederati*, → *socii* or *amici* (the terms are not strictly differentiated). Originally the *foedera* were probably signed by the → *fetiales* in the form of a *sponsio* (Liv. 1,24); later their role was confined to supervising the religious formalities. The *foedus* was usually signed by a magistrate or promagistrate in the field, but it had to be confirmed by the public assembly in Rome. In the Imperial period the right of signing a *foedus* was a prerogative of the emperor as attested in the *lex de imperio Vespasiani*.

The content of the *foedus* was a mutual duty of assistance. According to the later and probably not official systems in Proculus (Dig. 49,15,7,1) a distinction was made between the *foedera aequa* and the *foedera iniqua;* while the former established the duty of assistance between equals in the case of attacks by third parties, the latter obligated the partner – usually as a result of a *deditio* ('capitulation') – to acknowledge Rome's supremacy (*maiestatem populi Romani comiter conservare*; differently [1], who, however, rightly states that *foedus iniquum* was not a technical term). The originally clearly marked differences in the position of the → *foederati*, between those of varying power, and those within and outside of Italy, became increasingly blurred in proportion to the extent to which Rome became the only decisive power in the Mediterranean. In Italy the category of *foederati* disappeared with the Social War, and outside of Italy the *foedus* was increasingly replaced by Rome's unilateral declarations of freedom.

In late antiquity *foederati* were non-Roman troops (not necessarily of the same nationality), usually commanded by an aristocrat of the respective tribe, whereas *foedus* could denote virtually any treaty (POHL in [3. 8], cf. there also the contributions by WIRTH and HEATHER).

1 D.W. BARONOWSKI, Sub umbra foederis aequi, in: Phoenix 44, 1990, 345–369 2 L. DE LIBERO, Ut eosdem quos populus Romanus amicos atque hostes habeat, in: Historia 46, 1997, 270–305 3 P. HEATHER (ed.), The Goths, 1997 4 H. HORN, Foederati, Diss. 1929 5 StV, vols. 2 and 3.

H.GA.

Foedus Cassianum Alliance entered into with the Latins after the victory over them at the *Lacus Regillus* in 493 BC by the consul Sp. → Cassius [I 19] Vecellinus, which was extended to the Hernici in 486. The document was still preserved at the time of Cicero on a bronze column (the original?) in the Forum (Cic. Balb. 53). The historicity of the text is acknowledged today, as is the early dating, contrary to earlier research [1. 68f.; 2. 299–301]. The main conditions are found in Dion. Hal. Ant. Rom. 6,95: peace between Romans and Latins as long as heaven and earth exist; no support for third parties who intend to wage war against one of the parties, but mutual assistance; sharing the booty in equal parts; in international private lawsuits quick implementation within ten days; changes in the wording of the contract by mutual agreement only. Festus (p. 166, s.v. *nancitor*) quotes conditions concerning the *commercium* ('commerce') between Latins and Romans. Festus (p. 276, s.v. *praetor*) indicates that the supreme command in war alternated between the Romans and the Latins, though the order is unclear.

1 M. HUMBERT, Municipium et civitas sine suffragio, 1978 2 T. CORNELL, The Beginnings of Rome, 1995.

Stv 2, 22ff. no. 126; E. FERENCZY, Zum Problem des foedus Cassianum, in: RIDA 3, 22, 1975, 223–232; E. GABBA, La proposta di legge agraria di Sp. Cassio, in: Athenaeum 42, 1964, 29–41; H. GALSTERER, Herrschaft und Verwaltung im republikanischen Italien, 1976.

H.GA.

Foedus Gabinum Alleged treaty from the time of king Tarquinius Superbus (end 6th cent. BC), which was still extant in the Augustan period on a shield covered in cowhide in the temple of Semo Sancus; documented in Dion. Hal. Ant. Rom. 4,58,4 and on coins of two Antistii (family from Gabii, C. → Antistius [II 7] Vetus and C. Antistius Reginus) from the Augustan period: FOEDUS P.R. CUM GABINIS (RIC² 1, 68 no. 363 and 73 no. 411). Main content was an *isopoliteia* between Rome and Gabii. According to Varro (Ling. 5,33) the *ager Gabinus* represented an exceptional feature of augural law between the *ager Romanus* and the *ager peregrinus*. MOMMSEN believed, though hardly with justification, that in this case *ager Gabinus* as a 'technical exemplification' referred to each *ager Latinus* [1. 830f.].

1 MOMMSEN, STAATSRECHT 3.

F. BRUUN, The foedus Gabinum, in: Arctos 5, 1967, 51–66.

H.GA.

Foenum Graecum see → Fenugreek

Folius Roman *gentile* name (older form epigraphically *Foslius*, InscrIt 13,1,37, → folius [3]), attested in the early Republic solely for the family of the patrician Folii, which died out at the end of the 4th cent. BC; later common proper name of non-senatorial families.

TH. MOMMSEN, Röm. Forsch. 1, ²1864, 114f.

[1] Pontifex maximus, remained in Rome with other old men when Rome was taken by the Celts in 387 BC and was killed (Liv. 5,41,3).

[2] **F. Flaccinator, M.** Consular tribune in 433 BC (Liv. 4,25,2; Diod. Sic. 12,58,1), perhaps identical with F. [1].

[3] **Foslius Flaccinator, M.** Grandson of F. [2], *magister equitum* of the dictators C. Maenius (320 and 314 BC) and C. Poetelius (313), consul in 318 (Liv. 9,20,1; Diod. Sic. 19,2,1).

K.-L.E.

Folk songs It is not clear how to decide which ancient poems should be categorized as folk songs (FS). The category 'Greek FS' is a creation of modern publishers of Greek poetry; unlike poetic genres such as → *dithýrambos*, → *paián*, → *íambos* etc., FS do not reflect ancient classification. What remains of Greek FS (short poems and fragments) are collected under the customary modern title of *Carmina popularia* in modern publications of early Greek → lyric poetry [1; 3. 488–514; 4; 5. 463–482]. These texts probably stem from choral and monodic performance on a variety of occasions; they testify to the importance of song in Greek culture ('Song Culture': [6]). Metrically, they suggest an amazing variety, from simple iambi all the way to ionics and a variety of Aeolian kola [7. 146–149] (→ Kolon; → Metre).

Modern understanding of Greek FS is closely tied to the assumptions concerning the development of → lyric poetry, namely that there is a long oral tradition of folk songs behind the established lyrical forms. The earliest documentation comes from the 'Iliad', where songs that are known from the later lyrical tradition are mentioned: → *paián* (Hom. Il. 1,472–473; 22,391), → *thrênos* (24,720–722), → *aílinos* or → *línos* songs (18,570), as well as → *hyménaios*, the wedding song (18,493). Among the so-called *Carmina popularia* (see above) there are specimens of all these types of songs: 858 PMG is a paean to Eurus, the east wind; 878 PMG comes from a dirge; 880 PMG is quoted in schol. Hom. Il. 18,570 from the Linus Song; 881 PMG is comprised of fragments of a traditional wedding song.

All these songs are rooted in the religious traditions of Greek communities; ritual acts probably provided most of the occasions for the performance of songs. The majority of the passages ascribed to the *Carmina popularia* actually appear to belong within a cult framework. The evidence does not always reveal the role played by these songs in their specific rituals. In some cases the location of the cult is apparent: the → Anthesteria (883 PMG), → Lenaia (879 PMG), the Megalartia for Demeter (847 PMG), the Eleusinian → Mysteria (862 PMG). More often, however, there is only a vague allusion to a → hymnus to a specific deity (860 PMG), to singing 'at festivals of the gods' (ἐν ταῖς ἑορταῖς; Plut. Apophthegma Laconica 15 quotes 870 PMG), or to the bringing of a 'specific sacrifice' (Plut. Thes. 16,2 = fr. 868 PMG). In a few cases, the testimonia illuminate a context: Theognis of Rhodes (FGrH 526 F 1) passes on the Rhodian Swallow Song (848 PMG), a text that sheds light on ritualized begging on this island [8]; Plut. Quaest. Graec. 36 preserves the invocation of Dionysus by the women of Elis (871 PMG) at the Thyia or Dionysia [9]; in 851 PMG, Semus of Delos (FGrH 396 F 24) quotes a detailed description of cultic phallus worship [10. 137–144; 11. 31–35] (perhaps a parody of Eur. Hipp. 73 ff. [12. 36], but the similarity is only superficial and formal; the linking of lyrical salutation and iambic dedication in text passages of both Semus and Euripides probably indicate cultic occasions).

FS were also performed at many other occasions having nothing to do with cult worship: as an integral part of games (861, 875, 876 PMG; → Contests), as accompaniment to → dance (852 and 864 PMG) or to military marches (856 and 857 PMG); as song or recitation of a herald at athletic contests (863, 865, 866 PMG).

Plut. Amatorius 17 quotes a popular love song from Chalcis (873 PMG); Ath. 15,697b speaks of 'frivolous songs' (καπυρώτεραι ᾠδαί) and quotes 853 PMG as an example of 'songs of infidelity' (μοιχικαί). There seems to be a tradition of popular erotic songs behind the love duet in Aristoph. Eccl. 952–968 [13]. Also belonging to folk songs are → work songs; the Attic → *skólia* could also be regarded as FS.

The majority of texts in PMG have come down to us without being attributed to an author; perhaps some folk songs are hidden in the so-called *Adespota* of the PMG. Only those surviving texts on papyrus cause special difficulty in classification. D. Page places the paean to Eurus (858 PMG) in the *Carmina popularia*, the similarly constructed paean from Erythrae (933–934 PMG), on the other hand, in the *Adespota* (presumably because 858 PMG comes from Sparta, where traditional songs were repeatedly performed, cf. Plut. Lycurgus 21; [14. 3]). In the ancient tradition, some folk songs were also attributed to known poets: the hymnus to Hercules in Olympia was attributed to Archilochus (fr. spur. 324 West²) [12. 138 f.], the Swallow Song on Samos to Homerus [1] (Vita Homeri Herodotea 464 Allen) [15. 245–275]. Despite all these difficulties in classification 'FS' are a useful category for Greek poetry; they shed light on a tradition, within which the important Greek lyric poets worked.

→ Feasts; → Songs; → Lyric poetry

Editions: 1 PMG, 847–883 D. A. Campbell (ed.), Greek Lyric, vol. 5, 1993, 232–269 (with Engl. transl.) 3 H. W. Smyth, Greek Melic Poets, 1906.

Bibliography: 4 G. Lambin, La chanson grecque dans l'antiquité, 1992 5 F. Pordomingo, in: O. Pecere, A. Stramaglia (ed.), La letteratura di consumo nel mondo greco-latino, 1996 6 C. J. Herington, Poetry into Drama, 1985 7 M. L. West, Greek Metre, 1982 8 N. Robertson, Greek Ritual Begging in: TAPhA 113, 1983, 143–169 9 S. Scullion, Dionysus at Elis, in: Philologus 145, 2001, 203–218 10 A. Pickard-Cambridge, Dithyramb, Tragedy and Comedy, ²1962 11 C. G. Brown, Iambos, in: D. E. Gerber, A Companion to the Greek Lyric Poets, 1997 12 M. L. West, Studies in Greek Elegy and Iambus, 1974 13 C. M. Bowra, A Love Duet, in: AJPh 79, 1958, 376–391 (= Id., On Greek Margins, 1970, 149–163) 14 I. Rutherford, Pindar's Paeans, 2001 15 G. Markwald, Die homerischen Epigramme, 1986.

CH. BR.

Folk-tales

I. Term and genre II. Ancient Orient III. Greece IV. Roman Literature

I. Term and genre

In antiquity the folk-tale as a well-defined literary genre with unequivocally established terminology was not known. However, since oral narratives, partly put down in writing, that according to the modern meaning of the term can undoubtedly be designated as folk-tales, existed in all ages and all cultures, the issue of the folk-tale becomes a meaningful and inevitable subject also with regard to antiquity. The German word 'Märchen' is derived from OHG *māri*, MHG *diu/daz maere* = 'report', 'message', i.e. 'narrative', still entirely in the sense of a comment on events that were considered to be real. It was not until the late Middle Ages and the 15th cent. that the diminutive form acquired the meaning of 'invented story' (*fabula*) in contrast to the 'true event' (*historia*). This prose genre soon gained popularity as a literary form in European Baroque and in the Enlightenment. But it was Romanticism (Herder) that first recognized the oral tradition as a primary characteristic of the folk-tale and postulated a strict separation between 'artificial written poetry' (i.e. literature composed in writing) and 'natural written poetry' (i.e. oral folk tradition), which 'generates automatically', as it were (Herder). The Grimm brothers' 'Children's and Household Tales' [1] followed in the wake of this initial impetus. Using them as a model, a plethora of collections of European folk-tales was compiled in the 19th cent. Thereby, modern research into folk-tales, which studies folk-tales of all ages and cultures was initiated.

Defining the folk-tale is as difficult as ever. This is already evident from the absence of a semantically identical term in other languages (Engl. *fairytale*, *folk-tale*; French *conte*; Italian *fiaba*). Basic characteristics are the orality of the narrative, miraculous events as content, a Utopian idea of space, timelessness and a satisfactory end with poetic justice. The folk-tale is different from the → myth partly in that it was not invented, like the latter, for (religious) interpretation of the historical world (such as religious rites, social circumstances, topographical or other specific peculiarities of nature; → Aetiology), but exists purely for the sake of narration, of 'story-telling' – irrespective of the fact that social reality is also reflected in folk-tales [2. 79f.; 3. 17f.].

Research into folk-tales has followed two different routes in analyzing the material: a literary studies approach and a folkloristic-cultural studies approach. The literary studies approach is represented mainly by the works of the School of Russian Formalism, in particular by V. PROPP [4; 5]. For this school the focus of analysis was no longer the precisely documented text of the oral narrative, the recording of which had still been so important to the GRIMM brothers and which, subsequently had traditionally been studied with regard to its originality as a 'national' legacy of the 'early days of the nation', but the structure of the pragmatic coherence of the action. This folk-tale structure presents a small number of fixed motifs which form a variable series or sequence of motifs. Folk-tale analysis is therefore no longer analysis of individual texts, but of bodies of texts, reduced to basic structures, e.g. a hero sets off into the world, has to endure miraculous adventures, is thought to be dead and returns at the very last moment, before his wife/fiancée/mistress marries another man. It is difficult to draw a line between the folk-tale and other 'lesser' genres (saga, legend, myth) within this approach [6].

The folkloristic approach is pursued by the so-called 'Finnish School', in particular by A. AARNE and F. THOMPSON. Their main achievement is a comprehensive anthology of material and the compilation of a 'catalogue of types'. It is based on the idea that the folk-tale cannot be comprehended as a 'text', but as material organized in structures of meaning. Therefore it is only by collecting many variations that a 'type' can be abstracted [7; 8; 9; 10]. Aside from the 'catalogue of types' of folk-tale, an index of motifs can also be drawn up, which lists not only individual folk-tale motifs, but entire combinations of motifs that can also be found in other genres [9; 10]. According to AARNE-THOMPSON the three main types are the 'animal folk-tales', 'proper folk-tales' and 'comic folk-tales'. The proper folk-tales comprise 'magic-' or 'miracle folk-tales', 'legend-type', 'novella-type folk-tales' and 'folk-tales about stupid devils or giants'. They include chain or formulaic folk-tales, which become episodic due to repeated modification of the same motif. Finally, the 'comic folk-tales' are often represented in the form of 'liars' tales', of a 'world turned upside-down', 'Münchhausen tales', etc. [5]. Of the cultural studies approach only the psychological folk-tale research shall be mentioned here. In this context the school of C.G. JUNG deserves special mention. It regards the folk-tale as a symbol, as a cipher for dealing with the unknown [11].

1 Kinder- und Haus-M. der Brüder GRIMM, 3 vols. (1812–1822, [7]1857: final edition, with an appendix), ed. by H. RÖLLEKE, 1982 2 U. KINDL, s.v. M., HrwG 4, 78–84 3 NILSSON, GGR I, 17–23 4 V. PROPP, Morfologija skazki, 1928 ([2]1968) (English tr. by L.A. Wagner, Morphology of the Folk Tale, 1969) 5 Id., Istoriceskie korni volsebnoj skazki, 1946 (German: Die histor. Wurzeln des Zauber-M., 1987) 6 A. JOLLES, Einfache Formen, 1930 ([2]1956 et al.) 7 A. AARNE, S. THOMPSON, The Types of the Folktale (Folklore Fellows Communications = FFC 184), 1928 ([2]1961 et al.) 8 A. AARNE, Leitfaden der vergleichenden Märchen-Forsch. (FFC 13), 1913 9 S. THOMPSON, The Folktale, 1946 (repr. 1967 et al.) 10 Id., Motif-Index of Folk-Literature, 6 vols., 1955–1958 ([3]1975) 11 H. VON BEIT, Symbolik des M. Versuch einer Deutung, 3 vols., 1952–1957 ([4]1971).

M. LÜTHI, M., [9]1996; R. RANKE et al., Enzyklopädie des M., vol. 1ff., 1975ff. L.K.

II. Ancient Orient

A. Mesopotamia B. Syria/Palestine C. Hittite

A. Mesopotamia

No folk-tales have actually been handed down in the abundant cuneiform script literature. However, there is evidence of their existence in a mythical and epic context in extant folk-tale motifs, such as the fable of the 'eagle and snake' in Etana mythology, there also the 'ascension' of the hero; in the → Gilgamesh Epic episodes like the metamorphosis of Ištar's lovers into animals (→ Circe), the 'journey to the ends of the world', the 'garden of precious stones', the 'sea of death', the bearing away of the hero of the Flood into the 'land of the living'. The 'herb of life' is another such motif, which also occurs in the Sumerian Lugalbanda Epic I, and, in addition, there are the seven brothers and friends, the saving from death by 'good spirits'; in Lugalbanda II the assistance from the Anzu bird, etc. Various topoi in the legends about the Akkadian rulers, such as the abandonment of → Sargon after his birth and his rescue by Aqqi the water-drawer, the procession of the king into the 'fairytale Purušḫanda' through impenetrable forests and mountains, Narām-Sîns' battle against seven brothers, etc., have their parallels in folk literature. We can therefore assume that Mesopotamia also had an abundant folk-tale literature, now preserved only in such indirect pieces of evidence.

B. Syria/Palestine

Folk-tale motifs can also be found in Ugarit texts, for instance, in the → Keret Epic the loss and recovery of the children, the seven-day journey to Udum, and in the Aqhat text Anat's jealousy of a particularly precious bow. However, even the written tradition from Ugarit, like that of the OT, has no specific folk-tales.

→ Myth

E. BRUNNER-TRAUT, Altäg. M., [6]1983; Id., Altäg. Tiergeschichte und Fabel, 1968; R.M. DORSON (ed.), Folklore and Folklife, 1972; A. DUNDES (ed.), Sacred Narrative: Readings in the Theory of Myth, 1984; H. GUNKEL, Das M. im AT, 1921; H.-J. HERMISSON, s.v. M., TRE 21, 1995, 672–677; A. JOLLES, Einfache Formen, [2]1956; F. KARLINGER (ed.), Wege der M.-Forsch., 1973; M. LÜTHI, M., [9]1996; V. PROPP, Morphologie des M., 1972; L. RÖHRICH, M. und Wirklichkeit, [3]1974; W. RÖLLIG, Volkslit. in mesopot. Überl., in: K. HECKER, W. SOMMERFELD (ed.), Keilschriftl. Lit., 1968, 81–87; J.G. WESTENHOLZ, Legends of the Kings of Akkade, 1997.

W.R.

C. HITTITE

Several folk-tale type narratives and folk-tale motifs are preserved in Hittite literature. The story about the Queen of Neša and her thirty children, which takes place in the cities of Neša (→ Kaneš) and Zalpa (at the mouth of the Kızılırmak) and which is only partially extant, contains three folk-tale motifs: 1. the abandonment motif, 2. the marriage between brothers and sisters, and 3. the motif of the youngest (and most successful) child [1. 805–7]. The literature on the huntsman Kešši, handed down only in fragments in the Hittite, Hurrite and Akkadian languages, is more of an epic than a folk-tale. Kešši marries the beautiful Šintalimeni and therefore neglects his hunting and sacrificing. Ultimately, urged by his mother, he takes to the mountains, where, pursued by misfortune, he is threatened with being devoured by strange creatures [1. 851f.]. The story of the wealthy Appu, a Hurrite folk-tale figure, contains the motif of the two enemy brothers [1. 848–51].

In the folk-tale known as the 'tale of the fisherman' the sun god catches sight of a beautiful cow in the meadow which arouses his desire. In the form of a young man he descends from heaven and impregnates her. The cow bears a child in human form, but the angry mother threatens to kill it, whereupon the sun god takes it away from her. He ultimately arranges that the child is found by a childless fisherman and his wife. The fisherman's wife feigns a birth so that the neighbours believe the deception and bring gifts. The extant text ends here [1. 853–56]. In the story of Gurparanzaḫ, a Hurrite folk-tale figure, the hero kills a wild animal and enters into the Babylonian city of Akkade. After a banquet he beats 'sixty kings and seventy heroes' at archery. After he has gone to bed his wife Tatizuli appears. The story further tells how the personified Tigris (under its Hurrite name of Aranzaḫ) comes to Akkade through the air like an eagle, where he meets Gurparanzaḫ, whose marriage has caused difficulties. Therefore Aranzaḫ turns to the gods of fate [1. 852–853].

Typical motifs of folk-tale literature can also be found in myths and in incantations: in the myth of the god Telipinu [1. 815–821], animals as auxiliary spirits of the gods; in the Šedammu myth [1. 844–848], the motif of the fight with the dragon, which is also preserved in the myth of Illuyanka, the foolish dragon, and the weather god [1. 808–811]; finally the motif of the forbidden window; in the Ullikummi myth [1. 830–844] the stone monster, which lives on in the Phrygian Agdistis myth and in the Ossetic folk-tale of the fool; in incantations the motif of the impossible tasks, which is significant for folk-tale research: the 'abnormal people' are given the absurd task of making the long paths short and the short paths long, of making the high mountains flat and the flat mountains high, of catching the wolf with bare hands, catching the lion with their knees and stopping the flow of the river. The Hattic *hieros logos* of a Hittite storm ritual, which reports that the moon fell down from the sky into the marketplace, also has allusions to folk-tale.

1 TUAT 3, 1994.

V.H.

III. GREECE

There are no folk-tales in the above-defined sense in ancient Greece. The 'animal folk-tale' became literature as → fable (→ Aesop), while folk-tales in the stricter sense are extant only as folk-tale motifs in other genres (esp. → Epic). Whether 'children's stories' or 'stories told to children by wet-nurses' (Pl. Resp. 350e; Leg. 887d etc.) actually refer to folk-tales in the above-mentioned sense is hard to say. Their only specific characteristic seems to be that they are not true, in contrast to narrations for adults. However, there are no complete extant folk-tales from ancient Greece; this may be due to the fact that it was a purely oral genre, or because their motifs have been adopted by other genres.

There is, however, evidence of numerous folk-tale motifs in Greek mythology. A frequently occurring folk-tale motif is that of the adventure: the hero has to stand a series of battles and trials and to overcome giants and monsters or carry out superhuman tasks (e.g. → Iason, → Heracles, → Perseus, → Theseus). The sequence of adventures is often incorporated into a generic structure: the hero is forced by an enemy to brave dangers and is rewarded with the hand of the princess (→ Andromeda, → Iole, → Hippodamia); sometimes the woman is a widowed queen and with her hand the hero also gains the kingdom (→ Oedipus, → Odysseus). Sometimes the enamoured princess helps the hero to find his way to her (→ Ariadne with the thread, → Medea with the art of magic, and in the modern folk-tale by breadcrumbs eaten by birds, or small stones along the path). Magicians and witches, who turn people into animals etc., block the hero's way (→ Circe, → Medea). The hero is given miraculous aids (e.g. → Perseus: magic hood, winged shoes). The hero's life is magically linked to objects (→ Meleager [1], who dies as soon as the log has burned down). The list can be extended almost *ad infinitum*.

How productive a sensitive analysis of folk-tale motifs in other genres can be with regard to the specific interpretation of texts has been shown in recent research, after preliminary studies by L. RADERMACHER, D. PAGE (et al. [1; 2; 3;]), in particular by U. HÖLSCHER [4], who used the example of → Homer's 'Odyssey', consistently applying the methods of comparative folk-tale research. Whereas the research into the history of the subject matter behind this epic had always separated Odysseus as the hero of a seafarer folk-tale on the one hand from Odysseus as the hero of a homecoming novella on the other hand, thus differentiating between the 'miraculous' of the adventure and the realism of the events on Ithaca [5. 108], a decisive look at the pragmatic structures [6; 7] of the overall story of the 'Odyssey' shows a standard type of folk-tale, for which numerous parallels can be found, from ancient Egyptian miracle folk-tales, to Indian folk-tales and medieval legends: the protagonist leaves his wife, often to carry out heroic deeds as a 'seeker' or 'helper', is kept away from home for a long time, is involved in numerous adventures, leading him to the ends of the world and the afterlife, until he finally arrives at home, at first incognito, just in time to stop his wife from marrying another man [4]. Comparison with the plot of the 'Odyssey' shows that the epic follows this folk-tale structure in its overall outline. Many individual folk-tale motifs are incorporated into this structure: the individual adventures of the 'Odyssey' (the giant → Polyphemus, the witch Circe, lotus-eaters and → Calypso as versions of the realm of the dead, the bed as a secret sign of recognition, → Penelope's trick with the loom, etc.) [1]. The example of the 'Odyssey' shows particularly well that the structural approach of PROPP [6] combined with the analysis of motifs by AARNE-THOMPSON [8; 9] proves fruitful also with regard to ancient Greece (cf. also → Argonauts). Further, the characteristic absence of location situates the folk-tale near the → utopia: utopian folk-tale characteristics can already be found in the 'Odyssey' (→ Phaeaces); this connection is particularly prevalent in Hellenistic travel literature of the Imperial period and its caricature in Lucian (*Vera historia*) (e.g. → Antonius [3] Diogenes or → Iambulus).

→ Novel; → Utopia

1 L. RADERMACHER, Die Erzählungen in der Odyssee, SB Wien Philol.-histor. Klasse 178/1, 1915 2 Id., Mythos und Sage bei den Griechen, ²1934 3 D. PAGE, Folktales in Homer's Odyssey, 1973 4 U. HÖLSCHER, Die Odyssee. Epos zwischen M. und Roman, 1988 5 A. LESKY, s.v. Homeros, RE Suppl. 11, 795f. 6 V. PROPP, Morfologija skazki, 1928 (²1968) (English tr. by L.A. Wagner, Morphology of the Folk Tale, 1969) 7 Id., Istoriceskie korni volsebnoj skazki, 1946 (Ger.: Die histor. Wurzeln des Zauber-M., 1987) 8 A. AARNE, S. THOMPSON, The Types of the Folktale, ²1964ff. 9 S. THOMPSON, Motif-Index of Folk-Literature, 6 vols., 1955–1958 (³1975).

W. ALY, Volks-M., Sage und Novelle bei Herodot und seinen Zeitgenossen, 1921 (²1969); Id., s.v. M., RE 14, 254–281; G. GERLAND, Altgriech. M. in der Odyssee, 1869; K. MEULI, Odyssee und Argonautika, 1921, in: TH. GELZER (ed.), Gesammelte Schriften, 1975, 593–676; R. RANKE et al. (ed.), Enzyklopädie des M., Vol. 1ff., 1975ff. (s.v. of the ancient authors and mythological figures). L.K.

IV. ROMAN LITERATURE

In the family environment of the Roman household, much as in Greece, there was a widespread fund of stories (*fabulae aniles, f. nutricularum*, 'fairy tales'), whose motifs and formulas touch on those of modern era folk-tales (evidence from c. 200 BC onwards [1. 44–47]). The demarcation as regards content, especially compared with → myth and legend, is difficult and the terminology indistinct (*fabula*, similarly to German *Ammenmärchen*, can indicate various small narrative forms), and motifs appear only very sporadically. It is therefore difficult to decide whether there were any self-contained, orally handed-down texts independent of literary fixing and shaping, which could be considered Lat. equivalents of the popular folk-tales of modern era collections. Our knowledge of the fund of folk-tales familiar to the Romans is essentially confined to the recording, made possible by using motif and type catalogues, of relevant elements (e.g. animal metamorphosis and deliverance; grateful animals; jealous sisters and wicked stepmothers; virgin in the tower; magic herbs; the self-laying table) in Lat. texts from different literary genres (esp. → comedy, → epic, → fable, and later also → novella and → novel); proverb-like figures of speech also quite frequently allude to the subject matter of folk-tales [2. 95–97].

A special position is held by the 'Metamorphoses' of Apuleius (→ Ap(p)uleius [III]), which, with numerous individual motifs [3. 682f.] and the narrative of Cupid and → Psyche, probably intentionally placed in the centre (Apul. Met. 4,28–6,24), form, according to general opinion, the only complete extant ancient folk-tale. In spite of numerous attempts at explanation from the time of late antiquity, the question of the origin of the material, the genre of the narrative and the meaning intended by Apuleius as narrator (or inventor?) has not been satisfactorily solved [2; 4; 5]. Among the material from ancient literature recurring in more recent folk-tales that of Cupid and Psyche again stands out with regard to the number and wide range of its variations [6. 140–145; 7; 8; 9]. In more recent folk-tale research it is disputed whether these are cases of manifestations of age-old popular folk-tales [7; 8] or 'diminished cultural assets' which go back to literary models [10].

1 J. BOLTE, G. POLÍVKA, Anmerkungen zu den Kinder- und Haus-M. der Brüder Grimm, vol. 4, 1930, repr. 1992 2 O. WEINREICH, Das M. von Amor und Psyche und andere Volks-M. im Alt., in: FRIEDLÄNDER 4, 89–132 3 H. VAN THIEL, s.v. Apuleius, in: Enzyklopädie des M. (= EM) 1, 680–685 4 G. BINDER, R. MERKELBACH (ed.), Amor und Psyche, 1968 5 C. MORESCHINI, Il mito di Amore e Psiche in Apuleio, 1994 6 A. AARNE, S. THOMPSON (ed.), The Types of the Folktale, ²1964 7 J.-Ö. SWAHN, The Tale of Cupid and Psyche, 1955 8 G.A. MEGAS, Das M. von Amor und Psyche in der griech. Volksüberl., 1971 9 Id., s.v. Amor und Psyche, in: EM 1, 464–472 (with further bibliography) 10 D. FEHLING, Amor und Psyche, 1977. H.-P.S.

Follis

[1] (φῦσα/*phŷsa*, bellows). The blacksmith's tool already mentioned in Homer (Il. 18, 372; 412; 468–70) is associated in Greek art in particular with → Hephaestus (Siphnian Treasury, Delphi), but rarely appears in depictions of workshops. There were two (Hdt. I 68) or more (Hom. Il. 18,468–470) *folles* in a workshop. In Roman art the *follis* is also depicted relatively rarely; on a blacksmith's gravestone in Aquileia (Mus. inv. no. 166) the worker at the *follis* holds a protective shield in front of himself; a fresco in the house of the Vettii in Pompeii shows an Eros handling the *follis*.

H.G. NIEMEYER, 'Phönizische' Blasebalgdüsen. Die Funde im span. Toscanos im zeitgenössischen Vergleich, in: Der Anschnitt. Zschr. für Kunst und Kultur im Bergbau 35, 1983, 50–58; G. ZIMMER, Griech. Bronzegußwerkstätten. Zur Technologieentwicklung eines ant. Kunsthandwerks, 1990, 183–187; Id., Röm. Berufsdarstellungen, 1992, 186–187, no. 122. R.H.

[2] see → Ball games

[3] Lat. name originally for a bag, from the beginning of the 3rd cent. AD a bag of money (Ulp. Dig. 40,7,3,6). The contents, initially not fixed, was guaranteed by the seal of the person who last packed it (Paul. Dig. 16,3,29). Later the *follis* always contained the same sum. Payment in bags was always a sign of a shortage of currency and a preponderance of small change. *Follis* does not occur as a fixed accounting unit until the first half of the 4th cent. (CIL 3,743; 3,2240; 5,1880; 5,2046; 9,984; with dating between 300 and 338 P. Panopolis 2,302; Euseb. Hist. eccl. 10,6,1; Cod. Theod. 11,36,2–3; 7,20,3; 14,24,1; CIL 9,4215). The *follis* of the Tetrarchic period was probably worth 12,500 denarii [2. 99; 3. 34].

The meaning of *follis* changed only gradually to indicate individual coin traded in the bag. Today the name *follis* or → *nummus* refers to the copper coins with a thin coating of silver of *c.* 27–30 mm and 9–13 g. introduced by Diocletian's → coinage reform in *c.* 294. The rate of the *follis* fell rapidly, enforcing the Price Edict of 301 (→ Edictum Diocletiani). The *follis* lost both in size and in weight in the period after Diocletian (around 307: 25–26 mm, 7.5–8 g; 310–311: 20–21 mm, 4–5 g; 335: 15 mm, 1.5 g). The value of the *follis* in relation to gold and to the accounting unit → *denarius* is controversial. With the Price Edict of 301 copper coins were doubled in value. The *follis* probably had a value of 12 $^1/_2$ before 301, and afterwards of 25 denarii [1. 458; 2. 99]. There are only a few types, which were often replaced when the ruler changed. In 348 the → *maiorina* replaced the *follis*.

Follis as the name of a coin came to be used only gradually in the 4th cent. and not only for what is known today as a coin. The term → *nummus* also occurs several times for the same nominal. The earliest mention of a *follis* coin is P Mich. 126,8 (308–309); then Cod. Theod. 7,20,3 (326); 9,23,1,1 (352); 14,4,3 (363).

There is no further clear evidence of a *follis* coin until the → coinage reform of Anastasius in 498. The largest and most frequent nominal with value sign M was called *follis* in Lat. and probably *noúmmos* in Greek (Kedrenos I, 801) or *obolós* (Procop. Arc. 25; Suidas). Its value rose between 527 and 558 from $^1/_{210}$ to $^1/_{180}$ of the → *solidus* (Procop. Arc. 25,4). The Byzantine *follis* was minted up to 1100.

1 M.F. HENDY, Studies in the Byzantine Monetary Economy, Cambridge 1985 2 J. JAHN, Zur Geld-und Währungspolitik Diocletians, in: JNG 25, 1975, 91–105 3 A.H.M. JONES, The Origin and Early History of the Follis, in: JRS 49, 1959, 34–38.

J.P. CALLU, Genio Populi Romani, 1960; G. DEPEYROT, Le système monétaire de Dioclétien à la fin de l'Empire romain, in: RBN 138, 1992, 33–106; K.W. HARL, Coinage in the Roman Economy, 300 B.C. to A.D. 700, 1996; J.P.C. KENT, The Pattern of Bronze Coinage under Constantine I., NC 1957, 16–77; C.E. KING, The Fourth Century Coinage, in: L. CAMILLI (ed.), L''inflazione' nel quarto secolo d.C., 1993, 1–87; RIC vol. 6–8, 1966–81; SCHRÖTTER, 199ff.; O. SEECK, s.v. Follis, RE 6, 2829–2838. DI.K.

Fonteia Vestal virgin before 91 until after 68 BC, sister of Fonteius [I 2] (Cic. Font. 46–49). K.-L.E.

Fonteius Name of a Roman Plebeian family from Tusculum (who, as mint masters, liked to place on their coins the Dioscuri, who were particularly revered there, RRC 290, 307, cf. 353), whose members often held the office of praetor; the family did not attain the consulate until the early Imperial period.

I. REPUBLICAN PERIOD

[I 1] **F.** Legate of the proconsul Q. Servilius Caepio in Asculum; their murder by the local population triggered the → Social Wars [3] (Cic. Font. 41; 48; Vell. Pat. 2,15,1; App. B Civ. 1,173); perhaps identical with the mint master RRC 290 or 307.

[I 2] **F., M.** Biographical details are known only from Cicero's speech *Pro M. Fonteio*. Before 87 BC, F. was mint master, in 84 *quaestor urbanus* (Cic. Font. 1; 5; later accusations of embezzlement), in 81 legate of C. Annius [I 2] in the battle against Q. Sertorius (Cic. Font. 6; 45), then in 77/76 in Macedonia (Cic. Font. 44). After the praetorship in 75(?), he governed Gallia Narbonensis as propraetor from 74 to 72(?), where he undertook levies and requisitions for the wars in Spain and in the East (Cic. Font. 13; 16) and fought against Celtic tribes. Probably in 69 he was accused of blackmailing by the Allobroges led by Indutiomarus and represented by M. Plaetorius, and was defended by Cicero; the outcome of the trial is unknown.

[I 3] **F., P.** In 59, at the age of twenty, he adopted P. Clodius [I 4] Pulcher, so that he could join the *plebs* (Cic. Dom. 34–37). Perhaps in 55 mint master and supporter of Caesar (RRC 429, there cognomen *Capito*).

[I 4] F., Ti. Legate and camp commander of P. Cornelius [I 71] Scipio in 211 BC. After the death of the brothers Cn. and P. Scipio he took over the remains of the army, but then had to cede command to L. Marcius (Liv. 25,34–37; 26,17,3).

[I 5] F. Capito, C. In 169 BC praetor in Sardinia, which he governed as promagistrate until 167 (Liv. 43,11,7).

[I 6] F. Capito, C. Supporter of the triumvir M. Antonius [I 9], in 39 (?) BC as people's tribune (?), encouraged by Mark Antony, he introduced a law on the granting of civil rights (Roman Statutes 1, 1996, no. 36; cf. MRR 3,93; there designated as ἱερεύς; *hiereús* = *pontifex*?). In 37 in Italy he accompanied, among others, Maecenas to the conference of Tarentum between Antony and Octavian (Hor. Sat. 1,5,32, *iter Brundisinum*). In 37/36, on the orders of Antony, he brought Cleopatra from Egypt to him in Syria (Plut. Antonius 36,1); 33 *cos. suff.* (InscrIt 13,1,251). His son was probably F. [II 4]. He is perhaps identical to the antiquarian F. [I 9]. PIR² F 469.

[I 7] F. Capito, T. Praetor in 178 BC in Hispania ulterior, which he governed until 176 (Liv. 40,59,5; 41,15,11).

[I 8] F. Crassus, L. Was supposedly imprisoned in Spain by Hasdrubal, but managed to escape (Frontin. Str. 1,5,12; 4,5,8); perhaps identical with [I 4]. K.-L.E.

[I 9] A Roman writer on cults quoted only in Iohannes → Lydus. In the work Περὶ ἀγαλμάτων (*Perì agalmátōn*; *De simulacris*) he sees → Ianus allegorically as the lord of time (Lydus, Mens. 2,2); based on a sacred text (ἱερὸς λόγος; *hieròs lógos*), he derives the name of the month of May from → Maia, identifies her with → Gaia (Tellus) and interprets the rites as myths of nature (Mens. 4,80); he reports an oracle to Romulus (Mag. 2,12; 3,42 = Mens. Fr. 7) and, like (Ateius) Capito and Varro (Mens. 1,37), knows about Numa's introduction of the priestly art from Etruria. Equating him with → Ateius [6] Capito is not viable, even if a dating in the later Republican or Augustan period were possible. F.G.

II. Imperial period

[II 1] F. Agrippa. Senator, who in AD 16, together with others, accused Scribonius Libo Drusus of *maiestas* in the Senate. After the trial he received the praetorship *extra ordinem* as reward. As he had separated from his wife, his daughter was not elected *virgo Vestalis* in AD 19. PIR² F 465.

[II 2] C.F. Agrippa. Probably the son of F. [II 1]. *Cos. suff.* in AD 58; 66–68 *curator aquarum*; 68–69 proconsul of Asia. He allied himself to Vespasian, who at the end of 69 sent him to Moesia as governor, where he was killed in the following year in battle with the Sarmati. Vogel-Weidemann 465f.; PIR² F 466.

[II 3] F. Capito. Consular legate in the army of Lower Germany in AD 68; he could be identical to Capito, *cos. ord.* in 67; though identification with the *cos.* of 59 (→ F. [II 5]) is not impossible. He had the Batavi Claudius Paulus and Iulius Civilis arrested in Lower Germania. The former was executed, but Civilis simply remained in custody. Popular with the army of Lower Germany; allegedly on the order of Galba, the legionary legates Fabius Valens and Cornelius Aquinus had him murdered by a soldier. Eck, Statthalter 129f.; PIR² F 467, 468.

[II 4] C.F. Capito. Son of F. [I 5]. *Cos. ord.* in AD 12 jointly with Germanicus. Probably in 22–23 he governed the province of Asia as proconsul. In 25 he was accused by N. Vibius Serenus on grounds not known in greater detail, but was acquitted. PIR² F 470.

[II 5] C.F. Capito. Perhaps son or grandson of F. [II 4]. *Cos. ord.* in AD 59. Whether he is identical with F. [II 3] remains uncertain. PIR² F 471.

[II 6] D.F. Fronto. Proconsul of Lycia-Pamphylia in AD 164–165. AE 1992, 1663; 1993, 1548.

[II 7] D.F. Frontinianus L. Stertinius Rufinus. Praetorian legate of the *legio III Augusta* in Numidia from AD 160 to 162, where he is attested in numerous documents [1. 153ff.]. Married to Numisia Celerina. Probably in 162 (less likely in 163) he attained the office of suffect consul in the province. F. [II 6] could be his brother. PIR² F 472.

1 Thomasson, Fasti Africani.

[II 8] F. Maximus. Legate of the *legio I Italica*, attested in Novae in AD 233 (AE 1987, 862 = Inscr. Latines de Novae, 1992, 85f. no. 50).

[II 9] F. Magnus. One of the accusers of Varenus Rufus from the province of Bithynia. PIR² F 473. W.E.

Food (τροφαί/*trophaí*; Lat. *alimenta*). Name for nutritious solid and liquid substances which can sometimes be eaten or drunk raw, but which are not normally suitable for consumption without preparation and are therefore further processed into meals in the kitchen. A systematic classification of food is offered by Galen's treatise 'On the Powers of Food' (*De alimentorum facultatibus libri III*), one of the few ancient dietary specialized writings that are completely extant. Galen classifies food on the principle of its place in natural history in the following way: (1) seeds of plants (grain and pulses; ibid. 1,2–37); (2) fruits of plants (especially fruits and nuts, but also olives; ibid. 2,1–38); (3) roots, tips and shoots of plants (ibid. 2,39–69); (4) food originating from snails, four-legged animals, birds and aquatic animals, and additionally the eggs and milk and also the blood of some animals (ibid. 3,1–37); (5) honey (ibid. 3,38); (6) wine (ibid. 3,39). Within the individual categories Galen usually distinguishes strictly between cultivated food and wild food.

Galen's treatise shows that human beings gained the nutrients necessary for their survival from many different foods. Especially in Prehistoric times they were dependent on intensive use of the resources provided by their immediate environment. At first they lived only from hunting and gathering food, and it was not until the Neolithic period that they started growing plants and → domesticating animals. This changed in proportion to the extent to which procuring food was freed from the constraints of the environment (climate, composition of the soil) and the seasons. This process was well advanced by the beginning of the Historical period. In Homer, for example, the number of food actually consumed in a certain region no longer coincided at all with the number of food available there: the heroes lived mainly on grain, wine, oil and meat and did without many types of vegetables and fruits, especially wild plants [1. Q 34f.]. Here, a decline in the variety of food is indicated for the first time; this increased in the following centuries. This was in particular the result of progress in production of native food and its preservation and processing (e.g. Columella 12,4–59), but also of the imports of oriental useful plants (e.g. almonds, mulberries, peaches, quinces, walnuts) and domestic animals (esp. the domestic fowl) into the Mediterranean. They replaced less productive and tasty native food.

These developments reflect the evolution of new ways of life, which were less connected to agriculture. The urban population, in particular, wanted food which was cheap, non-perishable and easy to prepare. For this reason food rich in carbohydrate, such as pulses and especially grain (barley and wheat), gained increased significance from the time of ancient Greece and the early Roman Republic. The importance of other vegetable food, especially of wild plants, subsequently diminished; they were remembered only in times of famine (Gal. De alimentorum facultatibus 2,58). Meanwhile the demand for meat and fish increased everywhere; therefore the breeding of domestic animals, especially pigs, was intensified, and fishing techniques (→ Fishing, Fishing trade) were improved. The fact that in spite of these developments there was still a variety of food even in late antiquity is documented in the Price Edict of the Roman emperor Diocletian (Edictum Diocletiani 1,1a–6,96).

→ Dietetics; → Nutrition; → Meat, consumption of; → Beverages; → Grain; → Agriculture; → Meals

1 G. Bruns, Küchenwesen und Mahlzeiten (ArchHom 3), 1988, Q 1–69.

J. André, Essen und Trinken im alten Rom, 1998; P. and D. R. Brothwell, Manna und Hirse. Eine Kulturgesch. der Ernährung, 1984; A. Dalby, Essen und Trinken im alten Griechenland. Von Homer bis zur byz. Zeit, 1998; E. Fournier, s.v. Cibaria, DS 1, 1141–1169; V. Hehn, Kulturpflanzen und Haustiere in ihrem Übergang aus Asien nach Griechenland und Italien sowie in das übrige Europa. Histor.-linguistische Studien, [8]1911; O. Longo, P. Scarpi (ed.), Homo Edens. Regimi, miti e pratiche dell'alimentazione nella civiltà del mediterraneo, 1989; F. Mielentz, s.v. Mellona, Re 15, 558.

A.G.

Foot ornaments see → jewellery

Footstool (θρῆνυς/*thrēnys*, ὑποπόδιον/*hypopódion*, σφέλας/*sphélas*, rarely χελώνη/*chelṓnē*; Latin *scabellum*, *scamnum*). The footstool was used as a foot bench for a person sitting on the → klismos, → throne or a similar high seating (cf. Hom. Od. 17,409 f.), or as a step for climbing up on the → Kline or down from it. There were three footstool variants: rectangular footstools with simple vertical legs, rectangular footstools with curved legs that ended in animal feet (lion feet), sphinxes etc., as well as a bench without legs. The second and third variant in particular could sometimes be fairly long. In Greek, Etruscan and Roman art, footstools were frequently depicted, e.g. in symposium scenes where the shoes or boots of the symposiasts stand on them, as well as in the case of persons sitting enthroned: gods, kings, women etc. According to the literary tradition, the Thessalian women use footstools to slay the hetaera → Lais [2] out of jealousy (Ath. 13,589a) and Antinous throws a footstool at Odysseus (Hom. Od. 17,462–464). Since the Mycenaean period, fragmentary or completely extant footstools made of wood and other materials have been preserved – although they are few in number.

H. A. G. Brijder, An Etruscan Terracotta Footstool from the Fifth Century B. C. in Amsterdam, in: BABesch 62, 1987, 67–74; V. Karageorghis, Note on a Footstool from Salamis, in: Kadmos 6, 1967, 98–99; Richter, 49–54, 93, 104; Y. Sakellarakis, Mycenaean Footstools, in: G. Herrmann (ed.), The Furniture of Western Asia (Conference London, 1993), 1996, 105–110.

R.H.

Fordicidia Roman festival. On 15 April thirty pregnant cows (*fordae boves*) were sacrificed in the → curiae (Varro, Ling. 6,15; Ov. Fast. 4,629ff.; cf. Paul Fest. 74 and 91 L. – in this case the dialect form *Hordicidia* – and also Varro, Rust. 2,5,6 – *Hordicalia* – and Lydus, Mens. 4,72 Φορδικάλια; *Phordikália*). According to Ovid's account, a parallel sacrifice took place on the Capitol led by the *pontifices* (→ *pontifex*) (cf. Lydus ibid.). When the sacrificial servants had removed the unborn calf from the mother's body they offered up its entrails. Afterwards, the *virgo maxima* of the Vestals (→ Vesta) burned the calves (Ov. Fast. 4,639). Their ashes were part of the *februa* ('cleaning agents') distributed to the people on the occasion of the → *Parilia*.

Ovid explains the symbolism: because the earth and the cattle were both 'pregnant' at this time, this sacrifice was offered to → Tellus (633f.). The aetiological myth (641ff.) depicts the rigours to be encountered by the rite: if the soil is too wet or too dry the agricultural crop will rot and the cattle stock is threatened by premature births or the deaths of the mother animals. The incubation oracle of → Faunus is supposed to have revealed these correlations to king → Numa Pompilius.

The dual structure of the *Fordicidia* should not be written off as secondary and explained by a hypothesis of decay [1]; as with other rituals relating to the agricultural bases of existence of the state, the parallel (i.e. at the same time centralized and decentralized) celebrations at various levels of social organization illustrate their dependence on one another.

→ Ceres

1 Latte, 68f.

F. BÖMER, P. Ovidius Naso. Die Fasten, vol. 2: commentary, 1958, on 4,630; H. LE BONNIEC, Le culte de Cérès à Rome. Des origines à la fin de la République, 1958, 66–67. D.B.

Foreign peoples; foreigners see → Barbarians

Forentum City in Apulia (Φερέντη; *Pherénté*, Diod. Sic. 19,65,7; *Forentum*, Hor. Carm. 3,4,16; *Forentani*, Plin. HN 3,105). Roman from 317 BC (Liv. 9,20), a *municipium* from the time of Augustus. Identification with modern Forenza has been abandoned in favour of Lavello (in the northern Basilicata). The ancient settlement was located on the hill in Lavello. There is evidence of settlement from the Neolithic to the Imperial period, which receded in the 3rd cent. after the *colonia* of Venusia was established in 291 BC.

NISSEN 2, 831; E. GRECO, Magna Grecia, 1980, 276; M. GIORGI et al., F. vol. 1, 1988; A. BOTTINI et al., F. vol. 2, 1991; BTCGI 8, 455–460. M.G.

Forest Linguistically, a forest in Latin (Serv. Aen. 1,310) is differentiated according to the degree of human cultivation (*silva*, *nemus*, → *saltus*) and the associated religious sphere (*lucus*, → 'Grove'). On one hand, forests caused fear and discomfort (Cic. Nat. D. 2,6; Plin. HN 12,3), on the other hand they were valued as places of (even productive) rest and recuperation (Plin. Ep. 1,6,2; 9,10,2; Tac. Dial. 9,6; 12,1). Forests received an extremely negative connotation among Romans in the context of the military operations in Germania during the Augustan period (Tac. Germ. 5,1; Cass. Dio 56,19,5–20 on the campaign of P. Quinctilius [II 7] Varus; → Saltus Teutoburgiensis). Subsequently, it was attempted to neutralize the forest as a military obstacle by cutting clearances (*limites;* Frontin. Str. 1,3,10).

In antiquity the forest was significant in terms of economy. → Hunting was an important line of business but had also been a status activity of the → aristocracy since the Homeric period (Hom. Od. 19,418–458). The permanent high demand for → wood resulted in extensive clearances, which only locally decimated the rich forest stocks (cf. Str. 10,4,4 on Crete) despite the critical statements of contemporaries (Pl. Crit. 111a–e on the decline of Attic forests and their fertility for pasturing).

Legally, the forest was royal property in antiquity and → *ager publicus* or imperial property among the Romans. However, there also were privately owned forests.

→ Grove; → Wood; → Scenery (see addenda)

J. K. ANDERSON, Hunting in the Ancient World, 1985; A. CHANIOTIS, Die kretischen Berge als Wirtschaftsraum, in: E. OLSHAUSEN, H. SONNABEND (ed.), Gebirgsland als Lebensraum (Geographica Historica 8), 1996, 255–266; R. MEIGGS, Trees and Timber in the Ancient Mediterranean World, 1982; M. NENNINGER, s.v. Wald, in: H. SONNABEND (ed.), Mensch und Landschaft in der Ant., 1999, 593–595; Id., Die Römer und der Wald (Geographica Historica 16), 2001. H. SO.

Forma Urbis Romae Modern term for a graphical representation, albeit not to scale, of the City of Rome. It was created between AD 203 and 208 on a 235 m² marble wall in the Forum of Vespasian in Rome. The preserved fragments are an important record of the ancient topography of the city.

→ Rome (Topography)

G. CARETTONI et al., La pianta marmorea di Roma antica, 1960; E. RODRÍGUEZ-ALMEIDA, Forma Urbis Marmorea, 1981; J. P. HEISEL, Antike Bauzeichnungen, 1993, 193–197; K. BRODERSEN, Terra Cognita, 1995, 231–236. K.BRO.

Formiae City of the Aurunci in Latium with a harbour on the *Mare Tyrrhenum*; hence its name (Ὁρμίαι; *Hormíai* or Φορμίαι ; *Phormíai*... διὰ τὸ εὔορμον; *dià tò eúormon*, 'because of the good mooring': Str. 5,3,6; cf. Fest. 83); located on the *via Appia* 8 km north of Gaeta, 88 miles from Rome (mile stones: CIL X 6859–6863). Caieta also belonged to the territory of F. F. was formerly called Mola di Gaeta, but in 1862 it was renamed Formia (Latina province). In myths F. is associated with the Laestrygonians, Aeneas and Sparta. It was occupied early in the 5th cent. BC by the Volsci, in 334 it became a *civitas sine suffragio* like Fundi, but after 188 both were *civitas cum suffragio*, *tribus Aemilia*. It was plundered before 66 by pirates (Cic. Leg. Man. 33) and in 43 by Sex. Pompeius (Flor. 2,18). Under Hadrian it became the *colonia Aelia Hadriana Augusta F.*

Archaeological finds: city walls (in *opus polygonale*), temple from the Republican period [1], theatre, amphitheatre, pier in the harbour, *piscinae maritimae* (fish breeding pools). *Villae* are present from the 2nd cent. BC (belonging to L. Antistius Vetus, C. Laelius, Mamurra, Cn. Pompeius; to Munatius Plancus in Gaeta; the *Villa Rubino* was mistakenly considered to be Cicero's villa near which he was killed: Sen. Suas. 6,17; Plut. Cicero 50; Vir. ill. 81,7; at Piazza della Vittoria, owned by the Di Fava family, in Vindicio and Gianola). Also, monumental tombs, including the so-called tomb of Cicero (a columbarium of the Augustan period) on the *via Appia*, mausoleums (of L. Sempronius Atratinus, L. Munatius Plancus in Gaeta) and an antiquarium are preserved. The *Formianus sinus*, also called the Gulf of Caieta, between the foothills of Gaeta and Monte Scauri was named after F. (Symmachus Ep. 7,18; 8,23).

1 M. GUAITOLI, Un tempio di età repubblicana a F., in: Quaderni dell'Istituto di Topografia Antica della Università di Roma 6, 1974, 131–142.

S. AURIGEMMA, Gaeta, F., 1955; M. ZAMBELLI, Iscrizioni di Formia, Gaeta e Itri, in: Seconda Miscellanea greca e romana, 1968, 335–378; Formia archeologica. Guida per il turista e il studioso..., 1977; B. CONTICELLO, Antiquarium di F., 1978; BTCGI 7, 1989, 479–483; S. CICCONE (ed.), Formianum. Atti del Convegno di studi sull'antico territorio di Formia 1, 1993. G.U.

Formido

[1] A → personification of fear/horror that was etymologically equated with the bogey-man Μορμώ (→ Mormō), which then became a demon in its own right (Verg. Aen. 12, 335; Hygin. Fab. praef. 29; Claud. De consulatu Stilichonis 376; In Rufinum 1, 343–344). F. is the daughter of Mars (or his companion) and Venus, and the sister of → Harmonia. cf. Deimos and → Phobos as her precursors in Hes. Theog. 934–935.
W.-A.M.

[2] Analogue to οἶστρος (→ *oîstros*), the → gadfly, i.e. madness (Hyg. Fab. 145,4; Serv. Georg. 3,152) sent by Hera against Io. W.-A.M.

Formio (modern Rižana, more probably Osapska Reka). A small river east of Aegida (between Capra and Iustinianopolis, modern Koper/Capodistria), 6 miles from Tergeste. The name is perhaps derived from the language of the Veneti. The F. gained significance in 42–41 BC as the border river when Gallia Cisalpina was incorporated into Italy after the battle of Philippi. Between 18 and 12 BC this boundary was relocated to the Arsia (modern Raša). The stream is mentioned in Plin. HN 3,127 (*Formio amnis ... antiquus auctae Italiae terminus, nunc vero Histriae*) and Ptol. 3,1,27.

V. Vedaldi Iasbez, La Venetia orientale e l'Histria (Studi e Ricerche sulla Gallia Cisalpina 5), 1994, 127f. M.Š.K.

Formula The written *formula* is the essential component of the type of trial which replaced the → *legis actio* procedure; by means of the *lex Aebutia*, 2nd cent. BC, as well as the two *leges Iuliae*, 17 BC) and which consequently is generally described as a *formula* trial. Despite a slow development, this classical procedural type is distinguished from its predecessor by having far greater flexibility and by being more adaptable to individual cases in the late Republic and the Principate. The text of the suit was no longer ceremonial and immutably patterned on the wording of the law. Instead, the *formula* described the specific legal dispute, though it remained tied to a formal structure. The wording of the formula was jointly determined by both parties (→ *editio*, → *accipere*), occasionally even in co-operation with the court magistrate (cf. Gai. Inst. 4,30). The parties usually used as templates the promises of legal protection listed in the respective edict of the praetor (and the curule aediles or other court magistrates → *Edictum perpetuum*). In more complicated cases, they probably consulted jurists who spent much labour and thought on the formulation and subdivision of the *formula*. The *formula* had to be approved by the court magistrate. The first step was to appoint a judge. The *formula* constituted the obligatory programme of examining the fact for the judge and determined (alternative design, Gai. Inst. 4,43) the result of subsequent sentencing. The parts of the *formula* are the → *intentio*, → *demonstratio*, → *adiudicatio*, → *exceptio* (plea of the defendant), and → *condemnatio*. The flexibility of the *formula* is evident in that every part of it was more or less optional except for the *demonstratio*. The *formula* trial was officially abolished in AD 342 (Cod. Iust. 2,57,1) and replaced by the *cognitio* procedure, which had already been practised for centuries by imperial officials (→ *cognitio*).

→ litis actio

M. Kaser, K. Hackl, Das römische Zivilprozeßrecht, ²1997, 151ff. C.PA.

Fornacalia The → *feriae conceptivae* held in February in the → *curiae* whose date was set by the Curio Maximus (Ov. Fast. 2,527f.). The roasting of religiously symbolic 'primitive grain' → *far* (Paul. Fest. 73; 82 L.; Plin. HN 18,7f.) was celebrated. The 'oven goddess' (Ov. Fast. 6,313f.) Fornax (Ov. Fast. 2,525; Lact. Inst. 1,20,35) may be interpreted as a projection of the feast. Since the Vestals distributed → *mola salsa* on the → Lupercalia, for the preparation of which they needed roasted emmer, a date before 15 February may be assumed for the Fornacalia. Those who did not know to which *curia* they belonged, were permitted to celebrate the Fornacalia during the Quirinalia and, therefore, the festival bore the epithet → *stultorum feriae* (Fest. 418; 419 L.; Fest. 304; 305 L.; Ov. Fast. 2,513ff.; Plut. Quaest. Rom. 88, 285d = Iuba FGrH 275 F 94). This may be an indicator of the initiatory character of the feast.

F. Bömer, P. Ovidius Naso. Die Fasten 2: Kommentar, 1958, zu Ov. fast. 2, 475ff.; A. Brelich, Tre variazioni romane sul tema delle origini, in: Nuovi Saggi 14, 1955, 114ff.; Latte, 143; H. Le Bonniec, Le culte de Cérès à Rome. Des origines à la fin de la République, 1958, 125; 164; J. Rüpke, Kalender und Öffentlichkeit. Die Geschichte der Repräsentation und religiösen Qualifikation von Zeit in Rom, 1995, 300ff. D.B.

Fornix Latin term for 'arch'. As a technical term in ancient architecture, *fornix* describes the arch of a vault, the vault itself, or the masonry arch of a bridge or aqueduct; also arched gaps in masonry walls for doors and → windows (cf. also → vault and arch construction). A cellar vault or cellar floor may also be meant; the dirt and alleged disreputability of cellars are presumably the origin of the new meaning of the term *fornix* in the 1st cent. AD as 'brothel' (e.g. Hor. Ep. 1,14,21 and *passim*) or as a label for any form of misconduct. Presumably because of this negative change in meaning, streets and honorary arches in Rome were renamed; → triumphal and honorary arches were consistently called *arcus* from the 1st cent. AD. Some old arches in Rome retained the term *fornix*: the Calpurnianus Fornix (Oros. 5,9,2) as the upper end of the large flight of steps (→ *scala*) leading to the → Capitolium, the Fabianus Fornix, which spanned the *via sacra* between the *regia* and the house of the Vestals, built in 121 BC by Q. → Fabius Maximus to commemorate the victory over the Allobroges (Cic. Planc. 17; Cic. Verr. 1,19; Cic. Vatin. 28; Cic. Orat. 2,167; Sen. Dial. 2,1,2), the

Fornix Augusti (CIL 6.878), the Fornix Scipionis (Liv. 37,3,7) and the three Fornices Stertinii (Liv. 33,27,4).

LTUR, 262–267; RICHARDSON, 153–154; W.H. GROSS, s.v. F., KlP 2, 596f. C.HÖ.

Fors Fortuna see → Fortuna

Fortifications

I. GREECE II. EARLY HISTORY AND NEIGHBOURING CULTURES III. ROME

I. GREECE

After the massive Mycenaean fortified palaces had been abandoned, several centuries passed before larger fortifications were again built in Greece. During the Geometric Period fortification construction in the motherland remained modest. Simple structures were built that left few if any remains, and the ruins of Mycenaean fortifications sufficed for protection requirements. However, citadels (acropoleis), peninsulas, and other topographically suitable locations were fortified on the islands of the Aegean and in Ionia as protection against pirates (Thuc. 1,5) and military pressure from the interior of the mainland.

In the Archaic Period, with the origin of the → polis (8th/7th cents.), population growth, the colonization movement, and the threat of eastern Great Powers (Lydia, then Persia), which had a fully developed siege technology, went the transition to a proper defence of settlements. In the process, fortifications might become cores of settlements as in Old Smyrna or were abandoned in favour of new settlements, such as at Zagora on Andros. Late Archaic fortifications usually consisted only of mud-brick walls set on a stone foundation, or at best polygonal masonry. They might already have had two-storey towers such as at Burunçuk-Larissa in Aeolia (as for Samos cf. Hdt. 3,54). In the motherland this development only occurred when the Persian threat became evident there.

In the Classical Period the permanent state of war during the Persian and Peloponnesian Wars caused most poleis to build a city wall the size and strength of which depended as much on economic power as on the nature of the threat (Thuc. 1,7). A wall provided military protection, but was also a symbol of the autonomy (→ *autonomía*) of a polis. Aristotle (Pol. 1331a 10ff.) considered a wall a prerequisite for the successful defence of a city. Multiply embossed blocks or trapezoidal stones were often used as construction materials. Also, in this period extensive territorial walls ('territorial fortification'; such as the Euryalus Wall of Syracuse) were often built following closely the topography. Furthermore, there were systems to protect and guard the *chora*, consisting of a core of fortifications and watchtowers (Attica, Megaris). The period to *c.* 350 was characterized by a strategic superiority of defenders over attackers. Direct military means of attack such as storming and scaling walls with ladders, battering-rams, and the construction of ramps were inferior to the counterstrategies; treason, starvation, and surprise attacks achieved the objective more quickly. An impressive expression of this were the Long Walls of Athens which linked the fortified port of Piraeus with the main city and could not be taken by force (on wall construction in Argos cf. Thuc. 5,82,6). The invention of new siege engines (the simple catapult in 399 in Sicily, then the torsion catapult in the mid 4th cent., the *helepolis*, the tortoise, and others) and the development of further techniques (undermining) increased the chances of the besieging army, but defensive strategies changed at the same time (cf. Aristot. Pol. 1331a 10ff.; Aen. Tact. 32). In particular, Philip II, Alexander the Great, and their successors used siege engine depots because of increased financial means, etc.

During the Hellenistic Period, from which most still-visible and excavated wall remains derive, and which is therefore the best-documented era of Greek fortifications, defensive measures became more elaborate: outworks and ditches were built, walls received sally-ports, battlements were roofed over, and towers were built as artillery platforms. In this way active components were introduced beside the passive defensive strategies.

1 J.-P. ADAM, L'architecture militaire grecque, 1982 2 A.W. LAWRENCE, Greek Aims in Fortification, 1979 3 P. LERICHE, H. TRÉZINY (ed.), La Fortification dans l'histoire du monde grec, 1986 4 S. VAN DE MAELE, J.M. FOSSEY (ed.), Fortificationes anticae, 1992 5 F.G. MAIER, Griechische Mauerbauinschriften I, 1959; II, 1961 6 E.W. MARSDEN, Greek and Roman Artillery I, 1969; II, 1971 7 F.E. WINTER, Greek Fortifications, 1971. L.B.

II. EARLY HISTORY AND NEIGHBOURING CULTURES

A. PRE-ROMAN ITALY AND SARDINIA 1. PREHISTORY 2. SICILY AND MAGNA GRAECIA 3. ETRURIA 4. LATIUM 5. CENTRAL AND SOUTH ITALY 6. SARDINIA B. IBERIAN C. CELTO-GERMANIC

A. PRE-ROMAN ITALY AND SARDINIA

1. PREHISTORY

As long ago as the Neolithic there were settlements, mostly in the plains of Puglia and Sicily, which were defended by circular ditches. Beginning with the Bronze Age a tendency to fortify naturally protected locations on hilltops and peninsulas has been observed. Systems using large unworked stones, in part with ditches and towers, such as those of Thapsus, Coppa Nevigata, and Scoglio del Tonno, were possibly influenced by Mycenaean fortresses. Until the early Iron Age, small hilltop settlements with walls made of small unworked stones prevailed throughout Italy.

2. SICILY AND MAGNA GRAECIA

The number and dimensions of fortification systems increased with the Greek and Phoenician colonization of southern Italy and Sicily. In particular, the Phoenicians brought the system of offensive defence with tower-flanked sally-ports from the Orient to Sicily (Motya, Eryx, Lilybaeum), where it was adopted by the Greeks in the late 5th cent. BC, when new offensive weapons like the battering-ram and the torsion catapult made it necessary to keep attackers away from the walls.

The earliest Greek city walls are attested for the end of the 7th cent. BC (Siris, Leontini). Presumably, the original mud bricks (Siris) were later replaced by stone (perhaps also ashlar construction with alternation of headers and stretchers). The remarkable absence of special acropolis fortifications in the Greek colonies is a sign of the polis society that had been taking shape since the 8th cent. BC combined with an absence of ruling individuals. Conflicts between Greeks and Carthaginians also promoted the development of fortifications in Sicily and influenced the indigenous peoples of the hinterland, who began to wall their settlements in the early 6th cent. BC.

3. Etruria

From the 6th cent. BC, hilltops in North Etruria were surrounded with walls made mostly of unworked stone and, in a number of cases, they were repeatedly expanded up to the 3rd cent. BC (Volterra, Vetulonia, Populonia). In the northern interior of Etruria encircling fortifications made of large irregular blocks became customary only after the late 5th cent. BC (Perugia, Arezzo). Southern Etrurian settlements, usually located on the tuff spurs at the convergence of two valleys, were initially cut off from the hinterland by embankments and ditches. Later these earthworks were replaced by walls made of blocks of tuff that also extended around the entire settlement (Tarquinia, Caere, Veji). Only in the 4th cent. BC were innovations from Greek fortifications, such as towers and complicated gates with gate-houses, adopted there.

4. Latium

From the 5th cent. BC, encompassing fortifications made of polygonal limestone blocks were built by the cities of Latium, which lay on high ground, owing to the continuous threat from Rome (Norba, Cori, Segni, Alatri, Arpino, Ferentino, Artena). As in Rome, a separately fortified *arx* was apparently particularly important in the cities of Latium. South of Rome very early fortifications similar to those of southern Etruria are found (Castel di Decima, Ardea). Roman colonies in southern Etruria were apparently deliberately fortified with the same polygonal masonry as found in Latium (Cosa, Saturnia, Orbetello).

5. Central and South Italy

The Italian peoples of the central Apennines (Vestinians, Paelignians, Marsians, Aequians, Sabines and Umbrians), Samnium, Lucania, Apulia and Bruttium only fortified their settlements from the 4th cent. BC. In Umbria similarities to the city walls of the eastern interior of Etruria are evident (Bettona, Todi). The settlements on the heights of Samnium and the central Apennines were fortified with supporting walls on the slopes, made of unworked or only slightly worked stone. The settlements were located on long-distance droving tracks and may be differentiated into large centres and small dependent settlements. Securing the droving tracks apparently became necessary only with the increased threat from the Romans. In Lucania, Bruttium, and on the Salentinian peninsula, numerous settlements were fortified in the 4th cent. BC with regularly layered ashlar. Greek influence is apparent in the gate with gate-house and occasional towers. A federation similar to the one documented for the Bruttians (in 356 BC) may also be assumed for the Lucanians (around the sanctuary of → Rossano di Vaglio) and the Messapians. There is no precedent for the huge 6th-cent. earthworks of the Daunians in northern Apulia (Arpi).

6. Sardinia

The indigenous population of Sardinia settled around the *nuraghi* until the Iron Age. These began with tower-like free-standing buildings in the Bronze Age and were extended into increasingly complicated fortification complexes by *c.* 900 BC (Su Nuraxi, Losa, Santu Antine). New partly Oriental elements of fortification building (ditches, walls with outworks, batters, towers and sally-ports), which the Phoenician colonization brought to the island (Tharros, Sulcis, Monte Sirai, Nora) from the 9th cent. BC, apparently did not influence the indigenous population.

→ Siegecraft

1 M. Miller, Befestigungsanlagen in Italien vom 8. bis 3. Jh. v. Chr., 1995 2 G. Tore, Osservazioni sulle fortificazioni puniche in Sardegna, in: La fortification dans l'histoire du monde grec, Actes du Colloque International, Valbonne 1982, 1986, 229–240. M.M.

B. Iberian

Fortifications like Los Millares (Almería province) and Zambujal (Lisbon district) are attested since the Copper Age. Under Phoenician influence walls such as those of the port → Castillo Doña Blanca (Cádiz province, 2nd half of the 8th cent. BC) with bastions, casemates(?) and ditches were built. Greek influence is evident in city walls such as Ullastret (Gerona province, after 500 BC), also the orthogonal organization of La Picola, Santa Pola (Alicante province, 430–330 BC), the gateway flanked by pentagonal towers at Tivissa (Tarragona province, 3rd cent. BC) and others. While unique solutions existed (e.g. the gate system of El Castellar de Meca, Ayora, Valencia province), Iron Age fortifications continue the Bronze Age tradition: masonry shells made of worked fractured stone, massive bastions such as the fortifications of Tartessian Tejada la Vieja (Huelva province, late 8th cent. BC), while the number of hilltop settlements such as Plaza de Armas, Puente Tabla (Jaén province, 7th cent. BC) increased in leaps and bounds from the 5th cent. BC (cf. e.g. the fortified hamlet of Puntal dels Llops [Valencia province] with a massive tower). In the Mesetas *castros* such as Mesa de Miranda, Chamartín (Avila province) with settlement and refuge areas separated by walls, constitute a special group.

Simposio internacional d'arqueologia ibérica: Fortificaciones, Manresa 1990, 1991; Ruiz Mata, C.J. Pérez, El poblado fenicio del Castillo de Doña Blanca, 1995; P. Moret, Les fortifications ibériques, de la fin de l'âge du bronze à la conquête romaine, 1996. M.BL.

C. Celto-Germanic

Celto-Germanic fortifications have a long tradition beginning in the Neolithic and Bronze Ages. Hill settlements with walls made of wood, stone, and earth, predominate in the Celtic late Hallstatt and early La Tène periods (6th/5th cents. BC). Wooden platforms or reinforcing posts with stone facing '→ Preist construction' and earth embankments continue Bronze Age traditions. 'Aristocratic seats' associated with rich graves are found from Slovenia (Sticna) to Burgundy (Mt. Lassois), with the Heuneburg on the upper Danube being the best-researched of these bastions. Mediterranean elements, which characterize the fortifications, e.g. mudbrick walls and bastions, are important. These settlements are politically representational and economic centres, in addition to being the seats of the rulers. In the Germanic area fortifications also continue older traditions, e.g. the Lausitz culture. Fortifications that primarily functioned as economic and power centres and not places of refuge were built both on high ground and in plains from Scandinavia to the German uplands. In the late Iron Age of the 2nd–1st cents. BC, → *oppida* characterize the fortifications. Differentiation of these *oppida* and other hill fortifications (e.g. → *castellum*) from the Germanic fortified settlements towards the north is disputed because they have many common traits in the German upland region and were probably supported by similar demographic, economic, and social structures (e.g. the Alteburg near Niedenstein in North Hesse). In the proper Germanic territory of the late pre-Roman Iron Age in Scandinavia and North Germany, hilltop forts take second place to fortified lowland settlements (e.g. Heidenschanze near Bremerhaven).

→ Hallstatt culture; → Heuneburg; → La Tène culture; → Princes, tombs and residences of

D. Chropovský (ed.), Symposium zu Problemen der jüngeren Hallstattzeit in Mitteleuropa, 1974 (various contributions); G. Mildenberger, Germanische Burgen, 1978; H.G.H. Härke, Settlement Types and Settlement Patterns in the West Hallstatt Province. Brit. Arch. Reports Intant. Ser. 57, 1979; R.v. Uslar, RGA 4, 1981 s.v. Burg; F. Audouze, O. Buchsenschutz, Villes, Villages et Campagnes de l'Europe Celtique, 1989. V.P.

III. Rome

A. Early period and Roman Republic
B. Principate and Late Antiquity C. Military Fortifications

A. Early period and Roman Republic

Fortifications increased significantly in Italy with the onset of Greek and Etruscan colonization in the 8th cent. BC. Whether there was a fortification which enclosed Rome during the Etruscan period is debatable. The strongly fortified *arx* was built on the Capitol (→ Capitolium) and it alone was defended during the invasion of the Gauls in 387. Soon afterwards the first significant city wall, the Servian Wall, was built in Rome (2nd quarter of the 4th cent.). Roman fortifications developed from Greek and Etruscan components for the protection of Roman colonies founded after the mid 4th cent. The earth embankment (*agger*) that was often present behind a stone wall may be considered a peculiarity (e.g. the Servian Wall).

Fortification architecture reacted to advances in → siegecraft during the Hellenistic period with multiple walls and ditches, covered battlements, catapult stations, strong towers with flanking shooting ranges, and complex gate structures for which architectural forms were borrowed from the Assyrians and Persians. The Romans had been confronted with this fortification architecture, which was in use throughout the Hellenistic world and among the Carthaginians since the 3rd cent. BC. However, they merely took over those elements meeting their needs from Hellenistic models (e.g. regular spacing of towers on city walls, porticullises) and applied them to the city walls of the many colonies founded up to the Augustan period. Thus, Roman municipal fortifications did not receive the refined design and enormous magnitude of some Hellenistic fortifications. The vault (*concameratio*) and mortared rubble masonry (*structura caementicia, opus incertum*) were new construction elements of the 2nd cent. BC which permitted economic construction of very solid walls. The rubble masonry walls were often provided with shells of ashlar or brick, sometimes plastered, whitewashed, or even painted; gate buildings were often given a representational form (e.g. Verona, Turin, Nîmes, Autun, Trier).

Because the wall enclosed the city, it had legal and sacred functions from the earliest times. The city wall was usually the largest and most expensive public building; this confronted the city with difficult problems of financing, organization and maintenance of construction. The city wall and city gate developed into a symbol of identification for the city and during the Principate was represented on coins as a symbol of the city.

B. Principate and Late Antiquity

The architects of the Principate were always able to resort to Hellenistic models. However, because of the *pax Romana* most municipal fortifications lost their military significance for the time being. Only cities in endangered border provinces of the empire were an exception and became sites of new city wall construction (e.g. Nîmes, Cologne, Avenches, Trier, London). In Italy and provinces far from the borders old walls decayed or were outgrown by prospering cities (Rome, Pompeii, and others).

In the 3rd cent. AD, raids by neighbouring peoples forced the empire onto the defensive and resulted in a new period of fortification building. Many cities repaired their old walls or built new strong walls, often on a much smaller scale because of population decline. These city walls were designed for the massive deployment of long-range weapons such as catapults. They were therefore fitted with closely spaced strongly projecting defensive towers. Rome also received a strong fortification with the Aurelian Wall. As the only city wall in the West it had covered battlements and, as a result, would have been able to withstand an assault even by the technical means of the Roman army. Only the Sassanids were able to employ siege technology against Roman cities in the East. Covered battlements, multiple city walls and numerous projecting towers had been in use for some time there. These architectural elements were used by Roman cities in the East as well as in the large land wall of Constantinople.

C. Military Fortifications

The Republican army built only temporary lightly fortified camps of which the circumvallations are very well known (e.g. Numantia, Alesia). Permanent army camps developed only when the armies of the late Republic were in the field for longer periods. This became the rule when Augustus created the standing professional army. During wars the army continued to build field fortifications (route camps, circumvallations, linear blocks). The empire secured border provinces with *limites* (→ *limes*), which often had approach obstacles (earthen rampart and ditch, palisades, wall) and guarded the border, but only exceptionally had the character of a fortification (e.g. Hadrian's Wall, England). From the late 3rd cent. AD, army camps and border fortifications were built according to a new concept and provided with stronger defensive walls.
→ castellum

1 G. Brands, Republikanische Stadttore in It., BAR Int. Ser. 458, 1988 2 E. Gose, Die Porta Nigra in Trier, 1969 3 A. Johnson, Römische Kastelle, 1987 4 S. Johnson, Late Roman Fortifications, 1983 5 P. Leriche, Les fortifications grecques et romaines en Syrie, 1989 6 J. Maloney, B. Hobley (ed.), Roman Urban Defences in the West. Council of British Arch., Research Report 51, 1983 7 M. Todd, The Walls of Rome, 1978 8 P. Varène, L'enceinte gallo-romaine de Nîmes, 1992. D.BA.

Fortuna The goddess of fortune with an ancient cult in Italy; in the Republican period mostly understood as favourable chance but later considered increasingly negative, at least in literature. The myth of her relationship to Servius → Tullius demonstrates that this deification of an abstraction is to be understood in the full personal meaning (→ Personification).The multitude of her cultic specifications (lists: Plut. Mor. 281e; 322f.) makes a uniform interpretation of origin and function difficult (review of research [1. IX–XVII]); an interpretation promoted in particular by Wissowa [3] as originally a goddess of women or even a goddess of agricultural fertility, strongly based on the F. of Praeneste, is opposed by an interpretation based on the literal meaning as goddess of fate and chance, often the protector of certain groups or stages of life, while a separate solution (Greek or Etruscan import) must be sought for the cult of Praeneste. A survey of the historical development of the cult [1; 2] is more productive than attempting a uniform interpretation.

A. The cult outside Rome B. The cult in Rome C. Representation and Continuation

A. The cult outside Rome

Outside Rome – apart from isolated, often epigraphic mentions which take up aspects of the cult in Rome [1. 182–191] – old and independent cults of F. are attested in Antium and Praeneste. In Antium the cult of the two Fortunas (*veridicae sorores*: Mart. 5,1,3), which is well attested in iconography (coins) [1. 149–182], is only identifiable in outline in the sources. The sanctuary of → Praeneste, of which large temple ruins can still be seen [4, 5, 6], has been famous since the Hellenistic period. *F. Primigenia* ('First-born') was worshipped there as → Kourotrophos and an oracle deity (Liv. 45,44,8; Cic. Div. 2,85–87; Str. 5,3,11). The cultic statue of F. represents a maternal deity that is nursing a boy: the oldest dedication already identifies her as the goddess of birth, who was particularly worshipped by *matronae* (CIL I² 60). By contrast, since the 3rd cent. BC inscriptions name her as the daughter of Jupiter.

B. The cult in Rome

After initial resistance (Val. Max. epit. 1,3,2) official Rome also began to consult the → oracle of lots, and in 204 BC P. Sempronius vowed a F. sanctuary in the city to *F. Primigenia* (Liv. 29,36,8). The oldest F. sanctuaries in the city are associated with Servius → Tullius, that is, in the Roman imagination they were only created after → Numa had laid the foundations of the cult. However, this and Varro's thesis of Sabine origins (Ling. 5,74) should not be seen as evidence of a foreign import but rather as an indicator of a special ritual and religious status, especially since the close link of Servius to F. partially reflects Oriental mythologemes (Ov. Fast. 5,73–581, [7]). The F. cults of Servius are closely associated with women and their social role (its counterpart is the *F. Barbata* as a goddess of young men, who is only mentioned in Varro's Antiquitates fr. 143 Cardauns) and are generally located outside the → *pomerium*.

Servius is supposed to have founded the cult of *Fors F.*, whose feast on 24 June (Ov. Fast. 6,773–784) was celebrated in particular by craftsmen but also by slaves, across the Tiber (Varro, Ling. 6,17); a second temple was dedicated by Sp. Carvilius [4] in 238 BC (Liv. 10,46,14; not so in Ov. Fast. 6,783). The cult of F. by the Forum Boarium (near St. Omobono's at the foot of the Capitol) and the neighbouring temple of the → *Mater Matuta* (Ov. Fast. 6,475–636; Dion. Hal. Ant.

Rom. 4,27; both feasts on 11 June) are also considered founded by Servius.

The double temple of the early Republic (before the early 4th cent., for which literary sources estimate the building of → Camillus) was probably preceded by a double temple in two phases of the 6th cent. [8]. A wooden image of F. that had been donated by Servius and was completely wrapped in his togas survived the fire of 213 BC (Plin. HN 8,194; 197; Dion. Hal. Ant. Rom. 4,40,7; according to other sources it represented Servius: Varro Ap. Non. p. 189; Ov. Fast. 6,571). The fire, which is evident in literature and archaeology, was followed by reconstruction (Liv. 24,47,15; 27,7,5). The image was so sacred that it could not be touched even by the *matronae* who served the cult (Ov. Fast. 6,621). Since Varro calls the image *F. Virgo* (Ap. Non. p. 189), it was perhaps associated with the premarital rites of Roman brides, who dedicated their togas to *F. Virginalis* before marriage (Arnob. 2,67, cf. Plin. HN 8,194). Another foundation of Servius is the cult of *F. Virilis* (Plut. Mor. 281a), for which the main sacrifice falls on 1 April in the context of the feast of → Venus Verticordia, during which the women of Rome (both *matronae* and hetaeras) made offerings of incense to F. (Ov. Fast. 1,145–150). *F. Muliebris* is also connected to female sexuality. Her sanctuary at the fourth milestone of the *via Latina* was considered a donation of → Coriolanus in return for the support of women (Liv. 2,40,1–12). The women dedicated a second cultic image, which made itself known as being dedicated *rite* (Varro Antiquitates fr. 192 Cardauns; Dion. Hal. Ant. Rom. 8,55f.; Plut. Coriolanus 37) and which could only be wreathed and touched by the newly married.

In these three cults, F. is a goddess who watches over the important phases of the lives of women but in other cults she is a protector of individuals, families (epigraphy: e.g. *F. Crassiana*, *Iuveniana Lampadiana* and *F. Plotiana* [10]) and social groups – e.g. *F. Equestris* with a temple on the Field of Mars near the theatre of Pompey, which was vowed in 179 BC and dedicated in 173 BC (Vitr. De arch. 3,3,2; Liv. 40,44,8; 42,10,5) [9], and the all-embracing *F. Omnium*, whose feast on 1 January was founded by the emperor Trajan (Lydus, Mens. 4,7). Since Augustus established a sacrifice for *F. Redux* on 12 October after his return from the East in 19 BC and donated an altar (Cass. Dio 51,10; the date of donation is 15 December: Fasti Amiterni, Feriale Cumanum) [11], F. has been the protector of the emperor.

As the goddess of fortune in the sense of the Greek → Tyche, there were many cults dedicated to her in Rome and the provinces. These are occasionally only evident in epiclesis – *F. Bona* and *Mala* (Aug. Civ. 4,18; the altar of *F. Mala* on the Esquiline: Cic. Nat. D. 3,63), *F. Dubia* (altar on the Esquiline, CIL VI 675), *F. Brevis* (Plut. Mor. 281a; contrast: *F. Stabilis*: CIL III 5156a from Noricum), *F. Obsequens* (Plaut. Cas. 716), *F. Respiciens* (Cic. Leg. 2,28). Of some importance was her cult as protector of the present day, *F. Huiusce Diei*, with a temple on the Field of Mars vowed by Lutatius Catulus in 101 BC before Vercellae, probably at the site of an older temple of the same F., in which Aemilius Paullus dedicated statues (Plut. Marius 26,3; Plin. HN 34,54; [2. 154–170; 12]). F. was worshipped without epiclesis on the Quirinal, where three temples were located close to each other (*Tres F.e*, [13]), the oldest being that of *F. Publica Populi Romani Quiritium Primigenia* (Fasti Caeritani on 25 May), which had been adopted from Praeneste.

In the Isis mysteries, undependable and blind F. is contrasted with dependable and saving → Isis, as is frequently evident in literature (Apul. Met. 11,15) and iconography [14].

C. Representation and Continuation

F. had her own cultic and mythical character in Italy and Rome, but the literary evidence is largely dependent on the Greek → Tyche. F. is blind (Pacuvius 370; Cic. Phil. 13,10), capricious and undependable (Plin. HN 2,22), which is expressed in the depictions of F. precariously balancing on a sphere (Pacuvius 367; Ov. Tr. 5,8,7f.) and men are vulnerable to her continuously turning wheel (Cic. Pis. 10; Tac. Dial. 23). While literature emphasizes her negative aspects, the numerous pictorial images of F., who is responsible for unexpected luck and success, show the positive symbols of cornucopia and a rudder which is often leaning against a sphere [15]. However, Christian authors largely adhere to the negative assessment [16]. Under the tremendous influence of → Boethius (consolatio 2,1f.), the wheel became the most familiar image in mediaeval iconography [17; 18], while blind F. on the sphere became part of general European iconography through the allegories of the Renaissance and Baroque (not least in Baroque emblematics [19]).

1 J. Champeaux, F. Recherches sur le culte de la Fortune à Rome et dans le monde romain des origines à la mort de César. vol. 1: Fortune dans la religion archaïque, 1982 2 Id., ibid., vol. 2: Les transformations de Fortune sous la république, 1987 3 G. Wissowa, Religion und Kultus der Römer, 1912, 256–266 4 A. González Blanco et al., La Cueva Negra de F. (Murcia) y sus tituli picti. Un santuario de epoca romana, 1987 5 F. Fasolo, F.-G. Gullini, Il santuario della F. Primigenia a Palestrina, 1953 6 J. Aronen, LTUR 2, 273–275 7 C. Grottanelli, Servio Tullio, F. e l'Oriente, in: Dialoghi di archeologia 5.2, 1987, 71–110 8 F. Coarelli, Il Foro Boario, 1988, 205–244 9 Id., LTUR 2, 268f. 10 C. Lega, LTUR 2, 268; 271f.; 273 11 F. Coarelli, LTUR 2, 275f. 12 P. Gros, LTUR 2, 269f. 13 F. Coarelli, Tres F.e, LTUR 2, 285–287 14 Id., Iside e F. a Pompei e Palestrina, in: PdP 49, 1994, 119–129 15 F. Rausa, s.v. Tyche/F., LIMC 8.1, 125–141 16 I. Kajanto, s.v. F., RAC 8, 182–197 17 H. R. Patch, The Goddess F. in Medieval Literature, 1927 18 J. C. Frakes, The Fate of Fortune in the Early Middle Ages, 1988 19 G. Kirchner, F. in Dichtung und Emblematik des Barock, 1970.

J. B. Carter, The cognomina of the goddess F., in: TAPhA 31, 1900, 60–68; W. F. Otto, s.v. F., RE 7, 12–42; F. Castagnoli, Il culto di Mater Matuta e della F. nel Foro Boario, in: Studi Romani 27, 1979, 145–152; G. DUMÉZIL, Servius et la Fortune, 1943; I. KAJANTO, Epigraphical evidence of the cult of F. in Germania Romana, in: Latomus 47, 1988, 554–584; A. MILTENBERG, s.v. F., LMA 4, 665f.; K. MUSTAKALLIO, Some aspects of the story of Coriolanus and the women behind the cult of F. Muliebris, in: H. SOLIN, M. KAJAVA (ed.), Roman Eastern policy and other studies in Roman history, 1990, 125–131 · A. PASSERINI, Il concetto di F., in: Philologus 90, 1935, 90–97; H. RIEMANN, Praenestinae sorores. Tibur, Ostia, Antium, in: RhM 94, 1987, 131–162 and 95, 1988, 41–73; D. M. ROBINSON, The Wheel of Fortune, in: CPh 41, 1946, 207–216; M. J. STRAZZULLA, La F. Respiciens. Iconografia e culto, in: Rendiconti della Pontifica Accademia di Archeologia 63, 1990–91, 233–262. F.G.

Fortunatianus In AD 370–377 *comes rerum privatarum* in the East (Cod. Theod. 7,13,2; 10,16,3 and passim). In 371 he had subordinates who were accused of magic tortured (Amm. Marc. 29,1,5–7; Zos. 4,14,1). He may be identical with the pagan poet, rhetor, and philosopher of the same name (cf. Lib. Ep. 694,9; 1157; 1425), a correspondent of Libanius (Ep. 565; 644; 650 et passim). PLRE 1, 369 (F. 1). W.P.

Fortunat(ian)us F., an African, held office in 342–368/370 as bishop of → Aquileia. According to Jerome he wrote a gospel commentary *Titulis ordinatis brevi sermone rusticoque* (Jer. Vir. ill. 97,1) under Constantius [2] II (337–361). Perhaps three smaller fragments have been preserved (CPL 104); Jerome used the work for his own Matthew commentary (Praef.: PL 26,200 and Ep. 10,3). F. received → Athanasius in Aquileia in 345 but then pressured → Liberius of Rome to be lenient towards the Homoean movement (→ Arianism) under emperor Constantius II (thus Jer. Vir. ill. 97,2), which indicates a change of direction in his Church policy.

A. WILMART, B. BISCHOFF (ed.), Commentarii in Evangelia (= CCL 9), 1967, 365–370; L. DUCHESNE, Libère et Fortunatien, in: MEFRA 28, 1908, 31–78. C.M.

Foruli *Vicus* of the Sabini, *ager Amiterninus*, by the source of the Aternus (modern Pescara) on a rock spur (Str. 5,3,1), after 1204 Civitatomassa (Scoppito, L'Aquila). On a side road of the *via Salaria* (restored in AD 47 as the *via Claudia Nova*; CIL IX 5959; Tab. Peut. 5,5 erroneously *Erulos*), 13 miles after Interocrium (modern Antrodoco), 4 miles before Amiternum. Mentioned in 211 BC because of the passing of Hannibal (Liv. 26,11,11); *tribus Quirina*. Roman remains. Epigraphy: CIL IX p. 417–420; 4395–4435.

G. FILIPPI, s.v. F., EV 2, 567; G. FIORELLI, Civitatomassa, in: NSA 1885, 480; N. PERSICHETTI, Civitatomassa, in: NSA 1902, 122; G. RIVERA, Scoppito, in: NSA 1893, 436. G.U.

Forum

I. ARCHAEOLOGY AND URBAN STUDIES II. LEGAL HISTORY III. ROMAN FORUMS IV. PLACE NAMES

I. ARCHAEOLOGY AND URBAN STUDIES

A. DEFINITION AND FUNCTION B. THE FORUM IN VITRUVIUS C. TYPOLOGY D. IMPERIAL FORUMS

A. DEFINITION AND FUNCTION

Latin term for market, market place; rarely also the forecourt of a tomb (in the meaning of Greek *drómos*, e.g. Cic. Leg. 2,61) or part of a wine press (Varro, Rust. 1,54; Columella 11,2,71).

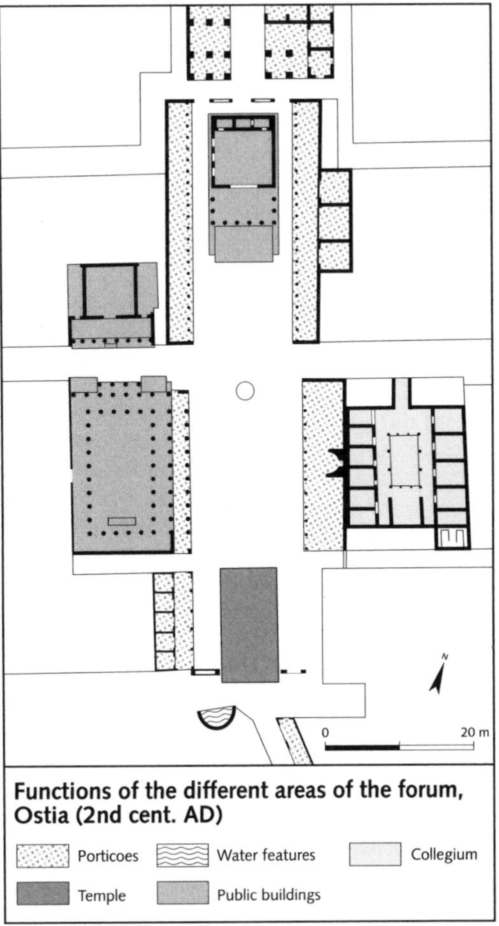

Functions of the different areas of the forum, Ostia (2nd cent. AD)

As the mercantile and administrative centre of a Roman city (→ Town/City), the forum, which took the form of a large open space framed by buildings, was essentially the equivalent of the Greek → agora. A location at the intersection of the → *decumanus* and → *cardo* in the city centre is the rule in all newly laid-out urban settlements of the Roman empire from the late Republican period (→ Town planning). The location as well as architectural and functional development of the → Forum [III 8] Romanum, the oldest forum of all, at the crossing of the *via sacra* and *vicus Tuscus* in Rome was the model. In 'unplanned' cities in the Greek cultural sphere, new forums were not necessarily built in the city centre but in a favourable location on main streets, near the main city gate or the harbour (e.g. Side, Gerasa, Palmyra), while newly built forums in old Greek cities were usually restricted to an economic function with the administration remaining at the old agora (e.g. Athens). On occasion the old agora was remodelled into a forum (Corinth). Larger cities usually had several forums, which were associated with specialization and hence a spatial separation of mercantile, administrative and religious functions that could even result in narrowing to specialized commercial activities (e.g. the Forum Boarium, Forum Suarium and Forum (H)olitorium in Rome). A special type of the forum reduced to mercantile functions is the → *macellum*.

The buildings and building groups framing the forum, usually a long rectangular square, were linked by roofed colonnades surrounding the area, but still clearly separated functionally; the peristyle-like surrounding building could be parcelled out into business areas and shops after the model of the Greek → stoa (e.g. Augusta Raurica [4], with plan). In addition to the Jupiter or Capitol temple and other cult sites and altars, the → basilica, various → assembly buildings for the magistrate and the administrative office buildings (*curia*, *comitium*, buildings for the *decuriones, duumviri* and *aediles*), often also the archive, calibration office and the → speaker's podium, also the → *horrea*, → latrines and occasionally also clubhouses and guild buildings (e.g. the Eumachia building in Pompeii) were located in the forum. In addition to trade and commerce, administration and worship, the forum was the centre of jurisdiction and site of legal business of all types (see below section II). During the Roman Republic before the construction of the first stone theatres, *munera* (→ Munus, munera) were held in the forum in temporary wooden buildings, as is frequently attested (→ Amphitheatre, → Theatre). The model for this amalgamation of buildings and functions was the → Forum [III 8] Romanum with the public hearth (temple of Vesta), administrative and assembly buildings, shops, → triumphal and honorary arches, and dismantable stages for *munera*.

As the city centre, which was also frequented by outside visitors, the forum was the most important site for representation. Private citizens of means drew attention to themselves there with donations, as the history of origin of the municipal basilicas of Rome, which have eternalized the names of the commissioning builders, demonstrates (→ Basilica Aemilia; → Basilica Fulvia; → Basilica Iulia). Wealth and communal spirit were most effectively demonstrated there with splendid temples and altars, official and administrative buildings as well as technological monuments such as sundials (Pompeii) and fountains (→ Well, fountains). Splendid rebuilding of porticas around the square in expensive materials became the custom in many Roman cities from the late 1st cent. BC, and this integrated the heterogeneous buildings at the edge of the forum into a unifying boundary. Furthermore, the forum was the preferred site for setting up honorary statues, arches and inscriptions. In many places it became a manifestation in stone of local history. If dedications and donations by the Imperial house or other superregional dignitaries were to honour a city, outstanding members of its administration or the citizenry as a whole, the forum was the frequently proposed and ideally suited location.

B. The Forum in Vitruvius

In two detailed passages Vitruvius describes the location as well as architectural and structural design of the Roman forum (1,7 and 5,1–2). For ports, he recommends a forum near the harbour, for inland cities as near as possible to the centre at the intersection of the main roads. In deliberate contrast to the Greek agora, Vitruvius particularly sees the forum square and its architectural surround as the traditional location of gladiatorial games; the colonnades around the square are to have wide intercolumnar spaces and easily accessible balconies in the upper stories to accommodate the audience and afford good views.

The size of the forum should correlate with the population of the city to avoid either crowding or the desolation of too large a square. For the layout Vitruvius recommends (again in contrast to the regular square layout of the Greek agora) a rectangle with sides in the proportion of 3:2. A → basilica should immediately adjoin the forum. It should be placed at the warmest location and the temple of Jupiter should be built opposite it. The treasury (*aerarium*), prison (*carcer*) and city hall (*curia*) should also be directly associated with the forum and be appropriate in size and proportion to the forum. Dividers for shops, money changers and other market functions were to be built into the basilica and the colonnades around the forum. The colonnades and the basilica are to have two storeys with the upper floor being three quarters the height of the ground floor. His complicated instructions for the elevation of the *curia* seek to set this building off from the surrounding architecture of the forum.

C. Typology

It immediately becomes clear when one considers the numerous preserved forums in the cities of the Roman empire that Vitruvius' representation is not universally applicable. In the organically developed cities of Italy the forum is often not at all or only partially integrated into the old city's structure of orthogonal street grids, which sometimes resulted in elongated or angular squares with complicated topography (e.g. the Forum Romanum in Rome). In Pompeii an elongated rectangular square in a ratio of almost 4:1 is bordered on the short sides by temples and offices. On the long sides the square is flanked in a rather irregular arrangement by the basilica, *horrea*, other communal buildings, temples, sanctuaries and guild buildings. An apparently complete rebuilding of a previously planned city area is

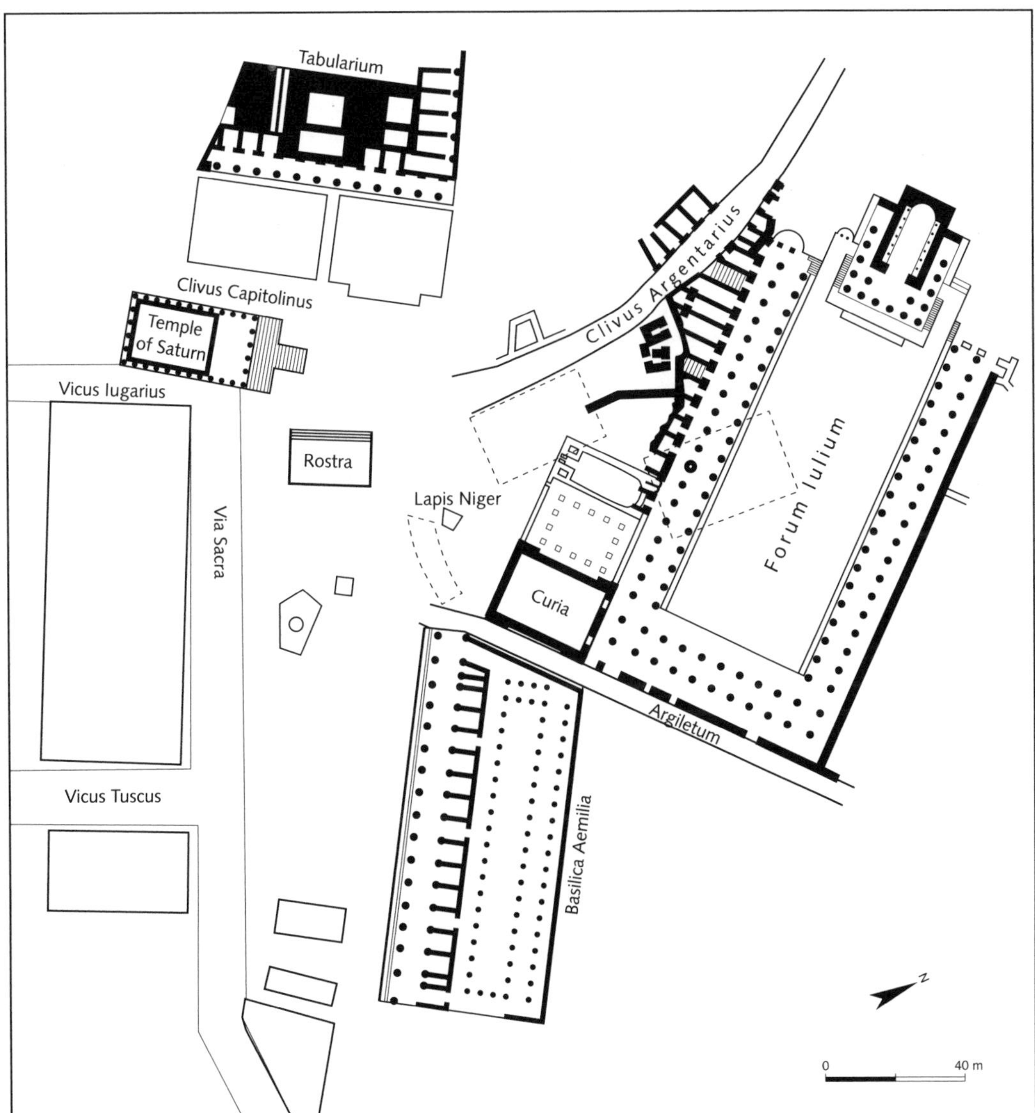

The Forum Romanum, state of 42 BC, with the area of the Comitium built over by the Forum Iulium.

found in the Greek city of Poseidonia after it was transformed in 273 BC into the Roman colony of Paestum. In entirely newly planned settlements in Italy, a forum 'cut from whole cloth', as Vitruvius describes it, is initially rare and in the foundation phase of the earliest Roman colonies it is often entirely absent. In Cosa, which was laid out in 273 BC, the capitol and forum were spatially separated from the start; its forum developed over more than a century from an unassuming open area, which was not central, into a district surrounded by buildings with structures for administration, worship (temple of Concordia), commerce and trade. Often a progressive merging of the capitol area with the market and assembly areas occurred in the development of early Italian forums (Minturnae, Ostia, Terracina). This development apparently went hand in hand with a politicization of the citizens during the reduction of aristocratic privileges enforced by the plebeians, the change in relationship of Roman Latin cities to Rome in the context of the Social Wars, and the increasing communal autonomy of settlements in the 2nd cent. BC. In late Italian city foundations of the 2nd and 1st cents. BC, a forum which merged religious, mercantile and administrative functions into a unit in a central location is consistently found, though with considerable variations in the building structure (Verona, Turin, Aosta).

The forums of cities newly founded outside Italy during the expansion of the Roman empire are all planned complexes built in one phase even though later they were frequently modified and the archaeological interpretation is sometimes ambiguous. These cities

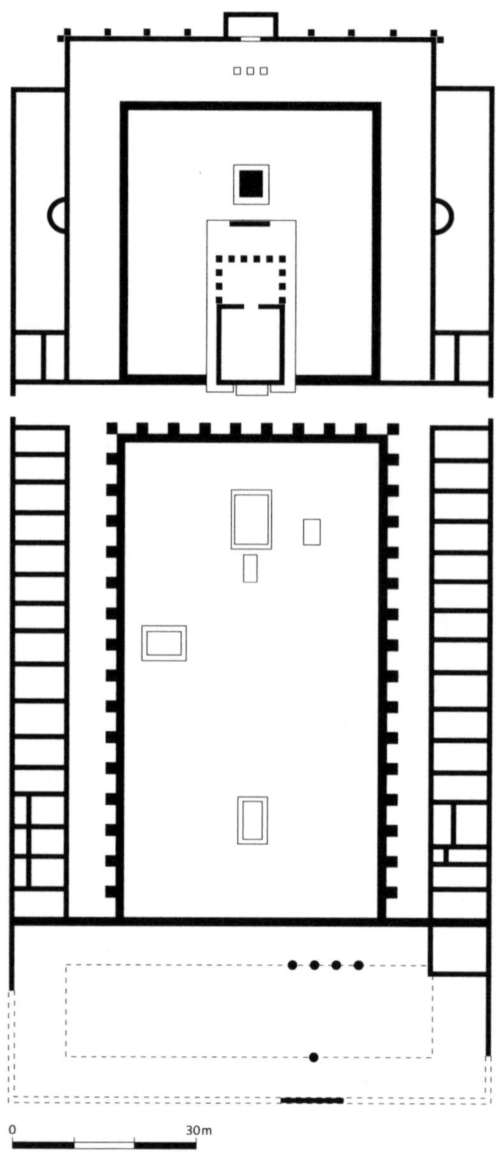

Gallo-Roman forum with, respectively, a temple and a transverse basilica at the two narrow sides. Lugdunum Convenarum/Saint-Bertrand-de-Comminges (1st-2nd cents. BC).

were often laid out according to the pattern of military camps (→ *castra*; → Town planning), with the forum at the centre of the settlement at the crossing of the two main roads, making it not only formally but also functionally equivalent to the *principia*, the centre of a military camp. Variations on three basic types of the Roman forum which also contradict the Vitruvian model forum are encountered: the peristyle forum is a square surrounded by colonnades with (Cyrene) or without (Ephesus, Athens, Miletus, St. Albans) a temple at the centre. Occasionally, the halls are limited to three sides and leave a short side open (Aosta, Arles). The temple forum completes a square bordered on three sides by colonnades with one or more temples on the open short side (Luni, Zadar, Vienne, Nîmes, Sbeitla, Ampurias, Tarragona). The basilica forum closes the open short side with a transverse basilica (Alise-Sainte-Reine, Martigny) rather than a temple; occasionally the basilica is on a long side (Dukla). A combination of the latter two types that matches Vitruvius' ideal with facing temple and basilica closing the short sides is found primarily in the Gallo-Hispanic northwest (Paris, Augst, Saint-Bertrand-de-Comminges, Lyons, Belo, Conimbriga), and occasionally in North Africa (Leptis Magna, Severian forum). Rare exceptional forms (an oval forum in Gerasa, apse forum in Thugga) do not fit into a typological classification.

D. Imperial forums

A special type of the forum reserved for the Imperial capitals of Rome and Constantinople are the imperial forums. In Rome they adjoined the Forum Romanum to the northwest: (→ Forum [III 5] Iulium, → Forum [III 1] Augustum, → Forum [III 10] Transitorium/Nervae, → Forum Traiani). However, they were scattered unlinked throughout Constantinople (Forum Arcadii, Forum Constantini, Forum Theodosii). These were spacious representational places created under the guidance of the ruler bearing their name and based on a politically and ideologically coherent concept of imperial self-representation. Not only the buildings but also the circumstances of their creation increased the donor's fame: an entire mountain, the former height of which was marked by Trajan's column, had to be removed to level the ground for the Forum of Trajan (→ Apollodorus [14]). In all cases this entailed significant costs for acquiring the required land and compensating those affected with a generosity visible to all the world.

How much these systems differed as 'private donations' from a traditional publicly furnished urban space like the neighbouring Forum Romanum in Rome, is made apparent with the repeated emphasis by Caesar (Cic. Att. 4,16,8) and Augustus (R. Gest. div. Aug. 21) that they had built their forums with their own private means on land bought specifically for the purpose. In accordance with this different initial situation, the architectural forms and functions of the city of Rome's imperial forums (the archaeology of those of Constantinople is only rudimentarily known) are very different from normal urban squares. These complexes, which are inserted into densely built-up areas, are sealed against the outside by high walls and focused internally upon themselves. They were closed to market activities and through traffic. Their functions were restricted to legal business, important acts of state, and musical and literary functions (→ Library). Also, the imperial forums with their representational endowments consisting of inscriptions, images, adjoining picture galleries, collections of books, cult objects, gems, and the like were an early form of museum (→ Art, interest in) as well as a manifestation of the patron's understanding

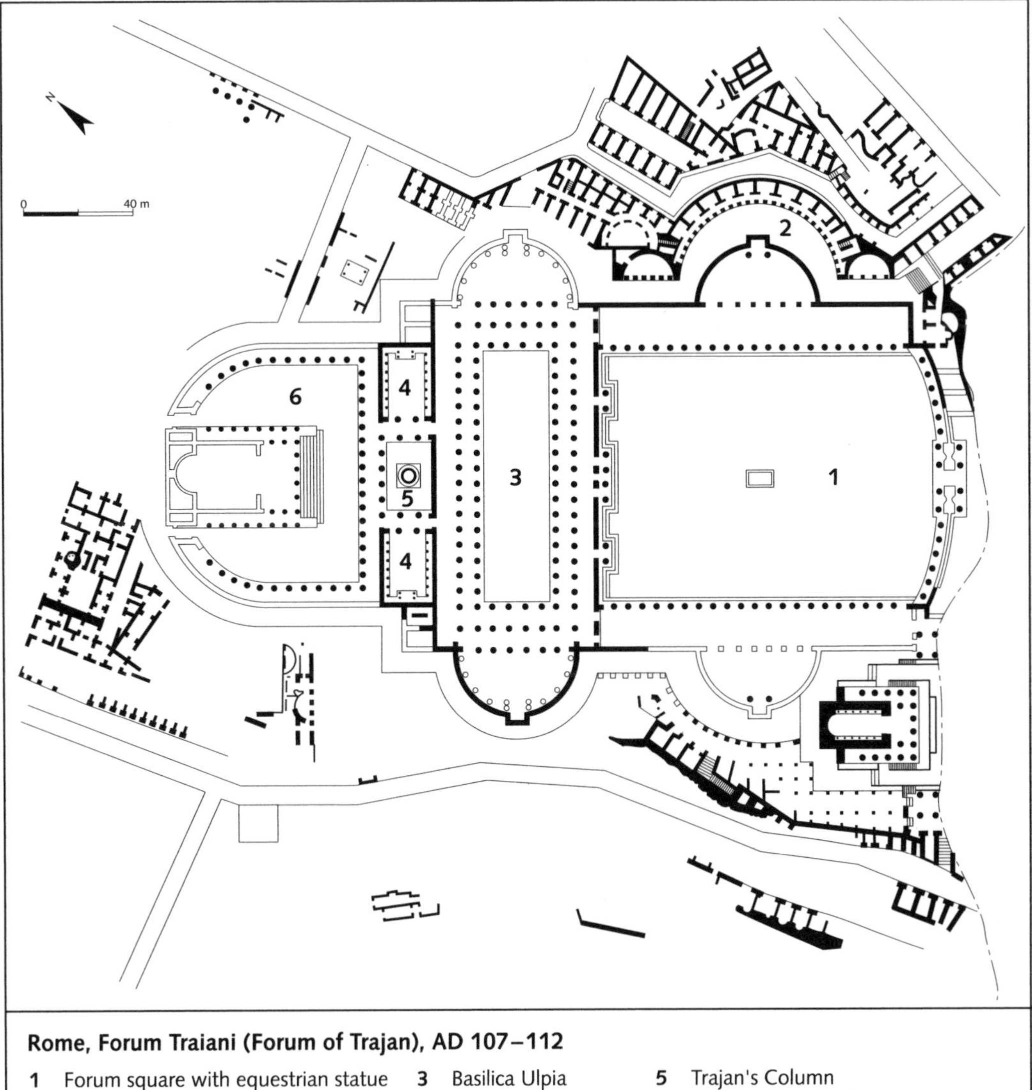

Rome, Forum Traiani (Forum of Trajan), AD 107–112

1 Forum square with equestrian statue
2 Mercati Traiani
3 Basilica Ulpia
4 Libraries
5 Trajan's Column
6 Open square with temple

of power. In this sense, the Augustus forum contains a very complex staging of Roman history that transcended various pictorial media and architectural components to unite the mythical past with the real reign of Augustus in a manner that was both seamless and beyond doubt for all viewers. Also in this sense, the Forum of Trajan was a complex ensemble of buildings and images that propagated the entire model function of the military in the Trajanic understanding of the state by means of group-specific, differentially received 'readings' and statement levels and attempted to relate it to the entire urban population of the city of Rome.

In its representational and ideological orientation towards the person or policy of the builder the imperial forum is a Roman invention; the theatre with large porticus built by Pompey (built in 61–55 BC) may be considered a precursor of this architectural idea – which in turn may have been the inspiration for Caesar's forum and is perhaps derived from Hellenistic temple sites like the sanctuary of Zeus in Priene. The three earliest examples, built respectively by Caesar, Augustus and Nerva, use the architectural structure of the temple forum (see section C). By contrast, Trajan's forum combined military architectural forms with structures of public squares into an entirely new whole, which incorporated a popular infrastructure component by attaching the *Mercati Traiani* to the imperial forum and in this way, creating an effective counterweight to the introverted ceremonial exclusivity of other examples.

→ FORUM

J.C. ANDERSON, The Historical Topography of the Imperial Fora, 1984; I.M. BARTON, Capitoline Temples in Italy and the Provinces, in: ANRW II 12.1, 259–333; F.A. BAUER, Stadt, Platz und Denkmal in der Spätantike, 1996;

J. BERGEMANN, Die röm. Kolonie von Butrint und die Romanisierung Griechenlands, 1998, 74–88; F.E. BROWN, Cosa. The Making of a Roman Town, 1980, 31–46; F. COARELLI, Il Foro Romano I/II, 1983/1985; J.J. DOBBINS, Problems of Chronology, Decoration, and Urban Design in the F. at Pompeii, in: AJA 98, 1994, 629–694; H. DRERUP, Zur Plangestaltung römischer Fora, in: P. ZANKER (ed.), Hellenismus in Mittelitalien, Kongreß Göttingen 1974, 1976, 398–412; J. EINGARTNER, Fora, Capitolia und Heiligtümer im westlichen Nordafrika, in: H.J. SCHALLES, H.v. HESBERG, P. ZANKER (eds.), Die römische Stadt im 2. Jh. n. Chr. Der Funktionswandel des öffentlichen Raumes, Kongreß Xanten 1990, 1992, 213–242; B. FEHR, Das Militär als Leitbild: Politische Funktion und gruppenspezifische Wahrnehmung des Traiansforums und der Traianssäule, in: Hephaistos 7/8, 1985/1986, 39–60; F. FELTEN, Heiligtümer oder Märkte?, in: AK 26, 1983, 84–105; A. FRAZER, The Imperial Fora. Their Dimensional Links, in: Eius virtutis studiosi. Classical and Postclassical Studies in Memory of F.E. Brown, 1993, 410–419; J. GANZERT, V. KOCKEL, Augustusforum und Mars-Ultor-Tempel, in: Kaiser Augustus und die verlorene Republik, exhibition catalogue Berlin 1988, 149–199; J. GRIFFITH PEDLEY, Paestum, 1990, 114–123; P. GROS, P. VARÈNE, Le forum et la basilique de Glanum, in: Gallia 42, 1984, 21–52; P. GROS, Les étapes de l'aménagement monumental du forum, in: La città nell'Italia Settentrionale in età romana, Kongreß Triest 1987, 1990, 29–68; P. GROS, L'architecture Romaine. Les monuments publics, 1996 (with detailed bibliography); M. HÜLSEMANN, Theater, Kult und bürgerlicher Widerstand, 1987; H. KNELL, Vitruvs Architekturtheorie, 1985, 115–128; V. KOCKEL, Ostia im 2. Jh. n.Chr. Beobachtungen zum Wandel eines Stadtbildes, in: H.J. SCHALLES, H.v. HESBERG, P. ZANKER (ed.), Die römische Stadt im 2. Jh. n. Chr. Der Funktionswandel des öffentlichen Raumes, Kongreß Xanten 1990, 1992, 99–117; H. KYRIELEIS, Bemerkungen zur Vorgeschichte der Kaiserfora, in: P. ZANKER (ed.), Hellenismus in Mittelitalien, Kongreß Göttingen 1974, 1976, 431–438; TH. LORENZ, Römische Städte, 1987; Los foros romanos de las provincias occidentales, Kongreß Valencia 1986, 1987; R. MARTIN, Agora et Forum, in: MEFRA 84, 1972, 903–933; W.L. MACDONALD, The Architecture of the Roman Empire II, 1986, 51–66; C. MORSELLI, s.v. Foro, EAA Suppl. II, 1994, 689–693 (with bibliography); E. RUOFF-VÄÄNÄNEN, Studies on the Italian Fora (Historia Einzelschriften 32), 1978; J. RUSSEL, The Origin and Development of Republican Forums, in: Phoenix 22, 1968, 304–336; H.J. SCHALLES, Forum und zentraler Tempel, in: H.J. SCHALLES, H.v. HESBERG, P. ZANKER (ed.), Die römische Stadt im 2. Jh. n. Chr. Der Funktionswandel des öffentlichen Raumes, Kongreß Xanten 1990, 1992, 183–221; M. TODD, Forum and Capitolium in the Early Empire, in: F. GREW, E. HOBLEY (ed.), Roman Urban Topography in Britain and the Western Empire, conference London 1985, 56–66; P. ZANKER, F. Augustum, 1986; Id., Das Trajansforum als Monument imperialer Selbstdarstellung, in: AA 1970, 499–544; P. ZUCKER, Town and Square, 1959. C.HÖ.

II. LEGAL HISTORY

In legal terminology, a *forum* (the term is still used in modern trial law) is usually that which is summarized in modern legal parlance as 'a court's responsibility'. However, sometimes it simply means the court location in a general sense, e.g. Gai. Dig. 1,2,1: *in foro causas dicere* ('to pronounce law in the forum') or (in criminal law) Ulp. Dig. 48,19,9,4: *nonnumquam cui forum interdicitur* ('on occasion someone will be barred from the forum'). The technical meaning refers to the question of which court or judge is competent to make the decision in a particular legal dispute. It is answered with a combination of factual and personal criteria.

The material criterion, which is rarely described as a *forum*, is a locational and material limitation which has not so far been entirely clarified, of the duties of the curule → aediles, municipal courts, the *praefecti* (→ *praefectus*), *iuridici*, provincial governors as well as the peregrine and city praetors (→ *praetor*). The latter was responsible at least in theory for all procedures concerning Roman citizens.

As far as the personal criteria are concerned, the principle that 'the plaintiff follows the defendant' (*actor rei forum sequatur*, Cod. Iust. 3,13,2; cf. also Cic. Verr. 3,38) applied for reasons of procedural fairness. It was always at the defendant's residence (→ *domicilium*), possibly also his place of origin (→ *origo*, Gai. Dig. 50,1,29). Apart from this general place of jurisdiction, there had been at least since late antiquity a number of special responsibilities for legal reasons or on grounds of agreement between the parties (the latter still called *prorogatio fori* in an un-Roman manner, but cf. Ulp. Dig. 5,1,2,2). An agreement of this sort may also be seen in the contractual determination of the location of payment (cf. Gai. Dig. 42,5,1 and 3). The *forum delicti commissi* (at the location of the offence committed) is one of the places of jurisdiction existing for legal reasons; Justinian (Nov. 69) says that he has introduced it universally. However, it may be assumed that an equivalent responsibility had occasionally existed previously (Cod. Iust. 3,16,1: Valentinian in 366; 3,15,1: Septimius Severus and Caracalla in 197: *satis notum est*, 'it is sufficiently known', concerning criminal law). Valentinian also established for suits concerning material claims the place of jurisdiction as location at which the object was located, the *forum rei sitae* (Cod. Iust. 3,19,3 in 385). Justinian also determined that a countersuit, regardless of its isolated responsibility could also be negotiated and decided upon at the location of the main suit and cites prior considerations by Papinian (Cod. Iust. 7,45,14). Special places of jurisdiction were created in late antiquity for certain persons and groups of persons, especially for senators, provincial governors, clerics, court officials and soldiers.

Of decisive importance was the responsibility at the time of determining the dispute, the → *litis contestatio* or even *in ius vocatio* (cf. Ulp. Dig. 5,1,7); ad hoc changes in factual matters were insignificant (un-Roman: *perpetuatio fori*, Iavolenus Dig. 5,1,34). The decision of a judge without responsibility was void (Ulp. Dig. 2,2,1,2 = Cod. Iust. 7,48,4: Valentinian in 379).

M. KASER, K. HACKL, Das römische Zivilprozeßrecht, [2]1997, 242ff. C.PA.

III. Roman forums

[III 1] Forum Augustum. In antiquity it was also occasionally called the *Forum Augusti*; the largest of numerous building projects by → Augustus in the city of → Rome, after Caesar's → Forum [III 5] Iulium the (chronologically) second large square with representational design, which complemented the space of the → Forum [III 8] Romanum to the north-east. Like Caesar's forum, the Forum Augustum was designed as a temple forum (see above Section I). Both were built with private funds on land bought specifically for this purpose (R. Gest. div. Aug. 21: *ex manibiis... in privato solo*), which in the case of the Forum Augustum was probably judged to be too small for the intended plan (Suet. Aug. 56,2). The Forum Augustum continues the basic ideas of the Forum Iulium. In their common character as 'private construction', both forums differed fundamentally from traditional public squares such as the Forum Romanum and the other forums of the city and constituted the ideological and conceptual germ for the later imperial forums of Nerva and Trajan.

The Forum Augustum consists of an oblong square which is focused on itself by being marked off from the neighbouring Subura by walls of up to 30 m high. It was bounded by two-storey colonnades and two facing → exedras on the long sides (dimensions of the Forum Augustum: *c.* 105 m wide including the exedras, *c.* 120 m long). At the centre stood the representational podium temple of Mars Ultor with eight Corinthian columns (a view is preserved in one of the 'Valle Medici reliefs') and open ptera (→ Temple) on the long sides, which had been vowed in 42 BC after the battle of Philippi. Construction of the Forum Augustum was probably not begun before 19 BC (construction and dedication of the 'Parthian Temple' on the Capitol for presentation of the recaptured field insignia, which were later transferred to the Temple of Mars Ultor). The Temple of Mars Ultor was dedicated in 2 BC (Ov. Fast. 5,549–552; Cass. Dio 55,10,1–3 and 60,5,3; Vell. Pat. 2,100,2), probably after the square had already been opened for use (Suet. Aug. 29,1).

The Forum Augustum was a place of state representation (reception of foreign delegations, location of the annual celebrations of the assumption of the *toga virilis* by Roman boys), for sacrifices (banquet of the → Salii, sacrifices of the → Arvales Fratres) and jurisdiction, not just market business. It was accessible only from the south side and not by vehicle. Overall, the buildings and images of the Forum Augustum constituted a highly complex visualization of the 'Golden Age' that Augustus proclaimed for his reign. The niches in the colonnades showed the 'greatest men' (*summi viri*) of the state. In the exedras as the culmination of the series, a programmatically purified 'narrative' history of Rome and the *gens Iulia* of Augustus was blended with great effect into one harmonious construct with Roman mythology and woven into Greek mythology by means of the Aeneas legend. The intertwining of the ruling family with mythology became equally apparent in the Temple of Mars Ultor, which contained statues of Mars (preserved, e.g. in an altar relief from Carthage in the Archaeological Museum in Algiers), Venus, and Divus Iulius and thus elevated the *gens Iulia* to the level of the highest state gods. The sculpted temple pediment hinted allegorically at Augustus' military successes; the → Caryatids, which support in endless repetition the upper colonnade, were copied from the korai of the Erechtheum of the Acropolis in Athens and symbolized by their uniform multitude the peoples subjected by Augustus. The highly representational claim of the square was underlined by numerous literal allusions to classical Greek art in sculptures, building ornaments, and architectural forms as well as the exorbitant opulence of the building materials: almost all available types of tuff, travertine, marble, and wood, as well as other stones were blended into a colourful whole.

The Forum Augustum remained a high-ranking site of state representation even after the death of Augustus and was subsequently only slightly modified and extended. Its details became often copied models (exedras of the → Forum [III 9] Traiani in Rome, statue galleries of the type of the *summi viri*, e.g. in Pompeii, Arezzo, Aventicum, Mérida). In the 9th cent. the site was converted into a monastery. The first survey of the buildings in their state during antiquity was compiled in the 16th cent. (Antonio da Sangallo) – today its value is disputed. A large scale dig, part of the excavation of the imperial forums in Rome 1924–1926, resulted in anastylosis, still without full documentation.

G. Alföldy, Zu den Monumenten der römischen Provinzen auf dem Augustusforum, in: FS für Th. Pékary, 1989, 226–234; F.A. Bauer, Stadt, Platz und Denkmal in der Spätantike, 1996, 86–89; J. Ganzert, Der Mars-Ultor-Tempel auf dem Augustus-Forum in Rom, 1996; J. Ganzert, V. Kockel, Augustusforum und Mars-Ultor-Tempel, in: Kaiser Augustus und die verlorene Republik, Ausst.-Kat. Berlin 1988, 149–199; V. Kockel, Beobachtungen zum Tempel des Mars Ultor und zum Forum des Augustus, in: MDAI(R) 90, 1983, 421–448; Id., F.A. in: LTUR 2, 1995, 289–295 (fundamental, with comprehensive bibliography); T.L. Luce, Livy, Augustus, and the Forum Augustum, in: K.A. Raaflaub (ed.), Between Republic and Empire. Interpretations of Augustus and his Principate, 1990, 123–138; A. Schmidt-Colinet, Exedra duplex. Überlegungen zum Augustusforum, in: Handlungen des Archäologischen Seminars der Universität Bern 14, 1991, 43–60; L. Schneider, Ch. Höcker, Die Akropolis von Athen, 1990, 222–242; B. Wesenberg, Augustusforum und Akropolis, in: JDAI 99, 1984, 161–185; P. Zanker, Forum Augustum, o.J. 1972).

C.HÖ.

[III 2] Forum Boarium see → Rome

[III 3] Forum Caesaris see → Forum [III 5] Iulium

[III 4] Forum (H)olitorium see → Rome

[III 5] Forum Iulium. In 54 BC Caesar had already bought the land for this forum northwest of the Capitol (Cic. Att. 4,16,8), which covered the area between the → *Mons Argentarius*, the → *Atrium Libertatis* and the → *Argiletum*. Nevertheless, construction of the first imperial forum could only begin in 51 BC. It was designed to lessen the burden on the → Forum [III 8] Romanum and to be used for routine administrative work and the courts (App. B Civ. 2,102). Its buildings replaced the area of the *comitium* in the Forum Romanum and connected the *curia,* the Senate's meeting place, as an annex building to the Forum Iulium. The rectangular square (160 × 75 m) was bordered on three sides by a double colonnade, while the Forum Iulium was accessed from the east through the *Argiletum* and the *Curia Iulia*, into the back wall of which two doors had been cut. A series of small *tabernae,* of which two acted as stairways, were located on the south side towards the *Mons Argentarius.* The temple of Venus Genetrix, which Caesar had originally vowed to Venus Victrix during the battle of Pharsalus, dominated the Forum Iulium. To this was added the Appiades fountain, mentioned in sources (Plin. HN 36,33; Ov. Ars am. 3,451f.; Ov. Rem. am. 660, cf. Ars am 1,82).

On his birthday (26 September), which was also the last day of his triumph in 46 BC, Caesar dedicated the forum and the temple though construction had not yet been completed. Augustus finished it in 44 BC (R. Gest. div. Aug, 19; Cass. Dio 45,6,4) and placed a star-crowned statue of Caesar (or Divus Iulius) into the temple because of the appearance of a comet (*sidus Iulium*) (Cass. Dio 45,7,1; 47,18,4). The remains of the Forum Iulium visible today are from a later period after a fire necessitated rebuilding the square, completed under Trajan in AD 113. At the time that square was extended by the → Basilica Argentaria on its western side. Diocletian rebuilt it again in AD 283.

P. Zanker, Forum Romanum, 1972; R.B. Ulrich, The Appiades fountain of the Forum Julium, in: MDAI(R) 93, 1986, 405–423; C.M. Amici, Il Foro di Cesare, 1991; Richardson, 165–167; P. Gros, s.v. Forum Iulium, LTUR 2, 1995, 306–307; F.A. Bauer, Stadt, Platz und Denkmal in der Spätantike, 1996, 81–86. R.H.

[III 6] Forum Nervae see → Forum Transitorium
[III 7] Forum Pacis see → Templum Pacis

[III 8] Forum Romanum
A. General B. The Republican Forum Romanum C. The Imperial Forum Romanum

A. General

The Forum Romanum, the centre of the city of Rome and, in the Ancient view, also the 'Navel of the World', lies in a valley at the intersection of the Vicus Tuscus and the *via sacra.* As the oldest forum of all, its name was synonymous with the term for centuries. The description *forum Romanum* is first found in Virgil (Aen. 8,361), but like its alternatives *forum magnum* (e.g. Cass. Dio 43,22,2) and *forum vetus* (e.g. Cic. Att. 4,16,14), it never completely entered official usage in antiquity. Until the 7th cent. BC, it was used as a burial ground but around 600 BC it became the common public area of the core settlements on the surrounding hills that were coalescing into a larger union. The Forum Romanum is, therefore, similar to the Athenian → Agora, the product of a → synoecism (→ Rome).

The early history of the square, which grew over more than twelve centuries with religious, economic, political, and social functions, was already mythologized in antiquity and topographically somewhat confused in part by arbitrary placements, e.g. by marking the grave of Romulus with the → *lapis niger* in the paving, the construction of the → *lacus Curtius* and, early in the 3rd cent. AD, the *umbilicus urbis* ('Navel of the City') as visualizations of mythical places. The Forum Romanum is integrated as a material version into the complex reformulation, falsification, and harmonization of Roman mythology and annalism during the middle and late Republic and, as a result, became a monumental testimony of a collective shaping of the past. Many topographical aspects remain obscure, owing to the considerable increase in ground level and the layering of phases of various architectural modifications and redesigns, which are somewhat difficult to distinguish, as well as the lack of clarity in what published findings there have been of large excavations since the middle of the 19th cent. More recent excavations have added little clarity. The overall representation of the place by Coarelli, Ammerman, and Purcell exemplify the dissension in modern archaeological research and only a basic outline of the historical and chronological development of the Forum Romanum is currently a matter of consensus.

B. The Republican Forum Romanum

As the centre not only of the city of Rome, but the entire Imperium Romanum, the Forum Romanum was already characterized in the 4th cent. BC by a transformation from the place of a communal administration and government to being the centre of religion, state, politics, and constitution of a great empire; the manifold and profound internal conflicts of this dynamic process materialized in the topography of the square in a more or less perceptible manner. The irregular layout of the Forum Romanum resulted from a succession of buildings up to the 2nd cent. BC with no overall plan. In the process two functionally separate parts of the square crystallized: the area of the *comitium* as the political and administrative centre and the forum proper with basilicas and temples for economic and religious activities.

The *comitium* (→ Assembly buildings), the ancient gathering place of the Roman people, was originally a *templum*, an open circular space dedicated and managed by the augurs. It was bordered by the *lapis niger*, subterranean heroon of the city's mythical founder Romulus, dating back to the 6th cent. and marked in the paving, by the → *senaculum*, meeting place of the senators as delegates of the tribes, by the *columna maenia* (→ Monumental column) as the location of juridical proclamations, and by the *carcer* as the site of punishment. The → speaker's podium (*rostra*) was immediately to the south of the square and the *curia* (→ Assembly buildings) as the meeting place of the Senate to the north. The individual components formed a functional whole that was a mirror image of the Roman constitution and its elements (assembly of the people, assembly of representatives by tribe, assembly of officials) until the 1st cent. BC and, therefore, also functioned as the political and judicial centre of the community.

Grouped around the forum square were the oldest temples of the Roman republic: the temple of Saturn (according to the annals dedicated in 498 BC) as the state treasury, the temple of the Dioscuri near the sanctuary and the source of the → Juturna, the temple programmatically dedicated after the class struggles of 366 BC to → Concordia, and somewhat apart the temple of Vesta with the Holy Fire, the house of the Vestals, and the *regia* with the official building of the *pontifex maximus* beside it; the temples, preserved after many building phases, will be discussed according to their origins. On the square itself stood several *tabernae*, temporary wooden buildings for trade and commerce, and numerous honorary statues, which were cleared out to some extent by the censors in 158 BC owing to lack of space (Plin. HN 34,30). The place was bounded and oriented in the 2nd cent. BC by the → Basilica Aemilia, the → Basilica Porcia and the → Basilica Sempronia. The forum square itself served also as the location of → *munera* and theatre performances, held in temporary wooden buildings of which numerous post holes, as soil discolorations, have been documented archaeologically (cf. also Liv. 23,30,15; Plut. C. Gracchus 33; see above Section I).

C. The Imperial Forum Romanum

The Forum Romanum underwent a drastic remodelling in the 2nd half of the 1st cent. BC, which transformed the lively character of the square into a stage of monarchical representation that was bereft of its Republican political significance. The stone → theatres of Marcellus and Pompey created a permanent space for stagings and games. Caesar's → Forum [III 5] Iulium obliterated the *comitium* by overbuilding, becoming the architectural manifestation of his political usurpation of the Republic. The new *Curia Iulia* became an annex to his forum, just as in his view the Senate had become an annex to his rule. The new rostra was deprived of its original function as the place of controversial debate and became a show stage at the front of the redesigned Forum Romanum, which was bordered on the south side by the → Basilica Iulia, also associated with Caesar's name, on the site of the demolished Basilica Sempronia. The eastern end of the square, the temple of Divus Julius, which had been vowed by the triumvirs in 42 BC, was built under Augustus and was furnished with an altar in the podium and a second rostra (with ship beaks from the battle of Actium). The dynastic nature as a monument of the *gens Iulia* was enhanced by an honorary arch to Augustus, which spanned the *via sacra* to the south of this building conglomeration and completely blocked off the *regia* and the Vesta temple from the Forum Romanum.

During the reign of Augustus and his successors, the Forum Romanum was completely redesigned as a representational square and gradually filled with monuments of the most diverse types: the single honorary arch to the south of the temple of Divus Julius were replaced (after 19 BC) by a structure with three arches on the occasion of recovering the standards lost to the Parthians. These arches bore inscriptions with the *fasti consulares* and *fasti triumphales*. It was probably augmented in 3 BC on the north side of the temple by the arch for the chosen throne pretenders Gaius and Lucius, which spanned a branch of the *via sacra*. The square, which was expensively paved in 10 BC in marble, first became a stage for symbolical and allegorical acts of rule by means of the exclusive renovation of the surrounding architecture, which for the first time included an *milliarium aureum*, a golden milestone with distances to the most important places in Italy. This tendency towards staging imperial omnipotence at the former centre of the Roman republic was the culmination of each period with the honorary arch for Tiberius built at the centre of the square (between the rostra and Basilica Iulia), the temples for Vespasian, Titus, and others, the monumental equestrian statue of Domitian (*equus Domitiani*), the elaborate honorary arches for the emperors Titus and Septimius Severus, the five-column monument of the Tetrarchs, the → Basilica Constantiniana (Maxentius Basilica), the equestrian statue of Constantine the Great, and the column of Phocas. The first Christian church buildings appeared in the 6th cent. AD (St. Maria Antiqua, Sts. Cosmas and Damian). → Forum

A. J. Ammerman, On the origins of the Forum Romanum, in: AJA 94, 1990, 627–645; Id., The Comitium in Rome from the Beginning, in: AJA 100, 1996, 121–136; Id., Forum Romanum, in: Richardson, 170–174; F. A. Bauer, Stadt, Platz und Denkmal in der Spätantike, 1996, 7–79; G. Carettoni, Topografia del Foro e del Palatino. Bilancio di un secolo di ricerche, in: Rivista di Studi Liguri 45, 1979, 209–219; F. Coarelli, Il Foro Romano, 1. Periodo arcaico, 1983; Id., Il Foro Romano, 2. Periodo repubblicano e augusteo, 1985; C. F. Giuliani, P. Verduchi, Foro Romano. L'area centrale, 1980 · C. F. Giuliani, P. Verduchi, L'area centrale del Foro Romano, 1987; M. Hoff, Rom. Vom Forum Romanum zum Campo Vaccino. Studien zur Darstellung des Forum Romanum im 16. und 17. Jh., 1987; M. Hülsemann, Theater, Kult und bürgerlicher Widerstand im antiken Rom, 1987; J. Isager, Forum Romanum og Palatin, 1977; R. T. Ridley, The monuments of the Roman Forum. The struggle for identity, in: Xenia 17, 1989; G. Tagliamonte, N. Purcell, C. F. Giuliani, P. Verduchi, Forum Romanum, in: LTUR 2, 1995, 313–345 (bibliography); P. Zanker, Forum Romanum, 1972. C.HÖ.

[III 9] **Forum Traiani.** The largest and chronologically last imperial forum of Rome. It completed the previously created conglomerate consisting of the → Forum

[III 5] Iulium, the → Forum [III 1] Augustum, the → Forum [III 10] Transitorium and the → Templum Pacis to the northwest and simultaneously lent the whole system the appearance of unity. Though probably begun by Domitian in the context of his modifications of the neighbouring Forum Iulium (Aur. Vict. Caes. 13,5), the Forum Traiani with its overall dimensions of about 300 × 185 m was built between AD 107 and 112 by the architect → Apollodorus [14] (Cass. Dio 69,4) in the area originally occupied by the ridge between the Capitol and the Quirinal, which was levelled at considerable expense to make a construction area. The elevation before levelling is marked by the height of Trajan's Column (dedicated in AD 113 together with the restored Forum Iulium; → Monumental column). To date most of the site is still unexcavated. The outline of the Basilica Ulpia is certain because of the → *forma urbis Romae*. Views of the Forum Traiani (especially also the equestrian statue of Trajan) have been identified on numerous coins (e.g. BMCRE III, pl. 16, 18, 21) and facilitate reconstruction of the unpreserved buildings (see above Section I with illustration of the Forum Traiani).

The overall layout of the Forum Traiani follows the pattern of a Roman military camp indicating the military aspect of Trajan's rule (Dacian wars; → Daci) – a theme that is also taken up in many details of the buildings and images and was in this manner conveyed to the late Roman urban population. The site is subdivided into three areas. The forum proper is located in the southeast: a rectangular square accessed through a representational propylon (→ Gates) with an equestrian statue (already much admired in antiquity) of Trajan at the centre and on the long sides two great → exedras opposite each other. The five-naved → basilica (*Basilica Ulpia*) with apses on the two short sides functioned as a massive architectural divide across the forum and was at that time the largest basilica in Rome. The northeastern side is completed by two → libraries (*Bibliotheca Divi Traiani*) and the column crowning the funerary monument to Trajan with its spirally rising relief. The detailed (though probably not historically accurate but symbolic) narration of the Dacian wars could also be read in a vertical segmented selection of scenes and images. Behind it lay the podium temple surrounded by U-shaped colonnades and separated by the basilica from the forum square proper. Its design was based on the Temple of Mars Ultor in the forum of Augustus with eight Corinthian columns and open ptera. The analogy of the concept with the central portion of a Roman military camp (→ *castra*) is evident and has repeatedly been emphasized in archaeological research: the basilica complex is equivalent to the → *principia*, the libraries, which probably also functioned as archives, to the legion archive. The column stood at the location of the standards (cf., e.g. the *principia* of Castra Vetera, Xanten in Germany).

Numerous preserved inscriptions, now often difficult to fit into their original architectural context, mosaics, multicoloured kinds of stone (granite, cipollino, travertine, marble, tuff, and many others), architectural ornaments and a rich furnishing with statuary (in part preserved by being reused as → spolia on the arch of Constantine in Rome (→ arcus [7]); both exemplified the immense splendour of imperial building donations and elevated the military as the model for society. Individual legions were honoured in inscriptions, while the subjugation of the Dacians was narrated in the meticulously realistic scenes on the relief band of the column, which will have been visible from the libraries at least in segments along its entire height, and was likewise illustrated in a gigantic frieze (→ Frieze; cf. fig. there) on the basilica (the attribution of fragments to the Forum Traiani is still debated) and free-standing statuary (statues of Dacian prisoners, some made of the most valuable green porphyry).

The essential purpose of the Forum Traiani was to establish another location for imperial jurisdiction, many aspects of which were relocated to the basilica of the Forum Traiani in AD 112. Acts of manumission occurred there, the → *congiaria* were distributed, and legal business of all types was recorded, while lessons were given in the exedras. The exclusivity of earlier Imperial forums was reduced with respect to activity and access. As an annex to the Forum Traiani, the five-storey *Mercati Traiani* were cut into a hillside on the steeply rising northeast along the *via Biberatica*, as a business quarter for the people on the edge of the → Subura. Today, its multistorey ruins are still among the most impressive remains of ancient architecture in Rome.

The effect of the Forum Traiani on later periods was significant but has not been examined in detail to date. The equestrian statue of Trajan and the *equus Domitiani* in the → Forum [III 8] Romanum represent the prototype of this type of monument, which became the image of the ruler embodying military virtues from antiquity (e.g. the equestrian statue of Marcus Aurelius) through to modernity (monuments of Kaiser Wilhelm among others). The concept of Trajan's Column was also adapted in the → monumental columns of Marcus Aurelius and Antoninus Pius, and in the modern period for the Victory column in Berlin, the Monument in London and the Napoleonic relief column in the Place Vendôme in Paris.

Even in the time of Constantius II in the mid–5th cent. AD, the Forum Traiani was the most important square in the city of Rome after the Forum Romanum. The circumstances in the early 4th cent. AD leading to a partial plundering of the buildings by removing the statuary and incorporating them into the arch of Constantine the Great are still unclear.

C. M. Amici, Foro di Traiano: Basilica Ulpia e biblioteche, 1982; J. C. Anderson Jr., Domitian's Building Program, Forum Julium and Markets of Trajan, in: Archaeological News 10, 1981, 41–48; F. A. Bauer, Stadt, Platz und Denkmal in der Spätantike, 1996, 93–100; A. Carandini, M. Medri, R. Volpe, Progetto per uno scavo nel Foro di Traiano, in: Roma. Archeologia nel centro Vol. 1, 1985, 272–298; B. Fehr, Das Militär als Leitbild. Politische

Funktion und gruppenspezifische Wahrnehmung des Traiansforums und der Traianssäule, in: Hephaistos 7–8, 1985–1986, 39–60; W. GAUER, Ein Dakerdenkmal Domitians, in: MDAI(R) 88, 1973, 318–350; C.F. GIULIANI, 'Mercati' e Foro Traiano. Un fatto di attribuzione, in: Saggi in onore di G. De Angelis d'Ossat, 1987, 25–28; C.F. LEON, Die Bauornamentik des Trajansforums und ihre Stellung in der früh- und mittelkaiserzeitlichen Architekturdekoration Roms, 1971; G. LUGLI, Date de la fondation du Forum de Trajan, in: CRAI 1965, 233–238; G.A. MANSUELLI, Osservazioni sull'iscrizione della Colonna Ulpia, in: Epigraphica 31, 1969, 124–138; R. MENEGHINI, M. MILELLA, Ricerche nel Foro di Traiano – Basilica Ulpia, in: Archéologie Médiévale 16, 1989, 541–559; J. PACKER, Numismatic Evidence for the Southeast (Forum) Façade of the Basilica Ulpia, in: Numismatic and other Studies in Honor of B.L. Trell, 1981, 57–67; J. PACKER, K.L. SARRING et al., Il Foro di Traiano, in: Archeo 7, 1992, No. 11, 62–93; J. PACKER, The West Library in the Forum of Trajan, in: Eius virtutis studiosi. Classical and postclassical studies in memory of F.E. Brown, 1993, 420–444; J. PACKER, Trajan's Forum again, in: Journal of Roman Archaeology 7, 194, 163–182; J. PACKER et al., in: LTUR 2, 1995, 348–359 (bibliography); P. PENSABENE et al., Foro Traiano. Contributi per una ricostruzione storica e architettonica, in: Archeologia Classica 41, 1989, 27–292; H. PLOMMER, Trajan's Forum, in: Antiquity 48, 1974, 126–130; RICHARDSON, 175–178; L. RICHARDSON JR., The Architecture of the Forum of Trajan, in: Archaeological News 6, 1977, 101–107; R. SCHNEIDER, Bunte Barbaren. Orientalenstatuen aus farbigem Marmor in der römischen Repräsentationskunst, 1986; Id., Kolossale Dakerstatuen aus grünem Porphyr, in: MDAI(R) 97, 1990, 235–260; S. SETTIS et al., La Colonna Traiana, 1988; R.A. STACCIOLI, I Mercati traianei, in: Capitolium 40, 1965, 584–593; S. STUCCHI, Tantis viribus. L'area della colonna nella concezione generale del Foro di Traiano, in: Archeologia Classica 41, 1989, 237–292; M. TRUNK, Das Traiansforum. Ein steinernes Heerlager in der Stadt?, in: AA 1993, 285–291; M. WAELKENS, From a Phrygian quarry. The provenance of the statues of the Dacian prisoners in Trajan's forum at Rome, in: AJA 89, 1985, 641–653; P. ZANKER, Das Trajansforum als Monument imperialer Selbstdarstellung, in: AA 1970, 499–544. C.HÖ.

[III 10] Forum Transitorium. Construction of the fourth imperial forum was begun by Domitian, but completed only under Nerva in AD 97 (or 98). The name of the site varied considerably in antiquity, but the complex received its name in late antiquity because of its location as the passage between the forums of Augustus and Caesar to the Templum Pacis on one hand, and from the → Subura to the Forum Romanum (S HA Alex. 28,6) on the other. In this way it replaced the → Argiletum. The temple of Minerva in the north-east and at the other end the temple of Janus (Mart. 10,28,5f., cf. Macrob. Sat. 1,9,13; Serv. Aen. 7,607), which was probably designed as a shrine open on all four sides, were the dominating short sides of the square (120 × 45 m). The Forum Transitorium was entered from the Subura through the horseshoe-shaped Porticus Absidiata, which bridged the space between the Templum Pacis and the eastern → exedra of the Forum of Augustus. The southern end of the Forum Transitorium was U-shaped towards the → Basilica Aemilia, which is also where the access to Caesar's forum and the Forum Romanum (Arcus Nervae?) was located.

RICHARDSON, 167–169; H. BAUER, C. MORSELLI, s.v. F.T., LTUR 2, 1995, 307–311; E. LA ROCCA, Das Forum Transitorium. Neues zu Bauplanung und Realisierung, in: Ant. Welt 29, 1998, 1–12; F.A. BAUER, Stadt, Platz und Denkmal in der Spätantike, 1996, 91–92. R.H.

IV. PLACE NAMES

[IV 1] Forum Clodii. A stopping-place on the *via Clodia* in southern Etruria between Careiae and → Blera on the western shore of the *lacus Sabatinus* (Lago di Bracciano), modern San Liberato. Probably named after the *censor* of 225 BC [1] or an ancestor of C. Clodius Vestalis (*monetalis* 41–29 BC; CIL XI 3310a); a *praefectura* with *IIviri*. Diocese from the 4th to the 6th cents.

1 NISSEN Vol. 2, 352.

L. GASPERINI, Un cippo al dio Termine dal territorio di Canale Monterano, in: ArchCl 10, 1958, 133–135; Id., Il Braccianese nell'antichità, in: Tuscia Archeologica 5–6, 1971, 4ff.; Id., Nuova dedica onoraria di Forum Clodii, in: Sesta Miscellanea Greca e Romana, 1978, 439–458; Id., Il monumento rupestre di Numerio Pullio nel Foroclodinense, in: ArchCl 36, 1984, 361–374; Id. (ed.), Antichità tardoromane e medioevali nel territorio di Bracciano, 1994; G. PACI, Senatori e cavalieri romani nelle iscrizioni di Forum Clodii, in: L. GASPERINI (ed.), Scritti in memoria di M. Zambelli, 1978, 261–314 (= Quaderni della Forum Clodii 4, 1977).

[IV 2] Forum Vibii. *Oppidum* of the Caburriates in the Transpadana (Alpes Cottiae) on the eastern slope of *Mons Vesulus*, 50 km southwest of Turin, by the source of the Padus (Plin. HN 3,117; 123); according to [1. 825; 2. 109; 3. 668] identical with Caburrum, modern Cavour (Torino).

1 CIL V 2 K.J. BELOCH, Der italische Bund, 1880 3 E. PAIS, Storia interna di Roma, 1931.

U. EVINS, The Early Colonisation of Cisalpine Gaul, in: PBSR 20, 1952, 66. G.U.

[IV 3] F. Gallorum. (Ἀγορὰ Κελτῶν; *Agorà Keltôn*). Settlement on the → via Aemilia, 8 Roman miles (*c.* 12 km) south-east of Mutina (Tab. Peut. 4,4; cf. Geogr. Rav. 4,33; Guido, Geographica 37) beside modern Castelfranco Emilia. Forum Gallorum (FG) is mentioned in literature in connection with the War of Mutina (→ Mutina, War of), when, on 14 April 43 BC, M. Antonius [I 9] defeated the consul C. Vibius [I 2] Pansa, only to be defeated in almost exactly the same location a few days later by the other consul, Hirtius (Frontin. Str. 2,5,39; App. B Civ. 3,67–70).

E. ANDREOLI, A. NEGRIOLI, Edizione archeologica della Carta d'Italia al 100000, sheet 87, 1938, 124. E.O.

[IV 4] **F. Iulii.** (Φόρος Ἰούλιος; *Phóros Ioúlios*). Harbour town of the Oxybii (→ Deciates) in Gallia → Narbonensis (Ptol. 2,10,8; It. Ant. 297,4; It. Burd. 505,1 ff.; Tab. Peut. 3,2; Geogr. Rav. 4,28; 5,3; Notitia Galliarum 16,4) at the mouth of the Argenteus (Ἀργέντιος/Argéntios, modern Argens) on the left bank, on the road from Italy to Hispania (later → via Aurelia), modern Fréjus (department of Var). Although numerous settlement traces exist in the surrounding country dating back to the Paleolithic, the settlement at Forum Iulii (FI) was only established in the 1st cent. BC (evident in letters of L. Munatius [I 4] Plancus of May 43 BC: Cic. Fam. 10,15,3; 10,17,1). The harbour had already been expanded on the initiative of the future Augustus (Str. 4,1,9), when he sent ships from the fleet of Antonius [I 9] to FI following the victory at → Actium in 31 BC (Tac. Ann. 4,5: *oppidum Foroiuliense*). At the same time, he is said also to have sent a *colonia* (*tribus Aniensis*: CIL XII 260; 290 ff.; 295; *duoviri*: CIL V 7907; X 4868; XII 261; *seviri Augustales*: CIL XII, 267–272) with men of his *legio VIII Hispana* to FI (cf. Plin. HN 3,35; Mela 2,77). Although FI, whose importance as a naval base in Augustus' time was fully comparable to that of Misenum or Ravenna, gradually relinquished its military significance, probably because of the silting up of its harbour, it remained into late antiquity an important centre for public administration, traffic and trade (cf. the placename *Forum I.*), and from the end of the 4th cent. was also a diocesan town (evidence from 374).

The harbour (*c.* 22 ha), today silted up, was linked to the sea by a canal *c.* 1 km long and 50–80 m wide. Of the Augustan city walls, which enclose more than twice the extent of the modern built-up area, large sections together with towers and two gates (at either end of the → *decumanus maximus*) are preserved. The orthogonal street plan, with building understructures, mosaics and, in the north, the theatre, is visible. Other ancient structures are found beyond the walls: the small amphitheatre (capacity *c.* 9,000; 1st/2nd cents. AD) in the north-west, baths and necropolis in the south-west ('La Tourrache'). A magnificently preserved aqueduct brings water over more than 40 km from Esterel, entering the town by the north-eastern gate.

→ Catualda, the rival of → Maroboduus, was interned at FI (Tac. Ann. 2,63). The elegist C. Cornelius [II 18] Gallus came from FI, as did Cn. Iulius [II 3] Agricola, the father-in-law of Tacitus (Tac. Agr. 4).

P.-A. Février, Fréjus (F.I.) et la basse vallée de l'Argens, 1977; A.L.F. Rivet, Gallia Narbonensis, 1988, 226–30; C. Goudineau, s.v. F.I., PE 335 ff. E.O.

Fossa

[1] **F. Augusta** Navigable → canal between the Padus and the harbour of Ravenna (Plin. HN 3,119); under Augustus diverted via the Padusa, a marshy branch of the Po. *Statio* on the *via Popilia*, later *Augusta*; traces in the Valle Mezzano in the drained Laguna di Comacchio.

G. Uggeri, Un insediamento a carratere industriale. Relazione preliminare degli scavi sull'argine d'Agosta 1971–1973, in: Boll. annuale. Centro di ... Musei Ferraresi 3, 1973, 174–179.

[2] **F. Claudia** Navigable → canal, built by Claudius between the Padus and the Altino to intensify inland navigation between Ravenna and Aquileia. Cf. modern Chioggia.

G. Uggeri, Vie di terra e vie d'acqua tra Aquileia e Ravenna in età romana, in: Antichità Altoadriatiche 13, 1978, 45–79.

[3] **F. Flavia** Navigable → canal in the Po delta, part of the water link running parallel to the coast between Ravenna and Altinum. Built under the Flavian emperors, it used an Etruscan canal that was diverted from the Sagis (branch of the Po) and crossed the swamps in the region of Adria (Plin. HN 3,120).

G. Uggeri, Vie di terra e vie d'acqua ... , in: Antichità Altoadriatiche 13, 1978, 45–79; Id., Interventi idraulici nell'Etruria padana, in: M. Bergamini, Gli Etruschi maestri di idraulica (Convegno Perugia 23–24 febbraio 1991), 1991, 69–72.

[4] **F. Neronia** 160 mile-long navigable → canal along the Latium coast, planned and partly built by Nero (Tac. Ann. 15,42; Plin. HN 14,61; Suet. Nero 31) to link the harbour of Ostia with the *lacus Avernus* and the *lacus Lucrinus* (Gulf of Puteoli). Its so-called *fossa Augusta* on Monte Circeo is still extant.

W. Johannowsky, Appunti su alcune infrastrutture dell'annona romana tra Nerone e Adriano, in: Bollettino di Archeologia 1990/4, 1ff.

[5] **F. Neronia** Navigable → canal in the ancient Po delta with a road station of the same name (Tab. Peut. 4,5 erroneously *Neroma*), possibly absorbed under the name *fossa Flavia* following the *damnatio memoriae* of Nero.

G. Uggeri, La romanizzazione dell'antico delta padano, 1975, 161–164; Id., Insediamenti, viabilità e commerci, in: N. Alfieri (ed.), Storia di Ferrara 3,1, 1989, 136f.

[6] **F. Philistina** Pre-Roman navigable → canal of the southern lagoon of Venice in the region of Adria (Plin. HN 3,121), built by using the Tartarus and the old Padus flow. The name (connection with Philistus of Syracuse?) is still to be found today in Pestrina (Rovigo) and Pellestrina south of Venice.

A. Karg, Die Ortsnamen des ant. Venetien und Istrien, in: Wörter und Sachen 22, 1941/2, 172; L. Braccesi, Grecità adriatica, 1977, 216; G. Uggeri, Le origini del popolamento, in: Storia di Cento 1, 1987, 99; G.B. Pellegrini, Ricerche di toponomastica veneta, 1987, 160. G.U.

[7] **F. regia** Demarcation line drawn by Scipio the Younger in 146 BC between the kingdom of the Numidian kings and the Roman province of *Africa*. It took ap-

proximately the following course: mouth of the river Tusca (modern Kébir) near → Thabraca (modern Tabarka) – eastern edge of the area of Vaga (modern Béja – close to Tichilla (modern Testour) – close to Thimissua (modern Gaffour) – close to Saradi (modern Henchir Seheli?) – close to Abthugni (modern Henchir es-Souar) – Thenai (modern Thyna). From 46 BC it formed the border between *Africa Vetus* and *Africa Nova*. In AD 73 and 74 Vespasian had it restored for fiscal reasons. Ten boundary stones bear witness to this measure: BCTH 1932–1933, 152; CIL VIII Suppl. 4, 25860; Bull. archéologique des travaux historiques, 1911, 402–404; CIL VIII Suppl. 4, 25967; BCTH 1934–1935, 391; BCTH 1938–1940, 204; CIL VIII Suppl. 4, 23084.
→ Limes

G. Di Vita-Evrard, La Fossa Regia et les diocèses d'Afrique proconsulaire, in: A. Mastino (ed.), L'Africa romana. Atti del III convegno di studio, 1986, 31–58 (with controversial interpretation of the area of Vaga); Ch. Saumagne, La Fossa Regia, in: Les Cahiers de Tunisie 10, 1962, 407–416. W.HU.

Fossae Papirianae Navigable → canal on the Etruscan coast (*regio VII*) between Pisae and Luna with a road station on the *via Aemilia Scauri* (Ptol. 3,1,43; It. Ant. 293; Tab. Peut. 4,1) near Massarosa (Lucca). The builder, a Republican official, is not identified.

A. Neppi Modona, Carta archeologica d'Italia 104, 1956, 16; Nissen 2, 287. G.U.

Fossatum The Cod. Theod. 7,15,1 mentions a ditch with a width of 4–10 m which, through aerial photographs, has been shown to be part of the African Limes secured by fortresses. Today it can best be seen near El-Kantara (Island of Djerba, Tunisia) and Gemellae (Batna, Algeria). It served not just military purposes but also to separate the cultivated land from the desert. Dating varies between Hadrian and the Four Emperors (2nd–3rd cents. AD).

J. Baradez, Fossatum Africae, 1949. C.HÜ.

Founder see → Ktistes

Foundry painter Attic red-figured vase painter working around 490–475 BC. Named after the external images on a bowl in Berlin, the foundry painter is the most independent of the 'ancillary painters' of the Brygos workshop. His work is primarily to be found on bowls that seldom, but then tersely, take up mythical themes (battles of the Centaurs, Theseus leaving Ariadne); the foundry painter prefers symposium and cosmos images that are full of sharply observed details.

Beazley, ARV[2], 400–404; Id., Paralipomena 369–371; Id., Addenda[2], 230–231; D.C. Kurtz (ed.), Greek Vases. Lectures by J.D. Beazley, 1989, 78–83; E.R. Knauer, Indiana University Museum. Occasional Papers, 1987. A.L.-H.

Four empires, theory of (the) see → Empires, Concept of empire

Four-man Commentary ('Viermännerkommentar') Modern term for a commentary, presumably early Byzantine, on the 'Iliad', being a compilation of the four exegetes of Homer → Aristonicus [5], → Didymus [1], Aelius → Herodianus [1] and → Nicanor [12] (cf. the subscription of the individual books of the Iliad in the Cod. Venetus A). The four-man commentary provides information on the factual and linguistic interpretation of Homer, as well as on the decisions of textual criticism of the Alexandrians in the circle of → Aristarchus [4] of Samothrace, and forms (alongside the exegetical → scholia) the primary model for scholia on Homer (especially the *Iliad*) as well as for the explanations of the text of Homer in the *Etymologicum Genuinum* (→ Etymologica), in → Eustathius [4] and in the → Suda.
→ Homer [1] VI.; → Scholia I.

H. Erbse, Beitrag zur Überlieferung der Iliasscholien (Zetemata 24), 1960; K. Lehrs, De Aristarchi studiis Homericis, [3]1882, 1–35; M. Schmidt, Die Erklärungen zum Weltbild Homers und zur Kultur der Heroenzeit in den bT-Scholien zur Ilias (Zetemata 62), 1976, 1–39; ScholiaIl. 1, XLV–LIX; M. van der Valk, Researches on the Text and Scholia of the Iliad, vol. 1, 1963. ST.MA.

Fox (ἀλώπηξ/*alṓpēx*; Lat. *volpes*, *vulpes*). Through outstanding adaptation to the human environment everywhere in Europe and North Africa, with the exception of the Mediterranean islands (Xen. Cyn. 5,24; Plin. HN 8,228), an ever-present predatory mammal. Pictorial representations [1. 88] on coins [2. pl. 2,1] and cameos [5. pl. 16,1–3 and 17,17] are relatively rare. In literature before Archilochus, i.e. in Homer and Hesiod, the fox is absent but it appears in the 5th cent., esp. in comedy. Its allegedly malicious cunning was proverbial (Archil. fragment 81 D.; Pind. I. 3,65; Aristoph. Pax 1067; 1189; Equ. 1069; Pl. Resp. 2,365c; Cic. Off. 1,41: *fraus quasi vulpeculae*; Hor. Sat. 2,3,186 et passim; see [3. 189, 379]) and was also applied to human beings (Theoc. 5,112; Plut. Solon 30,3 et passim). People therefore gave it many corresponding names like κερδώ/*kerdṓ*, κερδαλέος/*kerdaléos* (rogue, thief), κίδαφος/*kídaphos*, σκίνδαφος/*skíndaphos*, σκινδαφή/*skindaphḗ* (rascal), κόλουρις/*kólouris*, κοθοῦρις/*kothoûris*, (bobtail), λάμπουρις/*lámpouris*, (luminous tail, because of its striking red colouring), (σ)καφώρη/*(s)kaphṓrē* (the vixen; cf. Ael. NA 7,47), Sicilian κίναδος/*kínados*, Libyan βασσάρα/*bassára*, βασσάριον/*bassarion* (because the fox was almost always considered female, as in Semonides fragment 7). Its reproduction was described (Aristot. Hist. an. 2,1,500b 23; 6,34,580a 6; Plin. 10,176), and its prey, which comprised stolen poultry, young game, hares, mice, insects as well as honey and grapes (Aristot. Hist. an. 6,37,580b 25: mice; Xen. Cyn. 5,4 and 24; Plin. HN 10,207; Opp. Kyn. 3,460; Ael. NA 4,39; 6,24; 13,11). Only Opp. Kyn. 3,449f describes the fox's den. Crossing with the dog (Aristot. Hist. an. 8(9),28,607a 3; Xen. Cyn. 3,1) was said to have given rise to the esp. dangerous Laconian → dogs. Like the dog, the fox often had rabies (Plut. Mor. 963d). As a pest, and to obtain its fur (Hdt. 7,75; Xen. An. 7,4,4; Aristoph. Ach. 878), it was hunted with dogs, traps, nets and snares. Because of the supposed fine taste, and for therapeutic reasons, people ate its flesh in Greece in autumn (Orib. 1,181; Gal. 6,665; cf. Nic. Alex. 185). Plin. enumerates many sympathicolytic agents from the fox (HN 28,165ff.). In Rome it was hunted at the Cerealia (19th April) with a burning torch to the tail (Fest. 177; Ov. Fast. 4,681, in this regard [6. 197, 302]).

People attributed to the fox competition for food and hostility in relation to the lion, wolf and eagle and other diurnal birds of prey (Pind. I. 4,80; Aristot. Hist. an. 9(8), 1,609b 1ff.; Plin. HN 10,205), as opposed to friendship with the raven, crow and snake (Aristot. 8(9),609b 1ff.; Plin. HN 10,205; Plut. Mor. 981 B; Ael. NA 2,51). Hunters' jargon is to be found in Plin. HA 8,103; Ael. NA 4,24 and 6,64 etc. There are only a few fox legends (Paus. 4,18,4 and 9,19,1; Apollod. 2,8,4; Antoninus Liberalis 41 [4. 147]), but it plays a big part in the animal fable. It either outwits other animals (Aesop. fab. 9; 83; 126 and 269 HAUSRATH) or it is fooled or exposed by them (Aesop. fab. 17; 19; 41; 203; 245; 268; 323; 334). Its cunning, however, also enables it to see through things cleverly and to uncover difficult facts (Aesop. fab. 27; 98; 128; 135; 154; 252; 287; 335).

1 KELLER 2 F. IMHOOF-BLUMER, O. KELLER, Tier- und Pflanzenbilder auf Münzen und Gemmen des klass. Alt., 1889, repr. 1972 3 A. OTTO, Die Sprichwörter und sprichwörtlichen Redensarten der Römer, 1890, repr. 1988 4 PRELLER/ROBERT 5 F. BÖMER, P. Ovidius Naso: Die Fasten, 1957/58 6 G. WISSOWA, Religion und Kultus der Römer,²1912, repr. 1971, 197, 302. C.HÜ.

Fragmenta Vaticana A legal collection that was discovered in a → Palimpsest, overwritten with the text of the *Collationes* by Joh. → Cassianus, by Angelo Mai in the Vatican Library (Cod. Vat. no. 5766) in 1821. Of the Cod. in its original scope of at least 232 parchment pages there are only 28 partly highly damaged pages left. They contain not only fragments by Papinian, Paulus, Ulpian and perhaps other lawyers who cannot be individualized but also constitutions (→ *constitutiones*), particularly by Diocletian, as well as Constantine (Fragmenta Vaticana (FV) 35 and 249, probably also FV 36) and Valentinian (FV 37). The older constitutions come from the Cod. Gregorianus and Hermogenianus. The fact that orders of Maximian are recorded supports their origin and use in the west; the fact that Constantine's decrees do not take into consideration the → *damnatio memoriae* of Licinius, and the fact that they are unabridged indicates that they were compiled before AD 325, with the order of 372 inserted later [1. 404f.]. It is not very probable that the FV was compiled after 372; we can assume that it dates from before the Cod. Theod., which was not taken into account. The FV possibly were the model for the form of the original Theodosian codification project of 429 (Cod. Theod. 1,1,5); but they could scarcely have arisen from that project.

The FV are not the first edition of the collection. Nor do the numerous textual variants on the → *Corpus iuris* ('Confronti', cf. → Interpolation, critique of) reflect the original wording of the judicial writings: research (*Textstufenforschung*) reckons rather that since the first editions of the late Classical judicial writings there was at least one copy, possibly around 300, which had conveyed the original book roll texts into codices and can thus be regarded as the source for scribal errors and editorial interventions. No sensible arrangement of the incomplete title sequence, which is not even divided into books, can be discerned: *Ex empto et vendito* (1–40); *De usu fructu* (41–93); *De re uxoria ac dotibus* (94–122); *De excusatione* (123–247); *Quando donator intellegatur revocasse voluntatem* (248–259); *Ad legem Cinciam de donationibus* (260–341); *De cognitoribus et procuratoribus* (317–341). Whether the FV were used for practice or training is uncertain.

1 TH. MOMMSEN, Abh. der Berliner Akad. 1859/60.

W. FELGENTRAEGER, Zur Entstehungsgesch. der F.V., in: Romanische Studien, Freiburger Rechtsgesch. Abh. 5, 27ff.; F. WIEACKER, Textstufen klass. Juristen, 1960; Id., RRG, 134f. (more recent lit.). W.E.V.

Fragmentum Censorini The anonymous *Compendium disciplinarum*, a short encyclopaedia of 15 small ch., was considered until 1583 (L. CARRIO) to be the final part of *De die natali* by → Censorinus [4], as it joins on smoothly in his MSS, although it is probably garbled at the beginning. Cosmogony, astronomy, geography (Aristotelian-geocentric), geometry and postulates according to → Euclides, music theory (Aristoxian?) and metrics according to the theory of prototypes are treated, overall therefore approximately the quadrivium according to the Varronian model. The text, only used by the scholiast of → Germanicus, belongs to the period before the great encyclopaedias of late antiquity, most likely the 3rd cent. AD.

EDITION: K. SALLMANN, Censorinus, 1983, 61–86.
BIBLIOGRAPHY: Id., in: HLL, § 449.1. KL.SA.

Fragmentum (fragmenta) de iure fisci Two parchment pages from the chapter library of Verona written in two columns in half-uncial (→ writing) of the 5th/6th cents. AD. The text possibly dates from the 2nd or 3rd cents. AD. The upper edges of the pages are missing, and therefore the sequence of the pages is unclear. No one has yet convincingly succeeded in attributing the writings to a known author. No link with the text of the 'Institutions' by → Gaius [1] found in the same area is discernible. The subjects treated are the values, e.g. the *bona caduca* (→ *aerarium*), falling to the → *fiscus*, the duties of the *advocati fisci*, contracts with slaves of the *fiscus*, and the hereditary right of the emperor to his freedmen. For this reason, VON SAVIGNY, who first edited and commented on the text on the basis of NIEBUHR'S [1] reading, already considered classifying it with a work *De iure fisci*. The modern editions [2; 3] are primarily based on the edition of [4], which also offers a facsimile of the MS.

1 F. v. SAVIGNY, Neu entdeckte Quellen des röm. Rechts, in: Zschr. für gesch. Rechtswiss. 3, 1817, 150 2 FIRA 627–630 3 P.F. GIRARD, F. SENN, Textes du droit romain, [7]1967, 461 4 P. KRÜGER, Fragmentum de iure fisci, 1868.

R.WI.

Framea see → Pilum

Franci (the Franks). Initially a loose league of smaller Germanic tribes on the right-hand side of the Rhine that slowly arose from economic and cultic common ground as well as through relationship by marriage of the princes – e.g. the → Am(p)sivarii, → Bructeri, → Chamavi, → Chattuarii, possibly → Chatti, whose ethnicities as well as the general name used since the 3rd cent. AD (Pan. Lat. 11,5,4; 7,2; etymology 'those eager for battle', 'the daring') lived on (see Tab. Peut. 2,1–3). Since the start of the 4th cent. there is also evidence of *Francia*.

From *c*. AD 260 the F. repeatedly advanced, plundering as they went, to southern Gaul and Hispania (Aur. Vict. 33,3), but they also served early, esp. from the time of Constantine the Great (→ Constantinus [1]), in the Roman army (of → Postumus: S HA Gall. 7,1), where they reached positions of the highest command in the 4th cent. [1. 199–201]. As early as 275/6 Trier (→ Augusta [6] Treverorum) fell victim e.g. to the F., → Carausius set up his empire with their help; Frankish pirates (at times with the Saxons) made the North Sea insecure. Maximianus and Constantius settled the F. for the first time in regions of northern Gaul as → Laeti. After relative peace in the period of Constantine (Roman reactions under Crispus 320/1; Constans 341/2), the usurpation of → Magnentius changed the Rhine front significantly; in 355 Cologne (→ Colonia Agrippinensis) was destroyed. → Iulianus cleared the site by 360, settled Salian F. (→ Salii) in Toxandria [2] and through this policy of assimilation instituted their segregation. The usurpation of Maximus brought new ravages to Colonia Agrippinensis; the Frankish commander of the army → Arbogastes fought Bructeri and Chamavi and renewed treaties, as did → Stilicho later on [3]. From 406/7 the situation on the Rhine border became even more uncertain with the F. taking over Roman defence duties supporting usurpers like Constantinus III and Jovinus. Increasingly the Rhine F. (*Ripuarii*) stood out from the Salii. → Aetius [5] conquered the Lower Rhine F. who had settled around Colonia Agrippinensis and Vetera at the latest from 423, and entered into new *foedera*; in 445 he once again defeated the Salii who were spreading out under King

Chlodio, and allowed them to settle around Tournai as members of the federation. After 455 the Rhine was overrun on a wide front by F. from the right-hand side of the river who took → Mogontiacum (Mainz) and furthermore – in alliance with the Lower Rhine F. – Colonia Agrippinensis (456) and later became independent by turning to the Burgundian king overseeing the Gallic military government. At the same time, under → Childeric I (456) the development of the Salfrankish kingdom in alliance with the last Roman powerbrokers → Aegidius and → Syagrius took form. From the time of Childeric's son → Clovis I (481/2) the history of the F. can be followed continuously [4].

1 R. MACMULLEN, Corruption and the decline of Rome, 1988 2 P. BARCELÓ, Roms auswärtige Beziehungen unter der Constantinischen Dynastie, 1981 3 B. GUTMANN, Studien zur röm. Außenpolitik in der Spätant., 1991 4 H. AMENT et al., s.v. Franci, Frankenreich, LMA 4, 689–728.

H. BECK, H. H. ANTON et al., s.v. Franci, RGA 9, 373–461; A. WIECZOREK, P. PÉRIN, W. MENGHIN, K. v. WELCK (ed.), Die Franken – Wegbereiter Europas, 1997.

K.DI.

Fravitta (Fravitus). Tervingian army commander in the service of Rome, married to a Roman woman. In support of maintaining the Roman alliance with the Goths of AD 382, he killed Eriulf in 391 at the court of Theodosius I (Zos. 4,56,1–3; Eunapius fr. 60 FHG 4,41). In about 400 as the *magister militum* on behalf of Arcadius he prevented Gaenas from crossing the Hellespont (Zos. 5,20–21; Sozom. Hist. eccl. 8,4,19–21) and was rewarded for it in 401 with the consulate (Eunapius fr. 82 FHG 4,50). Around 403/4, however, he was accused of allowing Gaenas to escape and was overthrown in the same year (Zos. 5,21,5). PLRE 1, 372–73.

→ Tervingi

G. ALBERT, Goten in Konstantinopel, 1984; P. HEATHER, Goths and Romans 332–489, 1991; H. WOLFRAM, Die Goten, [3]1990.

M.MEI. and ME.STR.

Fredegar Chronicle A chronicle-like (→ Chronicles) collection of texts in 4 bks. written in the mid 7th cent. in France, *Ab orbe condito* (until 642), to which people wrongly attributed a Fredegar as the author in the 16th cent. The question of its authorship, like that of the number of people involved in the compilation (one editor: [1]), is unresolved. The Frankish orientation remains decisive. The entire compilation had little effect (38 MSS), and the only strong influence was the history of the Trojan origin of the Franks inserted in the collection. The Latin version shows clear signs of decadence. At best one can speak of a compilation in which different historiographic texts were linked (*Liber generationis*, lists of kings or popes, extracts from → Hieronymus and → Hydatius as well as the Frankish history of Gregory [4] of Tours). Only the 4th bk. appears to possess a certain autonomy and reliability.

1 W. GOFFART, The F. Problem Reconsidered, in: Speculum 38, 1963, 206–241 2 J. M. WALLACE-HADRILL, The 4th Book of the Chronicle of F. with its Continuations, 1960. U.E.

Fredericus (Frederick).

[1] Son of the West Gothic king Theoderic I, brother and co-ruler of Theoderic II, whom he helped to the throne in AD 453 after the murder of the eldest brother Thorismud (Chron. min. 1,483; 2,27 MOMMSEN; Greg. Tur. Franc. 2,7); after successful battles against the Spanish Bagauds (probably as *magister militum*, cf. Chron. min. 2,27; in this regard [1. 690f.]) he was involved in 455 in the rise of → Avitus [1] to the position of emperor (Sid. Apoll. Carm. 7,391ff.; 435ff.). In 463 he fell in battle fighting → Aegidius. PLRE 2, 484 (F. 1).

1 A. DEMANDT, s.v. magister militum, RE Suppl. 12, 553–790.

[2] Son of the Rugii king Feletheus (Fewa), fled after the latter's defeat by → Odoacer to the Ostrogoths under Theoderic (Eugippius 44), with whom he came into conflict in AD 491; he then went over to → Tufa who had revolted against Theoderic and gone over to Odoacer. In 492/3 he also came into conflict with Tufa in the course of which he probably died; his Rugii entourage then allied itself with Theoderic again (Ennod. Paneg. 55; vita Epiphanii 118f.; Chron. min. 1,320f. MOMMSEN).

PLRE 2, 484f. (F. 2); H. WOLFRAM, Die Goten, [3]1990, 278ff. M.MEI. and ME.STR.

Freedmen

I. GREECE II. ROME

I. GREECE

Documents show two different terms for the concept of a freedman: ἀπελεύθερος (*apeleútheros*) and ἐξελεύθερος (*exeleútheros*); according to Harpocration (p.31 BK), the latter referred not to those born as slaves, but to the freeborn sons of slaves. Pollux uses Demosthenes' terms *nómoi exeleútheroi* and *nómoi apeleútheroi* in his list of terminology on the topic of slavery. Thus, it is clear that the two terms refer to groups with different legal status. It also shows that private manumissions as well as other issues and facts regarding slavery were subject to legal rules [1]. In Athens, for instance, special court proceedings (*díkē apostasíou*) existed which offered a slave-owner the possibility of reversing the manumission of a slave. Freedmen usually did not receive full citizenship, but a legal status similar to that of a → *metoikos* [2]. Manumissions are documented epigraphically as early as the 6th and 5th cents. BC (SEG XXII 509, Chios; IEry 2B21). As indicated in Aristotle's explicit recommendation of promising manumission to slaves (Aristot. Pol. 1330a 32–34), it was probably not very common in the 4th cent. BC to free healthy and strong slaves; this is also confirmed by the fact that literary or documented sources of manumission are very rare. The type of manumission depended essentially on the respective form of → slavery and varied strongly among the different epochs and regions. People who ended up in slavery because of their debts generally needed only to pay back their debts in order to regain their freedom; Solon's ban on slavery due to debt, however, shows that it was regarded as humiliating [6].The manumission of → Helots and other groups enslaved by the community (bondsmen) required a formal act from the side of the community (Lex Gortyn. 5,25; 11,24; Ephoros ap. Str. 8,5,4). In exceptional political or military circumstances, slaves owned by individual citizens could be freed in large numbers. Prior to 360 BC, for instance, Euphron, the tyrant of Sicyon, not only freed the slaves of his political opponents but also granted them citizenship (Xen. Hell. 7,3,8; [3]); Philipp of Macedonia was cautious enough not to allow manumissions that would aid a *coup d'état* (Ps.-Demosth. 17,15). In the years 490 and 406 BC, the Athenians granted freedom to many slaves in return for military service (Marathon: Paus. 1,32,3; 7,15,7; Arginusae: Aristoph. Ran. 693) and compensated their owners [16]. The fate of a few of the well-educated slaves like Pasion and Phormion was exceptional; → Pasion, a skilful τραπεζίτης (*trapezítēs*; banker), was freed by his owners Antisthenes and Archestratus, while Phormion was not only freed by his owner Pasion, but even received his bank and married his widow according to instructions in the will (Dem. Or. 36,7–9; 36,43–49). The extraordinary economical influence of these freedmen is disproportionate to their small number; they even succeeded in gaining Athenian citizenship, thus overcoming the barrier between Athenian citizens and freedmen. In the time before the Roman rulership of Greece, it was equally extraordinary for female and male slaves to be treated as members of the family with equal rights, or to get epitaphs. It was more common, yet still a privilege, for slaves to work independently as well-trained craftsmen, with the permission of their owners (χωρὶς οἰκοῦντες; *chōrìs oikoûntes*), which afforded them the chance to buy their freedom with the profits of their work. Slave-owners had a number of options regarding the public announcement of their acts of manumission. For instance, the names of the few freedmen could be read out at the Great Dionysia in Athens (Aeschin. In Ctes. 41) or the names could be written on a certain wall of the sanctuary in Delphi [5; 8]. In all these cases, manumission took place in the context of religion. The Thessalian and Delphic manumissions were formally connected to the cult, since the former slaves were now owned by a god. The many mining slaves in the region of Laureion in Attica, however, had hardly any prospect of manumission; at best they could take the risk of freeing themselves by fleeing, as the 20,000 slaves did who unsuccessfully attempted to flee from Attica between the years 413 and 404 (Thuc. 7,27,5; Hell. Oxy. 12,4).

1 K.-D. Albrecht, Rechtsprobleme in der Freilassung der Böotier, Phoker, Dorier, Ost- und Westlokrer, 1978 2 A. Calderini, La manomissione e la condizione dei liberti in Grecia, 1908 3 P. Cartledge, The Greeks, [2]1997, 132 4 L. Delekat, Katoche, Hierodulie und Adoptionsfreilassung, 1964 5 R. Duncan-Jones, Problems of the Delphic manumission-payments 200–201 B.C., in: ZPE 57, 1984, 203–209 6 M.I. Finley, Debt-Bondage and the Problem of Slavery, in: Finley, Economy, 150–166 7 Y. Garlan, Les esclaves en Grèce ancienne, 1984 8 Hopkins, Conquerors, 133–171 9 D. Lewis, Attic manumissions, in: Hesperia 28, 1959, 208–238 10 Id., Dedications of phialai at Athens, in: Hesperia 37, 1968, 368–380 11 E. Perotti, Esclaves χωρὶς οἰκοῦντες, in: Actes du Colloque 1972 sur l'esclavage, 1974, 47–56 12 H. Raffeiner, Sklaven und Freigelassene: Eine soziologische Studie auf der Grundlage des griech. Grabepigramms, 1977 13 L. C. Reilly, Slaves in Ancient Greece: Slaves from Greek manumission inscriptions, 1978 14 S. Todd, The Shape of Athenian Law, 1993, 190–192 15 J. Trevett, Apollodorus the Son of Pasion, 1992 16 K.-W. Welwei, Unfreie im ant. Kriegsdienst, 2 vols., 1974–1977 17 W. L. Westermann, The Slave Systems of Greek and Roman Antiquity, 1955.

P.C.

II. Rome

A. Republic B. Imperial period C. Late antiquity D. Social Status

A. Republic

Freedmen and -women (*liberti/-ae*; regarding the term *libertini/-ae* cf. Suet. Claud. 24,1) already appear in the early Republic, as in the Law of Twelve Tables (7,12; regarding the Monarchic period cf. also Dion. Hal. Ant. Rom. 4,23). They enjoyed the care of the person who set them free (→ *patronus*), remained in his *familia* (Ulp. Dig. 50,16,195,1), and were allowed to enter his *clientela* with their children. In return, they owed their patron services (*operae*) and payments in kind (*dona*), whose type, size, and duration was negotiated for each case. As an alternative to the *operae* and *dona*, the amount for manumission could be demanded from the *peculium*, a special sum of money that had accumulated during bondage and usually remained in the possession of the freedman. Aside from this, the freedman had to pay a tax of 5% of his own market value (*vicesima libertatis*: Liv. 7,16,7, 357 BC), which had accumulated as an emergency fund to *c.* 4,000 Roman pounds of gold by 209 BC (Liv. 27,10,11). The estate left by a childless freedman went back to the patron or to the family heirs, however, the natural children of the freedman were entitled to all of it, while adopted children as well as daughters in another → *manus* were entitled to half of the estate (Gai. Inst. 3,39ff.).

In the Republic, manumission (*manumissio*) could take place publicly in cases of special achievements for the *res publica* (Cic. Balb. 24), but usually, it was done privately. It transferred Roman citizenship and led to the integration of the freedman into Roman society. In this respect, the Roman model differed markedly from the Greek-Hellenistic world (cf. Syll.3 543,33ff.) and from modern slave-holding societies, a fact that makes any parallelism methodologically doubtful. Roman law provided three options for formal private manumissions: firstly, the testamentary (*testamento*) option, which reduced the obligation of the freedman as *libertus orcinus* towards his patron to a merely formal level, secondly, the inclusion of the freedman's name in the citizens' list during the → *census*, and thirdly, a formal legal act in front of the *praetor* (*vindicta*). The freedman received the *nomen* → *gentile* (since Augustus, also the *praenomen*) of his patron. Aside from the formal *manumissio*, a permanent ostentative privileging of individual slaves by their masters resulted in a kind of unofficial manumission (*per mensam*, *per litteras*) and established a customary law that could be claimed in front of the *praetor*. This status was later legalized through the *lex Iunia* (*Norbana* of the year AD 19?), which granted Latin status to unofficial freedmen, but which allowed the persons who had set them free to transfer the rights of patronage also to unrelated heirs and denied the freedmen the right to make a will (Gai. Inst. 3,55–56).

Roman citizenship gained through manumission still entailed certain limitations: the inscription into only one of the four urban *tribus* resulted in an actual reduction of the right to vote, the access to offices (see below) and to legions was denied, not, however, access to the fleet. According to private law, the freedman remained under the patronage of the person who had set him free, and after his death under that of his family heirs; this established the freedman's obligation – and the patron's right – to *reverentia* (reverence) and, to a certain extent, to *obsequium* (obedience), and to use corporal punishment. Complaints of the freedman against the patron and his agnatic relatives were not permitted, furthermore, there existed a right to withhold testimony at the court. The patron's rights were increasingly limited during the Imperial period. Only the children of the freedman were regarded as freeborn (*ingenui*) and were no longer subject to the restrictions that resulted from manumission, except for limited access to higher offices (which was at times circumvented).

B. Imperial period

In the final phase of the Republic, the common practice of manumission became problematic due to a number of factors: the number of slaves had risen dramatically as a result of frequent wars, simultaneously, more and more slaves were freed who at best had been Romanized only superficially, patrons pursued criminal purposes through the purchase of freedom, and mass manumissions occurred through testaments (Dion. Hal. Ant. Rom. 4,24,4ff.). A response to this situation was the Augustan tightening of legal regulations of manumission. The *lex Fufia Caninia* of 2 BC decreed maximum limits in testamentary manumissions relative to the total number of slaves in the possession of a testator, lowering the permitted rate for a growing *familia* from 50% to 20%, with an absolute maximum of 100 persons that could be named (Gai. Inst. 1,42–43; revoked by Iustinianus: Cod. lust. 7,3).

The *lex Aelia Sentia* of AD 4 became the actual legal basis for manumissions during the Imperial period. It distinguished between three different categories of freedmen which were defined according to the status of their personal rights (Gai. Inst. 1,12; levelled out only under Justinian: Inst. Iust. 1,5,3): those with Roman citizenship (whose attainment, bound by certain requirements and a formal process, was no longer the rule: Gai. Inst. 1,18–20), those under Latin law (in informal manumissions *inter amicos*), and – concerning socially downgraded persons or slaves who had committed a criminal offence – those under peregrine law (in the precarious status of *dediticii*, with serious restrictions, for instance, regarding freedom of movement, and the threat of renewed enslavement upon violation of these restrictions: Gai. Inst. 1,13–15; 26f.). The minimum age was set at 30 years for the person to be freed, and 20 years for the patron; exceptions had to be approved by a commission (Gai. Inst. 1,36–38). The transition from Latin to Roman legal status was possible even without the participation of the patron, in cases when, for example, the freedman had children with a non-peregrine wife or if he took on socially desired tasks, whose spectrum was gradually broadened (Ulp. Reg. 3,1 and Gai. Inst. 1,32–34; on *manumissio in ecclesia*, the authorisation of clerics to grant formal manumissions, cf. Cod. Theod. 4,7,1, of 321). Marriage relationships between the members of the senatorial class and freedwomen were prohibited through the *lex Papia Poppaea* of AD 9, or they required an Imperial dispensation for the individual case. Furthermore, the *lex Visellia* of AD 24 (Cod. lust. 9,21) denied freedmen the access to Roman and municipal offices as well as access to the leading classes in Rome and in the cities of Roman and Latin law (*ordo senatorius, ordo decurionum*).

C. Late antiquity

In late antiquity, freedmen were completely excluded, their sons mostly excluded from holding court offices (Cod. Theod. 4,10,3, AD 426.), also from holding the office of a Christian priest (Council of Elvira, Canon 80, *c.* AD 306). Access to municipal → *curiae* was only granted to those freedmen who (by means of receiving the *anulus aureus* or *natalium restitutio*) were legally of a status similar to freeborn persons (Cod. lust. 10,33,1, under Diocletianus). The desire for social admiration so characteristic of Roman society also applied to freedmen, which is indicated by monuments and tomb reliefs for freedmen, and was taken into account as early as the 1st cent. AD with the establishment of colleges of priests for the cult of divinized Roman emperors (*seviri Augustales, Flaviales*). After holding office for one year, they conveyed lifelong membership of the municipal *ordo Augustalium*. Access to the equestrian class (→ *equites Romani*) was generally open to freedmen, but was hardly accepted socially and was always regarded as suspicious due to the presumptuous exaggeration of equestrian attributes (equestrian ring) common for freedmen (Plin. HN 33,33; Suet. Claud. 25,1). The striving for acceptance into the *ordo equester*, which required a minimum fortune of 400,000 sestertia, illustrates the economical rise of no small number of freedmen who at times owned considerable fortunes, often surpassing those of freeborn Romans (Plin. HN 33,134f.); numerous inscriptions of documented endowments are further evidence of this [7. no. 343ff.]. However, many freedmen were badly situated economically; this is indicated by the legal regulations concerning the support of needy freedmen by their patrons (Mod. Dig. 38,2,33; cf. ILS 2927).

D. Social Status

In general, Roman freedmen do not at all appear as a homogeneous group. The most fundamental differences result primarily from the relationship to the persons who set them free: according to Roman law, these could be single or several individuals, corporations of public law (cities, provinces, *collegia*), or the *princeps*. The social prestige of a freedman depended on his patron, and therefore, Imperial freedmen (*Augusti liberti*) had a higher rank than those set free by senators or by the city of Rome. Their importance grew with the increase of authority of the *princeps* in the public realm. Within hierarchically structured staffs, imperial freedmen had responsible functions, even leading entire departments within the closer circle around the emperor, as documented for → Pallas or → Narcissus as close confidants of Claudius. From the Flavian period, freedmen as co-ordinators of the central administration were gradually replaced by *equites*. However, together with imperial slaves, they still constituted the staff of the individual offices, which amounted to a total of several hundred people. Other imperial freedmen were entrusted with important functions in Italy and in the provinces, in particular with the administration of imperial assets. Structurally, this can be compared to a freedman's taking over the function of *procurator* or agent of his private patron.

In much greater numbers (and much less documented), we find freedmen who belonged to the lower or at best middle social classes, usually active in the service of their patrons, but often also independently, working as craftsmen, traders and service providers (such as doctors). Freedwomen are often the wives of their patrons, especially of veterans.

Freedmen were often condescendingly smiled at as upstarts (cf. esp. Petron. Sat. 28–78) but still absolutely accepted. For instance, in AD 56 a proposal for re-enslavement of ungrateful freedmen was rejected by the Senate and their significance for Roman society was emphasized (Tac. Ann. 13,27; cf. still Diocletianus and Maximianus: Cod. lust. 7,1,2, of the year 293). The legal requirements for this were not established until the rule of Constantinus I (Cod. Theod. 4,10,1, of AD 313?).

1 G. BOULVERT, Esclaves et affranchis impériaux sous le Haut-Empire romain, 1970 2 B. BOYCE, The language of the freedmen in Petronius' Cena Trimalchionis, 1991 3 K. BRADLEY, Slavery and society at Rome, 1994 4 A. DEMANDT, Die Spätant., 1989, 288ff. 5 A.M. DUFF, Freedmen in the early Roman Empire, [2]1958 6 R. DUTHOY, La fonction sociale de l'augustalité, in: Epigraphica 36, 1974, 134–154 7 W. ECK, J. HEINRICHS, Sklaven und F. in der Ges. der röm. Kaiserzeit, 1993 8 HIRSCHFELD 9 KASER, RPR 1, 293ff. 10 C. MASI DORIA, Bona libertorum, 1996 11 MOMMSEN, Staatsrecht 3, 420ff. 12 H. PAVIS D'ESURAC, Les effects juridiques de l'affranchissement sous le Haut-Empire, in: Ktema 6, 1981, 181–192 13 S. TREGGIARI, Roman Freedmen during the late Republic, 1969 14 P. VEYNE, Vie de Trimalcion, in: Annales ESC, 16, 1961, 213–247 15 VITTINGHOFF, 187ff. 16 W. WALDSTEIN, Operae libertorum, 1986 17 R.P.C. WEAVER, Familia Caesaris, 1972 18 P. ZANKER, Grabreliefs röm. F., in: JDAI 90, 1975, 267–315.

JO.H.

Fregellae Originally, the city of the Opici near the mouth of the river Trerus into the Liris, modern Rocca d'Arce. Until 354 BC, the city of the Volsci, destroyed by the Samnites (Liv. 8,23,6). In 328 BC, *colonia Latina* (Liv. 8,22,2; cf. 9,28,3). F. was loyal to Rome against Pyrrhus and Hannibal; the city took part in the outbreak of the 2nd war against the Samnites and was recaptured by the Samnites in 320 (Liv. 9,12,5–8), and recolonized by the Romans in 313 (Diod. Sic. 19,101,3). In 177, F.'s population increased by 4,000 families (Samnites and Paeligni: Liv. 41,8,8). The orator L. → Papirius was active there. Following a rebellion in 125, the city was ultimately destroyed by the *praetor* L. Opimius and was consequently subject to the *devotio*; F. was now a simple village, with a market and a few cults (Str. 5,3,6). A temple of Neptune is documented for 93 BC (Obseq. 52), also the cultivation of the tasty grape *nigra Fregellana* (Columella 3,2,27). In 124 BC, the Roman colony → Fabrateria [2] Nova was established in its vicinity.

Archaeological finds: fortress from the Volscian period (a wall in *opus polygonale*, finds from the Iron Age). The *colonia Latina* was located on the plateau of Opi near Ceprano (Frosinone), also on the left bank of the river Liris, crossed by the *via Latina*, which can be identified as → *cardo maximus* on the city layout. Excavations since 1978: the city centre from the 4th to the 2nd cents. with a 150 m long main forum, circular *comitium*, *curia*, and traces of processing of iron. At the north-western edge of the city, sanctuaries of Aesculapius and Salus [1]. From the Imperial period, a single *villa* is attested within the city area. The village Fregellanum from the Imperial period, a station on the *via Latina*, *c.* 14 miles from Frusino and three miles from Fabrateria (It. Ant. 303; 305), has been localized in Ceprano.

1 F. COARELLI, F., vol. 2, 1986.
G. COLASANTI, F., 1906; F. COARELLI, F. La storia e gli scavi, 1981; M.H. CRAWFORD, L. KEPPIE, J. PATTERSON, Excavations at Fregellae 1978–84, in: PBSR 54, 1986, 40–68; BTCGI 7, 1989, 505–513; P.G. MONTI, Un nuovo contributo alla ricostruzione della centuriazione romana nel Lazio meridionale, in: Terra dei Volsci. Contributi 1992,2, 14–21 (La provincia di Frosinone 10,2, suppl.).

G.U.

Freedom

I. POLITICAL II. PHILOSOPHICAL

I. POLITICAL

A. GREECE B. ROME

A. GREECE

The difference between 'free' and 'not free' in the sense of liberation from taxes or services is already to be found in the ancient Orient. A concept of political freedom on the basis of a citizenry with political rights is however opposed by an autocratic and divinely legitimized kingship as well as a graded status system that classifies society into groups of varying dependancy between freedom and slavery (Pollux).

Freedom (Greek *eleuthería*, ἐλευθερία, Roman *libertas*) in the political sense also appears late in Greece. The adjectives *eleútheros* and *liber* probably go back to Indo-European **leudh-* (presumably: 'to grow') and there is early evidence of them (in the Mycenaean period [Linear B], in Homer, e.g. Il. 6,455. 463, and in the Roman XII-Table Law). However freedom does not achieve political significance until the 6th and early 5th cents. BC when the Greeks confronted the expanding eastern empires of the Lydians and Persians – a confrontation which made them aware of the value of freedom. The advent at about the same time of commercial slavery probably reinforced still further the awareness of the distinction between freedom and lack of liberty.

A concept of political freedom was favoured as a result of the special situation after the collapse of the Mycenaean palace civilization. In the → Dark Ages that followed (12th–9th cents.) no central rule developed in sparsely settled Greece, in spite of social differentiation. Power remained widely stratified, early forms of equality continued to exist and were also maintained in the development of the → polis since the 8th cent., which had initially been supported by aristocrats. Although there is evidence of a political concept of servitude or slavery as a consequence of tyranny as early as Solon, the first signs of freedom as a political concept and the word *eleuthería* are not to be found prior to the Persian Wars of 480/479 BC. Referring to freedom from external rule, freedom also appears in the first Delian League, when Athens made the free allies into subjects and only allowed them self-administration (→ *autonomía*).

In addition, in Athens especially, there arose with the development of democracy a concept of freedom directed inwards that initially indicated freedom from tyranny, was then linked with the probably still aristocratic idea of equality (*isonomía*, ἰσονομία) and ultimately was extended to all citizens. In this way *isonomía* became synonymous with → *dēmokratía* (Hdt. 3,80,6). In confronting oligarchical concepts of order, the democrats took up for themselves the *eleuthería* as freedom of the citizens, with the consequence that the → *dḗmos* could only be free if it ruled itself (Ps.-Xen. Ath. pol. 1,6,9). Now along with 'equality of speech' (*isēgoría*, ἰσηγορία) there also came 'freedom of speech' (*parrhēsía*, παρρησία). The oligarchical concept of freedom accepted as 'free citizens' only wealthy people who could dedicate themselves to an education worthy of a free person (*eleuthérios paideía*, ἐλευθέριος παιδεία), an occupation (*eleuthérioi téchnai*, ἐλευθέριοι τέχναι) and political affairs. With the distinction between *eleuthérios* and *eleútheros,* the principle of proportional equality became alongside that of numerical equality a condition of freedom, a separation that was to play a role in the state philosophical discussion of the 4th cent. (see for instance Aristot. Eth. Nic. 4,1).

The outwardly directed concept of freedom quickly declined into political rhetoric: in the Peloponnesian War (431–404) Sparta propagated the idea of the freedom of the Greeks from Athenian tyranny, but did in turn behave like a tyrant after the war (→ Harmostai). In the 4th cent. freedom was used in the same way by Athens, Sparta and Thebes to find allies in the war against the respective ruling hegemonic power. The call of → Isocrates for a 'crusade' against Persia to liberate the Greeks, which was meant to reduce the social tensions in Greece and end the constant wars, was only taken up by → Alexander [4] after he had eliminated, in league with his father Philippus, the freedom of Greece at → Chaeronea in 338 BC. In the Hellenistic period, the declaration of the freedom of the Greeks became the catchphrase of monarchs trying to obtain political or material support. However, the Greek cities profited from the competition between the rulers who had to present themselves as protectors of Greek culture and freedom and thus allowed the cities a high level of internal autonomy (→ Euergetism). The declaration of the freedom of the Greeks of 196 BC by the Roman L. → Quinctius Flamininus after the victory over the Macedonians is also in line with this tradition.

B. Rome

The development of the political concept of freedom in Rome is less clear. It may have developed in connection with the expulsion of the Etruscan kings, who were regarded as foreign at the end of the 6th cent. BC or in the → struggle of the orders as a consequence of the dispute over the abolition of debtor slavery.

At the end of the Republic we encounter an aristocratic concept of political freedom developed by the political elite that stresses the equality of the governing class and is aimed against the rule of the king (*affectatio regni*) and power held by persons or groups (→ *factiones*). The freedom of the Roman people (*libertas populi*) is on the other hand not aimed at political participation by all citizens but at equality before the law and protection from the autocracy of magistrates. It is embodied in the right of the plebeian tribunes to → *provocatio* and their duty to provide assistance (*auxilium*; Liv. 3,54,6). This limited political meaning of freedom makes it easy for the Romans, in comparison with the Greeks, to grant → citizenship to freed slaves straight away. In the late Republic *libertas* became a catchphrase when the populares pretended to protect freedom from the optimates and cliques (*factiones paucorum*).

Amongst the emperors *libertas* remained a popular slogan that was also propagated on coins, although the aristocratization of the Principate gradually reduced freedom to personal safety and legal protection. With the reference of the emperors to divine protection from the 3rd cent. AD (→ Aurelianus [3]) and increasingly in the Christian emperorship of Byzantine colouring that was elevated to the level of the sacred, the political content of freedom was again dissolved.

→ Freedmen; → Manumission; → Slavery

J. Bleicken, Staatliche Ordnung und Freiheit in der röm. Republik, 1972; M.J. Finley, Economy and Society in Ancient Greece, 1982, ch. 7–9; R. Klein (ed.), Prinzipat und Freiheit, 1969; M. Pohlenz, Griech. Freiheit, 1955; K. Raaflaub, Freiheit in Athen und Rom, in: HZ 238, 1984, 529–567; Id., Die Entdeckung der Freiheit, 1985; D.C.A. Shotter, Principatus ac Libertas, in: AncSoc 9, 1978, 235–253; C. Wirszubski, Libertas als polit. Idee im Rom der späten Republik und des frühen Principats, 1967.

K.RA.

II. Philosophical

Freedom (*eleuthería*) as a political term is contrasted with the dependency on others: the contrast is between determination by others (heteronomy) and self-determination (autonomy). Philosophy adopts this concept of freedom. In → ethics the external (legal or physical) freedom from tyranny and slavery are replaced by internal, psychological freedom: to be free I must not be a slave to my passions or be subject to the tyranny of my desire for outward, material goods. This is freedom from certain influential factors in the soul that is regarded as a prerequisite for a good and happy life. Again heteronomy, this time the determination by desires (which are regarded as separate from the person), is contrasted with the control the person acting has over himself (e.g. the Socratic Antisthenes [1] and → cynicism). This concept of freedom in politics and ethics never involves the understanding of freedom in the way that people can decide between alternative options for action or perhaps to act in another manner, and it never has causal indetermination as its prerequisite. The Stoic concept of freedom has its origin in the metaphorical ethical use of 'free'. It is the concept of psychological freedom in the extreme, insofar as it demands the complete independence of the person from all emotions and from all false desires. Only the wise possess this freedom (Diog. Laert. 7,32–33). The political metaphor is also used in connection with the theory of fate: Epicurus, for example, calls fate a despot that enslaves us, and asserts that what happens on our account (παρ' ἡμᾶς) is subject to no despot (Diog. Laert. 10,133–134). The concept of that which lies 'with us' (ἐφ' ἡμῖν, *in nobis*) refers in the Hellenistic period to that which human beings (as rational creatures) cause themselves and for which they are themselves responsible (Cic. Fat. 41–43; Gell. NA 7,2). It presupposes freedom from compulsion and external influences.

In Roman philosophy, Lucretius, following Epicurus, bases freedom to act on a desire that is free from internal compulsion (2,251–293). Cicero, partly following Carneades, defends the freedom of humans from the necessity of fate (Fat. 23–28; 39–46), while Seneca, in line with contemporary Stoic doctrine, equates freedom (*libertas*) with submission to fate (De vita beata 15,6–7).

In the 1st–3rd cents. AD, building on elements of Aristotelian ethics and logic, Stoic psychology and perhaps Christian and Middle Platonic influences, a concept is developed from this of selective freedom that requires that the person not be causally predetermined in his actions (Alex. Aphr. De fato 6; 15; 29; Alex. Aphr. Mantissa 174,17–24, cf. [3]).

1 D. Nestle, Eleutheria, 1967 2 S. Bobzien, Determinism and Freedom in Stoic Philosophy, 1998 3 Id., The Inadvertent Conception and Late Birth of the Free-Will Problem, in: Phronesis 43, 1998. S.BO.

Fregenae City on the Tyrrhenian coast in South Etruria (*regio VII*) at the mouth of the Aro, which drains the *lacus Sabatinus*. Half-way (9 miles from → Ostia and → Alsium) between the *via Portuensis* and the *via Aurelia* (It. Ant. 300), modern Maccarese. In 245 BC, a *colonia* of Roman citizens (Liv. per. 19; Vell. Pat. 1,14,8). Inscriptions: CIL XI p. 549.

A. Branchini, F. e dintorni, 1991; Nissen 2, 350; Ruggiero 3, 216. G.U.

Frentani Samnite tribe on the Adriatic coast (Str. 5,4,2). The name is derived from the dissimilation of the place name [1] **Frentrum,* which in turn was inferred through numismatical (*Frentrei*) and inscriptional (*Frentra[ni]*) methods [2]. The F. settled on the slopes of the *regio VII* that fall away towards the Adriatic, between the Maiella mountains and the coastal region surrounded by Ortona, the valleys of the Sagrus (Sangro), the Trinius (Trigno), the Tifernus, and the Frento (Fortore). In the west, the tribal area bordered on that of the Paeligni, Caraceni, and Pentri, in the north, on that of the Marrucini, in the south on the Dauni. Centres of settlement were (from north to south) Ortona, Anxanum, and Iuvanum north of the Sagrus, Pallanum and Histonium up to the Trinius, Buca and Uscosium on the Tifernus. The southern branches of the area between Tifernus and Frento, the so-called *Larinates F.* with the towns of Larinum and Cliternia, were added to the *regio II* by Rome. The F. were subjugated by the Romans in 319 BC (Liv. 9,16,1). Following the Social War, they received citizenship (*tribus Arnensis*) [3. 41, 49]. Inscription: CIL IX p. 263–281.

1 G. Devoto, Gli antichi Italici, 1951, 137ff. 2 P. Fraccaro, Opuscula 3,1, 1957, 275 3 W. Kubitschek, Imperium Romanum tributim discriptum, 1889, 41, 49.

B. d'Agostino (ed.), Sannio, Pentri e F. dal VI al I sec. a.C., 1980; I. Raimondi, F., 1906; E.T. Salmon, Samnium and the Samnites, 1967. G.U.

Frequentative see → Word formation

Fresco From Italian *fresco, affresco intonaco*, 'on the fresh plaster'. Wall and ceiling paintings, in which the → pigments are applied to a damp base either in pure form or with the aid of a special binder such as diluted glue, casein, or marble powder. The composition of the covering varies; usually, it is a whitewash mortar mixed with different additives which are applied one after the other in several layers. Basically, the fresco technique lies in the fact that during the drying process of the plaster certain chemical reactions result in a kind of calcification of the surface and thus a highly durable bond between the painting and its base (see ill.).

Frescoes have long been common in many old cultures, also outside of Europe. Simple paintings of coloured outlines on loam or on a clay-like earthy plaster can be regarded as precursors of frescoes in earlier epochs. In antiquity, frescoes can be found from the early 2nd millennium in the Ancient Orient and in the Cretan-Mycenaean region, less often, however, in Egypt. Frescoes were also common in Graeco-Roman culture and Byzantine art. They were used in private and sacred architecture, in court and sepulchral. The ancient process, which today can be reconstructed to a great extent through chemical analyses, was already described in detail by Vitruvius (7,3ff.). Well researched are in particular the Roman-Campanian → wall paintings. They differ technically from the large fresco cycles that re-emerged from early Renaissance, and also from those of later times, in the handling and in the application of layers of mortar of varying thickness and in their grain. The special sheen of many Pompeian walls is due to a process of smoothing the uppermost layer of plaster with marble powder prior to painting it, and to polishing afterwards. On ancient frescoes, one can identify segments showing a 'day's work', also various techniques using sketches of red chalk or dotted lines of soot. → Pompeii

Bibliography: H. Béarat et al., Roman Wall Painting; Materials, Techniques, 1997; R. Biering, Die Odysseefresken vom Esquilin, 1994; K. Herold, Konservierung von Arch. Bodenfunden, Wandmalerei und Mosaik, 1994; S.A. Immerwahr, Aegean Painting in the Bronze Age, 1990; W. Klinkert, Bemerkungen zur Technik der pomp. Wanddekoration, in: MDAI(R) 64, 1957, 111–148; R. Ling, Roman Painting, 1991, 198–211.

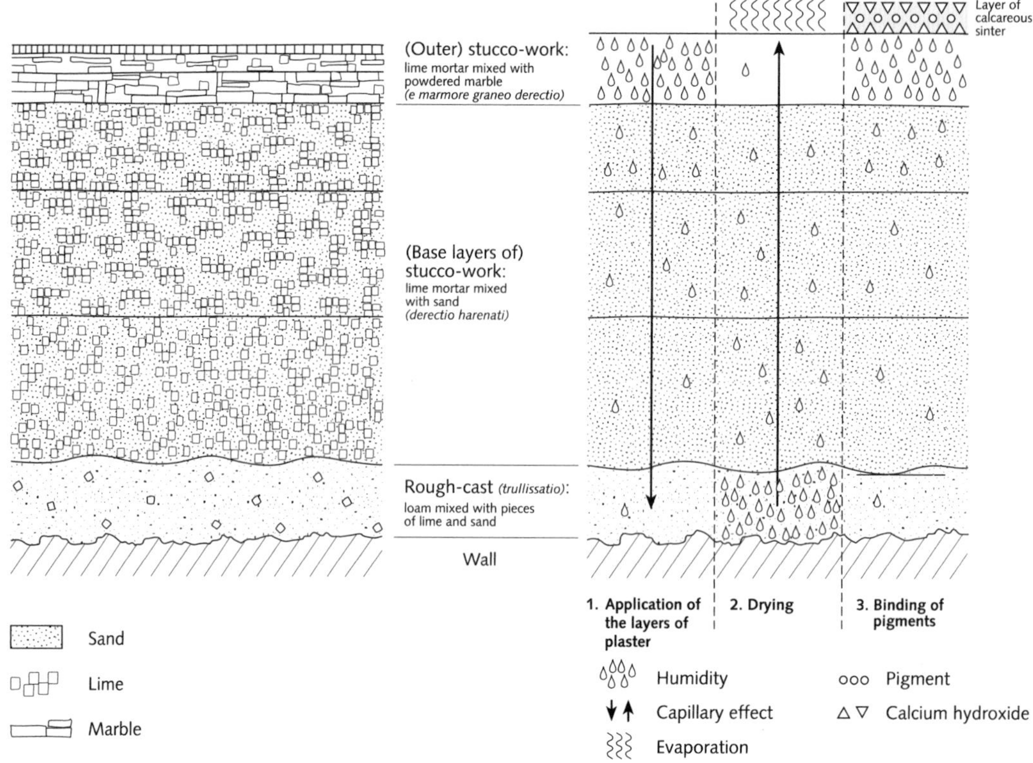

Layers of plaster in a Pompeian fresco, schematic representation.
The example, *regio* VIII, *insula* 2 no. 2 (Ist Pompeian style), possesses the qualities of the ideal stucco *(tectorium)* as described by Vitruvius (7.3).
This is made up of seven layers, the outer plaster work consisting of marble-stucco layers of decreasing thickness. Simpler stucco-work consists of two or three layers, with sand mortar used for the outer plaster work. Layers of Pompeian fresco have a thickness of 4 mm to 9 cm.

Setting of the mortar and binding of the pigments.
Each layer is applied damper than the preceding one. Because of the capillary effect - first in an inward direction, then outward - the outer plaster layer remains damp for a long time, and thus capable of binding the colours. The calcium hydroxide that has reached the surface binds the pigments in a calc-sinter layer. Because of the slow process of drying, the caustic lime contained in the mortar is exposed to large amounts of air, so that it is changed into calcium carbonate: the mortar hardens thoroughly.

M. HAA.

ILLUSTRATIONS: W. KLINKERT, Bemerkungen zur Technik der pompejanischen Wanddekoration, in: MDAI(R) 64, 1957, esp. 111–129. N.H.

Fretum Siculum Strait of Messina between Caenus and Pelorum, 12 *stadia* (Plin. HN 3,73) or 1,500 *passus* (Plin. HN 3,86), today 3 km wide, a rift valley, with frequent earthquakes, characterized by fluctuating tidal currents that result in dreaded whirlpools (cf. the myth of → Scylla and Charybdis).

E. MANNI, Geografia fisica e politica della Sicilia antica, 1981, 50f.; P. RADICI COLACE (ed.), Mito, Scienza e Mare: Animali fantastici, mostri e pesci del Mediterraneo (Meeting, Lipari 3.–4. Ottobre 1997), 1999. GI.MA. and E.O.

Friendship

I. SOCIAL HISTORY II. PHILOSOPHY

I. SOCIAL HISTORY

A. GREECE 1. PRIVATE FRIENDSHIP 2. FRIENDSHIP IN POLITICS

A. GREECE

1. PRIVATE FRIENDSHIP

For the Greeks, friendship was one of the most important social relationships, generally egalitarian and guided by two main norms of behaviour, the duty of → reciprocity and a thinking guided by agonal competition (Thgn. 105ff.; 857ff.; 1263ff.; Eur. Or. 449ff.; 646ff.; Xen. Mem. 2,6,35). Political actions and the idea of justice were largely based on the desire of helping one's friends and harming one's enemies to the best of one's ability (Hom. Il. 9,613ff.; Thgn. 879ff.; Sol.

1,3ff. D.; Soph. Ant. 643f.; Eur. HF 585f.; Med. 807ff.; IT 605ff.; IA 345ff.; Aristoph. Av. 420f.; Sympot. PMG 980; Gorg. DIELS/KRANZ B11a,25; Thuc. 1,41,1; Lys. 9,20; 19,59; Pl. Men. 71e; Rep. 332a-b; Isoc. Or. 1,16; 19,10ff.; Xen. An. 1,3,6; 1,9,11; Kyr.; 1,4,25; Hier. 2,2; M. 4,5,10; Pol. 1,14,4; Diod. Sic. 10,17,2; Plut. Mor. 807ab).

Friendship was therefore an affective bond expressed through emotional connectedness, leniency, care, and a special emotional affection that could occasionally show homoerotic overtones (Thgn. 93ff.; 213ff.; 323ff.; 1071ff.; 1164a-d; Eur. IT 497f.; IA 408), a bond that could be placed above that to the closest relatives (esp. Eur. Or. 804ff.); on the other hand, friendship was subject to obligatory norms and interests that were based on equality and reciprocity: particularly in hard times, a friend had to prove himself (Pl. Crit. 44b–45a; Eur. Or. 727f.) as loyal and faithful (Thgn. 416; 529f.; 811ff.; 1151f.). A friend had to be supported, in particular, in discharging his duties and rights (e.g. in court as *synḗgoros*, counsel for the defence); the same also applies to revenge (Lys. 13,41f.). In the pursuit of material interests, reciprocal help was also expected (Thgn. 561f.; 979ff.) so that the powerful, the respected, and the rich were regarded as those best qualified to discharge the duties of friends (Thgn. 411f.; Eur. IA 345ff.). The rules of friendship were socially sanctioned in that adherence to them brought honour, while their violation resulted in loss of honour (Hom. Il. 18,95ff.; Eur. IT 605ff.; Pl. Ap. 28cd) and provoked the revenge of the insulted friend instead of strengthening the reciprocal bonds through gratitude (*cháris*) (Archil. fr. 79a D.). A violation against the duties of friendship, esp. the betrayal of a friend, was regarded as a serious offence (Thgn. 851f.).

Friendship could also stretch across generations, and could, as it were, be inherited from fathers to sons. This was further supported by the practice of transforming close friendships into family relations by marrying sisters or daughters to friends (Isoc. Or. 19 offers impressive examples). In general, friendships were based on and strengthened anew by the sharing of common situations and experiences (military service, social events) and – esp. if it transcended the realm of the polis – it became even more regimented, 'ritualized' (→ Hospitality). In its last consequence, the strict obligations towards friends could lead to loyalty also in cases of wrongdoing (Eur. Or. 646ff.), just as enmity on the other hand could show a tendency towards excessiveness (Eur. Ion. 1045ff.). In any case, it was difficult to remain impartial, and the choice between conflicting obligations of friendship presented a serious dilemma (Aristoph. Ran. 1411f.). The limits of friendship were set not only by such conflicts of loyalty, but also when individual interests competed with friendship (Dem. Or. 23,122), and in particular, when one's own consciousness of status was affected, when envy and rivalry came into play (Aesch. Ag. 832ff.).

2. Friendship in Politics

Friendship was particularly important for social and political life if it led to the formation of a community of several individuals. Often, groups of friends formed (*hetairiai*) who met at a ritualized banquet (symposium), strengthened their ties through various joint activities (e.g. hunting), and who often took oaths. While the strong ties of friendship presented a general problem to the loyalty to the polis (Thuc. 8,50f.), the → *hetairiai* were an even greater problem, since they were often politically active and could be used as a political instrument by individual members of the group. The permanent threat to the integrity of the polis that came from violent interior disputes (→ Stasis) was also a result of the coherence of such groups of friends. In the Attic democracy of the 4th cent. on the other hand, this was replaced by the idea of self-protection of the people in which the same kind of solidarity should be developed (Dem. Or. 24,157). Contemporary political theory also regarded reciprocal friendships between citizens of the polis as an essential element for its inner cohesion (Pl. Leg. 757a; Aristot. Eth. Nic. 1161 b 13; 1167 b 2ff.).

Much more effective in terms of political reality was the transfer of the rules for friends and foes to the relationship between the poleis which could have friends and foes just like individuals. The corresponding formulation ('to have the same friends and foes') was a fixed component of Greek international treaties.

Since the monarchical forms of rulership in Greece (tyrannis, Macedonian kingship) adopted and developed the traditional social patterns of behaviour – esp. the symposium – in their ritualized social events, friendship also gained a new significance in this context: the friends (*phíloi*) of the ruler increasingly took on important tasks of functional elites. In Hellenism, they formed the closer circle around the king, which over time led to the development of a court hierarchy according to the ranks of friendship.

B. Rome

see → Amicitia.

1 E. Baltrusch, Symmachie und Spondai, 1994 2 M.W. Blundell, Helping Friends and Harming Enemies, 1989 3 F. Dirlmeier, φίλος und φιλία im vorhell. Griechentum, 1931 4 K.J. Dover, Greek Popular Morality in the Time of Plato and Aristotle, 1974 5 J.C. Fraisse, Philia: la notion d'amitié dans la philosophie antique, 1974 6 H.-J. Gehrke, Die Griechen und die Rache, in: Saeculum 38, 1987, 121–149 7 Id., Stasis, 1985 8 F.-P. Hager (ed.), Ethik und Politik des Aristoteles, 1972 9 G. Herman, Ritualized Friendship, 1987 10 H. Hutter, The Politics of Friendship, 1978 11 D. Konstan, Friendship in the Classical World, 1997.

H.-J.G.

II. Philosophy
A. Greece B. Rome

A. Greece

Friendship (φιλία/*philía*, *amicitia*) is a central concept and a constantly treated topic in ancient → ethics. In its social and political connotations, it goes far beyond the modern concept of friendship [7. 1–23].

Pre-philosophical reflection on friendship takes place in the realm of practical adages, cf. Hesiod (Op. 707–714) and esp. in Theognis' elegies [3; 5. 28 n. 54]. A theory of friendship handed down under Pythagoras' name appears to be a construct of a later, primarily Neo-Pythagorean tradition [5. 31–51]. The Pre-Socratics (Pherecydes of Samos, fr. 7 B 3 DK and esp. Empedocles, fr. 31 A 37 DK, 31 B 17 DK) make friendship into a cosmological principle [3]. Democritus (fr. 68 B 97–101, 106–107, 186 DK) formulates important aspects of later theories of friendship, such as *homophrosýnē*, tolerance, and the friendship as a requirement for a good life, but we do not know the systematic location of these considerations. In Sophism, the meaning of *philía* is reflected in the context of the polis. The concept of the φύσει φίλος (*phýsei phílos*; Hippias, Antiphon) developed within Sophism became the foundation for an anthropological view of friendship [3. 40ff.; 12. 25ff.].

The actual philosophical reflection on friendship begins with Plato and Aristotle. → Plato's dialogue *Lýsis*, the first systematic discussion of friendship, ends in aporia: the question raised by Socrates, the *philhetaíros,* of how to become someone's friend and what a friend is, remains without a definitive answer. However, the conversation provides a few qualifications: one can only be someone's friend if one is a friend to oneself (214c6ff.); to be one's own friend requires the right order of one's soul, its appropriate orientation towards the good; in this never-ending process we need friends in whom we can recognize a similar orientation towards the *prō̂ton phílon*, i.e., the good [18]. Already in the *Lýsis*, Plato deals with *philía* as inseparably linked to → *érōs*, and thereby lays the foundation for his discussion of (psychagogical) love in the *Phaedrus* and in the *Symposion*, despite the formal aporia [13].

Aristotle, in discussing Plato's approach, was the first to outline a comprehensive theory of friendship that was empirically grounded (Eth. Nic., B. 8 and 9; Eth. Eud., B. 7; cf. Mag.-mor., 2,11–17; Rhetoric 2,4,1380b 34–81b 37; 1,11,1371a 17–31; Pol. 2,4,1262b7–23). In his Nicomachean Ethics, he offers a three-step typology of friendship according to the criteria of usefulness, of pleasure, and of the good. Perfect friendship orients itself towards the moral value of the friend, who is defined as a 'second self'; it is characterized by goodwill and the desire for the happiness of the other good person; it is based on equality and reciprocity and is realized in a common life; its prerequisite is familiarity. It is a necessary precondition for *eudaimonia* (→ Happiness), because humans cannot be completely happy when they are confined to themselves – as social beings, they are anthropologically disposed towards friendship. Aside from developing his own concept of friendship, Aristotle's discussion of prior concepts and problems of friendship provides plenty of material on the tradition of the ancient discussion of friendship. His presentation became the starting-point for all later theories of friendship [5. 77–120].

→ Epicurus institutionalized his own friendship cult among his followers. For the members of his → *Kē̂pos*, friendship is realized in philosophizing together. It is cosmopolitan and independent of status or gender: men, women, and slaves can be joined in friendship [11]. Epicurus' statements on friendship (esp. Kyriai doxai 23; 27; Gnomologium Vaticanum 13; 23; 28; 34; 39; 52; 66; 78; cf. [2]) are – depending on whether one interprets his concept in a utilitarian or altruistic sense –, at odds with his concept of *eudaimonia*, which aims at the individual's → self-sufficiency [10]. Friendship provides security and dissolves fear, which is one of the preconditions of *eudaimonia* (Epicurus fr. 541 Usener). This is the most important thing that wisdom contributes to the happiness of a fulfilled life (Kyriai doxai 27) and is a good in itself (Gnomologium Vaticanum 23).

Although the Old Stoa (SVF 3, 716–726, supplemented by [5. 126, n. 374]; additional literature [5. 126, n. 375]) developed a typology of various kinds of friendship [12. 84f.], it only accepts friendship among the wise according to a rigourously logical derivation from its theory of virtues. Its criterion is agreement (*homodogmatía*). This type of friendship is free from emotions and tends to be impersonal or supra-personal, since it is understood to exist even among wise persons who do not know each other. Friendship is not an essential requirement for Stoic *eudaimonia*. Regarding the position of friendship in the design of the state by Zeno, cf. [14; 9]. Panaetius apparently aimed at moderating the rigorist Old Stoic concept of friendship in favour of considering emotional elements [15]. Virtue needs the support of friendship in order to realize *eudaimonia*.

B. Rome

In Roman-Latin thinking about friendship, Greek traditions are eclectically combined and centered on behavioural ethics. [12. 89–213]. → Cicero's considerations, above all, are essentially determined by the political and public significance of friendship ties within Roman society (→ *amicitia*). In the *Laelius* (other places in [5. 139]), Cicero discusses the ideal and the reality of friendship while leaning heavily on Stoic and Peripatetic traditions. His definition of friendship (§ 20) takes as a basic requirement the connection of intellectual and moral agreement (*consensio*) together with mutual affection (*cum benevolentia et caritate*). Necessary conditions for the realization of friendship are mutual favours, the recognition of affection, and the permanence of the relationship (§ 29). The boundary of friendship, however, is clearly defined by the primacy of *virtus* [15; 5. 138–182].

For Seneca (Epist. 3; 6; 9), friendship is a motivational force for self-perfection, a (self-)educational project based on reciprocity [9; 5. 187, n. 635]. Virtue, knowledge, and each single good becomes a gratifying possession only when shared with a friend (Epist. 6,4) – without necessarily contradicting the ideal of self-sufficiency of the Stoic wise (Epist. 9). Seneca devoted a special treatise to the preservation of friendship in case of conflict (*Quomodo amicitia continenda sit*; cf. [5. 188–192]).

The extensive writings on friendship from the Imperial period (Lucian, Plutarch, Maximus of Tyre, Libanius) have not yet received much attention within research [5. 184]. Especially → Plutarch presents, beside the rich material in the parallel biographies, in special writings (*De adulatore*; *De amicorum multitudine*; *De fraterno amore*) a systematic treatment of the traditions of friendship in ancient thought. In the Christian reflections on friendship (esp. Ambrosius, John Chrysostom, Jerome, Paulinus of Nola, Augustine), the worldly ideas of friendship become secondary to the idea of a friendship with God which comprises all believers [12. 215–338; 7. 149–173; 17].

1 Accademia di Studi italo-tedeschi Merano/L. Cotteri (ed.), Il concetto di amicizia nella storia della cultura europea, 1995 2 J. Bollack, Les Maximes de l'amitié, in: Id., La pensée du plaisir. Epicure: textes moraux, commentaires, 1975, 567–582 3 F. Dirlmeier, ΦΙΛΟΣ und ΦΙΛΙΑ im vorhell. Griechentum, 1931 4 J.-C. Fraisse, La notion d'amitié dans la philos. antique, 1974
5 A. Fürst, Streit unter Freunden. Ideal und Realität in der Freundschaftslehre der Ant., 1996 (with extensive bibliography) 6 O. Hiltbrunner (ed.), s.v. amicitia, Bibliogr. zur lat. Wortforsch., vol. 2, 1984, 171–190, 183–190
7 D. Konstan, Friendship in the classical world, 1997
8 U. Knoche, Der Gedanke der Freundschaft in Senecas Briefen an Lucilius, in: G. Maurach (ed.), Seneca als Philosoph, 1975, 149–166 9 G. Lesses, Austere Friends: The Stoics and Friendship, in: Apeiron 26.1, 1993, 57–75
10 Ph. Mitsis, Epicurus' Ethical theory. The pleasures of invulnerability, 1988 11 R. Müller, Die epikureische Gesellschaftstheorie, in: Schriften zur Gesch. und Kultur der Ant., ed. Akad. der Wiss. der DDR, 1972, 112–129
12 L. Pizzolato, L'idea di amicizia nel mondo classico e cristiano, 1993 13 A.W. Price, Love and friendship in Plato and Aristotle, 1989 14 M. Schofield, The Stoic Idea of the City, 1991 15 F.-A. Steinmetz, Die Freundschaftslehre des Panaitios, 1967 16 W. Suerbaum, Cicero (und Epikur) über die Freundschaft und ihre Probleme, in: [1.], 136–167 17 C. White, Christian Friendship in the fourth century, 1992 18 U. Wolf, Die Freundschaftskonzeption in Platons Lysis, in: E. Angehrn et al. (ed.), Dialektischer Negativismus. M. Theunissen zum 60. Geb., 1992. B.v.R.

Frieze Modern technical term, commonly used since the 17th cent. in the history of art and architecture (from French *frise*), which, as an architectonical term, designates that part of the stone entablature that rests

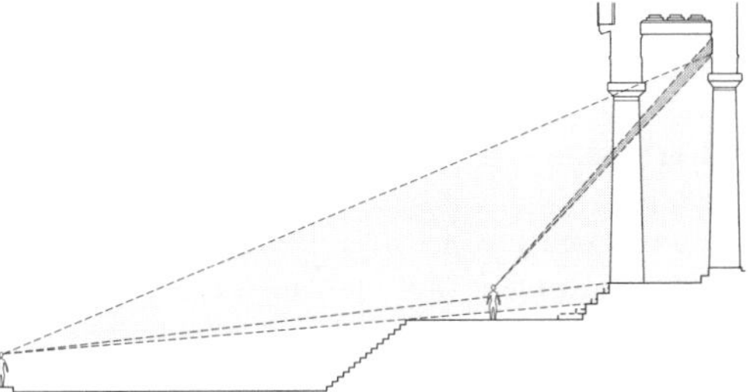

Possible visual angles for looking at the cella frieze of the Parthenon on the Athenian Acropolis.

on the architrave (→ Epistylion) in Greek column construction. The frieze of Doric buildings consists of an alternating sequence of → metope and → triglyphos (the whole of which is in Greek building inscriptions referred to as τρίγλυφος, *tríglyphos* [1. 29–30]), the frieze of Ionian buildings, which can (in contrast to that of the Doric order) be missing, consists of a smooth layer of ashlars, often decorated with a band of reliefs (according to Vitruvius 3,5,1, it was called *zophorus*, according to Attic and Delian building inscriptions, ζῷα (*zôia*), ζῷον (*zôion*), ζῳδίον (*zōidíon*) [1. 31]).

As a term in architecture and art history, 'frieze' can also refer to a decorative line, usually horizontal and decorated with ornamental or figurative paintings or reliefs, used to demarcate or separate surfaces or building elements, a line that was used in the most varied architectonic contexts, in sculpture (→ Sarcophagi, → Toreutics), and in two-dimensional pictorial media (→ Painting; → Mosaic; → Vase painters). The frieze with reliefs in → architectural sculpture is not restricted to the location of the architectonic frieze in the entablature, but can also cover, i.a. the architrave (Assus, temple of Athena), the cella (outside: → Parthenon; inside: Bassae, temple of Apollo), substructures (→ Mausolleum), as well as entire wall areas (Pergamon Altar).

1 Ebert.

F. Felten, Griech. tektonische Friese archa. und klass. Zeit, 1984; W. Müller-Wiener, Griech. Bauwesen der Ant., 1988, 216; B. Wesenberg, Vitruvs Vorstellung von der Entstehung des dor. Triglyphenfrieses, in: FS für F. Hiller, 1986, 143–157; N. Weickenmeier, Theoriebildung zur Genese des Triglyphon, 1985. C.HÖ.

Frigidarium see → Baths; → Thermal baths

Frigidus Left tributary of the river Sontius in East Venetia, modern Vipacco/Wippach, also a station on the *via Gemina*, 36 miles east of Aquileia (It. Ant. 18), modern Aidussina/Haidenschaft. Here, Theodosius defeated the usurper Eugenius in AD 394 (Claud. De III consulatu Honorii 99). G.U.

Frisii (the Frisians). A fairly ancient Germanic people (etymology not clear), first mentioned in Plin. HN 4,101, who, according to Tac. Germ. 34,1 comprised the *Frisii maiores* and *minores*; they could hardly have been the *Frisiavones* in Plin. (HN 4,101; 106) in the north of Belgica [1]. They lived to the north of the → Bructeri and to the west of the → Chauci, mainly between Oude Rijn and Ems. There were an estimated 1,500 to 2,000 settlements in the marshes and border regions of the moors of the provinces of Friesland and Groningen in the 1st cent. AD; Frisian influence subsequently declined in the east, while it increased in the west. The F. who had been obliged to pay tribute since Drusus in 12 BC (Tac. Ann. 4,72,1; Cass. Dio 54,32,2f.), revolted in AD 28, besieged the Roman harbour complex *castellum Flevum* and drove out the Romans (Tac. Ann. 4,72–74). → Domitius [II 11] Corbulo allocated to them new land in 47 and gave them a new state regime (Tac. Ann. 11,19,1; cf. [2]), but after the Roman troops were withdrawn to the south bank of the Rhine only the sections of the population on the left bank of the Rhine remained in the immediate Roman territory. In 58 the F. clashed again with Rome under their kings Verritus and Malorix (Tac. Ann. 13,54,1; 4), and the Am(p)sivarii tried to penetrate the territories on the right bank of the Rhine (ibid. 55,1). During the Batavian rebellion most of the F. were hostile to Rome (Tac. Hist. 4,15,2; 16,2; 79,2); subsequently they sometimes provided recruits for the *auxilia* or the imperial guard cavalry (CIL XVI 105; VI 3230), but were otherwise largely independent. In the 3rd cent. they probably co-operated with the Franks; they were defeated by Constantius Chlorus (Pan. Lat. 8,9,3). In the following cents. the F. spread out towards the west and the east and occupied the islands off the mouth of the Schelde and the North Sea coast.

1 G. Neumann, D. Timpe, s.v. Frisiavones, RGA 10, 82–84 2 J.P. A. van der Vin, Two new Roman Hoards, in: Bull. Antieke Beschaving 68, 1993, 247–253.

W. Will, Roms "Klientel-Randstaaten" am Rhein?, in: BJ 187, 1987, 1–61, esp. 24–30; P.D. Blok et al., s.v. Friesen, Friesland, LMA 4, 970–976; G. Neumann et al., s.v. Friesen, RGA 10, 2–68. K.DI.

Fritigern *Dux* (*reiks*) of the → Tervingi; in AD 376, with the permission of → Valens and under threat from the Huns, he led his tribe as *dediticii* (→ *deditio*) across the Danube to Thrace (Amm. Marc. 31,4,8; Iord. Get. 134), where the Arian won over parts of the indigenous population. After conflicts with the Romans the Goths defeated the Romans on 9 Sept. 378 in the battle of Hadrianople (Amm. Marc. 31,6,3–5; 11,5; 12,8 [1. 133–139]). F., who was not able to take advantage of the victory because his troops were splintered, invaded Macedonia and plundered it (Iord. Get. 140; Philostorgius 9,17) and in 381 eliminated his opponent → Athanaric by means of an intrigue (Socr. 4,33,1–4, Sozom. Hist. eccl. 6,37,6f.). F. is probably the *rex* on the side of the Goths in the → *foedus* with Theodosius I (3 Oct. 382, Chron. min. 1, 243 Mommsen [2. 126,6]). Nothing is known about his death.

1 H. Wolfram, Die Goten, [3]1990 2 A. Demandt, Die Spätantike, 1986.

PLRE 1, 374.; U. Wanke, Die Gotenkriege des Valens, 1990; S. Williams, G. Friell, Theodosius, 1994. M.MEI. and ME.STR.

Fritillus (φιμός, *phimós*). The shaker was used for throwing the dice and the → *astragaloi* in various → board games and → dice games (Hor. Sat. 2,7,17; Juv. 14,5; Mart. 4,14,7–9; 5,84,1–5 and passim; Sen. Apocol. 12,3,31; 14,4; 15,1; Sid. Apoll. Epist. 2,9,4 etc.). Besides shakers made of perishable material, there were some made of clay [1. fig. 15 from Mainz-Kastell, Wiesbaden] and bronze (Schol. Juv. 14,5 mentions horn). The playing-pieces in the shape of towers (called *turricula* or *pyrgus*) made of ivory, wood or copperplate, through which the dice were rolled on to the board over steps [2. fig. 3–13, 17–18], had a similar function (Mart. 14,16; Sid. Apoll. Epist. 8,12,5; Anth. Pal. 9,482,23f.),.

1 A. Rieche, Röm. Kinder- und Gesellschaftsspiele, Limesmuseum Aalen 34, 1984 2 H. G. Horn, Si per me misit, nil nisi vota feret. Ein röm. Spielturm aus Froitzheim, in: BJ 189, 1989, 139–159. R.H.

Fritte see → Faience

Frog (βάτραχος/*bátrachos*, Ionian βάθρακος/*bátrakos*, βρόταχος/*brótachos*, Lat. *rana*) is the collective name for frog amphibians (βατράχων γένος; *batráchōn génos*, Aristot. Hist. an. 7(8),2,589a 28f.) comprising the genuine frog species and the toad species.

A. The genuine frog species B. Toad species

A. The genuine frog species

The genuine frog species include the green water frog (Rana esculenta), the brown grass frog (Rana temporaria L.; the first two distinguished by Theophr. fr. 174,1; cf. *dioptes* Plin. HN 32,70 and 139) and the tree frog (Hyla arborea), which Pliny (HN 32,75; 92; 122) appropriately describes as *calamites* (cf. Ps.-Theophr. De signis tempestatum 15; Isid. Orig. 12,6,58). In literature usually the water frog is referred to: in Aristophanes' 'Frogs' its distinctive croaking (βοᾶν/*boân*, θορυβεῖν/*thorybeîn*, Lat. *coaxare*, *garrire*) is reproduced onomatopoeically as *brekekekéx koáx koáx*; the croaking annoyed both gods and people (Aristoph. Ran. 226ff; Batrachomyomachia 187ff.; Hor. Sat. 1,5,14). However, Pan and the Nymphs took pleasure in it (Aristoph. ibid.; Anth. Pal. 9,406). Non-croaking frogs are mentioned in Plin. HN 8,227 and there are legends about how they fell silent [1].

Frogs were admired as prophets of the weather, i.e. harbingers of rain (Arat. 946; Verg. G. 1,378); Pliny (HN 18,361) lists them among the *praesagia tempestatum* (cf. Aristot. Pr. 1,22,862a 10). Anxiety about plagues of frogs due to over-breeding are documented not only in Ex 8:1ff., but also by Varro in Plin. HN 8,104, who mentions the population of a Gaulish town being driven out by frogs (cf. Str. 16,772; Diod. Sic. 3,30). Theophr. fr. 174 did not believe in a rain of frogs. Aristotle describes the amphibian way of life of the frog (Hist. an. 1,1,487a 28), its tongue and the way it produces sounds (5,9,536a 8ff.; also Plin. HN 11,72) as well as its genitalia and reproduction (3,1,510b 35; 5,3,540a 30ff. and 6,14,568a 22ff.). Tadpoles (γύρινοι, *gýrinoi*) first appear in literature in Pl. Tht. 161d, further i.a. in Arat. 947 and Plin. HN 9,159. Aristotle claims that frogs hunt bees (Hist. an. 8(9),40,626a 9; cf. Ael. NA 1,58). Pliny knows that frogs hibernate in the mud (Plin. HN 9,159) from which they allegedly originate (Ov. Met. 15,375; Plut. Symp. 2,3). They live in hostility with snakes, storks, swans and other birds. By contrast with today's gourmets, people apparently did not enjoy eating the legs (Varro in Columella 8,16,4). Dioscorides (2,26 WELLMANN 1,130f. = 2,28 BERENDES 162) recommends them boiled in a broth with salt and oil as an antidote to snake venom, among other things.

The frog was seen as an animal of the Underworld (Aristoph. Ran. 207; Juv. 2,150); the many frog sculptures on buildings or implements (e.g. on the seal of Maecenas, Plin. HN 37,10) made from all kinds of materials have magic, i.e. apotropaic, significance. They appear as impure spirits in Apc. 16:13. Since time immemorial they have also been associated with Apollo as fortune-tellers (Plut. De Pyth. or. 12 = Mor. 25,399f.). Plut. Septem sapientes 21 (= Mor. 13,164a) mentions frogs grouped round a date palm in the house in Delphi which Cypselus had dedicated to the god. According to legend Latona turned the Lycian peasants into frogs because they did not let her drink from a pond (Ov. Met. 6,377ff.). Further legends about transformations are provided by Antoninus Liberalis in 35 and Probus, in Verg. G. 1,378. In the → *Batrachomyomachia*, an epic parody of Homer, the frogs – besides the mice – are the protagonists. In the animal fable (Aesop. Fab. 43f.; 70; 143; 146; 302; 307; 312; Phaedr. 1,6; 24 or 30) they appear as cowardly, stupid and arrogant.

B. TOAD SPECIES

The best known was the terrestrial toad (φρῦνος/*phrýnos*, φρύνη/*phrýnē*, Lat. *rubeta, bufo*; with two subspecies according to Plin. HN 32,49ff.; Nic. Alex. 567ff. and schol. to Aetios of Amida 13,37), but besides this also the toad known as λιμναία φρύνη/*limnaía phrýnē* (Nic. Alex. 567ff.; Theoc. 7,139). The toad behaves similarly to the frog: it lives an amphibian life (Plin. HN 8,110; Aetios of Amida 13,37), eats insects (Plin. HN 11,62) and dives into the water when rain is on the way (Ps.-Theophr. De signis tempestatum 15). The toxicity especially of their skin (Plin. HN 25,123) was greatly exaggerated (cf. Plin. HN 8,110; 11,196; 11,280; 32,50; Nic. Alex. 588; Ael. NA 17,12). Because of its eeriness and ugliness, but mainly because of its poison, it became the typical magic animal of peasants (Plin. HN 18,158; 294 and 303; Gp. 2,18,14) and witches (Hor. Epod. 5,19; Prop. 3,6,27; Juv. 1,70). Plin. HN 32,48ff. therefore provides a comprehensive catalogue of sympathetic remedies with regard to frogs and toads.

1 M. WELLMANN, s.v. F., RE 7, 114,30ff. 2 KELLER.

C.HÜ.

Frontality The term introduced by J. LANGE in 1892 as in the 'law of frontality' originally referred to a pre-Greek mode of portrayal, which, developed from the plane, displays all the essential individual forms paratactically in front view. Frontality was a label for an allegedly primitive form, which in evolutionary statements on style also seemed applicable to the early, pre-classical portrayal of people in Greek sculpture. In archaic statues frontality was supposedly expressed by mirror-symmetrical arrangement round a central axis, thus restricting the ability to move and distorting the anatomy. In the classical period frontality is supposedly overcome by the creation of a perspective and therefore a fictitious 'real space' round the sculpture. Structural research orientated towards the philosophy of art adopted the term frontality, though it saw in it less a stage in development than an 'artistic will', in which the form expressed a precedence of the transcendental over the realistic content. Thus, the term frontality also became applicable to the sculpture of late antiquity. After this transformation from inorganic form factor to bearer of a symbolic content, frontality lost its significance as a category of art criticism in favour of newer semiotic models for explaining the portrayal of the body. On manifestations and meaning of frontality in two-dimensional art, → relief.

J. LANGE, Die Darstellung des Menschen in der älteren griech. Kunst, 1899; R. BIANCHI-BANDINELLI, s.v. Frontalità, EAA 3, 1960, 742–744; B. SCHWEITZER, Strukturforsch. in Arch. und Vorgesch., in: Zur Kunst der Ant., 1, 1963, 179–197; H.H. WIMMER, Die Strukturforsch. in der klass. Arch., 1996.

R.N.

Frontier see vol. 6, Addenda

Frontinus, S. Iulius High state official under Domitian, Nerva and Trajan, military and technical specialist author. He probably began as an officer under → Domitius [II 10] Corbulo [1. 150], in AD 70 he was *praetor urbanus* (Tac. Hist. 4,39), i.e. in a prominent position in the absence of the consuls Titus and Vespasian, in 73 he became *cos. suff.*, then until 77/78 as successor to → Petilius Cerialis governor (*legatus Aug. pr. pr.*) in Britannia (Tac. Agr. 17,3), in 83 he campaigned against the Chatti together with Domitian (plans for the Low and Upper German limes? [1. 152f.; 2]); in 86 he became proconsul of Asia. Nerva appointed him *Vir publicis sumptibus minuendis* and *Curator aquarum*. He was *cos. II* together with Trajan in 98, in 100 *cos. III*, a rare honour, perhaps because of his merits in the context of Trajan's adoption and succession [3]. Many inscriptions testify to F.'s activities (e.g. ILS 6074; 1105), Pliny the Younger calls him *princeps vir* (Epist. 4,8,3) and quotes his instruction not to build a monument for him after his death, because his honour would be his *merita* (Epist. 9,19,6).

Still under Domitian he wrote his work on the art of land surveying (*De agri mensura libri II*), which is known only in fragments from quotations in Agennius Urbicus, and which is the first and trend-setting document of this genre; it deals with military and legal besides the geodetic issues. Only → Vegetius and the tactitian → Aelianus [1] testify to the professional competence of the document *De re militari*, whose loss is only partly compensated for by the four books, best documented in the Cod. Harleianus 2666 (9th/10th cents.), of the *Strategemata* (bk. 1 strategems before, bk. 2 during, bk. 3 after a siege; the authenticity of bk. 4 on historical cases is not certain in spite of [4]). The main achievement is the intelligence, circumspection and discipline of the *strategos*, with whom the author supposedly identifies latently. The work *De aquaeductu urbis Romae* (thus the title in the main codex Casinensis 361, 12th cent.) under Nerva is intended for personal training and general instruction. In the MSS it is divided into two bks. The history, capacity and purpose of the Roman aqueducts are competently explained, sometimes critically (e.g. improper removal of water); it is a first-rate archaeological and hydrological source. The style is almost historiographically narrative and apart from the many figures not very technical, the foreword is kept personal and programmatic.

EDITIONS: C.E. BENNETT, M.R. MCELWAIN, 1925; C.THULIN, De agri mens., 1913 (1971), 1–19; P.RESINA SOLA, 1984; R.I. IRELAND., Strat., 1990; C.KUNDEREWICZ, De aqu., 1973 (bibl.).
INDEX: J.C. RODRÍGUEZ, 1985 (bibl.).

1 K.CHRIST, S.I.F., princeps vir, in: Xenia 22, 1989, 149–160 2 G.PERL, F. und der Limes, in: Klio 63, 1981, 563–583 3 W.ECK, Die Gestalt Frontins, in: Wasserversorgung im ant. Rom: S.I.F., Curator Aquarum, ²1983, 47–62 4 G.BENDZ, Die Echtheitsfrage des 4. B. der Frontinischen Strategemata, 1938 5 PIR² 4, 322.

KL.SA.

Fronto Roman cognomen ('wide-browed'), first attested in the Imperial period.

KAJANTO, Cognomina 236. K.-L.E.

[1] A rich patron of Martial (1,55,2). He could be identical with Ti. Catius Caesius F., *cos. suff.* in AD 96.
[2] Praetorian governor of Galatia under Tiberius, perhaps AD 27–31.

S.MITCHELL, in: Chiron 16, 1986, 23ff.; PIR² F 485).

[3] **[...]us F.** *Cos. suff.* in AD 165, (VIDMAN, FO² 52; there also on possible identifications).
[4] **[...]rius F.** Praetorian governor of Thracia in AD 135; see Valerius F. W.E.
[5] see → Liternius Fronto.
[5a] Consular governor of Moesia *inferior*, already replaced by September/October AD 97, probably shortly before (RMD III 140 and [1]). Most likely to have been C. Caristanius [1] Fronto or C. Octavius Fronto; less probably Ti. Catius Caesius Fronto, *cos. suff.* 96.

1 D. MACDONALD, A.MIHAYLOVICH, A New Moesia Inferior Diploma of 97, in: ZPE 138, 2002, 225–228.

W.E.

[6] **M. Cornelius F.** Orator of the period of the adopted emperors, from Cirta in Numibia (Min. Fel. 9,6; 31,1). We learn most about his biography from his letters; the traditional *cursus honorum* (vigintivirate, quaestor in Sicily, i.e. senator still under Hadrian, plebeian aedile and praetor) is provided by ILS 2928 (before AD 138). Born in the early 2nd cent., trained by the philosopher Athenodotus and the orator Dionysius Tenuis, F. was active as a lawyer and orator, and by the end of Hadrian's rule he was regarded as Rome's premier administrator (Cass. Dio 69,18,3). He also seems to have become well known early on as a teacher of oratory, so that he was entrusted with the education of the princes M. Aurelius and L. Verus soon after Antoninus Pius came to power (July 138). His close links with the imperial family also remained decisive for his subsequent career. At the age of about 33 he was *consul suffectus* in July/August 143, but had to decline becoming governor of the prestigious province of Asia because of an illness. Although the extant correspondence covers only the years until about 166, his death is to be dated not until after 176; Marcus Aurelius commissioned a statue in honour of his former tutor.

Fronto's ancient reputation (Pan. Lat. 8,14,2: besides Cicero; Cass. Dio 69,18,3; Sid. Apoll. Epist. 8,10,3) is based in particular on his speeches, of which, however, we are unable to get a clear picture: ancient opinions are not united, and only fragments, of e.g. a *Gratiarum actio* on behalf of the Carthaginians have been preserved. Other Senate speeches were the *Laudes Hadriani* and the two *Gratiarum actiones de consulatu*, the speech *In Christianos* quoted by Min. Fel. 9,6; 31,2 is famous. F. sent a state speech in the *consilium principis* (*De testamentis transmarinis*) to Marcus Aurelius, who quoted it in his letter of reply. His prosecution speech against Herodes Atticus also caused a sensation.

Declamations and minor prose pieces in the collection of letters showing F. as a typical representative of the → Second Sophistic include the humorous panegyrics (*nugalia* p. 231,13 v.D. H.), *Laudes fumi et pulveris* (p. 215–217) and *Laudes neglegentiae* (p. 218–220), a letter essay *De feriis Alsiensibus* (p. 231,16–233,15) on both the spiritual and physical *otium*, and the letter replying to Marcus Aurelius' letter of condolence on the death (in 165) of F.'s grandson (*De nepote amisso*, p. 235–240). The *De bello Parthico* to Marcus Aurelius (162) after the defeat of the Romans by the Parthians is also a kind of consolatory writing. Finally, the *De eloquentia* on the value of rhetoric and *De orationibus* (p. 153–160) on stylistic exemplary figures for Marcus Aurelius' oratory practice are of a programmatic nature. The treatise *Principia historiae* about L. Verus returning victoriously from the Parthian war in 166, with the basic features of a panegyric historical work (p. 202–214), is in contrast to Lucian's *De historia conscribenda*. The letters themselves are preserved in a rescripted MS (end of 5th cent.; CLA 1,27; 3,19), divided today between Milan (Ambr. E 147 sup.) and Rome (Vat. Lat 5730), in total just under three-fifths of the original codex. Besides the minor prose there is also correspondence with Marcus Aurelius (*Ad Caesarum* and *Ad imperatorem* 5 bks. each) and L. Verus (2 bks.), and a more official correspondence with Antoninus Pius, besides two bks. *Ad amicos*. The fact that the letters have been handed down in duplicate form indicates that they were not published by F. himself. However, the private and contextual nature of the correspondence should not be used in a psychological generalization against the author. On the other hand, the pedagogic affection, sincerely reciprocated by his pupils, is to be taken seriously. F.'s didactics tends, though, towards an excessive cult of the form, corresponding to a rejection of philosophy. The recommendation especially of pre-classical authors (Plautus, Cato, Sallust; his attitude towards Cicero is ambivalent, that towards Seneca negative) makes F. one of the main representatives of the Second Sophistic appearing in Rome as → archaism.

F.'s status among his contemporaries was considerable. This reputation of the person and his works, especially in Gellius, congeals into an overall image of a great orator and favourite of the Antonines in late antiquity. The letters and speeches were lost in the early Middle Ages; it was not until 1815 or 1819 that A. Mai discovered the remains of the palimpsestic letter codex.

Editions: M.P. J. van den Hout, [2]1988 (256ff. fragments of the speeches).
Bibliography: PIR[2] C 1364; F. Portalupi, Marco Cornelio F., 1961; E. Champlin, F. and Antonine Rome, 1980; P. Steinmetz, Unt. zur röm. Lit. des 2. Jh., 1982, 173–186; P.V. Cova, M. Cornelio F., in: ANRW II.34,2, 873–918; M.A. Levi, Ricerche su F., 1994; K. Sallmann, in: HLL, § 456. P.L.S.

Fructus ('Fruits'). Objects extracted from another object ('mother object'), such as agricultural crops and tree fruits, wood, the young of animals, hair, wool, milk (Dig. 22,1,28 pr.; 7,1,48,1). *Fructi* belonged to the owner of the mother object before they were separated from it (Dig. 6,1,44), and basically also afterwards. A security (→ *pignus*) to the mother object was basically also extended to the *fructi*, if after separation they became the property of the person hypothecatinging the object (Dig. 20,1,1,2; 29,1); the hypothecary right of the lessor comprised also *fructi* which did not become the property of the tenant (Dig. 47,2,62,8; 19,2,53; 24,1). An usufruct (→ *usus fructus*) led immediately (Inst. Iust. 2,1,37) or on seizure (*percipere*, Dig. 7,4,13) to ownership of the *fructus* by the usufructuary. Yields from hunting and fishing were also regarded as *fructus* (Dig. 7,1,9,5; 22,1,26). Rental fees counted as *fructus* (*pro fructibus*) (Dig. 22,1,36), leasehold rents, the services of slaves, monies for crossings and haulage could replace *fructus* (*loco fructuum*) (Dig. 5,3,29). Broken marble was not included among *fructus*, unless the stone grew back (Dig. 24,3,7,13). → Interest (*usurae*) on loans, although not *in fructibus* (Dig. 50,16,121) was equated with *fructi* (Dig. 22,1,34).

A problem mentioned many times and already as an 'ancient question' (Ulp. Dig. 7,1,68 pr.) was the question to whom the child of a slave belonged (*partus ancillae*): in the opinion of the lawyer M. → Iunius Brutus, which became generally accepted, the child of an usufruct slave woman did not become the property of the usufructuary, 'because a person cannot be *in fructu* of a person' (Ulp. ibid.), similarly Gai. Dig. 22,1,28,1 with the philosophically influenced reasoning *cum omnes f. rerum natura hominum gratia comparaverit* ('as the nature of things brought forth all *fructi* for the people'). A hypothecary right on the mother, on the other hand, also included the child, even if did not devolve upon the lessor after selling (Dig. 13,7,18,2; 20,1,29,1). In a general sense *fructus* can denote an advantage such as the authority for hypothecation (Dig. 22,1,49) and in a figurative sense also 'wages' (*munificentia*, Dig. 50,10,2 pr.).

J. Filip-Fröschl, Partus et fetus et f., in: Ars boni et aequi, FS Waldstein, 1993, 99–121; Honsell/Mayer-Maly/Selb, 85f.; Kaser, RPR I, 284, 384, 425, 427f., 447–454, 464; Wieacker, RRG, 588. D.SCH.

Frugi Roman cognomen ('capable', 'upright', 'honourable', from *frux* [1]), within the Republican nobility among the Calpurnii (→ Calpurnius [I 20–23]; → [II 5; → 24]; → [III 1]) and M. Pupius Piso F. Calpurnianus, in the Imperial period also among the Licinii and other families.

1 Walde/Hofmann 1, 552.

Degrassi, FCIR 252; Kajanto, Cognomina 68, 253. K.-L.E.

Fruit (ὀπῶραι/*opôrai*, Lat. *poma*). Collective term for edible fruits or seed kernels (hazelnut, almond, pine kernel, etc.), usually from fruit trees. Ancient authors distinguish, according to the time of ripening of the fruit, early summer, summer and autumn fruits (e.g. Gal. de alimentorum facultatibus 2,2; 8). The most important cultivated fruits in the Roman imperial period were → apples, pears, dates, → figs, pomegranates, → plums, → quinces and grapes (→ Wine) with many respective subspecies (a list of these and other fruits in Plin. HN 15,35–105). For some the Mediterranean was already their natural habitat in prehistoric times, others, like the quince (and also the → apricot, cherry (→ Cherry tree), almond (→ *amygdálē*) and various kinds of nuts) did not arrive from the Orient until the archaic or classical periods, first in Greece and later in Italy, from where they spread into the western Mediterranean. Important fruits growing wild were wild pears, blackberries (→ Blackberry bush), acorns, rose hips, cornelian cherries, wild plums, sloes and bird cherries.

As most varieties of fruits quickly decay because of their high water content, fresh fruits were suitable almost only for the local market (Plin. HN 15,40). Nuts and dried fruit such as dates, figs, plums and raisins, on the other hand, played an important part in foreign trade (Edictum Diocletiani 6,49–55; 84–88; 93–94). The proportion of fruits in → nutrition was greater than today. They were served in fresh and preserved form as a side dish with bread and broths and also as a dessert (Mart. 5,78; Petron. 69,6). For fine cuisine Apicius provides complicated dishes with fruits, for e.g. puddings and fish or meat fricassees (Apicius 4,2,33–35; 4,3,4–6). Fruits were also an important medicine used by doctors for internal and external applications (Cels. Med. 3,7,2; Dioscorides 1,136–187 BERENDES).

J. ANDRÉ, Essen und Trinken im alten Rom, 1998; A. DALBY, Essen und Trinken im alten Griechenland. Von Homer bis zur byz. Zeit, 1998; V. HEHN, Kulturpflanzen und Haustiere in ihrem Übergang aus Asien nach Griechenland und Italien sowie in das übrige Europa. Histor.-linguistische Studien, [8]1911. A.G.

Frumentarii In the late Republic and in the early Principate *frumentarii* were soldiers possibly responsible for → logistics (providing food, escorting traders). From the 2nd cent. AD at the latest, however, they acted as imperial messengers, couriers, informers and policemen. Their name and activity is derived from the traders with whom they once collaborated, for these *frumentarii* were often also employed as spies. Military *frumentarii* were assigned to legions, but stationed in Rome in the *castra peregrina* and there under the command of the *praefectus praetorio*; *frumentarii* are epigraphically attested for Rome (ILS 2364–2367), Italy (Ostia: ILS 2223) and the provinces (ILS 2368; 2370; 8244). *Frumentarii* attested under governors also acted as police. In late antiquity the *frumentarii* were replaced by the → *agentes in rebus* (Aur. Vict. 39,44).

1 M. CLAUSS, Untersuchungen zu den principales des röm. Heeres von Augustus bis Diokletian. Cornicularii, speculatores, frumentarii, 1973 2 O. FIEBINGER, s.v. f., RE 7, 122–125. L.WI.

Frumentius Apostle of Ethiopia, born at the beginning of the 4th cent. AD in Tyre. The only source on him is Rufinus of Aquileia (Historia ecclesiastica 10,10). On a journey to India F. was captured by the Ethiopians, where he managed to gain the favour of the king of → Axum. After Athanasius of Alexandria had ordained him bishop of Ethiopia (Aksum) F. (from 340) was very active as missionary. On the beginnings of Christianity in Ethiopia cf. [3].

1 PL 21, 478f. 2 E. CERULLI, s.v. Äthiopien, LThK[2] 1, 999f. 3 B. B. W. DOMBROWSKI, F. A. DOMBROWSKI, F./ABBĀ SALĀMĀ, zu den Nachrichten über die Anfänge des Christentums in Äthiopien, in: Oriens Christianus 68, 1984, 114–169. RO.F.

Frusino (modern Frosinone). City in *Latium adiectum* on the *via Latina*, seven miles from Ferentinum on a hill (291 m) left of Cosa (modern Acquosa). In 306 BC it instigated a rebellion of the Hernici (Diod. Sic. 20,80), whose leaders were executed in 303; a third of F.'s territory was confiscated (Liv. 10,1,3) and F. was reduced to a *praefectura*. After the Social War *municipium*, *tribus oufentina*; in the Imperial period *colonia* (CIL X 5662f.; [1. 233]). Early historical finds, remains of city wall and amphitheatre; aqueduct (Ponte della Fontana).

1 F. BLUME, K. LACHMANN (ed.), Die Schriften der röm. Feldmesser 1, 1848.

I. BARBAGALLO, Frosinone, 1975, 12–44; E. M. BERANGER, Viaggio attraverso i musei, 1984; Id., Nuovi risultati di una indagine, 1992; BTCGI 7, 1989, 414–517. G.U.

Fucus (φῦκος; *phŷkos*, φυκίον; *phykíon*, φῦκος θαλάσσιος; *phŷkos thalássios*) originally denoted red algae used for dyeing clothes red and as a cosmetic (Lat. verb *fucare*): e.g. *Rytiphloea tinctoria* (*Clem.*) *Ag.*, but not the species *Fucus L.* The loan-word *phycos* (as bush *frutex*, Plin. HN 13,135) denotes not only the herb-like *algae*, but is extended to green algae like the sea lettuce (*Ulva lactuca*). Pliny distinguishes (HN 13,136) three species: 1. the orseille or litmus lichen (*Roccella tinctoria L.*), 2. perhaps some red algae (= Dioscorides 4,99 p. 2,255 WELLMANN = 4,98 p. 423 BERENDES: astringent effect) and 3. the eelgrass, a flowering plant (*Zostera marina L.*). Further species (Plin. HN 13,137 = Dioscorides 4,98 p. 2, 255 WELLMANN = 4,97 p. 423 BERENDES) are the sea lettuce and some indeterminate ones. Pliny understood Theophr. Hist. pl. 4,6,2–9 at the time partly only inadequately. Plin. HN 26,103 recommends *fucus marinus* in particular for gout and other joint diseases.

The drone is also called *Fucus* as is propolis, in Varro, Rust. 3,16,19; Verg. G. 4,244; Plin. HN 11,48 et al., while according to the physician Simeon Seth, φουκᾶς; *phoukâs*, like the Arabic *fokka*, designates a type of beer. C.HÜ.

Fuels

A. DEFINITION B. USE C. MATERIALS AND PRODUCTION

A. DEFINITION

Because of their ratio of hydrogen, fuels are easily inflammable organic substances, which emit the energy stored in their carbon compound as heat when burned. Controlling fire and generating heat was judged by the Greeks to be one of the most important cultural techniques. The myth of → Prometheus represents the availability of fire as a fundamental condition for human life; whereas in Hesiodus the guarantee of food is still at the centre of the myth (Hes. Theog. 535ff.; Op. 42ff.), in Aeschylus' tragedy the fire is regarded as διδάσκαλος τέχνης πάσης (*didáskalos téchnēs pásēs*, 'teacher of every techne'; Aesch. PV 110f.; cf. 254); the significance of fire for metallurgy and for producing glass and tiles was also emphasized by Pliny (HN 36,200f.).

B. USE

In antiquity fuels were firstly needed by households for preparing food and for heating and lighting living areas; besides, large quantities of fuel were also needed in industrial production. High temperatures and correspondingly large quantities of fuels were necessary for smelting ores, processing precious metals and bronze (bronze casting), forging iron and for producing ceramics and glass. Other branches of trade, e.g. lime burning plants, fabric dying workshops or bakeries, also relied on fuels. The need for fuel was exceptionally high in particular in metal processing and in the production of ceramics; experiments with Roman furnaces have proved that for the production of 8 kg of iron 40 kg of charcoal were needed, which were in turn extracted from *c.*150 kg of wood. In the Roman period large → thermal baths were heated by a wood fire; the wood supply was organized by the public administration.

C. MATERIALS AND PRODUCTION

Wood and charcoal were mainly used as fuels; wood was primarily cut in the forests, but the large estates also sold firewood at the city markets. The Athenian large-estate owner Phaenippus in the 4th cent. BC had wood worth 12 drachmas brought daily to Athens (Demosth. 42,7), and in the Roman period the sale of wood is mentioned in Cato (Cato Agr. 7,1; 38,4). Charcoal was already produced in the 5th cent. BC in the forests of the Parnes by charcoal burners from the deme of Acharnae (Aristoph. Ach. 321ff.). A precise description of the large charcoal kilns is provided by Theophrastus (Hist. pl. 9,3; cf. 5,9,4). The charcoal kilns were built up in layers of smooth logs on flat ground, which were then covered with firm clods of soil, so that the fire was invisible. As the wood gradually swelled, moisture, smoke and gases such as carbon dioxide, carbon monoxide and methane escaped. The pitch flowed out and was collected to be used as a sealing material. According to Theophrastus (Hist. pl. 5,9,1–3) the various branches of trade preferred different charcoals with special characteristics that had been extracted from a particular wood. The wood of young trees and that from trees which had grown in a sunny, dry location was thought to be particularly suitable for the production of charcoal in general. Charcoal is a black, porous, light substance and burns with a short, bluish flame and without smoke, the gases having escaped during carbonization. It is free of sulphur, has a high heating capacity and therefore makes very high temperatures possible. However, the temperature of 1535 degrees Celsius needed for smelting iron could not be achieved with charcoal in ancient furnaces, even with the aid of bellows.

Coal was used only in those regions where there were deposits close to the surface; in particular in Britannia the use of coal is attested in many sites where it was found. In this province coal was also transported to the settlements over fairly great distances. Olive oil, which was used to fill lamps made of clay, sometimes also bronze, served as lighting for living areas.

No new fuels were developed until late antiquity. In antiquity people limited themselves to generating thermal energy; it was not immediately redeployed for mechanical operation, thus the fuels were not used as motor fuels. The → automata constructed in Alexandria which converted heat energy into motion for display effects were an exception.

Forests close to larger cities or the centres of the production of metal and ceramics were cut down to produce fuels. Sometimes there was a shortage of fuels in such areas; in the 4th cent. BC Meidias, for instance, brought wood for the silver mines from Euboea to Laurium (Demosth. 21,167). There are calculations showing that 5,000 hectares of forest had to be cleared annually for the fuels required in Roman metal production.

→ Charcoal; → Commerce; → Energy; → Glass; → Heating; → Metallurgy; → Oil; → Pitch; → Pottery; → Prometheus; → Wood

1 BLÜMNER, Techn. 2, 347–356 2 M.J. DEARNE, K. BRANIGAN, The Use of Coal in Roman Britain, in: Antiquaries Journal 75, 1995, 71–105 3 J.F. HEALY, Mining and Metallurgy in the Greek and Roman World, 1978, 148–152 4 MEIGGS, 185, 192, 203ff., 237, 258
5 A. NESCHKE-HENTSCHKE, Gesch. und Geschichten. Zum Beispiel Prometheus bei Hesiod und Aischylos, in: Hermes 111, 1983, 385–402 6 PEACOCK, 25 7 D.W. REECE, The Technological Weakness of the Ancient World, in: Greece and Rome 16, 1969, 32–47, esp. 43ff.

AS.S.

Fuficius

[1] **Q.F. Cornutus.** Senator originating from the region of Histonium. His career started under Trajan or Hadrian. After the praetorate *iuridicus* of Asturia et Callaecia in the north of Spain, legionary legate in Moesia, praetorian governor in Pannonia inferior from at least AD 145 to 147, *cos. suff.* in 147; consular governor of Moesia inferior between 148 and 155. In Histonium a large monument, possibly a *quadriga*, was erected in his honour with public funds on the order of the council of *decuriones* (ILS 8975 = ALFÖLDY, FH 81ff.; THOMASSON I 113; 134). PIR[2] F 497. W.E.

[2] **F. Fango, C.** Veteran of Caesar (Cass. Dio 48,22,3), joined the Senate (Cic. Att. 14,10,2); perhaps already attacked by Catullus (54,5). After the battle of Phillippi in 41 BC, Octavian sent him to Africa as governor, to take over the province from a supporter of Antony, T. Sextius. After unsuccessful battles he committed suicide in the year 40 (App. B Civ. 5,102; Cass. Dio 48,22,1–23,3; MRR 2, 373, 382). K.-L.E.

[3] According to Vitr. De arch. 7 pr. 14 the oldest Roman author of a non-extant one-volume work on architecture. In the longest extant catalogue of ancient

architects → Vitruvius mentions → Varro (1 bk. *De architectura* in *De novem disciplinis*) and P. → Septimius (2 bks. *De architectura*) besides F. as his only Roman predecessors. Vitruvius gives the reason for his new complete works as the shortage of Roman → technical literature in spite of postulated equal ranking of Greek and Roman architecture. F.'s influence on Vitruvius is less important than that of Varro.

1 H.v. Hesberg, Vitruv und die ital. Tradition, in: H.Knell, B.Wesenberg (ed.), Vitruv-Kolloquium, 1984, 123–140, esp. 136f. 2 H.Knell, Vitruvs Architekturtheorie, 1985, 17ff. 3 L.Sontheimer, Vitruvius und seine Zeit, 1908, 61–71. UL.EG.-G.

Fufidius Name of a plebeian family (further development of *Fufius* [1]), prominent in Arpinum, the home town of Cicero.

1 Schulze 239, 428.

[1] Roman equestrian, in 57 BC creditor to Apollonia in Illyria (Cic. Pis. 86). Possibly identical with the F. from whom Cicero bought a country estate in Arpinum for his brother in 54 (Ad Q. fr. 3,1,3), who appointed Cicero joint heir in 47 (Att. 11,13,3) and whom Horace attacked as a profiteer (Sat. 1,2,12–22).

Nicolet 2, 882f.

[2] F., L. Allegedly ex-centurio (Oros. 5,21,3), is said to have pressed L. Cornelius [I 90] Sulla to publish the proscription lists in 82 BC (Plut. Sulla 31,3; cf. Sall. Hist. 1,55,21f.M), in 81 (?) praetor, in 80 *propraetor* in Hispania ulterior, where he was defeated by Q. Sertorius (Sall. Hist. 1,108M; Plut. Sertorius 12,3). K.-L.E.

[3] Lawyer from the 1st cent. AD, probably active under the Flavians [2], known only through four indirect quotations in later literature [1], i.a. from his *Quaestiones* (i.e. comments on legal cases, at least two bks.), the first work in legal literature handed down under this title [3].

1 O.Lenel, Palingenesia iuris civilis, 1889, 1, 177f. 2 Kunkel, 136 3 Schulz, 288. T.G.

Fufius Name of a plebeian family [1], perhaps from Cales, politically active from the 3rd cent. BC.

1 Schulze 239.

I. Republican period II. Imperial period

I. Republican period

[I 1] People's tribune (?) in the mid–2nd cent. BC, otherwise unknown author of a *lex Fufia* on the fixing of permissible days for public assemblies (usually mentioned together with the *lex Aelia*, → Aelius [I 1]). MRR 1,452f.; 3,3f. K.-L.E.

[I 2] F., L. Known as an orator in the 90s of the 1st cent. BC. Around 97 his speech in the prosecution of a blackmail case against M'. → Aquilius [I 4] gained him high esteem (Cic. Brut. 222; cf. De or. 2,194–196: the perspective of the counsel of defence M. Antonius); numerous (see Cic. Off. 2,50; De or. 1,179) later prosecution speeches were judged more derogatorily (Cic. De or. 2,91: *furit in re publica*, 'he raves'), the presentation of the material was reproached as muddled circumlocution (cf. ibid., 3,50).

ORF⁴, 277f.; G.V. Sumner, The Orators in Cicero's Brutus, 1973. J.R.

[I 3] F., M. Roman equestrian, mentioned in 59 BC in a speech by Cicero (Flacc. 46–48) as a moneylender. Confidant of Annius [I 14] Milo. F. accompanied Milo, when the latter had → Clodius [I 4] murdered on the *via Appia* on 18 Jan. 52 (Ascon. 31 Z. 26C). W.W.

[I 4] F. Calenus, Q. Born in Cales in Latium, probably brother of the former, mint master *c.* 70–68 BC (MRR 2, 440; 3, 94). His political career saw him as a consistent opponent of the Optimates. As people's tribune of 61 he supported P. → Clodius [I 4] Pulcher in the trial against him because of a religious sacrilege. The *plebiscitum* which he introduced decreed that judges should not be appointed by the praetor, but the lots should be cast by the three classes of senators, *equites* and *tribuni aerarii*, and he finally secured Clodius an acquittal [1. 125–129]. In 59 F. supported Caesar; a *lex Fufia* of this year again regulates the voting procedures (Cass. Dio 38,8,1; Schol. Bob. 97 St.). In 56 F. appeared in legal proceedings against Cicero's intimate, → Caelius [I 4], (Cic. Cael. 19) and in 52 after the murder of Clodius against P. Annius [I 14] Milo (Ascon. 44f. C).

In the following year F. went to Gallia as Caesar's legate (Caes. B Gall. 8,39,4), in 49 to Spain (MRR 2, 267). In the subsequent course of the Civil War he led reinforcements to Caesar in Epirus in 48. As *legatus pro praetore* in Achaea [2. 97ff.] he organized aid to Pharsalus for Caesar who was under attack in Alexandria (MRR 2, 281). On his return in Sept. 47 the latter honoured him with the consulate for the remaining months of the year (MRR 2, 286). As the son-in-law of the then consul Vibius Pansa, he occupied an influential position in the Senate in 43 and as an old friend of M. → Antonius [I 9] he opposed Cicero (Cic. Phil. *passim*). Through his influence on Anthony he was able to protect Terentius Varro, who had already been proscribed (App. B Civ. 4,202f.). In 42 during Anthony's absence in the East, F. commanded two legions for the protection of Italy (App. B Civ. 5,46); in 41 he was governor of Gallia Narbonensis and later also of the rest of Gallia. He died in mid 40 BC (MRR 2, 373, 382).

1 Ph. Moreau, Clodiana Religio, 1982 2 A.N. Oikonomides, Defeated Athens, the Land of Oropos, Caesar and Augustus, in: Ancient World 2, 1979, 97–103. W.W.

II Imperial period

[II 1] C.F.Geminus. Senator, probably originating from Urbs Salvia, father of F. [II 2]. *Cos. suff.* in 2 BC; he and his consulate colleague introduced the *lex Fufia Caninia*, PIR² F 510.

[II 2] **C.F. Geminus.** Son of F. [II 1]. Closely associated with Livia, the mother of Tiberius. Quaestor of Tiberius probably in AD 20, people's tribune; then already a member of the *VII viri epulonum*. In 29 *cos. ord.* With his sharp-tongued speeches he had often offended Tiberius, who never forgot. Between 29 and 31 F. was executed, probably in connection with the destruction of Seianus (→ Aelius [II 19]). He originated from Urbs Salvia, where he had the theatre erected.

L. GASPERINI, Ottava Miscellanea Gr. e Rom., 1982, 285ff.; W. ECK, in: Picus 12/13, 1992/3, 83ff.; PIR² F 511. W.E.

Fufluns (also Fuflunz, Fuflunsl, Fuflunsul, Fuflunus). The name of the god F. is attested from the beginning of the 5th cent. BC in inscriptions [1. vol. 1, 187]. It is not certain whether he is of Etruscan origin [4. 94ff.] or whether he belongs to the Umbrian substratum of Etruscan [2]; a mirror from Orvieto from the end of the 4th cent. on which he is depicted with the Umbrian goddess → Vesuna would support this [3. vol. 5, 35]. His connection with the name of the Etruscan city of Pupluna, Latin → Populonia [5; conversly 4. 97f.] is also contested. Mirror representations show F. with Thyrsus or Cantharus as the son of Semla (= Greek Semele) together with Areatha (= Greek Ariadne) and Apulu (= Greek Apollo); inscriptions define F. in greater detail through the epithet Pachies (= Bacchus) [1. vol. 2, 119 Vc 4.1], which suggests identifying F. with Dionysus/Bacchus for the 5th cent. His cult, which was introduced to Etruria from Greek southern Italy, was originally only reserved for women [6], but was later open to men as well. The worship centres of F. in → Tarquinii, for which there is evidence for the 3rd cent. BC, were called *pachana* [1. vol. 2, 56 Ta 1.184], the cult association was called *pachathuras*, and its head (in the 2nd cent. BC) *maru* [1. vol. 2, 70 AT 1.32]. F./Pachies was venerated together with Cath (cf. inscription and the joint depiction on the bronze liver of Piacenza [1. vol. 2, 329 Pa 4.2,23; vol. 2, 69 AT 1.1; 1.32]). With the banning of the → Bacchanalia in 186 BC by the → *senatus consultum de Bacchanalibus* the F. cult also seems to have disappeared. After this period there is an absence of datable evidence for F.

1 ET 2 G. MEISER, Lautgeschichte der umbr. Sprache, 1986, 215f. 3 E. GERHARD, G. KÖRTE, Etr. Spiegel, 1887–1897 4 M. M. T. WATMOUGH, Studies in the Etruscan loanwords in Latin, 1997 5 H. RIX, Annali della Fondazione per il Museo Claudio Faina 5 (1998), 207–229 6 PFIFFIG, fig. 1.

M. CRISTOFANI, s.v. Dionysos/F., LIMC 3.1, 531–540; M. PALLOTTINO, Etruskologie, 1988, 310; E. SIMON, Etr. Kultgottheiten, in: M. CRISTOFANI (ed.), Die Etrusker, 1995, 157, 163. L.A.-F.

Fulcinius Name of a Roman plebeian family (SCHULZE 169).

I. REPUBLICAN TIME II. IMPERIAL PERIOD

I. REPUBLICAN TIME

[I 1] **F., C.** Roman envoy, killed by the Fidenates in 438 BC (statue on the Rostra, Cic. Phil. 9,5; Liv. 4,17,2). K.-L.E.

II. IMPERIAL PERIOD

[II 1] **C.F. Fabius Maximus Optatus** Senator, probably from Cartennae, who certainly attained the praetorship and had a *legatio* in Baetica, probably at the end of the 2nd/beginning of the 3rd cents. AD. W.E.

LE GLAY, in: EOS II 777; PIR² F 514.

[II 2] **F. Priscus** Jurist, probably a contemporary of → Antistius [II 3] Labeo (Augustan period [2; 3]), known only because of 10 indirect quotations in the Digests of Justinian [1].

1 O. LENEL, Palingenesia iuris civilis 1, 1889, 179f. 2 C. FERRINI, Opere II, 1929, 81ff. 3 KUNKEL, 137. T.G.

[II 3] **C.F. Trio** *Praetor peregrinus* in AD 24, brother of F. [II 4]. PIR² F 516.

[II 4] **L.F. Trio** Ambitious young senator who in AD 16 appeared as one of the prosecutors of Libo Drusus. His reward was the praetorship *extra ordinem*, probably in 17. Involved in the indictment of Calpurnius [II 16] Piso in 20, but without great influence on the result [1. 134, 140, 148, 188, 203]. Tiberius promised him his support in the future. Praetorian governor of Lusitania, attested in 31; in the same year he was still *cos. suff.* He killed himself in 35 after he was denounced because of his friendship with Seianus (→ Aelius [II 19]). ALFÖLDY, FH 135f.; PIR² F 517.

1 W. ECK, A. CABALLOS, F. FERNÁNDEZ, Das senatus consultum de Cn. Pisone patre, 1996. W.E.

Fulcrum see → Kline

Fulgentius

[1] **F. Mythographus** (also F. Afer, Fabius Planciades F., Fabius Claudius Gordianus). Several prose works are extant by the Christian F. who lived around AD 500 and whose identification with → Fulgentius [2] is a matter of discussion [3]: *De aetatibus mundi et hominis* is an episodic outline of world history in which a particular letter of the alphabet is meant to be avoided (lipogram) in each of the planned 23 lemmata (of which only 14 were written). Lemmata 10, 11 and 14 deal with Greek and Roman episodes, the latter evidencing an anti-Roman attitude, while the remaining lemmata treat Biblical episodes. The 3 bks. of the *Mythologiae* interpret just 50 legends in a natural symbolic and moral manner (in the Platonic-Stoic tradition). Here F.

regards the priests and monks as those Christians continuing the contemplative life form of the pre-Christian philosophers. In the *Expositio Vergilianae continentiae* the *Aeneis* is allegorically interpreted cursively with the didactic goal of making it (and esp. Aeneas) into a mirror of the ethical perfection of man. In the *Expositio sermonum antiquorum* F. explains obsolete Latin words with evidence from old literature, in which → Nonius is used. The allegorical commentary on Statius' *Thebais* was possibly written by F. as well. As a whole F. endeavours to reclaim Graeco-Roman culture for Christian education [2]. The effect of the allegorical interpretations in his works was considerable in the Middle Ages, first in → Boethius' *Consolatio* [4. 56–69].
→ Allegoresis

EDITIONS: 1 R. HELM, J. PRÉAUX, 1970.
BIBLIOGRAPHY: 2 B. BALDWIN, F. and his sources, in: Traditio 44, 1988, 37–57 3 P. LANGLOIS, s.v. F., RAC 8, 1972, 632–661 4 S. LERER, Boethius and Dialogue, 1985.
K.P.

[2] F. of Ruspe
A. BIOGRAPHY B. WORKS C. THEOLOGY

A. BIOGRAPHY
F., born in AD 467 in Thelepte/Byzacena (= Medinet el-Khedima/Tunisia), came from a senatorial family and obviously enjoyed a respectable education. After a short time as procurator (tax collector) in Telepte he became a monk there and in 507 he was appointed bishop of the coastal town of Ruspe/Byzacena (= Rosfa/Tunisia). In 508, together with over sixty bishops who wanted to hold on to the new Nicene faith of the empire, he was exiled (508–515) to Sicily by the homoeian ('Arian') king of the Vandals Thrasamund (AD 496–523); in Calaris he founded a monastery. After his return F. taught in Carthage, and because of his success he was again banished by the king to Sardinia. He did not return to his diocese until after the king's death. After several years F. died in Ruspe, probably in 532 rather than 527 or 533. He is probably not identical to the mythographer of the same name (→ Fulgentius [1]). For the biography we have the Vita (CPL 847 = BHL 3280; ed. G. G. LAPEYRE) that was probably written by the Carthaginian deacon Ferrandus after all.

B. WORKS
A compendium of dogmatics written after 523 in Ruspe (*De fide ad Petrum*, CPL 826; [1]), cited in the Middle Ages under the name of Augustine, e.g. in the significant aphorisms of the Parisian bishop Petrus Lombardus († 1160). A series of writings of F. is directed against the subordinationist (= homoean) theology of the Vandals; F. answered ten questions of King Thrasamund with his *Contra Arianos liber* (CPL 815; [1]) and he continued the dialogue in his 3 bks. *Ad Thrasamundum* (CPL 816; [1]). The *Psalmus abecedarius* (CPL 827; [3]) is likewise directed against (Vandal) Homoeans. F. wrote the *Ad Monimum* (CPL 814; [1]) and the *De veritate praedestinationis et gratiae Dei* (CPL 823; [2]), both in three books, against the Gallic opponents of Augustine's theology of grace, who have been called Semipelagians since the 18th cent. The *sermones* passed down under the name of F. are only partly genuine (CPL 828–835; [2]); the corpus of letters also contains letters to F. (CPL 817; [2]).

C. THEOLOGY
F., as the 'abbreviated Augustine', defended the Augustinian theology of grace against attacks by the Gallic Semipelagians. He therefore taught dual predestination for salvation or disaster, and hereditary sin arising from the *concupiscentia* ('desire') of the parents. For his theology of the trinity he fell back upon → Ambrosius, Augustine (→ Augustinus, Aurelius) and → Hilarius.

EDITIONS: 1 J. FRAIPONT, CCL 91, 1968 2 Id., CCL 91A, 1968 3 A. ISOLA, Corona Patrum 9, 1983 (Ps.).

BIBLIOGRAPHY: R. J. H. COLLINS, s.v. F., TRE 11, 1983, 723–727; H. J. DIESNER, F. von Ruspe als Theologe und Kirchenpolitiker, 1966; G. KRÜGER, Ferrandus und F., in: Harnack-Ehrung, 1921, 219–231; P. LANGLOIS, s.v. F., RAC 8, 1972, 632–661; G. G. LAPEYRE, Saint F. de Ruspe, 1929; A. MANDOUZE, Prosopographie de l'Afrique chrétienne (303–533), 1980, 507–513; S. T. STEVENS, The Circle of Bishop F., in: Traditio 38, 1982, 327–341.
C.M.

Fulginiae Town in Umbria (*regio VI*) on the *via Flaminia* on the eastern edge of the plain of the Topino and Clitumno (*lacus Clitorius*), modern Foligno (Perugia). Conquered by Rome in 295 BC, *praefectura*, later *municipium*, *tribus Cornelia*. Without walls F. suffered in the Perusinian War; the town was abandoned in the 5th cent. AD in favour of the hill of San Valentino di Civitavecchia. Iron Age and Roman remains: amphitheatre, arch, thermal baths near Santa Maria del Sasso, necropoleis near Santa Maria in Campis, *villa* (Palace of Decius), four bridges over the Topino. Museo Civico (Palazzo Trinci).

G. DOMINICI, F. Questioni sulle antichità di F., 1935; L. SENSI, F., in: Bollettino storico della città di Foligno 8, 1984, 463–492; M. BERGAMINI, Foligno, la necropoli romana, 1988; P. FONTAINE, Cités et enceintes, 1990, 358f.
G.U.

Fulgurales libri see → Etrusci

Fulling, Fuller Woollen fabrics intended for the manufacture of → clothing were processed into cloth by means of fulling (κναφευτική/*knapheutikḗ* sc. τέχνη/*téchnē*; Lat. *fullonica*). This process endowed the fabric with greater strength and density. The fabric was trodden in a mixture of warm water, soda and human or animal urine (*urina fullonia*: Plin. HN 28,174; especially valued was the urine of → camels: Plin. HN 28,91; cf. also Mart. 6,93). The fabric was then treated with fuller's earth, a special clay (*creta fullonica*). The finest clay came from the islands of Cimolos (*creta Cimolia*: Plin. HN 35,36; 35,196), Samos and Lemnos. The fabric then had to be trodden once more in order to become felted. Once the material had been thoroughly washed to cleanse it of the fulling substances, then dried, it was napped (κνάπτειν/*knáptein*; Lat. *pectere*). This was achieved by using thistles or brushes; white fabrics were also treated with → sulphur for brightness. This was done by stretching them over a half-rounded frame (*viminea cavea*) beneath which the sulphur was burned (Apul. Met. 9,24; Plin. HN 35,198). The fabric was then clipped to remove jutting-out wool fibres, and finally smoothed in a cloth press (*prelum*).

Because domestic fulling was impossible owing to the lack of facilities, specialist fullers (κναφεῖς/*knapheîs*; Lat. *fullones*) undertook such work in their own workshops (κναφεῖα/*knapheîa*; Lat. *fullonicae*); evidence for this is provided by the *lex Metilia de fullonibus* of the late 3rd cent. BC (Plin. HN 35,197). Fullers also cleaned and washed used clothing. There were several fulling mills at Pompeii; the fuller's most important tasks as well as the cloth press are depicted on murals in the House of the Vettii, in the fulling mill of L. Veranius Hypsaeus (Pompeii VI VIII 20–21) and on a gravestone from Agedincum, modern Sens.

→ Clothing; → Textiles, production of; → Wool

1 Blümner, Techn. 1, 170–190 2 W. O. Moeller, The Wool Trade of Ancient Pompeii, 1976 3 J. P. Wild, Textile Manufacture in the Northern Roman Provinces, 1970, 18–27 4 Id., Textiles, in: Strong/Brown, 167–177.

A.P.-G.

Fullo see → Apustius [4] F.; see → Fuller

Fulvia

[1] From a noble family, friend and alleged mistress (perhaps because of defamatory accounts) of Catilinarian Q. Curius [3]. She informed Cicero of the conspiracy (Sall. Catil. 23,3–4; 26,3; 28,2). H.S.

[2] Daughter of M. → Fulvius [I 1] Bambalio and Sempronia, date of birth unknown, married until 52 BC to → Clodius [I 4] Pulcher, until 49 to C. → Scribonius Curio and then to Marcus → Antonius [I 9], the future triumvir. Five children were born to these unions [6. 152–154].

In antiquity, F. was considered to be a cold, cruel 'Fury', who acquired a strange position of power for herself next to Antony; today she is also considered to be an example of an exceptionally emancipated woman of the Roman upper classes and a forerunner of the powerful women at the imperial court [2. 89]. Direct political involvement can only be substantiated with certainty after the death of Caesar [1; 6. 155–160], but it must be noted that the information about F. is based on the propaganda directed by Cicero and Octavian against Antony, mirroring the view of the ideology of the Augustan age, which stylized F. as the counter image of the Roman matron [4; 5]. Her conduct, which damaged the traditional understanding of the female role, provided cause for this. She actively participated in the dealings concerning the *acta Caesaris* (→ Acta) 44 (Cic. Phil. 5,4,11; Att. 14,12,1), attended the execution of Antony's rioting soldiers in Brundisium (Cic. Phil. 5,8,22; 13,8,18; Cass. Dio 45,13,2) and clearly supported the financial objectives of the proscriptions, while she declined a request by Roman *matronae* not to tax their money (App. B Civ. 4,32) [6. 160–176].

Sources explain her actions as the result of character flaws, such as greed and capriciousness (Cic. Phil. 2,44,113), accuse her of an unbridled thirst for power by exaggerating her political role (Plut. Antonius 10; Cass. Dio 48,4,1; App. B Civ. 5,54), and paint a terrifying picture of her cruelty (Cic. Phil. 5,8,22). In addition, information, which is clearly intended as propaganda and to help exonerate Octavian and possibly Antony as well, is adorned with literary embellishments (e.g. Cass. Dio 47,8,2; App. B. Civ. 4,29) and to some extent it is grossly contorted (Cass. Dio 47,8,3–4: maltreatment of Cicero's corpse) [4; 5. 77–80]; the loyalty, which is usually expected of a Roman woman towards the objectives of her husband, was not taken into account. F. actually successfully defended the interests of the absent Antony in Rome in spite of fierce attacks (Nep. Att. 9,2–7) [2. 85; 3. 139–144; 5. 77–80; 6. 175–178; 210–214], e.g. in approximately 44/43 during the struggle against his impending declaration as public enemy (Cic. Phil. 12,1,2; App. B Civ. 3,51). As the wife of Antony and the mother of → Claudia [I 4], who was engaged to Octavian for a while (Suet. Aug. 62; Plut. Antonius 20; Cass. Dio 48,5,1–3), she had considerable political influence (for her portrait on coins see [6. 198–209]), but that does not mean that she became ruler of Rome (Cass. Dio 48,4,1–6) [4. 206–207; 5. 79–83].

The preservation of Antony's position of power (Cass. Dio 48,5,4; 6,2–7,4; App. B Civ. 5,14; 5,33) also helped her involvement in the Perusine War 41–40. The image of the wife who is jealous of Cleopatra (App. B Civ. 5,19; Plut. Antonius 30) and therefore starts the war and commands like a general (Cass. Dio 48,10,1–13,6; Plut. Antonius 28; Liv. Per. 125; 127; Flor. Epit. 2,16; Oros. 6,18,17–19), does not least have its cause in Octavian's interest, but also Antony's, to pass on the responsibility, to come to an agreement [4. 203–207; 6. 176–198]. Slingers' lead bullets from this war (CIL XI 6721,3–5.14) document Octavian's attempt to show F. as a virago (Vell. Pat. 2,74,2–3) who, not just in contrast to the ideal image of women of the Augustan age, engages in military affairs [2. 87–89; 5. 79–83]. F. died in 40 BC in Sicyon, paving the way for the marriage of Antony and → Octavia. Recently attempts have been made to vindicate F. and to recognize her role.

1 C. L. Babcock, The Early Career of Fulvia, in: AJPh 86, 1965, 1–32 2 R. A. Bauman, Women and Politics in Ancient Rome, 1992, 78–90 3 K. Christ, Die Frauen der Triumvirn, in: Il triumvirato constituente, Scritti in onore di M.A. Levi, 1993, 139–148 4 D. Delia, Fulvia Reconsidered, in: S. B. Pomeroy (ed.), Women's History and Ancient History, 1991, 197–217 5 B. v. Hesberg-Tonn, Coniunx carissima, 1983, 61–65; 77–83

6 B. Kreck, Untersuchungen zur polit. und sozialen Rolle der Frau in der späten röm. Republik, 1975, 152–214. H.S.

[3] **Pu(blia) F. Plautilla** Daughter of → Fulvius [II 11] Plautianus, the praetorian prefect of Septimius Severus. Probably systematically prepared for marriage to the imperial son Caracalla by her father; since AD 200 engaged to Caracalla, married in the year 202. She was then given the title Augusta, with which she also appears on coins of the realm and provincial minting. Numerous statues were erected of her alone or in a group with the other members of the *domus Augusta*. She participated in the journey of the emperor's family to North Africa, their native land, in 202–203. However, Caracalla despised his young wife from the beginning. When her father was killed in 205, she had to go into exile on the island of Lipara; her name was erased everywhere. She was murdered at the beginning of Caracalla's autocratic rule in 212; PIR² F 564. W.E.

Fulvius Roman plebeian gentes name, derived from *fulvus* ('reddish yellow, brownish yellow' [1. 1,561], probably named after hair colour); further evidence: [2. 170], inscriptions also *Folvius* (ILLRP 124 et passim). The Roman *gens* probably came from Tusculum (Cic. Planc. 20; cf. Cic. Phil. 3,16; Plin. HN 7,136), where F. [I 15] also had put up works of art from the spoils of war. The most important branches are initially the Centumali, Curvi and Paetini, since the 3rd cent. BC the Flacci and Nobiliores. Genealogical tree: [3. 231f.].

1 Walde-Hofmann 2 Schulze 3 Münzer, s.v. Fulvius, RE 7.

I. Republican period II. Imperial period
1. Rome 2. Municipalities

I. Republican period

[I 1] **F. Bambalio, M.** ('Stammerer'), probably a little respected descendant of the famous Fulvians, father of Fulvia [2] (Cic. Phil. 2,90; 3,16; Cass. Dio 45,47,4; 46,7,1).

[I 2] **F. Centumalus, Cn.** Consul in 229 BC with L. Postumius, landed on Corcyra, with his colleague he conquered and expelled the Illyrians from Apollonia and in 228 celebrated a naval triumph (MRR 1,228f.).

[I 3] **F. Centumalus, Cn.** As curulian aedile he put on four-day theatrical performances for the first time in 214 BC; praetor in 213; as consul in 211 with P. Sulpicius Galba, he protected Rome against Hannibal, then, in 210, remained in his area of office, Apulia, with extended imperium, and fell in battle against Hannibal during the siege of the rebellious town of Herdonea (Liv. 27,1,4–15; MRR 1,272; 280).

[I 4] **F. Curvus, L.** Consul in 322 BC with Q. Fabius [I 28] Maximus Rullianus. First bearer of the name to appear in the Roman magistrate lists, fought against the Samnites and is said to have triumphed (Liv. 8,38–40; MRR 1,149f.). In 316 he was *magister equitum* of the dictator L. Aemilius [I 24] Mamercinus Privernas and fought again against the Samnites.

[I 5] **F. Curvus Paetinus, M.** (Both cognomina based on physical characteristics, the second, 'the cross-eyed one', perhaps un-historical). In 305 BC *cos. suff.* in place of the fallen Consul Ti. Minucius Augurinus, triumphed over the Samnites (Liv. 9,44,15; InscrIt 13,1,71).

[I 6] **F. Flaccus, C.** Consul in 134 BC with P. Cornelius [I 70] Scipio Aemilianus, assumed leadership of the battles against the slaves on Sicily (Liv. per. 56; Obseq. 27; Oros. 5,9,6).

[I 7] **F. Flaccus, Cn.** Younger brother of F. [I 10], in 212 BC praetor with the command in Apulia, was beaten by Hannibal near Herdonea and fled; in 211 he was condemned for it and went into exile in Tarquinii (Liv. 26,2,7–3,12).

[I 8] **F. Flaccus, M.** First ancestor of this family, plebeian tribune in 271 or 270 BC (MRR 1,199), in 270 with M. → Curius [4] Dentatus Duumvir for the completion of the water pipe Anio vetus (Frontin. Aq. 1,6). As consul in 264 with Ap. Claudius [I 3] Caudex, he conquered the → Volsinii and triumphed; he took 2,000 bronze statues to Rome as booty (Plin. HN 34,34; booty dedication: [1. 103f.]) and took to Rome the cult of → Vertumnus, for whom he also built a temple (Fest. 228L; [2. 240]). In 246 he was cavalry colonel of the dictator Ti. Coruncanius (MRR 1,216), chosen for the holding of elections.

1 Roma medio repubblicana, 1973 2 Hölkeskamp.

[I 9] **F. Flaccus, M.** Supporter of Ti. and C. → Sempronius Gracchus. When the triumvirate for the implementation of the distribution of farm land, to which he had belonged since 130 BC (ILLRP 473), was no longer able to dispose autonomously of the land of the Roman confederates (→ Socii (Roman confederation)), on the instigation of P. Cornelius [I 70] Scipio Africanus, he as consul in 125 acted as advocate to allow the Italic peoples the choice between citizenship and provocation right (→ *provocatio*) so as to win them over for the reform (Val. Max. 9,5,1; MRR 1,510). The Senate therefore dispatched him to southern France to fight the Gauls; he defeated the Ligurians, Salluvians and Vocontians and triumphed after his return in 123. In support of C. Gracchus, and contrary to convention, he had himself elected plebeian tribune for 122; it is unclear whether he accompanied Gracchus to Africa to found a colony (App. B Civ. 1,102–106) or remained in Rome and resisted M. Livius Drusus, the opponent of Gracchus (Plut. C. Gracchus 10f.). After the consul L. Opimius had decided in 121 to mount a military campaign against Gracchus, both initially entrenched themselves on the Aventine. F. attempted in vain to negotiate with the Senate through his son and was finally killed while fleeing; his two sons also died. His house was torn down (Cic. Dom. 102; 114). His daughter Fulvia became the wife of L. Julius Caesar (*cos.* 90).

U. Hall, Notes on M. Fulvius Flaccus, in: Athenaeum N.S. 55, 1977, 280–288; W.L. Reiter, M. Fulvius Flaccus and the Gracchan Coalition, in: Athenaeum N.S. 56, 1978, 125–144; D. Stockton, The Gracchi, 1979, Index s.v. F.

[I 10] F. Flaccus, Q. The most important representative of the family at the time of the 2nd Punic War, and consul four times. As *cos. I* in 237 BC he fought the upper Italian Celts, together with his colleague L. Cornelius [I 45] Lentulus Caudinus. In 231 as censor he had to resign with his colleague T. Manlius Torquatus because of an election error. As *cos. II* in 224 (again with Torquatus) he was the first Roman to cross the Po in the battle against the Celts (Pol. 2,31,8). In 216 Pontifex, in 215 *praetor urbanus* (coastal protection, etc.), which he also remained in 214 (and without previous drawing of lots for the area of office). After serving as *magister equitum* for the elected dictator in 213, he became *cos. III* with Ap. Claudius [I 20] Pulcher in 212, conquered the Carthaginian camp of → Hanno at Benevent, and with his colleague encircled Capua, to which he also laid siege in 211 and 210 with an extended imperium; he warded off an attempt by Hannibal to obtain military relief, conquered the town and punished it harshly (Liv. 26,4–16). At the end of 210 he became dictator for the holding of elections, in 209 *cos. IV* with Q. Fabius [I 30] Maximus, he subjugated the Hirpinians and Lucanians, stood as proconsul in Bruttium in 208, and in 207, with an extended imperium, in Campania. In 205 he opposed in the Senate the plan by → Cornelius [I 71] Scipio Africanus to take the war to Africa (Liv. 28,45,2–7); he probably died shortly afterwards. He was married to Sulpicia, who on the occasion of the dedication of the temple of Venus Verticordia, was regarded as 'the most respectable woman' in Rome (Val. Max. 8,15,12; Plin. HN 7,120). His son: F. [I 12].

J. Briscoe, in: CAH 8, [2]1989, 54–73; H.H. Scullard, Roman Politics 220–150 B.C., [2]1973, Index s.v. F.; J. v. Ungern-Sternberg, Capua im Zweiten Punischen Krieg, 1975.

[I 11] F. Flaccus, Q. Son of F. [I 7]. Perhaps he brought Greek envoys to Rome in 197 BC on the order of T. → Quinctius Flamininus; in 189 he was plebeian aedile, in 187 praetor (Sardinia), and in 181 legate in the Ligurian War. After several election defeats he was *cos. suff.* in 180, he settled 7,000 Ligurian Apuanians in Samnium (MRR 1,387). Funeral games of the sons F. [I 6] and perhaps F. [I 13] in his honour are possibly attested by Lucilius 4,149M [1. 262–264].

1 C. Cichorius, Untersuchungen zu Lucilius, 1908.

[I 12] F. Flaccus, Q. Eldest son of F. [I 10]. In 184 BC curulian aedile, in 182 praetor with the province of Hispania citerior; there he also fought in 181/180 with pro-consular imperium against the Celtiberians (MRR 1,382; 385; 389). He celebrated a triumph in 180, became Pontifex and in 179 consul with his natural brother L. Manlius Acidinus Fulvianus. He was successful against the Ligurians and he triumphed again (MRR 1,391f.). In 174 he was censor with A. Postumius Albinus; during which time they also expelled a brother of F. from the Senate (MRR 1, 404). In 173 he dedicated the temple of Fortuna Equestris in Rome, which had been extolled in Spain, and for which the marble roof tiles of the Juno Lacinia Temple in Croton were going to be used; the Senate ordered their return (Liv. 42,3; Val. Max. 1,1,20; [1]). He committed suicide in 172, allegedly because of the loss of a son.

1 F. Coarelli, s.v. Fortuna Equestris, in: LTUR 2, 1995, 268f.

J. Briscoe, Q. Marcius Philippus and *nova sapientia*, in: JRS 64, 1964, 73f.

[I 13] F. Flaccus, Ser. Consul in 135 BC with Q. Calpurnius [I 15] Piso, he defeated the Ardeians in Illyria (MRR 1,488f.; 3,95). He probably also appeared as an orator (Cic. Brut. 81) and was perhaps the Consular F. who advised Ti. Sempronius Gracchus in 133 not to use any violence (Plut. Ti. Gracchus 11,1f.).

[I 14] F. Maximus Centumalus, Cn. In 302 BC legate of M. Valerius Maximus in the battle against the Etruscans, in 298 consul with L. Cornelius [I 76] Scipio Barbatus; fought successfully in Samnium and probably also in Etruria and triumphed (MRR 1,174); in 295, with pro-praetorian imperium, he defeated some of the Etruscans (MRR 1,178); 263 dictator for the building work at the Temple of Jupiter (inscription 13,1,73), 100 years after the first dictator with this responsibility [1. 156f.].

1 Mommsen, Staatsrecht vol. 2.

[I 15] F. Nobilior, M. In 196 BC curulian aedile with C. Flaminius [2], with whom he also held the praetorship in 193; in 193 and in the two subsequent years he distinguished himself, with an extended imperium, in Hispania ulterior and in 191 celebrated an Ovatio (MRR 1,347; 351; 354). In 189 he was consul with Cn. Manlius Vulso and led the war against the Aetolians (Liv. 38,3–11; [1]). He conquered Ambracia, and from there he took many works of art to Rome. Later they were put up in the Temple of Hercules Musarum, purpose-built in his censorship (179) (Pan. Lat. 9,7,3; Plin. HN 35,66; Base inscription: ILLRP 124; [2]), he also gave some of them to the home community of the family, Tusculum (ILLRP 332). Then he turned against Cephallenia, whose capture he was not able to complete until he was proconsul in 188, because of the siege of Same; he remained in Greece until the spring of 187, triumphed brilliantly after the return and held splendid festivals (Liv. 39,5,13–17). The poet Q. → Ennius [1] accompanied him on the campaign and celebrated his successes in the 15th book of the *Annales* and in the play *Ambracia* [3. 144–146, 553–559], while Cato [1] reproached him for having decorated soldiers for no convincing reason (Gell. NA 5,6,24–26). In 179 he was censor, reconciled himself with his former opponent and current colleague M. Aemilius [I 10] Lepidus (whose election to consul he had prevented twice), and implemented an extensive building programme that also included the → Basilica Fulvia (Liv. 40,45f.; 51f.).

1 V.M. Warrior, The Chronology of the Movements of M. Fulvius Nobilior (*cos.* 189) in 189/8 B.C., in: Chiron 18, 1988, 325–356 2 A. Viscogliosi, s.v. Hercules Musarum, in: LTUR 3, 1996, 17–19 3 O. Skutsch, The Annals of Ennius, 1985.

E. Badian, Ennius and his Friends, in: O. Skutsch (ed.), Ennius, 1972, 183–199; Gruen, Rome, Index s.v. F.

[I 16] **F. Nobilior, M.** Eldest son of F. [I 15], plebeian tribune in 171 BC, curulian aedile in 166 (performance of the *Andria* of P. → Terentius Afer at the *Ludi Megalenses*), consul with Cn. Cornelius [I 23] Dolabella 159, triumphed as proconsul in 158 over the eleatic Ligurians (MRR 1,446). He (not F. [I 12]) probably founded Forum Fulvi and built the road to go with it from Placentia to Ocelum, the so-called *via Fulvia* [1. 1599–1601].

1 G. Radke, s.v. Viae publicae Romanae, RE Suppl. 13.

[I 17] **F. Nobilior, Q.** Younger son of F. [I 15], in 160 BC curulian aedile, praetor at the latest in 156, in 153 consul with T. Annius [I 13] Luscus (the first consular pair to take up office on 1st January); he took over Spain but suffered heavy losses against the Celtiberians (App. Ib. 184–197; cf. Pol. 35,4,2), for which he was rigourously attacked in the Senate by → Cato [1]. In 149 he therefore defended Ser. Sulpicius Galba, who was reproached by Cato for serious misdemeanours in Spain (Liv. per. 49). In 136 he was censor together with Ap. Claudius [I 22] Pulcher (MRR 1,486).

[I 18] **F. Paetinus, M.** Consul in 299 BC with T. Manlius Torquatus, took Nequinum in Umbria, established the colony of Narnia there and triumphed (MRR 1,173).

[I 19] **F. Paetinus Nobilior, Ser.** In 255 BC consul, with his colleague M. Aemilius [I 34] Paullus he was supposed to evacuate the rest of the army of M. Atilius [I 21] Regulus from Africa. They occupied Cossyra (modern Pantelleria) and defeated the Carthaginians at Cape Bon, but on the return they lost most of the fleet and the army again in a storm off Sicily (Pol. 1,36,5–37,2); in spite of this as proconsuls they had a naval triumph in 254 (MRR 1, 209f.). K.-L.E.

II. Imperial period

[II 1] City prefect under Elagabalus. Shortly after the latter's death (11 March AD 222) he was killed by soldiers and the people. PIR² F 523. W.E.

[II 2] **L.F. Aburnius Valens** Jurist under Hadrian and Antoninus Pius [1], together with Tuscianus he was a successor of → Iavolenus and a predecessor of → Iulianus in the directorship of the Sabinian law school (Dig. 1,2,2,53). In the thirties of the 2nd cent. AD he wrote *Fideicommissorum libri* (7 b.; in this regard [2]).

1 R.A. Bauman, Lawyers and Politics in the Early Roman Empire, 1989, 231ff. 2 D. Liebs, Jurisprudenz, in: HLL 4, 129f. T.G.

[II 3] **F. Aemilianus** Patrician; *cos. ord.* in AD 206. Leunissen 135; PIR² F 528.

[II 4] **F. Aemilianus** *Cos. ord.* in AD 244 Dietz 160ff.

[II 5] **L.F. Gavius N[umisius] Aemilianus** Probably the brother of F. [II 4]. Patrician. Under Severus Alexander, he conducted a *dilectus* in the Transpadana; *cos. suff.* probably before AD 235; he is probably identical to the *cos. ord. II* of 249. Dietz 164f.; PIR² F 540.

[II 6] **M.F. Gillo** Came from Forum Novum; *cos. suff.* in AD 76, proconsul of Asia *c.* 89/90. IEph. II 232f.; 235; 238; 240; 242; 1498. PIR² F 543.

W. Eck, in: Chiron 12, 1982, 316; Thomasson III 35.

[II 7] **Q.F. Gillo Bittius Proculus** (Bittius is the main gentile.) Probably adopted by F. [II 6]. Prefect of *aerarium Saturni* in AD 96/7 together with Publicius Certus. When Pliny attacked the latter, Proculus defended him. Married to Pompeia Celerina, the mother of Pliny's second wife [cf. 1. VII 490]. *Cos. suff.* in Sept. 99 ([2] = RMD III 141), so not directly after the prefecture of *aerarium*, as could be assumed from Pliny Epist. 9,13,23. Frater Arvalis, proconsul of Asia 115/6, [3. 359]. Probably died in 119. Scheid, Collège 38f.; 351; PIR² F 544.

1 Syme, RP 2 W. Eck, in: Köln. Jb. 20, 1993, 445ff. 3 Id., in: Chiron 12, 1982. W.E.

[II 8] see → Macrianus

[II 9] **(T?) F. Macrianus** Under Emperor Valerian he had a rapid military career as an eques (SHA Tyr. Trig. 10,14; 12,1; 13,3); after being wounded – which made him unable to serve in the military – he became the leader of the → Fiscus (Euseb. Hist. eccl. 7,10,5; 7,10,8; Zon. 12,24 p. 145 D.). In AD 257 or 258 he is said to have persuaded the emperor to persecute the Christians (Euseb. Hist. eccl. 7,10,4–7). Responsible in the Persian War of Valerian for military funds and supplying the army (Petrus Patricius Exc. de sententiis p. 264 no. 159 Boissevain), he refused to come to the aid of Valerian after the latter's capture by the Persians (Euseb. Hist. eccl. 7,23,1). When the praetorian prefect → Ballista offered him the purple of office, he declined because of his age and infirmity in favour of his sons → Macrianus and → Quietus (Euseb. Hist. eccl. 7,10,8; SHA Tyr. Trig.12,7; Zon. 12,24 p. 145 D.), and with his elder son be moved to the west while the younger Quietus remained in the east. In Pannonia he was defeated and killed in the autumn of 261 by troops of → Gallienus under → Aureolus (SHA Gall. 2,6–7; 3,1; Tyr Trig. 11,2; 12,12–14; 13,3; 14,1; 15,4; Zon. 12,24, p. 145f. D.)

PIR² F 549; PLRE 1, 528f. 2; Kienast, ²1996, 224f. T.F.

[II 10] **C.F. Plautianus** Praetorian prefect of Septimius Severus. Came from Lepcis Magna; probably related to the mother of Septimius Severus, with whom he perhaps spent part of his youth. Beginning of his eques career unknown; if Inscriptions of Roman Tripolitania 572 refers to him, he was *praefectus vehiculorum* and *procurator XX hereditatium. Praefectus vigilum* in Rome, perhaps from AD 193, certainly from 195 [1. 493ff.]. From 197 *praefectus praetorio*, after the murder of Aemilius Saturninus he was sole prefect. Systematic strengthening of his position by forming ties with many senators and eques, particularly however with soldiers. The acquisition of a huge fortune also assisted him in this, and marble and oil trading contributed to his wealth. He made himself indispensable to Septimius Severus, and even his mother, Julia Domna, lost her influence over him. F. accompanied the emperor on all campaigns and journeys, against → Pescennius Niger, → Clodius [II 1] Albinus, the Parthians, and to Africa. In 201 betrothal of his daughter → Fulvia [3] Plautilla to → Caracalla, in 202 marriage. From that time he was called *necessarius dominorum nostrorum, socer et consocer Augustorum* (AE 1979, 294).

F. was considered to be the third ruler alongside → Septimius Severus and Caracalla. Larger numbers of statues were erected to him everywhere than to the emperors, also by the Senate – an expression of real power. First breach – though reconciled again – with the emperor during the visit to Lepcis Magna. In 203 *cos. ord. II*, after he had previously been given the *ornamenta consularia* and the title *clarissimus vir*, also senatorial priestly offices. The emperor's brother, → Septimius Geta, on his death bed warned his brother against F. Caracalla, who hated him, brought about his end: F. was accused of a fabricated murder plan, allegedly directed against Septimius Severus, and he was murdered on 22 January 205 at the palace. Mementos of him were removed, the statues destroyed, his name in inscriptions erased, many of his supporters were punished, for the fortune he had collected a separate *procurator ad bona Plautiani cogenda* was enacted, and his son and daughter were banished to Lipara. F. had occupied a position of power that was never achieved again by any other praetorian prefect.

1 R. Sablayrolles, Libertinus miles, 1996.

A.R. Birley, The African Emperor, ²1988, passim; G. Alföldy, Un' iscrizione di Patavium e la titolatura di C. Fulvio Plauziano, in: Aquileia nostra 50, 1979, 125ff.; PIR² F 554.

W.E.

[II 11] see → Quietus

Fulvus see → Aurelius [II 14–18]

Funale see → Lighting

Fundana see → Galeria

Fundania Daughter of Marcius Fundanius, presumably the second wife of M. Terentius Varro, who dedicated *De re rustica*, bk. 1 to her in 36 BC (Rust. 1,1,1; 2, praef. 6 with comm. in [1. *ad loc.*].

1 D. Flach, Gespräche über die Landwirtschaft, 1996 and 1997.

ME.STR.

Fundanius Widespread Roman plebeian gentes name (Schulze 357, 533, 542).

[1] F., C. Plebeian tribune in 68 BC (?), one of the originators of the *lex Antonia de Termessibus* (Roman Statutes 1, 1996, no. 19), at the same time *curator viarum* (ILLRP 465a). Probably identical to C.F. who was defended by Cicero in 66 or 65 (Q. Cic. comm. petitionis 19) and is still mentioned in 59 (Cic. Ad Q. Fr. 1,2,10). He was probably also the father-in-law of the antiquarian M. Terentius → Varro, who introduces him as a dialogue partner in *de re rustica* (1,2,1 et passim).

J.W. Crawford, M. Tullius Cicero: The Fragmentary Speeches, ²1994, 57–64.

K.-L.E.

[2] F., C. Roman eques, in 45 BC changed sides in Spain from supporting the sons of Pompey to supporting Caesar (Bell. Hisp. 11,3). Perhaps he is the comedy writer mentioned in Horace (Hor. Sat. 1,10,42; 2,8,19).

W.W.

[3] F., M. Plebeian tribune in 195 BC. With his colleague L. Valerius and despite the resistance of the consul → Cato [1], he succeeded in revoking the *lex Oppia* of 215 that was meant to limit the expenditure of women (Liv. 34,1,2; 2,6).

[4] F. Fundulus, C. *homo novus*, as plebeian tribune in 248 BC successfully denounced P. Claudius [I 29] Pulcher (*cos.* 249) for high treason (*perduellio*) after the lost naval battle against Carthage at Drepanum (Schol. Bobiensia p. 90St.; MRR 1, 215) and in 246 as plebeian aedile he denounced the latter's sister → Claudia [I 1] for despising the plebs (Liv. per. 19; Gell. NA 10,6,3f.; MRR 1, 217). In 243 as consul he successfully fought against Hamilcar Barca in Sicily (Diod. Sic. 24,9,2f.; tendentious).

K.-L.E.

Fundanus see → Minicius

Fundi Town of the Aurunci in *Latium adiectum* at the foot of the *montes Fundani* (Tac. Ann. 4,59) on the *via Appia* between Tarracina and Formiae, 74 miles from Rome, modern Fondi (Latina). In 338 or 332 BC together with → Formiae *civitas sine suffragio* (Liv. 8,14,10; Vell. Pat. 1,14,4), F. then sided with the Privernati (Liv. 8,19). In 188 BC F. and Formiae belonged to the *tribus Aemilia* (*cum suffragio*); F. was a *praefectura*; in 174 it obtained an aqueduct through the Roman *censores* (Liv. 41,27,11). F. was a *municipium* with three *aediles* and had a cult of Hercules. Under Augustus F. was a *colonia* and centuriation area [2. 234]. High quality wines were grown in F. Under a *procurator* (CIL VI 8583) F. was owned by the emperor. Off the coast was the *lacus Fundanus*.

Archaeological findings: the city wall (370 × 360 m) of *opus incertum* with four gates (traces of the preceding wall of *opus polygonale* with quadratic towers) is preserved; north-east tower (Portella) with inscription of the three *aediles*; portcullis as well as round and quadratic towers. Orthogonal floor plan [1],→ *decumanus maximus* paved with limestone. Temple under the cathedral of San Pietro, thermal baths at San Rocco. Traces of an amphitheatre and → *macellum*. In the territorium of F. there are villas (Frontinus, Phaon) and the so-called monument to Galba. Inscriptions: CIL X p. 617, 6219–6299.

1 F. Castagnoli, Ippodamo, 1956, 88 2 F. Blume, K. Lachmann (ed.), Die Schriften der röm. Feldmesser 1, 1848.

Nissen 2, 658; Ruggiero 3, 338; E. Pais, Storia della colonizzazione, 1923, 231f.; C.F. Giuliani, F., in: Quaderni dell' Istituto di Topografia Antica dell' Università di Roma 2, 1966, 71–78; E. Lissi Caronna, F., in: NSA 1971, 330–363; G. Pesiri, Amphitheatrum Fundanae civitatis, in: Athenaeum 55, 1977, 195–199; Id., Sul rito dell'amfiteatro di Fondi, in: Atene e Roma 23, 1978, 193–195; Id., Iscrizioni di Fondi e del circondario, in: Epigraphica 40, 1978, 162–184. G.U.

Funditores in the Roman army were manual catapult throwers who with the *funda*, a loop made of linen or horse hair (Veg. Mil. 2,23; 3,14; Sil. Pun. 1,314f.), catapulted small rocks or lead balls (Liv. 38,20,1; Tac. Ann. 13,39,3). They were mainly used on the wings to start the battle, to pursue the opponent and to cover the retreat (Veg. Mil. 1,20; 2,17; Caes. B Civ. 3,46,2); catapults were also used in the defence of a besieged city (Veg. Mil. 1,16; 4,22). The *funditores*, as lightly armed soldiers, were originally part of a Roman legion (Liv. 1,43,7; Veg. Mil. 1,20; 2,2; 2,15), but they were later provided by the *auxilia*; with the growing importance of the *funditores* from the 2nd cent. BC, their number in the Roman army also increased (cf. Liv. 38,21,2; 38,29,4). The inhabitants of the Balearic Islands were famous for their skill as catapult throwers (Str. 3,5,1); according to Vegetius the soldiers were carefully trained in catapult throwing (military 1,16; 2,23).

Th. Völling, Funditores, in: Saalburg-Jb. 45, 1990, 24–58. S.L.

Fundus see → Large estates/Latifundia

Funeral see → Burial; → Dead, cult of the

Funerary architecture

I. Definition II. Egypt and the Near East
III. Classical antiquity and neighbouring cultures

I. Definition

Funerary architecture (FA) refers to architectonically designed structures built above the contemporary ground level for the purpose of → burial, as opposed to underground hypogea, which have rooms for the cult of the dead and hero cult. Columbaria can combine both types. Hypogea with a ground level cult room influenced the early Christian martyria above the graves. Regarding further aspects of FA, cf. → Hypogaeum; → Maussolleum; → Necropoleis. H.K.-G.

II. Egypt and the Near East
A. Egypt B. Near East

A. Egypt

The Egyptian burial complex consists of three functional components: sepulture, cult site, and a monument-like marking that is usually integrated into a building complex. A separation between sepulture and cult site only occurs in exceptional cases, thus in the cenotaphs of esp. the Middle Kingdom in → Abydus [2] and, in the New Kingdom, in the separation between the king's FA and the temple of the dead. Since the early dynastic period (late 4th millennium BC), the FA of kings is morphologically strictly separated from private FA. Among the private FA, social status is the determining factor regarding the level of excessiveness and complexity.

From the predynastic period (4th millennium), we have documentation of tombs that are subdivided into several chambers and covered by a roof. The superstructures were probably built as tumuli, but the form of the cult site remains unknown. These gave rise to the Abydenic FA for the kings of the Thinite period, where the cult sites were marked by pairs of steles. This is the earliest period for which → mastaba are documented in private FA. In the 1st Dynasty (early 3rd millennium), these were occasionally surrounded by FA for servants similar to the FA of kings; boats as burial gifts are documented in several cases.

In the 3rd Dynasty (from 2700 BC), the shape of the → pyramids emerged in the FA of kings. Private FA usually took the shape of the mastaba in the Old Kingdom. Under the rule of → Chefren, a certain type of FA in cliff sides developed from the mastaba and became the standard form of FA for the elite in Upper Egypt in the late Old Kingdom: carved into the cliffs of the neighbouring mountains was a forecourt, a façade, and a widthways arrangement of cult rooms and burial shafts, sometimes organized by rows of columns. A special variation of cliff side FA can be found in the Saff-FA of Thebes from the 11th and early 12th Dynasties (9th cent.), where large forecourts were sunken into level ground and, in early times, distinguished by a façade of columns.

The style of royal FA returns to the pyramid shape in the Middle Kingdom; in addition, documents prove the existence of royal cenotaphs and temples of the dead in Abydus. Mastabas in an archaic style are documented as private FA. In regular cases, however, the FA of the elite continues with the Old Kingdom development of FA in cliff sides, but now it follows a strictly axial ground plan. The main cult site no longer appears as a false door, but as a shrine of statues. Towards the end of the Middle Kingdom, FA is clearly influenced by temple architecture.

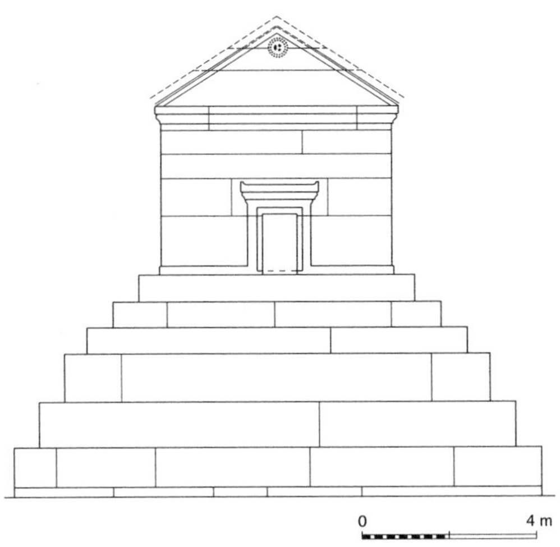

House tomb with gable roof. Tomb of Cyrus in Pasargadae (2nd half 6th cent. BC), north-west face.

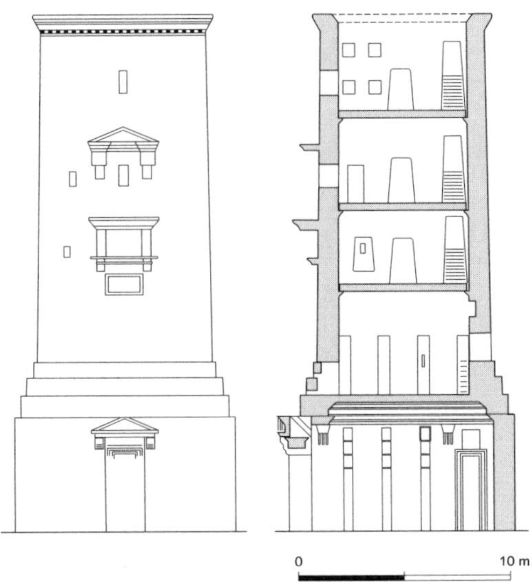

Funerary tower of Iamblichou, Palmyra (AD 83).

The New Kingdom brought an end to the shape of pyramids in royal FA. Now, FA takes the shape of long complexes of corridors hidden in the Valley of the Kings in Thebes; their temples of the dead are strung along in a row at the edge of the cultivated land. However, the shape of the pyramid is already adopted by private FA in the 18th Dynasty (*c.* 1550–1310 BC). The further development of FA in cliff sides leads to a series of new forms, esp. in the now dominating Theban necropolis, such as FA with a ground plan of T-shaped chapels, as well as a type of monumental FA with extensive columned halls. FA built on level ground such as that which was common for less important structures in Thebes but used for the highest dignitaries in the necropolis of Memphis are now designed in close adap-

Rock tomb façade from Petra; so-called Step Tomb (1st-2nd cents. AD).

tation of temple architecture – as a sequence of courtyards with pylon fronts and halls that lead to the cult chapel. The same is true for the FA in cliff sides, esp. in the later New Kingdom. The sepultures, formerly simple shafts or slanted ramps with a tomb chamber, turn into more and more complex series of rooms.

The monumental graves of the 3rd intermediate period and of the late period continue with the tradition of FA in the style of temples. This leads to the creation of innovative monumental structures in the Theban necropolis. FA of kings and royal family members is now documented in the temple districts of Tanis, Sais (Hdt. 2,169), and Thebes (Madīnat Habu).

→ Burial

D. Arnold, s.v. Grab, LÄ 2, 826–837; J. Vandier, Manuel d'archéologie Égyptienne, vol. 2, L'architecture funéraire, 1954.

S.S.

B. Near East

The purpose of special FA was to keep alive the memory of the dead, of their families, and of their prestige. They can be above ground and visible to everybody or they can be built underground. FA can serve individual persons, families, or clans, and is generally indicative of the deceased's high status. In the Near East, the different types of FA are usually determined by local conditions. While we find FA carved into cliffs on the Mediterranean coast, in → Urartu and in western Iran,

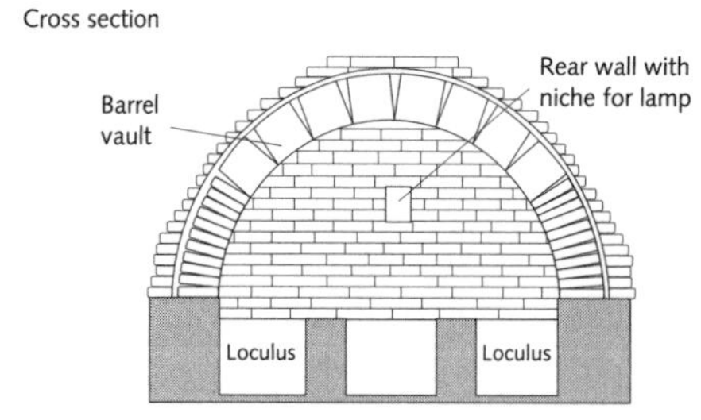

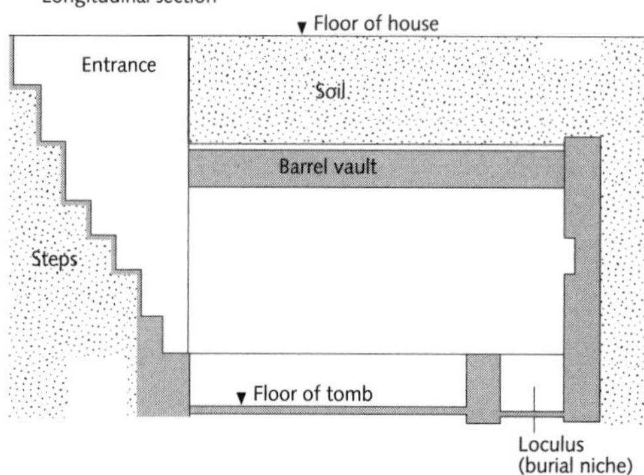

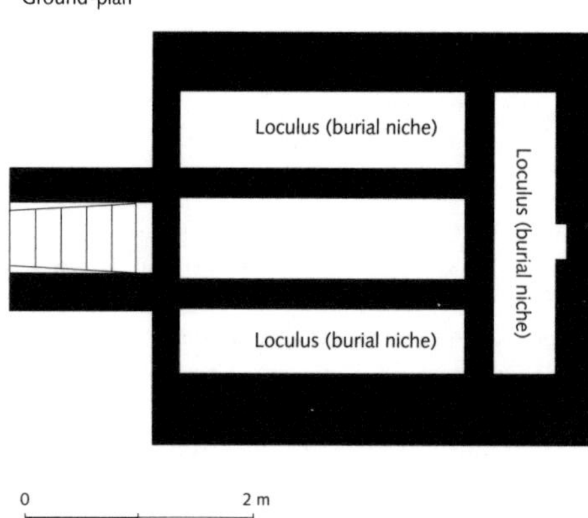

Underground brick-built tomb with barrel vault. Near Ctesiphon (2nd cent. AD).

the FA in Mesopotamia generally consists of brick underground structures. We must therefore distinguish between a) buildings above ground, b) structures carved horizontally into cliffs, and c) underground FA.

a) In the area of today's western Turkey (Yorgan), the northern Caucasus, and Bahrein (here, we find more than 150,000 tumuli dating from as late as the 2nd cent. AD), the building of tumuli (Russian Kurgans) goes back to the 3rd millennium BC. Compared to the numerous Kurgans in the northern Caucasus (→ Scythes) and the Middle East (for important burials of primarily the 2nd half of the 1st millennium BC), only few examples can be found in the Near East, in particular the tumulus necropoleis in Phrygia and Lydia. The tomb chambers of the Phrygian tumuli, which probably include King Midas' tomb (near → Gordium, Tumulus MM, *c.* 700 BC [1]), are made of wood, while stone graves with separate entrances are the dominant form in western Anatolia (e.g. Sardes, Bintepe). In addition to the tumuli, cliff side tombs with temple façades also appear in Anatolia since archaic times (esp. in Phrygia, Pontus/Paphlagonia, Lycia); → Antiochus [16] I of Commagene ordered the piling up of a hill for himself on the Nemrut Dağı in the 1st cent. BC. Unlike his successors, → Cyrus II chose the form of a house with a saddle roof on a base with six sets of steps for his grave in → Pasargadae (see fig.) [2. 24ff., 302f.]. Burial towers for families or clans such as those in → Palmyra and → Hatra are a typical form for northern Mesopotamia in the 1st to the early 2nd cents. [3] (see fig.). In Palmyra, they are replaced by temple architecture in the 2nd and 3rd cents. [4. 214–216].

b) Monumental cliff side tombs are common for the 1st millennium BC in Urartu, and still in the Sassanid period along the edge of the Zagros and in the Persis [5]. The façades of FA for Achaemenid kings in → Naqš-e Rostam and → Persepolis are more than 18 m wide and decorated with reliefs [6]. The fronts of the more than 600 cliff side tombs in → Petra (see fig.) and in Madāʾin Ṣāliḥ (Arabia) from the 1st cent. BC are designed in the style of temple or house façades.

c) In South Mesopotamia and Elam in the 3rd and 2nd millennia BC, underground FA was built of bricks (→ Ur; → Mari, 2nd millennium: → Uruk; Haft-tepe), occasionally with additional above-ground structures. Stone sarcophagi in brick FA below the palace served as burial places for the New Assyrian royal families in → Assur and Nimrud. Brick FA was also used by wealthy Assyrians since the 2nd millennium [7. 95–181]. These types of FA were widespread in Mesopotamia during the period of the Arsacides [8] (*c.* 250 BC to AD 224), but were replaced to the north by tombs in cliff side chambers, which – within the area of Roman influence – were at times painted over.

→ Gordium; → Tumulus

1 R.S. Young, Three Great Tumuli, 1981 2 D. Stronach, Pasargadae, 1978 3 S.R. Hauser, Hatra und das Königsreich der Araber, in: J. Wiesehöfer (ed.), Das Partherreich und seine Zeugnisse (Historia Einzelschriften), 1998 4 A. Schmidt-Colinet, Palmyren. Grabarchitektur, in: Palmyra, Kat. Linz, 1987 5 D. Huff, Zum Problem zoroastrischer Grabanlagen in Fars, in: AMI N.F. 21, 1988, 145–188 6 E.F. Schmidt, Persepolis III, 1970 7 A. von Haller, Die Gräber und Grüfte von Assur, 1954 8 S.R. Hauser, Eine arsakidenzeitliche Nekropole in Ktesiphon, in: BaM 24, 1993, 325–420.

S.HA.

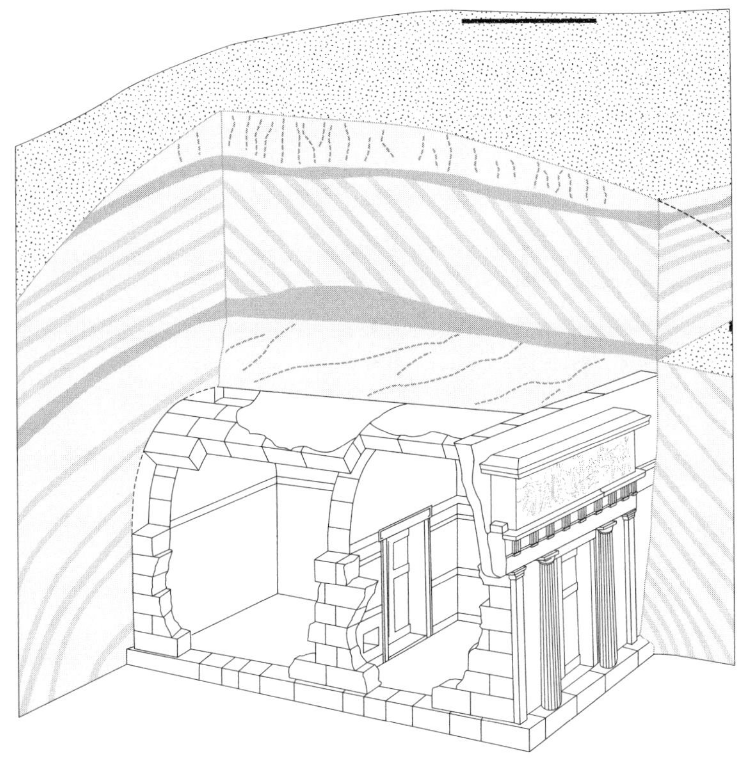

Vergina, so-called Tomb of Philip, burial chamber with vestibule and tumulus (4th-3rd cents. BC), reconstruction.

III. CLASSICAL ANTIQUITY AND NEIGHBOURING CULTURES
A. PHOENICIAN-PUNIC B. GREEK
1. CRETAN-MYCENAEAN 2. EARLY GREEK AND ARCHAIC 3. CLASSICAL 4. HELLENISTIC C. ITALIC
1. ETRUSCAN 2. ROME 2.1 TUMULUS AND EMPEROR'S TOMB 2.2 TOWER AND COLUMN MONUMENTS; RECEPTION OF THE 'MAUSOLEUM'
2.3 HOUSE-SHAPED FUNERARY ARCHITECTURE AND TEMPIETTO TOMBS 2.4 CENTRAL-PLAN FUNERARY ARCHITECTURE 2.5 SPECIAL FORMS
D. NORTHERN AFRICA AND THE WESTERN PROVINCES E. PALESTINE AND ISRAEL F. BEGINNINGS OF CHRISTIAN FUNERARY ARCHITECTURE
G. CELTIC-GERMANIC

A. PHOENICIAN-PUNIC

Phoenician-Punic culture did not develop a monumental FA of independent typology. There are, however, various types of tombs, such as Fossa graves and stone box graves for body burials, Pozzo graves for cremations, and furthermore, smaller and larger chamber tombs which were more or less artlessly lowered into the earth or into the bedrock. FA above ground – as structural architecture – is rare and appears rather late: The up to 10 m high tower tombs of Amrit (Greek → Marathus) known by the name of *meghazil* from the Persian period (6th–4th cents. BC) belong to a general Oriental-Egyptian typology [1]. Similarly, the monumental free-standing stone sarcophagus on a high base near Tyrus, falsely called 'Qabr Hiram' (Grave of Hiram) in the vernacular, can only be understood from the basis of the model presented in the monumental tombs of Cyrus II in → Pasargadae (see fig.).

Characteristic for the more extravagant FA of the archaic cents. are the carefully constructed underground chamber tombs with access by means of a shaft, a ramp, or stairs (Dromos), which at times are crowned by funerary tumuli (e.g. apparently in Trayamar, province of Málaga). They are esp. well documented in the west (Carthage, Sardinia, Andalusia), while in the east, the evidence appears in a broad spectrum of types (e.g. Sidon, Tambourit, Tyrus). Furthermore, they are evidenced indirectly in many fruitful adoptive forms (necropolis of → Salamis/Cyprus, Tamassus, etc.). This tradition remains alive in the west up into the 4th and 3rd cents. BC (e.g. Villaricos, province of Almería).

The range of influence of Phoenician-Punic tomb types is particularly obvious in Northern Africa, where the royal Numidic architecture has adopted the tower tomb as well as the tumulus tomb (e.g. Dougga, tower tomb of Atban; Batna, tumulus tomb 'Medracen'). A tower tomb is also documented in the → grave paintings of Tunesia (Djebel Mlezza).

→ Necropoleis, Thugga

1 A. HERMANN, Porphyra und Pyramide, in: JbAC 7, 1964, 117–138.

H. BENICHOU-SAFAR, Les tombes puniques de Carthage, 1982; E. DÍES CUSÍ, Architecture funéraire, in: V. KRINGS (ed.), La civilisation phénicienne et punique. Manuel de recherche (HbdOr I 20), 1995, 411–425; C. DOUMET,

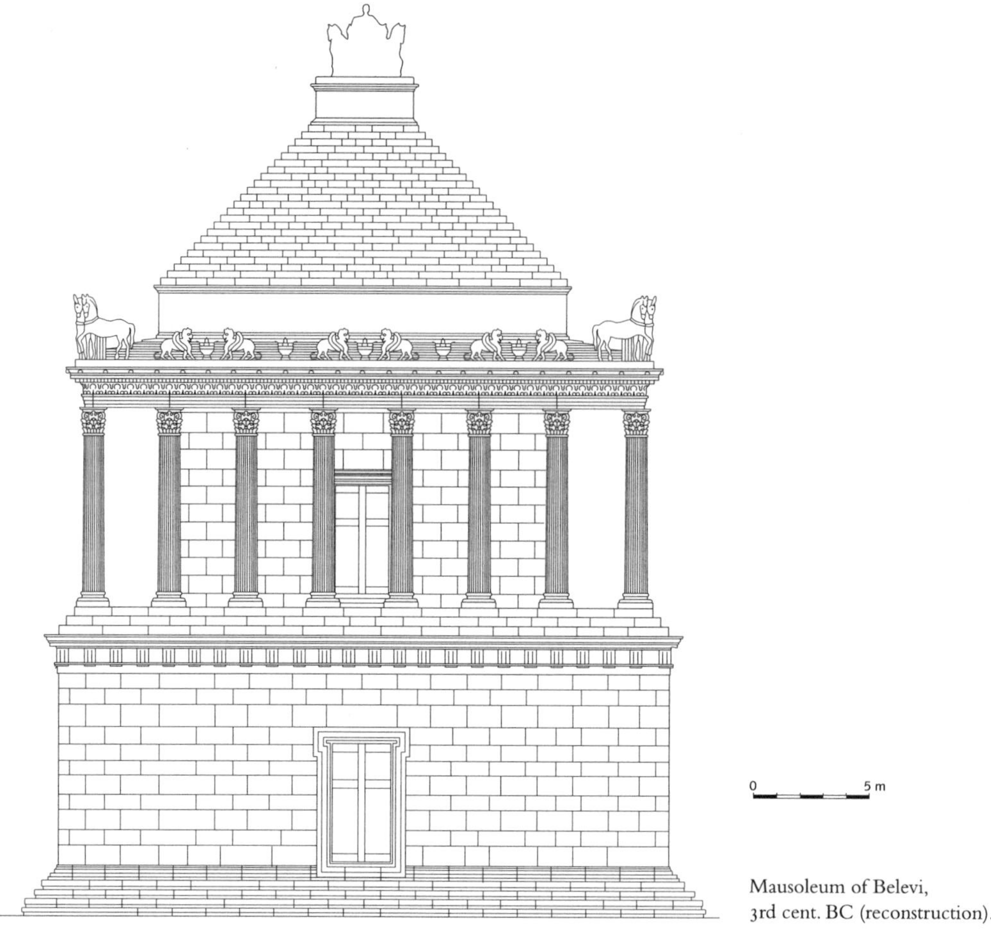

Mausoleum of Belevi, 3rd cent. BC (reconstruction).

H. Benichou-Safar, s.v. tombes, DCPP, 457–461; A. Tejera Gaspar, Las tumbas fenicias y púnicas del Mediterraneo Occidental, 1979. H.-G.N.

B. Greek

1. Cretan-Mycenaean

In the Cretan-Mycenaean cultural region, funerary architectonic installations can be found primarily below ground. In the Minoan regions, they were usually built in a rectangle and were integrated into palace architecture (cf. the two-storey temple tomb of Isopata near Cnossus). The leading form on the Greek mainland is the imperial cupola tomb with stone-enclosed Dromos (access) and false vaults in combination with the covering of the plate rings (e.g. treasure house of Atreus in Mycenae); → Vaults and arches, construction of.

2. Early Greek and Archaic

In the geometric period in Greece, earth piles were the dominant form, with mounds (→ Tumulus) reaching a diameter of 4–10 m and a height of *c.* 1,50 m. In Attica, the first FA was commonly box-shaped, rarely exceeding the body size of the deceased in its dimensions (Athens, Agora and Ceramicus). Mound and box/bank were conserved through a plaster covering; as the development progressed, clay bricks were used as well (Athens, Ceramicus). A change of the tumulus into a shape more suitable for stone can be found in the cylindrical FA of Menecrates on Korfu and in the tumulus in Vourva/Attica. In the course of the 7th cent. BC, the tumulus tombs greatly increased in size, at times causing a shortage of space in the necropoleis. Complete chambers below the tumuli can be found, for instance, in Ephesus and Olynthus; on Tenos we find a rectangular, roofed burial room with a cult room, probably intended for chthonic deities. Hero tombs usually show a sacred area that is strictly separated from the outside (Pelopium in Olympia; Neoptolemus district in Delphi; Aeacus-Temenos in the early Classical Theseium of Athens).

3. Classical

The burial mound survives as a venerable type of grave (e.g. tumulus of those fallen at Marathon, Soros 490 BC); one variant thereof is a mound with the addition of a tomb relief. Since the high classical period, we can detect a trend towards monumental FA in the increased use of stone. There are burial gifts of vessels, also figures of guardians and pillars. Until the end of the

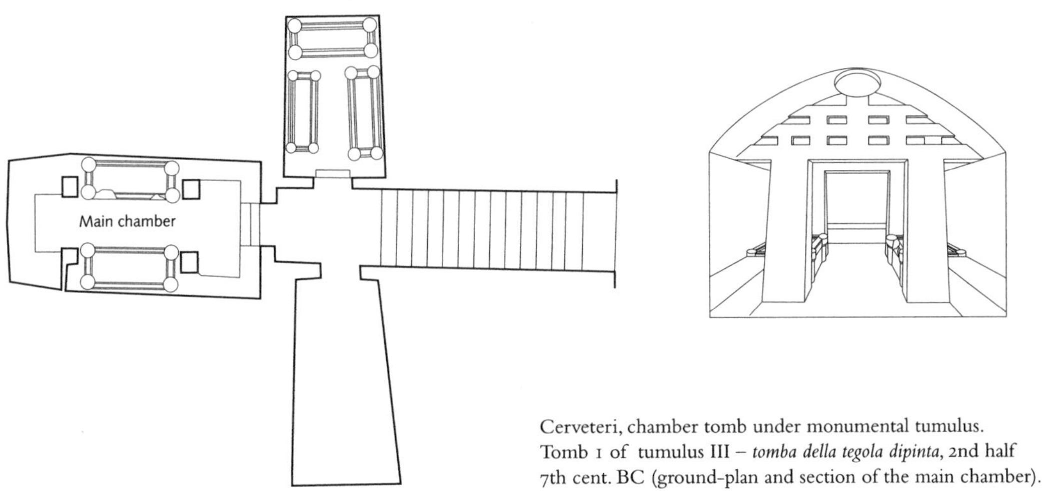

Cerveteri, chamber tomb under monumental tumulus. Tomb 1 of tumulus III – *tomba della tegola dipinta*, 2nd half 7th cent. BC (ground-plan and section of the main chamber).

late classical period (*c.* 300 BC), burials are primarily characterized by tables and boxes. Plato advises that citizens of outstanding merit should be buried in an underground 'polyandrion' (an oblong vault as communal grave, Leg. 12,4,947d). The special burial forms in Lycian Asia Minor determined the style for the ancient world: elevated burials (probably derived from Persias) in the form of a house, a sarcophagus, or a pillar with an elevated burial chamber (e.g., the early classical 'Harpies monument' with reliefs on the exterior sides). The 'Nereids monument' from Xanthus (London, BM, late 5th cent. BC) combines the pillar with the temple, while the burial site, the cella, is marked by stone klinai; on the heroon of Limyra, the → caryatid figures replace the columns. At the mausoleum of Halicarnassus (→ Maussolleum), the burial took place above ground on the level of the base, which – crowned by a step pyramid – carried the king's quadriga in the type of the ruler as chariot driver. The notion that the tomb was the house of the dead also determined the late classical cliff side tombs as well as the first façade or chamber tombs in Macedon in the late 4th cent. BC, which were first designed as large box tombs (Aeane, Vergina), later as buildings with many rooms, vaulted by casks (Lefkadia, Vergina; in Thrace: Svestari), at times also as a cupola with dromos (in Thrace, for instance, the tomb chamber of Kazanlak).

4. HELLENISTIC

Hellenistic FA reveals the continued influence of the forms developed in the classical period – thus we can find the mausoleum of Halicarnassus in that of Belevi near Ephesus (3rd cent. BC; see fig.). However, we can observe a tendency towards simpler forms: the family monument of the Charmyleion in Cos still has a temple façade of considerable depth; but in the lion monument of Cnidus, the 'Tomb of Theron' in Agrigent, and in the Numidic tower and pillar mausolea (Dougga), the column arrangements are reduced to the application of reliefs in face architecture. Simultaneously, columbaria-like burial complexes emerge in the eastern Hellenistic metropoleis (Alexandria, Mustafa Pasha necropolis) and in Rhodos. In the west, we can also observe the adoption of certain elements of temple construction in FA (cf. for instance the numerous representations of → naïskoi for the statues of the dead on south Italian vase images); the connection of tomb and → temple is also apparent in the temple-like façades of the cliff side tombs of Petra/Jordan (see fig.). Overall, we can ascertain the continued existence of a block-shaped monument, which also serves the function of a tomb altar, and the older form of the *trápeza* (→ Altar). Hellenistic FA increases in size and extravagance; correspondingly, there is an increase in the symbolic and practical value of such installations for the purpose of cult and memorial festivals (cf. for instance the family tomb in Calydon, *c.*100 BC).

M. ANDRONIKOS, Vergina, the Royal Tombs and the Ancient City, 1984; J. BORCHARD, Die Bauskulptur des Heroons von Limyra, 1976, 108–117; H. COLVIN, Architecture and the After-life, 1991; P. COUPEL, Le monument des Néréides (Fouilles de Xanthos, vol. 3), 1969; P. DEMARGNE, Les piliers funéraires (Fouilles des Xanthos, vol. 1), 1958; E. DYGGVE, F. POULSEN, K. RHOMAIOS, Das Heroon von Kalydon, 1934; J. FEDAK, Monumental Tombs of the Hellenistic Age, 1990; M. FRASER, Rhodian Funerary Monuments, 1977; H. V. GALL, Die paphlagonischen Felsgräber, 1. Beih. MDAI(Ist), 1966; B. GOSSEL-RAECK, Makedonische Kammergräber, 1980; U. KNIGGE, Der Kerameikos von Athen, 1988; F. KRISCHEN, Löwenmonument und Maussolleion, in: MDAI(R) 59, 1944, 173–181; K. KÜBLER, Der att. Grabbau, in: MDAI 2, 1949, 1–22; D.C. KURTZ, J. BOARDMAN, Thanatos. Tod und Jenseits bei den Griechen, 1985; M. MANSEL, Die Grabbauten von Side, Pamphylien, in: AA 1959, 364–402; P. MARCONI, Agrigento, 1929, 124–127; S.G. MILLER, Macedonian Tombs, in: B. BARR-SHERRAR (ed.), Macedonia and Greece in Late Classical and Hellenistic Times, 1982, 153–171; M. MÜLLER, Grabmal und Politik in der Archaik, in: W. HOEPFNER, G. ZIMMER (ed.), Die griech. Polis. Architektur und Politik, 1993, 58–75; W. MÜLLER-WIENER, Griech. Bauwesen in der Ant., 1988, 179–184; R. PAGENSTECHER, Nekropolis. Unt. über Gestalt und Entwicklung der alexandrinischen Grabanlagen, 1919;

O. Pelon, Tholoi, tumuli et cercles funéraires, 1976; H. Philipp, Archa. Gräber in Ostionien, in: MDAI(Ist) 31, 1981, 149–166; C. Praschniker, M. Theuer, Das Mausoleum von Belevi, FiE 6, 1979; L. Schneider, Ch. Höcker, P. Zazoff, Zur thrak. Kunst im Frühell., in: AA 1985, 595–643; L. Shivkova, Das Grabmal von Kasanlak, 1973; R. Stupperich, Staatsbegräbnis und Privatgrabmal im klass. Athen, 1977; P. G. Themelis, Frühgriech. G., 1976; J. Zahle, Lyk. Felsgräber, in: JDAI 94, 1979, 245–346. H.K.-G.

C. Italic

1. Etruscan

FA receives a special significance in the context of the Etruscan cult of the dead. In the → Villanova period since 900 BC, we find evidence of cremation in biconical or house-shaped urns (so called Pozzo tombs), but after the middle of the 8th cent., body burial in long, rectangular graves in the ground (Fossa tombs) becomes the prevalent custom. Both types of graves are covered by small mounds – tumuli. The social distinction of the dead is, at first, less obvious in the FA than in the burial gifts. A special type (influenced by Sardinia?) are the small cupola tombs (→ Tholoi) in → Populonia.

In the so-called oriental phase (late 8th–7th cents.), we find a transition from individual to collective burials and from individual tombs to chamber tombs made of several rooms, which in northern Etruria are made from square stone blocks (Populonia, → Vetulonia, → Cortona [1], etc.) while in the volcanic south, the FA was chiselled into the soft tuff rock. The necropolis of Cerveteri (→ Caere) offers an outstandingly clear chronology of FA up into the 2nd cent. BC. In the beginning (7th cent.), we find tombs that are half lowered, half built (Tomba Regolini-Galassi).

The tumulus consists of a profiled base of stone (→ Krepis) and the mound made of piled up earth. The large family tumuli later received additional chamber tombs. The interior of the FA essentially reflects the development and in part the furnishings of the contemporary residential architecture: we find huts (Tomba della Capanna), long houses with middle support and hipped roof (Tomba dei Leoni dipinti), wide houses with three back rooms (Tomba degli Scudi e Sedie), and since the 6th cent., adaptations of early forms of the house type with → atrium, tablinum, and cubicula (Tomba della Ripa), which also appear after the 5th cent. in Vulci (Tomba François) and in Perugia (tomb of the Volunmii). In the Tomba dei Rilievi in Cerveteri, which shows a vivid representation of household goods and weapons, the cubicula appear in the form of burial niches around the atrium.

In addition to the tumulus tomb, we also find the type of the cube tomb from as early as the 6th cent., characterized by a straight front and sides, oversized false door and rich elevation in the finish of the 'cube' (→ Blera, San Giuliano). The platform of the cube (with stone cippi) is accessible by stairs for the performance of cult activities.

In the so-called cliff side tomb necropoleis with cañon-like tuff ravines in the hinterland of Tarquinia and Vulci, the cube tombs gave rise to the development of new types of tombs in the 4th–2nd cents., which in form and detail could resemble either a temple (→ Sovana: Tomba Ildebranda) or the exterior of houses or palaces (→ Norchia, → Castel d'Asso), while the tomb chambers themselves were not decorated and only served for holding the sarcophagi and urns. Burials in Etruscan tombs can be documented into the early Imperial period.

G. Colonna, Architettura e urbanistica, in: G. Pugliese Carratelli (ed.), Rasenna. Storia e civiltà degli Etruschi, 1986, 371–532; A. Naso, Architetture dipinte. Decorazioni parietali non figurate nelle tombe a camera dell'Etruria Meridionale (VII–V sec. a. C.), 1996; J. P. Oleson, The Sources of Innovation in Later Etruscan Tomb Design (ca. 350–100 BC), 1982; F. Prayon, Frühetr. Grab- und Hausarchitektur, 1975. A.NA. and F.PR.

2. Rome

2.1 Tumulus and emperor's tomb

The oldest extant FA in Rome, the tomb of the Scipios on the *via Appia* (3rd cent. BC) refers to models from the Greek-Hellenistic period with its two storeys, figure paintings, and its arrangement of columns on the upper level. Furthermore, the basic forms of Etruscan FA show a continuity from the end of the Republic until the middle of the Imperial period (e.g. the tumulus of Sulla on the Campus Martius) and were also common in the provinces. The stone cylinder often shows ornamental decoration and a conical mound, (planting, statues?). The FA of Caecilia [9] Metella on the *via Appia* in Rome received the addition of an angular podium. The Roman tombs of emperors diversified the tumulus form. The stone FA of Augustus has two storeys and has niches for urns in the interior; the central column held the emperor's ashes. At the top of the mound, which was planted with black poplars, stood the statue of the emperor. The entrance was framed by obelisks, which refers back to the *Sēma* of Alexandria. The FA of Hadrianis (today's Castel S. Angelo) shows a marble cylinder within a quadratic podium, with access to the elevated tomb chamber. On it was the mound with Quadriga and emperor's statue.

2.2 Tower and column monuments; reception of the 'mausoleum'

Reminiscent of the mausoleum (→ Maussolleum) of Halicarnassus is the Roman tradition of column monuments in Italy and in the provinces – a cube with reliefs and an upper column front, similar to, for instance, the tombs in Aquileia, the tomb of Aefionius Rufus in Sarsina (see fig.), or of Lucius Poblicius in Cologne (with a curved roof pyramid and crowning pine cones). This is the model from which the type of the actual column tomb had been derived (FA of Igel on the Moselle). For private burials, FA modelled after the mausoleum of Halicarnassus was used, or else a FA in which the upper

Pillar monument with columned front above. Funerary monument of Aefonius Rufus in Sarsina (1st cent. BC).

storey was reduced to a column-bearing baldachin without → cella (cf. the three-storey FA of Saint Remy and the rectangular tempietto of Mylasa); an octagonal column arrangement above a square base is extant in Ephesus, so is an enclosed lantern at 'La Conocchia'

near S. Maria Capua Vetere. A link between monuments of burial and of honour can be found in the architectonically structured, two-storey Philopappus monument set on a levelling base in Athens, which has a decorated façade that opens out. The many variations in the typology of these architectures allow each builder the individual conception of his monument distinct from the existing buildings of a → necropolis, and thus the creation of a long-lasting *memoria* corresponding to his rank and his mental and social entitlement.

2.3 House-shaped funerary architecture and tempietto tombs

In the Roman period, both types can be found often and in many variations, illustrating the ambition for private deification. The 'rows of houses' of the necropoleis such as those below S. Sebastiano, S. Pietro, or on the Isola Sacra in Rome have house façades and are family tombs with boxes of ashes; later on, arcosolium tombs or sarcophagi were occasionally added. Often, we find a second underground level. Tombs with niches for urns have → loculi that identify them as columbaria. House tombs that occasionally have a second upper storey can be found not only in the city of Rome but in the provinces as well. These densely occupied rows of house tombs in the vicinity of the city gates on the major arterial roads give way to the FA of individual tombs in the periphery (Rome, Via Latina, → Necropoleis).

The *a tempietto* type develops particularly in the mid and late Imperial period, a good example in Rome is the so-called Deus Rediculus (see fig.) with podium and a superstructure including a prostyle column arrangement (mid–2nd cent. AD). The distinction between house and tempietto architecture is not clear and varies from landscape to landscape. Formally, it refers to the hero tombs of the early period with its cultic presence, and it is understood as *domus aeterna* ('eternal residence'). This type is difficult to distinguish from other forms of architectonic representation, also from the multilevel buildings with circular elements, which in literature are referred to as *templum*.

2.4 Central-plan funerary architecture

Since the mid Imperial period, we can observe a heightened development of the tempietto tomb into a central-plan building with → dome. An analogy to this is not the tumulus but the greater importance placed on the interior with a representative central cupola. The circular or polygonal mausolea are central-plan buildings with interiors organised into niches. Their precursors can be found in the architecture of the → palace and of → thermal baths; a similarity to the residential realm is maintained even in the most important representatives of the group (FA of Maxentius on the *via Appia*, the octagonal FA of Diocletian in Spalatum, the Galerius mausoleum in Thessalonica, the FA in Milan, the FA of Theoderic in Ravenna).

2.5 Special forms

Special forms of FA are either those with → exedra, or architectonically designed monumental tomb altars or tops of column. Completely unique is Trajan's FA

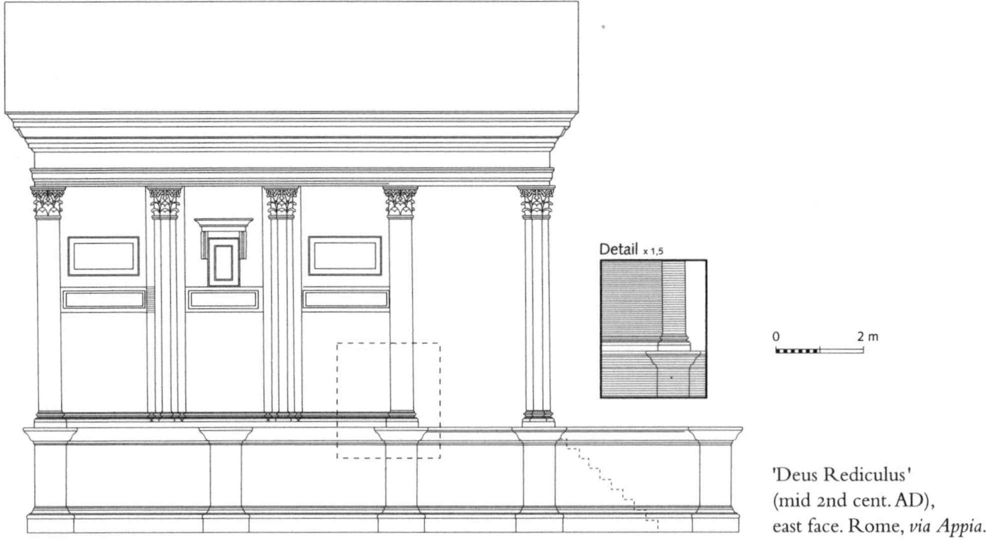

'Deus Rediculus' (mid 2nd cent. AD), east face. Rome, *via Appia*.

consisting of a column with a tomb chamber in the podium, also the *panarium* of Eurysaces, and the pyramid tomb of C. Cestius [I 4], or conical FA.

J.N. Andrikopoulou-Struck, G. des 1. Jh. n.Chr. im Rheingebiet, BJ 43. Beih., 1986; M. Eisner, Zur Typologie der G. im Suburbium Roms, MDAI(R) 26. Ergh., 1986; R. Fellmann, Das Grab des Lucius Munatius Plancus bei Gaeta, 1957; A. De Franciscis, R. Pane, Mausolei romani in Campania, 1957; H. v. Hesberg, Röm. Grabbauten, 1992; H. Gabelmann, Röm. Grabbauten der frühen Kaiserzeit, 1979; H. v. Hesberg, P. Zanker (ed.), Röm. Gräberstraßen. Selbstdarstellung, Status, Standard, Kongr. München 1987; H. Kammerer-Grothaus, Der Deus Rediculus im Triopion des Herodes Atticus ..., in: MDAI(R) 81, 1974, 162–199; V. Kockel, Die Grabbauten vor dem Herkulaner Tor in Pompeji, 1983; A. Machatschek, Die Nekropolen und Grabdenkmäler von Elaiussa Sebaste und Korykos im Rauhen Kilikien, 1967; J.C. Reeder, Typology and Ideology in the Mausoleum of Augustus. Tumulus and Tholos, in: Classical Antiquity 11, 1992, 265–307; L. Reekmans, Spätröm. Hypogea, in: FS für F.W. Deichmann vol. 2, 1986, 11–37; A. Pellegrino, Zu den antiken Gräberstraßen unter S. Sebastiano an der Via Appia Antica, in: MDAI(R) 85, 115–138; Id., Camere sepolcrali dei liberti e liberte di Livia Augusta ed altri Caesari, in: MelArchHist 91, 1979/1, 315–342; Id., Le Necropoli pagane di Ostia e Porto, 1984; J.C. Richard, Mausoleum. D'Halikarnasse à Rome, puis à Alexandrie, in: Latomus 29, 1970, 370–388; J.M. C. Toynbee, Death and Burial in the Roman World, 1971; Travlos, Athen, 462–465; G. Waurick, Untersuchung zur Lage der römischen Kaisergräber in der Zeit von Augustus bis Constantin, in: JRGZ 20, 1973, 107–146; A. Wigg, Grabhügel des 2. und 3. Jh. n.Chr. an Mittelrhein, Mosel und Saar, 1993; H. Wrede, Das Mausoleum der Claudia Semna und die bürgerliche Plastik der Kaiserzeit, in: MDAI(R) 78, 1971, 125–166.

D. Northern Africa and the western provinces

The Hellenistic-Roman metropoleis such as Alexandria are home to the distinctive underground burial complexes with → loculi corridors. Otherwise, high-ranking persons follow the models of FA used in the Hellenistic world (circular buildings such as medracens or the 'Tombeau de la Chrétienne' at Tipasa). Egyptian style architectural details evoke a conceptual connection to the Ptolemaic *Sēma* in Alexandria. Furthermore, there are Punic, Hellenistic, and Roman tower tombs with terraces, a base, and a pyramid roof. A → tumulus with a tall stone cylinder is the FA of the Lolli (Cirta, Algeria); also, we find → aedicula types (cf. Timgad), baldachins (Syria), octagonal forms, and other Italic and provincial FA.

M. Bouchenaki, Le mausolée royal de la Maurétanie, 1970; F. Coarelli, Y. Thébet, Architecture funéraire et pouvoir. Réflexions sur l'hellénisme numide, in: MEFRA 100, 1988, 761–818; F. Rakob, Numidische Königsarchitektur in Nordafrika, in: Die Numider, exhibition catalogue Bonn, 1979.

E. Palestine and Israel

The guiding model here is the underground FA or the cave, also cliff side tombs with an occasional façade showing architectonical structure. The free-standing monuments in the Kidron Valley/Jerusalem are carved from the adjacent rocks and do not have their own burial room. The so-called tombs of Zacharias and Absalom show a mixed style of Greek forms and Egyptian decorative elements. A type of mausoleum with surface columns on the base or real columns on the second level can be found in the Syrian region; it survives into late antiquity. The same is true for the Nabataean cliff façades in Petra of oriental-Egyptian influence (noticeable in the small obelisks and merlons), or the Graeco-Roman FA in Palmyra. There, we find tower tombs with hypogaeum (cf. Dura-Europus) as well as temple tombs.

M. GAWLIKOWSKI, Monuments funéraires de Palmyre, 1970, 18–30; J. MCKANZIE, The Architecture of Petra, 1990; J. BROWNING, Petra, 1974.

F. Beginnings of Christian funerary architecture

The alternation between cremation, sarcophagus burial and interment in the Roman empire and the corresponding uses of FA has not yet been sufficiently explained, neither have the beginnings of Christian burial sites in Rome. We know, however, that Callistus was entrusted with the administration of the first documented Christian community cemetery at the beginning of the 3rd cent. AD. It is probable that the Christians were somewhat tolerant of pagan installations, since sarcophagus burials of both Romans and Christians took place *sub divo* ('in open air'). We must assume the existence of a lengthy parallel development; → Catacombs; → Christianity [B II].

Bibliogr. → Catacombs. H.K.-G.

G. Celtic-Germanic

The FA of the Celts in central Europe does not show as many variations as that of the classical cultures; furthermore, its significance undergoes a change in the course of the cents. up to the birth of Christ. At first, the burial mound is the common form; in the late → Hallstatt and early → La Tène cultures (6th–4th cents. BC), they reach a monumental size (→ Princes, tombs and residences of). The deceased are buried in extravagantly built (wood) chambers, which are often covered by a thick layer of stones (to prevent grave robbery?). The mounds are usually made of piled up earth and are occasionally surrounded by ditches (e.g. → Glauberg) or by low stone walls (e.g.→ Hirschlanden). In several cases, close to the mounds stone steles were found, which sometimes represent Celtic warriors (Glauberg and Hirschlanden) and which originally stood on the mounds. In a few cases, there is evidence of further additions in the form of 'ramps' (→ Hochdorf), or 'processional roads' (Glauberg). 'Normal' entombment also took place primarily below mounds, which were somewhat simpler. Among the early Celts, the dead obviously distinguished themselves mainly through their FA, whose size, extravagance, location etc. corresponded to the social status of the dead. No other forms of FA have been documented in → Celtic archaeology.

In the course of the La Tène period (since the 4th cent. BC), the custom of burial below visible mounds is gradually lost, and the flat tomb on level ground becomes prevalent. However, the custom of smaller burial mounds continues in the form of smaller tomb enclosures such as square ditches or embankments ('grave gardens') esp. in the peripheral regions (→ Arras Culture) until the late Celtic period (late 1st cent. BC). At the same time, the Roman provinces have burial mounds that follow the Italic tradition and other Roman FA.

In → Germanic archaeology, extravagant FA is unknown in the pre-Roman period (→ Jastorf Culture) as well as in the 'Free Germania' of the 1st–3rd cents. AD; neither does it appear in the royal tombs of the Lübsow and Haßleben/Leuna group. Archaeological finds indicate that the social status of the dead among the Germanic people was documented through burial gifts rather than through FA.

→ Burial; → Stele; → Tumulus

W. EBEL, Die röm. Grabhügel des 1. Jh. im Treverergebiet, 1989; A. HAFFNER, Gräber – Spiegel des Lebens, 1989; H. LORENZ, Totenbrauchtum und Tracht, in: BRGK 59, 1978, 1–380, esp. 33ff.; G. A. WAIT, Burial and Otherworld, in: M. GREEN (ed.), The Celtic World, 1995, 489–511. V.P.

Funerary clubs see → Associations

Funerary epigrams see → Epigram; → Inscriptions

Funerary inscriptions Funerary inscriptions (FI) (now probably approaching a number of 200,000, cf. [3. 124,1]) emerged in the context of the cult of the dead with the purpose of marking the grave of a specific person so that sacrifices for the dead could be performed at the correct place. Furthermore, they soon took on the function of keeping alive the memory of this person and his achievements. They are located above ground at the burial site, or, in communal graves, on the urn holding the ashes, on the sarcophagus, or on the lid of the *loculus* (the burial niche). In addition to the inscription itself, we often find decorations of a general nature (plants, cherubs, etc.) or representations of the deceased in his life's surroundings, occasionally showing an attempt at true portraiture.

At a relatively late point in time, since the 1st cent. BC in Rome and soon thereafter in the provinces, FI began to spread rapidly. At first, they only gave the name of the deceased, later we also see the age of death and, above all, information about the office held by the deceased. This is frequently followed by authorizations of other persons entitled to burial and a mention of the person that put up the inscription. At the end, we usually find a formulaic phrase such as *s(it) t(ibi) t(erra) l(evis)* ('may earth be light for you'). More detailed FI can take on the form of an → elogium. The combination of FI and the cult of the dead early on led to the development of the altar tomb, which in the Imperial period is often dedicated to the *D(is) M(anibus)*.

The phraseology of FI changed over time: at first, the style was rather plain, but in the 2nd and 3rd cents. AD, it is characterized by many superlatives, in late antiquity again returning to brevity. The question of what type of statistical conclusions, if any, can be drawn from FI regarding gender, age, family relations etc., is still contested, cf. most recently [1].

Early Christian FI can hardly be distinguished from non-Christian FI and are only recognizable in occasional additions of Christian symbols or phrases such as *in pace* ('in peace') or *in deo* ('in God'). From the 4th cent. on, we see the emergence of an independent Christian funerary epigraphy. On Greek FI, see → epigram I.

1 E.A. Meyer, Explaining the Epigraphic Habit in the Roman Empire, in: JRS 80, 1990, 74–96 2 Ch. Pietri, s.v. Grabinschriften II, RAC 12, 514–590 3 R. Saller, B. Shaw, Tombstones and Roman Family Relations in the Principate, in: JRS 74, 1984, 124–156. H.GA.

Funerary literature

I. Mesopotamia II. Hattusa III. Egypt

I. Mesopotamia

Funerary literature (FL), intended to assist the deceased in accomplishing the journey and achieving admission into the Underworld, is rarely found in Mesopotamian graves. A prayer (found in a grave from the Middle Elamite period, 2nd half of 2nd millennium BC [1]) has a deceased person calling on a divinity to lead him into the → Underworld. In contrast to the Egyptian Books of the Afterlife, Mesopotamian sources exist which adopt such knowledge for use in earthly contexts. It is evident from a text describing the voyage of → Urnammu into the Underworld, that it was known which gifts were to be presented to the respective divinities of the Underworld [2]. The other texts found in funerary contexts do not constitute FL in the sense defined above: these are inscriptions on sections of grave architecture or burial gifts giving biographical details as well as curse and blessing formulae. Clay tablets are also found; their subject matter is highly diverse [1] and only seldom includes clear reference to the deceased or to → death in general.

II. Ḫattusa

There is, as yet, no evidence for text finds in graves from the Hittite Empire. As in Mesopotamia, texts concerned with the transition to the → underworld are located in 'earthly life', and they are only attested in courtly contexts, e.g. various funeral rituals, which derive from traditions dating back at least to the Middle Hittite period (14th cent. BC). One lengthy text describes the fourteen-day funeral ritual for members of the royal family, whose purpose was to transform the deceased into a god (→ Deification). The ritual also guaranteed his material existence. Another ritual describes the path of the deceased: a dialogue between priests and the divinities of the Underworld seems to accompany the deceased on a journey in which he is led into the underworld by his mother. Sacrifices to the sun goddess of the underworld are said to enable the deceased to ascend into the heavens.

1 J. Bottéro, Les inscriptions cunéiformes funéraires, in: G. Gnoli et al. (ed.), La mort, les morts dans les sociétés anciennes, 1982, 373–406 2 S. Lundström, Wenn Du in die Unterwelt hinabsteigen willst ..., in: Th. Richter et al. (ed.), Kulturgeschichten. FS V. Haas, 2001, 245–253.
S.LU.

III. Egypt

A. Introduction and Sources B. Pyramid Texts C. Coffin Texts D. The Book of the Dead E. Cosmographical Texts F. Others

A. Introduction and Sources

Throughout Egyptian history, individual texts or bodies of writings, either monumentalized or recorded on papyrus, were often placed in the grave with the deceased [13]. Egyptology categorizes such cases as FL, which creates the false impression that these texts were expressly composed for funerary purposes, whereas in many cases, evidence (of variable clarity) suggests their origin in the world of the temple cult, and their later adaptation for a funerary purpose [17; 18]. The most important bodies of writings are the Pyramid Texts (= PT), the 'Coffin Texts' (= CT), the Book of the Dead (= BD), the Books of the Underworld and Sky, the 'Opening of the Mouth Ritual' and the 'Books of Breathings'; there are also minor works such as the 'Book of Traversing Eternity' [9], *Que mon nom fleurisse* [16] etc., and texts such as the 'Book of the Heavenly Cow' [12]. Furthermore, particularly in the Late Period (from 664 BC), various Osirian rituals were adapted for use as FL, sometimes even by means of subsequently entering the name of the deceased in original disused temple Mss. The particularly propitious conditions for preservation in graves make FL disproportionately well known, and it constitutes one of the most important sources for Egyptian religion. Many FL texts are illustrated; in cosmographical texts, illustrations even predominate.

B. Pyramid Texts

PT is the modern title for a collection of well over 700 utterances [6. 21], first attested in the → pyramid of Unas (5th Dynasty, 2367–2347 BC) (no single pyramid contains all utterances). These texts are found chiselled into the walls of the burial spaces in pyramids of the late Old Kingdom (*c.* 2367–2190 BC) and the first intermediate period (*c.* 2190–1990 BC); they are here reserved for kings and queens. From the Middle Kingdom (*c.* 1990–1630 BC) they appear on the sarcophagi of private individuals along with CT. No decisive clarification of the relationship between these two text types has yet been presented. The royal pyramids were again undecorated during the Middle Kingdom. Over subsequent epochs up to the Roman period, excerpts from the PT are constantly found in temple rituals, private funerary texts, etc. [1]. The decoration of some private Late Period graves follows very precisely the pyramids of the Old Kingdom. In the late Ptolemaic period, PT were even transcribed into demotic script [22]. These texts are the oldest religious sources in Egypt, with the longest demonstrable tradition. Moreover, criteria of language and content suggest the dating of their archetype to before the 5th Dynasty, possibly to the pre-dynastic period.

In terms of content, the texts are highly variable: sacrificial rituals are, for example, found alongside protective charms against serpents. While some utterances clearly belong in a common context, and were always handed down in the same utterance sequence [14], others derive from quite different origins. In the pyramid, their common purpose was to secure the ascension of the dead king into the heavens. The content of the utterances is almost entirely located in the world of the gods, although earthly matters shine through in the realm of funeral and sacrificial rites. Allusions to various aspects of the → Osiris myth form a significant element. The astral nature of the religion is especially prominent [15], in that Orion and → Sothis (Sirius) constantly appear. In contrast, the solar cult, later to become so important, is noticeably less pronounced here.

C. Coffin Texts

The CT comprise an inhomogeneous body of 1,185 utterances, found predominantly on (mostly private) sarcophagi of the Middle Kingdom [4; 5]. The modern title encompasses all such texts, with the exception of PT also found on these sarcophagi. The CT may, at least in part, be of equal antiquity to the PT; only the selection changed. In the CT, the solar religion gradually took the place of the astral cult. Utterance sequences are also found among the CT; these can sometimes be separated in individual books (e.g. the 'Book of Two Ways' [10]). A considerable number of utterances, probably the later ones, are inspired by precursors among the PT, or form editorial revisions of existing utterances. Like the PT, the CT were handed down over long periods, and experienced revivals, notably during the 26th Dynasty.

D. The Book of the Dead

The so-called BD (in Egyptian: 'Spells for Coming Forth By Day') developed during the Second Intermediate Period (*c.* 1630–1550 BC) [11; 19]. At first also a disparate collection of utterances, it acquired a canonical structure during the Late Period [23]. More than 190 utterances are known in total. Most of the texts represent developments of precursors among the CT; some solar hymns are also traditionally included. The best-known utterance is BD 125, which concerns the judgment of the dead. The BD was used for kings and, especially, private individuals.

E. Cosmographical Texts

The Books of the Underworld and Sky, attested predominantly in royal graves from the New Kingdom (*c.* 1550–1070 BC), and increasingly also in priestly graves from the Third Intermediate Period (*c.* 1070–664 BC), may be considerably older than the New Kingdom, originating in the solar cult (cosmographical texts [3]). They concern the voyage of the Sun through the Underworld or the sky goddess → Nut, the 'Book of Nut' also dealing with the course of the stars and the Moon. Some of the texts are subdivided into the hours of the day. The most important identified Books of the Underworld are: *Amduat* ('That Which Is in the Underworld'), 'the Book of Gates', 'the Book of Caverns', 'the Book of the Earth'. The Books of the Sky are: 'the Book of the Day' and 'the Book of the Night'.

F. Others

The 'Opening of the Mouth Ritual' ([20], Original title) was originally a ritual of craftsmanship performed during the manufacture of a statue [7]. However, its animating function was also found especially suitable for → mummies, as well as for cultic equipment and buildings. The First and Second 'Books of Breathings' ([8], Original title) increasingly came in the final phase of Egyptian religion to supplement and replace the BD. They were said to have been composed by gods to inspire the deceased with breath.

→ Burial (B.); → Religion (III.)

1 T. G. Allen, Occurences of Pyramid Texts with Cross Indexes of These and Other Egyptian Mortuary Texts, 1950 2 H. Altenmüller, Texte zum Begräbnisritual in den Pyramiden des AR, 1972 3 J. Assmann, Der König als Sonnenpriester, 1970, 56 f. 4 P. Barguet, Les textes des sarcophages égyptiens du Moyen Empire, 1986 5 A. de Buck (ed.), The Egyptian CT, 1935–1961 6 R. O. Faulkner, The Ancient Egyptian Pyramid Texts, 1969 7 H.-W. Fischer-Elfert, Die Vision von der Statue im Stein, 1998 8 J.-C. Goyon, Rituels funéraires de l'ancienne Égypte, 1972, 183–317 9 F.-R. Herbin, Le livre de parcourir l'éternité, 1994 10 E. Hermsen, Die zwei Wege des Jenseits, 1992 11 E. Hornung, Das Totenbuch der Ägypter, 1979 12 Id., Der äg. Mythos von der Himmelskuh, [2]1991 13 Id., Altäg. Jenseitsbücher, 1997 14 J. Kahl, Steh auf, gib Horus deine Hand, 1996 15 R. Krauss, Astronomische Konzepte und Jenseitsvorstellungen in den PT, 1997 16 J. Lieblein, Le livre égyptien Que mon nom fleurisse, 1895 17 A. von Lieven, Book of the Dead, Book of the Living, in: S. Seidlmayer (ed.), Rel. in Context, 2002 18 Id., Mysterien des Kosmos. Kosmographie und Priesterwissenschaft, in: J. Assmann et al. (ed.), Äg. Mysterien?, 2000 19 E. Naville, Das äg. Todtenbuch der XVIII. bis XX. Dyn., 2 vols., 1886 (repr. 1971) 20 E. Otto, Das äg. Mundöffnungsritual, 1960 21 K. Sethe (ed.), Die altäg. PT, 4 vols., 1908–1922 (repr. 1960–1987) 22 M. Smith, New Middle Egyptian Texts in the Demotic Script, in: Sesto Congresso Internazionale di Egittologia, vol. 2, 1993, 492 f. 23 U. Verhoeven, Das saitische Totenbuch der Iahtesnacht, 3 vols., 1993.

A.v.L.

IV. Classical Antiquity

see Underworld; → Dialogues of the Dead

Funerary oration see → Epitaphios [2]; → Laudatio funebris

Funisulana Vettula Wife of Tettius Africanus, *praefectus Aegypti* in the year AD 82; probably the sister or the daughter of Funisulanus Vettonianus. PIR[2] F 571. W.E.

Funisulanus L.F.Vettonianus. Originally probably from Caesaraugusta in Spain. Was accepted into the Senate under Claudius; after the offices of quaestor, tribune of the people, and praetor, he became legate of the *legio IV Scythica* in Syria and Armenia in the year AD 62 (Tac. Ann. 15,7,1). Joined Vespasianus; in 78, he was appointed to the office of (among others) *praefectus aerarii Saturni* before becoming *cos. suff.* In the following, he became consular legate of Dalmatia (*c.* 79–82), Pannonia (82–86), and of the newly organized province of Moesia superior (86–88), from where he participated in the war against the Dacians; for this, he received the *dona militaria*. Proconsul of Africa *c.* 90/1. His tomb was erected on the *via Latina* (AE 1913, 224 = 1992, 238). On CIL XI 571 cf. AE 1992, 602.

W. Eck, in: Chiron 12, 1982, 302ff.; Thomasson, Fasti Africani, 47f.; Caballos, Senadores I, 146ff.; PIR² F 570. W.E.

Funus imaginarium Funus imaginarium (FI) was the name given in Rome (ILS 7212 II 4–5, dated AD 136; SHA Pert. 15,1) to a special type of → burial: since the dead body was usually visible on the bier during the funeral procession, a replacement body made of → wax (*imago* or *effigies*) was used when the body was not available, for instance in cases of death at sea or after cremation at war or in foreign countries. Tac. Ann. 3,5,2 correctly regards this custom as one of the 'customs of old time' (*veterum instituta*; taken for granted already in the Lex XII tab. 10,5: [1. 80]). The FI received special significance in the burials of emperors and their relatives; usually, the custom was connected to the ritual of apotheosis, which made the cremation of the body necessary. If the real body could not be burnt in Rome because interment was preferred (first mentioned in Tac. Ann. 16,6,2 for → Poppaea Sabina), or following death abroad (e.g. → Septimius Severus), the state burial was staged as a FI (description in Cass. Dio 74,4–5 and Hdn. 4,2).

1 H. Chantraine, "Doppelbestattungen" röm. Kaiser, in: Historia 29, 1980, 71–85. W.K.

Funus publicum (in the Imperial period also called *funus censorium*, Tac. Ann. 4,15,2 and passim) refers to a → burial whose costs and organization was covered by the state or the community, to honour the deceased.

1. Rome

In early times, foreign delegates (Plut. Quaest. Rom. 43) as well as royalty imprisoned by Rome (→ Syphax; → Perseus, cf. Val. Max. 5,1,1) were buried *publice* ('at public expense'). The funus publicum (FP) which became typical of prominent citizens probably did not emerge until the late Republic (certain documentation exists for L. → Sulla: App. B Civ. 1,493). It was held by order of the Senate (the exact wording in Cic. Phil. 9,16f.) and was similar to the traditional burial of the nobility; in general, it was even more extravagant than the traditional burial, with the role of the family (for instance, transporting the body; → *laudatio funebris*) taken on by state representatives [1. 337–339]. In the Imperial period, not only the emperors and their relatives but also deserving *privati* often received a FP (Cass. Dio 54,12,2; 58,19,5). In the course of time, the close connection between FP and apotheosis suggested that the FP be limited to the members of the emperor's house (often women as well) [2. 35–36]; the last known FP for a *privatus* was for L. → Licinius Sura (*c.* AD 110: Cass. Dio 68,15,3²).

2. Municipalities

At least since the Augustan period, many cities (esp. in Italy and Spain) staged FP – probably following the example of Rome – to honour local dignitaries, often their wives and children as well (inscriptional documents: [2. 125–211]). Often, the families were content with the decision of the decuriones (→ *decurio*) to honour their dead relative and did not insist on a public contribution to the costs.

1 F. Vollmer, De funere publico Romanorum, in: Jbb. für klass. Philol. Suppl. 19, 1893, 319–364 2 G. Wesch-Klein, F. p., 1993. W.K.

Furfanius Postumus, T. In 52 BC, judge in the case against Annius [I 14] Milo (Cic. Mil. 75) regarding the murder of → Clodius [I 4]. Praetor perhaps already in 55 or earlier ([1. 268f.]; MRR 2,295: 46 [?]), promagistrate in Sicily 50–49, proconsul there as well in 45 (MRR 3,96).

1 G. V. Sumner, The lex annalis under Caesar, in: Phoenix 25, 1971, 246–271. W.W.

Furfo *Vicus* of the Vestini (*regio IV*) on the upper reaches of the Aternus (Pescara), in the territorium of Peltuinum (CIL IX 3524), and near the church of Santa Maria di Furfona, 15 km south-east of L'Aquila; administered by two *aediles*. Cult of Jupiter Liber (58 BC; CIL I², 756). Located on the road between Prifernum and Peltuinum, later named *via Claudia Nova*. Inscriptions: CIL IX p. 333, 3513–3568.

Nissen 2, 442; Ruggiero 3, 1922, 353, s.v. F. G.U.

Furiae Ancient authors connect the F. etymologically with *furere* ('to rave', 'to rage'), *furia* ('fury', 'anger') and thereby equate them, as do Cicero (Nat. D. 3,46) and later authors, with the Eumenides/→ Erinys, but also, following the example set by Virgil (Aen. 3,252) and others, with the → Harpyies. Less importantly, the F. are regarded as the Latin translation of → *maníai*, which refers to the epiclesis of the Erinys (Paus. 8,34,1). The identification of the F. with the old Italic goddess → Furrina is contested. Dirae ('the horrific ones') is another designation for the F. (Serv. Aen. 4,609; 12,846). Acheron, Aether, or Pluto, and Nox or Terra are seen as the parents, the Underworld as the home of the F.; the derivation of the name of *furvus*, 'black', also indicates a chthonic quality (Paul. Fest. 74,11 L.).

Starting with Euripides (Or. 408; 1650; Tro. 457), the F. commonly appear as a trinity (Allecto/Alecto, Megaera, Tisiphone). The Etruscan, Greek, and Italian concepts of the F.'s appearance vary: they are depicted with snakes as top hair or as creatures with snakes in their hair or wound around their arms and breasts, with the result that the F. themselves are attributed with hissing (*sibila*) [1. 329 fig. 131]. The F. are pictured with wings, they carry burning torches and a scourge made of snakes (the whip is a symbol of lightning); flames burst out of hair and mouth, the robe is dripping with blood [2]. These attributes of horror and punishment correspond to the F.'s function as goddesses of vengeance. Correspondingly, the personifications of insania (madness), luctus (mourning), pavor (fear), and terror are their companions [3. 314]. Worship of the F. aims at punishment for breaking the law, contract violations, murder, and similar offences [4. 1614, l. 52–83; 3. 309, l. 19–21]. In research, the F. as figures of the Roman belief in ghosts were considered to be related to the ghosts in German popular belief [5. 1562, l. 52–59; 3. 314, l. 56–68]. Similar parallels can be established for other cultures as well [3. 314].

1 PFIFFIG (repr. 1998), 323–324 2 H. SARIAN, s.v. Erinys, LIMC 3.1, 825–843 3 O. WASER, s.v. F., RE 7, 308–314 4 J. RUBENBAUER, s.v. furia, ThlL 6.1, 1613–1617 5 A. RAPP, s.v. F., Roscher 1.2, 1559–1564.

F. ALTHEIM, Röm. Religionsgesch. I, 1931, 42–44; ERNOUT/MEILLET, s.v. furo, 263; RADKE 137. W.-A.M.

Furia Sabinia Tranquillina Daughter of C.F. Sabinius Aquila Timesitheus, from AD 241 wife of → Gordianus [3] III, who installed her as Augusta shortly before his Persian War (SHA Gord. 23,5–6; Eutr. 9,2,2; Zos. 1,17; Zon. 12, 18 p. 129 D.; CIL VI 2114; 130).

PIR² F 587; KIENAST, ²1996, 197. T.F.

Fur(r)ina Name of an ancient Roman goddess, the sources show both one and two *r* (cf. CIL I² p. 323: *Furrinalia*; the MSS vary). On the possible etymological emergence of the name from Etruscan, Oscan (here perhaps from **fursina*, **forsina*), or Umbrian, see [1. 137]. Her cult in earlier times is documented by a festival on 25 July, the *Fu(r)rinalia* or *Furnalia*, and a *flamen Furinalis* (→ *flamines*; Varro, Ling. 5,84; 6,19; Fest. 78 L). Myths or rites are unknown. The grove of F. was located in Rome on the other side of the Tiber (in today's Trastevere) on the southern slope of the Ianiculum (probably in the area of the Villa Sciarra [2. 315; 317]).

At the end of the Roman Republic, after the cult of F. had not been practised for a long time (cf. Varro, Ling. 6,19), the similarity of names probably led to an identification with the → *Furiae* (Cic. Nat. D. 3,46; cf. also Plut. C. Gracchus 17 as well as Mart. Cap. 2,163f.). The identification with the Furies may have continued, since Syrian deities were worshipped on the Ianiculum since the 1st cent. AD (as is suggested by the plural, CIL VI 422: consecration to Jupiter Optimus Maximus Heliopolitanus and to Genius Forinarum; cf., however, CIL VI 36802: Νυνφες Φορρινες and Ps.-Aur. Vict. De viris illustribus 65,5).

1 RADKE 2 F. COARELLI, Rome, ²1995, Germ. transl: Rom. Ein arch. Führer, 1975. HE.K.

Furius Name of an ancient Roman patrician lineage (on inscriptions also *Fourios*), derived from the praenomen *Fusus* and also occurring occasionally in the original form *Fusius* in the literary tradition; the family perhaps came from Tusculum (cf. the family grave of the Furii ILLRP 895–903). The numerous members of the gens from the early Republic in the 5th/4th cents. BC are scarcely tangible as historical persons, and their history is in part later annalistic invention. Most well known is the 'Saviour of Rome' after the catastrophe of the Gauls, M.F. [I 11] Camillus. The connection to the later F. is unknown.

I. REPUBLICAN PERIOD II. IMPERIAL PERIOD

I. REPUBLICAN PERIOD

[I 1] F., C. Perhaps people's tribune between 204 and 169 BC, introduced a law limiting the level of legacies to 1,000 asses (*lex Furia testamentaria*, Gai. Inst. 2,225).

KASER, RPR 2, 756.

[I 2] F., P. Son of a freedman, who in 102 BC was expelled from the equestrian class by Q. Caecilius [I 30] Metellus Numidicus and who therefore, as plebeian tribune in 100 (MRR 3,22), prevented Caecilius' return from exile. Furthermore, he wanted the inheritance of L. Appuleius [I 11] Saturninus confiscated (MRR 3,21f.); prosecuted unsuccessfully for this in 98, he was then killed by the enraged crowd before the end of a second trial (Cic. Rab. perd. 24; App. B Civ. 1,147, etc.).

[I 3] F. (Medullinus Fusus?), Sex. Consul in 488 BC with Sp. Nautius (Liv. 2,39,9).

[I 4] F., Sp. According to Livy (1,24,6) *pater patratus* under King Tullus Hostilius, probably invented.

[I 5] F., Sp. (or L.) Consular tribune in 378 BC.

[I 6] F. Aculeo, C. Quaestor of the consul L. Cornelius [I 72] Scipio in 190 BC, later accused and condemned with the same for bribery by Antiochus III, but then released on bail (Valerius Antias at Liv. 38,55,5–8; 58,1). K.-L.E.

[I 7] F. Antias A poet to whom → Lutatius Catulus (cos. 102) dedicated a work about his own consulate (Cic. Brut. 132). 6 v. of F. are quoted by Gell. NA 18,11. The hexameters are in epic style; perhaps F. used the work of Catulus as a source for an epic about the Cimbrian War, with Catulus as the hero. Gellius quotes the lines in order to refute the criticism of → Caesellius Vindex about F.'s neologisms, four of which are incohatives.

COURTNEY, 97–98. ED.C.

[I 8] F. Bibaculus, L. Praetor after 227 BC and before 218 (MRR 1,237); Salian; his father was *magister* of the Salian Collegium (Val. Max. 1,1,9). K.-L.E.

[I 9] F. Bibaculus, M. According to Hieronymus (Chron.1914), the → Neoteric poet was born in Cremona in 103 BC, but this date appears to be too early. He wrote → epigrams and iambi that contained → invectives against Julius Caesar and Octavian (Quint. Inst. 10,1,96; Tac. Ann. 4,34,5), as well as *Lucubrationes* in prose (Plin. HN praef. 24). The 11 bks. *Annales* by F. quoted by Macrob. Sat. 6,1,31–4,10 are probably the same work as the *Pragmatia Belli Gallici* that are ascribed to F. by Ps.-Acro (in Sat. 2,5,41; cf. 1,10,36 and Porph. Hor. comm. ad locos) perhaps they were never composed by the Neoteric poet at all, however it is also most unlikely they were composed by → Furius [I 7] Antias.

EDITIONS: FPL³, 197–204.
COMM.: COURTNEY, 192–200. J.A.R.

[I 10] (F.?) Camillus, C. Close friend and adviser of Cicero versed in the law, in whose correspondence between 51 and 45 BC he is often named. K.-L.E.

[I 11] F. Camillus, L. Son of F. [I 14] Camillus, he is supposed to have participated in his father's Volscian War in 389 BC (Plut. Camillus 35,1); as dictator in 350 he supervised the consular elections, probably in order to resist plebeian claims [1. 62f., 79f.]; his own election and that of Claudius [I 6] Crassus to consuls for 349 indicates this (MRR 1, 128). As consul he repulsed an invasion of the Gauls into Latium (the single combat of M. Valerius Corvus with a Gaul, probably invented by Valerius Antias, is legendary); a Syracusan fleet that co-operated with the Gauls [2. 68] retreated. A further dictatorship in 345 is disputed (→ F. [I 12]).

1 HÖLKESKAMP 2 M. SORDI, I rapporti romano-ceriti, 1960. W.ED.

[I 12] F. Camillus, L. Grandson of F. [I 14], perhaps the dictator of 345 BC who attacked the Aurunci and in the battle vowed a temple to Juno Moneta (Liv. 7,28,4; MRR 1,131). As consul in 338 in the Latin War (340–338), he triumphed over Pedum and Tibur and, according to Livy (8,13,10–18), played a leading role in the re-structuring of Latium (MRR 1,138). He and his colleague C. Maenius received the first honorary statues in the Forum [1. 338f.]. During the (second) Samnian War, having once again been elected consul in 325 with the plebeian D. Iunius Brutus Scaeva, he fell ill and appointed L. Papirius Cursor dictator in the war in Samnium (Liv. 8,29,6–9).

1 T. HÖLSCHER, Anfänge der röm. Repräsentationskunst, in: MDAI(R) 85, 1978, 315–357. W.ED.

[I 13] F. Camillus, M. Tradition, above all Livy, describes M. F. Camillus as the dominating figure in the first decades of the 4th cent. BC, the leader sent by fate (*dux fatalis*), second founder of Rome and 'father of the fatherland' (Liv. 7,1,10). He began his career as censor (in 403), served as consular tribune in the years 401, 398, 394, 386, 384 and 381, was appointed dictator in 396, 390, 389, 368 and 367, celebrated four triumphs (in 396 over → Veii, in 390 over the Gauls, in 389 over the → Volsci, → Aequi and Etruscans, in 367 again over the Gauls) and supposedly was *interrex* in 396, 391 and 389 (all sources in MRR 1 to the individual years). Reflected in and mixed in with his career, shaped predominantly by legend, are the efforts of Rome in the ten-year war against the Etruscan city of Veii (in 406–396; the duration is imitative of the Trojan War), the traumatic experience of the conquest and plundering of Rome by the Gauls (in 390; according to Pol. 1,6,1 and probably correct in 387–86), the problematic relationship of Rome with its neighbours after the assault by the Gauls, and the tense inner situation characterized by the striving of the plebeians for political equality (→ Struggle of orders).

Therefore, only the conquest of Veii in 396 by F., the resulting triumph and the sending of a votive offering to Delphi can be validated historically. Even the circumstances surrounding the victory are legendary (*evocatio* of Juno, the protective goddess of Veii; consecration of the temple of Juno Regina in Rome); the fashioning of the triumph (use of white horses) is a later invention like the trial over the mistaken use of spoils and the resulting exile, in order to explain the absence of F. during the Gallic assault. Further feasts belonging to the realm of legend are: winning back the gold paid to the Gauls (→ Brennus [1]) and the resulting dictatorships and triumphs of 390 and probably 367 as well, his resistance to moving the Roman settlement to Veii after the Gallic assault, and finally his reconciling role in the patrician-plebeian balance of 367, including the vow of a temple to Concordia. In spite of many individual inventions, his dedication in the fight against Rome's neighbours and with it the triumph of 389, mentioned on numerous occasions, is historically credible. He died in 365, according to Livy (7,1,8), of the plague.

E. BURCK, Die Gestalt des Camillus, in: Id. (ed.), Wege zu Livius, 1967, 310–328; T. J. CORNELL, The Beginnings of Rome, 1995, 309–326; R. M. OGILVIE, Commentary on Livy. Books 1–5, (1965) 1978 (comprehensive source-critical study to 390 BC). W.ED.

[I 14] F. Camillus, Sp. Son of F. [I 13], father of F. [I 12], first praetor in 366 BC according to the Licinio-Sextian rogations (Liv. 7,1,2).

[I 15] F. Chresimus, C. Freedman and farmer in the middle of the 2nd cent. BC, accused of magic because of a good harvest, but then acquitted (Piso at Plin. HN 18,41).

S. TREGGIARI, Roman Freedmen, 1969, 103.

[I 16] F. Crassipes (Praenomen unknown, cognomen 'Club foot', illustrated by the picture on a coin in 84 BC of a relative [?] P. F. Crassipes [RRC 356]). In 56 BC he was engaged to Cicero's daughter Tullia, from whom he separated again before 50 after a short marriage. In

51(?) he was quaestor in Bithynia (Cic. Fam. 13,9); in spite of the estrangement, he visited Cicero at his estate in Formiae (Cic. Att. 9,11,3). MRR 3,96.

[I 17] **F. Crassipes, L.** Probably a Roman official in Greece in the middle of the 2nd cent. BC, he allowed himself to be initiated into the Mysteries on Samothrace (ILLRP 213).

[I 18] **F. Crassipes, M.** Legate in Gallia in 200 BC (Liv. 31,21,8), probably the military tribune who set up several dedication gifts in Tusculum (ILLRP 100, 221). In 194–192 *IIIvir coloniae deducendae* (founding of Vibo Valentia in Bruttium in 192). As praetor in Gallia Cisalpina in 187, he unlawfully disarmed the *Cenomani*, for which the consul had him punished (Liv. 39,3,1–3; Diod. Sic. 29,14); therefore, possibly expelled from the Senate in the intervening period. In 173 he was praetor II in Sicily.

H.H. Scullard, Roman Politics, 220–150 B.C., [2]1973, 143.

[I 19] **F. Fusus, Agrippa** Consul with T. Quinctius Capitolinus Barbatus in 446 BC; allegedly a victory over the Volscii (Liv. 3,66–70; Diod. Sic. 12,30,6).

[I 20] **F. Medullinus, L.** (Cognomen from the town Medullia [1. 292]). As consul in 474 BC, together with C. Manlius Vulso, he allegedly resisted the implementation of the field law of Sp. Cassius [I 19] (Liv. 2,54f.; Dion. Hal. Ant. Rom. 9,37f.).

1 Th. Mommsen, Röm. Forschungen 2, 1879.

[I 21] **F. Medullinus, L.** Consular tribune in 432 BC, 425, 420, possibly *cos. I* 413, *cos. II* 409.

[I 22] **F. Medullinus, L.** Probably the son of F. [I 21] (*cos. I* in 413 BC, *cos. II* in 409), consular tribune in 407, 405, 398, 397, 395, 394, 391 BC.

[I 23] **F. Medullinus, L.** Consular tribune in 381 BC, in 370; censor in 363.

[I 24] **F. Medullinus Fusus, P.** In 472 BC consul with L. Pinarius Mamercinus Rufus, laid out the colony Antium in 467 as one of the first *triumviri* for land distribution (Liv. 3,1,6; Dion. Hal. Ant. Rom. 9,59,2); supposedly fell in 464 against the Aequi.

[I 25] **F. Medullinus Fusus, Sp.** Consul in 481 BC (MRR 1,24).

[I 26] **F. Medullinus Fusus, Sp.** Brother of F. [I 24], consul in 464 BC with A. Postumius Albus, is supposed to have been captured by the Aequi and freed by T. Quinctius (probably an annalistic invention). In 453 he was allegedly *cos. suff.* and like his predecessor died of the plague (Dion. Hal. Ant. Rom. 10,53,6).

[I 27] **F. Pacilus Fusus, C.** Consul in 441 BC; as censor in 435 with M. Geganius [1] Macerinus he took the census for the first time in the Villa Publica on the Field of Mars (Liv. 4,22,7), hence they were considered the first authentic joint censors; consular tribune in 426.

[I 28] **F. Philus, L.** Allegedly belonged to the circle of friends of P. Cornelius [I 70] Scipio Aemilianus and shared his cultural interests (Patron of the poet → Terentius, Suet. Vita Terentii 1); in 155 BC he is supposed to have attended to the Athenian philosophers legation in Rome (Cic. De or. 2,154f.). As a result, Cicero made him the speaker in *De re publica* and had him advocate the state doctrine of the → Carneades in bk. 3. In 136, as consul with Scipio and D. Laelius, he examined the contract of C. → Hostilius Mancinus (*cos.* 137) with the Numantians (Cic. Rep. 3,28); after the Senate turned down the contract, F. handed Mancinus over to the Numantians (Cic. Off. 3,109). He may have composed the text from which Macrobius (Sat. 3,9,6–11) records two formulae of the → *evocatio*.

[I 29] **F. Philus, P.** Was victorious as consul in 223 BC with his colleague C. Flaminius [1] over Gauls and Ligurians and celebrated a triumph (Plut. Marcellus 4; InscrIt 13,1,79). In 216 he was *praetor urbanus* (Liv. 22,35,5–7); after the defeat at Cannae he took over the fleet; however, an attempt to land in Africa failed (Liv. 22,57,8; 23,21,2). In 214, as censor with M. Atilius [I 22] Regulus, he punished conscientious objectors and defeatists severely (Liv. 24,11,6; 18), which is why in 213 he was sued (without success) by one of those he punished, M. Caecilius [I 12] Metellus. He became an augur and died in the same year.

[I 30] **F. Philus, P.** Praetor in 174 BC, propraetor in 173 in Hispania citerior; in 171 he was brought before a recuperative court for extortion on the basis of complaints by Spanish *socii*, but before the judgement he went into exile (Liv. 43,2,8–10; ORF I4, 59).

[I 31] **F. Purpureo, L.** (Cognomen 'Purple snail' illustrated on coins of a later relation, RRC 187). In 210 he was a military tribune and was victorious in 200 as praetor over the Celts and Ligurians and celebrated a triumph (MRR 1,323); F. was perhaps then a legate to the Aetolians (MRR 1,328). As consul in 196, with M. Claudius [I 12] Marcellus, F. again fought against the Celts and Ligurians (MRR 1, 335); during these battles, F. vowed a Jupiter Temple. In 189 he went to Asia Minor as a member of a commission of ten to bring local affairs in order after the victory over Antiochus [5] III under consul Cn. → Manlius Vulso (MRR 1, 363; 367); upon his return in 187, along with some of his colleagues he stubbornly put up resistance to Manlius' call for a triumph, but without success (Liv. 38,44,11–50,3). In 184 he competed for the position of censor for 183, also without success. In 183 he was envoy to the Celts who had invaded Upper Italy (Liv. 39,54,13).

K.-L.E.

II. Imperial period

[II 1] **F. Anthianus** Jurist from the 3rd cent. AD, possibly a freedperson active in the province [2]; he wrote a brief commentary *Ad edictum* (5 bks.), of which Justinian's digests contain three short fragments [1].

1 O.Lenel, Palingenesia iuris civilis 1, 1889, 179f.
2 D.Liebs, Jurisprudenz, in: HLL 4, 216.

T.G.

[II 2] **M.F. Camillus** He came from the family of F. [I 11] Camillus, who had become famous as dictator (Tac. Ann. 2,52,5). In AD 8 he was *cos. ord.*; his quaestor was M. Aedius [2] Celer (AE 1990, 222). In AD 17–18, as proconsul of Africa, he beat the rebellious → Tacfarinas, for which he received the triumphal insignia. He was also accepted into the arvales [1. 176f.]. He died in AD 37. His daughter Livia Medullina married the young Claudius [III 1].

VOGEL-WEIDEMANN 69ff.; PIR² F 576.

1 SCHEID, Recrutement.

[II 3] M. F. Camillus Co-opted Frater Arvalis in the year 37. Identical to Arruntius [II 8]. W.E.

[II 4] C. F. Octavianus (The Signum Amphilochius is questionable.) Probably from Ulpianum (Moesia superior), son of Furia Caecilia, CIL VI 1423 (= ILS 1169). *Clarissimus vir*, *pontifex*, patron of Canusium: CIL IX 338 (= ILS 6121). After he had apparently lost his father early on, he was under the guardianship of F. Alcimus, a *libertus* of his mother (Ulp. De officio praetoris tutelaris fragmentum Vaticanum 220, p. 69), and before 217 attained the suffect consulate. His family owned large estates near Ulpianum that were administered by his procurators F. Alcimus and Pontius Uranius: CIL III 14356, 3a (= ILS 9103).

PIR² F 580; L. SCHUMACHER, Prosopographische Untersuchungen zur Besetzung der vier hohen röm. Priesterkollegien, 1973, 38f., 241f.; LEUNISSEN, 67, 170. T.F.

[II 5] C. F. Sabinius Aquila Timesitheus A brilliant equestrian career allowed him to be promoted from a cohort prefecture in Hispania over numerous procuratorships in Gallia, Germania and the east of the empire as well as a few senatorial governor deputations to *praefectus praetorio* under Gordian [3] III in AD 241 (CIL XIII 1807 = ILS 1330). The young emperor made the experienced and educated man dependent on him by marrying his daughter → Furia (SHA Gord. 23,5;6; 24,2; 25,1), which was of particular importance against the backdrop of the looming war against the Sassanid Sapor, in which F. proved himself as successful army commander. He drove the Sassanids out of Antioch, pursued them up to the Tigris and in the process reconquered all the lost territories. On the way to Ctesiphon in 243 he succumbed to a mysterious illness (SHA Gord. 27,2; 4ff.; 28, 1; 6).

PIR² F 581; PFLAUM, vol. 2, 811ff. no. 317; LEUNISSEN, 124, 244, 268. T.F.

[II 6] P. Fu(rius?) Pontianus Governor of the province Moesia inferior between April AD 217 and July AD 218 according to the evidence of coins from Marcianopolis and Nicopolis.

PIR² F 496; B. PICK, Ant. Münzen Nordgriechenlands 1898, 1, 1, 234ff. no. 708–784; 432 no. 1680f. et al.; A. STEIN, Legaten Moesiens, 1940, 91. T.F.

[II 7] P. F. Saturninus Praetorian governor of Dacia superior *c.* AD 159–161; yet in the province he was given a suffect consulate, probably in 161. Fu[...] Pontianus, governor of Moesia inferior in 217, could be a descendant.

J. PISO Fasti provinciae Daciae, 1995, 74f.; PIR² F 583.

[II 8] T.F. Victorinus An equestrian, member of the → *tribus Palatina*, i.e. one of his ancestors could have been a slave. After the three equestrian officer positions he moved into the procurator career: procurator of Galatia *c.* AD 142 (cf. SEG 26, 1712), procurator of the Tarraconensis; *procurator ludi Magni* in Rome; prefect of the fleet of Ravenna *c.* 150, then of Misenum *c.* 154; *procurator a rationibus* in Rome; prefect of the Roman grain supply; prefect of Egypt in 159–160; praetorian prefect of Marcus Aurelius and Verus; participated in the Parthian War; for this he was honoured with *dona militaria* and a statue; furthermore he received the insignia of the office of a consul; he fell at the beginning of the Marcomannic War (CIL VI 39440 = ILS 9002 = CIL VI 41143).

PFLAUM I 326ff.; DEVIJVER F 100. W.E.

Furniture

I. ANCIENT ORIENT II. EGYPT III. CLASSICAL ANTIQUITY

I. ANCIENT ORIENT

Furniture can be documented for the Ancient Orient since the 6th millennium BC, in the form of a sculpture of a feminine figure from Çatal Hüyük that is enthroned on a chair flanked by felines. More substantial statements, however, are not possible until the 3rd millennium BC, as written sources are added. Of the furniture made mostly of wood, reed, woven textiles or leather, scarcely anything is preserved due to the aggressive climate in the Near East. Valuable individual pieces could be decorated by intarsia, appliqué and rounded three-dimensional figurines as well as by coverings and fittings of bronze and precious metals. Many furniture pieces may have served as a picture carrier in addition to their actual function.

Tables, sitting and lying furniture as well as shelves and boxes can all be found among ancient oriental furnishings. In addition to mobile goods in the houses, there were always stationary built-in pieces of clay that served as work surfaces, sleeping places or as storage space. Superior sitting furniture or beds could belong to the furnishings of a temple. The act of handing over or consecrating a throne to the gods could lead to the naming of a year. Beyond this, the empty throne could also receive food or libation sacrifices. The copying of small furniture models in clay, especially of tables and beds, as a votive offering was closely connected to the domestic cult or to private religious prayers. N.CH.

II. EGYPT

In Egypt, thanks to the climatic conditions, quite a few pieces of furniture have survived, mostly in the graves of kings and officials. Evidence of tables, chests,

Ancient furniture

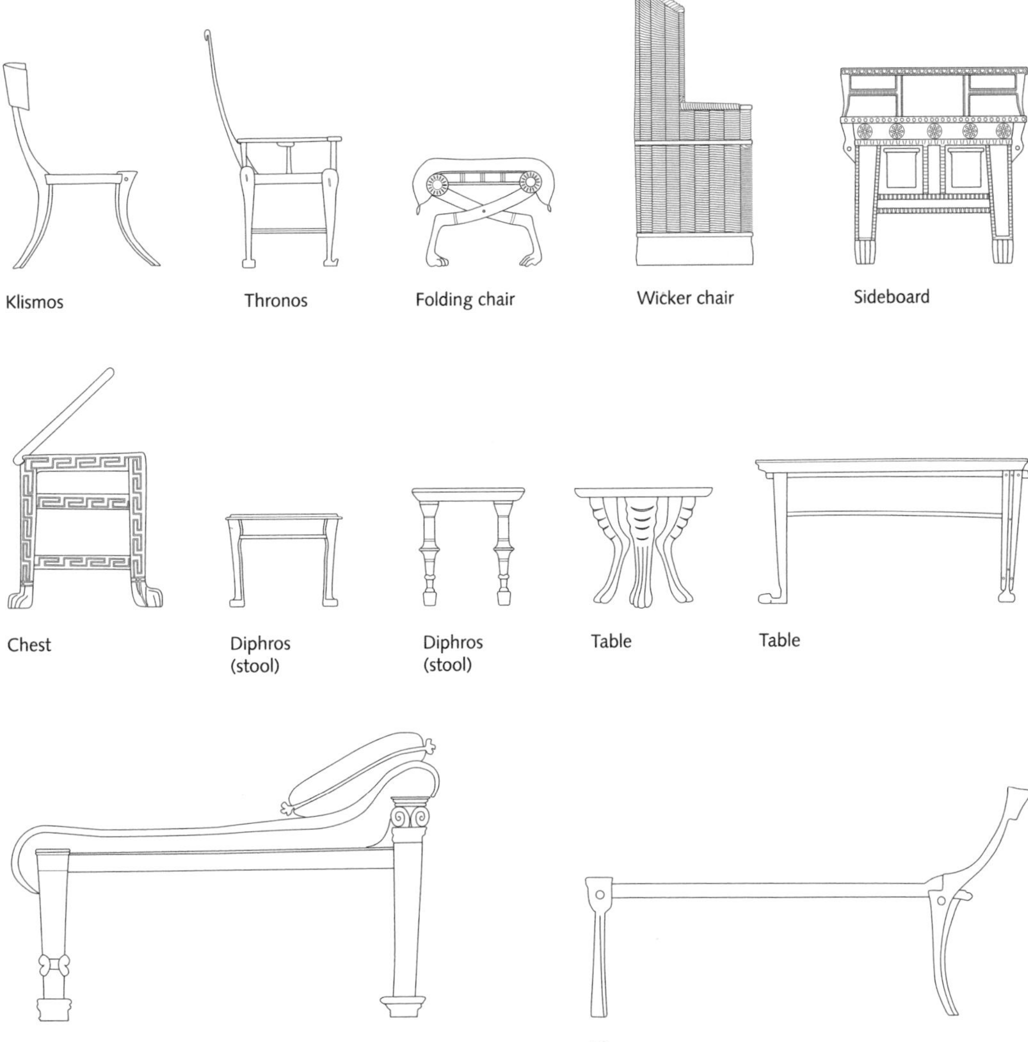

sitting and lying furniture (stools, chairs and beds) first documented in the grave of Hetepheres in → Giza (4th dynasty, around 2600 BC). Most of the furniture finds are from the New Kingdom (18th–20th dynasty, around 1530–1070 BC), and in contrast to the furnishings of previous epochs, stands out by a more curved design, increased technical ingenuity (e.g. collapsible beds) and richer decoration that goes from geometrical patterns to royal scenes. The grave of the architect Cha from the 18th dynasty (around 1400 BC) in addition to tables and chests also held ten stools, a chair, and two beds. These rich furnishings are surpassed only by the grave of → Tutankhamun from the 18th dynasty (around 1320 BC), which contained for instance, several of the king's thrones.

→ Ivory carvings

H.S. Baker, Furniture in the Ancient World, 1966; N. Cholidis, Möbel in Ton (Altertumskunde des Vorderen Orients 1), 1992; E. Gubel, Phoenician Furniture (Studia Phoenicia 7), 1987; G. Herrmann (ed.), The Furniture of Western Asia, 1996; G. Killen, Ancient Egyptian Furniture, vol. 1, 1980; vol. 2, 1994; Id., Egyptian Woodworking and Furniture, 1994; E. Simpson, Furniture in Ancient Western Asia, in: J.M. Sasson (ed.), Civilizations of the Ancient Near East, vol. 3, 1995, 1647–1671. IS.V.

III. Classical antiquity

A. General B. Greece C. Etruria and Rome

A. General

Ancient furnishings were limited predominantly to a few types of furniture: Chests, crates, boxes or baskets (→ *kálathos*) for storing utensils, → clothing or → jewellery, in addition to sitting and lying furniture as well as → tables, wall shelves and racks. Cupboards (→ *armarium*) were uncommon among the Greeks (e.g. book cupboards), and yet they were a common part of the Roman → household equipment (cf. Sarcophagus of Simpelveld, Leiden [1. fig. 586]) and, made of wood [2. 59f.] or of stone, they have survived to this day. Furthermore, looms (→ Textiles, production of), → hearths, → lamps and other lighting devices, → chamber pots, bathtubs or bathing ovens, cradles, cushions, → carpets, or → mattresses can be counted among the mobile furnishings of the house. Furniture pieces generally retained their actual purpose and design during Graeco-Roman antiquity; there is only one decisive change to be recorded: in the 6th cent. BC the original custom of sitting at meals was replaced by the oriental custom of lying on the → *kline*, which was retained until the end of antiquity. However, the usual custom for today of 'eating at the table' was not forgotten, but rather it was fostered e.g. at inns, as for instance, wall frescos in Pompeii show.

B. Greece

In addition to written sources, our knowledge of Greek furniture is based on its representations on grave reliefs and funerary frescoes, Locrian clay reliefs (→ Relief), vases and many other items; additionally, there are occasional examples of stone or bronze toy furniture or wooden furniture or furniture parts from sanctuaries (e.g. Samos; miniature furniture as burial objects, e.g. in Sindos); also worth mentioning is the wooden throne decorated with ivory from the Cypriot Salamis [3. 99–103] and the marble throne with a painting on the seat back from the 'grave of Eurydice' (around 340 BC) near Vergina (see [4]).

An important piece of furniture was the → kline; it served as a bed for night rest, but also as lying furniture at mealtime – the man ate while lying and the wife, to the extent she was present, sat at the foot. The kline consisted of a frame with four posts and interlaced straps upon which mattresses and blankets were laid. The head end was raised; in the 2nd half of the 5th cent. BC the foot end was similarly raised for cushions. Often, a small bench was placed in front of the kline, upon which one placed one's shoes, and that otherwise served as a footrest. The → table (*trápeza*) was an important furniture piece for putting down drinking vessels or foods. It was four-legged and rectangular or (mostly) three-legged and rectangular or round. Available as sitting furniture were the backless foot stool (→ *díphros*), the folding chair (*díphros okladías*), a large chair with a backrest but no armrests (→ *klismós*) and the throne with back and armrests (*thrónos*) as the most discriminating sitting furniture; the latter is found primarily in representations as the seat of rulers and gods. Often the legs of backed chairs and thrones end in animal paws. Chests (*kibōtós*, *lárnax)* were used for storing clothing etc., smaller boxes served for jewellery or money. Clothing or crockery cupboards in the sense they are known today were unknown to Greek antiquity. Dishes and utensils could be placed on step-like racks (*skeuothḗkē*) or on the *kylikeíon* (especially for crockery).

C. Etruria and Rome

Etruscan and Roman furniture is known by numerous representations on mirrors, vases, grave frescoes, urns etc.; in addition, there are metal fragments of furniture or stone items (e.g. in graves). To a great extent, Etruscan furnishings are comparable to those of the Greeks; they differ however, by exhibiting a richer ornamentation of the free surfaces on klines, boxes, or sitting furniture. Wood was the preferred material for Etruscan furniture, and yet bronze also played a large role (→ Praenestine Cistae, thrones etc.). Etruscan klines and chairs of the decades around 500 BC may be regarded as having exceptional quality; transport was considerably eased by wheels; the klines often exhibit an increase in height on both ends that is decorated on the sides with ornamental or figured *fulcra* (the ends of the headrest on the sides). As for the tables, there is often a second tabletop under the actual tabletop; one could, for instance, place drinking vessels there. Of the sitting furniture there is one Etruscan throne variation that is worth mentioning; it had a cylindrical or tapered lower part, a rounded sitting surface and a similar shape for the backrest; original items in stone or bronze are still extant.

In principle, Roman furniture does not differ from Greek or Etruscan, however what is noticeable is a striving for more elegant forms. Often more valuable materials are used (tortoise shell for a bed: Mart. 14,87; silver beds: Plin. HN 33,144–146), rare types of marble, precious stones, woods of all types (Plin. HN 13,91–102; 16,213; maple for tables: Mart. 14,89; ebony: Luc. 10,144–145); in the transalpine provinces, wicker furniture was also popular. In the Roman period, the cupboard becomes a popular piece of furniture, as witnessed by wall frescoes from the Vesuvius cities as well as extant remains. Dishes, smaller statues of bronze or stone, and books were stored in it.

→ Árca; → Armarium; → Cista; → Delphica; → Diphros; → Household equipment; → Loculi; → Monopodium; → Chair; → Throne; → Table; → Furniture

1 Richter, Furniture 2 R. Holloway, The Town of Hercules, 1995 3 V. Karageorghis, Appendix II to S. Laser, Hausrat (ArchHom 2.8), 1968 4 M. Andronikos, Οι Μακεδονικοί τάφοι, in: R. Ginouvès (ed.), Μακεδονία, 1993, 145–190.

E. Brümmer, Griech. Truhenbehälter, in: JDAI 100, 1985, 1–168; S. Faust, Fulcra. Figürlicher und ornamentaler Schmuck an ant. Betten (MDAI(R), 30. Ergh.), 1989; A.R. Furger, Der Inhalt eines Geschirr- oder Vorratsschrankes aus dem 3. Jh. von Kaiseraugst-Schildmatt, in: Jahresber. aus Augst 10, 1989, 213–268; W. Höpfner, Zu griech. Bibliotheken und Bücherschränken, in: AA 1996, 25–36; J. McIntosh, Reprensentations of Furniture on the Frieze Plaques from Poggio Civitate, in: MDAI(R) 81, 1974, 15–40; St. Mols, Houten Meubles in Herculaneum. Vorm, Techniek en Functie, 1994; P. Muhly, Furniture from the Shaft Graves: the Occurence of Wood in Aegean Burials in the Bronze Age, in: ABSA 91, 1996, 197–215; S. Steingräber, Etr. Mödel, 1979.

R.H.

Furnius Plebeian family name, perhaps connected with Etruscan *furnial* (Schulze 217, with epigraphical evidence). K.-L.E.

[1] F., C. Like his son F. [2], a famous Roman orator (*Furnii ... clari oratores*; Jer. Chron. ad annum 1980–81). People's tribune in 50 BC, legate in 44–43, praetor in 42 (?), envoy in 40 and 39, promagistrate in Asia in 36–35, *consul designatus* for 29 (MRR 2, 249, 331, 353, 359, 376, 389, 402, 408; 3, 97). At first, an admirer of the orator Cicero, he placed himself politically in the Civil War on the side of Caesar since 49, later on that of L. or M. Antonius [I 9]. Octavian pardoned him after his victory (Sen. Benef. 2,25,1). Terminus post quem for his death is 17 BC (Jer. loc. cit.). W.W.

[2] F., C. Son of F. [1], from 22–19 BC he was *legatus Augusti pro praetore* in Hispania Tarraconensis (Cass. Dio 54,5,1–3 [2. 829; 839]); *cos. ord.* in 17. Like his father (whom he preceded in death) he was an important orator (Jer. Chron. 159H), friend and supporter of Horace (Hor. Sat. 1,10,86).

1 PIR² F 591 2 Syme, RP 2. K.-L.E.

[3] M.F. Augurinus. *Cos. suff.* probably AD 40 or 41.

G. Camodeca, I consoli del 43, in: ZPE 140, 2002. W.E.

Furnus

[1] Maius City in *Africa proconsularis*, southwest of Thuburbo Maius, modern Aïn Fourna. *Municipium* since an indefinite period (CIL VIII Suppl. 1, 12039). Epigraphical evidence: CIL VIII 1, 752f.; Suppl. 1, 12030; 12039; Suppl. 4, 23798–23811; ILTun 617–620.

AATun 100, sheet 25, no. 187.

[2] Minus City in *Africa proconsularis*, southwest of Carthage, modern Henchir Msaadine. *Municipium* since Caracalla (AD 211–217) (CIL VIII Suppl. 4, 25808b). Epigraphical evidence: CIL VIII 2, 10609f.; Suppl. 1, 14751–14753; Suppl. 4, 25807–25818; AE 1991, 468 no. 1672.

AATun 050, sheet 19, no. 235. W.HU.

Furor The expression for → mental illness in Roman law. The person affected by this, the *furiosus*, according to the Twelve Tables (*c.* 450 BC), found himself in a special relationship of authority and dependence (foster-care, *cura furiosi*). The agnate (→ *agnatio*) and, when needed, in early times the gentile (→ *gens*) were entitled to the office of the *curator* (Cic. Inv. 2,148; Rhet. Her. 1,23). The position of the *curator*, similar to that of a trustee, corresponded to a great extent to that of a guardian (→ *tutela*) and was valid not only for the person but also for the property of the *furiosus*. Nevertheless, there was no separate legal action provided for this relationship; instead, it was covered by the *actio negotiorum gestorum* (→ *gestio*). The *furiosus* was not legally competent, nor could he be held liable (Gai. Inst. 3,106). *Furor* was in addition an impediment to marriage (Paulus, Sent. 2,19,7). All of these limitations were likely not appropriate for the harmless mentally disturbed, but rather only for those severely and obviously ill (Cic. Tusc. 3,11). Business transactions that the *furiosus* undertook in lucid moments were valid.

Honsell/Mayer-Maly/Selb, 96, 430f.; Kaser, RPR I, 84, 278, 371f. G.S.

Furtum

A. Overview B. Twelve Tables C. Furtum in classical Roman law

A. Overview

Furtum is the offence against property in Roman law. At least in the classical period (1st–3rd cents. AD) the term *furtum* includes not only theft and embezzlement, but also the mere use of items that are not one's own (*furti usus*), the removal of one's own property, e.g. from a collateral creditor (*furtum possessionis*, possession theft), fraud, receiving stolen goods and aiding and abetting the perpetrator of a *furtum*. The object of *furtum* could in addition to *res corporales* be slaves and persons under paternal authority. In the classical period, the condition of *furtum* is fulfilled only when the person responsible acted intentionally and fraudulently. The term for the person responsible is *fur*. Like other offences that were directed against private objects protected by law, *furtum* was first prosecuted only under civil law. Probably at the beginning of the Imperial period, the acquisition of money belonging to the state or religious institutions was subject to prosecution in public criminal proceedings (*iudicium publicum*) (→ *peculatus*). Theft of livestock (*abigeatus*) and burglary (→ *effractor*) were probably punished since Trajan and Marcus Aurelius (2nd cent. AD) as → *crimen extraordinarium* by the state. Since the 3rd cent. AD, public and civil prosecutions of *furtum* ran simultaneously.

B. Twelve Tables

The eighth of the 12 Tables (*c.* 450 BC, → *tabulae duodecim*) contained a series of regulations about *furtum* that were presumably already valid law earlier. The law differentiates between obvious *furtum manifestum* and not obvious *furtum nec manifestum*. If the person responsible for the *furtum* was caught in the act, the victim was allowed to kill him (Gai. Inst. 3,184; 3,189). In the case of theft at night, or if the thief defended himself with a weapon, he could be killed out of hand (Table 8,12f.). However, the killing was lawful only if the injured party announced the deed by crying out to neighbours (*endoplorare*). The injured party was allowed to drag other thieves caught in the act before the magistrate. Then they were flogged (*verberari*) and handed over to the victim of the theft (as a slave or as a son of the house), who had the right to kill him (*addictio*, Table 8,14). It was also considered *furtum manifestum* when the victim found the stolen goods in a formal house search. This had to occur with → *lanx* and → *licium* ('with bowl and string'). Even Festus (104,5–8 L.) in interpreting this *quaestio lance et licio* only knew to submit 'foolish acts' [1. 798]. Perhaps the bowl and string served to measure the exact quantity and size of the stolen goods [2. 177f.].

If the *furtum* was not obvious but first had to be proven, the injured party was entitled to damages at double the value (Table 8,16). After the 12 Table period (5th cent. BC), killing for *furtum manifestum* was abandoned in favour of damages that in these cases amounted to four times the value (Gai. Inst. 3,189).

C. Furtum in classical Roman law

According to the digests, in the period of classical Roman law (1st–3rd cents. AD), the victim of *furtum* was entitled to quadruple, resp. double the value as penalty suit for *actiones furti manifesti* or *nec manifesti*. In place of the house search with bowl and string, in this period the simple house search with the consultation of witnesses was used. If the stolen goods were found in the process, the *fur* owed triple the value from an *actio furti concepti*. This held true even when he himself had not committed the *furtum* intentionally; in this case he could take recourse with the real *fur* with an *actio furti oblati*. Gai. Inst. 3,186–188,191f. describes how different complications of search requests led to further praetorian legal actions. All of this is redressed by Justinian with the right of the victim to search.

Preserved up until Justinian in the 6th cent., the possibility remained, in addition to the penalty suit, of raising a prosecuting action against the unjustified enrichment of the *fur*: a → *condictio furtiva* (Dig. 13,1,1), which remained as before even in the event of accidental destruction of the stolen goods (*fur semper in mora*: the thief is liable like a debtor in default). The *actio furti* was barred between spouses. Instead the praetor granted the husband an *actio rerum amotarum* on the simple intrinsic value of the items his wife, expecting a divorce, had for instance taken out of her dowry (→ *dos*) (Dig. 25,2,1).

1 Mommsen, Strafrecht 2 D. Flach, Die Gesetze der frühen röm. Republik, 1994.

Honsell/Mayer-Maly/Selb, 358ff.; Kaser, RPR I, 157ff., 614ff.; A. Berger, Dig. IX 2,4,1 und das "endoplorato" der Zwölftafeln, in: P. Ciapessoni (ed.), Studi A. Albertoni I, 1935, 379–397; K. Hackl, Gaius 4,37 und die Formeln der actio furti, in: Ars boni et aequi, FS W. Waldstein, 1993, 127–139; A. Wacke, Actio rerum amotarum, 1963; J. G. Wolf, Lanx und licium, in: Sympotica Wieacker, 1970, 59–79. G.S.

Furtum tabularum A criminal offence that corresponds with modern obstruction of evidence and so implies a more or less definite obstruction of evidence in Roman civil procedure. *Tabulae* are written notes that served, e.g., to safeguard evidence; as such they belong to the evidence classified by Quintilian (*instrumenta*, Inst. 5,5,1ff.).

G. Klingenberg, Das Beweisproblem beim Urkundendiebstahl, in: ZRG 96, 1979, 229–257; C. Paulus, Die Beweisvereitelung in der Struktur des dt. Zivilprozesses, in: Archiv für die civilistische Praxis 197, 1997, 136–160; J. A. C. Thomas, Furtum of Documents, in: RIDA 15, 1968, 429–444; F. Wieacker, F.t., in: Synteleia V. Arangio-Ruiz, 1964, 562–576. C.PA.

Fuscus, Arellius Rhetor in the Augustan period; came from Asia (Sen. Controv. 9,6,16). In the twenties BC, at the latest, he probably taught in Rome, more often in Greek than in Latin (Sen. Suas. 4,5). Amongst his outstanding students were → Papirius Fabianus (who later turned away again from F.'s style) and Ovid; close contact with the imperial house is shown by F.'s homage to Maecenas (through the frequent quoting of Vergil's verses, Sen. Suas. 3,5) and probably also by the fact that Seneca mentions an important student of F. without naming him (Suas. 4,5); presumably he was awarded the rank of *eques* (cf. Plin. HN 33,152 about the son of F.). F. was a supporter of → Asianism; Seneca the Elder, through whom alone we know about F., quite a few times provides detailed stylistic samples and a characterization (Controv. 2, pr. 1; 1,1,16: *color ... religionis*); he considers him to be one of the four best orators (Controv. 10, pr. 13).

J. Brzoska, s.v. Arellius 3, RE 2, 635–637; F. G. Lindner, De A.F., Programm Breslau, 1862; PIR² A 1030; J. Fearweather, Seneca the Elder, 1981, 211f. J.R.

Fusius Roman proper name, → Furius.

Fussala Fort on the border of the region of Hippo Regius. The precise location is unknown. Augustine appointed a bishop in F. who had mastered the Punic language (Aug. Epist. 209,2). F. remained a bishop's see (Not. Episc. Num. 21[a]). Inscription: AE 1983, 283 no. 980.

AAAlg, sheet 9, no. 59; J. Desanges, S. Lancel, L'apport des nouvelles lettres à la géographie historique de l'Afrique antique et de l'Église d'Afrique, in: C. Lepelley (ed.), Les lettres de saint Augustin découvertes par Johannes Divjak, 1983, 87–98 and 99, here 92–98. W.HU.

Futius

[1] **Q. Futius** *Cos. suff.* probably in the time of Claudius. PIR² F 605; Vidman, FO² 72.

[2] **F. Longus** Proconsul of Achaea; the period cannot be established precisely (AE 1973, 495 = 1974, 601).

[3] **Q.F. Lusius Saturninus** *Cos. suff.* with M. Seius Varanus, probably in July AD 41 ([1] = AE 1984, 228). At the instigation of Suillius, Claudius had him executed in 43. PIR² L 449.

1 G. Camodeca, Puteoli 6, 1982, 4ff. W.E.

G

G (linguistics) The letter G is a Latin peculiarity. Because the Latin → C, which had taken the place of the Greek Gamma, had acquired the phonetic value/k/, there was a need for a letter to represent the common Latin phoneme/g/; the new letter was produced by adding a line to the letter C, and in the Latin alphabet took the place of the redundant → Z. This major achievement is ascribed to a certain Sp. → Carvilius [2] (GRF 3 [5. 324–333; 3. 70–72]).

In words with Indo-European roots, the Greek and Latin media/g/ as a rule continues from the proto-Indo-European *g* (velar) or *ǵ* (palatal) [4. 83; 2. 150f.]: τέγ-ος *teg-o* < **teg-*; ἄγ-ω *ag-o* < **ə₂eǵ-*; γίγνομαι *gign-or* (< **ǵiǵn-*) was pronounced [giŋn-] in both languages [4. 94; 2. 200]. In Latin, the initial *g-* disappeared in front of *n*: *nōsco*, but *co-gnōsco* (cf. Greek γι-γνώσκω).

In loan words, too, the g-sounds in both languages generally correspond: *geographia*; λεγιών/λεγεών [1. 232].

→ Gutturals; → Centum languages

1 H. Hofmann, Die lat. Wörter im Griech. bis 600 n.Chr., thesis Erlangen-Nuremberg 1989 2 Leumann 3 G. Radke, Beobachtungen zum Elogium auf L. Cornelius Scipio Barbatus, in: RhM 134, 1991, 69–79 4 Rix, HGG 5 Wachter.

B.F.

Gaba (Canaanite **gabʿ*, 'hill'). Settlement 5 km north-west of → Megiddo in the Valley of Jezreel, modern Tall Abī Šūša. The name first appears as *qbʿ* (no. 114) on → Thutmosis' III (1479–1425 BC) list of conquered Palestine cities, and is probably identical with Γαιβαι (Γεβαι, Γαβαι) in Jdt 3,10.

Under → Alexander [16] Iannaeus (103–76 BC), G. was part of the Hasmonaean kingdom (Sync. 558,17–559,3). According to Josephus (Jos. BI 1,166; Ant. Iud. 14,88), the settlement was 'restored' by Gabinius between 57 and 55 BC; however, according to numismatic evidence dating from 36 BC as well as from Claudius to Elagabalus (AD 50–219), the 'freedom' of the Γαβηνοι dates back to 61/0 BC, when Marcus Philippus served as *proconsul* in Syria: on the oldest coins, the citizens of G. adopt his name, referring to themselves as 'Philippans'. After 36 BC, the Romans returned G. to Herod the Great. (37–4 BC), who settled horsemen of his guard there (Jos. BI 3,36; Ant. Iud. 15,294). After his death, G. came under the Galilean rule of Herod Antipas (Georgios Kedrenos 1,333; PG 121,369; read *ΓΑΒΑΑΝ instead of ΠΑΡΝΑΝ). At the beginning of the Jewish uprising (AD 66–70), the town was considered non-Jewish (Jos. BI 2,459). It was the operational base of a *decurio*, who was unsuccessful against Josephus, the Galilean *strategos* (Jos. Vit. 115; 116–118).

The dominant deity on the town's coins is the Phrygian moon god Mên, an indication that (former) soldiers still constituted a large proportion of its inhabitants. At the beginning of the 4th cent, Eus. On. 70,8 G. refers to a πολίχνη ('small town') on the edge of the plain of el-Lejjun (Legio). The bishop of Gabai, a city of *Palaestina Secunda* (Hierocles or Georgios Kyprios, Synekdemos 43,720,11; 67,1037), took part in the second Jerusalem synod of 536.

The settlement of *Geba*, mentioned by Pliny in HN 5,17,75, is probably not G./Tall Abī Šūša, but Ǧabaʿ/Ḥurvat Gevaʿ west of the Carmel.

1 Y. Meshorer, City Coins of Eretz-Israel and the Decapolis, 1985, 38 2 G. Schmitt, G., Getta und Gintikirmil, in: ZPalV 103, 1987, 22–48.

E.A.K.

Gabali Gallic tribe in Aquitania, south of the Arverni, north of the Ruteni, on the north-western foot of the Cevennes. Source references: Caes. B Gall. 7,7,2; 64,6; 75,2; Γαβαλεῖς (*Gabaleîs*): Str. 4,2,2; *Gabales*: Plin. HN 4,109; *civitas Gabalum* of *Aquitania I*: *notitia Galliarum* 12,8, modern Gévaudan, Lozère. The Gabali were miners (silver mines) and bred cattle (cheese: Plin. HN 11,240). Main town: Anderitum (Ptol. 2,7,11; Sid. Apoll. Epist. 5,13,2; 7,6,7).

D. Fabrié, Carte archéologique de la Gaule. 48 (Lozère), 1989.

Y.L.

Gabara (Γαβαρα; *Gabara*, also Γαβαρωθ, Γαδαρα, Γαμαλα, Γαραβα, Γαβαρους; *Gabarōth*, *Gadara*, *Gamala*, *Garaba*, *Gabarous* [1]; from the Semitic *ǧrb* 'to bear a grudge against someone' or 'to be angry', which is the root of all variations of the name – apart from orthographic mistakes). Settlement in Lower Galilee, more likely the modern ʿArrāba/ʿArāv than Ḫirbat al-Qabra. At the beginning of the Jewish War (AD 66–70), G. sympathized with Josephus' opponent John of Gischala (Jos BI 2,629; Vita 82; 123f.; 203; 229–243; 265; 313); it was the first insurgent settlement to be captured and destroyed by Vespasianus (Jos. BI 3,132–134). Euseb. On. 16,13 mentions it as the village of Αραβα (*Araba*).

1 B. Lifshitz, Beth Sheʿarim II, no. 46 2 C. Möller, G. Schmitt, Siedlungen Palästinas nach Flavius Josephus, 1976, 56f.

E.A.K.

Gabii City of the Latini east of Rome on the south-eastern banks of the Lago di Castiglione (a volcanic crater) left of the Anio, 12 miles from Rome, modern Gabi (Roma). According to legend, it was of Siculan origin or a foundation by Alba Longa. It was here that Romulus and Remus allegedly were instructed in literature, music, and the use of Greek weapons (links with Greece, culturally dominating position amongst the Latin cities). The text of a *foedus* with Rome, concluded under Tarquinius Priscus, was preserved on a leather shield in the Quirinal temple of Semo Sancus (Dion.

Hal. Ant. Rom. 4,58). Allegedly, it was by treason that G. fell to Sex. Tarquinius (Liv. 1,53,4). In 382 BC, G. was allied with Rome against Praeneste; it became a *municipium* and the subject of Sullan land assignations [1. 234]. In 54 BC, G. did not take part in the *feriae Latinae* (Cic. Planc. 23) and declined to a mere *statio* on the *via Praenestina* (Liv. 1,53,4; 2,11,7; Str. 5,3,10; It. Ant. 302; Tab. Peut. 5,5). The town walls and gates as well as temples of Juno, Apollo, and Venus are extant. Some restoration work was carried out under Hadrian. Within the territory of the town there were cold mineral springs and quarries, where the *lapis Gabinus* was extracted, which was considered to be fireproof. *Cinctus Gabinus* is a technical term for a certain way of belting e.g. the Roman war toga, *ager Gabinus* is a technical term of Augural lore (Varro, Ling. 5,33); G. also appears in a damnation formula (Macrob. Sat. 3,9,13).

Archaeological data: bronze and iron age settlements with necropolis 2 km west of G. (Osteria dell'Osa); from the 8th cent. BC, the centre of the settlement was near Torre di Castiglione. Dating from the town's period of bloom in the 6th cent. BC, there are remnants of the town walls and the forum, which was lined on three sides by arcades and housed the *curia* as well as a large peripteros temple without a *posticum* (for Apollo?, dating from the 2nd cent., generally referred to as the temple of Juno Gabina). The *Fasti Gabini* and the 'Artemis of Gabii' (a copy of the statue by Praxiteles, now in the Louvre) originate from there. A sanctuary (of Juno? 7th–2nd cents. BC) was located east of the town walls.

1 F. Blume, K. Lachmann (ed.), Die Schriften der röm. Feldmesser 1, 1848.

P. Bruun, The foedus Gabinum, in: Arctos 5, 1967, 51–66; E. Peruzzi, Origini di Roma 2, 1973, 9; M. Guaitoli, G., in: PdP 36, 1981, 152–173; Id., G. Osservazioni sulle fasi di sviluppo dell'abitato, in: Quaderni dell'Istituto di Topografia Antica dell' Università di Roma 9, 1981, 23–57; M. Almagro Gorbea, El Santuario de Juno en Gabii, 1982; BTCGI 7, 1989, 520–528; A.M. Bietti Sestieri (ed.), La necropoli laziale di Osteria dell'Osa, 1992. G.U.

Gabinius Roman family name, probably related to Gabii (Schulze 532f.), widespread in Latium, and documented from the 3rd cent. BC; during the 2nd cent. BC, the family gained senatorial rank.

C. F. Konrad, On the Stemma of the Gabinii Capitones, in: Klio 66, 1984, 151–156.

I. Republican Period II. Imperial Period

I. Republican Period

[I 1] G., A. Allegedly the grandson of a slave (Liv. Per. Oxyrhynch. 54; cf. Cic. Leg. 3,35), in 146 BC envoy to the Achaeans; as people's tribune he introduced the secret ballot with voting tablets (*tabellae*) for the election of officials in 139 (1. *lex tabellaria*, Cic. loc. cit.; Lael. 41).

M. Jehne, Geheime Abstimmung und Bindungswesen in der röm. Republik, in: HZ 257, 1993, 593–613.

[I 2] G., A. Served perhaps as early as 86 BC as military tribune under L. Cornelius [I 90] Sulla in the war against Mithridates VI, and repeatedly in diplomatic missions. As people's tribune of 67, he had the supreme command against Mithridates transferred from L. → Licinius Lucullus to M'. Acilius [I 13] Glabrio, and discharged the *Fimbriani* (C. Flavius [I 6] Fimbria). Against considerable resistance from the Senate, he succeeded in passing a further law, that set up a special command against the pirates in the Mediterranean, intended for Cn. → Pompeius (Sall. Hist. 5,13; Cic. Leg. Man. 32–35; 52, et al. [1. 71ff.]). A ban on loans for provincials might belong in the same context (Cic. Att. 5,21,12; 6,2,7). In 66, G. went to the east as Pompey's legate, and in Iudaea mediated between Hyrcanus and Aristobulus, both pretenders to the Hasmonaean throne [2]. He probably served as praetor in 61, and in 58, with the support of Pompey, Caesar, and Crassus, he acceded to the consulship together with L. Calpurnius [I 19] Piso. He continued to support openly Clodius' [I 4] actions against Cicero until he was stopped by Pompey (MRR 2,193f.). The inscription of a law in favour of Delos is extant (Roman Statutes 1, 1996, no. 22). G. received the wealthy province of Syria as a reward, which he administered until 54 with military ambition and considerable skill; however, the Senate denied permission for a planned campaign across the Euphrates against the Parthians.

In 55 he led → Ptolemaeus XII Auletes back to Egypt and left behind occupational troops, for which the king paid him 10,000 talents in return. On his journey back, he pacified insurgent Judaea (Jos. Ant. Iud. 14,82–87). G. fell out with the tax leaseholders (*publicani*) by claiming the profits from his province for himself. Therefore, he did not succeed in being granted a triumph after his return to Rome (Cic. Pis. 48); he also got involved in a number of lawsuits. He was acquitted of the charge of treason (*maiestas*) because of Ptolemy's repatriation, but convicted of bribery in an extortion trial, even though Cicero had been forced by Pompey to defend him [2]. He went into exile, returned in 49 with Caesar's approval, and fought for him in Illyria, where he died of a disease at Salona in 47.

In the shadows of the powerful rulers Pompey and Caesar, G. became quite a talented politician; his image is distorted by Cicero's attacks in his speeches following his return from exile in 57.

1 M. Gelzer, Pompeius, ²1958 2 Alexander, 145; 148f.

E. Badian, The Career of A.G., in: Philologus 103, 1959, 87–99; Gruen, Last Gen.; Cl. Nicolet (ed.), Insula sacra, 1980, 45–57.

[I 3] G., P. Praetor in 89 BC (?), then governor of Achaea (MRR 3,98), in 76 *XVvir sacris faciundis*, later probably convicted in a *repetundae* lawsuit (Cic. Div. Caec. 64; Arch. 9; [1. 86f.]).

1 ALEXANDER.

[I 4] **G. Capito, P.** Eques, executed on 5 Dec. 63 BC as one of the most important followers of Catalina (Cic. Cat. 3,6; 12; 14 et al.; Sall. Catil. 17,4; 47,4; 55,5 et al.). K.-L.E.

II. IMPERIAL PERIOD

[II 1] **C. G. Barbarus Pompeianus.** Following his service as suffect consul in *c.* AD 194, he became consular governor of Moesia superior from 195 to 199 (CIL III 14507; [1]; AE 1976, 610); under Caracella, he became proconsul of Asia, probably in 211/212 [2. 224, 254]. He probably came from Venafrum.

1 W. ECK, in: ZPE 51, 1983, 291ff. 2 LEUNISSEN. W. ECK, RE Suppl. 14, 125.

[II 2] **G. Modestus.** Epistrategos of the → Heptanomia in AD 206/207 (POxy. 3341; 2131).

D. THOMAS, The epistrategos in Ptolemaic and Roman Egypt 2, 1982, 190, 203.

[II 3] **A. G. Secundus.** Regarding the name, see [1]. *Cos. suff.* in AD 35; appointed legate of the army in Germania inferior by Calligula. He defeated the Chauci, and was granted permission to bear the honorary cognomen Chaucius. Probably the father of G. [II 4].

1 G. CAMODECA, in: Athenaeum 65, 1987, 586f. W. ECK, Statthalter 114f. PIR² G 9.

[II 4] **A. G. Secundus.** *Cos. suff. c.* AD 43/44; probably son of G. [II 3]. PIR² G 8. W.E.

[II 5] King of the Quadi, treacherously murdered in *c.* AD 373 by Marcellianus, the *dux per Valeriam*; this resulted in a Quadian incursion into the Roman empire (Amm. Marc. 29,6,5f.; Zos. 4,16,4). PLRE 1, 377. W.P.

Gable Greek ἀ(ι)ετός/*a(i)etós* (architectural inscriptions: [1. 33f.]); Latin *fastigium, fronton*; triangular front, framed by the horizontal and raking cornices, of the saddleback roof of a typical Greek columned building; sacred architecture, the gable field (tympanon, for the terminology see: Vitr. De arch. 3,5,12; 4,3,2) is frequently decorated with sculptures; cf. → architectural sculpture. The pitch and hight of a gable in → proportion to the columns and the entablature provide some indication with regard to the buildings' position within the chronology of Greek temples. The heavy and high gables of the early archaic temples (Corfu, temple of Artemis; Syracuse, temple of Apollo) are reduced in the course of the developmental history of the Greek temple to the lower, lighter forms of the 4th and early 3rd cents. BC (Olympia, Metroon; Kournò, Peripteros). Even though the typological and functional expansion of columned buildings in the late 5th cent. BC led to an increasing occurrence of gables in secular contexts (e.g. on buildings with halls and archways; façades on → funerary architecture), they still bore the connotation of sacred dignity. Caesar was permitted to embellish his house with a gable only after a formal decree from the Senate (Cic. Phil. 2,110; Suet. Iul. 81; Plut. Caesar 63). As part of the architecture of walls and façades, which developed from the early Hellenistic period, gables also increasingly became ornamental elements to provide structure (Ptolemais, Palazzo delle Colonne; Tyndaris, skene of the theatre; earliest 'broken' gables in the rock tombs of Petra). In Roman representational architecture, gables developed more and more into features comparable to arches in the design of gates, façades, niches, windows, and aedicules.

1 EBERT.

H. LAUTER, Die Architektur des Hell., 1986, 113–232; S. MARINATOS, Ἀετός, in: FS für A.K. Orlandos I, 1965, 12–22; W. MÜLLER-WIENER, Griech. Bauwesen in der Ant., 1988, 112–156; J.B. WARD-PERKINS, Roman Imperial Architecture, 1970. C.HÖ.

Gabriel

[1] **(Archangel)** In the Jewish tradition, the angel G. ('man of God') is one of the six archangels, together with Uriel, Rafael, Raguel, Michael, and Sariel (1 Enoch, 20:1–7; for seven archangels cf. Tob 12:12–15; for four archangels: 1 Enoch 9–10; 40:9f.). In the biblical tradition, G. appears already together with Michael in the role of *angelus interpres*, who interprets the seer's visions (Dan 8:16; 9:21), and who announces the births of John the Baptist and Jesus (Lc 1:19.26). According to 1 Enoch 20:7, G. is placed above the snakes of paradise and the cherubs; this is an early indication of the hierarchization of the angelic world, which was subsequently even more differentiated. According to the Rabbinic tradition, his body is made of fire (cf. bPes 118a-b). As the archangel Michael, G. also appears as advocate and champion of Israel (e.g. bYom 77b), but he could also take the part of the avenging angel (bSan 19b). In the Greek magic papyri, Apollo is invoked as 'Michael, Gabriel, πρωτάγγελε ('first of the angels')' (PGM 1,300ff.; see also PGM 3,145ff.).

G. DAVIDSON, s.v. G., A Dictionary of Angels, 1967, 117–119; H.L. GINSBERG, s.v. Michael und Daniel, Encyclopaedia Judaica 11, 1487–1490; L. GINZBERG, The Legends of the Jews, 7, 1909–1938, index s.v. G.; M. MACH, Entwicklungsstadien des jüd. Engelglaubens in vorrabbinischer Zeit, 1992, 61, 177, 225, 264f., 299f. B.E.

[2] Author of an equally short and witty epigram, describing an Eros engraved on a pepper caster as – though sleeping – not far from the 'fiery bites' (Anth. Pal 16,208). As indicated by the lemma (Γαβριηλίου Ὑπάρχου; *Gabriēlíou Hypárchou*), he was probably the prefect of Constantinople (AD 543), whose portrait was praised by Leontios Scholastikos (Anth. Pal. 16,32). The poem may originate from the 'Kyklos' of Agathias.

Av. & A. Cameron, The Cycle of Agathias, in: JHS 86, 1966, 14. M.G.A.

Gabrielus *Praefectus urbis Constantinopolitanae* in AD 543; while in office, he resumed charge of the capital's grain supply, which John the Cappadocian (→ Iohannes [16]) had assigned to the *praefectus praetorio Orientis* (Lydus, Mag. 3,38; Nov. Iust. 125).

PLRE 3 A, 498; Stein, Spätröm. R., vol. 2, 441. K.P.J.

Gadara (modern Umm Qais). Town in north-eastern Transjordania, east of Lake Gennesareth; traces of settlement date back to the 7th cent. BC. After the fall of the Achaemenid kingdom (→ Achaemenids), the district of G. came under the control of the Ptolemies for a short period, but became part of the Seleucid kingdom under → Antiochus [5] III in 198 BC. For some time, the name of the town appears on coins as Seleucea or Antioch. Under Roman supremacy from 63 BC, G. was counted as one of the towns of the → Decapolis in the 1st and 2nd cents. AD. In the late imperial period, it held the title of a Roman colony and commanded an extensive hinterland. Archaeological remains indicate G.'s wealth and importance: two temples, two theatres, and two thermal baths, the fortified acropolis, a street of colonnades, as well as the necropolis with two mausolea. As early as the beginning of the 4th cent. AD, G. had developed into an important Transjordanian Christian centre with an episcopal see and a basilica. However, an earthquake in *c.* AD 400 initiated the decline of the city. The modest dimensions of restored public buildings indicate the decline in its economic power. The descendants of the 7th cent. Muslim conquerors were content with converting part of the thermal baths to a mosque.

S. Holm-Nielsen et al., Umm Qeis (Gadara), in: Archaeology of Jordan 2, 1989, 597–611; Th. Weber, Umm Qeis, Gadara of the Decapolis, 1990. T.L.

Gades (oldest Phoenician form of the name *ʾGdr*, 'wall', 'citadel', 'fortress', cf. Avien. 85, 267, 269, and [1. I 119; 3. 101f.], Greek Γάδειρα (*Gádeira*), Latin *Gades*, modern Cádiz). The date of its foundation is linked to the foundations of Utica and Carthage; according to literary sources, it is estimated for *c.* 1100 BC (Vell. Pat. 1,2; Iust. 44,5,2; Mela 3,46; Plin. HN 16,216; cf. [3. 5–12; 4. I 35ff., 44 n. 1, 47), but archaeological sources date back only to the 8th cent. BC [3. 17–21; 4. I 44 n. 1, 47 n. 1]. Ancient G. was located on three islands. The Phoenician settlement was on the island of Erythea, now as S. Sebastián part of the mainland (Plin. HN 4,120). It contained a temple of Astarte (*Venus Marina*, Avien. 315) with an oracular cave (near the so-called Torre Tavira); therefore the island was also known as Aphrodisias (Plin. HN 4,120; Steph. Byz. s.v. G.). It was also named after Hera (Plin. loc. cit.), the equivalent to the Phoenician goddess Tinnit [5. 263]. To the east of Erythea, orientated from NNW to SSE, lies a long, larger island, separated from the mainland by the Sancti Petri channel. It is about 18 km in length, and housed the Roman settlement of *Gades nova*. Old and new town together were known as *Gades gemina* (Str. 3,5,3; [5. 264; 7. 210f.]; for the most recent maps, see [8]). 18 km south of Cádiz lies the island of Santi Petri, in the south of which stood a temple of Heracles, originally dedicated to the Tyrian god Melqart; Hannibal visited this temple before setting out on his march on Rome. Most information about it comes from Posidonius, who visited it during his one-month stay in G. (cf. Str. 3,5,7; 9; Philostr. VA 5,1–7, on Apollonius of Tyana's stay in G., and Sil. Pun. 3,14ff.). Very little remains of the temple, because a fort was built on its site in the 17th cent. There is evidence of two wells, famous for their fluctuating water levels.

Modelled on the Melqart temple of Tyrus (Hdt. 2,44; cf. also Jachin and Boaz in front of the temple of Solomon, 1 Kgs 7:7ff.), two pillars stood in front of the temple [12. 100], referred to as the 'Pillars of Heracles' (the identification with the rocky headlands of Ǧabal Mūsā and Gibraltar, Ǧabal aṭ-Ṭāriq, which line the straits, is wrong [13. 14–26]). The finds from the Phoenician period, both from the town and from the necropolis to its south-east, near the Punta de la Vaca, are important; i.a., two anthropoid 'Sidonian' sarcophagi (1st half of the 5th cent. BC), a partly gilded bronze statuette of a priest or a praying figure, and golden jewellery [14. 47ff.]. Numerous coins have been found [2. I 51–60 with pl. IXf., III 8–14 with pl. LXXIV–LXXIX], whereas inscriptions from the Roman period are less informative (CIL II Suppl. p. 1145).

No clear conclusion is possible regarding G.'s legal status under Barcid rule (→ Barcids, with stemma). Undoubtedly, the city played an important part as starting point of the military campaigns of → Hamilcar (Diod. Sic. 25,10,1) and Mago (206 BC, Liv. 28,16,8; 13; 28,36,1; App. Ib. 28; 31). G. submitted to Roman rule in good time (Liv. 28,37,10). The city is frequently mentioned in the context of the later Spanish campaigns; it gave valuable support to Caesar in his fight against Pompey (Caes. B Civ. 2,18–21). After 206, G. presumably became a *civitas foederata*; Caesar granted its inhabitants Roman citizenship; under Augustus, it became an *oppidum civium Romanorum qui appellantur Augustani urbe Iulia Gaditana* (Plin. HN 4,119). G. was also a *municipium*; however, the dating of attaining this status is contested [6. 45; 11. 439ff.; 9. 246ff.]. L. Cornelius Balbus expanded his home town by building the new town and a port (Str. 3,5,3). For many cents., G. was a blooming and wealthy city, based on shipping, fishing industry, and the fertility of its environs ([1. II 42,46f.; VIII 325], Str. 3,5,3; Avien. 270). Its female dancers were famous [1. VIII 252, 259, 267; 3. 107–109]. G. was the capital of a *conventus* (Plin. HN 3,7; 15); with regard to the size of its population, it ranked second only to Rome (Str. 3,5,3). It remains an unsolved mystery, why G. in the 4th cent. – as described in Avien. 271–274 – was partially destroyed and was insignificant and poor. This information is confirmed by the fact that subsequently G. is no longer mentioned in literary sources, apart from the fact that for the Greeks it was the proverbial 'end of the world' [1. IX 432, 439]. The only possible explanation seems to be the incursion of an African tribe [1. VIII 41f.]. Only in the 8th cent. AD, under ʿAbd ar-Raḥmān, did it regain its (strategic) importance [10. 331].

1 A. Schulten, Fontes Hispaniae Antiquae I–IX, 1925–1959 2 A. Vives, La moneda hispánica, 1924 3 A. Garcia y Bellido, Fenicios y Carthagineses en Occidente, 1942 4 Id., Hispania Graeca, 2 vols., 1948 5 Schulten, Landeskunde 6 Tovar 2 7 A. Schulten, Forschungen in Spanien 1927, in: AA 1927, 197–235 (with city map) 8 A. Alvarez Rojas, Sobre la localización del Cádiz fenicio, in: Boletín del Museo de Cádiz 5, 1992, 17–30 9 J. L. López Castro, Hispania Poena, 1995 10 Enciclopedia Universal Ilustrada 10 11 E. Hübner, s.v. Gades, RE 7, 439–451 12 H. G. Niemeyer, Zum Thymiaterion vom Cerro del Peñón, in: Madrider Mitt. 11, 1970, 96–101 13 H. Walter, Zum Ursprung und Nachleben der Sage von den Säulen des Herakles, in: R. Stupperich (ed.), Lebendige Antike. Koll. W. Schiering, 1992, 14–26 14 J. A. Martín Ruiz, Catálogo documental de los Fenicios en Andalucía, 1995.

P. Rouillard, s.v. G., DCPP, 181–183; M. Cruz Marin, La Ciudad de Cádiz, in: Cité et Territoire, 1994, 219–226; H. G. Niemeyer, Anno octogesimo Troiam captam ... Tyria classis Gadis condidit? Polemische Gedanken zum Gründungsdatum von Gades (Cádiz), in: Hamburger Beitr. zur Arch. 8, 1981, 9–33. P.B. and H.G.N.

Gadfly (οἶστρος; *oîstros*, *tabanus bovinus*, substituted in Verg. G. 3,147 by *asilus*, later considered antiquated by Seneca in Epist. 58,2). Earlier authors generally equated it with the horsefly μύωψ (*mýōps*) (cf. Aesch. Suppl. 511 and 308; Prom. 567 and 675), but Aristotle distinguishes between the two (Hist. an. 1,5,490a20 and 8,11,596b14, without description). As the μύωψ in Aristot. Hist. an. 5,19,552a30, are described in the *tabanus* and the *cossus* (Pliny HN 11,113) as originating from wood. Apparently, the gadfly was only properly identified in Augustean times by Sostratus [1. 344]. Gadflies drive cows to frenzy (Hom. Od. 22,300; Verg. G. 3,147; Varro, Rust. 2,5,14), as for example Io, who was transformed into a cow at the orders of Hera. Therefore, the tragedians used the name metaphorically for any tormenting passion (e.g. Eur. HF 862; IT 1456; cf. Soph. Trach. 1254) and the suffering resulting from it (Hdt. 2,93; Eur. Hipp. 1300); as such it was personified in the visual arts (Munich Medea vase [2. 163ff. and pl. 90], cf. [3]).

→ Insects

1 Wellmann, Sostratos. Ein Beitrag zur Quellenanalyse des Aelian, in: Hermes 26, 1891, 321–350
2 Furtwängler/Reichhold vol. 2 3 J. Schmidt, s.v. B., RE 17, 2286f. C.HÜ.

Gaesati According to Polybius (Pol. 2,22,1; 2,34), the G. were a Gallic tribe, living in the Alps and along the Rhône; G. went into service as mercenaries, hence their name (Pol. 2,22,1). They took part in the Gallic invasion of Italy in 225 BC, but were beaten off, and subsequently defeated in 222 BC. *Gaesum* is also the name of a Gallic spear (Caes. B Gall. 3,4), sometimes carried by lightly armed Roman troops (Liv. 8,8,5). In the early Principate, auxiliary troops recruited from Raetia and apparently equipped with this kind of spear were referred to as *gaesati*. They were stationed in a fortress within that province under the command of a cavalry veteran (CIL XIII 1081; ILS 2531). Later, a unit described as *vexillatio Retorum Gaesa(torum)* is evident in the Scottish Jedburgh (ILS 2623); alongside naval soldiers, G. were involved in the construction of a water pipe in Africa (Saldae) (ILS 5795).

D. Vaglieri, s.v. G. Ruggiero 3, 357. J.CA.

Gaeson (Γαίσων; *Gaísōn*). Small river on the southern slopes of the Mycale mountains (Samsun Dağı), cf. Hdt. 9,97; Mela 1,87 (*Gaesus*); Plin. HN 5,113 (*Gessus*). Scolopoeis (Σκολοπόεις) with a temple of the Eleusinian Demeter was located at the G.; it was the location of the battle between Greeks and Persians in 479 BC (Hdt. 9,97). A lake named after the river (Γαισωνὶς λίμνη; *Gaisōnìs límnē*, Ath. 7,311e) is also to be located in the vicinity. E.O.

Gaetuli Berber tribe, whose numerous clans lived in the area between the Syrtis Minor and the Atlantic Ocean. Source references: Str. 2,5,33; 17,3,2; 9; 19; Mela 1,23; 3,104; Plin. HN 5,9f.; 17; 30; 43; Apul. Apol. 24,1; 41,4; Dimensuratio provinciarum 25; Aug. De ordine 2,5,15; Aug. In psalmos 148,10; Divisio orbis terrarum 26; Steph. Byz. s.v. Γαιτοῦλοι; Anon. Geographia compendiaria 15 (GGM II 497); Eust. epit. de commentariis in Dionysium Periegeten 215 (GGM II 254). A branch of the G., who had intermarried with black Africans, was called the *Melanogaitoûloi* (Μελανογαιτοῦλοι, Ptol. 4,6,16; cf. Anon. Geographia compendiaria 16 [GGM II 498]). There are several reports on their (nomadic) way of life (Sall. Iug. 18; 19,5–7; Varro, Rust. 2,11,11; Mela 3,104; Plin. HN 5,12; 6,201; 8,20; 48; 54; 9,127; 10,201; 21,77; 25,79; 35,45; Ath. 2,62e). Gaetulian soldiers served in the armies of Hannibal and Jugurtha (Liv. 23,18; Sall. Iug. 19,7; 80; 88; 97; 99; Cass. Dio 43,4,2), and in 46 BC they fought on Juba's as well as on the Caesarians' side (Bell. Afr. 25,2f.; 35; 56,3; 61; Cass. Dio 43,3,4). In AD 6, Cossus Cornelius Lentulus, the *proconsul Africae*, was forced to take action against Gaetulian units (Vell. Pat. 2,116,2; Tac. Ann. 4,42,3; Flor. Epit. 4,12,40; Cass. Dio 53,26,2; 55,28,3f.; Oros. 6,21,18). Because of his success, he – or his younger son Cn. – were given the cognomen → Gaetulicus. In later times, Gaetulian tribes in Numidia were under the control of a Roman officer (ILS I 2721; Tert. Adv. Iudaeos 7). In the 2nd or 3rd cent., G.

threatened Cirta (ILS II 1, 6860). However, there were also Gaetulian *alae* and *cohortes* serving in the Roman army (cf. e.g. Not. Dign. Or. 35,32).

J. DESANGES, Pline l'Ancien. Histoire Naturelle. Livre V, 1–46, 1980, 342–346; S. GSELL, Histoire ancienne de l'Afrique du Nord 5, ²1929, 109–112; A. LUISI, Getuli, dei popoli libici il più grande (Strab. 17,826), in: CISA 18, 1992, 145–151. W.HU.

Gaetulicus [I] (Γαιτουλικός; *Gaitoulikós*). Epigrammatist, to whom ten poems are ascribed in the *Anthologia Palatina* (not authentic, however, Anth. Pal. 7,245 and perhaps 6,154), which in style and topics (but not by their arrangement) bear resemblance to the 'Garlands' of Meleager or Philippus; however, 11,409 originates from the *Anthologion* of Diogenianus [2] of Heraclea. The identification with the poet Cn. → Cornelius [II 29] Lentulus Gaetulicus, who was *cos.* in AD 26 and executed by Caligula in 39, is controversial. G.'s poetry is without originality. It is based on the successful, sometimes literal, imitation of other works, esp. by → Leonidas of Tarentum (mentioned in Anth. Pal. 6,190,2), → Chaeremon [3] (7,244,4), and → Dioscorides [3] (11,409).

FGE 49–60. M.G.A.

Gaetulicus [II] 'Victor over the Gaetuli', cognomen of Cossus → Cornelius [II 26] Lentulus G. and his son Cn. → Cornelius [II 29] Lentulus G., as well as C. → Iulius Tiro G. and D. (→ Iunius) Silanus G.

KAJANTO, Cognomina 206. K.-L.E.

Gaia (Γαῖα, Γῆ; *Gaîa, Gê*). Greek personification of the earth as the basis of all existence; her name can be interpreted possibly in Indo-European as 'she who gives birth' [1]. From Hesiod (Theog. 117ff.), she is seen in theogonic poetry as a primal power, who first gave birth to → Uranus, the sky, and Pontus, the Sea, then became the mother of the subsequent generation of deities as well as that of a number of monsters, whose birth even posed a threat to the order of Zeus (→ Giants, → Typhoeus). Later theogonies followed this pattern which had already been established in the Ancient Orient, but with some variations: Orpheus' theogonies place a generation of earlier beings before G., and the Derveni Papyrus places greater emphasis on the role of → Nyx; Pherecydes of Syrus replaces G. with Chtonie, the deity of the elemental depth of the earth (DIELS/KRANZ 7 B 1). Whereas Hesiod emphasized the anthropomorphous aspect of her character, which is not easily reduced to an allegory of nature, later works used the images of the wedding between G. and Uranus as an allegory of natural processes (Aesch. fr. 44 TrGF; Eur. fr. 839 TGF). In the Delphian myth, G. is seen as the first owner of the oracle, prior to → Themis and Apollo (Aesch. Eum. 2–4); in local mythology, she is also linked to the oracles of Dodona (Paus. 10,12,10) and Olympia (Paus. 5,14,10), which testifies to the claim of these locations with regard to antiquity and authenticity.

In keeping with her ambivalent position in the theogonic myth, in which she is seen as a primal power but outside of the current order as established by Zeus and even a threat to it, she rarely appears in the cult of the polis; however, where she does, some extraordinary rites are associated with her. It is said that in Athens → Erichthonius introduced presacrifices prior to any sacrifice to G. Kourotrophos as the nurturer of the young (Suda s.v. κουροτρόφος; *kourotróphos*); as Ge Karpophoros, she was able to mediate with Zeus in times of extraordinary drought (IG III[1] 166; Paus. 1,24,3). She was frequently invoked in oaths, not only in poetry (Hom. Il. 3,278–280), often together with the all-seeing Helius (→ Sol) and with Zeus as the guarantors of all order; the same connection is still evident in the Anatolian grave curses of the Imperial period [2]. However, none of these confirm the Romantic notion of an all-embracing 'mother earth', at least not in the Greek or Roman (→ Tellus) tradition [3].

1 M. MEIER-BRÜGGER, Zu griech. γῆ und γαῖα, in: Münchner Stud. zur Sprachwissenschaft 53, 1992, 113–116
2 M. TÜRKTÜZÜN, M. WÖRRLE, Eine neue Türgrabstele aus dem phrygischen Alioi, in: Chiron 24, 1994, 95–101
3 A. DIETERICH, Mutter Erde, 1905.

R. RENEHAN, Hera and Earth Goddess, in: RhM 117, 1974, 193–201; CH. SOURVINOU-INWOOD, Myth as History. The Previous Owners of the Delphic Oracle, in: Id., "Reading" Greek Culture. Texts and Images, Rituals and Myths, 1991, 217–243; W. STAUDACHER, Die Trennung von Himmel und Erde. Ein vorgriech. Schöpfungsmythos bei Hesiod und den Vorsokratikern, 1942. F.G.

Gaianus A Tyrian (Lib. Ep. 336), a friend of → Libanius, also not a Christian (Lib. Ep. 1364); he is only known from Libanius' letters. G. was a lawyer (Lib. Ep. 119; 336); in 360, he became assessor to a magistrate in Antioch (Lib. Ep. 780; 799), and in 362 he was promoted to the office of *consularis Phoenices* (Lib. Ep. 780; 799; 800 et al.), from which he resigned in 363 (Lib. Ep. 1218). He died after 388 (Lib. Ep. 881). PLRE 1, 378f. (G. 6). M.R.

Gaia Taracia (or Gaia Fufetia). A Vestal, who donated to the city of Rome the *campus Tiberinus* (the Tiber island according to Plut. Publicola 8,8,101b, or rather the Campus Martius according to Gell. NA 7,7,4); therefore, she was not only honoured with a statue (Plin. HN 34,11,25), but also with a law which set out the central prerogatives of the vestals (*lex Horatia*, Gell. NA 7,7,2–4). This story is the *aition* for these rather unusual privileges, which in many aspects gave the Vestals an equal standing with men.

A. MOMIGLIANO, Tre figure mitiche. Tanaquilla, Gaia Cecilia, Acca Larenzia, in: Momigliano 4, 1989, 455–485. F.G.

Gaieochos (γαιήοχος; *Gaiēochos*). Ep. epithet meaning 'earth shaker', used in Homer as a metric substitute or complimentary cognomen for Poseidon (especially in conjunction with γαιήοχος ἐννοσίγαιος; *gaiēochos ennosígaios*). Only late antique texts extend the reference of *gaieochos* beyond Poseidon to Zeus (Opp. Hal. 1,74) and Oceanus (Quint. Smyrn. 2,208). In antiquity, it was generally understood as a composite of γαῖα and ἔχειν (etymologically not tenable) or ὀχεῖσθαι (either in the form of the earth carrying Poseidon as a river or Poseidon flowing as an underground river). Nowadays, it is undoubtedly seen as linked to the root ὀχεῖσθαι (*ocheîsthai*; Latin vehere, 'move'), but the exact meaning is unclear.

W. Beck, s.v. γαιήοχος, LFE; Chantraine, s.v. G., 282; Frisk, s.v. γῆ, 219. E.V.

Gainas Tervingian Goth of low birth, Arian. Recruited by Theodosius I in AD 378, he led eastern troops to support Arcadius in Constantinople as *comes rei militaris* (for his military career, see Socr. 6,6,2; Sozom. Hist. eccl. 8,4,1), at the order of → Stilicho, after Theodosius' victory over Eugenios in 394. As Stilicho's confidant, he was involved in the death of → Rufinus in 399 ([1. 107,99], Zos. 5,7,4; Philostorgius 11,3, Iohannes Antiochenus 190 FHG 4,610). In 399, he was elevated to *magister utriusque militiae*, and was sent by → Eutropius to Phrygia against the rebellious Gruthongs under → Tribigild, with whom he however joined forces and eliminated Eutropius (Zos. 5,13,1f.; 17,4). In 400, G. occupied Constantinople against the resistance of its inhabitants. When he demanded a Catholic church for his Arians against the will of Iohannes Chrysostomos (Theod. Hist. eccl. 5,32), his soldiers were massacred. G. fled with the remainder of his troops to Thrace; in his attempt to return to Asia Minor, he was defeated by → Fravitta. G. retreated across the Danube, where he was killed by the Huns (regarding the date of death, see [3. 427,63]). As a consequence of G.'s uprising, the Eastern empire no longer followed politics sympathetic to the Goths, but turned towards the Huns. For source material, see [1. 14–17]. PLRE 1, 379–380.
→ Tervingi

1 G. Albert, Goten in Konstantinopel, 1984
2 P. Heather, Goths and Romans, 1991, 332–489
3 H. Wolfram, Die Goten, ³1990. ME.STR.

Gaiso

[1] In AD 350, possibly as *magister militum* of the usurper Magnentius, he pursued the fleeing emperor Constans, and killed him during his arrest in the Pyrenean town of Helena ([Aur. Vict.] Epit. Caes. 41,23; Zos. 2,42,5). In 351, he was *consul* together with Magnentius (Chron. min. 1, 69 Mommsen). PLRE 1, 380. W.P.

[2] *Comes sacrarum largitionum* under Honorius probably in AD 409, and *comes et magister officiorum* in 410 (Cod. Iust. 4,61,12; Cod. Theod. 9,38,11). He was probably of Germanic descent. PLRE 2, 490. K.P.J.

Gaius [I] (Γάϊος; *Gáïos*). Platonic philosopher of the early 2nd cent. AD. The physician → Galen studied with two of his students [3. 34f.]. No works are extant. His commentary on the myth of → Er [1. 18, 205] and his comments on Plato's dual teaching methods [1. 213; 2.98, 357ff.] were most likely part of (lost) lecture notes taken by his student → Albinus [1. 28, 182ff.]. He was held in high regard particularly by Plotinus, Porphyrius, and Priscian; Proclus saw him as one of the great authorities amongst the Platonists [1. 18, 151ff., 161f.]. He was given an honorary inscription in Delphi [1. 144f.; 3. 36ff.].

1 Dörrie/Baltes, III, 1993 2 Id., IV, 1996
3 T. Göransson, Albinus, Alcinous, Arius Didymus, 1995.

Fragments: T. Göransson [s. 3], 28–30
Bibliography: K. Praechter, Zum Platoniker G., in: Hermes 51, 1916, 510–529 = KS 1973, 81–100; L. Deitz, Bibliographie du platonisme impérial antérieur à Plotin: 1926–1986, in: ANRW II 36.1, 1987, 149.
M.BA. and M.-L.L.

Gaius [II] Widespread Roman *praenomen* (probably connected with the Latin family name *Gavius*, but not related to *gaudere*), abbreviated as C., more rarely G.; in late Greek inscriptions also Γα (*Ga*).

Salomies 28f. K.-L.E.

[1] Physician of the school of Herophilus, probably 1st cent. BC or AD, wrote about hydrophobia (Caelius Aurelianus morb. ac. 3,113–4). He explained that this disease affected the brain as well as the meninges, because the nerves surrounding the stomach and responsible for involuntary movement originated in the brain. It remains uncertain whether he is identical with the oculist from Naples, whose prescriptions are extant in the Asclepiades Pharmakion from the end of the 1st cent. AD (Gal. 12,628; 771; 13,830). V.N.

[2] Jurist of the Antonine period, known only by the praenomen.
A. Person B. Works 1. General 2. The Institutes C. Appreciation and Later Reception

A. Person

G., a pupil of the Sabinian school of law, worked between *c.* AD 140 and 180 [7. 188]; there is no documentary evidence showing him either as an office holder or as a respondent. Even though G. left behind a sizeable opus of 100 scrolls, he was never quoted by his fellow jurists (*Gaius noster* in Dig. 45,3,39 may have been coined by Justinianus: [6. 91ff.]). This led to assumptions that G. may have been identical with another jurist, such as e.g. C. → Cassius [II 14] Longinus, → Laelius Felix (critical discussion in [1. 295ff.]), or

Sex. → Pomponius [6. 83ff.]; however, the hypothesis that after his studies in Rome he worked as a provincial law teacher [7. 188] should be preferred.

B. Works

1. General

G. wrote the commentaries *Ad edictum praetoris urbani* (10 bks.), and *Ad edictum aedilium curulium* (2 bks.), and also the only commentary in legal literature on the provincial edict *Ad edictum provinciale* (30 bks.; for these works, see [7. 189f.]); author of the legal commentary *Ad legem Iuliam et Papiam* (15 bks.) and *Ad legem duodecim tabularum* (6 bks., the first commentary after → Antistius [II 3] Labeo), also of the monographs *De manumissionibus* (3 bks.), *De verborum obligationibus* (3 bks.), *De fideicommissis* (2 bks.), and the ' individual treatises' *Dotalicion, Ad senatus consultum Tertullianum, Ad senatus consultum Orfitianum, De tacitis fideicommissis, De formula hypothecaria* (see [1. 328ff.], and *De casibus*. Of the 'individual treatise' *Ad legem Glitiam*, only a short fragment (Dig. 5,2,4) is extant [7. 194]. His work *Ex Quinto Mucio* is only mentioned by G. himself (Gai. Inst. 1,188).

2. The Institutes

G. achieved his greatest success with his textbook *Institutiones* (4 bks.; see [2; 7. 191f.]). These lecture notes, which were presumably published by his students, based on his lectures of AD 161, are the only other almost completely extant example of the legal literature of the Principate apart from Justinian's compilation. Initially, the text was only known as the model for Justinian's Institutes, and from excerpts in the *Collatio legum Mosaicarum et Romanarum* as well as in Justinian's digests; then, in 1816, it was discovered on a 5th cent. → palimpsest in Verona; fragments were also found on papyri in 1927 (POxy. XVII 2103) and 1933 (PSI XI 1182) [2. 1 ff., 46ff.]. The *Institutiones* offer the only extant ancient Roman synopsis of civil law, in the order of (Gai. Inst. 1,8) *personae* (private and family law) – *res* (property law) – *actiones* (procedural law). 'Persons' (1,9ff.) are subdivided into freeborn and slave, 'tangibles' (2,12ff.) into *res corporales* and *incorporales* such as *hereditas, usus fructus,* and *obligatio*, 'actions ' (4,1ff.) into material actions (*actiones in rem*) and obligatory actions (*actiones in personam*). Obligations are subdivided into contractual (*ex contractu*) and delictual responsibilities (*ex delicto*); contracts are subdivided into real, verbal, literal, and consensual ones (3,88ff.). This classification in accordance with Hellenistic textbooks replaced Massurius → Sabinus' associative system with one based on logic, and the antiquated focus on actions with a clear separation of material law and legal procedures. This involved combining the *ius civile* and *ius honorarium* as well as imperial law, which had traditionally been dealt with separately in the commentaries of Sabinus and on edicts. This 'system of institutes', rooted in the teaching practices of the Sabinian law school [2. 370ff.], is followed by all modern private law systems [4; 7. 195].

G. himself extended and refined the systematics of the *Institutiones* in his *Res cottidianae sive aurea* (7 bks.; see [5. 94ff.; 7. 192f.]). This work completes the bipartition of obligations with the introduction of 'other motives' (Dig. 44,7,1 pr.: *variae causarum figurae*), subsequently further divided by Justinian (Inst. Iust. 3,13,2) into quasi contracts and quasi offences. Apart from his understanding of systematics, G. exhibits an interest in legal history (Dig. 1,2,1) and in comparative law (Gai. Inst. 1,52ff.; 1,189ff.), unusual in Roman jurisprudence. The universal applicability of the *ius gentium* irrespective of citizenship is explained by G. with the legal philosophical argument of 'natural law' (Gai. Inst. 1,1: *naturalis ratio*; see [5. 20ff., 40ff., 98ff.]).

C. Appreciation and Later Reception

In late antiquity, G. enjoyed great popularity: he was one of five jurists listed in the Law of Citations (→ Citations, law governing [vol. 4 add.]) of 426 (Cod. Theod. 1,4,3); in the west, his *Institutiones* were the basis for the 4th cent. elementary paraphrase (*Fragmenta Augustodunensia* [3. 71f.]), and their adaptation by the Visigoths in the 5th cent., the *Epitome Gai* [2. 123ff.]; in the east, they were used in their complete form in legal instructions (*Omnem* § 1), and served as a basis for Justinian's own Institutes (*Imperatoriam* § 6) [2. 182ff.]. However, in view of the paucity of transmitted material, it is uncertain whether G.'s *Regulae*, excerpted in Justinian's digests, are pseudepigraphical [3. 68f.].

1 D. Liebs, Röm. Provinzialjurisprudenz, in: ANRW II 15, 288–362 2 H. L. W. Nelson, Überlieferung, Aufbau und Stil von Gai Institutiones, 1981 3 D. Liebs, Recht und Rechtslit., in: HLL 5, 55–73 4 D. R. Kelley, Gaius noster: Substructures of Western Social Thought, in: C. Varga (ed.), Comparative Legal Cultures, 1992, 39–68 5 M. Kaser, Ius gentium, 1993 6 D. Pugsley, Justinian's Digest and the Compilers, 1995 7 D. Liebs, s.v. Jurisprudenz, in: HLL 4, 83–217. T.G.

[3] G. of Rome. Theologian of the end of the 2nd cent. AD, who wrote in Greek. According to Eus. Hist. eccl. II,25,6f., at the time of pope Zephyrinus (198–217) he wrote a (fragmentarily preserved) dialogue with Proclus, in which he pointed out the tombs of Peter and Paul, who had been executed in the course of Nero's persecutions; he also spoke against both the Chiliasm and the → Montanism of → Cerinthus (ibid. III,28,1f.). In G.'s view, the epistle to the Hebrews was not written by Paul (ibid. VI,20,3), and he also did not recognize John the Apostle as the author of Revelation, for which he was reproached by Hippolytus of Rome.

Hippolytos, Kapitel gegen G.: GCS I/2, 239–247; Dionysios Bar Salibi, In Apocalipsim: CSCO 53,60,1f.; E. Kirschbaum, Die Gräber der Apostelfürsten, [3]1974; K. H. Schelkle, Das Neue Testament, [4]1970, 242ff.; J. D. Smith, G. and the Controversy over the Johannine Literature, diss. Yale Univ. 1979. RO.F.

Gaizatorix (Γαιζατόριξ, Γεζατόριος; *Gaizatórix*, *Gezatórios*). Celtic name, 'lord of the Gaesati (spear bearers)' [2. 215]. Leader of the Galates, who in 180 BC together with → Cassignatus approached Eumenes II for help against → Pharnaces of Pontus. Eumenes refused, as the Galates had previously sided with the latter (Pol. 24,14; 25,2). A region in western Paphlagonia may also have been named after G. (Str. 12,3,41). Regarding a forged silver coin of the 'Boian king' Gesatorix, see [1. 77–79].

1 R. Göbl, Typologie und Chronologie der kelt. Münzprägungen in Noricum, 1973 2 Schmidt.

F. Stähelin, Gesch. der kleinasiatischen Galater, [2]1907. W.SP.

Galaad (Γαλαάδ; *Galaád*, LXX, Eus.), Gilead (Hebrew *gilʿad*).

[1] Town in eastern Jordan (Judg. 10:17; Hos. 6:8; 12:12), the modern *Ḫirbat Ǧalʿad* south of the Jabboq 10 km north-northeast of *as-Salt*, on the homonymous mountain range (Gen. 31:21, et al.: *hăr [hăg]gilʿad*, modern *Ǧabal Ǧalʿad*) (cf. Euseb. On. 62,1f.).

[2] Region east of the Jordan (LXX alongside Γ. also Γαλαδ[ε]ῖτις; *Galad[e]ītis*; Jos. Ant. Iud. 1,324 et al. Γαλαδηνή; *Galadēnē*; 5,164 et al., Γαλα[α]δῖτις; *Gala[a]dītis*; 12,336 et al. Γαλάτις; *Galátis*). Originally, the land of 'Gilead' was limited to an area south of the Jabboq extending westward (cf. Gen. 31; Judg. 10:17; see also [3. 30ff.]) from Mt. Gilʿād (cf. → G. [1]; hence the name). The Israelites apparently extended the term 'Gilead' to denote their area of settlement between the *ʿAǧlūn* mountains and the Yarmuk river, cf. the towns Yabes-Gilead (1 Sam. 11:1ff. et al.), Ramoth-Gilead (1 Kgs 4:13 et al.), Camon (Judg. 10:5), and Thisbe-Gilead (LXX, 1 Kgs 17:1). Finally, G. comprised the land between the rivers Arnon and Yarmuk (Deut. 3:10; 2 Kgs 10:33), possibly also including Bāšān (between Yarmuk and Mt. Hermon) (Deut. 34:1; Euseb. On. 60,15ff., 44,9ff.). In the Aramaic wars of the 9th and 8th cents. BC, G. came under the rule of Damascus for some time (2 Kgs 10:33, Am 1:3; differently 2 Kgs 14:25, Am. 6:13); it became an Assyrian province in 733 BC. → Alexander [16] Iannaios conquered large parts of the region (Jos. Ant. Iud. 13,356; 393f. et al.; cf. 13,397). Following Pompey's subjugation, the Jews were left with only a narrow strip of land called Peraea.

1 N. Glueck, Explorations in Eastern Palestine III (AASO 18/19), 1939, 151–251 2 Id., Explorations in Eastern Palestine IV (AASO 25/28), 1951 3 M. Noth, Gilead und Gad, in: ZPalV 75, 1959, 14–73. ER.K.

Galactophagi (Γαλακτοφάγοι/*Galaktophágoi*, 'milk eaters') are fist mentioned in Hom. Il. 13,5f. together with the Hippemolgi ('mare-milkers') and → Abii as neighbours of the Thracians. Ancient literature offers three different views on the identity of the G.: 1. G., Hippemolgi, and Abii as three fabulous tribes who live on the edge of the inhabited world (Str. 7,3,7; 12,3,27). 2. G. and Hippemolgi as Scythian or Sarmatian nomadic tribes (Str. 7,3,7–9), or 3. G. as a real, geographically locatable Scythian tribe (Ptol. 6,14,12). C.U.-K.

Galaei (Γαλαῖοι; *Galaîoi*). The G., who appear in the Athenian tribute lists from 436/435 BC, were the citizens of a town on the western coast of Sithonia, close to the modern Neos Marmaras, referred to by Herodotus (Hdt. 7,122), probably erroneously, as Galepsos in his description of Xerxes' campaign. In 432, the G. seceded from Athens and resettled in the enlarged city of Olynthus, but their town was recaptured by Athens before 425, and declared independent in the peace of Nicias of 421. After that, the sources no longer mention it.

M. Zahrnt, Olynth und die Chalkidier, 1971, 178f. M.Z.

Galaesus River, also known as Eurotas (Pol. 8,35,8), 40 stades (Pol. loc. cit.) or 5 miles (Liv. 25,11,8) from Tarentum. In 212 BC, Hannibal built a camp on its banks. Mentioned in Virgil (Georg. 4,12,6), Horace (Carm. 2,6,10), and Propertius (2,34,67). Its water is praised as particularly suited for the washing of wool (Mart. 2,43,3; 4,28,3; 5,37,2; 8,28,3; 12,63,6; Stat. Silv. 3,3,93).

Nissen 2, 870. H.SO.

Galanthis see → Galinthias

Galaria Town of the Siculi, localized by Rizzo [1. 67] near the Sicilian S. Mauro di Caltagirone. Only mentioned by Diodorus twice: in the context of the battle against the Carthaginians alongside → Entella in 334 BC (Diod. Sic. 16,67,3) and in the context of the 312/311 BC revolt against Agathocles (Diod. Sic. 19,104). Archaeological finds: rare silver *lítrai*, originating from the area north-west of Mineo (cf. [2. 84–87; 3. 36–39]).

1 G.E. Rizzo, Monete greche di Sicilia, 1946 2 K. Jenkins, in: Atti di IV Convegno di Studi Numismatici Napoli, Annali del Istituto Italiano per gli Studi Storici, Suppl. 20, 1975 3 G. Manganaro, in: Annali del Istituto Italiano per gli Studi Storici 21–22, 1974/5.

E. Manni, Geografia fisica e politica della Sicilia antica, 1981, 175f.; BTCGI 7, 535–539. GI.MA.

Galata Small island off the north African coast between Karalis and Thabraca (modern Tabarka), formed from volcanic rocks, modern Galita. Source references: Mela 2,120; Plin. HN 3,92; 5,42; 35,202; Ptol. 4,3,44 (Καλάθη; *Kaláthē*); It. Ant. 494,7–495,1; 514,4–8 (providing some wrong distances); Tab. Peut. 3,4; Liber generationis, Chron. min. 1, p. 103,134; 109,212; Liber genealogus, Chron. min. 1, p. 168,165; Mart. Cap. 6,645; Geogr. Rav. p. 102,1.

J. Toutain, Note sur l'île de la Galite, in: MEFRA 11, 1891, 454–456. W.HU.

Galatea (Γαλατεία; Galateía).

[1] Nereid, daughter of → Nereus and → Doris (Hom. Il. 18,45; Hes. Theog. 250; Apollod. 1,11), whose name probably refers to the milky-white colour, i.e. either to sea-foam or milk in its important role in pasture farming (Lucian 14,3; Eust. 1131,5 ad Hom. Il. 18,42). In Sicily, G. was venerated as the protector of herds (Duris FGrH 76 F 58). The love story between the Cyclops → Polyphemus and G. also originates from Sicily (Prop. 3,2,7f.; Nonnus, Dion. 39,257–264); this union produced a son named Gala(te)s (Timaeus FGrH 566 F 69). The story is first evident in a Dithyrambus of Philoxenus of the 5th/4th cents. (Phaenias of Eresus fr. 13 Wehrli = Ath. 1,6e–7a), who, according to Duris, was also its creator. Of the comedies on this subject, almost nothing is extant (Nicochares PCG VII fr. 3–6; Antiphanes PCG II fr. 129–131; Alexis PCG II fr. 37–40). The motif of the giant's unrequited love was very popular in Hellenistic poetry (Theoc. 6,6–19; 11; Callim. Fr. 378f.; Bion, Apospasmata 16; later Verg. Ecl. 7,37–40; 9,39; Lucian 78,1; Niketas Eugenianos 6,503–537), whereas Odysseus as Polyphemus' rival became less significant or was replaced altogether by the shepherd Acis (Ov. Met. 13,750–897).

Bibliography: J. Farrell, Dialogue of genres in Ovid's "Lovesong of Polyphemus" (Met. 13,719–897), in: AJPh 113, 1992, 235–268; G. R. Holland, De Polyphemo et G., in: Leipziger Stud. zur class. Philol. 7, 1884, 141–312; S. Montón Subias, s.v. G., LIMC 5.1, 1000; G. Weicker, s.v. G. (1), RE 7, 517–518

fig.: S. Montón Subias, s.v. G., LIMC 5.2, 628–631. R.HA.

[2] Daughter of Eurytios, wife of Lamprus in Phaestus (Crete), who ordered her to kill her unborn child after birth, if it was a girl. She pretended that her daughter was a boy and reared her under the name of → Leucippus. As the discovery of her deceit became increasingly likely as her daughter grew up, G. asked → Leto to turn the girl into a young man. According to Antoninus Liberalis 17,6 (as stated by Nicander), the *Ekdýsia* were celebrated in Phaestus in honour of Leto Phytia to commemorate the fulfilment of this wish. Furthermore, brides lay down next to the statue of Leucippus before their wedding.

G. Weicker, s.v. G. (2), RE 7, 518–519. R.HA.

Galates (ὁ Γαλάτης; *Galátēs*). Plut. Phocion 33,4 mentions G. as the then current name for the Acrurium mountains, part of the → Callidromus range, on whose southern slopes Phocion and Polyperchon met in 318 BC. The change of name is perhaps linked to the invasion by the Celts in 279 BC. HE.KR.

Galatia

I. Region II. Roman Province

I. Region

A. Definition B. Geography C. Culture

A. Definition

Region in central Anatolia; it received its ethnically derived name following the conquest, settlement, and formation of states by the Celtic → Tolistobogii, → Tectosages, and → Trocmi, thus replacing the older names for its constituent regions (Phrygia, Cappadocia).

B. Geography

Before 188 BC, the tribal states of G. included, in the north, peripheral areas of → Paphlagonia and the territory of the → Mariandyni (basins of Bolu and Gerede), the zone – rich in woodlands and high pastures – of the Köroğlu Dağları from about the Çatak Çayı to the border of the Paphlagonian kingdom of → Gangra (Adyos Dağı), the north-eastern part of Phrygia (initially without → Ancyra and its basin) east of → Dorylaeum to the → Halys range, and in the south to the → Dindymum and the area of → Pessinus, furthermore the land between Emir Dağları and the northern part of the Tuz Gölü (→ Axylus), but without the territory to the north-west of the latter (Proseilemmene). The Tolistobogii, whose territory was the largest and located in the west, expanded their settlement area eastward to the eastern edge of the Murted Ovası, below Ancyra to the basin south of Gölbaşı, the uplands west of Haymana, the central course of the Demirözü, and in the south to → Vetissos. The territory of the central Tectosages extended in the east across the Halys by incorporating the basin of Kirrikale. Eastern G., the territory of the Trocmi, taken out of Cappadocia, comprised the region of the central and lower course of the → Cappadox together with its tributaries up to the defile east of Yerköy, the mountains south-east of Yozgat, as well as the Sorgun region including the northern part of the Kanak Çayı. In 179 BC, the northern basins fell to → Bithynia and Paphlagonia, and, probably in 183, the southern area stretching from around Amorion to west of → Tolastochora and Ak Göl to Pergamum. In 65/64 BC, the former Pontic territory of Alaca Çayı, including the fortress of Mithridation, came under Trocmi rule. From 25/24 to 21/20, Roman G. was reorganized as the urban territories of Ancyra, Tavium, and Pessinus; the latter became an integral part of G. and main place of the Tolistobogii.

G.'s great importance was based on both its road system and its agriculture. Agricultural lands were especially located around the central course of the Sangarius, the lower course of the Trembris, around Ova and Ankara Çayı, on the Siberis, southwest and south of Ankara, north of the Paşa Dağı, along the Halys, along the central and lower course of the Cappadox including its tributaries, around Sulakyurt, between Sungurlu and Boğazkale, as well as around Sorgun.

Eastern G. had richly forested mountains; in western G., forested mountain ranges originally also extended far southward to about Vetissos and towards the north and west of the Tuz Gölü.

Until 189 BC, the Tolistobogii had an important urban settlement in → Gordium, which had been rebuilt in the early Hellenistic period. Characteristic for eastern G. are fortified central settlements (Tavium, Ekkobriga/Kalekişla, Podanala/Kuşaklı Höyük, Boğazkale, Ceritkale), for the tetrarchies of the Tectosages and Tolistobogii after the mid 2nd cent. representative central fortresses (Sirkeli, Gorbeus, Güzelcekale, Odunboğazı; Oyaca, Blucion, Peium, Basri, Çanakçı, and probably also Balkuyumcu).

C. Culture

The settlement of the comparatively small Celtic migratory groups in the 2nd half of the 70s of the 3rd cent. BC resulted in the ethnogenesis of the three Galatian tribes, in the course of which the Anatolian population was absorbed into the social structure of the tribes, their branches and clans. The whole region underwent a process of Galatization. The new ethnic identity of the Galates originated with the Celtic groups, and remained self-evident as late as the mid 6th cent. AD. The Continental Celtic Galatian became the language of the entire region (Str. 12,5,1); Greek became the written language and the second language of the Galatian elite, in whose onomatology Greek and Anatolian elements appeared alongside traditional Celtic names as early as the 2nd cent. BC. In the 4th cent. AD, Galatian is evident as the spoken language of a large part of the population alongside the universally spoken Greek, and in the 6th cent. AD, it is again recorded as a living colloquial language [1. 139ff.]. The continued survival of Celtic traditions is evident in the recently recognized sacrificial area in Gordium including the literary evidence of human sacrifices. Early fortifications with circular ramparts and earth banks are *mons Olympus*/Çile Dağı, Cuballum/Ortakışla, Aşaği Karaören, and Selâmetli); early fortresses Karacasu near Bolu (lost in 179 BC) and Yalnızçam (archaic wall structure, imported ceramics). Galatian finding places of the 3rd to 1st cents. are rich in imported ceramics. 'Galatian ware' developed in eastern G. from the pre-Hellenistic painted pottery and Hellenistic forms and decors. The Hellenization of central Anatolia received an important impulse with the formation of the Galatian states (evident in the Roman terminology: *Gallograeci* or *Gallograecia* respectively). The typical form of Hellenistic-Anatolian tombs was adopted (*tumuli* of the elite). Indigenous cults such as that of Cybele (statuette of the goddess with painted torques, from Gordium) and of Teššop/Zeus Tavianos (important sanctuary with a colossal bronze statue in Tavium; Str. 12,5,2) were adopted, probably by equation with Celtic deities, but in their Greek appearance.

Christian congregations developed in the wake of Paul's two missionary journeys, presumably to the south and west of G.; however, he was not active in the Galatian towns ([1. 117ff.], differently in [2. 3ff.]). Alongside, a Petrine, Jewish-Christian evangelization took place (1 Peter is a reflection of the proximity of pagan and Jewish Christians, probably also with regard to G. at the end of the 1st cent. [3]). Characteristic is the strong presence of heretical groups, amongst them the Montanists (2nd–4th cents.; → Montanism) or the Novatians (→ Novatianus); → Arianism was at times strong [2. 91ff.; 4. 84ff.]. For the middle Byzantine period, only sporadical information is available regarding non-orthodox movements. From the 4th cent., monastic life experienced an upsurge. At the Council of Nicaea in 325, G. was represented by bishops from Ancyra, Tavium, Gdanmaa, Iuliopolis, and probably also Cinna; the church provinces of G. *I* and G. *II* existed from the early 5th cent.

→ Celts (history and map)

1 K. Strobel, Die Galater 1, 1996 2 Mitchell II 3 E. Cothenet, La Première de Pierre, in: ANRW II 25,5, 1988, 3685–3712 4 Belke.

J. Darrouzès, Notitiae episcopatuum Ecclesiae Constantinopolitanae, 1981; R. Janin, D. Stiernon, G., DHGE 19, 1980, 714–731; Magie; Mitchell; Id., Regional Epigraphic Cat. of Asia Minor II. The Ankara District. The Inscriptions of North G., 1982; K. Strobel, Die Galater I, 1996; II, 1998; Id., G. und seine Grenzregionen, in: E. Schwertheim (ed.), Forsch. in G. (Asia Minor Stud. 12), 1994, 29–96; Id., Galatica I. Ostgalatien in: Orbis Terrarum 3, 1997, 131–153; Id., Galatica II. Die Tolistobogier, III. Die Tektosagen, in: Orbis Terrarum 4, 1998.

K.ST.

II. Roman Province

Following the death of → Amyntas [9], his entire empire was confiscated and in 25/4 BC (beginning of the provincial era [1. 398ff.]) instituted as the province of G. (first praetorian legate M. Lollius 25/4–22). The tribal areas of the Galatians were organized as urban territories (*Sebasteni Tectosages Ancyrani, Sebasteni Tolistobogii Pessinuntii*), completing the process in 21/0 with the institution of the *pólis* Tavium (differently [1. 410ff.]) for the territory of the → Trocmi (*Sebasteni Trocmi Taviani*). They constituted the *koinón* of the Galatians. The territory of the Tolistobogii suffered some losses: Iuliopolis fell to → Bithynia, and the Roman colony of → Germa was founded (its territory between Sündiken and west of Sivrihisar Dağları including Vindia, the Roman settlement succeeding → Gordium, but excluding the area of Çardaközü Deresi); the remaining territory in the north-east, up to the lower course of the → Siberis and including the valley of Ankara Çayı fell to the *pólis* Ancyra, which also got the land north-west of Lake Tatta under the name of Proseilemmene (*regio attributa*). From 25/4, the province had a legionary garrison (*legio VII* at the latest from 20/19 BC with some interruptions to AD 13/4 in northern Pisidia; presumably very early also the *III Cyrenaica*); under the consular successors of Lollius, several legions were stationed in the province. In 6/5 BC, the kingdom of Paphlagonia was added to G., in 3/2 Amasea with Karanitis (*Pontus Galaticus*), in AD 34/5 the hierocratic state of *Comana Pontica*, and in 64/5 the annexed Pontic empire under the name of *Pontus Polemoniacus*. The province Cappadocia was united with G. in 55–65/6, and again presumably from 70/71. The province of G. was subdivided into several *eparchíai* (districts): the actual region of G. (the *koinón* of the Galatians), Paphlagonia, Pontus Galaticus, Pontus Polemoniacus, Phrygia (Paroreius), Pisidia, Isauria, Lycaonia, Pamphylia, later Cappadocia and Armenia Minor. In 20 BC, → Archelaus [7] obtained the coastal region of Cilicia Tracheia, and in AD 43, Pamphylia with the central and southern part of Pisidia was added to the newly formed province of Lycia-Pamphylia (under Nero up to AD 70, Pamphylia was once again for a time part of G.). Cappadocia, Pontus Polemoniacus, and Pontus Galaticus were separated in 113. Early in the reign of M. Aurelius, the coastal region including Abonutichus/Ionopolis, Sinope, and Amisus was joined to G. (→ Bithynia et Pontus). Prior to the period from 226/229 to 250, eastern G. (Tavium) belonged to Cappadocia. In 250, the province of Pontus (the former district of Pontus Galaticus) was united with G., but from 279 it is again documented as a separate province, inclusive of Neoclaudiopolis. Before 305/6, the Paphlagonian *eparchía* (Pompeiopolis, Gangra, Hadrianopolis) was split off to form the separate province of Paphlagonia. Diocletianus separated the entire south (Phrygia Paroreius, northern Lycaonia) from G.; in the west, Iuliopolis was added, and also the territory of the Troknades west of Pessinus at the end of the 3rd cent. In 371, the area west of Lake Tatta, including the diocese of Gdanmaa (Çeşmelisebil) became part of the province of Lycaonia. At the end of the 4th cent., G. was divided into *Galatia I* (with the metropolis of Ancyra) and *Galatia II* (or *Salutaris*). *Galatia II* included the metropolis of Pessinus, also Troknada, Eudoxias, Germa, Petenissos, Therma (Myrikion, near Haymana), and on the upper course of the Sangarius also Amorion and Orcistus. The territory of Cinna – the Proseilemmene organized as a municipality under the Antonines – formed the southern border of *Galatia I*. As a civic administrative unit, G. existed until the 8th cent.; the territory was initially part of the theme of Opsikion, then of the theme of Bukellarion.

1 W. Leschhorn, Ant. Ären, 1993.

RPC 1, 535–549; C. Foss, s.v. G., ODB 2, 816; Mitchell 1, 61ff.; 2, 151ff.; Id., Population and Land in Roman G., in: ANRW II 7,2, 1053–1081; B. Rémy, L'évolution administrative de l'Anatolie aux trois premiers s., 1986 (review: S. Mitchell, in: CR 38, 1988, 437f.); Id., Les carrières sénatoriales dans les prov. rom. d'Anatolie aux Haut-Empire, 1989 (review: W. Ameling, in: Gnomon 67, 1995, 697); K. Strobel, Die Galater 2, 1998. K.ST.

Galaxaure (Γαλαξαύρη; *Galaxaúrē*). → Oceanid, mentioned in Hes. Theog. 353 (alongside Plexaure) and in H. Hom. 5,423 (based on that Orph. Fr. 49,26) where she picks flowers with Persephone when the latter is abducted by Hades. The etymology of the name is uncertain (for hypotheses see [1; 2]).

1 E. Maass, Aglaurion, in: MDAI(A) 35, 1910, 338 2 P. Kretschmer, Mythische Namen, in: Glotta 10, 1920, 51ff. A.A.

Galaxia (τὰ Γαλάξια; *tà Galáxia*). Athenian festival in honour of the mother of the gods, named after the milk gruel served on the occasion (Hsch. s.v. G.). The importance of the festival is indicated by the evidence provided by ephebic inscriptions, that in the Hellenistic period the *epheboi* offered sacrifices for the goddess and dedicated a golden bowl to her (from IG II^2 470,13). F.G.

Galba

[1] King of the → Suessiones and commander-in-chief of the coalition of Belgic tribes against Caesar in 57 BC. Following his victory over the Belgae and the capture of → Noviodunum, the main town of the Suessiones, Caesar took two of G.'s son as hostages (Caes. B Gall. 2,4,7; 2,13,1; Cass. Dio 39,1,2). 'Galba' appears frequently as a cognomen of the Roman *gens Sulpicia*, but its Celtic origin (Suet. Galba 3,1) is not certain [1. 1621ff.; 2. 349–350].

1 Holder 1 2 Evans. W.SP.

[2] Roman emperor from AD 68 to 69, originally named Ser. Sulpicius G. He was born on 24 Dec. (probably) 3 BC near Tarracina as a son of Sulpicius G. (*cos. suff.* 5 BC) and Mummia Achaica; the family belonged to the Republican patriciate. He was adopted by his father's second wife, Livia Ocellina; thus, he became her heir and adopted her name: L. Livius Ocella Ser. Sulpicius Galba. Her family, too, owned estates near Tarracina [1]. Thereby, he was closer to Livia, Tiberius' mother, who supported him in his career. If he really took up offices earlier than usual, this applies only to the praetorship. Prior to his regular consulate of AD 33, he served as praetorian governor of Aquitani for a year. In 39, Caligula appointed him successor to the rebellious Cornelius [II 29] Gaetulicus as commander of the army in Upper Germania; there, he exercised strict military discipline. Claudius took him to Brittania as *comes*. Probably from 44 to 46, he was appointed proconsul of Africa without drawing the lots to tame the insurgent tribes. For his actions in Germania and Africa, he was awarded the *ornamenta triumphalia* and three priestly offices; all this indicates his exceptional position within the senatorial society of his time. In 60, Nero sent him as governor to Hispania Tarraconensis, which can be interpreted as a precautionary measure; for G.'s career, see [2. 138ff.].

As early as 67, G. became involved in the rebellious movement in Gallia through Iulius Vindex, but only in early 68 he declared himself against Nero. He was acclaimed emperor by soldiers and provincials in Carthago Nova; he called himself *legatus Senatus Populique Romani*, in order to leave the final decision to the Senate, who, however, at first declared him *hostis publicus*, following Nero's proposal. G. levied new troops, the *legio VII Galbiana* as well as auxiliary troops [3; 4]. Even though G. had sent letters to the other provincial governors, only Salvius Otho of Lusitania and Caecina [II 1] Alienus, quaestor of Baetica, joined him. Regarding his other followers, see [5]. After Vindex' defeat by the army from Upper Germania, G. withdrew to Clunia, where he eventually received news of Nero's death and of his own recognition by the praetorians and the Senate on 8 June by his freedman Icelus. Since then he was known as Ser. G. Imperator Caesar Augustus, i.e. the last two components – originally names – were used almost as titles. Afterwards, he took over the *tribunicia potestas*; he probably became *pontifex max.* only in Rome, and *pater patriae* perhaps only on the occasion of the adoption of Calpurnius [II 24] Piso in January 69. The legions and governors in the provinces recognized him as emperor.

G.'s basic attitude was aristocratic-authoritarian. He had no political sensitivity as far as the requirements of his situation were concerned. Thus, he refused the praetorians in Rome the promised → *donativum*; in Gallia, he granted Roman citizenship to the tribes who had supported Vindex – an affront to the legions from Upper Germania, further compounded by the simultaneous replacement of their commander Verginius Rufus. In Rome, a newly formed legion was decimated upon his arrival and thus driven to oppose him. G. was not even able to win over the Senate, because he had the designated consul Cingonius Varro, who had, however, conspired with the praetorian prefect Nymphidius Sabinus, executed without sentence, and also → Clodius [II 7] Macer, who had risen against Nero in Africa. In addition, G. was far too reliant on his freedmen, particularly Icelus, whom he had made an equestrian. The people rejected him because of his thriftiness. In order to reclaim money given away by Nero, a financial commission was formed; it had little success but created massive resentment amongst those affected.

On 1 January 69, G. began his second consulate, together with the unpopular T. Vinius. On the same day, the legions in Mainz in Upper Germania refused their oath of allegiance and destroyed G.'s images. On 2 January, governor A. Vitellius was proclaimed emperor in Cologne, at the instigation of → Fabius [II 19] Valens, whose conduct G. had not recognized after his elevation, and of Caecina Alienus. In reaction to the news of the legion's mutiny in Mainz, G. adopted → Calpurnius [II 24] Piso, who was no relative, on 10 January 69 thus designating him as his successor, once again without a *donativum* for the praetorians. The news from Germania regarding Vitellius were suppressed. Otho, who had hoped that his services to G. might have merited his own adoption, was driven to rebellion; on 15 January, he was acclaimed by the praetorians, who were joined by other troops encamped in Rome. On the Forum, G. was killed by mutinous soldiers. His body was buried in his gardens on the via Aurelia. Initially, his memory was erased, but restored under Vespasian by the Senate on 1 January 70.

1 W. Eck, in: Listy Filologické 114, 1991, 93ff. 2 Vogel-Weidemann 3 P. Le Roux, L'armée romaine ... des provinces Iberiques ..., 1982, 131f. 4 W. Eck, in: Chiron 27, 1997, 203ff. 5 Syme, RP IV 115ff.

Coins: RIC I² 216ff.; PIR1 S 723; E.P. Nicolas, De Néron à Vespasien 1, 1979, 431ff.; Kienast², 102f. W.E.

Galea see → Armour

Galen of Pergamum (Γαλήνος; *Galēnos*)

A. Life B. Philosophy C. Physiology D. Anatomy E. Surgery F. Medical Theory G. Therapy H. Pharmacology I. Galen and medical tradition J. Linguistic studies K. Medical ethics L. Later reception

A. Life

AD 129 to *c.* 216, Greek doctor and philosopher. As the son of a prosperous architect named Aelius or Iulius Nicon (not Claudius, as older accounts have it), G. enjoyed a wide education, especially in philosophy. When he was 17, Asclepius appeared to Nicon in a dream which turned G. towards a medical career. After studying with Satyrus, Aiphicianus and Stratonicus in Pergamum, G. went to Smyrna *c.* 149 to learn from Pelops, a pupil of the Hippocratic Quintus. From there he journeyed to Corinth to find Numisianus, another pupil of Quintus. Numisianus, however, had already left for Alexandria, where he died before G. arrived there around 151. In Alexandria, G. attended lectures given by Heracleianus and Iulianus, extended his anatomical and surgical knowledge, travelled and conducted research into drugs [1]. In 157 he returned to Pergamum, where he was appointed as doctor to the gladiators of the high priest of Asia and was extremely successful in that position. In 162 he set off for Rome, where he initially made a name for himself as a philosopher. Curing his erstwhile philosophy teacher Eudemus gained him entry to the highest circles, where he made the acquaintance of *coss.* → Flavius Boethus, Sergius Paulus and Cn. Claudius Severus. His public autopsies also caused a sensation but, fearing the enmity of his rivals, he later carried them out only in front of a private audience.

In 166 G. left Rome unnoticed to return to Pergamum, either for fear of being killed by jealous rivals (De praecognitione 14,648 Kühn), or, as he wrote later (De libris propriis 19,15 Kühn), because of the outbreak of the plague. Neither of those explanations is entirely convincing: in Pergamum, civic unrest (*stásis*) had recently been settled, and as a result G. was able to return at no risk. His stay, however, was only brief. He went travelling to find medicinal herbs and as a doctor. At the end of 168, G. was ordered to the winter quarters of M. Aurelius and L. Verus at Aquileia, arriving shortly before Verus' death. In the summer of 169 he returned to Rome and thereafter remained continuously in the emperor's service in Italy. [2]. At first he looked after the young Commodus and other members of the court but he also attended the emperors themselves into the Severian period. Of his life after 169 little authenticated information has survived, apart from a few case histories. G. continued to treat patients and was a highly productive writer. A large part of his library was burnt in 191. In the nineties he paid Pergamum at least one more visit, but later accounts that he died in Sicily or Egypt do not stand up to scrutiny. The Suda (s.v. G.) maintains that G. reached the age of 70, and thus died in 199/200, but that year for his death is contradicted by *i.a.* the work *De theriaca (ad Pisonem)*, composed between 204 and 209, and a biographical tradition, preserved in Arabic sources in particular, according to which he died at the age of 87, after spending 17 years as a student and 70 years as a practising doctor [3].

B. Philosophy

From early youth G. was familiar with the great philosophical schools of his period. Study of geometry saved him from aporia. That was the origin of his interest in logic, on which he composed various treatises, of which only the *Institutio logica* (ed. [20]) survived in entirety. G. was later credited with discovering the fourth figure of the syllogism. His main philosophical work was *De demonstratione* (fr., ed. [21]). In it he expounded that knowledge was only certain if one had started from suitable premisses, especially those that were 'clearly visible'. On material issues, his world vision was influenced by Aristotelian physics; on the doctrine of the soul, however, he followed the Platonic doctrine of a tripartite soul that seemed to correspond to his anatomical discovery of a bodily system governed by brain, heart and liver. He was a supporter of teleology and firmly believed in creation methodically designed by a divinity (hence his dislike of Christian and Jewish belief in miracles) [4; 5]. In his eyes, medical discoveries confirmed, on an empirical level, a number of philosophical speculations. He rejected as useless philosophical debates that could not be resolved either logically or empirically. In *De placitis Hippocratis et Platonis* he explained his anatomy in Platonic terms, but in *De usu partium*, on the other hand, in Aristotelian terms. As he was always convinced of a strong interaction between body and soul, he also composed works on ethics (*De moribus*), and in the work *Quod animi mores*, conceived towards the end of his life, he even flirted with the notion of a soul entirely dependent on the physical make-up of the body [6].

C. Physiology

G. regarded Hippocrates as his medical master and closely followed his theory, developed in *De natura hominis*, of the four bodily humours that are derived from the four elements and the four primary qualities of hot, cold, wet and dry. All parts of the body consist of these humours. Illness G. defines as an imbalance or a discontinuity between the parts of the body. Each part of the body has a potential for activity (faculty) and any impairment to the balance in terms of qualities or humours destroys this potential and the function dependent on it. Moreover, every body part has within itself the primary faculties of genesis, growth and nutrition.

The body consists of three systems that are dependent on the brain, heart and liver respectively (a theory that links G. to Hippocrates and Plato) and that respectively control thought and feeling through the nervous system, movement through the arteries, and nourishment through the veins. Blood produced in the liver provides nutriment, while any excess is eliminated. A small part of this blood reaches the left half of the heart, where it is mixed with air (*pneûma*) and thus transformed into arterial blood. Under the influence of a pulsative faculty to be found in their wall-lining, the heart and arteries beat synchronously. In a net of vessels at the base of the brain that is possibly to be identified with the venous 'miracle net' (*rete mirabile*), a portion of this arterial blood is further processed to form, in the ventricular system of the brain, the soul pneuma that flows through the nerves as bearer of sensation [7]. G. distinguished intentional from unintentional movements and in *De motibus dubiis* (ed. princeps [22]) paid special attention to those bodily parts in which both forms of movement seem to occur, as for example the eyelid.

D. Anatomy

G. was trained by teachers who were steeped in Alexandrian anatomy. Added to that was the technical skill that his father had passed on to him. G. regarded anatomical knowledge as fundamental, not just in a surgical context but in terms of medicine as a whole. He conducted a complicated series of anatomical experiments on animals, especially monkeys, sheep, pigs and goats, to explore the nervous system. He stated that he consistently performed dissections throughout his entire life. Out of respect for the achievements of → Herophilus and → Erasistratus in anatomy, he repeated some of their experiments, in particular on the brains and the eyes. Although he advocated a research program based on human anatomy, he was unable to achieve it – apart from observations on the human skeleton or in the course of surgical operations. Nevertheless, his committed concern with anatomy seems to have distinguished him from everyone else and to have lent added authority to his descriptions of the human body [8].

E. Surgery

Although G. did not complete his planned book on surgery, his recommendations for an ideal surgeon in *De medico examinando* (ed. princeps [23]) show that he mastered a large number of surgical operations, from the removal of polyps and the cleaning of ulcers to the treatment of complicated fractures. Among his case notes there are accounts of the removal of a suppurating breast bone, as well as the re-positioning of the 'large net', that had protruded from the abdominal cavity through a sword wound. His commentary on the Hippocratic treatise *De articulis* displays a familiarity with sprains and fractures that in part stems from his experience with wounds occurring in the wrestling-school [9].

F. Medical Theory

Even if G. as a rule defined specific illnesses, e.g. marasmus, as a combination of different symptoms, he did not accord them any independent ontological existence but saw them as the result of changes within the body or – in the case of wounds – as the result of external influences. He developed a theory of causality that set out an order of precedence of causes with a long-term or sudden influences. The immediate change was generally to be attributed to a shifting of balance within a particular part of the body and could be treated, or possibly forestalled, by the application of allopathic medicines. Diagnosis depended on sensory perception: talking to the patient, touching, observing, and using the sense of taste and smell. In his writing on the pulse, G. developed the theories of → Archigenes as the basis for identifying and diagnosing illness. G. even regarded examination of urine as useful, though he did not always carry it out in practice. He advised against relying exclusively on any one diagnostic procedure, no matter which. By examination, a doctor who was capable of accurate and informed observation could establish the cause of an illness, especially if he then proceeded logically – G.'s clinical logic is faultless – to an appropriate prescription of treatment that attacked the cause of the illness, and could, finally, predict the further course of the illness. This frequently followed a predictable pattern – deterioration until it reached the crisis, with either a cure or death as its consequence. The whole procedure came under the generic term of prognosis that G. traced back to Hippocrates and that, to the astonishment of his contemporaries, he regarded as a clear and simple undertaking (*De praecognitione*, ed. [24]). It applied equally to both bodily and mental illnesses, the interplay of which constituted one of G.'s main research interests (→ Mental illness).

G. Therapy

Preventing illness was more important to G. than curing it. Thus, in his treatise *De sanitate tuenda* and in other works on nutrition, he set out rules for a healthy lifestyle, based on his deep knowledge of life in the eastern Mediterranean. They included sporting activity. As a treatment method he preferred dietary measures (→ Dietetics), followed by medication and finally surgical intervention, which was considered a last resort as it was always dangerous. In contrast to contemporary Erasistrateans, G. upheld the value of bloodletting for removing excess or peccant material from the body, though his careful restrictions with regard to age and sex of the patients show that he did not always perform it in practice. His patients came from all social classes, from peasants to successors to the throne, and people living hundreds of kilometres away wrote to him asking for advice. The spectacular cases documented in *De praecognitione*, *De locis affectis* and *Methodus medendi* are still today impressive testimony to his skill as a doctor and would have justified the respect that several successive emperors had for him.

H. Pharmacology

G.'s extensive writings on pharmacology (vols. 11–14 K.) represent compilations from the works of earlier authors. He simply added information on additional medicines that he had been able to collect thanks to his wide-ranging contacts and his depth of experience. He visited the mines in Cyprus to look for usable minerals. In Rome he was able to draw on the stocks of the emperor's own stores of drugs especially from Crete. He attempted to classify medicines according to the intensity of their action, and to correlate their use with the intensity of the condition. Although he did not complete the research, his classification of numerous plants into so-called grades of intensity offered successive authors of pharmacological works a model of classification, especially in the Arab world [10; 11].

I. Galen and medical tradition

In a world where → Methodists, → Empiricists and advocates of natural therapy were probably more numerous and more successful, G. insisted on the superiority of Hippocratic teaching. G.'s commitment to Hippocratic medicine, the value of which was attested not only by practical results but also by Plato's endorsement, helped to achieve its breakthrough to become the most important in Western medical tradition. G. expounded the Hippocratic doctrine in a long series of commentaries (produced over a period of over twenty years) on individual Hippocratic writings. In that project he used earlier commentaries, especially those of Heraclides of Tarentum and Rufus of Samaria. His own teachers, themselves followers of Hippocrates, exercised a special influence on him. G.'s efforts to trace back to Hippocrates everything that he regarded as fundamental in medicine – including anatomy – appears, however, not to have gained undivided support. He established rules for determining to what degree Hippocratic texts accurately reflected the words and teachings of Hippocrates, as set out in *De natura hominis* and confirmed by G.'s own experience. His remarkable knowledge of the older language and literature enabled him to comment on Hippocratic terminology and compile a glossary. As G. makes it clear in all his medical writings whenever he disagrees with another author, but keeps silent when he borrows something, however, it is hard to pinpoint exactly his dependence on earlier authors [12; 13]. G. had a large personal library and quoted extensively from a wide range of works. How many of those he knew from first-hand experience is unclear, but for the verbatim borrowings in his pharmacological writings he certainly relied on a much narrower range of sources than appears at first glance [14]. Many of these authors are known today only because of G., but the presentation of their views was no doubt influenced by his own perspective as a combative philosopher-physician. The way that ancient medicine is widely seen by modern historians of medicine often simply reflects G.'s own point of view, with all of its idiosyncrasies. Modern accounts of Erasistratus or the Methodists often repeat G.'s accusations uncritically. G.'s own idea of 'good' medicine – both in theory and practice – has influenced the Western medical tradition and the view that it was based on Hippocrates [15. 408].

J. Linguistic studies

G. produced a whole range of lexicographical works on Attic Comedy, as well as his studies into the ambiguity of language (*De captionibus*) and specialized medical terminology (*De nominibus medicis*, ed. [25]). Most have been lost but G. gives the titles in the catalogue of his own works *De libris propriis* (19,8–48 Kühn). As clarity was all-important to him, he rejected Atticism and much of the newer specialist terminology. His own style, varying according to the context, is generally fluid and elegant but marred by didactically motivated repetition. The structure of his works composed in the 190s is less taut than in those of the 170s.

K. Medical ethics

Throughout his whole career G. emphasized the fundamental unity of all branches of medicine, exhorting doctors to use both reason and experience. He saw Hippocrates and Asclepius (*In Hippocratis Iusiurandum commentarii*, ed. [26]) as model doctors. In *De medico examinando* he set down what he expected of the accomplished practitioner. Successful medicine was for him synonymous with ethically defensible medicine, and thus a good doctor was, consciously or not, also a philosopher.

L. Later reception

G.'s standing as an imperial physician and the praise of his medicine from Athenaeus of Naucratis and Alexander of Aphrodisias attest to the medical authority that he enjoyed during his own lifetime. Egyptian papyri dated to before AD 250 give testimony of the wide dissemination of his ideas. His philosophical works were more controversial but many were still being quoted well into the 6th cent. [16]. His agnostic attitude towards creation and the nature of the human soul, espoused in *De demonstratione* and his last work, *De sententiis* [27], aroused criticism from pagan, Christian and Muslim circles alike. In G.'s lifetime a shoemaker named Theodotus was led into heresy by trying to modify Christian doctrine in such a way as to accommodate G.'s criticism.

Around the middle of the 4th cent., G. already had a central position within the Hippocratic tradition as represented by Oribasius. A considerable number of passages quoted by the latter come from G. and this number increased in later encyclopaedists, as other authors were either overlooked or appeared in entries that essentially went back to G. Something similar can generally be seen in the MSS tradition, in which material from G. or transmitted under his name is accorded priority. The range of authors who were quoted by G. and were read in G.'s lifetime gave way to an exclusive dependence on G. Non-Galenic texts survived in significant quantity only if they had been strongly recommended by G. – as for example the *Corpus Hippocraticum* – or treated subject areas that G. himself had not worked on, such as gynaecology, veterinary medicine or botany.

In the 5th cent., a canon of Galenic texts was compiled in Alexandria that later represented the basis for training doctors in the Byzantine world and Ravenna and the Near East. G. enjoyed a much less extensive influence in the Latin West. He was quoted by Gargilius Martialis in the 3rd cent., by Cassius Felix in the 5th, but until the revival of ancient medicine in southern Italy in the 11th cent., his fame rested almost exclusively on his discovery of a remedy, the so-called *hiera Galeni*. Only later did G. become *the* dominant figure, thanks to Latin translations of Greek works or to renderings in Arabic. Knowledge of the Greek originals on medical subjects, rekindled after 1470 and especially after publication of the Aldine edition (editio princeps, Venice 1525), quickly re-established G.'s position as the greatest doctor of antiquity. At the same time, though, errors and contradictions were discovered in G.'s works, especially those dealing with anatomy. Around 1600, G. was replaced by Hippocrates as *the* source of reliable medical knowledge of antiquity [17].

→ Dietetics; → Empiricists; → Galenism

1 V. Nutton, Galen and Egypt, in: J. Kollesch, D. Nickel (ed.), Galen und das hell. Erbe, 1993, 11–32 2 Nutton, 2, 158–171 3 V. Nutton, Galen ad multos annos, in: Dynamis 15, 1995, 25–40 4 R. Walzer, Galen on Jews and Christians, 1949 5 S. Gero, Galen on the Christians, in: Orientalia Christiana Periodica 56, 1990, 171–411 6 Moraux, 2, 607–808 7 C. R. S. Harris, The Heart and the Vascular System in Ancient Greek Medicine, 1973, 267–431 8 M. T. May, Galen, On the Usefulness of Parts of the Body, 1968 9 G. Majno, The healing hand, 1975 10 G. Harig, Bestimmung der Intensität im medizinischen System Galens, 1974 11 A. Touwaide, Galien et la Toxicologie, in: ANRW II 37.2, 1887–1986 12 G. E. R. Lloyd, Methods and Problems in Greek Science, 1991 13 D. Manetti, A. Roselli, Galeno Commentatore di Ippocrate, in: ANRW II 37.2, 1530–1635 14 C. Fabricius, Galens Exzerpte aus älteren Pharmakologen, 1972 15 W. D. Smith, Erasistratus' Dietetic Medicine, in: BHM 56, 1982, 398–409 16 Nutton, 3, 315–324 17 O. Temkin, Galenism, 1973.

Complete edition: 18 C. G. Kühn, Claudii Galeni Opera Omnia, 1821–1833.

EDITIONS OF SEPARATE WORKS: 19 H. DIELS et al., CMG 5,9,1914– (since 1964 with transl. and comm.; since 1934 supplements with editions of medieval transl. of Galenic writings lost in the original) 20 K. KALBFLEISCH, Institutio logica, 1896 21 I. MÜLLER, De demonstratione, in: ABAW 1895, 403–478 22 C. LARRAIN, De motibus dubiis (editio princeps), in: Traditio 49, 1994, 171–233 23 A. Z. ISKANDAR, De medico examinando, 1988 24 V. NUTTON, De praecognitione, 1979 25 M. MEYERHOF, J. SCHACHT, De nominibus medicis, ADAW 1931 26 F. ROSENTHAL, In Hippocratis Iusiurandum commentarii, in: BHM 30, 1956, 52–87 27 V. NUTTON, On My Own Opinions (De sententiis), CMG 3,2, 1999
BIBLIOGR.: K. SCHUBRING, Bibliogr. references, in: C. G. KÜHN, Claudii Galeni Opera Omnia, repr. 1960, vol. 20 G. FICHTNER, Corpus Galenicum, 1990 J. KOLLESCH, D. NICKEL, Bibliographia Galeniana, in: ANRW II 37.2, 1077–1253.
TRANSL.: (no transl. of the complete works available, but important separate translations which surpass Kühn's Latin transl., by:) CH. DAREMBERG (French), 1854 E. BEINTKER, W. KAHLENBERG (German), 1939–1954 I. GAROFALO, M. VEGETTI (Italian), 1978 D. J. FURLEY, M. WILKIE (breathing, Engl.), 1984 P. MORAUX (French), 1985 P. BRAIN (phlebotomy, Engl.), 1986 I. GAROFALO (anatomy, Italian), 1991 R. J. HANKINSON (therapeutics, Engl.), 1991 P. N. SINGER (Engl.), 1997.
LEXIKON: R. J. DURLING, A Dictionary of Medical Terms in Galen, 1993.
GENERAL OVERVIEWS: J. ILBERG, Über die Schriftstellerei des Klaudios Galenos, 1889–1897, repr. 1974 J. MEWALDT, s.v. G., RE 7, 578–791 L. GARCIA BALLESTER, Galeno, 1972 SMITH. V.N.

Galene (Γαλήνη/*Galḗne*, 'calmness of the sea'). → Nereid in Hes. Theog. 244; according to the Euhemerist Mnaseas, daughter of Ichthys and Hesychia (FHG 3 155,33). As embodiment of the sea's brighter aspect, G. smoothes the waves in Anth. Pal. 5,156 (Meleager) and 7,668 (Leonidas) as well as in Lucian 5. 'Conversation of the sea-gods'. An epigram by Adaeus (Anth. Pal. 9,544) describes a cameo of Tryphon with the portrait of G. that, however, cannot be unequivocally identified with extant models [1]. Paus. 2,1,9 mentions a statue of G. in the temple of Poseidon at the Isthmus. In vase inscriptions G. is attested as the name of a Nereid [1] and Maenad [2]. Variants are Galaneia (in Eur. Hel. 1458 daughter of Pontus) and Galenaie (epithet of Aphrodite in Philod. in Anth. Pal. 10,21,1; personified in Callim. Epigr. 5,5).

1 N. ICARD-GIANOLIO, s.v. G. I, LIMC 4.1, 151–153
2 A. KOSSATZ-DEISSMANN, s.v. G. II, ibid., 153. A.A.

Galeoi see → Galeotae

Galeos see → Shark

Galeotae (Γαλεῶται; *Galeôtai*). Name of a Sicilian family of seers, probably from Hybla Galeatis/Gereatis (Paus. 5,23,6), whose members are linked with prophecies relating to the rule of → Dionysius I (Philistus FGrH 556 F 57 in Cic. Div. 1,39; Ael. VH 12,46). Myth associates them with → Telmissus, the location in Caria famous for its prophecy (Cic. Div. 1,91): the eponymous Galeos was said to be, like his brother Telmissus, the son of → Apollo and the Hyperborean princess Themisto. On the advice of the Dodonan oracle, Galeos is said to have made his way to Sicily, and Telmissus to Caria (Steph. Byz. s.v. G.). A pun from comedy associated the name with γάλεος (*gáleos*), a variety of fish or lizard (Rhinton fr. 17 CGF, cf. Phanodemus FGrH 325 F 20 with JACOBY's supplement); however, no close connection between lizard and prophecy can be inferred from that.

A. S. PEASE, M. Tulli Ciceronis De Divinatione, 1963 (1920), 163 (on 1,39). F.G.

Galepsos (Γάληψος; *Gálēpsos*).
[1] Settlement east of the point where the Strymon flows into the Aegean, probably east of Orfani, at the mouth of a water-course between the Pangaeum and the Symvolon. G. was part of the settlement of the Peraea of Thasos. Archaeologically attested from the 7th cent. BC and attested in literature since Hecataeus (FGrH 1 F 152). Scyl. 67 et al. call G. a *pólis*. Together with the small neighbouring cities of Amphipolis (Thuc. 4,107,3), G. was captured in 424 BC by Brasidas, with the aid of Perdiccas, and in 422 by Cleon (Thuc. 5,6,1). Around 359 BC, G. was part of the territory controlled by Berisades. In 356 it was destroyed by Philip II but was later rebuilt (Str. 7, fr. 35). In 168 BC Perseus fled from G. to Samothrace (Liv. 44,45,14).

B. ISAAK, The Greek Settlement in Thrace until the Macedonian Conquest, 1989. I.v.B.

[2] see → Galaei

Galeria
[1] **Annia G. Faustina.** see → Faustina [1]
[2] **G. Fundana.** Daughter of a senator of praetorian rank, related also to Galerius [4] [1]. Married A. Vitellius, the later emperor, no later than around AD 60. In 69 she joined her husband in Gaul. After his death she took care of the funeral. PIR² G 33.

1 W. ECK, in: ZPE 101, 1994, 229f. W.E.

Galerianus see → Calpurnius

Galerius
[1] **C. G.** Eques, who probably came from Ariminum. Of his public offices only the *praefectus Aegypti* is known, which he held for 16 years, probably AD 16–31. [1; 2]; P. Oxy 3807. Died returning from Egypt. Married to Helvia, Seneca's aunt. PIR² G 25.

1 G. BASTIANINI, in: ZPE 17, 1975, 270 2 I. CAZZANIGA, in: Analecta Papyrologica 4, 1992, 5ff.

[2] **M. G. Aurelius Antoninus.** Son of the later emperor Antoninus [1] Pius and of Annia Galeria Faustina; died before AD 138. Later buried in the Mausoleum Hadriani (CIL VI 989). PIR² G 26.

[3] **G. Maximus.** Senator, proconsul of Africa AD 258, who had Bishop Cyprian arrested because of the Valerian edict on Christians. He died shortly after 13 September 258, before the end of the proceedings. Possibly of patrician rank [1]. PIR² G 28.

1 M. CHRISTOL, Essai sur l'évolution des carrières sénatoriales, 1986, 198f.

[4] **P. G. Trachalus.** Probably descendant of G. [1], came from Ariminum. Related to → Galeria Fundana, wife of the later emperor Vitellius. Famous as an orator in the Senate (Quint. Inst. 12,5,5). Of his career we know only of the regular consulate in AD 68. After Otho's death he was saved from punishment through Vitellius by Galeria Fundana. Proconsul of Africa *c.* 78/79.

THOMASSON, Fasti Africani 45; W. ECK, in: ZPE 101, 1994, 229f.; PIR² G 30. W.E.

[5] **C. G. Valerius Maximianus.** AD 293–305 *Caesar*, 305–311 *Augustus*, often named Maximianus in historiographical sources. Born probably around 250 in *Dacia ripensis* ([Aur. Vict.] epit. Caes. 40,16; unspecific in Eutr. 10,2,1). Like other Illyrian soldier emperors, he came from the thinly Romanized rural population, which earned him the nickname Armentarius ('cowherd') in late sources (Aur. Vict. Caes. 39,24). Because of his military qualities, aided by his impressive height ([Aur. Vict.] epit. Caes. 40,15; caricature in Lact. mort. pers. 9,3f.; cf. now also the portrait discovered in Gamzigrad [1]), he quickly moved into the closer military surroundings (*protectores*) of emperors like Aurelianus and Probus (Aur. Vict. Caes. 39,28), and this finally led to his elevation on 1 March 293 as *Caesar* together with Constantius (→ Tetrarchy). As adoptive son of Diocletian, he became a member of the Iovii family and, after dissolution of an earlier relationship (that apparently produced Maximilla, who was later to be the wife of Maxentius), he married Diocletian's daughter, Galeria Valeria (Aur. Vict. Caes. 39,24f.).

As *Caesar*, G. probably had no legislative power (contrary view in [2]). A lasting allocation of a share of the empire had still not taken place in 293, in contrast to 305 (anachronistic Aur. Vict. Caes. 39,30). Instead, G. still had to intervene wherever Diocletian thought necessary (Amm. Marc. 14,11,9). Initially G. was assigned tasks on the Danube border against Sarmatians and Carpi (according to Lactant. De mort. pers. 18,6 and Pan. Lat. 8,5,1f.). In the autumn of 293 he was probably in Egypt to put down the rebellion in the Busiris and Coptus settlements [3. 62]. After an invasion into Armenia by the Sassanid ruler Narseh, G. was sent to the Syrian-Mesopotamian border, where he (perhaps in the autumn of 296; for the disputed chronology see [3] and [4]) he had to accept defeat at a point between Callinicum and Carrhae. Thereafter, the further campaign was coordinated in Antioch with Diocletian, who rushed over from Egypt. The account that G. preceded Diocletian's carriage on foot during the ceremonial entry into Antioch should not be interpreted, in spite of a late tradition (Amm. Marc. 14,11,10; 22,7,1; Eutr. 9,24; Fest. 25), as a denigration of the *Caesar* (contrary view in [5. 172–175]). With fresh troops assembled from Illyricum and Moesia, G. invaded Armenia and was able to defeat Narseh at Satala and take his encampment, including the harem, as booty (Lactant. De mort. pers. 9,7; Eutr. 9,25). Whether G. pursued the Persians across Media as far as Ctesiphon is still an open question. Constantine's assertion (Or. ad sanct. coet. 16) that he himself (accompanying G.?) had seen the ruins of Babylon is scarcely enough to attest to the historicity of such a risky and logistically complicated campaign. The victory was in any case so overwhelming that the Persians had to sue for peace (Petrus Patricius fr. 12). The negotiations conducted jointly by Diocletian and G. in Nisibis (Petrus Patricius fr. 14) resulted in the cession of East Mesopotamia and the final restoration of the Arsacid regime in Armenia. This victory over the Persians was the crowning moment for the Tetrarchy's prestige and was celebrated in imperial propaganda as for example in the decoration of the arch in the palace complex at Thessalonica (see [6]).

According to the well-informed but highly tendentious account by Lactantius, the victory even changed the balance of power within the Tetrarchy, in that G. demanded the succession from Diocletian and was the guiding force behind the latter's policy towards Christians (Lactant. De mort. pers. 9,8–9). Giving rise to the rumour of incipient discord between Diocletian and G. may have been G.'s attempt to establish, apart from the Joviate (→ Tetrarchy), his own forms of sacral self-representation, attaching special significance to his claimed descent from the union of Mars with his mother Romula ([Aur. Vict.] Epit. Caes. 40,16; Lactant. De mort. pers. 9f.). The discovery of Romuliana/Gamzigrad, named after G.'s mother, has confirmed the conspicuous prominence of Romula [7]. At the same time, though, the imagery of this palace complex demonstrates in itself G.'s integration into the tetrarchic ideology, so that we should probably not join Lactantius in seeing the Joviate and descent from Mars as necessarily being in conflict with each other.

With Diocletian's abdication in 305, G., now *Augustus*, received Asia Minor and Illyricum as his immediate share of the empire. After the death of → Constantius [1] he became the highest ranking *Augustus* (from July 306) in the so-called 3rd Tetrarchy. His efforts to continue the tetrarchic program, however, were in vain. He did indeed acknowledge as *Caesar* Constantius' son who was elevated to *Augustus* without his consent, but a little later he sent Severus against the usurper

Maxentius, his son-in-law. After the former's capture (307), he himself headed for Rome where a threatened mutiny by his troops forced his retreat. In the Conference of Carnuntum (November 308) the *Senior Augustus* Diocletian and G. sought to restore the tetrarchic system, with Diocletian appointing Licinius as *Augustus* of the West. Finally, in 310, G. had to acknowledge the *Caesar* of the East, his nephew Maximinus Daia, and Constantine [1] as *Augusti* of equal ranking. With the system's collapse, persecution of Christians also lost the important motive of ideological-religious consolidation of the Tetrarchy. For that reason, and in view of its technical impracticability, G. called the persecution off in April 311 (Lactant. De mort. pers. 34; Euseb. Hist. eccl. 8,17,1–11). Shortly before his retirement to Romuliana that he had planned for 312, G. died of cancer in Serdica in May 311. His portion of the empire was taken over by Licinius and Maximinus Daia and his family was put to death.

1 D. Srejovic, The Representations of Tetrarchs in Romuliana, in: Antiquité Tardive 2, 1994, 143–152 2 S. Corcoran, The Empire of the Tetrarchs, 1996 3 T. D. Barnes, The New Empire of Diocletian and Constantine, 1982 4 F. Kolb, Chronologie und Ideologie der Tetrarchie, in: Antiquité Tardive 3, 1995, 21–31 5 J. Lehnen, Adventus Principis, 1997 6 K. L. Laubscher, Der Reliefschmuck des Galeriusbogens in Thessaloniki, 1975 7 D. Srejovic, C. Vasic, Emperor G.' Buildings in Romuliana, in: Antiquité Tardive 2, 1994, 123–142. B.BL.

Galestes (Γαλέστης; *Galéstēs*). Son of the Athamanian king → Amynander, fled to Pydna to Ptolemy VI, whose *phílos* (φίλος) he became. In 150 BC G. led an expeditionary corps against Demetrius [7] I, and in 145 against Alexander [13] Balas. In 144 Ptolemy VIII took his *dōreaí* (δωρεαί, 'benefices'; *i.a.* in Herakleopolites) away from him; G. fled to Hellas and gathered exiles; he died in an attempt to return to Alexandria and enthrone an alleged son of Ptolemy VI.

W. Schäfer, PKöln V 223/4; L. Criscuolo, L'archivo di Philô (PKöln V 222–225), in: ZPE 64, 1986, 83–86. W.A.

Galgala (Biblical *Gilgāl*, 'circle of stones', probably not a settlement). Pre-Israelite sanctuary (Judg. 3:19) on the eastern shore of the oasis of Jericho (Jos 4:19), probably the site of Saul's elevation as king (1 Sam 11:15) and a pilgrimage centre of the 8th/7th cents. BC (Amos 4:4; 5:5; Hos 4:15; 9:15; 12:12), historicized as a memorial for the crossing of the Jordan under Joshua (Jos 4:20–24, hence Δωδεκαλιθον (*Dōdekalithon*), 'place of twelve stones' on the Madaba map). The Jewish-Christian topographical tradition is continued in *Tosefta Sōṭa* 8,6 (2nd cent. AD ?) and in the *Pilgrim of Bordeaux* 19 (AD 333), as well as in Jerome (Epist. 108,12; AD 404), et al. According to Euseb. On. 66,4–6 (beginning of 4th cent.) the place was, as probably always before, barren and venerated also by pagans. The *Anon. Placentinus* (It. Plac. 13; *c.* 570) first mentions a memorial church over the stones; this is also depicted on the appr. contemporary Madaba mosaic, as Γαλγαλα το και Δωδεκαλιθον (*Galgala to kai Dōdekalithon*). Bishop Arculf (Adamnan, De locis sanctis 2, xiv–xv) still saw the church, rebuilt or renovated, at the end of the 7th cent., but not Bishop Willibald in 724.

O. Keel, M. Küchler, Orte und Landschaften der Bibel 2, 1982, 520–527. E.A.K.

Galilaea Most northern region of → Palaestina. Under Ptolemaic rule (→ Ptolemaeus) after the death of → Alexander [4] the Great, together with all of Palestine, G. became a Seleucid territory at the beginning of the 2nd cent. BC. Urbanization, and the → Hellenization that came along with it, resulted in an antagonism between the Hellenized cities and the Judaism in rural G. In 164 BC, in the context of the Maccabaean (→ Judas Maccabaeus) rebellion against the Seleucids and the Hellenistic cities, the Jewish population was evacuated to Judaea by Simeon. The Hasmonaean → Aristobulus [1] I (104–103 BC) conquered G., which initiated an extensive Judaization by the Hasmonaean kings (→ Hasmonaeans).

After Pompey transformed the Hasmonaean kingdom into a Roman client state in 63 BC, → Antipater [4] appointed his son Herodes governor of G. in 47 BC. As a supporter of Rome, he assisted in suppressing unrest amongst the Jewish population directed against Roman rule. G. became part of the Herodean kingdom and, in keeping with Herodes' will, fell to his son → Herodes Antipas in 4 BC. During Antipas' rule Jesus, who came from the village of Nazareth, was active as an itinerant preacher in G. In the possession of Agrippa I from AD 39 to 44, G. became part of the *prov. Iudaea* after his death. After the initial success of the Jewish revolt of AD 66, organization of the military resistance in G. was taken over by Flavius → Iosephus, who, however, was defeated by Vespasian's troops in AD 67.

As a result of the → Bar Kochba revolt (AD 132–135), which did not affect G., and consequently the expulsion of the Jews from Judaea, G. became the centre of Judaism, under the leadership of the Patriarchs who were recognized by Rome. The seat of the Sanhedrin and the Patriarch was initially → Beth Shearim, and from the middle of the 3rd cent. → Tiberias. Even after the Christianization of the Roman Empire there were no tensions between Christians and Jews; but then, Christianity began to spread in G. only from the 5th cent. onwards. The revolt against Gallus (around AD 350) had probably no far-reaching consequences. Around AD 400, G. and the → Decapolis formed the newly constituted *prov. Palaestina secunda*. Cultivation of olives and flax for textile production were G.'s main economic sectors.

→ Synagogue

W. Bösen, Galiläa als Lebensraum und Wirkungsfeld Jesu, [2]1990; M. Goodman, State and Society in Roman

Galilee, A.D. 132–212, 1983; A. KASHER, Jews and Hellenistic Cities in Eretz-Israel, 1990; L. I. LEVINE (ed.), The Galilee in Late Antiquity, 1992; G. STEMBERGER, Juden und Christen im Heiligen Land, 1987. J.P.

Galinthias (Γαλινθιάς; *Galinthiás*). According to Nicander (Heteroiumena 4 = Antoninus Liberalis 29) G. (Galanthis in Ov. Met. 9,285–323 [5. 469f.]; → Historis in Paus. 9,11,3; Akalanthis in Lib. narrationes 8, s. [1]), daughter of Proetus, helped → Alcmene when the Moirai and Eilithyia, on Hera's behalf (cf. Hom. Il. 19,119), delayed the birth of → Hercules by folding their hands. With her false report of his birth, G. alarmed them so much that they broke the magical spell and Hercules was born. Angered, they transformed G. into a → weasel, which gives birth through its mouth (aition of a popular belief; cf. Anaxagoras 59A 114 D/K = Aristot. Gen. an. 3,6,756b14ff. [6. 136 n.16]). → Hecate, the goddess of birth, appointed the animal as a temple servant (cf. [6. 137 n. 20]). Hercules donated a statue and sacrificed to it (cult aition for preliminary sacrifice in the Theban Hercules festival, the Iolaeia [2]). According to Istros (FGrH 334F72 = schol. T Il. 19,119, cf. Eust. p. 1175,44; Ael. NA 12,5), however, the goddesses broke the magic spell because they were frightened by a real weasel; Gale (according to [4. 614], a short form of G.) is supposed to have been Hercules' wet-nurse.

1 E. K. BORTHWICK, Beetle, Bell, Goldfinch and Weasel in Aristoteles' Peace, in: CR 18, 1968, 134–139 2 NILSSON, Feste, 447 3 J. LOEHR, Ovids Mehrfacherklärungen in der Tradition aitiologischen Dichtens, 1996, 58; 136; 145 n. 232; 150; 152; 156 4 E. MAASS, Mythische Kurznamen, in: Hermes 23, 1888, 613–621 5 F. BÖMER, Komm. zu P. Ovidius Naso, Metamorphosen, B. 8–9, 1977, 360–374 (rich anthology of sources) 6 M. PAPATHOMOPOULOS (ed.), Antoninus Liberalis, Les Métamorphoses, 1968. T.H.

Galla

[1] First wife of Julius Constantius [4], a son of emperor Constantius [5] I. She was mother of Constantius Gallus, Caesar from AD 351–354 (Amm. Marc. 14,11,27). PLRE 1, 382 (G. 1). W.P.

[2] Youngest daughter of → Valentinianus I, sister of Valentinianus II. In AD 387 she fled, together with him and her mother Iustina, from the usurper Maximus to Constantinople, where she married Theodosius I (their daughter: G. [3] Placidia). In 390 she is said to have expelled her stepson Arcadius from the palace after an argument. She died in 394 during a miscarriage. PLRE 1, 382 (G. 2). K.G.-A.

[3] **G. Placidia.** Daughter of Theodosius I and his second wife Galla [2], born between AD 391 and 394 [5; 6]. After her father's death she was cared for by his niece Serena, → Stilicho's wife, in Rome. In 408 she became a hostage of Alarich (→ Alaricus [2]) and his successor Athaulf (Zos. 6,12,3), whom she reluctantly married in Gaul at the beginning of 414. Her son Theodosius, who was born in Barcelona, died soon, as did Athaulf, in 415. In early 416 the Goths concluded a treaty with the Romans and returned G. In 417 Honorius married his half-sister, against her will, to the army commander Constantius [6]. They had two children: Iusta Grata Honoria and the later emperor Valentinianus III. G., who had been elevated to Augusta, was at first on the losing side in the court intrigues, occasionally erupting into street fighting, that followed the death of her husband, shortly after he had been elevated to co-regent (421). Consequently, she was exiled to Rome. She finally fled to Constantinople, where she remained until Johannes usurped the throne in the west in 423. G. was supposed to conduct government business on behalf of Valentinianus, who had then been appointed Caesar. On 23 October 425 he was proclaimed Augustus in Rome, but G. continued to exercise the regency, while the next ten years were marked by power struggles, in which Aetius [2] featured prominently. G., who was anxious to have good legislation (e.g. Cod. Theod. 1,4,3), sought the church's support at this time. She retired after Valentinianus' marriage in 437, but probably continued to exert significant influence. G. died in Rome on 27 Nov. 450. Her burial place is unknown.

As an orthodox Christian and staunch supporter of Roman primacy, she intervened in church politics on several occasions, as in 419 in the Roman schism between Bonifatius and Eulalius, and in 450 in favour of the primacy that had been disputed in Ephesus in 449. G. is credited with the construction and adornment of a number of churches in Ravenna and Rome, such as the church of John the Baptist, promised during a stormy voyage to Constantinople, though none of its decoration has survived (the mosaic inscription CIL XI 276 = ILS 818 = ILCV 20), or the mausoleum attributed to her.

1 PLRE 1, 382 (G. 2) 2 E. DEMOUGEOT, L'évolution politique de G., in: Gerion 3, 1985, 183–210 3 W. ENSSLIN, s.v. Placidia (1), RE 20, 1910–1931 4 S. I. OOST, G., 1968 5 S. REBENICH, Gratian, a Son of Theodosius, and the Birth of G. Placidia, in: Historia 34, 1985, 372–385 6 Id., Gratianus Redivivus, in: Historia 38, 1989, 376–379 7 V. A. SIRAGO, G., 1961 8 L. STORONI MAZZOLANI, Una donna tra mondo antico e Medio Evo, in: R. UGLIONE (ed.), Atti del Convegno nazionale di studi sulla donna nel mondo antico, 1987, 195–205. K.G.-A.

Galli (Γάλλοι/*Gálloi*). 'Servants', 'attendants' and 'worshippers' of the → Mater Magna [1] chiefly in late Republican and Imperial Rome, described consistently as 'priests' only in Christian contexts. They first arose, along with the → Metragyrtae, in Asia Minor, late 3rd/early 2nd cent. BC (Pol. 21,6,6 and 21,37,5, 190 and 189 BC; as literary figures: Dioscorides, Anth. Pal. 6,220). The derivation of the name from Gauls or Galatians is now favoured by [4. 229; 3; 2. 118–120]; only from the end of the 2nd cent. BC, however, do they appear to have become a Roman cultic phenomenon involving voluntary castration (earliest reference:

Obseq. 44a, 101 BC; Val. Max. 7,7,6, 77 BC), at which time their status as a marginal group evidently offered some security of social advantage. Earlier theories of the cult as a Stone Age remnant, and of its supposed Syrosemitic or Phrygian origin, must be weighed against the lack of evidence for ritual eunuchry in pre-Roman Phrygia or Greece. At Rome, the G., in the retinue of the priest and priestess of the Mater Magna, appeared particularly in connection with the latter's feast in April, in a procession with the cult statue, during which they danced ecstatically (→ Ecstasy) to the music of flutes, tambourines and cymbals, begging alms (Lucr. 2,600–660). During the Imperial period, they were also seen at the feast of their mythological role model, → Attis, in March (instructive fig.: [1. vol. 2, 211]). Controversy engendered state control (ban on castration for Roman citizens), and from the Imperial period, the G. were led by an *archigallus*, an uncastrated Roman citizen. Interference with the Christian discussion of eunuchry (→ Montanism) and celibacy in [2. 139–142]. The anthropological parallels with the Hijras of the Hindu → mother goddess Mata are striking [4. 320–325].

→ Attis; → Cybele; → Magna Mater; → Religion

1 M. Beard, J. North, S. Price, Religions of Rome, 2 vols., 1998 2 Ph. Borgeaud, La Mère des dieux, 1996 (bibliography) 3 E. N. Lane, The Name of Cybele's Priests the "Galloi", in: Id. (ed.), Cybele, Attis and Related Cults, 1996, 117–133 4 L. E. Roller, In Search of God the Mother, 1999 (bibliography). T.H.

Gallia/Gaul

A. Land and population in pre-Roman times
B. Roman period 1. Roman conquest 2. Romanization

A. Land and population in pre-Roman times

G. comprises the most western part of the European rump, between the Rhine, the Alps, the Mediterranean, the Pyrenees and the Atlantic. Five large river-systems supply the land with water: the Garumna (Garonne) in the south-west, the Liger (Loire) in the centre and the west, the Sequana (Seine) in the north, the Mosa (Maas) with a tributary of the Rhine, the Mosella (Mosel), in the north-east, and the most important water vein, the Rhodanus (Rhône) with its tributary, the Arar (Saône), both navigable, in the south-east. Prior to the Roman conquest these regions formed neither a geographic, nor a linguistic nor a political unity. The use of the Latin term *Gallia* to refer to this heterogeneous group of tribes and cultures is anachronistic, even if it has become established over time. Two events marked Gallic territory between the 4th and 2nd cents. BC: the expansion of the Celtic population and culture, and the development of trade with the Mediterranean countries. In this context the south of G. had a special position. As this region was at the same time subject to Ligurian (between the Rhône and Italy), Iberian (Languedoc) and Hellenistic influence (→ Massalia and other Greek trading settlements), with the arrival of the Celts in the 5th cent. G. became the birthplace of Celto-Ligurian culture, significant for the development of *oppida*. Powerful tribal groups (Volcae Arecomici, Salluvii, Vocontii, Arverni) formed there in the 3rd and 2nd cents. The rest of G. can be divided into four large parts: central G. around the *Massif Central* as far as the Loire and Lake Geneva covered the territories of some of the largest Gallic tribes (Arverni, Bituriges, Haedui, Sequani and Helvetii); Aremorica between Aquitania and Belgium; Aquitania, where the Celtic tribes that had been settling there since the 3rd cent. controlled the main axis of the trade route from the Atlantic to the Mediterranean; G. Belgica with the Seine and Marne forming the boundary in the south, and the Rhine in the north, which, however, probably did not mark any ethnic or linguistic boundary. Ancient authors and archaeological discoveries show that G. Belgica differed from the rest of G. in terms of language, population, pattern of settlement and social structure.

B. Roman period

1. Roman conquest

After several military campaigns from 125–121 BC, provoked by Massilia's appeals for help, G. on the Mediterranean became a Roman province, named *G. Narbonensis* or *G. togata* to distinguish it from *G. comata* (independent until its subjugation by Caesar). In 118 BC the first civilian colony was brought to → Narbo (Vell. Pat. 1,15; 2,7,8; Eutr. 4,23; Cic. Brut. 43). The history of the new province until Caesar was marked by several revolts and abuse of office by an unscrupulous administration. Caesar's conquest of G. (58–51) opened up for Rome the control of countries between the Mediterranean, the Atlantic, the North Sea and the Rhine and unified the heterogeneous fabric of Celtic G. Three colonies (→ Noviodunum, → Lugdunum and Raurica) were founded on the eastern border of the country as a protection against possible Germanic invasions from the Rhine.

2. Romanization

Restructuring of the province of Gaul took place under Augustus: cession of the *prov. Narbonensis* to Senate administration (22 BC) and division of the country (27 or between 16 and 13 BC) into the *Tres Galliae* (*Lugdunensis*, *Belgica*, *Aquitania*), imperial praetorian provinces with their centre *Ara Romae et Augusti* near Lugdunum. The *concilium Galliarum* met there. The restructuring of the province was part of a series of measures to organize the territory, including the construction of road networks and the institution of *civitates*. Under Augustus many colonies were founded with his name. Many monuments date back to Tiberius' reign. Claudius granted the *Tres G.* the *ius honorum* (CIL XIII 1668; Tac. Ann. 11,25). Several rebellions (Florus and Sacrovir under Tiberius, Vindex under Nero, Civilis under Vitellius) clearly distinguish the militant Gauls in the north-east from the rest of the country. In the period

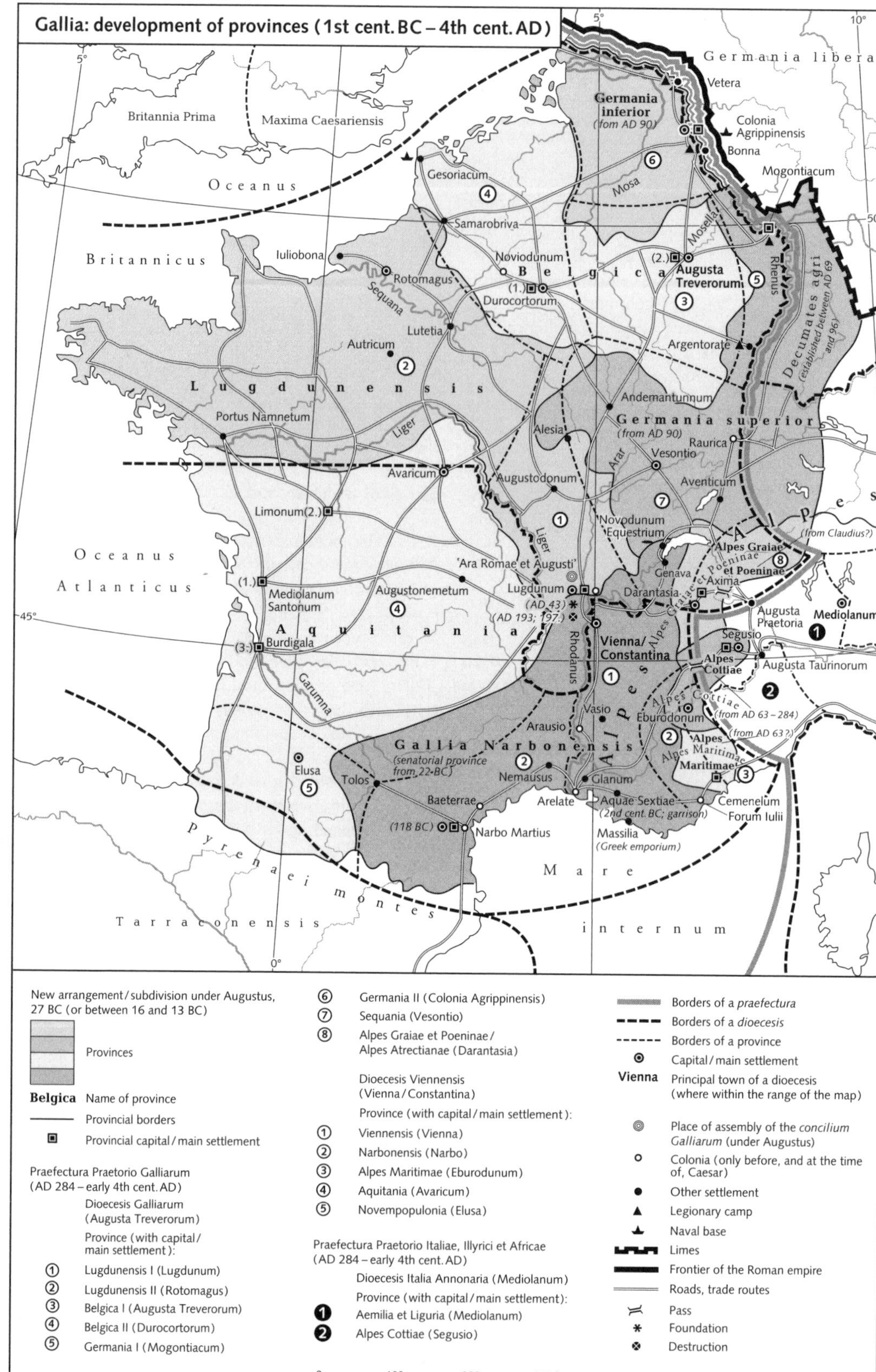

Gallia: development of provinces (1st cent. BC – 4th cent. AD)

of the Flavians and later the Antonines, the Roman peace gave the three provinces a degree of affluence, notwithstanding their insignificant political role. Archaeological evidence provides a highly accurate picture of urban development and the rise in social status of the trading class. Germans invaded G. for the first time during the reign of Marcus Aurelius. In 197 Lugdunum was seriously affected by the war between Septimius Severus and Clodius Albinus. Consequently, German incursions became even more frequent. From 258 to 274 a special Gallic territory was formed (under Postumus and Tetricus) for the purpose of protecting the Rhine border against the Germans. The last third of the 3rd cent. is marked by the advance of the barbarians and by depredations (→ *bagaudae*). Restructuring of the whole imperial administration under Diocletian resulted in the establishment of two dioceses: the one with ten provinces (with → Augusta [6] Treverorum, i.e. Trier, as its capital) comprised *i.a.* the *prov. Lugdunensis*, the old *G. Celtica* and the *G. Belgica*. The *dioecesis Viennensis* (with Vienna, named *Constantina urbs* from the time of Constantine, as its capital) consisted of the entire south-east of the former province and of *Aquitania*. This *renovatio imperii* was accompanied by a strengthening of the defensive fortifications (*limes*). Under Constantine the *praefectura Galliarum* (Trier) was instituted with the dioceses of Hispania, Britannia and the two Gallic dioceses. Barbaric kingdoms were formed in the 5th cent. after a number of invasions: the Franks settled in the north between the Rhine and the Somme; the Alamanni settled in Helvetia and the north-east; the Burgundians in the plains of the Saône and the Rhône; West Goths had settled throughout the Gallic south-west. Clovis (→ Chlodovechus) unified the majority of G. (*regnum Francorum*) towards the end of the 5th cent.

→ Lugdunum; → Narbo; → Aquitania; → Aremorica; → Belgica; → Gallia Cisalpina, → Augustus; → Caesar; → Celtic archaeology

C. Delaplace, J. France, Histoire des Gaules, 1995; J. F. Drinkwater, H. Helton (ed.), Fifth-Century Gaul, 1992; P. M. Duval, Gallien, 1979; J. J. Hatt, Histoire de la Gaule romaine, 1970; M. Py, Les Gaulois du midi, 1993; D. Roman, Y. Roman, Histoire de la Gaule, 1997. Maps: R. Chevallier, G. Narbonensis, in: ANRW II 3, 686–828; Id., G. Lugdunensis, in: ANRW II 3, 860–1060; J. F. Drinkwater, in: R. J. A. Talbert (ed.) Atlas of Classical History, 1985 (repr. 1994), 136; M.-Th. Raepsaet-Charlier, G. Raepsaet, G. Belgica et Germania Inferior, in: ANRW II 4, 3–299; J. Prieur, L'histoire des régions alpestres (Alpes Maritimes, Cottiennes, Graies et Pennines) sous le haut-empire romain (Ier-IIIe siècle après J.C.), in: ANRW II 5, 630–656; Ch.-M. Ternes, Die Provincia Germania Superior im Bilde der jüngeren Forsch., in: ANRW II 5, 721–1260. Y.L.

Gallia Cisalpina

A. Location B. Waves of migration C. Romanization D. Traffic routes E. Cultural development

A. Location

The Roman province in northern Italy borders on the Alps in the north and west, the Apennines in the south and the Adriatic in the east. Traversed by the Padus (Po) (*Gallia Transpadana* to the north and *Gallia Cispadana* to the south of the Padus), *Gallia Cisalpina (GC)* was identified with the Po valley (*latissima pars Italiae*, Tac. Hist. 1,70,1).

In antiquity the geomorphological structure of *GC* was in many respects quite different from today, especially with regard to the riverbeds of the Padus (which ran further south) and the Atesis (the Adige), the lagoons of the upper Adriatic, and the Adriatic coastline (then without today's delta silt of the Padus). The rivers had great economic importance (transport of goods), especially the Padus with its left tributaries and their lakes (*lacus Verbanus* on the Ticinus, *lacus Larius* on the Addua, *lacus Sebinus* on the Ollius, *lacus Benacus* on the Mincius) and the Atesis, the transport link to the Adriatic for Trentino and the city of Verona.

B. Waves of migration

A centre of highly developed cultures from the Bronze Age, *GC* came under the influence of the Etruscans (→ Etrusci), who invaded the territory between the Liguri in the west and the Veneti in the east and introduced urban culture (Felsina, Spina, Marzabotto). The province's name derives from the Galli, who crossed over the Alps in the 6th/5th cents. BC, and reached the Apennines and the Adriatic. In the process they drove back the Etruscans, from whom they acquired viticulture (Liv. 5,33) [1] and many other elements that were absorbed into the La Tène Culture [2–10]. For the first time Gauls appeared north of Milan (Lepontic inscription of Prestino). During the invasion of 386–385 they penetrated as far as Rome. The → Insubres settled in the north-west between the Ticinus and Ollius [11], the → Cenomanni [3] in the north-east, the → Boii in Aemilia, the → Lingones in Romagna, the → Senones in the Marches as far as the Aesis; they had contacts with → Umbri [12], who were assimilated as early as the 4th cent. However, isolated waves of migration continued into the 3rd cent. (225 as far as Talamone, 222 defeat of the Insubres against M. Claudius Marcellus). In the 2nd cent. the → Carni (186–183), the → Cimbri and the → Teutoni immigrated, the latter being defeated in 101 at Vercellae [13]. In 180, some 47,000 Ligures Apuani were deported to Hirpinia. After 168 the territory of the Senones was colonized by the Romans. The region of the → Ligures was restructured in 125–123 BC.

C. Romanization

The south-eastern foothills of *GC* were the first to be Romanized, i.e. the region between the Aesis and

Ravenna traversed by the rivers from the Apennines; then the fertile Po valley and the plains of the Veneti in the north between the Atesis and the Isontius. The Celts and Ligures of the Apennines were subjugated in succession, and in the Augustan period, the various Alpine peoples with the result that the Alpine passes were accessible for the Romans.

In the 3rd/2nd cents. BC the consular province was named *Gallia* or *Ariminum* (Liv. 28,38,13: *Ariminum, ita Galliam appellabant*). After the conquest of *Gallia Narbonensis* in 125 different names were required to distinguish the Celtic territory on both sides of the Alps – *GC* (in contrast to *Transalpina*) from the time of Sulla, or *Gallia Citerior* (Caes. B Gall. 1,24,3). The province was granted the *ius Latii* by Cn. Pompeius Strabo in 89, and the *civitas Romana* with the *lex Roscia* in 49 (Cass. Dio 41,36,3) [14]; therefore, it was called *Gallia togata*. Its borders were formed by the Verus in the west, the Formio in the east, Luca in the south-west and the Rubicon in the south-east. In 42 BC the last military command in Italia was dissolved and the province *GC* was divided into four regions by Augustus: *VIII Aemilia*, *IX Liguria*, *X Venetia et Histria* and *XI Transpadana*. The new borders were the Arsia in the east, Ariminum in the south-east and the Macra in the south-west. The cities thrived, especially Aquileia and Verona. With the restructuring under Diocletian the province became part of *Italia annonaria*. Between AD 286 and 404, first Mediolanum, and then Ravenna were the imperial seats of residence [15].

D. Traffic routes

Military roads, which developed into general traffic arteries, were of special significance for the process of Romanization: the *via Flaminia* (220 BC) to → Fanum Fortunae and → Ariminum, the *via Aemilia* from Ariminum to → Bononia [1] and Placentia and the *via Flaminia minor* from → Arretium to Bononia (187 BC); the *via Aemilia Altinate* (175 BC); the *via Postumia* (148 BC), a connecting road across the Apennines and the foothills of the Alps from Genoa through Dertona, Placentia and Verona to Aquileia; the *via Popilia* from Ariminum to Hadria (132 BC); the *via Annia* in the Veneto (131 BC ?); the *via Fulvia* (124 BC) and the *via Aemilia Scauri* (115 BC). Augustus organized the → *cursus publicus* and from 27 BC rebuilt many roads; in particular he began the construction of roads over the Alps (the *via Iulia Augusta*: in the west on the coast to *Gallia Narbonensis*, in 13–12, in the east over the Alpes Carnicae, 2 BC). Claudius continued the construction of roads with the branchlines of the *via Claudia Augusta* (AD 46–47) to Raetia; Vespasian built the *via Flavia* (AD 78; Tergeste-Pola). The inland waterways retained their great economic significance; by the *cursus publicus* the Padus and, in Etruscan tradition (cf. → *fossa Philistina*), navigable canals were used, which, apart from the Padus and the Atesis via the Laguna Veneta (*VII Maria*), connected Ravenna with Altinum, Concordia and Aquileia through the *fossae Augusta*, *Claudia*, *Flavia* and *Neronia*.

E. Cultural development

The Etruscan cities of Hadria, Spina, Felsina (later Bononia Celtica) and Marzabotto showed a remarkable stage of development. The town of Acerrae (Insubres) was termed *pólis* by Polybius (2,34). The *coloniae Latinae* adopted the regular city structure that can still be seen in the cities Ariminum (268 BC), Placentia, Cremona (218 BC) and Bononia (189 BC). Aquileia (181 BC) was the last city to receive the *ius XII coloniarum* (*ius Arimini*) [16; 17]. The other settlements were Roman *coloniae*: Mutina and Parma 183 BC, Dertona 109, Eporedia 100, Comum 89 or 59; *coloniae III virales*: Ariminum and Cremona, Tergeste and Pola (33 BC); Augustan *coloniae*: Ariminum, Ateste, Augusta Praetoria (25 BC), Augusta Taurinorum (27 BC), Bononia, Brixellum, Brixia, Concordia, Dertona, Parma and Placentia; Claudian *coloniae*: Iulium Carnicum and Opitergium. Many of the *fora* that were constructed on the roads prospered and achieved a status similar to that of cities, as for example the *fora Cornelii*, *Iuli*, *Livi*, *Novum* and *Popili*.

Colonization and the development of traffic routes resulted in the particularly agricultural, cultural and economic wealth of *GC*, as described by Polybius (2,15,1–7) in the 2nd cent. BC and by Strabo (5,1,4–12) in the 1st cent.

In the *GC* of the 2nd cent. BC Celts, Ligures, Etruscans and Veneti were assimilated, apart from linguistic aspects (Pol. 2,17,9). The Latin language and official religious doctrines became obligatory in 89. The upper classes produced significant *poetae novi* (Helvius Cinna, Licinius Calvus, Furius Bibaculus, Cornificius, Ticida, Caecilius, Catullus) and Virgil, the historians Livy, Cornelius Nepos, Pliny and the agronomist Saserna (Cic. De or. 34, Phil. 3,5: *flos Italiae*; *firmamentum imperii populi Romani*) [18].

1 M. Sordi, La leggenda di Arunte Chiusino, in: Rivista Storica dell'Antichità 6–7, 1976/7, 111–118 2 M. Zuffa, I Celti nell'Italia adriatica, in: Introduzione alle Antichità Adriatiche (Convegno di studi sulle antichità adriatiche Chieti-Francavilla al Mare 27–30 giugnio 1971), 1975, 97–159 3 J. Loicq, Les Celtes en Italie, in: Études Celtiques 15, 1978, 655–703 4 E. Arslan, Celti e Romani in Transpadana, in: Études Celtiques 15, 1978, 441–481 5 P. Santoro (ed.), I Galli e l'Italia, 1978 6 V. Kruta, Celtes de Cispadane et Transalpins, in: SE 46, 1978, 149–174 7 C. Peyre, La Cisalpine Gauloise, 1979 8 E. Campanile (ed.), I Celti d'Italia, 1982 9 D. Vitali (ed.), Celti ed Etruschi, 1987 10 E. Arslan, D. Vitali (ed.), I Celti, 1991 11 P. Piana Agostinetti, Per una definizione dei confini delle civitates celtiche, in: Scienze dell'Antichità 2, 1988, 137–218 12 J. J. Hatt, De Denys d'Halicarnasse à Tite-Live ..., in: Soc. Archéologique de l'Aube (ed.), Hommage J. Carcopino, 1977, 157ff. 13 F. Sartori, Catullo e Sirmione, 1994 14 U. Ewins, The Enfranchisement of Cisalpine Gaul, in: PBSR 23, 1955, 73–98 15 L. Ruggini, Economia e società nell' Italia annonaria, 1961 16 U. Ewins, The Early Colonisation of Cisalpine Gaul, in: PBSR 20, 1952, 54–71 17 E.T. Salmon, Roman Colonization, 1969, 92, 111 18 S. Mratschek, Lit. und Ges. in der Transpadana, in: Athenaeum 72, 1984, 154–198.

G.E.F. Chilver, Cisalpine Gaule, 1941; G.A. Mansuelli (ed.), Arte e civiltà romana nell'Italia Settentrionale, 1964; G.Tozzi, Storia padana antica, 1972; E.Gabba (ed.), L'Italia Settentrionale nell'età antica, 1976; G.Tibiletti, Storie locali, 1978; G.Uggeri, La romanizzazione dell'antico delta padano, 1975; Id., La navigazione interna della Cisalpina in età romana, in: Antichità altoadriatiche 2, 1987, 305–350; R.Chevallier, La Romanisation de la Celtique du Pô, 1983; G.Bandinelli, Problemi storici e archeologici, 1983/4; V.Vedaldi Iasbez, La problematica sulla romanizzazione della Transpadana, in: Quaderni Giuliani 1, 1985, 7–47; La città nell'Italia Settentrionale in età romana, Atti di Convegno Trieste 1987 (Collection de l'École française de Rome 130), 1990; M.Denti, I Romani a N del Po, 1991; L.Bosio, Le strade romane della Venetia et Histria, 1991.

G.U.

Gallic see → Celtic languages

Gallica see → Shoes

Gallic Wars see → Caesar

Gallienus Imp. Caes. P. Licinius Egnatius G. Augustus, born *c.* AD 218 near Milan ([Aur. Vict.] epit. Caes. 33,3), son of the later emperor P. Licinius Valerianus and Egnatia Mariniana. Valerian, who had himself proclaimed emperor in September/October 253, immediately appointed G. Caesar, then Augustus, and had this confirmed by the Senate with a territorial allocation of responsibilities: Valerian went to the east to confront the Persian threat, G. went to the west to defend the Rhine and Danube borders. Until 257 he secured the Balkan from Sirmium and transferred this task to his generals, but left behind his son Cornelius Valerianus as Caesar (from 255) and went to the Rhine border (Zos. 1,30,1; [Aur. Vict.] epit. Caes. 32,2; CIL VIII 10132; XVI 155; AE 1967, 584). He appears on coins in 257–258 as *restitutor Galliarum*, recalling the *victoria Germanica* (RIC 5,1,70ff. no. 27–35, 39–50, 61–63, et al.) and no later than 257 declared himself *Germanicus maximus* and *Dacicus maximus* (CIL II 2200 [1. 199ff.]). On 24/25 April 260 the Iuthungi, who had penetrated into northern Italy, were decisively defeated on their retreat to Raetia [2. 369ff.], and in the same year a victory was won over the Alamanni near Milan and, at roughly the same time, over the Franks who had penetrated to Tarragona (Zos. 1,37; Zon. 12,24; Eutr. 9,8). The death of his son Cornelius Valerianus in Illyria, in whose place he immediately appointed his younger son Saloninus Caesar in Cologne, resulted in the usurpation by Ingenuus in Pannonia. It was suppressed by Aureolus probably still in 259. The capture of G.'s father Valerianus by the Persians in 260 led to further imperial proclamations by individual parts of the army, as for example that of Regalianus at the lower Danube. He, too, was eliminated by Aureolus (Aur. Vict. Caes. 33,2; [Aur. Vict.] epit. Caes. 32,2f.; Eutr. 9,8). On the Rhine, Postumus, who was in command of the army, had Saloninus murdered in 260, elevated himself to Augustus and established the Gallic special territory, which existed until 274 (S HA Tyr. Trig. 3 [3. 66ff.]).

From 260 G. was in fact the absolute ruler. Attempts at usurpation by Macrianus and his sons in the east and by Aemilianus in Egypt were only ephemeral occurrences (S HA Gall. 2ff.). In Byzantium, G. suppressed a mutiny of the army in 262 and then rushed to Rome to celebrate the Decennalia festivities (→ *decennalia*) (SHA Gall. 6,8ff.; 7,4ff.). It was probably only then that G. implemented his comprehensive reform of the army by creating an independent cavalry as a tactical reserve in the rear echelon. He also excluded members of the Senate from all senior military commands and appointed equestrians [4. 13ff.]. In 264 or 265 G. journeyed to Greece and was initiated into the Eleusinian mysteries (S HA Gall. 10,3ff. [5. 235ff.]). In 265 he started the unsuccessful war against Postumus in Gaul and was consequently wounded by an arrow (Zon. 12,23; S HA Tyr. Trig. 3,5; S HA Gall. 4,4–6). In the meantime the Persians had overrun the east, but with G.'s approval Odaenathus of Palmyra opposed them (S HA Gall. 3,3; 10,1ff.; 12,1; Zos. 1,39,1f.; Zon. 12,3; CIL VIII 22765 [262/263]). When Odaenathus was murdered in 267 and a special Palmyrenian territory (→ Palmyra) under the rule of his wife Zenobia was established, G. dispatched an army under his general Heraclianus, which, however, was wiped out (S HA Gall. 13,1ff.). Meanwhile, the Herulians had invaded Moesia and Greece and penetrated as far as Athens, so that G. had to entrust the war against Postumus in Gaul to his general Aureolus in order to oppose them (S HA Gall. 13,9; Zos. 1,39,1; Zon. 12,24). An intervention against the Goths, who had invaded Asia Minor, was thwarted by Aureolus' usurpation in Milan (Zos. 1,40,1). G. held him captive in the city but fell victim to a conspiracy of his generals, including Aurelianus [3] and Claudius [III 2] Gothicus (Aur. Vict. Caes. 33,21ff.; Zon. 12,25) probably in September 268. Besides the two sons mentioned above, he had another son, Marinianus, *cos.* in 268, by his wife Cornelia Salonina.

As absolute ruler, G. rescinded his father's anti-Christian edicts; for his relationship with the Christians, cf. Euseb. Hist. eccl. 7,23. He was friendly with Plotinus (Porph. Vita Plotini 12). To counter his disparaging evaluation in the sources, in terms of administration and military structures G. paved the way for → Diocletian's reforms. Although he did not succeed in restoring the Imperium's unity, for 15 years he successfully faced the empire's internal and external problems that Aurelianus [3] and Diocletian were finally able to resolve.

1 H.Koethe, Zur Geschichte Galliens im dritten Viertel des 3. Jh., in: BRGK 32, 1942, 199–224 2 L.Bakker, Raetien unter Postumus, in: Germania 71, 1993, 369–386 3 C.Patti, Cronologia degli imperatori gallici, in: Epigraphica 15, 1953, 66–89 4 M.R. Alföldi, Zu den Militärreformen des Kaisers G., Limes-Stud., 1959, 13–18 5 D.Armstrong, G. in Athens, 264, in: ZPE 70, 1987, 235–258.

PIR² L 197; PLRE 383f. G. (1); L. DE BLOIS, The Policy of the Emperor G., 1976; KIENAST ²1996, 218–230; W. KUHOFF, Herrschertum und Reichskrise, 1979; E. MANNI, L'impero di Gallieno, 1949; G. WALSER, TH. PEKÁRY, Die Krise des Röm. Reiches, 1962, 28–50. T.F.

Gallinaria

[1] (modern Gallinara). Small uninhabited island in the Ligurian Sea (Varro, Rust. 3,9); place of refuge for St. Martinus and Hilarius (Sulp. Sev. Sanctus Martinus 6,5; Sozom. Hist. eccl. 3,14; Ven. Fort. Sanctus Hilarius 35). Archaeological finds in the sea off the coast.

G. FORNI (ed.), Fontes Ligurum et Liguriae Antiquae (Atti della Società ligure di storia patria 16), 1976; G. SPADEA, Archeologia Subacquea in Liguria, in: Bollettino di Archeologia Subacquea 2–3, 1995/6, 103. R.PE.

[2] Wooded (*silva*, *pinus*) territory in Campania, south of Volturnum, notorious hide-out for robbers and bandits (Cic. Fam. 9,23; Str. 5,4,4; Juv. 3,307, mentioned there with the marshes in the *ager Pomptinus*).

NISSEN 2, 713. H.SO.

Gallio see → Iunius Gallio Annaeanus

Gallius Latin family name (SCHULZE 424), possibly originally denoting descent from a Gallus.

[1] **G., M.** Praetor in 44 BC or earlier, served under M. Antonius at Mutina in 43 [I 9] and also fought against Octavian; in his will he adopted the later emperor Tiberius (Cic. Phil. 13,26; Suet. Tib. 6,3).

[2] **G., Q.** *Aedilis plebis* in 67 BC, held magnificent games in 66, as praetor he chaired the trial against C. Cornelius [I 2] in 65 and was probably successfully defended by Cicero in proceedings initiated by M. Calidius [I 2] for bribing voters in 64 (or 66) (Q. Cic. Comm. pet. 19; Cic. Brut. 277f.; Ascon. 88C). Father of G. [1] and [3].

J.W. CRAWFORD, M. Tullius Cicero: The Fragmentary Speeches, ²1994, 145–158; P. NADIG, Ardet ambitus, 1997, 164f.

[3] **G., Q.** Praetor (peregrinus?) in 43 BC, removed from office by Octavian, sentenced to death for conspiracy and exiled (Suet. Aug. 27,4; App. B Civ. 3,394f.). K.-L.E.

Gallonius Family name, also Galonius, Calonius (SCHULZE 171); bearers of this name are attested several times but are of little historical significance.

[1] **G., C.** Roman *eques*, was sent by L. Domitius [I 8] Ahenobarbus to Gades to administer an inheritance in 49 BC, became city leader in the Civil War there, but withdrew in favour of Caesar (Caes. B Civ. 2,18,2; 20,2f.).

[2] **G., P.** Made proverbial by Lucilius (1238 M.) as a gourmet and glutton. K.-L.E.

Gallunianum *Praedium* (estate) in Etruria, then a centre of settlement with *ecclesia*, modern Galognano near Siena, mentioned in inscriptions on liturgical silver objects (6th cent. AD, now in the Pinacoteca of Siena).

O. VON HESSEN, W. KURZE, C.A. MASTRELLI, Il tesoro ecclesiastico di Galognano, 1977; M.M. MANGO, Silver from Early Byzantium, 1986, 250–254; S.A. BOYD, M.M. MANGO, Ecclesiastical Silver Plate, 1992, 134. G.U.

Gallus [I] (Γάλλος; *Gállos*).

[1] River in Bithynia, modern Mudurnu Çayı, rises near Modrene (modern Mudurnu) in Phrygia Epictetus (Str. 12,3,7; [2], differently [1]) and flows into the lower course of the → Sangarius.

[2] Small river that originally flowed through → Pessinus to the → Sangarius [3].

1 W. RUGE, s.v. G., RE 7, 674 2 S. ŞAHIN, Stud. über die Probleme der histor. Geogr. Kleinasiens, in: EA 7, 1986, 125–151 3 BELKE, 165f. K.ST.

[3] Writer of epigrams, to whom the *Anthologia Palatina* ascribes a love poem (Anth. Pal. 5,49) that, by virtue of its style and vocabulary (though not because of its obscene tone), appears to belong to the 'Garland' of Philip, and also an ecphrastic epigram, a polished description of a Tantalus figure on a cup (16,89). In the first case the lemmatist added a τοῦ δικαίου to Γάλλου; that probably conceals the *nomen gentile* Tudicius (cf. Cic. Clu. 70) – but it is not evidence that it is the same writer. As author or addressee of the second epigram, Cornelius [II 18] Gallus (Virgil's friend, who committed suicide in 26 BC) has been suggested.

FGE 60–62. M.G.A.

Gallus [II] Widespread Roman cognomen ('Gaul').

DEGRASSI, FCIR 253; KAJANTO, Cognomina 195. K.-L.E.

[1] see → Cornelius [II 18] Gallus

[2] **P.G.** *Eques*, who was friendly with the *praef. praet.* → Faenius Rufus and the consular → Antistius [II 12] Vetus and was therefore exiled in AD 65 (PIR² G 66). In Tacitus the name is rendered as Publius Gallus, but that is out of the question. A *nomen gentile* is concealed behind Publius, perhaps Publilius?

W. ECK, in: Splendidissima civitas. Études ... en hommage à F. JACQUES, 1996, 74. W.E.

[3] see → Trebonianus

[4] see → Constantius [5]

Galus Roman cognomen (orthographic variation of → Gallus?) in the → Sulpicii family.

DEGRASSI, FCIR 253; Id., FCap 149; KAJANTO, Cognomina 195. K.-L.E.

Gamala (modern Ḫirbat ehdeb). Town in lower Gaulanitis (→ Batanaea; Jos. BI 4,1,1) with a large Jewish component in the population (Jos. Ant. Iud. 13,15,3; BI 1,4,8) because of the settlement policy of → Alexander [16] Iannaios. Under the Zealots and → Iosephus (cf. Vita passim), G. therefore became a bulwark against the Romans (Jos. BI 2,20, 4; 6). After an uprising in AD 68, the town was captured by Vespasian, who had all the inhabitants put to death as punishment (Jos. BI 4,1,3–10).

O. KEEL, M. KÜCHLER, Orte und Landschaften der Bibel 2, 1982, s.v. G. C.C.

Gamaliel

[1] G. I. Also called 'the Old Man' (died *c.* AD 50), a grandson of Hillel. G. was a Pharisee (→ Pharisaei) and member of the Sanhedrin (→ Synhedrion). G., about whom little is known historically (for discussion of the problem, cf. [1]), is thought to have been → Paulus' teacher prior to his conversion to Christianity (Acts 22:3). According to Acts 5:34–39 his intervention saved Peter and other apostles from prosecution by the Sanhedrin.

[2] G. II. Grandson of [1], active in Jamnia from *c.* AD 80 as successor to Rabbi Jochanan ben Zakkai and played an important role in establishing rabbinic Judaism after the destruction of the Temple and at the beginning of Jewish self-government. G. is reported to have made a journey to Rome (ySan 7,19 [11] 25d). He died between AD 100 and 120.

[3] G. III. (*c.* AD 217–230), second eldest son of Rabbi Jehuda ha-Nasi. According to his father's will, he obtained the office of Patriarch (bKet 103b), while his brother Simeon received that of Ḥahham, the highest doctrinal authority. G. resided in → Sepphoris in upper Galilee. As two unusually decorated sarcophagi were found in the necropolis of → Beth Shearim with the names Simeon and G., it is assumed the brothers were buried there.

1 M. HENGEL, Der vorchristl. Paulus, in: M. HENGEL, U. HECKEL, Paulus und das ant. Judentum, 1991, 177–294, here 242ff. 2 s.v. G., Rabban, Encyclopaedia Judaica 7, 1972, 295–299 (Lit.) 3 E. SCHÜRER, The History of the Jewish People in the age of Jesus Christ 2, 1979, 367ff., 372f. B.E.

Gambrium (Γάμβρειον; *Gámbreion*). Xenophon (Hell. 3,1,6f.) mentions G. and Palaigambreion as seats of dynasties that allied with the Spartans in 399 BC. Both places are assumed east of Pergamum near today's Kınık. Nothing is known of its earlier history; there is no reference in the Attic tribute lists. However, coins are attested in the 4th and 3rd cents. An inscription (CIG 3562) mentions a king Alexander of G. in 326–325 BC and a temple for a certain Artemis Lochia, with remains still extant.

L. BÜRCHNER, s.v. G., RE 7, 691. E.SCH.

Gambrivi Germanic tribe that Str. 7,1,3 counts among the weaker tribes, together with the Cherusci, Chatti and Chattuari. A version of the Mannus-genealogy (→ Herminones) ranked the G., together with the Marsi, Suebi and Vandili, among the original Germanic tribes (Tac. Germ. 2,2). A connection with the Sugambri seems to be linguistically indicated, but the fact that Str. loc. cit. mentions both names in the same context argues against their being identical.

G. NEUMANN, D. TIMPE, s.v. G., RGA 10, 406–409. K.DI.

Gamedes Boeotian potter, active around the middle of the 6th cent. BC, who twice signed a jug now in Paris (LV, inventory no. MNB 501): ΓΑΜΕΔΕΣ ΕΠΟΕΣΕ (*GAMEDES EPOESE*). The clover-leaf jug, with its conical body and knurled rim and its high neck divided by a sharply ridged ring design, can be linked to the shape of other Boeotian jugs. The signatures of G. and Polon are the only ones preserved in Boeotian black-figured vase painting. Named after G. is the G.-painter, who painted the jug in the Louvre (shepherd with bull and sheep) in his uncomplicated style, as well as a kantharos in Athens (Num., inventory no. 499, horseman, cows).

M. DENOYELLE, Chefs-d'œuvre de la céramique Grecque dans les collections du Louvre, 1994, 46f., no. 18; N. HIMMELMANN, Über das Hirten-Genre in der ant. Kunst, 1980, 55. M.ST.

Games

I. EGYPT AND ANCIENT ORIENT II. CLASSICAL ANTIQUITY

I. EGYPT AND ANCIENT ORIENT

The boundaries between games and → sport are fluid; here only relaxation games (→ Board games) are treated that are very well known e.g. for Egypt as originals from tomb contexts and pictorial representations e.g. the Senet board game (*znt*) was popular. The position regarding the sources for the Ancient Orient is very limited for climatic reasons (wood barely preserved). We can make only assumptions about the rules of games. In addition to the game boards there are game stones, *astragaloi* (→ Astragalos [2]), dice and little dice rods that indicate a considerably larger variety of games than was once known. It is debatable whether the numerous models of figures and everyday objects from Egypt and the many animal figures and wagon models made of clay from the Ancient Orient should be regarded as toys for children.

→ Board games

E. BRUNNER-TRAUT, s. v. Spielzeug, LÄ 5, 1152–1156; N. CHOLIDIS, Tiere und tierförmige Gefäße auf Rädern. Gedanken zum Spielzeug im Alten Orient, in: MDOG 121, 1989, 197–220; W. DECKER, s. v. S., LÄ 5, 1150–1152; U. HÜBNER, Spiel und Spielzeug im ant. Palästina, 1992; E. KLENGEL-BRANDT, Spielbretter und Würfel aus Assur, in: Altorientalische Forsch. 7, 1980, 119–126;

M. Stol, Private Life in Ancient Mesopotamia, in: J. M. Sasson (ed.), Civilizations of the Ancient Near East, vol. 1, 1995, 498–499. H. J. N.

J. RE.

II. Classical antiquity

A. General B. Children's games C. Erotic games D. Games with animals E. Depictions

A. General

Greek and Latin literature regarding games or their rules has only scantily been passed down to us: the most important source is considered to be the information – though only lexicographical – in Poll. 9,94–129 about individual games. The work by Suetonius [2] 'On Children's Games among the Greeks', the treatise of emperor → Claudius [III 1] on → Dice games listed in Suet. Claud. 33,2, the play *Paidiaí* ('Children's Games') of Crates [1] (Ath. 11,478f) and the didactic poems about → ball games, → board games and → dice games about which Ovid (Ov. Tr. 2,471–485) reports have been lost.

In all social classes and age groups games were popular. As in ancient times there were no playgrounds in the modern sense, children, young people and adults attempted to pursue their joy in and passion for games in the most varied of places: people played in the house (Verg. Aen. 7,379; Plut. Cato minor 2,5 f.), on the roads and squares (Mart. 14,169; Plut. Alcibiades 2,2), in palaestrae, thermal baths and inns etc. Especially in Roman times people looked for free areas to play with hoops, balls or discuses or set up such areas (Sen. Ep. 80,2; Hor. Sat. 1,6,126; 2,6,48f.; Hor. Epist. 1,7,59; Hor. Ars P. 379–381), so as to offer also spectators sufficient room. Furthermore there were areas or open places for the ball games known as *sphaeristeria* (Plin. Ep. 2,17,12; 5,6,27; Suet. Vesp. 20) at the → thermal baths. There were also bars or private dwellings for many games and entertaining diversions.

Characteristic for the pleasure that games provided in antiquity, is the story in Hdt. 1,94 according to which games helped the Lydians to get over a famine. The propensity for playing games increased into a passion for dice, board and other games of luck, and sometimes large sums of money were also wagered, the loss of which could drive the players to ruin (Hor. Epist. 1,18,21). The games for two players (e.g. board games) was just as popular as group games (e.g. ball games, Sen. Ep. 80,1; Hor. Ars P. 379–381). People played as recreation after tiring work (Ael. VH 12,15; Hor. Sat. 2,1,73; Suet. Aug. 83), which is already recommended by Aristotle [6] (Aristot. Pol. 8,3,1337b), also for mental relaxation and diversion (Phaedr. 3,14; Cic. De or. 2,22; 3,58) and naturally for entertainment too (Hor. Sat. 2,1,71–77), especially at symposia (→ Banquet). A game which the Greeks liked to play in this context was → *kóttabos*, whereas the Romans threw dice (Suet. Aug. 71,1–4). In addition Greeks and Romans passed the time at drinking sprees (→ *comissatio*) with → guessing games. Ball games and other motion games were played after the end of the day's work (Hor. Epist. 1,7,59; Petron. Sat. 27,1–3; in the thermal baths before going into the bath: Hor. Sat. 1,6,123–126). Board and dice games could be played at home, in the tavernas, on streets and squares or at the theatre etc.; the game board necessary for this was scratched into the road cobbles, the temple and theatre steps or people carried portable game boards (*tabulae lusoriae*) around with them (made of wood, small stone slabs, simple tile slabs).

B. Children's games

Children played at all times of the day and would also play truant from school sometimes for this purpose (Pers. 3,45–51); it was also common for adults to play games with children (Ael. VH 12,15; Suet. Aug. 83). On feast days (→ *feriae*) children had a particularly good opportunity to play games (Hor. Epist. 2,2,197). They had available to them a considerable selection of toys, from rattles and clappers for the small child to nuts, *astragaloi* (→ Astragalos [2]), hoops, little carts, → dolls, hobbyhorses, → tops and other toys for the older children (→ Children's games). Games with animals (Plin. Ep. 4,2,3; Plaut. Capt. 1002–1004) could sometimes degenerate into cruelty to animals (Aristoph. Nub. 763f.; Aristoph. Vesp. 1341f.). Even adults kept animals for game and pleasure: monkeys, parrots (Mart. 14,73) and other birds, dogs and cats and even snakes (Suet. Tib. 72). All classes and age groups liked to play ball games often. Whilst → running and catching games as well as → games of dexterity were primarily considered to be children's pleasures, board and dice games were preferred by adults.

C. Erotic games

Erotic games and beauty contests should also be counted among the games in which the attractiveness of a part of the body was foregrounded (Alci. 4,14; Lucian. Dialogi meretricii 3; Ath. 13,609e–610b; Anth. Pal. 5,35; 5,36; Plin. HN 10,172). The kissing games κυνητίνδα/*kynētínda* (Crates 23) and χύτρα/*chýtra*, in which a person held his or her partner by the ears when kissing (Eunicus 1), and also of course the Kottabos game (→ Kiss II. C.2.) were among the erotic games.

D. Games with animals

Animal fights are frequently mentioned and depicted in literature and art; they were popular with the Greeks, Etruscans and Romans. The animals were set upon each other in → palaestrae, → gymnasiums or in the 'game casinos' (Aeschin. In Tim. 53) known as κυβεῖα/*kybeîa*. According to Ael. VH 2,28, these agons took place after the → Persian Wars even in the Dionysus theatre of Athens (cf. Lucian, Anach. 37). For → cockfighting bets were placed and prizes offered. There were also quail fights (Plut. Mor. 319f; Poll. 9,107–109), in which the birds fought each other on a table with a raised edge (Aeschin. In Tim. 53). By plucking feathers or hitting the birds on the head (Aristoph. Av. 1297–1299) people incited the animals to fight each other. We also know from the sources that there were crane fights (Aristot. Hist. an. 9,12; Cass. Dio 66,25,1). People set dogs and cats on each other, as a funerary stele from the Ceramicus shows [1].

E. Depictions

Depictions of human beings playing games are extant from as early as the Mycenaean-Minoan culture (miniature clay model of a swing with a child from Hagia Triada [2. 113 fig. 42a]). From the 8th cent. BC toy horses on wheels, so-called Boeotian bell dolls, tops, rattles and other toys are known (→ Children's games). From the archaic period, aside from preserved toys, scenes on vases in particular are worthy of mention that take up the motif of the 'boardgame-playing heroes' in which Ajax [1] and Achilles are discernible. From the classical period come numerous representations of people playing games, of which the Attic → choes pitchers with the games of small children are especially noteworthy [3]. Of the games of the adults, the kottabos game particularly was depicted in many cases on vases from Athens and lower Italy. In addition, children and adults are shown playing ball games, on swings or on the seesaw, with hoops, and playing games with *astragaloi* and dice. More rarely the game is to be found as a motif in sculpture and here Attic grave reliefs are worthy of mention; dead children in particular are depicted with their toys. Noteworthy are also free-standing sculptures ('Dice player' of → Polyclitus [1]) among which the female 'Knuckle players' became a genre motif of Hellenistic and Roman art.

From Etruscan art only a few game scenes are known, whilst from Roman art on the other hand, particularly from the Imperial period, a wealth of pictorial material is known. Among these we should name in particular the wall frescos of Pompeii and Herculaneum with playing children, with men playing dice games, and adults playing ball games, and other representations. A further pictorial source are the Roman sarcophagi of the 1st and 2nd cent. AD which show children playing games with nuts, *astralagoi*, playing disc games or cockfighting. Also playing Cupids exist: wall frescos and sarcophagi show them driving carts, racing and hiding etc. Our knowledge is also enriched by mosaic representations of which the ball-playing girls from the villa of → Piazza Armerina are particularly well known [4. pl. 11 f.]. From late antiquity there are also book illustrations (→ Book illustration) as conveyors of images which in many cases have as their theme board and dice games. An enormous wealth (especially since the Hellenistic period) of toys for children and adults are preserved, among these clay or tin soldiers, gladiators, animals, miniature furniture, dice, dolls and marbles.

→ Abacus; → Askoliasmos; → Duodecim scripta; → Ephedrismos; → Epostrakismos; → Leisure; → Fritillus; → Harpaston; → Latrunculorum ludus; → Ostracinda; → Puppet theatre; → Tabula; → Trigon; → Tropa; → Games

1 R. Lullies, Griech. Plastik, [4]1979, fig. 57 2 S. Laser, Sport und Spiel (ArchHom III T), 1987 3 G. Horn, Choes and Anthesteria, 1951 4 M. Dolch, Wettkampf, Wasserrevue oder diätetische Übung? Das Mosaik mit den zehn Mädchen in der röm. Villa bei Piazza Armerina auf Sizilien, in: Nikephoros 5, 1992, 333 f.

R. Amedick, Die Sarkophage mit Darstellungen aus dem Menschenleben (ASR 4,1 Vita Privata), 1991, 97–104; M. Fittà, Spiele und Spielzeug in der Antike. Unterhaltung und Vergnügen im Alt., 1998; N. Hanel, Sonderkeramik in der Militärziegelei? Zu einer tabula lusoria mit Mühles. und Legionsstempel, in: Kölner Jb. für Vor- und Frühgesch. 30, 1997, 317–321; O. Höckmann, Brettspiele im Didymeion, in: MDAI(IST) 46, 1996, 251–262; A. Rieche, So spielten die Alten Römer. Röm. Spiele im Arch. Park Xanten, [3]1991; J. Väterlein, Roma ludens. Kinder und Erwachsene beim Spiel im antiken Rom (Heuremata 5), 1976.

R. H.

Games of dexterity were primarily performed by children. With some of these games → astragaloi (knucklebones), nuts, pebbles, coins, small balls or potsherds were used as toys (→ Children's games), with others, sticks, discs, wheels, etc.

A favourite was the so-called πεντάλιθα (*pentálitha*) (Poll. 9,126), in which five stones (nuts, balls, etc.) were thrown up in the air and caught in the palm of the hand or on the back of the hand. In another, the *orca*-game, nuts, stones etc. were thrown into a narrow-necked container (Ps.-Ov. Nux 85f.; Pers. 3,50). Similar to this game was the ἐς βόθυνον (*es bóthynon*, → *trópa*), but in this case the nuts, astragaloi, etc. were thrown into a hole. In another game players tried to knock down a cone-shaped pile of nuts or nut-halves ([1. 97] mentions walnuts) (Ps.-Ov. Nux 75f.) with a well-aimed shot of a nut. A nut could also be rolled down a steep slope to scatter nuts lying on the ground (the winner being the one who hit most nuts; Ps.-Ov. Nux 77f.); balls or rings could also be used in this game. In the 'Delta'-game several lines were drawn on the ground parallel to the base of the Greek letter Δ, after which a nut was rolled to cross over as many lines as possible (Ps.-Ov. Nux 81–84). The game εἰς ὤμιλλαν (*eis ṓmillan*) was similar but here a circle was drawn, into which *astragaloi*, nuts et al. were thrown from some distance (cf. the terra cotta group in [2]), to eject from the circle those belonging to the other player (Poll. 9,102).

'Beating the hoop' deserves mention as a children's game that also gained popularity amongst adults in the Roman Imperial period (Hor. Carm. 3,24,57 calls it *Graeco trocho*, Hor. Ars P. 380; Ov. Ars am. 3,383; Mart. 14,168f.; Prop. 3,14,6), furthermore the beating of the → top. A variation of beating the hoop was the game with a disc-shaped wheel that was set into motion by beating the wheel-hub with a rod; several players employed it as a competition [1. 101f.].

Ov. Ars am. 3,361f. describes a game for adults in which balls had to be taken out of a net without moving the others. The winner was the one who succeeded in removing the most balls. Included among the games of dexterity is also the στρεπτίνδα game (*streptínda*, 'turn around'), where a piece of wood was thrown to turn around a piece of wood lying on the ground (Poll. 9,117), and the κυνδαλισμός (*kyndalismós*, Poll. 9,120), played in a similar fashion but with a wooden stake upright in the ground that was to be thrust aside with a well-aimed throw. Of the games of dexterity listed in Poll. 9,114–120 using fingers, the χαλκισμός (*chalkismós*) game should be mentioned, in which a gold coin spinning like a top is brought to a standstill before it falls over.

→ Askoliasmos; → Epostrakismos; → Kottabos; → Games

1 R. AMEDICK, Die Sarkophage mit Darstellungen aus dem Menschenleben, 4. Vita Privata, in: ASR 14, 1991, 97–104 2 DS vol. 5, 28, fig. 6737.

A. RIECHE, Röm. Kinder- und Gesellschaftsspiele, Limesmuseum Aalen 34, 1984; J. VÄTERLEIN, Roma ludens. Kinder und Erwachsene beim Spiel im ant. Rom, 1976, 34–50. R.H.

Gamos see → Marriage

Gandaridae also Gangaridae. Mentioned in accounts of Alexander's campaign (→ Alexander [4], with map) and in Megasthenes as a powerful people in India. They lived east of the → Prasii on the lower Ganges. Also mentioned in Ptol. 7,1,81.

D. C. SIRCAR, Studies in the Geography of Ancient and Medieval India, 1971, 213ff. K.K.

Gandaritis (Greek Γανδαρικὴ χώρα/*Gandaríkē chṓra*; Ethnic groups: *Gandarai*, *Gandarioi*), district on the Kābul. According to Herodotus (3,91), the Gandarioi, together with the tribes of the Sattagydai, Aparytai and Dadikai, formed the ancient Persian Empire's seventh satrapy, which essentially covered the Kabulistan alpine territory intersected by the Cophen, between Paropanisos (Hindu Kush) and the upper Indus, and the mountain range itself.

In spite of difficult passes along the Cophen, the routes through G. were used, from at least the 4th cent. BC onwards, as trade routes westwards and northwards from the Indus valley, and also as invasion routes for numerous conquerors, Indo-Aryan 'Indians', Achaemenids, Macedonians under Alexander the Great, Sakians, Parthians, Arabs, Turks, Afghans and Mongols. A powerful Greek-Indian empire, with → Menander (*c.* 100 BC) as its most influential king, developed here.

Under the → Graeco-Bactrians and the Kushans (→ Kushan), G. was a flourishing Buddhist cultural region, in which Graeco-Roman and nomadic art combined with Indian tradition and subject material to form Gandhara art (2nd–3rd cents.). Its stylistic repertoire influenced certain artistic styles of northern India and played an important role in spreading Buddhism to central Asia and China.

J. AUBOYER, Afghanistan und seine Kunst, 1968; J. M. ROSENFELD, The Art of the Kushans, 1967. B.B. and J.D.-G.

Gandhara see → Gandaritis

Ganges (Γάγγης; *Gángēs*, Sanskrit *Gaṅga*). The largest river in India, known to the west (Arr. Anab. 5,4,1; 5,6,7; 5,9,4; 5,26,1; Curt. 8,9,5, et passim) since Alexander's campaign (→ Alexander [4], with map), if not already in Ktesias (in Plin. HN 37,39). Its length was measured in the early Hellenistic period and calculated to be 10,000 *stadia* (Str. 15,689). According to Str. 15,719 its source lay in the *Ēmōdá órē* (Himalaya). The G. is mentioned several times by Ptolemy (7,1,29; 30; 42; 51 NOBBE, et passim), its delta described as having five arms (7,1,18), and also the *Gangētikós kólpos* (Bay of Bengal), into which the G. flows, is also named (1,13,6 MÜLLER-FISCHER, 7,1,16 NOBBE, et passim; cf. Str. 15,690). The largest tributary, Yamunā or Jumna, was known as *Iomanes* (Plin. HN 6,69; 71ff.), *Iobares* (Arr. loc. cit.) or *Diamunas* (Ptol. 7,1,29). Other tributaries mentioned by Pliny (HN 6,64f.) and Arrian (Arr. Ind. 4; Megasthenes FGrH 715 F 9a) are often hard to identify. From the time of Ptolemy, the G. was important in geography as the border between *India intra Gangem* and *India extra Gangem*. The → Prasii and → Gandaridae lived on the banks of the G. At the confluence of the G. and the → Erannoboas the capital of the Maurya kingdom, → Palimbothra/Pāṭaliputra (near today's Patna) was located. H.T. and K.K.

Gangra Town in Paphlagonia south of the Olgassys (modern Ilgaz-Dağları), modern Çankırı. This toponym remained almost unchanged until the present: Kanġırı, Çangrı, Çangra. According to Str. 12,3,41 the town included the old basileion of the Paphlagonian dynasts, a fortress and a settlement. In 3 BC the Paphlagonian delegates met here to swear the imperial oath to Augustus [1] after in 5 BC he had elevated G. to a *pólis* and established the *eparchía* Paphlagonia. While the acropolis kept the old name, the town soon became known as 'Germanicopolis near Gangra'. On imperial coins it styled itself as 'the Oldest of Paphlagonia'. The coin inscription ἑστία θεῶν associated its origin with Greek mythology: Tantalus took part in the banquet of the gods on the Olgassys, his son Pelops was considered the ancestor of the Paphlagonians (Diod. Sic. 4,74; Apoll. Rhod. 2,357ff.; 792f.; Schol. Pind. Ol. 1,37). Gangra possessed an extensive territory with numerous rural sanctuaries (Str. 12,3,40) and became a diocese in the Christian period.

1 P. HERRMANN, Der röm. Kaisereid, 1968.

L. ROBERT, À travers l'Asie Mineure, 1980, 203–219. C.MA.

Gannascus A Canninefate, who deserted from Roman service and together with the Chauci laid waste to Lower Germania and the Gallic bank of the Rhine after the death of → Sanquinius Maximus, the governor of Lower Germania, in AD 47. The new governor → Domitius [II 11] Corbulo drove G. away and restored order. When he had G. murdered by a ruse, unrest again broke out among the Chauci, causing Claudius to pull the advance troops back to the west bank of the Rhine (Tac. Ann. 11,18f.). PIR² G 73. M.MEI. and ME.STR.

Gannys (Γάννυς; *Gánnys*). G. was raised in the house of → Iulia Maesa and had a relationship with her daughter → Iulia Soaemias, who made him the tutor of her son → Elagabalus [2] (Cass. Dio 79,6,1f. BOISSEVAIN). G. and → Valerius Comazon had the troops elevate Elagabalus to emperor in Emesa in May AD 218 (Cass. Dio 78,31,2–4). Despite a lack of military experience, G. defeated → Macrinus in June, but was eliminated in the winter of 218–219 by Elagabalus, who had toyed with the idea of marrying him to Soaemias (Cass. Dio 78,38,3; 79,6,1–3). In the mediaeval Dio tradition (78,31,1) G. was either confused or identified with a certain Eutychianus (who contrary to PIR V 42 is not identical to Comazon; thus in PIR² G 74; also BOISSEVAIN, apparatus on the passage). PIR² G 74.

M.MEI. and ME.STR.

Ganus (Γάνος; *Gános*). A mountain above modern Gaziköy on the European Propontis coast, modern Ganos Dağı (945 m). Its region was *Ganiás* (Γανιάς) with the local deity *theà Ganéa* (θεὰ Γανήα). A fortified settlement was located below the mountain *tò Gános* (τὸ Γάνος, Scyl. 67). In the 5th cent. BC, G. was part of the Thynian tribal territory under Seuthes II, who promised → Bisanthe, G. and Neon Teichos to Xenophon (400–399 BC., Xen. An. 7,5,8). G. is also mentioned in association with the advance of Philip II into Propontis against Kersebleptes (346 BC, Aeschin. In Ctes. 3,82).

ERRINGTON, 55. I.v.B.

Ganyctor (Γανύκτωρ; *Ganýktōr*). Person in the → competition between Homer and Hesiod; information on his role and genealogical position varies:

[1] The son of king Amphidamas [5] of Chalcis (Certamen l. 63), as such perhaps the judge in the poetic competition (Vita Hesiodi l. 10).

[2] Son of the Locrian Phegeus of Oenoë, the brother of Amphiphanes. Together they killed Hesiod for seducing their sister Ctimene, who then gave birth to Stesichorus (Vita Hesiodi l. 51; Certamen l. 226–227). The brothers fled the anger of their fellow citizens across the sea and, according to Tzetzes, perished in a storm (Vita Tzetzae l. 34–42 SOLMSEN); according to Alcidamas they are struck down by Zeus' lightening (Certamen l. 238–240).

[3] Naupactian, father of Ctimenus and Antiphus, who murder Hesiod for the same reason as in [2] (Plut. Mor. 969e; Certamen l. 240–242). Rhion (Plut. Mor. 162c-e) and Molycria (Paus. 9,31,6) are given as locations for their death. According to Herodian (1,44,26; 2,742,32 LENTZ) in Eratosthenes the form of the name is Γάνυξ.

T.W. ALLEN (ed.), Certamen Homeri et Hesiodi, in: Homeri opera 5, 225; Id. (ed.), Vita Hesiodi, in: ibid.

JO.S.

Ganymeda (Γανυμήδα; *Ganyméda*). Female deity in Phleius, patroness of prisoners, later equated with → Hebe because of the linguistic similarity to → Ganymede, the cup-bearer of the gods. The only source is Paus. 2,13,3f. E.V.

Ganymede (Γανυμήδης; *Ganymédēs*, Etruscan *Catmite*, Latin apart from G. also *Catamitus*).

[1] In Greek mythology (main source: Hom. Il 20,231–235) the son of the Dardanian king Tros (Iliad parva 29,4 PEG I: son of Laomedon), who as the most beautiful human was abducted to the Olympus to serve Zeus as cupbearer in eternal youth and to delight the gods with his beauty. He is either abducted in a windstorm (H. Hom. 5,202), by → Iris (in art, possibly already in Ibycus PMG Fr. 289), by → Hermes or by an eagle (in art; this is the starting point for taking Zeus himself as the abductor). As compensation (ποινή) for the abduction, Zeus gives → Tros divine horses (or → Laomedon a golden vine). Eratosthenes (*Katasterismoí* 26) speaks of G. being placed into the firmament as the ὑδροφόρος (*hydrophóros*, 'water carrier'). While the erotic motive for the abduction can only be surmized in the epic version, this aspect is clearly emphasized in the lyrics (Ibycus, loc. cit.; Pind. Ol. 1,144; 10,105); the myth is also used to sanction abductions in the context of homoerotic relationships (Hes. Theog. 1345–1348; Soph. 345 TrGF). The popularity of the G. tale as motif in love poetry is evident in the large number of preserved Greek love epigrams; Middle Comedy repeatedly picked up this theme. In Roman and especially in Christian literature the relationship of Zeus to G. is severely criticized: there the abduction of G. is seen as an example of sexual excess and G. himself as the symbol of an effeminate and morally spoiled youth.

The G. myth plays no role in archaic art. Only at the beginning of the 5th cent. BC does the subject appear on several vases. A particularly significant image of this period is the terracotta group '*Zeus and Ganymede*' from Olympia. With the bronze group by Leochares (about 350 BC), the eagle figure takes its place in the iconography of this myth. An essential element of the G. myth is its homoerotic aspect, but the figure of the youthful cupbearer is also significant as a reflection of certain initiation rites. Despite G.'s possibly Greek name, the myth's region of origin is probably Thrace or Phrygia.

J. BREMMER, Adolescents, Symposion, and Pederasty, in: O. MURRAY (ed.), Sympotica. A Symposium on the "Symposium", 1990, 135ff.; P. FRIEDLÄNDER, s.v. G., RE 6, 737–749; H. SICHTERMANN, G., Mythos und Gestalt in der ant. Kunst, 1953; Id., s.v. G., LIMC 4.1, 154–169.

E.V.

[2] Eunuch, *nutricius* of Arsinoë [II 6] IV, who in 48/7 BC fled with her from Alexandria and Caesar's safe-keeping to the troops of → Achillas. He played a significant part in the death of Achillas, then assumed his position in the army and also handled the government in Arsinoë's name. G. achieved significant successes against Caesar, but he and Arsinoë nevertheless lost the confidence of the Alexandrians, who pleaded for and were granted the release of Ptolemy XIII from Caesar. Nothing further is heard of G. but he must have lost his position; he died fleeing the victorious Caesar.

H. Heinen, Rom und Ägypten von 51–47 v.Chr., 1966, 106ff. W.A.

Gaon (Hebrew *gā'ōn*, 'Eminence', later 'Excellency'; pl.: Gəōnīm). Official title of the head of the Rabbinic academies in Babylonian → Sura and → Pumbedita. There the gaons functioned from the 6th cent. AD to the end of the academies in the 11th cent. as the highest teaching authorities (cf. the name of this period as the 'Gaonic period'). The most important representatives of this office were Amram ben Sheshna (died about AD 875; author of the earliest preserved prayer book), Saadiah ben Joseph (882–942; numerous philosophical writings; author of an Arabic Bible translation, → Bible translations), Sherira ben Hananiah (*c.* 906–1006; author of a letter to the community of Qairawān regarding the period of authorship of the Rabbinic writings), Samuel ben Hophni (died 1013; author of Bible commentaries and philosophical writings) and Hai ben Sherira Gaon (939–1038; author of halakhic works and religious poetry). Their halakhic decisions (→ Halakhah) were sometimes accepted as far away as Spain ('Responsa').

In the 10th and 11th cent. the title was also used for academy heads in Palestine, and in the 12th and 13th cents. eventually also for the heads of schools in Damascus, Baġdād and Egypt. In the later period the title functioned as a kind of honorary designation for anyone with unusual knowledge of religious literature.

S. Asaf, J. Brand, s.v. G., Encyclopaedia Judaica 7, 315–324 (with list of the various G.); R. Brody, s.v. Ga'on, The Oxford Dictionary of the Jewish Religion, 265f. B.E.

Garama Main town of the → Garamantes, northeast of Mursuk (Fezzan), modern Djerma. References: Plin. HN 5,36; Ptol. 1,8,5; 10,2; 4,6,30; 8,16,7; Solin. 29,5. L. Cornelius Balbus, *procos. Africae*, led an expedition in 20 BC that certainly reached Garama. Subsequently, there was a close but sometimes stormy relationship between Garama and Rome. Many archaeological finds attest to this close relationship.

Ch. M. Daniels, Garamantian Excavations..., in: Libya Antiqua 5, 1968, 113–194, T. LXXIII–LXXX. W.HU.

Garamantes A Berber tribe in the Libyan interior centered on → Garama. References: Hdt. 4,174; 183,1–184,1; Str. 2,5,33; 17,3,19; 23; Liv. 29,33,9; Mela 1,23; 45; Plin. HN 5,26; 36; 38; 6,209; 8,142; 178; 13,111; Flor. Epit. 2,31; Ptol. 1,8,5–7; 9,9; 10,2; 4,6,16; Solin. 29,7; 30,2; Arnob. 6,5; Tab. Peut. 7,4; Amm. Marc. 22,15,2; Oros. 1,2,88; 90; Iulius Honorius, Cosmographia A 48; B 47; Chronicum Alexandrinum in: Chron. min. 1, p. 107,167; Isid. Orig. 9,2,128; Geogr. Rav. p. 36,22–40.

The influence of the G., who perhaps included a sub-Saharan racial element, extended to the territory of → Agisymba. Contacts with the Punic and Neo-Punic sphere were of considerable importance. In 20 BC L. Cornelius Balbus, *procos. Africae*, fought against the G.; in AD 22 and 69 they appeared before Leptis Magna (Tac. Ann. 3,74,2; Hist. 4,50,4; cf. also Tac. Ann. 4,23,2; 26,2). In 569 they converted to Christianity. They are also mentioned by → Iohannes Biclarensis (Chron. Min. 2, p. 212,569,1). For mention of the G. in poetic works cf. [1. 95 note 7, 96 note 1].

1 J. Desanges, Catalogue des tribus africaines ..., 1962.

C. Daniels, The Garamantes of Southern Libya, 1970; E. Lipiński, s.v. G., DCPP, 184; E.M. Ruprechtsberger, Die Garamanten (Zaberns Bildbände zur Archäologie), 1997. W.HU.

Garden rocket (εὔζωμον/*eúzōmon*, Latin *eruca*), of the Cruciferae family with few species, the most important being the common rocket (*Eruca sativa*), cultivated in the Mediterranean region, with a lignified stem (Theophr. Hist. pl. 7,2,8). According to Plin. HN 19,117 the seeds open after only three days (cf. Theophr. Hist. pl. 7,1,3). Its popularity as a spice gave rocket its Greek name according to Plin. HN 20,126 (literally 'good for soups'). It was enjoyed raw and with onions and was considered an aphrodisiac for which the only antidote was to simultaneously eat lettuce (→ *lactuca* [1], Plin. HN 19,127 and 154 f.; Dioscurides 2,140 Wellmann = 2,169 Berendes, cf. Ov. Rem. am. 799: *erucas salaces*, 'horny rocket'). The seeds were prescribed against scorpion poison (→ Arachnids), → shrews and skin parasites (Plin. HN 20,125). Pastes made from the seeds with vinegar and milk for spicing could be stored for extensive periods (Dioscurides loc. cit.).

F. Orth, s. v. R., RE 1 A, 287. C.HÜ.

Gardens

[1] Horticulture. s. → Horticulture

[2] Gardens

I. Ancient Orient and Egypt II. Greece and Rome

I. Ancient Orient and Egypt

In the immediate proximity of homes, gardens were important providers of shade for humans and livestock. Pleasure gardens as part of palace grounds enhanced prestige. As part of the temple grounds they symbolized the cosmos. The Garden of Eden is a mythological invention (Gen 2,8; 2,15). Gardens were depicted in reliefs (Assyria) and wall paintings (Egypt). Assyrian kings recorded planting gardens with exotic trees and plants. The description of the → 'Hanging Gardens' of Babylon by ancient writers probably reflects an idealized pleasure garden established by → Sanherib in Nineveh, which was watered by a *c.* 16 km long aqueduct that is still visible. Gardens of Persian kings (*pardēsu*; → Paradeisos) are attested in Sippar, Uruk and Nippur.

M.A. Dandamayev, Royal *paradeisoi* in Babylonia, in: Orientalia J. Duchesne-Guillemin ... oblata, 1984, 113–117; W. Fauth, Der königliche Gärtner und Jäger im Paradeisos. Beobachtungen zur Rolle des Herrschers in der vorderasiat. Hortikultur, in: Persien 8, 1979, 1–53; H. Forkl, J. Kalter, T. Leisten, M. Pavaloi (ed.), Die Gärten des Islam. Ausstellungskat. Lindenmus. Stuttgart, 1993; J.-J. Glassner, À propos des jardins mésopotamiens, in: R. Gyselen (ed.), Jardins d'Orient (Res Orientales III), 1991, 9–17; D.J. Wiseman, Palace and Temple Gardens in the Ancient Near East, in: Bull. of the Middle Eastern Culture Center in Japan 1, 1984, 37–43 (with fig.); D. Wildung, s.v. G., LÄ 2, 376–378. J.RE.

II. Greece and Rome

A. Greece B. Rome C. Gardens as a literary motif

A. Greece

In Classical Greece a garden (κῆπος, *kêpos*) was rarely part of an urban home. Gardens were usually located outside the town near a source of water. However, there was a limited greening of the inner town area because gardens and groves were established in sanctuaries and the agorai were planted (Paus. 2,15,2; 8,31,4f.; Plut. Cimon 13). Greek gardens included commercial gardens of all types, parks, groves, sanctuary and cemetery gardens. Ornamental gardens are not documented. Parts of Theophrastus' garden near the Gymnasium in the Athenian suburb of Lyceum were dedicated to the Muses and allotted for grave sites, therefore, walkways, statues, lawns and beds in this garden hint at an ornamental garden only at first sight (Diog. Laert. 5,51–54; IG II/III 2613f.). Floral decoration using ornamental plants were restricted to wreaths and garlands on festive occasions. In the Hellenistic period the demand for flowers increased especially by the monarchs who used them to opulently decorate their imaginative festivals. This included the festive tent of Ptolemy Philadelphus, which was decorated with roses, myrtles and white violets (Ath. 5, 196d; 12, 542c-d) in Alexandria. These garden products mostly came from royal lands in Egypt.

The town of Rhodes, which was refounded in the late 5th cent. and rebuilt after an earthquake in the 3rd cent., was given a more generous territorial outlay than the old organically grown towns. Large areas within the city walls were reserved for developing temples and nymphaea with groves and fields (Aristid. 25,6). New foundations in the Hellenistic period were also able to lay out a generous green area. In Alexandria, groves (ἄλση, *álsē*) were located near the dikasterion in the town centre (Str. 17,1,10), and in Memphis a grove was situated by a lake (Str. 17,1,31f.). Under Alexander the Great, Greece's contact with Egypt and the Orient increased. Influenced by eastern traditions, Hellenistic kings had large palaces (βασίλεια, *basíleia*) built in their residence cities incorporating residential and representational buildings of the ruler, cultural institutions, sanctuaries and gymnasia that dominated entire city quarters. For example, groves with the Ptolemaic royal tombs, the Museion and sanctuaries, which were traditionally planted, were located in the palace district of Alexandria (Str. 17,1,8f.). This green zone was doubtlessly representational in character and reminiscent of old Egyptian gardens of Pharaonic palaces. Royal arboretums (παράδεισος, → *parádeisos*) for hunting and ceremonial acts based on Persian court mores were particularly maintained in the Seleucid kingdom (Plut. Demetrios 50, 7ff.). However, these *parádeisoi* differed from the large fruit plantations and wine gardens of Hellenistic Egypt and Syria, which also received the same appellation. The lead pipes installed by king Hieron II of Syracuse in the 3rd cent. to water gardens on his palace ship (Ath. 5,207d) were a rarity in Hellenistic gardens.

The preferred location for urban Hellenistic gardens continued to be an area outside the town, often immediately by the city wall. Funerary gardens were located in the suburb Necropolis to the west of the city of Alexandria (κηποτάφια, kēpotáphia), as presumably were private domestic and commercial gardens whose irrigation benefited from proximity to the Canopus canal (Str. 17,1,10). These suburban gardens served the city's demand for vegetables, fruits and flowers (Cato Agr. 9,10). Hellenistic and classical sources do not state that gardens increased the quality of life in a home. In this respect the Roman concept of residential style was fundamentally different.

B. Rome

Ornamental and pleasure gardens in the modern sense are only attested in the Roman period – it can be said that gardening as an art is a Roman invention. The increasing construction of aqueducts in the 1st cent. BC in Italy supplied for the first time a sufficient and constant amount of water for artificial irrigation. While Plato (Leg. 761c) still recommended in the 4th cent. BC that the superfluous water from well houses be conducted into public and sacred green areas, Pliny noted (HN 36,24,121ff.) that aqueduct water was used in his age for public grounds as well as for private homes, villas and gardens. Gardeners (κηπουροί, *kēpouroí*) had been familiar for some time (Plut. Aratus 5–9; Pol. 18,6), the profession of a garden artist (*topiarius*) is found from the mid-1st cent. BC (Cic. Ad Q. Fr. 3,1,5; Plin. HN 12,11,22). Beginning in the Augustan period, art gar-

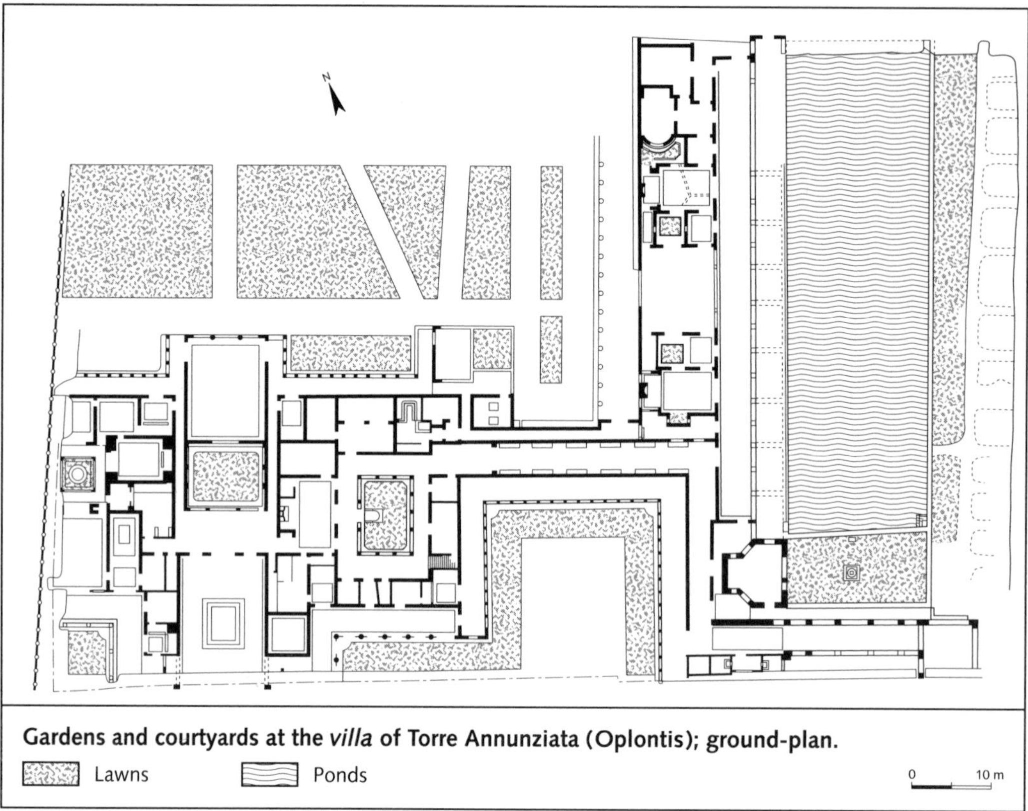

Gardens and courtyards at the *villa* of Torre Annunziata (Oplontis); ground-plan.

dens enriched by pruning trees into shapes and figures (*opera topiaria*) became very popular (Plin. HN 12,6,13; 16,60,140; Plin. Ep. 5,6,35f.), while concurrently artful ornamental gardens became a favourite subject of → wall paintings. The plant inventory of these gardens included ivy, boxwood, laurel, cypress, myrtle, acanthus, dwarf plantain and rosemary.

The garden (*hortus*) of the early Roman house in the 4th and 3rd cents. BC traditionally was a kitchen garden. After the 2nd cent. BC the peristyle court, which was adopted from Greek architecture, as an elaborate garden supplanted this small utility garden. In addition to domestic gardens, Roman towns were also characterized by gardens associated with temples, gymnasia and inns. Some peristyle gardens were planted with an open scattering of fruit trees while others had a strictly planned, symmetrical design. For the most part they were planted with evergreens. Flowering shrubs and seasonal flowers such as myrtles, lilies, chrysanthemums, roses and violets provided small accents of colour. Water from fountains and statues as well as basins, canals and ponds were the essential elements of design. Large water courses that were supposed to be reminiscent of ancient monuments such as the Canopus canal in Alexandria or the Nile often formed a decorative centre piece of gardens. Gardens were also decorated with sculptures, craters, furniture, pergolas and fences. Imitations of Greek statues as well as genuine classical and Hellenistic art were redeployed as garden sculpture in a profane context (Plin. Ep. 3,6; Cic. Att. 1,4–6; 8–11). This affirms the Roman adoption of Greek art and the desire of Roman owners to create a culturally suitable ambiance and show off their education, especially when Greek education sites such as gymnasia were to be imitated (Cic. Orat. 2,9,10). The rooms around the garden often possessed large windows with a view towards the green inner court. If a small garden was to appear optically larger, paintings representing lush gardens were applied to the back wall. Triclinia (→ Triclinium) in the garden permitted open air dining. They were particularly frequent in inns with adjoining gardens. In rental housing residents normally had to make do with potted plants on the balcony or a view of the gardens of affluent residents. However, occasionally rental housing and multi-family units such as those in Ostia were surrounded by a green strip or built around a garden court.

Roman villas in the country were often enriched by gardens and parks. The interplay between nature and → architecture began in the Hellenistic period but the Romans implemented it in domestic architecture. The rural villa of Poppaea near Oplontis had several gardens ranging from tiny planted light shafts, smaller and larger peristyle gardens to parks planted with oleander, citrus trees and plantains, that were interspersed with water basins, sculptural arrangements and walkways (cf. illustration). The axes of view from the villa's rooms are always oriented towards the gardens. The architectural design of the hippodrome was also reconfigured into a complicated, planted garden with promenades in the context of extensive villas and palaces, e.g. the Tuscan villa of Pliny and the palace of Domitian on the Palatine in Rome (Plin. Ep. 5,6,15 and 32ff.). The furnishing of gardens in town and country houses with statuary (*ornamenta*) and murals makes it clear that Greek sanctuaries, gymnasia, parks and palaces as well as Oriental *parádeisoi* were being evoked. Gardens were a place in which owners could dedicate themselves to leisure and represent themselves socially.

Imperial palaces included entire park landscapes with architectural ensembles, pavilions, promenades and sculptures. Many of these parks and gardens (*horti*) of the emperor, the wealthy elite of Rome and its environs are known. The *horti* and privately financed public gardens such as the *porticus Pompeiana* (Mart. 2,14,10) greatly contributed to the greening of the capital. Some private parks were willed to the people for recreation (Suet. Iul. 83). The largest of all imperial palaces, the rural Villa Hadriana near Tivoli, included a multitude of gardens decorated with statues, waterfalls, fountains, grottoes and nymphaea. In other parts of the empire, especially the Mediterranean regions, gardens of the Italian type became part of the private and public sphere. Even in the northern provinces, with a harsher climate, the romanized population adopted the Roman horticultural tradition.

→ GARDENS; → Irrigation; → Wells, fountains; → Houses; → Canals; → Palace; → Town planning; → Villa

B. ANDREAE, Am Birnbaum. Gärten und Parks im antiken Rom, 1996; M. CARROLL-SPILLECKE, ΚΗΠΟΣ. Der antike griech. Garten, 1989; Id. (ed.), Der Garten von der Antike bis zum MA, 1992; K. L. GLEASON, Porticus Pompeiana: A New Perspective on the First Public Park of Ancient Rome, in: Journal of Garden History 14.1, 1994, 13–27; W. F. JASHEMSKI, The Gardens of Pompeii, Herculaneum and the Villas destroyed by Vesuvius, 2 vols., 1979/1993; E. B. MACDOUGALL, W. F. JASHEMSKI (ed.), Ancient Roman Gardens. Dumbarton Oaks Colloquium on the History of Landscape Architecture 7, 1981; E. B. MACDOUGALL (ed.), Ancient Roman Villa Gardens. Dumbarton Oaks Colloquium on the History of Landscape Architecture 10, 1987; I. NIELSEN, Hellenistic Palaces, 1994; W. SONNE, Hell. Herrschaftsgärten, in: W. HOEPFNER, G. BRANDS (ed.), Basileia. Die Paläste der hell. Könige, 1996, 136–143. M.C.-S.

C. GARDENS AS A LITERARY MOTIF

Gardens in the context of temples, palaces and → villas have been a favourite subject of → ekphrasis since Homer. The garden is differentiated from the *locus amoenus* and an idealized bucolic scenery (→ Bucolics) by its limitedness (e.g. walls and porticoes) and its artificial design.

Homer's description of the orchard near the palace of Alcinous (Hom. Od. 7,112ff.) has been very influential, although it emphasizes, apart from the abundance of fruits, the garden's utilitarian aspect (cf. Hom. Od. 24,230ff.). By contrast, Sappho (Fr. 192 PAGE) evoked a festive mood and the grove's sacred aspect by using divine hymns, fire altar and feast. Fruits and flowers (apples, roses) are attributed to Aphrodite and represent the goddess' charm. Sophocles' description of the grove of the Eumenides in Colonus prepares by the praise of Attica and the death of Oedipus (Soph. OC 16ff.; [3. 232ff.]). The prohibition on entry is a typical provision of sacred groves ([7]; cf. Plin. Ep. 8,8,6 on *Clitumnus fons*). In Hellenism architecture dominated gardens: in the palace of Aeetes the garden is part of a frontal display (Apoll. Rhod. 3,215ff.), and in Longus (Proemium and 4,2) only the melding of nature with art makes the garden an enjoyable experience. Romance and epic describe the garden from the perspective of the loving: plants and flowers are personified and 'erotisized', the beloved is inversely 'vegetalized' in metaphoric language (Ach. Tat. 1,15 and 1,19,1; Nonnus, Dion. 3,140ff. [3. 420ff.]).

In Roman literature the → villa is cast as educational scenery with reference to Greek models by means of statues, buildings and imaginary names (Cicero's 'Academy' and 'Amalthea', Cic. Att. 1,5,2; 2,1,11; cf. Leg. 2,7) that reflects the owner's character, becomes an invitation to retreat for philosophical discussion (Cic. De or. 1,28f.; Sen. Ep. 55; Stat. Silv. 1,3; [2]) and serves as source for literary inspiration (Plin. Ep. 1,3; 1,9; [6]). Also, the urbanite is delighted by the (short-term!) participation in a simple country life, which he observes in part with amused detachment (Plin. Ep. 9,20; [11]) and in part as an ideal life (Tib. 1,5,19ff.).

According to Pliny (Ep. 2,17; 5,6) villa gardens are nature that has been shaped, moderated and artificially 'improved' to keep all uncontrolled obnoxiousness away. Free nature is reduced to a charming scenery and kept at a distance by using porticoes, windows and doors as frames [5]. This well-proportioned aesthetic enjoyment of nature with associations to (literary) education continues to exert influence in the landscape gardens of the 17th to 20th cent. (e.g., Pope's garden with the 'Poet's Parnassus' and Girardin's park with the 'cabin of Philemon and Baucis' [1; 8. 32ff.]).

→ Grove; → Nature; → natural philosophy; → Environment

1 A. VON BUTTLAR, Der Landschafts-Garten, 1980
2 H. CANCIK, Tibur Vopisci, in: Boreas 1, 1978, 116–134
3 W. ELLIGER, Die Darstellung der Landschaft in der griech. Dichtung, 1975
4 P. GRIMAL, Les jardins romains, 1984
5 E. LEFÈVRE, Röm. Baugesinnung und Landschaftsauffassung in den Villenbriefen, in: Gymnasium 84, 1977, 519–541
6 Id., Die Villa als geistiger Lebensraum, in: Gymnasium 94, 1987, 247–262
7 Les Bois sacrés, 1993
8 P. DE LA RUFFINIÈRE DU PREY, The Villas of Pliny from Antiquity to Posterity, 1994
9 K. SCHNEIDER, Villa und Natur, thesis 1994
10 G. SCHÖNBECK, Der locus amoenus von Homer bis Horaz, 1962
11 E. STÄRK, Vindemia, in: Gymnasium 97, 1990, 193–211. UL.EG.-G.

Gardens, hanging see → Hanging Gardens; → Semiramis; → Wonders of the World

Gargaphia (Γαργαφία; *Gargaphía*). Source fountain near → Plataeae, from which the Greek army drew water before the battle in 479 BC until it was filled in by the Persians (Hdt. 9,25,2; 49,2–51,1; 52; Paus. 9,4,3; Plin. HN 4,25); located by [2. 557; 3. 113–115]; regarding G.'s identification as the place where → Actaeon surprised Artemis while bathing [1. 757].

1 F. Bölte, s.v. G. 2), RE 7, 757 2 Müller 3 Pritchett, 1. P.F.

Gargara, Gargaris (Γάργαρα, Γαργαρίς; *Gárgara, Gargarís*), town in Aeolis on the 780 m high crest of Koca Kaya, a western extension of the Ida range (Hom. Il. 8,48; 14,292; 14,352 Γάργαρον ἄκρον; Plin. HN 5,122 *Gargara mons*). Founded by Assus (Str. 13,1,58) and inhabited by Leleges (EM s.v. Γ.; Steph. Byz. s.v. Γ.), G. already existed in the mid-6th cent. BC, as temple finds on the acropolis indicate [1]. G. is mentioned in the Attic tribute lists with an amount of 4,500 drachmes. When the, probably only partial, resettlement to a coastal town, which Strabo mentions, occurred in the Hellenistic period is uncertain. Due to an insufficient population number, the inhabitants of Miletupolis were relocated there in the Hellenistic period (Str. 13,1,58). G. participated in the founding of the *koinón* of Athena Ilias [2. no. 1], but was no longer a member in 77 BC [2. No. 10]. It appears to have still been a port of significance in the Roman period: G. is mentioned in the tariff law of Ephesus [3. 62]. In the Byzantine period it was important as a diocese (Hierocles 20).

1 R. Stupperich, Ein archaisches Kriegerrelief aus G., in: Stud. zum antiken Kleinasien 3 (Asia Minor Stud. 16), 1995, 127ff. 2 P. Frisch, in: IK 3 (Ilion) 3 H. Engelmann, D. Knibbe (ed.), Das Zollgesetz der Prov. Asia, in: EA 14, 1989.

L. Bürchner, s.v. G., RE 7, 757f.; W. Leaf, Strabo on the Troad, 1923, 258ff.; J. M. Cook, The Troad, 1973, 251ff. E.SCH.

Gargettus (Γαργηττός; *Gargēttós*). Attic *Mesogea* deme in the Aegeis phyle, after 307/6 BC in the Antigonis. It provided four (already in IG I³ 1040), later seven → *bouleutaí*. Name pre-Greek [1. 1336]. A decree on the demes of Hagios Giorgios near Ieraka locates it in the marching order between Hymettus and Pentelicum east of Pallene and attests a Dionysus sanctuary as the mustering ground [2. 41; 3. 127]. G. was with Acharnae, Paeania and Pallene a member of the cultic federation of Athena Pallenis (Ath. 234f–235c; [4. 185[46]]), the hero G. was considered the father of Ion, the hero of Ionidae (Paus. 6,22,7).

1 G. Neumann, s.v. Vorgriech. Sprachen, KlP 5, 1334–1338 2 Traill, Attica 7, 17, 33, 41, 59, 68, 110 no. 47, table 2, 11 3 J. S. Traill, Demos and Trittys, 1986 4 Whitehead, Index s.v. G. H.LO.

Gargilius

[1] **Q. Coredius Gallus G. Antiquus.** His father was perhaps G. Antiquus (AE 1954, 63). Praetorian governor of the Province of Arabia, *c.* AD 116–118/9; *cos. suff.* late in 119; *proconsul Asiae* probably in 134/5 [1; 2. 148ff., 176]. If he is identical with M. Paccius Silvanus Q. Coredius Gallus G. Antiquus ([3. 260ff.] = AE 1991, 1576), he was either consular governor of Iudaea or of Syria. Cf. also [4].

1 W. Eck, in: Chiron 12, 1982, 361 2 Id., in: Chiron 13, 1983 3 D. Gera, H. Cotton, in: IEJ 41, 1991 4 E. Dąbrowa, in: Nunc de Suebis dicendum est. Studia ... G. Kolendo dicata, 1995, 99ff.

[2] **M. Paccius Silvanus Coredius Gallus L. Pullaienus G. Antiquus.** Senator, whose career is known up to his consulate from CIL III 7394 = ILS 1093. Praetorian legate of Thracia *c.* AD 159–161, *c.* 162 *cos. suff.*

G. Alföldy, in: Chiron 8, 1978, 370f.; PIR² G 79.

[3] **L. Pullaienus G. Antiquus.** Probably the son of G. [2]. Patrician, consul towards the end of Commodus' reign. Participated in the Secular Games of AD 204.

Leunissen, Konsuln 150; PIR² G 80. W.E.

[4] **Q. G. Martialis.** A horticultural and pharmaceutical writer who was admired for completing Virgil (Serv. Georg. 4,148). He lived in the 3rd cent. AD (SHA Alex. 37,9) and may be identical with the *eques Romanus* of Auzia/Mauretania, who died in 260 (CIL 8,9047 = ILS 2767). The work (*De hortis* ?) was together with the Roman agronomists part of the Florentine Cod. Marcianus but had already been removed from this collection before the codex was completely lost in the 16th cent. Gargilius probably discussed in his work the cultivation of garden plants and trees as well as their healing properties (cf. Cassiod. Inst. 1,28,6). Parts are preserved in Palladius' books of the months under the headings *De hortis* and *De pomis*; the Neapolitan Fr. *De arboribus pomiferis* (*pom.*) of the 6th cent. (on quince, peach, almond, chestnut) as well as reworkings and excerpts, especially the *Medicinae ex oleribus et pomis* (*med.*), contain more material. Important sources for G. were Pliny, Celsus and Columella. The *curae boum ex corpore Gargili Martialis* are now considered forgeries on linguistic grounds. According to [1] they are a collection of excerpts of the 4th–6th cents. that do not contain any material by G.

Individual editions: S. Condorelli, Fragmenta ad holera arboresque pertinentia, 1978 I. Mazzini, De hortis, ²1988 V. Rose, Plinii Secundi medicina, 1875, 129–222 (med.).

Bibliography: 1 K.-D. Fischer, G. Martialis, in: HLL 8.4, 1997, 269–273 2 White, Farming, 29f. E.C.

Gargonius Rhetoric teacher of the Augustan period, student of Buteo [1. 156f.], then his successor, who is perhaps identical with the example of lacking hygiene cited in Hor. Sat. 1,2,27 (= 1,4,92). His voice was rough and aggressive (Sen. Controv. 1,7,18). The older Seneca always connects the quotes form G. that illustrate his *Colores* with harsh reproach (*stultitia* contr. 10,5,25; *cacozelia* 9,1,15, *insaniens* Suas. 2,16).

1 H. Bornecque, Les Déclamations, 1902, 168. P.L.S.

Gargoris Name derived from an uncertain Indo-European root [1. 118–119]. Legendary king of the Curetes (?) in → Tartessus, who allegedly invented honey gathering. He repeatedly attempted to have his grandson Habis, who was born after a slip by his daughter, killed by wild animals but they spared and even nursed him. G. recognized his growing grandchild and made him his successor (Iust. 44,4,1–14).
→ Exposure, myths of

1 M. Lourdes Albertos Firmat, La onomastica personal primitiva, 1966.

H.J. Rose, Griech. Mythologie, [5]1978, 284. W.SP.

Garizim see → Samaria, Samaritans

Garsaura, Garsauira (Γαρσάουρα, Γαρσαύιρα; *Garsáoura, Garsaúira*). Main town of the Cappadocian strategia Garsauritis, modern Aksaray; refounded by → Archelaus [7] as → Archelais (later *colonia Claudia Augusta;* in Str. 12,2,6 called κωμόπολις). From AD 325 to the 14th cent. attested as a bishopric. The original name was preserved (in the Seljuq period Aqsarā).

Hild/Restle, 205f.; Mitchell 1, 95f. K.ST.

Garsyeris (Γαρσύηρις; *Garsýeris*, because of -υηρις/υερις late Hittite-Luwian? [1. 669]). As a cast-out officer of Achaeus [5], he advised the latter in 221/0 BC to secede from Antiochus III. In the dispute of the Pisidian towns Pednelissus and Selge in 218, he intervened against Pednelissus together with several other towns of the region, but without the help of Side. Together with Achaeus he forced Selge to accept a peace and pay money (Pol. 5,57; 72–76).

1 Zgusta.

A. Bouché-Leclercq, Histoire des Séleucides (323–64 avant J.-C.), 1913/14, 140, 148; H.H. Schmitt, Untersuchungen zur Geschichte Antiochos' d. Gr. und seiner Zeit, 1964, 172f. A.ME.

Garum see → Fish dishes

Garumna (Garunna, Γαρούνας/*Garoúnas*). One of the main rivers of Gaul (Tib. 1,7,11), the modern Garonne and Gironde, the boundary between the Gauls and the Aquitanians (Caes. Gall. 1,1,1; 5; 7; Str. 4,1,1; 2,1f.; 3,3; 5,2; Mela 3,20f.; Plin. HN 4,105; Amm. Marc. 15,11,2). According to Str. 4,2,1 navigable over more than 370 km.

R. Boudet (ed.), Les Celtes, la Garonne et les Pays aquitains, 1992; Y. Roman, Les Celtes, les sources antiques et la Garonne, in: Aquitania 12, 1994, 213–219; H. Sion, Carte archéologique de la Gaule. 33/1 (Gironde), 1994. Y.L.

Gastaldi Administrators of goods and representatives of the king's interests in the Lombardic kingdom, first attested under Authari (AD 584–590). Since the 7th cent. they watched over the dukes (cf. *Edictus Rothari* 23); in the 8th cent. they could preside over courts of law. They were directly subject to the king in their non-inheritable office. In the Duchies of Spoleto and Benevent they administered the most important towns for the dukes.

C.G. Mor, Lo stato longobardo nel VII secolo, 1969, 1, 271ff. M.MEI. and ME.STR.

Gastronomical poetry
I. Greek II. Latin

I. Greek

Gastronomical poetry (GP) may be considered a special stream of the parodistic poetry that → Hegemon of Thasos turned into a genuine literary genre in the late 5th cent. BC: light, jesting poetry (though resulting from artistic dedication) sings the delights of the stomach and the table. The lost Δεῖπνον (*Deîpnon*, 'Feast') of Hegemon was the description of a banquet (*anagraphḗ*, Ath. 1,5a; s. also → symposium literature), as are the works of the same name by Numenius of Heraclia (3rd cent. BC, cf. SH 596) and Timachidas of Rhodes (2nd–1st cents. BC, at least 11 books in hexameter; cf. SH 769–773). The *Deîpnon Attikón* ('Attic Feast') of → Matron of Pitane, is an amusing listing of foods. The linguistic elements and means of expression are all taken from the epic, which is the major (though not only) formal point of reference for this type of poetry. A unique *divertissement* in dactyloepitrites (instead of hexameters) was composed by the dithyrambographer Philoxenus of Cythera (*c.* 435–380 BC). Many, though often poorly preserved, fragments remain of his *Deîpnon*, which describes an infinite variety of delicacies. The choice of the Doric language and numerous long dithyrambic compounds are characteristic (PMG 836 is unjustifiably ascribed to Philoxenus of Leucas, cf. [1]).

In the 4th cent. BC, a different type of GP experienced great popularity. Rules and recipes take the place of descriptions in this parody of didactic poetry. Terpsion, the teacher of Archestratus, introduced the new tendency with his *Gastrología*, the first gastronomic reference work. Philoxenus of Leucas is known from a fragment of the comedian Plato, who in his *Pháon* of 391 BC reproduced (with some comical distortions) twelve informative hexameters, which contain short but serious cooking instructions (Fr. 189 K.-A.). In turn Philoxenus, as is demonstrated by numerous similarities, was a favourite model of → Archestratus [2] of

Gela, the 'father of Greek gastronomy' [2]; the latter lived about 330 BC and was the author of the work Ἡδυπάθεια (*Hēdypátheia*, 'Life of Culinary Delight '), which had a significant success in the Graeco-Roman world.

1 E. Degani, La poesia gastronomica greca (I), in: Eikasmos 9, 1998 2 A. Rapp, The Father of Western Gastronomy, in: CJ 51, 1955, 43–48.

P. Brandt, Corpusculum poesis epicae Graecae ludibundae, I, Lipsiae 1888; SH 132–192 (Archestratos), 534–540 (Matro); E. Degani, Alma Mater Studiorum 3/2, 1990, 33–50 und 4/1, 1991, 147–155. O.M.

II. Latin

Latin GP probably began with a translation in hexameters of the *Hēdypátheia* of Archestratus: → Ennius' *Hedyphagetica* (title according to Apul. Apol. 39) probably preceded his *Annales*. As a long didactic poem, it was not productive in Latin literature though a number of small texts are devoted to the topic of eating and drinking (e.g., Hor. Sat. 2,2. 8; *Copa* and → *Moretum* in the Appendix Vergiliana; Juv. 5; 11; numerous epigrams by Martial). They cannot be separated from the rest of the → symposium literature; their success is based on the sociological importance of the banquet, which in Rome emphasized eating more than drinking and must be considered the primary place of publication for these texts. The literary reflection permits self-deprecation of the institution and its participants – in satirical GP as well as prose texts (Petron. Sat.; *Testamentum porcelli*) – and a metaphorical treatment of the dishes and the dining process, which especially criticizes food excesses. This finally results in its opposite: a representation of asceticism.

→ Symposium literature

J. André, L'alimentation et la cuisine a Rome, 1981 (Semantik); S. Döpp, Saturnalien und lat. Lit., in: Id. (ed.), Karnevaleske Phänomene in ant. und nachant. Kulturen und Lit. (Bochumer Altertumswiss. Colloquium 13), 1993, 145–177; E. Gowers, The Loaded Table, 1993; J. Rüpke, Kommensalität und Ges.-Struktur, in: Saeculum 49, 1998. J.R.

Gastronomy

A. Origins B. Hellenistic-Roman period

A. Origins

The art of cooking, which is the search for a balance of flavours, the preference for certain kinds of wine etc., in short, good taste in matters of nourishment, probably always existed in the ancient world but only became the subject of scientific discourse in the classical period. (This impression is based on the current state of documentation.) In antiquity the development of a true art of cooking was considered in a contradictory way both a sign of a high degree of civilized maturity and – in the case of excessive extravagance – a possible sign of decadence in a political system. As a result Greek authors ascribed to their forebears of the Homeric period a preference for fried food and the total absence of a refined culinary art in order to underline the primitiveness of their customs as well as the deeply rooted egalitarianism of their society. It is therefore difficult to outline a history of gastronomy in the early period when the phenomenon has already been subjected to strong interpretation by Classical authors.

Greek gastronomy was above all based on the quality of the ingredients eaten; in the numerous statements in ancient texts about various foodstuffs a link is established between the quality of a product and its geographical origin; the text of the 'Deipnosophists' by → Athenaeus [3] (about AD 200) is an almost inexhaustible treasure trove on this subject. Food preparation – which today we call the culinary art – is merely an additional facet of gastronomy in antiquity. The influence of neighbouring cultures plays a major role in the gastronomy of Greeks and Romans: the Lydians, for example, were considered the people who taught the Greeks to make a spicy sauce (*karýkē*: Ath. 516c) and *kándaulos* (probably a kind of cheese or soft cheese soufflé or cake: Ath. 516c–517a), which had been very highly esteemed since the 4th cent.; another sauce probably came from the Hellespont, the *myttōtós* (based on garlic, leek, cheese, honey, olive oil, and eggs: Schol. Theophr. Hist. pl. 7,4,11), which was served particularly with fish. The first recipe collections were created in the 4th cent. BC in the Greek towns of Sicily (→ Cookery books). If one attempts to develop a geography of Greek gastronomy in this period [1], it soon becomes evident that there is little information regarding most Greek regions and cities. Only a list of local products can be established. Outside Sicily, Athens seems to have developed cooking the furthest, as is well attested by the comedians of the 4th cent. BC.

B. Hellenistic-Roman period

In the Hellenistic and Roman period the opening up of the world affected gastronomy. Spices and aromatics such as different types of pepper, ginger, cloves, caraway, cinnamon, cassia, and asafoetida were imported from the Orient and were introduced into sauce preparation and wine making. With Alexander's campaigns new fruits and nuts such as lemons, apricots, jujubes, and pistachios became known. The ordinary cooking habits of the poor, the majority of the population, probably barely changed, but those of princes at the Hellenistic courts reflected the increased range of ingredients and flavours. The wedding banquet arranged by the Macedonian king Caranus included an overabundance of dishes during the entire meal in which several courses followed one another (Ath. 128a–130e). The feast organized in 271/70 BC by Ptolemy II in Alexandria was preceded by a procession displaying all the courses that were later served: this ostentatious display of dishes was a form of exercizing power in which gastronomy became part of the discourse of political behaviour (Ath. 196a–203b).

The feast, i.e. the consumption of food and gastronomy, stands at the centre of social action and elite culture from the Hellenistic period. The Roman world furthered this development. Roman cuisine surpassed everything before it with the variety of ingredients employed and the high quality of aesthetic presentation. The banquet described in the 1st cent. AD by C. → Petronius in the *Satyricon* and the book of recipes compiled in the 4th cent. AD by Caelius [II 8] Apicius are testimony to this. The cuisine of the Empire combined Greek gastronomy with western influences (e.g. the eating of rabbits and dormice).

It appears that ancient gastronomy remained an elite art; its cultural significance is echoed in other arts, especially literature, in which the discourse on the *sympósion* merges into a discourse on → *cena* [2]. Modern attempts to reconstruct ancient gastronomy can only arrive at approximately correct results because we lack an exact knowledge of ingredients, methods of preparation and the cooks' techniques. Furthermore, an assessment of various tastes from sweet/sour to very salty is culturally dependent.

→ Nutrition; → Table culture; → Banquet; → Cookery books

1 A. Dalby, Siren feasts, A History of Food and Gastronomy in Greece, 1996 2 F. Dupont, Le plaisir et la loi, 1977.

P.S.-P.

Gate, deities associated with The three most important Greek deities associated with gates (for Rome see → Ianus, → Carna) were → Hecate (and → Artemis, who was closely associated with her), → Hermes and → Hercules. Hecataea (small statues or shrines to Hecate) were to be found in front of the gates of private houses and in front of city gates (Aeschyl. TrGF 388; Aristoph. Vesp. 804, Hsch. s. v. προπύλαια). Corresponding with this is the association between Hecate and additional liminal places, particularly road-forks (*tríhodoi*), which is in turn connected with her role as protector from the threat posed by spirits and → demons. Set up in front of a house door, Hecate and her Thracian parallel Enodia (→ Hecate) were supposed to protect the children in the house in particular [1. 205–215]. As *Propylaía,* Artemis often protected city gates (Paus. 1,38,6), and the same applied from time to time to her brother → Apollo as *Propýlaios* [2. 173–176].

Hermes stood in front of the gates of private and public buildings (Theoc. 25,4; Aristoph. Plut. 1153; Paus. 1,22,8) and on the roads of the city and took the form of a → Herm (a pillar at whose top was chiselled in the head of the god and that was decorated below with his phallus). Just how important the protective power of the herms for the Athenians was, is shown by the dismay caused by their desecration on the evening before the Sicilian expedition (Thuc. 6,27; [3]; → Herms, mutilation of the). Herms and hecataea were crowned with a wreath and purified on nights of the new moon (Theopompus FGrH 115 F 344). Hercules too was placed on gates, for instance as *Kallínikos* ('Conquering hero') or *Alexíkakos* ('Defender against disaster'). Inscriptions stating that he was living in the house were, however, more common than statues of the god [2. 173–176].

1 S. I. Johnston, Restless Dead, 1999 2 Graf 3 D. Furley, Andokides and the Herms, 1996.

S. I. J.

Gates People in Aquitaine between the Elusates and the Ausci (only in Caes. B Gall. 3,27).

Y.L.

Gates; porches Gates that went beyond purely military aspects (for these cf. → Fortifications) are to be found in Greek architecture from the 6th cent. BC onwards – initially as imposingly designed entrances to sanctuaries, and from about 400 BC also in secular contexts (entrances to the → Agora, → Gymnasium, → Stadium or → Assembly buildings, e.g. in Miletus, Priene, Olympia).

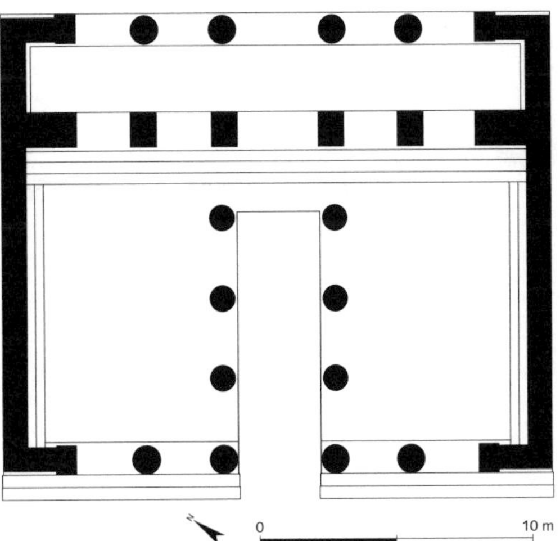

Athens, Acropolis: Propylaea, *c.* 530 BC (reconstructed ground-plan).

The development and extension of the *própylon* as a decorative entrance gate to a → sanctuary can be reconstructed, for example, from the Acropolis of Athens (cf. → Athens II. with location plan): hand in hand with the loss of the fortification functions of the old Mycenaean fortress gate, there initially arose in the 7th cent. AD in the west, a wide, cobbled court that was superseded in the 2nd half of the 6th cent. BC by a roofed gate construction that in the ground plan was almost square and in the shape of a temple (with six Doric front columns). In order to achieve a better optical effect from this earliest Greek monumental gate, the orientation of the body of the building was changed compared to the previous layout by rotation on its axis. A new dimension was achieved with the Acropolis Propylaea (*Propýlaia*) by the architect → Mnesicles [1]

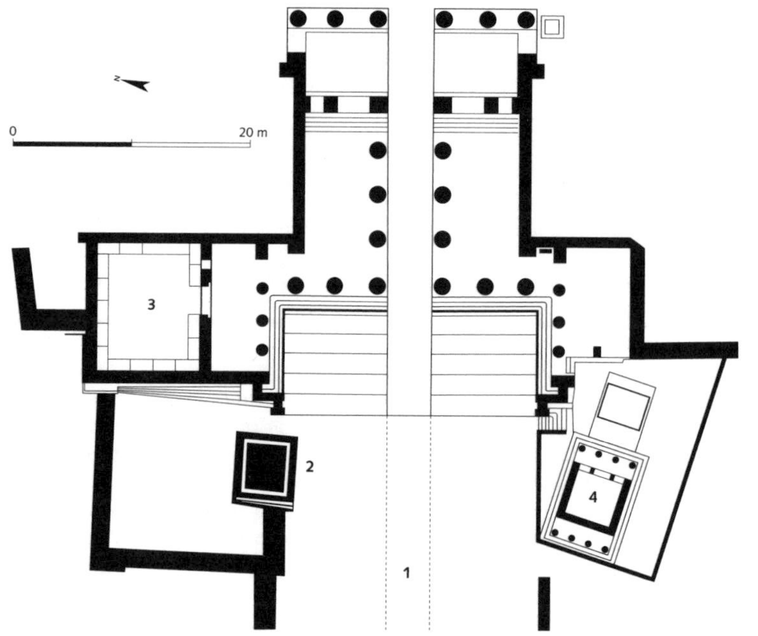

Athens, Acropolis: Propylaea, 437–432 BC (ground-plan).

1 Ramp
2 Monument of Agrippa
3 Pinakotheke
4 Temple of Athena Nike

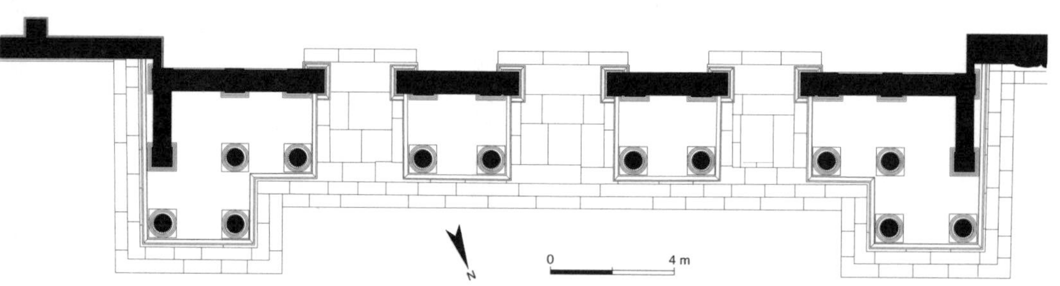

Miletus: Market gate, *c.* AD 120 (ground-plan).

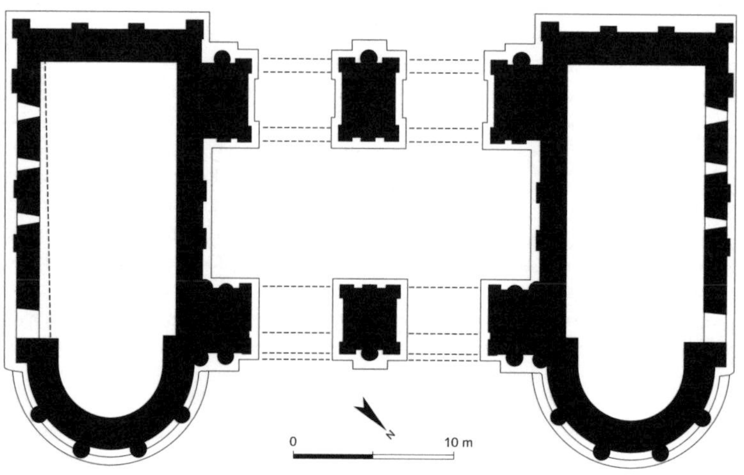

Augusta Treverorum (Trier): Porta Nigra, 2nd half 2nd cent. AD (plan of the ground floor).

(built in 437–432/1 BC), a multi-part, technically – because of the level differences to be overcome and the width of the column bays to be spanned – highly complicated building conglomerate, its actual gate passageway reminiscent of a temple with six Doric front columns and rows of four Ionian pillars each in the passageway; the northern annex building presumably served as a → Pinakotheke.

This gate became the much-quoted – and sometimes copied (e.g. in → Eleusis [1]) – model of the imposing entrance gate to a sanctuary. Echoes of this layout are still to be found in the ressaut gate or the wing gate of the sanctuaries of Samothrace (185/180 BC) and in the propylaea of the Athena sanctuary of Lindus/Rhodes (3rd cent. BC). The gate construction of the Athena sanctuary of Pergamum, on the other hand, with its two-storey facade (stepping of Doric and Ionic columns over each other) is already in the tradition of the Hellenistic multi-storey building, where the architectural concern is with the effect made by the facade (similarly also the market gate of Miletus, around AD 120).

Not rarely did Roman gates, especially in the relatively safer periods of the 1st and 2nd cents. AD, have an imposing image which overshadowed with the military function, e.g. the Porta Nigra in Trier (→ Augusta [6] Treverorum; → TRIER). In the Imperium Romanum, magnificent gates as entrances to public squares were in general a common and indispensable element of → town planning (e.g. Hadrian's Gate in Athens).
→ Door; → GATES

R. CARPENTER, The Propylon in Greek and Hellenistic Architecture, 1970; H. EITELJORG, The Entrance of the Athenian Acropolis before Mnesikles, 1995; A. FRAZER, The Propylon (Samothrace, vol. 10), 1990; D. GIRAUD, The Greater Propylaia at Eleusis – a Copy of Mnesikles' Propylaia, in: S. WALKER (ed.), The Greek Renaissance in the Roman Empire (Congress London 1986), 1989, 69–75; H. LAUTER, Die Architektur des Hell., 1986, 201–205; M. M. MILES, The Propylon to the Sanctuary of Demeter Malophoros at Selinous, in: AJA 102, 1998, 35–57; W. MÜLLER-WIENER, Griech. Bauwesen in der Ant., 1988, 154; A. POST, Zum Hadrianstor in Athen, in: Boreas 21/22, 1998/99, 171–183; L. SCHNEIDER, CH. HÖCKER, Die Akropolis von Athen, 2001, 160–166; V. M. STROCKA, Das Markttor von Milet, 1981; H. THÜR, Ein dorischer Torbau am Staatsmarkt in Ephesos, in: F. BLAKOLMER et al. (ed.), Fremde Zeiten. FS J. Borchhardt, 1996, 345–361; R. F. TOWNSEND, The Roman Rebuilding of Philon's Porch and the Telesterion at Eleusis, in: Boreas 10, 1987, 97–106; J. DE WAELE, The Propylaia of the Akropolis in Athens. The Project of Mnesikles, 1990. C. HÖ.

Gauanes (Γαυάνης/*Gauánēs*; etymology doubtful). According to Herodotus (8,137f.) the son of the Heraclid Temenus of Argos, predecessor of the Macedonian king → Alexander [2]. Together with his brothers → Aeropus [1] and → Perdiccas, G. subjected the whole of Macedonia and founded a new dynasty (Hdt. ibid.). With this aetiology the origin of the Macedonian royal family can be traced through the Temenids to → Hercules. J.S.-A.

Gauda Son of the Numidian king Mastanabal, grandson of Massinissa, brother of → Jugurtha, claimed rule despite his mental and physical debility during the war between Rome and Jugurtha. After the war in 105 BC he succeeded his uncle Micipsa with the support of Marius and obtained eastern Numidia (Sall. Iug. 65,1–4).

CAH 9 [2]1994, 30; V. WERNER, Quantum bello optimus, tantum pace pessimus, 1995, 35. ME.STR.

Gaudentius (Γαυδέντιος; *Gaudéntios*).
[1] G. Philosophus. Author of an introduction to harmony, Ἁρμονικὴ εἰσαγωγή (*Harmonikḕ eisagōgḗ*) – probably written in line with Claudius Ptolemy's – translated into Latin by Cassiodorus' friend Mutianus (Cassiod. Inst. 2,5,142 MYNORS). The incompletely preserved work (in 23 chapters) contains traditional teachings in a slightly modified form, especially from Aristoxenus and the Pythagoreans: voice, sound, interval, modes, composition (1–7), unison, concord, ratio (8–10), Pythagoras legend, experiment with 2 strings, 12-part canon, whole tone, major/minor semi-tone, and so on (11–17), fourths and fifths, 7 octave modes with names such as Dorian (18f.); of the teachings on notations, resembling those of → Alypius [3] (20–23), only the introduction and the beginning of the table are preserved. Modulation and melody formation [1. 327,7] are lost. G. counts from low to high pitches.

1 MSG 317–356 2 CH.-E. RUELLE, Alypius et Gaudence, 1895 (French trans. with comm.) 3 L. ZANONCELLI, La manualistica musicale greca, 1990, 307–369 (Ed. after MSG, with Italian trans. and comm.). F.Z.

[2] A 4th cent. AD rhetor from Arabia (Lib. Ep. 543), known only from comments by Libanius (he is called an 'old man' in 362, Ep. 749), later a teacher of rhetoric in Antioch (Ep. 174). Libanius always speaks of G. with deep affection (Ep. 174; 224), supports his relatives (Ep. 329; 543), and even composes a speech against G.'s son Silvanus (Or. 38) for mistreating him. If the attribution of a funerary epigram (III 2031 LE BAS-WADDINGTON = 1974 PEEK) to G. is correct, he paid for a tomb for his parents and himself in Migdala out of his income as a lawyer. M.W.

[3] As *agens in rebus* under Constantine II, in AD 355 G. denounced the *consularis Pannoniae* Africanus (Amm. Marc.: 15,3,8; 16,8,3). In 358–361 he was *notarius* and was spying on Julian in Gaul at the emperor's behest (Amm. Marc. 17,9,7; Iul. Ep. 282b/c). In 361 he defended Africa against a potential attack by Julian (Amm. Marc. 21,7,2–4). In 362 Julian had him executed (Amm. Marc. 22,11,1; Artemii passio 21 [in Philostorgius, ed. BIDEZ, S. 75]). PLRE 1, 386 (Gaudentius 3). W.P.

[4] The father of → Aetius [2], aristocrat of Durostorum in the province of Scythia. As the *Comes Africae* from AD 399 to 401 he destroyed pagan temples and idols especially in Carthage (Chron. min. 1,246 MOMMSEN;

Aug. Civ. 18,54; Cod. Theod. 11,17,3). Later he rose to *magister militum per Gallias* and was killed before 425 in a soldier uprising (Greg. Tur. Franc. 2,8; Chron. min. 1,658; Merobaudes paneg. 2,110–114).

PLRE 2, 493f., 1316; A. DEMANDT, s.v. magister militum, RE Suppl. 12, 641. K.P.J.

[5] **Gaudentius.** In 386/7 bishop of Brixia (Brescia), who participated under Simplicianus at the Synod of Milan against Rufinus and Origen (397–401). According to Palladius (CPG 6037: IV,2, ed. MALINGREY) he belonged to a delegation sent by Pope Innocent I (407–417) to emperor Arcadius to recall John Chrysostom from exile. G. was thanked by the exile (died 14 September 407) for his involvement (Ep. 184, PG 52,715–716). 21 homilies by G. are preserved (CPL 215) of which he edited at least 15 based on shorthand notes. He died in about 410 and is venerated as a saint (feast day: 25 October).

Y.-M. DUVAL, Saint Léon le Grand et saint G. de Brescia, in: Journal of Theological Studies n.s. 11, 1960, 82–84; Id., Le *Liber Hieronymi ad G.*, in: Revue Bénédictine 97, 1987, 163–186; F. TRISOGLIO, Appunti per una ricerca delle fonti di S.G. da Brescia, in: RSC 24, 1976, 50–125; C. TRUZZI, Zeno, G. e Cromazio, 1985. K.U.

[6] **Gaudentius.** In the *Scholia Bernensia* he is cited 58 times as a commentator on Vergil's *Bucolica* and *Georgica*, mostly in association with → Iunius Filargyrius, though not always agreeing with him. He was used mainly to explain grammatical and geographical facts. He knew → Servius (the only evidence for his dates) and apparently was a Christian (Serv. Georg. 4,493 *ridiculosa gentilitas*). Mediaeval commentaries on Orosius and Priscianus both mention his name once.

EDITIONS: H. HAGEN, Scholia Bernensia, 1867.
BIBLIOGRAPHY: R. A. KASTER, Guardians of Language, 1988, 409f. (no. 223). K.P.

Gaugamela Large village (κώμη μεγάλη, probably modern Tall Gōmil near Ǧabal Maqlūb, 35 km north-east of Mosul) on the river Bumelos in northern Mesopotamia (Arr. Anab. 6,11,6), near which (cf. Arr. Anab. 3,8,7) the battle between → Alexander [4] the Great and → Darius [3] III took place on 1 October 331 (Arr. Anab. 3,11–15; Curt. 4,13,26–16; Plut. Alexander 31–33; Diod. Sic. 17,56–61; Iust. 11,14). After Alexander stalled a flanking manoeuvre by the Persian cavalry, he directed his attack against the opponent's centre and Darius' royal chariot. The latter then fled the battle field pursued by Alexander. The transiently successful attack by the Persian right flank, which reached the Macedonian camp at the rear, was stopped by Alexander doubling back, upon which the leaderless Persian army disbanded.

A. B. BOSWORTH, Conquest and Empire, 1988, 75–85. J.W.

Gaulanitis see → Batanaea

Gauls see → Gallia; → Gallia Cisalpina; → Celts; → Celtic archaeology; → Celtic languages

Gauls, fear of see → Metus

Gaulus (Γαῦλος, Γαῦδος; *Gaûlos*, *Gaûdos*). North-western island of the Malta group (modern Gozo), first mentioned by Hecataeus (FGrH 1 F 341; cf. Str. 6,2,11; Diod. Sic. 5,12,4: located in the open sea with good harbours; Procop. Vand. 1,14; Plin. HN 3,92). Name probably Phoenician: γαῦλος/*gaûlos*, 'round cargo boat'. In the 8th cent. it was colonized by Phoenicians, later in Carthaginian, Greek, and after 220 BC Roman possession. Inland there was a settlement of the same name. Coins with Greek and Punic legends (HN 883). In Ggantija two temples with a clover-leaf shaped plan are incorporated into the orthostatic city walls (3500–3000 BC); a settlement contemporary with the erection of the temple consisting of huts of unburnt bricks and dry stone walls has been found; also subterranean burial chambers from the Zebbug (*c.* 4000 BC) and the Tarxien periods (*c.* 3000–2500 BC). From the Carthaginian period: a burial chamber in the region of Rabat; from the Roman period: a *villa* with peristyle (in Rabat), a cistern, the remains of a ring wall, thermal baths (in Ramba).

S. STODDARD, s.v. Malta, EAA II Suppl., 525ff.; T. ASHBY, Roman Malta, in: JRS 5, 1915, 23ff.; A. BONANNO, Distribution of Villas and Some Aspects of the Maltese Economy in the Roman Period, in: Journal of the Faculty of Arts 6, 1977, 73ff.; D. H. TRUMP, Malta, 1972, 146ff. GI.F.

Gaumata (Old Persian *Gōmāta*; Elamitic *Kammadda*; Akkadian *Gumātu*). A magus (→ Magi) [3. DB 39], who seized power after Cambyses had his brother → Bardiya [1] assassinated, on Cambyses' absence on campaign in Egypt. To justify his usurpation he claimed to be Bardiya. After Cambyses' death → Darius [1] I. and six noble Persians (Aspathines, → Hydarnes, → Intaphernes, → Gobryas, → Megabyzus, and → Otanes) brought the rule of G./Bardiya to an end and killed him (522 BC). A detailed description is in the → Bisutun inscription of Darius I, which in content is largely identical with Hdt. 3,88. However, it is uncertain to what extent Hdt. is dependent on the Bisutun inscription. Researchers have expressed doubt in the existence of a usurper and his murder by Darius. Herodotus' claim (not in [3. DB]) that the usurper strongly resembled Bardiya does not appear very credible. Justinus (1,9) and Ctesias (FGrH 688 F 13, F 29,8–14) provide variants but add nothing reliable. The problem probably cannot be resolved because the literary and epigraphical sources (especially Hdt., Ctesias and the Bisutun inscription) often contradict each other. More recent literature has rejected the formerly accepted religious and nationalistic motivation for G./Bardiya's struggle for control of the Persian empire.

1 D. Asheri, Erodoto, Le storie, 1990 2 M. A. Dandamaev, A Political History of the Achaemenid Empire, 1989, 83–113 3 R. Kent, Old Persian, 1953, 116–135 4 H. Sancisi-Weerdenburg, Yaunā en Persai, 1980, 84–121 5 J. Wiesehöfer, Der Aufstand Gaumatas und die Anfänge Dareios' I., 1978. A.KU. and H.S.-W.

Gauradas (Γαυράδας). Author of an ingenious epigram in iambic trimeters in the form of a dialogue between Echo and her lover (Anth. Pal. 16,152). The popular theme (cf. also Archias, Anth. Pal. 9,27; Evodus, ibid. 16,155; Satyrus, ibid. 16,153; Anon., ibid. 16,156) is developed in an original fashion; dating the poet, whose obviously barbarous name is unique, is impossible.

FGE 111f. M.G.A.

Gaurium (Γαύρειον, Γαύριον; *Gaúreion, Gaúrion*). The name of a settlement with a deep harbour on the north-western side of the island of Andros in the Cyclades. In the Hellenistic period, G. served as a port and is mentioned in association with various events in wars: Xen. Hell. 1,4,22; Diod. Sic. 13,69,4f.; Liv. 31,45,3ff.; GGM 1,500. Inland at Hagios Petros are the remains of a Hellenistic round tower, probably used to protect the nearby mines.

J. T. Bent, Aegean Islands, [2]1966, 291ff.; Lauffer, Griechenland, 230; L. Ross, Reisen auf den griechischen Inseln des ägäischen Meeres 2, 1843, 12ff.; Philippson/Kirsten 4, 1959, 92ff. H.KAL.

Gavius Roman family name, frequently attested in inscriptions, also in the form *Cavius* [1. 76f.]; in the Republican period its bearers are still politically insignificant; also a Faliscan *praenomen* [2. 103].

1 Schulze 2 Salomies

I. Republican period II. Imperial period

I. Republican period

[I 1] G., P. from Compsa (Lower Italy), was captured and crucified in Sicily in 72 BC by C. → Verres as an alleged spy of the slave leader → Spartacus (Cic. Verr. 2,5,158–170). K.-L.E.

[I 2] G. Bassus. Roman grammarian and antiquarian of the late Republic. His main work *Commentarii de origine verborum et vocabulorum* in at least seven books was used by Verrius Flaccus (via Verrius and Donatus, then Macrob. Sat. 3,18,2f., and, thus quoted here as *De significatione verborum*), Quintilian (Inst. 1,6,36), and frequently by Gellius (2,4; 3,9; 18; 19; 5,7; 11,17: *libro VII*). Explanations of words and etymologies seem to have been listed alphabetically. Stoic influence has been assumed both here and in his second work *De dis* (Macrob. Sat. 1,9,13, direct source Cornelius Labeo, cf. 3,6,17, again via Verrius as well as Lactant. Div. inst. 1,22,9). Little trust may be placed in Fulg. Expositio sermonum antiquorum 33 (*Gavius Bassus in satiris ait*).

Fr.: L. Lersch, G.B., in: Philologus 1, 1846, 615–622; GRF, 486–491.
Bibliography: G. Funaioli, s.v. G. 11, RE 7,866f.; P. Mastandrea, Un neoplatonico latino. Cornelio Labeone, 1979, 29ff. P.L.S.

II. Imperial period

[II 0] Q.G. Atticus. Suffect consul with L. Aelius Oculatus, attested on 30 May AD 85 (CIL XVI 18 and one unpublished diploma). On the duration of the consulate cf. → Aelius [II 17 a] Oculatus. W.E.

[II 1] P.G. Balbus. Equestrian officer and procurator, who rose to obtain at least the procurature over the province of Chersonesus (IEph VII 1, 3048). The brother of G. [II 2].

W. Eck, in: Id. (ed.), Prosopographie und Sozialgeschichte, 1993, 368ff.

[II 2] M.G. Bassus. Brother of G. [II 1], the father of G. [II 6]. Equestrian whose *origo* was Rome but whose family had settled in Ephesus. After his equestrian military service, during which he was decorated by Trajan in the Dacian war, he became *praefectus orae Ponticae maritimae* under Pliny in about AD 110–112 (IEph III 680). PIR[2] G 96.

[II 3] M. (G.) Cornelius Cethegus. *Cos. ord.* in 170; son of G. [II 2]. Regarding his person [1].

1 G. Alföldy, in: Chiron 9, 1979, 536f.

[II 4] M.G. Crispus Numisius Iunior. Senator whose career probably took place in the last decades of the 2nd cent., including a praetorship, the command over a legion, the proconsulate over Lycia-Pamphylia, and a suffect consulate. Later he was proconsul of Asia, IEph III 682; CIL XIV 4238; X 6663 + 6665 + 8292 = [1].

1 W. Eck, in: ZPE 37, 1980, 31ff.

[II 5] (M.G.) Gallicanus. *Cos. suff.* probably under Commodus, proconsul of Asia or Africa, *pontifex, flamen Augustalis* CIL V 3223 = [1].

1 G. Alföldy, in: Chiron 9, 1979, 507ff., 538.

[II 6] M.G. Maximus. The son of G. [II 2]. He owned property in Firmum Picenum, which however was not his place of origin [1]. He probably was a praetorian tribune and *primus pilus II*, then had a procuratorial career, which took him from the governorship of Mauretania Tingitana and the command of the fleet of Ravenna and later of Misenum to the praetorian praefecture; *praefectus praetorio* probably in AD 138–158. He received the *ornamenta consularia*.

1 W. Eck, in: Picus 8, 1988 [1992], 157ff.
PIR[2] G 104; Pflaum Suppl. 32f.; W. Eck, s.v. G. (18), RE Suppl. 15, 109f. W.E.

[II 7] G. Sabinus. In the Augustan period, a Latin orator of minor importance, about whose activity a few quotations in Seneca Rhetor provide information: apart from the fact that G. adhered to the emotionally charged and pointed style of his period, no characterization of his style and presentation can be made (Controv. 7,1,16; 2,1; 6,19f.; Suas. 2,5). PIR² G 109 C.W.

[II 8] G. Silo. Latin orator of the early Augustan period in Tarraco. Seneca the Elder equates him in terms of quality with the Clodii Turrini, orators of the city of Rome (Sen. Controv. 10, pr., 13; 16). His stance of hiding his rhetorical professionalism supposedly caused Augustus, who heard him repeatedly in Tarraco (probably about 25 BC), to exclaim: 'Never have I heard a more well-spoken head of a family' (ibid., 14). The few preserved quotes (ibid., 10,2,7; 16; 3,14; 4,7; 5,1) permit no further assessment.

PIR² G 111; J. FAIRWEATHER, Seneca the Elder, 1981, 142. J.R.

[II 9] C.G. Silvanus. From Augusta Taurinorum. Long-term service in the Roman army, eventually praetorian tribune. Participated in the Pisonian conspiracy; when it was uncovered he was acquitted but then committed suicide (Tac. Ann. 15,50; 60f.; 71). PIR² G 112.

[II 10] M.G. Squilla Gallicanus. AE 1971, 534. Perhaps a patrician, from Verona. The father of G. [II 11]. *Cos. ord.* in 127.

PIR² G 113; G. ALFÖLDY, in: Chiron 9, 1979, 535.

[II 11] M.G. Squilla Gallicanus. The son of G. [II 10]. *Cos. ord.* in AD 150, proconsul of Asia about 165. About 177 he participated in the *consilium* of Marcus Aurelius (AE 1971, 534). Pompeia Agrippinilla, who was honoured by the Bacchic mystics, was his wife (IGUR I 160; [1. 535f.] regarding the entire Gavii family from Verona). PIR² G 114.

1 G. ALFÖLDY, in: Chiron 9, 1979.

[II 12] G. Tranquillus. Proconsul of Lycia-Pamphylia, probably in AD 212/3 (AE 1989, 721 = 1994, 1725). W.E.

Gaza (Arabic *Ġazza*, Hebrew *ʿAzzā*, from Semitic *ǧzz*, 'being thorny'). From → Thutmosis III (1457 BC) to Ramses IV (mid 12th cent. BC) an Egyptian administrative centre in southern Palestine [1], under the Ramessids 'the town of Canaan', short 'Canaan' (Κάδυτις, Hdt. 2,159; 3,5); under → Ramses II also the 'town of Ramses in Canaan'. Taken over in the 12th cent. BC by the Philistines (Dt 2,23; Statue of Peteese, 22nd Dynasty: '[Town] of Canaan of the Philistines'), up to the 8th cent. BC G. rose to being the chief town of the Philistine Pentapolis because of its favourable traffic location (1 Sam 6,17f.) (Judg. 13–16; Am 1,6–8). When Tiglatpilesar III took G. in 734 BC, it was the terminal of the → Incense Road from Southern Arabia to the Mediterranean (Plin. HN 12,64). Though in revolt in 722–720, G. remained loyal to Assyria in 705–701 and received territorial compensation for Judaean attacks (2 Kg 18,8) [5. 31–34]. In 609 G. went back to being Egyptian (Hdt. 2,159; Jer 47,1), but became part of the Neo-Babylonian kingdom in 605/4 (Jer 25,20; 47,2–7). G. opposed the Persian advance on Egypt in 525 BC (Pol. 16,22a [=40]) and enjoyed autonomy under the → Achaemenids because of its Arabian trade relations (Hdt. 3,5). G. minted its own coins as well as those of Arabic client princes in southern Palestine and north-western Arabia by proxy. In the 5th(?) to 3rd(?) cents. the largest Minaean merchant colony on the Incense Road was located in G., as attested by the 'Hierodoule lists [actually: marriage documents] of Maʿin'.

1 O. KEEL, M. KÜCHLER, Orte und Landschaften der Bibel 2, 1982, 76–96 2 E.A. KNAUF, Ismael, ²1989 3 L. MILDENBERG, Vestigia Leonis, 1998, 64f., 77–94 4 NEAEHL 2, 464–467 5 TUAT 1, 390. E.A.K.

During the Hellenistic period, Ptolemies and Seleucids repeatedly disputed over G. In Seleucid possession for good from 200 BC, its economic decline began. After its complete destruction by → Alexander [16] Iannaeus (98 BC), reconstruction as 'New G.' south of the old town mound was promoted by the Roman *proconsul* Gabinius no earlier than 58 BC.

As a centre of Hellenistic culture, G. was home to a renowned school of rhetoric; the pre-Christian cult of Mārnā ('Our Lord ') of G. continued alongside rising Christianity up to AD 406. In the 2nd half of the 6th cent. the mosaic map of Mādabā shows G. as the second largest town after Jerusalem with forums, theatres, stoas and a church. Early in the 7th cent. G. traded with Mecca, but played no significant role in the early Islamic period until it was elevated by the Fāṭimids (10th cent.). The ancient town is now covered by the modern one.

K.B. STARK, Gaza und die philistäische Küste, 1852; G. DOWNEY, Gaza in the Early Sixth Century, 1963; M. MEYER, History of the City of Gaza, 1966; C. GLUKKER, The City of Gaza in the Roman and Byzantine Periods, 1987. T.L.

Gazelle The dorcas gazelle (*Gazella dorcas*, formerly *Antilope dorcas* or *Gazella africana*) represents the antilope subfamily, which also includes the wildebeest and the oryx), in North Africa and the Middle East (ζορκάς, δορκάς, δόρκων, δόρκος, δόρξ, or ζόρξ; *zorkás, dorkás, dórkōn, dórkos, dórx* or *zórx, damma* or *dorcas*). The gazelle is a typical desert dweller (Hdt. 4,192), e.g. in Libya (Theophr. Hist. pl. 4,3,5), and lives in harmony with partridges (πέρδικες; *pérdikes*) and in herds together with wild asses (ὄναγροι; *ónagroi*, Timothy of Gaza *c.* 17 [1. 27f.]). Gazelles, which are timid (Grattius cynegetica 200; Ael. NA 7,19) but slower than wild asses (Arr. Cyn. 24,1), were hunted on horseback with dogs, using nets, lassoes, arrows, and spears (Arr. Cyn. 24,1). In Egypt and the Roman empire they were bred in enclosures (Columella 9,1,1) as delicacies (Juv. 11,121). The ankle bones (δορκάδειοι ἀστράγαλοι; *dorkádeioi astragaloi*, Theophr. Char. 5,9) were prized as dice (Lucian Amores 16; Ath. 5,194a), the curved horns (Plin. HN 11,124) were made into tools and the leather into expensive parchment. On a hunt mosaic in

Utica (now in London) they are shown together with ostriches, in a painting in Pompeii gazelles hang in a butcher's [2nd vol. 1, 287f.] and the house of the Vettii in Pompeii contained a wall frieze depicting amorettos on a light cart drawn by gazelles [3. 135 and Fig. 69].

1 F.S. Bodenheimer, A. Rabinowitz (ed.), Timotheus of Gaza on animals, 1948 2 Keller 3 Toynbee. C.HÜ.

Gazioura (Γαζίουρα). Fortress of the Pontic kings in Zelitis on an isolated mountain peak near Turhal with a flight of steps from the Hellenistic period and late Byzantine wall remains. Also an inscription from the time of Mithridates VI, and two Roman milestones on the road from → Amasea to Nicopolis [1. 251–253 no. 278; 2. 348f. no. 960f.].

1 Anderson/Cumont/Grégoire 3,1 2 D. French, Roman Roads and Milestones of Asia Minor 2 (British Institute of Archaeology at Ankara, Monograph 9), 1988.

H. v. Gall, Zu den kleinasiatischen Treppentunneln, in: AA 82, 1967, 515; Olshausen/Biller/Wagner, 132; W.H. Waddington, E. Babelon, Th. Reinach, Recueil général des monnaies grecques d'Asie Mineure 1,1, ²1925, 112f.; H. Weimert, Wirtschaft als landschaftsgebundenes Phänomen, 1984, 60ff.; D.R. Wilson, The Historical Geography of Bithynia, Paphlagonia, and Pontus in the Greek and Roman Periods, thesis Oxford 1960 (typescript), 216; L. Zgusta, Kleinasiatische Ortsnamen, 1984, 132. E.O.

Gedrosia, Gadrosia Area in south-eastern Iran and south-western Pakistan, roughly equivalent to modern Baluchistan. Now a largely arid mountainous area with deep valleys, known from Arrian's account of the difficulties encountered by Alexander's army on its return march. The coast is described in detail in the Voyage of Nearchus (Arr. Anab. 6,22–26; Str. 15,723). Bearers of various cultures since the 8th millennium, they were possibly the ancestors of the Brahui, who are linguistically close to the Dravidians, but were largely assimilated by the dominant Baluchi who speak an Iranian language. The Baluchi presumably migrated from the north during the Bronze Age, possibly in association with the migration of the Aryans to India. They settled in oases and lived mostly as nomads.

In the 6th and 5th cents. BC the Myci or Maca, who, as the Makara, the Bṛihatsaṁhitā of Varāhamihira enumerates among the western neighbours of India, lived in the western G. The Persian administration extended their name to all of G., as the cuneiform inscriptions of → Darius [1] I tell. G. was part of the Sassanid empire for a time. In the Islamic period the tribes were mostly independent and formed khanates and federations. Ruins of the castles and fortifications, which are comparatively well preserved owing to the arid climate, remain mostly unstudied. B.B.

Gegania A Roman lady, who entered into a relationship with an ugly slave by the name of Clesippus and eventually made him her heir (probably in the 2nd half of the 1st cent. BC). After her death he called himself Clesippus Geganius and had built for himself an expensive tomb of which the inscription is still preserved (Plin. HN 34,11f.; ILLRP 696). This widespread story may underlie the character of Trimalchio in → Petronius. K.-L.E.

Geganius Name of a Roman patrician family, which according to tradition was politically significant in Rome during the 5th cent. BC, but then entirely disappeared. The *gens* supposedly came to Rome from Alba Longa under king Tullus Hostilius (Liv. 1,30,2; Dion. Hal. Ant. Rom. 3,29,7); a later construction traced the family back to → Gyas, a companion of Aeneas (Serv. Aen. 5,117).

[1] **G. Macerinus, M.** Consul I in 447 BC, II in 443 (triumph over the Volsci, InscrIt 13,1,67; Liv. 4,9f.), III in 437, censor in 435 with C. Furius [I 25] Pacilus; legate in 431.

[2] **G. Macerinus, Proculus.** Consul in 440.

[3] **G. Macerinus, T.** Consul in 492 BC with P. Minucius Augurinus. K.-L.E.

Gegeneis (Γηγενεῖς, 'Earth Born ').

[1] Epithet of the Aloads (Schol. Apoll. Rhod. 1,482), → Orion (Apollod. 1,25 Wagner), the Spartans (Eur. Bacch. 264), Argus [I 5] (Aesch. PV 567), and the → giants (Batr. 7; Soph. Trach. 1058f.; Eur. Phoen. 1131). As a noun = giants (Aristoph. Nub. 853; Lycoph. 1408; explained in Diod. Sic. 4,21,7).

[2] Mythical people living near Cyzicus, mentioned by Apoll. Rhod. (1,941–3; 989–91 with schola). Dei(l)ochus of Proconnesus called them ἐγχειρογάστορες (*Encheirogástores*) (FGrH III B 471, 7b from Schol. Apoll. Rhod. 1,989).

[3] Equivalent in meaning with αὐτόχθονες (*autóchthones*, 'indigenous'), attested for the Argive king Pelasgus (Aesch. Supp. 251) and the Attic king Erechtheus (Lycoph. 111; Hdt. 8,55). Similar names such as 'Son of the Earth' (e.g. in Antoninus Liberalis 6 for Cecrops) are also often found. In Athens in particular, indigenous status was used for political propaganda (Thuc. 2,36,1; Isoc. Or. 4,24–25; 12,124–125). JO.S.

Geidumni A people of Gallia Belgica mentioned only in Caes. B Gall. 5,39,1 as being subject to the Nervii. Their home in Flanders cannot be located with certainty. F.SCH.

Geisericus (Geiseric) Regarding the name [5. 394]. King of the Vandals and Alani AD 428–477, successor to his half-brother → Gundericus. In 429 G. crossed from the south of Spain to north Africa with 80,000 others (Victor Vitensis 1,2), possibly called in by the *Comes Africae* → Bonifatius [1], who fell from grace in 427, but ultimately he went because the wealth of the country. Neither Boniface nor an eastern Roman auxiliary corps commanded by Aspar (→ Ardabur [2]) were able to stop the Vandals' advance; in 431 G. conquered Hippo (→ Augustinus died in 430 during the siege; Procop. Vand. 3,3,30ff.; Possidius vita Aug. 28). As → *foederati*, the Vandals obtained in 435 Numidia, parts of Mauretania, and the province of Africa Proconsularis *ad habitandum* (Chron. min. 1,474; 3,458 MOMMSEN). Nevertheless, G. conquered Carthage in 439 and plundered Sicily in 440. When in 441 an eastern Roman fleet sent against him had to turn back because of the Hunnic and Persian threat in the east, G. received the Proconsularis, Byzacena, eastern Numidia, and a part of Tripolitania [5. 171ff.] in a treaty with Valentinian III in 442. For the first time Roman territory was not just granted for settlement but ceded, as a result of which G.'s full sovereignty was recognized as fact (cf. [5. 173]; not so in [2. 53]). He had committed himself to annual tribute payments and sent his son → Hunericus as a hostage to Rome, but minted his own coins and reckoned his own regnal years (beginning in 439).

When the engagement of Valentinian's eldest daughter → Eudocia to Hunericus was dissolved by the new government after her father's death, G. took Rome in 455. After a fourteen day sacking in which Pope Leo was able to prevent only the worst excesses, the Vandals left with a rich booty, Valentinian's widow and her two daughters (Proc. Vand. 3,5,1ff.); in 456 Hunericus married Eudocia. Despite Rome's inability to act in Africa, G. did not significantly extend his realm there after 442. However, he repeatedly plundered the Italian coast and conquered the Balearic islands, Sardinia, Corsica, and Sicily (Victor Vitensis 1,13). A campaign planned by Majorian against the Vandal kingdom (460) failed as did a large joint naval expedition by both halves of the empire under → Basiliscus (468) (Priscus FHG 4, fr. 27; Proc. Vand. 3,6,10ff.). When the Vandals devastated even the coasts of Illyria and Greece, their conquests were finally recognized by the eastern empire (474), and this caused G. to cease his raids [6. 175].

It was G.'s objective to establish a sovereign Vandal kingdom in Africa. His foreign policy was not limited to raiding with his powerful fleet ('Vandalism'); in 472 Olybrius, a candidate supported by G., briefly ascended the Western imperial throne. In 476/7 G. attempted to bind → Odoacer to him by ceding Sicily, which was important to Italy's grain supply, in return for tribute (Victor Vitensis 1,14). After G.'s death, activity in the Vandal's foreign policy declined.

After 435 G. probably considered himself king of the Vandals as well as the formerly Roman population in his territory, i.e. he clearly considered his rule to be territorial. However, there were considerable tensions between the two groups, which G. and his successors were never able to eradicate and this was a continual weakness in the structure of the Vandal empire [3]. Thus, the Vandals acquired the best lands in the Proconsularis, whereas the Roman owners were expelled or had to work their land as *coloni* (Procop. Vand. 1,5,11ff.). The anti-Catholic policies of the Arian Vandal kings began with G. and intensified under his successors. Since Italy continued to depend on African grain, G.'s power had a solid economic foundation. He also used his military successes to strengthen his position against the Vandal nobility, leading to a revolt in 442 (?), which was brutally suppressed (Chron. min. 1,479 MOMMSEN; cf. [7. 59ff.]).

Among the Germanic rulers of late antiquity, G. occupies an outstanding position owing to his military and organizational ability and his tactical skill.

1 PLRE 2, 496ff. 2 F. CLOVER, Flavius Merobaudes, 1971 3 Id., The Symbiosis of Romans and Vandals in Africa, in: E.K. CHRYSOS, A. SCHWARCZ (ed.), Das Reich und die Barbaren, 1989, 57–73 4 Id., The Late Roman West and the Vandals, 1993 5 CHR. COURTOIS, Les Vandales et l'Afrique, 1955 6 A. DEMANDT, Die Spätantike, 1989 7 H.-J. DIESNER, Das Vandalenreich, 1966, 44ff.

M.MEI.

Geison (γεῖσον; *geîson*). Ancient architectural term (instances from Greek antiquity in [1. 32f.]) designating the cornice, the upper section of the entablature, originally in columned buildings with a hipped or saddleback roof, later also in storey and wall construction. The compact, monolithic or many-stone, horizontal cornice runs around the whole colonnade. Used since the first Doric peripteral temples, imitates the overhang of roof beams providing shelter from rain water in buildings and forms the abutment of the truss. The cornice blocks are firmly attached to the → frieze and the epistyle (→ epistylion) underneath and they buttress the horizontal thrust of the wooden rafters. In contrast, the sloping edge of the gables of the canonical → temple is called a 'sloping cornice'. In the 'stone-built' Doric order the protruding overhang of the horizontal geison is decoratively emphasized by a regular sequence of the → *mutulus* and the → *via*. Numerous structurally unweighted terracotta sidings of beams of the 7th and 6th cents. BC (Thermus, Korfu, Metapontus etc.) follow this scheme or, as bearer and base of the → sima, were executed as box geisons.

The geison of the Ionian and Corinthian orders was set above the dentil usually offset by an ornamental frieze) and also was the base of the sima blocks; it usually ended in a 'suspended plate' with downward-facing profile. In the 2nd cent. BC the independent variant of the console geison originated in the eastern Mediterranean, which became a standard form in the Roman Imperial period. In the process it largely lost its original structural significance and was progressively transformed into a decorative and ornamental building component.

1 EBERT.

O. BINGÖL, Überlegungen zum ion. Gebälk, in: MDAI(Ist) 40, 1990, 101–108; H.v. HESBERG, Konsolengeisa des Hell. und der frühen Kaiserzeit, 24. Ergh. MDAI(R), 1980; W. MÜLLER-WIENER, Griech. Bauwesen in der Ant., 1988, 113, 119f., 129f.; W.v. SYDOW, Die hell.

Gebälke in Sizilien, in: MDAI(R) 91, 1984, 239–358; B. Wesenberg, Griech. Säulen- und Gebälkformen in der lit. Überlieferung, in: DiskAB 6, 1997, 1–15. C.HÖ.

Gela (Γέλα; *Géla*)
A. History B. Archaeology

A. History

City on the south-west coast of Sicily, named after the river Gelas, at the mouth of which G. lies. G. was founded as a Dorian colony with the name 'Lindioi' by Antiphemus of Rhodes and the Cretan Entimus forty-five years after the founding of → Syracusae (Thuc. 6,4,3), in other words in 690 BC. Herodotus also names as founder Gelon of Telos (Hdt. 7,153), an ancestor of the tyrant of the same name (on the founding oracle from Delphi cf. Diod. Sic. 8,23). Battles with the indigenous Siculi are reported by schol. Pind. Ol. 2,16 and Paus. 8,46,2. In 582 BC inhabitants from G. under Aristonus and Pystilus founded the city of Acragas (Thuc. 6,4,4). In 505, with the help of Sicilian mercenaries, Cleander, the son of the Olympic champion Pantares, set himself up as tyrant of G. In 498 his brother Hippocrates succeeded him in the tyranny and conquered a large part of eastern Sicily; at Helorus he defeated a Syracusan army, thus acquiring Camarina. After the death of Hippocrates his head of cavalry → Gelon, son of Deinomenes, acquired rulership of G., now the most powerful city on the island. Gelon succeeded in acquiring Syracuse and transferred his residence there; he put G. under the control of his brother → Hieron (Hdt. 7,154–156). In 466 inhabitants of G. took part in the fall of the Deinomenids (Thuc. 6,5,3; Diod. Sic. 11,68,1; 76,5). Aeschylus spent the last years of his life in G. and it was here that he was buried in 456/5 (cf. Vita Aeschyli 11). In 422 G. opposed the suggestion by Phaeax of Athens of forming an alliance against Syracuse (Thuc. 5,4,6). G. supported Syracuse in the battle against Athens with a few troops (Thuc. 7,1,5; 33,1; 58,1; Diod. Sic. 13,4,2). Soon afterwards G. became a victim of the Carthaginian offensive under Himilco, which began in 409: in 405, in spite of the support of Dionysius of Syracuse, the city was conquered and destroyed (Diod. Sic. 13,108–111). Uninhabited for some time, G. was repopulated after 338 BC under the Corinthian Timoleon (Plut. Timoleon 35,2). In 311/0, → Agathocles [2] used G. as an operational base in the battle against Carthage (Diod. Sic. 19,107; 110). Between 285 and 282 G. was destroyed by Phintias, the tyrant of Acragas, with the help of Mamertine mercenaries and the population of G. was moved to the newly founded city of Phintias (modern Licata) (Diod. Sic. 22,4); however, the inhabitants continued to call themselves Γελῷοι (*Gelôioi*) there (cf. IG XIV 256).

It was Frederic II who first had the hill of G. repopulated in 1233 (Terranova); since 1927 the place has gone by the name G. again.

B. Archaeology

The ancient city of G. extends parallel to the seashore on a low, narrow hill, the main part of which is taken up by the medieval settlement of Terranova and the modern city, under whose buildings are the ancient necropoleis; the oldest are below the Borgo and the Villa Garibaldi, where the tombs of the first colonists from Rhodes and Crete were discovered; particularly worthy of mention are the burial sites dating from the 6th and 5th cents. BC, when the cemetery area stretched as far as the western end of the hill of G. and as far as the Cape of Soprano.

In the eastern area of the hill (Mulino a Vento) above G. was the acropolis of the ancient city. There the remains of homes and sacred precincts from the beginnings of the city are preserved; in the archaic and classical periods the city was developed on a regular ground plan, concentrated round a large square towards which various streets run at right angles. On the acropolis are numerous sacred precincts, including that of Athena, in which two temples encased in clay were built in succession between the 7th and 6th cents. A Dorian temple (temple C), also dedicated to Athena, was erected around 480 BC together with other smaller sacred buildings; from one of them comes the head of a clay horse; a series of magnificent Silenian mask antefixes comes from a nearby sanctuary at Molino Di Pietro.

For the period after its destruction by Carthage in 405 BC and during the era of Dionysius of Syracuse, the acropolis shows immediate readoption and continuation of the cults in sacred precincts, in which representations of Athena in the style borrowed from Lindus have been found. On the other hand, at the time of Timoleon and Agathocles the city seems to have gained particular importance in the arts, when the city centre was moved to the western part of the hill, which was surrounded by a wide circle of walls made of bare bricks made into walls pseudoisodomically, erected in the cent. after Timoleon. The walls are still excellently preserved, as they escaped the final destruction of 280 BC and in the following cents. gradually became buried in sand.

After centuries of exploitative excavations in the necropoleis, which have equipped museums and private collections all over Europe with precious Greek vases since the 18th cent., excavation work was started in G. in 1900 by P. Orsi, paying particular attention to the burial sites and sacred precincts; resumed in the post-war period with important studies by P. Griffo, P. Orlandini and D. Adamesteanu, they have been continued up to the present day mainly by E. De Miro and G. Fiorentini and R. Panvini. Today G. is one of the best researched Greek cities in Sicily, as far as its aspects of urban development, its large number of monuments and its extensive craft production is concerned, expressed as much in the architectural ornamentation made of clay and the art of pottery as in the numerous series of coins. The sea in front of Gela has retained many well-preserved remains, including a very rare example of a ship from the 5th cent. BC.

P. Orsi, G., in: Monumenti Antichi 17, 1906; P. Griffo, L. von Matt, G., 1964; H. Berve, Die Tyrannis bei den Griechen 1, 1967, 137ff.; E. De Miro, G. Fiorentini, in: Cronache di archeologia 17, 1978; G. Fiorentini, G., 1985; R. Panvini, Γέλα, 1996; Omaggio a G., 1997.
DA.P. and E.O.

Gelanor (Γελάνωρ; *Gelánōr*). Mythical original king of Argus, son of Sthenelus (Paus. 2,16,1), whose only significance is that he abdicated the rulership to → Danaus (Apollod. 2,13); in Aesch. Supp. 266 he is called → Pelasgus. The change in dynasty took place either after a battle (Plut. Pyrrhus 32,9f., 404e-f) or by referendum (Paus. 2,19,3f.). A battle, understood as an omen, between a bull and a wolf, which the wolf wins, is crucial on both occasions. Danaus is in this way connected to Argus' chief god, Apollo → Lykeios; a relief in front of the temple of the god represents the clash (Paus. 2,19,3). F.G.

Gelasius

[1] Bishop of → Caesarea [2] Maritima/Palaestina (died before AD 400). The nephew of → Cyrillus of Jerusalem, installed as bishop around 365/367, took part in the Council of Constantinople in 381 and in the synod there in 394. At the wish of his uncle, G. wrote a continuation of the Church history by → Eusebius [7] of Caesarea, going as far as 395, which had a long-lasting effect (Gelasius of Cyzicus, hagiographic lives, etc.). Parts of the lost script can be reconstructed ([3. 18–69], synopsis [3. 117–123]). Bks. 10 and 11 of the Church history by → Rufinus of Aquileia may possibly be borrowings from this work which is well-disposed towards Constantinus [1] the Great ([3. 104]; on the other hand [2]). Seventeen fragments of G.'s dogmatic writings are extant [1. 44–49].

1 F. Diekamp, Analecta Patristica, 1938, 32–49 2 J. Schamp, Gélase ou Rufin: un fait nouveau, in: Byzantion 57, 1987, 360–381 3 F. Winkelmann, Unt. zur Kirchengesch. des G. von Kaisareia, 1966.
J.RI.

[2] **G. of Cyzicus.** A work handed down in the MSS as anonymous and usually under the title of σύνταγμα τῶν κατὰ τὴν ἐν Νικαίᾳ ἁγίαν σύνοδον πραχθέντων ('summary of the events at the holy synod in Nicaea') about the Church history of the east under Constantinus [1] the Great is traditionally connected, owing to the same *initium*, with details by → Photius on a three-volume depiction of the Council of Nicaea (AD 325), which he ascribes to a G. (bibl. cod. 15 [4 b 23f.]); individual MSS were, however, apparently often already circulated at that time anonymously (bibl. cod. 88 [66 b 30f.]) or in the name of G. [1] of Caesarea [2]/Palaestina as ἱστορίας ἐκκλησιαστικῆς λόγοι γ' ('3 bks. of Church history') (ibid. [66 b 32f./67 a 3f.]). Since the author introduces himself as a Bithynian and son of a priest from Cyzicus (prooemium 2), an otherwise unknown 'Gelasius of Cyzicus' has been postulated as author (firstly Fr. Pithou, 1599, and then A. Ceriani, 1861; by contrast now G. Chr. Hansen). As well as → Eusebius [7] of Caesarea, → Socrates, → Theodoretus and → Rufinus, sources now lost have been used for the portrayal.

CPG 3, 6034; G. Loeschcke, M. Heinemann, Gelasius. Kirchengesch. (GCS 18), 1918 (new ed. by G. Chr. Hansen, Anonyme Kirchengeschichte (Gelasius Cyzicenus, CPGG034), 2000; G. Loeschcke, Das Syntagma des Gelasius Cyzicenus, 1906; P. Nautin, La continuation de l'«histoire ecclésiastique» d'Eusèbe par Gélase de Césarée, in: REByz 50, 1992, 164–183; F. Winkelmann, Die Quellen der Historia Ecclesiastica des Gelasius von Cyzicus, in: Byzantinoslavica 27, 1966, 104–130.
C.M.

[3] G. I, Pope from 1 March 492 to 19 November 496, who, during the dispute between the Eastern Roman emperor → Anastasius [1] I and the patriarch of Constantinople, developed the 'doctrine of the two powers' (Epist. 12). He recognized the competence of 'Imperial power' (*regalis potestas*) in the worldly sphere, but subordinated this, with regard to spiritual responsibility, to the 'sacred authority of the bishops' (*auctoritas sacrata pontificum*). The doctrine of the two powers, in the form of the doctrine of the two swords, was of decisive importance in the Middle Ages in determining the relationship between Emperor and Pope. Literary works: letters [1], six treatises, of which four oppose → Monophysitism and one Pelagianism (cf. → Pelagius [4]; → Semipelagianism). One treatise [2. 161–189] comes out against the→ *Lupercalia*.

1 PL 59, 13–116 2 G. Pomarès (ed.), SChr 65, 1959.
R.BR.

Gelduba (modern Krefeld-Gellep). Place in *Germania inferior*, field camp and battle site of the Batavian wars (Tac. Hist. 4,26,3; 32,1; 35,3; 36,1; 58,4); after AD 70 auxiliary fort (Plin. HN 19,90), which after three wood and earth stages was converted into stone before 150. The occupying force was for a long time the *cohors II Varcinorum equitata*. In the wake of Postumus' uprising in 259 (tombs of the fallen!) and in 275/6 G. was destroyed by the Franks, redesigned into a fortress around 295 and in 353 to 355 again fell victim to the Franks. Nevertheless, G. remained militarily occupied for some time to come. The *vicus* renovated at the beginning of the 5th cent. was destroyed by a fire only at the beginning of the 6th cent. The uninterrupted settlement of the place is assured by graveyards even up to the 2nd half of the 8th cent. AD (also Frankish tombs with rich findings).

H. Tiefenbach, R. Pirling, s.v. G., RGA 10, 636–646.
K.DI.

Geleontes see → Iones

G(a)eli (Γῆλαι/*Gēlai*, Str. 11,5,1, cf. 11,7,1; 11,8,1; Γηλύς/*Gēlýs*, Steph. Byz. s.v. Γ.; Γηλοί/*Gēloí*, Dionys. Per. 1019 [GGM II, 167]). Median tribe of Scythian origins, first mentioned by Strabo (according to Theophanes of Mytilene), who inhabited the south-western shores of the Caspian Sea. Some ancient authors (Plin. HN 6,48; Ptol. 6,2,5) identified them with the → Cadusii. The tribe's name lives on in the region's (or rather the Sassanid province's) modern name of Gīlān (middle Persian Gēlān).

R. Gyselen, La géographie administrative de l'Empire sassanide, 1989, 49f., 81f.; F.H. Weissbach, s.v. Geli, RE 7, 986f. J.W.

Gelimer Grandson of → Geisericus, last of the Vandal kings (AD 530–4), took over rulership in 530 after the fall of Hildericus (Procop. Vand. 1,9,8–9; Greg. Tur. Franc. 2,3). His adamant refusal of any intervention by Justinian in internal affairs led to war (Procop. Vand. 1,9,10–24). Since G. had dispatched his troops to Sardinia against the rebellious Godas, he could not defend himself either against Pudentius, who was in revolt in Tripolitania, or against → Belisarius, who had landed in Sicily in 533 (Procop. Vand. 1,10,24–27). He secured his retreat by an alliance with the Visigoths in Spain. After the battle at *Ad Decimum* (near Carthage) in Sept. 533 G. fled, acquired new allies, attacked again Belisarius with the army, which had returned from Sardinia, but was defeated in mid-December 533 at Tricamarum and retreated into the Pappua mountains (Procop. Vand. 2,3,1–28). In March 534 Belisarius took him prisoner and paraded him in triumph as he entered Constantinople (Iord. Get. 171; Procop. Vand. 1,23,20;21). Justinian left him properties in Galatia, but did not elevate the Arian to a *patricius*. The sources portray G. as the last ruler of a kingdom with the typical features of an epigone and tyrant.

PLRE 3, 506–508; F.H. Clover, The Late Roman West and the Vandals, 1993; H.-J. Diesner, Das Vandalenreich, 1966, 98–104; J.A.S. Evans, The Age of Justinian, 1996, 126–133. ME.STR.

Gellias (Γελλίας; *Gellías*). Wealthy Acragantian, whose unique hospitality and generosity were extolled by Diodorus (13,83) when portraying the prosperity of Acragas in the 5th cent. BC (Diod. Sic. 13,81,4–84,7 = Timaeus FGrH 566 F 26a). Cf. also Ath. I 4 and Val. Max. 4,8 ext. 2. G. died when Acragas was destroyed by the Carthaginians in 406/5. K.MEI.

Gellius Roman *nomen gentile*, which can almost certainly be traced back to the praenomen G. attested from the beginning of the 3rd cent. BC. There is evidence of the bearers of the name in the political life of Rome from the 2nd cent. BC.

Salomies 104; Schulze 519.

[1] Stepbrother of L. Marcius Philippus (*cos.* 56 BC), otherwise unknown supporter of P. Clodius [I 4] from the equestrian class, defamed by Cicero as 'the wet-nurse of all revolutionaries' (Cic. Vatin. 4; Cic. Sest. 110–112). K.-L.E.

[2] **G., Cn.** Roman historian, probably identical to the mint master of the denarius RRC 232 (*c.* 138 BC): [2. 268; 3. 20]. G. wrote *annales*, which ranged from the early Roman period to at least 146 BC (fr. 28 Peter [= HRR 12, 156]), probably towards the end of the 2nd cent. The unusually large scope of the work (fr. 26 from bk. 33 [= HRR 12, 155] relates to the year 216; bk. 97 in fr. 29 [= HRR 12, 156] also need not be a misquotation) is less likely to have been based on the first use of the → *Annales maximi* (thus, though [1. 12]) than on the large-scale incorporation of mythologems and cultural-historical speculations, strict annalistic working out to the last detail (even of the period of the kings: fr. 11; 18 [= HRR 12, 151, 153]) and imaginative supplementing of the sparse tradition with orations, motivations and elements of action which were invented according to the rules of plausibility (*eikós*; εἰκός) [3. 21f.]. G. in this way anticipates the characteristics of late → annalists. His language is relatively inconspicuous apart from a few extravagances (predilection for forms ending in *-abus*; gen. *lapiderum*). – Of later historians C. → Licinius Macer (Dion. Hal. Ant. Rom. 6,11,2; 7,1,4) and → Dionysius [18] of Halicarnassus (who censures gross chronological errors) used G., but Livy did not; later quotations (e.g. in Aulus Gellius and Servius) have perhaps been conveyed by Varro.

Fr: HRR 1² 148–157.

1 E. Badian, The Early Historians, in: T.A. Dorey et al. (ed.), Latin Historians, 1966, 1–38, esp. 11–13 2 Rawson, Culture, 267–271 3 T.P. Wiseman, Clio's Cosmetics, 1979. W.K.

[3] **G., Statius.** Samnite commander, defeated and taken captive at Bovianum in 305 BC (Liv. 9,44,13–15).

[4] **G., L.** (The cognomen Poblicola was first held by his adoptive son G. [5].) *Homo novus*, aedile in 96 BC at the latest, *praetor peregrinus* in 94 (mentioned in Rome's contract of alliance with Thyrreum in Arcadia, Syll.³ 732), then in 93 promagistrate in one of the eastern provinces, probably Asia (MRR 3,99); he tried, to the derision of his peers, to mediate in the arguments of the Athenian schools of philosophy (Cic. Leg. 1,53). Not until 73 did he become consul with L. Cornelius [I 48] Lentulus Clodianus. He first defeated a group of rebellious slaves of Spartacus under Crixus, but was then himself defeated by Spartacus and afterwards dismissed from the command with his colleague by the Senate (MRR 2, 116), but, in spite of this, he became censor in 70 with Cn. Cornelius [I 48] Lentulus (ejection of 64 senators from the Senate, Liv. Per. 98). In 67 to 65 he was legate of Pompey in the war against the pirates and entrusted with guarding the Italian coast and supervision of the Tyrrhenian Sea. In 63 he supported Cicero's action against the Catilinarians, in 59 he opposed Caesar's law on agriculture (Plut. Cicero 26,2) and appeared in the Senate again in 57 and 55. His adopted son G. [5] is said to have committed adultery with his second wife (Val. Max. 5,9,1).

[5] **G. Poblicola, L.** Brother of M. Valerius Messalla Corvinus (*cos.* 31 BC) and adopted son of G. [4] [1. 8]. In the 50s he belonged to the circle around P. Clodius [I 4] and was therefore sharply attacked by Catullus as a rival for the favours of his sister Clodia [1] (74; 80; 88–91; accusation of incest). In 43 he was first on the side of Caesar's murderer M. Iunius Brutus, but after a failed attempt on Brutus' life went over to the triumvir Marcus Antonius [I 9] (Cass. Dio 47,24,3–5; Liv. Per. 122). In 41 as *quaestor p(ro praetore)* (?) under Antony he minted coins (RRC 517). In 36 consul, in 35 mentioned in praise by Horace (Sat. 1,10,85); in 31 at Actium with Antony he commanded the right wing of the fleet (Plut. Antonius 65,1; 66,2); he probably died in the battle or shortly afterwards.

1 E. BADIAN, The Clever and the Wise, in: BICS Suppl. 51, 1988 2 SYME, RR, Index s.v. G. 3 T.P. WISEMAN, Cinna the Poet and Other Essays, 1974, 119–129 (family).

K.-L.E.

[6] **A.G.** Author of the *Noctes Atticae*, probably born in Rome between AD 125 and 130 (Gell. NA 7,6,12). The sparse information about his life that can be gleaned from the work relates primarily to education and spiritual development (exception: Gell. NA 14,2,1 – function as *iudex extra ordinem*). G. names → Sulpicius Apollinaris, Antonius → Iulianus and Ti. → Castricius as his first teachers. On an educational trip to Greece (probably 147/8) he heard the Platonist Lucius Calvenus Taurus and met the wealthy patron and illustrious orator → Herodes Atticus. G. (praef. 4) also traces his literary collection activities and the title of his miscellaneous work *Noctes Atticae* back to this trip. Further important friends and teachers are the princes' tutor → Fronto and in particular → Favorinus of Arelate, in whom G. saw the ideal image of an intellectual versed in all areas of Greek and Roman culture.

G.'s only work, comprising 20 bks., which he himself placed in the tradition of → *Buntschriftstellerei* (praef. 4–10), purports to be a kind of reading list and contains information from the poetic and rhetorical literature of the Greeks and Romans, from historiography, philosophy and all the important disciplines of specialist writing (in particular grammar, jurisprudence and medicine). In general, as is usual in → archaism, an interest in linguistic matters (especially lexicography and etymology) dominates. The material is presented not systematically, but in individual chapters of self-contained subject matter in varied sequence. Sources, as well as the originals, are other encyclopaedias and miscellanies (e.g. M. Terentius → Varro, → Plinius the Elder, → Suetonius). The work, which the author dedicates to his children (praef. 23), is aimed at his averagely educated contemporaries. The declared pedagogical goal is to convey correct conduct within the contemporary culture of conversation. By an anecdotal type of narrative and the frequent framing of individual chapters in narrative scenes G. exemplifies, over and above the mere content, the code of conduct he demands and demonstrates it in situations. In this way G. also greatly differs from other *Buntschriftsteller*. G. is therefore of significance not only because of his numerous quotations from literature otherwise lost, but primarily as a representative of the urban culture of the 2nd cent., in which education becomes an essential component of social prestige.

G. was used as a literary model in late antiquity. Particularly important in this respect are → Nonius Marcellus and → Macrobius, whose *Saturnalia* are also close to G. in form. The manuscript tradition was a main focus in the 12th cent. and then in close association with its adoption by the Humanists, by whom G. is regarded not least as a model of academic miscellany writing (e.g. Angelo Poliziano's *Miscellanea*), in the 15th cent.

→ Second Sophistic

EDITIONS: P.K. MARSHALL, 1968.
TRANSL.: F. WEISS, 1875/6 (reprint 1992).
BIBLIOGRAPHY: M.L. ASTARITA, La cultura nelle Noctes Atticae, 1993; S.M. BEALL, Civilis eruditio, thesis Berkeley, 1988; H. BERTHOLD, A.G., Auswahl und Aufgliederung seiner Themen, 1959; L. HOLFORD-STREVENS, A.G., 1988; P.L. SCHMIDT, in: HLL, § 408; D.W.T. VESSEY, A.G. and the Cult of the Past, in: ANRW II.34,2, 1863–1917.

H.KR.

Gello (Γελλώ; *Gellṓ*) designates the spirit of a girl who died single, which kills unmarried or pregnant women and small children; it is first mentioned in Sappho (fr. 178 L.P. = 168 V.) [1]; G. is also the name of a mythological creature with these characteristics (Suda s.v.). It was still feared in the Byzantine period (Johannes Damascenus *Perì Stryngôn*, PG 94, 1904 C; Psellos *Dihḗgesis perì Gellṓs* [2]), something that has survived to the present day in rural Greece [3]. G. has often been associated with → Lamia and → Mormo, two similar spirits, and the *strix*. Rites to fend off G. – a 'creature of the night', which 'strangles children and harms those in labour' – are known to the Cyranides (2,31,20–23) and Byzantine authors [4].

1 S.I. JOHNSTON, Restless Dead, (1999, ch. 5)
2 K. SATHAS (ed.), Μεσαιωνικὴ Βιβλιοθήκη 5, 1876, 572–573 3 C. STEWART, Demons and the Devil, 1991
4 P. PERDRIZET, Negotium Perambulans in Tenebris, 1922, 16–38.

S.I.J.

Gelon (Γέλων; *Gélōn*).

[1] Son of Deinomenes from Gela, greatest Sicilian tyrant prior to Dionysius I, period of reign *c.* 491–478 BC. Firstly bodyguard, later master-of-horse of Hippocrates of Gela, after whose death in 491 he usurped the tyrannis over Gela and brought the east Sicilian *archḗ* of his predecessor, comprising Gela, Camarina, Callipolis, Leontini, Catana, Naxos and numerous Sicilian communities, into his power (Hdt. 7,154). Called to help around 485 by the Syracusan *gamoroi* (land owners), who had been driven out to Casmenae, against the people and Cyllyrians (bondsmen), he led the *gamoroi* back to Syracuse and in doing so also took control of

this city (Hdt. 7,155f.). By forcible resettlements from Gela, Camarina and Megara Hyblaea he made Syracuse the 'greatest city in Sicily' (Hdt. 7,156; Thuc. 6,5,3) and also his residence, while entrusting the rulership of Gela to his brother Hieron.

By contrast with most ancient tyrants, G. did not rely on the common people, but on the land-owning aristocracy. Moreover, he granted citizenship to 10,000 mercenaries (Diod. Sic. 11,72,3) and created a significant war fleet. Allied to the tyrant Theron of Acragas, whose daughter Damarete was G.'s wife, he had already campaigned successfully against the Carthaginians after the end of Dorieus in the period before 485 (Hdt. 7,158). In 481 he declined membership of the Hellenic League, not because he was refused the supreme command (according to Hdt. 7,158–162), but because invasion of Sicily by the Carthaginians was immediately imminent: responding to the cry for help from Terillus (who had been driven out of Himera by Theron) and his father-in-law Anaxilaus of Rhegium, the Carthaginians under Hamilcar landed at Himera in 480 with large land and naval fighting forces. There G. won a splendid victory which freed the island from the threat of the Carthaginians for *c.* 70 years and helped it to flourish and achieve great prosperity (Hdt. 7,165–167; Diod. Sic. 11,20–26). G. erected magnificent buildings in Himera and Syracuse as a memorial to his victory and was fêted as a 'benefactor and saviour' (Diod. Sic. 11,26,6). That he held the office of an 'authorized *strategos*' (according to Diod. Sic. 13,94,5), is a later invention. He died in 478 of a disease and was succeeded by his brother Hieron.
Sources: Hdt. 7,153–167; Diod. Sic. 11,20–38,3 (mostly from Timaeus).

W. AMELING, Karthago, 1993, 15ff.; D. ASHERI, CAH 4, ²1988, 766–775; H. BERVE, Die Tyrannis bei den Griechen, 1967; vol. 1, 142ff.; 2, 598ff.; S. N. CONSOLO LANGHER, Siracusa e la Sicilia greca, 1996, 218ff.; W. HUSS, Geschichte der Karthager, 1985, 93ff.; A. VON STAUFFENBERG, Trinakria, 1963, 176ff.; M. ZAHRNT, Die Schlacht bei Himera und die sizilische Historiographie, in: Chiron 23, 1993, 353–390.

[2] Son and co-regent of King Hieron II of Syracuse, died before his father in 216/15 BC. K.MEI.
[3] Supporter of Neoptolemus, king of Epirus, who ruled the country from about 297 BC with Pyrrhus in joint rulership. G. entered into intrigues to bring about the fall of Pyrrhus. However, this occasioned only the fall of Neoptolemus (Plut. Pyrrhus 5), at the latest in the winter of 296/5, for in 295 Pyrrhus intervened in the dispute over the succession to the Macedonian throne. BO.D.

Geloni (Γελωνοί; *Gelōnoí*). According to Hdt. (4,102; 108f.; 120; 136), agricultural Scythian tribe in the neighbourhood of the → Budini and speaking a Graeco-Scythian hybrid language; descendants of Gelonus; originally Greek refugees from Greek trade settlements.

They apparently took part in the battle against → Darius [1] I. J.W.

Gelonus (Γελωνός; *Gelōnós*).
[1] Son of Hercules and the snake maiden → Echidna, brother of Agathyrsus and of → Scythes, eponym of the Graeco-Scythian Geloni (Hdt. 4,10). JO.S.
[2] City of the Budini, mentioned only by Hdt. 4,108, according to the context of the highly contested passage, north of the Melanchlaeni on the upper Donec. Herodotus describes a city built of wood with Greek architecture and a Greek life-style. The inhabitants spoke partly Scythian, partly Greek. This makes G. the first literary attested example of a Greek city in the barbarian hinterland of the Pontus areas and of the Mixhellenes. The name system (*Gelōnoí*, *Gelōnós* as mythological personal name and G.) seems to be of Greek structure, however.

B. N. GRAKOW, Die Skythen, 1978, 14, 122, 148. I.v.B.

Gem cutting

I. ANCIENT ORIENT
see → Seals

II. PHOENICIAN
Phoenician and Punic gem cutting (GC) (= glyptography) is known almost exclusively through stamp seals in the form of scarabees (→ Scarabee) or scaraboids that were very widespread in the ancient world; the body of the beetle is graphically linear in the Phoenician east, whilst in the Punic west – under the Ionian-Etruscan influence – it is structured much more three-dimensionally. Here Greek motifs (Hercules and the lion, warriors, satyrs, heads of deities and others) also entered the iconography of the sealing plate, that otherwise mainly remained reserved for the Egyptian pictorial world (winged goddess, Horus, god on papyrus bark and others), and to a lesser extent for the Oriental (sphinx, cow with calf) pictorial world. As material, not just common gemstones (steatite, carneole, green jasper) but also paste and faience were used on many occasions. According to the finds and their stylistic differentiation, an important centre for Punic GC existed in → Tharrus on Sardinia.

As in the other ancient cultures, GC developed in the Phoenician and Punic world for the primary purpose of sealing → documents (on clay bullae, as are e.g. extant from a temple archive in → Carthage with over 4,000 specimens partly excavated from 1989 to 1993). To the same extent it was used for the illustration of the talismanic-magical quality of the → seal that ensured the identity of the individual. This property also explains the frequent use of cut stones as personal adornment and as funerary gifts.
→ Phoenicians, Poeni

D. BERGES, Die Tonsiegel aus dem karthagischen Tempelarchiv, in: F. RAKOB (ed.), Karthago 2. Die deutschen Ausgrabungen in Karthago, 1997, 1–214, esp. 14–19, 41–57; D. CIAFALONI, Glyptique, in: V. KRINGS (ed.), La civilisation phénicienne et punique, 1995 (= HbdOr I, vol. 20), 501–508; E. GUBEL, s. v. Glyptique, DCPP, 191–194; ZAZOFF, AG, 85–98. H. G. N.

III. CLASSICAL ANTIQUITY

A. MATERIAL, TECHNIQUE, GEM CUTTER B. HISTORICAL DEVELOPMENT 1. MINOAN-MYCENAEAN (*c.* 2600–*c.* 1050 BC) 2. GREEK-GEOMETRIC (9TH–7TH CENTS. BC) 3. 'ISLAND STONES'(7TH/6TH CENTS. BC); ARCHAIC (6TH/EARLY 5TH CENT. BC) 4. GREEK-CLASSICAL (5TH/4TH CENTS. BC) 5. HELLENISTIC (3RD/2ND CENTS. BC) 6. ITALIAN AND ROMAN REPUBLICAN (1ST CENT. BC–1ST CENT. AD) 7. IMPERIAL PERIOD (2ND–4TH CENTS. AD) 8. MAGICAL INTAGLIOS (2ND–4TH CENTS. AD)

A. MATERIAL, TECHNIQUE, GEM CUTTER

In GC (glyptography, from Greek γλύφειν/*glýphein*, 'to cut') – i.e. in the processing of precious stones and gemstones as well as pastes (fashioning, smoothing, decoration) – the term refers to cut stones with the image and/or inscription in hollowed-out (in the case of seal stones, negative) relief work as an intaglio (= I.), executed in embossed relief work (high cut) as a cameo (= C.). Stone or glass vessels (Tazza Farnese, → Portland vase) cut with the C. technique are also among the products of GC. The country of origin of GC is Mesopotamia (5th millennium BC) with the manufacture of stamp seals and cylinder seals (→ Seals). For I. and C., stones of the oxide and hydroxide class were mostly used, particularly the varieties like chalcedony, jasper or carneole that belong to the quartz group, very rarely those of the corundum group (diamond, ruby). Material formation and the design depended on the varying popularity in the individual epochs. Facetting is only attested since the Middle Ages.

In the older Minoan phase and then again in the geometric period, people scratched soft stones (steatite, serpentine) with the engraving tool, and later they also cut 'hard' stones like carneole, chalcedony, agate, jasper and quartz using a bow drill. The I. image of an Etruscan carneole scarabee (London, BM) [1. 233 n. 95 pl. 59,1] illustrates drilling with the bow drill, cf. also the tombstone fragment of the gem cutter Dorus of Sardes [2. 399; 5. 381 fig. 316]: looped around a rod running horizontally with an engraving instrument ('Pointer') at the tip is the leather strap chord of a bow so that the rod was set in rotation by means of the bow. The bow could be moved by an assistant or by the I. cutter himself with one hand while the other hand guided the stone stuck onto a piece of wood towards the rotating drill. As a grinding agent, an oil-corundum mixture was used (Plin. HN 37,10). In the Hellenistic and Roman period, people used small diamond splinters set in iron (Plin. HN 37,15) that produced sharp, fine lines [2]. Finally the I. was polished, and here methods and predilections differed among the various periods. The principle of magnification by focussing rays was known (e.g. Plin. HN 36,67; 37,10), but the use of magnifying glasses is improbable. According to Plin. HN 37,16, looking through concave, green emeralds allowed the gem cutter's eyes to recover. Workshops in the Minoan-Mycenaean period were unearthed during excavations in Mallia, and additional ones – with stones from the early Imperial period and the Republican epoch – came to light in Pompeii [1. 31[43], 33[59], 266[35]].

Gem cutters are known from written evidence passed down to us or autographs, with signing not common in all periods and genres of glyptography. The topics of GC are primarily mythological, religious and political (portraits) and works of contemporary sculpture have likewise been taken up as themes. Replicas of master I.s show that these were already admired in antiquity. Stylistic peculiarities sometimes allow us to discern the origin of the I. cutter.

B. HISTORICAL DEVELOPMENT

1. MINOAN-MYCENAEAN (*c.* 2600–*c.* 1050 BC)

Typical of the early Minoan period are seals scratched with the hand graver and made of soft steatite with asymmetrical lines, later a cross, grid or spiral pattern, [1. 25 ff.; 3]. Because of advanced technology with the rotating drill, hard stones are also used in the Minoan period (e.g. jasper, chalcedony). Popular shapes are four-sided prisms, signets (seal plates or sealing stones on a short handle) as well as theriomorphic sealing moulds, on the basis of pictographic characters presumably amulets rather than pure sealing stones [1. 44f.; 3]. These were superseded during the last Minoan phase by 'talismanic' I.s that in the late Minoan period progressed to become the mass product of the amulet that continued to be in demand: perforated amygdaloids (almond-shaped) and lentoids (lens-shaped) of jasper or quartz with symbols (fish, fishing gear, sacrifice requisites). The patterns of 'Architecture I.s' are reminiscent of combinations of architectural details. In late Minoan-Mycenaean GC a naturalistic tendency is conspicuous. The images of the hunt, animals, mythological beings, gods and humans are characterized by fine modelling and flowing shapes.

2. GREEK-GEOMETRIC (9TH–7TH CENTS. BC)

Initially people fell back again on soft stones and scratching gravers. GC determined by the scratching style passes through a trend from matchstick man to geometric figures. The seal shapes resemble those of the Minoan-Mycenaean phase: theriomorphic shapes, foot amulets, face seals, plates with a handle, pyramids, prisms as well as the disc shape (discus) that already approaches the scarabee shape. This is followed by scarabees, cylinders, amygdaloids and steatite rectangular solids [1. 51–56]. Because of imprinting on clay, the I.s that were mostly perforated were used as sealing stones but could also be worn as an amulet, especially the *c.* 300 serpentine scarabees of the 'Lyre player group' with musicians and fishermen motifs [1. 61 f.; 5. 109 f., 398]. The finding places of the geometric I.s show that the area of distribution was the Greek mainland, the Aegean islands, Cyprus, Asia Minor, Syria, Etruria and Ischia; the production centres are unclear [1. 59 f.].

3. 'Island stones'(7th/6th cents. BC); archaic (6th/early 5th cent. BC)

The shapes and themes of the 'Island stones' ('Melic I.s') of the 7th/6th cents. BC cut in the Orientalizing Greek style resemble the Minoan-Mycenaean ones: lentoids, amygdaloids, disci or hemispheres, signets, cylinders, animal sealing stones – only shaped somewhat more flatly and tending rather to be ps.-scarabees and anthropomorphic shapes – mostly of whitish green to brownish steatite, furthermore carneole, quartz, jasper and chalcedony. Animals and mythological beings, later also humans and heroes are depicted [1. 80–82; 4]. The oldest autograph of a master is considered to be that of → Syries, and subsequently Onesimus. The island of Melos was probably the manufacturing centre, whilst the wide distribution across the whole of Greece is indicative of the popularity of the stones [1. 77].

At the beginning of the 6th cent. the upswing in trade brought the practice of sealing with it into everyday Attic life. Scarabees or scaraboids on a golden frame were used for the sealing e.g. of containers as well as being worn on the finger as jewellery (ring of Polycrates: Hdt. 3,40; 3,41, Diog. Laert. 8,1,17). Aside from green jasper, carneole, chalcedony and then also sardonyx, agate and quartz in particular were preferred. The main form is the very small scarabee that is differentiated in its development from Egyptian and Phoenician models, furthermore the variants with a sculptured animal or mask as the back. The pictorial field always framed by bands of strokes shows heroes, animal fighting groups (lions), satyrs and Maenads, gods, winged demons and mythological beings as well as secular themes like a youth with a dog, artisans, warriors or athletes [1. 105–112; 4]. Master autographs from the archaic period are the names written in the nominative case of the Ionians Epimenes and Anacles (480–460 BC) and of the Cypriot Aristoteiches [1. 103f. n. 19–21 pl. 23,2; 5; 8].

4. Greek-Classical (5th/4th cents. BC)

In the classical period the scarabee declines in favour of the scaraboid, blueish chalcedony is preferred, then quartz and carneole, as well as agate, colourfully speckled jasper and – as a surrogate for quartz or chalcedony – white glass. The animal image (see → Dexamenus [2]), the female lyre player, women making their toilet or Odysseus were popular, furthermore works of contemporary sculpture are cited [1. 146–150 pl. 34; 35]. The masterpieces include the signed works of → Onatas [2], Dexamenus and → Pergamus with gem cutters now also attested as coin-stamp cutters, e.g.: 'Olympius' (380–360 BC), Phrygillus (for Sicilian towns *c.* 430–399 BC), Sosias (coins from Syracuse 430–400 BC) [1. 137–141 pl. 32, 6; 10; 11].

5. Hellenistic (3rd/2nd cents. BC)

Through the campaigns of Alexander [4] the Great and new trade relations, new materials become accessible: garnet, almandine, amethyst, emerald, aquamarine and topaz. Ring stone is preferred, convex, narrow high oval, commonly of sard (brown carneole) or brown glass with an image on the convex side. Colourful glass casts prove the popularity of the sealing stones set in large gold, silver or bronze rings (→ Seals II.). Now popular are portraits, motifs of Sarapis, Isis or Zeus-Ammon, frequently Alexander the Great himself, river deities and Nereids – mostly in a bust cut-out and in the back view – as well as Muses or Maenads with a narrow upper body, Hellenistic arrangement of folds, delicate profile and a bun hairstyle [1. 199–205 pl. 46–52; 2; 5; 6; 7]. The I. images are also influenced by sculpture: e.g. Alexander the Great as Zeus in the type of the Lysippus statues [1. 200f.[49] pl. 48, 3]. The technique of C. cutting was rejuvenated and reached its first high point with Athenion [3], Boethus [13] and Protarchus [5]. Plin. HN 7,125 passes down to us information about → Pyrgoteles, the court gem cutter, and Apollonius [22], → Onesas, Daedalus, Gelon, Lycomedes, Nicander, Nicias, Phidias and Sosis are known from their autographs [1. general index s. v. gem cutters' names, antiquity].

6. Italian and Roman Republican (1st cent. BC–1st cent. AD)

The development of Italian glyptography was initially decisively shaped by Etruscan GC [1. 214–259]. The main object of Italian and Roman-Republican GC is the ring stone. Especially popular are agates with different coloured layers, also mostly circular-shaped carneoles and sard (brown carneole) as well as chalcedony and nicolo. Paste was manufactured through mass production. The rings made of gold or bronze are smooth, sometimes also solid with a raised representation in the ring plate [1. 268–274]. Aside from their use as sealing stones, utilization for the purpose of jewellery and use as an amulet or decoration are foregrounded [10. 57 n. 3, 59]. Popular are Dionysian themes, Hercules mingens, the stealing of the Palladion, rural sacrifice scenes, images of philosophers, actors and musicians as an expression of the glorification of wisdom and art, skeletons and insect men as allegories of the transitory nature of things, ears of grain, the poppy, horn of plenty or rudder as symbols of blessings [1. 290–302 pl. 82–89; 9; 11]. Gem cutters well known through their autographs from the Roman Republican period are Agathangelus [1], → Alexas, Aulus [2] and Quintus, Felix [1], Anterus, → Gnaeus, → Scopas [4], Menophilus, Pamphilus, Sosocles and Teucer [1. general index s. v. gem cutters' names, antiquity]. Diodotus, Tryphon, Rufus and → Sostratus [4] [8. 131ff.; → 9. 139–141] worked as cameoglypthographers.

7. Imperial period (2nd–4th cents. AD)

According to Plin. HN 37,196, in the Imperial period, flat stones were more valuable than convex ones, the valuation of the shapes was ranked in the order oblong, lens-shaped, round and square. A relationship between design and material can also be established (Plin. HN 37,76). Often the choice of material is linked with particular motifs [1. 344 f.]. Chalcedony, jasper and nicolo are common, but the most commonly used stone was carneole, although prase, garnet, hyacinth and amethyst also gained greatly in popularity. As a mass medium of political → propaganda, pastes are widespread from the Augustan period onwards. The Imperial period I.s – initially small to tiny – almost always set in rings of iron, bronze, silver and gold or as medallions [1. 344–348 fig. 69–71]. With the State-C., the C. technology reaches its second high point (Gemma Augustea, Grand Camée de France) [12]. Chosen gem cutters – particularly resident Greeks or Greeks who had migrated there – obtained in Rome Imperial state orders (→ Dioscorides [8]). Ancient sources report on the motifs of the private seals of Caesar, Galba, Trajan or Augustus but none of these is preserved in the original or copy [1. 315 f.]. As to its themes, portraits were accorded primary status [1. 323–328 pl. 97–100,3; 10], and there were also representations of myths that refer to Roman history as well as propagandistic symbols [1. 328–337]. The masters of the early Imperial period known by name are: Solon [3], Cleon [7], Dioscorides, Eutyches [1], Herophilus [2], Hyllus [3], Agathopus, Saturninus, Epitynchanus, Polyclitus, Gaius, Lucius (Leucius), Agathamerus, Dalion and probably Mycon [1. general index s. v. gem cutters' names, antiquity]. Included in this is also the contentious autograph of → Thamyras. Scylax [2] belongs to the period of Claudius [III 1] and Evodus to the Flavian period [1. 321 n. 100 Taf. 95,4]. Well known gem cutters of the Hadrian epoch are Antonianus, Plato and probably Coenus [1st general reg. s. v. gem cutters' names, antiquity]. The time classification of Aspasius is a matter of contention [4]. The work of → Hyperechius and of another Aspasius was done during the Antoninian period. Romulus is known to have lived in the first third of the 5th cent. AD because of the autographed sardonyx with the investiture of Valentinianus III by Honorius in 423 [1. 323[108], pl. 96,7].

8. Magical intaglios (2nd–4th cents. AD)

The magical I.s that were widespread across the entire empire particularly under Septimius Severus (so-called 'gnostic, basilidianic I.s', 'Abraxes'; → Magic; → *phylaktḗrion*) [1. 350–362; 13; 14; 15] were not sealing stones but amulets and talismans. Images and inscriptions are positively cut legibly on the stone that was presumably set as a ring stone or medallion, rubbed in the hand as a stroking stone or worn under the clothing [14. 23 f.]. The effectiveness of the amulets was based on the synthesis of motif, inscription and material/colour (e.g. all colours of jasper, chalcedony, carneole, haematite, magnetite, lapis lazuli) [15]. The stones corresponding with magical texts (→ Magic papyri; PGM) and sorcery refer particularly to the areas of belief in the afterworld, medical-magical healing remedies and love charms [13; 15]. Based on numerous syncretistic influences in image and inscription, Alexandria [1] is assumed to be the place of manufacture of these gems with a mostly unknown finding place [13. 22 ff.; 14. 8–10[18]]. Passed down through the Middle Ages and in the context of alchemy, the magical I.s achieved a second period of flourishing in the Modern Age [15. 345 ff. pl. 89–95, 603–649].

→ Precious stones; → Magic; → Phylakterion; → Jewellery; → Sphragis; → Seals; → Gem cutting/intaglios

1 Zazoff, AG 2 Furtwängler 3 CMS
4 J. Boardman, Archaic Greek Gems. Schools and Artists in the Sixth and Early Fifth Centuries BC, 1968 5 Id., Greek Gems and Finger Rings, 1970 6 Richter, Portraits 7 G. M. A. Richter, The Engraved Gems of the Greeks and Etruscans, 1968 8 Id., The Engraved Gems of the Romans, 1971 9 M.-L. Vollenweider, Die S. und ihre Künstler in spätrepublikanischer und augusteischer Zeit, 1966 10 Id., Die Porträtgemmen der röm. Republik, 1972–1974 11 R. Fellmann-Brogli, Gemmen und Kameen mit ländlichen Kultszenen. Unt. zur Glyptik der ausgehenden röm. Republik und der Kaiserzeit, 1996 12 W. R. Megow, Kameen von Augustus bis Alexander Severus, 1987 13 C. Bonner, Studies in Magical Amulets, Chiefly Graeco-Egyptian, 1950 14 H. Philipp, Mira et Magica. Gemmen im Äg. Mus. der Staatl. Museen Preußischer Kulturbesitz, 1986 15 S. Michel, Die magischen Gemmen im Britischen Mus. (ed. H. and P. Zazoff), 2001.

AGD; A. D'Agostini, Gemme del Museo Civico di Ferrara, 1984; R. Casal García, Colección de glíptica del museo arqueológico nacional (Madrid). Serie de entalles romanos, 1990; S. Finogenova (ed.), Die Slg. ant. Gemmen im Staatl. Mus. für bildende Kunst A. S. Puschkin, 1993 (Russ.); M. Henig, Classical Gems. Ancient and Modern Intaglios and Cameos in the Fitzwilliam Mus., Cambridge, 1994; A. R. Mandrioli Bizzarri, La collezione di gemme del Museo Civico Archeologico di Bologna, 1987; U. Pannuti, Catalogo della collezione glittica, Museo Archeologico Nazionale di Napoli, vol. 2, 1994; G. Platz-Horster, Die ant. Gemmen aus Xanten, 1987; E. Zwierlein-Diehl, Die ant. Gemmen des Kunsthistor. Mus. in Wien, vol. 3, 1991. S. MI.

Gemellae Camp and city in *Numidia*, situated 25 km south-west of Biskra, modern El-Kasbat. G. was part of the fortification system of the *fossatum*. A detachment of the *legio III Augusta* and the *ala I Pannoniorum* were here at various times. In the 4th cent. the *praepositus limitis Gemellensis* had its quarters in G. Evidence: Tab. Peut. 5,1; Not. Dign. Occ. 25,24. Inscriptions: CIL VIII 1, 2482; Suppl. 2, 17976–17985; AE 1969–1970, 222 no. 741(?); 1989, 287 no. 883.

→ Limes

J. Baradez, G., in: Revue Africaine 93, 1949, 5–26. W.HU.

Gemellus

[1] Friend of King Herod I. Entrusted with political and diplomatic commissions and with the education of Alexander, the eldest son of the king of Mariamme, he

accompanied him in 23 BC to Rome for five years. When in 14 BC Herod began to distrust his son, G. fell from grace (Jos. Ant. Iud. 16,241–243). K.BR.

[2] Son of Anatolius, Cilician, brother of Apolinarius, with whom he accompanied his father, the governor, in AD 361 to Phoenicia (Lib. Ep. 304; 637). Pupil of Libanius, whose son he looked after in 391 (Lib. Ep. 233; 806; 1023; Or. 1,279). In 404/408 *praef. urbi Constantinopolitanae* (Ioh. Chrys. Ep. 79; 124; 132; 194). PLRE 1, 388 G. (2). M.MEI. and ME.STR.

Gemini see → Constellations

Geminius Roman family name, probably derived from, and in manuscripts often confused with, *Geminus* (SCHULZE 108).

I. REPUBLICAN PERIOD II. IMPERIAL PERIOD

I. REPUBLICAN PERIOD

[I 1] G. Friend of Pompey, on whose orders he murdered M. Iunius Brutus in 77 BC (Plut. Pompeius 2,6; 16,6).

[I 2] G. Friend of the triumvir Marcus Antonius [I 9], who tried in vain to persuade the latter to return to Rome in 32 BC and become reconciled with Octavian (Plut. Antonius 59,1). K.-L.E.

II. IMPERIAL PERIOD

[II 1] G. Equestrian. *Amicus* of Seianus; executed for his participation in the latter's 'conspiracy'. PIR² G 142.

[II 2] G. Chrestus. Equestrian. *Praefectus Aegypti* in AD 219/220 [1. 308; 2. 86]. According to Zos. 1,11,2, Severus Alexander made him *praefectus praetorio* together with Flavianus; but at the instigation of Mamaea → Ulpianus. was appointed as a higher *praefectus*.They were removed because of a plot against Ulpian. PIR² G 144.

1 G. BASTIANINI, in: ZPE 17, 1975 2 G. BASTIANINI, in: ZPE 38, 1980.

[II 3] G. Modestus. → Gabinius [II 2]. W.E.

Geminus (Γέμινος; *Géminos*) [I].

[1] Astronomer and mathematician from the school of Posidonius. Almost nothing is known about his life. The height of his creativity was around 70 BC. It is generally accepted that he lived in Rhodes. The only fully extant treatise by G. is the 'Introduction to Astronomy' (Εἰσαγωγὴ εἰς τὰ φαινόμενα). It is in the tradition of → Eudoxus and → Aratus [4]. Similarly to the later writing by → Cleomedes, it is an elementary textbook on astronomy which was supposed to serve as a preparation for the more demanding specialist literature (e.g. → Hipparchus). G. gives an easily understood, clear and almost entirely accurate description of the basic principles of astronomy; he omits the mathematical details and calculations. For the planets only the periods are stated; epicycles and eccentrics are not mentioned (apart from the eccentricity of the orbit of the sun in respect of the earth). Ch. 1 describes the zodiac and explains the annual anomaly of the sun by the eccentricity of its sphere. Ch. 2 illustrates the astrological aspects of the signs of the → zodiac and points out errors in the astrology of the nativity. Chs. 3 to 5 describe the fixed star sky, the main cycles and the celestial co-ordinates. Chs. 6 to 7 deal with the difference between a solar and a sidereal day, the length of the days in the various latitudes and seasons and also the laws for the ascent times of the signs of the zodiac. Ch. 8 describes the various calendar systems with the different attempts to bring the lunar and solar year into harmony. Ch. 9 explains the phases of the moon, chs. 10 and 11 the eclipses of the sun and the moon and ch. 12 the general motions of the planets. Chs. 13 and 14 deal with the ascents and settings and the daily course of the fixed stars and chs. 15 and 16 the division of the earth into zones based on → Eratosthenes. Ch. 17 brings comments on weather signs and ch. 18 the theory of forecasting eclipses of the moon (using the so-called Sarus cycle). The conclusion is formed by a calendar in which the weather signs and phases of the fixed stars are listed for the individual zodiac months; this section probably did not belong to the original text.

Not preserved is a comm. by G. on the *Meteōrologiká* of → Posidonius (mentioned by Simpl. in Aristot. Ph. p.291,22 DIELS).

G. also wrote a 'Theory of mathematics' (Μαθημάτων θεωρία) consisting of more than six bks. In this work, from which e.g. Proclus (Euclid comm.), Pappus and Eutocius quote, G. dealt with the logical basic principles of mathematics according to Euclid's pattern from the Stoic point of view. In his efforts to classify the basic terms, G. examined, among other things, the meaning of logical terms such as 'hypothesis', 'theorem', 'postulate' and 'axiom' and the definitions of mathematical terms (line, area, figure, angle). G. criticized Euclid's concept of the so-called parallels postulate, which he wanted to replace with a different formulation. However, the attempt at evidence, ascribed in Arabic texts to an 'Aganis', probably originates from a different author.

EDITIONS: K. MANITIUS, Gemini Elementa astronomiae, 1898 (Greek and German with suppl. to life and works) E.J. DIJKSTERHUIS, Gemini Elementorum astronomiae capita I, III–VI, VIII–XVI (with glossary), 1957 G. AUJAC, Geminus. Introduction aux phénomènes (with French transl.), 1975.

BIBLIOGRAPHY: D.R. DICKS, s.v. G., Dictionary of Scientific Biography 5, 1972, 344–347 T.L. HEATH, History of Greek Mathematics, vol.2, 1921, 222–234 A.I. SABRA, Thābit ibn Qurra on Euclid's parallels postulate, in: Journal of the Warburg and Courtauld Institutes 31, 1968, 12–32 C.R. TITTEL, s.v. Geminos 1, RE 7,1026–1050. M.F.

[2] Epigram poet, to whom the *Anthologia Palatina* attributes ten epigrams; sometimes with the *nomen gentile* Tullius in front (Anth. Pal. 9,410, however, is ascribed to Tullius Sabinus). The author could be the

Τούλλιος from the 'Garland' of Philippus (Anth. Pal. 4,2,9), perhaps identical with C. Terentius Tullius Geminus (*cos. suff.* AD 46). The epigrams mainly describe works of art, but do not rise above the commonplace and are sometimes awkwardly expressed (e.g. 6,260; 16,205). 16,205,4 seems to be a translation from Latin. The original praise of the Thracian-Macedonian River Strymon (9,707) suggests first-hand observation.

GA II 1,260–266; 2,294–299. M.G.A.

Geminus [II] Cognomen ('twin') of the Tusculan → Maecius G.; in the *fasti* of the Republican period otherwise used by the Servilii and Veturii; widespread in the Imperial period.

Degrassi, FCap. 145; Id., FCIR 253; Kajanto, Cognomina 294; Walde/Hofmann 1, 586f. K.-L.E.

Gems, Gem and cameo cutters see → Gem cutting

Genauni Alpine tribe in Raetia (Hor. Carm. 4,14,10), subjugated by Drusus in 15 BC, which, like the Breuni, was thought of as Illyrian (Str. 4,6,8); Plin. HN 3,137 has *Caenauni*, Ptol. 2,12,4 Βένλαυνοι (*Bénlaunoi*). It is thought that their dwelling places were, e.g., in the eastern Inn Valley in the Tyrol. Allocation by Paus. 8,43,4 (Britannia) is uncertain [1].

1 J.G.F. Hind, The 'Genounian' part of Britain, in: Britannia 8, 1977, 229–234.

R. Frei-Stolba, Die Räter in den ant. Quellen, in: B. Frei (ed.), Das Räterproblem in gesch., sprachl. und arch. Sicht, 1984, 6–21, esp. 13. K.DI.

Genava Most northerly *oppidum* of the Celtic tribe of the → Allobroges in the hilly area between the embouchure of the Rhône, Arve and Lake Geneva, modern Geneva. The name, like Genoa, is Ligurian. Even in the pre-Roman period the place was significant from the point of view of traffic policy: harbour complex on the south side of the embouchure of the Rhône for navigation on the Rhône and Lake Geneva, wooden bridge over the Rhône (at Pont de l'Isle) into the territory of the Helvetii. From 121 BC, G. was part of the Roman province of → Gallia Narbonensis. Caesar used the location as the starting-point for his Gallic conquests (Caes. B Gall. 1,6,3; 1,7,1). The restructuring of the Celtic fortified *oppidum* into a Roman *vicus* began in the 1st cent. BC: residential buildings in the region of the Grande Rue, the churches Cathédrale St. Pierre and La Madeleine stand on Roman foundations. It was not until late antiquity that G. acquired a city wall and at the same time became a bishop's seat. At the end of the 4th cent. G. became a *civitas* (notitia Galliarum 11: *civitas Genavensium*), but did not possess a city charter, which, with the *colonia*'s civil service, remained the preserve solely of the suburb of Vienna. The only official inscription to date from G. is the tomb inscription for an *aedilis*, probably a local police officer (CIL XII 2611; fig. in [1. no. 19]). Imperial officials with residence in G. are a tax collector [2. 369] (fig. in [1. no. 32]) and the lance corporal of a legion as harbour commandant (CIL XII 5878; fig. in [1. no. 38]). In 443 the Roman army commander Aëtius assigned the upper Rhône district to the Germanic Burgundiones as confederates, which is why the Burgundian king resided for a time in G.

1 G. Walser, Römische Inschriften der Schweiz 1, 1979
2 A. Cartier, Inscriptions romaines trouvées à Genève 1917, Anz. Schweiz. Alt. 20, 1918, 139 (= J.-L. Maier, Genavae Augustae, 1983, no. 77).

W. Drack, R. Fellmann, Die Römer in der Schweiz, 1988, 398–407; Id., Die Schweiz zur Römerzeit, 1991, 123–131; F. Staehelin, Die Schweiz in röm. Zeit, ³1948, 614f.; E. Howald, E. Meyer, Die röm. Schweiz, 1940, 219–235; L. Blondel, Le développement urbain de Genève à travers les siècles, 1946; J.-L. Maier, Genavae Augustae, 1983. G.W.

Gender see → Sex

Gender roles

I. Society II. Medicine

I. Society

A. Greece 1. Rites of Initiation for Girls and Boys 2. Gender Roles in Literature 3. Sexual Norms B. Rome

A. Greece

It was a characteristic of Greek society that the spheres of the two genders were strictly separated in a way that has little in common with the modern distinction between a private, domestic sphere and a public, political one. Neither should the house (→ *oíkos*) be seen as a purely private sphere, nor can gender roles (GR) be limited to one area only. There were divisions both within the house and within the public sphere of ancient cities. The ancient discourse on GR was characterized both by complimentariness and by demarcation.

1. Rites of Initiation for Girls and Boys

Sexual maturity was the landmark in the organization of gender relations. A number of rites marked the life of both girls (κόρη; *kórē* or respectively παρθένος; *parthénos*) and boys (κοῦρος; *koûros* or respectively νέος; *néos*), until they reached sexual maturity. In Athens, the festival of → *Ōschophória*, centring around a ritual swapping of GR, marked the end of childhood for boys and their subsequent complete integration into the citizenry as well as the *oíkos*. For young girls, their integration into the polis structure was signified by the cultic service in honour of the city goddess Athena. The ritual integration of Spartan boys and girls into the polis took place through service to Artemis Orthia and during the festivals of → *Hyakínthia*, → *Kárneia*, and *Gymnopaidíai*, amongst others. Whereas the cultic activities of girls – in Athens performed vicariously by individuals

– were targeted towards their future tasks within the *oíkos*, those of boys pointed to their participation in the → hoplite society and consisted of agones as well as the performance of sacrificial slaughter. They were prepared for these tasks in the *gymnásion* and the *palaístra*.

The wedding ritual marked the final determination of GR (→ Wedding Customs). In its centre stood the transfer of the bride (νύμφη; *nýmphē*) to the house of the bridegroom, a scene depicted on numerous wedding vessels. Only after the birth of a child was a bride referred to as γυνή (*gyné*; woman), which also included the status of a female citizen; the adult male was referred to as ἀνήρ (*anḗr*). In the view of philosophers, girls were seen as marriageable from the age of 16; for men, a later age at marriage of about 30 was recommended, an age which in Athens also marked their admittance to active political life (Pl. Leg. 785b; Aristot. Pol. 1335a 6–35). According to the evidence in forensic speeches, this was common practice in Attica; for Sparta and Crete, a lesser difference in age is transmitted (Ath. 555c; Str. 10,4,20; inscription of Gortyn VIII 35 and VII 18–19). For women, marriage meant taking over the management of the *oíkos*; in that way, the spheres of activity of men and women were defined (Xen. Oec. 7,30). The degree to which husband or wife could dispose of the dowry was subject to regionally varying regulations, as was its total amount.

2. Gender Roles in Literature

From very early on, Greek literature and philosophy reflected upon GR and relationships between the genders, and provided normative descriptions. In Homer, Telemachus directs his mother Penelope to textile work, to spinning and weaving, as her sphere of activity, whereas the spoken word was up to men; in that way, he explicitly claimed the authority within the *oíkos* for himself (Hom. Od. 1,356–359; cf. Hom. Il. 6,490–493). In Hesiod's myth of Prometheus, women are described as nothing but a plague (κακόν) for men, inflicted upon humans by Zeus in punishment for the theft of fire. In Hesiod's view, it is impossible for man to avoid marriage, because without it he would lack care in his old age, and there would be no direct descendants to inherit his possessions; at best, marriage was characterized by a balance of bad and good. Women were no helpmeets in poverty, but like drones, they devoured what men had toiled for (Hes. Theog. 570–612). In the version of the *Érga*, the first woman, → Pandora, carried with her in a large casket all manner of evils, and from then on, earth was full of evil for mankind (men) (Hes. Op. 53–105).

Such negative view of gender relations and thus the role of women not only found expression in tragedies as well as comedies, but also led to repeated learned discussions (cf. e.g. Eur. Med.; Aristoph. Thesm.). Catalogues of negative female qualities were compiled, culminating in the accusations of unfaithfulness, of unrestrained eating, and the inclination to drink undiluted wine (Aristoph. Eccl. 220–238). Aristophanes describes how Euripides was accused by the women at the Thesmophoria because of his allegedly anti-female tragedies (Thesm. 383–431). However, comedy is also the literary genre, in which the transgression of traditional GR can go the furthest; in Aristophanes' *Lysistrátē*, women refuse to fulfil their sexual role, and in his *Ekklēsiázousai*, women take over the running of the polis, having first dressed up as men. Conversely, men appeared on stage in women's clothes, such as the poet Agathon (Aristoph. Thesm. 91–267).

In his *Oeconomicus* of the 4th cent. BC, Xenophon provides a clear definition of the competencies of the genders within the domestic sphere in reference to conditions within nature, while emphasizing the complimentariness of GR. His demarcation is based on a spatial division into an outer and an inner sphere. Provision and storage, care for children or the sick, as well as textile production were the responsibility of the mistress of the house, the δέσποινα (*déspoina*); whereas agricultural work and martial activities were male domains (Xen. Oec. 7,22–43; similar in Aristot. Oec. 1,1343b–1344a). These descriptions depicted an ideal type, e.g. in reference to conditions in Attica, but these ideals were at the same time frustrated by a vast range of social practices. Thus it was quite common for women to work in a number of professions, including some where they worked in public, e.g. on the Agora (Dem. Or. 57,30–36; 57,45). Furthermore, competing images of the ideal state existed. Plato, for example, rather tended towards an abolition of GR in favour of a model, in which responsibilities were not ordered according to gender, but social status, and both men and women would go to war and be involved in the government of the polis (Pl. Resp. 451c–458b; Leg. 806a f.).

3. Sexual Norms

The adherence to GR included the compliance with certain sexual norms, which were defined differently for both sexes. In classical Greece, women were expected to abstain from sexual intercourse before and outside of marriage (Plut. Solon 23,2; Aeschin. In Tim. 183; Demosth. 59,85ff.; Lys. 1); men, by contrast, were free to mix with → *hetaerae* or prostitutes (Xen. Mem. 2,2,4; Demosth. 59,122). In the extreme, a man could even take *hetaerae* and prostitutes into the shared marital home (And. 4,14; Plut. Alcibiades 8), an act reflected upon in tragedies (Soph. Trach. 531ff.). At least in ethics, the demand for mutual marital faithfulness prevailed in the course of the 4th cent. BC (Pl. Leg. 840d–841e), the unfaithfulness of a man was seen as a wrong (ἀδικία δὲ ἀνδρὸς αἱ θύραζε συνουσίαι γιγνόμεναι, Aristot. Oec. 1344a). Furthermore, male prostitution was seen as a violation of behavioural norms and perceived as effemination (Aeschin. In Tim. 185).

Also important for the understanding of GR are Aristotle's fundamental observations in his zoological works on male and female nature; in these, he described the opposition of the genders as that of motion and matter, of activity and passivity (Aristot. Gen. an. 716a; 729b). The world of women – the sphere of the *oíkos*, textile production, but also wedding rites – as well as the sphere of men – war and battle, but also symposion

and sports – were frequently the subject of vase paintings, an important additional source of material for the analysis of GR in Greece alongside literary texts.
→ Work; → Marriage; → Woman

1 C. Bérard et al., Die Bilderwelt der Griechen, 1985, 127–153 2 P. Brulé, La fille d'Athènes, 1987 3 C. Calame, Les chœurs des jeunes filles, 1977 4 D. Cohen, Law, Sexuality and Society, 1991 5 H. P. Foley (ed.), Reflections of Women in Antiquity, 1981 6 L. Foxhall, Household, Gender and Property in Classical Athens, in: CQ 39, 1989, 22–44 7 R. Hawley, B. Levick (ed.), Women in Antiquity, 1995 8 D. W. K. Lacey, The Family in Classical Greece, 1968 9 J. J. Winkler, The Constraints of Desire, 1990 10 R. Zoepffel, Aufgaben, Rollen und Räume von Mann und Frau im archa. und klass. Griechenland, in: Id., J. Martin (ed.), Aufgaben, Rollen und Räume von Mann und Frau, 1989, 443–500. B.W.-H.

B. Rome

In Rome, a clear separation in the spheres of the genders set in at the age of seven, the end of childhood: for as long as education was a family matter, sons accompanied their fathers and were thus introduced to their future tasks, and girls stayed with their mothers and learnt about the management of a household. Only from about 150 BC onwards was the teaching of children of upper-class families handed over to specialists. With sexual maturity, the *puella* became a *virgo*, the *puer* a *pubens*. Boys were garbed in the *toga virilis*, and led to the forum in a solemn procession (*deductio in forum*). Girls, by contrast, only discarded their *bulla* as part of the wedding ceremony, an indication that they were originally married soon after reaching sexual maturity. However, that changed at the time of the Principate. In parallel with a boy's procession to the forum, a girl was conducted to the house of her husband (*deductio in domum*). For young men of the elite, this was followed by a period of military and political training, before they entered marriage. As indicated by the Latin term for marriage – *matrimonium* (derived from *mater*) – it was seen as the most important task of a wife to provide her husband with descendants. However, it was not necessary for a woman to have children of her own in order to attain the highest social standing as *mater familias* or as *matrona*. The status of *pater familias*, too, most importantly depended on the fact that the man in question was no longer under the power of a relative (→ Family).

It seems to have been a serious problem in the relationship of the sexes that some men were socially unable to feed a family, and a negative attitude towards marriage seems to have been widespread; even before 131 BC, the censor Q. Caecilius Metellus felt the need to encourage Roman men to get married and to raise children (Liv. Per. 59; Gell. NA 1,6). Prostitution and concubinate offered unmarried men the opportunity for sexual relations. Anti-marriage positions were often expressed in literature, as by Juvenal, who advised against marriage particularly with reference to female unfaithfulness (Juv. 6,25–37); Lucretius, in turn, warned against any kind of amorous relationship (Lucr. 4,1040–1207). On the other hand, the perception of marriage from the late Republic onwards also included increasingly mutual affection, understanding, and solidarity between husband and wife; an example for this is provided by the → *Laudatio Turiae*, and both Tacitus and Pliny quote the examples of women who chose to die with their husbands, when the latter were persecuted by the *principes* (Tac. Ann. 16,34; Plin. Ep. 3,16,6–13). In the description of his own marriage, Pliny emphasizes the mutual interest in literature (Plin. Ep. 4,19); Musonius Rufus and Plutarch both stipulate the need for the husband to be faithful in marriage (Musonius 12; Plut. Mor. 144).

In accordance with the traditional ideal, women were expected to 'spin wool, be pious, modest, thrifty, chaste, and home-loving' (CIL VI 11602 = ILS 8402: *lanifica, pia, pudica, frugi, casta, domiseda*). However, this ideal did not always match with reality: in large aristocratic households, the textile work of the woman became largely demonstrative in character (Suet. Aug. 73). In the agrarian context, by contrast, this kind of work was still wide spread, and the women of the house was also responsible for provisions and storage, food preparation, and the education of the children; on large estates, women worked on the fields or supervised the household as *vilicae* (Cato Agr. 143,2; Verg. G. 1,293–297; 1,390–392; Varro, Rust. 2,10,6–9; Columella 12 praef. 4–8; 12,3,6). For the great number of small and medium-sized artisans and traders, an involvement of the wives in their husband's profession has to be assumed; independent female owners of workshops and enterprises are also documented. The wide range of women's spheres of work is also evident in grave inscriptions.
→ Woman

1 M.-L. Deissmann, Aufgaben, Rollen und Räume von Mann und Frau im ant. Rom, in: J. Martin, R. Zöpffel (ed.), Aufgaben, Rollen und Räume von Frau und Mann, 1989, 501–564 2 J. F. Gardner, Women in Roman Law and Society, 1986 3 N. Kampen, Image and Status. Roman Working Women in Ostia, 1981 4 A. Mette-Dittmann, Die Ehegesetze des Augustus, 1991 5 B. D. Shaw, The Age of Roman Girls at Marriage. Some Reconsiderations, in: JRS 77, 1987, 30–46 6 T. Späth, Männlichkeit und Weiblichkeit bei Tacitus, 1994 7 S. Treggari, Jobs for Women, in: AJAH 1, 1976, 76–104 8 Id., Roman Marriage. Iusti coniuges from the Time of Cicero to the Time of Ulpian, 1991. I.ST.

II. Medicine

The hierarchization of the genders and the culture-specific roles of men and women were supported in a variety of ways by ancient medical authors; however, some of their anatomic models suggest that in view of the fundamental similarity between the male and the female body, genders were less perceived as complete opposites, but rather as the result of different degrees of heat within the body (→ Sex). The contrast between 'active' and 'passive' was linked to the gender problem through comparisons such as Aristotle's, that in conception, man was the carpenter and woman the wood (with his seed giving form to the material which she provided, Gen. an. 729a25–35; 729b12–21). In sexual intercourse, women were assigned the passive role in ancient Greece.

'Strength' and 'weakness' characterized the genders in the medical theories of many Hippocratic authors. It was assumed that in differentiation and formation, the male foetus developed faster than the female one (i.e. in 30 days as opposed to the 42 for girls), also corresponding with the duration of lochia after the birth of a boy, i.e. 30 days, but 42 after the birth of a girl (De natura pueri 18 = 7,504–6 L.). Even though a female foetus developed more slowly, after their birth, girls, because of their physical weakness and their way of life, were quicker than boys in reaching puberty and the power of judgement, but also old age (De octomensuali 9,7 = 7,450 L.). Soranus (Gyn. 1,45) reports on the widespread belief amongst his contemporaries that a male foetus moved more actively than a female one, thus making it possible to deduce from a pregnant woman's rosy face that she was carrying a boy. The gynaecological treatises of the *Corpus Hippocraticum* generally describe women as warmer and moister than men. In Aristotle's view, however, warmth is associated with the positive end of the temperature scale; for that reason, women are classified as the colder and moister sex, as the female body is seen in every aspect as physiologically inferior to the male one. Aristotle claimed that women lacked the necessary inner heat required to turn blood into semen (Part. an. 650a8ff.; Gen. an. 775a14–20). Because of this lack of warmth, women also aged faster than men; as inferior beings, their life-span expired sooner (Gen. an. 775a14ff.). They were also exhausted by the experience of childbirth (Hist. an. 583b23–8; 582a21–4; cf. Sor. Gyn. 1,42).

The different bodily features of men and women were reflected on the social level in women being responsible for the 'interior', and men for the 'exterior'. It was believed that the nature of women was such that their innate qualities best fitted their social roles as housewives and mothers (Xen. Oec. 7,20–43), whereas men were made to withstand extreme temperatures, enabling them to travel outside their home regions. Woman were seen as soft and moist, and leading a sedentary life, in contrast with men whose flesh was firm and dry (→ Gynaecology).

Female medical practitioners only rarely appear in the Hippocratic works (e.g. De mulierum affectibus 1,68 = 8,144 L.), but were more common in the post-Hellenistic periods; the role of the physician was seen as ideally suited to men, because illness was associated with the loss of control in male members of the social elite. A man showed moral greatness by issuing orders, a woman by obedience (Aristot. Pol. 1260a 20–23); for that reason, the obvious loss of control of his own body as a consequence of illness would disqualify a man from his role as commander. In such instance, women, who were traditionally seen as incapable even to strive for self-control, would be unable to assist a sick man. With reference to the metaphorical language of poetry and tragedy with its analogies of women and sacrificial animals, Greek physicians drew parallels between the blood lost by a sacrificial animal and that by a woman during menstruation or after childbirth. In their suggestion that only men could shed the blood of others, whereas women shed their own blood, these texts emphasized sacrifice and war as symbols of the role of men, while within the polis, whose defence was again part of the male role, women were allocated the task of reproduction [1].

1 H. King, Sacrificial Blood, in: Helios 13, 1987, 117–126.

G.E.R. Lloyd, Science, Folklore and Ideology, 1983, 86–94. H.K.

Genealogy In early societies, largely based on family organizations, genealogy as a derivation of a person's descent in the form of a pedigree is often used as a means of legitimation and (pseudo-historical) memory, which was always also directed at publicity (genealogy from Greek γενεαλογεῖν; *genealogeîn*, 'to talk about [one's] origin').

I. Near East and Egypt II. Greece III. Rome

I. Near East and Egypt

The purpose of lineage, transmitted in the form of a genealogy (generally patrilineal; exceptions in the case of Egyptian rulers), was to legitimate a claim to rulership, to tenure of a particular office (priests, high-ranking officials), to professional status (e.g. scribe), or to property rights (→ Succession, law of), with the length of the pedigree adding weight to the claim. This is illustrated e.g. by the naming of ancestors of scribes and priests (Egypt, OT), the lists of kings (Mesopotamian, OT, Egypt), the pedigrees listed in the inscriptions of the → Achaemenids, and the claims of rulers to divine descent and the like, the fictitiousness of which must have been apparent to their contemporaries (→ Gilgamesh Epic). Concepts of prehistory were also presented as genealogies (Gen. 4,1–5,32), as were historical facts ([2]; 'Table of Nations' in Gen. 10; a political 'map' at the time of David) and theology (genealogy of the gods in Mesopotamia and Egypt; 'Genealogy of Jesus Christ' in Mt 1,1–17). As it was the purpose of genealogies to pass on historical memories in oral or written form and to provide explanations of complex correlations and developments, it is very difficult in individual cases to ascertain the relationship between knowledge [2] – confirmed by primary sources – and fiction.

→ Historiography; → Manetho

1 H. Brunner, s.v. Abstammung, LÄ 1, 13–18
2 C. Wilcke, Genealogical and Geographical Thought in the Sumerian King List, in: H. Behrens et al. (ed.), Studies

in Honor of A.W. Sjöberg, 1989, 557–571 3 R.R. Wilson, Genealogy and History in the Biblical World, 1977 (with bibliography). J.RE.

II. Greece

In the Greek archaic period, the awareness of mythical descent was a source of particular status and pride: in Homer (cf. e.g. Il. 6,145–211), the heroes vaunt their pedigree prior to battle, listing up to eight generations; in his 'Theogony' as well as in the 'Catalogue of Women', Hesiod has the pedigrees of male and female lines reaching far back into mythical times. But genealogies retain their importance in the classical period (cf. Pol. 9,1,4). In Athens, aristocrats emphasized their descent from heroes and even gods: the → Philaids, to whom Miltiades and Cimon belonged, traced their descent back to Ajax [1] (Pherecydes, FGrH 3 F 2; Marcellinus, Thuc. 3); the orator Andocides [1] claimed to have descended through Odysseus from Hermes (Hellanicus, FGrH 323 a F 24), Alcibiades [3] through Eurysaces from Zeus (Plut. Alcibiades 1); Plato's family was linked with Solon and Codrus (Plut. Solon 1,2). Even in Sparta with its emphasis on equality, genealogies enjoyed general popularity (Pl. Hp. mai. 285d); they were not merely the privilege of kings, but widely spread, e.g. in the Talthybiad family of heralds (Hdt. 7,134,1; → Talthybius). Mythical or heroic descent was also claimed by cities, esp. colonies (→ *apoikía*) or tribes (→ Phyle; → Attica, map of Attic phyles).

The great importance which early beginnings, and the qualities and deeds of distant ancestors had for the social status, political claims, and moral attitudes of subsequent generations soon gave rise to a literary form of genealogy in early prose, e.g. in Hecataeus of Miletus, Acusilaus of Argus, Pherecydes of Athens, and Hellanicus of Lesbos. As the oral tradition placed the greatest emphasis on the mystical forefathers and often ignored the intermediate links, the authors of genealogies often employed a rather fierce rationalism to force the fragmentary or contradictory tradition into a system and a pseudo-historical whole, in order to generate a complete pedigree. The image of early Greek history remains to a high degree coloured by the explanatory model and systematic order of genealogy.

F. Jacoby, Abhandlungen zur griechischen Geschichtsschreibung, 1956; W. Leschhorn, Gründer der Stadt, 1984; P. Philippson, G. als mythische Form (Symbolae Osloenses, Suppl. 7), 1936; R. Thomas, Oral Tradition and Written Record in Classical Athens, 1989; M.L. West, The Hesiodic Catalogue of Women, 1985. K.MEI.

III. Rome

Typical of the Roman form of genealogy is the presence of patrilineal ancestors (agnates) in the name, extending to the inheritability of the → cognomen. Furthermore, in line with the development of a patrician-plebeian nobility (see also [3]), the magistrateship held by ancestors played a central role in genealogically based social standing: in the most important public memorial ritual of the elite, the funeral procession (*pompa funebris*), in which dead ancestors were introduced in the funeral oration (→ *laudatio funebris*) and represented by wearers of ancestral masks (→ *imagines*), those ancestors who did not achieve curule office (→ *cursus honorum*) were ignored [4]. In contrast, claims based on divine ancestry were of lesser importance by the later years of the Republic [1]. As early as the 3rd cent. BC, it was an important motive of early forms of → historiography to secure such claims; in the 2nd cent. a massive number of false claims to important ancestors, esp. boasting early or multiple consulates, must have arisen (in detail in [6]). The → *fasti*, listing the highest officials in chronological order, later provided an ordered way to formulate and settle such claims [5]. In the Imperial period, genealogical constructs played an important role in securing dynastic claims, which in turn were propagated by name forms and a corresponding selection of imperial feast days [2].

1 C. Koch, Der röm. Juppiter, 1937 2 P. Herz, Kaiserfeste der Prinzipatszeit, in: ANRW II.16/2, 1135–1200 3 K.J. Hölkeskamp, Die Entstehung der Nobilität, 1987 4 E. Flaig, Die Pompa Funebris, in: O.G. Oexle (ed.), Memoria als Kultur, 1995, 115–148 5 J. Rüpke, Fasti, in: Klio 77, 1995, 184–202 6 F. Mora, Fasti e schemi chronologici, 1998. J.R.

Geneleus Sculptor of the archaic period, famous for the family group with his signature in the Heraion on → Samos (560–550 BC). The group consists of the reclining figure of the founder ...ιλάρχος, three standing girls (unknown name, Philippe, Ornithe), the fragments of a young man, and the enthroned mother Phileia; apart from Ornithe (Berlin, SM, Inv. 1739), all the figures are on Samos (Vathy, Mus. Inv. 768). G. proves himself a master of Ionian sculpture because of the minute detail to which he worked: the folds of the garments and the voluptuous body structures and mass of material, typical of eastern Greek sculpture, especially noticeable in the reclining figure. The need to gather a garment because of its length (cf. Ath. 12,525f) as well as the light stance of the *korai*, show G. to be a progressive artist. A further *kore* on Samos (Vathy, Mus.) is also seen as connected to G.

B. Freyer-Schauenburg, Bildwerke der archaischen Zeit und des Strengen Stils, in: Samos 11, 1974, 106–130, no. 58–63; W. Fuchs, J. Floren, Die griechische Plastik 1. Die geometrische und archaische Plastik, HbdA 1987, 345; H.v. Steuben, Die Geneleosgruppe in Samos, in: Armagani. FS J. Inan, 1989, 137–144; W. Martini, Die archaische Plastik der Griechen, 1990; H.J. Kienast, Die Basis der Geneleos-Gruppe, in: JDAI(A) 107, 1992, 29–42; B. Fehr, Kouroi e korai, in: S. Settis et al. (ed.), I Greci. Storia, Cultura, Arte, Società 1, 1996, 810–813. R.H.

Genera causarum (γένη τῶν λόγων ῥητορικῶν; *génē tôn lógōn rhētorikôn*).

A. The Branches of Oratory B. The individual genres of speech

A. The Branches of Oratory

The doctrine of the *genera causarum* (*GC*) was developed in particular by Aristotle, who divided all oratorical topics into three groups (Rh. 1,3 = 1358b6–8), whereas his predecessors distinguished several types (*eídē, species*) and only considered two *GC*, i.e. the deliberative and the judicial. Two *GC* are mentioned in Pl. Phdr. 261b [7. 170; 4. 258], and the same two *GC* together with seven *eídē* appear in the → *Rhetorica ad Alexandrum* (1,1 = 1421b6–12), written in *c.* 340 BC before Aristotle's 'Rhetoric' [8. 114; 1. 233]. In its teachings, the *Rhetorica ad Alexandrum* is based partly on Isocrates, partly on Theodectes [1. 224–230; 47–55]. Of the initial division into three (the version τρία γένη of the MSS has been restored by M. Fuhrmann in contrast to Spengel), only two points are developed later on, because the *génos epideiktikón* (*genus demonstrativum*; epideictic oratory) is no longer extant. The wording in [Aristot.] Rh. Alex. corresponds with Quint. Inst. 3,4,9 and Syrianus in Hermog. II 2,17–21 Rabe with the exception that Quintilian cites Anaximenes as the source for his quote, whereas Syrianus attributes it to Aristotle (cf. [2. 189–198; 205–207]; opposing view in [1. 212–218; 6. 684–688; and 10. 56–61]). It seems therefore likely that the *GC* were either created or systematized by Aristotle and only introduced into the Rh. Alex. with the interpolation of the *génos epideiktikón* in accordance with Syrianus [1. 218].

Aristotle (Rh. 1,3 = 1358b 13ff.) offers a justification of the division into three groups, based on the time the oratorical topic refers to: the *génos symbouleutikón* (*genus deliberativum*; political speeches/deliberative genre) with the future, the *dikanikón* (*genus iudiciale*; forensic speeches) with the past, and the *epideiktikón* with the present. This classification also corresponds to the role of the listener, who can be either spectator or judge: if he has to judge on future actions, he is referred to as a member of the public assembly (deliberative *genus*), if he judges on past deeds, he is seen as a member of a court of law (forensic *genus*), if he judges on the orator's ability, he is taken to be a spectator ('ceremonial oratory of display'). In this way, Aristotle provides philosophical and rational reasons for the tripartition. The order in which Aristotle names them in his introduction is noteworthy – *génos symbouleutikón, dikanikón, epideiktikón* – though the order of the latter two is reversed in his more detailed treatment.

Among Latin authors, the doctrine of the *GC* first appears in Cicero (Inv. 1,7) and in the → *Rhetorica ad C. Herennium* (1,2), in both instances in the order *demonstrativum, deliberativum, iudiciale*. This order is attributed by [12. 32] to the Stoics. Apart from the above-mentioned instances, it can also be found in Cic. Inv. 2,12; Part. 69; Quint. Inst. 3,3,14 and passim, Consultus Fortunatianus 1,1; Mar. Vict. Ars grammatica 192,45H.; Cassiod. Inst. 2,2,3; Albinus 526,35H.; Emporius Rhetor 570,26H. However, it is striking that it is possible for Cicero after only a few lines to switch to a different order of *GC*: *genus iudiciale, deliberativum, demonstrativum* (Inv. 1,8, also De orat. 1,141; 2,341; Part. 10; Top. 91; Quint. Inst. 2,21,23; 3,8,54; Mart. Cap. 220,17f. Dick 4.259f.). It is therefore justifiable to state that the Aristotelian development of this rhetorical doctrine was adopted by all subsequent rhetors, with the exception of Hermagoras of Temnos ([13. 4f.; 9. 81[1]]; for the non-acceptance of his position in Rhet. Her. and Cic. Inv. see [3. 219]).

B. The individual genres of speech

The *genus demonstrativum* is subdivided into *laus* and *vituperatio*, corresponding to Anaximenes' *eídos enkōmiastikón* and *psektikón* ([Aristot.] Rh. Alex. 1421b6ff.) (Cic. Inv. 1,7); the division into praise and rebuke is also found in Aristot. Rh. 1358b 12f. The concept of a 'ceremonial oratory of display' (from *epídeixis*) was introduced by Aristotle and Theophrastus in order to separate it from true rhetoric, whereas in Rome an orator also had to perform other duties such as giving the → *laudationes funebres*, assessing a defendant or witnesses, and blaming a political opponent [2. 120ff.]. The particular characteristic of the *genus demonstrativum* rests on the difference between a spectator and a judge, the latter being under real pressure to come to a decision, and on the absence of any competitive aspect; its aesthetic character had been emphasized by Isocrates (Or. 4,11) [7. 173]. In substitution for *epideiktikón*, the Stoics introduced the term *enkōmiastikón* (according to Diog. Laert. 7,42; cf. [14. 21; 12. 31; 2. 126[4]; 4. 261f.]). The corresponding term used by Latin authors is *laudativum* (Cic. Part. or. 10; 70; Quint. Inst. 3,3,14; 3,4,12; 3,7,28).

As far as the *genus deliberativum* is concerned, the term *dēmēgorikón* is used in the pre-Aristotelian rhetoric of Plato and Anaximenes (Pl. Soph. 222e; Resp. 365d; Rh. Alex. 1354b 23ff.), translated in Quint. Inst. 3,4,9–14; 9,4,130 as *contionalis*; the most common terminology, however, is *symbouleutikón*. According to the Rh. Alex. (1421b 21ff.), attributable to Anaximenes [2], and Aristotle (Rh. 1358b8f.), the fundamental elements of this *genus* are persuasion and dissuasion (*protropḗ* and *apotropḗ*, Lat. *suasio* and *dissuasio*: Rhet. Her. 1,2; Quint. Inst. 3,6,8; Cassiod. Inst. 2,2,3; Isid. Orig. 2,4,3; alternative view in Cic. Inv. 1,7, see also [4. 263]). According to Cicero (Inv. 2,156; De orat. 2,335), its main points are *honestas* and *utilitas* (slightly different in Rhet. Her. 3,3, see also [9. 150; 8. 310ff.; 3. 257; 4. 262f.]).

The *genus iudiciale* (*dikanikón/ḗ* in Pl. Soph. 222c) concerns legal disputes, *causae forenses* (see also Cic. Brut. 44; Or. 12; 30; 120), and comprises the most important area of rhetoric. It consists of accusation and defence (*accusatio* and *defensio*). Its link to the doctrine of → *status* is provided by the *krinómenon* theory: in the interplay of accusation and defence, the *quaestio* 'point of contention' is defined as the basis of each *status*. The *status* doctrine developed by Hermagoras, was still applied only to the *genus iudiciale* in the Rhet. Her., whereas later rhetors such as Martianus Capella (232,1f. DICK) recognized *status* in all three *GC* (see also in detail [5. 29–50]).

1 K. BARWICK, Die Rhetorik ad Alexandrum und Anaximenes ..., in: Philologus 110, 1966, 212–245; Philologus 111, 1967, 45–55 2 V. BUCHHEIT, Untersuchung zur Theorie des Genos Epideiktikon von Gorgias bis Aristoteles, 1960 3 G. CALBOLI, Cornifici Rhetorica ad Herennium, ²1993 4 L. CALBOLI MONTEFUSCO, Consulti Fortunatiani Ars Rhetorica, 1979 5 Id., La dottrina degli "status" nella retorica greca e romana, 1986 6 M. FUHRMANN, Untersuchung zur Textgeschichte der pseudo-aristotelischen Alexander-Rhetorik (AAWM 7), 1965, 547–747 7 D. A. G. HINKS, Tria G.C., in: CQ 30, 1936, 170–176 8 G. A. KENNEDY, The Art of Persuasion in Greece, 1963 9 D. MATTHES, Hermagoras von Temnos 1904–1955, in: Lustrum 3, 1958, 58–214 10 D. C. MIRHADY, Aristotle, the Rhetorica ad Alexandrum and the tria g.c., in: W. W. FORTENBAUGH, D. C. MIRHADY (ed.), Peripatetic Rhetoric after Aristotle, 1994, 54–65 11 L. PERNOT, La rhétorique de l'éloge dans le monde gréco-romain, 1993 12 F. STRILLER, De Stoicorum studiis rhetoricis, 1886 13 G. THIELE, Hermagoras, 1893 14 R. VOLKMANN, Die Rhetorik der Griechen und Römer in systematischer Übersicht, ²1885. G.C.

Genera dicendi (χαρακτῆρες τῆς λέξεως, *charaktêres tês léxeōs*).

A. CONCEPT AND CLASSIFICATIONS B. DEVELOPMENT C. LATER RECEPTION

A. CONCEPT AND CLASSIFICATIONS

Genera dicendi (*GD*) is taken as the usual term for the doctrine of style (as in Cic. Orat. 20; 69; Quint. Inst. 12,10,58; Isid. Orig. 2,17 H.), alongside *elocutionis genera* (Iul. Vict. rhet. 22 p. 438,8 H., 92,12 GIOM.-CELENTANO; Aquila rhet. 27,10f.H.; Mart. Cap. 479,5 H.; Consultus Fortunatianus 3,8 [5. 510,5f.] as sing. *genus e.*). In the earliest Latin attestation (Rhet. Her. 4,11), *elocutio* and *genera* are linked, albeit separated by twelve words; *genera elocutionis* does not exist as a fixed expression. The *GD* are referred to as *figurae*, a hitherto unused term, because the Greek *schêma* was not translated as *figura*, but as *exornatio* [3. 287]. In Greek, alongside the standard expression *charaktêres* [11. 80], we also find the term *plasmata* being used (e.g. Dion. Hal. Demosthenes 33, p. 203,9–24 U.-R.; Ps.-Plut. Vita Homeri 72 [13. 68–70; 12. 331–333]). As a concept, the *GD* first appear in Rhet. Her. 4,11–16, referred to as *virtutes* or respectively *vitia orationis* ('virtues' or respectively 'flaws of speech', *aretaí* or respectively *kakíai tês léxeōs*); a distinction is made between 1) *genus grave* or respectively *grande* (*charaktḗr hadrós* or respectively *hypsēlós*); 2) *genus mediocre* (*ch. mésos*); 3) *genus humile* or respectively *extenuatum* (*ischnós*; for the terminology, see [5. 449]), and negatively (Rhet. Her. 4,15f.) between 1) *genus sufflatum* or respectively *inflatum*; 2) *dissolutum* or respectively *fluctuans*; 3) *exile* or respectively *aridum* or *exangue*. The flaws (*vitia*) are the result of violations of the *prépon* [3. 294], one of the four → *virtutes dicendi* in Theophrastus' system. Alongside the three *GD* was a fourth, *floridum* (*anthērón*), close to both the middle and the high style (Quint. Inst. 12,10,58; also schol. Dion. 449,30f. HILGARD). Demetrius Phalereus' De elocutione 36 lists four *GD* of Peripatetic origin, of whom *megaloprepḗs* and *deinós* seem to correspond with *ch. hadrós*, and *glaphyrós* with *anthērón* (cf. Dion. Hal. Comp. epit. 21, p. 95,16 U.-R.). Macrob. Sat. 5,1,7 mentions alongside *copiosum*, *breve*, *siccum* also a *genus pingue et floridum* ('rich and flowering'), and Diom. 1,483,7 distinguishes four *poḗmatos charaktêres: makrós, brachýs, mésos,* and *anthērós* ('grand, brief, middle, flowering'); the latter, however, is also seen as a feature common to all three *GD* (Ps.-Plut. Vita Homeri 72f.; schol. Theocr. p. 11,11), or alternatively as a particular feature of *hadrós* and *ischnós* (a Stoic peculiarity; comprehensively discussed in [5. 447–452]).

B. DEVELOPMENT

The questions of when and by whom the theory of the *GD* was developed are both contentious [13. 55–111]. It is frequently attributed to Theophrastus, or to educational exercises of *grammatici* and *rhetores* [16. 93]. The strongest objectors against its Peripatetic origins [9. 136; 16. 107–111] maintain that the Peripatetic tenet of *mesótēs*, the 'golden' mean, would only have permitted the development of a middle *genus*. However, Aristotle himself distinguished between three styles of speech as part of *hypókrisis* (*pronuntiatio*; *officia orationis*, officium [7]) – high, middle, and low (Rh. 3,1 = 1403b 26ff.; [4]). Even though in principle *hypókrisis* lies outside of the discipline of rhetorics, it still remains connected with *téchnē* through the use of language (1404a 15f.). In Rh. 2,7 = 1408a 10f., Aristotle draws a clear distinction between two different styles: a plain style should not be used for great subject matters, a grand style not for trivial ones. This congruence of subject matter and style is a recommendation later also adopted by Roman orators beginning with Cicero (Orat. 100), as part of the theory of the three styles of speech and in the same manner as Aristotle, i.e. based on the tenet of *decorum* ('appropriateness'); this stipulation develops into a topos of the *GD* [14. 8f.]. This also confirms the proximity of Aristotle's text to the doctrine of the three *GD*. In practice, most Peripatetics may well have had a preference for *mesótēs*, but in theory, at least, they were probably also acquainted with the other two styles.

An important innovation at the time of Cicero was the establishment of a link between the *GD* and the *officia oratoris* (emphasized in [6. 76f.]). With references to Quint. Inst. 12,10,58ff. and Ps.-Plut. Vita

Homeri 72, [15. xxxvf.] lists the following: 1) *genus subtile – officium docendi* ('to teach') – represented by the orators Lysias, Xenophon, Menelaus; 2) *genus medium – delectare vel conciliare* ('to please' or 'to persuade') – Isocrates, Herodotus, Nestor; 3) *genus grande – movere* ('to move emotionally') – Gorgias, Thucydides, Ulyxes. According to recent research [1. 108; 6; 7; 8], the three *officia* of Cicero's early works – *docere, conciliare, movere* – (Orat. 2,115 *et passim*) were superseded by the later triad of *docere, delectare, movere* (Cic. Brut. 185; 197ff.; 276; Orat. 69; Opt. gen. 3).

C. LATER RECEPTION

The link of the *GD* with the *officia oratoris* was continued by St. Augustine (Doctr. christ. 4,12,27). The (Ciceronian-)Augustinian tradition demanded of a good orator to have mastered all three styles (Cic. Orat. 101; Aug. Doctr. christ. 4,17,34).

The non-Augustinian tradition is split into two strands: (a) the Virgilian tradition (Donat. vita Vergilii 14 BRUMMER; Servius p. 1f. THILO), according to which Virgil's three works mark the three different styles. In this, the terminology is frequently Servian (*humilis, medius, grandiloquus*); the cultural-philosophical theory of the *ordo temporum* ('order of occupations': herdsmen: *pastores – Bucolica*, followed by farmers: *agricolae – Georgica*, and finally the battle for *culta rura*: *bellatores – Aeneid*) is found in Philargyrius and Donatus (Vita Vergilii p. 46 [14. 10f., 159]). Due to Virgil's importance, this theory found the widest recognition in the Middle Ages. (b) The Horatian tradition (Hor. Ars 26–28; 93–98; [2. 108–113, 177–181]) which, with reference to Rhet. Her. 4,15f., focusses particularly on the *vitia* as characteristic features, is later continued in Fortunatianus' (3,9; cf. [5. 452]) provision of antitypes to each style. In the Middle Ages, this theory was taken on in particular by Matthew of Vendôme (Ars versificatoria 1,30) [14. 73f.].

1 K. ADAM, Docere – delectare – movere, Diss. 1971
2 C.O. BRINK, Horace on Poetry, 1971
3 G. CALBOLI, Cornifici Rhetorica ad Herennium, ²1993
4 Id., From Aristotelian λέξις to *elocutio*, in: Rhetorica 16, 1998, 47–80
5 L. CALBOLI MONTEFUSCO, Consulti Fortunatiani Ars Rhetorica, 1979
6 Id., Aristotle and Cicero on the *officia oratoris*, in: W.W. FORTENBAUGH, D.C. MIRHADY (ed.), Peripatetic Rhetoric after Aristotle, vol. 6, 1994, 66–94
7 E. FANTHAM, Ciceronian "conciliare" and Aristotelian Ethos, in: Phoenix 27, 1973, 262–275
8 W. FORTENBAUGH, "Benevolentiam conciliare" and "animos permovere", in: Rhetorica 6, 1988, 259–273
9 G.L. HENDRICKSON, The Peripatetic Mean of Style and the Three Stylistic Characters, in: AJPh 25, 1904, 125–146
10 D.C. INNES, Theophrastus and the Theory of Style, in: W.W. FORTENBAUGH, P.M. HUBY, A.A. LONG (ed.), Theophrastus of Eresus, 1985, 251–267
11 A. KÖRTE, ΧΑΡΑΚΤΗΡ, in: Hermes 64, 1929, 69–86
12 J. MARTIN, Ant. Rhet., 1974
13 F. QUADLBAUER, Die G.D. bis Plinius d.J., in: WS 71, 1958, 55–111
14 Id., Die ant. Theorie der G.D. im lat. MA (SAWW 12), 1962
15 D.A. RUSSELL, "Longinus", On the Sublime, 1964
16 J. STROUX, De Theophrasti virtutibus dicendi, 1912
17 L. VOIT, ΔΕΙΝΟΤΗΣ, 1934. G.C.

Genesia (τὰ Γενέσια; *tà Genésia*). Name of a Greek family festival in honour of a dead ancestor (Hdt. 4,26). In Athens, it became – allegedly at Solon's instigation – a public festival of the dead, the celebrations of which on the 5th Boedromion also included a sacrifice to → Gaia (Philochorus FGrH 328 F 168).

F. JACOBY, Γενέσια. A forgotten festival of the dead, in: CQ 38, 1944, 65–75. F.G.

Genesis poetry see → Biblical poetry

Genethliakon

I. GREEK II. LATIN

I. GREEK

A *genethliakón* (γενεθλιακόν, sc. μέλος, ᾆσμα) is a poem in honour of a birthday (γενέθλιος ἡμέρα, γενέθλιον ἦμαρ), in association with a gift or standing alone. Callim. Fr. 202 is a iamb to a friend in celebration of the seventh day after the birth of his daughter. There is an isopsephic epigram written by Leonides of Alexandria (Anth. Pal. 6,321) as a birthday present to Caesar γενεθλιακαῖσιν ἐν ὥραις. Other epigrams, particularly by → Crinagoras, accompanied birthday gifts: in Anth. Pal. 6,227 Proclus is given a silver stylus, in 6,261 Simon's son receives a small bronze oil cruet, in 6,345 an unnamed lady about to be married is given roses, and in 9,239 Antonia receives poems by Anacreon on an unspecified occasion which may have been her birthday. The *genethliakòs lógos* was an important part of epideictic rhetoric. Only two examples survive: Aristid. 10 (1,113–125 DINDORF) and Himerius 44 COLONNA. The latter is closely modelled on the *tópoi*, as presented in the rhetoric treatises of Menander Rhetor 8 (= 3,413ff. SPENGEL) and Dion. Hal. Rhet. 3,1–5 (= 266,19ff. USENER-RADERMACHER). They stipulate that a birthday speech should begin with praise of the family and the place of origin, then continue by extolling the person's physical and spiritual strengths, and conclude with a prayer for the future and a long life. The existence of such treatises indicates that the genre was quite a common one, despite the limited number of extant examples. Lucian of Samosate dedicated his *Makróbioi* to Quintillus as a birthday present.

T.C. BURGESS, Epideictic Literature, 1902, 142–144; K. BURKHARD, Das antike Geburtstagsgedicht, 1991; FGE 514; GA 2,II, 214–217; J. MARTIN, Antike Rhetorik (Handbuch der Altertumswissenschaft II,3), 1974. E.R.

II. LATIN

In Roman literature, the *genethliakon* (sc. *carmen*) was a separate genre, closely linked to the customs of the *dies natalis* and the veneration of the *genius*. The earliest example is Tib. 1,7 for Messala. Hor. Carm. 4,11 is an invitation to celebrate the birthday of Maecenas. Other examples are Prop. 3,10; Ov. Tr. 3,13; 5,5; Stat. Silv. 2,3, and Pers. 2. Martial demonstrates in some of his epigrams – sometimes in a teasing tone – the importance given to birthdays (7,86; 8,64; 9,52f.; 10,24; 27; 87; 11,65; 12,60). 12,67 was dedicated to Virgil's birthday, three epigrams addressed to Lucan's widow remembered his anniversary (7,21–23; cf. Stat. Silv. 2,7). The last non-Christian example is Ausonius' *genethliacos* [*sic*] to his grandson. Christian writers tended to celebrate the day of death as a new birthday: thirteen poems by → Paulinus of Nola are *natalicia* in honour of St Felix as the patron of his home town.

F. Cairns, Generic Composition in Greek and Roman Poetry, 1972; E. Cesario, Il carme natalizio nella poesia latina, 1929. E.R.

Genethlius (Γενέθλιος; *Genéthlios*). Greek rhetor from Petra, a pupil of Minocianus and Agapetus, 2nd half of the 3rd cent. AD. He taught in Athens in rivalry to Callinicus, and died there aged 28. He wrote epideictic orations and was praised for his talent and his astounding memory (Suda s.v.). The fact that he is mentioned four times in the Schol. Demosth. (18,8; 52; 19,148; 22,3) supports the assumption that G. had written a commentary on that rhetor. Two treatises on the classification of epideictic orations are generally transmitted under the name of → Menander of Laodicea, but in the best manuscript (Par. Gr. 1741) also with the annotation Μενάνδρου ῥήτορος ἢ Γενεθλίου. As it is hardly likely that both these treatises were written by the same author and as the style of the second points with some certainty to Menander, G. comes into consideration as the author of the first.

Ed. (with commentary): D.A. Russel, N.G. Wilson, 1981. M.W.

Genetyllis (Γενετυλλίς; *Genetyllís*). The Genetyllides (pl.) were Attic goddesses, linked, as their name indicates, to birth and fertility. Their sanctuary was situated on Cape Colias. They were venerated by women in an exuberant celebration and received the sacrifice of a dog. Closely related in function were the Phocaean Gennaides (Paus. 1,1,5), and in particular → Eileithyia, who also received canine sacrifices. Documentary evidence: Aristoph. Lys. 2; Aristoph. Nub. 52; Aristoph. Thesm. 130 with schol.; Paus. 1,1,5 with schol.; Hsch., Suda s.v. G.

S. Hadzisteliou-Price, Kourotrophos, 1978, 126f.; Graf 421f. F.G.

Genita Mana Goddess, mentioned by Plutarch (Quaest. Rom. 52,277a) and Pliny (HN 29,14,58) in conjunction with a canine sacrifice. According to Plutarch, the prayer during the sacrifice was for 'none of the house slaves to become good (χρηστός, *chrēstós*)', interpreted as a euphemism for 'dead'. Plutarch links the name of the goddess to childbirth. Modern interpretations proceed hardly any further [1; 2]. A Diva Geneta appears in Agnone (mid–3rd cent. BC [3]), whereas Mana is referred to as a deity of the Underworld in Mart. Cap. 2,164; the unusual sacrifice of a dog, in any case, fits in with the link to childbirth, as is documented for various birth deities, albeit only in Greece (→ Genetyllis, → Hecate).

1 G. Wissowa, Religion und Kultus der Römer, 1912, 240 2 Latte, 95; 379 3 Vetter, 147,13. F.G.

Genius

A. Roman Development B. Christian Development

A. Roman Development

Genius is etymologically interpreted as the tutelary deity external to a man (ἀγαθὸς δαίμων, *agathòs daímōn*) or alternatively his internal power of procreation and in other life events. Academic research [2. 23; 5. 11] has resulted in a synthesis, as no prototype can be assumed for the cult of the *genius*; the *genius* is seen as a deified personality/concept located in the forehead, as manifest in an individual's innate qualities: the procreational force within each man, the power embracing his personality. The *genius* is divine and responsible for the 'life-force of all things yet to be born' (*vim omnium rerum gignendarum*, Isid. Orig. 8,11,88f.) (Apul. De deo Socratis 15,151f.; Fest. 84,3–7; Mart. Cap. 2,152). It is linked to a person (Censorinus, DN 3,1f.), not to a location like the *lares*, and in antiquity it was attributed to both men and women (Serv. Auct. Aen. 2,351); thus Juno was not originally the counterpart of the *genius*, and the link with the 'marital bed' (*lectus genialis*) does not have to be taken as absolute (Varro in Aug. Civ. 7,13). The feast of the *genius* was celebrated on the → birthday of the → *pater familias* under his protection. The housekeeper (*vilica*) made a sacrifice of flowers, consecrated wafers, and wine to him, and his forehead was touched in a gesture of veneration (Serv. Aen. 3,607); he was seen as the divine guardian of the house, being depicted as a male figure wearing a toga *(togatus: t.),* his head veiled (*capite velato*: *c.v.*), holding a *patera* (*pt.*) in his right hand and a *cornucopia* (*co.*) in the left. The depictions of the *genius* accompanied by one or more snakes [1. pl. 13,2], or as a snake himself, are clear indications of Greek religious influences (→ *agathòs daímōn*) on the development of a specific iconography [2. pl. 7 and 8,3; 10], whereas any Etruscan influence remains doubtful. It is assumed that in the early Roman period the genius was venerated aniconically. Several different types of *genius* are to be distinguished:

1) *genius familiaris*: in the *aedicula alae atrii* (small household shrine in the atrium) with images of the *penates* and both *lares* [2. pl. 8,3];

2) *genius publicus*: first venerated in the winter of 218/17 BC; iconographically the same as the personification of the *demos*: a) *Genius Augusti* (imperial geni-

us): as *t.*, *c.v.* or in full armour between two *lares*; part of the ritual staging of the Principate; the oath on the genius of the emperor/Augustus (*genius imperatoris/Augusti*) was considered sacred in the public-private sector. b) *genius populi Romani*; see no. 2): personified as a youth wearing a toga (*t. iuvenilis*) or a military cloak (*paludamentum*: *pl.*). In the Imperial period, the *genius* was seen as a symbol of wealth and success. c) *genius senatus:* artists of the 1st to 3rd cent. AD [3. pl. 1,8 and 3,2] depict the genius of the Roman Senate as a bare-chested bearded man, wearing a cloak, *pt.* and *co.*, or *t.* holding a sceptre and a laurel branch. d) *genius hominum mortuorum* (of the deceased) or respectively *genius funerarius* (of the funeral procession): as *t.*, *c.v.*, standing at the altar or resting at the 'funeral feast'; e) *genius legionis/militaris* (of the legions or of war): standing, with cloak or breast armour, *pl.*, boots, mural crown. The *genius exercitus* (of the army) appears on coins with *pl.*, *pt.*, *co.*, and mural crown (*modius*) [4. 603, 607 no. 28*]. f). The *genius loci* is depicted as a snake, standing or reclined, with cloak, *pt.*, *co.*, as a hybrid of *genius* and *lar*. g) *genius urbis Romae* (of the city of Rome); h) *genius oppidi* (of the town). i) *genius theatri*: as *t.*, with *pt.*, *co.* and as (?) a snake [5. pl. 74,3]. j) *genius coloniae/ provinciae*. k) *genius fatalis* (Symmachus, Relat. 3,8) as a guardian protector.

3) *genii cucullati:* trio of hooded male figures.

4) genii of the gods: a) *genii deorum*: *genius Apollinis*, *Iovis*, *Martis*, *numinis Priapi*, *Veiovis*; b) with Apollo, Hercules, Minerva, Vulcanus, Zeus as *t.*, *c.v.*, holding a sceptre, with nimbus/mural crown, *pt.*, *co.*, or bearing wheat grains for a burnt offering [4. 604–605, 607 no. 45–49*].

B. Christian Development

After the prohibition of the old cults by Theodosius I (AD 392), the notion of the *genius* lived on as a spiritual concept (a moral-spiritual companion) as well as in the Christian interpretation of ambiguous terms (e.g. *salus*, 'health', but also 'salvation'). Beginning with Origen (Homilia in numeris 20,3), the concept of a 'guardian angel' was amalgamated with the notions of the *genius*. It remains a contentious issue whether this guardian angel appears at the birth or the baptism of his ward. The inclusion of the *genius* into oaths was taken over (*per genium tuum*, 'on your genius' replaced by *per angelum tuum*, 'on your angel'; see above *genius* no. 2a), the touching of the forehead survived in the sign of the cross (Serv. Aen. 3,607; see above); he appeared on funerary inscriptions (*genius* no. 2d), and interceded in ways unique to *genii* (Mart. Cap. 2,153). Even the symbolic snakes made a reappearance in a speech by Ambrosius (Expos. Psalmi 118,6,16 CSEL 62,116). The *genius* became the angel of peoples (see no. 2) and of the Church (see no. 2h, 2j). Other angelic forms of the *genius* included youthful male winged figures and Cupids.

→ Lares; → Penates

1 Pfiffig, 412 s.v. G. 2 Th. Fröhlich, Lararien- und Fassadenbilder in den Vesuvstädten, 1991, 367 3 Alföldi, 290f. 4 I. Romeo, s.v. G., LIMC 8.1, 599–607 5 H. Kunckel, Der römische G., 1974.

V. Bulhart, s.v. g., ThlL 6.2, 1826–1842; H. Cancik, J. Rüpke (ed.), Röm. Reichsreligion und Provinzialreligion, 1997; D. Martens, s.v. Genii Cucullati, LIMC 8.1, 598f.; R. Muth, Einführung in die griech. und römische Religion, 1988; J. Rüpke, Kalender und Öffentlichkeit, 1995; R. Schilling, s.v. G., RAC 10, 52–83. W.-A.M.

Genizah In Judaism, a *genizah* ('safekeeping', from Aramaic *gənaz*, 'to hide') is a repository for books which are no longer in use but which contain the name of God, or for ritual objects, in order to prevent misuse or profanation. Such rooms were frequently found in synagogues; if the synagogue itself was demolished, the books and objects were 'interred' in the cemetery.

Of particular importance amongst the multitude of *genizahs* in the Jewish world is the *genizah* of the Esra synagogue in Fusṭāṭ (Old Cairo), whose academic evaluation was due mainly to the British scholar S. Schechter. In 1987, he was able to move to Cambridge a considerable part of the total of about 200,000 complete or fragmentary documents. The remainder is spread among libraries all over the world (though an almost complete microfilm collection is housed in the National Library in Jerusalem). The majority of the texts found in the Cairo *genizah* date from the 9th–13th cents.; some fragments, however, are undoubtedly older and date back to the 6th/7th cents. Among the most important finds are a Hebrew manuscript of the book of Ben Sira, previously extant only in Greek ('Jesus Sirach'), a fragment of the Greek translation of the Bible by → Aquila [3], the Covenant of Damascus, biblical texts with pre-Masoretic (→ Masorah) Palestinian and Babylonian pointing, rabbinical works and examples of → Hekhalot literature, ancient Palestinian and Babylonian *piyyuṭim* (liturgical hymns), numerous documents on the history of the Jews in Palestine and Egypt for the period between the Arab conquest and the First Crusade, material on the history of the → Karaites, Yiddish literature, legal documents such as marriage certificates, divorce letters, and sales contracts, business and private letters, amulets, writing exercises, etc. The documents are of inestimable value for the understanding of Old Testament knowledge, but also for further insights into the history of ancient and mediaeval Judaism.

D. Goitein, A Mediterranean Society 1, 1967, 1–28; A. M. Habermann, s.v. Genizah, Encyclopaedia Judaica 7, 404–407; G. A. Khan, Twenty Years of Geniza Research, in: Encyclopaedia Judaica Year Book 1983–1985, 163–169; S. Reif, Genizah Material at Cambridge University, in: Encyclopaedia Judaica Year Book 1983–1985, 170f. B.E.

Gennadius

[1] Patriarch of → Constantinople AD 458–471. As an advocate at the Council of → Calchedon (451), he opposed acceptance of the Christology of → Cyrillus of Alexandria.

F. Diekamp, Analecta Patristica, 1938, 54–72 (73–108). K.SA.

[2] Priest in Marseilles associated with the Semipelagians, who died between 492 and 505. Complementary to → Hieronymus' *De viris illustribus*, he compiled under the same title a catalogue of Christian authors, providing reliable information on Christian literature of the 5th cent.; beginning with Cassiodorus (Inst. 1,17,2), both works were transmitted together. G. is also seen as the author of the theological tractates *Liber sive diffinitio ecclesiasticorum dogmatum* and *Adversus omnes haereses* in 8 books (largely lost). The attribution to him of the *Statuta ecclesiae antiqua* is uncertain.

Bibliography: CPL 957–960; 1776; Duval, in: HLL, § 768.1; S. Pricoco, Storia ecclesiastica e storia letteraria, in: La storiografia ecclesiastica nella tarda antichità, 1980, 241–273. J.GR.

Gennesar see → Tiberias

Genoa (ancient Genua, modern Genova). Ligurian fortress on the harbour of Mandraccio, used in pre-Roman times by Etruscans and Massiliotes: pre-urban phase end of the 6th cent. BC; settled from the mid 5th cent. BC (wall remains, pottery, bronze and lead, statuette of a discus thrower, Etruscan inscriptions; necropoleis, cremations in 'well graves'). It was an *oppidum* allied with Rome, in 218 BC the base of P. → Cornelius [I 68] Scipio against → Hannibal (Liv. 21,32,1; Amm. Marc. 15,10,10); in 205 BC, it was destroyed by Mago (Liv. 28,46,7), and rebuilt in 203 BC by Sp. Lucretius (Liv. 30,1,10); in 197 BC, it served as base for Q. Minucius Rufus against the Liguri (Liv. 32,29,5); from 148 BC, it was the starting-point of the *via Postumia* (CIL V 8045); in 137 BC, it harboured the fleet of C. Hostilius Mancinus destined for Numantia (Val. Max. 1,6,7); it was probably not crossed by the *via Aemilia Scauri* (Str. 5,1,11). G. was the trading port of the Liguri, used for wood, animals, skins, honey, but also olive oil and Italian wine (Str. 4,6,2); possibly a *colonia Latina* 89 BC, G. was a *municipium* from 49 BC (CIL V 7153), perhaps *IVviralis*, belonging to the *tribus Galeria* (CIL VI 2867; AE 1939, 130), as part of the *regio IX Liguria* (Plin. HN 3,5,46).

Remains from the Roman period: buildings, graves, aqueduct, amphitheatre (?), statuette of Cerberus, pottery, inscriptions, coins. A diocese possibly as early as the 3rd cent., the city was represented by its bishop at the Council of Aquileia in 381, the Synod of Milan in 451, and the Synod of Rome in 680; from 569 to 643, it was the residence of the archbishop of Milan. Apart from inscriptions, remains of the early Christian period are the earliest churches (San Siro), cemeteries, and a synagogue (Cassiod. Var. 2,27). After the capture by the Goths (→ Goti) (Iord. Get. 30,154), G. became a Byzantine garrison town in 544 (Procop. Goth. 3,10,14); in 643, it was destroyed by the Langobard king Rothari.

Fontes Ligurum et Liguriae antiquae, 1976, s.v. Genua; M.G. Angeli Bertinelli, Genova antica, in: L. Borzani (ed.), Storia illustrata di Genova 1, 1993, 1–32; Id., La città ritrovata. Archeologia urbana a Genova 1984–1994, 1996. M.G.A.B.

Genos (γένος; *génos*, pl. γένη/*génē*). The term has been used commonly in archaic Greece with the meaning 'of aristocratic origin', in addition in the sense of house, family, generation, species etc. [1]. In the research Attic *génē* were for a long time regarded as exclusive noble clans whose former dominance was still demonstrated in the later privileges (supervision of admission to the phratria and exclusive holding of positions as priests). According to the investigation by [2] and [3], the *génē* are today regarded as local village communities which arose in archaic Greece in the process of polis formation. We cannot discern whether it rests on older forms of organization. The *génē* were integrated into the → polis and took on religious roles in particular; some were presumably part of → phratria (Aristot. Pol. 1252b 16–18; Philochorus, FGrH 328 F 35). Not all Athenian citizens belonged to a *génos* (on Aristot. Pol. fr. 3 cf. [4]).

In the 4th cent. BC the term *génos* was used for a group of individuals who felt that they belonged to a → family. The size, composition and function of the *génē* [5], over 60 of which are attested in Athens, are debated. Members of *génē* held priestly positions (e.g. Eumolpidae: IG I³ 6; Praxiergidae: IG I³ 7), were responsible for cults and the holding of → festivals and were active as pilgrims. Outside Athens *génē* are attested e.g. on Crete (Aristot. Pol. 1272a 34), in Sicilian Naxos (cf. [6]) and on Cos (cf. [7]).

→ Phratria; → Polis

1 M. Schmidt, s. v. γένος, LFE 2, 1991, 130–133 2 F. Burriot, Recherches sur la nature du genos, 2 vols., 1976 3 D. Roussel, Tribu et cité, 1976 4 S. Lambert, The Phratries of Attica, ²1998, 371–381 5 R. Parker, Athenian Religion, 1996, 284–327 6 I. Rutherford, The Amphikleidai of Sicilian Naxos, in: ZPE 122, 1998, 81–89 7 M. Sherwin-White, Ancient Cos, 1978, 299–230.

S. Lambert, The Attic Genos, in: CQ 49, 1999, 484–489; Id., The Attic Genos Salaminioi and the Island of Salamis, in: ZPE 119, 1997, 85–106. K. F.

Gens

A. Politics and Society B. Religion and Cult

A. Politics and Society

The Roman *gens* comprised the members of a → family who descended from a common ancestor and under whose *potestas* they would have been, if he had still been alive (Varro, Ling. 8,4). The main distinction between *gentiles* and *agnati* lay in the fact that the latter could prove their blood relationship with their progenitor, whereas for the former, this relationship was only a fictitious assumption.

The origins of the *gens* are a matter of scholarly dispute, and will likely remain so because of the lack of source material from Rome's earliest period. Probably, the *gentes* were 'clans' which had formed in the 9th/8th cents. BC, but initially only assembled under their respective leader on special occasions. It is likely that the political importance of the *gentes* decreased with the ascent of the Roman monarchy, but it seems that the *patres*, who formed the Senate at that time, were representatives of gentilicial associations. According to ancient tradition, the Etruscan kings increased the number of *patres*, i.e. the members of the Senate, through the addition of the leaders of the *minores gentes*; however, their number, the date, and also the question of whether these were plebeian *gentes*, were already a matter of contention in ancient debates (Liv. 1,35,6; Cic. Rep. 2,35; Dion. Hal. Ant. Rom. 2,47,1f.; 3,67,1; Tac. Ann. 11,25,2). The *maiores gentes* comprised the Aemilii, Claudii, Cornelii, Fabii, Manlii, and Valerii, of whom both the Claudii and Cornelii later also had a plebeian branch. Scholars assume that the distinction between *gentes maiores* and *minores* dates back to the claim of particular *gentes* to the tenure of certain *maiora* or *minora flaminia* respectively (great and small priestly offices, → *flamines*). Furthermore, the relationship between *gentes* and → *curiae* also remains unclear, as the *curiae*, too, were obviously formed by groups of extended families, though not, however, necessarily identical with the *gentes*. The *nomen* → *gentile* as an addition to the previously only single name is first evident in the 6th cent. BC in Etruria, later also in Latium; it marks the bearer as a member of a particular *gens*. As the membership of a *gens* could only be ascertained by the name (Fest. 94: *Gens Aemilia apellatur quae ex multis familiis conficitur*), it was a punishable offence to assume a false name (Papin. Dig. 48, 10,13,pr.). The → *cognomen*, indicating a subdivision within a *gens* (*stirps*; *familia*), was added only later. It is noticeable that even in subsequent periods, the number of *praenomina* used within a particular *gens* remained limited.

Even as early as the late Republic, common usage no longer made a strict distinction between *gens* and *familia* (Cic. S.Rosc. 15; Ulpian Dig. 50,16,195,4), but the term *gens* was still used in oratory (cf. e.g. Cic. Dom. 35). According to the Law of the Twelve Tables, *gentiles* had to be considered in the law of inheritance (→ Succession, law of) (Gaius 3,17) as well as the law of guardianship, in each case right after the *agnatus proximus*. From the late Republican period onwards, the → *tutela* of the *gentiles* is only rarely evident, but is still claimed in the → *laudatio Turiae* (*c.* 40 BC) (1,21). If therefore the membership of a *gens* required particular proof (Dig. 22,3,1), it follows that not every citizen was a member of one (cf. Liv. 10,8,9). Neither → freedmen nor their descendants were members of *gentes* – even though they adopted the *nomen gentile* of their former masters –, but were counted among the → *clientes* (Cic. Top. 29 with reference to Scaevola; but cf. Fest. 83 L).

Even in the early Republic, the *gentes* still showed great unity, as demonstrated by the independent campaign of the *gens Fabia* against Veii and the former's subsequent annihilation on the banks of the Cremera in 477 BC (Liv. 2,48,8–50,11). We cannot ascertain conclusively when and how the division into patrician and plebeian *gentes* took place: it is possible that it was only with in the early years of the Republic that the patrician *gentes* closed ranks against lower-ranking *gentes*, whereas prior to that the integration of foreign *gentes*, as e.g. the *gens Claudia*, was effortlessly achieved. The evidence of plebeian *nomina gentilia* in early consular lists further supports the assumption that these *gentes* already existed in Rome at the time of the Monarchy. In the Republic, the patrician *gentes*, who had more power, laid claim to the two politically important monopolies of *imperium* (supreme power of command) and *auspicia*. It is even likely that in the Conflict of the Orders the plebeian *gentes* were denied the right of being constituted as a *gens* (Liv. 10,8,9). While most of the patrician privileges were renounced in the early years of the Republic, the patrician *gentes* held on to the offices of the → *interrex* as well as the three major *flaminia* (→ Flamines); furthermore, the → Salii and → Luperci remained purely patrician.

B. Religion and Cult

As a general rule, the originally important role of the *gentes*, so difficult to grasp within the political sphere, is clearly reflected in the sphere of religious law. Already during the Monarchy, individual *gentes* were charged with the performance of *sacra publica* (public cults), which they carried out alongside their own *sacra privata* (private cults). The *gens Potitia* shared responsibility with the *gens Pinaria* for the sacrifices introduced by Hercules (Fest. 270 L). It seems that initially the responsibility for the *lupercalia* lay in the hands of the Quinctii and Fabii, before their role was taken over by *sodalitates* (priestly colleges), while the (plebeian!) *gens Aurelia* was responsible for the cult of → Sol and the *gens Horatia* for the *Tigillum Sororium*. The *Titii sodales* (→ Sodales) and the → *Arvales fratres* also probably got their names from the *gentes* originally performing these cults. They were later replaced by *collegia* and *sodalitates*.

From very early on, each *gens* also seems to have performed *privata sacra*, which are still evident in historical times: the *gens Fabia* was obliged to perform *sacra gentilicia* on the Quirinal (Liv. 5,46,1–3; 5,52,3). The sanctuary of the *gens Iulia* was in Bovillae, that of the *gens Claudia* and the *gens Domitia* in Antium (cf. Plin. HN 34,137 on the *sacra* of the *gens Servilia*). The rites, in which *clientes* possibly also participated, took place annually on set dates (*feriae gentiliciae*). The *sacra gentilicia* (gentilicial cults) were not restricted to the patrician *gentes*, even though they are less well documented for the plebeian ones. It was the task of the *pontifices* to ensure that the *sacra* of a *gens* were not neglected or abandoned. Graves were also a common and unifying concern of a *gens*, which apparently also applied to the plebeian *gentes* (Cic. Leg. 2,55 on the *gens Popillia*). Certain *gentes* also favoured a particular form of burial; thus the *gens Cornelia* spurned the tradition of cremation (Plin. HN 7,187).

Even though in the middle and later years of the Republic the *gentes* no longer immediately intervened in political life as a collective force, it remained a source of public prestige in Rome's aristocratically structured society to belong to a powerful *gens* steeped in tradition: during a *pompa funebris* (funeral procession), the *imagines* (ancestral masks) of outstanding members of the *gens*, normally on display in the *atrium*, were paraded in public (Pol. 6,53,1–54,3; Plin. HN 35,6–7). In the later years of the Republic, aristocratic families not only commissioned the recording of their family history, but they also traced the origins of their *gens* back to a divine forefather or a Trojan hero; Dionysius of Halicarnassus still knew of 50 contemporary families who claimed to be of Trojan descent (Dion. Hal. Ant. Rom. 1,85,3); this is a clear manifestation of the social prestige that was associated with the membership in a *gens*.

As a consequence of civil wars and proscriptions, the number of patrician *gentes* had dwindled by the onset of the Principate. Later, the *principes* had the right to make someone a patrician.

→ Agnatio; → Family, B. Rome

1 G. Franciosi, Famiglia e persone in Roma antica dall'età arcaica al principato, 1989 2 Id., Ricerche sulla organizzazione gentilizia romana, I and II, 1984–1988 3 R.E. Mitchell, Patricians and Plebeians, 1980 4 J. Poucet, Les origines de Rome, 1985 5 K.A. Raaflaub (ed.), Social Struggles in Archaic Rome, 1986 6 H. Rix, Zum Ursprung des röm.-mittelitalischen Gentilnamensystems, in: ANRW 1,2, 1972, 700–758 7 Chr. J. Smith, Early Rome and Latium, 1996. M.D.M.

Gens Bacchuiana Settlement in *Africa proconsularis*, in the valley of Oued Siliana near Tichilla and → Thubursicum Bure, modern Bou Djelida. Chief place of the *gens Bacchuiana*, under Antoninus Pius (AD 86–161), its administration lay in the hands of *undecimprimi*. Inscriptions: CIL VIII Suppl. 1, 12331–12340a; Suppl. 4, 23922–23930.

AATun 050, sheet 34, no. 74. W.HU.

Genthius (Γένθιος; *Génthios*). King of the → Labeates *c.* 181–168 BC, allegedly a drunkard and fratricide (Pol. 29,13; Liv. 44,30,2–5); he also supposedly encouraged the activities of the (previously defeated) Illyrian pirates (Liv. 40,42,1–5). G. distanced himself from the pro-Rome policies of his predecessor and father → Pleuratus, and refused to enter into an alliance with Rome on the eve of the Third Macedonian War (Liv. 42,37,1f.; 45,8); in 170, he had to accept the requisitioning of 54 *lembi* (→ Navigation) by M. Lucretius in Dyrrhachium (Liv. 42,48,8). Even though G. was already said to be on very good terms with Macedonia as early as 172 BC (Liv. 42,26,2–7), he only consented to an alliance in 169, having received three legations and the payment of 300 talents; in this → Perseus is said to have let his stinginess (?) loose him strategic advantages against the Romans (Pol. 28,8f.; Liv. 43,19,13–20,3; 44,23. 27,8–12; Diod. Sic. 30,9). After G. had immediately taken two Roman legates prisoner and attacked the coastline near Dyrrhachium and Apollonia with 80 *lembi* (Liv. 44,30; App. Mac. 18,1; Ill. 9,25; Plut. Aem. 13,1–3), in 168 BC he encountered the newly appointed praetor L. → Anicius [I 4] Gallus near Bassiana, who put him under siege in his residency of Skodra and forced him into capitulation (App. Ill. 9,26). G., his wife Etuta and his sons Pleuratus and Scerdilaedas were paraded in Anicius' triumph in Rome and subsequently incarcerated in Spoletum and Iguvium (Liv. 44,30; 45,43; App. Ill. 9,27).

P. Cabanes, Les Illyriens, 1988, 311–322. L.-M.G.

Gentiana (gentian). Greece boasts seven, Italy more than 20 species of this family with about 200 species in total. According to Dioscorides (3,3 p.2,4 Wellmann = p.262f. Berendes), the medicinal properties of these species, generally identified as γεντιανή/*gentianḗ* (*gentiana*: Pliny), were allegedly discovered by an Illyrian king called Gentis (= Gentius: Plin. HN 25,71). In medicine, *gentiana* found a multitude of applications (Plin. HN 26,29 and *passim*): Even in antiquity, juice was extracted from the root of the yellow *Gentiana lutea L.* and related species – ascribed by Dioscorides with heating and astringent powers – and made into gentian-wine (Plin. HN 14,111), from the late Middle Ages also distilled to make bitters. Pregnant women were warned against the consumption of the root extract (Plin. HN 25,71). Less attention was paid to the blue flowering varieties with smaller roots, such as *Gentiana cruciata L.* (Late Lat. *basilica* or *basilisca*, Cross Gentian), *Pneumonanthe L.* (Marsh Gentian) and *Asclepiadea L.* (Willow Gentian). C.HÜ.

Gentile The *gentile* – signifying membership to a family (→ *Gens*) – is bequeathed by the father to the children and kept by the wife after marriage. It is the defining element in the Roman and Middle Italian system of personal names (→ Personal names: Rome and Italia), occupying second place after the *praenomen* in the formula for names. Aside from birth, other possibilities existed of attaining a *gentile*: a) through → adoption, wherein the adopted person receives the *gentile* of the adoptive father; his prior *gentile* added as a suffix at first (*P. Cornelius Scipio Aemilianus*, son of *L. Aemilius Paullus*), later carried as a (heritable) → *cognomen* (*C.*

Plinius Caecilius Secundus, son of a *Caecilius*); b) through → manumission, wherein the slave adopts his patron's *gentile*: *Nico*, slave of *M. Antonius*, becomes *C. Antonius M. l(ibertus) Nico*; c) through granting of citizenship to → *peregrini*, who were free to choose their own *gentile* at first (the poet *Q. Ennius*; the Etruscan *Aθ Unata* called himself *Mn. Otacilius*), but later adopted the *gentile* of the person who assisted them in attaining citizenship. The abuse of these three possibilities led to a devaluation of the *gentile* as a means of identification: repeated adoptions in a family led to numerous *gentilia* within one name; mass manumissions of imperial slaves as well as the universal granting of citizenship in, for instance, the → Constitutio Antoniniana of AD 212 led to a large number of identical *gentilia* such as *Iulius*, *Claudius*, *Ulpius*, *Aurelius*. The heritable family name as an institution disappeared towards the end of antiquity, not to be revived again until the Middle Ages.

The morphological structure of the *gentile* shows that it emerged patronymically – as an adjectival derivation from the name of the father – probably in the 8th/7th cents. BC on the lower Tiber in the region of contact between Etruscans, Latini, Falisci, and Sabelli. In order to derive the patronymic *gentile* from the individual names that had become the → *praenomina*, Latin and Faliscan uses *-io-* and (in *-io-stems*) *-īlio-*: *Marcus – Marcius* (Faliscan *Marco – Marcio*), *Lūcius – Lūcīlius*, the Sabellan *-io-*: Oscan *Heírens – Heírennis*, *Lúvkis – Lúvkiís*; Umbrian also *-ēno-*: *Uois(is) – Uoisien(s)*, the Etruscan *-na* and *-ni(e)*: *Larice Laricena*, *Latine – Latinie*. A secondary source of the *gentile* useful for foreigners were designations of origin (ethnica): Latin *Norbānus – Norba*, Oscan *Aadirans – (H)Atria*, Etruscan *Laθite – Latium*. In cases of language change by the name bearer, the *gentile* was often matched only superficially with the new language: Etruscan *Velimna* – Latin *Volumnius*. For many *gentilia*, for example, *Fabius*, *Cornelius*, *Vipsanius*, the individual or place name at its origin is unknown.

G. Colonna, Nome gentilizio e società, in: SE 45, 1977, 175–192; B. Doer, Die röm. Namengebung, 1937 (repr. 1974); J. Reichmuth, Die lat. Gentilizia und ihre Beziehungen zu den röm. Individualnamen, 1956 (thesis); H. Rix, Zum Ursprung des röm.-mittelital. Gentilnamensystems, in: ANRW I 2, 1972, 700–758; H. Rix, Röm. PN, in: E. Eichler et al. (ed.), Namenforschung 1, 1995, 724–732; Solin/Salomies. H.R.

Gentunis (Genzon). Son of → Geisericus, brother of Hunericus, father of Gunthamundus, Gelaridus, and Thrasamund (Procop. Vand. 1,5,11; 8,6–8; 9,6). In AD 468, he participated in the naval battle against → Basiliscus (Procop. Vand. 1,6,24), only to die in 477, preceding his father in death. PLRE 2,502–503 (Genton 1).

M.MEI. and ME.STR.

Genucius Name of an old family, perhaps immigrants from Etruria [1. 456f.]. One of the leading families of plebeian nobility in the 4th and 3rd cents. BC: G. [9] occupied the office of consul immediately after it was opened up to plebeians (in 367/6), G. [1] belonged to the first plebeian augurs. The historicity of the patrician name-bearers of G. [5]–[7] is contested [2. 111; 3. 12f.]. The family died out at the end of the 3rd cent. BC.

1 R.M. Ogilvie, A Commentary on Livy. Books 1 – 5, 1965 2 Th. Mommsen, Röm. Forschungen 1, ²1864 3 Münzer.

[1] **G., C.** One of the first plebeian augurs appointed following the *lex Ogulnia* of 300 BC (Liv. 10,9,2). The cognomen *Augurinus* of earlier family members [6] and [7] of the G., later added to the *fasti*, probably refers to him.

[2] **G., Cn.** People's tribune in 473 BC. Annalistic tradition holds that he had intended to bring the consuls of the previous year to court due to their hostility against Sp. Cassius [I 19] Vecellinus' agricultural law, but was found dead on the day of the proceedings (Liv. 2,54f.; Dion. Hal. Ant. Rom. 9,37f.).

[3] **G., L.** People's tribune in 342 BC, imposed a prohibition against charging interest (Liv. 7,42,1) still known as late as the 2nd cent. BC (App. B Civ. 1,54). Additional plebiscites – attributed to G. if not with certainty – prohibited holding the same office within 10 years as well as holding two offices simultaneously and made it possible for both consuls to be plebeians (Liv. 7,42,2). The historicity of these plebiscites is contested; the latter of the rules may have helped enforce the Licinian-Sextian laws of 367/6 BC.

T.J. Cornell, in: CAH 7,2, ²1989, 333, 337, 345; Id., The Beginnings of Rome, 1995, Index s.v. G.; K.-J. Hölkeskamp, Die Entstehung der Nobilität, 1987, 92–95, 105–108.

[4] **G., T.** People's tribune in 476 BC, oldest known bearer of the name (MRR 1, 27); regarding the person see Q. → Considius [I 1].

[5] **G. Augurinus, Cn.** (regarding the *cognomen* see [1. 12f.]). Consular tribune in 399 and 396 BC who is said to have fallen in the battle against the Falerii and Capua (Liv. 5,18,2f.). He might be the G. described in a speech by C. → Sempronius Gracchus as the victim of vituperation by the Falisci (Plut. C. Gracchus 3,5; there he erroneously appears as people's tribune, probably due to a mistake in the transmission).

1 Münzer 2 MRR 1,85, 87.

[6] **G. Augurinus, M.** According to the *fasti*, consul in 445 BC with C. Curtius [I 3] Chilo, and allegedly an enemy of the *lex Canuleia* (Liv. 4,1–6), although this may be an invention.

[7] **G. Augurinus, T.** According to annalistic tradition, consul in 451 BC with Ap. Claudius [I 5] Crassus; afterwards, they both headed the assembly of the *decemviri* (Liv. 3,33,4; Dion. Hal. Ant. Rom. 10,54,4; 56,2).

[8] **C. Aventinensis, Cn.** (According to later tradition, the *cognomen* is derived from the Roman hill most important to plebeians), consul in 363 BC (MRR 1,116).

[9] **G. Aventinensis, L.** *Cos. I* 365 BC, *cos. II* 362, with Q. Servilius Ahala in both cases; said to have fallen in the battle against the Hernici (Liv. 7,6,7ff.).

[10] **G. Aventinensis, L.** Consul in 303 BC (MRR 1,169).

[11] **G. Clepsina, C.** *Cos. I* 276 BC, *II* in 270; supposedly conquered Rhegium (Dion. Hal. Ant. Rom. 20,16,1; Oros. 4,3,5).

[12] **G. Clepsina, L.** Consul in 271 BC, may have initiated the campaign against Rhegium, → G. [11] (MRR 1,198). K.-L.E.

Genus see → Literary genre

Genusia (modern Ginosa). City west of Tarentum – the original centre of the Peucetii; Roman *municipium* (*Genusini*, Plin. HN 3,105). Settlements existed from the Iron Age until the late Roman period; funerary finds.

E. DE JULIIS, L'attività archeologica in Puglia nel 1983, Atti del XXIII Convegno di Taranto (1983), 1984, 421–446, 429–431; Id., Magna Grecia, 1996, 266; T. SCHOLJER, Notiziario delle Attività di Tutela, Settembre 1987–Agosto 1988. Ginosa (Taranto), via S. Francesco Saverio, Taras, VIII, 1–2, 1988, 114f.; M.T. GIANNOTTA, s.v. G., BTCGI 8, 1990, 137–142. M.G.

Geographical names

A. TYPES: PLACE NAMES AND VOCABULARY
B. WORD FORMATION, MOTIFS C. OLD AGE, AFTERLIFE D. PLACE NAMES AND GREEK PREHISTORY E. PLACE NAMES AND ITALIC PREHISTORY

A. TYPES: PLACE NAMES AND VOCABULARY

In antiquity, the different types of place names (esp. names of regions and cities or settlements, also names of mountains, lakes, rivers, islands, fields, and roads) are thoroughly documented and transmitted in Greek and Latin, however, there are many variations in form, e.g. Πιθηκοῦσσα : *Aenāria* (today *Ischia*). If a place name cannot be interpreted from within the vocabulary of the language in which it is documented, it usually goes back to the language(s) of prehistorical populations. On the other hand, place names that can be interpreted in Greek or Latin (occasionally through a comparison with other Indo-European languages) are highly instructive sources of forms as well as motifs found in place names.

B. WORD FORMATION, MOTIFS

Appellatives and their derivatives as well as adjectives are used as place names. Several suffixes: **-i̯o-/-i̯eh₂-*; Greek *–(o)Ϝεντ- (also Mycenaean */-wont-/*) or F. –(o)Ϝεσσα from **-u̯ent-/*-u̯n̥t-i̯h₂-* (Old Indian, Old Indo-Aryan *-vant-*, Anatolian *-u̯ant-* 'to equip') and –ών from **-h₃on-*; Lat. *-V̆li-*, *-no-/-nā-*. Pre-Greek or pre-Italic words also serve as a basis, e.g. Σελινοῦς in Triphylia, Arcadia (Mycenaean PY *se-ri-no/nu-wo-te/-wont-ei/?*), etc. 'rich in celery, parsley, araliaceae' (: σέλινος) : *Selinus* (today *Selinonte*, Sicily).

The following typical motifs can be identified: a) localities, b) names of plants or animals, c) physical characteristics or objects, shapes, and the like, d) personal names, names of gods, and ethnica.

In regard to a) cf. Ἦλις ('valley', cf. Lat. *uallis*), Ἤπειρος ('mainland'); settlements Ἄκρα, -αι *passim*, Δειράς ('hill') in Corinth, Λίμναι and Ἕλος ('swamp') in Laconia (Mycenaean PY loc. *e-re-i*), Κρῆναι 'fountain' in the Argolid (in Thessaly Κράννων, in Elis Κρουνοί), Πύλος 'palace', 'fortress' in Messenia (Mycenaean PY *pu-ro*), Elis and Triphylia or Ῥίον ('mountain top', Mycenaean PY *ri-jo*) in Achaea; Εὔριπος 'arm of the sea' ('having wide water[courses]' [3]), cf. *Fretum Siculum*. Cf. also the Greek types Νέα πόλις (today *Napoli*), Ὀλβία (πόλις), Ἡλίου πόλις, Μητρόπολις. In Italia, cf. *Ocriculum* in Umbria (in the case of *ocris* 'rocky mountain'), *Fānum* ('grove'), the harbours *Ostia, -ium* (passim) or the river *Rhēnus* in northern Italy (as in German *Rhein*, cf. Old Irish *rían* 'current'). Agricultural designations also serve as place names, e.g. Δώτιον πεδίον in Thessaly, *ager Gallicus* on the Adriatic coast.

In regard to b) cf. the mountains (Boeotian) Ἑλικών or (Roman) *Vīminālis* (: ἑλίκη or *uīmen* 'pasture)'), Boeotian rivers Σχοῖνος, Προβατ/σία (σχοῖνος 'bulrush', πρόβατα 'livestock'), the islands Εὔβοια, Πιτυοῦσσαι, Πιθηκοῦσσα (: βοῦς 'cattle', πίτυς 'spruce', πίθηξ 'monkey'), the plain of Μαραθών 'fennel field' (μάραθος 'fennel'). Cf. also *Italia*, originally only Bruttium (: *uitulus* 'calf', according to a lower Italic Greek form without *u̯*), *Fagifulae* in Samnium, *Pīcēnum* (: *fāgus* 'beech', *pīcus* 'woodpecker').

In regard to c) cf. the rivers Ἀλφειός in Elis and *Albula* in Latium (: ἀλφούς· λευκούς, *albus* 'white, bright'), Ἴσ-τρος (today Danube) in Thrace (**is-ró-* 'to give an impulse', cf. Homer. ἱερὸς ποταμός from **is-eró-*, Ger. *Isar*, French *Isère*) or the springs Θέρμη, -αι (passim). Cf. also the ὁδὸς Σιωπῆς (Elis) or the Roman *via Lāta*. Homeric influence can be detected in city names like Πάνορμος (today *Palermo*) or Ἀμαθοῦς (Cyprus), Τειχιοῦσσα (Ionia) (cf. Homeric εὔορμος λιμήν, ἠμαθόεις 'sandy' and τειχιόεσσα 'with a city wall' as an epithet of cities [4. 196ff.]). Geographical shape serves as the basis for naming, for example, the Laconian foothills: Ὄνου Γνάθος 'donkey's jawbone', the municipium *Corniculum* or the city of Ζάγκλη 'sickle' (τὸ δὲ δρέπανον οἱ Σικελοὶ ζάγκλον καλοῦσιν Thuc. 6,4,5).

In regard to d) Concerning personal names, cf. Ἀλεξάνδρεια, Ἀντιόχεια and passim, *Co(n)silinum* in Bruttium. Concerning ethnica, cf. Λοκροί, Λεοντῖνοι, (Etruscan) *Volsiniī* (today *Bolsena*), *Tarquiniī* and derivativa such as Βοιωτία, Κυδωνία, *Campānia*, *Tuscia* after Βοιωτοί, Κύδωνες, *Campānī*, *Tuscī*. Concerning names of gods, cf. the mountains Ἥραιον (Corinth),

Quirīnālis after Ἥρα, *Quirīnus*; the cities Ἀθῆναι, Ὀλύμπια based on Ἀθήνη, (Zeus) Ὀλύμπιος (also the type Ἀπολλωνία, Ἡράκλεια, Ποσ/τειδω/ανία, Ποτειδαία); *Lymphaeum*, *Mamertium* after *Nymphae*, (Etruscan) *Mamers*; also Πελοπόννησος (: Πέλοπος νῆσος).

Names of mountains, rivers, etc. are often applied to settlements, for instance Σκιλλοῦς (σκίλλα 'squill'), the river in Elis, the city in Triphylia; Πυξοῦς (πύξος 'boxwood') : *Buxentum*, the city, foothills, and river in Lucania. There are other motifs as well: Roman roads are named after the family of the builder (e.g. *via Appia*) or after the destination city (e.g. *via Ardeatina*).

C. Old Age, afterlife

Place names defying interpretation are usually regarded as very ancient, while those understandable from within their language are considered younger. In a few cases, it is possible to establish an absolute chronology. Greek place names transplanted to Italy (see below E.), for instance, go back to the period of → colonization, the type of Ἀλεξάνδρεια to the Hellenistic period, the type of Ἁδριανόπολις to the Imperial period.

Toponomy is generally very conservative. In general, place names continue to live on – at times with phonetic modification – cf. the place names mentioned above, and, for example, Ἀντίπολις (today *Antibes*), *Carthāgō Nova* (today *Cartagena*), *Colonia* (modern *Köln*), (*Colonia*) *Batāva* (today *Passau*), *Gratiānopolis* (today *Grenoble*), Ὑδροῦς (: *Hydruntum, Odruntum* : today *Otranto*), etc. Place names may also be translated (e.g. Ἄκρα Λευκή : *Lucentum* : today *Alicante/Alacant*), or adapted by folk etymology, cf. Εὔξεινος 'hospitable' (sc. πόντος: Black Sea), a tabooistic reformation from Ἄξεινος, based on the reinterpretation of a Scythian word (equivalent to Avestian *axšaēna*- corresponds to 'dark'), or Ἱππώνιον (southern Italy), such as 'horse market', after *Vibo Valentia* (ethnicon Ϝειπωνιεύς: today *Bivona*); a (partial) adaptation is likely, cf. the affix (Cretan) Ἱε/αρα-πύτνα (suffix Πύδ/τνα pre-Greek!). Occurrences of renaming are documented as well: Ζάγκλη was named Μεσσάνα (today *Messina*) by the Greeks; (Gall.) *Bonōnia* (today *Bologna*) was formerly called (Etruscan) *Felsina*; the Messenian Πύλος was called Κορυφάσιον in archaic times.

D. Place names and Greek prehistory

Place names that are impossible to interpret as Greek go back to (insufficiently known) pre-Greek populations and are a) completely opaque, or b) have identifiable suffixes that also appear in appellativa. Regarding a) cf. Θῆβαι (Mycenaean *te-qa*), Ὄλυμπος, Ἴτανος (Mycenaean KN *u-ta-no*). Some were adapted (e.g. Ἄπτερα 'wingless' from Mycenaean *a-pa-ta-wa* /*Aptarwā*/) or occasionally translated (e.g. Θερμόπυλαι [1. 83]).

In regard to b) cf. the suffixes -*ānā*- (e.g. Μεσσᾱ́νᾱ, Ἀθήνα, -αι), cf. ἀπήνη 'wagon'; -*Vnt^h^os* (e.g. Κόρινθος, Ζάκυνθος), cf. ἀσάμινθος 'bathtub'; -*V̆ssos*/Attic Boeotian -*V̆ttos* (e.g. Ἁλικαρνασσός/Λυκαβηττός), cf. κυπάρισσ/ττος 'cypress' which is not identical with -*sos* (Attic river Κηφισός, [Argive] Κνῶhιαν with *-*s*- > -^{h}-). -νθος may correspond to Anatol. -*(a)nda*, -νδα; -σσ/ττος can hardly be separated from Luwian -*šša*- and indicates (at least) one Indo-European Luwian substratum in Greece (cf. to Παρνα-σσός Luwian *parna*- 'house, temple'). Incidentally, more than one suffix appears with the same basis, e.g. Πύρανθος (Crete), Πύρασος (Thessaly), Πύρινδος (Caria), Luwian *Puranda*.

The appearance of a place name in more than one region may (not necessarily) indicate population shifts: following the destruction of the Mycenaean kingdom which did not reach beyond Messenia [2], several place names documented for Mycenaean Pylos (e.g. *e-ko-meno*, *pi-*82*, *ro-u-so*) were transferred to Arcadia (Ἐ/Ορχομενοί, Λουσοί) or to Elis (Πῖσα); however, Boeotian (pre-Greek) Ἐ/Ορχομενοί is independent thereof. Also, correspondences between place names of Thessaly and those of the western Peloponnese may go back to pre-Greek substrata and are not necessarily indicative of population shifts.

E. Place names and Italic prehistory

In addition to place names that can be interpreted in Latin, others are documented in Italy that are a) not associated with any known language, associated b) with non Indo-European languages, or c) with Indo-European languages. Place names under a) must be attributed to a mysterious 'Mediterranean' substratum, those under c) correspond to a number of languages that are non-Latin substrata or adstrata. The latter languages – despite their fragmented character (exceptions are the Italic languages and Greek) – suggest the existence of populations from various origins who had settled in Italy during prehistorical and early historical times.

In regard to a) cf. *Arretium* (today *Arezzo*), *Capua*, *Cumae* (: Κύμη), *Salernum*.

In regard to b) cf. Etruscan place names in northern and middle Italy: *Felsina* (later *Bonōnia*), perhaps after the gentile *felzna*, and *Volsiniī* (today *Bolsena*) after the ethnicon Etruscan *velsna*; *Feltria*, *Mantua*, *Mutina* (today *Modena*), *Tarquinia*; also, the rivers *Volturnus*, *Tīcinus* or the place names *Volturnum*, *Tīcinum* (today Pavia), if not pre-Etruscan. In principle, Ligurian place names (*Tauromenium*?) are not to be found in north-west Italy, and Siculan (Ζάγκλη?, see above) or Elymite place names in Sicily, even considering the uncertain status of these languages.

In regard to c) cf. names of rivers that are considered to be Indo-European-'ancient European', e.g. Αἴσαρος (today *Esaro*) in Bruttium, *Albin(i)a* (today *Albegna*) in Etruria, *Duria* (today *Dora Baltea*) in Liguria, *Liquentia* (today *Livenza*) in Venetia. Northern Italy has place names of Gallic origin (e.g. *Mediolānium* : today *Milano*, cf. *-*plāno*- 'smooth' with Celtic **p*- > ∅; *Bonōnia*, cf. Gallic *bona* 'founding'; *Eporedia* : today *Ivrea*, cf. Gallic *epo-* ‘equus’, *reda* ‘crowd, flock’, the personal name *Epo-redo-rix*), perhaps even of Lepontic origin (*Genua*, *Aquae Bormiae*?). Of Venetian origin are, for instance, *Tarvisium* (today *Treviso*), *Opitergium* (today *Oderzo*), *Tergeste* (today *Trieste*), cf. Venetian *tarvos* ‘taurus’, **terg-i̯o-* ‘market’, **terg-es-* ‘market’. On the Salentinian peninsula, Messapian place names are documented, such as *Barium* (today *Bari*, cf. βᾶρις· οἰκία), *Brundisium* : Βρεντέσιον (today *Brindisi*, cf. **b*^{h}*rentó-* ‘deer’, βρένδον· ἔλαφον, *brunda* : *caput cerui* and the ethnica Βρέττιοι, *Frentānī* or *Bruttiī* ‘deer people’ [5]), *Rudiae*: ῾Ρωδίαι (**rud*^{h}*-i̯ā-* ‘red earth’?). Much evidence exists for Italic place names in middle and southern Italy, those of Greek origin can also be found in Sicily. Regarding Italic place names, cf. *Aequum Tuticum* (Oscan *touticum* ‘publicum’, Umbrian *totam* ‘populum’, ‘cīuitātem’), *Bouiānum Uetus*, *Pompēiī*, *Nōla* with the Oscan ethnicon *BÚVAIANÚD* (cf., also, Umbrian *bum* ‘bouem’), *PÚMPAIIANS* (cf. Oscan *pomtis* ‘quinquiēns’ and **pompe* ‘five’), *NÚVLANÚS* (**nou̯olāno-*), also, *Samnium* (or *SAFINIM*, Greek Σαύνιον) from **sab*^{h}*-n-i̯o-* (cf. ethn. *Samnītēs*, Σαυνῖται; without *-n-* cf. *Sabīnī*, *Sabellī* [6]). Among place names imported from Greece to Italy are pre-Greek names (e.g. *Cūmae*, *Messānā*), names with a Pre-Greek root (for example *Selīnūs*), and genuine Greek place names (e.g. *Heraclea*, *Metapontum*, *Neapolis*, *Panormus*).

→ Ancient European; → Onomatology; → Ethnic names

1 J. CHADWICK, Greek and Pre-Greek, in: TPhS 1968, 80–98 2 Id., Arcadia in the Pylos Tablets?, in: Minos 16, 1977, 219–227 3 B. FORSSMAN, Mykenisch *e-wi-ri-po* und εὔριπος, in: Münchener Stud. zur Sprachwiss. 49, 1988, 5–12 4 E. RISCH, Ein Gang durch die Gesch. der griech. ON, in: MH 22, 1965, 194–205 (= KS 145–157) 5 H. RIX, *Bruttii*, *Brundisium* und das illyrische Wort für “Hirsch”, in: BN 5, 1954, 115–129 6 Id., *Sabini*, *Sabelli*, *Samnium*, in: BN 8, 1957, 127–143.

A. FICK, Vorgriech. ON, 1906 (useful as collection of references); D. A. HESTER, Pre-Greek Place Names in Greece and Asia Minor, in: RHA 61, 1957, 107–119; H. KIEPERT, Lehrbuch der alten Geogr., 1878; A. LANDI, Etnici e toponimi dell'Italia antica. Rassegna bibliografica, in: AION (Sez. ling.) 8, 1986, 307–317; 11, 1989, 237–243; J.K. MCARTHUR, A Tentative Lexicon of Mycenaean Place-Names. I: The Cnossos Tablets, Minos 19, 1985; Id., Place-Names in the Knossos Tablets, 1993; A. MORPURGO DAVIES, The linguistic evidence: is there any?, in: G. CADOGAN (ed.), The End of the Early Bronze Age in the Aegean, 1986, 93–123; G. NENCI, G. VALLET (ed.), Bibliografia topografica della colonizzazione greca in Italia e nelle isole tirreniche (since 1977); NISSEN 2, 968–1004 (ch. ‘Antike ON’); G.B. PELLEGRINI, Toponimi ed etnici dell'Italia antica, in: PROSDOCIMI, 79–127; PHILIPPSON/KIRSTEN; P. POCCETTI, Per un progetto di bibliografia su “Etnici e toponimi dell'Italia antica”: Decennio 1951–1960, in: AION (Sez. ling.) 11, 1989, 211–235; A.P. SAINER, An Index of the Place Names at Pylos, in: SMEA 17, 1976, 17–63; F. SCHACHERMEYR, s.v. Prähistor. Kulturen Griechenlands, RE 22, 1954, 1350–1548; F. SOLMSEN, Idg. Eigennamen als Spiegel der Kulturgesch., 1922; J. TISCHLER, Kleinasiat. Hydronymie, 1977; ZGUSTA.

J.G.-R.

Geographus Ravennas Anonymous, apparently clerical, author of the 8th cent. AD from Ravenna (4,31), also referred to as *Anonymus Ravennas*. His *Cosmographia* describes the entire world as it was known in his time in 5 bks. Bk. 1 argues – in observance of Biblical and patristical traditions – for a view of the earth as a flat disc surrounded by oceans, with the sun running along the southern rim during the day. Bks. 2–5 present lists of 5,000 place names, organized by regions and, in part, by Roman provinces (regions, cities, rivers) in Asia, Africa, Europa, on the Mediterranean, and on ocean islands.

The author consulted many (today mostly lost) works; parallels to the → Tabula Peutingeriana suggest that the same sources were used by both authors. The GR's influence can be found in later interpolations in the transmitted text as well as in the fact that Guido of Pisa consulted it as a source for his work *De variis historiis* (written in 1119), wherein he excerpts an older version of the GR.

J. SCHNETZ, Itineraria Romana 2, 1940, 1–110 (ed.; repr. with new index 1990; ibid. 113–142 Guidonis Geographica); Id., Ravennas Anonymus, 1951 (Germ. transl.); F. STAAB, Ostrogothic Geographers at the Court of Theodoric the Great, in: Viator 7, 1976, 27–58; O.R. BORODIN, Die Kosmographie des Anonymus Ravennas und ihre Stellung in der Geogr.-Gesch. [Russian], in: Vizantijskij vremennik 43, 1982, 54–63.

K.BRO.

Geography

I. ANCIENT ORIENT AND EGYPT II. GREECE AND ROME

I. ANCIENT ORIENT AND EGYPT

The oldest sources for the geography of Mesopotamia consist of topographical lists (3rd millennium BC), of which one lists a total of 289 eastern and central Mesopotamian places. Clay plates from the 3rd to the 1st millennium BC occasionally show schematised city maps with labels (Babylon, Nippur, Uruk, Sippar) as well as regional area maps (Nuzi, Tellō, Nippur, Euphratis region, Sippar). These were probably created in the context of land surveying. A world map exists which is unique in its central orientation towards Babylon (*c.* 5th cent. BC). A disk-shaped earth (several cities, water courses, and mountain ranges are named) is surrounded by a belt of bitter water. Beyond it are eight further regions. Astral geography was developed only rudimentarily. Surprising for Mesopotamia is the lack of detailed descriptions of territories and borders as they are known from the Bible (Num. 34,1–12; Jos. 15,1 i.a.). The table of nations in Gen. 10 became important for the post-Biblical period as well (cf. Jubilees 8–10; Jos. Ant. Iud. 1,122–147).

The Egyptian worldview is characterized by the north-south axis of the Nile and the desert to the east and west. The outside world is partially referenced through toponymies in so-called apotropaic texts. From the time of the 18th Dynasty (1550–1314 BC), lists of place names appear based primarily on military campaigns (by Thutmosis III i.a.). A Turin papyrus contains the map of a region of gold mines. The papyrus Anastasi I contains excerpts from a handbook with information about road conditions.

Systematic geographical research is not attested in the Ancient Orient until the 7th/6th cents. BC. It was undertaken primarily for the benefit of commerce (Phoenician ships) and has been transmitted exclusively through Greek sources such as the → Periplous of Africa under → Necho II, the Phoenician sea enterprises of → Hanno and → Hamilcar, or the Arabia-India expedition by → Scylax of Caryanda under → Darius [1] I.

P. ALEXANDER, s.v. Geography and the Bible, The Anchor Bible Dictionary 2, 977–88; D. FRAYNE, The Early Dynastic List of Geographical Names, 1992; R. GIVEON, s.v. Ortsnamenslisten, LÄ 4, 621f.; R. GUNDLACH, s.v. Landkarte, LÄ 3, 922f.; W. RÖLLIG, s.v. Landkarten, RLA 6, 464–467; W. WESTENDORF, s.v. Weltbild, LÄ 6, 1211–1213. K.KE.

II. Greece and Rome

Geographical knowledge was important for both Greeks and Romans; the ancient concept of *geōgraphía*, however, was broader and less clearly defined than the modern concept, encompassing esp. ethnography as well. Geography was also often treated as a literary genre which – corresponding to the ancient ideal of education – connected the real and the imaginary worlds in a creative way. An objective treatment of scientific and technical aspects of geography or even an education therein was largely limited to a few exceptional Greek personalities: these were the individuals who coined the term geography (γεωγραφία) and its derivations in the 3rd cent. BC [1. 9[2]].

The Homeric epics are pervaded by a strong sense of geography, for instance, in the so-called catalogue of ships (Hom. Il 2), in the description of Achilles' shield (Hom. Il 18), and in the description of Odysseus' journey (Hom. Od.). The earth is regarded as a limited realm of islands surrounded by an endless Oceanus – a view that resonates through all of antiquity despite considerable evidence to the contrary: → Crates of Mallus, for instance, could therefore refer to the above-mentioned description of the shield as an 'imitation of the world' (κόσμου μίμημα, Str. 1,1,7, cf. [1. 14]). The colonization movement and its consequential interaction with other populations in the archaic period resulted in the Greeks' increased consciousness and interest in geography. In the 6th cent. BC in Ionia, → Anaximander and → Hecataeus of Miletus founded the literary genre of a 'path around the world' (περίοδος γῆς, Anaximand. 2 A 2 DK; Hecat. FGrH 1 F 37–359), which aimed at an ordered and comprehensive description of the world (at times supported by maps) in poetry or prose. These maps are not extant. There is no lack, however, of imaginative modern 'reconstructions' (see [2] as an example). Apparently, a constant demand for this type of 'panoramic' literature emerged, obviously written for an audience who preferred pleasant descriptions of miracles and myths over accurate contemporary information. This type of literature flourished in the Hellenistic period, reaching its peak in the 2nd cent. AD in the *Peri[h]egesis* by → Dionysius [27], translated and edited by → Avienus in the 4th cent. for a Latin audience. Both works are extant, as is the earliest work of this kind in Latin prose, written by → Pomponius Mela in the early 40s of the 1st cent. AD, probably an armchair scholar who wrote for people like himself.

In the 5th cent. BC, Herodotus was able to utilize new discoveries about the Persian Empire, Northern Africa, and the western Mediterranean region, thus questioning the view that Oceanus surrounds all of these regions – described by him with the new term *oikouménē* (οἰκουμένη). This term literally refers to the 'inhabited' world, although the content refers more to the world 'as known to be inhabited' or to the 'familiar' world (Hdt. 2,32; 2,34; 3,114; 4,36). This gives rise to the possibility that other parts of the world may be inhabited as well, even if the populations are unknown there, without any contact to the Oikoumene. Such regions are bordered – with the exception of the west – by remote empty space rather than the sea. As persuasive as this new view may have been, it did not result in a revision of the older Homeric view of a world surrounded by ocean. Furthermore, the report by the Seleucid governor Patrocles stating that the Caspian Sea and the Indian Ocean are connected by a stretch of water (Plin. HN 6,58) convinced → Eratosthenes of the accuracy of the Homeric view. Strabo followed this course of thinking as well, and begins his work with a new articulation of the Homeric view. A renewed confirmation of the Herodotean view of the world does not emerge until the 2nd cent. AD in the *Geographia* by Claudius → Ptolemaeus (Ptol. 7,5,2).

The Ionians saw the world as a flat, slightly concave disc three times as wide as it was deep (Democr. 55 B 15 DK). The idea that the earth is a sphere and part of the solar system originated in Pythagorean theory (Diog. Laert. 8,26) and continued to spread. In the 4th cent., the globe was, for the first time, assumed to be divided into five zones – arctic, moderate, equatorial, moderate again, and antarctic. At the same time, it was attempted to determine the earth's circumference, a fact that confirmed the idea that the Oikoumene was only a small part of the entire world. It also supported the speculation that other inhabited parts of the world existed, separated from the Oikoumene by sea or desert, that is, they existed beyond the Atlantic (Pl. Ti. 24e–25a) or south of the equator as a mirror image of the Oikoumene inhabited by Antichthons ('counter-earth-inhabitants') or by the Antipods ('counter-peds'). This scheme was preferred by Aristotle and refined by Cratus of Mallus in the 2nd cent. BC, who assumed two further worlds that correspond to each other in the north and south of the western hemisphere, thus altogether four worlds separated from each other by parts of the Oceanus (Aristot. Mete. 2,5; Str. 2,5,10).

Even before → Alexander [4] the Great, the Greeks (→ Scylax among them) had undertaken voyages of → exploration with the explicit goal of furthering geographical knowledge, but Alexander's campaigns greatly surpassed all previous enterprises and provided an inexhaustible source of stimulation for scientific as well literary endeavours. Geography became a particularly important area of interest in the Mouseion of Alexandria, where Eratosthenes first shaped it into a coherent and rigorous discipline in the 3rd cent. BC. His works, known to us only through secondary sources [3], comprised calculations of the earth's circumference and instructions for the cartographical recording of the world. Eratosthenes' methodology was well founded; he was conscious of the necessity of gaining precise physical and astronomic data, which, however, was hard to attain: the problem of exactly determining longitude was still unsolved (remaining so until the 18th cent.), a problem that interfered with the reliability of the data. Still, Eratosthenes' data became fundamental for the geography of Claudius Ptolemy. His work constitutes the most comprehensive attempt of projecting the physical and cultural landscape onto the curved surface of the world; it provides (not always correct) information about co-ordinates and gives instructions for the creation of a world map as well as 26 regional maps. It is not clear whether these maps were distributed by Ptolemy himself (cf. the posthumously published volume of maps in the unfinished edition of C. MÜLLER, 1813–1894).

If we define maps as graphic representations that aid in the understanding of spatial conditions, we can ascertain that such maps had been produced by Greeks and Romans since earliest times. However, these maps played a relatively insignificant role among the practical means that were employed to organise and comprehend physical surroundings. Their visual attributes were quite varied and remained inconsistent, probably due to the fact that a universal concept of 'map' was yet to be developed. Furthermore, there were no 'maps' available for general use, since large numbers of copies simply could not be produced. The 'cartographical' data (→ Cartography) most commonly collected consisted of lists of place names and the distances between these places on well-known routes. For this purpose, *períploi* (Peripl. m.r., ed. L. CASSON, 1989; Stadiasmus maris magni, GGM I 427–514) were created for sea voyages, and *itineraria* [4] for overland journeys, allowing only a linear representation of the spatial conditions when transferred into (carto)graphical form. The most extensive and refined example of this among the few surviving documents of this kind is the → *Tabula Peutingeriana* [5]. The source of the latter document dates to the 4th cent. AD but it contains elements from as early as the 1st or 2nd cent. and was surely produced in the context of precursors or comparable documents. Despite a lack of trueness to scale and a lack in projection, this graphic offers a lot of correct topographical information. Its main purpose, however, is the representation of land routes through the known world from Britannia to Taprobane (Ceylon/Sri Lanka). The author as well as the original purpose of this 'map' remain uncertain.

The descriptive geographical works by Eratosthenes also inspired a number of Greek authors who reacted in various ways to the expansion of Roman power up into the period of Augustus: → Polybius, → Posidonius, → Diodorus [18], and, above all, → Strabo, who characterizes the work he completed under Tiberius with good reasons as a 'tremendous task' (κολοσσουργία) (1,1,23): In 17 books, it presents a comprehensive *chōrographía*, a mixture of regional geography and ethnography, with the purpose of justifying and supporting Roman Imperial rule (Str. 1,1,16f.). However, not all the information from Strabo's sources was current – esp. concerning remote regions such as India; furthermore, the work apparently had only little influence on Roman readers.

Among the leading Romans, → Caesar's interest for geography and ethnography – manifested in his *Commentarii de bello Gallico* – remained an exception. Following the empire's rapid expansion during the Augustan period, a phenomenon which was exploited by contemporary propaganda in many ways, the Romans saw little cause for investigating the geography of regions beyond the boundaries of the empire, esp. in the absence of incentives such as the need for land, economical exploitation, or missionary zeal. Still, knowledge of geography was deemed important – the encyclopaedia by → Plinius the Elder or the historical work by → Ammianus Marcellinus testify to this. Geography was appreciated in its ability to entertain, to stimulate, and to instil a sense of cultural superiority within a fixed framework of knowledge. Geography was practised only rarely in the sense of a continuous quest for deeper, more precise, or more empathetic insights into populations and places.

→ GEOGRAPHY

1 J. S. ROMM, The Edges of the Earth in Ancient Thought, 1992 2 J. B. HARLE, D. WOODWARD (ed.), The History of Cartography I 2, 1978 3 D. R. DICKS, The Geographical Fragments of Hipparchus, 1960 4 O. CUNTZ, J. SCHNETZ, Itineraria Romana, 1929–1940 (expanded repr. 1990) 5 E. WEBER, Tabula Peutingeriana, 1976.

W. WOLSKA-CONUS, s.v. G., RAC 10, 155–222; E. RAWSON, Intellectual Life in the Late Roman Republic, 1985, ch. 17; C. JACOB, Géographie et ethnographie en Grèce ancienne, 1991; K. BRODERSEN, Terra Cognita, 1995; M. T. RILEY, Ptolemy's use of his predecessor's data, in: TAPhA 125, 1995, 221–250. RI.T.

Geology Geology, in modern understanding, is the science of physical nature (mineralogy, metallurgy) and of the structure, formation, and development of earth's crust (tectonics) as well as the forces that shaped this development ('dynamic geology'). Antiquity only knew the first beginnings of a comparable scientific discipline [1. 8–50; 2]. Geological technologies (→ Mining,

→ Quarries) were implemented even before specific geological questions began to be studied in Near Eastern theories of the world's origin (→ World, creation of the; Egypt, Mesopotamia, Phoenicians, Hittites), early Greek → cosmogonies, and by Ionian natural philosophers (→ Thales, → Anaximander, → Anaximenes [1]; → Geography), who often deliberately contradicted the former's mythical ideas. Topics such as the origin of the world (cf. Pl. Criti. 110f.; Aristot. Mete. 1,14; 2,7f.) and the nature of petrification were fascinating to science since Plato, Aristotle, and Theophrastus, but also to religious trends in popular beliefs (→ Orphic poetry; lithomancy, → Divination). Of similar interest were problems of mineralogy (cf. Aristot. Mete. 3,6; Theophr. *perì líthōn*, 'About Stones'; [3. 1963–1966]) and metallurgy (cf. Pl. Leg. 678d; Plin. HN 33,59ff.; 34,94ff.; 35,183; Diod. Sic. 3,11ff.; [4–8]). Further topics were → volcanic activity (cf. Lucr. 6,535–702; Str. 6,1,5; 2,3; 8; Sen. Q Nat. 2,16,5; 30,1), → earthquakes cf. Aristot. Mete. 2,7, Mund. 395b,30–396a,16; Theophr. Meteor., trans. by Ibn al-Ḫammār DAIBER; Lucr. 6,535–608; Sen. Q Nat. 6; Plin. HN 2,81–89; Amm. Marc. 17,7,9–14; [9–14]), and the effects of water (cf. Str. 1,3,6–8; 17; 15,1,16; Sen. Q Nat. 2,6,5) and of wind (→ Winds).

→ GEOLOGY

1 F.D. ADAMS, The Birth and Development of Geological Sciences, [2]1954 2 A. NEUBURGER, The Technical Arts and Sciences of the Ancients, 1930 3 F. KRAFFT, s.v. Mineralogie (and G.), LAW, 1963–1966 4 L. AITCHISON, A History of Metals, 2 vols., 1960 5 R.J. FORBES, Metallurgy in Antiquity, 2 vols., [2]1964 6 J.F. HEALY, Mining and Metallurgy in the Greek and Roman World, 1978 7 H. SCHNEIDER, Einführung in die ant. Technikgesch., 1992, 71–95 8 R.F. TYLECOTE, A History of Metallurgy, [2]1992 9 W. CAPELLE, s.v. Erdbebenforschung, RE Suppl. 4, 344–374 10 E. GUIDOBONI (ed.), I terremoti prima del Mille in Italia e nell'area mediterranea, 1989, 622–673 (list of earth- and seaquakes) 11 A. HERMANN, s.v. Erdbeben, RAC 5, 1070–1113 12 E. OLSHAUSEN, H. SONNABEND (ed.), Naturkatastrophen in der ant. Welt. Akten des 6. Histor. Geogr. Kolloquiums in Stuttgart 1996 (Geographica Historica 10), 1998 13 W.C. PUTNAM, Geologie. Einführung in ihre Grundlagen, 1969 14 G.H. WALDHERR, Erdbeben (Geographica Historica 8), 1997.

E.O.

Geometric pottery From the time of *c.* 900 BC, the geometric style emerged seamlessly from proto-geometric vase painting in Athens. The previous rather bulbous shapes, decorated with curvy ornaments, were replaced by more slender shapes on which outlines were accentuated through straight-lined systems of decorations, esp. through hatched maeanders and multifarious zigzag bands (→ Ornaments). Closed vessel types were primarily painted on the neck and belly areas, open types primarily around the handle. During the 9th and 8th cents. BC, the geometric style was common throughout the entire Aegean region. Until the 2nd half of the 8th cent. BC, Athens was the centre of this development. Later, we find more and more independent workshops and an increased Corinthian influence (→ Corinthian vases). Geometric pottery (GP) began to decline in the late 8th cent. BC; in the 1st half of the 7th cent., geometric decorations were superseded by oriental-style motifs (→ Orientalizing vase painting) and a growing interest in figural scenes.

GP receives its name from the simple geometric line drawings of figures such as circles, triangles and rectangles that decorate the vessels in encircling horizontal bands or figurative scenes. Aside from various maeanders, ornaments in the shape of lozenges, angles, zigzags, and teeth were popular. Curved shapes only appear in later phases. A high point of GP can be found in the magnificent vases of the tombs at the Dipylon Gate in Athens (→ Burial; → Pottery). Remarkable are the complex arrangements of simple patterns, the placement of the ornamental bands on the vessels that clearly defines their outlines as well the exceedingly precise detail in painting. Generations of geometric potterers dealt with the fundamental stereotype of endlessly repeated patterns by creating many variations of individually styled ornamental friezes, but their precision in painting began to fade in the last third of the 8th cent. BC.

GP is generally divided into three periods (early, middle, late geometric), and these in turn are subdivided. This development can be traced best in Athens. In the early Geometric period (*c.* 900–850 BC), closed vessels became more slender and show ornamental bands on a black background around neck and belly. The open vessels in this period appear sturdy and heavy; the few ornamental bands they show – if any – are quite narrow. The tendency towards more slender vase shapes with clearly accented vessel zones and a growing variety of ornaments continues in the middle Geometric period (*c.* 850–760 BC). The use of figurative scenes and the number of horizontal bands increases until a balance is achieved between light and dark and the ornamental zones alternating with the black-based body of the vessel – in which, however, the previously close relationship between decoration and shape of the vessel is gradually fading.

The 1st half of the 8th cent. gives rise to the first figure drawings of humans and animals adapted to the repertoire of geometrical ornament bands in their simplicity and abstraction of form. Particularly popular were representations of horses, painted or in the form of sculpted handles. The late Geometric period (*c.* 760–700 BC) in Attica produced the first individual artist in Greek art history identifiable by research, the → Dipylon Painter and his workshop, attributed, for instance, with the great belly amphora (Athens, NM 804; *c.* 760/750 BC). With a height of *c.* 1,5 m, this vase stood as a burial monument near the Dipylon Gate in the Kerameikos of Athens. It is decorated with ornamental bands painted with utter precision and discipline. At the same time, the Dipylon Painter marks the beginning of the decline of GP in his frequent use of figural scenes on the main zones of the vessel. Many successive vase painters followed this trend and increasingly neglected ornamental decor. Several figural scenes from this period appear to show first attempts at depicting narrative images of mythical or heroic content, but the lack of characteristic details disallows any clear identifications.

In the Attic late Geometric period, we can distinguish between *c.* two dozen painters, groups of painters, and workshops within or outside the Dipylon Painter's surroundings. Compared to these, other regional 'schools' of GP are of only secondary importance. Aside from Athens, another important centre was Argus, although it followed Attic styles and motifs well into the late period (*c.* 750–690 BC). Typical for Argus are figurative scenes depicting horses or men with horses. The background often consists of fishes and waterfowl. The ornamentation consists of boldly stepped maeanders and occasionally orientalizing motifs. In Corinth, a simple and tasteful style emerged; the vessels show narrow horizontal lines on the sides and decorated figurative scenes along neck, shoulder and handle areas, all done in a precise and well-ordered way. Horizontal zigzag patterns, angles, rare maeanders, and later, antithetical pairs or rows of waterfowl are the ornaments. The introduction of orientalizing motifs in the last quarter of the 8th cent. BC particularly influenced the Corinthian geometric style and led to the development of Proto-Corinthian vase painting.

Other painting schools on the Greek mainland, such as those in Boeotia, Thessaly, Laconia, and western Greece, produced rather inanimate, often imitative products that are quite 'provincial' compared to Athens. Euboea (Eretria/Lefkandi) produced high-quality vessels, sometimes covered with a thick, cream-coloured finishing layer. In the middle and late periods, the decorations imitated Attic patterns, later Corinthian kotyles as well. Specifically Euboean in style are bowls decorated with hanging, concentric half-circles, so is the use of white paint or white paste for framing or filling ornaments.

On the Cyclades, Attic influence is particularly obvious in the early and middle phases. In the late period, workshops from Naxos, Paros, Melos, and Thera can be distinguished through the materials used, the shapes of the vessels, and the ornamental decor. Cretan vase painting quickly adopted the geometric style in the 9th cent. BC; here it was of Attic character esp. in the middle phase, while Corinthian models were preferred later. Attic influence can also be found in the east Greek ceramics of the middle Geometric period, when hatched maeanders, triangles and rhombi are common. In the late period, we find waterfowl as well, becoming a tradition still to be found on sub-Geometric east Greek vases of the 7th cent. BC.

J. Boardman, Symbol and Story in Geometric Art, in: W. Moon (ed.), Ancient Greek Art and Iconography, 1983, 15–36; J.N. Coldstream, Greek Geometric Pottery, 1968; Id., The Geometric Style: Birth of the Picture, in: T. Rasmussen, N. Spivey (ed.), Looking at Greek Vases, 1991, 37–56; R.M. Cook, Greek Painted Pottery, ³1997, 15–40.

G.P.S.

Geometry see → Mathematics

Geomoroi (γεωμόροι; *geōmóroi*, Dor. γαμόροι; *gamóroi*), technical term for the social elite in archaic and classical Samos and Syracuse. As is suggested literally in the name itself, the status of this elite was based on land ownership assumed to have been in this group's possession from the time of the earliest settlements. As the ruling class, the geomoroi probably enjoyed legal privileges for a while, a status clearly designated by the term. *C.* 600 BC or shortly thereafter, their pre-eminence was threatened on Samos (Plut. Quaest. Graec. 303e–304c), but they were able to maintain a dominant position for two more cents. A more radical democratic development on Samos in 412 BC was primarily directed against the geomoroi: some were killed, exiled, or demoted in their legal status (Thuc. 8,21).

In Syracuse, the privileges of the geomoroi included authority over enslaved agricultural workers, the Cillyrians (who were identified with the Spartan → Helots). These workers together with the population (i.e., underprivileged Syracusan groups) drove out the geomoroi in the early 5th cent. BC, but Gelon brought them back from their exile in Casmenae shortly thereafter (485 BC), thus establishing his rulership over Syracuse (Hdt. 7,155; Aristot. fr. 586 R; Timaeus FGrH 566 F 8; Diod. Sic. 10,28,1f.; Dion. Hal. Ant. Rom. 6,62,1f.).

In later reconstruction of Attic early history, the geomoroi appear as the peasant class between → Eupatridae and → Demiourgoi (Aristot. fr. 384 R; Hecataeus of Abdera, FGrH 264 F 25, 222ff.; Plut. Thes. 25,1ff.; Poll. 8,111). Generally, the term is used as a synonym to *geōrgós* ('farmer') with undertones of venerability (e.g. Hsch. s.v. γαμόροι). Referring to Rome, the term geomoroi may designate an official committee for the assignment of land property (Dion. Hal. Ant. Rom. 9,52,2).

1 B. Bravo, Citoyens et libres non-citoyens dans les cités coloniales à l'époque archaïque, in: L'Étranger dans le monde grec, 1992, 43–85 2 H.-J. Gehrke, Stasis, 1985 3 D. Lotze, ΜΕΤΑΞΥ ΕΛΕΥΘΕΡΩΝ ΚΑΙ ΔΟΥΛΩΝ, 1959 4 N. Luraghi, Tirannidi archaiche in Sicilia e Magna Grecia, 1994 5 G. Shipley, A History of Samos 800–188 BC, 1987.

H.-J.G.

Geoponica

I. Collective term for agricultural technical literature II. 10th-cent. AD compilation

I. Collective term for agricultural technical literature

In the broader sense, G. refers to a genre of → technical literature, represented by numerous writings, which aims at a systematic representation of 'scientific' knowledge about all types of agriculture [1; 2; 3. 427ff.]. The spectrum of knowledge contained therein is very broad: it reaches from naïve peasant magic to speculative attempts at classifying types of soil, useful plants, and animals. Aside from the experiental knowledge, some of the material consists of very old superstitions, a fact that makes it very difficult to prove specific textual references or the existence of lost books.

The history of texts must proceed from the fact that no original Greek work is extant from before the 10th cent. [3. 427ff.] and that the original sources can only be reconstructed through Latin, Syriac, Arabic, and Armenian [4] translations. Although even → Aristotle [6] and → Androtion were already attributed with lost works bearing titles such as γεωργικά (*geōrgiká*), we only enter secure territory in the Hellenistic period. WELLMANN's [5] older view that perceived Bolus of Mendes, the Democritean (3rd cent. BC), to be the author of all magical traditions in this context (so still occasionally in [3. 428f.]) was proven wrong. But the fundamental work by → Mago of Carthage, translated by → Cato [1] into Latin, offers some rough insights. Its systematic structure [6] became normative for all later works (esp. for → Columella and for the Arabic works as well [3. 429f.; 7]): the agricultural estate and its organization (bk. 1 in Columella); farming (bk. 2); tree cultivation (bks. 3–5, always: wine – olives – other trees); animal husbandry (bks. 6–7, from large to small animals); chickens (bk. 8); bees (bk. 9); horticulture (bk. 10); the duties of *villicus* and *villica* (that is, to manage the estate, bk. 11–12). This structure is also used by → Vergilius in his *Georgica* (cf. the title itself), with the exception that apiculture appears at the end. The content of this most artful work of its tradition is almost completely indebted to the lost sources that can, however, be reconstructed through Syriac and Arabic translations, and the same holds true for the famous *bougonia* (Verg. G. 4,281ff.). Later compilations still carefully refer back to their models. The most important of these is the lost (yet still known to → Photius) Greek work by Vindanius Anatolius (4th or 5th cent. [3. 429f.; 1. 66ff.]), extant in Syriac [8; 9; 10] and Arabic, although inadequately edited [11]. Here, we can identify the most stringent parallel to Virgil's *bougonia*. Also lost, but again reconstructible through Syriac and Arabic translations, is the compilation by Cassianus Bassus, who wrote in the 6th cent. [3. 433ff; 1. III, 24ff.]. The only surviving Greek source is a compilation transmitted under the name of the scholarly emperor → Constantinus VII Porphyrogennetus (see below II).

1 E. ODER, Beiträge zur Gesch. der Landwirtschaft bei den Griechen I, in: RhM N.F. 45, 1890, 58ff.; II, 212ff.; III, RhM 48, 1893, 1ff. 2 E. FEHRLE, Studien zu den griech. Geoponikern (Stoicheia, H. 3), 1920 3 M. ULLMANN, Die Natur- und Geheimwiss. im Islam (HbdOr 1,6,2), 1972 4 C. BROCKELMANN, Die armen. Übersetzung der Geoponica, in: ByzZ 5, 1896, 385ff. 5 M. WELLMANN, Die Georgika des Demokritos (Abh. der preuss. Akad. der Wiss. 1921/4), 1921, 3ff. 6 J. NIEHOFF-PANAGIOTIDIS, Landwirtschaft und ihre Fachsprache: eine Übersicht, in: H. KALVERKÄMPER (ed.), Hdb. der Sprach- und Kommunikationswiss., 1998 7 IRFAN HABIB, s.v. Filāḥa, EI² 2, 899a–910b 8 P. LAGARDE (ed.), Geoponicon in sermonem syriacum versorum quae supersunt, 1860 9 A. BAUMSTARK, Lucubrationes syrograecae, 1894 (A. FUCKEISEN [ed.], Jahrbücher für classische Philologie, Suppl. 21) 10 G. SPRENGER, Darlegung der Grundsätze, nach denen die syr. Übersetzung der griech. G. gearbeitet worden ist, 1889 11 M.C. VÁZQUEZ DE BENITO, El manuscrito n. XXX de la colección de Gayangos, 1974 12 HUNGER, Literatur 2. J.N.

II. 10TH-CENT. AD COMPILATION

The agricultural compilation αἱ περὶ γεωργίας ἐκλογαί is part of an encyclopaedic program by Emperor Constantine VII Porphyrogennetus (944–959). The unknown Byzantine editor attributed the G. to the emperor as the actual author (*c.* 950) in a dedication (transmitted only through MS F, Laurentianus 59,32 of the 11th cent). It is an adaptation of an older compilation by Cassianus Bassus Scholasticus of the 6th cent. Apparently, he had analyzed two 4th-cent. works: the compilation συναγωγὴ γεωργικῶν ἐπιτηδευμάτων in 12 bks. by Vindanius Anatolius from Berytus and the Γεωργικά in 15 bks. by Didymus from Alexandria. Cassianus' work was soon translated into Persian and in the 9th cent. into Arabic as well, that is, prior to the edition of the G. But Vindanius Anatolius' work continued to co-exist: Photius (Bibliotheca 163) read it and praised it as late as the 9th cent. It had been translated into Syriac and Arabic, later also into Armenian. Vindanius still exerted an influence in the Spanish-Arabic Middle Ages.

The 20 bks. of the surviving G. offer lessons in all areas of agriculture, in farming (13 bks.), and animal husbandry (7 bks.). The following subjects are treated individually: calendar and weather (Gp. 1), farming (2), monthly calendar of work schedules (3), viticulture (4–8), olive trees (9), pomiculture (10; the longest bk.), ornamental plants (11), vegetables (12), insect control (13), poultry (14), bees (15), horses (16), cattle (17), small animals (18), dogs and wild game (19), fishes (20). The bks. begin with a *hypothesis* that includes a table of content. Each chapter is preceded by a heading which briefly states the topic, often including the source in a genitival mention of the author. However, in individual cases it is still contested who had added these names and whether the named author really is the source of parts of the subsequent chapter. Quotations and authors' names within the chapters have greater credibility; these could be confirmed in a few verifiable cases.

Even though the work begins with grain cultivation as the traditional core subject (Gp. 2), the main focus is on viticulture, trees and horticulture, areas that still needed development according to ancient views (Gp. 4–12). A tendency towards entertainment – already noticeable in Hellenistic agricultural theory – is apparent in numerous references to the magical and the miraculous (for example, natural miracles in grafting and

crossing; in the cultivation of fruit with the appearance of faces or animals) and in legends of transformations (esp. Gp. 11).
→ Agrarian writers

EDITIONS: I.N. NICLAS, 1781 (with Lat. transl., comm.) H. BECKH, 1895 ST. GEORGOUDI, Des chevaux et des boeufs dans le monde grec, 1990 (on Gp. 16 and 17; with important introd. to the problems of G., p.18–89).
BIBLIOGRAPHY: 1 J. KODER, Gemüse in Byzanz, 1993 2 M. ULLMANN, Die Natur- und Geheimschriften im Islam (HbdOr 1,6,2), 1972, 429–436. E.C.

Georgia, Georgians (Georgian *Sak'art'velo*, Persian *Gurğistān*, Arabic *al-Kurğ* or *Ğurzān*, Turkish *Gürcistan*, Russian *Gruzija*).
I. GEOGRAPHICAL LOCATION II. HISTORICAL DEVELOPMENT

I. GEOGRAPHICAL LOCATION

Land in west and central Caucasia south of the main range of the Great → Caucasus. It is divided into two parts by the Liḫi-(Surami) mountain range that runs north-south from the Great to the Small Caucasus: → Colchis in the west, a humid and unhealthy region until the drainage projects of the early 20th cent. which also includes the river system of the Rioni/ → Phasis in the west, and, in the east, the more arid valleys of the Kura/Cyrus and their tributaries. This geographical division was matched by two states of differing characters, Colchis (→ Lazika, Egrisi) in the west and → Iberia (K'art'li) in the east including the mountainous area south of Colchis. The name Sak'art'velo/G. for the entire kingdom unified under King Bagrat III was first used in AD 1008. A.P.-L.

II. HISTORICAL DEVELOPMENT

In the Hellenistic period, the area of modern G. was divided into a western part, Egrisi, known by the Greeks as → Colchis, and an eastern part, → Iberia. Politically, West G. stood under Macedonian rule, while East G. was under Parthian influence. In 65 BC, Cn. Pompeius Magnus conquered West and East G. and placed both sides under a Roman protectorate. In this period, the cities of → Dioscurias (Suḫumi), → Phasis (P'ot'i), Pityus (Pizunda), and Wani were the economic and cultural centres of Colchis. Mc'ḫet'a was regarded as the metropolis of the Iberian kingdom. Excavations reveal a wealthy city of merchants and craftsmen with a high level of education, as documented in the Georgian chronicle, *K'art'lis C'ḫovreba*. The Iberian royal court maintained ambivalent relationships to the Parthian and Roman empires, whose spheres of influence varied due to enemy incursions. In the 1st cent. AD, the noble line of Lazes rose to power in West G. and formed the kingdom of → Lazica, strongly influenced by Rome. The Romans were able to extend their influence up into the 3rd cent. into Iberia due to a changeover of power in the Persian region: the → Sassanids took over the rulership from the → Parthians in 224 and their ruler Shapur I (241–71) (→ Sapor) was able to push back Roman dominance in East G.

Christianization led to an important break in the history of G. during the 1st half of the 4th cent. Tradition has it that St. Nino, after growing up in Jerusalem as a Christian, came to G. by way of Armenia. In Mc'ḫet'a, she encountered various pagan religions such as the worship of ancient nature and tribal deities, also fire worship spread through Persian influence, as well as Judaism. Her special healing abilities are claimed to have brought her much recognition in the Jewish quarter. Her reputation later spread to the Georgian royal court, with the result that King Mirian adopted Christianity and proclaimed it as the state religion in 337. It established itself completely under Vachtang Gorgasal in the 2nd half of the 5th cent. During his period of rulership, the state borders were fortified and interior peace was attained. Vachtang moved the capital from Mc'ḫet'a to T'bilisi, with Mc'ḫet'a remaining a religious centre.

In the 6th cent., battles for G. erupted between the Byzantine and Sassanid empires. Finally, the Byzantine emperor → Heraclius succeeded in conquering the capital of T'bilisi in the year 622. The long-lasting Byzantine-Sassanid feuds had exhausted the military forces in East G. to such an extent that the Arabs could invade unhindered in the middle of the 7th cent., plundering and devastating the land. West G. remained firmly in Byzantine hands after the fall of the kingdom of Lazika. → Iconoclasm and the new Dynasty of the Bagratids, rising to power after the middle of the 8th cent., caused the decline of Byzantine power in West G.
→ Georgian; → GEORGIA

D. BRAUND, Georgia in Antiquity: a history of Colchis and Transcaucasian Iberia 550 BC – AD 562, 1994; K'art'uli sabč'ot'a encik'lop'edia [Encyclopedia of Soviet Georgia], 1994; Očerki istorii Gruzii [Studies in the History of Georgia; Russian], 1989; Sak'art'velos ist'oria. ACH.S.

Georgian
I. LANGUAGE II. SCRIPT III. LITERATURE

I. LANGUAGE

The Kartvelic (or south Caucasian) family of languages and peoples (Strabo's Ἴβηρες) is formed by G. alongside Mingrelian-Lazic and Swanic, but its further genetic classification is not clear (→ Caucasian languages). The oldest G. monuments in old-G. script (see II. below) date to the 4th cent. AD [1. 12]. Old-G. texts are primarily kept in Georgia but also in the Near East, in Europe, and in the USA [2. 5].

The structure of the language shows the following phonetic characteristics [1; 2]: a) simple vowels (*i*, *u*, *e*, *o*, *a*, no long vowels or diphthongs); b) a complex consonant system with three-part opposition (voiced versus unvoiced and aspirated versus ejective [= with glottal stop]) in plosives and affricates; uvular fricatives and plosives; extensive combinations of consonants, ablaut, and syncope.

Morphologic characteristics include a lack of genera in nouns, fully developed nominal inflections with distinctions of pure stem case (only Old-G.), nominative and ergative (agent case with transitive verbs and patiens in nominative), genitive, dat.-acc., and four to six additional, sometimes local cases.

The pronominal deixis corresponds to that of Greek, Latin, and Armenian.

The verb is poly-personal (subject and objects can be marked on the verb) and expresses aspect, versions (actant orientation) as well as the diathesis of active and passive voice. Stem formation is similar to several Indo-European languages in that it distinguishes between presence, aorist, and perfect tenses,

An interesting aspect of the syntax lies in the fact that transitive verbs are constructed according to tempus sequences, which show, in the present tense, the nominative-accusative construction common to Indo-European languages, in the aorist sequence, the ergative-nominative construction, and in the perfect tense, a dative-nominative construction.

Lexically, G. has been influenced strongly by neighbouring languages. Already in Old-G., numerous Greek loan words are documented (i.e. *ek'lesiay* 'church', *p'at'roni* 'patron', *angelozi* 'angel', *mankanay* 'machine, device', *melani* 'ink' in addition to borrowings from Armenian and Iranian [2. 250]).

1 H. Fähnrich, Kurze Gramm. der g. Sprache, [3]1993 2 Id., Gramm. der altg. Sprache, 1994. M.J.

II. Script

G. script is of unknown origin with letters running to the right [1. 5ff.]. The hypothesis that it developed from a pre-Christian script for which no direct evidence exists cannot be proven, neither – despite several similarities – its origin from Armenian script. The sequence (*a*, *b*, *g*, *d*, *e*) and the shape of individual letters (for example, digraphic [*u*]) can partially be traced back to Greek influence, as is the case for the assignment of number values. The oldest form (with 38 letters) is a majuscule script (*Asomtavruli*, 4th–11th cents.), while in the 9th and 10th cents., scripts in minuscules appear that sometimes differ greatly from the former: *Nusxuri* (into the 19th cent.) and the 'warrior script' *Mxedruli* in use today, with a strictly phonological system of 33 letters.

1 H. Fähnrich, Gramm. der altg. Sprache, 1994. M.J.

III. Literature

G. script is documented in building inscriptions from the 4th cent. AD and in MSS of Church literature. The oldest known coherent inscription is found in the former G. monastery Bi'r al-Quṭṭ near Bethlehem. The inscription has survived in the form of a mosaic and is dated to the 30s of the 5th cent. This inscription not only serves to attest G. script but also the early relationships of Georgians to other Christian populations. The oldest document in G. literature in its own region exists on the basilica of Bolnisi and dates to the year 493/4.

One of the oldest original G. literary documents is authored by Iakob Curtaveli, probably a court minister, entitled 'Martyrium of St. Šušanik' from the 5th cent. This *vita* traces the life of a woman of Armenian descent who was married to a G. governor. Varsken, her husband, was enticed to break with Christianity through Sassanid influence and demanded the same from his court. After Šušanik's steadfast refusal, he had her thrown into the dungeon and tortured. Despite the terrible torture, she held on to Christianity until her death in *c.* 475. This early yet in a qualitative sense highly developed work of G. literary art suggests the existence of a long literary tradition. Other martyr acts and *vitae* give testimony to a great literary creativity in the G. language. For instance, we still have the 'Martyrdom of St. Eustathius of Mc'ẖet'a' from the middle of the 6th cent. An outstanding work of 8th cent. G. literature is authored by Ioane Sabaniʒe and entitled 'Martyrdom of St. Abo of T'bilisi', from the period of Arab rule. In this work, Sabaniʒe reports the conditions at the time, describing the rule of power by Arabs and the attitude of the people towards religion. The work focusses on Abo, an Arab who had converted to Christianity and who was tortured to death for his conversion by the Arabic emir of T'bilisi. Christian G. literature reached its peak in the 11th cent.

Important centres of religious and cultural life outside of Georgia emerged – thanks to a thriving monasticism – in Jerusalem, on the Athos and the Sinai, and still other places, resulting in excellent translations. These translations are esp. valuable since the G. versions have survived while the original works had been altered or lost altogether. They are based on Armenian, Arabic, Greek, or Syrian originals, among others.

The history of Georgia is described in a more recent work which describes the time period from 300–1200, entitled *K'art'lis C'ẖovreba*. Little is known about the history of this chronicle's origins. The work had been forgotten over a long period of time, its MSS neglected, but the 18th cent. brought a renewed interest in reviving and reconstructing the lost parts of this work. Several original authors are named, each reporting about a certain time period. The chronicle largely consists of a list of G. kings, framed by a description of historical events. Emphasis is placed on important persons and events such as the ancestors of the Georgians, the conversion of the Georgians to Christianity, martyrs, commendable kings, and wars. Until today, the chronicle is baffling for researchers and an important source for historians at the same time.

→ Georgia; → Georgia

J. Assfalg, G. Handschriften, 1963; K. Kekeliʒe, ʒveli k'art'uli literaturis istoria, 1951; O. Lordkipaniʒe, Antikuri samqaro da k'art'lis samep'o, 1968; G. Pätsch (ed.), Das Leben Kartlis: Eine Chronik aus Georgien 300–1200, 1985; S. Qauẖčišvili (ed.), K'art'lis Cẖovreba, 1955–1973; P. M. Tarchnischwili, Gesch. der kirchlichen g. Lit., 1955. ACH.S.

Georgius

[1] Bishop of → Laodicea (died *c.* AD 360). The Alexandrine presbyter G., dismissed by his local bishop Alexander in *c.* 320 because of his radical → Arianism, became bishop of Syrian Laodicea *c.* 330 following his stay in Antioch. In persistent animosity to → Athanasius, he and Basilius of Ancyra gathered the Trinitarian Church Party of the Homoeousians (slogan: 'The father resembles the son in essence' ὅμοιος κατ' οὐσίαν) in 358/9. Also, he played a role in drafting the 4th Sirman Creed (22 May 359). The so-called 'Letter of G.' (Epiphanius, Panarion 73,12–22 [GCS 37,284–295]), a Homoeousian manifest of 358 may have been co-authored by him in parts [1. 366]. The last appearance of this friend of → Eusebius [9] from Emesa was at the synod of Seleucia (September 359).

1 R. P. C. Hanson, The Search for the Christian Doctrine of God, 1988, 365–371 and passim (s. index)
2 P. Nautin, s.v. Georges 46, DHGE 20, 629f. J.RI.

[2] Confidant of → Belisarius in Iustinian I's Second Persian War, negotiated the peaceful handing over of the fortress Sisauranon at Nisibis in AD 541. In 547, he thwarted an attack planned by the Persian King Chosroes [5] I on the city of Dara with the aid of his delegate Isdigusnas. (PLRE 3, 514 [Georgius 4]). F.T.

[3] **G. Continuatus.** Continuation of the chronicle by → Georgius [5] Monachos up to AD 948; probably written under → Romanus II (959–963). The possible author is → Symeon Magistros. Several MSS continue the chronicle further up to 1081 or 1143.

I. Bekker (ed.), Theophanes Continuatus, 1838, 763–924 (text). AL.B.

[4] **G. Cyprius.** Byzantine saint, born *c.* AD 550 (?) on Cyprus. He supposedly fled from an arranged marriage to Palestine, to his brother Heraclides in the monastery of Kalamon, then became a monk in the monastery of Choziba, only to return to Kalamon later; at the time of the Persian conquest of Jerusalem (614), he returned to Choziba and died there alone in the ruins of the monastery. The only biographical source is the almost contemporary *vita* by Antonius Chozibites.

Vita S. Georgii Chozebitae, Analecta Bollandiana 7, 1888, 97–144, 336–359. AL.B.

[5] **G. Monachos.** Also known as G. Hamartolos ('the sinner'), author of a Byzantine chronicle from the creation of the world up to AD 842. His biographical dates are unknown, the creation of the chronicle was formerly dated to *c.* 867, but today scholars assume a slightly later date still in the 9th cent. (cf. [1. 259; 2. 252]).

The chronicle of G. is a typical example of so-called 'monk's chronicles' in religious and Church history, also of religious polemics, which – from the point of view of Greek orthodoxy – greatly outweighed political history in importance. It contains numerous citations from the texts of Church Fathers. The representation varies strongly in its breadth; for the Byzantine period, G. consults primarily → Iohannes Malalas and → Theophanes. The chronicle is of independent value only for the period from 813 to 842. It is extant in several MSS, but has been edited according to only one codex so far (cf. [3. 39]). The text was also translated into → Georgian and → Church Slavonic.

1 P. Lemerle, Thomas le Slave, in: Travaux et Mémoires (Centre de recherche ... byzantines) 1, 1965, 255–297
2 A. Markopulos, Βίος τῆς αὐτοκράτειρας Θεοδώρας, in: Symmeikta 5, 1983, 249–285
3 P. Odorico, Excerpta di Giorgio Monaco nel Cod. Marc. Gr. 501, in: Jahrbuch der österr. Byzantinistik 32/4, 1982, 39–48.

C. de Boor (ed.), Georgius Monachus, Chronicon, 2 vol., 1904 (repr. 1978, with corr. by P. Wirth); V. M. Istrin, Chronika Georgija Amartola, 3 vols., 1920–1930; Hunger, Literatur 1, 347–350. AL.B.

[6] **G. Pisides.** Born in Pisidia, died in *c.* AD 631/634. *Diákonos*, *skeuophýlax* and *referendários* at the church of St. Sophia in Constantinople, one of the greatest Byzantine poets. Highly revered and often imitated, G. treats the Persian campaign of Emperor → Heraclius (*Expeditio Persica*, *Bellum Avaricum*, *Heraclias*, etc.) in his epic-encomiastic [1] poems, and deals in part with philosophical, in part with purely dogmatic topics in his theological works (*Hexaemeron*, a didactic poem that was translated also into Armenian and Slavic, *Contra Severum*, *De vanitate vitae* [2], *De vita humana*, his only writing in hexameter [3], numerous epigrams [4] etc.). His iambic trimeter marks the transition to accentuated metrics (Byzantine twelve-syllable metrics).

1 A. Pertusi, Giorgio di Pisidia, Poemi I. Panegirici epici, 1959
2 PG 92 1373–1754
3 F. Gonnelli, Il *De vita humana* di Giorgio Pisida, in: Bollettino dei Classici III,12, 1991, 118–138
4 L. Sternbach, Carmina inedita, in: WS 13, 1891, 1–62; 14, 1892, 51–68.

J. D. C. Frendo, The Poetic Achievement of George of Pisidia, in: Maistor. FS R.Browning, 1984, 159–187; H. Hunger, s.v. G.P., LMA 4, 1287f.; B. Baldwin, s.v. G., ODB 2, 838. I.V.

Gepidae, Gepidi (Γήπαιδες; *Gḗpaides*). Germanic tribe, related to the → Goti according to Iord. Get. 17,94. The original area of settlement was located in the Vistula-Nogat Delta. Groups of G. began to move south-east from the 2nd half of the 3rd cent. AD onward. In 249, the son of Philippus Arabs was defeated by the G. in Dacia (Chron. pasch. 503 de Boor). The G. participated in the great anti-Roman coalition of the Germani in *c.* 263. *C.* 290, battles erupted between the G. and the Vandali against the Taifali and the Visigoths (Pan. Lat. 287 Baerens). The G. took part in numerous Germanic invasions into the west (Jer. Ep. ad Agerichiam). Between 418 and 454, they were under Hun rulership (Iord. De summa temporum vel origine actibusque gentis Romanae 331). In 451, they invaded Gallia as part of Attila's army. Under Ardaric, they achieved independence with the battle on the Nedao in

454 (Iord. Get. 50,259ff.). Under the latter's rule, they converted to Arianism. The heart of their kingdom was located between the Danube, the Theiß, and the Olt (?). They established a contract with Byzantium. In *c.* 473, as the Goti were leaving Pannonia, the G. crossed the Danube and conquered Sirmium, which became their area of residence (Ennod. Pan. Lat. 12,60). In 488/9, Theoderic defeated the G. on his march to Italia (Ennod. Pan. Lat. 12,60). The G. kingdom divided between 489 and 504 to be ruled by two kings (in Pannonia and Transdanubia). In 504, they were forced to surrender Sirmium and Singidunum to Theoderic (Procop. Vand. 1,2; Goth. 3,33f.) and were pushed back to their Trans-Danubian region. The Langobards, who settled north-west of the Theiß in the early 6th cent., presented an acute danger to the G. Both sides tried to win the favour of Byzantium, with the result that Justinian instigated intrigues between the two sides (Procop. Goth. 7,34f.). Justinian II formed an alliance with the Avares against the G. in 567. After the G. were destroyed by Avars and the Langobards (Menander, fr. 24f.; Paulus Diaconus 1,27), the surviving parts of the population were absorbed into the victorious tribes.

C. Diculescu, Die Gepiden, 1922; L. Schmidt, Die Ostgermanen, 1941, 529ff.; B. Hänsel (ed.), Die Völker Südosteuropas im 6.–8. Jh., 1987; H. Wolfram, F. Daim, Die Völker an der mittleren und unteren Donau im 5. und 6. Jh., 1980. I.v.B.

Geraestus (Γεραιστός; *Geraistós*).

[1] In antiquity, G. was the name for the southernmost tip of Euboea: Hdt. 8,7,1; 9,105; Str. 10,1,2; Plin. HN 4,63; GGM I, 500; Scyl. 58. Called Cape Tzeraso in the Middle Ages, it became an anchorage for Genoan and Venetian ships (remnants of fortifications). Today Cape Mandelo.

F. Geyer, Top. und Gesch. der Insel Euboia 1, 1903, 111ff.; Lauffer, Griechenland, 231. H.KAL.

[2] The only safe harbour on the dreaded southern coast of Euboea, *c.* 3 km north of the cape by the same name [1], today (Porto) Kastri (Eur. Or. 993; Hom. Od. 3,177; Eur. Cyc. 295; Thuc. 3,3,5; Dem. Or. 4,34; Str. 10,1,7; Plin. HN 4,51; 64; Arr. Anab. 2,1,2; Liv. 31,45,10; Ptol. 3,14,22). G. Busolt was mistaken to add G. to the Attic lists of tribute quotas; most likely, G. was never independent, belonging to Carystus most of the time. G. is the place where Agesilaus gathered army and fleet in 396 BC before sailing to Ephesus in the war against the Persians (Xen. Hell. 5,4,61; Plut. Agesilaus 6,4). In 376, when the Spartans closed Piraeus, ships with grain anchored there (Xen. Hell. 5,4,61). In the 2nd Roman-Macedonian War (200–197), G. was a stronghold for the Roman-Pergamene fleet (Liv. 31,45,10). The Poseidon sanctuary was famous (Hom. Od. 3,177; Str. 10,1,7; Aristoph. Equ. 561; Apoll. Rhod. 3,1244; Steph. Byz. s.v. G.; schol. Pind. Ol. 13,159; Lucian. Jupiter tragoedus 25; Procop. Goth. 4,22,27f.; EM 227,42ff). Few ancient remnants (IG XII 9,9f. no. 44–49).

F. Geyer, Top. und Gesch. der Insel Euboia 1, 1903, 111ff.; Philippson/Kirsten 1, 629; Koder/Hild, 186, 212, 281; ATL 1, 1939, 478; Lauffer, Griechenland, 231. H.KAL.

Gerana (Γεράνα; *Gerána*, 'Crane woman'), a Pygmy woman, also called Oenoe (Antoninus Liberalis 16). She scorns Hera and Artemis and was worshipped like a goddess by her peers. Hera changed her into a crane and made her into an enemy of the → Pygmies (Ath. 9,394e; Ov. Met. 6,90). Her death led to a war between Pygmies and cranes (Hom. Il. 3,3ff.; Ael. NA 15,29). Three versions of the myth have been transmitted, all going back i.a. to the 'Ornithogony' by Boeus [1].

1 A. Ballabriga, Le malheur des nains, in: REA 83, 1981, 57–74. RE.ZI.

Gerania (Γεράνεια; *Geráneia*). Mountain range formed primarily by lime and dolomites of the Trias and the Lower Jura as well as (in the west) by ophiolites (serpentinites), reaching across today's Nomos boundary between Attica and Corinth. In the west, it flattens out in Akron Melankavi (and Akron Heraion) into the Gulf of Corinth; in the east, it drops off steeply to the Gulf of Megara (part of the Saronic Gulf), forming the Scironian Cliffs. In Makriplagi, at the border between Attica and Corinth, it reaches a height of 1351 m. In the north, it closes off the Isthmus of Corinth. In the middle, a single pass leads across the mountains (Megalo Derveni 820 m). The dangerous footpath of the Scironian Cliffs (*Kaki Skala*), notorious still in modern times and expanded by Hadrian into a road, runs along the southern drop to the Saronic Gulf. Today, it accommodates train tracks and a highway. Similarly, in the north on the coast of the Corinthian Gulf, the mountains could be circumvented only on difficult trails with long detours (Xen. Hell. 5,4,16ff.; 6,4,26). The αἰγίπλαγκτον ὄρος (*aigíplankton óros*) in Aesch. Ag. 303 probably refers to the G., differing: [1. 129f.]. The northern side of the mountain range was home to a small fort named G. (according to Scyl. 39; Plin. HN 4,23; Suda s.v.), location unknown [2]. On the height above the Scironian Cliffs was a sanctuary of Zeus Aphesios (Paus. 1,44,9), whose excavated remnants have disappeared [2].

1 J. H. Quincey, The Beacon-Sites in the *Agamemnon*, in: JHS 83, 1963, 118–132 2 E. Meyer, s.v. Megara (2), RE 15, 167.

A. Philippson, s.v. G., RE 7, 1236ff.; E. Meyer, s.v. Megara (2), RE 15, 158; 169ff.; Philippson/Kirsten 1, 948ff. C.L.

Geranor (Γεράνωρ; *Geránōr*). Spartiate, former *polemarchos*, fell in 369/8 BC during the defence of Asine against the Arcadians (Xen. Hell. 7,1,25). K.-W.WEL.

Gerar(a) Probably Tall Abī Huraira/Tall Haror between → Gaza and Be'eršeba. Important settlement of the 18th–11th cents. and the 7th–4th cents. BC. The sources 1 Chr 4,39–40 and 2 Chr 14,8–14 refer to the events of the 4th or 3rd cent. BC, although it remains unclear, where the authors were looking for G. 2 Macc 13,24 no longer refers to G., only to 'Gerrenians'. In the 4th–6th cents. AD, there is mention of a *saltus Geraritícus*, seat of the bishop of Orda in 518.

1 O. Keel, M. Küchler, Orte und Landschaften der Bibel, vol. 2, 1982, 134–137 2 NEAEHL 2, 553–560 3 P. Thomsen, Loca Sancta, 1907, 51. E.A.K.

Geras (Γῆρας; *Gêras*, Lat. Senectus). Personification of hated old age, often depicted as a small, naked, wrinkly old man with a long, drooping penis who is defeated by → Hercules in a burlesque way [1]. As a creature of the night (Hes. Theog. 225), G. belongs to the creatures of horror found at the entrance to the Underworld (Verg. Aen. 6,275; Sen. Herc. f. 696), although he resides on Olympus (Aristoph. Av. 606). Sisyphus is brought back to the Underworld by G. (Eust. Od. 11,592). A sanctuary is attested only for the extremely pious residents of Gades (Philostr. VA 5,4).

1 H. A. Shapiro, s.v. G., LIMC 4.1, 180ff.

F. Preisshofen, Unt. zur Darstellung des Greisenalters in der frühgriech. Dichtung, 1977. B.SCH.

Gerasa (modern Ǧaraš). City located 34 km north of ʿAmmān. Thanks to a stream with the ancient name of Chrysorrhoas, G. was a place of settlement from the time of the early Stone Age. It is therefore reasonable to assume that a settlement already existed when the Macedonians, mentioned in a Roman inscription, introduced the Greek element – contrary to legends that → Alexander [4] the Great, → Perdiccas, or → Antiochus [2] I were the city's founders. In the Seleucid period, the Aramaic name of Garšu was common, in addition to the official name of Antioch on the Chrysorrhoas. During the Hasmonaean uprising of 173–164 BC, G. remained in Greek hands but ended up under Roman rulership with the other cities of the → Decapolis in 63 BC. After this, the city's name was changed to G. Graeco-Nabataean inscriptions attest to the close connection between G. and → Petra in this time period. When G. was annexed to *prov. Arabia* in AD 106, the link to the *via Nova Traiana* resulted in even more lucrative economical contacts to Nabataea. From the Augustan age, but esp. from the 2nd cent. AD on, the city was changed through an ambitious building programme supported by local patrons. The old cult site was replaced by the terraced grounds of the temple of Zeus (AD 162–166), a monumental Artemisium (AD 150–180) was consecrated to the city goddess, two theatres were built, a *cardo maximus* and two *decumani* created a strictly axial groundplan surrounded by a city wall. Even though the rise of → Palmyra brought economical setbacks, G. still prospered into the post-Justinianic period. Numerous churches were built within the city (5th/6th cents. AD). No important buildings stem from the time period following the Sassanid occupation (AD 614) or the Islamic conquest (AD 635). The city was destroyed by a series of earthquakes in the 8th cent. AD.

I. Browning, Jerash and the Decapolis, 1982; C. Kraeling (ed.), G., City of the Decapolis, 1938; F. Zayadine (ed.), Jerash Archaeological Project vol. 2, 1989.
Maps: B. Andreae, Röm. Kunst, ²1999, 572f.; C. Kraeling (ed.), G., City of the Decapolis, 1938. T.L.

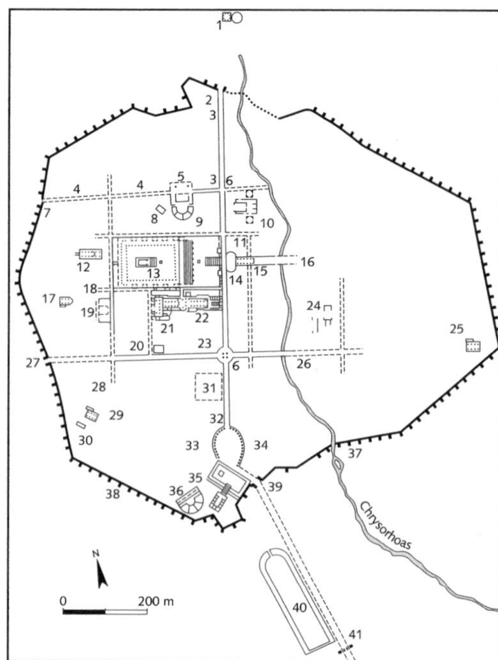

Gerasa

1 Octagonal church
2 North Gate
3 Northern cardo
4 Northern decumanus
5 Square in front of the north theatre
6 Tetrapylon
7 Northwest Gate
8 Church of Isaiah
9 North theatre
10 West Baths
11 Atrium mosque
12 Synagogue church
13 Temple of Artemis
14 Propylaea court (Atrium), Nymphaeum
15 Viaduct church
16 North bridge (destroyed)
17 Church of St. Genesius
18 Stairway
19 Complex of three churches (St. Cosmas and Damian, St. John, St. George)
20 Omayyad building (?)
21 St. Theodorus
22 Cathedral
23 Square around the south tetrapylon
24 East Baths
25 Church of Procopius
26 South bridge
27 Southwest Gate
28 Southern decumanus
29 St. Peter and Paul
30 Memorial church
31 State Agora (?)
32 Southern cardo
33 'Oval Forum'
34 Hellenistic settlement mound
35 Temple of Zeus
36 South theatre
37 Sluice-gate
38 City wall
39 South Gate
40 Circus
41 Triumphal Arch of Hadrian

Gerellanus Praetorian tribune, who instigated the killing of consul Iulius Vestinus in AD 65 under Nero's orders (Tac. Ann. 15,69). His brother is possibly L.G. Fronto (CIL III 14387 g.h = IGLS VI 2786/7).

B. Dobson, Die Primipilares, 1978, 201f. W.E.

Gerenia (In Str. also Γέρηνα; *Gérēna*, on inscriptions ἁ πόλις τῶν Γερηνῶν, formerly *Enópē*). Spartan perioecic city on the west side of the Taygetus peninsula, member of the league of → Eleutherolakones during the Imperial period. The location is documented on an inscription (finding-place of a decree with the mention τὸ ἱερὸν τοῦ Μαχάονος, 'the sanctuary of Machaon') near today's Kambos, 15 km south-west of Kalamata, home also to a Mycenaean cupola tomb. The relationship to → Nestor, who is said to have spent time there in his youth or later as a fugitive, is a pure fabrication spun from his epithet *Gerḗnios*, which must be explained in a different way ('old, venerable' or as patronymic). Sources: Hom. Il. 9,150; 292; Str. 8,3,7; 29; 8,4,4f.; Paus. 3,21,7; 26,8–11; Ptol. 3,14,43.

E. Meyer, s.v. Messenien, RE Suppl. 15, 177; B. Sergent, La situation politique de la Méssenie du Sud-Est à l'époque mycénienne, in: RA, 1978, 3–26. Y.L.

Gerga (Γέργα; *Gérga*). Village in northern → Caria, south-east of Eskiçine on the Marsyas [4], near Incekemer (formerly Gâvurdamları). The name G. (also *Gergas*, *G. kṓmē*) is to be found many times in uniquely large clumsy Greek (on one occasion also Latin) letters on boulders, rock stelae hewn in a pyramid shape and idol-like colossal statues (fragmentary) in the vicinity of a small temple (?) built of solid granite blocks, on the temple itself and carved into one of the low well-houses (?). Several parts that have been worked over in the rock (cult devices?) are enigmatic; the inscription *G. énbolo* on a rock sheet perhaps designated the place for the speaker of the community. The rough buildings and sculptures appear primeval, but like the inscriptions, they are from the Imperial period (2nd/3rd cents., archaizing?). The secluded sanctuary to a Carian god (G.?) or the *Mḗtēr oreía* ('Mountain mother'; → Asia Minor IV. E.) obviously maintained little contact with the Hellenistic-Roman high culture.

In a rock formation close to the Roman aqueduct of Incekemer south of G., the *Leukaí Stḗlai* ('white pillars', Hdt. 5,118) of the Cares can possibly be detected.

G. E. Bean, G. in Caria, in: AS 19, 1969, 179–182; Id., Kleinasien 3, 1974, 211–217; R. P. Harper, Two Carian Notes, in: S. Şahin et al. (ed.), Stud. zu Rel. und Kultur Kleinasiens. FS K. F. Dörner, vol. 1, 1978, 384–388, esp. 386–388; W. Koenigs, Westtürkei, 1991, 159 f.; A. Laumonier, Les cultes indigènes en Carie, 1958, 446–451; R. T. Marchese, The Historical Archaeology of Northern Caria, 1989, 39 f.; Archaeological Reports 45, 1998–99, 158; Zgusta § 202–1; D. Müller, Bildkomm. zu den Historien Herodots: Kleinasien, 1997, 333. H. KA.

Gergis (Γέργις; *Gérgis*, *Gérgitha*, *Gergíthion*, *Gérgithos*). City in the Troad, not located at the foot of the Balli Dağı as formerly assumed but at the Karıncalı on the Kursak deresi [1. 349]. According to Ath. 6,256 C, it was founded by the descendants of the Troes (Teucri) under the leadership of a Gergithes. In the context of Xerxes' campaign, Herodotus mentions the *Gérgithes Teukroí* (7,43), to whom he had referred earlier as the successor tribe of the Teucri (Hdt. 5,122). Ceramic finds from Karıncalı go back to the 6th cent. BC. G. is not mentioned in the Attic lists of tribute quotas. In the 5th cent. BC, the city was apparently the seat of the dynast, which was conquered in 399 BC by Dercylidas after the victory over the dynast Mania (Xen. Hell. 3,1,15). Dercylidas sacrificed in the Athena sanctuary located there (Xen. Hell. 3,1,22f.). G. apparently remained free up to the peace of Apamea, when it became subject to Ilium (Liv. 38,39,10). Strabo (13,1,70) reports of Gergitha, the place where the residents of Gergithion were relocated from the Troad after the destruction of their city by a certain Attalus. If there is any truth to this (thus already [2. 106]), then G. was destroyed by Attalus. I, a group of residents was resettled in a newly founded Gergitha, and the region was annexed to Ilium in 188 BC. In any case. the youngest pottery finds belong to the 2nd cent. BC [1. 347f.]. G. no longer existed in Pliny's time (HN 5,122).

1 J.M. Cook, The Troad, 1973 2 W. Leaf, Strabo on the Troad, 1923. L. Bürchner, s.v. G., RE 7, 1248f. E.SCH.

Gergovia City of Gallia Celtica in the region of the → Arverni, later in Aquitania, west of the Elaver, 6 km south of → Augustonemetum on a high plateau that is hard to reach, today Gergovie. Besieged unsuccessfully by Caesar in 52 BC (Vercingetorix: Caes. B Gall. 7,34; Liv. Per. 107; Str. 4,2,3; Suet. Iul. 25; Polyaenus 8,23,9; Cass. Dio 40,35; Sid. Apoll. Carm. 7,152). Excavations of the large and the small camp and the connecting double trench. Three surrounding walls on the Merdogne-Plateau (Gaulish before the siege, Gaulish-Roman after the siege and in the early Imperial period). In the interior: houses and two temples in a peribolos. Prosperity under Augustus (pottery workshops, market, sanctuaries), decline since Tiberius; the *oppidum* remained vacant from the time of Claudius.

P. Eychart, L'oppidum des côtes, Augustonemetum, Gergovie, 1961; Grenier, vol. 1, 198–200; J. Harmand, Vercingétorix, 1984; M. Provost, C. Jouannet, Carte archéologique de la Gaule. 63,2 (Puy-de-Dôme), 1994. Y.L.

Germa, Germokoloneia (Γέρμα κολωνία, Γερμοκολώνεια; *Gérma kolōnía*, *Germakolṓneia*). *Colonia Iulia Augusta Felix Germenorum*, founded between 25/24 and 21/20 BC; at the crossing of the roads Ancyra – Dorylaeum/Ancyra – Pessinus. Attested as a suffragan diocese until the 12th cent. Ruins near modern Babadat.

H. v. Aulock, Die röm. Kolonie G., in: MDAI(Ist) 18, 1968, 221–237; Belke, 168f.; Mitchell I, 87–90, 151f., 155; M. Waelkens, G., Germokoloneia, Germia, in: Byzantion 49, 1979, 447–464. K.ST.

Germani, Germania G. is a collective noun attested in various regions of Europe and West Asia and was disseminated, at least in part, by the migrations of splinter groups. Linguistically, Germanic belongs to the Indo-European language family (→ Germanic languages); the term 'Germanic' was attributed from outside. Countering popular, Romantically influenced ideas that assumed a parallelism of language and material culture, as well as a lasting ethnic constancy, and countering an inherently racist concept of the unity of the G. that has been misused for ideological purposes, the problem of the Germanic ethnogenesis is posed anew today (→ Germanic archaeology). This covers the historical reality as well as the classification of the G., evident in self-description and in external definition, as an expression of unity. According to the understanding in antiquity, this classification was not based on any specific characteristic but was the result of a general evaluation based on a state of affairs, real or imagined, that could also be mutually contradictory with regard to details.

[1] G. on the right side of the Rhine
I. Historical-Ethnical II. Historical-Geographical

I. Historical-Ethnical
A. Ancient Definitions B. Germani, Rome and modern research

A. Ancient Definitions

While in the earlier Greek tradition the area north of the *oikoumene* was seen as shared between the Celts and Scythians, later geographic transmission fixes the area of settlement of the G. as being bounded by the Rhine and Danube to the west and south (Tac. Germ. 1,2) and the Vistula in the east (Mela 3,33; Plin. HN 4,81; 97), including the → Suebi. Posidonius knew obviously of a group of G., north of the low mountain area (Mittelgebirge) and east of the Rhine, whom he saw as related to the Celts but distinct from them (Ath. 4,39 p. 153e Kaibel = FGrH 87 F 22; cf. Str. 7,1,2). This group's self-assertion during the migrations of the → Cimbri seems to be an argument for extending the name of G., and for their identification with neighbouring tribes, rather than adopting the notion deriving from Tacitus (Germ. 2,3) of G. settling west of the Rhine [see II], which, however, is clearly marked as hearsay, to which Tacitus does not commit himself. Even the Mannus genealogy (Tac. Germ. 2,2), probably first formulated by Posidonius, is no evidence of an original ethnic unity. Only in Caesar does the concept of G. start to take shape but, as Cicero (Prov. 13,33; 56 BC) points out, he neither created it for political purposes nor was the first to make it known in Rome. However, Caesar significantly promoted the spread and acceptance of the name G. Consequently, the tribes settling west of the Rhine became a historical reality as G.

B. Germani, Rome and modern research

In the pre-Roman phase, it was partly by force and partly with the consent of the Celtic population that the G. crossed over the rivers Rhine and Danube that were later regarded as borders. Contacts between Romans, Celts and G. resulted in a process of acculturation, especially in the border areas. Germanic tribes or groups of tribes were repeatedly settled on imperial Roman territory from the time of Augustus. As the border was pushed forward over the Rhine and the Danube and the → *limes* was established, other G. entered into territory directly controlled by Rome, although they are not easily discernible in the material culture of the early and middle Imperial period. From the time of Caesar, G. served in the Roman forces as auxiliary troops, either formed or called up *ad hoc*. In Rome, G. formed the emperor's bodyguard, from Caesar and Augustus to Galba as *G. corporis custodes,* and from Trajan to Septimius Severus exclusively then partly, as *equites singulares Augusti*. For the Romans, the *furor Teutonicus* (Luc. 1,255) became an ideological cliché, regardless of actual experience and greater understanding through a wide range of contacts, and this is also evident in portrayals of the G. On the other hand this corresponds with the repeated emphasis that the Romans gave to their victories over the G.

The history of the G. is primarily a history of individual tribes in their respective historical settings. Accordingly, generalized comments on the economic, social and political structure of 'the G.' are naturally undifferentiated and do not reflect the complex historical reality. In general, especially, Caesar's excursus on the Germans (Gall. 6,21–28) and Tacitus' *Germania* are taken as the basis for an oversimplified statement on common Germanic characteristics. Both accounts, however, are conditioned by the times and need to be interpreted in the context of the respective motivations of the authors. Literary transmission and archaeological research are thus to be analyzed first, according to their respective preconditions, before they can be related to each other. In this context, research has been keen to develop an interdisciplinary concept of the G.

Tribal hierarchy, the structure of rulership and society, including allegiances, as well as economic conditions in *Germania magna,* are discussed in the context of studies in Germanic antiquity (see the relevant articles in RGA). For Roman policy towards the Germani see II C. below.

→ Germani, image of the

J. Herrmann (ed.), Griech. und lat. Quellen zur Frühgesch. Mitteleuropas bis zur Mitte des 1. Jt. u.Z. (Schriften und Quellen der Alten Welt 37,1–4), 1988–1992; H. Ament, Der Rhein und die Ethnogenese der Germanen, in: PrZ 59, 1984, 37–47; H. Beck (ed.), Germanenprobleme in heutiger Sicht, RGA, suppl. vol. 1, 1986; H. Birkhan, Germanen und Kelten bis zum Ausgang der Römerzeit (SB der österr. Akad. der Wiss., philol.-histor. Kl. 272), 1970; A. Demandt, Die westgerman. Stammesbünde, in: Klio 75, 1993, 387–406; G. Dobesch, Zur Ausbreitung des Germanennamens, in: W. Alzinger et

al., Pro arte antiqua. FS H. Kenner, vol. 1, 1982, 77–99; B. KRÜGER (ed.), Die Germanen: Gesch. und Kultur der german. Stämme in Mitteleuropa (Veröffentlichung des Zentralinst. für Alte Gesch. und Arch. Akad. Wiss. DDR 4,1–2), 51986–1988; A.A. LUND, Die ersten Germanen: Ethnizität und Ethnogenese, 1998; RGA, s.v. G., 1998 (forthcoming); H. STEUER, Frühgesch. Sozialstruktur in Mitteleuropa (AAWG 3.F., no. 129), 1982; D. TIMPE, Die Söhne des Mannus, in: Chiron 21, 1991, 69–125; Id., Der Namensatz der taciteischen Germania, in: Chiron 23, 1993, 323–352; M. TODD, The Early Germans, 1992 (repr. 1995); R. WENSKUS, Stammesbildung und Verfassung. Das Werden der frühmittelalterlichen Gentes, 1961 (repr. 1977); H. WOLFRAM, Die Germanen, 31997; K. DÜWEL, H. JANKUHN, H. SIENS, D. TIMPE (ed.), Unt. zu Handel und Verkehr der vor- und frühgesch. Zeit in Mittelund Nordeuropa, Teil I (AAWG 3. F., no.143), 1985; H. JANKUHN, Siedlung, Wirtschaft und Gesellschaftsordnung der german. Stämme in der Zeit der röm. Angriffskriege, in: ANRW II 5.1, 65–125; II 5.2, 1262–1265.
RA.WI.

II. Historical-Geographical

A. GEOGRAPHY AND REGIONAL STUDIES B. ROME AND GERMANIA UNTIL THE ESTABLISHMENT OF THE ROMAN PROVINCE C. THE ROMAN PROVINCE AND ITS HISTORICAL DEVELOPMENT

A. Geography and regional studies

Greek and Roman ideas of the size, geographical segmentation and the population of northern Europe were vague until the time of Caesar. They held that, north of the Danube, the → *Hercynia silva* traversed the whole continent whose boundary in the north was the Oceanus, which extended eastwards into the unknown. According to Caesar, for whom the G. east of the Rhine were a reality, Gaul and the Roman empire were threatened especially by uprisings of aggressive tribal alliances of the → Suebi (Caes. B Gall. 1,37,3f.; 1,54,1; 4,1–4; 4,16,5; 4,19,1–4; 6,29,1). Historical prototypes were the → Cimbri and the → Teutoni, counted among the G., whose migration to the west was stylized as a myth and trauma of the threat to Italy from the peoples of the north (Caes. B Gall. 1,33,3f.; 2,29,4f.; Tac. Germ. 37,1f.; Plut. Marius 11–27 etc.). Not until → Agrippa [1] in the early Augustan period was a firmly geographical description of G. undertaken, which consequently influenced geographic reports on the G. Thus, G. was bordered by the Rhine, the Danube (or the Alps), the Vistula and the Ocean (Str. 1,1,17; 1,2,1; 2,5,28–30; 4,4,2f.; 7,1,1; 7,2,3f.; Strabo, however, describes only the area as far as the Elbe as really known; Mela 3,24–33; Plin. HN 4,80, cf. 4,98–100,8; Tac. Germ. 1,1f.). In the east, instead of the Vistula (Mela 3,33; Plin. HN 4,81; Dimensuratio provinciarum 8,19), tribes (Getae, Bastarni, Sarmatae, Daci) are also mentioned whose areas of settlement, not accurately established, separate them from G. According to Tacitus (Germ. 46,1), the Suebi, by then settled, mark the northern limits not only of G., but also of peoples about whom concrete knowledge is available. Into the Germanic area, additional information on the type of country, the climate, the tribes and their origins is introduced, frequently linked to accounts on the customs and practices of the inhabitants. The information, generally acquired secondhand, is on the one hand mixed with topoi and generalizations and, on the other hand, has its focus narrowly concentrated on what seems to be unusual in Roman view and thus, not infrequently, on what is rather marginal in historical perspective.

B. Rome and Germania until the establishment of the Roman Province

Literary tradition of military conflicts and peaceful relations between Rome and G. reports almost exclusively from the Roman-Mediterranean perspective. Moreover, it is fragmentary, subject to Roman conditions of historiography and ethnography, in accordance with the contemporary taste of Graeco-Roman readers and heavily dependent on available, often officially filtered information.

Political and military contacts between Rome and G. began with Caesar's crossing the Rhine twice, in 55 and 53 BC. They were a demonstration of Roman power, although there had previously been partly peaceful negotiations, partly hostile encounters with tribes and tribal princes from the Germanic area. From the late Republic and the early Imperial period until late antiquity, the Roman-Germanic relationship was not characterized by constant conflict, and such a state of affairs did not really exist between Rome on the one hand and a homogenous G. on the other hand. With → Claudius [II 24] Drusus a new phase began in 13/12 BC, in which the protection of Gaul and Roman imperial territory was aimed at by securing the region on the right bank of the Rhine as far as the Elbe with political and military actions. Thereby, a political G. extending to the Elbe (cf. for example R. Gest. div. Aug. 26,2) was added to the geographic G. Whether, and to what extent, internal political considerations and concessions and to the idea of a 'world domination' may have influenced the decision to take the offensive remains contented. Nevertheless, we need to separate the concrete, practically motivated decisions from an interpretation of the procedure in terms of ideological imperatives designed to appeal to the imperial fantasy of the Roman public. Statements defining the inhabitants of G. as potential rivals with regard to world domination (Tac. Germ. 37,2–6; cf. already Sen. De ira 1,11,3f.) can be attributed to the latter category. After the death of Drusus in 9 BC and the subsequent operations by → Tiberius in 8/7 BC, the goal of turning this G. into a province (Vell. Pat. 2,105,4) seemed close, but a *provincia* G. was not formally instituted. Only the kingdom of the → Marcomanni under → Maroboduus which had gained strength was regarded as a threat, but the Pannonian uprising in AD 6–9 necessitated an agreement. Relying on their base camps, especially those of the legions on the Rhine, the Romans made thrusts into the interior of G. along well-known routes, with the course of rivers and the sea route, as well as the traditional overland invasion routes from the Upper Rhine to the Lower Rhine dictating their direction. After the defeat of P. Quinctilius Varus against a Germanic tribal group under → Arminius in AD 9, the number of legions stationed on the Rhine front was increased from six to eight, and at the same time a twofold area command was established, the *exercitus Germanicus superior* and *inferior*. The principles of Rome's Germania policy, however, were not abandoned in the process. Not until → Germanicus was recalled by Tiberius in AD 16 did Rome's Germania policy undergo a new orientation, with more limited goals, similar to those before Drusus' campaigns. The troops were still used to pacify Gaul internally and guard it against external threats. The more or less direct control of the border zones directly beyond the Rhine was aimed principally at consolidating what had been gained and was determined by tactical military concerns. This includes the advancement of the border on the Upper, Lower and Middle Rhine from Claudian times but especially from the Flavian period, with the inclusion of Wetterau, Odenwald and the → *decumates agri* in imperial territory, not least to ensure a closer link between the Rhine and Danube. Establishment of the → *limes* in the Domitian period, with the – from an overall perspective – nonessential extensions under Hadrian and Antoninus Pius, was aimed essentially at border control but was also the expression of a rather lower evaluation of danger from the G. That is reflected in the successive reduction in the number of legions, down to four for both G. together. Protection of imperial territory became the responsibility of reinforced auxiliary troops stationed along the border.

C. The Roman Province and its historical development

Official establishment of the provinces of *Germania superior* and *inferior* in the early Domitian period brought a formal conclusion to the goals of Roman Germania policy. Thereafter, the military focus shifted from the Rhine front to the Danube. The two provinces formed a third, now Roman G. The Vinxt river south of Remagen formed the border between the two provinces. *G. inferior* almost exclusively, and *G. superior* to a great extent, comprised large sections of Gallic territory, but how territories in the west were allocated to both G. is an issue partly unresolved. The capitals were → Colonia Agrippinensis and → Mogontiacum. At the height of the Imperial period, each of the provinces was under the control of a *legatus Augusti pro praetore* of consular rank, who was in charge of the military command and the civil administration. Financial administration was the responsibility of an equestrian *procurator provinciae Belgicae utriusque Germaniae*, who resided in → Augusta [6] Treverorum. In both provinces distinct corporate bodies, such as *coloniae*, *municipia* or *civitates*, existed, or were established in the course of time.

Around the middle of the 2nd cent. new offensives were launched on the Roman imperial borders from the territory of *G. magna*, but the two Germanic provinces were largely spared. Incursions by the → Alamanni in the course of the 3rd cent., which Rome sought to ward off with clearing operations, led to the abandonment of the *limes* and of the Roman territory on the right bank of the Rhine around the middle of the century. Although this did not result in a complete break in continuity, the decline in terms of economy and civilization, not only in the former imperial territories on the right bank of the Rhine, were evident. At that time, the → Franci were also penetrating the Roman provincial territory on the Central and Lower Rhine. Both provinces were then part of the so-called Gallic Empire. Following → Diocletian's measures of stabilization, the Germanic provinces were divided into smaller units. In the course of the 4th cent., Rome occasionally ventured into the territory on the right bank of the Rhine but its territorial gains were limited to small bridgeheads. At the beginning of the 5th cent., further heavy incursions by Germanic tribes took place, sounding the death knell for Roman domination.

While the Roman military was initially the decisive driving force for economic, civilizing and cultural changes in the 1st cent., a partly independent civil process got underway from the end of that century, culminating in the heyday for Rome's Germanic provinces in the 2nd and early 3rd cents. Evidence for this is provided by bustling construction activity, economic productivity, combined with extensive trade, artistic creativity and an abundance of textual and non-textual evidence of every kind. Even after this period, however, the cities on the left bank of the Rhine maintained their earlier significance. Acculturation processes led to a mixed Gallo-Roman culture also in the Germanic provinces, which in places preserved its unique identity well beyond the period of late antiquity.

Sources: H.-W. Goetz, K.-W. Welwei (ed.), Altes G., 1995; J. Herrmann (ed.), Griech. und lat. Quellen zur Frühgesch. Mitteleuropas bis zur Mitte des 1. Jt. u.Z. (Schriften und Quellen der Alten Welt 37, 1–4), 1988–1992; A. Riese, Das röm. G. in den ant. Inschr., 1914.

Research reports: M.-Th. Raepsaet-Charlier, G. Raepsaet-Charlier, Gallia Belgica et G. Inferior, in: ANRW II 4, 11–299; Ch.-M. Ternes, Die Prov. G. Superior im Bilde der jüngeren Forsch., in: ANRW II 5.2, 726–1260.

Bibliography for A.: A.A. Lund, Zum Germanenbild der Römer, 1990; G. Neumann, H. Seemann (ed.), Beitr. zum Verständnis der Germania des Tacitus, Teil II (AAWG 3. F. no. 195), 1992; D. Timpe, Geogr. Faktoren und polit. Entscheidungen in der Gesch. der Varuszeit, in: R. Wiegels, W. Woesler (ed.), Arminius und die Varusschlacht, 1995, 13–28.

Bibliography for B. and C.: D. Baatz, F.-R. Herrmann (ed.), Die Römer in Hessen, [2]1989; A. Becker, Rom und die Chatten (Quellen und Forsch. hess. Gesch. 88), 1992; H. Cüppers (ed.), Die Römer in Rheinland-Pfalz, 1990; W. Czysk, K. Dietz, Th. Fischer, H.-J. Kellner (ed.), Die Römer in Bayern, 1995; R. Fellmann, La Suisse gallo-romaine, 1992; PH. FILTZINGER, D. PLANCK, B. CÄMMERER (ed.), Die Römer in Baden-Württemberg, 31986; H.G. HORN (ed.), Die Römer in Nordrhein-Westfalen, 1987; J.-S. KÜHLBORN (ed.), Germaniam pacavi, 1995; G.A. LEHMANN, Das Ende der röm. Herrschaft über das „westelbische" G., in: ZPE 86, 1991, 79–96; H. NESSELHAUF, Die spätröm. Verwaltung der gall.-german. Länder, 1938; M.L. OKUN, The Early Roman Frontier in the Upper Rhine Area, 1989; B. TRIER (ed.), Die röm. Okkupation nördl. der Alpen. Kolloquium Bergkamen 1989 (Bodenaltertümer Westfalens 26), 1991; C. RÜGER, Germany, in: CAH X2, 1996, 517–534; H. SCHÖNBERGER, Die röm. Truppenlager der frühen und mittleren Kaiserzeit zw. Nordsee und Inn, in: BRGK 66, 1985, 321–497; K.E. STROHEKER, Germanentum und Spätant., 1965; D. TIMPE, Arminius-Studien, 1970; Id., Der Triumph des Germanicus (Antiquitas 1,16), 1968; W.A. VAN ES, De Romeinen in Nederland, 31981; G. WALSER, Caesar und die Germanen (Historia Einzelschr. 1), 1956; C.M. WELLS, The German Policy of Augustus, 1972; K.-W. WELWEI, Röm. Weltherrschaftsideologie und augusteische Germanienpolitik, in: Gymnasium 93, 1986, 118–137; R. WIEGELS, Rom und Germanien in augusteischer und frühtiberischer Zeit, in: W. SCHLÜTER (ed.), Kalkriese – Römer im Osnabrücker Land, Arch. Forsch. zur Varusschlacht, 31994, 231–265; R. WOLTERS, Röm. Eroberung und Herrschaftsorganisation in Gallien und G. (Bochumer hist. Stud., Alte Gesch. 8), 1990. RA.WI.

III. RELIGION

Ancient sources transmit little on the religion of the G.: a short account by Strabo about human sacrifice amongst the → Cimbri and → Teutoni (Str. 7,294); the most important evidence can be found in Caesar and Tacitus. Caesar paints the picture of a primitive natural religion that extends especially to the veneration of fire and the stars (Caes. B Gall. 6,21). By contrast Tacitus mentions deities with Roman (Mercurius, Hercules, Mars and Isis) and Germanic names (e.g. Tuisto, → Nerthus, → Tamfana, Baduhenna), whom the G. worshipped in groves without sacred architecture and cult images (Germ. 2; 9; 40; Ann. 1,51; 4,73). While Caesar denies their existence, Tacitus repeatedly mentions priests and priestesses who perform human sacrifice (Germ. 7; 8; 10; 11; 43). Neither author is free of positive and negative prejudices about the religion of primitive peoples. Tacitus in particular wants to highlight the superior value of G.'s sacred groves and the absence of images [1. 452–453]. Recent archaeological findings show that, while most cult activity obviously took place in sacred groves, the G. also had smaller primitive, partly anthropomorphic cult images and cult buildings. Also, findings in marshland indicate human sacrifice. From the Germanic names of gods attested from about the middle of the 2nd cent. AD and their identification with Roman gods, a differentiated Germanic heaven of the gods results, with a principal god of heaven (Wodanaz/Mercury), a god of war (Tiwaz/Mars), a weather god (Thor/Jupiter/Hercules) and goddesses of fertility like Frîja/Isis. There were also a large number of locally venerated tribal gods.

Evidence of religion in the Roman Rhine provinces is primarily epigraphical and archaeological in character. We have *c.* 1400 votive inscriptions from Germania superior and *c.* 1600 from Germania inferior, most of which were *c.* AD 150–240. From at least the 2nd cent. AD, a separate regional religion developed here, in the course of Romanization by a process of reciprocal influence (→ *interpretatio*), because the mixed population on the Rhine, through various settlement activities and the influx of soldiers in particular, was hardly able to draw on homogenous traditions. On the basis of Roman, Celtic and Germanic religious ideas, a system developed with new divinities, such as e.g. the → Matres or Matronae, who were venerated especially in Germania inferior, and votive memorials like the 'Jupiter-giant-columns', which were especially common in Germania superior. The Roman religion survived in the imperial and army religion. Besides, there were many eastern cults that reached Germania through Roman mediation. Christianity gained full acceptance late, in the 6th/7th cents. AD, and the Germanic religion came to an end in the non-Roman area of G. only through Charlemagne's Saxonian mission. After the 'German Mythology' of J. GRIMM (1835), research into the religion of the G. was never free of the nationalistic tendencies that culminated in National Socialism.

→ Germanic archaeology; → Germanic languages

1 D. TIMPE, Tacitus' Germania als rel.gesch. Quelle, in: H. BECK, D. ELLMERS, K. SCHIER (ed.), German. Rel.gesch. Quellen und Quellenprobleme 1992, 434–485
2 H. BECK, D. ELLMERS, K. SCHIER, (ed.) German. Rel.gesch. Quellen und Quellenprobleme, 1992
3 F. DREXEL, Die Götterverehrung im röm. Germanien, in: BRGK 14, 1923, 1–68
4 W. SPICKERMANN, Götter und Kulte in Germanien zur Römerzeit, in: G. FRANZIUS (ed.), Aspekte röm.-german. Beziehungen in der frühen Kaiserzeit, 1995, 119–154
5 B.H. STOLTE, Die rel. Verhältnisse in Niedergermanien, in: ANRW II 18.1, 591–671. W.SP.

[2] G. on the left bank of the Rhine. Caesar referred to a group of tribes between the Rhine and the Meuse as *G. cis Rhenum* (Caes. B Gall. 2,3,4), *cisrhenani G.* (Caes. B Gall. 6,2,3) and *G. citra Rhenum* (Caes. B Gall. 6,32,1). They include the → Condrusi, → Eburones, Caerosi, Paemani and → Segni (Caes. B Gall. 2,4,10; 6,32,1). Caesar distinguished this tribal federation from other G. on the left bank of the Rhine. Its members belonged also to the general alliance of the → Belgae, but were also partly dependent on other tribes (Caes. B Gall. 2,3,4; 4,6,4). The tribal federation was obviously destroyed by Caesar's annihilation of the Eburones (Caes. B Gall. 6,34,8). West of the → Ubii it was replaced, *i.a.*, by the Sunuci and the → Tungri (Plin. HN 4,106), although the territorial borders were not identical. These were probably the G. mentioned by Livy (Per. 139) as the opponents of Drusus on the left bank of the Rhine. According to Tacitus (Germ. 2,2f.), it was from them that the German name derived. These G. are no longer found amongst the ethnicities of the early Imperial period. Obviously, they were absorbed into the *civitates* of the Imperial period. Nowadays, all the G. who settled in the north of Gaul are often summarized as the *G. cisrhenani*. Caesar's nomenclature has thus given way to a more general use of the term and concept.

1 H. v. PETRIKOVITS, Germani Cisrhenani, in: Germanenprobleme in heutiger Sicht, 1986, 88–106 2 G. NEUMANN, Germani cisrhenani. Die Aussagen der Namen, in: loc. cit., 107–129 3 D. TIMPE, Der Namensatz der taciteischen Germania, in: Chiron 23, 1993, 323–352.

RA.WI.

[3] Iberian G. According to Plin. HN 3,25 (cf. Pol. 3,33,9: Ὀρῆτες Ἴβηρες; *Orêtes Íbēres*), the G. were a subgroup of the Iberian Oretani; according to Ptol. 2,6,58 there was also a city of the G., named *Ṓrēton Germanôn* (Ὤρητον Γερμανῶν). In general, the correspondence between this name and that of the G. of the north is considered accidental [1. 545]. It is striking, however, that a *dea Poemana* is attested (CIL II 2573) on a stone from Lugo (= Lucus Augusti on the Miño), while the Paemani were one of the four tribes of the Germanic Belgae, according to Caes. B Gall. 2,4,10. Furthermore, despite their designation as Celts, the Spanish Cempsi could be identified with the *Kampsianoí* (Καμψιανοί), whom Strabo (7,1,3) defines as a Germanic tribe. It is thus not improbable that individual Germanic splinter groups reached Spain together with the Celts [2. I 104; III 47; VI 201; VIII 258].

1 R. MUCH, s.v. G., RE Suppl. 3, 545 2 A. SCHULTEN, Fontes Hispaniae Antiquae, 1925ff.

P.B.

Germania libera see → Germanic archaeology

Germanianus

[1] Decimius G. Under Constantius II he was *consularis* of the province Baetica (CIL II 2206). In AD 361, he was temporarily *praefectus praetorio Galliarum* in place of Nebridius, who had refused to give allegiance to Julian, and then again in 363–366 (Amm. Marc. 21,8,1; 26,5,5). PLRE 1, 392 (G. 4).

[2] *Comes sacrarum largitionum* at the court of Valentinian I in AD 366–368 (Cod. Theod. 7,7,1; Cod. Iust. 11,62,3) and probably responsible also for the *res privata* (only three of the laws submitted to him relate to the *largitiones*, the rest, to the *res privata*). PLRE 1, 391 (G. 1).

→ Comes, comites K.G.-A.

Germanicaea (Γερμανίκεια; *Germaníkeia*). City (modern Maraş) in the northern Syrian region of → Commagene mentioned by Ptol. 5,14,8, as well as in Roman itineraries and lists of bishops of late antiquity. The name (on coins Καισαρεία Γερμανική; *Kaisareía Germanikḗ*) is evidence of the gratitude of the Commagenian king → Antiochus [18] IV towards the emperors Caligula and Claudius, who in AD 38 and 41 restored the indigenous dynasty as rulers of the kingdom of Commagene that had been defeated in AD 17 and annexed to the province of Syria. The city was significant in the Byzantine-Arab wars over the Taurus border, since two mountain passes led from it to the Anatolian highlands.

D. FRENCH, Commagene, in: Asia Minor Studies 3, 1991, 11–19; F. HILD, Das byz. Straßensystem in Kappadokien, 1977, 126ff., 137ff.

J.WA.

Germanic archaeology

A. GENERAL B. PRE-ROMAN IRON AGE C. ROMAN IMPERIAL PERIOD D. PERIOD OF MIGRATIONS

A. GENERAL

Germanic archeology (GA) seeks to study the evolution, development and organization of the tribes and ethnicities of the → Germani by drawing on archaeological sources and methods [5; 7; 8]. Thereby, historical and linguistic knowledge about the Germani can be supplemented and extended. Presently, GA is focussing on two aspects: a) the evolution of the Germani in the undocumented pre-Roman period; b) analysis of archaeological sources on patterns of settlement, everyday life, economy, cult of the dead, etc., in order to study those subject areas covered partly incorrectly, fragmentarily, or not at all by the historical and literary sources.

GA's starting-point are always the historic Germani, in order to investigate the archaeological source material (especially burial grounds and settlement sites, but also finds of sacrifices and treasure). For the pre-Roman Iron Age, continuity is assumed for the use of settlements, burial grounds and entire settlement areas. There is a debate as to how reliable this approach is and especially also as to how far it can be traced back chronologically [1; 5; 8]. There is also no way of verifying whether archaeological groupings can be equated to ethnic units. The archaeological picture of the Germani is supplemented by well-preserved bodies found in → swamps. Reference to the Celts and, in particular, to Rome aids in drawing up the chronological relationships.

GA has a long historical tradition of research, as archaeological finds were used from very early on to distinguish and characterize the Germani – often by contrast with the Celts and Romans. In the Third Reich, GA was ideologically biased and was used to promote a thesis of Germanization extending way back into the past [2. 298–320; 6].

B. PRE-ROMAN IRON AGE

At the centre of discussion of the Germani's archaeological roots lies the → Jastorf culture, which in the second half of the last millennium BC comprised the vast area from the west of the Elbe to the Oder and from the edge of the low mountain region (Mittelgebirge) to Jutland (cf. map) [5. vol. 1, 86–202; 6; 7, 131–158]. Common features in the archaeological finds, especially

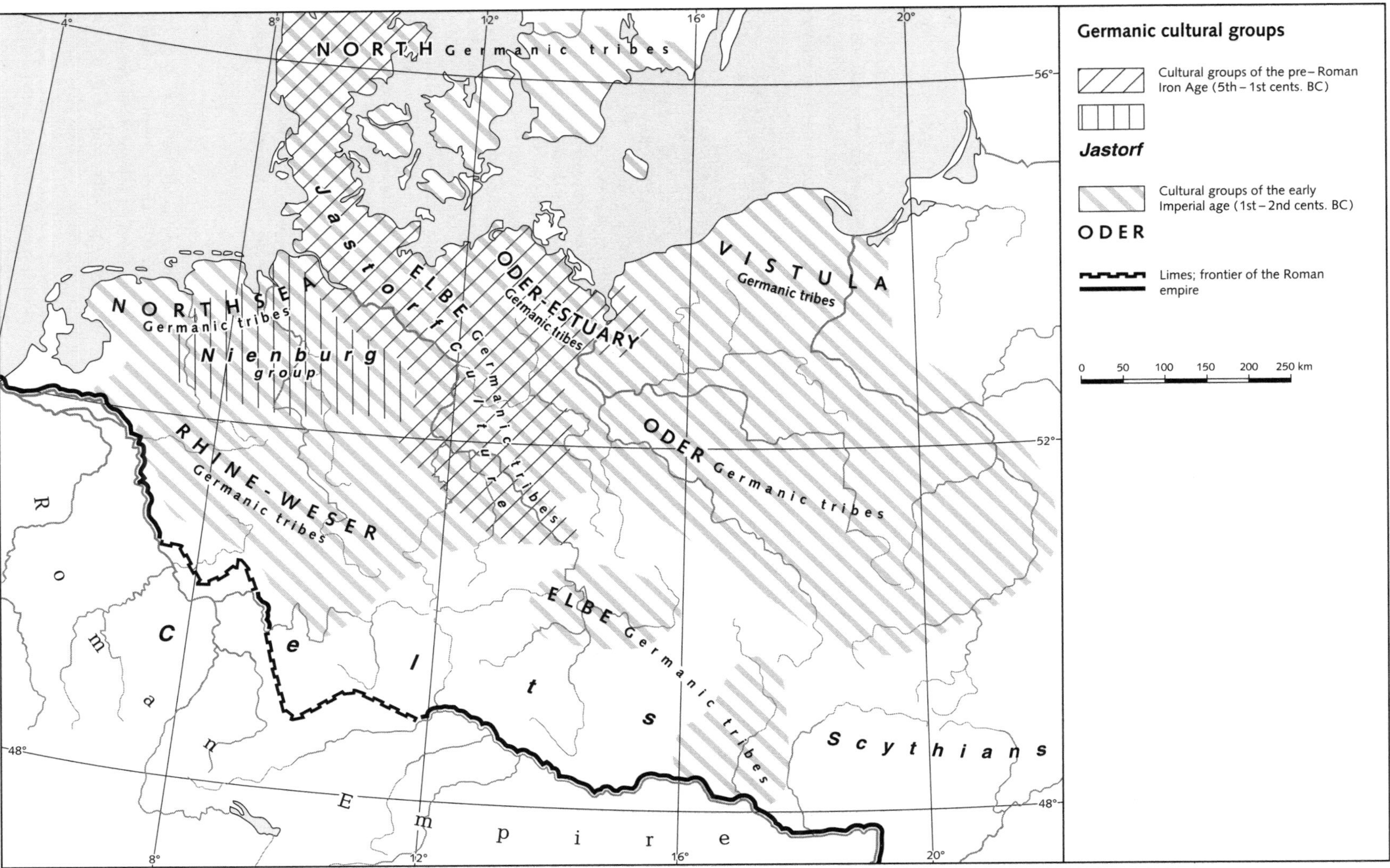
Germanic cultural groups
Cultural groups of the pre–Roman Iron Age (5th – 1st cents. BC)
Jastorf
Cultural groups of the early Imperial age (1st – 2nd cents. BC)
ODER
Limes; frontier of the Roman empire
0 50 100 150 200 250 km
NORTH Germanic tribes
Jastorf culture
ELBE Germanic tribes
ODER-ESTUARY Germanic tribes
VISTULA Germanic tribes
NORTH SEA Germanic tribes
Nienburg group
RHINE-WESER Germanic tribes
ODER Germanic tribes
ELBE Germanic tribes
Celts
Scythians
Roman Empire
4°
8°
12°
16°
20°
56°
52°
48°

in ceramics, particular shapes of needles, fibulae, torques, parts of belts etc., that generally come from flat-grave burial grounds with cremation graves (often in urns protected by stones), suggest the attribution to several regional groupings. The archaeologically distinct → 'Nienburg group' in north-west Germany, on the left bank of the Elbe, has to be included also in the circle of these decidedly rural cultural groups, in which the continuity of the burial grounds (often with several hundred graves) and of traditions of settlement are evident for the period of the historically attested Germani. It remains uncertain whether, and to what extent, these traditions and common features point to an ethnic unity that was also experienced as such by its members and was termed 'Germani' [1; 4].

Over the centuries the Jastorf culture had varied (trade-)contacts with the Celtic world in southern Europe, as attested by a large number of finds [5. vol. 1, 241–263]. Towards the end of the 2nd and in the 1st cent. BC – for reasons unknown to us – fairly large groups (→ Cimbri and → Teutoni, → Suebi of → Ariovistus, etc.), moved south, an event reflected in the first historical accounts that first mention the term Germani. Further incursions remain unrecorded but find archaeological expression for the last cent. BC in southern Bavaria, Bohemia or in the Wetterau [10. 183–202].

C. Roman imperial period

The activities embodied in reflected incursions involves an expansion of the Jastorf culture and at the same time result in the further differentiation of archaeological groups around the time of Christ's birth [7, 157–177; 8]. Again, it is especially grave finds that attest to the transition from the Jastorf culture to the Elbe-Germanic group and also show the respective characteristics of the other Germanic groups. Different forms of cremation graves, the wealth and contents of burial offerings, ceramics and types of adornment (→ Fibulae, etc.) are the most important criteria.

To the west of the centrally located and archaeologically strongest represented Elbe Germani (cf. map), the North-Sea Germani and the Rhine-Weser Germani can be traced archaeologically; to the east there are the Oder, Oder-estuary and Vistula Germani, as well as the North Germani in Scandinavia. Views differ as to the extent to which these groupings can be brought into accordance with further differentiated historically described tribes [7; 8; 9].

The period from the 1st to the 3rd cents. AD is marked, with differing degrees of intensity, by the permanent proximity to the Roman Empire. Around the turn of the eras, attacks take place against Germania, which ultimately result in the foundation of the two German provinces and the construction of the → *limes*; incursions into Germanic territory proper, however, were not substantial. Contacts through → commerce, → mercenaries, etc. strongly colour the archaeological picture of the different Germanic groups. Abundant imports of luxury goods and the adoption of techniques and lifestyles are reflected in the grave finds of *Germania libera* in the form of aristocratic graves (→ Princes, tombs and residences of) or of rich → hoard finds (e.g. the Hildesheim silver treasure) [7]. Due to these imports, H. J. Eggers was able to work out the generally adopted archaeological model of dividing the Imperial period in 'Free Germania' into four or five stages [3]. In the 3rd cent. AD, the formation of larger cultural entities can be discerned in the archaeological finds.

D. Period of migrations

The reasons for the concentration of archaeological groups in the 3rd–4th cents. AD are not clear but connections with the onset of the migrations have often been mentioned; these migrations eventually sealed the end of the Roman Empire in Germania and shaped the events of the 4th–5th cents. in Europe. Ethnicities like the → Alamanni, → Franci, → Goti, → Saxones, etc. manifest themselves here for the first time, also archaeologically attested [5. vol. 2, 336–631; 7]. Archaeological features in common, as e.g. cemetery with row-graves, stand in contrast to the different forms of ceramics, grave furnishings, weaponry, etc. which, however, provide only a limited archaeological basis for mapping out the migratory movements of individual tribal groups.

→ Germani; → Celtic archaeology; → Jewellery; → Settlement, continuity of

1 H. Ament, Der Rhein und die Ethnogenese der Germanen, in: PrZ 59, 1984, 37–47 2 H. Beck (ed.), Germanenprobleme in heutiger Sicht, 1986 3 H. J. Eggers, Zur absoluten Chronologie der röm. Kaiserzeit im freien Germanien, in: ANRW II 5, 3–64 4 R. Hachmann, G. Kossack, H. Kuhn, Völker zw. Germanen und Kelten, 1962 5 B. Krüger (ed.), Die Germanen: Gesch. und Kultur der german. Stämme in Mitteleuropa, vols. 1–2, [5]1986–1988 6 W. Künnemann, Jastorf: Gesch. und Inhalt eines arch. Kulturbegriffs, in: Die Kunde N.F. 46, 1995, 61–122 7 W. Menghin, Kelten, Römer und Germanen: Arch. und Gesch., 1980 8 G. Mildenberger, Sozial- und Kulturgesch. der Germanen, 1972 9 K. Motykova, Die ältere röm. Kaiserzeit in Böhmen, in: ANRW II 5, 143–199 10 S. Rieckhoff, Süddeutschland im Spannungsfeld von Kelten, Germanen und Römern, 1995.
Maps: H. Jankuhn, Siedlung, Wirtschaft und Gesellschaftsordnung der germ. Stämme in der Zeit der röm. Angriffskriege, ANRW II 5, 65–126, fig. 5 B. Krüger (ed.), Die Germanen: Gesch. und Kultur der german. Stämme in Mitteleuropa, vol. 1, [5]1986, 86–105, 191–240 G. Mildenberger, Sozial- und Kulturgesch. der Germanen, 1972, fig. 1 und 2.

V.P.

Germanic languages Original Germanic can be reconstructed from the individual Germanic languages (GL). Like Latin and Greek, it belongs to the group of → Centum languages within the genetically related → Indo-European languages (e.g. Lat. *fer-o*, Greek φέϱ-ω; *phérō*, 'carry, bear', Gothic *baír-an* 'carry, give birth to', Old High German *ber-an* 'give birth to'). The transition to proto-Germanic as a preliminary stage of

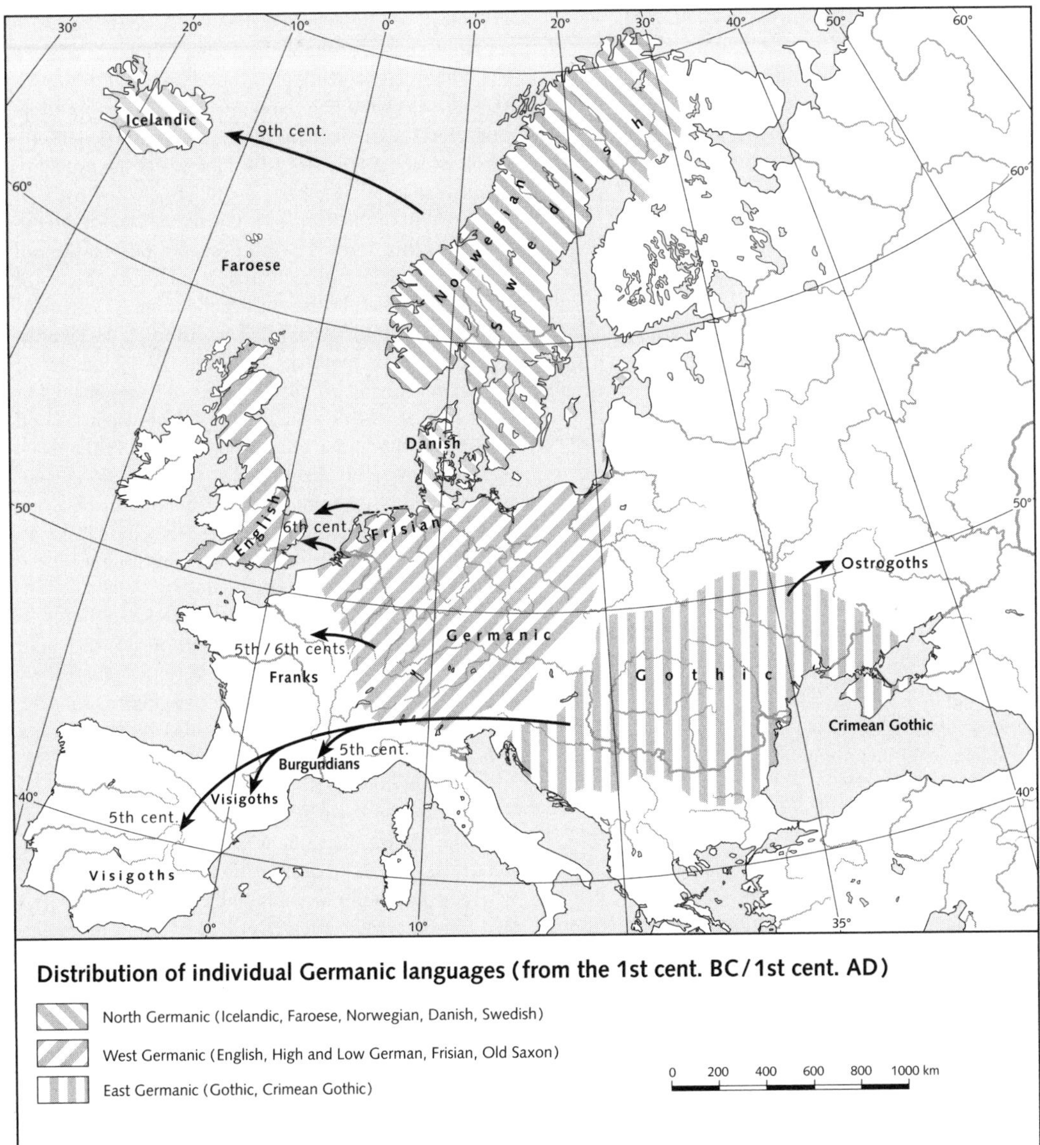

Distribution of individual Germanic languages (from the 1st cent. BC/1st cent. AD)

North Germanic (Icelandic, Faroese, Norwegian, Danish, Swedish)

West Germanic (English, High and Low German, Frisian, Old Saxon)

East Germanic (Gothic, Crimean Gothic)

the individual GL was probably completed around the middle of the 1st millennium BC. Proto-Germanic (*c.* 500 BC until the birth of Christ) differs from other Indo-European languages in characteristic linguistical changes (primarily the Germanic sound shift, accent shift to the first syllable, preterite of weak verbs). However, with proto-Germanic we are not entirely dependent on reconstruction. First written evidence of Germanic words can already be found in ancient authors (e.g. in Caesar, *alces* 'elk', *urus* 'aurochs'; in Tacitus, *glesum* 'amber' > New High German *Glas*; in Pliny, *ganta* 'goose', *sapo* 'make-up' > New High German *Seife* [1. 16]). Personal names are very frequently transmitted (e.g. *Chariovalda* > *Harald* [2; 4]). German loan words have also entered other languages, especially Finnish (e.g. *rengas* 'ring', *saippua* 'soap') and Slavonic (e.g. Old Church Slavonic къnęʒь 'king'). Moreover, Germanic words can be found in Latin documents and law books (e.g. Lex Alamannorum: '... quod Alamanni *mortaudo* (murder and death) dicunt ...' [3. 448]). In the course of their evolution, individual GL in turn have adopted a great number of loan words from Latin (e.g. Ger. *Kiste* from *cista*; Ger. *Pfund*, English *pound* from *pondus*) and Greek (e.g. *Pfingsten* from πεντηκοστή (*pentē-kostḗ*), 'fiftieth [day after Easter]'; often via Latin) [1. 9–30]. The GL are divided into three sub-groups: North Germanic (Icelandic, Norwegian, Danish, Swedish and their precursors); West German (English, High and Low German, Frisian, with their precursors, and Old Saxon); East German (→ Gothic, Crimean Gothic). The formation of the individual GL took place in the first half of the first millennium AD. The earliest linguistically distinct evidence are the runic inscriptions (→ Runes). Gothic linguistic evidence dates back to the

4th cent. AD (→ Ulfila's translation of the Bible, written in → Gothic script). Crimean Gothic is known only from a list of words from the 16th cent. AD (e.g. *schlipen*: *dormire*; *waghen*: *currus*). Nordic evidence from the 3rd cent. AD (so-called Old Norse Runic). West Germanic: English from the 7th cent; Frisian from the 13th cent.; Dutch and Low German from the 8th cent.; High German from the 8th cent.

→ Gothi; → Gothic script; → Indo-European languages; → Centum languages; → Runes; → Ulfilas

1 F. KLUGE, Urgermanisch, in: H. PAUL (ed.), Grundriß der german. Philol. 2, 31913 2 H. REICHERT, Lex. der altgerman. Namen, 2 Teile 1987/1990 3 R. SCHMIDT-WIEGAND, Stammesrecht und Volkssprache. Ausgewählte Aufsätze zu den Leges barbarorum, 1991 4 M. SCHÖNFELD, WB der altgerman. Personen- und Völkernamen, 1911.

H. BECK (ed.), Germanenprobleme in heutiger Sicht, 1986; Id. (ed.), German. Rest- und Trümmersprachen, 1989; H. BIRKHAN, Germanen und Kelten bis zum Ausgang der Römerzeit, 1970; W. BRAUNE, Althochdt. Gramm., 121987; A. HEUSLER, Altisländisches Elementarbuch, 1931 (repr. 1977); H. KRAHE, W. MEID, German. Sprachwiss., 3 vols., 1965–1969; W. KRAUSE, Hdb. des Got., 1968; Id., Runen, 1970; O. W. ROBINSON, Old English and its closest relatives. A survey of the earliest Germanic languages, 1992; W. STREITBERG, Urgerman. Gramm., 1895 (repr. 1974); J. B. VOYLES, Early Germanic grammar: pre-, proto-, and post-Germanic languages, 1992.

MAPS: H. KRAHE, W. MEID, German. Sprachwiss., 3 vols., 1965–1969. S.ZI.

Germanicopolis (Γερμανικόπολις; *Germanikópolis*, Hierocles, Synekdemos 710,2). City in Isauria, modern Ermenek, 67 km north of → Anemurium, probably founded by → Antiochus [18] IV of Commagene [1. 960f.]. G. played a leading role in the Isaurian wars of the 4th cent. AD (Amm. Marc. 27,9,7). G. is attested as a diocese from the middle of the 5th cent. Parts of a necropolis are preserved in the north of the modern city [2].

1 D. STIERNON, L. STIERNON, s.v. Germanicopolis, DHGE 20, 1984, 960–964 2 H. HELLENKEMPER, F. HILD, s.v. G., TIB 5, 1990. K.T.

Germanicus

[1] Epithet, first conferred to Nero → Claudius [II 24] Drusus posthumously by the Senate in 9 BC, for his victories over Germanic tribes; adopted by his successors G. [2], Caligula, Claudius, Nero. Vitellius gave the name to his son. From the time of Domitian, it was again granted by the Senate for victories over Germanic tribes, namely to Nerva, Trajan, and Marcus Aurelius. The intensification 'G. maximus' is found from Commodus to Gratianus.

P. KNEISSL, Die Siegestitulatur der röm. Kaiser, 1969, passim, esp. 246f. W.E.

[2] Son of → Claudius [II 24] and → Antonia [4]. Born 24 May 15 BC, probably in Rome. His name was initially Nero Claudius Drusus, but after the death of his father, Nero Claudius Germanicus, and after his adoption in AD 4, Germanicus Iulius Caesar. He was adopted on 26 or 27 June AD 4 by Tiberius at the urging of Augustus, so as to anchor the newly created form of government of the Principate within the *domus Augusta* for the long term. The *ara Providentiae* was erected on the *campus Agrippae* in memory of the double act of adoption, probably still during the reign of Augustus (*SC. de Cn. Pisone patre* l. 83f. [7. 199ff.]). As Tiberius already had his own son, → Drusus [II 1], the act of adoption probably entailed a degree of compulsion, but even later on no tension developed between G. and Drusus on that score (Tac. Ann. 2,43,6). Probably in AD 5, G. married Agrippina [2] the Elder, Augustus' grand-daughter, who bore him a total of nine children, of whom six outlived their father: Nero Julius Caesar, Drusus [II 2] Caesar, → Caligula, → Agrippina [3] the Younger, Iulia Drusilla, Iulia Livilla.

Through a privilege granted by the Senate, G. was able to take up offices of the magistrature earlier than the legally defined age and thus became *quaestor* already in AD 7. He took part in the campaign against the Illyrian uprising from 7–9 and was awarded *ornamenta triumphalia*. In 11 he was sent to Germania with Tiberius. Whether he already had proconsular powers then is contested; he must have had them by AD 13 at the latest [8. 168ff.]. In 12 he was an ordinary consul for the whole year. Subsequently, he was sent to Germania, where he had supreme command over two armies and two consular *legati Augusti*. Still in 13, or at the beginning of 14, he was acclaimed *imperator*; he thus had his own *imperium* [3. 56ff.]. At the death of Augustus, G. stayed in Belgica to conduct a *census*; on receiving news of the mutiny of the legions in Lower Germany, he returned to the Rhine. The situation was particularly dangerous because the mutineers offered to carry out a putsch against Tiberius in favour of G. G. rejected the offer on principle. Tiberius, however, may have continued to nurture a certain mistrust. G. was able to pacify the mutineers with financial concessions and by releasing the oldest serving soldiers; the mutiny was finally quelled only after Agrippina's withdrawal to Trier (Tac. Ann. 1,31ff.).

In AD 14 the *imperium proconsulare* for G. was renewed by the Senate. In 14 and 15 he marched against the Germani on the right bank of the Rhine and had the remains of Varus' legions buried. He was able to free Segestes from the siege by → Arminius, but generally had no success against the Cheruscans. The triumph that he was accorded to G. in AD 15 recognized the victory of AD 13 or 14 [3. 56ff.]. In 16 he once again campaigned against the Cheruscans; despite the victory, the battle at Idistaviso did not decide the course of events. In the winter of 16–17 G. at last returned to Rome, where, on 26 May 17, he celebrated the triumph over the Cheruscans, Chatti, Angrivarii and all the tribes as far as the Elbe (Tac. Ann. 2, 41, 2; Tab. Siarensis fr. a 12ff.; [6. 515]). An arch to commemorate the recapture of an eagle lost in the battle of Varus was erected already in AD 16 for Tiberius and Germanicus near the temple of Saturn; coins with references to this success were minted only after the death of Tiberius.

In Rome, G. was then apparently seen as a counterpart to Tiberius: a young, universally popular 'prince', who was able to win over the affections of the masses. It may have been for that reason that Tiberius is thought to have hatched the plan to remove G. from Rome. By a Senate decree, the *transmarinae provinciae*, i.e. the provinces east of the Adriatic or east of the Hellespont, were assigned to him, as a new regime was to be installed there that necessitated 'the presence of the *princeps* or one of his two sons' (*SC de Cn. Pisone* l. 31f.). Problems had arisen in particular because of the death in AD 17 of the Cappadocian king whose kingdom Tiberius seized as a province. Furthermore, difficulties with the Parthians over Armenia had to be resolved. By decree of the Assembly G. received an *imperium*, that, according to *SC de Cn. Pisone* l. 33ff., was superior to all proconsuls and, according to Tac. Ann. 2,43,1, to all governors (*imperium maius*). However, the *imperium* of Tiberius was always to be superior to G.'s; this was probably the reaction to G.'s behaviour in Germania when he undertook campaigns against the Germani against Tiberius' advice.

Cn. → Calpurnius [II 16] Piso was appointed as G.'s *adiutor* and, probably through the *mandata* of Tiberius, had exclusive command over the troops in Syria. Still in the autumn of AD 17, G. set off to the east with Agrippina and some of his children. He started his second consulate, which he held together with Tiberius, in Nicopolis in Epirus on 1 January 18. After a slow journey via Ilium and Rhodes he arrived in Syria in early summer and immediately headed for Armenia, where he installed Artaxias as the new king. On his return to Syria in the late summer of AD 18, he came into conflict with Piso, which was intensified by people in the entourage of both. In the spring of 19, he travelled to Egypt and was severely reprimanded by Tiberius for this, as the ban on entering Egypt without the approval of the *princeps* applied also to G. He endeared himself to the population of Alexandria by putting state-owned grain on the market during a famine. His journey took him as far as Elephantine, and in the middle of the summer he returned to Syria. There, he got into open conflict with Piso, whose rights G. obviously sharply curtailed without authority. When G. fell ill in Antioch in early autumn, he broke off the *amicitia* with Piso (*SC de Cn. Pisone* l. 27ff.). Shortly afterwards, G. died on 10 October AD 19, allegedly from poison and magic. Before his death G. himself had declared Piso responsible for it. The corpse was cremated in the forum in Antioch and Agrippina took the ashes back to Italy by ship in the winter of 19/20. In January/February AD 20, G.'s remains were interred in the Mausoleum Augusti. News of G.'s death had caused a highly emotional reaction among the population of Rome which continued until April 20. The Senate and the Assembly accorded him honours, similar to those bestowed earlier on Gaius and Lucius Caesar: they are recorded in the *tabula Siarensis* and *tabula Hebana* [6. 507ff.]. The trial of the alleged murderer, Cn. Piso, did not come to an end until 10 December 20. The final verdict of the Senate was published in Rome, in all provincial capitals and all legion encampments, so as to disseminate the Senate's ruling on Germanicus and Piso. The *SC* was discovered in six copies in the province Baetica [7].

G. as writer: he composed 725 lines of hexameter verse under the title *Claudi Caesaris Arati Phaenomena*, an adaptation of → Aratus [4], see [5].

Coins: RIC I² 110ff.
Portraits: Fittschen-Zanker Catalogue I no. 23ff.
Editions: Les Phénomènes d'Aratos, ed. Le Boeuffle (Coll. Budé), 1975.
Bibliography: 1 PIR² J 221 2 D.G. Weingärtner, Die Ägyptenreise des Germanicus, 1969 3 R. Syme, History in Ovid, 1978 4 G. Bonamante, M.P. Segoloni (ed.), Germanico, 1987 5 C. Santini, L'astronomia e Germanico nell' Antologia Palatina, 1991 6 M. Crawford (ed.), Roman Statutes, vol. 1, 1996, 507ff. 7 W. Eck, A. Caballos, F. Fernández, Das s.c. de Cn. Pisone patre, 1996 8 F. Hurlet, Les collègues du prince sous Auguste Tibère, 1997, 163–208.

W.E.

Germanus

[1] Son of a sister of Justin I, cousin of Justinian I, Byzantine general, as *magister militum per Thracias* under Justin I he conquered the people of the Anti who had invaded the Empire from the lower Danube. As *patricius* and *primus magister militum praesentalis,* he successfully combated the military revolt of Stotzas in North Africa in 536–537, on the orders of Justinian I. In a deployment in 540 against the first assault by Chosroes [5] I after the 'eternal peace' of 532, a shortage of troops prevented him from achieving any notable success. Because of empress Theodora's intrigues against him (Procop. Arc. 5; for the novelistic character of this part of the HA, however, see → Belisarius), he fell from favour, possibly for a few years. We do not hear of him again until 548, in connection with a conspiracy against Justinian, in which he was allegedly involved together with his son → Iustinus. In the ensuing trial, however, he was able to make a credible plea of his innocence. Thereafter Justinian gave him Matasuntha, the widow of the defeated Gothic king Witigis (died in 542) and grand-daughter of Theoderic, as wife, and appointed him commander-in-chief in the war against the Goths. G., however, died in 550, even before crossing to Italy.

PLRE 2, 505–507 (G. 4); Rubin vol. 2, 1995, 276 (Index s.v.).

F.T.

[2] from Iustiniana Prima, son of Dorotheus, still quite young, he defeated the Huns in the region of the Thracian Chersonnesos in AD 559 on the orders of emperor Justinian I, who had had him brought up (PLRE 3, 528 [G. 4]).

F.T.

[3] Patriarch of Constantinople AD 715–730, saint of the Orthodox church. The year of his birth is contested (reckoned between *c.* 630 and 670, cf. [3. v-vii; 6. 157]). G. was possibly related to the imperial family [10] and after his father's involvement in the murder of → Constans [2] II in 668 he was made a eunuch. From 705 he was bishop of → Cyzicus, supported → monotheletism under emperor Philippicus (711–713), but after his overthrow he supported orthodoxy again. As patriarch he came into conflict with emperor → Leo III, according to later Byzantine tradition because of the iconoclastic controversy that began in 726, but actually probably because of Leo's interference with Church administration (the so-called transfer of Illyricum, [8. 154]). G. had to resign in 730 and then lived on his estate Platanion near Constantinople. The year of his death is unknown, but he probably still lived after 746 [9. 267–281].

The theological works and ecclesiastical writings transmitted in his name are only partly authentic. His anonymous *vita* [6. 200–240] originated only in the 11th cent.

EDITIONS: 1 PG 98, 39–454.
BIBLIOGRAPHY: 2 C. GARTON, L. WESTERINK (ed.), Germanos I. On Predestined Terms of Life, 1979 3 L.G. WESTERINK, Germanos on Predestined terms of Life, 1979 4 J. DARROUZÈS, Deux textes inédits du patriarche Germain, in: REByz 45, 1987, 5–13 5 H.-G. BECK, Kirche und theologische Lit. im byz. Reich, 1959, 473–475 6 L. LAMZA, Patriarch Germanos. I. von Konstantinopel, 1975 7 P. SPECK, Klassizismus im achten Jahrhundert?, in: REByz 44, 1986, 209–227 8 Id., Die Affäre um Konstantin von Nakoleia, in: ByzZ 88, 1995, 148–154 9 Id., Artabasdos, 1981 10 E. STEIN, Die Abstammung des ökumenischen Patriarchen Germanus. I., in: Klio 16, 1920, 207. AL.B.

Germia (Γέρμια; *Gérmia*). Town on the northern edge of the Dindymon in *Galatia II*, modern Gümüşkonak (previously Yürme; different [1]); attested from 553 as a suffragan diocese, then as an archdiocese.
→ Eudoxias

1 M. WAELKENS, Germa, Germokoloneia, G., in: Byzantion 49, 1979, 447–464.

K. BELKE, G. und Eudoxias, in: W. HÖRANDNER, Byzantios. FS H. Hunger, 1984, 1–11; BELKE, 166–168, 247; MITCHELL II, 129. K.ST.

Germinius (Germanios). Bishop of Sirmium from 351, belonged to the *principes Arianorum* (→ Arianism); together with Valens of Mursa and Ursacius of Singidunum he drafted a creed that mentioned only the 'similarity' (ὅμοιος, *hómoios*), not the identical nature (ὁμοούσιος, *homooúsios*) of the Son and God-the-Father (4th Sirmic Creed). The (5th) Synod of Rimini (359) imposed anathema (excommunication) on the authors. Consequently, emperor Constantius II enforced revisions and further synods, until the Synod of 378 in Rimini, after G.'s death, finally adopted the Nicene version.

PL 10, 487; PG 26, 742; Handb. der Kg II/1 (1973), 46; A. JÜLICHER, s.v. G., RE 7, 1262f.; R. ROGOSIC, s.v. Sirmium, LThK², vol. 9, 795f. RO.F.

Germisara (CIL III 1395; Γερμίζερα; *Germízera* Ptol. 3,8,4; cf. *Germigera* Geogr. Rav. 4,7; *Germizera* Tab. Peut. 8,1). Roman fortress and civilian settlement in Dacia superior, modern Geoagiu (Romania). G. lay in the Marisus valley and was administratively dependent on Sarmizegetusa. Tile of the *Legio XIII Gemina* (CIL III 8065; 14h). Thermal baths at the site (cult of nymphs) and a quarry in the vicinity.

TIR L 34, 1968, 60 (Bibliogr.). J.BU.

Gerontes (γέροντες; *gérontes*). 'Elders', in the Homeric epic not only the aged advisers of a city-king (Hom. Il. 3,149) but also high-ranking dignitaries (→ Basileus, I. B. Homeric) with leadership functions in war and peace (Hom. Il. 2,404–408). From the advisory assemblies in early Greek pre-city settlements and defensive communities, committees with distinct competencies and criteria of admission developed along with city structures. An indication of this process is the trial scene in Hom. Il. 18,497–508, in which *gerontes* resolve a dispute over compensation [1; 2. 10]. From the archaic period, for example, members of the → *gerousía* in Sparta were termed *gerontes*.

1 R. WESTBROOK, The Trial Scene in the Iliad, in: HSPh 94, 1992, 53–76 2 K.-J. HÖLKESKAMP, Agorai bei Homer, in: W. EDER, K.-J. HÖLKESKAMP (ed.), Volk und Verfassung im vorhell. Griechenland, 1997, 1–19. K.-W.WEL.

Geronthrae (Γερόνθραι; *Gerónthrai*). Spartan *perioikoi* town on the western edge of the Parnon above the Eurotas valley, later part of the league of the → Eleutherolakones, near modern Geraki, still inhabited in the Imperial period and thus even named in Hierocles (Synekdemos 647,9). Paus. 3,22,6f. mentions a temple of Ares with a grove, an agora with a fountain house and a temple of Apollo on the acropolis. Further evidence: Steph. Byz. s.v. Γεράνθραι; *Geránthrai*; IG V 1, 1110–1141.

C. LE ROY, Inscriptions de Laconie inédites ou revues. I: Inscriptions de Géronthrai, in: Mél. G. Daux, 1974, 219–229; A.J.B. WACE, F.W. HASLUCK, H.J.W. TILLYARD, Laconia. Geraki, in: ABSA 11, 1904/5, 91–123; 15, 1908/9, 163f.; 16, 1909/10, 72–75; 55, 1960, 85f. Y.L.

Gerontius

[1] Armenian, held his first office in the imperial administration in AD 356–357 (Lib. Ep. 538 FOERSTER), *praefectus Aegypti* in 361–362. In 364–365 (without office) he had great influence at the court in Constantinople (Lib. Ep. 1484 etc.). PLRE 1, 393 (G. 2).
[2] Commander of the city of Tomi in AD 384–387. He had barbarians in Roman service executed for planning an assault on the city. Charged for that act, he was able to escape only by bribery (Zos. 4,40). PLRE 1, 393f. (G. 4).

He is perhaps identical to the commander in Achaea (PLRE 1, 394 [G. 6]), who in 395 deliberately did not prevent Alaricus [2] from marching through Greece. K.G.-A.

[3] Briton, *comes et magister militum* of the usurper → Constantinus [3] III, whom he freed from Valentia together with → Edobicus in AD 408 (Zos. 6,2,4f.). On the usurper's behalf he subjugated Spain in 408 (Zos. 6,4,2; 6,5,1), but when the usurper tried to dismiss him in 409, he had his *domesticus* Maximus proclaimed emperor. Still the army commander, he expelled Constantinus' son from Spain in 411, pursued him to Vienna and had him executed there. G. besieged Constantinus III in Arelate, but when an army of Honorius advanced, many of his soldiers went over to the latter. G. fled to Spain, was defeated there still in 411 by the troops who had deserted him and committed suicide (Sozom. Hist. eccl. 9,12,6; 9,13,1–7; Olympiodoros fr. 16 FHG IV 60f.; Oros. 7,42,4; Greg. Tur. Franc. 2,9).

PLRE 2, 508; A. Demandt, s.v. magister militum, RE Suppl. 12, 647f. K.P.J.

Gerousia (γερουσία; *gerousía*, 'Council of Elders'). I. Graeco-Roman II. Jewish

I. Graeco-Roman

In Sparta the *gerousia* was probably originally an assembly of representatives from leading families. There it gained its institutional character from early on and consisted of the two kings and 28 → *gérontes* (γέροντες), who were appointed for life and were at least 60 years old. Election took place on the basis of the volume of the acclamation in the → *apélla* (ἀπέλλα), with 'electoral officials' in a closed room deciding who got the strongest applause (Plut. Lycurgus 26) [1]. According to the Great → Rhetra (Plut. Lycurgus 6), the Spartan *gerousia* could submit proposals to the *apélla* as early as the 7th cent., but did not have to accept the decision of the *dâmos* (δᾶμος) based on the acclamation; thus, decisions could only be made with the consent of all organs of the *polis* (except for the not yet mentioned ephors). This consensus-oriented procedure is characteristic of pre-state societies. The powers of the *gerousia* were never formally rescinded, but it is hardly evident in the transmission of political decisions in the classical period. As far as that is concerned, the Spartan *gérontes* were neither 'rulers of the crowd' (δεσπόται τῶν πολλῶν; *despótai tôn pollôn*: Dem. Or. 20,107) nor 'helmsmen of the state' (Pol. 6,45,5), however, this did not exclude consultations between the → *éphoroi* and the *gérontes* in critical situations (Xen. Hell. 3,3,8). The *gerousia* had political importance primarily as the tribunal hearing cases against military commanders and Spartan kings, as well as capital offences (Xen. Lac. 10,2; Aristot. Pol. 1275b 10; Paus. 3,5,2). Their corruptibility (Aristot. Pol. 1270b 35ff.) is evident in recorded trials (Xen. Hell. 5,4,24–33). Their function, however, was obviously only formal during the Hellenistic period in the context of the affirmation by oath of an alliance with Athens in 268 BC (Stv 3,476, l. 91) [2. 117ff.]. As a consultative body the *gerousia* was 're-activated' in 243–242 for political reasons (Plut. Agis 11), when it supported the intentions of → Agis [4] IVs opponents with a majority of one vote and did not present the latter's reform plans to the public assembly.

Aristotle (Pol. 1272a7–8; 34–35) and Ephorus (FGrH 70 F 149 [Str. 10,4,17]) compared the Spartan *gérontes* to the council members in Cretan *poleis* elected from the former → *kósmoi* who, however, were officially described as *preígistoi* (πρείγιστοι; StV 2,216) in an agreement between Gortyn and Rhittenia (end of the 5th cent.) and, several times elsewhere, collectively as *bōlá* (βωλά = βουλή, → *boulḗ*) [3. 112ff.]. According to Ephorus (in Str. 10,4,22), they were regarded as advisers to the highest-ranking officials. Legally, their powers lay primarily in the area of controlling the civil service. In Elis, until the institution of a council of the 500 privileged families in the 5th cent., they formed a council of *gérontes,* appointed for life and limited to 90 (Aristot. Pol. 1306a 12ff.). Originated from similar councils of elders probably also were the *amnḗmones* (ἀμνήμονες) in Cnidus (Plut. Mor. 291d) and the so-called Eighty in Argos [4. 56ff.], who in 420 BC still participated in the swearing of oaths for a state treaty (StV 2,193; Thuc. 5,47,8). According to Diodorus (16,65,6–8), a *gerousia* existed in Corinth at the time of Timoleon which was responsible for criminal cases and for decisions on foreign policy. It was probably identical to the eighty-member *boulḗ*, to which a pre-advisor and nine other *bouleutaí* (βουλευταί) were appointed from each of the eight historical phyles of Corinth.

After the battle of Ipsos, a *gerousia* was instituted by Lysimachus in Ephesus (and probably in other *poleis* of his kingdom) (Syll.³ 353; Str. 14,1,21), which, however, did not gain importance in its own right. The *gerousia* mentioned by Polybius (38,13,1) in the Achaean League in 146 BC was probably identical to the college of *dāmiorgoí* of that time [5. 231]. A member of the *gerousia* in the Arcadian Orchomenus performed official duties as a witness in acquittal proceedings that took place after 146 (IG V 2, 345). The *gerousia* is frequently mentioned as communal body in inscriptions of the Imperial period from Thrace and Asia Minor, as well as from the Mediterranean area. Greek authors also used the term *gerousia* to designate the Carthaginian and Roman Senates. In the rules of the Iobacchae in Eleusis, the *gerousia* had a private character, Syll.³ 1109 (*c.* AD 178).

1 E. Flaig, Die spartanische Abstimmung nach Lautstärke, in: Historia 42, 1993, 139–160 2 H. Heinen, Untersuchungen zur hell. Geschichte des 3. Jh. v.Chr., 1972 3 St. Link, Das griech. Kreta, 1994 4 M. Wörrle, Unters. zur Verfassungsgesch. von Argos im 5. Jh. v.Chr., (thesis) 1964 5 J. A. O. Larsen, Greek Federal States, 1968.

St. Link, Der Kosmos Sparta, 1994, 76–79; L. Thommen, Lakedaimonion Politeia, 1996, 37f. K.-W.WEL.

II. Jewish

In the Hellenistic period the *gerousia* was the official body representing the population of Judaea (→ Palaestina). Its origins probably go back to Persian times (cf. Ezra 5:5; 5:9; 6:7; 6:14; 10:8, et al.). The *gerousia* was mainly recruited from the nobility (the proportion from the priestly nobility is contested) and first appears as a regular committee in a decree of → Antiochus [5] III (223–187 BC), who had been respectfully welcomed by the *gerousia* after the 5th Syrian War (201–200 BC) and in return granted them, the priests, the temple scribes and temple singers exemption from taxation, in recognition of their loyalty and with regard to a speedy rebuilding of Jerusalem (Jos. Ant. Iud. 12,138–144). → Antiochus [6] IV also addressed the *gerousia* in a letter (2 Macc 11:27). With Jonathan (High Priest from 153 BC), the High Priest seems to have been ranked with the *gerousia* as the people's representative (cf. 1 Macc 12:6; Jos. Ant. Iud. 13,166). Many scholars assume that the *gerousia* was continued in the institution of the Sanhedrin (→ Synhedrion).

M. Hengel, Judentum und Hellenismus. Studien zu ihrer Begegnung unter bes. Berücksichtigung Palästinas bis zur Mitte des 2. Jh. v.Chr., ³1988, 48f.; E. Schürer, The history of the Jewish People in the Age of Jesus Christ, vol. 2, 1979, 202–204. B.E.

Gerrha The most important trading post in north-east Arabia at the time of the Seleucids (304–64 BC), at the intersection of India in the east, Mesopotamia in the north, Arabia in the south-west and the Levant in the north-west. Spices and incense were the commodities predominantly traded. The location of the ancient G. is uncertain. Two places on the eastern coast of modern Saudi Arabia, Ǧubail, right on the banks of the Persian Gulf, and Ṯağ, *c.* 100 km to the east inland [1. 89], might correspond to the harbour G. (HN 6,32,147) and the city G. [1. 89] mentioned by Pliny.

Trade with G. is mentioned in a large number of Greek written sources [1. 90]. In the late 4th cent. BC, G. had close trading contacts by sea with Babylonia. During the 3rd cent. BC incense from B. arrived overland in Ptolemaic Egypt and Syria-Palestine controlled by the Ptolemies. G.'s economic and political activities suffered after → Antiochus [5] III's victory (222–187 BC) over the Ptolemies, who presumably forced their rulers to resume their trade with Babylon on an increased scale [1. 94]. In the middle of the century, Syria-Palestine again belonged to G.'s trading zone; trade with the Nabataeans is attested. As the Parthians grew in strength (AD 247–227), G. finally re-oriented its trading links by turning to → Charax Spasinou as a new important trading partner.

→ Nabataei

1 D. Potts, The Arabian Gulf in Antiquity 2, 1990. M.H.

Gerrhus (Γέῤῥος; *Gérrhos*).

[1] River in the north Pontus between → Borysthenes and → Maeotis, the border between the monarchic and nomadic Scythians, identified as modern Moločnaja voda (Ptol. 3,5,4; Plin. HN 4,84, *Gerrhus*).

[2] Region around modern Nicopol/Ukraine, in the 5th/4th cents. BC centre of the monarchic Scythians and seat of their rulers, who were buried in large kurgans (→ Funerary architecture) (Hdt. 4,71).

[3] River in Caucasian Albania on the northern edge of the Great Caucasus, flowing into the Hyrcanian (Caspian) Sea, south of the Albanian border river Soana (Terek?), possibly identical to modern Sulak in Dāġestān (Ptol. 5,12,2 and 7).

A. Akopjan, Albanija-Aluank v greko-rimskich i drevnearmjanskich istočnikach [Albania-Alvank in Graeco-Roman and Old Armenian Sources], 1977, 32f.; F. Gajdukevič, Das Bosporanische Reich, 1970, 288; E. Kiessling, s.v. G. 1)–3), RE 7, 1273ff. A.P.-L.

Gerrunium Fortress in Dassaretia near Antigonea (modern Berat); captured in 200 BC by L. Apustius (Liv. 31,27,2). Probably identical to Gerus (Γεροῦς; *Geroûs*), that was conquered by Philip V in 217 BC (Pol. 5,108,8).

N. G. L. Hammond, Illyris, Rome and Macedon in 229–205 B.C., in: JRS 58, 1968, 16. MA.ER.

Gerulata (It. Ant. 247,3; *Gerolate* Not. Dign. Occ. 34,21). Roman military encampment established in Pannonia superior between Carnuntum and Ad Flexum before 116 BC, once located on a tributary of the Danuvius, modern Bratislava-Rusovce. In the 2nd and 3rd cents. the *ala I Cannenefatium* was stationed in G. (CIL III 4391; XVI 64; 76f.; 84; 96f.; 104; 178). The *equites sagittarii* were mentioned as garrison there during the 4th cent. (Not. Dign. Occ. 34,21). Rich archaeological finds from the 2nd–4th cents.: temple of Jupiter, remains of buildings, burial ground, ceramics, metal vessels, inscriptions, coins.

J. Fitz, s.v. G., RE Suppl. 9, 72f.; TIR M 33, 1986, 39f. (bibliography). J.BU.

Geruli see → Communications

Gerunda (modern Gerona). The place name is probably Iberian (an almost complete collection of toponymical evidence in [1. 2015]). It is debatable whether the Iberian coins with *Krsa* (?) on it refer to G. [2. 81]. The place is frequently mentioned in inscriptions (CIL II p. 614; Suppl. p. 1145). According to Plin. HN 3,23, G. was an *oppidum civium Latinorum*. In the Christian period G. played a role as the city of the martyr Felix (died during the reign of Diocletian; Prudent. 4,29f.), as a diocese and as a Visigothic mint [3. 448]. In AD 713, G. fell temporarily into the hands of the Moors. For G.'s later fate, see [4. 1476].

1 HOLDER I 2 A. VIVES, La moneda hispánica 2, 1924 3 A. SCHULTEN, Fontes Hispaniae Antiquae 9, 1958 4 Enciclopedia Universal Ilustrada 25.

TOVAR 3, 449f. P.B.

Gerunium Town in Apulia, 200 stadia (= 24 miles) from → Luceria (Pol. 3,100,3) on a side-road reaching the coastal road between Larinum and Teanum Apulum (Tab. Peut. 6,3), can probably be located near Castel Dragona to the south of Fortore. In 217–216 BC, it served as Hannibal's winter quarters (Pol. 3,100ff.; Liv. 22,18ff.; App. Hann. 15f).

NISSEN 2, 785. E.O.

Geryoneus (Γηρυονεύς; *Gēryoneús*; also *Gerýónēs*, *Gerýōn*, Γηρυόνης, Γηρυών; Etruscan *Cerun*). Mythical giant with three heads and three bodies, residing on the island → Erytheia in the far west of the inhabited world (later generally identified with Gadeira/Cadiz: Hdt. 4,8, et al., in Ptolemy's Geographia 4,1,16, identified with Mauretania, euhemeristically relocated to Ambracia by Hecataeus FGrH 1 F 26), where he tends an especially splendid breed of red cattle. His father is Chrysaor, originated from Medusa, and his mother, an → Oceanid (Callirhoe).

In the Greek myth, G.'s role consists in being → Hercules' adversary in the tenth of the Twelve Labours. In spite of the increasing level of difficulty of the labours assigned to Hercules, in spite of G.'s monstrous figure and the aid of a shepherd named Eurytion and the dog Orthus, G. does not, however, represent a significantly dangerous opponent: Hercules defeats him without great difficulty with the shot of an arrow. The dangers inherent in this adventure lie instead in the journey to the western edge of the world and back. They are particularly evident in Hercules' dispute with Helios and in the necessity to use a miraculous vehicle, i.e. the sun god's sun chalice, to reach Erytheia across the Oceanus. The G. myth is thus primarily an elaboration of the mythological motif of the 'journey to the end of the world'.

Hercules' adventure with G. was probably already a subject in Greek oral poetry (last but not least indicated by the variations of names). The earliest extant version of the myth can be found in Hes. Theog. 287–294. The choral lyricist Stesichorus extensively elaborated the material at the beginning of the 6th cent. BC. Individual fragments of this *Gēryonēís* are extant (SLG S 13,4 and 14,8). The most intensive iconographic representation of the G.-myth comes from this period. A complete paraphrase, however, is not extant until Apollod. 2,106–109. Apart from the Hercules myth, G. is generally mentioned in later Greek literature, because of his monstrous appearance and thus features in allegories (especially in comedy and the rhetorics of the Second Sophistic). In the Roman sphere, G. appears, apart from references to the Hercules myth, as a form of Underworld demon (Verg. Aen. 6,289; Hor. Carm. 2,14,7f.; with Agyrion and Patavium he had two sanctuaries on Sicily and in northern Italy).

The geographic context of the G.-myth suggests that this figure was originally an independent Celtic deity (of death?), with whom the Greeks probably became familiar through their trading links with the western Mediterranean, and the Romans in northern Italy through the Etruscans.

P. BRIZE, s.v. G., LIMC 4.1, 186–190; M. DAVIES, Stesichoros' Geryoneis and its Folk-tale Origins, in: CQ 38, 1988, 277ff.; G. WEICKER, s.v. G., RE 7, 1286–1296. E.V.

Gesalicus (Gesalech; also Gesalecus, Gisaleicus). Illegitimate son of → Alaricus [3] II; after the latter's death at Vouillé in AD 507 he was elected king of the Visigoths, as his legitimate half-brother → Amalaricus, grandson of the Ostrogothic king Theoderic, was still a minor (Procop. Goth. 5,12,43). G. was soon forced to retreat to Spain by the Burgundians and Franks (Chron. min. 1,665f. MOMMSEN). When Theoderic contested his leadership on behalf of Amalaricus (Procop. Goth. 5,12,46), G. fled to Africa in 511. With money from the Vandal king → Thrasamund, he first went to Aquitania (Cassiod. Var. 43f.), but was later defeated by the Ostrogoths near Barcelona and captured on his flight to the Burgundians in 511–512 or 513–514 and killed (Chron. min. 2,223; 282; 3,465).

PLRE 2, 509f.; W. ENSSLIN, Theoderich d. Gr. [2]1960, index s.v.; H. WOLFRAM, Die Goten, [3]1990, 245–247. M.MEI. and ME.STR.

Ges anadasmos (γῆς ἀναδασμός; *gês anadasmós*). The term *ges andasmos* (*GA*); ('apportioning of land', 'land distribution') was generally applied to a redistribution of agricultural land ('land reform'). Such measures were important not only socially and economically but were also highly important politically, as landownership and citizenship were closely connected in the Greek polis. In the context of other measures, especially χρεῶν ἀποκοπή (*chreṓn apokopḗ*, liquidation of debts) the *ges andasmos* was also the means and the objective in internal power struggles and in times of social unrest. It was accordingly characterized as a revolutionary factor and not infrequently explicitly banned.

The earliest credible reference to demands for land redistribution can be found in the context of → Solon's reforms (Aristot. Ath. Pol. 11,2; Plut. Solon 16,1). Solon did not, however, yield to the people's pressure (Aristot. ibid.; Sol. fr. 5,23 D.). As early as the archaic period, the *GA* played an important role, as may be deduced from later political campaigning and efforts for agricultural laws (Aristot. Pol. 1319a 12ff.; 1265b 12ff.; 1274a 31ff.). Closely related to the *ges andasmos* was the notion of equality of property, which was also discussed in philosophical thought and in legal concepts (Aristot. Pol. 1266a 37ff.; Archytas 47 B 3 DK; cf. Aristot. Pol. 1320b9ff. on Tarent). That is probably the reason why the equality of the landless Spartans was later traced back to a *GA* of Lycurgus (Plut. Solon 16,1f.; comparatio Lycurgi et Numae 2,6; Mor. 226b) and why possibly the *GA* is also mentioned with regard to the Doric conquest and settlement on the Peloponnese (Paus. 2,13,2).

In Herodotus the term is applied to the plans of Arcesilaus of Cyrene, who planned his return from his Samian exile *c.* 530 BC and intended to win over supporters with the prospect of a *GA* (Hdt. 4,163,1). It was thus not so much a social revolution in Cyrene as the acquisition of foreign helpers. Something similar seems to have happened more often also in the classical period, as the examples of a *GA* in Sicily indicate. Linked to the tyranny there, strong shifts of population (indigenous population and colonists, old and new settlers, bondsmen and enslaved groups, mercenaries, emigrants) took place, with a corresponding mobility. Under these conditions, political upheavals were often linked to a *GA* (Diod. Sic. 11,86,3): a link between a *GA* and resettlements is attested in the case of Leontini (423–422 BC; Thuc. 5,4,1ff.). Large shifts in property occurred under Dionysius I, and in the struggle against his son, Dionysius II, Heraclides and Hippon demanded a *GA* and this was contested by Dion (Nep. Dion 7,1f.; Plut. Dion 37,5; 48,6f.). In 317 BC Agathocles was still able to promise to put such a program into effect in Syracuse (Diod. Sic. 19,9,5). Together with liquidation of debts, *GA* played a similar role in the developements before the tyranny of Clearchus in Heraclea Pontike *c.* 364 BC (Iust. 16,4,1ff.).

Evidently *GA* became a policy demand, at times realized during periods of demographic, social and political crisis. As it – or resistance to it – was also relevant to the political regime and together with other measures, especially liquidation of debts, was considered a symptom of upheaval, safeguards against it were frequently formulated in oaths or agreements sealed by sworn oaths, that are attested for Athens (Heliast oath), Delphi, the Corinthian League (337 BC) and Itanus on Crete (Dem. Or. 24,149; FdD III 294, col. VII 5; Ps.-Dem. Or. 17,15; ICret III, IV 8,21f.).

In political theory from the 4th cent. BC, the connection between radical democracy, demagogic tyranny and *GA* is quite common and treated as a theme (Isoc. Or. 4,104f.; 8,79; 12,259; Pl. Resp. 566a; Aristot. Pol. 1305a 2ff.; 1309a 14ff.; Polyb. 6,9,8f.; Schol. Dem. Or. 24,149). Even earlier events could be reconstructed accordingly (on Cyme, cf. Dion. Hal. Ant. Rom. 7,3ff.; especially 7,7,5ff.).

In the Hellenistic period a *GA* was put into effect by the reform kings, Agis IV and Cleomenes III (Pol. 4,17,4f.; Plut. Agis/Cleomenes 13,2f.; 24,5ff.; 31,10ff.; 38,5) by drawing on old concepts of equality, and in the War of Cleomenes (227–222) it was systematically used as a weapon against the Achaean League, though evidently without any great success (Pol. 2,52,1; 4,17,4f.; Plut. Aratus 39,5; Agis/Cleomenes 38,5). Greek authors used the concept of *GA* to describe the agrarian reform of Tib. Gracchus, in a quite conventional fashion, by linking it to the theme of tyranny (Posidon. FGrH 87 F 112 = Diod. Sic. 35,33,6; Plut. Tib. Gracchus 9,3); it was also used in this way in recounting the Social Wars (Dion. Hal. Ant. Rom. 9,52,3).

1 Aristoteles, Politik Buch IV–VI, transl. and introd. by E. Schütrumpf, annotated by E. Schütrumpf and H.-J. Gehrke, 1996 2 D. Asheri, Distribuzioni di terre nell'antica Grecia, 1966 3 S. Berger, Revolution and Society in Greek Sicily and Southern Italy, 1992 4 P. Cartledge, A. Spawforth, Hellenistic and Roman Sparta, 1989 5 H.-J. Gehrke, Stasis, 1985 6 M. Jehne, Koine Eirene, 1994 7 A. Lintott, Violence, Civil Strife and Revolution in the Classical City, 1982 8 A. Passerini, Reforme sociali e divisioni di beni nella Grecia del IV secolo A.C., in: Athenaeum N.S. 8, 1930, 273–298 9 A. J. M. Talbert, Timoleon and the Revival of Greek Sicily, 1971 10 R. Urban, Das Verbot innenpolit. Umwälzungen durch den Korinthischen Bund (338/37) in antimaked. Argumentation, in: Historia 30, 1981, 13–21 11 Id., Wachstum und Krise des Achäischen Bundes, 1979. H.-J.G.

Gesatorix see → Gaizatorix

Gesimund Son of Hunimund the Elder, first Gothic king under Hunnish rule. In AD 376 he helped the Hunnish king Balamber to victory over the Amalian Vinitharius (Iord. Get. 248). Perhaps identical to Gensimund, who, although the kingship was offered to him as Amalian *magister militum*, declined in favour of the legitimate successors (Cassiod. Var. 8,9). PLRE 2,510 and [1. 26f.] consider the two to be identical; contrary [2. 254f.].

1 P. Heather, Goths and Romans 332–489, 1991 2 H. Wolfram, Die Goten, ³1990. M.MEI. and ME.STR.

Gesius or Gessios, from Petra (Steph. Byz. s.v. Γέα/ *Géa*), physician and teacher, end of the 5th/early 6th cent. AD, close friend of Aeneas [3] (Epist. 19; 20) and Procopius of Gaza (Epist. 38; 58; 123; 134). He studied medicine under the Jew Domnos (Suda s.v. Γέσιος/ *Gésios*) in Alexandria, where he practised as → *iatrosophistḗs* (teacher of medicine). Although opposed to Christianity, he was baptized at the instigation of the emperor Zeno but retained a cynically negative attitude towards his new religion. He protected the philosopher Heraescus in his home and arranged for the burial of his non-Christian friend. He wanted to explain the incubation healings (cure through sleep) of Saints Cyrus and Johannes in Menuthis near Alexandria by the application of the methods of Greek profane medicine. Patriarch Sophronios (Miracula SS Cyri et Johannis 30) describes how G. had to seek healing at the same sanatorium after having unsuccessfully tried all other forms of treatment for his back condition. As a highly esteemed master of 'everyone who wanted to philosophize in medicine', G. received large sums of money and 'extraordinary honours' from emperor Zeno (Zacharias of Mytilene, De opifice mundi, PG 75, col. 1016, 1060). He commented on many texts of the *Corpus Hippocraticum*, especially *De natura pueri* ('On the Nature of the Embryo') [1. 36]. In the Cod. Vat. pal. 1090, foll. 1^r–42^v a commentary on Galen's *De sectis* is ascribed to G., while elsewhere → Agnellus of Ravenna or → Iohannes Alexandrinus is named as the author [2. 7f.]. G. is also renowned in Arabic medicine as the author of the so-called → *Summaria Alexandrinorum* [3. 51, 71–75].

1 G. Bergsträsser, Hunain ibn Ishaq, AKM 17,2, 1925 2 C.D. Pritchet, Iohannis Alexandrini Commentaria in Librum De sectis Galeni, 1982 3 O. Temkin, Gesch. d. Hippokratismus im ausgehenden Altertum, Kyklos 4, 1932, 1–80. V.N.

Geskon Carthaginian name (*Grskn = 'protégé of Skn'; Γέσκων, Γίσκων, Γίσγω; *Géskōn, Gískōn, Gísgō*; Lat. *Gisgo, Gisco*).

[1] Son of the Magonid → Hamilcar [1]; after 480 BC he lived as an exile in Selinus, as did probably also his son Hannibal [1] for a while (Diod. Sic. 13,43,5) [1. 30f.; 2. 40].

[2] Carthaginian commander in 343–339 BC in the war against → Timoleon, for which he had been recalled from exile (Diod. Sic. 16,81,3; Polyaenus, Strat. 5,11). In 341 G. crossed over to Sicily as an ally of → Hicetas and → Mamercus and operated there not unsuccessfully until the peace treaty (Diod. Sic. 16,81,4; Plut. Timoleon 30; 34; Stv 2,344) [1. 31–33; 3. 165f.].

[3] Father of → Hasdrubal [5], Carthaginian strategist in Lilybaeum at the end of the 1st Punic War (Pol. 1,66; Diod. Sic. 24,13). G. was involved as a mediator at the beginning of the so-called Mercenaries' War and was eventually savagely killed as a prisoner of the rebels (Pol. 1,69f.; 79–81; Diod. Sic. 25,3) [1. 33f.; 3. 255, 261; 4. 48f., et al.].

[4] Carthaginian emissary to the Macedonian king → Philippus V, on behalf of → Hannibal [4], together with → Bostar [3] and → Mago (Liv. 23,34; 38) [1. 35].

[5] G. Strytanos. [1. 222, 1300], Carthaginian emissary to Rome in 149 BC, together with Gillimas, → Hamilcar [5], Misdes and → Mago (Pol. 36,3–4) [1. 36; 3. 440].

1 Geus 2 L.M. Hans, Karthago und Sizilien, 1983 3 Huss 4 L. Loreto, La grande insurrezione libica..., 1995. L.-M.G.

Gesoriacum Harbour city of the Morini in Gallia Belgica, modern Boulogne-sur-mer, also attested as Bononia. Both names, which were used contemporaneously (Flor. Epit. 2,30), actually refer only to parts of the site. According to the traditional view, G. is the lower part of the city, while Bononia is the upper part (contrary [1. 63]). During his stay in AD 4, Tiberius called the place Bononia (ILS 9463); thereafter, until the beginning of the 4th cent., only the name G. is used (Mela 3,25; Plin. HN 4,102; 106; Suet. Claud. 17; Ptol. 2,9,1; It. Ant. 356; 363; 376; 463; 496). At the beginning of the imperial period, G., situated at the mouth of the Liane, extended from the Vallon des Tintelleries in the north to the Val St. Martin in the south, a valley that ended in the now largely silted-up bay of Bréquerecque, where a military base of the *classis Britannica* for the crossing to Britain was established under Caligula or Claudius. The oldest section of the civilian settlement was located on the southern side of the valley in today's Bréquerecque. The area of development is bounded by the two necropoleis of Bréquerecque in the south and by Veil Atre in the east (*c.* 60 ha; *c.* 40 ha of civilian settlement). At the beginning of the Flavian period an encampment of stones (*c.* 400 × 300 m). was erected on the plateau above the harbour for the *classis Britannica*. Around 270 the lower part of the city fell victim to a conflagration; the camp of the upper city was abandoned. The old core section of the civilian settlement was never re-inhabited. → Carausius is regarded as the founder of the new settlement on what used to be the encampment grounds. He was surrounded and defeated in G. in 293 during his rebellion against → Constantius [1] Chlorus (Panegyricus Constantii Chlori 4,6,1; 14,4). The city was thenceforth known exclusively as Bononia (Pan. Lat. Constantine 7,5 [from 310]; Eutr. 9,21,1; Tab. Peut. 2,1/2; Cod. Theod. 11,16,5) and became the main city of the *civitas Bononensium* (Notitia Galliarum 6,13). Even the harbour achieved new prosperity in the 4th cent. (Amm. Marc. 20,1,3; 9,9; 27,8,6). The course of the fortification walls of the upper city corresponded roughly to that of the earlier fort and was unprotected only on the south-west side towards the harbour. Bononia was mentioned for the last time in 407, when → Constantinus [3] III landed there with Britannic troops (Zos. 6,2,2; Sozom. Hist. eccl. 9,11,3; Olympiodoros, fr. 12). Recently discovered: warehouses, parts of the enclosure walls, from the middle imperial period and late antiquity, in the 'Terrain Landrot' in the former port district [2]. Regular reports on excavations in [3; 4].

1 R. Brulet, The Continental Litus Saxonicum, 1989, 6–72 2 E. Belot, Le renouveau de l'archéologie Boulonaise, in: Archéologia 301, 1994, 42–51 3 Archéologia 4 Revue du Nord (esp. vol. 75, 1993).

J.J. Gosselin, C. Seilier, G.-Bononia, in: Revue archéologique de Picardie 1984, 3/4, 259–264; J. Heurgon, De G. à Bononia, in: (without ed.), Hommages à J. Bidez et F. Cumont (Coll. Latomus 2), 1949, 127–133. F.SCH.

Gessius Florus The last of seven procurators who administered most of Palestine as a Roman province after the death of Agrippa I in AD 44 under the supreme command of the Syrian governor. Born in Clazomenae, he obviously obtained his office through the links between his wife Cleopatra and the empress Poppaea Sabina (Jos. Ant. Iud. 20,252f.). His rule lasted only two years (AD 64–66) and ended with the outbreak of the 1st Jewish uprising against Rome (Tac. Hist. 5,10).

Josephus Flavius whose *Bellum Iudaicum* is the most important source for Gessius Florus (GF) (cf. Jos. BI 2,14,2–2,17,6 = § 277–429), mentions as one of the decisive reasons for the outbreak of Jewish-Roman hostilities the administration of GF, the cruelty of which far exceeded that of his predecessors and that culminated in the plunder of the temple treasure (April/May AD 66) – presumably in order to compensate for the falling tax revenue. GF had to withdraw to Caesarea from the rebellious people of Jerusalem, and the attempts at mediation by the Syrian governor Cestius Gallus failed; simultaneously the Zealots captured Masada, the daily sacrifice for the emperor in Jerusalem was stopped and fighting also broke out against the troops of Agrippa II who was on the side of the party mediating for peace. Cestius Gallus blamed GF for the outbreak of the uprising; he informed Nero to this effect (Jos. BI 2,20 = § 558). Nothing is known of the dismissal from office and death of GF.

A.H.M. Jones, Procurators and Prefects, in: Studies in Roman Government and Law, 1960, 115–125; Schürer 1, 369, 470, 485f.; E.M. Smallwood, The Jews under Roman Rule. From Pompey to Diocletian, 1976. I.WA.

Gesta In the Republican period in Rome the records (also → *commentarii*) that a magistrate made or had made regarding the orders decreed by him (→ *acta*). They were personally archived by the magistrate after the end of his period in office (Cic. Sull. 42). From the 3rd cent. AD the term *gesta* superseded the expression *commentarii* for the official records. Apart from *gesta* the word *cottidiana* occurs in the same sense. With this meaning *gesta* can be found in all levels of the administration of late antiquity. Ultimately the recording of official files and negotiations by *gesta* was transferred to the church (*gesta ecclesiastica*).

Apart from the *gesta* within the administration there were also *gesta* of private individuals in late antiquity. This initially described notices and petitions to the authorities and vice versa – official decisions to private individuals (Cod. Iust. 1,2,14,7; 10,13,1 pr.; Cod. Theod. 11,30,31). Finally *gesta* (as earlier, already *acta*) are official collaborative acts in the Latin language area in the case of private legal transactions: until the early Middle Ages, this facilitates the submission (*insinuatio*) for the official files of contracts, and in the case of gifts of a record regarding the completion of the transaction (*gesta municipalia*) and is even demanded as a prerequisite for effectiveness (Nov. Valentiniani 32). Wills too can be set up in this way (Cod. Iust. 6,23,19,1). In spite of this, the declarations themselves can be made to the authority orally for recording.

B. Hirschfeld, Die gesta municipalia, PhD thesis 1904 A. Steinwenter, Beiträge zum öffentlichen Urkundenwesen der Römer, 1915 P. Classen, Fortleben und Wandel spätröm. Urkundenwesens im frühen MA, in: Id. (ed.), Recht und Schrift im MA, 1977, 13–54 M. Amelotti, Il documento nel diritto giustinianeo, in: G.G. Archi (ed.), Il mondo nell' epoca giustinianea, 1985, 125–137 Kaser, RPR II, 80f. M. Kaser, K. Hackl, Das röm. Zivilprozeßrecht, [2]1997, 601 W. Kunkel, Staatsordnung und Staatspraxis der röm. Republik, 1995, 106. G.S.

Gestio (also *gesta*). Generally an expression for transactions relevant to business (not necessarily legal transactions). In Roman civil law the following are significant: (1) the *pro herede gestio* (behaviour as an heir), informal behaviour (e.g. taking possession) as an expression of the desire to come into an inheritance (→ Succession, law of). (2) the *negotiorum gestio* (modern law: conducting business without a commission). In Roman law it concerns all affairs in the conduct of someone else's transactions that are not commissioned (→ *mandatum*) or result of guardianship (→ *tutela*). This includes the exercise of the authority of the private *curator* (e.g. over the mentally ill, → *furor*) as well as the socially dependent property administrator or trustee in individual business transactions (*procurator*). In the period of the classical jurists (1st–3rd cents. AD) the essence of the *negotiorum gestio* was commerce based on voluntary readiness to help. Justinian classified this *gestio* with quasi-contracts (Inst. Iust. 3,27,1). In addition he expressly demanded of the manager the will (*animus*) to conduct business for another person.

The legal consequence of the *negotiorum gestio* for the owner of a business (in whose favour the *gestio* was effected) was an *actio negotiorum gestorum directa*. With it the owner of the business could demand the return of whatever the *gestor* acquired through the *gestio*. If the *gestor* damaged the owner of the business in a culpable manner, the latter was able to demand compensation (Dig. 3,5,31 pr.; 47,2,54,3). The manager was entitled to an *actio negotiorum gestorum contraria* if he wished to demand reimbursement (*animus recipiendi*). If the *gestio* was in the interest of the owner of the business, the manager could demand reimbursement of outlays and compensation for damages.

Kaser, RPR I, 586–590 H. Honsell, Th. Mayer-Maly, W. Selb, Röm. Recht, 4 1978, 348–350 H.H. Seiler, Der Tatbestand der negotiorum gestio, 1968. G.S.

Gestures

I. Ancient Orient II. Egypt III. Greece and Rome

I. Ancient Orient

The forms of expression in ancient Oriental art were reinforced by a marked language of gestures that was especially useful in the communication between mortals and gods as well as between subordinate and higher-ranking persons. In the sacred sphere gestures expressed individual feelings and wishes; in the profane sphere their official information content was foregrounded more strongly. Prayer gestures were frequently represented by hands placed together in front of the chest [1. 175f.], even though this was not described in the texts. Prayer directed to the gods was however

Speaking and calling

Musician

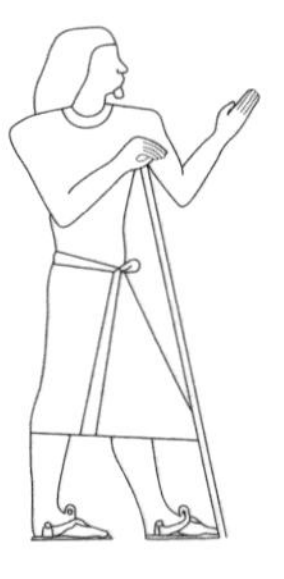

1

2

3

4

Worship and salutation

5

6

7

8

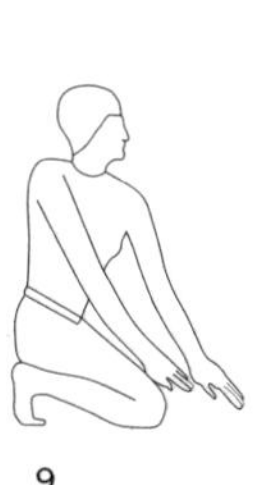

9

Lamentation and mourning

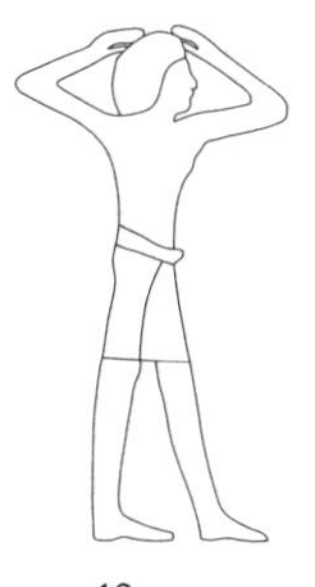

10

11

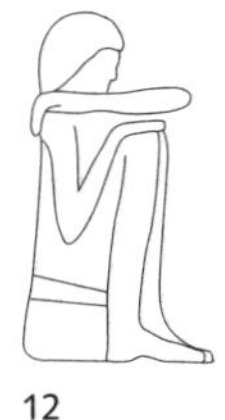

12

13

14

Selection of Egyptian gestures, based on the iconography of the Old and Middle Kingdoms (for the exact references, see [1])

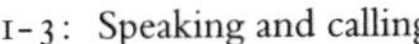

1-3: Speaking and calling
1 The tomb owner speaking [1. 78]
2 Man calling, from a market scene [1. 128]
3 Recitation accompanying the sacrifice in the context of the burial ritual [1. 128]
4: Musician giving a sign to the instrumentalists [1. 170]
5-9: Worship and salutation
5 Invoking the gods [1. 29]
6 Worshipping woman (from a false door) [1. 29]
7; 8 Servants facing persons of higher rank[1. 8; 22]
9 Stranger facing a person of higher rank [1. 22]
10-14: Lamentation and mounring [1. 68]
10 'Raising the arms to the head'
11 Grasping the hem of the garment
12 'Head resting on the knee'
13 Covering one's face with one's hands
14 'Tearing one's hair'

M. HAA.

described as 'raising the hand' whilst 'opening the fists' expressed the beseeching plea ([2. 50–64]; for comparison [6. fig. 453]). The gestures of deference, e.g. throwing oneself down and bowing, were originally characteristic forms of homage and of imploring the gods [3. 161], later they were secularized as signs of political submission or loyalty [2. 178–181, 238–254]. In this connection gestures such as falling at the feet of the king, repeated kissing of the ground in front of people, kissing the foot or grasping the feet of persons ([2. 257–284] were also often used in Assyrian pictorial propaganda; for comparison [6. fig. 355, 371]). Phatic gestures such as extending the finger describes direct speech contact through which important content – particularly in the communication between man and the gods – is conveyed [4. 45–55, 94–104]. A body language develops to express literary and figurative events [2. 313, 318]. In the 1st millennium BC this increasingly becomes part of political propaganda. In this way Assyrian relief art uses gestures to express a marked consciousness of power whereas the rather more dignified language of gestures in the art of the Achaemenid court alludes to the phatic community of the great empire (cf. [5. pl. 17] and [6. fig. 355]; for gestures in the Assyrian region cf. e.g. the stele of King Tukultininurta I (13th cent. BC) in prayer and speech gestures in front of an altar [7]).

1 M. Falkner, s.v. Gebetsgebärden und Gebetsgesten, RLA 3, 175–177 2 M.I. Gruber, Nonverbal Communication (Studia Pohl 12/1), 1980 3 W. v. Soden, s.v. Gebet II, RLA 3, 160–170 4 U. Magen, Assyr. Königsdarstellungen Aspekte der Herrschaft (BaF 9), 1986 5 M.C. Root, The King and Kingship in Achaemenid Art (Acta Iranica 19), 1979 6 ANET 7 W. Orthmann, Propyläen Kunstgeschichte 14: Der Alte Orient, 1975, fig. 195.

DO.BO.

II. Egypt

Representations of gestures are passed down in ancient Egyptian tombs and cult sites; inscriptions explain their general and special meaning. Aside from general and specific accompaniments for speeches, calls and recitation [1. 77–178], there are those that express an inner attitude [1. 5–75; 2. 49–66; 3. 115–129; 4]. General gestures are the outstretched arm with the hand directed upwards or downwards or the hand on the mouth as in the determinatives of the verbs and verbal nouns of speech [1. 77]. In the ritual of sacrifice an oration gesture can be combined with certain words: raising/stretching out the arm, bending the hand/the arm [1. 86–87]. Specific gestures such as the raised fist and the outstretched index finger are found in magical averting of evil [1. 131–150]. Gestures as determinatives are attested for verbs and verbal nouns expressing worship (bowing) and greeting (glorifying, welcoming), mourning and lamentation (wailing), joy and rejoicing (celebrating) [1. 5–75]. The gestures of the determinatives are represented and described with rich differentiation, for example for worship and greeting: bending the arms/the back, 'putting the arms on the body, stretching out the arms' [1. 23–31, 43–48]. Silence as a means of showing respect is designated by placing the hand on the mouth [1. 19]. Mourning and lamentation give rise to a wide range of the gestures represented: the arms/the hand on the head, the arms towards the face, the head on the knee/the arms around the knee [1. 65–75].

1 B. Dominicus, Gesten und Gebärden in Darstellungen des Alten und Mittleren Reiches, 1994 2 A. Hermann, Jubel bei der Audienz, in: ZÄS 90, 1963, 49–66 3 A. Radwan, Der Trauergestus als Datierungsmittel, in: MDAI(K) 30, 1974, 115–129 4 M. Werbrouck, Les pleureuses dans l'Egypte ancienne, 1938.
Representations: B. Dominicus, Gesten und Gebärden in Darstellungen des Alten und Mittleren Reiches, 1994.

B.DO.

III. Greece and Rome

A. Introduction

Gestures are considered to be movements of the arms, hands and fingers (in this regard Quint. Inst. 11,3,92–121; → *gestus*), in contrast with movements of the body (*motus*) with the head (and eyes), legs or feet. Here no distinction is made between gesticulation and gestures, as the boundaries between the two are fluid. Gestures and movements of the hand served to intensify words and actions, to express psychological feelings, wishes, fears and hopes or even to make situations understandable at all; in Roman culture they can also be an expression of legal occurrences or signs of virtue. On the other hand gestures can also be so intensely expressive that explanatory words can be dispensed with, i.e. a gesture can suffice to define and clarify a situation. In art the gesture serves as an aid to bringing a scene presented into sharper focus and explaining it to the observer. It is, however, essential to consider that a gesture can make the understanding of a scene more difficult or even impossible because of its possible double meaning. Many gestures have also taken on a new meaning over time so that this too makes true understanding more difficult.

B. Communication gestures

Emphasis could be added to a conversation between two or more people by means of a wide range of gestures; among the most common was the stretching out of the index and middle finger of the right hand (the other fingers were clasped) in the direction of the discussion partner; the person could also stretch forward his thumb at the same time. A simple communication gesture was also the raised, opened hand, corresponding to the gesture when → greeting. In a further gesture a person pointed forwards with the index finger and the little finger, with the other fingers clasped (*corna* gesture). Admonition or reprimand is expressed by the raised index finger (e.g. crater in Vienna, KM 466 [1. vol. 1, pl. 88,1]); this admonishing gesture can intensify into a command or a directive if the outstretched index finger is directed towards the floor or the discussion partner.

C. Erotic gestures

With the thumb and the index finger a circle is formed (→ Greeting); this gesture is encountered in hetaera scenes (e.g. cup London, BM E 51 [2. 12, fig. 3]), and the same applies to the outstretching of the middle finger with a clenched fist. The so-called up-and-down gesture of the *erastḗs* with his right hand pointing to the penis of the *erṓmenos* and the left – as a gesture of tenderness – to his chin is to be found particularly on vases depicting ἐρασταί (*erastaí*, 'lovers') and ἐρώμενοι (*erṓmenoi*, 'sweethearts') (e.g. hydria Munich, SA 1468, CVA (7) pl. 343; [3]); occasionally this gesture is attested for the man and the woman (e.g. oinochoe Irakleion, Mus. [4]). Women baring their bottom, especially hetaerae (Alci. 4,14,4; Ath. 12,554c-e; Anth. Pal. 5,35; Lucian, Dial. Mer. 3,2), are mentioned in literature, although is it only rarely represented such as by the well-known statue of Aphrodite Callipygus in Naples [5]. Showing the sexual parts by lifting the clothes is exhibitionist in nature in the case of men (Theophr. Char. 11,2) or is an indication of manly potency (Hdt. 2,30,4); in women the exposure can be a sexual invitation and also an expression of contempt for cowards. The complex of erotic gestures also includes spectators of erotic or sexual acts placing their right arm on heads [6. 157, pl. 22, catalogue A 34; pl. 25, catalogue L 7] or pressing nipples [6. 18, n. 23].

D. Gestures of tenderness

Aside from the above-mentioned touching of the chin, the → kiss should be mentioned along with laying the hand or the finger on the chin and cheek of the other person [7. 462 no. 88, vase lost] as a caress, mutual embrace, and also the intimate laying of the arm on the shoulder of another person (e.g. Tib. 1,8,33 should be listed; this gesture also expresses harmony and closeness, e.g. among the Graces, see [8]); in sepulchral art this gesture symbolizes – as with intertwined hands – matrimonial *concordia* and *fides*. The kiss on the hand also serves as a sign of mutual love (Hom. Od. 23,87; Theoc. 11,55).

E. Gestures of supplication

As early as Hom. Il. 1,500; 8,371, the touching of the knee and chin with the right hand are mentioned as a pleading gesture (cf. Eur. IT 362f.), which is intensified by enfolding the knees. Petronius (17,9), Virgil (Aen. 3,607), Aristaenetus (1,13) and others also list in this regard the kissing of the breast by the person making the plea. On Greek and Roman statues supplication or throwing oneself down are represented by kneeling on the ground with open hands stretched forwards, e.g. [9. vol. 2, pl. 17 6,1; 10. 153 fig. 128, skyphos from Boscoreale]). In scenes of pursuit and abduction, the arms stretched far forward characterize the person seeking help; in addition this position of the arms can also serve as a defensive gesture (crater Boston, MFA 63,1246 [11. fig. 174, 1.2]) or in the case of arms outstretched far in the opposite direction, it can represent the attempt to separate quarrelling parties (cup London, BM E 69 [11. fig. 247]). A further pleading gesture involved the person making the request laying his or her hand on the cheek of the other person (Eur. El. 1214–1217). Pleading gestures also include a kiss on the hand (→ Kiss; Hom. Il. 24,478; 506; Phaedr. 5,1,4f.), as this also expresses thanks (Plut. Brutus 991) or homage (Tac. Hist. 1,45) (→ *salutatio*). The person to whom the supplication is made grants the plea or shows mercy with a handshake (Hom Il. 24,508; Verg. Aen. 3,610) or by stretching out his or her hand to the suppliant (e.g. skyphos from Boscoreale [10. 153 fig. 128]). In Roman culture this gesture simultaneously expresses the virtue of *clementia* [12].

F. Dexiosis/Dextrarum iunctio

The handshake with the right hand between two people is a gesture that goes beyond the situation and also means a warm closeness between them, as in the case of greeting and farewell (→ Greeting; e.g. Plut. Caesar 708). The *dexíōsis* is attested on Greek monuments from the 3rd quarter of the 7th cent. BC and is performed by mythical (Hercules-Athena; Perseus-Athena, etc.) and non-mythical figures; in the so-called warrior's farewell scenes in particular (→ Greeting), this gesture becomes a significant form of representation for the first time. On Greek grave reliefs of the Classical period it is a highly expressive gesture of the last farewell, of familial closeness and the feeling of a common bond. This gesture is represented differently on the Attic document reliefs and symbolizes here steadfast agreement between the contractual partners [13].

The same applies in Roman culture: *renovare dextras* means 'to renew contracts' (Tac. Ann. 2,58); *dextras iungere* as a gesture of the sealing of a friendship or a contract can be found on several occasions in Virgil (cf. Verg. Aen. 7,266). As a symbol of harmony this gesture appears e.g. from the 2nd half of the 1st cent. AD on Roman coins depicting the following: soldiers shaking hands, emperors reigning simultaneously, members of the imperial family, etc. (with corresponding inscriptions: *fides exercituum*, *consensus exercitus*, *fides militum*, *concordia Augustorum* etc. [14. 88–108]). This also includes the handshake between a man and a woman at Roman weddings – it is unknown in Greek wedding ceremonies – just as the *dextrarum iunctio* between a man and a woman on Etruscan (here from the 4th cent. BC) and Roman monuments, especially tomb monuments, is a symbol of matrimonial *fides* and *concordia* (→ Wedding customs). We should differentiate from the *dexíōsis/dextrarum iunctio* the grasp around the wrist (cf. Hom. Il. 1,323; Hom. Od. 18,258, here at the farewell, e.g. Zeus-Hera metope from Selinunte, Palermo) that signifies taking possession of a person or ownership of the person and is attested both for mythical figures and in Greek scenes of daily life. This includes particularly Attic wedding images with the bridegroom leading the bride home to his house (e.g. loutrophoros, Athens, NM [15. 59, fig. 13]). This grasp is also encountered in abduction scenes and in Hermes Psychopompos who escorts the deceased to the Underworld.

G. Reflecting, pondering, considering

This includes the gestures made by the hand or individual fingers into the direction of the head or on the head. Very commonly the hand grasping the beard is used, as e.g. in the case of the seer in the eastern pediment of the Temple of Zeus at Olympia [16. pl. 52] or in scenes of arming or of the warrior's farewell for the relative looking worriedly into the future. An additional gesture of pondering involves laying the flat hand on the cheek with a slightly inclined head; on many occasions in the case of standing figures, the left arm is then laid on the stomach and the right one is supported on the left hand, with the inclined head resting on the back of the hand (Peliad relief Rome, MV [17]; Calypso, wall painting from the Macellum, Pompeii). Frequently the pondering figure is depicted in an en-face perspective which is to be interpreted as intensifying the pondering or as intensifying a strongly emotional event. The head supported on the back of the hand (e.g. Oedipus in front of the Theban sphinx, cup Rome MV [11. fig. 301,2]) in the case of sitting or lying figures also characterizes those represented in such a way as reflecting or as attentive listeners (e.g. crater, Berlin SM, 3172 [2. 116, fig. 55]). A finger guided to the mouth – mostly the index finger – is an expression of thinking something over or of amazement, whilst the index finger laid over the mouth (Harpocrates motif: Plut. Mor. 378c) signifies silence. Fingers only lightly touching the chin or resting bent on it express being deeply lost in oneself or absent-mindedness; this gesture is also attested on grave monuments (→ Mourning) (stele from Rhamnus, Athens, NM). Deep reflection and inner concentration are conveyed by arms hanging down with folded hands and clasped fingers (statue of Demosthenes, Copenhagen), likewise strong mental effort (Medea, wall painting from Herculaneum, Naples, MN).

H. Finger gestures

Finger gestures are extremely numerous and the development of sign language is essentially based on the movement of individual fingers (cf. Nonnus, Dion. 19,156f.; according to Ov. Am. 2,5,18 the fingers of lovers form *litteras* for secret messages); this was also the origin of the pantomime. The ancient orators were trained in finger gestures (Cic. De or. 3,220; Quint. Inst. 11,3,65–137; → *gestus*); calculating and counting were likewise accompanied by individual finger signals and many and varied → games of dexterity were played with the fingers. To mention only a few of the repertoire of finger gestures: chewing on the fingers or finger nails characterizes the furious person (Hor. Epod. 5,47; Sat. 1,10,71; Prop. 2,4,3) or the person in mourning (Prop. 3,25,4). Anyone who scratches his or her head is embarrassed (Apul. Met. 10,10); using only one finger signifies an aristocratic dandy (Plut. Caesar 709) or someone in love (Plut. Pompey 645); the furious Venus (Apul. Met. 6,9) scratches her ear. People snapped their fingers to call a slave with the vessel for passing water (Petron. Sat. 27; Mart. 3,82,15; 6,89,1f.), however, this gesture can also be understood apotropaically (Ov. Fast. 5,433). The individual fingers had different functions. In this way the middle finger formed magic symbols, the index finger was primarily important in rhetorical gestures etc., and showing it also expressed contempt (Mart. 6,70,5).

I. Apotropaic gestures

Among the protective gestures are the spreading out of the fingers with a raised forearm or outstretched arms (this gesture can also mean a curse [18]), likewise the *fica* gesture (the thumb is placed between the index finger and the middle finger; Ov. Fast. 5,433) that is meant to provide particular protection from the evil eye (→ Deisidaimonia; → Superstitio; → Magic); the already mentioned baring of the bottom can also be of an apotropaic nature (Plin. HN 28,78; Plut. Mor. 248b). The protective gesture of raised arms is directed against an attacker (e.g. with a weapon) and is on many occasions combined with a fleeing movement.

J. Other gestures

Placing the hand over the head: connected with people asleep (Anth. Pal. 5,275; Lucian, Dial. D. 11; Ariadne [19]; Endymion [20] etc.) and the dead (cup, formerly New York [11. fig. 246]; Adamclisi, Tropaeum Traiani [10. 231, fig. 196]) from the ancient period to late antiquity, this gesture expresses relaxation and peace (Apollo Lykeios in Lucian, Anach. 7); the aspect of relaxation or the enjoyment connected with it is also encountered in banqueting images when the carousers are shown in this posture listening to the flute-playing of a hetaera or singing along with it or watching the undressing of a hetaera ([6. 37f.], see above) or having coitus with her (e.g. painting from Pompeii, Naples, MN [21]; → Eroticism). This gesture also expresses the visionary beholding of deities [22].

Surprise/dismay: raised arms with the hands open and the fingers spread characterize surprise or dismay, on many occasions accompanied by a movement of flight from the unexpected (running away, turning away, etc.); the gesture of surprise is emphasized by wide open eyes and a slightly open mouth [2. 97f.].

Ἀποσκοπεῖν (*aposkopeîn*): shading the eyes with the right hand is typical of a person peering sharply at an event taking place in the distance and of a person looking out at the unexpected (e.g. the appearance of a deity); gestures of this kind are frequently found in → epiphanies. As a gesture of lasciviousness, it is primarily connected with satyrs creeping up on and secretly observing Maenads or Ariadne [23], and it can also be found in representations of Pan and others who have occasion to gaze at something appearing in the distance.

Ἀνακάλυψις (*anakálypsis*, opening the bridal veil): the gesture of removing the veil is performed on the wedding night when the bride shows herself to the groom for the first time [15. 57–70]. This gesture is often represented in Greek wedding images; certainly, on a large number of monuments, women perform this gesture without the wedding aspect being perceptible so that the gesture becomes more a sign of 'womanliness', perhaps even a gesture of coquetry (hardly a greeting gesture, as is the opinion of [2. 41 n. 134]). Men are rarely represented with this gesture (cf. however Dionysus).

Raised and outstretched right arm: the gesture attested in Roman statues, particularly armour and equestrian statues has several antecedents in south Italian vase painting and in Hellenism and is initially a gesture of greeting and speech (Cic. De or. 3,59,220; Arringatore in Florence, MA [24]); in addition it should be interpreted as a gesture of peace at least for the Roman statues, according to Stat. Silv. 1,1,37 *dextra vetat pugnas* (cf. Procop. Aed. 1,2,12) [25].

Hand on the hip: encountered in art particularly in representations of women to describe tension-charged situations [2. 118, fig. 55] and those that depict insistent, intensive speech on the basis of the scenery (cf. Aristaen. 2,20); this gesture is also to be found for women standing quietly, e.g. Atalante [11. fig. 369]; the earliest(?) example of this is the statue of Athena in Athens (AM 140 [26], around 480 BC). This gesture is also not unusual for men, e.g. in the case of Zeus in the eastern pediment of the Temple of Zeus at Olympia [16. pl. 51], and describes intensive listening or a moment of tension. In Roman culture it is however also encountered amongst people standing in a relaxed manner.

→ Acclamatio; → Applause; → Eroticism; → Prayer; → Gestus; → Greeting; → Kiss; → Salutatio; → Mourning

1 TRENDALL/CAMBITOGLOU 2 G. NEUMANN, Gesten und Gebärden in der griech. Kunst, 1965 3 G. KOCH-HARNACK, Knabenliebe und Tiergeschenke, 1983, 55 4 K. SCHEFOLD, Frühgriech. Sagenbilder, 1964, pl. 27b 5 G. SÄFLUND, Aphrodite Kallipygos, 1963 6 R. HURSCHMANN, Symposienszenen auf unteritalischen Vasen, 1985 7 TRENDALL, Lucania 8 H. SICHTERMANN, s.v. Gratiae, LIMC 3.1, 203–210 9 TRENDALL/CAMBITOGLOU 10 D. E. E. KLEINER, Roman Sculpture, 1992 11 J. BOARDMAN, Athenian Red Figure Vases. The Archaic Period, 1975 12 H. GABELMANN, Antike Audienz- und Tribunalszenen, 1984, 132–138 13 M. MEYER, Die att. Urkundenreliefs, in: MDAI(A) 13. Beih., 1988/89, 140–145 14 R. BRILLIANT, Gesture and Rank in Roman Art, 1963 15 C. REINSBERG, Ehe, Hetärentum und Knabenliebe im antiken Griechenland, 1989 16 H. V. HERRMANN, Olympia. Heiligtum und Wettkampfstätte, 1972 17 W. FUCHS, Die Skulptur der Griechen, 1969, 519, fig. 607 18 E. KUNZE, 5. Bericht über die Ausgrabungen in Olympia, 1956, 62f. 19 M.-L. BERNHARD, W.A. DASZEWSKI, s.v. Ariadne, LIMC 3, 1050–1070 20 H. SICHTERMANN, Späte Endymion-Sarkophage, 1966 21 J. MARCADÉ, Roma amor, 1977, 79, fig. 177 22 N. HIMMELMANN, Zur Eigenart des klass. Götterbildes, 1959, 17, n. 29 23 H. JUCKER, Der Gestus des Aposkopein, 1956 24 H. KÄHLER, Rom und seine Welt, 1958, pl. 60, 62 links 25 D. KREIKENBOM, Canovas Ferdinand IV. von Neapel, in: Städel-Jahrbuch 13, 1991, 227–244 26 J. BOARDMAN, Greek Sculpture. The Archaic Period, 1978, fig. 173.

P. J. CONNOR, The Dead Hero and the Sleeping Giant by the Nikosthenes Painter. At the beginnings of a motif, in: AA, 1984, 387–394; G. DAVIES, The Significance of the Handshake Motif in Classical Funerary Art, in: AJA 89, 1985, 627–640; H. DEMISCH, Erhobene Hände. Gesch. einer Gebärde in der bildenden Kunst, 1984; T. DOHRN, Gefaltete und verschränkte Hände, in: MDAI 70, 1955, 50–87; S. EITREM, Die Gestensprache – Abwehr oder Kontakt, in: Geras A. Kerampulu, 1959, 598–608; J. ENGEMANN, Der 'corna'-Gestus – ein antiker und frühchristlicher Abwehr- und Spottgestus?, in: Pietas. FS für B. Kötting, JbAC, Ergh. 8, 1980, 483–498; B. FORSÉN, E. SIRONEN, Zur Symbolik von dargestellten Händen, in: Arctos 23, 1989, 55–66; G. FREYBURGER, Supplication grecque et supplication romaine, in: Latomus 47, 1988, 501–525; K. GROSS, Menschenhand und Gotteshand in Antike und Christentum, 1985; A. HERMANN, 'Mit der Hand singen', in: JbAC 1, 1958, 105–108; S. HUMMEL, Etr. Miszellen II. Die Lex Gestus bei den Etruskern, in: JÖAI 57, 1986/7, 7–12; N.B. KAMPEN, Biographical narration in Roman funerary art, in: AJA 85, 1981, 47–58; F. KIENER, Hand, Gebärde und Charakter, 1962; K.R. KRIERER, Sieg oder Niederlage, 1995; T. J. MCNIVEN, Gestures in Attic Vase-Painting: Use and Meaning, 1982; R. MERKELBACH, Die Zahl 9999 in der Magie und der 'comptus digitorum', in: ZPE 63, 1986, 305–308; G. NEUMANN, Gesten und Gebärden in der griech. Kunst, 1965; D. OHLY, Δῖα Γυναικῶν, in: R. BOEHRINGER, Eine Freundesgabe, 1957, 433–460; J. PAPAOIKONOMOU, Une pleureuse crétoise, in: REA 85, 1983, 5–14; E. G. PEMBERTON, The Dexiosis on Attic Gravestones, in: Mediterranean Archaeology 2, 1989, 45–50; A. RIECHE, Computatio romana. Fingerzählen auf provinzialröm. Reliefs, in: BJ 186, 1986, 165–192; L. ROSSI, Le geste 'favete linguis' dans la personification de la Constantia sur les monnaies claudiennes, in: Caesarodunum 23, 1988, 187–189; K. SCHEFOLD, Pandions Sorge, in: Boreas 5, 1982, 67–69; B. SCHMALTZ, Griech. Grabreliefs, 1983; A. SCHOLL, Die attischen Bildfeldstelen des 4. Jhs. v.Chr., in: MDAI(A) 17. Beih., 1996, 164–170; S. F. SCHRÖDER, Röm. Bacchusbilder in der Tradition des Apollon Lykeios, 1989; C. SITTL, Die Gebärden der Griechen und Römer, 1890; P. SOMVILLE, Le signe d' extase et la musique, in: Kernos 5, 1992, 173–181; R. STUPPERICH, Zur *dextrarum iunctio* auf frühen röm. Grabreliefs, in: Boreas 6, 1983, 143–154; P. VEYNE, Les saluts aux dieux, le voyage de cette vie et la 'réception' en iconographie, in: RA 1985, 47–61; P. WÜLFING, Antike und moderne Redegestik, in: G. BINDER, K. EHLICH (ed.), Kommunikation durch Zeichen und Wort, Bochumer Altertumswissenschaftliches Colloquium 23, 1995, 71–90. R.H.

Gestus

A. Definition B. Example C. Teachings D. Historical factors E. Modern approach

A. Definition

Gestus is the → gesture accompanying an oration; in rhetorics this part of the → *actio* is described in greatest detail by → Quintilianus. Quintilian (Inst. 11,3,1) divides the *actio*, as does the → Rhetorica ad Herennium 3,19, into *vox* (voice) and *motus* (movement). Whilst however the *motus* is otherwise further subdivided into *vultus* (→ Facial expression) and *gestus*, Quintilian (Inst. 11,3,14) calls the entire second part of the *actio gestus* (as does Cic. Brut. 141), and so has *gestus* encompassing all visual things. The Greek models have to be reconstructed from later writings (→ Actio[1]): the parts πάθη τῆς φωνῆς (*páthē tês phōnês*; voice registers) and σχήματα τοῦ σώματος (*schḗmata toû sṓmatos*; body postures) were probably already named (Dion. Hal. Demosthenes 53; cf. Eust. re Hom. Od. 4, p.1496 Romana).

Quintilian (Inst. 11,3,65–135) describes in sequence the movements of the head, the face (*vultus*) and especially of the eyes and eyebrows (→ Facial expression) and shoulders. He devotes the main part (11,3,84–124) to the hands and fingers, with the arms being understood as being involved although they are not mentioned especially; then he describes the stance and stride (*status* and *incessus*) of the feet. Rules for clothing complete the passage. For the evaluation of ancient theory it is decisive that the whole figure of the orator who mostly stood on a platform with his hands free was entirely visible. His upper garment (→ *himátion* or → *toga*) was thrown with one end over his left shoulder, leaving his right shoulder and arm free.

B. Example

Quint. Inst. 11,3,92f.: 'That very widespread *gestus* in which the middle finger is drawn towards the thumb but the three other fingers remain outstretched, is useful for the → *prooemium* when it is done with a gentle movement and in a measured manner to both sides and with the head and shoulders gently following the hand; it also has an elucidating effect in the → *narratio* but must then be done further forward and sharply and passionately in the case of accusation and refutation (in the → *argumentatio*); in these parts people allow the *gestus* to go further afield and without restriction'. Quintilian then warns: it has the incorrect effect if people in the process hold their arm diagonally forwards 'as if they were talking with the elbow'.

C. Teachings

Quintilian's text demonstrates the will and ability of the author to verbalize movements (drawings were not used); it shows that hand, head, eye and shoulder movements are included. It is paradigmatic that the middle finger does not point into the audience, for instance, but is caught by the thumb: the 'broken' *gestus* and the warning about theatrical exaggeration are predominant. All *gestus* are directly related to oration; here the *gestus* is applied through variation to three different oration situations. The tenor is advisory, especially clear in the warning about clumsiness. From the context of Quintilian's text, further insights can be gained: an oration without *gestus* would be garbled (*trunca*) and weak (*debilis*) (Inst. 11,3,85). *Gestus* and word must harmonize; Quintilian however rejects regulation, the *gestus* should in each case change after three words (Inst. 11,3,106f.). A *gestus* is always made with the right hand, the left one can intensify this (Inst. 11,3,114); gesticulation with the left arm could make the garment untidy. We learn about styles: from the time of Cicero, i.e. in the 150 years that had passed by since then, the style of movement had become more passionate (*agitatior*); in this way an orator could however lose the authority of a person of rank (*viri boni*) and respectability (Inst. 11,3,184). Quintilian's exhortations are in keeping with the ideal of the *elegantia* of that social class which was called to oratory and to which oration and its theory were directed. Many Greek schools of oratory taught more dramatic gestures than were tolerated in Rome (Inst. 11,3,102). In general cultural differences are denied: the *gestus* was the common language of all people (Inst. 11,3,87).

D. Historical factors

Reference is made for a gesture-less art of oration in the archaic period to a statement by the Spartan → Chilon, one of the Seven Sages, who said that the orator should not move the hand, it was μανικόν (*manikón*, 'exalted', cf. Diog. Laert. 70), which however presupposes the existence of oration gestures; the comment amounts to the well-known exhortation to restraint. → Solon is said to have spoken without movements of the hand; this is the conclusion of → Aeschines (In Tim. 25) based on a statue in Salamis, representing Solon with his right hand in his garment. For Classical and especially for Athenian orators, however, it was known that they were even guided by theatrical art: → Demosthenes took lessons from the actor Satyrus (Plut. Demosthenes 7,849); → Aeschines himself had acting experience (Plut. Mor. 840b).

A theory of *hypókrisis* (= *actio*) was first written by → Theophrastus (→ Actio[1]); we do not know what treatment the *gestus* was given there; he attached great value to it for himself (Ath. 1,21a-b). The earliest extant text about *gestus* is in Rhet. Her. 3,26f.; the author considers his short expositions to be an important achievement and leaves everything else to practice (*exercitatio*). Cic. De or. 3,220 and Or. at 59 touch very briefly on the actual *gestus*. For the Middle Ages and the modern period see below and [1].

Gestus is a field that – together with the entire *actio* and → *memoria* (recitation from memory) – belonged to practical and oral ancient rhetoric when it was still one school of successful pleading. With the reduction of rhetoric to the theory of style and composition of written texts from late antiquity (culminating in LAUSBERG), they were no longer part of rhetorical instruction. Fundamentally descriptive ways of teaching separate us today from a type of instruction that is intent only on making recommendations: Quintilian comments, not fully, on twenty *gesta* of the hand without using specialized terms; only parts of the → speech allow for the connection with oration in a systematic order.

E. MODERN APPROACH

For us, too, a stiff orator is intolerable; but modern research (psychology, art history) treats *gestus* separately from language or as opposed to it [2; 3]; it emphasizes sociological differences [4] and often behaves in an investigative and denouncing manner [5]. A functional systematization through classification by groups appears to be indispensable, e.g. of gestures concerned with offering, for instance the upward, open, flat hand and gestures that demand attention, for instance the 'refined posture' [6]: the speaker holds his hand in front of him with fingers joined together, a *gestus* that is also described by Quintilian (Inst. 11,3,96).

→ Actio; → Gestures; → Facial expression; → Rhetoric

1 D. BARNETT, s.v. Gestus, HWdR 3, 972–989, esp. 984f. and 987–989 2 S. MOLCHO, Körpersprache, 1984 3 D. MORRIS, Körpersignale, 1986 4 M. WEX, Weibliche und männliche Körpersprache als Folge patriarchalischer Machtverhältnisse, 1980 5 P. EKMAN, W. FRIESEN, K.R. SCHERER, in: K.R. SCHERER, H. WALBOTT (ed.), Nonverbale Kommunikation, ²1984, 271–275 6 F. KIENER, Hand, Gebärde und Charakter, 1962, ch. II B 1.

U. MAIER-EICHHORN, Die Gestikulation in Quintilians Rhetorik, 1989; R. VOLKMANN, Rhetorik der Griechen und Römer, 1885, repr. 1963, 573–580; P. WÜLFING, Antike und moderne Redegestik, in: G. BINDER, K. EHLICH (ed.), Kommunikation durch Zeichen und Wort, Bochumer Altertumswissenschaftliches Colloquium 23, 1995, 71–90. P.WÜ.

Geta

[1] see → Hosidius, Lusius, Septimius, Vitorius

[2] **Imp. Caesar P. Septimius Geta Augustus.** Born in March AD 189 in Rome, the son of L. → Septimius Severus and → Iulia Domna, younger brother of → Caracalla (Cass. Dio 57,2,5; SHA Sept. Sev. 4,2; Get. 3,1 [27 May 189]; [2. 522ff.]). In 197 he went with his father, together with his mother and brother, to the 'Second Parthian War' (AE 1942,11), and at the same time as his brother was appointed Augustus (co-ruler with his father) in mid 198, he was elevated to *Caesar nobilissimus* (SHA Sept. Sev. 16,3,4; CIL III 218 = ILS 422; e.g. AE 1981, 921; 1984, 833) and probably *princeps iuventutis* (ILS 8916) and in 199 (?) to *pontifex*. In 199/200 with his family he visited Alexandria and Egypt and returned to Rome with them via Syria, Asia Minor and the Balkans [3] in mid 202 (SHA Sept. Sev. 17,4; CIL III 6581; IGR 1, 1113). In 203/4 G. accompanied his father to the latter's homeland Africa, took part in mid 204 in the secular games in Rome (CIL VI 32329) and became consul (*cos. I*) in 205 together with his brother (*cos. II*) (CIL VI 1670).

The relationship between the two brothers had never been good, and it worsened – after the execution of C. → Fulvius [II 10] Plautianus at the instigation of Caracalla – to the point of acts of violence in full view of the public (Cass. Dio 76,7,1–3). When attempts to keep them away from Rome (in 205–207 mostly in Campania) or to show unity (in 208 G. *cos. II*, Caracalla *cos. III*), proved relatively unfruitful, Septimius took the brothers with him on a campaign to Britain (Cass. Dio 76,11,1; Hdn. 3,14). In 209 G. was granted jurisdiction over Roman Britain (Hdn. 3,14,9) and at the end of the year finally the title of Augustus (AE 1950, 136; RIC 4/1, p. 323 no. 67f.), probably also in order to protect him from Caracalla. In 210 he also called himself Britannicus (RIC 4/1, p. 323 no. 69b). After the death of their father (4 February 211) Caracalla accepted G. as co-ruler out of consideration for the army (Cass. Dio 77,1,1; SHA Sept. Sev. 23,3–7), but, after an unsuccessful murder plot, he finally murdered him himself in December 211 during a feigned attempt at reconciliation in the arms of their mother (Cass. Dio 77,2,1–6; Hdn. 4,4,3). Then Caracalla had 20,000 friends and supporters of G. murdered, and his name fell into disrepute in *damnatio memoriae* (Cass. Dio 77,4,1; Hdn. 4,6,1–2).

1 PIR S 325 2 T.D. BARNES, Pre-Dacian Acta Martyrum, in: Journal of Theological Studies, 19, 1968, 509–531 3 J. FITZ, Der Besuch des Septimius Severus in Pannonien, in: Acta Arch. Acad. Scientiarum Hungaricae 11, 1959, 237–263 4 KIENAST, ²1996, 166f. T.F.

Get(h)a Roman cognomen ('the Getan'), in the Republican period of C. Licinius G. (*cos.* in 116 BC) and C. Hosidius G., in the Imperial period – in the form Geta – also among the Hosidii and Septimii.

DEGRASSI, FCIR 253; KAJANTO, Cognomina 204. K.-L.E.

Getae (Γέται; *Gétai*). Greek term for the Thracian tribes south of the Lower Danube in modern Dobrudža and in the hinterland of the north-western Greek colonies on the Black Sea coast. Their region shows traces of settlement from the Stone Age onwards and was the centre of highly developed cultures from the time of the Copper Stone Age (cf. Varna, Durankulag). On the basis of the written sources and the language remnants attested in the Onomastikon, the G. are shown to be the northern Thracian branch. The names of some of their partial tribes have been passed down, cf. Crobyzi, Troglodytae (Hdt. 4,49), Terizi (Hellanicus, FGrH 4 F 73). Only the Iron Age finds can be attributed to the G. with certainty. Important Hallstatt settlements and necropolises have e.g. been discovered at Carev brod, Dălgopol and Belogradec.

They are mentioned for the first time together with the Scythian campaign of → Darius [1] I in 513 BC (Hdt. 4,93ff.) who had to break down their fierce resistance. Herodotus characterizes the G. in the following manner – which is reiterated right through to late antiquity: they are the bravest and most just among the Thracians and differ from them in their religion, the focus of which is the god (*daimon*) Zalmoxis (Gebeleizis) (Hdt. 4,94–97). Through the establishment of the western Pontic colonies they came into economic and cultural contact with the Greeks from the 7th cent. BC, as attested by Getic trading posts. However they were only rarely to be found in the Greek poleis until the 2nd cent. BC. During the period when the Odrysae flourished they became part of their territory; they had to do military service. Their cavalry divisions were famous. After the disintegration of the Odrysian kingdom, smaller Getic principalities began to consolidate themselves. In 339 BC the Scythian king Atheas marched against the G., so that the Getic prince Cothelas allied himself with Philip II; Philip married the Getic princess Meda (Ath. 13,557d). In 335 Alexander the Great defeated the G. (Arr. Anab. 1,2ff.), but he was unable to subjugate them once and for all. In 313 the G. allied themselves with the western Pontic colonies under the leadership of Callatis against Lysimachus who finally defeated the G. and built a fortress against them on Tirizis Akra (modern Kalliakra). Around the turn of the 4th to the 3rd cent. the principality of Dromichaites (Diod. Sic. 21,11f.; Str. 7,3,8) rose up in rebellion and held King Lysimachus captive for a short period in 292.

The 1st half of the 3rd cent. BC was the period when the G. flourished: residences and sanctuaries attest to the high culture as well as the wealth and power acquired by these rulers particularly through trade with the Greeks (cf. Svestari, Borovo, Adzighol). Literary and epigraphical sources also bear witness to this (cf. the legendary wealth of the Getic king Isanthus in Ath. 12,536d). An inscription from Histria around 200 BC (SEG 18,288) shows the dependence of this colony on the Getic prince Zalmodegicus, another one the dependence on a certain prince Zoltes and an equally strong Getic ruler Rhemaxos (about 180 BC). Numerous Getic princes had their own coins minted. The tombs of the kings and also the details provided by Strabo (16,2,38f.) and Cassius Dio (68,9) show that there was a marked ruler cult. The G. were probably little more than peripherally affected by the incursions of the Celts. In the 2nd/1st cents. BC, aside from the Getic settlements there were also numerous Scythian and Bastarnian enclaves (Ps.-Scymn. 756f.; Str. 7,4,5; for the Getic presence in the Greek poleis: Ov. Pont. 4,1,67–84; Tr. 5,10,15–44). M. Terentius Varro Lucullus was the first Roman commander to march against the G. (72/1 BC) in order to strike the western Pontic allies of Mithridates VI, without having much success. Ten years later C. Antonius Hybrida was beaten at Histria by a coalition of Scythae, G., Bastarnae and Greek colonists (Liv. per. 103; Cass. Dio 38,10,1–3). This victory over the Romans allowed the tribes under → Byrebista to dominate for a short period (60–50 BC) in the Getic and Dacian regions. After his death the G. became independent again. Augustus however continued to pursue the plan of subjugating the entire Balkan peninsula. His excuse was an incursion of Bastarnae over the Danube, devastating the Getic and Thracian areas right through to modern southern Bulgaria. M. Licinius Crassus assumed control of the implementation of the plan. In 29 BC he defeated the Bastarnae in the Getic area with the help of the Getic (and Dacian) prince Rholes (Cass. Dio 52,24,7; 26,1) who promised him help for his support against the Getic ruler Dapyx (Cass. Dio 51,26). The G. suffered a devastating defeat. After Crassus had reached the Danube delta, he appointed Rholes as Roman-dependent *regulus* and returned to Rome. In 16 BC Sarmatae invaded the Getic area and were repulsed by Roman troops (Cass. Dio 54,20,1–3). The Getic region was placed under the control of the Roman vassal king in Thrace, Rhoemetalces I, who was supposed to secure the *ripa Thraciae*. In AD 12 and 15 these garrisons were fortified with Roman troops. In AD 45 the province of Moesia was founded to which the G. belonged.

The demographic picture changed considerably during the Roman Imperial period: the incursion of foreign tribes over the Danube, the numerous Roman camps and towns to which many people also moved from other areas of the Roman empire, displaced the G. more and more. In the literature of late antiquity there is no longer a distinction between G. and → Daci. The remainder of the population was absorbed into the Germanic, Avar, Bulgarian and Slavic tribes.

D.M. Pippidi, Scythica minora, 1975; Id., Epigraph. Beiträge zur Gesch. Histrias in hell. und röm. Zeit, 1962, 75–88; J. Iouroukova, Nouvelles données sur la chronologie des rois scythes en Dobroudja, in: Thrakia 4, 1977, 105–121; D.M. Pippidi, D. Berciu, Dĭn istoria dobrugei 1, 1965; A. Fol, S. Dimitrov (ed.), Istorija na Dobrudža 1, 1984; A. Avram, Unters. zur Gesch. des Territoriums von Kallatis in griech. Zeit, in: Dacia N.S. 35, 1991, 103–137. I.v.B.

Geth Gat (Canaanitic *gint*, Hebrew *gat*, 'winepress'). In Syria-Palestine frequent place name of the late Bronze and Iron Age.

[1] The Philistine Gat, the south-eastern corner of the Pentapolis (1 Sam 7,14; 17,52), probably Tall aṣ-Ṣāfī. As the direct neighbour of Judah, G. was involved in the 10th cent. BC in the uprising of David who as a *condottiere* received Ziklag (Tall as-Sabaʿ/Tel Bəʾer Ševaʿ) as a fief from G. (1 Sam 27). Perhaps already conquered by Hasaël of Damascus as early as the 2nd half of the 9th cent. BC as part of his power politics between the Euphrates and the Nile (2 Kg 12,18f.), G. finally lost its independence in 720 BC under Sargon II (cf. Am 6,2). Before 702/1 [3] and again in the 7th cent. BC, G. belonged to Judah (2 Chr 11,8; 26,6). In the 4th cent. AD it is only named as a village (*vicus*, Jer. Comm. in Michaeam 1,10).

[2] The Γεθηνυν Γιττα (*Gethēnyn Gitta*) mentioned in the Madaba map (6th cent. AD) and in Eusebius (On. 72,2–4) and Jerome (Comm. in Ionam praef.) should, according to [4], be identified with the unnamed field of ruins at Rīšôn lə Ṣijjôn between Lydda/Diospolis and Tall Yūnni on the Mediterranean Sea.
[3] The homeland of the prophet Jonah, G.-Hefer (2 Kg 14,25) in Galilee (modern al-Mašhad) is known by Jerome (Comm. in Ionam praef.) under the name G.

1 M. Görg, s.v. G., Neues Bibel-Lexikon 5, 731f. 2 O. Keel, M. Küchler, Orte und Landschaften der Bibel 2, 1982 3 N. Na'aman, Sennacherib's 'Letter to God', in: BASO 214, 1974, 25–29 4 G. Schmitt, G., Gittaim und Gitta, in: R. Cohen, G. Schmitt, Drei Stud. zur Arch. und Top. Altisraels, 1980, 77–138 5 P. Thomsen, Loca Sancta, 1907, 50. E.A.K.

Gethsemane see → Jerusalem

Gezer City(state) of Palestine in the Bronze and Iron Age that controlled the exit of the road from Jerusalem to the coast out of the mountains. Conquered from the 15th to the 10th cents. BC. by Egypt, acquired and fortified by Solomon (1 Kg 9,16–18; 9,15 is anachronistic). It is impossible to decide whether G. was Israelitic, Judaic, Philistine or independent in the period that followed. From 734 it was under Assyrian rule, and in the 7th cent. BC it served as an Assyrian administrative centre. In 142 BC G. was conquered by the Maccabeans (1 Macc 13,43–48; one of the first applications of the Deuteronomic excommunication laws in practice); in the Herodian period, the town consisted just of the estate of an Alcius whose boundary stones have facilitated the identification of G. with the Tell Ǧazar.

E. A. Knauf, in: L. K. Handy (ed.), The Age of Solomon, 1997, 81–95. E.A.K.

Ghazni Finds of coins from the period of the Indo-Greek kings → Artemidorus [1], Peucolas and → Archebius (around 130 BC) and the Saka king Azes I (around 70 BC) prove that G. was an important centre in the Graeco-Bactrian period. The Buddhist monastery of Tapa Sardar (2nd–4th cents. AD) discovered closeby and buildings of the Islamic Ghaznowid dynasty of the 11th–12th cents. attest to the continuous importance of the region.

F.R. Allchin, N. Hammond, The Archaeology of Afghanistan from the earliest times to the Timurid period, 1978. B.B.

Ghiaccio Forte In antiquity the Etruscan settlement situated on a hill that was flat on top and fell away steeply on the edges, 14 km south-east of Scansano, probably belonged to the area of influence of Vulci. In the 6th cent. BC there was a rural sanctuary here. A settlement can only be proven for the late 4th and early 3rd cents. BC. The settlement that was fortified by a surrounding wall made of large blocks with rough stone filling was violently destroyed in about 280 BC. American excavations in 1972/1973 uncovered remains of houses with stone foundations and clay brick walls, roads, a drainage system and a votive deposit.

M. A. Del Chiaro, Etruscan G.F., 1976; A. Talocchini, Il G.F., 1986. M.M.

Giants (Γίγαντες; *Gígantes*).
I. Mythology II. Iconography

I. Mythology
Giants are usually huge, clumsy beings from primeval times; according to the commonest myth, the → Gigantomachy, they attempted unsuccessfully to deprive Zeus and the Olympians of power. In Homer the Giants are a lawless and arrogant marginal people destroyed because of their king → Eurymedon (Hom. Od. 7,59–61); they settled close to the → Cyclopes and → Phaeaces (Hom. Od. 7,205f.). According to Hesiod, during the castration of → Uranus, drops of blood fall on the earth (→ Gaia) and fertilize her: she gives birth to the huge giants equipped as warriors as well as to → Erinys and the Melic nymphs (Hes. Theog. 183–187). The birth of the Giants armed with weapons (→ Spartoi) is a pointer to their essentially war-like character; but only in the post-Hesiodic appendix to the 'Theogony' is reference made indirectly to the Gigantomachy and the role of → Heracles in it (Theog. 954).

Since the late ancient period, tales of Gigantomachy are well-known, and the Hesiodic catalogues refer to Heracles' victorious battle in Phlegra (Hes. fr. 43a 65, cf. Pind. Nem. 1,67f.; the king of the Giants is called, as often later on, → Porphyrion: Pind. Pyth. 8,12). For Xenophanes (21 B. 1,21 DK) such stories belong to the myths that were rejected because they were ethically unacceptable. Especially among the tragedians of the 5th cent. BC there are frequent allusions to this myth, on many occasions to an artistic representation: it was depicted on the peplos of Athena [1. 210]. The only detailed tale is not offered until Apollodorus (1,34–38): out of fury at the death of the → Titans, Gaia gives birth to the enormous, long-haired and snake-footed Giants (in Phlegrai or Pallene). They attack the Olympians; because an oracle had foretold victory for them only on the condition that a mortal fought with them, they ask Heracles for help; a long series of single combats follows in which it is not just → Zeus and Heracles but especially → Poseidon and → Athena who stand out. The tale of the Gigantomachy was popular from early on and was often represented; the variation in the detail is correspondingly great. Originally, like the battles with the Titans (with whom they are often later confused) and with → Typhoeus or as in the Mesopotamian myth of the battle of → Marduk against Tiamat, it must have depicted the assertion of the ruling order of Zeus over the chaos of threats. Probably since the late archaic period, the myth had been politically interpreted as the victory of Greeks over threats from barbarians (Persians in Attic art of the 5th cent. BC; Gauls on the Pergamum altar; perhaps also the fragmentary *Gigantomachia* of → Claudianus [2]). In the Hellenistic period, the myth is related in a mythological manner to natural phenomena like the vulcanoes of Campania and is set in the Campi Phlegraei (Diod. Sic. 7,71,4; Str. 5,4,4).

1 F. Vian, s.v. Giganten, LIMC 4.1, 191–270.

O. Waser, s.v. Giganten, RE Suppl. 3, 655–759; F. Vian, La guerre des Géants. Le mythe avant l'époque hellénistique, 1952; C. Calame, Les figures grecques du gigantesque, in: Communications 42, 1985, 147–172. F.G.

II. Iconography

The first certain representations of Giants are preserved from the period around 580/570 BC: cf. Corinthian pinakes, Berlin, SM, 575/550 BC. On early Attic vases from the Athenian Acropolis Giants appear around 560/550 BC, when the → Gigantomachy as the greatest battle of the gods of Greek myth becomes an important pictorial motif in Greek art, which aims to make visible the superiority of Greek concepts of order over the uncivilized nature of the barbarians (cf. further representations on black-figured and red-figured vases of the 6th and 5th cents. BC). An early handling of the theme in architectural sculpture is possibly attested in the battle group with Zeus in the western pediment of the Temple of Artemis on Cercyra (590/580 BC: interpretation of the opponents of Zeus as G. or Titan). Paus. 3,18,11 mentions the battle of Heracles against a Giants on the so-called Throne of Amyclae (end of the 6th cent. BC). Battles with Giants are certainly passed down on the northern frieze of the Siphnian treasury at Delphi (around 525 BC), in the Gigantomachy pediment of the Peisistratid Temple of Athena on the Athenian Acropolis (around 530/520 BC), in the eastern pediment of the Megarian treasury at Olympia (around 510 BC), and in the western pediment of the Temple of Apollo of the Alcmaeonids at Delphi (510/500 BC).

For the 5th cent. BC the following are mentioned in particular: from the Athenian Acropolis the eastern metopes of the Parthenon (445/ 440 BC), presumably the eastern pediment of the Temple of Athena-Nike (about 425 BC), the non-preserved interior painting of the shield of Athena Parthenos (438 BC; in this regard cf. the Gigantomachy scene on the crater fragment in Naples, MN, 430/410 BC); from Selinonte metopes of Temple F (1st quarter of the 5th cent. BC, with Dionysus) and E (2nd quarter of the 5th cent. BC, with Athena); in Sounion the pronaos frieze of the Temple of Poseidon (460/440 BC), from Argos the eastern metopes of the Heraeum (420/400 BC). Probably the most impressive example of a Gigantomachy in ancient art is passed down to us in the Pergamum Altar (180 BC; according to recent, newly proposed later dating: about 160 BC): first depicted in the surrounding frieze, the theme of the triumph of the gods, of order and civilization over disorderly wildness becomes here the symbol of the victory of the world of Hellenistic states over the barbarians threatening it.

Initially represented as → hoplitai or 'wild' warriors, the Giants also appear from about 400 BC as snake-legged monsters; on the Pergamum Altar some of the Giants are for the first time – borrowing from ancient Near Eastern monsters? – depicted in the shape of birds, lions or bulls. In Roman antiquity too the pictorial motif of Gigantomachy remains current, cf. e.g. the frieze of the *scenae frons* in the theatre of Corinth (2nd half of the 2nd cent. AD), the frieze in the theatre of Hierapolis (1st/2nd cents. AD). Snake-legged Giants are to be found particularly on monumental colums depicting Jupiter fighting a giant (→ Monumental column) of the Upper Germanic provinces.

M. Barbanera, Il significato della gigantomachia sui templi greci in Sicilia, in: Scritti di antichità in memoria di S. Stucchi 2, 1996, 149–153; H. Knell, Mythos und Polis, 1990; M. B. Moore, The central group in the Gigantomachy of the Old Athena Temple on the Acropolis, in: AJA 99, 1995, 633–639; H. Schaaf, M. Zelle, Reichsadler und Giganten. Neue Funde röm. Wandmalerei aus der Colonia Ulpia Traiana, in: Antike Welt 28, 1997, 519–521; H.J. Schalles, Der Pergamonaltar, 1986; B. Schmidt-Dounas, Anklänge an altoriental. Mischwesen im Gigantomachiefries des Pergamonaltars, in: Boreas 16, 1993, 5–17; Th. M. Schmidt, Der späte Beginn und der vorzeitige Abbruch der Arbeiten am Pergamonaltar, in: B. Andreae et al. (ed.), Phyromachos-Probleme, 1990, 141–162; F. Vian, M.B. Moore, s.v. Gigantes, LIMC 4.1, 191–270 (with older bibliography). A.L.

Gibeon Town in the Ephraimitic mountains. G. was one of the Canaanite city states of the southern transverse run that separated the northern and southern part of the Israelite settlement area in Palestine (Jos 9 and passim). According to the literary testimonies (OT, Hellenistic-Roman and Byzantine authors; e.g. Eus. On. 66,11–16), it must have been settled at least from the late Bronze Age (2nd half of the 2nd millennium BC) until after the beginning of the Common Era. It is true that the identification with *al-Ǧib c.* 9 km north-west of Jerusalem has not been proven with certainty by American excavations (1956–1962) but it has become a probability. The excavations yielded Bronze Age shaft graves (from the 2nd millennium BC), water supply facilities, the 'industrial area' of the wine-makers and Iron Age city walls.

A. Alt, Neue Erwägungen über die Lage von Mizpa, Ataroth, Beeroth und G., in: ZpalV 69, 1953, 1–27; J. B. Pritchard, Gibeon. Where the Sun Stood Still, 1962; Id., The Bronze Age Cemetery of Gibeon, 1963. H.D.

Gift exchange see → Prsents, gifts

Gigantomachy (γιγαντομαχία; *gigantomachía*, Plato and others, γιγαντία; *gigantía*, Philostratus; *Gigantomachia* Claudianus and others). Battle of the → Giants against the (Olympian) gods for the rule of the world, usually set in Phlegrae or → Phlegra (e.g. Aesch. Eum.

295; Eur. HF 1194; Ion 988) that was, in a second step, equated with the peninsula of → Pallene (e.g. Hdt. 7,123); won by the gods with the help of → Heracles (the role of Heracles probably mentioned for the first time in Hes. Theog. 954 [1. 419], clearly in Hes. Cat. fr. 43a 65 M-W). The Gigantomachy is part of the myth of securing the well-ordered world (under Zeus) against repeated uprisings by uncivilized representatives of an elemental world condition in which brute force reigns. As a variant on this pattern, aside from → Titanomachy, Typhonomachy, attack of the heaven by the → Aloads among others, it increasingly gains a growing symbolic power – especially a political one: destruction of the attacking primeval forces of chaos by the orderly powers of free states (→ Panathenaea), kings (Pergamum Altar) and emperors (Augustus, Domitian, Maximian etc.: [2]) – and develops great metaphorical potential (e.g. 'Gigantomachy' of ontological factions: Pl. Soph. 246a4). Thanks to its highly effective referential nature as a result of succinct vividness, Gigantomachy as the substitution for conceptual facts – the 'ultimate decisive battle between utter violence and the norm' – becomes a topos especially in art (representations in all art forms [3; 4. 191–270], and literature (countless uses in poetry and prose [5; 6]). The first literary mention of Gigantomachy is probably to be found in Hes. Theog. (see above), then, clearly in Xenophanes 21 B. 1,21 DK. A literary work with the title Gigantomachy is first attested for → Claudianus [2] (previously a Γιγαντιάς/*Gigantiás* for → Dionysius [32] and a Γιγαντία/*Gigantía* for → Scopelianus). Short description of the course of the battle in → Apollodorus 1,6,1–2 [7], detailed representation in Claudianus.

1 M.L. West, Hesiod, Theogony, 1966 2 G. Kleiner, Das Nachleben des Pergamenischen Gigantomachie-Kampfes. Berliner Winckelmann-Programm 105, 1949 3 F. Vian, Répertoire des Gigantomachies figurées dans l'art grec et romain, 1951 4 Id., s.v. Gigantes, LIMC 4.1, 191–270 5 Id., La guerre des géants devant les penseurs de l'antiquité, in: REG 65, 1952, 1–39 6 Id., s.v. Gigantes, LIMC 4.1, 191–196 7 Apollodorus, The Library of Greek Mythology, translated by R. Hard, 1997. J.L.

Gigonus (Γίγωνος; *Gígōnos*). The town situated close to Cape Gigonis, that is probably to be found north-west of modern Nea Kallikrateia on the west coast of the Chalcidian Peninsula, is mentioned in Hdt. 7,123,2 with regard to the campaign of Xerxes; G. is also mentioned in the Athenian tribute quota lists between 434/3 and 421 BC and for 432 as the line of communication of an Athenian army marching from Macedonia to Poteidaia (Thuc. 1,61,5; 62,2), then however, like the cape, it is only mentioned again in the geographical literature.

F. Papazoglou, Les villes de Macedoine à l'époque romaine, 1988, 417; M. Zahrnt, Olynth und die Chalkidier, 1971, 179f. M.Z.

Gigthis Town on the Lesser Syrte, 30 km north-east of Medenine, modern Bou Grara. Evidence: Ptol. 4,3,11; It. Ant. 60,1; 518,5; Tab. Peut. 6,5. G. was presumably a Phoenician or Punic settlement and in later times perhaps the outlying area of the Cinithi, the allies of → Tacfarinas. Under Hadrian or Antoninus Pius the town was accorded *ius Latii maius*, and under Antoninus Pius (AD 138–161) it became a *municipium* (CIL VIII Suppl. 4, 22707). Further inscriptions: CIL VIII 1, 25–34; Suppl. 1, 11017–11047; Suppl. 4, 22691–22757.

S. Lancel, E. Lipiński, s.v. G., DCPP, 190; K. Vössing, Unt. zur röm. Schule, Bildung, Schulbildung im Nordafrika der Kaiserzeit, 1991, 54f. W.HU.

Gigurri (Georres, Giorres). In Valdeorras on the upper Sil (Province of Orense) the inscription ILS I 2079 was found on which a Roman soldier with the Celtic epithet (according to [2. 1089]) *Reburrus* is called *Gigurrus Calubrigensis*. Calubriga is the (according to [1. 705]) Celtic name of an unknown town (assumptions in this regard in [3. 95]). The Asturian tribe of the G. is mentioned on several occasions (Plin. HN 3,28; Ptol. 2,6,37; Geogr. Rav. 4,45). As Valdeorras was called Val de Geurrez or Jurrez in the Middle Ages (see [3] and ILS), it is undoubtedly the case that the G. were often settled here – further evidence is that the frequently mentioned western Gothic mint Georres or Giorres [4. 13, 237, 253, 281] is identical to Valdeorras; see also [5. 24].

1 Holder 1 2 Holder 2 3 A. Schulten, Los Cántabros y Astures y su guerra con Roma, 1943 4 A. Schulten, Fontes Hispaniae Antiquae 9, 1947 5 Enciclopedia Universal Ilustrada 26.

Tovar 3, 112f. P.B.

Gilda Town in *Mauretania Tingitana*, north-west of Volubilis, perhaps identifiable with Souk el-Arba of Sidi Slimane. Evidence: Mela 3,107; Ptol. 4,1,13 (Σίλδα; *Sílda*); It. Ant. 23,4; Steph. Byz. s.v. Γίλδα; Geogr. Rav. p. 43,3 (?).

M. Euzennat, Les voies romaines du Maroc ..., in: M. Renard (ed.), Hommages à A. Grenier II (Coll. Latomus 58), 1962, 599f. W.HU.

Gildas Oldest historian of the Britons with the epithet *Sapiens*. G. was a Romanized Celt from western Britain, was born before AD 504 and wrote before 547, as a Christian who was fully committed to Roman culture, the work *De excidio et conquestu Britanniae* that was important for the history of the island during and after the decline of Roman rule. A description of the topography is followed by the history in Roman times, emphasizing the events of Church history. The invasion of the Anglo-Saxons is interpreted as a punishment from God and the immorality of the ruling classes is interpreted as having caused the misery of the post-Roman period. G.

died in 569; he is said to have founded the Monastery of St. Gildas de Rhuys in Brittany and was made a saint.

EDITIONS: MGH AA 13.
BIBLIOGRAPHY: M. WINTERBOTTOM, The Ruin of Britain and Other Works, 1978. K.P.J.

Gildilas Eastern Goth, *comes Syracusanae civitatis* in AD 526/7, commander of the province of Sicilia, known from two letters of → Athalaric (Cassiod. Var. 9,11; 14) who threatened the *comes Gotharum* G. with dismissal from office because of serious irregularities in the levying of taxes and in legal decisions.

M.MEI. and ME.STR.

Gildo Son of the Moorish king Nubel and brother of Firmus (Amm. Marc. 29,5,6), born before AD 330, executed on 31 July 398. In the rebellion of his brother Firmus, G. supported the *magister militum* Theodosius in 373–375 and distinguished himself by arresting the *vicarius* of Romanus, Vincentius, and two rebellious leaders, Belles and Fericius (Amm. Marc. 29,5,6; 21; 24). In about 386 G. was elevated to the position of *comes Africae* (Oros. 7,36). He was initially on friendly terms with the usurper Maximus, with whom he had served in the battle against Firmus. However, when Maximus invaded Italy in 388, Emperor Theodosius I succeeded in winning G. over to his side. After the successful suppression of the usurper, G. received – probably as thanks – the extraordinary title of *comes et magister utriusque militiae per Africam,* as attested by a law of 393 (Cod. Theod. 9,7,9). Theodosius also attempted to consolidate the hesitant loyalty of the Mauretanian by marrying G.'s daughter Salvina to Nebridius, the nephew of → Flacilla.

From 386 G. ruled in Africa like a king (Claud. Bellum Gildonicum 157: *privato iure*). From 388 he supported the Donatist bishop Optatus and in this way contributed decisively to Donatism increasing in importance to become the strongest denomination of Africa.

In the years that followed G. cleverly managed in his own way to manipulate and weaken the power of the emperor. When Eugenius rebelled in 393/4, he initially allowed the grain deliveries to continue to come to the usurper and in the war that followed he gave Theodosius, to whom he was still formally subject, no military assistance (Cod. Theod. 9,7,9) but adopted a neutral stance, awaiting the outcome of the disputes (Claud. bellum Gildonicum 241–252). After Theodosius' death G. put Honorius under pressure by allowing the grain supplies to be sent off only irregularly, so causing constant shortages in Rome (Claud. ibid. 17f.; 34). G. sold the production surplus in favour of his private casket and so amassed huge wealth. When Stilicho planned a military reaction, G. broke off his allegiance to Honorius in 397 and became a subject of the eastern emperor Arcadius; the Roman Senate then declared him to be an enemy of the state (*hostis publicus*) (Symmachus, Ep. 4,5). In winter 397/8 an advance detachment under G.'s brother Mascezel was sent to Africa which surprisingly defeated G.'s troops near Theueste. After G.'s execution his assets were confiscated and these were so extensive that the office of *comes Gildoniaci patrimonii* was set up to manage them.

PLRE 1, 395f.; H.J. DIESNER, Gildos Herrschaft und die Niederlage bei Theueste (Tebessa), in: Klio 40, 1962, 178–186; W.H.C. FREND, The Donatist Church, 1952; C. GEBBIA, Ancora sulle 'rivolte' di Firmo e Gildone, in: A. MASTINO (ed.), Atti del V convegno di studio su 'L'Africa romana', 1988, 117–129; Y. MODÉRAN, Gildon, les Maures et l'Afrique, in: MEFRA 101,2, 1989, 821–867. M.R.

Gilgamesh, Gilgamesh Epic (Gilgameš, Gilgameš Epic). G., legendary ruler of → Uruk in southern Mesopotamia; linked in the sources passed down to us with the construction of the 9-km long city wall of Uruk around 2900 BC. Non-literary sources already mention G. about 2700 BC. The rulers of the 3rd dynasty of Ur (21st cent. BC) originating in Uruk maintained that they were genealogically connected with G. and therefore fostered the stories passed down about G. and his equally legendary predecessors (→ Epic) in order to glorify and legitimize the dynasty (→ Genealogy). The written form of the Epic of G. in five individual epics in the Sumerian language, known from copies from the 18th cent. BC [2. 540–559], was produced in the 21st cent. In the 19th/18th cents. a uniform, Akkadian version comprising *c.* 1,000 verses arose, which is the basis of further tradition that can be followed in a unique manner over more than 1,500 years [2. 640–744]. The Epic of G. was also known outside Mesopotamia. Apart from Akkadian fragments (15th cent. BC), tablets were found in Asia Minor in → Ḫattuša with a Hittite and a Hurritic version (13th cent. BC), and an Akkadian fragment (14th cent. BC) was found in Megiddo (Palestine). The most extensive and complete version (12 tablets with *c.* 3,000 verses) that originates in the 13th/12th cents. BC comes from the library of → Assurbanipal (7th cent. BC). A certain Sin-leqe-uninni is considered to be its creator. These or other slightly different versions from southern Mesopotamia (7th–4th cent. BC) influenced Greek (Ael. NA 12,21) and Syrian writers [3. 87–89].

The central theme of the epic is G.'s search for lasting fame. For this purpose he goes with his companion Enkidu to the cedarwood (Lebanon) to fell trees for a temple door as a votive offering for the god → Enlil. In the process they kill Ḫuwawa, the watchman of the forest. After their return Ištar (→ Astarte), the city goddess of Uruk, desires G. as her husband. Rejected by him, she has the celestial bull fight G. but the bull is killed by G. and Enkidu. As a consequence of this wicked deed, Enkidu wastes away and dies. G., whose search for fame is suddenly halted and who is confronted with the reality of death, embarks upon a futile search for eternal life. The 11th tablet that among other things also contains the tale of the Flood (→ Atraḫasis), ends with the reference to the city wall of Uruk built by G. that was meant to announce his fame to those who came after him. The 12th tablet, a translation of the Sumerian epic 'Death of G.', is appended. The Akkadian version of the G. Epic represents in comparison with the Sumerian precursors – with primarily historical aetiologies and those related to the cult – a transformation to a literary genre whose goal is of a didactic nature: behaviour which pleases the gods is rewarded, wicked behaviour is punished; no one can escape death because it is the fate of human beings. What remains is the memory of outstanding deeds.

Since the epic became known at the end of the 19th cent. the subject has attracted great attention (among others R. M. Rilke, A. Strindberg, H. H. Jahnn). The stories about G. are the object of drama performances (R. Wilson, The Forrest), historicizing novels and (illustrated) books for children and young people; translated into all the important world languages.

1 D. O. Edzard et al., s.v. Gilgamesch-Epos, Kindler 18, 636–647 (with bibliography) 2 D. O. Edzard, K. Hekker, W. H. P. Römer, TUAT 3, 1993/4 (transl., with lit.) 3 T. Jacobsen, The Sumerian Kinglist, 1939. J.RE.

Gilgamos see → Gilgamesh Epic

Gillium Town in *Africa proconsularis*, situated west of → Thubursicum Bure, modern Henchir Frass. Inscriptions: Revue Tunisienne 6, 1899, 447 (new Punic); CIL VIII suppl. 4, 26222–26236 (*decuriones Gillitani*, 3rd cent. AD). Victor Tonnennensis mentions an abbot of the *monasterium Gillense* or *Gillitanum* (Chron. min. II p. 203, 553,1; 204, 557,2) for the years 553 and 557.

AATun (1:50 000), sheet 32, no. 11. W.HU.

Ginger Through Plin. HN 12,28 we know that the Romans did not import the rhizome of the *zingiber* or *zimpiber* (Zingiber officinalis L.), a bitter-tasting spice, from Asia like today but from Arabia and Troglodytia (southern Egypt). Palladius used it to spice preserved quinces (Agric. 11,20,2). Dioscorides attributes to the *zingíberi* a warming, stomach-friendly effect (2,160 Wellmann = 2,189 Berendes). It helped with cataracts and in antidotes.

R. Stadler, s.v. Ingwer, RE IX 2, 1554. C.HÜ.

Gir River that has its source in the high Atlas Mountains, presumably the Oued Guir. C. → Suetonius Paullinus advanced to it with his troops in AD 42. References: Plin. HN 5,15 (*Ger*); Ptol. 4,6,13; 16; 31 (Γεὶρ; *Geír*); Geogr. Rav. p. 2,69; 3,14; 36,28; 37,11 (*Ger*); Claud. Carm. 21,252 (*Gir*); Anon. Geographia Compendiaria 31 (GGM II 502; Γὶρ; *Gír*).

H. Dessau, s.v. G., RE VII 1, 1366. W.HU.

Giraffe The ancient sources give varying accounts of the place of origin of the giraffe (*Camelopardalis girafa*): Agatharchides (De mare rubro = Phot. bibl. 250,455b 4 B.) considers that it was among the Troglodytae in Nubia, Plin. HN 8,69 under the name *nabun* it had there in Ethiopia, Artemidorus of Ephesus (Str. 16,775) locates it in Arabia, whilst Paus. 9,21,2 places it in India. The name καμηλοπάρδαλις, *camelopardalis* (*-parda*, *-pardala*) comes from similarities with the camel and panther: 'it has the figure of a camel but the spots of a panther' (Varro, Ling. 5,100; cf. Agatharchides; Hor. Epist. 2,1,195: *diversum confusa genus panthera camelo*; Plin. HN 8,69). Agatharchides gives a good description, among other things, of the excessively long neck suited to grazing on trees, whilst Artemidorus praises the unsurpassable quickness and wildness (doubted by Strabo) (cf. Opp. Kyn. 3,461ff. and in detail Heliodorus, Aethiopiaca 10,27f.).

In Egypt they were hunted for millennia [1] but they are not mentioned until Agatharchides and Artemidorus (2nd/1st cents. BC). Ptolemy II's procession displayed a specimen for the first time (Ath. 5,201c). In 46 BC it was a special showpiece in the Roman triumphal procession of Caesar, according to Hor. Epist. 2,1,198 (cf. Varro; Pliny and Cass. Dio 43,23,1–2). 10 giraffes appeared at the secular games in AD 247. The precise descriptions indicate that there were several showings. A wall painting in Rome [2. vol. 1, 284f., fig. 90] shows them realistically, with a bell on the neck, led by a black man. A sarcophagus with the Indian triumph of Dionysus provides a successful representation [3. 128 and pl. 65].

1 H. Kees, HbdOr, 1. Abt., 1. vol. 2 Keller 3 Toynbee, Tierwelt. C.HÜ.

Gisco, Giscon see → Geskon

Gitiades Bronze sculptor from Sparta, where he created the temple and cult image of Athena *Polioúchos kaì Chalkíoikos* as well as extensive mythological scenes in bronze reliefs (Paus. 3,17,2). The latter were presumably displayed on the walls of the temple, and according to later coin reproductions, the gown of the Athena statue was also provided with reliefs. G. had also written a hymn to Athena. Also on view in Amyclae were two bronze tripods by him with Aphrodite and Artemis as supporting figures that were dedicated from the booty of a Messenian War (Paus. 3,18,7). However, historical data are lacking so we can only estimate the period of G.'s creativity as the 6th cent. BC, based on the coin image.

Overbeck, no. 357–359 (sources); L. Lacroix, Les reproductions de statues sur les monnaies grecques. La statuaire archaïque et classique, 1949, 217–218, pl. 18, 1; B. S. Ridgway, The Severe Style in Greek Sculpture, 1970, 72, no. 6–7; M. Herfort-Koch, Archaische Bronzeplastik Lakoniens, Boreas, suppl. 1, 1986, 26, 69; Fuchs/Floren, 215; J. J. Pollitt, The Art of Ancient Greece. Sources and Documents 2, 1990, 26, 241. R.N.

Gizeh Egyptian necropolis for the residence of the Old Kingdom (2700–2190 BC) on a plateau in the Libyan desert west of Cairo that juts out prominently. The pyramid complexes of the Kings → Cheops, → Chefren and → Mycerinus from the 4th dynasty (*c.* 2600–2400 BC) characterize the place; they are surrounded by the → mastabas and cliff tombs of the members of the royal family and high officials. After the 4th dynasty the cemetery was, by the end of the Old Kingdom, intensively occupied further by private tombs, particularly by the graves of the priests working in the old cults of the dead. In the Middle Kingdom (1900–1680 BC) G. was practically deserted, whilst in the New Kingdom (1550–1070 BC) the place became popular again because of its proximity to the northern capital city of → Memphis, with the worship of → Harmachis at the Great Sphinx. As → Wonders of the World the pyramids of G. were a lively tourist destination in the Graeco-Roman period and were described and commented on frequently (e.g. Hdt. 2,124–135; Diod. Sic. 1,63–64; Str. 17,1,33–34; Plin. HN 36,12).

C. M. Zivie, s.v. Gisa, LÄ 2, 602–614. S.S.

Glabrio Roman cognomen ('bald-head', cf. *glaber*) in the family of the Acilii (→ Acilius [I 10–13]; [II 6–9]), in the Imperial period also in other families.

Degrassi, FCIR 254; Kajanto, Cognomina 236. K.-L.E.

Gladiator The Romans took over the custom from the Etruscan Campania of having gladiators fight at funerals in honour of the person who had died. Gladiators first appeared in Rome on the occasion of the burial of Brutus Pera in 264 BC (Val. Max. 2,4,7). The aristocratic *gentes* outdid each other in the arrangement of their funerals; therefore the number of gladiators in use steadily increased. Sharp competition for offices supported the tendency in the late Republic for separating the gladiatorial combats (→ *munus, munera*) from the funerals, in order to repeat them at a later stage as soon as an election was imminent. The attempt was made to stop this practice (*lex Tullia de ambitu*, Cic. Sest. 133). Starting in 42 BC, certain magistrates held gladiatorial combats at official games (Cass. Dio 47,40,6; 54,2,3f.; Suet. Claud. 24,2). From the time of Caesar its implementation was regulated throughout the empire (ILS 6087,70f.; Suet. Tib. 34,1). Prisoners of war, condemned criminals, slaves and also volunteers who had taken an oath for the duration of their contract to serve in conditions similar to slavery all served as gladiators (Sen. Ep. 37,1f.). They were trained in a *ludus gladiatorius*, whose owner rented them to games-promoters (*editores*). Since the early Principate period, the gladiators were equipped and armed in various ways: the *retiarii* fought with net and trident, the *myrmillones* with a short sword and round shield. During combats gladiators stood – often in pairs, but also in larger groups – across from each other with different weapons (Suet. Calig. 30,3). If gladiators survived three years, they no longer needed to go into the arena and they received a wooden sword (*rudis*) as a symbol; they remained in the *ludus* another two years until their → manumission (Coll. 11,7,4). After that they were subject to → *infamia*, so they were excluded from all public activity (ILS 6085) and even from military service.

Gladiatorial combats were mostly carried out in → amphitheatres, in the Greek east also in the theatre. They were ceremonially connected neither with the cult of the gods nor with that of the dead. The combat ended as soon as a gladiator raised a finger (Mart. Liber spectaculorum 27). The spectators signalled whether the one defeated deserved mercy (*missio*) or death; the *editor* made the decision (Mart. ibid. 20). Gladiatorial combat represented the superiority of the Roman order over its enemies; discipline, technique and fearlessness in the face of death – the warlike values of the Roman culture – guaranteed victory (Cic. Tusc. 2,41; Plin. Pan. 33). Even outcasts were worthy of being accepted into Roman society (again) if they had proven in the arena that they had internalized these values. Citizens and games-promoters celebrated their attachment with the basic Roman inalienable values; the citizens checked whether the games-promoters had the same idea of *virtus* (bravery), of *clementia* (leniency) and finally of *iustitia* (justice) as they had (Tac. Ann. 1,76,3f.). No other ritual could so powerfully demonstrate the citizens' political consensus – in Rome with the emperor, in the provinces with the local aristocracy; therefore, although Roman authors expressed their disgust over the theatre, almost to a man they judged the gladiator system highly.

Gladiatorial games quickly spread throughout the entire Imperium; it also found enthusiastic acceptance in the Greek east. Gladiatorial combats were even put on in the towns of Italy (Petron. Sat. 45,11–13), and in Pompeii gladiators have been archaeologically documented in numerous ways. In order to retain the political symbolism of gladiatorial games, the emperors repeatedly intervened legally; they forbade combats *sine missione* (without mercy, cf. Suet. Aug. 45,3), because this robbed the ritual of its political meaning; they attempted to stop members of the imperial aristocracy from appearing as gladiators because this softened the political dividing line between the ostracized and the citizens, and disqualified the entire aristocracy in the eyes of the citizens (Cass. Dio 48,43,3). Individual *principes*, such as Titus or Domitian, favoured certain groups of gladiators (Suet. Tit. 8,2; Dom. 10,1). Commodus, as the only *princeps*, fought openly as a gladiator, however with a wooden sword and without killing (Cass. Dio 72,17,2); he wanted to add the victor's aura of the arena to the imperial majesty; but the people of the capital city left the amphitheatre on such appearances of the emperor (Cass. Dio 72,17,2; 72,20,2; 72,22,3). Members of the upper class who trained as gladiators, or women who gave up their marriage because of a gladiator, were sharply criticized in literature (Juv. 8,199–210; 2,143–148; 6,78–113). Even though there were critical voices to individual harmful consequences (Cic. Tusc. 2,42; Sen. Ep. 7), gladiatorial games were never fundamentally rejected. Christian authors denounced them because they damaged the soul of the spectators; they were not concerned about the gladiators themselves. The practice died out at the beginning of the 5th cent. AD because acquiring gladiators became more and more difficult and the events became too expensive.

Numerous mosaics with scenes of gladiatorial combats from villas in Italy and the provinces (e.g. Tusculum, 3rd cent. AD, Rome, Villa Borghese; Nennig; Augst; Villa di Dar Buc Amméra, Africa Proconsularis) are evidence for the attractiveness of this subject area. → Munera; → Spectacles

1 J.-C. Golvin, C. Landes, Amphithéâtres et gladiateurs, 1990 2 K. Schneider, s.v. Gladiatores, RE Suppl. 3, 760–784 3 G. Ville, La gladiature en occident, 1981 4 Id., Les jeux de gladiateurs dans l'empire chrétien, in: MEFRA 72, 1960, 273–335 5 Th. Wiedemann, Emperors and Gladiators, 1992. E.F.

Gladiatorius ludus see → Gladiator, see → Munus, Munera

Gladius see → Sword

Glagolitic (Glagolica). The older of the two Slavonic alphabets that was invented by Constantine (with the monk's name → Cyrillus). Until the 18th cent. the origin of G. was connected with the activity of Jerome (342–429) as *doctor maximus* and patron saint of Dalmatia [13. 111], to whom a few slavonic apocrypha [12. 7, 26, 27] were ascribed. Assemanus [1] was the first to establish the theory that Constantine-Cyrillus certainly was the inventor of G.; this is generally accepted today.

The *Vita Constantini* (VC) [6] is the only source to report about how one year before his vocation to do missionary work in Moravia (863) Constantine designed the Slavonic characters and translated the Gospel kerygma into Slavonic – 'thanks to the revelation of God' (VC 14,9). The controversial date of origin comes from the treatise *O pis'meněch* of the monk (with pseudonym) Chrabr ('in the year 6363 of creation') or the *Skazanie iz 'javlenno o pismenech* by Konstantinos Kostenečki, from the end of the 14th–15th cents. ('in the year 6370 of creation'). The date (AD) can be calculated according to the authoritative era in Constantinople 'from the creation of the world', which dates Christ's birth in the year 5508, or according to the era of Antioch and Alexandria (Christ's birth in the year 5500). According to the research of the older Slavonic chronology by Ratkoš [11. 350–357], the period for the date of origin of the G. would in that case be between 1 September 861 and 24 March 863.

There is no lack of sources from which one has 'derived' the G. characters. A wide spectrum of explanations – from the mystic power of the revelation that, with the hand of Constantine, 'sealed' 100 years of Bulgarian history in each G. letter [15. 128–135], to the geometrical figure module 'thought out by Constantine' [9. 118–142] and the integrated Christian symbolism (cross, circle, triangle), to the graphic impact of Greek, Latin, Phoenician, Aramaic, Hebrew i.a. scripts – obscures the 'mystery' of the origin.

The oldest G. inscriptions (9th–10th cents.) have been found in the 'round church' and in the czar's palace in Preslav (eastern Bulgaria), e.g. the oldest G. *Abecedarium Bulgaricum* (10th cent.) [5. 45; 10. 139–164]. G. was widespread from the 9th–12th cents. in the south-west of Bulgaria (Ochrid), in Dalmatia and on the Adriatic islands, however, not so much in the east of Bulgaria (Preslav) and in Greater Moravia; later G. was also used as a secret writing system (tajnopis') [14. 1929].

1 J. Assemanus, Kalendaria ecclesiae universae, 1755 2 I. Duridanov et al., Gramatika na starobălgarskija ezik, 1991, 19–73 3 T. Eckhardt, Azbuka. Versuch einer Einführung in das Studium der slav. Paläographie, 1989 (esp. 31–48 and epilogue) 4 Id., Theorien über den Ursprung der Glagolica, in: Slovo (Zagreb) 13, 1963, 87–117 5 I. Gošev, Starobălgarskite glagoličeski i kirilski nadpisi ot IX i X vek, 1961 6 F. Grivec, F. Tomšič, Constantinus et Methodius Thessalonicenses. Fontes, 1960 7 V. Jagić, Enciklopedija slavjanskoj filologii. III. Glagoličeskoe pis'mo, 1911, 51–229 8 P. Ilčev, Azbuki, Glagolica, in: P. Dinekov, Kirilo-Metodievska Enciklopedija, 1985, 34–49, 491–509 9 V. Ončev, O. Ončeva, Dreven i săvremenen bălgarski šrift, 1982 10 R. Marti, Slav. Alphabete in nicht-slav. Hss., in: Kirilo-Metodievski studii, knižka 8, 1991, 139–164 11 P. Ratkoš, L'ère d'Antiochie et l'ère de Constantinople dans quelques ouvrages vieux slaves, in: Byzantinoslavica 27, 1966, 350–357 12 F. Repp, Untersuchungen zu den Apokryphen der Österreichischen Nationalbibliothek, in: Wiener Slavistischer Almanach 6, 1957/8, 5–34 13 K. Rösler, St. Hieronymus, ein Mittelpunkt der Kroaten in Rom, in: Wiener Slavistischer Almanach 5, 1956, 110–115 14 M. Speranskij, Tajnopis' v jugoslavjanskich i russkich pamjatnikach pis'ma, in: Enciklopedija slavjanskoj filologii, 4,3, 1929 15 M. Vezneva, Svrăchsetivno poznanie. Zapiski na edin extrasens, 1991, 85–135 16 J. Vereecken, Nazvanija glagoličeskich bukv i judeo-christianskaja tradicija, in: Palaeobulgarica 19,1, 1995, 5–14. L.D.

Glanis

[1] The silurid (*silurus glanis*), an (up to 3 metres long) freshwater fish. Aristot. Hist. an. 8(9),37,691 a20–b2 describes the care of the brood of the *glánis*, whose name was passed on to Thomas of Cantimpré (*glamanez monstrum* [1] 6,26) and Albertus Magnus (*garcanez*, animal. 24,35 [2]) via the Arabian-Latin translation of Michael Scotus as *glanieuz* without real knowledge of the animal. A connection to evil demons was ascribed to it, perhaps due to its supposed attacks on fishing nets [3. 1 § 458].

1 H. BOESE (ed.), Thomas Cantimpratensis, Liber de natura rerum, 1973 2 H. STADLER (ed.), Albertus Magnus, De animalibus, 2, 1920 3 HOPFNER. C.HÜ.

[2] (Γλάνις; *Glánis*). In Aristophanes (Equ. 1004; 1035; 1097; cf. Suda s.v.), the name of a prophet; his younger brother's name is Bacis. The name is likely fictitious and can be classified (see *glánis* [1]) among the ἄνδρες ἰχθυομάντεις (*ándres ichthyománteis*, 'fish fortune-tellers'), mentioned in Athenaeus (8,333d) for Lycia. JO.S.

Glannaventa (probably modern Ravenglass/Cumbria). The camp was laid out at the beginning of Hadrian's rule at an anchorage at the river (not excavated); especially striking is a bathhouse outside the walls; the building's walls with windows 3.5 metres high are still extant. G. was likely abandoned in the late 4th cent.

E. BIRLEY, The Roman Fort at Ravenglass (Transactions of the Cumberland and Westmorland Archaeological Society 58), 1958, 14–30. M.TO.

Glanum Town in *Gallia Narbonensis* (modern Saint-Rémy-de-Provence) in the region of the → Salluvii. Located on the great trade route running east-west that connected Italy with Spain (later the *via Domitia*), G.'s importance was also due to its location at the end of the north-south road which provided G. control over the direct access to the Crau plain. A Celtic-Ligurian sanctuary that was dedicated to the god Glan and the → *Matres* [1] was located in the vicinity of a mineral spring. The residential area and civic or cultural public facilities developed especially in the 2nd cent. BC so that G. had the appearance of a small city of the Greek type already before the Roman conquest. Possibly it belonged to → Massalia. Although G. is considered the most Hellenized town of the Provence, recent excavations have proven its Salluvian character [2; 3]. Therefore, the destructions in the Hellenistic period are to be seen in relation to the Roman interventions of 125–124 and 90 BC. The actual Gallic-Roman era (49 BC until the end of the 3rd cent. AD) is characterized by profound changes in the city's transit traffic. Presumably, G. had the status of an *oppidum Latinum* from the end of the Republic. Among the Roman remains are a bouleuterion, sanctuaries, houses, a triumphal arch, and the memorial of the Iulii [4]. The Roman town was pillaged around AD 270; Christian cemetery near the thermal baths.

1 M. LEJEUNE, Recueil des Inscriptions gauloises 1, 1985, 76–78 2 A. ROTH CONGÈS, Nouvelles fouilles à G. (1982–1990), in: Journal of Roman Archaeology 5, 1992, 39–55 3 Id., Le centre monumental de G., ou les derniers feux de la civilisation salyenne, in: M. BATS et al. (ed.), Marseille grecque et la Gaule, 1992, 351–367 4 P. GROS, Le mausolée des Julii et le statut de G., in: Revue archéologique de Narbonnaise 19, 1986, 65–80.

C. GOUDINEAU, s.v. Glanon, PE, 356f.; P. GROS, s.v. G., EAA 2, 795–797; F. SALVIAT, G. et les Antiques, 1990. Y.L.

Glaphyra

[1] Courtesan of the priest-king Archelaus [6] of Comana and mother of Archelaus [7], whom → Antonius [I 9] elevated to king of Cappadocia in 36 BC (Cass. Dio 49,32,3; App. B Civ. 5,7). Octavianus criticized the relationship of Antonius with G. (Mart. 11,20). OGIS 361. ME.STR.

[2] Daughter of king Archelaus [7] of Cappadocia, granddaughter of G. [1], in her first marriage G. was married to Alexander, the eldest son of king Herod I by Mariamme, and was caught up in the family intrigues at court. After the execution of her husband (7 BC), Herod sent her back to her father. She married king Juba II of Mauretania and after their divorce the stepbrother of her first husband, Herod Archelaus, the tetrarch of Judaea and Samaria. The marriage gave offence to pious Jews because G. had children by Archelaus' half-brother, Tigranes and Alexander (Jos. Ant. Iud. 16,11; 193; 206ff.; 261ff.; 303; 328ff.; 17,11f.; 341; 349ff.; BI 1,476ff.; 499ff.; 552f.; 2,114). K.BR.

Glaphyrae (Γλαφύραι; *Glaphýrai*). The catalogue of ships of the *Iliad* (Hom. Il. 2,711ff.) mentions the town together with → Boebe and → Iolcus. Its mythological founder was Glaphyros, son of Magnes and father of Boibos. In historical time, the ethnic term Γλαφυρεύς (*Glaphyreús*) is documented for officials from → Demetrias [1]. Therefore, it can be assumed that G. existed until the Hellenistic period, although Str. 9,15,5 does not mention G. at the Synoikismos for Demetrias. The exact location of G. at the southern bank of the former Boebe Lake is not certain.

M. DI SALVATORE, Ricerche sul territorio di Pherai, in: La Thessalie, quinze années de recherches archéologiques (1975–1990). Actes du colloque international, Lyon 1990, 1994, vol. 2, 92–124; F. STÄHLIN, Das hellenische Thessalien, 1924, 61. HE.KR.

Glass (ὕαλος; *hýalos* or ὕελος; *hýelos*, *vitrum*)
I. METHODS OF GLASS PRODUCTION II. GLASS IN THE ANCIENT ORIENT III. EARLY TECHNIQUES OF PRODUCING GLASS OBJECTS IV. TECHNIQUES OF GLASS BLOWING V. FURTHER TECHNIQUES OF GLASS PROCESSING VI. GLASS WINDOWS VII. GLASS IN LITERATURE AND ART VIII. CELTIC-GERMANIC

I. METHODS OF GLASS PRODUCTION

Glass is a mixture of silicic acid (silicon dioxide, quartz or quartz sand) and alkali (soda, sodium bicarbonate or potash) as flux [2; 7; 8]. Since it was apparently unknown in antiquity that alkali makes the mixture water-soluble, only glass with sufficient lime to neutralize this reaction is preserved. Producers of raw glass (ὑελέψης; *hyelépsēs* or ὑαλοψός; *hyalopsós*) knew from experience which sand (ψάμμος ὑαλικός; *psámmos hyalikós*) or which calcareous plant ashes made the glass durable.

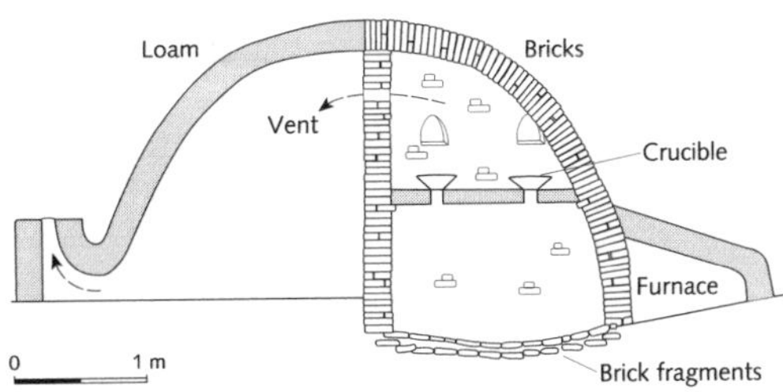

Roman glassworks near Niederzier, district of Düren. Cross-section of a reconstructed furnace (4th cent. AD).

Up into the Roman period, raw glass was produced only in a few specialized centres in the Near East, later in Egypt, and exported in ingots to the processors (ὑαλουργός; *hyalourgós*, *vitrearius*). It was produced in two stages: first, fritting was slowly vitrified from the crushed ingredients at a low temperature of around 850°C; after cooling, it was ground and then melted to pure glass at 1000–1100°C. The natural colour of glass is a transparent green with a yellow to blue paleness as a result of the impurities due to iron; however, due to the low melting temperatures, early glass is mostly almost opaque. Since the 16th cent. BC, glass was produced in bright colours by the addition of metal oxides, and since the 8th cent. BC the colour was taken out of the glass by adding antimony or manganese to the raw material.

Glass was discovered in the late 3rd millennium BC in Mesopotamia, likely by experiments with faience, but vessels are known only from the 16th cent. BC. In Egypt, glass was processed from the beginning of the 18th dynasty. G.PL.

II. Glass in the Ancient Orient

Up to the 1st millennium BC, all objects made of glass were sodium-calcium glass, produced from the raw materials sand, limestone and soda (in Egypt; in the Near East alternatively plant ash); metal oxides were added to give colour. The material glass was viewed as an artificial imitation of semi-precious stones. In cuneiform script texts (recipes for the production of glass) glass is appropriately characterized; the terminology of lexical lists refers to older (Sumerian) precursors of glass technology, thus to its roots in the 3rd millennium BC. No larger objects of glass are documented before the 2nd millennium BC; recipes for its production are first known from this period.

A. Lucas, Ancient Egyptian Materials and Industries, 1989; P. R. S. Moorey, Ancient Mesopotamian Materials and Industries, 1994, 189–215. R.W.

III. Early Techniques of Producing Glass Objects

The earliest glass objects are inlays melted in an open form, pendants and seals. Vessels were at first formed over a core of clay and sand; this core could be coated with cold pulverised glass, marbled in glass chunks or

rewound with hot glass threads and then be combed to diverse decorations. After cooling the glass skin, the core was removed. Such small ointment vessels were distributed in the entire Mediterranean between 550 BC and the Augustan period.

Since the 8th cent. BC, vessels of clear glass were melted in a solid clay form: this was filled with glass bits, heated and then broken off after cooling. The massive blank was then drilled out on the inside like a vessel made of precious stone (Sargon vase from Nimrud). Mosaic and reticella glass was produced from drawn and twisted canes of different colours of glass that was laid and melted into patterns with disks or strips in the form. *Zwischengoldglas* was heat-fused by two bleached bowls. Large footed bowls and the Berlin amphora from Olbia required a multi-step fusion process. This risky and complicated procedure characterizes the highly esteemed Hellenistic luxury glass as found intact and in various forms in the graves of Canosa in Apulia. The clear raw glass preferred here presumably came from Sidon, famous for the melting of especially pure glass from the sand of Belos (Str. 16,2,25; Plin. HN 5,76).

IV. Techniques of Glass Blowing

Sidon is considered the cradle of glass (Plin. HN 36,190ff.); the earliest attempts at glass-blowing have been archaeologically documented in the Jewish quarter of Jerusalem (2nd quarter of the 1st cent. BC). The development of the blowpipe was a technical revolution that made possible the serial production of vessels of varying size and function. The new technique was widespread already around the middle of the 1st cent. BC, and in the Augustan period throughout the entire Roman Empire. Especially tumblers and small bottles were blown into richly decorated moulds of clay, gypsum, metal, stone or wood consisting of two or more parts; for the first time, manufacturers signed their widely desired products (Ennion, Aristeas et al.).

In addition to the invention of the blowpipe, the prerequisite for the quick distribution of glass was the production of molten glass in closed ovens with constant high temperatures over 1000° C. Brisk trade and the immigration of craftsmen from Palestine resulted in the blossom of new glass centres in Italy, and soon after even in the new provinces of the Roman Empire, e.g. in Cologne with the pure quartz sand of its surroundings. In addition to serial dishes (*vitrea*) and large urns, old as well as new glass workshops produced vessels from clear glass blown freehand, whereby a rich range of colours and a large variety of forms were developed; the decoration consisted of contrasting colours of marbled strips, grains or prunts, of patterns and representations engraved, painted or cut in gold foil, of threads laid in a zigzag, as a net or in wavy lines.

V. Further Techniques of Glass Processing

Glass-blowing did not immediately displace earlier techniques such as form-melting and slumping; rather, mosaic, gold-band and reticella glass were produced far into the 1st cent. AD. Cameo glass, opaque white or multi-coloured relief on blue clear glass, was melted from fine frit and cullet in the form for flat glass cameos and the large Ariadne panels from Pompeii. Contested, however, is the production of the → 'Portland Vase' and other vessels of cameo glass, for which a procedure based on the division of labour of mould casting and cutting is to be assumed. The ancient art of glass-cutting and engraving achieved a new prosperity in the high-relief cut glass of the early Principate period, but especially in the net tumblers and cups of the 3rd/4th cents. AD.

The ancient technique of *zwischengoldglass* was also revived in late antiquity, especially in the *fondi d'oro*, vessel bases often with Christian subjects that were used as grave decoration in the Roman catacombs. In the migration period, glass processing was cultivated in the Frankish-Merovingian and Anglo-Saxon and in the Byzantine and Islamic spheres of influence. After the fall of Byzantium in 1204, precious glass made it into the treasury of San Marco in Venice and revitalized the glass production resident there since the early Roman period.

VI. Glass Windows

Glass windows (*specularia*) made of clear glass are known for the thermal baths of the cities buried by Vesuvius in AD 79, but even the great thermal baths of Agrippa (around 19 BC) and of Nero (around AD 62) in Rome could only function glazed (Sen. Ep. 86,8; 86,11; 90,25). The oven developed for glass-blowing was the prerequisite for the pouring and drawing of liquid glass in a metal or wooden form. Panes of 20–100 cm long and 3–6 mm thick were set in glazing bar frames of bronze, lead, stone or wood. They also changed the façades of the villas (Plin. Ep. 2,17,11; 2,17,21), then of the castles and palaces especially in the northern provinces where thin cylinder-blown window glass is found (1.5–3 mm). In late antiquity, round blown 'bull's-eye panes' (diameter 12–27 cm) appeared that as colourful elements decorated also Byzantine and Islamic buildings.

VII. Glass in Literature and Art

The development of glass production found great resonance in literature and art; numerous transparent glass bowls with fruit are portrayed on wall paintings in Pompeii, and an anecdote about a glass-maker who supposedly could produce unbreakable glass was told by several authors (Petron. Sat. 51; Plin. HN 36,195; Cass. Dio 57,21,7). The invention of glass-blowing is referred to in philosophical discourse (Sen. Ep. 90,31), and a poem describes the work of the glass-maker at the oven (Anth. Gr. 16,323). Pliny offers a comprehensive description of glass production (HN 36,189–199). Glass-makers are documented epigraphically, for example Iulius Alexander from Carthage who died in Lugdunum (ILS 7648; cf. 7647; 7649; in Rome: ILS 1778; 1779). In late antiquity glass-makers were freed from *munera* (Cod. Theod. 13,4,2).

1 D. Baatz, Fensterglas, Glasfenster und Architektur, in: A. Hoffmann et al. (ed.), Bautechnik der Ant., 1991, 4–13 2 D.F. Grose, Early Ancient Glass. The Toledo Museum of Art, 1989 3 D.B. Harden (ed.), Glas der Caesaren, 1988 4 M. Newby, K. Painter (ed.), Roman Glass: Two Centuries of Art and Invention, 1991 5 J. Price, Glass, in: Strong/Brown, 111–125 6 E.M. Stern, Roman Mold-blown Glass. The Toledo Museum of Art, 1995 7 E.M. Stern, B. Schlick-Nolte, Frühes Glas der alten Welt, 1600 v.Chr.–50 n.Chr. Sammlung E. Wolf, 1994 8 M. Sternini, La fenice di sabbia. Storia e tecnologia del vetro antico, 1995 9 H. Tait (ed.), Glass, 5000 years, 1991 10 J. Welzel, Becher aus Flechtwerk von Kristall, 1994. G.PL.

VIII. Celtic-Germanic

Glass beads occur sporadically north of the Alps in barrows in the middle Bronze Age (15th–13th cents. BC). In the late Bronze Age (→ Urnfield culture) glass beads are already produced locally in Switzerland and south-west Germany on a large scale from the 10th to the 8th cents. BC. In the older → Hallstatt Culture of the south-east Alpine region (Carniola) a glass centre is to be presumed in the 7th–6th cents. BC. In the younger Hallstatt and the early → La Tène period (5th–4th cents. BC) the rich princely graves (→ Princes, tombs and residences of) contain substantial glass bead finds that perhaps had a production centre at the → Dürrnberg. In the late La Tène period (end of the 2nd until the middle of the 1st cent. BC) glass jewellery (beads and armlets in the most varying colours and forms) is produced professionally (chunks of raw glass) in → *oppida* (e.g. → Manching). Occasionally, glass vessels (bowls and small bottles) were also produced or imported from the south. Glass production does not play a role for the ancient Germans; however, Roman glass vessels (tumblers) are frequently found as burial offerings in the princely graves of the 2nd or 3rd/4th cents. AD. Frankish glass production goes back to the Roman glass tradition. By determining glass components with modern scientific methods of analysis, the attempt is being made – in larger series – to ascertain the procedures of production (colouring, etc.) and the centres of production.
→ Germanic archaeology; → Crafts, trades; → Celtic archaeology; → Jewellery

M. Feugère (ed.), Le verre préromain en Europe occidentale, 1989; Th.E. Haevernick, Beiträge zur Glasforschung, 1981; K. Kunter, Schichtaugenperlen: Glasperlen der vorröm. Eisenzeit IV, 1995; N. Venclová, Prehistoric Glass in Bohemia, 1990; M.A. Zepezauer, Mittelund spätlatènezeitliche Perlen: Glasperlen der vorröm. Eisenzeit III, 1993. V.P.

Glauberg The G. is an early Celtic (5th cent. BC) princely seat with a princely grave (→ Princes, tombs and residences of; s. also the map) that lies a good 30 km north of Frankfurt/Main on the eastern edge of Wetterau in Hesse. The G. rises as a high plateau *c.* 150 m over the plain; it comprises an area of *c.* 8 ha. Initial excavations took place already in the 1930s and were continued in the 1980s and 1990s, only then truly shedding light on the importance of the place. The G. was already settled in the Neolithic period (5th/4th millennia BC) and the late Bronze Age (10th–8th cents. BC). In the late → Hallstatt Culture and early → La Tène period (5th cent.), the G. was surrounded by fortification made of wood, stone and earth. A gigantic annex embankment (additional embankment) included a spring at the foot of the mountain. It played an important role as a fortress still in the late Celtic period (2nd/1st cents. BC → *oppidum*?), in the period of the → migrations of peoples (*Völkerwanderung*) and the Merovingian period, as well as in the High Middle Ages.

In the 1990s, the remains of a gigantic barrow were found at the southern foot of the G. with a circular ditch of almost 70 m. diameter in which two Celtic warriors from the 5th cent. were buried with rich furnishings – gold, bronze vessels, weapons, burial chamber structure etc. (one bodily and one cremated). Therefore they were regarded as 'princes'. Even before completion of the restoration, rich gold jewellery (neck, arm and finger rings), a bronze pot of Celtic production in each grave, splendid weapons (→ sword, → shield, lances), → belts, → fibulas etc. are discernible, among which many Mediterranean elements have been adopted, but up to now no actual imports have been documented.

Of outstanding exceptional quality on the G. are two → stelae of sandstone, one of which lay in the trench at the edge of the hill – an approximately life-size warrior figure (height *c.* 1.80 m) almost completely preserved. The powerfully modelled legs contrast with the simply formed upper body. The figure displays equipment commensurate with the two graves: shield, sword, as well as neck, arm and finger rings, and a suit of composite armour that up to now had been unknown in this context. It wears a crown of leaves on its head.

A 'procession road', *c.* 350 m long and lined by deep ditches, leads from the barrow to the south. It evidently leads out of a huge 'holy precinct' that stretches south of the G. and is bordered to the south by a 'façade' over 1 km long made of embankment and ditches. This complex – located at the very northern edge of the Celtic world (!) –, whose research is still in process, represents an isolated case up to now and opens up new categories of interpretation for Celtic ritual and burial complexes. → Fortifications; → Gold; → Funerary architecture; → Armour; → Jewellery

F.-R. Herrmann, O.-H. Frey, Die Keltenfürsten vom G.: Ein frühkelt. Fürstengrabhügel am Hang des G. bei Glauburg-G., Wetteraukreis, in: Arch. Denkmäler in Hessen 128/129, 1996; F.-R. Herrmann, Die Statue eines kelt. Fürsten vom G., in: Denkmalpflege in Hessen 1/2, 1996, 2–7; F.-R. Herrmann et al., Ein frühkelt. Fürstenhügel am G. im Wetteraukreis, Hessen: Ber. über die Forsch. 1994–1996, in: Germania 75, 1997, 459–550. V.P.

Glauce (Γλαύκη; *Glaúkē*).

[1] Nereid (Hom. Il. 18,39; Hes. Theog. 244; Hyg. Praef. 8), whose name describes the glossy blue as well as comparable colour shades of the sea (Hom. Il. 16,34; Hes. Theog. 440) and whose masculine counterpart is → Glaucus. G. is also represented as a nymph at various locations (Paus. 8,47,2f.; Tzetz. Theogony 100–102).

[2] Spring nymph in Corinth, equated by some authors with the daughter of the local king → Creon, who otherwise is called → Creusa. After she, as the bride of → Iason, had received poisoned gifts, causing firy torments, from his abandoned wife → Medea, she is said to have plunged into the spring (Paus. 2,3,6) and drowned (Diod. Sic. 4,54; Hyg. Fab. 25; Apollod. 1,145; Lucian 45,80; Ath. 13,560d).

[3] Amazon, who, abducted by → Theseus and made his wife, becomes the mother of → Hippolytus (Hyg. Fab. 163; Apollod. epit. 5,2).

Bibliography: C. Lochin, s.v. G. (1), LIMC 4.1, 270; G. Weicker, s.v. G. (1), (3)–(7), (9), RE 7, 1394–1396. fig.: A. Kauffmann-Samaras, s.v. Amazones no. 7, 16, LIMC 1.2, 441f.; C. Lochin, s.v. G. (1), LIMC 4.2, 159f. R.HA.

[4] **G. of Chios.** Cithara player of questionable reputation, at the time of → Ptolemaeus Philadelphus (she is supposed to have been his mistress), mentioned by Hedylus (in Ath. 4, 176d) and Theocritus (4,31). She was said to have an unnatural propensity for animals (Plut. Mor. 972f., Ael. VH 9,39; Plin. HN 10,51). A gravestone inscription (Anth. Pal. 7,262), wrongly ascribed to Theocritus, was most likely meant for her.

P. Maas, s.v. G. 13), RE 7, 1396. F.Z.

[5] Anchorage on the west coast of the peninsula Mycale (modern Samsun Dağı), where Samos is very close to the mainland (Steph. Byz. s.v. G.; Str. 14,1,12); a fleet of Athenians with 82 ships dropped anchor there in 411 BC (Thuc. 8,79,2). G. can be located in the area of the Dip Burnu. E.O.

Glaucia Roman *cognomen* (the identification with the Greek proper name Γλαυκίας (*Glaukías*) is disputed, [1]) in the family of the Servilii (known is the praetor in 100 BC C. → Servilius Glaucia).

1 Schulze 343. K.-L.E.

Glaucias (Γλαυκίας; *Glaukías*).

[1] Bronze sculptor from Aegina. According to Pausanias, he created statues of the boxers Glaucus, Philo and Theagenes in Olympia, whose victories or honours occurred in the 1st quarter of the 5th cent. BC. According to the description, they were depicted in motion, some of them at shadow-boxing; small bronze statues give at least an idea of this. He created a monument for Gelon of Syracuse after his chariot victory in 488 BC; parts of the base with inscriptions are preserved.

OVERBECK, no. 429–432 (sources); LOEWY, no. 28; P. ORLANDINI, s.v. G., EAA 3, 954; F. ECKSTEIN, Anathemata, 54–60; E. WALTER-KARYDI, Die äginetische Bildhauerschule, 1987, 35–39; J.J. POLLITT, The Art of Ancient Greece. Sources and Documents 2, 1990, 39–41. R.N.

[2] King of the → Taulantii, dates of birth and death are unknown. In 335 BC he supported → Cleitus against → Alexander [4] and granted him asylum after their joint defeat (Arr. Anab. 1,5f.). After the expulsion of → Aeacides [2], related to his wife, by the → Molossi, he protected → Pyrrhus, the son of the latter, against → Cassander in 317, who could neither buy nor force his being handed over; he adopted Pyrrhus and led him back to the Molossian throne in 306 (Diod. Sic. 19,67,5f.; 88f.; Plut. Pyrrhus 3,1–5; Iust. 17,3,16–21). In 313–312 he supported Epidamnos and → Apollonia [1] in a revolt against Cassander, he occupied both cities and held Apollonia against an attack by Cassander (Diod. Sic. 19,78,1; 89,1). E.B.

[3] **G. of Tarentum.** Active around 175 BC as a physician of the Empiricist school and successor of Serapion of Alexandria; author of an extensive work with the title Τρίπους (*Trípous*, 'tripod kettle') as well as of a commentary and glossary on Hippocrates. Galen and Oribasius record recommendations for bandaging by G., Pliny and Athenaeus record a few of his remedies [1]. G. is not to be confused with the physician G., whom Alexander had executed in 324 BC after the failed attempt at healing his friend Hephaestion (Arr. Anab. 7,14,4; Plut. Alexander 72).
→ Empiricists

1 DEICHGRÄBER, 168–170. V.N.

Glaucon (Γλαύκων; *Glaúkōn*).
[1] Son of Leagoras, Athenian → *stratēgós* at Samos in 441–440 BC (Androtion FGrH 324 F 38 with comm.); in 439–438 and 435–434 *stratēgós*, in 433–432 commander of the fleet sent to Corcyra (Thuc. 1,51; Syll.[3] 72). Often mentioned on Attic → *kalos*-inscriptions in 480–450 BC. TRAILL, PAA 277035.

[2] Son of → Critias, father of Charmides and of Plato's mother Perictione (Pl. Prt. 315a; Charm. 154ab; Symp. 222b; Thgn. 128d; Xen. Mem. 3,6,1; 7,1; Diog. Laert. 3,1). TRAILL, PAA 276785. M.MEI.

[3] Son of Ariston and of → Perictione, one of the two brothers of → Plato. Dialogue partner of Socrates in the main dialogue of Plato's *Politeia* and in Xenophon's *Memorabilia* (3,6). Diog. Laert. (2,124) lists the titles of nine dialogues that G. is supposed to have authored.

DAVIES 332–333. K.D.

[4] Athenian, agon competitor in 282–281 BC, Olympic victor in the four-horse chariot race (Paus. 6,16,9), → *próxenos* ('host?') of Delphi, Rhodes and Orchomenus in Arcadia, honoured in Plataeae by the assembled Hellenes, in Olympia by → Ptolemaeus III (1st Olympia in 296) and in Orchomenus (MORETTI 1,53). With his brother → Chremonides he was *pár(h)edros* (πάρεδρος) of Ptolemy II.
→ Chremonidean War

PA 3019; TRAILL, PAA 276950; R. ETIENNE, M. PIÉRART, Un décret du koinon des Héllènes, in: BCH 99, 1975, 51–75; HABICHT, 141, 149, 159. J.E.

[5] Son of Ptolemy (PP III 5238), Ἀλεξανδρεύς; *Alexandreús*, πρόξενος; *próxenos* of Delphi in 185 BC, where he functioned as the envoy of Ptolemy V.

E. OLSHAUSEN, Prosopographie der hell. Königsgesandten, 1, 1974, 53 no. 31. W.A.

[6] **from Ephesus.** Son of Glaucon. Tragedic poet. A victory at the Rhomaea in Magnesia at the Maeander in appr. 150 BC can be ascertained (DID A 13,2).

METTE, 47; TrGF 135. F.P.

[7] Physician, friend of Galen, active around AD 190. He convinced Galen to investigate a case of inflammation of the liver, which brought Galen great status (Gal. 8,364). G. received from Galen the shorter treatise *De methodo medendi* (Gal. 11,1) as a summary of what he had seen Galen perform in his practice. V.N.

Glauconome (Γλαυκονόμη; *Glaukonómē*). → Nereid at Hes. Theog. 256 and Apollod. 1,11. Her name means 'she who lives/rules in the glossy (γλαυκός; cf. → Glauce) sea' [1]. For the word formation, cf. the names Amphinome: 'she who rules widely' and Eurynome: 'she who rules for miles around' (Hom. Il. 18,44; 398f.).

1 G. HERZOG-HAUSER, s.v. Nereiden, RE 17, 15. A.A.

Glaucus (Γλαῦκος; *Glaûkos*). The name means 'glossy blue', also 'luminous' [1]; → Glauce: Hom. Il 16,34).
[1] A sea demon, into which a Boeotian fisherman from Anthedon was transformed after consuming a magical herb. The place of his jump into the sea after the transformation, Γλαύκου πήδημα (*Glaúkou pḗdēma*, 'Glaucus' jump'), was indicated (Paus. 9,22,6–7). Representations are known by Evanthes, Hedyle and Nicander (Ath. 7,295b–297c), by Callimachus (Suda s.v.), Q. Cornificius (Macrob. Sat. 6,5,13) and Cicero (Plut. Cic. 2,3,861); the description by Ovid (Ov. Met. 13,904–14,74) has survived. G. is part fish (Pl. Resp. 611d; Philostr. Imag. 2,15; Ov. Met. 13,915), has prophetic powers (Paus. 9,22,7), and is considered the least of the gods (Claud. Rapt. Pros. 3,12). G. accompanies Dionysus on the India expedition (Nonnus, Dion. 13,75; 42,478 and passim). He appears to the → Argonauts (Apoll. Rhod. 1,1310). G. is the father of the Sibyl Deiphobe (Verg. Aen. 6,36). He is loved by the Nereids → Nesaea and Cymothoe (Prop. 2,26,13–16), also by → Circe, whom he rejects due to his love for → Scylla (Ov. Met. 14,1–74). Nonetheless he is regarded as an old man of the sea (Verg. Aen. 5,823; schol. Apoll. Rhod. 2,767; → Halios geron). On Delos he has an oracle with the → Nereids

(Aristot. fr. 490 Rose). A Satyr play by Aeschylus, G. *Póntios* ('G. from the sea', fr. 25c–35 Radt) is documented, as well as several comedies (Anaxilas fr. 7 PCG II; Antiphanes fr. 76 PCG II; Eubulus fr. 18–19 PCG V) [2; 3. 1408–1412].

[2] G. of Potniae in Boeotia, king of Corinth, son of → Sisyphus and of Merope, husband of Eurynome or Eurymede, father of → Bellerophon, and therefore great-grandfather of G. [4] (Hom. Il. 6,154f.; Apollod. 1,85; 2,30 Wagner; Hyg. Fab. 157; 250; 273). His mares kept in Potniae grew wild, a punishment from Aphrodite because in order to increase their speed he kept them from mating with the stallions as she desired; G. lost control over the cart, fell and was torn to pieces (Verg. G. 3,267–268 with Serv. schol.; Ov. Ib. 553). The spring waters there are also given as a reason for the frenzy of the horses (Paus. 9,8,2). Aeschylus treats the material in *G. Potnieús* ('G. from Potniae'), the 3rd piece of the Persian trilogy (fr. 36–42a Radt) [3. 1412–1413].

[3] G. from Crete, son of → Minos and of → Pasiphae, falls into a jar of honey as a child and suffocates (Apollod. 3,17–20 Wagner; Hyg. Fab. 136; Schol. Lycoph. 811). His finding and revival is promised by Apollo (in Hyginus) or the Curetes (in Apollodorus) to him who finds a fitting comparison for a magical calf in Minos' herds that changes its colour three times daily (white, red, black). The prophet → Polyidus solves the riddle by citing the blackberry and finds the boy. Forced by Minos to also awaken G., he is locked in a tomb chamber with G. and can revive him by means of a magical herb whose effect is shown to him by a snake, whose companion he had struck dead (revived by Asclepius at Hyg. Fab. 49). Polyidus is then richly rewarded by Minos and released (Hyginus) or forced by Minos to teach G. his prophetic gift. He does this, but then upon taking leave from G. has him spit into his mouth and receives the gift back (Apollodorus) [4. 887; 5. 175 with n.]. The tale points out peculiarities of the Minoan culture such as embalming in honey and burial in *píthoi* [6. 9–22]. The material was treated by Aeschylus in the *Krẽssai* ('Cretans', fr. 116–120 Radt), by Sophocles in the *Mánteis* ('Prophet', fr. 389a–400 Radt) as well as in the *Polýidos* of Euripides (fr. 634–646 Nauck), which is criticized by the eponymous comedy by Aristophanes (fr. 468–476 PCG).

[4] G. of Lycia, son of Hippolochus, grandson of → Bellerophon, therefore great-grandson of G. [2] (Hom. Il. 6,119; 144; 12,309 and *passim*). Leader of the Lycians together with → Sarpedon (Hom. Il. 2,876). Due to long inherited guest-friendship, it does not come to a duel with Diomedes before Troy, but rather to an unequal exchange of arms (Hom. Il. 6,119–236; Apollod. epit. 4,2 Wagner; Hyg. Fab. 112). Wounded by Ajax (Hom. Il. 12,387–389), called to be the avenger by the dying Sarpedon (Hom. Il. 16,492–501), he is healed by → Apollo (Hom. Il. 16,508–526) and killed at the battle for the dead body of Achilles by Ajax (Apollod. epit. 5,4 Wagner; Quint. Smyrn. 3,277; at Hyg. Fab. 113 of Agamemnon). His body is saved by Apollo from the burning woodpile and carried by winds to Lycia (Quint. Smyrn. 4,4–6).

[5] Name of several other Trojans: a) Son of Antenor, saved by Odysseus and Menelaus at the destruction of Troy (Apollod. epit. 5,21 Wagner; represented on Polygnotus' *Ilioupersis* in the → *lesche* of the Cnidians in Delphi: Paus. 10,27,3). Perhaps also named by Homer (Hom. Il. 17,216; cf. also Verg. Aen. 6,483) [7. 326]. b) Son of → Priamus, killed by Diomedes (Apollod. 3,152 Wagner; Hyg. Fab. 112; Hyg. Fab. 90: conjecture from the Apollodorus passage, handed down is Hilagus). c) Son of the Lycian Imbrasus, companion of → Aeneas I, killed by → Turnus (Verg. Aen. 12,342–344).

1 Frisk s.v. 2 F. Bömer, P. Ovidius Naso, Metamorphosen, vols. 12–13, 1982, 453–454 3 G. Weicker, s.v. G. (9), RE 7, 1412–1413 4 O. Gruppe, Griechische Mythologie und Religionsgeschichte, HdbA 5,2, 1906 5 H.J. Rose, Griech. Myth. [A Handbook of Greek Mythology], [7]1988 6 A.W. Persson, The Rel. of Greece in Prehistoric Times, Sather Classical Lectures 17, 1942 7 W. Kullmann, Die Quellen der Ilias (Troischer Sagenkreis), Hermes ES 14, 1960. JO.S.

[6] Bronze sculptor from Argus, active in the middle of the 5th cent. BC. Of the two multi-figured consecrations of Micythus in Olympia, he created the one that according to the information from Pausanias was erected in the east hall of the temple to Zeus. According to Pausanias, it encompassed the larger-than-life-sized statues of Poseidon, Amphitrite and Hestia. The return of Micythus from Rhegium in 467 BC delivers the only clue for the creative period of G., since nothing of the group is preserved.

→ Dionysius [1]

Overbeck, no. 401 (sources); Loewy, no. 31; Lippold, 103; F. Eckstein, Anathemata, 1969, 33. R.N.

[7] **of Rhegium** or generally 'from Italy', 5th–4th cents. BC, contemporary of → Democritus (Diog. Laert. 9,38 = fr. 5 Lanata). Author of a treatise 'On the Ancient Poets and Musicians' (Περὶ τῶν ἀρχαίων ποιητῶν τε καὶ μουσικῶν; Ps.-Plut. De musica 4, 1132e = fr. 1 Lanata; ibid. 4 and 7, 1133f = fr. 1 and 2 Lanata). The work is also attributed to the sophist Antiphon [4] (Ps.-Plut. Vita decem oratorum 833d; cf. Diels/ Kranz II 337 and II 369, 26 n.). That is why it has been suspected that it was written in Attic dialect [11. 1419], but literary Ionian has also been considered [10. 54]. It is one of the first works on the history of lyric poetry and Greek music. It was expressly organized in an antiquarian and biographical fashion [14; 13. 31, 156]; G.'s role is perhaps overstated by Bergk (on G. as a key figure, see also [16. 228]). Even if the hypothesis by Müller that G. concerned himself above all with Italian or Sicilian personalities [cf. 9. 405] were not valid, his town of origin could substantiate a connection to the Homer biographer → Theagenes [cf. 7; 10. 52]. G.'s work is described

as a 'little book' (σύγγραμμα/*sýngramma*, ἀναγραφή/*anagraphḗ* and βιβλίον/*biblíon*): its scope, therefore, was rather modest, and it was more like a catalogue than a treatise, according to its contents analogous to the 'Catalogue of Musicians' (Συναγωγὴ τῶν ἐν μουσικῇ) by → Heraclides Ponticus. G. mainly defined the relative chronology among the poets and perhaps drew upon → Archilochus as a fixed point of comparison, whose dating is considered certain due to his contemporaneity with Gyges [13. 156]. G. also connected the 'imitation' of a poet by a successor with the chronological order [2. 273].

The fragments of the work, commented in detail by LANATA [2], have been handed down almost exclusively by the ps.-Plut. treatise *De musica*. The muddled handling by the editor of *De musica* of his sources makes any reconstruction of the content uncertain (it is also uncertain whether he knew G. directly or only through the mediation of → Heraclides Ponticus). What is certain, however, is that G. advocated the preference of playing the aulos over the lyre (cf. also [17]). Perhaps G. possessed musical experience himself [7; 18. XIII; 10. 1419], especially if he is to be equated with the Pythagorean G. of Rhegium, who according to Aristoxenus, fr. 90 WEHRLI (= schol. Pl. Phd. 108d = Hippasus, fr. 12 DK) carried out experiments with the percussion discs of Hippasus [20. 128, 234[38]; 4. 377[33]] and to whom the proverbial expression 'Glaucus-Art' (Γλαύκου τέχνη; *Glaúkou téchnē*) in the scholion refers; cf. [18. 77–78] and [10. 51].

G. also concerned himself with → Musaeus (Harpocr. s.v. Μουσαῖος = fr. 4 LANATA), → Empedocles (Diog. Laert. 8,52 = fr. 6 LANATA) and Democritus: according to the evidence of G., the latter was 'hearer' of a Pythagorean (Diog. Laert. 9,38 = fr. 5 LANATA, cf. [4. 215 and 292]). HILLER [9. 428] would like to allow these quotes to go back to other works. For chronological reasons as well [11. 1418], it is difficult to equate G. with the 'Homer critic' Glaucon mentioned by Pl. Ion 530d and Aristot. Poet. 25,1461b1 (= fr. 9 and 10 LANATA); in contrast, the G. mentioned in the scholion of Porphyrius (1,168,10) at Hom. Il. 11,636 (fr. 8 LANATA; cf. [5. 246 n.]) is likely to refer to G. of Rhegium. G. is probably also the author of the treatise 'On the Myths of Aeschylus' (Περὶ Αἰσχύλου μύθων), that is mentioned in the hypothesis to Aeschylus' 'Persians' (fr. 7 LANATA) [9. 428–429]. Equating G. with the G. of schol. Eur. Hec. 41 = Cypria fr. 34 PEG I (cf. also the scholion A on the same verse) is uncertain, see [11].

EDITIONS: 1 C. MÜLLER, FHG II, 23–24 2 G. LANATA, Poetica pre-platonica, 1963, 270–281.
BIBLIOGRAPHY: 3 TH. BERGK, Griech. Literaturgesch. I, 1872, 265 and 398 4 W. BURKERT, Lore and Science in Ancient Pythagoreanism, 1972 5 H. ERBSE, Scholia Graeca in Homeri Iliadem, vol. 3, 1974, 246 6 B. GENTILI, Poesia e pubblico nella Grecia antica, [3]1995, 238 7 M. GIGANTE, La civiltà letteraria nell' antica Calabria, in: S. SETTIS (ed.), Storia della Calabria antica, 1987, 542–543 8 A. GOSTOLI, Terpander, 1990 9 E. HILLER, Die Fragmente des G., in: RhM 41, 1886, 398–436 10 G. HUXLEY, G. of Rhegion, in: GRBS 9, 1968, 47–54 11 F. JACOBY, s.v. G. (36), RE 7, 1417–1420 12 F. JOUAN, Euripide et les légendes des Chants Cypriens, 1966, 368, n. 2 13 F. LASSERRE, Plutarque, De la musique, 1954 14 A. MOMIGLIANO, The Development of Greek Biography, 1971, 28 15 G.A. PRIVITERA, Il ditirambo come spettacolo musicale, in: B. GENTILI, R. PRETAGOSTINI (ed.), La musica in Grecia, 1988 16 L.E. ROSSI, in: Atti del XXII Convegno di studi sulla Magna Grecia e mondo miceneo 1983, 1985 17 SCHMID/STÄHLIN I, 330, 2 18 F. WEHRLI, Aristoxenos, 1975 19 H. WEIL, TH. REINACH, Plutarque, De la musique, 1900, XI–XIII 20 M.L. WEST, Ancient Greek Music, 1992. S.FO.

[8] **of Samos** Grammarian presumably from the pre-Alexandrian period (before Aristophanes of Byzantium: [9]; peripatetic from the beginning of the 3rd cent. BC: [3. 123]). He was one of Varro's sources for phonology and the theory of accentuation (*De prosodia*: cf. [10]), of which we learn more through the Donatus-commentary of so-called Sergius (GL IV 528,28–533,27; GRF 282). G. differentiated between six different types of accent; in addition to the grave (ἀνειμένη/*aneiménē*, Lat. *gravis*) and the acute (ἐπιτεταμένη/*epitetaménē*, Lat. *acutus*), he also recognized a middle tone (μέση/*mésē*, Lat. *media*) (cf. [2]), as well as presumably three sub-types of the circumflex (κεκλασμένη/*keklasménē*, ἀνακλωμένη/*anaklōménē*, ἀντανακλωμένη/*antanaklōménē*, according to SCHÖLL's constitution of the text: see Varro, Ling. 215 GÖTZ-SCHÖLL; different [3. 121–123]). A Τέχνη γραμμάτων (*Téchnē grammátōn*) was more than likely ascribed to the same G. according to schol. Pl. Phd. 108d; he is perhaps identical to the G. named in schol. Hom. Il. 16,414: cf. [4].

BIBLIOGRAPHY: 1 H. EHRLICH, Untersuchungen über die Natur der griech. Betonung, 1912, 253–254 2 W. HAAS, SGLG 3, 169–171 3 P. HANSCHKE, De accentuum Graecorum nominibus, 1914, 119–123 4 E. HILLER, Die Fragmente des G., in: RhM 41, 1886, 434–435 5 A.N. JANNARIS, An Historical Greek Grammar, 1897, 507–508, 537 6 B. LAUM, Das Alexandrinische Akzentuationssystem, 1928, 9 7 B.A. MÜLLER, s.v. G. (44), RE 7, 1421 8 E. PÖHLMANN, Der Peripatetiker Athenodor, in: WS 79, 1966, 206–207 9 SCHMID/STÄHLIN II, 262[8] 10 H. USENER, KS II, 281–282 11 J. VENDRYES, Traité d'accentuation Grecque, 1904, 51. S.FO.

[9] see → Cookery books

[10] **of Athens** Author of three ekphrastic epigrams, perhaps belonging to the 'Garland' of Philippus: Anth. Pal. 9,774 consists of a vivid description of a marble bacchante of → Scopas using rare new terms. Metric-lexical difficulties lead to the view that 9,775 (an imitation of this epigram that is scarcely successful) is not genuine. Without reference to its city of origin, 16,111 is finally a conventional description of an otherwise unknown painting by → Parrhasius.

GA II 1, 430f.; 2, 457f.; GA I 2,286. M.G.A.

[11] **of Nicopolis** Epigrammatist of the 'Garland' of Meleager, author of an epitaph (Anth. Pal. 7,285) per-

haps known to Propertius (Prop. 3,7,11). Despite the missing reference to his town of origin, two further poems are probably to be ascribed to this G.: a dialogue between Pan and nymphs, in which the former receives news of his beloved Daphnis (Anth. Pal. 9,341), and an amusing lament about the unruliness of the greedy boys of today (12,44).

GA I 1, 99f.; GA I 2, 286–288. M.G.A.

Glaukopis (γλαυκῶπις; *glaukôpis*). Epic epithet. In Homer used as a metrical substitute or complementary for the name Athene, above all in the connection γλαυκῶπις Ἀθήνη (*glaukôpis Athḗnē*). The noun μήνη (*mḗnē*, 'moon') is also documented several times as a reference word for *glaukopis* (first in Empedocles, 31 B 42 DIELS/KRANZ). The epithet can be interpreted in two ways: either as 'owl-eyed' (from γλαῦξ, *glaûx*, 'owl') or 'with a sparkling look' (from γλαυκός, *glaukós*, 'sparkling'). Both interpretations were already represented in antiquity. The suffix limb -ωπις (-ōpis) is formed with regard to ὄψ (*óps*) 'eye, look' (etc.). Comparable epithets are βοῶπις (*boôpis*, 'cow-eyed') and κυνῶπις (*kynôpis*, 'dog-eyed').

W. BECK, s.v. g., LFE. E.V.

Glaukytes see → Little-master cups

Glaze Modern technical term for a special surface treatment in the production of → pottery, that consists of a flux of lead and silicon-oxide. Glaze is found only in a few ancient ceramic forms; earliest examples occur in Mesopotamia of the 3rd millennium BC. Glaze is mostly used erroneously as a technical term for ancient surface treatments that are based on a strongly levigated shiny clay [1]; glaze is furthermore to be separated from vessels and objects of silicic ceramics made of quartz sand with a surface similar to glaze and containing copper (→ Faience).

Between 50 BC and AD 50 there is → relief ware from Asia Minor that is coated with a blue-green or yellow glaze. These ceramics were fired twice; the glaze was applied after the first firing. The green glaze was achieved by the addition of iron and copper oxide in a relation of 1:3, the yellow glaze by a higher iron oxide percentage. Production is attested for Tarsus and Smyrna. The glazed vessels (skyphoi, kantharoi, goblets and jugs) allude to simultaneous silver ware; later examples also exhibit connections to simultaneous ceramic forms. A third group of western Asia Minor workshops begins with simple vessel forms in the late 1st cent. BC. In the first half of the 1st cent. AD, production is also taken up in Northern Italy and Gallia. The distribution of the glazed ceramics from the workshops of Asia Minor encompasses the entire Mediterranean region and even regions north of the Alps; the Northern Italian workshops mainly supplied northern Alpine towns.

1 A. WINTER, Die antike Glanztonkeramik. Praktische Versuche, 1978.

A. HOCHULI-GYSEL, Kleinasiatische glasierte Reliefkeramik (50 v.Chr. bis 50 n.Chr.) und ihre oberitalischen Nachahmungen, 1977; O.S. REYE, Pottery Technology. Principles and Reconstruction, 1981, 40–56. R.D.

Glevum The region around Gloucester, located at the lowest lying crossing-point over the Severn, was first occupied by the Roman army in *c.* AD 50. A legion base was erected in Kingsholm, probably by the *legio XX Valeria Victrix* [1]; this was abandoned in *c.* AD 60 and replaced towards the end of the rulership of Nero by a fortress on the ground of modern Gloucester, which itself was abandoned in *c.* AD 74/5. On the grounds of the fortress, the *colonia Glevum* was founded using the fortress' building materials, apparently under Nerva. A *frumentarius* of the *legio VI* originated from G.: *origo ... Ner(viana) Glevi* (CIL VI 3346). Early development of the town proceeded slowly, probably due to the small number of veterans that had been settled here. Large structures were erected in the 2nd cent. when the *forum* was rebuilt. The city defence complex was reconstructed by using material from older buildings in the late 3rd and again in the 4th cent. [2]. Fallen into disrepair in the late 4th cent., G. was not completely abandoned. A Britannic community existed here until the Saxon conquest in AD 577.

1 H.R. HURST, Kingsholm, 1985 2 Id., Gloucester, 1988. M.TO.

Glicia Cognomen of M. → Claudius [I 29] Glicia.

Glinditiones One of the Illyrian tribes in the province Dalmatia, subjugated with the greatest difficulty in 35–33 BC together with the Docleatae, Carni, Interphrurini, Naresii and the Taurisci by the future Augustus and forced to pay overdue taxes (App. Ill. 47: Γλιντιδίωνες; *Glintidíōnes*); thus they had already been subjugated previously. According to Plin. HN 3,143, the G. belonged with 44 *decuriae* to the *conventus* of Narona. It is not known where they settled, not even whether they are in some way to be connected with the *Ditiones*. Different localizations in the valleys of the rivers Krka, Una and Unac continue to be discussed, for instance as neighbours of the *Ditiones* in Sandžak, more recently in Nevesinjsko polje.

I. BOJANOVSKI, Bosna i Hercegovina u antičko doba [Bosnia and Herzegovina in antiquity], Akademija nauka i umjetnosti Bosne i Hercegovine, Djela 66, Centar zu balkanološka ispitivanja 6 [Monographies, Académie des sciences et des arts de Bosnie-Herzegovine 66, Centre d'études balk. 6], 1988, 106–108. M.Š.K.

Glisas (Γλίσ[σ]ας/*Glís[s]as*, Γλισ[σ]άς/*Glis[s]ás*). Town already mentioned in the Homeric catalogue of ships (Il. 2,504), located on the southern slope of the Hypatus mountain range by modern Hypaton (formerly Sirtzi) *c.*

10 km northeast of Thebae, to which G. belonged (Hdt. 9,43,2; Str. 9,2,31; Paus. 9,19,2f.; Stat. Theb. 7,306; Steph. Byz. s.v. G.); settlement traces reach back into the Neolithic period; extant are graves from the Early Helladic, geometric and classical period; remains of polygonal fortress walls are to be found on the hill Tourleza north of the modern town. The Argive Epigoni defeated the Thebans at G. (schol. Pind. Pyth. 8,68; Paus. 1,44,4; 9,5,13; 8,6; 9,4; 19,2); Plut. Mor. 774e–775b tells of the heroon of a Phocus.

Fossey, 217–223; H. G. Lolling, Reisenotizen aus Griechenland (1876/7), 1989, 504f.; Müller, 493f.; Schachter, I, 124; II, 202; P. W. Wallace, Strabo's description of Boiotia, 1979, 127f. P.F.

Glitius

[1] Q.G. Atilius Agricola. An Atilius by birth, presumably adopted by a G., from Augusta Taurinorum, where he was honoured by various cities, also by means of *trapezophora.* Probably of senatorial origin; the fact that he became quaestor of Vespasianus indicates imperial patronage; under Domitianus he was *iuridicus* in Spain, *legatus legionis VI Ferratae* in Syria and praetorian governor of Belgica, also under Nerva, then *cos. suff.* in September/October AD 97, when Trajan was adopted. Consular governor of Pannonia in 101–2, participant in the Dacian War of Trajan; received → *dona militaria* for this. *Cos. suff. II* as successor of Trajan, probably on the 13th of January 103. Finally *praefectus urbi*; the timing is uncertain. Although coming from Transpadana, he does not appear in the correspondence of Pliny the Younger.

Syme, RP VII 629ff.; PIR² G 181.

[2] P.G. Gallus. Senator, first husband of Vistilia (Plin. HN 7,39); probably admitted to the patriciate under Claudius [1]; father of G. [3]. He could be identical to the senator whom Nero banned in AD 65. He went into exile with his wife Egnatia Maximilla on the island of Andros. He returned under Galba; restitution of his fortune under Otho. PIR² G 184.

1 Syme, RP IV 399.

[3] P.G. Gallus. Son of G. [2]; patrician. Probably *quaestor Titi Caesaris, praetor, flamen Augustalis* and *cos. suff.*, perhaps in AD 84. Syme, RP IV 399f.; PIR² G 185. W.E.

Globus see → Cartography

Gloriosus (and *gloriosissimus*). Unofficial epithet of the Roman emperor and of high officials in correspondence and in the *intitulatio* of laws, having the same meaning as the official *inclitus*, Greek *éndoxos* (ἔνδοξος), a result of translating the Greek word back into Latin.

G. Rösch, Ὄνομα βασιλείας, 1978. F.T.

Glos (Γλῶς/*Glôs*, Diod. Sic. 14,19,6; Γλοῦς/*Gloûs*, Xen. An. 2,1,3). Son of the 'Egyptian' Tamos of Memphis (probably the Carian Tamos, born in Memphis), marched with Cyrus the Younger against his brother Artaxerxes II in 401 BC and after Cyrus' death defected to the other side (Xen. An. 1,4,16; 1,5,7; 2,1,3; 2,4,24). As commander of the fleet and son-in-law of the satrap → Tiribazus, G. organized the grain transport from Cilicia in the war against Evagoras of Salamis and defeated him in 381 at Citium (Diod. Sic. 15,3,2ff.; 9,3; Polyaenus, Strat. 7,20; Aen. Tact. 31,35). To avoid being connected with the fall of Tiribazus, G. allied himself with Sparta and the Egyptian King Hacoris against the Great King, but was murdered in 380 (Diod. Sic. 15,9,3ff.; 18,1).

P. Briant, AchHist 3, 1988, 161; Briant, s.v. Glous. J.W.

Glossary, Glosses see → Glossography

Glossography

I. Greek II. Latin

I. Greek

A. The ancient concept of 'Glosses' B. Alexandrian Glossography C. Glossography and Exegesis

A. The ancient concept of 'Glosses'

Glosses (γλῶσσαι; *glôssai*) are words that are rare and difficult to explain. The Greeks' interest in such words dates back to the earliest periods: even in works of archaic and classical poets, glosses were accompanied by more common synonyms ('glossarial synonymity'); this kind of 'self-exegesis' is perhaps already evident in the first two verses of the *Odyssey* (Hom. Od. 1.1–2).

→ Antisthenes [1] and the Sophists saw the exact interpretation of words as the root of all teaching (παίδευσις, *paídeusis*). For that reason, glosses attracted special attention; → Prodicus in particular studied subtle differences in semantics and regionally variant expressions of the same meaning. Alongside Prodicus, Democritus' treatise on Περὶ Ὁμήρου ἢ ὀρθοεπείης καὶ γλωσσέων apparently constituted an investigation into Homer, distinguishing between 'terms used in the exact sense of their meaning' and 'glosses'. Such material was used in lessons, as shown by Aristophanes' fragment of 'The Banqueters' (Δαιταλῆς; *Daitalḗs*, fr. 233 PCG III 2). Echoes of the Sophist debate on the various expressions and terminology used in different parts of the Greek world are still evident in Plato's *Cratylus*.

The first precise – and subsequently greatly influential – definition of meaning was attempted by Aristotle (cf. Poet. 1457b4–7; 1459a 9–1460b 11; Rh. 3,1406a 7–b 12; Top. 140a 5): he defined a word as a gloss, if it was not clear in its meaning because of its remoteness either in time (archaic expressions which had fallen out of use) or in space (an expression commonly used by other peoples); furthermore, he saw the term 'gloss' as relative, because one person might perceive something as a gloss which to another was very familiar. For that reason, Aristotle sought to limit the use of glosses to the language of poetry (particularly in epics and tragedies) and to exclude philosophical-scientific usage.

B. Alexandrian Glossography

The Aristotelian concept formed the basis for the Alexandrian glossography. Its attention was always directed towards both aspects, i.e. the particular linguistic features of the poetic tradition as well as regional dialects; because poetry, not philosophy, was its main focus, the exclusion of the latter was of no consequence. These studies were reflected mainly in works such as → Philetas' Ἄτακτοι γλῶσσαι (*Átaktoi glōssai*), but also in numerous others such as → Simias of Rhodes' Γλῶσσαι; *Glōssai* (in three bks.), and those of → Zenodotus: whereas Philetas' main focus was undoubtedly on ethnographic glosses, it is likely that Zenodotus, alongside his editorial work, mainly produced annotations. (The Ἐθνικαὶ λέξεις (*Ethnikaí léxeis*), an anthology of dialectal glosses listed amongst Zenodotus' works, is not an independent work, but, as suggested by K. Nickau, a section from the *Glō̃ssai*). Other anthologies of glosses of certain dialectal regions are also known of. Thus → Neoptolemus compiled Phrygian glosses, and → Antigonus [7] of Carystus Aeolian ones. Furthermore, dialectal variations were also listed in the onomastic anthologies of λέξεις (*léxeis*), well-known to Alexandrian philologists. The lasting interest in literary glosses also resulted in glossarial anthologies for individual authors (e.g. Hippocrates). Some indications of the debates on the literary character and the exemplariness of some unusual terms are contained in the fragments of → Aristophanes [4] of Byzantium's tractate on Περὶ ὑποπτευομένων μὴ εἰρῆσθαι τοῖς παλαιοῖς.

C. Glossography and Exegesis

The close connection between the exegesis of Homer and the development of glossaries was born from the need to explain difficult words in Homer's works. For that reason, interpreters of Homer also include the glossographers (γλωσσογράφοι; *glōssográphoi*), i.e. various exegetes without affiliation to any particular homogenous school of thought, who used derivations from the immediate context or daring etymologies in their attempts to reach plausible explanations of difficult words. It is quite probable that over time these glosses with their added explanations were compiled as independent scholarly aids, i.e. 'glossaries', initially in the order of appearance of the words in the commentated text, but later also independent from it, possibly in alphabetical order. These glossaries are almost entirely lost. Following – in view of the papyrus finds – the definition by F. Montanari, the term 'glossary' should be limited to anthologies which adhere to the order of the text, so that they can be clearly distinguished from the early beginnings of true lexicography.

A similar arrangement, not yet completely independent from the original text, is found in a 'commentary' on Callimachus (POxy. 3328) and also in the Homer→ Scholia, preserved on papyrus, of which numerous examples from the 1st cent. AD onwards are extant. The glossographical element, understood as a translation of rare words into more common synonyms, began to dominate the history of exegesis, especially that of Homer: traces of it can also be found in important *hypomnḗmata* as e.g. POxy. 1086 and 1087. It would thus be wrong to say that glossography was no more than a 'school teaching aid'. From the Hellenistic period onwards, glossographical interpretations began to develop into different directions: alongside the actual glossographical tradition (represented for Homer by → Apollonius [12] Sophistes, the D-scholia, and the *Léxeis Homērikaí*), glossographical elements are therefore evident in all manifestations of the Byzantine exegetical tradition, particularly in the field of lexicography, i.e. glossography's direct heir. However, in lexicography, the subject matter was frequently presented prescriptively and its adaptation influenced by Atticist interests.

→ Lexicography; → Philology; → Scholia

Edition: A.R. Dyck, The Glossographoi, in: HSPh 91, 1987, 119–60.

Bibliography: K. Latte, Glossographika, in: Philologus 80, 1924, 136–175 = KS, 1968, 631–666; Pfeiffer, KP I; R. Tosi, La lessicografia e la paremiografia, in: Entretiens Hardt XL, 1993, 143–209; F. Montanari, Studi di filologia omerica antica, II, 1995; Id., L'erudizione, la filologia e la grammatica, in: G. Cambiano, Lo spazio letterario della Grecia antica, I 2, 1993, 235–281; E. Degani, La lessicografia, in: ibid. II, 1995, 505–527. R.T.

II. Latin

In the history of Latin language research and editions, glossography (as explanations of rare, mostly obsolete words) and lexicography (as the comprehensive study of the vocabulary) have generally been treated jointly. In both, diachrony (i.e. the increasing bilingualism, esp. in the Imperial period) as well as synchrony (i.e. the separate developments in late antiquity of spoken and cultured Latin) always have to be taken into consideration. – (1) The explanation of older, uncommon, and thus incomprehensible *glossae, glossemata* (Quint. 1,1,35; 1,8,15), particularly taken from the language of poetry (Diom. 1,426,25f.), but also of Greek words and rare flective forms, signified the first step in the reception of Hellenistic grammar in *c.*100 BC. Varro's references to *qui glossas scripserunt* (Ling. 7,10, cf. 34: *qui glossemata interpretati* or respectively *glossematorum scriptores* in Fest. 166,13f. L.) referred to such authors as Aelius Stilo, who 'glossed' archaic texts such as the → *Carmen Saliare* and the Twelve Tables, Aurelius Opillus (*Musae*), L. Ateius Praetextatus (*Pinaces*), or L. Cincius (*De verbis priscis*): sometimes under precious titles, they explained older language material, especially of earlier poets, as indicated in Varro, Ling.

7 –, thus turning erudition into education. – (2) Beginning with Verrius Flaccus, in a slight change of function, a second trend can be discerned, directed at orthography and orthoepy, i.e. the grammaticality in correct common usage and cultured written language; for the associated didactic practice, cf. Suet. Gram. 22. – (3) Transcending true glossography, Verrius Flaccus' *De verborum significatu*, developed from Varro's *Antiquitates*, was presented in alphabetical order, complimenting the topical order of the *Res memoria dignae* and in contrast with *De orthographia* (see 2 above). Its dictionarial or encyclopaedial character was further emphasized by Verrius' epitomist Festus (2nd cent.), who split it between the dictionary *De verborum significatione* and the (lost) *Priscorum verborum cum exemplis libri* (cf. 242,28ff. L.). Of greatest importance in this context, as also for (2), is the documentary evidence, generally acknowledged as a mine of information for fragment collections and the history of language. – (4) The trend outlined in (2) continued with Pliny's *Dubii sermonis libri* and subsequently in the Archaism of the 2nd cent., represented by Terentius Scaurus and Velius Longus (both *De orthographia*), Caesellius Vindex (Στρωματεῖς, *Strōmateís*) and particularly Flavius Caper (*De Latinitate*); they in turn built on the glossographers listed under (1) (cf. Charisius, Gramm. p. 297,24; 315,25ff. BARWICK), whose material surfaced again in the → Buntschriftstellerei (Gellius; Suetonius' *Pratum*) as well as the commentaries (Aemilius Asper, Donatus), and also in the systematically structured *artes*, e.g. by Charisius and later Nonius; the alphabetical order – e.g. the list of adverbs in Charisius, Gramm. p. 253ff. (according to Iulius Romanus) – is rather incidental. – (5) As a special subgroup, true language dictionaries developed in late antiquity in the form of *differentiae* as well as bilingual dictionaries such as the (topically ordered) Greek-Latin or respectively Latin-Greek bilingual glossaries (*hermeneumata*) and also the *idiomata*, which lead into syntax. – (6) The early medieval dictionaries, in rival editions by GOETZ and LINDSAY, served as (monolingual) dictionaries mainly to uphold a lexical norm; they mixed texts listed above under (2) (controversial the extent of Festus' influence) and (3); source references were generally omitted, as in the Carolingian epitome of Festus by Paulus Diaconus. In that period, the tradition continued with the *Liber Glossarum*, later Papias (11th cent.), Osbern of Gloucester, Uguccione da Pisa (12th cent.), and also the *Catholicon* of Johannes Balbus of Genoa.

→ Differentiarum scriptores; → Encyclopaedia; → Lexicography

FR.: GRF, 51ff., 111ff.

BILINGUAL TEXTS: J. KRAMER, Glossaria bilinguia, 1983.

EARLY MEDIEVAL GLOSSARIES: G. GOETZ et al., CGL 1–7, 1888–1923; W. M. LINDSAY et al., Glossaria Latina 1–5, 1926–1931.

RESEARCH REPORTS: G. GOETZ, P. WESSNER, F. LAMMERT, in: Bursian's Jahresbericht für die Altertumswiss. 68, 1891–252, 1936.

BIBLIOGRAPHY: ThlL 6, 2108f. s.v. glossa, glossema; G. GOETZ, s.v. G., RE 7,1, 1433–1466; F. STOK, Appendix Probi 4, 1997, 27ff.; A. C. DIONISOTTI, Greek Grammars and Dictionaries in Carolingian Europe, in: M. W. HERREN, The Sacred Nectar of the Greeks, 1988, 1–56; J. HAMESSE (ed.), Les Mss. des lexiques et glossaires de l'Antiquité Tardive à la fin du Moyen Age, 1996. P.L.S.

Glow-worm Thomas of Cantimpré 9,11 [1. 300] clearly described the glow-worm with the name *cicendula* (= firefly) as a beetle (*scarabeus*) the size of a small fly that occurs mainly in Italy and flies 15 days before and after the summer solstice. The glowing, which is only visible at night as sparks (*scintillarum modo*), is especially noticeable at the tail but not after the wings have been folded. He adopted the name and etymology (*cicindela ... quod volans vel gradiens lucet*) from Isid. Orig. 12,8,6, but the remainder of the context from Plin. HN 11,98 and 18,250. There, *cicindela* is equivalent to λαμπουρίς; *lampourís*, 'glowing'. This insect is otherwise only encountered in the Greek [2] and Latin *Koiranides* 3, elem. L (no. 2) [3. 161] in magical and medicinal use.

1 Thomas Cantimpratensis, Liber de natura rerum, ed. H. BOESE, 1973 2 Koiranides ed. F. DE MÉLY, M. CH and E. RUELLE, in: Les lapidaires grecs, 1898 3 L. DELATTE, Textes latins et vieux français relatifs aux Cyranides, 1942. C.HÜ.

Glycera (Γλυκέρα; *Glykéra*).

[1] Famous Athenian hetaera (→ Hetaerae) of the late 4th cent. BC. After the death of → Pythionike, she was summoned to Tarsus by → Harpalus, who awarded her royal honours. This was met with mockery and contempt by the Greeks. However, Harpalus supported Athens with grain because she acted as an intermediary, and he acquired the citizenship there. G. appears to have accompanied him on his flight and spent the remainder of her life in Athens, where she allegedly was, e.g., the lover of the poet → Menander (Ath. 13,584a; 586c-d; 594d; 595d–596a).

BERVE 2, no. 231. E.B.

[2] see → Pausias

Glycerius West Roman emperor from AD March 473 to June 474. In 472/3 he was *comes domesticorum* and was proclaimed Augustus in Ravenna at the behest of the supreme imperial general → Gundobad. He persuaded Ostrogoths who had invaded Italy to withdraw by giving them gifts. The East Roman emperor → Leo I did not recognize him and sent a fleet under → Iulius Nepos to whom G. submitted without battle. He became bishop of Salona and allegedly instigated the murder of Nepos in 480 (Iohannes Antiochenus Fr. 209,2 FHG IV 617f.; Iord. Get. 45,239; 241; 56,283f.; Anon. Valesianus 7,36).

PLRE 2, 514; A. DEMANDT, Die Spätantike, 1989, 175. K.P.J.

Glycon (Γλύκων; *Glýkōn*).
[1] Named by Heph. 10,2 CONSBRUCH as the inventor of Glyconic verse (→ Metre). His existence is disputed and the three verses ascribed to him (= 1029 PMG) are generally viewed as alexandrine in terms of metre: G. could hardly have lived before Sappho (late 7th cent. BC), who used this meter. Choeroboscus names G. (in his Comm. on St. In Heph. CONSBRUCH) as a comedic poet, but probably mistook him for Leucon (PCG V 612). Anth. Pal. 10,124, a two-liner on the futility of all things, is attributed to G., but its poet is probably even more recent than the author cited by Hephaestion (FGE 112). S.FO.
[2] Nicknamed *Spyridion* ('Little Basket'), Greek rhetor, early 1st cent. BC, perhaps from Pergamum. Seneca praised him (Controv. 1,7,18; Suas. 1,11 etc.), but also criticized his tastelessness (Controv. 10,5,27; Suas. 1,16). Quintilian (6,1,41) only notes an embarrassing situation. Anth. Pal. 11,399 is probably attacking a *grammatikós* of same name.

PIR G 188. E.BO.

[3] According to Lucian (Alexander 1,9f.) a serpent who took → Alexander [27] from Macedonia to → Abonuteichos about AD 160 and was worshipped there as an apparition of *Neos Asklepios*. The cult site flourished as an oracle and place of healing, especially during the campaigns of Marcus Aurelius and during the Antonine plague. On municipal coins G. is depicted as a serpent with a human head. Statues, dedications and coins with depictions dating from at least half a cent. later than Lucian's massive attack on the cult and its founder Alexander were found in the Danubian region, near the Black Sea and in Syria.
→ Healing deities; → Healing cults V.N.
[4] Sculptor from Athens. G. signed the so-called Hercules Farnese, a copy of a work by → Lysippus found in 1546 in the baths of Caracalla in Rome and now kept in Naples (NM). Created in the early 3rd cent. AD, this work was highly esteemed in the Baroque period because of its expressive representation of the musculature.

LOEWY, no. 345; S. FERRI, s.v. G., EAA 3, 1960, 965; D. KRULL, Der Herakles vom Typus Farnese. Kopienkritische Untersuchung einer Schöpfung des Lysipp, 1985. R.N.

Glykyrrhiza (γλυκύρριζα; *glykýrriza*, liquorice). This thirst-quenching asthma, throat and cold medication was produced from the rootstock of certain representatives of the 12-species liquorice genus (Leguminosae), especially G. glabra L. and echinata L. As Σκυθική (*Skythikḗ*) or γλυκεῖα (*glykeîa*) (sc. ῥίζα; *ríza*) it supposedly came from Scythia (Theophr. Hist. pl. 9,13,2). Dioscurides 3,5 p. 2,8–10 WELLMANN = p. 265 BERENDES also recommended it for chest and liver ailments. According to Plin. HN 22,24–26, who knew several prescriptions (cf. 25,82 *Scythice* = Theophr. ibid.), the best variety came from Cilicia, the second-best from the Black Sea. In the MA *liquiritia* or *liguricia* played an important role in pharmaceutics (e.g., in the pharmaceutical book *Circa instans* [1. 65; 2]). Today, liquorice is more a treat food.

1 H. WÖLFEL (ed.), Das Arzneidrogenbuch Circa instans, PhD thesis Berlin 1939 2 M. PUTSCHER, Das Süßholz und seine Gesch., PhD thesis Köln 1968. C.HÜ.

Glympeis (Γλυμπεῖς; *Glympeîs*; by Paus. 3,22,8 Γλυππία; *Glyppía*). Cynurian settlement on the boundary of the Argolis with Laconia (Pol. 5,20) in the Parnon mountains, the ruins of Palaeochora near modern Hagios Vasilios.

J. CHRISTIEN, De Sparte à la côte orientale du Péloponnèse, in: M. PIÉRART (ed.), Polydipsion Argos, 1992, 157–170. Y.L.

Gnaeus Glyptographer/gem engraver of the Roman republic, signatures on a sardonyx with the theft of the palladion (Diomedes at the altar, Collection of the Duke of Devonshire), amethyst with a portrait of the young M. Antonius (Ionides Collection) and a hyacinth with a copy of the Polycletic encaser (formerly the Marlborough Collection, lost). A characteristic of G. is the slanted positioning of attributes behind a bust, e.g., an aquamarine of Hercules with a club (*c.* 20 BC, London, BM) and a cornelian of a queen with a scepter (New York, MMA).
→ Gem cutting

M. L. VOLLENWEIDER, Die Steinschneidekunst und ihre Künstler in spätrepublikan. und augusteischer Zeit, 1966, 45[49], pl. 43,1–3; ZAZOFF, AG, 288f.[132ff.], pl. 81,7–82,3. S.MI.

Gnathia (also *Egnatia*, *Ignatia*). Peucetic port town in Apulia between Barium and Brundisium (Str. 6,3,7; Ptol. 3,1,15; *in Sallentino oppido G.*, Plin. HN 2,240) on the *via Minucia* (Tab. Peut. 6,5). Station on Horace's journey to Brundisium, who mocks alleged incense miracles in Sat. 1,5,97–100 (cf. Plin. loc. cit.). Ruins near modern Torre d'Egnazia (land wall, necropoleis, basilicas). Remains of Oriental cults (ILS 4178: *Sacerdos Matris Magnae et Suriae deae et sacrorum Isidis*).

NISSEN, 860. H.SO.

Gnathia ware Modern archaeological technical term, derived from the place name (ancient → Gnathia) in eastern Apulia, where the first vases of this type were found in the mid-19th cent. Unlike red-figured vases, in Gnathia ware (GN) the decoration was applied in various opaque colours on the fired vessel body. In addition, details on persons and objects depicted could be indicated or entirely represented by grooving. The production of GN began about 370/360 BC in Apulia, probably triggered by the onset of polychrome decoration on Apulian red-figured vases (→ Apulian vases). A comparison of vessels produced in the Gnathian and the red-figured technique reveals a close relationship between both types.

Popular themes of early GN are scenes of Eroses and women, theatre scenes and Dionysian motifs; major types are the bell krater, pelike, oinochoe and scyphus. Often figurative decoration is restricted to the upper vessel half or one side of the vase while the other only bears ornamentation. Outstanding artists are the Konnakis and the rose painters.

The original polychrome decoration (white, yellow, orange, red, brown, green etc.) winds down after 330 BC in an excessive use of white; the thematic range also narrows: wine, ivy and laurel vines, theatre masks, heads of men and women in vines, pigeons and swans became the dominant motifs. Another innovation is grooving of the lower vessel half. Preferred shapes and types of → pottery are the oinochoe, scyphus, pelike, cantharus, bowl, lekythos and flask. The important painters of this phase include the painter of the Louvre flask and the Dunedin painter. In the last production phase of GN, which lasts about 25 years, the return of figurated imagery is remarkable, with depictions of Eroses predominating. The preferred vessel type of painters was the cantharus, a bowl with painted-on handles; grooving of vessels and excessive use of white were retained though the addition of yellow attempted a shading effect.

In contrast to the red-figured vases of Lower Italy, GN was traded in the Mediterranean and Black Sea region, where it had considerable influence on native pottery production (e.g., → West slope pottery ?). In Italy, GN from Campania, Sicily and Paestum has been found. It was produced in the period from 330 to 300/280 BC. Imitations were only sporadically produced in Lucania. The Pocolum type, which was produced by an emigrant GN painter in Etruria, is significant.

J. R. Green, Ears of corn and other offerings, in: FS A.D. Trendall, 1979, 81–90; Id., Gnathia, in: M. E. Mayo, K. Hamma (ed.), The Art of South Italy. Vases from Magna Graecia, exhibition catalogue Richmond, 1982, 244–285 · I. McPhee, Stemless bell-kraters from ancient Corinth, in: Hesperia 66, 1997, 99–145. R.H.

Gnesippus (Γνήσιππος; *Gnḗsippos*). Perhaps identical with the tragedian → Nothippus (5th cent. BC; cf. TrGF 26; DID A3,14 and TrGF 8) [1. 481, 18ff.]; the name G. was possibly used jestingly for Nothippus [2. 399]. In Athenaeus (8,344c f. and 14,638d ff.) they are used for two different persons: in 14,638d ff., due to his new 'soft' style, G. is mocked on one hand as a 'paigniagraphos of the merry muse' by contemporary comedians (e.g., Cratinus), on the other hand – if the transition in 14,638e is to be understood in this meaning [1. 1480,35ff] – he is mocked for his lasciviousness as a tragedian, a competitor of → Sophocles and son of → Cleomachus.

1 P. Maas, s.v. G., RE 7, 1479–1481 2 U. v. Wilamowitz-Moellendorff, KS V.1. F.P.

Gnipho Roman cognomen (from Greek Γνίφων; *Gníphōn*, 'miser'), epithet of Mark Antony [I 12] G., the teacher of Caesar and Cicero. K.-L.E.

Gnome

[1] Literary history

I. Greek II. Roman Reception: Sententia III. Later history of reception

I. Greek

A. Meaning of the word B. Gnome as a literary phenomenon 1. Individual gnomai 2. Gnomics

A. Meaning of the word

As a nomen actionis the noun γνώμη (not found in Homer or Hesiod), with its originally extraordinary comprehensive range of meaning must be considered together with the verb γιγνώσκω (*gignṓskō*) [11; 37. 491; 27. 32 (also with regard to etymology)]. The verb with its meanings 'to recognize', 'to form an opinion', 'to decide' and 'to judge' falls between two poles: 'the ability to recognize a state of affairs' and 'the consequences of this recognition' [40. 20–39, esp. 32f.]. Therefore, its meaning includes orientation in the world and the resulting decision to act'. Consequently, the noun gnome has cognitive, deliberative and voluntary elements: 'recognition', 'insight', 'opinion', 'decision' (even 'will'), 'instruction', 'decisive judgment', 'petition', 'resolution' and 'judge's verdict'. An interplay of these heterogeneous elements of recognition – in general not on a theoretical and speculative level –, of forming an opinion and of resolving is characteristic of the original semantic field of the word gnome and later also of the literary form called gnome (though with restrictions). The meaning 'characteristic' (LSJ s.v. Γνώμη I on Thgn. 60: γνώμας εἰδότες [27. 36]) is modified to 'relevant judgment' ([20. 264, n. 1], cf. [40. 34, n. 4], similar 31. 77]), probably also in Heraclitus (22 B 78 DK = vol. 1, 168). Compared to gnome, the semantic field of the nomen actionis γνῶσις (→ *gnṓsis*), which is derived from the same root, is narrower, meaning 'recognition' and later 'knowledge'.

The meaning of gnome as the ability and act of recognizing, forming an opinion and deciding of individual persons or groups of persons confronted with very different real situations (similar [27. 32–33]) is attested from the earliest references to gnome in developed archaic literature (6th cent. to mid–5th cent. BC) with author-specific nuances in meaning [23] to the literature of the imperial period [24. s.v.]. For example, the Syrian Tatian (Ad Graecos 7,3 Marcovich) speaks of αὐτεξούσιος γνώμη, the 'free decision' of humans. Regarding the meaning of gnome in the political, public and legal areas, see → Gnome [2].

B. Gnome as a literary phenomenon

1. Individual gnomai

In Sophocles (Aj. 1091), Euripides (Fr. 362,3 Nauck/Snell) and Aristophanes (Nub. 889–1114, esp. 923/4) gnome is used for the first time in the sense of 'maxim' [3. 54–56; 19. 112–114]. The sayings known as Δημοκράτους γνῶμαι ('The Maxims of Democrates'), which also use gnome in this sense (68 B 35 DK = vol. 2, 153; different: [3. 53]), are probably mostly by Democritus. This literary and rhetorical gnome (in English best translated as 'aphorism', 'maxim', 'wise saying', 'epigram') represents one meaning of gnome although the Greeks could already find the literary phenomenon in Homer. In the personal and the political-social areas it offered guidance with respect to the meaning and conduct of life by establishing a factual state and prescribing contingent duties [25. 431–434 (§§872–879)]. Therefore, the association of cognition and the resulting direction of action characteristic of the original meaning of gnome is not necessarily found in the exact wording of the gnome but in the functional context of the text. The didactic element was clearly evident because 'the *gnṓmai* of wise men makes those who acquire it rich in ἀρετή/*aretḗ*' (Xen. Mem. 4,2,9).

This literary gnome, however, is already determined before the specific situation to which it is applied; this is a new aspect compared to the original meaning of the word in which a specific situation called for a gnome. The content of literary gnomai may be determined by certain political and social groups (e.g. the gnomai in Theognis), but it calls for the approval of all and general validity beyond the circle of persons addressed. Formally, the literary and rhetorical gnome in its simple form consists only of one sentence: a statement or, less often, a request or a rhetorical question. An explanation may also be added (this is why Aristotle treated it as an enthymem). This gnome is related to other literary forms: in Greek and especially in modern literature ([41] with citation of texts more commonly considered to be gnomai) they are occasionally considered gnomai (in a wider sense) although, to be precise, they are classified differently or more precisely in terms of form and content than the literary gnomai found in Greek literature [18. 75–76; 14]: the → a*enus* [2] directly affects the person addressed; the → a*phorismos* is originally a brief description of an illness or a prognosis; the → apophthegma designates an often humorous but apt saying with claiming the speaker's authenticity; the → chreia is more varied than the gnome and relates to the sayings or actions of a particular person [12. 88/9; 42. 53/4]; the *hypothḗkai* (ὑποθῆκαι) are clearly advice and instructions by a person in authority [3. 5]; closely related to them but more general are the παραγγέλματα (*parangélmata*), Latin *praecepta*, which include moral teachings that could be read at the sanctuary in Delphi or in the gymnasia and which resembled the sayings of the → Seven Wise Men (Diels in Syll³ 1268; [36. 3–5]; in a figurative sense gnomon (γνώμων) can mean, similar to the gnome, a 'rule of life' (Thgn. 543; Lucian Hermotimus 76); the → priamel with its enhancing series of statements on facts is rather a special case of the proverb than the gnome; due to its anonymous origin, the proverb (παροιμία/→ *paroimía*, Latin *adagium*, *proverbium*), with its claim to convey a general human experience, which has a wider sense than the gnome may often be attributed to a specific author and may address a specific person or group; also, the instruction for action that is typical of the gnome becomes secondary in the gnome. However, the fluent difference between the proverb and the gnome increasingly disappeared in Hellenism (Aristot. Rh. 2,21,1395a 19) [18. 76–77; 13; 15].

The literary element called gnome ('aphorism' or 'maxim') since the 5th cent. appeared already in the speeches of the Homeric epics (e.g., 'No good thing is a multitude of lords; let there be one lord!' Hom. Il. 2,204; cf. Aristot. Pol. 1292a 13; Aristid. 31,7; Suet. Calig. 22,1; also Hom. Il. 12,243 and 18,309; Aristot. Rh. 2,21,1395a 14 and 16). Generally formulated statements, especially when they were introduced with τοι, ἀτάρ or τε (e.g., Hom. Il. 11,779 and Od. 9,268 [6. 239–240]) called for a generalizing use in a quotation [43. 85–96]. When used as gnomai, the quoted words were later separated from their respective functional context, where they structured the speech in epic poetry and were especially used at the beginning or the end. On the other hand, these gnomai retained their affinity to rhetorical application. Literary gnomai must be differentiated into general statements that were originally incorporated in speeches taken from Homer and others, and gnomai whose form and content became increasingly independent, especially in Hesiod, and then also in Pindar [4], in Euripides, the stage philosopher, and in the comedian Epicharmus. At the end of this development the deliberately created individual monostichic gnome appears as an independent literary form, e.g. in a collection of 'gnomai of Menander' [9. 900–903], which was begun in the 2nd cent. BC and extended until the Byzantine era. Even originally non-gnomic or only loosely formulated γνωμολογίαι (*gnōmologíai*; regarding the meaning [18. 75]) were reformulated as monostichic gnomai [16. 143–149]. The collection of → Stobaeus contains ἐκλογαί (*eklogaí*; prose excerpts), ἀποφθέγματα (*apophthégmata*) and ὑποθῆκαι (*hypothêkai*). The so-called Gnomologium Vaticanum is actually a collection of apophthegmata [28. IX].

The extension of the semantic field of gnome to include the meaning 'epigram' (see above), which is associated with this literary process and observable since the 5th cent. BC, had also far-reaching consequences for the theory. Henceforth, gnome had a general meaning and was not related to a specific situation. A definition on a general level is found in Aristotle; he discusses this rhetorical gnome (Rh. 2,21,1394a 19 – 1395b 20) as part of the enthymeme [3. 59–73; 29. 122–124] and classifies it as a general statement (1394a 21–25), though not with regard to all facts, e.g. straight being the opposite of curved, but which refers to what is chosen and what is avoidable in human behaviour. In spite of the emphasis on action, it nevertheless originated – according to the sense of the word gnome – from an insight, because apart from the gnome that is generally recognized and immediately understandable, Aristotle knows those gnomai that require an explanatory addition (1394b 7–26). Therefore, he classified gnomai as enthymemes [21. 99]. An orator would be particularly successful using gnomai because of the intellectual inflexibility of the audience (1395b 1–3): they would be delighted to hear their preconceived opinion in a particular case as a universal statement. These rhetorical gnomai – a variant of the literary gnomai – were rarely used by the rhetoricians of the classical period [44. 453] and served, as described by Aristotle, to express an ethical way of thinking. However, a change occurred in the rhetorical gnome that paralleled the development in the literary gnomai. In archaic and especially classical poetry (Euripides) the independent use of the gnome as a literary form to be reformulated anew increased. Therefore, it is not surprising that,in addition to the generally recognized gnomai, which he cites as examples, Aristotle knows others that were formulated by the orator himself (Rh. 2,21,1395a 2–11 and 1395b 5–9). In the *Ars rhetorica* of Anaximenes (11,1 FUHRMANN) the gnome is even defined as revealing one's own opinion.

Since Theophrastus the gnomai as a witty formulation were used as an ornament of speech. Thus, in his definition of the gnome (WALZ 7,2. 1154,23), he omits Aristotle's link to the enthymem (see above) [34; 7. 100–102]. The gnomai were used on a larger scale only in the Asianic rhetoric (Cic. Brut. 95,325; [44. 454]). The rhetorical gnome had lost its restriction to ethics and became a standard feature of textbooks of rhetorics (in the sense of a general saying). For example, Hermogenes (Progymnasmata 4,24–27 RABE) defined gnomai not just as means of ethical warning and encouragement but also explanation of the quality of a factual state (ὁποῖον, 4,24). Sopater (Progymnasmatum fragmenta ed. RABE p. 60–61; Ad Aphthonium 7,2) even defined the gnome as merely a ἀπόφανσις καθολικὴ περὶ ποιότητος. Thus, the gnome only refers to a factual state and is no longer distinguishable from the proverb (*paroimía*). (Regarding other rhetorical definitions of the gnome [10; 29. 122–124, 257f.])

2. GNOMICS

Gnomics is the deliberate use of gnomai as elements of a literary work. The Greek adjective underlying this word and attested since Hellenism, γνωμικός (*gnōmikós*, 'leading to insight' [27. 35]) belongs to the literary gnome (as defined above; Philod. Hom. p. 15 OLIVIERI; Hermog. De inventione 4,3, p. 177,3 RABE, et al.). Based on this ancient view, gnomics is understood as the use of gnomai and of series of gnomai when they are characteristic of the narrative context of a literary text, e.g., Hesiod, Theognis [3. 21–51], Phocylides (quoted by Isoc. Or. 2,43/44), Aeschylus, Pindar [4], Euripides (in Raisonnements, e.g., Eur. Hipp. 380–387), Thucydides [30] and Menander [16. 5–101]. This results in special formal and argumentative structures, especially since these gnomai can also serve as markers for listeners in texts defined by an elaborate orality. Gnomai are used in the following functions: as starting points of a line of thought, as highlights of an argument, as transitions between groups of thought, and as the conclusion of a line of thought. The author presents the ethical background of his statements by using gnomics.

II. ROMAN RECEPTION: SENTENTIA

A. MEANING OF THE WORD B. SENTENTIA AS A RHETORICAL-LITERARY PHENOMENON

A. MEANING OF THE WORD

Compared with the associated verb *sentire* ('to perceive', 'judge', 'think', 'vote for something'), the element of perception is missing in the semantic field of the noun *sententia* ('opinion, view, judgment, petition, meaning, thought'), which has been attested since Cicero. This meaning is represented by Latin *sensus* and is thus an equivalent element to 'recognition' (cf. Quint. Inst. 8,5,1 and 2), which is the first link in the chain of meaning associated with the late archaic and classical Greek word gnome (see above I.A.). Thus, *sententia* corresponds more to the Hellenistic meaning of gnome as 'saying', 'maxim', and, therefore, is suitable to denote in Latin the literary feature that is equivalent to the literary and rhetorical gnome in Greek (see above I.B.1.). The *sententia* differs from the *proverbium* and *adagium* (*paroimía*) with their strict anonymity insofar as it also makes a statement on a general fact but can still be attributed to an author (regarding a similar situation with gnomai, see above). The forensic meanings of *sententia* ('opinion', 'vote' and 'judgement') are also attested in the semantic field of gnome in the Hellenistic period. The literary gnomai with increasingly deliberately created forms and their claim to universality, and gnomics consisting of series of gnomai together with closely related forms of wise sayings as mentioned above, merge in Latin into a broader term of *sententia* and, thus loose their distinctive characteristic as attested in Greek literature.

B. SENTENTIA AS A RHETORICAL-LITERARY PHENOMENON

The elder Cato (Plut. Cato maior 2,6) incorporated Greek gnomai in his sentences rich in *sententiae*. In Roman rhetorical teaching *sententia* has a meaning and function very similar to that of the Hellenistic gnomai but, in typical Roman fashion, is especially realistic. In the *Rhetorica ad Herennium* (4,24/5) in the Hellenistic tradition the *sententiae* are defined as a significant ornament of speech but on the other hand they also have a content taken from life and morality that does not require explanation [7. 102]. Cicero (Orat. 79), and Theophrastes classified the *sententiae* among the ornaments of speech (*ornatus*); they should be used often and aptly formulated (*acutae;* De or. 2,34). Subsequently, Roman orators had a big reservoir of *sententiae translaticiae*, i.e., commonplaces, whose application was part of their training (Sen. Controv. 1, pr. 23) [8. 103f.]. Quintilian (Inst. 8,5, esp. 2 and 34) [26. 1, 301f.; 7. 104–124] stated that at his time *sententiae* were considered rhetorical highlights that had their place especially in the *clausulae* and contrasts them (8,5,3) somehow with the 'earliest' form of the *sententiae*, 'a general statement that can find approval independent of the context' and was called gnome by the Greek. He called, among other things, (Inst. 8,5,6), and in contrast to Aristotle, those *sententiae* more powerful that were not formulated in general terms but reflected individual situations. In pursuing this argument further (8,5,9–14), Quintilian considered the enthymem as much an ornament of speech as the epiphonem, an exclamation as a climax at the end of the explication, and the *nóēma*, in which what has not been mentioned must also be included. That a *sententia* occasionally appears also as *clausula* is welcomed by Quintilian, but he distances himself from striving for applause for a humorous comment before every breathing pause, which was quite common then. These newer *sententiae* were not so much characterized by their ethical content as by the form of their statement (Inst. 8,5,15–19). Quintilian recommends a moderate use if one wishes to be better than the ancients (Inst. 8,5,34). However, he is not thinking (Inst. 12,10,48) of their points but of those found in Cicero and praises them as follows: 'They affect the listener, often give a sudden impetus, stick (in one's mind) because of their brevity and persuade because of the delight.'

With the older gnome and *sententia*, as described by Aristotle (see above I.B.1.), the mentally rigid audience was delighted to find its own judgement in a general gnome presented by the orator. At the latest with the beginning of the imperial period, the delight in a witty form became a serious rival. Besides the ethical orientation, there was the intellectual play in front of a rhetorically well versed audience. Seneca the Younger already attempted refined epigrammatic *sententiae* [26. 1, 266, 272]. In the second speech of Aper in the *Dialogus* of Tacitus (esp. 20,4), brevity is emphasized as a requirement of modern rhetoric; the receptive audience welcomes it when a thought lights up in a shrewd and brief *sententia,* which it then reports on in the affiliated cities and provinces. Speeches should contain excerptable *sententiae* (ibid. 22,3). The *sententiae* found their place proper in Roman literature because of the role that rhetorics played in education and society. Thus, the *sententiae* in other prose literature and in poetry are influenced by rhetorics but their characteristic is not only due to the personalities of the authors but also to Greek models, which in part (from Homer to the classical poets) were older than the rhetorical gnomai, which were deliberately used only at the beginning of the Hellenistic period (see above I.B.1.). For example, Horace used *sententiae* equivalent to the type of gnome found in early Greek lyrics for division and transition between thought groups (Hor. Carm. 3,1,14–16; 25; 37–40; 3,2,13f; 25; 3,5,29f.). In contrast, Lucan structured the speeches in his epic by using *sententiae* of the kind that Quintilian called modern (and therefore praises him [Inst. 10,1,90] as *sententiis clarissimus* [5. 260, 269]). The influence of modern rhetorical training was already obvious in the numerous *sententiae* that Ovid adopted from his teacher Latro [22. 405–419, esp. 406]. In prose too, even in the deliberately simple prose of Caesar, *sententiae* [33] are found, and in Tacitus *sententiae* that are rich in points particularly occur in the *Agricola* as markers of division at the end of a context (Quintilian's *clausulae*).

The didactic element, which is associated with literary gnomai/*sententiae* from the very beginning is already evident in the *sententia*-like verses in the satires of Lucilius (e.g., 1326ff. MARX: *virtus, Albine, est ...*). The *sententiae* of the mime poet Publilius Syrus (a contemporary of Caesar) are simple and didactic iambic senaries and trochaic septenaries [38. 1926f.]. The → *Dicta (Disticha) Catonis*, a collection composed in hexameters in the 3rd cent. AD, also belongs in this context [35].

III. LATER HISTORY OF RECEPTION

Around AD 500, Priscianus (Praeexercitamina 3,11 HALM) defines the *sententiae,* like Hermogenes in the 2nd cent. AD the *gnomai* (see above I.B.1), as 'statements whose contents is a general message that admonishes with regard to a certain issue, or warns of it, or shows its nature'. The *Liber sententiarum* (mainly from the works of Augustine) of Prosper of Aquitaine and the *Sententiarum libri tres* of Isidore of Seville (*c.* 600), who incorporated the *sententiae* of other Church Fathers, conform to this definition. He provided the model for collections in which excerpts (= *sententiae*) from the work of the Church Father or short medieval comments were systematically compiled from the 12th cent. onwards. These literary *sententiae* are later represented in particular by Peter Lombard's *Libri IV sententiarum* [17] with the 'aphoristic commentaries' of later centuries.

Outside theological literature, the *Dicta (Disticha) Catonis* had a particularly strong influence in the Middle Ages [39; 23]. They were first received by Alcuin in his *Praecepta vivendi*, then, among others, by 'Freidank' [32]. In the Humanistic period, Erasmus' *Adagia* (proverbs, see above I.B.1.), which include many *sententiae,* can be mentioned. In modern language, *sententia* can largely be used to denote a → proverb and, therefore, it is part of the proverb's history of reception. However, the characteristic of the gnomai/*sententiae*, a general liability with instructions for conduct based on knowledge, continued into the MA and the modern period in collections of sayings [2] and in other literary forms such as didactic poetry [1. 54–74]. In his 'Lecture on Aesthetics' (vol. 3, part 2) G.W.F. Hegel considered these gnomai as a characteristic of the epic. Modern scholarship finds the ancient Greek gnomai e.g., in Shakespeare's dramas [8. esp. 1–21] and in the 'gnomic' type of the German epigram in the 17th cent. [45. 80–98].

→ GNOME

1 L.L. ALBERTSEN, Das Lehrgedicht, 1967 2 B. BAUER, Sprüche in Prognostiken des 16. Jh., in: W. HAUG, B. WACHINGER (ed.), Kleinstformen der Lit., 1994, 165–204 3 K. BIELOHLAWEK, Hypotheke und Gnome (Philologus, Suppl. 32, 3), 1940 4 H. BISCHOFF, Gnomen Pindars, 1938 5 S.F. BONNER, Lucan and the Declamation Schools, in: AJPh 87, 1966, 257–289 6 P. CHANTRAINE, Grammaire homerique, 2, [2]1963 7 F. DELARUE, La sententia chez Quintilien, in: La Licorne 3, 1979, 97–124 8 M. DONKER, Shakespeare's Proverbial Themes, 1992 9 J.M. EDMONDS (ed.), The Fragments of Attic Comedy, III B: Menander, 1961 10 H. FRAMM, Quomodo oratores Attici sententiis usi sint, 1909 11 FRISK 12 K.v. FRITZ, s.v. G., Gnomendichtung, Gnomologien. Zusatz 1, RE Suppl. 6, 87–89 13 H. GÄRTNER, s.v. Paroimia, in KlP 4, 523–524 14 O. GIGON, K. RUPPRECHT, s.v. G., LAW 1099–1100 15 Id., s.v. Sprichwort, LAW 2873–2874 16 W. GÖRLER, Μενάνδρου γνῶμαι, 1963 17 L. HÖDL, s.v. Petrus Lombardus, TRE 26, 296–303 18 K. HORNA, s.v. G., Gnomendichtung, Gnomologien, RE Suppl. 6, 74–87 19 P. HUART, Γνώμη chez Thucydide et ses contemporains, 1973 20 W. JAEGER, Paideia 1, [2]1936, repr. 1973 21 G. KENNEDY, The Art of Persuasion in Greece, 1963 22 Id., The Art of Rhetoric in the Roman World, 1972 23 P. KESTING, s.v. Cato, Die dt. Lit. des MA. Verfasserlex. 1, 1192–1196 24 G.W.H. LAMPE, A Patristic Greek Lexicon, [12]1995 25 LAUSBERG 26 A.D. LEEMAN, Orationis ratio, 1963 27 J.P. LEVET, Ῥήτωρ et γνώμη. Présentation sémantique et recherches isocratiques, in: La Licorne 3, 1979, 9–40 28 O. LUSCHNAT, Vorwort zum Neudruck, in: Gnomologium Vaticanum, ed. L. STERNBACH, 1963 29 J. MARTIN, Ant. Rhet., 1974 30 C. MEISTER, Die Gnomik im Geschichtswerk des Thukydides, 1955 31 S.N. MOURAVIEV, Gnōmē, in: Glotta 51, 1973, 69–78 32 F. NEUMANN, s.v. Freidank, Die dt. Lit. des MA. Verfasserlex. 2, 897–903 33 R. PREISWERK, "Sententiae" in Cäsars Commentarien, in: MH 2, 1945, 213–226 34 G. ROSENTHAL, Ein vergessenes Theophrastfragment, in: Hermes 32, 1897, 317–320 35 P.L. SCHMIDT, s.v. Dicta Catonis, KlP 2, 1–2 36 E. SCHWERTHEIM, Die Inschr. von Kyzikos und Umgebung, 2, 1983 37 E. SCHWYZER, Griech. Gramm., 1, [3]1959 38 O. SKUTSCH, s.v. Publilius Syrus, RE 23, 1920–1928 39 Id., s.v. Dicta Catonis, RE 5, 358–370 40 B. SNELL, Die Ausdrücke für den Begriff des Wissens in der vorplatonischen Philos., in: PhU 29, 1924 41 W. SPOERRI, s.v. Gnome 2, in: KlP 2, 823–829 42 F. TROUILLET, Le sens du mot χρεία des origines à son emploi rhétorique, in: La Licorne 3, 1979, 41–64 43 J. VILLEMONTEIX, Remarques sur les sentences homériques, in: La Licorne 3, 1979, 85–96 44 R. VOLKMANN, Die Rhet. der Griechen und Römer, 1885 45 J. WEISZ, Das dt. Epigramm des 17. Jh., 1979. H.A.G.

[2] Legal. The noun *gnṓmē* has a number of particular meanings in Greek law. (1) The 'insights' of a collegial body gained by voting by the council (→ *boulḗ*), the public assembly (→ *ekklēsía*) or a jury court (→ *dikastḗrion*). Depending on the content, the *gnome* may be called an 'experts' opinion', a 'resolution' or a 'judgement'. For Athens it must be kept in mind that the Council of the Five Hundred (such as the one on the → Areopagus) as well as the public assembly had also judicial functions and passed 'verdicts'. (2) Several formularies of judges' oaths are preserved from Greek poleis in which the → *dikastḗs* commits himself to judging according to the laws (→ *dikázein*) and, when no such laws exist (sometimes also when there are no witnesses), 'to act upon the most just conviction' (γνώμη δικαιοτάτῃ, *gnṓmē dikaiotátē*). The juror's own *gnome* is regarded as a correction to strict judicial positivism as it is known from Athens. (3) The latter principle continued to be effective under very different conditions in the Ptolemaean empire (P. Gūrob 2 [1]).

1 J.G. SUYLY (ed.), Greek Papyri from Gūrob, Royal Irish Academy, Cunningham Memoirs 12, 1921.

H.J. WOLFF, Gewohnheitsrecht und Gesetzesrecht in der griech. Rechtsauffassung, in: Dt. Landesreferate zum VI. Intern. Kongreß für Rechtsvergleichung in Hamburg, 1965, 3ff.; J. TRIANTAPHYLLOPOULOS, Das Rechtsdenken der Griechen, 1985, 174ff. 220ff. G.T.

Gnomon

[1] see → Groma (surveying)

[2] see → Clocks (time measurement)

[3] Arithmetic technical term from Greek numerical theory. The term was adopted from geometry, where the *gnomon* describes the shape of an angle bar that remains when a smaller square is removed from a larger square. The Pythagoreans represented arithmetic series with geometrically arranged dots (pebbles) in the form of figures, so that the sum of the elements beginning with one forms a regular n-angular shape (figurate numbers). Series with the difference of 1 produce triangles (triangular numbers), with the difference of 2 squares (square numbers), with the difference of 3 pentagons (pentangular numbers), etc. The *gnomon* is the piece to be added to a shape representing an n-angular number to produce the next biggest number. For example, the square number $3^2 = 9$ produces the square number $4^2 = 16$ by adding the gnomon $3+1+3 = 7$. By transferring this concept to bodies, three-dimensional gnomons are derived. According to Pseudo-Iamblichus (Theologoumena arithmeticae p. 61 AST = p. 82 DE FALCO), Speusippus laid out the theory in general, including for irregular n-angular shapes and bodies. The arithmetic gnomon is mentioned in Aristotle (Phys. 3,4,203a 14; Metaph. N 5,1092b 11). The theory of figurate numbers was stated by Nicomachus of Gerasa (Arithmetica introductio 2, chs. 7–29), whose work made it widely known in the MA.

O. BECKER, Das mathematische Denken in der Ant., 1957, 40–44 T.L. HEATH, History of Greek Mathematics, vol. 1, 78–82 B.L. VAN DER WAERDEN, Erwachende Wissenschaft, 1956, 162–164. M.F.

Gnosis, Gnostics, Gnosticism

A. Definition, names B. Sources, literature C. Basic concepts D. Beginnings and history E. After-effects, history of research

A. Definition, names

The term Gnosticism that is common today in the German-speaking areas (γνῶσις; *gnôsis*, 'insight, knowledge') has to a large extent superseded the older term 'Gnosticism' that is, however, used in English and French. It goes back to the early Christian period (1. Tim 6, 20; Iren. Adversus haereses I, 6.2) and has a heresiological meaning; its representatives are called 'Gnostics' (γνωστικοί; *gnōstikoí*, Iren. Adversus haereses I, 2.1), i.e. people who represent and disseminate particular 'insights' and also ways of behaving that diverge from the official Church and its theological tradition.

Apart from the 'gnoseological' meaning in Greek philosophy, the term has remained a positive one in Christianity since Paul and John the Evangelist – it is not seen as being in opposition to pure 'faith' (*pístis*) but as defining the recognition of salvation, as it regarded the dominant school of thought in early Christianity. Origen and Clemens [3] Alexandrinus understood the term in the sense of Christian theology, placing it against heresiological Gnosticism. Certainly the primarily negative usage in polemics continued to exist.

Gnostic sources claim the true 'insight' about the position of man and his redemption from the material world that is often equated with darkness; in spite of this, 'Gnostic' is not a constant self-description. Other names, as we now know from the Nağʿ Ḥammādī texts demonstrate this: 'Lineage, children or descendants of Seth', 'Children of the light', 'Children of the bridal chamber', 'Chosen ones', 'Saints', 'Perfect ones', 'Outsiders', 'Possessors of the spirit' (Pneumatics), 'Unconvertable race', 'Kingless race', also simply 'Church' [1].

The names that appear in the heresiological sources primarily refer to the founders of the school (Simonians, Valentinians, Basilidians, Marcosians) or to obvious points in their teachings (Archonts, Barbelo-Gnostics, Ophites or Naasenes, i.e. snake worshippers, Sethians, or similar). It was not until modern research that the term Gnosticism was introduced as a general description of the world view common to these groups (see E. below).

B. Sources, literature

By 1945/46 there were only relatively few original documents that could be attributed to Gnosticism [9; 10; 11]. These include the texts of the Codex Ascew (Pistis Sophia) and Codex Brucianus (2 books of Jeu, untitled writing) that are only preserved in Coptic, the Coptic papyrus Berolinensis 8502 (Evangelium Mariae, Apocryphon Johannis, Sophia Jesu Christi) that has been known since 1896 but was not edited until 1955, also some parts of the → Corpus Hermeticum (especially the 1st tract 'Poimandres'), the 'Odes of Solomon' and passages of → apocryphal apostle literature (Acta Johannis, Acta Thomae with the 'Song of the Pearl'). Also the polemic literature of the apologists and Church Fathers of the 2nd–4th cents. (Justin, Irenaeus of Lyon, Hippolytus of Rome, Tertullian, Clement of Alexandria, Origen, Epiphanius of Salamis) contains relatively long quotations and summaries of Gnostic writings and poetic works (e.g. the book of the Gnostic → Iustinus, the Naassene homily, the 'Great revelation' of → Simon Magus, the letter of Ptolemy to Flora, extracts from the comm. of Heracleon on Io, fragments of Valentinus among others).

However it was not until the appearance of the 13 Coptic codices with 51 writings, not all completely preserved, that were found in 1945 at → Nağʿ Ḥammādī (Upper Egypt), that there was a turning point in the literary documentation of Gnosticism [6–8; 12; 13]. Of these, 45 texts are shown to be clearly Gnostic, and 39 of them were previously unknown. They are still being edited and evaluated. They contain not just a known wide variety of Gnostic teachings, primarily Valentinian, 'Sethian' or 'Barbelo-Gnostic' and also of Hermetic origin (in Codex 6), but they partly reveal a literary process that stretches from the preliminary phases of the Greek originals of the 2nd/3rd cents. to the Coptic translation in the 4th/5th cents. AD. On many occasions these are compilations, which is why classification with the Gnostic schools known from the heresiological data often remains uncertain. In some texts the secondary Christian adaptation becomes clear (Apocryphon Johannis, Sophia Jesu Christi or Eugnostus Letter; three-fold Protennoia) whilst others work on (middle) Platonic traditions. The breadth of content is flanked by a literary one: aside from 'Revelations' (Apocalypses), like those of 'Adam to his son Seth', of 'Dositheus' (Three Steles of Seth), of Zostrianus (Zoroaster), of Peter and Paul, or 'Secret writings' (*Apókryphoi*), that are available particularly in the form of 'Dialogues' between the Redeemer (*Sōtḗr*, Jesus Christ) and his disciples (*Apókryphoi* of John, of Jacob; Dialogue of *Sōtḗr*), there are collections of proverbs or didactic texts as 'Gospels' (of Thomas, of Philip, of the Egyptians, of truth), letters (of Jacob, Rheginus, Eugnostus), tracts (so-called Tripartite Treatise, Authenticus Logos, Exegesis of the Soul, Nature [*hypóstasis*] of the Archonts), prayers and homilies.

The → Mandaeans, whose extensive Aramaic literature increasingly attracted the attention of Gnostic research at the end of the 19th cent., form an autonomous Oriental branch of Gnosticism. Manichaeism is also part of Gnosticism in the widest sense (→ Mani, Manichaeans).

C. Basic concepts

Like other ancient and early Christian movements, Gnosticism attempts to provide answers to the problems of evil in the world, its origin, the position of man in the cosmos and his destiny, but it does so in a truly radical way. Here dualistic views in particular play a decisive part leading to the parlous state of the world being traced back to an accident in its creation and the discrepancy between spirit and matter (body) being depicted as unbridgeable antitheses. Taking as the starting-point faith in an absolutely transcendent God (→ *ágnostos theós*, often called 'Father'), the origin of the world is traced back to a subordinate, hybrid creator (demiurge, also called 'Fool') who with his 'Powers' (angels, archonts, planets) also undertakes the creation of man (Adam). In order to control this process that had been set in motion, God takes several counter-measures revolving around the salvation of man as the centre of the cosmos. Without the knowledge of the demiurge and his helpers, the body of Adam that is not viable, is fed a supra-worldly 'divine' substance called either 'Spirit' (*pneûma*, *énnoia*), 'Soul' (*psychḗ*, Aramaic *nisimta*), 'Spark' (*spinthḗr*) or something similar. This part of man not only enables him to recognize the true God and to comprehend the work of the creator as having turned out badly but also to recognize the true goal of man as the return to the spiritual realm of the true God, often called 'Fullness' (*plḗrōma*) or 'Realm of light', to 'know' – at the same time however to recognize the frailty of the cosmos as a topsy-turvy creation based on evil intentions.

This 'insight' (*gnṓsis*) with regard to cosmological and anthropological correlations is a 'supernatural one' that is imparted to the 'knowing one' (*gnōstikós*) through revelations, be it through heavenly messengers appearing in the name of the true God, or through the traditional form of the myths of ancient times (primarily of Biblical origin). The occurrences of ancient times determine the fate of the present-day world. The process of liberation of the supraworldly (divine, spiritual, enlightened) core of man from the chains of the 'dark' material cosmos destined for decline determines the (hidden) course of history right to the end, i.e. soteriology and eschatology ultimately coincide. It is not 'redemption' from individual guilt and sin but the rescue of the 'Soul' or the 'Spirit' from body and matter (*hýlē*) that sets the agenda of Gnosticism. The whole apparatus of Gnostic mythology or theology that is also documented primarily in the 'protest exegesis' of older traditions (especially Biblical ones) serves this purpose that also guides world-denying behaviours.

The Gnostics therefore regard themselves as a 'chosen race', an elite, as opposed to people who are earth- and world-minded. The communities are correspondingly structured: the 'Pneumatics' (amongst the Manichaeans the *electi*) are the core, the 'Psychics' (the *auditores* or *katechoúmenoi* among the Manichaeans) are the simple members of the community, often identical to the 'Church Christians' who were open to Gnosticism without accepting the ultimate consequences; very much on the outside are the 'Earthly ones' (*choikoí*) who correspond to the 'Heathens'. Although only insight guarantees salvation, rituals and sacraments are available; however the sources (apart from the Mandaean and Manichaean ones) provide little information: there were baptisms, banquets, incantations, initiations, dedications and death ceremonies [25. 235–261]. The focus however was on the didactic teachings by the 'Pneumatics'. It therefore took the form of a 'school' or a 'mysteries club' of Gnostics, which then under Christian conditions became 'parish churches'. The reproaches originating in heresiological literature (→ Heresiology) regarding libertine practices that could certainly be deduced from the anti-cosmic ideology, have not been able to be proven to date in the original texts.

D. Beginnings and history

In the opinion of the Church Fathers, Gnosticism originates in the devil, who wanted to destroy the Church through it. → Simon 'the Magician' (*mágos*) from Acts 8 is designated as the first earthly representative; his pupil Menander passed the Gnostic heresy on to Saturninus (or Saturnilus) of Antioch and to Basilides of Alexandria. This chain of religious obedience was used for centuries to explain the origin and dissemination of Gnosticism although it is based more on legend than history. At any rate, those named were obviously familiar with Gnostic thought; to Simon is attributed not just (secondarily?) a revelatory writing ('Great Proclamation') but also his own school of Gnostic thought (see B. above). As no historical Gnostic writing has turned up to date, research has to rely on reconstructions and hypotheses based on the remaining source material. This has occurred many times over the last decades without having led to a generally recognized viewpoint. Today the predominant opinion of researchers into Gnosticism is, however, that the origins of Gnosticism are not primarily Christian, i.e. Gnosticism is not purely a Christian heresy but a relatively independent development with a new 'understanding of existence' [19] that is fed in a literary and religious historical sense by various sources, primarily however it is connected with early Jewish traditions (especially of Wisdom and apocalyptic writings) (this links in with its preoccupation with Jewish [OT] writings [26. 123–209; 31]). In addition, the Greek-Hellenistic as well as the Iranian (especially in Mandaean and Manichaean Gnosticism) background has a part to play in its further course in increasingly influencing early Christian ideas of the world; although early Christianity ultimately considered Gnosticism to be a → heresy, it had already influenced Christian theology with its deeply probing questions stemming from its *curiositas*.

The ideological prerequisites of Gnosticism in Hellenistic individualism and syncretism are accompanied by the socio-economic and political-historical conditions in the east of the Roman empire that were characterized by exploitation, repression and fear as well as the resistance of the (Oriental) population. The idea of the 'inner man' served self-identification beyond the official cult religions and the earthly, social ties. The world is understood as lack of order (chaos), no longer as a cosmos ruled by → *logos*, as in the political philosophy of the Greeks. This protest, discernible in the mythological constructions and ascetic behaviour, is one of the most radical of ancient times: in its concentration on the sole salvation of the 'inner man' (Spirit, Soul), it represents utter rejection of this world [25. 294–315].

The early schools and comments are known to us only in a fragmentary way and can be understood well as the prerequisites of the later systems (from the 2nd cent. AD). These include the following concepts: the contrast between God or creator and creation (world), the emanation of spiritual powers (*énnoia*, *epínoia*, *pneûma*) from God for the salvation of man, the sending of one or several 'Redeemers' who can be identical to the founders of the school (Simon Magus), the soteriological power of 'insight', the anti-cosmic state and types of behaviour. The adoption of the figure of Christ as the dominant figure of redemption is clear in the more or less anti-Gnostic polemic of early Christian literature (pastoral letters, Ignatius of Antioch), as well as the reverse process: the influence of Gnostic theologoumena on the Christian intellectual world, above all on the shaping of Christ as a heavenly ambassador (already discernible in Paul [Eph, Col] and in John) the rejection of the resurrection 'in the flesh', the emphasis on the 'possession of pneuma' and anti-worldly characteristics (Jude; revelation of John). So-called Docetism (→ Doketai), i.e. the only 'apparent' (*dokéō*, *dókēsis*) appearance of Christ in the earthly-physical world, is a product of heresiological polemics. Gnosticism, too, does not dispute the incarnation of the Redeemer, namely of the immortal, supraworldly 'spiritual' ambassador of God in the earthly Jesus, but the cosmic powers have not received any power over him: only his body declines into death, not the actual redeeming power [25. 172–186; 26. 266–272].

If the beginnings of Gnosticism in the 1st. cent. AD can be pinpointed initially in Syria and Asia Minor, then Alexandria and Rome become its centres in the 2nd cent. without the older areas becoming insignificant in the process, as the origin of Manichaeism shows. The 2nd cent. is the period when the great systems and schools flourished in the form of Christian Gnosticism, which in the course of the gradual development of 'apostolic' orthodoxy becomes heresy with the aid of the hierarchical bishop system from the middle of the 2nd cent.; the Church wins out against Gnosticism in the 3rd cent. and with Emperor Constantine I in the 4th cent. is also able to draw upon state funds for this purpose. The dispute between the 'Great Church' and Gnosticism determines in many ways the discussion about central topics in early Christian theology. The most recent research has for the first time acknowledged here the contribution of Gnosticism to this field (especially Basilides and Valentinus as well as Marcion). The essential features are preserved but are varied and developed in many forms and legitimized with emphatically exegetic references back to the Biblical writings, including references back to the NT, which was in the process of evolving. Parallel to the Church development of the 'Apostolic succession', Gnosticism also follows a similar concern; its writings are traced back to the known Christian authorities: Paul (who therefore becomes the 'Apostle of the heretics'), John, Peter, Thomas and Philip; they are the witnesses of Gnostic ideology, as Christ 'revealed' it as higher esoteric wisdom and the witnesses to his spiritually, not hierarchically determined 'Church' [26. 220–243].

Listed as the first and best-known theologian and Gnostic school founder is → Basilides [2], who lived at the time of the Emperors Hadrian and Antoninus Pius in Alexandria (117–161). Several works are attributed to him, among these a gospel, an 'Exegesis' in 24 books, psalms or odes; only a little of this is extant in the form of extracts. His son(?) also wrote several books that have been lost. The teaching of Basilides can only be reconstructed with difficulty as the few extant fragments of his writings do not suffice to decide between the divergent reports. It is therefore said that he taught the 'emergence' (*emanatio*) of six paired spiritual powers from the 'Unbegotten father' from which a further 365 angelic beings arose with their 'Heavens' which together form the world year (aeon). The God of the Jews → 'Abraxas (Abrasax)' (= 365) created the world with the lowest class of angelic powers. To save man, i.e. only his soul, from its tyranny, the 'Father' sent the Christ-*nous* that appeared in Jesus. Instead of him, Simon of Cyrene was crucified. The community of Basilides regarded itself as a 'selection' of ascetically living 'Pneumatics', as 'Outsiders' *vis-à-vis* the world and mankind. With regard to the debatable position of the contemporary → Marcion in respect of Gnosticism, see that section.

The most important Gnostic theologian before Mani is → Valentinus, also an Egyptian. Brought up in Alexandria and converted to Christianity, he went to Rome in 140 where he founded a school and played a part in the church disputes about leadership roles. After an interlude in Cyprus (?) he died in Rome in about 160. Only a few (11) quotations from him are extant, primarily from sermons, songs (hymns) and letters. It turned out that attributing the texts of the Naǧʿ Ḥammādī Codices 'Gospel of Truth' and 'Three-Part Tract' to him was a mistake so that as before we are unclear about the system that was attributed to him by the heresiologists. It is said primarily to have consisted in the primeval beginning of becoming lying in the divine 'depths' (*bythós*) and its emanations of 15 pairs of spiritual powers (aeons) of which the first four are of particular importance. The last aeon is 'Wisdom' (*Sophía*) that through its 'ignorance' or its 'error' disturbs the harmony of the *pleroma* and that – only through the aeon pair 'Christ' and the 'Holy Spirit' – is returned to the 'All'; its 'passion' (*enthýmēsis*) however becomes the cause of the origin of the world, i.e. from it originates the demiurge who with his powers controls the material and psychic world. Only the 'Spirit' (*pneûma*) or 'Seed of light' is capable of redemption by being activated through 'insight' (*gnṓsis*), imparted through Jesus Christ, in the 'Spiritual carrier' (Pneumatic). The 'Soul' (*psychḗ*) can have a part in the liberation only with the help of remoulding through the 'Spirit'. The extent to which the highly complicated system of the school passed down to us in various versions goes back to Valentinus is a problem that is still unresolved in research. Of the texts of the Nağ' Ḥammādī Codices, the Apocryphon of John that was also used by Irenaeus [2] (Adversus haereses I, 29) gives an idea of the older stages of this.

Incontestable is the great influence of Valentine on his pupils, of whom several are well known and were described by the Church Fathers as dangerous competitors. According to this they have been classified into 'Oriental' or 'Anatolian' and 'Italian' schools of thought that differ in matters of Christology. Mark belonged to the former group active in Egypt, Syria and Asia Minor that dedicated itself particularly to 'mysticism of the letters of the alphabet' and created their own ceremonies for this purpose, and there was also Theodotus, whose views are known to us from the 'Excerpts' of Clement of Alexandria. The other school that had its centre in Rome is represented by Ptolemy (Irenaeus of Lyon describes his teachings) and Heracleon; the latter wrote a commentary on the gospel of John, which was examined by Origen and Clement of Alexandria. We are informed about the activities of the Valentinian Gnosticism, especially in the East, up to the 5th cent.; undoubtedly it was one of the strongest and most widely disseminated schools of Gnostic thought whose influence is also obvious in several texts of the Nağ' Ḥammādī Codices. With its testimonies we also reach the end of 'western' Gnosticism. Other sources do not originally offer anything new and do not go beyond the often far-reaching repetitions of the mythological guidelines (e.g. the 'Pistis Sophia'); unfortunately we know nothing about who disseminated them. The reports of the enthusiastic Epiphanius [1] of Salamis (5th cent.) in his 'Medical box' (*Panarion*) to stop the poison of the heresies are both very constructive and often very much divorced from reality (especially regarding the Borborites) [2].

E. AFTER-EFFECTS, HISTORY OF RESEARCH

The effect of Gnosticism with regard to the questions about the world (cosmos, creation), redemption and the Redeemer (soteriology), the relationship between God and the redeemer (Christology), faith and knowledge, body and spirit or soul, good and evil, death and resurrection – that were often raised by it for the first time – is mirrored in the answers of the heresiologists provoked in this way, often affecting the very structure of their works (especially noticeable in Irenaeus). J.G. HERDER already therefore saw in Gnosticism the first religious philosophy of Christianity. F.C. BAUR and also A. VON HARNACK, with the emphasis on the 'Hellenization' of Christianity that then took place, made similar judgements. The more or less direct continuation of Gnosticism occurred particularly in the Orient in the form of the world religion of → Manichaeism and in the Islamic period among several of the Shiite groups [3]. The → Mandaeans are still today the last heirs of Gnosticism in the Orient. In the West the after-effects can be shown in the dualistic movements of the → Bogomils, Cathars and Albigensians, the combating of which led to the institution of the Church inquisition and to the appearance of the concept of 'heretic' (from *cathari*, *gazari*, Italian *gazaro*). With the rediscovery of the → Corpus Hermeticum in the 15th cent. and its interpretation, Gnostic ideas also again gained importance and they then played a part in mystic, neo-Cabbalistic, theosophic, alchemistic and other doctrines. These effects which are not always easy to demonstrate range from the cosmological, anthropological, soteriological and eschatological field to revolutionary ideology of psychological and philosophical systems [4].

The history of research also contributed and contributes to revitalizing interest in Gnosticism [25. 35–58; 27. texts]. The change in the view of Church history that came about with the Reformation and the end of the subsequent interdenominational wars also included historical writings regarding heretics. First discernible in the 'impartial Church history and history of heretics' of the Pietistic minister Gottfried ARNOLD (1699), then in the monumental work of the Hugenot Isaak DE BEAUSOBRE about Manichaeism (1734/39) and in the works of the Church historian Joh. Lorenz VON MOSHEIM ('Attempt at an Impartial and Thorough History of Heretics', 1746). The relevant books by F.C. BAUR ('The Manichaean System of Religion', 1831; 'Christian Gnosis or Christian Philosophy of Religion', 1835) then constitute the beginning of modern research. The investigations that then started which were critical of the sources led to a fairer evaluation of Gnosticism within the framework of the history of the Church and the history of articles of faith, as particularly in Adolf von HARNACK (1886). However, only the religious history school around 1900 broke with the pure Church history view of Gnosticism by placing greater importance on its non-Christian roots that had already been assumed previously, whilst at the same time however recognizing the repercussions of Gnosticism for early Christian literature and the development of teachings (W. BOUSSET, R. REITZENSTEIN, W. WREDE). In this tradition are also the works of R. BULTMANN and his pupil Hans JONAS, who in 1934 presented his pioneering book 'Gnosis and the Spirit of Late Antiquity'. The discovery of the → Nağ' Ḥammādī Codices signified a further turning-point in research into Gnosticism (see B. above), as well as the unexpected revival in interest in this phenomenon of late antiquity and its new documents, a revival that has been sustained right through to the present time without interruption.

→ GNOSTICISM

1 F. SIEGERT, Selbstbezeichnungen der Gnostiker in den Nağ'-Ḥammādī-Texten, in: Zschr. für die nt. Wissenschaft 71, 1980, 129–132 2 A. POURKIER, L'hérésiologie

chez Épiphane de Salamine, 1992 3 H. HALM, Die islamische G., Zürich 1982 4 P. SLOTERDIJK, T. H. MACHO, Weltrevolution der Seele, 1993 (texts).

BIBLIOGR.: 5 D. M. SCHOLER, Nağʿ Ḥammādī Bibliography 1948–1969, 1971; 1970–1994, 1997 (concerns the entire field of research on Gnosticism).
ED. AND TRANSL.: 6 The Facsimile Edition of the Nağʿ Ḥammādī Codices. Introduction. Codex I – XIII, 1972 – 1979 7 The Coptic Gnostic Library ed. with English transl.; intr. and notes publ. under the auspices of the Institute for Antiquity and Christianity, 15 vols., 1975 –1996 8 Bibliothèque copte de Nağʿ Ḥammādī. Section "Textes", Collection éd. par J. E. MÉNARD, P.-H. POIRIER, M. ROBERGE, 1977ff. 9 W. FOERSTER (ed.), Die Gnosis, 3 vols., 1977, 21995 (special edition 1997) 10 R. HAARDT, Die G., 1997 11 B. LAYTON, The Gnostic Scriptures, 1987 12 J. M. ROBINSON (ed.), The Nağʿ Ḥammādī Library in English, 1977, 31988 13 G. LÜDEMANN, M. JANSSEN (ed.), Bibel der Häretiker. Die gnostischen Schriften aus Nağʿ Ḥammādī, 1997.
BIBLIOGRAPHY: 14 U. BIANCHI (ed.), Le origini dello gnosticismo. Colloquio di Messina 13–18 Aprile 1966, 1967, 21970 15 A. BÖHLIG, Mysterion und Wahrheit, 1968 16 Id., G. und Synkretismus, 2 parts, 1989 17 W. BOUSSET, Hauptprobleme der G., 1907, 21973 18 G. FILORAMO, A History of Gnosticism, 1990, 21991 19 H. JONAS, G. und spätant. Geist. Teil 1: Die myth. G., 1934, 41988; Teil 2/1.2: Von der Myth. zur mystischen Philos., ed. by K. RUDOLPH, 1993 20 K. KOSCHORKE, Die Polemik der Gnostiker gegen das kirchliche Christentum, 1978 21 B. LAYTON (ed.), The Rediscovery of Gnosticism, vol. 1–2, 1981 22 H. LEISEGANG, Die G., 1924, 41955 23 A. MAGRIS, La logica del pensiero gnostico, 1997 24 H.- CH. PUECH, En quête de la Gnose, 2 vols., 1978 25 K. RUDOLPH, Die G., 1977, 31990 26 Id., G. und spätant. Rel.gesch., 1996 27 Id. (ed.), G. und Gnostizismus, 1975 28 W. SCHMITHALS, Neues Testament und G., 1984 29 G. STROUMSA, Another Seed: Stud. in Gnostic Mythology, 1984 30 K.-W. TRÖGER (ed.), G. und Neues Testament, 1973 31 Id. (ed.), Altes Testament – Frühjudentum – G., 1980 32 J. D. TURNER, A. MCGUIRE (ed.), The Nağʿ Ḥammādī Library after Fifty Years, 1997 33 R. MCL. WILSON, The Gnostic Problem, 1958, 21964. KU.R.

Goat

[1] (αἴξ *aíx*). According to the post-Hesiodic myth, Zeus was fed and nourished as a child in the Cretan cave by a goat (→ Amalthea) or a nymph by the name of 'Goat'. Zeus kills her, uses her coat as a shield (→ Aegis) in the battle of the Titans and in gratitude sets her among the stars (Eratosth. Catast. 13 CAPELLA; Ant. Lib. 36). The nymph is the mother of Aegipan and Aegocerus (Capricorn, Eratosth. Catast. 27). The representation of the constellation of Ἡνίοχος (*Hēníochos*; Auriga) bearing the goat on the shoulder and her two male kids (ἔριφοι; *ériphoi*) on the arm (Arat. 156–67) links two originally separate interpretations of the constellations. – The word is used proverbially in Αἴξ οὐρανία (*Aíx Ouranía*), 'the heavenly goat', in the ancient Attic comedy (Cratinus in Zenob. 1,26; Antiphanes in Ath. 9,66,402e). F.G.

[2] (αἶξ/*aîx*; τράγος/*trágos*: billy-goat; Latin *caper, capra, hircus*).
I. ANCIENT ORIENT AND EGYPT II. GREECE III. ROME

I. ANCIENT ORIENT AND EGYPT

Goats (Sumerian ùz, female goat; Akkadian *enzu* that could be used to describe both the female goat and goats as a genus (then mostly pl. *enzāte*); Sumerian máš, Akkadian *urīṣu* billy goat) are attested in inscriptions in Mesopotamia from the beginning of the 3rd millennium BC. The texts distinguish conceptually according to breed, age, sex and also purpose of use (sacrifice goats, wool goats). Goats were described as 'black' and pictorial representations also show piebald animals (white/dark brown) [5. vol. 14. pl. XXX]. Goats were kept as a rule in mixed herds together with → sheep and then usually under the collective term 'small livestock' (Akkadian *ṣēnu*). The proportion of goats in a herd of such kind was small (usually less than 25 %). Because of their higher intelligence compared with the sheep, billy-goats were often used as lead animals (Sumerian en.zi). The animals from temple herds were branded in the neo-Babylonian period. Goats supplied (through shearing) hair that was used, among other things, for the production of tent materials and felt as well as to stuff mattresses. In the early 3rd millennium it appears that billy-goats were used for extispicy (later sheep). Pictorial representations show a behaviour typical of goats: they stand up straight on their hind legs on a tree eating its green leaves [3. pl. 47b; 4. pl. 86a].

In Egypt goats were as a rule more numerous than sheep, and they were tended together with sheep. Goats served as milk suppliers, and as animals for slaughter they were important particularly for the common people.

→ Husbandry

1 Chicago Assyrian Dictionary, vol. E, 1958, 180–182, s. v. *enzu* 2 B. HROUDA, Der Alte Orient, 1991 3 F. VON LUSCHAN, Sendschirli, vol. 5, 1945 4 A. MOORTGAT, Tell Halaf, vol. 3, 1955 5 PropKg 6 P. STEINKELLER, Sheep and Goat Terminology in Ur III Sources from Drehem, in: Bull. on Sumerian Agriculture 8, 1995, 49–70 7 L. STÖRK, s. v. Z., LÄ 6, 1400 f. J. RE.

II. GREECE

Goats, like → sheep, were introduced to the Aegaean area and Greece in the Neolithic Age. As it is hard to distinguish between the bones of goats and sheep, the contribution made by palaeozoology to the history of the goat in antiquity is limited. A lot of information is therefore based essentially on knowledge of the lifestyle of these animals and on the keeping of goats in later periods. Goats require far less water than sheep and their agility and capacity to eat the most varied of plants make it possible to keep them in marginal soil areas of the Mediterranean landscape – on mountain slopes situated relatively high up or on deserted islands. Before

1936, when the reforestation programme was commenced, there were more than three times as many goats as sheep in Greece.

The characteristics of the goat are described in detail in the zoological writings of → Aristotle [6] where former errors are also corrected (respiration through the ears: Aristot. Hist. an. 492a); reproduction receives a lot of attention; according to Aristotle, goats reached the age of eight years (Aristot. Hist. an. 573b–574a). The → milk as an economically important product and the suitable feed are a topic in literature (ibid. 521b–523a; 569a-b). → Eupolis in his comedy *Aîges* ('The Goats') vividly characterizes the eating behaviour of the animals.

In the late Bronze Age, goats also appear in the → Linear B tablets aside from sheep that undoubtedly predominated, for instance in → Knos(s)os. The keeping of goats is also attested for the Homeric age: Odysseus had numerous goat herds on Ithaca (Hom. Od. 14,103f. and 17,212–225); wild goats were hunted (Hom. Od. 9,152–162). In the 5th and 4th cents. BC, goats were likewise kept in Attica in large herds; the possessions of Panaetius [3] confiscated in 414 BC included not just 84 sheep but also 68 goats, and → Philoctemon sold a herd of goats with the goatherd for 1,300 drachmai (ML 79B, 71 ff.; Isaeus 6,33; cf. also 11,41: stock of Theophon, 60 sheep and 100 goats; Dem. Or. 47,52: herd of 50 sheep with a shepherd; Xenophon in Scillus: Xen. An. 5,3,11).

In addition to the meat and milk that is more nutritious in the long term than that of sheep and was mostly consumed as → cheese (meat: Hom. Il. 9,207; Hom. Od. 2,56; 17,213 f.; milk and cheese: Aristot. Hist. an. 521b–523a; cf. Hom. Od. 9,216–251; Hes. Op. 585–590), goat hair and goat skins were always important for rural Greece. There were wineskins made of goat → leather (Hom. Il. 3,247; Hom. Od. 6,78), and bags of goat hair were used for pressing olives; clothing made of goat skins was characteristic in antiquity of slaves and poor people in rural regions (Hom. Od. 14,530; Theoc. 7,15 ff.); goat pelts were used at night as covering (Hom. Od. 14,519).

Goats were important in the classical period as sacrificial animals and they are frequently mentioned in connection with → sacrifices to → Aphrodite, → Artemis and → Dionysus. In the cult of → Apollo, goats were commonly used as sacrificial animals but it was forbidden to sacrifice them in the great Asclepieum of Epidaurus (Paus. 2,26,9; cf. 10,32,12 for the temple of Asclepius near Tithorea), perhaps because of their unrestrained behaviour and their bad odour (Plut. Quaest. Rom. 111). A red or black billy-goat was sacrificed to Dionysus in Thoricus in Attica (SEG 33, 147,33 f.) and a white goat was sacrificed in a reconciliation ceremony with a neighbouring polis in Sicilian Nacone (SEG 30, 1119,27f.). The piling up of the horns of sacrificed goats is remarkable; these horns partly formed an accumulation or even an altar – in a building complex in Drerus and in Halieis, in the open air in Ephesus and attested epigraphically. As a symbol goats are connected especially with Aphrodite, Artemis and Dionysus, the deities to whom they were mainly sacrificed. Aphrodite is sometimes represented riding on a goat (bronze sculpture of Scopas [1] in Elis: Paus. 6,25,1), and she shares with the animal dangerous, uncontrollable desire (ἀφροδισιαστικός/*aphrodisiastikós*: Gal. De temperamentis 1,624,10).

On campaigns of war, Spartan armies always kept with them for the sacrifice a herd of sheep at whose head went goats (Paus. 9,13,4). Before the Spartan army began a battle, goats were sacrificed to → Artemis Agrotera, the goddess of wild animals (Xen. Hell. 4,2,20; Xen. Lac. pol. 13,8; Plut. Lycurgus 22,4). In gratitude for the victory at → Marathon (490 BC), the Athenians likewise sacrificed 500 goats to Artemis Agrotera every year (Xen. An. 3,2,11–12).

The antisocial, dangerous characteristics of the goat were associated in turn with Dionysus. The image of the mythological companions of the god, the → satyrs, is derived from the stubborn, lascivious billy-goat; → Pan, a god with billy-goat feet and goat horns, is said to have assisted the goatherds in the mountains of Arcadia. For the urban Athenians, Pan, like D., was a figure of the exotic wilderness. The well known problem of the meaning of the word 'tragedy' ('billy-goat song', cf. → Tragedy I. A.) should also be viewed in this connection, since the tragedies were performed at the → Dionysia.

The goatherd (αἰπόλος/*aipólos*), often a slave, had only low social status in Greece; it was the goatherd in particular who had the hardest job of all the shepherds but the lowest social position, as the goat was certainly the least tame domesticated animal. It is therefore no coincidence that Melanthius [1], the goatherd in the 'Odyssey', appears as a malicious character who is horribly punished at the end of the epic (Hom. Od. 17,212–238; 17,369–373; 22,474–479).

1 A. Burford, Land and Labour in the Greek World, 1993, 144–156 2 H. Grassl, Zur Gesch. des Viehhandels im klass. Griechenland, in: MBAH 4, 1985, 77–88 3 P. Halstead, Pastoralism or Household Herding? Problems of Scale and Specialization in Early Greek Animal Husbandry, in: World Archaeology 28, 1996, 20–42 4 S. Hodkinson, Animal Husbandry in the Greek Polis, in: Whittaker, 35–74 5 Isager/Skysgaard, 91–93; 96–107 6 M. H. Jameson, Sacrifice and Animal Husbandry in Classical Greece, in: Whittaker, 87–119 7 Id., C. N. Runnels, Tj. van Andel, A Greek Countryside: The Southern Argolid from Prehistory to the Present Day, 1994, 290–301 8 D. Mackenzie, Goat Husbandry, [3]1970 9 Osborne, 189–192 10 W. Richter, Die Landwirtschaft im homerischen Zeitalter (ArchHom 2 H), 1968, 44–53.

MI. JA.

III. Rome

The goat was important for the farming industry and was also part of small animal husbandry in Roman tenant farming. Varro and Columella dedicate relatively long sections to the keeping of goats (Varro, Rust. 2,3;

Columella 7,6–8; cf. in addition Verg. G. 3,300–326; Plin. HN 8,199–204). Goats were considered to be less demanding than → sheep, as they were not dependent upon open grazing land but could also be kept in forested regions and in areas covered with spiny plants; acorns were also added to their diet (Varro, Rust. 2,3,6–7; Columella 7,6,1; 7,6,5). Autumn to December at the latest was recommended as the suitable period for reproduction, as the kids were then born in spring when young leaves of bushes and trees were available (Varro, Rust. 2,3,8; Columella 7,6,6; Pall. Agric. 12,13,7). The kids were supposed to be given elm seeds, medick, ivy, mastic shoots or other young foliage as additional feed for as long as they suckled from their mothers (Columella 7,6,7). Because of their love of eating, kids were regarded as a danger to young plants in cultivated fields, which is why, according to Varro, leaseholders were forbidden to allow them to graze there (Varro, Rust. 2,3,7).

Owners of large estates in Italy kept 50–100 animals under the control of one shepherd; there were herds that consisted exclusively of goats; there were about 10 to 20 female goats to one billy-goat (Varro, Rust. 2,3,10; Columella 7,6,5). For Roman Egypt small-livestock declarations and indentures of leases attest to herds of goats and the existence of herds made up purely of goats. The goatherd (*caprarius*: Varro, Rust. 2,3,10; *magister pecoris*: Columella 7,6,9) had to be physically very resilient and hardy.

The keeping of goats primarily served the purpose of making → cheese from the → milk. According to modern information, the goat supplies, in relation to its body weight, four times the milk yield of the sheep and three times that of the cow (→ Cattle). The meat of the kid that was said in Rome to have cost one → *denarius*, was a highly desired food (Varro, Rust. 2,3,10; Edictum [3] Diocletiani 4,3; 4,48); Goat meat traders are epigraphically attested (*caprinarii*: CIL VI 9231; X 7185). The long-haired goats (Columella 1 pr. 26) were shorn like sheep (Verg. G. 3,311–313; Columella 7,6,2); their hair was used to manufacture felt, ship's ropes, cables for catapults and carpets (Varro, Rust. 2,11,11 f.); pelts and skins of goats were used not only as → clothing for the poor (Verg. Moretum 22; Varro, Rust. 2,11,11) but also for sitting and lying on (Sen. Ep. 95,72) as well as for the production of wineskins (Plin. HN 28,240). The Roman army also used large amounts of goat leather; for the tents of a legion, people needed the skins of over 70,000 goats. The fact that goats were sacrificed in numerous cults likewise promoted the keeping and sale of goats.

→ Nutrition; → Meat, consumption of; → Cheese; → Clothing; → Agriculture; → Leather; → Milk; → Sacrifices; → Sheep; → Stables, keeping of animals in; → Husbandry

1 L. Chioffi, Caro: il mercato della carne nell'occidente romano, 1999 2 H.-J. Drexhage, Preise, Mieten/Pachten, Kosten und Löhne im röm. Äg. bis zum Regierungsantritt Diokletians, 1991, 302–305 3 W. Habermann, Die Deklarationen von Kleinvieh (Schafe und Ziegen) im röm. Äg. Quantitative Aspekte, in: P. Herz, G. Waldherr (ed.), Landwirtschaft im Imperium Romanum, 2000, 77–100 4 P. Herz, Der Aufstand des Iulius Sacrovir (21 n. Chr.), in: Laverna 3, 1992, 42–93, esp. 66 f. 5 J. Peters, Röm. Tierhaltung und Tierzucht, 1998, 71–76; 83–93; 101–107 6 M. Schnebel, Die Landwirtschaft im hell. Äg., 1925, 327–328 7 White, Farming, 313–316.

K. RU.

Gobazes (Γωβάζης; *Gōbázēs*). King of the Lazes, abdicated in *c.* AD 456 in favour of his son under pressure from the Roman government, visited Constantinople in 465/6 for negotiations with Emperor Leo I, in which Daniel the Stylite, who lived there and whom he revered, supported him in a mediating role.

PLRE 2, 515; ODB 1, 585, s.v. Daniel the Stylite. F.T.

Gobryas (Γωβρύας; *Gōbrýas*, Akkadian *Gu/Gú-ba/bar-ru(-ʾu*; Elamite *Kam-bar-ma*, ancient Persian *Gaubaruva-*). Name of various Achaemenid dignitaries.

[1] 'Governor' of Cyrus the Great known from the Nabonidus Chronicle (3,20 [4]) who after the conquest of Babylonia appointed administrative officials there. Presumably identical to Ugbaru, the 'Governor of Gutium' mentioned in 3,15 who captured Babylon for the Persian king and died there a few days after Cyrus' arrival. In this case it is probable that the G. in Xenophon (Cyr. 4,6,1) is based on this person.

[2] Not identical to G. [1]. Attested to from the 4th year of the rule of Cyrus for at least 10 years as 'Governor of Babylonia and Transeuphratene (*Ebir nāri*)'. He is known from numerous Babylonian texts in political, legal and economic contexts.

[3] A contemporary of → Darius [1] I, son of Mardonius (ancient Persian *Marduniya-*), who according to information from the inscription of → Bīsutūn [5. DB IV 84] helped Darius murder → Gaumāta (cf. also Hdt. 3,70ff.; Just. 1,9; Plut. De fratrum amore 7,904). He is identical to *G. Pātišuvariš* ('from the tribe of the Patishorians', cf. Str. 15,3,1), the 'spear bearer of King Darius' from an inscription on the tomb of Darius I in → Naqš-e Rostam [5. DNc], and the army commander sent by the king to put down an uprising in → Elam [5. DB V 7.9.11]. He and his famous son Mardonius (from a marriage to Darius' sister, Elamite *Raduš-dukda* [?], married to Darius' daughter Artazostra, Hdt. 6,43 and passim) are known to us from the Elamite tablets from Persepolis [3; 10. 106f., 364].

[4] Son of Darius I and → Artystone, commander in Xerxes' campaign against Greece (Hdt. 7,72).

[5] Governor of Babylonia at the time of Darius [2] II, perhaps – then in another role – identical to the commander in the army of → Artaxerxes [2] II (Xen. An. 1,7,12) [7; 9].

1 P.-A. Beaulieu, The Reign of Nabonidus, King of Babylon, 1989 2 Briant 3 M. Brosius, Women in Ancient

Persia, 1996 4 A.K. GRAYSON, Assyrian and Babylonian Chronicles, 1975 5 R.G. KENT, Old Persian, ²1953 6 A. KUHRT, Babylonia from Cyrus to Xerxes, in: CAH IV², 1988, 112–138 7 W. RÖLLIG, s.v. Gubaru, RLA 3, 671f. 8 R. SCHMITT, Zur babylon. Version der Bisutun-Inschr., in: AfO 27, 1980, 106–126 9 M.W. STOLPER, Mesopotamia, 482–330 B.C., in: CAH VI², 1994, 234–260 10 J. WIESEHÖFER, Das ant. Persien, 1994. J.W.

Godigisclus (Godigisel, Godegisel). Burgundian king, son of → Gundiok, lived from *c.* AD 474 in Geneva, always in the shadow of his older brother → Gundobad (Ennod. Vita Epiphanii 174). In 500, together with the king of the Franks, Chlodovechus (→ Clovis I), he defeated Gundobad at Dijon, but in 501 he was killed by the latter when Chlodovechus had to turn against the Visigoths (Greg. Tur. Franc. 2,32f; Chron. min. 2,234 MOMMSEN).

PLRE 2, 516 (Godigisel 2); STEIN, Spätröm. R., 2, 144 with n. 2. M.MEI. and ME.STR.

Godigiselus King of the Vandal Hasdingians around AD 400, father of → Gundericus and → Geisericus. Under G. the Hasdingians moved from Pannonia via Vindelicia and Noricum to the Rhine-Neckar area where G. fell in battle in 406 fighting the Franks, who were defending the Roman Rhine border (Greg. Tur. Franc. 2,9); Procop. (Vand. 3,3,2; 22f.) and Theophanes (5931; 6026) erroneously report that G. led the Hasdingians to Spain.

PLRE 2, 515f.; F. CLOVER, The Late Roman West and the Vandals, 1993; CHR. COURTOIS, Les vandales et l'Afrique, 1955, esp. 392f.; H.-J. DIESNER, Das Vandalenreich, 1966, 23f. M.MEI. and ME.STR.

Godomarus (Gundomarus, Gundomar). Son of → Gundobad, after the death of his brother Sigismundus (Greg. Tur. Franc. 3,6) in AD 524 he was elevated to the position of king of the Burgundians (Chron. min. 2,235 MOMMSEN). He defeated the Franks under Chlodomer at Vienne on 25 June 524, entered in 530 into an alliance with → Amalasuntha and bought the freedom of prisoners of war (CIL XII 2584). In 533 the Franks under Chlothachar and Childebert defeated G. at Autun and in 534 divided up the Burgundian kingdom amongst themselves (Greg. Tur. Franc. 3,11). PLRE 2, 517 G. (2). M.MEI. and ME.STR.

Gods, names of

A. GREEK AND ITALIAN NAMES OF GODS – SUBSIDIARY TRADITION B. AGE, EXPLANATION, INTERPRETATIONS IN ANTIQUITY C. SUBSIDIARY FORMS D. SEVERAL EXAMPLES E. LATER NAMES OF GODS

A. GREEK AND ITALIAN NAMES OF GODS – SUBSIDIARY TRADITION

Although important Greek gods or heroes were adopted in Italy (including Etruria), the Italian names of gods are as a rule different from the Greek ones, cf. Ἄρης : *Mārs* (Etruscan *Laran*); Ἀφροδίτη : *Venus* (Etruscan *Turan*); Ἑρμῆς : *Mercurius* (Etruscan *Turms*), whose traits have a parallel in Vedic *Pūṣán-* [8]; or Ἥφαιστος : *Vulcānus* (Etruscan *Śeθlans*). There are formal correspondences or similarities only in the case of the subsidiary tradition of Greek names of gods or heroes in Italy. The shared religion of the Italians and Etruscans at the beginning of the 1st millennium BC does not always allow us to determine in which language the adoption took place – in Latin (for the name Apollo see below, Πολυδεύκης : Latin *Pollux*, ancient Latin dat. *Podlouqei*) or in Etruscan (e.g. Ἄρτε/αμις : Etruscan *Aritimi*, *Artumes*; Ἡρακλῆς : Etruscan *Hercle* and, assuming, Latin *Herculēs*, ancient Latin *hercle*, Oscan *herekleís*; Περσεφόνη : Etruscan *Φersipnai*, *Φersipnei* [5. 292]). Greek names of gods could also be translated (e.g. *Dīs* : Πλοῦτος) or adapted (*Lātōna*, *Morta* from Λᾱτώ, Μοῖρα). Italian names of gods are also passed down in Etruscan, cf. Etruscan *Menelarua*, *Neθuns*, *Seluans*, *Tivs*, *Uni* from Latin Faliscan (or Umbrian) *Minerua*, Latin Umbrian *Neptūnus*, Latin *Siluānus*, Latin *Dīus*, **Iūnī* (see below).

B. AGE, EXPLANATION, INTERPRETATIONS IN ANTIQUITY

The age of the names of gods, that does not absolutely correspond to that of the respective god (because Indo-European or pre-Indo-European gods are renamed), can be estimated to some extent by the degree to which they can be understood. The following can be differentiated: a) Greek and Latin names of gods that are etymologically related; b) single-language names of gods that prove to be Indo-European (or consisting of Indo-European material) or c) *ex Graeco* or *Latino ipso* are understandable, even if they are not based on Indo-European common nouns; d) utterly uninterpretable names of gods. As a rule, names under d) are ancient (of pre-Greek or pre-Italian origin), names under a) are older than those under b)-c); the latter are often hard to distinguish.

For a) cf. Ζεύς : *Iuppiter*, *Diēspiter* (Indo-European **di̯eu̯-* 'Sky', Vedic *dyáuṣ pitā́*), Ἥλιος : *Sōl* (re **seh₂u̯el-* or **sh₂u̯ol-* 'Sun'), Ἠώς : *Aurōr-a* (**h₂usos-* 'Dawn') in comparison with Etruscan *Tinia*, *Uśil*, *Θesan*; also Ἑστία 'Hearth': *Vesta*, perhaps also Δῖα (Mycenaean *di-wi-ja*, Pamphylian ΔιϜια) : *Dea Dia* (**di̯u̯ih₂-*) and, with different suffixes, Διώνη and *Diāna*.

The Greek names of gods tend to belong to d) rather than to b)-c). For b) cf. Ἥρα (Mycenaean *e-ra*), if from **i̯ēr-* [4. 67] 'Year, time of flourishing'; Διόνυσος, if from **diu̯ós sūnos* 'of Zeus/Heaven's Son' [6. 665]; attempts to interpret Demeter or Poseidon as 'Mother Earth' (Δᾶ-μάτηρ) or 'Master of Earth' (*Ποσι-δᾶ-ων) are hardly convincing. To c) cf. Ἀπέλλων (see below), Ἑρμῆς, -έας (Mycenaean *e-ma-a₂*), if related to ἕρμα 'Support', Ἄρης (Mycenaean *a-re*), if related to ἄρος · βλάβος. For d) cf. e.g. Ἀθήνᾱ, Ἀθηνᾶ (Mycenaean *a-ta-na*), Ἥφαιστος, Ἄρτε/αμις (Mycenaean *a-te/i-mi-*, cf. Lydian *Artimuś*). On the other hand, most local epicleses of alphabetic Greek that relate to an aspect of the deity or a place of worship belong to b) or c). For b) cf. e.g. Demeter Χαμύνη (χαμαί, εὐνή) 'Having the earth as a bed' [7], for c) cf. e.g. Apollo Αἰγλάτας (αἴγλη 'Shine'). Some of them were originally names of gods, e.g. Ἐν(ν)οδία ('Being/going on the way'), epiclesis of Hecate and of Artemis, was originally a Thessalian goddess. In Mycenaean names of gods are attested that are in keeping with b) even if they describe pre-Greek deities (several *po-ti-ni-ja /Potnia-/* especially in Crete, the *po-ti-ni-ja i-qe-ja /(ʰ)ikkʷeiā-/*'Mistress of the Horses'), *do-po-ta* (from **doms-potā-*) 'Master of the house', *ko-ma-we-te-ja /komāweteiā-/*'Long-haired woman'; also to c), cf. dat. *ti-ri-se-ro-e /Tris-ʰērōʰei/*'To the three-times hero', Mycenaean *si-to-po-ti-ni-ja* (cf. Σιτώ in Sicily); others are pre-Greek, e.g. *e-ri-nu* or *e-nu-wa-ri-jo*, dat. *pa-ja-wo-ne* (cf. Ἐρινύς, Ἐνυάλιος or Παιᾶν as names for Ares or Apollo), *e-ne-si-da-o-ne /-dāʰonei/*.

The names of the more important Latin gods tend to belong to b) and/or c) rather than to d) and correspond to conspicuous traits of the respective Greek gods. To b) and c) cf. *Cerēs* 'Growth' (**kerh₁-es-*, cf. *crēscō*), *Diāna* (see above), *Iūnō* 'The lively one' (see below), *Mercurius* (cf. *merx* 'Ware'), *Minerua* 'Having a powerful spirit' (from **menes-u̯ā-*, cf. Greek μένος, Glossian *promeneruat : promonet*) [3. 111f.], *Neptūnus* 'Master of moisture' (**nebʰ-* 'Be moist', Greek νεφέλη), *Venus* 'Charm' (ancient Indian *vánas-* 'Charm'); also most indigenous names of gods, cf. *Iānus* (: *iānus* 'Door'), *Sēmō* 'He who causes sowing' (: *sēmen*), *Volcānus* (if re ancient Indian *ulkā́* 'Flame'), the names of gods on *–(V)no/ā-* (*Siluānus* re *silua* 'Forest'), especially the one on *-ōna* (*Bellōna*, *Duellōna* re *bellum*, *Pōmōna* re *pōma*), the double names (e.g. *Anna Perenna* 'Beginning and end of the year') and the designations (e.g. *Lubentīna* re Venus, *L(o)ucīna* re Juno, cf. *lubet* 'It pleases', *lūcus* 'Grove', or *[Māter] Mātūta*, goddess of the early morning, cf. *mātūrus* 'in good time', Hittite *meḫur* 'Time' [1. 63ff.]). Also in the area outside Latin Italy, cf. Oscan *Herentas* (= Venus, cf. *herest* 'Wishes') or Picenian, Umbrian *Cupra mater* (cf. Latin *cupiō*?). To d) cf. *Mārs*, *Sāturnus* or the Italian names of gods *Fērōnia Lar(ēs)* from **Lasēs* (family gods, hardly from *lārua* 'Evil spirit' or from Etruscan *Lasa*), *Falacer*, the names of gods in *-mnus* (*Vertumnus*, *Vitumnus* etc.) or the name *Grādīuus* of Mars.

Ancient attempts at explanation were mostly unsuccessful, cf. the absurd interpretations in Plato (Crat. 401bff., if meant seriously), in Hesiod (Theog. 188f., Ἀφροδίτην / ἀφρογενέα 'Foam-born', re ἀφρός 'Foam') or in the Etymologicum magnum. Cf. also Festus' interpretations of *Mātūta* (re *mānes*: *-am antiqui ob bonitatem appellabant*), of *Sāturnus* (*ab satu*) or of *Grādīuus* (*a gradiendo in bello*).

C. Subsidiary forms

In several names of gods subsidiary forms are attested (e.g. *Iuppiter / Diēspiter*). Some are dialectal (e.g. eastern Greek Ἄρτε/ιμις / western Greek Ἄρταμις; Attic Ποσειδῶν, Mycenaean dat. *po-se-da-o-ne /Poseidāʰonei/* / Arcadian Ποσοιδᾶν / Doric Ποτιδᾶν; 'Elean' Ζᾶνες 'Zeus statuettes' alongside Ζην-), others are based on phonetic fluctuations in foreign names of gods (e.g. Mycenaean *e-re-u-ti-ja /Eleutʰia/*, Laconian ⟨Ελευθ/σια⟩, Cretan ⟨Ελευθυια⟩, Homeric Εἰλείθυια and others), on folk etymology (Ἀπόλλων see below, *Prōserpina* instead of **Persepona* based on *prōserpō*): in both cases there are attempts to clarify the name of the god (or part of it, e.g. –φόνη, -φόνεια instead of –φασσα, -φαττα in the name of Persephone). Often however they remain an enigma, e.g. *Māuors*, *Sīspita* alongside *Mārs*, *Sōspes*. Other subsidiary forms are based on suffix varieties (Ἀθάνα / -αία, Πλοῦτος / -ων, *Angerōna* /*-nia*, *Mellōna* /*-nia*).

D. Several examples

Apollo: originally Ἀπέλλων (Doric, Cypriot dat. *a-pe-i-lo-ni*, name of the month Ἀπελλαῖος) related to ἀπέλλα (·σηκοί, ἐκκλησίαι), cf. Oscan *Apellun*; then Ἀπόλλων (based on ἀπόλλυμι) that was passed into Latin (*Apollō*) and, assuming this, into Etruscan (*Ap[u]lu*) [2; 3. 126⁷⁹].

Asclepius: The name Ἀσκλᾶπιός is considered to be pre-Greek because of the sound fluctuations in its local variants (Αι-/ Αἰ-, κ/χ, π/β); Αἰγλᾶπιός (Laconia) is based on crossing with Αἴγλα (αἴγλη 'Shine'), the name of his mother; the variant Αἰσκλᾶπιός (Epidaurus, Troezen) is adopted from Latin as *Aesculapius* (gen. *Aisclapi* 3rd cent. BC).

Juno: *Iūnō* is a subsidiary formation with an 'individualizing' *-ōn-* suffix related to **Iūn-ī* (Latin *iūnī-x* feminine 'Young, lively' with the basic stem **iūn-*, cf. Vedic gen. *yū́naḥ* 'of the boy'); the latter must be the original Italian form that was adopted as Etruscan *Uni* [3. 108ff.].

E. Later names of gods

From the Hellenistic period onwards, abstract names of gods developed (Τύχη, *Fortūna*). Oriental gods with their respective names, which were previously attested sparsely were adopted: Egyptian (Ἶσις, Σέ/άραπις), Indo-Iranian (Μίθρας: ancient Indian *mitrá-*, Avestian *miθra-*), from Asia Minor (Κυβέλη/Κυβήβη), Phoenician (Ἄδωνις/Ἄδων, Thracian-Phrygian (Σα/εβάζιος, Κάβειροι). These names were reproduced in Latin according to the usual substitution rules (e.g. *Cybelē/Cybēbē*, but *Mithrās/Mithrēs*).

1 H. EICHNER, Die Etym. von hethit. *mehur*, in: Münchener Stud. zur Sprachwiss. 31, 1973, 53–107, 63ff. 2 A. HEUBECK, Noch einmal zum Namen des Apollon, in: Glotta 65, 1987, 179–182 3 H. RIX, Rapporti onomastici fra il panteone etrusco e quello romano, in: G. COLONNA et al. (ed.), Gli etruschi e Roma, 1981, 104–126 4 F. R. SCHRÖDER, Hera, in: Gymnasium 63, 1956, 57–78 5 C. DE SIMONE, Die griech. Entlehnungen im Etr. 2, 1968 6 O. SZEMERÉNYI, review of CHANTRAINE 1–2, in: Gnomon 43, 1972, 641–675 7 A. VEGAS, Χαμύνη, ein Beiname der Demeter in Olympia, in: Glotta 70, 1992, 166–180 8 C. WATKINS, An Indo-European God of Exchange and Reciprocity?, in: G. CARDONA et al. (ed.), Indo-European and Indo-Europeans, 1970, 345–354 (= Id., Selected Writings, 1994, 446–455).

L. BAUMBACH, Greek Religion in the Bronze Age, in: SMEA 20, 1979, 143–160; BRUCHMANN; P. CHANTRAINE, Reflexions sur les noms des dieux helléniques, in: AC 22, 1953, 65–78; G.E. DUNKEL, Vater Himmels Gattin, in: Die Sprache 34, 1988–1990, 1–26; W. MEID, Das Suffix *-no-* in Götternamen, in: BN 8, 1957, 71–108, 113–126; RADKE (useful as collection of references); H. USENER, Götternamen, 1896. J.G.-R.

Goes see → Magic

Gogarene (Γωγαρηνή; *Gōgarēnḗ*), Str. 11,14,4f.; Ptol. 5,12,4; χωρίον μεταξὺ Κόλχων καὶ Ἰβήρων ανατολικῶν, Steph. Byz. 216; Armenian *Gugarkʿ*, AŠX 5,22 [1]). Fertile plateau in ancient times (olive-growing, etc.) in the Little Caucasus south-east of Cyrus bend, possibly corresponding to modern southern Georgia and parts of northern Armenia; frontier district between Armenia and Iberia with changing ownership: in the 5th/4th cents. BC G. belonged to Armenia, in the 3rd cent. to Iberia, in the 2nd cent. G. was an Armenian frontier province as an Iberian territory with a prince from Gugarkʿ; around the time of Christ the region belonged to Iberia again, at the end of the 1st cent. AD it went to Armenia, and in 387 G. belonged fully to Iberia.

1 R.H. HEWSEN (ed.), The Geography of Ananias of Širak (AŠX), 1992, 200ff., map XXII 2 TAVO B VI 14. A.P.-L.

Golan see → Batanaea

Golasecca culture Chronologically, the Golasecca culture (GC) encompasses the 12th to the 4th cents. BC, with the proto-GC (12th–11th cents. BC) regarded as the first stage that was still Bronze Age; spatially the GC stretches from the source region of the Ticino via Lago Maggiore and Lago di Como to the Po. This culture which can mainly be understood through tomb inventories is divided up into three groups that initially all favoured cremation. The western group with the important necropoleis Sesto Calende and Castelletto Ticino at the finding place Golasecca that has given its name to the culture is distinguished, among other things, by rich warrior tombs and should be linked with the → Insubres. The eastern group had its centre around Como-Cà Morta and is identified as the core of the Orobii. The northern group around Bellinzona (Cerinasca, Molinazzo; Giubiasco) is regarded as the core territory of the → Lepontii. The last is distinguished from the others by the transition to body burial from the 6th cent. BC. Stamp-decorated clay vessels, biconical or also partly in the shape of birds, are among the physical legacy. There were particularly close ties with the → Este culture, as well as with the → Hallstatt culture and with Etruria (→ Etruscan, Etruria). The Celtic invasion signified the end of the GC in the 4th cent. BC. → Comum; → Etruscan Archaeology; → Veneti; → Villanova culture

M. PRIMAS, Die südschweizerischen Grabfunde der älteren Eisenzeit und ihre Chronologie, 1970; L. PAULI, Studien zur G., 1971; R. DE MARINIS, La cultura di Golasecca: Insubri, Orobi e Leponzi, in: G. PUGLIESE CARRATELLI (ed.) Italia omnium terrarum alumna, 1988, 159–247. C.KO.

Gold

I. GENERAL II. HISTORICAL OVERVIEW

I. GENERAL

A. GOLD AND GOLD DEPOSITS B. GOLD EXTRACTION C. TECHNIQUES OF GOLD PROCESSING D. METHODS OF MATERIAL ANALYSIS

A. GOLD AND GOLD DEPOSITS

Gold is a soft precious metal that can be shaped well mechanically and so can be worked easily into sheets and wires, but it has a relatively high melting point at 1063°C that makes casting difficult. It is relatively rare in nature where it is present in the form of gold aggregates in solid rock from which it is extracted through mining methods, or it is present in the form of gold particles or grains in sandy deposits of weathered primary rock, from which it can be separated out through gold panning because of its higher specific weight. The gold extracted from river sands is not pure gold but contains to a greater or lesser extent large proportions of silver (Plin. HN 33,80), copper, platinum and elements related to platinum whose concentration can provide indications of the site of the deposit. The silver content can rise to 30%, and the copper content to 5%. Gold, like the other metals, is discussed in detail by Pliny, whose topics include not just natural historical and technical aspects but also cultural, social and economic historical matters (Plin. HN 33,1–85).

The gold deposits in the Mediterranean Sea area are limited to some few regions. In Greece in ancient and classical times the deposits on the island of Siphnos (up to 516 BC; Hdt. 3,57; Paus. 10,11,2) and in Thrace (Hdt. 6,46f.; Thuc. 4,105,1; Pangaeum Mountains: Xen. Hell. 5,2,17; Str. 7 fr. 34) were particularly important; the wealth of the Lydians was also based on the alluvial gold that was extracted in relatively large quantities from the Pactolus, a river in Asia Minor, during the 6th cent. BC (Str. 13,4,5). Philip II of Macedonia re-organized the gold mines in Thrace after 356 BC and was able in this way to boost their yield considerably (Diod. Sic. 16,8,6f.), and Philip V also attempted at the beginning of the 2nd cent. BC to increase his income by reactivating gold extraction (Liv. 39,24,2). The gold mines in Nubia supplied the Ptolemies with gold that was also needed for minting (Diod. Sic. 3,12–14). In the western Mediterranean region it was the rivers with their sources in the Alps and the Pyrenees in particular that supplied gold (Str. 4,2,1; 4,6,12; Ath. 233d). The Celts had such large quantities of gold available to them that some was used for jewellery and some for votive offerings; the temple treasures of Tolosa, for instance, that were plundered in 106 BC by the *cos.* Q. Servilius Caepio were famous (Diod. Sic. 5,27; Str. 4,1,13). Even Caesar was able during his campaigns in Gaul to sell so much gold from the spoils of war in Italy and in the provinces that the price of gold decreased sharply (Suet. Iul. 54,2). In the Roman period the most important centres of gold extraction were in the Spanish provinces, especially in the south-west, in the province of Baetica (Diod. Sic. 5,36,4; 5,37,2; Str. 3,2,3; 3,2,8f.; 3,4,2), and in the north-west where the exploitation of the alluvial gold deposits began under Augustus (Flor. Epit. 2,33; Plin. HN 33,76–78). In Italy gold mining had to a large extent already stopped in the Augustan period (Vercellae: Str. 5,1,12; Plin. HN 33,78); during the Principate, new provinces, Britannia (Tac. Agr. 12,6), Noricum and Dacia, then also supplied relatively large quantities of gold. Today the mining district of Dolaucothi in Wales still gives us a good impression of Roman gold mining.

B. Gold extraction

Pliny mentions three methods of extracting gold: panning the river sand, mining and open-cut mining (Plin. HN 33,66–78). The methods used by the Romans in north-western Spain to exploit alluvial gold were technically particularly extravagant. Above the gold deposits, large quantities of water that were often brought in via pipes more than ten kilometres in length were first collected in tanks; when these were opened, the water fell on the top layers of soil and washed it away. Through a continuous water stream, the deposit was then washed out and the heavy metal was caught in ditches. To accelerate this process, the miners also forced the caving in of entire mountains by digging under them and then the water was fed over the rock rubble. Through these activities, vast mountain landscapes in north-western Spain were changed by the Romans and this is still obvious today. Techniques for removing the silver and the copper from the gold with the goal of obtaining a purer, higher quality gold had been known since the middle of the 2nd millennium BC, but had only been used to a relatively great extent from the Hellenistic-Roman period. Diodorus (3,14,3f.) describes a method of such kind for the gold mines in Nubia.

C. Techniques of gold processing

Gold was either processed in the composition in which it had been extracted or as an alloy with other metals. In antiquity the usual alloy element was silver that could be mixed with the gold completely so that it was possible to achieve all the mixing ratios between pure gold and pure silver. Alloys that consist of about equal parts of gold and silver were called *electron* (Plin. HN 33,80). The addition of silver increases the hardness and in this way the durability of gold, changes its colour to a lighter golden yellow and decreases the value of the metal. Gold was processed by casting or by mechanical shaping through hammering, rolling, drawing or moulding. The high melting temperature and the preciousness of gold meant that initially only small pendants, amulets and statuettes were cast. More widespread than casting was, however, the hammering out of gold into sheets and foils with which other materials like stone, ceramics or wood were covered or that were laid on other metals. According to Pliny, one *uncia* of gold (27.3 g) could in this way be used to make 750 small quadratic gold leaves (*bratteae*) with a lateral length of *c.* 7.4 cm and a weight in each case of less than 0.04 g (Plin. HN 33,61). A further technique applied in antiquity was granulation. Experimental investigations show that the little balls could be made by cutting off fine gold shreds from sheets or wires that were put into charcoal powder and melted. The granulation balls and the base were combined at high temperatures, either by applying a copper salt or using the surface formation of gold carbide, which also lowered the melting point. Aside from the formation of gold compounds by welding using melting-point-lowering compounds, soldering techniques were also common in antiquity, whereby low-melting silver-copper or gold-silver-copper alloys and lead-tin solders were used.

The use of gold in other materials goes back to the early cultures of the Middle East when objects from the most varied of materials were overlaid with gold foils of varying strength, with the gold leaf either directly overlaid or combined with the base through an organic binding agent. Thin gold foils were also hammered onto metal objects and combined with these through heating. In Roman times fire-gilding became more important, and in this way either gold amalgam, made through rubbing in gold powder with mercury, or a gold foil coated with mercury, was put on the metal that was to be gilded (Plin. HN 33,64f.; 33,100). By applying heat, the mercury evaporated, and the gold bonded in this way with the base. Gold objects were decorated by chasing, engraving and working; a microscopic analysis of the traces of tools can provide revealing information about the working technique.

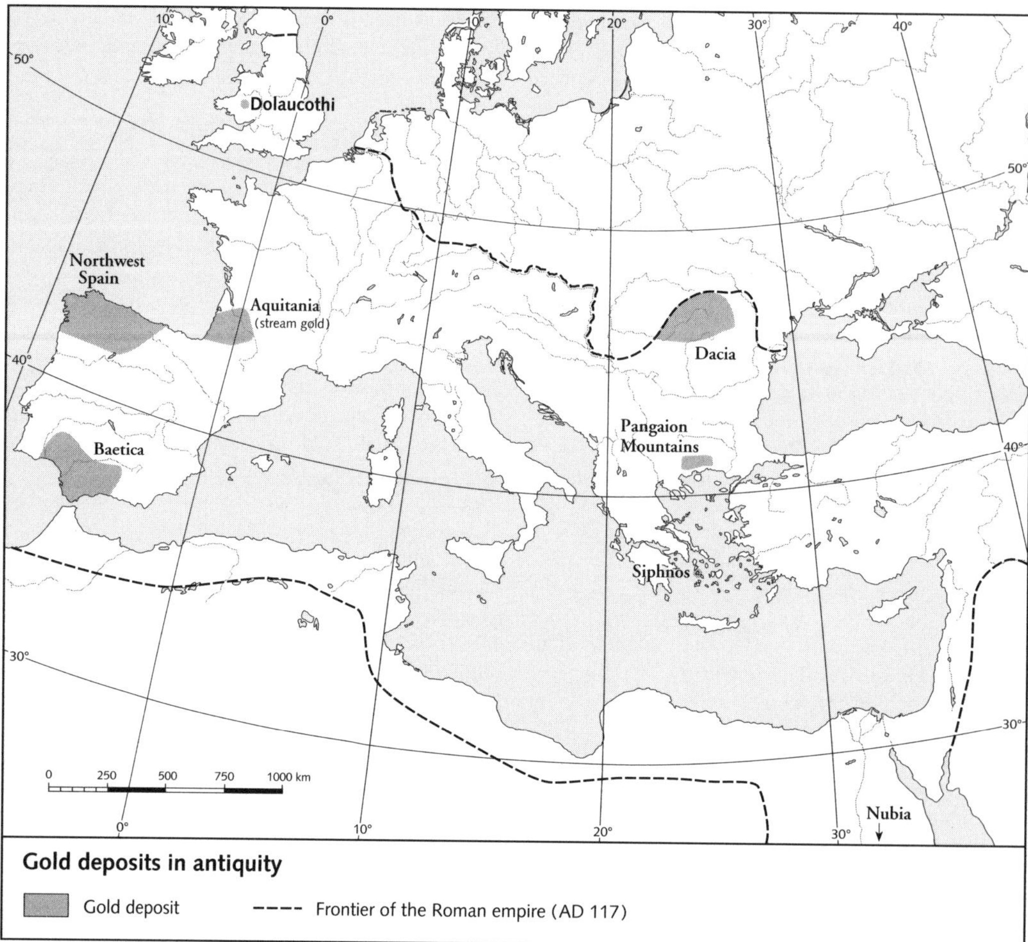

D. Methods of material analysis

With regard to the technology of ancient gold alloys, recent material investigations have been carried out particularly with the help of scanning electron microscopy. In the meantime there have also been numerous analyses of the composition of gold objects; for this purpose several methods are available that do not require any taking of samples, for instance activation analysis, X-ray fluorescence analysis or more lavish techniques of the PIXE kind (Proton Induced X-Ray Emission); here, however, it must be considered that the composition of the surface can be changed by lixiviation in the soil. If a particularly precise analysis is required, methods that manage with very small samples, atom absorption analysis or emission spectral analysis, for instance, are preferred. The material analysis provides information about the type of alloy whose silver and copper content can fluctuate within wide limits, about the origin of the gold – whether it be from mining or river deposits – about the region of origin of the gold – although there are limits to this –, about economic developments, for instance the worsening in the composition of gold coins, or about the genuineness of gold objects, through comparison with objects whose origin is certain or through providing evidence of chemical elements that can be proven in the gold by modern processing technologies. JO.R.

II. Historical overview

A. Middle East and Egypt B. Celtic-Germanic cultural area C. Greece D. Italy
III. Economy and politics IV. Literature and myth

A. Middle East and Egypt

In the Middle East and Egypt gold already played a special part in prehistory. There were deposits of gold in Egypt and Nubia, and it was imported to Mesopotamia from there as well as via the Iranian highlands and the Gulf region. Objects made of gold were primarily concentrated in the hands of the rulers and in the temples. Gold was the most prestigious metal and it served particularly as representation. It was coveted as booty and tribute, was important as trading capital and a method of payment and was very suitable for accumulation. Egyptian sources report of huge quantities of gold with which various pharaohs endowed the gods (among others 15,000 kg for the Temple of Amun donated by

Thutmosis III [2. 727]). In the private sphere gold played a minor role. In its shaped form gold was mostly used for jewellery, vessels, weapons/tools, reliefs, statues/statuettes or for decoration (e.g. of furniture); it could also be the script base for documents. Gold-finds from the tombs of the kings of Ur (middle of the 3rd millennium BC), from the tomb of the pharaoh Tutankhamon in western Thebes (18th dynasty, *c.* 1346–1336 BC) and from the royal crypts in Nimrud (9th/8th cents. BC), for example, attest to the high status involved in controlling the material. Both the melting technologies and just about all gold-smithing technologies practised today can already be proven for the middle of the 3rd millennium BC in the Middle East, particularly hammering, beating, plating, chasing and engraving, casting, inlay-decorating, soldering and welding, granulation, filigree (*à jour* or on a solid underlay). Only for *émail cloisonné* and *niello* techniques is the first evidence from Egypt.

→ Elektron

1 P. R. S. Moorey, Ancient Mesopotamian Materials and Industries, 1994, 217–232 2 L. Störk et al., s.v. G., LÄ 2, 725–755.

R.W.

B. Celtic-Germanic cultural area

From the end of the 3rd millennium BC gold was a common material in central Europe used in almost all periods for valuable tomb objects, particularly jewellery. In the central German and western European → princes' tombs of the early Bronze Age (1st half of the 2nd millennium BC) gold was also used for sumptuous objects (axes etc.) and vessels.

Gold vessels play a big role in the region of the Nordic Bronze Age (Denmark, northern Germany; 10th–8th cents.BC) in → hoard finds as cult objects, and the same applies to the 'gold hat' in southern German finds. At least in the north gold had to be imported, as there were no deposits. During this period the alloying of gold begins (additions of silver and copper), and we know of the first gold-smithing workshops (→ Ingots, touchstones, raw pieces).

In the Celtic late Hallstatt/early La Tène period (6th/5th cents. BC) most of the gold finds again come from the tombs of princes as evidence of wealth and power, e.g. neck rings (→ Torques), drinking bowls, decoration of weapons (→ Swords, Daggers, → Helmets etc.). The gold objects partly show strong Mediterranean influences (imitation of granulation, filigree technique etc.). Throughout the entire La Tène period (5th–1st cents. BC) hoard finds with jewellery (neck rings) and also Celtic coins (→ Regenbogenschüsselchen) are widespread. In the Germanic cultural groups of the pre-Roman and Roman period gold does not play a significant role, aside from the rich tombs of princes. Tombs of goldsmiths (→ Tools, touchstones) are known from the Roman period and the early Middle Ages.

→ Germanic archaeology; → Crafts; → Hochdorf; → Celtic archaeology; → Vix; → Waldalgesheim

A. Hartmann, Prähistor. Goldfunde aus Europa vol. 1, 1970; vol. 2, 1982; J. Driehaus, Zum Problem merowingerzeitlicher Goldschmiede, 1972; B. Hardmeyer, Prähistor. G. Europas im 3. und 2. Jt. v.Chr., 1976; Ch. Eluère, Das G. der Kelten, 1987; V. Pingel s.v. Goldgefäße, RGA 12/1998, 327–333.

V.P.

C. Greece

In Greece and in the northern and north-eastern bordering areas, individual gold objects can already be proven for the late 4th millennium BC. Towards the end of the 3rd millennium, in this area too, particularly in the region of the rich gold deposits of Thrace, with individual regional focal points in the Dacian and Scythian area, gold starts to be widely used in the manufacture of jewellery and vessels, large numbers of which are extant from hoard finds. In the middle of the 2nd millennium the production of gold vessels was highly developed in this area. As tomb objects show, the Mycenaean world had a great wealth of jewellery and drinking vessels made of gold; consumer goods and weapons often have golden decorations. Gold goblets or small gold dishes show figured scenes made with chasing work, for instance the two gold goblets from the tholos tomb at Vaphio (*c.* 1500 BC). Representations of bull catching; in Mycenae the faces of dead kings were covered with golden death masks. On clay tablets from Pylos and Knossos golden vessels and offerings of gold are recorded on several occasions. This wide range of artefacts made of gold is reflected in the epics of Homer which often mention the precious metal (Il. 9,122ff.; 23,196; 23,219; 23,253; 23,269; 23,614; 23,796; Od. 1,136f.; 1,142; 3,40f.; 3,425f.; 3,435ff.; 4,52f.; 4,58; 4,615f.; 7,90f.; 7,100; 8,430f.; 8,440; 13,11; 13,136; 13,218; 17,91f.; 18,293ff.). From the Dark Ages to the end of the classical period gold was a rare metal in Greece that was only used to a small extent in the manufacture of jewellery or crockery (Ath. 231bff.). The gold-smithing trade reached a particularly high point in the classical period through the development of diverse decorating techniques in the production of gold jewellery. In sculpture gold was used for the monumental gold-ivory statues of the 5th cent. BC (Paus. 1,24,5–7; 5,11; Plut. Pericles 13,14; 31,2–5); for the statue of Athena Parthenos 40 talents of gold are said to have been processed that were probably removable especially as parts of its garment and could therefore be counted by Pericles as among the financial reserves of Athens (Thuc. 2,13,5).

D. Italy

In Italy there are hardly any gold finds extant from the prehistoric period; only with the Etruscans did the processing of gold into jewellery objects and vessels commence in the 7th cent. BC; in the techniques of chasing work and granulation, great perfection was achieved quickly and impressive examples of this are the gold jewellery from the Tomba Regolini-Galassi in Cerveteri or from the Tomba Bernardini in Praeneste

(1st half of the 7th cent. BC). Bronze statues were gilded from the early Principate period onwards. The use of mercury in the gilding of silver or copper is already attested in Vitruvius (Vitr. De arch. 7,8,4). According to Pliny, Nero had a statue of Alexander gilded, which was still rather unusual, as the later removal of the gold shows (Plin. HN 34,63f.). In the period that followed, however, portraits of rulers were increasingly gilded, for instance the equestrian statue of Marcus Aurelius in Rome and the portrait busts *of principes* from Brescia from the 3rd cent. AD. A goldsmith (*aurifex brattiarius*) at work is represented pictorially on a relief in the Vatican (room no. 124), a small wall-painting in the house of the Vettii in Pompeii shows Erotes in a gold-smithing workshop. JO.R.

III. Economy and politics

The political and economic importance of gold in antiquity was based on its role as a means of accumulating wealth as well as on it being a coin metal; in the Greek period the poleis hoarded not just silver coins but also unminted gold in temples. This was often in votive offerings or decor and costumes for holding festivals (Ath.: Thuc. 2,13,2–6). Before the 3rd Punic War 17,410 Roman pounds of gold (5703 kg) were stored in the *aerarium*. The most important coins of the Greek poleis and the Roman Republic, the drachma and denarius, however, consisted of silver, and so ancient currencies up to the Principate period can be regarded essentially as silver currencies. During Hellenism the minting of gold coins was limited, to a large extent, to the period of Alexander, who after the capture of Persepolis had the gold treasures of the Persians at his disposal (Diod. Sic. 17,71,1), and to the kingdom of the Ptolemies. From the time of Caesar onwards, a gold coin, the *aureus*, was minted regularly; its weight was reduced by Nero to *c.* 7.25 g. After the crisis in the Roman precious-metal currency in the 3rd cent. AD, Constantine created the *solidus*, a new gold coin whose weight (4.5 g) and fine metal content remained stable until the early Byzantine period. Gold was an important element of monarchical representation of the Hellenistic kings (Ath. 197c ff. on the splendour of Ptolemy II), and gold wreaths were preferred gifts of honour for the rulers (Plin. HN 33,38; 33,54) in the Hellenistic period and later in the Principate. In Roman society, the possession of gold bestowed social prestige: gold jewellery was an important status symbol for women, as their role in the revocation of the *lex Oppia* of 215 BC makes clear (Liv. 34,1–8,3). For rich Romans golden rings and other pieces of jewellery made of gold had the same function; in Petronius, Trimalchio displays his rings and his golden arm bangle demonstratively (Petron. Sat. 32; cf. Plin. HN 33,39–41).

IV. Literature and myth

The word gold is often used metaphorically in ancient literature; in this way, Hesiod describes the oldest human race as 'golden' (χρύσεον); these people lived free of disease and worries, they did not have to work to feed themselves, as the earth made everything grow by itself (Hes. Op. 109–120; cf. Ov. Met. 1,89–112). In many contexts gold appears as the symbol for great wealth (Lucr. 2,24; 2,27f.) and as the object of greed that brings ill fortune to human beings: the desire of Midas to have everything he touched turn to gold proves disastrous for him (Aristot. Pol. 1257b 15ff.; Ov. Met. 11,100–145; cf. also Plut. Mor. 262d–263a). For this reason gold itself could be described as more harmful even than iron (Ov. Met. 1,141; cf. Lucr. 5,1113ff.; 5,1423f.); the first minting of gold coins is considered by Pliny to be *scelus* (Plin. HN 33,42), as with the money and the usury connected with it, it was the origin of avarice (*avaritia*) and even of a hunger for gold (*fames auri*). In this context the murder of M'. Aquillius, into whose mouth Mithridates had gold poured, can be understood as a symbolic act (Plin. HN 33,48; cf. App. Mithr. 21). The ban on precious-metal minting in Sparta was consistently regarded as positive, as so many crimes like bribery and robbery had disappeared from Sparta (Plut. Lycurgus 9; cf. Xen. Lac. pol. 7), and Pliny even praises Spartacus, because he forbade the possession of gold at his camp (Plin. HN 33,49).
→ Aureus; → Aurum coronarium; → Mining; → Natural resources; → Solidus H.SCHN.

Bibliography: Blümner, Techn., 4,10ff., 110ff., 302ff.; D.L. Caroll, A Classification for Granulation in Ancient Metalwork, in: AJA 78, 1974, 33–39; D.L. Caroll, Wire Drawing in Antiquity, in: AJA 77, 1972, 321–323; P.T. Craddock, Early Metal Mining and Production, 1996; E. Folz, Einige Beobachtungen zu ant. G.- und Silberschmiedetechniken, Arch. Korrespondenzbl. 9, 1979, 213–233; J.F. Healy, Mining and Metallurgy in the Greek and Roman World, 1978; I. Lang, M. Hughes, Joining Techniques, in: W. A. Oddy (ed.), Aspects of Early Metallurgy, 1980; G. Morteani, J. P. Northover (ed.), Prehistoric Gold in Europe. Mines, Metallurgy and Manufacture, 1995; W.A. Oddy (ed.), Aspects of Early Metallurgy, 1980; Id., Gilding through the Ages. Gold. Bull. 14, 1981, 75–79; W.A. Oddy, L. Borelli Vlad, N.D. Meeks, Die Vergoldung von Bronzestatuen bei den Griechen und Römern, in: Die Pferde von San Marco, 1982, 107–112; J. Riederer, Arch. und Chemie, 1987; R.F. Tylecote, A History of Metallurgy, 1976; R.F. Tylecote, The Early History of Metallurgy in Europe, 1987; J. Wolters, Die Granulation. Geschichte und Technik einer alten Goldschmiedekunst, 1983.
Maps: P.T. Craddock, Early Metal Mining and Production, 1996; J. F. Healy, Mining and Metallurgy in the Greek and Roman World, 1978; J. Riederer, Arch. und Chemie, 1987. JO.R.

Golden Age see → Origin myths; → Period, Era

Golden Ass see → Ap(p)uleius [II 8]

Gold-ivory technique (also called Chryselephantine technique). The naked parts of a statue were primarily worked from → ivory; and the garments and hair from sheet-gold, and materials like glass, precious stones and

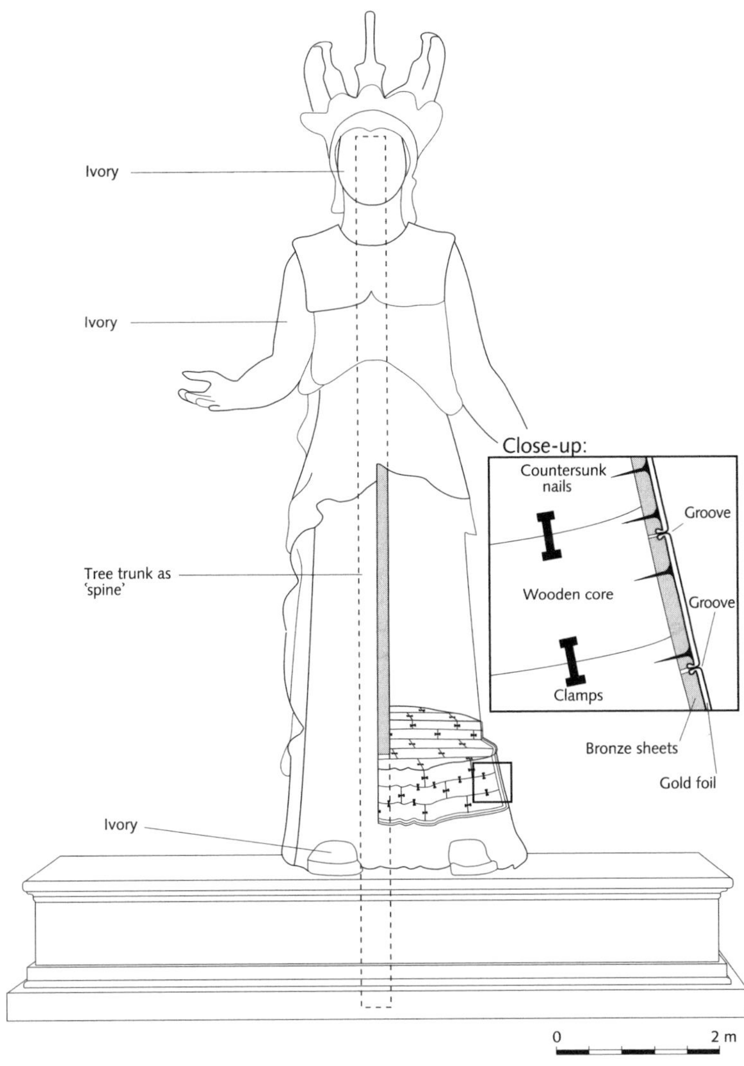

Inside view of the statue of Athena Parthenos: hypothetical reconstruction based on G.P. Stevens. According to ancient accounts, the gold foil was detachable. The indentation for the 'spine' can still be seen in the floor of the Parthenon cella. The bronze sheets and gold foil provided the artistic design of the surface.

M. HAA.

coloured metals were also used. Chryselephantine works were rare because of the value of their materials and are only extant in fragmentary form. The manufacturing technique is therefore not known in detail and appears to be mainly dependent on the size of the work. If the work was life-size, ivory was used in compact form and sheet-gold was overlaid on it, and the detail was put on using other materials (votive group in Delphi, head of Athena in Rome). Statues of enormous proportions were made in a similar manner to an → akrolithon by means of a bearing wooden scaffold or wood core whose construction, as with the manner in which ivory strips and gold plates were attached (cf. STEVENS and fig.) can be reconstructed only hypothetically. Possibly the inside was visible or could be entered for maintenance purposes (Lucian., Gallus 24 regarding the colossal Zeus image of Phidias in Olympia), and the gold plates could be removed for inspection (Thuc. 2,13 regarding the *c.* 1 ton of gold on the Athena Parthenos).

Imitations of gold-ivory technique (GT) are found in dolls made of bone with gold overlays and in partially gilded marble statues. GT had already been known in Mesopotamia since early times, but was used for secular subjects. Because of the primarily religious context, we should think of Greek GT rather in terms of an autonomous combination of → sphyrelata, → ivory carvings and Orientalizing gold sheets from the 7th cent. BC. Because, according to the testimonies of the ancient authors, almost exclusively images of gods were represented in GT, for example the cult image of Hera and statues of the Dioscuri in Argus from archaic time. Reliefs were also worked in GT (Cypselus Chest in Olympia, 6th cent. BC). The heads of a Delphic Triad (in Delphi), which should perhaps be related to the Croesus dedication, show this. The most famous works in GT were the statue of Zeus in Olympia and the Athena Parthenos in Athens by → Phidias. The workshop of Phidias in Olympia provided evidence of glass parts in the statue; on the Parthenos, painting was also used on the shield. In Hellenism, Serapis was added to the statues of the gods in GT, whilst the statues of Philip II and his family in Olympia are considered to be an exceptional self-representation. In the Imperial period gods continued to be sculpted in GT, for instance by order of Hadrian, a Zeus at the Olympieion, for Herodes Atticus a Tyche in Athens and Poseidon with Amphitrite in Corinth.

→ Akrolithon; → Sculpting, technique of; → Cypselus Chest

P. Amandry, Rapport préliminaire sur les statues chryséléphantines de Delphes, in: BCH 63, 1939, 86–119; G. P. Stevens, How the Parthenos was made, in: Hesperia 26, 1957, 350–361; C. Albizzati, s.v. criselefantina, in: EAA 2, 1959, 939–941; P. Amandry, Plaques d'or de Delphes, in: MDAI(A) 77, 1962, 35–71; N. Leipen, Athena Parthenos, a Reconstruction, 1971; Fuchs/Floren, 21–22, 394–395; W. Schiering, Die Werkstatt des Pheidias in Olympia 2, Die Werkstattfunde, OlF 18, 1991.

Literature to figure: G.P. Stevens, How the Parthenos was made, in: Hesperia 26, 1957, 350–361; N. Leipen, Athena Parthenos, a Reconstruction, 1971. R.N.

Golgi (Γολγοί; *Golgoí*). Town on Cyprus that is considered by the scholarly Alexandrian writers to be one of the main cult centres of → Aphrodite (Theoc. 15,100 and Lycophr. 589; Catull. 36,14; 64,69); its eponymous hero Golgus is considered to be the son of Aphrodite and → Adonis (Schol. Theoc. 15,100). According to Paus. 8,15,2, the sanctuary was the oldest on Cyprus; it was founded long before the establishment of the sanctuary in Paphus by Agapenor; the town itself was regarded as a colony of → Sicyon (Steph. Byz. s.v.). Since 1851 the town has been identified with a ruined settlement north-east of the village of Athienou near Nicosia; neither the excavations of the 19th cent. (summary [1. 306f.]) nor various excavations carried out since 1971 in the town area [2], in a Bronze Age temple district [3] and in a rural sanctuary outside the town (Hagios Photios) [4], have yet created certainty in this regard.

1 O. Masson, Kypriaka IX. Recherches sur les antiquités de Golgoi, in: BCH 95, 1971, 305–334 2 G. Bakalakis, Anaskaphé sto lopho Giorkous, B.A. tēs Athēainou, Kupros 1988 3 T. Dothan, A. Ben-Tor, Excavations at Athienou, Cyprus 1971–1972, 1983 F.G.

Golgotha see → Jerusalem

Gomoarius Of Germanic descent; *tribunus scutariorum* in AD 350.; a follower of → Vetranio, whom he betrayed to → Constantius [2] II. In 360 *magister militum* of the emperor → Iulianus; when the emperor removed him from office in the following spring, G. switched his allegiance to Constantius II. In 365/366, G. served as *magister militum* of the usurper → Procopius, in whose defeat G.'s switch of allegiance to → Valens played a decisive part. PLRE 1, 397f. H.L.

Gomphi (Γόμφοι; *Gómphoi*). Settlement created by synoecism in the 4th cent. BC; its location close to the modern G. (formerly Mouzaki) is verified. Together with → Metropolis, Pelinnaion, and → Tricca, G. formed the belt of fortifications of the Thessalian Hestiaeotis on the Pindus passes to Dolopia, Athamania, and Epirus. On coins from the 4th and 2nd cents., G. bears the name of Philippopolis (HN 295). Towards the end of the 3rd cent., G. was under Aetolian rule; during the wars of the early 2nd cent., it changed hands frequently, and in 186/185 BC, Philip V ultimately had to return it to the Thessalians (Liv. 39,23–26), in whose league (founded in 196 BC) G. often provided the annual chief magistrates. In 171 BC, the Roman army rested in G. after its crossing of Mt. Pindus. Caesar (B Civ. 3,80) ordered the looting of G. shortly before the battle of Pharsalus. In the Imperial period, G. became an episcopal see, thus explaining its Byzantine name of Episkopi. Under Justinian I, the town walls were rebuilt. It is likely that G. was destroyed in the course of the Slavic invasion of the 7th cent.

N. Chatzangelakis, in: AD 42, 1987, II 264f. and 43, 1988, II 253 (reports of finds); G. St. Karagiannis, Γόμφοι Επισκοπή – Μουζάκι, in: Θεσσαλικό Ημερολόγιο 9, 1986, 97–106; H. Kramolisch, Die Strategen des Thessal. Bundes, 1978, 36f.; F. Stählin, Das hellenische Thessalien, 1924, 124ff.; TIB 1, 1976, 166. HE.KR.

Gonnus, Gonni (Γόννος; *Gónnos*, Γόννοι; *Gónnoi*). Town of the → Perrhaebi, located on three hills to the north of the Peneius at the western entry to the Tempe valley. Evidence of settlement dates back to the Neolithic. In historical times, after initial domination by Larissa, the town gained in strategic importance in the course of the 4th cent. BC, following Philip II's conquest of Thessalia. It became a Macedonian fortress with a garrison and influx of Macedonian population, and experienced a period of economic bloom. After 196 BC, it was a member of the newly formed Perrhaebi league, dissolved again in 146. In the Roman imperial period, G. was part of the province of Achaea, but its location was no longer of strategic importance, and it was once again overshadowed by Larissa. There is no knowledge of any bishop.

B. Helly, Gonnoi, 1973 (with the inscriptions). MA.ER.

Goose (χήν; *chḗn*, *anser*, derived from its voice according to Varro, Ling. 5,75). Family of waterfowl found throughout the world with numerous wild species. The Mediterranean cultures knew only the bean goose (*anser fabalis*) and the larger greylag goose (*anser anser*) – which Aristotle (Hist. an. 7(8),3,593b 22 and 7(8),12,597b 30) first distinguished by size – as birds of passage (proof in Troy II and Swiss pile-dwellings). They caused considerable damage to sown fields during the migration period (cf. among others Plaut. Truc. 252; Verg. G. 1,119: *improbus anser*; Priap. 61,11). Pliny mentions their V-formation (HN 10,63), in which they supposedly forced themselves to be silent with stones in their beaks (Plut. De sollertia animalium 10 = Mor. 63,967b; De garrulitate 14 = Mor. 35.510ab; Dionysii Ixeuticon 2,19 [1. 36]; Ael. NA. 5,29). They rested in wetlands (e.g. Hom. Il. 2,460f.; 15,692; Nemesianus, Cynegetica 315). Most characteristics apply to both the wild and the domestic goose, thus also the description of the web between the toes (Aristot. Hist. an. 2,1,499a 27f.), the broad, flat gullet (2,17,509a 3–5), the resulting unpleasant voice (Aristot. Aud. 800b 22–24) and the appendages (ἀποφυάδες, Aristot. Hist. an. 2,17,509a 21). Their loud and ugly gaggling (*clangere, gingrire, gliccire, graccitare*) was disliked (among others Verg. Ecl. 9.36; Prop. 2,34,84).

The goose was justifiably regarded as shy (Aristot. Hist. an. 1,1,488b 24; Plin. HN 10.44) and was supposed to have a keen sense of smell (Lucr. 4.682f.; Serv. Aen. 8.652 = Isid. Orig. 12,7,52), with the help of which, according to legend, the Capitol in Rome was saved from the Gauls in 390 BC. Their frequent calls of contact among themselves led to their characterization as garrulous (Eubul. in Ath. 12,519a; Dionysii Ixeuticon 2,19 on the night-watch; Mart. 3,58,13). Their voracity (Varro, Rust. 3,10,5; Plin. HN 10.163) made them easy to fatten (already in Cato Agr. 89; cf. [2, 256f.]). They were caught with nets and traps (Dionysii Ixeuticon 2,19; Longus 2,12).

The somewhat smaller fox-goose (χηναλώπηξ; *chēnalṓpēx*, modern Egyptian goose, *alopochen aegyptiacus*, Aristot. Hist. an. 6,2,559b 29 and 7(8)593b 22f.; Ath. 9,395d; Plin. HN 10,56 and 166) from Egypt was known from hearsay. Aelianus ascribed the qualities of the fox to it (NA 5,30) and called the young χηναλωπηκιδεῖς (NA 7,47). According to Hdt. 2,72, they were sacred to the god of the Nile, but according to a painting [3. 2,226, Fig. 89] they were used as bait for hunting birds of prey, and they were occasionally mummified.

The taming of the greylag goose as the white domestic goose has been proven for Egypt (goose as food for pharaohs and priests according to Hdt. 2,37 and Diod.Sic. 1,71, but also for sacred animals according to Diod. Sic.1,84), India (according to Ael. HN 13,25 a gift for kings) and Greece. There, particularly tame white geese were considered the favourite animals of certain people (Hom. Od. 15,160; 19,536ff.: Penelope; Plin. HN 10,51; Plut. De sollertia animalium 18 = Mor. 63,972f.; Ael. HN 1,6 and 7,41; Ath. 13,606c).

The liver was enlarged by force-feeding the confined goose (Gp. 14,12,12ff.; Pers. 6,71; Stat. Silv. 4,6,9; Juv. 5,114; Gal. De alimentorum facultatibus 3,20,2 among others), according to Plin. HN 10,52 an invention of Caecilius [I 32] Metellus Scipio (*cos.* 52 BC). Pliny also mentions the use of its fat for medicine and its down for beds (HN 10, 51–55, cf. also Columella 8,13,3) as well as the fattening (Plin. HN 8,209). The poor digestibility of goose, for which Caelius [II 10] Apicius provided recipes (6,5,5 no. 229 and 6,8 no. 235 ANDRÉ), did not detract from the enjoyment of the meat, which is as tasty as it is nutritious (Cels. 2,18; Gal. De alim. fac. 3,19 and passim). Breast and wings were particularly desired (Aesop. 277 HAUSRATH; Eur. in Ath. 14,640b; Petron. Sat. 69; Gal. De alim. fac. 3,20,3). Geese were quite affordable (Ov. Met. 8,684ff.; Petron. Sat. 93,2). The meat was also mixed with that of other animals (Ath. 14,664e).

The quill served to induce vomiting (Alexander of Tralles 1,417 PUSCHMANN). Since at least Theoderic (around AD 500) it was used for writing on parchment (Anon. Vales. 79; Isid. Orig. 6,14,3; Paul of Aegina 6,91). In organotherapy, besides blood, testicles and tongue, the fat was an important component in prescriptions (Dioscorides 2,76,1f. and 13 WELLMANN 1,151 and 156 = 2,86 and 91 BERENDES 184 and 187; Plin. HN 29,55 and 134). In veterinary medicine it was used for bandages (Pelag. 336; Veg. Mulomedicina 6,28.24). The eggs, whose consumption was not highly regarded by Galen (De alim. fac. 3,22,1) and Oribasius (Coll. 2,45,1) among others, were only of interest to breeders (Varro, Rust. 3,10,3; Columella 8,14,4; Plin. HN 10,162f.; Gp. 14,22,9f.). Unfertilized 'wind eggs' (ᾠὰ ὑπηνέμια) were already known to Aristotle (Hist. an. 6,2,559b 23; Gen. an. 3,1,751a 12f.).

The goose was one of the six classical sacrificial animals [4. 226f.], primarily for Isis (Paus. 10,32,16; Ov. Fast. 1,453f.; Juv. 6,540), but not a sacred bird. Only on the Capitol were geese kept in memory of the Gaulish attack in 390 BC (among others Lucr. 4,682f.; Prop. 3,3,12; Verg. Aen. 8.655; Liv. 5,47,4; Dion. Hal. Ant Rom. 13,7; for interpretation see Plut. De fortuna Romanorum 12; Ael. NA 12,33; Isid. Orig. 12,7,52). The affiliation with Juno is not generally accepted. The connection to Priapus in Petron.Sat. 136 is a spontaneous notion. One swore 'by the goose' (so-called oath of Rhadamanthys) out of consideration for the names of the gods, but without any actual legal relevance [5. 96[2], 100[1]]. As with almost all birds, the goose was also used in dream interpretation (Artem. 4,83), however its behaviour was also considered an omen of stormy weather (Ps.-Theophr. De sign. 39; Arat. 1021; Plin. HN 18,363). In fables the goose lays golden eggs (Aesop. 89 H.) and is a symbol of wealth (Aesop. 256 H.). In ancient art it was very commonly depicted on Mycenaean and Geometric vases (among others in 'single file' bands and as a filler for ornamental fields), and also on late antique terracottas and genre-pictures [7. 723–735], as well as, among others, on landscape pictures (cf. Philostr. Imag. 1,9,2) and corresponding mosaics such as in an apsidal mosaic of the 4th cent. from Tabarka, Tunisia, next to a *villa rustica* [8. 248, cf. 455], furthermore on coins and gems [9. pl. 6, 21–23 and 33; 17,6; 22,19 and 22,30–32]. Geese were a favoured decoration on women's items. Jugs and vessels were given the shape of geese; arms on thrones and seats were often extended in the form of geese (cheniskoi).

→ Breeding of small domestic animals

1 A. GARZYA (ed.), Dionysii Ixeuticon libri, 1963 2 TOYNBEE, Tierwelt 3 KELLER 4 P. STENGEL, Opferbräuche der Griechen, 1910, repr. 1972 5 R. HIRZEL, Der Eid, 1902, repr. 1966 6 ROSCHER 7 F. OLCK, s.v. G., RE 7, 709–735 8 C.W. HÜNEMÖRDER, Phasianus. Studien zur Kulturgeschichte des Fasans, 1970 9 F. IMHOOF-BLUMER, O. KELLER, Tier- und Pflanzenbilder auf Münzen und Gemmen des klass. Alt., 1889, repr. 1972. C.HÜ.

Gophna Town *c.* 22 km north of Jerusalem on the Roman trade route to Neapolis, the modern Arabic Ǧifnā. At the time of → Herod, G. was the chief town of one of the eleven Jewish toparchies. In 44 BC, → Cassius sold the inhabitants of G. into slavery because they were not able to raise the tribute demanded. Mark Antony rescinded this measure shortly thereafter. Vespasian conquered the city in AD 69 during the course of the First Jewish War.

M. AVI-YONAH, E. ORNI, s.v. Gofnah, Encyclopaedia Judaica 7, 691. J.P.

Gorbeus, Corbeuntus (Γορβεῦς, Κορβεῦντος; *Gorbeûs, Korbeûntos*). Residence of Castor the Elder, the tetrarch of the Tectosages, who was murdered here along with his wife by his father-in-law → Deiotarus; the latter destroyed the castle and large parts of the settlement (Str. 12,5,3). Later a road station (Ptol. 5,4,6; It. Ant. 143,2; 205,9); SE of Oğulbey, 29 km south of Ankara.

BELKE, 171; K. STROBEL, Die Galater 2, 1998. K.ST.

Gordianus

[1] Imp. Caes. M. Antonius G. Sempronianus Romanus Africanus Aug. (G.I.), born in *c.* AD 159, the son of Maecius Marullus and Ulpia Gordiana (Hdn. 7,5,2; SHA Gord. 2,2; Zon. 12,17 p. 127 D.). After a successful *cursus honorum* (SHA Gord. 3,5–8; 4,1), he became suffect consul, probably under Elagabalus. In 216, he was governor in *Britannia inferior* (RIB 1, 1049), soon after in Achaea [2. 181ff.], perhaps also in Syria. In 237, he was allotted the proconsulate of the province of *Africa* [5; 6. 89f. N. 21]. In Thysdrus (modern El Djem, Tunesia) in 238, an angry mob, incensed by the burden of taxes imposed by the emperor Maximinus Thrax, murdered one of his revenue officers and proclaimed the popular G. emperor and Augustus (SHA Gord. 5–9; Hdn. 7,5). G. immediately moved to Carthage, made his son → G. [2] his joint-ruler, whereupon both were readily recognized by the Senate in Rome (SHA Gord. 9–11; Aur. Vict. Caes. 26; Hdn. 7,6–7). However, after his son was defeated and killed at Carthage by → Capellianus, Maximinus' governor in Numidia, G. hanged himself after only three weeks as emperor; both father and son were consecrated in Rome (SHA Gord. 15–16; Zon. 12,17 p. 128 D.; Hdn. 7,9; Amm. Marc. 26,6,20).

1 PIR[2] A 833 2 BIRLEY 3 K. DIETZ, Senatus contra principem, 1980, 56ff. 4 KIENAST, [2]1996, 188f. 5 B.E. THOMASSON, Die Statthalter der röm. Provinzen Nordafrikas, vol. 2, 1960, 120f. 6 Id., Fasti Africani. T.F.

[2] Imp. Caes. M. Antonius G. Sempronianus Romanus Africanus Aug. (G. II.), born in *c.* AD 192, the son of M. Antonius G. [1] and Fabia Orestilla (SHA Gord. 17,4; 4,2). Following his service as quaestor, praetor, and consul (SHA Gord. 18,5), he accompanied his father to Africa in 237 in the role of *legatus consularis*. Together with his father he was proclaimed Augustus in 238 (AE 1971, 475; SHA Gord. 18,6; 7,2; 9,6; 11,4; 15,2; Zos. 1,14; Hdn. 7,7,2) and recognized by the Senate. After only a short rule, he was killed in battle against Capellianus (→ G. [1]). PIR[2] A 834 T.F.

[3] Imp. Caes. M. Antonius G. Aug. (G. III.), born early AD 225 in Rome, the son of Maecia Faustina and Iunius Balbus, a nephew of G. [2] II and grandson of G. [1] I (SHA Gord. 4,2; 22,4; Hdn. 7,10,7; ILS 496–497; AE 1942, 40; 1956, 127a). Under the senatorial emperors → Pupienus and → Balbinus [1], he was proclaimed Caesar in early 238 by the people of Rome, mobilized probably at the instigation of friends of G. (Hdn. 7,10,6–9; AE 1951, 48). Following the praetorians' murder of the two emperors in early May or June 238, they gave G. the title of Augustus with the consent of the Senate (SHA Gord. 22,5; Hdn. 8,8; for the chronology cf. [3. 195]). Legal and financial reforms helped to stabilize the situation. Militarily, G.'s general → Tullius Menophilus succeeded in keeping Carpi and Goths out of the Balkan provinces (Petrus Patricius fr. 8, FHG 4, 186f.), and an uprising of the usurper Sabinianus in Africa was successfully crushed in 240 (SHA Gord. 23,4). Supported (from 241) by the able praetorian prefect C.F. Sabinius Aquila Timesitheus, whose daughter → Furia Tranquillina he married, G. prepared a major campaign against the Persians with great military expenditure and idealistic rhetoric (SHA Gord. 23,6–7). After the death (in late 242) of Timesitheus (succeeded by the prefect → Philippus Arabs who may have been involved in his death: SHA Gord. 28,1; 29,1), G. led his troops across the Balkan into Asia, secured Syria, pushed Sapor I back and subjugated all of Mesopotamia (SHA Gord. 26,4–6; 27,2–8). G. died in early 244 during the decisive battle near Ctesiphon, either from his wounds or as victim of an attack by Philippus Arabs (SHA Gord. 29; [Aur. Vict.] Epit. Caes. 27). His body was transported back to Rome, and he himself consecrated (SHA Gord. 31,3; Eutr. 9,2). A cenotaph for him was erected near Dura Europos (SHA Gord. 34,2; Amm. Marc. 23,5,7).

1 PIR[2] A 835 2 E. KETTENHOFEN, Die röm.-persischen Kriege des 3. Jh. n.Chr., 1982 3 KIENAST, [2]1996, 195f. 4 A. NICOLETTI, Sulla politica legislativa di Gordiano III, 1981 5 T. SPAGNUOLO VIGORITA, Secta temporum meorum, 1978. T.F.

Gordium Pre-classical city near Yassıhüyük west-south-west of Ankara on the eastern bank of the Sangarius, located at a ford of the road from Pessinus to Ancyra (ruins visible). Apparently founded as a residence by its eponym, Gordius, the first Phrygian king. Excavations uncovered rich royal tombs in wooden chambers under *tumuli* (cf. map), further a citadel which was fortified in the 8th and 6th cents. BC, later to be destroyed by the Cimmerii who also caused the suicide of Midas, the last Phrygian king. G. was still of importance in the Persian empire: the satrap Pharnabazus spent the winter of 407 BC there (Xen. Hell. 1,4,1), as did Alexander the Gr. in 334 BC, when – as legend holds – he cut the 'Gordian knot' (Arr. Anab. 2,3,6–8; Curt. 3,1,12–18) in order to legitimize his rulership over Asia. In the Hellenistic period, G. was no longer a big city, but rather an important market, located in equal distance to the Hellespont, the Black Sea, and the Mediterranean (cf. Liv. 38,18,12). It was plundered by Manlius Vulso (Liv. 38,18), who camped there during his campaign against the Galatai in 189 BC. In the Greek-Roman period, G. was no more than a village (Str. 12,5,3; only smaller Roman and Byzantine finds) on the territory of the Tolistobogii in the province of Galatia, possibly identical to the road station of Vindia (Ptol. 5,4,5; It. Ant. 201,5; 202,9).

G.K. SAMS, G. and the Kingdom of Phrygia, in: M. SALVINI (ed.), Atti del 1° Simposio Internazionale "Frigi e Frigio" (16–17 ottobre 1995), 1997, 239–248; BELKE, 171. T.D.-B.

MAPS: R.S. YOUNG et al., G. Excavations Reports 1, Three Great Early Tumuli, 1981; M.M. VOIGT, Excavations at Gordion, 1988–1989: The Yassıhöyük Stratigraphic Sequence, in: A. ÇILINGIROĞLU, D.H. FRENCH (ed.), The Proc. of the Third Anatolian Iron Ages Colloquium 1990, 1994, 265–293; M.M. VOIGT et al., Fieldwork at Gordion: 1993–1995, in: Anatolica 23, 1997, 1–59, esp. 39.

Gordius (Γόρδιος; *Górdios*).

[1] Mythical founder of the Phrygian state and eponymous hero of its capital → Gordium. When birds flew around him as he was ploughing, he wanted to find out the significance of the sign from the seers in the city. A beautiful girl from a family of seers whom he asked for information at the city gate interpreted the sign as a promise of royal honour and offered to marry him. In order to end a civil war, the → Phrygians followed Zeus' oracle and proclaimed the first wagon driver to come their way as the king: it is G., who then dedicated the wagon in the temple and tied the shaft with an insoluble ('Gordian') knot; whoever untied it would become ruler of Asia. Only Alexander [4] the Great succeeded by cutting the knot in half (Iust. 11,7,5–16, briefly: Curt. 3,2; Aristobulus FGrH 139 F 7b). In divergent stories, G.'s son → Midas, the founder of the city (Hdt. 1,14; 8,138), is portrayed as king and donator of his father's wagon, to whom an eagle appeared while ploughing (Arr. Anab. 2,3,1–5, the prophetess comes from → Telmessus; Ael. NA 13,1; very briefly: Plut. Alexander 18,1–4,674bc).

P. FREI, Der Wagen von G., in: MH 29, 1972, 110–123; A. BORGHINI, La scena del carro e la donna divina. Gordio, Pisistrato e Tarquinio Prisco, in: Materiali e discussioni per l'analisi dei testi classici, 12, 1984, 61–115. F.G.

[2] Cappadocian nobleman who murdered the Cappadocian king Ariarathes VI in 111 BC on behalf of Mithridates VI of Pontus and fled to Pontus. Mithridates also eliminated the successor Ariarathes VII and eventually installed one of his own sons as king (*c.* 100) under the name of Ariarathes (IX) under his own tutelage. In Rome, he tried in vain to advocate his ward's claim against a counter candidate nominated by Nicomedes III from Bithynia. Although G. considered taking over the rulership himself, Rome supported the installation of Ariobarzanes [3] I. As a consequence, Mithridates prompted Tigranes II of Armenia, his son-in-law, to expel Ariobarzanes and to appoint G. as regent of Cappadocia. Soon thereafter, however, G. was chased away by Cornelius [I 90] Sulla, who reinstated Ariobarzanes. G. remained in Mithridates' service, still commanding the advance unit of his army in the war against Murena (83/2).

B.C. McGING, The Foreign Policy of Mithradates VI Eupator, King of Pontus, 1986; R.D. SULLIVAN, The Dynasty of Cappadocia, in: ANRW II 7.2, 1980, 1125–1168; H. SWOBODA, H. WILLRICH, s.v. G. (5) and (7), RE 7, 1592f. M.SCH.

Gordyaea (Γορδυηνή/*Gordyēnḗ*, Plut. Lucullus 21; 26; 29 and passim; Plut. Pompey 36; Ptol. 5,12,9; Str. 11,14,2; 14,8; 14,15; App. Mith. 105; Γορδυαία/*Gordyaía*, Str. 16,1,8; 1,21; 2,5). Region on the border of Armenia, the Adiabene, and the Atropatene on the upper course of the Tigris, south of Lake Van, with the poleis Sareisa (modern Šārīš), Satalka, and Pinaka (modern Finek) (Str. 16,1,24). Strabo identifies the inhabitants of the region, the *Gordyaíoi* (Γορδυαῖοι), with the → *Carduchi* (Καρδοῦχοι) (cf. Xen. An. 4,1,8; Plin. HN 6,44). After the region was incorporated into the Armenian empire under → Tigranes II, Zarbienus, the last king, was executed because of his co-operation with → Lucullus (Plut. Lucullus 29). After the rulership over the region was exchanged several times between the Armenians, Parthians, and Rome in the wake of Tigranes' defeat (69 BC), Pompey finally handed G. back to Tigranes (Cass. Dio 37,5,3). As part of the Parthian empire, the region was later occupied by Traianus, finally to be ceded to the Sassanids by Iovianus (Amm. Marc. 25,7,8f.).

R.D. SULLIVAN, Near Eastern Royalty and Rome, 1990, s.v. Gordyene. J.W.

Gorgasus and Nicomachus Healing heroes in a sanctuary in Messenian Pharae. They are regarded as the sons of → Machaon and Anticlea, the daughter of king

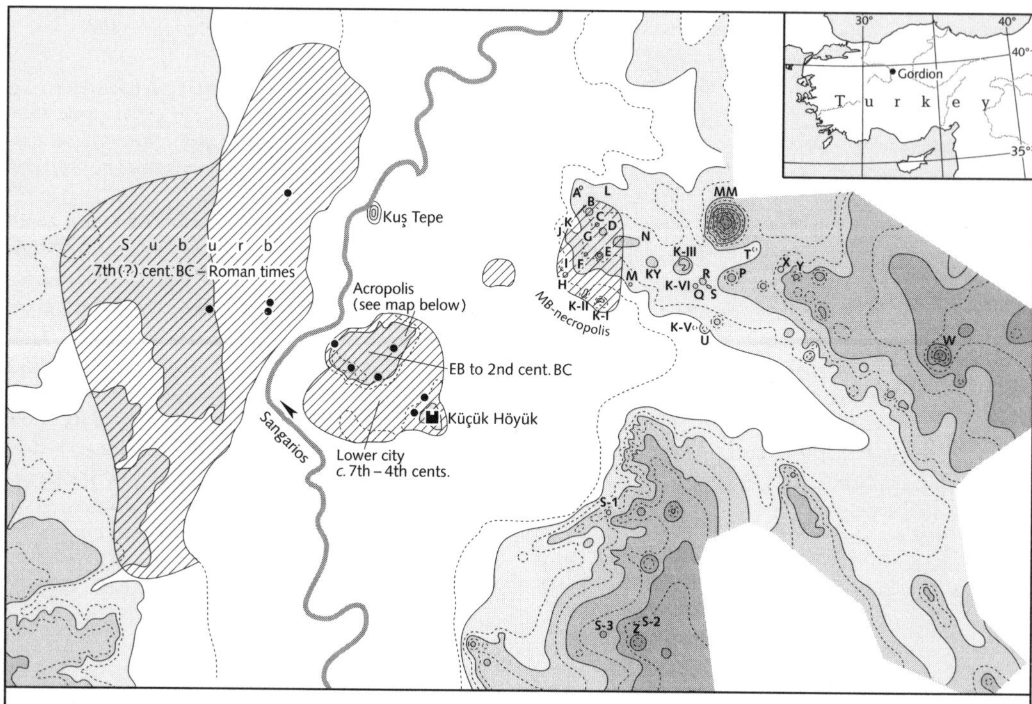

Gordium: site-map

Settlement areas

Fortress (Lydian, late 7th/early 6th cents. – Persian)

K-III Tumulus

Dates of the tumuli:

8th cent.: MM, G, K-III, K-IV, KY, P, Q, S, W, X, Y

7th cent.: B, D, F, H, J, N, S-I, Z

6th cent.: A, C, E, I, K, K-I, K-II, K-V, S-2, S-3, U(?)

? L, R, T,

Ancient course of the river

Excavated areas (1993–1995)

Settlement phases:

YHSS 10 Middle Bronze Age (MB) (before 1400 BC)

YHSS 9 Late Bronze Age (c. 1400 – 1200 BC)

YHSS 8 Late Bronze Age (c. 1200 BC; hiatus?)

YHSS 7B Early Iron Age (c. 1100 – 1000 BC; hiatus?)

YHSS 7A Early Iron Age (c. 1000 – 950/900 BC)

YHSS 6B Early Phrygian (c. 950/900 – 700 BC)

YHSS 6A Early Phrygian: destruction level (c. 700/early 7th cent. BC)

YHSS 5 Middle Phrygian I – II (c. 1st half 7th – 1st half 6th cents. BC)

YHSS 4 Middle Phrygian III (c. 550 – 300 BC)

YHSS 3–1 Late Phrygian – Roman

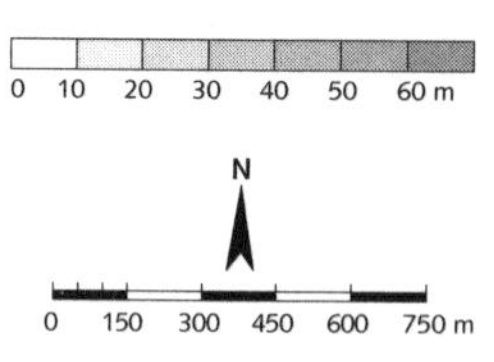

Acropolis, c. 700 BC
(eastern part)

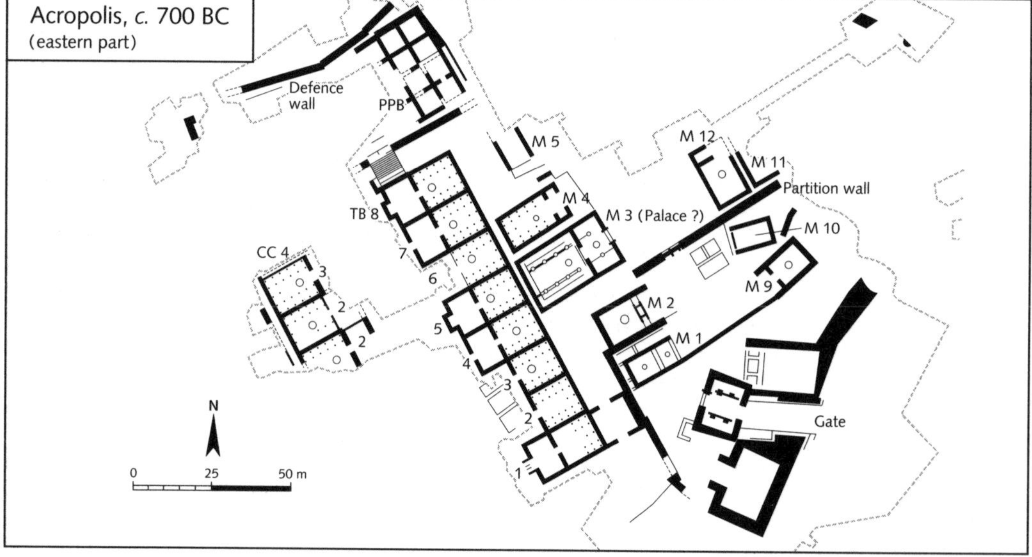

Diocles (Paus. 4,30,3). Their sanctuary was donated by Isthmius, son of the Glaucus who initiated the cultic worship of Machaon (Paus. 4,3,10). Through these myths, an independent healing cult is obviously incorporated into the cult of → Asclepius so central to Messenia. F.G.

Gorgias (Γοργίας; *Gorgías*).

[1] Sculptor who created bronze and marble votive offerings on the Athenian acropolis in the late 6th cent. BC. The bases are the only extant parts and suggest mostly statues of horses or riders. Pliny (HN 34,49) refers to G. with wrong biographical dates, or perhaps refers to a homonymous sculptor.

Overbeck, no. 356a (sources); Loewy, no. 36; A.E. Raubitschek, Dedications from the Athenian Akropolis, 1949, no. 5, 65, 77, 147; B.S. Ridgway, The Archaic Style in Greek Sculpture, 1977, 284–298; Fuchs/Floren, 300. R.N.

[2] **G. of Leontini** According to Philostratus, he was the 'father' of Sophistic (Philostr. VS 1,9,1), but according to Plato and the Suda, he was a rhetor (Pl. Grg. 449a; cf. Pl. Hp. mai. 282b: 'The sophist of Leontini').
A. Life B. Works

A. Life

Born *c.* 480, died *c.* 380 BC. The dates have been inferred from the only confirmed year of 427 BC, when G. led the legation of his city in order to plead for help from Athens against the neighbouring city of Syracuse – a role reserved for an older man. Furthermore, the sources agree that he lived to the age of 100. G. was Socrates' contemporary and is said to have still known the young Plato: according to Ath. 505d, he still read the latter's *Gorgias*. The *setting* of *Gorgias* can only refer to a visit to Athens after the legation, a fact confirmed by Plato's *Menon* (71c). G. travelled around the Greek mainland: Philostratus (Philostr. VS 1,9,4) mentions a *Pythian* (= held in Delphi) and an *Olympic* (= held in Olympia) *speech* and also reports the impression left on the Thessalians to have been so strong (epist. 73 = 82A35 DK) that 'making a public speech' (ῥητορεύειν; *rhetoreúein*) was thereafter referred to as 'gorgianizing' (γοργιάζειν; *gorgiázein*). Also, at the beginning of *Menon* (70a-b), G.'s stay in Thessaly is mentioned as well as the success he probably had there in old age; he may have died there. He had a brother who was a doctor (Suda s.v. Γοργίας; cf. Pl. Grg. 448b) and was a student of → Empedocles (Suda, ibid. and s.v. Ἐμπεδοκλῆς; Diog. Laert. 8,58; Olympiodorus in Gorg. p. 8, 2–3 Westerink; schol. Pl. Grg. 465d = p. 140 Greene). In Athens, → Alcidamas and → Isocrates were students of G.

B. Works

Two works have been transmitted: the *Praise of Helena* and the *Defence of Palamedes*. In the first, G. acquits Helena of having caused the Trojan War through her infidelity. He shows that she cannot be held responsible at all for her behaviour, no matter how it is explained: she fell victim either to the will of the gods or to the power of her abductor, to his fluent speech, or finally to her desire, i.e., to the psychological effect of visual impressions not subject to her own will. Thus, G. is able to conclude that 'through my speech, I have cleared the bad reputation of a woman'. He thus praises not only Helena but also his own profession as an orator. In the *Defence of Palamedes*, he proves the latter's innocence against Odysseus' charge of high treason by means of a *reductio ad absurdum*. He employs the same method for all the conditions under which the crime could have been committed, then for all imaginable motives. Furthermore, he argues that the accuser – and words in general – cannot possibly convey the truth to the audience. This rhetorical exercise goes beyond a mere demonstration of a number of argumentative strategies – later to become classic – such as the principle of consistence (25). The view that it is not possible to communicate facts through speech coupled with the dialectic strategy of first demonstrating the absurdity of a thesis only to accept it later on in order to prove the absurdity of another thesis, moves *Palamedes* into an argumentative position that refutes Eleatism. This view is also apparent in a text attributed to G. entitled *On Non-Being or On Nature*.

This text exists in two versions: one was transmitted by Sextus Empiricus (Adversus math. 7,65–87), the other in the ps.-Aristotelian treatise *De Melisso Xenophane Gorgia* (979a 12–980b 21). It is based on the following reasoning: nothing exists; if something existed, it could not be recognized; if it could be recognized, it could not be communicated. An argument against attributing this text to G. is the fact that Plato and Aristotle do not mention it with a single word: whenever G. is mentioned, they refer to his activity as a rhetor or to his rhetorical works. The argumentative similarity between this philosophical text and *Palamedes*, however, supports G.'s authorship, which today is generally accepted. Interpreters are divided into two opposing factions. According to the first point of view – still represented primarily by H. Gomperz [7] – G. was a rhetor and has no place in the history of philosophy: the text on Non-Being is a rhetorical exercise, a 'game' (παίγνιον; *paígnion*, to say it with a word used by G. himself in reference to the *Praise of Helena* (21)). Those arguing the other point of view (W. Nestle [8], G. Calogero [9]) regard the text as a serious polemic against Eleatism, and *Helena* and *Palamedes* as a utilization of a system of logic developed in the field of philosophy for rhetorical purposes. This dichotomy can be resolved in two different ways: one can either adopt the genetic interpretation by H. Diels [5] – G. was at first a philosopher of nature in the school of Empedocles, then became an Eristic dialectician through contact with Eleatic dialectics, which led him to concentrate exclusively on oration – or, on the other hand, one can follow the interpretation by Dupréel [10], who sees the text on

Non-Being as a philosophical introduction into rhetoric which replaces the science of nature with the art of oration and which eliminates the methods of the first with those of the second.

→ Eleatic School; → Rhetoric; → Sophists

EDITIONS: 1 TH. BUCHHEIM, G. von Leontinoi: Reden, Fragmente und Testimonien, ed. with transl. and comm., 1989 2 H. DIELS (ed.), Aristotelis qui fertur de Melisso Xenophane Gorgia. Philos. und histor. Abh. der königlichen Akad. der Wiss. zu Berlin, 1900, I, 3–40 3 DIELS/KRANZ vol. 2, no. 82 (Version des Sextos Empeirikos über das Nicht-Seiende, die beiden Reden und Slg. der indirekt überlieferten Fr.) 4 B. CASSIN, Si Parménide. Le traité anonyme *De Melisso Xenophane Gorgia*. Édition critique et commentaire, 1980.

BIBLIOGRAPHY: 5 H. DIELS, G. und Empedokles, 1884, in: C. J. CLASSEN, Sophistik, 1976, 351–383 6 O. APELT, G. bei Pseudo-Aristoteles und bei Sextus Empiricus, in: RhM 44, 1888, 203–219 7 H. GOMPERZ, Sophistik und Rhet., 1912 (repr. 1965), 1–35 8 W. NESTLE, Die Schrift des G. 'Über die Natur oder über das Nichtseiende', 1922, in: Id., Griech. Studien, 1948, 240–252 9 G. CALOGERO, Studien über den Eleatismus, 1970, esp. 171–242 (orig. Ital. 1932) 10 E. DUPRÉEL, Les Sophistes, 1948, 59–113 11 G. CALOGERO, G. and the Socratic Principle Nemo Sua Sponte Peccat, 1957, in: C.J. CLASSEN, Sophistik, 1976, 408–421 12 C. M. J. SICKING, G. und die Philosophen, 1964, in: C.J. CLASSEN, Sophistik, 1976, 384–407 13 M. MIGLIORI, La Filosofia di Gorgia. Contributi per una riscoperta del sofista di Lentini, 1973 14 H. J. NEWIGER, Unt. zu G.' Schrift über das Nichtseiende, 1973 15 L. MONTONERI, F. ROMANO (ed.), Gorgia e la sofistica, 2 vols., 1985 MI.NA.

[3] Seleucid → *stratēgós* from Idumaea under Antiochus IV, mentioned in 2 Macc 8:9 as a subordinate of Nicanor. He was ordered by Ptolemy (*stratēgós* of Coele Syria and Phoenice, son of Dorymenes) to overthrow the revolt of the Maccabaeans that began in 167/6 BC. G. is the main character in the parallel account 1 Macc 3:38–4:25.

BENGTSON 1, 170f. K.BR.

[4] Greek rhetor of the 1st cent. BC, probably from Athens. He was the younger Cicero's teacher in 44 until the latter's father forbade their contact (Cic. Fam. 16,21,6; Plut. Cicero 873ab). Seneca (Controv. 1,4,7) mentions G., but the Greek quotations have been lost in the transmission. G. wrote a work on → figures of speech (περὶ σχημάτων; *perì schēmátōn*) in 4 bks., translated into Latin by his contemporary → Rutilius Lupus (Quint. Inst. 9,2,102: *in usum suum transtulit* [AHRENS] instead of *unum* [codd.]); the extant text consists of only two bks. and deals only with word figures, not the figures of meaning. It is therefore uncertain whether Rutilius' translation has survived in its entirety or only in parts, whether it is the original text or an epitome. 41 word figures are presented in an unsystematic order; a definition is usually followed by examples from Attic orators or by those of a later time such as Demetrius of Phalerum and Hegesias; G. was apparently still unaffected by → Atticism and represented the asianistically shaped rhetorical tradition of Hellenism. The Latin translation of his work became the basis of the → *Carmen de figuris* (4th cent.). The attribution of a work mentioned by Poll. (9,1) entitled *Onomastikón biblíon* to G. remains uncertain.

EDITIONS: G. BARABINO, 1967; E. BROOKS, Mnemosyne Suppl. 11, 1970.

BIBLIOGRAPHY: K. MÜNSCHER, s.v. G. 9, RE 7, 1604–1619. M.W.

Gorgidas (Γοργίδας/*Gorgídas*, or Γοργίας/*Gorgías* in Diodorus). The most important Theban politician and commander of the 4th cent. BC (cf. Diod. Sic. 15,39,2) alongside → Epaminondas and → Pelopidas, Hipparchus in *c.* 383. After the Spartan seizure of the Cadmeia, G. remained in contact with Theban fugitives in Athens (Plut. Mor. 578BC; 576A). He is said to have organized the resistance against Sparta by forming the 'holy throng' (*hieròs lóchos*, ἱερὸς λόχος) (Plut. Mor. 594AB; Plut. Pel. 12; 18f.; Polyaenus, Strat. 2,5,1; in Ath. 13,602a attributed to Epaminondas). In 379–378, G. became Boeotarch (Plut. Pel. 14,2; cf. also 13,1, where Pelopidas, Melon, and Charon were elected to this office [1. 41]). In 378, he commanded the Theban cavalry in the campaign against Thespia (Xen. Hell. 5,4,42–45; Diod. Sic. 15,33,6; Polyaenus, Strat. 2,5,2).

1 J. BUCKLER, The Theban Hegemony, 1980. M.MEI.

Gorgippia Military colony in the area of the → Sindi in the north-west Pontus Euxinus (Str. 11,2,10; Steph. Byz. s.v. Γοργιππία; *civitas Sindica*, Plin. HN 6,1) in the place of modern Anapa. Founded in the late 6th cent. BC [1. 7], the city had a harbour (originally Σινδική, Σινδικὸς λιμήν; *Sindikḗ, Sindikòs limḗn*, Ps.-Scymn. 888f.; Peripl. m. Eux. 65; Arr. Peripl. p. eux. 29) and was officially named after the Spartocid Gorgippus after its integration into the Bosporus Kingdom (→ *Regnum Bosporanum*) in the 4th cent. BC. In the 5th cent. AD, the city had Gothic inhabitants and was renamed Eudusia (Peripl. m. Eux. 63).

In the Hellenistic period, G. was one of the most important trade centres on the Bosporus. It experienced a second peak during the Roman period through the shipping of cerealia from the Kuban region. The city never recovered from a catastrophic fire shortly after 239 BC, which occurred as a result of the beginning migration of the steppe population.

Excavations show seven different settlement phases separated by burnt layers [1. 5–19]. The earth huts of the first settlers were followed by clay brick houses with stone foundations and storage cellars, as they are found in the entire northern Pontus. Following the integration into the Bosporus Kingdom in the early 4th cent. BC, the city area was significantly extended with a unified and apparently radial city planning. In the Roman period until *c.* 239, the entire city was reconstructed on 40 ha: peristyle houses (up to 700 m^2) with large cellars and monumental public buildings with marble decorations date from this time. The economic base was primarily grain production and – in the Roman period – viticulture; the Chous, that is, the rural surroundings, extended *c.* 25 km around the city with many settlements. → Amphora stamps attest to intensive trade with the cities in the south Pontus, esp. with → Heraclea Pontika. Black-glazed Attic ceramics popular in the 4th/3rd cents. were replaced in the 3rd cent. by relief ware from Asia minor. For the Roman period, there is evidence of imports from the north-western provinces.

Beginning in the 5th cent. BC, coins circulate esp. from Pontic cities. G. minted its own coins only under Mithridates VI of Pontus (1st half of the 1st cent. BC), otherwise (4th cent. BC – 3rd cent. AD) we find the minting of Bosporus kings. From the 4th cent. BC, there are many inscriptions: aside from royal rescripts, we find religious/professional *thiasoi* of citizens, usually in the context of the munificence for cult buildings. Most gods of the Greek Pantheon were venerated with a greater focus on Chthonic aspects. For the 3rd cent. BC, Hermaea with agons are attested.

→ Pontus Euxinus; → Heraclea Pontika; → Mithridates [6].; → Regnum Bosporanum

1 E.M. Alekseeva, Antičnyj gorod Gorgippija, 1990 2 V.F. Gajdukevič, Das Bosporanische Reich, 1971, 228–238 3 Z.E. Charaldina, A.M. Novočikin, Ancient Collections of the Anapa Mus., in: VDI 1994.2, 200–212. A.P.-L.

Gorgippus (Γόργιππος; *Górgippos*).

[1] Eponym of → Gorgippia, regent of the Sindian region after his father → Satyrus I 's war against the Maeotae (Polyaenus, Strat. 8,55). High government official at the time of his uncle → Paerisades. A statue was erected for him in Athens (Din. in Demosthenem 43).

→ Maiotae, → Sindi

V.F. Gaidukevič, Das Bosporanische Reich, 1971, 72; 43; 232. I.v.B.

[2] Son of Pythippos, author of satyr plays. His victory at the Soteria in Acraephia in the 1st cent. BC (DID A 9) is attested. He may have been a brother of the tragedian (?) Dorotheus (TrGF 160, cf. DID A 7 app. crit.).

Mette, 61; TrGF 175. F.P.

Gorgo

[1] Female monster in Greek mythology. According to the canonical version of the myth (Apollod. 2,4,1–2), → Perseus must get the head of → Medusa, the mortal sister of Sthenno and Euryale (Hes. Theog. 276f.; POxy. 61, 4099), the daughters of Phorcys and Ceto (cf. Aeschylus' drama *Phorcides*, TrGF 262). The three sisters live on the island of Sarpedon in the ocean (Cypria, fr. 23; Pherecydes FGrH 3 F 11), although Pindar (Pyth. 10,44–48) located them among the Hyperboraeans (→ Hyperborei). Their connection to the sea is still apparent in Sophocles (TrGF 163) and Hesychius (s.v. Gorgides). The Gorgos' terrifying shape (snake hair, fangs) transforms into stone whoever looks at them (their ugliness was so notorious that Aristoph. [Ran. 477] referred to the women of the Athenian deme Teithras as *Gorgones*). In the divine battle against the Titans, Athena also kills a G., whose blood was later attributed with the power to heal as well as to poison (Eur. Ion 989–991; 1003ff.; Paus. 8,47,5; Apollod. 3,10,3). With the aid of Athena, Hermes, and the Nymphs, who equipped him with winged sandals, Hades' helmet of invisibility, and a sickle (*hárpē*), Perseus is able to decapitate Medusa in her sleep (Pherecydes FGrH 3 F 11). From her neck rise Chrysaor [4] and the winged horse → Pegasus. Perseus is pursued by Medusa's sisters, but he escapes and, in the end, turns his enemy → Polydectes to stone by using G.'s head.

The myth was already known to Hesiodus (Theog. 270–282) and shows oriental influences: the iconography of the G. has borrowed traits from Mesopotamian Lamaštu. Perseus saves Andromeda in Ioppe-Jaffa (Mela 1,64), and an oriental seal shows a young hero holding a *hárpē* and seizing a demonic creature [1. 83–87]. In Etruria, Perseus' adventure was already popular in the 5th cent. [3]. Roman authors like Ovidius (Men. 4,604–5,249) – who change Medusa into a stunningly beautiful young girl – and Lucan (9,624–733) focussed in particular on the frightening head of Medusa [cf. 4].

In Mycenae, Perseus was seen in the context of initiation. His killing of Medusa reflects the testing of young warriors [2]. In fact, the descriptions of G.'s head recall certain elements of the archaic battle vehemence: the horrifying appearance, broad grin, grinding teeth, and powerful battle screams [6]. The popularity of G.'s head, the → Gorgoneion, as attested on Athena's → *aegis* and on warriors' shields (as early as Hom. Il. 5,741; 11,35–37) as well as in Aristoph. Ach. 1124, indicates the frightening effect and the protection of the Delphic → *omphalós* (Eur. Ion 224) and the Delian *thēsaurós* (thesauros: IG XIV 1247) by the Gorgos. The myth of Perseus and Medusa is therefore an important example of the complex interrelation of narrative and iconographic motifs between Greece and the Orient during the archaic period.

1 W. Burkert, The Orientalizing Revolution, 1992 2 M. Jameson, Perseus, the Hero of Mykenai, in: R. Hägg, G. Nordquist (ed.), Celebrations of Death and Divinity in the Bronze Age Argolid, 1990, 213–230 3 I. Krauskopf, S.-C. Dahlinger, s.v. G., Gorgones, LIMC 4.1, 285–330 4 I. Krauskopf, s.v. Gorgones (in Etrurien), LIMC 4.1, 330–345 5 O. Paoletti, s.v. Gorgones Romanae, LIMC 4.1, 345–362 6 J.-P. Vernant, Mortals and Immortals, 1991, 111–149. J.B.

[2] Daughter of Spartan king Cleomenes I (*c.* 525–490 BC), whom she is said to have warned as a child about Aristagoras [3] of Miletus when the latter requested assistance in Sparta for the Ionians, who were rebelling against Persia (Hdt. 5,51). Wife of King → Leonidas

(Hdt. 7,205), is said to have deciphered a secret message by the exiled king Damaratus about the invasion planned by Xerxes (Hdt. 7,239). K.-W.WEL.

Gorgobina (Modern La Guerche/Nièvre). City of Gallia Celtica in the region of the → Arverni, later of Aquitania, east of Elaver, south of Aquae Bormonis. The → Boii settled in G. in 58 BC, after the defeat of the Helvetii in the battle against Caesar. G. became *Boiorum oppidum* (Caes. B Gall. 7,9,6).

H. Bigeard, A. Bouthier, Carte archéologique de la Gaule 58 (Nièvre), 1996. Y.L.

Gorgone (Rut. Namat. 1,515; Γοργόνη/*Gorgónē*, Ptol. 3,1,78; Ὀργών/*Orgṓn*, Steph. Byz. s.v.; Lat. *Urgo*, Plin. HN 3,81; *Gorgona* from the time of Gregory the Great). Small island in the *mare Ligusticum* between Pisa and Corsica; modern Gorgona. Eneolithic (early 2nd millennium BC) finds in the Grotta di San Gorgonio. A bronze crater from Vulci was found on the coast (late 6th cent. BC, today in the Vatican Museum). In the north, ruins of a Roman *villa*.

BTCGI 8, 1990, 161–163. G.U.

Gorgoneion According to the myth, the G. is the head of the → Gorgo [1] Medusa killed by Perseus which could still turn people into stone after Medusa's death. Perseus finally handed it to Athena, who attached it to her → *aegis*. The significance of the G. as an object of representation, however, far exceeds the myth of Perseus and has complex older foundations. It belongs to the group of grotesque masks whose polyvalent functions go far beyond those of causing terror and deterring evil. Even though there are certain similarities, common opinion holds that no obvious derivation from oriental patterns can be established in the representational type of the oldest Greek Gorgoneia [1].

The G. as a powerful demonic appearance or as a pictorial formula more or less bereft of content was used in various ways all over the ancient world, e.g. as a sign on shields, on other weapons, on roof tiles, gems, coins, equipment of all kinds, and, particularly telling, on burial monuments. On older archaic G., animalistic traits dominate (wide open mouth, long teeth, protruding tongue, mane-like hair with snakes) within the basic shape of a human face. From the late 6th cent. BC, these slowly give way to an 'anthropomorphization', and beginning in the mid 5th cent., the type of the 'beautiful Gorgo' develops, yet the old grimace never quite disappears, esp. in minor arts and always identifiable through the snakes in the hair. During the Hellenistic period, emphasis is placed on the suffering expression of the beautiful demonic being, now seen as victim and corruptress at the same time. This tendency dominates in the famous 'Medusa Rondanini', a marble work in the Munich Glyptothek, which today is regarded as a classicistic work from the Roman Empire.

1 J. Boardman, Archaic Greek Gems, 1968, 37f.

J. Floren, Studien zur Typologie des G., 1977; Th. Karagiora, Γοργείη Κεφαλή, 1970; I. Krauskopf, s.v. Gorgo, Gorgones, LIMC 4.1, 285–345; O. Paoletti, s.v. Gorgones (Romanae), LIMC 4.1, 345–362; G. Riccioni, Origine e sviluppo del G. e del mito della Gorgone-Medusa nell'arte Greca, in: RIA N.S. 9, 1960, 127ff.; J.-P. Vernant, L'autre de l'homme: la face de Gorgo, in: M. Olender (ed.), Pour L. Poliakov. Le racisme – mythe et sciences, 1981, 141ff. MA.SCH.

Gorgo Painter Attic black-figured vase painter of *c.* 600–580 BC, named after his main work – a *dinos* on a tall base in the Louvre depicting Perseus' escape from the Gorgos. The Gorgo Painter (GP) is the first representative of the animal frieze style in Athens. He was a successor of the → Nettos painter, into who's 'monstrous' style he brings order by following the Corinthian model of capturing the demonic world of animals in friezes and arranging them in symmetrical groups. He utilizes the blank picture area – in early stages used only as a window for horse heads or women's heads – for the depiction of whole animals as well. Characteristic for the GP are his lions with box-like muzzle, red flaming mane, and hatched forehead hair. He depicted humans only rarely, and complete scenes have only survived on the above mentioned *dinos*. The tradition established by his workshop can be traced further esp. in olpes (pitchers).

Beazley, ABV, 8–10, 679; Id., Paralipomena, 6–7; Id., Addenda, 2f.; J. Boardman, Athenian Black Figure Vases, 1974, 17–18; I. Scheibler, Olpen und Amphoren des Gorgo-Malers, in: JDAI 76, 1961, 1–47. H.M.

Gorgopas (Γοργώπας; *Gorgṓpas*). Spartiate, in 389/8 BC. *Epistoleús* of the nauarch Hierax, who assigned to him the defence of the polis Aegina under the siege of Athens. He operated successfully against Athenian forces and against Attic coastal regions, accompanied the new nauarch Antalcidas to Ephesus in 388, and got into difficulties in a battle against an Athenian squadron on his return. He won the counter attack in a night battle at Cape Zoe, but was not up to the surprise attack of the Athenian Peltastai under → Chabrias in 387, and was killed in action. (Xen. Hell. 5,1,5–13; Dem. Or. 20,76).

Ch. D. Hamilton, Sparta's Bitter Victories, 1979, 297, 302f. K.-W.WEL.

Gorgophone (Γοργοφόνη; *Gorgophónē*).
[1] Epithet of Athena in the sense of 'killer of Gorgo' (Eur. Ion 1478; Orph. H. 32,8 Quandt after the passage in Euripides, although γοργοφόνος is transmitted in the vocative); the name can also be interpreted as 'glowing terribly' (cf. → Persephone).

1 F. Bräuninger, s.v. Persephone, RE 19, 946–947. JO.S.

[2] One of the Danaids (→ Danaus, Danaids) natural sister of Hypermestra. Her husband is Proteus (Apollod. 2,16 WAGNER), whose wife is also named Scylla (Hyg. Fab. 170).
[3] Daughter of → Perseus, wife of Perieres; their children are Tyndareus, Aphareus, Leucippus, and Icarius (Apollod. 1,87; 3,117 WAGNER refers to Stesichorus). After Perieres' death, she was the first Greek wife not to remain a widow; she married Oebalus (Paus. 2,21,7). Contrary to Apollodorus, Pausanias (3,1,4) regards Tyndareus as the son of the second marriage. Alcaeus, Sthenelus, Helius, Mestor, and Electryon are understood to be her brothers (Apollod. 2,49 WAGNER). Her tomb was in Argus next to that of the Gorgo's head (Paus. 2,21,7). JO.S.

Gorgophonus/-os
[1] ('killer of Gorgo'). Epithet of Athena in Orph. H. 32,8 (but see → Gorgophone [1]).
[2] Epithet of Perseus (Eur. fr. 985 NAUCK; Nonnus, Dion. 18,305; 30,269; 31,12; 47,506; 47,536).
[3] Son of → Electryon and Anaxo, Alcaeus' daughter, thus Perseus' grandson. → Alcmene is mentioned as his sister, his brothers' names are listed as Stratobates, Phylonomos, Celaeno, Amphimachus, Lysinomus, Cheirimachus, Anaktor, and Archelaus (Apollod. 2,52 WAGNER). JO.S.

Gorgopis limne (Γοργῶπις λίμνη; *Gorgôpis límnē*). In Aesch. Ag. 302, it belongs to the chain of fire signals from Ida to Mycenae between → Cithaeron and Aigiplanktos (→ Gerania in the Megaris) and is therefore regarded as identical with the eastern part of the gulf of Corinth, the bay of Eleusis, and several lakes on the Isthmus of Corinth (Limni Vouliagmenis to the west of the Gerania, cf. Xen. Hell. 4,5,6; Limni Psatho to the east of Schinos).

F. BÖLTE, s.v. G. 1), RE 7, 1658f.; W. LEINER, Die Signaltechnik der Ant., 1982, 59ff.; PHILIPPSON/KIRSTEN 1, 954f. E.O.

Gorgus (Γόργος; *Górgos*). In 324 BC, G. of Iasos – in the role of the 'keeper of weapons' (*hoplophýlax*, ὁπλοφύλαξ) – interceded with → Alexander [4] the Great on behalf of the Samians expelled by the Athenians and tried to persuade Alexander to start a campaign against Athens (Ath. 12,538b). After the latter's death, G. had Iasos allow the return of Samians to Athens at the city's expense. The newly created community of Samos honoured him and his brother → Minnion for their merits by granting them citizenship among other things (Syll.[3] 312). The brothers had succeeded in obtaining a lake from Alexander for Iasos, an act for which they were honoured by fellow citizens (Syll.[3] 307).

BERVE 2, no. 236. E.B.

Gorsium (It. Ant. 264,4; 265,1; CIL III 3342f.; 3346; 11345). Roman camp and civil settlement in Pannonia inferior, modern Tác/Fejér (near Székesfehérvár/Hungary). Originally, G. was the centre of the Celtic Aravisci; during the Roman period, it was the intersection of the roads Sopianae–Aquincum and Sopianae–Brigetio. Rich archaeological finds attest to the importance of G. (remnants of buildings, burial ground). In the 1st cent. AD the camp which harboured the *ala I Scubulorum* was installed. The garrison was discharged in the early 2nd cent., after which the civil settlement enjoyed a period of prosperity. During the wars against the Marcomanni and in the 3rd cent. time of crisis (*c.* 260), G. suffered invasions by the Sarmatae. In honour of → Maximianus, the settlement was renamed Herculia. G. enjoyed its last period of prosperity in the mid 4th cent. (reconstruction of destroyed buildings).

J. FITZ, s.v. G., RE Suppl. 9, 73–75; E. B. THOMAS, Röm. Villen in Pannonien, 1964, 299–328; TIR L 34, 1968, 62f. (bibliogr.). J.BU.

Gortyn
I. LOCATION II. HISTORICAL DEVELOPMENT
III. THE GREAT LAW INSCRIPTION

I. LOCATION
One of the biggest and most important cities of Crete, in the Mesara plain on the river Lethaeus, between the villages of Agi Deka and Mitropolis, 16 km (Str. 10,4,7: 90 stadia) from the Libyan Sea, also transmitted as *Gortyna* and *Gortyne*.

II. HISTORICAL DEVELOPMENT
The earliest literary mention of G. is found in Hom. Il. 2,646 (a comment on its fortress-like character; Hom. Od. 3,294). However, records indicate the existence of a settlement as early as the Minoan period (acropolis, also with Neolithic traces; *villa* near Mitropolis [1]). Although G. was founded in pre-Doric times (cf. the tradition of legends in Paus. 8,53,4: founding by Gortys, son of Tegeates, while the Cretan version holds that Gortys was the son of Rhadamanthys), the actual history of Greek G. begins with the Doric conquest and settlement in the 7th cent. BC. The temple of Athena Poliouchos on the acropolis and the temple of Apollo Pythius in the lower city date from this period. There is almost no information from the classical period. The famous Law Code of G., however, dates from the mid 5th cent.: a 12 columned boustrophedon inscription in Doric dialect discovered in 1884, containing information about personal and family law, laws of succession, property and obligations unique in the Greek world both with regard to detail and comprehensiveness ([2; 3; 4] see below). The plates are located in the ambulatory of a Roman odeum which had replaced an older building in *c.*100 BC (possibly an ekklesiasterion), the text was inscribed in its apsidial outer wall.

In the Hellenistic period, G. played an increasingly dominant role on Crete, maintaining its place as the second greatest power next to → Knosos in an unstable political situation marked by various interior rivalries. Numerous international contracts attested by inscriptions document this process [5]. Furthermore, G. had extensive contacts in the way of coalitions or military conflicts to the Greek mainland (Sparta), to the Hellenistic empires (Macedonia, and esp. Ptolemaic Egypt), and also to the Romans from the 2nd cent. BC. The report by Polybius (4,53f.) about a conflict (220 BC) between the 'Younger' (sympathizers of → Lyctus) and the 'Older' (sympathizers of Knossos) provides insight into G.'s domestic policy, although it remains vague due to its historically conditioned nature. Fleeing from the Romans in 189 BC, Hannibal stayed in G. (Nep. Hann. 9; cf. Iust. 32,4,3f.).

After the Roman conquest of Crete, G. became the capital of the senatorial double province → *Creta et Cyrenae*. Now the city enjoyed its urban hey day which is still evident in numerous, partially extant public buildings: praetorium, theatre, amphitheatre, circus, thermal baths, two nymphaea (mid 2nd cent. AD), temples of the Egyptian god Serapis and goddess Isis (possibly also Hermes Anubis; 1st/2nd cents. AD). The residential area (hardly researched as of today) extended far to the south-east, bordered by two large necropoleis. The entire terrain of the city comprised an area of *c.*150 ha.

During the same period, G. developed into a stronghold of early Christianity on Crete. In AD 59, the Apostle Paul visited the city (Acts 27:7) and installed Titus as the first bishop. He is remembered in the 6th cent. three-naved basilica of Titus, one of the best preserved buildings in G. The name of the modern village Mitropolis preserves the memory of the former status of G. as a metropolis of the Church. The name of the town Agi Deka refers to the martyr's death of 10 Christians during the persecutions by emperor → Decius [II 1].

In the Byzantine period, G. was initially able to maintain its outstanding position. G. was further developed and new basilicas were constructed. When the Arabs turned G. into their base for attacks on Constantinople in *c.* 670, many inhabitants fled or retreated into the then heavily fortified acropolis. Following the invasion of the Arabs in 824, G. was abandoned by its inhabitants, not to be resettled even after the recapture of Crete by the Byzantines. Excavations began in 1880 first by German (F. Halbherr) and then Italian archaeologists.

1 D. Levi, La villa rurale minoica di Gortina, in: BA 44, 1959, 237–265 2 J. Kohler, E. Ziebarth, Das Stadtrecht von G., 1912 3 R.F. Willets, The Law Code of G., 1967 4 S. Avramovic, Die "Epiballontes" als Erben im Gesetz von G., in: ZRG 107, 1990, 363–370 5 A. Chaniotis, Die Verträge zw. kret. Poleis in der hell. Zeit, 1996, passim.

N. Allegro, M. Ricciardi, Le fortificazione di Gortina in età ellenistica, in: Cretan Studies 1, 1988, 1–16; H. van Effenterre, La Crète et le monde Grec de Platon à Polybe, 1948; M. Guarducci, Inscriptiones Creticae 4, 1950; Lauffer, Griechenland, 237–239; I.F. Sanders, Roman Crete, 1982, 156–159; A. di Vita (ed.), Gortina I, 1988.

H.SO.

III. The great law inscription

The most important law inscription of archaic Greece, also called 'Law Code of G.', presents in 12 columns (often erroneously referred to as '12 tables') of about 55 lines each a coherent, though according to modern standards not systematically structured legal text with general legal rules. The inscription was chiselled into a wall of ashlars in the 5th cent. BC in → *boustrophēdón* manner (systematic alternation of the script direction from one line to the next within a column, → Script). In the 1st cent. AD the stones were numbered, dismantled, and built into the back wall of the Roman Odeum (where they can still be read today below a protective roof). First fragments were discovered in 1857 but not read until 1884 by F. Halbherr and E. Fabricius while standing in the water of a mill canal. Many more inscripted stones with similar content were found, partly in sequential columns. They show that the recording of legal norms became usual practice in the 2nd half of the 7th cent. BC (collected and translated by Koerner [1] in no. 116–162, the great inscription of G. in no. 163–181).

The reason for these recordings were probably social tensions within the nobility. Written laws were meant to keep the individual officials who were active as δικαστάς (*dikastás*, Doric for → *dikastḗs*) in their place. There are no indications of the existence of jury courts in G. (→ *dikastḗrion*), as they existed e.g. in Athens to restrict the decision-making power of the archontes. Therefore, the legal inscription consistently prescribes two methods of decision-making for the bearer of jurisdiction in the state (*dikastḗs*), each strictly determined in content: either δικάδδεν (*dikádden*, Doric for → *dikázein*), by demanding an oath that settled the dispute from one of the parties of the case or from a certain number of witnesses, or ὀμνύντα κρίνεν (*omnýnta krínen*), by decision of the *dikastḗs* himself under oath.

A brief synopsis of the contents of the great law inscription of G.: prohibition to act on one's own authority in a dispute on the status of freedom and on the ownership of a slave, the proceedings in such disputes. Rape and adultery. Distribution of property after a divorce, property rights in marriage. Children born after divorce or out of wedlock. Law of succession for freely available family property, sale in somebody's lifetime. Buying the freedom of a prisoner. Marriage between a free person and a slave. Purchase of a slave. Daughter heiress (→ *epíklēros*). Surety and money debt. Adoption (→ *eispoíēsis*).

1 R. Koerner, Inschr. Gesetzestexte der frühen griech. Polis, 1993.

M. Guarducci (ed.), Inscriptiones Creticae 4, 72; J. Kohler, E. Ziebarth, Das Stadtrecht von G., 1912; R.F. E. Willetts, The Law Code of G., 1967; R.R. Metzger,

Unters. zum Haftungs- und Vermögensrecht von G., 1973; A. MAFFI, Studi di epigrafia giuridica greca, 1983; H. VAN EFFENTERRE, F. RUZÉ, Nomima II, 1995, 357–389; G. THÜR, Oaths and Dispute Settlement, in: L. FOXHALL, A. D. E. LEWIS (ed.), Greek Law in its Political Setting, 1996, 57–72. G.T.

Gortys (Γόρτυς; *Górtys*). Settlement in Arcadia near the modern Atsicholo between Dimitsana and Karytaina, where the valley widens on the right bank of the Gortynius, a tributary of the → Alpheius [1]. G. comprised a fortified acropolis which controlled the northern access to the plain of Megalopolis, and north-east of the acropolis a terrace towering over the gorge of the Gortynius. According to Paus. 8,27,4, it was one of a number of settlements whose inhabitants came from → Cynuria. G. became part of the territory of Megalopolis, but retained its status as a *kṓmē* [1]. In the early 2nd cent. BC, G. was a member of the Achaean League (cf. copper coins). Two walled circles are well preserved [2], a larger one (100 by 425 m) to the north, probably dating from the mid 4th cent. BC, and a smaller one in the south (*c.* 57 by 131 m), no longer inhabited during the Imperial period. Right south of this smaller walled circle was a sanctuary of Asclepius. The sanctuary of Asclepius mentioned by Pausanias [3], comprising a temple and several outbuildings, amongst them large Hellenistic baths, was located about half an hour to the north on the terrace overlooking the Gortynius, with wealthy private dwellings adjacent to the south (Paus. 5,7,1; 8,28,1–3).

1 M. JOST, Villages de l'Arcadie antique, in: Ktema 11, 1986 (1990), 150–155 2 R. MARTIN, Les enceintes de G. d'Arcadie, in: BCH 71–72, 1947–1948, 81–147 3 JOST, 202–210. Y.L.

Goshawk It is almost impossible to distinguish exactly whether ἱέραξ/*hiérax* (ἴρηξ, in Homer) in each individual instance refers to the goshawk (*Accipiter gentilis*), the sparrowhawk (*A. nisus*) or a species of the Falconidae. A commonly used synonym was κίρκος/*kírkos* (e.g. Hom. Il. 22,139). The pigeon-killer φασσοφόνος/*phassophónos* in Hom. Il. 15,237 apparently refers to the goshawk, *írēx*, however, to the sparrowhawk. In popular etymology, the Latin name *accipiter* (*acceptor* in Lucil. 1130) is derived from *accipere* (Isid. Orig. 12,7,55, cf. Plaut. Persa 406f.).

Aristot. Hist. an. 8(9),3,592b 2f. differentiated by size between the φαβοτύπος/*phabotýpos* and the σπιζίας/*spizías*. In Aristot. Hist. an. 8(9),36,620a 17–b 5, they are listed among 11 species of raptors, amongst 16 in Plin. HN 10,21f. A characteristic feature of the goshawk and related raptors is the combination of nimbleness and speed (Hom. Il. 13,62 and 819; 15,237; 16,582; 18,616; Od. 13,86; cf. Paus. 7,12,2), as well as their predatory nature (e.g. Pl. Phd. 82a; Lucr. 4,1009; Ov. Ars am. 2,147; see Dial. 4,16,1). The goshawk predominantly hunts smaller birds, up to the size of a pigeon (Hom. Il. 13,62–64; 15,237f.; 16,582f.; 21,493f.; 22,139f.; Eur. Andr. 1141; Alcm. frg. 15 D.; Aristot. Hist. an. 8(9),11, 615 a 6; Varro, Sat. Men. 289, rust. 3,7,6; Verg. Aen. 11,721f.; Hor. Carm. 1,37,17f.; Ov. Met. 11,344f., Trist. 1,1,75; Sen. Oed. 903; Dionysius 1,6 [1. 6f.]), but sometimes also mice (Batrachomyomachia 49) and other animals. Several myths existed: the goshawk would not eat the heart of a bird (Aristot. Hist. an. 8(9),11,615a 5; Plin. HN 10,24), its cry differed with the seasons (Lucr. 5,1079–81) and caused hen's eggs to die (Plin. HN 10,152), it would at times metamorphose into a cuckoo (Aristot. Hist. an. 6,7,563b 14–28; Plin. HN 10,25) or a hoopoe (Gp. 15,1,22), and was persecuted by other birds of prey and the chamaeleon (Paul Fest. 32; Plin. HN 10,109; 28,113; Gell. NA 10,12,2).

Because goshawks were a danger for poultry farming, nets or lime-twigs were used to catch them (Ter. Phorm. 330; Varro, Rust. 3,7,7; Hor. Epist. 1,16,50f.). In the oldest Greek fable, too, the goshawk is presented as a robber (Hes. Op. 203ff.; cf. Aesop. 4 HAUSRATH; Plut. Mor. 158 b), and the bird was used as a symbol for robbery by Plato (Phd. 82a) and Plautus (Persa 409), as well as in paradoxes, e.g. by Lucretius (3,752: *accipiter fugiens veniente columba*) and Ovid (Fast. 2,90: *accipitri iuncta columba*). The proper name Hierax is applied ambiguously in Aristoph. Equ. 1052 to Cleon. Because of its excellent visual ability (Polemon of Laodicea, Physiognomia 1,184,10 FOERSTER et al.), a goshawk should be boiled in lard to produce an eye ointment (Gal. 14,243; cf. Marcellus, De medicamentis 8,66), and according to Plin. HN 29,125, it was not only the meat boiled in rose oil, but also the droppings mixed with ash and Attic honey, which were considered beneficial in the treatment of eye illnesses.

In antiquity, only falcons were used in hunting, as in Ctesias frg. 11 with reference to India, and in Aristot. Hist. an. 8(9),3,6,620a 30ff. (cf. Antigonus of Carystus, Rerum mirabilium collectio 28; Plin. HN 10,23; Ael. NA 2,42) for Thrace. Generally, falconry was of little importance prior to the 5th cent. AD [2. vol. 2, 24f.]. It is not clear to what extent the alleged sanctity to Apollo (Aristoph. Av. 516) or Mars (Serv. Aen. 11,721) and also the mantic role (Iambl. Myst. 6,3 p.243 PARTHEY; Cic. Nat. D. 3,19; Obseq. 58; Sil. Pun. 4,104; Stat. Theb. 3,503) referred not just to falcons, but also included the goshawk. In any case, such references generally refer to Egypt (e.g. Hdt. 2,65; Ael. NA 10,14, and 12,4; Hecat. 73 B 6 D.-K.; Str. 17,1,40,812 and 17,1,47,817; Diod. Sic. 1,87,8) and thus to the → Horus falcon [3. 117f.]. This is supported by Aristotle's statement (Hist. an. 7(8),28,606a 21–24) that smaller members of the species lived there. In the interpretation of dreams, birds represented thievery or robbery (Artem. 2,20 p.137 and 4,56 p.279 PACK), a reference once again to the goshawk.

1 A. GARZYA (ed.), Dionysii Ixeuticon libri, 1963 2 KELLER 3 D'ARCY W. THOMPSON, A Glossary of Greek Birds, 1936, repr. 1966. C.HÜ.

Gospel book see → Liturgical manuscripts

Gospels (literary forms)
A. DEFINITIONS B. ANCIENT GOSPELS C. GOSPEL AND BIOGRAPHY D. GOSPEL AND HISTORIOGRAPHY

A. DEFINITIONS

The term Gospel (Greek εὐαγγέλιον; *euangélion*, good news, OE *god spel*, 'glad tidings'; → Euangelion) is generally understood to refer to the four books of the NT, dealing with the life, the teachings and the death of → Jesus of Nazareth; they are attributed to the four 'Evangelists' (Mt, Mk, Lc, Jo). The (reconstructed) Gospel source Q (*c.* AD 50–60) only seems to know the verb (εὐαγγελίζονται; *euangelízontai*, Mt 11:5; Lc 7:23), a reference to Jesus' oral 'evangelizing', not to a genre; in the NT itself, the noun is never used as a generic term either; early documentary evidence: Didache 8:2; 15:3; 5:12; Justin. Apol. 1,66,3; as inscriptio in MSS: P66 of *c.* 200 [13]. The literary character of the genre Gospel was disputed time and again – not least for theological reasons [6; 14]. Of great influence was OVERBECK's thesis (1880ff.) that the Gospels were *Urliteratur*, utilitarian literature for the congregations, and thus on principle set apart from contemporary literature [12]. By contrast, alongside literary-historical references regarding individual literary forms within the Gospels – anecdote, apophthegma, 'last words', parable (simile), fictitious speeches (didactic and promotional speech, → Protreptics) and dialogues (debates), stories of conversions and callings (cf. Apul. Met. XI; → Novel), Itineraries, summaries, alternation between mass and individual scenes [3; 4] –, great emphasis is placed particularly on the relationship between the Gospels and the 'grand genres' of ancient historiography.

B. ANCIENT GOSPELS

More than fifty works are transmitted which could be described as Gospels, either because of their title or as sources for the Gospels, or on the basis of the criterion of content: 'Jesus appears speaking (and acting)' [8. 91]. Early Gospels, presupposing the canonical Gospels, are the Gospels of Peter and of Thomas, as well as the Egerton Gospel. The Gospel of Peter reports on Jesus' trial, and defends Pilatus' innocence; the description of Jesus' last days seems to be dependent on Mt [5. 2,1317–1349]. The extant text of the Gospel of Thomas is gnostic (chs. 8; 20; 49; 96; 107): sayings of the 'living Jesus', not the earthly Jesus. The Jesus in the Gospel of Thomas rejects the prophets of Israel (52) as well as women for not being male (114). Five of these sayings (42; 81f.; 97f.) may go back to Jesus; saying 5 seems to be dependent on Lc 8,17. The four papyrus fragments of the Egerton Gospel, dating from the mid 2nd cent., contain reminiscences of Jo 5 and 7–10, probably as a result of oral tradition.

The dating of the four canonical Gospels: Mk was written in Rome or Syria between *c.* 60 and 75; Mt *c.* 80–90 in Syria; Lc *c.* 80–100; Jo 85–100, before of after the letters of John, either in Ephesus or Syria. John differs from the three synoptic Gospels with regard to the following points: Jesus is mainly active in Jerusalem, the motif of the kingdom of God is not central; long speeches take the place of parables, there are no → exorcisms and only few miracles. The beginning with John the Baptist and the end with the Passion and the narratives of the empty tomb are similar in all four Gospels.

C. GOSPEL AND BIOGRAPHY

Amongst the historiographic genres of Greek literature, → biographies show clear parallels with the Gospels. → Lucianus, for example, wrote i.a. an 'autobiography' as well as six *Bíoi* of philosophers, ascetics, and founders of cults. An analysis of the history of the genre and the tradition, e.g. of the 'Life of Demonax', leads to models predating Mk [8. 115–130]. Lucian recorded as an eyewitness of Demonax's teachings [3] the latter's life and death (3–11; 63–67), also his anecdotes and sayings (12–62), a combination of life and teaching (βίος; *bíos* and διδαχή; *didaché*). The 'Demonax' is the programmatic script of the 'Greek Renaissance'; it has a *kerygma*, and it is a protreptic on philosophy. Similarities as well as differences to the Gospels can advance the debate on what constitutes the genre Gospel. The generalizing statement that Lucian's *vitae* are entirely unsuitable for any comparison with the genre Gospel [6. 399f.; 14. 350], needs to be modified [8. 127–129].

To prove that the Gospels are *bíoi* of Jesus, a wide-ranging research into Greek and Roman *vitae* has been presented, investigating the sociological (formation of groups around a charismatic leader) and literary criteria (title, subject matter, length of text, structures and topic) of ancient biographies, i.a. using word statistics [7], and comparing them with the Gospels. Presupposing a certain range of variation [7. 197–199, cf. 77, 165–167, 179], the structure of the Gospels – chronological narration with geographical movement (most obviously in Lc) and the insertion of a variety of material – equates to that of several Greek *Bíoi*. The literary units, anecdotes, speeches, are similar [7. 168; 172; 204], the topics familiar: the lack of a birth narrative is easier to explain than the absence of Jesus' genealogy and education. The purpose of the Gospels was clearly didactic and apologetic, in common with most other ancient *bíoi*.

D. GOSPEL AND HISTORIOGRAPHY

For Luke's historical work in particular, consisting of the Gospel (Lc) as part one (λόγος; *lógos*) and Acts as part two, the comparison with historiographies in the stricter sense seems more suggestive [1; 8; 9] (→ Historiography). Counter arguments based on the length of the works – Mt comprises 18,305 words, Mk 11,242, Lc 19,428 [7. 199] – seem unsound. In view of both size and structure, the comparison with the Augustan historiographer → Dionysius [18] of Halicarnassus seems beneficial. (a) The average length of Dionysius' portrayals of Roman kings is comparable: Romulus (Ant. 1,76–2,56) – *c.* 20,000 words, Numa (Ant. 2,57–76) – *c.* 6,000 words, Tullus Hostilius (Ant. 3,1–35) – *c.* 13,500 words etc. Dionysius does not emphasize the individual character of the kings, but their social, political and religious acts, e.g. in respect to the 'growth' of Rome and the relations between the poor and the rich, patricians and plebeians, two topics which are also central to Luke's historical work [2]. Equally, the focus on one individual (a criterion for a *bíos* [7. 116]: In Mk, Jesus is the subject of 24 % of all verbs, thus comparable to the 18 % of Tacitus' *Agricola*) is also found in Dionysius: Tarquinius Superbus is the subject of 24,7 % of all sentences. The much lower percentage in Herodotus' works applying to the kings Darius and Xerxes (bks. 6 and 7) is thus not a valid counter argument.

(b) Dionysius' *Antiquitates Romanae* tell the story of Rome's prehistory (1,9–70), its regal period – the 'biographies' of the seven kings (1,71–4,85) – and finally that of their successors, the annually changing consuls (5–20). A comparison can be drawn between these three historical epochs and the three stages of the history of salvation in Lc/Acts: (1) Israel, the ancestors (Lc 3:23–38; cf. Acts 7:1–53; 13:16–41, 46f.), (2) Jesus, the central period (Lc), and (3) the Church (Acts). In the third stage, the successors put into practice the founders' political inheritance: Rome, or the Church, 'grows', wealthy citizens, or the disciples, 'waive the debts of the poor'. Thus the Gospels of Mk, Mt, and Jo are related to Graeco-Roman biographies, and Lc and Acts to (political) historiography.

1 D.E. Aune, The New Testament in its Literary Environment, 1987 2 D.L. Balch, Cultural Ideology. A Comparison of Dionysius of Halicarnassus, Roman Antiquities, and Luke-Acts, in: B.W. Winter (ed.), The Book of Acts in its First Century Setting, vol. 4: The Book of Acts in its Theological Setting, 1998 3 K. Berger, Hell. Gattungen im Neuen Testament, in: ANRW II 25.2, 1034–1880 4 H.D. Betz, The Sermon on the Mount, 1995 5 R. Brown, Death of the Messiah, 1993 6 R. Bultmann, Die Gesch. der synoptischen Tradition, 1921. repr. 1987 7 R.A. Burridge, What are the Gospels? A Comparison with Graeco-Roman Biography, 1992 8 H. Cancik (ed.), Markus-Philologie. Histor., literargesch. und stilistische Unt. zum zweiten E., 1984, there: Id., Die Gattung E. (1981) and Id., Bios und Logos 9 Id., The History of Culture, Rel., and Institutions in Ancient Historiography: Philological Observations Concerning Luke's History, in: Journ. of Biblical Literature 116, 1997, 681–703 10 A. Dihle, Die Entstehung der histor. Biographie, in: SB der Akad. der Wiss. Heidelberg 3, 1987, 1–83 11 H. Koester, Ancient Christian Gospels: Their History and Development, 1990 12 F. Overbeck, Werke und Nachlaß, ed. by E.W. Stegemann et al., 1994ff. (vols. 1–3: works until 1898) 13 G. Stanton, The Fourfold Gospel, in: New Testament Studies 43, 1997, 317–346 14 P. Vielhauer, Gesch. der urchristl. Lit., 1975.

DA.B.

Gossypium see → Cotton

Gotarzes II After the death of King Artabanus II [5] which did not occur before AD 39, the empire of the Parthians was shaken by battles for the throne that filled the entire period of the reign of his successor G. His relationship to his predecessor and to the Arsacids is unclear: whilst he is usually regarded in the literary sources as the son of Artabanus (Tac. Ann. 11,8f.; Jos. Ant. Iud. 20,3,4), various pieces of circumstantial evidence lead us to conclude that he was only the foster-son of the former king and that he came from a wealthy line of the Arsacids in Hyrcania. He began his rule with the murder of Artabanus [6], the eldest natural son of his 'father', and the murder of the latter's family. The younger brother Vardanes was able to flee, gather an army and expel G. to Hyrcania. The latter, however, soon returned with troops consisting of Dahae and Hyrcanians and went into battle. The plan of a party hostile to the two 'brothers' to murder → Vardanes, which was discovered by G., led to an agreement: G. acknowledged Vardanes as the Parthian king while he retained uncontested rule over the Hyrcanians. In a new attempt to gain the crown, G. initially got the worse deal: Vardanes defeated G. on the Erindes and drove him to Hyrcania. He was, however, forced to turn around by his battle-weary soldiers and fell victim soon afterwards (summer of 45) to an attack by G.

At first, G. was recognized as the king of the Parthians, but in 49/50 he had to ward off the invasion of the Arsacid → Meherdates who had been brought in from Rome. From the outset, however, the latter's position was not very promising, as the only serious support he had was from the head of the noble house of Karîn, whilst his other allies, the vassal kings Abgar V of Osrhoene and Izates II of Adiabene had a secret alliance with G. After Meherdates was betrayed by his allies and after the death in battle of Karîn, Meherdates fell into the hands of G. who rendered him incapable of rule by cutting off his ears. With regard to the end of G.'s life, there are contradictions between the accounts of Tacitus (Ann. 12,14,4: death by illness) and Josephus (Ant. Iud. 20,3,4: murder). The matter is decided by evidence of Parthian coins that show that G. and Vologaeses I competed for rule from autumn 50 onwards and that the former succumbed to his rival in the summer of 51. It is now impossible to link with G. the inscriptions that are part of the rock relief at → Bisutun and that contain the names 'Gotarzes' and 'Gotarses' (OGIS 431 b+c) [1. 61–71]. On the other hand, his shimmering figure in an idealized form probably entered Iranian heroic legend, made tangible in the work of Ṭabarī and in the book of kings of Firdausī.

1 H.v. Gall, Die parthischen Felsreliefs unterhalb des Dariusmonumentes, in: W. Kleiss, P. Calmeyer (ed.), Bisutun, 1996 2 M. Schottky, Parther, Meder und Hyrkanier, in: MDAI(I) 24, 1991, 61–134.

M.SCH.

Gothic language The Gothic language, the sole representative of the eastern Germanic group within the → Germanic languages together with Crimean Gothic [6], is only known from a few testimonials in the language itself. The most important text – recorded in → Gothic script – is → Ulfila's translation of the Bible (NT, 4th cent. AD, [7]). Some additional linguistic monuments of the Gothic language are only extant in parts [7. 456–487]. Furthermore, there is evidence of Gothic names passed down to us in a secondary manner, e.g. *Visigot(h)ae*, *-i* and *Austro-*, *Ostrogot(h)ae*, *-i* (usually reproduced as 'Visigoths' and 'Ostrogoths'; see [1. 1]); *Augis*, *Mathesventha* (personal name in Jordanes) [4; 5]. In the Christian context, Greek words were adopted into Gothic, e.g. *aikklesjo* 'parish, church' (ἐκκλησία; *ekklēsía*), *aipistaule* 'letter' (ἐπιστολή; *epistolḗ*), *paintekusten* (acc. sing.) 'Pentecost' (πεντηκοστή; *pentēkostḗ*), *rabbei* 'Master, Rabbi' (ῥαββεί; *rabbeí*, Hebrew transmitted via Greek) [2. 35–37; 3]. Latin and Greek words were also absorbed into Gothic from other word fields, e.g. *aketis* (gen. sing.) 'vinegar' (Latin *acetum*), *sinapis* (gen. sing.) 'mustard' (σίναπι; *sínapi*), *lukarn* 'lamp' (Latin *lucerna*) [3].

→ Gothic script; → Germanic languages; → Ulfila

1 W. Braune, E.A. Ebbinghaus, Gotische Gramm., ¹⁹1981 2 F. Kluge, Urgermanisch, in: H. Paul (ed.), Grundriß der german. Philologie 2, ³1913 3 W.P. Lehmann, A Gothic Etymological Dictionary, 1986 4 H. Reichert, Lex. der altgerman. Namen, 2 parts, 1987/1990 5 M. Schönfeld, WB der altgerman. Personenund Völkernamen, 1911 6 M.D. Stearns, Crimean Gothic. Analysis and Etymology of the Corpus, 1978 7 W. Streitberg, Die gotische Bibel, 1950.

W. Griepentrog, Zur Text- und Überlieferungsgesch. der gotischen Evangelientexte, 1990; F. Holthausen, Gotisches etymologisches WB, 1934; F. de Tollenaere, R.L. Jones, Word-Indices and Word-Lists to the Gothic Bible and Minor Fragments, 1976; N. Wagner, Getica. Untersuchungen zum Leben des Jordanes und der frühen Gesch. der Goten, 1967. S.ZI.

Gothic script

[1] The linguistic monuments of → Gothic are written in their own alphabetical script. It was created about the middle of the 4th cent. AD by the Gothic bishop Wulfila (→ Ulfila) in Moesia (modern Bulgaria) for the purpose of translating the Bible. The extant manuscript tradition starts about AD 500 and is divided into two slightly different script variants of different ages. Most letters are taken directly from the Greek → alphabet. The reasons for deviations from it lie in special Gothic sounds and sound combinations, for instance q, j and ƕ that are written 𐌵 𐌾 𐍈 in Gothic, which could not have been reproduced in the Greek alphabet. How strong the influence of the Latin alphabet was in the emergence of these differing letters is a matter of debate and depends on whether a co-effect is also attributed to the Germanic runic alphabet (→ Runes) or not. The problem depends on the fact that the MS of Wulfila himself is not extant and so we do not know what effect the Latin alphabet had already had in (partially Romanized) Moesia or only later in Italy.

W. Braune, Gotische Gramm., ¹⁹1981, 11–18; F. Cercignani, The elaboration of the Gothic alphabet and orthography, in: IF 93, 1988, 168–185; H.B. Rosén, Zur Erschließung der Quellen und der Lautwerte des got. Alphabets, in: W. Smoczyński (ed.), Kuryłowicz Memorial Volume, vol. 1, 1995, 469–481. N.O.

[2] In the 12th cent. the last and final change in the Carolingian → minuscule took place that led to a new script, the so-called Gothic script (GS). In the sources of the 14th and 15th cents. it is called *littera textualis, textura, textus, littera formata, lettre de forme*; however the term 'Gothic' does not occur until later. This new script is attested from the mid 12th cent. onwards in southern England, in Belgium and in northern France and spread in the first decades of the 13th cent. throughout the whole of Europe. The transformation of late Carolingian miniscule to Gothic brought with it no significant change to the form and structure of the letters. The entire image of this new bookhand is, however, characterized by clear stylistic innovation. In the GS type there are narrow letters that join each other (with primarily vertical stems standing on the line), strongly reduced ascenders and descenders, a general break in the arcs in straight strokes, steep upstrokes and downstrokes (that sometimes also become quadrilaterals), as well as the change from hair-strokes and shadow strokes. In the transformation of late Carolingian minuscule it is not just the new formation of the letters themselves but also the organization of the spaces in between that is worthy of note. This leads to a script image of word blocks with broader parts clearly separated from each other. So-called GS shows regional differences: the German, French and English GS remains narrow and angular, whilst in Italy and Spain it allows for round and wide forms. There are also differences in the degree of stylization: better known are its formal strictly stylized forms, but GS was generally widespread in a wide variety of simplified forms.

GS was used from the 13th to the 15th cents. usually for copying Latin classics; from the 14th cent. onwards it, however, lost importance because of the spread of the → cursive and the → bastarda and finally the → Humanist script. In the late 15th cent. the GS was used particularly for liturgical books and university MSS (theology, scholastic philosophy, medicine, law), so that it was finally taken up by book printing.

→ Bastarda

B. Bischoff, Paläographie des röm. Altertums und des abendländischen Mittelalters, ²1986, 171–183; E. Casamassima, Tradizione corsiva e tradizione libraria nella scrittura latina del Medioevo, 1988, 95–126; J. Destrez, La Pecia, 1935, 43–61, pl. 1–36; J.P. Gumbert, Die Utrechter Kartäuser und ihre Bücher, 1974, 215–241; J. Kirchner, Scriptura gothica libraria, 1966, pl. 1–36; W. Meyer, Die Buchstaben-Verbindungen der sog. gothischen Schrift, 1897; S. H. Thomson, Latin Bookhands of the Later Middle Ages, 1100–1500, 1969, pl. 3–17, 23, 28, 34–44, 47, 59–71, 74, 75, 77, 79, 85–93, 96, 98–100, 102, 103, 106, 112–120, 122, 126, 128, 131; S. ZAMPONI, La scrittura del libro nel Duecento, in: Civiltà Comunale: Scrittura, libro, documento, 1989, 317–354. N.G.

[3] Gothic script (GS) also refers to a particular script stylization that arose in the German cultural region at the beginning of the 16th cent. and was used in German book printing up to the mid 20th cent. This type of script can also be called 'broken script' (*Fraktur*) because of the breaking of its stems. It was practically regarded as the German national script of the modern age.

GS is derived from the → chancellery script and was influenced by textura, i.e. by the *Littera textualis* of the late Middle Ages; it became the German, Gothic broken script type. The perfect image of GS is characterized by heavy and especially long narrow letters: in this way the tapering descenders of *F, P, Q* and *S* are extended below the line. The capital letters are decorated and their upswings are in the form of an 'elephant's trunk'.

German palaeographical research traces GS back to the stylized forms of the chancellery script, otherwise it is assumed that GS originated in a developed → bastarda. This is not necessarily a contradiction, as the chancellery scripts of the late medieval script types of the Occident – provided that they do not imitate the forms of the Italian Humanist → minuscule – are guided by the model of the bastarda.

G. CENCETTI, Lineamenti di storia della scrittura latina, [2]1997, 287–291; H. FICHTENAU, Die Lehrbücher Maximilians I. und die Anfänge der Frakturschrift, 1961; H. A. GENZSCH, Kalligraphische Stilmerkmale in der Schrift der Luxemburg-habsburgischen Reichskanzlei. Ein Beitrag zur Vorgesch. der Fraktur, in: Mitt. des Öst. Inst. für Geschichtsforsch., 45, 1931, 205–214; A. HESSEL, Die Schrift der Reichskanzlei seit dem Interregnum und die Entstehung der Fraktur, in: Nachr. von der Göttinger Ges. der Wiss., Philol.-histor. Kl., N.F. 2/3, 1937, 43–59. N.G.

Goti (Gutones, 'Goths'). Germanic people whose very small traditional core of people supposedly left Scandinavia (Iord. Get. 25f.; [1]; archaeological evidence for a migration overseas are lacking) under 'King' Berig (important: not one of the → Amali!). At the beginning of the common era the G. settled in the Oder area (cf. Str. 7,1,3); their ethnogenesis obviously took place in the area of the Wielbark culture, next to (Ulmi)rugic-Lemovian neighbours, north of the Lugic-Vandal Przeworsk culture and west of the western Baltic cultures (→ Aestii). The G. who are counted among the Germanic eastern tribes (Tac. Germ. 43) had particularly powerful kingdoms who relied upon the fealty structure of the wandering army, which meant that it did not succumb to the influence of → Maroboduus. Detached from the Lugic-Vandal cult association, the G. as an entire tribe moved out of Pommerania and Greater Poland between 150 and 230, into the regions east of the middle course of the Vistula (Ptol. 2,11,16; 3,5,8; cf. Iord. Get. 26f.). Under Filimer (not one of the Amali!) smaller groups (*exploratores*) moved to the south and south-east and around 220/230 increasingly covered the whole area of Wolhynia and northern Moldavia, so that around the middle of the 3rd cent. they had the rest of Moldavia and the Ukraine in their possession, although the first expansion area remained occupied by G. until around 400. During this formative phase of the Černjachov culture (= late Č3) that existed until about 370/380, the G. attacked the Balkans from 238 over several decades and received annual funds from the Roman emperor (cf. Petrus Patricius FHG 4,184ff, fr. 8); under Kniva (249) they mostly attacked Moesia (victory at Abrittus over → Decius [II 1]), in 254 for the first time also Thessalonica; from 257 their naval campaigns were supported by logistical bases in the north and north-east of the Pontus Euxinus (from 268 Tyras was Gothic) [2]. It was not until Claudius II and Aurelianus that decisive successes were achieved against the G. who were allied with the Heruli [3; 4]. After the stabilization of the Goth settlement area in *Oium* ('in the leas') the separation into so-called Ostro- and Visigoths took place that was first attested in 291 (cf. Pan. Lat. 11[3]17,1), whereby the latter extended their expansion area west of the Pruth (= Sîntana de Mureş culture in Romanian Moldavia, in Vlachia, in Muntenia and Transylvania for which there is evidence until late Č3). → Gothic script; → Gothic language; → Greuthungi; → Ostrogoths; → Tervingi; → West Goths

1 N. WAGNER, *Optila**, *Accila**, *Thraufstila** und die *Gaut(h)igoth*, in: BN 29/30, 1994/5, 358–370 2 A. SCHWARCZ, Die gotischen Seezüge des 3. Jh., in: H. PILLINGER, A. PÜNZ, H. VETTERS (ed.), Die Schwarzmeerküste in der Spätantike und im frühen Mittelalter, 1992, 47–57 3 T. KOTULA, Νέσσος et Νάισσος, in: Eos 79, 1991, 237–243 4 E. KETTENHOFEN, Die Einfälle der Heruler ins Röm. Reich im 3. Jh. n.Chr., in: Klio 74, 1992, 291–313.

H. WOLFRAM, Die Goten, [3]1990; V. BIERBRAUER, Arch. und Gesch. der Goten vom 1.–7. Jh., in: FMS 28, 1994, 51–171; I Goti, Palazzo Reale, Milano (exhibition catalogue), 1994. K.DI.

Got(h)icus Cognomen *ex virtute* given to the victorious general deriving from the Goths; the Roman emperors from Claudius II (AD 268–270) onwards bore it – last used by Justinian and Mauricius (without *maximus*).

P. KNEISSL, Die Siegestitulatur der röm. Kaiser, 1969, passim; 247. W.E.

Government see → Political administration

Government, theories of forms of see → Aristokratia; → Basileus; → Demokratia; → Mixed constitution; → Monarchia; → Oligarchia; → Tyrannis; → Theory of constitution

Gracchus Roman cognomen probably of Etruscan origin, as a praenomen passed down for the Aequian king G. Cloelius in 458 BC (Liv. 3,25,5). As cognomen prominent in the family of the Sempronii, especially with the people's tribunes Ti. and C. → Sempronius Gracchus.

SALOMIES 72 SCHULZE 172, 354, 519 WALDE/HOFMANN 1, 615. K.-L.E.

[1] Writer of Latin tragedies (*Thyestes*, *Atalanta*, *Peliades*), only a short fragment of each is extant (for Inc. inc. fab. 120–124 ²R see [4]); Ov. Pont. 4,16,31 names him together with L. → Varius Rufus in a catalogue of contemporary writers. This presumably refers to Sempronius G., the lover of Augustus' daughter Iulia (Tac. Ann. 1,53).

EDITIONS: TRF p. 230 (³266).

BIBLIOGRAPHY: 1 BARDON 2, 48f. 2 E. GROAG, s.v. Sempronius 41, RE IIA 2,1371–1374 3 I. LANA, L'Atreo di Accio e la leggenda di Atreo e Tieste nel teatro tragico romano, in: Atti della Accademia delle Scienze di Torino 93, 1958–59, 293–385, esp. 327f. 4 J. SOUBIRAN, Les débuts du trimètre tragique à Rome 2, in: Studi F. della Corte 3, 1987, 109–124, esp. 120ff. W.-L.L.

Grac(c)urris Town in the upper Ebro valley; precise location unknown. In 179 BC founded as a Gracchuris by Tib. Sempronius Gracchus in place of the Iberian town of Ilurcis (Liv. Epitome 41; Festus p. 86,5). G. is mentioned later in the war against Sertorius in 76 BC (Liv. Epitome 41). Pliny (HN 3,24) names G. among the *oppida Latii veteris* of the *conventus* of Caesaraugusta. There are no inscriptions, but G. appears on several coins from the time of Tiberius as a *municipium* [1. 113f.]. Later G. is no longer mentioned.

1 A. VIVES, La moneda hispánica 4, 1924.

TOVAR 3, 391f.; A. SCHULTEN, Fontes Hispaniae Antiquae 3, 1935, 223f.; 4, 1937, 189; 8, 1959, 134; E. HÜBNER, s.v. G., RE VII 2, 1687. P.B.

Graeae (Γραῖαι; *Graîai*). The G. (Pemphredo, → Enyo, Deino/Perso) are daughters of Ceto and the sea god Phorcys, after whom they are also called Phorcides or Phorciades. Their number varies from two to three. They are grey-haired (Greek *graía*), swan-like (Ps.-Aesch. PV 795), beautifully dressed (Hes. Theog. 273) maidens living on the far side of Oceanus in Atlas' cave. Between them, they possess only one eye and one tooth, which they use alternately.

They are known through their connection to the Gorgon adventure in the myth of Perseus: according to one version, → Perseus steals the G.'s eye and tooth to make them tell him how to find the Nymphs who are to lend him the bag, the winged sandals, and the cap of invisibility for his battle against the G.'s sisters, the Gorgons (→ Gorgo). According to another version, Perseus – already in possession of the magical accoutrements – overcomes the G., who are guarding the entrance to the land of the Gorgons. The original meaning of the G., no longer immediately apparent in the myth, is disputed. Older interpretations saw them as sea goddesses, based on the etymology of the name and on their ancestry. However, it is probably more correct to regard them, parallel to the Gorgons, as cloud goddesses and to understand their light-coloured vestments and swan-like shape as symbols of the storm cloud. The single eye and tooth may be understood as a symbol of lightning (cf. Lat. *fulmen* meaning 'boar's tooth'). C.U.-K.

Graecia Magna see → Katepanate; → Magna Graecia

Graecinius P.G. Laco. Knight from Verona. Successor of Sutorius Macro as *praefectus vigilum* in AD 31; he supported him in the elimination of Seianus (→ Aelius [II 19]); therefore, the Senate bestowed upon him the *ornamenta quaestoria*. He was *procurator* in Gallia under Claudius during the Britannia campaign, possibly entrusted with a special logistic function for the campaign. He was honoured with a statue and *ornamenta consularia* by the Senate in 44 at the request of Claudius; in addition, he received a seat in the Senate as often as he escorted Claudius there (in which capacity is not clear).

R. SABLAYROLLES, Libertinus Miles, 1996, 476f. · PIR² G 202. W.E.

Graeco-Babyloniaca Babylonian clay tablets with cuneiform script text in Sumerian or Akkadian on one side and its transliteration in Greek on the other side are called Graeco-Babyloniaca. The total of less than 30 tablets and fragments of tablets were written between the 2nd cent. BC and the 2nd cent. AD and come from Babylon, as far as their origin is known. They contain excerpts from lexical texts as well as prayers and incantations. The choice of texts and their arrangement on the clay tablets corresponds exactly with the traditional cuneiform school texts of the new and late Babylonian era. The scribes of Graeco-Babyloniaca were Babylonian students, who had not yet mastered actively the cuneiform script and rendered the cuneiform script text, written by the teacher, in Greek letters that could be learned easily. A standardized transcription system was obviously not developed.

The significance of the Graeco-Babyloniaca lies in the fact that they confirm the assumed readings of cuneiform script characters. On the other hand they give reason to believe that traditional Mesopotamian texts in the Hellenized Orient could also have been transliterated into Greek (comparable to Coptic) and recorded on perishable writing materials, however with no extant traces, after clay tablets were no longer used after the first cent. AD.

M.J. GELLER, The last wedge, in: ZA 87, 1997, 43–95. S.M.

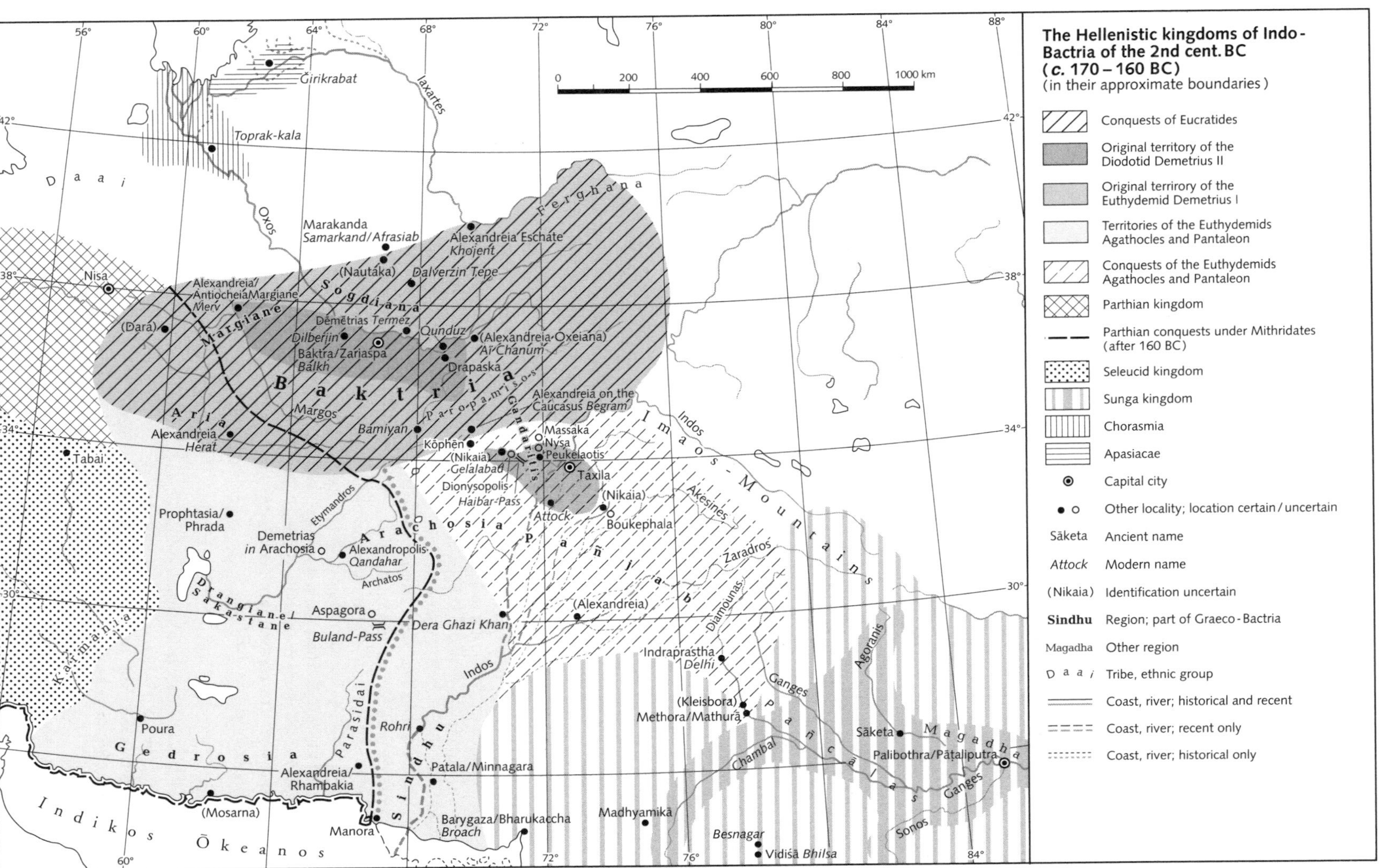
The Hellenistic kingdoms of Indo-Bactria of the 2nd cent. BC (c. 170 – 160 BC)
(in their approximate boundaries)
Conquests of Eucratides
Original territory of the Diodotid Demetrius II
Original terrirory of the Euthydemid Demetrius I
Territories of the Euthydemids Agathocles and Pantaleon
Conquests of the Euthydemids Agathocles and Pantaleon
Parthian kingdom
Parthian conquests under Mithridates (after 160 BC)
Seleucid kingdom
Sunga kingdom
Chorasmia
Apasiacae
Capital city
Other locality; location certain / uncertain
Sāketa Ancient name
Attock Modern name
(Nikaia) Identification uncertain
Sindhu Region; part of Graeco-Bactria
Magadha Other region
Daai Tribe, ethnic group
Coast, river; historical and recent
Coast, river; recent only
Coast, river; historical only
0 200 400 600 800 1000 km
Čirikrabat
Toprak-kala
Iaxartes
Oxos
Daai
Nisa
Marakanda Samarkand/Afrasiab
Alexandreia Eschate Khojent
(Nautaka)
Dalverzin Tepe
Fergh ana
Sogdiana
Alexandreia/Antiocheia Margiane Merv
Margiane
(Dara)
Dēmētrias Termez
Dilberjin
Baktra/Zariaspa Balkh
Qunduz
(Alexandreia Oxeiana) Ai Chanum
Drapaska
Baktria
Paropamisos
Alexandreia on the Caucasus Begram
Margos
Aria
Alexandreia Herat
Bamiyan
Kōphēn
Massaka
Nysa
Peukelaotis
Gandaritis
(Nikaia) Gelalabad
Taxila
Dionysopolis
Haibar-Pass
Attock
(Nikaia)
Boukephala
Tabai
Prophtasia/Phrada
Etymandros
Demetrias in Arachosia
Alexandropolis Qandahar
Archatos
Arachosia
Drangiane/Sakastane
Aspagora
Buland-Pass
Dera Ghazi Khan
Karmania
Pañjab
Imaos-Mountains
Indos
Akesines
Zaradros
(Alexandreia)
Diamounas
Indraprastha Delhi
Agoranis
Ganges
(Kleisbora)
Methora/Mathurā
Pañcālas
Sāketa
Magadha
Palibothra/Pāṭaliputra
Chambal
Sonos
Poura
Gedrosia
Parasidai
Rohri
Sindhu
Patala/Minnagara
Alexandreia/Rhambakia
(Mosarna)
Manora
Barygaza/Bharukaccha Broach
Madhyamikā
Besnagar
Vidiśā Bhilsa
Indikos Ōkeanos

Graeco-Bactria

A. History B. Archaeology C. Society

A. History

The area of → Bactria in north-east Iran is a country with an old culture with an early developed city culture and an Iranian population. Greeks settled there sporadically as early as under the → Achaemenids [2]; however, one cannot as yet speak of a Greek population, with [1]. Not until under Alexander [4] the Great, who conquered the country in a gruelling two-year war, were several settlements started for the veterans of his army. Bactria became a Hellenistic satrapy under the early Seleucids and obtained further Greek settlements. The satrap Diodotus [2] became independent around the middle of the 3rd cent. BC and created a Graeco-Bactrian kingdom. An attempt by Antiochus [5] III. to recapture Bactria was brought to an end through an agreement with king → Euthydemus [2] in 206. Euthydemus and his son Demetrius [10] conquered extensive areas in north-west India, but the kingdom fell to Eucratides, who had instigated a revolt in Bactria during the war. After he was murdered by his son, two dynasties were created, the Eucratids in the north-west, the actual Bactrians, and the Euthydemids in the south-east of the Hindu Kush. Around the middle of the 2nd cent. BC or shortly thereafter, the area was conquered by the nomadic Indo-Scythians, but in the north-east the principalities of the → Indo-Greeks were able to hold out for about another 150 years. The written records until the time of Eucratides are already very sparse, after that there are just numismatic and archaeological sources.

B. Archaeology

The most important site where objects of the Hellenistic period were found is undoubtedly → Ai Khanum on the Oxus (Araxes [2]); only sparse remains of the old capital Bactra (modern Balḫ) are known; some remains of a Dioscuri temple were found in Dil'berdžin. Finds in the north (Uzbekistan and Tajikistan) and in Termez (Demetrias), Dal'verzin Tepe and Ḫalchayan originate mostly from the Indo-Scythian period; Hellenistic wall remains are known from Afrasyab (old Samarkand) in the north (Sogdiana). Greek inscriptions in larger numbers were only found in Ai-Khanum, at other sites (such as Juga Tepe near Dil'berdžin) only here and there. The numismatic sources have considerably increased by extensive hoard finds (e.g. in Qunduz).

C. Society

Because Alexander and the Seleucids established numerous settlements and fortresses next to the old city cultures, the country had an Iranian-Greek mixed population during the 3rd and 2nd cents., expanded by Macedonian and Thracian settlers. Thus the Greek religious tradition is evident on coins, the Iranian in the temple ruins, while the river cult of the Oxus exhibits mixed forms. The artistically very distinguished coinage shows purely Hellenistic characteristics. Most of the known artistic remains from Ai Khanum are partially of pure Greek, partially of Iranian origin and often represent mixed forms. The so-called Gandhara art (→ Gandaritis), a fusion of Hellenistic and Buddhistic styles mostly found in modern Pakistan probably originated here.

→ Bactria

1 A.K. Narain, The Indo-Greeks, 1957.

P. Bernard, Fouilles d'Aï Khanoum 4, 1985 (hoard finds of coins); Bopearachchi; F.L. Holt, Alexander the Great and Bactria, 1989; W. Posch, Baktrien zwischen Griechen und Kuschan, 1995; S. Sherwin-White, A. Kuhrt, From Samarkand to Sardis, 1993; W.W. Tarn, The Greeks in Bactria and India, [2]1951 (1938).
Maps: W.W. Tarn, The Greeks in Bactria and India, [3]1985; H. Waldmann, Vorderer Orient. Die hell. Staatenwelt im 2. Jh. v.Chr., TAVO B V 4, 1985. K.K.

Graecus (Γραικός; *Graikós*). According to Hes. fr. 5, 3 M.-W., the son of Zeus and Pandora (or the brother of Latinus, though according to Theog. 1013 the latter's mother is Circe) and the eponymous hero of the Greeks before they acquired the name Hellenes from → Hellen. The name suggests an Illyrian origin [1].

1 Chantraine, s.v. G., 234.

P. Dräger, Untersuchungen zu den Frauenkatalogen Hesiods, 1997, 27–42. E.V.

Graffiti An imprecise term: for antiquity it is primarily taken to mean 'incised inscription' – especially in contrast to the '*dipinti*', painted inscriptions. On the one hand, though, not everything scratched on was thought of as graffiti (e.g. a letter on a → writing tablet, a Mycenaean clay tablet with → Linear B or an inscription on Etruscan → mirrors and → Praenestine cistae), and on the other, hardly any ancient type of text or any ancient writing medium (concerning form and → writing utensils) is limited exclusively to graffiti. Finally, sketches can also be labelled as graffiti, no less than text [1; 2]. A common characteristic of graffiti is speedy and spontaneous execution (graffiti technique is therefore ideally suited for it because the implements needed are available almost everywhere and at any time). By the same token, though, lack of care taken in the execution is a rather unsuitable criterion – many graffiti were extremely carefully executed (and many *dipinti*, very carelessly). For a scholarly analysis (epigraphical, linguistic, historical etc.), therefore, graffiti cannot be considered in isolation.

The best known corpus of graffiti and *dipinti* is to be found in the wall inscriptions of → Pompeii ([3], and still indispensable as *editio minor*, [4]), mostly in Latin, rarely in Greek and language combinations, with a great variety in content: election propaganda (mostly *dipinti*) [5], gladiatorial inscriptions of all kinds (mostly graffiti) [6], advertisements for different goods and ser-

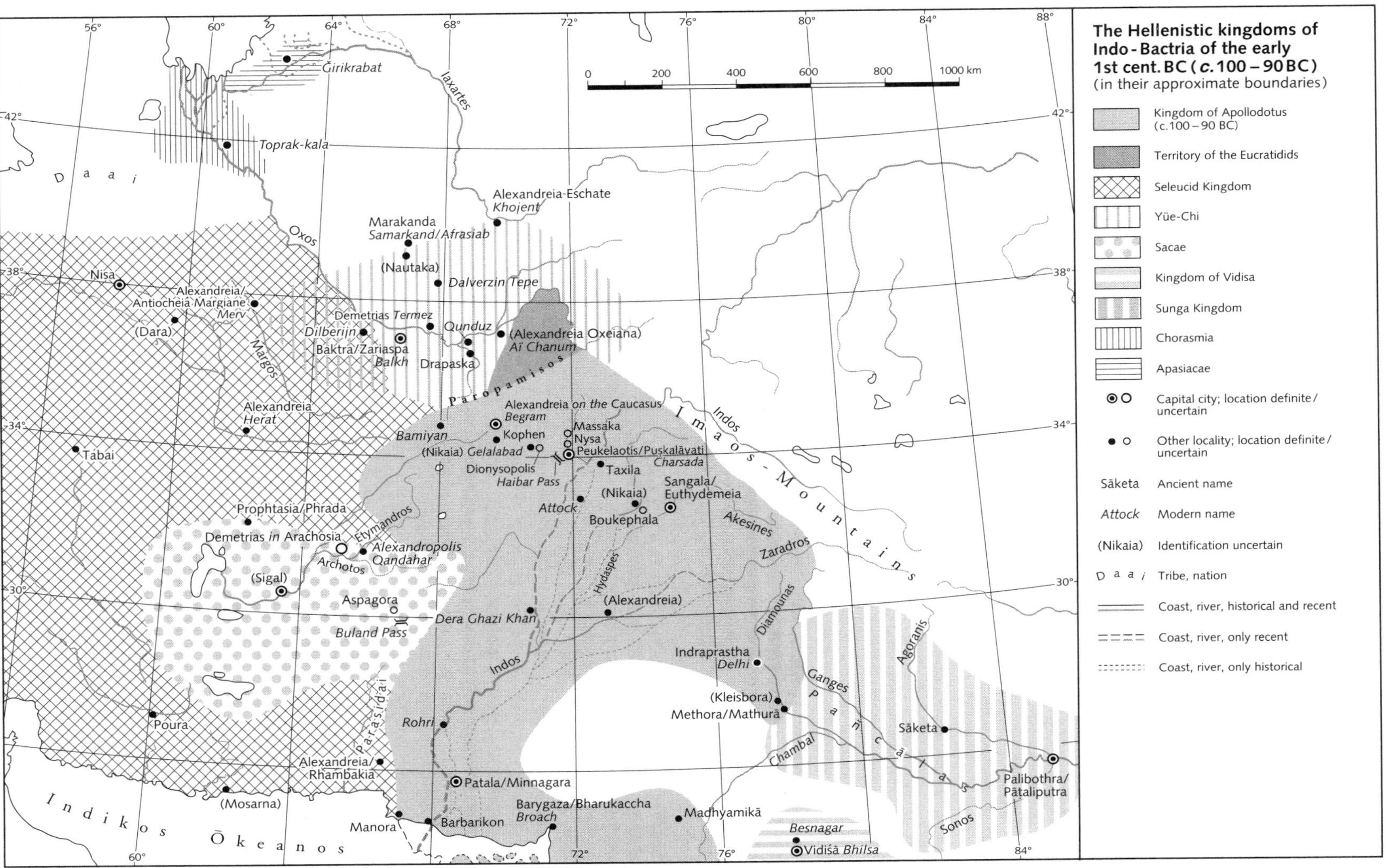
The Hellenistic kingdoms of Indo-Bactria of the early 1st cent. BC (c. 100–90 BC)
(in their approximate boundaries)
Kingdom of Apollodotus (c.100–90 BC)
Territory of the Eucratidids
Seleucid Kingdom
Yüe-Chi
Sacae
Kingdom of Vidisa
Sunga Kingdom
Chorasmia
Apasiacae
Capital city; location definite / uncertain
Other locality; location definite / uncertain
Sāketa Ancient name
Attock Modern name
(Nikaia) Identification uncertain
D a a i Tribe, nation
Coast, river, historical and recent
Coast, river, only recent
Coast, river, only historical
0 200 400 600 800 1000 km
Girikrabat
Iaxartes
Toprak-kala
D a a i
Alexandreia-Eschate
Khojent
Marakanda
Samarkand/Afrasiab
Oxos
(Nautaka)
Dalverzin Tepe
Nisa
Alexandreia/
Antiocheia Margiane
Merv
(Dara)
Demetrias Termez
Dilberjin
Qunduz
(Alexandreia Oxeiana)
Aï Chanum
Baktra/Zariaspa
Balkh
Drapaska
Margos
Paropamisos
Alexandreia
Herat
Alexandreia on the Caucasus
Begram
Bamiyan
Kophen
Massaka
Nysa
Indos
Imaos - Mountains
Tabai
(Nikaia) Gelalabad
Peukelaotis/Puskalāvati
Charsada
Dionysopolis
Haibar Pass
Taxila
Sangala/
Euthydemeia
(Nikaia)
Attock
Boukephala
Prophtasia/Phrada
Etymandros
Akesines
Demetrias in Arachosia
Alexandropolis
Qandahar
Archotos
Zaradros
(Sigal)
Hydaspes
Aspagora
(Alexandreia)
Buland Pass
Dera Ghazi Khan
Diamounas
Agoranis
Indraprastha
Delhi
Ganges
Poura
Parasidai
Rohri
(Kleisbora)
Methora/Mathurā
Sāketa
Chambal
Alexandreia/
Rhambakia
Patala/Minnagara
Palibothra/
Pātaliputra
Indikos Ōkeanos
(Mosarna)
Barygaza/Bharukaccha
Broach
Madhyamikā
Manora
Barbarikon
Besnagar
Vidiśā Bhilsa
Sonos

vices (mostly graffiti), literary quotations and popular poetry (mostly graffiti), from which stock even the Augustan poets occasionally drew inspiration [7]. They are in the Latin cursive script (→ Writing, styles of III.), with its special letter forms (e.g. | | = E, |' = F) and special symbols (in particular, i-longa and the apex), though largely without ligatures, as used in the early Augustan writing tablets (alphabet table: [8. pl. I]). The language of the wall-inscriptions at Pompeii displays both backwards-looking features, with links to pre-classical colloquial → Latin from the comedies of Plautus in particular (→ Plautus; cf. → Vulgar Latin), and forward-looking elements, moving towards the Romance languages [9; 10]. Similar graffiti have been found at other locations, e. g. in Rome [11; 12]. On the walls at Pompeii there also appear Oscan graffiti, including model alphabets [13].

In the Greek domain, the ostraka (→ Ostrakon) deserve special mention as a graffiti medium, mostly ceramic shards used and re-used as 'note-paper', not infrequently, though, written (and painted) in ink or dye. The ostraka from the Athenian Agora (→ Ostrakismos) are a historically important corpus, providing moreover – together with other Attic graffiti and *dipinti* [14] and vase-inscriptions (cf. especially [15]) – surprising insights into the colloquial language of pre-Classical Athens.

Finally, deserving of mention as specific genres are commercial trademarks – generally short combinations of letters or abbreviations of the names of merchants and carriers – on the base of (especially Attic) Greek vases [16], and the curse tablets (→ *defixio*), mostly of lead and mainly in Greek, Oscan [17] and Latin.

Graffiti on clay(-shards) was probably an especially early form of alphabetical writing in the West: the surviving pieces from the 8th cent. BC are almost without exception graffiti on clay: → Nestor's Cup admittedly presupposes fairly long epic texts on another medium. Also, the standard Greek word for 'write', γράφειν/*gráphein*, first meant 'incise'. A large number of early Greek and Latin inscriptions are graffiti (e.g. inscriptions of dedication or ownership) [18; 19]. The same goes for items in many other languages in the Greek cultural sphere that used alphabets early on, for example → Etruscan with numerous vessel-inscriptions from the 7th/6th cents. (a well-studied corpus: [20]), in particular a number of model alphabets with syllable lists, reflecting the teaching of writing (→ Italy, alphabetical scripts, B. and E.). Later, too, however, numerous graffiti are to be found amongst inscriptions on everyday objects.

→ Inscriptions; → Pompeii (with a further bibliography); Script; → GREEK EPIGRAPHY; → CLASSICAL ARCHAEOLOGY III. C.; → LATIN INSCRIPTIONS

1 M. LANGNER, Ant. G.-Zeichnungen (Palilia 11), 2001 (with CD-ROM) 2 F. P. MAULUCCI VIVOLO, Pompei: i graffiti figurati, 1993 3 CIL IV (and suppl., now 3 parts) 4 E. DIEHL (ed.), Vulgärlat. Inschr. (Kleine Texte für Vorlesungen und Übungen 62), [2]1930 5 R. A. STACCIOLI, Manifesti elettorali nell'antica Pompei, 1992 6 P. SABBATINI TUMOLESI, Gladiatorum paria: annunci di spettacoli gladiatorii a Pompei, 1980 7 R. WACHTER, "Oral Poetry" in ungewohntem Kontext: Hinweise auf mündliche Dichtungstechnik in den pompejanischen Wandinschr., in: ZPE 121, 1998, 73–89 8 CIL IV 9 V. VÄÄNÄNEN, Le latin vulgaire des inscriptions pompéiennes, [2]1959 10 Id., Introduction au latin vulgaire, [3]1981 11 Id. (ed.), Graffiti del Palatino, vol. 1, 1966: Paedagogium; vol. 2, 1970: Domus Tiberiana (Acta Instituti Romani Finlandiae 3–4) 12 L. CANALI, Graffiti latini: scrivere sui muri a Roma antica, [2]1999 13 VETTER, no. 58–69 14 M. L. LANG, G. and D. (Agora 21), 1976 15 L. THREATTE, The Grammar of Attic Inscriptions, 2 vols., 1980–1996 16 A. W. JOHNSTON, Trademarks on Greek Vases, 1979 17 VETTER, no. 3–7 18 LSAG, passim 19 WACHTER 20 G. SASSATELLI (ed.), Iscrizioni e graffiti della città etrusca di Marzabotto, 1994. R. WA.

Grai, Graeci (Γραί; *Graí*, Γραικοί; *Graikoí*). In Latin the Greeks were called *Graei* (singular *Graius*) and (often in a form expanded by the ethnicon suffix *-ko*) *Graeci*. It seems reasonable that this name was originally applied to a tribe neighbouring an Italic one, i.e. probably a north-western Greek tribe. It is identified as the *Graikoí* of Thessaly who disappeared at an early date. Their eponym *Graecus* was considered by some to be a son of a sister of Hellen (Hes. Cat. 5), so that the *Graikoí* were not Greeks but their near relatives (much as according to Hes. Cat. 7 the Magnetes and the Macedonians); others considered him to be a son of Thessalus (Steph. Byz. s.v. Γραικός); later scholars, perhaps already with a view towards Latin *Graeci*, saw in the *Graikoí* the later (Thessalian) Hellenes (→ Hellas [1] Hellenes) and surmised that their original home was in southern Thessaly (Marmor Parium FGrH 239 A 6: Apollod. 1,7,3,1), in part (because of the similarity in sound with Hellopes [→ Hellopia] and Helloi) near → Dodona (Aristot. Mete. 1,352a). The *Graikes* (→ Aeolians) in Parion on the Hellespont (Steph. Byz. s.v. Γραικός) were probably a splinter of this tribe; the expansion of ethnic names by *-o-* is common in north-western Greece. Therefore, the existence of the proto-historical *Graikoi* in Thessaly is almost certain but their equation with the Latin *Graeci* remains difficult because only forms with *-k(o)-* are attested from the Greek area (the Boeotian placename → Graia, Hom. Il. 2,498, is almost certainly not relevant), but *Grai* must be assumed as the original form in Latin.

J. MILLER, s.v. Grai, RE 7, 1693–1696. F.GSCH.

Graia (Γραία/*Graía*, Γραῖα/*Graîa*). A settlement in Boeotia mentioned in the Homeric catalogue of ships (Il. 2,498), located between Oropus and Tanagra. Its location was probably known as far back as the archaic period but then lost. There were already several identifications in antiquity; possibly located on the Boeotian coast of the Euboean Gulf west of Oropus. References: Str. 9,2,10; Paus. 9,20,1; Steph. Byz. s.v. Γ., s.v. Ὠρωπός.

H. Beister, Auf der Suche nach dem homer. G. in Böotien, in: E. Olshausen (ed.), Stuttgarter Kolloquium zur histor. Geogr. des Altertums 1, 1980, 51–80 (= Geographica Historica 4, 1987); Id., Probleme bei der Lokalisierung des homer. G. in Böotien, in: La Béotie Antique, 1985, 131–136; Fossey, 66f.; J.M. Fossey, The Identification of G., in: Euphrosyne 4, 1970, 3–22; P.W. Wallace, Strabo's description of Boiotia, 1979, 42f. M.FE.

Grain

I. Ancient Orient II. Graeco-Roman Antiquity III. Species of Grain

I. Ancient Orient

The various species of hulled and naked wheat (*triticum* = *t.*) and barley (*hordeum*) are among the earliest domesticated plants of the Middle East (Q. Ǧarmu; Çatal H.; → Faiyum). Besides → emmer (*t. dicoccum*) and einkorn (*t. monococcum*), both hulled, the common or bread wheat (naked; *t. aestivum*) are also species of wheat. The fact that the hulled sorts, which require more work (removal of the hull through roasting), also predominated in later millennia is ascribed to their better storability [1. 35]. The species of wheat usually took second place to barley; this is often explained by barley's greater tolerance for the often salty soils in the Middle East, but also by a greater reliability and higher yield [2]. In Egypt, → emmer appears to have played a more important role in the New Kingdom (1550–1070 BC) [3. 587ff.]. The view that of the two-rowed and six-rowed forms of *hordeum distichum* the latter gained the upper hand through inclusion in the irrigation economy and was then selected out and thus gave the food economy the decisive impulse, has recently been questioned [4. 57ff.].

Wheat and barley served, above all, for the production of → bread and groats; barley also for the brewing of → beer (for Mesopotamian texts of the 4th millennium [5]; general [6]; for Egypt [7]).

The productivity of grain cultivation in Egypt and Babylonia was inordinately overestimated by ancient authors; thus Herodotus speaks of 200–fold, in exceptional cases even of 300–fold production (Hdt. 1,193; cf. Str. 16,1,14; Theophr. Hist. pl. 8,7,4) [8].

1 J.M. Renfrew, Cereals cultivated in ancient Iraq, in: Bull. Sumerian Agriculture 1, 1984, 32–44 2 M.A. Powell, Salt, Seeds and Yields in Sumerian Agriculture, in: ZA 75, 1985, 7–38 3 W. Helck, s.v. G., LÄ 2, 586f. 4 D.T. Potts, Mesopotamian Civilization, 1997 5 H.J. Nissen, P. Damerow, R.K. Englund, Frühe Schrift und Techniken der Wirtschaftsverwaltung, 1991 6 W. Röllig, Das Bier im alten Mesopot., 1970 7 W. Helck, Das Bier im alten Ägypten, 1971 8 K. Butz, P. Schröder, Zu Getreideerträgen in Mesopot. und dem Mittelmeergebiet, in: BaM 16, 1985, 165–209.

W. Helck, s.v. G., LÄ 2, 586f.; RLA 3, s.v. G., 308–318. H.J.N.

II. Graeco-Roman Antiquity

For most people in the ancient Mediterranean area, grain was the most important food. Our information about the species of grain, cultivation of grain and the significance of grain for human nutrition in antiquity is based both on palaeobotanic remains which have been found in archaeological excavations, and on literary witnesses, particularly the works of Theophrastus (Theophr. Hist. pl. 8; Caus. pl. 4,8–9), Xenophon (Oec. 16–18), the Roman agronomists (Varro, Rust. 1,44–53; 1,57; Columella 2,6; 2,8–9; 2,11–12; 2,20; Plin. HN 18,48–116), of Galen as well as other doctors. The following species of grain were cultivated in antiquity: wheat, barley, oats, rye, millet and rice. Maize (*zea mays*) came to Europe only after 1492.

The Greek and Latin terms for the different species of grain already were confusing for ancient authors (cf. e.g. Hdt. 2,36,2). Until the Price Edict of Diocletian (→ Edictum Diocletiani, AD 301), the increasing significance of all the different species of wheat led to the suppression of the original names for wheat (πυρός; *pyrós* and *triticum*) by terms which had previously referred to grain in general: σῖτος (*sîtos*) and *frumentum*. It was difficult to distinguish clearly between the individual species of grain, which were often very similar. The predominant differentiation in antiquity between naked wheat and hulled wheat, for example, is no longer considered correct today, because it only accounted for external characteristics. Another problem was that grain sown in a foreign region very often took on the typical characteristics of the local grains within three years. This occurred through natural selection, if seeds of different species of grain were accidentally mixed (cf. Theophr. Hist. pl. 8,8,1; Caus. pl. 1,9,3; 2,13,3; 4,1,6; Columella 2,9,13; Plin. HN 18,93). Because the interpretation of the literary witnesses is often problematic under these conditions, the archaeological material is of greater importance. Grain seeds have been found in excavations in charred condition; in the dry climate of Egypt sometimes also in dried, uncharred condition. In addition to the palaeobotanic research of ancient grain seeds for the last century, the biochemical analysis of ancient DNA, which can be extracted from ancient seeds, is now providing new insights.

III. Species of Grain

A. Wheat B. Naked Wheat C. Emmer and Spelt D. Einkorn E. Barley F. Oats G. Rye H. Millet I. Rice J. Sorghum

A. Wheat

There are three species of wheat, all of which were already cultivated in antiquity: 1. diploid wheat (14 chromosomes), generally called einkorn (*triticum monococcum*); 2. tetraploid species of wheat (28 chromosomes), emmer (*t. dicoccum*), durum wheat (*t. durum*) and rivet wheat (*t. turgidum*); 3. hexaploid species of wheat (42 chromosomes), above all common wheat (*t. aestivum*) and spelt (*t. spelta*). With species of wheat of the second and third groups, there is a distinction between the so-called naked or threshing wheat (*t. durum*, *t. turgidum* and *t. aestivum*) and the hulled wheat (*t. dicoccum* and *t. spelta*). In naked wheat, the seed husk is only loosely connected to the seed and can be easily removed by threshing; in hulled wheat, the husks are tightly bound to the seed and can only be removed by roasting and crushing the ears (Plin. HN 18,97). The differentiation between naked and hulled wheat was fundamental for the preparation of food and has therefore determined the subdivision of species of wheat since antiquity, until modern genetics finally showed the significance of a small number of genes for classification.

The most important developments in the history of ancient grain cultivation were first the decline of barley in many regions, while at the same time wheat was increasingly cultivated, and the tendency to replace hulled wheat with naked wheat. *Triticum dicoccum* was displaced in regions with a semi-arid Mediterranean climate by *t. durum* and *t. turgidum*; in the colder regions of the north, the cultivation of *t. aestivum* gained acceptance over that of *t. spelta*. These changes were the result of the different characteristics of the species of grain. Thus, wheat, whose higher concentration of gluten allows → bread to rise during the baking process, was preferred over barley. Of the naked species of wheat, *t. aestivum* (a soft grain with high water content) was well-suited for the production of fine flour for bread, while *t. durum* (a hard grain with low water content) could easily be crushed to semolina, but could not be further processed to fine flour with the primitive milling techniques of antiquity. With the simple cultivation methods of antiquity, the highest yields could be achieved through sowing *t. turgidum*, which was therefore preferentially cultivated in some regions. The seed of *t. turgidum*, however, is softer than that of *t. durum* and therefore not suited for the production of semolina, the flour, on the other hand, is less suited for baking bread than that of *t. aestivum*.

The great popularity of common wheat (Lat. *siligo*) with the Romans is connected to the ever more widely spreading practice of baking bread from sourdough, for which *triticum aestivum* was best suited. In Roman times, common wheat was primarily cultivated in northern Italy, Gallia and Britain. The Roman upper classes ate *panis siligneus*, the lower classes, however, ate *panis plebeius* (Sen. Ep. 119,3) which was prepared from *triticum durum* or other species of grain. The invention of the rotary mill and finer sieves made it possible to produce fine, white flour; however, even the best bread in antiquity was far coarser and more contaminated than modern bread. Galen (6, p. 494 KÜHN) recommended strongly leavened bread as the most easily digestible food for most people. Before the spread of the cultivation of common wheat in Roman times, flat bread from unleavened dough, which was prepared from flour from *t. durum* or *t. diccocum*, was predominantly eaten.

B. NAKED WHEAT

As palaeobotanic finds for the period from 1000 BC show, the Crimea and bordering regions on the northern coast of the Black Sea were the only areas in which *t. aestivum* had been the most important type of grain even before the *Imperium Romanum*. Theophrastus (Hist. pl. 8,4,5) describes a very soft, light common wheat from the Pontus region, which was sown in the autumn and which the Athenians of the 5th and 4th cents. BC preferred to the wheat of Sicily and Egypt. The better quality of the wheat from the Pontus region was the reason why the grain trade with the rulers of this region gained such importance for classical Athens (Dem. Or. 20,30–33; Str. 7,4,6). However, the cultivation of common wheat in antiquity was always difficult because it did not ripen uniformly, and the ripe ears also lost their grains quickly (Plin. HN 18,91). This problem was dealt with in Roman Gallia with the use of the *vallus* during harvest, a tool with which the grain could be harvested more quickly than with the sickle (Plin. HN 18,296; Pall. Agric. 7,1,1–4; 8,1). Also, *t. aestivum* did not thrive as well as *t. durum* in the Mediterranean climate.

Although Columella explicitly states that the best bread could be baked from *siligo* (common wheat), he nevertheless recommends the cultivation of *triticum* (by which *t. durum* is to be understood here), which has larger and heavier grains (Columella 2,6,2; 2,9,13). The species of wheat of antiquity had a higher concentration of protein and a lower concentration of carbohydrates than modern wheat; they were therefore more nutritious, but also produced a significantly lower yield per hectare. The Roman agrarian writers considered a careful selection of the seed-corn to be necessary to prevent degeneration of the grain (Verg. G. 1,197–200; Varro, Rust. 1,52,1; Columella 2,9,11; Plin. HN 18,195); there was, however, no deliberate culturing with the goal of developing new types in antiquity.

According to Galen (6, pp. 480–481 KÜHN) and Oribasius (1,2,2–3), the *semidalítēs pyrós* (*triticum*) had glassy seeds; furthermore, they state that even the best wheat has seeds that are glassy (*diaphanḗs*). These comments confirm that in the Mediterranean region of the Roman period *triticum durum* was the most widespread, because only this species of wheat exhibits these types of seeds, independent of regional conditions. Basilius offers a precise description of *t. durum* for Cappadocia (Basil. Homiliae in hexaemeron 5,290–291 GIET), in which he mentions the strong stalks and long awns which are characteristic of tetraploid species of wheat. Particularly in Byzacium (North Africa), *triticum* is said to have produced high yields (Plin. HN 17,41; 18,94). The wheat in Numidia mentioned by Strabo (17,3,11) is probably *triticum turgidum*. Because of its low water content, hard wheat could be stored for many years (Varro, Rust. 1,57 for Spain; Jos. BI 7,295–298 for Masada in Palestine). According to Theophrastus (Hist. pl. 8,11,5–6), this was also true for Cappadocian wheat. For the assessment of the yield in the cultivation of grain in antiquity, the ratio between sowing and harvest was considered crucial, and not the ratio between the cultivated area and the yield as today. It was by no means considered extraordinary if 400 grains grew on a single stalk, as Pliny reported (HN 18,94). Nevertheless, the hectare yields in ancient North Africa were probably very low, because the relatively thin sowing (25 kg per hectare) could not be balanced out by the growth of the plants.

C. Emmer and Spelt

Emmer (*triticum dicoccum*) – Greek ζειά (*zeiá*), ὄλυρα (*ólyra*), Lat. *far*, *semen* and *arinca* – was cultivated in many regions in antiquity; according to Herodotus (2,36,2), however, it was unusual to bake bread from emmer in classical Greece, unlike in Egypt. The emmer cultivated in Egypt was easier to thresh than the Greek emmer, whose preparation was very laborious (Plin. HN 18,92). This explains why the Egyptians still cultivated emmer in the 1st millennium BC, while the Greeks had already moved on to the cultivation of naked wheat. In the time of the Ptolemies, the Greeks brought *t. durum* to Egypt and thus replaced the native emmer. As palaeobotanic finds prove, emmer was the most important grain in the Argolid during the Mycenaean epoch; in classical Greece, however, emmer appears to have been unimportant for human nutrition (Plin. HN 18,84). According to Theophrastus (Hist. pl. 8,9,2), emmer was used as fodder in this period. Palaeobotanic finds and literary documents (Dion. Hal. Ant. Rom. 2,25,2; XII Tabulae 3,4; Liv. 2,5,2–3; 5,47,8; 6,17,5; 7,37,3; Plin. HN 18,15–17) show that emmer was the most important wheat in Latium at the beginning of the Iron Age; however, it was later increasingly displaced by *t. turgidum*. According to Pliny (HN 18,111), emmer was still of great significance in Campania in the 1st cent. AD, which has been confirmed by new excavations in Pompeii, although earlier excavations also provided indications of naked wheat. Pliny (HN 18,109–116) mentions the production of husked wheat from emmer in Italy and North Africa (*alica*; χόνδρος; *chóndros*; cf. Dioscorides Materia medica 2,96; Gp. 3,7 Beckh). Two types of emmer are distinguished in Europe: *t. dicoccum varietas farrum* and *t. dicoccum varietas rufum*; these two types are probably identical with the Greek types ζειά (*zeiá*) and ὄλυρα (*ólyra*). Emmer was the hulled wheat which flourished best in the Mediterranean climate, while in northern Europe, in Britain e.g., spelt (*t. spelta*) grew best. Because classical authors wrote primarily about the Mediterranean region, there are few references to spelt (cf. Edictum Diocletiani 1,7–8; *Carmen de mensuris et ponderibus*, around AD 400). Hulled wheat required the same amount of work as naked wheat (Columella 2,12,1–2), although twice as much hulled wheat was sown as naked wheat (Columella 2,9,1).

D. Einkorn

Einkorn (*triticum monococcum*; τίφη/*típhē*), which was also known in Greece (Theophr. Hist. pl. 8,9,2; Aristot. Hist. an. 603b26), had a greater significance primarily in the prehistoric epoch; in the area of Pergamum, the cultivation of einkorn was still widespread in the 2nd cent. AD (Gal. 6, p. 518 Kühn). Galen (6, p. 522 Kühn) correctly describes it as wheat with short ears and believed that the πυρός (*pyrós*) mentioned by Homer (Il. 8,188; 10,569) was einkorn. This diploid type of wheat was, to a large extent, resistant to frost and disease, but less productive than emmer; in the western Mediterranean, einkorn never belonged to the important types of grain.

For all species of wheat, autumn was the most favourable time for sowing (Plin. HN 18,49). It had already been recognized in antiquity that grain sown in the autumn produced higher yields than that sown in the spring (Theophr. Caus. pl. 4,9,1; 4,11,1–3; Plut. Mor. 915d-e). Xenophon (Oec. 17,1–6) recommended for Attica that the grain be sown over a longer period and thus adapt the sowing to the unpredictable weather conditions as best as possible. Particularly when the winter sowing did not meet expectations, there was a new sowing in the spring (Hes. Op. 485–490; Columella 2,6,2; 2,9,7–8; Plin. HN 18,69; 18,239–240; 18,201–205). Common wheat is more suited for spring sowing than hard wheat, which requires a lot of moisture at the beginning of its growth, although later it is resistant to drought. Therefore, common wheat was sometimes called 'three-month-wheat' or σιτάνιος πυρός (*sitánios pyrós*, wheat which is harvested in the year of sowing). Theophrastus (Caus. pl. 4,9,6) and Dioscorides (Materia medica 2,101) mention this wheat for Lemnos and Crete.

E. Barley

Barley (κριθή/*krithḗ*; *hordeum*), which counts as the oldest cultivated grain in Greece (Plin. HN 18,72; Philochorus FGrH 328 F73), was also of great significance in antiquity. The inscription IG II[2] 1672 cites a ratio of barley to wheat harvests of 9.3:1 in Attica for the year 329/328 BC. This inscription perhaps indicates a poor harvest caused by little rainfall, with a particularly low yield of wheat as a consequence, while barley, which requires considerably less rainfall, produced average yields. Other texts, however, indicate that in Attica barley was primarily cultivated. Thus the Attic orators mention country estates producing large amounts of barley, but no wheat (Isaeus 11,43; Dem. Or. 42,20). A law of Solon ordered that those who ate at public expense in the Prytaneion should receive only meals of barley on normal days, and only receive wheat on feast days (Ath. 137e). Barley was also the prize for the victor at the Eleusinian Games (schol. Pind. Ol. 9,150). Homer (H. Hom. to Demeter 309; 452) mentions the cultivation of white barley in Eleusis, and the sacred Rharian Field brought a lease of 619 *medimnoi* of barley (IG II[2] 1672,252–254; Paus. 1,38,6). Homer and

Aristophanes mention dishes of barley more often than those of wheat. In Athens, the contractual capacity of women was limited to one → *medimnos* of barley (Isaeus 10,10). According to Theophrastus (Hist. pl. 8,8,2), Attica was particularly well-suited for the cultivation of barley.

In Laconia and Messenia, the helots had to deliver 82 *medimnoi* of barley for every → *kleros* (Plut. Lycurgus 8,7) to the Spartans, so that the Spartans were in turn able to make their contribution of barley to the *syssitia* (Plut. ibid. 12,3; Dicaearchus fr. 72 WEHRLI; Aristotle. frg 611,13 ROSE; Hdt. 6,57,3). Wealthy Spartans, however, now and then contributed wheat rather than barley (Xen. Lac. 5,3). Hecataeus (FGrH 1 F9) proves that barley was the basis of nutrition in Arcadia. Barley was also of great significance in the Cyrenaica, a region of very little precipitation.

The Greeks mainly cultivated six-rowed barley, which was normally sown in the autumn. Columella (2,9,14–16) knew the six-rowed and two-rowed barley as the original sorts; two-rowed barley was particularly suited for the spring sowing in mountainous regions, for example. According to Theophrastus (Hist. pl. 8,4,2) there also existed a three-rowed, a four-rowed and a five-rowed type. Barley cultivation was less labour-intensive in comparison to wheat cultivation (Columella 2,12,1–2); therefore, barley was probably cheaper than wheat in antiquity. The Greeks preferred pearl barley (Plin. HN 18,72); in Egypt → beer was produced from barley. Also attested is the use of barley as fodder (Aristot. Hist. an. 573b 10–11; 595a 28–29; 595b 6–10). The Roman army, finally, gave up barley in favour of wheat (Pol. 6,38,3–4; Gal. 6, p. 507 KÜHN). Barley was often the food of the poor and the slaves (Columella 2,9,16). In Palestine of the 1st cent. AD, the poor ate barley, the rich ate wheat (Jos. BI 5,427).

F. OATS

Oats (βρόμος/*brómos*) was cultivated later than wheat and barley, because wild oats, which were found as weeds in the emmer crops, produced smaller yields than wild wheat or wild barley (Theophr. Hist. pl. 8,9,2; Caus. pl. 4,5,2). Oats was not an important field crop in southern Greece in the classical epoch; sometimes it was sown together with barley as a part of *farrago* (mixed grain) in order to produce fodder (Plin. HN 18,149; Columella 2,10,24; 2,10,31–32). The cultivation of oats is also verified in the 2nd cent. AD for Mysia in Asia Minor (Gal. 6,522–523 KÜHN) and in the 4th cent. AD for Thrace (Serv. Georg. 5,37). Pliny mentions the *avena Graeca* (the modern *avena byzantina*, a hexaploid species of grain), whose seed did not easily come off (HN 18,143), and furthermore the half-cultivated tetraploid grain *avena abyssinica* (Plin. HN 6,188), which today is associated with emmer and barley.

G. RYE

Rye (*secale cereale* – Lat. *secale* or *asia*) was not cultivated in southern Greece, because it does not grow well in the Mediterranean climate. In northern Greece, however, rye was an important field crop during the 1st millennium BC. Although it has not been archaeologically attested for the early Iron Age, Galen (Gal. 6,514 KÜHN) indicates that rye (βρίζα/*bríza*) was significant in Thrace and Macedonia in the 2nd cent. AD at the latest. Rye cultivation is also attested for northern Italy as well as for central and northern Europe (Plin. HN 18,141); furthermore it is also mentioned in the → Edictum Diocletiani (1,3). According to Pliny, rye was bitter and not easy digestible. Rye never achieved the significance in antiquity that it had in Europe in the early modern era.

H. MILLET

The only species of grain in antiquity that could also be cultivated in Europe during the summer was millet. Therefore, it also played a rather important role in ancient agriculture, although it produced a lower yield than all other grains. If millet appeared to someone in a dream, this was a sign of future poverty (Artem. 1,68). There were two cultivated species of millet, namely *setaria italica* (μελίνη/*melínē*: Xen. An. 2,4,13) and *panicum miliaceum* (κέγχρος/*kénchros*: Hes. Sc. 398–399). Both are mentioned in Theophrastus (Hist. pl. 8,7,3; 8,11,6; Caus. pl. 4,15) and Columella (2,9,17–19). According to Aristotle (Hist. an. 595a 26–29), *panicum miliaceum* was used as fodder. Millet was cultivated from south-western France and across central Europe as far as China; in northern Italy the cultivation of millet was concentrated in the plain of the river Po (Pol. 2,15,2; Str. 5,1,12), where there was enough water for artificial irrigation of the fields even in summer (Diod. Sic. 2,36,3–4; Gp. 2,38,2). Demosthenes also mentions cultivation of millet in Thrace (Or. 8,45).

I. RICE

Rice (*oryza sativa*) was cultivated in the 1st millennium BC in the Middle East in regions such as Anatolia and Mesopotamia, which were first annexed by the Hellenistic kingdoms and then by the Imperium Romanum. Rice is cited in the *Triptólemos* of Sophocles (fr. 552 NAUCK). Theophrastus (Hist. pl. 4,4,10) got his information about rice from Greek scholars who had accompanied Alexander the Great to India (Aristobulus FGrH139 fr. 35). Jewish texts, the *Mishnah* and *Talmud*, mention cultivation of rice for the Roman era in the Huleh marshes in the Jordan valley. At times, rice also found its way farther to the west through long-distance trade. In Greece, a grain of rice was found in the Mycenaean palace of Tiryns, and a significant amount of rice was found in a Roman military camp in Germany of the 1st cent. AD. However, there is no proof that, in antiquity, rice was cultivated west of the Middle East, although it was more productive than all other grains. This is due to the fact that facilities for the constant irrigation of rice fields were unknown in antiquity, and this is true even for Egypt. Greek traders in the 1st cent AD had knowledge of cultivation of rice in Persia and India (Peripl. m. r. 37; 41).

J. Sorghum

Sorghum, a grain from sub-Saharan Africa, reached India in the Bronze Age, where it was noted by Greek scholars who accompanied Alexander the Great on his campaigns (Theophr. Hist. pl. 4,4,9); in the 1st cent. AD, sorghum was imported to Rome (Plin. HN 18,55). However, nothing indicates that it was cultivated in the Mediterranean region in antiquity. According to palaeobotanic finds, in antiquity sorghum was the most important grain in the kingdom of → Meroë in Sudan, where, however, millet and barley were also cultivated (Str. 17,2,2; Diod. Sic. 1,33,4; Plin. HN 18,100).

→ Agrarian writers; → Bakeries; → Bread; → Threshing; → Fertilizer; → Nutrition; → Plough; → Sickle

1 M.C. Amouretti, Le pain et l'huile dans la Grèce antique, 1986 2 C. Ampolo, Le condizioni materiali della produzione, in: Dialoghi d'Archeologia 11, 1980, 15–46 3 Blümner, Techn. 1, 1–57 4 T. Brown et al., DNA in wheat seeds from European archaeological sites, in: Experientia 50, 1994, 571–575 5 D.J. Crawford, Food: tradition and change in Hellenistic Egypt, in: World Archaeology, 11, 1979, 136–146 6 L. Gallo, Alimentazioni e classi sociali: una nota su orzo e frumento in Grecia, in: Opus 2, 1983, 449–472 7 S. Gansiniec, Cereals in early archaic Greece, in: Archeologia 8, 1956, 1–48 (in Polish) 8 Garnsey 9 J.R. Harlan, The early history of wheat, in: L.T. Evans, W.J. Peacock (ed.), Wheat Science: Today and Tomorrow, 1981, 1–15 10 F.M. Heichelheim, s.v. Sitos, RE Suppl. 6, 819–892 11 Z.V. Janushevitch, Die Kulturpflanzen Skythiens, in: Zschr. für Arch. 15, 1981, 87–96 12 A. Jardé, Les céréales dans l'antiquité grecque, 1925 13 N. Jasny, Competition among grains in classical antiquity, in: American Historical Review 47, 1942, 747–764 14 N. Jasny, The Wheats of Classical Antiquity, 1944 15 M.E. Kisley, A barley store of the Bar-Kochba rebels (Roman period), in: Israel Journal of Botany 35, 1986, 183–196 16 K.-H. Knorzer, Römerzeitliche Pflanzenfunde aus Xanten, 1981 17 Id., Über Funde römischer Importfrüchte in Novaesium (Neuss am Rhein), in: BJ 166, 1966, 433–443 18 H. Kroll, Kastanas. Ausgrabungen in einem Siedlungshügel der Bronze- und Eisenzeit Makedoniens 1975–1979. Die Pflanzenfunde, 1983 19 Id., Kulturpflanzen Tiryns, in: AA, 1982, 476–485 20 F.G. Mayer, Carbonised food plants of Pompeii, Herculaneum, and the villa at Torre Annunziata, in: Economic Botany 34, 1980, 401–437 21 L.A. Moritz, Grainmills and Flour in Classical Antiquity, 1958 22 J. Percival, The Wheat Plant: a Monograph, 1921 23 M. Rostovtzeff, s.v. Frumentum, RE 7, 126–187 24 R. Sallares, The Ecology of the Ancient Greek world, 1991 25 M.S. Spurr, Arable Cultivation in Roman Italy, 1986 26 H.-P. Stika, Römerzeitliche Pflanzenreste aus Baden-Württemberg, 1996. 27 M. Voigt, Die verschiedenen Sorten von Triticum, Weizen-Mehl und Brot bei den Römern, in: RhM 31, 1876, 105–128 28 White, Farming 29 K.D. White, The parable of the sower, in: Journal of Theological Studies 15, 1964, 300–307 31 L. Wittmack, Die in Pompeji gefundenen pflanzlichen Reste, in: Botanische Jbb. für Systematik, Pflanzengesch. und Pflanzengeographie, Beiblatt 33 no. 73, 1904, 38–66. R.SA.

Grain laws (*leges frumentariae*). Laws for the handing out of grain at a reduced price or free of charge in the city of Rome. Supply crises and attempts to eliminate these are recorded already for the first century of the Republic although these are based only on vague recollection [16. 25f.]. A *praefectus annonae* in 440 BC (Liv. 4,12,8) is anachronistic, and even the grain purchase by the *aediles* in 299 BC (Liv. 10,11,9) is very doubtful [3. 31ff.]. For the 2nd cent. BC an increase of the state's interference with matters concerning the supply sector is attested[4. 193f.]; possibly there was a law against grain profiteering [6. 29f.].

The first *lex frumentaria* was introduced by the tribune C. Gracchus in 123 BC in order to win the *plebs urbana* for his reform programme and at the same time as a reaction to a price increase [5. 20ff.]. For the cost of 6 $^{1}/_{3}$ *as* per *modius* (schol. Bob. p.135 ST) each citizen in Rome could buy grain, and probably for around 2 denarius per month, each citizen could buy the 5 *modii* (Granius Licinianus p.27 Criniti) first attested for the proposed law of the consul M. Aemilius Lepidus in 78 BC. The grain law of C. Gracchus was rejected by the Optimates as an encouragement to idleness (Cic. Sest. 103), *largitio* (Cic. Off. 2,72) and plundering of the state treasury (Cic. Tusc. 3,48). Nevertheless it was necessary to ensure that the basic needs of the metropolis Rome were met (C. Gracchus fr. 51 ORF; Plut. C. Gracchus 5). To share profits of the government seemed rightful (Flor. Epit. 2,1,3) and considering its large income this was possible to finance [16. 31ff.].

Marius as tribune in 119 BC prevented a further grain law through his veto (Plut. Marius 4,7). Towards the end of the 2nd cent. the grain policy became the object of Optimate and popular competition with the Optimates preferring individual measures to statutory regulations [2. 243ff.]. In 104 the *princeps senatus* M. Aemilius Scaurus was entrusted with the job of looking after grain matters instead of the *quaestor Ostiensis* L. Appuleius Saturninus (Cic. Har. resp. 43; Cic. Sest. 39; Diod. Sic. 36,12). A grain law of the people's tribune Saturninus in 103 or 100 BC that was meant to lower the price per *modius* to the symbolic $^{5}/_{6}$ *as* was foiled violently by the *quaestor urbanus* Q. Servilius Caepio (Rhet. Her. 1,21). To compensate for this Caepio and his colleague L. Calpurnius Piso had coins minted – *AD FRU(mentum) EMU(ndum) EX SC* (RRC 330). Only the grain law of the people's tribune M. Octavius in the 90s [14. 235ff.] replaced the *lex Sempronia* with the aim of relieving the *aerarium* (Cic. Brut. 222; Off. 2,72); the grain law of the tribune M. Livius Drusus in 91 BC was probably meant to restore the former situation (Liv. per. 71), but was revoked after his death together with his other laws.

There is little evidence for the total revocation of the grain laws by Sulla (Sall. Hist. 1,55,11 M); it is likely that he reduced the amount of 5 *modii* per month that was mentioned several times in the subsequent years. The grain law of Aemilius Lepidus who was declared *hostis* in 77 was only valid for a short time but it is remarkable as it was the first Consular *lex frumentaria*. Around the year 75 BC rising prices and riots in Rome forced individuals to seek alleviation (Sall. Hist. 2,45 M) (Cic. Verr. 2,3,215; Cic. Planc. 64; Cic. Off. 2,58; Plin. HN 18,16). According to Cicero, in what is certainly a rhetorical passage (Cic. Verr. 2,3,72), a consular *lex Terentia Cassia* provided in 73 BC the handing over of 5 *modii* (Sall. Hist. 3,48,19 M) – to *c.* 40,000 people entitled to receive it. As, in addition to the grain tithe, 3.8 million *modii* were apparently purchased (Cic. Verr. 2,3,163; 2,3,227), this low figure is really doubtful.

M. Porcius Cato, as tribune in 62 BC, by a decision of the Senate increased the expense for grain supply considerably in the difficult political situation after the execution of the Catilinarians (Plut. Cato minor 26,1; Plut. Caesar 8,4). In 58 BC the tribune P. Clodius Pulcher took the last step towards the handover of grain free of charge instead of the previously valid price of 6 $^{1}/_{3}$ *ases* per *modius* (Cic. Sest. 55) and at the same time ensured financing through the annexation of Cyprus and the organization of grain procurement [8. 282ff.]. Shortage (with supply) and severe price fluctuations in the years 58/57 required Cn. Pompey to be entrusted with the → *cura annonae* [12. 75ff.] on the basis of a consular *lex Cornelia Caecilia* with pro-consular *imperium* for five years. The Senate granted him 40 million HS for the purchase of grain in 58 (Cic. Ad Q. Fr. 2,6,1).

Although Pompey tried to compile a list of names of those entitled to receive it (Cass. Dio 39,24,1; [9.29ff.]), their number rose to 320,000. The meaning of a *rogatio alimentaria* of the tribune C. Scribonius Curio in 50 BC aiming to transfer the allotment of the grain to the *aediles* remains unclear (Cic. Fam. 8,6,5). In 46 Caesar reduced the number of entitled recipients to a maximum of 150,000 (Suet. Iul. 41,3), with the list of those entitled to receive it being completed again by lot. 80,000 Proletarian citizens were settled instead in overseas colonies (Suet. Iul. 42,1). In 44 BC Caesar increased the aedileship by two *aediles plebis Ceriales* from the following year on for the purposes of grain supply (Cass. Dio 43,51,3). After his murder the Senate in 43 wanted to exclude the possibility of grain purchasing or the *cura annonae* being transferred to a sole person for the future (Cass. Dio 46,39,3).

Nevertheless Augustus took over the *curatio annonae* in 22 BC (R. Gest. div. Aug. 5) and in the subsequent period institutionalized the procurement and distribution as part of his legitimation: *Ubi ... populum annona ... pellexit* (Tac. Ann. 1,2,1). Initially donations went to 250,000, once even to 320,000 citizens (R. Gest. div. Aug. 15), the number was reduced in 2 BC to 200,000 (Cass. Dio 55,10) and because of the crisis in AD 6 (Cass. Dio 55,25) to 150,000 [20. 46ff.]. But still the grain distributions were not a social measure but gratuities for a privileged social group [1. 55ff.]. Responsible for grain distribution from 22 BC on were initially two, then four praetorian *curatores* (later: *praefecti*) *frumenti dandi ex s.c.* The purchase was taken over in about AD 7 or 8 by a *praefectus annonae* of equestrian status. A simultaneous *lex Iulia de annona* was directed against grain speculation and obstruction of transportation [6. 81ff.].

1 D. van Berchem, Les distributions de blé et d'argent à la plèbe romaine sous l'Empire, 1939 2 L.A. Burckhardt, Polit. Strategien der Optimaten in der späten röm. Republik, 1988 3 M. Ernst, Die Entstehung des Ädilenamtes, thesis Paderborn 1990 4 Garnsey 5 P. Garnsey, D. Rathbone, The Background to the Grain Law of Gaius Gracchus, in: JRS 75, 1985, 20–25 6 P. Herz, Studien zur röm. Wirtschaftsgesetzgebung, 1988 7 J. Martin, Die Popularen in der Geschichte der Späten Republik, 1965 8 C. Nicolet, La *Lex Gabinia – Calpurnia de insula Delo* et la loi "annonaire" de Clodius (58 av. J.-C.), CRAI 1980, 260–292 9 Id., Le temple des Nymphes et les distributions frumentaires à Rome à l'époque républicaine d'après des découvertes récentes, CRAI 1976, 29–51 10 G. Rickman, The Corn Supply of Ancient Rome, 1980 11 M. Rostowzew, s.v. Frumentum, RE 7, 126–187 12 K. Ruffing, Ein Fall von polit. Getreidespekulation im Jahr 57 v.Chr. in Rom?, in: Münstersche Beitr. z. ant. Handelsgesch. 12, 1993, 75–93 13 H. Schneider, Wirtschaft und Politik, 1974, 361–391 14 J. G. Schovánek, The Date of M. Octavius and his Lex Frumentaria, in: Historia 21, 1972, 235–243 15 L. Thommen, Das Volkstribunat der späten röm. Republik, 1989 16 J. v. Ungern-Sternberg, Die polit. und soziale Bedeutung der spätrepublikanischen *leges frumentariae*, in: A. Giovannini (ed.), Nourrir la plèbe, 1991, 19–42 17 Id., Überlegungen zum Sozialprogramm der Gracchen, in: H. Kloft (ed.), Sozialmaßnahmen und Fürsorge. Zur Eigenart ant. Sozialpolitik (Grazer Beitr. Suppl. 3), 1988, 167–185 18 P. Veyne, Le pain et le cirque, 1976 19 C. Virlouvet, Famines et émeutes à Rome des origines de la république à la mort de Néron, 1985 20 Id., La plèbe frumentaire à l'époque d'Auguste: Une tentative de définition, in: A. Giovannini (ed.), Nourrir la plèbe, 1991, 43–65.

J.v.U.-S.

Grain Trade, Grain Import

I. General II. Greece III. Rome

I. General

In the ancient world, grain was the most important commodity in supraregional trade. Three different forms of this trade can be distinguished: 1. regular imports to supply a large urban population whose food requirements could not be met sufficiently by the agriculture of its surrounding countryside, such as in the case of Rome at the time of the late Republic and the Principate; 2. irregular imports into regions in which the population was usually self-sufficient, but which were temporarily afflicted by war or crop failure due to bad weather; 3. grain trade to satisfy particularly demanding eating habits, e.g. when wheat was imported into a region whose climate favoured the predominant cultivation of barley – a crop which was seen as less

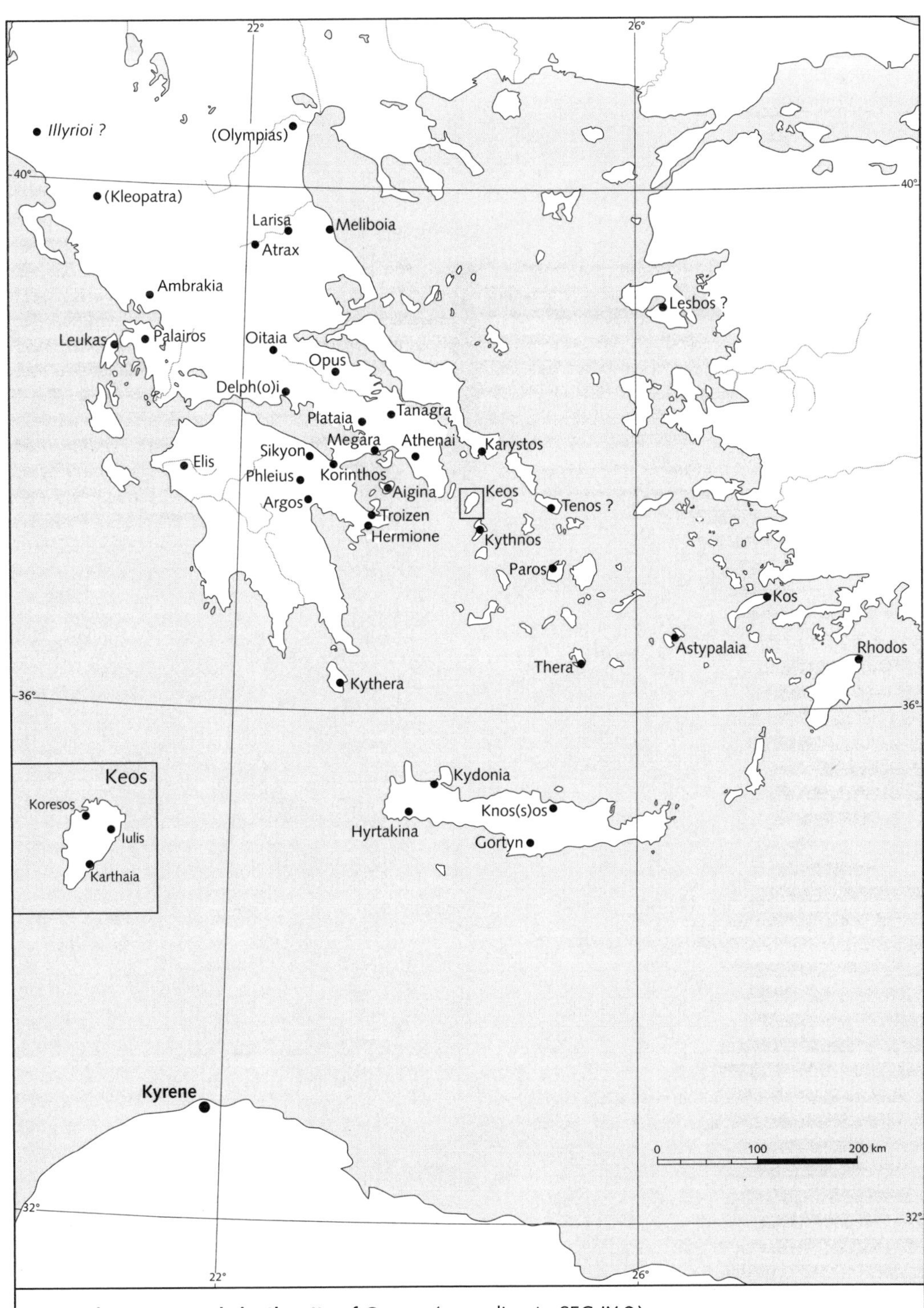

Grain donations made by the city of Cyrene (according to SEG IX 2)

Ambrakia	Polis	Gifts of grain (a total of 805,000 Aeginetan *medimnoi*) made in *c.* 330 BC by the city of Cyrene to Greek poleis and ethnic groups, as well as to Olympias and Cleopatra, because of grain shortages.
Illyrioi	Ethnic group	
(Olympias), (Kleopatra)	Mother/sister (respectively) of Alexander the Great	

nutritious and not much liked. The often low and irregular rainfall in the Mediterranean frequently caused crop failures and food shortages even in regions known for their grain exports. For that reason, in the 2nd cent. BC, grain was sometimes traded from the Black Sea to the Aegean, but at other times also in the reverse direction (Pol. 4,38,5).

II. Greece

No direct documentary evidence exists for Athenian grain imports in the Archaic period, and only sporadic archaeological evidence for trade between the Greek *apoikiai* on the northern shore of the Black Sea and the Scythian farmers, who in the 5th cent. BC produced seed wheat for export (Hdt. 4,17–19). In 480 BC, ships laden with grain sailed through the Hellespont to Aegina and the Peloponnese, but no mention is made of imports to Athens (Hdt. 7,147,2).

With the growth in population, the grain trade became more important in Classical Greece. In 446/445 BC, Athens received 30,000 or 40,000 *medimnoi* of grain from the Egyptian king Psammetichus (Philochorus FGrH398 F90; Plut. Pericles 37,4). During the Peloponnesian War, Athens depended almost entirely on imported grain (Thuc. 6,20,4); with its fleet, Athens controlled the grain imports to its allies (IG I^3 61, 32–41 = Syll.3 75), and it intervened militarily in Sicily's internal affairs in order to prevent the export of Sicilian grain to the Peloponnese (Thuc. 3,86,4). The grain trade of the 4th cent. BC is much better documented. Athens imported grain from Egypt and Sicily (Dem. Or. 56,3–10), Syria and Phoenicia (Diod. Sic. 20,46,4), as well as from the Po valley (IG II/III^2 1629). However, Athens' most important imports came from the Bosporan kingdom, whose king Leucon sent 400,000 *medimnoi* to Attica (probably at a time of food shortages), an amount as large as that of all other regions combined (Dem. Or. 20,31–33). Altogether, he exported 2,100,000 *medimnoi* to Athens (Str. 7,4,6). It is for this reason that the kings of the Bosporan kingdom were honoured in Athens (Syll.3 206). Between about 330 and 320 BC, Cyrene supplied Athens and 40 other cities with about 805,000 Aeginetan *medimnoi* during an extended period of food shortages in Greece, probably caused by drought (SEG IX 2). The Athenian public assembly discussed grain supply ten times in each year (Aristot. Ath. Pol. 43,4). It was the task of the σιτοφύλακες (*sitophýlakes*) to supervise the grain markets in Athens and the Piraeus (Aristot. Ath. Pol. 51,3–4). There were several laws regulating the grain trade (Dem. Or. 34,37; 35,50–51; Lysias 22,6). In order to ease this trade, special procedural provisions were passed in cases concerning merchant shipping (Dem. Or. 32,1; 33,1).

III. Rome

As reported in the historiographic records, probably dating back to the *annales maximi* (Cato fr. 77), 5th-cent. Rome experienced frequent supply crises, mainly as a result of war, drought, or epidemics. In such situations, the Romans tried to receive grain from other Italian regions, mainly Etruria and Campania, but also from Sicily (508 BC: Liv. 2,9,6; 2,12,1; 492 BC: Liv. 2,34,1–5; 477 BC: Liv. 2,52,1; 440 BC: Liv. 4,12,9; 433 BC: Liv. 4,25,1–4). For the period of Rome's expansion in central Italy beginning with the conquest of Veii, no records exist regarding any supply crises which may have necessitated grain imports.

Grain imports once again gained in importance in the late 3rd cent. BC because of the growth of Rome's urban population and the burdens of the Punic Wars. As it was very expensive to transport grain overland from fertile, but distant regions such as Apulia or the Po valley, the import by sea from much more distant regions of the Roman Empire became increasingly indispensable to ensure the grain supply of the city of Rome. From 263 BC, Hiero II of Syracuse delivered grain to Rome in times of supply crises (Pol. 1,16,6–10; Diod. Sic. 25,14; Liv. 22,37; 23,21,5; 24,21,9). After the annexation of Syracuse in 211 BC, Sicily paid a regular grain tithe to Rome (*Expositio totius mundi* 65 Rougé; Cic. Verr. 2,2,5). The tithe amounted to 3 million *modii*, but it was quite common for more grain to be available in some years: after 73, the Romans thus bought a further 3.8 million *modii* for grain distribution in Rome (Cic. Verr. 2,3,163). Between 200 and 170 BC, Masinissa of Numidia donated considerable amounts of grain to Rome (Liv. 31,19,4; 32,27,2; 36,4,8; 43,6,11). After Rome's annexation of the Carthaginian territory as a province in 146 BC, grain from northern Africa satisfied Rome's demand for eight months of every year (Jos. BI 2,383). Sardinia, too, supplied grain to Rome (Plin. HN 18,66). In the 1st cent. BC, Sicily, North Africa, and Sardinia formed the *tria frumentaria subsidia rei publicae* (Cic. Leg. Man. 34). Because of this, in the later years of the Republic, slave revolts or crop failures in the provinces, but also bad weather or piracy could easily result in interruptions of Rome's grain supply. From the Augustan period onwards, Egypt, too, contributed significantly to the grain supply of the city of Rome, meeting its demands for four months in each year (Jos. BI 2,386; Plin. Pan. 31,2). A late-antique text states that under Augustus, 20 million *modii* of grain were imported annually from Egypt to Rome (Ps.-Aur. Vict. epit. de Caes. 1,6). In late antiquity, the Egyptian grain was then exported to Constantinople. From 123 BC, the supply of Roman citizens resident in Rome was regulated by grain laws and later by the *cura annonae*; nevertheless, the population remained dependent on the grain trade. The interest of the traders in maximizing profits and increasing prices sometimes led to artificial grain shortages in Rome as a result of stockpiling (Cic. Dom. 10f.). Even as late as the Principate, the population reacted to price increases with unrest (Tac. Ann. 6,13; 12,43; Suet. Claud. 18,2). Claudius granted privileges to ship owners if they made their ships available for the transport of grain to Rome (Suet. Claud. 18–19); it was only in late antiquity that

the transport of grain to Rome became a compulsory public duty (Cod. Theod. 13,5).
→ Cura annonae; → Grain laws

1 L. CASSON, The Grain Trade of the Hellenistic World, in: TAPhA 85, 1954, 168–187 2 GARNSEY 3 L. GERNET, L'approvisionnement d'Athènes en blé au Ve et IVe siècle, 1909 4 P. HERZ, Stud. zur röm. Wirtschaftsgesetzgebung Die Lebensmittelversorgung, 1988 5 JONES, LRE, 695–705 6 Le ravitaillement en blé de Rome et des centres urbains des débuts de la République jusqu'au Haut Empire, 1994 7 G. RICKMAN, The Corn Supply of Ancient Rome, 1980 8 B. SIRKS, Food for Rome, 1991 9 E. TENGSTRÖM, Bread for the People, 1974.
MAPS: GARNSEY, 160. R.SA.

Graminea Amongst the herbs (*herbae*, ποιώδη; *poiṓdē*), Gramineae or Poaceae represent the grass family (Glumiflorae, πόαι; *póai*, in Theophr. Hist. pl. 7,8,3); in antiquity, however, the reeds (Cyperaceae) and rushes (Juncaceae) were not differentiated (→ Bulrush; → Byblus). Besides the meadow grass (ἄγρωστις; *ágrōstis*, e.g. Theophr. Hist. pl. 1,6,7 et passim) and the grass proper (→ grain; *frumenta*), other members of the Graminea family are, 1. the cat's tail Arundo (δόναξ, κάλαμος; *dónax, kálamos*, i.a. in Theophr. Hist. pl. 4,11,11 and elsewhere), esp. Arundo donax L. (Giant Reed) which, from its introduction from Asia Minor, was frequently used to make flutes (*kálamos syringías*, cf. Dioscorides 1,85 p. 1,81 WELLMANN = 1,114 p. 104 BERENDES; Plin. HN 32,141: *Cyprius qui et donax vocatur*) or fences; 2. Phragmites (*kálamos ho plókimos* Theophr. Hist. pl. 4,11,1; Plin. HN 32,141), including probably *órophos lachnḗeis* used as a roofing material already mentioned in Hom. Il. 24,451, and 3. Ampelodesmos (Plin. HN 17,209), perhaps Lygeum spartum, used from antiquity, as suggested by its name (according to Pliny from Sicily), to tie vines, like the Spanish → broom (*genista*). It is contested whether the genuine sugar cane (*Saccharum officinarum*), which also belongs to this group, existed already in the Mediterranean in antiquity [1. 20f.].

1 J. BILLERBECK, Flora classica, 1824, repr. 1972. C.HÜ.

Grammarians

I. ANCIENT ORIENT II. GREECE III. ROME

I. ANCIENT ORIENT

In the Ancient Orient, Akkadian scribes acted as grammarians, adding Sumerian translations to Akkadian flective forms, or who provided abstract grammatical explanations for Sumerian syllables. Grammatical texts took the form of a two-columned list; there were no grammatical rules expressed in sentence form. In order to achieve congruence between the non-isomorphic languages of Sumeria and Akkadia, grammarians made up artificial Sumerian forms, neglected morpho-syntactic rules, and used false allomorphs. However, the works of these grammarians presupposes a metalinguistic awareness of language and an abstractive ability in dealing with language as early as the 2nd millennium BC.

J. A. BLACK, Sumerian Grammar in Babylonian Theory (Studia Pohl: Ser. Maior 12), 1984; P. ATTINGER, Éléments de linguistique sumérienne (OBO Sonderbd.), 1993, 59f. M.S.

II. GREECE

The earliest documentary evidence for a Greek interest in linguistics dates back to the 5th cent. BC: a fragment of Euripides' *Palamḗdēs* (578,2 NAUCK[2]) and a title by Democritus (2,91,26; 2,146,18 DK) document the first attempts at a phonetic classification, whereas Protagoras (2,262,12f. DK) differentiated the gender of nouns. Plato achieved significant advances: the *Cratylus* contains a discussion on whether language is a natural phenomenon or based on convention. Plato distinguished between three classes of sound (Crat. 424c; Tht. 203b) as well as two kinds of intonation and accent (the acute and the grave: Crat. 399b). The distinction between ὀνόματα (*onómata*) and ῥήματα (*rhḗmata*) constitutes the core of the analysis of the parts of speech (Soph. 261d), which was to develop into one of the fundamental topics of Greek and Roman grammatical reflections. Aristotle contributed the clear distinction between vowels and consonants, the definition of the circumflex, and a more complex subdivision of the elements of language (λέξις; *léxis*): ὄνομα (*ónoma*), ῥῆμα (*rhêma*), σύνδεσμος (*sýndesmos*), ἄρθρον (*árthron*) appear together with στοιχεῖον (*stoicheîon*), συλλαβή (*syllabḗ*), πτῶσις (*ptôsis*), λόγος (*lógos*) (Poet. 20), in a linguistic analysis which does not concern itself with the logical distinction between true and false statements.

The Stoic school of philosophers played an important part in the history of Greek grammar. Their basic principle was → anomaly, i.e. the interest in linguistic irregularities, and their main criterion usage (συνήθεια, *synḗtheia*). Undoubtedly, they also discussed theoretical problems, such as the ambiguity of language and the relationships between form and meaning, but it is not always possible to make clear attributions of the concrete progress within individual problems: → Diogenes of Babylon added προσηγορία (*nomen appellativum*) to the parts of speech, → Antipater [10] of Tarsus added μεσότης or πανδέκτης which correspond to the adverb. The main advances subsequent to → Chrysippus [2] concerned terminology: the terms for tenses, diatheses, and cases were defined.

The study of grammar received a decisive impulse in the environment of Alexandria, where Aristotle's legacy was taken up. However, it was not really a discipline in its own rights, but closely linked to → philology (a γραμματικός/*grammatikós* was someone who studied texts, i.e. a philologist; Eratosthenes defined γραμματική/*grammatikḗ* as the complete expert knowledge of literature). The influences of the Stoic school on the Alexandrians is undeniable, and not to be limited to the post-Aristarchan period or the work of → Apollodorus [7] of Athens. However, the main interest of the Alexandrians was not of a logical or philosophical nature, but had its focus on linguistics and formalities (as in Aristot. Poet. 20 it was focussed on the word); special attention was paid to morphological regularities and the formation of words (→ Analogy). Without any doubt, the foundations for the development of a coherent normative grammar were laid in Alexandria. The theoretical bases were provided by → Aristophanes [4] of Byzantium and → Aristarchus [4] of Samothrace, but the question of the actual creation of the first normative system remains open. According to one point of view, Aristarchus gained an awareness of morphological regularities, but not for a system of rules; extant fragments show various grammatical elements, always as exegetical instruments, but without any sign indicating a desire towards systemization. In the view of others, the first normative grammar has been written by Aristophanes' immediate successors on the basis of his material and that of other teachers. The solution of this question depends on the assumed authenticity of Τέχνη γραμματική (*Téchnē grammatikḗ*; 'grammar'), attributed to → Dionysius [17] Thrax (*c.* 170–90 BC), a direct pupil of Aristarchus; however, only the first four chapters of this work are undoubtedly authentic. Those who do not think this work authentic maintain that for the subsequent period (from Dionysius of Halicarnassus to Sextus Empiricus) Dionysius Thrax was less influential than e.g. → Asclepiades [8] of Myrleia or Tryphon (Dionysius' division of speech into eight parts, for example, was not taken up); for that reason, they date the earliest grammars to Tyrannion, Philoxenus, and Tryphon in the 1st cent. BC.

In the 2nd cent. AD, this tradition of grammatical studies flows into the works of → Apollonius [I 11] Dyscolus and of his son → Herodianus: the former devoted individual treatises to all aspects of grammar and various dialectal characteristics, and wrote the first systematic tractate on → syntax. This part of grammar had previously been neglected or had only been investigated from a philosophical-logical or rather rhetorical point of view, and even afterwards it was to remain in the background for a long time to come. Herodianus, by contrast, made the impressive attempt to systematize the entire available material. Of his main work, the *Katholikḗ prosōidia*, only excerpts and revisions by later authors are extant, prominent amongst them the works of Ps.-Arcadius. In this way, grammar finally established itself as an independent discipline, even though the link to classical texts and their exegesis remained a close one. At the same time, the question of what constituted good Greek (ἑλληνισμός, *hellēnismós*) became increasingly important; it was a quality that was to be determined by certain clearly defined criteria and to be protected from signs of potential decay. The main criterion was analogy, joined by etymology and the usage by Attic authors. This explains the cultural requirement of a series of increasingly strict rules (cf. the rigid rules by Phrynichus in the 2nd cent. AD).

Subsequent grammarians took up the 'grammar' attributed to → Dionysius [17] Thrax as well as Herodianus' work and provided commentaries. Amongst these, mention should be made particularly of Theodosius of Alexandria (4th cent. AD), Choeroboscus of Constantinople (6th–7th cents.), the author i.a. of a commentary on the works of Theodosius, and Theognostus (9th cent.), who compiled more than 1,000 orthographical rules (κανόνες; *kanónes*). Other important forms of grammatical works are the → epimerismi, grammatical commentaries on individual works (esp. Homer's), which originally followed the text verbatim, but whose material could also be ordered alphabetically, and also the → etymologica, which gained in importance after their renaissance through Photius in the 9th cent.

EDITIONS: Grammatici Graeci, I/1–2, Dionysii Thracis Ars Grammatica, ed. G. UHLIG; Ibid. I/3: Scholia in Dionysii Thracis Artem Grammaticam, ed. A. HILGARD, 1883–1901; Ibid. II/1–3: Apollonii Dyscoli quae supersunt, ed. R. SCHNEIDER, G. UHLIG, 1878–1910; III/1–, Herodiani Technici Reliquiae, ed. A. LENTZ, 1867–1870; Ibid. IV/1–2: Theodosii Alexandrini Canones. Georgii Choerobosci Scholia. Sophronii Patriarchae Alexandrini Excerpta, ed. A. HILGARD, 1889–1894.

BIBLIOGRAPHY: H. STEINTHAL, Geschichte der Sprachwissenschaft bei den Griechen und Römern mit besonderer Rücksicht auf die Logik, 2 vols., [2]1890–1891 (repr. 1961); V. DI BENEDETTO, in: ASNP 27, 1958, 169–210; ASNP 28, 1959, 87–118; R. PFEIFFER, History of Classical Scholarship, 1968; E. SIEBENBORN, Die Lehre von der Sprachrichtigkeit und ihren Kriterien, 1976; I. SLUITER, Ancient Grammar in Context, 1990; F. MONTANARI, L'erudizione, la filologia e la grammatica, in: G. CAMBIANO (ed.), Lo Spazio letterario nella Grecia antica I/2, 1993, 235–281; D.M. SCHENKEVELD, Scholarship and Grammar, in: Entretiens XL, 1993, 263–306.

R.T.

III. ROME

Within the framework of Roman → philology, the study of grammatical topics in the stricter sense, esp. flectional morphology and syntax, represented but one area of activity; in addition, the philological activities of a *grammaticus* also comprised editing of and commenting (→ Commentary) on 'classical works', formulating theories on → metre and style (frequently works in the pattern of *De latinitate*; → Rhetoric, → Figures, → Style, stylistic figures). Theoretical research concentrated on the level of the word, and found its expression in the form of orthographical treatises (*De orthographia*), glossaries (→ Glossography), as well as lexica or lists of synonyms (often with a focus on etymology) (→ Lexicography, → Verrius Flaccus; → Differentiarum scriptores).

For Latin, the earliest evidence of grammatical works in a stricter sense sets in from the mid 1st cent. BC with → Varro's only partially extant books *De lingua latina*. The dispute between analogists (e.g. → Caesar) and anomalists, as described by Varro, subsequently presents itself as a dominance of the anomalistic position (see → Anomaly). Documentary evidence of the earliest actual *Ars grammatica* (as a handbook-like representation of Latin grammar with only minor attention to syntax) only came with → Remmius Palaemon's *Ars* at the end of the 1st cent. AD. The tradition exemplified in this work extends to the grammar of Aelius → Donatus [3] (Rome, mid 4th cent.), split in transmission and usage into *Ars minor* and *Ars maior*, a work that remained influential into the Middle Ages. The works within this tradition (from single-volume school grammars to many-volumed accounts, all based in their basic layout on → Dionysius [17] Thrax) are not characterized by originality; typically, they provide a pragmatic combination of parts from various works, while incorporating older accounts and falsely attributing works to certain authors, or changing previous attributions, often distorting the names of authors. The main strand of this tradition leads from Remmius via Q. → Terentius Scaurus and excerpts of his grammar, and Marius Plotius → Sacerdos to the *Artes*, written by → Cominianus for a Greek audience (in Byzantium) in the first half of the 4th cent. AD, followed in the 2nd half by Flavius Sosipater → Charisius [3] and → Diomedes [4]. Diomedes' work was still widely known in the Middle Ages, whereas Charisius' *Ars* was generally known under Cominianus' name; a proper bilingual layout can be found in → Dositheus' grammar (late 4th cent.). This eastern strand of the tradition concludes with the 18 volumes of the *Institutio grammatica* by → Priscianus, the most comprehensive extant treatise on Latin grammar, which was known throughout the Middle Ages. Other well-known grammars in the western sphere for the 3rd cent. are C. → Iulius Romanus' *Aphormaí sive De analogia* (taking up i.a. the works of L. → Caesellius Vindex and → Flavius [II 13] Caper) and → Censorinus' [4] *Ars grammatica*, followed later in a new wave of grammatical works from the early 4th cent. onwards by Palladius (Ps.-Probus). Donatus, who subsequently became himself the subject of commentaries, concludes this strand.

→ GRAMMAR

EDITIONS: GRF (and add.); GL.
RESEARCH REPORT: A. DELLA CASA, Rassegna di studi sui grammatici latini (1934–1984), in: Bollettino di Studi Latini 15, 1985, 85–113.
BIBLIOGRAPHY: K. BARWICK, Remmius Palaemon und die röm. Ars grammatica, 1922; L. HOLTZ, Donat et la tradition de l'enseignement grammatical, 1981; R.A. KASTER, Guardians of Language, 1988; P. L. SCHMIDT, in: HLL, § 432–446; 520–527 (bibliography). J.R.

Grammateis (γραμματεῖς; *grammateîs*). In the Greek world, *grammateis* were protocolists, secretaries with a wide range of tasks. Generally, they are distinguished from the *árchontes* ('officials'), but like them, they were appointed by the citizenry for a set period of time, either by election or by lot.

In Athens, the chief secretary of the state was referred to as the 'council secretary' or 'secretary at the prytany'. He was responsible for the publication of documents resulting from the activities of the council or the citizens' assembly. Until the 360s BC, he was a member of the council (→ *boulḗ*), elected for the period of one → *prytaneía*, but subsequently, he was appointed (probably in the interest of greater efficiency) by lot from citizens who volunteered for the position ([Aristot.] Ath. Pol. 54,3). The appointments were made from the phyles, according to their official order. This rotation is an important tool for the definition of chronology in Hellenistic Athens; a break in the rotation is seen as a sign for a change of government in Athens [5; 6].

Numerous other secretaries are also evident in Athens. The author of the Aristotelian *Athenaíōn Politeía* (54,4) mentions a 'secretary in charge of matters of law' (*nómoi*); in the 4th cent., there is epigraphical evidence for a secretary 'in charge of decrees' (*psēphísmata*) (both documented in [1. 62] for 303/2 BC). The *Athenaíōn Politeía* (54,5) also refers to an elected secretary, whose task it is to read aloud documents to the council and the citizens' assembly; he is presumably identical with the 'secretary of the council and the people', known from inscriptions (cf. [1. 12, 64]). Amongst other documented secretaries are the *anagrapheús* and the *antigrapheús*; from 321/0 to 319/8 and again 294/3 to 292/1, the chief secretary bore the title *anagrapheús* [4]. Courts of law and various colleges of officials had their own secretaries. In addition, there were numerous under-secretaries (*hypogrammateís*) – even though Demosthenes seems to use this term derogatorily with reference to Aeschines (e.g. Dem. Or. 19,70) –, as well as public slaves (→ *dēmósioi*) who assisted the secretaries (cf. [Aristot.] Ath. Pol. 47,5–48,1).

In the Achaean League, the chief secretary was an important official (perhaps only up to 255); the Aetolian League initially only had one chief secretary, but before the end of the 3rd cent. he was joined by a 'council secretary' (documented for 207: SEG 38, 412) [2]. In Orcistus in Phrygia, the secretary was still an important official in AD 237; he chaired the citizens' assembly [3].

1 Agora, vol. 15 2 A. AYMARD, Recherches sur les secrétaires des confédérations aitolienne et achaïenne, in: Mélanges Iorga, 1933, 71–108 3 W.H. BUCKLER, A Charitable Foundation of A.D. 237, in: JHS 57, 1937, 1–10 4 S. DOW, The Athenian Anagrapheis, in: HSPh 67, 1963, 37–54 5 W.S. FERGUSON, The Athenian Secretaries, 1898 6 P.J. RHODES, The Athenian Boule, 1972, 134–141 7 RHODES, 603–605. P.J.R.

Grammaticus (γραμματικός; *grammatikós*). The profession of the *grammaticus* formed in the course of the 3rd cent. BC. These teachers taught the children of the upper citizenry. The *grammaticus* took over from the elementary teacher (*grammatistḗs*/*grammatodidáskalos*) the children of the well-to-do, in order to lay the foundations for a rhetorical education by means of language and literature lessons [1. 235–257]. In Rome the custom developed after the adoption of Greek education in the 2nd cent. BC – Roman education was bilingual from then on – to first visit the *grammaticus Grae-*

cus and then the *grammaticus Latinus* [2. 47–64]. If not employed by a gymnasium in the Hellenistic and Imperial periods, the *grammaticus* was a 'private entrepreneur' who usually only received a modest pay [2. 146–162] and little respect [1. 401f.] (which is why many slaves and freedmen were in this profession [3. 211–228; 4. 192–201]), but this eventually improved in Imperial society and due to Imperial education policy (tax privileges, occasionally state salaries) [1. 435–448; 3. 228–245]. 'Philologist' was not a professional designation in antiquity [4. 45]; on occasion *grammaticus* had the same meaning as *grammatistḗs* (Hippoc. epidemiae 4,37; Plut. Mor. 59f) and the other way around (Lucian De mercede 4).
→ Education; → School

1 Marrou 2 Bonner 3 J. Christes, Bildung und Ges., 1975 4 Id., Sklaven und Freigelassene als Grammatiker und Philologen im antiken Rom, in: Forsch. zur antiken Sklaverei, vol. 10, 1979.

A. Gwynn, Roman Education. From Cicero to Quintilian, 1926; R. A. Kaster, Guardians of Language. The Grammarian and Society in Late Antiquity, 1988; M. P. Nilsson, Die hell. Schule, 1955. J.C.

Grammatistes see → Grammaticus; → Education

Gramme (γραμμή; *grammḗ*). A component of the start and finish line in the Greek stadium (→ *balbís*), which indicated the start and finish marking. It usually consisted of two parallel lines carved into stone and sunk into the ground. Examples are preserved, e.g., in Olympia, Delphi, Epidaurus and Priene.

W. Zschietzschmann, Wettkampf- und Übungsstätten in Griechenland I. Das Stadion, 1960, 35–39; O. Broneer, Isthmia II, 1973, 137–142; P. Roos, Wiederverwendete Startblöcke vom Stadion in Ephesos, in: JÖAI 52, 1979/80, 109–113. C.HÖ.

Granarium see → Horrea

Grand Far from any significant roads on the inhospitable high plateau between Marne and Maas (Mosa) (Dept. Vosges), G. owed its existence to a forest sanctuary of the Leuci of interregional importance. After the Roman conquest, the healing god → Grannus, who had been absorbed by the Apollo cult (Claudius Marius Victor, Alethia 3,204–209), gave his name to the new *vicus* (AE 1937, 55). Laid out orthogonally, G. was enclosed by a circular *pomerium* ('sacred city boundary'), today *voie close*; inside, there is an 18-ha. precinct surrounded by an irregular, six-sided enclosure wall; there is possibly on the → *cardo maximus* a large temple complex dedicated to the Apollo cult (CIL XIII 5933; 5942; AE 1937, 55); fragments of a colossal imperial statue (CIL XIII 5940); Fortuna, Jupiter, Mars and Mercurius were also worshipped (CIL XIII 5934–5939). On the opposite side stands a basilica with mosaic from the Severan period; on the extension of the → *decumanus maximus* lies an amphitheatre *extra muros*; two thermal bath complexes. It may be the Apollo Grannus of G. (Cass. Dio 78,15,5f.) from whom the emperor Caracalla requested advice. In the year 309, Constantine the Great visited G., where he had a prophetic vision (Paneg. Constantini 7,21,3f.). At the beginning of the 4th cent., G. replaced Tullum as capital of the *civitas* [1]; in the Middle Ages, the cult centre survived as a place of pilgrimage for St. Libara. Of particular interest are the zodiac tablets [2] found in G., as well as the network of artificial underground canals explored by modern geophysical methods [3].

1 R. Billard, Découvertes de deux bornes milliaires à Soulosse, in: Revue archéologique de l'Est 20, 1969, 223f. 2 J.-H. Abry, A. Buisson (ed.), Les tablettes astrologiques de G. (Vosges) et l'astrologie en Gaule romaine (Collection du Centre d'Études Romaines et Gallo-Romaines 12), 1993 3 J.-P. Bertaux, P. Delétie, Y. Lemoine (ed.), De la truelle ... au radar, in: Blesa 1, 1993, 235–246.

E. Frézouls, Les villes antiques de la France, I. Belgique 1, 1982, 177–234; G., Dossier d'archéologie Paris 162, 1991 (suppl.); esp. 1–83. F.SCH.

Granicus (Γράνικος; *Gránikos*). River in Asia Minor which has its source in the Ida mountains (Kaz Dağları) and flows through the Troad along the Mysian border. North of Biga (where the river is known today as Biga Çayı) it flows into the Propontis. It is famous for the battle which Alexander the Great won here against the Persian satrap Memnon in summer 334 BC. The site of the battle is sought today not far from Biga, near the road from Zelia to Lampsacus.

1 L. Bürchner, s.v. G. 3), RE 7, 1814f. E.SCH.

Granite This widespread primary rock from the interior of the earth only received its name in the modern age, derived from the Italian 'granito' (from Lat. *granum*, 'grain'). The Greeks took their name *lithotomíai Thēbaikṓn* from its source in quarries in Egyptian Thebes (Theophr. De lapidibus 6 [1. 58]; according to Plin. HN 36,63 suited to the manufacture of small hand mortars, *coticulae*). According to Hdt. 2,127 the lowest level of Chefren's pyramid consists of granite. Because of its colourful nature, competing terms were πυρροποίκιλος (*pyrrhopoíkilos; pyrrhopoecilos*, Plin. HN 36.63), συηνίτης (*syēnítēs*; Plin. HN 36,63; Stat. Silv. 4,2,27) or ψάρανος (*psáranos*). The designation *lapis claudianus* leads one to suppose that the Romans began to quarry and use granite under Claudius. Signed granite blocks from the time of Septimius Severus (2nd/3rd cents. AD) have been found.

1 Theophrastus de lapidibus, ed. D. E. Eichholz, 1965. C.HÜ.

Granius Name of a Latin family which belonged to the upper class in Puteoli (Schulze 480).

I. Republican Period II. Imperial Period

I. Republican Period

[I 1] As *duumvir* of Puteoli, he entered into a dispute with Cornelius [I 90] → Sulla in 78 BC, who was so upset that he died (Val.Max. 9,3,8; Plut. Sulla 37,3).

[I 2] **G., Q.** Public crier and auctioneer (*praeco*) in the late Republican period (Cicero claims to have known him, Brut. 172). Many anecdotes about his wit and repartee (Cic. De or. 2,244; 281ff.; Att. 6,3,7; Planc. 33) circulated, such as in connection with P. Cornelius [I 85] Scipio Nasica (*cos.* 111) and the plebeian tribune of 91, M. Livius Drusus. He was a close friend of the orator L. Licinius Crassus (Cic. De or. 2,254; Brut. 160). Lucilius (bk. 20) describes a banquet at his house (Cic. Brut. 160). K.-L.E.

[I 3] **G. Flaccus.** Author of a commentary on a collection of cult laws of the pontifices (the so-called *leges regiae*; Dig. 50,14,142) titled *De iure Papiriano ad Caesarem.* This commentary, of which only the title is known, was used primarily by writers of the Imperial period as a collection of the above-named pontifical cult canons [1. 308f., 533]. Because G. is supposed to have written a work on the → *indigitamenta* (sacred books of the pontifices) dedicated to C. Iulius → Caesar, he is assumed to have lived in the 1st cent. BC [2. 73; 3. 625]. This work, mentioned by Censorinus, DN 3.2, did not survive either. G.'s authorship of additional works on religious subjects is disputed; because only the name Flaccus or G. is handed down, one or more other person(s) may be implied (frg. in [4]).

1 Wieacker, RRG 2 G. Wissowa, Religion und Kultus der Römer, ²1912 3 Schanz/Hosius 4 P. Huschke, Iurisprudentiae anteiustinianae reliquae, 1908, 53ff.
C.F.

II. Imperial Period

[II 1] **Q. G. Caelestinus** Senator from Leptis Magna (Inscriptions of Roman Tripolitania 532). Belonged to the family of the Granii of which Apuleius spoke.

M. Corbier, in: EOS II 722. W.E.

[II 2] **G. Licinianus** Historian, probably of the 2nd cent. AD (cf. G.L. 28,11); he was only known from references in Solinus (2,12), Macrobius (Sat. 1,16,30) and Servius (Aen. 1,737) until 1853, when twelve palimpsest sheets of a compendium of Roman history were discovered (see [2. 156ff.]) in London (British Library Add. 17212; CLA (E.A. LOWE, Codices Latini Antiquiores) II, 167, saec. V) with parts of bks. 26, 28, 33, 35 (conflict between the young Cn. Pompeius and Cinna in the 80s), and 36. They deal with events of the years 177–163 BC and show an 'annalistic' structure; Livy certainly served as the basis [2. 173ff.]. Therefore, the work probably also began with the foundation of Rome; the important question where it ended appears to be insoluble. The narrative (cf. [1]) is dry and shows a preference for anecdotes, while Sallust's excursuses are criticized as rhetoric (36,30–32); for the senatorial viewpoint cf. [3]. Only Servius (see above) definitely refers to a further antiquarian work *Cena sua*, which is discernibly a successor to the *Noctes Atticae* of Gellius.

1 P. Steinmetz, Unt. zur röm. Literatur des 2. Jh. n.Chr., 1982, 139–145 2 N. Criniti, Granio Liciniano, in: ANRW II 34.1, 184–197 3 M. Hose, Erneuerung der Vergangenheit, 1994, 454–462 4 K. Sallmann, in: HLL 4, § 463.

Editions: N. Criniti, 1981 (bibliography XVII–XXII); B. Scardigli, A.R. Berardi, 1983 (transl. and comm.; bibliography 149–170). P.L.S.

[II 3] **M. G. Marcellus** Senator from Allifae (AE 1990, 222). Praetorian proconsul of Pontus-Bithynia at the end of the reign of Augustus (AD 14/15 is unlikely). In 15, he was accused of *maiestas* in the Senate by his quaestor, but acquitted. A charge of extortion came before a special court. He had property near Tifernum Tiberinum, where he had bricks manufactured in the years 2 BC, AD 5 and 15. Later, the estate passed into the hands of Pliny the Younger. PIR² G 211.

[II 4] **G. Marcianus.** Related to G. [II 2], perhaps his son. Proconsul of Baetica under Tiberius *c.* AD 22 (AE 1990, 222). Accused of *maiestas* in the year 35, he killed himself. PIR² G 212. W.E.

Grannus Celtic god equated through the → *interpretatio romana* with → Apollo, whom Caesar ranks second among the gods most worshipped by the Gauls in his function as healer (Caes. B Gall. 6,1f.). This attribution is based on the specifically Roman conception of the Greek Apollo as Apollo Medicus, the healing god who drives away disease. With one exception (CIL XIII 8007), G.'s name always appears as an epithet to Apollo. That the deity is nonetheless the Celtic healing god is suggested by the far-flung dispersal of the epigraphical dedications to him in the Imperial period (14 in Raetia, in the two German provinces and in Belgica, one each in Rome and Britain). Among his devotees and worshippers were some high ranking civil and military officials – indeed, even the Emperor Caracalla (Cass. Dio 78,15,6). The existence of shrines to Apollo G. has been substantiated through the inscriptions from Großbottwar, in Hochscheid, and in the vicinity of Faimingen, and is suspected in Aachen and → Grand. Apollo G. is mentioned and represented together with the Nymphs, with Sancta Hygia, and particularly with the Celtic deity Sirona. Thus, the dedications to an epithetless Apollo and Sirona probably also refer to the Celtic G., especially when they are located near water sources, spring shrines, therapeutic springs, etc. – just as the above-mentioned dedications to G. The representations depict Apollo G. along the lines of the Graeco-Roman model, with his classical attributes (cithara, griffin, tripod, omphalos). However, on the relief from the Altbachtal in Trier, the indigenous god can be identified by the presence of the water jug.

G. Bauchhenss, s.v. Apollo G., LIMC 2.1, 458f.; M. Ihm, s.v. G., RE 7, 1823ff.; K. Goethert, Zwei Religionen treffen aufeinander: Die galloröm. Götterwelt, in: H.-P. Kuhnen, Religio Romana 1996, 166–178; H. Nesselhauf, H. v. Petrikovits, Ein Weihaltar für Apollo aus Aachen-Burtscheid, in: BJ 167, 1967, 268ff.; G. Weber, Zur Verehrung des Apollo G. in Faimingen, zu Phoebiana und Caracalla, in: J. Eingartner, P. Eschbaumer, G. Weber, Faimingen-Phoebiana 1, 1993, 122ff.; G. Weisgerber, Das Pilgerheiligtum des Apollo und der Sirona von Hochscheid im Hunsrück, 1975. M.E.

Graphe (γραφή; *graphḗ*).

[1] Literally 'script', in adjective law in Greek poleis *graphe* generally had the meaning 'statement of claim' (Dem. Or. 45; 46; cf. also IPArk 17; 114/5; 178 from Stymphalus and SEG 27, 545, 27 and 33 from Samos). Especially in Athens *graphe* was used in the actual sense of 'complaint document' that each blameless citizen (ὁ βουλόμενος, 'each person who wishes') could lodge against persons who harmed certain public interests, whilst a party whose rights had been infringed in a private sense could defend himself with → *díkē* [2]. This difference does not parallel the modern one between 'public' or 'criminal law' and 'civil law': only the closest relatives were allowed, for example, to bring a (private) action for murder, the victim of theft could only make a (private) theft complaint; against the embezzlement of public monies, there was the corresponding *graphe* (→ *klopḗ*). Persons in need of assistance against attacks by close relatives (parents, orphans, heiresses, → *kákōsis*) were also protected by *graphe*. Aside from the *graphe*, in Athens in special cases, there were also additional procedures against public criminals (→ *eisangelía*, → *phásis*, → *éndeixis* and → *apagōgḗ*). Public criminal law in the Greek poleis was based in principle on individuals taking action for the state in 'popular complaints': only rarely were the general officeholders obligated to do so. The state did not have its own public prosecution complaint authorities.

[2] In the papyri of Egypt *graphe* simply means 'list', e.g. of priests or offices.

E. Gerner, Zur Unterscheidbarkeit von Zivil- und Straftatbeständen im att. Recht, 1934; A. R. W. Harrison, The Law of Athens II, 1971, 76–78; H.-A. Rupprecht, Einführung in die Papyruskunde, 1994, 62, 88. G.T.

Grapheion, Graphis, Graphium see → Stylus

Grasshoppers The word ἀκρίς/*akrís* (from κρίζειν, 'to scream') attested since Hom. Il. 21,12 describes all species of *Saltatoria* same as *locusta* (since Naevius in Varro, Ling. 7,39 basic meaning 'equipped with joints' or 'jumping'). This also applies to the synonyms βροῦχος/*broûchos* = *bruc(h)us*, βρύκος/*brýkos*, μάσταξ/*mástax*, πάρνοψ/*párnops* (Aristoph. Ach. 150 and Av. 588; Ael. NA 6,19; Paus. 1,24,8) or κόρνοψ (*kórnops*; Str. 13,1,64 [613]) and ἀττέλαβος (*attélabos*; Hdt. 4,172) = *attelebus* (Plin. HN 29,92). Regarding their biology, Aristot. Hist. an. 5,28,555b 18–556a 7 (= Plin. HN 11,101f.) reports that grasshoppers after mating in a manner common to insects lay their eggs in autumn just underneath the ploughed farmland soil in a 'pod' from which – after spending the winter under the surface of the earth – egg-like soft larvae (μαλακὰ κυήματα) hatch. As small dark *akrídes*, they then come to the surface, shed their skin and die at the end of summer after laying their eggs. Aristotle explains that they hop by stretching their back legs (Part. an. 4,6,683a 33–b 3). Grasshoppers eat ears of grain (Nic. Ther. 803) and the flowers of the vine (Aristoph. Av. 588). They are in turn eaten by owls and kestrels (Aristoph. ibid.) as well as jackdaws (κολοιοί, Ael. NA 3,12; *graculi*, Plin. HN 11,106). The chirping produced by rubbing the back legs on the front wings (Aristot. Hist. an. 4,9,535b 11–12; Plin. HN 11,107) is emphasized repeatedly in poems in the *Anthologia Palatina* (7,189; 7,192ff.; 197f.; 7,190: memorial for a grasshopper and a cricket, τέττιξ; cf. Plin. HN 34,57).

The swarms (*nubes locustarum*, Pall. Agric. 1,35,12), probably of species of locusts, that plagued Italy, North Africa, Syria (Plin. HN 11, 104–106), Ethiopia (Agatharchides in Phot. Bibl. c. 250) and Egypt (Ex 10,4ff.) blacked out the sun. Some of these invasions can be dated historically (125 BC in Africa: Iulius Obsequens 30; 202 and 173/72 BC in Italy: Liv. 30,2,10; 42,2,4; 42,10,7) or inferred (Ath.: Paus. 1,24,8; the Oitaeans revered Hercules as their liberator from plagues of grasshoppers: Str. 13,1,64 [613]).

As a food grasshoppers are mentioned In the OT (Lv 11,22; cf. [1. 492]) and in relation to John the Baptist Mt 3,4 and Mk 1,6. Hdt. 4,172 report that the Nasamonians in Lybia ingested them as a pulverized additive to milk. In Ethiopia there was a people of so-called 'grasshopper-eaters' (ἀκριδοφάγοι, Diod. Sic. 3,29 and Str. 16,4,12 [772]). The Parthians (Plin. HN 11,107) and occasionally the Greeks (Aristoph. Ach. 116) regarded them as a delicacy.

1 V. Pöschl, H. Gärtner et al., Bibliographie zur ant. Bildersprache, 1964.

H. Gossen, s.v. H., RE 8,1381ff.; Id., s.v. H., RE Suppl. 8,179ff., 1956. C.HÜ.

Graßmann's law Also aspirate dissimilation law. Sound changes discovered in 1862 by the mathematician and language researcher Hermann Grassmann (1809–1877): of two aspirated consonants appearing in consecutive syllables in the same word, the first loses its aspiration. This de-aspiration should be understood as dissimulation with a regressive effect. Graßmann's law applies to ancient Indian (or Sanskrit), and – historically independent of it – to post-Mycenaean Greek.

Consequently in Greek /p^h, t^h, k^h/φ, θ, χ that begin a syllable are replaced by /p, t, k/π, τ, κ if in the same word the following syllable begins with /p^h, t^h, k^h/φ, θ, χ: πέφευγα < *φέφευγα, τίθημι < *θίθημι, ἐκεχειρία < *ἐχεχειρία. Equally /h/ (Spiritus asper; mostly < */s/) that begins a word gets left out: ἔχω < *ἕχω (< *σέχω).

The paradigmatic change in the aspirated and non-aspirated consonant is preserved in some cases: τριχός etc. as opposed to θρίξ, θριξί, and changed through systemic coercion in others: πείσ-θη-τι with progressive dissimilation instead of *πείστηθι because of ἐπείσ-θη-ν etc., or completely cancelled: πείσω instead of *φείσω < *φείθσω because of πείθω etc.

H. GRASSMANN, Ueber die Aspiraten und ihr gleichzeitiges Vorhandensein im An- und Auslaute der Wurzeln ..., in: ZVS 12, 1863, 81–138; N.E. COLLINGE, The Laws of Indo-European, 1985, 47–61; W. COWGILL, M. MAYRHOFER, Idg. Gramm. 1, 1986, 112–115; RIX, HGG, 97 (§ 107); R. PLATH, Hauchdissimilation im Myk.?, in: Münchener Stud. zur Sprachwiss. 48, 1987, 187–193.

C.H.

Gratiae see → Charites

Gratianus

[1] The father of emperors → Valens and → Valentinianus. Born near Cibalae. A man of low origins who rose in the military: between AD 305 and 316 he was *protector domesticus* in Salona, in about 321 *tribunus* in Illyricum, later *comes* in Africa and Britain. In 350/1 he was as a private person host to the usurper → Magnentius and was punished with confiscation of his property. His sons arranged for an honourable memorial. PLRE 1, 400f.

[2] Flavius G. Roman emperor in the West AD 367–383, grandson of G. [1]. Born in 359 in Sirmium as the son of → Valentinianus I and → Marina. In 374 married to → Constantia [3], the daughter of → Constantius [2] II, after her death married in 383 to → Laeta; a son from his first marriage died before him. Already in 366 G. was consul for the first time (later consulates in 371, 374, 377 and 380). On 24 August 367 he was proclaimed Augustus. Carefully educated, e.g. by → Ausonius, he ruled independently in the West after 375 (death of his father; → Valens ruled in the East); → Valentinianus II who had been proclaimed emperor by the soldiers in reality remained without any power of his own. The *magister militum* → Merobaudes acted quite independently. In the emperor's circle, Ausonius as *quaestor sacri palatii* was very influential and acquired high offices for his relatives. Using a variety of measures, G. defused the conflicts that had arisen under Valentinian I, especially the tensions with the Senate: amnesty, tax debt relief, return of confiscated wealth; → Maximinus who was particularly hated resigned his office and was eventually executed.

Trier was initially the most important residence city, and G. repeatedly and on the whole successfully fought the Alamanni from there. A visit by G. to Rome in 376 is uncertain (disputed by [1. 88]). In 378 he went to Sirmium because of the Gothic threat but was not able to intervene in time to help Valens. After the latter's death in the battle of Adrianopolis, G. attempted to use → Theodosius, whom he had elevated to emperor on 19 January 379 after initial successes (on the background: [2]), but Theodosius became increasingly independent. After 379 G. often stayed in Milan, where bishop → Ambrosius made his influence felt though this should not be overrated [1. 79ff.]. In 383 a famine broke out and a Germanic incursion occurred. During the march to counter it, G. heard of the usurpation of → Maximus in Britain. G. campaigned against Maximus, but a large part of his soldiers deserted him when the two armies faced each other near Paris. G. did not risk a battle and was murdered through trickery on 25 August 383 while fleeing. Theodosius' loyalty during these events is doubtful.

G. was educated as a Christian and was personally pious but remained unbaptized. He appears to have been interested in questions of dogma; he requested a dogmatic treatise from Ambrose (*De fide*, also *De spiritu sancto* are dedicated to the emperor; on this [3]). Initially, he continued the tolerant policies of Valentinian I, but increasingly supported Nicaean Orthodoxy, which asserted itself in 381 at the Council of Aquileia. However, G. only fought hard against Donatists (→ Donatus I), Priscillianists (→ Priscillianus) and Manichaeans (→ Mani, Manichaeans); he was also stricter towards the Homoeans than Theodosius. The power of the bishop of Rome in ecclesiastic jurisdiction was strengthened.

The policy towards non-Christians became harsher, as under Theodosius: probably in 382 rather than 379 G. refused to act as *pontifex maximus* (regarding the problematic record in Zos. 4,36,5 s. [4]). In 382 he discontinued the grants for traditional Roman cults, revoked their privileges and had the altar of Victory removed from the curia. A protest delegation was not permitted to see him. The emperor had broken with traditional religion.

Several panegyrics on G. are preserved (Symmachus, Or. 3; Them. Or. 13; Auson. Gratiani Acta). Contemporary authors describe him as talented but not capable of asserting himself ([Aur. Vict.] Epit. Caes. 47,4–6) and immature (Amm. Marc. 27,6,15; 31,10,18). Later Christian tradition portrays him as a strict Orthodox ruler (Rufin. Historia Ecclesiastica 11,13), but he plays no major role in ecclesiastical historiography [5. 103].

1 N. MCLYNN, Ambrose of Milan, 1994 2 R. M. ERRINGTON, The Accession of Theodosius I, in: Klio 78, 1996, 438–453 3 C. MARKSCHIES, Ambrosius von Mailand und die Trinitätstheologie, 1995, 165ff. 4 A. CAMERON, Gratian's Repudiation of the Pontifical Robe, in: JRS 58, 1968, 96–102 5 H. LEPPIN, Von Constantin dem Großen zu Theodosius II., 1996.

PLRE 1,401f. (G. 2); M. FORTINA, L'imperatore Graziano, 1953; G. GOTTLIEB, s.v. G., RAC 12, 718–732.

H.L.

Gratidia

[1] The sister of M. Gratidius [2], married to M. Tullius Cicero, the grandfather of the orator (Cic. Leg. 3,36).

[2] The true name of the sorceress → Canidia, who is repeatedly named in Horace.

K.-L.E.

Gratidianus see M. → Marius G. (praetor 85/4 BC).

Gratidius Name of a Roman family originating from Arpinum (epigraphically also *Grattidius*) from a development of the name *Grattius* (SCHULZE 427).
[1] In 88 BC, G. was supposed to take over the army of the consul Cornelius [I 90] Sulla on behalf of C. Marius and, therefore, was murdered by his soldiers (first victim of the civil wars; Val. Max. 9,7b,1; Oros. 5,19,4).
[2] G., M. A relative of Cicero, died in 102 BC as the *praefectus* of Marcus → Antonius [I 7] fighting pirates in Cilicia. His brother-in-law M. Tullius Cicero, the grandfather of the orator (Cic. Leg. 3,36), opposed the attempt to introduce secret ballots on the Roman model in Arpinum. He unsuccessfully sued C. Flavius [I 5] Fimbria for blackmail (Cic. Font. 24; 26; Brut. 168). His son (*praet.* 85/4) was adopted by a brother of C. Marius and killed by → Catilina during Sulla's proscriptions. K.-L.E.

Grattius Writer of an informative Latin → didactic poem about the → hunt (*Cynegetica* = *Cyn.*) in several bks., of which one fragment of 541 hexameters from the first bk. is extant. G. was perhaps of Faliscan (→ Falisci) origin (Cyn. 40). Ovid mentions him and his didactic poem in the *Epistulae ex Ponto* (4,16,35); in the case of the spelling *Gratius* attested by the Ovid MSS, it is probably a matter of an historically incorrect variation. As the *Cyn.* presuppose the 'Georgica' of → Vergilius [5] and the 'Metamorphoses' of → Ovidius, we can limit their origin precisely to the years between AD 1 and 8. In the extant fragment, after the Prooemium (1–23) the poet deals with the equipment of a hunter with hunting nets and hunting spears (24–149) as well as his utilitarian animals: hunting dogs (150–496) and horses (497–541). The didactic material is repeatedly made less monotonous by minor narrative insertions and excursuses. In this way the *Cyn.* contain the depiction of remote myths of archegetes of the hunt (Dercylus: 95–126; Hagnon: 213–252), an excursus on the corrupting influence of luxury (310–325), and the description of a grotto at the foot of Etna (Aetne [1]) that the poet claims to have visited himself (430–460), and of a sacrifice to Diana (480–496).

G.'s didactic poem was denied a major afterlife. However his influence on Nemesianus' [1] *Cynegetica* can be regarded as certain. The most important textual testimonial to the tradition of G. is the Cod. Vindobonensis 277 written in the 9th cent., upon which all further textual testimonials depend.
→ Hunt; → Didactic poetry

EDITIONS: GEORGIUS LOGUS, Venice 1534 (ed. princeps); P. J. ENK, 1918 (with commentary); R. VERDIÈRE, 2 vols., 1964 (with French transl. and comm.); C. FORMICOLA, 1988 (with It. transl. and comm.).
BIBLIOGRAPHY: G. CURCIO, Grazio poeta didattico, in: RFIC 26, 1898, 55–69; F. VOLLMER, s. v. G. (2), RE 7, 1841–1846; B. EFFE, Dichtung und Lehre, 1977, 154–165; C. FORMICOLA, Studi sull'esametro del Cynegeticon di Grattio, 1995. C. SCHI.

Gratus
[1] Pro-Roman commander of the infantry of Herod the Great (Jos. BI 2,3,4; 4,2,3; 5,2; Ant. Iud. 17,10,3; 17,10,6f.; 17,10,9).
[2] Valerius G. In AD 15–26 *procurator* of Judaea as successor of Annius Rufus (Jos. Ant. Iud. 18,2,2; 18,6,5) under emperor Tiberius. He was in turn succeeded by Pontius Pilate.

PIR², 123, no. 146 (G. 1); 3, 357, no. 58. J.RI.

Grave-mound see → Funerary architecture

Grave offerings see → Etrusci, Etruria II. C4

Grave paintings Interior or exterior painting of funerary architecture built from stone or carved into rock existed in antiquity and throughout the entire Mediterranean region, also images on wood and stone steles; sarcophagi rarely bore paintings. Each region and period had its own particular programmes of pictures, which are interpreted as realistic or symbolic, and referring to this or the next world depending on the state of research. Due to the perishable nature of the genre, much has been lost. However, significant new finds have also been made in recent years.

Grave paintings (GP) are, despite their often craft-like rather than artistic character, often evidence of the state of development of grand → painting, which is often no longer preserved. Grave painting was already customary in royal and private tombs in Egypt's Old Kingdom. Initially, painted flat reliefs on false doors or on free-standing wood or stone plates prevailed. The grave owner was shown in sepulchral and cultic acts. Other techniques were coloured outline drawings on stucco and 'paste mosaics'. The themes were expanded by fishing and fowling scenes, agriculture and daily life, as well as historical topics. Independent grave painting that was formally and stylistically freed of the relief only developed in the 15th cent. BC in Egyptian Thebes. Painted friezes lost their abstract symbolic appearance; composition and colour became freer and the content more private.

Grave painting particularly flowered in Etruria, where it is preserved for the period from the 7th to the 2nd cents. BC especially in Tarquinia, in many of the chamber tombs that were customary there. The frescoes, which are usually applied on a lime whitewash (→ Fresco) range from simple architectural dividers to floral and other ornaments as well as animal pictures; they also depict Etruscan religious customs and Other World concepts. Images of ritual games during the funeral as well as from daily life and feasts relate to the deceased and were meant to embellish life in the hereafter in the 'funerary house', but at the same time represented worldly status. Similar statements may be made with respect to the preserved GP at the northern borders of Greece, e.g., Macedonia, Thrace and southern Russia, the western Greek colonies including neighbouring parts of Italy and Asia Minor. Status, military, athletic and hunting skills, feminine beauty and virtues as well as claims to education by a small elite are expressed in figured images and ornamental friezes. Images of the cult of the dead and symbols of the belief in the Beyond also appear and generally resemble the themes and representation style of the expanding Hellenistic *koinḗ*. N.H.

The few preserved GP of the Phoenician and Punic necropoleis, which are part of simple folk art, belong in this range of themes, e.g., in → Sidon, Cagliari/Sardinia, → Kerkouane/north-eastern Tunisia (and the derivative 'haouanet', which probably are Numidic rock chambers, in Carthaginian northern Africa). H.G.N.

GP in an architectural context were rather uncharacteristic in the Greek mother country because of the differing style of burial. Nevertheless, painted archaic Attic steles indicate a certain familiarity.

Roman grave painting, which in some respects betrays an Etruscan influence and currently is mostly interpreted in historical and representational terms, is known from a few Republican and later contexts, especially the numerous → catacombs of the late Imperial period and late antiquity. However, fully painted tombs are also found everywhere in the colonies.

B. D.'Agostino, La necropoli e i rituali della morte, in: S. Settis (ed.), I Greci II/1, 1996, 435–470; M. Andronikos, Vergina II, 1994; O. Bingöl, Malerei und Mosaik der Ant. in der Türkei, 1997; J. Balty, s.v. Peintures, DCPP, 344f.; S. M. Cecchini, L'Art. "Arts mineurs", in: V. Krings (ed.), La civilisation phénicienne et punique. Manuel de recherche (HbdOr I 20), 1995, 528f.; Mh. H. Fantar, La décoration peinte dans les tombes puniques et les Houanets libyques de Tunisie, in: Africa 10, 1988, 28–49; H. v. Hesberg, Röm. Grabbauten, 1992, passim; S. G. Miller, The Tomb of Lyson and Kallikles, 1993 B. Otto, Die Fresken der "Tomba del Tuffatore" in Paestum, in: Echo. FS G. Trentini, 1990; A. Pontrandolfo, A. Rouveret, Le tombe dipinte di Paestum, 1992; R. T. Ridley, The praetor and the pyramid, in: BA 13–15, 1992, 1–29; I. Scheibler, Griech. Malerei der Ant., 1994; L. Schneider, Ch. Höcker, P. Zazoff, Zur thrakischen Kunst im Frühhellenismus, in: AA 1985, 616–643; S. Steingräber, Etrusk.-hell. G., in: Die Welt der Etrusker, 1990; Id., Zu Entstehung, Verbreitung und architekt. Kontext der unterital. G., in: JDAI 106, 1991, 1–36. N.H.

Grave relief see → Relief

Graviscae A harbour town on the Etruscan coast south of the mouth of the Marta, connected to the *via Aurelia* by a byway; known today as Porto Clementino (municipality of Tarquinia). Commercial trading post for Tarquinii, prone to malaria (Cato Orig. 2: 46). In 181 BC, it becomes a Roman *colonia*, *Tribus Stellatina*, whose territory was divided into parcels of land of five *iugera*; later *colonia Augusta*, *regio VII*. Wine production and trade in red coral (Plin. HN 14, 67; 32, 21). Destroyed in AD 408 (Rut. Namat. 1, 281; cf. coin find with 174 *solidi*). Diocese in AD 504.

Excavations since 1969: large Etruscan settlement (end of 7th cent.), Greek-Etruscan marketplace (580–480 BC) with small sanctuary and numerous votive offerings to Hera-Uni, Aphrodite-Turan, Apollo and Demeter; stone anchor with inscribed dedication to Apollo of Aegina by Sostratos, a merchant mentioned in Herodotus (4,152). Two periods of Etruscan dominance ensued in 480 and around 400; G. declined in the 3rd cent. and was given up with the founding of the *colonia*. The territory of the *colonia* was limited to the promontory: the harbour, the city walls of *opus incertum*, and the regular ground-plan, as well as the *insulae* ($^1/_2$ *actus*: 17.7 m wide) are recognizable. In the east, there is a necropolis with a mausoleum.

L. Quilici, G., in: Quaderni dell'Istituto di Topografia dell'Università di Roma 4, 1968, 107–120; I. Moretti, M. Torelli, G., in: NSA 1971, 195–299; M. Torelli, Il santuario di Hera a G., in: PdP 26, 1971, 44–77; Id., Il santuario greco di G., in: PdP 32, 1977, 398–458; Id., Il caso di G., in: PdP 37, 1982, 304–326; BTCGI 8, 1990, 172–176; V. Valentini, G., 1993. G.U.

Grease-drop script Greek script type of the 2nd half of the 13th cent. to the beginning of the 14th cent. (contemporary with the first Paleologi Period) that is characterized by a striking contrast between the small, rounded and often crooked core of most letters and the oversized curves of omikron, sigma, beta, ypsilon, alpha and omega as well as by the inscribing of small letters into omikron, ypsilon and omega and in this way best represents the complete crumbling of the ancient minuscule canon (→ Minuscule). The script therefore gives the impression of grease drops on a soup [1. 101–102]. This style that should be seen as being derived from the middle Byzantine → chancellery script and also occasionally appears in the documents of the early Paleologi Period is mainly used in MSS of secular authors. Influences or elements of grease-drop script can also be demonstrated in other book types, such as the Otrantine Baroque script (→ Southern Italian script) and the → 'Metochites style' and can be found later with individual copyists of the 15th and 16th cents.

1 H. Hunger, Ant. und ma. Buch- und Schriftwesen, in: Gesch. der Textüberlieferung der ant. und ma. Lit. I, 1961.

H. Hunger, Die sog. F.-Mode in griech. Hss. des 13. und 14. Jh, in: Byz. Forsch. 4, 1972, 105–113 (repr. with addenda: Byz. Grundlagenforsch., 1973, II). P.E.

Great Goddess see → Cybele; → Mater Magna; → Mother goddesses

Great Gods see → Theoi Megaloi; → Theai Megalai

Great King The title Great King in the ancient Oriental tradition (from the 2nd millennium BC to the Achaemenids [1]) was adopted by Hellenistic rulers as μέγας βασιλεύς; *megas basileûs* (and continued as *rex magnus* [2. 253]). It is attested for the Seleucids → Antiochus [5] III, who did not use it on coins and in royal letters, but tolerated (or even promoted) its use elsewhere [3. 75–77], → Antiochus [9] VII (Iust. 38,10,6), Ptolemy III (OGIS I 54) and IV [5. 71–74], and later also for other Hellenistic kings and petty princes such as Antiochus I of Commagene [6]. By claiming this title, often after great military or political successes (eastern campaigns of Antiochus III and Ptolemy III, success of Antiochus I in 65/4 BC), the kings were trying to create a kingship of special rank (above other kings, empires, possibly even former Achaemenid territories). The Greek form of the name is also attested in Elymaic (Kamnaskires I) and especially in Parthian coin legends (since Mithridates I) but βασιλεὺς βασιλέων; *basileùs basiléōn* (already since the 13th cent. in Assyria, later also used by Darius I), soon became more common there.

As μέγας βασιλεύς the title was a component of the Greek version of the *njswt-bjtj* name in Ptolemaic Egypt (attested since the Rapheia decree, 217 BC) [4. 106].
→ Ruler

1 P. Artzi, A. Malamat, The Great King, in: M.E. Cohen et al. (ed.), The Tablet and the Scroll, 1993, 28–40 2 J.E. Bogaers, King Cogibdubnus in Chichester, in: Britannia 10, 1979, 243–254 3 K. Brodersen, Appians Antiochike, 1991 4 G. Hölbl, Gesch. des Ptolemäerreiches, 1994 5 W. Huss, Untersuchungen zur Außenpol. Ptolemaios' IV., 1976 6 J. Wagner, Dynastie und Herrscherkult in Kommagene. Forschungsgesch. und neuere Funde, in: Istanbuler Mitt. 33, 1983, 177–224.

J.W.

Greece, languages Before the arrival of the Greeks (beginning of the 2nd millennium BC) and the consequent spread of the Greek language in Greece (mainland, Peloponnese, Aegean) already in the Mycenaean period, other → pre-Greek languages were spoken; they have left traces especially in the vocabulary and → onomatology and they co-existed with the Greek language in conditions that varied from region to region until the classical period.

Written materials of the second millennium are limited to a hieroglyphic-pictographic script (Crete, end of the third millennium until about 1500; → Hieroglyphic script, Crete) that has not been deciphered until today, → Linear A (Crete, about 1650 until about 1400: transliterated, but the language has not been deciphered) and the Cypro-Minoan clay tablets (esp. Enkomi, 1500 until the end of the 13th cent.; → Cypro-Minoan scripts). The language of the → Discus of Phaestus (origin, time and type of writing system unknown) remains a complete mystery. Antique sources mention autochthonal populations in practically every Greek region: for example Eteo-Cretans (→ Eteo-Cretan) and the Cydonians (→ Cydonia) in Crete, the Carians (→ Caria, Cares) in Crete and on the Cyclades, the Tyrseni (→ Tyrrheni) in Delos, as well as the → Leleges, just about everywhere, also on the western coast of Asia Minor and the → Pelasgians (Thessaly, but also in other regions). It is impossible to associate concrete languages with these many tribes. Some signs seem to point to the → Anatolian languages; but one has to reckon with (at least) one non-Indo-European language, from which certain words can be derived (for example ἔλαιον < **elaiuom* 'olive oil'). In any case the geographical distribution cannot be determined. The attempt to determine phonological rules for an Indo-European pre-Greek language ('Pelasgian') (V. Georgiev, W. Merlingen, A.J. van Windekens), is considered a complete failure today. On the other hand neighbouring languages from the southern part of the Balkan Peninsula (→ Balkans, languages [with map]) could have coexisted with Greek in some Greek regions because of the migrations in prehistoric times: the tradition about Thracians in Boeotia and Phocis, the place name Φρυγία (*Phrygía*) in Boeotia (Thuc. 2,22,2) or the signs of non-Greek populations in Macedonia (cf. Βίλιππος; *Bílippos*, Βερενίκη; *Bereníkē* = Φίλιππος; *Phílippos*, Φερενίκη; *Pherenı́kē*) can be interpreted in this way. An Illyrian language stratum in Greece, esp. in the northwest (Δωδώνα; *Dōdṓna*) and in Thessaly (Πενέσται; *Penéstai*, Δώτιον πεδίον; *Dṓtion pedíon*), but also in Laconia and in the Doric area (cf. the phyle Ὑλλεῖς; *Hylleîs*) can barely be accounted for, already since the expression 'Illyrian' is linguistically unclear; in antiquity it was used for all peoples east of → Illyricum as well [1].

Non-Greek languages still lived on in the first millennium, as written evidence shows: the fragments of so-called → Eteo-Cretan in East Crete (Praesus, Drerus: 6th–3rd cents.), some inscriptions in → Eteo-Cyprian (since 700: esp. in → Am(m)athous [3]) and Cypriot-Phoenician bilingual inscriptions (4th cent.) as well as the bilingual → Lemnos Stele (6th cent.), which shows an alphabetical script and language that is related to → Etruscan (AFIZ = Etr. *avils* 'years'). The non-Greek → personal names in many areas and the antique references to βάρβαροι (*bárbaroi*) and similar terms in regions whose inscriptions are written in Greek: Epirus (Thuc. 2,80,5; 81 passim), Aetolia (2,68,5; ἀγνωστότατοι δὲ γλῶσσαν; *agnōstótatoi dè glôssan*, 3,94,5), a few cities on the Athos Peninsula (βάρβαροι δίγλωσσοι; *bárbaroi díglōssoi*, 4,109,4) or the Propontis (Hdt. 1,57,2). The unique features of → Pamphylian point indirectly to the existence of a native Asian population. In any case it cannot be ruled out that the speakers of non-Greek languages also spoke Greek to varying degrees at least in the Greece of the classical period.

1 H. Kronasser, Illyrier und Illyricum, in: Die Sprache 11, 1965, 155–183.

Heubeck 2ff., 6ff., 11ff., 54ff., 67f.; R. Hiersche, Grundzüge der griech. Sprachgesch. 1970, 30ff.; O. Hoffmann, A. Scherer, Gesch. der griech. Sprache 1,

1969, 9ff.; A. Morpurgo Davies, The linguistic evidence: is there any?, in: G. Cadogan (ed.), The End of the Early Bronze Age in the Aegean, 1986, 93–123. J.G.-R.

Greece, systems of writing The history of → writing shows that throughout the world there are fundamentally only three ways of transcribing the spoken word: pictograms, syllabic scripts and phonetic alphabets (in that order). All known scripts use either one of those techniques or a combination of them. Only the last of the three is suitable for an adequate representation of sound patterns. The consonantal script that was adopted mainly in the East constitutes a special form of phonetic script.

In Hellas and the Aegean the oldest textual evidence comes from Crete [2]: the hieroglyphic-pictographical script (*c*. 2000–1450, → Hieroglyphic scripts, Crete) consists of pictorial symbols (ideograms) representing objects that are generally recognizable. From it derives the 'proto-linear' script (found predominantly at Phaestus), from which → Linear A (*c*. 1650–1450) then probably developed. Hieroglyphs on seals continued in use until 1450 (partly contemporaneously with Linear A). The language of the Linear-A texts and that of the even older texts has so far not been identified (probably that of the pre-Greek 'Minoan' population). Linear A, probably a mostly syllabic script, was succeeded by → Linear B (used until *c*. 1200), a syllabic script that was invented by the Mycenaean Greeks and that is also attested in the south and the central mainland regions [5]. Both linear scripts consist of simplified characters; both contain signs in whose case formal similarity clearly shows which earlier symbol they developed from, even though there is no simple imitation anywhere. In addition to syllabic signs, Linear A and B also use ideograms, and symbols for numbers, weights and measures. Linear B's simple signs for vowels or open syllables only are not very suitable for rendering Greek word forms.

Unique within the Cretan script is the → Discus of Phaestus (*c*. 1650–1550): despite its pronounced pictorial character, its 45 signs suggest a (still undeciphered) syllabic script.

On Cyprus, the → Cypro-Minoan scripts (= CM) 1–3 were modelled on the Cretan scripts [3]: while CM 1 was dispersed throughout Cyprus from the 16th–11th cents., CM 2 (Enkomi, at the turn of the 13th/12th cents., probably in the Hurrite language) and CM 3 (Ugarit, 14th/13th cents., introduced by Cypriot settlers) represent special forms that are chronologically and geographically limited. The roughly 85 signs identify CM 1–3 as syllabic scripts. On the basis of this script of a non-Greek population from the 2nd millennium the → Cypriot script was formed. It was used on Cyprus from the last years of the 8th to the 3rd cent. for texts of the indigenous and immigrant Greek population. Because of the improved writing rules (and the resulting abandoning of pictograms), this syllabic script (about 60 signs) was better suited for rendering Greek than Linear B.

The → alphabet stands at the end of this development: it is based on the Phoenician consonantal script, which was not adopted by the Greeks without alteration (probably at the beginning of the 8th cent.), but was transformed into a phonetic script by creating vowel signs from superfluous symbols. It is first attested in inscriptions from the 2nd half of the 8th cent.

→ Greek; → Crete; → Cyprus; → Pre-Greek languages

1 Heubeck 2 J.-P. Olivier, Cretan writing in the second millennium B.C., in: World Archaeology 17, 1985/6, 377–389 3 Th. G. Palaima, Ideograms and Supplementals and Regional Interaction among Aegean and Cypriot Scripts, in: Minos 24, 1989, 29–54 4 L. Godart, Le pouvoir de l'écrit, 1990 5 J. Chadwick, Linear B and related scripts, (Reading the Past 1), 1987, 137–195. R.P.

Greek

I. Ancient Greek II. Middle and Modern Greek

I. Ancient Greek

A. Age, Sources B. Greek as an Indo-European language C. Proto-Greek D. Historical Period E. Language area F. Characteristics G. Contacts

A. Age, Sources

The earliest extant Greek texts date from around 1400 BC. Greek is thus the oldest known language transmitted in Europe and takes second place (after → Hittite) amongst the Indo-European languages. As Greek has a partly accessible prehistory (see B., C. below) and survives today, its linguistic history can be traced over about 5,000 years.

The most important linguistic sources of Ancient Greek are textual. They range from functional (→ Mycenaean, → Papyri) to literary texts. The latter are transmitted, sometimes with corruption, in medieval manuscripts; the numerous authentic → inscriptions serve an important controlling function. Refined style is the rule; colloquial language and slang are the exception (→ *defixio*).

Greek texts have been transmitted either in two syllabic scripts of limited life-span (→ Cypriot script, → Linear B) or, predominantly, in the Greek → alphabet. As a phonetic script, the latter is far better suited for Greek, although it imperfectly conveys vowel quantity and the /h/. Even in the classical period, moreover, spelling is occasionally historical: 'spurious': ει ου ⟨ἔμεινα δοῦλος⟩ = */emēna dūlos/* (→ Pronunciation). Additional useful information is provided, along with useless detail, by the ancient → grammarians and lexicographers (→ Lexicography): e.g. the length of the *ā*- in ἄρδω is not evident in texts (Hdn. 2,109,15); and the Indo-European derivative ἔορ< **s̯uesor-* 'sister' (Hesych. E 4048f.) does not appear at all in textual transmission. Secondary transmission occasionally furnishes additional details (see below G.).

1 Hieroglyphic-pictographic script; four-sided seal (Crete)

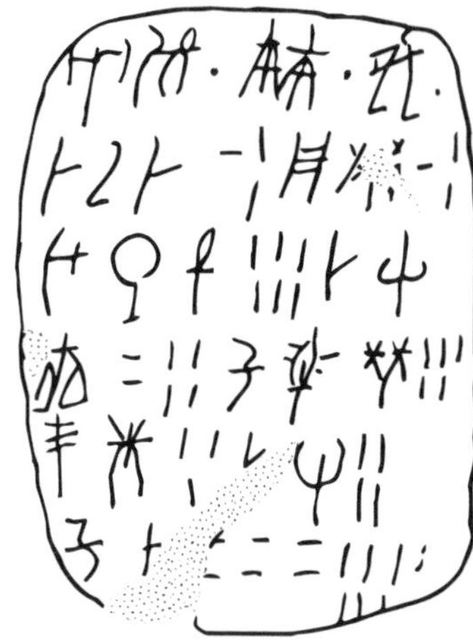

2 Linear A tablet from Agia Triada

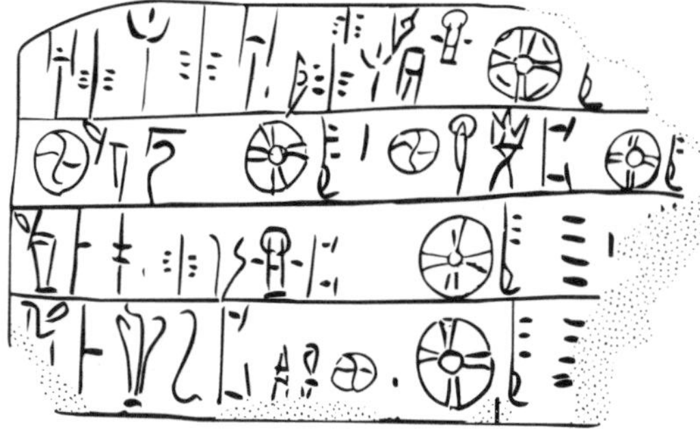

3 Linear B tablet from Knossos (KN So 894)

4 Cypro-Minoan script; clay cylinder from Enkomi

5 Cypric syllabary (Paphos); funerary inscription of King Echetimus

6 Alphabetic script: Nestor's Cup

B. Greek as an Indo-European language

As an → Indo-European language, Greek can be traced back to proto-Indo-European, which possibly started to break up around 3000 BC. Like Latin, Greek also belongs to the → Centum languages but a closer relationship between the two can neither be deduced from this [7. 104f.], nor be established otherwise [9. 57f.]. A closer relationship is occasionally postulated with → Armenian [2], → Phrygian, → Tocharic and, most plausibly perhaps, with → Macedonian. Greek's Indo-European credentials are established from numerous items of evidence on all linguistic levels down to style and textual structure (→ Indo-European poetic language).

Its most important point of comparison is the even more ancient Old Indic (= OI). That is evident, *i.a.*, in vocabulary and word forms (for the system see F. below). Substantives: βοῦς, acc. βῶν (OI. *gáuḥ gā́m*); Ζεύς Ζῆν (OI *dyáuḥ dyā́m*); νηῦς νῆα (OI *náuḥ nā́vam*). Adjectives: νέ(ϝ)ος (OI *návaḥ*). Cardinal numbers: δύο, τρεῖς (OI *dvā́*, *tráyaḥ*). Pronouns: ὁ ἡ τό (OI *sá sā́ tát*). – Verbal ending *-ti* in ἔσ-τι (OI *ás-ti*). – Verbal stems in the present tense: ἄγε-, τανυ- (OI *ája-*, *tanu-*); in the aorist: θή-, φύ- (OI *dhā́-*, *bhū́-*); in the perfect: ἐγρήγορ- (OI

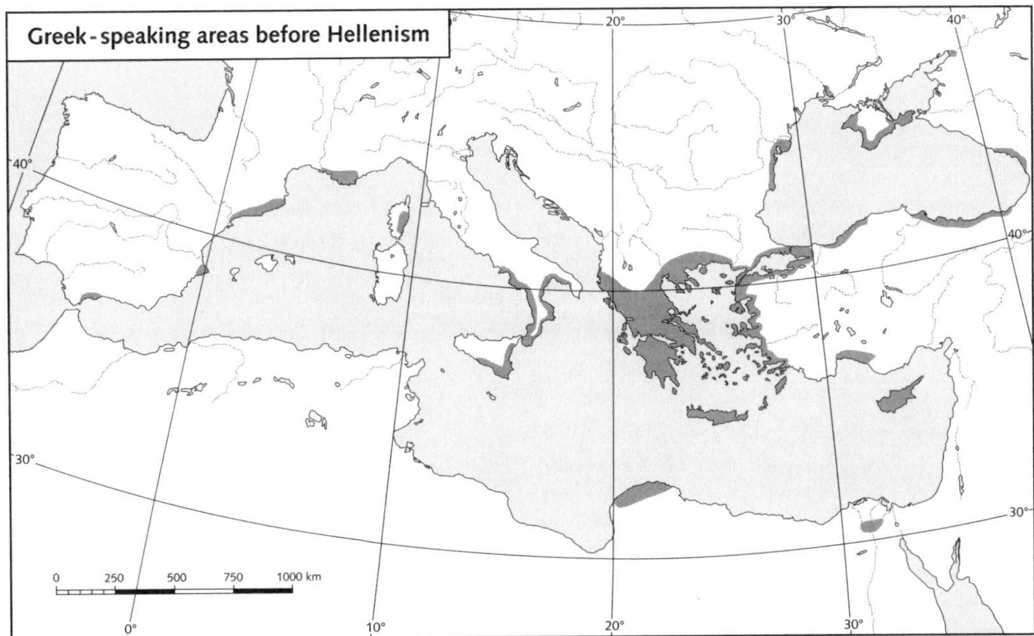

jāgár-). Form words: τε unaccented, μή as a prohibition (OI *ca*, *mā́* identically).

C. Proto-Greek

The still prehistoric proto-Greek developed gradually in the 3rd millennium BC. It contained those features that were inherited in common by the later dialects (such as φέρω φέρετε < proto-Gk. **pherō pherete*), rather than coming into being through later diffusion or parallel innovation; other features can be reconstructed through dialectal comparison: Doric φέροντι, Arcadian φερονσι, Aeolic φέροισι, Attic-Ionic φέρουσι derive from proto-Gk. **pheronti*; Mycenaean 〈*-qe*〉, Attic-Ionic (etc.) τε from **k^we*. The Indo-European languages also play a role in establishing data for proto-Greek : **pheronti* is confirmed by OI *bháranti*, **k^we* by Latin *-que*. The proto-Greek form is, however, uncertain for the 1st person plural active of the verb: Doric φέρομες, Attic-Ionic etc. φέρομεν. Features that certainly did belong to proto-Greek are: the resonants *l̥ r̥ m̥ n̥*, the labio-velars *k^w g^w k^wh*; *u̯* (Ϝ) in all positions, *i̯* initially and intervocalically; both the instrumental and locative cases; **hem-* 'one' (> ἕν-); **u̯ekh* 'move, shift' (Latin *ueh-ere*); **-u̯oh-* in the perfect active participle (later -Ϝοτ- > -οτ-, e.g. ἑστα-ότ-).

Proto-Greek also includes a large number of innovations that had generally penetrated even earlier and thus comprehensively influenced the whole of Greek [8. 7]: *bh* > *ph* etc. (**bheronti* > **pheronti*); the vowels *e*/*a*/*o*-as the continuants of the → laryngeals; palatalized consonants from clusters involving *i̯* (**phulačō* vel sim. < **phulak-i̯ō* 'guard' : φυλάσσω); *s* > *h* in several positions (**septm̥* > ἑπτά); restriction of the non-vocalic final sounds to *-n -r -s* (**ebher-om -et* > ἔφερ-ον -ε); *-si* in the locative plural (ποσ-σί); *-tato-* in the superlative; *-sth-* in the Middle Voice endings; *kappa* aorist (ἔθηκα) and *kappa* perfect (ἕστακα). In addition, there also are new vocabulary items and syntagmata.

D. Historical Period

The historical period of Greek begins with Mycenaean around 1400 BC, a few cents. after the Greek immigration. An identifiable sound change in Mycenaean is evidence of an already existing first dialectal split (→ Greek dialects): the southern Greek innovation of **pheronsi* (> φέρουσι), while northern Greek maintained **pheronti* (> Doric φέροντι). The → Dark Ages [1], that began at the end of the Mycenaean period (around 1200), then saw the → Doric migration; in this process southern Greek was partly split and partly pushed eastwards, likewise Aeolic, which originally probably belonged to northern Greek. The linguistic material that was again and very abundantly reappearing after 750 demonstrates a very colourful panorama of dialects, fostered by the smallness of geographical and political scale. These differences were transferred from the homeland to the colonies. Linguistic developments throughout the whole language area, isoglosses between clearly distinct neighbouring dialects (e.g. Attic and Boeotian) attest to the enduring unity. Even though the differences are very noticeable indeed, they are in many cases not very far-reaching (*i.a.*, vocalism, pronouns, formation of the infinitive; vocabulary). While the literary dialects were recognized throughout the Greek world (→ Greek literary languages), a universal standard language did not develop until the 4th cent.

Elevated by the political and cultural pre-eminence of Athens in the 5th cent., → Attic filled this gap by providing the basis of the → Koine. Other dialects, however, left their legacy in this common language; a short-lived 'Koinā' (→ Doric/Northwest Greek) developed as a variant in Doric territory. The Koine became the dominant language of Alexander's empire. The old dialects of the ancestral territories were driven back or even out, first in Ionic territory. A far-reaching countermovement, beginning in the 1st cent BC, can be seen in → Atticism; it led, for example, to a revival of the → dual, which had died out some time earlier, and of Classical Attic vocabulary.

E. Language area

The post-proto-Indo-European precursors of proto-Greek (see C. above) developed to the north of Greece, probably on the Balkan peninsula. Proto-Greek might well have developed there or already in north-west Greece. Greek immigrants soon reached the southernmost parts of Greece, and Crete. Western Asian Minor, Pamphilia and Cyprus were settled after the Mycenaean period. Coastal cities in Italy, Sicily, Spain, North Africa and the Black Sea area (see map) developed in the 2nd wave of → colonization. Through Alexander's empire (→ Alexander [4] with map) and → Hellenism Greek, as language of culture, trade and of the cities, was taken as far as India in the east and as far as Nubia in the south, though without establishing itself everywhere on a long-term basis. Apart from Asia Minor, Greece subsequently lost the Orient. In the West it had to give way to Latin; it was however recognized in the eastern part of the Roman empire and after the schism was made the official language. In Greece, Greek has thus been spoken for over 3,500 years.

F. Characteristics

The Romans found Greek melodious (Quint. Inst. 12,10,27); it had a musical → accent and was rich in vowels: the five syllables in Ἠελίοιο (*Ēelíoio*) 'of Helios' (Hom. Od. 1,8) contain only one non-vowel. As well as the five short and seven long vowels of Attic, there were, *i.a.*, three classes of plosives, e.g. *b* – *p* – *ph*. The vocabulary is extensive. In addition to → ablaut (λέγω : λόγος, τέμνω : τομή) inherited from proto-Indo-European, some prefixes (ἄ-λογος, δύσ-τομος) and a great many suffixes (λογ-ικός -ίζομαι) were available for word formation. Even outside the realm of poetry, nominal composition (determinative, possessive and governing compounds) was very productive; this ensured the survival of the inherited practice of forming full names (Θρασύ-βουλος, Μενέ-λαος; → Personal names). The use of prepositions increases, *i.a.* as a replacement for the local cases that had been lost. Of the three numbers the dual is receding.

The verbal system is extensive. The inherited active and middle voices are supplemented by new passive forms (ποιη-θῆναι, -θήσεσθαι). Present and aorist stems represent the inherited strong contrast of the two → aspects; they are supplemented by future and perfect stems. Four moods were inherited, an imperative was lost, and the injunctive only partly preserved; the Ionic iterative mood (φέρεσκον) is an innovation. The non-finite parts of the verbal system were also strongly developed; the infinitive and participle are both used in periodic construction. In the historical period a definite article developed from the demonstrative pronoun. Particles, used partly for nuancing, partly in fixed phrases, were numerous and in common use: ἄρα 'therefore', γε 'at least, at any rate', δή 'just' (emphasizing: temporal), etc.

G. Contacts

Even in the Mycenaean period, → loan-words of differing origin (→ Pre-Greek languages, also → Semitic languages) were to be found. Among them are names of plants (σήσαμον, σῦκον), materials (ἐλέφας, χρυσός) and others (ἀσάμινθος, Ϝάναξ, θώραξ, χιτών). Other loanwords, in some cases probably just as old, are attested only later on (ἀψίνθιον, μνᾶ, μόλυβδος, τύραννος). In later periods, it was only on the geographical fringes (→ Hipponax) and in the vernacular that Greek was similarly receptive. Latin borrowings are to be found in the NT (κεντυρίων, μόδιος), but only rarely in higher literature [5]. Greek influence on other languages, however, is disproportionately stronger – as a result, we find '*die Nebenüberlieferung des Griechischen*', the 'secondary transmission of Greek' [9. 150–165]. The Italic languages, namely Latin (*poena* as early as the Twelve Table Law) [1], and also Etruscan [3], began to borrow from Greek at an early stage. Latin, for example, provides evidence of *-h-* in medial position (Lat. *sun-* or *syn-hodus* = σύνοδος [6. 175]) that is insufficiently attested in Greek. Many Greek words are attested only, or attested earlier, in Latin texts [4]. Christianity opened up new areas of influence for Greek, e.g. in → Armenian and → Syriac.

→ Greek dialects; → Greek literary languages

1 F. Biville, Les emprunts du latin au grec, 2 vols., 1990–1995 2 J. Clackson, The linguistic relationship between Armenian and Greek, 1994 3 C. De Simone, Die g. Entlehnungen im Etrusk., 2 vols., 1968–1970 4 S. Frei-Korsunsky, G. Wörter aus lat. Überlieferung, thesis Zurich 1969 5 H. Hofmann, Die lat. Wörter im G. bis 600 n.Chr., thesis Erlangen-Nuremberg 1989 6 Leumann 7 M. Mayrhofer, Indogermanische Gramm. I 2, 1986 8 Rix, HGG 9 Schwyzer, Gramm.

Chantraine; Frisk; Kühner/Blass; Kühner/Gerth; M. Lejeune, Phonétique historique du mycénien et du grec ancien, 1972; LSJ; M. Meier-Brügger, G. Sprachwissenschaft, 2 vols., 1992 (bibl.); Rix, HGG; Schwyzer, Gramm.; Schwyzer/Debrunner; ThGL.

Maps: Schwyzer, Gramm., 83. B.F.

II. Middle and Modern Greek

To a large extent, the linguistic evolution from Ancient to Modern Greek remains concealed behind texts that conform to sets of rules, but evidence can still be found, even in antiquity, especially in Koinē texts (→ Koinē), papyri, quotations of spoken discourse or of less high-brow literature. There is, thus, little point in attempting to define a distinct 'Middle Greek' linguistic period. Moreover, the decisive point of departure in the written language falls between the written dialects (or Attic prose in particular) and literary Koinē, which was, however, later abandoned for an Atticizing norm. It is therefore more useful to use 'Middle Greek' as a term for medieval Greek, while remembering that this includes texts of a very heterogeneous character, ranging from prose that comes up to Atticist standards to literature in the vernacular. The most important linguistic differences between ancient and modern Greek are as follows:

1. Phonology

1) the collapse of quantity, i.e. the breakdown of the phonological distinction between long and short vowels; 2) the iotacism that merges the sounds differentiated classically as ⟨η⟩, ⟨ει⟩ and ⟨ι⟩ into/i/ (⟨υ⟩ is added later, shifting from/y/ to/i/, even if ⟨υ⟩ survives dialectally as /u/ even today); 3) the monophthongization of the diphthong/ai/ to /ę/. 4) within the consonantal system, the change of the old voiceless aspirated stops to voiceless fricatives (⟨θ⟩ : /t^h/> /þ/; ⟨φ⟩ : /p^h/>/f/; ⟨χ⟩ : k^h/> /χ/ or /ç/ depending on the following vowel; the pronunciation endorsed by Erasmus is not consistent in this respect), in which new geminates develop (modern Greek νύφη < ancient Greek νύμφη by way of *νύφφη) by a process of assimilation after nasals (a cluster of nasal + fricative is not admitted at any stage of Greek linguistic history; cf. e.g. the acc. pl. in –ους < *–ονς); 5) the change of the old voiced consonants to voiced stops (⟨δ⟩ : /d/> /ð/; ⟨β⟩ :/b/>/v/; ⟨γ⟩ : /g/>/j/ and /γ/ depending on the following vowel); 6) the voicing of stops after a nasal (⟨ντ⟩,/nt/>/nd/ etc.) and the change of fricative + fricative or stop + stop clusters into fricative + stop, e.g. in αἰσθάνομαι > αἰστάνομαι or ἑπτά > ἑφτά. There were serious morphological consequences from the phonological simplification (not extending to all modern Greek dialects!) of geminates, as in the weakening of –/n/ as accusative morpheme, which led to a metaplasm in the system of declension. The transcription errors encountered on papyri, as in ⟨γ⟩ for ⟨κ⟩ etc. and *vice versa,* have no basis in Greek linguistic history and can be traced back to the influence of a Coptic substratum.

2. Morphology and Morphosyntax

The gender system survives apart from the removal of exceptions such as ἡ νῆσος; the Attic declension had already largely been abandoned in Koinē times; the same also happened to the i-stem declension (Modern Greek όρεξη < Ancient Greek ὄρεξις, evident already in papyri from the Imperial period). Accusatives from the consonantal declension in –αν, foreshadowing the adoption of consonantal stems into the thematic declension (cf. Modern Greek άντρας < Ancient Greek ἀνήρ), are found already in the Hellenistic period. Together with new inflectional endings, such as –ες for the nominative plural of agent nouns in –της (e.g. κλέφτες for κλέφτης), the decline of the dative is especially important to the declensional system; it partly merges with the genitive but is also formed periphrastically with the preposition σε < εἰς. In the verb, the distinction between middle and passive, relevant even in Ancient Greek only in the aorist stem, disappeared (uncertainty about the use of deponent verbs was already quite frequent in the NT), the Ancient Greek perfect was abandoned for a periphrastic construction, as was the future, that is then formed with the particle θά < θέλει ἵνα, in parallel with the disappearance of the infinitive (rudimentally surviving in dialect forms) in favour of νά < ἵνα plus an inflected verbal form. The augment was preserved only when accented, and the distinction between imperfect, aorist and perfect endings likewise broke down: Modern Greek has a unified paradigm with the endings –α/-ες/-ε/-αμε/-ατε/-ανε. The optative also disappeared, although it survived in the written language until well into the Byzantine period as a flourish of refinement. Amongst the morphosyntactic innovations, the formation of an indefinite article ένας < εἷς should be mentioned furthermore the merging of the interrogatives 'where' and 'to where', and the accusative used universally as the case after prepositions.

3. Vocabulary

Apart from the generally observable tendency of the vernacular to a) replace words that are poorly anchored morphologically (replacement of athematic verbs, unless they had already been transferred to the thematic conjugation, as e.g. modern Greek χορτάζω for ancient Greek κορέννυμι; abandoning heteroclitic forms, cf. modern Greek νερό for ancient Greek ὕδωρ) and b) employ diminutives as standard words (cf. modern Greek αυτί < ὠτίον for ancient Greek οὖς), the influence of foreign languages should be mentioned in this context. Latin, which even provided derivative morphemes such as –άτος < *-atus* or –άρης < *-arius*, deserves special mention, and later on, Italian also (not in the Pontic dialect), French (especially on Cyprus) and Turkish (not in the dialects of Lower Italy or the Ionian islands). The acceptance of *dhimotikí* over *katharévusa* required linguistic expansion, e.g. with the creation of abstract specialist/technical vocabularies, and even elevated borrowings have been absorbed into the modern standard language, cf. for example pairs such as the inherited θωριά 'face' and the *mot savant* θεωρία 'theory'.

→ Greek [I]

G. Böhlig, Das Verhältnis von Volks- und Reinsprache im griech. MA, in: Berliner Byzantinistische Arbeiten 5, 1957, 1–13; R. Browning, Medieval and Modern Greek, ²1983; A. Debrunner, A. Scherer, Gesch. der griech. Sprache II. Grundfragen und Grundzüge des nachklass. Griech., 1969; K. Dieterich, Untersuchungen zur Gesch. der griech. Sprache von der hell. Zeit bis zum 10. Jh. n.Chr., 1898 (= Byz. Archiv 1); W. Dietrich, Griech. und Romanisch. Parallelen und Divergenzen in Entwicklung, Variation und Strukturen (Münstersche Beiträge zur Romanischen Philol. 11), 1995; G.N. Hatzidakis, Einleitung in die neugriech. Gramm., 1892; H. KAHANE, R. KAHANE, Abendland und Byzanz: Sprache, in: P. WIRTH (ed.), Reallex. der Byzantinistik 1, 1970–1976 (repr. in H. KAHANE, R. KAHANE, Graeca et Romanica. Scripta Selecta vol. 2. Byzantium and the West, Hellenistic Heritage in the West, Structural and Sociolinguistics, 1981, 1–148); J. KALITSUNAKIS, Gramm. der neugriech. Volkssprache, [3]1963; J. KRAMER, Ant. Sprachform und moderne Normsprache. Part Two: Griech., in: Balkanarchiv N.F. 11, 1986, 117–210; G. MEYER, Neugriech. Studien III. Die lat. Lehnworte im Neugriech., in: SAWW 132, 1895; J. NIEHOFF-PANAGIOTIDIS, Koine und Diglossie, 1995; S. PSALTES, Gramm. der byz. Chroniken, 1913; S.T. TEODORSSON, The Phonology of Ptolemaic Koine (Studia Graeca et Latina Gothoburgensia 36), 1977; M. TRIANDAPHYLLIDES, Die Lehnworte der mittelgriech. Vulgärlit., 1909.

V.BI.

Greek dialects

I. Ancient Greek dialects

A. Dialect and standard language

Greek is attested in dialectal form from the first texts in → Linear B onwards. Local dialects are used in every city or region from the Archaic to the Hellenistic period (in competition with the → Koinē and regional Koinaí). In the Imperial period some dialects (e.g. → Aeolic [Lesbian], Laconian (→ Doric/Northwest Greek, Tsakonian) are used in a rather archaizing manner. Variants of the old dialects still survive today in Laconia (Tsaconian) and Lower Italy. A unified form of Greek did not exist before the Koinḗ, although the Greeks were conscious, even in the Classical period, of speaking a common language [15].

B. Distribution

The geographical distribution of the Greek dialects (GD) corresponds to that of the Greek tribes from the beginning of the 2nd millennium BC (migration into Greece) up to the great → colonization (8th–6th cents): Greece and the Aegean, then the coast of the Black Sea, the west coast of Anatolia (Aeolis, Ionia, Doris) together with Pamphylia, Cyprus and Cyrene; Lower Italy and Sicily were settled from the Doric north-western regions of Greece, north-east Spain (Emporion) and southern France (Pech Mahó), from Ionia. Traditions about migrations (e.g. the Thessalian origin of the Boeotians, cf. Thuc. 1,12,3) or settlements (e.g. Heraclea from the Laconian settlement of Tarentum) are often confirmed by linguistic agreements between non-neighbouring dialects.

C. Sources

The most important sources are epigraphical: in the 2nd millennium, the Linear-B tablets (also vases and small lumps of clay) from Crete (especially Cnossos: rather *c.*1400 than *c.* 1200), Pylos, Mycenae, Tiryns and Thebes (*c.* 1200); in the 1st millennium the inscriptions from the 8th cent. onwards: until the end of the 5th cent. we find local → alphabets, then the Ionic-Milesian alphabet (from 403 in Athens, from the 4th cent. in other regions); in Cyprus, a syllabary related to Linear B is used (first text: *o-pe-re-ta-u /Op^{h}eltau/* 11th cent.?), from the 3rd cent. on also the alphabet. Despite their uncertain transmission, the glosses are also interesting (primarily from literary writers but also dialectal, sometimes with information concerning their origin, → glossography), as comparison with inscriptions often demonstrates. The → Greek literary languages, on which the information of Greek grammarians is largely dependent [7], do contain some genuine dialectal material but are partly artificial [12].

D. Difficulties

Our knowledge of the GD is full of gaps. The Mycenaean texts are extremely short, and many words cannot be interpreted. Even the description of many dialects from the 1st millennium is beset with considerable difficulties: long inscriptions from the archaic period are rare; private inscriptions are generally too short or composed in literary style, and official documents – even in the Classical period but especially from the 4th cent. – show a strong influence from the standard languages shaped by Attic-Ionic. It can thus not always be determined whether the syntax and vocabulary of inscriptions derive from genuine dialect forms or whether instead they reflect some dialect colouring. On top of that, there is the influence of orthography: the actual pronunciation is often given away only by 'spelling errors' (e.g. ⟨ΣΤ⟩ for [st^h]). We are also lacking the evidence for many aspects of morphology, syntax and vocabulary of those dialects for which there is no literature. Even for well-documented dialects it is hard to sketch dialectal geography, as relevant features are often not synchronically attested in all places. Attempts to trace sociolinguistic variations [4. 184ff.] have mostly been illusory.

E. Groupings in the 1st millennium BC

There are nevertheless features attested in virtually all dialects: they permit a grouping based on an inter-dialectal comparison and enable us, with the assistance of chronological criteria (see below), to draw conclusions about their prehistory. Even if there is the possibility of parallel developments that are of no importance to the comparison (e.g. replacement of –[ν]τοι by –[ν]ται in all dialects except Mycenaean, Arcadian, Cypriot), isoglosses between geographically remote dialects generally indicate original unity or prehistoric proximity, especially in the case of an innovation (e.g. nominative singular –ής for –εύς in Arcadian and Cyp-

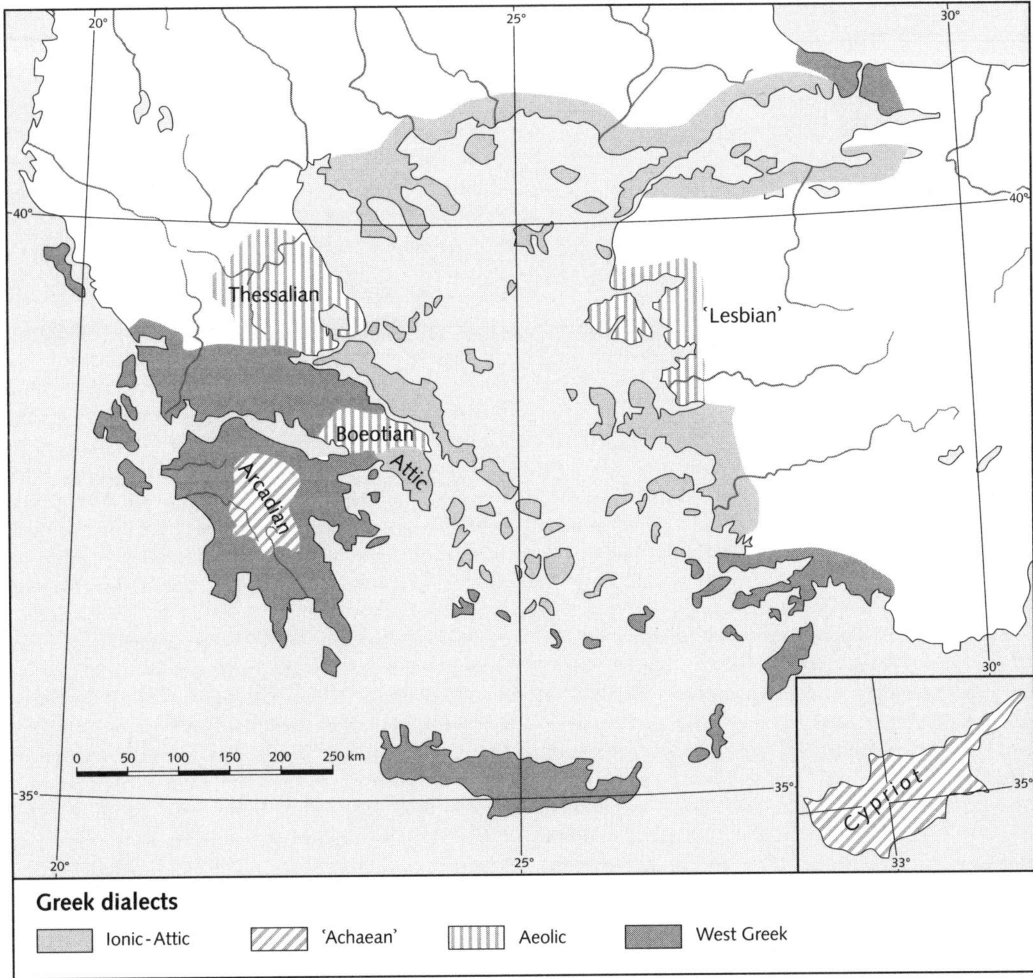

riot) or of a choice between two alternatives (levelling of the thematic or athematic inflection of the *verba vocalia*: –άω, -έω or –ᾶμι, -ημι) [1. 46ff., 27ff.]. Conversely, isoglosses between neighbouring dialects (e.g. Arcadian., Laconian ἠμί, βωλᾶ́) suggest a development that took place after the final settlement of the dialects. Which developments belong to the pre- and which to the post-Mycenaean age can often be determined from the evidence offered by Mycenaean. Even the relative chronology of isoglosses can be established in some cases: e.g. Ionic-Attic **ā* > *ǟ* (**dāmos* > δῆμος) is later than the first compensatory lengthening (**VRsV* > *V̄RV*: because **éphansa* > *éphāna* > ἔφηνα) and earlier than the second **VntiV*, **-Vns* > *V̄sV*, *-V̄s* (because **pantia*, **tans* > πᾶσα, τᾶ́ς) or than *a+e* > *ā* (ἐτίμᾶ). In the Classical period the dialects, with the exception of → Pamphylian, can be broken down into four main categories which suggest original continua in the prehistorical period (at around the end of the 2nd millennium):

a) 'Attic-Ionic' (with Ionic from Euboea, the Ionian Cyclades and Ionia): **ā* > *ǟ*; metathesis **āo* > *eō* (with the so-called 'Attic' declension λεώς) or **ēa* > *eā*; **r̥* > *ra* in the context of C*r̥*C; early loss of **u̯-*; genitive πόλεως (but Ionic also –ιος); ἡμεῖς, ὑμεῖς; 3rd singular ἦν 'he was'; 3rd plural –σαν (ἔθε-σαν); *verba vocalia* in –άω, -έω; ἀπό, πρός, *ἐν-ς with accusative.

b) 'Arcado-Cypriot' (or by convention 'Achaean'): raising of *e*, *o* before a nasal (ἰν = ἐν, ὀν-/ὐν- = ἀν-) and of *o* (genitive singular in –αυ, 3rd singular plural in –[ν]τυ); **r̥* > *ro*; **kʷi* > *t'i-*; ἱερής; ὅνυ (= -εύς, οὗτος); 3rd plural –αν (ἔθε/ι-αν); *verba vocalia* in –ᾶμι, -ημι; ἀπύ/ἐς with dative, πός, κάς (= ἀπό/ἐξ with genitive, πρός, καί), ἐν with accusative.

c) 'Aeolic' (Lesbian, Thessalian, Boeotian): **r̥* > *ro*; **kʷe* > *pe*; athematic dative plural in –εσσι; ἴα (Lesbian ἴα) 'one'; perfect participle with *-nt-*; patronymics. Probably also thematic infinitive in –έμεν, ἐν with accusative (Lesbian –ην, εἰς); ἀπύ; αἴ κε (Boeotian ἀπό, κα). Genuine 'Aeolic' is hard to establish as Lesbian is under Ionic influence [17. 151ff.; 18. 70ff.] and Boeotian has a lot in common with Northwest Greek.

d) 'Doric/Northwest/Greek ': *ā* + *ŏ̄* > *ā*, *ā* + *e* > *ē* (genitive singular –ᾶ, plural –ᾶν, 3rd singular ἐνίκη); **r̥* > *ra*; 1. plural in –μες; 3rd plural ἔθεν (= ἔθεσαν); 3rd singular ἦς 'he was'; *verba vocalia* in –άω, -έω; 'Doric' future in –σέω (*-sé̯io/e-); aorist and future with –ξ- and present in *–di̯o/e- (aorist ψᾶφιξα-, δικαξα-/δικασσα-); τέτορες 'four'; ἀπό. With respect to some features (e.g. ἐν with the accusative, athematic dative plural in –οις or –εσσι), the North-West dialects are unique.

F. Groupings in the 2nd millennium BC

Moreover, important parallels exist between a) and b) in comparison with d), and partly also with c), which suggest links in an even earlier period (middle of the 2nd millennium): *-ti(–) > -si(–); *t(ʰ)i̯ (the τόσος type), *ts > s, but *t(ʰ)-i̯, *k(ʰ)i̯ (present in –σσω, Attic Euboean –ττω), *tu̯ > ss (Attic Euboean tt); nominative plural οἱ, αἱ; 1st plural in –μεν; athematic infinitive in –ναι; ὅτε; εἰ (ἠ) ἄν (but Cypriot κε); βούλομαι / βόλομαι 'to want' (*gᵘ̯ol-); πρῶτος; ἱερός (but East Ionic ἱρός); εἴκοσι 'twenty'. These can be traced back to an original continuum ('East-' or 'South Greek'), regarded as the precursor to a) and b) [17; 18]. The concordances in d) point in each case to a 'West-' or 'North-Greek' continuum: preserved -ti(–), *t(ʰ)i̯ (the τόσσος type) as well as *t(ʰ)-i̯, *k(ʰ)i̯ (present in –σσω), *tu̯, *ts > ss (in Cretan still tˢ); nominative plural τοι, ται; athematic infinitive in –μεν; ὄκα; αἴ κα; δήλομαι/δείλομαι (*gᵘ̯el-); πρᾶτος; ἱαρός; (Ϝ)ίκατι 'twenty'. For c) we can postulate a combination of East- (1st plural –μεν, πρῶτος, ἱερός) and predominantly West-Greek elements (-ti[–], *totˢos, athematic infinitive in –μεν, αἰ, *gᵘ̯el-). Mycenaean (di-do-si /-onsi/, o-te, i-je-ro, also to-so / toso-/ rather than /tosso-/) belongs to 'East Greek': it has important isoglosses with b) (⟨ro⟩, ⟨Co-ro⟩ for *r̥, -to /–(n)to(i)/, a-pu, po-si /posi/ as an early stage of Arcado-Cypriot πός, perhaps also pa-ro with locative, personal name ka-ke /Kʰalkēs/) and is therefore thought to be closely related to b)'s precursor in the 2nd millennium. Despite a few peculiarities (e.g. i-jo/i-ju 'son' [but in Thebes also u-jo /ʰuios/], no augment except for a single occurrence of a-pe-do-ke), Mycenaean hardly merits special categorization.

In any event, there is no clear family-tree structure; this is demonstrated by the isoglosses that do not correspond to the a)-d) distribution: *r̥ > ra, the verba vocalia in –άω and –έω, ἀπό are common to a) and d) in contrast to b) and c); a) and the Doric dialects have *ἐν-ς with the accusative, in contrast to b), c) and the North-West GD; a) and a portion of d) have εἰμί, βουλᾱ́, τρεῖς, τοῦ, b) and a portion of d) ἠμί, βωλᾱ́, τρῆς, τῶ. This suggests the conclusion that there were contacts between a) and d) somewhere around the end of the 1st millennium and that shared developments trace back to it, before individual dialects, after settling in their historic locations, acquired the form that is reflected in inscriptions.

G. Prehistory

The often advanced notion [1. 68] that the GD developed outside Greece and arrived in three migrations can be discarded. Instead, the first dialectal splintering of early Greek took place around 1600, after the Greeks had migrated into Greek territory (around 2000/1900). The Mycenaean area (including Thessaly) was home to East Greek, to which (at least) the early stages of a) (in Attica and Euboea, and perhaps in Boeotia as well?) and b) (Peloponnese and the islands) can be traced back; variations are traceable even in the almost homogeneously attested Mycenaean (thus in Pylos the 'standard' Mycenaean with the dative in e /-ei/, pe-mo for *spermn̥, ti-mi-ti-ja, also *-ti(–) > -si(–) in contrast to the 'special' Mycenaean with -i /-i/, pe-ma, te-mi-ti-ja and (–)ti (only in proper names) [19. 97ff.]. Whether the latter corresponds to Doric as the dialect of the lower orders in Greek society [7] is hardly capable of proof [19. 101ff.]. By contrast, West Greek remained in the border areas of north-west Greece: whether, or to what extent, North-West Greek or 'proto-Aeolic' occupied a special position at that time remains a mystery. With the spread of West-Greek tribes into most areas of East-Greek territory (around 1200/1100) and the consequential tribal movements in the course of the → Dark Ages, the dialect map of Greece was fundamentally altered by the breaking-down of earlier continua, the development of new, more recent (: post-Mycenaean) isoglosses and the mixture of dialects within each region. Before their geographical separation Arcadian and Cypriot, in which East Greek, namely 'standard' Mycenaean continued, had undergone b) changes that were partly post-Mycenaean and common to both: traces of an Arcado-Cypriot substratum are recognizable, for example, in Laconian and in Cretan (→ Doric/Northwest Greek). 'Attic-Ionic' and Doric/Northwest Greek each underwent specific changes, cf. a) and d); others are common to both (see above) and derive from contacts of both groups somewhere in central Greece. 'Proto-Aeolic', which sprang up in Thessaly and had East- and, in particular, West-Greek features, underwent a series of probably post-Mycenaean c) changes there and then spread to Boeotia (around 1250) and Aeolis (around 1000) [10].

→ Aeolic (Lesbian); → Arcadian; → Attic; → Boeotian; → Dialect; → Doric/Northwest Greek; → Greek literary languages; → Ionic; → Koine; → Cypriot; → Mycenaean; → Pamphylian; → Thessalian

1 F.R. Adrados, La dialectología griega como fuente para el estudio de las migraciones indoeuropeas en Grecia, 1952 (²1997) 2 A. Bartoněk, Greek Dialects between 1000 and 300 B.C., in: SMEA 20, 1979, 113–130 3 Bechtel, Dial. 4 M. Bile, C. Brixhe, R. Hodot, Les dialectes grecs, ces inconnus, in: BSL 79, 1984, 155–203 5 C. Brixhe et al., Bulletin de dialectologie grecque, in: REG 98, 1985, 260–314; 101, 1988, 74–112 (research report) 6 C.D. Buck, The Greek Dialects, 1955 7 A.C. Cassio, Parlate locali, dialetti delle stirpi e fonti letterarie nei grammatici greci, in: E. Crespo et al. (ed.), Dialectologica Graeca Miraflores 1993, 74–88 8 J. Chadwick, Who were the Dorians?, in: PdP 166, 1976, 103–177 9 C. Consani, Διάλεκτος. Contributi alla storia del concetto di "dialetto", 1991 10 J.L. García-Ramón, Les origines postmycéniennes du groupe dialectal éolien, 1975 11 Id., El micénico 1982–1983, in: Actualización

científica en filología griega, 1984, 239–274 (research report) 12 M. García Teijeiro, Vestigios de acentuación dialectal en textos dóricos y eólicos, in: Dialectologica Graeca Miraflores 1993, 147–165 (esp. 156–162) 13 O. Hoffmann, A. Scherer, Geschichte der griech. Sprache I, 1969 14 J. Méndez Dosuna, Los dialectos dorios del Nordeste. Gramática y estudio dialectal, 1985 15 A. Morpurgo Davies, The Greek Notion of Dialect, in: Verbum 10, 1987, 7–28 16 Id., Mycenaean, Arcadian, Cyprian and some questions of method in Dialectology, in: J.-P. Olivier (ed.), Mykenaika, 1992, 415–432 17 W. Porzig, Sprachgeographische Untersuchungen zu den altgriech. Dial., in: IF 61, 1954, 147–169 18 E. Risch, Die Gliederung der griech. Dial. in neuer Sicht, in: MH 12, 1955, 61–76 (= KS 207–221) 19 Id., Die griech. Dial. im 2. vorchristl. Jt., in: SMEA 20, 1979, 91–110 (= KS, 269–289) 20 Thumb/Kieckers 21 Thumb/Scherer.

Maps: Thumb/Kieckers Thumb/Scherer. J.G.-R.

II. Modern Greek dialects

One of the crucial questions of Greek dialectology is the relationship between the ancient and the modern GD. The *communis opinio* that the → Koinē forms the basis of modern Greek and has pushed out all of the old dialects needs to be modified in that it holds completely true only for the written language: in modern GD significant vestiges of the old dialects are still to be found, even if only as relics. This suggests that they were still spoken even after they had disappeared from written tradition and that on the other hand differentiation of modern dialects began at a point of time when the Koinē had not established itself in every region.

In this connection, the most important isogloss is the preservation of geminate consonants, in the wake of which even new geminates arose in the dialects in question: although degemination is attested even in → Attic, which in this respect behaves differently from other ancient GD (e.g. Attic μέσος versus Ionic μέσσος; it can be understood as the consequence of a general tendency towards open syllables, giving rise also to the so-called *correptio Attica*, and thus to the reading of the first syllable of e.g. πατρός as short, therefore a shift in syllabification from πατ-ρός to πα-τρός), double consonants have survived until now, especially in the modern Greek of Lower Italy, Cyprus and the largely defunct Cappadocian. It is precisely the geographical distribution, the fact that the phenomenon occurs on the fringes of the Greek linguistic area, that makes the case for the survival of an archaism that goes back beyond the Koinē. Consistent with that, the Greek of Lower Italy still displays distinct traces of Doric that could not have been transmitted through Latin (e.g. *nasída* < νᾶσος or *lanó* < λανός; the latter is at the same time a lexical archaism: the standard word in modern Greek is πατητήρι); there also are other innovations of modern Greek that we do not find in this dialect (e.g. the survival of the infinitive after the word for 'to be able to', if only in a rudimentary form).

On the whole, Doric (→ Doric/Northwest Greek) has shown itself to be particularly resistant: Tsaconian with its archaic appearance is sometimes justly described as modern Doric, cf. e.g. the survival of /ā/ in *fonā* < φωνά, of/w/ in *vanne* < Ϝαρνίον, of/u/ in *psjuχā* < ψυχά, and the rhotacism as in *tar amer* for τᾶς ἁμέρας, which first appears in recent Laconian. Similarly, in addition to general archaisms such as the partial preservation of ⟨η⟩ as/e/ as in *pegádin* < πηγάδιον – in modern Greek, ⟨η⟩ avoids iotacism only in front of/r/ as in ξερός < ξηρός – or the preservation of the original location of the accent in forms like *paidía* instead of modern Greek παιδιά, Pontic also retains not insignificant features of old Ionic, hence e.g. forms without α *impurum* as in *forí* < φορή versus modern Greek φορά, the negative κί < οὐκί for modern Greek δέν, the shift in aspiration e.g. in βοθράκα 'frog'; cf. κιθών for χιτών in Herodotus.

Inside of this 'fringe' of geminating dialects, we find the area of dialects that open up syllables, standard modern Greek among them. Under Slavic influence, the dialects of the north are going their own, novel way: unaccented /e/ and /o/ become /i/ and /u/ and unaccented /i/ and /u/ are syncopated, giving rise to new consonantal groups otherwise not permissible in Greek, and thus to new closed syllables (e.g. *mlar* for μουλάρι).

Unlike in Latin/Romance, the modern GD have not developed into separate languages: neither the popular-dialectal Cretan (particularly 16th/17th cents.) nor Cypriot literature (e.g. the so-called Assizes from the 14th cent. and the Chronicle of Leontius Machairas from the 15th cent.) were able to establish a lasting, independent tradition; nor was this achieved in the Soviet Union in the Thirties by the introduction of the Pontic dialect in schools as a language for dialect speakers, with its own spelling, e.g. the replacement of ⟨ψ⟩/⟨ξ⟩ by ⟨πς⟩/⟨κς⟩ and the use of ⟨ι⟩ to render all sounds affected by iotacism.

N. Andriotis, Lex. der Archaismen in den neugriech. Dial., 1974; R. Browning, Medieval and Modern Greek, [2]1983; S. Caratzas, Die Entstehung der neugriech. Literatursprache, in: Glotta 36, 1958, 194–208; Id., L'origine des dialectes néogrecs de l'Italie méridionale, 1958; N. Kontosopoulos, Διάλεκτοι και ιδιώματα της νέας ελληνικής, 1981; J. Niehoff-Panagiotidis, Koine und Diglossie, 1995; D.E. Oikonomides, Lautlehre des Pontischen, 1908; H. Pernot, Introduction à l'étude du dialecte tsakonien, 1934; G. Rohlfs, L'antico Ellenismo nell'Italia di oggi, in: Id., Latinità ed Ellenismo nel Mezzogiorno d'Italia, 1985, 33–54; Id., Grammatica storica dei dialetti italogreci, [2]1977; H. Sailer, Das Problem der sog. Geminaten in den neugriech. Dial. mit esp. Berücksichtigung einiger Dodekanesdial., in: Glotta 36, 1958, 194–208; A. Semenov, Der nordpontische Dial. des Neugriech., in: Glotta 23, 1935, 91–107; A. Thumb, Die griech. Sprache im Zeitalter des Hellenismus, 1901. V.BI.

Greek fire see vol. 6, Addenda

Greek literary languages

A. GENERAL AND HISTORICAL B. OVERVIEW
C. TRANSMISSION AND CRITICISM

A. GENERAL AND HISTORICAL

Only utility texts have survived from the Mycenaean period. The oldest extant literary texts, Homer's *Iliad* and *Odyssey* (8th cent. BC), are written in the epic literary language. While predominantly in the Ionic dialect, the language also displays the influences of earlier, partly linguistically different (Aeolic), sources and artificialities. Consequently, the epic literary language does not correspond to any particular local dialect. Even after Homer, however, it displays an essentially similar form in works of the same or related genres, up until the time of Nonnus in the 5th cent. AD.

Beside the epic literary language, or the dialect of the epic genre, others gradually appear in the course of the following centuries. Compared to the epic literary language, they all contain a far smaller share of the traditional linguistic heritage derived from literary precursors. As in the epic, however, the linguistic model of important earlier genres continued even here to exercise an influence. In this way several genres became attached to particular literary languages. Consequently, writers from different dialect areas often used the same literary language (see below B. 2). Conversely, it could happen that one and the same author could use different literary languages for the same genre, e.g. the tragedians (see below B. 5 and B. 6). Despite these conventions, there was adequate scope in the literary languages, especially in poetry, for individual stylistic feeling and distinctive features. The latter came about in different ways: for example, through linguistic innovations, literary models from other genres, allusions, and the spoken dialect forms of the author's home and elsewhere. Every Greek literary language is therefore rich in both variants and supra-regional forms, much more in poetry than in prose, but nevertheless rooted in one particular primary dialect.

Most important of the basic dialects in literature were Doric, → Ionic, and especially → Attic, which was largely dominant in prose from an early stage and was the basis for the → Koinē. → Aeolic and → Boeotian were less significant; traces of other dialects, however, did enter the literary languages. Research into the origin of linguistic phenomena in Greek literary languages certainly has its appeal but is occasionally difficult. Many contrary patterns of influence are to be found in the literary languages. The epic literary language – that of Homer – had the most effect on other literary languages, extending to prose; this influence was strongest in poetic works using the same or a related (dactylic) metre [4. 291]. Where other sources are thought to have caused departures from the primary dialect, various explanations often need to be considered; e.g. certain Aeolic elements in the lyricist Pindar (see below B. 5), who wrote in Doric, may derive from Aeolic lyrics or from epic also influenced by Aeolic (or may even be indigenous). As a result of the variety of sources there also arose hybrid or mixed forms [1. 388; 2. 170], in which features from various dialects are combined: φήμα 'report' (Eur. Hipp. 572) consists of the Doric inflectional ending -ᾱ and the Attic root form φημ-; the Doric φάμα was common in Euripides (Med. 420), but he also uses the pure Attic φήμη (Hel. 820) [1. 368].

Hellenistic writers made free use of the linguistic material from established literary languages, even in new genres.

B. OVERVIEW

The following concise references each contain: a) author or texts of a genre, b) the primary dialect, c) other dialects involved, d) some characteristic forms of the primary dialect (→ Greek dialects), e) some deviations and peculiarities, especially with respect to c), without the customary epic features in other literary languages.

1. Epic and related material (→ Homeric language): a) Narrative epic (Homer etc.), didactic poetry (Hesiod etc.), Homeric hymns, Delphic oracular utterances, inscriptions and literary epigrams, b) Ionic, c) earlier Aeolic, Doric (see below), d) τιμή, βίη, Ἀτρείδεω, θυρέων, μευ, φυλάσσω, μοῦνος, πρός, τόσος, φέρουσι, εἶναι, εἰ, ἄν, ὅτε, οἱ αἱ nominative plural, πᾶσα, ποσί dative plural; e) Aeolic probably Ἀτρείδαο, θυράων, π(ρ)οτί, τόσσος, ἔμμεναι, αἰ, κε, τοί ταί nominative plural, πόδεσσι. Doric was also used in epigrams, e.g. στονοϝεσαν αϝυταν, κλεϝος απθιτον αιϝει.

2. Elegy (could also be included under 1.): a) Callinus from Ephesus, Solon from Athens, Theognis from Megara, b) Ionic, c) see e), d) τιμή, βίη, Μίδεω, κοτε = ποτε, e) Solon Attic ἡμετέρα, ἀδικοῦσι (?), Theognis Doric ἦμεν = εἶναι.

3. Iambic poetry: a) Archilochus, Hipponax, Herodas, b) Ionic, d) ἑτέρη, ὁκοῖος.

4. Monodic lyrics: without unifying literary languages, Sappho and Alcaeus, Aeolic-Lesbian: τίμα = τιμή (with barytone → accent), βία, Κρονίδα genitive singular, ξάνθαν genitive plural feminine, φυλάσσω, μόνος, τόσσος, φέροισι, ἔμμεναι, αἰ, κε, ὄτα = ὅτε (with → psilosis), οἰ αἰ nominative plural, παῖσα = πᾶσα, πόδεσσι; Corinna, Boeotian: τάττω, ποκα = ποτε, τύ = τοί nominative plural οὑμές = ὑμεῖς, κή = καί, πατείρ = πατήρ, βανά = γυνή; Anacreon, Ionic: Θρηικίη, Ἀίδεω, μευ, κου.

5. Choral lyrics: a) Alcman, Pindar, Bacchylides; Songs in Attic drama: Aeschylus, Sophocles, Euripides (Tragedy), Aristophanes (Comedy, parodistic), b) Doric, c) late Aeolic (Lesbian), d) τιμά, βία, Ἀίδα genitive singular, Ἀτρειδᾶν genitive plural; Pindar: τύ = σύ, φέροντι 3rd plural, κε, τόκα, τοί ταί nominative plural, πᾶσα, ποσσί, e) Pindar, Aeolic: φέροισι, Μοῖσα, πόδεσσι (?).

6. Drama in Athens, metre: a) Aeschylus etc. see 5.a), b) Attic, c) in tragedy also Ionic, Doric (partly of uncertain origin), d) τιμή, βία, Ἅιδου, θυρῶν, μου, νεώς 'temple', μόνος; Comedy: φυλάττω, ἄρρην, e) Ionic Tragedy: φυλάσσω, ἄρσην; Doric: Ἀθάνα, ἕκατι, ναός = νεώς.

7. Comedy in Sicily and Italy: a) Epicharmus, Sophron, Rhinthon, b) Doric, d) ἅδιστον, καλέομες, ἐντί = εἰσί, ἦν 3rd plural.

8. Ionic prose: a) Hecataeus, Heraclitus, Democritus, Herodotus, Hippocrates, Aretaeus, Arrian, b) Ionic, c) see e), d) κατήκω (→ Psilosis), τιμή, βίη, νεηνίεω, νεηνιέων, εὔνοος, μευ, φυλάσσω, μοῦνος, πρός, τόσος, φέρουσι, εἶναι, εἰ, ἄν, ὅτε (ὄτε?), οἱ αἱ (οἰ αἰ?), πᾶσα, ποσί, κοτε, e) Herodotus, Attic: διάνοια; Hippocrates, Doric: ποτί.

9. Attic prose: a) Gorgias, Thucydides, Xenophon, orators, etc., b) Attic c) Ionic, d) τιμή, βία, Ἅιδου genitive, θυρῶν, μου, φυλάττω, ἄρρην, μόνος, πρός, τόσος, φέρουσι, εἶναι, εἰ, ἄν, ὅτε, οἱ αἱ, πᾶσα, ποσί. e) Thucydides, Ionic: φυλάσσω, ἄρσην.

10. Doric prose: a) *Dissoi logoi*, Pythagoreans, Archimedes, b) Doric, c) –, d) ἁδονά, ἐκ τῶ βίω, τὼς φίλως, ποτί, ἐσθίεν infinitive, ἦμεν = εἶναι, ἐντί = εἰσί, αἰ, κα = ἄν, e) τέτμακε, κίνασις (unclear).

C. Transmission and criticism

Ancient philologists (→ Aristarchus [4]) were aware of the colourful variety in literary languages and took great care with the texts. That they even recorded peculiar word accents, e.g. in Homer, Sappho and Alcaeus (see above B. 4) and Alcman, indicates analysis of oral transmission as well. It is a matter of contention, however, to what extent they also consciously altered the texts, apart from the usual unintentional transcription errors, including standardization into the later dominant Attic. Hyperdialectisms, for example, also played a part, as in the insertion of Doric Aeolic *ā* for authentic *ē* [2. 36–85] or of Aeolic-Lesbian *ais* for authentic *ās* [3. 24f.]. In critical editions, though, it is necessary to present the complete range of transmitted material and to examine it without prejudice. Contrary to many assumptions, authors did not employ linguistic consistency – in poetry the metre would have made that more difficult – or use so-called 'pure dialect' as a guiding principle. At every point account has to be taken of individual changes, as well as of individual choice from the full range of available linguistic options: φήμα/φάμα/φήμη (see above A. end), φέροντι/φέροισι (see above B. 5), νεώς/ναός (see above B. 6).

→ Greek dialects; → Homeric language; → Indo-European poetic language

1 G. Björck, Das Alpha impurum und die tragische Kunstsprache, 1950 2 B. Forssman, Unt. zur Sprache Pindars, 1966 3 E.-M. Hamm, Gramm. zu Sappho und Alkaios, [2]1958 4 E. Risch, KS, 1981.

R. Hiersche, Grundzüge der griech. Sprachgesch. bis zur klassischen Zeit, 1970; O. Hoffmann, A. Debrunner, A. Scherer, Gesch. der griech. Sprache, [4]1969; M. Meier-Brügger, Griech. Sprachwiss. 1, 1992, 80–86; Schmid/Stählin 1; Schwyzer, Gramm., 100–116; Thumb/Kieckers; Thumb/Scherer. B.F.

Greeting

I. Gestures of greeting II. Verbal Forms of Greeting

I. Gestures of greeting

A. Handshake B. Kiss and Embrace C. Raising One's Right Hand D. Showing Respect towards Elders and People of Senior Rank

A. Handshake

According to Greek and Roman custom, one would shake the right hand of guests, family members, close acquaintances or friends and squeeze it firmly (Hom. Il. 10,542 et passim; Xen. Cyr. 3,2,14; Aristoph. Nub. 81; Plut. Cicero 879; Plut. Antonius 952; Plut. De amicorum multitudine 94b), both as a greeting (according to Plut. Caesar 708 more a form of affability) and to say good-bye. Shaking hands was seen as a sign of friendship and trust (Xen. Cyr. 3,2,14; Liv. 30,12,18); it was saved for special people to whom one felt close and whose unexpected return (from war or a journey) caused delight (Hom. Il. 10,542; Hom. Od. 24,409; Aesch. Ag. 34f.; Ov. Met. 7,495f.). This form of greeting could go as far as leading the person who had just arrived by the hand into the house or to his seat (Hom. Od. 1,119–121). One also shook hands when saying good-bye for a long time (Xen. Cyr. 3,2,14) or when expecting someone to die (Eur. Alc. 193; Plut. Themistocles 127; Plut. Brutus 1008). According to Tac. Hist. 2,49 soldiers even kissed the hand of the dead Emperor Otho: the idea of showing respect and mourning is also involved here. In accordance with the meaning of the handshake, people who seized someone's hand for no apparent reason were considered to be flatterers (Hor. Sat. 1,9,4; Plaut. Aul. 115f.).

B. Kiss and Embrace

A greeting sometimes also included an embrace (ἀσπασμός, *aspasmós*; Lat. *complexus*) and a → kiss (φίλημα, *phílēma*; Lat. *osculum*, Hom. Od. 17,38f.), often on the head and shoulders, or on the hand (Hom. Od. 24,397; → Gestures; → *salutatio*); one also said good-bye by kissing and embracing, especially before death (Lucian. Verae Historiae 1,30 with a particularly imaginative story). Kissing as a form of greeting, a Persian custom (Hdt. 1,134), had advanced through the Greek east and had spread during Hellenism; it had already established itself for the most varied occasions (when visiting, when returning from a journey, etc.) at the beginning of the Roman Imperial Period. Plin. HN 26,2f. attributes a then common facial rash (eczema, a disease he called *mentagra*) to kissing when greeting or departing, and Tac. Ann. 4,57 mentions Tiberius' aversion to kissing – perhaps for this reason; the same Emperor tried in vain to forbid kissing, which was getting out of hand (Suet. Tib. 34,2) and to which one was even exposed when meeting on the street, a fact about which Mart. 2,10; 2,12; 10,22; 11,95; 11,98 et passim held forth polemically.

C. Raising One's Right Hand

Another form of greeting was to raise one's right hand (→ Gestures; cf. the Trier [1] relief depicting a classroom scene), occasionally also to the deity when praying and sacrificing. Sometimes one raised the index finger of the right hand as a sign of greeting (Aristaen. 2,14; Suet. Aug. 80, hence called *digitus salutaris*).

D. Showing Respect towards Elders and People of Senior Rank

It was considered inappropriate to incline one's head in greeting (Hor. Sat. 2,5,91f.; cf. SHA Alex. Sev. 18,1f.), as this was seen as a sign of slavery. Courtesy and respect among Greeks and Romans, however, demanded that younger people rose or made room for older people, and that one rose for people of senior rank (Hom. Il. 1,533f.; Hdt. 2,80; Juv. 13,55). Accordingly, one also rose in the theatre when the Emperor entered (Suet. Aug. 53; 56; → *acclamatio*; → Applause), and even for teachers (Lucian Convivium 7). To this – the realm of respect or flattery – also belongs the uncovering of one's head in the presence of people of senior rank.

II. Verbal Forms of Greeting

The above gestures would be accompanied by verbal greeting formulae, whereby the Greek literally said 'fare well' (χαῖρε, *chaîre*; Amphora Rome, MV [2]; cf. [3]) when greeting and saying good-bye, the Roman correspondingly said *salve* (cf. Lucian pro lapsu 13) or *ave* (or *have*) when greeting (cf. the gladiators' greeting *Ave, Imperator, morituri te salutant*, which was answered with *Avete, vos* Suet. Claud. 21,6) and took leave with 'fare well' (*vale*, also *ave*); *vale* could also be used as a greeting in the evening. All of these originated as blessings. Both Greeks and Romans also added the name or title of the person to be greeted;Romans would also frequently address someone as 'Sir' (*domine*, cf. Suet. Aug. 53; Mart. 5,57). Care for the well-being of the person to be greeted is found already at Hom. Od. 24,402; this is also continued later, so that the greeting was expanded through the question about the well-being or the wish of good health for the person addressed (πῶς ἔχετε; *pôs échete*, 'how are you'; ὑγίαινε; *hygíaine*, 'may you fare well'; similarly εὖ πράττειν; *eû práttein* and καλῶς ἔχε; *kalôs éche*, meaning 'all the best', used also for the sick, Lucian pro lapsu 4; Lucian De saltatione 76; cf. Pseudo-Plato epist. 3,315a-c). According to Lucian pro lapsu (1; 2; 14; cf. 8) *chaíre*, *chaírete* was used at the first greeting, and in the morning. One should also mention the greeting formulae involving the use of *chaíre* that are found on Attic drinking vessels; these are often found with addenda such as 'and drink well' [4] etc. Note also epigrams on gravestones with greeting and counter-greeting by the deceased and the passers-by [5]. The situation in Rome is similar [5; 6]; even the runner Philippides is supposed to have saluted before he conveyed the news of the victory at Marathon (Lucian pro lapsu 3). The Romans have also developed their greeting formulae correspondingly: one expanded – this can e.g. be gathered from comedy – the courteous greeting *salve* with a *di te bene ament* (equalling something like: 'the Gods be with you!': Plaut. Capt. 138); one could ask the question *quid fit, quid agitur?* (something like 'how are you, how is it going?'), which would be answered with *recte* ('very well, thank you' or 'alright': cf. Ter. Ad. 883f.).

Sometimes trained birds would sing the greeting for an approaching person (Mart. 14,73; Pers. section 8; cf. Petron. Sat. 28), sometimes one wrote the greeting on the floor (cf. the pavement in front of the Casa del Fauno [7]).

→ Gestures; → Prayer; → Gestus; → Mourning

1 R. Schindler, Führer durch das Landesmuseum Trier, 1977, fig. 141 2 JHS 30, 1910, pl. 3 J.D. Beazley, The Kleophrades-Painter, 1974, 14, no.2 4 W. Hornbostel, Aus der Glanzzeit Athens, 1986, 50, no. 13 5 G. Pfohl, Griech. Inschr., [2]1980, no. 20,28 6 H. Geist, Röm. Grabinschr., 1969, 25–28, esp. no. 25 7 E. Pernice, Pavimente und figürliche Mosaiken, in: Die hell. Kunst in Pompeji VI, 1938, 90, pl. 42,1.

K. Bogen, Gesten in Begrüßungsszenen auf att. Vasen, 1969; E. Brandt, Gruß und Gebet, 1965; C. Sittl, Die Gebärden der Griechen und Römer, 1890; A.B. Spiess, Der Kriegerabschied auf att. Vasen der archa. Zeit, 1992; D. Stutzinger, Der Adventus des Kaisers und der Einzug Christi in Jerusalem, in: H. Beck, C. Bol(ed.), Spätant. und frühes Christentum, Ausstellung Frankfurt a. M. 1983–1984, 1983, 284–307; P. Veyne, Les saluts aux dieux, in: RA, 1985, 47–61.

R.H.

Gregentius of Safar see → Leges Homeritarum

Gregorius [1] (Γρηγόριος; *Grēgórios*)

[1] Thaumaturgus G. was born between AD 210 and 213, as the son of a wealthy pagan family in Neocaesarea/ Pontus (modern Niksar), probably under the name of Theodorus. In 232/3 (or 239), after a thorough elementary education G. actually wanted to study law in → Berytus/Beirut but before this in → Caesarea [2] (Palestine) got to know → Origen who taught there and then studied under his supervision the 'Christian sciences' (initially dialectics, physiology, ethics, philosophy, then also exegesis and theology). After five years he returned to his native city, is said to have worked there as a lawyer and at an unknown time became bishop in his home town. Here his work that partly resembled the administration of a justice of the peace made the very small community grow enormously; the rich property assets of the family were probably also of some importance in this development.

G. was deeply impressed by Origen for whom he held a panegyric of gratitude (probably in 238/9 for the departure from Caesarea) [1. 1763]. In addition an *Epistula canonica* [1. 1765] and a metaphrase for the book Kohelet [1. 1766] have been passed down to us. The authenticity of other texts, especially of his profession of the faith [1. 1764] and his letter to Theopompus

[1. 1767] handed down to us in Syrian is rather improbable ([7]; different in [8; 10]); besides that there are all kinds of texts that are certainly pseudepigraphical [1. 1772–1794]. → Gregorius [2] of Nyssa wrote a *vita* [2. 3184; 3. 715/715b] containing not just legendary tradition (from which his nickname Θαυματουργός, 'Miracle-worker' among others stems) but also important historical information.

1 CPG 1 2 CPG 2 3 Bibliotheca Hagiographica Graeca 4 P. Guyot, R. Klein, Gregor der Wundertäter, Oratio prosphonetica ac panegyrica in Origenem/Dankrede an Origenes (Fontes Christiani 24), 1996 5 K. M. Fouskas, Γρηγορίου Θαυματουργοῦ ἡ κανονικὴ ἐπιστολή, 1978 6 J. Jarik, Gregory Thaumaturgos' Paraphrase of Ecclesiastes (Society of Biblical Literature. Septuaginta and Cognate Studies 29), 1990 7 L. Abramowski, Formula and Context: Studies in Early Christian Thought, 1992, no. VII/VIII 8 H. Crouzel, s.v. Gregor I (Gregor der Wundertäter), RAC 12, 779–793 9 V. Ryssel, Gregorius Thaumaturgus. Sein Leben und seine Schriften, 1880 10 M. Simonetti, Una nuova ipotesi su Gregorio il Taumaturgo, in: Recherches de science religieuse 24, 1988, 17–41 11 M. Slusser, s.v. Gregor der Wundertäter, TRE 14, 188–191. C.M.

[2] G. of Nyssa

A. Biography B. Works C. Theology

A. Biography

G., the younger brother of → Basil [1] the Great, comes from the urban upper class of Cappadocia, was born after AD 335 and was probably named after → Gregorius [1] Thaumaturgus. His older brother and his eldest sister Macrina had a deep influence on him. Probably he was married until 381(De virginitate 3) and pursued a secular career (as a rhetorician?). After 372 he became bishop of Nyssa (location of the town not yet pinpointed without ambiguity) in Basil's metropolitan system of Cappadocia and in this office his ideas initially did not always seem to match those of his brother (Basil. Epist. 58, 100 and 215). In 376 he was dismissed by the Homoean opposition in Nyssa (Greg. Naz. Epist. 72) and was only able to return in 378 after the death of the emperor → Valens. Only after the death of his brother he became more and more an influential church politician, a celebrated orator and a revered theologian and attempted successfully to make Basil's doctrines and teachings obligatory in the Church. For a short time G. hold office as metropolitan of Sebaste/ Armenia (modern Sivas); since the Council of → Constantinople in 381 he was one of the bishops (Cod. Theod. 16,1,3) who defined the empire-wide obligatory standard of the neo-Nicene orthodoxy. In 385/6 he held the funeral speeches for the wife of the emperor → Theodosius, → Flacilla, and their daughter Pulcheria ([1. 3182; 2. 1548; 4. 475–490] or [1. 3181; 4. 461–472]). G. died soon after 394.

B. Works

G. wrote exegetic treatises and homilies (e.g. a commentary on the Song of Songs: [1. 3158; 5]), also writings on the controversies concerning trinitarian theology and Christology (e.g. a detailed refutation of the Neo-Arian → Eunomius: [1. 3135; 6]), hagiographic writings (among these a *vita* of his sister: [1. 3166; 2. 1012; 7]) as well as sermons, speeches (e.g. *De deitate adversus Euagrium* on the synod of 381: [1. 3179; 8. 331–341]) and letters [1. 3167; 9]. The *Oratio Catechetica* [1. 3150; 10] is a summary of the fundamental teachings of the Christian faith for catechetic purposes that was rather unusual for its time because it was not motivated by polemical theology. The critical edition of his works [3] was set up by W. Jaeger and comprises 14 volumes to date.

C. Theology

G. attempted from 372 at the latest to realize in his life the ideal of the 'philosophical life' as Christian asceticism and to propagate it through individual works. The goal was of course not *hénōsis* (ἕνωσις, 'Union'), but only *homoíōsis theôi* (ὁμοίωσις θεῷ, 'becoming similar to God'). G. is considered to be one of the originators of a 'mystical theology': truths of the faith understandable with rationality lead *mystikôs* (μυστικῶς) above and beyond themselves to certain additional theological insights or ascetic ideas [12. 877–884]; further one has to separate from this the question of whether G. developed his theology on the basis of 'mystical experiences' [17. 63–73]. He attempted to disprove the logical and (language-) philosophical basis of neo-Arian trinitarian theology; he further developed the philosophical concept of God with the emphasis on the eternity and infinity of God [18. passim]. Ascetic and theological ideas are directly connected because the endless *prokopḗ* (προκοπή, 'progress') of man as a self-responsible perfection of ethical behaviour and *gnôsis theoû* (γνῶσις θεοῦ) corresponds with the unlimited nature of God. Even if G. adopted much from → Origenes (e.g. the allegorical → exegesis of the Bible as well as the teaching of universal reconciliation), as well as adopting from → Plato and → Plotinus, his theology will be understood, depending on the point of view, as the end point or perfection of Christian metaphysics based on Plato. The effect of his literature remained limited to the East.

Editions: 1 CPG 2 2 F. Halkin (ed.), Bibliotheca Hagiographia Graeca, ³1957 3 W. Jaeger, Gregorii Nysseni Opera (= GNO), 1921ff. 4 A. Spira (ed.), GNO 9, 1967 5 H. Langerbeck (ed.), GNO 6, 1961 6 W. Jaeger (ed.), GNO 1/2, ²1960 7 P. Maraval (ed.), SChr 178, 1971 8 E. Gebhardt (ed.), GNO 9, 1967 9 G. Pasquali (ed.), GNO 8/2, ²1959 10 E. Mühlenberg (ed.), GNO 3/2, 1996.
Bibliography: 11 M. Altenburger, F. Mann, Bibliographie zu Gregor von Nyssa. Editionen – Übersetzungen – Literatur, 1988 12 H. Dörrie, s.v. Gregor III (Gregor von Nyssa), RAC 12, 863–895 13 H. R. Drobner, Bibelindex zu den Werken Gregors von Nyssa, 1988

14 C. Fabricius, D. Ridings, A Concordance to Gregory of Nyssa, 1989 15 Ch. Klock, Untersuchungen zu Stil und Rhythmus bei Gregor von Nyssa (Beitr. zur klass. Philol. 173), 1987 16 G. May, Gregor von Nyssa in der Kirchenpol. seiner Zeit, in: Jahrbuch der Österr. byz. Ges. 15, 1966, 105–132 17 E. Mühlenberg, Die Sprache der rel. Erfahrung bei Gregor von Nyssa, in: W. Haug, D. Mieth (ed.), Rel. Erfahrung, 1992, 63–73 18 E. Mühlenberg, Die Unendlichkeit Gottes bei Gregor von Nyssa. Gregors Kritik am Gottesbegriff der klass. Metaphysik, 1966. C.M.

[3] G. of Nazianzus. Born in Arianzus in AD 329/30 on an estate of his wealthy parents near → Nazianzus in → Cappadocia. He was brought up as a Christian at the instigation of his mother. His father by the same name was bishop of Nazianzus. G. attended schools in → Caesarea/Cappadocia in → Palestine, in → Alexandria [1] and the Academy in Athens (→ Academy). There he got to know → Basilius [1] the Great with whom he formed a close friendship. Together they devoted themselves to the study of antiquity. His inclination towards rhetoric became decisive for his work. He wrote his ceremonial speeches and encomia in the richly adorned Asian style (→ Asianism).

Theologically G. took a stance against the Arians (→ Arianism). For him the teaching about God, the doctrine of the Trinity, is essential to the Christian faith: in the Trinity we pray to the divine and the Trinity is brought together as a unity (Or. 6,22). Contrary to the → Pneumatomachians he adheres to the divinity of the Holy Spirit. G. takes up elements of cosmology (→ Origenes): religion relates to what is intelligible in the world and to the spirit.

After his studies he dedicated himself to asceticism. On the estate of Basil on the → Iris both of them engrossed themselves in the Origenist writings (editing of the *Philokalía*). He got baptized and ordained by his father as a priest. After a short time however he left his parish. (Apology for his 'flight': Or. 1–3; Carm. 1,1,11; De vita sua 354).

He energetically took a stance against the emperor Julian who was making it more and more difficult for the Christians to teach classical antiquity. Persuaded by Basil, he became bishop of Stasima. However, after his ordination G. fled again. After the death of the emperor → Valens G. successfully took on the leadership of the Nicene community in Constantinople and was involved in the preparation of the 2nd Oecumenical Synod in 381. For a short time he was patriarch of Constantinople. Until his death (389/90) he dedicated his life to the art of poetry and asceticism. He used metrics to control his own inclination towards excessiveness, as well as for catechetic and therapeutic reasons in order to alleviate to some extent the burden of ageing (Carm. 2,1,33–57). The art of writing he uses in his letters still follows the pagan tradition. His language contains Atticisms as well as poetic and contemporary vocabulary. The eastern Church honours him as 'the Theologian', alongside John the Evangelist and Symeon the New Theologian.

Editions: CPG, 140–178.

Bibliography: H. Althaus, Die Heilslehre des hl. G., 1972; S. Bergmann, Geist, der Natur befreit: die trinitarische Kosmologie Gregors von Nazianz im Horizont einer ökologischen Theologie der Befreiung, 1995; J. Mossay (ed.), II. Symposium Nazianzenum. Louvain-la-Neuve, 25–28 août 1981, 1983. K.SA.

[4] G. of Corinth Possibly a teacher (of grammar and rhetoric) at the school of the patriarch of Constantinople [3. 167], definitely bishop of Corinth; G. is also known by the name Georgius (his baptismal name, G. probably his religious name?) and by his patronym Pardus. Initially scholars dated him around AD 1200 [11. 1849], then at the end of the 11th cent. or the 1st half of the 12th cent. [8. 32–33; 4. 13], mainly based on the fact that his episcopate can be dated to the period after 1092 and before 1156, perhaps the 2nd quarter of the 12th cent. [9. 290]. Recently however he has been placed in the 1st half of the 10th cent. [1. 248], although dating him in the 11th/12th cents. seems to be more likely [13].

G. is the author of a work that is still not very well known, at present not satisfactorily edited, and, considering that some of his works were unknown until recent times [1], is problematical. To date we know of his grammatical and rhetorical treatises that are placed in the context of his teaching activities; these are: a treatise on dialects [12. 1–624; 2], a commentary on the writing *Perì methódou deinótētos* by Hermogenes [14. vol. 7/2. 1090–1352], a treatise on syntax [4. 163–229] and a treatise on tropes [14. vol. 8. 761–778] of which the authenticity still has to be approved [4. 15]; the treatise on the dialect of Sappho appears not to be authentic [4. 15]. In addition G. wrote an exegesis on the liturgical canons that scholars attribute to Cosmas of Jerusalem and → John of Damascus [10. 1–85] – a work that because of its didactic character does not necessarily have to be connected with his episcopate – and religious poetry [7].

The reception of the grammatical, rhetorical and exegetic works in Byzantium appears to have suffered from the personal rivalries between G. and → Theodorus Prodromos [10. LV–LVI], whilst Eusthathius of Thessaloniki seems to have had a high regard for them [10. LVI–LVIII].

G. was regarded as a good systematician of language [2] as well as a Christian humanist [6. 85] and also as an unoriginal compiler who took his material from various sources without necessarily having had direct contact with the works themselves. Although a more recent investigation has already been able to prove the opposite in at least one case [5], we have to wait for the edition of his works and a more thorough investigation before we can form a fair judgment on him [15].

1 V. Becares, Ein unbekanntes Werk des Gregorios von Korinth und seine Lebenszeit, in: ByzZ 81, 1988, 247f. 2 G.C. Bolognesi, Sul PERI DIALEKTON di Gregorio di Corintho, in: Aevum 27, 1953, 97–120 3 R.B. Bro-

WNING, The Patriarchal School of Constantinople in the twelfth Century, in: Byzantion 32, 1962, 167–202 4 D. DONNET, Le traité PERI SYNTAXEOS LOGOU de Grégoire de Corinthe, 1967 5 J. GLUKER, Thukydides I 29, 3, Gregory of Corinth and the Ars interpretandi, in: Mnemosyne 4/23, 1970, 127–161 6 HUNGER, Literatur 1 7 H. HUNGER, G. von Korinth, Epigramme auf die Feste des Dodekaorton, in: Analecta Bollandiana 100, 1982, 637–651 8 A. KOMINIS, Gregorio Pardos Metropolita di Corinto e la sua opera, 1960 9 V. LAURENT, review of A. KOMINIS, in: REByz 21, 1963, 290f. 10 F. MONTANA, Gregorio di Corinto, Esegesi al canone giambico per la Pentecoste attribuito a Giovanni Damasceno, 1995 11 B.A. MUELLER, G. von Korinth, RE 7, 1848–1852 12 G.H. SCHAEFER, Gregorius Corinthius et alii De dialectis linguae graecae, 1811 13 H. VAN DER VALK, On the lexicographer Gregorius Corinthus, in: Mnemosyne 39, 1986, 399 14 WALZ 15 N.G. WILSON, Scholars of Byzantium, 1983. A.TO.

Gregorius [II]

[1] Lawyer, *magister libellorum* ('master of petitions', head of the office that dealt with written petitions from private persons to the emperor and drafted replies to them) under Diocletian [1]. Published the *Codex Gregorianus* (→ Codex II) presumably in AD 291: a semi-official collection of imperial constitutions meant for judicial practice, mainly rescripts, from the period from Hadrian to Diocletian. The collection from which excerpts were frequently taken in the pre-Justinianic period (→ *Fragmenta Vaticana*; *Collatio legum Mosaicarum et Romanarum*; *Consultatio*) formed the basis for the *Codex Justinianus* (*Haec* pr.; *Summa* § 1) [2].

1 PLRE I, 403 2 D. LIEBS, Recht und Rechtslit., in: HLL 5, 60ff. T.G.

[2] **G. of Elvira (Illiberis)** Bishop of Baetica, who died at an advanced age after 392. Admirer but not an adherent of Lucifer of Caligari. On the basis of Jer. Vir. ill. 105, homilies with allegorical scriptural exegeses (CPL 546–550) and a defence of the Nicene creed, written after the Synod of Rimini (359) are attributed to him (CPL 551).

H. KOCH, Zu G.' v. E. Schrifttum und Quellen, in: ZKG 51, 1932, 238–272; J. DOIGNON, in: HLL, § 579. K.U.

[3] **G. I. the Great** 540–604, pope from 590. Came from wealthy, senatorial aristocracy (Felix III and Agapetus I come from the same family), in 572/3 *praefectus urbi*, in 575 retreat to a monastery which he himself had founded, 579–585 apocrisarius (i.e. nuntius) of Pelagius II in Constantinople. As pope G. developed his political, administrative and writing activities. Against the will of East Rome he made peace in 592/3 with the → Langobardi. In 596 he delegated monks (Augustinus) to take the gospel to the Anglo-Saxons. He rearranged the church properties (*patrimonium Petri*) stretching to Sicily, Dalmatia, and North Africa. The basis of his theological works is the Bible and its meaning is understood through allegorical and moral interpretation (dual meaning of Scripture). His claim to hold full leadership authority over the entire Church is manifested clearly (Epist. 3,57; 5,20; 13,37). Since Boniface VIII (1295) he is considered, together with Jerome, Ambrosius and Augustine, to be one of the four great doctors of the Latin Church.

PL 75–79; MG epist. I–II (854 erh. Letters); LThK[3] 4, 1010ff.; J. RICHARDS, G. d.Gr., sein Leben – seine Zeit, 1983; R. GODDING, Bibliografia di G. Magno (1890–1989), 1990. RO.F.

[4] **G. of Tours** (30 November AD 538/9–17 November AD 594). Comes from a Gallo-Roman family from the senatorial upper class. He appears to have changed his original name of Georgius Florentius to G. with regard to his great-grandfather Gregorius, bishop of Langres. From the age of 8 he got a certain education in literature, but he admitted constantly that there were gaps in it in comparison with the language norm of Late Antique Latinity. He played an important part in Merovingian society and was made bishop of Tours in 573. His literary activity falls within the period of his episcopate and is documented in a list of his works at the end of the *Historia Francorum* (10,31). It is important to differentiate between his theological and hagiographical works and his historiography. The first group encompasses the commentaries on the Psalms and a piece of writing which G. called *De cursibus ecclesiasticis*, and the second encompasses the *Libri miraculorum* (I–VII), the *Vitae patrum* (VIII), *In gloria martyrum* (I), *De virtutibus s. Iuliani martyris* (II), *De virtutibus s. Martini* (III–VI). In the *vita* of St. Martin G. continues → Sulpicius Severus and → Paulinus of Périgueux with a presentation of the miracles recorded after the death of Martin. There is also a *Passio septem dormientium*. The main work is the *Historia Francorum*, a popular history with a strong Gallic focus, although he chooses not to write the history of a sole people, as → Cassiodorus and → Iordanes had done. G. primarily writes a Christian history in which contemporary history is strongly accentuated but always remains tied to the history of salvation with the institution of the Church in its centre [1]. Therefore, bk. 1 *ab orbe condito* covers the period to the death of St. Martin (397), and bks. 2–9 then go up to 594. These books are the most important source for the history of the Merovingian period and are of high quality.

→ Historiography [V], Christian-Lat.

1 M. HEINZELMANN, G.v.T. (538–594), 1994. U.E.

Gresham's law Modern technical term for the inflation-driving phenomenon in which bad money displaces good money that is then exported, melted down or hoarded. Not until the 19th cent. was it named after Thomas GRESHAM (1519–1579), the founder of the London Stock Exchange and royal financial agent.

The main source of knowledge of the circulation of money and the disappearance of good coins in antiquity are the treasure finds. As an example (with a weakening of Gresham's law [GL] due to the higher valuation of minted silver), the better of the pre-Neronian *denarii* disappeared from circulation up to the Flavians and the heavily worn pieces up to Trajan after the reduction in weight of the → *denarius* under Nero (→ Coinage reforms), whilst the lower-valued legion *denarius* of Mark Antony was circulated until the beginning of the 3rd cent. The overvaluation of minted silver also delayed the effect of GL for the post-Neronian *denarius* despite the continuing decline, as it was only worth melting the coins down once there was a noticeable change to the worse. Sometimes emissions were meant to entice the old money back into circulation. Examples are the restored Republican *denarius* of Trajan and the large bronze coins from the middle of the 4th cent. (→ Centenionalis; → Maiorina).

S. BOLIN, Der röm. Denar und Greshams Gesetz, in: Congrès International de Numismatique, Rapports, Paris 1953, 577–588; Id., State and Currency in the Roman Empire to 300 A.D., 1958; Les Dévaluations à Rome, Rom 1978; G. HENNEQUIN, Bonne ou mauvaise monnaie?, in: L'information historique 39/5, 203–212; S.P. NOE, Hoard-Evidence and its Importance, in: Hesperia Suppl. 8, 1949, 235–242; SCHRÖTTER, 236. DI.K.

Greuthungi Gothic people of the 4th cent. AD, also called *Grauthingi* (S HA Probus 18,2), *Greothingi* (Hydatius, Chronica, sub anno 385; Chron. min. 2,15), *Greothyngi* (Chron. min. 1,244) or *Gruthungi* (Claud. in Eutropium 2, 153; 196; 399; 576; Claud. Panegyricus de IV consulatu Honorii 623ff.) or Γρουθίγγοι (Suda s.v. Σκήψας) and often considered to be Scythians. Also named *Ostrogothi* or *Austrogoti* (S HA Clod. 6,2) with whom they occur mixed, for instance by Claudianus (Pan. Lat. de IV consulatu Honorii 624–636). Under their king Ermanaric from the *stirps regia* of the → Amali, they settled, according to Amm. Marc. 31,3,1, in modern Moldavia and in the Ukraine east of the Carpathian Arc up to the Don. When their kingdom fell apart under the attack of the Huns, some of the G. under Alatheus and Saphrac fled across the Danube in 376 and after violent battles were stationed in Pannonia in 380 [1]. The remainder came under Hunnic rule. Stragglers under Odotheus were defeated in 386 and settled in Phrygia. Cf. also Zos. 4,25,1; 38f.

1 H. WOLFRAM, Die Goten, [3]1990, 95–98, 125–140.

P. HEATHER, The Goths, 1996, 52–58, 97–104; L. SCHMIDT, Die Ostgermanen, [2]1941, 240–243, 249–265. A.SCH.

Griffin Composite creature with the head of a bird of prey and the body of a lion, usually winged, presumed to have been conceived of in the early → Elam period and to have reached predynastic Egypt, where it developed independently. In the 1st quarter of the 2nd millennium the ancient Syrian G. (characterized by a curl on the nape of its neck), which emerged under Egyptian influence, spread to Anatolia and the Aegean; established in Crete since the MM II/III era, it was adapted to the Minoan style. Neo-Assyrian and neo-Babylonian depictions more strongly emphasize the avian element with a feathered body and the tail and hind legs of a bird. The forms which arose in late Hittite art such as erect ears, side curl and open beak served as models for the G. in the orientalizing art of Greece. An important intermediary role is also played by the frequent depiction of the G. in Phoenician art, e.g. on ivory reliefs (Nimrud), on the so-called Cypro-Phoenician bronze bowls exported as far as Etruria, and in glyptics.

The G. is usually depicted as either hunter or hunted. The anthropomorphous figure with a griffin's head which developed in parallel in the Orient was associated with the solar disk in the second millennium.

W. BARTA, Der G. als bildhafter Ausdruck einer altägypt. Religionsvorstellung, in: Jaarbericht Ex oriente lux 23, 1973/4, 335–357; A. M. BISI, Il Grifone, Studi Semitici 13, 1965; Id., s.v. Griffon, DCPP, 196; I. FLAGGE, Untersuchungen zur Bed. des Greifen, 1975; E. EGGEBRECHT, s.v. Greif, LÄ 2, 895f. U.SE. and H.-G.N.

Grillius Latin grammarian and rhetor, probably from the 5th cent. AD. Extant by him is part of a commentary on Cicero's *De inventione* which is preceded by an *argumentum artis rhetoricae*, a synopsis of the *Rhetorica ad Herennium*. Priscian (Inst. gramm. 2,35,27; 36,1f.) mentions (probably our) G. as the author of a (nonextant) work *Ad Vergilium de accentibus*, which must be considered a grammar dedicated to a certain Virgilius, rather than a study of Virgilian verses. Included in numerous medieval catalogues, G. was used frequently by, among others, Anselm of Besate, Thierry of Chartres (whose commentary on Cic. Inv. may be directly dependent on it; both Thierry and G. were in turn used in the *Rhetorica* of Brunetto Latini [2. 41–48]), an anonymous commentator on *De inv.* in MS. Oxford, Bodleiana, Canon. Class. Lat. 201 (12th cent.) [1. 8, 30] as well as Dionysius of Burgos in the 14th cent. G. is also mentioned by Benzo of Alba.

1 M. DICKEY, Some Commentaries on the De inventione and Ad Herennium of the 11th and Early 12th Centuries, in: Mediaeval and Renaissance Studies 6, 1968, 1–41 2 G. BALDASSARRI, Ancora sulle fonti della Rettorica, in: Studi e problemi di critica testuale 19, 1979, 41–69.

EDITIONS: J. MARTIN, G., 1927, 1–94; P. COURCELLE, Pages inédites de G. sur le De inventione, in: RPh 81, 1955, 34–38.
BIBLIOGRAPHY: K. MÜNSCHER, s.v. G., RE 7, 1876–1879; SCHANZ/HOSIUS, 4,2,263f. P.G.

Grinario (modern Köngen). Fort (2.4 ha) on the Augsburg-Mainz road probably founded around AD 90/95. In about 160 the unit was moved to Lorch but the old camp probably still served as a base for supplies. The *vicus G.* (CIL XIII 11726f.; Tab. Peut. 4,1) that was *c.* 20 ha. in size flourished to around the middle of the 3rd cent. and belonged to the *civitas Sumelocennensis* (modern Rottenburg; CIL XIII 6384; 11727).

C. Unz, G., 1982; M. Luik, F. Reutti, Der Römerpark in Köngen, 1988; D. Planck, Neues zum röm. Vicus G.-Köngen, in: Arch. Ausgrabungen in Baden-Württemberg 1993, 158–162; M. Luik, Köngen G. 1, 1996. K.DI.

Groma (Greek γνώμων; *gnṓmōn*). Name of the Roman → surveyors' device for determining straight lines and right angles when surveying a terrain. It consists of a pole about the height of a man (*ferramentum*) and a rotatable cross of four horizontal rods (*stella*) attached to it at right angles. On the four ends were attached plumb-lines (*perpendicula*) almost down to the ground.

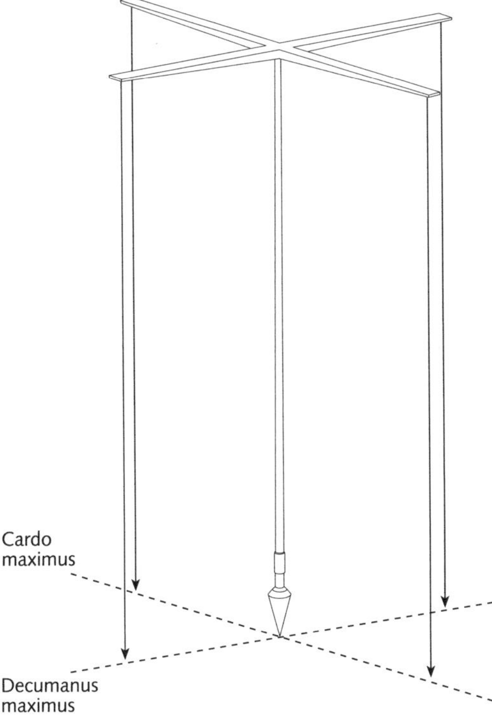

Groma (schematic depiction).

The plumb attached to the centre point of the rotary cross (*umbilicus soli*) was aligned above the measurement point by a slight slanting of the *ferramentum* [3]. The application is known through Heron of Alexandria, the construction and appearance through a specimen found in Pompeii [1. 202] and through depictions on the tombstones of the *mensores* L. Aebutius Faustus [1. 201] and Popidius Nicostratus [1. 200]. It was initially set up in the centre of the terrain to be surveyed to determine → *cardo* and → *decumanus*, then on these axes at regular intervals boundary stones were set through which the parallel lines were drawn (→ Limitation).

1 K. Brodersen, Terra cognita (Spudasmata 59), 1995 2 M. della Corte, G., in: Monumenti Antichi 28, 1922, 5–100 3 T. Schiøler, The Pompeji-Groma in new light, in: Analecta Romana 22, 1994, 45–60.
O. Behrends, L. Capogrossi Colognesi (ed.), Die röm. Feldmeßkunst, 1992; O. Dilke, Archaeological and epigraphic evidence of Roman land survey, in: ANRW 2,1, 564–592; U. Heimberg, Röm. Landvermessung, 1977; A. Schulten, s.v. G., RE 7, 1881–1886. H.-J.S.

Großromstedt (district of Apolda/Thüringen). Germanic burial site of the pre-Roman Iron Age that was excavated between 1907 and 1913. It comprises over 600 graves containing cremation burials from the 2nd half of the last pre-Christian cent. and the time of Christ as well as some graves from the 2nd/3rd cents. AD. The graves contain typical ceramics (→ Situla, wheelmade pottery), weapons (→ Sword, → Shield and lance) as well as → fibulae that are taken to be stereotypes for the subdivision of this period. The burial area of G. also shows the influences of Celtic and Roman culture (imported bronze vessels etc.) but is considered to be typical for the Germanic 'G.-culture' of the Elbe that plays an important role in Germania around the time of Christ.

→ Germanic archaeology

K. Peschel, G., in: J. Herrmann (ed.), Arch. in der Deutschen Demokratischen Republik 2, 1989, 507–511; S. Rieckhoff, Süddeutschland im Spannungsfeld von Kelten, Germanen und Römern, 1995, esp. 151–168, 192–197. V.P.

Grotta Regina A cult cave on the north-eastern slope of Monte Gallo near Palermo (*c.* 180 m above sea-level) used since prehistoric times. According to Punic inscriptions and paintings (5th–1st cents. BC, among these Tinnit symbols) on the walls, underworld and fertility gods were worshipped here.

→ Tinnit

G. Coacci Polselli, M.G. Guzzo Amadasi, V. Tusa, Grotta Regina – II, 1979. H.-G.N.

Grotto The word grotto is borrowed from Greek *kryptós* ('concealed, hidden'; Italian *grotta*, French *grotte*). Grotto is occasionally used as a synonym for cave but it mostly describes in particular caves with natural or artificially irrigation. In religious history grottos appear in the following contexts:

1. Grotto sanctuaries of the prehistoric period: here it is worth mentioning the cult sites of north-western European peoples that were situated in grottos and often painted with religious and mythological motifs of the hunt [1; 2], as well as the grotto sanctuaries of the Minoan palace culture on Crete. Here especially the grotto of Psychro has become known because of the rich votive finds [3. 55f.; 4. 54ff.].

2. Grotto cults in conjunction with the → Nymphs and the reception within Greece of the Arcadian god → Pan: characteristic of the cult sites is their position outside urban civilization that was partly consciously chosen because of the 'wild' and 'anti-civilized' character of the deities [5. 75ff.], unless these were older (spring) sanc-

tuaries that were situated in the 'wilderness' anyway [6.509ff.]. Between the 5th and 3rd cents. BC there is evidence, starting from Athens, of a series of privately used grotto sanctuaries in Attica that were frequented exclusively by (free) women (cf. Men. Dys. 260ff.; 407–418) [5. 233ff.].

3. Grotto as an 'imaginary place' in poetry and architecture: to this belongs, for example, the so-called Grotta di Tiberio near Terracina, an artificially laid out grotto that served as mythological scenery for banquets within the scope of villa architecture (a total of four marble groups, of which three depicted adventures of Odysseus) [7. 32f.] or the so-called Blue Grotto on Capri, probably a sea nymphaeum belonging to a Roman villa that is possibly also meant in Sil. 7,419ff. [8. 137f.]. In Renaissance and Baroque gardens (e.g. garden of the Villa d'Este, Tivoli) as well as in Romanticism grottos fulfilled decorative purposes following this ancient tradition.

→ Cave sanctuaries

1 B. Delluc, G. Delluc, La place des représentations animales dans le dispositif parietal des grottes ornées magdaléniennes du Haut Périgord. Grottes de Villars, La Croix, Teyat, Fronsac et La Font Bargeix, Dordogne, in: P. Meniel (ed.), Animal et pratiques religieuses, 1989, 27–36 2 A. Vignola, L'uomo e gli animali preistorici nelle caverne, grotte e cave del Salento, in: Studi Salentini 68, 1991, 176–184 3 Burkert 4 W. Pötscher, Aspekte und Probleme der minoischen Rel., 1990 5 Ph. Borgeaud, Recherches sur le dieu Pan, 1979 6 R. Bloch, s.v. Nymphen, Roscher 3.1, 500–567 7 N. Himmelmann, Ansichten von Sperlonga, in: Gymnasium 103, 1996, 32–41 8 E. Stärk, Liebhabereien des Silius Italicus: Die G. des Proteus auf Capri, in: A&A; 39, 1996, 132–143. C.F.

Group R A group of Attic lekythoi with white-grounded polychromatic dull-coloured painting from the time between 420 and 410 BC. According to the shape of the vessel, the ornamental decoration, painting technique and colours (red contour lines, blackish grey ornament drawing), they come from the same workshop as the lekythoi of the Reed Painter but are bigger than those and of significantly higher quality in the drawing of the figures. Beazley therefore separated them from the lekythoi of the Reed Painter and combined them under the auxiliary name Group R = Group of the R(eed painter). Classification in the group does not mean that all these lekythoi have to originate from the same painter; only the two most famous ones (Athens, NM, inventory no. 1816/1817) are certainly the work of one hand.

Characteristics of the images of the group are: three-figure compositions (mostly funeral scenes), an extremely careful and subtle drawing of outlines, a graphic volume of the figures achieved by movement in contour and body rotation and an expression of melancholy and worried seriousness that is often noticeable over the faces, mainly depicted in a three-quarter view, and also defines their body posture. Scholars linked the images of Group R with the painter → Parrhasius and interpreted them as reflections of his art.

Beazley, ARV², 1383–1384, no. 1–22; 1692; Beazley, Addenda², 371–372; D.C. Kurtz, Athenian White Lekythoi-Patterns and Painters, 1975, 58–68, pl. 49–50; A. Rumpf, Parrhasios, in: AJA 55, 1951, 1–12, fig. 1.3–4.; I. Wehgartner, Att. wgr. Keramik, 1983, 29. J.d.B.

Grove (ἄλσος/*álsos*, Latin *lucus*). In Greece and Italy a sacred area characterized by its stand of trees (cf. Str. 9,2,33); although *lucus* originally meant 'glade'. A grove had at least one altar, often also votive offerings; often a grove could also be part of a larger sacred area with a temple: as in the Apollo sanctuary of → Didyma (Str. 14,1,5), the Samian Heraeum (LSCG, Suppl. 18) or in the Roman grove of the → Dea Dia. The grove was sacred because it was considered to be the place where a deity resided; Roman authors like Verg. Aen. 8,352 or Sen. Ep. 41,3 express this concisely and from the form in which the grove appeared draw the conclusion of an (unknown) deity. In Rome grammarians defined differences that have no equivalents in the Greek sources [1. 14–20]: *lucus* is contrasted with *nemus* (a place with a cultivated plantation of trees) and with *silva* (the untended forest) as sacred (Serv. Auct. 1,310). The grove as a place of 'sacralized nature' was occasionally an environment where people could experience an especially intense encounter with the divine; oracle sanctuaries therefore often had groves (Dodona: Soph. Trach. 171; for Didyma, Clarus and Gryneion [1. 23–29]; Myra in Lycia: Ath. 8,8,333d-e), likewise healing sanctuaries (Cos: LSCG 150 and [2] ED 181). The grove was in possession of the deity; therefore it could be forbidden to let animals graze in it, particularly however to cut timber in it (for instance Korope: LSCG 84; Cos: LSCG 150; Rom: CIL I 366); violation brought on divine punishment [3. no. 7]. In Rome any interference with the trees necessitated an expiatory sacrifice (Cato Agr. 139; Dea Dia [4. 95–172]). However, neat categorization is not possible, neither in Greece nor in Rome. Groves could be situated outside of towns (in a *nemus* of the grove of → Diana Nemorensis of Aricia: Cato Orig. 58; in a *silva* for instance Liv. 24,3,4), as well as in a town (grove around the Hephaisteion of Athens [5], in Rome, e.g. groves of → Bellona, → Mefitis, → Strenae and → Vesta). Groves were not tied to particular deities – although Apollo and Artemis/Diana appear often – and were not planted with particular trees (often the laurel is mentioned; list in [1. 41]). In the wake of Romanticism the grove was linked repeatedly with → tree cult (not least by Frazer). This is however not tenable: the trees of a grove were holy and inviolable in themselves because they were in the possession of a deity [1. 15–18, 171–180].

→ Sanctuary

1 de Cazanove, J. Scheid (ed.), Les bois sacrés, 1993 2 M. Segre, Iscrizioni di Cos (ed. by D. Pepas-Delmousou, M.A. Rizza), 1994 3 G. Petzl, Die Beichtinschr. Westkleinasiens, 1994 4 J. Scheid, Romulus et ses frères. Le collège des frères arvales, modèle du culte public dans la Rome des empereurs, 1990 5 J.M. Camp, The Athenian Agora,1986, 87.

D.E. BIRGE, Sacred groves in the ancient Greek world, thesis Berkeley 1982; B. JORDAN, J. PERLIN, On the protection of sacred groves, in: Studies presented to St. Dow, 1984, 153–159; D. BIRGE, Sacred groves and the nature of Apollo, in: J. SOLOMON (ed.), Apollo. Origins and Influences, 1994, 9–18. F.G.

Grudii One of the five tribes in Gallia Belgica dependent on the → Nervii (the others being the → Ceutrones [1], → Levaci, → Pleumoxii and → Geidumni: Caes. B Gall. 5,39,1). Their area of settlement lay in what is now Flanders.

TIR M 31 Paris, 1975, 133; H. BOONE, Ceutrones et Nervii, in: Mémoires de la Societé d'Emulation de Cambrai 73, 1926, 105–206. E.O.

Grumentum Town in Lucania (→ Lucani) where the Sora (modern Sciaura) flows into the Aciris (modern Agri) (cf. Str. 6,1,3; Ptol. 3,1,70); ruins 1.5 km east of Grumento. Place of fierce battles in the 2nd Punic War (Liv. 23,37,10; 27,41,3) and in the Social War (cf. App. B Civ. 1,41). *Municipium, tribus Pomptina* (*regio III*). Pliny speaks of the good wine from Lagarina near G. (HN 14,69). E.O.

Grylloi According to Pliny (HN 35,114), the name for caricature depictions in painting since Antiphilus [4] of Alexandria represented a certain Gryllus in that way. Originally these were dancers with grotesque physical proportions and contortions. As *gryllographeîn* and *grylloeídēs* later generally referred to ridiculously proportioned bodies, small-format free-standing sculpture representations can also be described as *grylloi*. Today the genre is no longer attributed to Alexandrian art only. To cover all animal caricatures and monstrous figures as well as the parodies of gods depicted in the wall painting of Pompeii with the term *grylloi* is dubious as well. On the other hand, the historical identification of ancient *grylloi* is increasingly replaced by cultural sociological interpretations of all kinds of representations of misshapen and absurd people (→ Caricatures; realism as a means of expression).

K. LATTE, G., in: Glotta 34, 1955, 190–192; W. BINSFELD, G., 1956; G. BECATTI, s.v. G., EAA 3, 1960, 1065–1066; J.P. CÈBE, La caricature et la parodie dans le monde romain antique des origines à Juvénal, 1966; N. HIMMELMANN, Alexandria und der Realismus in der griech. Kunst, 1983; L. GIULIANI, Die seligen Krüppel. Zur Deutung von Mißgestalten in der hell. Kleinkunst, in: AA 1987, 701–721; H. WREDE, Die tanzenden Musikanten von Mahdia und der alexandrinische Götter- und Heroenkult, in: MDAI(R) 95, 1988, 97–114. R.N.

Gryllus (Γρύλλος; *Grýllos*).

[1] Athenian; father of → Xenophon. TRAILL, PAA 281935.

[2] Son of → Xenophon, born after 399 BC. G. was brought up with his brother Diodorus in Sparta. In 362 both fought in the Athenian army as allies of Sparta; G. died fighting on horseback in a skirmish before the battle of Mantinea and was greatly honoured for this (Xen. Hell. 7,5,15–17; Diog. Laert. 2,52–55; Paus. 8,9,5). In Athens a painting of the battle showed G. and the Boeotian general → Epaminondas (Paus. 1,3,4; 8,11,6). TRAILL, PAA 281945.

J.K. ANDERSON, Xenophon, 1974, 193–195. W.S.

Grynium (Γρύν(ε)ιον; *Grýn(e)ion*). Aeolian town in the north of Cyme. According to Herodotus, G. was one of the 11 old Aeolian towns (1,149). Further testimonies: Ἀχαιῶν λιμήν ('Achaean harbour'), Scyl. 98; cf. *portus Grynia*, Plin. HN 5,121. As a member of the → Delian League G. paid 1/3 talent. At the end of the 5th cent. BC Gongylus of Eretria, to whom Darius had given the town as a seat for his dynasty (Xen. Hell. 3,1,6), ruled here and in Myrina. In 335 BC Parmenion conquered G. and sold the inhabitants into slavery (Diod. Sic. 17,7,9). However the town continued to exist, as its own coin minting in the 3rd cent. shows; at the time of Strabo, G. already belonged to the territory of Myrina (13,3,5). The sanctuary of Apollo that is already mentioned in the middle of the 3rd cent. BC and that the rhetor Aristides still visited in the 2nd cent. AD seemed to have been of supraregional importance. The temple was said to have been built totally in white marble (Str. 13,3,5). An oracle also belonged to the sanctuary (Verg. Aen. 4,345).

W. KROLL, L. BÜRCHNER, s.v. G., RE 7, 1900f.; O. JESSEN, s.v. Gryneios, RE 7, 1901f. E.SCH.

Gryps see → Griffin

Gubla see → Byblus

Guessing games Only a small number of these are known from antiquity (→ Riddles). In order to determine who should start, people liked to choose the game *capita aut navia*. It is named after the ancient Roman coins with the head of → Ianus (*capita*) and a ship's prow (*navia*, probably a plural paralleling *capita*). People threw a coin up into the air: one had to guess (as in the modern game 'heads or tails') which image came to lay on top. A guessing game for two players was *par-impar* (ἀρτιάζειν/*artiázein* or ποσίνδα/*posínda*): the first person holds in his right hand a number of relatively small objects (→ astragaloi, beans, nuts or similar) and shows his partner his closed fist; the latter now has to guess whether an even (*par*) or an odd (*impar*) number of objects are in the fist; then it is the turn of the second player. Who guesses correctly receives the objects hidden in the hand. The game ends when one of the two has no more nuts, beans etc. left. The game was played by children (Hor. Sat. 2,3,248; Aristoph. Plut. 1057; Ov. Nux 79) and adults (Aristoph. Plut. 816; Suet. Aug. 71,4) who certainly took coins as wagers.

Another popular game was *micare digitis* (διὰ δακτύλων κλῆρος/*diá daktýlōn klêros*; also λαχμός/*lachmós*, according to Nonnus, Dion. 33,77–78) that is mostly called *morra* to date. Again it was played by two people who simultaneously quickly raised the right hand with some, all or no fingers and at the same time tried to guess the correct number of outstretched fingers of the other person. On Greek representations the two players hold a staff together in their hands; the one who guessed the right number was probably allowed to move up on the staff.

K. OHLERT, Rätsel und Gesellschaftsspiele der alten Griechen, [2]1912; K. SCHAUENBURG, Erotenspiele, in: Ant. Welt 7.3, 1976, 40 f.; H. A. CAHN, Morra: Drei Silene beim Knobeln, in: H. FRONING (ed.), Kotinos. FS E. Simon, 1992, 214–217. R.H.

Guide see → Travels, travelling

Guido Latin author, identified as G. Pisanus ([4], a different view in [6]); *c.* 1119 he wrote an encyclopaedic compilation *De variis historiis* ('On various historical matters') in 6 books. For the sections *Geographica* and *Descriptio totius maris* he excerpted the → Geographus Ravennas, following him very closely. In the *Geographica* he copied the latter's personal reference to Ravenna as his hometown (Geographica 20,20), but apart from that, as evidence of his education, he displays his knowledge of Classical writers and historians, as well as of the traditions of saints and martyrs, as in e.g. the excursus on Epidaurus (Geographica 113) [3]. He provides us with a first-hand experience of his own, some of it based on autopsy, in discussing Apulia [6]. G. used a more detailed Codex of the Geogr. Rav. than the versions we have today; thus, starting from the *Geographica*, it has been possible to assume an original MS of Geogr. Rav. in Greek [1; 2. 309].

1 H. BERGER, s. v. G., RE 14, 1931 f. 2 G. FUNAIOLI, s. v. Ravennas Geographus, RE 1 A, 305–310 3 G. A. MANSUELLI, I geografi ravennati, in: Corsi di cultura sull'arte ravennate e bizantina 20, 1973, 331–346 4 Repertorium Fontium Historiae Mediaevi 5, 1984, 282 f. 5 J. SCHNETZ (ed.), Itineraria Romana vol. 2, Ravennatis Anonymi Cosmographia et Guidonis Geographica, 1940 (repr. with index, 1990) 6 G. UGGERI, Topografia antica nella Puglia medioevale, in: Brundisii res 6, 1974, 133–154 (bibliography). H. A. G.

Guineafowl The ancient names (μελεαγρίς/*meleagrís*, Latin *meleagris*, synonym: *gallinae Africanae* or *Numididae*) actually only meant the common guineafowl (*Numida meleagris L.*) – in spite of Columella 8,2,2 (cf. [1. 19]) – among the total of 23 species spread over southern Asia and the Middle East as well as North and West Africa. The guineafowl was probably introduced to Greece in the 4th cent. BC and only in the 1st cent. BC to Italy (Varro, Rust. 3,9,18, cf. Plin. HN 10,74: 'the last of the southern birds brought to the table'). Its rarity was probably the reason why it was displayed with many other expensive animals in the procession of Ptolemy III Euergetes in Alexandria (Ath. 5,201b). In Ath. 14,655c-e, the Peripatetic Clytus of Miletus gives an excellent description of the birds kept around the sanctuary of Artemis on Leros. Aristot. Hist. an. 6,2,559a 25 (= Plin. HN 10,144) mentions only the speckled eggs, not the birds themselves. Plin. HN 10,74 asserts (because of the white drops on the plumage and the shrill voice) that they were famous through the grave of Meleager because the latter's sisters who were mourning him were turned into guineafowls (cf. Ael. NA 4,42; Ov. Met. 8,525–46 and Plin. HN 37,40). Apart from their role in the Artemis cult on Leros, they played a part in the Isis cult (Paus. 10,32,16). In decorative art they are rarely represented, for instance between the vine shoots on the mosaic floor of the church of Justinian in Sabratha [2. 246 and fig. 125] or in a fresco in Pompeii [3. 155, Fig. 44].

1 B. LORENTZ, Kulturgesch. Beitr. zur Tierkunde des Alt., Progr. Gymnasium Wurzen 1904 2 TOYNBEE, Tierwelt 3 KELLER, vol. 2, 154–156. C.HÜ.

Gulussa Second son of → Massinissa; envoy to Rome (Liv. 42,23–24; 43,3,5–7; Liv. per. 48) [3. 429f.; 433]. In 150 BC envoy of → Massinissa to Carthage, on which occasion the attack on envoys led to war (App. Lib. 317–319; 336–339; Liv. per. 49) [2. 54; 3. 434]. When the inheritance was divided in 149 BC, military commander; in the 3rd Punic War on the side of Rome (App. Lib. 500–527; 596–604; Liv. per. 50) [3. 447ff.; 454]. Negotiation with Hasdrubal; acquainted with Scipio and Polybius (Pol. 34,16; 38,7–8; Diod. Sic. 32,22) [1. 638; 677; 695–699]. Death before 118 BC. His son: Massiva (Sall. Iug. 5; 35,1).

→ Africa; → Mauretania; → Numidae, Numidia

1 F. W. WALBANK, A Historical Commentary on Polybius, vol. 3, 1979 2 M.-R. ALFÖLDI, Die Gesch. des numidischen Königreiches und seiner Nachfolger, in: H. G. HORN, C. B. RÜGER (ed.), Die Numider, 1979, 43–74 3 HUSS. B.M.

Gum (kommi) As a loan-word from Egyptian, κόμμι (*kómmi*) first appears in Hdt. 2,86 as an adhesive for the linen bandages of embalmed corpses. It was extracted from the so-called Egyptian thorn *Acacia arabica* = nilotica (→ Acacia) that is already described by Theophr. Hist. pl. 4,2,8 (cf. *spina nigra*, Plin. HN 13,63). Plin. HN 13,66 mentions further suppliers of gum. Dioscorides 1,133 p. 1, 205 WELLMANN = 1,160 p. 225 BERENDES knows gum from the skeletonweed, *Chondrilla iuncea L.* (*Compositae*). The medical importance of various *cummi*, for eyes and wounds among other things, is summarized by Plin. HN 24,105. C.HÜ.

Gundericus (Gunderic). In AD 406 G. was chosen as king of the Vandal Hasdingians after the death of his father → Godigiselus; he united his troops with the Alani under Respendial (Greg. Tur. Franc. 2,9), defeated the Franks and by the end of 406 crossed the Rhine. Without facing organized resistance, he plundered Gaul (Oros. 7,40,3; Chron. min. 1,299; 465 MOMMSEN; Zos. 6,3), crossed the Pyrenees in 409 (Chron. min. 2,17; Soz. 9,12; Greg. Tur. Franc. 2,2) and secured for himself the east of the province of Gallaecia (Chron. min. 2,18) in 411. In 418 the Vandal Silingians and the Alani placed themselves under his control. In 418/9 he successfully fought against the Suebi and considerably extended his domain of power in Spain despite Roman resistance (Chron. min. 1,469; 2,18ff.; Salv. Gub. 7,66). He died in 428 while plundering Seville; his successor was his half-brother → Geisericus (Chron. min. 2,21).

PLRE 2, 522; F. CLOVER, The Late Roman West and the Vandals, 1993; CHR. COURTOIS, Les vandales et l'afrique, 1955, esp. 393; H.-J. DIESNER, Das Vandalenreich, 1966, 24ff. M.MEI. and ME.STR.

Gundeshapur (*Ǧundīsābūr*, 'Place of the army of Šāpūr'; middle Persian *Veh-Andiyōk-Šābūr*, 'Šāpūr [made this city] better than Antioch'; Syrian *Bēṯ Lāpāṭ*). City located about 30 km east of Susa in which the Sassanid Šāpur (→ Sapor) I settled artisans and specialists deported from Syria in the 3rd cent. AD. The town soon became a cultural and scientific centre with its own 'university' (important especially in the field of medicine), a main location for Persian silk manufacturing and a centre for the Christians of Ḫūzistān. The founder of a religion, → Mani, died in the Sassanid jail of G.

J. WIESEHÖFER, Das ant. Persien, 1994, s.v. Ǧundaisābūr. J.W.

Gundestrup On the G. moor, Ålborg district in northern Jutland, a large dismantled cauldron made of 13 partially gilded silver plates and a frame rack was found in 1891 (diameter almost 70 cm, weight *c.* 9 kg). The plates in repoussé technique show depictions of gods, scenes of sacrifice, mythical beasts etc. represented in a characteristic form. The questions of dating, origin and function of the G. cauldron have been the subject of controversy and debate from the time when it was found to the present. The cultic nature as well as the deposition in the Germanic north are beyond dispute. The manufacture and place of original use are however seen in Gaul (whether it be in the north or in the Hellenized south), furthermore in south-eastern Europe (in turn alternating between the Thracians/Dacians and the rather Celtic → Scordisci) or (an opinion held by very few today) in the Germanic north. The time of manufacture is mostly thought to have been the 2nd half of the 1st cent. BC; but here too the dating fluctuates between the 2nd cent. BC and the prehistoric period. The G. cauldron provides manifold insights into the art and religion of the Celtic world and its south-eastern neighbours.

→ Dacians; → Celtic archaeology; → Thracians

R. HACHMANN, G.-Studien, in: BRGK 71, 1990 (1991), 565–903; F. KAUL, G.-kedlen, 1991; G. S. OLMSTEDT, The G. Cauldron, 1979; R. PITTIONI, Wer hat wann und wo den Silberkessel von G. angefertigt?, 1984. V.P.

Gundicharius (Gundahar, Gundihar, Guntiar). Traditionally the son of Gibica; king of the Burgundians. In AD 411 with the king of the Alanians Goar, G. elevated the Gaulish senator → Jovinus in Mainz to the status of emperor (Olympiodorus FHG 4, 61 fr. 17). After the latter's death in 417, he entered into a → *foedus* with → Honorius (Chron. min. 1,467; 2,155 MOMMSEN), but in 435 invaded the province of Belgica I where → Aetius [2] defeated him (Sid. Apoll. Carm. 7,234f.). In 436 G., allegedly with 20,000 Burgundians, was killed in an attack of the Huns, that was perhaps launched by Aetius (Chron. min. 1,475; 660; 2,22f.; 156). This forms the historical core of the Burgundian heroic legend and is also treated in the Nibelungenlied (there G. = Gunther) [2].

1 PLRE 2, 523 2 A. HEUSLER, Nibelungensage und Nibelungenlied, 61965 3 STEIN, Spätröm. R., 400; 480f. M.MEI.

Gundiok (Gundovech). King of the Burgundians in AD 457–470, from the family of → Athanaric [1. 44], married a sister of Ricimer (Malalas 374–75; Johannes Antiochenus fr. 209), his sons are Gundobad, Godigisclus, Chilperic and Godomer (Greg. Tur. Franc. 2,28). As an ally of Theoderic II he attacked in 455 with his brother Chilperic I the Suebians in Gaul and settled there after the victory of Theoderic in 457. In 463 he was *magister utriusque militiae (per Gallias)*; in the same year he informed Pope Hilarius about the irregular administration of the bishop of *Vienna* (Hilarius Epist. 9 THIEL). PLRE 2,523f. (Gundiocus).

1 H. WOLFRAM, Die Goten, [3]1990. M.MEI. and ME.STR.

Gundobad Son of Gundiok, king of the Burgundians in AD 474–516, Arian. On the side of → Ricimer he, as *magister utriusque militiae* in 472, killed Anthemius [2] (Chron. min. 1,306 MOMMSEN), administered the western empire and in 473 elevated Glycerius to the status of *Augustus* (Chron. min. 1,664). In 474 he – in the meantime *comes* and *patricius* – returned to Gaul and succeeded Ricimer in *Vienna*. He defeated the Alemanni and around 490 invaded Liguria (Ennod. 80). In 496 he married his son Sigismundus to Areagni, a daughter of Theoderic. In 501 he defeated his brother Godigisclus – who in 500 in the dispute for rulership had allied himself with → Chlodovechus – and he assumed sole rule (Johannes Antiochenus fr. 209,2; Greg. Tur. Franc. 2,32f.). The battles against the West Goths and then the East Goths ended in 507–9 with great losses including losses of territory. G. now sought closer ties with the Catholics (cf. the dispute with Avitus, the bishop of *Vienna*, Avitus Epist. 4 and 5; MGH AA 7).

G. died in 516 (Greg. Tur. Franc. 3,5; Chron. min. 2,234).

The *lex Burgundionum* (*lex Gundobada*), a collection of older laws with *Novellae* of G. (MGH leges 1,1,1), can be traced back to him.

PLRE 2, 524f.; A. Demandt, Die Spätantike, 1989, Index s.v.; H. Wolfram, Die Goten [3]1990, 311f.

M.MEI. and ME.STR.

Guneus (Γουνεύς; *Gouneús*). Leader of the 28th contingent described in the Homeric catalogue of ships (Hom. Il. 2,748–755). His territory, clearly defined by the place names Kyphos and Dodona as well as the tribal names of the Aenianes and Peraebians, comprises approximately the centre of the Pindus Massif and links Thessaly with Epirus. In the epic Kyklos, G. then only reappears in the → Nostoi; here it told of a shipwreck off the coast of Cape Caphereus, perhaps also of migration to Libya. According to this, G. obviously played no part in pre-Homeric myth; his name was probably rather derived from the Thessalian town → Gonnos and his large territory was not stipulated until it was designated in the catalogue of ships.

E. Visser, Homers Kat. der Schiffe, 1997, 721–735. E.V.

Gunthamundus Son of Gentunis, king of the Vandals in AD 484–496 (Iord. Get. 170; Procop. Vand. 1,8,6f.), fought successfully against the Moors. In 491 his attempt to reconquer Sicily failed (Ennod. Panegyricus 70). He showed tolerance to the Catholics after initially persecuting them. PLRE 2, 525f.

H.-J. Diesner, Das Vandalenreich, 1966, 84–88.

M.MEI. and ME.STR.

Guntharith (Guntharis, Gundarus, Gontharis). *Bucellarius* of → Solomon I, *magister militum* and *dux Numidiae* from AD 545 (Iord. De origine actibusque Romanorum 384). G., whom Solomon had sent out in advance to Bagae on the River Abigas with an army to fight the Moors, escaped defeat only through the latter's rapid assistance (Procop. Vand. 2,19,6–16). In a secret alliance with the prince of the Moors Antalas, G. decided in 546 to remove → Areobindus [3], which also occurred (Procop. Vand. 2,25,1–28). G. occupied Carthage and after only 36 days of rule was stabbed to death (Procop. Vand. 2,27–28) by → Artabannes [2] (Johannes Antiochenus FHG 4,232–237).

PLRE 3, 574–76 (Guntharis 2); J. A. S. Evans, The Age of Justinian, 1996, 152, 170, 189; Rubin, vol. 2, 1995, 41, 47–49.

M.MEI. and ME.STR.

Gunther see → Gundicharius

Gunugu (New Punic *Gngn*). Punic or Punic-influenced trading post west of Caesarea, modern Sidi Brahim near Gouraya. Under Augustus G. rose to become a *colonia* whose citizens were allocated to the *tribus Quirina*. Evidence: Plin. HN 5,20; Ptol. 4,2,5 (Κανουκκίς); It. Ant. 15,1 (*Gunugus*); Geogr. Rav. p. 40,45 (*Gunubus*); 88,10 (*Gunagus*); 132,19 (*Cunagus*). In the *Notitia episcopatuum Mauretaniae Caesariensis* (111[a]) an *episcopus Gunugitanus* is mentioned for the year 484. Inscriptions: Répertoire d'épigraphie sémitique III 1979–2000; CIL VIII 2, 9071; 9423; Suppl. 3, 21447–21452; AE 1976, 235 no. 751.

S. Lancel, E. Lipiński, s.v. G., DCPP, 202. W.HU.

Guraeus (Γουραῖος; *Gouraîos*, Arr. Anab. 4,25,7; Γαροίας; *Garoías*, Arr. Ind. 4,11, according to Megasthenes; Old Indo-Aryan Gaurī). River (modern Pañkorā) whose source is in the 'Indian Caucasus' (Hindukush) and which flows into the Cophen (modern Kābul) in a deep gorge that → Alexander [4] the Great crossed on his campaign. In the G. area lived the *Guraîoi* (Γουραῖοι, Arr. Anab. 4,23,1; 25,6), who raised cattle and whose land, according to Ptolemy, was called *Gōryaîa* (Γωρυαία, 7,1,42) with the town of *Gôrya* (Γωρύα, 7,1,43), perhaps modern Ǧalālābād.

TAVO B V 1. A.P.-L.

Gurgenes In Procopius (Pers. 1,12,4ff.), king of Caucasian Iberia who asked Justin I for help against the introduction of the fire cult demanded by Kavad I and who fled from the Persians to the Lazian mountainous countryside. Toumanoff [1] considers him to be the legendary Vaḫtang Gorgasal of Georgian and Armenian tradition although this is rejected by Martin-Hisard [2].

1 C. Toumanoff, Studies in Christian Caucasian History, 1963, 362–378 2 B. Martin-Hisard, Le roi Vaxtang Gorgasal, in: Temps, mémoire, tradition au Moyen Âge: Aix-en-Provence, 4–5 juin 1982 (Actes du 13e congrès de la Société des Historiens Médiévistes ...), 1983, 207–242.

A.P.-L.

Gurges Roman cognomen ('Throat', pejorative 'Spendthrift', Macrob. Sat. 3,13,7; cf. *gurgulio*), in the Republican period in the family of the Fabii.

Kajanto, Cognomina 269; Walde/Hofmann 1, 627f.

K.-L.E.

Gurnard Seven of the probably 15 identified representatives of the family of the Cottidae are of major significance: 1) The armed gurnard (Peristedion cataphractum C.) that growls after being caught is – according to Aelianos (NA 13,26), who calls it τέττιξ ἐνάλιος/*téttix enálios* ('Sea Cicada') –, darker than the κάραβος/*kárabos*, the lobster. The inhabitants of Seriphus are said to have spared it because it was dedicated to Perseus. 2) The flying gurnard (Dactylopterus volitans L.) is said, as ἱέραξ ὁ θαλάττιος/ *hiérax ho thaláttios*, Latin *accipiter* ('Marine goshawk'), to glide shallowly above the water (Ael. NA 9,52; Opp. Hal. 1,428–437, [1. 287]). 3) The grey G. (Eutrigla gurnardus L.), as the gloriously colourful κάνθαρος θαλάττιος/*kántharos thaláttios* ('Sea beetle'), according to Opp. Hal. 3,339–370, is caught with a good bait. 4) The proper G., κόκκυξ/*kókkyx* ('Cuckoo'), Trigla hirundo L., is said to have received its name from its reputation (Aristot. Hist. an. 4,9,535b 19f.). 5) Athenaeus (7,320f.) states that he often ate the small dragon head (Scorpaena porcus L.), σκόρπαινα/*skórpaina*. According to Plin. HN 9,162 the *scorpaena* spawns twice a year. 6) The reddish brown (Ov. Halieuticorum 116) scorpion fish (Scorpaena scrofa L.), σκορπίος/*skorpíos*, is often identified with the 7) sea scorpion (Cottus scorpius L.) of the same name. It lives in rocks (Opp. Hal. 2,458f.) and has poisonous barbs. Caelius [II 10] Apicius recommends its broth (10,3,10).

1 D'Arcy W. Thompson, A Glossary of Greek Fishes, 1947 2 H. Gossen, s.v. K., RE Suppl. 8,250f. C.HÜ.

Gurza Town in *Africa Byzacena*, 12 km north-west of → Hadrumetum, modern Kalaa Kebira (for the location cf. Tab. Peut. 6,2: *Gurra*). G. was under Punic influence. Patronage deeds are extant from the years 12 BC (CIL VIII 1,68) and AD 65 (CIL VIII 1,69). Inscriptions: CIL VI 4,2, 32757; 36277; VIII 1, 68–72; Suppl. 4, 23021. The town attested in Pol. 1,74,13, Γόρζα/ Gorza, was not very far from Utica [1. 258].
→ Patronage

1 Huss.

E. Lipiński, s.v. G./Gorza, DCPP, 202. W.HU.

Gustatio see → Cena

Gutta Roman cognomen (gentes name?) of an otherwise unknown family.
[1] **G.** from Capua, as commander in 82 BC supported the Marianians in the Civil War against Sulla (App. B Civ. 1,416).
[2] **G.** (possible nickname?), praetor around 55 BC and together with T. Annius [I 14] Milo contender for the consulate for 52 BC (Cic. Ad Q. Fr. 3,6,6; MRR 3,100). K.-L.E.

Guttae Latin for drops (pl.); in the architectonic sense, ancient technical term only attested in Vitruvius (4,1,2 and 4,3,6) for the drop-like cylindrical shapes that are found on parts of the stone entablature of the Doric building style and that as imitated nails or nail heads attest to the anachronistic transformation of the only wooden building form into the canonical Doric stone temple [1. 53–55; 3. 10–13]. *Guttae* are to be found (mostly) in three parallel rows of six on the → *mutulus* of the → *geison* and on the architrave as the bottom completion of the → *regula* [2. 112–120].

1 Ch. Höcker, Architektur als Metapher. Überlegungen zur Bed. des dor. Ringhallentempels, in: Hephaistos 14, 1996, 45–79 2 W. Müller-Wiener, Griech. Bauwesen in der Ant., 1988 3 B. Wesenberg, Griech. Säulen- und Gebälkformen in der lit. Überlieferung, in: DiskAB 6, 1997, 1–15. C.HÖ.

Gutturals The Neo-Latin *terminus technicus* gutturals ('guttural sounds') for a class of consonants is traditional (nouns that before the endings have a g, k/c or χ are called guttural stems). Today research prefers the more appropriate term 'Tectals', as in the articulation of this consonant the back of the tongue is pressed against the roof of the mouth (Latin *tectum*) in order to obstruct the stream of air through constriction or blockage, so producing the sound typical of gutturals. To the proto-Indo-European are attributed nine or ten tectal phonemes. The guttural stops are divided into three series according to the respective place of articulation: in the front palate (Latin *palatum*) the palatals $\hat{k}$, $\hat{g}$, $\hat{g}^h$ are formed, in the back palate (Latin *velum*) the velars k, g, g^h, and just there with the same rounding of the lips the → labio-velars k^w, g^w, g^{wh}. Depending on the type of articulation, unvoiced (= tenues, k etc.), voiced (= *mediae*, g etc.) and voiced aspirate (= *mediae aspiratae*, g^h etc.) can be differentiated. The → Laryngeal h_2 was probably a tectal fricative /x/. The conspicuously large number of proto-Indo-European gutturals is reduced in all historical Indo-European languages. The coincidence of the palatal and velar series ($*\hat{k}$, $*k > k \sim$ Greek κ, Latin *c*) characterizes the → Centum languages to which Greek and Latin also belong.
→ Indo-European languages; → Phonetics; → Satem language

W. Cowgill, M. Mayrhofer, Idg. Gramm. I 1/2, 1986, 102–109, 121f.; Leumann, 146–153; Rix, Historische Grammatik des Griechischen, 1976, 82–97. D.ST.

Guttus see → Vessels, shapes and types

Gyarus (Γύαρος; *Gýaros*). Island 17 km² in size, uninhabited today (micaceous slate) of the north-western Cyclades, modern Jura or Gioura. On the eastern side there are traces of old terrace cultures, and close to a spring and an old mole are the remains of the ancient town of G. that minted its own copper coins in the 3rd cent. BC; at the time of Strabo G. was still only a poor fishing village, in the Imperial period it was a feared place of exile (Tac. Ann. 3,68; 4,30; Plut. Mor. 602c.; Juv. 1,73; 10,170; Lucian. Toxaris 17f.; Philostr. VA. 7,16,2; Str. 10,5,3; Plin. HN 4,69; 8,104; 222; IG XII 5, 651; XII Suppl., 117). From 1573 to 1617 G. was in the duchy of Naxos and then came under Turkish rule. Under Papadopoulos it was a place of exile for opponents of the regime (1967–1974).

HN, 486; Lauffer, Griechenland, 241; Philippson/Kirsten 4, 81; IG XII 5, S. XXXI. H.KAL.

Gyas
[1] Companion of → Aeneas (Verg. Aen. 1,222; 1,612; 12,460). As a skipper he took part in the regatta in honour of Anchises (Verg. Aen. 5,114f.; Hyg. Fab. 273). The patrician house of the Geganii, was, according to Servius (Aen. 5,117) descended from him, although this is probably a later fabrication.
[2] A Latin, a giant with a club, son of Melampus, who for his part is said to have come to Italy with Hercules. He and his brother Cisseus were killed in battle by Aeneas (Verg. Aen. 10,317). RE.ZI.

Gye (γύη, γύης; *Gýē, Gýēs*) is mentioned in Homer (Il. 9,579, Od. 7,113; 18,374) as the multiple of a land measure. The exact size of the measure cannot be determined, as in later commentaries (Eust.) and Lexica (Hsch.) different information is to be found. In this way *gye* could be equated on the one hand with $^1/_2$ → *pléthron* and also 1 Roman → *iugerum* or 1 *pléthron*. In Il. 9,579 and Od. 18,374 it probably corresponds approximately to the *pléthron*, whilst in Od. 7,113 it is at least 12 *pléthra*. In lower Italy there is a *gye* with 50 *pléthra*.

F. Hultsch, Griech. und röm. Metrologie, [2]1882, 40–42; 668–669. GE.S.

Gyenus (Γυηνός; *Gyēnós*). Town in the → Colchis (Ps.-Scyl. 81). Now linked with the ancient settlement (6th cent. BC – 6th cent. AD) near Očamčire on the Georgian Pontus coast, discovered in 1935/6 during the construction of the harbour. The ancient finding points to three man-made hills surrounded by ditches with remains of wooden architecture with a pounded clay floor; apart from Colchic ceramics, fragments of ancient Ionian and Attic red-figured ceramics as well as black-glazed ceramics were found. Worthy of mention as the latest building is a hall church with pastophoria (*opus mixtum*) from the 6th cent. AD.

D. Kačarava, G. Kvirkvelia, Goroda i poselenija Pričernomor'ja antičnoj epochi, 1991, 76ff. A.P.-L.

Gyes (Γύης; *Gýēs*). According to the MSS [1], probably the incorrectly written form of Gyges, one of the → Hecatoncheires.

1 M. L. West, Hesiod, Theogony, 1966, 210. RE.ZI.

Gygaie limne (Γυγαίη λίμνη; *Gygaíē límnē*). Lake in Lydia north of → Hermus and of → Sardis, to which in the south adjoin the Lydian royal necropolis (modern Bintepe, 'Thousand Hills') with the tomb tumuli of → Alyattes, → Gyges and other princes (Hipponax fr. 42 Masson); possibly called after the ancestors of → Gyges (Nicolaus of Damascus FGrH 90 F 46) by the same name or a legendary figure. Gygaiae limne (GL) is already mentioned in Homer (Hom. Il. 20,390f.; cf. 2,865), mythographical fantastic stories are to be found in Lycoph. Alexandra 1353 ('Typhon's camp') and Prop. 3,11,17 ('Omphale's bath'). The lake was filled all year round (Hdt. 1,93,5) and was used as a (supposedly man-made) storage pond against the high tides in the Hermus Plain that abounded in rivers (Str. 13,4,7); later it was also called Lake Coloe (Κολόη λίμνη) after the temple of Artemis Coloene nearby (Str. 13,4,5); it was partly silted up (*Gygaeum stagnum*, Plin. HN 5,110). Today it is called Marmara gölü ('Marble lake').

On the southern bank there are (on the Ahlatlı tepecik) burial places from a prehistoric settlement – with Neolithic and early Byzantine finds (Pithus tombs and cists, 3rd millennium) – that was also inhabited in the Lydian period (7th/6th cents. BC).

G. M. A. Hanfmann, Letters from Sardis, 1972, Index; Id., Sardis und Lydien, in: AAWM 1960, 6; Id., The Seventh Campaign at Sardis (1964), in: BASO 177, 1965, 2–37; Id., The Ninth Campaign at Sardis (1966), in: BASO 186, 1967, 40–42; D. G. Mitten, in: BASO 191, 1969, 7–10; J. G. Peadley, Ancient Literary Sources on Sardis (Archaeological Exploration of Sardis, Monograph 2), 1972, 69f. and index; L. Robert, Documents d'Asie Mineure, 1987, 296–321, 341f. H.KA.

Gyges (Γύγης; *Gýgēs*).
[1] Lydian king (*c.* 680–644 BC) and founder of the Mermnade Dynasty, is said, according to Herodotus (1,12), to have married the wife of his predecessor → Candaules, murdered by him, and (in this way) to have won rule in Sardis. It is uncertain from where the Lydian-speaking Mermnades came (from Maionia/Mysia?). In any case they were probably not in Sardis until the 1st millennium. Their relationship with the Luvian-speaking ([1. 384,10] → Luvian, → Lydian) earlier inhabitants (Heraclidae?, Hdt. 1,7) probably tended to be hostile. For us the Lydian history of Sardis and the country that the Assyrians called *māt Luddi* (7th cent.) and the Ionians (6th/5th cents.) *Lydíē* (→ Lydia) begins with G. His name probably goes back to an abbreviated Luvian PN compositum with *ḫūḫa-*, 'Grandfather'. G. is called a *týrannos* (cf. *tyrannís* Archil. fr. 19 West) that is glossed in Hesychius as Lydian **laila*, which is in turn etymologically connected with Hittite *laḫḫijala-*, 'War Hero'. He actually lived from war: against Ionian cities like Milet he conducted raids (Hdt. 1,14) and to Psammetichus I he sold off Ionian and Carian subjects as mercenaries (Assurbanipal Prisma A II 111ff.; Diod. Sic. 1,66, cf. Hdt. 2,152). Through this G. became proverbially rich ('Show-off with his gold': Archil. fr. 19 West, cf. Hdt. 1,14). However war also sealed his fate: under pressure from the Cimmerians, Indo-European horsemen, against whom the Lydian dynasts were still going into action with the chariot and their Ionian mercenaries in the phalanx (Sappho fr. 16 Voigt), G. turned to → Assurbanipal, subjugated himself, paid tribute (Assurbanipal Prisma E) and was able in this way to ward off the danger from the Cimmerians. However G. then threw off the yoke of Assurbanipal rashly whereupon the Cimmerians mas-

sively increased their pressure. Sardis was finally conquered by them (Str. 14,1,40 quoting Call. fr. 3 G.-P.), and G. suffered a cruel death (Assurbanipal Prisma A II 16ff.). The dynasty remained in power; G.'s son Ardys was able to ascend the throne (Hdt. 1,15) but because of the Cimmerians he could only rule as a vassal of the Assyrians (Assurbanipal Prisma A II 18ff.).

1 F. Starke, Sprachen und Schriften ..., in: B. Pongratz-Leisten et al. (ed.), FS Röllig, 1997, 381–395.

M. Cogan, H. Tadmor, Gyges and Ashurbanipal, in: Orientalia 46, 1977, 65–85; H. Gelzer, Das Zeitalter des G., in: RhM 30, 1875, 230–268; E. Lipiński, Gygès et Lygdamis, in: Orientalia Lovaniensia Periodica 24, 1993, 65–71; G. Radet, Lydie, 1893. PE.HÖ.

[2] Primeval being, see → Hecatonchiron

Gylippus (Γύλιππος; *Gýlippos*). Spartiate, son of Cleandridas. His education (→ *agōgé*) was perhaps (at times?) made possible by an affluent Spartan, as Aelianus (Var. 12,43) calls him *mothax* ('Bastard') [1. 434]. When Syracuse asked Sparta for help against the Athenians, he was sent to Sicily (Thuc. 6,93; 104), reached Himera in the summer of 414 BC with a small force, reinforced his army there considerably, broke through to Syracuse, organized the resistance and prevented the encircling of the city (Thuc. 7,1–7). After preliminary rounds of battles in the harbour and on the plateau of Epipolae and with reinforcements found in summer 413 in Sicily (Thuc. 7,46), he forced the Athenians, after further battles in the harbour, to retreat to the interior of the island (Thuc. 7,51–87); he supposedly tolerated this retreat (Thuc. 7,81,1). When the Athenian forces had capitulated, he tried in vain to prevent the execution of the Athenian *strategoi* Demosthenes [1] and Nicias (Thuc. 7,86,2; Plut. Nicias 27f.). Probably exaggerated is the reproach in Plutarch (comparatio Timoleonis et Aemilii 2) adopted from Timaeus of insatiable greed that was supposedly made against the unpopular G. in Syracuse. It could go back to stories reporting a legal proceeding against his father in 446 on account of corruption (Plut. Pericles 22) and the embezzlement of booty funds that G. was supposed to take from Athens to Sparta on behalf of Lysander in 404 (Plut. Lysander 16–17,1). It remains an unanswered question whether G. committed suicide after the scandal was uncovered (Ath. 6,234a) or fled Sparta and was condemned to death (Diod. Sic. 13,106,8–10).

1 D. Lotze, Μόθακες, in: Historia 11, 1962.

D. Kagan, The Peace of Nicias and the Sicilian Expedition, 1981, Index s.v. K.-W.WEL.

Gylis (Γῦλις; *Gŷlis*). Spartiate, in 394 BC polemarch, assumed command of the army of Agesilaus [2] II after the battle of Coronea and advanced to Locris. He fell in battle after the retreat (Xen. Ages. 2,15; Hell. 4,3,21–23). K.-W.WEL.

Gylon (Γύλων; *Gýlōn*). Athenian, is said at the end of the 5th cent. BC to have been responsible for the northern Pontic → Nymphaeum that belonged to Athens being 'Handed to the enemies', for which he was given the death penalty (Aeschin. In Ctes. 171); probably his offence was less serious (Dem. Or. 28,3). G. was allocated by the Bosporanian rulers the town of Kepoi with its territory, from which he collected high taxes. He married a rich Scythian and returned to Athens with her. One of his daughters was the mother of → Demosthenes [2] (Traill, PAA 282005).

V. F. Gajdukevič, Das Bosporanische Reich, 1971, 189f. I.v.B.

Gymnasiarchus see → Gymnasiarchy

Gymnasiarchy (γυμνασιαρχία; *Gymnasiarchía*). Supervision of a → gymnasium by a gymnasiarchus, whose functions varied in scope and importance depending on the place and time. In Athens the gymnasiarchy in the 5th and 4th cents. BC was a one-year → *leitoûrgía* (λειτουργία; And. 1,132; Dem. Or. 20,21), the task being to train a certain number of runners for torch competitions at the Great Panathenaea, Hephaistia, Promethia and festivals of Pan and to supply them with all their requisites. At the end of the 4th cent. the gymnasiarchy became here a type of office that could be bestowed again. Outside Athens as well, its term was one year with diverse and changing tasks for gymnasia, which in the classical period imparted to broader circles aristocratic values and in the Hellenistic and Roman period were not just places for training athletes but – primarily for Greeks of the diaspora in the Middle East and in Egypt – were centres of culture and social life.

W. Decker, Zum Gymnasiarchengesetz im antiken Griechenland, in: S. Yaldai et al. (ed.), Menschen im Sport. FS H.-E. Rösch, 1997, 12–19; Ph. Gauthier, M. B. Hatzopoulos, La loi gymnasiarchique de Beroia, 1993; H. W. Pleket, Sport und Leibesübungen in der griech. Welt des hell.-röm. Zeitalters, in: H. Überhorst (ed.), Geschichte der Leibesübungen, vol. 2, 1978, 280–311; P. J. Sijpesteijn, Liste des gymnasiarques de métropoles de l'Égypte romaine, 1967; I. Weiler, Der Sport bei den Völkern der Alten Welt, 1981, 91ff. K.-W.WEL.

Gymnasium (γυμνάσιον; *gymnásion*).
I. Building style II. The Hellenistic Gymnasium

I. Building style

Public facility for sporting and musical leisure activities in the Greek polis; the term is derived from γυμνός/*gymnós* (naked) and refers to the → nakedness at sports practices and competitions. Synonymous with gymnasium for the period from the 4th cent. BC in ancient written sources as well as in modern specialized literature is the concept of the → palaistra (cf. Vitruvius 5,11). This as the 'Wrestler school' originally referred only to a functionally determined partial building field

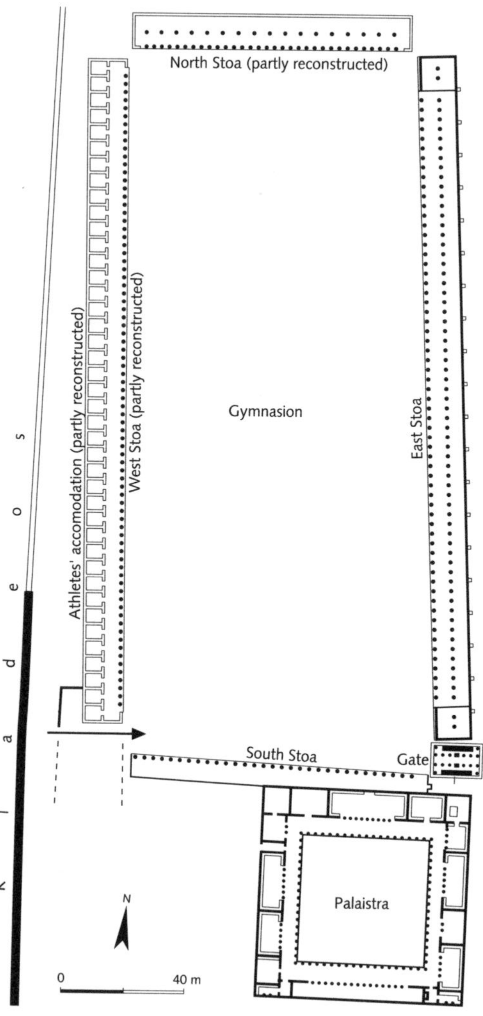

Olympia. Gymnasion and palaistra (reconstructed ground-plan).

of the gymnasium, namely the large peristyle court with a sand area for the wrestlers in the centre that however became in the architectonic development of the gymnasium from about 400 BC the visually characteristic and regularly best-preserved element of these facilities.

The gymnasium of the 6th cent. BC was initially an architectonically little developed area, mostly in a grove shaded by trees in which the long racetrack (*drómos*) dominated; this gymnasium was enclosed from about the middle of the century by a low wall and can therefore also be understood as a place that was distinctive from a building point of view (Athens). In the 5th cent. BC, as part of the gymnasium, the palaistra developed as a big, mostly approximately square peristyle court; this structure became the most prominent part of gymnasium architecture, as it arose from the 4th cent. BC in numerous Greek poleis and sanctuaries (early examples: Thera, Nemea, Delphi).

The gymnasium as a functionally connected conglomerate of various architectonic elements became in the late classical and Hellenistic period one of the greatest building 'styles' in the Greek world; often it occupied an area of over two hectares. Around a large free space the individual building elements were grouped: an open racetrack (*drómos*), mostly a → stadium long, a roofed racetrack (→ *xystós*) and long columned halls, in which the various exercise and instruction rooms were housed: the change room (*apodytḗrion*), an ointment room (*elaiothḗsion*), the wash room (*loutrón*), cold and hot baths (baths as early developments in public → Thermal baths), a hearth room (*pyriatḗrion*), → latrines and the various rooms for the preparations for sports competitions; then, outside the columned halls, → exedra for residence and instruction, now and then a ball game area (Delphi) and small sanctuaries (mostly to Hermes, Hercules or the Muses). The palaistra with its peristyle court that as a rule was approximately square often formed an annex for these facilities (e.g. Olympia) and was surrounded on all four sides with groups of rooms that were used for special preparation for combat sports.

In Hellenism the gymnasium became a central public building project and in this way at the same time a favourite representational object for the respective building authorities (→ Building trade). Lavish propylon buildings marked the accesses to the gymnasium facilities and to the palaistra (Olympia) that were now separated from them more and more by buildings; the columned halls and the peristyle courts were built out of expensive building materials and were decorated richly with → architectural sculpture. The Asia Minor 'Sumptuous Gymnasia' of Priene, Miletus or Ephesus showed in this sense considerable building luxury, covered a huge area at times and supplemented the gymnasium with new fields (→ Library, → Theatre, e.g. the gymnasium of Pergamum or Rhodes).

In contrast with the palaistra that was isolated from the original building context of the gymnasium, the gymnasium as an autonomous building conglomerate in Roman architecture experienced no passing down of ideas but was replaced as multifunctional sporting and leisure architecture by the → thermal baths that adapted all the tasks of the gymnasium but at the same time reweighed them in keeping with the needs of Roman culture. An exception were the restorations and extensions of existing, traditional facilities in the Greek-Asia Minor cultural area (e.g. the Eudemus gymnasium in Miletus) and occasional new buildings that were in no way inferior in the magnificence of their development to the thermal baths and that became an allusion to the exemplarily understood Greek cultural tradition (e.g. the harbour gymnasium in Ephesus; cf. on the other hand Vitr. De arch. 5,11).

From the change in the three great gymnasia that go back to the 6th cent. BC in Athens, i.e. Academy (→ Academeia), Cynosarges and Lyceion – which became schools of philosophy of Plato, Antisthenes and

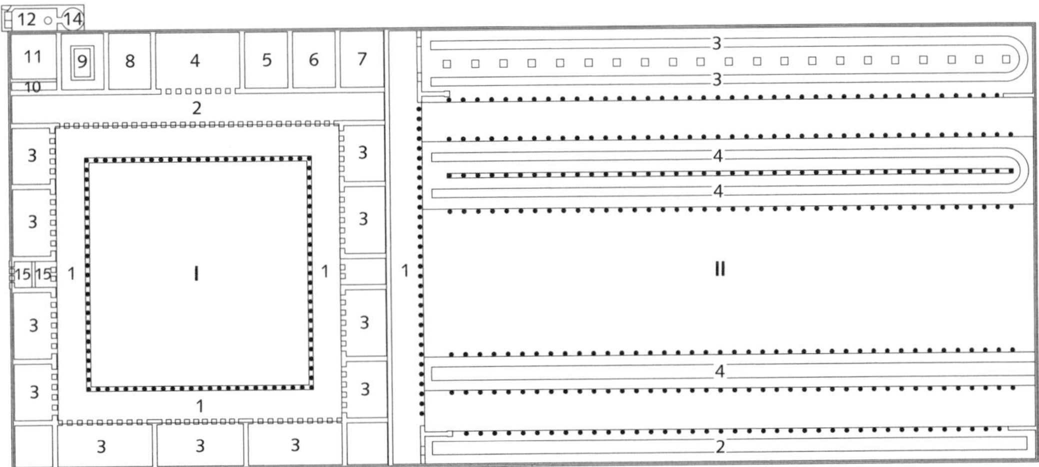

The gymnasium according to Vitruvius (5.11).

I. Palaestra
1./2. Peristylon (1. Porticus simplices 2. Porticus duplex)
3. Exedrae
4. Ephebeum
5. Coryceum
6. Conisterium
7. Lutron
8. Elaeothesium
9. Frigidarium
10. Iter in propnigeum
11. Propnigeum
12. Sudatio
13. Calida Lavatio
14. Laconicum
15. Gate structure

Peristylon	Circumference	2 stadia
Ephebeum	Width: Depth	3 : 2
Xystus	Length of track	1 stadium
	Clear width	10+12+10= 32 feet

II. Actual gymnasium
1. Porticus
2. Xystus
3. Porticus (Xystus) duplex
4. Paradromides

Aristotle – grew in modern times the humanistic understanding of the gymnasium as a high-standing educational facility for the social elite.

J. Delorme, Gymnasion, 1960; P. Gauthier, Notes sur le rôle du gymnasion dans les cités helléniques, in: M. Wörrle, P. Zanker (ed.), Stadtbild und Bürgerbild im Hell., Congr. München 1993, 1995, 1–11; S.L. Glass, Palaistra and G. in Greek Architecture, 1981; Id., The Greek G. Some Problems, in: The Archaeology of the Olympics, Congr. Los Angeles 1984, 1988, 155–173; H.v. Hesberg, Das griech. G. im 2. Jh. v.Chr., in: M. Wörrle, P. Zanker (ed.), Stadtbild und Bürgerbild im Hell., Congr. München 1993, 1995, 13–27; H. Lauter, Die Architektur des Hell., 1986, 132–148; M. Maass, Das ant. Delphi, 1993, 62–67; A. Mallwitz, Olympia und seine Bauten, 1972, 268–289; W. Martini, Das G. von Samos (Samos 16), 1984; W. Müller-Wiener, Griech. Bauwesen in der Ant., 1988, 166–170; W. Radt, Pergamon, 1988, 131–146; P. Schazmann, Altertümer von Pergamon VI, Das G., 1923; Travlos, Athen, 42–51, 340f., 345–347; Ch. Wacker, Das G. in Olympia. Gesch. und Funktion, 1996; W. Zschietzschmann, Wettkampfund Übungsstätten in Griechenland, vol.2: Palästra-Gymnasium, 1961.

C.HÖ.

II. The Hellenistic Gymnasium

A. General B. Special cases C. The significance for the cults D. The gymnasium as the headquarters for clubs E. Historical development F. Cultural effects of the gymnasium on the peoples ruled

A. General

The Greek gymnasium was used in the classical period particularly for physical fitness and pre-military exercises (→ Ephebeia). Testimonials that could provide information beyond that (→ School) [3. 1–16] are few and far between. It was only in the Hellenistic period that the gymnasium increasingly developed into a teaching institution that also taught skills in music (playing an instrument and singing) and basic literary knowledge but did not provide instruction in the mathematical subjects like geometry, astronomy and arithmetic [1; 2; 3]. The cycle of the 'Seven free arts' (grammar, rhetoric, dialectics, geometry, arithmetic, astronomy, theoretical music) that originated in Neoplatonism provided the basics of general youth instruction neither in the Hellenistic nor in the Imperial period [1; 2]. It is inappropriate to describe the gymnasia as universities [4. 316] and so to attribute to them indiscriminately a high educational level; this can at best only be accurate for Athens that occupies a special position. The Greek towns of the Oekumene had no uniform educational system. Each town looked after the education of the youth of the freeborn and only supplied education for these according to their financial assets [3. 40, 42, 60]. Frequently the gymnasia owed their foundation and maintenance to private endowments (cf. e.g. the endowment deed of Coressus on Ceos: Syll.[3] 958; the boys' school endowments of Polythrus in Teos: Syll.[3] 578) were however always administered publicly by the town. The teachers like the gymnasiarchs were selected by the public assembly annually for one year. The educational level depended on the duration and quality of the instruction imparted at the gymnasium. Many towns could afford to set up separate gymnasia for boys (*paîdes*, παῖδες), young people (ephebes [*éphēboi*, ἔφηβοι]: boys before the onset of puberty, i.e. from about 15 to 18 years of age) and for young men (*néoi*, νέοι = 18 to 19 year olds) [cf. 3. 34–42], and the period of instruction that was therefore about eight years must have been very successful. Poorer towns could generally only maintain one gymnasium, the one for the ephebes and sometimes none at all (Paus. 10,4,1). In these cases reading and writing had to be learnt privately [3. 28, 40, 42]; for Egypt [5. 17f.]. The short period of public instruction of about 3 years could in itself not achieve a high level of education. In every Greek town, however small, private instruction was available for affluent people from wandering teachers who were occasionally also invited to hold guest lectures at the gymnasium [3. 50–51; 1. 304] that could also be visited by outsiders. In many towns there arose from the 2nd cent. BC onwards additional private institutions that were often of a high level and that gave instruction in grammar (= Greek literature) and rhetoric. In the towns in which a philosopher had established himself knowledge could also be acquired within the framework of this instruction in the mathematical sciences that otherwise only belonged to vocational training e.g. of architects and geometers [1. 41–44].

B. Special cases

In Egypt, as opposed to the already mentioned classification by age groups, the ephebes commenced at the gymnasium one year earlier – previously the instruction was private –, which was connected with the special tax conditions in this country [3. 90f.]. In addition this instruction (probably only sports instruction) in the gymnasium appears to have only lasted one year [3. 91].

In Athens, the ephebes institution was, as an exception, for young men between 18 and 19 years of age and this sole municipally organized instruction lasted only one year [3. 34]. The principal of this institution was also not called *gymnasíarchos* (γυμνασίαρχος) as in most Greek towns but *kosmētḗs* (κοσμητής) (4th cent. BC: IG II 478; 3rd cent. BC: IG II 1350–1352; 2nd cent. BC: IG II[2] 900; 930; 991; 1006; 1008; 1027 etc.; 1st cent. BC: IG II[2] 1028–1030; 1039–1043 etc.). The teaching programme was demanding befitting the age of the young men. They listened to lectures in philosophy, grammar and rhetoric. This institution enjoyed a high status and the sons of rich parents came from far afield to be accepted by it ([3. 26]; cf. IG II 1[2] 1028 (100/99 BC) and IG II[2] 2097 (169/70)), which confirms the role of Athens as a Greek cultural centre.

The gymnasium in Teos, the seat of the Dionysian → Technites had a special position; this is because the winners' lists from there (CIG II 3088) mention, among other things, teaching subjects (Rhythmography, Melography, Comedy, Tragedy) that were not offered anywhere else and were probably targeted especially at training to become an actor.

C. The significance for the cults

The gymnasium was also a cult centre. The god of science, Hermes, as well as Hercules, and frequently often the Muses, were venerated in the gymnasium as protective gods and had altars there [4. 453ff.]. The → hero cult too played a really important part in the gymnasium. In the gymnasium founders and outstanding students and others were buried who therefore had the status of heroes and were accorded appropriate cult worship [3. 64–71; 4. 448–449]. To an increasing extent the gymnasium was also however decorated, especially from the end of the Roman Republic, with secular statues of gods as pure artworks (*ornamenta* γυμνασιώδη, cf. Cic. Att. 1,6). The young people of the school were regularly brought in for municipal festivals of the gods and cults of the rulers; the youth provided the choirs that sang the hymns, the prerequisite for which was musical training [6. 115, 214–216, 380–382]. The young people also had to take part in the numerous processions [3. 67–71] and so were heavily involved in public life. Competitions and the winners' honours connected with them likewise played a very big part in the gymnasium. The Hellenistic gymnasium had no examinations but instead held competitions (before an audience) in all teaching subjects: military exercises, endurance running, stadium running, double running, wrestling, boxing, all-round fighting (Pancratium), zither playing, singing, reading, recitation of epic poems. There were also prizes for good conduct. The names of the winners were put up publicly by the town clerk or were even recorded in inscriptions (Syll.[3] 958, especially 40f.). Most of the information about the running of the school comes from the winners' lists that are unfortunately preserved in very few inscriptions (from Coressus on Cos, 3rd cent. BC: Syll.[3] 958; from Chios: Syll.[3] 959 etc.) and the decrees of honour for the principal of the gymnasium, mostly called the gymnasiarch (occasionally called ephebarch/ἐφήβαρχος or cosmet). The gymnasiarch had, aside from the supervision of the educational enterprise, also to provide a large part of the operating costs. We also have information about paedonomes (παιδονόμοι) who had charge of the boys' schools wherever necessary.

D. THE GYMNASIUM AS THE HEADQUARTERS FOR CLUBS

Student clubs too, which were modelled on those of the adults, had their headquarters at the gymnasium. They made decisions on honours for teachers of particularly outstanding merit or other personalities or endeavoured to uphold the memory of dead comrades; the latter can be regarded as part of the cult of the hero [3. 75–78].

E. HISTORICAL DEVELOPMENT

Gradually, especially under Roman rule, the gymnasium lost its role as an educational centre. The daily physical exercises became unfashionable: the Romans rejected naked sports, the paedophiles connected with them (cf. Cic. Rep. 4,4,4; Tusc. 4,70), and musical instruction [2]; and even among most foreign peoples (Egyptians, Syrians) sport did not enjoy high status. Gymnasia became → thermal baths. Professional sport, which was establishing itself more and more, also contributed to this. Public instruction (elementary instruction, instruction in grammar, rhetoric and – very rarely – philosophy) was organized in the Imperial period (the first signs are already to be found in the 1st cent. BC) by the individual towns independently of the gymnasium. This development was completed at the beginning of the 2nd cent. AD [1. 215–261].

F. CULTURAL EFFECTS OF THE GYMNASIUM ON THE PEOPLES RULED

The Hellenistic gymnasium played a large cultural part especially in the areas conquered by Alexander [4] and ruled after him by his Macedonian generals and their successors (from Asia Minor to Bactria and Persia, Mesopotamia and Egypt). The towns established or conquered by the Seleucids and the Lagidae became centres of Greek culture, with the gymnasium becoming the symbol and preserver of national identity. The Greeks were known to be not interested in the language and culture of the peoples ruled by them – in the gymnasium neither the language nor the history of the subjugated people was taught even to a small extent; it was up to the subjects to come closer to them and the language of administration was Greek. It is debatable whether and to what extent the Greek gymnasium was open at least to the 'cultural Greeks' although the question should probably by and large be answered in the negative. Occasional admissions of foreigners to Greek gymnasia, like the rare participation of non-Greeks in the Panhellenic Games, should probably be explained by the fact that the cultural Greeks or whole towns in question had endeavoured to provide proof of their Greekness on the basis of Greek mythology. Rome, for example, traced its origin to Troy (Aeneas), and the Phoenician town of Sidon to Argus [7]. The leading citizens of those towns that had also demonstrably assimilated with Greek culture were then no longer considered by the Greeks to be foreigners.

The → Hellenization of the upper class of foreign peoples occurred with differing levels of success. The Phoenician coastal towns like Aradus, Tyrus, Sidon and Byblus that had already for a long time maintained trading links with the Greeks and under Greek rule had not been renamed were probably Hellenized the most quickly and the most completely even if they always remained conscious of their own culture there [8]. Probably some Phoenician cities had also been accorded the right to establish and maintain gymnasia according to the Greek model (with Greek language and Greek literature). A bilingual, Phoenician-Greek inscription (IGLS VII, no. 4001) from 25/24 BC suggests this. Its client is a Phoenician who calls himself a gymnasiarch, and the protective gods typical of the Greek gymnasium, Hermes and Hercules/Melqart, are mentioned. The Aramaic-speaking Syrians too had been accorded similar rights by the Seleucid kings [9. 64]; this is also referred to in the critical remark (Ath. 5,210f) by the Stoic philosopher from Apamea, Posidonius (*c.* 151–35 BC), that the Syrians mainly used the gymnasia for bathing, oiling themselves, perfuming themselves and holding banquets there, as if the gymnasia were private houses. It is hard to imagine that the Greeks would have tolerated such abuse of their own gymnasia. If we believe the 2nd Book of the Maccabees (4,9ff.) (which is the case for the most part), a faction of Hellenized Jews under their high priest Joshua, who typically changed his name to Jason, won the right in 175/174 BC from the Seleucid king Antiochus IV to change Jerusalem to a Greek polis with the name Antiochia, to dedicate the temple (the centre of ancient Judaism) to Zeus Olympius and to set up a gymnasium (different in [10.103f.]). The fact that the Bible had to be translated into Greek (Septuaginta) is further evidence that the Jews of the diaspora were to a large extent Hellenized and could no longer read Hebrew. In Egypt, Hellenization does not appear to have been as universal, which can probably be attributed, among other things, to the fact that this country had for a long time not been as 'urbanized' as Asia Minor and Syria. In most cases we cannot determine the extent to which the numerous papyrus finds and shard finds there that contain, among other things, Greek grammar exercises and writing exercises should be attributed to instruction at Greek gymnasia or to private teaching [5].

The Greek gymnasium therefore had – in the areas in which the people were Greek subjects – no direct influence on the Hellenization process that would have involved its teaching being open to as many indigenous people as possible (the opposite was the case); rather the influence was indirect in that its teaching subjects were emulated widely in the striving for social advancement among the foreign peoples in the private sphere and in the gymnasia for non-Greeks.

→ Hellenization

1 I. HADOT, Arts libéraux et philosophie dans la pensée antique, 1984 2 Id., Geschichte der Bildung. Artes liberales, in: F. GRAF (ed.), Einleitung in die lat. Philol., 1997

3 M.P. NILSSON, Die hell. Schule, 1955 4 J. DELORME, Gymnasion. Étude sur les monuments consacrés à l'éducation en Grèce, 1960 5 R. CRIBOIRE, Teachers and Students in Graeco-Roman Egypt, 1996 6 L. ROBERT, J. ROBERT, La Carie, vol. 2, 1954 7 E. BIKERMANN, Sur une inscription grecque de Sidon, in: Mélanges Syriens offerts à R. Dussaud, 1939, 91–99 8 F. MILLAR, The Phoenician Cities. A Case-Study of Hellenisation, in: PCPhS 209, 1983, 55–71 9 A. MEHL, Erziehung zum Hellenen – Erziehung zum Weltbürger, in: Nikephoros 5, 1992, 43–73 10 A. MOMIGLIANO, Sagesses barbares. Les limites de l'hellénisation, 1980 (controversial). I.H.

Gymnastics see → Sports

Gymnetes (γυμνῆτες; *Gymnêtes*). Lightly-armed men. Pollux (3,83) describes the lower-ranking people in Argus as *gymnetes* and compares them with the → helots in Sparta, the → penestae in Thessaly and the → korynephoroi in Sicyon. However in Argus (as in Sicyon) they tended to be dependents rather than slaves, and Stephanus of Byzantium (s.v. χίος) probably describes them correctly as *gymnḗsioi*. The error of Pollux should perhaps be explained by the fact that the helots often fought as lightly-armed soldiers (*psíloi*, Hdt. 9,29), for whom the Greeks used the term *gymnetes*. The *gymnetes* and *gymnomáchoi* are mentioned for the first time in Tyrtaeus (fr. 11,35–8; P.Oxy. 3316,14); they were probably poorer Spartans who stood behind the protective shields of the → hoplites. In the battle of Plataeae (479 BC) the helots were the lightly-armed troops of Sparta who were said to have been 35,000 strong (Hdt. 9,29). The *gymnetes* fought on both sides in the battle of Delium in 424 BC (Thuc. 4,90,4; 4,93,3); at that time they were placed with the cavalry on the flanks. In all these cases, the deployment of the *gymnetes* was only of secondary importance, probably for political and social reasons. Only in Syracuse did the lightly-armed infantry (ἡ γυμνητεία, *gymnēteía*; Thuc. 7,37,2) play an important part under the leadership of the Spartan Gylippus in 414 BC, perhaps as a consequence of the special situation of the siege of the city by the Athenians or because of the democratic system. The *gymnetes* are also attested for the early years of the → Corinthian War (Xen. Hell. 4,2,14); among the lightly-armed troops, the → peltasts, initially under the command of Iphicrates, certainly soon became more important (Xen. Hell. 4,5,13–17; Nep. 11). When war was waged in the Hellenistic period, the deployment of lightly-armed mercenaries was favoured because of political as well as strategic and economic factors.

1 P. CARTLEDGE, Hopliten und Helden: Spartas Beitrag zur Technik der ant. Kriegskunst, in: K. CHRIST (ed.), Sparta, 1986, 387–425, 470 2 O. LIPPELT, Die griech. Leichtbewaffneten bis auf Alexander den Großen, 1910 3 D. LOTZE, Μεταξὺ Ἐλευθέρων καὶ Δούλων, 1959 4 L. THOMMEN, Lakedaimonion Politeia, 1996. P.C.

Gymnias (Γυμνιάς; *Gymniás*, Xen. An. 4,7,19). Large, heavily populated and affluent town of the *Skythēnoí* on the left bank of the Harpasus (modern Çoruh su), at the location of or near modern Bayburt.

O. LENDLE, Kommentar zu Xenophons Anabasis, 1995, 270–272. A.P.-L.

Gymnosophists (Γυμνοσοφισταί; *Gymnosophistaí*). Literally: 'the naked wise men'; the word appears for the first time in the papyrus Berol. 13044 (1st cent. BC) to describe the ten Indian wise men with whom Alexander the Great is said to have held a conversation that was most certainly legendary [3] [1]. The first nine of these wise men each had to answer a question posed by Alexander that was of a scientific or metaphysical nature, whilst the tenth wise man had to assess the value of these responses. (Plut. Alexander 64; 65,1; Clem. Al. Strom. 6,4,38; Ps.-Callisthenes 3,5–7 KROLL). According to several biographies about Alexander from the Imperial period, Greek wise men had already previously gone for instruction to the gymnosophists – namely Lycurgus, Pythagoras, Democritus, Socrates and Plato; also philosophers from the later period, particularly Pyrrho and Plotin, are said to have wanted to establish contact with the gymnosophists.

The lifestyle of the gymnosophists is distinguished, according to the sources mentioned, by a reverence for nature and a rejection of the achievements of civilization. The teaching of the gymnosophists is all the more difficult to summarize because it is accessible to us only via the circuitous route of Greek philosophy – especially cynic philosophy – that may have acted as a filter here [3]. In numerous texts from the Roman period the Indian gymnosophists appear only as a model of courage and piety (Phil. De Abrahamo 1,82; Proclus in Tim. 1,208 DIEHL) or as examples of a simple life close to nature (Phil. De Somniis 2,56). In the stereotypical records of the barbarian wise men or in the discussions about the Greek or foreign origin of the philosophy, only the bare name 'gymnosophist' (Diog. Laert. 1,1 and 6; Clem. Al. Strom. 6,7,57) appears. The Ethiopian gymnosophists appear more rarely in the sources than the Indian gymnosophists. In the *Aithiopiká* of Helodorus, the gymnosophists appear as a caste of wise priests. In Philostr. VA 6 they are represented as less talented doubles of the Indian Brahmans [4].

1 U. WILCKEN, Alexander der Große und die indischen Gymnosophisten, in: SPrAW 1923, philol.-histor. Klasse, 150–183 2 H. VAN THIEL, Alexanders Gespräch mit den Gymnosophisten, in: Hermes 100, 1972, 343–358 3 C. MUCKENSTURM, Les Gymnosophistes étaient-ils des cyniques modèles?, in: Id., Le cynisme ancien et ses prolongements, 1993, 225–239 4 P. ROBIANO, Les gymnosophistes éthiopiens chez Philostrate et chez Héliodore, in: REA 94, 1992, 3–4, 413–428. C.M.-P.

Gynaecocracy (γυναικοκρατία; *gynaikokratía*). The term gynaecocracy ('Rule of women', from Greek γυνή/ *gyné*, 'woman' and κρατεῖν/*kratein*, 'to rule'; cf. *gynaikokrateísthai*, 'to be ruled by women') is first attested in philosophical texts from the 4th cent. BC. The use is almost always polemical. In Aristotle the gynaecocracy becomes a theme in the context of criticism of the *politeía* (constitution) of the Spartans and was considered as the prerequisite for greed and an extremely unequal distribution of land (Aristot. Pol. 1269b 12–1270a 31; cf. also Plut. Lycurgus 14,1). For Aristotle there is no difference between women ruling themselves or the leading politicians being ruled by women (καίτοι τί διαφέρει γυναῖκας ἄρχειν ἢ τοὺς ἄρχοντας ὑπὸ τῶν γυναικῶν ἄρχεσθαι: Pol. 1269b 23–34); in the section about the tyrants he speaks of the gynaecocracy inside the home that is also typical of a perfected democracy (Pol. 1313b 32–35). The topos of the man ruled by his wife is said to go back to a saying of Themistocles; later Cato is said to have expressed something similar (Plut. Themistocles 18; Cato maior 8,2–3); in late antiquity the term gynaecocracy appears in the critical remarks of Procopius about Belisarius (Procop. Arc. 5,26). Gynaecocracy was also a theme of comedy; a comedy by Amphis bore the title ' Gynaecocracy' (Ath. 336c). In Aristophane (*Lysistrate*, *Ekklesiazusai*, late 5th/early 4th cent. BC) the way in which women attempt to exercise political power is also depicted (cf. especially Eccl. 105–109), and in this manner the roles of the sexes and their reversal are problematized. According to a late version of the tale of the quarrel between Athena and Poseidon that is attributed to Varro, women took part in early Athens in ballots and children bore the names of their mothers (Aug. Civ. 18,9). The pupil of Aristotle, Clearchus, reports with regard to the Lydians that → Omphale had succeeded as a woman in establishing tyrannical rule over effeminate men who increasingly behaved like women (Ath. 515d–516a). There were also tales of foreign peoples, mostly living in the marginal zones of the known world, where the women ruled over the men or at least had as much power as they did (Hdt. 4,26,2 about the Issedones). The idea that the peoples of the east were ruled by women is also encountered in the literature of late antiquity (S HA Tyr. Trig. 30,1; Claudianus, in Eutropium 1,321–323).

Apart from such notions of the rule of women in the early period or amongst far-away peoples, there are also references in Greek literature to matrilineal family structures. In this way Herodotus notes that among the Lydians there was a custom of deriving origin from the mother and the female ancestors; the legal status of a child therefore depended on that of the mother, not that of the father (Hdt. 1,173,4–5; cf. Plut. Mor. 248d). In the same way attention was paid to the fact that the emphasis amongst aristocratic families in the lower Italian Locri Epizephyrii was on origin being derived from women Pol. 12,5–6).

→ Amazons; → Woman; → Gender roles;→ MATRIARCHY

A.S. BRADFORD, Gynaikokratoumenoi: Did Spartan Women Rule Spartan Men?, in: Ancient World 14, 1986, 13–18; M.H. DETTENHOFER, Die Frauen von Sparta. Ökonomische Kompetenz und polit. Relevanz, in: Id. (ed.), Reine Männersache? Frauen in Männerdomänen der ant. Welt, 1994, 15–40; B.WAGNER-HASEL (ed.), Matriarchatstheorien der Altertumswissenschaft, 1992.

H.SCHN.

Gynaecology

A. SPECIALIZED FIELD IN THE HIPPOCRATIC SCHOOL B. TREATMENT METHODS C. FERTILITY AND PREGNANCY D. TREND IN GYNAECOLOGICAL THEORIES FROM HEROPHILUS

A. SPECIALIZED FIELD IN THE HIPPOCRATIC SCHOOL

The question whether gynaecology should be regarded as a field of medical specialization was a matter of controversy in antiquity. This debate whose rudiments can be reconstructed and can be traced back to Hesiod who programmatically represents the descendants of → Pandora, the first woman, as their own 'race' (γένος γυναικῶν; Theog. 585–590). *Gynaikeía* (which can be used to describe the female sex organs, menstruation as well as the treatment of women's diseases) is the Greek title of the two long texts from the Corpus Hippocraticum that are concerned exclusively with women's diseases (Hippoc. *De mulierum affectibus* 1 and 2 = Mul.; re the abbreviations of the titles of the work, Corpus Hippocraticum, see → Hippocrates). In Mul. 1,62 (8,126 L.) a warning is issued that sick women should be treated like men; the author assures us rather that the healing of women's diseases is significantly different from that of men's diseases and this is the first actual justification, according to [1. 154], for Greek gynaecology. The Corpus Hippocraticum also contains a treatise on the problem of infertility (*De sterilibus*), a divergent edition of material from Mul. 1 and 2 (*De natura muliebri*), texts on conception and the growth of the foetus (*De genitura*, *De natura pueri*), a discussion on the risks of premature birth (*De octimestri partu* = Oct.), the description of the removal of a dead foetus from the womb (*De exsectione foetus*) as well as a short treatise on the diseases of young girls (*De virginum morbis*). All these treatises show that women are different from men to such an extent that a medical approach specific to them is justified; certainly it also states in texts like Oct. that the same prognostic and therapeutic principles that relate to the disease, health and death of all people, e.g. the theory of the 'Critical days' according to which certain days during a phase are particularly decisive, are just as applicable to conception, miscarriage and birth in women (Oct. 9 = 7,446 L.).

What then makes the nature of a woman different? The Hippocratic writings refer in answering this question by no means only to the function of the bearing of children and the organs necessary for this but see the most important criterion of difference as being the texture of the flesh of the body. Women are moist and flabby whilst the flesh of a man, on the other hand, is dryer and more solid. To illustrate this principal difference, a comparison was made between female flesh and wool on the one hand, and male flesh and densely woven clothing on the other hand (Mul. 1,1 = 8,10–14 L.; Gland. 16 = 8,572 L.); the idea behind this is that the woman is the raw material and the man the finished product made in an artisan manufacturing process. Because of the looser texture of the flesh of women, they drew from their food more liquid, the accumulated excess of which they had to expel again with the help of menstruation. If menstruation fails to occur, the excess blood continues to rise in the body and puts pressure on various organs until the woman dies. According to this model, it is even conceivable that the heat arising from the constant accumulation of menstrual blood leads to a change of sex before the onset of death; in a tale of illness in the Hippocratic books *Epidemiarum* (= Epid.), it is said that Phaethusa of Abdera's periods stopped after the departure of her husband and that she then grew hair on her body and developed a deep voice (Epid. 6,8,32 = 5,356 L.).

Stories of sick female patients are to be found in all seven books of *Epidemiarum*, whilst other Hippocratic writings that deal with illness in general devote an individual chapter to women's diseases (e.g. Aph. 5, Coac. 503–544 = 5,700–708 L. and the last part of Loc. Hom.). Whilst in Mul. 1 and 2 the failure of menstruation to occur is considered to be the main cause of a whole series of symptoms of disease in women, the movements of the womb are held responsible in Loc. Hom. 47 (6,344 L.) in particular for women's illnesses. Here a movement forward is considered to be particularly serious, not just because of the pain produced by this but also because it blocks the menstrual flow; an upward movement can draw organs of the body up to the head in sympathy. The uterus was presented as jug-shaped and this is how it was pictorially represented in the Mustio manuscript form the 9th cent.

Excessive or untimely menstrual flow was likewise considered unhealthy (Aph. 5.57 = 4,552 L.). As it was assumed that there were links between the uterus and the female breasts (Gland. 16 = 8,572 L.), so that mother's milk could be described as 'the sister of menstruation' (Epid. 2,3,17 = 3,118 L.), an attempt was made to bring heavy menstrual bleeding to a standstill by placing cupping glasses on the chest (Aph. 5.50 = 4,550 L.). Aristotle, according to whom women were 'cold' and men were 'hot', developed this line of argument further; he maintained that menstrual blood, mother's milk and semen were refining products of a single substance that followed one upon the other, whereby only the male part of a species had enough heat to be able to create the end stage of the transformation process, i.e. the sperm (e.g. Aristot. Part. an. 650a8ff.; Gen. an. 774a1).

The field of the medical care of women awakened interest among the most varied of practitioners. In Hippocratic texts a 'Healing woman' (ἡ ἰητρεύουσα, Mul. 1,68 = 8,144 L.) and 'Female healers' (αἱ ἀκεστρίδες, Carn. 19 = 8,614 L.) are mentioned as midwives but in all probability they – aside from providing midwifery services at the side of Hippocratic doctors – also independently assisted women with health problems. Women could also take advice from family members or people in the neighbourhood or go to a temple in search of healing. In view of the remedies passed down to us in the Corpus Hippocraticum, it was assumed that they bore testimony to an oral healing tradition nurtured amongst women (→ Woman; Birth).

B. Treatment methods

The treatment of women's illnesses mainly consisted of influencing the intensity of the blood production through dietary measures, removing retained blood or moving the womb back from an unsuitable place – for instance the liver, to which it had wandered in search of additional moisture. As a rule, people decided on a combination of measures. A fluid-withdrawing diet was prescribed for women with mucous-containing menstrual bleeding, as well as steam baths, vomitives and purifying uterine inserts (Mul. 1,11 = 8,44–46 L.). The Hippocratic gynaecology had a whole range of pharmacological substances, among these being substances like sulphur, asphalt, squill and laurel as well as animal excrement that were all used in cleansing rituals (→ Purification) [2]. To fragrant substances e.g. myrrh were attributed warming properties (they draw, for instance, retained blood from the body), and they were administered with the aid of hot poultices, steam baths and tampons. In a procedure known as aromatic substance burning, steam was fed through the cervix into the uterus to open it and, in case it had moved on further, to bring it back to its usual anatomical location, or to drive out substances that – like retained menstrual blood – caused illnesses. The womb could be enticed downwards through sweet fragrances rising in the vagina, whereby unpleasant odours inhaled via the nose further assisted with the descent (e.g. Mul. 2,123 = 8,266 L.; 2,154 = 8,330 L.); in the case of prolapse of the uterus, the fragrant substances effective via the nose and vagina were reversed (e.g. Mul. 2,125 = 8,268 L.). Vomiting or sneezing could likewise serve to give a push to the uterus (Mul. 2,142 = 8,314 L.); cf. also → Hysteria.

The upper and lower part of the female body were explicitly related to each other, not just in the terminology which is still mirrored in our current language usage (cf. 'Uterine neck' and 'Pudendal lip'), but also from a theoretical point of view; Ps.-Aristotle maintained that the womb also 'breathed' the sperm 'in', just as the mouth and nose breathe in substances, and the region of the vulva right through to the inside of the womb resembled the area between the nostrils and the larynx (Steril. 643b 35; 636b 17–18; 637a 21–35). The conviction amongst Greek and Roman authors too that the loss of virginity could be detected by the development of a deeper voice in a girl can also be traced back to this idea [3].

C. Fertility and pregnancy

The potential fertility of a woman was tested with the aid of fragrant substances, the idea being to find out whether the fragrances could spread out freely in the body (Aph. 5,59 = 4,554 L.). An obstacle to birth was considered to be an extremely dense, hot, cold, dry or moist womb (Aph. 5,62 = 4,554 L.), as sperm could not survive in such an environment. Obesity – thought to constrict the opening of the uterus and block the entry of the male sperm – was considered a further obstacle to birth (Aph. 5,46 = 4,548 L.). According to Aristotle, obese women did not menstruate because all the excess blood was consumed by the body (Aristot. Gen. an. 746b27–29). Absence of menstruation in conjunction with nausea was known to be a symptom of pregnancy (Aph. 5,61 = 4,554 L.), which was confirmed by prescribing hydromel; if the woman then developed intestinal gripes, it was certain that she was expecting a child (Aph. 5,41 = 4,546 L.). People believed that the opening of the uterus closed during pregnancy (Aph. 5,51 = 4,550 L.). A conclusion about the → sex of the unborn child could be drawn from the facial colouring of the mother: paleness indicated that the child would be a girl (Aph. 5,42 = 4,546 L. and Steril. 216 = 8,416 L.).

D. Trend in gynaecological theories from Herophilus

In the context of Alexandrian anatomy that is associated particularly with the name → Herophilus, women tended to be viewed as 'topsy-turvy' men rather than their own 'breed'. The reproductive organs that were outside in the man were analogously inside the female body. Herophilus discovered the ovaries (fr. 61 von Staden), even if their function remained a mystery to him. A branch of ancient gynaecology describes the woman as a receptacle in which the male semen could ascend, whilst other texts assume that men like women contribute sperm to produce the foetus (e.g. *De genitura*, *De natura pueri*). Although Herophilus had seen the fallopian tubes, he did not however know their function and believed that they ran to the bladder; apparently → Galenus discovered for the first time that they are inserted in the womb (De uteri diss. 9 = CMG 5,2,1,48). Herophilus described the retaining ligaments of the womb that allowed the enormous mobility of the womb, as advocated by Hippocratic gynaecology, to become a technical impossibility (fr. 114 von Staden); the theory of the 'Wandering womb' was however only reformulated in the sense of a theory of sympathy between the upper and lower body regions, according to which the latter could cause symptoms in the former. With regard to therapy, hardly any innovations arose from the anatomical progress in Alexandria; the fact that Hippocratic prescriptions for women's illnesses continued to be passed down, even if, depending on availability, there were slight changes with regard to the components, is proven by papyri. The fragrance therapy of the 'Wandering womb' was now interpreted differently by some authors; Celsus, for example, who realized that the uterus is attached to the iliac bones (5,1,12), thought that the significance of the fragrance theory lay in waking up an unconscious female patient (4,27,1).

→ Soranus posed the question whether women experience conditions that are reserved exclusively for their gender (Gyn. 3,1), and summarized the positions of his predecessors with regard to this question: authors like Diocles [6] of Carystus (fr. 169 Wellmann), who was active in the 4th cent. BC, and the school of the Empiricists had believed that there were physical conditions specific to women whilst Erasistratus and Herophilus in the 3rd cent. BC as well as the school of the Methodists rejected this thesis. The Methodists believed rather that as men and women consisted of the same substance and reacted in accordance with the same rules, all diseases too were determined by the same natural laws. Soranus himself maintained that the womb consisted of the same material as the rest of the body, even if it was women-specific and fulfilled its own functions; although some conditions were therefore specific to women like pregnancy and lactation, their illnesses did not differ fundamentally from those of men. → Aretaeus supported a similar point of view (2,11 = CMG 2,34) although he conceded that the mobility of the womb led to certain health disorders like hysterical choking attacks, prolapse of the uterus and discharge that women did not share with men.

Galenic gynaecology (→ Galenus) is distinguished from Hippocratic gynaecology in that it is now no longer considered to be the menstrual blood but the 'Female semen' that is the fluid whose retention represents the greatest danger to the body (Loc. Aff. 6,5 = 8,420–424, 432 K.). Whilst the Hippocratics regarded the sedentary lifestyle and the moist and flabby nature of the woman as factors contributing to blood containment and in this way to menstruation, Galenus was of the opinion that a change in lifestyle in combination with climatic influences could theoretically reverse male-female norms: in De caus. puls. 3,2 (9,109–110 K.) we read that the pulse of a warm-dry woman living in Egypt and working in the open air was stronger than that of a cold-moist man living an inactive life in Pontus.

In the Greek east the gynaecological thought of Soranus survived because it was adopted and adapted in the work of the encyclopaedists Oribasius, Aetius [3] and Paulus of Aegina. An independent Greek text, the book of the → Metrodora, is extant in a MS from the 9th cent. In the Latin west in the late 4th and early 5th cent. Caelius [II 11] Aurelianus based his work on that of Soranus. A dialogue recorded in the *Liber ad Soteris* between Soranus and a midwife was also passed down, possibly as a catechism for obstetrics. In the west the focus appears to have been on practical instruction in the art of healing rather than on medical theory [4].

→ Woman; → Birth; → Gender roles; → Hippocrates (with → abbreviation list of the titles of the works)

1 P. Manuli, Donne mascoline, femmine sterili, vergini perpetue, in: S. Campese, P. Manuli, G. Sissa (ed.), Madre Materia, 1983, 147–192 2 H. von Staden, Women and dirt, in: Helios 19, 1990, 7–30 3 A. E. Hanson, D. Armstrong, Vox virginis, in: BICS 33, 1986, 97–100 4 A. E. Hanson, M. H. Green, Soranus of Ephesus: Methodicorum Princeps, in: ANRW II 37.2, 1994, 1042–1061.

L. A. Dean-Jones, Women's Bodies in Classical Greek Science, 1994; N. Demand, Birth, Death, and Motherhood in Classical Greece, 1994; P. Diepgen, Die Frauenheilkunde der alten Welt, 1937; D. Gourevitch, Le mal d'être femme, 1984; H. Grensemann, Hippokratische Gynäkologie, 1982; A. E. Hanson, Hippocrates: Diseases of Women I, in: Signs 1, 1975, 567–584; G. E. R. Lloyd, Science, Folklore and Ideology, 1983; A. Rousselle, Images médicales du corps. Observation féminine et idéologie masculine: le corps de la femme d'après les médecins grecs, in: Annales: économies, sociétés, civilisations 35, 1980, 1089–1115; H. von Staden, Apud nos foediora verba: Celsus' Reluctant Construction of the Female Body, in: G. Sabbah (ed.), Le Latin médical, 1991, 271–296. H.K.

Gynaikonitis (γυναικωνῖτις; *gynaikōnîtis*). In contrast to the → *andrṓn* [4], *gynaikonitis* describes the introverted women's wing in the Greek → house that as a rule was closed off in the upper floor from the rather extroverted area of the world of men and that also held the tools of economic production of the woman (weaving stool, spinning wheel etc.); the inferior position of the → woman in the patriarchal society of Greece was expressed in this hierarchization of building conditions.

W. Hoepfner, E. L. Schwandner, Haus und Stadt im klass. Griechenland, 1986, 290. C.HÖ.

Gynaikonomoi (γυναικονόμοι; *gynaikonómoi*). The officials who were responsible in various Greek towns for compliance with laws regarding the behaviour of women, especially at festivals and at funerals, were called *gynaikonomoi* ('Women's overseers'). Aristotle regarded this office as neither democratic nor oligarchical but as aristocratic (Pol. 4, 1300a4–8; 6, 1323a3–6). Actually *gynaikonomoi* are however found in states in varying ways, for instance in Thasos ([2. no. 141, 154–155]; 4th–3rd cents. BC), Gambrea (Syll.[3] 1219; 3rd cent. BC) or Sparta (IG V 1, 170; 3rd cent. AD), and even in Egypt where they apparently play a part in the registration of male citizens (PHibeh II 196; 3rd cent. BC). Philochorus mentions *gynaikonomoi* (FGrH 328 F 65) for Athens: the office had presumably been introduced by Demetrius [4] of Phalerum.

1 D. Ogden, Greek Bastardy, 1996, 352–353 (Egypt), 363–375 (general) 2 J. Pouilloux, Recherches sur l'histoire et les cultes de Thasos, vol. 1, 1954 3 C. Wehrli, Les gynéconomes, in: MH 19, 1962, 33–38. P.J.R.

Gyndes (Γύνδης; *Gýndēs*). According to Herodotus (1,189; 202; 5,52) a Mesopotamian river name. The Persian king Cyrus is said, before the capture of Babylon in 539 BC, to have diverted the water of the G. into 360 canals. Herodotus describes the → Araxes that was geographically untenable as the source area of the G. as well as describing the Persian region → Matiane. Because of the direction in which Cyrus marched, a link with the Diyālā (Babylonian *Turan/Turnat*; Latin *Tornadotus*, Plin. HN 6,132) and the canal system between Diyālā and → Tigris is the most probable.

M. Streck, s.v. G., RE 6, 2091f. K.KE.

Gypsum (γύψος; *gýpsos*, *gypsum*) is the name both for the mineral anhydrite and for the mass manufactured from it by heating until red-hot and mixable with water. Quarrying was carried out in many places, according to Theophrastus (De lapidibus 64, [1. 82]), who also provides details on the properties of gypsum, among these on Cyprus, in Phoenicia and Syria, in Thurii, Tymphaia and Perrhaebia, and according to Plutarch (Mor. 914c) also on Zacynthus. Theophr. l.c. 69 and Plin. HN 36,182 describe the process of heating until red-hot. Gypsum was used for plastering walls and ceilings and with the addition of lime and sand for the *opus albarium*, the material for cornices and profiles (Plin. HN 36,183; Vitr. De arch. 7,3–4). Stucco decorations of such kinds can still be seen today in Pompeii and Rome. Sculptures of gypsum were replacement pieces only rarely used (for the Zeus image in Megara, according to Paus. 1,40,3; for Dionysus in Creusis, according to Paus. 9,32,1) or non-durable decorations (S HA Sev. 22,3). Small sculptures too were made out of gypsum (Anecd. Bekk. 272,31; EM 530,11). Mummy portraits in Roman Egypt consisted of painted gypsum. Goldsmiths made models and casts out of it for their pieces of jewellery [2; 3. 97].

We cannot determine exactly when gypsum started to be used for casting statues (cf. Plin. HN 35,153), but at the latest it was from the late Hellenistic period. The first certain information about it mentions the casting of a statue in Kirrha for Ptolemy Soter about 300 BC (Plut. Mor. 984b). A first face mask made of gypsum of a living person is said to have been taken from Lysistratus of Sicyon, the brother of Lysippus (Plin. HN 35,153). A similar method, but with a wax cast of a gypsum form, was used for the Roman ancestor masks. For the technique, iron was protected from rust with a coating of white lead, pitch and gypsum (Plin. HN 34,150), and tailors used tymphaic gypsum instead of chalk for finishing clothes (Plin. HN 35,198). Pungent wine was made milder by adding gypsum or lime (Plin. HN 14,120; Columella 12,28,3) and amphoras, barrels and other containers were made airtight with gypsum (Columella 2,10,16; 12,10,4 and passim). Fruit was also placed in gypsum as a preservative (Theophr. l.c. 67) or grapes were for example sprinkled with it (Columella 12,44,4) and apples coated with it (Plin. HN 15,64).

→ Minerals

1 D. E. Eichholz (ed.), Theophrastus, De lapidibus, 1965
2 O. Rubensohn, Hell. Silbergerät in ant. Gipsabgüssen, 1911 3 A. Ippel, Guß- und Treibarbeit in Silber, 1937.
C.HÜ.

Gyrton(e) (Γυρτών[η]; *Gyrtṓn[ē]*). Lapithae from G. appear both in the Argonaut legend (→ Argonautae; Apoll. Rhod. 1,57) and in The *Iliad* (Hom. Il. 2,738). The town originally belonged to Perrhaebia, but in historical times was an important place of the Thessalian Pelasgiotis. In 431 BC among the Thessalian reinforcement troops for Athens there was also a contingent from G. (Thuc. 2,22). In 215 at the behest of Philip V at least 60 Gyrtonians became citizens of the neighbouring → Larisa (IG IX 2, 517). In 191 and 171 the town resisted the sieges of Antiochus [5] III and of Perseus (Liv. 36,10; 42,54). Right through to the 1st cent. BC G. from time to time positioned itself the Thessalian federal *strategos*. For the Imperial period there is no longer evidence of the town. G. was situated north-east of Larisa, in the area of the Erimon mountain range on the right bank of the Peneius. The precise location of G. is however uncertain; the allocation of the name to the modern village of Bakraina goes back to Stählin, who later doubted this himself (→ Mopsion, → Dotium).

H. Kramolisch, Die Strategen des Thessal. Bundes, 1978, 32f.; Philippson/Kirsten 1, 271 n. 1; F. Stählin, Das hellenische Thessalien, 1924, 91f.
HE.KR.

Gytheumium (Γύθ(ε)ιον; *Gýth(e)ion*). Laconian perioikoi town on the north-western coast of the innermost Laconian gulf in a relatively protected position with good communications links. In the historical period the main harbour for → Sparta (*c.* 45 km from G.), fortified, with shipyards and an artificially laid out harbour (in the Bronze Age the naval bases of the region were Las and Helus). Evidence: Scyl. 46; Xen. Hell. 1,4,11; 6,5,32; Pol. 5,19,6; Str. 8,3,12; 5,2; Ptol. 3,14,32; Paus. 3,21,6–9. Off the coast lies the island of Kranae (modern Marathonisi, connected with the mainland by a causeway), on which Paris first cohabited with Helena (Hom. Il. 3,445; Paus. 3,22,1; Steph. Byz. s.v. G.) and from which come the oldest ancient remains. After it was captured in 369 BC by the Thebans (Xen. Hell. 6,5,32), G. fell briefly into the hands of the Spartans again before 362 (Polyaenus, Strat. 2,9). The town was captured in 192 BC by Nabis, then it remained under Achaean control until 146. In Roman times G. belonged to the league of the → Eleutherolakones and experienced the period of its greatest flourishing: G. was the natural southern exit of the Eurotas Plain, and marble mining in Laconia by Rome increased the town's importance even more. From the Imperial period come most of the numerous inscriptions, the coins and most of the extensive but minor important ruins north of modern G., the most impressive being the theatre on the slopes of the Acropolis. In late antiquity G. is no longer mentioned.

W. Cavanagh et al., The Laconia Survey, in: ABSA Suppl. 27, 1996, 296f.; H. Edgerton, N. Skouphopoulos, Sonar Search at Gytheion Harbor, in: AAA 5, 1972, 202–206; E. S. Forster, Gythium and Nordwestern Coast of the Laconian Gulf, in: ABSA 13, 1906–1907, 219–237; C. Le Roy, s.v. G., PE, 369; Id., Richesse et exploitation en Laconie au Ier siècle av. J.-C., in: Ktema 3, 1978, 261–266; D. Musti, M. Torelli, Pausania. Guida della Grecia. III, 1991, 262–266.
Y.L.

H (linguistics)

A. History of writing B. Occurrence of /h/ C. Origin of /h/

A. History of writing

The eighth letter of the Greek alphabet is based on the Semitic consonant letter *ḥet*. Consequently ⟨H⟩ described the consonant phoneme/h/ in several local Greek alphabets, e.g. in ancient Attic HOPOΣ = ὅρος; from this stems also the Latin use of ⟨H⟩. In other Greek alphabets, e.g. that of Miletus (where/h-/ had disappeared), ⟨H⟩ was used for e-vowels. Occasionally ⟨H⟩ in the early period is also a symbol for the syllable /hē/ or /he/; hence in the Naxian Nicander inscription CEG I 403 [1. 124f.], in which four different uses of ⟨H⟩ are discernible. Eventually in the standard alphabet of Miletus, the use of ⟨H⟩ for /ę̄/ caught on. As this now left no letter for the/h/, a new symbol * =/h/ was created from *H⟩, which was printed as the 'spiritus asper' over vowel letters and ϱ.

B. Occurrence of/h/

In Greek /h/ occurs primarily at the beginning of words, but, although omitted in print, also at the juncture of a compound word ('interaspiration': P Oxy. 2442 fr. 105,10 παρέδρος; Latin *synhodus*); interjections like εὐάν are isolated cases. Similarly in Latin: *habēre ad-hibēre*, *hērēs ex-hērēdāre*; also interjections like *āh*, *prōh*, but also additional individual cases like *ahēnus*, *mihi*, *uehere*.

In both languages /h/ was spoken more weakly than other consonants; in → sandhi – apart from the aspiration in Greek (ἀφ' οὗ) – it had no consonant effect: *maior honos* –˘˘– (Ov. Met. 13,96). Consequently /h/ was under threat of disappearing from the outset. In Latin inscriptions it is often absent or is incorrectly present: *ostes hocidit* (CIL III 3800) = *hostis occīdit*. Ultimately the Greek and Latin /h/ was generally eliminated.

C. Origin of /h/

The /h/ in Greek words derived from Indo-European has a different origin from that in Latin. While the Latin *h* usually continues an aspirated voiced stop *gh*, Greek *h* can be traced back to *s*, *i̯*, *u̯*, *su̯* or the aspiration of a beginning *u-* (*u-* > *hu-*): ἑπτά < **septm̥*; ὅς (relative pronoun) < **i̯os*; ἕσται 'is dressed' < **u̯estai̯*; ὅς (possessive pronoun) < **su̯os*; ὕδωρ < **udōr*. On the other hand: Latin *ueh-ere* < **u̯eg̑h-*; *hostis* < **ghostis* (cf. Modern High German *be-weg-en*; *Gast*).

→ E (linguistics); → Itacism; → Psilosis

1 Heubeck.

Leumann, 173–175; LSAG, 28f., 427; Alfred Schmitt, Der Buchstabe H im Griech., 1952 (= Id., KS, 477–522); Schwyzer, Gramm., 145–147, 218–222, 303–306; ThLL 6,3, 2389–2391. B.F.

H

Habitancum Roman camp near modern Risingham (Northumberland), one of the outposts north of Hadrian's Wall in the Rede valley. Little is known about the early phases of occupation; there is no evidence that the fort was built at the same time as Hadrian's boundary wall. A camp certainly existed in the 140s; in the Severan period it was a major base for the occupation of the north. The garrison of H. was the *Cohors IIII Gallorum* in the 2nd cent. and the *cohors I Vangionum* in the 3rd cent., accompanied by a *numerus exploratorum* and a *vexillatio Raetorum Gaesatorum*. Inside the camp there is evidence of the *principia* (command headquarters) and a bathhouse [1. 235–40].

1 E. Birley, Research on Hadrian's Wall, 1961. M.TO.

Habitatio Initially means home, e.g. as the object of purchase and sale (→ *locatio conductio*; Dig. 2,14,4; 19,2,5) or a protective object of the *lex Cornelia de iniuriis* (Dig. 47,10,5,5). *Habitatio* also means the right to live, which is founded in part on legacy (→ *legatum*) (Dig. 7,8,10 pr.). The relationship of the *habitatio* to the → *usus* and the → *usus fructus* (usufruct) was doubtful. In effect (*effectu quidem*) the *habitatio legata* 'almost' (*paene*) was covered by the *usus legatus* (Papin./Ulp. Dig. 7,8,10 pr.). The Roman jurists occupied themselves with questions like: how should the legacy of a χρῆσις (→ *chresis*) be understood? Like that of an *usus* or *usus fructus habitandi causa* (home usufruct)? And for how long should a *habitatio* be granted? (a dispute of the *veteres*; P. Rutilius Rufus, Dig. 7,8,10 pr.–3 is in favour of gift for life). The *habitatio* is part of the *alimenta legata* (maintenance legacies, Dig. 34,1,6). The bequeathed *habitatio* could be the object of a settlement (→ *transactio*) (Dig. 2,15,8,1; 12,13,25). Justinian separates the *habitatio* from *usus* and *usus fructus* and decides certain questions of doubt (Inst. Just. 2,5,5; Cod. Just. 3,33,13). On conditional terms for the sale of a house Dig. 19,1,21,6, in the case of transfer of ownership Dig. 7,1,32.

Honsell/Mayer-Maly/Selb, 188; Kaser, RPR I, 454; II 306. D.SCH.

Habitus Roman cognomen in the family of the Cluentii (→ Cluentius [2]) and others. K.-L.E.

Habron (Ἅβρων; *Hábrōn*). Greek grammarian, a slave of Phrygian origin, taught (and perhaps also studied) first on Rhodes, then in Rome in the 1st half of the 1st cent. AD (Suda α 97 Adler). He was a student of the Aristarchian → Tryphon and dealt with the same topics as the former although he took another position and also criticized the teaching of Aristarchus [4] of Samothrace in regard to pronouns (cf. [1. 1520; 7. 91]). Nine quotations from his work Περὶ ἀντωνυμίας ('On the pronoun') are cited by Apollonius [11] Dyscolus (cf. Syntaxis 245,6 n. UHLIG); almost all the fragments of the script Περὶ παρωνύμων ('On noun derivations'; cf. [10]) on the other hand rely on Aelius → Herodianus. In the scholia to the *Téchnē* of → Dionysus [17] Thrax (371,7–9 and 532,33–36 HILGARD) there is a work Περὶ κτητικῶν (*On possessive pronouns*: the term had been used by Tryphon, cf. Apollonius Dyscolus GG II/1, De pronominibus 16,14–18 and [3. 192]). H. also occupied himself with dialect forms (cf. ibid. 51,9 –16), etymology and word formation. H., together with → Tryphon, appears to have had a decisive role in the systematization of Greek grammar before Apollonius Dyscolus, particularly if the *Téchnē* of Dionysius Thrax is regarded as spurious: [3; 4; 8].

1 R. BERNDT, Die Fragmente des Gramm. H., in: Berliner philologische Wochenschrift 1915, 1451–1455, 1483–1488, 1514–1520 2 J. CHRISTES, Sklaven und Freigelassene als Grammatiker und Philologen im antiken Rom, 1979, 92–93 3 V. DI BENEDETTO, Dionisio Trace e la techne a lui attribuita, in: ASNP 27, 1958, 169–210 and 28, 1959, 87–118 4 P.M. FRASER, Ptolemaic Alexandria, 1972, 475, 810 5 H. FUNAIOLI, s.v. H., RE 7, 2155–2156 6 A. HILLSCHER, Hominum Litteratorum Graecorum, 1891, 386–387 7 F.W. HOUSEHOLDER, The Syntax of Apollonius Dyscolus, 1981, 5 and passim 8 J. PINBORG, Current Trends in Linguistics 13, 1975, 115 9 A. DE VELSEN, Tryphonis ... fragmenta, 1853 (repr. 1965), 2 10 C. WENDEL, s.v. Tryphon, RE 8A, 732–733.

S.FO.

Habronichus (Ἁβρώνιχος, also Ἀβρώνιχος; *Habrṓn, Habrṓnichos*). Son of Lysicles, Athenian from the Lamptrae deme (on the form of the name [1]). He brought the news of the defeat of → Leonidas at Thermopylae (Hdt. 8,21) to the Greek fleet at Artemisium in 480 BC. In 479 he was sent to Sparta with → Aristides [1] to inform → Themistocles of the progress of the wall construction (Thuc. 1,91,3). Later H. was a candidate for → ostrakismos, his name (with demotikon) is found on several *ostraca* (ML 21).

1 A.E. RAUBITSCHEK, (H)abronichos, in: CR 70, 1956, 199–200.

DAVIES 20; TRAILL, PAA 101650.

HA.BE.

Habur (Akkadian *Ḫābūr*, Greek Χαβώρας/*Chabṓras*; not identical with Araxes [1. 43]). Largest tributary in north-eastern Syria of the → Euphrates, on the lefthand side. Fed by karst springs that come to the surface in 13 basins near Rā's al-ʿAin (Rēšʿainā). Initially the H. runs south-east to Hassaka (upper reaches), and is then diverted to the south by the Kaukab volcano (lower reaches); the mouth is close to the town of Buṣaira (Circesium). The H. catchment area ('H. triangle') drains the southern Taurus foothills (Mardin, Ṭūr ʿAbdīn). The course of the rainfed agriculture boundary south of Hassaka determines the pattern of settlement and economic use: in the H. triangle, rich settled farming is possible, while along the lower reaches, there is pasture farming with transhumance.

The upper H. has not yet been systematically researched archaeologically; the lower H. was investigated by H. KÜHNE and W. RÖLLIG in 1975 and 1977 (TAVO). The first signs of settlement date from the middle Palaeolithic Age (Moustérien) on the lower H. Isolated settlements are attested from the aceramic (8th–7th millennium BC) and ceramic Neolithic Age (*c.* 6000–4500 BC, Ḥalaf period), as well as from the Chalcolithic period (*c.* 4500–3000 BC, Ubaid and Uruk period). At the time of urbanization (3rd millennium BC), only small and medium-sized settlements were created throughout the entire river area, the large centres being situated in the steppe and in the H. triangle. The first cuneiform evidence (2nd half of the 3rd millennium) indicates the formation of a Ḫurrian kingdom of Urkiš (Tall Mūzān) and Nawar (Tall Birāk) (→ Ḫurrians). The occupation by the Akkadians occurred in the same period. In the old Babylonian period, the dependence of the territory of the lower H. on the kingdom of → Mari is attested, while the H. triangle belonged to the Old Assyrian kingdom (19th/18th cents. BC). The capital city of the kingdom of → Mittani (1550–1350 BC), Waššukanni, which has not yet been rediscovered, should perhaps be located in Tall Faḫarīya, on the upper H. In the Middle Assyrian empire (1350–932 BC), the important provincial centre of Dūr-Katlimmu was set up on the lower H., from where the steppe areas and the western part of the kingdom were controlled. While the upper H. and the central Euphrates fell into the hands of the invading → Aramaeans, the lower H. remained under Assyrian control. At the time of the Neo-Assyrian empire (932–612 BC), the H. belonged to the core of the empire's territory. In the Achaemenid empire (→ Achaemenids) and in the empire of Alexander (→ Alexander [4], with map), the region became less important. From the Seleucid period not much is known. From the 2nd cent. BC to the 2nd cent. AD, the H. area belonged to the Parthian kingdom. From the 2nd cent. on, the eastern border of the Roman empire ran along the H. The region was a bone of contention between Byzantium and the Persian Sassanids until the conquest of Syria by the Arabs (AD 632).

1 O. LENDLE, Komm. zu Xenophons Anabasis, 1995 2 TAVO, Karten B I 16, B I 17, B II 7, B II 8, B II 12, B III 7, B IV 10, B IV 13, B V 3, B V 4, B V 6, B V 7, B V 8, B V 13, B VI 5, B VII 2.

H.KÜ.

Hacoris Son of Herieus, father of Euphron (Greek for Herieus) (OGIS 94; PKöln 4,186). Commanded troops under Comanus against Anchwennefer in 187 BC, probably as the *strategos* of Hermopolites or Cynopolites. Appellation of the town of Acoris [1].

W. CLARYSSE, Hakoris, in: AncSoc 22, 1991, 235ff.

W.A.

Hadad (the name should perhaps be regarded as etymologically related to Arabic *hadda* 'break, hit', *haddat*, 'thunder'). Evidence: Jos. Ant. Iud. 9,93 (Ἄδαδος); Phil. Bybl. FGH 3, 569, 24 (Ἄδωδος); Plin. HN 37,186

(*Adadu*); Macr. Sat. 1,23,17 (*Adad*). Western Semitic name of the → weather god venerated in cult worship as Adad in Akkadian, as Tarhu(a)n(t) in cuneiform Luwian and Hittite, from the middle of the 3rd millennium in numerous local formulations (especially as Ḫadda of Ḫalab/Aleppo [1]). Iconographically he appears as a bull or in connection with bull(s) and (two) mountain(s) [2] as well as with a thunder club or axe and a two- or three-pointed thunderbolt in his hands [3]. In the rainfed-farming cultures of Mesopotamia he was experienced as a 'dike reeve of the sky', as well as a storm god with destructive power (Cod. Hammurabi 47,64–80, TUAT 1), whilst in the rainfed cultures of northern Mesopotamia, Anatolia, and Syria in particular, he was seen as the rain-bringer promoting the vegetation; in addition he united the cosmic and chthonic aspects [4].

Adad is encountered in (the onomasticons of) Māri, Ebla, Alalaḫ and Emar [5]. In → Ugarit the weather god appears in the mythological texts mainly under the title → Baal, which became firmly established as his own name. Names of Ugaritic kings as well as from the southern Syrio-Palestinian area (see the personal names in the → Amarna Letters [6]) with the divine element (*h*)*addu* show that H. was venerated there too.

In the Aramaic inscriptions of the 1st half of the 1st millennium H. plays a role at the top of local pantheons ([7]; KAI no. 214; 215,22; 216,5 and passim) and in the death cult for the deceased king (KAI no. 215 [8]).

In the Hellenistic-Roman period H. was often equated with → Zeus (Keraunios, e.g. CIG 4520) and → Jupiter Optimus Maximus. In → Baalbek the iconography (Macr. Sat. 1,23,12 and [9]) shows Jupiter → Heliopolitanus as a solarized H. In the form of Jupiter Optimus Maximus, H. reached Rome (CIL VI 117; 399). H. of Doliche as Jupiter → Dolichenus became even more widespread amongst the Roman soldiers in the Severan period [10].

1 H. Klengel, Der Wettergott von Halab, in: JCS 19, 1965, 87–93 2 K. Koch, Hazzi-Safôn-Kasion. Die Gesch. eines Berges und seiner Gottheiten, in: B. Janowski, K. Koch, G. Wilhelm (ed.), Religionsgesch. Beziehungen zwischen Kleinasien, Nordsyrien und dem AT, 1993, 171–224 3 A. Abou Assaf, Die Ikonographie des altbabylonischen Wettergottes, in: BaM 14, 1983, 43–66 4 N. Wyatt, The Relationship of the Deities Dagan and Hadad, in: Ugarit-Forschung 12, 1980, 377 5 H.B. Huffmon, Amorite Personal Names in the Mari Texts, 1965 M. Krebernik, Die Personennamen der Ebla-Texte, 1988 6 R.S. Hess, Amarna Personal Names, 1993 7 J. Tropper, Die Inschriften von Zincirli, 1993 8 H. Niehr, Zum Totenkult der Könige von Sam'ol im 9. und 8. Jh. v.Chr., in: Studi epigrafici e linguistici 11, 1994, 57–73 9 Y. Hajjar, La triade d'Héliopolis-Baalbek, 1977 10 M. Hörig, Jupiter Dolichenus, in: ANRW II.17/4, 1984, 2136–2179.

H. Gese, Die Religionen Altsyriens, 1970, 1–232; J.C. Greenfield, Aspects of Aramean Religion, in: P.D. Miller (ed.), Ancient Israelite Religion. FS Cross, 1987, 67–78; V. Haas, Gesch. der hethitischen Rel., 1994; P.W. Haider, M. Hutter, S. Kreuzer (ed.), Religionsgesch. Syriens von der Frühzeit bis zur Gegenwart, 1996; J. Teixidor, The Pagan God. Popular Religion in the Graeco-Roman Near East, 1977. M.K.

Hades (Ἅιδης; *Háidēs*). Greek term for the Underworld and its ruler. Various spellings are attested: Aides, Ais and Aedoneus in Homer, H. (aspirated) only in Attica. The etymology is unclear; the most recent proposal is that H. should be traced back to *a-wid 'invisible' [1. 575f.], cf. however [2. 302]. Outside Attica, for instance in Homer (Il. 23,244; Od. 11,623), the word can also designate the → Underworld, whose gates are guarded by the hell-hound → Cerberus (Il. 5,646; 8,368). In Homer H. is situated under the world but people also reach it if they travel to the western end of the earth, i.e. here various underworld concepts coincide [3. 60]. A river separates this 'unpleasant place' (Hom. Od. 11,94; Hes. Op. 152ff.) from the world of the living (Hom. Il. 23,70–101; Od. 11,51ff.); the figure of the ferryman → Charon is certainly only a post-Homeric invention [3. 303–361]. Without burial the dead could not enter H. (Hom. Il. 23,71ff.; Eur. Hec. 28–54).

According to Hom. Il. 5,395ff., H. is wounded by → Hercules 'in Pylus among the dead'. This dark myth is probably part of Hercules' role as 'Lord of the animals' [4. 86] and indicates that H. was already personified in the Bronze Age. In any case H. in Greece was a shadowy god who had few myths and even fewer rites; his depiction on ancient vases cannot be demonstrated with certainty [5. 389]. According to Hom. Il. 15,187–193, he receives the Underworld when he draws lots with his brothers Zeus and Poseidon; this passage can probably ultimately be traced back to the Akkadian epic → *Atrahasis* [6. 90f.]. H. does already control the Underworld in Homer, but does not appear as the judge of the dead until the post-Homeric period (Aeschyl. Suppl. 228–231; Eum. 273ff.), a role that was later transferred to Minus, Aeacus and Rhadamanthys (Pl. Ap. 41a; Pl. Grg. 523e–24a; Dem. Or. 18,127). Although this is not obvious in art [5. 367–406], his link with the Underworld makes H. 'hated' (Il. 8,368), 'irreconcilable' and 'uncompromising' (Il. 9,158); this aspect can be seen particularly in the later curse tablets [7. 53; 84; 89; 110; 134]. Often he was indirectly referred to as 'Zeus of the Underworld' (Hom. Il. 9,457), 'King of those living under the Earth' (Aeschyl. Pers. 629) or 'God of the Underworld' (Soph. Aj. 571). As death makes no exception, he was also described as *polydégmōn*, 'taking up many' (Hom. h. 2,17), *pasiánax*, 'Lord of all' [8. no. 43f.] and *hagēsílaos*, 'Leader of people' (Aeschyl. fr. 406 TrGF). He was even the epitome of death personified (Semonides 1,14 IEG; Pind. Pyth. 5,96; Nem. 10,67; I.6,15).

Paradoxically he was also regarded as a 'good and wise god' (Pl. Phd. 80d7) who sent good things up to human beings from below (Aristoph. fr. 504 PCG; Pl. Crat. 403a3–5). This belief led in the 5th cent. BC to his epithet → Pluto (Soph. fr. 273; 283 TrGF [9. 105–113], which was connected with the Eleusinian cult figures

→ Plutus [9. 49–55] and Eubuleus [9. 56–59]. Despite the link with 'affluence' the association with the Underworld was not lost and later the entrances of the Underworld were called *ploutṓnia* (Str. 5,4,5). As H. is so hard to comprehend and could not be limited to one function, he had no cult (Soph. Ant. 777–780); people also believed that he was indifferent to their prayers and gifts (Aeschyl. fr. 161 TrGF; Eur. Alc. 424). In Greece there appears to have been only one H. temple in Elis, which significantly was open only once a year (Str. 8,3,14; Paus. 6,25,2).

The most famous H. myth is his abduction of → Persephone; this story was localized in various places in the Greek world [10. 74–78]. As Persephone was connected with love and marriage [11. 147–188] and abduction was part of the Spartan wedding rite, the myth was probably originally a narrative representation of prenuptial rites for girls. The union of H. and Persephone became an emblem of marriage itself so that girls who died unmarried were called 'Brides of H.' [3. 250]. Because of H.'s 'hellish' nature it is not surprising that the couple remained childless (Apollod. FGrH 244 F 102a2). The two continued to be venerated together, usually as Pluto and → Kore (IG II[3] 1620c); in Eleusis even as gods *par excellence*, Theus and Thea [9. 114f.]. Only a later myth tells of H.'s lover → Minthe who was transformed by Persephone into mint (Str. 8,3,14; Ov. Met. 10,728ff.).

H. lost its significance as a general destination in the 5th cent. BC with the appearance of the idea of souls that make their way to the upper layer of the air while bodies are absorbed by the Earth (CEG 1. 10,6f.); this belief is already evident in the tragedies of Euripides and refers there to mortals (Eur. Suppl. 531–534; Eur. Hel. 1013–1016) and deified mortals (Eur. Erechtheus fr. 65, 71f. AUSTIN). On late and post-Classical Apulian vases H. is often linked with → Orpheus. This can perhaps be regarded as a sign of a changed role in the religious concepts in southern Italy [5. 394].

→ Afterlife, concepts of

1 C.J. RUIJGH, Scripta Minora I, 1991 2 BURKERT 3 C.SOURVINOU-INWOOD, 'Reading' Greek Death to the End of the Classical Period, 1995 4 W.BURKERT, Structure and History in Greek Mythology and Ritual, 1979 5 S.F. DALINGER et al., s.v. H., LIMC 4.1 6 W.BURKERT, The Orientalizing Revolution, 1992 7 J.GAGER, Curse Tablets and Binding Spells from the Ancient World, 1992 8 A.AUDOLLENT, Defixionum Tabellae, 1904 9 K. CLINTON, Myth and Cult. The Iconography of the Eleusinian Mysteries, 1992 10 N.J. RICHARDSON, The Homeric Hymn to Demeter, 1973 11 C.SOURVINOU-INWOOD, 'Reading' Greek Culture, 1991.

A.HENRICHS, s.v. H., OCD, [3]1996, 661f.

J.B.

Ḥâḏra ware Modern technical term designating the Hellenistic painted → hydriae, which were produced mainly between 270 and 180 BC; named after the Egyptian place where they were found, Ḥâḏra near → Alexandria, where the majority of the around 300 known examples came to light. They are derived from white-ground hydriae, which were formerly also counted as belonging to this type. Their provenance from central Crete is today considered certain on the basis of scientific analyses. Production continued here with unpainted examples until into the 1st cent. BC.

Four main groups (workshops) were distinguished, based on the way they are painted, of which the 'laurel group' with fourteen vase painters has been best researched. Eight vase painters are differentiated within the 'dolphin group'. A third group is called the 'simple group', owing to its unassuming decoration, and thought to be the oldest. Between 240 and 120 BC Alexandria finally had its own production of Ḥâḏra ware (HW) ('group of laurel leaves without branches') with at least two vase painters.

In Crete HW was principally used in the domestic sphere. However, the majority of HW was exported to Alexandria, where they were used as urns for ashes in the cult of the dead. Among these about thirty Ḥâḏra vases stand out, as they state the name of the dead person with rank and origin, the name of the Ptolemaic official in charge of the funeral, and the date. The dead were either ambassadors or leaders of the mercenary troops who died in Alexandria and were given a state burial.

L.GUERRINI, Vasi di Hadra, Tentativo di sistemazione cronologica di una classe ceramica, 1964; A.ENKLAAR, Chronologie et peintres des hydries de Hadra, in: BABesch 60, 1985, 106–151; Id., Les hydries de Hadra II: Formes et ateliers, in: BABesch 61, 1986, 41–65.

R.D.

Hadramaut (Arabic Ḥaḍramaut, Ḥaḍramōt, Ḥaḍramūt; Ἀδραμύτα; *Hadramýta*, Theophr. Hist. pl. 9,4). Ancient southern Arabian kingdom with capital Sabota, i.e. Šabwa(t) in the west; its residents are the easternmost people of Arabia Felix, the so-called *Chadramōtítai* (Str. 16,4) or *Atramitae* (Plin. HN 6,155). In ancient times H. was not only the valley of that name with its catchment areas but comprised the entire region up to the Arabian Sea. The kingdom of H. is attested from the 7th cent. BC in Ancient Southern Arabic inscriptions, initially as a vassal of → Saba. Through the capture of the bordering incense land to the east, H. also achieved economic importance (connection with the trading Minaeans). Its greatest expansion brought with it in the 2nd cent. AD the incorporation of the remainder of Qatabān in the west. At the end of the 3rd cent. the Himjarian kings conquered H., united southern Arabia into a large kingdom and also gave themselves the title of kings of H.

→ Ancient Southern Arabian

H.v. WISSMANN, Zur Arch. und antike Geogr. von Südarabien. Ḥaḍramaut, Qatabān und das ʿAden-Gebiet in der Antike, 1968; P.A. GRJAZNECIČ, A.V. SEDOV (ed.), Chadramaut. Archeologičeskie, ėtnografičeskie i istoriko-kul'turnyje issledovanija, vol. 1, 1995; Hadramawt, la vallée inspirée. Saba, Arabie méridionale 3–4, 1997.

W.W.M.

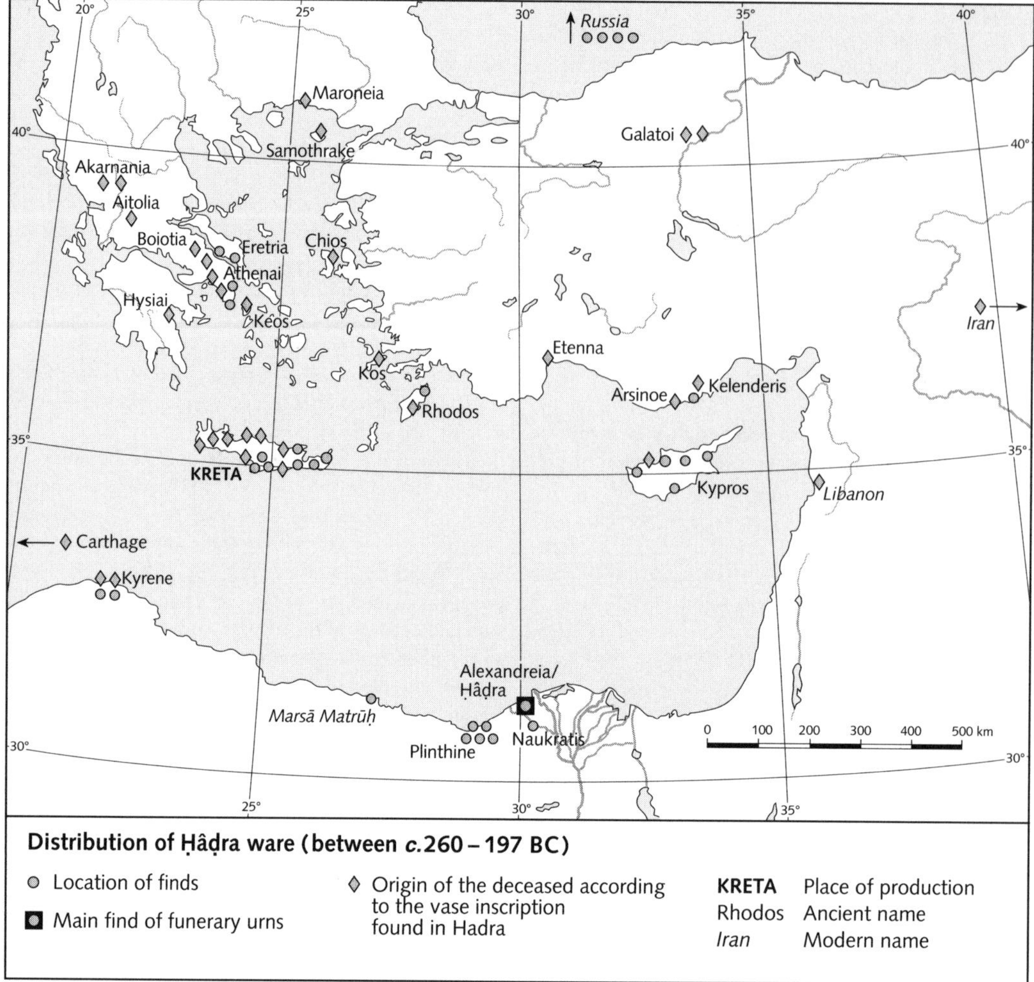

Distribution of Ḥâḍra ware (between *c.*260–197 BC)

Hadria (modern Atri). At first Hatria, later H., town 7 km west of the Adriatic coast in the south of Picenum (*regio V*) between the Vomanus (modern Vomano; Sil. Pun. 8,438) and the Matrinus (modern Piomba). Founded by the Siculi and Liburni, captured by the Piceni. After its subjugation a *colonia Latina* was founded (289 BC; Liv. per. 11) that minted coins bearing the legend *HAT(ria)* (cf. Steph. Byz. s.v. Ἀτρία). *Municipium*, *tribus Maecia* [1. 64], recolonized by Sulla or Augustus. The amphoras from H. were famous (Plin. HN 35,161). Hadrian had restoration work done here (family relationships: S HA Hadr. 1; 19). Traces of settlement from the 6th cent. BC can be found (Picenian necropoleis on the Colle di Giustizia and in Pretara). The ruins of the Roman town are beneath the modern one; its layout is based on the streets of the regular Roman city, *insulae* (1 *actus*). The walls consist of *opus quadratum* made of flint conglomerate. The square cistern with pilasters in the area of the thermal baths today forms the crypt of the cathedral; a further cistern is located in the forum under the Palazzo Acquaviva. In the northeast are a sanctuary and a theatre; a *villa suburbana* and kilns for ceramics and terracotta are preserved.

1 W. Kubitschek, Imperium Romanum tributim discriptum, 1889.

G. Azzena, Atri, forma e urbanistica, 1987; L. Sorricchio, H., 1911.

G.U.

Hadrianis (Ἁδριανίς; *Hadrianís*). Last of the five post-Cleisthenian → phyles of Attica, set up in AD 127/8 in honour of emperor Hadrian. Each of the 12 phyles at the time (10 Cleisthenian, Ptolemais, Attalis) gave the H. a deme. To this the new deme → Antinoeis was added in AD 130 after the death of → Antinous [2]. The trittyes played no part in the formation of the post-Cleisthenian phyles. The proportional representation of the demes in the phyles had been abandoned in 201/200 BC. The imperial lists of *bouleutai* for the individual demes therefore show an inhomogenous picture.

→ Antigonis; → Demetrias; → Ptolemais

W.K. Pritchett, The Five Attic Tribes After Kleisthenes, 1943; Traill, Attica, 25ff., esp. 31, 34, table 15. H.LO.

Hadrianopolis (Ἁδριανόπολις; *Hadrianópolis*).
[1] Caesarea (Καισάρεια; *Kaisáreia*). City in Paphlagonia in the basin of Eskipazar (formerly Viranşehir), close to the fortress of Semail, the centre of the Paphlagonian region of Sanisene [2]. In 6/5 BC this, together with Potamia and Marmolitis, became a *regio attributa* [1. 116ff.] of the Paphlagonian *eparchía* of the province of Galatia, which was soon organized as the *pólis* of H. (originally Καισαρεῖς Προσειλημμενεῖται [1. no. 1]). Before AD 305/6 H. was defeated and became the province of Paphlagonia and in 384/7 of Honorias ([1. no. 10], 6th cent.); from 451 until into the 12th cent. it is attested as a bishopric.

1 C. Marek, Stadt, Ära und Territorium in Pontus-Bithynia und Nord-Galatia, 1993, 100–125, 187–210 2 K. Strobel, Galatien und seine Grenzregionen, in: E. Schwertheim (ed.), Forschung in Galatien (Asia Minor Stud. 12), 1994, 29–65.

K. Belke, Paphlagonien und Honorias, 1996, 63, 155f. K.ST.

[2] A town founded by emperor Hadrian probably to promote urbanization [1]. In antiquity partly included in Phrygia, partly in Lycaonia, and in the early Byzantine period in the province of Pisidia. It has been located on a direct road from → Philomelium (Akşehir) to → Iconium more likely near modern Koçaş (24 km south-east of Philomelium) than near Adaras 20 km to the southeast [2. 456f.]. Coins mention a River Karmeios [3. 74], probably modern Koçaş (also Ağık or Adıyan). H. was a diocese (suffragan of the Pisidian → Antioch [5]) from AD 325 (at the latest) [4. 47, 134] until the 11th/12th cents. Numerous inscriptions. [5].

1 Magie 1, 622; 2, 1484. 2 W.M. Calder, Inscriptions of Southern Galatia, in: AJA 36, 1932, 452–464 3 J. Tischler, Kleinasiatischische Hydronymie, 1977 4 E. Honigmann, La liste originale des pères de Nicée, in: Byzantion 14, 1939, 17–76 5 MAMA 7, 30–37.

K. Belke, N. Mersich, Phrygien und Pisidien (TIB 7), 79, 145f., 171. K.BE.

[3] Town in Thrace, at the confluence of Tuntza and Maritza (= Hebrus) that is navigable from here onwards, modern Edirne (Turkey). Founded by emperor Hadrian with the incorporation of a prior settlement, for which the Thracian (*Uscudama*) and Greek (Ὀρεστίας and others, according to [5. 161f.] archaizing usage) names have been passed on. Situated on the road from Serdica to Byzantium (It. Ant. 175,6; 322,8; Tab. Peut. 7,3 Weber), H. was of particular military significance: as the capital of the province of Haemimontus, centre of weapons production and as the location of two decisive battles for the emperorship – in AD 313 (victory of Licinius over Maximinus Daia at Tzirallum [5. 63; 6. 14]) and in 324 (victory of Constantine over Licinius [6. 18]) – and the defeat of Emperor Valens fighting against the Goths in 378, which Amm. Marc. (31,12–16) considered a turning-point of history ([6. 35–37, 116, 166] with additional comments).

The strategic position on the road to Constantinople made H. on the one hand a goal of attack by the Avaro-Slavs (6th/7th cents.), Bulgarians (especially in the 9th/10th cents. but also later) and Crusaders (11th–13th cents.), on the other hand until the conquest by the Turks (about 1370) it made it an important town for Byzantine military administration (details in [5. 162–165]). Bishops are attested from the 4th cent. [2. 1453ff.], but H. was of secondary status despite its position as the metropolis of Haemimontus in the Byzantine Church. There are hardly any remains left of the ancient town, from Byzantine times there are only a few, particularly of the fortifications and several churches [3. 167; 4. 23; 5. 165f.].

1 E. Oberhummer, s.v. H., RE 7, 2174f. 2 D. Stiernon s.v. H., DHGE 22, 1442–1466 3 J. Gruber, G. Weiss, K. Kreiser, s.v. Adrianopel, LMA 1, 167f. 4 T.E. Gregory, N. Patterson Ševčenko, A. Kazhdan, s.v. Adrianople, s.v. Adrianople, battle of, ODB 1, 23f. 5 Soustal, Thrakien (TIB 6, 161–167 (additional bibliography) 6 J. Martin, Spätantike und Völkerwanderung, ³1995. E.W.

Hadrianus (Ἀδριανός; *Hadrianós*) [1].
[1] Sophist from Tyre, at 18 years of age a favourite pupil of → Herodes Atticus (Philostr. VS 2,10,585–586). With → Flavius Boethus (also from Phoenicia) he attended the anatomy lectures of → Galen in Rome in AD 162–166 (Gal. 14,627; 629 Kuhn). He may perhaps have been the target of mockery in Lucian's *Pseudologístēs* [1]. He taught in Ephesus (Philostr. VS 2,23,605) and (163–169) [2] honoured his patron there, the consular Cn. → Claudius [II 64] Severus, with a statue and a poem [3; 4]. From 176 at the latest he held the imperial professorship in Athens [5], where he had citizenship and gave the funeral oration to Herod (177/8). From the first years after 180 he held the chair in Rome where his voice even attracted those who had not mastered Greek (Philostr. VS 2,10,589). One oration led emperor Marcus Aurelius to bestow honours and gifts; shortly before his death at the age of about 80, Commodus bestowed upon him the office of *ab* → *epistulis Graecis* (Philostr. VS 590). Works: Suda α 528 Adler mentions 'Metamorphoses' (7 bks.); two works on the technique of rhetoric (3 and 5 bks.); *Phalaris*; letters; speeches; a *consolatio* for Celer (the teacher of Marcus Aurelius and Verus?, S HA Aur. 2,4 and *ab epistulis Graecis*, Philostr. VS 1,22,524; Aristid. 50,57). A short (fragmentary?) speech is extant [6], which demands the burning of a woman who had burnt a witch. Libanius (Or. 64,41) knows of a funeral speech for an actor by the name of Maximinus.
→ Philostratus; → Second Sophistic

1 C.P. Jones, Two Enemies of Lucian, in: GRBS 13, 1972, 478–86 2 R. Syme, The Ummidii, in: Roman Papers 2, 1979, 690 3 IK 15, 1539 4 FGE 566–8 5 I. Avotins,

Holders of the Chairs of Rhetoric at Athens, in: HSPh 79, 1975, 320–321 6 H. HINCK, Polemonis declamationes, 1873, 44f. (Ed.).

G. W. BOWERSOCK, Greek Sophists in the Roman Empire, 1969, 55–63; 82–4; 91–2; PIR H 4. E.BO.

[2] A Greek presumed to have lived in Syria, perhaps identical with a monk to whom → Neilus addressed three letters (Epist. 2,60; 3,118; 3,266), wrote before AD 440 a concise 'Introduction to the Holy Scriptures' (*Eisagōgḗ*), the first work with that title. It was also known in the west (Cassiod. Inst. 1,10); it is his goal to comment on figurative styles of speaking, particularly that of the Old Testament: meaning, word, and sentence forms. The work tries to explain characteristic peculiarities of the Hebrew language on the basis of the Greek Biblical text (§ 1) and ends with concise remarks on general hermeneutics (§ 132–134). If follows basic principles of the → Antiochene School, especially → Theodorus of Mopsuestia, → Iohannes Chrysostomus and → Theodoretus of Cyrrhus. As numerous catena fragments not taken into account in [3] are extant [1. 6527; 2. 24, 28, 39, 48, 53f., 324], the text is in need of a new edition. Possibly only the epitome or just a part of a more extensive work has been edited to date.

1 CPG 3 2 G. KARO, H. LIETZMANN, Catenarum Graecarum Catalogus, 1901 3 F. GOESSLING (ed.), Adrians ΕΙΣΑΓΩΓΗ ΕΙΣ ΤΑΣ ΘΕΙΑΣ ΓΡΑΦΑΣ aus neu aufgefundenen Handschriften, 1887 4 L. DIESTEL, Gesch. des Alten Testamentes in der christlichen Kirche, 1869, 110 5 G. MERCATI, Pro Adriano, in: RBi 11, 1914, 246–255 (= Id., Opere Minore 3, Studi e Testi 78, 1937, 383–392). C.M.

[II]

A. ORIGIN AND SENATORIAL CAREER

Roman Emperor AD 117–138. Son of Senator P. Aelius Hadrianus Afer and one Domitia Paulina; his home town was → Italica in the Spanish province of Baetica. Born on 24 January 76 probably in Rome as P. Aelius Hadrianus. When he was 10 years of age he lost his father, who had achieved the rank of praetor. The *eques* Acilius Attianus and the senator (later emperor) M. Ulpius Traianus, his great-uncle (see stemma in [1. 308]), both likewise from Italica, became his guardians. At an early age he was made acquainted with Greek literature and culture. Before starting his senatorial career he lived only a short time in Italica.

About 94 he began his career as *decemvir stlitibus iudicandis*, *praefectus urbi feriarum Latinarum* and *sevir*. Then he was senatorial military tribune for three legions: in the *legio II Adiutrix* in Pannonia, the *V Macedonica* in Moesia inferior in 96/7. When Trajan, at that time governor of Germania superior, was adopted by Nerva and made the designated successor, H. delivered the congratulations from the Lower Moesian army. Then he was tribune of the *legio XXII Primigenia* in Mainz. At the beginning of February 98 at the death of Nerva he hurried to Trajan in Cologne to be the first to bring him the news; H.'s brother-in-law Julius Servianus, legate of Germania superior, supposedly attempted to prevent that. From then on H. was always close to Trajan as the nearest male relative; in addition he married Sabina, the grandniece of Trajan in 100. There was little unusual about H.'s senatorial career (ILS 308; HA Hadr. 3,1–10) under Trajan: participation in the 1st Dacian War as *quaestor* of the emperor, people's tribune, in 104 *praetor*; participation in the 2nd Dacian War in 105 as legate of the *legio I Minervia* (in both wars he was distinguished with *dona militaria*); in 106–108 praetorian governor of Pannonia inferior. In May 108 he became *cos. suff.* at the age of 32 – exceptional for a non-patrician. At that time he was allegedly informed that Trajan wanted to adopt him, but no extraordinary official sign followed. During this period he stayed in Greece and was archon in Athens in 112.

B. ASSUMPTION OF POWER

H. took part in the Parthian War as *comes* of Trajan; in the first six months of 117 at the latest he was appointed governor of Syria; whether he was really designated *cos. II* for 118 is uncertain. As Trajan fell ill, H's governorship in Syria was however a clear message as to who Trajan wanted as his successor; but an adoption only took place in Selinus in Cilicia where Trajan died on 7 (?) August 117. H. received the news in Syria on 9 August. Allegedly Trajan's letter was forged, only after his death, by his wife Plotina, who had been supporting H. for a long time, and the *praefectus praetorio* Acilius [II 1] Attianus. Today we cannot be certain in detail of what really happened. But all social and political factors indicate that Trajan did want H. as his successor. On 11 August H. was acclaimed emperor by the troops in Syria (*dies imperii*). His name was now Imperator Caesar Traianus Hadrianus Augustus. He did not take on Trajan's *nomen gentile*, Ulpius, which is why new citizens and freedmen bore the name P. Aelius.

The beginning of H.'s reign was difficult: the lack of success of Trajan against the Parthians was acknowledged by also surrendering the last remnant of the conquests and withdrawing support from the dependent Parthian king Trajan had appointed. In Dacia and on the middle course of the Danube, in Britain and Mauretania uprisings broke out; Marcius Turbo, the *praefectus praetorio*, kept a special detachment for this purpose in the Danube region (RMD I 21). The rest of those involved in the revolts of the Jews in the east, in Egypt, and Cyrenaica were defeated. Allegedly four consuls embarked upon a conspiracy: Avidius Nigrinus, Cornelius Palma, Publilius Celsus and ultimately Lusius Quietus of Mauretania, whom Trajan had appointed in

Judea in 116/7; by order of the *praefectus praetorio* all four were executed after they were condemned by the Senate; H.'s relationship with the Senate was strained in this way all his life. Presumably all were indeed opponents of H's new policy on the borders of the empire but not conspirators.

After H.'s return to the capital on 9 July 118 he developed a plan involving a particular endeavour for the Senate and the people of Rome: remission of the 900 million sesterces debt for the years 104–118 in the *fiscus*; the scene is represented on the *Anaglypha Traiani*. The assets of condemned people were to go to the → *aerarium*, not the → *patrimonium* of the emperor. Impoverished senators received financial assistance; the conditions were improved for the recipients of → *alimenta* in Italy. Only a total of twice did H. take on the consulate again (in 118 and 119, so as a whole only *cos. III*) – a sign of *moderatio*. He generally rejected the victor's title of Trajan which was conferred upon him as well as the title *pater patriae*; he did not accept it until 128. Outwardly the climate improved in this way; but the majority of senators nursed feelings of resentment until after H's death.

C. Border policy and military undertakings

In Roman policy with respect to the empire H. made a decisive change from the time of Trajan. He emphatically dispensed with military expansion and surrendered several regions acquired by Trajan: in the east all the Parthian territories, then the eastern part of Dacia reorganized by H. (modern southeastern Romania and Moldavia), a consequence of fierce attacks by the Roxolani and Sarmati, during which the governor C. Iulius Quadratus Bassus fell. Some senatorial circles opposed the surrender of the conquered territories. The building up of the border installations in Upper Germania and Raetia, in North Africa and particularly in Britain (H.'s Wall) could be understood as a sign of outward military restraint. No expansionist war was conducted under H. Nevertheless H. did not neglect the army; on his journeys through the provinces he inspected the troops, for which there is evidence particularly in the manoeuvre criticism of Lambaesis as well as the setting up of the cult of Disciplina (ILS 2487; 9133–5), the same, however, also applies to coins on which his visit to the provincial armies is immortalized. Whenever necessary, he also sent in the army as a threat, for example in 123 against the Parthians, though the crisis was resolved through talks on the Euphrates with the Parthian king. H.'s military restraint is also discernible in his dispensing with the *Imperator* acclamations. The only exception is the assumption of the title of *Imperator II* after the lengthy → Bar Kochba War, probably for the first time in spring 136. This revolt, probably triggered by the foundation of the colony of Aelia Capitolina instead of Jerusalem and possibly by a ban on circumcision, caused immense losses among the Roman troops. Only through the deployment of the armies of Judaea, Arabia, and Syria and additional commandeered units was the war against Bar Kochba's guerrillas successfully ended after about four years. H. bestowed triumphal decorations on Sex. Julius Severus, T. Haterius Nepos, and C. Publicius Marcellus (ILS 1056; IGR III 175; ILS 1058); for H. himself the Senate probably erected a triumphal arch in southern Galilee near Tel Shalem (unpublished inscription).

D. Concern for the empire – the journeys

The emphasis of H.'s policy was on the internal development of the empire. His means of achieving this were his extensive travels through almost every province [4. 188ff.]. The first journey, begun after 21 April 121, went through Gaul, Germania superior, Raetia, Noricum, and Germania inferior to Britain, where he arranged for the building of the *Vallum Hadriani* between Ituna and Tina by the governor Platorius Nepos. His return took him to Tarraco, although it appears that he did not visit his home province of Baetica. In the spring of 123 at the latest he travelled to the east because of the Parthian crisis. From Syria he went to Cappadocia and the Black Sea and spent the period from the end of 123 to autumn 124 in Bithynia, then primarily in Asia. From October 124 to the summer of 125 in Greece, especially Athens; return through Sicily to Rome in the summer of 125. A journey through Italy began on 3 March 127 (Vidman, FO^2 49; cf. [12. II 695; VI 349]: possibly only northern Italy); at the beginning of August 127 back in Rome. In early summer 128 he set out for North Africa and a visit to the *legio III Augusta*, then by way of Rome to Greece where he spent the winter of 128/9 in Athens again. In spring 129 to Ephesus, through Asia Minor to Antioch in Syria, Palmyra; winter of 129/130 in Syria. Visit to Arabia and Judaea; summer 130 to Egypt where in October his lover → Antinous [2] drowned in the Nile. In spring 131 left Alexandria to go to Syria, through Thrace and Moesia to Athens with a winter stay in 131/2. Whether he then returned to Rome or went to the east again, to Judaea, which was in revolt and other places, is disputed.

The journeys gave H. the widest possible knowledge of the local and supraregional problems of the empire. He strengthened the self-awareness of the provinces, whose status was enhanced with respect to Italy by their appearing on imperial coinage as independent units; H. appointed on the other hand four *legati Augusti pro praetore* as decentralized office bearers, who in actual fact had the role of provincial governors (Antoninus Pius revoked this regulation [13]). Town life was promoted in particular: through the new foundation of towns like the poleis of Hadrianoutherae, Hadriani, and Hadriania in Asia, the *municipium* of Choba in Mauretania, the elevation of Italica in Baetica and Mursa in Pannonia to the status of *colonia*, and the founding of Antinoopolis as a memorial to Antinous in Egypt, which was accorded privileges to an extraordinary extent; through financing numerous buildings, e.g. in Gabii (CIL XIV 2747), Ostia (CIL XIV 95), Athens

[1. 219], Alexandria in the Troad (Philostr. VS 2,1,8), and Caesarea Maritima (e.g. AE 1928, 136; 137); through allocating the more extensive *ius Latii maius*, through which all decurions of a Latin community received Roman citizenship. The numerous letters to towns passed down to us show directly the intensity of his endeavours [14].

Although H. cared for all the regions of the empire, the eastern, mostly Greek-speaking provinces profited the most. The Greek element received a new centre through the foundation of the Panhellenion in Athens. Members were Greek cities from the entire empire; the centre was the gigantic temple of Panhellenic Zeus that was now finally finished after many prior attempts. The inauguration of the temple occurred in the presence of H. in 131/2. In the east H. himself was called Olympius (from 128/9), Panhellenius (from 132) and Panionius, and this characterizes a core part of his political dealings. The initiation to the Eleusinian Mysteries is also related to this. However he was not the first to increase considerably the proportion of senators from the Greek east; rather, this had already happened in the time of the Flavians, but the first consul from the Greek motherland was under H.: Ti. Claudius Atticus Herodes, *c.* 132/3. Nevertheless he neglected the west, particularly Rome. Numerous buildings were financed by him there, a temple for his 'parents' Trajan and Plotina, the → Pantheon, the dual temple of Venus and Rome, establishing their cult in the capital city of the empire.

H. had begun early to build a quite unique residence at Tivoli which was spread over 1.5 km², the *villa Hadriana* (→ Villa, → Tibur). It is incontestable that he gave shape there to memories of his journeys.

E. Administration

The special feature of H.'s style of rule were his journeys; however the systematization of the administration of the empire frequently attributed to him, particularly the regions managed by *equites*, was not his work; rather, he only to a limited extent supplemented the measures of his predecessors Domitian and Trajan. Possibly the role of an *advocatus fisci* was introduced by him; the first known incumbent however, contrary to HA Hadr. 20,6, had assumed a military role (AE 1975, 408). The supposed reorganization of the imperial council, the *consilium principis*, is an invention of late antiquity. However, the recording of the praetorian edict collection (→ *Edictum* [2] *perpetuum*), which H. Salvius Julianus transcribed (ILS 8973) was significant, if only symbolically, and documents the concentration on further development of the law by the emperor. In the field of institutionalized organization of the empire, H. otherwise continued to follow in the footsteps of his predecessors.

F. Organization of the succession

H. had no children from his marriage with Sabina. His relationship with her is said to have also been very strained; whether this is true or only a reflection of court gossip is hard to decide. However, H.'s paedophile inclinations, especially his relations with Antinous [2], probably damaged the relationship. After his return from the last great journey, the question of the succession arose for H., who was increasingly suffering from illnesses. In 136 he adopted one of the consuls of the year, L. Ceionius Commodus, who took the name of L. Aelius Caesar. The choice is surprising, especially as the chosen one was suffering from tuberculosis; the reason is unknown, despite much speculation. The choice aroused resistance amongst H.'s relatives, L. Iulius Ursus Servianus, *cos. III* in 134, and Pedanius Fuscus, H.'s grandnephew; a 'revolt' against H. was discovered and the 'conspirators' were executed. But Aelius Caesar also died on 31 December 137. On 24 January 138 H. named the 51-year-old senator T. Aurelius Fulvus Boionius Arrius Antoninus (Antoninus [1] Pius) as his successor; the adoption was completed on 25 February. Antoninus for his part had to adopt the son of the deceased Aelius Caesar, the later Lucius Verus, and the young Marcus Aurelius, whom H. called Verissimus and regarded highly; this ensured the continuation of rule for two generations. On 10 July 138 H. died after a long illness in Baiae. His ashes were later interred in his mausoleum (modern Castel Sant'Angelo) on the other side of the Tiber. His divinization by the Senate did not happen until Antoninus Pius enforced this with the threat that otherwise his adoption too would be untenable. It was the final consequence of the latent ever-present tension between H. and the Senate.

Coins: RIC II 314ff.

Portraits: Fittschen/Zanker Katalog I no. 46ff. M. Bergmann, Zu den Porträts des Traian und Hadrian, in: A. Caballos, P. León (ed.), Itálica MMCC, 1997, 137ff.

Bibliography: 1 A. R. Birley, Hadrian. The Restless Emperor, 1997 (with extensive bibliography) 2 Id., Hadrian and Greek Senators, in: ZPE 116, 1997, 209ff. 3 E. Champlin, Hadrian's Heir, in: ZPE 21, 1976, 79ff. 4 H. Halfmann, Itinera principum, 1986 5 C. P. Jones, The Panhellenion, in: Chiron 26, 1996, 29ff. 6 O. Lenel, Edictum perpetuum, ³1927 7 R. Syme, Hadrian, the Intellectual, in: Id., RP VI 103ff. 8 Id., Hadrian as Philhellene. Neglected Aspects, in: Id., RP V 546ff. 9 M. Tagliaferro Boatwright, Hadrian and the City of Rome, 1990 10 D. Willers, Hadrians panhellenisches Programm, 1990 11 M. Zahrnt, Hadrian, in: M. Clauss (ed.), Die röm. Kaiser, 1997, 124ff. 12 Syme, RP 13 W. Eck, Die Verwaltung des röm. Reiches 1, 1995, 315ff. 14 J. H. Oliver, Greek Constitutions, 1989, 150ff.

W.E.

Hadrumetum (Ἀδρύμης; *Hadrýmēs*). Phoenician trading centre on the east coast of Tunisia, modern Sousse. Evidence: Ps.-Scyl. 110 (GGM I 88); Sall. Iug. 19,1; Solin. 27,9. From the Punic or Neo-Punic period come the Tofet (with prominent steles), a necropolis (with various tomb offerings) and over 60 inscriptions. In 310 BC H. went over to the side of → Agathocles [2] (Diod. Sic. 20,17,3–5). In 203 BC → Hannibal chose H. as his base; after the defeat of Naraggara he went back there (Pol. 15,5,3; 15,3; Nep. Hann. 6,3f.; Liv. 30,29,1; 35,4; App. Lib. 33, 139; 47,206). At the beginning of the 3rd Punic War H. entered into an alliance with the Romans and was therefore accorded the status of a *populus liber* after the end of the war (App. Lib. 94,446). At the time of Caesar the town lost its freedom but won it back again as early as 36 BC (Plin. HN 5,25). Trajan elevated it to a *colonia* (CIL VI 1, 1687). Still in the 2nd cent. H. became the seat of the *procurator regionis Hadrumetinae*. It is debatable whether H. was also the seat of a *legatus proconsulis Africae*. The town flourished in the Severan period. Under Diocletian H. rose to become the capital city of the new *Provincia Valeria Byzacena*. The ancient monuments that are preserved are significant inscriptions: CIL VIII 1, 59–67; 2, 10503–10510; Suppl. 1, 11137–11150; Suppl. 4, 22909–23020; AE 1977, 258 no. 863; 1989, 285 no. 879; 287 no. 885; 290 no. 893; 1991, 461 no. 1639.

L. Foucher, H., 1964; S. Lancel, E. Lipiński, s.v. Hadrumète, DCPP, 203f.; C. G. Piccard, Catalogue du Musée Alaoui. Nouvelle série. vol. I 1, n.d., 298–300; K. Vössing, Unt. zur röm. Schule, Bildung, Schulbildung im Nordafrika der Kaiserzeit, 1991, 92–102. W.HU.

Hadylium (Ἁδύλιον, Ἡδύλε[ι]ον; *Hadýlion, Hēdyle[i]on*). Mountain range (modern Vetritza) with an average ridge height of 300–400 m (highest point: 543 m) on the northern border of Phocis and Boeotia. In the west at Parapotamioi separated from → Parnassus by the Kephisos. In the east and southeast bordering on the mountains Palaiovouna (ancient Hyphanteion?) and Akontion. Evidence: Dem. Or. 19,148 (with schol.); Theopomp. FGrH 115 F 157; Str. 9,3,16; Plin. HN 4,25; Plut. Sulla 16f.

Philippson/Kirsten, I,2, 425. P.F.

Haedui Powerful, rich people of the *Gallia Celtica* (later Lugdunensis; → Gallia). In the west the region of the H. was essentially bounded by the rivers Doubs and Saône; in the north their neighbours were the → Senones, the → Mandubii, and the → Lingones. Alliances with the → Bituriges in the west and the Senones, → Parisii, and → Bellovaci in the north made it possible for the H. to control trade from the Mediterranean to the English Channel; close relations with the → Boii gave them access to the rich Celts of central Europe. According to Liv. 5,34, the H. took part in the Gallic migration to upper Italy in the 6th cent. BC. This tradition presumably explains that of all the Gallic peoples the H. were the only ones to have a great diversity of other ethnic groups both in the interior of the country and in their border regions (Caes. B Gall. 1,11,4; 2,14,2; 6,4,2; 7,5,2; 7,75,2). Early on they became friends with the Romans and were called by them 'brothers and blood relations', *fratres consanguineique* (Caes. B Gall. 1,33,2). After a long period of supremacy they were subjugated by the → Sequani, but Caesar restored them to their former state. They rebelled against Rome possibly as early as 54, certainly however in 52 BC and in AD 21. At the time of the Augustan new order, the H. together with the → Segusiavi and the → Ambarri formed the connecting link between the province of Lugdunensis in the north of the Rhône and the province of Narbonensis. When emperor Claudius gave the Gauls the *ius honorum*, they were the first to attain the Senate (Tac. Ann. 11,25). In the Carolingian period the *civitas Aeduorum* established three dioceses with sees in Autun, Chalon, and Mâcon.

→ Augustodunum; → Bibracte

C. Goudineau, C. Peyre, Bibracte et les Eduens, 1993; M. Pinette et al., Autun-Augustodunum, 1987; E. Thévenot, Les Eduens n'ont pas trahi, 1960. Y.L.

Haematite Haematite (αἱματίτης; *haimatítēs, haematites*) is seen today as a form of red iron ore. Theophrastus (De lapidibus 37, [1. 70]) derives its name from the appearance of dried blood (*haîma*). In the ancient kingdoms of the Orient it was highly valued as a precious stone. Pliny recommends it among other things for treating blood-shot eyes (HN 36,144–148), and for staunching blood flow in consumptives and women. Following Sotacus, a Greek lithologist of the 4th cent. BC, he distinguishes five kinds, and referring to one Zachalias, he tells of magic practices of Babylonian magicians with haematite (37,169). Through Dioscorides (5,126, Wellmann 3,94f. = 5,143, Berendes 545), Isidore (Orig. 16,8,5) and the gem treatises (*Lithica*), for instance that of Marbode of Rennes (11th cent. AD, V. 467–486 [2. 70ff.]), haematite became very well known in the Middle Ages (e.g. Thomas of Cantimpré 14,27 [3. 361]). It is also discussed in detail in Kitāb al-Muršid al-Tamīnī (10th cent. AD), *c.* 14 [4. 65–70].

→ Precious stones

1 D. E. Eichholz (ed.), Theophrastus de lapidibus, 1965 2 J. M. Riddle (ed.), Marbode of Rennes' De lapidibus, 1977 3 H. Boese (ed.), Thomas Cantimpratensis, Liber de natura rerum, 1973 4 J. Schönfeld, Über die Steine. Das 14. Kap. aus dem 'K. a. M' ..., 1976 (Islamkundliche Untersuchungen 38). C.HÜ.

Haemimontus One of the six provinces of the diocese of Thrace with the capital → Hadrianopolis [3]. It comprised the territory on the Danube between the confluence with the Vit and the delta, the western Pontic coast up to Constantinople (excluding the city itself), the Propontis and the northern Aegean to the mouth of the Nestus.

V. Velkov, Cities in Thrace and Dacia in Late Antiquity, 1977, 61; Soustal, Thrakien. I.v.B.

Haemon (Αἵμων; *Haímōn*, 'skilful'), name of heroes.

[1] Eponym of the Thessalian Haemones, son of → Pelasgus, father of → Thessalus (Rhianus of Bene, FGrH

265 F 30), or son of Zeus and Melia (IG IX 2, 582: 1st cent. BC, Larisa [1]), or son of Ares (Schol. Apoll. Rhod. 2,527e).

[2] Son of → Lycaon, founder of Haemoniae in Arcadia (Paus. 8,44,1; Apollod. 3,97).

[3] Leader of the Pylians, companion of → Nestor (Hom. Il. 4,296).

[4] Theban, father of → Maeon (Hom. Il. 4,394ff.).

[5] Theban, son of → Creon, in ancient myth victim of the → Sphinx (Apollod. 3,54; → *Oedipodea* fr. 1 PEG I [2. 7; 17]). As a result, despite BETHE [3], H.'s love for → Antigone cannot belong to the ancient legend; Sophocles was the first to make H. into her fiancé and in this way invents the father-son conflict, in the course of which H. kills himself beside the body of his bride (Soph. Ant. 1234ff.). In Eur. Antigone, fr. 157–178 TGF [4] H. marries Antigone, who has probably been freed from the death penalty by Dionysus, and fathers → Maeon with her; in Eur. Phoen. 1672–1682 on the other hand, Creon renounces the marriage only after Antigone's threat to murder H. on the wedding night. According to Hyg. Fab. 72 H. hides his bride delivered to him for killing and they have a son, after whose murder by Creon H. kills himself and Antigone.

1 WILAMOWITZ 1, 186 with n. 2 2 E. BETHE, Thebanische Heldenlieder, 1891 3 Id., s.v. Antigone (3), RE 1, 2403 4 A. LESKY, Die tragische Dichtung der Hellenen, [3]1972, 328f.

O. KERN, s.v. H. (1)–(12), RE 7, 2217f.; I. KRAUSKOPF, s.v. Antigone, LIMC 1.1, 818–828; Id., s.v. H., LIMC 4.1, 406; CH. ZIMMERMANN, Der Antigone-Mythos in der antiken Literatur und Kunst, 1993. P.D.

[6] A stream which flows into the Cephisus east of Chaeronea, also sometimes equated with the Thermodon (Plut. Demosthenes 19; Plut. Thes. 27). Its exact location remains uncertain [1].

1 F. BÖLTE, s.v. H. 13), RE 7, 2218f. P.F.

Haemus (Αἷμος; *Haîmos*). Mountain range in Thrace, the Balkan mountains (Turkish Balkan, Bulgarian Stara Planina. The name is probably Thracian). The H. stretches from Timacus to Pontus and represents a distinctive watershed. According to ancient opinion the H. began at the Adriatic (Str. 7, fr. 10). As it is not very high but hard to cross it was often also an ethnic and political border. The first mention is in Hecataeus (FGrH 1 F 169). Numerous myths are connected with the H. (Apollod. 1,6,3; Ps.-Plut. De fluviis 11,3; Serv. Aen. 1,317; 321; Steph. Byz. s.v. Αἶ.). I.v.B.

Ovid gives the aetiology of the mountains (Met. 6,88): H. and Rhodope, the children of Boreas and Oreithyia, became a couple and called themselves Zeus and Hera. As punishment for this sacrilege they were turned into mountains. C.W.

In antiquity the roads went from Oescus to Philippopolis and from the Danube to Cabyle and Aenus over the H.; at the time of Hdt., there were various Thracian tribes living south of the H. and to the north were the Getae. The Odrysae were the first to conquer territories situated north of this. → Alexander [4] the Great too crossed the H. on his campaigns of conquest against the Getae and Triballi. In the H. there were ore deposits, dense forests and good grazing areas; the H. also offered protection against attackers. This led to a considerable economic and cultural standard amongst the indigenous tribes particularly in the Hellenistic period, as is attested by many ancient sites. In Roman times fortresses were built on the passes of the H. that were extended after the 3rd cent. to form a second line of defence (behind the Danube *limes*). The H. was for a long time the border between the Byzantine empire and the tribes invading across the Danube, later the Bulgarian-Slavonic empire.

CH. DANOFF, Zu den historischen Umrissen Altthrakiens I, 1944. I.v.B.

Hagesarchus of Megalopolis, father of the Cypriot *strategos* Ptolemy (PP 6,14778), himself Ptolemaic *stratēgòs epì Karías* (στρατηγὸς ἐπὶ Καρίας) under Ptolemy III, was also responsible for Samos; attested in 225/4 BC as an eponymous officer of a military unit.

K. HALLOF, CH. MILETA, Samos und Ptolemaios III., in: Chiron 27, 1997, 255–283, esp. 268ff. W.A.

Haggadah The term *Haggadah* (the *Hifʿil* of the Hebrew root *ngd* 'say, tell') or its Aramaic equivalent *Aggada* refers to all non-Halachic traditions from Rabbinic literature and is therefore a collective term for all in the widest sense narrative materials in this extensive corpus of literature. Such a negative definition of the term can already be found in the Middle Ages in Šmuel ha-Nagid (993–1055): 'Haggadah is any interpretation in the Talmud on any topic which is not a commandment.' Quite particular importance is accorded here to the scriptural exegesis, which for its part is in turn based on quite specific hermeneutical and methodical premises (cf. the 32 *Middot* of Rabbi Eliezer). Among the central themes of these interpretations, which provide narrative embellishment and interpretation of the text of the Biblical stories – often on individual words, striking expressions and style are a) the unity and uniqueness of God, b) the significance of the Torah as a revelation of God to his people, c) the love of God for Israel, which finds its most manifest expression in the presentation of the *sympátheia theoú*, d) Israel's liberation from hated Roman rule in the near future, and e) the belief in a just world order, which – despite all reality that appears different – will not deny the pious their reward. Aside from these literary commentaries, other literary genres also occur like stories, anecdotes, fairytales, fables, proverbs, etc., which are subsumed under this term. In this way paraenesis and paraclesis supplement each other in a complementary manner: the study of and adherence to the Torah and the practice of prayer and deeds of neighbourly love are inculcated, and at the same time a future is heralded in which Israel can live in direct communion with God without need or oppression. The most important *Haggadah* collections to mention are the various Midrash works like Midraš Rabba (on the Pentateuch and the *Megillot*), the Pesiqta Rabbati, the Pesiqta de Rav Kahana or Midraš Tanchuma among others, the traditions of which were compiled in the period from the 4th cent. AD into the early Middle Ages. The two Talmuds too, the Palestinian and particularly the Babylonian Talmud, contain numerous Haggadic traditions.

→ Halakhah; → Rabbinical literature; → Talmud

H. Bietenhard, s.v. Haggada, TRE 30 (30), 351–354; L. Ginzberg, The Legends of the Jews, 1909–1938; G. Stemberger, Der Talmudische Einführung, Texte, Erläuterungen, 1982, 158–285. B.E.

Hagia Irini

A. Location B. Archaeological remains

A. Location

Near the modern village of Hagia Irini (HI) on the northwest coast of → Cyprus there are remains of an ancient port, inhabited from the late Bronze Age to the middle Imperial period. On the altar of a sanctuary outside the town a large number of clay votives was found *in situ*.

E. Gjerstadt et al., Ajia Irini, in: The Swedish Cyprus Expedition, vol. 2, 1935, 642–824; L. Quilici et al., Rapporti di scavo ad Aghia Irini. Studi ciprioti e rapporti di scavo 1, 1971, 9–170; S. Törnquist, Arms, Armour and Dress of the Terracotta Sculpture from Ajia Irini, Cyprus, in: Medelhavsmuseet Bulletin 6, 1972, 7–55. R.SE.

B. Archaeological remains

The sanctuary (fertility cult) of HI originates from the end of the late Bronze Age and with alterations in the Cypro-geometric period was used until about 500 BC; revival of the cult in the Hellenistic period. Swedish excavations (1929/1930) produced not just architectural remains but also an abundance of sculpture (mostly made of → terracotta) of various sizes from all eras (among these Phoenician *ex votos*, evidence of the Cypro-Egyptian style and Ionian influences). Away from the sanctuary there are remains of the municipal settlement from the Cypro-archaic period. Italian excavations (since 1970) in the coastal necropolis of Palaiokastro uncovered many tombs from the late Bronze Age which were reused in ancient times (rich ceramic finds, including Mycenaean, Greek and eastern Greek imports, and Phoenician inscriptions). Further necropoleis with proto-geometric ceramics and Syrian-Palestinian influence.

V. Karageorghis, Archaeology in Cyprus 1960–1985, The Cyprus Department of Antiquities 1935–1983, 1985. A.W.

Hagia Sophia

Hagia Sophia The most important church of Constantinople, built on the site of the church Μεγάλη Ἐκκλησία (*Megálē Ekklēsía*; 1st half of the 4th cent.). It was destroyed in AD 532 in an uprising, instigated and paid for by Justinian based on designs by the architect Anthemius of Tralles and → Isidorus [9] of Miletus as a combination of nave and → central-plan building of gigantic dimensions. The huge dome rests on four pillars with foundations in rock. Dedicated on 27 December 537 in the presence of the emperor (Procop. Aed. 1,1,20–78; Malalas 479 B), the dome collapsed in early summer 558; ancient research frequently presumed that there was a connection with the earthquake of December 557. The building of a → dome was based not on static calculations but on a trial-and-error method and the striking changes in the profile of the rebuilt dome justify the assumption that the collapse of the dome was caused rather by vaulting that was too shallow and the resultant stress was too great.

The rebuilding of the dome under the direction of the younger → Isidorus [10] provided for a profile almost 7 m steeper above an additionally reinforced support – with a diameter of about 33 m (the dome base deviates strikingly from a circle). The form of the church is known from a poem by → Paulus Silentiarios written on the occasion of the rededication (24 December 563), which describes the building in detail; the rich decoration in late antiquity with mosaics, frescoes, and → incrustations is however only preserved in small parts because of the numerous later changes and extensions in architecture and decoration that lasted into the 12th cent.

Plundered and then Latinized during the western conquest in the Fourth Crusade (1204), the building was restored for the orthodox rite after the city was regained in 1261; directly after the Islamic conquest of Constantinople by Mehmet II (29 May 1453) the function of the Hagia Sophia was changed to become the principal mosque of the city.

C. Fossati, U. Peschlow, Die Hagia Sophia: nach dem Tafelwerk von 1852, 1980; H. Kähler, Die H.S., 1967; A. Kleinert, Die Inkrustationen der Hagia Sophia, 1979; W. Kleiss, Beobachtungen zur Hagia Sophia in Istanbul, in: MDAI (Ist) 15, 1965, 168–185; R. Mark, A.S. Cakmak (ed.), Hagia Sophia from the Age of Justinian to the Present, 1992; W. Müller-Wiener, Bildlexikon zur Top. Istanbuls, 1977, 84–96; O. Veh, W. Pülhorn (ed.), Prokop, Bauten. Paulos Silentiarios, Beschreibung der H.S., 1977. C.HÖ.

Hagia Thekla

Hagia Thekla (Ἁγία Θέκλα; *Hagía Thékla*), modern Ayatekla, Meryemlik. Important place of pilgrimage extended in the manner of a city with a wall, cisterns, an aqueduct and several huge churches (monasteries) south of Seleucia on the Calycadnus in western Cilicia with a cult tradition involving older sanctuaries of Apollo Sarpedonius, Athene, and Artemis (as πότνια θηρῶν, 'Mistress of beasts'). Aside from the apocryphal Acts (*Pauli*) *et Theclae*, the *vita* and *miracula* of St

Thecla are preserved from the middle of the 4th cent. [1]. Gregory of Nazianzus stayed here from 376 to 379, and the nun Egeria in 384. Emperor Zeno had a new church built after 476 for St Thecla (over her burial cave?). With the end of Christian-Armenian rule in Cilicia (1375), memory of the saint was lost. The place name *Meryemlik* means 'Place of St Mary'.

1 G. DAGRON, Vie et miracles de Sainte Thècle, 1978.

F. HILD, H. HELLENKEMPER, Kilikien und Isaurien, TIB 5, 441–443; H. HELLENKEMPER, Frühe christliche Wallfahrtsstätten in Kleinasien, in: Akt. XII. Int. Kongr. für christl. Arch. (JbAC Erg. vol. 20,1, 1995), 262–264.

F.H.

Hagiography In modern parlance hagiography denotes all the literature covering Christian veneration of → saints, as well as the scientific, philological-historical research into related issues. The origins and development of hagiography reflect changes in the early Church's conception of sainthood, in so far as saints (ἅγιοι/*hágioi*; Lat. *sancti*) are no longer regarded as being, as in the NT, the community of Christians but, instead, distinguished individuals, who in their life and death are exemplary representatives of the fundamental tenets of Christian belief and who are therefore venerated in cult and invoked: at first → martyrs, then confessors (cf. as well → martyrs), ascetics (→ Asceticism), virgins, bishops (→ *epískopos* [2]), miracle-workers (→ Miracles), missionaries (→ Mission II.), and finally even secular rulers.

The oldest evidence of hagiography is to be found in the cult of martyrs, for the official celebration of which calendar lists of memorial dates were drawn up and accounts of martyrdom (→ Martyrdom, literature of) kept for reading aloud in public. The fluid literary genre of saints' lives (→ *Vitae sanctorum*), originating at the end of the period of persecution, marked an expansion of hagiography, a special case of 'spiritual biography', which constitutes the largest proportion of the hagiographic tradition. In a narrative mode, it praises the saint's life, not just his death, as a testimony of faith, to serve to glorify and accredit its hero and promote religious edification in a conscious propagation of a hagiographic ideal image. As well as individual *vitae,* there soon appeared works conceived from the outset as collection of saints' lives. Other literary forms relevant to hagiography, such as eulogies, → sermons (III.), hymns (→ Hymnus III.), epigrams and accounts of → pilgrimage, as well as books of → miracles and lists of discovery and transference of → relics, could serve a hagiographical purpose. Not infrequently, ecclesiastical-political interests, aiming to gain prestige, came into play as well.

After many preliminary steps, in the wake of liturgical reform after the turmoil of the iconoclastic controversy (→ Cult image IV.; → Syrian dynasty), the Greek Church arranged all hagiographic material to fit the context of the Church festival calendar and adapted it in liturgical books, annual collections and menologies (→ *mēnológion*) for reading in church services. As traditions evolved, the editorial activity of Symeon Metaphrastes (*c.* 1000), called for by the imperial court in Constantinople, marked a turning-point and had a standardizing effect. A similar development took place in the West (but cf. the Papal canonization, taking place for the first time in 993), starting with the so-called *Martyrologium Hieronymianum* of *c.* AD 450 and culminating with the *Legenda aurea* of Jacobus de Voragine (1263–1267).
→ Acta Sanctorum; → Literature (Christian); → BYZANTIUM II.C.-D.

R. AIGRAIN, L'Hagiographie. Ses sources, ses méthodes, son histoire, 1953.

D. W.

Hagnias (Ἁγνίας; *Hagnías*). Father of → Tiphys who was the helmsman of the → Argo, reconstructed from the Patronymikon Hagniades (Apoll. Rhod. 1,105; 560; Orph. A. 122; 542; 690; Apollod. 1,111). J.S.-A.

Hagnon (Ἅγνων; *Hágnōn*).

[1] Father of Theramenes [1. 191], in 440 BC *stratēgós* in the war of Athens against rebellious Samos (Thuc. 1,117,2). H. founded Amphipolis in 437/6 (Thuc. 4,102,3; 5,11,1). At the beginning of the Peloponnesian War he held the office of *strategos* again in 431/0 and 429/8 (Thuc. 2,58,1; 6,31,2; 2,95,3 [2. 117, 121]). According to Plutarch (Pericles 32) he was one of the opponents of → Pericles. In April 421 he signed, among other things, the peace treaty (Peace of Nicias) between Athens and Sparta (Thuc. 5,19,2; 24,1). After the Sicilian catastrophe H. was elected to a council of elders (Lys. 12,65), who were to 'deliberate in advance on measures as occasioned by the situation' (Thuc. 8,1,3). TRAILL, PAA 107380.

1 S. HORNBLOWER, Commentary on Thucydides, 1, 1991
2 DEVELIN.

W.W.

[2] of Teos, one of the → Hetairoi of → Alexander [4]. With regard to him, the sources report mainly of luxury and flattery. He was hardly suitable for war service.

BERVE 2, no. 17.

E.B.

[3] **of Tarsus.** Probably one of the oldest students of → Carneades, who is depicted as responsible for a considerable part of the lecture notes of his teacher (Philod. index Academicorum XXIII 4); Cic. Acad. 2,16 considers him to be of equal rank with Cleitomachus. The indictment of rhetoric in Quint. 2,17,15 reflects the rhetoric-critical stance widespread in the Academy at this time. It is no longer certain what academic connection there is with individual statements probably attributable to H. (Ath. 13,602d; Plut. De sollertia animalium 12,968d and Schol. Hom. Il. 4,101). K.-H.S.

Hagnonides (Ἁγνωνίδης; *Hagnōnídēs*). Son of Nicoxenus of Pergase. In 325/4 BC claimant in a naval document (IG II2 1629a 14f.). Accused in the Harpalus affair by Dinarchus (Hyp. in Demosthenem 40; Dion. Hal. de Dinarcho, 10f.). After the defeat of Athens in 322, the banished H. was able to stay in the Peloponnese through the mediation of Phocion. Later however H. instigated the latter's execution (May 318; Plut. Phocion 33–37; Nepos Phocion 3,3). Attested as the claimant again in 318/7 (IG II2 448B l. 39), he was condemned to death after 317 (Plut. Phocion 38). (Possibly the accuser of the philosopher Theophrastus?, see Diog. Laert. 5,37). PA 176; TRAILL, PAA 107455.

HABICHT 58ff. BO.D.

Hagnus (Ἁγνοῦς; *Hagnoûs*, originally Ἀγνοῦς; *Agnoûs*). Attic *mesogeia* deme of the Acamantis phyle, from 307/6 BC of Demetrias, from 200/199 BC of Attalis; it provided five → *bouleutaí*. Formerly located near Dankla east of Markopoulo [1. 48], now to the southwest near Dardiste [2. 132], on the basis of the finding-place of the deme decree IG II[2] 1083 attributed erroneously in this collection to Myrrhinus. Leon, who had betrayed to Theseus the ambush of the Pallantids at Gargettus, was accorded a cult in H. (Steph. Byz. s.v. Ἁ.) [3. 12]. The old quarrel was considered to be the cause of the marriage ban with Pallene (Plut. Thes. 13,2f.) [3. 224[5]].

1 TRAILL, Attica 9, 48, 67, 110 no. 48, table 5, 12, 14 2 Id., Demos and Trittys, 1986, 132 3 WHITEHEAD, Index s.v. H. H.LO.

Hairesis (αἵρεσις; *haíresis*). Important term in the historiography of ancient philosophy and medicine, later in the history of Christian dogma. Its original meaning is 'selection', either concretely (e.g. 'election' of an official), or rather abstractly (e.g. 'decision'). In a first extension of meaning *hairesis* means 'disposition' or 'inclination' based on repeated decisions or choices; in a second extension of meaning *hairesis* means 'line of thought' or 'school of thought' and plays an important part in the historiography of ancient philosophy. Latin equivalents are *disciplina* or *secta*. The ancient Greek and Latin terms are more abstract in meaning and do not refer to any institution *per se*. The modern term often used for *hairesis*, 'sects', used for a strictly defined group of persons, is therefore misleading (→ Heresy).

In his preface to the history of philosophy, → Diogenes Laertius states that in ethical philosophy there were ten *hairéseis*: Academics, Cyrenaics, Elians, Megarians, Cynics, Eretrians, Dialectics, Peripatetics, Stoics and Epicureans (1,18). In his list of nine *hairéseis* (dating back to → Hippobotus), he notes that the description of the Pyrrhonians as *hairesis* is contentious as they did not have any clear doctrine (*asapheía*), and he adds that a new Eclectic *hairesis* was recently founded by Potamo of Alexandria (→ Eclecticism).

Obviously only post-Socratic schools are described as *hairesis*. Relevant here is the Hellenistic literature 'On the schools' (Περὶ αἱρέσεων; *Perì hairéseōn*), with its systematic presentation of the doctrines of the various schools or rather of their founders ([2]; → Doxography). For post-Socratic philosophy Diogenes Laertius typically offers only an outline of the doctrines of the founder of each *hairesis* (cf. 7,38). The most important *hairéseis* of around the 2nd cent. AD are the Platonics (successors to the Academic), the Peripatetics, Stoics, Epicureans and (Neo-) Pythagoreans. A philosopher was expected to show allegiance to one of the *hairéseis*, which meant in practice that the writings of the founders and of the members who succeeded them (διαδοχή, *diadochḗ*) were studied thoroughly [3].

The term *hairesis* is also found in ancient medicine: around the 1st cent. BC the doctors confessed their membership of three 'schools', the Dogmatists, the Empiricists and the Methodists (cf. → Galen, 'On *hairéseis* for beginners'); they were mainly differentiated by their methods of diagnosis and therapy ([4]; → Medicine).

In his description of contemporary Judaism, → Iosephus states that there are three *hairéseis* – Pharisees, Sadducees and Essenes – and presents their primary characteristics (BI 2,119–162). By analogy in the NT the Christian movement is called by its opponents 'the *hairesis* of the Nazarene' (Acts 24:5, cf. 14). In both cases the term is still used primarily neutral, as in Greek philosophy and medicine. In the 2nd cent. the two early Christian theologians → Iustinus and → Irenaeus use *hairesis* to refer to those 'lines of thought' which deviate from the doctrine of the Church as formulated in the apostolic succession. This negative interpretation is developed further by → Clemens [3] and → Origenes and becomes the starting-point for the important ideological concept of → heresy. Greek heresiography thus becomes Christian → heresiology (e.g. → Hippolytus, *Refutatio omnium haeresium*, 'Refutation of all *hairéseis*'), and followers of a *hairesis* become heretics (cf. e.g. → Tertullianus, *De praescriptione haereticorum*).

1 J. GLUCKER, Antiochus and the Late Academy, 1978, 166–206 2 J. MEJER, Diogenes Laërtius and his Hellenistic Background, 1978, 75–81 3 D. SEDLEY, Philosophical Allegiance in the Greco-Roman World, in: M. GRIFFIN, J. BARNES (ed.), Philosophia Togata: Essays on Philosophy and Roman Society, 1989, 97–119 4 H. VON STADEN, H. and Heresy: The Case of the *haireseis iatrikai*, in: B.F. MEYER, E.P. SANDERS (ed.), Jewish and Christian Self-Definition, vol 3: Self-Definition in the Greco-Roman World, 1982, 76–100 5 A. LE BOULLUEC, La notion d' hérésie dans la littérature grecque, IIe-IIIe siècles, Tome I: De Justin à Irénée, Tome II: Clément d' Alexandrie et Origène, 1985.

H. BROX, s.v. Häresie, RAC 13, 248–297. D.T.R.

Hair-net see → Phenake

Hairpin see → Needle

Hair sacrifice see → Sacrifice

Hair-stroke see → Writing, styles of

Hairstyle
I. Ancient Orient II. Greece and Italy

I. Ancient Orient
In the Ancient Orient differences existed between male and female hairstyles as well as human and divine hairstyles. Ancient Oriental hairstyles were usually based on long hair. With the exception of goddesses who were portrayed *en face* with long curls, braided hairstyles were usually worn up to the 1st millennium. Men preferred knots and women braided crown styles. The form and size of knots and braided crowns were used to differentiate between gods and humans. Shaved heads as a special style were frequenly associated with cultic roles. In the 1st millennium, hair was often worn loose with a cluster of curls at the end. Hairstyles were subject to fashion and could change from generation to generation. Male and female hairstyles can no longer be differentiated in the Neo-Assyrian period. Finds of wigs prove that artificial hairstyles were also known. Hairpins and ribbons were used as fastening and decoration. Individual hairstyles or a great abundance of hair served as a name-giving characteristic for various demons and certain classes of women.

J. Börker-Klähn, s.v. H., RLA 4, 1–22. G.CO.

II. Greece and Italy
A. General B. Greece C. Etruria D. Rome

A. General
Among the peoples of antiquity, hair was considered a special seat of life and strength that must be cared for and protected (→ *phenake*, → Needle). Hair loss signified old age and disease; shortening or cutting symbolized loss of freedom and servitude. On the other hand, voluntary cutting was a sign of surrender, e.g., to the service of a deity. The life- and strength-imbuing quality of hair or individual locks is related in several myths of which the tale of Samson and Delilah is the most famous. This symbolism was also well-known in the Greek sphere: Nisus/Scylla, Pterelaus/Comaetho and the hair of → Gorgo that → Athena gave to → Cepheus, to name but a few examples. Hair was also the subject of → magic and superstition: hair sacrifices and consecrations as part of taking a vow, penance and mourning, at marriages and sexual maturity were common. It was mandatory when making a promise or vow at the grave or in honour of the gods. Also, unusual hairstyles were considered noteworthy, e.g., the hair of the Abantes, Maxyges and Pramnae. The peculiarities, state and colour of their hair were assigned to historical persons as names, in Rome even as names of the *gens* and as epithets: Calvus, Chrysa, Cincinnatus, Crispinus, Flav(i)us, Hirtius, Helva, Pyrrha/Pyrrhus, Rufus, Rutilus, etc.

B. Greece
Men in Minoan Crete wore medium-long hair frequently divided into strands with a single long strand often hanging over the base of the nose, but wavy shoulder-length and short hair were also popular. Minoan women had long hair that was divided into thick strands that rested on the shoulders and upper arms and extended to the waist. They also wore their hair in loops, either with a simple twist or in knots, and in braids. Ribbons were often woven into the hair of Minoan and Mycenaean men and women (Hom. Il. 12,52 [1]), while ornaments at the temples adorned women's cheeks. The complicated Minoan women's hairstyle with a cross part, loose locks or knots was adopted by Mycenaean women during the palace period. During the '→ Dark Ages' short and long hairstyles were worn loosely or braided.

The 'stepped wig' in which the hair, which until that time is hanging down at the same length, was made to stand from the head in a compact mass and structured horizontally by means of cloth or metal bands [2] is attested from the 2nd half of the 8th cent. The hair of the Lady of Auxerre was divided into strands as a variant of this style and resulted in a diamond-shaped pattern. The 'stepped wig' developed in Crete from the Egyptian style and from there spread throughout the entire Greek world. Late evidence for it can be found in the 6th cent. About 600 BC, the full and occasionally wavy, hanging hair of men and women was often divided using ribbons (e.g., Sappho 98 a D) or sometimes hair in single strands was preferred: hair spirals, of which many are preserved, provided the necessary support. Individual strands could hang down freely at the temples or on the back. Using rings and decorative ribbon, hair was held above the forehead, over which wavy curls extended. In the 'pearl style', individual strands are also divided by bands and rings (e.g., the archaic kouros figures); the forehead is framed by arched curls. In the late 6th cent. the use of → *phenake* and hair parts spread, which resulted in more complicated arrangements [3]. Spiral and jagged curls became fashionable. Around the middle of the 6th cent., long hair was collected on the nape and tucked in under a headband (→ *krobylos*) while the hair ends hung down freely (fig. I A). In another style, the hair was twisted into a braid and held together by a spiral (→ *tettix* [2]) or tied in a knot.

In the last third of the 6th cent. BC, a period of short hair began among men, probably as a bourgeois reaction against long aristocratic hair (also called 'athlete's hairstyle'): the hair ended at the nape and could lie on the head in curls, short strands or strained smoothly back. Aristocrats and portraits of gods mostly retained long hair, but the short hairstyle prevailed by the 2nd half of the 5th cent. Women continued to prefer long

I. Greek women's hairstyles (5th–1st cents. BC).

II. Roman women's hairstyles (1st cent. BC–4st cent. AD).

hair: images show that it was held together by bands, nets or pins (→ Needle) and tied (fig. I B). Parted hair covered the forehead in loose wavy strands or was combed tightly to the nape. In the 2nd half of the 5th cent., the '*lampadion* style' (flame style) emerged: the hair was bound upward and ended in a peak above the crest of the head so that it was reminiscent of a flame (fig. I C). The 'ponytail' was also popular.

Even before the 4th cent., the 'Greek bun style' (or 'melon style') was introduced and lasted to the end of antiquity: the hair was divided into segments and taken tightly to the back of the head or formed into a braided crown or a bun (fig. I D). The beginning of the 4th cent. also saw the introduction of the hair band. The parted hair was pulled back over the head and bound with a band with the hair ends hanging freely on the head. This hairstyle was – just as the Greek bun style – a mark of youth and the preferred style for youthful deities (Apollo, Artemis, Aphrodite). In the final centuries, a host of other new hairstyles appeared. The most popular were parted hair with a high knot, Greek bun style with a high knot, the roll on the nape with the hair pulled tightly back, and the centre parting with temple roll and knot (fig. I E). The hairstyles of philosophers, children (from the 4th cent. also with a *Scheitelzopf*), slaves and artisans must be considered separately.

The hairstyle of Alexander the Great (→ Alexander [4]) with raised frontal hair (ἀναστολή, *anastolḗ*), which was often imitated (e.g., by → Pompeius), is noteworthy as a peculiarity; it has some precursors among images of → satyrs, but Alexander adopted it from heroic iconography (→ Achilles). The effect of this apparently dishevelled hair was caused by ἀναστολή, often combined with strands taken from the crown to the forehead and long hair at the nape; it was deliberately used by later rulers to symbolize strength and energy similar to that of Alexander.

C. Etruria

Etruscan hairstyles were similar to Greek styles. Generally, long hair was preferred and was either unbound, braided or arranged in the pearl style. Often, arched curls frame the forehead of the person pictured. However, unlike in Greece, women would also wear short styles where the hair was taken around the head in curls. In the 5th and 4th cents., hairstyles largely followed those of the Greeks. For example, women wore the melon style while men wore short hair. Often the hair was combed forward from the crown in strands and laid in heavy flame-like comma curls on the forehead. The 'Arringatore' statue of the early 1st cent. (Florence, AM) shows a short hairstyle with bundles of curls layered in rows lying flat on the forehead, whereas at the crown they are radially arranged.

D. Rome

In the early period, men wore a long hairstyle (cf. Varro, Rust. 2,11,10) that probably was similar in appearance to Greek and Etruscan styles. Presumably, a corresponding shift to short hair occurred in the 5th cent. In the early 2nd cent. BC, the coin image of T. Quinctius → Flamininus shows a development towards the style worn by Hellenistic rulers. During the late Republic men's hair was generally combed in loose, smooth strands from the crown to the forehead and far down the nape. In the Roman Imperial period the hairstyle was for the most part set by the imperial house. The differing hairstyles of the emperors and empresses were distributed through portraits and coins and adapted in numerous variants by citizens and provincials. Generally, it was fashion for men up to the 2nd cent. AD to wear short hair, unparted and combed over the forehead. Also, images of Nero, Domitian etc. show hair in crescent-shaped, wavy curls layered in several rows (*coma in gradus formata*, Suet. Nero 51). → Augustus' style pointed towards the future – especially for members of his family. The striking tongue-and-fork division of his frontal hair created a characteristic hairstyle later copied by the emperor Trajan, whereas otherwise hair was combed evenly into the forehead. A new style arrived with Hadrian: his hair was rather flat, but the frontal hair consisted of moving curls or bulging rolls (→ Beard). This changed among his successors when the hair was raised in many small curls. The soldier emperors of the 3rd cent. AD wore short hair, but in the Constantinian period longer hair was back in style. It was combed from the crown into the forehead and encircled it in a gentle arch, or the hair would lie on the forehead in a wave and cover the ears.

Roman female hairstyles were infinitely more complex and varied (Ov. Ars am. 3, 151f., cf. Ov. Ars am. 3,133–149 with notes on which hairstyle fits which face). While Roman women in the Republican period simply combed their hair back or wore styles based on Greek models, the hairstyles were enhanced by intricate patterns such as a looped fringe and braids on the calotte by the end of the Republican period. In the early Augustan period, 'Octavia's hairstyle' was the fashion: the hair was pulled tightly over the nape and formed into a knot while a second strand was pulled forward over the crest and ended in a flat knot (Ov. Ars am. 3,139f.; fig. II A). Subsequently, the (braided) hair could be tied at the nape and embellished by a bunch of curls in the 1st cent. AD. Later in the century, these curls then grew into a high, round bulge (s. Juv. 6,502f.; Mart. 2,66), which required → *phenake* and hair parts (fig. II B).

At the beginning of the 2nd cent., a change to simpler hairstyles occurred: women wrapped their hair, which was gathered in braids, several times around the head. The Hadrianic and Antonine periods favoured frontal hair layered in loops or pressed together in a flat roll. The hair mass was taken to the back of the head in a type of melon style with a knot or a hive [4] (fig. II C). A complete change occurred with Iulia Domna (→ *phenake*) whose compact hair mass was collected in horizontal waves and often did not have a centre parting (fig. II D). The forehead was occasionally framed by small corkscrew curls. The typical hairstyle of the 1st third of the 3rd cent. was the *Scheitelzopf*: the hair was combed back on both sides from the centre parting, folded over broadly at the nape, taken up and pinned at the top of the head (fig. II E). Towards the end of the cent. *Scheitelzopf* could form a loop on the forehead with the frontal hair divided in a melon style pattern [5].

→ Beard; → Mourning

1 H. Reusch, Die zeichnerische Rekonstruktion des Frauenfrieses im boiot. Theben, 1956, pl. 15 2 C. Davaras, Die Statue von Astritsi, in: AK 8. Beih., 1972, 24–25, 58. 3 Richter, Korai, fig. 411–419 4 M. Wegner, Datier. röm. Haartrachten, in: AA 1938, 276–325 5 K. Wessel, Röm. Frauenfrisuren von der severischen bis zur konstantinischen Zeit, in: AA 1946/7, 62–76.

L. Bonfante, Etruscan Dress, 1975, 67–80; R. Brilliant, Hairiness. A Matter of Style and Substance in Roman Portraits, in: FS F.E. Brown, 1993, 302–312; L. Byvanck-Quarles van Ufford, La coiffure des jeunes dames d'Athènes au second quart du 5ème siècle av. J.C., in: FS J.M.Hemelrijk, 1986, 135–140; E. David, Sparta's social hair, in: Eranos 90, 1992, 11–21; W.H. Gross, s.v. Haartracht, Haarschmuck, in: KlP 2, 1967, 897–899; E.B. Harrison, Greek Sculptured Coiffures and Ritual Haircuts, in: R. Hägg (ed.), Early Greek Cult Practice, 1988, 247–254; S.A.H. Kennell, Women's Hair and the Law. Two Cases from Late Antiquity, in: Klio 73, 1991, 526–536; A. Klein, Child Life in Greek Art, 1932, 36f.; J.H. Krause, Plotina oder die Kostüme des Haupthaares bei den Völkern der alten Welt mit Berücksichtigung einiger Kostüme neuerer Völker ..., 1858; I. Jenkins, D. Williams, Sprang Hair Nets. Their Manufacture and Use in Ancient Greece, in: AJA 89, 1985, 411–418; H.P. Laubscher, Fischer und Landleute. Stud. zur hell. Genreplastik, 1982, 44, 51–53; S. Marinatos, Kleidung, Haarund Barttracht, (ArchHom vol. 1 B), 1967; J. Meischner, Das Frauenporträt der Severerzeit, 1964; A. Onassoglou, Ein Klappspiegel aus einem Grab in der Ostlokris, in: AA 1988, 439–459; K. Polaschek, Stud. zu einem Frauenkopf im Landesmuseum Trier und zur weibl. Haartracht der iulisch-claudischen Zeit, in: TZ 35, 1972, 141–210; H. Rühfel, Das Kind in der griech. Kunst, 1984; A.V. Siebert, Quellenanalytische Bemerkungen zu Haartracht und Kopfschmuck röm. Priesterinnen, in: Boreas 18, 1995, 77–92. R.H.

Halae (Ἁλαί; *Halaí*). 'Salt pans', name of several settlements, in Attica of two demes.

[1] H. Aixonides (Ἁλαὶ Αἰξωνίδες; *Halaì Aixōnídes*), Attic deme, which constituted together with Aexone the *paralia* trittys of the phyle Cecropis. Therefore, (only administratively? [3. 148[476]]) distinguished by 'Aixonides' from H. [2] on the east coast of Attica. H. provided six (ten) → *bouleutaí*. H. (modern Voula and Vouliagmeni [7. 466 fig. 588]) bordered in the north on Aexone (modern Glyphada) and in the east on Anagyrus (modern Vari) (Str. 9,1,21). Its eastern boundary was marked by *horos* inscriptions on the Kaminia [1; 2; 3. 63ff. pl. 35].

Decrees from H. document an → agora (IG II² 1174 l. 13–15), a → dḗmarchos [3] [8. 58[84], 410f. no. 15f.], *tamíai* [8. 143], an *eúthynos* ([8. 117f.], etc.; more at [8. 380f. no. 50–58 and Index s.v. H. Aixonides]; → *eúthynai*). The decree IG II² 1175 (*c.* 360 BC) is reacting to an internal (religious?) scandal [8. 97, 182f., 380 no. 53].

Several cults are documented for H. [8. 206]: Apollo Zoster [8. 380f. no. 55], Aphrodite (IG II² 2820), Artemis, Athena (Paus. 1,31,1), Dionysus Anthios (IG II² 1356 l. 9f.), Poseidon? (Ath. 297e *Halae* [8. 208]).

Ancient remains: prehistoric settlements and graves are found in several locations [3. 66f.], Mycenaean graves (SH III A-C) near Glyphada [7. 467 fig. 589–594]. In the area of Voula/Ano Voula two village-like settlement concentrations from the classical period [3. 27–70 pl. 34; 5. 129ff. fig. 16–18 pl. 88,3.4, 89, 90;

7. 467, 474ff. fig. 595–597] as well as numerous farmsteads and graves are preserved. The sanctuary of Zoster (Steph. Byz. s.v. Ζωστήρ) with the archaic Apollo temple [3. 58; 7. 467, 477 fig. 599f.], which was dedicated to Apollo, Artemis, Leto and Athena (Paus. 1,31,1), is located north of the cape on the narrow land bridge, which is now submerged [5. 14f.]. The late classical (!) 'priest's residence' is interpreted by LAUTER as a 'villa' [3. 59ff.]. During the → Chremonidean War (267–262 BC) a fortification was created over a prehistoric settlement on Cape Zoster [3. 68; 6] as well as the early Hellenistic Kastro Vouliagmenis at the western end of the defile of Vari [4. 95ff. Abb. 3]. Settlement has declined drastically since the early Hellenistic period [3. 67; 8. 360].

1 H.R. GOETTE, Neue att. Felsinschr., in: Klio 76, 1994, 120–134 2 H. LAUTER, Zwei Horosinschr. bei Vari, in: AA 1982, 299–315 3 Id., Att. Landgemeinden in klass. Zeit, in: MarbWPr 1991, 1–161 4 H. LAUTER-BUFÉ, Die Festung auf Koroni und die Bucht von Porto Raphti, in: MarbWPr 1988, 67–102 5 H. LOHMANN, Atene, 1993 6 J.R. MCCREDIE, Fortified Military Camps in Attica (Hesperia Suppl. 11), 1966, 30ff. 7 TRAVLOS, Attika, 466–479 fig. 588–602 8 WHITEHEAD.

C.W.J. ELIOT, Coastal Demes, 1962; TRAILL, Attica, 20, 50, 59, 67, 110 no. 49, 124 table 7; WHITEHEAD, Index s.v. H. Aixonides. H.LO.

[2] H. Araphenides (Ἁλαὶ Ἀραφενίδες; *Halaì Araphenídes*). An Attic *paralia* deme of the phyle Aegeis; it provided five (nine) → *bouleutaí*. Near Loutsa on the east coast of Attica between Brauron in the south (Str. 9,1,22; Steph. Byz. s.v. Ἁ.) and Araphen in the north [2]. Therefore, (only administratively?) distinguished by 'Araphenides' from H. [1]. Three demes decrees [5. 381 no. 59–61] document several functionaries and (indirectly) a theatre in which agons were held during the Rural Dionysia [4. 211; 5. 123[12], 141[118], 212, 220[263], 222]. The cults (aition: Eur. IT 1449ff.) and temple [2; 3] of Artemis Tauropolos and the Tauropolia (Hsch. s.v. T.; Men. Epit. 234, 255, 260, 300, 479, 685; [1–3; 4. 211])were of superregional significance. Ath. 297e records a Poseidon cult at H. The lost comedy *Halaieîs* (Ἁλαιεῖς) by Menander was set in H. [5. 338[76], 341[81]].

1 L. DEUBNER, Att. Feste, ³1969, 208f. 2 C.W.J. ELIOT, s.v. H. Araphenides, PE, 373f. 3 H. KNELL, Der Tempel der Artemis Tauropolos in Lutsa, in: AA 1983, 39–43 4 TRAVLOS, Attika 5 WHITEHEAD.

TRAILL, Attica, 16, 40, 59, 67, 110 no. 50, 124 table 2; TRAVLOS, Attika, 211–215 fig. 264–268; WHITEHEAD, Index s.v. H. Araphenides. H.LO.

[3] Originally belonging to Locris Opuntia, H. was the northernmost Boeotian port on the Gulf of Euboea from *c.* 270 BC (Str. 9,2,13; 4,2; Paus. 9,24,5; Steph. Byz. s.v. Ἁ.). Traces of the settlement on the eastern side of the bay of Opus (modern Atalanti), NW of modern Theologos immediately by the sea range from the Neolithic to the Byzantine period. The municipal fortifications from the period about 600 BC were destroyed in 426/5 by an earthquake, but were renewed and expanded in the 4th cent.; even after the destruction by Sulla's troops in 86/5 BC, it was quickly resettled (Plut. Sulla 26). The walls are still well-preserved in sections, as are intramural buildings (e.g., the temple of Athena Poliouchos in three construction phases of the archaic and classical periods; late Roman baths) and necropoleis.

J.E. COLEMAN, Excavations at Halai, 1990–1991, in: Hesperia 61, 1992, 265–289; LAUFFER, Griechenland, 253; N.D. PAPACHATZIS, Παυσανίου Ἑλλάδος Περιήγησις 5, ²1981, 167f.; P. ROESCH, Thespies et la confédération béotienne, 1965, 66f.; SCHACHTER, vol. 1, 114f.; vol. 3, 100, 161f.; P.W. WALLACE, Strabo's description of Boiotia, 1979, 59f. P.F.

Halaesa (Ἅλαισα; *Hálaisa*). Place name ascribed to several cities (Diod. Sic. 14,16,2); one lay south of → Tauromenium, another near St. Agata di Militello [3. 394, n. 45; 5. 142]; the best known, Ἁ. Ἀρχωνίδειος, founded 403 BC by → Archonides [2], the dynast in → Herbita, with the help of mercenaries, near the small church of St. Maria di Palatii located near Tusa (8 stadia from the sea: Diod. Sic. 14, 16, 1–4). This town submitted to the Romans in 263 BC (Diod. Sic. 23,4), became *civitas libera et immunis* (Cic. Verr. 2,3,13; Diod. Sic. 14,16,3 f.), in the Augustan age → *municipium* (CIL X 7458). Italian traders, who set up a dedicatory inscription to a L. Cornelius Scipio (CIL X 2, 7459), settled in H. It appeared in the lists of the Delphic theorodokoi (→ Theoria [1]) [6. 24 f.; 4. 421, Z. 115]. Still quite prosperous in the 2nd/3rd cents., it declined in the Byzantine era [1. 26ff; 2. 293 ff.].

INSCHR.: IG XIV 352–358 [7]; CIL X 2, 7458–60. 1 M. BOLLANI, Imola, in: Notizie degli scavi di antichità 1961, 26–32 2 G. CARETTONI, Tusa, in: Notizie degli scavi di antichità, 1959, 293–349 3 A. HOLM, Gesch. Siziliens im Alt. 3, 1898 4 G. MANGANARO, Città di Sicilia e santuari panellenici nell III e II sec. a. C., in: Historia 13, 1964, 415–439 5 E. MANNI, Geografia fisica e politica della Sicilia antica (Kokalos Suppl. 4), 1981 6 A. PLASSART, La liste des thèorodoques, in: BCH 45, 1921, 1–85 7 G. SCIBONA, Epigraphica Halaesina, in: Kokalos 17, 1971, 3–20.

R. CALCIATI (ed.), Corpus Nummorum Siculorum vol. 1, 1983, 59–63; G. LANCILLOTTO CASTELLI, La storia di Alesa, 1753. C.GIU./M.B.

Halakhah The term (derived from the Hebrew root *hlk*, 'to go') describes both a particular Jewish legal requirement or fixed regulation as well as the entire system of legal requirements dictated by Jewish tradition. The fundamental principles of these requirements, traditionally considered to be the 'Oral Torah' (*Tora shebe-al-peh*) and the revelations to Moses on Mt. Sinai, form the legal corpora of the Pentateuch (e.g., the so-called 'Book of the Covenant' [Ex 20,22–23,19], Deuteronomic law [Dt 12,1–26,15] or the Holiness Code

[Lv 17–26]). After the canonization of the Pentateuch in the post-exile and Early Judaic periods individual regulations were standardized, updated, and expanded, in the course of which vastly diverging opinions and conceptions could arise among the various factions of early Judaism, such as the Saducees, the Pharisees, or the Essenes (cf. e.g., 4Q Ma'aseh Miqzat ha-Torah). The earliest authoritative, post-biblical collection of laws is the Mišna, which was codified – again, on the basis of older traditions – by the patriarch Jehuda ha Nasi *c.* AD 200. It is made up of six different orders (Hebrew *sedarīm*) with a total of 63 tractates (Hebrew *peraqīm*) and contains the laws governing ritual, purity, cultic rites (and agricultural offerings in particular), times and customs of the festivals, as well as questions pertaining to the calendar, dealings with the poor, and family law and torts – thus covering all spheres of human life.

Further early Jewish compilations of Halakhic content worthy of note are the Tosefta, as well as the so-called Halakhic Midrašim Mekhilta of Rabbi Ishmaʿel (on Ex), the Sifra (on Lv) and the Sifre on Numbers or on Deuteronomy. The Mišna forms the basis for further Halakhic reifications, supplements, and discussions, which were later compiled in the two Talmudīm: the Palestinian (codified *c.* end of 5th cent. AD) and the Babylonian (codified *c.* 6th cent.). The foundation of the Halakhah is scriptural exposition, in accordance with a very specific methodological and hermeneutic apparatus (the so-called seven Middot, or Rules of Hillel – which, for their part, show clear influences of ancient rhetoric). In terms of modernizing the Halakhah, however, rabbinical authorities can issue entirely new regulations, which may, on occasion, represent a radical reinterpretation of the existing biblical law (so-called *Taqqanot*). Finally, long-standing customs may also be regarded as binding law and even replace older *Halakhot* (*Minhag*).

The necessity of updating the Halakhah, as well as the tendency to safeguard the observance of the Torah through additional regulations (cf. mAv 1,1: 'Make a fence around the Torah') led to a continual growth of the body of traditions. Due to the significant role played by the Babylonian Jews in late antiquity and the early Middle Ages, the Babylonian Talmud became the highest Halakhic authority. However, the material tends to be organized rather unsystematically and appears confusing. Thus, the desire for, and necessity of, a clear summary of the individual regulations was soon felt (cf., e.g., the 'Book of Laws' of Isaac Alfasi [1013–1103], the *Mishne Torah* of Maimonides [1135–1204], or the *Šulchan Aruch* of Joseph Karo [1488–1575]). In addition, since the early Middle Ages, it was common practice in difficult cases to appeal to the scholars for individual judgements – so-called responsa. The question of how to substantiate the legal requirements, which often cannot be comprehended rationally, was already under discussion in antiquity. No definite answer has as yet been found. In general, it is pointed out that God gave Israel the Torah with its Halakhic regulations so that it might earn merit. At the same time, warning is given against observing the Halakhah in a manner that is calculating and intent on reward. Rather, Israel should be like 'servants who serve the master out of love' (mAv 1,3). In addition to the practical function of the Halakhah, great significance is also ascribed to its theoretical study – for it is considered to be a form of religious service that is graced with the presence (*Šekhina*) of God (cf., e.g., bBer 17a). Thus, ultimately, it is the study of the Halakhah that continues to offer direct contact with God even after the destruction of the temple.

→ Haggadah; → Rabbinical Literature; → Talmud

L. Jacobs, s.v. Halacha, TRE 30 (30), 384–388; L. Jacob, J. and B. De-Vries, s.v. Halakhah, Encyclopaedia Judaica 2, 1156–1166; G. Stemberger, Der Talmud. Einführung, Texte, Erläuterungen, 1982, 71–158; Id., Das klass. Judentum, 1979, 126–160. B.E.

Halcyone see → Alcyone

Halcyoneus (Ἁλκυονεύς/*Halkyoneús* or Ἀλκυονεύς/*Alkyoneús*). Son of → Antigonus [2] Gonatas, to whom he brought the head of his fallen archrival → Pyrrhus in Argos in 272 BC; rebuked by his father as a barbarian, H. treated Pyrrhus' son Helenus honourably (Plut. Pyrrhus 34; Plut. Mor. 119C; Ael. VH 3,5). L.-M.G.

Hales (modern Alento). River in Lucania, at whose mouth lay the gradually silting up anchorage of Elea (Str. 6,1,1; Cic. Att. 16,7,5; [2]), probably named for a native deity [1].

1 L. Ronconi, La ninfa Hyele, in: Atti e Memorie dell'Accademia Patavina 95, 1982/3, 65–72 2 G. Schmiedt, Contributo alla recostruzione della situazione geotopografica di Velia nell'antichità, in: PdP 25, 1970, 65–92.

D. Musti, Le fonti per la storia di Velia, in: PdP 21, 1966, 318–335, esp. 321. M.I.G.

Halesus (usually spelled Halaesus). Italic hero, companion or illegitimate son of → Agamemnon, who fled to Italy (Serv. Aen. 7,723). He is regarded as the founder of → Falerii and the eponymous hero of the → Falisci, and imported the local cult of Juno from Argos (Ov. Am. 3,13,31–35; Fast. 4,73f.; connection of Falerii with Argos: Cato fr. 47 HRR). Alternatively, he is the founder of Alsium (Sil. Pun. 8,474). The former case presupposes the Faliscan sound change *f* > *h* [1]; the latter assumes the name takes the form **Alesus*. In Virgil, H., the companion of Agamemnon (Aen. 7,723), supplies Turnus with 'a thousand men' from the northern campaigns (Auruncans, Sidicinians, Oscans etc., Aen. 7,725–730; 10,352f. [2]). His father, a seer, kept H. hidden in the forest to prevent him from going to war (Aen. 10,417, possibly Virgil's own invention). H., the son of → Neptunus, is celebrated by the Veiians in a hymn of the local Salian priests (Serv. Aen. 8,285). The diversity of traditions can generally be explained by the various attempts of Italic communities to provide themselves with Homeric ancestry, though it may in some cases be a matter of poetic invention.

1 A. NEHRING, Lat. Gramm., in: Glotta 14, 1925, 233–275 2 J. PERRET, H. ou Messapus (A propos d'Aeneis VII 641–871), in: Mélanges de philosophie, de littérature et d'histoire ancienne offerts à Pierre Boyancé, 1974, 557–568.

G. GARBUGINO, s.v. H., EV 1,90. F.G.

Halex (Ἅληξ; *Hálēx*). River in southern Bruttium, modern Alice. According to Timaeus (FGrH 566 F 43b) and Strabo (6,1,9) the border river between Rhegium and Locri (Paus. 6,6,4, however, says Caecinus). In the Peloponnesian War (426 BC) scene of an Athenian expedition against Locri (Thuc. 3,99).

NISSEN 2, 955. H.SO.

Halia (Ἁλία, Ἁλίη; *Halía, Halíē*), 'belonging to the sea' [1].
[1] → Nereid catalogued [2] in Hom. Il. 18,40, Hes. Theog. 245 (θ' Ἁλίη [3]; but Θαλίη [4]) and Apollod. 1,11. A female figure on the lid of an Attic red-figured lekanis is labelled H. [5].
[2] According to a Rhodian myth in Diod. Sic. 5,55, sister of the → Telchines, who raised Poseidon. H. had seven children by the latter – six sons and a daughter, Rhodos. The sons were driven insane by Aphrodite as punishment for their hubris and raped their mother, H. In consequence, she threw herself into the sea. Thereafter, she was worshipped as a goddess under the name of → Leucothea.

1 KAMPTZ, 268 2 R. WACHTER, Nereiden und Neoanalyse: ein Blick hinter die Ilias, in: WJA, 1990, 19–31 3 Hesiodi Theogonia, Opera et dies, Scutum, ed. F. SOLMSEN, 31990 4 Hesiod, Theogony, ed. M.L. WEST, 1966, with comm. 5 R. VOLLKOMMER, s.v. H., LIMC 4.1, 407f. A.A.

Haliacmon (Ἁλιάκμων; *Haliákmōn*). Largest southern Macedonian river, flows through the lands of Orestis, Elimea and Pieria and empties into the Thermaic Gulf. An important route to Thessaly ran through the lower H. valley.

E. MEYER, s.v. H. (2), RE Suppl. 11, 674f. MA.ER.

Haliartus (Ἁλίαρτος, Ἀρίαρτος, Ἁρίαρτος; *Halíartos, Aríartos, Haríartos* [1. 483]). Boeotian city on the southern edge of Lake Copais, 20 km west of Thebes. The acropolis with archaic Athena sanctuary is located on the hill Kastri Mazíou, which was settled from the Middle Helladic to the Roman period and was adjoined by the fortified lower city. In the 6th cent. BC, H. – mentioned by Homer (Il. 2,503) – struck coins with the league emblem, the 'Shield of the Boeotians' [2. 345]. In its territory lay the league sanctuary of Poseidon of Onchestus. Beginning in 446 (?), H. formed a district of the Boeotian League with Coronea and Lebadea (Hell. Oxy. 19,3,392). The Spartan Lysander fell in the battle near H. in 394 (Xen. Hell. 3,5,17f.). On the side of Rome's enemies in the 3rd Macedonian War, H. was destroyed in 172 BC by the Romans, the land transferred to Athens (Pol. 27,1,5; 30,21; Liv. 42,44,1; 46,9f.; 56,3–5; 63,3). Athens sent settlers and managed the area (Str. 9,2,30) through *epimelētaí* [3. 168–171]. Also cf. to H. Heraclides Criticus 1,25 and Paus. 9,32f.

1 W. SPOERRI, s.v. H., LFE 1 2 HN 3 P. ROESCH, Études Béotiennes, 1982.

FOSSEY, 301–308. K.F.

Halicarnassus (Ἁλικαρνασσός; *Halikarnassós*).
I. LOCATION II. HISTORICAL DEVELOPMENT III. ARCHAEOLOGICAL FINDINGS IV. LITERARY NOTABLES

I. LOCATION

Coastal city in the south of → Caria on the Gulf of Ceramus, modern Bodrum. The plan of the city (Str. 14,2,16; Steph. Byz. s.v. Ἁ.; Vitr. De arch. 2,8,10–14) resembled the seating arrangement of a theatre: a circular harbour bay, the 'enclosed harbour' (λιμὴν κλειστός, Ps.-Scyl. 98a), framed on both sides by rocky, raised land projections, in the east by Zephyrion (originally an island, Plin. HN 2,204), in the west by Salmacis (Arr. Anab. 1,23,3); the city rises step-like in the background. Up to the 4th cent. BC, settlement was concentrated on Zephyrion and Salmacis, the centre of the city of Maussollos was still a necropolis (esp. in the area of the → Maussolleum).

II. HISTORICAL DEVELOPMENT

A. EARLY HISTORY B. GREEK AND ROMAN PERIOD C. BYZANTINE PERIOD

A. EARLY HISTORY

This very old Carian city was alleged to have already received Greek settlers from Argolis (Troezen: Hdt. 7,99; Paus. 2,30,8; Argos: Vitr. De arch. 12,8,12; Mela 1,16,3) in the 12th cent. BC (1175: Tac. Ann. 4,55), probably, however, not before the 11th/10th cents. in the bounds of the 'Ionian colonisation' (→ Ionic migration). Regarding the pre-Greek population, besides the Carians there is mention of Leleges north and west of H., especially on the ' peninsula of H.' which stretches west to → Myndus. These probably had early contact with Mycenaean Greeks (necropolis of Müskebi) and persisted around H. into → Maussollos' time. The oldest Greek settlement in H. was probably located on Zephyrion, while Salmacis or the spring of the same name appears (in mythic-aetiological fables, Vitr. De arch. 2,8,11f.; Str. 14,2,16; cf. Ov. Met. 4,285ff.) to be connected with the Carian substrate which had been driven inland. Judging from personal names, the Carian portion of the population was still strong in the mid 5th cent. H., although to a large extent Hellenized; despite Doric traditions which still flourished in the 4th cent. (oecist Anthes from Troezen with mixed Greek colonists, Str. 14,2,16; Paus. 2,30,10) and Doric institutions, the Doric element (Hdt. 7,99,3) was always weak; Ionic Greek was the colloquial and official language.

B. Greek and Roman Period

Expelled early on from the Doric Hexapolis (Hdt. 1,145), H. probably came under the rule of Croesus after 560 BC, 546 under that of the Persians (Hdt. 1,174f.; 2,178; 3,4; 3,11) and was the seat of the Carian-Greek dynastic family of Lygdamis, whose daughter → Artemisia [1] was praised by Herodotus. Probably around 468, at the time of Cimon's expedition to southern Asia Minor, H. became a member of the → Delian League. After a failed uprising against the namesake (great?)grandson Lygdamis (around the mid–5th cent.), → Herodotus fled H. for Samos (Suda s.v. Herodotus); afterwards, the tyrant was successfully removed. A law from this period concerning disputed house and property ownership (ML 32) still names Lygdamis alongside the constitutional bodies of H. and the then still semi-autonomous community of Salmacis. Towards the end of the Peloponnesian War, H. again fell under Persian suzerainty, but before 390 belonged to the newly created satrapy Caria under the dynasts of → Mylasa. Phormion of H., Olympic boxing champion in 392, was sentenced with two other boxers to a heavy fine in Olympia for bribery in 388 (Paus. 5,21,3). H. lodged a successful complaint against the customs duty imposed in 389 by Thrasybulus on Athens' regained ally (Lys. 28,12; 17), the renewed orientation to Athens remained an interlude. After the King's Peace of 386, H. came under control of Hecatomnus of Mylasa.

H. first gained importance when the latter's son → Maussollos made H. his capital in place of Mylasa (Diod. Sic. 15,90,3), enhanced its population by that of six small towns of the Leleges on the basis of a synoecism (Callisthenes FGrH 124 F 25; Str. 13,1,58f.) and built H. into a large city with naval prestige: The hillside territory between Zephyrion and Salmacis was developed following a Hippodamian plan: the agora near the harbour. Above, in the terraced city area, a main street was laid out running across and cut by side streets going uphill (Vitr. De arch. 2,8,11); the tomb of Maussollos rose at its midpoint. It lay exactly in the centre of a circle whose diameter corresponded to the length of the main street between the two city gates (10 stadia, *c.* 1.76 km), and which circumscribed the entire area from the harbour to the heights north of the city – making the whole city a monument to its new founder. On Zephyrion, where in the 5th cent. the city's temple of Apollo probably stood, rose the palace of Maussollos (Vitr. De arch. 2,8,10; Plin. HN 36,47); hidden behind the walls on the 'isthmus' to the mainland was the naval harbour (*portus secretus*, Vitr. De arch. 2,8,13f.) with access to the palace (which perhaps also lay north of the isthmus on the mainland?) and a channel to the outer harbour.

The attempt by Rhodes to seize the city and its harbours in a surprise attack after Maussollos' death in 353 was thwarted by Artemisia [2] (Vitr. De arch. 2,8,14). In 334, the city, defended by Memnon of Rhodes against Alexander the Great, was conquered after a short siege and destroyed (Arr. Anab. 1,20,5–23,6; Diod. Sic. 17,23,4–27,6). The female dynast → Ada took part in the battle on Alexander's side and captured one of the two acropoleis of H. (Str. 14,2,17; Zephyrion, Salmacis or mountain fortresses in the ring wall?). In the Hellenistic era, H. was mostly under Ptolemaic influence at first, was free in 192 BC and on the side of Rome (Liv. 37,10,16); in 88 BC, the city came under the rule of Mithridates VI (App. Mith. 21); in 80/79 it fell victim to the rapacity of Verres, then legate of the governor of Cilicia (Cic. Verr. 2,1,49); attacked by pirates in 62–58, H. recovered thanks to the care of Q. Tullius Cicero, the governor of Asia (Cic. Ad Q. Fr. 1,1,25); in 58 BC, H. was incorporated into the Roman province. The request to be granted a → neocoria in AD 26 was refused by Tiberius (Tac. Ann. 4,55). The Jewish community in H. was guaranteed free religious practice (Jos. Ant. Iud. 14,10,23).

C. Byzantine Period

H. became a city of the eastern Roman Empire in AD 395; in the 13th cent., H. came under the rule of the Seljuk Menteşe emirs of Milâs (Mylasa), 1402 the city was taken over by the Knights of St. John of Rhodes: construction of the fortress S. Pietro, 'Petronion', on Zephyrion by the German Heinrich Schlegelholt. During its reinforcement in 1495, stone was once again taken from the → Maussolleum, so that this, ruined by earthquakes, was now levelled to the ground (exposure of the tomb chamber). In the Middle Ages, H. was no more than a small town named Mese (Μέση, 'lying amid') or Tabia ('fortification'). It finally came under Turkish rule in 1523 after the withdrawal of the Knights of St. John.

III. Archaeological Findings

Among the ancient structures identified and partially uncovered in the 19th cent. by Newton (1856–1858) and others, still extant are, at the top of the eastern slope of Göktepe, a large platform for a temple of Ares or Mars (Roman), in which a colossal acrolithic statue by Leochares or Timotheus once stood (Vitr. De arch. 2,8,11; Plin. HN 36,4); on the southern slope of Göktepe is the theatre (3rd cent.? with alterations from the Imperial era) for 13,000 spectators; in the west of the city, a Roman house with mosaic floors was found, the same were also uncovered in the southern part of the peribolus of the Maussolleum. Awaiting rediscovery or systematic excavation in the eastern part of the city are a Roman stoa (on large terrace, 30 columns), a Hellenistic stoa, a gymnasium (?), a temple of Demeter and Persephone. Probably near the Salmacis spring above the Turkish arsenal not far from a *türbe* (Turkish funerary tower) – probably not on the Kaplan kalesi ('Tiger palace'), which lies farther south and has only shown prehistoric surface finds – a sanctuary of Aphrodite and Hermes (or of Hermaphroditus) is suspected. The over 6 km long city wall, which surrounded the city mountains to the north, still exists in many places (countless chamber tombs above the theatre in peak cliffs, mostly of Hellenistic-Roman period); in the east, the gate to Mylasa is visible (Arr. Anab. 1,20,4; 21,1; today destroyed), in the west, where the road to Myndus begins, is the Tripylon with a deep ditch in front of it; Alexander broke through at this weakest point (Arr. Anab. 1,20,8; 22,4–7). The ancient principal axis between the gates is still followed today by the Turgut-Reis road, on whose southern side lies the excavation field of the → Maussolleum (today with museum). Archaeologically speaking, H. is today a Scandinavian domain: research, excavations and surveys have been carried out by Danes and Swedes since the 1980s.

IV. Literary notables

Besides the 'Father of History', Herodotus (Cic. Leg. 1,1,5), literary notables who came from H. include, in the 2nd half of the 1st cent. BC, the historian → Dionysius [18], as well as, in the Hadrianic period, the musicologist → Dionysius [20] Musicus, possibly identical with the lexicographer Aelius → Dionysius [21]. H.KA.

G.E. Bean, J.M. Cook, The H. Peninsula, in: ABSA 50, 1955, 85–108; G.Bockisch, Die Karer und ihre Dynasten, in: Klio 51, 1969, 117–175; L.Bürchner, s.v. H., RE 7, 2253–2264; W.Hoepfner, H., die Hauptstadt des Maussollos, in: Ant. Welt 18/4, 1987, 51–54; Id., Haus und Stadt im klass. Griechenland, 1994, 226–234; S.Hornblower, Mausolus, 1982; J.Isager (ed.), Hecatomnid Caria and the Ionian Renaissance (Congr. Odense 1991), 1994; W.Judeich, Kleinasiat. Studien, 1892; G.Jürgens, De rebus Halicarnassensium 1, 1877; T.Linders (ed.), Architecture and Society in Hecatomnid Caria (Congr. Upsala 1987), 1989; Magie 2, 909ff.; Ch.Th. Newton, A History of Discoveries at H., Cnidus, and Branchidae, 1862; P.Pedersen, The Fortifications of H., in: REA 96, 1994, 215–235; L.Rocchetti, EAA 1, 251–253. H.KA. and C.HÖ.

Halicyae (Ἁλικύαι; *Halikýai*). Town of the → Elymi between Lilybaeum and → Entella [1. 168–171] in the Carthaginian sphere of influence. Allied with Athens during the Peloponnesian War (Thuc. 7,32,1; IG I², 20), in 278/7 conquered by Pyrrhus, in 263 by the Romans (Diod. Sic. 22,10,2; 23,5). Cicero counted the *Halicyenses* among the *civitates immunes ac liberae* (Cic. Verr. 3,13; 91; 5,15), Pliny among the *stipendiarii* (Plin. HN 91).

1 BTCGI 3.

G.Bejor, Città di Sicilia, in: ASNP 12/3, 1982, 838f.; G.Manganaro, La Sicilia da Sesto Pompeo a Diocleziano, in: ANRW II 11.1, 1988, 78 n. 429. GI.MA.

Halieis (Ἁλιεῖς, Ἁλιαί; *Halieîs*, *Haliaí*). Harbour town on the Bay of Porto Cheli in the Argolis, founded by exiles from → Tiryns, instigated by Hermione, shortly after 479 BC (Hdt. 7,137). The remains of the ancient city, partially sunken into the sea, were found opposite the modern town on a small cape dominating the harbour entrance. H. was probably destroyed at the end of the 4th cent. BC. References: Scyl. 52; Str. 8,6,11; Paus. 2,36,1 (Ἁλίκη).

B.Bergquist, Primary or Secondary Temple Function: the Case of H., in: OpAth 18, 1990, 23–37; M.H. Jameson, s.v. H., EAA², 21–23; M.H. McAllister, The Fortifications of Ancient H., 1973. Y.L.

Halieuticon Plin. HN 32,11. 152 mentions a work with this title ('Fishing', probably a gen. pl., Ἁλιευτικῶν; *Halieutikôn*), which he says → Ovid began in exile. Pliny's citations appear to paraphrase the 130 or so *Versus Ovidi de piscibus et feris* that have been handed down in two MSS of the 8th/9th and 10th cents. On stylistic, linguistic, and metric grounds, the brief fragment cannot be attributed to Ovid. However, it seems very unlikely that it is a post-Plinian forgery. Ultimately, it draws on the ancient zoological tradition.

Editions: E.de Saint-Denis, Ovide, Halieutiques, 1975.
Bibliography: J.Richmond, Chapters on Greek Fish-Lore, 1973; Id., The authorship of the H. ascribed to Ovid, in: Philologus 120, 1976, 92–106. J.A.R.

Halimus (Ἁλιμοῦς; *Halimoûs*). Attic asty-deme of the phyle Leontis, with three → *bouleutaí* (for population size [4. 286]), according to Str. 9,1,21 located on the west coast of Attica between Phalerum and Aexone 35 stadia (= 6.2 km) from the city (Dem. Or. 57,10). H., which bordered Euonymon in the east, lay near the modern Halimos and Hagios Kosmas, the ancient cape → Colias with the sanctuary of Demeter Thesmophoros and Kore (Paus. 1,31,1; Hsch. s.v. Κωλιάς; [1–3]; prehistorical settlement: [5]). Thesmophoria are documented for H. (Schol. Aristoph. Thesm. 80 [6. 80]) as well as the following cults [6. 207[172]]: Hercules (Dem. Or. 57, 46–48; 62 [6. 114[147], 181f.]), Hestia (SEG 21, 813), Dionysus (SEG 2, 7 l. 23 [2; 6. 204[172], 221[268]]). The cult of Aphrodite Colias was incorrectly located by Strabo (9,1,21) in Anaphlystus [6. 207[172]]. Five → *dḗmarchoi* are known by name [6. 411f. no. 18–22]. The historian → Thucydides came from H. Demosthenes dealt with a judicial scandal in H. (Or. 57; [6. 105ff. 296ff.]).

1 J.Day, Cape Colias, Phalerum and the Phaleric Wall, in: AJA 36, 1932, 1–11 2 J.J. Hondius, A New Inscription of the Deme Halimous, in: ABSA 24, 1919/21, 151–160
3 G.Karo, Arch. Funde, in: AA 1930, 100
4 H.Lohmann, Atene, 1993 5 G.Mylonas, Agios Kosmas, 1959 6 Whitehead.

Traill, Attica, 43, 62, 68, 110 no. 51, table 4; J.S. Traill, Demos and Trittys, 1986, 130; Whitehead, Index s.v. H. H.LO.

Halios geron (ἅλιος γέρων; *hálios gérōn*, 'Old Man of the Sea'). Old sea deity, originally without a name of his own, later identified with → Nereus, → Proteus, → Phorcys and → Glaucus, with whom he shares the characteristics of old age, gift of prophecy, and ability to change shape [1; 2]. In the *Iliad*, *Halios geron (HG)* appears as the father of → Thetis and the → Nereids (Hom. Il. 1,358; 538 = 556; 18,141; 20,107; 24,562; Hom. Od. 24,58), but he is not explicitly equated with Nereus until Hesiod (Theog. 234; 1003; cf. schol. Pind. Pyth. 9,164 DRACHMANN and Cornutus, De natura deorum 23). In Hom. Od. 4,365; 384 Proteus is given the epithet *HG*, in 13,96 (345) it is Phorcys. There are isolated examples of a cult of *HG* – i.e., of the respective local deity: in Laconian Gytheum (Paus. 3,21,9: Nereus), among the Iberians (schol. Apoll. Rhod. 2,767: Glaucos; cf. Avien. 263) and on the Bosporus (Dionysius of Byzantium 49 p. 20 GÜNGERICH: Nereus, Phorcys, Proteus or the father of the nymph Semistra). Two pictorial representations with inscriptions survive, one of which shows *HG* (Nereus) with a fishtail battling Hercules [3; 4].

1 NILSSON, GGR, 240–244 2 A. LESKY, Thalatta, 1947, 112f. 3 R. GLYNN, s.v. H.G., LIMC 4.1, 409–410 4 E. BUSCHOR, Meermänner, 1941. A.A.

Halipedon (Ἁλίπεδον, Ἁλαί; *Halípedon, Halaí*). Swampy plain (Hsch. s.v. Ἁ.) North of the main harbour of the Piraeus [1; 2], in 403 BC scene of a defeat of Thrasybulus by the Spartan king Pausanias (Xen. Hell. 2,4,30–34).

1 W. JUDEICH, Top. von Athen, ^{2}1931, 425, 426 n. 1 2 W. KOLBE, s.v. H., RE 7, 2268 3 TRAVLOS, Athen 3, 164 fig. 213 (Neophaliron). H.LO.

Halirrhothius (Ἁλιρρόθιος; *Halirrhóthios*). Attic hero, son of Poseidon and a nymph, whose death was the subject of the first trial before the → Areopagus. In the most common form of the myth, which explains the role of the Areopagus as a homicide court, he rapes the daughter of Ares and Aglaurus, Alcippe, and is struck down by Ares; the site of both deeds is the spring in the later Asclepium above the theatre of Dionysus. Poseidon indicts Ares, the court of the twelve gods acquits him (Eur. El. 1258–1262; Apollod. 3,180; Paus. 1,21,4; Dem. Or. 23,66; Marmor Parium FGrH 239,3; Aristid. Panathenaicus 46).

Another tale connects him with the task of the Areopagus to protect the Attic olive trees: to avenge his father on Athena, H. tries to cut down Athena's olive trees (μορίαι). He accidentally kills himself with his axe in the process, and Poseidon indicts Ares as the master of iron (Serv. Georg. 1,18; Schol. Aristoph. Nub. 1005). Perhaps the punishment of Ares with servitude to a mortal belongs to this (cf. Apollo in Admetus, Panyassis fr. 16 EpGF). F.G.

Halisarna (Ἁλίσαρνα; *Halísarna*).

[1] Small city, dynastic seat in the border region of the regions of Mysia and the Troad. In Xenophon (Hell. 3,1,6; An. 7,8,17) H. is mentioned in connection with the Spartan-Persian war 400–396 BC. The dynast Procles named there is the descendant of the Spartan king Damaratus, who was exiled there at the beginning of the 5th cent. BC and received H. along with Pergamum and Teuthrania from Darius I as a gift (Paus. 3,7,8). The exact location and further history are unknown.

L. BÜRCHNER, s.v. H. (1), RE 7, 2270. E.SCH.

[2] Town in the south-east of Cos (Str. 14,2,19), in the area of Kardamena.

PHILIPPSON/KIRSTEN 4, 297. H.SO.

Halitherses (Ἁλιθέρσης; *Halithérsēs*), 'having courage on the sea' [1; 2].

[1] Son of → Ancaeus [2] and Samia (Asius EpGF fr. 7; PEG I).

[2] Soothsayer in the *Odyssey*, son of Mastor (2,157f.), old friend of Odysseus and Telemachus (2,253; 17,68). Divining a bird sign in light of an earlier prophesy, he warns the suitors, in vain, of the return of Odysseus (2,161ff.). After the suitors are murdered, he advises against a civil war (24,451ff.) [3; 4].

1 KAMPTZ, 88; 2 E. RISCH, Wortbildung der homerischen Sprache, ^{2}1974, 78 3 ST. WEST, in: A Commentary on Homer's Odyssey, vol. 1, 1988, 142 4 A. HEUBECK, ibid., vol. 3, 1992, 409f. A.A.

Hallstatt Culture The early Iron Age in central Europe is called the Hallstatt Culture (HC), after the town of Hallstatt in the Austrian Salzkammergut. In the middle of the 19th cent., a large cemetery (over 1,000 burials) was found there with extensive find material, which was viewed as typical and led to the definition of the HC in the 19th cent. The find site has a very special significance, because there is a salt mine there which was already extensively worked in the Bronze Age [5; 11. 67–79].

The HC includes the period from the middle of the 8th cent. to the middle of the 5th cent. BC. An early phase (= early HC) lasted to the end of the 7th cent., afterwards came the more recent HC (= late HC) [4; 10; 12. 35–64]. The main area of the spread of the HC reached from central France to western Hungary and Slovenia, and from the Alps to the German central mountain region. Based on varying development and archaeological forms, an eastern and western HC are distinguished [1; 3; 6; 10; 11. 80–116; 12. 65–158].

The HC developed from the Bronze Age → Urnfield culture and is marked by, among other things, the development of iron technology. In connection with this came evident social, economic and also religious changes, which brought about a lavish grave cult (hills, chamber structures, preferred physical burial), a differentiation in the population structure (wealthy graves, first imported items, etc.) and a decline in the custom of hoards. Altogether, the HC is marked by farming, which however is joined by increasing trade, crafts and complex forms of settlement [1; 10; 11. 389–398].

In the eastern HC, clear elements from the mounted nomads advancing from the east (→ Cimmerians, → Scythians, etc.) are already tangible in the early phase in graves furnished with corresponding horse tack; in addition, there are → helmets (Italic shapes) and axes as characteristic grave goods, which are also occasionally combined with bronze vessels and massive grave mound structures, which reach the status of → princes' tombs (e.g. Klein-Klein in Styria) [6; 11. 29–137; 12. 185–204]. Krain is also an important centre of the eastern HC, likewise with especially wealthy graves [1; 6; 12. 241–260]. Additional forms of the grave furnishings (jewellery, traditional clothing, ceramics) characterize the various regional groups in the entire area of the HC.

A fundamentally similar development towards wealthy grave mound burials can be observed in the western HC, distinguished here above all by the inclusion of four-wheeled carts and longswords of bronze or iron. Occasionally bronze vessels (in part Etruscan imports) also appear already in graves of the early HC [1; 3; 4; 9].

The high point of this development lies, however, in the late HC of the 6th/5th cents. BC, in which the princes' tombs (→ Princes, tombs and residences of; see also map there) from south-west Germany to Burgundy define the picture. Changes in other areas can also be recognized in the late HC, thus for example in the weaponry, in which the sword is replaced by the dagger, or in the shapes of fibulae, ceramics, etc. [3; 4; 10]. A typical warrior of the late HC is recorded in the stone sculpture of → Hirschlanden. In the HC, the representation of figures (sculpture, toreutics, ceramics) gained in significance, which can be traced to Mediterranean stimuli and communication with upper Italian groups (situla district). Here, the representations of Greek/Etruscan elements (mythological beings, etc.) intermingle with those of the HC (weapons, etc.) on bronze vessels (situlae), belts, etc. [2; 12. 261–298].

At least in the eastern HC, fortified settlements on heights with wood-stone-earth walls are more frequently found (e.g. Sticna, Slovenia); these were already in use in the early HC and were only abandoned with the end of the period [6; 8; 12]. In the western HC such fortified heights are only known in the late phase; their most distinctive representatives are the partially Mediterranean influenced princes' residences (→ Princes, tombs and residences of) [3; 8; 10]. These settlements show an intensive contact (trade etc.) with the Mediterranean region (Etruria, Greek colonies), which determines lifestyle (luxury goods, wine, textiles, etc.), technology (knowledge of → potter's wheel and → lathe) and settlement type (clay bricks, bastions, building structure). In south Germany (Bavaria) the so-called *Herrenhöfe* ('lords' manors'; squares surrounded by a wall and ditch) can be regarded as large farmsteads and an expression of a farming aristocracy [7].

Based on Greek information, the late western HC is identified with the early → Celts. Neighbouring regions of the HC, on the other hand, can hardly be categorized ethnically, apart from the east (Cimmerians/Scythians) and the south (→ Etruscans, other Italic tribes, Illyrians, etc.) [3; 6]. In the west and north of the HC, Bronze Age cultures for whom iron technology is still unknown continue to exist; in north Germany these may be the forerunners of the Germanic → Jastorf culture [1; 12. 297–332]. In the 5th cent. BC, the HC was replaced by the → La Tène culture; how, where and why this process occurred has been difficult to understand to this point [3; 10].

→ Fortifications; → Dürrnberg; → Etrusci (with map); → Germanic archaeology; → Commerce; → Heuneburg (with map); → Hochdorf; → Hoard finds; → Illyricum; → Celtic archaeology (with map); → Salt; → Vix

1 M. Egg, C. Pare, Die Metallzeiten in Europa und im Vorderen Orient, in: Die Abteilung Vorgeschichte im Röm.-German. Zentralmuseum, 1995, 160–192 2 O.-H. Frey, Die Entstehung der Situlenkunst, in: Röm.-German. Forsch. 31, 1969 3 W. Kimmig, Die griech. Kolonisation im westl. Mittelmeergebiet und ihre Wirkung auf die Landschaften des westl. Mitteleuropa, in: JRGZ 30, 1983, 5–78 4 G. Kossack, Südbayern während der Hallstattzeit, in: Röm.-German. Forsch. 24, 1959 5 K. Kromer, Das Gräberfeld von Hallstatt, 1959 6 Id., Das östl. Mitteleuropa in der frühen Eisenzeit (7.–5. Jh. v.Chr.), in: JRGZ 33, 1986, 3–93 7 K. Leidorf, Herrenhöfe, Bauernhöfe und Tempelbezirke der frühen Eisenzeit, in: H. Becker (ed.), Arch. Prospektion, 1996, 143–154 8 E. Lessing, Hallstatt: Bilder aus der Frühzeit Europas, 1980 9 C. Pare, Wagons and Wagon-Graves of the Early Iron Age in Central Europe, 1992
10 K. Spindler, Die frühen Kelten, 1983 11 Die Hallstattkultur: Frühform europäischer Einheit. Internationale Ausst., Steyr, 1980 (without ed.) 12 Die Hallstattkultur. Ber. über das Symposium in Steyr, 1981 (without ed.). V.P.

Halonnesos (Ἁλόννησος; *Halónnēsos*). This island in the north Aegean (Str. 9,5,16; Mela 2,106; Harpocr. s.v.), modern Hag. Eustratios, Hagistrati or Strati, was the object of a conflict between Philip II and Athens: Demosth. 7 hypoth.; 7,2; 12,12; 18,69; Aesch. 3,83; Plut. Demosthenes 9,5; Dion. Hal. Demosthenes 9; 13; Ath. 6,223d–224b. The island, which belonged to Athens, was occupied by pirates; Philip II drove them out, but did not return the island to the Athenians. Traces of ancient settlement.

L. Bürchner, H. (2), in: RE Suppl. 3, 880–883; IG XII 8, S. 17f.; Kirsten-Kraiker, 807. H.KAL.

Halosydne (Ἁλοσύδνη; *Halosýdnē*).

[1] Name of the sea or a sea goddess (→ Amphitrite, according to schol. ad loc.) in Hom. Od. 4,404, where the seals appear as the 'offspring of H.'

[2] The epithet of → Thetis (Hom. Il. 20,207) and the → Nereids as a whole (Apoll. Rhod. 4,1599). The etymology was disputed in antiquity ('daughter of the sea', among other meanings; cf. Hsch. s.v. ὕδναι); today, H. is defined as 'sea-wave' (with gen. ἁλός and *n*-stem from ὕδωρ) [1; 2; 3]. The reference may be as early as Mycenaean (PY Ta 642 a_2-ro-u-do-pi/halos hudo[r]phi/: 'with aquamarines') [4].

1 FRISK, s.v. 2 CHANTRAINE, s.v. 3 E. RISCH, Wortbildung der homerischen Sprache, [2]1974, 219, 228 4 VENTRIS/CHADWICK, 339f. A.A.

Halotus Eunuch, who was the food taster of → Claudius [III 1], and is supposed to have given him the poison from which he died at the order of → Agrippina [3]. Although he was found guilty under Nero, Galba protected him and conferred a financially lucrative procuratorship on him. PIR[2] H 11. W.E.

Haluntium (Ἀλόντιον; *Halóntion*). City on the north coast of Sicily (Dion. Hal. Ant. Rom. 1,51; Cic. Verr. 2,3,103; 2,4,51; Plin. HN 3,90; 14,80: viticulture), modern San Marco d'Anunzio. For the gymnasium of H., cf. SEG 26, 1060 (revision in [1]). For coin production cf. [2. 5–16].

1 G. MANGANARO, Sikelika, 1988 2 F. BIANCO, Archeologia Storica di Messina, 1993. GI.MA.

Halus (Ἅλος; *Hálos*). The remains of H. lie at the south end of the Κρόκιον πεδίον (Krokion plain) and on the north foot of a foothill of Othrys, where the passage from the Malian Gulf to the Gulf of Pagasae was easy to block, because the coasts were only a few hundred metres apart (today *c.* 2 km). H. owes its name to the rich saline spring of Amphrysus at the foot of the town hill. Already named in the catalogue of ships in the Iliad (Hom. Il. 2,682), it was an important Thessalian harbour during the Persian Wars (Hdt. 7,173). Bronze coins from the 4th cent. BC are known (HN 295). In 346 Philip II destroyed H. and gave the city territory to Pharsalus (Str. 9,5). In the early Hellenistic period, a new foundation occurred on the plain, probably as a harbour town for Achaea Phthiotis. A border agreement with Thebes in the north is known from the middle of the 2nd cent. (IG IX 2 add. ult. 205). There is no information for the Imperial period; in the early Byzantine era, however, the name is cited (Steph. Byz. s.v.). The successor settlement Halmyros (*c.* 6 km north of H.) played an important role in the age of the crusades.

H. had an ancient cult of Zeus Laphystius (Hdt. 7,197: human sacrifices in times of drought), also a temple of Artemis Panachaea (IG IX 2, add. ult. 205). The walls on the town hill above the spring are, according to modern view, not STÄHLIN's 'Old H.', but rather a Byzantine fortress and a small acropolis of the Hellenistic town in the plain. This latter, with almost square city walls (*c.* 750 m) and orthogonal road system, shows only a single settlement horizon and had already been destroyed around 260 BC (possibly by earthquake). The harbour of H. (and with it probably the continuously occupied settlement) is suspected to be closer to the sea, near the former village of Tsengeli, whose area is today a restricted military zone.

BCH 114, 1990, 773 (excavation report); P. PANTOS, R. REINDERS, in: Ἀρχαιολογία 3, 1982, 94 (excavation report); R. REINDERS, Earthquakes in the Almirós Plain and the Abandonment of New Halos, in: E. OLSHAUSEN, H. SONNABEND (ed.), Stuttgarter Kolloquium zur Histor. Geographie des Altertums 6, 1996. Naturkatastrophen in der ant. Welt (Geographica Historica 10), 1998; F. STÄHLIN, Das hell. Thessalien, 1924, 177ff.; TIB 1, 1976, 170f. s.v. Halmyros. HE.KR.

Halycus (Ἅλυκος; *Halykos*). River (84 km long) on the south-west coast of Sicily, empties into the sea northwest of Capo Bianco near Heraclea Minoa, modern Plátani. The H. was mentioned in the treaties between Dionysius I (376 or 374 BC: Stv 2, no. 261) and Timoleon (339 BC: Stv 2, no. 344) respectively and the Carthaginians as the demarcation line between the two spheres of control. E.O.

Halys (Ἅλυς; *Hálys*). Longest river in Asia Minor (over 900 km), modern Kızıl İrmak ('red river'). Its headstreams joining in the countryside of Kamisene (east of Sivas), the H. flows in a wide arc stretching to the south through Cappadocia; east of the Tuz Gölü ('salt lake') it turns to the north, touches Galatia (in more ancient times Phrygia) and breaks through the mountains as the border river between the countries of Paphlagonia and Pontus to its mouth on the Black Sea. The Greek form of the name was connected with the salt beds in the country of Ximene; pre-Greek names are unknown, and the identification of the language to which the name of the river traces back is disputed [1. 60]. First named by Aesch. Pers. 865, the H. is often mentioned in ancient literature (esp. Hdt. 1,6; 5,52; Str. 12,3,12; Plin. HN 6,6); the story of the crossing of the H. by the Lydian king → Croesus is famous (Hdt. 1,75; Aristot. Rh. 3,5).

1 J. TISCHLER, Kleinasiat. Hydronomie, 1977.

D. J. GEORGACAS, From the River Systems in Anatolia, in: Journ. of the American Name Society 12, 1964, 197–214.
C.MA.

Ham (Hebrew: *cham*, meaning approximately 'hot'). Together with Shem (→ Semites) and Japheth one of → Noah's three sons and, according to Gen. 10, the progenitor of the four nations Kush, Miṣrayīm, Put and Canaan who were later called Hamites. The tale of Ham, who according to Gen. 9,22ff. shamed his father Noah, was treated in various ways in post-Biblical Rabbinic and Haggadic writings. Y.D.

Hamadryads (ἁμαδρυάδες/*hamadryádes*, later also: ἀδρυάδες/*adryádes*, ἁδρυάδες/*hadryádes*), tree nymphs. In contrast to the Dryads who reside in the vicinity of trees, the H. are intimately connected to their trees (δρῦς, *drys*): they come into being and die at the same time (ἅμα, *hama*) as the tree in which they live (schol. Apoll. Rhod. 2,477; Serv. Ecl. 10,62, cf. Pind. Fr. 165). The name is first documented in Apoll. Rhod. 2,477 (and Anth. Pal. 9,823,6), but the idea appears already in H. Hom. 5,256ff. The concept of the H. might go back to the ash-tree nymphs mentioned by Hesiod (Μελίαι, → *Melíae*, Hes. Theog. 187; cf. Hes. Op. 145) [1. 186]. The sympathetic relationship between the nymphs and their trees is expressed particularly clearly in Callim. H. 4,79ff. and in narratives about tree sacrilege (e.g. Erysichthon) (Callim. H. 6,31ff.; Ov. Met. 8,725ff.). The motif of the bleeding tree (Ov. Met. 8,762ff.; 9,325ff.) might reflect the old belief in trees as spirited beings (cf. [2. 92]). However, animistic interpretations of the H. such as we find in MANNHARDT [3], for example, fail to consider the Graeco-Roman notion of nature as anthropomorphous (thus [4. 249]; opposing [5. 187; 6]). Unlike for nymphs in general, little evidence points to a cultic worship of the H. (cf., however, Apoll. Rhod. 2,477ff. and Nonnus, Dion. 44,88f.). In later periods, the relationship between the H. and their trees was regarded as less symbiotic – thus in several legends of transformation (Ov. Met. 1,690: Syrinx; Nonnus, Dion. 2,98: Daphne). In the *Dionysiaká* by Nonnus, which mentions the H. the most frequently, the H. leave their trees and continue to live after the trees have died (e.g. 37,20). As early as Propertius (1,20) and Ovid (Fast. 4,231), the H. are no longer strictly differentiated from other nymphs. There is no evidence for an iconography specific to the H.

→ Tree cult; → Erysichthon; → Nymphs

1 WILAMOWITZ, 1, 184–187 2 A. HENRICHS, "Thou shalt not kill a tree": Greek, Manichaean and Indian tales, in: Bulletin of the American Society of Papyrologists 16, 1979, 85–108 3 W. MANNHARDT, Antike Wald- und Feldkulte, 1877, vol. 2, 1–38 4 NILSSON, GGR 1, 244–255 5 C. BOETTICHER, Der Baumkultus der Hellenen, 1856 6 L. MALTEN, Motivgesch. Untersuchungen zur Sagenforsch., in: Hermes 74, 1939, 200ff. S.G.

Hamaxantia (Ἁμαξάντεια; *hamaxánteia*). Attic *paralia*? deme of the Hippothontis phyle, supplying one → *bouleutḗs*, unknown location.

TRAILL, Attica, 51, 68, 110 no. 52, table 8; J.S. TRAILL, Demos and Trittys, 1986, 138; WHITEHEAD, 372 n. 6. H.LO.

Hamaxia (Ἁμαξία/*Hamaxía*, Stadiasmus maris magni 208). City in western Cilicia, modern Sinekkale (6 km west of Coracesium) [1. 78f.]. The name might have been derived from ἅμαξα (*hámaxa*, 'wooden cart') [2. 250f.]. H. was one of Antonius' gifts to Cleopatra (Str. 14,5,3). There is no secure evidence about its status of polis [1. 79]. Archaeology: well preserved, walled-in settlement with an arched gate in the south, three-naved church in the west, necropolis in the north-west.

1 G.E. BEAN, T.B. MITFORD, Journeys in Rough Cilicia 1964–1968, 1970, 78ff. 2 J. NOLLÉ, Pamphylische Studien 6–10, in: Chiron 17, 1987, 235–276. K.T.

Hamaxitus (Ἁμαξιτός; *Hamaxitós*). Small city in the Troad, located, according to COOK ([1. 231ff.], also incl. older attempts at localisation) on the coast in the Beşik Tepesı area north-west of modern Gülpınar. Presumably founded by the Achaeans, H. was settled by the Cilician residents of Chrysa (Str. 13,1,63). After 427 BC, H. was probably dependent on Mytilene, and, in the Attic lists of tribute quotas, was listed among the Actaeic poleis with a *phoros* of 4 talents. In *c.* 400 BC, H. was under the rulership of the dynast Mania before Dercylidas' peaceful capture of H. in 399 BC (Xen. Hell. 3,1,15f.). → Antigonus [1] Monophthalmus annexed H. to Alexandreia Troas in a *synoikismos*, but nevertheless, H. was not relinquished: the harbour H. is still mentioned in the customs law of Ephesus [2. 61], also by Pliny (HN 5,124). The temple of Apollo Smintheios/Smintheus was famous, its ruins from the Roman period are still visible today in Gülpınar. The worship of mice in H., however, is older still (cf. Ael. VH 12,4; Str. 13,1,63).

1 J.M. COOK, The Troad, 1973, 227ff.
2 H. ENGELMANN, D. KNIBBE (ed.), Das Zollgesetz der Prov. Asia, in: EA 14, 1989.

W. LEAF, Strabo on the Troad, 1923, 227ff. E.SCH.

Hamilcar (Carthaginian name Hmlk = 'grace is to mlk'; Gk. Ἀμίλκας/*Hamílkas*).

[1] Son of Hanno and a Syracusan woman (Hdt. 7,165), grandson of → Mago [1. 36,183f.], father of → Geskon [1]; Carthaginian commander in *c.* 500–480 BC, whose role in his brother Hasdrubal's campaign against Sardinia remains unclear (Iust. 19,1,6f.) [1. 37]. It is seriously disputed whether he was king, or rather suffete [2. 459–461; 3. 70f., 90–97]. In 480, H. undertook a military expedition against → Himera, which had been seized by → Theron and defended with the aid of → Gelon [1]. Himera's previous ruler → Terillus, who was H.'s friend and host as well as → Anaxilaus [1] had requested H.'s military assistance (Hdt. 7,165). The expedition ended with Carthage's defeat, and H. choosing death in a ritualistic self-sacrifice (Hdt. 7,167) [3. 51–64]. The legend that the battle at Himera took place parallel to the Greek victory at Salamis (Hdt. 7,166) as well as the report that H. attacked the Greeks of Sicily under orders of → Xerxes (Diod. Sic. 11,1,4f.; 20; Stv 2,129) [1. 38; 2. 97f.] must be regarded in the context of Sicilian propaganda [3. 15–48].

[2] Carthaginian *strategos* for western Sicily, who in 318 and 315 intervened in favour of the exiled oligarchs surrounding → Deinocrates [1] in the Syracusan civil war against → Agathocles [2] (Iust. 22,2,2–4) [2. 178f.; 4. 55]. The claim that H. had clandestinely hoped in 318 to count on Agathocles' help with his own coup (Iust. 22,2,5f.) was only a rumour [1. 44; 4. 56]. After H. mediated a peace agreement in the Sicilian war in 314/3, confirming the hegemony of the Syracusan tyrant (Diod. Sic. 19,65; 71,6f.; Stv 3,424), the exiled Syracusans brought a complaint against H. in Carthage: he was removed from office and convicted, but meanwhile had died in Sicily (Iust. 22,3) [1. 43f.; 2. 181–183; 4. 55–57].

[3] **H. Barkas.** ('Lightning'). Founder of the → Barcids, father of → Hannibal [4], → Hasdrubal [3], and → Mago; brilliant Carthaginian commander. In the 1st Punic War, H., as nauarch and successor of → Carthalo [2] since 247, attacked – partisan style – the Bruttian and Lucanian coastal region as well as Roman positions on Sicily and entrenched himself on the coast of northern Sicily near Panormus on the → Heircte (today Monte Castellaccio?). In 244, he captured the city of → Eryx and led a tough, ongoing battle full of privation against Roman → Drepanon [4] (Pol. 1,56; 58; Diod. Sic. 24,6; 8f.; Zon. 8,16). Following the loss of → Hanno [5]'s fleet in the spring of 241, H. – as plenipotentiary *strategos* – negotiated the preliminary conditions for peace, including his own free and honourable withdrawal, then resigned his command in Lilybaeum, leaving → Geskon [3] with the task of demobilizing the mercenary army (Pol. 1,62f.; 66; 68,12; 3,9,7; 27; Stv 3,493) [1. 51f.; 2. 246–252; 5. 9–12].

H.'s motives for relinquishing his office as well as his role on the eve of the so-called Mercenaries' War are equally unclear. In the year 240 during the war, H. was given supreme command against the rebels. He operated successfully alongside → Hanno [6], the *strategos* for Libya, despite various disputes over their respective areas of responsibility: he relieved → Utica, defeated → Spendius several times – as in the spectacular battle at Prion (which, to a large extent, was due to the assistance of the Numidian ruler Naravas, with whom H. was related by marriage), and in the end overpowered (together with Hanno) → Mathus, the leader of the revolt (Pol. 1,75–78; 81f.; 84–88; Zon. 8,17,8) [1. 52–54; 2. 252–266; 5. 13–23]. Meanwhile, the Romans annexed Sardinia [2. 266–268; 5. 23f.], an event which influenced H.'s further life in the following way: as *strategos* for Libya for life (!) since 238, he strove once again to establish Carthage's economical and political stability after the loss of its sea power. Thus, in 237, he crossed over to Gades (today Cadiz) along with his army and family in order to establish Carthage's direct rulership in southern Spain, an area rich in iron and silver ore. Through a series of resolute campaigns against Tartessian and Celtiberian tribal leaders, H. succeeded in reaching his ambitious goal. He fell in 299 against the Orissans, but left his successor → Hasdrubal [2] with an established rulership, the new centre of which was the newly-founded Leuke Acron (= Alicante?) (Pol. 2,1,7; Diod. Sic. 25,10; Liv. 21,1f.) [1. 56–58; 2. 270–274; 5. 25–39].

[4] Carthaginian officer of → Hasdrubal [3] (?, cf. Liv. 31,11,5) [1. 62, 360], who, on his own accord, organized a revolt of the → Cenomanni [3] and the → Insubres in Upper Italy as late as 200 BC. He was then exiled following a Roman representation in Carthage but could not be defeated until the year 197 by C. → Cornelius [I 11] Cethegus (Liv. 31,10f.; 19) [1. 62f.].

[5] Carthaginian delegate who brought Carthage's offer of surrender to Rome in 149 BC along with → Gescon [5] and → Mago (Pol. 36,3,7f.) [1. 65].

[6] **H. Phameas.** (Pol. 36,8,1) erroneously for → Himilkon [5] Phameas [1. 64, 371].

1 Geus 2 Huss 3 W. Ameling, Karthago, 1993 4 L. M. Hans, Die Göttin mit der Tiara, in: SNR 66, 1987, 45–58 5 J. Seibert, Hannibal, 1993.

L.-M.G.

Hamites, Hamitic see → Afro-Asian

Hammon see → Ammon

Ḫammurapi (Ḫammurabi). Most important ruler of the 1st Dynasty of → Babylon, in office from 1792 to 1750 BC. Following extended battles with rival powers in Mesopotamia as well as with the rulers of → Elam who all claimed sovereignty over the states of Mesopotamia, Ḫ. ruled over all of Mesopotamia from Mari on the middle reaches of the Euphrates and the region surrounding modern Mossul to the Persian Gulf from 1755 BC on. In over 200 of his letters and in numerous reports by delegates of Zimrilim of Mari, one of H.'s allies and a future rival, their actions and behaviours are described in great detail, a rarity with regards to rulers of antiquity. In Mesopotamia, Ḫ.'s fame as a great ruler lived on into the 1st millennium (→ Amulet). This resulted primarily from his collection of legal norms recorded on a stele, found in 1902 in → Susa, which had been carried off there in the 13th cent. BC (trans.: [1]). With more than 280 paragraphs, the stele is one of the oldest and most comprehensive 'law books'. It is therefore of great importance for the legal history of Mesopotamia and of antiquity in general.

→ Cuneiform, legal texts in

1 TUAT 1, 39–80.

H. Klengel, König Ḫ. und der Alltag Babylons, 1991; J. Renger, Noch einmal: Was war der "Kodex" Ḫ. – ein erlassenes Gesetz oder ein Rechtsbuch?, in: H.-J. Gehrke (ed.), Rechtskodifikation und soziale Normen, 1994, 27–59 (with bibliography).

J.RE.

Hampsicora High-ranking Sardinian, who in 215 BC, along with his son Hostus, acted as organizer and military leader of the revolt by Sardinian tribes against the Roman rulership. H. received only insufficient Carthaginian assistance through → Hasdrubal [4] and killed himself after a devastating defeat against T. → Manlius Torquatus (Liv. 23,32,7–10; 40,3–41,6).

Huss, 348f.

L.-M.G.

Hamster The hamster (*Cricetus cricetus*) occurs only in grain fields north of the Alps and was unknown to Greeks or Romans. The hibernating μυωξός/ *myōxós* in Opp. Kyn. 2,574 and 585 was formerly identified with the hamster [1], but actually refers to the → dormouse. The *crichetus* in Thomas of Cantimpré 4,26 (according to the as yet undiscovered *Liber rerum*) is well described, but the description of its size (similar to a squirrel) and its habitat (*Apulea*) do not match those of a hamster. In Albertus Magnus' De animalibus 22,47 [3. 1375], the term *cricetus* is confirmed in the gloss *hamester Germanice*.

1 LAMER, s.v. H., RE Suppl. 3, 885 2 H. BOESE (ed.), Thomas Cantimpratensis, Liber de natura rerum, 1973 3 H. STADLER (ed.), Albertus Magnus, De animalibus, 2, 1921. C.HÜ.

Hanging gardens Built by → Semiramis (9th/8th cents. BC) in → Babylon (or Nineveh [2]), one of the Seven → Wonders of the World, mentioned neither in the cuneiform tradition nor in the city's description by Herodotus (1,178ff.). Records only begin to appear in the 4th cent. BC [1. 48f.]. The view that it was Queen Semiramis who had them built contradicts Diodorus (3,10,1ff.); Josephus (Ant. Iud. 10,11,225f.) refers to Nebuchadnezzar II (605–562 BC) as the builder. The hanging gardens (HG) were regarded as a wonder of the world because of their size, their building style, and their irrigation technology, and were described by ancient authors as a tall, quadratic terraced structure of multiple steps that rested on vaults (Str. 16,1,5). Concerning the HG's appearance and location, several possibilities of reconstruction have been proposed [3. 44ff.; 4. 19ff.]; however, no definite archaeological findings exist as yet.

→ Bīsutūn; → Garden; → WONDERS OF THE WORLD

1 K. BRODERSEN, Die Sieben Weltwunder, [2]1997 2 S. DALLEY, Niniveh, Babylon and the Hanging Gardens: Cuneiform and Classical Sources Reconciled, in: Iraq 56, 1994, 48–58 3 W. EKSCHMITT, Die Sieben Weltwunder, [10]1995 4 W. NAGEL, Wo lagen die Hängenden Gärten von Babylon?, in: MDOG 110, 1978, 19–28. J.BÄ.

Hannas (NT Ἄννας; *'Annas*, Jos. Ἄνανος/*Ánanos*, Rabbinic literature *Elḥanan*, *Ḥanin*).

[1] Jewish high priest in AD 6–15, the first to have been appointed to this office by the Romans (Jos. Ant. Iud. 18,26). Even after he was deposed (ibid. 18,34), he maintained great political influence, being a member of the → Synhedrion as former high priest. He played a significant role along with his son-in-law Caiphas in the trial against Jesus (Jo 18: 13; 24; cf. [1]), as well as against the apostles Peter and John (Acts 4,6). He was the head of one of the most powerful yet infamous (Babylonian Talmud Pesaḥim 57a; Siphre Dt 14,22 § 105) non-Sadducean families of high priests. Among his descendants, five sons and one grandson held the office of high priest (Jos. Ant. Iud. 20,197; 223).

[2] Son of H. [1]. He held the office of high priest for three months in AD 62 (Jos. Ant. Iud. 20,197). He was deposed (ibid. 20,203) because he had misused the absence of the procurator Albinus by using the → Synhedrion to instigate the death penalty for several persons who had fallen out of favour with him. Among them was Jacob, the brother of Jesus, who was accused of lawlessness (ibid. 20,200; this report can hardly be regarded as Christian interpolation, cf. [2]). In the Jewish War, H. played a leading role in Jerusalem (Jos. BI 2,563; 647). His efforts to remove the dictatorship of the Zelots and to guide the revolt into a more moderate direction failed after initial successes (ibid. 4,151–313). H. fell in AD 68 in Jerusalem during the battles with the Idumaeans who had been called in by the Zelots (ibid. 4,315–316).

1 J. BLINZLER, Der Prozeß Jesu, [3]1960, 85–94
2 M. DIBELIUS, Der Brief des Jakobus, [8]1956, 12–14.

SCHÜRER 1, [3/4]1901, 581–583; 2, [4]1907, 256, 270–275; J. JEREMIAS, Jerusalem z.Z. Jesu, [3]1962, 216–223 and passim BE.SCH.

Hannibal (*Ḥnbʿl* = 'grace of Bʿl'; Ἀννίβας; *Anníbas*).

[1] Successful Carthaginian commander, son of → Gescon [1], the Magonid. Having grown up in exile in Selinunt among other places, he established the Punic 'province' in western Sicily ('epicracy') through military campaigns in 410/9 and 406/5 BC. The politics of Carthaginian intervention which H. inaugurated were initially occasioned by a call for help from Segesta but the true cause lies in Syracuse's hegemonic expansion [1. 107–114; 2. 37, 41, 119]. Due to the merciless sieges of Selinunt, Himera, and Acragas (Diod. Sic. 13,43f.; 54–62), but primarily due to H.'s sacrifice of 3,000 prisoners at Himera in an act of revenge for the defeat of → Hamilcar [1] in 480 (Diod. Sic. 13,62,4f.), H. is regarded as a 'hater of Greeks' [cf., however, 1. 109, 112; 3. 69, 409] and is even said to have aimed at the subjugation of all of Sicily through the campaign of 406 (Diod. Sic. 13,79f.; 85f.) [3. 68]. H.'s far-sighted diplomacy included negotiations with Athens (SEG 10,136 = Stv 2,208) [1. 117f.]. Upon H.'s death at the gates of Acragas (406), his fellow commander and relative → Himilkon [1] assumed the supreme command [1. 119; 3. 69].

[2] Carthaginian nauarch and *strategos c.* 269–258 BC, father (?) of → Hanno [4], his colleague in office. In 269, H. secured Messana against → Hieron [2] through a garrison which, on the eve (?) of the 1st Punic War, was expelled by the → Mamertini (Pol. 1,10f.; Diod. Sic. 22,13,7f.) [2. 102, 112]. In the following period, H. defended Acragas against the Romans until early 261, withdrew from the city after Hanno was seriously defeated (Pol. 1,17–19) [3. 70, 414 and p. 112], and then operated with his fleet in the Tyrrhenian sea (Zon. 8,10). In 260, H.'s officer Bodo brought in the Roman consul L. → Cornelius [I 74] Scipio Asina (Pol. 1,21,6–8) [cf. 3. 15], but H. himself suffered a deva-

stating defeat soon thereafter at Mylae, at the hands of C. → Duilius [1] (Pol. 1,23). Thus stripped of his command (Vir. ill. 38,2f.; Zon. 8,11), H. was entrusted with defending Sardinia in 258, but lost his life in his luckless defeat at the hands of C. Sulpicius Paterculus (Pol. 1,24,5–7; Zon. 8,12) [3. 71, 422].

[3] H. 'the Rhodian' [3. 221, 1297]. High-ranking Carthaginian owner of an extremely fast (pirate?) quinquereme, who by his own decision repeatedly broke the Roman naval blockade of Lilybaeum in 250/49 BC. When H. was caught, the Romans built a new fleet modelled after his ship (Pol. 1,46,4–47,10; 59,8) [3. 73; 4. 134–137].

1 Huss 2 L.M. Hans, Karthago und Sizilien, 1983
3 Geus 4 W. Ameling, Karthago, 1993. L.-M.G.

[4] Son of → Hamilcar [3] Barkas, the → Barcid, 247/46–183 BC. Most famous Carthaginian, brilliant commander, and lifelong enemy of Rome, after whom the 2nd Punic War was called H.'s War. In 237, while accompanying his father to Iberia, H. is said to have sworn relentless hatred of Rome (Liv. 35,19; App. Hisp. 9,34). Until 224, H. appears to have lived at times in Spain, at times in Carthage. After that, he became a subcommander of his brother-in-law → Hasdrubal [2] (Liv. 21,3,2–4,2), and following the latter's death (221), the troops proclaimed H. the succeeding *strategos* for Libya and Iberia, the appointment also being confirmed in Carthage (Pol. 3,13,3f.; Liv. 21,3,1; Diod. Sic. 25,15; App. Hisp. 8,29). After conducting successful campaigns against Celtiberian tribes (→ Carpetani, → Olcades, → Vaccaei), H. aimed at breaking the resistance of Saguntum, an effort that a Roman representation tried to prevent in Carthago Nova in 220/19 and subsequently in Carthage (Pol. 3,13–15; Liv. 21,5–6; 9,3). The Carthaginian Senate rejected the Romans, granting H. free rein (App. Hisp. 10,37). The conflict surrounding the capture of the city, which H. achieved after a siege of eight months (Pol. 3,17), gave rise to the 2nd Punic War (218–201 BC): the Romans had unsuccessfully demanded H.'s extradition in Carthage – H. having captured the area north of the Ebro in the spring of 218 – and declared war. H. then thwarted the Roman strategic plans by swiftly and boldly advancing across the Pyrenees and the Alps into Upper Italy, where he arrived in October. The crossing of the Alps with 38,000 troops, 8,000 cavalrymen, and elephants incurred heavy losses and is much discussed in its topographical details. H.'s triumphal march, marked by the Roman defeats of P. → Cornelius [I 68] Scipio on the Ticinus and Ti. Sempronius Longus on the Trebia (218), then of C. → Flaminius [1] on Lake Trasimene (217) and L. → Aemilius [I 31] Paullus at Cannae (216) did, however, end up in inglorious positional warfare in Southern Italy because the Romans refused to engage in negotiations and H. refused to besiege Rome. H., who had hoped to dismantle the Roman confederation system with his call for freedom, managed in 216–213 to win over cities such as Capua, Locri, Tarentium, even entering alliances with the Macedon King → Philippus V and with Syracuse (Stv 3,524; 525; 527–529; 531), but in the end he failed to succeed. Beginning with the recapture of Syracuse, Capua, etc. (212–209), the victory over → Hasdrubal [3] (207), and the successes of P. → Cornelius [I 71] Scipio in Spain (209–206), the Romans clearly were gaining the upper hand. Although H. returned undefeated to North Africa in 203 in order – now as omnipotentiary *strategos* – to fight against the Roman invasion led by Scipio, whose invading troops had been successful since 204 and were allied with → Massinissa, H.'s defeat at Zama (autumn 202) resulted in the capitulation of Carthage (Stv 3,548).

H., recalled from his supreme command due to Roman pressure in 200/199, did not emerge again until 196. As elected suffete, he cut back the membership of the court of justice of the one hundred and four with a constitutional reform and stabilized state revenues through strict enforcement of taxation (Liv. 33,45,6–47,3). Following this, his political enemies instigated the Romans to intervene in Carthage's interior affairs by raising suspicions that H. was part of an anti-Roman conspiracy along with → Antiochus [5] III the Great. H., outlawed in Carthage and with his house destroyed (Liv. 33,47–49; Nep. Hann. 7; Iust. 31,1–2), evaded a Roman investigative delegation in 195 by fleeing to the Seleucid kingdom. H. gained access to the royal council in Ephesus as a competent informant against the Romans on the eve of the war, but was not regarded as a serious advisor and was left to operate without much luck as commander over a small fleet in the southern Aegean (Liv. 37,23–24; App. Syr. 22,108–109; Iust. 31,6,7–10). Because the Romans demanded H.'s extradition in 189/88 from defeated Antioch, the exiled Carthaginian fled via Crete and Armenia – where he is claimed to have organized the founding of Artaxata – to Bithynia (Nep. Hann. 9–10; Plut. Lucullus 31,4–5; Iust. 32,4–5). There, H. served king → Prusias I as admiral in the war against → Eumenes [3] II (186–183) of Pergamum, a friend of the Romans, and assisted in the founding of Prusa (Plin. HN 5,148). At the end of the war, when a Roman delegation under Ti. → Quinctius Flamininus demanded H.'s extradition from Prusias, H. poisoned himself in → Libyssa (Pol. 23,5,1; App. Syr. 11,43; Plut. Flamininus 20; Liv. 39,51; Nep. Hann. 12). In AD 200, Septimius Severus, Roman emperor from North Africa, ordered the building of a monumental tomb for H. near the place of the latter's death in Bithynia (Hdn. 4,8,5). In more recent times, Ataturk ordered the construction of a memorial for H. above the coast near Gebze.

H.'s personality and military/political achievements were already described by the historiographers → Silenus and → Sosylus who had accompanied H.'s army. These works, although no longer extant, were the sources for later authors (e.g. Polybius, Livy, Nepos). The ancient image of H. either as brilliant commander reminiscent of Alexander the Great or an incarnation of a Carthage forever hostile to Rome has become more differentiated in recent times. Regardless of the continuing discussions whether H. failed as a statesman in situations when he should have gained politically from his victories, or whether H. was not primarily a loyal representative of Carthage, but rather an independent political agent following the Hellenistic model, H.'s historical importance lies in the fact that he brought to light to his contemporaries and to later generations the relentlessness of Rome's politics of alliances and expansion, which proved fatal to its enemies.

→ Punic Wars (incl. map)

GEUS 75–94; E. GROAG, Hannibal als Politiker, 1929; L. M. GÜNTHER, Hannibal im Exil, in: H. DEVIJVER, E. LIPIŃSKI (ed.), Punic Wars, 1989, 241–250; W. HOFFMANN, Hannibal, 1962; HUSS; D. A. KUKOFKA, Süditalien im Zweiten Punischen Krieg, 1990; T. SCHMITT, Hannibals Siegeszug, 1991; K. H. SCHWARTE, Der Ausbruch des Zweiten Punischen Krieges, 1983; J. SEIBERT, Der Alpenübergang Hannibals, in: Gymnasium 95, 1988, 21–73; Id., Hannibal. Feldherr und Staatsmann, 1993; Id., Forschungen zu Hannibal, 1993; Id., Hannibal, 1997.

L.-M.G.

Hannibalianus

[1] **Afranius H.** Officer in Probus' staff (HA Probus 22,3), in AD 285, *praefectus praetorio* alongside Asclepiodotus, in 292 *consul ordinarius* again with Asclepiodotus, in 297–8 *praefectus urbi*. Perhaps the father of Maximian's stepdaughter → Theodora.

[2] Half-brother of → Constantinus [1] († AD 337) from the marriage between Constantius [1] and Theodora. Unlike his brothers Dalmatius [1] and Iulius Constantius [4], H. did not play a role at the end of Constantius' reign, probably because he had already died at that point.

[3] **Flavius H.** Son of Dalmatius [1], nephew of → Constantinus [1]. In AD 335, he was included in Constantinus' agenda for multiple rulers and succession. He was married to Constantina and assigned to rule – as a *rex regum* dependent on Rome – over Armenia and the bordering Caucasus monarchies (RIC VII 589, no. 145, Anon. Vales. 35; Ps.-Aur. Vict. epit. Caes. 41,20). He was murdered in 337 along with other members of this sideline of Contantinus' imperial family. B.BL.

Hanno

[1] 'King' (suffete) of Carthage, probably in the early 5th cent. BC, only known for his sea expedition along the western coast of Africa intended to create and secure Carthaginian colonies. It led from the 'Columns of Hercules' (Straight of Gibraltar) to the island of Kerne (near modern Mauretania?), and – for the purpose of discovering passages – further to the Bay of Notou Keras ('Horn of the Southern Wind', modern Cameroon?).

References to H.'s voyage begin to appear in the 3rd cent. BC (Aristot. Mir. 833a 11), esp. in Mela (3,90; 93), Pliny (HN 2,169; 5,8), and Arrianus (Ind. 43,11f.). Added to these must be a short text with the title *Ánnōnos Karchēdoníōn basileṓs períplous* ('The Voyage of Carthage's King Hanno') in the Cod. Palatinus graecus 398 (9th cent.), translated probably from a Punic original into Greek at an unknown time. This text, first edited by S. Gelenius in 1533 and rich in wondrous details, is primarily responsible for H.'s fame after his death. For instance, the reference to savages (§ 18) as γορίλλαι (*gorillai*) led to the modern term for a type of great ape.

→ Exploration, voyages of

GGM 1, 1–14; J. BLOMQUIST, The Date and Origin of the Greek Version of Hanno's Periplus, 1979; K. BAYER, in: G. WINKLER, R. KÖNIG (ed.), C. Plinius Secundus d.Ä., Naturkunde B. 5, 1993, 337–353 (Ed., transl., comm.; lit. ibid. 360–363). K.BRO.

[2] **H. Sabellus.** Carthaginian commander claimed to have subjugated North Africa *c.* 500 BC (?) (Pomp. Trog. prol. 19) [1. 97]; H. is often falsely identified with → H. [1] and with H., the son of → Hamilcar [1], Mago's grandson [1. 97f., 556–558 and 105, 609].

[3] **H. 'the Great'** (Punic *rb*) [1. 223]. Carthaginian *strategos* in 368–362 (?) BC on Sicily. He led a surprise attack against the fleet of → Dionysius [1] at Eryx (Diod. Sic. 15,73,4; Iust. 20,5,11) and later also had military success in North Africa (Pomp. Trog. prol. 20) [1. 106f.]; often falsely identified with H., the 'person guilty of high treason' [1. 107, 618], who was claimed to have planned the poisoning of the Carthaginian Senate in the mid 4th cent. (Iust. 21,4).

[4] Carthaginian *strategos* in the 1st Punic War on Sicily 264–261, probably the son of → Hannibal [2]. H. ordered the fortification of Acragas, an allied city, later besieged Messana alongside → Hieron [2], with whom he had formed an alliance, withdrew into the western Sicilian epicracy in 263, after the Romans had enjoyed a few successes, and operated successfully there (Pol. 1,11; Diod. Sic. 22,13,9) [2. 223f.]. In early 261, he suffered a serious defeat at the gates of occupied Acragas, for which he had to pay a fine of 6000 pieces of gold in Carthage (Pol. 1,12; 15; 18; Diod. Sic. 23,3; 5; 8; 9,2; Zon. 8,9) [2. 228]. H. apparently received the command over another fleet in 258 and led it successfully near Sardinia [1. 113, 648]. In 256, he appears as a luckless nauarch in a defeat on the Eknomon (Pol. 1,27f.), then encounters Roman invasion troops and fights them in North Africa, where he also commanded land troops at Clupea (Pol. 1,36,10–12; Oros. 4,9,7; Zon. 8,12; 14) [1. 113, 654].

[5] Carthaginian nauarch in the 1st Punic War. His supply fleet for the troops of → Hamilcar [3] Barkas on the Eryx was seized and defeated by C. Lutatius Catulus in March of 241 BC near the westernmost of the Aegates Islands [1. 119, 681]. As a result, H. was executed (Pol. 1,60f.; Zon. 8,17,1–3) [2. 248f.]. An identification with H. [4] is spurious [1. 119, 679].

[6] **H. 'the Great'** (Punic *rb*) [1. 116, 662]. Prominent Carthaginian politician in the 2nd half of the 3rd cent., who, as *strategos*, had captured Theveste (modern Té-

bessa) for Libya in *c.* 247 (Diod. Sic. 24,10) [2. 246, 232] and, in 241, received supreme command for the suppression of the Libyan revolt at the start of the so-called Mercenaries' War following his failed negotiations in Sicca (modern El Kef) (Pol. 1,66f.; 73) [2. 254, 257f.]. As a result of luckless warfare, H. was forced to hand his command of the Carthaginian army over to → Hamilcar [3] Barkas in 240. Despite frequent disputes between the two *strategoi*, they joined forces to win a decisive victory in 238 over → Mathus (Pol. 1,74; 82; 87f.) [1. 116f.]. When the command for Libya was transferred to H.'s rival at the end of the war, H. took the lead among the political critics of the → Barcids [cf. 1. 117f.] and features in the transmission on the 2nd Punic War as opponent of → Hannibal [4] whose extradition to the Romans he demanded in 219. He also pushed for a quick peace in 216 after the victory at Cannae (Liv. 21,10; 23,12,6–13,6) [3. 216]. In 202, H. went to the Romans as peace negotiator alongside → Hasdrubal [6], with whom he had shielded a Roman delegation in Carthage as early as 203 (App. Lib. 34,145; 49,213).

[7] H., or (more accurately?): Banno [1. 120], Carthaginian officer in the Second Punic War. In 218 BC, he was then taken captive by Cn. → Cornelius [I 77] Scipio as → Hannibal [4]'s deputy in the newly conquered area between the Ebro and the Pyrenees (Pol. 3,35,4f.; 76,5f.; Liv. 21,60, 5–9; Zon. 8,25,1) [1. 12f.].

[8] Carthaginian commander of the occupation of → Capua in 212–211 BC, alleged to have written an entreaty to → Hannibal [4] requesting assistance against the Roman occupation. After the fall of the city, H. was brought to Rome as prisoner (Liv. 26,5,6; 12,10–19; App. Hann. 36,153; 43,185) [1. 125f.].

[9] Carthaginian *strategos* for Sicily in 212–210 as successor of → Himilkon [4]. In 212, he suffered a serious defeat against M. → Claudius [I 11] Marcellus at the Himeras because he had arrogantly (?) turned away help from the Numidic cavalry under the Libyo-Phoenician → Myttones. When Myttones, relieved from command of the cavalry by H. in the meantime, betrayed the city of Acragas to M. → Valerius Laevinus, H. was able to flee from besieged Acragas to North Africa in 211/0 (Liv. 25,40f.; 26,40) [1. 124f.; 3. 317, 335f.].

[10] Carthaginian *strategos* in the 2nd Punic War in 208/7 BC. Successor of → Hasdrubal [3] in Spain, where his army of 9000 Celtiberian recruits surprisingly lost to M. → Iunius [I 31] Silanus. H. was brought to Rome as prisoner (Liv. 28,1,4; 2,11; 4,4) [1. 126].

[11] Officer (*praefectus*) of → Mago, who in 206 BC was defeated by the Roman legate L. → Marcius Septimus on the Baetis (modern Guadalquivir) yet managed to escape imprisonment (Liv. 28,30,1; cf. App. Hisp. 31,121–126) [1. 126f.].

[12] Carthaginian *nobilis iuvenis*, cavalry officer for → Hasdrubal [5], who recruited several thousand cavalrymen in 204 BC in Numidia for the opposition to the Roman invasion troops. H. captured the city of Salaeca (modern Henchir el Bey?) but was later defeated in a trap set up by P. → Cornelius [I 71] Scipio and → Massinissa (Liv. 29,28f.; 34). It is unclear whether H. was killed or whether he was exchanged as high-ranking prisoner for Massinissa's mother who was held by Hasdrubal (App. Lib. 14,60; Zon. 9,12) [1. 127f.].

1 Geus 2 Huss 3 J. Seibert, Hannibal, 1993.

L.-M.G.

Haoma see → Zoroaster

Hapax legomenon (ἅπαξ λεγόμενον; *hápax legómenon*, 'said only once', also referred to as ἅπαξ εἰρημένον/*hápax eirēménon*): in the strictest sense, *hapax legomenon* is a technical term for a word that is attested in only one place within the entire textual corpus of a language (literature, inscriptions, *i.a.*). One must distinguish between the following: (a) actual creations of new expressions, that is, forms created poetically, esp. those supported through the metre, (b) words that only appear once due to the nature of the sources (mainly specialized vocabulary), and (c), archaic words extant in early texts (e.g. → Homer [1], → Plautus) or taken from them by ancient → grammarians (such as → Hesychius [1], → Festus [6]; → Lexicography). The meaning of such singular words can usually be delineated to some extent by means of their context and word analysis. Examples: for (a): the noun *glandiōnida* ('piece of glandular meat') occurs in Latin only in Plaut. Men. 210: it is a jokingly extended form of *glandium* in a form modelled after Greek patronyms (→ personal names II. B.). For (b): in Latin, the noun *latiārius* (CIL VIII 19994) is attested only on an inscription, the suffix *-ārius* suggesting the name of a profession. For (c): in Greek, the feminine noun μύνη (*mýnē*, Hom. Od. 21,111) occurs only in Homer, the context of the sentence ἀλλ' ἄγε μὴ μύνῃσι παρέλκετε (instrumental dat. to the predicate, thus a means of delay) suggesting the meaning of 'excuse, resistance' or 'dawdling'.

In a larger sense, *hapax legomenon* can also be applied to smaller groups of texts such as the collected or partial works of an author [2] or a group of authors [3].

1 Schwyzer, Gramm., 36 2 M.M. Kumpf, Four Indices of the Homeric h.l., 1984 3 I. Kazik-Zawadska, Les hapax eiremena et les mots rares dans les fragments papyrologiques des trois grands tragiques grecs, 1962.

R.P.

Haplology see → Phonetics

Happiness (εὐδαιμονία/*eudaimonía*, μακαριότης/*makariótēs*, Lat. *felicitas, beatitudo*).

A. Definition and background B. Plato and Aristotle C. Hellenistic and Roman philosophy

A. Definition and background

The etymological meaning of the Greek word *eudaimonía* is 'to have a good demon', 'to be blessed with good fortune', that is, simply to be doing well, particularly in regard to external well-being such as the possession of beauty, wealth, power etc. However, the philosophers soon emphasized the idea that happiness is not to be found in exterior goods but within the soul (e.g. → Heraclitus 22 B 4 DK; → Democritus 68 B 170 DK). How exactly this is meant by these early philosophers is no longer clearly discernible due to the fragmentary transmission of their works. A clear picture emerges only with the philosophers of the classical period. In general, the ancient concept of happiness can be defined as the realization of all intended goals.

B. Plato and Aristotle

For the philosophers of the classical period, the goals to be realized were predetermined by the cosmic order. → Plato sees happiness in the virtue of → justice, which is a result of everyone 'doing their bit' (Resp. 354a; 433b). Thus, the state does well when each social class is content with exactly fulfilling the task assigned to it by the natural order, and in an analogous manner, the individual is happy when each part of his soul is content with its natural function. This line of thinking leads to the conclusion that reason must be the guiding force in human life, just as a happy state is guided by philosopher kings. → Aristotle defines happiness in a similar manner as an 'activity of the soul in accordance with its essential ability', which he understands as the accomplished realization of the role that man plays within the cosmic order based on his essence (Eth. Nic. 1098a 16, trans. Dirlmeier). What makes a human being and what distinguishes him from all other transitory beings is the possession of reason. He is therefore happy when he lives according to his reason. As a consequence, the philosopher lives the happiest life, since he devotes himself completely to reason and obeys it in all his actions. When the soul is governed by fully developed reason, the result is virtue (ἀρετή/*aretḗ*). Thus, Aristotle also locates happiness in virtue. However, exterior goods are necessary as well, and happiness must last a lifetime (Eth. Nic. 1099a 31ff.; 1098a 18).

For Plato (Resp. 473 c-e) as well as Aristotle (Eth. Nic. 1094b 7–10), happiness is the highest good, especially happiness of the community, the polis, which includes happiness of the individual. Because happiness lies in the harmony with the natural world order, it is an objective state for classical thinkers. Subjective feeling – pleasure – only plays a secondary role. For Plato, it occupies the fifth and last place, the same holding true only for the 'pure pleasures of the soul itself' (Phil. 66 c); for Aristotle, it is only an 'additional accomplishment' (Eth. Nic. 1174 b 33). Both reject contemporary hedonism as represented by → Eudoxus of Cnidus and → Aristippus of Cyrene, who is anti-eudaemonistic (→ Cyrenaics) [3. 29ff].

C. Hellenistic and Roman Philosophy

The Hellenistic epoch that followed is marked by individualism. Not happiness of the polis is the highest good, but that of the individual. As a result, goals are no longer regarded as predetermined by a comprehensive order, but must be determined by the individual himself. Happiness is the realization of all self-determined purposes, a view that entails a radically subjective conception of happiness. Only the individual himself can judge his own happiness [4. 32ff.]. 'All good and bad lies in perception' (Epicurus Epist. ad Menoeceum 124) and 'nobody is happy who does not deem himself happy' (Sen. Ep. 9,21). This view has essentially shaped the idea of happiness until today. Psychologically, the Hellenistic philosophers regard happiness as freedom from inner tension, the Stoics call it *apatheia*, the Epicureans and Pyrrhoneans → *ataraxia* (→ Affects). The meaning is the same in both cases, namely, inner peace, a soul at rest. Since this state can only be achieved by reaching goals that were chosen by the individual himself, it is all-important that only such goals are chosen that the individual himself is capable of realizing at any time – only that which is available should be regarded as the true good, everything else should be regarded with indifference [4. 23ff.].

The Stoics – as part of the Socratic-Cynic tradition – are the most radical in employing this programme. Because they regard everything as ultimately unavailable except for the inner attitude towards things, they teach indifference to all exterior things as such. The only true good is insight into the indifference of things. And it is this insight wherein lies virtue, which in turn is the path to happiness. → Epicurus proceeds more questioningly. He does not believe that all values can be neutralized through rational insight, rather, that our feelings of pleasure or reluctance indicate judgements given to us and that they cannot be explained away. He therefore tries to realize the Hellenistic concept of happiness by proving, with the aid of a restrictive concept of pleasure, that one can dispose freely and at any time over pleasure and reluctance. In this manner he arrives at hedonism. The Pyrrhoneans, finally, are even more cautious. They believe that happiness is ultimately not at one's disposal, therefore it must not be desired. However, as the highest good it cannot be regarded as indifferent, so they try to exclude it as a goal of human striving altogether by showing that it is impossible to discern what it consists of. For this purpose, they develop → Scepticism (→ Epoche).

Hellenistic thinking also determines the concept of happiness in Neoplatonism and in early Christianity. Plotinus sees happiness in an accomplished life, that is, a life guided by reason, a view that seems classical at first sight. His proof, however, lies in the idea that whoever lives such a life desires nothing more than this (Enneades 1,4,4). Similarly, for Augustine, happiness lies in God, because He is the fulfilment of all wishes (Civ. 22,30).

→ Ethics; → Pleasure; → Practical philosophy

1 M. Forschner, Über das Glück des Menschen. Aristoteles, Epikur, Stoa, Thomas von Aquin, Kant, [2]1994
2 M. Hossenfelder, Ant. Glückslehren. Kynismus und Kyrenaismus. Stoa, Epikureismus und Skepsis. Quellen in

deutscher Übersetzung mit Einführungen, 1996 3 Id., Epikur, [2]1998 4 Id., Stoa, Epikureismus und Skepsis, [2]1995. M.HO.

Harappa see → Indus Culture

Harbours, docks

A. General B. Greece and Hellenism C. Rome D. The economic importance of harbours E. Harbours in literature

A. General

Docks were terrestrial constructions (moles, breakwaters and harbour basins) which served as protection of ships against surf and storms and which were meant to simultaneously facilitate the loading operations as well as storage of freight (stores). In the ships-sheds (νεώσοικοι; *neṓsoikoi, navalia*) of the ancient naval ports, warships were moored between engagements. Ancient commercial ports were the location of the annona and customs authorities, of associations of ship owners, merchants and dock workers, of marine courts, money changers, sanctuaries, inns and brothels.

In the Mediterranean region, where the exchange of goods over long distances depended on sea transport, harbours were important economic centres necessary for supplying cities and sanctuaries with food, building materials, raw materials and wood as well as for transport. No later than the 6th cent. BC, they also gained importance as bases for naval fleets. The prerequisite for the development of harbours and docks was, on the one hand, the coastal shape, such as the lack of a natural harbour, and, on the other hand, the construction of bigger ships. Beach harbours – if possible on both sides of a peninsula in order to offer protection against storm and surf in all weather conditions (cf. e.g. Hom. Od. 6,263ff.) – were common until the 1st millennium BC.

B. Greece and Hellenism

The oldest archaeologically attested harbour, a basin in Thebes-West (Birkat Habu) on the Nile from the 2nd millennium BC, shows, just as depictions of harbours do, that shipping on the Nile in Ancient Egypt required harbours. In the 2nd millennium BC, Phoenician cities created harbours which have now been discovered for the first time on Crete (e.g. in Amnissos and Kommos). For this period, the wrecks of Ulu Burun and of Cape Gelidonya in Lycia attest to shipping in the eastern Mediterranean. Naval traffic, already highly developed in the eastern Mediterranean during the Bronze Age, collapsed around 1200 BC and, only after the 8th cent. BC, again reached a level that required harbours. An impressive constructional achievement in the 6th cent. was the construction of the port of → Samos with a mole of *c.* 300 m in length and with ship-sheds for the fleet of Polycrates (Hdt. 3,45; 3,60); this harbour was already integrated into the city's fortifications. In the 6th cent. BC, the two harbours of Corinth were probably connected across the isthmus through the *diolkos*, a tow path.

Up to the early 5th cent. BC, the harbour of Athens was located on the shallow bay of Phalerum. During the time of the Persian Wars, on Themistocles' initiative, the Athenians fortified the → Piraeus which possessed three bays suitable as harbours, and they developed the peninsula into a commercial and naval port (Hdt. 6,116; Thuc. 1,93,3; Paus. 1,1,2; Plut. Themistocles 19,3). Under Cimon, the 'Long Walls' (μακρὰ τείχη; *makrà teíchē*) were started, which linked Athens and the Piraeus. Athens and its harbour thus became one single fortress which could be supplied from the sea (Plut. Cimon 13,6; Thuc. 1,107,1; 1,108,3; 2,13,6f.; 7,28,1; Str. 9,1,15). In classical times, the two smaller bays in the east served as bases for the naval fleet (harbours of Munychia and of Zea); there were more than 250 ship-sheds and the *skeuotheke* of Philo (after 350 BC), a long hall where oars and other equipment for the triremes were stored (cf. Syll.[3] 969). In the west, the harbour of Cantharus was the commercial port of Athens, separated from the open sea by the Eëtionia peninsula. In the immediate vicinity, there were a large stoa (Thuc. 8,90,5), which probably served as a grain store, and the Deigma (Xen. Hell. 5,1,21), a commercial centre. The Emporion on the east side of the port of Cantharus was separated from the city by a wall. Megara was also linked to the port of Nisaea by 'long walls', which had been erected by the Athenians during the 1st Peloponnesian War (Thuc. 1,103,4). What importance was attributed to a suitable harbour during the 5th cent. BC, is demonstrated in particular by the *synoikismos* of the towns on the island of Rhodes between 411 and 408 BC (Diod. Sic. 13,75,1); the new city of → Rhodes was built after the model of Piraeus (Str. 14,2,9) on the northern cape of the island, where two harbours could be constructed; the bigger harbour was protected against the sea by a mole which was intensively fought over during the siege by Demetrius Poliorcetes in 305 BC (Diod. Sic. 20,85,4–88,8).

In Hellenistic times, artificial harbours were constructed with great engineering efforts. A prominent example is → Alexandria where, by constructing a seven stadia long dam (Heptastadion) between the mainland and the offshore island of Pharos, two protected harbours were created, the 'Great Harbour' in the east and the Eunostos harbour in the west; here, a further harbour basin was dug up (the Kibotos harbour). Further docks belonged to the royal palaces on the Lochias peninsula. Within the 'Great Harbour' the emporion and the ship-sheds extended from the mole of Antony to the Heptastadion. The lighthouse, erected at the beginning of the 3rd cent. BC, stood at the eastern end of the island of → Pharos, after which it was named (Str. 17,1,6–10; Plin. HN 36,83). In antiquity, the Pharos became the model for all later lighthouses.

The harbours constructed by the Carthaginians were often dug-up basins lined with blocks of stones, which were connected to the sea by a canal (κώθων; *kṓthōn*); there is archaeological proof for such harbours at Motya on Sicily and for Carthage itself. In Carthage, there was a rectangular basin serving as the commercial port, and behind it a circular naval port with a round island in the middle and more than 200 ship-sheds on both sides; this construction was probably built in the 4th cent. BC (Str. 17,3,14).

C. Rome

Already at an early stage, the growth of the city of Rome required the extension of the harbour and the docks, with construction activities after the Second Punic War initially concentrating on the Emporium on the Tiber in the immediate vicinity of the city (Liv. 35,10,12; 35,41,10). In 179 and 174 BC, the *censores* had the Emporium in front of the Porta Trigemina extended and had porticos erected there (Liv. 40,51,6; 41,27,8); among these buildings was the *porticus Aemilia*, which is identified with the large storage complex south of the Aventine. However, during the time of the Republic, Rome did not have a maritime harbour at the mouth of the Tiber suitable for grain ships. The grain from the provinces was brought to → Puteoli, whose harbour was extended by a 370 m long and 15 m wide mole in Augustan times; the mole of Puteoli was not a dam of stones, but consisted of 15 pillars joined by arches. Cast mortar (*opus caementicium*) which hardens under water, was used as a building material (Str. 5,4,6; Vitr. De arch. 2,6; 5,12; Plin. HN 35,166; Cass. Dio 48,51,4). Only Claudius initiated the construction of a monumental mole harbour at the mouth of the Tiber after a famine revolt in Rome. As a foundation for the moles and the lighthouse freight ships were used, which were sunk for that purpose; amongst them was the ship that had been used under Gaius for the transport of an obelisk from Egypt to Rome (Tac. Ann. 12,43; Suet. Claud. 18; 20; Plin. HN 16,201f.; 36,70; Cass. Dio 60,11,1–5). However, Nero's project to build a canal from Puteoli to Rome, and thus to create a safe inland waterway for the grain supply, had to be abandoned (Tac. Ann. 15,42,2). Later Trajan extended the harbour constructed under Claudius inland by digging up a hexagonal basin. The Portus ('the harbour') with its numerous storage halls and administrative buildings became the centre of the *annona*. At the Portus, the grain was transferred to tow boats (*caudicariae*) and transported on the Tiber to Rome, where the river port was improved further during the time of the Principate.

The building activities of Roman magistrates or the *principes* was by no means limited to the city of Rome, but also extended to Italy and the provinces. In 179 BC, the censor M. Aemilius Lepidus had a mole constructed near Tarracina (Liv. 40,51,2), and Nero made sure that his birth town Antium was provided with a spacious harbour (Suet. Nero 9). Under Trajan, the harbours of Centumcellae (Plin. Ep. 6,31,15–17) and Ancona were further developed. Numerous harbour buildings and in particular lighthouses, such as those of La Coruña (Brigantium; cf. Oros. 1,2,71) or of Dover bear witness to Roman building activities in the provinces: amongst the buildings of Septimius Severus, which gave a new look to → Leptis Magna, were a harbour basin with storage halls and a lighthouse. The entrance to a Roman harbour could be blocked with chains by using mechanical devices (*machinae*) (Vitr. De arch. 5,12,1). Client kings followed the Roman example. Thus, in *c.* 20 BC, king Herod gave orders for the construction of the harbour at Caesarea Maritima; at the exposed coastline, a harbour basin was created which was protected by moles, whereby the cast-mortar technique was already applied. This shows how fast the use of *opus caementicium* as a building material spread in the Mediterranean (cf. Jos. BI 1,408–415).

Inland navigation on the great rivers of the northwestern provinces also depended on moorings and harbours. Especially on the Rhine and the Danube, a large number of quays are archaeologically attested. In Cologne, the Roman harbour was well protected between the city and an offshore island in the Rhine. For such quays, oak trunks were frequently used as, for example, in Xanten or in London. In late antiquity, moorings on rivers forming a border were often protected on the land side by walls, while on the enemy bank a tower fortress was erected. During the time of the Principate, the Roman fleets were not stationed in the big commercial ports, but had their own bases in Misenum (Str. 5,4,5f.; Cass. Dio 48,50) and Ravenna.

Harbours were often furnished impressively with monuments or lavish buildings; the monumental statue of Helios of Rhodes probably stood at the entrance to the harbour and thus gave an impression of the wealth of the city. On each side of the harbour entrance at Caesarea Maritima three colossi were erected (Jos. BI 1,413). In Roman harbours – e.g. in Ancona – triumphal arches and inscriptions referred to the person who had commissioned the construction and mentioned the purpose of the buildings (*quod accessum Italiae hoc etiam addito ex pecunia sua portu tutiorem navigantibus reddiderit*; CIL IX 5894 = ILS 298). The completion of the harbour at the mouth of the Tiber was celebrated with an image on a coin. The construction of docks certainly attracted the attention and admiration of the public; thus, the mole of Puteoli was praised in epigrams (Anth. Gr. 7,379; 9,708).

In harbour basins cut off from currents in the sea, there was always the risk of silting. Therefore, the mole of Puteoli rested on great pillars in order to maintain the water currents. In Cosa, canals allowed flowing water into the harbour, and the harbours at the mouth of the Tiber were connected with the river by a canal. For Ephesus, repeated attempts to keep the harbour open are documented (Tac. Ann. 16,23,1; IEph I a 23).

D. The economic importance of harbours

While the harbours of Athens and Rome primarily had the function of guaranteeing the supply for the urban population, there were also harbour cities which principally exported goods from the hinterland. Gades, for example, which had been provided with a hew harbour by Cornelius Balbus, was important for the export of grain, wine and oil from the province of Baetica to Rome (Str. 3,2,4–6; 3,5,3); Alexandria is said to have exported more goods than it imported (Str. 17,1,7). Other harbour cities were centres of trade with regions outside the Imperium Romanum. This applies to Aquileia, for example, which played a decisive role in the exchange of goods with the Danube region (Str. 5,1,8). The starting-point of the trade with India was the harbour town Myos Hormos on the Red Sea (Peripl. maris Erythraei 1; Str. 2,5,12; 17,1,45). What range the exchange of goods reached in the harbours, becomes evident from the amount of harbour duties which were leased for 36 talents (216,000 drachmas; And. 1,133ff.) in Piraeus at the beginning of the 4th cent. BC: on that basis, the value of goods imported into or exported from Piraeus amounted to *c.* 1,800 talents (10.8 million drachmas). The harbour duties significantly contributed to the revenue of ancient cities; in this context, they are expressly mentioned in Ps.-Aristotle ([Ps.]Aristot. Oec. 1346a). Prior to Delos being declared a free port by the Romans, the greatest part of the public revenue of Rhodes came from such duties (1 million drachmas; Pol. 31,7,10).

E. Harbours in literature

In political theory, the question as to whether the proximity to the sea and to a harbour was advantageous for a polis, was assessed in various ways. While Plato regards the commercial activities and financial dealings related to a harbour as a danger for the city and consequently recommends limitations for imports and exports (Pl. Leg. 704d–705b; 847b-e), Aristotle considers a connection to the sea as rather favourable since all important goods can be obtained easily only in that way (Aristot. Pol. 1327a). Finally, Cicero counts the expenses for *navalia* and *portus* amongst the useful expenditures of a *res publica* (Cic. Off. 2,60). Amongst the topics of ancient eulogies belongs the reference to harbours and the variety of the goods offered there (Piraeus: Isoc. Or. 4,42; Portus: Aristid. 26,11–13; for Antioch cf. also Lib. Or. 11,34–41). Pliny in his Panegyricus lists the construction of harbours amongst the merits of a ruler (Plin. Pan. 29,2). In his theory of architecture (Vitr. De arch. 5,12), Vitruvius primarily deals with aspects of building technology in the construction of harbours. Amongst the pictorial representations of Roman harbours, apart from those on coins, the relief in the Museo Torlonia (Portus, *c.* AD 200) and a wall painting from Stabiae (harbour of Puteoli, 1st cent. AD, now Naples, MN) are to be mentioned.

→ Alexandria; → Inland navigation; → Caesarea Maritima; → Horrea; → Carthage; → Leptis Magna (with illustration); → Ostia (with illustration); → Piraeus; → Portus; → Puteoli; → Rhodes

1 R. Bartoccini, Il porto romano di Leptis Magna, 1958 2 D.J. Blackman, Ancient Harbours in the Mediterranean, in: International Journ. of Nautical Archaeology 11, 1982, 79–104; 185–211 3 Casson, Ships, 361–370 4 L. Casson, Harbour and River Boats of ancient Rome, in: JRS 55, 1965, 31–39 5 F. Castagnoli, Installazioni portuali a Roma, in: D'Arms/Kopff, 35–42 6 A.M. Colini, Il porto fluviale del Foro Boario a Roma, in: D'Arms/Kopff, 43–53 7 O. Höckmann, Ant. Seefahrt, 1985, 144–156 8 G.W. Houston, Ports in Perspective: Some Comparative Materials on Roman Merchant Ships and Ports, in: AJA 92, 1988, 553–564 9 J. Le Gall, Le Tibre fleuve de Rome dans l'antiquité, 1953 10 K. Lehmann-Hartleben, Die ant. Hafenanlagen des Mittelmeeres, 1923 11 A.M. McCann, J. Bourgeois, E.K. Gazda, The Roman Port and Fishery of Cosa, 1987 12 R. Meiggs, Roman Ostia, [2]1973 13 G. Milne, The Port of Roman London, 1985 14 J.P. Oleson, G. Branton, The Technology of King Herod's Harbour, in: R.L. Vann (ed.), Caesarea Papers, JRA Suppl. 5, 1992, 49–67 15 A. Raban (ed.), Harbour Archaeology, British Archaeological Reports, International Series 257, 1985 16 J.W. Shaw, Bronze Age Aegean harboursides, in: D.A. Hardy (ed.), Thera and the Aegean World, 3, 1990, 420–436 17 Id., Greek and Roman harbourworks, in: G.F. Bass (ed.), A History of Seafaring Based on Underwater Archaeology, 1972, 87–112 18 O. Testaguzza, Portus, 1970 19 Travlos, Attica, 258–287; 340–363 20 White, Technology, 104–110.

O.H.

Hare (*Lepus europaeus Pallas*). The hare can be found from Central Europe to the Near East and South Africa in cultivated steppe lands and in forests. Its name: λαγωός (*lagōós*; Homeric), λαγώς, λαγῶς (*lagṓs*, *lagôs*; Attic), λαγός (*lagós*; Ionian, Doric), λέπορις (*léporis*; Aeolian, Sicilian: Varro, Rust. 3,12,6), Latin *lepus* or the derivatives thereof λαγίον; *lagíon*, λαγίδιον; *lagídion*, λαγιδεύς; *lagideús*, furthermore special appellations according to characteristic features such as 'ducker' (πτώξ; *ptṓx*; Hom. Il. 17,676; Aesch. Eum. 326; Theophr. Hist. pl. 4,3,5; Theocrit 1,110), 'rough-foot' (δασύπους; *dasýpous*; in comedies of Xen. and Aristot.), 'the fast' (ταχίνας; *tachínas*; Lacon. according to Ael. NA 7,47) and 'the jumper' (κέκην; *kékēn*, Cretan according to Hsch.).

In the Mediterranean area, the hare was found almost everywhere, even on islands, with the exception of Ithaca (Aristot. Hist. an. 7(8),28, 606a 2–5; Plin. HN 8,226), Cyrnos (Corsica; Pol. 12,3,10 against the historian Timaeus) and others. In Attica, it was perhaps rarer (Nausicrates comicus in Ath. 9,399 f = CAF 2,296). Its appearance on some islands is at times historically documented, for Astypalaea by Hegesander of Delphi (Ath. 9,400 d) and for Sicily by Aristotle (res publica Rheginensium 1565a 7). Local species were differentiated, e.g. for Macedonia (Aristot. Hist. an. 2,17,507a 16–19; cf. Plin. HN 11,190), Egypt (Aristot. ibid. 7(8),28,606a 24), Scythia (Aristot. Hist. an. 8(9),33,619b 15), Crastonia (Aristot. Mir. 122, 842a 15f.) and Sicily (Mir. 82, 836b 19) as well as Italy (Varro, Rust. 3,12,5). The snow hare of the Alps is mentioned by Varro, Rust. 3,12,5 and Plin. HN 11,190, but, with the exception of the white winter coat, without any special characteristics. Xenophon (Cyn. 5), similar to Aelianus (Ael. NA 13,14f.), excellently describes the two hare species (the bigger one = Macedonian, the smaller one = Italian, the latter probably identical with the χελιδόνειος λαγωός;

chelidóneios lagōós in Diphilus fragment 1, cf. Ath. 9,401a, who identifies it with the rabbit), including their behaviour.

In terms of zoology, many special features of these rodents with upper and lower incisors (ἀμφόδοντες, *amphódontes* in Aristot. Hist. an. 3,1,511a 30f.; 3,21, 522b 9) were observed: their swiftness and the forward placement of the significantly longer hind legs when running (Hom. Il. 17,676; Hes. Sc. 302; Xen. Cyn. 5; Ael. NA 13,14f), the strong, soft hair even in its mouth and under its feet (Aristot. Hist. an. 3,12, 519a 22f.; Gen. an. 4,5,774a 35; Xen. Cyn. 5; Plin. HN 11,229: here, this feature is related to their randiness by Trogus), the incomplete blood-clotting because of the lack of fibrin (ἶνες; *înes*, Aristot. Hist. an. 3,6,515b 35–516a 5), the reported presence of suction nipples within the female's uterus (3,11,511a 29–31), a two-part liver in some areas of distribution (2,17,507a 16–19, Plin. HN 11,190; Ael. NA 5,27 and 11,40; Gell. NA 16,115), the presence of rennin in the stomach as in ruminants (3,21,522b 8f.; Plin. HN 11,239) as well as their enormous fecundity (Aristot. Hist. an. 6,33,579b 30–580a 5; Hor. Sat. 2,4,44). Even the superfecundation [1. 156], now a proven fact, was known (Hdt. 3,108,3; Aristot. Hist. an. 5,9,542b 30f.; Gen. an. 4,5,774a 30–32; Plin. HN 8,219), but a parthenogenesis as stated by Archelaus in Plin. HN 8,218 and the formation of embryos in the male (Ael. NA 13,12) are pure fantasy. The supposed sleeping with open eyes was often repeated (Xen. Cyn. 5,11; Plin. HN 11,147; Ael. NA 2,12 and 13,13). The cunning cowardice of hares was quite legendary (cf. Hdt. 3,108; Aristot. Hist. an. 1,1,488b 15; Xen. Cyn. 5; Ael. NA 7,19): 'more cowardly than a Phrygian hare' (δειλότερον λαγὼ Φρυγός; *deilóteron lagṓ Phrygós*, Str. 1,36) and 'an (apparently) sleeping hare' (λαγὼς καθεύδων; *lagṓs katheúdōn*, Zenob. 4,84). Fables presented hares as dumb and cowardly (Aesop. 143; 169 and 254; Syntipas 10 Hausrath). In Aristot. Pol. 3,15,1284a 15f., Antisthenes describes the hare's claim of equal rights for all animals as absurd.

Many predators hunted hares, such as eagles (Hom. Il. 17,676 and 22,310; Aesop. 3 and 273; Aristot. Hist. an. 8 (9),33,619b 9), dogs (Hom. Il. 10,360–2; Hom. Od. 17,295; Aesop. 139), lions (Aesop. 153, cf. chasing hares with lions in a Roman circus in Ov. Fast. 5,371f.) and foxes (Ael. NA 13,11; cf. Aesop. 169). But their greatest enemy were humans who always hunted them for their lean meat (recipes in Ath. 9,399d f. with quotes from comedians; about hunting mosaics e.g. in Piazza Armerina [2. fig. 102–104]). Allegedly, the consumption of hare was to enhance beauty for several days (Plin. HN 28,260; Mart. 5,29 and 13,92; cf. a witty poem about Alexander Severus, S HA Alex. Sev. 19) and to help against numerous diseases of almost all parts of the body (cf. Plin. HN 28,166; 178f; 199; 215 *et passim*) or have a magic effect. Therefore, in the Edictum Diocletiani, a hare cost up to 150 denars, a rabbit only 40. Thus, it is easy to understand that, already in the days of the Roman Republic, it was popular to keep hares together with other wild animals in large enclosures (*leporaria*, Varro, Rust. 3,3,2 and 3,12,1–7; Columella 9,1,8f.; Gell. NA 2,20). According to Xenophon (Cyn. 5), an individual or many animals were hunted with large upright nets (δίκτυον; *díktyon*, πάναγρον; *pánagron*) during a battue or with cross-path or drop nets (ἐνόδιον; *enódion*, ἄρκυς; *árkys*) or just with dogs (cf. Verg. G. 1,308). Consequently, the Eumenids (Aesch. Eum. 326) call Orestes, who was chased by them, a hare (πτώξ; *ptṓx*). The animals caught were killed with a club (καλαῦροψ; *kalaûrops*, Homeric; λαγωβόλον; *lagōbólon*).

Its calm behaviour, but also its erotic nature also made the hare a sought-after pet, just like the sparrow, e.g. in Melagros (Anth. Pal. 7,207), as is suggested in many illustrations (e.g. in Roman wall paintings [2. 190] in the company of Bacchus) of cupids and girls. Plautus (Cas. 138) uses *lepus* alongside *columba* ('domestic dove') and *passer* ('sparrow') as a term of affection. A cultic meaning cannot be found for the hare amongst the Greeks and Romans; it is regarded as unclean in the OT (Lv 11:6; Dt 14:7).

The rabbit (*Oryctolagus cuniculus Lilljeborg*; cf. a wall painting from Herculaneum [2. 192 and fig. 105]), with the Iberian name *cuniculus* adopted by the Romans, originates from Spain and was called κ(ο)ύνικλος (*koíniklos*, *kýniklos*) by Pol. 12,3,10, Posidonius as well as Theopompus in Ath. 9,400 f–401 a. Strabo (3,144: λαγιδεύς; *lagideús*) calls it λεβηρίς; *lebērís* and (γεώρυχος; *geṓrychos*) λαγιδεύς (*lagideús*) or also δασύπους (*dasýpous*) in Massilian (in spite of the correct identification with the hare in Aristot. Hist. an. 7(8),28, 606a 24), which is incorrectly adopted by Plin. HN 8,219. The Romans not only registered its origins (Catull. 37,18: *cuniculosa Celtiberia*), but also its spread into Gallia, the Balearic Islands and the islands to the west of Italy. The sources (i.a. Varro, Rust. 3,12,6; cf. Mart. 13,60) refer to it as a different kind of hare, similar to the Italian one but smaller, and mention their extensive networks of burrows (Plin. HN 8,217f.) that undermine whole cities (Iberian *cuniculi*). A population explosion on the Balearic islands at the time of Augustus lead to a famine which, with state support and among other measures, the introduction of the → ferret (*viverra*; Str. 3,144: γαλῆ ἀγρία; *galê agría* from Libya), was kept in check by intensive hunting (Plin. HN 8,218). The almost mature foetus (Iberian *laurex* in Plin. HN 8,217) was regarded as a delicacy right into the Middle Ages (cf. Gregory of Tours, Historia Francorum 5,4). Breeding rabbits was apparently never practised in antiquity.

→ Hunting

1 J. Niethammer, Säugetiere, 1979 2 Toynbee, Tierwelt.

H. Gossen, s.v. H., RE 7, 2477; Id., s.v. Kaninchen, RE 10, 1867; Keller 1, 210–218; F. Orth, s.v. Jagd, RE 9,558; Id., s.v. Leporarium, RE 12, 2068; Id., s.v. Lepus, RE 12, 2079.

C.HÜ.

Harem (*ḥarīm*). A sacred, inviolable, prohibited place, i.e. those parts of the house where the women (mother, wife/wives, daughters, unmarried sisters, concubines) of a family live and which can only be entered by those male members of the family who have a particular family relationship. Also a term for the female members of a family. The segregation of the sexes is based on statements in the Koran (Surah 33,53–59). In Europe, an erotically-exotic image of the harem prevailed for a long time, influenced especially by the descriptions in the 'Arabian Nights', paintings and accounts of travellers, all shaped by the knowledge of the harem in the Ottoman sultan's palace.

EI 3, s.v. Ḥarīm, 209a-b; N.M. PENZER, The Ḥarēm, [2]1966 (about the sultan's palace in Istanbul). H.SCHÖ.

Haremhab (῞Αρμαις; *Hármais*). As a generalissimo under Tutanchamun and Eje, H. served the last of the Amarna rulers. As a king, he suppressed the memory of all Amarna rulers, in particular of Akhnaton and Eje, while he spared Tutanchamun's tomb [2]. In the pseudo-Manetho tradition, H. is regarded as → Danaus (Jos. Ap. 1,26).

1 J.v. BECKERATH, s.v. H., LÄ 2, 962–4 2 M. EATON-KRAUSS, Tutankhamun at Karnak, in: MDAI(K) 44, 1988, 10f. R.K.

Harii Alongside the → Helvecones, Manimi, Halisiones and Nahanarvali, the H. are a powerful branch of the Vandali-Lugii tribe (Tac. Germ. 43,2). The identification with the Charini (Plin. HN 4,99) [1] is uncertain; the old conjecture of reading the hand-written *alii* (Tac. Germ. 43,4) as *(H)arii* must be abandoned. Thus, the conclusions related to the supposed *ferialis exercitus* ('army of ghosts', 'army of the dead') of the H. are invalid. [2].

1 G. NEUMANN, s.v. Charini, RGA 4, 371f. 2 A.A. LUND, Kritischer Forsch.-Ber. zur *Germania* des Tacitus, in: ANRW II 33.3, 1989–2222, esp. 2171f.

D. TIMPE, Romano-Germanica, 1995, 127–129. K.DI.

Harioli The etymology and meaning of the term *harioli* are not clear: *harioli* is either a diminutive formation of *haruspex* (→ *Haruspices*) or it is derived from Latin *ara* ('altar') [1. 886]. In ancient Rome, persons were referred to as *harioli*, who were knowledgeable in the various forms of → divination and who told fortunes for private persons. Since the term is always used in a derogatory sense (e.g. Cato Agr. 5,4; Catull. 90,2; in the comedy amongst others Plaut. Cist. 746; Plaut. Men. 76; Plaut. Mostell. 571 and 791; Plaut. Rud. 326, 347, 377, 1139ff.; Ter. Phorm. 492, 708 et passim), the assumption presents itself that the *harioli* cannot be attributed any specific abilities or functions, but that the word is only a 'term of abuse'. This conclusion is noteworthy in that, in Roman antiquity, there is apparently no area outside the officially sanctioned divination – i.e. no linguistic one either – that is defined (in a positive sense) for private fortune-telling.

1 G. THIELE, s.v. Harioli, RE Suppl. 3, 886–888.

S. MONTERO, Mántica inspirada y demonologica. Los "harioli", in: AC 62, 1993, 115–129. C.F.

Harma (῞Αρμα; *Hárma*). Boeotian settlement on the Thebae – Chalcis [1] road between Teumessus and Mycalessus, already listed in the Homeric catalogue of ships (Hom. Il. 2,499; Str. 9,2,26); mentioned in connection with the disappearance of → Amphiaraus or the rescue of → Adrastus [1] (Str. 9,2,11; Paus. 1,34,2; 9,19,4). For some time, H. together with Eleon, Mycalessus and Pharae formed an association of villages subordinate to Tanagra; in Roman times, the place was abandoned (Str. 9,2,11; 14). H. is identified with modern Kastron (polygonal ring of walls; finds from early Helladic to Hellenistic periods) on the south-eastern end of the south-eastern foothills, called Lykovouni, of the Messapion mountains, *c.* 4 km north of modern H.

FOSSEY, 85–89; J.M. FOSSEY, Η αρχαία τοπογραφία τῆς Βοιωτίας, in: Id., Papers in Boiotian Topography and History, 1990, 16–18; LAUFFER, Griechenland, 258; N.D. PAPACHATZIS, Παυσανίου Ἑλλάδος Περιήγησις 5, [2]1981, 126–128; P.W. WALLACE, Strabo's Description of Boiotia, 1979, 49f. P.F.

Harmachis (Egyptian *Ḥrw-m-ꜣḫ.t*, 'Horus in the horizon').

[1] Name under which the great → Sphinx of → Gizeh was venerated as the embodiment of the sun god since the beginning of the New Kingdom (*c.* 1500 BC). Many votive steles document the popularity of the cult amongst private people as well as kings.

J. ASSMANN, s.v. H., LÄ2, 992–996. S.S.

[2] Son of Anemhor, father of Nesysti III; high priest of Ptah of Memphis (*c.* 260 – after 194–193 BC); sometimes identified with the rebel king → Harwennefer, which, however, is improbable for chronological reasons.

PP 3,5358.; J. QUAEGEBEUR, The Genealogy of the Memphite High Priest Family in the Hellenistic Period, in: D.J. CRAWFORD (ed.), Studies on Ptolemaic Memphis, 1980, 43–81, esp. 67f., no. 16; 81.

[3] Agent of the *oikonomos* Horus in the south of the Herakleopolites *nomos*; his official archive has records of transactions from April 215 to February 214 BC

W. CLARYSSE, Harmachis, Agent of the Oikonomos, in: AncSoc 7, 1976, 185–207. W.A.

[4] Rebellious native Egyptian ruler in southern Upper Egypt at the time of Ptolemy V (210–180 BC).

J. ASSMANN, s.v. H., LÄ 2, 992–996. S.S.

Harmodius (Ἁρμόδιος; *Harmódios*).

[1] **Harmodius of Athens** conspired with → Aristogiton [1] and others in order to murder the tyrants → Hippias [1] and → Hipparchus [1] during the Panathenaea in 514 BC. However, they only managed to kill Hipparchus. H. was also killed during this assassination attempt (Hdt. 5,55–58; Thuc. 1,20; 6,54–59; Aristot. Ath. Pol. 18). For Thucydides, the motivation for the conspiracy was purely personal: H. and his sister had suffered humiliation after H. had rejected the homoerotic advances of Hipparchus. In Athens, soon after the overthrow of Hippias in 511–510, H. and Aristogiton were celebrated as freedom fighters and founders of the democracy and were honoured with the erection of the statue of → Antenor [2] on the Agora.

H. Berve, Die Tyrannis bei den Griechen 1, 1967, 68–74; Davies 12267, III; B. Fehr, Die Tyrannentöter, 1984; Traill, PAA 203425. E.S.-H.

[2] **Harmodius of Tarsus.** (TrGF I 156), son of one of the Asclepiads; in the 1st cent. BC, with the satyr play 'Protesilaus' he was the winner at the Romaea in Magnesia at the Maeander (TrGF I: DID A 13,4). B.Z.

Harmonia (Ἁρμονία; *Harmonía*). Daughter of Ares and Aphrodite, wife of → Cadmus, mother of → Ino, → Semele, → Agave, → Autonoe and → Polydorus (Hes. Theog. 933–937; 975–978; Apollod. 3,25). The wedding of Cadmus and H., for which the gods bring along opulent presents (i.a. a necklace made by Hephaestus and a → peplos, in Alcmaeon [1], Amphiaraus), was a popular topic (Pind. Pyth. 3,88–92; Paus. 3,18,12; Apollod. 3,25). The bridal song is sung by the Muses (Thgn. 15–18). At the end of their life, Cadmus and H. are transferred to the island of the blessed (Eur. Bacch. 1338f.; Pind. Ol. 2,78), according to some they are (first) turned into snakes (Eur. Bacch. 1330–1332; Ov. Met. 4,563–603). In Thebes, the *thalamos* ('bridal chamber') of H. and the place of the song of the Muses (Paus. 9,12,3) as well as the three *xóana* (→ Xoanon) of Aphrodite (Paus. 9,16,3) donated by H. were shown. Together with the Charites, Horae, Hebe, Aphrodite and others, H. is also the embodiment of the characteristic referred to by her name (H. Hom. 3,194–196; Aesch. Supp. 1039–1042). She also appears as the daughter of Zeus (Aesch. PV 551) and mother of the Muses (Eur. Med. 831f.). Since the 5th cent. BC, H. was associated with the mystery cult in Samothrace, where she is regarded as the daughter of Zeus and → Electra (or → Electryone) and where, after her abduction by Cadmus, she is being looked for by her mother, just as → Kore/Persephone by → Demeter (Hellanicus FGrH 4 F 23; Ephoros FGrH 70 F 120; Diod. Sic. 5,48–49).

E. Paribeni, s.v. H., LIMC 4.1, 412–414; M. Rocchi, Kadmos e H.: Un matrimonio problematico, 1989. K.WA.

Harmostai (ἁρμοσταί; *harmostaí*, Ionian ἁρμοστῆρες; *harmostêres*: Xen. Hell. 4,8,39).

[1] Spartan military commanders responsible for the supervision of certain areas. The 20 *harmostai* of the Lacedaemonians, mentioned in the scholia to Pindar (Ol. 6,154), cannot be identified with certainty as supervisory officials over the poleis of the *perioikoi* and should rather be regarded as 'governors' residing outside the Spartan polis area [1. 11f.; 2. 62f.]. The *harmostḗs* (IG V 1,937), documented in the early 4th cent. for Cythera, probably represents an exception for military reasons. After the Peloponnesian War, garrisons led by *harmostai* were stationed at vulnerable locations of Sparta's external sphere of influence (Xen. Hell. 1,1,32; 1,2,18; 1,3,5; 1,3,15; 2,3,14; 4,8,3ff.), partly as a result of → Lysander's initiative who attempted to support the oligarchic → dekadarchia [1] in dependent poleis [3. 66ff.; 4. 152f.].

[2] Commanders of Theban garrisons who were appointed in Achaean poleis for the expulsion of oligarchs, first in 369 BC during the 2nd Peloponnesian Campaign of → Epaminondas in Sicyon (Xen. Hell. 7,2,11; 7,3,4 and 9), then in 366 as a result of the Boeotian League's resolution, but they could not prevent the renewed rise to power of the exulants (Xen. Hell. 7,1,43) [5. 191ff.; 6. 61].

[3] A *harmostḗs* from Sinope was a garrison commander in Cytyora around 400 BC (Xen. An. 5,5,19).

1 St. Link, Der Kosmos Sparta, 1994 2 L. Thommen, Lakedaimonion Politeia, 1996 3 D. Lotze, Lysander und der Peloponnesische Krieg, 1964 4 J.-P. Bommelaer, Lysandre de Sparte, 1981 5 J. Buckler, The Theban Hegemony 371–362 BC, 1980 6 H. Beck, Polis und Koinon, 1997. K.-W.WEL.

Harmozice (Ἁρμοζική; *Harmozikḗ* Str. 11,3,5; Ἀρμάκτικα; *Harmáktika* Ptol. 5,11,3; 8,19,4; *Hermastis iuxta Cyrum* Plin. HN 6,29; *Armastika* Geogr. Rav. 2,8; Georgian *Armazʿiẖe*, 'fortress of the Armazi').

Residence of the kings of the Caucasian → Iberia on the Bagineti hill in modern Mccheta south opposite the confluence of the → Aragus into the → Cyrus; conquered by Pompey in 65 BC.

Excavations since 1937 have revealed buildings of Hellenistic and Roman times: fortress wall (clay brick wall on a stone block foundation), transverse stoa (stone block walling, timber columns with bases and capitals of stone), two baths (Roman provincial type, rubble masonry), cult(?) complex with architectural elements of unusual form and decoration as well as a necropolis of Roman times with opulent graves: i.a. a silver dish with Marcus Aurelius' portrait and a horse in front of an altar, gold jewellery with polychrome incrustation, silver fittings for furniture feet (cf. Plut. Pompey 34). On the opposite side, on the northern bank of the Cyrus, Iberia's capital → Mestleta was situated.

A. Apakidze (ed.), Mccheta. Archeologičeskie raskopki, 1958ff.; O. Lordkipanidse, Archäologie, 1991, 159f.; W. Tomaschek, s.v. Armastika, RE 2, 1177. A.P.-L.

Harpagus (῞Αρπαγος; *Hárpagos*).
[1] Median who, from *c.* 550 BC, fought as a field marshal in Cyrus' service against the Lydians, Ionians, Carians and Lycians (Hdt. 1,80; 162–169; 171–176). Against the Ionian cities, he built earth walls (Hdt. 1,162) and employed the first catapults in history during their conquest; this is documented for Phocaea.
[2] Persian field marshal who, during the → Ionian Revolt (499–497 BC), captured Histiaeus in Miletus, and who was then crucified by the Satrap Artaphernes [2] of Sardeis (Hdt. 6,28–30).

P. Briant, L'histoire de l'empire Perse, 1996, 111–113; J. Cobet, Milet 1994–1995, in: AA 1997, 249–284, esp. 260. PE.HÖ.

Harpalus (῞Αρπαλος; *Hárpalos*). Son of Machatas, nephew of → Derdas [3] and → Phila from the dynasty of → Elimea (Ath. 13,557c), in his youth a friend of → Alexander [4] the Great and, in 337 BC, banned by → Philippus II together with the others. Physically unfit for active service, he became Alexander's treasurer (Arr. Anab. 3,6,6). At the end of 334, he fled to Megara for reasons unknown, but he was given back his old post by Alexander in the spring of 331. In 330, he remained in → Ecbatana for guarding the booty transported from Persepolis and, together with his countryman → Cleander, probably took part in murdering → Parmenion. Assigned to Babylon, where the main part of the royal treasure was stored, he resided in the palace and became notorious for his indulgent lifestyle at the expense of the treasure, mainly because of his Athenian → hetaerae → Pythionice and → Glycera [1] whom he showered with honours and precious objects. He was conscientious about providing supplies and fulfilled Alexander's personal wishes (Curt. 9,3,21; Plut. Alexander 8,3). He sent grain to Athens and was rewarded by being granted citizenship.

When, after Alexander's return from India, Cleander became a victim of the purge, H. fled with 30 ships, 6,000 mercenaries and 3,000 silver talents and, in mid-324, demanded entry into Athens. Rejected due to fears of his army, he left his army and fleet in → Taenarum and, with three ships and 700 talents, was accepted as a citizen in danger. When Alexander demanded his extradition, he was put in jail and his silver was confiscated. But he soon escaped, which, in Athens, led to the sentencing of → Demosthenes [2] and other prominent politicians. When assembling his forces on Crete, he was murdered by → Thibron; otherwise, he probably would have become the first of the Diadochi (→ Diadochi and Epigoni).

E. Badian, Harpalus, in: JHS 81, 1961, 16–43; Berve 2, no. 143; Heckel, 213–221; S. Jaschinski, Alexander und Griechenland unter dem Eindruck der Flucht des Harpalos, 1981. E.B.

Harpalyce (῾Αρπαλύκη; *Harpalýkē*).
[1] Daughter of the Thracian king Harpalycus who, after the death of her mother, raises her with cow's and mare's milk and trains her to be a warrior. After his death, she lives as a livestock thief and hunter until she is captured with a net and killed. Ritual fighting took place at her grave (Serv. Auct. Aen. 1,317; Hyg. Fab. 193). The oldest reference to her can be found in Virgil (Aen. 1,317) for whom H. served as a model of → Camilla (Verg. Aen. 11,532–915).
[2] Daughter of Epicaste and the Arcadian Clymenus who abuses her sexually in an incestuous relationship (Euphorion fr. 24a v. Groningen; Parthenius 13). When he prevents her marriage to Alastor, she kills her younger brother in revenge (Euphorion; Parthenius) and, according to others, her son begotten by Clymenus (Lact. Placidus; Stat. Theb. 5,120; Hyg. Fab. 206), and presents him to her father as a meal. H. is transformed into a bird called χαλκίς (*chalkís*) (Parthenius) or killed by her father (Hyg. Fab. 206) who subsequently commits suicide. The parallel to the myth of → Tereus is striking.
[3] According to Ath. 14,619e, a virgin who dies of grief because her love for a certain Iphis is unrequited. In memory of her, a song contest carried out by young women is called *harpalýkē*.

O. Crusius, s.v. H., Roscher 1, 1835–1841; J. Eitrem, s.v. H., RE 7, 2401–2404. K.WA.

Harpalycus (῾Αρπάλυκος; *Harpálykos*).
[1] Thracian king, father of → Harpalyce.
[2] From Panopeus. Son of → Hermes, teacher of → Hercules in wrestling, boxing and pancratium (Theoc. 24,111–118).
[3] Trojan, killed by → Camilla with a lance (Verg. Aen. 11,675).
[4] Son of → Lycaon (Apollod. 3,97). According to [1] to be compared with the giant Harpolycus.

1 A.S.F. Gow (ed.), Theocritus, 1952, for 24,115f.
2 K.J. Dover, Theocritus, 1971, for 24,116; 2,16. T.H.

Harpaston (ἁρπαστόν/*harpastón*; *harpastón*; *harpastum*). Name for a small, firm ball, then also for a catch ball game using such a ball (Poll. 9,105; Ath. 1,14f.), similar to the → *phainínda* (cf. Clem. Al. 3,10,50 [and schol.]). The *harpaston* was a very physical combat game; details of the game are not known. One party attacks the player of the other side, who is in possession of the ball, and attempts to wrest the ball from him (ἁρπάζειν; *harpázein*, '[hastily] grasp', 'snatch', 'rob'). This player strives to pass the ball to his team mates who in turn are prevented by the attackers from catching the ball. The side in possession of the ball tries to dominate the middle part of the playing field, while the opposing side tries to gain possession of the ball and themselves penetrate the middle part of the field. This resulted in obstructions because of pushing,

tripping up or kicking and wrestling over the ball, in the course of which apparently all actions were permissible (Sen. Ep. 80,1–3; Epict. 2,5,16; Mart. 4,19,6; 7,32,10; 14,48). The *harpaston* required a high degree of skill and physical agility.
→ Ball games; → Play

E. WAGNER, Kritische Bemerkungen zum Harpastum-Spiel, in: Gymnasium 70, 1963, 356–366; I. WEILER, Der Sport bei den Völkern der Alten Welt, 1981, 212. R.H.

Harpasus (Ἅρπασος; *Hárpasos*).
[1] Southern tributary of the Maeander in Caria (Plin. HN 2,210; 5,109; Ptol. 5,2,15; Quint. Smyrn. 10,141–146; Steph. Byz. s.v. H.), modern Akçay, narrow like a canyon along its middle course, today with a dam further south (Kemer dam). Old Ionian settlement area, ruins of ancient settlements near its banks (e.g. Neapolis, Harpasa, modern Arpaz near Esenköy). In the summer of 228 BC, → Attalus [4] I beat Antiochus → Hierax at the H., in 189, Cn. Manlius Vulso made camp at the H. (Liv. 38,13,2ff.). Inscriptions and coins reaching into the Imperial period.

W. M. CALDER, G. E. BEAN, A Classical Map of Asia Minor, 1958; Map Türkiye-Türkei, Turkish Ministry of Defence, Ryborsch, Obertshausen bei Frankfurt/M. 1994, sheet 2; W. M. RAMSAY, The Historical Geography of Asia Minor, 1890, 423; MAGIE 2, 738f.; L. ROBERT, A travers l'Asie Mineure, 1980, 355–362. H.KA.

[2] River in → Colchis (Xen. An. 7,18; Ἄψαρος; *Ápsaros*, Arr. Peripl. p. eux. 9r45 DILLER), modern Čoroḫi (Turkish Çoruh Nehri), originating at the Karakaban Dağı/Turkey, it flows into the Black Sea south of Batʿumi/Georgia. The H. was navigable for light ships. Situated at its upper course was → Gymnias (Xen. An. 7,19; modern Bayburt), a station along the caravan route to Trapezus. The plains along the H. were very fertile and well suitable for growing crops and keeping livestock. Rich Bronze Age finds (Pitšwnari). In historic times, the Chalybes and Taoches had settlements on the right bank and the Scythenes on the left bank. The Romans fortified the mouth of the H. (Apsarus) against pirates. Later, five cohorts were stationed there, amongst them the *cohors II Claudiana* (CIL X 1202).

M. I. MAKSIMOVA, Antičnye goroda jugovostočnogo Pricernomor'a [Ancient cities on the southern shore of the Black Sea], 1956; O. LENDLE, Komm. zu Xen. an., 1995, 270–273. I.v.B.

Harpies (Ἅρπυιαι; *Hárpyiai*, Latin *Harpyiae*). Female monsters of Greek mythology who, as daughters of Thaumas and Electra (Apollod. 1,2,6), belong to an older generation of gods. These 'snatchers' (< ἁρπάζω, *harpázō* = 'snatch', 'rob'), who are never described in detail, are personifications of the demonic forces of storms and are always represented as winged women. Homer uses them in order to explain the disappearance without a trace of Odysseus (Hom. Od. 1,241; 14,371) or the sudden death of → Pandareus' daughters (Od. 20,66–78). Their names – Podarge (Hom. Il. 16,149–151) or Aello and Ocypete (Hes. Theog. 267) – refer to their speed. Usually, as in Hesiod, there are only two harpies, later sources, however, mention three (possibly influenced by the theatre) or leave their number indeterminate. Iris, the fast messenger of the gods, is their sister (Apollod. 1,2,6). The H. play their most important mythological role in the legend of the Argonauts: they torment the Thracian king → Phineus by snatching his meals until they are finally chased away by Boreas' sons (already in Hes. fr. 150–156 M-W; Aesch. Eum. 50f.; especially popular during Hellenism: detailed representations in Apoll. Rhod. 2,234–434). In Virgil, who for the first time calls a harpy Celaeno, they play a role in Aeneas' adventure on the islands of the Strophades (Verg. Aen. 3,209–277) [1].

1 R. J. RABEL, The Harpyiae in the Aeneid, in: CJ 80, 1984–5, 317–325.

L. KAHIL, s.v. H., LIMC 4.1, 445–450. J.B.

Harpocras Freedman of Claudius, who is said to have honoured him by permitting him the use of a litter and the holding of games in Rome, which was normally the prerogative of the magistrates. PIR² H 16. W.E.

Harpocration (Ἁρποκρατίων; *Harpokratíōn*).
[1] Platonic philosopher from Argos, 2nd cent. AD, pupil of → Atticus, called 'top Platonist' (Πλατωνικῶν κορυφαῖος; *Platōnikôn koryphaîos*) by Proclus [1. 18]. Important was his commentary on Plato (24 bks.) [1. 28, 152, 180ff., 191, 194, 197, 206, 216f.] and his lexicon on Plato (2 bks.) [1. 28, 235]. Just as Atticus and Plutarch, H. supported the idea of the world's origin in a single (temporal) act, but, in his understanding of the → Demiourgos [3] and the immortality of all souls, he strongly followed the example of → Numenius. According to H., the evil in the soul originates from visible bodies [2. 190, 512].

1 DÖRRIE/BALTES, III, 1993 2 Id., IV, 1996.

FRAGMENTS: J. DILLON, H.'s Commentary on Plato, in: Californian Studies in Classical Antiquity 4, 1971, 125–146. BIBLIOGRAPHY: Id., The Middle Platonists, 1977, 258–262. M.BA. and M.-L.L.

[2] **(Valerius) H.** Greek rhetor and lexicographer from Alexandria, 2nd cent. AD.
A. PERSON B. WORKS

A. PERSON

Little is known about his life; the Suda merely mentions his place of origin, his name and the title of two works: 'Lexicon on the ten orators' (Λέξεις τῶν δέκα ῥητόρων; *Léxeis tôn déka rhētórōn*) and 'Collection of "colourful" expressions' (Ἀνθηρῶν συναγωγή; *Anthērôn synagōgḗ*) (Suda α 4014). The dating is confirmed by POxy. 2192, col. II 28–38 (2nd cent. AD): the letter mentions H. looking for scrolls; SHA Verus 2,5 names a

H. as teacher of the emperor L. Verus. Thus, H. lived in a culturally interested environment which also included Pollio and the son of Diodorus.

B. Works

The 'collection of showpieces' must have belonged to the genre of *Florida* (made known by → Apuleius); of these, not even fragments have survived. The 'Lexicon' contains glosses of the ten orators of the Hellenistic Canon and is, apart from → Galen's lexicon on Hippocrates, the first lexicographic work in fairly strict alphabetical order (the 10% of lemmata deviating therefrom can probably be attributed to later tradition). The extensive explanations on the glosses contain numerous quotations of other Attic authors as well, e.g. of Aristophanes and the 'minor' comedians as well as of Aristotle (H. often refers to the *Athenaíōn politeía* and also hands down otherwise unknown fragments); from his work, important information can be derived, e.g. regarding the handing down of *Hellēniká* and of *Anábasis* by Xenophon. This is a lexicon which was created as reading material for authors and not as a prescription of Atticist norms; his sources are based in Hellenism (e.g. Aristophanes [4] of Byzantium and Aristarchus [4] of Samothrace) and the Imperial period (e.g. Didymus [1] of Alexandria), but some reports also go back to earlier authors (Hecataeus, Hellanicus, Theopompus, Ister). The 'Lexicon' has survived in two editions: the epitome was prepared even before Photius and shows a strong relationship to his lexica and the Suda. It is documented by four MSS (amongst which the Cod. Parisinus Graecus 2552 from the year 1496 contains peculiarities which indicate a contamination from a different edition) as well as by excerpts in the Cod. Baroccianus 50 (cf. [3]). The more complete edition has been handed down in numerous MSS; the Cod. Marcianus Gr. 444 (14th cent.) with 71 glosses, which cannot be found in the remaining tradition, and the Cod. Ricciard. 12 (15th cent.), which was identified by Keaney as the Codex acquired in 1491–1492 by I. Laskaris for Lorenzo de' Medici deserve special mention. But the lexicon was most probably interpolated in the 13th–14th cents., possibly by Manuel Moschopoulos. A papyrus fragment has also survived (PRylands 532 = Pack[2] 458, end of 2nd, beginning of 3rd cent. AD).
→ Glossography; → Lexicography

Editions: 1 G. Dindorf (ed.), Harpocrationis Lexicon in decem oratores Atticos, I–II, 1853 2 J.J. Keaney (ed.), Harpocration. Lexeis of the Ten Orators, 1991.
Bibliography: 3 J.A. Cramer, Anecdota Graeca e codd. manuscriptis bibliothecarum Oxoniensium I–IV, 1835–37, in: AO 2, 488–500 4 B. Hemmerdinger, Les papyrus et la datation d'Harpocration, in: REG 72, 1959, 107–109 5 J.J. Keaney, Moschopoulos and Harpocration, in: TAPhA 100, 1969, 201–207 6 Id., Alphabetization in Harpocration's Lexicon, in: GRBS 14, 1973, 415–423 7 Id., John Lascaris and Harpocration, in: GRBS 23, 1982, 93–95 8 R. Otranto, Rec. Harpocration, ed. Keaney, in: Quaderni di Storia 38, 1993, 225–231. R.T.

[3] Alexandrian author of texts on astrology and the magic healing powers of plants, animals and stones, 2nd and 3rd cents. AD. Some coinciding parts can be found in the Cyranids and in the Corpus Hermeticum. Some MSS contain a dedicational letter for an emperor, in which the author mentions having taught grammar in Asia Minor before coming to Alexandria. However, it appears that this letter originally belonged to a work lost today and was possibly not even composed by H.
→ Corpus Hermeticum V.N.

Ḥarran Settlement 40 km south-east of Edessa, old Oriental Ḫarrān(u), Greek Κάρραι; *Kárrai*, Latin Carrhae, Aramaic Ḥrn, modern Harran, important commercial centre and important cult centre of the moon god → Sin; documented since the 3rd millennium BC, Assyrian provincial capital and, from 611–610 BC, residence of the last Neo-Assyrian king; new temple construction under → Nabonid (finds of steles). In the biblical tradition, H. was Abraham's place of residence (Gn. 11:31). Macedonian settlers of H. supported the Romans in their campaign against the Parthians (Cass. Dio 37,5,5), but in 53 BC the defeat and death of Crassus occurred near Ḥ. (Plut. Crassus 17–29; Cass. Dio 40,17–27). The consequences of the battle, the capture of the soldiers and in particular the loss of the Roman ensigns left their mark on Roman policies towards the Parthians until their return was achieved diplomatically under Augustus. Ḥ. remained Parthian as part of the kingdom of Osrhoëne (→ Edessa [2]), and became a Roman *colonia* and *Metropolis Mesopotamiae* as of AD 214.

Caracalla planned visiting the temple of the moon god whose cult (Sabian sect) still existed in the Middle Ages (Cass. Dio 79,5,4); emperor Julian, too, sacrificed in the temple (Amm. Marc. 23,3,2). Syrian sources (Doctrina Addai, Acta Šarbel, Jacob of Sarug) know Ḥ. as a multi-ethnic centre of paganism; alongside Sin and his wife Nikkal, there were, i.a., the cults of Atargatis and of Tyche (Aramaic Gad, Arabic Allat).

W. Cramer, s.v. Ḥ., RAC 15, 634–50; H.J.W. Drivers, Cults and Beliefs at Edessa, 1980; J.N. Postgate, s.v. Ḥ., RLA 4, 1972–75, 122–124; F.H. Weissbach, s.v. Κάρραι, RE 10, 2009–21. K.KE.

Harrow The verb *occare* (cf. also the noun *occatio*; Cato Agr. 33,2; Varro, Rust. 1,29,2; 1,31,1; Columella 2,12,1–6; 11,2,60; Plin. HN 18,180; 18,185), frequently used by Roman agrarian writers, is often translated as 'to harrow'; however, it referred to work with a hoe (*rastrum*). The breaking up of lumps of soil in the vineyard or on a crop field was the aim of this work (Varro, Rust. 1,31,1: *occare, id est comminuere, ne sit glaeba*; Columella 11,2,60: *pulverationem faciunt, quam vocant rustici occationem*). According to Columella, ploughing should be carried out repeatedly and carefully so that a further treatment of the soil would no longer be required (Columella 2,4,1–2, cf. Plin. HN 18,179). As a primitive form of harrow, the 'wicker-work harrow' first occurs in Virgil (*cratis*; Verg. G. 1,94f.; cf. 1,165f.), which served the purpose of levelling and smoothing the soil; in Columella, the *cratis* is mentioned as an instrument which was used for the same purpose when working on meadows after ploughing (Columella 2,17,4); in Pliny, too, the *occatio* follows after ploughing, while the implements are alternatively called *cratis* or *rastrum* (Plin. HN 18,180). In Cato, a harrow (*irpex*) is listed in the inventory of an olive tree plantation; according to Varro, this wooden implement, which was fitted with teeth, was pulled across the field by oxen in order to eradicate weeds (Cato Agr. 10,3; Varro, Ling. 5,136; cf. Fest. 93). Furthermore, Pliny talks of a *cratis* 'fitted with iron teeth' (Plin. HN 18,186; cf. *cratis dentata*: Plin. HN 18,173); this implement is probably to be regarded also as a frame harrow.

Apart from the breaking up of lumps of soil and the eradication of weeds, the *occatio*, carried out after sowing, had the purpose of covering the seeds with soil (Plin. HN 18,180). Columella only mentions this explicitly for the sowing of beans, lucerne, etc. (Columella 2,10,5; 2,10,27; 2,10,33; 2,12,6).

→ Agrarian writers; → Grain

1 M.-CL. AMOURETTI, Le pain et l'huile dans la Grèce antique, 1986, 107f. 2 F. OLCK, s.v. E., RE 5, 1983–1986 3 M.S. SPURR, Arable Cultivation in Roman Italy c. 200 B.C.- c. A.D. 100, 1986, 48–56 4 K.D. WHITE, Agricultural Implements of the Roman World, 1967, 59, 146–151 5 Id., Farm Equipment of the Roman World, 1975, 3–5, 77–79 6 Id., Roman Farming, 1970.

E.C.

Harsiesis Son of Paious (?), established himself during the Civil War (132–124 BC) as counter-pharaoh and was the last Egyptian who carried the title 'Pharaoh'. He was presumably supported by the Theban priests; between 26 June and November 131 BC, dating was based on him in Thebes, but already on 10 November, he was no longer recognized there. He fled to the north, where his rebellion came to an end before 15 September 130.

K. VANDORPE, City of Many a Gate, in: S.P. VLEEMING (ed.), Hundred-Gated Thebes, 1995, 203–239, esp. 233ff.; B.C. MCGING, Revolt Egyptian Style, in: APF 43, 1997, 273–314, esp. 295f.

W.A.

Harun al-Rashid (*Hārūn ar-Rašīd*). Fifth Abbasid (→ Abbasids) → Caliph (AD 786–809). Popular because of the narratives from the 'Arabian Nights'. His term of office was characterized by political unrest in the Arab lands from North Africa to Yemen, by difficulties in consolidating → Islam in the eastern parts of his realm, as well as by wars against Byzantium. His main achievement in the cultural area is the promotion of translations into Arabic of Greek natural scientific and philosophical literature.

F. OMAR, s.v. Hārūn al-Rashīd, EI 3, 232b–234b.

H.SCHÖ.

Haruspices

I. ANCIENT ORIENT
see → Divination

II.
A. INTRODUCTION AND DEFINITION B. LATIN RECORDS 1. ETRUSCAN HARUSPICES 2. ROMAN HARUSPICES C. ETRUSCAN RECORDS 1. INSCRIPTIONS AND IMAGES 2. LIVER MODELS – ETRUSCAN AND ANCIENT ORIENTAL HARUSPICY

A. INTRODUCTION AND DEFINITION

Haruspices is the Latin term for viewers and interpreters of entrails (of animals) in various ancient cultures, mostly from Etruria (Cic. Div. 1,3). The etymology of the word's first syllable is unclear; amongst others, *hira* ('intestines') and *hostia* (from *haruga*, 'sacrificial animal') have been assumed [1. 45]. In Roman Republican times, the viewing of entrails (*haruspicina*) was regarded as an *ars*, an 'empirical science' based on observation (Cic. Div. 1,24f.), whose mastery and maintenance enabled various poleis, families and peoples to practice → divination (Cic. Div. 1,91f.: Telmessus in Caria, clans of the Iamids and Clutids in Elis/ Peloponnese, Etruscans).

B. LATIN RECORDS

1. ETRUSCAN HARUSPICES

The extant ancient literary reports on the Etruscan haruspices are almost exclusively handed down by Roman, i.e. Latin-speaking, authors. Livy reports (1,56,4) that the haruspices had already been engaged during the period of the Monarchy for advice on and expiation of omens, → *prodigia* (*publica*); according to MACBAIN, it is more likely that the haruspices were only consulted regularly as of the 3rd cent. BC (280/278) after the Romans had gained the majority of the Etruscan cities as political allies in the Punic Wars [3. 43ff.]: upon request by the Roman Senate, they provided *responsa* ('expert advice') in which both the deities, who were being linked to the omens, as well as the means of expiation were mentioned. However, the interpretation and implementation of the *responsa* was the responsibility of members of the Senate and the Roman priests (Cic. Har. resp. 20ff., 34f.; Cic. Div. 2,21). Whether the *ordo* (*LX haruspicum*) of the haruspices, documented for Republican times by inscriptions and literary sources, had been founded as a result of Roman initiatives or whether the Etruscans organized themselves, is not clear; it is also debated whether its headquarters were in Rome (cf. CIL VI 2161) or whether they merely had an 'office' there (on the disputed questions [3. 47ff.; 4.10f.]).

For how long haruspicy was only practised by Etruscans in Rome, is not clear; well into the 1st cent. BC, the Roman emperors appear to have preferred Etruscan personal haruspices [5. 2441]. In addition, there were itinerant haruspices (probably also Etruscan) who were

Terminology of ancient haruspicy

Sheep's liver *(facies visceralis)*

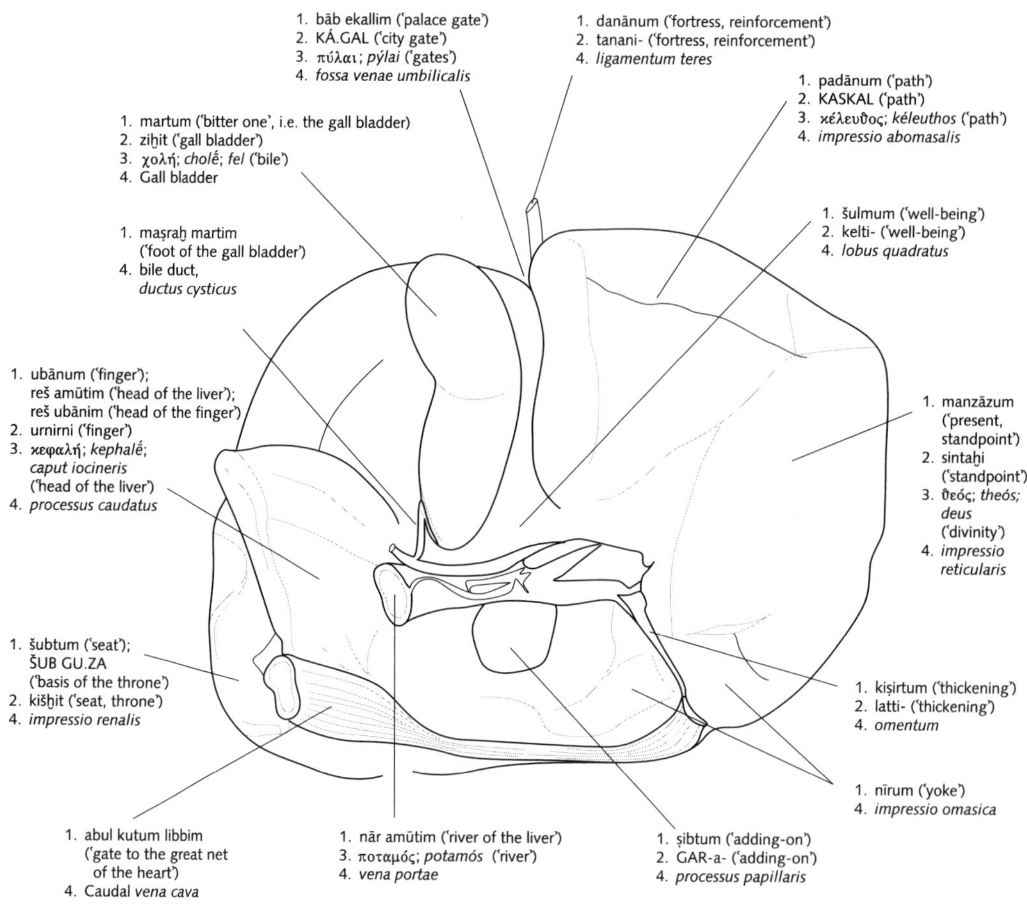

Position of the *haruspex*

As far as known, the following are stated:

1. the terms used in Akkadian texts
2. the terms used in Hittite texts
3. Greek/Latin terms
4. the modern medical term

M. HAA.

engaged by private persons (Plin. HN 8,102; Hdn. 8,3,7).

2. Roman haruspices

With the translation of the (Ps.-)Tagetic (→ Tages) texts, the Romans were theoretically able to practise haruspicy themselves. Proof of such Roman haruspicy are inscriptions, mainly originating from north-western provinces, and the *lex coloniae* of the city of Urso (CIL II 5439, ch. 62). However, neither the inscriptions nor the constitution of the city of Urso reveal anything about the activity of the haruspices; the haruspices mentioned in the constitution are merely characterized as subordinate officials of the municipal magistrate (*aediles, duoviri*).

From the 3rd cent. AD, so-called 'legionary haruspices' appear on inscriptions (e.g. CIL VIII 2567; 2586; 2809; North Africa) who possibly had the task to perform viewing the entrails prior to military action. Whether the haruspices mentioned quite often in the *Historia Augusta* are Romans, is not certain (S HA Alex. Sev. 13,2; 27,6; 44,4; S HA Maximini Duo 30,2; S HA Tac. 15,2 and 4). C.F.

C. Etruscan records

1. Inscriptions and images

The possible Etruscan word for haruspices appears as a name or office title [6. 139, 274f.] in grave inscriptions in northern Etruria and in Umbria. In the bilingual inscription of Pesaro (end of 1st cent. BC; CIL XI 6363; ET Um 1.7; [7. 105]; cf. ET CL 1.1036, Ta 1.17), the Etruscan *netsvis trutnvt frontac* corresponds with Latin *haruspex fulguriator*; here, *netsvis* quite probably reflects one syllable or both syllables of *haruspex* [6. 274; 8. 190f.]. Thus, the haruspices were specialists not only for entrails but also for viewing lightning and probably for the interpretation of omens in general. If *natis* on a scarabee (ET VT G.1; cf. ET AS 1.314, CL 1.1461) of the 4th/3rd cents. BC [9. 52; but cf. 10. 278, 305] is connected with *netsvis* [1. 117], this is probably the earliest epigraphical record.

Possible Etruscan depictions of haruspices can be found from *c.* 500 to 100 BC on urns, sarcophagi, mirrors, scarabees, coins, vessels of bronze and clay, and as votive statuettes [9; 11; 12]. Regarded as characteristics are the clothing (tall head covering, coat with clasp), the utensils (→ *lituus*, → *liber linteus*), the specific posture (bowed upper body, leg resting on something). The identification is not always certain, particularly since pictorial, epigraphical and literary records can rarely be associated directly (but → Umbricius Melior).

2. Liver models – Etruscan and Ancient Oriental haruspicy

While the bronze model of Piacenza (around 100 BC; [13]) can be explained by the spread of oriental mantics in Hellenistic times [14. 109f.], the use of the Etruscan clay liver from Falerii (before 241 BC; [7. 146 no. 194]) by Etruscan haruspices would presuppose knowledge of the oriental liver models of the 2nd millennium BC [14. 107f., 110] and of the associated systems of symbols. Mycenaean finds [15] provide evidence of Italy being a sphere of influence of the → Aegean Koine from the middle of the 2nd millennium: it may be assumed that Etruscan haruspicy preserved these older cultural layers; this could also be confirmed by equivalencies in the terminology of symbols; cf. also [11] for official robes of haruspices in 'early history'. The tradition could (so [14]; different e.g. [16. 642–645; 17. 46–53]: oriental 'influence' in the 8th/7th cents. BC or in Hellenistic times) lead from Babylonian haruspicy via Hurrite [18] to Hittite or south-west Anatolian and thus, after 1200 BC, to Etruscan haruspicy.

→ Divination; → Etrusci, Etruria III M.HAA.

1 Pfiffig 2 O. Thulin, s.v. Etrusca disciplina, RE 6, 725–730 3 B. MacBain, Prodigy and Expiation: A Study in Religion and Politics in Republican Rome, 1982 4 S. Montero, Política y adivinación en el Bajo Imperio Romano. Emperadores y harúspices (193 D.C.- 408 D.C.), 1991 5 O. Thulin, s.v. H., RE 7, 2431–2468 6 H. Rix, Das etr. Cognomen, 1963 7 Die Etrusker und Europa, catalogue Berlin, 1993 8 M. Hano, Le témoignage des inscriptions latines sur les h., in: La divination dans le monde étrusco-italique 6, 1995, 184–199 9 L. B. van der Meer, Iecur Placentinum..., in: BABesch 54, 1979, 49–64 10 Zazoff, AG 11 F. Roncalli, Die Tracht des H. ..., in: Die Aufnahme fremder Kultureinflüsse in Etrurien..., congress Mannheim 1981, 124–132 12 A. Maggiani, Immagini di aruspici, in: 2° Congr. Internazionale Etrusco III, 1989, 1557–1563 13 Id., Qualche osservazione sul fegato di Piacenza, in: SE 50, 1982, 53–88 14 J. W. Meyer, Zur Herkunft der etr. Lebermodelle, in: Phoenicia and Its Neighbours, conference Brussels, 1985, 105–120 15 L. Vagnetti, Primi contatti..., in: I Greci in Occidente, catalogue Venice 1996, 109–116 16 Dumézil 17 W. Burkert, The Orientalizing Revolution, 1992 18 M. Schuol, Die Terminologie des hethit. SU-Orakels, in: Altoriental. Forsch. 21, 1994, 73–124; 247–304.

R. Bloch, Réflexions sur le destin et la divination haruspicinale en Grèce et en Étrurie, in: Iconographie classique et identités régionales, 1986, 77–83; La divination dans le monde étrusco-italique, 1–7 = Caesarodunum Suppl. 52, 1985; 54, 1986; 56, 1986; 61, 1991; 63, 1993; 64, 1995; 65, 1996. C.F.and M.HAA.

Maps: C. Thulin, Die etr. Disziplin II. Die Haruspicin, 1906, repr. 1968, 46f.; 50–54; R.D. Biggs, G.-W. Meyer, s.v. Lebermodelle, RLA 6, 1980–3, 518–527; Ch. Guittard, Haruspicine et *devotio*: »Caput iocineris a familiari parte caesum« (Tite-Live 8,9,1), in: La divination dans le monde étr.-italique 3, Caesarodunum Suppl. 56, 1986, 49–67; W. Burkert, The Orientalizing Revolution, 1992, 49f. with n. 21. M.HAA.

Haruspicy see → Divination

Harwennefer (= *Haronnophris*, Greek *Hourgonaphor*). Leader of an indigenous uprising who was crowned as Pharaoh in Thebes in October/November 205 BC; his rulership also included Abydus and Pathyris; a Ptolemaic offensive displaced him from Abydus (and Ptolemais) only in 201–200. In the summer of 199, → Anchwennefer is recorded as his successor.

P. W. Pestman, Haronnophris and Chaonnophris, in: S. P. Vleeming (ed.), Hundred-Gated Thebes, 1995, 101–134; B. C. McGing, in: APF 43, 1997, 285ff. W.A.

Hasai(ti)c early north-Arabic dialect (→ Arabic). Its inscriptions, written in a slightly modified ancient south-Arabic → alphabet, are predominantly grave inscriptions, amongst them two Hasaitic-Aramaic → bilingual inscriptions from north-eastern Saudi Arabia (*c.* between 5th and 2nd cents. BC).

→ Ancient south-Arabic; → Semitic languages

W. W. Müller, Das Altarab. und das klass. Arabisch, Hasaitisch, in: W.-D. Fischer (ed.), Grundriß der arab. Philol., 1982, 25–26. C.K.

Hasdrubal (*ʿzrbʿl* = 'Help is Bʿl'; Ἀσδρούβας/*Asdroúbas*).

[1] Carthaginian field marshal in the First Punic War. Together with → Bostar [1] he was defeated near Adys by the Roman invasion troops of consul M. → Atilius [I 21] Regulus in 256 BC, under → Xanthippus he probably took part in the victory near Tynes in 255 (Pol. 1,30; 32; Diod. Sic. 23,11) [1. 48, 264 and 132, 751] and from 251 he was active i.a. in Sicily with 140 elephants, until he suffered a crushing defeat near Panormis by the Roman consul L. → Caecilius [I 11] Metellus (Pol. 1,38; 40; Diod. Sic. 23,21). In Carthage, H. was executed for his failure (Zon. 8,14,12) [2. 241].

[2] Prominent Carthaginian politician and general (cf. Liv. 21,2,3–7), possibly father of → Mago [1. 188,

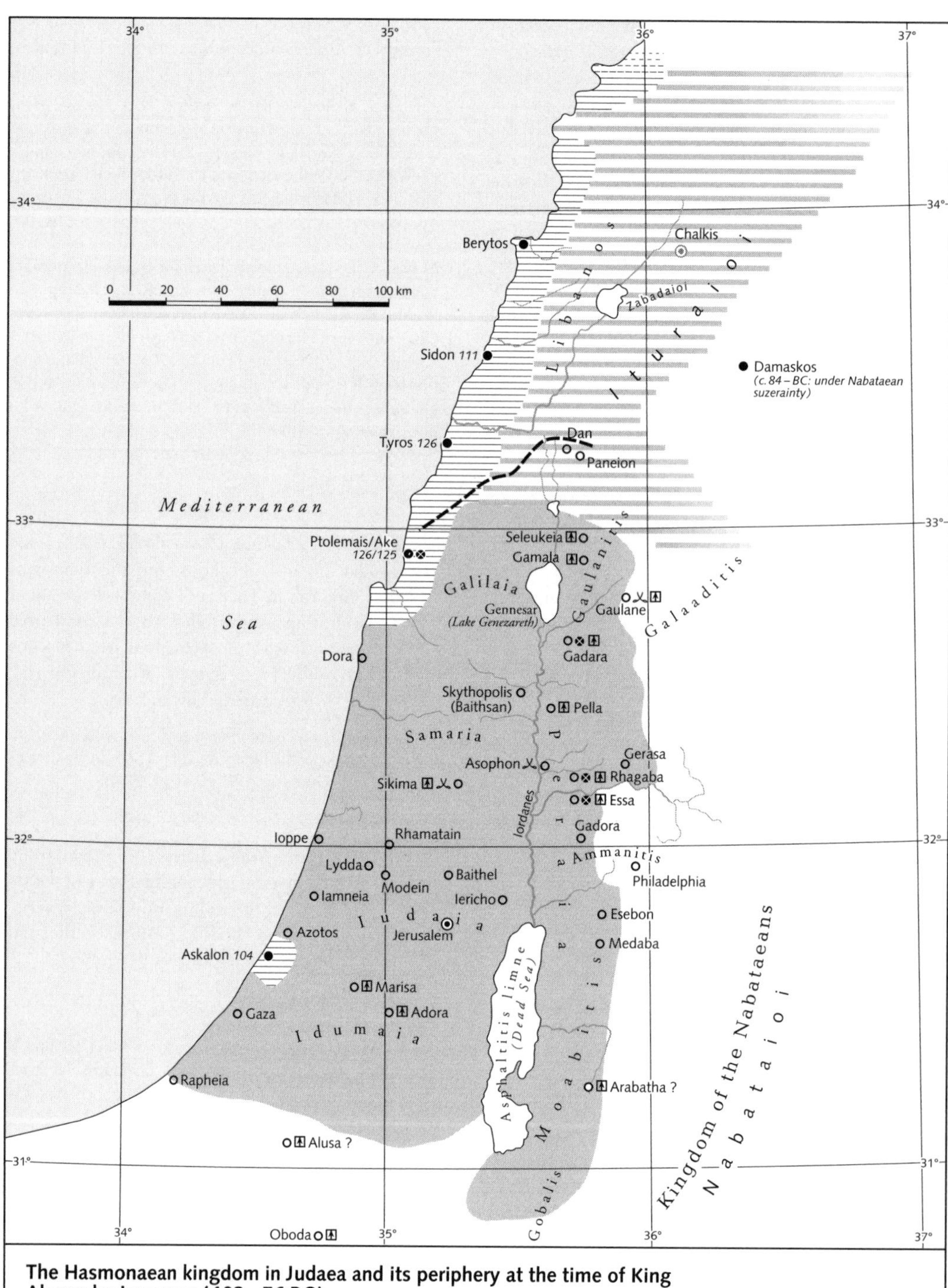

The Hasmonaean kingdom in Judaea and its periphery at the time of King Alexander Iannaeus (103 – 76 BC)

Kingdom of the Hasmonaeans *(Hasamonaioi/Makkabaioi)*

Conjectural northern border of Galilee under Alexander Iannaeus

Kingdom of the Ituraeans *(Itouraioi)*

Territory of the autonomous Phoenician cities

Capital

Free city (with date of independence)

Other city

? Identification uncertain

Location uncertain

Battle under Alexander Iannaeus

Siege under Alexander Iannaeus

Conquest under Alexander Iannaeus

Gobalis Region, area, mountain range

Ituraioi Ethnic group, tribe

? Identification uncertain

Location uncertain

Battle under Alexander Iannaeus

Siege under Alexander Iannaeus

Conquest under Alexander Iannaeus

Gobalis Region, area, mountain range

Ituraioi Ethnic group, tribe

1115], son-in-law of and, as general for Africa and Iberia, successor of → Hamilcar [3] Barkas (Pol. 2,1,9) whom H. accompanied to Gades in 237 BC after he had already supported him in 240 as an exponent of the 'people's party' (App. Ib. 4,16–5,17). Sent to North Africa to restore the Numidic allegiance (Diod. Sic. 25,10,3) [1. 133; 2. 272, 274], H. only returned to Spain in the year 229 after Hamilcar had been killed in action. The troops chose H. as his successor, which was also confirmed in Carthage (App. Ib. 6,22; Liv. 21,2,4) [1. 133f.]. Up to his murder in the year 221 (Pol. 2,36,1; App. Hann. 2,8), H. consolidated by military and diplomatic means, int. al. by marrying an Iberian princess, the position of Spain as a Carthaginian province, in the course of which the rule of the → Barcids assumed a monarchic profile [3. 149; 4. 40–42], e.g. with the foundation of the seat of royal power → Carthago Nova (modern Cartagena) in the year 227 (?) [3. 134; 4. 43f.]. To be rejected as historically unreliable are not only reports about H.'s homosexuality (Liv. 21,2,4; 3,4) and separatist-subversive designs (Pol. 3,8; 10,10,9) [1. 135; 2. 275f., 56; 4. 41f.], but probably also the tradition of the so-called Ebro agreement which H. is said to have signed with Rome in 226 (Stv 3,503) [4. 44–47].

[3] Son of → Hamilcar [3] Barkas, famous Carthaginian strategist alongside his brother → Hannibal [4] (cf. Pol. 11,2). As supreme commander in Spain (Liv. 21,22) in 218–216 BC, he fought without much success against rebellious Celtiberians (Liv. 22,21,5–8) and against Cn. → Cornelius [I 77] Scipio near Ibera, Saguntum, Iliturgi and Intibili (Liv. 22,19f.; 23,26–29; 49,5–14) [1. 137f.; 4. 250f.]. After H. had beaten the disloyal → Syphax in Numidia in the year 214 (App. Ib. 15,58–16,60) [2. 357; 4. 284[84]], H. also succeeded, together with → Mago and → Hasdrubal [5], in recapturing Spain in 211 [1. 138f.] and, in 208, after the loss of → Carthago Nova to P. → Cornelius [I 71] Scipio, in crossing into Gaul [4. 369–373]. In the spring of 207, H. advanced as far as Umbria with a large army reinforced by Celts, where his crushing defeat against M. → Livius Salinator near the → Metaurus finally reversed his luck in war (Liv. 27,43–49) [1. 140–142; 4. 385–390].

[4] **Hasdrubal 'the Bald'** (*Calvus*: Liv. 23,34,16) [1. 225]. Carthaginian commander in the Second Punic War; he became a Roman prisoner of war on Sardinia in 215 when his army, which was meant to reinforce → Hampsicora but had arrived late due to damage sustained in storms at sea, was annihilated by T. → Manlius Torquatus (Liv. 23,40f.; Zon. 9,4) [1. 148f.; 2. 348f.].

[5] Son of → Geskon [3], renowned Carthaginian field marshal in the Second Punic War in Spain and Africa. After joint successes with Hasdrubal [3] and → Mago in Iberia in the year 211 (Liv. 25,32; 34–36; App. Ib. 16) [2. 373f.; 4. 319f.], H. as supreme field marshal was defeated near → Ilipa in 206 by P. → Cornelius [I 71] Scipio (Pol. 11,20–24; Liv. 28,12–16; App. Ib. 27). H. then negotiated the Carthaginian-Numidian alliance in Africa and gave his daughter → Sophonisba to → Syphax in marriage with whom he, after occasional joint successes against the Roman invasion troops under P. Cornelius Scipio, was defeated in the Medjerda valley ('on the Large Fields') in the year 204 (Pol. 14,6; 8; Liv. 29,35; 30,4–8; App. Lib. 18–24) [1. 146f.; 4. 433–442]. Further reports about H. habving been deposed and sentenced to death (?), covering the time to his suicide in the year 202, are unreliable [1. 147; 2. 411, 56].

[6] **Hasdrubal 'the He-goat'** (ἔριφος; *ériphos*, *haedus*) [1. 225, 1317], opponent of the → Barcids in internal politics (cf. Liv. 30,44) [1. 150; 2. 242, 166]. In the year 202, together with → Hanno [6], he travelled to P. → Cornelius [I 71] Scipio and to Rome as a peace negotiator (App. Lib. 49,213–53,229; Liv. 30,42,12–19).

[7] Carthaginian commander in the Third Punic War; together with → Carthalo Boetharch against → Massinissa, H. was sentenced to death after the defeat in the year 150 (Pol. 36,16,12; Diod. Sic. 32,3; App. Lib. 70,319–74,341) [2. 439], but then, after he laid siege to Carthage with a private army, he was appointed as a general at the beginning of the war against Rome (App. Lib. 80,374; 93,439) [1. 153f.; 2. 443f.]. After varied fortunes of battle and the treacherous liquidation of his colleague Hasdrubal, the grandson of Massinissa, H. obtained sole command which he exercised in a despotic fashion (cf. Pol. 38,7) [1. 154f.]. After H. had opened the capitulation negotiations employing → Gulussa, he finally switched over to P. Cornelius [I 70] Scipio and later died in Roman honorary custody (Zon. 9,30) [2. 456].

1 Geus 2 Huss 3 P. Barceló, Karthago und die Iberische Halbinsel vor den Barkiden, 1988 4 J. Seibert, Hannibal, 1993.

L.-M.G.

Hasmonaeans Jewish family of priests from Modeïn, belonging to the Joarib class of priests; the name, which is recorded only in Iosephus and in the Talmud, refers to a not clearly identifiable Ḥašmōn (according to Jos. BI 1,36 father of Mattathias, according to Jos. Ant. Iud. 12,265 his great grandfather). The armed resistance against religious coercion imposed by → Antiochus [6] IV., began with Mattathias in 167 BC. In 165, his son → Iudas Maccabaeus achieved the recapture and reconsecration of the Temple of Jerusalem. After → Antiochus [7] V had restituted the Jewish theocracy under the high priest Alcimus in 163, the H. gradually gained control over Judaea despite some setbacks and annexed large parts of the periphery of the Jewish settlement area by taking advantage of the dynastic conflicts and foreign-policy problems of the Seleucid suzerains (largest expansion under → Alexander [16] Iannaeus, see map). The Seleucid pretender to the throne, → Alexander [13] Balas, appointed Ionathan as high priest in 152, and after gaining freedom, i.e. the end of tribute obligations, and the conquest of the Seleucid citadel in Jerusalem (143–142), the people bestowed the hereditary rank of high priest on Simon in 141.

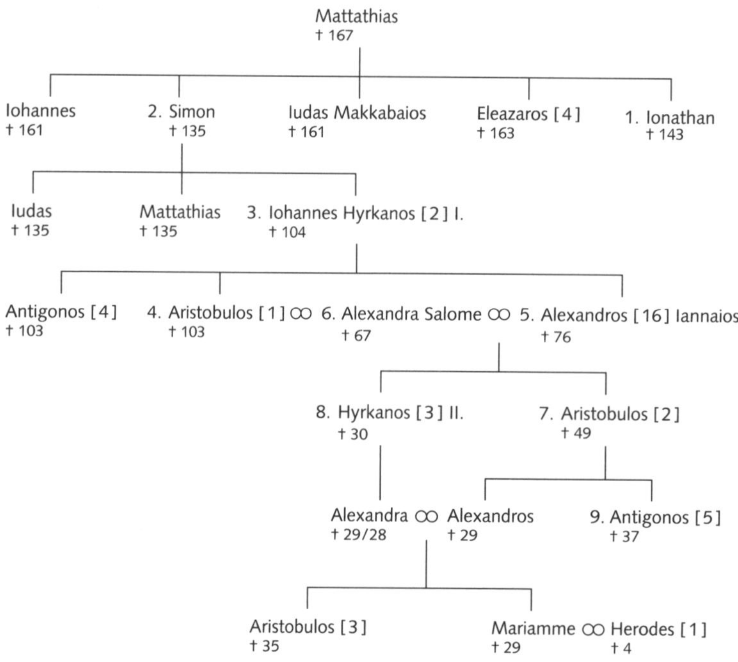

The numbers in brackets indicate the order of regency of those who ruled as high priests or as kings and high priests; for more details on these, see the individual entries.

The title of king was perhaps already adopted by Aristobulus I, but certainly by Alexander Iannaeus. The proximity to Hellenistic kingship, thus also demonstrated outwardly, resulted in serious internal conflicts. Already after the restitution of the theocracy under Antiochus V, the association of pious scribes had renounced the pact with the H. Under Alexander Iannaeus, open civil war broke out with the → Pharisaei. After the death of → Alexandra Salome, a dynastic conflict broke out between Aristobulus [2] II and → Hyrcanus [3] II, which was a decisive condition for the subordination of the reduced Jewish state under the Roman governor of Syria as of the year 63. Hyrcanus II was deprived of his royal title, and actual power was transferred to the representative of the Romans, → Antipater [4], the father of → Herod [1] I In the course of the Parthian invasion and the Roman reconquest of the Orient (40–37), the rule of the H. was abolished. Sources: 1 and 2 Macc; Jos. BI 1,36–437; Ant. Iud. 12,265–15,56.
→ Judaism

1 Schürer, vol. 1 2 J. Wellhausen, Israelitische und jüdische Geschichte, [8]1921 3 E. Bickermann, Der Gott der Makkabäer, 1937 4 Id., From Ezra to the Last of the Maccabees, 1962 5 F.-M. Abel, Histoire de la Palestine 1, 1952 6 K. Bringmann, Hell. Reform und Religionsverfolgung in Judäa, 1983. K.BR.

Maps: H. Waldmann, Syrien und Palästina in hell. Zeit. TAVO B V 16.2. Die Makkabäer und die Hasmonäer (167–37 v.Chr.), 1987.

Hassan (*Ḥasan*). Grandson of the prophet → Muhammad, son of his daughter → Fatima and his cousin → Ali, brother of → Husain; 624–625 until after AD 670. After Ali's murder, H. relinquished the Caliphate after negotiations in favour of the → Umayyad → Muʿāwiya (in 661) and thereafter remained politically unimportant. For the → Shiites, he is the second → imam after his father Ali.

L. Veccia Vaglieri, s.v. Ḥasan b. ʿAlī b. Abī Ṭālib, EI 3, 240b–243b. H.SCHÖ.

Hasta

[1] Hasta, hastati. In the Roman army of the middle Republic, the *hasta* served primarily as a thrust lance for close combat although it could also be thrown; it had a wooden shaft and an iron point. The *hasta* was adapted to the fighting style of the → phalanx, but it remained in use when, in the 4th cent. BC, the Romans adopted a more flexible set-up in maniples (→ *manipulus*). According to Livy (Liv. 8,8,5–13), whose account, however, is not without its problems, in 340 BC the Roman army consisted of three battle rows, the *hastati*, the *principes* and the *triarii*. The *triarii* were armed with the *hasta*; it can be assumed that the *hastati* were also equipped with the *hasta*. The spear (→ *pilum*), on the other hand, is not mentioned here. Polybius, in his description of the Roman army, which probably reflects the situation in the 2nd cent. BC, refers to property and age as the criteria for the recruitment of soldiers: the *hastati*, younger men, wore the full armour and stood in the first battle row, the *principes* stood in the second row, while the older and battle-hardened soldiers were placed as *triarii* in the third row (Pol. 6,21–23). The *hastati* and *principes* were equipped with an oval shield, a sword and probably two *pila, a*nd wore bronze breast plates and greaves; the *hastati* had bronze helmets with long feathers which made them appear larger. Only the *triarii* were still armed with the *hasta*; the *hasta* of the lightly armed (*velites*) had a sling added to it and was thus suitable for throwing (*hasta amentata*; Cic. Brut. 271). Despite these changes, the *hastati* kept their name.

Hastati and *principes* of a legion were each divided into ten maniples of 120 men, while the ten maniples of the *triarii* consisted of 60 men each. In battle, the *hastati* started with close combat and, if beaten off, retreated through the rows of the *principes*. In legionary camps (→ *castra*), the *hastati* occupied a fixed place on the *via quintana* and formed their own column during marches (Pol. 6,28f.; 6,40).

Although the maniples were replaced by the *cohortes* (→ *cohors*) up to the time of Caesar, the names of the old battle rows remained in the titles of the *centuriones* (*hastatus prior* and *hastatus posterior*). Since this reorganization, the *hasta* was no longer used; henceforth, all soldiers were armed with the *pilum*. During the Principate, the term *hasta* was used for various spears of the → *auxilia*. The *hasta pura* was part of the military decorations (→ *dona militaria*) for officers from the *ordo equester* and the *ordo senatorius*.

1 M.C. Bishop, J.C.N. Coulston, Roman Military Equipment, 1993, 52–53; 69 2 L. Keppie, The Making of the Roman Army, 1984, 14–67. J.CA.

[2] In a legal sense, according to Gai. Inst. 4,16, *hasta* has the same meaning as *festuca*. In the → *legis actio sacramento in rem*, both appear as symbols of the claim of possession *iusti dominii* (of the legally justified ownership) over the contentious subject matter as asserted by the parties. This explains why in the centumviral court responsible for the → *vindicatio*, a *hasta* was displayed (Dig. 1,2,2,29). Later on, the *hasta* became the overall symbol for the disposal of property initiated by the state (Cic. Phil. 2,64).

M. Kaser, K. Hackl, Das röm. Zivilprozeßrecht, [2]1997, 14, 97. C.PA.

[3] Wooden ritual instrument with an iron point and a burnt and bloody shaft, which the → *fetiales* hurled into enemy territory in accordance with the old Roman ritual of a declaration of war or with which they carried out the symbolic act before the Bellona Temple (cf. *hastiferi* = followers of the Bellona cult [1]) in Rome. The *hasta* was also regarded as a symbol for the god → Mars (*hasta Martis,* which was kept in the sacrarium of the regia: Serv. Aen. 8,3) or as an attribute of the → Salii (Dion. Hal. Ant. Rom. 2,70: λόγχη; *lónchē*) [2]. However, whether it was an attribute of the *flamines* is uncertain (differently: [3]).

1 AE 48,8; 48,29 2 A.V. Siebert, Instrumenta sacra, in print 3 Th. Schäfer, Flaminat und h., in: Scritti in ricordo di G. Massari Gaballo e di U. Tocchetti Pollini (Comune di Milano, Ripartizione Cultura, Raccolte Archeologiche Numismatiche), 1986, 129f. with n. 42.

F. Klingmüller, s.v. H. (1), RE 7, 2502. A.V.S.

[4] *Oppidum* on the Tanaro in Liguria, *municipium II virale* or *colonia* (Ptol. 3,1,45) of the *regio IX*, *tribus Pollia*, on the *via Fulvia* (Tab. Peut. 3,5), modern Asti in Piemont; *dioecesis*, Lombard duchy. Famous for ceramics (Plin. HN 35,160; Anth. Pal. 11,27,3). In AD 402, H. resisted Alaricus [2] (Claud. Carm. 27f., 203), in 480, attack by the Burgundiones, supported by the Ostrogoths in AD 534 (Cassiod. Var. 11,15,2). Extant are Torre Rosso, thermal baths, theatre, *domus*, necropoleis. On the Ligurian coast and in Etruria, two homonymous *mansiones* (Tab. Peut. 3,5; 4,3; Geogr. Rav. 4,32; 5,2).

S. Giorcelli Bersani, Alla periferia dell'impero, 1994, 45–76; M. Somà, Note topografiche su Asti romana, in: Bollettino storico-bibliografico subalpino 93, 1995, 219–243; E. Zanda, A. Crosetto, L. Pejrani, Asti. Interventi archeologici e ricerche in centro storico (1981–1986), in: Quaderni della Soprintendenza Archeologica del Piemonte 5, 1986, 67–121. E.S.G.

[5] Town in the Baetica (Plin. HN 3,1; Str. 3,1,9; Liv. 39,21), remains on the hill Mesa de Asta 25 km north of Puerto San Maria. First mentioned in 189 BC (CIL II 5041). In 187 BC, conquered by C. → Atinius [2] (Liv. 39,21), constituted by Caesar as *colonia Hasta Regia* (on bronze coins: *Felix*) in 45 BC (cf. Plin. HN 3,11). Last mentioned in the *Acta Sanctorum* by Marcellus; destroyed in Arab times.

M. Esteve Guerrero, Miscellanea arqueologica Jerezana, 1979; M. Ferrero, Apuntes para una interpretación estadística de la cerámica aparecida en Asta Regia, in: Boletín del Museo de Cádiz 2, 1979–1980, 37–44; P. Piernaveja, Sobre Marcial y un pretendido Romanus, in: Archivo Español de Arqueología 48, 1975, 181f.; Tovar 2, 148–150. M.F.P.L. and P.B.

Addenda

Economy

I. Mesopotamia II. Egypt III. Levant IV. Iran V. Classical Antiquity

I. Mesopotamia

Mesopotamia's economy was based on → agriculture, with animal → husbandry integrated into it. Craft production (→ Crafts) was only supplementary in character and catered for internal demand as well as external trade (production of high-quality textiles for → Commerce). Agriculture in southern Mesopotamia (Babylonia) was entirely dependent on artificial → irrigation; in northern Mesopotamia (Assyria) it was generally rainfed.

Varying agricultural regimes led to different patterns of land tenure. Large production units are attested in documents from the end of the 4th millennium BC. The predominant form of agricultural organization was that of the redistributive [12. 178 f.] → *oikos* economy, which was replaced at the start of the 2nd millennium by tributary forms of economy [15]. In areas with artificial irrigation private ownership of farmland was available only occasionally (mainly only from the 19th cent. BC) and to a limited extent [13]; its quantitative role as an economic factor cannot be assessed. Agricultural production took place essentially on small areas (fields for subsistence farming and leasehold property of a → palace or → temple; cf. → Leasehold I.), which were just adequate for a rural family's subsistence. In regions with predominantly rainfed agriculture (*i.a.* Assyria) the village community played the decisive role as a production unit, in conditions of subsistence farming, up until the middle of the 2nd millennium. From then on the increasing indebtedness (→ Debts) of the small producers within a village community began to lead to a gradual consolidation of land in the hands of a few large estate owners from the circle of elite city officials from the capital → Assur. The rural population was absorbed into these large estate holdings ('manors') as *glebae adscripti* ('tied to the soil') (→ Social structure I.) [13].

The principal agricultural product was barley (in monoculture; → Grain), along with oil-producing fruits (→ Oils I.), bulbous plants (→ Leek I.) and, on a smaller scale, other types of vegetable. Date-palm cultivation (→ Horticulture I.) played an outstanding role, in southern Mesopotamia in particular, as a source of sweeteners (syrup), date wine and the by-products, raffia (for ropes etc.), leaf panicles (as building material), leaves (for weaving mats and baskets) [4]. Natural resources such as reeds and clay and, for → nutrition, fish and game birds were harvested to the full.

In southern Mesopotamia, craft production was closely linked to institutional households (temple, palace) and largely geared to their needs [14]. For trade with other regions which were the source of important ('strategic') goods (especially metals and wood) and prestige items (precious stones, aromatic substances, etc.) for resource-poor Mesopotamia, it was almost exclusively high-quality textiles, which were predominantly produced in institutional workshops (Ergasteria; → Textiles, production of).

The method of meeting material needs within Mesopotamia (by internal production or trade) was determined in each case by the prevailing patterns of production [9]. The *oikos* economy was characterized by a redistributive system in which all members of the *oíkos* were actively involved in production and the products were apportioned in the form of → rations according to status. The tributary form of economy, which was based on individual production, was essentially, from the start of the 2nd millennium BC, subsistence production. Substantial surpluses, which would have been available for export, were not achieved (→ Commerce; → Market; [11; 12. 174–176]).

In particular, theories about ways of meeting needs have led to various and much-debated models of trading patterns. In this respect, views based on K. Polanyi are at odds with those based on neo-classical economic theory (→ Money; → Commerce; → Market; cf. [8; 12]) that point to fundamental differences in assessing premodern society and its economy [8; 11; 12]. The representatives of neo-classical theory are thus criticized for applying to the totally different economic systems of antiquity an analytical system derived from the practices of a modern economic system exclusively geared to monetary and market economics. The economic systems of antiquity, argue the critics, were embedded in social structures, processes and rationales in a quite different way and were shaped by them rather than by modern patterns of market economics.

A distinguishing feature of both the redistributive (3rd millennium BC) and tributary (2nd/1st millennia BC) economic forms in Mesopotamia is the absence – either entirely or as essentially quantitative factors – of elements, structures and processes of monetary and market economics. There are no allusions to → loans for productive purposes; credit played a role especially in trading concerns. It was generally extended for a single undertaking, in the form of silver or of goods, and brought to account by the two parties at the conclusion of the undertaking [12. 189–203, especially 198]. Another feature of the Mesopotamian economy was the absence of steady technological progress as a motor for economic growth. Moreover, for a relatively long period of time, overall economic growth was held back by the limited availability of the principal means of production, arable land. That problem was linked to the demographic situation, as a consequence of which a given arable surface could sustain only a limited number of people. Regular and adequate subsistence production was guaranteed by optimal use of available

Addenda

Economy

I. Mesopotamia II. Egypt III. Levant IV. Iran V. Classical Antiquity

I. Mesopotamia

Mesopotamia's economy was based on → agriculture, with animal → husbandry integrated into it. Craft production (→ Crafts) was only supplementary in character and catered for internal demand as well as external trade (production of high-quality textiles for → Commerce). Agriculture in southern Mesopotamia (Babylonia) was entirely dependent on artificial → irrigation; in northern Mesopotamia (Assyria) it was generally rainfed.

Varying agricultural regimes led to different patterns of land tenure. Large production units are attested in documents from the end of the 4th millennium BC. The predominant form of agricultural organization was that of the redistributive [12. 178 f.] → *oikos* economy, which was replaced at the start of the 2nd millennium by tributary forms of economy [15]. In areas with artificial irrigation private ownership of farmland was available only occasionally (mainly only from the 19th cent. BC) and to a limited extent [13]; its quantitative role as an economic factor cannot be assessed. Agricultural production took place essentially on small areas (fields for subsistence farming and leasehold property of a → palace or → temple; cf. → Leasehold I.), which were just adequate for a rural family's subsistence. In regions with predominantly rainfed agriculture (*i.a.* Assyria) the village community played the decisive role as a production unit, in conditions of subsistence farming, up until the middle of the 2nd millennium. From then on the increasing indebtedness (→ Debts) of the small producers within a village community began to lead to a gradual consolidation of land in the hands of a few large estate owners from the circle of elite city officials from the capital → Assur. The rural population was absorbed into these large estate holdings ('manors') as *glebae adscripti* ('tied to the soil') (→ Social structure I.) [13].

The principal agricultural product was barley (in monoculture; → Grain), along with oil-producing fruits (→ Oils I.), bulbous plants (→ Leek I.) and, on a smaller scale, other types of vegetable. Date-palm cultivation (→ Horticulture I.) played an outstanding role, in southern Mesopotamia in particular, as a source of sweeteners (syrup), date wine and the by-products, raffia (for ropes etc.), leaf panicles (as building material), leaves (for weaving mats and baskets) [4]. Natural resources such as reeds and clay and, for → nutrition, fish and game birds were harvested to the full.

In southern Mesopotamia, craft production was closely linked to institutional households (temple, palace) and largely geared to their needs [14]. For trade with other regions which were the source of important ('strategic') goods (especially metals and wood) and prestige items (precious stones, aromatic substances, etc.) for resource-poor Mesopotamia, it was almost exclusively high-quality textiles, which were predominantly produced in institutional workshops (Ergasteria; → Textiles, production of).

The method of meeting material needs within Mesopotamia (by internal production or trade) was determined in each case by the prevailing patterns of production [9]. The *oikos* economy was characterized by a redistributive system in which all members of the *oíkos* were actively involved in production and the products were apportioned in the form of → rations according to status. The tributary form of economy, which was based on individual production, was essentially, from the start of the 2nd millennium BC, subsistence production. Substantial surpluses, which would have been available for export, were not achieved (→ Commerce; → Market; [11; 12. 174–176]).

In particular, theories about ways of meeting needs have led to various and much-debated models of trading patterns. In this respect, views based on K. Polanyi are at odds with those based on neo-classical economic theory (→ Money; → Commerce; → Market; cf. [8; 12]) that point to fundamental differences in assessing pre-modern society and its economy [8; 11; 12]. The representatives of neo-classical theory are thus criticized for applying to the totally different economic systems of antiquity an analytical system derived from the practices of a modern economic system exclusively geared to monetary and market economics. The economic systems of antiquity, argue the critics, were embedded in social structures, processes and rationales in a quite different way and were shaped by them rather than by modern patterns of market economics.

A distinguishing feature of both the redistributive (3rd millennium BC) and tributary (2nd/1st millennia BC) economic forms in Mesopotamia is the absence – either entirely or as essentially quantitative factors – of elements, structures and processes of monetary and market economics. There are no allusions to → loans for productive purposes; credit played a role especially in trading concerns. It was generally extended for a single undertaking, in the form of silver or of goods, and brought to account by the two parties at the conclusion of the undertaking [12. 189–203, especially 198]. Another feature of the Mesopotamian economy was the absence of steady technological progress as a motor for economic growth. Moreover, for a relatively long period of time, overall economic growth was held back by the limited availability of the principal means of production, arable land. That problem was linked to the demographic situation, as a consequence of which a given arable surface could sustain only a limited number of people. Regular and adequate subsistence production was guaranteed by optimal use of available and stood in the first battle row, the *principes* stood in the second row, while the older and battle-hardened soldiers were placed as *triarii* in the third row (Pol. 6,21–23). The *hastati* and *principes* were equipped with an oval shield, a sword and probably two *pila, a*nd wore bronze breast plates and greaves; the *hastati* had bronze helmets with long feathers which made them appear larger. Only the *triarii* were still armed with the *hasta*; the *hasta* of the lightly armed (*velites*) had a sling added to it and was thus suitable for throwing (*hasta amentata*; Cic. Brut. 271). Despite these changes, the *hastati* kept their name.

Hastati and *principes* of a legion were each divided into ten maniples of 120 men, while the ten maniples of the *triarii* consisted of 60 men each. In battle, the *hastati* started with close combat and, if beaten off, retreated through the rows of the *principes*. In legionary camps (→ *castra*), the *hastati* occupied a fixed place on the *via quintana* and formed their own column during marches (Pol. 6,28f.; 6,40).

Although the maniples were replaced by the *cohortes* (→ *cohors*) up to the time of Caesar, the names of the old battle rows remained in the titles of the *centuriones* (*hastatus prior* and *hastatus posterior*). Since this reorganization, the *hasta* was no longer used; henceforth, all soldiers were armed with the *pilum*. During the Principate, the term *hasta* was used for various spears of the → *auxilia*. The *hasta pura* was part of the military decorations (→ *dona militaria*) for officers from the *ordo equester* and the *ordo senatorius*.

1 M.C. Bishop, J.C.N. Coulston, Roman Military Equipment, 1993, 52–53; 69 2 L. Keppie, The Making of the Roman Army, 1984, 14–67. J.CA.

[2] In a legal sense, according to Gai. Inst. 4,16, *hasta* has the same meaning as *festuca*. In the → *legis actio sacramento in rem*, both appear as symbols of the claim of possession *iusti dominii* (of the legally justified ownership) over the contentious subject matter as asserted by the parties. This explains why in the centumviral court responsible for the → *vindicatio*, a *hasta* was displayed (Dig. 1,2,2,29). Later on, the *hasta* became the overall symbol for the disposal of property initiated by the state (Cic. Phil. 2,64).

M. Kaser, K. Hackl, Das röm. Zivilprozeßrecht, [2]1997, 14, 97. C.PA.

[3] Wooden ritual instrument with an iron point and a burnt and bloody shaft, which the → *fetiales* hurled into enemy territory in accordance with the old Roman ritual of a declaration of war or with which they carried out the symbolic act before the Bellona Temple (cf. *hastiferi* = followers of the Bellona cult [1]) in Rome. The *hasta* was also regarded as a symbol for the god → Mars (*hasta Martis,* which was kept in the sacrarium of the regia: Serv. Aen. 8,3) or as an attribute of the → Salii (Dion. Hal. Ant. Rom. 2,70: λόγχη; *lónchē*) [2]. However, whether it was an attribute of the *flamines* is uncertain (differently: [3]).

1 AE 48,8; 48,29 2 A.V. Siebert, Instrumenta sacra, in print 3 Th. Schäfer, Flaminat und h., in: Scritti in ricordo di G. Massari Gaballo e di U. Tocchetti Pollini (Comune di Milano, Ripartizione Cultura, Raccolte Archeologiche Numismatiche), 1986, 129f. with n. 42.

F. Klingmüller, s.v. H. (1), RE 7, 2502. A.V.S.

[4] *Oppidum* on the Tanaro in Liguria, *municipium II virale* or *colonia* (Ptol. 3,1,45) of the *regio IX*, *tribus Pollia*, on the *via Fulvia* (Tab. Peut. 3,5), modern Asti in Piemont; *dioecesis*, Lombard duchy. Famous for ceramics (Plin. HN 35,160; Anth. Pal. 11,27,3). In AD 402, H. resisted Alaricus [2] (Claud. Carm. 27f., 203), in 480, attack by the Burgundiones, supported by the Ostrogoths in AD 534 (Cassiod. Var. 11,15,2). Extant are Torre Rosso, thermal baths, theatre, *domus*, necropoleis. On the Ligurian coast and in Etruria, two homonymous *mansiones* (Tab. Peut. 3,5; 4,3; Geogr. Rav. 4,32; 5,2).

S. Giorcelli Bersani, Alla periferia dell'impero, 1994, 45–76; M. Somà, Note topografiche su Asti romana, in: Bollettino storico-bibliografico subalpino 93, 1995, 219–243; E. Zanda, A. Crosetto, L. Pejrani, Asti. Interventi archeologici e ricerche in centro storico (1981–1986), in: Quaderni della Soprintendenza Archeologica del Piemonte 5, 1986, 67–121. E.S.G.

[5] Town in the Baetica (Plin. HN 3,1; Str. 3,1,9; Liv. 39,21), remains on the hill Mesa de Asta 25 km north of Puerto San Maria. First mentioned in 189 BC (CIL II 5041). In 187 BC, conquered by C. → Atinius [2] (Liv. 39,21), constituted by Caesar as *colonia Hasta Regia* (on bronze coins: *Felix*) in 45 BC (cf. Plin. HN 3,11). Last mentioned in the *Acta Sanctorum* by Marcellus; destroyed in Arab times.

M. Esteve Guerrero, Miscellanea arqueologica Jerezana, 1979; M. Ferrero, Apuntes para una interpretación estadística de la cerámica aparecida en Asta Regia, in: Boletín del Museo de Cádiz 2, 1979–1980, 37–44; P. Piernaveja, Sobre Marcial y un pretendido Romanus, in: Archivo Español de Arqueología 48, 1975, 181f.; Tovar 2, 148–150. M.F.P.L. and P.B.

resources, i.e. of manpower in particular (→ Work I.; → Social structure I.). In none of the Ancient Eastern economic systems was → slavery a key economic factor. → Deportation of population groups in the Neo-Assyrian period (8th/7th cents. BC) increased workforce capacity only to a limited extent. A limited number of specialized artisans from conquered lands was engaged only for the prestige buildings of the Neo-Assyrian rulers.

The economy of the Neo-Assyrian state (9th–7th cents. BC) was determined by, and very closely linked to, the demands of unbridled military expansion. It called for the tapping of ever newer and more extensive human and material resources than the sovereign territory was capable of providing. It was thus, at one and the same time, the cause and consequence of the expansion. When the Assyrians had exhausted the geographic limits of their expansionism, in the 2nd half of the 7th cent. BC, the sudden collapse of their kingdom (caused by external enemies) was inevitable.

→ Agriculture I.; → Banks I.; → Commerce I.; → Crafts I.; → Grain I.; → Irrigation I.; → Leasehold I.; → Market I.; → Money I.; → Oikos economy; → Palace II. B.; → State II.; → Supply economy; → Taxes I.; → Work

1 A. Gadders, Economy and Society in Northern Babylonia in the Early Old Babylonian Period, 2002 2 J. G. Dercksen (ed.), Finance in the Ancient Near East, 1999 3 M. Hudson, M. van de Mieroop, Debt and Economic Renewal in the Ancient Near East, 2002 4 B. Landsberger, The Date-Palm and Its By-Products, 1967 5 M. Liverani, Prestige and Interest. International Relations in the Near East ca. 1600–1100 B. C., 1990 6 M. van de Mieroop, Economic History, in: Id., Cuneiform Texts and the Writing of History, 1999, 106–137 7 J. N. Postgate, Early Mesopotamia. Society and Economy at the Dawn of History, 1992 8 J. Renger, Probleme und Perspektiven einer W.-Gesch. Mesopot.s, in: Saeculum 40, 1989, 166–178 9 Id., Different Economic Spheres in the Urban Economy of Ancient Mesopotamia – Traditional Solidarity, Redistribution and Market Elements as the Means of Access to the Necessities of Life, in: E. Aerts, H. Klengel (ed.), The Town as Regional Economic Centre in the Ancient Near East, 1990, 20–28 10 Id., W. und Ges., in: B. Hrouda (ed.), Der Alte Orient, 1991, 187–215 11 Id., Formen des Zugangs zu den lebensnotwendigen Gütern: Die Austauschverhältnisse in der altbabylonischen Zeit, in: Altoriental. Forsch. 20, 1993, 87–114 12 Id., On Economic Structures in Ancient Mesopotamia, in: Orientalia 63, 1994, 157–208 13 Id., Institutional, Communal, and Individual Ownership or Possession of Arable Land in Ancient Mesopotamia, in: Chicago-Kent Law Review 71, 1995, 269–319 14 Id., Handwerk und Handwerker im alten Mesopot., in: Altoriental. Forsch. 23, 1996, 211–231 15 Id., W.-Gesch. des alten Mesopot. Versuch einer Standortbestimmung, in: A. Hausleiter et al. (ed.), Material Culture and Mental Spheres-Rezeption archäologischer Denkrichtungen in der Vorderasiatischen Altertumskunde, Int. Symposium f. H.J. Nissen, Berlin 23.–24. Juni 2002 (= AOAT, vol. 293), 2002, 239–265.

K. Polanyi et al. (ed.), Trade and Market in Early Empires – Economies in History and Theory, 1957; Id., The Livelihood of Man, 1977.

II. Egypt

Egypt's economy, just like Mesopotamia's, was based on → agriculture with → animal husbandry integrated into it [1; 2. 204 f.]. Craft production (→ Crafts) loomed as an important complementary factor in the course of Egyptian history [2. 205 f.]. In the Egyptian early period (1st Dynasty/start of the 3rd millennium BC), originally self-sufficient rural households were gradually absorbed into royal lands. As early as the 4th Dynasty (2570–2450 BC) land from the land reserves accumulated in that way was bestowed on officials – in order to ensure their loyalty – and members of the ruling clan [2. 198]. This led to individual large estates in the hands of an upper class consisting essentially of officials (functionaries) of the state. Even → temples, however, received extensive allotments and endowments of land, with the result that in the New Kingdom the temple of → Amun in → Thebes [1], for example, represented the most important economic force in Egypt [2. 202].

The regime of land tenure patterns was governed by the fact that availability of arable farmland – in contrast to Mesopotamia (organization of irrigation and thus control of arable land) – required only a certain level of state measures; because of the annual flooding of the → Nile, the soil's fertility was essentially assured without any organizational effort on the part of the state. The ruler's rights in respect of his subjects were based on other factors.

The central role of the → ruler in the Egyptian economy was based on a state system constructed hierarchically so as to culminate in the ruler [5. 232 f.]. Essential sectors of the economy (other than direct agricultural production) seem to have been controlled directly by the ruler in all periods of Egyptian history (transport system, regulation of wages and prices [2. 209–212; 5. 250–253], establishing of the work quota in all sectors of the economy). The pharaoh was entitled to the fruit of his subjects' labour, as well as their → taxes and duties, especially on the output of agricultural production. They were used for dealing with tasks concerning the entire state (*i.a.*, the erection of prestige buildings, payment of workers, maintenance of a civil service, the military). The use of considerable economic resources to fund prestige items of expenditure (buildings, running the court, cult rites) has been described as a distinguishing feature of the Egyptian economy [7].

Supplementary revenue, which was of importance to the Egyptian economy, derived from military expeditions (building material, gold from → Nubia in particular), booty or tribute from other regions (*i.a.*, gregarious animals; animal → husbandry). In contrast to Mesopotamia, where long-distance trade was a substantial theme in the texts, the official Egyptian sources often describe it in ideological phraseology as exchange of gifts, or even as tribute [6. 240–266]. In this way, the power, status and prestige of the ruler were given expression. To that extent the Egyptian economy – like the economy in areas with rainfed agriculture, where the fertility of arable land was not dependent on measures undertaken by the state – contained forms of an economic system of tribute. However, the Egyptian economy also contained redistributive elements to a considerable extent. In that respect it was fundamentally different from the patrimonial *oíkos*-system of Mesopotamia in the third millennium BC.

There is widespread agreement that the Egyptian economy had the character of a regimented system [1; 2; 3; 4; 5. 231 f.; 6.17 f.]. Its redistributive character is highlighted, as well as the absence of features of a monetary and market economy. There is also agreement that a redistributive model cannot account for all aspects of Egyptian economy. Alternating periods of stronger and weaker state central authority required an ability to adjust to changing economic conditions [5. 259 f.]. In periods of a weak central government that was incapable of comprehensively ensuring the population's needs by redistribution, barter between individuals played an important role [5. 259], with social obligations determining the patterns of exchange. Grave-robbing was apparently an important and widespread source of income for members of the lower class in some regions [2. 213 f.].

→ Agriculture I.; → Commerce I.; → Crafts I.; → Grain I.; → Irrigation I.; → Leasehold I.; → Market I.; → Money I.; → Palace III.; → State III.; → Taxes II.

1 M. Gutgesell, s. v. W., LÄ 6, 1275–1278 2 Id., W., Landw., Handwerk, in: A. Eggebrecht, (ed.), Das Alte Äg., ²1988, 197–225 3 W. Helck, W.-Gesch. Äg.s, 1975 4 J. J. Janssen, Die Struktur der pharaonischen W., in: Göttinger Miszellen 48, 1981, 59–77 5 B. J. Kemp, The Birth of Economic Man, in: Id., Ancient Egypt, 1989, 231–260 6 M. Liverani, Prestige and Interest. International Relations in the Near East ca. 1600–1100 B. C., 1990 7 S. Morenz, Prestige-W. im alten Äg., 1969.

III. Levant

The strong agricultural fragmentation of Syria and the Levant led to the formation of numerous smaller or larger palace-oriented states, which encompassed a more or less large, arable hinterland, as well as the city itself (*i.a.* → Alalaḫ, → Byblus, → Ebla, Ḫalab/ → Aleppo, → Sidon, → Tyre, → Ugarit). The Levant economy was based on rainfed agriculture and animal husbandry. Its principal products were grain, wine, olive oil, fruits and wool. The pattern of economic organization was distinguished by two different economic spheres: the rural sphere was characterized by village communities with individual rural households – independent or integrated into the palace households of urban centres [8; 10]. These village communities had to surrender part of their production as duty to the palace, which from it paid for its own upkeep, satisfied its demand for prestige goods and also provided for the urban elite. In contrast to Mesopotamia and Egypt, temples played no significant role as economically relevant institutions.

The Levantine cities owed their extraordinary wealth to two factors: their position as entrepots at the crossroads of important trade routes, east-west and north-south [4], and to their own range of goods in demand. These latter included wine and olive oil and, especially, products crafted in metal and ivory (→ Ivory carvings I.) and → purple-dyed fabrics [3]. The long-distance trade undertaken by the Levantine cities was generally organized by the palaces, whose objective was the import of prestige goods for ostentatious projects.

Long-distance trade was very risky by land and by sea, and thus very costly. Various efforts were therefore made to keep the high transaction costs [7. 159 f.] to a minimum: → state contracts, which furnished security for the trading agents, contracts between a trading agent and a silent partner, absolving the former from claims for compensation in event of shipwreck (so-called bottomry loans, developed in Ugarit), setting up trading warehouses or depots in other cities, and a system of intermediary trade in which a trading agent's goods were transported only from point A to point B; onward trade with point C was the responsibility of trading agents at point B (e.g. tin from Elam to Mari, Mari to Karkemiš, Karkemiš to Anatolia). Phoenician traders occasionally formed associations to equip a fleet and stock it with goods; with the protection of a powerful city-prince they were thus able to counter the danger of piracy. Trade by land may have been organized in a similar manner. Transaction costs could also be limited by specializing or even by a monopoly in certain goods (e.g. → purple in Ugarit, Sidon and Tyre; → shipbuilding in Byblus), that guaranteed exorbitant profits (between 100% and 200%). These latter depended on a supply and demand situation between different parts of the Aegean, the Near East, Anatolia and Egypt. Profits were often invested in agricultural properties that sometimes reached the scale of large estates. Income from these agricultural enterprises brought in supplementary income and thus further reduced the risks from long-distance trade.

→ Commerce; → Silver

1 J.-P. Grégoire, J. Renger, Die Interdependenz der wirtschaftl. und gesellschaftl.-polit. Strukturen von Ebla, in: H. Hauptmann, H. Waetzoldt (ed.), W. und Ges. von Ebla, 1988, 211–224 2 M. Heltzer, The Economy of Ugarit, in: W. G. E. Watson, G. Wyatt (ed.), Handbook of Ugaritic Studies, 1999, 423–445 3 H. J. Katzenstein, The History of Tyre, 1973 4 H. Klengel, Near Eastern Trade and the Emergence of Interaction with Crete in the Third Millennium, in: SMEA 24, 1984, 7–31 5 M. Liverani, Prestige and Interest: International Relations in the Near East ca. 1600–1100 B. C., 1990 6 J. D. Muhly, Phoenicia and the Phoenicians, in: J. Amitai (ed.), Biblical Archaeology Today, 1985, 177–191 7 J. Renger, On Economic Structures in Ancient Mesopotamia, in: Orientalia 63, 1994, 157–208 8 J. D. Schloen, The House of the Father as Fact and Symbol. Patrimonialism in Ugarit and the Ancient Near East, 2001 9 J.-P. Vita, The Society of Ugarit, in: see [2], 455–498 10 F. Zeeb, Die Palast-W. in Altsyrien, 2001.

IV. Iran

In the absence of adequate textual sources for large periods of time, we are missing a coherent economic history of → Iran. As in other areas of the Ancient East, the economy in Iran depended essentially on agriculture, to which a strong pastoral farming element was later added. The economic systems of Iran assumed different forms over the centuries – corresponding to the prevailing political and social relationships at a given time and also independently of the individual regions.

Under the Elamite dynasty from the 3rd to well into the 2nd millennium BC (→ Elam), a dimorphic economy was a feature, in so far as an irrigation system was possible for agriculture in → Susiana, whereas only rainfed agriculture was feasible in the empire's other regions. Large institutional households, possibly resembling the → *oikos* economy familiar from southern Mesopotamia, can be discerned in early Elamite texts[2]. On the Iranian plateau it was more a case of nomadic pastoral economy and of agrarian production, organized in village communities, existing side by side in mutual dependence. In the course of history the village communities were gradually absorbed into the large property holdings of the ruling upper classes. This form of economy predominated until the Sassanid period (3rd cent. BC–7th cent. AD) and beyond [5. 255 f.]. The land was cultivated by dependent leaseholders who had to hand over part of their production to the landowners. The latter in turn were obliged to hand over a portion to the → ruler – and to that extent we can describe it as a tributary form of economy. Following the political expansion of Iranian dynasties beyond Iranian core territory (6th cent. BC), the tributary economy was based not only on the internal system of duty payable but substantially on the tribute payments from individual parts of the empire. According to Hdt. 3,88–117, these tribute payments largely consisted of gold and silver. From Achaemenid administrative documents at → Persepolis [5. 98–101] elements of a redistributive economy can be discerned, as well as those of tributary economic forms [5. 109–114].

As a thoroughfare of important trading routes, Iran's economy always benefited from intermediary trade in raw materials and prestige goods [5. 116, 161, 185, 195–197]. Especially from the Hellenistic period onwards, after the campaigns of → Alexander ([4] the Great), Iran became an important centre of trade between China and India (→ India, trade with) on the one hand and with the Mediterranean world on the other. From along the → Silk Road, in particular, silks, silk garments, spices and aromatic substances, jewellery and other craft products of high value, exotic animals and their pelts, as well as slaves (eunuchs) found their way into the Roman empire [5. 225–265]. The oasis city of → Palmyra served as → port of trade between the Parthian empire (→ Parthia) and the Roman empire. Palmyrene traders maintained trading bases in several cities of the Parthian empire, in → Bahrain and in the Indus delta (→ Indus [1]). Iran itself obtained, in particular, silk, steel and fruits (apricots, peaches) from the east and exported silver vessels (in the 4th–6th cents. AD a royal monopoly), linen clothing, pomegranates, wines and vines, and horses (from → Nisaea [2]).

Iranian dynasties used their strategic position in east-west trade to impose tolls on goods passing through. For this reason, Rome and Byzantium sought to avoid passing through Iran by using the sea-route from the → Persian Gulf to India (→ Charax Spasinu). At a relatively early stage, money was introduced into Iran by Darius [1] I. The → dareikos played a part in traffic with the Mediterranean world in particular. The Attic currency was adopted under the → Seleucids and was then consolidated under the Arsacids (→ Arsaces) and → Sassanids. As far as we can establish, the monetarization of taxes and duties seems to have taken place then also [5. 253 f.].

1 R. McC. Adams, Agriculture and Urban Life in Early South-Western Iran, in: Science 136, 1962, 109–122 2 E. Carter, M. W. Stolper, Elam, Surveys of Political History and Archaeology, 1984 3 M. A. Dandamayev, V. G. Lukonin, The Culture and Social Institutions of Ancient Iran, 1989 4 I. Gershevitch (ed.), The Cambridge History of Iran, vol. 2: The Median and Achaemenian Periods, 1985 5 J. Wiesehöfer, Das ant. Persien, [3]1998.

J. RE.

V. Classical Antiquity

A. General Structures B. Economic development in Greece and the Imperium Romanum VI. Byzantium

A. General Structures

The term οἰκονομία/*oikonomía* derives from → *oíkos* ('house') and originally meant 'household economy', having nothing at all to do with political economy. That fact alone demonstrates that economy in antiquity cannot be equated to modern patterns. According to the research of K. Bücher, J. Hasebroek, K. Polanyi and M. I. Finley, study of ancient economics should always bear in mind that modern systems of economics developed during the industrial era and modern economic structures should by no means be imposed on antiquity.

First of all, it needs to be stressed that ancient societies were agrarian and two-thirds of the population worked on the land to produce → food, but also raw materials like → wool, for themselves and for the urban population. On this basis, production in antiquity should be thought of as being comprehensively directed at → subsistence. Rural families produced primarily for their own consumption and the workers on large estates were initially provided with what they had produced themselves. This also applied to additional workers who were hired for the harvest; they usually received a share of the harvest. Even households of rich upper-class families can be assumed to have been largely self-sufficient. Consequently, → markets had only a limited function, as not everyone in ancient societies took part in market activity or went there to satisfy their needs. Only in the larger cities, where the population had no direct link with agrarian production, was self-sufficiency no longer possible, with the result that many people there were obliged to purchase their essential commodities. Urban craftsmen (→ Crafts) produced basically to meet local demand and many items were produced on commission. Crafts productivity remained at a low level, as technical innovations were introduced only on a limited scale and did not in any way replace human labour using → tools. Owners of largish workshops were able to reach a certain level of affluence, but their wealth did not match that of large-estate owners (→ large estates / latifundia), who were the largest holders of wealth (→ wealth, distribution of).

Urban wealth depended largely on agrarian production within the city territory, and the property of the social and political elite consisted mainly of rural landholdings and, to a certain extent also, of urban real estate. → Commerce was mainly geared to supplying the towns and was thus import-oriented, though it did also handle high-value luxury goods that were produced only in certain regions. That trade seems to have been of little economic importance.

→ Slavery was a distinctive feature of ancient society and economy. Although it by no means prevailed in all periods and regions of the ancient world, its economic importance should not be underestimated. In classical Greece, in the late Republic and in the early Principate, slaves occupied a large part of the workforce that was active in → agriculture and crafts. It must also be said, though, that in the rural areas of Hellenistic kingdoms and the Imperium Romanum of late antiquity agrarian production was largely dependent on the labour of semi-free → farmers or leaseholders (*coloni*) who were tied to the soil, and slave-labour lost importance in the rural sector. With few exceptions, mineral resources – especially metal deposits and marble quarries – remained in the public domain. There was thus no possibility for property owners to acquire large wealth through mining gold and silver (→ Mining). Mines were usually operated by small leaseholders – or, in the Roman period, by lease-holding associations – and during the Principate this gave rise to the trend to have mining districts placed under imperial administration.

Economic patterns were in each case dependent on certain geographic conditions. Cultivation was concentrated on the few fertile plains in river valleys or in areas with soil of volcanic origin. Precipitation and winter temperatures were important factors in the choice of plants to cultivate. Animal → husbandry was assigned to forest areas that were also suitable as summer meadows. As metal deposits are distributed unevenly in the Mediterranean region and restricted to just a few areas, only a small number of cities communities and kingdoms were in a position to increase their wealth by mining precious metals and → minting coins. Those cities and kingdoms with access to precious mineral deposits thus had at their disposal an economic resource that could be used to develop their power base. That was true of Athens first of all, then Macedonia and finally Carthage and Rome.

B. Economic development in Greece and the Imperium Romanum

The description and analysis of economic structures in antiquity should not view ancient societies as being static and deny them the prospect of any economic development. K. Hopkins has emphatically pointed out that the society and economy of the Homeric period clearly differed from those of the Principate. There the economic development was influenced by various factors. The first of these to warrant mention is the population growth, then an increase in the size of cities, social differentiation that led to greater wealth (Money; money economy) in the upper classes and thus to a growing demand for manufacture of luxury goods, a wide-spread acceptance of → monetary economy, an intensification of trading links within the Mediterranean area, and an increase in trade with the regions outside it.

Undoubtedly, a considerable economic dynamics developed in larger cities that were both political and economic centres. On the one hand, the urban population could no longer be supplied with → foodstuffs from its immediate surroundings, and so trading links became necessary so as to be able to obtain essential items. On the other hand, goods had to be exported in the exchange or else the imports had to be paid for with precious metals. In Athens, which was dependent on grain imports and had the silver deposits at → Laurium at its disposal, trade developed under those conditions and, in connection with → fenus nauticum, monetary transactions and banking (→ Banks) as well; → Piraeus became a commercial and business centre of supra-regional importance, in which rich metics (→ *métoikoi*) were involved in banking and owned large workshops.

In the Hellenistic period, completely novel opportunities for trade were opened up through Alexander's [4] conquests. The → Ptolemies promoted trade with India, Alexandria [1] became the most important harbour in the eastern Mediterranean. Rhodes, which supplanted Piraeus as Aegean trading centre in the 3rd cent. BC, lost that position when the Romans made Delos a free port in 166 BC. Delos thus became a centre of Roman commercial activity, and especially of the → slave trade, in the Greek east. Monetary circulation was stimulated through the minting of Persian precious metals under Alexander.

Through contacts with the Greek cities in Lower Italy and Sicily, as well as the Hellenistic kingdoms in the east, Rome, which had been rather agrarian in character up to the 3rd cent. BC, was absorbed into the Hellenistic economic area. Evidence of that is the beginning of Roman minting, with Roman nominal value, following Greek standards. Following the victories over Carthage in the 1st and 2nd → Punic Wars, the Romans annexed provinces that brought in considerable taxes and in particular provided access to Spanish precious metal deposits.

Rome's economic development was quite substantially marked by its political contexts. By virtue of the military victories over → Carthage and Hellenistic rulers in the east, extraordinarily large quantities of money and precious metals reached Rome, where the small senatorial elite acquired great wealth. At the same time, new fields of business opened up for well-to-do Roman citizens – including the → *equites Romani* – in the provinces. The lucrative tax farming in Sicily or the province of Asia opened up opportunities for enrichment for the Roman → *negotiatores* as well. In order to satisfy the financial demands of tax farming, the → *publicani* founded associations (*societates publicorum*). The growth of Rome and the cities of central Italy resulted in a substantial demand for agricultural products and in this way promoted the growth and establishment of a market-oriented agrarian economy in central Italy. The economic dynamics of Rome and of Italy was undoubtedly a consequence of the political development that, in the period between the 1st Punic War and the start of the Civil War in 49 BC, made Rome the leading political power of the Mediterranean area.

Political events also exerted considerable influence over economic development in the Principate. The administration of the → *principes* had to ensure the provision of supplies not only for the city of Rome but also for the legions that were stationed on the borders of the Imperium Romanum (→ *legio*). While the city of Rome received grain brought in from Africa and Egypt as → taxes, the legions on the Rhine and later in Britain had to be supplied with olive oil in particular from the Mediterranean. For this purpose transport of bulk goods had to be organized on a large scale by the bureaucracy. Free trade nevertheless still had a role to play in supplying foodstuffs and consumer goods to the markets in other cities.

A distinguishing aspect of the Principate was the rise of large craft-production centres, for example in → pottery production. Thus → terra sigillata was produced in Arretium in the late Republic, and in southern and central Gallic pottery centres in the early Principate. Something comparable happened in glass and → textile production. Despite the concentration of production in such centres, it was never a case of large businesses being created or even of manufactures. Those centres should be seen as an agglomeration of many small workshops that could also co-operate in individual production processes, such as the firing of pottery. The Gallic potteries produced quality items that were sold in many provinces of the Imperium Romanum. In the area of → agriculture a distinct supra-regional division of labour occurred: in the especially fertile regions large surpluses were produced of → wine and olive oil (→ Oils II. Thus, the province of Baetica supplied large quantities of olive oil not only to the legions in the north-west provinces but also to Rome. Wine was similarly transported over large distances. Luxury goods were imported on a steadily increasing scale from regions outside the empire, as for example → ivory from Ethiopia and India, as well as → spices and → silk from India and China. In addition to the sea-route to India through the Red Sea, the → caravan trade – via Palmyra, for example – played an important part in that.

In this period the traffic routes in the Imperium Romanum were also developed in a systematic way. Although military perspectives were also important in this program, the effect of intensified → road construction on trade and → communication should not be underestimated. A road network was created that opened up even the large interior of the north-western provinces and connected Italy to the provinces north of the Alps and to the Danube provinces (→ Roads). The development of harbours – not only at the mouth of the Tiber – gave a special boost to shipping (→ Navigation).

An essential condition for urban prosperity in the 1st and 2nd cents. AD was the long period of peace that the political system of the Principate had been able to ensure for the Imperium Romanum. The end of the wars that had been waged incessantly in the Classical and Hellenistic periods, with permanent damage to property, frequent destruction of cities and large-scale human enslavement, favoured economic activity and an improvement in living standards. It must be emphasized, though, that even in the Principate cities remained islands in an agriculturally oriented world and that in agriculture → slavery was only slowly and partly displaced by forms of leasehold. As is shown by the archaeological finds of money hoards, the → monetary economy was widely accepted in the provinces. It depended, however, on the extraction of precious metals in the Spanish mining areas, and the Roman currency system was severely affected when the gold and silver deposits there were exhausted.

The political crisis of the 3rd cent. AD, caused by the incursions of Germanic tribes into the Roman provinces, led to far-reaching disturbances, to a breakdown of lines of communication and to a growing taxation burden on the unaffected areas of the Imperium Romanum. Financing the military and → administrative structures was possible only by increasing and systematizing → taxes; the currency system was stabilized again only for gold coins under Constantinus [1] (→ *solidus*), with the result that the Imperium Romanum increasingly demanded payment in kind in lieu of taxation. Taxing of property ownership resulted in the *coloni* (→ *coloniae*) being tied to the soil, and there was also a discernible trend for people in the cities to become tied to their trades through edicts. Services to the population of Rome were extended to the point that supplies of wine and meat were now organized by the administration. Moreover, Constantinople was incorporated into this system in the 4th cent. AD. The economic system that had evolved in the Principate finally broke down completely when the Germanic tribes conquered the north-western provinces and Africa in the 5th cent. AD, blocked the sea-routes in the

western Mediterranean and cut off Rome's supply-line from the western provinces.
→ ECONOMY; → ECONOMIC DOCTRINE

1 J. ANDREAU, Banking and Business in the Roman World, 1999 2 K. BÜCHER, Die Entstehung der Volkswirtschaft, 1893 3 E. E. COHEN, Athenian Economy and Society. A Banking Perspektive, 1992 4 D'ARMS 5 DUNCAN-JONES, Economy 6 D'ARMS/KOPFF 7 FINLEY, Ancient Slavery 8 FINLEY, Property 9 FINLEY, Ancient Economy 10 M. I. FINLEY, The World of Odyseus, 1977 11 ESAR 12 J. M. FRAYN, Subsistence Farming in Roman Italy, 1979 13 P. GARNSEY, Cities, Peasants and Food in Classical Antiquity, 1998 14 GARNSEY 15 P. GARNSEY (ed.), Non-Slave Labour in the Greco-Roman World, 1980 16 GARNSEY/HOPKINS/WHITTAKER 17 W. V. HARRIS (ed.), The Inscribed Economy, 1993 18 HASEBROEK 19 J. HASEBROEK, Staat und Handel im alten Griechenland, 1928 20 F. M. HEICHELHEIM, An Ancient Economic History, 3 vols., 1964–65 21 R. HODGES, Primitive and Peasant Markets, 1988 22 K. HOPKINS, Economic Growth and Towns in Classical Antiquity, in: P. ABRAMS, E. A. WRIGLEY (ed.), Towns and Society, 1978, 35–77 23 Id., Taxes and Trade in the Roman Empire (200 B. C.-A. D. 400), in: JRS 70, 1980, 101–125 24 JONES, Economy 25 JONES, LRE 26 D. J. MATTINGLY, J. SALMON (ed.), Economies beyond Agriculture in the Classical World, 2001 27 E. MEYER, Die wirtschaftliche Entwicklung des Alt., in: Id., KS 1, ²1924, 79–168 28 MILLET 29 K. POLANYI, The Great Transformation, 1944 30 PRÉAUX 31 G. RICKMAN, The Corn Supply of Ancient Rom, 1980 32 ROSTOVTZEFF, Hellenistic World 33 ROSTOVTZEFF, Roman Empire 34 P. VEYNE, Mythe et réalité de l'autarchie à Rome, in: REA 81, 1979, 261–280 35 P. VIDAL-NAQUET, Economic and Social History of Ancient Greece, 1977 36 M. WEBER, Gesammelte Aufsätze zur Sozial- und W.-Geschichte, 1924 37 WHITTAKER 38 H.-J. DREXHAGE et al., Die W. des röm. Reiches (1.–3. Jh.), 2002 39 W. SCHEIDEL, S. v. REDEN, The Ancient Economy, 2002.

J. M. A.-N.

VI. BYZANTIUM

At first glance the period of Justinian [1] (527–565) seems to be the last cultural, economic, political and military flourishing of late antiquity, and yet even then signs were evident of the decline that eventuated with great violence in the course of the 7th cent. AD. The 6th cent. can thus be described as Janus-like: on the one hand certain regions of the Eastern Empire prospered, while others were already caught up in unmistakable decline.

A key economic factor – even if its exact ramifications are the subject of academic controversy – was the state with its central policy of finance and taxation. From roughly AD 500 (at the time of Emperor Anastasius [1], 491–518) the transition from paying taxes in kind to cash taxation (→ *adaeratio*) was largely, though not fully, in place. The demand for natural produce, for example for the army, was now increasingly covered by the *coemptio* (compulsory acquisition by the state at fixed prices).

Agricultural production flourished on the extensive imperial, state- and Church-owned and aristocratic → large estates. The extensive holdings of the Church, in particular, were leased (→ *emphýteusis*). As well, in certain regions of the empire there were free farmers, for example in Asia Minor or Syria. Until its fall to the Persians in 617, Constantinople was supplied with grain shipments from Egypt. The sharp drop in the Byzantine capital's population, however, prevented a famine when those supplies ceased. Byzantine crafts maintained a high technical level into the first half of the 7th cent. In the large cities (Constantinople, Antioch [1], Alexandria [1], Ephesus), → crafts and → commerce were organized into guilds (→ *collegia*, συστήματα/ *systēmata*) and subject to state control (→ professional associations). State workshops (→ *fabricae*) for textiles, including also luxury items like → silk, or for weapons had to meet the state's needs, especially those of the military. Urban life was affected as early as the 6th cent. by the decline of the social class of the → *curiales* [2]. Various reform attempts by the state, to keep that trend in check, were unsuccessful.

The outbreak of the bubonic plague that ravaged the Mediterranean area for the first time in 541/2 had grave repercussions. Although the demographic losses cannot really be quantified – estimates range from 25% to 50% of the population – the plague undeniably had far-reaching consequences (cf. → Epidemic diseases IV.). As the plague continued to erupt until 746/748, regular population losses can be assumed. Amongst the consequences of this catastrophe, the enormous loss of taxation needs to be mentioned first of all. The cities in particular seem to have suffered, while rural areas – at least in some regions – were less affected.

Traditional internal and long-distance trade links seem to have survived until the start of the 7th cent. The large churches, too – well attested in the case of Alexandria by the *vita* of → Iohannes [32] Eleemon (Patriarch 610–619), composed by → Leontius [8] of Neapolis (Bibliotheca Hagiographica Graeca 886b-c) – developed comprehensive economic activities. Thereafter, as modern pottery studies show, an almost complete collapse of long-distance trade occurred.

The Eastern Empire experienced extensive upheavals from the start of the 7th cent. The periods of crisis that had already been taking place up to that point expanded then into a widespread collapse of late antiquity's social and economic structures. After Phocas [4] (602–610) ousted → Mauricius in 602, a decades-long war took place with the Sassanid Persians and came to an end only in 627/8 under Emperor Heraclius (610–640) (→ Parthian and Persian wars). Coming on top of the ravages of the plague, the conduct of the war with the Persians caused considerable damage to urban institutional infrastructure. The expansion of → Islam began only a few years later. In the space of few years Byzantium lost its economically important provinces in Egypt, Syria, Palaestine and Mesopotamia. Arab incursions into Byzantine Asia Minor, sometimes on an annual basis, led to considerable population loss and the abandonment of many villages.

The almost century-long defence against the relentlessly attacking Islamic → Arabs (674–678 and 716–717 sieges of → Constantinople) caused a fundamental change in the social and economic structure. In the course of the 7th cent. the old estate-owning aristocracy disappeared and even the system of imperial and state → domains had to accept heavy losses. In the 9th cent. crown and state disposed of only a fraction of the estates attested in the 6th cent. Apparently only the Church succeeded in retaining its property (→ Church property). The notorious lack of source material for the 7th and 8th cents. precludes any more detailed pronouncement. What is discernible is a pronounced swing towards a barter economy. In 668 the minting of smaller denominations – the hallmark of a functioning market economy – was drastically reduced. At the same time the administration of state finances and taxation was fundamentally transformed. From the middle of the 7th cent. until *c.* 730 payment in kind was collected once again and passed on to the army. Along with that, taxes in cash continued to be imposed, especially in relatively prosperous regions (environs of Constantinople, Lower Italy, and Sicily).

The axis of the city-country relationship now shifted in favour of the country. While Constantinople and the capital's environs (Thrace, Bithynia) were able to maintain a certain level of craft and agricultural production even in this period, the situation appeared very different in Asia Minor, which had now become the heartland of the Byzantine empire. The lack of sources does not allow any authoritative pronouncements but all the indications suggest that Byzantium changed into a state with especially strongly fortified *kástra* (fortified towns) that were no longer able to fulfil the functions of urban settlement based on a division of labour but were primarily dedicated to military protection. As well, there were scattered villages with agricultural production in which pasture farming acquired great importance. Only a few *civitates/póleis* were able to maintain their urban character: Constantinople and Thessalonica, Ephesus and perhaps Trapezus.

After external danger was largely removed from the middle of the 8th cent., there was an economic upswing, which within a few decades made Byzantium once again an economically dominant power, second only to the Arab Caliphate. There was an increase in agricultural and commercial production and correspondingly intensified market relationships. This allowed the gradual reintroduction of monetary taxes and resulted in the dominance of → monetary economy in Byzantium in the following years. However, taxes paid in kind were never fully abolished. By *c.* 800, the economic situation had been stabilized to the point that it was again possible to compile an estate register.

→ Church property; → Commerce VI.; → Crafts VI.; → Domain; → Money, money economy IV.

1 W. BRANDES, Finanzverwaltung in Krisenzeiten, 2002 2 Id., Die Städte Kleinasiens im 7. und 8. Jh., 1989 3 Id., J. HALDON, Towns, Tax and Transformation: State, Cities and Their Hinterlands in the East Roman World, ca. 500–800, in: G. P. BROGIOLO et al. (ed.), Towns and Their Territories between Late Antiquity and the Early Middle Ages, 2000, 141–172 4 A. CAMERON et al. (ed.), Late Antiquity. Empire and Successors, A. D. 425–600 (CAH 14), 2000 5 J. DURLIAT, De la ville antique à la ville byzantine, 1990 6 J. F. HALDON, Byzantium in the Seventh Century, [2]1997 7 Id., State, Army and Society in Byzantium, 1995 8 M. HENDY, Studies in the Byzantine Monetary Economy, 1985 9 J. H. LIEBESCHUETZ, Decline and Fall of the Roman City, 2001 10 JONES, LRE 11 A. CH. JOHNSON, L. C. WEST, Byzantine Egypt: Economic Studies, 1949 12 M. KAPLAN, Les hommes et la terre à Byzance, 1992 13 P. LEMERLE, The Agrarian History of Byzantium from the Origins to the Twelfth Century, 1979 14 M. MCCORMICK, Origins of the European Economy. Communications and Commerce, A. D. 300–900, 2001 15 F. MITTHOF, Annona militaris. Die Heeresversorgung im spätant. Äg., 2 vols., 2001 16 E. PATLAGEAN, Pauvreté économique et pauvreté sociale à Byzance, 1977 17 B. SIRKS, Food for Rome. The Legal Structure of the Transportation and Processing of Supplies for the Imperial Distributions in Rome and Constantinople, 1991 18 E. WIPSZYSKA, Les ressources et les activités économiques des églises en Egypte du IVe au VIIIe siécles, 1972.

W. BR.